The Prayer Book Concordance

The Prayer Book Concordance

Edited by Galen Bushey

THE CHURCH HYMNAL CORPORATION, NEW YORK

The Church Hymnal Corporation
800 Second Avenue
New York, NY 10017

10 9 8 7 6 5 4 3 2 1

Table of Contents

Preface vii

Introduction ix

Section One:

Spoken Text 1

Section Two:

Rubrics, Notes, Historical Documents 557

Glossary 789

Table of Deletions & Retentions 975

Preface

Since the approval of the current edition of *The Book of Common Prayer* in 1979, there has been an expressed need to have a concordance to the Prayer Book. The question posed by this desire was, "Just how can such a concordance be produced accurately and economically?" Over the last nine years, there have been many discussions and proposals of methods to accomplish this massive task. However, each plan was found to be unworkable for various reasons, and the subject would rest until a new idea was presented.

The Church Hymnal Corporation then approached Paragraphics Press, opening the discussions that led to this volume. Paragraphics Press is a firm that specializes in the production of musical scores, Latin and foreign text, indices, and other reference and scholarly works. Mr. Stephen Severson of Paragraphics spent a great deal of time researching the various methods currently being used to prepare other concordances. No commercial computer software was available which met the sophisticated needs posed by this project. Paragraphics therefore wrote their own concordance software specifically to address these needs. A satisfactory balance between automated functions and human editors was thus maintained.

Since the computer had to have a data base from which to construct the concordance, the entire Prayer Book (minus the Lectionary) was newly input to the computer. This new data base was then proofread before work on the concordance could begin. From the finished data base, a glossary was produced, showing every word in the Prayer Book and the number of occurrences (See page 789). After decisions were made on the words that would be excluded (and, of, in,...), each word to be included had to be extracted separately from the data base in order to compile the entries for that word. The report thus generated was the rough basis for this volume. However, the rough report had to be refined due to certain problems in the Prayer Book.

The main problem presented by the 1979 Prayer Book is its mix of prose and poetry, with prose printed as running text and the poetry printed in "sense" lines. The software program would only refer to the precise printed line in which a given word appeared. This meant that the context printed by the computer was not always acceptable, since there are places in the Prayer Book prose where there is only one word on a line. This would obviously give no context at all. In the unique mix of poetry and prose found in the BCP Collects and the Historical Documents, there are occasions where subordinate clauses separate two halves of a thought, making a useful context difficult to supply without printing a paragraph. In addition, many of the poetic sections contain lines that are too long to fit in any concordance of reasonable size.

To overcome these drawbacks, the rough computer-generated Concordance had to be edited so that the context of each word was clear, yet would fit into a manageable format. Editorial guidelines were developed and followed scrupulously in the preliminary editing process. The second-generation computer printouts were re-edited and then typeset, rechecked, and appear on the following pages. Much thanks goes to Kathleen Forbes, Eric Gordon, Sydney Cohen, and Randal Tupper for their invaluable assistance.

Throughout this process, the goal has been to make the Concordance clear, concise, and easy to use. It is the hope of the Publisher that *The Prayer Book Concordance* will find a place in our Church, and will help to further both understanding and knowledge of *The Book of Common Prayer 1979.*

Introduction

This Concordance is divided into two parts: the first section is a concordance of all of the *spoken* text found in BCP. The second section contains *all* word references for the rubrics, notes, and Historical Documents; that is, those parts of the Prayer Book which are never heard aloud in a service of worship. This was done to make the Concordance more useful and flexible, so that the theological and spiritual texts of the Prayer Book are separated from the mechanical and historical texts. It is the hope of the Editors that this will make it easier to find references in each type of text by making entries in each section smaller and more manageable.

Plural forms of nouns are listed separately from their singular forms. In addition, a distinction has been made between the following words because of theological and / or source differentiation: GOD / God; LORD / Lord; Mark (proper noun) / mark (verb / noun); Name / name.

In each section, the key words are followed by all of the occurrences of that word in an appropriate context. Following the context is first the page number on which this line is found, followed by the line number which contains the key word. Some contexts may begin on the previous line in the Prayer Book. This was done in order to have an understandable context for reference.

With only one exception, every occurrence of a key word is listed in this Concordance. The exception deals with repetitive phrases, as in the Great Litany. In this case, only the first occurrence of the response on a given page is listed.

Because of the way in which the computer recognizes each of the two types of text, line numbers relate only to the text used in each section. That is, when looking for a line number in Section One, the reader should count only the lines of spoken text on the given page, ignoring rubrics, headings, and other non-spoken text.

In Section Two, line numbers were a considerable problem, given the number of different types of text recognized by the computer as non-spoken text. Therefore, line numbers are given only for pages that are 80% or more given to rubrics and related text. On these pages, it is important to count headings and other notes.

Section One

Spoken Text

A

Aaron

by the hand of Moses and *A*. 694 18
Moses and *A* among his priests, 729 11
and *A* whom he had chosen. 740 6
and *A*, the holy one of the LORD. 743 4
O house of *A*, trust in the LORD, * 758 8
he will bless the house of *A*; 758 14
Let the house of *A* now proclaim, * 761 1
Upon the beard of *A*, * 787 1
O house of *A*, bless the LORD. 789 14
for Moses, the lawgiver, and *A*, the priest; 838 11

abandon

you did not *a* us to the power of death. 373 22
For you will not *a* me to the grave, * 600 17
The LORD will not *a* them to their hand, * 636 1
For the LORD will not *a* his people, * 723 21
do not *a* the works of your hands. 793 21

abhor

the bloodthirsty and deceitful, O LORD, you *a*. 589 2
For he does not despise nor *a* the poor 612 1
he does not *a* that which is evil. 632 11
all paths of falsehood I *a*. 774 4
As for lies, I hate and *a* them, * 777 5

abhored

you have made me to be *a* by them; * 712 18
and he *a* his inheritance. 745 5
They *a* all manner of food * 747 17

abhors

but those who delight in violence he *a*. 596 20

abide

a in his presence and rejoice 171 13
to cleave to those who *a* 182 9
Grant us during our earthly pilgrimage to *a* 198 25
who hast given the Holy Spirit to *a* with us for ever: 204 9
a in his presence and rejoice 223 7
during our earthly pilgrimage to *a* in their fellowship, 250 10
you have given the Holy Spirit to *a* with us for ever: 255 7
Jesus said, "*a* in me, as I in you. 397 7
neither can you, unless you *a* in me. 397 9
so have I loved you; *a* in my love." 397 12
Go (or *a*) in peace, and pray for me, a sinner. 448 14
Go (or *a*) in peace. The Lord has put away all 451 19
O Lord, who may *a* it? 474 6
who may *a* upon your holy hill? 599 5
a haughty look and a proud heart I cannot *a*. 730 19
may thy peace which passeth understanding *a* 830 17

abides

a under the shadow of the Almighty. 129 22
he *a* with his Church on earth, 226 4
Whoever eats my flesh and drinks my blood *a* in me, 397 5
cannot bear fruit by itself, unless it *a* in the vine, 397 8
and the place where your glory *a*. 616 23
a under the shadow of the Almighty. 719 11
you established the earth, and it *a*. 770 23

abideth

he *a* with his Church on earth, 174 11

abiding

the *a* witness in the sky.'" 716 16
grant them a sense of your *a* presence 823 6

Abiram

and covered the company of *A*. 743 6

ablaze

like the flame that sets mountains *a*. 707 6

able

without thee we are not *a* to please 182 1
without you we are not *a* to please you, 233 14
we are *a* to triumph over every evil, 346 6
By his grace we are *a* to triumph over every evil, 379 2
a stronger and more *a* minister of Christ? 532 7
they are cast down and shall not be *a* to rise. 633 4
but is he *a* to give bread or to provide meat 696 15
Send us honest and *a* leaders. 825 10
to know Christ and be *a* to follow him. 859 4

abolish

and to *a* poverty and crime. 839 18

abominable

All are corrupt and commit *a* acts; 598 13
All are corrupt and commit *a* acts; 658 22

abound

our joy may *a* in the morning as we celebrate 134 3

abounding

thine *a* grace may increase among us; 71 8
slow to anger and *a* in steadfast love, 76 15
long-suffering, and *a* in mercy. 91 6
that in companionship with one another your *a* grace 125 3

above

seek those things which are *a*, 39 14
and a great King *a* all gods. 44 15
O ye waters that be *a* the firmament, 47 10
praised and exalted *a* all for ever. 49 10
but *a* all for thine inestimable love 58 21
but *a* all for thine inestimable love 71 17
seek the things that are *a*, 77 13
and a great King *a* all gods. 82 10
O heavens and all waters *a* the heavens. 88 10
but *a* all for your immeasurable love 101 13
but *a* all for your immeasurable love 125 11
The Lord is high *a* all nations, * 138 7
and his glory *a* the heavens. 138 8
and a great King *a* all gods. 146 6
loving thee in all things and *a* all things, 174 4
Christ ascended far *a* all heavens 174 9
loving you in all things and *a* all things, 225 16
Christ ascended far *a* all heavens 226 2
likeness of any thing that is in heaven *a*, 318 2
thou art exalted as head *a* all. 344 11
and *a* all in the Word made flesh, Jesus, 368 4
For the peace from *a*, 383 3
a mine enemies round about me. 477 24
your majesty is praised *a* the heavens. 592 10

your judgments are far *a* out of their sight; * 595 2
my good *a* all other." 599 21
you exalted me *a* those who rose against me; * 606 8
A all, keep your servant from presumptuous sins; 607 24
a my enemies round about me. 618 6
The LORD sits enthroned *a* the flood; * 620 25
with the oil of gladness *a* your fellows. 648 5
He calls the heavens and the earth from *a* * 654 9
Exalt yourself *a* the heavens, O God, * 664 8
Exalt yourself *a* the heavens, O God, * 664 19
So he commanded the clouds *a* * 696 22
and a great King *a* all gods. 724 19
you are exalted far *a* all gods. 727 16
he is high *a* all peoples. 729 2
For as the heavens are high *a* the earth, * 734 3
You lay the beams of your chambers in the waters *a*; * 735 6
Exalt yourself *a* the heavens, O God, * 750 3
The LORD is high *a* all nations, * 756 8
and his glory *a* the heavens. 756 9
and that our Lord is *a* all gods. 788 11
if I do not set Jerusalem *a* my highest joy. 792 14
and your word *a* all things. 793 7
and you waters *a* the heavens. 806 2
you are exalted as head *a* all. 822 16
A all, we thank you for your Son Jesus Christ; 836 12
A all, we give you thanks for the great mercies 837 21

Abraham

A and his seed for ever. 50 19
oath which he swore to our forefather *A*, * 51 5
A and his seed for ever. 65 22
God of *A*, Isaac, and Jacob, 90 18
to *A* and his children for ever. 92 15
This was the oath he swore to our father *A*, * 92 27
to *A* and his children for ever. 119 21
to see fulfilled your promise to our father *A*; 289 9
numbered among the offspring of *A*, and rejoice in 289 17
Lord God of our Fathers; God of *A*, Isaac, and 372 1
to *A* and his children for ever. 442 10
heirs of the covenant of *A*, 520 16
with the people of the God of *A*. 650 23
O offspring of *A* his servant, * 738 11
The covenant he made with *A*, * 738 17
his holy word and *A* his servant. 741 10
for *A*, the father of believers, 838 10

abroad

Shed *a* this gift throughout the world 175 10
Shed *a* this gift throughout the world 227 3
and shall spread *a* like a cedar of Lebanon. 721 22
So mightily spread *a* your Spirit, 815 24
our armed forces at home and *a*. 823 3

absent

those who are *a*, that we may be delivered from 391 2
those whom we love, now *a* from us. 830 21

absolution

The Almighty and merciful Lord grant you *a* 42 11
The Almighty and merciful Lord grant you *a* 63 14
was put in mind of the message of pardon and *a* 265 7
the *a* and remission of their sins. 269 7
receive the benefit of *a*, and spiritual counsel 317 14
The Almighty and merciful Lord grant you *a* 321 14
For the *a* and remission of our sins 385 4
and ask you for counsel, direction, and *a*. 447 11
assurance of pardon and the grace of *a*. 861 12

absolve

a all sinners who truly repent and believe in him, 448 2
authority committed to me, I *a* you 448 4
to forgive sins, *a* you through my ministry 448 9
to forgive sins, *a* you through my ministry 451 8
a all sinners who truly repent and believe in him, 451 12
authority committed to me, I *a* you 451 14

absolves

He pardons and *a* all those who truly 269 8

abundance

Pour down upon us the *a* 182 20
Pour upon us the *a* 234 14
and for an *a* of the fruits 384 11
pour out the *a* of your blessing upon this 430 15
They feast upon the *a* of your house; * 632 20
they will delight in *a* of peace. 634 6
there shall be *a* of peace till the moon shall 685 22
May there be *a* of grain on the earth, 686 17
nor remember the *a* of your love; * 742 12

abundant

that *a* life which thou hast manifested 164 7
that *a* life which you have made known 216 2
that they may bring forth *a* fruit 290 11
grateful enjoyment of your *a* creation, 840 12

abundantly

Give *a* to all pastors the gifts 197 6
Give *a* to all pastors the gifts 248 17
has poured his gifts *a* upon your people, 533 7
You visit the earth and water it *a*; 673 4

abuse

that no one may suffer from our *a* of them, 827 20

abyss

in dark places, and in the *a*. 712 14

accept

A, O LORD, the willing tribute of my lips, * 104 3
Mercifully *a* our prayers; 164 12
Mercifully *a* our prayers; 216 7
Give us grace to *a* 220 15
A our repentance, Lord, for the wrongs we have done: 268 16
A our repentance, Lord. 268 19
Holy Father, *a* our evening sacrifice, 287 23
Do you turn to Jesus Christ and *a* him 302 16
A this our sacrifice of praise and thanksgiving; 335 25
yet we beseech thee to *a* this our bounden duty 336 10
desire thy fatherly goodness to *a* this 342 21
A these prayers and praises, Father, 372 10
A and fulfill our petitions, 394 5
Mercifully *a* the prayers of your people, 394 10
O Lord our God, *a* the fervent prayers 395 3
A, O Lord, our sacrifice of praise, 405 13
Mercifully *a* our prayers, and grant to your servant 458 12
and gracefully *a* your healing 461 3
A our prayers on behalf of thy servant 470 1

A our prayers on behalf of your servant 493 10
Will you *a* this call and fulfill this trust 518 1
A this Bible, and be among us 561 1
A us now, as we dedicate this place 568 8
A our prayers and intercessions 572 10
A and bless all we have done, 573 4
A here the continual recalling 574 3
and *a* the work of our hands, 578 5
and *a* your burnt sacrifice; 608 6
A, O LORD, the willing tribute of my lips, * 772 9
A their responsibilities to their fellow citizens, 822 11
and the willingness to *a* help; 830 4
A, O Lord, our thanks and praise for all 836 1
benefits of true freedom and gladly *a* its disciplines. 839 25
repent of our sins and *a* Jesus as our Lord and Savior. 858 23

acceptable

be always *a* in thy sight, O Lord, 40 14
be *a* in your sight, O Lord, 78 13
that we may be made an holy temple *a* unto thee; 179 1
intercessions are *a* through the Spirit, 199 10
that we may be made a holy temple *a* to you; 230 16
Jesus Christ, in whom all our intercessions are *a* 250 19
as a living sacrifice, holy and *a* to God, 343 15
that we may be *a* through him, 369 7
as a living sacrifice, holy and *a* to God, 376 11
intercessions are *a* through the Spirit, 395 23
In all things may he present before you the *a* 521 14
offer spiritual sacrifices *a* to you; 534 2
Be *a* to you, O Lord our God. 571 6
the meditation of my heart be *a* in your sight, * 607 29

accepted

you have graciously *a* us as living members 365 10
you have graciously *a* the ministry 520 18

accepting

and bear what he has to bear; that, *a* your healing 459 13

accepts

the LORD *a* my prayer. 590 17

acclaim

You are the Lord: we *a* you; 95 16
voice to every creature under heaven, we *a* you, 373 10
We *a* you, holy Lord, glorious in power. 373 17

acclaiming

their trust in you by *a* your election. 517 2

acclaims

Throughout the world the holy Church *a* you; 95 26

accomplish

But it will *a* that which I have purposed, * 87 7
with free hearts *a* those things 177 6
both in mind and body, may *a* with free hearts 229 1
grace and power faithfully to *a* them; 231 7
A in us the work of your salvation, 268 29
confusion to *a* your purposes on earth; 815 18
courage to pursue it and the grace to *a* it; 818 6

accomplishments

and for leading us to *a* which satisfy 836 8

accord

with one *a* to make our common supplication 59 13
with one *a* to make our common supplication 72 10
with one *a* to make our common supplication to you; 102 2
with one *a* to make our common supplication to you; 126 2
when they are in *a* with the Scriptures. 853 4

accordance

in *a* with your great mercy, * 91 23
that we may use our liberty in *a* 207 4
a with your gracious will; 258 5
in *a* with the Scriptures; 327 7
in *a* with the Scriptures; 358 23
and in *a* with the purposes for which it 423 15
united in marriage lawfully, and in *a* with God's 424 6
in *a* with the Scriptures; 519 26
Has he been selected in *a* with the canons 526 4
a with the canons of this Church, obey 526 11
in *a* with the Scriptures; 530 17
a with its precepts. 531 10
a with the teachings of Christ, 532 21
Has he been selected in *a* with the canons 538 4
a with the canons of this Church, obey 538 11
in *a* with the Scriptures; 542 17
a with the teachings of Christ, 544 9
and relented in *a* with his great mercy. 745 16
making provision for its future in *a* 828 20
we are called to enjoy it and to care for it in *a* 846 11

according

a to thy promises declared unto mankind 42 6
a to thy word; 51 24
a to thy promises declared unto mankind 63 9
a to thy word; 66 2
preserve my life, O LORD, *a* to your word. 104 2
direct and rule us *a* to your will, 107 5
neither reward us *a* to our sins. 148 10
a to thy holy Word, 152 6
which we have asked faithfully *a* to thy will, 153 23
Mercifully give us faith to perceive that, *a* to 174 10
may by thee be enabled to live *a* to thy 180 16
may truly repent *a* to his preaching; 190 5
Mercifully give us faith to perceive that, *a* to 226 3
be enabled to live *a* to your will; 232 8
may truly repent *a* to his preaching; 241 14
Have mercy on me, O God, *a* to your 266 1
Passion of our Lord Jesus Christ *a* to ________. 272 15
The Passion of our Lord Jesus Christ *a* to John. 277 1
for people everywhere *a* to their 277 7
Gospel of our Lord Jesus Christ *a* to ________. 300 6
a to thy promises declared unto mankind 321 9
Gospel of our Lord Jesus Christ *a* to________. 326 2
and the third day he rose again *a* to the Scriptures, 328 7
Wherefore, O Lord and heavenly Father, *a* to the 335 8
a to thy Son our Savior 335 21
Through Jesus Christ our Lord; *a* to whose true 347 6
Gospel of our Lord Jesus Christ *a* to ________. 357 9
Therefore, *a* to his command, O Father, 368 19
Gospel of our Lord Jesus Christ *a* to ________. 414 6
Gospel of our Lord Jesus Christ *a* to ________. 426 2
cherish, till death do us part, *a* to God's holy 436 9
may live faithfully *a* to your will 444 5

O God, *a* to your loving-kindness; 449 1
heal me *a* to your will; 461 9
Remember me, O LORD, *a* to the favor 478 17
a to John. 479 21
into the arms of thy mercy, and remember him *a* 481 18
Remember thy servant, O Lord, *a* to the favor 488 21
Gospel of our Lord Jesus Christ *a* to John. 495 2
Gospel of our Lord Jesus Christ *a* to ________. 516 6
Gospel of our Lord Jesus Christ *a* to ________. 529 5
Gospel of our Lord Jesus Christ *a* to ________. 541 5
Give judgment for me *a* to my 591 12
and *a* to my innocence, O Most High. 591 14
Therefore the LORD rewarded me *a* to my 604 11
remember me *a* to your love, 615 2
Repay them *a* to their deeds, * 619 14
and *a* to the wickedness of their actions. 619 15
A to the work of their hands repay them, * 619 16
a to your righteousness; * 631 19
Have mercy on me, O God, *a* to your 656 5
for you repay everyone *a* to his deeds. 670 11
and do not walk *a* to my judgments; 716 2
He has not dealt with us *a* to our sins, * 734 1
nor rewarded us *a* to our wickedness. 734 2
To instruct his princes *a* to his will * 739 21
oh, deal with me *a* to your Name; * 752 17
give me life *a* to your word. 765 10
strengthen me *a* to your word. 765 16
and your salvation, *a* to your promise. 766 18
be merciful to me *a* to your promise. 768 4
with your servant, *a* to your word. 768 18
preserve my life, O LORD, *a* to your word. 772 8
Sustain me *a* to your promise, 773 5
Deal with your servant *a* to your loving-kindness * 773 21
Hear my voice, O LORD, *a* to your loving-kindness; * 776 1
a to your judgments, give me life. 776 2
a to your promise, give me life. 776 12
preserve my life, *a* to your judgments. 776 16
give me understanding, *a* to your word. 777 18
deliver me, *a* to your promise. 777 20
relieve them *a* to their several necessities, 815 10
fashion our lives *a* to the example 817 15
and amendment of life *a* to your will, 826 19
which we have faithfully asked *a* to thy will, 834 5
may live in this world *a* to thy will, 841 11
and, *a* to the gifts given them, to carry on 855 17
and wine, given and received *a* to Christ's 859 20

accordingly

set it forth, and show it *a*, 150 8
those who *a* have a good understanding; 755 2

accords

Help us to ask only what *a* with your will; 394 13

account

remembering the *a* that we must one day give, 208 12
remembering the *a* that we must one day give, 259 14
what happens to me here is of little *a* 461 10
of little *a*, and sojourners in the land, 739 2
I am small and of little *a*, * 775 7
to whom we must *a* for all our powers 822 23
remembering the *a* which we must 827 3

accounted

without which whoever lives is *a* 216 16
we may be *a* worthy to enter 280 11
we are *a* as sheep for the slaughter. 647 2

accusation

"I have made my *a*; * 655 24

accuse

I do not *a* you because of your sacrifices; * 654 19
He will not always *a* us, * 733 25
Despite my love, they *a* me; * 751 4

accused

when they are *a*, save them 823 10

accuser

and let an *a* stand at his right hand. 751 9

accusers

Let this be the recompense from the LORD to my *a*, * 752 14
Let my *a* be clothed with disgrace * 753 6

acknowledge

we *a* thee to be the Lord. 52 23
all the world doth *a* thee, 53 7
a the glory of the eternal Trinity, 176 3
a the glory of the eternal Trinity, 228 3
And *a* your sins before 317 4
We *a* one baptism for the forgiveness of sins. 327 17
I *a* one Baptism for the remission of sins; 328 19
We *a* and bewail our manifold sins 331 4
the fruit of lips that *a* his Name. 344 2
We *a* one baptism for the forgiveness of sins. 359 8
the fruit of lips that *a* his Name. 376 18
to recognize and *a* their fault, 429 15
A, we humbly beseech you, a sheep 465 2
A, we humbly beseech thee, a sheep 483 7
A, we humbly beseech you, a sheep 499 14
We *a* one baptism for the forgiveness of sins. 520 8
We *a* one baptism for the forgiveness of sins. 530 27
We *a* one baptism for the forgiveness of sins. 542 27
that lead us to *a* our dependence on you alone. 836 11
to *a* the holiness of God, to hear God's Word, 857 23

acknowledged

Then I *a* my sin to you, * 625 7

acknowledging

worthily lamenting our sins and *a* 166 4
lamenting our sins and *a* 217 17
lamenting our sins and *a* 264 5

acquaintance

a dismay to those of my *a*; * 623 12

acquainted

and art *a* with all my ways. 474 22
and are *a* with all my ways. 794 5

across

surely, you will strike all my enemies *a* the face, 587 16

act

but repays to the full those who *a* haughtily. 624 20
Those who *a* deceitfully shall not dwell in my house, * 730 24

Happy are those who *a* with justice * 742 1
those who *a* accordingly have a good understanding; 755 2
It is time for you to *a*, O LORD, * 773 25
Redemption is the *a* of God which sets us free 849 5
We mean that by God's own *a*, his divine Son 849 28
to proclaim the Word of God; to *a* in Christ's name 855 25

acted

On this day the Lord has *a;* we will rejoice 77 8
On this day the LORD has *a;* * 762 19

acting

he has left off *a* wisely and doing good. 632 8

action

an effective example in word and *a*, 523 6
an effective example in word and *a*, 535 6
an effective example in word and *a*, 547 2
an effective example in word and *a*, 564 6

actions

a for the welfare and peace of the world. 329 21
and according to the wickedness of their *a*. 619 15
They provoked him to anger with their *a*, * 744 5
Thus they were polluted by their *a* * 745 1

activity

Is God's *a* limited to these rites? 861 17

acts

of those mighty *a*, whereby you have given us life 270 6
It is right to praise you, Almighty God, for the *a* 271 5
Who can express the noble *a* of the LORD, * 478 13
Holy Scripture. Here we read about your mighty *a* 570 24
The LORD is known by his *a* of justice; * 594 9
All are corrupt and commit abominable *a*; 598 13
All are corrupt and commit abominable *a*; 658 22
My mouth shall recount your mighty *a* 684 9
I will meditate on all your *a* * 693 24
For you have made me glad by your *a*, O LORD; * 721 3
Who can declare the mighty *a* of the LORD * 741 21
and tell of his *a* with shouts of joy. 747 26
They shall speak of the might of your wondrous *a*, * 801 22
Praise him for his mighty *a;* * 808 1

Adam

For as in *A* all die, * 46 17
For as in *A* all die, * 83 25
paid for us the debt of *A*'s sin, 287 4

add

sense of his weakness may *a* strength 460 2
A length of days to the king's life; * 668 24
and *a* to the pain of those whom you have pierced. 681 17

added

a to your household, as we grow in grace 569 6

adder

You shall tread upon the lion and *a*; * 130 23
they are like the deaf *a* which stops its ears, 665 2
You shall tread upon the lion and *a*; * 720 11
a's poison is under their lips. 796 6

addiction

with compassion upon all who through *a* have lost 831 19

additional

The Apocrypha is a collection of *a* books 853 20

administer

and rightly and duly *a* thy holy Sacraments. 329 12
and rightly *a* the sacraments of 534 3
preach the Word of God and to *a* his holy 534 11
and grant that I may faithfully *a* your 563 2
and impartially *a* the law in the fear 821 12
proclaim the Gospel; to *a* the sacraments; 856 5

administered

faithfully *a* and faithfully received. 817 14

administration

to celebrate and to provide for the *a* 517 8
to share in the *a* of Holy Baptism 531 14
that, by faithful *a* and wise laws, 822 26
and the *a* of the sacraments. 856 11

administrative

Mayors of Cities, and to all in *a* 821 20

admirable

pure, lovable and gracious, excellent and *a*, 443 28

admonish

Hear, O my people, and I will *a* you: * 704 17

admonishes

He who *a* the nations, will he not punish? * 723 13

ado

The nations make much *a*, 649 15

adopted

beings might be *a* as children of God, 850 3

adopting

a us as your own children, 311 16

adoption

children by *a* and grace, 161 10
that Spirit of *a* which is given 170 18
your children by *a* and grace, 213 4
Spirit of *a* which is given 222 10
Spirit of *a* which is given 295 10
As God has made us his children by *a* and grace, 441 5
For making us your children by *a* and grace, 578 16

adopts

May God the Father, who by Baptism *a* us 445 3
Holy Baptism is the sacrament by which God *a* 858 9

adorable

thine *a*, true, and only Son, 53 9

adoration

The principal kinds of prayer are *a*, 856 27
What is *a*? 857 1
A is the lifting up 857 2

adore

O come, let us *a* him. 43 1
O God and Father of all, whom the whole heavens *a*: 70 15
Come let us *a* him. 80 10

O God and Father of all, whom the whole heavens *a*: 124 12
We *a* you, O Christ, and we bless you, 281 15
We *a* you, O Christ, and we bless you, 282 1

adorn

you *a* him with glory and honor; 592 18

adorned

an image of the heavenly Jerusalem, *a* as a bride 349 2
an image of the heavenly Jerusalem, *a* as a bride 381 17
Jesus Christ *a* this manner of life 423 5
that they may be *a* with all Christian virtues, 549 13
a with the gold of Ophir. 648 10

adornment

for the building (rebuilding, or *a*) 567 4

adorns

and holiness *a* your house, O Lord, 722 16
and *a* the poor with victory. 807 9

adulterers

and you cast in your lot with *a*. 655 17

adultery

Thou shalt not commit *a*. 318 19
You shall not commit *a*. 350 15

adversaries

may not fear the power of any *a*; 57 5
may not fear the power of any *a*; 99 24
Lord, how many *a* I have! * 587 3
You have set up a stronghold against your *a*, * 592 11
you have cast down my *a* beneath me; 605 19
it was they, my foes and my *a*, 617 12
Deliver me not into the hand of my *a*, * 618 23
Through you we pushed back our *a*; * 645 20
Surely, you gave us victory over our *a* * 645 25
my *a* are all in your sight." 681 2
Your *a* roared in your holy place; * 689 16
Forget not the clamor of your *a*, * 691 1

adversary

Your *a* the devil prowls 132 8
You have made us fall back before our *a*, * 646 5
For had it been an *a* who taunted me, 661 6
How long, O God, will the *a* scoff? * 690 4
his glory into the *a*'s hand. 700 2

adversities

from all *a* which may happen to the body, 167 6
from all *a* which may happen to the body, 218 16
You have showed me great troubles and *a*, * 684 23

adversity

fall into sin, not be overcome by *a*; 100 4
fall into sin, not be overcome by *a*; 137 17
sickness, or any other *a*. 329 29
given one another in prosperity and *a*; 423 11
Look upon my *a* and misery * 615 24
and the years in which we suffered *a*. 719 4
through stress of *a* and sorrow, 749 8
patient in suffering and faithful in *a*, 837 15

advice

absolution, and spiritual counsel and *a*; 317 14

advocate

and the Holy Spirit, *a* and guide. 95 29
our only Mediator and *A*, Jesus Christ our Lord. 155 13
our only Mediator and *A*. 330 8
If any man sin, we have an *A* with the Father, 332 15
our only Mediator and *A*. 395 16
If any man sin, we have an *A* with the Father, 450 1
our only Mediator and *A*. 487 23
through Jesus Christ, our Mediator and *A*. 572 12
Grant this, O Lord, for the honor of our *A* 817 8

afar

my neighbors stand *a* off. 637 19
he perceives the haughty from *a*. 793 15
you discern my thoughts from *a*. 794 3

affairs

and to manage their *a* with justice. 755 14

affecteth

that all we do *a*, for good or ill, 210 11

affection

and united to one another with pure *a*; 179 7
and united to one another with pure *a*; 231 1
Give them such fulfillment of their mutual *a* 429 23
may live together in love and *a*; 441 9
Knit together in constant *a* 829 3

affectioned

that we may evermore be kindly *a* 829 7

affections

From all inordinate and sinful *a*; 149 5
the unruly wills and *a* of sinful men: 167 16
the unruly wills and *a* of sinners: 219 7
with steadfast thoughts and kindled *a* 833 22

affects

that all we do *a*, for good or ill, 261 16

affirm

are penitent for their sins, and are ready to *a* 860 25

affirmed

My brother, the people have chosen you and have *a* 517 1

afflict

and *a* your chosen nation. 723 4
thou dost not willingly *a* or grieve 831 12

afflicted

wherewith the Lord hath *a* me. 39 6
soothe the suffering, pity the *a*, 71 4
whom the Lord has *a*. 77 5
soothe the suffering, pity the *a*, 124 20
soothe the suffering, pity the *a*, 134 9
Let us pray for all who suffer and are *a* 279 3
he will not forget the cry of the *a*. 593 24
do not forget the *a*. 595 20
Their aim is to confound the plans of the *a*, * 598 26
Though I am poor and *a*, * 641 19
As for me, I am *a* and in pain; * 681 22
The *a* shall see and be glad; * 682 1
they are not *a* as others are; 687 10
I have been *a* all day long, * 688 5

by the measure of the days that you *a* us * 719 3
they were *a* because of their sins. 747 16
Before I was *a* I went astray, * 768 21
It is good for me that I have been *a*, * 769 5
and that in faithfulness you have *a* me. 769 15
all those who are in any ways *a* 815 7

affliction

and give him patience under his *a*. 458 6
may be unto us a comfort in *a*, 482 5
Sacrament may be to us a comfort in *a*, 498 16
for you have seen my *a*; 622 23
my strength fails me because of *a*, 623 8
I called in my *a* and the LORD heard me * 628 5
My friends and companions draw back from my *a*; * 637 18
Take your *a* from me; * 639 15
and forgotten our *a* and oppression? 647 6
I should have perished in my *a*. 771 4
Behold my *a* and deliver me, * 776 9

afflictions

to comfort us in all our *a*, 107 6
Graciously behold our *a*. 154 16
your mercy present with them in all their *a*; 279 17
happy issue out of all their *a*. 815 12

aflame

Grant that we also may be *a* with the spirit 198 11
Grant that we also may be *a* with the spirit 249 20

afraid

I will trust in him and not be *a*. 86 2
You shall not be *a* of any terror by night, * 130 6
those things whereof our conscience is *a*, 183 2
those things of which our conscience is *a*, 234 15
though at times he may be *a*, he yet may 459 10
and are *a* at thy wrathful indignation. 472 24
of whom then shall I be *a*? 477 15
and the torrents of oblivion made me *a*. 602 15
of whom then shall I be *a*? 617 10
yet my heart shall not be *a*; 617 15
Why should I be *a* in evil days, * 652 13
Whenever I am *a*, * 662 17
in God I trust and will not be *a*, * 662 20
in God I trust and will not be *a*, * 663 12
they shoot without warning and are not *a*. 671 17
the earth was *a* and was still; 692 17
He led them to safety, and they were not *a*; * 699 11
we are *a* because of your wrathful indignation. 718 14
You shall not be *a* of any terror by night, * 719 20
the earth sees it and is *a*. 727 4
because they were *a* of them. 741 2
They will not be *a* of any evil rumors; * 755 17
I am *a* of your judgments. 773 14

after

Jesus said, "Whosoever will come *a* me, 38 24
a that the Holy Ghost is come upon you; 39 18
who *a* the creation of the world didst rest 56 11
people everywhere may seek *a* thee and find thee; 58 4
teacheth me, night *a* night. 61 11
and awake up *a* thy likeness; 69 10
Jesus said, "If anyone would come *a* me, 76 23
who *a* the creation of the world rested · 99 6
people everywhere may seek *a* you and find you; 100 20
my heart teaches me, night *a* night. 115 11
and run *a* false gods?" 128 13
and diligently to live *a* thy commandments, 150 23
and *a* his example constantly speak the truth, 190 5
and we pray that, *a* his example, 192 21
that *a* the example of thy servant James the Just, 193 18
people everywhere may seek *a* thee and find thee, 206 12
a his example, we may with ready wills 244 9
people everywhere may seek *a* you and find you, 257 8
concern for those who come *a* us, 268 25
Likewise, *a* supper, he took the cup; 335 3
Likewise, *a* supper, he took the cup; 342 5
a his glorious resurrection manifestly appeared 347 2
who *a* his resurrection sent forth his apostles 348 12
A supper he took the cup of wine; 363 1
A supper he took the cup of wine; 368 14
A supper, he took the cup of wine, 371 14
A supper he took the cup of wine; 374 19
A his glorious resurrection he openly appeared 379 21
who *a* his resurrection sent forth his apostles 381 6
A supper, he took the cup of wine, 403 8
A supper he took the cup of wine; 405 6
so longeth my soul *a* thee, O God. 471 2
A my awaking, he will raise me up; 491 9
and may thirst *a* righteousness, 548 22
and run *a* false gods?" 588 3
and grief in my heart, day *a* day? * 598 2
if there is one who seeks *a* God. 598 17
But those who run *a* other gods * 600 3
my heart teaches me, night *a* night. 600 12
Let those who seek *a* my life be shamed and humbled; 629 20
Those who seek *a* my life lay snares for me; * 637 20
who seek *a* my life to destroy it; * 641 11
a her the bridesmaids follow in procession. 648 20
that you may tell those who come *a*. 652 3
and leave their wealth to those who come *a* them. 652 25
though they call the lands *a* their own names. 653 3
if there is one who seeks *a* God. 659 3
But it was you, a man *a* my own heart, * 661 10
The singers go before, musicians follow *a*, * 678 7
Trample down those who lust *a* silver; * 678 20
go *a* him and seize him; * 683 23
The lions roar *a* their prey * 736 19
"You are a priest for ever *a* the order of Melchizedek." 753 20
you and your children *a* you. 758 18
you is better than chasing *a* selfish goals. 829 17
For all valiant seekers *a* truth, liberty, and justice, 837 17

afterwards

nd *a* receive me with glory. 688 26

against

"Father, I have sinned *a* heaven, 38 18
though we have rebelled *a* him; 38 21
we have offended *a* thy holy laws, 41 20
as we forgive those who trespass *a* us. 54 21
we have offended *a* thy holy laws, 63 1
as we forgive those who trespass *a* us. 67 11
"Father, I have sinned *a* heaven and before you; 76 17
we have rebelled *a* him and have not obeyed 76 20
Let us confess our sins *a* God and our neighbor. 79 9
we confess that we have sinned *a* you 79 11

who trespass *a* us. 97 12
who trespass *a* us. 106 22
Let us confess our sins *a* God and our neighbor. 116 11
we confess that we have sinned *a* you 116 13
who trespass *a* us. 121 12
We have sinned *a* you, 127 7
lest you dash your foot *a* a stone. 130 22
who trespass *a* us. 133 4
as we forgive those who trespass *a* us. 153 13
Grant us grace fearlessly to contend *a* evil 209 2
Grant us grace fearlessly to contend *a* evil 260 9
A you only have I sinned * 266 8
of wickedness that rebel *a* God? 302 9
who trespass *a* us. 311 9
Thou shalt not bear false witness *a* thy neighbor. 318 25
we confess that we have sinned *a* thee 320 11
we have offended *a* thy holy laws, 321 1
by thought, word, and deed, *a* thy divine Majesty, 331 7
provoking most justly thy wrath and indignation *a* us. 331 8
we confess that we have sinned *a* thee 331 22
as we forgive those who trespass *a* us. 336 25
thy brother hath aught *a* thee, 343 18
Let us confess our sins *a* God and our neighbor. 352 9
we confess that we have sinned *a* you 352 11
Let us confess our sins *a* God and our neighbor. 360 1
we confess that we have sinned *a* you 360 3
who trespass *a* us. 364 9
But we turned *a* you, and betrayed 370 14
and we turned *a* one another. 370 15
that your brother has something *a* you, 376 14
we confess that we have sinned *a* you 397 20
who trespass *a* us. 398 20
who trespass *a* us. 428 16
Do you, then, forgive those who have sinned *a* you? 451 1
we confess that we have sinned *a* you 454 2
who trespass *a* us. 464 12
as we forgive those who trespass *a* us. 486 2
who trespass *a* us. 502 9
a the LORD and *a* his Anointed? 586 5
how many there are who rise up *a* me! 587 4
who set themselves *a* me all around. 587 14
for they have rebelled *a* you. 589 16
rise up *a* the fury of my enemies. 591 7
You have set up a stronghold *a* your adversaries, * 592 11
nor does he take a bribe *a* the innocent. 599 16
from those who rise up *a* them. 601 13
and have not offended *a* my God; 604 6
you exalted me above those who rose *a* me; * 606 8
Though they intend evil *a* you 609 20
and they bear a violent hatred *a* me. 615 27
Though an army should encamp *a* me, * 617 14
And though war should rise up *a* me, * 617 16
for false witnesses have risen up *a* me, 618 24
they put their head together *a* me; 623 18
Let the lying lips be silenced which speak *a* 624 1
The face of the LORD is *a* those who do evil, * 628 25
Draw the sword and bar the way *a* those 629 17
Malicious witnesses rise up *a* me; * 630 13
they gathered *a* me; * 630 24
but invent deceitful schemes *a* the quiet 631 10
let those who boast *a* me be clothed 631 25
The wicked plot *a* the righteous * 634 7
heal me, for I have sinned *a* you." 642 7
and devise evil *a* me. 642 14
has lifted up his heel and turned *a* me. 642 19
and defend my cause *a* an ungodly people; * 644 15
rose up *a* us. 645 22
"O Israel, I will bear witness *a* you; * 654 17
A you only have I sinned * 656 12
a the godly all day long? 657 24
For the arrogant have risen up *a* me, 659 21
and are set *a* me in fury. 660 12
or had it been an enemy who vaunted himself *a* me, 661 8
the battle waged *a* me; * 661 23
companion stretched forth his hand *a* his comrade; * 661 28
truly there are many who fight *a* me, O Most High. 662 16
protect me from those who rise up *a* me. 665 19
how the mighty gather together *a* me; * 665 23
Grant us your help *a* the enemy, * 668 8
a strong tower *a* the enemy. 668 18
let no rebel rise up *a* him. 674 8
Those who sit at the gate murmur *a* me, * 680 11
For my enemies are talking *a* me, * 683 20
Let those who set themselves *a* me be put to shame 684 3
They set their mouths *a* the heavens, * 687 17
why is your wrath so hot *a* the sheep of your pasture? 689 10
the unending tumult of those who rise up *a* you. 691 2
But they went on sinning *a* him, * 696 7
rebelling in the desert *a* the Most High. 696 8
They railed *a* God and said, * 696 11
a fire was kindled *a* Jacob, 696 18
and his anger mounted *a* Israel; 696 19
So God's anger mounted *a* them; * 697 11
and was angered *a* his inheritance. 700 4
and turn my hand *a* their foes. 705 4
They take secret counsel *a* your people * 706 7
and plot *a* those whom you protect. 706 8
they have made an alliance *a* you: 706 13
The arrogant rise up *a* me, O God, 711 1
lest you dash your foot *a* a stone. 720 10
rise up *a* me. 721 20
Who rose up for me *a* the wicked? * 723 25
who took my part *a* the evildoers? 723 26
They conspire *a* the life of the just * 724 7
and those who scoff at me have taken an oath *a* me. 731 16
but the Egyptians rebelled *a* his words. 740 10
Fire blazed up *a* their company, * 743 7
So he lifted his hand *a* them, * 743 24
Therefore the wrath of the LORD was kindled *a* 745 3
Because they rebelled *a* the words of God * 747 3
Grant us your help *a* the enemy, * 750 19
the mouth of the deceitful, is opened *a* me. 750 25
and fight *a* me without a cause. 751 3
Set a wicked man *a* him, * 751 8
and to those who speak evil *a* me. 752 15
let those who rise up *a* me be put to shame, 753 4
that I may not sin *a* you. 764 6
Even though rulers sit and plot *a* me, * 765 5
when will you give judgment *a* those who 770 10
when enemies rose up *a* us; 781 4
but they have not prevailed *a* me." 784 4
a Pharaoh and all his servants. 788 20
a the people of Edom, * 792 16
and dashes them *a* the rock! 792 23

you stretch forth your hand *a* the fury of my enemies; 793 17
They speak despitefully *a* you; * 795 18
and do I not loathe those who rise up *a* you? 795 21
for my prayer is continually *a* their wicked deeds. 797 14
who can stand *a* his cold? 805 12
Because we rebel *a* God, 845 13

age

and his faithfulness endures from *a* to *a*. 83 9
and in the *a* to come life everlasting. 102 7
and in the *a* to come life everlasting. 126 7
and attain to the riches of the *a* to come; 198 5
and attain to the riches of the *a* to come; 249 15
in the *a* to come have life everlasting. 431 13
As he grows in *a*, may he grow in grace, 445 1
The days of our *a* are threescore years and ten; 473 3
Father, in every *a* you have spoken through the voices 571 9
and the designs of his heart from *a* to *a*. 626 22
Blessed be the Lord God of Israel, from *a* to *a*. 642 27
Do not cast me off in my old *a*; * 683 18
and show forth your praise from *a* to *a*. 702 11
will you prolong your anger from *a* to *a*? 709 4
from *a* to *a* my mouth will proclaim your faithfulness. 713 18
from *a* to *a* you are God. 718 3
They shall still bear fruit in old *a*; * 721 25
and his faithfulness endures from *a* to *a*. 730 6
and your Name from *a* to *a*. 731 24
your renown, O LORD, endures from *a* to *a*. 789 2
you proclaim your truth in every *a* 827 6
martyrs and saints in every *a* and in every land. 838 17

aged

For the *a* and infirm, 384 20

agents

those whom you chose as the *a* of your will. 571 1

ages

and yours is the glory to *a* of *a*. 91 26
O King of all the *a*. 94 13
be honor and glory throughout all *a*. 101 24
To you be glory for endless *a*. 113 8
to eternal life and to the *a* of *a*. 113 15
be honor and glory throughout all *a*. 125 22
even unto the end of the *a*; 174 12
even to the end of the *a*; 226 5
he saved his people in *a* past; 288 2
be with them always, even unto the end of the *a*. 348 14
saints who have found favor with you in *a* past. 375 24
be with them always, even to the end of the *a*. 381 8
the Holy Spirit, to the *a* of *a*. 498 7
Through the *a*, Almighty God has moved his people 567 1
now and for endless *a*. 574 9
your dominion endures throughout all *a*. 802 12

ago

your congregation that you purchased long *a*, * 689 11

agony

By thine *A* and Bloody Sweat; 149 22
willingly endured the *a* and shame of the cross 201 8
whose beloved Son willingly endured the *a* 252 12

agree

thy holy Name may *a* in the truth of thy holy Word, 329 7

aha

"*A*! we saw it with our own eyes." 631 13
"*A*! just what we want!" * 631 22
Let those who say "*A*!" and gloat 641 14
Let those who say to me "*A*!" and gloat 682 17

ahead

that they may have strength to meet the days *a* 481 11

aided

encouraged by their examples, *a* by their prayers, 489 19
encouraged by their examples, *a* by their prayers, 504 17

ailed

What *a* you, O sea, that you fled? * 757 5

aim

Their *a* is to confound the plans of the afflicted, * 598 26
and *a* your arrows at them. 609 24
and *a* their bitter words like arrows, 671 15

air

O all ye fowls of the *a*, bless ye the Lord; * 48 25
All birds of the *a*, glorify the Lord, * 89 12
For those who travel on land, on water, or in the *a* 384 17
The birds of the *a*, the fish of the sea, * 592 23
as food for the birds of the *a*, * 701 5
Beside them the birds of the *a* make their nests * 735 25

alarm

Yet I said in my *a*, 624 14

alien

an *a* to my mother's children. 680 4
upon an *a* soil? 792 9

alike

darkness and light to thee are both *a*. 62 8
darkness and light to you are both *a*. 110 10
darkness and light to you are both *a*. 116 4
the darkness and light to thee are both *a*. 475 17
caring *a* for young and 531 11
all *a* have turned bad; * 598 19
all *a* have turned bad; * 659 5
darkness and light to you are both *a*. 794 24

alive

but *a* unto God through Jesus Christ our Lord. 46 12
even so in Christ shall all be made *a*. 46 18
and *a* to God in Jesus Christ our Lord. 83 20
so also in Christ shall all be made *a*. 83 26
you were dead, and are now *a* in Christ 451 18
For if we have life, we are *a* in the Lord, 491 15
without a cause they have dug a pit to take me *a*. 630 4
The LORD preserves them and keeps them *a*, 642 1
let them go down *a* into the grave; * 661 15
Then would they have swallowed us up *a* * 781 5
and to keep *a* their joy in your creation; 829 20

all

and *a* flesh shall see it togaether. 37 6
great joy, which shall be to *a* people. 37 9
and to cleanse us from *a* unrighteousness, 38 12
A we like sheep have gone astray; 39 1
the Lord hath laid on him the iniquity of us *a*. 39 3
Is it nothing to you, *a* ye that pass by? 39 4

all

and in *a* Judaea, and in Samaria, 39 20
Their sound is gone out into *a* lands; 40 5
let *a* the earth keep silence 40 18
remission of *a* your sins, 42 12
and a great King above *a* gods. 44 15
In his hand are *a* the corners of the earth, * 44 16
O be joyful in the Lord *a* ye lands; * 45 11
For as in Adam *a* die, * 46 17
even so in Christ shall *a* be made alive. 46 18
O *a* ye works of the Lord, bless ye the Lord; * 47 5
O *a* ye powers of the Lord, bless ye the Lord; * 47 11
O *a* ye green things upon the earth, bless ye the Lord; 48 19
O ye whales and *a* that move in the waters, 48 23
O *a* ye fowls of the air, bless ye the Lord; * 48 25
O *a* ye beasts and cattle, bless ye the Lord; 48 26
praised and exalted above *a* for ever. 49 10
a generations shall call me blessed. 50 6
throughout *a* generations. 50 10
and from the hand of *a* that hate us; 51 2
a the days of our life. 51 10
which thou hast prepared before the face of *a* people, 51 26
A the earth doth worship thee, the Father everlasting. 52 24
To thee *a* Angels cry aloud, 52 25
the Heavens and *a* the Powers therein. 52 26
The holy Church throughout *a* the world 53 6
thou didst open the kingdom of heaven to *a* believers. 53 16
Give peace, O Lord, in *a* the world; 55 5
Thy saving health among *a* nations. 55 10
rest from *a* thy works and sanctify a day of rest 56 12
Grant that we, putting away *a* earthly anxieties, 56 13
Drive far from us *a* wrong desires, 56 20
Defend us, thy humble servants, in *a* assaults 57 3
that in *a* the cares and occupations of our life 57 16
for *a* members of thy holy Church, 57 22
who hast made of one blood *a* the peoples 58 1
pour out thy Spirit upon *a* flesh; 58 5
Almighty God, Father of *a* mercies 58 14
for *a* thy goodness and loving-kindness 58 17
to us and to *a* men. 58 18
and *a* the blessings of this life; 58 20
but above *a* for thine inestimable love 58 21
give us that due sense of *a* thy mercies, 59 2
in holiness and righteousness *a* our days; 59 8
be *a* honor and glory, world without end. 59 11
the fellowship of the Holy Ghost, be with us *a* 59 23
May the God of hope fill us with *a* joy and peace 60 1
Thou hast fixed *a* the boundaries of the earth; 61 8
remission of *a* your sins, 63 15
Thou art worthy at *a* times to be praised 64 7
and to be glorified through *a* the worlds. 64 9
a generations shall call me blessed. 65 9
throughout *a* generations. 65 13
which thou hast prepared before the face of *a* people, 66 4
Give peace, O Lord, in *a* the world; 67 20
Thy saving health among *a* nations. 68 2
the communion of [________ and] *a* thy saints, 68 23
entrusting one another and *a* our life to Christ, 68 24
O God, from whom *a* holy desires, *a* good counsels, 69 16
a just works do proceed: 69 17
defended from the fear of *a* enemies, 69 20
great mercy defend us from *a* perils and dangers 70 2
O God, who art the life of *a* who live, 70 4
beseech thy merciful protection *a* the night. 70 7
O God and Father of *a*, 70 15
Let the whole earth also worship thee, *a* nations obey 70 16
a tongues confess and bless thee, 70 17
and *a* for thy love's sake. 71 5
Almighty God, Father of *a* mercies, 71 10
for *a* thy goodness and loving-kindness 71 13
to us and to *a* men. 71 14
and *a* the blessings of this life; 71 16
but above *a* for thine inestimable love 71 17
give us that due sense of *a* thy mercies, 71 21
in holiness and righteousness *a* our days; 72 5
be *a* honor and glory, world without end. 72 8
the fellowship of the Holy Ghost, be with us *a* 72 20
May the God of hope fill us with *a* joy and peace 73 1
and *a* flesh shall see it together. 75 6
a great joy which will come to *a* the people; 75 9
and cleanse us from *a* unrighteousness. 76 11
A we like sheep have gone astray; 76 25
the Lord has laid on him the iniquity of us *a*. 77 2
Is it nothing to you, *a* you who pass by? 77 3
and in *a* Judea, and Samaria, 77 18
Their sound has gone out into *a* lands, 78 4
let *a* the earth keep silence 78 17
forgive you *a* your sins 80 1
strengthen you in *a* goodness, 80 2
and a great King above *a* gods. 82 10
Be joyful in the Lord, *a* you lands; * 82 20
The death that he died, he died to sin, once for *a*; * 83 17
For as in Adam *a* die, * 83 25
so also in Christ shall *a* be made alive. 83 26
and this is known in *a* the world. 86 12
and *a* your portals, Praise. 87 26
Glorify the Lord, *a* you works of the Lord, * 88 5
Glorify the Lord, you angels and *a* powers of the Lord, 88 9
O heavens and *a* waters above the heavens. 88 10
a winds and fire and heat. 88 14
and *a* that grows upon the earth, * 89 8
O whales and *a* that move in the waters. 89 11
A birds of the air, glorify the Lord, * 89 12
and *a* you flocks and herds. 89 15
and of *a* their righteous offspring: 90 19
with *a* their vast array. 90 21
A things quake with fear at your presence; * 91 1
But your merciful promise is beyond *a* measure; * 91 3
it surpasses *a* that our minds can fathom. 91 4
I will praise you without ceasing *a* the days of my life. 91 24
For *a* the powers of heaven sing your praises, * 91 25
From this day *a* generations will call me blessed: * 92 1
from the hands of *a* who hate us. 92 24
a the days of our life. 92 31
whom you have prepared for *a* the world to see: 93 15
O King of *a* the ages. 94 13
A creation worships you. 95 18
To you *a* angels, *a* the powers of heaven, 95 19
your true and only Son, worthy of *a* worship, 95 28
and opened the kingdom of heaven to *a* believers. 96 6
Give peace, O Lord, in *a* the world; 97 22
Your saving health among *a* nations. 98 4
Lord, keep us from *a* sin today; 98 13
and sanctified a day of rest for *a* your creatures: 99 7
Grant that we, putting away *a* earthly anxieties, 99 8
Drive far from us *a* wrong desires, 99 15
in *a* assaults of our enemies; 99 22

and in *a* we do, direct us to the fulfilling 100 4
that in *a* the cares and occupations 100 8
for *a* members of your holy Church, 100 14
O God, you have made of one blood *a* the peoples 100 17
pour out your Spirit upon *a* flesh; 100 21
Almighty God, Father of *a* mercies, 101 7
for *a* your goodness and loving-kindness 101 9
to us and to *a* whom you have made. 101 10
and *a* the blessings of this life; 101 12
but above *a* for your immeasurable love 101 13
in holiness and righteousness *a* our days; 101 21
be honor and glory throughout *a* ages. 101 24
the fellowship of the Holy Spirit, be with us *a* 102 11
May the God of hope fill us with *a* joy and peace 102 12
The Lord shall preserve you from *a* evil; * 104 25
A this is from God, 106 2
to comfort us in *a* our afflictions, 107 5
to defend us from *a* error, 107 6
and to lead us into *a* truth; 107 7
Grant that *a* the peoples of the earth may look 107 9
that *a* nations may come and worship you; 107 14
Bless the Lord who forgives *a* our sins. 109 5
defend us from *a* perils and dangers 111 2
by its cleansing flame we may be purged of *a* our sins 111 5
You are worthy at *a* times to be praised 112 7
and to be glorified through *a* the worlds. 112 9
You fixed *a* the boundaries 115 8
forgive you *a* your sins 117 6
strengthen you in *a* goodness, 117 7
You are worthy at *a* times to be praised 118 7
and to be glorified through *a* the worlds. 118 9
From this day *a* generations will call me blessed: * 119 7
whom you have prepared for *a* the world to see: 120 4
Give peace, O Lord, in *a* the world; 121 22
Your saving health among *a* nations. 122 4
the communion of [_________ and] *a* your saints, 122 25
entrusting one another and *a* our life to Christ, 122 26
Most holy God, the source of *a* good desires, 123 15
a right judgements, and *a* just works: 123 16
being delivered from the fear of *a* enemies, 123 19
defend us from *a* perils and dangers of this night; 123 22
O God, the life of *a* who live, 124 1
O God and Father of *a*, 124 12
Let the whole earth also worship you, *a* nations obey 124 13
a tongues confess and bless you, 124 14
and *a* for your love's sake. 124 21
Almighty God, Father of *a* mercies, 125 5
for *a* your goodness and loving-kindness 125 7
to us and to *a* whom you have made. 125 8
and *a* the blessings of this life; 125 10
but above *a* for your immeasurable love 125 11
in holiness and righteousness *a* our days; 125 19
be honor and glory throughout *a* ages. 125 22
the fellowship of the Holy Spirit, be with us *a* 126 11
May the God of hope fill us with *a* joy and peace 126 12
forgive us *a* our offenses; 127 12
Almighty God grant us forgiveness of *a* our sins, 128 1
to keep you in *a* your ways. 130 20
bless the Lord, *a* you servants of the Lord, * 131 6
Come to me, *a* who labor and are heavy-laden, 131 15
defend us from *a* perils and dangers of this night; 133 11
Visit this place, O Lord, and drive far from it *a* snares 133 21
and *a* for your love's sake. 134 10
whom you have prepared for *a* the world to see: 135 4
and in *a* we do, direct us to the fulfilling 137 17
The Lord is high above *a* nations, * 138 7
Grant that *a* the peoples of the earth 138 13
You are worthy at *a* times to be praised 139 7
and to be glorified through *a* the worlds. 139 9
bless the Lord, *a* you servants of the Lord, * 140 1
whom you have prepared for *a* the world to see: 140 10
Visit this place, O Lord, and drive far from it *a* snares 140 13
and a great King above *a* gods. 146 6
In his hand are *a* the corners of the earth, * 146 7
From *a* evil and wickedness; 148 15
From *a* blindness of heart; 149 1
and from *a* want of chairity, 149 2
From *a* inordinate and sinful affections; 149 5
and from *a* the deceits of the world, 149 5
From *a* false doctrine, heresy, and schism; 149 8
From *a* oppression, conspiracy, and rebellion; 149 14
In *a* time of our tribulation; 149 26
in *a* time of our prosperity; 149 26
That it may please thee to illumine *a* bishops, 150 5
it may please thee to bless and keep *a* thy people, 150 10
and to draw *a* mankind into thy kingdom, 150 13
That it may please thee to give to *a* people 150 15
bring into the way of truth *a* such as have erred, 150 19
and *a* others in authority, 150 26
to make wars to cease in *a* the world; 151 1
to give to *a* nations unity, peace, and concord; 151 2
bestow freedom upon *a* peoples, 151 3
it may please thee to show thy pity upon *a* prisoners 151 5
and *a* who are desolate and oppressed, 151 6
so that in due time *a* may enjoy 151 10
it may please thee to preserve *a* who are in danger 151 17
and provide for, *a* women in childbirth, 151 20
and *a* whose homes are broken or torn by strife, 151 22
to strengthen *a* who suffer in mind, body, and spirit; 151 24
and comfort *a* who are in danger, 151 28
it may please thee to have mercy upon *a* mankind, 152 1
forgive us *a* our sins, negligences, and ignorances; 152 4
it may please thee to grant to *a* the faithful departed 152 15
in the fellowship of [_________ and] *a* the saints, 152 19
the fellowship of the Holy Ghost, be with us *a* 154 2
a those evils that we most justly have deserved; 155 9
that in *a* our troubles we may put our whole trust 155 10
Grant that *a* who are baptized 163 3
and proclaim to *a* people the Good News 163 15
that we and *a* the whole world may perceive the glory 163 16
who dost govern *a* things in heaven and earth: 164 1
the strength of *a* those who put their trust in thee: 164 11
a our doings without charity are nothing worth: 164 18
the very bond of peace and of *a* virtues, 165 2
who willest us to give thanks for *a* things, 165 6
and to cast *a* our care on thee 165 7
and dost forgive the sins of *a* those who are penitent: 166 2
may obtain of thee, the God of *a* mercy, 166 5
to *a* who have gone astray from thy ways, 166 17
that we may be defended from *a* adversities 167 5
and from *a* evil thoughts 167 6
that *a* mankind should follow the example 168 4
that we may behold him in *a* his redeeming work; 171 19
that *a* who have been reborn into the fellowship 172 3

that we may behold him in *a* his redeeming work;	173	7
that we, loving thee in *a* things and above *a* things,	174	3
exceed *a* that we can desire;	174	5
ascended far above *a* heavens	174	9
that he might fill *a* things:	174	9
the same Spirit to have a right judgment in *a* things,	175	17
we beseech thee, from *a* things that may hurt us,	177	4
whose never-failing providence ordereth *a* things	177	14
put away from us *a* hurtful things,	177	16
O God, from whom *a* good doth come:	178	1
who hast taught us to keep *a* thy commandments	179	4
Almighty God, the fountain of *a* wisdom,	179	16
O God, the protector of *a* that trust in thee,	180	1
manifest thy power among *a* peoples,	181	7
Lord of *a* power and might,	181	11
the author and giver of *a* good things:	181	12
nourish us with *a* goodness,	181	13
we pray thee, to trust in thee with *a* our heart;	181	17
grant that thy Holy Spirit may in *a* things direct	182	2
and make us continually to be given to *a* good works;	183	7
hast caused *a* holy Scriptures to be written	184	15
whose will it is to restore *a* things	185	1
into the arms of thy mercy *a* innocent victims;	186	15
that we and *a* the people of this land may have grace	190	20
be healed of *a* our infirmities	191	4
a who are at variance and enmity;	193	21
saints in *a* virtuous and godly living,	194	11
the relief of *a* who are in need,	194	20
Give abundantly to *a* pastors the gifts	197	6
in whom *a* our intercessions are acceptable	199	9
Grant, O Lord God, to *a* who have been baptized	201	12
O eternal Lord God, who holdest *a* souls in life:	202	1
with *a* who have faithfully served thee in the past,	202	12
whose will it is to restore *a* things	202	16
may live in righteousness and holiness *a* our days;	203	8
a who seek thee here may find thee,	204	4
may fulfill *a* the mind of him who loved it	204	13
Almighty God, the giver of *a* good gifts,	205	4
to *a* who are [now] called to any office	205	6
thee for *a* members of thy holy Church,	206	4
O God, who hast made of one blood *a* the peoples	206	9
pour out thy Spirit upon *a* flesh,	206	13
O God of *a* the nations of the earth:	206	17
Lord God Almighty, who hast made *a* peoples	207	1
and may prosper *a* who labor to gather them,	207	18
and give to us *a* a pride in what we do,	208	5
Bless, we beseech thee, *a* who, following	209	10
Almighty God, the fountain of *a* wisdom:	209	17
that *a* we do affecteth, for good or ill, *a* other lives:	210	11
Grant that *a* who are baptized into his Name	214	14
and proclaim to *a* people the Good News	215	9
Almighty and everlasting God, you govern *a* things	215	13
O God, the strength of *a* who put their trust in you:	216	6
and of *a* virtue, without which whoever lives	216	16
to give thanks for *a* things,	216	21
and to cast *a* our care on you	216	21
made and forgive the sins of *a* who are penitent:	217	15
obtain of you, the God of *a* mercy, perfect remission	217	18
to *a* who have gone astray from your ways,	218	8
that we may be defended from *a* adversities	218	15
and from *a* evil thoughts	218	16
that we may behold him in *a* his redeeming work;	223	12
Grant that *a* who have been reborn	223	16
Grant that *a* who have been reborn	224	14
that we may behold him in *a* his redeeming work;	224	21
loving you in *a* things and abaove *a* things,	225	16
your promises, which exceed *a* that we can desire;	225	17
far above *a* heavens that he might fill *a* things:	226	2
the same Spirit to have a right judgment in *a* things,	227	10
keep us, we pray, from *a* things that may hurt us,	228	15
your never-failing providence sets in order *a* things	229	10
Put away from us, we entreat you, *a* hurtful things,	229	12
O God, from whom *a* good proceeds:	229	15
you have taught us to keep *a* your commandments	230	19
Almighty God, the fountain of *a* wisdom,	231	10
O God, the protector of *a* who trust in you,	231	17
show forth your power among *a* peoples,	232	19
Lord of *a* power and might,	233	3
the author and giver of *a* good things:	233	3
nourish us with *a* goodness;	233	5
Grant us, O Lord, to trust in you with *a* our hearts;	233	9
grant that your Holy Spirit may in *a* things direct	233	15
who caused *a* holy Scriptures to be written	236	8
whose will it is to restore *a* things	236	14
into the arms of your mercy *a* innocent victims;	238	9
a the people of this land may have grace	242	4
may be healed from *a* our infirmities	242	11
and to the reconciliation of *a* who are at variance	245	6
follow your blessed saints in *a* virtuous	245	19
the relief of *a* who are in need,	246	5
Give abundantly to *a* pastors the gifts	248	17
in whom *a* our intercessions are acceptable	250	19
Grant, Lord God, to *a* who have been baptized	252	16
Eternal Lord God, you hold *a* souls in life:	253	6
that, with *a* who have faithfully served you	253	16
whose will it is to restore *a* things	254	1
live in righteousness and holiness *a* our days;	254	10
a who seek you here may find you,	255	2
may fulfill *a* the mind of him who loved it	255	11
Almighty God, the giver of *a* good gifts,	256	1
Give your grace, we humbly pray, to *a*	256	3
for *a* members of your holy Church,	257	1
O God, you have made of one blood *a* the peoples	257	5
pour out your Spirit upon *a* flesh,	257	9
O God of *a* the nations of the earth:	257	13
Lord God Almighty, you have made *a* the peoples	258	1
and may prosper *a* who labor to gather them,	258	18
to us *a* a pride in what we do,	259	7
Bless *a* who, following in his steps, give	260	16
Almighty God, the fountain of *a* wisdom:	261	1
that *a* we do affects, for good or ill, *a* other lives:	261	16
and forgive the sins of *a* who are penitent:	264	3
obtain of you, the God of *a* mercy, perfect remission	264	6
and of the need which *a* Christians continually have	265	8
and blot out *a* my iniquities.	266	21
We confess to you, Lord, *a* our past unfaithfulness:	268	1
For *a* false judgments,	268	20
Bring us with *a* your saints to the joy	269	2
He pardons and absolves *a* those who truly repent,	269	8
that *a* who believe in him might be delivered	277	4
For *a* bishops and other ministers	278	4
For N., our Bishop, and *a* the people of this diocese	278	6
For *a* Christians in this community	278	7
for *a* members of your holy Church,	278	14

all

Let us pray for *a* nations and peoples of the earth,	278	17
For *a* who serve the common good	278	22
Let us pray for *a* who suffer and are afflicted	279	3
Gracious God, the comfort of *a* who sorrow,	279	14
the strength of *a* who suffer:	279	15
your mercy present with them in *a* their afflictions;	279	16
Let us pray for *a* who have not received the Gospel	279	20
Creator of *a* the peoples of the earth	280	1
Have compassion on *a* who do not know you	280	2
that, with *a* who have departed this world	280	9
a things are being brought to their perfection	280	20
by him through whom *a* things were made,	280	21
your saving health among *a* nations.	281	8
let *a* the peoples praise you.	281	10
Rejoice and sing now, *a* the round earth,	286	4
A you who stand near this marvelous and holy flame,	286	10
when *a* who believe in Christ are delivered	287	9
to drive away *a* darkness.	287	25
he who gives his light to *a*	287	26
covenant with *a* living things:	289	2
God and Father of *a* believers,	289	6
sign for us of the salvation of *a* nations by the water	289	15
Grant that *a* the peoples of the earth	289	16
where *a* tears are wiped away	290	5
O God, you have created *a* things by the power	290	8
Grant that *a* who are reborn	290	15
and power to proclaim you to *a* the world;	291	8
a things are being brought to their perfection	291	17
by him through whom *a* things were made,	291	18
renounced Satan and *a* his works,	292	6
Will you seek and serve Christ in *a* persons,	293	29
Will you strive for justice and peace among *a* people,	294	1
Bless the Lord who forgives *a* our sins.	299	5
One God and Father of *a*.	299	10
Do you renounce Satan and *a* the spiritual forces	302	8
Do you renounce *a* sinful desires that draw you	302	14
Will you who witness these vows do *a* in your power	303	17
Will you seek and serve Christ in *a* persons,	305	4
Will you strive for justice and peace among *a* people,	305	7
Grant, O Lord, that *a* who are baptized into the death	306	5
be *a* honor and glory,	307	7
Holy Spirit to be the Savior and servant of *a*,	307	10
and wonder in *a* your works.	308	8
and sustain him *a* the days	309	13
A praise and thanks to you,	311	15
you may be filled with *a* the fullness of God.	311	24
for his love for *a* mankind,	316	12
to consider how Saint Paul exhorts *a* persons	316	20
ready to make restitution for *a* injuries and wrongs	317	6
and write *a* these thy laws in our hearts,	318	30
Bless the Lord who forgiveth *a* our sins.	319	6
Thou shalt love the Lord thy God with *a* thy heart,	319	9
with *a* thy soul, and with *a* thy mind.	319	10
hang *a* the Law and the Prophets.	319	13
and to cleanse us from *a* unrighteousness.	320	3
remission of *a* your sins,	321	15
Bless the Lord who forgiveth *a* our sins.	323	5
unto whom *a* hearts are open, *a* desires known,	323	7
Thou shalt love the Lord thy God with *a* thy heart,	324	2
with *a* thy soul, and with *a* thy mind.	324	3
hang *a* the Law and the Prophets.	324	6
of *a* that is, seen and unseen.	326	9

Through him *a* things were made.	326	17
and of *a* things visible and invisible;	327	23
begotten of his Father before *a* worlds,	327	26
by whom *a* things were made;	327	31
and to give thanks for *a* men:	329	3
and grant that *a* those who do confess	329	6
Give grace, O heavenly Father, to *a* bishops	329	9
And to *a* thy people give thy heavenly grace,	329	13
in holiness and righteousness *a* the days of their life.	329	16
Open, O Lord, the eyes of *a* people to behold	329	22
behold thy gracious hand in *a* thy works,	329	23
to comfort and succor [and] *a* those who,	329	27
And we also bless thy holy Name for *a* thy servants	330	1
examples of [and of] *a* thy saints,	330	5
maker of *a* things, judge of *a* men:	331	3
forgive us *a* that is past;	331	16
hath promised forgiveness of sins to *a* those	332	2
pardon and deliver you from *a* your sins,	332	4
and strengthen you in *a* goodness,	332	5
Hear the Word of God to *a* who truly turn to him.	332	7
Come unto me, *a* ye that travail and are heavy laden,	332	8
that *a* that believe in him should not perish,	332	11
and worthy of *a* men to be received,	332	13
at *a* times, and in *a* places, give thanks unto thee,	333	8
and with *a* the company of heaven,	334	1
A glory be to thee, Almighty God,	334	9
saying, "Drink ye *a* of this;	335	4
we, and *a* thy whole Church, may obtain remission	335	28
and *a* other benefits of his passion.	335	29
humbly beseeching thee that we, and *a* others	336	3
a honor and glory be unto thee,	336	14
blessed company of *a* faithful people;	339	8
a such good works as thou hast prepared for us	339	12
Holy Ghost, be *a* honor and glory,	339	14
The peace of God, which passeth *a* understanding,	339	15
at *a* times, and in *a* places, give thanks unto thee,	341	2
and with *a* the company of heaven,	341	4
A glory be to thee, O Lord our God,	341	12
saying, "Drink this, *a* of	342	6
Grant, we beseech thee, that *a* who partake	342	24
and also that we and *a* thy whole Church	342	27
Holy Ghost *a* honor and glory be unto thee,	343	4
for thou hast created *a* things,	344	6
For *a* that is in the heaven	344	9
thou art exalted as head above *a*.	344	11
to show forth thy glory in *a* the world.	345	6
eternal salvation for *a* who put their trust in him.	346	16
and to lead them into *a* truth;	347	9
preach the Gospel to *a* nations.	347	12
grace and virtue declared in *a* thy saints,	348	1
A thy creatures praise thee,	348	8
preach the Gospel and to teach *a* nations;	348	13
given us the Holy Spirit to guide us into *a* truth.	348	22
Bless the Lord who forgives *a* our sins.	351	5
Love the Lord your God with *a* your heart,	351	9
with *a* your soul, with *a* your mind,	351	9
and with *a* your strength.	351	10
and cleanse us from *a* unrighteousness.	352	3
God have mercy on you, forgive you *a* your sins	353	1
strengthen you in *a* goodness,	353	2
Bless the Lord who forgives *a* our sins.	355	5
to you *a* hearts are open, *a* desires known,	355	7

all

of *a* that is, seen and unseen.	358	6
Through him *a* things were made.	358	14
God have mercy on you, forgive you *a* your sins	360	15
strengthen you in *a* goodness,	360	16
and with *a* the company of heaven,	362	2
God and Father of *a*.	362	14
and said, "Drink this, *a* of you:	363	2
and at the last day bring us with *a* your saints	363	17
A this we ask through your Son Jesus Christ.	363	19
in the unity of the Holy Spirit *a* honor and glory	363	20
and with *a* the company of heaven,	367	11
and above *a* in the Word made flesh, Jesus,	368	4
and said, "Drink this, *a* of you:	368	15
thanksgiving to you, O Lord of *a*;	369	2
put *a* things in subjection under your Christ,	369	9
where, with [and] *a* your saints,	369	10
the firstborn of *a* creation,	369	12
the Holy Spirit *a* honor and glory is yours,	369	16
God of *a* power, Ruler of the Universe,	370	5
At your command *a* things came to be:	370	8
martyrs, and with *a* those in every generation	370	24
and said, "Drink this, *a* of you:	371	15
Fountain of life and source of *a* goodness,	373	4
our Creator, we might rule and serve *a*	373	20
and to bring to fulfillment the sanctification of *a*.	374	12
and said, "Drink this, *a* of you:	374	20
Grant that *a* who share this bread	375	9
[Remember (NN. and) *a* who minister	375	15
[Remember *a* your people, and those who seek	375	16
[Remember *a* who have died in the peace of Christ,	375	18
and] *a* the saints who have found favor	375	23
and in Christ, *a* honor and glory are yours,	375	26
because you have created *a* things,	377	4
exalted as head over *a*.	377	9
show forth your glory in *a* the world.	378	3
salvation for *a* who put their trust in him.	379	13
and to lead them into *a* truth;	380	4
preach the Gospel to *a* nations.	380	7
and virtue declared in *a* your saints,	380	17
A your creatures praise you,	381	2
preach the Gospel and to teach *a* nations;	381	7
given us the Holy Spirit to guide us into *a* truth.	381	15
With *a* our heart and with *a* our mind,	383	1
and for the unity of *a* peoples,	383	7
For our Bishop, and for *a* the clergy and people,	384	1
for the leaders of the nations, and for *a* in authority,	384	4
and for *a* who remember and care for them,	384	26
For *a* who have died in the hope of the resurrection,	384	29
and for *a* the departed,	384	30
For deliverance from *a* danger,	385	1
In the communion of [and of *a* the] saints,	385	13
commend ourselves, and one another, and *a* our life,	385	14
and for *a* ministers and people.	385	18
and for the well-being of *a* people.	386	2
I ask your prayers for *a* who seek God,	386	7
That we *a* may be one.	387	2
That your Name may be glorified by *a* people.	387	5
We pray for *a* bishops, priests, and deacons;	387	6
We pray for *a* who govern and hold authority	387	9
Give us grace to do your will in *a* that we undertake;	387	12
Grant, Almighty God, that *a* who confess your Name	388	2
Guide the people of this land, and of *a* the nations,	388	7
Give us *a* a reverence for the earth	388	12
Bless *a* whose lives are closely linked with ours,	388	17
Comfort and heal *a* those who suffer in body,	389	3
We commend to your mercy *a* who have died,	389	8
with *a* your saints in your eternal kingdom.	389	10
for *a* bishops and other ministers,	390	2
and for *a* the holy people of God,	390	2
For *a* who fear God and believe in you,	390	4
and that *a* may be one as you and the Father are one,	390	5
For *a* who live and work in this community	390	19
For a blessing upon *a* human labor,	390	21
For the poor, the persecuted, the sick, and *a*	390	24
for refugees, prisoners, and *a* who are in danger;	390	25
and show forth your glory in *a* that we do,	391	3
and for *a* whom we have injured	391	5
For *a* who have commended themselves	391	10
For *a* who have died in the communion	391	15
faith is known to you alone, that, with *a* the saints,	391	16
(blessed N.) and] *a* the saints,	391	20
and *a* our life to Christ our God.	391	21
For *a* people in their daily life and work;	392	2
For *a* who work for justice, freedom, and peace.	392	6
For *a* who are in danger, sorrow,	392	9
For *a* who proclaim the Gospel,	392	13
and *a* who seek the Truth.	392	13
for] *a* bishops and other ministers;	392	15
For *a* who serve God in his Church.	392	16
We thank you, Lord, for *a* the blessings of this life.	393	1
We pray for *a* who have died,	393	4
Almighty and eternal God, ruler of *a* things in heaven	394	9
and *a* who turn to you for help;	395	5
in whom *a* our intercessions are acceptable	395	22
have mercy on you, forgive you *a* your sins	398	7
strengthen you in *a* goodness,	398	8
and said, "Drink this, *a* of you:	403	9
the Holy Spirit *a* honor and glory is yours,	403	20
the Holy Spirit be with you *a*.	404	3
and said, "Drink this, *a* of you:	405	7
A this we ask through your Son Jesus Christ.	405	19
the Holy Spirit *a* honor and glory is yours,	405	20
Bless the Lord who forgives *a* our sins.	413	5
One God and Father of *a*.	413	10
Will you who witness these vows do *a* in your power	416	1
Will you seek and serve Christ in *a* persons,	417	14
Will you strive for justice and peace among *a* people,	417	17
and sustain him *a* the days of his life.	418	11
strengthen you, that in this, and in *a* things,	420	2
strengthen us *a* in our Christian vocation of witness	421	5
Scripture commends it to be honored among *a* people.	423	8
and, forsaking *a* others, be faithful to him	424	11
and, forsaking *a* others, be faithful to her	424	17
Will *a* of you witnessing these promises	425	1
do *a* in your power to uphold these two persons	425	1
and with *a* that I am, and *a* that I have, I honor you,	427	13
Eternal God, creator and preserver of *a* life,	429	2
author of salvation, and giver of *a* grace:	429	3
peace with you and one another *a* the days	429	13
Grant that *a* married persons who have witnessed	430	1
by which *a* your children are united	430	4
Lead them into *a* peace.	430	17
and fill you with *a* spiritual benediction	431	11
the giver of *a* that is true and lovely and gracious:	432	1

and obtain those eternal joys prepared for *a* 432 6
and, forsaking *a* others, to be faithful to her 433 7
and, forsaking *a* others, to be faithful to him 433 12
do *a* in your power to uphold these two persons 434 1
heavenly Father, the Lord of *a* life, 440 5
May God, the Father of *a*, bless our child 441 7
From this day *a* generations will call me blessed:* 441 15
for *a* the good things he has done for me? 442 20
in the presence of *a* his people, 442 24
your goodness and mercy shall follow me *a* the days 443 15
bring this child to love *a* that is true and noble, 443 27
love and peace *a* the days of their life; 444 14
and *a* other sins which I cannot now remember, 447 8
absolve *a* sinners who truly repent and believe in him, 448 2
his great mercy forgive you *a* your offenses; 448 3
I absolve you from *a* your sins: 448 4
The Lord has put away *a* your sins. 448 12
remember in truth *a* your sins and his unfailing mercy. 449 11
Hear the Word of God to *a* who truly turn to him. 449 12
Come unto me, *a* ye that travail and are heavy laden, 449 13
that *a* that believe in him should not perish, 449 16
a true saying, and worthy of *a* men to be received, 449 18
Therefore, O Lord, from these and *a* other sins 450 16
strengthen you in *a* goodness, 451 4
absolve *a* sinners who truly repent and believe in him, 451 12
his great mercy forgive you *a* your offenses; 451 13
I absolve you from *a* your sins: 451 14
The Lord has put away *a* your sins. 451 19
Peace be to this house (place), and to *a* who dwell 453 1
forgive you *a* your sins 455 6
strengthen you in *a* goodness, 455 7
to drive away *a* sickness of body and spirit, 456 3
May he deliver you from *a* evil, 456 17
preserve you in *a* goodness, 456 17
a strong tower to *a* who put their trust in him, 456 20
to whom *a* things in heaven, on earth, 456 21
O Father of mercies and God of *a* comfort, 458 1
drive away from our bodies *a* sickness and *a* infirmity: 458 17
guard him from *a* danger, restore to him your gifts 459 4
O God, the source of *a* health: 461 1
From *a* evil, from *a* sin, from *a* tribulation, 463 3
mercifully to pardon *a* his sins, 463 15
O Sovereign Lord Christ, from *a* evil, 464 16
rest with *a* your saints in the eternal habitations; 464 18
May his soul and the souls of *a* the departed, 465 7
"Come to me, *a* you who labor and are burdened, 465 10
before whom live *a* who die in the Lord: 466 7
O Sovereign Lord Christ, from *a* evil, 466 16
a your saints in the eternal habitations; 466 18
Let us also pray for *a* who mourn, 467 1
bring us *a* to thy heavenly kingdom; 470 10
For when thou art angry *a* our days are gone; * 473 1
The LORD shall preserve thee from *a* evil; * 473 21
redeem Israel * from *a* his sins. 474 17
and art acquainted with *a* my ways. 474 22
mercy shall follow me *a* the days 476 16
mercy shall follow me *a* the days 477 9
dwell in the house of the LORD *a* the days 477 17
or show forth *a* his praise? 478 14
I will pay my vows now in the presence of *a* 479 18
Grant that *a* who have been baptized 480 8
lead us in holiness and righteousness *a* our days. 481 3
be cleansed from *a* our sins, 481 5
Grant to *a* who mourn a sure confidence 481 7
that, casting *a* their grief on thee, 481 8
Grant us, with *a* who have died in the hope 481 23
a thy saints, to receive the crown of life 481 26
promise to *a* who share in the victory 481 27
but the fullness of joy with *a* thy saints; 482 7
A we go down to the dust; 482 15
Christ will open the kingdom of heaven to *a* 483 20
A that the Father giveth me shall come to me; 484 18
O Almighty God, the God of the spirits of *a* flesh, 486 7
May his soul, and the souls of *a* the departed, 486 19
virtue declared in *a* thy saints, 487 12
with *a* those who are of the mystical body 487 17
good examples of *a* those thy servants, 488 5
beseech thee that we, with *a* those who are departed 488 7
We give thee thanks for *a* thy servants 488 27
lead us in holiness and righteousness *a* our days; 489 6
A which we ask through Jesus 489 12
for *a* thy servants who have finished their course 489 15
and for *a* other thy righteous servants, 489 17
Father of mercies and giver of *a* comfort: 489 30
Deal graciously, we pray thee, with *a* those who mourn, 489 31
and bring us *a* to your heavenly kingdom; 494 3
give him fellowship with *a* your saints. 497 17
and for *a* those whom we love but see no longer. 498 8
and the souls of *a* the departed, 498 11
but the fullness of joy with *a* your saints; 498 18
A of us go down to the dust; 499 7
Christ will open the kingdom of heaven to *a* 500 9
May his soul, and the souls of *a* the departed, 502 17
for the good examples of *a* your servants, 503 15
with *a* who have died in the true faith 503 17
lead us in holiness and righteousness *a* our days; 504 4
A this we ask through Jesus 504 10
for *a* your servants who have finished their course 504 13
and for *a* your other righteous servants, 504 15
Father of *a*, we pray to you for those we love, 504 26
Grant, O Lord, to *a* who are bereaved the spirit 505 10
graciously, we pray, with *a* who mourn; 505 18
that, casting *a* their care on you, 505 18
Bless the Lord who forgives *a* our sins. 512 5
to you *a* hearts are open, *a* desires known, 512 7
and to contain *a* things necessary to salvation; 513 10
a things are being brought to their perfection 515 10
by him through whom *a* things were made, 515 11
and to be in *a* things a faithful pastor 517 10
support *a* baptized people in their gifts 518 13
guide and strengthen the deacons and *a* others 518 25
Will you be merciful to *a*, 518 28
of *a* that is, seen and unseen. 519 9
Through him *a* things were made. 519 17
Father of mercies and God of *a* comfort, 520 12
knowing *a* things before they come to pass: 520 13
To you, O Father, *a* hearts are open; 521 6
with such love of you and of *a* the people, 521 8
In *a* things may he present before you 521 14
Bless the Lord who forgives *a* our sins. 525 5
to you *a* hearts are open, *a* desires known, 525 7
and to contain *a* things necessary to salvation; 526 16
a things are being brought to their perfection 528 8

by him through whom *a* things were made,	528	9
of *a* that is, seen and unseen.	529	12
Through him *a* things were made.	530	8
A baptized people are called to make Christ known	531	2
In *a* that you do, you are to nourish Christ's people	531	18
Will you undertake to be a faithful pastor to *a*	532	14
offering *a* your labors to God,	532	26
God and Father of *a*, we praise you	533	1
Grant that in *a* things he may serve	534	5
and your Name glorified in *a* the world.	534	7
A this we ask through Jesus	534	7
Bless the Lord who forgives *a* our sins.	537	5
to you *a* hearts are open, *a* desires known,	537	7
and to contain *a* things necessary to salvation;	538	16
things are being brought to their perfection	540	8
by him through whom *a* things were made,	540	9
of *a* that is, seen and unseen.	541	12
Through him *a* things were made.	542	8
to serve *a* people, particularly the poor,	543	5
At *a* times, your life and teaching are to show	543	16
Will you look for Christ in *a* others,	544	4
may be a wholesome example to *a* people?	544	10
Will you in *a* things seek not your glory	544	12
and made him Lord of *a*;	545	5
that whoever would be great must be servant of *a*.	545	6
For *a* members of your Church in their vocation	548	16
For N., our Presiding Bishop, and for *a* bishops,	548	20
that they may be adorned with *a* Christian virtues,	549	13
For *a* who fear God and believe in you,	549	16
our divisions may cease and that *a* may be one	549	17
For a blessing upon *a* human labor,	550	6
For the poor, the persecuted, the sick, and *a*	550	11
for refugees, prisoners, and *a* who are in danger;	550	12
For *a* who have died in the communion	550	20
faith is known to you alone, that, with *a* the saints,	550	21
(blessed N.) and] *a* the saints,	550	27
and *a* our life to Christ our God.	550	28
and good shepherd of us *a*, Jesus Christ our Lord.	552	12
Let us then offer our prayers to God for *a* his people,	560	1
let the doors of this place be open to *a* people.	562	2
let *a* these be signs of the ministry which is mine	562	7
and may *a* the desires of my heart	562	14
a the world may be drawn	563	8
A this I ask for the sake of your Son	563	9
Grace be to this house, and to *a* who enter here:	568	2
A that we are and *a* that we have is yours.	568	8
One God and Father of *a*.	569	20
the Holy Spirit, be *a* honor and glory,	570	21
Almighty God, *a* times are your seasons,	572	9
and *a* occasions invite your tender mercies:	572	9
Accept and bless *a* we have done,	573	4
Grant that *a* who eat and drink	574	4
of [N., our patron, and of] *a* your Saints,	579	10
Happy are they *a* *	587	1
who set themselves against me *a* around.	587	14
surely, you will strike *a* my enemies across the face,	587	16
you hate *a* those who work wickedness.	588	26
But *a* who take refuge in you will be glad; *	589	17
and worn away because of *a* my enemies.	590	13
Depart from me, *a* evildoers, *	590	14
save and deliver me from *a* who pursue me;	590	21
how exalted is your Name in *a* the world!	592	8
you put *a* things under his feet:	592	20
A sheep and oxen, *	592	21
how exalted is your Name in *a* the world!	592	26
I will tell of *a* your marvelous works.	593	2
So that I may tell of *a* your praises	594	4
and also *a* the peoples that forget God.	594	12
Their ways are devious at *a* times;	595	1
they defy *a* their enemies.	595	3
Oh, that the LORD would cut off *a* smooth tongues, *	597	5
A are corrupt and commit abominable acts;	598	13
The LORD looks down from heaven upon us *a*, *	598	15
a alike have turned bad; *	598	19
Have they no knowledge, *a* those evildoers *	598	21
my good above *a* other."	599	21
A my delight is upon the godly that are in the land, *	600	1
For *a* his judgments are before my eyes, *	604	7
he is a shield to *a* who trust in him.	604	26
Their sound has gone out into *a* lands, *	606	21
Above *a*, keep your servant from presumptuous sins;	607	24
Remember *a* your offerings *	608	5
and prosper *a* your plans.	608	8
may the LORD grant *a* your requests.	608	11
Your hand will lay hold upon *a* your enemies; *	609	12
your right hand will seize *a* those who hate you.	609	13
scorned by *a* and despised by the people.	610	13
A who see me laugh me to scorn; *	610	14
a my bones are out of joint; *	611	6
I can count *a* my bones.	611	14
a you of Jacob's line, give glory.	611	28
A the ends of the earth shall remember and turn	612	10
and *a* the families of the nations shall bow	612	12
To him alone *a* who sleep in the earth bow down	612	15
a who go down to the dust fall before him.	612	17
your goodness and mercy shall follow me *a* the days	613	11
The earth is the LORD's and *a* that is in it, *	613	14
the world and *a* who dwell therein.	613	15
in you have I trusted *a* the day long.	614	23
A the paths of the LORD are love and faithfulness *	615	8
and forgive me *a* my sin.	615	25
out of *a* his troubles.	616	6
and recounting *a* your wonderful deeds.	616	21
that I may dwell in the house of the LORD *a* the days	617	20
a are crying, "Glory!"	620	24
I have become a reproach to *a* my enemies	623	10
fear is *a* around; *	623	17
hich you have done in the sight of *a*	624	6
Love the LORD, *a* you who worship him; *	624	18
a you who wait for the LORD.	624	22
because of my groaning *a* day long.	625	4
Therefore *a* the faithful will make their prayers to you	625	11
shout for joy, *a* who are true of heart.	625	26
sound a fanfare with *a* your skill upon the trumpet.	626	6
and *a* his works are sure.	626	8
by the breath of his mouth *a* the heavenly hosts.	626	12
Let *a* the earth fear the LORD; *	626	15
let *a* who dwell in the world stand in awe of him.	626	16
and beholds *a* the people in the world.	627	2
on *a* who dwell on the earth.	627	4
He fashions *a* the hearts of them *	627	5
and understands *a* their works.	627	6
for *a* its strength it cannot save.	627	10
I will bless the LORD at *a* times; *	627	21

and delivered me out of *a* my terror.	628	2
and saved me from *a* my troubles.	628	6
and delivers them from *a* their troubles.	629	2
but the LORD will deliver him out of them *a*.	629	6
He will keep safe *a* his bones; *	629	7
Let *a* who rejoice at my ruin be ashamed	631	24
and of your praise *a* the day long.	632	2
Transgressors shall be destroyed, one and *a*; *	636	13
I go about in mourning *a* the day long.	637	9
O LORD, you know *a* my desires, *	637	14
and plot treachery *a* the day long.	637	22
Deliver me from *a* my transgressions *	639	11
like a moth you eat away *a* that is dear to us; *	639	18
a wayfarer, as *a* my forebears were.	639	24
Let *a* who seek you rejoice in you and be glad; *	641	16
A my enemies whisper together about me *	642	13
while *a* day long they say to me,	643	6
a your rapids and floods have gone over me.	643	22
A day long they mock me *	644	7
A this has come upon us; *	646	19
Indeed, for your sake we are killed *a* the day long; *	647	1
A your garments are fragrant with myrrh,	648	6
A glorious is the princess as she enters; *	648	17
you shall make them princes over *a* the earth.	648	24
It is he who makes war to cease in *a* the world; *	649	21
Clap your hands, *a* you peoples; *	650	6
he is the great King over *a* the earth.	650	9
For God is King of *a* the earth; *	650	18
sing praises with *a* your skill.	650	19
Beautiful and lofty, the joy of *a* the earth,	651	3
Hear this, *a* you peoples;	652	6
hearken, *a* you who dwell in the world, *	652	7
For *a* the beasts of the forest are mine, *	654	23
for the whole world is mine and *a* that is in it.	655	4
and blot out *a* my iniquities.	656	25
against the godly *a* day long?	657	24
You love *a* words that hurt, *	658	6
A are corrupt and commit abominable acts;	658	22
God looks down from heaven upon us *a*, *	659	1
a alike have turned bad; *	659	5
a day long they assault and oppress me.	662	14
They hound me *a* the day long; *	662	15
A day long they damage my cause; *	662	22
and your glory over *a* the earth.	664	9
and your glory over *a* the earth.	664	20
Awake, and punish *a* the ungodly; *	666	5
you laugh *a* the ungodly to scorn.	666	13
a of you together, *	669	10
a of them together.	670	4
a those who swear by him will be glad; *	671	8
and *a* who see them will shake their heads.	672	2
and *a* who are true of heart will glory.	672	6
O Hope of *a* the ends of the earth	672	19
Be joyful in God, *a* you lands; *	673	18
A the earth bows down before you, *	673	24
how wonderful he is in his doing toward *a* people.	674	2
Come and listen, *a* you who fear God, *	674	27
your saving health among *a* nations.	675	12
let *a* the peoples praise you.	675	14
and guide *a* the nations upon earth.	675	17
let *a* the peoples praise you.	675	19
and may *a* the ends of the earth stand in awe of him.	675	23
my adversaries are *a* in your sight."	681	2
the seas and *a* that moves in them;	682	6
Let *a* who seek you rejoice and be glad in you; *	682	19
and your glory *a* the day long.	683	17
and saving deeds *a* day long; *	684	10
and your power to *a* who are to come.	684	19
My tongue will proclaim your righteousness *a* day	685	6
A kings shall bow down before him, *	686	5
and *a* the nations do him service.	686	6
and may they bless him *a* the day long.	686	16
may *a* the nations bless themselves in him	686	23
and may *a* the earth be filled with his glory.	686	28
I have been afflicted *a* day long, *	688	5
you destroy *a* who are unfaithful.	689	4
I will speak of *a* your works *	689	7
they broke down *a* your carved work with hatchets	689	19
They burned down *a* the meeting-places of God	689	25
You fixed *a* the boundaries of the earth; *	690	18
remember how fools revile you *a* day long.	690	29
and declaring *a* your wonderful deeds.	691	4
Though the earth and *a* its inhabitants are quaking, *	691	8
and *a* the wicked of the earth shall drink and	691	20
He shall break off *a* the horns of the wicked; *	691	24
and to save *a* the oppressed of the earth.	692	19
let *a* around him bring gifts to him who is worthy	692	23
I will meditate on *a* your acts *	693	24
and *a* the night through with a glow of fire.	696	2
In spite of *a* this, they went on sinning *	697	14
He struck down *a* the firstborn of Egypt, *	699	7
so that *a* who pass by pluck off its grapes?	703	12
a the foundations of the earth are shaken.	705	19
and *a* of you children of the Most High;	705	21
for you shall take *a* nations for your own.	706	2
and *a* their commanders like Zebah and Zalmunna,	706	25
you alone are the Most High over *a* the earth.	707	14
and blotted out *a* their sins.	708	23
You have withdrawn *a* your fury *	708	24
I call upon you *a* the day long.	710	4
and great is your love toward *a* who call upon you.	710	8
A nations you have made will come	710	15
I will thank you, O LORD my God, with *a* my heart, *	710	24
more than *a* the dwellings of Jacob.	711	14
"*A* my fresh springs are in you."	711	25
and *a* your great waves overwhelm me.	712	16
or your righteousness in the country where *a*	713	2
They surround me *a* day long like a flood; *	713	13
and preserve your throne for *a* generations.'"	714	2
great and terrible to *a* those round about him.	714	8
O mighty LORD, your faithfulness is *a* around you.	714	10
laid the foundations of the world and *a* that is in it.	714	16
Once for *a* I have sworn by my holiness: *	716	11
You have breached *a* his walls *	716	21
A who pass by despoil him; *	716	23
and made *a* his enemies rejoice.	716	26
how frail you have made *a* flesh.	717	9
When you are angry, *a* our days are gone: *	718	17
so shall we rejoice and be glad *a* the days of our life.	719	2
to keep you in *a* your ways.	720	8
and *a* the workers of iniquity flourish,	721	10
and *a* the workers of iniquity shall be scattered.	721	15
a evildoers are full of boasting.	723	2
he who teaches *a* the world, has he no knowledge?	723	14

and *a* the true of heart will follow it. 723 24
and a great King above *a* gods. 724 19
sing to the LORD, *a* the whole earth. 725 18
and his wonders among *a* peoples. 725 22
he is more to be feared than *a* gods. 725 24
As for *a* the gods of the nations, they are but idols; * 726 1
let the sea thunder and *a* that is in it; * 726 15
let the field be joyful and *a* that is therein. 726 16
Then shall *a* the trees of the wood shout for joy 726 17
and *a* the peoples see his glory. 727 8
Confounded be *a* who worship carved images 727 9
Bow down before him, *a* you gods. 727 11
most high over *a* the earth; * 727 15
you are exalted far above *a* gods. 727 16
and *a* the ends of the earth have seen 728 8
Shout with joy to the LORD *a* you lands; * 728 10
Let the sea make a noise and *a* that is in it, * 728 16
he is high above *a* peoples. 729 2
Be joyful in the LORD, *a* you lands; * 729 22
I will soon destroy *a* the wicked in the land, * 730 26
root out *a* evildoers from the city of the LORD. 730 27
My enemies revile me *a* day long, * 731 15
and *a* the kings of the earth your glory. 732 7
your years endure throughout *a* generations. 732 26
they *a* shall wear out like a garment; * 733 2
and *a* that is within me, bless his holy Name. 733 10
and forget not *a* his benefits. 733 12
He forgives *a* your sins * 733 13
and heals *a* your infirmities; 733 14
and judgment for *a* who are oppressed. 733 20
and his kingship has dominion over *a*. 734 21
Bless the LORD, *a* you his hosts, * 734 25
Bless the LORD, *a* you works of his, 734 27
in *a* places of his dominion; * 734 28
A the beasts of the field drink their fill from them, * 735 23
in which *a* the beasts of the forest prowl. 736 18
in wisdom you have made them *a*; 736 26
A of them look to you * 737 7
may the LORD rejoice in *a* his works. 737 17
and speak of *a* his marvelous works. 738 4
his judgments prevail in *a* the world. 738 14
as a ruler over *a* his possessions, 739 20
and gnats within *a* their borders. 740 16
Which ate up *a* the green plants in their land * 740 23
the firstfruits of *a* their strength. 740 26
in *a* their tribes there was not one that stumbled. 740 28
or show forth *a* his praise? 741 22
throughout *a* generations for ever. 744 10
and let *a* the people say, "Amen!" 745 25
Let *a* those whom the LORD has redeemed proclaim * 746 3
They abhorred *a* manner of food * 747 17
but *a* wickedness will shut its mouth. 749 14
and your glory over *a* the earth. 750 4
they are studied by *a* who delight in them. 754 9
a his commandments are sure. 754 19
The LORD is high above *a* nations, * 756 8
and so are *a* who put their trust in them. 758 5
nor *a* those who go down into silence; 758 24
for *a* the good things he has done for me? 759 24
in the presence of *a* his people. 760 2
Praise the LORD, *a* you nations; * 760 15
laud him, *a* you peoples. 760 16
A the ungodly encompass me; * 761 15
and seek him with *a* their hearts! 763 8
when I regard *a* your commandments. 763 16
a the judgments of your mouth. 764 10
than in *a* manner of riches. 764 12
My soul is consumed at *a* times * 764 23
I shall keep it with *a* my heart. 766 4
I entreat you with *a* my heart, * 768 3
I am a companion of *a* who fear you * 768 13
A your commandments are true; * 770 14
for *a* things are your servants. 771 2
I see that *a* things come to an end, * 771 11
a the day long it is in my mind. 771 14
I have more understanding than *a* my teachers, * 771 17
You spurn *a* who stray from your statutes; * 773 9
a the wicked of the earth are but dross; * 773 11
I hold *a* your commandments to be right for me; * 774 3
a paths of falsehood I abhor. 774 4
therefore I obey them with *a* my heart. 774 6
and *a* your commandments are true. 776 6
a your righteous judgments endure for evermore. 776 24
for *a* my ways are before you. 777 16
for *a* your commandments are righteous. 777 24
The LORD shall preserve you from *a* evil; * 779 13
Happy are they *a* who fear the LORD, * 783 13
may you see the prosperity of Jerusalem *a* the days 783 22
a those who are enemies of Zion. 784 10
and he shall redeem Israel from *a* their sins. 785 9
and *a* the hardships he endured; 785 20
bless the LORD, *a* you servants of the LORD, * 787 19
and that our Lord is above *a* gods. 788 11
in the seas and *a* the deeps. 788 13
against Pharaoh and *a* his servants. 788 20
and *a* the kingdoms of Canaan. 788 25
and so are *a* who put their trust in them. 789 12
Who gives food to *a* creatures, * 791 19
and your word above *a* things. 793 7
A the kings of the earth will praise you, O LORD, * 793 10
and are acquainted with *a* my ways. 794 5
a of them were written in your book; * 795 7
to count them *a*, my life span 795 14
and stir up strife *a* day long. 796 4
and tell him *a* my trouble. 798 4
I muse upon *a* your deeds; * 799 8
and bring *a* my foes to naught, * 799 26
May our barns be filled to overflowing with *a* manner 801 3
and *a* your marvelous works. 801 21
and his compassion is over *a* his works. 802 4
A your works praise you, O LORD, * 802 5
your dominion endures throughout *a* ages. 802 12
The LORD is faithful in *a* his words * 802 13
and merciful in *a* his deeds. 802 14
The LORD upholds *a* those who fall; * 802 15
The eyes of *a* wait upon you, O LORD, * 802 17
The LORD is righteous in *a* his ways * 802 21
and loving in *a* his works. 802 22
to *a* who call upon him faithfully. 802 24
The LORD preserves *a* those who love him, * 802 27
but he destroys *a* the wicked. 802 28
let *a* flesh bless his holy Name for ever and ever. 803 2
earth, the seas, and *a* that is in them; * 803 13
your God, O Zion, throughout *a* generations. 803 25

and calls them *a* by their names.	804	9
Praise him, *a* you angels of his; *	805	23
praise him, *a* his host.	805	24
praise him, *a* you shining stars.	805	26
you sea-monsters and *a* deeps;	806	8
Mountains and *a* hills, *	806	11
fruit trees and *a* cedars;	806	12
Wild beasts and *a* cattle, *	806	13
Kings of the earth and *a* peoples, *	806	15
princes and *a* rulers of the world;	806	16
and praise for *a* his loyal servants, *	806	23
this is glory for *a* his faithful people.	807	19
to behold thy gracious hand in *a* thy works;	814	2
him through whom *a* things were made,	814	4
O God, the creator and preserver of *a* mankind,	814	6
beseech thee for *a* sorts and conditions of men;	814	7
thy saving health unto *a* nations.	815	1
that *a* who profess and call themselves Christians	815	3
a those who are in any ways afflicted or distressed,	815	7
and a happy issue out of *a* their afflictions.	815	11
a nations and races may serve you	815	19
a peoples may be gathered under the banner	815	25
Father of *a*, whose Son commanded us to love	816	5
your good time enable us *a* to stand reconciled	816	8
with *a* truth, in *a* truth with *a* peace.	816	11
whose will it is that *a* should come to you	816	16
that *a* may know the power of his forgiveness	816	18
and other clergy, and *a* our people.	817	12
love to *a* among whom we live;	817	17
ruler of *a* things in heaven	817	18
Grant us *a* things necessary for our common life,	817	21
and bring us *a* to be of one heart and mind	817	22
Almighty and everliving God, source of *a* wisdom	818	1
Teach us in *a* things to seek first your honor	818	4
take away *a* hatred and prejudice,	818	17
one God and Father of us *a*,	818	20
so we may be *a* of one heart	818	20
a which we ask through Jesus Christ our Lord.	820	15
O Lord our Governor, whose glory is in *a* the world:	820	16
and to *a* in authority,	820	20
the magistrates in *a* this land;	821	10
and to *a* in administrative authority,	821	20
foresight to provide for the needs of *a* our people,	822	3
you are exalted as head above *a*.	822	16
offices to promote the well-being of *a* people;	822	21
to whom we must account for *a* our powers	822	23
a may be protected and our nation be enabled	822	27
a the men and women of our armed forces at home	823	2
we may *a* share the fruits of the earth,	824	9
that *a* may find suitable and fulfilling employment,	824	13
bless *a* schools, colleges, and universities	824	16
you to be the source of *a* truth;	824	20
Have mercy upon *a* of us who live and work	825	19
and grant that *a* the people of our nation	825	20
and *a* other bodily necessities of life,	825	22
A this we ask in your holy Name.	825	24
remember before you *a* poor and neglected persons	826	2
and *a* who have none to care for them.	826	4
and equal opportunities for *a*.	826	13
Remember *a* prisoners,	826	18
A this we ask for your mercy's sake.	826	25
whose loving hand hath given us *a* that we possess:	827	1
with *a* its marvelous order,	827	12
openest thine hand and fillest *a* things	828	1
hast promised to *a* those who seek thy kingdom	828	10
a things necessary to sustain their life:	828	11
and given us dominion over *a* the earth:	828	17
enkindle fervent charity among us *a*,	829	7
Look with mercy, O God our Father, on *a*	830	1
trust in your goodness *a* the days of his life;	830	11
passeth understanding abide *a* the days of his life;	830	17
Defend them from *a* dangers of soul and body;	830	22
Almighty God, we entrust *a* who are dear to us	831	7
O blessed Lord, you ministered to *a* who came to you:	831	18
upon *a* who through addiction have lost	831	19
Direct us, O Lord, in *a* our doings	832	1
that in *a* our works begun,	832	2
Grant us, in *a* our doubts	832	7
save us from *a* false choices,	832	10
that, among *a* the changes	832	20
O Lord, support us *a* the day long,	833	14
O Almighty God, who pourest out on *a* who desire it	833	19
Redeem *a* our days by this victory;	835	3
Give us grateful hearts, our Father, for *a* thy mercies,	835	8
For these and *a* his mercies,	835	16
Accept, O Lord, our thanks and praise for *a*	836	1
Above *a*, we thank you for your Son Jesus Christ;	836	12
and through him, at *a* times and in *a* places,	836	18
may give thanks to you in *a* things.	836	19
Let us give thanks to God our Father for *a* his gifts	837	1
For *a* that is gracious in the lives of men and women,	837	6
For *a* valiant seekers after truth, liberty, and justice,	837	17
For the communion of saints, in *a* times and places,	837	19
Above *a*, we give you thanks for the great mercies	837	21
preach the Gospel to *a* nations.	838	4
We thank you that in *a* parts of the earth	838	4
thanks to you, O Lord our God, for *a* your servants	838	9
for Isaiah and *a* the prophets;	838	13
for Peter and Paul and *a* the apostles;	838	14
and *a* the martyrs and saints in every age	838	16
Almighty God, giver of *a* good things:	838	21
the faith we have inherited in *a* its rich variety.	839	12
a our people, with many voices in one united chorus,	839	19
that we may not rest until *a* the people of this land	839	24
O God, who created *a* peoples in your image,	840	1
your love is made perfect in our love for *a*	840	5
for *a* the other blessings of thy merciful providence	840	18
walking before thee *a* our days;	840	22
with thee and the Holy Ghost be *a* glory and honor,	840	23
Help us to remember that we are *a* your children,	841	3
of *a* that is, seen and unseen.	846	4
It means that *a* people are worthy of respect	846	14
because *a* are created in the image of God,	846	15
a can respond to the love of God.	846	16
a the nations of the world to him.	847	2
be kind to *a* the creatures of God;	848	10
To use *a* our bodily desires as God intended;	848	11
and the necessities of life for *a* people;	848	13
Since we do not fully obey them, are they useful at *a*?	848	25
with other people, and with *a* creation.	848	31
and with *a* creation.	849	15
through them, to *a* who believe in him.	850	29
and give us life in *a* its fullness.	851	3
You shall love the Lord your God with *a* your heart,	851	11

with *a* your soul, and with *a* your mind. 851 12
a truth and enables us to grow in the likeness 852 22
with our neighbors, and with *a* creation. 852 29
the Good News of the Kingdom for *a* people. 853 18
Christ is the Head and of which *a* baptized persons 854 7
Faith to *a* people, to the end of time. 854 23
to carry out Christ's mission to *a* people. 854 27
The mission of the Church is to restore *a* people 855 2
through the ministry of *a* its members. 855 10
What is the duty of *a* Christians? 856 12
The duty of *a* Christians is to follow Christ; 856 13
Thanksgiving is offered to God for *a* the blessings 857 8
and be in love and charity with *a* people. 860 6
necessary for *a* persons in the same way that Baptism 860 15
and will make *a* things new. 862 4
are united with *a* the people of God, 862 27

alleluia

A! Christ is risen. 39 7
The Lord is risen indeed. *A*! 39 8
A 42 18
A. Unto us a child is born: 43 2
[*A*.] The Word was made flesh 44 6
A. 46 1
the unleavened bread of sincerity and truth. *A*. 46 6
A! Christ is risen 77 6
The Lord is risen indeed. *A*! 77 7
A. 80 9
A. To us a child is born: 80 11
A. The Lord is risen indeed: 81 4
[*A*.] The Word was made flesh 82 1
A. 83 10
the unleavened bread of sincerity and truth. *A*. 83 14
A. 103 5
A. Christ is risen. 109 3
The Lord is risen indeed. *A*. 109 4
Thanks be to God. *A*, *A*. 114 7
A. 117 14
A. 128 7
A, *a*, *a*. 134 18
A, *a*, *a*. 135 11
A. Christ is risen. 294 8
The Lord is risen indeed. *A*. 294 9
A. Christ is risen. 299 3
The Lord is risen indeed. *A*. 299 4
A. Christ is risen. 319 4
The Lord is risen indeed. *A*. 319 5
The Lord is risen indeed. *A*. 323 3
[*A*.] Christ our Passover is sacrificed for us; 337 1
Therefore let us keep the feast [*A*.] 337 2
Thanks be to God. *A*, *a*. 340 8
A. Christ is risen. 351 3
The Lord is risen indeed. *A*. 351 4
A. Christ is risen. 355 3
The Lord is risen indeed. *A*. 355 4
[*A*.] Christ our Passover is sacrificed for us; 364 15
Therefore let us keep the feast. [*A*.] 364 16
Thanks be to God. *A*, *a*. 366 23
A. Christ is risen. 413 3
The Lord is risen indeed. *A*. 413 4
at the grave we make our song: *A*, 483 2
at the grave we make our song: *A*, 499 8
A. Christ is risen. 502 19
The Lord is risen indeed. *A*. 502 20
A. Christ is risen. 512 3
The Lord is risen indeed. *A*. 512 4
A. Christ is risen. 525 3
The Lord is risen indeed. *A*. 525 4
A. Christ is risen. 537 3
The Lord is risen indeed. *A*. 537 4

alliance

they have made an *a* against you: 706 13

allotted

Canaan * to be your *a* inheritance." 738 22
hold sway over the land *a* to the just, * 781 23

allow

and will not *a* our feet to slip. 674 12
I will not *a* my eyes to sleep, * 786 5

almighty

Holy, holy, holy, Lord God *A*, 39 22
A God our heavenly Father, to render thanks 41 6
Let us humbly confess our sins unto *A* God. 41 15
A and most merciful Father, 41 16
The *A* and merciful Lord grant you absolution 42 11
O Lord God, heavenly King, God the Father *A*. 52 9
I believe in God, the Father *a*, 53 23
and sitteth on the right hand of God the Father *a*. 54 3
A God, whose most dear Son went not up to joy 56 6
A God, who after the creation of the world 56 11
O Lord, our heavenly Father, *a* and everlasting God, 57 7
A and everlasting God, by whose Spirit 57 19
A God, Father of all mercies 58 14
A God, who hast given us grace 59 12
here in the presence of *A* God, 62 11
Let us humbly confess our sins unto *A* God. 62 15
A and most merciful Father, 62 16
The *A* and merciful Lord grant you absolution and 63 14
I believe in God, the Father *a*, 66 9
on the right hand of God the Father *a*. 66 19
A God, Father of all mercies, 71 10
A God, who hast given us grace 72 9
Holy, holy, holy is the Lord God *A*, 77 20
A God our heavenly Father, to set forth his praise, 79 2
A God have mercy on you, forgive you 80 1
the *A* has done great things for me, 92 2
heavenly King, *a* God and Father, 94 24
I believe in God, the Father *a*, 96 13
A God, whose most dear Son went not up to joy 99 1
A God, who after the creation of the world 99 6
Lord God, *a* and everlasting Father, 100 1
A and everlasting God, by whose Spirit 100 11
A God, Father of all mercies, 101 7
A God, you have given us grace 102 1
A Savior, who at noonday called your servant 107 12
A God, we give you thanks 110 12
O Lord God *A*, as you have taught us 110 23
A and most merciful God, kindle within us 111 4
A, everlasting God, let our prayer 113 9
here in the presence of *A* God, 116 7
A God have mercy on you, 117 6
the *A* has done great things for me, 119 8

I believe in God, the Father *a*, 120 9
A God, Father of all mercies, 125 5
A God, you have given us grace 126 1
The Lord *A* grant us a peaceful night 127 1
A God, our heavenly Father: We have sinned 127 6
May the *A* God grant us forgiveness 128 1
abides under the shadow of the *A*. 129 22
The *a* and merciful Lord, Father, Son, and Holy 135 14
Lord God, *a* and everlasting Father, you have brought 137 14
The *a* and merciful Lord, 140 17
A God, who hast promised to hear the petitions 153 19
A God, give us grace that we may cast away 159 1
We beseech thee, *A* God, to purify our consciences 160 6
A God, who has given us thy only-begotten Son 161 7
A God, who hast poured upon us the new light 161 14
A God, whose Son our Savior Jesus Christ 163 7
A and everlasting God, who dost govern 164 1
A and everlasting God, who hatest nothing 166 1
A God, whose blessed Son was led 166 9
A God, who seest that we have no power 167 3
O *A* God, who alone canst order the unruly wills 167 15
A and everlasting God, who, of thy tender love 168 1
A God, whose most dear Son went not up to joy 168 10
A Father, whose dear Son, on the night before he 169 7
A God, we beseech thee graciously to behold 169 14
A God, who through thine only-begotten Son 170 23
we beseech thee, *A* God, that we who celebrate 171 5
A and everlasting God, who in the Paschal 172 1
A Father, who hast given thine only Son to die 172 8
A and everlasting God, who in the Paschal 172 20
O *A* God, whom truly to know 173 16
O *A* God, whose blessed Son 174 8
Grant, we beseech thee, *A* God, that like as we 174 15
A God, who on this day didst open 175 8
A and everlasting God, who hast given 176 1
O *A* and most merciful God, of thy bountiful 177 3
O *A* God, who hast built thy Church 178 18
A God, the fountain of all wisdom, 179 16
A God, who hast given thy only Son 180 19
O God, who declarest thy *a* power 182 12
A and everlasting God, who art always more ready 182 18
A and everlasting God, who in Christ hast revealed 183 11
A and everlasting God, give unto us the increase 183 17
A and merciful God, of whose only gift 184 1
A and everlasting God, whose will it is 185 1
A God, who didst give such grace to thine apostle 185 7
A Father, who didst inspire Simon Peter, 187 1
A and everliving God, we humbly beseech thee 187 16
O *A* God, who into the place of Judas didst choose 188 1
A God, who by the hand of Mark 188 21
A God, who didst give to thine apostles Philip 189 5
A God, by whose providence thy servant John 190 1
A God, whose blessed apostles Peter and Paul 190 10
Lord God *A*, in whose Name the founders 190 17
A God, whose blessed Son restored Mary Magdalene 191 1
O *A* and everlasting God, who didst give 192 7
A God, whose Son our Savior Jesus Christ was lifted 192 13
A God, who didst inspire thy servant Luke 193 11
O *A* God, who hast knit together thine elect 194 8
A and gracious Father, we give thee thanks 194 16
O *A* God, who didst give to thy servant 195 1
O *A* God, by whose grace and power thy holy martyr 195 8
A and everlasting God, who didst enkindle 196 1
A and everlasting God, we thank thee 196 7
A God, who willest to be glorified in thy saints, 196 15
O *A* God, who didst give to thy servant 197 19
O *A* God, who hast compassed us about 198 16
O *A* God, who by thy Holy Spirit 199 4
A God, who hast revealed to thy Church 199 12
A and most merciful God, grant, we beseech thee, 200 1
A God, whose beloved Son willingly endured 201 7
A God, we remember this day before thee 202 9
A and everlasting God, whose will it is 202 16
A God, who by our baptism into the death 203 5
Grant, *A* God, that we, who have been redeemed 203 12
O *A* God, to whose glory we celebrate the dedication 204 1
A and everlasting Father, who hast given 204 8
A Father, whose blessed Son before his passion 204 17
A God, the giver of all good gifts, 205 4
A and everlasting God, by whose Spirit 206 1
Lord God *A*, who hast made all peoples 207 1
O *A* God, kindle, we beseech thee, 207 8
A God, Lord of heaven and earth: We humbly pray 207 15
A God, whose Son Jesus Christ in his earthly life 208 1
A God, who hast created us in thine own image: 209 1
A God, the fountain of all wisdom: Enlighten 209 17
A God our heavenly Father, who declarest thy glory 210 1
A God, who hast so linked our lives 210 10
A God, give us grace to cast away the works 211 1
Purify our conscience, *A* God, 212 6
A God, you have given your only-begotten Son 213 1
A God, you have poured upon us the new light 213 8
A God, whose Son our Savior Jesus Christ is the light 215 1
A and everlasting God, you govern 215 13
A and everlasting God, you hate nothing 217 14
A God, whose blessed Son was led by the Spirit 218 1
A God, you know that we have no power 218 13
A God, you alone can bring into order the unruly 219 6
A and everliving God, in your tender love 219 13
A God, whose most dear Son went not up to joy 220 1
A Father, whose dear Son, on the night before 221 1
A God, we pray you graciously to behold 221 8
A God, who through your only-begotten Son 222 15
we pray, *A* God, that we who celebrate 222 22
A and everlasting God, who in the Paschal 223 15
A Father, who gave your only Son to die 224 1
A and everlasting God, who in the Paschal 224 13
A God, whom truly to know is everlasting life: 225 8
A God, whose blessed Son our Savior 226 1
Grant, we pray, *A* God, that as we believe 226 8
A God, on this day you opened the way 227 1
A and everlasting God, you have given 228 1
A and merciful God, in your goodness keep us, 228 14
A God, you have built your Church 230 12
A God, the fountain of all wisdom, 231 10
A God, you have given your only Son 232 11
O God, you declare your *a* power 234 6
A and everlasting God, you are always more ready 234 12
A and everlasting God, in Christ you have revealed 235 3
A and everlasting God, increase in us the gifts 235 9
A and merciful God, it is only by your gift 235 14
A and everlasting God, whose will it is 236 14
A God, who gave such grace to your apostle Andrew 237 1
A Father, who inspired Simon Peter, 238 14

A and everliving God, we humbly pray	239	6
A God, who in the place of Judas chose	239	11
A God, by the hand of Mark	240	7
A God, who gave to your apostles Philip and James	240	13
A God, by whose providence your servant John	241	10
A God, whose blessed apostles Peter and Paul	241	19
Lord God *A*, in whose Name the founders	242	1
A God, whose blessed Son restored Mary Magdalene	242	8
A and everlasting God, who gave to your apostle	243	14
A God, whose Son our Savior Jesus Christ was lifted	244	1
A God, who inspired your servant Luke	244	20
A God, you have knit together your elect	245	16
A and gracious Father, we give you thanks	246	1
A God, who gave to your servant	246	8
A God, by whose grace and power your holy martyr	247	6
A and everlasting God, who kindled the flame	247	13
A and everlasting God, we thank you	247	19
A God, whose will it is to be glorified	248	1
A God, you gave to your servant	249	5
A God, you have surrounded us	250	1
A God, by your Holy Spirit you have made us one	250	14
A God, you have revealed to your Church	251	1
A and most merciful God, grant that	251	7
A God, whose beloved Son willingly endured	252	12
A God, we remember before you today	253	13
A and everlasting God, whose will it is to restore	254	1
A God, by our baptism into the death	254	7
Grant, *A* God, that we, who have been redeemed	254	13
A God, to whose glory we celebrate the dedication	254	19
A and everlasting Father, you have given	255	6
A Father, whose blessed Son before his passion	255	15
A God, the giver of all good gifts,	256	1
A and everlasting God, by whose Spirit	256	19
Lord God *A*, you have made all the peoples	258	1
A God, kindle, we pray, in every heart	258	8
A God, Lord of heaven and earth: We humbly pray	258	15
A God, whose Son Jesus Christ in his earthly life	259	3
A God, who created us in your own image:	260	8
A God, the fountain of all wisdom: Enlighten	261	1
A God our heavenly Father, you declare your glory	261	7
A God, you have so linked our lives	261	15
A and everlasting God, you hate nothing	264	2
A God, you have created us out of the dust	265	16
A God, the Father of our Lord Jesus Christ,	269	3
It is right to praise you, *A* God, for the acts	271	5
A God, whose most dear Son went not up to joy	272	1
A and everliving God, in your tender love	272	7
A Father, whose dear Son, on the night before	274	1
A God, we pray you graciously to behold	276	4
A and everlasting God, by whose Spirit	278	11
A God, kindle, we pray, in every heart	278	25
pray with me to God the *A*	286	11
praise you, the invisible, *a*, and eternal God,	287	2
A God, you have placed in the skies the sign	289	1
A and everlasting God, who in the Paschal	290	14
A God, by the Passover of your Son	291	5
I believe in God, the Father *a*,	292	12
May *A* God, the Father of our Lord	294	4
A God, who for our redemption gave	295	1
I believe in God, the Father *a*,	304	2
We thank you, *A* God, for the gift of water.	306	13
A God, we thank you that by the death	309	3

A and everliving God, let your fatherly hand	310	8
A God, the Father of our Lord Jesus Christ,	311	21
obedience to his command, his Church renders to *A*	316	9
A God, with full purpose of amendment of life,	317	5
[and humbly confess our sins to *A* God].	317	23
Let us humbly confess our sins unto *A* God.	320	9
A and most merciful Father,	320	23
The *A* and merciful Lord grant you absolution	321	14
A God, unto whom all hearts are open,	323	6
O Lord God, heavenly King, God the Father *A*.	324	20
We believe in one God, the Father, the *A*,	326	7
I believe in one God, the Father *A*,	327	21
A and everliving God, who in thy holy Word	329	1
and make your humble confession to *A* God,	330	13
Let us humbly confess our sins unto *A* God.	330	15
A God, Father of our Lord Jesus Christ,	331	1
A God, our heavenly Father, who of his great mercy	332	1
holy Father, *a*, everlasting God.	333	9
All glory be to thee, *A* God, our heavenly Father,	334	9
and, of thy *a* goodness, vouchsafe to bless	335	18
all honor and glory be unto thee, O Father *A*,	336	14
A and everliving God, we most heartily thank thee	339	2
the blessing of God *A*,	339	18
The blessing of God *A*,	339	20
holy Father, *a*, everlasting God.	341	3
be unto thee, O Father *A*, world without end.	343	5
A God have mercy on you, forgive you	353	1
A God, to you all hearts are open,	355	7
Lord God, heavenly King, *a* God and Father,	356	4
We believe in one God, the Father, the *A*,	358	4
A God have mercy on you, forgive you	360	15
to give thanks to you, Father *A*,	361	8
glory is yours, *A* Father, now and for ever.	363	21
A and everliving God, we thank you	366	1
to give thanks to you, Father *A*,	367	8
all honor and glory is yours, *A* Father,	369	16
glory are yours, *A* God and Father, in the unity	375	27
Grant, *A* God, that all who confess your Name	388	2
A and eternal God, ruler of all things in heaven	394	9
A God, to whom our needs are known	394	12
A God, by your Holy Spirit you have made us one	395	17
A Father, whose dear Son, on the night before	397	13
A God have mercy on you, forgive you	398	7
all honor and glory is yours, *A* Father,	403	20
glory is yours, *A* Father, now and for ever.	405	21
I believe in God, the Father *a*,	416	7
A God, we thank you that by the death	418	1
A and everliving God, let your fatherly hand	419	4
A God, look with favor upon this person	421	2
to join in giving thanks to *A* God	440	4
the *A* has done great things for me,	441	16
A God, giver of life and love, bless	444	8
I confess to *A* God, to his Church, and to you,	447	5
A God, our Creator and our Redeemer.	450	7
May *A* God in mercy receive your confession	451	3
A God have mercy on you, forgive you	455	6
The *A* Lord, who is a strong tower to all	456	20
A God our heavenly Father, graciously comfort	459	7
A God, look on this your servant, lying in great	462	1
In the Name of God the Father *A* who created you;	464	22
A God, our Father in heaven, before whom live all	466	7
A God, look with pity upon the sorrows	467	3

A God, who hast knit together thine elect 480 4
A God, we thank thee that in thy great love 482 1
through our Lord Jesus Christ, we commend to *A* 485 10
O *A* God, the God of the spirits of all flesh, 486 7
A and everlasting God, we yield unto thee 487 10
A God, with whom do live the spirits of those 488 1
A God, our heavenly Father, in whose hands are 488 26
A God, Father of mercies and giver of all comfort: 489 30
I believe in God, the Father *a*, 496 3
A God, we thank you that in your great love 498 12
through our Lord Jesus Christ, we commend to *A* 501 12
A God, with whom still live the spirits of those 503 12
in your loving wisdom and *a* power, 504 28
A God, Father of mercies and giver of comfort: 505 17
A God, to you all hearts are open, 512 7
and offer our prayers to *A* God before 514 16
We believe in one God, the Father, the *A*, 519 7
A Father, we thank you for feeding us 523 1
The blessing, mercy, and grace of God *A*, 523 15
A God, to you all hearts are open, 525 7
We believe in one God, the Father, the *A*, 529 10
A Father, we thank you for feeding us 535 1
The blessing of God *A*, 535 11
A God, to you all hearts are open, 537 7
We believe in one God, the Father, the *A*, 541 10
A Father, we thank you for feeding us 546 3
A Father, we thank you for feeding us 564 1
Through the ages, *A* God has moved his people 567 1
A God, we thank you for making us in your image, 567 8
We thank you, *A* God, for the gift of water. 570 5
A God, all times are your seasons, 572 9
We praise you, *A* and eternal God, 573 8
When the *A* scattered kings, * 677 8
abides under the shadow of the *A*. 719 11
A God our heavenly Father, guide the nations 816 1
A and everlasting God, from whom cometh 817 3
A and everliving God, ruler of all things 817 18
A and everliving God, source of all wisdom 818 1
A God, giver of every good gift: Look graciously 818 8
A God, who hast given us this good land 820 1
A God, who sittest in the throne judging right: 821 8
A God our heavenly Father, send down 822 17
A God, to whom we must account 822 23
A God, we commend to your gracious care 823 1
A God, we thank you for making the earth fruitful, 824 6
A and most merciful God, we remember before you 826 1
A God, whose loving hand hath given us 827 1
A God, you proclaim your truth in every age 827 6
A and everlasting God, you made the universe 827 11
A God, in giving us dominion 827 17
A God, our heavenly Father, who settest the solitary 828 22
A God, heavenly Father, you have blessed us 829 9
A God, whose Son had nowhere to lay his head: 829 22
A God, we entrust all who are dear to us 831 7
A and eternal God, so draw our hearts 832 24
O *A* God, who pourest out on all who desire 833 19
A God, who hast promised to hear 834 1
A God, that the words which we have heard 834 18
A God, you sent your Son Jesus Christ 838 1
A God, giver of all good things: 838 21
A God and heavenly Father, we give thee humble 841 7
We learn that there is one God, the Father *A*, 846 3

almost
I had *a* tripped and fallen; 687 4
I was pressed so hard that I *a* fell, * 761 22
They had *a* made an end of me on earth, * 770 16

aloes
All your garments are fragrant with myrrh, *a*, 648 6

alone
For you *a* are the Holy One, 95 9
you *a* are the Lord, 95 10
you *a* are the Most High, 95 11
O Almighty God, who *a* canst order 167 15
of self-denying service by which *a* 191 11
from the service of self *a*, that we may do the work 210 4
that we may do it not for self *a*, 210 12
Almighty God, you *a* can bring into order 219 6
service by which *a* they may have true authority 242 18
from the service of self *a*, that we may do the work 261 10
that we may do it not for self *a*, 261 17
those whose faith is known to God *a*, 280 11
For you *a* are the Holy One, 356 13
you *a* are the Lord, 356 14
you *a* are the Most High, 356 15
for you *a* are God, living and true, 373 2
those whose faith is known to you *a*; 375 19
to live no longer for ourselves *a*, 379 4
those whose faith is known to you *a*, 391 16
for those who are *a*. 392 4
health which it is yours *a* to give; 458 24
From you *a*, O Lord, 492 7
those whose faith is known to you *a*, 550 21
Draw us to you, when we come *a* 568 16
To him *a* all who sleep in the earth bow down 612 15
for I am left *a* and in misery. 615 21
Refrain from anger, leave rage *a*; * 633 21
For God *a* my soul in silence waits; * 669 5
He *a* is my rock and my salvation, * 669 7
For God *a* my soul in silence waits; * 669 16
He *a* is my rock and my salvation, * 669 18
I will recall your righteousness, yours *a*. 684 13
who *a* does wondrous deeds! 686 26
you *a* are the Most High over all the earth. 707 14
and you *a* are God. 710 20
administer the law in the fear of thee *a*; 821 12
Grant that those who live *a* may not be lonely 829 23
acknowledge our dependence on you *a*. 836 11

along
garments and branches of palm *a* his way. 271 9
and guides me *a* right pathways 443 6
and guides me *a* right pathways 613 2
a with hot glowing coals. 778 17
they have set traps for me *a* the path. 796 12

aloud
To thee all Angels cry *a*, 52 25
Cry *a*, inhabitants of Zion, ring out your joy, * 86 13
I call *a* upon the LORD, * 587 9
Singing *a* a song of thanksgiving * 616 20
I will cry *a* to God; * 693 1
I will cry *a*, and he will hear me. 693 2

altar

If thou bring thy gift to the *a*, 343 17
leave there thy gift before the *a*, 343 19
If you are offering your gift at the *a*, 376 13
leave your gift there before the *a* 376 15
and to serve at your *a*. 562 11
Let us now pray for the setting apart of the *A*. 573 7
a sign of the heavenly *A* 574 2
that I may go in procession round your *a*, 616 19
That I may go to the *a* of God, 644 24
then shall they offer young bullocks upon your *a*. 657 22
procession with branches up to the horns of the *a*. 762 26

altars

They grieved him with their hill-*a* * 699 22
by the side of your *a*, O LORD of hosts, 707 21

although

And *a* we are unworthy, 336 9
A they have no words or language, * 606 19
A they are means of grace, 860 14

altogether

but thou, O LORD, knowest it *a*. 474 24
true and righteous *a*. 607 15
Let them be ashamed and *a* dismayed 641 10
be ashamed and *a* dismayed; * 682 14
"Let us destroy them *a*." * 689 24
but you, O LORD, know it *a*. 794 7

alway

as thou dost *a* resist the proud 181 18
Blessed are they that *a* keep judgment, * 478 15

always

a acceptable in thy sight, 40 14
do *a* what is righteous in thy sight; 57 12
I have set the Lord *a* before me; 61 11
Your gates will *a* be open; * 87 19
Govern and uphold them, now and *a*. 98 10
My life is *a* in my hand, * 104 5
I have set the Lord *a* before me; 115 11
and let your blessing be upon us *a*; 133 23
and let your blessing be upon us *a*; 140 15
O God, whose glory it is *a* to have mercy: 166 16
that we may *a* serve thee 172 10
think and do *a* such things 180 15
Give us grace that we may *a* 180 21
Almighty and everlasting God, who art *a* 182 18
Lord, we pray thee that thy grace may *a* 183 6
may *a* be ordered and guided 188 4
as thy holy angels *a* serve and worship 193 6
may *a* be ready to give a reason 195 4
as thy holy angels *a* serve and worship 200 8
may *a* give thee thanks; 207 19
O God, whose glory it is *a* to have mercy: 218 7
that we may *a* serve you 224 3
protect and govern it *a* by your goodness; 232 3
the spirit to think and do *a* 232 6
you *a* resist the proud 233 10
Almighty and everlasting God, you are *a* 234 12
Lord, we pray that your grace may *a* 234 20
may *a* be guided and governed 239 13
as your holy angels *a* serve and worship 244 15
may *a* be ready to give a reason 247 2
we may *a* be supported by this fellowship 250 16
as your holy angels *a* serve and worship 251 14
receiving good things from your hand, may *a* 258 19
Make us *a* thankful for 259 12
It is truly right and good, *a* and everywhere, 286 22
The peace of the Lord be *a* with you. 308 15
The peace of the Lord be *a* with you. 310 13
The peace of the Lord be *a* with you. 332 19
whose property is *a* to have mercy. 337 13
and remain with you *a*. 339 19
be with them *a*, 348 14
The peace of the Lord be *a* with you. 360 19
It is right, and a good and joyful thing, *a* 361 7
It is right, and a good and joyful thing, *a* 367 7
be with them *a*, 381 8
we may *a* be supported by this fellowship 395 19
The peace of the Lord be *a* with you. 419 9
The peace of the Lord be *a* with you. 431 14
that he may *a* think and do 460 22
and help me *a* to believe 461 9
The peace of the Lord be *a* with you. 522 1
and *a* rejoice in your glory; 523 8
The peace of the Lord be *a* with you. 534 14
and *a* rejoice in your glory; 535 8
be among you, and remain with you *a*. 535 12
The peace of the Lord be *a* with you. 546 1
and *a* rejoice in your glory; 547 4
Be *a* with me in carrying out 563 4
The peace of the Lord be *a* with you. 563 12
and *a* rejoice in your glory; 564 8
Be present *a* to guide 568 12
Be *a* near us when we seek you 568 15
The peace of the Lord be *a* with you. 574 10
For the needy shall not *a* be forgotten, * 594 13
I have set the LORD *a* before me; * 600 13
let them say *a*, "Great is the LORD, 631 28
The righteous are *a* generous in their lending, * 635 12
and my pain is *a* with me. 638 4
your offerings are *a* before me. 654 20
You are *a* speaking evil of your brother * 655 20
So will I *a* sing the praise of your Name, * 669 3
Put your trust in him *a*, O people, * 669 22
my praise shall be *a* of you. 683 13
But I shall *a* wait in patience, * 684 7
may prayer be made for him *a*, 686 15
a at ease, they increase their wealth. 688 2
Yet I am *a* with you; * 688 23
they will *a* be praising you. 707 24
But you are *a* the same, * 733 5
He will not *a* accuse us, * 733 25
He has *a* been mindful of his covenant, * 738 15
and *a* do what is right! 742 2
Let their sin be *a* before the LORD; * 751 27
but *a* walk in his ways. 763 10
which I have *a* loved. 767 8
and it is *a* with me. 771 16
My life is *a* in my hand, * 772 11
as you *a* do to those who love your Name. 774 12
We humbly beseech thee that we may *a* prove 820 2
as thou wilt, and *a* to thy glory 833 2

Amalek

Gebal, and Ammon, and *A*; * 706 16

ambush

They lurk in *a* in public squares 595 8
to shoot from *a* at the true of heart. 596 12
That they may shoot down the blameless from *a*; * 671 16

amend

grace of thy Holy Spirit to *a* our lives 152 5
grace of the Holy Spirit to *a* our lives, 391 8
grace of the Holy Spirit to *a* our lives, 550 17
with the intention to *a* our lives. 857 13

amendment

remission of all your sins, true repentance, *a* 42 12
remission of all your sins, true repentance, *a* 63 15
with full purpose of *a* of life, 317 5
remission of all your sins, true repentance, *a* 321 15
I firmly intend *a* of life, 447 10
a of life according to your will, 826 19

amiss

wilt be extreme to mark what is done *a*, * 474 5
If you, LORD, were to note what is done *a*, * 784 21
where in any thing it is *a*, reform it. 816 13

Ammon

Gebal, and *A*, and Amalek; * 706 16

among

my Name shall be great *a* the Gentiles, 38 6
for my Name shall be great *a* the heathen, 38 8
The Word was made flesh and dwelt *a* us: 44 6
Thy saving health *a* all nations. 55 10
Thy saving health *a* all nations. 68 2
abounding grace may increase *a* us; 71 9
my Name shall be great *a* the nations, 76 6
my Name shall be great *a* the nations, 76 8
his deeds *a* the peoples. 78 7
The Word was made flesh and dwelt *a* us: 82 1
compared with you, O Lord, *a* the gods? * 85 16
Make his deeds known *a* the peoples; * 86 9
Your saving health *a* all nations. 98 4
Then they said *a* the nations, * 105 8
my Name shall be great *a* the nations, 106 7
my Name shall be great *a* the nations, 106 9
like the lamp, must shed light *a* 109 10
Your saving health *a* all nations. 122 4
abounding grace may increase *a* us; 125 4
with great might come *a* us; 160 2
that so, *a* the sundry and manifold changes 167 18
manifest thy power *a* all peoples, 181 7
and even now, while we are placed *a* things 182 7
revealed thy glory *a* the nations: 183 12
inspire Simon Peter, first *a* the apostles, 187 1
apostle James, first *a* the Twelve 191 8
may have true authority *a* thy people; 191 12
justice in our communities and *a* the nations, 209 5
for the sake of him who came *a* us 210 6
with great might come *a* us; 212 2
a the swift and varied changes of the world, 219 9
show forth your power *a* all peoples, 232 19
and even now, while we are placed *a* things 234 2
revealed your glory *a* the nations: 235 4
Simon Peter, first *a* the apostles, 238 14
Matthias to be numbered *a* the Twelve: 239 12
James, first *a* the Twelve 242 15
may have true authority *a* your people; 242 18
justice in our communities and *a* the nations, 260 12
him who came *a* us as one who serves, 261 12
and for those in authority *a* them; 278 18
your saving health *a* all nations. 281 8
numbered *a* the offspring of Abraham, 289 17
Will you strive for justice and peace *a* all 294 1
Will you strive for justice and peace *a* all 305 7
Recalling Christ's death and his descent *a* the dead, 374 25
for goodwill *a* nations; 386 1
forbearance may grow *a* nations 390 14
Will you strive for justice and peace *a* all 417 17
Scripture commends it to be honored *a* all people. 423 8
in sending Jesus Christ to come *a* us, 430 11
and established me *a* your children 450 12
a such as keep holy-day. 471 11
I will be exalted *a* the nations, 472 5
for raising up *a* us faithful servants 523 4
serve the people *a* whom you work, 531 11
the firstborn *a* many brethren, 533 4
for raising up *a* us faithful servants 535 4
be *a* you, and remain with you always. 535 12
a whom you live, and work, and worship. 543 11
for raising up *a* us faithful servants 546 6
forbearance may grow *a* nations 549 30
accept this Bible, and be *a* us 561 1
receive this stole, and be *a* us 561 4
receive this book, and be *a* us 561 5
use this oil, and be *a* us 561 6
obey these Canons, and be *a* us 562 3
take this bread and wine, and be *a* us 562 5
for raising up *a* us faithful servants 564 4
Son Jesus Christ to be born *a* us, 573 10
the faithful have vanished from *a* us. 597 2
upon those who are noble *a* the people. 600 2
Therefore will I extol you *a* the nations, O LORD, * 606 10
and their descendants from *a* the peoples of the earth. 609 19
they divide my garments *a* them; 611 16
Who *a* you loves life * 628 17
a those who keep holy-day. 643 12
and from the peak of Mizar *a* the heights of Hermon. 643 20
and have scattered us *a* the nations. 646 8
You have made us a byword *a* the nations, * 646 13
laughing-stock *a* the peoples. 646 14
Kings' daughters stand *a* the ladies of the court; * 648 8
the rich *a* the people seek your favor." 648 16
I will be exalted *a* the nations; 650 2
I will confess you *a* the peoples, O LORD; * 664 15
I will sing praise to you *a* the nations. 664 16
your saving health *a* all nations. 675 12
Though you lingered among the sheepfolds, * 677 5
that the LORD God might dwell *a* them. 677 20
and became a byword *a* them. 680 10
and not be written *a* the righteous. 681 21
He shall defend the needy *a* the people; * 685 15
there is not one *a* us who knows how long. 690 3
and have declared your power *a* the peoples. 694 2
He sent swarms of flies *a* them, which ate them up, * 698 17

the tabernacle where he had lived *a* his people. 699 27
Let it be known *a* the heathen and in our sight 702 2
There shall be no strange god *a* you; * 704 19
They have said, "Come, let us wipe them out from *a* 706 9
A the gods there is none like you, O LORD, * 710 13
I count Egypt and Babylon *a* those who know me; * 711 17
I am counted *a* those who go down to the Pit; * 712 7
Lost *a* the dead, * 712 9
who is like the LORD *a* the gods? 714 6
Consider well, you dullards *a* the people; * 723 9
Declare his glory *a* the nations * 725 21
and his wonders *a* all peoples. 725 22
Tell it out *a* the nations: "The LORD is King! * 726 11
Moses and Aaron *a* his priests, 729 11
and Samuel *a* those who call upon his Name, * 729 12
like an owl *a* the ruins. 731 12
and sing *a* the branches. 735 26
make known his deeds *a* the peoples. 738 2
They worked his signs *a* them, * 740 7
To cast out their seed *a* the nations, * 744 1
and a plague broke out *a* them. 744 6
and gather us from *a* the nations, * 745 20
I will confess you *a* the peoples, O LORD; * 749 22
I will sing praises to you *a* the nations. 749 23
and dwell *a* the tents of Kedar! 778 19
I had to live *a* the enemies of peace. 778 21
Then they said *a* the nations, * 782 10
And brought out Israel from *a* them, * 790 17
and establish *a* them that peace 816 2
your love to all *a* whom we live; 817 17
may show forth thy praise *a* the nations 820 12
may be a people at peace *a* ourselves 821 16
Lord Christ, when you came *a* us, 825 16
and so enkindle fervent charity *a* us all 829 6
that, *a* all the changes and chances 832 20

amongst

be *a* you, and remain with you always. 339 19

Amorites

Sihon, king of the *A*, 788 23
Sihon, king of the *A*, * 791 7

ancestors

we may be gathered to our *a*, 504 6

ancient

who led your *a* people into freedom 111 8
you led your *a* people by a pillar of cloud 290 2
He rides in the heavens, the *a* heavens; * 678 26
Yet God is my King from *a* times, * 690 8
I will declare the mysteries of *a* times. 694 22
The Apostles' Creed is the *a* creed of Baptism; 852 2
The Athanasian Creed is an *a* document 852 9

Andrew

who didst give such grace to thine apostle *A* 185 8
who gave such grace to your apostle *A* 237 1

anew

By his great mercy we have been born *a* 137 12

angel

announced by an *a* to the Virgin Mary, 188 17
announced by an *a* to the Virgin Mary, 240 3
The *a* of the LORD encompasses those 628 7
and let the *a* of the LORD drive them away. 629 23
and let the *a* of the LORD pursue them. 630 2

angels

O ye *a* of the Lord, bless ye the Lord; * 47 7
To thee all Angels cry aloud, 52 25
That thy holy *a* may lead us 68 9
and give thine *a* charge over those 71 2
Glorify the Lord, you *a* 88 9
To you all *a*, all the powers of heaven, 95 19
That your holy *a* may lead us 122 11
and give your *a* charge over those 124 18
For he shall give his *a* charge over you, * 130 19
let your holy *a* dwell with us 133 22
and give your *a* charge over those 134 7
let your holy *a* dwell with us 140 14
constituted the ministries of *a* and men 193 5
as thy holy *a* always serve and worship 193 6
near to an innumerable company of *a* 198 24
constituted the ministries of *a* and men 200 7
as thy holy *a* always serve and worship 200 8
order the ministries of *a* and mortals: 244 14
as your holy *a* always serve and worship 244 15
near to an innumerable company of *a*, 250 9
order the ministries of *a* and mortals: 251 13
as your holy *a* always serve and worship 251 14
Rejoice now, heavenly hosts and choirs of *a*, 286 1
Therefore with *A* and Archangels, 334 1
Therefore with *A* and Archangels, 341 4
we praise you, joining our voices with *A* 362 1
we praise you, joining our voices with *A* 367 10
Countless throngs of *a* stand before you 373 7
And so we join the saints and *a* 402 7
And so we join the saints and *a* 404 9
May *a* surround him, 466 5
Into paradise may the *a* lead thee; 484 1
Into paradise may the *a* lead you. 500 12
saints and *a* praise you for ever. 574 3
You have made him but little lower than the *a*; * 592 17
So mortals ate the bread of *a*; * 696 26
a troop of destroying *a*. 699 3
For he shall give his *a* charge over you, * 720 7
Bless the LORD, you *a* of his, 734 22
Praise him, all you *a* of his; * 805 23
O God, whom saints and *a* 819 13

anger

slow to *a* and of great kindness, 38 16
for he is gracious and merciful, slow to *a* 76 14
Our *a* at our own frustration, 268 7
and let your *a* depart from us; 268 27
LORD, do not rebuke me in your *a*; * 589 23
they reeled because of his *a*. 603 3
Refrain from *a*, leave rage alone; * 633 21
O LORD, do not rebuke me in your *a*; * 636 20
O God, in your *a*, cast down the peoples. 663 5
and let the fierceness of your *a* overtake them. 681 13
has he, in his *a*, withheld his compassion? 693 19

and his *a* mounted against Israel; 696 19
So God's *a* mounted against them; * 697 11
many times he held back his *a* 698 3
He poured out upon them his blazing *a*: * 699 1
He gave full rein to his *a*; 699 4
let your *a* depart from us. 709 2
will you prolong your *a* from age to age? 709 4
slow to *a*, and full of kindness and truth. 711 5
Your *a* weighs upon me heavily, * 712 15
Your blazing *a* has swept over me; * 713 11
how long will your *a* burn like fire? 717 7
slow to *a* and of great kindness. 733 24
nor will he keep his *a* for ever. 733 26
They provoked him to *a* with their actions, * 744 5
Again they provoked his *a* at the waters of Meribah, * 744 11
in their fierce *a* toward us; 781 6
slow to *a* and of great kindness. 802 2

angered

who by our sins are justly *a*. 492 8
and was *a* against his inheritance. 700 4
how long will you be *a* 702 19

angry

For when thou art *a* all our days are gone; * 473 1
Lest he be *a* and you perish; * 586 26
you have been *a*; 667 10
who can stand before you when you are *a*? 692 15
When God heard this, he was *a* * 699 24
How long will you be *a*, O LORD? * 701 13
When you are *a*, all our days are gone: * 718 17
The wicked will see it and be *a*; 755 25

anguish

For those in loneliness, fear, and *a* 279 7
my cry of *a* came to his ears. 602 21

ankles

and my *a* do not give way. 605 13

announce

Let me *a* the decree of the LORD: * 586 14
and to *a* the coming of the Messiah. 849 9

announced

a by an angel to the Virgin Mary, 188 17
a by an angel to the Virgin Mary, 240 2

anoint

didst proclaim him thy beloved Son and *a* him 163 2
I *a* you with oil in the Name of 456 11
let not the oil of the unrighteous *a* my head; * 797 13

anointed

proclaimed him your beloved Son and *a* him 214 13
received the baptism of John and was *a* 306 17
Eternal Father, whose blessed Son was *a* 307 9
you have *a* my head with oil, 443 13
a many that were sick and healed them, 455 11
As you are outwardly *a* with this holy oil, 456 13
thou hast *a* my head with oil, 476 14
Our brother (sister) was washed in Baptism and *a* 497 16
received the baptism of John and was *a* 570 9
against the LORD and against his *A*? 586 5
he shows loving-kindness to his *a*, 606 13
Now I know that the LORD gives victory to his *a*: * 608 12
you have *a* my head with oil, 613 9
a safe refuge for his *a*. 620 2
Therefore God, your God, has *a* you * 648 4
and look upon the face of your *A*. 708 9
with my holy oil have I *a* him. 715 7
But you have cast off and rejected your *a*; * 716 17
which they hurled at the heels of your *a*. 717 17
I am *a* with fresh oil. 721 17
Saying, "Do not touch my *a* * 739 7
do not turn away the face of your *A*. 786 18
I have prepared a lamp for my *A*. 787 6

anointest

thou *a* my head with oil; 477 7

anointing

heavenly Father grant you the inward *a* 456 14
Unction is the rite of *a* the sick with oil, 861 14

another

entrusting one *a* and all our life to Christ, 68 24
companionship with one *a* thine abounding grace 71 8
entrusting one *a* and all our life to Christ, 122 26
companionship with one *a* your abounding grace 125 3
and united to one *a* with pure affection; 179 7
who hast so linked our lives one with *a* 210 10
and united to one *a* with pure affection; 231 1
you have so linked our lives one with *a* 261 15
We confess to you and to one *a*, 267 13
Love one *a* as I have 275 3
you have love for one *a*. 275 8
and members one of *a*. 316 7
And then, being reconciled with one *a*, 317 9
and we turned against one *a*. 370 15
commend ourselves, and one *a*, 385 14
that we may honor one *a* 388 8
that we may serve Christ in them, and love one *a* 388 18
commend ourselves, and one *a*, 391 21
given one *a* in prosperity and adversity; 423 11
and peace with you and one *a* all the days 429 13
your children are united one to *a*, 430 5
This is *a* day, O Lord. 461 19
from one generation to *a*. 472 10
commend ourselves, and one *a*, 550 28
one with you and with one *a*, 569 1
be forgiven for their sins, united with one *a*, 574 6
One day tells its tale to *a*, * 606 17
and one night imparts knowledge to *a*. 606 18
One deep calls to *a* in the noise of your cataracts; * 643 21
from one generation to *a*; * 648 26
from one generation to *a*. 685 18
he puts down one and lifts up *a*. 691 17
from one generation to *a*. 717 21
and from one kingdom to *a*, 739 4
and let *a* take his office. 751 13
Your faithfulness remains from one generation to *a*; * 770 22
One generation shall praise your works to *a* * 801 18
one *a* without hatred or bitterness, and to work 824 3
find with one *a* the fulfillment of their humanity; 825 14
kindly affectioned one to *a*; 829 8

as he begins *a* year. 830 9
The New Commandment is that we love one *a* 851 16
union with Christ and one *a*, 860 2

answer

A me when I call, 128 8
He shall call upon me, and I will *a* him; * 131 1
Give us grace, O Lord, to *a* readily 163 14
Give us grace, O Lord, to *a* readily 215 7
a the earnest prayers 440 9
A me when I call, 587 20
Look upon me and *a* me, 598 4
I call upon you, O God, for you will *a* me; * 601 9
they cry to the LORD, but he does not *a*. 605 23
May the LORD *a* you in the day of trouble, * 608 1
he will *a* him out of his holy heaven, 608 13
and *a* us when we call. 608 20
I cry in the daytime, but you do not *a*; * 610 4
have mercy on me and *a* me. 618 11
you will *a* me, O Lord my God. 637 28
Listen to me and *a* me; * 660 7
Save us by your right hand and *a* us, * 667 18
a me with your unfailing help. 680 16
A me, O LORD, for your love is kind; * 680 23
be swift and *a* me, for I am in distress. 680 26
Bow down your ear, O LORD, and *a* me, * 709 22
for you will *a* me. 710 12
He shall call upon me, and I will *a* him; * 720 17
when I call, make haste to *a* me, 731 4
save with your right hand and *a* me. 750 6
a me, O LORD, that I may keep your statutes. 775 16
a me in your righteousness. 798 20
O LORD, make haste to *a* me; 799 12
as ones who must *a* for them to God; 848 15

answered

I sought the LORD, and he *a* me * 628 1
I *a* you from the secret place of thunder 704 15
they called upon the LORD, and he *a* them. 729 13
"O LORD our God, you *a* them indeed; * 729 16
the LORD *a* by setting me free. 761 6
I will give thanks to you, for you *a* me * 762 13
I have confessed my ways, and you *a* me; * 765 11
I called to the LORD, and he *a* me. 778 11
When I called, you *a* me; * 793 8

answers

and he *a* me from his holy hill; 587 10

anticipate

Sacraments sustain our present hope and *a* 861 22

anxieties

putting away all earthly *a*, 56 13
putting away all earthly *a*, 99 8
from faithless fears and worldly *a*, 165 9
from faithless fears and worldly *a*, 217 2

anxiety

that being freed from *a*, 391 12
the pain and *a* of childbirth 444 2
want and *a* from lack of work. 824 12

anxious

Grant us, Lord, not to be *a* 234 1

any

there be *a* sorrow like unto my sorrow 39 5
may not fear the power of *a* adversaries; 57 5
fall into no sin, neither run into *a* kind 57 10
there is *a* sorrow like my sorrow 77 4
may not fear the power of *a* adversaries; 99 24
You shall not be afraid of *a* terror by night, * 130 6
neither shall *a* plague come near your dwelling. 130 18
called to *a* office and ministry 205 7
called to *a* office and ministry 256 4
Thou shalt not make to thyself *a* graven image, 318 1
likeness of *a* thing that is in heaven above, 318 2
sickness, or *a* other adversity. 329 28
If *a* man sin, we have an Advocate 332 15
to offer unto thee *a* sacrifice, 336 10
You shall not make for yourself *a* idol. 350 5
Pray for those in *a* need or trouble. 386 6
Have compassion on those who suffer from *a* grief 387 14
sorrow, or *a* kind of trouble; 392 9
If *a* of you can show just cause 424 2
that if either of you know *a* reason 424 5
If *a* of you know just cause 437 2
If *a* man sin, we have an Advocate 450 1
through *a* pains of death, 484 17
if *a* of you know *a* reason 514 6
if *a* of you know *a* impediment 527 4
if *a* of you know *a* impediment 539 4
if there is *a* wickedness in my hands, 590 25
there is none who does *a* good. 598 14
to see if there is *a* who is wise, 598 16
with the help of my God I will scale *a* wall. 604 23
there is none who does *a* good. 658 23
to see if there is *a* who is wise, 659 2
not for *a* offense or fault of mine, O LORD. 665 24
Not because of *a* guilt of mine * 666 1
and fall like *a* prince.'" 705 23
nor *a* wicked man bring him down. 715 11
You shall not be afraid of *a* terror by night, * 719 20
neither shall *a* plague come near your dwelling. 720 6
Can a corrupt tribunal have *a* part with you, * 724 5
so that it never shall move at *a* time. 735 12
They will not be afraid of *a* evil rumors; * 755 17
than to put *a* trust in flesh. 761 12
than to put *a* trust in rulers. 761 14
Who never do *a* wrong, * 763 9
neither is there *a* breath in their mouth. 789 10
Look well whether there be *a* wickedness in me * 795 26
let not my heart incline to *a* evil thing. 797 9
Put not your trust in rulers, nor in *a* child of earth, * 803 7
He has not done so to *a* other nation; * 805 17
all those who are in *a* ways afflicted 815 7
where in *a* thing it is amiss 816 12
When *a* are held unjustly, 826 20

anyone

Jesus said, "If *a* would come after me, 76 23
If *a* is in Christ he is a new creation; 106 1
if *a* eats of this bread, he will live for ever; 397 2

I will never turn away *a* who believes in me. 501 2
what can *a* do to me? 761 8

anything

You shall not covet *a* that belongs to your neighbor. 350 21
nor *a* like your works. 710 14
We praise God, not to obtain *a*, 857 5

apart

and to set *a* places 567 2
now to be set *a* for your worship, 567 10
Let us now pray for the setting *a* of the Altar. 573 7
Why then do we live *a* from God 845 8

Apocrypha

called the *A*, are often included in the Bible. 853 8
What is the *A*? 853 19
The *A* is a collection of additional books 853 20

apostle

Paul to be an *a* to the Gentiles: 107 13
who didst give such grace to thine *a* 185 7
who didst strengthen thine *a* Thomas 185 14
teaching of thine *a* and evangelist John, 186 8
O God, who, by the preaching of thine *a* Paul, 187 8
servant and *a* James, first among the Twelve 191 8
a Bartholomew grace truly to believe 192 8
witness of thine *a* and evangelist Matthew 192 20
who gave such grace to your *a* Andrew 237 1
who strengthened your *a* Thomas 237 8
being illumined by the teachings of your *a* 238 2
O God, by the preaching of your *a* Paul 238 20
servant and *a* James, first among the Twelve 242 15
who gave to your *a* Bartholomew 243 14
for the witness of your *a* and evangelist 244 7
particularly as *a*, chief priest, 855 23

apostles

The glorious company of the *a* praise thee. 53 3
The glorious company of *a* praise you. 95 23
you said to your *a*, "Peace I give 107 17
you said to your *a*, "Peace I give 138 16
foundation of the *a* and prophets, 178 19
Simon Peter, first among the *a*, 187 2
being delivered from false *a*, 188 3
who didst give to thine *a* Philip 189 5
whose blessed *a* Peter and Paul 190 10
company of the *a*, and especially on this day 194 2
didst lead thy holy *a* to ordain ministers 205 14
foundation of the *a* and prophets, 230 13
Simon Peter, first among the *a*, 238 15
being delivered from false *a*, 239 13
who gave to your *a* Philip 240 13
whose blessed *a* Peter and Paul 241 19
we thank you for the glorious company of the *a*, 245 10
you led your holy *a* to ordain ministers 256 11
Will you continue in the *a*' teaching 293 19
Will you continue in the *a*' teaching 304 22
after his resurrection sent forth his *a* 348 12
with prophets, *a*, and martyrs, 370 24
with patriarchs, prophets, *a*, and martyrs, 375 22
after his resurrection sent forth his *a* 381 6
you said to your *a*, "Peace I give 395 8
Will you continue in the *a*' teaching 417 4
as your holy *a* anointed many 455 10
patriarchs, prophets, *a*, and martyrs; 489 17
patriarchs, prophets, *a*, and martyrs; 504 15
Likewise, the *a* prayed 514 14
Church is called to be one with the *a* 517 3
patriarchs, prophets, *a*, and martyrs, 517 15
with whom he endowed the *a*, 521 4
making some *a*, some prophets, 533 7
Peter and Paul and all the *a*; 838 15
given by Jesus Christ, the Messiah, to the *a*; 850 28
This Church uses two creeds: The *A*' Creed 851 25
What is the *A*' Creed? 852 1
The *A*' Creed is the ancient creed of Baptism; 852 2
teaching and fellowship of the *a* 854 26

apostolic

member of the one holy catholic and *a* Church, 310 2
We believe in one holy catholic and *a* Church. 327 16
And I believe one holy Catholic and *A* Church; 328 18
We believe in one holy catholic and *a* Church. 359 7
Remember, Lord, your one holy catholic and *a* 375 12
member of the one holy catholic and *a* Church, 418 18
bishop in the one, holy, catholic, and *a* Church. 513 6
We believe in one holy catholic and *a* Church. 520 7
We believe in one holy catholic and *a* Church. 530 26
We believe in one holy catholic and *a* Church. 542 26
described as one, holy, catholic, and *a*. 854 13
Why is the Church described as *a*? 854 24
The Church is *a*, because it continues 854 25

apparel

In embroidered *a* she is brought to the king; * 648 19
he has put on splendid *a*; * 722 2
the LORD has put on his *a* 722 3

appeal

and make my *a*, sure of your gracious goodness. 91 13
I *a* to you, brethren, by the mercies of God, 376 10
early in the morning I make my *a* and watch for you. 588 22
and let his *a* be in vain. 751 11

appear

to *a* in the presence of God for us. 39 17
now to *a* in the presence of God 77 15
and his glory will *a* upon you. 87 16
when he shall *a* again with power 184 11
when shall I come to *a* before the presence of God? 471 4
when shall I come to *a* before the presence of God? 643 4
and his glory will *a*. 732 9
these great mercies, such as may *a* 840 20

appeared

after his glorious resurrection manifestly *a* 347 2
After his glorious resurrection he openly *a* 379 21
They asked, and quails *a*, * 741 5

appearing

behold his *a*. 345 12
behold his *a*. 378 8
at the time of your *a*, O LORD; 609 15

appetites

Our self-indulgent *a* and ways, 268 4

apple

Keep us, O Lord, as the *a* of your eye; 132 14
Keep me as the *a* of your eye; * 601 14

applied

I have *a* my heart to fulfill your statutes * 104 11
I have *a* my heart to fulfill your statutes * 772 17

apply

that we may *a* our hearts unto wisdom. 473 8
that we may *a* our hearts to wisdom. 718 26
I will *a* my mind to your decrees. 771 10

appoint

"I will *a* a time," says God; * 691 6

appointed

Offer the *a* sacrifices * 128 18
providence hast *a* various orders in thy Church: 205 5
providence you have *a* various orders in your 256 2
the apostles prayed before they *a* 514 14
Offer the *a* sacrifices * 588 8
Then you will be pleased with the *a* sacrifices, 657 20
indeed, the *a* time has come. 732 3
to the places you had *a* for them. 735 18
You *a* the moon to mark the seasons, * 736 15

appointment

so by thy *a* they may help and defend us 193 7
so by thy *a* they may help and defend us 200 9
so by your *a* they may help and defend us 244 16
so by your *a* they may help and defend us 251 15

apportioned

and *a* an inheritance to them by lot; * 699 16

approved

has *a* him for this sacred responsibility. 514 5

Arabia

and the kings of *A* and Saba offer gifts. 686 4
and may there be given to him gold from *A*; * 686 14

archangels

Therefore with Angels and *A*, 334 1
Therefore with Angels and *A*, 341 4
joining our voices with Angels and *A* 362 2
joining our voices with Angels and *A* 367 11

ardent

with *a* devotion make known the love and mercy 194 4
with *a* devotion make known the love and mercy 245 13

areas

live and work in rural *a* 825 20

arise

I will *a* and go to my father, 38 17
I will *a* and go to my father, 76 16
A, shine, for your light has come, * 87 11
O Lord, *a*, help us; 154 3
A, O LORD; confront them and bring them down; * 601 25
but we will *a* and stand upright. 608 18
Awake, *a* to my cause! * 631 16
A! do not reject us for ever. 647 4
Let God *a*, and let his enemies be scattered; * 676 1
when you *a* you will make their image vanish. 688 18
A, O God, maintain your cause; * 690 28
A, O God, and rule the earth, * 706 1
You will *a* and have compassion on Zion, 732 1
A, O LORD, into your resting-place, * 786 13

ark

He delivered the *a* into captivity, * 700 1
"The *a*! We heard it was in Ephratah; * 786 9
you and the *a* of your strength. 786 14

arm

He hath showed strength with his *a*; * 50 11
he hath showed strength with his *a*; * 65 14
He has shown the strength of his *a*, * 92 6
He has shown the strength of his *a*, * 119 12
by the power of your mighty *a* your chosen 289 14
He has shown the strength of his *a*,* 442 1
nor did their *a* win the victory for them; * 645 14
but your right hand, your *a*, 645 15
you have scattered your enemies with your mighty *a*. 714 14
You have a mighty *a*; * 714 19
and my *a* will make him strong. 715 9
With his right hand and his holy *a* * 728 1
With a mighty hand and a stretched-out *a*, * 790 19

armed

The people of Ephraim, *a* with the bow, * 695 20
keeping all the men and women of our *a* forces 823 2

armies

and do not go forth with our *a*. 646 4
you no longer go out, O God, with our *a*. 668 7
"Kings with their *a* are fleeing away; * 677 3
you no longer go out, O God, with our *a*. 750 18

armor

the finest of those who bear *a* 85 10
and put upon us the *a* of light, 159 2
and put on the *a* of light, 211 2
Take up shield and *a* * 629 15

arms

Christ, who didst stretch out thine *a* 58 8
Christ, you stretched out your *a* 101 1
upon the cross, stretching out your loving *a*: 107 9
upon the cross, stretching out your loving *a*: 138 13
Receive, we beseech thee, into the *a* of thy mercy 186 15
Receive we pray, into the *a* of your mercy 238 9
enfold him in the *a* of your mercy, 314 5
He stretched out his *a* upon the cross, 362 15
Receive me again into the *a* of your mercy, 450 18
you gather the lambs in your *a* 459 2
Receive him into the *a* of your mercy, 465 4
children into his *a* and bless them: 470 8
receive him into the *a* of thy mercy, 481 18
Receive him into the *a* of thy mercy, 483 9
whose beloved Son took children into his *a* 494 1
Receive him into the *a* of your mercy, 499 16
and my *a* for bending even a bow of bronze. 605 8

army

The noble *a* of martyrs praise thee. 53 5
The chariots of Pharaoh and his *a* 85 9

The white-robed *a* of martyrs praise you. 95 25
Though an *a* should encamp against me, * 617 14
There is no king that can be saved by a mighty *a*; * 627 7
But swept Pharaoh and his *a* into the Red Sea, * 790 25

arose

Then he spoke, and a stormy wind *a*, * 748 5

around

and the light *a* me turn to night," 62 6
and the light *a* me turn to night," 110 8
and shed its light on those *a* us, 110 19
and to recognize you in the lives of those *a* 113 12
and the light *a* me turn to night," 116 2
the devil prowls *a* like a roaring lion, 132 9
who set themselves against me all *a*. 587 14
and gangs of evildoers circle *a* me; * 611 12
fear is all *a*; * 623 17
a mockery and derision to those *a* us. 646 12
let all *a* him bring gifts to him 692 23
an object of scorn and derision to those *a* us. 701 12
O mighty LORD, your faithfulness is all *a* you. 714 10
cloak which he wraps *a* himself, * 752 12
and the light *a* me turn to night," 794 21
the righteous will gather *a* me. 798 17
serve you in harmony *a* your heavenly throne; 815 20

arouse

and *a* our concern for those who are out 210 15
and *a* our concern for those who are out 261 20
a the careless, 817 20

array

heavens and the earth, with all their vast *a*. 90 21

arrogance

I have seen the wicked in their *a*, * 636 6
take away the *a* and hatred which 815 15
from pride and *a*, and from every evil way. 820 6

arrogant

For the *a* have risen up against me, 659 21
The *a* rise up against me, O God, 711 1
give the *a* their just deserts. 722 21
Let the *a* be put to shame, for they wrong me 769 20

arrogantly

The wicked *a* persecute the poor, * 594 21

arrow

nor of the *a* that flies by day; 130 7
but God will loose an *a* at them, 671 24
nor of the *a* that flies by day; 719 21

arrows

he makes his *a* shafts of fire. 591 25
and fit their *a* to the string, * 596 11
He loosed his *a* and scattered them; * 603 17
and aim your *a* at them. 609 24
For your *a* have already pierced me, * 636 22
your *a* are very sharp, O mighty warrior. 647 22
their teeth are spears and *a*, 664 2
and aim their bitter words like *a*, 671 15
There he broke the flashing *a*, * 692 5
your *a* flashed to and fro; 694 10
The sharpened *a* of a warrior, * 778 16
Like *a* in the hand of a warrior * 783 8
shoot out your *a* and rout them. 800 13

art

Blessed *a* thou, O Lord God of our fathers; * 49 9
Blessed *a* thou for the Name of thy Majesty; * 49 11
Blessed *a* thou in the temple of thy holiness; * 49 13
Blessed *a* thou that beholdest the depths, 49 15
Blessed *a* thou on the glorious throne 49 18
Blessed *a* thou in the firmament of heaven; * 49 20
Blessed *a* thou, O Father, Son, and Holy Spirit; * 49 22
For thou only *a* holy, 52 18
thou only *a* the Lord, 52 19
a most high in the glory of God the Father. 52 22
Thou *a* the King of glory, O Christ. 53 11
Thou *a* the everlasting Son of the Father. 53 12
Our Father, who *a* in heaven, 54 14
O God, who *a* the author of peace 57 1
Thou *a* worthy at all times to be praised 64 7
Our Father, who *a* in heaven, 67 4
O God, who *a* the life of all who live, 70 4
that we may know thee as thou *a* revealed in 70 12
Our Father, who *a* in heaven, 97 4
Our Father, who *a* in heaven, 106 14
Our Father, who *a* in heaven, 121 4
Our Father, who *a* in heaven, 132 19
Our Father, who *a* in heaven, 153 6
Lord of all power and might, who *a* 181 11
Almighty and everlasting God, who *a* 182 18
and *a* wont to give more than either 182 19
Our Father, who *a* in heaven, 311 1
For thou only *a* holy; 325 5
thou only *a* the Lord; 325 6
a most high in the glory of God the Father. 325 9
Our Father, who *a* in heaven, 336 18
But thou *a* the same Lord 337 12
Worthy *a* thou, O Lord our God, 344 5
thou are exalted as head above all. 344 11
thou *a* one God, 347 13
Because thou *a* greatly glorified 348 7
Our Father, who *a* in heaven, 364 1
Our Father, who *a* in heaven, 398 12
Our Father, who *a* in heaven, 428 8
Our Father, who *a* in heaven, 464 4
Why *a* thou so full of heaviness, O my soul? * 471 12
and why *a* thou so disquieted within me? 471 13
thou *a* God from everlasting, and world without end. 472 13
For when thou *a* angry all our days are gone; * 473 1
Thou *a* about my path, and about my bed, * 474 21
and *a* acquainted with all my ways. 474 22
If I climb up into heaven, thou *a* there; * 475 7
if I go down to hell, thou *a* there also. 475 8
for thou *a* with me; 476 10
for thou *a* with me; 477 3
Thou only *a* immortal, the creator 482 12
"Dust thou *a*, and unto dust shalt thou return." 482 15
who for our sins *a* justly displeased? 484 7
Our Father, who *a* in heaven, 485 20
Our Father, who *a* in heaven, 502 1

a and music to perfect the praises offered 819 15
thou *a* doing for them better things 831 9
and know that thou *a* God; 832 17

arts

and practice of the *a* of healing, 460 11

ascend

thither *a*, and with him continually dwell; 174 18
so we may also in heart and mind there *a*, 226 10
"Who can *a* the hill of the LORD? * 613 18

ascended

He *a* into heaven, 54 2
He *a* into heaven, 66 18
Christ the Lord has *a* into heaven: 81 6
He *a* into heaven, 96 22
He *a* into heaven, 120 18
Christ *a* far above all heavens 174 9
Jesus Christ to have *a* into the heavens, 174 17
Christ *a* far above all heavens 226 2
Christ to have *a* into heaven, 226 9
he *a* into heaven, 293 9
He *a* into heaven, 304 12
he *a* into heaven 327 8
and *a* into heaven, 328 8
and in their sight *a* into heaven, 347 3
he *a* into heaven 358 24
and in their sight *a* into heaven, 379 22
He *a* into heaven, 416 17
He *a* into heaven, 496 12
he *a* into heaven, 519 27
he *a* into heaven 530 18
and, having *a* into heaven, 533 6
he *a* into heaven 542 18
What do we mean when we say that he *a* into 850 17

ascendeth

Christ the Lord *a* into heaven: 43 10

ascension

by thy glorious Ressurrection and *A*; 149 24
his mighty resurrection and glorious *a*; 335 14
his mighty resurrection and glorious *a*; 342 14
Recalling his death, resurrection, and *a*, 363 12
proclaiming his resurrection and *a* 374 26
celebrating his resurrection and *a*, 405 12
By your glorious Resurrection and *A*, 463 8

ascribe

A to the Lord the honor due his Name; 343 10
A to the Lord the honor due his Name; 376 6
A to the LORD, you gods, * 620 5
a to the LORD glory and strength. 620 6
A to the LORD the glory due his Name; * 620 7
A power to God; * 679 1
A to the LORD, you families of the peoples; * 726 5
a to the LORD honor and power. 726 6
A to the LORD the honor due his Name; * 726 7

ashamed

LORD, let me not be *a* for having called upon you; * 623 27
and let not your faces be *a*. 628 4
Let all who rejoice at my ruin be *a* 631 24
They shall not be *a* in bad times, * 634 22
Let them be *a* and altogether dismayed 641 10
because they are *a*. 641 15
Let those who seek my life be *a* 682 13
because they are *a*. 682 18
let me never be *a*. 683 2
for they are *a* and disgraced who sought 685 7
Let not the oppressed turn away *a*; * 690 26
so that those who hate me may see it and be *a*; * 711 10
and will not be *a*. 767 6

ashes

Grant that these *a* may be to us a sign 265 17
earth to earth, *a* to *a*, dust to dust. 485 12
earth to earth, *a* to *a*, dust to dust. 501 14
For I have eaten *a* for bread * 731 17
and lifts up the poor from the *a*. 756 13
he scatters hoarfrost like *a*. 805 10

aside

nor the hand of the wicked push me *a*. 633 2
As for those who turn *a* to crooked ways, 782 3
And to set *a* regular times for worship, 847 26

ask

to hear his holy Word, and to *a*, 41 8
more than we can *a* or imagine: 60 4
more than we can *a* or imagine: 73 4
to hear his holy Word, and to *a*, 79 3
more than we can *a* or imagine: 102 15
humbly *a* for your protection 124 4
more than we can *a* or imagine: 126 15
those who *a* in thy Son's Name: 153 20
before we *a* and our ignorance in asking: 179 17
for our blindness we cannot *a*, 179 20
good things which we are not worthy to *a*, 183 3
We *a* this for the sake of Jesus Christ, 199 9
before we *a* and our ignorance in asking: 231 11
for our blindness we cannot *a*; 231 14
for which we are not worthy to *a*, 234 17
We *a* this for the sake of Jesus Christ 250 18
All this we *a* through your Son Jesus Christ. 363 19
I *a* your prayers for God's people 385 17
I *a* your prayers for peace; 386 1
I *a* your prayers for the poor, 386 4
I *a* your prayers for all who seek God, 386 7
I *a* your prayers for the departed 386 10
I *a* your prayers for __________. 386 12
I *a* your thanksgiving for __________. 386 13
you have promised to hear what we *a* 394 4
not as we *a* in our ignorance, nor as we deserve in our 394 6
to whom our needs are known before we *a*: 394 12
Help us to *a* only what accords with your will; 394 13
dare not, or in our blindness cannot *a*, 395 2
a this for the sake of Jesus Christ, 395 22
All this we *a* through your Son Jesus Christ. 405 19
and *a* you for counsel, direction, and absolution. 447 11
This we *a* through Christ our Lord. 466 11
All which we *a* through Jesus Christ 489 12
All this we *a* through Jesus Christ 504 10
And this we *a* in the Name of Jesus Christ 505 15
a you to lay your hands upon him 513 4
this we *a* through Jesus Christ our Lord, 534 8

All this I *a* for the sake of your Son	563	9
to *a* your forgiveness, to know your healing	568	10
Ask of me, and I will give you the nations	586	17
all which we *a* through Jesus Christ our Lord.	820	15
This we *a* for the sake of Jesus	823	15
All this we *a* in your holy Name.	825	224
this we *a* for your mercy's sake.	826	26
This we *a* in the name of Jesus Christ	830	6
the grace to *a* what thou wouldst have us	832	8
petitions of those who *a* in thy Son's Name:	834	2
we *a* in the Name of Jesus Christ our Lord.	839	26

asked

which we have *a* faithfully according to thy will,	153	23
what we have *a* faithfully,	394	2
He *a* you for life, and you gave it to him: *	609	3
One thing have I *a* of the LORD;	617	18
They *a*, and quails appeared, *	741	5
He gave them what they *a*, *	743	1
For those who led us away captive *a* us for a song,	792	5
have faithfully *a* according to thy will,	834	5

asking

before we ask and our ignorance in *a*:	179	17
before we ask and our ignorance in *a*:	231	11
first time of *a*.	437	5
a God's grace, both for yourself	532	25
a nothing but to enjoy God's presence.	857	3

asleep

may at length fall *a* peacefully in thee,	69	10
lest he come suddenly and find you *a*.	75	3
the first fruits of those who have fallen *a*.	83	22
and he who watches over you will not fall *a*.	104	18
you have led the way, that we may at length fall *a*	123	8
I lie down in peace; at once I fall *a*; *	129	6
and *a* we may rest in peace.	134	17
and *a* we may rest in peace.	135	10
you have led the way, that we may at length fall *a*	504	23
I lie down in peace; at once I fall *a*; *	588	15
and he who watches over you will not fall *a*.	779	6

aspirations

make us mindful of the rightful *a*	210	14
make us mindful of the rightful *a*	261	19

assail

How long will you *a* me to crush me,	669	9

assault

thoughts which may *a* and hurt the soul;	167	7
thoughts which may *a* and hurt the soul;	218	17
From the wicked who *a* me, *	601	16
all day long they *a* and oppress me.	662	14

assaulted

servants who are *a* by manifold temptations;	166	11
Come quickly to help us who are *a*	218	2

assaults

Defend us, thy humble servants, in all *a*	57	4
Defend us, your humble servants, in all *a*	99	22
from the crafts and *a* of the devil;	148	16

assembled

the laity here (or now, or soon to be) *a*	204	11
the laity here (or now, or soon to be) *a*	255	9
friends wish us, here *a*, to witness	440	15
Behold, the kings of the earth *a* *	651	8
Representatives in Congress *a*	821	4

assembly

thou art greatly glorified in the *a* of thy saints.	348	7
you are greatly glorified in the *a* of your saints.	381	1
let the *a* of the peoples gather round you.	591	9
My praise is of him in the great *a*; *	612	4
in the full *a* I will bless the LORD.	617	6
and to your faithfulness in the *a* of the holy ones;	714	4
in the *a* of the upright, in the congregation.	754	7
tribes of the LORD, * the *a* of Israel,	780	3

asses

and the wild *a* quench their thirst.	735	24

assigned

and you are to carry out other duties *a*	543	15

assist

beseech thee, O heavenly Father, so to *a* us	339	10
and *a* them with your grace	425	9
You are to *a* the bishop and priests in public	543	13
and to *a* in the ministration of his holy Sacraments.	545	20
to *a* bishops and priests in the proclamation	856	10

assurance

in full *a* of the glory	169	4
removal of scruple and doubt, the *a* of pardon,	317	15
I may enjoy the blessed *a* of your love;	461	17
In the *a* of eternal life given at Baptism,	496	1
increase their faith and their *a*	830	5
Restore to them the *a* of your unfailing mercy;	831	20
and receive the *a* of pardon	861	12
What, then is our *a* as Christians?	862	29
Our *a* as Christians is that nothing,	862	30

assure

and dost *a* us thereby of thy favor	339	5

assured

You have been *a* of his suitability	514	4

assuring

and for *a* us in these holy mysteries	366	5

Assyrians

The *A* also have joined them, *	706	18

astounded

They looked and were *a*; *	651	10

astray

All we like sheep have gone *a*;	39	1
All we like sheep have gone *a*;	76	25
to all who have gone *a* from thy ways,	166	17
to all who have gone *a* from your ways,	218	8
home to your fold those who have gone *a*;	280	6
liars go *a* from their birth.	664	26
Before I was afflicted I went *a*, *	768	21
I have gone *a* like a sheep that is lost; *	778	7

asunder

whom God has joined together let no one put *a*. 428 6
whom God has joined together let no one put *a*. 434 7
and broke their bonds *a*. 747 10

ate

So mortals *a* the bread of angels; * 696 26
So they *a* and were well filled, * 697 7
He sent swarms of flies among them, which *a* them 698 17
Which *a* up all the green plants in their land * 740 23
and *a* sacrifices offered to the dead. 744 4

Athanasian

What, then, is the *A* Creed? 852 8
The *A* Creed is an ancient document 852 9

athirst

My soul is *a* for God, yea, even for the living God; * 471 3
My soul is *a* for God, athirst for the living God; * 643 3

atoms

all its marvelous order, its *a*, worlds, and galaxies, 827 12

attack

a those who are attacking me. 629 14

attacking

attack those who are *a* me. 629 14

attain

we may *a* to thy heavenly kingdom, 152 19
be found worthy to *a* to everlasting joys; 171 7
that we may at length *a* to the fullness of life 186 9
and *a* to the riches of the age to come; 198 5
we may with him *a* to thine eternal joy; 198 20
be found worthy to *a* to everlasting joys; 222 23
at length we may *a* to the fullness of eternal life; 238 4
and *a* to the riches of the age to come; 249 14
until at last we may with him *a* to your eternal 250 4
that with pure minds we may *a* to the festival 285 11
I cannot *a* unto it. 475 4
it is so high that I cannot *a* to it. 794 11
that he may *a* to that full stature 841 4

attainment

towards the *a* of everlasting salvation; 832 20

attend

and *a* to the voice of my supplications. 710 10

attended

he has *a* to the voice of my prayer. 675 6

attention

and give *a* to your ways. 764 14

aught

rememberest that thy brother hath *a* against thee, 343 18

author

O God, who art the *a* of peace 57 1
O God, the *a* of peace 99 20
Lord of all power and might, who art the *a* 181 11
Christ, the *a* and perfecter of our faith, 198 21
Lord of all power and might, the *a* 233 3
who by his suffering and death became the *a* 346 15
and the *a* of our salvation. 369 13
preserver of all life, *a* of salvation, 429 2

authority

all others in *a*, that they may do justice, 150 27
service by which alone they may have true *a* 191 12
service by which alone they may have true *a* 242 18
those in *a* among them; 278 18
the *a* of government in this and every land 329 19
for all in *a*, let us pray to the Lord. 384 5
We pray for all who govern and hold *a* 387 9
and by his *a* committed to me, I absolve 448 4
and by his *a* committed to me, I absolve 451 14
and other ministers who may have *a* over you 526 12
Receive this Bible as a sign of the *a* given 534 10
and other ministers who may have *a* over you 538 12
Receive this Bible as the sign of your *a* to 545 19
the *a* of government, that there may be justice 820 10
and to all in *a*, wisdom and strength to know 820 20
to all in administrative *a*, grant wisdom 821 21
to honor those in *a*, and to meet 848 5
Ordination is the rite in which God gives *a* 860 28

authors

because God inspired their human *a* 853 25

avenge

that you *a* the shedding of your servants' blood. 702 3

avenger

to quell the enemy and the *a*. 592 12
The *A* of blood will remember them; * 593 23
because of the enemy and *a*. 646 18

avoid

when they see me in the street they *a* me. 623 13

await

may *a* with him the coming of the third 170 3
may *a* with him the coming of the third 221 15
may *a* with him the coming of the third 283 3
We *a* his coming in glory; 368 22
as we *a* the day of his coming. 371 22
we *a* his coming in glory. 405 12
O tarry and *a* the LORD's pleasure; 619 1
in those who *a* his gracious favor. 804 25
and to *a* the coming of Christ in glory 861 26

awaiting

a his coming in glory; and offering to you, 374 27

awake

fall asleep peacefully in thee, and *a* up 69 10
that *a* we may watch with Christ, 134 16
that *a* we may watch with Christ, 135 9
A, O my God, decree justice; * 591 8
when I *a*, I shall be satisfied, beholding 602 5
A, arise to my cause! * 631 16
A, O Lord! why are you sleeping? * 647 3
a, lute and harp; * 664 13
A, and punish all the ungodly; * 666 5
I lie *a* and groan; * 731 13
a, lute and harp; * 749 20

awaken

kindle our hearts, and *a* hope, 70 12
kindle our hearts, and *a* hope, 124 9
kindle our hearts, and *a* hope, 139 18

awakens

Like a dream when one *a*, O Lord, * 688 17

awaking

After my *a*, he will raise me up; 491 9

aware

Make us, we pray, deeply *a* 504 2

awareness

And, we pray, give us such an *a* of your mercies, 101 16
And, we pray, give us such an *a* of your mercies, 125 14

away

and the rich he hath sent empty *a*. 50 16
Father, that takest *a* the sins of the world, 52 12
Thou that takest *a* the sins of the world, 52 14
Nor the hope of the poor be taken *a*. 55 12
Grant that we, putting *a* all earthly anxieties, 56 13
and the rich he hath sent empty *a*. 65 19
Nor the hope of the poor be taken *a*. 68 4
O Lord Jesus Christ, who by thy death didst take *a* 69 7
and the rich he has sent *a* empty. 92 11
you take *a* the sin of the world: 95 5
Nor the hope of the poor be taken *a*. 98 6
Grant that we, putting *a* all earthly anxieties, 99 8
the old has passed *a*, behold the new has come. 106 2
and the rich he has sent *a* empty. 119 17
Nor the hope of the poor be taken *a*. 122 6
Lord Jesus Christ, by your death you took *a* 123 6
Cast me not *a* from your presence * 137 5
O Lamb of God, that takest *a* the sins 152 24
give us grace that we may cast *a* 159 1
so to put *a* the leaven of malice 172 10
put *a* from us all hurtful things, 177 16
while we are placed among things that are passing *a*, 182 8
as we have put *a* the old life of sin, 253 2
Almighty God, give us grace to cast *a* the works 211 1
so to put *a* the leaven of malice 224 2
Put *a* from us, we entreat you, 229 11
while we are placed among things that are passing *a*, 234 3
as we have put *a* the old life of sin, 253 2
Cast me not *a* from your presence * 266 24
wickedness is put to flight, and sin is washed *a*. 287 18
May it shine continually to drive *a* 287 24
where all tears are wiped *a* 290 5
that takest *a* the sins of the world, 324 23
Thou that takest *a* the sins of the world, 325 1
O Lamb of God, that takest *a* the sins 337 3
taken *a* the sin of the world; who by his death 346 20
that fadeth not *a*. 347 21
you take *a* the sin of the world: 356 9
and has taken *a* the sin of the world. 379 17
receive the crown of glory that never fades *a*. 380 16
Lamb of God, you take *a* the sins 407 1
and the rich he has sent *a* empty. 442 6
The Lord has put *a* all your sins. 448 12
The Lord has put *a* all your sins. 451 19
to drive *a* all sickness of body 456 3
you drive *a* from our bodies all sickness 458 17
and fade *a* suddenly like the grass. 472 20
For we consume *a* in thy displeasure, * 472 23
so soon passeth it *a*, and we are gone. 473 6
nor cast thy servant *a* in displeasure. 478 4
having taken *a* the sin of the world. 483 19
Lamb that was slain to take *a* the sins 488 16
of this earthly life being purged and done *a*, 488 18
do not let the pains of death turn us *a* 492 20
taken *a* the sin of the world. 500 8
I will never turn *a* anyone who believes in me. 501 2
Lord Jesus Christ, by your death you took *a* 504 21
they are like chaff which the wind blows *a*. 585 11
and worn *a* because of all my enemies. 590 13
and snatch me *a* with none to deliver me. 590 23
they seize the lowly and drag them *a* in their net. 595 13
"Fly *a* like a bird to the hilltop; 596 9
and his decrees I have not put *a* from me; 604 8
Be not far *a*, O LORD; * 611 18
Do not sweep me *a* with sinners, * 616 24
nor turn *a* your servant in displeasure. 618 15
cast me not *a*; * 618 17
Do not snatch me *a* with the wicked or with the 619 10
and whose sin is put *a*! 624 24
While I held my tongue, my bones withered *a*, * 625 3
and let the angel of the LORD drive them *a*. 629 23
and like the green grass fade *a*. 633 8
like a moth you eat *a* all that is dear to us; * 639 18
God has spoken, and the earth shall melt *a*. 649 16
Their form shall waste *a*, * 653 11
For they will carry nothing *a* at their death, * 653 17
Cast me not *a* from your presence * 657 3
I would fly *a* and be at rest. 660 18
Let them be like the snail that melts *a*, * 665 9
like thorns and thistles let them be swept *a*. 665 12
and of the seas that are far *a*. 672 20
like smoke when the wind drives it *a*; * 676 3
"Kings with their armies are fleeing *a*; * 677 3
Though my flesh and my heart should waste *a*, * 689 1
Let not the oppressed turn *a* ashamed; * 690 26
They turned *a* and were disloyal like their fathers; * 699 20
and took him *a* from the sheepfolds. 700 20
And so will we never turn *a* from you; * 703 22
my neighbor you have put *a* from me, * 713 15
You sweep us *a* like a dream; * 718 9
we fade *a* suddenly like the grass. 718 10
For we consume *a* in your displeasure; * 718 13
for they pass *a* quickly and we are gone. 718 22
For my days drift *a* like smoke, * 731 5
you have lifted me up and thrown me *a*. 731 20
My days pass *a* like a shadow, * 731 21
do not take me *a* in the midst of my days; * 732 25
at the voice of your thunder they hastened *a*. 735 16
The sun rises, and they slip *a* * 736 21
you take *a* their breath, 737 12
to turn *a* his wrath from consuming them. 743 19
I have faded *a* like a shadow when it lengthens; * 752 21
they will gnash their teeth and pine *a*; * 755 26
My soul melts *a* for sorrow; * 765 15
Turn *a* the reproach which I dread, * 766 13
A from me, you wicked! * 773 3

the Lord will lead them _a_ with the evildoers; * 782 4
do not turn _a_ the face of your Anointed. 786 18
And gave _a_ their lands for an inheritance, * 791 11
For those who led us _a_ captive asked us for a song, 792 5
he gave them a law which shall not pass _a_. 806 6
take _a_ the arrogance and hatred which 815 15
take _a_ all hatred and prejudice, 818 16

awe

let the whole earth stand in _a_ of him. 45 7
let the whole earth stand in _a_ of him. 61 6
that we who celebrate with _a_ the Paschal 222 23
I will bow down toward your holy temple in _a_ of you. 589 5
stand in _a_ of him, O offspring of Israel; 611 27
let all who dwell in the world stand in _a_ of him. 626 16
many shall see, and stand in _a_, 640 7
Everyone will stand in _a_ and declare God's deeds; * 672 3
and may all the ends of the earth stand in _a_ of him. 675 23
but my heart stands in _a_ of your word. 777 2

awesome

_a_ in renown, and worker of wonders? 85 18
what _a_ things he has done on earth. 649 20
_A_ things will you show us in your righteousness, 672 17
Say to God, "How _a_ are your deeds! * 673 21
Let them confess his Name, which is great and _a_; * 729 3
holy and _a_ is his Name. 754 24

axes

They were like men coming up with _a_ to a grove 689 18

B

Baal

They joined themselves to _B_-Peor * 744 3

Babylon

I count Egypt and _B_ among those who know me; * 711 17
By the waters of _B_ we sat down and wept, * 792 1
O Daughter of _B_, doomed to destruction, * 792 19

back

You hold _b_ your hand; * 91 7
our Savior gave his _b_ to the smithers 169 1
they shall turn _b_ and suddenly be put to shame. 590 19
Their malice turns _b_ upon their own head; * 592 3
When my enemies are driven _b_, * 593 5
and does not take _b_ his word. 599 14
I will not turn _b_ till I have destroyed them. 605 15
let those who plot my ruin fall _b_ and be dismayed. 629 21
companions draw _b_ from my affliction; * 637 18
let them draw _b_ and be disgraced 641 12
Through you we pushed _b_ our adversaries; * 645 20
You have made us fall _b_ before our adversary, * 646 5
Our heart never turned _b_, * 646 22
and toss my words behind your _b_? 655 15
He will bring me safely _b_ from the battle 661 22
oh, take us _b_ to you again. 667 11
"I will bring them _b_ from Bashan; * 678 1
I will bring them _b_ from the depths of the sea; 678 2
Must I then give _b_ what I never stole? 679 19
draw _b_ and be disgraced. 682 16
who say to me "Aha!" and gloat over me turn _b_, * 682 17
Why do you draw _b_ your hand? * 690 6
turned _b_ in the day of battle; 695 21
many times he held _b_ his anger 698 3
You have turned _b_ the edge of his sword * 716 27
You turn us _b_ to the dust and say, * 718 4
"Go _b_, O child of earth." 718 5
He will turn their wickedness _b_ upon them 724 11
to the heavens and fell _b_ to the depths; * 748 7
Jordan turned and went _b_. 757 2
O Jordan, that you turned _b_? 757 6
The plowmen plowed upon my _b_ * 784 5
Let them be put to shame and thrown _b_, * 784 9
happy the one who pays you _b_ 792 20
God sent the prophets to call us _b_ to himself, 849 8

backs

you laid heavy burdens upon our _b_. 674 16

backside

He struck his enemies on the _b_ * 700 11

bad

all alike have turned _b_; * 598 19
They shall not be ashamed in _b_ times, * 634 22
all alike have turned _b_; * 659 5

badgers

and the stony cliffs for the rock _b_. 736 14

band

They _b_ together; they lie in wait; * 663 1
and a _b_ of violent men seeks my life; * 711 2

banish

forgive our sins, _b_ our fears, 835 4

banished

weakness may be _b_ and his strength restored; 458 19

banner

You have set up a _b_ for those who fear you, * 667 16
all peoples may be gathered under the _b_ of the Prince 815 25

banners

they set up their _b_ as tokens of victory. 689 17

Banns

I publish the _B_ of Marriage between 437 1

banquet

come to the _b_ of that most heavenly Food. 317 10
foretaste of thy heavenly _b_. 482 4
foretaste of your heavenly _b_. 498 15
and the foretaste of the heavenly _b_ which 860 2

baptism

by thy _B_, Fasting, and Temptation, 149 19
Father in heaven, who at the _b_ of Jesus 163 1
Spirit of adoption which is given to us in _B_, 170 18
Almighty God, who by our _b_ into the death 203 5
from the old life of sin by our _b_ into the death 203 13
Father in heaven, who at the _b_ of Jesus 214 12
Spirit of adoption which is given to us in _B_, 222 10
Almighty God, by our _b_ into the death 254 7
from the old life of sin by our _b_ into the death 254 14

converts to the faith were prepared for Holy *B*. 265 3
salvation of all nations by the water of *B*: 289 16
by *B* into his death, and raised with him 292 2
vows of Holy *B*, by which we once renounced 292 5
Spirit of adoption which is given to us in *B*, 295 10
One Lord, one Faith, one *B*; 299 9
The Candidate(s) for Holy *B* will now be presented. 301 1
I present N. to receive the Sacrament of *B*. 301 2
I present N. to receive the Sacrament of *B*. 301 5
received the *b* of John and was anointed 306 17
We thank you, Father, for the water of *B*. 306 20
N., you are sealed by the Holy Spirit in *B* 308 9
covenant you made with them at their *B*. 309 8
We acknowledge one *b* for the forgiveness of sins. 327 17
I acknowledge one *B* for the remission of sins; 328 19
We acknowledge one *b* for the forgiveness of sins. 359 8
One Lord, one Faith, one *B*; 413 9
covenant you made with them at their *B*. 418 6
that through the Sacrament of *B* he may 444 18
May God the Father, who by *B* adopts us 445 3
Through the water of *b* you clothed me 450 11
In the assurance of eternal life given at *B*, 496 1
Our brother (sister) was washed in *B* and anointed 497 16
who was reborn by water and the Spirit in Holy *B*. 498 2
We acknowledge one *b* for the forgiveness of sins. 520 8
We acknowledge one *b* for the forgiveness of sins. 530 27
to share in the administration of Holy *B* 531 15
We acknowledge one *b* for the forgiveness of sins. 542 27
Father, we thank you that through the waters of *B* we 569 15
There is one Lord, one Faith, one *B*; 569 19
Jesus received the *b* of John and was anointed 570 9
We thank you, Father, for the water of *B*. 570 12
one *B*, one God and Father of us all, 818 20
The Apostles' Creed is the ancient creed of *B*; 852 2
are Holy *B* and the Holy Eucharist. 858 7
What is Holy *B*? 858 8
Holy *B* is the sacrament by which God adopts 858 9
What is the outward and visible sign in *B*? 858 12
The outward and visible sign in *B* is water, 858 13
What is the inward and spiritual grace in *B*? 858 16
The inward and spiritual grace in *B* is union 858 17
What is required of us at *B*? 858 21
necessary for all persons in the same way that *B* 860 15

baptismal

desire to reaffirm their *b* vows. 303 9
to Christ and renew our own *b* covenant. 303 19
desire to reaffirm their *b* vows. 415 8
to Christ and renew our own *b* covenant. 416 5
to recall our *b* Covenant. 852 4

Baptist

John the *B* was wonderfully born, and sent 190 2
John the *B* was wonderfully born, and sent 241 11

baptize

I *b* you in the Name of the Father, 307 14
If you are not already baptized, N., I *b* you 313 1
I *b* you in the Name of the Father, and of the Son, 313 3
take this water, and help me (help the bishop) *b* 561 1

baptized

Grant that all who are *b* 163 3
Grant, O Lord God, to all who have been *b* 201 12
Grant that all who are *b* 214 14
Grant, Lord God, to all who have been *b* 252 16
For those about to be *b* (particularly ________.) 278 8
Do you desire to be *b*? 301 3
Grant, O Lord, that all who are *b* 306 5
Let us welcome the newly *b*. 308 11
If you are not already *b*, N., I baptize you 313 1
Grant that all who have been *b* into Christ's death 480 8
support all *b* people in their gifts 518 13
All *b* people are called to make Christ known 531 2
that those *b* here may enjoy the liberty 569 17
We share in his victory when we are *b* 850 24
Christ is the Head and of which all *b* persons 854 7
the person is *b* in the Name of the Father, 858 14
Why then are infants *b*? 858 24
Infants are *b* so that they can share citizenship 858 25
that they have been *b*, are sufficiently instructed 860 24

baptizing

those who come to him in faith, *b* them 307 1
those who come to him in faith, *b* them 570 16

bar

Draw the sword and *b* the way against those 629 17

bare

and the foundations of the world laid *b*, * 603 20
and strips the forests *b*. 620 22

Barnabas

servant *B*, who, seeking not his own renown 189 18
servant *B*, who, seeking not his own renown 241 4

barns

May our *b* be filled to overflowing 801 3

barren

as in a *b* and dry land where there is no water. 670 14

barriers

that *b* which divide us may crumble 823 19

bars

and breaks in two the iron *b*. 747 14
For he has strengthened the *b* of your gates; * 805 3

Bartholomew

B grace truly to believe and to preach 192 8
B grace truly to believe and to preach 243 15

Bashan

strong bulls of *B* surround me. 611 2
O mighty mountain, O hill of *B*! * 677 10
O rugged mountain, O hill of *B*! 677 11
The LORD has said, "I will bring them back from *B*; * 678 1
and Og, the king of *B*, * 788 24
And Og, the king of *B*, * 791 9

basic

The creeds are statements of our *b* beliefs about God. 851 23

basin

Moab is my wash-*b*, 668 1

bathe

they will *b* their feet in the blood of the wicked. 665 14

battle

from violence, *b*, and murder; and from dying 149 15
at your *b* cry, O LORD, 603 21
He trains my hands for *b* * 605 7
You have girded me with strength for the *b*; * 605 18
the LORD, mighty in *b*." 614 6
He will bring me safely back from the *b* 661 22
they run and prepare themselves for *b*. 666 2
the shield, the sword, and the weapons of *b*. 692 6
turned back in the day of *b*; 695 21
and have not sustained him in *b*. 716 28
you have covered my head in the day of *b*. 796 16
who trains my hands to fight and my fingers to *b*; 800 2

beams

You lay the *b* of your chambers in the waters above; * 735 6

bear

the finest of those who *b* armor have been 85 10
They shall *b* you in their hands, * 130 21
be strengthened to *b* our cross, 165 17
James grace and strength to *b* witness to the truth: 189 6
strengthened to *b* our cross, 217 10
and strength to *b* witness to the truth: 240 14
we who *b* them in his name may ever hail him 271 11
Thou shalt not *b* false witness against thy neighbor. 318 25
rule the hearts of those who *b* 329 18
As the branch cannot *b* fruit by itself, 397 8
By this my Father is glorified, that you *b* much fruit 397 10
to do what he has to do and *b* what he has to *b*; 459 13
I will *b* witness that the LORD is righteous; * 592 5
and they *b* a violent hatred against me. 615 27
like a heavy burden they are too much for me to *b*. 637 5
"O Israel, I will *b* witness against you; * 654 17
Before they *b* fruit, let them be cut down * 665 11
The heavens *b* witness to your wonders, O LORD, * 714 3
They shall *b* you in their hands, * 720 9
They shall still *b* fruit in old age; * 721 25
to *b* no malice, predjudice, or hatred 848 8
to *b* witness to him wherever they may be; 855 16

beard

that runs down upon the *b*, 787 12
Upon the *b* of Aaron, * 787 13

bearer

Jesus, *b* of our sins: 463 25

bearest

favor that thou *b* unto thy people; * 478 18
favor which thou *b* unto thy people. 481 19
favor which thou *b* unto thy people; 488 22

bearing

mother of thy incarnate Son was blessed in *b* 189 12
mother of your incarnate Son was blessed in *b* 240 19
b fruit in due season, * 585 8
his hands were set free from *b* the load." 704 13

bears

leadership in your Church, and *b* these signs, 552 9
the God of our salvation, who *b* our burdens. 677 22

beast

you save both man and *b*, O LORD. 632 16
Rebuke the wild *b* of the reeds, * 678 18
I was like a brute *b* in your presence. 688 22
the firstborn both of man and *b*. 788 18

beasts

O all ye *b* and cattle, bless ye the Lord; 48 26
Glorify the Lord, O *b* of the wild, * 89 14
even the wild *b* of the field, 592 22
rescue me from the roaring *b*, 631 2
they are like the *b* that perish. 653 5
understanding, are like the *b* that perish. 653 24
For all the *b* of the forest are mine, * 654 23
I will offer you sacrifices of fat *b* 674 24
Do not hand over the life of your dove to wild *b*; * 690 22
and the flesh of your faithful ones to the *b* 701 6
and the *b* of the field have grazed upon it. 703 14
All the *b* of the field drink their fill from them, * 735 23
in which all the *b* of the forest prowl. 736 18
Wild *b* and all cattle, * 806 13

beat

and finally to *b* down Satan under our feet, 152 13
I *b* them like dust before the wind; * 605 24

beautified

for the work of many hands, which have *b* 573 2

beautiful

B and lofty, the joy of all the earth, 651 3

beauty

Worship the Lord in the *b* of holiness: 44 3
O worship the Lord in the *b* of holiness; * 45 6
O worship the Lord in the *b* of holiness; 61 5
Worship the Lord in the *b* of holiness: 81 12
Worship the Lord in the *b* of holiness; 115 5
behold the King in his *b*; 191 19
which thou givest us to do, in truth and *b* 210 5
behold the King in his *b*; 243 5
you give us to do in truth and *b* 261 11
to behold the fair *b* of the LORD, 477 19
we may behold the order and *b* of things 573 5
Let us thank God whom we worship here in the *b* 578 1
To behold the fair *b* of the LORD * 617 22
worship the LORD in the *b* of holiness. 620 8
The king will have pleasure in your *b*; * 648 13
Out of Zion, perfect in its *b*, * 654 4
they will be satisfied by the *b* of your house, 672 15
Worship the LORD in the *b* of holiness; * 726 9
in the *b* of holiness have I begotten you, 753 17
O heavenly Father, who hast filled the world with *b*: 814 1
and grant to them even now glimpses of your *b*, 819 16
for the *b* of this world, 836 3
For the *b* and wonder of your creation, 837 3
for the natural majesty and *b* of this land. 838 22
for the *b* of earth and sky and sea; 840 7

became

When you *b* man to set us free 96 3
O God, whose blessed Son *b* poor 198 1
b a burning and a shining light 198 10

O God, whose blessed Son *b* poor 249 11
b a burning and a shining light 249 19
it *b* the custom of the Church to prepare 264 12
he *b* incarnate from the Virgin Mary, 327 2
who by his suffering and death *b* the author 346 16
he *b* incarnate from the Virgin Mary, 358 18
by his suffering and death, he *b* the source 379 12
he *b* incarnate from the Virgin Mary, 519 21
he *b* incarnate from the Virgin Mary, 530 12
he *b* incarnate from the Virgin Mary, 542 12
but my pain *b* unbearable. 638 21
and *b* a byword among them. 680 10
When my mind *b* embittered, * 688 19
they *b* like dung upon the ground. 706 23
and Jacob *b* a sojourner in the land of Ham. 739 24
which *b* a snare to them. 744 20
Judah *b* God's sanctuary * 756 21
O Lord Jesus Christ, you *b* poor for our sake, 819 6
Son, who for our sake *b* poor, 826 7
by the power of the Holy Spirit and *b* incarnate 849 26
The divine Son *b* human, 850 2

become

and *b* the first fruits of them that slept. 46 14
the Lord has *b* my Savior. 85 4
and in our heavenly country to *b* 198 26
to obtain your promises, may *b* partakers 234 8
in our heavenly country to *b* partakers 250 11
b heirs with him of everlasting life. 277 6
and receive power to *b* thy children. 345 18
when we had fallen into sin and *b* 362 10
that all who share this bread and cup may *b* one 375 9
receive power to *b* your children. 378 13
Matrimony, may *b* one in heart and soul, 432 5
Baptism, he may *b* the child of God; 444 19
we might *b* your sons and daughters 573 10
I *b* like those who go down to the Pit. 619 7
I have *b* a reproach to all my enemies 623 10
I have *b* like one who does not hear * 637 25
Do not be envious when some *b* rich, * 653 15
For you have *b* my stronghold, * 667 5
I have *b* a stranger to my own kindred, * 680 3
I have *b* a portent to many; * 683 14
We have *b* a reproach to our neighbors, * 701 11
I have *b* like one who has no strength; 712 8
you have *b* enraged at him. 716 18
he has *b* the scorn of his neighbors. 716 24
But the Lord has *b* my stronghold, * 724 9
I have *b* like a vulture in the wilderness, * 731 11
and his wife *b* a widow. 751 15
I have *b* a reproach to them; * 752 24
and he has *b* my salvation. 761 25
and have *b* my salvation. 762 14
has *b* the chief cornerstone. 762 16
I have *b* like a leather flask in the smoke, * 770 7
they have *b* my own enemies. 795 23
they may *b* the kingdom of our Lord 816 4
New Covenant and *b* living members of Christ. 850 25

becomes

and none *b* his own master when he dies. 491 14

becoming

and humbled himself, *b* obedient even to death 545 3
and save them from *b* brutal or callous 826 23

bed

speak to your heart in silence upon your *b*. 128 17
Thou art about my path, and about my *b*, * 474 21
speak to your heart in silence upon your *b*. 588 7
every night I drench my *b* 590 10
He thinks up wickedness upon his *b* 632 9
he has taken to his *b* and will never get up again." 642 16
When I remember you upon my *b*, * 670 23
It is in vain that you rise so early and go to *b* so late; * 783 3
nor climb up into my *b*; 786 4
if I make the grave my *b*, you are there also. 794 15

beds

The *b* of the seas were uncovered, 603 19
let them be joyful on their *b*. 807 11

bees

They swarm about me like *b*; 761 19

before

"Father, I have sinned against heaven, and *b* thee, 38 18
walk in his laws which he set *b* us. 38 23
let all the earth keep silence *b* him. 40 19
Let us come *b* his presence with thanksgiving, * 44 12
and kneel *b* the Lord our Maker. 45 2
and come *b* his presence with a song. 45 13
In holiness and righteousness *b* him, * 51 9
for thou shalt go *b* the face of the Lord 51 12
which thou hast prepared *b* the face of all people, 51 26
supplications and prayers which we offer *b* thee 57 21
and by walking *b* thee 59 7
I have set the Lord always *b* me; 61 12
which thou hast prepared *b* the face of all people, 66 4
not be condemned *b* the great judgment seat 68 19
and by walking *b* thee 72 4
"Father, I have sinned against heaven and *b* you; 76 17
by following his laws which he set *b* us. 76 22
let all the earth keep silence *b* him. 78 18
Let us come *b* his presence with thanksgiving * 82 7
and kneel *b* the Lord our Maker. 82 16
and come *b* his presence with a song. 82 22
for you will go *b* the Lord to prepare his way, 93 2
All nations will draw near and fall down *b* you, * 94 17
supplications and prayers which we offer *b* you 100 13
and by walking *b* you 101 20
let the whole earth tremble *b* him. 115 6
I have set the Lord always *b* me; 115 11
and not be condemned *b* the great judgment seat 122 21
and by walking *b* you 125 18
Let us come *b* his presence with thanksgiving, * 146 3
and kneel *b* the Lord our Maker. 146 12
and in the old time *b* them. 154 7
whosoever liveth is counted dead *b* thee. 165 3
the same place whither our Savior Christ is gone *b*; 175 5
O gracious God, we remember *b* thee this day 191 7
confess the Name of our Savior Jesus Christ *b* the rulers 195 2
and may ever walk *b* thee as children of light; 198 12
set *b* us, until at length, through thy mercy, 198 19

Almighty God, we remember this day *b* thee 202 9
that they may faithfully serve *b* thee, 205 9
supplications and prayers, which we offer *b* thee 206 3
whoever lives is accounted dead *b* you. 216 17
that place where our Savior Christ has gone *b*; 226 17
O gracious God, we remember *b* you today 242 14
confess the Name of our Savior Jesus Christ *b* the rulers 246 9
and walk *b* you as children of light; 249 21
running the race that is set *b* us, 250 4
Almighty God, we remember *b* you today 253 13
that they may faithfully serve *b* you, 256 6
supplications and prayers, which we offer *b* you 256 21
kneel *b* the Lord, our maker and redeemer. 265 15
and my sin is ever *b* me. 266 7
supplications and prayers which we offer *b* you 278 13
perform the service you set *b* them; 309 9
And acknowledge your sins *b* Almighty God, 317 4
come boldly *b* the throne of grace 317 22
begotten of his Father *b* all worlds, 327 26
do celebrate and make here *b* thy divine Majesty, 335 10
leave there thy gift *b* the altar, 343 19
run with patience the race that is set *b* us; 347 19
confessing *b* the rulers of this world the great Name 348 9
b thee a sacrifice of praise and prayer 348 17
and made us worthy to stand *b* you. 368 8
now bring *b* you these gifts. 371 7
Countless throngs of angels stand *b* you 373 7
leave your gift there *b* the altar and go; 376 15
run with endurance the race that is set *b* us; 380 14
confessing *b* the rulers of this world 381 3
b you a sacrifice of praise and prayer 381 11
perform the service you set *b* them; 418 7
You spread a table *b* me in the presence 443 11
and my sin is ever *b* me. 449 6
b whom live all who die in the Lord: 466 7
when shall I come to appear *b* the presence of God? 471 4
Thou hast set our misdeeds *b* thee, * 472 25
Thou hast beset me behind and *b*, * 475 1
Thou shalt prepare a table *b* me in the presence 476 12
Thou preparest a table *b* me in the presence 477 5
I will walk *b* the LORD * 479 16
he may be presented pure and without spot *b* thee; 488 19
O God of grace and glory, we remember *b* you 493 16
serving *b* you day and night in the ministry 521 11
In all things may he present *b* you the acceptable 521 14
whose power is limitless, we place *b* you, 552 6
For the faith of those who have gone *b* us 579 7
and with trembling bow *b* him; 586 25
make your way straight *b* me. 589 8
let them be judged *b* you. 594 16
The innocent are broken and humbled *b* them; * 595 14
the helpless fall *b* their power. 595 15
I have set the LORD always *b* me; * 600 13
For all his judgments are *b* my eyes, * 604 7
I beat them like dust *b* the wind; * 605 24
strangers will cringe *b* me. 605 30
and all the families of the nations shall bow *b* him. 612 12
all who go down to the dust fall *b* him. 612 17
You spread a table *b* me in the presence 613 7
For your love is *b* my eyes; * 616 12
Let them be like chaff *b* the wind, * 629 22
there is no fear of God *b* his eyes. 632 4
Be still *b* the LORD * 633 17
and shall set me *b* your face for ever. 642 25
when shall I come to appear *b* the presence of God? 643 4
You have made us fall back *b* our adversary, * 646 5
My humiliation is daily *b* me, * 646 15
b him there is a consuming flame, 654 7
"Gather *b* me my loyal followers, * 654 11
your offerings are always *b* me. 654 20
I have put my case in order *b* your eyes. 655 25
and my sin is ever *b* me. 656 11
that I may walk *b* God in the light of the living. 663 18
they have dug a pit *b* me, 664 6
Let him sit enthroned *b* God for ever; * 669 1
pour out your hearts *b* him, for God is our refuge. 669 23
cringe *b* you. 673 23
All the earth bows down *b* you, * 673 24
let those who hate him flee *b* him. 676 2
But let the righteous be glad and rejoice *b* God; * 676 6
YAHWEH is his Name, rejoice *b* him! 676 10
O God, when you went forth *b* your people, * 676 16
The singers go *b*, musicians follow after, * 678 7
Let the table *b* them be a trap * 681 8
His foes shall bow down *b* him, * 686 1
All kings shall bow down *b* him, * 686 5
who can stand *b* you when you are angry? 692 15
He drove out the Canaanites *b* them 699 15
Let the sorrowful sighing of the prisoners come *b* you, 702 4
Those who hate the LORD would cringe *b* him, * 705 5
and like chaff *b* the wind; 707 4
Righteousness shall go *b* him, * 709 20
they have not set you *b* their eyes. 711 3
in the morning my prayer comes *b* you. 713 5
love and truth go *b* your face. 714 22
I will crush his foes *b* him * 715 12
and his throne as the sun *b* me; 716 14
Our iniquities you have set *b* you, * 718 15
Let us come *b* his presence with thanksgiving * 724 16
and kneel *b* the LORD our Maker. 725 2
let the whole earth tremble *b* him. 726 10
b the LORD when he comes, * 726 18
A fire goes *b* him * 727 1
Bow down *b* him, all you gods. 727 11
shout with joy *b* the King, the LORD. 728 15
and let the hills ring out with joy *b* the LORD, 728 19
and fall down *b* his footstool; * 729 9
and come *b* his presence with a song. 729 24
I will set no worthless thing *b* my eyes; * 730 12
LORD, hear my prayer, and let my cry come *b* you; * 731 1
He has brought down my strength *b* my time; * 732 22
He sent a man *b* them, * 739 11
had not Moses his chosen stood *b* him in the breach, 743 18
Let the wickedness of his fathers be remembered *b* 751 24
Let their sin be always *b* the LORD; * 751 27
I have set your judgments *b* me. 765 20
I will tell of your decrees *b* kings * 767 5
for all my ways are *b* you. 777 16
Let my cry come *b* you, O LORD; * 777 17
Let my supplication come *b* you; * 777 19
let us fall upon our knees *b* his footstool." 786 12
b the gods I will sing your praise. 793 2
You press upon me behind and *b* * 794 8

Set a watch *b* my mouth, O Lord, 797 7
I pour out my complaint *b* him * 798 3
enable us all to stand reconciled *b* you; 816 8
we remember *b* you those who suffer 824 11
we remember *b* you all poor 826 1
Increase our reverence *b* the mystery of life; 828 17
we remember *b* you with grateful hearts 839 21
by a humble, holy, and obedient walking *b* thee 840 21
Intercession brings *b* God the needs of others; 857 18
vows *b* God and the Church, 861 6

beg

and I humbly *b* forgiveness of God 447 11
And this we *b* for Jesus Christ's sake. 815 12

began

which have been since the world *b*: 50 27
Ever since the world *b*, your throne 722 7

beggars

Let his children be waifs and *b*; * 751 16

begging

or their children *b* bread. 635 11

begin

work which thou didst *b* in them may be made perfect 486 11
I will *b* with the mighty works of the Lord God; * 684 12

beginning

as it was in the *b*, is now, and will be for ever. 42 17
as it was in the *b*, is now, and will be for ever. 46 20
as it was in the *b*, is now, and will be for ever. 50 21
as it was in the *b*, is now, and will be for ever. 51 22
as it was in the *b*, is now, and will be for ever. 52 2
who hast safely brought us to the *b* of this day: 57 8
as it was in the *b*, is now, and will be for ever. 63 20
as it was in the *b*, is now, and will be for ever. 64 11
as it was in the *b*, is now, and will be for ever. 65 24
as it was in the *b*, is now, and will be for ever. 66 8
it was in the *b*, is now, and will be for ever. 80 8
as it was in the *b*, is now, and will be for ever. 84 2
as it was in the *b*, is now, and will be for ever. 85 31
as it was in the *b*, is now, and will be for ever. 86 16
as it was in the *b*, is now, and will be for ever. 87 10
as it was in the *b*, is now, and will be for ever. 88 4
as it was in the *b*, is now, and will be for ever. 92 17
as it was in the *b*, is now, and will be for ever. 93 11
as it was in the *b*, is now, and will be for ever. 93 19
as it was in the *b*, is now, and will be for ever. 94 20
as it was in the *b*, is now, and will be for ever. 103 4
as it was in the *b*, is now, and will be for ever. 105 19
as it was in the *b*, is now, and will be for ever. 117 13
as it was in the *b*, is now, and will be for ever. 118 11
as it was in the *b*, is now, and will be for ever. 119 23
as it was in the *b*, is now, and will be for ever. 120 8
as it was in the *b*, is now, and will be for ever. 128 6
as it was in the *b*, is now, and will be for ever. 131 11
as it was in the *b*, is now, and will be for ever. 135 8
as it was in the *b*, is now, and will be for ever. 137 10
As it was in the *b*, is now, * 141 3
As it was in the *b*, is now, and ever shall be, * 141 7
as it was in the *b*, is now, and ever shall be, 154 11
And, to make a right *b* of repentance, 265 13
Over it the Holy Spirit moved in the *b* of creation. 306 14
As it was in the *b*, is now, and ever shall be,* 406 3
as it was in the *b*, is now, and will be for ever. 442 12
as it was in the *b*, is now, and will be for ever. 442 29
as it was in the *b*, is now, and will be for ever. 443 19
kingdom prepared for you from the *b* of the world." 505 7
We give you thanks that from the *b* you have 520 14
Will you who witness this new *b* support 559 8
the Holy Spirit moved in the *b* of creation. 570 6
In the *b*, O Lord, you laid the foundations 732 27
The fear of the Lord is the *b* of wisdom; * 755 1
From the *b*, human beings have misused 845 10

begins

on your servant N. as he *b* another year. 830 9

begotten

O Lord, the only-*b* Son, Jesus Christ; 52 10
Almighty God, who has given us thy only-*b* Son 161 7
manifest thy only-*b* Son to the peoples 162 14
O God, who before the passion of thy only-*b* Son 165 14
didst give thine only-*b* Son to the death 170 8
Almighty God, who through thine only-*b* Son 170 21
as we do believe thy only-*b* Son 174 16
as thy only-*b* Son was this day presented 187 17
Almighty God, you have given your only-*b* Son 213 1
O God, who before the passion of your only-*b* Son 217 7
Almighty God, who through your only-*b* Son Jesus 222 15
for our redemption gave your only-*b* Son 222 1
only-*b* Son our Lord Jesus Christ to have ascended 226 9
only-*b* Son was this day presented 239 7
almighty, and eternal God, and your only-*b* Son, 287 2
gave your only-*b* Son to the death 295 2
O Lord, the only-*b* Son, Jesus Christ; 324 21
eternally *b* of the Father, 326 12
b, not made, 326 15
the only-*b* Son of God, 327 25
b of his Father before all worlds, 327 26
b, not made, 327 29
God so loved the world, that he gave his only-*b* 332 10
eternally *b* of the Father, 358 9
b, not made, 358 12
God so loved the world, that he gave his only-*b* 449 15
eternally *b* of the Father, 519 12
b, not made, 519 15
eternally *b* of the Father, 530 3
b, not made, 530 6
eternally *b* of the Father, 542 3
b, not made, 542 6
this day have I *b* you. 586 16
in the beauty of holiness have I *b* you, 753 17

begun

may the Holy Spirit, who has *b* a good work in you, 310 5
may the Holy Spirit, who has *b* a good work in you, 419 1
the good work you have *b*; 460 20
work which thou hast *b* in them may be perfected; 489 1
in all our works *b*, continued, and ended in thee, 832 3
Help us, O Lord, to finish the good work here *b*. 839 16

behalf

and to ask, for ourselves and on *b* of others, 41 9
to appear in the presence of God on our *b*. 77 16
to ask, for ourselves and on *b* of others 79 3
Accept our prayers on *b* of thy servant 470 2
Accept our prayers on *b* of your servant 493 11
Bishop in the Church of God, on *b* of the clergy 526 1
Bishop in the Church of God, on *b* of the clergy 538 1
from his sickness thy servant N., in whose *b* 841 9

behaved

I *b* like one who mourns for his mother, 630 21

beheld

from the heavens he *b* the earth; 732 15
They *b* the works of the LORD * 748 3
The sea *b* it and fled; * 757 1
Your eyes *b* my limbs, yet unfinished in the womb; 795 6

behind

Thou hast beset me *b* and before, * 475 1
and toss my words *b* your back? 655 15
You press upon me *b* and before * 794 8

behold

B, I bring you good tidings of great joy, 37 8
B, the tabernacle of God is with men, 37 11
B and see if there be any sorrow 39 4
For *b* from henceforth * 50 5
and our eyes *b* the vesper light, 64 5
For *b* from henceforth * 65 8
B, I bring you good news of a great joy 75 8
B, the dwelling of God is with mankind. 75 11
For *b*, darkness covers the land; * 87 13
B, he who keeps watch over Israel * 104 19
b the new has come. 106 2
and our eyes *b* the vesper light, 112 5
Give us grace to *b* you, 113 11
and our eyes *b* the vesper light, 118 5
Your eyes have only to *b* * 130 13
B now, bless the Lord, all you servants 131 6
and our eyes *b* the vesper light, 139 5
B now, bless the Lord, all you servants 140 1
Graciously *b* our afflictions. 154 16
With pity *b* the sorrows of our hearts; 154 17
b him when he shall come to be our Judge; 160 15
where we may *b* thy glory face to face 162 15
we beseech thee graciously to *b* 169 14
that we may *b* him in all his redeeming work; 171 19
that we may *b* him in all his redeeming work; 173 7
b the King in his beauty; 191 19
b him when he comes to be our Judge; 212 13
we pray you graciously to *b* 221 8
that we may *b* him in all his redeeming work; 223 12
that we may *b* him in all his redeeming work; 224 21
b the King in his beauty; 243 5
For *b*, you look for truth deep within me, * 266 14
we pray you graciously to *b* 276 4
Open, O Lord, the eyes of all people to *b* 329 22
or fear rejoice to *b* his appearing. 345 11
or fear rejoice to *b* his appearing. 378 8
may with joy *b* thy Son at his coming 395 14
b, visit, and relieve thy sick servant 458 2
whom I shall see for myself and mine eyes shall *b*, 469 7
B, he that keepeth Israel * 473 15
to *b* the fair beauty of the LORD, 477 19
I myself shall see, and my eyes *b* him 491 11
we may *b* the order and beauty of things 573 5
Surely, you *b* trouble and misery; * 595 23
His eyes *b* the inhabited world; * 596 17
To *b* the fair beauty of the LORD * 617 22
B, the eye of the LORD is upon those who fear him, * 627 11
I went by, and *b*, they were not there; * 636 8
and so I said, "*B*, I come. 640 19
b, I did not restrain my lips; 640 24
B, the kings of the earth assembled * 651 8
For *b*, you look for truth deep within me, * 656 18
B, God is my helper; * 659 24
B, they boast with their mouths, 666 9
that I might *b* your power and your glory. 670 16
b and tend this vine; * 703 16
B our defender, O God; * 708 8
B Philistia, Tyre, and Ethiopia: 711 18
our eyes have only to *b* * 720 1
but stoops to *b* the heavens and the earth? 756 11
B, I long for your commandments; * 766 15
B my affliction and deliver me, * 776 9
B, he who keeps watch over Israel * 779 7
B now, bless the LORD, all you servants 787 19
Open our eyes to *b* thy gracious hand 814 2
and make them worthy at length to *b* it unveiled 819 17
B and visit, we pray, the cities of the earth. 825 8
We humbly beseech thee graciously to *b* and bless 830 20

beholdest

Blessed art thou that *b* the depths, 49 15

beholding

Glory to you, *b* the depths; * 90 13
that we, *b* by faith the light of his countenance, 165 16
that we, *b* by faith the light of his countenance, 217 9
and, *b* the glory of your presence, 373 8
I shall be satisfied, *b* your likeness 602 5

beholds

and *b* all the people in the world. 627 2

being

Christ *b* raised from the dead dieth no more; * 46 7
That we *b* delivered out of the hand of our enemies * 51 7
but that we, *b* ordered by thy governance, 57 11
in whom we live and move and have our *b*: 57 15
b defended from the fear of all enemies, 69 19
Christ *b* raised from the dead will never die again; * 83 15
by your will they were created and have their *b*; 93 23
in you we live and move and have our *b*: 100 7
b delivered from the fear of all enemies 123 18
Grant that we, *b* regenerate 161 9
we, *b* renewed both in body and mind, 170 19
we, *b* ready both in body and soul, 177 5
Christ himself *b* the chief cornerstone: 178 20
thou *b* our ruler and guide, 180 3
b gathered together in unity by thy Holy Spirit, 181 6
that we, *b* illumined by the teaching 186 7
thy Church, *b* delivered from false apostles, 188 3
that we, *b* mindful of their victory of faith, 189 7

not his own renown but the well-*b* of thy Church, 189 19
we, *b* delivered from the disquietude 191 17
B of glorious majesty and perfect love as one God 199 13
Grant that we, *b* reborn to new life in him, 203 7
thy Church, *b* preserved in true faith 204 12
Grant that thy Church, *b* bound together 204 19
we, *b* renewed both in body and mind, 222 11
b ready both in mind and body 228 15
Christ himself *b* the chief cornerstone: 230 14
your Church, *b* gathered together 232 17
we, *b* illumined by the teachings 238 2
your Church, *b* delivered from false apostles, 239 13
b mindful of their victory 240 14
not his own renown but the well-*b* of your Church, 241 5
we, *b* delivered from the disquietude 243 3
B of glorious majesty and perfect love as one God 251 2
Grant that we, *b* reborn to new life in him, 254 9
your Church, *b* preserved in true faith 255 10
Grant that your Church, *b* bound together 255 17
to his people, *b* penitent, the absolution 269 7
which were cast down are *b* raised up 280 18
which had grown old are *b* made new, 280 19
all things are *b* brought to their perfection 280 20
which were cast down are *b* raised up 291 15
which had grown old are *b* made new, 291 16
all things are *b* brought to their perfection 291 17
and respect the dignity of every human *b*? 294 2
we, *b* renewed both in body and mind, 295 11
respect the dignity of every human *b*? 305 9
b ready to make restitution for all injuries 317 5
and also *b* ready to forgive those 317 7
b reconciled with one another, 317 9
of one *b* with the Father. 326 16
b of one substance with the Father; 327 30
they were created and have their *b*. 344 7
of one *b* with the Father. 358 13
b sanctified by the Holy Spirit. 369 8
By your will they were created and have their *b*. 370 11
they were created and have their *b*. 377 5
in Trinity of Persons and in Unity of *b*; 380 9
and for the well-*b* of all people. 386 2
that *b* freed from anxiety 391 11
and respect the dignity of every human *b*? 417 18
his health *b* renewed, he may bless 458 20
in the midst of this earthly life *b* purged 488 18
that your servant N., *b* raised with him, 493 6
which were cast down are *b* raised up 515 8
which had grown old are *b* made new, 515 9
all things are *b* brought to their perfection 515 10
of one *b* with the Father. 519 16
which were cast down are *b* raised up, 528 6
which had grown old are *b* made new, 528 7
all things are *b* brought to their perfection 528 8
of one *b* with the Father. 530 7
which were cast down are *b* raised up, 540 6
which had grown old are *b* made new, 540 7
all things are *b* brought to their perfection 540 8
of one *b* with the Father. 542 7
Will you look for Christ in all others, *b* ready 544 4
When the foundations are *b* destroyed, * 596 13
While my bones are *b* broken, * 644 5
I will praise my God while I have my *b*. 737 21
while I was *b* made in secret 795 4
I will sing praises to my God while I have my *b*. 803 6
b guided by thy Providence, we may dwell 820 17
wide decisions for the well-*b* of our society; 822 13
offices to promote the well-*b* of all people; 822 21
our divisions *b* healed, we may live in justice 823 21
God's *b* draws praise from us. 857 6
grace of the Holy Spirit to those *b* made bishops, 860 29
from death in the fullness of our *b*, 862 18

beings

From the beginning, human *b* have misused 845 10
human *b* might be adopted as children of God, 850 3

beliefs

The creeds are statements of our basic *b* 851 23

believe

We *b* that thou shalt come to be our judge. 53 18
I *b* in God, the Father almighty, 53 23
I *b* in the Holy Ghost, 54 5
I *b* in God, the Father almighty, 66 9
I *b* in the Holy Ghost, 66 21
We *b* that you will come and be our judge. 96 8
I *b* in God, the Father almighty, 96 13
I *b* in Jesus Christ, his only Son, our Lord. 96 15
I *b* in the Holy Spirit, 96 25
I *b* in God, the Father almighty, 120 9
I *b* in Jesus Christ, his only Son, our Lord. 120 11
I *b* in the Holy Spirit, 120 21
we do *b* thy only-begotten Son our Lord 174 16
perfectly and without doubt to *b* in Jesus Christ, 185 16
apostle Bartholomew grace truly to *b* and to preach 192 8
that the world may *b* in him whom thou didst send 204 21
that as we *b* your only-begotten Son 226 8
perfectly and without doubt to *b* in Jesus Christ, 237 10
Bartholomew grace truly to *b* and to preach 243 15
that the world may *b* in him whom you have sent, 255 19
and with sincere hearts *b* his holy Gospel. 269 9
that all who *b* in him might be delivered 277 4
This is the night, when all who *b* in Christ 287 9
Do you *b* in God the Father? 292 11
I *b* in God, the Father almighty, 292 12
Do you *b* in Jesus Christ, the Son of God? 293 1
I *b* in Jesus Christ, his only Son, our Lord. 293 2
Do you *b* in God the Holy Spirit? 293 12
I *b* in the Holy Spirit, 293 13
Do you *b* in God the Father? 304 1
I *b* in God, the Father almighty, 304 2
Do you *b* in Jesus Christ, the Son of God? 304 4
I *b* in Jesus Christ, his only Son, our Lord 304 5
Do you *b* in God the Holy Spirit? 304 15
I *b* in the Holy Spirit, 304 16
We *b* in one God, 326 6
We *b* in one Lord, Jesus Christ, 326 10
We *b* in the Holy Spirit, the Lord, 327 12
We *b* in one holy catholic and apostolic Church. 327 16
I *b* in one God, 327 20
And I *b* in the Holy Ghost the Lord, 328 13
And I *b* one holy Catholic and Apostolic Church; 328 18
all that *b* in him should not perish, 332 11
We *b* in one God, 358 3
We *b* in one Lord, Jesus Christ, 358 7

We *b* in the Holy Spirit, the Lord, 359 3
We *b* in one holy catholic and apostolic Church. 359 7
his own first gift for those who *b*, 374 11
For all who fear God and *b* in you, Lord Christ, 390 4
For those who do not yet *b*, 390 10
Do you *b* in God the Father? 416 6
I *b* in God, the Father almighty, 416 7
Do you *b* in Jesus Christ, the Son of God? 416 9
I *b* in Jesus Christ, his only Son, our Lord. 416 10
Do you *b* in God the Holy Spirit? 416 20
I *b* in the Holy Spirit, 416 21
absolve all sinners who truly repent and *b* in him, 448 2
to the end that all that *b* in him should not perish, 449 16
absolve all sinners who truly repent and *b* in him, 451 12
b that what happens to me here is of little account 461 10
I *b* verily to see the goodness of the LORD 478 6
to *b* and trust in the communion of saints, 481 15
Christ will open the kingdom of heaven to all who *b* 483 20
I *b* in God, the Father almighty, 496 3
I *b* in Jesus Christ, his only Son, our Lord. 496 5
I *b* in the Holy Spirit, 496 15
Christ will open the kingdom of heaven to all who *b* 500 9
I do *b* the Holy Scriptures 513 9
We *b* in one God. 519 5
We *b* in one God, 519 6
We *b* in one Lord, Jesus Christ, 519 10
We *b* in the Holy Spirit, the Lord, 520 3
We *b* in one holy catholic and apostolic Church. 520 7
And do you *b* his manner of life to be suitable 526 5
and we *b* him to be qualified for this order. 526 8
I do *b* the Holy Scriptures 526 15
We *b* in one God, 529 9
We *b* in one Lord, Jesus Christ, 530 1
We *b* in the Holy Spirit, the Lord, 530 22
We *b* in one holy catholic and apostolic Church. 530 26
My brother, do you *b* that you are truly called by 531 21
I *b* I am so called. 531 23
And do you *b* his manner of life to be suitable 538 5
and we *b* him qualified for this order. 538 8
I do *b* the Holy Scriptures 538 15
We *b* in one God, 541 9
We *b* in one Lord, Jesus Christ, 542 1
We *b* in the Holy Spirit, the Lord, 542 22
We *b* in one holy catholic and apostolic Church. 542 26
My brother, do you *b* that you are truly called 543 19
I *b* I am so called. 543 21
For all who fear God and *b* in you, Lord Christ, 549 16
For those who do not yet *b*, 549 25
We *b* that he is well qualified, 559 3
and would not *b* his promise. 743 21
Our duty is to *b* and trust in God; 847 20
Who do we *b* is the Messiah? 849 16
apostles; and, through them, to all who *b* 850 29
Christ commanded us to *b* in him 851 5
Where may we find what Christians *b* 851 18
What Christians *b* about Christ is found 851 20
We *b* that Christ will come in glory 862 14

believed

to love what he *b* and to preach 192 10
Grant that your Church may love what he *b* 243 16
What if I had not *b* 618 26
Then they *b* his words * 742 22
I *b*, even when I said, 759 20
for I have *b* in your commandments. 768 20

believers

thou didst open the kingdom of heaven to all *b*. 53 16
and opened the kingdom of heaven to all *b*. 96 6
God and Father of all *b*, 289 6
for Abraham, the father of *b*, 838 10

believes

whoever *b* in him should not perish, but have eternal 396 2
and whoever *b* in me shall never thirst." 396 5
I will never turn away anyone who *b* in me. 501 2

believeth

he that *b* in me, though he were dead, 469 2
whosoever liveth and *b* in me shall never die. 469 3

believing

b through the power of the Holy Spirit. 60 2
b through the power of the Holy Spirit. 73 2
b through the power of the Holy Spirit. 102 13
b through the power of the Holy Spirit. 126 13

bellies

Whose *b* you fill with your treasure, * 602 1

belly

and also my throat and my *b*. 623 5

belong

To the Lord our God *b* mercies and forgivenesses, 38 20
To the Lord our God *b* mercy and forgiveness, 76 19
accomplish those things which *b* to thy purpose; 177 6
free hearts those things which *b* to your purpose; 229 2
The rulers of the earth *b* to God, * 650 24

belongs

anything that *b* to your neighbor. 350 21
Deliverance *b* to the LORD. * 587 18
For kingship *b* to the LORD; * 612 13
that power *b* to God. 670 9
It means that the world *b* to its creator; 846 10

beloved

Dearly *b*, we have come together 41 5
hast promised through thy well-*b* Son 59 14
hast promised through thy well-*b* Son 72 11
Dearly *b*, we have come together 79 1
have promised through your well-*b* Son 102 3
have promised through your well-*b* Son 126 3
didst proclaim him thy *b* Son 163 2
restore all things in thy well-*b* Son, 185 2
reveal to chosen witnesses thy well-*b* Son, 191 16
whose *b* Son willingly endured 201 7
restore all things in thy well-*b* Son, 202 17
proclaimed him your *b* Son 214 13
restore all things in your well-*b* Son, 236 15
revealed to chosen witnesses your well-*b* Son, 243 2
whose *b* Son willingly endured 252 12
restore all things in your well-*b* Son, 254 2
B in the Lord: 316 1
institution of thy dearly *b* Son 335 9
the Body and Blood of thy dearly-*b* Son 342 19

Because thou didst send thy *b* Son to redeem us 345 8
Through thy dearly *b* Son 347 1
Because you sent your *b* Son to redeem us 378 4
Through your dearly *b* Son 379 20
Communion of the Body and Blood of your *b* Son 399 8
Dearly *b*: We have come together 423 1
Communion of the Body and Blood of your *b* Son 457 6
O God, whose *b* Son did take little children 470 7
O God, whose *b* Son took children 494 1
that blessing which your well-*b* Son 505 5
Spirit, whom you bestowed upon your *b* Son 521 3
for he gives to his *b* sleep. 783 5

belt

and like the *b* that he wears continually. 752 12

bend

Come, let us bow down, and *b* the knee, * 82 15
And now, O Lord, I *b* the knee of my heart, * 91 12
he will *b* his bow and make it ready. 591 23
For see how the wicked *b* the bow 596 10
The wicked draw their sword and *b* their bow 634 11
Come, let us bow down, and *b* the knee, * 725 1

bending

and my arms for *b* even a bow of bronze. 605 8

beneath

heaven above or in the earth *b*, 318 3
You lengthen my stride *b* me, * 605 12
you have cast down my adversaries *b* me; 605 19
and cast down the peoples *b* me. 606 6
into the hills and down to the valleys *b*, * 735 17

benediction

be filled with thy grace and heavenly *b*, 336 6
be filled with thy grace and heavenly *b*; 342 27
and fill you with all spiritual *b* 431 11

benefit

thankfully receive that his inestimable *b*, 180 22
and for the *b* of thy holy Church 205 10
and for the *b* of your holy Church 256 7
For, as the *b* is great, if with penitent hearts 316 23
and confess your sins, that you may receive the *b* 317 13

benefits

great *b* that we have received at his hands, 41 7
innumberable *b* procured unto us by the same. 335 16
and all other *b* of his passion. 335 29
and forget not all his *b*. 733 12
people of this land share the *b* of true freedom 839 25
offered them also the *b* of redemption. 850 16
What are the *b* which we receive 859 27
The *b* we receive are the forgiveness 859 29

Benjamin

There is *B*, least of the tribes, at the head; 678 11
In the presence of Ephraim, *B*, and Manasseh, * 702 14

bereaved

For the sorrowful and *b* 279 9
Give courage and faith to those who are *b*, 481 10
to all who are *b* the spirit 505 10

beseech

we *b* thee, 59 1
Lighten our darkness, we *b* thee, 70 1
And, we *b* thee, 71 20
Lighten our darkness, we *b* thee, 111 1
We sinners do *b* thee to hear us, 150 1
We *b* thee to hear us, good Lord. 150 4
Son of God, we *b* thee to hear us. 152 22
We *b* thee mercifully 153 20
We humbly *b* thee, 155 7
We *b* thee, 160 6
we *b* thee, 161 2
we *b* thee, 162 3
we *b* thee, 164 7
we *b* thee graciously to behold this thy family 169 14
we *b* thee, Almighty God, that we who celebrate 171 5
we *b* thee, Almighty God, that like as we do 174 15
We *b* thee, leave us not comfortless, 175 3
We *b* thee that thou wouldest keep us 176 4
we *b* thee, from all things 177 4
we *b* thee, that the course of this world 177 9
We humbly *b* thee to put away from us 177 15
Keep, O Lord, we *b* thee, thy household the Church 178 6
we *b* thee, make us to have a perpetual fear 178 12
we *b* thee mercifully to receive the prayers 179 10
Have compassion, we *b* thee, upon our infirmities, 179 18
we *b* thee, let thy continual pity cleanse 180 8
Grant to us, Lord, we *b* thee, the spirit to think 180 14
we *b* thee, merciful God, that thy Church, 181 5
we *b* thee, that we may run without stumbling 184 3
we *b* thee, that, having this hope 184 9
Shed upon thy Church, we *b* thee, 186 6
Receive, we *b* thee, into the arms of thy mercy 186 15
we *b* thee, that we, having his wonderful 187 10
we humbly *b* thee that, 187 16
We *b* thee, O Lord, pour thy grace into our hearts, 188 15
we *b* thee, that we and all the people 190 19
we *b* thee, 192 9
we *b* thee, 193 18
Make us, we *b* thee, faithful stewards 194 18
we *b* thee, in this and every land evangelists 196 10
we *b* thee, that by this teaching we 197 21
we *b* thee, that by the indwelling of thy Holy Spirit 200 1
we *b* thee, to take up our cross 201 9
we *b* thee, to thy whole Church in paradise 202 2
we *b* thee, with his grace and presence 204 9
we humbly *b* thee, to all who are [now] called to any office 205 6
we *b* thee, in every heart the true love of peace 207 8
we *b* thee, ever thankful for thy loving providence; 208 10
we *b* thee, all who, following in his steps, give themselves 209 10
we *b* thee, in our several occupations 210 3
Therefore we *b* him to grant us true repentance 269 10
Save us and help us, we humbly *b* thee, 282 5
write all these thy laws in our hearts, we *b* thee. 318 30
We *b* thee also so to rule the hearts 329 18
b thee, of thy goodness, O Lord, to comfort 329 26
b thee, O merciful Father, to hear us; 335 17
yet we *b* thee to accept this our bounden duty 336 10
And we humbly *b* thee, O heavenly Father, so to assist 339 10

b thee, O merciful Father, to hear us 342 16
we *b* thee, that all who partake of this Holy Communion 342 24
I *b* you, brethren, by the mercies of God, 343 14
Save us, and help us, we humbly *b* you, 455 18
We humbly *b* thee to behold, 458 2
We sinners *b* you to hear us, 463 11
We *b* you to hear us, good Lord. 463 14
Acknowledge, we humbly *b* you, a sheep 465 2
we *b* thee, to entrust this child 470 8
I *b* thee, deliver my soul. 479 7
we *b* thee, to thy whole Church 480 6
we humbly *b* thee, a sheep of thine 483 7
we *b* thee, to those who rest 486 9
And we *b* thee that we, 488 7
we *b* thee, 489 4
and we *b* thee that, 489 19
Acknowledge, we humbly *b* you, a sheep 499 14
we humbly *b* thee for all sorts 814 7
We humbly *b* thee that we may always prove 820 2
We *b* thee so to guide and bless 821 2
We humbly *b* thee to bless the courts 821 9
we *b* thee, every root of bitterness 828 24
We humbly *b* thee graciously to behold and bless 830 20
We *b* thee mercifully to incline thine ear to us 834 2
we *b* thee, so to venerate the sacred mysteries 834 13
we *b* thee, Almighty God, that the words 834 18
we *b* thee, give us a just sense 840 19

beseeching

b thee to inspire 329 4
b thee to grant them continual growth 330 3
humbly *b* thee to grant that, 335 26
humbly *b* thee that we, 336 3
b our Lord 456 2
b him to uphold you 456 8
most humbly *b* thee to give us grace 487 14
b thee that he may be precious 488 14

beset

Thou hast *b* me behind and before, * 475 1
give them courage to face the perils which *b* them; 823 5
remove from them the fears that *b* them; 831 21

beside

and leads me *b* still waters. 443 4
and lead me forth *b* the waters of comfort. 476 4
he leadeth me *b* the still waters. 476 22
and leads me *b* still waters. 612 26
B them the birds of the air make their nests * 735 25
He will drink from the brook *b* the road; * 754 3

besides

What shall be done to you, and what more *b*, * 778 14

besieged

wonders of his love in a *b* city. 624 13

best

petitions of thy servants as may be *b* for us; 59 17
petitions of thy servants as may be *b* for us; 72 14
petitions as may be *b* for us; 102 6
petitions as may be *b* for us; 126 6
Will you do your *b* to pattern your life 532 19
Will you do your *b* to pattern your life 544 7
petitions as you see *b* for us, 578 22
Even my *b* friend, whom I trusted, 642 17
for setting us at tasks which demand our *b* efforts 836 7

bestow

b freedom upon all peoples, 151 3
B on them, if it is your will, the gift 429 20
Since it has pleased God to *b* 441 10

bestowed

through your Son you have *b* 285 8
and *b* upon us the forgiveness of sins, 294 6
you have *b* upon these your servants 308 3
you have *b* upon this your servant 314 2
you have *b* upon this family 443 24
whom you *b* upon your beloved Son 521 3
splendor and majesty have you *b* upon him. 609 6
freely *b* upon us. 837 2
thy merciful providence *b* upon this nation 840 19

bestowing

b upon us occasions of song 113 3

Bethlehem

the slaughter of the holy innocents of *B* 186 14
the slaughter of the holy innocents of *B* 238 8

betrayed

Christ was contented to be *b*, 169 16
Christ was willing to be *b*, 221 10
Christ was willing to be *b*, 276 6
For in the night in which he was *b*, 334 17
For in the night in which he was *b*, 342 1
and *b* your trust 370 14
On the night he was *b* he took bread, 371 10
On the night he was *b* he took bread, 403 4
nor have we *b* your covenant. 646 21
I should have *b* the generation 688 8

better

"Oh, that we might see *b* times!" * 129 2
for *b* for worse, 427 2
for *b* for worse, 436 3
"Oh, that we might see *b* times!" * 588 11
is *b* than great riches of the wicked. 634 17
For your loving-kindness is *b* than life itself; * 670 17
For one day in your courts is *b* than 708 10
It is *b* to rely on the LORD * 761 11
It is *b* to rely on the LORD * 761 13
following you is *b* than chasing after selfish goals. 829 17
thou art doing for them *b* things 831 9

between

and dwellest *b* the Cherubim; * 49 16
Glory to you, seated *b* the Cherubim; * 90 11
your passion, cross, and death *b* your judgment 282 7
the mystery of the union *b* Christ and his Church, 423 7
the spiritual unity *b* Christ and his Church 431 2
I publish the Banns of Marriage *b* 437 1
b thy judgment and our souls 489 24
they flow *b* the mountains. 735 22

bewail

We acknowledge and *b* our manifold sins 331 4

beyond

But your merciful promise is *b* all measure; * 91 3
How wonderful and *b* our knowing, 287 12
whose wisdom is *b* our understanding, 494 7

Bible

Receive this *B* as a sign of the authority 534 10
Receive this *B* as the sign of your authority 545 19
accept this *B*, and be among us 561 1
The Holy Scriptures, commonly called the *B*, 853 6
are often included in the *B*. 853 8
God still speaks to us through the *B*. 853 26
How do we understand the meaning of the *B*? 853 27
We understand the meaning of the *B* 853 28
How is the Church described in the *B*? 854 5

bid

Who dost *b* thy faithful people cleanse their hearts, 346 9
You *b* your faithful people cleanse their hearts, 379 5
I *b* you, 440 3
I *b* you join with them 440 10
b love and faithfulness watch over him. 669 2

bidden

b to declare it. 437 4

bidding

you mighty ones who do his *b*, * 734 23

bind

To *b* their kings in chains * 807 16

binding

We give you thanks for *b* us together 432 2

binds

nor the bosom of him who *b* the sheaves; 784 14
and *b* up their wounds. 804 7

bird

"Fly away like a *b* to the hilltop; 596 9
I know every *b* in the sky, * 655 1
We have escaped like a *b* 781 13

birds

All *b* of the air, glorify the Lord, * 89 12
The *b* of the air, the fish of the sea, * 592 23
and winged *b* like the sand of the sea. 697 4
as food for the *b* of the air, * 701 5
Beside them the *b* of the air make their nests * 735 25
In which the *b* build their nests, * 736 11
creeping things and winged *b*; 806 14
for the songs of *b* 840 9

birth

the yearly remembrance of the *b* 160 13
you make us glad by the yearly festival of the *b* 212 10
I have been wicked from my *b*, * 266 12
a new *b* by water and the Holy Spirit, 294 5
to receive the Sacrament of new *b* 305 12
The *b* of a child 440 1
and give *b* to a lie. 591 27
I have been wicked from my *b*, * 656 16
liars go astray from their *b*. 664 26
from the day of your *b*; * 753 16
b into God's family the Church 858 18

bishop

to be a [*b* and] pastor in thy Church 197 5
Shepherd and *B* of our souls, 205 19
to be a [*b* and] pastor in your Church 248 16
and *B* of our souls, 256 16
our *B*, 278 6
For our *B*, 384 1
for our *B*(s); 385 18
For our Presiding *B*, for our own *B*(s), 390 1
For [our *B*(s); 392 14
B in the Church of God, 513 1
have chosen to be a *b* and chief pastor. 513 3
to consecrate him a *b* 513 5
chosen *B* of the Church 513 8
elected to be a *b* of the Church of God 514 3
Is it your will that we ordain a *b*? 514 8
Will you uphold as *b*? 514 10
A *b* in God's Holy Church 517 2
to the office of *b*? 517 20
B of our souls. 518 18
to serve his Church in the office of *b*. 519 2
make a *b* in your Church. 521 1
to be a *b* in your Church 521 7
B in the Church of God, 526 1
obey your *b* and other ministers 526 11
b and fellow presbyters, 531 6
direction and leadership of your *b*? 532 2
B in the Church of God, on behalf of the clergy and 538 1
obey your *b* and other ministers 538 11
servanthood directly under your *b*. 543 4
You are to assist the *b* and priests 543 13
direction and leadership of your *b*? 543 26
For our Presiding *B*, 548 20
chosen *b* (priest, deacon) in your Church, 549 1
B N., we have come together today 559 1
and help me (help the *b*) baptize 561 3
yours (the *B*'s and yours) 562 8
Bless our *B*(s) 817 11
choose a *b* for this Diocese 818 10
What is the ministry of a *b*? 855 21
The ministry of a *b* is to represent Christ 855 22
to share with the *b* in the overseeing 856 4
and the laying on of hands by a *b*. 860 21

bishops

That it may please thee to illumine all *b*, 150 5
the *b* and the other clergy 204 10
the *b* and the other clergy 255 8
For all *b* and other ministers 278 4
to all *b* and other ministers 329 9
We pray for all *b*, 387 6
for all *b* and other ministers, 390 2
for] all *b* and other ministers; 392 14
and to join in ordaining *b*; 517 10
With your fellow *b* you will share in the leadership 517 13
Will you share with your fellow *b* in the government 518 22
and for all *b*, priests, and deacons 548 20
Send down upon our *b*, 817 4
The ministers of the Church are lay persons, *b*, 855 12

to assist *b* and priests in the proclamation 856 10
Spirit to those being made *b*, 860 29
the laying on of hands by *b*. 861 2

bit

who must be fitted with *b* and bridle, 625 21

bitter

deliver us not into the *b* pains of eternal death. 484 10
and aim their *b* words like arrows, 671 15

bitterness

deliver us not into the *b* of eternal death. 492 11
save them from *b*; 823 12
one another without hatred or *b*, 824 3
every root of *b*, 829 1

blameless

Whoever leads a *b* life 599 6
For I have been *b* with him * 604 9
That they may shoot down the *b* from ambush; * 671 16
I will strive to follow a *b* course; 730 9
and only those who lead a *b* life shall 730 22
Happy are those whose way is *b*, * 763 5

blaspheme

will the enemy *b* your Name for ever? 690 5

blasphemers

Because of the taunts of the mockers and *b*, * 646 17

blast

at the *b* of the breath of your nostrils. 603 22
Praise him with the *b* of the ram's-horn; * 808 3

blasted

He *b* their vines and their fig trees * 740 19

blaze

will your fury *b* like fire for ever? 701 14
they *b* like a fire of thorns; * 761 20

blazed

hot burning coals *b* forth from him. 603 6
Fire *b* up against their company, * 743 7

blazing

He poured out upon them his *b* anger: * 699 1
Your *b* anger has swept over me; * 713 11

bless

b ye the Lord; * 47 5
O let the earth *b* the Lord; * 48 17
O ye mountains and hills, *b* ye the Lord; 48 18
O ye holy and humble men of heart, *b* ye the Lord; 49 6
Let us *b* the Father, the Son, and the Holy Spirit; * 49 7
We praise thee, we *b* thee, 52 5
and *b* thine heritage; 55 15
We *b* thee for our creation, 58 19
Let us *b* the Lord. 59 20
I will *b* the Lord who giveth me counsel; 61 10
our lives may *b* thee, 69 14
all tongues confess and *b* thee, 70 17
b the dying, 71 3
We *b* thee for our creation, 71 15
Let us *b* the Lord. 72 17
and *b* your inheritance; 98 9
Day by day we *b* you; 98 11
We *b* you for our creation, 101 11
Let us *b* the Lord. 102 8
Let us *b* the Lord. 107 22
B the Lord who forgives all our sins. 109 5
The Lord *b* you and keep you. 114 1
I will *b* the Lord who gives me counsel; 115 10
our lives may *b* you, 123 13
all tongues confess and *b* you, 124 14
b the dying, 124 19
We *b* you for our creation, 125 9
Let us *b* the Lord. 126 8
b the Lord, all you servants 131 6
and *b* the Lord; * 131 8
b you out of Zion. 131 9
b the dying, 134 8
Let us *b* the Lord. 135 12
b us and keep us. 135 15
b the Lord, all you servants 140 1
and *b* the Lord; * 140 3
b you out of Zion. 140 4
b us and keep us. 140 18
to *b* and keep all thy people, 150 10
B, we beseech thee, with his grace 204 9
B, we beseech thee, all who, 209 10
B, we pray, with his grace and presence, 255 7
B all who, following in his steps, 260 16
May God be merciful to us and *b* us, 281 5
We adore you, O Christ, and we *b* you, 281 15
We adore you, O Christ, and we *b* you, 282 1
B the Lord who forgives all our sins. 299 5
b, preserve, and keep you. 310 4
B the Lord who forgiveth all our sins. 319 6
B the Lord who forgiveth all our sins. 323 4
We praise thee, we *b* thee, 324 16
And we also *b* thy holy Name 330 1
vouchsafe to *b* and sanctify, 335 18
Let us *b* the Lord. 340 6
to *b* and sanctify 342 17
and thy faithful servants *b* thee, 348 8
B the Lord who forgives all our sins. 351 5
B the Lord who forgives all our sins. 355 5
Let us *b* the Lord. 366 21
and we *b* you. 374 29
We praise you, we *b* you, 375 1
and your faithful servants *b* you, 381 3
B all whose lives are closely linked with ours, 388 17
Let us *b* the Lord. 399 13
Holy Spirit *b* and sanctify this bread (wine) 408 2
B the Lord who forgives all our sins. 413 5
b, preserve, and keep you. 418 20
and *b* the joining together 423 2
B, O Lord, this ring 427 10
B them in their work 430 19
b, preserve, and keep you; 431 9
B, O Lord, this ring 434 4
b our child 441 7
giver of life and love, *b* 444 8
B this child 444 16
B me, for I have sinned. 447 1
Let us *b* the Lord. 457 11
he may *b* your holy Name; 458 20

and *b* the means made use	459	8
May God the Father *b* you,	460	5
children into his arms and *b* them:	470	8
The Lord *b* him	485	12
B, we pray, this grave,	487	6
The Lord *b* him	501	14
B, we pray, this grave,	503	8
B the Lord who forgives all our sins.	512	5
B the Lord who forgives all our sins.	525	5
B the Lord who forgives all our sins.	537	5
break the Bread and *b* the Cup.	562	6
to illumine and to *b* your people.	568	13
Accept and *b* all we have done,	573	4
For you, O Lord, will *b* the righteous; *	589	21
I will *b* the Lord who gives me counsel; *	600	11
in the full assembly I will *b* the Lord.	617	6
Save your people and *b* your inheritance; *	620	3
I will *b* the Lord at all times; *	627	21
They *b* with their lips, *	669	14
So will I *b* you as long as I live *	670	19
you soften the ground and *b* its increase.	673	10
B our God, you peoples; *	674	9
May God be merciful to us and *b* us, *	675	9
B God in the congregation; *	678	9
b the Lord, you that are of the fountain of Israel.	678	10
and may they *b* him all the day long.	686	16
may all the nations *b* themselves in him and	686	23
Sing to the Lord and *b* his Name; *	725	19
B the Lord, O my soul, *	733	9
and all that is within me, *b* his holy Name.	733	10
B the Lord, O my soul, *	733	11
B the Lord, you angels of his,	734	22
B the Lord, all you his hosts, *	734	25
B the Lord, all you works of his,	734	27
b the Lord, O my soul.	734	29
B the Lord, O my soul; *	735	1
B the Lord, O my soul. *	737	26
They may curse, but you will *b*; *	753	3
The Lord has been mindful of us, and he will *b* us; *	758	12
he will *b* the house of Israel;	758	13
he will *b* the house of Aaron;	758	14
He will *b* those who fear the Lord, *	758	15
But we will *b* the Lord, *	758	25
we *b* you from the house of the Lord.	762	24
The Lord *b* you from Zion, *	783	21
I will surely *b* her provisions, *	787	1
b the Lord, all you servants of the Lord, *	787	19
in the holy place and *b* the Lord; *	787	21
b you out of Zion.	787	22
B the Lord, O house of Israel; *	789	13
O house of Aaron, *b* the Lord.	789	14
B the Lord, O house of Levi; *	789	15
you who fear the Lord, *b* the Lord.	789	16
and *b* your Name for ever and ever.	801	13
Every day will I *b* you *	801	14
and your faithful servants *b* you.	802	6
let all flesh *b* his holy Name	803	2
B our Bishop(s)	817	11
B our land with honorable industry,	820	4
and *b* our Senators and Representatives	821	3
to *b* the courts of justice	821	9
b the leaders of our land,	821	15
B those who work in the fields;	824	7
b all schools,	824	16
B the lands and waters,	828	2
b and guide him	830	13
and *b* those whom we love,	830	21
B, O Lord, thy gifts	835	11
We praise and *b* you	838	2
we *b* and praise thy Name.	841	9
to *b* and declare pardon	856	6

blessed

B art thou, O Lord God of our fathers; *	49	9
B art thou for the Name of thy Majesty; *	49	11
B art thou in the temple of thy holiness; *	49	13
B art thou that beholdest the depths,	49	15
B art thou on the glorious throne of thy kingdom; *	49	18
B art thou in the firmament of heaven; *	49	20
B art thou, O Father, Son, and Holy Spirit; *	49	22
all generations shall call me *b*.	50	6
B be the Lord God of Israel, *	50	22
and didst send thy *b* Son	58	2
O Jesus Christ, holy and *b*!	64	3
all generations shall call me *b*.	65	9
From this day all generations will call me *b*: *	92	1
B be the Lord, the God of Israel; *	92	18
and sent your *b* Son	100	18
B Savior, at this hour you hung upon the cross,	107	8
O Jesus Christ, holy and *b*!	112	3
B are you, O Lord,	113	1
O Jesus Christ, holy and *b*!	118	3
From this day all generations will call me *b*: *	119	7
B be the God and Father	137	11
Let the Name of the Lord be *b*, *	138	3
B Savior, at this hour you hung upon the cross,	138	12
O Jesus Christ, holy and *b*!	139	3
O holy, *b*, and glorious Trinity, one God,	148	7
whose *b* Son was led by the Spirit	166	9
whose *b* Son Jesus Christ came down	167	10
who by the passion of thy *b* Son	168	17
whose *b* Son our Savior gave his back	169	1
whose *b* Son did manifest himself	171	17
whose *b* Son did manifest himself	173	5
whose *b* Son our Savior	174	8
to follow the *b* steps	181	1
whose *b* Son was manifested	184	7
B Lord, who hast caused all holy Scriptures	184	15
the *b* hope of everlasting life,	184	19
the virgin mother of thy incarnate Son was *b*	189	12
but still more *b* in keeping thy word:	189	12
whose *b* apostles Peter and Paul	190	10
whose *b* Son restored Mary Magdalene	191	1
who hast taken to thyself the *b* Virgin Mary,	192	1
Grant us grace so to follow thy *b* saints	194	10
whose *b* Son became poor	198	1
whose *b* Son before his passion	204	17
and didst send thy *b* Son to preach peace	206	10
whose *b* Son came not to be ministered	209	9
whose *b* Son was led by the Spirit	218	1
whose *b* Son Jesus Christ came down from heaven	219	1
by the passion of your *b* Son	220	8
whose *b* Son our Savior gave his body	220	14
whose *b* Son made himself known	223	10

whose *b* Son made himself known	224	19
whose *b* Son our Savior	226	1
and to follow daily in the *b* steps	232	14
whose *b* Son came into the world	236	1
B Lord, who caused all holy Scriptures	236	8
hold fast the *b* hope of everlasting life,	236	11
your incarnate Son was *b* in bearing him,	240	19
but still more *b* in keeping your word:	240	20
whose *b* apostles Peter and Paul	241	19
whose *b* Son restored Mary Magdalene	242	8
you have taken to yourself the *b* Virgin Mary,	243	8
Give us grace so to follow your *b* saints	245	18
whose *b* Son became poor	249	11
whose *b* Son before his passion	255	15
and sent your *b* Son to preach peace	257	6
whose *b* Son came not to be served	260	15
B is the King who comes	270	1
B is he who comes	271	15
B by our God.	276	1
How *b* is this night,	287	19
B be God: Father, Son, and Holy Spirit.	299	1
whose *b* Son was anointed	307	9
B be God: Father, Son, and Holy Spirit	319	1
And *b* be his kingdom,	319	2
B be God: Father, Son, and Holy Spirit.	323	1
And *b* be his kingdom,	323	2
B is he that cometh	334	7
having in remembrance his *b* passion	335	13
of his most *b* Body and Blood.	335	23
the *b* company of all faithful people;	339	8
B is he that cometh	341	10
having in remembrance his *b* passion	342	13
the *b* hope of everlasting life;	349	7
B be God: Father, Son, and Holy Spirit.	351	1
And *b* be his kingdom,	351	2
B by God: Father, Son, and Holy Spirit.	355	1
And *b* be his kingdom,	355	2
B is he who comes	362	7
B is he who comes	367	16
and *b* us with memory, reason, and skill.	370	13
B is he who comes	371	4
B is he who comes	373	15
find our inheritance with [the *b* Virgin Mary,	375	21
the *b* hope of everlasting	382	2
the fellowship of [the ever-*b* Virgin Mary,	391	19
(*b* N.) and] all the saints,	391	20
B is he who comes	402	12
B is he who comes	404	14
B be God: Father, Son, and Holy Spirit.	413	1
From this day all generations will call me *b*:*	441	15
you have taught us through your *b* Son	443	21
to the *b* company of your faithful people;	450	19
enjoy the *b* assurance of your love;	461	17
into the *b* rest of everlasting peace,	465	5
"Come, you *b* of	465	21
B are the dead who die in the Lord;	469	14
B are they that alway keep judgment, *	478	15
with [*b* N. and] all thy saints,	481	25
into the *b* rest of everlasting peace,	483	10
O *b* of my Father;	483	21
B are the dead who die in the Lord:	486	8
whose *b* Son was laid in a sepulcher	487	5

"Come, ye *b* of my Father,	487	19
for the *b* Virgin Mary;	489	16
into his arms and *b* them:	494	2
into the *b* rest of everlasting peace,	499	17
Come, O *b* of my Father;	500	10
whose *b* Son was laid in a sepulcher	503	7
for the *b* Virgin Mary;	504	14
"Come, you *b* of my Father,	505	6
B be God: Father, Son, and Holy Spirit.	512	1
And *b* be his kingdom,	512	2
B be the Name of the Lord;	523	13
B be God: Father, Son, and Holy Spirit.	525	1
And *b* be his kingdom,	525	2
B be God: Father, Son, and Holy Spirit.	537	1
the fellowship of [the ever-*b* Virgin Mary,	550	26
(*b* N.) and] all the saints,	550	27
be drawn into your *b* kingdom.	563	9
B be your Name, Lord God.	573	12
B be your Name, Father, Son, and Holy Spirit;	574	8
The LORD lives! *B* is my Rock! *	606	3
B is the LORD! *	619	22
B be the LORD! *	624	11
Those who are *b* by God shall possess the land, *	635	3
B be the LORD God of Israel, *	642	26
because God has *b* you for ever.	647	16
B be God, who has not rejected my prayer, *	675	7
B be the Lord day by day, *	677	21
B be God!	679	6
call him *b*.	686	24
B be the Lord GOD, the God of Israel, *	686	25
And *b* be his glorious Name for ever! *	686	27
B be the LORD for evermore! *	717	18
B be the LORD, the God of Israel,	745	23
He *b* them, so that they increased greatly; *	749	5
the generation of the upright will be *b*.	755	8
Let the Name of the LORD be *b*, *	756	4
May you be *b* by the LORD, *	758	19
B is he who comes in the name of the Lord; *	762	23
B are you, O LORD; *	764	7
B be the LORD! *	781	11
shall thus indeed be *b*.	783	20
B be the LORD out of Zion, *	789	17
B be the LORD my rock! *	800	1
he has *b* your children within you.	805	4
Father, you have *b* us	828	16
Father, you have *b* us	829	9
O *b* Lord, you ministered	831	18
B are you, O Lord God, King of the Universe,	835	13
God's holy Name be *b*	835	16

blessedness

and everlasting *b*,	463	18
and taste the *b* of perfect rest.	466	2

blessing

such *b* through our worship of thee,	56	3
such *b* through our worship of you,	98	21
and let your *b* be upon us always;	133	19
and let your *b* be upon us always;	140	15
and the *b* of God Almighty,	339	17
The *b* of God Almighty,	339	20
said the *b*,	371	11

and fill them with your *b*; 373 5
For a *b* upon all human labor, 390 21
said the *b*, 403 5
who come to you seeking your *b*, 425 9
pour out the abundance of your *b* 430 15
Send therefore your *b* 431 3
that their home may be a haven of *b* and peace; 431 6
to seek the *b* of God 433 1
We give you thanks for the *b* 443 23
that *b* which your well-beloved Son 505 5
The *b*, mercy, and grace of God Almighty, 523 15
to pronounce God's *b*, 531 14
The *b* of God Almighty, 535 11
For a *b* upon all human labor, 550 6
For the *b* of our vows 579 4
Your *b* be upon your people! 587 19
They shall receive a *b* from the LORD * 613 23
the LORD shall give his people the *b* of peace. 621 2
and their children shall be a *b*. 635 13
may God, our own God, give us his *b*. 675 21
May God give us his *b*, * 675 22
he took no delight in *b*, 752 6
For there the LORD has ordained the *b*: * 787 17
the continual dew of thy *b*. 817 8
blessing of the Holy Spirit, 819 4
and a *b* to other nations 821 16
We thank you for the *b* of family and friends, 836 5
and *b* of God to help them fulfill their vows. 861 7

blessings

and all the *b* of this life; 58 20
We thank thee for the timely *b* of the day, 70 6
and all the *b* of this life; 71 16
and all the *b* of this life; 101 12
thank you for the *b* of the day that is past, 124 3
and all the *b* of this life; 125 10
for all the *b* of this life. 393 1
in Jesus the manifold *b* of thy love, 486 10
For you meet him with *b* of prosperity, * 609 1
and for all the other *b* 840 18
for all the *b* of this life, 857 8

blind

the LORD opens the eyes of the *b*; * 803 18

blindness

From all *b* of heart; 149 1
and for our *b* we cannot ask, 179 20
and for our *b* we cannot ask; 231 14
for our *b* to human need and suffering, 268 17
or in our *b* cannot ask, 395 1

bliss

to have our consummation and *b* 481 24
our perfect consummation and *b*, 488 9
have perfect fulfillment and *b* 503 18

block

for them there is no stumbling *b*. 777 10

blood

whom thou hast redeemed with thy precious *b*. 53 20
who hast made of one *b* all the peoples 58 1
for with your *b* you have redeemed for God, 94 2
bought with the price of your own *b*, 96 10
you have made of one *b* all the peoples 100 17
by the *b* of the eternal covenant, 132 2
redeemed with thy most precious *b*, 148 12
did institute the Sacrament of his Body and *B*: 169 8
who have been redeemed by his *b*, 192 3
the sacred mysteries of his Body and *B*, 201 4
who hast made of one *b* all the peoples 206 9
instituted the Sacrament of his Body and *B*: 221 2
who have been redeemed by his *b*, 243 10
the sacred mysteries of his Body and *B*, 252 9
you have made of one *b* all the peoples 257 5
instituted the Sacrament of his Body and *B*: 274 2
who by thy cross and precious *b* hast redeemed us: 282 4
and by his *b* delivered your faithful people. 287 5
B as a sign and pledge of his love, 316 3
and washed us in his own *b*, 317 18
for this is my *B* of the New Testament, 335 5
of his most blessed Body and *B*. 335 23
and through faith in his *b*, 335 27
receive the most precious Body and *B* of thy Son 336 5
and to drink his *b*, 337 15
The *B* of our Lord 338 9
remembrance that Christ's *B* was shed for thee, 338 11
The Body (*B*) of our Lord 338 13
The *B* of Christ, the cup of salvation. 338 16
the most precious Body and *B* 339 4
for this is my *B* of the New Covenant, 342 7
the Body and *B* of thy dearly-beloved Son 342 19
receive the most precious Body and *B* of thy Son 342 26
This is my *B* of the new Covenant, 363 3
the Body and *B* of your Son, 363 14
The Body (*B*) of our Lord 365 4
The *B* of Christ, the cup of salvation. 365 7
in the Sacrament of his Body and *B*. 365 13
of the most precious Body and *B* 366 3
This is my *B* of the new Covenant, 368 16
and his *B* of the new Covenant. 369 6
By his *b*, he reconciled us. 370 21
the Body and *B* of Jesus Christ our Lord. 371 9
This is my *B* of the new Covenant, 371 15
This is my *B* of the new Covenant, 374 21
the Body and *B* of your Son 375 7
redeemed by the *b* of your Christ. 375 13
and my *b* is drink 397 4
Whoever eats my flesh and drinks my *b* 397 5
instituted the Sacrament of his Body and *B*: 397 14
The Body (*B*) of our Lord 399 5
Communion of the Body and *B* of your beloved Son 399 8
to be for your people the Body and *B* 403 2
This is my *B* of the new Covenant, 403 9
This is my *B* of the new Covenant, 405 8
the Body and *B* of your Son. 405 16
the precious Body (*B*) of thy (your) Son 408 3
"This is my Body (*B*)." 408 5
these holy mysteries of the Body and *B* 432 3
by your cross and precious *b* 455 16
Communion of the Body and *B* 457 6
B of thy Son Jesus Christ, 482 3
the *b* of the everlasting covenant: 487 1
in the *b* of that immaculate Lamb 488 15
He was nourished with your Body and *B*; 497 19

B of your Son Jesus Christ, 498 14
the *b* of the everlasting covenant: 503 3
the holy food of the Body and *B* of your Son, 523 2
the mysteries of Christ's Body and *B*, 531 16
the holy food of the Body and *B* of your Son, 535 2
the holy food of the Body and *B* of your Son, 546 4
the holy food of the Body and *B* of your Son, 564 2
the Body and *B* of your Son. 568 12
refreshed by his flesh and *b*, 574 6
The Avenger of *b* will remember them; * 593 23
Their libations of *b* I will not offer, * 600 5
nor my life with those who thirst for *b*, 616 25
"What profit is there in my *b*, 621 24
or drink the *b* of goats? 655 6
they will bathe their feet in the *b* of the wicked. 665 14
and save me from those who thirst for my *b*. 665 21
That your foot may be dipped in *b*, * 678 3
the tongues of your dogs in the *b* of your enemies." 678 4
and dear shall their *b* be in his sight. 686 12
He turned their rivers into *b*, * 698 15
They have shed their *b* like water on every side 701 8
that you avenge the shedding of your servants' *b*. 702 3
He turned their waters into *b* * 740 11
They shed innocent *b*, 744 23
the *b* of their sons and daughters, * 744 24
and the land was defiled with *b*. 744 26
You that thirst for *b*, depart from me. 795 17
the sacred mysteries of thy Body and *B*, 834 15
the Body and *B* of Christ 859 25

bloodthirsty

the *b* and deceitful, O Lord, you abhor. 589 2
For you will bring the *b* and deceitful * 662 8

bloody

By thine Agony and *B* Sweat; 149 22

blot

in your great compassion *b* out my offenses. 266 3
and *b* out all my iniquities. 266 21
in your great compassion *b* out my offenses. 449 2
in your great compassion *b* out my offenses. 656 7
and *b* out all my iniquities. 656 25
but you will *b* them out. 672 12
Strengthen our efforts to *b* our ignorance 839 17

blotted

you have *b* out their name for ever and ever. 593 10
and *b* out all their sins. 708 23
and his name be *b* out in the next generation. 751 23
and his mother's sin not be *b* out; 751 26

blow

He caused the east wind to *b* in the heavens * 697 1
B the ram's-horn at the new moon, * 704 5

blows

they are like chaff which the wind *b* away. 585 11
I am worn down by the *b* of your hand. 639 16
he *b* with his wind, and the waters flow. 805 14

bluster

They *b* in their insolence; * 723 1

boar

The wild *b* of the forest has ravaged it, * 703 13

boast

who make their *b* of thy mercy; 181 20
make their *b* of your mercy; 233 11
The wicked *b* of their heart's desire; * 594 23
let those who *b* against me be clothed with 631 25
and *b* of their great riches? 652 16
You tyrant, why do you *b* of wickedness * 657 23
Behold, they *b* with their mouths, 666 9
I will say to the boasters, '*B* no more,' * 691 10

boasters

I will say to the *b*, 'Boast no more,' * 691 10

boasting

all evildoers are full of *b*. 723 2

boasts

and close the lips that utter proud *b*! 597 6

bodies

Keep us both outwardly in our *b* 167 4
Keep us both outwardly in our *b* 218 14
our souls and *b*, 336 2
souls and *b*. 342 24
you drive away from our *b* all sickness 458 17
will also give life to our mortal *b*, 485 2
will also give new life to our mortal *b* 501 4
and their *b* are sleek and sound; 687 8
They have given the *b* of your servants as food 701 4
to rebuild our *b* and renew our minds, 825 3

bodily

daily increasing in *b* strength, 460 20
all other *b* necessities of life, 825 22
To use all our *b* desires as God intended; 848 11

body

the resurrection of the *b*, 54 9
the whole *b* of thy faithful people is governed 57 20
the resurrection of the *b*, 66 25
the resurrection of the *b*, 96 29
the whole *b* of your faithful people is governed 100 12
the resurrection of the *b*, 120 25
who suffer in mind, *b*, and spirit; 151 25
adversities which may happen to the *b*, 167 6
did institute the Sacrament of his *B* and Blood: 169 8
the crucified *b* of thy dear Son 170 2
being renewed both in *b* and mind, 170 17
the fellowship of Christ's *B* 172 4
the fellowship of Christ's *B* 173 1
being ready both in *b* and soul, 177 5
to health of *b* and mind, 191 2
fellowship in the mystical *b* of thy Son 194 9
the sacred mysteries of his *B* and Blood, 201 4
may be united in one *b* 204 20
the whole *b* of thy faithful people is governed 206 2
from all adversities which may happen to the *B*, 218 16
our Savior gave his *b* to be whipped 220 14
instituted the Sacrament of his *B* and Blood: 221 2
the crucified *b* of your dear Son 221 14
being renewed both in *b* and mind, 222 11

reborn into the fellowship of Christ's *B* 223 17
reborn into the fellowship of Christ's *B* 224 15
we, being ready both in mind and *b*, 229 1
to health of *b* and of mind, 242 9
fellowship in the mystical *b* of your Son 245 17
the sacred mysteries of his *B* 252 8
may be united in one *b* by the one Spirit, 255 18
the whole *b* of your faithful people is governed 256 20
had been separated from the *b* of the faithful 265 4
that the *b* you have broken may rejoice. 266 19
instituted the Sacrament of his *B* and Blood: 274 2
the whole *b* of your faithful people is governed 278 12
afflicted in *b* or in mind; 279 3
the crucified *b* of your dear Son 283 2
the fellowship of Christ's *B* 291 1
the resurrection of the *b*, 293 17
being renewed both in *b* and mind, 295 11
There is one *B* and one Spirit; 299 7
the resurrection of the *b*, 304 20
instituted the Sacrament of his *B* 316 2
we are made one *b* in him, 316 7
not recognizing the Lord's *B*. 316 25
"Take, eat, this is my *B*, 335 1
of his most blessed *B* and Blood. 335 23
receive the most precious *B* and Blood 336 5
and made one *b* with him, 336 7
The *B* of our Lord 338 5
preserve thy *b* and soul unto everlasting life. 338 6
preserve thy *b* and soul unto everlasting life. 338 10
The *B* (Blood) of our Lord 338 13
The *B* of Christ, the bread of heaven. 338 15
spiritual food of the most precious *B* and Blood 339 4
members incorporate in the mystical *b* of thy Son, 339 7
"Take, eat, this is my *B*, 342 3
the *B* and Blood of thy dearly-beloved Son 342 19
the most precious *B* and Blood of thy Son 342 26
thy whole Church may be made one *b* with him, 342 28
and when our mortal *b* doth lie in death, 349 9
This is my *B*, which is given for you. 362 21
the *B* and Blood of your Son, 363 14
The *B* (Blood) of our Lord Jesus Christ keep you 365 4
The *B* of Christ, the bread of heaven. 365 6
in the Sacrament of his *B* and Blood. 365 13
of the most precious *B* and Blood 366 3
living members of the *B* of your Son, 366 6
"Take, eat: This is my *B*, 368 12
the Sacrament of the *B* of Christ 369 5
the *B* and Blood of Jesus Christ our Lord. 371 9
"Take, eat: This is my *B*, 371 12
make us one *b*, 372 7
"Take, eat: This is my *B*, 374 17
the *B* and Blood of your Son 375 7
become one *b* and one spirit, 375 10
and when our mortal *b* lies in death, 382 4
Comfort and heal all those who suffer in *b*, 389 3
instituted the Sacrament of his *B* and Blood: 397 14
The *B* (Blood) of our Lord 399 5
Communion of the *B* and Blood 399 8
to be for your people the *B* and Blood of Jesus 403 2
"Take, eat: This is my *B*, 403 6
this Holy Communion into one *b* in your Son 403 17
"Take, eat: This is my *B*, 405 4
the *B* and Blood of your Son. 405 16
the precious *B* (Blood) of thy (your) Son 408 3
"This is my *B* (Blood)." 408 5
There is one *B* and one Spirit; 413 7
the resurrection of the *b*, 417 2
The union of husband and wife in heart, *b*, and mind 423 9
mysteries of the *B* and Blood of your Son 432 3
drive away all sickness of *b* and spirit, 456 4
Communion of the *B* and Blood of your beloved Son 457 6
undivided Trinity guard your *b*, 460 7
sleep for the refreshing of soul and *b*: 461 13
we receive the *b* of our brother 466 13
and though this *b* be destroyed, 469 6
fellowship, in the mystical *b* of thy Son 480 5
the spiritual food and drink of the *B* and Blood 482 2
and we commit his *b* to the ground;* 485 11
b is (is to be) buried 487 7
the mystical *b* of thy Son, 487 18
both in *b* and soul, 488 9
and in my *b* I shall see God. 491 10
the resurrection of the *b*, 496 19
He was nourished with your *B* and Blood; 497 19
the spiritual food and drink of the *B* and Blood 498 13
my *b* also shall rest in hope. 501 7
and we commit his *b* to the ground;* 501 13
he whose *b* is (is to be) buried 503 9
the holy food of the *B* and Blood of your Son, 523 2
the *b* of Christ 531 1
Christ's *B* and Blood, 531 16
the building up of his *b*. 533 10
the holy food of the *B* and Blood of your Son, 535 2
the holy food of the *B* and Blood of your Son, 546 4
I devote myself, *b*, soul, and spirit. 562 12
the holy food of the *B* and Blood of your Son, 564 2
to be nourished by the *B* and Blood of your Son. 568 11
my *b* also shall rest in hope. 600 16
my wretched *b* from the horns of wild bulls. 611 23
there is no soundness in my *b*, 637 3
there is no health in my *b*. 637 11
our *b* cleaves to the ground. 647 8
that the *b* you have broken may rejoice. 656 23
let it soak into his *b* like water 752 8
"A son, the fruit of your *b* * 786 21
My *b* was not hidden from you, * 795 3
in mind, *b*, or estate; 815 8
as there is but one *B* 818 18
to heal those who are broken in *b* or spirit, 826 5
Defend them from all dangers of soul and *b*; 830 22
to venerate the sacred mysteries of thy *B* and Blood, 834 14
a *b* of people responds in faith. 846 22
The Church is described as the *B* 854 6
The Church is one, because it is one *B*, 854 15
and makes us members of Christ's *B*, 858 10
the *B* and Blood of Christ 859 25
of spirit, mind, and *b*. 861 16
What do we mean by the resurrection of the *b*? 862 16

bold

we are *b* to say, 336 16
we are *b* to say, 343 6
we are *b* to say, 363 24
we are *b* to say, 369 20

we are *b* to say, 372 16
we are *b* to say, 376 3
make us *b* to praise you 835 5

boldly

and *b* confess him as Lord 163 4
b rebuke vice, 190 6
and *b* confess him as Lord 214 15
b rebuke vice, 241 15
b before the throne of grace 317 22
let us come *b* unto the throne 320 6
Will you *b* proclaim and interpret the Gospel 518 8
b proclaim the gospel of salvation; 534 2

boldness

proclaim thy truth with *b*, 178 8
who didst give to thy servant N. *b* 195 1
proclaim your truth with *b*, 230 3
who gave to your servant N. *b* 246 8

bond

the very *b* of peace and of all virtues, 165 2
love, the true *b* of peace 216 15
The *b* and covenant of marriage 423 3
and set him free from every *b*; 464 17
and set him free from every *b*; 466 17
in the *b* of peace, 815 5
united in one holy *b* of truth 818 21

bondage

Set us free, O God, from the *b* of our sins 164 6
Set us free, O God, from the *b* of our sins, 216 1
Israel, out of *b* in Egypt, 287 7
you led the children of Israel out of their *b* 306 15
from the *b* of sin into everlasting life. 306 19
out of the house of *b*. 317 26
that we might be delivered from the *b* of sin, 345 17
who brought you out of *b*. 350 2
from the *b* of sin, 378 12
led the children of Israel out of their *b* 570 7
from the *b* of sin into everlasting life. 570 11

bonds

Christ broke the *b* of death and hell, 287 12
Grant that the *b* of our common humanity, 430 4
"let us cast off their *b* from us." 586 7
and broke their *b* asunder. 747 10
you have freed me from my *b*. 760 7
unite us in *b* of love; 815 17

bones

heal me, LORD, for my *b* are racked. 590 2
all my *b* are out of joint; * 611 6
I can count all my *b*. 611 14
and my *b* are consumed. 623 9
While I held my tongue, my *b* withered away, * 625 3
He will keep safe all his *b*; * 629 7
My very *b* will say, "LORD, who is like you? * 630 10
While my *b* are being broken, * 644 5
for God has scattered the *b* of the enemy; 659 12
and my *b* are hot as burning coals. 731 6
I am but skin and *b*. 731 10
and into his *b* like oil; 752 9
let their *b* be scattered at the mouth of the grave. 797 18

book

receive this *b*, and be among us as a man of prayer. 561 5
In the roll of the *b* it is written concerning me: * 640 20
are they not recorded in your *b*? 663 8
Let them be wiped out of the *b* of the living * 681 20
all of them were written in your *b*; * 795 7

books

the *b* which we call the Old Testament. 847 8
the *b* of the Old and New Testaments; 853 7
other *b*, called the Apocrypha, 853 7
The Old Testament consists of *b* 853 10
The New Testament consists of *b* 853 14
The Apocrypha is a collection of additional *b* 853 20

borders

ruin or destruction within your *b*. 87 24
and gnats within all their *b*. 740 16
He has established peace on your *b*; * 805 5

bore

the heart of your Son as he *b* his passion, 113 14
great was the company of women who *b* the tidings: 677 2

born

For unto you is *b* this day 37 9
Unto us a child is *b*: 43 2
to be *b* of a Virgin. 53 14
b of the Virgin Mary, 53 27
b of the Virgin Mary, 66 13
for to you is *b* this day 75 9
To us a child is *b*: 80 11
b of the house of his servant David. 92 21
and *b* of the Virgin Mary. 96 17
and *b* of the Virgin Mary. 120 13
By his great mercy we have been *b* anew 137 12
and as at this time to be *b* of a pure virgin: 161 8
John the Baptist was wonderfully *b*, 190 2
and to be *b* [this day] of a pure virgin: 213 2
who have been *b* again 213 3
Baptist was wonderfully *b*, 241 11
and *b* of the Virgin Mary. 293 4
and *b* of the Virgin Mary. 304 7
cleansed from sin and *b* again 307 5
to be *b* for us; 345 15
your only Son, *b* of a woman, 370 19
b of the Virgin Mary, 374 3
Because you gave Jesus Christ, your only Son, to be *b* 378 9
and *b* of the Virgin Mary. 416 12
to be *b* of a human mother, 430 11
and *b* of the Virgin Mary. 496 7
are cleansed from sin and *b* again 570 19
to be *b* among us, 573 9
I have been entrusted to you ever since I was *b*; * 610 20
I have been sustained by you ever since I was *b*; 683 11
in Zion were they *b*. 711 19
"Everyone was *b* in her, * 711 20
"These also were *b* there." 711 23
or the land and the earth were *b*, * 718 2
are *b* to eternal life. 833 13
first-*b* of many from the dead. 838 20

borne

then I could have *b* it; * 661 7
I have *b* your terrors with a troubled mind. 713 10

borrow

The wicked *b* and do not repay, * 635 1

bosom

the lambs in your arms and carry them in your *b*: 459 2
why is your right hand hidden in your *b*? 690 7
how I carry in my *b* the taunts of many peoples, 717 15
nor the *b* of him who binds the sheaves; 784 14

bosoms

return seven-fold into their *b*. 702 8

both

witnesses unto me *b* in Jerusalem, 39 19
darkness and light to thee are *b* alike. 62 8
darkness and light to you are *b* alike. 110 10
you made *b* summer and winter. 115 9
darkness and light to you are *b* alike. 116 4
Watch over those, *b* night and day, 134 12
and that *b* by their preaching and living, 150 7
B now and ever vouchsafe to hear us, 155 3
to judge *b* the quick and the dead, 159 5
b in will and deed; 164 15
Keep us *b* outwardly in our bodies and inwardly in our souls, 167 4
that we may *b* follow the example of his 168 5
being renewed *b* in body and mind, 170 17
being ready *b* in body and soul, 177 5
ordereth all things *b* in heaven and earth: 177 15
that they may *b* perceive and know 179 11
b a sacrifice for sin and also an example 180 20
to judge *b* the living and the dead, 211 5
b in heaven and on earth: 215 13
b in will and deed; 216 10
b outwardly in our bodies and inwardly in our souls, 218 14
being renewed *b* in body and mind, may worship 222 11
being ready *b* in mind and body, may accomplish 229 1
sets in order all things *b* in heaven and earth: 229 11
being renewed *b* in body and mind, may worship 295 11
to judge *b* the quick and the dead; 328 11
b by their life and doctrine, 329 10
I require and charge you *b*, 424 4
as long as you *b* shall live? 424 12
as you *b* shall live? 433 8
will enable you to serve him *b* now and evermore. 456 5
b relief from pain and hope of health 460 18
the darkness and light to thee are *b* alike. 475 17
consummation and bliss, *b* in body and soul, 488 9
persevere in prayer, *b* in public and in private, 532 24
asking God's grace, *b* for yourself 532 25
you save *b* man and beast, O LORD. 632 16
you made *b* summer and winter. 690 19
b horse and rider lie stunned. 692 13
For the LORD God is *b* sun and shield; * 708 14
creatures *b* small and great. 737 3
b small and great together. 758 16
the firstborn *b* of man and beast. 788 18
darkness and light to you are *b* alike. 794 24
grant us *b* the courage to pursue it 818 5
and grant that *b* they and we, 830 22

bottle

put my tears into your *b*; * 663 7

boughs

and the towering cedar trees by its *b*. 703 8

bought

b with the price of your own blood, 96 10

bound

That we may be *b* together by thy Holy Spirit 68 22
That we may be *b* together by your Holy Spirit 122 24
Because he is *b* to me in love, 130 26
b together in love and obedience to thee, 204 19
b together in love and obedience to you, 255 17
you have *b* us to your service. 309 6
But chiefly are we *b* to praise thee 346 19
But chiefly are we *b* to praise you 379 14
you have *b* us to your service. 418 4
this man and this woman have *b* themselves 427 11
this man and this woman have *b* themselves 434 5
I am *b* by the vow I made to you, O God; * 663 14
Because he is *b* to me in love, 720 14
b fast in misery and iron; 747 2
and he brought them to the harbor they were *b* for. 748 16
you have *b* us together in a common life. 824 1
may be *b* together by thy love 830 23
b together in Christ by sacrament, 862 23

boundaries

b of the earth; 61 9
You fixed all the *b* of the earth; 115 8
My *b* enclose a pleasant land; * 600 9
You fixed all the *b* of the earth; * 690 18

bounden

which is our *b* duty and service, 317 21
It is very meet, right, and our *b* duty, 333 7
this our *b* duty and service, 336 11
It is very meet, right, and our *b* duty, 341 1

boundless

In your *b* compassion, 493 19

bounds

but your commandment has no *b*. 771 12

bountiful

and sustain me with your *b* Spirit. 137 8
the *b* fruits of the earth, 151 10
let thy *b* grace and mercy speedily help 160 3
of thy *b* goodness keep us, 177 3
let your *b* grace and mercy speedily help and deliver 212 3
and sustain me with your *b* Spirit. 266 27
and sustain me with your *b* Spirit. 657 6

bountifully

Deal *b* with your servant, * 764 17
when you have dealt *b* with me, 798 16

bounty

of thy great *b*, 194 19
may be faithful stewards of thy *b*; 208 13

faithful stewards of your great *b* 246 4
and be faithful stewards of thy *b*. 329 25
may be faithful stewards of thy *b*, 827 4
may continue to praise you for your *b*; 827 21

bow

let us *b* down, and bend the knee, * 82 15
thou shalt not *b* down to them, 318 3
and under the earth *b* and obey: 457 1
and with trembling *b* before him; 586 25
I will *b* down toward your holy temple in awe of you. 589 5
he will bend his *b* and make it ready. 591 23
For see how the wicked bend the *b* 596 10
and my arms for bending even a *b* of bronze. 605 8
and all the families of the nations shall *b* before him. 612 12
To him alone all who sleep in the earth *b* down 612 15
The wicked draw their sword and bend their *b* 634 11
and their *b* shall be broken. 634 15
For I do not rely on my *b*, * 645 23
he breaks the *b*, and shatters the spear, 649 22
to be a refuge from the power of the *b*. 667 17
His foes shall *b* down before him, * 686 1
All kings shall *b* down before him, * 686 5
The people of Ephraim, armed with the *b*, * 695 20
they were undependable like a warped *b*. 699 21
B down your ear, O LORD, and answer me, * 709 22
Come, let us *b* down, and bend the knee, * 725 1
B down before him, all you gods. 727 11
I will *b* down toward your holy temple 793 3
B your heavens, O LORD, and come down; * 800 10

bowed

b down and grieving. 630 22
I am utterly *b* down and prostrate; * 637 8
and I am *b* low; * 664 5
he lifts up those who are *b* down. 802 16
the LORD lifts up those who are *b* down; 803 19

bowls

you have given them *b* of tears to drink. 702 22

bows

All the earth *b* down before you, * 673 24

braggarts

B cannot stand in your sight; * 588 25

brake

and when he had given thanks, he *b* it, 334 18

branch

As the *b* cannot bear fruit by itself, 397 7

branches

and *b* of palm along his way. 271 9
Let these *b* be for us signs of his victory, 271 10
I am the vine, you are the *b*. 397 10
and its *b* to the River. 703 10
and sing among the *b*. 735 26
form a procession with *b* 762 26

brave

For the *b* and courageous, 837 14

bravely

help me to stand *b*. 461 21

breach

his chosen stood before him in the *b*, * 743 18

breached

You have *b* all his walls * 716 21

breaching

May there be no *b* of the walls, 801 8

bread

but with the unleavened *b* of sincerity and truth. 46 6
Give us this day our daily *b*. 54 19
Give us this day our daily *b*. 67 9
and the breaking of *b*. 70 13
but with the unleavened *b* of sincerity and truth. 83 14
seed for sowing and *b* for eating, 87 4
Give us this day our daily *b*. 97 9
Give us this day our daily *b*. 106 19
Give us this day our daily *b*. 121 9
and the breaking of *b*. 124 10
Give us this day our daily *b*. 133 1
and the breaking of *b*. 139 19
Give us this day our daily *b*. 153 11
the true *b* which giveth life 167 11
Evermore give us this *b*, 167 12
to his disciples in the breaking of *b*: 171 18
to his disciples in the breaking of *b*: 173 6
to be the true *b* which gives life 219 2
Evermore give us this *b*, 219 3
to his disciples in the breaking of *b*: 223 11
to his disciples in the breaking of *b*: 224 20
in the breaking of *b*, 293 20
in the breaking of *b*, 304 23
Give us this day our daily *B*. 311 6
prepare themselves carefully before eating of that *b* 316 21
in the night in which he was betrayed, he took *b*; 334 17
and creatures of *b* and wine; 335 20
Give us this day our daily *b*. 336 23
The Body of Christ, the *b* of heaven. 338 15
in the night in which he was betrayed, he took *b*; 342 1
sanctify these gifts of *b* and wine, 342 18
Lord Jesus Christ took *b*; 362 19
Give us this day our daily *b*. 364 6
The Body of Christ, the *b* of heaven. 365 6
our Lord Jesus Christ took *b*; 368 11
this *b* and this wine. 369 3
On the night he was betrayed he took *b*, 371 10
broke the *b*, and gave it to his friends, 371 11
be known to us in the breaking of the *B*. 372 9
supper with them he took *b*, 374 16
from the gifts you have given us, this *b* and this cup, 374 28
the *b* of life and the cup of salvation, 375 7
Grant that all who share this *b* and cup 375 9
"I am the *b* of life; 396 4
"I am the living *b* which came down from heaven; 397 1
if anyone eats of this *b*, he will live for ever; 397 2
the *b* which I shall give for the life 397 3
Give us this day our daily *b*. 398 17
On the night he was betrayed he took *b*, 403 4
broke the *b*, and gave it to his friends, 403 5
means of this holy *b* and cup, 403 14
Lord Jesus Christ took *b*; 405 2
And grant that we who eat this *b* 405 17

bless and sanctify this *b* (wine) 408 2
who took *b* (the cup) 408 4
in the breaking of *b*, 417 5
Give us this day our daily *b*. 428 13
Give us this day our daily *b*. 464 9
Give us this day our daily *b*. 485 25
Give us this day our daily *b*. 502 6
take this *b* and wine, 562 5
break the *b* and bless the Cup. 562 6
refreshing us day by day with the *b* of life. 578 17
who eat up my people like *b* 598 22
or their children begging *b*. 635 11
who broke *b* with me, * 642 18
who eat up my people like *b* 659 8
but is he able to give *b* 696 15
So mortals ate the *b* of angels; * 696 26
You have fed them with the *b* of tears; * 702 21
so that I forget to eat my *b*. 731 8
For I have eaten ashes for *b* * 731 17
and *b* to strengthen the heart. 736 8
and destroyed the supply of *b*. 739 10
and he satisfied them with *b* from heaven. 741 6
vain, too, to eat the *b* of toil, 783 4
and satisfy her poor with *b*. 787 2
He scatters his hail like *b* crumbs; * 805 11
and be known to us in the breaking of *b*; 834 10
The outward and visible sign in the Eucharist is *b* 859 19

break

the dawn from on high shall *b* upon us, 93 6
and be among us to *b* the Bread 562 5
"Let us *b* their yoke," they say; * 586 6
you will *b* the teeth of the wicked. 587 17
B the power of the wicked and evil; * 595 27
With you I will *b* down an enclosure; * 604 22
therefore he will *b* them down and not 619 20
God shall help her at the *b* of day. 649 14
O God, *b* their teeth in their mouths; * 665 5
He shall *b* off all the horns of the wicked; * 691 24
If they *b* my statutes * 716 3
I will not *b* my covenant, * 716 9
in truth, he will not *b* it: 786 20
b down the walls that separate us; 815 16

breakers

The *b* of death rolled over me, * 602 14
mightier than the *b* of the sea, * 722 13

breaking

and the *b* of bread. 70 13
and the *b* of bread. 124 10
and the *b* of bread. 139 19
to his disciples in the *b* of bread: 171 18
to his disciples in the *b* of bread: 173 6
to his disciples in the *b* of bread: 223 11
to his disciples in the *b* of bread: 224 20
in the *b* of bread, 293 20
in the *b* of bread, 304 23
be known to us in the *b* of the Bread. 372 9
in the *b* of bread, 417 5
and be known to us in the *b* of bread; 834 10

breaks

The voice of the LORD *b* the cedar trees; * 620 14
the LORD *b* the cedars of Lebanon; 620 15
he *b* the bow, and shatters the spear, 649 22
He *b* the spirit of princes, * 692 25
and *b* in two the iron bars. 747 14

breast

and kept me safe upon my mother's *b*. 610 19
my heart within my *b* is melting wax. 611 7
like a child upon its mother's *b*; * 785 15

breath

at the blast of the *b* of your nostrils. 603 22
by the *b* of his mouth all the heavenly hosts. 626 12
Those of high degree are but a fleeting *b*, * 670 1
On the scales they are lighter than a *b*, * 670 3
So he brought their days to an end like a *b* * 697 16
a *b* that goes forth and does not return. 698 6
you take away their *b*, 737 12
neither is there any *b* in their mouth. 789 10
Let everything that has *b* * 808 9

breathe

When they *b* their last, they return to earth, * 803 9

brethren

I beseech you, *b*, by the mercies of God, 343 14
I appeal to you, *b*, by the mercies of God, 376 10
the firstborn among many *b*, 533 4
I will declare your Name to my *b*; * 611 24
For my *b* and companions' sake, * 780 11
when *b* live together in unity! 787 10

bribe

nor does he take a *b* against the innocent. 599 16

bribes

and their right hand full of *b*. 617 2

bride

heavenly Jerusalem, adorned as a *b* 349 2
heavenly Jerusalem, adorned as a *b* 381 17

bridegroom

adorned as a bride for her *b*, 349 3
adorned as a bride for her *b*, 381 18
it comes forth like a *b* out of his chamber; 606 24

bridesmaids

after her the *b* follow in procession. 648 20

bridle

who must be fitted with bit and *b*, 625 21

brier

let them be cut down like a *b*; * 665 11

bright

the night is as *b* as the day; 62 7
the night is as *b* as the day; 110 9
the night is as *b* as the day; 116 3
b with a glorious splendor, 286 5
my God, you make my darkness *b*. 604 21
the night is as *b* as the day; * 794 23

brightness

and kings to the *b* of thy rising. 38 1
pure *b* of the everliving Father in heaven, 64 2
and kings to the *b* of your rising. 76 1
and kings to the *b* of your dawning. 87 18
by night you will not need the *b* of the moon. 87 28
with the *b* of the vesper light; 110 13
the *b* of your holy Spirit; 110 16
that by its *b* we may have a vision 110 20
that by your *b* we may know you 110 26
pure *b* of the everliving Father 112 2
pure *b* of the everliving Father 118 2
pure *b* of the everliving Father 139 2
the *b* of thy light; 186 7
to shine with the *b* of the true Light: 212 17
the *b* of your light, 238 1
bestowed upon your people the *b* of your light: 285 9
by the clearness and *b* of your holy Word, 563 8
From the *b* of his presence, 603 13
and the *b* of my eyes is gone from me. 637 17

bring

I *b* you good tidings of great joy, 37 8
and *b* me unto thy holy hill, and to thy dwelling. 40 17
b the nations into thy fold; 58 4
may *b* those who do not know thee 58 11
B us, we pray thee, in safety 70 7
I *b* you good news of a great joy 75 8
and *b* me to your holy hill and to your dwelling. 78 16
You will *b* them in and plant them * 85 24
and *b* us with your saints 96 11
b the nations into your fold; 100 20
may *b* those who do not know you 101 4
B us in safety to the morning hours; 124 5
I will rescue him and *b* him to honor. 131 3
and to *b* forth the fruits 150 16
That it may please thee to *b* into the way of truth 150 19
and *b* them again with penitent hearts 166 17
Christ didst destroy death and *b* life 171 11
and *b* us at last to see thee 176 6
and *b* forth in us the fruit of good works: 181 14
and to *b* those near to us into his gracious presence; 185 11
b the nations into thy fold, 206 12
and *b* them again with penitent hearts 218 8
you alone can *b* into order the unruly wills 219 6
and *b* us at last to see you 228 5
and *b* forth in us the fruit of good works; 233 5
b those near to us into his gracious presence; 237 5
b the nations into your fold, 257 8
B us with all your saints to the joy 269 2
and *b* home to your fold 280 5
b each of us to the fullness of redemption. 288 3
that they may *b* forth abundant fruit 290 10
B them to the fullness of your peace and glory. 306 3
we *b* into his fellowship 306 23
and *b* you to everlasting life; 332 5
b offerings and come into his courts. 343 10
If thou *b* thy gift to the altar, 343 17
and at the last day *b* us with all your saints 363 17
and *b* us to that heavenly country 369 9
now *b* before you these gifts. 371 7
and to *b* to fulfillment the sanctification of all. 374 12
b them into the place of eternal joy 375 19
b offerings and come into his courts. 376 6
b them the joy of your salvation. 389 5
it may *b* us forgiveness of our sins, 399 10
we *b* you these gifts. 403 1
and the grace to *b* them up to know you, 429 21
b them to that table 430 22
b this child to love all that is true and noble, 443 27
and *b* you to everlasting life; 456 18
it may *b* us forgiveness of our sins, 457 8
and *b* you safely to his heavenly country; 460 7
I know now what it will *b* forth, 461 19
b us all to thy heavenly kingdom; 470 10
we *b* our years to an end, 473 2
and *b* me forth in the paths of righteousness 476 6
and *b* thee into the holy city Jerusalem. 484 2
and *b* us all to your heavenly kingdom; 494 3
b our brother (sister) to the joys of heaven. 497 13
and *b* you into the holy city Jerusalem. 500 13
we *b* into his fellowship those who come to him 570 15
confront them and *b* them down; * 601 25
b me out of my troubles. 615 23
and he will *b* it to pass. 633 14
and *b* me to your holy hill 644 22
He will *b* me safely back from the battle 661 22
b them down; * 661 26
For you will *b* the bloodthirsty and deceitful * 662 8
who will *b* me into Edom? 668 5
They seek only to *b* me down 669 12
"I will *b* them back from Bashan; * 678 1
I will *b* them back from the depths of the sea; 678 2
Kings shall *b* gifts to you, * 678 16
and *b* me up again from the deep places of the earth. 684 25
That the mountains may *b* prosperity to the people, * 685 13
and the little hills *b* righteousness. 685 14
let all around him *b* gifts to him who is worthy 692 23
nor any wicked man *b* him down. 715 11
we *b* our years to an end like a sigh. 718 18
I will rescue him and *b* him to honor. 720 19
b offerings and come into his courts. 726 8
That they may *b* forth food from the earth, * 736 5
who will *b* me into Edom? 750 16
You are good and you *b* forth good; * 768 23
B me out of prison, 798 15
b me out of trouble. 799 24
and *b* all my foes to naught, * 799 26
and *b* us all to be of one heart 817 21
to which the nations of the world *b* their glory: 825 7
and *b* the guilty to repentance 826 18
When any are held unjustly, *b* them release; 826 20
and patient wisdom as we *b* them up, 829 11
b them weakness, distress, or isolation. 830 2
and *b* them in safety to their journey's end; 831 5
b forth in us the fruit of good living, 834 21
to *b* all the nations of the world to him. 847 1
and to *b* others to know him; 847 21
Christ promised to *b* us into the kingdom of God 851 2

bringing

B forth life and giving growth, * 87 3

brings

and *b* peace and concord. 287 17
The LORD *b* the will of the nations to naught; * 626 19
God gives the solitary a home and *b* forth prisoners 676 13
He *b* up rain clouds from the ends of the earth; * 788 14
and *b* the winds out of his storehouse. 788 16
Intercession *b* before God the needs of others; in 857 18

brink

my life is at the *b* of the grave. 712 6

broke

Christ *b* the bonds of death and hell, 287 12
he *b* it, and gave it to his disciples 342 2
he *b* it, and gave it to his disciples, 362 20
he *b* it, and gave it to his disciples, 368 11
b the bread, and gave it to his friends, 371 11
he *b* it, and gave it to his disciples, 374 16
b the bread, and gave it to his friends, 403 5
he *b* it, and gave it to his disciples, 405 3
who *b* bread with me, * 642 18
they *b* down all your carved work with hatchets 689 19
There he *b* the flashing arrows, * 692 5
and a plague *b* out among them. 744 6
and *b* their bonds asunder. 747 10

broken

and all whose homes are *b* or torn by strife, 151 22
that the body you have *b* may rejoice. 266 19
a *b* and contrite heart, 267 11
to this sinful and *b* world, 429 18
The innocent are *b* and humbled before them; * 595 14
I am as useless as a *b* pot. 623 15
not one of them shall be *b*. 629 8
and their bow shall be *b*. 634 15
For the power of the wicked shall be *b*, * 634 18
While my bones are being *b*, * 644 5
that the body you have *b* may rejoice. 656 23
a *b* and contrite heart, 657 17
he has *b* his covenant. 661 29
O God, you have cast us off and *b* us; * 667 9
Reproach has *b* my heart, and it cannot be healed; * 681 3
Why have you *b* down its wall, * 703 11
You have *b* your covenant with your servant, * 716 19
for they have *b* your law. 773 26
the snare is *b*, and we have escaped. 781 14
who are *b* in body or spirit, 826 5
the depths are *b* up and the clouds drop down the dew: 840 15

brokenhearted

The LORD is near to the *b* * 629 3
and sought to kill the *b*. 752 3
He heals the *b* * 804 6

bronze

and my arms for bending even a bow of *b*. 605 8
For he shatters the doors of *b* * 747 13

brook

He will drink from the *b* beside the road; * 754 3

brooks

Like as the hart desireth the water-*b*, * 471 1
As the deer longs for the water-*b*, * 643 1

brother

and brought his *b* with him: 185 9
James the Just, *b* of our Lord, 193 19
and brought his *b* with him: 237 3
James the Just, *b* of our Lord, 245 5
thy *b* hath aught against thee, 343 18
first be reconciled to thy *b*, 343 20
that your *b* has something against you, 376 14
first be reconciled to your *b*, 376 16
for a new *b* (sister)]. 440 7
who now has a new *b* (sister) 440 11
b (sister) N. both relief from pain 460 18
Let us pray, then, for our *b* (sister) 465 11
we commend our *b* (sister) 465 16
we commend our *b* (sister) 465 20
we commend our *b* (sister) 465 24
we commend our *b* (sister) 466 4
Receive our *b* into the courts 466 8
we receive the body of our *b* (sister) 466 13
our *b* and we commit his body to the ground;* 485 11
our dear *b*, as into the hands 488 13
we remember before you this day our *b* (sister) . 493 17
For our *b* (sister) N., let us pray 497 1
give to our *b* (sister) eternal life. 497 10
bring our *b* (sister) to the joys of heaven. 497 14
Our *b* (sister) was washed in Baptism 497 16
at the death of our *b* (sister) 497 22
we commend to you our *b* (sister) 498 1
our *b* and we commit his body to the ground;* 501 13
My *b*, the people have chosen you 517 1
My *b*, the Church is the family of God, 531 1
My *b*, do you believe 531 21
My *b*, every Christian is called 543 1
My *b*, do you believe 543 19
as one would for a friend or a *b*; * 630 20
You are always speaking evil of your *b* * 655 20

brothers

B and sisters in Christ Jesus, 514 1

brought

hast safely *b* us to the beginning of this day: 57 8
my sorrow which was *b* upon me, 77 4
with your might you *b* them in safety 85 22
you have *b* us in safety 100 2
who *b* again from the dead 132 1
you have *b* us in safety 137 14
and hast *b* us into the kingdom 172 15
freed and *b* together under his most gracious rule; 185 4
and *b* his brother with him: 185 9
his cross and passion be *b* unto the glory 188 18
who hast *b* us near 198 23
may be freed and *b* together 203 2
may be *b* to know and worship thee 206 21
Christ destroyed death and *b* life 223 5
and *b* us into the kingdom 224 8
and *b* together under his most gracious rule; 236 17
and *b* his brother with him: 237 3
be *b* to the glory of his resurrection; 240 4
you have *b* us near to an innumerable company 250 8
and *b* together under his most gracious rule; 254 4
may be *b* to know and worship you 257 17

things are being *b* to their perfection 280 20
when you *b* our fathers, the children of Israel, 287 6
you have *b* us out of sin 291 5
things are being *b* to their perfection 291 17
b up in the Christian faith and life? 302 2
you have overcome sin and *b* us to yourself, 309 5
who *b* thee out of the land of Egypt, 317 25
who *b* you out of bondage. 350 2
you have *b* us out of error 368 8
you *b* forth the human race, 370 12
you have overcome sin and *b* us to yourself, 418 3
and *b* them forth into the house of God; 471 8
Before the mountains were *b* forth, 472 11
who *b* again from the dead 486 21
Christ destroyed death, and *b* life 493 5
who *b* again from the dead our Lord 503 1
all things are being *b* to their perfection 515 10
all things are being *b* to their perfection 528 8
all things are being *b* to their perfection 540 8
He *b* me out into an open place; * 604 1
You *b* me up, O LORD, from the dead; * 621 8
nor let them be found guilty when *b* to trial. 636 2
In embroidered apparel she is *b* to the king; * 648 19
With joy and gladness they are *b*, * 648 21
You *b* us into the snare; * 674 15
but you *b* us out into a place of refreshment. 674 19
The earth has *b* forth her increase; * 675 20
Let tribute be *b* out of Egypt; * 678 22
He *b* streams out of the cliff, * 696 5
So he *b* their days to an end like a breath * 697 16
He *b* them to his holy land, * 699 13
He *b* him from following the ewes, * 700 21
for we have been *b* very low. 701 23
You have *b* a vine out of Egypt; * 703 3
who *b* you out of the land of Egypt and said, * 704 22
Before the mountains were *b* forth, 718 1
He has *b* down my strength before my time; * 732 22
and were *b* down in their iniquity. 745 12
and he *b* them to the harbor they were bound for. 748 16
and *b* in a fruitful harvest. 749 4
Yet when they were diminished and *b* low, * 749 7
I was *b* very low, and he helped me. 759 13
"I have been *b* very low." * 759 21
And *b* out Israel from among them, * 790 17
for I have been *b* very low; * 798 12
b hither out of many kindreds and tongues. 820 8
and are *b* into love 852 27
b up within the Church, 859 3

bruised
They *b* his feet in fetters; * 739 13

brutal
and save them from becoming *b* or callous. 826 24

brute
I was like a *b* beast in your presence. 688 22

bucket
to put it under a *b*, 109 9

buckler
his faithfulness shall be a shield and *b*. 130 5
his faithfulness shall be a shield and *b*. 719 19

build
to *b* up the family of God? 532 16
b up your Church, 549 4
to *b* houses of prayer and praise, 567 2
and not *b* them up. 619 21
For the LORD will *b* up Zion, * 732 8
In which the birds *b* their nests, * 736 11
their labor is in vain who *b* it. 782 21

builders
The same stone which the *b* rejected * 762 15

building
and the *b* up of his body. 533 9
for the *b* (rebuilding, or adornment) 567 4
the *b* up of the living, 567 11
the *b* up of the Church; 855 27

buildings
of which these visible *b* are the symbol, 578 7

builds
Unless the LORD *b* the house, * 782 20

built
A city *b* on a hill cannot be hid. 109 7
who hast *b* thy Church upon the foundation 178 18
you have *b* your Church upon the foundation 230 12
we are *b* up as living stones of a holy temple, 348 16
we are *b* up as living stones of a holy temple, 381 10
and by whom your Church is *b* up in every place, 521 4
He *b* his sanctuary like the heights of heaven, * 700 17
Jerusalem is *b* as a city * 779 22

bull
I will take no *b*-calf from your stalls, * 654 21
Israel made a *b*-calf at Horeb * 743 9

bullocks
then shall they offer young *b* upon your altar. 657 22
more than *b* with horns and hoofs. 681 27

bulls
Many young *b* encircle me; * 611 1
strong *b* of Bashan surround me. 611 2
my wretched body from the horns of wild *b*. 611 23
Do you think I eat the flesh of *b*, * 655 5
a herd of wild *b* with its calves. 678 19
exalted like the horns of wild *b*; * 721 16

bulwarks
Consider well her *b*; 652 1

burden
For my yoke is easy, and my *b* is light. 131 18
the *b* of them is intolerable. 331 12
after they are delivered from the *b* of the flesh, 488 3
like a heavy *b* they are too much for me to bear. 637 5
Cast your *b* upon the LORD, 662 5
"I eased his shoulder from the *b*; 704 12

burdened
"Come to me, all you who labor and are *b*, 465 10

burdens
you laid heavy *b* upon our backs. 674 16
the God of our salvation, who bears our *b*. 677 22

burial
by thy precious Death and *B*; 149 23
by your precious Death and *B*, 463 6
the body of our brother (sister) N. for *b*. 466 14

buried
was crucified, dead, and *b*. 53 29
was crucified, dead, and *b*. 66 15
was crucified, died, and was *b*. 96 19
was crucified, died, and was *b*. 120 15
Paschal mystery, dear friends, we are *b* 292 1
was crucified, died, and was *b*. 293 6
was crucified, died, and was *b*. 304 9
b with Christ in his death. 306 21
he suffered death and was *b*. 327 5
he suffered and was *b*; 328 6
he suffered death and was *b*. 358 21
was crucified, died, and was *b*. 416 14
he whose body is (is to be) *b* 487 7
was crucified, died, and was *b*. 496 9
he whose body is (is to be) *b* 503 9
he suffered death and was *b*. 519 24
he suffered death and was *b*. 530 15
he suffered death and was *b*. 542 15
In it we are *b* with Christ. 570 13

burn
may *b* in us and shed its light on those around us, 110 19
and let it *b* in us to eternal life 113 14
we may so *b* with heavenly desires, 285 10
So that the sun shall not *b* thee by day, * 473 19
They *b* it with fire like rubbish; * 703 18
how long will your anger *b* like fire? 717 7

burned
Stir up in us the flame of that love which *b* 113 13
They *b* down all the meeting-places of God 689 25

burning
became a *b* and a shining light 198 10
became a *b* and a shining light 249 19
find it ever *b*— 287 24
he shall rain coals of fire and *b* sulphur; * 596 22
hot *b* coals blazed forth from him. 603 6
nothing is hidden from its *b* heat. 607 3
and my bones are hot as *b* coals. 731 6
I am filled with a *b* rage, * 767 19
Let hot *b* coals fall upon them; * 796 21

burns
and *b* the shields with fire. 649 23
Like fire that *b* down a forest, * 707 5
and *b* up his enemies on every side. 727 2

burnt
but you take no delight in *b*-offerings. 267 9
and accept your *b* sacrifice; 608 6
B-offering and sin-offering you have not required, * 640 18
but you take no delight in *b*-offerings. 657 15
with *b*-offerings and oblations; * 657 21
I will enter your house with *b*-offerings 674 20

burst
b hailstones and coals of fire. 603 14
while I pondered, the fire *b* into flame; * 638 23

bury
and there was no one to *b* them. 701 10

busy
in the course of this *b* life, 825 1
and the *b* world is hushed, 833 15

butter
His speech is softer than *b*, * 662 1

byword
You have made us a *b* among the nations, * 646 13
and became a *b* among them. 680 10

C

cabinet
To the President and members of the *C*, 821 19

calf
He makes Lebanon skip like a *c*, * 620 16
I will take no bull-*c* from your stalls, * 654 21
Israel made a bull-*c* at Horeb * 743 9

call
and *c* upon his Name; 40 7
all generations shall *c* me blessed. 50 6
all generations shall *c* me blessed. 65 9
and *c* upon his Name; 78 6
and *c* upon his Name. 83 6
and *c* upon his Name; 86 8
c upon him when he draws near. 86 18
They will *c* you, The City of the Lord, * 87 21
You will *c* your walls, Salvation, * 87 25
all generations will *c* me blessed: * 92 1
as you have taught us to *c* the evening, 110 23
all generations will *c* me blessed: * 119 7
Answer me when I *c*, O God, defender of my cause; * 128 8
when I *c* upon the Lord, he will hear me. 128 15
He shall *c* upon me, and I will answer him; * 131 1
Give us grace, O Lord, to answer readily the *c* 163 14
the prayers of thy people who *c* upon thee, 179 11
Andrew that he readily obeyed the *c* 185 8
whom thou didst *c* to preach the Gospel 196 8
Give us grace, O Lord, to answer readily the *c* 215 7
prayers of your people who *c* upon you, 231 5
Andrew that he readily obeyed the *c* 237 2
We have been deaf to your *c* to serve, 267 23
I *c* upon you, 292 3
There is one hope in God's *c* to us; 299 8
I therefore *c* upon you to consider 316 19
There is one hope in God's *c* to us; 413 8
all generations will *c* me blessed:* 441 15
and *c* upon the Name of the LORD, 442 22
therefore will I *c* upon him as long as I live. 479 2
by your *c*, we are reunited 493 22

Will you accept this *c* and fulfill this trust 518 1
We therefore *c* upon you, chosen to be a guardian 519 3
I *c* aloud upon the LORD, * 587 9
Answer me when I *c*, O God, defender of my cause; * 587 20
when I *c* upon the LORD, he will hear me. 588 5
and do not *c* upon the LORD? 598 23
I *c* upon you, O God, for you will answer me; * 601 9
I will *c* upon the LORD, * 602 12
but we will *c* upon the Name of the LORD our God. 608 16
and answer us when we *c*. 608 20
Hearken to my voice, O LORD, when I *c*; * 618 10
O LORD, I *c* to you; 619 4
though they *c* the lands after their own names. 653 3
C upon me in the day of trouble; * 655 9
and do not *c* upon God? 659 9
But I will *c* upon God, * 661 17
Whenever I *c* upon you, 663 9
I will *c* upon the Most High God, * 663 23
I *c* upon you from the ends of the earth 668 14
bless themselves in him and *c* him blessed. 686 24
and *c* to mind your wonders of old time. 693 23
give us life, that we may *c* upon your Name. 703 23
I *c* upon you all the day long. 710 4
and great is your love toward all who *c* upon you. 710 8
In the time of my trouble I will *c* upon you, * 710 11
He shall *c* upon me, and I will answer him; * 720 17
and Samuel among those who *c* upon his Name, * 729 12
give thanks to him and *c* upon his Name. 730 3
when I *c*, make haste to answer me, 731 4
Give thanks to the LORD and *c* upon his Name; * 738 1
and *c* upon the Name of the LORD. 759 26
and *c* upon the Name of the LORD. 760 9
I *c* with my whole heart; * 775 15
I *c* to you; 775 17
O LORD, I *c* to you; come to me quickly; * 797 3
The LORD is near to those who *c* upon him, * 802 23
to all who *c* upon him faithfully. 802 24
that all who profess and *c* themselves Christians 815 3
those whom you *c* to follow you under the vows 819 8
in every place your servants *c* upon your Name; 838 7
the books which we *c* the Old Testament. 847 8
God sent the prophets to *c* us back to himself, 849 8
Why do we *c* the Holy Scriptures the Word of God? 853 23
We *c* them the Word of God 853 24

called

am no more worthy to be *c* thy son." 38 19
And thou, child, shalt be *c* the prophet 51 11
I am no longer worthy to be *c* your son." 76 18
You, my child, shall be *c* the prophet 93 1
who at noonday *c* your servant Saint Paul 107 12
and we are *c* by your Name: 131 12
and we are *c* by your Name: 140 5
and, as thou hast *c* us to thy service, 176 10
are *c* by thy Word, 185 10
and *c* her to be a witness 191 2
who hast *c* us out of darkness 196 18
to all who are [now] *c* to any office 205 7
as you have *c* us to your service, 228 10
Give us, who are *c* by your Holy Word, 237 3
and *c* her to be a witness 242 9
whom you *c* to preach the Gospel 247 20
who *c* us out of darkness 248 4
to all who are [now] *c* to any office 256 4
made us in thine image, and *c* us to new life 344 15
Again and again, you *c* us to return. 370 17
Again and again you *c* us into covenant 373 24
image, and *c* us to new life 377 13
because he has inclined his ear to me whenever I *c* 442 15
Sanctify, O Lord, those whom you have *c* 460 10
Out of the deep have I *c* unto thee, O LORD; * 474 1
then *c* I upon the Name of the LORD; * 479 6
we trust the Holy Spirit has *c* him. 514 18
God's holy Church is *c* to be one with the apostles 517 3
You are *c* to guard the faith, 517 7
Are you persuaded that God has *c* you 517 19
priesthood to which you have *c* him, 521 11
All baptized people are *c* to make Christ known 531 3
Now you are *c* to work as a pastor, 531 4
do you believe that you are truly *c* by God 531 21
I believe I am so *c*. 531 23
whom you are *c* to serve, 532 15
every Christian is *c* to follow Jesus 543 1
do you believe that you are truly *c* by God 543 19
I believe I am so *c*. 543 21
who has been *c* to leadership in your Church, 552 9
yet you have *c* your servant to stand 562 14
I *c* upon the LORD in my distress * 602 18
let me not be ashamed for having *c* upon you; * 623 27
I *c* in my affliction and the LORD heard me * 628 5
he has *c* the earth from the rising of the sun to 654 2
I *c* out to him with my mouth, * 675 1
and upon the kingdoms that have not *c* upon 701 17
You *c* on me in trouble, and I saved you; * 704 14
LORD, I have *c* upon you daily; 712 21
they *c* upon the LORD, and he answered them. 729 13
Then he *c* for a famine in the land * 739 9
I *c* upon him. 759 4
Then I *c* upon the Name of the LORD: * 759 8
I *c* to the LORD in my distress; * 761 5
When I was in trouble, I *c* to the LORD; * 778 10
I *c* to the LORD, and he answered me. 778 11
Out of the depths have I *c* to you, O LORD; 784 18
and our oppressors *c* for mirth: * 792 6
When I *c*, you answered me; * 793 8
by your grace you have *c* us in this Diocese 817 10
we are *c* to enjoy it and to care for it 846 11
who has *c* us into fellowship with him. 848 21
The Holy Scriptures, commonly *c* the Bible, 853 6
other books, *c* the Apocrypha, 853 8
It is *c* the People of God, the New Israel, 854 8
Why is the Eucharist *c* a sacrifice? 859 9
The Holy Eucharist is *c* the Lord's Supper, 859 15

calleth

that *c* for the waters of the sea, 62 3
who *c* us each by name, 173 13

calling

make us worthy of our *c*; 176 11
ready wills and hearts obey the *c* of our Lord 193 1
make us worthy of our *c*; 228 11
ready wills and hearts obey the *c* of our Lord 244 10
a glorious pledge of the hope of our *c*. 348 6

in the *c* of Israel to be your people; 368 2
a glorious pledge of the hope of our *c*. 380 22
c us to be a holy people 533 2
and for *c* this your servant to the order 545 7
c upon your Name 691 4
one hope of our *c*, one Lord, one Faith, 818 19
and make them ever mindful of their *c* 820 23

callings

to inspire us, in our several *c*, 151 13

callous

and save them from becoming brutal or *c*. 826 24

calls

who *c* for the waters of the sea 115 15
who *c* us each by name, 225 5
God now *c* you to a special ministry 543 3
One deep *c* to another in the noise 643 21
He *c* the heavens and the earth from above * 654 9
and *c* them all by their names. 804 9

calm

give them *c* strength and patient wisdom 443 26
that with *c* expectancy I may make room 461 2
Then were they glad because of the *c*, * 748 15
Give us *c* strength and patient wisdom 829 10

calves

a herd of wild bulls with its *c*. 678 19

came

For since by man *c* death, * 46 15
by man *c* also the resurrection of the dead. 46 16
For since by a man *c* death, * 83 23
Christ *c* to visit us in great humility; 159 4
Christ *c* down from heaven 167 10
whose blessed Son *c* not to be ministered unto 209 9
for the sake of him who *c* among us 210 6
Christ *c* to visit us in great humility; 211 3
Christ *c* down from heaven 219 1
whose blessed Son *c* into the world 236 1
whose blessed Son *c* not to be served but to serve: 260 15
him who *c* among us as one who serves, 261 12
he *c* down from heaven: 326 19
salvation *c* down from heaven, 328 2
Jesus *c* into the world to save sinners. 332 14
the Holy Ghost *c* down [on this day] 347 8
he *c* down from heaven: 358 16
At your command all things *c* to be: 370 8
you *c* to our help, 373 23
the Holy Spirit *c* down [on this day] 380 2
"I am the living bread which *c* down from heaven; 397 1
Jesus *c* into the world to save sinners. 449 19
who *c*, not to be served, but to serve, 517 17
he *c* down from heaven: 519 19
he *c* down from heaven: 530 10
he *c* down from heaven: 542 10
As your Son *c* not to be served but to serve, 545 15
my cry of anguish *c* to his ears. 602 21
He parted the heavens and *c* down * 603 7
When evildoers *c* upon me to eat up my flesh, * 617 11
For he spoke, and it *c* to pass; * 626 17
when he *c* out of the land of Egypt. 704 10
Until his prediction *c* to pass, * 739 15
Israel *c* into Egypt, * 739 23
He spoke, and there *c* swarms of insects * 740 15
He spoke, and the locust *c*, * 740 21
and the plague *c* to an end. 744 8
When Israel *c* out of Egypt, * 756 19
I *c* to grief and sorrow. 759 7
but the LORD *c* to my help. 761 23
when you *c* among us, you proclaimed the kingdom 825 16
you ministered to all who *c* to you: 831 18

camp

Let their *c* be desolate, * 681 14
He let it fall in the midst of their *c* * 697 5
They envied Moses in the *c*, * 743 3

Cana

first miracle at a wedding in C of Galilee. 423 6

Canaan

"To you will I give the land of C * 738 21
which they offered to the idols of C, 744 25
and all the kingdoms of C. 788 25

Canaanites

He drove out the C before them 699 15

candidate

The C(s) for Holy Baptism will now be presented. 301 1
The other C(s) will now be presented. 303 4
The C(s) will now be presented. 415 3

candle

the offering of this *c* in your honor. 287 22

canons

Has he been selected in accordance with the *c* 526 4
the requirements of the *c*, 526 8
in accordance with the *c* of this Church, 526 11
Has he been selected in accordance with the *c* 538 4
the requirements of the *c*, 538 8
in accordance with the *c* of this Church, 538 11
obey these C, and be among us 562 4

canst

God, who alone *c* order the unruly wills 167 15

captive

You have gone up on high and led captivity *c*; 677 18
That he might hear the groan of the *c* * 732 16
by those who held them *c*. 745 18
For those who led us away *c* asked us for a song, 792 5

captives

pity upon all prisoners and *c*, 151 6
For prisoners and *c*, 279 10
for prisoners and *c*, 384 26

captivity

You have gone up on high and led *c* captive; 677 18
He delivered the ark into *c*, * 700 1

care

Lord, keep this nation under thy *c*; 55 7
Lord, keep this nation under thy *c*; 67 22
Lord, keep this nation under your *c*; 98 1

Lord, keep this nation under your *c*; 122 1
cast all our *c* on thee who carest for us: 165 8
who was faithful in the *c* and nurture of thy flock; 196 23
and have confidence in thy loving *c*; 208 20
cast all our *c* on you who *c* for us: 217 1
who was faithful in the *c* and nurture of your flock; 248 9
and have confidence in your loving *c*; 260 5
giving the whole world into our *c*, 373 19
for all who remember and *c* for them, 384 27
We commend to your loving *c* this child 459 3
and have confidence in your loving *c*; 459 20
that they may cast their *c* on God, 467 2
entrust this child to thy never-failing *c* and love, 470 9
a sure confidence in thy fatherly *c*, 481 8
casting every *c* on thee, 489 32
to your never-failing *c* and love, 494 3
casting all their *c* on you, 505 19
and understanding he may love and *c* for your people; 560 7
your salvation for the people entrusted to my *c*, 563 2
The wicked are so proud that they *c* not for God; * 594 25
why should they say in their heart, "You do not *c*"? 595 22
your loving *c* makes me great. 605 11
so does the LORD *c* for those who fear him. 734 8
O LORD, what are we that you should *c* for us? * 800 6
pastor, who will *c* for your people 818 11
We commend this nation to thy merciful *c*, 820 17
keep this nation under your *c*. 821 18
we commend to your gracious *c* 823 1
and all who have none to *c* for them. 826 4
We commend to thy continual *c* the homes 828 23
you have blessed us with the joy and *c* of children: 829 10
whose fatherly *c* reacheth to the uttermost parts 830 19
surround them with your loving *c*; 831 4
thy never-failing *c* and love, 831 8
and to those who *c* for them, 831 23
the loving *c* which surrounds us on every side. 836 6
this child, entrusted to our *c*. 841 2
we are called to enjoy it and to *c* for it 846 11

carefully

prepare themselves *c* before eating of that Bread 316 21

careless

arouse the *c*, and restore the penitent. 817 20

cares

that in all the *c* and occupations of our life 57 16
that in all the *c* and occupations of our life 100 8
The LORD *c* for the lives of the godly, * 634 20
I have no peace, because of my *c*. 660 8
When many *c* fill my mind, * 724 3
As a father *c* for his children, * 734 7
Though the LORD be high, he *c* for the lowly; * 793 14
I have no place to flee to, and no one *c* for me. 798 8
the LORD *c* for the stranger; * 803 21

carest

to cast all our care on thee who *c* for us: 165 8

caring

c alike for young and old, 531 11
Everliving Father, watchful and *c*, our source 568 7

carried

and though the hills be *c* into the midst 471 20
How are the promises for infants made and *c* out? 858 28

carries

The Church *c* out its mission through the ministry 855 9

carry

make those who *c* on the industries 208 3
make those who *c* on the industries 259 5
c out in tranquillity the plan of salvation; 280 16
c out in tranquillity the plan of salvation; 291 13
and *c* them in your bosom: 459 2
c out in tranquillity the plan of salvation; 515 6
c out in tranquillity the plan of salvation; 528 4
c out in tranquillity the plan of salvation; 540 4
and you are to *c* out other duties 543 15
shepherd them and *c* them for ever. 620 4
For they will *c* nothing away at their death, * 653 17
how I *c* in my bosom the taunts of many peoples, 717 15
to *c* out Christ's mission to all people. 854 27
Through whom does the Church *c* out its mission? 855 8
to *c* on Christ's work of reconciliation 855 17

carrying

Those who go out weeping, *c* the seed, * 105 16
Be always with me in *c* out the duties 563 4
Those who go out weeping, *c* the seed, * 782 18

carved

they broke down all your *c* work with hatchets 689 19
Confounded be all who worship *c* images 727 9

case

I have put my *c* in order before your eyes. 655 25

cassia

fragrant with myrrh, aloes, and *c*, * 648 6

cast

He has *c* down the mighty from their thrones, * 92 8
he has *c* down the mighty from their thrones, * 119 14
C me not away from your presence * 137 5
that we may *c* away the works of darkness, 159 1
and to *c* all our care on thee 165 7
to *c* away the works of darkness, 211 1
and to *c* all our care on you 216 21
C me not away from your presence * 266 24
things which were *c* down are being raised up, 280 18
things which were *c* down are being raised up, 291 15
He has *c* down the mighty from their thrones,* 442 3
that they may *c* their care on God, 467 1
nor *c* thy servant away in displeasure. 478 4
him that cometh to me I will in no wise *c* out. 484 19
things which were *c* down are being raised up, 515 8
things which were *c* down are being raised up, 528 6
things which were *c* down are being raised up, 540 6
"let us *c* off their bonds from us." 586 7
Because of their many transgressions *c* them out, * 589 15
watching how they may *c* me to the ground, 601 22
you have *c* down my adversaries beneath me; 605 19
and *c* down the peoples beneath me. 606 6
they *c* lots for my clothing. 611 17
c me not away; * 618 17

they are *c* down and shall not be able to rise. 633 4
and you *c* in your lot with adulterers. 655 17
C me not away from your presence * 657 3
For they have *c* an evil spell upon me * 660 11
C your burden upon the LORD, 662 5
O God, in your anger, *c* down the peoples. 663 5
O God, you have *c* us off and broken us; * 667 9
Have you not *c* us off, O God? * 668 6
Do not *c* me off in my old age; * 683 18
you *c* them down in ruin. 688 14
O God, why have you utterly *c* us off? * 689 9
Will the Lord *c* me off for ever? * 693 14
you *c* out the nations and planted it. 703 4
But you have *c* off and rejected your anointed; * 716 17
and *c* his throne to the ground. 717 2
To *c* out their seed among the nations, * 744 1
Have you not *c* us off, O God? * 750 17
let them be *c* into the mire, 796 22

casting

c all their grief on thee, they may know 481 8
c every care on thee, they may know 489 32
c all their care on you, they may know 505 18

castle

Be my strong rock, a *c* to keep me safe, 129 13
Be my strong rock, a *c* to keep me safe, 622 12
Be my strong rock, a *c* to keep me safe; * 683 5

casts

It *c* out pride and hatred, 287 17
but *c* the wicked to the ground. 804 13

cataracts

in the noise of your *c*; * 643 21

caterpillar

He gave their crops to the *c*, * 698 19

catholic

the holy *c* Church, 54 6
the holy *c* Church, 66 22
the holy *c* Church, 96 26
the holy *c* Church, 120 22
Let us pray for the holy C Church 278 1
in his holy C Church. 292 7
the holy *c* Church, 293 14
the holy *c* Church, 304 17
as a member of the one holy *c* and apostolic Church, 310 1
We believe in one holy *c* and apostolic Church. 327 16
And I believe one holy C and Apostolic Church; 328 18
We believe in one holy *c* and apostolic Church. 359 7
your one holy *c* and apostolic Church, 375 12
we pray for your holy C Church; 387 1
the holy *c* Church, 416 22
as a member of the one holy *c* and apostolic Church, 418 17
in the communion of the C Church; 489 9
the holy *c* Church, 496 16
in the communion of the C Church, 504 7
a bishop in the one, holy, *c*, and apostolic Church. 513 6
We believe in one holy *c* and apostolic Church. 520 7
ordained a priest in Christ's holy *c* Church. 526 3
We believe in one holy *c* and apostolic Church. 530 26
ordained a deacon in Christ's holy *c* Church. 538 3
We believe in one holy *c* and apostolic Church. 542 26
we pray for thy holy C Church. 816 10
The Church is described as one, holy, *c*, 854 12
Why is the Church described as *c*? 854 21
The Church is *c*, because it proclaims 854 22

cattle

O all ye beasts and *c*, bless ye the Lord; 48 26
He delivered their *c* to hailstones * 698 23
may our *c* be fat and sleek. 801 7
Wild beasts and all *c*, * 806 13

caught

and in the snare they set is their own foot *c*. 594 8
let them be *c* in the net they hid; 630 6
let them be *c* in their pride. 666 23

cause

Answer me when I call, O God, defender of my *c*; * 128 8
just *c* why they may not lawfully be married, 424 2
just *c* why they may not be joined together 437 2
Answer me when I call, O God, defender of my *c*; * 587 20
or plundered him who without *c* is my enemy; 591 2
For you have maintained my right and my *c*; * 593 7
secretly spread a net for me without a *c*; * 630 3
without a *c* they have dug a pit to take me alive. 630 4
nor let those who hate me without a *c* 631 7
Awake, arise to my *c*! * 631 16
Let those who favor my *c* sing out with joy 631 27
Those who are my enemies without *c* are mighty, * 638 7
and defend my *c* against an ungodly people; * 644 15
Ride out and conquer in the *c* of truth * 647 19
Let the heavens declare the rightness of his *c*; * 654 14
in your might, defend my *c*. 659 18
All day long they damage my *c*; * 662 22
the God who maintains my *c*. 663 24
Those who hate me without a *c* are more 679 16
Arise, O God, maintain your *c*; * 690 28
and fight against me without a *c*. 751 3
Plead my *c* and redeem me; * 776 11
Rulers have persecuted me without a *c*, * 777 1
the LORD will maintain the *c* of the poor * 796 25

caused

has *c* his light to shine within us, 110 4
has *c* his light to shine within us, 139 13
who hast *c* this holy night to shine with the illumination 161 1
who hast *c* all holy Scriptures to be written 184 15
hast *c* the light of the Gospel to shine 187 9
you have *c* this holy night to shine 212 16
who *c* all holy Scriptures to be written 236 8
have *c* the light of the Gospel to shine 238 21
hast *c* a new light to shine in our hearts, 346 2
have *c* a new light to shine in our hearts, 378 15
He *c* the east wind to blow in the heavens * 697 1
and *c* their fish to die. 740 12
He *c* them to be pitied * 745 17

caverns

In his hand are the *c* of the earth, * 82 11
In his hand are the *c* of the earth, * 724 20

cease

to make wars to *c* in all the world; 151 1
that our divisions may *c*, 390 5
that our divisions may *c* 549 17
It is he who makes war to *c* in all the world; * 649 21
suspicions disappear, and hatreds *c*; 823 20

ceasing

and I will praise you without *c* all the days 91 24
pray for them without *c*, 518 15
Therefore my heart sings to you without *c*; * 622 5

cedar

The voice of the LORD breaks the *c* trees; * 620 14
and the towering *c* trees by its boughs. 703 8
and shall spread abroad like a *c* of Lebanon. 721 22

cedars

the LORD breaks the *c* of Lebanon; 620 15
the *c* of Lebanon which he planted, 736 10
fruit trees and all *c*; 806 12

celebrate

as we *c* the Paschal mystery; 134 4
who *c* with joy the day of the Lord's resurrection, 170 23
who *c* with reverence the Paschal feast 171 5
we *c* the dedication of this house of prayer: 204 1
who *c* with joy the day of the Lord's resurrection, 222 17
that we who *c* with awe the Paschal feast 222 22
we *c* the dedication of this house of prayer: 254 19
do *c* and make here before thy divine Majesty, 335 10
we thy people do *c* and make, 342 11
and we *c* the one and equal glory of thee, 347 16
We *c* the memorial of our redemption, 363 10
We *c* his death and resurrection, 371 21
we now *c* this memorial of our redemption. 374 24
and we *c* the one and equal glory of you, 380 10
we now *c* the memorial of your Son. 403 13
to *c* and to provide for the administration 517 8
and *c* with them the sacraments 518 15
I will *c* your love in the morning; 667 4
and to *c* the sacraments. 857 24

celebrating

by hearing his Word and *c* his Sacraments, 285 5
and *c* his resurrection and ascension, 405 11

celebration

if we are to share rightly in the *c* 316 17
and in the *c* of the mysteries 531 15
for the *c* of your holy mysteries. 573 3

center

and will *c* in what you would have me do. 562 15
the hill of Zion, the very *c* of the world 651 5

centers

that they may be lively *c* for sound learning, 824 17

certain

with sure and *c* faith in thy Son's resurrection: 185 15
with firm and *c* faith in your Son's resurrection: 237 9
In sure and *c* hope of the resurrection 485 9
in the confidence of a *c* faith; 489 10
In sure and *c* hope of the resurrection 501 11
in the confidence of a *c* faith, 504 8
given by Christ as sure and *c* means 857 27

certify

We *c* to you that he has satisfied the requirements 526 7
We *c* to you that he has satisfied the requirements 538 7

chaff

they are like *c* which the wind blows away. 585 11
Let them be like *c* before the wind, * 629 22
and like *c* before the wind; 707 4

chains

To bind their kings in *c* * 807 16

chamber

it comes forth like a bridegroom out of his *c*; 606 24

chambers

You lay the beams of your *c* 735 6
in the very *c* of their kings. 740 14

champion

it rejoices like a *c* to run its course. 606 25

chance

but as a *c* for a new start. 829 18

chances

the changes and *c* of this life 133 15
changes and *c* of this mortal life, 832 21

change

they never *c*; they do not fear God. 661 27
nor *c* what has gone out of my lips. 716 10
as clothing you will *c* them, 733 3

changed

and be *c* into his likeness 165 17
and be *c* into his likeness 217 10
life is *c*, not ended; 349 9
life is *c*, not ended; 382 3
and they shall be *c*; 733 4
The LORD *c* rivers into deserts, * 748 21
He *c* deserts into pools of water * 748 25

changelessness

this life may rest in your eternal *c*; 133 15

changes

creator of the *c* of day and night, 113 2
we who are wearied by the *c* and chances of this life 133 14
among the sundry and manifold *c* of the world, 167 19
among the swift and varied *c* of the world, 219 9
among all the *c* and chances of this mortal life, 832 21

charge

and give thine angels *c* over those who sleep. 71 2
and give your angels *c* over those who sleep. 124 18
For he shall give his angels *c* over you, * 130 19
and give your angels *c* over those who sleep. 134 7
I require and *c* you both, 424 4
flock of Christ committed to your *c*, 521 19
they *c* me with matters I know nothing about. 630 14
Lay to their *c* guilt upon guilt, * 681 18
He laid it as a solemn *c* upon Joseph, * 704 9

For he shall give his angels *c* over you, * 720 7
congregations committed to their *c*, 817 6

chariot

you make the clouds your *c*; 735 7

chariots

The *c* of Pharaoh and his army has he hurled 85 9
Some put their trust in *c* and some in horses, * 608 15
The *c* of God are twenty thousand, 677 15

charity

Lord, the lamp of *c* which never fails, 110 18
and from all want of *c*, 149 3
all our doings without *c* are nothing worth: 164 19
into our hearts that most excellent gift of *c*, 165 1
the increase of faith, hope, and *c*; 183 18
the gifts of faith, hope, and *c*; 235 10
and are in love and *c* with your neighbors, 330 10
and in perfect *c* with the world. 489 12
and in perfect *c* with the world. 504 9
holy bond of truth and peace, of faith and *c*, 818 22
the spirit of wisdom, *c*, and justice; 822 19
and so enkindle fervent *c* 829 6
and be in love and *c* with all people. 860 6

charmer

Which does not heed the voice of the *c*, * 665 3

charming

no matter how skillful his *c*. 665 4

chasing

following you is better than *c* after selfish goals. 829 17

chastity

the vows of poverty, *c*, and obedience, 819 9

cheer

your consolations *c* my soul. 724 4

cheerful

Oil to make a *c* countenance, * 736 7

cheerfulness

having done thy will with *c* while it was day, 56 22
having done your will with *c* during the day, 99 17

cherish

to love and to *c*, 427 4
to love and to *c*, 427 8
that they may so love, honor, and *c* each other 431 4
to love and to *c*, 436 4
to love and to *c*, 436 9

cherubim

and dwellest between the C; * 49 16
To thee C and Seraphim continually do cry: 52 27
Glory to you, seated between the C; * 90 11
C and Seraphim, sing in endless praise: 95 20
He mounted on *c* and flew; * 603 9
you that are enthroned upon the *c*. 702 13
he is enthroned upon the *c*; 728 25

chief

Christ himself being the *c* cornerstone: 178 20
Christ himself being the *c* cornerstone: 230 14
to be a bishop and *c* pastor. 513 3
As a *c* priest and pastor, will you encourage 518 12
lies are their *c* delight. 669 13
has become the *c* cornerstone. 762 16
particularly as apostle, *c* priest, 855 23

chiefly

c in showing mercy and pity: 182 12
c in showing mercy and pity: 234 6
But *c* are we bound to praise thee 346 19
But *c* are we bound to praise you 379 14

child

Unto us a *c* is born: 43 2
And thou, *c*, shalt be called the prophet 51 11
To us a *c* is born: 80 11
You, my *c*, shall be called the prophet 93 1
Will you be responsible for seeing that the *c* 302 1
Will you by your prayers and witness help this *c* 302 4
The birth of a *c* is a joyous and solemn occasion 440 1
for the gift of a *c*. 440 10
do you take this *c* for your own? 440 17
May God, the Father of all, bless our *c* 441 7
the gift of a *c*, 441 11
whoever receives a little *c* in the name of Christ 443 22
bestowed upon this family in giving them a *c*. 443 24
bring this *c* to love all that is true and noble, 443 27
Bless this *c* and preserve his life; 444 17
he may become the *c* of God; 444 19
Into your hands, O God, we place your *c* 444 20
Heavenly Father, watch with us over your *c* 458 22
We commend to your loving care this *c* 459 3
entrust this *c* to thy never-failing care 470 9
like a stillborn *c* that never sees the sun. 665 10
and save the *c* of your handmaid. 711 8
"Go back, O *c* of earth." 718 5
I am your servant and the *c* of your handmaid; 760 6
like a *c* upon its mother's breast; * 785 15
Put not your trust in rulers, nor in any *c* 803 7
Watch over thy *c*, O Lord, as his days increase; 830 13
thank you for the life of this *c*, 841 2

childbirth

and provide for, all, women in *c*, 151 21
the pain and anxiety of *c* 444 2
they writhed like a woman in *c*, 651 13

childless

He makes the woman of a *c* house * 756 16

children

O ye *c* of men, bless ye the Lord; * 48 27
to Abraham and his *c* for ever. 92 15
rejoice in the liberty of the *c* of God; 111 11
to Abraham and his *c* for ever. 119 21
women in childbirth, young *c* and orphans, 151 21
and made thy *c* by adoption and grace, 161 10
and make us the *c* of God 184 8
and may ever walk before thee as *c* of light; 198 13
again and made your *c* by adoption and grace, 213 4
and make us *c* of God 236 2
and walk before you as *c* of light; 249 21
when you brought our fathers, the *c* of Israel, 287 6
the number of your *c*; 289 8

you led the *c* of Israel out of their bondage	306	15
for adopting us as your own *c*,	311	16
that he might make us the *c* of God	316	15
and receive power to become thy *c*.	345	18
and receive power to become your *c*.	378	13
for the procreation of *c*	423	12
the gift and heritage of *c*,	429	21
your *c* are united one to another,	430	5
As God has made us his *c* by adoption and grace,	441	5
to Abraham and his *c* for ever.	442	10
who by Baptism adopts us as his *c*,	445	4
and established me among your *c*	450	12
you give your *c* sleep	461	12
Son did take little *c* into his arms	470	7
Come again, ye *c* of men.	472	15
Son took *c* into his arms	494	1
enjoy the liberty and splendor of the *c* of God.	569	18
you led the *c* of Israel out of their bondage	570	7
For making us your *c* by adoption and grace,	578	16
Out of the mouths of infants and *c* *	592	9
who are well supplied with *c*	602	2
Come, *c*, and listen to me; *	628	15
or their *c* begging bread.	635	11
and their *c* shall be a blessing.	635	13
an alien to my mother's *c*.	680	4
The *c* of his servants will inherit it, *	682	9
I should have betrayed the generation of your *c*.	688	8
the *c* of Jacob and Joseph.	694	4
we will not hide from their *c*.	695	3
which he commanded them to teach their *c*;	695	9
and the *c* yet unborn; *	695	11
in their turn might tell it to their *c*;	695	12
and all of you *c* of the Most High;	705	21
"If his *c* forsake my law, *	716	1
and your splendor to their *c*.	719	6
The *c* of your servants shall continue, *	733	7
and his works to the *c* of Israel.	733	22
As a father cares for his *c*, *	734	7
and his righteousness on *c*'s *c*;	734	17
O *c* of Jacob his chosen.	738	12
and the wonders he does for his *c*.	746	17
and the wonders he does for his *c*.	747	12
and the wonders he does for his *c*.	748	18
Let his *c* be fatherless, *	751	14
Let his *c* be waifs and beggars; *	751	16
and none to pity his fatherless *c*.	751	21
to be a joyful mother of *c*.	756	17
you and your *c* after you.	758	18
C are a heritage from the LORD, *	783	6
are the *c* of one's youth.	783	9
your *c* like olive shoots round about your table.	783	18
May you live to see your *c*'s *c*; *	783	24
If your *c* keep my covenant	786	23
their *c* will sit upon your throne	786	25
he has blessed your *c* within you.	805	4
the *c* of Israel, a people who are near him.	806	24
let the *c* of Zion be joyful	807	5
of the Prince of Peace, as *c* of one Father;	815	26
Turn the hearts of the parents to the *c*,	829	5
and the hearts of the *c* to the parents;	829	6
you have blessed us with the joy and care of *c*:	829	10
you see your *c* growing up	829	14
thou dost not willingly afflict or grieve the *c*	831	12
in our love for all your *c*;	840	6
Help us to remember that we are all your *c*,	841	3
human beings might be adopted as *c* of God,	850	3
God adopts us as his *c*	858	10
chill		
Glorify the Lord, O *c* and cold, *	88	17
choice		
thy saints, who have been the *c* vessels	487	12
nor eat of their *c* foods.	797	11
choices		
save us from all false *c*,	832	10
It means that we are free to make *c*:	845	5
have misused their freedom and made wrong *c*.	845	11
choirs		
Rejoice now, heavenly hosts and *c* of angels,	286	1
choose		
didst *c* thy faithful servant Matthias	188	1
may *c* suitable persons for the ministry	205	16
may *c* suitable persons for the ministry	256	13
he will teach them the way that they should *c*.	615	13
Happy are they whom you *c*	672	13
and did not *c* the tribe of Ephraim;	700	14
those who shall *c* a bishop	818	10
chooses		
He *c* our inheritance for us, *	650	12
chorus		
joining with the heavenly *c*,	370	24
with many voices in one united *c*,	839	19
chose		
c your faithful servant Matthias	239	11
Christ spent the whole night in prayer before he *c*	514	13
whom you *c* as the agents of your will.	570	25
at the hill which God *c* for his resting place? *	677	13
He *c* instead the tribe of Judah *	700	15
He *c* David his servant, *	700	19
chosen		
And make thy *c* people joyful.	55	4
And make thy *c* people joyful.	67	19
who on the holy mount didst reveal to *c* witnesses	191	15
who on the holy mount revealed to *c* witnesses	243	1
your *c* people from slavery under Pharaoh,	289	14
who have been the *c* vessels of thy grace,	348	2
who have been the *c* vessels of your grace,	380	18
That I may see the felicity of thy *c*, *	478	20
have *c* to be a bishop and chief pastor.	513	3
I, *c* Bishop of the Church	513	8
the people have *c* you	517	1
c to be a guardian of the Church's faith,	519	3
accepted the ministry of those whom you have *c*.	520	19
this your servant whom you have *c* to be a bishop	521	7
For *c* bishop (priest, deacon) in your Church,	549	1
who has been *c* to serve as Rector	559	2
happy the people he has *c* to be his own!	626	24
"I have made a covenant with my *c* one; *	713	21
and have exalted one *c* out of the people.	715	5

and afflict your *c* nation. 723 4
O children of Jacob his *c*. 738 12
and Aaron whom he had *c*. 740 6
his *c* with shouts of joy. 741 12
had not Moses his *c* stood before him 743 18
I have *c* the way of faithfulness; * 765 19
for I have *c* your commandments. 778 2
For the LORD has *c* Zion; * 786 26
For the LORD has *c* Jacob for himself * 788 8
What response did God require from the *c* people? 847 3
God required the *c* people to be faithful; 847 4
those who have *c* to serve him will grow in his love, 862 11

Christ

a Savior, which is C the Lord. 37 10
C is risen. 39 7
the victory through our Lord Jesus C. 39 12
If ye then be risen with C, 39 13
where C sitteth on the right hand of God. 39 14
C is not entered into the holy places 39 15
and from the Lord Jesus C. 40 10
declared unto mankind in C Jesus our Lord; 42 7
C the Lord ascendeth into heaven: 43 10
C our Passover is sacrificed for us, * 46 2
C being raised from the dead dieth no more; * 46 7
but alive unto God through Jesus C our Lord. 46 12
C is risen from the dead, * 46 13
in C shall all be made alive. 46 18
the only-begotten Son, Jesus C; 52 10
thou only, O C, 52 20
Thou art the King of glory, O C. 53 11
And in Jesus C his only Son our Lord; 53 25
through the same Jesus C our Lord. 56 5
through the same thy Son Jesus C our Lord. 56 10
through Jesus C our Lord. 56 17
the might of Jesus C our Lord. 57 6
through Jesus C our Lord. 57 12
through our Lord and Savior Jesus C. 57 24
through the same thy Son Jesus C our Lord. 58 7
Lord Jesus C, who didst stretch out thine arms 58 8
the redemption of the world by our Lord Jesus C, 58 22
through Jesus C our Lord, 59 9
The grace of our Lord Jesus C, 59 22
in the Church, and in C Jesus 60 5
and from the Lord Jesus C. 61 4
Dear friends in C, here in the presence 62 11
in C Jesus our Lord; 63 10
O Jesus C, holy and blessed! 64 3
And in Jesus C his only Son our Lord; 66 11
the great judgement seat of C, 68 20
entrusting one another and all our life to C, 68 24
whose Son our Savior Jesus C triumphed 69 1
O Lord Jesus C, who by thy death 69 7
through Jesus C our Lord. 69 15
through the merits of Jesus C our Savior. 69 21
for the love of thy only Son, our Savior Jesus C. 70 3
and rose again, thy Son our Savior Jesus C. 70 9
through Jesus C our Lord. 70 18
Tend the sick, Lord C; 71 3
through Jesus C our Lord. 71 9
in the redemption of the world by our Lord Jesus C, 71 18
through Jesus C our Lord, 72 6
The grace of our Lord Jesus C, 72 19
in the Church, and in C Jesus 73 5
a Savior, who is C the Lord. 75 10
C is risen. 77 6
the victory through our Lord Jesus C. 77 11
If then you have been raised with C, 77 12
where C is, seated at the right hand of God. 77 13
C has entered, not into a sanctuary 77 14
and the Lord Jesus C. 78 9
For the sake of your Son Jesus C, 79 18
our Lord Jesus C, strengthen you 80 2
C the Lord has ascended into heaven: 81 6
C our Passover has been sacrificed for us; * 83 11
C being raised from the dead 83 15
and alive to God in Jesus C our Lord. 83 20
C has been raised from the dead, * 83 21
in C shall all be made alive. 83 26
and to C the Lamb, 94 6
Lord Jesus C, only Son of the Father, 95 3
you alone are the Most High, Jesus C, 95 12
You, C, are the king of glory, 96 1
I believe in Jesus C, his only Son, our Lord. 96 15
through Jesus C our Lord. 98 22
through Jesus C your Son our Lord. 99 5
through the might of Jesus C our Lord. 99 24
through Jesus C our Lord. 100 5
through our Lord and Savior Jesus C. 100 16
Lord Jesus C, you stretched out your arms of love 101 1
the redemption of the world by our Lord Jesus C; 101 14
through Jesus C our Lord, 101 22
The grace of our Lord Jesus C, 102 10
in the Church, and in C Jesus 102 16
If anyone is in C he is a new creation; 106 1
through C reconciled us to himself 106 3
C, have mercy. 106 12
through Jesus C our Lord. 107 7
Lord Jesus C, you said to your apostles, 107 17
Light and peace, in Jesus C our Lord. 109 1
C is risen. 109 3
we proclaim C Jesus as Lord, 110 1
the glory of God in the face of Jesus C. 110 6
through Jesus C our Lord. 110 16
the true and never-failing Light, Jesus C 110 21
for the love of thy only Son, our Savior, Jesus C. 111 3
through Jesus C our Lord. 111 7
Lord C, your saints have been the lights 111 12
O Jesus C, holy and blessed! 112 3
and from the Lord Jesus C. 115 4
Dear friends in C, here in the presence 116 7
For the sake of your Son Jesus C, 117 1
our Lord Jesus C, strengthen you 117 7
O Jesus C, holy and blessed! 118 3
I believe in Jesus C, his only Son, our Lord. 120 11
the great judgement seat of C, 122 22
entrusting one another and all our life to C, 122 26
whose Son our Savior Jesus C triumphed 123 1
Lord Jesus C, by your death 123 6
through Jesus C our Lord. 123 14
through the mercies of C Jesus our Savior. 123 20
of your only Son, our Savior Jesus C. 123 23
your Son our Savior Jesus C. 124 6
through Jesus C our Lord. 124 16

Christ

Tend the sick, Lord C;	124	19
through Jesus C our Lord.	125	4
in redemption of the world by our Lord Jesus C;	125	12
The grace of our Lord Jesus C,	126	10
in the Church, and in C Jesus	126	16
For the sake of your Son our Lord Jesus C,	127	11
through Jesus C, to whom be glory	132	5
C, have mercy.	132	17
love of your only Son, our Savior Jesus C.	133	12
through Jesus C our Lord.	133	16
through Jesus C our Lord.	133	20
for revealing your Son Jesus C to us	134	2
through Jesus C our Lord.	134	5
Tend the sick, Lord C;	134	8
that awake we may watch with C,	134	17
that awake we may watch with C,	135	10
Blessed be the God and Father of our Lord Jesus C!	137	11
through the resurrection of Jesus C from the dead.	137	13
through Jesus C our Lord.	137	18
Lord Jesus C, you said to your apostles,	138	16
O Jesus C, holy and blessed!	139	3
we proclaim C Jesus as Lord,	139	10
the glory of God in the face of Jesus C.	139	15
through Jesus C our Lord.	140	16
Remember not, Lord C, our offenses,	148	9
O C, hear us.	153	1
C, have mercy upon us.	153	4
through Jesus C our Lord.	153	25
The grace of our Lord Jesus C,	154	1
From our enemies defend us, O C;	154	15
Both now and ever vouchsafe to hear us, O C;	155	3
Graciously hear us, O C;	155	4
hear us, O Lord C.	155	5
our only Mediator and Advocate, Jesus C	155	13
in which thy Son Jesus C came to visit us	159	3
the coming of Jesus C our Redeemer;	159	12
through Jesus C our Lord,	160	4
through the same Jesus C our Lord,	160	9
the birth of thy only Son Jesus C:	160	13
through the same our Lord Jesus C,	161	11
same Jesus C our Lord, who liveth	161	17
even our Lord Jesus C;	162	4
to share our humanity, thy Son Jesus C;	162	10
through the same Jesus C our Lord,	162	16
our Savior Jesus C is the light of the world:	163	7
may shine with the radiance of C's glory,	163	9
through the same Jesus C our Lord,	163	11
the call of our Savior Jesus C and proclaim	163	15
Jesus C our Lord, who liveth and reigneth	164	4
manifested to us in thy Son our Savior Jesus C;	164	8
through Jesus C our Lord,	164	16
for thine only Son Jesus C's sake,	165	4
in thy Son Jesus C our Lord;	165	12
through the same Jesus C our Lord,	165	18
through Jesus C our Lord,	166	6
through Jesus C thy Son our Lord,	166	13
truth of thy Word, Jesus C thy Son;	166	19
through Jesus C our Lord,	167	8
Son Jesus C came down from heaven	167	10
hast sent thy Son our Savior Jesus C	168	2
through the same Jesus C our Lord,	168	7
through the same thy Son Jesus C our Lord,	168	14
Grant us so to glory in the cross of C,	168	19
for the sake of thy Son our Savior Jesus C;	168	21
through the same thy Son Jesus C our Lord,	169	5
the same thy Son Jesus C our Lord;	169	11
for which our Lord Jesus C was contented	169	15
through the same thy Son C our Lord,	170	12
through the same Jesus C our Lord,	170	18
C hast overcome death and opened unto us	170	22
through the same Jesus C our Lord,	171	2
through Jesus C our Lord,	171	7
C didst destroy death and bring life	171	11
reborn into the fellowship of C's Body	172	3
through the same Jesus C our Lord,	172	5
through the same thy Son Jesus C our Lord,	172	12
through the same Jesus C our Lord,	173	2
through the same thy Son Jesus C our Lord,	173	8
Grant us so perfectly to know thy Son Jesus C	173	17
through Jesus C our Lord,	174	5
whose blessed Son our Savior Jesus C	174	8
through the same Jesus C our Lord,	174	12
thy only-begotten Son our Lord Jesus C	174	16
Jesus C with great triumph unto thy kingdom	175	2
the same place whither our Savior C is gone before;	175	5
through Jesus C our Lord,	175	12
through the merits of C Jesus our Savior,	175	19
through Jesus C our Lord,	176	11
through Jesus C our Lord,	177	7
through Jesus C our Lord,	178	4
for the sake of our Savior Jesus C,	178	10
Jesus C himself being the chief cornerstone:	178	19
through the same Jesus C our Lord,	179	2
through Jesus C our Lord,	179	8
for the worthiness of thy Son Jesus C our Lord;	179	21
through Jesus C our Lord,	180	5
through the same thy Son Jesus C our Lord,	181	2
through Jesus C our Lord,	181	8
through Jesus C our Lord,	182	3
but through the merits and mediation of Jesus C	183	4
who in C hast revealed thy glory	183	11
through the same Jesus C our Lord,	183	15
through Jesus C our Lord,	184	4
which thou hast given us in our Savior Jesus C;	184	20
obeyed the call of thy Son Jesus C,	185	9
and without doubt to believe in Jesus C,	185	16
for his persecutors to thy Son Jesus C,	186	3
through Jesus C our Lord,	186	10
follow the one Lord, our Savior Jesus C;	187	5
through Jesus C our Lord,	187	13
clean hearts by the same thy Son Jesus C our Lord;	187	19
through Jesus C our Lord,	188	5
through the same thy Son Jesus C our Lord,	188	12
the incarnation of thy Son Jesus C,	188	16
hast given to thy Church the Gospel of Jesus C	188	22
through the same Jesus C our Lord,	189	2
life and death the Name of our Lord Jesus C;	189	8
through the same Jesus C our Lord	189	15
through Jesus C our Lord,	189	21
through the same thy Son Jesus C our Lord,	190	7
which is Jesus C our Lord;	190	14
through Jesus C our Lord,	190	22
martyrdom for the Name of Jesus C;	191	9
through the same Jesus C our Lord,	191	12

through the same thy Son Jesus C our Lord, 192 4
through Jesus C our Lord, 192 11
Jesus C was lifted high upon the cross 192 13
through Jesus C our Lord, 193 2
through the same thy Son Jesus C our Lord, 193 15
through the same our Lord Jesus C, 193 22
the love and mercy of our Lord and Savior Jesus C; 194 5
the mystical body of thy Son C our Lord: 194 10
through the same Jesus C our Lord, 194 13
through Jesus C our Lord, 194 21
confess the Name of our Savior Jesus C 195 2
of the same our Lord Jesus C; 195 6
through Jesus C 195 12
through Jesus C our Lord, 196 5
unsearchable riches of our Savior Jesus C; 196 12
through Jesus C our Lord, 196 19
of the fullness of our Lord and Savior Jesus C; 197 2
minister in thy household as true servants of C 197 8
through the same Jesus C our Lord, 197 9
through Jesus C our Lord, 197 16
and teach the truth as it is in C Jesus: 197 21
and Jesus C whom thou hast sent; 197 22
through the same thy Son Jesus C our Lord, 198 6
through Jesus C our Lord, with 198 13
Jesus C, the author and perfecter of our faith, 198 20
through Jesus C our Lord, 199 1
We ask this for the sake of Jesus C, 199 9
through Jesus C our Lord, 200 3
to share our humanity, thy Son Jesus C; 200 16
C in a wonderful Sacrament hath left unto us a memorial 201 1
the death and resurrection of thy Son Jesus C, 201 13
through the same Jesus C our Lord, 201 16
through Jesus C our Lord, 202 6
the eternal victory of Jesus C our Lord; 202 13
the death and resurrection of thy Son Jesus C 203 6
through the same thy Son Jesus C our Lord, 203 9
through the same Jesus C our Lord, 203 16
through Jesus C our Lord, 204 5
thy Son Jesus C our Saviour; 204 14
didst send, the same thy Son Jesus C our Lord; 205 1
through Jesus C our Lord, 205 11
and Bishop of our souls, Jesus C our Lord, 205 19
through our Lord and Savior Jesus C, 206 6
through the same thy Son Jesus C our Lord, 206 15
the redeeming work of our Savior Jesus C; 206 19
through Jesus C our Lord, 207 5
whose Son Jesus C in his earthly life 208 1
through Jesus C our Lord, 208 6
through Jesus C our Lord, 209 6
the same thy Son our Saviour Jesus C, 209 15
one that serveth, thy Son Jesus C our Lord, 210 7
through Jesus C our Lord, 210 16
in which your Son Jesus C came to visit 211 3
that we may greet with joy the coming of Jesus C 211 12
through Jesus C our Lord, 212 4
that your Son Jesus C, at his coming, 212 7
the birth of your only Son Jesus C: 212 11
through our Lord Jesus C, 213 5
through Jesus C our Lord, 213 10
the Savior of the world, our Lord Jesus C; 213 16
share our humanity, your Son Jesus C; 214 4
through Jesus C our Lord, 214 10
whose Son our Savior Jesus C is the light 215 1
may shine with the radiance of C's glory, 215 3
through Jesus C our Lord, 215 5
to answer readily the call of our Savior Jesus C 215 8
made known to us in your Son our Savior Jesus C; 216 3
through Jesus C our Lord, 216 10
for the sake of your only Son Jesus C, 216 18
have manifested to us in your Son Jesus C 217 4
through Jesus C our Lord, 217 11
through Jesus C our Lord, 217 19
through Jesus C your Son our Lord, 218 5
the unchangeable truth of your Word, Jesus C 218 10
whose blessed Son Jesus C came down from heaven 219 1
through Jesus C our Lord, 219 11
you sent your Son our Savior Jesus C 219 14
through Jesus C your son our Lord, 220 5
Grant us so to glory in the cross of C, 220 10
our Savior Jesus C; 220 12
in remembrance of Jesus C our Lord, 221 4
for whom our Lord Jesus C was willing 221 9
through Jesus C your Son our Lord, 222 5
through Jesus C our Lord, 222 12
C overcame death and opened to us the gate 222 16
through Jesus C our Lord, 223 1
C destroyed death and brought life 223 5
reborn into the fellowship of C's Body 223 17
through Jesus C your Son our Lord, 224 5
reborn into the fellowship of C's Body 224 15
through Jesus C our Lord, 224 17
to know your Son Jesus C to be the way, 225 9
through Jesus C your Son our Lord, 225 11
through Jesus C our Lord, 225 18
C ascended far above all heavens that 226 1
through Jesus C our Lord, 226 5
C to have ascended into heaven, 226 9
C with great triumph to your kingdom in heaven: 226 14
where our Savior C has gone before; 226 17
through Jesus C our Lord, 227 5
through Jesus C your Son our Lord, 227 12
through Jesus C our Lord, 228 11
through Jesus C our Lord, 229 3
for the sake of our Savior Jesus C, 230 4
through Jesus C our Lord, 230 10
Jesus C himself being the chief cornerstone: 230 13
through Jesus C our Lord, 231 2
through Jesus C our Lord, 232 4
through Jesus C our Lord, 233 1
through Jesus C our Lord, 234 4
through the merits and mediation of Jesus C 234 18
through Jesus C our Lord, 235 1
in C you have revealed your glory 235 3
which you have given us in our Savior Jesus C; 236 12
he readily obeyed the call of your Son Jesus C, 237 2
and without doubt to believe in Jesus C, 237 10
for his persecutors to your Son Jesus C, 237 16
through Jesus C our Lord, 238 5
follow the one Lord, our Savior Jesus C; 238 18
through Jesus C our Lord, 239 3
the incarnation of your Son Jesus C, 240 2
the Gospel of Jesus C the Son of God: 240 8
through Jesus C our Lord, 240 10

Christ

in life and death the Name of our Lord Jesus C;	240	16
through Jesus C our Lord,	241	7
through Jesus C your Son our Lord,	241	16
foundation, which is Jesus C our Lord;	241	23
through Jesus C our Lord,	242	5
to suffer martyrdom for the Name of Jesus C;	242	16
through Jesus C our Lord,	243	11
C was lifted high upon the cross	244	1
through Jesus C our Lord,	244	11
through Jesus C our Lord,	245	7
the love and mercy of our Lord and Savior Jesus C;	245	14
the mystical body of your Son C our Lord:	245	18
through Jesus C our Lord,	246	6
confess the Name of our Savior Jesus C	246	9
to suffer gladly for the sake of our Lord Jesus C;	247	3
through Jesus C our Lord,	247	10
the unsearchable riches of our Savior Jesus C;	247	24
through Jesus C our Lord,	248	5
the fullness of our Lord and Savior Jesus C;	248	12
minister in your household as true servants of C	248	19
through Jesus C our Lord,	249	2
and teach the truth as it is in C Jesus:	249	6
and Jesus C whom you have sent;	249	8
through Jesus C, the pioneer and perfecter	250	5
through Jesus C our Lord,	250	12
We ask this for the sake of Jesus C,	250	19
through Jesus C our Lord,	251	9
through Jesus C our Lord,	251	16
to share our humanity, your Son Jesus C;	252	4
C in a wonderful Sacrament has left us a memorial	252	6
the death and resurrection of your Son Jesus C,	253	1
through Jesus C our Lord,	253	4
he may share in the eternal victory of Jesus C	253	17
the death and resurrection of your Son Jesus C,	254	8
through Jesus C our Lord,	254	10
the death and resurrection of your Son Jesus C,	254	15
through Jesus C our Lord,	255	3
your Son Jesus C our Savior;	255	12
your Son Jesus C our Lord;	255	20
through Jesus C our Lord,	256	8
the Shepherd and Bishop of our souls, Jesus C	256	16
through our Lord and Savior Jesus C,	257	3
the redeeming work of our Savior Jesus C;	257	15
through Jesus C our Lord,	258	5
through Jesus C our Lord,	258	12
through Jesus C our Lord,	259	1
C in his earthly life shared our toil	259	3
through Jesus C our Lord,	260	6
your Son our Savior Jesus C,	260	21
through Jesus C our Lord,	261	5
your Son Jesus C our Lord,	261	13
through Jesus C our Lord,	264	7
through Jesus C our Savior.	265	20
deaf to your call to serve, as C served us.	267	23
We have not been true to the mind of C.	267	24
the Father of our Lord Jesus C,	269	3
through Jesus C our Lord.	269	14
through Jesus C our Lord.	270	7
you have redeemed us through your Son Jesus C	271	6
In the name of C.	271	18
through Jesus C our Lord.	272	5
you sent your Son our Savior Jesus C	272	8

The Passion of our Lord Jesus C according to	272	15
in remembrance of Jesus C our Lord,	274	4
for whom our Lord Jesus C was willing to be betrayed,	276	5
The Passion of our Lord Jesus C according to John.	277	1
Let us pray for the holy Catholic Church of C	278	1
through our Lord and Savior Jesus C.	278	16
through Jesus C our Lord.	279	2
your Son Jesus C our Lord.	279	19
for all who have not received the Gospel of C;	279	20
For those who are enemies of the cross of C	279	25
For those who in the name of C have persecuted	279	27
as you are revealed in your Son Jesus C;	280	3
one flock under one shepherd, Jesus C	280	7
this world and have died in the peace of C,	280	10
your Son Jesus C our Lord;	280	22
We adore you, O C, and we bless you,	281	15
We adore you, O C, and we bless you,	282	1
Lord Jesus C, Son of the living God,	282	6
Dear friends in C:	285	1
through Jesus C our Lord.	285	12
The light of C.	285	13
through Jesus C his Son our Lord,	286	13
and your only-begotten Son Jesus C our Lord;	287	3
all who believe in C are delivered	287	9
C broke the bonds of death and hell,	287	12
May C, the Morning Star who knows no setting,	287	25
to share our humanity, your Son Jesus C our Lord.	288	8
through Jesus C our Lord.	289	4
through Jesus C our Lord.	290	6
reborn into the fellowship of C's Body	291	1
through Jesus C our Lord.	291	3
we are buried with C by Baptism	292	2
renew your commitment to Jesus C?	292	9
Do you believe in Jesus C, the Son of God?	293	1
I believe in Jesus C, his only Son, our Lord.	293	2
News of God in C?	293	27
Will you seek and serve C in all persons,	293	29
the Father of our Lord Jesus C,	294	4
in C Jesus our Lord.	294	7
C is risen.	294	8
through Jesus C your Son our Lord,	295	5
through Jesus C our Lord,	295	12
C is risen.	299	3
The Holy Gospel of our Lord Jesus C	300	5
Glory to you, Lord C.	300	7
Praise to you, Lord C.	300	9
into the full stature of C?	302	5
Do you turn to Jesus C and accept him	302	16
Do you renew you commitment to Jesus C?	303	12
to support these persons in their life in C?	303	15
join with those who are committing themselves to C	303	17
Do you believe in Jesus C, the Son of God?	304	4
I believe in Jesus C, his only Son, our Lord	304	5
the Good News of God in C?	305	2
Will you seek and serve C in all persons,	305	4
who have renewed their commitment to C.]	305	13
baptized into the death of Jesus C	306	6
anointed by the Holy Spirit as the Messiah, the C,	306	18
In it we are buried with C in his death.	306	21
in the risen life of Jesus C our Savior.	307	6
share in the royal priesthood of Jesus C;	307	12
as C's own for ever.	308	10

Confess the faith of C crucified,	308	13
have renewed their commitment to C.	309	2
by the death and resurrection of your Son Jesus C	309	4
through Jesus C your Son our Lord,	309	9
direct and uphold you in the service of C	310	6
through Jesus C our Lord.	310	12
through Jesus C your Son	311	18
the Father of our Lord Jesus C,	311	21
C dwelling in your hearts by faith,	311	23
Our Savior C, on the night before he suffered,	316	1
made one with C, and C with us;	316	6
for the redemption of the world by our Savior C,	316	13
To C our Lord who loves us,	317	17
C is risen.	319	4
Hear what our Lord Jesus C saith:	319	8
For the sake of thy Son Jesus C,	320	18
declared unto mankind in C Jesus our Lord;	321	10
through C our Lord.	323	10
Hear what our Lord Jesus C saith:	324	1
C, have mercy upon us.	324	8
O Lord, the only-begotten Son, Jesus C;	324	21
thou only, O C,	325	7
The Holy Gospel of our Lord Jesus C	326	1
Praise be to thee, O C.	326	5
We believe in one Lord, Jesus C,	326	10
And in one Lord Jesus C,	327	24
Let us pray for the whole state of C's Church	328	22
these our prayers, O Father, for Jesus C's sake,	330	7
Father of our Lord Jesus C,	331	2
for thy Son our Lord Jesus C's sake,	331	15
through Jesus C our Lord.	331	20
For the sake of thy Son Jesus C,	331	29
through Jesus C our Lord.	332	6
that C Jesus came into the world to save sinners.	332	14
Jesus C the righteous;	332	16
didst give thine only Son Jesus C to suffer	334	11
thy dearly beloved Son our Savior Jesus C,	335	9
thy Son our Savior Jesus C's holy institution,	335	21
by the merits and death of thy Son Jesus C,	335	27
Body and Blood of thy Son Jesus C,	336	6
through Jesus C our Lord;	336	12
as our Savior C hath taught us,	336	16
C our Passover is sacrificed for us;	337	1
so to eat the flesh of thy dear Son Jesus C,	337	14
Take them in remembrance that C died for you,	338	2
The Body of our Lord Jesus C,	338	5
in remembrance that C died for thee,	338	7
The Blood of our Lord Jesus C,	338	9
in remembrance that C's Blood was shed for thee,	338	11
The Body (Blood) of our Lord Jesus C	338	13
The Body of C, the bread of heaven.	338	15
The Blood of C, the cup of salvation.	338	16
Body and Blood of thy Son our Savior Jesus C;	339	5
through Jesus C our Lord,	339	13
and of his Son Jesus C our Lord;	339	17
Let us go forth in the name of C.	339	22
didst give thine only Son Jesus C	341	15
Body and Blood of thy dearly-beloved Son Jesus C.	342	20
Body and Blood of thy Son Jesus C,	342	26
through the same Jesus C our Lord;	343	2
as our Savior C hath taught us,	343	6
as C loved us and gave himself for us,	343	12
Through C let us continually offer to God	344	1
and called us to new life in Jesus C	344	15
Through Jesus C our Lord;	345	1
in Jesus C our Lord,	345	5
Because thou didst give Jesus C, thine only Son,	345	14
of thy glory in the face of thy Son Jesus C	346	3
Through Jesus C our Lord;	346	5
resurrection of thy Son Jesus C our Lord;	346	20
Through thy dearly beloved Son Jesus C our Lord;	347	1
Through Jesus C our Lord;	347	6
Through the great shepherd of thy flock, Jesus C	348	11
Through Jesus C our great High Priest;	348	15
Because in Jesus C our Lord thou hast received us	348	20
her bridegroom, thy Son Jesus C our Lord;	349	3
Through Jesus C our Lord;	349	6
C is risen.	351	3
For the sake of your Son Jesus C,	352	18
through our Lord Jesus C, strengthen you	353	2
C is risen.	355	3
through C our Lord.	355	11
Lord Jesus C, only Son of the Father,	356	7
you alone are the Most High, Jesus C,	356	16
C, have mercy.	356	20
The Holy Gospel of our Lord Jesus C	357	8
Glory to you, Lord C.	357	10
Praise to you, Lord C.	358	2
We believe in one Lord, Jesus C,	358	7
For the sake of your Son Jesus C,	360	10
through our Lord Jesus C, strengthen you	360	16
you, in your mercy, sent Jesus C,	362	12
our Lord Jesus C took bread;	362	19
C has died	363	7
C is risen.	363	8
C will come again.	363	9
All this we ask through your Son Jesus C.	363	19
As our Savior C	363	22
C has taught us,	363	23
C our Passover is sacrificed for us;	364	15
Take them in remembrance that C died for you,	365	1
The Body (Blood) of our Lord Jesus C	365	4
The Body of C, the bread of heaven.	365	6
The Blood of C, the cup of salvation.	365	7
living members of your Son our Savior Jesus C,	365	11
through C our Lord.	365	18
Blood of your Son our Savior Jesus C;	366	4
as faithful witnesses of C our Lord.	366	11
Let us go forth in the name of C.	366	14
our Lord Jesus C took bread;	368	10
the Sacrament of the Body of C	369	6
put all things in subjection under your C,	369	9
through Jesus C our Lord,	369	12
As our Savior C	369	18
C has taught us,	369	19
Body and Blood of Jesus C our Lord.	371	9
God and Father of our Lord Jesus C:	372	2
make us one body, one spirit in C,	372	7
through Jesus C our great High Priest,	372	11
As our Savior C	372	13
C has taught us,	372	14
Recalling C's death and his descent	374	25
the Body and Blood of your Son Jesus C.	375	8
spirit, a living sacrifice in C,	375	10

redeemed by the blood of your C.	375	13
[Remember all who have died in the peace of C,	375	18
and give you glory through your Son Jesus C	375	25
Through C, and with C, and in C,	375	26
As our Savior C	376	1
C has taught us,	376	2
Walk in love, as C loved us	376	8
Through C let us continually offer to God	376	17
and called us to new life in Jesus C	377	13
Through Jesus C our Lord;	377	14
a new people in Jesus C our Lord,	378	2
Because you gave Jesus C, your only Son,	378	9
your glory in the face of your Son Jesus C	378	16
Through Jesus C our Lord,	379	1
glorious resurrection of your Son Jesus C	379	15
Through your dearly beloved Son Jesus C	379	20
Through Jesus C our Lord.	380	1
great shepherd of your flock, Jesus C	381	5
Through Jesus C our great High Priest;	381	9
Because in Jesus C our Lord you have received us	381	13
her bridegroom, your Son Jesus C our Lord;	381	18
Through Jesus C our Lord;	382	1
and all our life, to C our God.	385	15
in whom C has been honored	386	14
Pray that we may have grace to glorify C	386	17
that we may serve C in them,	388	18
For all who fear God and believe in you, Lord C,	390	4
and all our life to C our God.	391	21
through Jesus C our Lord.	393	16
through Jesus C our Lord.	394	3
and love us in your Son Jesus C our Lord.	394	8
through Jesus C our Lord.	394	11
grant us for the sake of your Son Jesus C	395	2
Lord Jesus C, you said to your apostles,	395	8
even Jesus C, our only Mediator and Advocate.	395	15
ask this for the sake of Jesus C,	395	22
in remembrance of Jesus C our Lord,	397	16
For the sake of your Son Jesus C,	398	2
our Lord Jesus C, strengthen you	398	8
Let us pray in the words our Savior C	398	11
Take them in remembrance that C died	399	2
The Body (Blood) of our Lord Jesus C	399	5
Son Jesus C,	399	9
through Jesus C our Lord.	399	11
Body and Blood of Jesus C our Lord.	403	3
into one body in your Son Jesus C.	403	18
The grace of our Lord Jesus C	404	1
our Lord Jesus C took bread;	405	2
All this we ask through your Son Jesus C.	405	19
Body (Blood) of thy (your) Son Jesus C	408	4
C is risen.	413	3
The Holy Gospel of our Lord Jesus C	414	5
Glory to you, Lord C.	414	7
Praise to you, Lord C.	415	2
Do you renew your commitment to Jesus C?	415	11
support these persons in their life in C?	416	2
committing themselves to C	416	5
Do you believe in Jesus C, the Son of God?	416	9
I believe in Jesus C, his only Son, our Lord.	416	10
the Good News of God in C?	417	12
Will you seek and serve C in all persons,	417	14
renewed their commitment to C.	417	21
and resurrection of your Son Jesus C	418	2
through Jesus C your Son our Lord,	418	7
direct and uphold you in the service of C	419	2
through Jesus C our Lord.	419	8
in the service of the kingdom of his C.	420	3
reaffirmed his commitment to follow C	421	3
through Jesus C our Lord.	421	6
Jesus C adorned this manner of life	423	5
mystery of the union between C and his Church,	423	7
through Jesus C our Lord,	425	12
The Holy Gospel of our Lord Jesus C	426	1
Glory to you, Lord C.	426	3
Praise to you, Lord C.	426	5
through Jesus C our Lord.	427	12
Make their life together a sign of C's love	429	17
in sending Jesus C to come among us,	430	11
through Jesus C our Lord,	430	24
the spiritual unity between C and his Church:	431	2
through Jesus C our Lord,	431	7
Body and Blood of your Son Jesus C.	432	3
for the sake of Jesus C our Lord.	432	7
through Jesus C our Lord.	434	6
through Jesus C our Lord.	441	9
whoever receives a little child in the name of C	443	22
receives C himself:	443	23
the example of our Lord and Savior, Jesus C.	443	29
through Jesus C our Lord.	444	7
the knowledge of his Savior Jesus C.	445	2
Our Lord Jesus C, who has left power	448	1
Our Lord Jesus C, who offered himself	448	7
C Jesus came into the world to save sinners.	449	19
we have an Advocate with the Father, Jesus C	450	2
in the presence of C, and of me, his minister,	450	5
Death by the cross of your Son Jesus C.	450	10
your Son our Savior Jesus C.	450	21
Will you turn again to C as your Lord?	450	22
Our Lord Jesus C, who offered himself	451	6
Our Lord Jesus C, who has left power	451	11
you were dead, and are now alive in C	451	18
Our Lord Jesus C, who offered himself	452	1
For the sake of your Son Jesus C,	455	1
our Lord Jesus C, strengthen you	455	7
through Jesus C our Lord,	455	13
C to sustain you with his presence,	456	3
in the Name of our Lord and Savior Jesus C,	456	8
through Jesus C our Lord.	456	19
and salvation is the Name of our Lord Jesus C.	457	4
Body and Blood of your beloved Son Jesus C,	457	7
through Jesus C our Lord.	457	9
through Jesus C our Lord.	458	10
Lord Jesus C, Good Shepherd of the sheep,	459	1
through Jesus C our Lord.	459	11
through Jesus C our Lord.	460	4
healing; through Jesus C our Lord.	461	4
Lord Jesus C, by your patience in suffering	461	5
Son Jesus C our Lord.	462	4
We sinners beseech you to hear us, Lord C:	463	11
C, have mercy.	464	2
Deliver your servant, O Sovereign Lord C,	464	16
In the Name of Jesus C who redeemed you;	464	23
This we ask through C our Lord.	466	11
With faith in Jesus C, we receive the body	466	12

Deliver your servant, O Sovereign Lord C,	466	16
through Jesus C our Lord.	467	7
through Jesus C thy Son our Lord,	470	4
through the same thy Son Jesus C our Lord,	470	11
The Holy Gospel of our Lord Jesus C	479	20
Praise be to thee, O C.	480	2
in the mystical body of thy Son C our Lord:	480	6
Grant that all who have been baptized into C's death	480	8
share in the victory of thy Son Jesus C;	481	28
Body and Blood of thy Son Jesus C,	482	3
through Jesus C our Savior.	482	8
Give rest, O C, to thy servant(s)	482	9
Give rest, O C, to thy servant(s)	483	3
Let us go forth in the name of C.	483	12
C is risen from the dead,	483	14
C will open the kingdom of heaven	483	20
through our Lord Jesus C,	485	10
unto the day of Jesus C.	486	12
for the sake of thy Son Jesus C our Lord.	486	15
from the dead our Lord Jesus C,	486	22
through Jesus C, to whom be glory	487	3
buried here may dwell with C in paradise,	487	7
thy son Jesus C our Lord.	487	9
for the sake of the same thy Son Jesus C,	487	22
through Jesus C our Lord.	488	10
through the merits of Jesus C	488	20
through Jesus C our Lord.	488	25
through Jesus C thy Son our Lord.	489	2
through Jesus C our Lord.	489	13
through the merits of thy Son Jesus C our Lord.	489	22
O Lord Jesus C, Son of the living God,	489	23
through Jesus C our Lord.	489	33
C destroyed death, and brought life	493	5
through Jesus C our Lord,	493	13
through Jesus C our Lord,	494	4
The Holy Gospel of our Lord Jesus C	495	1
Glory to you, Lord C.	495	3
Praise to you, Lord C.	495	5
I believe in Jesus C, his only Son, our Lord.	496	5
C who said, "I am Resurrection and I am Life."	497	2
Lord Jesus C, we commend to you	498	1
Body and Blood of your Son Jesus C,	498	14
through Jesus C our Savior.	498	19
Give rest, O C, to your servant(s)	499	1
Give rest, O C, to your servant(s)	499	10
Let us go forth in the name of C.	500	1
C is risen from the dead,	500	3
C will open the kingdom of heaven	500	9
He who raised Jesus C from the dead	501	3
through our Lord Jesus C,	501	12
C is risen.	502	19
Let us go forth in the name of C.	502	21
Lord Jesus C, the great Shepherd of the sheep,	503	2
through Jesus C,	503	5
buried here may dwell with C in paradise,	503	9
your Son Jesus C our Lord.	503	11
through Jesus C our Lord.	503	19
All this we ask through Jesus C our Lord.	504	10
through the merits of your Son Jesus C our Lord.	504	20
Lord Jesus C, by your death	504	21
through Jesus C our Lord.	504	30
Jesus C who is the Resurrection and the Life:	505	1
Grant this, O merciful Father, through Jesus C,	505	8
And this we ask in the Name of Jesus C	505	15
through Jesus C our Lord.	505	20
C is risen.	512	3
through C our Lord.	512	11
Brothers and sisters in C Jesus,	514	1
C spent the whole night in prayer	514	12
Son Jesus C our Lord;	515	12
The Holy Gospel of our Lord Jesus C	516	5
Glory to you, Lord C.	516	7
Praise to you, Lord C.	516	9
with the apostles in proclaiming C's resurrection	517	4
to testify to C's sovereignty as Lord of lords	517	5
example for the entire flock of C.	517	12
in obedience to C?	518	2
I will obey C, and will serve in his name.	518	3
that you may have the mind of C?	518	6
and interpret the Gospel of C,	518	9
I will, in the name of C, the Shepherd	518	17
I will, for the sake of C Jesus.	518	31
We believe in one Lord, Jesus C,	519	10
God and Father of our Lord Jesus C,	520	11
whom you bestowed upon your beloved Son Jesus C,	521	3
he may feed and tend the flock of C,	521	9
through Jesus C your Son,	521	16
Feed the flock of C	521	18
through Jesus C your Son our Lord,	523	9
C is risen.	525	3
through C our Lord.	525	11
ordained a priest in C's holy catholic Church.	526	3
and worship of C as this Church has received them?	526	10
Dear friends in C, you know the importance	527	1
your Son Jesus C our Lord;	528	10
The Holy Gospel of our Lord Jesus C	529	4
Glory to you, Lord C.	529	6
Praise to you, Lord C.	529	8
We believe in one Lord, Jesus C,	530	1
the body of C, and the temple of the Holy Spirit.	531	2
All baptized people are called to make C known	531	3
proclaim by word and deed the Gospel of Jesus C,	531	9
the mysteries of C's Body and Blood,	531	15
you are to nourish C's people	531	18
a stronger and more able minister of C?	532	7
that the reconciling love of C may be known	532	11
in accordance with the teachings of C,	532	21
through the mediation of Jesus C,	532	27
through Jesus C your Son, give your Holy Spirit	533	11
this we ask through Jesus C our Lord,	534	8
Jesus C your Son our Lord,	535	9
C is risen.	537	3
through C our Lord.	537	11
ordained a deacon in C's holy catholic Church.	538	3
the doctrine, discipline, and worship of C	538	10
Dear friends in C, you know the importance	539	1
your Son Jesus C our Lord;	540	10
The Holy Gospel of our Lord Jesus C	541	4
Glory to you, Lord C.	541	6
Praise to you, Lord C.	541	8
We believe in one Lord, Jesus C,	542	1
every Christian is called to follow Jesus C,	543	1
In the name of Jesus C, you are to serve	543	4
You are to make C and his redemptive love known,	543	9

Christ

your life and teaching are to show C's people 543 17
in serving the helpless they are serving C himself. 543 18
Will you look for C in all others, 544 4
in accordance with the teachings of C, 544 9
but the glory of the Lord C? 544 13
we praise you for sending your Son Jesus C, 545 2
through Jesus C your Son, 545 9
to observe the discipline of C. 545 13
may this deacon share in C's service, 545 16
through Jesus C your Son our Lord, 547 5
We pray to you, Lord C. 548 9
For all who fear God and believe in you, Lord C, 549 16
and all our life to C our God. 550 28
C, have mercy. 551 2
Jesus C our Lord. 552 12
grant that together they may follow Jesus C, 560 8
for the sake of your Son our Savior Jesus C. 563 10
through Jesus C your Son our Lord, 564 9
through Jesus C our Lord. 567 12
Lord Jesus C, make this a temple of your presence 568 14
Lord C, that we are made one with you 568 19
we die to sin and are made new in C. 569 16
the Holy Spirit as the Messiah, the C, to lead us, 570 10
we are buried with C in his death. 570 13
in the risen life of Jesus C our Savior. 570 20
through Jesus C, our Mediator and Advocate. 572 12
through Jesus C our Lord. 573 6
you sent your Son Jesus C to be born 573 9
thy Son Jesus C our Lord. 814 5
And this we beg for Jesus C's sake. 815 12
through Jesus C 815 20
become the kingdom of our Lord and Savior Jesus C. 816 4
through Jesus C our Lord. 816 9
of Jesus C thy Son our Savior. 816 15
through your Son Jesus C: 816 17
our Advocate and Mediator, Jesus C. 817 9
through Jesus C our Lord. 817 17
through Jesus C our Lord. 818 6
O God the Father of our Lord Jesus C, 818 14
through the teaching of your Son Jesus C: 819 2
through Jesus C our Lord. 819 5
O Lord Jesus C, you became poor for our sake, 819 6
through Jesus C our Lord, 820 24
through Jesus C our Lord. 821 7
thy Son our Savior Jesus C. 821 14
through Jesus C our Lord. 822 22
through Jesus C our Lord. 823 7
Jesus C, our merciful and righteous Judge. 823 16
through Jesus C our Lord. 824 5
through Jesus C our Lord. 825 5
Lord C, when you came among us, you proclaimed 825 16
for our sake became poor, Jesus C our Lord. 826 7
through Jesus C our Lord. 826 15
through Jesus C our Lord. 827 5
to the honor of Jesus C our Lord. 827 10
in the name of Jesus C our Lord. 827 16
through C our Lord. 828 7
who by thy Son Jesus C hast promised 828 9
through Jesus C our Lord. 828 14
through Jesus C our Lord. 829 8
of our Savior Jesus C. 829 13
This we ask in the name of Jesus C 830 6
through Jesus C our Lord. 830 12
through Jesus C our Lord. 831 6
through Jesus C our Lord. 832 5
through our Lord and Savior Jesus C. 833 4
through Jesus C our Lord. 833 23
through Jesus C our Lord. 834 7
O Lord Jesus C, who in a wonderful Sacrament 834 12
by the resurrection of your Son Jesus C 835 1
through the same Jesus C our Lord. 835 7
through Jesus C our Lord. 835 9
for C's sake. 835 12
we thank you for your Son Jesus C; 836 12
revealing the image of C, 837 7
promises given to us in C Jesus our Lord; 837 22
you sent your Son Jesus C to reconcile 838 1
through Jesus C our Lord, 838 19
we ask in the Name of Jesus C our Lord. 839 26
through Jesus C our Lord. 840 6
your dear Son, Jesus C our Lord. 841 6
through Jesus C our Lord. 841 13
The Messiah, or C, is Jesus of Nazareth, 849 17
and become living members of C. 850 25
given by Jesus C, the Messiah, to the apostles; 850 28
C promised to bring us into the kingdom of God 851 2
What response did C require? 851 4
C commanded us to believe in him 851 5
What are the commandments taught by C? 851 7
C taught us the Summary of the Law 851 8
C loved us. 851 17
what Christians believe about C? 851 19
What Christians believe about C is found 851 20
to grow in the likeness of C. 852 23
we confess Jesus C as Lord 852 27
the Body of which Jesus C is the Head 854 7
under one Head, our Lord Jesus C. 854 16
to carry out C's mission to all people. 854 27
unity with God and each other in C. 855 3
The ministry of lay persons is to represent C 855 15
to carry on C's work of reconciliation in the world; 855 18
The ministry of a bishop is to represent C 855 22
to act in C's name for the reconciliation 855 26
to ordain others to continue C's ministry. 855 28
The ministry of a priest is to represent C 856 2
The ministry of a deacon is to represent C 856 8
The duty of all Christians is to follow C; 856 13
through Jesus C, in the power of the Holy Spirit. 856 22
What prayer did C teach us? 856 23
in union with C, for the purposes of God. 857 16
and spiritual grace, given by C 857 27
The two great sacraments given by C to his Church 858 6
and makes us members of C's Body, 858 10
Baptism is union with C in his death 858 18
membership in C, and redemption by God. 858 26
to know C and be able to follow him. 859 3
the sacrament commanded by C 859 7
is the way by which the sacrifice of C is made present, 859 11
given and received according to C's command. 859 20
Holy Communion is the Body and Blood of C 859 25
the strengthening of our union with C 860 1
a mature commitment to C, 860 19
their confession of Jesus C as Savior and Lord. 860 26
and to await the coming of C in glory, 861 26

What do we mean by the coming of C in glory? 862 1
By the coming of C in glory, 862 2
we mean that C will come, 862 2
We believe that C will come in glory 862 14
we may live with C in the communion of the saints. 862 18
bound together in C by sacrament, 862 23
the love of God which is in C Jesus our Lord. 862 32

Christe

C eleison. 153 4
C eleison. 324 8
C eleison. 356 20

Christian

brought up in the C faith and life? 302 2
strengthen us all in our C vocation of witness 421 5
the obligations which C Marriage demands. 433 4
rejoicing in the C community. 440 3
C family, for the gift of a child. 440 10
Depart, O C soul, out of this world; 464 21
every C is called to follow Jesus Christ, 543 1
that they may be adorned with all C virtues, 549 13
and used in the C Church. 853 22
What is C Prayer? 856 20
C prayer is response to God the Father, 856 21
are sufficiently instructed in the C Faith, 860 24
Holy Matrimony is C marriage, 861 4
How are the sacraments related to our C hope? 861 21
What is the C hope? 861 24
The C hope is to live with confidence 861 25

Christians

The first C observed with great devotion 264 10
C continually have to renew their repentance 265 9
For all C in this community 278 7
themselves C may be led into the way of truth, 815 4
Where may we find what C believe about Christ? 851 18
What C believe about Christ 851 20
What is the duty of all C? 856 12
The duty of all C is to follow Christ; 856 13
What, then is our assurance as C? 862 29
Our assurance as C is that nothing, 862 30

church

The holy C throughout all the world 53 6
the holy catholic C, 54 6
for all members of thy holy C, 57 22
from generation to generation in the C, 60 5
the holy catholic C, 66 22
That there may be peace to thy C 68 15
from generation to generation in the C, 73 5
Throughout the world the holy C acclaims you; 95 26
the holy catholic C, 96 26
for all members of your holy C, 100 14
from generation to generation in the C, 102 16
Regard not our sins, but the faith of your C, 107 19
the holy catholic C, 120 22
That there may be peace to your C 122 17
from generation to generation in the C, 126 16
but the faith of your C, 138 18
it may please thee to rule and govern thy holy C 150 2
Stir up in thy C that Spirit of adoption 170 15
he abideth with his C on earth, 174 11
and that thy C may joyfully serve thee 177 11
Keep, O Lord, we beseech thee, thy household the C 178 6
who hast built thy C upon the foundation 178 18
let thy continual pity cleanse and defend thy C, 180 9
Grant, we beseech thee, merciful God, that thy C, 181 5
that thy C throughout the world may persevere 183 13
Shed upon thy C, we beseech thee, O Lord, 186 6
Keep thy C steadfast upon the rock of this faith, 187 3
Grant that thy C, being delivered 188 3
given to thy C the Gospel of Jesus Christ 188 22
not his own renown but the well-being of thy C, 189 19
Grant that thy C, instructed by 190 11
thou wilt pour out upon the leaders of thy C 191 10
Grant, we beseech thee, unto thy C to love 192 9
Graciously continue in thy C the like love 193 13
thy C may give itself continually to prayer 193 19
that thy C may proclaim the unsearchable riches 196 11
pastor in thy C and to feed thy flock: 197 5
and we pray that thy C may never be destitute 197 15
became a burning and a shining light in thy C: 198 11
who hast revealed to thy C thine eternal Being 199 12
to thy whole C in paradise and on earth 202 2
that thy C, being preserved in true faith 204 12
Grant that thy C, being bound together 204 19
providence hast appointed various orders in thy C: 205 5
for the benefit of thy holy C; 205 11
Grant that thy C, under the guidance 205 15
thee for all members of thy holy C, that in their 206 4
by the prayers and labors of thy holy C, 206 20
Stir up in your C that Spirit 222 9
he abides with his C on earth, 226 4
your C may joyfully serve you 229 7
Keep, O Lord, your household the C 230 1
you have built your C upon the foundation 230 12
cleanse and defend your C; 232 2
that your C, being gathered together 232 17
that your C throughout the world may 235 5
Shed upon your C, O Lord, the brightness 238 1
Keep your C steadfast upon the rock of this faith, 238 16
your C, being delivered from false apostles, 239 13
you have given to your C the Gospel of Jesus Christ 240 8
not his own renown but the well-being of your C, 241 5
Grant that your C, instructed by their teaching 241 20
pour out upon the leaders of your C that spirit 242 17
Grant that your C may love what he believed 243 16
Graciously continue in your C this love 244 22
your C may give itself continually to prayer 245 5
that your C may proclaim the unsearchable 247 23
to be a [bishop and] pastor in your C 248 16
and we pray that your C may never be destitute 249 1
a shining light in your C: 249 20
you have revealed to your C your eternal Being 251 1
Give to your whole C in paradise 253 7
your C, being preserved in true faith 255 10
Grant that your C, being bound together in love 255 17
you have appointed various orders in your C: 256 3
for the benefit of your holy C; 256 8
Grant that your C, under the guidance 256 12
before you for all members of your holy C, 257 1
by the prayers and labors of your holy C, 257 16
it became the custom of the C to prepare 264 12
and restored to the fellowship of the C. 265 6

church

I invite you, therefore, in the name of the C,	265	10
Let us pray for the holy Catholic C	278	1
That God will confirm his C in faith,	278	9
for all members of your holy C,	278	14
Look favorably on your whole C,	280	15
to your holy C peace and concord;	282	10
the C invites her members,	285	2
Rejoice and be glad now, Mother C,	286	7
that your C may rejoice to see fulfilled	289	8
Look favorably on your whole C,	291	12
in his holy Catholic C.	292	7
the holy catholic C,	293	14
Stir up in your C that Spirit of adoption	295	9
the holy catholic C,	304	17
and communion of your holy C.	305	22
the one holy catholic and apostolic C,	310	2
for incorporating us into your holy C,	311	17
in obedience to his command, his C renders	316	9
to him be glory in the C evermore.	317	19
We believe in one holy catholic and apostolic C.	327	16
And I believe one holy Catholic and Apostolic C;	328	18
Let us pray for the whole state of Christ's C	328	22
the Universal C with the spirit of truth,	329	5
we, and all thy whole C, may obtain remission	335	28
thy whole C may be made one body with him,	342	28
and giving to thy C the power to serve thee	347	10
We believe in one holy catholic and apostolic C.	359	7
the head of the C, and the author	369	13
your C gives honor, glory, and worship,	372	12
your one holy catholic and apostolic C,	375	13
[Remember (NN. and) all who minister in your C.]	375	15
and giving to your C the power to serve you	380	5
for the welfare of the holy C of God,	383	6
Pray for the C.	385	20
we pray for your holy Catholic C;	387	1
Grant that every member of the C may truly	387	3
Let us pray for the C and for the world.	388	1
For the holy C of God,	389	15
For the mission of the C,	390	7
For all who have died in the communion of your C,	391	15
For the peace and unity of the C of God;	392	12
For all who serve God in his C.	392	16
Regard not our sins, but the faith of your C,	395	10
the holy catholic C,	416	22
the one holy catholic and apostolic C,	418	18
the mystery of the union between Christ and his C,	423	7
the spiritual unity between Christ and his C:	431	3
the blessing of God and of his C upon his marriage.	433	2
May God the Holy Spirit, who has made the C one	445	7
I confess to Almighty God, to his C, and to you,	447	5
I humbly beg forgiveness of God and his C,	447	11
who has left power to his C to absolve all sinners	448	1
and who conferred power on his C to forgive sins,	448	8
in the perfect peace of the C.	448	11
I confess to you and to the C...	450	15
and who conferred power on his C to forgive sins,	451	7
in the perfect peace of the C.	451	10
who has left power to his C to absolve all sinners	451	11
to thy whole C in paradise and on earth,	480	7
in the communion of the Catholic C;	489	9
to thy holy C peace and concord,	489	27
the holy catholic C,	496	16
in the communion of the Catholic C,	504	7
Bishop in the C of God,	513	1
the one, holy, catholic, and apostolic C.	513	6
chosen Bishop of the C	513	8
and worship of The Episcopal C.	513	13
bishop of the C of God to serve in the Diocese	514	3
the C has approved him for this sacred responsibility.	514	4
Look favorably on your whole C,	515	5
God's holy C is called to be one with the apostles	517	3
and discipline of the C;	517	8
the leadership of the C throughout the world.	517	14
And discipline of the C?	518	20
in the government of the whole C;	518	23
others who minister in the C?	518	26
to serve his C in the office of bishop.	519	2
chosen to be a guardian of the C's faith,	519	3
We believe in one holy catholic and apostolic C.	520	7
Therefore, Father, make a bishop in your C.	521	1
and by whom your C is built up	521	4
to be a bishop in your C,	521	8
overseeing the life and work of the C.	521	14
and power and glory in the C,	521	17
Bishop in the C of God, on behalf of the clergy	526	1
to be ordained a priest in Christ's holy catholic C.	526	3
in accordance with the canons of this C?	526	5
worship of Christ as this C has received them?	526	10
in accordance with the canons of this C, obey	526	11
discipline, and worship of The Episcopal C.	526	18
Look favorably on your whole C,	528	3
We believe in one holy catholic and apostolic C.	530	26
My brother, the C is the family of God,	531	1
your share in the councils of the C.	531	7
and his C to this priesthood?	531	22
in the presence of the C commit yourself	531	24
and the head of the C.	533	5
make him a priest in your C.	533	13
priest of the C of God.	534	13
Bishop in the C of God,	538	1
ordained a deacon in Christ's holy catholic C.	538	3
accordance with the canons of this C?	538	5
worship of Christ as this C has received them?	538	10
in accordance with the canons of this C, obey	538	11
discipline, and worship of The Episcopal C.	538	18
Look favorably on your whole C,	540	3
We believe in one holy catholic and apostolic C.	542	26
As a deacon in the C,	543	7
interpret to the C the needs, concerns, and hopes	543	12
that you are truly called by God and his C	543	20
Do you now in the presence of the C commit	543	22
We praise you for the many ministries in your C,	545	7
and make him a deacon in your C.	545	11
For the holy C of God,	548	11
For all members of your C in their vocation	548	16
For chosen bishop (priest, deacon) in your C,	549	1
build up your C, and glorify your Name,	549	5
For the mission of the C,	549	21
For all who have died in the communion of your C,	550	20
called to leadership in your C,	552	9
to serve as Rector of (name of *c*).	559	2
c), we are now gathered to dedicate	567	5
and to unite us in your holy C.	573	20
For the C universal,	578	7

pray for thy holy C universal; 815 2
we pray for thy holy Catholic C. 816 10
to be of one heart and mind within your holy C; 817 22
for the renewal and mission of your C. 818 3
Look graciously on your C, 818 9
by their prayer and service they may enrich your C, 819 10
How many creeds does this C use in its worship? 851 24
This C uses two creeds: 851 25
it is used in the C's daily worship 852 3
The Nicene Creed is the creed of the universal C 852 6
in the world and in the C even now. 852 16
and used in the Christian C. 853 22
the Holy Spirit, who guides the C 854 1
What is the C? 854 3
The C is the community of the New Covenant. 854 4
How is the C described in the Bible? 854 5
The C is described as the Body 854 6
How is the C described in the creeds? 854 11
The C is described as one, holy, catholic, 854 12
Why is the C described as one? 854 14
The C is one, because it is one Body, 854 15
Why is the C described as holy? 854 17
The C is holy, because the Holy Spirit 854 18
Why is the C described as catholic? 854 21
The C is catholic, because it proclaims 854 22
Why is the C described as apostolic? 854 24
The C is apostolic, because it continues 854 25
What is the mission of the C? 855 1
The mission of the C is to restore all people 855 2
How does the C pursue its mission? 855 4
The C pursues its mission as it prays 855 5
Through whom does the C carry out its mission? 855 8
The C carries out its mission through the ministry 855 9
Who are the ministers of the C? 855 11
The ministers of the C are lay persons, 855 12
to represent Christ and his C; 855 16
And governance of the C. 855 20
to represent Christ and his C, 855 23
and discipline of the whole C; 855 25
and the building up of the C; 855 27
represent Christ and his C, 856 3
with the bishop in the overseeing of the C; 856 4
to represent Christ and his C, 856 9
The two great sacraments given by Christ to his C 858 6
members of Christ's Body, the C, 858 11
birth into God's family the C, 858 19
the infants will be brought up within the C, 859 3
Because the Eucharist, the C's sacrifice 859 10
What other sacramental rites evolved in the C 860 7
Other sacramental rites which evolved in the C 860 9
vows before God and the C, 861 6

circle

and gangs of evildoers *c* around me; * 611 12

circles

Enrich our lives by ever-widening *c* of fellowship, 840 3

circuit

Make the *c* of Zion; 651 26

citadels

God is in her *c*; * 651 6

cities

their *c* plowed under, the memory of them perished; 593 12
and the *c* of Judah rejoice, * 651 24
For God will save Zion and rebuild the *c* 682 7
Zion hears and is glad, and the *c* 727 12
Mayors of C, and to all in administrative 821 20
and those who make our laws in States, C, 822 2
visit, we pray, the *c* of the earth. 825 8

citizens

but fellow-*c* with the saints 40 3
but fellow *c* with the saints 78 2
made us *c* of thy kingdom, 348 21
made us *c* of your kingdom, 381 14
accept their responsibilities to their fellow *c*, 822 11

citizenship

Infants are baptized so that they can share *c* 858 25

city

For unto you is born this day in the *c* of David 37 9
may praise thee in that C of which he is the light; 69 4
for to you is born this day in the *c* of David, 75 9
They will call you, The C of the Lord, * 87 21
give to us the peace and unity of that heavenly C, 107 20
A *c* built on a hill cannot be hid. 109 7
by its brightness we may have a vision of that holy C, 110 20
may praise you in that C of which he is the light, 123 4
peace and unity of that heavenly C, 138 19
On this day he entered the holy *c* of Jerusalem 271 7
For this *c* (town, village,), for every *c* 384 7
peace and unity of that heavenly C, 395 11
the streams whereof make glad the *c* of God, * 471 23
and bring thee into the holy *c* Jerusalem. 484 3
and bring you into the holy *c* Jerusalem. 500 13
in the gates of the *c* of Zion. 594 6
the wonders of his love in a besieged *c*. 624 13
whose streams make glad the *c* of God, * 649 10
in the *c* of our God is his holy hill. 651 2
of the world and the *c* of the great King. 651 5
in the *c* of the LORD of hosts, 651 16
in the *c* of our God; * 651 16
for I have seen violence and strife in the *c*. 660 25
they snarl like dogs and run about the *c*. 666 8
Who will lead me into the strong *c*? * 668 4
in the gates of the *c* of Zion. 689 8
On the holy mountain stands the *c* 711 12
O *c* of our God. 711 16
that I may root out all evildoers from the *c* 730 27
they found no way to a *c* where they might dwell. 746 9
to go to a *c* where they might dwell. 746 15
and they founded a *c* to dwell in. 749 2
Who will lead me into the strong *c*? * 750 15
Jerusalem is built as a *c* * 779 22
Unless the LORD watches over the *c*, * 783 1
who hold office in this State (Commonwealth, C, 822 18
that holy C to which the nations of the world 825 7

civic

ties of mutual regard which form our *c* life. 825 9

claim

on Edom I throw down my sandal to *c* it, * 668 2
on Edom I throw down my sandal to *c* it, * 750 13

clamor

and the *c* of the peoples. 672 25
Forget not the *c* of your adversaries, * 691 1

clanging

praise him with loud-*c* cymbals. 808 8

clap

C your hands, all you peoples; * 650 6
Let the rivers *c* their hands, * 728 18

clay

out of the mire and *c*; * 640 3

clean

Create in us *c* hearts, O God; 55 13
Create in us *c* hearts, O God; 68 5
Create in us *c* hearts, O God; 98 7
Create in us *c* hearts, O God; 122 7
Create in me a *c* heart, O God, * 137 3
presented unto thee with pure and *c* hearts 187 19
presented to you with pure and *c* hearts 239 8
wash me, and I shall be *c* indeed. 266 17
Create in me a *c* heart, O God, * 266 22
because my hands were *c* he rewarded me; 604 4
The fear of the LORD is *c* 607 12
"Those who have *c* hands and a pure heart, * 613 20
wash me, and I shall be *c* indeed. 656 21
Create in me a *c* heart, O God, * 657 1
In vain have I kept my heart *c*, * 688 3

cleanness

because of the *c* of my hands in his sight. 604 13

cleanse

and to *c* us from all unrighteousness. 38 12
and *c* us from all unrighteousness. 76 11
c and defend thy Church, 180 8
c and defend your Church; 232 1
and *c* me from my sin. 266 5
and to *c* us from all unrighteousness. 320 3
C the thoughts of our hearts 323 8
Who dost bid thy faithful people *c* their hearts, 346 9
will forgive our sins and *c* us 352 3
C the thoughts of our hearts 355 8
You bid your faithful people *c* their hearts, 379 5
and *c* me from my sin. 449 4
C the thoughts of our hearts 512 8
C the thoughts of our hearts 525 8
C the thoughts of our hearts 537 8
c me from my secret faults. 607 23
and *c* me from my sin. 656 9
How shall a young man *c* his way? * 764 1

cleansed

that those who here are *c* from sin 307 4
that we may be *c* from all our sins, 481 5
are *c* from sin and born again 570 19
that our society may be *c* and strengthened. 823 15

cleansing

that by its *c* flame we may be purged 111 5

clear

but the night is as *c* as day; * 475 16
the commandment of the LORD is *c* 607 10
He will make your righteousness as *c* as the light * 633 15

clearly

God's will for us shown most *c*? 847 10
God's will for us is shown most *c* 847 11
we see more *c* our sin 848 26

clearness

by the *c* and brightness of your holy Word, 563 8

cleave

to *c* to those that shall abide; 182 8
Let my tongue *c* to the roof of my mouth 792 12

cleaves

our body *c* to the ground. 647 8
My soul *c* to the dust; * 765 9

clergy

the bishops and the other *c* 204 10
the bishops and the other *c* 255 8
and for all the *c* and people, 384 1
the *c* and people of the Diocese 513 1
on behalf of the *c* and people of the Diocese 526 1
on behalf of the *c* and people of the Diocese 538 1
Send down upon our bishops, and other *c*, 817 5
Bless our Bishop(s) and other *c*, 817 12

cliff

set my feet upon a high *c* and made my footing 640 4
He brought streams out of the *c*, * 696 5

cliffs

and the stony *c* for the rock badgers. 736 14

climb

If I *c* up into heaven, thou art there; * 475 7
They will *c* from height to height, * 708 4
nor *c* up into my bed; 786 4
If I *c* up to heaven, you are there; * 794 14

cling

I hate those who *c* to worthless idols, * 622 20

clings

My soul *c* to you; * 671 1

cloak

and the valleys *c* themselves with grain; * 673 16
and wrap their violence about them like a *c*. 687 12
You wrap yourself with light as with a *c* * 735 4
Let it be to him like the *c* 752 10
and wrap themselves in their shame as in a *c*. 753 7

close

sing your glory at the *c* of this day, 134 3
and *c* the lips that utter proud boasts! 597 6
Packs of dogs *c* me in, 611 11
You will not let my eyelids *c*; * 693 8

closed
They have *c* their heart to pity, * 601 18

closely
Bless all whose lives are *c* linked with ours, 388 17
"Hear, O daughter; consider and listen *c*; * 648 11

closer
that we may grow *c* to you through joy 569 4
and for whatever draws us *c* to God. 857 10

cloth
you have put off my sack-*c* and clothed me with joy. 622 4
But when they were sick I dressed in sack-*c* * 630 17
her gown is *c*-of-gold. 648 18
I put on sack-*c* also, * 680 9

clothe
So *c* us in thy Spirit 58 10
C your ministers with righteousness; 97 20
So *c* us in your Spirit 101 3
C your ministers with righteousness; 121 20
and *c* them with holiness of life, 205 8
and *c* them with holiness of life, 256 5
and *c* him in his heavenly wedding garment. 465 17
I will *c* her priests with salvation, * 787 3
As for his enemies, I will *c* them with shame; * 787 7

clothed
you *c* me with the shining garment 450 11
you have put off my sack-cloth and *c* me with joy. 622 4
who boast against me be *c* with dismay 631 25
and the hills be *c* with joy. 673 14
you are *c* with majesty and splendor. 735 3
Let my accusers be *c* with disgrace * 753 6
Let your priests be *c* with righteousness; * 786 15

clothing
they cast lots for my *c*. 611 17
as *c* you will change them, 733 3

cloud
a pillar of *c* by day and a pillar of fire by night: 111 9
with so great a *c* of witnesses: 198 17
with a great *c* of witnesses: 250 1
a pillar of *c* by day and a pillar of fire by night: 290 2
with so great a *c* of witnesses, 347 19
with a great *c* of witnesses, 380 13
with a storm *c* under his feet. 603 8
He led them with a *c* by day, * 696 1
He spoke to them out of the pillar of *c*; * 729 14
He spread out a *c* for a covering * 741 3

clouds
O ye lightnings and *c*, bless ye the Lord; * 48 15
Storm *c* and thunderbolts, glorify the Lord, * 89 3
that no *c* of this mortal life 165 9
that no *c* of this mortal life 217 2
he made dark waters and thick *c* his pavilion. 603 12
From the brightness of his presence, through the *c*, * 603 13
and your faithfulness to the *c*. 632 13
and your faithfulness reaches to the *c*. 664 18
The *c* poured out water; 694 8
So he commanded the *c* above * 696 22
C and darkness are round about him, * 726 25
you make the *c* your chariot; 735 7
and your faithfulness reaches to the *c*. 750 2
He brings up rain *c* from the ends of the earth; * 788 14
He covers the heavens with *c* * 804 16
and the *c* drop down the dew: 840 15

clutches
from the *c* of the evildoer and the oppressor. 683 8

coals
Upon the wicked he shall rain *c* of fire and 596 21
hot burning *c* blazed forth from him. 603 6
burst hailstones and *c* of fire. 603 14
and my bones are hot as burning *c*. 731 6
along with hot glowing *c*. 778 17
Let hot burning *c* fall upon them; * 796 21

cock
at even, or at midnight, or at the *c*-crowing, 37 2

cockcrow
in the evening, or at midnight, or at *c*, 75 2

cold
O ye frost and *c*, bless ye the Lord; 48 10
Glorify the Lord, O chill and *c*, * 88 17
Frost and *c*, ice and sleet, glorify the Lord, * 88 19
who can stand against his *c*? 805 12

coldness
from *c* of heart and wanderings of mind, 833 21

collapse
They *c* and fall down, * 608 17

collar
his neck they put in an iron *c*. 739 14
and runs down upon the *c* of his robe. 787 14

collection
The Apocrypha is a *c* of additional books 853 20

collects
their heart *c* false rumors; 642 11

colleges
bless all schools, *c*, and universities 824 16

comb
than honey in the *c*. 607 19

come
The Gentiles shall *c* to thy light, 38 1
"Whosoever will *c* after me, let him deny himself, 38 24
after that the Holy Ghost is *c* upon you; 39 18
which was, and is, and is to *c*. 39 23
we have *c* together in the presence of 41 5
O *c*, let us adore him. 43 1
O *c*, let us sing unto the Lord; * 44 10
Let us *c* before his presence with thanksgiving, * 44 12
O *c*, let us worship and fall down * 45 1
and *c* before his presence with a song. 45 13
We believe that thou shalt *c* to be our judge. 53 18
he shall *c* to judge the quick and the dead. 54 4
thy kingdom *c*, 54 16
that the days to *c* may be spent in thy favor; 56 4
that everyone might *c* within the reach 58 9

and in the world to *c* life everlasting. 59 18
Now as we *c* to the setting of the sun, 64 4
he shall *c* to judge the quick and the dead. 66 20
thy kingdom *c*, 67 6
and in the world to *c* life everlasting. 72 15
when the master of the house will *c*, 75 2
lest he *c* suddenly and find you asleep. 75 3
a great joy which will *c* to all the people; 75 8
Nations shall *c* to your light, 76 1
"If anyone would *c* after me, let him deny himself 76 23
when the Holy Spirit has *c* upon you; 77 17
who was, and is, and is to *c*! 77 21
we have *c* together in the presence 79 1
C let us adore him. 80 10
C, let us sing to the Lord; * 82 5
Let us *c* before his presence with thanksgiving * 82 7
C, let us bow down, and bend the knee, * 82 15
and *c* before his presence with a song. 82 22
by a man has *c* also the resurrection of the dead. 83 24
Arise, shine, for your light has *c*, * 87 11
He has *c* to the help of his servant Israel, * 92 12
he has *c* to his people and set them free. 92 19
We believe that you will *c* and be our judge. 96 8
C then, Lord, and help your people, 96 9
He will *c* again to judge the living and the dead. 96 24
thy kingdom *c*, 97 6
that the week to *c* may be spent in your favor; 98 22
that everyone might *c* within the reach 101 2
and in the age to *c* life everlasting. 102 7
from where is my help to *c*? 104 14
will *c* again with joy, shouldering their sheaves. 105 17
behold the new has *c*. 106 2
thy kingdom *c*, 106 16
And let our cry *c* to you. 107 2
that all nations may *c* and worship you; 107 15
Now as we *c* to the setting of the sun, 112 4
Now as we *c* to the setting of the sun, 118 4
He has *c* to the help of his servant Israel, * 119 18
He will *c* again to judge the living and the dead. 120 20
thy kingdom *c*, 121 6
and in the age to *c* life everlasting. 126 7
but it shall not *c* near you. 130 12
neither shall any plague *c* near your dwelling. 130 18
C to me, all who labor and are heavy-laden, 131 15
thy kingdom *c*, 132 21
And let our cry *c* to you. 133 8
Now as we *c* to the setting of the sun, 139 4
O *c*, let us sing unto the Lord; * 146 1
Let us *c* before his presence with thanksgiving, * 146 3
O *c*, let us worship and fall down * 146 11
thy kingdom *c*, 153 8
he shall *c* again in his glorious majesty to judge 159 5
and with great might *c* among us; 160 1
he shall *c* to be our Judge; 160 15
from whom all good doth *c*: 178 1
that we may *c* to those ineffable joys 194 11
and attain to the riches of the age to *c*; 198 5
that in the last day, when he shall *c* again 211 4
and with great might *c* among us; 212 1
C quickly to help us who are assaulted 218 2
that we may *c* to those ineffable joys 245 19
and attain to the riches of the age to *c*; 249 15
concern for those who *c* after us, 268 25
so that at the last we may *c* to his eternal joy; 269 13
those in misery and need *c* to you, 279 15
joy has *c* to the whole world. 281 4
show us the light of his countenance, and *c* to us. 281 6
joy has *c* to the whole world. 281 14
may *c* to the joy of that heavenly Jerusalem, 290 4
He will *c* again to judge the living and the dead. 293 11
He will *c* again to judge the living and the dead. 304 14
and look for him to *c* again in glory; 306 7
we bring into his fellowship those who *c* to him 307 1
and dwell with you in the life to *c*; 310 12
thy kingdom *c*, 311 3
c to the banquet of that most heavenly Food. 317 9
c boldly before the throne of grace 317 21
let us *c* boldly unto the throne of grace, 320 6
He will *c* again in glory to judge 327 10
and the life of the world to *c*. 327 19
and he shall *c* again, with glory, to judge 328 10
and the life of the world to *c*. 328 21
C unto me, all ye that travail and are heavy laden, 332 8
thy kingdom *c*, 336 20
We do not presume to *c* to this thy Table, 337 9
and *c* into his courts. 343 11
and then *c* and offer thy gift. 343 20
that when he shall *c* again in power 345 10
they may *c* to the fullness of grace 346 12
He will *c* again in glory to judge 359 1
and the life of the world to *c*. 359 10
Christ will *c* again. 363 9
thy kingdom *c*, 364 3
When the hour had *c* for him to be glorified by you, 374 13
bring offerings and *c* into his courts. 376 7
and then *c* and offer your gift. 376 16
when he shall *c* again in power and great triumph 378 6
they may *c* to the fullness of grace 379 8
May we also *c* to share in your heavenly kingdom. 387 20
thy kingdom *c*, 398 14
He will *c* again to judge the living and the dead. 416 19
and dwell with you in the life to *c*; 419 8
We have *c* together in the presence of God 423 1
Into this holy union now *c* to be joined. 424 1
and this woman who *c* to you seeking your blessing, 425 9
thy kingdom *c*, 428 10
in sending Jesus Christ to *c* among us, 430 11
in the age to *c* have life everlasting. 431 13
you have *c* here today to seek the blessing 433 1
He has *c* to the help of his servant Israel, * 442 7
partake of everlasting glory in the life to *c*; 444 6
C unto me, all ye that travail and are heavy laden, 449 13
thy kingdom *c*, 464 6
"*C* to me, all you who labor and are burdened, 465 10
"*C*, you blessed of my Father." 465 21
when shall I *c* to appear before the presence of God? 471 4
C again, ye children of men. 472 15
so strong that they *c* to fourscore years, * 473 4
C, O blessed of my Father; 483 21
All that the Father giveth me shall *c* to me; 484 18
thy kingdom *c*, 485 22
and may *c* to thy heavenly kingdom; 487 8
"*C*, ye blessed of my Father, 487 19
and strength to meet the days to *c*; 494 11

He will *c* again to judge the living and the dead. 496 14
C, O blessed of my Father; 500 10
Everyone the Father gives to me will *c* to me; 501 1
thy kingdom *c*, 502 3
and may *c* to your heavenly kingdom; 503 10
"C, you blessed of my Father, 505 6
to *c* with steadfastness and patience; 505 12
He will *c* again in glory to judge 520 1
and the life of the world to *c*. 520 10
knowing all things before they *c* to pass: 520 13
c forward now, and make it known. 527 5
He will *c* again in glory to judge 530 20
and the life of the world to *c*. 530 29
and in the life to *c*. 531 20
c forward now and make it known. 539 5
He will *c* again in glory to judge 542 20
and the life of the world to *c*. 542 29
that through him many may *c* to know you 545 15
and *c* to the unending glory of him 545 17
we have *c* together today to welcome 559 1
I am not worthy to have you *c* under my roof; 562 9
as we dedicate this place to which we *c* 568 9
Draw us to you, when we *c* alone 568 16
when we *c* with others, to find comfort and wisdom, 568 17
bring into his fellowship those who *c* to him in faith, 570 16
and in the days to *c*; 572 12
Let the malice of the wicked *c* to an end, 591 15
Oh, that Israel's deliverance would *c* out of Zion! * 599 1
my prayer, which does not *c* from lying lips. 600 24
Let my vindication *c* forth from your presence; * 601 1
they shall *c* trembling out of their strongholds. 606 2
They shall *c* and make known to a people yet unborn 612 21
and the King of glory shall *c* in. 614 3
C, children, and listen to me; * 628 15
Let ruin *c* upon them unawares; * 630 5
Let not the foot of the proud *c* near me, * 633 1
because he sees that their day will *c*. 634 10
and so I said, "Behold, I *c*. 640 19
Even if they *c* to see me, they speak empty words; * 642 10
when shall I *c* to appear before the presence of God? 643 4
All this has *c* upon us; * 646 19
C now and look upon the works of the LORD, * 649 19
that you may tell those who *c* after. 652 3
leave their wealth to those who *c* after them. 652 25
Our God will *c* and will not keep silence; * 654 6
that Israel's deliverance would *c* out of Zion! * 659 14
Fear and trembling have *c* over me, * 660 15
Let death *c* upon them suddenly; 661 14
Rouse yourself, *c* to my side, and see; * 666 3
To you that hear prayer shall all flesh *c*, * 672 9
C now and see the works of God, * 674 1
C and listen, all you who fear God, * 674 27
show us the light of his countenance and *c* to us. 675 10
I have *c* into deep waters, * 679 11
c to me speedily, O God. 682 23
c quickly to help me, O my God. 684 2
and your power to all who are to *c*. 684 19
He shall *c* down like rain upon the mown field, * 685 19
Oh, how suddenly do they *c* to destruction, * 688 15
c to an end, and perish from terror! 688 16
Has his loving-kindness *c* to an end for ever? * 693 16
We will recount to generations to *c* 695 4
That the generations to *c* might know, 695 10
O God, the heathen have *c* into your inheritance; 701 1
sighing of the prisoners *c* before you, * 702 4
stir up your strength and *c* to help us. 702 15
They have said, "C, let us wipe them out from among 706 9
and have *c* to help the people of Lot. 706 19
All nations you have made will *c* and 710 15
but it shall not *c* near you. 719 26
neither shall any plague *c* near your dwelling. 720 6
If the LORD had not *c* to my help, * 723 27
C, let us sing to the LORD; * 724 14
Let us *c* before his presence with thanksgiving * 724 16
C, let us bow down, and bend the knee, * 725 1
bring offerings and *c* into his courts. 726 8
and *c* before his presence with a song. 729 24
oh, when will you *c* to me? * 730 10
LORD, hear my prayer, and let my cry *c* before you; * 731 1
indeed, the appointed time has *c*. 732 3
let it *c* upon him; * 752 5
Let your loving-kindness *c* to me, O LORD, * 766 17
Let your compassion *c* to me, that I may live, * 769 18
I see that all things *c* to an end, * 771 11
Trouble and distress have *c* upon me, * 775 11
Let my cry *c* before you, O LORD; * 777 17
Let my supplication *c* before you; * 777 19
from where is my help to *c*? 779 2
will *c* again with joy, shouldering their sheaves. 782 19
"I will not *c* under the roof of my house, * 786 3
O LORD, I call to you; *c* to me quickly; * 797 3
Bow your heavens, O LORD, and *c* down; * 800 10
whose will it is that all should *c* to you 816 16
through him who shall *c* to be our Judge, 821 13
and the water from which these good things *c*. 825 24
we may *c* to know you more truly, 827 14
generations yet to *c* may continue to praise you 827 21
for this life and the life to *c*, 831 8
be partaker of everlasting glory in the life to *c*; 841 12
to *c* together week by week 856 13
What is required of us when we *c* to the Eucharist? 860 4
Christ will *c*, not in weakness but in power, 862 3
We believe that Christ will *c* in glory 862 14

comes

when night *c*, rejoice to give you thanks; 99 18
My help *c* from the LORD, * 104 15
behold him when he *c* to be our Judge; 212 13
when he *c* again with power 236 4
Blessed is the King who *c* in the name of the Lord. 270 1
Blessed is he who *c* in the name of the Lord. 271 15
until he *c* to your everlasting kingdom. 309 17
Blessed is he who *c* in the name of the Lord. 362 7
Blessed is he who *c* in the name of the Lord. 367 16
Blessed is he who *c* in the name of the Lord. 371 4
Blessed is he who *c* in the name of the Lord. 373 15
whoever *c* to me shall not hunger, 396 4
Blessed is he who *c* in the name of the Lord. 402 12
and proclaim his resurrection, until he *c* 403 15
Blessed is he who *c* in the name of the Lord. 404 14
until he *c* to your everlasting kingdom. 418 15
not stand upright when judgment *c*, * 585 13
it *c* forth like a bridegroom out of his chamber; 606 24
but joy *c* in the morning. 621 15

the deliverance of the righteous *c* from the LORD; * 636 15
and from whose mouth *c* no defense. 637 26
My merciful God *c* to meet me; * 666 16
from him *c* my salvation. 669 6
the Lord *c* in holiness from Sinai. 677 17
Their iniquity *c* from gross minds, * 687 13
in the morning my prayer *c* before you. 713 5
before the LORD when he *c*, * 726 18
when he *c* to judge the earth. 726 19
when he *c* to judge the earth. 728 20
Blessed is he who *c* in the name of the Lord; * 762 23
My help *c* from the LORD, * 779 3
until the shadows lengthen, and the evening *c*, 833 15

cometh

when the master of the house *c*, 37 2
The hour *c*, and now is, 40 20
For he *c*, for he *c* to judge the earth, * 45 8
when the night *c*, rejoice to give thee thanks; 56 23
that when thy Son our Lord *c* 160 7
of whose only gift it *c* 184 1
Blessed is he that *c* in the name of the Lord. 334 7
Blessed is he that *c* in the name of the Lord. 341 10
from whence *c* my help? 473 10
My help *c* even from the LORD, * 473 11
and him that *c* to me I will in no wise cast out. 484 19
from whom *c* every good and perfect gift: 817 3

comfort

to *c* us in all our afflictions, 107 5
and the grace and *c* of the Holy Spirit. 128 2
and to *c* with thy presence 151 25
and *c* all who are in danger, 151 28
to *c* and help the weak-hearted; 152 12
but send to us thine Holy Ghost to *c* us, 175 4
and evermore to rejoice in his holy *c*; 175 18
by patience and *c* of thy holy Word, 184 18
C and relieve thy sick servants, 208 16
and evermore to rejoice in his holy *c*; 227 11
C and relieve your sick servants, 260 1
That God in his mercy will *c* and relieve them, 279 11
Gracious God, the *c* of all who sorrow, 279 14
to *c* and succor 329 27
and doth *c* us with the blessed hope 349 7
C and heal all those who suffer 389 3
for the help and *c* given one another in prosperity 423 10
Will you love him, *c* him, 424 10
Will you love her, *c* her, 424 16
a counselor in perplexity, a *c* in sorrow, 429 9
Do you promise to love her, *c* her, 433 6
Do you promise to love him, *c* him, 433 11
your rod and your staff, they *c* me. 443 10
a counselor in perplexity, a *c* in sorrow, 444 11
O Father of mercies and God of all *c*, 458 1
c him with a sense of thy goodness; 458 4
the strength of the weak and the *c* of sufferers: 458 11
graciously *c* your servant 459 7
C and relieve your sick servant 459 17
and *c* him with the promise of life everlasting, 462 2
c them with a sense of your goodness; 467 5
and lead me forth beside the waters of *c*. 476 4
thy rod and thy staff *c* me. 476 11
thy rod and thy staff, they *c* me. 477 4
be strong, and he shall *c* thine heart; 478 9
in the *c* of a reasonable and holy hope, 481 11
may be unto us a *c* in affliction, 482 5
in the *c* of a reasonable, religious, and holy hope; 489 10
Father of mercies and giver of all *c*: 489 30
c us in our sorrow. 497 7
C us in our sorrows at the death 497 22
be to us a *c* in affliction, 498 16
in the *c* of a religious 504 8
Father of mercies and giver of *c*: 505 17
and God of all *c*, 520 12
come with others, to find *c* and wisdom, 568 17
your rod and your staff, they *c* me. 613 6
be strong, and he shall *c* your heart; * 619 2
you enfold and *c* me, 684 27
This is my *c* in my trouble, * 767 13
O LORD, I take great *c*. 767 18
Let your loving-kindness be my *c*, * 769 16
"When will you *c* me?" 770 6
that it may please thee to *c* 815 9
to our *c* and to thy honor; 828 14
c him when discouraged or sorrowful; 830 15
c him with a sense of thy goodness, 831 15

comforted

I refused to be *c*. 693 5
because you, O LORD, have helped me and *c* me. 711 11

comforter

also the Holy Ghost the *C*. 53 10

comforters

for *c*, but I could find no one. 681 5

comfortless

leave us not *c*, 175 3
Do not leave us *c*, 226 15

comforts

Our intemperate love of worldly goods and *c*, 268 10
and *c* us with the blessed hope 382 2

coming

lest *c* suddenly he find you sleeping. 37 3
and hasten the *c* of thy kingdom; 58 6
The hour is *c*, 78 19
and hasten the *c* of your kingdom; 100 22
your going out and your *c* in, * 105 2
so be with us in the *c* night; 113 6
your protection through the *c* night. 124 4
and by the *C* of the Holy Ghost, 149 24
that we may greet with joy the *c* of Jesus Christ 159 12
await with him the *c* of the third day, 170 4
and hasten the *c* of thy kingdom; 206 14
that we may greet with joy the *c* of Jesus Christ 211 12
at his *c*, may find in us a mansion 212 7
await with him the *c* of the third day, 221 16
and hasten the *c* of your kingdom; 257 10
await with him the *c* of the third day, 283 4
death and sacrifice, until his *c* again. 334 16
death and sacrifice, until his *c* again. 341 20
his *c* again with power and great glory. 342 15
We await his *c* in glory; 368 22

as we await the day of his *c*. 371 22
the presumption of *c* to this Table for solace 372 4
awaiting his *c* in glory; 374 27
at the day of your *c*, 389 17
Hasten, O Father, the *c* of thy kingdom; 395 13
may with joy behold thy Son at his *c* 395 15
we await his *c* in glory. 405 12
by the *c* of N. to be a member of their family. 440 13
and by the C of the Holy Spirit, 463 9
thy going out, and thy *c* in, * 473 23
and at thy *c* may the martyrs receive thee, 484 1
At your *c* may the martyrs receive you, 500 12
at the Day of your C, 548 13
They were like men *c* up with axes 689 18
over your going out and your *c* in, * 779 16
you prepared your disciples for the *c* of the Spirit 819 1
and to announce the *c* of the Messiah. 849 10
until his *c* again. 859 8
and to await the *c* of Christ 861 26
What do we mean by the *c* of Christ in glory? 862 1
By the *c* of Christ in glory, 862 2

command

make us to love that which thou dost *c*; 183 20
to love what you *c* and desire what you promise; 219 8
make us love what you *c*; 235 11
and in obedience to his *c*, 316 9
Gospel *c* us to continue, a perpetual memory of that 334 15
did institute, and in his holy Gospel *c* us to continue, 341 18
Therefore, according to his *c*, 368 19
At your *c* all things came to be: 370 8
by the might of your *c* 458 16
you *c* victories for Jacob. 645 19
He sends out his *c* to the earth, * 805 7
according to Christ's *c*. 859 21

commanded

the memorial thy Son hath *c* us to make; 335 12
the memorial thy Son hath *c* us to make; 342 12
he *c*, and it stood fast. 626 18
which he *c* them to teach their children; 695 9
So he *c* the clouds above * 696 22
as the LORD had *c* them. 744 16
he *c* his covenant for ever; * 754 23
for he *c*, and they were created. 806 4
whose Son *c* us to love our enemies: 816 5
Christ *c* us to believe in him 851 5
the sacrament *c* by Christ 859 6

commanders

and all their *c* like Zebah and Zalmunna, 706 25

commandest

love the thing which thou *c*, 167 17

commandment

and contempt of thy Word and *c*, 149 9
has given power and *c* to his ministers 269 6
I give you a new *c*: Love one another 275 3
This is the first and great *c*. 319 11
This is the first and great *c*. 324 4
"The first *c* is this: 351 7
There is no other *c* greater than these." 351 11
the *c* of the LORD is clear 607 10
but your *c* has no bounds. 771 12
Your *c* has made me wiser than my enemies, * 771 15
and gave us the New C. 851 9
This is the first and the great *c*. 851 13
What is the New C? 851 15
The New C is that we love one another 851 16

commandments

that our hearts may be set to obey thy *c*, 69 19
but I have not strayed from your *c*. 104 8
and diligently to live after thy *c*, 150 23
that in keeping thy *c* we may please thee 164 15
who hast taught us to keep all thy *c* 179 4
that in keeping your *c* we may please you 216 9
you have taught us to keep all your *c* 230 19
by the rule of God's *c*, 317 2
On these two *c* hang all the Law 319 12
On these two *c* hang all the Law 324 5
lead a new life, following the *c* of God, 330 11
Hear the *c* of God to his people: 350 1
and obedience to thy holy *c*, 487 16
Let his life and teaching so reflect your *c*, 545 14
but keep his *c*; 695 15
and did not keep his *c*. 699 19
and do not keep my *c*; 716 4
and remember his *c* and do them. 734 19
all his *c* are sure. 754 19
and have great delight in his *c*! 755 6
You laid down your *c*, * 763 11
when I regard all your *c*. 763 16
let me not stray from your *c*. 764 4
I will meditate on your *c* * 764 13
do not hide your *c* from me. 764 22
cursed are they who stray from your *c*! 765 2
Make me understand the way of your *c*, * 765 13
I will run the way of your *c*, * 765 23
Make me go in the path of your *c*, * 766 5
Behold, I long for your *c*; * 766 15
because I study your *c*. 767 4
I delight in your *c*, * 767 7
I will lift up my hands to your *c*, * 767 9
because I have kept your *c*. 767 26
to keep your *c*. 768 8
and of those who keep your *c*. 768 14
for I have believed in your *c*. 768 20
but I will keep your *c* with my whole heart. 769 2
that I may learn your *c*. 769 11
but I will meditate on your *c*. 769 22
All your *c* are true; * 770 14
but I have not forsaken your *c*. 770 17
I will never forget your *c*, * 771 5
for I study your *c*. 771 8
because I observe your *c*. 771 20
Through your *c* I gain understanding; * 772 1
but I have not strayed from your *c*. 772 14
I will keep the *c* of my God. 773 4
Truly, I love your *c* * 774 1
I hold all your *c* to be right for me; * 774 3
I long for your *c*. 774 10
and I will keep your *c*. 774 16
yet I do not forget your *c*. 775 8
yet your *c* are my delight. 775 12

and all your *c* are true. 776 6
See how I love your *c*! * 776 21
and I have fulfilled your *c*. 777 12
I have kept your *c* and decrees, * 777 15
for all your *c* are righteous. 777 24
for I have chosen your *c*. 778 2
for I do not forget your *c*. 778 9
is shown most clearly in the Ten C. 847 12
What are the Ten C? 847 13
The Ten C are the laws given to Moses 847 14
What do we learn from these *c*? 847 16
What is the purpose of the Ten C? 848 22
The Ten C were given to define 848 23
and to keep his *c*. 851 6
What are the *c* taught by Christ? 851 7

commands

and his obedience to thy *c*; 188 11
and his obedience to your *c*; 239 20

commend

Into your hands I *c* my spirit, * 129 18
Into your hands, O Lord, I *c* my spirit; 132 12
c the faith that is in us, 268 14
let us *c* ourselves, and one another, 385 14
We *c* to your mercy all who have died, 389 8
let us *c* ourselves, and one another, 391 20
I *c* you to this work, 420 4
We *c* to your loving care this child 459 3
we *c* your servant 465 1
we *c* our brother (sister) 465 16
we *c* our brother (sister) 465 20
we *c* our brother (sister) 465 24
we *c* our brother (sister) 466 4
we *c* thy servant 483 6
we *c* to Almighty God 485 10
we *c* thy servant 488 12
we *c* to you our brother (sister) 498 1
we *c* your servant 499 13
we *c* to Almighty God 501 12
let us *c* ourselves, 550 27
Into your hands I *c* my spirit, * 622 17
we *c* to thy fatherly goodness 815 6
We *c* this nation to thy merciful care, 820 17
we *c* to your gracious care 823 1
We *c* to thy continual care the homes 828 23

commended

For all who have *c* themselves to our prayers; 391 10

commends

Holy Scripture *c* it to be honored 423 8

commerce

the industries and *c* of this land 208 4
the industries and *c* of this land 259 6

commit

Let us *c* ourselves to our God, 280 8
Thou shalt not *c* adultery. 318 19
You shall not *c* murder. 350 13
You shall not *c* adultery. 350 15
and we *c* his body to the ground; * 485 11
and we *c* his body to the ground; * 501 13

Do you now in the presence of the Church *c* 531 24
Do you now in the presence of the Church *c* 543 22
do you, in the presence of this congregation, *c* 559 5
The helpless *c* themselves to you, * 595 25
All are corrupt and *c* abominable acts; 598 13
C your way to the LORD and put your trust in him, * 633 13
All are corrupt and *c* abominable acts; 658 22

commitment

evil and renew your *c* to Jesus Christ? 292 9
Do you renew you *c* to Jesus Christ? 303 12
who have renewed their *c* to Christ.] 305 13
who have renewed their *c* to Christ. 309 2
Do you renew your *c* to Jesus Christ? 415 11
who have renewed their *c* to Christ. 417 21
who has now reaffirmed his *c* to follow Christ 421 3
we express a mature *c* to Christ, 860 19

committed

from time to time most grievously have *c*, 331 6
and by his authority *c* to me, 448 4
and by his authority *c* to me, 451 14
and has *c* himself to me in faith, 491 5
through these promises you have *c* yourself 519 1
Feed the flock of Christ *c* to your charge, 521 19
Do not forget the trust *c* to you 534 12
when we are *c* into the Father's hands. 569 9
and upon the congregations *c* to their charge, 817 5

committing

Let us join with those who are *c* themselves 303 17
Let us join with those who are *c* themselves 416 4

common

to make our *c* supplication unto thee, 59 13
to make our *c* supplication unto thee, 72 10
to make our *c* supplication to you; 102 2
to make our *c* supplication to you; 126 2
our *c* life depends upon each other's toil; 134 14
and for the *c* good, 151 15
and for the *c* good; 210 6
and for the *c* good; 261 11
For all who serve the *c* good 278 22
and serve the *c* good. 388 9
in the ordering of their *c* life, 429 8
Grant that the bonds of our *c* humanity, 430 4
in the ordering of their *c* life, 444 9
Grant us all things necessary for our *c* life, 817 21
you have bound us together in a *c* life. 824 1

commonly

The Holy Scriptures, *c* called the Bible, 853 6

Commonwealth

State (or C), 820 20
(or in the Legislature of this State, or C), 821 4
in this State (C, City, County, 822 18

commune

I *c* with my heart in the night; * 693 12

communion

the *c* of saints, 54 7
the *c* of saints, 66 23
the *c* of [_________ and] all thy saints, 68 23

the *c* of saints, 96 27
the *c* of saints, 120 23
the *c* of [_________ and] all your saints, 122 25
c and fellowship in the mystical body of thy Son 194 9
c and fellowship in the mystical body of your Son 245 17
and to the whole *c* of saints 267 14
the *c* of saints, 293 15
to be received into this C. 303 7
the *c* of saints, 304 18
in the faith and *c* of your holy Church. 305 21
into the fellowship of this C. 310 3
who shall be partakers of this Holy C, 336 4
that all who partake of this Holy C 342 25
Let the grace of this Holy C make us one body, 372 6
In the *c* of [and of all the] saints, 385 13
For all who have died in the *c* of your Church, 391 15
and thanks for this Holy C of the Body and Blood 399 8
Gather us by this Holy C into one body 403 17
to be received into this C. 415 6
the *c* of saints, 416 23
into the fellowship of this C. 418 19
and thanks for this Holy C of the Body and Blood 457 6
c and fellowship, in the mystical body 480 5
to believe and trust in the *c* of saints, 481 15
in the *c* of the Catholic Church; 489 9
the *c* of saints, 496 17
in the *c* of the Catholic Church, 504 7
For all who have died in the *c* of your Church, 550 20
in the *c* of thy Holy Spirit, 830 24
For the *c* of saints, 837 19
the Lord's Supper, and Holy C; 859 16
The inward and spiritual grace in the Holy C 859 24
in the *c* of the saints. 862 19
What is the *c* of saints? 862 20
The *c* of saints is the whole family of God, 862 21

communities

justice in our *c* and among the nations, 209 5
justice in our *c* and among the nations, 260 12

community

For all Christians in this *c* 278 7
for every city and *c*, 384 8
For all who live and work in this *c* 390 19
For this *c*, the nation, and the world; 392 5
rejoicing in the Christian *c*. 440 3
the health of the *c* may be promoted 460 13
of your family, or household, or *c*] 532 20
of your family, or household, or *c*] 544 8
For his family [the members of his household or *c*], 549 12
fulfill our obligations in the *c* of nations. 822 4
the people of the United States (or of this *c*) 822 25
a *c* of love has been gathered together 838 5
a *c* created by a covenant with God. 846 19
The Church is the *c* of the New Covenant. 854 4

companion

be our *c* in the way, 70 11
be our *c* in the way, 124 8
be our *c* in the way, 139 17
and a *c* in joy. 429 9
and a *c* in joy. 444 11
as a *c* on our earthly pilgrimage. 493 18
my *c*, my own familiar friend. 661 11
My *c* stretched forth his hand 661 28
and darkness is my only *c*. 713 16
I am a *c* of all who fear you * 768 13

companions

My friends and *c* draw back from my affliction; * 637 18
For my brethren and *c*' sake, * 780 11
and death as their constant *c*. 826 10

companionship

that in *c* with one another 71 8
that in *c* with one another 125 3
in their work and in their *c*; 430 20

company

The glorious *c* of the apostles praise thee. 53 3
The glorious *c* of apostles praise you. 95 23
we thank thee for the glorious *c* 194 1
near to an innumerable *c* of angels 198 24
we thank you for the glorious *c* of the apostles, 245 10
to an innumerable *c* of angels, 250 8
and with all the *c* of heaven, 334 2
the blessed *c* of all faithful people; 339 8
and with all the *c* of heaven, 341 5
Archangels and with all the *c* of heaven, 362 2
Archangels and with all the *c* of heaven, 367 11
to the blessed *c* of your faithful people; 450 19
the glorious *c* of the saints in light. 465 6
the *c* of the saints. 466 15
glorious *c* of the saints in light. 483 11
the glorious *c* of the saints in light. 499 18
which restores us to the *c* of your faithful people, 579 1
because God is in the *c* of the righteous. 598 25
I have hated the *c* of evildoers; * 616 16
They shall join the *c* of their forebears, * 653 21
great was the *c* of women who bore the tidings: 677 2
the princes of Judah in a *c*; * 678 12
and covered the *c* of Abiram. 743 6
Fire blazed up against their *c*, * 743 7

compared

Who can be *c* with you, O Lord, among the gods? * 85 16
there is none who can be *c* with you. 640 13
For who in the skies can be *c* to the LORD? * 714 5

compassed

God, who hast *c* us about 198 16
hast *c* us about 347 18
The snares of death *c* me round about, * 479 3

compassion

The Lord is full of *c* and mercy: 43 6
The Lord is full of *c* and mercy: 81 2
and he will have *c*, * 86 21
you are full of *c*, * 91 5
In the tender *c* of our God * 93 5
and minister thy justice with *c*; 178 9
Have *c*, 179 18
and minister your justice with *c*; 230 4
Have *c* on our weakness, 231 12
in your great *c* blot out my offenses. 266 3
Have *c* on all who do not know you 280 2
Defend us, deliver us, and in thy *c* protect us, 385 10

Have *c* on those who suffer	387	14
in your *c* forgive us our sins,	393	10
look with *c* upon us	395	4
our God is full of *c*.	442	18
in your great *c* blot out my offenses.	449	2
In your boundless *c*,	493	19
show *c* to the poor and strangers,	518	28
Remember, O LORD, your *c* and love, *	614	24
do not withhold your *c* from me; *	641	2
in your great *c* blot out my offenses.	656	7
in your great *c*, turn to me."	680	24
has he, in his anger, withheld his *c*?	693	19
let your *c* be swift to meet us; *	701	22
But you, O LORD, are gracious and full of *c*, *	711	4
You will arise and have *c* on Zion,	732	1
The LORD is full of *c* and mercy, *	733	23
the LORD is gracious and full of *c*.	754	13
the righteous are merciful and full of *c*.	755	12
our God is full of *c*.	759	11
Let your *c* come to me, that I may live, *	769	18
Great is your *c*, O LORD; *	776	15
and shows *c* to his servants.	789	4
The LORD is gracious and full of *c*, *	802	1
and his *c* is over all his works.	802	4
Look with *c* on the whole human family;	815	14
Look with *c* upon all who through addiction	831	19

compassionate

keep them humane and *c*;	826	23

compassions

O Lord, your *c* never fail	460	16

complain

I will *c* and lament, *	661	20
Hear my voice, O God, when I *c*; *	671	10

complaint

the voice of my *c*.	474	4
I pour out my *c* before him *	798	3

complete

to *c* his work in the world,	374	11

completion

and the *c* of God's purpose	861	27

complexity

the infinite *c* of living creatures:	827	13

comrade

stretched forth his hand against his *c*; *	661	28

conceal

and did not *c* my guilt.	625	8

concealed

I have not *c* your love and faithfulness	640	28

conceit

he has scattered the proud in their *c*.	92	7
he has scattered the proud in their *c*.	119	13
he has scattered the proud in their *c*.	442	2

conceive

who *c* evil, and give birth to a lie.	591	27

conceived

who was *c* by the Holy Ghost,	53	26
who was *c* by the Holy Ghost,	66	12
He was *c* by the power of the Holy Spirit	96	16
He was *c* by the power of the Holy Spirit	120	12
He was *c* by the power of the Holy Spirit	293	3
He was *c* by the power of the Holy Spirit	304	6
He was *c* by the power of the Holy Spirit	416	11
He was *c* by the power of the Holy Spirit	496	6
Jesus was *c* by the power of the Holy Spirit	849	26

concern

and arouse our *c* for those	210	15
and arouse our *c* for those	261	20
our lack of *c* for those	268	25
reach out in love and *c* for others.	429	24

concerning

In the roll of the book it is written *c* me: *	640	20

concerns

For the special needs and *c* of this congregation.	392	17
interpret to the Church the needs, *c*, and hopes	543	12

concord

who art the author of peace and lover of *c*,	57	1
the author of peace and lover of *c*,	99	20
to give to all nations unity, peace, and *c*;	151	2
and live in peace and *c*.	278	24
to your holy Church peace and *c*;	282	10
and brings peace and *c*.	287	18
with the spirit of truth, unity, and *c*;	329	6
to thy holy Church peace and *c*,	489	27
else may hinder us from godly union and *c*;	818	18

condemn

nor *c* me to the depths of the earth.	91	19
not to *c* the world, but that the world	277	3
and *c* the innocent to death.	724	8
to save his life from those who would *c* him.	753	11

condemned

not be *c* before the great judgment seat	68	19
not be *c* before the great judgment seat	122	21
spare those who are *c* to die.	702	6
and set free those *c* to die;	732	17
Jesus, for our sake you were *c* as a criminal:	826	16

conditions

beseech thee for all sorts and *c* of men;	814	7

conduct

Examine your lives and *c* by the rule	317	1
may so order his life and *c*	460	21

conferred

and who *c* power on his Church	448	8
and who *c* power on his Church	451	7

confess

but if we *c* our sins, God is faithful	38	11
c our sins, that we may obtain forgiveness	41	13
Let us humbly *c* our sins unto Almighty God.	41	15
spare thou those who *c* their faults,	42	4
c our sins, so that we may obtain forgiveness	62	13
Let us humbly *c* our sins unto Almighty God.	62	15
spare thou those who *c* their faults,	63	7
all tongues *c* and bless thee,	70	17
but if we *c* our sins, God, who is faithful	76	10

penitent and obedient hearts *c* our sins, 79 7
Let us *c* our sins against God and our neighbor. 79 9
we *c* that we have sinned against you 79 11
c our sins, so that we may obtain forgiveness 116 9
Let us *c* our sins against God and our neighbor. 116 11
we *c* that we have sinned against you 116 13
all tongues *c* and bless you, 124 14
Let us *c* our sins to God. 127 5
c him as Lord and Savior; 163 5
to *c* Jesus as Messiah and Son 187 2
c the Name of our Savior Jesus Christ 195 2
c him as Lord and Savior; 214 16
to *c* Jesus as Messiah and Son of the living God: 238 15
c the Name of our Savior Jesus Christ 246 9
We *c* to you and to one another, 267 13
We *c* to you, Lord, all our past unfaithfulness: 268 1
We *c* to you, Lord. 268 3
C the faith of Christ crucified, 308 12
and *c* your sins, 317 13
[and humbly *c* our sins to Almighty God]. 317 22
but if we *c* our sins, God is faithful 320 2
Let us humbly *c* our sins unto Almighty God. 320 9
we *c* that we have sinned against thee 320 11
spare thou those who *c* their faults, 321 7
and grant that all those who do *c* 329 6
Let us humbly *c* our sins unto Almighty God. 330 15
we *c* that we have sinned against thee 331 22
But if we *c* our sins, God, who is faithful 352 2
Let us *c* our sins against God and our neighbor. 352 9
we *c* that we have sinned against you 352 11
Let us *c* our sins against God and our neighbor. 360 1
we *c* that we have sinned against you 360 3
Grant, Almighty God, that all who *c* your Name 388 2
we *c* that we have sinned against you 397 20
Word, you do now *c* it. 424 7
truly and humbly *c* your sins: 447 3
I *c* to Almighty God, to his Church, and to you, 447 5
c your sins with a humble and obedient heart 450 6
Especially, I *c* to you and to the Church... 450 15
we *c* that we have sinned against you 454 2
I said, "I will *c* my transgressions to the LORD." * 625 9
I will *c* my iniquity * 638 5
I will *c* you among the peoples, O LORD; * 664 15
Let them *c* his Name, which is great and awesome; * 729 3
I will *c* you among the peoples, O LORD; * 749 22
c Jesus Christ as Lord and are brought into love 852 27
In penitence, we *c* our sins and make restitution 857 12
which those who repent of their sins may *c* them 861 10

confessed

I have *c* my ways, and you answered me; * 765 11

confessing

c before the rulers of this world 348 9
c before the rulers of this world 381 3
to lead us in *c* that faith. 519 4

confession

by the *c* of a true faith, 176 2
with steadfast faith in the *c* of thy Name; 183 14
to continue steadfast in the *c* of this faith, 199 15
by the *c* of a true faith, 228 2
in the *c* of your Name; 235 6
to continue steadfast in the *c* of this faith, 251 4
and make your humble *c* to Almighty God, 330 13
in the *c* of one faith, 347 11
in the *c* of one faith, 380 5
May Almighty God in mercy receive your *c* 451 3
to affirm their *c* of Jesus Christ 860 26

confide

resist the proud who *c* in their own strength, 181 19
resist the proud who *c* in their own strength, 233 10

confidence

put our whole trust and *c* in thy mercy, 155 11
so we may with sure *c* behold him 160 15
thy Church may joyfully serve thee in *c* 177 11
and have *c* in thy loving care; 208 20
may with sure *c* behold him 212 12
your Church may joyfully serve you in *c* 229 7
and have *c* in your loving care; 260 5
let us with *c* draw near to the throne of grace, 352 6
Fill his heart with *c* 459 9
and have *c* in your loving care; 459 20
Let us pray with *c* to God, 466 13
Grant to all who mourn a sure *c* 481 7
in the *c* of a certain faith; 489 10
so that in quiet *c* we may continue 493 21
but have *c* in your goodness, 494 10
in the *c* of a certain faith, 504 8
my *c* since I was young. 683 10
in *c* shall be our strength: 832 14
The Christian hope is to live with *c* 861 25

confident

c of the glory that shall be revealed; 220 16

confirm

That God will *c* his Church in faith, 278 9
c and strengthen you in all goodness, 332 4
C their joy 443 24

confirmation

I present these persons for *C*. 303 5
I present these persons for *C*. 415 4
include *c*, ordination, holy matrimony, 860 10
What is *C*? 860 17
C is the rite in which we express 860 18

confirmed

and their loyalties *c*. 430 3
What is required of those to be *c*? 860 22
It is required of those to be *c* 860 23

conform

c to the doctrine, discipline, and worship 513 12
and I do solemnly engage to *c* to the doctrine, 526 17
and I do solemnly engage to *c* to the doctrine, 538 17

confound

Their aim is to *c* the plans of the afflicted, * 598 26
c their speech; * 660 24
he will *c* those who trample upon me; * 663 26

confounded

Let me never be *c*. 55 24
my enemies shall be *c* and quake with fear; * 590 18
and gloat over me be *c*, * 641 14
C be all who worship carved images 727 9

confront

c them and bring them down; * 601 25
to *c* one another without hatred 824 2

confronted

They *c* me in the day of my disaster; * 603 28

confusing

growing up in an unsteady and *c* world: 829 15

confusion

let them be put to *c* and perish. 707 12
and work through our struggle and *c* 815 18
Save us from violence, discord, and *c*; 820 5

congregation

the whole *c* 265 6
to this *c* here present; 329 14
For this *c* 391 1
For the special needs and concerns of this *c*. 392 17
In the name of this *c* 420 4
in the presence of this *c*, 559 5
for this *c*, 560 2
in the midst of the *c* I will praise you. 611 25
I will give you thanks in the great *c*; * 631 4
I proclaimed righteousness in the great *c*; * 640 23
from the great *c*. 640 29
Bless God in the *c*; * 678 9
your *c* that you purchased long ago, * 689 11
Let them exalt him in the *c* of the people * 748 19
in the assembly of the upright, in the *c*. 754 7
sing his praise in the *c* of the faithful. 807 3

congregations

upon the *c* committed to their charge, 817 5

Congress

For the C and the Supreme Court 278 20
and bless our Senators and Representatives in C 821 3

conquer

forgiveness heal guilt, and joy *c* despair. 429 19
Ride out and *c* in the cause of truth * 647 19

conquered

on the first day of the week, you *c* sin, 835 2

conscience

things whereof our *c* is afraid, 183 1
Purify our *c*, Almighty God, 212 6
things of which our *c* is afraid, 234 15
having the testimony of a good *c*; 489 9
having the testimony of a good *c*, 504 7
and stirring up the *c* of your people? 518 10
Strengthen those who suffer for the sake of *c*; 823 10

consciences

to purify our *c* by thy daily visitation, 160 6

consecrate

we pray you to *c* this oil, 307 11
to *c* him a bishop 513 5
we are now gathered to dedicate and *c* it 567 5

consecrated

you have so *c* the covenant of marriage 431 1

consecrates

c its members, 854 19

consecrating

for *c* the union of man and woman 430 13

conserve

and for the wisdom and will to *c* it, 384 15

consider

So also *c* yourselves dead to sin, * 83 19
to *c* how Saint Paul exhorts all persons 316 20
O let thine ears *c* well * 474 3
c my meditation. 588 18
When I *c* your heavens, 592 13
Happy are they who *c* the poor and needy! * 641 23
"Hear, O daughter; *c* and listen closely; * 648 11
C well her bulwarks; 652 1
C this well, you who forget God, * 655 26
I *c* the days of old; * 693 10
C well, you dullards among the people; * 723 9
In Egypt they did not *c* your marvelous works, 742 11
and *c* well the mercies of the LORD. 749 16
let your ears *c* well the voice 784 20
I *c* the works of your hands. 799 9

considered

I have *c* my ways * 768 5

consists

The Old Testament *c* of books written 853 10
The New Testament *c* of books written 853 14

consolation

and the grace and *c* of his Holy Spirit. 42 13
and the grace and *c* of his Holy Spirit. 63 16
and the grace and *c* of his Holy Spirit. 321 16
and know the *c* of his love. 467 2
may know the *c* of thy love. 481 9
they may know the *c* of thy love; 489 32
let our faith be our *c*, 497 23
they may know the *c* of your love; 505 19

consolations

your *c* cheer my soul. 724 4

console

c us who mourn. 493 20
not so much seek to be consoled as to *c*; 833 10

consoled

you *c* Martha and Mary in their distress; 497 3
not so much seek to be *c* as to console; 833 10

consort

nor do I *c* with the deceitful. 616 15

conspiracy
From all oppression, *c*, and rebellion; 149 14
Hide me from the *c* of the wicked, * 671 12

conspire
They *c* against the life of the just * 724 7

conspired
They have *c* together; * 706 12

constancy
and serve you in unity, *c*, and peace; 363 16

constant
With your *c* love you led the people 85 21
and *c* in our worship of thee, 199 15
and *c* in our worship of you, 251 4
modest and humble, strong and *c*, 545 12
and death as their *c* companions. 826 10
Knit together in *c* affection 829 3

constantly
after his example *c* speak the truth, 190 5
who *c* receive good things from thy hand, 207 18
following his example, *c* speak the truth, 241 15
who are *c* receiving good things 258 18

constituted
and *c* the ministries of angels 193 4
and *c* the ministries of angels 200 6
and *c* in a wonderful order 244 13
and *c* in a wonderful order 251 12

constrain
c us to improve their lot. 826 25

consume
For we *c* away in thy displeasure, * 472 23
and fire shall *c* them. 609 17
For we *c* away in your displeasure; * 718 13

consumed
my eye is *c* with sorrow, 623 4
and my bones are *c*. 623 9
The fire *c* their young men; * 700 5
Let sinners be *c* out of the earth, * 737 24
My soul is *c* at all times * 764 23
My indignation has *c* me, * 775 3

consuming
and a *c* fire out of his mouth; * 603 5
before him there is a *c* flame, 654 7
to turn away his wrath from *c* them. 743 19

consummation
to have our *c* and bliss 481 24
our perfect *c* and bliss, 488 9
to wait for the *c* of your kingdom 835 6

contain
and to *c* all things necessary to salvation; 513 10
and to *c* all things necessary to salvation; 526 16
and to *c* all things necessary to salvation; 538 16
the heaven of heavens cannot *c* you, 578 3

contemplation
the *c* of those mighty acts, 270 5

contempt
and *c* of thy Word and commandment, 149 9
and *c* toward those who differ from us, 268 21
he does not heap *c* upon his neighbor. 599 10
haughtily, disdainfully, and with *c*. 624 3
(He pours *c* on princes * 749 9
for we have had more than enough of *c*. 780 22

contemptuous
For the *c* and the scornful 279 24

contend
Grant us grace fearlessly to *c* against evil 209 2
Grant us grace fearlessly to *c* against evil 260 9

contends
when he *c* with his enemies in the gate. 783 12

content
My soul is *c*, as with marrow and fatness, * 670 21

contented
Christ was *c* to be betrayed, 169 15

continual
let thy *c* pity cleanse 180 8
Let your *c* mercy, O Lord, cleanse 232 1
for the *c* remembrance 316 3
for his *c* providence over us, 316 11
to grant them *c* growth in thy love 330 3
the *c* recalling of the sacrifice 574 3
and give them *c* trembling in their loins. 681 11
pour upon them the *c* dew 817 7
We commend to thy *c* care 828 23
and further us with thy *c* help; 832 2
for the *c* remembrance of his life, 859 7

continually
To thee Cherubim and Seraphim *c* do cry: 52 27
and with him *c* dwell; 174 18
and make us *c* to be given to all good works; 183 7
thy Church may give itself *c* to prayer 193 20
and with him *c* dwell; 226 11
that we may *c* be given to good works; 234 21
your Church may give itself *c* to prayer 245 6
Christians *c* have to renew their repentance 265 9
May it shine *c* to drive away all darkness. 287 22
let us offer *c* the sacrifice of praise, 317 20
inspire *c* the Universal Church 329 5
Through Christ let us *c* offer to God 344 1
Through Christ let us *c* offer to God 376 17
let those who love your salvation *c* say, 641 17
c seek his face. 738 8
and like the belt that he wears *c*. 752 12
for my prayer is *c* against their wicked deeds. 797 14

continue
because it cannot *c* in safety 180 9
Graciously *c* in thy Church 193 13
Give us grace to *c* steadfast 199 14
because it cannot *c* in safety 232 2
Graciously *c* in your Church this love 244 22
Give us grace to *c* steadfast 251 3
Will you *c* in the apostles' teaching 293 19
Will you *c* in the apostles' teaching 304 22

may *c* for ever in the risen life 307 5
that he may *c* yours for ever, 309 16
command us to *c*, a perpetual memory 334 15
that we may *c* in that holy fellowship, 339 11
command us to *c*, a perpetual memory 341 18
Will you *c* in the apostles' teaching 417 4
that he may *c* yours for ever, 418 14
C in him, we pray, the good work 460 19
we may *c* our course on earth, 493 21
may *c* for ever in the risen life 570 19
C your loving-kindness to those who know you, * 632 24
those who tell lies shall not *c* in my sight. 730 25
The children of your servants shall *c*, * 733 7
I shall *c* to keep your law; * 767 1
By your decree these *c* to this day, * 771 1
and the upright shall *c* in your sight. 797 2
and that generations yet to come may *c* to praise you 827 21
Grant that we may *c* to grow 840 11
to ordain others to *c* Christ's ministry. 855 28

continued

works begun, *c*, and ended in thee, 832 3

continues

The Church is apostolic, because it *c* 854 25

contracted

whatsoever defilements he may have *c* 488 17

contrite

that is of a *c* and humble spirit, 41 2
and to revive the heart of the *c* 41 3
also with the one who has a *c* and humble spirit, 78 24
and to revive the heart of the *c*." 78 26
make in us new and *c* hearts, 166 3
make in us new and *c* hearts, 217 16
make in us new and *c* hearts, 264 4
a broken and *c* heart, 267 11
a broken and *c* heart, 657 17

control

so fill our imaginations, so *c* our wills, 832 25

conversion

having his wonderful *c* in remembrance, 187 11
having his wonderful *c* in remembrance, 239 1

convert

He shall *c* my soul, * 476 5

converts

a time in which *c* to the faith were prepared 265 2

copy

a *c* of the true one, but into heaven itself, 77 15

cords

The *c* of hell entangled me, * 602 16
The *c* of death entangled me; 759 5
Though the *c* of the wicked entangle me, * 768 9
has cut the *c* of the wicked. 784 8
and stretched out a net of *c*; * 796 11

corners

In his hand are all the *c* of the earth, * 44 16
In his hand are all the *c* of the earth, * 146 7
and our daughters like sculptured *c* of a palace. 801 2

cornerstone

Jesus Christ himself being the chief *c*: 178 20
Jesus Christ himself being the chief *c*: 230 14
has become the chief *c*. 762 16

corporate

together week by week for *c* worship; 856 14
What is *c* worship? 857 21
In *c* worship, we unite ourselves with others 857 22

corpses

He will heap high the *c*; * 754 1

corrupt

which *c* and destroy the creatures of God? 302 11
All are *c* and commit abominable acts; 598 13
All are *c* and commit abominable acts; 658 22
Can a *c* tribunal have any part with you, * 724 5
Where it is *c*, purify it; 816 11

corruption

There is *c* at her heart; * 661 4

couch

and flood my *c* with tears. 590 11

council

nor the sinner in the *c* of the righteous. 585 14
God takes his stand in the *c* of heaven; * 705 9
God is much to be feared in the *c* of the holy ones, * 714 7
and praise him in the *c* of the elders. 748 20

councilor

a patient teacher, and a wise *c*. 534 5

councils

and to take your share in the *c* of the Church. 531 7
share in the *c* of this diocese. 562 4

counsel

I will bless the Lord who giveth me *c*; 61 10
I will bless the Lord who gives me *c*; 115 10
take *c* for the nations of the earth, 207 10
take *c* for the nations of the earth, 258 9
take *c* for the nations of the earth; 278 26
you need help and *c*, 317 11
and spiritual *c* and advice; 317 14
and ask you for *c*, direction, and absolution. 447 12
your fellow presbyters and take *c* with them; 518 24
Happy are they who have not walked in the *c* 585 1
I will bless the LORD who gives me *c*; * 600 11
We took sweet *c* together, * 661 12
who lie in wait for my life take *c* together. 683 21
You will guide me by your *c*, * 688 25
They take secret *c* against your people * 706 7
and did not wait for his *c*. 742 25
and despised the *c* of the Most High. 747 4
be present with those who take *c* 818 2

counselor
a *c* in perplexity, a comfort in sorrow, 429 9
a *c* in perplexity, a comfort in sorrow, 444 11

counselors
and they are my *c*. 765 8

counsels
from whom all holy desires, all good *c*, 69 16

count
I can *c* all my bones. 611 14
but they are more than I can *c*. 640 15
c the number of her towers. 651 28
I *c* Egypt and Babylon among those who know me; * 711 17
If I were to *c* them, they would be more in number 795 12
to *c* them all, 795 14

counted
whosoever liveth is *c* dead before thee. 165 3
I am *c* among those who go down to the Pit; * 712 7

countenance
The Lord lift upon his *c* upon you 114 4
Lift up the light of your *c* upon us, 129 3
beholding by faith the light of his *c*, 165 16
beholding by faith the light of his *c*, 217 9
show us the light of his *c*, 281 6
lift up your *c* upon them; 467 6
which is the help of my *c*, and my God. 471 16
and our secret sins in the light of thy *c*. 472 26
the Lord lift up his *c* upon him 485 14
the Lord lift up his *c* upon him 501 15
Lift up the light of your *c* upon us, 588 12
who is the help of my *c*, and my God. 643 17
who is the help of my *c*, and my God. 644 13
who is the help of my *c*, and my God. 645 5
and the light of your *c*, 645 16
show us the light of his *c* 675 10
show the light of your *c*, 702 17
show the light of your *c*, 703 2
at the rebuke of your *c* let them perish. 703 19
show the light of your *c*, 703 25
and our secret sins in the light of your *c*. 718 16
Oil to make a cheerful *c*, * 736 7
Let your *c* shine upon your servant * 774 17
lift up thy *c* upon him, 831 16

countless
C throngs of angels stand before you 373 7
of *c* ways by which God uses material things 861 19

country
into that heavenly *c* where you live and reign 111 15
the founders of this *c* won liberty for themselves 190 18
and in our heavenly *c* 198 26
Grant to the people of our *c* a zeal for justice 207 3
the founders of this *c* won liberty for themselves 242 2
and in our heavenly *c* 250 11
Give to the people of our *c* a zeal for justice 258 3
and bring us to that heavenly *c* 369 10
and bring you safely to his heavenly *c*; 460 8
laid down their lives in the service of our *c*. 488 28
in the *c* where all is forgotten? 713 2
and shattered every tree in their *c*. 740 20
who have made this *c* strong. 839 5
the men and women of our *c* 839 22

counts
He *c* the number of the stars * 804 8

county
hold office in this State (Commonwealth, City, C, 822 18

courage
and *c* to die for this faith: 195 3
Give us *c*, we beseech thee, to take up our cross 201 9
that with wisdom, patience, and *c*, 209 12
and *c* to die for this faith: 247 1
Give us *c* to take up our cross 252 13
that with wisdom, patience, and *c*, 260 18
the *c* to will and to persevere, 308 6
and grant us strength and *c* to love and serve you 365 15
give them *c* and hope in their troubles, 389 4
Give him *c*, patience, and vision; 421 4
that my strength and *c* may not fail; 461 8
Give *c* and faith to those who are bereaved, 481 10
who are bereaved the spirit of faith and *c*, 505 11
Be strong and let your heart take *c*, * 624 21
and grant us both the *c* 818 5
give *c*, wisdom, and foresight to provide 822 2
give them *c* to face the perils which beset them; 823 5

courageous
For the brave and *c*, 837 14

course
that the *c* of this world may be peaceably governed 177 9
that the *c* of this world may be peaceably governed 229 5
having finished their *c* in faith, 488 6
have finished their *c* in thy faith 489 15
we may continue our *c* on earth, 493 22
having finished their *c* in faith, 503 16
have finished their *c* in your faith 504 13
it rejoices like a champion to run its *c*. 606 25
because I follow the *c* that is right. 638 10
They hold fast to their evil *c*; * 671 18
I will strive to follow a blameless *c*; 730 9
in the *c* of this busy life, give us times 825 1

courses
the planets in their *c*, 370 9
the moon and the stars you have set in their *c*, 592 14

court
For the Congress and the Supreme C 278 20
Kings' daughters stand among the ladies of the *c*; * 648 8

courts
and into his *c* with praise; * 45 18
go into his *c* with praise; * 83 5
and let your holy *c*, in radiant light, 286 8
and come into his *c* 343 11
offerings and come into his *c*. 376 7
In the *c* of the LORD's house,* 442 25
into the *c* of your heavenly dwelling place. 466 8
and draw to your *c* to dwell there! * 672 14
for the *c* of the Lord; 707 16
For one day in your *c* is better 708 10

shall flourish in the *c* of our God; 721 24
bring offerings and come into his *c*. 726 8
go into his *c* with praise; * 730 2
In the *c* of the LORD's house, * 760 12
in the *c* of the house of our God. 788 5
bless the *c* of justice 821 9
To the Judges and officers of our *c* 822 6

covenant

and to remember his holy *c*; 51 4
and to remember his holy *c*. 92 26
by the blood of the eternal *c*, 132 3
keep the *c* they have made, 163 4
hast established the new *c* of reconciliation: 172 2
hast established the new *c* of reconciliation: 172 21
keep the *c* they have made, 214 15
mystery established the new *c* of reconciliation: 223 16
mystery established the new *c* of reconciliation: 224 14
the sign of your *c* with all living things: 289 2
mystery established the new *c* of reconciliation: 290 15
and renew our own baptismal *c*. 303 18
the *c* you made with them 309 7
for this is my Blood of the New C, 342 7
This is my Blood of the new C, 363 3
This is my Blood of the new C, 368 16
and his Blood of the new C. 369 6
This is my Blood of the new C, 371 16
Again and again you called us into *c* with you, 373 24
This is my Blood of the new C, 374 21
This is my Blood of the new C, 403 10
This is my Blood of the new C, 405 8
and renew our own baptismal *c*. 416 5
the *c* you made with them 418 5
The bond and *c* of marriage 423 3
to live together in the *c* of marriage? 424 9
to live together in the *c* of marriage? 424 15
you have so consecrated the *c* of marriage 431 1
the blood of the everlasting *c*: 487 1
the blood of the everlasting *c*: 503 3
the sacraments of the New C; 517 9
a people to be heirs of the *c* 520 15
the sacraments of the New C, 532 10
the sacraments of the New C. 534 4
to those who keep his *c* and his testimonies. 615 9
and will show them his *c*. 615 17
nor have we betrayed your *c*. 646 21
those who have made a *c* with me 654 12
and take my *c* upon your lips; 655 13
he has broken his *c*. 661 29
Look upon your *c*; * 690 24
They did not keep the *c* of God, * 695 22
and they were not faithful to his *c*. 697 25
"I have made a *c* with my chosen one; * 713 21
and my *c* will stand firm for him. 715 23
I will not break my *c*, * 716 9
You have broken your *c* with your servant, * 716 19
On those who keep his *c* * 734 18
He has always been mindful of his *c*, * 738 15
The *c* he made with Abraham, * 738 17
an everlasting *c* for Israel, 738 20
He remembered his *c* with them * 745 15
he is ever mindful of his *c*. 754 15
he commanded his *c* for ever; * 754 23
If your children keep my *c* 786 23
community created by a *c* with God. 846 19
What is meant by a *c* with God? 846 20
A *c* is a relationship initiated by God, 846 21
What is the Old C? 846 23
The Old C is the one given by God 846 24
Where is this Old C to be found? 847 6
The *c* with the Hebrew people 847 7
when we are baptized into the New C 850 25
What is the New C? 850 26
The New C is the new relationship with God 850 27
What did the Messiah promise in the New C? 851 1
to recall our Baptismal C. 852 4
How is the Holy Spirit revealed in the Old C? 852 17
The Holy Spirit is revealed in the Old C 852 18
How is the Holy Spirit revealed in the New C? 852 20
books written by the people of the Old C, 853 11
The Church is the community of the New C. 854 4
they can share citizenship in the *c*, 858 26

cover

"Surely the darkness will *c* me, 62 5
"Surely the darkness will *c* me, 110 7
"Surely the darkness will *c* me, 116 1
He shall *c* you with his pinions, 130 3
Peradventure the darkness shall *c* me, * 475 13
I will take refuge under the *c* of your wings. 668 20
May the meadows *c* themselves with flocks, 673 15
C their faces with shame, O LORD, * 707 9
He shall *c* you with his pinions, 719 17
they shall not again *c* the earth. 735 20
"Surely the darkness will *c* me, * 794 20

covered

and shame has *c* my face; 646 16
and *c* us over with deep darkness. 646 25
like a dove whose wings are *c* with silver, 677 6
and shame has *c* my face. 680 2
let those who seek to do me evil be *c* with scorn 684 5
The mountains were *c* by its shadow * 703 7
for the early rains have *c* it with pools of water. 708 3
and have *c* him with shame. 717 4
You *c* it with the Deep as with a mantle; * 735 13
The waters *c* their oppressors; * 742 20
and *c* the company of Abiram. 743 6
you have *c* my head in the day of battle. 796 16

covering

He spread out a cloud for a *c* * 741 3

covers

For behold, darkness *c* the land; * 87 13
He *c* the heavens with clouds * 804 16

covert

They lie in wait, like a lion in a *c*; 595 11
You hide them in the *c* of your presence 624 8

covet

Thou shalt not *c*. 318 28
You shall not *c* anything that belongs 350 21

covetous
the *c* curse and revile the LORD. 594 24

cracks
repair the *c* in it, for it totters. 667 13

crafts
from the *c* and assaults of the devil; 148 15

crag
for you are my *c* and my stronghold; * 129 14
O LORD my stronghold, my *c*, and my haven. 602 8
for you are my *c* and my stronghold; * 622 13
you are my *c* and my stronghold. 683 6

craved
for he gave them what they *c*. 697 8

craving
demanding food for their *c*. 696 10
But they did not stop their *c*, * 697 9
A *c* seized them in the wilderness, * 742 26

create
C in us clean hearts, O God; 55 13
C in us clean hearts, O God; 68 5
C in us clean hearts, O God; 98 7
C in us clean hearts, O God; 122 7
C in me a clean heart, O God, * 137 3
who didst wonderfully *c*, 162 7
C and make in us new and contrite hearts, 166 3
who didst wonderfully *c*, 200 13
C and make in us new and contrite hearts, 217 15
C and make in us new and contrite hearts, 264 3
C in me a clean heart, O God, * 266 22
for that thou didst *c* heaven and earth, 341 13
C in me a clean heart, O God, * 657 1
to love, to *c*, to reason, 845 6

created
For you *c* everything that is, * 93 22
and by your will they were *c* 93 23
multitudes who have been *c* in thine image 206 18
who hast *c* us in thine own image: 209 1
who wonderfully *c*, 214 1
who wonderfully *c*, 252 1
multitudes who have been *c* in your image 257 14
who *c* us in your own image: 260 8
you have *c* us out of the dust 265 16
who wonderfully *c*, 288 5
you have *c* all things by the power 290 8
for thou hast *c* all things, 344 6
they were *c* and have their being. 344 7
By your will they were *c* and have their being. 370 11
you *c* them to rejoice 373 5
because you have *c* all things, 377 4
they were *c* and have their being. 377 5
you have *c* us male and female 425 7
In the Name of God the Father Almighty who *c* you; 464 22
For so did you ordain when you *c* me, 499 6
You send forth your Spirit, and they are *c*; * 737 14
Who *c* great lights, * 790 9
For you yourself *c* my inmost parts; * 794 25
for he commanded, and they were *c*. 806 4
who *c* all peoples in your image, 840 1
What does it mean to be *c* in the image of God? 845 4
because all are *c* in the image of God, 846 15
a community *c* by a covenant with God. 846 19

createdst
For so thou didst ordain when thou *c* me, 482 14

creates
a single loving God who *c*, sustains, and directs 846 8

creation
who after the *c* of the world didst rest 56 11
We bless thee for our *c*, 58 19
We bless thee for our *c*, 71 15
All *c* worships you. 95 18
who after the *c* of the world rested 99 6
We bless you for our *c*, 101 11
If anyone is in Christ he is a new *c*; 106 1
We bless you for our *c*, 125 9
For our waste and pollution of your *c*, 268 24
he who gives his light to all *c*, 287 27
Spirit moved in the beginning of *c*. 306 14
thanks for the *c* of the world, 316 11
rejoicing in thy whole *c*, 329 23
that he might make the whole *c* new. 349 5
which you have made known to us in *c*; 368 2
presenting to you, from your *c*, 369 2
the firstborn of all *c*, the head of the Church, 369 13
You made us the rulers of *c*. 370 14
and made the whole *c* new. 374 8
might make the whole *c* new. 381 20
a reverence for the earth as your own *c*, 388 12
of the riches of *c*, 390 22
For the just and proper use of your *c*; 392 7
marriage was established by God in *c*, 423 4
and your *c* glorified; 460 14
from the *c* you have graciously accepted 520 18
of the riches of *c*, 550 7
Spirit moved in the beginning of *c*. 570 6
of your *c* in the music we make 572 3
rejoicing in thy whole *c*, we may learn to serve 814 3
be opened to the goodness of your *c*; 825 4
probe the mysteries of your *c*, 827 14
you made us fellow workers in your *c*: 827 18
and to keep alive their joy in your *c*; 829 20
whose glory fills the whole *c*, 831 2
for the splendor of the whole *c*, 836 3
For the beauty and wonder of your *c*, 837 3
in our grateful enjoyment of your abundant *c*, 840 12
We are part of God's *c*, 845 2
and to live in harmony with *c* 845 6
and out of harmony with *c*? 845 9
with other people, and with all *c*. 848 31
with our neighbors, and with all *c*. 849 15
with our neighbors, and with all *c*. 852 29

creator
c of heaven and earth. 96 14
c of the changes of 113 1
c of heaven and earth. 120 10
C of heaven and earth, 148 1
C of heaven and earth: 170 1

O merciful *C*, whose hand is open wide 208 9
C of heaven and earth: 221 13
O merciful *C*, your hand is open wide 259 11
C of all the peoples of the earth 280 1
C of heaven and earth: 283 1
c of heaven and earth. 292 13
c of heaven and earth. 304 3
C of the light and source of life, 344 14
C of heaven and earth. 361 8
C of heaven and earth. 367 8
obedience to you, our *C*, 373 20
c of heaven and earth. 416 8
c and preserver of all life, 429 2
our *C* and our Redeemer. 450 7
the *c* and maker of mankind; 482 12
as into the hands of a faithful *C* 488 13
c of heaven and earth. 496 4
the *c* and maker of mankind; 499 4
the *c* and preserver of all mankind, 814 6
What do we learn about God as *c* 846 1
c of heaven and earth, 846 4
It means that the world belongs to its *c*; 846 10

creature

to satisfy the needs of every living *c*: 208 10
to satisfy the needs of every living *c*: 259 12
giving voice to every *c* under heaven, 373 10
and satisfy the needs of every living *c*. 802 20

creatures

a day of rest for all thy *c*: 56 13
a day of rest for all your *c*: 99 8
which corrupt and destroy the *c* of God? 302 11
and *c* of bread and wine; 335 20
All thy *c* praise thee, 348 8
we might rule and serve all your *c*. 373 21
All your *c* praise you, 381 2
and the *c* of the fields are in my sight. 655 2
the earth is full of your *c*. 736 27
c both small and great. 737 3
Who gives food to all *c*, * 791 19
the infinite complexity of living *c*: 827 13
kind to all the *c* of God; 848 10

creditor

Let the *c* seize everything he has; * 751 18

creed

The Apostles' *C* and the Nicene *C*. 851 25
What is the Apostles' *C*? 852 1
The Apostles' *C* is the ancient *c* of Baptism; 852 2
What is the Nicene *C*? 852 5
The Nicene *C* is the *c* of the universal Church 852 6
What, then, is the Athanasian *C*? 852 8
The Athanasian *C* is an ancient document 852 9

creeds

and summed up in the *c*. 851 21
What are the *c*? 851 22
The *c* are statements of our basic beliefs about God. 851 23
How many *c* does this Church use in its worship? 851 24
This Church uses two *c*: 851 25
How is the Church described in the *c*? 854 11

creeping

c things and winged birds; 806 14

cried

and *c* out to my God for help. 602 19
They *c* out to you and were delivered; * 610 10
O LORD my God, I *c* out to you, * 621 6
I *c* to you, O LORD; * 621 22
when I *c* out to you. 624 17
Then they *c* to the LORD in their trouble, * 746 12
Then they *c* to the LORD in their trouble, * 747 7
Then they *c* to the LORD in their trouble, * 748 11

cries

he shall deliver the poor who *c* out in distress, * 686 7

crime

if any of you know any impediment or *c* 527 4
if any of you know any impediment or *c* 539 4
and to abolish poverty and *c*. 839 18

crimes

who will find out our *c*? * 671 21

criminal

for our sake you were condemned as a *c*: 826 16

cringe

strangers will *c* before me. 605 30
your enemies *c* before you. 673 23
Those who hate the LORD would *c* before him, * 705 5

crippled

For the sick, the wounded, and the *c* 279 6

crooked

but with the *c* you are wily. 604 17
A *c* heart shall be far from me; * 730 15
As for those who turn aside to *c* ways, 782 3

crops

He gave their *c* to the caterpillar, * 698 19
with all manner of *c*; * 801 4

cross

and take up his *c*, and follow me." 38 25
walking in the way of the *c*, 56 9
on the hard wood of the *c* 58 9
and take up his *c* and follow me." 76 24
walking in the way of the *c*, 99 4
on the hard wood of the *c* 101 2
at this hour you hung upon the *c*, 107 8
at this hour you hung upon the *c*, 138 12
by thy *C* and Passion; 149 22
be strengthened to bear our *c*, 165 17
and to suffer death upon the *c*, 168 4
walking in the way of the *c*, 168 13
Grant us so to glory in the *c* of Christ, 168 19
and to suffer death upon the *c*; 169 17
Son to the death of the *c*, 170 8
may by his *c* and passion 188 17
Christ was lifted high upon the *c* 192 14
may have grace to take up our *c* 192 16
and shame of the *c* for our redemption: 201 8
to take up our *c* and follow 201 9

may be strengthened to bear our *c*, 217 10
and to suffer death upon the *c*, 219 15
walking in the way of the *c*, 220 4
Grant us so to glory in the *c* of Christ, 220 10
and to suffer death upon the *c*; 221 11
Son to the death of the *c*, 222 2
may by his *c* and passion 240 3
Christ was lifted high upon the *c* 244 2
may have grace to take up our *c* 244 4
and shame of the *c* for our redemption: 252 13
take up our *c* and follow him; 252 14
By the *c* and passion of your Son our Lord, 269 1
walking in the way of the *c*, 272 4
and to suffer death upon the *c*, 272 9
and to suffer death upon the *c*; 276 7
For those who are enemies of the *c* of Christ 279 25
We glory in your *c*, O Lord, 281 1
for by virtue of your *c* 281 3
We glory in your *c*, O Lord, 281 11
for by virtue of your *c* 281 13
because by your holy *c* you have redeemed the world. 281 16
because by your holy *c* you have redeemed the world. 282 2
who by thy *c* and precious blood hast redeemed us: 282 4
your passion, *c*, and death between your judgment 282 7
Son to the death of the *c*, 295 2
and humbled himself even to death on the *c*, 316 14
Christ to suffer death upon the *c* for our redemption; 334 11
and to suffer death upon the *c* for our redemption. 341 16
sins was lifted high upon the *c*, 346 15
He stretched out his arms upon the *c*, 362 15
he was lifted high upon the *c*, 379 11
and to make the way of the *c* 430 12
from sin and death by the *c* of your Son Jesus Christ. 450 10
by your *c* and precious blood 455 16
By your holy Incarnation, by your C and Passion, 463 5
set thy passion, *c*, and death, between thy judgment 489 24
becoming obedient even to death on the *c*. 545 4
and for his death upon the *c*, 573 14

crowd
For I have heard the whispering of the *c*; 623 16

crowded
For innumerable troubles have *c* upon me; 641 4

crowing
at even, or at midnight, or at the cock-*c*, 37 2

crown
may receive with him the *c* of life; 195 12
may receive with him the *c* of life; 195 19
may receive with him the *c* of life; 247 10
and receive the *c* of life 280 12
may receive the *c* of glory 347 21
receive the *c* of glory 380 15
and a *c* upon their foreheads. 430 19
to receive the *c* of life 481 26
and set a *c* of fine gold upon his head. 609 2
You *c* the year with your goodness, * 673 11
"I have set the *c* upon a warrior 715 4
defiled his *c*, and hurled it to the ground. 716 20
but as for him, his *c* will shine." 787 8

crowning
and the *c* of our years 579 4

crowns
and *c* you with mercy and loving-kindness; 733 16

crucified
was *c*, dead, and buried. 53 29
and entered not into glory before he was *c*: 56 8
was *c*, dead, and buried. 66 15
was *c*, died, and was buried. 96 19
and entered not into glory before he was *c*: 99 3
was *c*, died, and was buried. 120 15
and entered not into glory before he was *c*: 168 12
the *c* body of thy dear Son was laid in the tomb 170 2
and entered not into glory before he was *c*: 220 3
the *c* body of your dear Son was laid in the tomb 221 14
and entered not into glory before he was *c*: 272 3
the *c* body of your dear Son was laid in the tomb 283 2
was *c*, died, and was buried. 293 6
was *c*, died, and was buried. 304 9
Confess the faith of Christ *c*, 308 13
For our sake he was *c* under Pontius Pilate; 327 4
and was *c* also for us under Pontius Pilate; 328 5
For our sake he was *c* under Pontius Pilate; 358 20
was *c*, died, and was buried. 416 14
was *c*, died, and was buried. 496 9
For our sake he was *c* under Pontius Pilate; 519 23
For our sake he was *c* under Pontius Pilate; 530 14
For our sake he was *c* under Pontius Pilate; 542 14

cruelly
The proud have derided me *c*, * 767 15

cruelty
indifference to injustice and *c*, 268 18
deliver them and us from hatred, *c*, and revenge; 816 7
eliminate our *c* to these our neighbors. 826 11

crumble
that barriers which divide us may *c*, 823 20

crumbs
as to gather up the *c* under thy Table. 337 12
He scatters his hail like bread *c*; * 805 11

crush
You shall *c* them with an iron rod * 586 20
How long will you assail me to *c* me, 669 9
God shall *c* the heads of his enemies, * 677 25
he shall rescue the poor and *c* the oppressor. 685 16
I will *c* his foes before him * 715 12
They *c* your people, O LORD, * 723 3

crushed
and will save those whose spirits are *c*. 629 4
I am utterly numb and *c*; * 637 12
You *c* the heads of Leviathan * 690 12
You have *c* Rahab of the deep with a deadly wound; * 714 13
he has *c* me to the ground; * 799 2

cry
To thee all Angels *c* aloud, 52 25
To thee Cherubim and Seraphim continually do *c*: 52 27
C aloud, inhabitants of Zion, ring out your joy, * 86 13

And let our *c* come to you. 107 2
And let our *c* come to you. 133 8
Let the *c* of those in misery 279 15
Hearken unto my voice, O LORD, when I *c* unto thee; 477 28
Hearken to my *c* for help, my King and my God, * 588 19
he will not forget the *c* of the afflicted. 593 24
and the poor *c* out in misery, * 597 10
give heed to my *c*; * 600 23
my *c* of anguish came to his ears. 602 21
at your battle *c*, O LORD, 603 21
they *c* out, but there is none to help them; * 605 22
they *c* to the LORD, but he does not answer. 605 23
and are so far from my *c* 610 2
O my God, I *c* in the daytime, but you do not answer; 610 4
but when they *c* to him he hears them. 612 3
my Rock, do not be deaf to my *c*; * 619 5
Hear the voice of my prayer when I *c* out to you, * 619 8
and his ears are open to their *c*. 628 24
The righteous *c*, and the LORD hears them * 629 1
and give ear to my *c*; * 639 21
he stooped to me and heard my *c*. 640 2
shout to God with a *c* of joy. 650 7
Hear my *c*, O God, * 668 12
I will *c* aloud to God; * 693 1
I will *c* aloud, and he will hear me. 693 2
by day and night I *c* to you. 712 2
But as for me, O LORD, I *c* to you for help; * 713 4
LORD, hear my prayer, and let my *c* come before you; 731 1
Early in the morning I *c* out to you, * 775 20
Let my *c* come before you, O LORD; * 777 17
hear my voice when I *c* to you. 797 4
I *c* to the LORD with my voice; * 798 1
I *c* out to you, O LORD; * 798 9
Listen to my *c* for help, for I have been brought very low; * 798 12
he hears their *c* and helps them. 802 26
and for the young ravens when they *c*. 804 21

crying

sorrow nor *c*, but the fullness of joy 482 7
sorrow nor *c*, but the fullness of joy 498 18
all are *c*, "Glory!" 620 24
I have grown weary with my *c*; 679 13

cultures

women from different *c* 825 13
diversity of races and *c* in this world. 840 2

cup

and drinking of that C. 316 22
Likewise, after supper, he took the *c*; 335 3
The Blood of Christ, the *c* of salvation. 338 16
Likewise, after supper, he took the *c*; 342 5
After supper he took the *c* of wine; 363 1
The Blood of Christ, the *c* of salvation. 365 7
After supper he took the *c* of wine; 368 14
After supper, he took the *c* of wine, 371 14
After supper he took the *c* of wine; 374 19
the gifts you have given us, this bread and this *c*, 374 28
the bread of life and the *c* of salvation, 375 7
Grant that all who share this bread and *c* 375 9
After supper, he took the *c* of wine, gave thanks, 403 8
By means of this holy bread and *c*, 403 14
After supper he took the *c* of wine; 405 6
and drink this *c* may be filled with your life 405 17
who took bread (the *c*) 408 4
I will lift up the *c* of salvation * 442 21
and my *c* is running over. 443 14
and my *c* shall be full. 476 15
my *c* runneth over. 477 8
and bless the C. 562 6
O LORD, you are my portion and my *c*; * 600 7
and my *c* is running over. 613 10
For in the LORD's hand there is a *c*, 691 18
I will lift up the *c* of salvation * 759 25

cure

and bless the means made use of for his *c*. 459 9

curl

they *c* their lips and wag their heads, 610 15

curse

the covetous *c* and revile the LORD. 594 24
but in their hearts they *c*. 669 15
They may *c*, but you will bless; * 753 3

cursed

but those who are *c* by him shall be destroyed. 635 4
c are they who stray from your commandments! 765 2

cursing

Their mouth is full of *c*, deceit, and oppression; * 595 6
for the *c* and lies that they utter, * 666 22
He loved *c*, 752 4
He put on *c* like a garment, * 752 7

curtain

and spread out the heavens like a *c*. 735 5

custom

it became the *c* of the Church to prepare for them 264 12

cut

it is *c* down, dried up, and withered. 472 22
Oh, that the LORD would *c* off all smooth tongues, * 597 5
"I have been *c* off from the sight of your eyes." * 624 15
For evildoers shall be *c* off, * 634 1
and when the wicked are *c* off, you will see it. 636 5
the future of the wicked is *c* off. 636 14
Before they bear fruit, let them be *c* down 665 11
for they are *c* off from your hand. 712 12
You have *c* short the days of his youth * 717 3
has *c* the cords of the wicked. 784 8

cymbals

Praise him with resounding *c*; * 808 7
praise him with loud-clanging *c*. 808 8

D

daily

Give us this day our *d* bread. 54 19
Give us this day our *d* bread. 67 9
Give us this day our *d* bread. 97 9
Give us this day our *d* bread. 106 19
Give us this day our *d* bread. 121 9

Give us this day our *d* bread. 133 1
Give us this day our *d* bread. 153 11
purify our consciences by thy *d* visitation, 160 7
may *d* be renewed by thy Holy Spirit; 161 10
Grant us so to die *d* to sin, 170 10
and also *d* endeavor ourselves to follow 180 22
Purify our conscience, Almighty God, by your *d* visitation, 212 6
may *d* be renewed by your Holy Spirit; 213 4
Grant us so to die *d* to sin, 222 4
follow *d* in the blessed steps of his most holy life; 232 14
our dishonesty in *d* life and work, 268 11
Grant us so to die *d* to sin, 295 4
and *d* increase in your Holy Spirit 309 16
Give us this day our *d* bread. 311 6
Give us this day our *d* bread. 336 23
Give us this day our *d* bread. 364 6
For all people in their *d* life and work; 392 2
Give us this day our *d* bread. 398 17
and *d* increase in your Holy Spirit 418 14
Give us this day our *d* bread. 428 13
d increasing in bodily strength, 460 20
Give us this day our *d* bread. 464 9
while they *d* say unto me, 471 6
Give us this day our *d* bread. 485 25
Give us this day our *d* bread. 502 6
My humiliation is *d* before me, * 646 15
LORD, I have called upon you *d*; 712 21
They rejoice *d* in your Name; * 714 25
For our *d* food and drink, 837 9
Church's *d* worship to recall our Baptismal Covenant. 852 3

damage
All day long they *d* my cause; * 662 22

damnation
and from everlasting *d*, 148 16

dance
Let them praise his Name in the *d*; * 807 6
Praise him with timbrel and *d*; * 808 5

dancers
The singers and the *d* will say, * 711 24

dances
Therefore my heart *d* for joy, * 619 26

dancing
You have turned my wailing into *d*; * 622 3

danger
neither run into any kind of *d*; 57 11
preserve all who are in *d* 151 17
comfort all who are in *d*, 151 29
For prisoners and captives, and those in mortal *d* 279 10
so is the *d* great, if we receive it improperly, 316 24
For deliverance from all *d*, violence, oppression, 385 1
refugees, prisoners, and all who are in *d*; 390 25
For all who are in *d*, sorrow, or any kind 392 9
guard him from all *d*, 459 4
refugees, prisoners, and all who are in *d*; 550 12
protect them from every *d*; 831 4

dangers
defend us from all perils and *d* 70 2
defend us from all perils and *d* 111 2
defend us from all perils and *d* 123 22
defend us from all perils and *d* 133 11
great *d* we are in by our unhappy divisions; 818 16
Defend them from all *d* of soul and body; 830 22

dare
things which for our unworthiness we *d* not, 179 19
things which for our unworthiness we *d* not, 231 13
good things which we *d* not, 395 1

dark
"darkness is not *d* to thee, 62 6
O shining light and enfolding *d*. 89 2
"darkness is not *d* to you, 110 8
"darkness is not *d* to you, 116 2
he made *d* waters and thick clouds his pavilion. 603 12
Let their way be *d* and slippery, * 630 1
the *d* places of the earth are haunts of violence. 690 25
in *d* places, and in the abyss. 712 14
Will your wonders be known in the *d*? * 713 1
He sent darkness, and it grew *d*; * 740 9
Darkness is not *d* to you; 794 22
he has made me live in *d* places 799 3

darkened
Let their eyes be *d*, that they may not see, * 681 10

darkeneth
and *d* the day into night; 62 2

darkens
and *d* the day into night; 115 14

darkness
O ye light and *d*, bless ye the Lord; 48 14
To give light to them that sit in *d* 51 18
turneth deep *d* into the morning, 62 2
"Surely the *d* will cover me, 62 5
d is not dark to thee, 62 6
d and light to thee are both alike. 62 7
he that followeth me shall not walk in *d*, 62 10
Lighten our *d*, we beseech thee, 70 1
For behold, *d* covers the land; * 87 13
To shine on those who dwell in *d* 93 7
"Out of *d* let light shine," 110 3
"Surely the *d* will cover me, 110 7
d is not dark to you, 110 8
d and light to you are both alike. 110 9
Dispel the *d* of our hearts, 110 25
Lighten our *d*, we beseech thee, 111 1
turns deep *d* into the morning, 115 14
"Surely the *d* will cover me, 116 1
d is not dark to you, 116 2
d and light to you are both alike. 116 3
whoever follows me will not walk in *d*, 116 6
Be our light in the *d*, 123 21
Of the plague that stalks in the *d*, * 130 8
Be our light in the *d*, 133 10
"Out of *d* let light shine," 139 12
cast away the works of *d*, 159 2
who hast called us out of *d* 196 18

cast away the works of *d*, 211 2
who called us out of *d* 248 4
for *d* has been vanquished by our eternal King. 286 6
drive away all *d*. 287 25
Peradventure the *d* shall cover me, * 475 13
Yea, the *d* is no *d* with thee, 475 15
d and light to thee are both alike. 475 17
giving light to those who sat in *d* 483 17
giving light to those who sat in *d* 500 6
He wrapped *d* about him; * 603 11
you make my *d* bright. 604 21
and covered us over with deep *d*. 646 25
they go about in *d*; * 705 18
and *d* is my only companion. 713 16
Of the plague that stalks in the *d*, * 719 22
Clouds and *d* are round about him, * 726 25
You make *d* that it may be night, * 736 17
He sent *d*, and it grew dark; * 740 9
Some sat in *d* and deep gloom, * 747 1
He led them out of *d* and deep gloom * 747 9
Light shines in the *d* for the upright; * 755 11
"Surely the *d* will cover me, * 794 20
d is not dark to you; 794 22
d and light to you are both alike. 794 24
light riseth up in *d* for the godly: 832 7
where there is *d*, light; 833 8

dash

lest you *d* your foot against a stone. 130 22
lest you *d* your foot against a stone. 720 10

dashes

and *d* them against the rock! 792 23

Dathan

The earth opened and swallowed *D* * 743 5

daughter

to be their son (*d*) 440 6
may you receive as your own son (*d*). 441 6
"Hear, O *d*; consider and listen closely; * 648 11
O *D* of Babylon, doomed to destruction, * 792 19

daughters

thou hast received us as thy sons and *d*, 348 21
everlasting heritage as your sons and *d*; 369 12
you have received us as your sons and *d*, 381 14
we might become your sons and *d*. 573 11
Kings' *d* stand among the ladies of the court; * 648 8
and their *d* to evil spirits. 744 22
the blood of their sons and *d*, * 744 24
and our *d* like sculptured corners of a palace. 801 2

David

D a Savior, which is Christ the Lord. 37 10
in the house of his servant *D*, 50 25
D, a Savior, who is Christ the Lord. 75 10
born of the house of his servant *D*. 92 21
O Son of *D*, have mercy upon us. 155 2
from the family of thy servant *D* 188 8
from the family of your servant *D* 239 17
to *D* and his descendants for ever. 606 14
He chose *D* his servant, * 700 19
I have sworn an oath to *D* my servant: 713 22
I have found *D* my servant; * 715 6
"I will not lie to *D*. 716 12
which you promised *D* in your faithfulness? 717 13
the thrones of the house of *D*. 780 6
LORD, remember *D*, * 785 19
For your servant *D*'s sake, * 786 17
The LORD has sworn an oath to *D*; * 786 19
There will I make the horn of *D* flourish; * 787 5
and have rescued *D* your servant. 800 22

dawn

the *d* from on high shall break upon us, 93 6
I myself will waken the *d*. 664 14
you make the *d* and the dusk to sing for joy. 673 3
I myself will waken the *d*. 749 21

dawned

and the glory of the Lord has *d* upon you. 87 12

dawning

and kings to the brightness of your *d*. 87 18

day

For unto you is born this *d* 37 9
This is the *d* which the Lord hath made; 39 9
The third *d* he rose again from the dead. 54 1
Give us this *d* our daily bread. 54 19
D by *d* we magnify thee; 55 17
to keep us this *d* without sin; 55 19
Grant us this *d* such blessing 56 3
sanctify a *d* of rest for all thy creatures: 56 12
who dividest the *d* from the night 56 18
having done thy will with cheerfulness while it was *d*, 56 22
who hast safely brought us to the beginning of this *d*: 57 8
grant that this *d* we fall into no sin, 57 10
Thine is the *d*, O God, thine also the night; 61 7
and darkeneth the *d* into night; 62 2
the night is as bright as the *d*; 62 7
The third *d* he rose again from the dead. 66 17
Give us this *d* our daily bread. 67 9
this *d* given thanks for his resurrection, 69 3
Shed forth thine unending *d* upon us who watch 69 13
We thank thee for the timely blessings of the *d*, 70 6
for evening is at hand and the *d* is past; 70 10
for to you is born this *d* 75 9
On this *d* the Lord has acted; 77 8
And on that *d* you shall say, * 86 7
by *d* or night they will never be shut. 87 20
The sun will no more be your light by *d*; * 87 27
From this *d* all generations will call me blessed: * 92 1
On the third *d* he rose again. 96 21
Give us this *d* our daily bread. 97 9
D by *d* we bless you; 98 11
Give us this *d* such blessing 98 21
and sanctified a *d* of rest 99 7
whose light divides the *d* from the night 99 13
having done your will with cheerfulness during the *d*, 99 17
you have brought us in safety to this new *d*: 100 2
So that the sun shall not strike you by *d*, * 104 23
Give us this *d* our daily bread. 106 19
the night is as bright as the *d*; 110 9
the evening, the morning, and the noonday one *d*; 110 24
a pillar of cloud by *d* 111 9

creator of the changes of *d* and night,	113	2
As you have protected us in the *d* that is past,	113	5
Yours is the *d*, O God, yours also the night;	115	7
and darkens the *d* into night;	115	14
the night is as bright as the *d*;	116	3
From this *d* all generations will call me blessed: *	119	7
On the third *d* he rose again.	120	17
Give us this *d* our daily bread.	121	9
this *d* given thanks for his resurrection,	123	3
Shed forth your unending *d* upon us	123	12
thank you for the blessings of the *d* that is past,	124	3
for evening is at hand and the *d* is past;	124	7
nor of the arrow that flies by *d*;	130	7
nor of the sickness that lays waste at mid-*d*.	130	9
Give us this *d* our daily bread.	133	1
sing your glory at the close of this *d*,	134	3
Watch over those, both night and *d*,	134	12
you have brought us in safety to this new *d*:	137	15
for evening is at hand and the *d* is past;	139	16
and as in the *d* of temptation in the wilderness;	146	18
and in the *d* of judgment,	149	27
Give us this *d* our daily bread.	153	11
that in the last *d*, when he shall come again	159	4
await with him the coming of the third *d*,	170	4
celebrate with joy the *d* of the Lord's resurrection,	171	1
who on this *d* didst open the way	175	8
who on this *d* didst teach the hearts	175	15
We remember this *d*, O God, the slaughter	186	13
this *d* presented in the temple,	187	17
we remember before thee this *d* thy servant	191	7
and especially on this *d* for Simon and Jude;	194	2
we remember this *d* before thee thy faithful servant	202	9
remembering the account that we must one *d* give,	208	12
that in the last *d*, when he shall come again	211	4
and to be born [this *d*] of a pure virgin:	213	2
await with him the coming of the third *d*,	221	16
celebrate with joy the *d* of the Lord's resurrection,	222	18
on this *d* you opened the way	227	1
who on this *d* taught the hearts of your faithful	227	8
this *d* presented in the temple,	239	7
and especially on this *d* for Simon and Jude;	245	11
remembering the account that we must one *d* give,	259	14
please him which we do on this *d*,	269	12
On this *d* he entered the holy city of Jerusalem in	271	7
receive the crown of life in the *d* of resurrection.	280	13
await with him the coming of the third *d*,	283	4
deeds of old shine forth even to our own *d*,	289	13
you led your ancient people by a pillar of cloud by *d*	290	2
On the third *d* he rose again.	293	8
On the third *d* he rose again.	304	11
Give us this *d* our daily bread.	311	6
Remember that thou keep holy the Sabbath *d*.	318	10
On the third *d* he rose again	327	6
and the third *d* he rose again	328	7
Give us this *d* our daily bread.	336	23
who on the first *d* of the week	345	1
the Holy Ghost came down [on this *d*]	347	8
Remember the Sabbath *d* and keep it holy.	350	9
On the third *d* he rose again	358	22
and at the last *d* bring us with all your saints	363	17
Give us this *d* our daily bread.	364	6
as we await the *d* of his coming.	371	22
angels stand before you to serve you night and *d*;	373	8
who on the first *d* of the week	377	14
the Holy Spirit came down [on this *d*]	380	2
we may have grace to glorify Christ in our own *d*.	386	17
and be found without fault at the *d* of your coming,	389	16
Give us this *d* our daily bread.	398	17
On the third *d* he rose again.	416	16
have and to hold from this *d* forward,	427	2
to have and to hold from this *d* forward,	427	6
Give us this *d* our daily bread.	428	13
to have and to hold from this *d* forward,	436	2
to hold from this *d* forward,	436	7
From this *d* all generations will call me blessed:*	441	15
This is another *d*, O Lord.	461	19
Give us this *d* our daily bread.	464	9
May your rest be this *d* in peace,	464	25
he shall stand at the latter *d* upon the earth;	469	5
My tears have been my meat *d* and night, *	471	5
among such as keep holy-*d*.	471	11
So that the sun shall not burn thee by *d*, *	473	19
then shall my night be turned to *d*.	475	14
but the night is as clear as *d*; *	475	16
Give us this *d* our daily bread.	485	25
be made perfect unto the *d* of Jesus Christ.	486	12
that at the *d* of the general resurrection,	487	16
we remember before you this *d* our brother (sister)	493	16
On the third *d* he rose again.	496	11
Give us this *d* our daily bread.	502	6
On the third *d* he rose again	519	25
serving before you *d* and night	521	11
On the third *d* he rose again	530	16
On the third *d* he rose again	542	16
and be found without fault at the *D* of your Coming,	548	12
refreshing us *d* by *d* with the bread of life.	578	17
and they meditate on his law *d* and night.	585	6
this *d* have I begotten you.	586	16
God sits in judgment every *d*.	591	21
and grief in my heart, *d* after *d*? *	598	2
They confronted me in the *d* of my disaster; *	603	28
One *d* tells its tale to another, *	606	17
May the LORD answer you in the *d* of trouble, *	608	1
in you have I trusted all the *d* long.	614	23
For in the *d* of trouble he shall keep me safe	618	1
because of my groaning all *d* long.	625	4
For your hand was heavy upon me *d* and night; *	625	5
and of your praise all the *d* long.	632	2
because he sees that their *d* will come.	634	10
I go about in mourning all the *d* long.	637	9
and plot treachery all the *d* long.	637	22
My tears have been my food *d* and night, *	643	5
while all *d* long they say to me,	643	6
among those who keep holy-*d*.	643	12
All *d* long they mock me *	644	7
Every *d* we gloried in God, *	646	1
Indeed, for your sake we are killed all the *d* long; *	647	1
God shall help her at the break of *d*.	649	14
Call upon me in the *d* of trouble; *	655	9
against the godly all *d* long?	657	24
D and night the watchmen make their rounds	661	1
all *d* long they assault and oppress me.	662	14
They hound me all the *d* long; *	662	15
All *d* long they damage my cause; *	662	22

a refuge in the *d* of my trouble. 667 6
and *d* by *d* I will fulfill my vows. 669 4
Blessed be the Lord *d* by *d*, * 677 21
and your glory all the *d* long. 683 17
and saving deeds all *d* long; * 684 10
and to this *d* I tell of your wonderful works. 684 15
My tongue will proclaim your righteousness all *d* 685 6
and may they bless him all the *d* long. 686 16
I have been afflicted all *d* long, * 688 5
Yours is the *d*, yours also the night; * 690 16
remember how fools revile you all *d* long. 690 29
In the *d* of my trouble I sought the Lord; * 693 3
turned back in the *d* of battle; 695 21
He led them with a cloud by *d*, * 696 1
in the *d* when he ransomed them from the enemy; 698 12
and at the full moon, the *d* of our feast. 704 6
For one *d* in your courts is better than 708 10
I call upon you all the *d* long. 710 4
by *d* and night I cry to you. 712 2
They surround me all *d* long like a flood; * 713 13
nor of the arrow that flies by *d*; 719 21
nor of the sickness that lays waste at mid-*d*. 719 23
at Meribah, and on that *d* at Massah, 725 8
proclaim the good news of his salvation from *d* to *d*. 725 20
hide not your face from me in the *d* of my trouble. 731 2
My enemies revile me all *d* long, * 731 15
Princely state has been yours from the *d* of your birth; 753 16
will smite kings in the *d* of his wrath; * 753 22
On this *d* the LORD has acted; * 762 19
By your decree these continue to this *d*, * 771 1
all the *d* long it is in my mind. 771 14
Seven times a *d* do I praise you, * 777 7
So that the sun shall not strike you by *d*, * 779 11
The sun to rule the *d*, * 790 11
Remember the *d* of Jerusalem, O LORD, 792 15
the night is as bright as the *d*; * 794 23
they were fashioned *d* by *d*, 795 8
and stir up strife all *d* long. 796 4
you have covered my head in the *d* of battle. 796 16
Every *d* will I bless you * 801 14
and in that *d* their thoughts perish. 803 10
and in the *d* of trouble, suffer not our trust 820 14
Defend them *d* by *d* with your heavenly grace; 823 3
remembering the account which we must one *d* give, 827 4
support us all the *d* long, 833 14
we have heard this *d* with our outward ears, 834 19
on the first *d* of the week, you conquered sin, 835 2
consummation of your kingdom on the last great *D*; 835 7
And hasten the *d* when all our people, 839 18
who in the *d* of decision ventured much 839 22

daylight

d fades, with the brightness of the vesper light; 110 13

days

O ye nights and *d*, bless ye the Lord; * 48 13
all the *d* of our life. 51 10
that the *d* to come may be spent in thy favor; 56 3
in holiness and righteousness all our *d*; 59 8
in holiness and righteousness all our *d*; 72 5
Glorify the Lord, O nights and *d*, * 89 1
all the *d* of my life. 91 24
all the *d* of our life. 92 31
in holiness and righteousness all our *d*; 101 21
in holiness and righteousness all our *d*; 125 19
the noble works that thou didst in their *d*, 154 7
may live in righteousness and holiness all our *d*; 203 8
may live in righteousness and holiness all our *d*; 254 10
the *d* of our Lord's passion and resurrection, 264 11
and sustain him all the *d* of his life. 309 13
and righteousness all the *d* of their life. 329 16
For in these last *d* you sent him to be incarnate 368 5
and sustain him all the *d* of his life. 418 11
all the *d* of their life. 429 13
all the *d* of my life,* 443 16
all the *d* of their life; 444 14
For when thou art angry all our *d* are gone; * 473 1
The *d* of our age are threescore years and ten; 473 3
So teach us to number our *d*, * 473 7
all the *d* of my life; * 476 17
shall follow me all the *d* of my life, 477 9
all the *d* of my life, 477 18
and righteousness all our *d*. 481 3
that they may have strength to meet the *d* ahead 481 11
whose *d* are without end, 489 3
lead us in holiness and righteousness all our *d*; 489 6
and strength to meet the *d* to come; 494 11
whose *d* are without end, 504 1
lead us in holiness and righteousness all our *d*; 504 4
have strength to meet the *d* to come 505 11
and in the *d* to come; 572 11
length of *d*, for ever and ever. 609 4
all the *d* of my life, 613 11
all the *d* of my life; 617 20
and in *d* of famine they shall have enough. 634 23
let me know my end and the number of my *d*, * 639 1
You have given me a mere handful of *d*, 639 3
the deeds you did in their *d*, 645 8
in the *d* of old. 645 9
Why should I be afraid in evil *d*, * 652 13
They shall not live out half their *d*, * 662 10
Add length of *d* to the king's life; * 668 24
I consider the *d* of old; * 693 10
So he brought their *d* to an end like a breath * 697 16
and his throne as the *d* of heaven." 715 25
You have cut short the *d* of his youth * 717 3
When you are angry, all our *d* are gone: * 718 17
So teach us to number our *d* * 718 25
so shall we rejoice and be glad all the *d* of our life. 719 2
by the measure of the *d* that you afflicted us * 719 3
To give them rest in evil *d*, * 723 19
For my *d* drift away like smoke, * 731 5
My *d* pass away like a shadow, * 731 21
he has shortened the number of my *d*; 732 23
do not take me away in the midst of my *d*; * 732 25
Our *d* are like the grass; * 734 11
Let his *d* be few, * 751 12
all the *d* of your life. 783 22
our *d* are like a passing shadow. 800 9
all the *d* of his life; 830 11
Watch over thy child, O Lord, as his *d* increase; 830 13
abide all the *d* of his life; 830 17
Redeem all our *d* by this victory; 835 4
obedient walking before thee all our *d*; 840 22

dayspring
whereby the *d* from on high hath visited us; 51 17

daytime
I cry in the *d*, but you do not answer; * 610 4
The LORD grants his loving-kindness in the *d*; * 643 23

deacon
to be ordained a *d* 538 3
Is it your will that N. be ordained a *d*? 539 7
As a *d* in the Church, you are to study 543 7
to the life and work of a *d*? 543 20
and make him a *d* in your Church. 545 11
may this *d* share in Christ's service, 545 16
For chosen bishop (priest, *d*) in your Church, 549 1
What is the ministry of a *d*? 856 7
The ministry of a *d* is to represent Christ 856 8

deacons
illumine all bishops, priests, and *d*, 150 6
We pray for all bishops, priests, and *d*; 387 6
to ordain priests and *d* 517 10
guide and strengthen the *d* 518 25
for ordination to the sacred order of *d*. 539 3
calling this your servant to the order of *d*. 545 8
and for all bishops, priests, and *d*, 548 21
lay persons, bishops, priests, and *d*. 855 13
being made bishops, priests, and *d*, 861 1

dead
Christ being raised from the *d* dieth no more; * 46 7
yourselves to be *d* indeed unto sin, * 46 11
Christ is risen from the *d*, * 46 13
by man came also the resurrection of the *d*. 46 16
was crucified, *d*, and buried. 53 29
The third day he rose again from the *d*. 54 1
he shall come to judge the quick and the *d*. 54 4
was crucified, *d*, and buried. 66 15
The third day he rose again from the *d*. 66 17
he shall come to judge the quick and the *d*. 66 20
and the repose of the *d*: 70 5
Christ being raised from the *d* 83 15
So also consider yourselves *d* to sin, * 83 19
Christ has been raised from the *d*, * 83 21
by a man has come also the resurrection of the *d*. 83 24
He descended to the *d*. 96 20
to judge the living and the *d*. 96 24
He descended to the *d*. 120 16
to judge the living and the *d*. 120 20
and the repose of the *d*: We 124 2
who brought again from the *d* our Lord Jesus, 132 1
the resurrection of Jesus Christ from the *d*. 137 13
to judge both the quick and the *d*, 159 6
whosoever liveth is counted *d* before thee. 165 3
to judge both the living and the *d*, 211 6
whoever lives is accounted *d* before you. 216 17
pardon and rest to the *d*; 282 9
He descended to the *d*. 293 7
to judge the living and the *d*. 293 11
He descended to the *d*. 304 10
to judge the living and the *d*. 304 14
to judge the living and the *d*, 327 10
We look for the resurrection of the *d*, 327 18
to judge both the quick and the *d*; 328 11
the resurrection of the *d*, 328 20
who rose victorious from the *d*, 349 7
to judge the living and the *d*, 359 1
We look for the resurrection of the *d*, 359 9
his descent among the *d*, 374 25
who rose victorious from the *d*, 382 2
He descended to the *d*. 416 15
to judge the living and the *d*. 416 19
and the living to the *d*, 430 6
you were *d*, and are now alive 451 18
though he were *d*, yet shall he live; 469 2
Blessed are the *d* who die in the Lord; 469 14
Christ is risen from the *d*, 483 14
He that raised up Jesus from the *d* 485 1
Blessed are the *d* who die in the Lord: 486 8
who brought again from the *d* our Lord 486 21
in whose hands are the living and the *d*: 488 27
pardon and rest to the *d*, 489 26
He descended to the *d*. 496 10
to judge the living and the *d*. 496 14
You raised the *d* to life; 497 10
Christ is risen from the *d*, 500 3
He who raised Jesus Christ from the *d* 501 3
who brought again from the *d* our Lord 503 1
to judge the living and the *d*, 520 1
We look for the resurrection of the *d*, 520 9
to judge the living and the *d*, 530 20
We look for the resurrection of the *d*, 530 28
to judge the living and the *d*, 542 20
We look for the resurrection of the *d*, 542 28
and the remembrance of the *d*, 567 11
We praise you for raising him from the *d*, 573 16
You brought me up, O LORD, from the *d*; * 621 8
I am forgotten like a *d* man, out of mind; * 623 14
and the land of the *d* shall be their home. 653 12
Lost among the *d*, * 712 9
Do you work wonders for the *d*? * 712 23
and ate sacrifices offered to the *d*. 744 4
The *d* do not praise the LORD, * 758 23
like those who are long *d*. 799 4
first-born of many from the *d*. 838 20
he descended to the *d*? 850 14
Why do we pray for the *d*? 862 8
and judge the living and the *d*. 862 15
the living and the *d*, 862 22

deadly
and from the *d* pestilence. 130 2
from my *d* enemies who surround me. 601 17
you saved me from my *d* foe. 606 9
"A *d* thing," they say, "has fastened on him; * 642 15
crushed Rahab of the deep with a *d* wound; * 714 13
and from the *d* pestilence. 719 16

deaf
We have been *d* to your call to serve, 267 23
my Rock, do not be *d* to my cry; * 619 5
But I am like the *d* who do not hear, * 637 23
they are like the *d* adder which stops its ears, 665 2

deal

D graciously, we pray thee, with all those who mourn, 489 31
D graciously with NN. in their grief. 494 8
D graciously, we pray, with all who mourn; 505 17
and your hands *d* out violence in the land. 664 24
oh, *d* with me according to your Name; * 752 16
D bountifully with your servant, * 764 17
D with your servant according to your loving-kindness * 773 21

dealing

The LORD rewarded me because of my righteous *d*; * 604 3
the Lord rewarded me according to my righteous *d*, * 604 12
and your just *d* as the noonday. 633 16

dealings

To be honest and fair in our *d*; 848 12

dealt

I will sing to the LORD, for he has *d* with me richly; * 598 10
He has not *d* with us according to our sins, * 734 1
and *d* unjustly with his servants. 740 4
we have done wrong and *d* wickedly. 742 10
O LORD, you have *d* graciously with your servant, * 768 17
when you have *d* bountifully with me, 798 16

dear

whose most *d* Son went not up to joy 56 6
D friends in Christ, 62 11
Keep watch, *d* Lord, with those who work, 71 1
whose most *d* Son went not up to joy 99 1
D friends in Christ, 116 7
Keep watch, *d* Lord, with those who work, 124 17
Keep watch, *d* Lord, with those who work, 134 6
whose most *d* Son went not up to joy 168 10
whose *d* Son, on the night before he suffered, 169 7
thy *d* Son was laid in the tomb 170 2
whose most *d* Son went not up to joy 220 1
whose *d* Son, on the night before he suffered, 221 1
your *d* Son was laid in the tomb 221 14
D People of God: 264 10
whose most *d* Son went not up to joy 272 1
whose *d* Son, on the night before he suffered, 274 1
D People of God: 277 2
your *d* Son was laid in the tomb 283 2
D friends in Christ: 285 1
Through the Paschal mystery, *d* friends, 292 1
so to eat the flesh of thy *d* Son Jesus Christ, 337 14
whose *d* Son, on the night before he suffered, 397 13
D Friends: 440 1
D Friends: 440 8
Hear us, we pray, for your *d* Name's sake. 459 6
D Friends: 465 9
right *d* in the sight of the LORD 479 19
our *d* brother, as into the hands of a faithful Creator 488 13
D friends in Christ, 527 1
D friends in Christ, 539 1
like a moth you eat away all that is *d* to us; * 639 18
that those who are *d* to you may be delivered. 667 19
and *d* shall their blood be in his sight. 686 12
How *d* to me is your dwelling, O LORD of hosts! * 707 15
So that those who are *d* to you may be delivered, * 750 5
and your servant holds it *d*. 775 6
we entrust all who are *d* to us 831 7
for the sake of your *d* Son, 841 6

dearer

The law of your mouth is *d* to me * 769 7

dearly

D beloved, we have come together 41 5
D beloved, we have come together 79 1
according to the institution of thy *d* beloved Son 335 9
the Body and Blood of thy *d*-beloved Son 342 19
Through thy *d* beloved Son 347 1
Through your *d* beloved Son 379 20
D beloved: 423 1

death

d hath no more dominion over him. 46 8
For since by man came *d*, * 46 15
and in the shadow of *d*, * 51 19
When thou hadst overcome the sharpness of *d*, 53 15
and turnest the shadow of *d* into the morning: 56 19
Christ triumphed over the powers of *d* 69 2
who by thy *d* didst take away the sting of *d*: 69 7
d no longer has dominion over him. 83 16
The *d* that he died, he died to sin, once for all; * 83 17
For since by a man came *d*, * 83 23
who dwell in darkness and the shadow of *d*, * 93 8
You overcame the sting of *d* 96 5
and turns the shadow of *d* into the morning: 99 14
Christ triumphed over the powers of *d* 123 2
by your *d* you took away the sting of *d*: 123 6
by thy precious *D* and Burial; 149 23
the hour of *d*, and in the day of judgment, 149 27
and to suffer *d* upon the cross, 168 3
shameful *d* to be unto us the means of life: 168 18
and to suffer *d* upon the cross; 169 17
only-begotten Son to the *d* of the cross, 170 8
Christ hast overcome *d* 170 22
may be raised from the *d* of sin 171 1
Christ didst destroy *d* and bring life 171 11
thou hast delivered us from the dominion of sin and *d* 172 15
as by his *d* he hath recalled us to life, 172 17
in life and *d* the Name of our Lord Jesus Christ; 189 8
was faithful even unto *d*: 195 10
who have been baptized into the *d* and resurrection 201 13
by our baptism into the *d* and resurrection 203 5
by our baptism into the *d* and resurrection 203 13
and to suffer *d* upon the cross, 219 15
shameful *d* to be for us the means of life: 220 9
and to suffer *d* upon the cross; 221 11
Son to the *d* of the cross, 222 2
Christ overcame *d* 222 16
may be raised from the *d* of sin 222 18
Christ destroyed *d* and brought life 223 5
delivered us from the dominion of sin and *d* 224 8
as by his *d* he has recalled us to life, 224 9
may glorify in life and *d* 240 15
and was faithful even to *d*: 247 7
baptized into the *d* and resurrection 253 1
by our baptism into the *d* and resurrection 254 7
by our baptism into the *d* and resurrection 254 14
Deliver me from *d*, O God, * 267 3

who desires not the *d* of sinners, 269 4
and to suffer *d* upon the cross, 272 9
and to suffer *d* upon the cross; 276 7
be delivered from the power of sin and *d*, 277 5
set your passion, cross, and *d* 282 7
now and in the hour of our *d*. 282 8
Jesus passed over from *d* to life, 285 2
in his victory over *d*. 285 6
Christ broke the bonds of *d* and hell, 287 12
and out of *d* into life: 291 6
with Christ by Baptism into his *d*, 292 2
to the *d* of the cross, 295 2
from the way of sin and *d*. 305 15
all who are baptized into the *d* 306 5
through his *d* and resurrection, 306 18
In it we are buried with Christ in his *d*. 306 21
we thank you that by the *d* and resurrection 309 3
remembrance of the sacrifice of his *d*, 316 4
and humbled himself even to *d* on the cross, 316 14
he suffered *d* and was buried. 327 5
Christ to suffer *d* upon the cross for our redemption; 334 11
his precious *d* and sacrifice, 334 16
in remembrance his blessed passion and precious *d*, 335 14
in remembrance of his *d* and passion, 335 22
by the merits and *d* of thy Son 335 27
and to suffer *d* upon the cross 341 15
memory of that his precious *d* and sacrifice, 341 19
in remembrance his blessed passion and precious *d*, 342 14
overcame *d* and the grave, 345 2
sin and *d*, 345 8
who by his suffering and *d* 346 16
who by his *d* hath destroyed *d*, 346 22
and when our mortal body doth lie in *d*, 349 10
he suffered *d* and was buried. 358 21
become subject to evil and *d*, 362 11
On the night he was handed over to suffering and *d*, 362 18
Recalling his *d*, resurrection, and ascension, 363 11
out of *d* into life. 368 9
We remember his *d*, 368 20
We celebrate his *d* and resurrection, 371 21
you did not abandon us to the power of *d*. 373 22
fulfill your purpose he gave himself up to *d*; 374 6
from the grave, destroyed *d*, 374 7
Recalling Christ's *d* and his descent among the dead, 374 25
who on the first day of the week overcame *d* 377 15
to redeem us from sin and *d*, 378 5
by his suffering and *d*, 379 12
By his *d* he has destroyed *d*, 379 17
and when our mortal body lies in *d*, 382 4
we show forth the sacrifice of his *d*, 403 15
On the night he was handed over to suffering and *d*, 405 1
Recalling now his suffering and *d*, 405 11
we thank you that by the *d* and resurrection 418 1
until we are parted by *d*. 427 4
until we are parted by *d*. 427 8
in their life and in their *d*. 430 21
until we are parted by *d*. 436 4
till *d* do us part, 436 9
Though I walk through the valley of the shadow of *d*, 443 7
and redeemed me from sin and *d* 450 10
your precious *D* and Burial, 463 6
and from eternal *d*, 463 13
though I walk through the valley of the shadow of *d*, 476 8
though I walk through the valley of the shadow of *d*, 477 1
The snares of *d* compassed me round about, * 479 3
thou hast delivered my soul from *d*, * 479 14
in the sight of the LORD is the *d* of his saints. 479 19
baptized into Christ's *d* and resurrection 480 8
through the grave and gate of *d* we may pass 480 10
inheritance in that kingdom where there is no *d*, 482 6
trampling down *d* by *d*, 483 14
and in the shadow of *d*. 483 17
In the midst of life we are in *d*; 484 4
deliver us not into the bitter pains of eternal *d*. 484 10
through any pains of *d*, 484 17
set thy passion, cross, and *d*, 489 24
now and in the hour of our *d*. 489 25
In the midst of life we are in *d*; 492 5
deliver us not into the bitterness of eternal *d*. 492 11
deliver us not into the bitterness of eternal *d*. 492 17
do not let the pains of *d* turn us away from you 492 19
deliver us not into the bitterness of eternal *d*. 492 23
Christ destroyed *d*, and brought life 493 5
Give us faith to see in *d* the gate of eternal life, 493 20
at the *d* of our brother (sister); 497 22
his *d* may recall to us your victory over *d*, 498 3
in that kingdom where there is no *d*, 498 17
trampling down *d* by *d*, 500 3
those who sat in darkness and in the shadow of *d*. 500 6
by your *d* you took away the sting of *d*: 504 21
the *d* of sin to the life of righteousness; 505 3
he suffered *d* and was buried. 519 24
he suffered *d* and was buried. 530 15
We thank you that by his *d* he has overcome *d*, 533 5
he suffered *d* and was buried. 542 15
becoming obedient even to *d* on the cross. 545 3
to lead us, through his *d* and resurrection, 570 10
we are buried with Christ in his *d*. 570 13
and for his *d* upon the cross, 573 13
For in *d* no one remembers you; * 590 7
He has prepared his weapons of *d*; * 591 24
O you who lift me up from the gate of *d*; 594 3
give light to my eyes, lest I sleep in *d*; 598 5
The breakers of *d* rolled over me, * 602 14
and the snares of *d* were set for me. 602 17
Though I walk through the valley of the shadow of *d*, 613 3
To pluck their lives from *d*, * 627 13
D is their shepherd; * 653 9
he will snatch me from the grasp of *d*. 653 14
For they will carry nothing away at their *d*, * 653 17
Deliver me from *d*, O God, * 657 9
and the terrors of *d* have fallen upon me. 660 14
Let *d* come upon them suddenly; 661 14
For you have rescued my soul from *d* and my feet 663 16
God is the LORD, by whom we escape *d*. 677 24
he did not spare their souls from *d*; * 699 5
and at the point of *d*; * 713 9
Who can live and not see *d*? * 717 10
and put the orphans to *d*. 723 6
and condemn the innocent to *d*. 724 8
and drew near to *d*'s door. 747 18
The cords of *d* entangled me; 759 5
For you have rescued my life from *d*, * 759 16
is the *d* of his servants. 760 4
but he did not hand me over to *d*. 762 7

and put mighty kings to *d*: 788 22
while he was suffering shame and *d*: 823 9
live with injustice, terror, disease, and *d* 826 9
put *d* to flight, 835 2
through which he overcame *d*; 836 15
sets us free from the power of evil, sin, and *d*. 849 6
Jesus' suffering and *d*? 850 6
even to suffering and *d*, 850 7
Jesus overcame *d* 850 11
victory over sin, suffering, and *d*? 850 23
Christ in his *d* and resurrection, 858 18
remembrance of his life, *d*, and resurrection, 859 7
by hell, we mean eternal *d* in our rejection of God. 862 7
We mean that God will raise us from *d* 862 17
not even *d*, shall separate us 862 31

Deborah

for Miriam and Joshua, *D* and Gideon, 838 12

debt

paid for us the *d* of Adam's sin, 287 4

deceit

Their mouth is full of cursing, *d*, and oppression; * 595 6
her streets are never free of oppression and *d*. 661 5

deceitful

the bloodthirsty and *d*, O LORD, you abhor. 589 2
nor do I consort with the *d*. 616 15
but invent *d* schemes against the quiet 631 10
The words of his mouth are wicked and *d*; * 632 7
deliver me from the *d* and the wicked. 644 16
O you *d* tongue. 658 7
For you will bring the bloodthirsty and *d* * 662 8
the mouth of the *d*, is opened against me. 750 25
and from the *d* tongue. 778 13
O you *d* tongue? 778 15

deceitfully

Those who act *d* shall not dwell in my house, * 730 24
Whose mouths speak *d* * 800 17
Whose mouths speak *d* * 800 25

deceitfulness

their *d* is in vain. 773 10

deceits

and from all the *d* of the world, 149 6

deceive

If we say that we have no sin, we *d* ourselves, 38 10
If we say we have no sin, we *d* ourselves, 76 9
If we say that we have no sin, we *d* ourselves, 320 1
If we say that we have no sin, we *d* ourselves, 352 1
No enemy shall *d* him, * 715 10

deceived

all such as have erred, and are *d*, 150 20

deception

O worker of *d*. 658 3

decision

the day of *d* ventured much 839 23

decisions

they may be led to wise *d* 329 20
elect trustworthy leaders and make wise *d* 822 12

declare

you *d* your almighty power 234 6
you *d* your glory 261 7
d and pronounce to his people, 269 6
you are bidden to *d* it. 437 4
d that I do believe the Holy Scriptures 513 9
d that I do believe the Holy Scriptures 526 14
d God's forgiveness to penitent sinners, 531 13
d that I do believe the Holy Scriptures 538 14
D them guilty, O God; * 589 13
The heavens *d* the glory of God, * 606 15
I will *d* your Name to my brethren; * 611 24
will the dust praise you or *d* your faithfulness? 621 25
Let the heavens *d* the rightness of his cause; * 654 14
and *d* the goodness of your Name in the presence 658 19
Everyone will stand in awe and *d* God's deeds; * 672 3
I will *d* the mysteries of ancient times. 694 22
D his glory among the nations * 725 21
The heavens *d* his righteousness, * 727 7
That they may *d* in Zion the Name of the LORD, * 732 18
Who can *d* the mighty acts of the LORD * 741 21
and *d* the works of the LORD. 762 5
and shall *d* your power. 801 19
to bless and *d* pardon in the name of God. 856 6

declared

according to thy promises *d* unto mankind 42 6
according to thy promises *d* unto mankind 63 9
our fathers have *d* unto us, the noble works 154 6
according to thy promises *d* unto mankind 321 9
grace and virtue *d* in all thy saints, 348 1
grace and virtue *d* in all your saints, 380 17
grace and virtue *d* in all thy saints, 487 12
and have *d* your power among the peoples. 694 2
Will your loving-kindness be *d* in the grave? * 712 25

declares

He *d* his word to Jacob, * 805 15

declarest

who *d* thy almighty power 182 12
who *d* thy glory 210 1

declaring

d pardon in your Name, 521 12
and *d* all your wonderful deeds. 691 4

decrease

he did not let their herds *d*. 749 6

decree

Let me announce the *d* of the LORD: * 586 14
Awake, O my God, *d* justice; * 591 8
Do you indeed *d* righteousness, you rulers? * 664 21
they kept his testimonies and the *d* that he gave them. 729 15
By your *d* these continue to this day, * 771 1

decreed

To inflict on them the judgment *d*; * 807 18

decrees

Your _d_ are my inheritance for ever; * 104 9
and his _d_ I have not put away from me; 604 8
He gave his _d_ to Jacob 695 7
Happy are they who observe his _d_ * 763 7
I have taken greater delight in the way of your _d_ * 764 11
for I have kept your _d_. 765 4
For your _d_ are my delight, * 765 7
I hold fast to your _d_; * 765 21
Incline my heart to your _d_ * 766 7
I will tell of your _d_ before kings * 767 5
and turned my feet toward your _d_. 768 6
and also those who know your _d_. 769 24
that I may keep the _d_ of your mouth. 770 19
I will apply my mind to your _d_. 771 10
for your _d_ are my study. 771 18
Your _d_ are my inheritance for ever; * 772 15
therefore I love your _d_. 773 12
that I may know your _d_. 773 24
Your _d_ are wonderful; * 774 5
You have issued your _d_ * 775 1
The righteousness of your _d_ is everlasting; * 775 13
I will keep your _d_. 775 19
Long have I known from your _d_ * 776 7
yet I have not swerved from your _d_. 776 18
I have kept your _d_ * 777 13
I have kept your commandments and _d_, * 777 15

dedicate

we are now gathered to _d_ and consecrate 567 5
as we _d_ this place 568 9
We _d_ this Font 569 21
We _d_ this Pulpit 571 15
We _d_ this (name of instrument) 572 7

dedicated

We _d_ this Lectern 571 7
Sanctify this Table _d_ to you. Let 574 1
utterly _d_ unto thee; 833 1

dedication

the _d_ of this house of prayer: 204 1
the _d_ of this house of prayer: 254 19

deed

in thought, word, and _d_, 79 12
in thought, word, and _d_, 116 14
in thought, and word, and _d_, 127 9
in will and _d_; 164 15
in will and _d_; 216 10
in thought, word, and _d_; 267 17
in thought, word, or _d_. 317 4
in thought, word, and _d_, 320 12
by thought, word, and _d_, 331 7
in thought, word, and _d_, 331 23
in thought, word, and _d_, 352 12
in thought, word, and _d_, 360 4
in thought, word, and _d_, 397 21
in thought, word, and _d_, 447 7
in thought, word, and _d_, 454 3
to proclaim by word and _d_ 531 8
in thought, word, and _d_; 847 25

deeds

make known his _d_ among the peoples. 78 7
Make his _d_ known among the peoples; * 86 9
great _d_ are they that you have done, * 94 10
Let us hear the record of God's saving _d_ in history, 288 1
whose wonderful _d_ of old shine forth 289 12
he delights in righteous _d_; * 596 25
the saving _d_ that he has done. 612 22
and recounting all your wonderful _d_. 616 21
Repay them according to their _d_, * 619 14
the _d_ you did in their days, 645 8
With God we will do valiant _d_, * 668 10
for you repay everyone according to his _d_. 670 11
Everyone will stand in awe and declare God's _d_; * 672 3
"How awesome are your _d_! * 673 21
and saving _d_ all day long; * 684 10
who alone does wondrous _d_! 686 26
and declaring all your wonderful _d_. 691 5
and ponder your mighty _d_. 693 25
the praiseworthy _d_ and the power of the LORD, * 695 5
and not forget the _d_ of God, 695 14
yet punished them for their evil _d_." 729 18
I hate the doers of evil _d_; 730 13
make known his _d_ among the peoples. 738 2
But they soon forgot his _d_ * 742 24
Wonderful _d_ in the land of Ham, * 743 15
and went whoring in their evil _d_. 745 2
With God we will do valiant _d_, * 750 21
Great are the _d_ of the LORD! * 754 8
for my prayer is continually against their wicked _d_. 797 14
I muse upon all your _d_; * 799 8
they shall sing of your righteous _d_. 801 25
and merciful in all his _d_. 802 14
Prayer is responding to God, by thought and by _d_, 856 18

deep

that turneth _d_ darkness into the morning, 62 1
The fathomless _d_ has overwhelmed them; * 85 12
_d_ gloom enshrouds the peoples. 87 14
and turns _d_ darkness into the morning, 115 13
For behold, you look for truth _d_ within me, * 266 14
Out of the _d_ have I called unto thee, O LORD; * 474 1
*Or the _d_, or the elements, or its resting place. 485 16
*Or the _d_, or the elements, or its resting place. 501 17
They dig a pit and make it _d_ * 592 1
In the _d_ has he set a pavilion for the sun; * 606 23
and made it firm upon the rivers of the _d_. 613 17
rebellion _d_ in the heart 632 3
your justice like the great _d_; * 632 15
your law is _d_ in my heart.'" 640 22
One _d_ calls to another in the noise 643 21
and covered us over with _d_ darkness. 646 25
you look for truth _d_ within me, * 656 18
I am sinking in _d_ mire, * 679 9
I have come into _d_ waters, * 679 11
and out of the _d_ waters. 680 19
neither let the _d_ swallow me up; * 680 21
from the _d_ places of the earth. 684 25
and gave them drink as from the great _d_. 696 4
You have crushed Rahab of the _d_ 714 13
your thoughts are very _d_. 721 6
You covered it with the _D_ as with a mantle; * 735 13

and he led them through the *d* as through a desert. 742 17
Some sat in darkness and *d* gloom, * 747 1
He led them out of darkness and *d* gloom * 747 9
and plied their trade in *d* waters; 748 2
and his wonders in the *d*. 748 4
How *d* I find your thoughts, O God! * 795 10

deeper

or a *d* knowledge of him. 386 7

deeply

I am *d* troubled; * 104 1
d sensible of the shortness and uncertainty of life; 489 4
d aware of the shortness and uncertainty of human life; 504 2
I am *d* troubled; * 772 7
and I have loved them *d*. 777 14

deeps

in the seas and all the *d*. 788 13
you sea-monsters and all *d*; 806 8

deer

He makes me sure-footed like a *d* * 605 5
As the *d* longs for the water-brooks, * 643 1

defeated

they fall *d* at my feet. 605 17

defend

D us, thy humble servants, 57 3
D us in the same with thy mighty power; 57 9
d us from all perils and dangers 70 2
D us, your humble servants, 99 21
to *d* us from all error, 107 6
d us from all perils and dangers 111 2
d us from all perils and dangers 123 22
d us from all perils and dangers 133 11
From our enemies *d* us, 154 15
d thy Church, 180 9
so by thy appointment they may help and *d* us 193 7
so by thy appointment they may help and *d* us 200 9
cleanse and *d* your Church; 232 1
help and *d* us here on earth; 244 17
help and *d* us here on earth; 251 16
D, O Lord, your servant 309 15
D us, deliver us, and in thy compassion protect us, O 385 10
D, O Lord, your servant 418 13
D them from every enemy. 430 16
and *d* those who have no helper? 518 29
guard and *d* them in his truth, 521 19
you will *d* them with your favor as with a shield. 589 22
the Name of the God of Jacob *d* you; 608 2
and *d* my cause against an ungodly people; * 644 15
in your might, *d* my cause. 659 18
He shall *d* the needy among the people; * 685 15
d the humble and needy; 705 14
D our liberties, 820 6
D them day by day 823 3
D them from all dangers of soul and body; 830 21

defended

being *d* from the fear of all enemies, 69 20
that we may be *d* from all adversities 167 5
that we may be *d* from all adversities 218 15
be *d* by thy gracious and ready help; 832 22

defender

Answer me when I call, O God, *d* of my cause; * 128 8
Answer me when I call, O God, *d* of my cause; * 587 20
Father of orphans, *d* of widows, * 676 11
Behold our *d*, O God; * 708 8

defense

surely trusting in thy *d*, 57 5
For the Lord is my stronghold and my sure *d*, * 86 3
surely trusting in your *d*, 99 23
Be now and evermore your *d*, 457 1
the LORD is thy *d* upon thy right hand; 473 18
God is my shield and *d*; * 591 18
to my *d*, my God and my Lord! 631 17
and from whose mouth comes no *d*. 637 26

defied

But they tested the Most High God, and *d* him, * 699 18
they *d* the Most High at the Red Sea. 742 13

defiled

they *d* the dwelling-place of your Name 689 22
d his crown, and hurled it to the ground. 716 20
and the land was *d* with blood. 744 26

defilements

whatsoever *d* he may have contracted 488 17

define

The Ten Commandments were given to *d* 848 23

defy

they *d* all their enemies. 595 3

degradation

all danger, violence, oppression, and *d*, 385 2

degree

you of high *d* and low, rich and poor together. 652 8
Those of high *d* are but a fleeting breath, * 670 1

delay

to follow him without *d*, 185 10
to follow him without *d*, 237 4

deliberately

d, and in accordance with the purposes 423 15

delight

that we may *d* in your will, 79 20
that we may *d* in your will, 117 3
but you take no *d* in burnt-offerings. 267 9
that we may *d* in thy will, 320 20
that we may *d* in thy will, 331 31
that we may *d* in your will, 352 20
that we may *d* in your will, 360 12
that we may *d* in your will, 398 4
that we may *d* in your will, 455 3
My *d* is in the LORD, * 478 23
Their *d* is in the law of the LORD, * 585 5
but those who *d* in violence he abhors. 596 20
All my *d* is upon the godly that are in the land, * 600 1
Take *d* in the LORD, * 633 11

and the end of those who *d* in their own words. 653 7
but you take no *d* in burnt-offerings. 657 15
lies are their chief *d*. 669 13
scatter the peoples that *d* in war. 678 21
and *d* in false gods! * 727 10
he took no *d* in blessing, let it depart from him. 752 6
they are studied by all who *d* in them. 754 9
and have great *d* in his commandments! 755 6
I have taken greater *d* in the way of your decrees * 764 11
My *d* is in your statutes; * 764 15
For your decrees are my *d*, * 765 7
I *d* in your commandments, * 767 7
but my *d* is in your law. 769 4
for your law is my *d*. 769 19
If my *d* had not been in your law, * 771 3
and my *d* shall be ever in your statutes. 773 8
yet your commandments are my *d*. 775 12
and your law is my *d*. 778 4
here will I dwell, for I *d* in her. 786 29
O God, whom saints and angels *d* to worship in 819 13
which satisfy and *d* us. 836 9

delighted

he rescued me because he *d* in me. 604 2

delights

he *d* in righteous deeds; * 596 25
let him rescue him, if he *d* in him." 610 17
you give them drink from the river of your *d*. 632 21
he strengthens those in whose way he *d*. 635 6

deliver

When thou tookest upon thee to *d* man, 53 13
but *d* us from evil. 54 23
but *d* us from evil. 67 13
but *d* us from evil. 97 14
but *d* us from evil. 106 24
but *d* us from evil. 121 14
d me in your righteousness. 129 10
make haste to *d* me. 129 12
He shall *d* you from the snare of the hunter * 130 1
therefore will I *d* him; * 130 27
but *d* us from evil. 133 6
Good Lord, *d* us. 148 17
Good Lord, *d* us. 149 4
but *d* us from evil. 153 15
And *d* us for thy Name's sake. 154 4
help and *d* us; 160 3
D us, we pray thee, from an inordinate love 198 2
D us, we beseech thee, in our several occupations 210 3
help and *d* us; 212 3
D us from an inordinate love of this world, 249 12
D us in our various occupations 261 9
D me from death, O God, * 267 3
D them, O Lord, from the way of sin and 305 14
but *d* us from evil. 311 11
and *d* you from all your sins, 332 4
but *d* us from evil. 336 27
but *d* us from evil. 364 11
D us from the presumption of coming to this Table 372 3
Defend us, *d* us, and in thy compassion 385 10
but *d* us from evil. 398 22
but *d* us from evil. 428 18
May he *d* you from all evil, 456 17
Good Lord, *d* him. 463 4
Good Lord, *d* him. 463 10
to *d* the soul of your servant 463 12
but *d* us from evil. 464 14
D your servant, 464 16
D your servant, 466 16
d my soul. 479 7
d us not into the bitter pains of eternal death. 484 10
but *d* us from evil. 486 4
d us not into the bitterness of eternal death. 492 11
but *d* us from evil. 502 11
Turn, O LORD, and *d* me; * 590 5
save and *d* me from all who pursue me; 590 21
and snatch me away with none to *d* me. 590 23
d me from the wicked by your sword. 601 26
D me, O LORD, by your hand * 601 27
You *d* me from the strife of the peoples; * 605 26
"He trusted in the LORD; let him *d* him; * 610 16
Protect my life and *d* me; * 616 1
D Israel, O God, * 616 5
D me not into the hand of my adversaries, * 618 23
d me in your righteousness. 622 9
make haste to *d* me. 622 11
and he will *d* them. 628 8
but the LORD will *d* him out of them all. 629 6
You *d* the poor from those who are too strong 630 11
he will rescue them from the wicked and *d* them, 636 18
D me from all my transgressions * 639 11
Be pleased, O LORD, to *d* me; * 641 8
the LORD will *d* them in the time of trouble. 641 24
d me from the deceitful and the wicked. 644 16
or *d* to God the price of our life; 652 18
I will *d* you, and you shall honor me." 655 10
lest I rend you and there be none to *d* you. 655 27
D me from death, O God, * 657 9
and the LORD will *d* me. 661 18
because of my enemies *d* me. 680 28
Be pleased, O God, to *d* me; * 682 11
In your righteousness, *d* me and set me free; * 683 3
D me, my God, from the hand of the wicked, * 683 7
For he shall *d* the poor who cries out in distress, * 686 7
d us and forgive us our sins, for your Name's sake. 701 25
d them from the power of the wicked. 705 16
He shall *d* you from the snare of the hunter * 719 15
therefore will I *d* him; * 720 15
Many a time did he *d* them, 745 10
for your tender mercy's sake, *d* me. 752 17
do not *d* me to my oppressors. 773 16
Behold my affliction and *d* me, * 776 9
d me, according to your promise. 777 20
D me, O LORD, from lying lips * 778 12
D me, O LORD, from evildoers; * 796 1
D me from my enemies, O LORD, * 799 19
rescue me and *d* me from the great waters, 800 15
and *d* me from the hand of foreign peoples, 800 24
d them and us from hatred, 816 7
D us, when we draw near to thee, 833 20
d from his sickness thy servant 841 8

deliverance

For *d* from all danger, 385 1
D belongs to the LORD. * 587 18
Oh, that Israel's *d* would come out of Zion! * 599 1
you surround me with shouts of *d*. 625 16
The horse is a vain hope for *d*; * 627 9
d of the righteous comes from the LORD; * 636 15
your faithfulness and your *d*; * 640 27
Oh, that Israel's *d* would come out of Zion! * 659 14
D is far from the wicked, * 776 13

delivered

That we being *d* out of the hand 51 7
being *d* from the fear of all enemies, 123 18
resurrection hast *d* us 170 9
for that thou hast *d* us 172 14
being *d* from false apostles, 188 3
d from the disquietude of this world, 191 18
d us from the power of our enemy: 222 3
d us from the dominion of sin and death 224 7
being *d* from false apostles, 239 13
d from the disquietude of this world, 243 4
might be *d* from the power of sin and death, 277 5
and by his blood *d* your faithful people. 287 5
are *d* from the gloom of sin, 287 9
you once *d* by the power of your mighty arm 289 13
resurrection *d* us from the power of your enemy: 295 3
that we might be *d* from the bondage of sin, 345 17
you have *d* us from evil, 368 7
that we might be *d* from the bondage of sin, 378 12
That they may be *d* from their distress. 387 16
that we may be *d* from hardness of heart, 391 2
thou hast *d* my soul from death, * 479 14
after they are *d* from the burden of the flesh, 488 3
He *d* me from my strong enemies 603 25
they trusted, and you *d* them. 610 9
They cried out to you and were *d*; * 610 10
a strong man is not *d* by his great strength. 627 8
and *d* me out of all my terror. 628 2
that those who are dear to you may be *d*. 667 19
He *d* their cattle to hailstones * 698 23
but *d* their lives to the plague. 699 6
He *d* the ark into captivity, * 700 1
you have *d* me from the nethermost Pit. 710 27
and he *d* them from their distress. 746 13
and he *d* them from their distress. 747 8
and he *d* them from their distress. 747 20
and he *d* them from their distress. 748 12
So that those who are dear to you may be *d*, * 750 5
And *d* us from our enemies, * 791 17

deliverer

You are my helper and my *d*; * 641 21
You are my helper and my *d*; * 682 24
my stronghold and my *d*, * 800 3

delivers

and *d* them from all their troubles. 629 2
and *d* them from the hand of the wicked. 727 19

demand

tasks which *d* our best 836 7

demanding

d food for their craving. 696 10

demands

the obligations which Christian Marriage *d*. 433 4

demolish

Oh, that God would *d* you utterly, * 658 8

denial

by prayer, fasting, and self-*d*; 265 12

denied

you have not *d* him the request of his lips. 608 24

dens

and lay themselves down in their *d*. 736 22

deny

"Whosoever will come after me, let him *d* 38 24
"If anyone would come after me, let him *d* 76 23

denying

of self-*d* service 191 11
of self-*d* service 242 17

depart

now lettest thou thy servant *d* in peace, * 51 23
now lettest thou thy servant *d* in peace, * 66 1
That we may *d* this life in thy faith and fear, 68 18
That we may *d* this life in your faith and fear, 122 20
and let your anger *d* from us; 268 27
D, O Christian soul, out of this world; 464 21
the spirits of those who *d* hence 488 2
that when we *d* this life 505 4
D from me, all evildoers, * 590 14
let your anger *d* from us. 709 2
let it *d* from him. 752 6
You that thirst for blood, *d* from me. 795 17

departed

to all the faithful *d* 152 15
with all who have *d* this world 280 9
d this life in thy faith 330 2
and for all the *d*, 384 30
I ask your prayers for the *d* 386 10
Give to the *d* eternal rest; 387 17
and the souls of all the *d*, 465 7
and the souls of all the *d*, 486 19
with all those who are *d* 488 7
and the souls of all the *d*, 498 11
and the souls of all the *d*, 502 17
We mean that he went to the *d* 850 15

dependence

to acknowledge our *d* on you alone. 836 11

depends

our common life *d* upon each other's toil; 134 14

depths

Blessed art thou that beholdest the *d*, 49 15
they sank into the *d* like a stone. 85 13
Glory to you, beholding the *d*; * 90 13
nor condemn me to the *d* of the earth. 91 19
and stores up the *d* of the sea. 626 14

be toppled into the *d* of the sea; 649 5
go down into the *d* of the earth; 671 4
I will bring them back from the *d* of the sea; 678 2
the very *d* were shaken. 694 7
You have laid me in the *d* of the Pit, * 712 13
and fell back to the *d*; * 748 7
Out of the *d* have I called to you, O LORD; 784 18
and woven in the *d* of the earth. 795 5
by whose knowledge the *d* are broken up 840 14

derided

The proud have *d* me cruelly, * 767 15

derision

the Lord has them in *d*. 586 9
a mockery and *d* to those around us. 646 12
an object of scorn and *d* to those around us. 701 12
You have made us the *d* of our neighbors, * 702 23
and of the *d* of the proud. 780 24

descend

Spirit may *d* upon us, 375 5

descendants

to David and his *d* for ever. 606 14
and their *d* from among the peoples 609 19
my *d* shall serve him; * 612 19
Let his *d* be destroyed, * 751 22
Their *d* will be mighty in the land; * 755 7

descended

He *d* into hell. 53 30
He *d* into hell. 66 16
He *d* to the dead. 96 20
He *d* to the dead. 120 16
He *d* to the dead. 293 7
He *d* to the dead. 304 10
He *d* to the dead. 416 15
He *d* to the dead. 496 10
he *d* to the dead? 850 13

descent

Recalling Christ's death and his *d* among the dead, 374 25

described

How is the Church *d* in the Bible? 854 5
The Church is *d* as the Body 854 6
How is the Church *d* in the creeds? 854 11
The Church is *d* 854 12
Why is the Church *d* as one? 854 14
Why is the Church *d* as holy? 854 17
Why is the Church *d* as catholic? 854 21
Why is the Church *d* as apostolic? 854 24

desert

make straight in the *d* 37 4
in the *d* a highway for our God. 75 5
and gave him to the people of the *d* for food. 690 13
rebelling in the *d* against the Most High. 696 8
and offended him in the *d*! 698 8
and he led them through the deep as through a *d*. 742 17
and they put God to the test in the *d*. 742 27
Some wandered in *d* wastes; * 746 8

deserts

and give them their just *d*. 619 17
give the arrogant their just *d*. 722 21
The LORD changed rivers into *d*, * 748 21
He changed *d* into pools of water * 748 25

deserve

you do not punish as we *d*. 91 8
and not what we *d*; 176 10
we desire or *d*: 182 20
and not what we *d*; 228 10
give more than we either desire or *d*: 234 14
nor as we *d* in our sinfulness, 394 6

deserved

all those evils that we most justly have *d*; 155 9

designs

frustrate the *d* of evil tyrants 186 16
frustrate the *d* of evil tyrants 238 10
he thwarts the *d* of the peoples. 626 20
and the *d* of his heart from age to age. 626 22

desire

and *d* that which thou dost promise; 167 17
exceed all that we can *d*; 174 5
we *d* or deserve: 182 20
and *d* what you promise; 219 8
which exceed all that we can *d*; 225 18
give more than we either *d* or deserve: 234 13
Do you *d* to be baptized? 301 3
who *d* to reaffirm their baptismal vows. 303 8
And we earnestly *d* thy fatherly goodness 335 24
And we earnestly *d* thy fatherly goodness 342 21
who *d* to reaffirm their baptismal vows. 415 7
The wicked boast of their heart's *d*; * 594 23
The LORD will hear the *d* of the humble; * 596 3
Grant you your heart's *d* * 608 7
You have given him his heart's *d*; * 608 23
and he shall give you your heart's *d*. 633 12
and having you I *d* nothing upon earth. 688 28
My soul has a *d* and longing for the courts of 707 16
until they see their *d* upon their enemies. 755 21
for that is my *d*. 766 6
He fulfills the *d* of those who fear him; * 802 25
the *d* of vainglory, 829 1
better things than we can *d* or pray for; 831 10
who pourest out on all who *d* it 833 19

desired

Had you *d* it, I would have offered sacrifice; * 267 8
for whom our prayers are *d*. 458 3
One thing have I *d* of the LORD, 477 16
More to be *d* are they than gold, 607 16
Had you *d* it, I would have offered sacrifice, * 657 14
he has *d* her for his habitation: 786 27
for whom our prayers are *d*]; 815 9

desires

the devices and *d* of our own hearts, 41 18
Drive far from us all wrong *d*, 56 20
the *d* and petitions of thy servants 59 16
the devices and *d* of our own hearts, 62 18
from whom all holy *d*, 69 16

the *d* and petitions of thy servants 72 13
far from us all wrong *d*, 99 15
our *d* and petitions as may be 102 5
the source of all good *d*, 123 15
our *d* and petitions as may be 126 5
who *d* not the death of sinners, 269 4
burn with heavenly *d*, 285 11
Do you renounce all sinful *d* 302 13
the devices and *d* of our own hearts, 320 25
all *d* known, 323 6
all *d* known, and from you no secrets are hid: 355 7
who *d* now to offer you her praises 444 3
all *d* known, and from you no secrets are hid: 512 7
all *d* known, and from you no secrets are hid: 525 7
all *d* known, and from you no secrets are hid: 537 7
and may all the *d* of my heart 562 18
For the fulfilling of our *d* 578 21
and *d* long life to enjoy prosperity? 628 18
who *d* the prosperity of his servant." 631 29
O LORD, you know all my *d*, * 637 14
the *d* of the wicked will perish. 755 27
Do not grant the *d* of the wicked, O LORD, * 796 17
To use all our bodily *d* as God intended; 848 11

desireth

Like as the hart *d* the water-brooks, * 471 1

desolate

d and oppressed, 151 7
He lifted me out of the *d* pit, 640 3
Let their camp be *d*, * 681 14
Those who go through the *d* valley 708 1
my heart within me is *d*. 799 6

despair

For those who face temptation, doubt, and *d* 279 8
forgiveness heal guilt, and joy conquer *d*. 429 19
my soul is full of *d*. 630 16
save them from *d*; 823 13
where there is *d*, hope; 833 8

despise

you will not *d*. 267 11
For he does not *d* nor abhor the poor 612 1
you will not *d*. 657 17
and his prisoners he does not *d*. 682 4
he will not *d* their plea. 732 11

despised

scorned by all and *d* by the people. 610 13
how a foolish people *d* your Name. 690 21
and *d* the counsel of the Most High. 747 4

despite

Shall they escape *d* their wickedness? * 663 4
d the prayers of your people? 702 20
D my love, they accuse me; * 751 4

despitefully

They speak *d* against you; * 795 18

despoil

All who pass by *d* him; * 716 23

despoiled

The strong of heart have been *d*; 692 9

destined

Like a flock of sheep they are *d* to die; 653 8

destitute

thy Church may never be *d* of such gifts; 197 16
your Church may never be *d* of such gifts; 249 2
the *d* and the oppressed 279 4
for the unemployed and the *d*, 384 26
the homeless and the *d*, 826 3

destroy

Christ didst *d* death 171 11
d the works of the devil 184 8
d the works of the devil 236 2
which corrupt and *d* the creatures of God? 302 11
You *d* those who speak lies; * 589 1
I *d* those who hate me; 605 21
You will *d* their offspring from the land * 609 18
who seek after my life to *d* it; * 641 11
in your faithfulness, *d* them. 659 27
May those who seek my life to *d* it * 671 3
my lying foes who would *d* me are mighty. * 679 18
you *d* all who are unfaithful. 689 4
"Let us *d* them altogether." * 689 24
and did not *d* them; * 698 2
and *d* them in their own malice; * 724 12
the LORD our God will *d* them. 724 13
in secret slander their neighbors I will *d*; * 730 17
I will soon *d* all the wicked in the land, * 730 26
They did not *d* the peoples * 744 15
Though the wicked lie in wait for me to *d* me, * 771 9
Of your goodness, *d* my enemies 799 25
They restore us, though we often *d* them. 838 23

destroyed

Christ *d* death 223 5
his death hath *d* death, 346 21
rising from the grave, *d* death, 374 7
By his death he has *d* death, 379 17
and though this body be *d*, 469 6
Christ *d* death, 493 5
rebuked the ungodly and *d* the wicked; * 593 9
When the foundations are being *d*, * 596 13
I will not turn back till I have *d* them. 605 15
but those who are cursed by him shall be *d*. 635 4
but the offspring of the wicked shall be *d*. 635 19
Transgressors shall be *d*, one and all; * 636 13
how you *d* nations and made your people flourish. 645 12
and frogs, which *d* them. 698 18
They were *d* at Endor; * 706 22
your terrors have *d* me; 713 12
They flourish only to be *d* for ever; * 721 11
and *d* the supply of bread. 739 10
So he would have *d* them, 743 17
Let his descendants be *d*, * 751 22

destroying

a troop of *d* angels. 699 3

destroys

but he *d* all the wicked. 802 28

destruction
ruin or *d* within your borders. 87 24
Thou turnest man to *d*; * 472 14
there is *d* in their heart; 589 10
down to the pit of *d*, O God. 662 9
Oh, how suddenly do they come to *d*, * 688 15
your faithfulness in the land of *d*? 712 26
O Daughter of Babylon, doomed to *d*, * 792 19

determination
d in making provision for its future 828 19

determined
I have sworn and am *d* * 103 8
I have sworn and am *d* * 772 5
who are *d* to trip me up. 796 9

detested
Forty years long I *d* that generation and said, * 725 12

devices
we have followed too much the *d* and desires 41 18
we have followed too much the *d* and desires 62 18
we have followed too much the *d* and desires 320 25
to follow their own *d*. 704 27
but they rebelled through their own *d*, * 745 11

devil
Your adversary the *d* prowls 132 8
assaults of the *d*; 148 16
deceits of the world, the flesh, and the *d*, 149 6
destroy the works of the *d* 184 8
destroy the works of the *d* 236 2

devious
Their ways are *d* at all times; 595 1

devise
and *d* wicked schemes, * 609 21
and *d* evil against me. 642 14
you *d* evil in your hearts, * 664 23
Who *d* evil in their hearts * 796 3

devised
trapped in the schemes they have *d*. 594 22

devote
I *d* myself, body, soul, and spirit. 562 12

devoted
that we may be *d* to thee 179 6
that we may be *d* to you 230 21

devotion
to follow the example of her *d* to thy will; 189 14
so we may with ardent *d* 194 4
inspired by the *d* of thy servant 198 3
the example of her *d* to your will: 240 22
may with ardent *d* make known the love 245 13
inspired by the *d* of your servant 249 13
Christians observed with great *d* 264 11
Give them wisdom and *d* 429 7
Grant them wisdom and *d* 444 9
In prayer, quicken my *d*; 563 5

devour
seeking someone to *d*. 132 9
I lie in the midst of lions that *d* the people; * 664 1

devoured
For they have *d* Jacob * 701 19
and *d* the fruit of their soil. 740 24
and flames *d* the wicked. 743 8

devoutly
they may truly and *d* serve you; 100 15
they may truly and *d* serve you; 257 2
they may truly and *d* serve you; 278 15
d kneeling. 330 14

dew
O ye showers and *d*, bless ye the Lord; * 48 3
every shower of rain and fall of *d*, * 88 13
drops of *d* and flakes of snow. 88 18
like *d* from the womb of the morning." 753 18
It is like the *d* of Hermon * 787 15
pour upon them the continual *d* 817 7
and the clouds drop down the *d*: 840 15

dews
O ye *d* and frosts, bless ye the Lord; * 48 9

die
For as in Adam all *d*, * 46 17
Christ being raised from the dead will never *d* again; * 83 15
For as in Adam all *d*, * 83 25
Grant us so to *d* daily to sin, 170 10
who hast given thine only Son to *d* 172 8
and courage to *d* for this faith: 195 3
Grant us so to *d* daily to sin, 222 3
who gave your only Son to *d* for our sins 224 1
and courage to *d* for this faith: 247 1
Grant us so to *d* daily to sin, 295 4
to live and *d* as one of us, 362 13
before whom live all who *d* in the Lord: 466 9
and believeth in me shall never *d*. 469 3
and if we *d*, we *d* unto the Lord. 469 12
Whether we live, therefore, or *d*, we are the Lord's. 469 13
Blessed are the dead who *d* in the Lord; 469 14
d to sin and rise to newness of life, 480 9
Blessed are the dead who *d* in the Lord: 486 9
even though he *d*. 491 3
shall not *d* for ever. 491 6
and if we *d*, we *d* in the Lord. 491 16
So, then, whether we live or *d*, 491 17
are those who *d* in the Lord! 492 2
still live the spirits of those who *d* in the Lord, 503 13
d to sin and are made new in Christ. 569 16
"When will he *d*, and his name perish?" 642 9
For we see that the wise *d* also; 652 23
Like a flock of sheep they are destined to *d*; 653 8
condemned to *d*. 702 6
Nevertheless, you shall *d* like mortals, * 705 22
and set free those condemned to *d*; 732 17
and they *d* and return to their dust. 737 13
and caused their fish to *d*. 740 12
I shall not *d*, but live, * 762 4

died

For in that he *d*, he *d* unto sin once; 46 9
through him who *d* for us and rose again, 70 9
The death that he *d*, he *d* to sin, 83 17
was crucified, *d*, and was buried. 96 19
was crucified, *d*, and was buried. 120 15
d and rose again for us, 124 6
have *d* in the peace of Christ, 280 10
If we have *d* with him, 281 17
was crucified, *d*, and was buried. 293 6
was crucified, *d*, and was buried. 304 9
Christ *d* for you, 338 2
Christ *d* for thee, 338 7
but unto him who *d* for us and rose again. 346 8
Christ has *d*. 363 7
Christ *d* for you, 365 1
On the night before he *d* for us, 368 10
who *d* and rose for us, 374 10
[Remember all who have *d* in the peace of Christ, 375 18
but for him who *d* for us and rose again. 379 4
For all who have *d* in the hope of the resurrection, 384 29
Pray for those who have *d*. 386 11
We commend to your mercy all who have *d*, 389 8
For all who have *d* in the communion 391 15
We pray for all who have *d*, 393 4
Christ *d* for you, 399 2
was crucified, *d*, and was buried. 416 14
with all who have *d* in the hope of the resurrection, 481 23
was crucified, *d*, and was buried. 496 9
all who have *d* in the true faith 503 17
For all who have *d* in the communion of your Church, 550 20
will those who have *d* stand up and give you thanks? 712 24

dies

and none becomes his own master when he *d*. 491 14

dieth

Christ being raised from the dead *d* no more; * 46 7
and no man *d* to himself. 469 10

differ

contempt toward those who *d* from us, 268 22
show us your presence in those who *d* most from us, 840 4
How do they *d* from the two sacraments 860 12

different

women from *d* cultures 825 13

differing

and with *d* talents 825 13

dig

They *d* a pit and make it deep * 592 1

digest

and inwardly *d* them; 184 17
and inwardly *d* them, 236 10

dignity

the *d* of human nature: 162 8
the *d* of human nature: 200 14
the *d* of human nature: 214 2
the *d* of human nature: 252 2
the *d* of human nature: 288 6
and respect the *d* of every human being? 294 2
and respect the *d* of every human 305 8
remember the *d* of that holy Sacrament. 316 19
and promote the *d* and freedom of every person, 390 17
and respect the *d* of every human being? 417 18
and promote the *d* and freedom of every person, 550 2
of your servant's ministry and *d*. 552 8
Provide for them homes of *d* and peace; 830 3

diligent

Will you be *d* in the reading and study of the 532 4

diligently

and *d* to live after thy commandments, 150 23
and *d* search for God. 697 19

diminished

Yet when they were *d* and brought low, * 749 7

diminishes

as their strength *d*, increase their faith 830 5

diocese

and all the people of this *d* 278 6
the clergy and people of the *D* 513 2
to serve in the *D* 514 3
on behalf of the clergy and people of the *D* 526 2
on behalf of the clergy and people of the *D* 538 2
share in the councils of this *d*. 562 5
you have called us in this *D* 817 10
choose a bishop for this *D* 818 10
and pastor of a *d*; 855 24

dipped

That your foot may be *d* in blood, * 678 3

direct

d us to the fulfilling of your purpose; 100 4
d and rule us according to your will, 107 5
d us to the fulfilling of your purpose; 137 17
d and rule our hearts; 182 3
d and rule our hearts; 233 15
d and uphold you in the service 310 6
d and uphold you in the service 419 2
Oh, that my ways were made so *d* * 763 13
where it is in error, *d* it; 816 12
D, in our time, we pray, those who speak 827 7
D us, O Lord, in all our doings 832 1

directed

Our steps are *d* by the LORD; * 635 5

direction

and ask you for counsel, *d*, and absolution. 447 12
d and leadership of your bishop? 532 2
Will you be guided by the pastoral *d* 543 25

directly

ministry of servanthood *d* under your bishop. 543 4

directs

who creates, sustains, and *d* it. 846 8

disappear

suspicions *d*, and hatreds cease; 823 20

disappointed
let the treacherous be *d* in their schemes. 614 18
and let me not be *d* in my hope. 773 6

disappointments
We thank you also for those *d* 836 10

disaster
poverty, famine, and *d*, 390 23
poverty, famine, and *d*, 550 8
They confronted me in the day of my *d*; * 603 28

discern
you *d* my thoughts from afar. 794 3
that they may *d* the truth, 821 11
and to *d* the truth, 823 14

discerned
and *d* the end of the wicked. 688 12

discerning
an inquiring and *d* heart, 308 6

discernment
Teach me *d* and knowledge, * 768 19

disciples
did manifest himself to his *d* 171 17
did manifest himself to his *d* 173 5
prayed for his *d* that they might be one, 204 18
made himself known to his *d* 223 11
made himself known to his *d* 224 20
prayed for his *d* that they might be one, 255 16
after he had supped with his *d* 274 8
By this shall the world know that you are my *d*: 275 7
persecutors of his *d* 279 26
and gave it to his *d*, 335 1
and gave it to his *d*, 342 3
appeared to his *d*; 347 3
lighting upon the *d*, to teach them 347 8
and gave it to his *d*, 362 20
and gave it to his *d*, 368 12
and gave it to his *d*, 374 17
appeared to his *d*, 379 22
lighting upon the *d*, to teach them 380 3
and so prove to be my *d*. 397 11
and gave it to his *d*, 405 3
you prepared your *d* for the coming 819 1
as you were present with your *d*, 834 9

discipline
with the spirit of love and *d*, 198 12
and godly *d*, 204 13
with the spirit of love and *d*, 249 21
and godly *d*, 255 11
conform to the doctrine, *d*, and worship 513 12
You are called to guard the faith, unity, and *d* 517 7
Will you guard the faith, unity, and *d* 518 19
Will you be loyal to the doctrine, *d*, and worship 526 9
conform to the doctrine, *d*, and worship 526 18
Will you be loyal to the doctrine, *d*, and worship 538 9
conform to the doctrine, *d*, and worship 538 18
to observe the *d* of Christ. 545 13
Since you refuse *d*, * 655 14
to guard the faith, unity, and *d* 855 24

disciplines
and gladly accept its *d*. 839 25

discord
Save us from violence, *d*, and confusion; 820 5
where there is *d*, union; 833 7

discouraged
comfort him when *d* or sorrowful; 830 15

discovery
new *d*, and the pursuit of wisdom; 824 18

discreet
open your grief to a *d* and understanding priest, 317 12

disdainfully
haughtily, *d*, and with contempt. 624 3

disease
the prevention of *d* and pain. 460 12
who live with injustice, terror, *d*, and death 826 9

disgrace
Let my accusers be clothed with *d* * 753 6

disgraced
Let all who rejoice at my ruin be ashamed and *d*; * 631 24
let them draw back and be *d* 641 12
let not those who seek you be *d* because of me, 679 24
my misfortune draw back and be *d*. 682 16
put to shame and be *d*; * 684 4
for they are ashamed and *d* 685 7
Let them be *d* and terrified for ever; * 707 11

dishonesty
our *d* in daily life and work, 268 11

dishonor
"You mortals, how long will you *d* my glory? * 128 11
"You mortals, how long will you *d* my glory; * 588 1
You know my reproach, my shame, and my *d*; * 681 1

disloyal
They turned away and were *d* like their fathers; * 699 20

dismay
a *d* to those of my acquaintance; * 623 12
clothed with *d* and shame. 631 26

dismayed
let those who plot my ruin fall back and be *d*. 629 21
Let them be ashamed and altogether *d* 641 10
be ashamed and altogether *d*; * 682 14

disobedience
When our *d* took us far from you, 373 21

disobeyed
How often the people *d* him in the wilderness * 698 7

dispel
D the darkness of our hearts, 110 25

dispersed
d throughout the world, 285 3

displeased
who for our sins art justly *d*? 484 7
Will you be *d* with us for ever? * 709 3

displeasure
For we consume away in thy *d*, * 472 23
nor cast thy servant away in *d*. 478 4
nor turn away your servant in *d*. 618 15
and provoked his *d* with their idols. 699 23
For we consume away in your *d*; * 718 13

dispose
and *d* the way of thy servants 832 19

disquieted
and why art thou so *d* within me? 471 13
and why are you so *d* within me? 643 14
and why are you so *d* within me? 644 10
and why are you so *d* within me? 645 2

disquietude
delivered from the *d* of this world, 191 18
delivered from the *d* of this world, 243 4

distorted
our relationship with God is *d*. 849 3

distorting
thus *d* our relationship with God, 848 30

distress
That they may be delivered from their *d*. 387 16
you consoled Martha and Mary in their *d*; 497 3
I called upon the LORD in my *d* * 602 18
and from the words of my *d*? 610 3
you know my *d*. 622 24
be swift and answer me, for I am in *d*. 680 26
For he shall deliver the poor who cries out in *d*, * 686 7
fury, indignation, and *d*, 699 2
Nevertheless, he saw their *d*, * 745 13
and he delivered them from their *d*. 746 13
and he delivered them from their *d*. 747 8
and he delivered them from their *d*. 748 12
In my *d* I said, "No one can be trusted." 759 22
I called to the LORD in my *d*; * 761 5
Trouble and *d* have come upon me, * 775 11
bring them weakness, *d*, or isolation. 830 2

distressed
who are in any ways afflicted or *d*, 815 7

distribute
But to do good and to *d*, forget not; 344 3

disturbed
"I shall never be *d*. * 621 17

diversity
for the wonderful *d* of races and cultures 840 2

divide
they *d* my garments among them; 611 16
I will *d* the valley of Succoth. 667 22
I will *d* the valley of Succoth. 750 9
that barriers which *d* us 823 19

divided
d and enslaved by sin, 185 3
d and enslaved by sin, 203 1
d and enslaved by sin, 236 16
d and enslaved by sin, 254 4
You *d* the sea by your might * 690 10
I hate those who have a *d* heart, * 772 19
Who *d* the Red Sea in two, * 790 21
where it is *d*, reunite it; 816 14

divides
whose light *d* the day from the night 99 13

dividest
who *d* the day from the night 56 18

dividing
the women at home are *d* the spoils." 677 4

divine
that we may share the *d* life 162 9
and in the power of the *D* Majesty 176 4
and stewards of thy *d* mysteries; 197 8
that we may share the *d* life 200 15
who of thy *d* providence 205 4
that we may share the *d* life 214 3
and in the power of your *d* Majesty 228 4
and stewards of your *d* mysteries; 248 19
that we may share the *d* life 252 3
in your *d* providence 256 1
that we may share the *d* life 288 7
which we offer unto thy *d* Majesty, 329 4
by thought, word, and deed, against thy *d* Majesty, 331 7
and make here before thy *d* Majesty, 335 11
his *d* Son received our human nature 849 28
The *d* Son became human, 850 2
it is also known as the *D* Liturgy, 859 16

divisions
that our *d* may cease, 390 5
that our *d* may cease 549 17
great dangers we are in by our unhappy *d*; 818 16
that our *d* being healed, 823 21

doctrine
From all false *d*, heresy, and schism; 149 8
in unity of spirit by their *d*, 178 21
by following the holy *d* 187 12
follow his *d* and holy life, 190 4
and so fill them with the truth of thy *d* 205 8
and so fill them with the truth of your *d* 256 5
both by their life and *d*, 329 11
conform to the *d*, discipline, and worship 513 12
Will you be loyal to the *d*, discipline, and worship 526 9
and I do solemnly engage to conform to the *d*, 526 17
Will you be loyal to the *d*, discipline, and worship 538 9
and I do solemnly engage to conform to the *d*, 538 17

document
The Athanasian Creed is an ancient *d* 852 9

doers
I hate the *d* of evil deeds; 730 13

dog
my life from the power of the *d*. 611 21

dogs
Packs of *d* close me in, 611 11
they snarl like *d* and run about the city. 666 8
the tongues of your *d* in the blood of your enemies." 678 4

doing

how wonderful he is in his *d* toward all people. 674 2
This is the LORD's *d*, * 762 17

doings

O Lord, who has taught us that all our *d* 164 18
They have no understanding of the LORD's *d*, 619 18
Direct us, O Lord, in all our *d* 832 1

dominion

death hath no more *d* over him. 46 8
death no longer has *d* over him. 83 16
Be worship and praise, *d* and splendor, * 94 7
be *d* and praise for ever 171 15
from the *d* of sin and death 172 15
thy *d* may increase till the earth is filled 207 11
be *d* and praise for ever and ever. 223 9
from the *d* of sin and death 224 8
that in tranquillity your *d* may increase 258 10
that in tranquillity your *d* may increase, 278 27
let them not get *d* over me; * 607 25
I shall make his *d* extend * 715 16
and his kingship has *d* over all. 734 21
in all places of his *d*; * 734 28
and Israel his *d*. 756 22
let no iniquity have *d* over me. 774 14
your *d* endures throughout all ages. 802 12
to whom be *d* and glory, 815 26
in giving us *d* over things on earth, 827 17
and given us *d* over all the earth: 828 17

doom

and my ears rejoice to hear the *d* of the wicked 721 19

doomed

but the way of the wicked is *d*. 585 16
O Daughter of Babylon, *d* to destruction, * 792 19

door

Let the *d*(s) be opened. 568 1
and drew near to death's *d*. 747 18
and guard the *d* of my lips; * 797 8

doors

and let the *d* of this place be open 562 1
lift them high, O everlasting *d*; * 614 2
lift them high, O everlasting *d*; * 614 8
and opened the *d* of heaven. 696 23
For he shatters the *d* of bronze * 747 13

double

with a smooth tongue they speak from a *d* heart. 597 4

doubt

and without *d* to believe in Jesus 185 16
and without *d* to believe in Jesus 237 10
For those who face temptation, *d*, and despair 279 8
to the removal of scruple and *d*, 317 15
where there is *d*, faith; 833 7

doubts

in all our *d* and uncertainties, 832 8

dove

"Oh, that I had wings like a *d*! * 660 17
you shall be like a *d* 677 6
Do not hand over the life of your *d* 690 22

down

From the rising of the sun even unto the going *d* 38 5
O come, let us worship and fall *d* * 45 1
He hath put *d* the mighty from their seat, * 50 13
He hath put *d* the mighty from their seat, * 65 16
Come, let us bow *d*, and bend the knee, * 82 15
He has cast *d* the mighty from their thrones, * 92 8
All nations will draw near and fall *d* before you, * 94 17
and have made the sun to know its going *d*: 110 25
he has cast *d* the mighty from their thrones, * 119 14
I lie *d* in peace; at once I fall asleep; * 129 6
Look *d*, O Lord, from your heavenly throne, and 133 17
From the rising of the sun to its going *d* * 138 5
O come, let us worship and fall *d* * 146 11
and finally to beat *d* Satan under our feet, 152 13
Gracious Father, whose blessed Son Jesus Christ came *d* 167 10
Pour *d* upon us the abundance of thy mercy, 182 20
for the love of him who laid *d* his life for us, 209 14
Gracious Father, whose blessed Son Jesus Christ came *d* 219 1
for the love of him who laid *d* his life for us, 260 20
see and know that things which were cast *d* 280 18
see and know that things which were cast *d* 291 15
thou shalt not bow *d* to them, nor worship them. 318 4
he came *d* from heaven: 326 19
came *d* from heaven, 328 2
the Holy Ghost came *d* [on this day] from heaven, 347 7
he came *d* from heaven: 358 16
the Holy Spirit came *d* [on this day] from heaven, 380 2
"I am the living bread which came *d* from heaven; 397 1
He has cast *d* the mighty from their thrones,* 442 3
He makes me lie *d* in green pastures* 443 3
but in the evening it is cut *d*, dried up, and withered. 472 22
Thou knowest my *d*-sitting and mine up-rising; 474 19
if I go *d* to hell, thou art there also. 475 8
He maketh me to lie *d* in green pastures; * 476 21
All we go *d* to the dust; 483 1
trampling *d* death by death, 483 14
who have laid *d* their lives in the service 488 28
All of us go *d* to the dust; 499 7
trampling *d* death by death, 500 3
see and know that things which were cast *d* 515 8
he came *d* from heaven: 519 19
see and know that things which were cast *d* 528 6
he came *d* from heaven: 530 10
see and know that things which were cast *d* 540 6
he came *d* from heaven: 542 10
I lie *d* and go to sleep; * 587 11
I lie *d* in peace; at once I fall asleep; * 588 15
I will bow *d* toward your holy temple in awe of you. 589 5
The LORD looks *d* from heaven upon us all, * 598 15
melt me *d*; you will find no impurity in me. 601 4
Arise, O LORD; confront them and bring them *d*; * 601 25
He parted the heavens and came *d* * 603 7
He reached *d* from on high and grasped me; * 603 23
With you I will break *d* an enclosure; * 604 22

I strike them *d*, and they cannot rise; * 605 16
you have cast *d* my adversaries beneath me; 605 19
and cast *d* the peoples beneath me. 606 6
They collapse and fall *d*, * 608 17
To him alone all who sleep in the earth bow *d* 612 15
all who go *d* to the dust fall before him. 612 17
He makes me lie *d* in green pastures * 612 25
I will not sit *d* with the wicked. 616 17
I become like those who go *d* to the Pit. 619 7
therefore he will break them *d* and not 619 20
you restored my life as I was going *d* to the grave. 621 9
if I go *d* to the Pit? * 621 24
The LORD looks *d* from heaven, * 627 1
bowed *d* and grieving. 630 22
they are cast *d* and shall not be able to rise. 633 4
to strike *d* the poor and needy, * 634 12
I am utterly bowed *d* and prostrate; * 637 8
I am worn *d* by the blows of your hand. 639 16
Though you thrust us *d* into a place of misery, * 646 24
We sink *d* into the dust; * 647 7
they go *d* straightway to the grave. 653 10
God looks *d* from heaven upon us all, * 659 1
let them go *d* alive into the grave; * 661 15
and bring them *d*; * 661 26
d to the pit of destruction, O God. 662 9
O God, in your anger, cast *d* the peoples. 663 5
let them be cut *d* like a brier; * 665 11
and put them *d*, O Lord our shield. 666 20
on Edom I throw *d* my sandal to claim it, * 668 2
They seek only to bring me *d* from my place 669 12
go *d* into the depths of the earth; 671 4
That they may shoot *d* the blameless from ambush; * 671 16
All the earth bows *d* before you, * 673 24
The earth shook, and the skies poured *d* rain, 676 18
Trample *d* those who lust after silver; * 678 20
He shall come *d* like rain upon the mown field, * 685 19
His foes shall bow *d* before him, * 686 1
All kings shall bow *d* before him, * 686 5
you cast them *d* in ruin. 688 14
they broke *d* all your carved work with hatchets 689 19
They burned *d* all the meeting-places of God 689 25
he puts *d* one and lifts up another. 691 17
He rained *d* manna upon them to eat * 696 24
He rained *d* flesh upon them like dust * 697 3
He struck *d* all the firstborn of Egypt, * 699 7
Why have you broken *d* its wall, * 703 11
Turn now, O God of hosts, look *d* from heaven; 703 15
Like fire that burns *d* a forest, * 707 5
and righteousness shall look *d* from heaven. 709 17
Bow *d* your ear, O LORD, and answer me, * 709 22
I am counted among those who go *d* to the Pit; * 712 7
nor any wicked man bring him *d*. 715 11
and strike *d* those who hate him. 715 13
Come, let us bow *d*, and bend the knee, * 725 1
Bow *d* before him, all you gods. 727 11
and fall *d* before his footstool; * 729 9
For the LORD looked *d* from his holy place on high; * 732 14
He has brought *d* my strength before my time; * 732 22
They went up into the hills and *d* to the valleys 735 17
and lay themselves *d* in their dens. 736 22
He struck *d* the firstborn of their land, * 740 25
and were brought *d* in their iniquity. 745 12
Some went *d* to the sea in ships * 748 1
on Edom I throw *d* my sandal to claim it, * 750 13
From the rising of the sun to its going *d* * 756 6
nor all those who go *d* into silence; 758 24
You laid *d* your commandments, * 763 11
that runs *d* upon the beard, 787 12
and runs *d* upon the collar of his robe. 787 14
It was he who struck *d* the firstborn of Egypt, * 788 17
Who struck *d* the firstborn of Egypt, * 790 15
Who struck *d* great kings, * 791 3
By the waters of Babylon we sat *d* and wept, * 792 1
who said, "*D* with it! *d* with it! 792 17
I will bow *d* toward your holy temple 793 3
you know my sitting *d* and my rising up; 794 2
and evil shall hunt *d* the lawless. 796 24
or I shall be like those who go *d* to the Pit. 799 14
Bow your heavens, O LORD, and come *d*; * 800 10
he lifts up those who are bowed *d*. 802 16
the LORD lifts up those who are bowed *d*; 803 19
break *d* the walls that separate us; 815 16
Send *d* upon our bishops, 817 4
Father, send *d* upon those who hold office 822 17
broken up and the clouds drop *d* the dew: 840 15
How was this revelation handed *d* to us? 846 17
This revelation was handed *d* to us 846 18

drag

they seize the lowly and *d* them away in their net. 595 13

dragons

and shattered the heads of the *d* upon the waters; 690 11

drain

wicked of the earth shall drink and *d* the dregs. 691 21

draw

Therefore you shall *d* water with rejoicing * 86 5
All nations will *d* near and fall down before you, * 94 17
and to *d* all mankind into thy kingdom, 150 13
that he might *d* the whole world unto himself: 192 14
that he might *d* the whole world to himself: 244 2
that *d* you from the love of God? 302 13
D near with faith, 330 12
that he might *d* the whole world to himself; 346 15
let us with confidence *d* near to the throne 352 6
that he might *d* the whole world to himself; 379 11
d near to us who mourn 497 3
D us to you, 568 16
D the sword and bar the way 629 17
The wicked *d* their sword and bend their bow 634 11
companions *d* back from my affliction; * 637 18
let them *d* back and be disgraced 641 12
and *d* to your courts to dwell there! * 672 14
D near to me and redeem me; * 680 27
d back and be disgraced. 682 16
Why do you *d* back your hand? * 690 6
They *d* near who in malice persecute me; * 776 3
so *d* our hearts to thee, 832 24
Deliver us, when we *d* near to thee, 833 20

draweth

Our King and Savior *d* nigh: 43 1

drawing
d nearer to thee, may be bound together 830 23

drawn
be *d* into your blessed kingdom. 563 9
but they are *d* swords. 662 4
in whose perfect kingdom no sword is *d* 815 22
It has *d* people from every nation, 839 9

draws
Our King and Savior now *d* near: 80 10
call upon him when he *d* near. 86 18
God's Being *d* praise from us. 857 6
and for whatever *d* us closer to God. 857 9

dread
to *d* nothing but the loss of thee, 165 7
Turn away the reproach which I *d*, * 766 13
My flesh trembles with *d* of you; * 773 13

dream
then were we like those who *d*. 105 5
Like a *d* when one awakens, O Lord, * 688 17
You sweep us away like a *d*; * 718 9
then were we like those who *d*. 782 7

dregs
wicked of the earth shall drink and drain the *d*. 691 21

drench
every night I *d* my bed 590 10
You *d* the furrows and smooth out the ridges; * 673 9

dressed
But when they were sick I *d* in sack-cloth * 630 17

drew
he *d* me out of great waters. 603 24
and *d* near to death's door. 747 18

dried
but in the evening it is cut down, *d* up, and withered. 472 22
My mouth is *d* out like a pot-sherd; 611 8
my moisture was *d* up as in the heat of summer. 625 6
you *d* up ever-flowing rivers. 690 15
in the evening it is *d* up and withered. 718 12
He rebuked the Red Sea, and it *d* up, * 742 16

drift
For my days *d* away like smoke, * 731 5

drink
"*D* ye all of this; 335 4
as oft as ye shall *d* it, in remembrance of me." 335 7
and to *d* his blood, 337 15
D this in remembrance 338 10
"*D* this, all of you; 342 6
as oft as ye shall *d* it, in remembrance of me." 342 9
"*D* this, all of you: 363 2
Whenever you *d* it, 363 4
the holy food and *d* of new and unending life 363 14
"*D* this, all of you: 368 15
Whenever you *d* it, 368 17
"*D* this, all of you: 371 15
Whenever you *d* it, 371 17
"*D* this, all of you: 374 20
Whenever you *d* it, 374 22
and my blood is *d* indeed. 397 4
"*D* this, all of you: 403 9
Whenever you *d* it, 403 11
"*D* this, all of you: 405 7
Whenever you *d* it, 405 9
we who eat this bread and *d* this cup 405 17
fed us with the spiritual food and *d* 482 2
fed us with the spiritual food and *d* 498 13
Grant that all who eat and *d* at this holy Table 574 4
d from the river of your delights. 632 21
or *d* the blood of goats? 655 6
and when I was thirsty, they gave me vinegar to *d*. 681 7
and all the wicked of the earth shall *d* 691 20
and gave them *d* as from the great deep. 696 4
so that they could not *d* of their streams. 698 16
you have given them bowls of tears to *d*. 702 22
and mingled my *d* with weeping. 731 18
All the beasts of the field *d* their fill 735 23
He will *d* from the brook beside the road; * 754 3
give thanks to you for food and *d* 825 21
For our daily food and *d*, 837 9

drinking
eating of that Bread and *d* of that Cup. 316 22

drinks
Whoever eats my flesh and *d* my blood 397 5

drive
D far from us all wrong desires, 56 20
D far from us all wrong desires, 99 14
and *d* far from it all snares 133 17
and *d* far from it all snares 140 13
May it shine continually to *d* away all darkness. 287 22
to *d* away all sickness of body and spirit, 456 3
you *d* away from our bodies all sickness 458 17
and let the angel of the LORD *d* them away. 629 23
D them with your tempest * 707 7

driven
When my enemies are *d* back, * 593 5
let them be *d* from the ruins of their homes. 751 17

drives
like smoke when the wind *d* it away; * 676 3

drop
and the clouds *d* down the dew: 840 15

drops
d of dew and flakes of snow. 88 18

dross
all the wicked of the earth are but *d*; * 773 11

drove
How with your hand you *d* the peoples out 645 10
He *d* out the Canaanites before them 699 15

drowned
have been *d* in the Red Sea. 85 11

drums
in the midst of maidens playing upon the hand-*d*. 678 8

drunkards

and the *d* make songs about me. 680 12
They reeled and staggered like *d* * 748 9

dry

and his hands prepared the *d* land. 44 19
and his hands have molded the *d* land. 82 14
and his hands prepared the *d* land. 146 10
through the Red Sea on *d* land. 287 8
and *d* the tears of those who weep. 497 4
as in a barren and *d* land where there is no water. 670 14
He turned the sea into *d* land, 674 3
but the rebels shall live in *d* places. 676 15
and his hands have molded the *d* land. 724 23
so the river ran in the *d* places. 741 8
and *d* land into water-springs. 748 26

due

give us that *d* sense of all thy mercies, 59 2
give us that *d* sense of all thy mercies, 71 21
so that in *d* time all may enjoy them, 151 10
with meek heart and *d* reverence, 329 15
Ascribe to the Lord the honor *d* his Name; 343 10
Ascribe to the Lord the honor *d* his Name; 376 6
bearing fruit in *d* season, 585 8
Ascribe to the LORD the glory *d* his Name; * 620 7
Ascribe to the LORD the honor *d* his Name; * 726 7
to give them their food in *d* season. 737 8
and you give them their food in *d* season. 802 18

dug

The ungodly have fallen into the pit they *d*, * 594 7
without a cause they have *d* a pit to take me alive. 630 4
let them fall into the pit they *d*. 630 7
they have *d* a pit before me, 664 6
until a pit is *d* for the wicked. 723 20
The proud have *d* pits for me; * 770 12

dull

like the *d* and stupid they perish * 652 24

dullard

The *d* does not know, 721 7

dullards

Consider well, you *d* among the people; * 723 9

duly

may be *d* prepared for the service 56 14
may be *d* prepared for the service 99 9
and rightly and *d* administer thy holy Sacraments. 329 12
has been *d* and lawfully elected 514 2

dumb

how long will you worship *d* idols 128 12
how long will you worship *d* idols 588 2

dung

they became like *d* upon the ground. 706 23

during

done your will with cheerfulness *d* the day, 99 17
Grant us *d* our earthly pilgrimage 198 25
Grant us *d* our earthly pilgrimage 250 10

dusk

you make the dawn and the *d* to sing for joy. 673 3

dust

you have created us out of the *d* 265 16
Remember that you are *d*, and to *d* you shall return. 265 21
you formed me from the *d* 450 8
"*D* thou art, and unto *d* shalt thou return." 482 15
All we go down to the *d*; 483 1
earth to earth, ashes to ashes, *d* to *d*. 485 12
"You are *d*, and to *d* you shall return." 499 7
All of us go down to the *d*; 499 8
earth to earth, ashes to ashes, *d* to *d*. 501 14
and lay my honor in the *d*. 591 5
I beat them like *d* before the wind; * 605 24
and you have laid me in the *d* of the grave. 611 10
all who go down to the *d* fall before him. 612 17
will the *d* praise you or declare your faithfulness? 621 25
We sink down into the *d*; * 647 7
and his enemies lick the *d*. 686 2
He rained down flesh upon them like *d* * 697 3
O my God, make them like whirling *d* * 707 3
You turn us back to the *d* and say, * 718 4
and are moved to pity even for her *d*. 732 5
he remembers that we are but *d*. 734 10
and they die and return to their *d*. 737 13
He takes up the weak out of the *d* * 756 12
My soul cleaves to the *d*; * 765 9

duties

and you are to carry out other *d* 543 15
That he may faithfully fulfill the *d* of this ministry, 549 4
carrying out the *d* of my ministry. 563 5
in the exercise of their *d*. 821 22

duty

our bounden *d* and service, 317 21
It is very meet, right, and our bounden *d*, 333 7
this our bounden *d* and service, 336 11
It is very meet, right, and our bounden *d*, 341 1
our *d* to God, and our *d* to our neighbors. 847 17
What is our *d* to God? 847 19
Our *d* is to believe and trust in God; 847 20
What is our *d* to our neighbors? 848 1
Our *d* to our neighbors is to love them as ourselves, 848 2
and to do our *d* for the love of God, 848 20
What is the *d* of all Christians? 856 12
The *d* of all Christians is to follow Christ; 856 13

dwell

and he will *d* with them, 37 11
"I *d* in the high and holy place, 41 1
He will *d* with them, 75 11
"I *d* in the high and holy place 78 23
To shine on those who *d* in darkness 93 7
make me *d* in safety. 129 7
let your holy angels *d* with us 133 18
let your holy angels *d* with us 140 14
and with him continually *d*; 174 18
and with him continually *d*; 226 11
and *d* with you in the life to come; 310 11
that he may *d* in us, 336 7
that we may evermore *d* in him, 337 15

that he may *d* in us, and we in him; 343 1
and *d* with you in the life to come; 419 7
and I will *d* in the house of the LORD for ever. 443 17
and to all who *d* in it. 453 1
that finally he may *d* with thee in life everlasting; 458 9
and I will *d* in the house of the LORD for ever. 476 18
and I will *d* in the house of the LORD for ever. 477 11
even that I may *d* in the house of the LORD 477 17
may *d* with Christ in paradise, 487 7
may *d* with Christ in paradise, 503 9
make me *d* in safety. 588 16
and evil cannot *d* with you. 588 24
LORD, who may *d* in your tabernacle? * 599 4
and I will *d* in the house of the LORD for ever. 613 13
the world and all who *d* therein. 613 15
They shall *d* in prosperity, * 615 14
LORD, I love the house in which you *d* * 616 22
that I may *d* in the house of the LORD 617 20
let all who *d* in the world stand in awe of him. 626 16
on all who *d* on the earth. 627 4
d in the land and feed on its riches. 633 10
and *d* in the land for ever. 635 15
and *d* in it for ever. 635 21
hearken, all you who *d* in the world, * 652 7
I will *d* in your house for ever; * 668 19
and draw to your courts to *d* there! * 672 14
Those who *d* at the ends of the earth 673 1
the LORD will *d* there for ever. 677 14
that the LORD God might *d* among them. 677 20
and let there be none to *d* in their tents. 681 15
and those who love his Name will *d* therein. 682 10
and Mount Zion where you *d*. 689 13
he made the tribes of Israel to *d* in their tents. 699 17
the Philistines and those who *d* in Tyre. 706 17
Happy are they who *d* in your house! * 707 23
than to *d* in the tents of the wicked. 708 13
that his glory may *d* in our land. 709 13
the lands and those who *d* therein. 728 17
that they may *d* with me, * 730 21
who act deceitfully shall not *d* in my house, * 730 24
they found no way to a city where they might *d*. 746 9
to go to a city where they might *d*. 746 15
because of the wickedness of those who *d* there. 748 24
and they founded a city to *d* in. 749 2
and *d* upon your law. 767 24
and *d* among the tents of Kedar! 778 19
here will I *d*, for I delight in her. 786 29
and *d* in the uttermost parts of the sea, 794 17
we may *d* secure in thy peace. 820 18
the homes in which thy people *d*. 828 24

dwellest

and *d* between the Cherubim; * 49 16

dwelleth

by his Spirit that *d* in us. 485 3

dwelling

and bring me unto thy holy hill, and to thy *d*. 40 17
the *d* of God is with mankind. 75 11
and bring me to your holy hill and to your *d*. 78 16
in safety to your holy *d*. 85 23
neither shall any plague come near your *d*. 130 18
Christ *d* in your hearts by faith, 311 24
there is prepared for us a *d* place eternal 349 10
d in light inaccessible before time 373 2
there is prepared for us a *d* place eternal 382 5
and your *d* place in the Paradise of God. 464 26
into the courts of your heavenly *d* place. 466 10
in the secret place of his *d* shall he hide me, 477 21
Therefore will I offer in his *d* 477 25
God of all comfort, *d* on high 520 12
He heard my voice from his heavenly *d*; * 602 20
he shall hide me in the secrecy of his *d* 618 3
Therefore I will offer in his *d* 618 7
bring me to your holy hill and to your *d*; 644 23
their *d* places from generation to generation, * 653 2
and snatch you from your *d*, 658 9
they defiled the *d*-place of your Name 689 22
and his *d* is in Zion. 692 4
and made his *d* a ruin. 701 20
How dear to me is your *d*, O LORD of hosts! * 707 15
neither shall any plague come near your *d*. 720 6
You water the mountains from your *d* on high; * 736 1
and in whose tops the stork makes his *d*. 736 12
a *d* for the Mighty One of Jacob." 786 8
Let us go to God's *d* place; * 786 11

dwellings

for wickedness is in their *d*, 661 16
and round about their *d*. 697 6
the flower of manhood in the *d* of Ham. 699 8
more than all the *d* of Jacob. 711 14

dwells

where *d* the true and never-failing Light, 110 21
He who *d* in the shelter of the Most High * 129 21
Sing praise to the LORD who *d* in Zion; * 593 21
He who *d* in the shelter of the Most High, * 719 10
mightier is the LORD who *d* on high. 722 14
who *d* in Jerusalem. 789 18
because the Holy Spirit *d* in it, 854 18

dwelt

The Word was made flesh and *d* among us: 44 6
The Word was made flesh and *d* among us: 82 1
I should soon have *d* in the land of silence. 723 28

dying

bless the *d*, 71 4
bless the *d*, 124 20
bless the *d*, 134 9
and from *d* suddenly and unprepared, 149 15
and it is in *d* that we are born 833 12
for his *d*, through which he overcame death; 836 14

E

each

our common life depends upon *e* other's toil; 134 14
let *e* one find thee mighty to save; 166 12
who calleth us *e* by name, 173 13
as you know the weaknesses of *e* of us, 218 4
let *e* one find you mighty to save; 218 4
who calls us *e* by name, 225 5

will bring *e* of us to the fullness of redemption. 288 3
have bound themselves to *e* other; 427 11
have given themselves to *e* other 428 1
that *e* may be to the other a strength in need, a 429 8
when they hurt *e* other, 429 14
and to seek *e* other's forgiveness 429 15
Let their love for *e* other be a seal 430 17
that they may so love, honor, and cherish *e* other 431 4
have bound themselves to *e* other; 434 5
to be married to *e* other? 437 8
that *e* may be to the other a strength in need, 444 10
who hate me without a cause wink at *e* other. 631 8
righteousness and peace have kissed *e* other. 709 15
unity with God and *e* other in Christ. 855 3
knowing and loving God and *e* other. 862 28

eagerly

O God, you are my God; *e* I seek you; * 670 12

eagle

and your youth is renewed like an *e*'s. 733 18

ear

Incline your *e* to me; * 129 11
to incline thine *e* to us 153 21
because he has inclined his *e* to me 442 15
Because he hath inclined his *e* unto me, * 479 1
Give *e* to my words, O Lord; * 588 17
incline your *e* to me and hear my words. 601 10
Incline your *e* to me; * 622 10
and give *e* to my cry; * 639 21
I will incline my *e* to a proverb * 652 11
give *e* to the words of my mouth. 659 20
incline your *e* to me and save me. 683 4
Bow down your *e*, O Lord, and answer me, * 709 22
Give *e*, O Lord, to my prayer, * 710 9
incline your *e* to my lamentation. 712 4
He that planted the *e*, does he not hear? * 723 11
Incline your *e* to me; * 731 3
because he has inclined his *e* to me 759 3
to incline thine *e* to us 834 3

early

God shall help her, and that right *e*. 472 3
e in the morning I make my appeal and watch 588 22
for the *e* rains have covered it with pools 708 3
To tell of your loving-kindness *e* in the morning * 720 24
e in the morning I cry out to you, * 775 20
It is in vain that you rise so *e* 783 3

earnest

answer the *e* prayers 440 9

earnestly

Ye who do truly and *e* repent 330 9
We do *e* repent, 331 9
And we *e* desire thy fatherly goodness 335 24
And we *e* desire thy fatherly goodness 342 21

ears

we have heard with our *e*, 154 5
O let thine *e* consider well * 474 3
shut not thy merciful *e* to our prayer; 484 12
shut not your *e* to our prayers, 492 13
open our eyes, our *e*, and our hearts, 569 3
Give us *e* to hear 571 2
strengthen their heart and your *e* shall hear; 596 4
my cry of anguish came to his *e*. 602 21
and his *e* are open to their cry. 628 24
(you have given me *e* to hear you); 640 17
We have heard with our *e*, O God, 645 6
they are like the deaf adder which stops its *e*, 665 2
incline your *e* to the words of my mouth. 694 20
and my *e* rejoice to hear the doom of the wicked 721 19
They have *e*, but they cannot hear; * 757 24
let your *e* consider well the voice of my supplication. 784 20
They have *e*, but they cannot hear; * 789 9
we have heard this day with our outward *e*, 834 19

earth

my salvation unto the end of the *e*. 38 4
uttermost part of the *e*. 39 21
let all the *e* keep silence 40 18
The *e* is the Lord's for he made it: 44 1
In his hand are all the corners of the *e*, * 44 16
let the whole *e* stand in awe of him. 45 7
For he cometh, for he cometh to judge the *e*, * 45 8
O let the *e* bless the Lord; * 48 17
O all ye green things upon the *e*, 48 19
and on *e* peace, good will towards men. 52 4
All the *e* doth worship thee, 52 24
Heaven and *e* are full of the majesty of thy glory. 53 2
maker of heaven and *e*; 53 24
on *e* as it is in heaven. 54 18
Let thy way be known upon *e*; 55 9
that our rest here upon *e* may be a preparation 56 15
of one blood all the peoples of the *e*, 58 2
let the whole *e* stand in awe of him. 61 6
Thou hast fixed all the boundaries of the *e*; 61 9
and poureth them out upon the face of the *e*: 62 4
maker of heaven and *e*; 66 10
on *e* as it is in heaven. 67 8
Let thy way be known upon *e*; 68 1
Let the whole *e* also worship thee, 70 16
reach to the end of the *e*. 76 4
Judea, and Samaria, and to the ends of the *e*. 77 19
let all the *e* keep silence 78 17
The Spirit of the Lord renews the face of the *e*: 81 8
The *e* is the Lord's for he made it: 81 11
In his hand are the caverns of the *e*, * 82 11
the *e* swallowed them up. 85 20
For as the heavens are higher than the *e*, * 86 25
and return not again, but water the *e*, 87 2
Let the *e* glorify the Lord, * 89 5
and all that grows upon the *e*, * 89 8
You made the heavens and the *e*, * 90 20
nor condemn me to the depths of the *e*. 91 19
and peace to his people on *e*. 94 22
heaven and *e* are full of your glory. 95 22
creator of heaven and *e*. 96 14
on *e* as it is in heaven. 97 8
Let your way be known upon *e*; 98 3
that our rest here upon the *e* may be a preparation 99 10
of one blood all the peoples of the *e*, 100 18
the maker of heaven and *e*. 104 16
on *e* as it is in heaven. 106 18

the *e* may look to you and be saved;	107	10
let the whole *e* tremble before him.	115	5
You fixed all the boundaries of the *e*;	115	9
and pours them out upon the surface of the *e*:	115	16
creator of heaven and *e*.	120	10
on *e* as it is in heaven.	121	8
Let your way be known upon *e*;	122	3
Let the whole *e* also worship you,	124	13
The maker of heaven and *e*.	127	4
the Lord who made heaven and *e* bless you	131	9
on *e* as it is in heaven.	132	23
the *e* may look to you and be saved;	138	14
the Lord who made heaven and *e* bless you	140	4
In his hand are all the corners of the *e*, *	146	7
Creator of heaven and *e*,	148	1
bountiful fruits of the *e*,	151	10
on *e* as it is in heaven.	153	10
the mystery of that Light upon *e*,	161	3
begotten Son to the peoples of the *e*:	162	14
and obeyed to the ends of the *e*;	163	11
who dost govern all things in heaven and *e*:	164	2
Creator of heaven and *e*: Grant that,	170	1
he abideth with his Church on *e*,	174	11
that it may reach to the ends of the *e*;	175	12
both in heaven and *e*:	177	15
Mercifully grant that the peoples of the *e*,	185	3
and defend us on *e*;	193	8
fruits of the *e* in their season	194	17
with thy saints in heaven and on *e*:	199	5
and defend us on *e*;	200	10
to thy whole Church in paradise and on *e*	202	2
Mercifully grant that the peoples of the *e*,	203	1
of one blood all the peoples of the *e*,	206	10
O God of all the nations of the *e*:	206	17
who hast made all peoples of the *e*	207	1
take counsel for the nations of the *e*,	207	10
thy dominion may increase till the *e* is filled	207	11
Lord of heaven and *e*:	207	15
thy handiwork in the heavens and in the *e*:	210	3
the mystery of that Light on *e*,	212	18
to the peoples of the *e*:	214	8
and obeyed to the ends of the *e*;	215	5
you govern all things both in heaven and on *e*:	215	13
Creator of heaven and *e*:	221	13
he abides with his Church on *e*,	226	4
that it may reach to the ends of the *e*;	227	5
sets in order all things both in heaven and *e*:	229	11
Mercifully grant that the peoples of the *e*,	236	16
help and defend us here on *e*;	244	17
fruits of the *e* in their season	246	2
help and defend us here on *e*;	251	16
whole Church in paradise and on *e*	253	7
Mercifully grant that the peoples of the *e*,	254	3
of one blood all the peoples of the *e*,	257	6
O God of all the nations of the *e*:	257	13
all the peoples of the *e* for your glory,	258	2
for the nations of the *e*,	258	10
until the *e* is filled with the knowledge	258	11
Lord of heaven and *e*:	258	15
your handiwork in the heavens and in the *e*:	261	9
created us out of the dust of the *e*:	265	17
in heaven and on *e*,	267	15
Let us pray for all nations and peoples of the *e*,	278	17
for the nations of the *e*;	278	27
until the *e* is filled with the knowledge	279	1
Creator of all the peoples of the *e*	280	1
Let your ways be known upon *e*,	281	7
Creator of heaven and *e*:	283	1
Rejoice and sing now, all the round *e*,	286	4
when *e* and heaven are joined	287	19
Grant that all the peoples of the *e*	289	16
who serve you now on *e*,	290	4
and you renew the *e* by your Spirit:	290	9
creator of heaven and *e*.	292	13
creator of heaven and *e*.	304	3
on *e* as it is in heaven.	311	5
whom every family in heaven and *e* is named,	311	22
that is in heaven above, or in the *e*	318	2
or in the water under the *e*;	318	3
and on *e* peace, good will towards men.	324	15
maker of heaven and *e*,	326	8
maker of heaven and *e*,	327	22
Heaven and *e* are full of thy glory.	334	5
on *e* as it is in heaven.	336	22
Heaven and *e* are full of thy glory.	341	8
for that thou didst create heaven and *e*,	341	13
For all that is in the heaven and in the *e* is thine.	344	10
and peace to his people on *e*.	356	2
maker of heaven and *e*,	358	5
Creator of heaven and *e*.	361	9
heaven and *e* are full of your glory.	362	5
on *e* as it is in heaven.	364	5
Creator of heaven and *e*.	367	9
heaven and *e* are full of your glory.	367	14
and this fragile *e*, our island home.	370	10
heaven and *e* are full of your glory.	371	2
heaven and *e* are full of your glory.	373	13
For everything in heaven and on *e* is yours.	377	8
an abundance of the fruits of the *e*,	384	12
For the good *e* which God has given us,	384	14
That there may be justice and peace on the *e*.	387	11
Give us all a reverence for the *e*	388	12
preach the Gospel to the ends of the *e*,	390	8
ruler of all things in heaven and *e*:	394	10
with your saints in heaven and on *e*:	395	18
on *e* as it is in heaven.	398	16
heaven and *e* are full of your glory.	402	10
heaven and *e* are full of your glory.	404	12
creator of heaven and *e*.	416	8
on *e* as it is in heaven.	428	12
be done on *e* as it is in heaven;	430	7
to whom all things in heaven, on *e*,	456	21
the *e* bow and obey:	457	1
on *e* as it is in heaven.	464	8
he shall stand at the latter day upon the *e*;	469	5
Therefore will we not fear, though the *e* be moved, *	471	19
and I will be exalted in the *e*.	472	6
or ever the *e* and the world were made, *	472	12
who hath made heaven and *e*.	473	12
Church in paradise and on *e*,	480	7
formed of the *e*, and unto *e* shall we return.	482	13
e to *e*, ashes to ashes, dust to dust.	485	12
on *e* as it is in heaven.	485	24
who now serve thee on *e*,	486	13

earth

and that at the last he will stand upon the *e*. 491 8
we may continue our course on *e*, 493 22
creator of heaven and *e*. 496 4
formed of the *e*, and to *e* shall we return. 499 5
e to *e*, ashes to ashes, dust to dust. 501 14
on *e* as it is in heaven. 502 5
maker of heaven and *e*, 519 8
The maker of heaven and *e*. 523 12
maker of heaven and *e*, 529 11
maker of heaven and *e*, 541 11
preach the Gospel to the ends of the *e*, 549 22
The maker of heaven and *e*. 552 2
The maker of heaven and *e*. 568 5
For everything in heaven and on *e* is yours. 569 12
We praise you for his life on *e*, 573 13
For everything in heaven and on *e* is yours. 579 15
Why do the kings of the *e* rise up in revolt, 586 3
and the ends of the *e* for your possession. 586 19
be warned, you rulers of the *e*. 586 23
The *e* reeled and rocked; * 603 1
descendants from among the peoples of the *e*. 609 19
All the ends of the *e* shall remember 612 10
To him alone all who sleep in the *e* bow down 612 15
The *e* is the LORD's and all that is in it, * 613 14
the loving-kindness of the LORD fills the whole *e*. 626 10
Let all the *e* fear the LORD; * 626 15
on all who dwell on the *e*. 627 4
to root out the remembrance of them from the *e*. 628 26
you shall make them princes over all the *e*. 648 24
Therefore we will not fear, though the *e* be moved, * 649 3
God has spoken, and the *e* shall melt away. 649 16
what awesome things he has done on *e*. 649 20
I will be exalted in the *e*." 650 3
he is the great King over all the *e*. 650 9
For God is King of all the *e*; * 650 18
The rulers of the *e* belong to God, * 650 24
the joy of all the *e*, is the hill of Zion, 651 3
Behold, the kings of the *e* assembled * 651 8
he has called the *e* from the rising 654 2
He calls the heavens and the *e* from above * 654 9
and your glory over all the *e*. 664 9
and your glory over all the *e*. 664 20
surely, there is a God who rules in the *e*." 665 17
and to the ends of the *e*. 666 27
You have shaken the *e* and split it open; * 667 12
I call upon you from the ends of the *e* 668 14
go down into the depths of the *e*; 671 4
O Hope of all the ends of the *e* 672 19
Those who dwell at the ends of the *e* will tremble 673 1
You visit the *e* and water it abundantly; 673 4
for so you provide for the *e*. 673 8
All the *e* bows down before you, * 673 24
Let your ways be known upon *e*, * 675 11
and guide all the nations upon *e*. 675 17
The *e* has brought forth her increase; * 675 20
and may all the ends of the *e* stand in awe of him. 675 23
The *e* shook, and the skies poured down rain, 676 18
Sing to God, O kingdoms of the *e*; * 678 24
Let the heavens and the *e* praise him, * 682 5
bring me up again from the deep places of the *e*. 684 25
like showers that water the *e*. 685 20
and from the River to the ends of the *e*. 685 25
May there be abundance of grain on the *e*, 686 17
and its grain like grass upon the *e*. 686 20
and may all the *e* be filled with his glory. 686 28
and having you I desire nothing upon *e*. 688 28
victorious in the midst of the *e*. 690 9
You fixed all the boundaries of the *e*; * 690 18
the dark places of the *e* are haunts of violence. 690 25
Though the *e* and all its inhabitants are quaking, * 691 8
and all the wicked of the *e* shall drink and 691 20
the *e* was afraid and was still; 692 17
and to save all the oppressed of the *e*. 692 19
and strikes terror in the kings of the *e*. 692 26
the *e* trembled and shook. 694 13
like the *e* which he founded for ever. 700 18
all the foundations of the *e* are shaken. 705 19
Arise, O God, and rule the *e*, * 706 1
you alone are the Most High over all the *e*. 707 14
Truth shall spring up from the *e*, * 709 16
Yours are the heavens; the *e* also is yours; * 714 15
and higher than the kings of the *e*. 715 21
or the land and the *e* were born, * 718 2
"Go back, O child of *e*." 718 5
In his hand are the caverns of the *e*, * 724 20
sing to the LORD, all the whole *e*. 725 18
let the whole *e* tremble before him. 726 10
Let the heavens rejoice, and let the *e* be glad; 726 14
when he comes to judge the *e*. 726 19
let the *e* rejoice; * 726 23
the *e* sees it and is afraid. 727 4
at the presence of the Lord of the whole *e*. 727 6
most high over all the *e*; * 727 15
and all the ends of the *e* have seen the 728 8
when he comes to judge the *e*. 728 20
let the *e* shake. 728 26
and all the kings of the *e* your glory. 732 7
from the heavens he beheld the *e*; 732 15
you laid the foundations of the *e*, * 732 28
For as the heavens are high above the *e*, * 734 3
You have set the *e* upon its foundations, * 735 11
they shall not again cover the *e*. 735 20
the *e* is fully satisfied by the fruit of your works. 736 2
That they may bring forth food from the *e*, * 736 5
the *e* is full of your creatures. 736 27
and so you renew the face of the *e*. 737 15
He looks at the *e* and it trembles; * 737 18
Let sinners be consumed out of the *e*, * 737 24
The *e* opened and swallowed Dathan * 743 5
and your glory over all the *e*. 750 4
but let him root out their names from the *e*; 751 28
he will smash heads over the wide *e*. 754 2
but stoops to behold the heavens and the *e*? 756 11
Tremble, O *e*, at the presence of the Lord, * 757 9
the maker of heaven and *e*. 758 20
but he entrusted the *e* to its peoples. 758 22
I am a stranger here on *e*; * 764 21
The *e*, O LORD, is full of your love; * 768 15
They had almost made an end of me on *e*, * 770 16
you established the *e*, and it abides. 770 23
all the wicked of the *e* are but dross; * 773 11
the maker of heaven and *e*. 779 4
the maker of heaven and *e*. 781 16
the LORD who made heaven and *e* bless 787 22

does whatever pleases him, in heaven and on *e,* * 788 12
He brings up rain clouds from the ends of the *e;* * 788 14
Who spread out the *e* upon the waters, * 790 7
All the kings of the *e* will praise you, O LORD, * 793 10
and woven in the depths of the *e.* 795 5
A slanderer shall not be established on the *e,* * 796 23
As when a plowman turns over the *e* in furrows, * 797 17
Put not your trust in rulers, nor in any child of *e,* * 803 7
When they breathe their last, they return to *e,* * 803 9
Who made heaven and *e,* the seas, and all 803 13
and prepares rain for the *e;* 804 17
He sends out his command to the *e,* * 805 7
Praise the LORD from the *e,* * 806 7
Kings of the *e* and all peoples, * 806 15
his splendor is over *e* and heaven. 806 21
to accomplish your purposes on *e;* 815 18
ruler of all things in heaven and *e,* 817 19
to perfect the praises offered by your people on *e;* 819 16
show forth thy praise among the nations of the *e.* 820 12
other nations of the *e.* 821 17
we thank you for making the *e* fruitful, 824 6
that we may all share the fruits of the *e,* 824 9
Behold and visit, we pray, the cities of the *e.* 825 8
in giving us dominion over things on *e,* 827 17
Spirit go forth, that it may renew the face of the *e;* 828 4
that we may receive the fruits of the *e,* 828 13
and given us dominion over all the *e:* 828 17
to the uppermost parts of the *e:* 830 20
and wonder of your creation, in *e* 837 3
in all parts of the *e* a community 838 5
for the beauty of *e* and sky and sea; 840 8
creator of heaven and *e,* of all that is, 846 4

earthly

putting away all *e* anxieties, 56 13
putting away all *e* anxieties, 99 8
not to mind *e* things, but to love things heavenly; 182 6
during our *e* pilgrimage to abide in their fellowship, 198 25
in our *e* pilgrimage we may ever be supported 199 6
Christ in his *e* life shared our toil 208 1
not to be anxious about *e* things, 234 1
during our *e* pilgrimage to abide in their fellowship, 250 10
Grant that in our *e* pilgrimage 250 15
Christ in his *e* life shared our toil 259 3
in our *e* pilgrimage we may always be supported 395 19
in suffering you hallowed *e* pain 461 6
in the midst of this *e* life being purged 488 18
love as a companion on our *e* pilgrimage. 493 19
in these *e* things we may behold the order 573 5

earthquake

from *e,* fire, and flood; 149 11

ease

always at *e,* they increase their wealth. 688 2

eased

"I *e* his shoulder from the burden; 704 12

east

like ships of the sea when the *e* wind shatters them. 651 14
judgment is neither from the *e* nor from the west, * 691 14
He caused the *e* wind to blow in the heavens * 697 1

As far as the *e* is from the west, * 734 5
out of the lands; * from the *e* and from the west, 746 6

easy

For my yoke is *e,* and my burden is light. 131 18
whom it would be *e* for us to forget: 826 2

eat

"Take, *e,* this is my Body, 335 1
so to *e* the flesh of thy dear Son Jesus Christ, 337 14
Take and *e* this in remembrance that 338 6
"Take, *e,* this is my Body, 342 3
"Take, *e*: This is my Body, 362 21
"Take, *e*: This is my Body, 368 12
"Take, *e*: This is my Body, 371 12
"Take, *e*: This is my Body, 374 17
"Take, *e*: This is my Body, 403 6
"Take, *e*: This is my Body, 405 4
we who *e* this bread and drink this cup 405 16
all who *e* and drink at this holy Table 574 4
who *e* up my people like bread 598 22
The poor shall *e* and be satisfied, 612 7
When evildoers came upon me to *e* up my flesh, * 617 11
like a moth you *e* away all that is dear to us; * 639 18
Do you think I *e* the flesh of bulls, * 655 5
who *e* up my people like bread 659 8
They gave me gall to *e,* * 681 6
He rained down manna upon them to *e* * 696 24
so that I forget to *e* my bread. 731 8
vain, too, to *e* the bread of toil, 783 4
You shall *e* the fruit of your labor; * 783 15
nor *e* of their choice foods. 797 11

eaten

You have made us like sheep to be *e* * 646 7
Zeal for your house has *e* me up; * 680 5
For I have *e* ashes for bread * 731 17

eating

seed for sowing and bread for *e,* 87 4
to prepare themselves carefully before *e* 316 21

eats

if anyone *e* of this bread, he will live for ever; 397 2
Whoever *e* my flesh and drinks my blood abides in me, 397 5

edge

It goes forth from the uttermost *e* of the heavens 607 1
Let them fall upon the *e* of the sword, * 671 5
You have turned back the *e* of his sword * 716 27

edged

and a two-*e* sword in their hand; 807 13

Edom

on *E* I throw down my sandal to claim it, * 668 2
who will bring me into *E*? 668 5
Truly, wrathful *E* will give you thanks, * 692 20
The tents of *E* and the Ishmaelites; * 706 14
on *E* I throw down my sandal to claim it, * 750 13
who will bring me into *E*? 750 16
against the people of *E,* * 792 16

effective
an *e* example in word and action, 523 6
an *e* example in word and action, 535 6
an *e* example in word and action, 547 2
an *e* example in word and action, 564 6

effectual
by the *e* working of your providence, 280 16
by the *e* working of your providence, 291 13
by the *e* working of your providence, 515 6
by the *e* working of your providence, 528 4
by the *e* working of your providence, 540 4

effectually
obtained *e*, to the relief of our necessity, 153 24
obtain *e*, to the glory of thy Name; 394 2
may *e* be obtained, to the relief of our necessity, 834 5

efforts
tasks which demand our best *e*, 836 8
Strengthen our *e* to blot our ignorance 839 17

Egypt
the children of Israel, out of bondage in *E*, 287 7
out of their bondage in *E* into the land of promise. 306 16
out of the land of *E*, out of the house of bondage. 317 26
the children of Israel out of their bondage in *E* 570 7
Let tribute be brought out of *E*; * 678 22
in the land of *E*, in the field of Zoan. 695 27
How he wrought his signs in *E* * 698 13
He struck down all the firstborn of *E*, * 699 7
You have brought a vine out of *E*; * 703 3
when he came out of the land of *E*. 704 10
who brought you out of the land of *E* and said, * 704 22
I count *E* and Babylon among those who know me; * 711 17
Israel came into *E*, * 739 23
E was glad of their going, * 741 1
In *E* they did not consider your marvelous works, 742 11
who had done great things in *E*, 743 14
When Israel came out of *E*, * 756 19
It was he who struck down the firstborn of *E*, * 788 17
signs and wonders into the midst of you, O *E*, * 788 19
Who struck down the firstborn of *E*, * 790 15

Egyptians
but the *E* rebelled against his words. 740 10

eighty
perhaps in strength even *e*; * 718 20

either
to give more than *e* we desire or deserve: 182 19
and to give more than we *e* desire or deserve: 234 13
if *e* of you know any reason 424 5

elders
and to teach his *e* wisdom. 739 22
and praise him in the council of the *e*. 748 20
I am wiser than the *e*, * 771 19

elect
who hast knit together thine *e* in one communion 194 8
you have knit together your *e* in one communion 245 16
who hast knit together thine *e* in one communion 480 4
That I may see the prosperity of your *e* 742 6
e trustworthy leaders and make wise decisions 822 12

elected
has been duly and lawfully *e* to be a bishop 514 2

election
their trust in you by acclaiming your *e*. 517 2
in the *e* of officials and representatives; 822 25

eleison
Kyrie *e*. 153 3
Christe *e*. 153 4
Kyrie *e*. 324 7
Christe *e*. 324 8
Kyrie *e*. 356 19
Christe *e*. 356 20
(or "Kyrie *e*"). 389 14
Kyrie *e*. 389 18

elements
From the primal *e* you brought forth 370 12
*Or the deep, or the *e*, or its resting place. 485 16
*Or the deep, or the *e*, or its resting place. 501 17

eliminate
Enable us to *e* poverty, 825 10
Help us to *e* our cruelty to these our neighbors. 826 11

else
speak now; or *e* for ever hold your peace. 424 3
or *e* they will not stay near you." 625 22
and whatever *e* may hinder us 818 17

embittered
When my mind became *e*, * 688 19
For they so *e* his spirit * 744 13

embrace
within the reach of thy saving *e*: 58 10
the reach of your saving *e*: 101 3
to *e* and hold fast the unchangeable truth 166 18
e and ever hold fast the blessed hope 184 18
to *e* and hold fast the unchangeable truth 218 9
e and ever hold fast the blessed hope 236 10

embraces
but mercy *e* those who trust in the LORD. 625 24

embroidered
In *e* apparel she is brought to the king; * 648 19

employ
our freedom, help us to *e* it 209 4
our freedom, help us to *e* it 260 11

employment
that all may find suitable and fulfilling *e*, 824 14

empower
e him for your service; 309 13
e him for your service; 418 11

empty
and the rich he hath sent *e* away. 50 16
and the rich he hath sent *e* away. 65 19
it will not return to me *e*; 87 6

and the rich he has sent away *e*. 92 11
and the rich he has sent away *e*. 119 17
and the rich he has sent away *e*. 442 6
Why do the peoples mutter *e* threats? 586 2
Even if they come to see me, they speak *e* words; * 642 10
in robbery take no *e* pride; * 670 6

enable
receive him and *e* him to receive you, 444 17
and peace which will *e* you to serve him 456 5
restore him to health, and *e* him to lead 458 7
e us all to stand reconciled before you; 816 8
E us to eliminate poverty, 825 10

enabled
may by thee be *e* to live according to thy will; 180 16
may by you be *e* to live according to your will; 232 8
and our nation be *e* to fulfill your purposes; 822 27

enables
and *e* us to grow in the likeness of Christ. 852 22

enact
that they may *e* such laws as shall please thee, 821 5

encamp
Though an army should *e* against me, * 617 14

encircle
Many young bulls *e* me; * 611 1

enclose
My boundaries *e* a pleasant land; * 600 9

enclosure
With you I will break down an *e*; * 604 22

encompass
they *e* me on every side. 713 14
they *e* me with hateful words 751 2
All the ungodly *e* me; * 761 15

encompasses
The angel of the LORD *e* those who fear him, * 628 7

encourage
As a chief priest and pastor, will you *e* 518 12

encouraged
e by the good example of thy servant 198 17
e by the good example of your servant 250 2
e by their examples, aided by their prayers, 489 19
e by their examples, aided by their prayers, 504 17
and *e* to persevere to the end, 549 9

encouragement
and pledge you our prayers, *e*, and support. 420 5
and for our *e* by their perseverance, 579 8

end
my salvation unto the *e* of the earth. 38 4
And we worship thy Name ever, world without *e*. 55 18
be all honor and glory, world without *e*. 59 11
be all honor and glory, world without *e*. 72 8
reach to the *e* of the earth. 76 4
for ever and to the *e*. 104 12
a peaceful night and a perfect *e*. 127 2
world without *e*. 141 8
world without *e*. 154 12
be honor and glory, world without *e*. 160 5
one God, world without *e*. 160 17
one God, world without *e*. 161 13
one God, world without *e*. 169 13
one God, world without *e*. 169 18
one God, world without *e*. 171 4
even unto the *e* of the ages; 174 12
one God, world without *e*. 174 20
one God, world without *e*. 175 7
one God, world without *e*. 181 10
one God, world without *e*. 184 14
one God, world without *e*. 191 21
one God, world without *e*. 200 5
even to the *e* of the ages; 226 4
and his kingdom will have no *e*. 327 11
whose kingdom shall have no *e*. 328 12
to the *e* that all that believe in him should not perish, 332 11
world without *e*. 336 15
be all honor and glory, world without *e*. 339 14
world without *e*. 343 5
be with them always, even unto the *e* of the ages. 348 14
and his kingdom will have no *e*. 359 2
he loved them to the *e*; 374 15
with them always, even to the *e* of the ages. 381 8
That we may *e* our lives in faith and hope, 385 7
world without *e*. 406 4
to the *e* that all that believe in him 449 16
thou art God from everlasting, and world without *e*. 472 13
we bring our years to an *e*, as it were a tale 473 2
whose days are without *e*, 489 3
whose days are without *e*, 504 1
and his kingdom will have no *e*. 520 2
and his kingdom will have no *e*. 530 21
and his kingdom will have no *e*. 542 21
and encouraged to persevere to the *e*, 549 9
our source and our *e*: 568 8
Let the malice of the wicked come to an *e*, 591 15
and runs about to the *e* of it again; * 607 2
let me know my *e* and the number of my days, * 639 1
reaches to the world's *e*; * 651 21
and the *e* of those who delight in their own words. 653 7
Make an *e* of them in your wrath; * 666 24
make an *e* of them, and they shall be no more. 666 25
and discerned the *e* of the wicked. 688 12
come to an *e*, and perish from terror! 688 16
Has his loving-kindness come to an *e* for ever? * 693 16
So he brought their days to an *e* like a breath * 697 16
You have put an *e* to his splendor * 717 1
we bring our years to an *e* like a sigh. 718 18
and your years will never *e*. 733 6
and the plague came to an *e*. 744 8
and were at their wits' *e*. 748 10
and I shall keep it to the *e*. 766 2
They had almost made an *e* of me on earth, * 770 16
I see that all things come to an *e*, * 771 11
for ever and to the *e*. 772 18
there is no *e* to his greatness. 801 17
one God, world without *e*. 820 25

and bring them in safety to their journey's *e*; 831 5
all glory and honor, world without *e*. 840 24
Faith to all people, to the *e* of time. 854 23

endeavor

and also daily *e* ourselves to follow 180 22
Will you *e* so to minister the Word of God 532 9

ended

Lenten observance is *e*, 292 4
life is changed, not *e*; 349 9
life is changed, not *e*; 382 4
works begun, continued, and *e* in thee, 832 3

endeth

Here *e* the Lesson (Reading). 47 4
Here *e* the Lesson (Reading). 65 3
Here *e* the Reading (Epistle). 325 16

ending

never-*e* thanks for the creation of the world, 316 10

endless

Cherubim and Seraphim, sing in *e* praise: 95 20
To you be glory for *e* ages. 113 8
and know thee in the power of his *e* life; 191 5
and for *e* ages. 574 9
Turn your steps toward the *e* ruins; * 689 14

Endor

They were destroyed at *E*; * 706 22

endowed

with whom he *e* the apostles, 521 4

ends

and their words into the *e* of the world. 40 6
Judea, and Samaria, and to the *e* of the earth. 77 19
and their message to the *e* of the world. 78 5
Here *e* the Lesson (Reading). 84 6
Here *e* the Lesson (Reading). 119 3
and obeyed to the *e* of the earth; 163 11
that it may reach to the *e* of the earth; 175 11
and obeyed to the *e* of the earth; 215 5
that it may reach to the *e* of the earth; 227 4
Here *e* the Reading (Epistle). 300 4
Here *e* the Reading (Epistle). 357 7
preach the Gospel to the *e* of the earth, 390 8
Here *e* the Reading (Epistle). 414 4
Here *e* the Reading (Epistle). 516 4
Here *e* the Reading (Epistle). 529 3
Here *e* the Reading (Epistle). 541 3
preach the Gospel to the *e* of the earth, 549 22
and the *e* of the earth for your possession. 586 19
and their message to the *e* of the world. 606 22
All the *e* of the earth shall remember 612 10
and to the *e* of the earth. 666 27
I call upon you from the *e* of the earth 668 14
O Hope of all the *e* of the earth 672 19
Those who dwell at the *e* of the earth will tremble 673 1
and may all the *e* of the earth stand in awe of him. 675 23
and from the River to the *e* of the earth. 685 25
and all the *e* of the earth have seen the 728 8
He brings up rain clouds from the *e* of the earth; * 788 14

endue

E thy ministers with righteousness; 55 3
E thy ministers with righteousness; 67 18
and to *e* us with the grace of thy Holy Spirit 152 4
E with the spirit of wisdom 820 8

endurance

and run with *e* the race that is set 380 14

endure

hold fast to those that shall *e*; 234 4
if we *e*, we shall also reign with him. 281 18
He shall live as long as the sun and moon *e*, * 685 17
His line shall *e* for ever * 716 13
But you, O LORD, *e* for ever, * 731 23
your years *e* throughout all generations. 732 26
They shall perish, but you will *e*; 733 1
May the glory of the LORD *e* for ever; * 737 16
all your righteous judgments *e* for evermore. 776 24

endured

whose beloved Son willingly *e* the agony 201 7
whose beloved Son willingly *e* the agony 252 12
and all the hardships he *e*; 785 20

endures

and his faithfulness *e* from age to age. 83 9
His mercy *e* for ever. 109 6
His mercy *e* for ever. 299 6
His mercy *e* for ever. 351 6
His mercy *e* for ever. 355 6
His mercy *e* for ever. 413 6
His mercy *e* for ever. 512 6
His mercy *e* for ever. 525 6
His mercy *e* for ever. 537 6
and *e* for ever; * 607 13
For his wrath *e* but the twinkling of an eye, * 621 12
Your throne, O God, *e* for ever and ever, * 648 1
and be established as long as the sun *e*; * 686 22
and his faithfulness *e* from age to age. 730 6
But the merciful goodness of the LORD *e* for ever 734 15
for his mercy *e* for ever. 741 20
and his mercy *e* for ever. 746 2
and his righteousness *e* for ever. 754 11
his praise *e* for ever. 755 3
and the faithfulness of the LORD *e* for ever. 760 18
his mercy *e* for ever. 760 21
"His mercy *e* for ever." 760 23
"His mercy *e* for ever." 761 2
his mercy *e* for ever. 763 4
your renown, O LORD, *e* from age to age. 789 2
for his mercy *e* for ever. 789 21
O LORD, your love *e* for ever; 793 20
your dominion *e* throughout all ages. 802 12

endureth

and his truth *e* from generation to generation. 45 22
His mercy *e* for ever. 319 7
His mercy *e* for ever. 323 5
and his mercy *e* for ever. 478 12

enemies

That we should be saved from our *e*, * 51 1
That we being delivered out of the hand of our *e* * 51 7

in all assaults of our *e*; 57 4
defended from the fear of all *e*, 69 20
that he would save us from our *e*, * 92 23
to set us free from the hands of our *e*, 92 28
in all assaults of our *e*; 99 22
being delivered from the fear of all *e*, 123 19
That it may please thee to forgive our *e*, 152 8
From our *e* defend us, O Christ; 154 15
For those who are *e* of the cross of Christ 279 25
For our *e* and those who wish us harm; 391 5
in the presence of mine *e*; * 477 6
above mine *e* round about me. 477 24
you will strike all my *e* across the face, 587 16
and worn away because of all my *e*. 590 13
All my *e* shall be confounded and quake with fear; * 590 18
rise up against the fury of my *e*. 591 7
When my *e* are driven back, * 593 5
they defy all their *e*. 595 3
from my deadly *e* who surround me. 601 17
and so shall I be saved from my *e*. 602 13
He delivered me from my strong *e* 603 25
I pursue my *e* and overtake them; * 605 14
you have put my *e* to flight. 605 20
You rescued me from the fury of my *e*; 606 7
Your hand will lay hold upon all your *e*; * 609 12
nor let my *e* triumph over me. 614 16
Look upon my *e*, for they are many, * 615 26
above my *e* round about me. 618 6
lead me on a level path, because of my *e*. 618 22
and have not let my *e* triumph over me. 621 5
I have become a reproach to all my *e* and 623 10
rescue me from the hand of my *e*, 623 23
and the *e* of the LORD, 634 25
Those who are my *e* without cause are mighty, * 638 7
he does not hand them over to the will of their *e*. 642 3
My *e* are saying wicked things about me: * 642 8
All my *e* whisper together about me * 642 13
my *e* mock me to my face; 644 6
and our *e* have plundered us. 646 6
and the king's *e* are losing heart. 647 24
for my *e* are hounding me; * 662 13
my *e* will be put to flight; * 663 9
Rescue me from my *e*, O God; * 665 18
God will let me look in triumph on my *e*. 666 17
and he shall tread our *e* under foot. 668 11
because of your great strength your *e* 673 22
You let *e* ride over our heads; 674 17
Let God arise, and let his *e* be scattered; * 676 1
you have received gifts even from your *e*, * 677 19
God shall crush the heads of his *e*, * 677 25
the tongues of your dogs in the blood of your *e*." 678 4
because of my *e* deliver me. 680 28
For my *e* are talking against me, * 683 20
and his *e* lick the dust. 686 2
but the sea overwhelmed their *e*. 699 12
He struck his *e* on the backside * 700 11
and our *e* laugh us to scorn. 702 24
I should soon subdue their *e* * 705 3
For your *e* are in tumult, * 706 5
you have scattered your *e* with your mighty arm. 714 14
and made all his *e* rejoice. 716 26
The taunts your *e* have hurled, O LORD, * 717 16
For lo, your *e*, O LORD, 721 13
lo, your *e* shall perish, * 721 14
My eyes also gloat over my *e*, * 721 18
and burns up his *e* on every side. 727 2
My *e* revile me all day long, * 731 15
he made them stronger than their *e*; 740 2
Their *e* oppressed them, * 745 8
and he shall tread our *e* under foot. 750 22
until I make your *e* your footstool." 753 13
"Rule over your *e* round about you. 753 15
until they see their desire upon their *e*. 755 21
Your commandment has made me wiser than my *e*, * 771 15
because my *e* forget your words. 775 4
among the *e* of peace. 778 21
when *e* rose up against us; 781 4
when he contends with his *e* in the gate. 783 12
all those who are *e* of Zion. 784 10
As for his *e*, I will clothe them with shame; * 787 7
And delivered us from our *e*, * 791 17
you stretch forth your hand against the fury of my *e*; 793 17
your *e* take your Name in vain. 795 19
they have become my own *e*. 795 23
Deliver me from my *e*, O LORD, * 799 19
Of your goodness, destroy my *e* 799 25
commanded us to love our *e*: 816 6
forgave his *e* while he was suffering shame 823 8

enemy

your right hand, O Lord, has overthrown the *e*. 85 15
and drive far from it all snares of the *e*; 133 18
and drive far from it all snares of the *e*; 140 14
delivered us from the power of our *e*: 170 10
delivered us from the power of our *e*: 222 3
delivered us from the power of your *e*: 295 3
Defend them from every *e*. 430 16
preserve him from the temptations of the *e*; 458 6
or plundered him who without cause is my *e*; 591 2
Then let my *e* pursue and overtake me, * 591 3
to quell the *e* and the avenger. 592 12
As for the *e*, they are finished, 593 11
how long shall my *e* triumph over me? 598 3
Lest my *e* say, "I have prevailed over him," * 598 6
You have not shut me up in the power of the *e*; * 623 1
that my *e* does not triumph over me. 642 23
while the *e* oppresses me?" 644 3
because of the *e* and avenger. 646 18
for God has scattered the bones of the *e*; 659 12
I am shaken by the noise of the *e* * 660 9
or had it been an *e* who vaunted himself against me, 661 8
Grant us your help against the *e*, * 668 8
a strong tower against the *e*. 668 18
protect my life from fear of the *e*. 671 11
the *e* has laid waste everything in your sanctuary. 689 15
will the *e* blaspheme your Name for ever? 690 5
Remember, O LORD, how the *e* scoffed, * 690 20
in the day when he ransomed them from the *e*; 698 12
No *e* shall deceive him, * 715 10
and redeemed them from the hand of the *e*. 742 19
Grant us your help against the *e*, * 750 19
For my *e* has sought my life; 799 1

enfold

as you *e* us with the radiance 110 14
e him in the arms of your mercy, 314 4
you *e* and comfort me, 684 27

enfolding

O shining light and *e* dark. 89 2

engage

and I do solemnly *e* to conform to the doctrine, 513 11
and I do solemnly *e* to conform to the doctrine, 526 17
and I do solemnly *e* to conform to the doctrine, 538 17

enjoy

so that in due time all may *e* them, 151 10
so may we also perfectly *e* him in heaven; 161 4
may also *e* him perfectly in heaven; 212 18
I may *e* the blessed assurance of your love; 461 16
that those baptized here may *e* the liberty 569 17
and desires long life to *e* prosperity? 628 18
may *e* a fair portion of the riches of this land; 826 14
ventured much for the liberties we now *e*. 839 23
we are called to *e* it and to care for it 846 11
asking nothing but to *e* God's presence. 857 3

enjoyment

to grow in our grateful *e* of your abundant creation, 840 12
By heaven, we mean eternal life in our *e* of God; 862 6

enkindle

God, who didst *e* the flame 196 1
and so *e* fervent charity among us all, 829 6

enkindled

Grant that the same light, *e* in our hearts, 161 15
e with the fire of thy love, 198 9
Grant that this light, *e* in our hearts, 213 9

enlighten

A Light to *e* the nations, * 93 16
A Light to *e* the nations, * 120 5
A Light to *e* the nations, * 135 5
A Light to *e* the nations, * 140 11
E by thy Holy Spirit 209 17
E by your Holy Spirit 261 1
May God in his love *e* your heart, 449 10
e my understanding with the light of your Holy Spirit 562 13
E us. 839 11

enlightened

that by the indwelling of thy Holy Spirit we may be *e* 200 2
that by the indwelling of your Holy Spirit we may be *e* 251 8
By them also is your servant *e*, * 607 20

enlightening

e the minds and stirring up the conscience 518 9

enlightens

by grace God forgives our sins, *e* our minds, 858 3

enmity

reconciliation of all who are at variance and *e*; 193 21
reconciliation of all who are at variance and *e*; 245 7

enough

and in days of famine they shall have *e*. 634 23
that we should never have *e* to pay it, 652 20
he provided for them food *e*. 696 27
for we have had more than *e* of contempt. 780 22

enraged

you have become *e* at him. 716 18

enrich

by their prayer and service they may *e* your Church, 819 10
E our lives by ever-widening circles 840 3

enrolls

The LORD will record as he *e* the peoples, * 711 22

enshrouds

deep gloom *e* the peoples. 87 14

enslaved

divided and *e* by sin, 185 4
divided and *e* by sin, 203 2
divided and *e* by sin, 236 17
divided and *e* by sin, 254 4

entangle

Though the cords of the wicked *e* me, * 768 9

entangled

The cords of hell *e* me, * 602 16
The cords of death *e* me; 759 5

enter

e his gates with thanksgiving; 83 4
worthy to *e* with them into that heavenly country 111 14
that they should not *e* into my rest. 146 25
may at the last *e* with them into thine unending joy; 202 5
may at the last *e* with them into your unending joy; 253 10
that we may *e* with joy upon the contemplation 270 5
we may be accounted worthy to *e* 280 11
we may *e* the everlasting heritage 369 11
that he may rest from his labors, and *e* into the light 465 12
Grace be to this house, and to all who *e* here: 568 2
and *e* into the palace of the king. 648 22
I will *e* your house with burnt-offerings 674 20
Let my prayer *e* into your presence; * 712 3
"They shall not *e* into my rest." 725 16
E his gates with thanksgiving; 730 1
I will *e* them; 762 9
he who is righteous may *e*." 762 12
E not into judgment with your servant, * 798 21
the woman and man *e* into a life-long union, 861 5

entered

Christ is not *e* into the holy places made with hands, 39 15
and *e* not into glory before he was crucified: 56 7
Christ has *e*, not into a sanctuary made with hands, 77 14
and *e* not into glory before he was crucified: 99 2
and *e* not into glory before he was crucified: 168 11
and *e* not into glory before he was crucified: 220 2
On this day he *e* the holy city of Jerusalem 271 7
and *e* not into glory before he was crucified: 272 2
We praise you for your saints who have *e* into joy; 387 19
not to be *e* into unadvisedly or lightly, but reverently, 423 14
Until I *e* the sanctuary of God * 688 11

enters
All glorious is the princess as she *e*; * 648 17

enthroned
But the LORD is *e* for ever; * 593 13
e upon the praises of Israel. 610 7
The LORD sits *e* above the flood; * 620 25
the LORD sits *e* as King for evermore. 620 26
From where he sits *e* he turns his gaze * 627 3
God, who is *e* of old, will hear me and 661 25
Let him sit *e* before God for ever; * 669 1
you that are *e* upon the cherubim. 702 13
he is *e* upon the cherubim; 728 25
the LORD our God, who sits *e* on high, * 756 10
to you *e* in the heavens. 780 16

entire
wholesome example for the *e* flock of Christ. 517 12

entrance
an *e* into the land of light and joy, 470 3
an *e* into the land of light and joy, 493 12

entreat
We *e* thee, O Lord. 68 8
Put away from us, we *e* you, 229 11
I *e* you with all my heart, * 768 3
we *e* thee, in this time of need, such moderate rain 828 12

entreaty
Nevertheless, you heard the sound of my *e* 624 16

entrust
e this child to thy never-failing care and love, 470 9
Grant us grace to *e* to thy never-failing love; 481 17
Give us grace to *e* to your never-failing care 494 2
in thy Name we *e* the authority 820 9
we *e* all who are dear to us 831 7

entrusted
perform the other ministrations *e* to you. 531 17
your salvation for the people *e* to my care, 563 1
I have been *e* to you ever since I was born; * 610 20
but he *e* the earth to its peoples. 758 22
thank you for the life of this child, *e* to our care. 841 2

entrusting
e one another and all our life to Christ, 68 24
e one another and all our life to Christ, 122 26

envied
Because I *e* the proud * 687 5
They *e* Moses in the camp, * 743 3

envious
Do not be *e* when some become rich, * 653 15

envy
from *e*, hatred, and malice; 149 2
and our *e* of those more fortunate than ourselves, 268 7
Why do you look with *e*, O rugged mountain, 677 12
To resist temptations to *e*, greed, and 848 18

Ephraim
E is my helmet and Judah my scepter. 667 24
The people of *E*, armed with the bow, * 695 20
and did not choose the tribe of *E*; 700 14
In the presence of *E*, Benjamin, and Manasseh, * 702 14
E is my helmet and Judah my scepter. 750 11

Ephratah
"The ark! We heard it was in *E*; * 786 9

Episcopal
and worship of The *E* Church. 513 13
and worship of The *E* Church. 526 18
and worship of The *E* Church. 538 18

epistle
Here ends the Reading (*E*). 300 4
Here endeth the Reading (*E*). 325 16
Here ends the Reading (*E*). 357 7
Here ends the Reading (*E*). 414 4
Here ends the Reading (*E*). 516 4
Here ends the Reading (*E*). 529 3
Here ends the Reading (*E*). 541 3

equal
and we celebrate the one and *e* glory of thee, 347 16
and we celebrate the one and *e* glory of you, 380 10
who spend their lives establishing *e* protection 826 12
and *e* opportunities for all. 826 13

equip
the eternal covenant, *e* you with everything good 132 3
e the saints for the work of ministry 533 9
and *e* us for our ministries; 818 12

equity
he judges the peoples with *e*. 593 16
do you judge the peoples with *e*? 664 22
for you judge the peoples with *e* 675 16
"I will judge with *e*. 691 7
he will judge the peoples with *e*." 726 13
and the peoples with *e*. 728 22
you have established *e*; * 729 6
because they are done in truth and *e*. 754 21

erect
even those who stand *e* are but a puff of wind. 639 5

err
It is a people that do *e* in their hearts, 146 22

erred
we have *e* and strayed from thy ways like lost sheep, 41 17
we have *e* and strayed from thy ways like lost sheep, 62 17
all such as have *e*, and are deceived, 150 20
we have *e* and strayed from thy ways like lost sheep, 320 24

error
to defend us from all *e*, and to lead us into all truth; 107 6
In him, you have brought us out of *e* 368 8
where it is in *e*, direct it; 816 12

escape
I would hasten to *e* * 660 21
Shall they *e* despite their wickedness? * 663 4
God is the LORD, by whom we *e* death. 677 24
while I myself *e*. 797 25

escaped

We have *e* like a bird from the snare 781 13
the snare is broken, and we have *e*. 781 14

especially

and *e* on this day for Simon and Jude; 194 2
and *e* on this day for Simon and Jude; 245 11
to all bishops and other ministers [*e* __________], 329 10
give thy heavenly grace, and *e* to this congregation 329 13
government in this and every land [*e* __________], 329 19
departed this life in thy faith and fear [*e* __________], 330 2
I ask your prayers for the departed [*e* __________]. 386 10
in whom Christ has been honored [*e* __________] 386 15
For those in positions of public trust [*e* __________] 390 16
For all who live and work in this community [*e* __________] 390 19
and *e* upon this man and this woman 429 5
things done and left undone; *e* __________. For these 447 8
E, I confess to you and to the Church... 450 15
For those in positions of public trust [*e* __________] 550 1
More *e* we pray for thy holy Church universal; 815 1
[*e* those for whom our prayers are desired]; 815 8
[and *e* the hearts of the people of this land], 823 18
bless all schools, colleges, and universities [and *e* __________], 824 17
who live and work in rural areas [*e* __________]; 825 20
and *e* through the prophets of Israel. 845 20

establish

and *e* thy rule of justice, love, and peace; 186 17
and *e* your rule of justice, 238 10
but *e* the righteous; * 591 16
e, O God, what you have wrought for us. 678 15
"I will *e* your line for ever, * 714 1
I will *e* his line for ever * 715 24
and *e* among them that peace 816 2

established

thou hast *e* the moon and the sun. 61 8
the sanctuary, O Lord, that your hand has *e*. 85 27
you *e* the moon and the sun. 115 7
hast *e* the new covenant of reconciliation: 172 2
e the new covenant of reconciliation: 223 16
e the new covenant of reconciliation: 224 14
e the new covenant of reconciliation: 290 15
marriage was *e* by God in creation, 423 4
and *e* me among your children 450 12
God has *e* her for ever. 651 17
and be *e* as long as the sun endures; * 686 22
you *e* the moon and the sun. 690 17
and *e* a law for Israel, * 695 8
For I am persuaded that your love is *e* for ever; * 713 19
Ever since the world began, your throne has been *e*; * 722 7
you have *e* equity; * 729 6
Which he *e* as a statute for Jacob, * 738 19
Their heart is *e* and will not shrink, * 755 20
you *e* the earth, and it abides. 770 23
that you have *e* them for ever. 776 8
A slanderer shall not be *e* on the earth, * 796 23
He has *e* peace on your borders; * 805 5

establishing

who spend their lives *e* equal protection 826 12

estate

even those of low *e* cannot be trusted. 670 2
Who remembered us in our low *e*, * 791 15
afflicted or distressed, in mind, body, or *e*; 815 8

estrangement

that unity may overcome *e*, 429 18

eternal

the *e* rest promised to thy people in heaven; 56 16
O God, the King *e*, who dividest the day 56 18
in knowledge of whom standeth our *e* life, 57 2
O God, the source of *e* light: 69 12
Spirit keep you in *e* life. 80 4
You are the *e* Father: 95 17
the *e* Son of the Father. 96 2
the *e* rest promised to your people in heaven; 99 11
O God, the King *e*, whose light divides the day 99 13
to know you is *e* life 99 21
the true God and *e* light, living and reigning 110 27
E God, who led your ancient people into freedom 111 8
to *e* life and to the ages of ages. 113 15
Spirit keep you in *e* life. 117 9
O God, the source of *e* light: 123 11
by the blood of the *e* covenant, 132 3
this life may rest in your *e* changelessness; 133 15
faithful departed *e* life and peace, 152 16
E Father, who didst give to thine incarnate Son 162 1
holy mysteries giveth us a pledge of life *e*, 169 11
and rejoice in the hope of *e* glory; 171 13
he may raise us to joys *e*; 172 18
steps in the way that leadeth to *e* life; 173 19
who on this day didst open the way of *e* life 175 8
acknowledge the glory of the *e* Trinity, 176 3
bring us at last to see thee in thy one and *e* glory, 176 6
that we finally lose not the things *e*; 180 5
make us the children of God and heirs of *e* life: 184 9
made like unto him in his *e* and glorious kingdom; 184 12
share with her the glory of thine *e* kingdom; 192 4
with him attain to thine *e* joy; 198 20
who hast revealed to thy Church thine *e* Being 199 12
O *e* Lord God, who holdest all souls in life: 202 1
he may share in the *e* victory of Jesus Christ 202 13
E Father, you gave to your incarnate Son 213 13
these holy mysteries gives us a pledge of *e* life; 221 5
and rejoice in the hope of *e* glory; 223 7
so by his love he may raise us to *e* joys; 224 10
steps in the way that leads to *e* life; 225 11
on this day you opened the way of *e* life 227 1
acknowledge the glory of the *e* Trinity, 228 3
see you in your one and *e* glory, O Father; 228 6
that we lose not the things *e*; 231 20
make us children of God and heirs of *e* life: 236 3
made like him in his *e* and glorious kingdom; 236 6
at length we may attain to the fullness of *e* life; 238 4
share with her the glory of your *e* kingdom; 243 11
until at last we may with him attain to your *e* joy; 250 4
you have revealed to your Church your *e* Being 251 1
E Lord God, you hold all souls in life: 253 6
he may share in the *e* victory of Jesus Christ 253 17
so that at the last we may come to his *e* joy; 269 13
and follow him in the way that leads to *e* life; 271 12

these holy mysteries gives us a pledge of *e* life; 274 5
O God of unchangeable power and *e* light: 280 14
for darkness has been vanquished by our *e* King. 286 6
almighty, and *e* God, and your only-begotten Son, 287 2
O God of unchangeable power and *e* light: 291 11
keep us in *e* life by his grace, 294 6
E Father, whose blessed Son was anointed 307 9
share with us in his *e* priesthood. 308 14
e salvation for all who put their trust in him. 346 17
For with thy co-*e* Son and Holy Spirit, 347 14
and in their *e* joy a glorious pledge of the hope 348 5
there is prepared for us a dwelling place *e* 349 10
Spirit keep you in *e* life. 353 4
Spirit keep you in *e* life. 360 18
sent Jesus Christ, your only and *e* Son, 362 12
into the joy of your *e* kingdom. 363 18
E God, heavenly Father, 365 9
and heirs of your *e* kingdom. 366 7
the place of *e* joy and light.] 375 20
e salvation for all who put their trust in him. 379 13
For with your co-*e* Son and Holy Spirit, 380 8
and in their *e* joy a glorious pledge 380 21
there is prepared for us a dwelling place *e* 382 5
Give to the departed *e* rest; 387 17
with all your saints in your *e* kingdom. 389 10
where there is no pain or grief, but life *e*, 391 18
a place in your *e* kingdom. 393 5
Almighty and *e* God, ruler of all things in heaven 394 9
not perish, but have *e* life. 396 2
these holy mysteries gives us a pledge of *e* life; 397 17
Spirit keep you in *e* life. 398 10
E God, creator and preserver of all life, 429 2
and obtain those *e* joys prepared for all 432 6
O *e* God, you have promised to be a father 444 15
Spirit keep you in *e* life. 451 5
Spirit keep you in *e* life. 455 8
you hold me in *e* life, my Lord and my God. 461 11
from the power of evil, and from *e* death, 463 13
rest with all your saints in the *e* habitations; 464 18
enter into the light of God's *e* sabbath rest. 465 13
all your saints in the *e* habitations; 466 18
in the joyful expectation of *e* life 481 12
and bliss in thy *e* and everlasting glory, 481 25
deliver us not into the bitter pains of *e* death. 484 10
thou most worthy Judge *e*. 484 15
In sure and certain hope of the resurrection to *e* life 485 9
Rest *e* grant to him, O Lord: 486 17
in thy *e* and everlasting glory; 488 10
deliver us not into the bitterness of *e* death. 492 11
O worthy and *e* Judge, 492 18
and rejoice in his *e* glory; 493 7
faith to see in death the gate of *e* life, 493 21
In the assurance of *e* life given at Baptism, 496 1
give to our brother (sister) *e* life. 497 10
let our faith be our consolation, and *e* life our hope. 497 23
Grant to them *e* rest. 498 9
In sure and certain hope of the resurrection to *e* life 501 11
Rest *e* grant to him, O Lord; 502 15
bliss in your *e* and everlasting glory; 503 18
and in the joyful expectation of *e* life 505 14
O God of unchangeable power and *e* light: 515 4
O God of unchangeable power and *e* light: 528 2
who is the image of your *e* and invisible glory, 533 3
O God of unchangeable power and *e* light: 540 2
where there is no pain or grief, but life *e*, 550 23
your *e* Word speaks to us 570 23
We praise you, Almighty and *e* God, 573 8
E God, the heaven of heavens cannot contain you, 578 3
E God, in whose perfect kingdom no sword is drawn 815 22
O *E* God, bless all schools, colleges, and universities 824 16
fulfill our role in your *e* purpose; 827 16
Almighty and *e* God, so draw our hearts to thee, 832 24
in dying that we are born to *e* life. 833 13
the hope of salvation and the promise of *e* life; 838 19
that full stature intended for him in your *e* kingdom; 841 5
and opened for us the way of *e* life. 850 12
our nourishment in *e* life. 860 3
By heaven, we mean *e* life in our enjoyment of God; 862 6
by hell, we mean *e* death in our rejection of God. 862 7

eternally

e begotten of the Father, 326 12
e begotten of the Father, 358 9
e begotten of the Father, 519 12
e begotten of the Father, 530 3
e begotten of the Father, 542 3

eternity

Thus saith the high and lofty One that inhabiteth *e*, 40 23
Thus says the high and lofty One who inhabits *e*, 78 22

Ethiopia

let *E* stretch out her hands to God. 678 23
behold Philistia, Tyre, and *E*: 711 18

Eucharist

and is used at the *E*. 852 7
Holy Baptism and the Holy *E*. 858 7
What is the Holy *E*? 859 5
The Holy *E* is the sacrament commanded by Christ 859 6
Why is the *E* called a sacrifice? 859 9
Because the *E*, the Church's sacrifice 859 10
The Holy *E* is called the Lord's Supper, 859 15
What is the outward and visible sign in the *E*? 859 18
The outward and visible sign in the *E* 859 19
spiritual grace given in the *E*? 859 23
What is required of us when we come to the *E*? 860 4
Baptism and the *E* are. 860 16

evangelist

the teaching of thine apostle and *e* John, 186 8
who by the hand of Mark the *e* hast given 188 21
for the witness of thine apostle and *e* Matthew 192 20
the teaching of your apostle and *e* John, 238 3
by the hand of Mark the *e* you have given 240 7
for the witness of your apostle and *e* Matthew 244 8

evangelists

e and heralds of thy kingdom, 196 10
e and heralds of your kingdom, 247 22
some *e*, some pastors and teachers, 533 8

even

at *e*, or at midnight, or at the cock-crowing, 37 2
From the rising of the sun *e* unto the going down 38 5
e so in Christ shall all be made alive. 46 18

e our Lord Jesus Christ;	162	4
his Church on earth, *e* unto the end	174	11
and *e* now, while we are placed among things	182	7
we may purify ourselves *e* as he is pure;	184	10
and was faithful *e* unto death:	195	9
e as thou and he are one:	204	18
his Church on earth, *e* to the end	226	4
and *e* now, while we are placed among things	234	2
and was faithful *e* to death:	247	7
deeds of old shine forth *e* to our own day,	289	12
and humbled himself *e* to death on the cross,	316	14
e unto the end of the ages.	348	14
e to the end of the ages.	381	8
e Jesus Christ, our only Mediator and Advocate.	395	15
e so saith the Spirit, for they rest from their labors.	469	15
My soul is athirst for God, yea, *e* for the living God; *	471	3
As soon as thou scatterest them they are *e* as a sleep, *	472	19
My help cometh *e* from the LORD, *	473	11
yea, it is *e* he that shall keep thy soul.	473	22
E there also shall thy hand lead me, *	475	11
e that I may dwell in the house of the LORD	477	17
yet *e* at the grave we make our song:	483	1
e though he die.	491	3
yet *e* at the grave we make our song: Alleluia,	499	8
becoming obedient *e* to death	545	3
e the wild beasts of the field,	592	22
and my arms for bending *e* a bow of bronze.	605	8
E now he lifts up my head *	618	5
reproach to all my enemies and *e* to my neighbors,	623	11
e those who stand erect are but a puff of wind.	639	5
E if they come to see me, they speak empty words; *	642	10
E my best friend, whom I trusted,	642	17
E though honored, they cannot live for ever; *	653	4
e those of low estate cannot be trusted.	670	2
e thousands of thousands; *	677	16
you have received gifts *e* from your enemies, *	677	19
growing thick *e* on the hilltops; *	686	18
perhaps in strength *e* eighty; *	718	20
and are moved to pity *e* for her dust.	732	5
I believed, *e* when I said,	759	20
E though rulers sit and plot against me, *	765	5
down with it! *e* to the ground!"	792	18
E there your hand will lead me *	794	18
and grant to them *e* now glimpses of your beauty,	819	16
By his obedience, *e* to suffering and death,	850	7
work in the world and in the Church *e* now.	852	16
nothing, not *e* death, shall separate us	862	30

evening

the lifting up of my hands be an *e* sacrifice.	61	2
That this *e* may be holy, good, and peaceful,	68	7
Lord Jesus, stay with us, for *e* is at hand	70	10
in the *e*, or at midnight, or at cockcrow,	75	2
call the *e*, the morning, and the noonday one day;	110	24
bestowing upon us occasions of song in the *e*.	113	4
the lifting up of our hands as the *e* sacrifice.	113	10
the lifting up of my hands as the *e* sacrifice.	115	2
That this *e* may be holy, good, and peaceful,	122	9
Lord Jesus, stay with us, for *e* is at hand	124	7
Lord Jesus, stay with us, for *e* is at hand	139	16
Holy Father, accept our *e* sacrifice,	287	21
but in the *e* it is cut down, dried up, and withered.	472	22
In the *e*, in the morning, and at noonday,	661	19
They go to and fro in the *e*; *	666	7
They go to and fro in the *e*; *	666	28
in the *e* it is dried up and withered.	718	12
and to his labor until the *e*.	736	24
the lifting up of my hands as the *e* sacrifice.	797	6
and the *e* comes, and the busy world is hushed,	833	15

ever

as it was in the beginning, is now, and will be for *e*.	42	17
as it was in the beginning, is now, and will be for *e*.	46	20
praise him and magnify him for *e*.	47	6
praised and exalted above all for *e*.	49	10
Abraham and his seed for *e*.	50	19
as it was in the beginning, is now, and will be for *e*.	50	21
as it was in the beginning, is now, and will be for *e*.	51	22
as it was in the beginning, is now, and will be for *e*.	52	2
for *e* and *e*.	54	25
Govern them and lift them up for *e*.	55	16
And we worship thy Name *e*, world without end.	55	18
we are *e* walking in thy sight;	57	17
for *e* and *e*.	60	6
as it was in the beginning, is now, and will be for *e*.	63	20
as it was in the beginning, is now, and will be for *e*.	64	11
Abraham and his seed for *e*.	65	22
as it was in the beginning, is now, and will be for *e*.	65	24
as it was in the beginning, is now, and will be for *e*.	66	8
for *e* and *e*.	67	15
for *e* and *e*.	69	5
for *e* and *e*.	73	6
as it was in the beginning, is now, and will be for *e*.	80	8
as it was in the beginning, is now, and will be for *e*.	84	2
for *e* and *e*.	85	29
as it was in the beginning, is now, and will be for *e*.	85	31
as it was in the beginning, is now, and will be for *e*.	86	16
as it was in the beginning, is now, and will be for *e*.	87	10
as it was in the beginning, is now, and will be for *e*.	88	4
praise him and highly exalt him for *e*.	88	6
we will praise you and highly exalt you for *e*.	90	8
to Abraham and his children for *e*.	92	15
as it was in the beginning, is now, and will be for *e*.	92	17
as it was in the beginning, is now, and will be for *e*.	93	11
for *e* and for evermore.	94	8
as it was in the beginning, is now, and will be for *e*.	94	20
for *e* and *e*.	97	17
We praise your Name for *e*.	98	12
we are *e* walking in your sight;	100	10
for *e* and *e*.	102	17
it was in the beginning, is now, and will be for *e*.	103	4
Your decrees are my inheritance for *e*; *	104	9
for *e* and to the end.	104	12
as it was in the beginning, is now, and will be for *e*.	105	19
for you live and reign for *e* and *e*.	107	15
Spirit you live and reign, now and for *e*.	107	21
His mercy endures for *e*.	109	6
living and reigning for *e* and *e*.	110	27
heavenly country where you live and reign for *e* and *e*.	111	15
it was in the beginning, is now, and will be for *e*.	117	13
as it was in the beginning, is now, and will be for *e*.	118	11
to Abraham and his children for *e*.	119	21

as it was in the beginning, is now, and will be for *e*. 119 23
as it was in the beginning, is now, and will be for *e*. 120 8
for *e* and *e*. 121 17
and where he lives and reigns for *e* and *e*. 123 5
for *e* and *e*. 126 17
it was in the beginning, is now, and will be for *e*. 128 6
as it was in the beginning, is now, and will be for *e*. 131 11
to whom be glory for *e* and *e*. 132 5
as it was in the beginning, is now, and will be for *e*. 135 8
as it was in the beginning, is now, and will be for *e*. 137 10
Spirit you live and reign, now and for *e*. 138 20
and will be for *e*. 141 4
As it was in the beginning, is now, and *e* shall be, * 141 7
preserve us for *e*. 148 13
as it was in the beginning, is now, and *e* shall be, 154 11
Both now and *e* vouchsafe to hear us, O Christ; 155 3
one God, now and for *e*. 159 8
one God, now and for *e*. 159 14
one God, now and for *e*. 160 11
e, one God, world without end. 161 12
one God, now and for *e*. 161 18
one God, for *e* and *e*. 162 12
one God, now and for *e*. 162 18
one God, now and for *e*. 163 13
one God, for *e* and *e*. 163 18
one God, for *e* and *e*. 164 5
one God, now and for *e*. 164 10
one God, for *e* and *e*. 164 17
one God, now and for *e*. 165 5
one God, for *e* and *e*. 166 8
one God, now and for *e*. 166 15
one God, for *e* and *e*. 167 2
one God, now and for *e*. 167 14
for *e* and *e*. 168 9
one God, for *e* and *e*. 168 22
one God, for *e* and *e*. 169 6
e, one God, world without end. 169 13
one God, for *e* and *e*. 170 6
one God, now and for *e*. 170 13
e, one God, world without end. 171 4
one God, now and for *e*. 171 9
be dominion and praise for *e* and *e*. 171 15
one God, for *e* and *e*. 172 6
one God, now and for *e*. 172 13
one God, for *e* and *e*. 173 3
one God, now and for *e*. 173 10
one God, for *e* and *e*. 174 7
one God, for *e* and *e*. 175 13
one God, for *e* and *e*. 176 8
one God, now and for *e*. 177 2
one God, for *e* and *e*. 177 13
one God, for *e* and *e*. 178 5
one God, now and for *e*. 178 11
for *e* and *e*. 178 17
one God, for *e* and *e*. 179 3
thee and the Holy Spirit, one God, now and for *e*. 179 22
one God, for *e* and *e*. 180 6
one God, for *e* and *e*. 181 4
one God, now and for *e*. 181 22
one God, now and for *e*. 182 5
one God, for *e* and *e*. 182 10
one God, for *e* and *e*. 183 5
one God, now and for *e*. 183 10
one God, now and for *e*. 184 6
he liveth and reigneth *e*, one God, world without end. 184 14
and *e* hold fast the blessed hope of everlasting life, 184 19
one God, for *e* and *e*. 184 21
one God, now and for *e*. 185 6
one God, for *e* and *e*. 186 12
one God, now and for *e*. 187 7
one God, now and for *e*. 188 7
one God, for *e* and *e*. 188 13
one God, for *e* and *e*. 189 4
one God, now and for *e*. 189 10
one God, for *e* and *e*. 190 9
may *e* stand firm upon the one foundation, 190 13
one God, now and for *e*. 191 6
one God, now and for *e*. 192 6
one God, for *e* and *e*. 192 12
one God, now and for *e*. 193 3
one God, for *e* and *e*. 193 9
one God, for *e* and *e*. 194 7
one God, now and for *e*. 194 22
one God, for *e* and *e*. 195 7
one God, for *e* and *e*. 196 6
one God, now and for *e*. 196 14
one God, for *e* and *e*. 197 3
one God, for *e* and *e*. 197 10
one God, now and for *e*. 198 8
and may *e* walk before thee as children of light; 198 12
one God, for *e* and *e*. 198 22
one God, now and for *e*. 199 3
we may *e* be supported by this fellowship 199 6
for *e* and *e*. 199 11
one God, now and for *e*. 199 17
one God, world without end. 200 5
one God, for *e* and *e*. 200 11
that we may *e* perceive within ourselves 201 4
one God, for *e* and *e*. 201 6
one God, now and for *e*. 201 11
one God, now and for *e*. 202 8
one God, for *e* and *e*. 202 15
one God, now and for *e*. 203 4
one God, now and for *e*. 204 7
Spirit to abide with us for *e*: 204 9
one God, now and for *e*. 204 16
one God, now and for *e*. 205 3
one God, now and for *e*. 205 13
God, for *e* and *e*. 205 21
one God, now and for *e*. 206 8
one God, now and for *e*. 206 16
one God, for *e* and *e*. 206 23
for *e* and *e*. 207 7
one God, now and for *e*. 207 14
one God, for *e* and *e*. 207 21
one God, now and for *e*. 208 8
e thankful for thy loving providence; 208 11
one God, for *e* and *e*. 208 15
one God, now and for *e*. 208 22
one God, now and for *e*. 209 8
one God, for *e* and *e*. 209 16
one God, for *e* and *e*. 210 8
one God, now and for *e*. 211 8
be honor and glory, now and for *e*. 212 5

one God, now and for *e*. 212 9
be honor and glory, now and for *e*. 213 7
one God, now and for *e*. 213 12
one God, for *e* and *e*. 214 5
one God, now and for *e*. 214 11
one God, now and for *e*. 215 6
one God, for *e* and *e*. 215 11
one God, now and for *e*. 216 5
one God, for *e* and *e*. 216 12
one God, now and for *e*. 217 6
one God, for *e* and *e*. 217 13
one God, now and for *e*. 218 6
one God, for *e* and *e*. 218 12
one God, now and for *e*. 219 5
one God, for *e* and *e*. 219 19
one God, for *e* and *e*. 220 6
one God, for *e* and *e*. 221 6
one God, now and for *e*. 222 7
one God, now and for *e*. 223 3
be dominion and praise for *e* and *e*. 223 9
one God, for *e* and *e*. 223 20
one God, now and for *e*. 224 6
one God, for *e* and *e*. 224 18
one God, now and for *e*. 225 2
one God, for *e* and *e*. 225 6
one God, for *e* and *e*. 226 12
one God, for *e* and *e*. 227 6
one God, for *e* and *e*. 228 7
one God, now and for *e*. 228 13
one God, now and for *e*. 229 4
one God, for *e* and *e*. 229 9
one God, now and for *e*. 230 6
one God, for *e* and *e*. 230 11
one God, for *e* and *e*. 231 3
one God, now and for *e*. 231 9
one God, for *e* and *e*. 232 5
one God, now and for *e*. 232 16
one God, for *e* and *e*. 233 8
one God, now and for *e*. 233 13
one God, for *e* and *e*. 234 5
one God, now and for *e*. 235 2
one God, for *e* and *e*. 235 8
one God, for *e* and *e*. 236 7
and *e* hold fast the blessed hope of everlasting life, 236 10
one God, now and for *e*. 236 19
one God, now and for *e*. 237 7
one God, for *e* and *e*. 238 6
one God, now and for *e*. 238 19
one God, now and for *e*. 239 5
one God, for *e* and *e*. 239 22
one God, now and for *e*. 240 6
one God, for *e* and *e*. 240 12
one God, for *e* and *e*. 241 2
may *e* stand firm upon the one foundation, 241 22
one God, now and for *e*. 241 24
one God, for *e* and *e*. 242 7
one God, now and for *e*. 242 13
one God, for *e* and *e*. 243 6
one God, now and for *e*. 243 13
one God, now and for *e*. 244 12
one God, for *e* and *e*. 244 19
one God, now and for *e*. 245 3
one God, for *e* and *e*. 245 15
one God, now and for *e*. 246 7
one God, for *e* and *e*. 247 5
one God, now and for *e*. 247 25
one God, now and for *e*. 248 7
one God, for *e* and *e*. 248 14
God, for *e* and *e*. 249 4
one God, now and for *e*. 249 17
one God, for *e* and *e*. 250 7
one God, now and for *e*. 250 13
and who lives and reigns for *e* and *e*. 250 20
one God, now and for *e*. 251 6
one God, for *e* and *e*. 251 18
one God, for *e* and *e*. 252 5
that we may *e* perceive within ourselves the fruit 252 9
one God, now and for *e*. 252 15
one God, now and for *e*. 253 5
one God, for *e* and *e*. 253 19
one God, now and for *e*. 254 6
one God, now and for *e*. 255 5
Spirit to abide with us for *e*: 255 7
one God, now and for *e*. 256 10
one God, for *e* and *e*. 256 17
one God, now and for *e*. 257 4
one God, for *e* and *e*. 257 19
one God, for *e* and *e*. 258 7
one God, now and for *e*. 258 14
one God, for *e* and *e*. 259 2
one God, now and for *e*. 259 10
one God, for *e* and *e*. 260 7
one God, now and for *e*. 260 14
one God, for *e* and *e*. 261 6
one God, for *e* 264 8
and my sin is *e* before me. 266 7
in his name may *e* hail him as our King, 271 11
you and the Holy Spirit, now and for *e*. 271 14
one God, for *e* and *e*. 272 13
one God, for *e* and *e*. 274 6
For *e* and *e*. 276 2
one God, for *e* and *e*. 276 8
one God, for *e* and *e*. 280 23
one God, now and for *e*. 282 12
one God, for *e* and *e*. 283 6
one God, for *e* and *e*. 286 16
find it *e* burning—he who gives his light 287 24
who lives and reigns for *e* and *e*. 287 25
and where your saints for *e* sing your praise; 290 5
one God, now and for *e*. 295 7
His mercy endures for *e*. 299 6
lives and reigns now and for *e*. 306 8
born again may continue for *e* in the risen life 307 5
be all honor and glory, now and for *e*. 307 8
with you and the Holy Spirit, for *e* and *e*. 307 13
as Christ's own for *e*. 308 10
one God, now and for *e*. 309 11
that he may continue yours for *e*, 309 16
let your fatherly hand *e* be over these your servants; 310 8
let your Holy Spirit *e* be with them; 310 9
for *e* and *e*. 311 14
one God, for *e* and *e*. 311 20
and keep him safe for *e*. 314 5
And blessed be his kingdom, now and for *e*. 319 2

His mercy endureth for *e*.	319	7
And blessed be his kingdom, now and for *e*.	323	2
His mercy endureth for *e*.	323	5
grant that we may *e* hereafter serve and please thee	331	17
and the glory, for *e* and *e*.	336	29
be upon you and remain with you for *e*.	339	21
And blessed be his kingdom, now and for *e*.	351	2
His mercy endures for *e*.	351	6
And blessed be his kingdom, now and for *e*.	355	2
His mercy endures for *e*.	355	6
all the company of heaven, who for *e* sing this hymn	362	2
and glory is yours, Almighty Father, now and for *e*.	363	21
for *e* and *e*.	364	14
now and for *e*.	364	14
be honor and glory, now and for *e*.	366	13
all the company of heaven, who for *e* sing this hymn	367	11
and glory is yours, Almighty Father, now and for *e*.	369	17
Glory to you for *e* and *e*.	370	7
inaccessible from before time and for *e*.	373	3
in the unity of the Holy Spirit, for *e* and *e*.	375	28
the fellowship of [the *e*-blessed Virgin Mary,	391	19
the power and the glory, now and for *e*.	391	25
And praise your Name for *e* and *e*.	393	3
Holy Spirit, now and for *e*.	395	7
live and reign, now and for *e*.	395	12
lives and reigns for *e* and *e*.	395	24
if anyone eats of this bread, he will live for *e*;	397	2
lives and reigns for *e* and *e*.	397	18
for *e* and *e*.	398	25
and glory is yours, Almighy Father, now and for *e*.	403	21
and glory is yours, Almighty Father, now and for *e*.	405	21
As it was in the beginning, is now, and *e* shall be, *	406	3
His mercy endures for *e*.	413	6
one God, now and for *e*.	418	9
that he may continue yours for *e*,	418	14
let your fatherly hand *e* be over these your servants;	419	4
let your Holy Spirit *e* be with them;	419	5
speak now; or else for *e* hold your peace.	424	3
one God, for *e* and *e*.	425	13
for *e* and *e*.	428	21
live and reign in perfect unity, now and for *e*.	430	9
where your saints feast for *e* in your heavenly home;	430	23
one God, for *e* and *e*.	430	25
one God, now and for *e*.	431	8
to Abraham and his children for *e*.	442	10
as it was in the beginning, is now, and will be for *e*.	442	12
and I will dwell in the house of the LORD for *e*.	443	17
as it was in the beginning, is now, and will be for *e*.	443	19
and my sin is *e* before me.	449	6
one God, for *e* and *e*.	455	14
where he lives and reigns for *e* and *e*.	460	9
one God, for *e* and *e*.	464	20
one God, for *e* and *e*.	466	20
one God, now and for *e*.	470	6
or *e* the earth and the world were made, *	472	12
and I will dwell in the house of the LORD for *e*.	476	18
and I will dwell in the house of the LORD for *e*.	477	11
and his mercy endureth for *e*.	478	12
one God, for *e* and *e*.	481	29
and the glory, for *e* and *e*.	486	6
to whom be glory for *e* and *e*.	487	4
one God, now and for *e*.	489	29
shall not die for *e*.	491	6
one God, for *e* and *e*.	493	9
one God, now and for *e*.	493	15
one God, now and for *e*.	494	6
for *e* and *e*.	502	14
to whom be glory for *e* and *e*.	503	6
And blessed be his kingdom, now and for *e*.	512	2
His mercy endures for *e*.	512	6
one God, for *e* and *e*.	515	13
power and glory in the Church, now and for *e*.	521	17
one God, now and for *e*.	523	10
and remain with you for *e*.	523	17
And blessed be his kingdom, now and for *e*.	525	2
His mercy endures for *e*.	525	6
one God, for *e* and *e*.	528	11
one God, for *e* and *e*.	534	9
one God, now and for *e*.	535	10
His mercy endures for *e*.	537	6
one God, for *e* and *e*.	540	11
one God, for *e* and *e*.	545	18
one God, now and for *e*.	547	6
the fellowship of [the *e*-blessed Virgin Mary,	550	26
one God, for *e* and *e*.	560	10
one God, now and for *e*.	564	10
born again may continue for *e* in the risen life	570	19
be all honor and glory, now and for *e*.	570	22
Altar where your saints and angels praise you for *e*.	574	3
they will sing out their joy for *e*.	589	18
you have blotted out their name for *e* and *e*.	593	10
But the LORD is enthroned for *e*; *	593	13
and the hope of the poor shall not perish for *e*.	594	14
no harm shall happen to me *e*."	595	5
The LORD is King for *e* and *e*; *	596	1
and save us from this generation for *e*.	597	17
will you forget me for *e*? *	597	21
to David and his descendants for *e*.	606	14
The fear of the Lord is clean and endures for *e*; *	607	13
length of days, for *e* and *e*.	609	4
I have been entrusted to you *e* since I was born; *	610	20
"May your heart live for *e*!"	612	9
they shall be known as the LORD's for *e*.	612	20
and I will dwell in the house of the LORD for *e*.	613	13
My eyes are *e* looking to the LORD, *	615	18
shepherd them and carry them for *e*.	620	4
O LORD my God, I will give you thanks for *e*.	622	6
But the LORD's will stands fast for *e*, *	626	21
his praise shall *e* be in my mouth.	627	22
and their inheritance shall last for *e*.	634	21
and dwell in the land for *e*.	635	15
They shall be kept safe for *e*, *	635	18
and dwell in it for *e*.	635	21
let your love and your faithfulness keep me safe for *e*,	641	3
and shall set me before your face for *e*.	642	25
and we will praise your Name for *e*.	646	2
Arise! do not reject us for *e*.	647	4
because God has blessed you for *e*.	647	16
Your throne, O God, endures for *e* and *e*, *	648	1
therefore nations will praise you for *e* and *e*."	648	27
God has established her for *e*.	651	17
This God is our God for *e* and *e*; *	652	4
In order to live for *e* and *e*, *	652	21
Their graves shall be their homes for *e*,	653	1

Even though honored, they cannot live for *e*; *	653	4
and my sin is *e* before me.	656	11
I trust in the mercy of God for *e* and *e*.	658	17
I will dwell in your house for *e*; *	668	19
Let him sit enthroned before God for *e*; *	669	1
In his might he rules for *e*;	674	6
truly, the LORD will dwell there for *e*.	677	14
let those who love your salvation say for *e*,	682	20
I have been sustained by you *e* since I was born;	683	11
May his Name remain for *e*,	686	21
And blessed be his glorious Name for *e*! *	686	27
God is the strength of my heart and my portion for *e*.	689	2
will the enemy blaspheme your Name for *e*?	690	5
you dried up *e*-flowing rivers.	690	15
But I will rejoice for *e*; *	691	22
Will the Lord cast me off for *e*? *	693	14
Has his loving-kindness come to an end for *e*? *	693	16
like the earth which he founded for *e*.	700	18
will your fury blaze like fire for *e*?	701	14
we will give you thanks for *e*	702	10
and their punishment would last for *e*.	705	6
Let them be disgraced and terrified for *e*; *	707	11
Will you be displeased with us for *e*? *	709	3
E since my youth, I have been wretched and at the	713	8
Your love, O LORD, for *e* will I sing; *	713	17
persuaded that your love is established for *e*; *	713	19
"I will establish your line for *e*, *	714	1
I will keep my love for him for *e*, *	715	22
I will establish his line for *e* *	715	24
His line shall endure for *e* *	716	13
will you hide yourself for *e*? *	717	6
They flourish only to be destroyed for *e*; *	721	11
E since the world began, your throne has been established; *	722	7
for *e* and for evermore.	722	17
But you, O LORD, endure for *e*, *	731	23
nor will he keep his anger for *e*.	733	26
But the merciful goodness of the LORD endures for *e*	734	15
May the glory of the LORD endure for *e*; *	737	16
for his mercy endures for *e*.	741	20
throughout all generations for *e*.	744	10
and his mercy endures for *e*.	746	2
a priest for *e* after the order of Melchizedek."	753	20
and his righteousness endures for *e*.	754	11
he is *e* mindful of his covenant.	754	15
They stand fast for *e* and *e*, *	754	20
he commanded his covenant for *e*; *	754	23
his praise endures for *e*.	755	3
and their righteousness will last for *e*.	755	10
and their righteousness stands fast for *e*;	755	23
and the faithfulness of the LORD endures for *e*.	760	18
his mercy endures for *e*.	760	21
"His mercy endures for *e*."	760	23
"His mercy endures for *e*."	761	2
his mercy endures for *e*.	763	4
I shall keep it for *e* and *e*.	767	2
Your decrees are my inheritance for *e*; *	772	15
for *e* and to the end.	772	18
and my delight shall be *e* in your statutes.	773	8
that you have established them for *e*.	776	8
which cannot be moved, but stands fast for *e*.	781	18
"This shall be my resting-place for *e*; *	786	28
for his mercy endures for *e*.	789	21
O LORD, your love endures for *e*;	793	20
and bless your Name for *e* and *e*.	801	13
and praise your Name for *e* and *e*.	801	15
let all flesh bless his holy Name for *e* and *e*.	803	2
who keeps his promise for *e*;	803	14
The LORD shall reign for *e*, *	803	24
He made them stand fast for *e* and *e*; *	806	5
to whom be dominion and glory, now and for *e*.	815	27
one God, now and for *e*.	817	2
one God, now and for *e*.	819	12
Be *e* present with your servants	819	14
and make them *e* mindful of their calling	820	22
may *e* be defended by thy gracious and ready help;	832	21
the Holy Spirit, now and for *e*.	834	11
that we may *e* perceive within ourselves the fruit	834	15
one God, for *e* and *e*.	834	17
the Holy Spirit, now and for *e*.	837	24
the glory are yours for *e*.	838	8
Enrich our lives by *e*-widening circles of fellowship,	840	3
and glory of your Name, now and for *e*.	840	13

everlasting

The mercy of the Lord is *e*:	44	5
his mercy is *e*; *	45	21
All the earth doth worship thee, the Father *e*.	52	24
Thou art the *e* Son of the Father.	53	12
in glory *e*.	53	22
and the life *e*.	54	10
almighty and *e* God, who hast safely brought	57	7
Almighty and *e* God, by whose Spirit	57	19
and in the world to come life *e*.	59	19
and the life *e*.	66	26
and in the world to come life *e*.	72	16
The mercy of the Lord is *e*:	81	14
his mercy is *e*; *	83	8
The Lord will be your *e* light, *	88	1
to glory *e*.	96	12
and the life *e*.	96	30
almighty and *e* Father, you have brought	100	1
Almighty and *e* God, by whose Spirit	100	11
your truth, and in the age to come life *e*.	102	7
Almighty, *e* God, let our prayer	113	9
and the life *e*.	120	26
your truth, and in the age to come life *e*.	126	7
almighty and *e* Father, you have brought	137	14
assaults of the devil; and from *e* damnation	148	16
one God, in glory *e*.	161	6
one God, in glory *e*.	162	6
Spirit liveth and reigneth, one God, in glory *e*.	163	6
Almighty and *e* God, who dost govern	164	1
Almighty and *e* God, who hatest nothing	166	1
Almighty and *e* God, who, of thy tender love	168	1
and opened unto us the gate of *e* life:	170	23
found worthy to attain to *e* joys;	171	7
Almighty and *e* God, who in the Paschal mystery	172	1
whom truly to know is *e* life:	173	16
one God, in glory *e*.	174	14
Almighty and *e* God, who hast given	176	1
Almighty and *e* God, who art always	182	18
Almighty and *e* God, who in Christ hast revealed	183	11
Almighty and *e* God, give unto us	183	17

and ever hold fast the blessed hope of *e* life,	184	19
Almighty and *e* God, whose will it is to restore	185	1
the Holy Spirit, one God, in glory *e*.	186	5
attain to the fullness of life *e*;	186	10
O Almighty and *e* God, who didst give	192	7
one God, in glory *e*.	192	18
O *e* God, who hast ordained	193	4
one God, in glory *e*.	194	15
Almighty and *e* God, who didst enkindle	196	1
Almighty and *e* God, we thank thee	196	7
O *e* God, who hast ordained	200	6
Almighty and *e* God, whose will it is to restore	202	16
Almighty and *e* Father, who hast given	204	8
Almighty and *e* God, by whose Spirit	206	1
one God, in glory *e*.	212	20
one God, in glory *e*.	213	17
one God, in glory *e*.	214	17
Almighty and *e* God, you govern	215	12
Almighty and *e* God, you hate nothing	217	14
opened to us the gate of *e* life:	222	17
found worthy to attain to *e* joys;	223	1
Almighty and *e* God, who in the Paschal mystery	223	15
Almighty and *e* God, who in the Paschal mystery	224	13
God, whom truly to know is *e* life:	225	8
one God, in glory *e*.	226	7
one God, in glory *e*.	226	18
Almighty and *e* God, you have given	228	1
Almighty and *e* God, you are always more ready	234	12
Almighty and *e* God, in Christ you have revealed	235	3
Almighty and *e* God, increase	235	9
hold fast the blessed hope of *e* life,	236	11
Almighty and *e* God, whose will it is to restore	236	14
one God, in glory *e*.	237	18
Almighty and *e* God, who gave to your apostle	243	14
one God, in glory *e*.	244	6
e God, you have ordained	244	13
one God, in glory *e*.	245	22
Almighty and *e* God, who kindled	247	13
Almighty and *e* God, we thank	247	19
e God, you have ordained	251	12
Almighty and *e* God, whose will it is to restore	254	1
Almighty and *e* Father, you have given	255	6
Almighty and *e* God, by whose Spirit	256	19
Almighty and *e* God, you hate nothing	264	2
only by your gracious gift that we are given *e* life;	265	19
become heirs with him of *e* life.	277	6
Almighty and *e* God, by whose Spirit	278	11
and to us sinners *e* life and glory;	282	10
attain to the festival of *e* light;	285	12
Almighty and *e* God, who in the Paschal mystery	290	14
and the life *e*.	293	18
and the life *e*.	304	21
from the bondage of sin into *e* life.	306	19
until he comes to your *e* kingdom.	309	18
and exalt us to *e* life.	316	16
and bring you to *e* life;	332	6
should not perish, but have *e* life.	332	12
holy Father, almighty, *e* God.	333	9
preserve thy body and soul unto *e* life.	338	6
preserve thy body and soul unto *e* life.	338	10
Christ keep you in *e* life.	338	14
through hope, of thy *e* kingdom.	339	9

holy Father, almighty, *e* God.	341	3
resurrection opened to us the way of *e* life.	345	3
and to make us heirs in him of *e* life;	345	9
rising to life again hath won for us *e* life.	346	24
comfort us with the blessed hope of *e* life;	349	8
Christ keep you in *e* life.	365	5
we may enter the *e* heritage of your sons	369	11
resurrection opened to us the way of *e* life.	377	16
and to make us heirs in him of *e* life;	378	5
rising to life again he has won for us *e* life.	379	19
and comforts us with the blessed hope of *e* life.	382	2
Christ keep you in *e* life.	399	6
strength in our weakness, and *e* salvation;	399	11
and the life *e*.	417	3
until he comes to your *e* kingdom.	418	16
in the age to come have life *e*.	431	13
partake of *e* glory in the life to come;	444	6
should not perish, but have *e* life.	449	17
and bring you to *e* life;	456	18
strength in our weakness, and *e* salvation;	457	9
he may dwell with thee in life *e*;	458	9
he may live with you in *e* life;	460	4
comfort him with the promise of life *e*,	462	3
a place of refreshment and *e* blessedness,	463	18
into the blessed rest of *e* peace,	465	5
Wash him in the holy font of *e* life,	465	17
thou art God from *e*, and world without end.	472	13
and the resurrection to life *e*.	481	16
bliss in thy eternal and *e* glory,	481	25
neither sighing, but life *e*.	482	11
neither sighing, but life *e*.	483	5
into the blessed rest of *e* peace,	483	10
the blood of the *e* covenant:	487	1
Almighty and *e* God, we yield	487	10
in thy eternal and *e* glory;	488	10
and to us sinners *e* life and glory;	489	27
and the life *e*.	496	20
neither sighing, but life *e*.	499	3
into the blessed rest of *e* peace,	499	17
the blood of the *e* covenant:	503	3
bliss in your eternal and *e* glory;	503	18
from the bondage of sin into *e* life.	570	11
For you will give him *e* felicity *	609	7
lift them high, O *e* doors; *	614	2
for they are from *e*.	614	25
more splendid than the *e* mountains!	692	8
you are from *e*.	722	8
his mercy is *e*; *	730	5
an *e* covenant for Israel,	738	20
from *e* and to *e*; *	745	24
the righteous will be kept in *e* remembrance.	755	16
O LORD, your word is *e*; *	770	20
Your justice is an *e* justice *	775	9
The righteousness of your decrees is *e*; *	775	13
O LORD, your Name is *e*; *	789	1
and lead me in the way that is *e*.	795	27
Your kingdom is an *e* kingdom; *	802	11
Almighty and *e* God, from whom cometh	817	3
Almighty and *e* God, you made	827	11
by thy mercy, obtain *e* life;	832	4
towards the attainment of *e* salvation;	832	20
and gave us the hope of *e* life:	835	3

and also be partaker of *e* glory in the life to come; 841 12
What do we mean by *e* life? 862 25
By *e* life, we mean a new existence, 862 26

everliving

pure brightness of the *e* Father in heaven, 64 2
pure brightness of the *e* Father in heaven, 112 2
pure brightness of the *e* Father in heaven, 118 2
pure brightness of the *e* Father in heaven, 139 2
E God, who didst strengthen thine apostle Thomas 185 14
Almighty and *e* God, we humbly beseech 187 16
Almighty and *e* God, in your tender love 219 13
E God, who strengthened your apostle Thomas 237 8
Almighty and *e* God, we humbly pray 239 6
Almighty and *e* God, in your tender love 272 7
Almighty and *e* God, let your fatherly hand 310 8
Almighty and *e* God, who in thy holy Word hast 329 1
Almighty and *e* God, we most heartily thank 339 2
Almighty and *e* God, we thank you 366 1
Almighty and *e* God, let your fatherly hand 419 4
O gracious and *e* God, you have created 425 7
E God, whose power is limitless, 552 6
E God, strengthen and sustain 560 6
E Father, watchful and caring, 568 7
E God, whose will 816 16
Almighty and *e* God, ruler of all things 817 18
Almighty and *e* God, source of all wisdom 818 1

evermore

the fellowship of the Holy Ghost, be with us all *e*. 59 23
the fellowship of the Holy Ghost, be with us all *e*. 72 20
for ever and for *e*. 94 8
the fellowship of the Holy Spirit, be with us all *e*. 102 11
from this time forth for *e*. 105 3
the fellowship of the Holy Spirit, be with us all *e*. 126 11
from this time forth for *e*. 138 4
the fellowship of the Holy Ghost, be with us all *e*. 154 2
and *e* serve thee in holiness 155 11
E give us this bread, that he may live in us, 167 12
that we may *e* live with him 170 11
and *e* to rejoice in his holy comfort; 175 18
without thy succor, preserve it *e* by thy help 180 10
E give us this bread, that he may live in us, 219 3
that we may *e* live with him 222 4
and *e* to rejoice in his holy comfort; 227 11
that we may *e* live with him 295 4
to him be glory in the Church *e*. 317 19
e praising thee, 334 3
that we may *e* dwell in him, 337 15
e praising thee, 341 6
serve him both now and *e*. 456 6
Be now and *e* your defense, 457 1
from this time forth for *e*. 473 24
and at thy right hand there is pleasure for *e*. 485 8
and in your right hand are pleasures for *e*. 501 10
From this time forth for *e*. 523 14
and in your right hand are pleasures for *e*. 600 21
the LORD sits enthroned as King for *e*. 620 26
he shall be our guide for *e*. 652 5
has his promise failed for *e*? 693 17
and glorify your Name for *e*. 710 25
It shall stand fast for *e* like the moon, * 716 15
Blessed be the LORD for *e*! * 717 18
but you, O LORD, are exalted for *e*. 721 12
for ever and for *e*. 722 17
from this time forth for *e*. 756 5
from this time forth for *e*. 758 26
all your righteous judgments endure for *e*. 776 24
from this time forth for *e*. 779 17
from this time forth for *e*. 781 21
from this time forth for *e*. 785 18
their children will sit upon your throne for *e*." 786 25
ordained the blessing: * life for *e*. 787 18
behold it unveiled for *e*; 819 18
that we may *e* be kindly affectioned one to another; 829 7

every

and in *e* place incense shall be offered unto my Name, 38 7
we have turned *e* one to his own way; 39 1
and in *e* place incense shall be offered to my Name, 76 6
we have turned *e* one to his own way; 76 25
Glorify the Lord, *e* shower of rain and fall of dew, * 88 13
mercy on those who fear him * in *e* generation. 92 5
From *e* family, language, people, and nation, * 94 3
and in *e* place incense shall be offered to my Name, 106 7
the lights of the world in *e* generation: 111 13
keep us from *e* sin, *e* evil, and *e* fear; 113 6
mercy on those who fear him * in *e* generation. 119 11
Plant in *e* heart, 162 2
eternal life to *e* race and nation by the promised gift 175 9
in this and *e* land evangelists 196 10
to ordain ministers in *e* place: 205 15
in *e* heart the true love of peace, 207 8
satisfy the needs of *e* living creature: 208 10
Plant in *e* heart, 213 14
eternal life to *e* race and nation by the promised gift 227 2
in this and *e* land evangelists 247 22
ordain ministers in *e* place: 256 11
in *e* heart the true love of peace, 258 8
satisfy the needs of *e* living creature: 259 12
in *e* heart the true love of peace, 278 25
and respect the dignity of *e* human being? 294 2
and respect the dignity of *e* human being? 305 8
whom *e* family in heaven and earth is named, 311 22
the authority of government in this and *e* land 329 19
who was in *e* way tempted as we are, 346 4
we are able to triumph over *e* evil, 346 6
those in *e* generation who have looked to you in hope, 370 25
giving voice to *e* creature under heaven, 373 10
who was tempted in *e* way as we are, 379 1
we are able to triumph over *e* evil, 379 3
for *e* city and community, 384 7
for those in *e* generation in whom Christ has been honored 386 14
Grant that *e* member of the Church may truly 387 3
promote the dignity and freedom of *e* person, 390 18
and respect the dignity of *e* human being? 417 18
Defend them from *e* enemy. 430 16
those who fear him * in *e* generation. 441 19
your mercies are new *e* morning: 460 17
and set him free from *e* bond; 464 17
and set him free from *e* bond; 466 17
e good work to do his will, 487 2
casting *e* care on thee, 489 32

e good work to do his will, 503 4
e generation who have looked to God in hope. 517 16
your Church is built up in *e* place, 521 5
My brother, *e* Christian is called to follow 543 1
the dignity and freedom of *e* person, 550 3
Father, in *e* age you have spoken through the voices 571 9
e night I drench my bed 590 10
God sits in judgment *e* day. 591 21
The wicked prowl on *e* side, * 597 18
E one has proved faithless; 598 18
E day we gloried in God, * 646 1
I know *e* bird in the sky, * 655 1
E one has proved faithless; 659 4
For you have rescued me from *e* trouble, * 660 3
and punished *e* morning. 688 6
They have shed their blood like water on *e* side 701 8
they encompass me on *e* side. 713 14
and burns up his enemies on *e* side. 727 2
and shattered *e* tree in their country. 740 20
They hem me in, they hem me in on *e* side; * 761 17
I restrain my feet from *e* evil way, * 771 21
therefore I hate *e* lying way. 772 2
E day will I bless you * 801 14
satisfy the needs of *e* living creature. 802 20
from whom cometh *e* good and perfect gift: 817 3
giver of *e* good gift: 818 8
from pride and arrogance, and from *e* evil way. 820 6
Spirit may so move *e* human heart 823 18
grant that *e* one of us may enjoy a fair portion 826 13
you proclaim your truth in *e* age 827 6
e root of bitterness, the desire of vainglory, 829 1
protect them from *e* danger; 831 4
the loving care which surrounds us on *e* side. 836 6
that in *e* place your servants call upon your Name; 838 6
all the martyrs and saints in *e* age and in *e* land. 838 17
It has drawn people from *e* nation, 839 9

everyone
e might come within the reach of thy saving embrace: 58 9
e might come within the reach of your saving embrace: 101 2
but on a lamp-stand where it gives light for *e* 109 9
And *e* who has life, 491 4
E the Father gives to me will come to me; 501 1
E speaks falsely with his neighbor; * 597 3
and that which is worthless is highly prized by *e*. 597 19
truly, *e* is but a puff of wind. 639 19
Let *e* know that God rules in Jacob, * 666 26
for you repay *e* according to his deeds. 670 11
E will stand in awe and declare God's deeds; * 672 3
Of Zion it shall be said, "*E* was born in her, * 711 20
The LORD is loving to *e* * 802 3

everything
For you created *e* that is, * 93 22
equip you with *e* good that you may do his will, 132 3
For *e* in heaven and on earth is yours. 377 7
For *e* in heaven and on earth is yours. 569 12
For *e* in heaven and on earth is yours. 579 15
e they do shall prosper. 585 9
the enemy has laid waste *e* in your sanctuary. 689 15
Let the creditor seize *e* he has; * 751 18
Let *e* that has breath * 808 9

everywhere
Grant that people *e* may seek after thee 58 4
men and women *e* love thee 70 17
O men and women *e*, glorify the Lord, * 89 16
Grant that people *e* may seek after you 100 20
men and women *e* love you and serve you in peace; 124 15
Grant that people *e* may seek after thee 206 12
Grant that people *e* may seek after you 257 8
for people *e* according to their needs. 277 7
It is truly right and good, always and *e*, 286 22
always and *e* to give thanks to you, 361 7
always and *e* to give thanks to you, 367 7
men and women *e* may give thee thanks; 828 7

evil
and repenteth him of the *e*. 38 16
but deliver us from *e*. 54 23
but deliver us from *e*. 67 13
abounding in steadfast love, and repents of *e*. 76 15
Not with the old leaven, the leaven of malice and *e*, * 83 13
and the *e* ones their thoughts; 86 20
but deliver us from *e*. 97 14
The LORD shall preserve you from all *e*; * 104 25
but deliver us from *e*. 106 24
keep us from every sin, every *e*, 113 6
but deliver us from *e*. 121 14
There shall no *e* happen to you, * 130 17
but deliver us from *e*. 133 6
From all *e* and wickedness; 148 15
but deliver us from *e*. 153 15
and from all *e* thoughts 167 6
and by thy great might frustrate the designs of *e* 186 16
Grant us grace fearlessly to contend against *e* 209 2
and from all *e* thoughts 218 16
frustrate the designs of *e* tyrants 238 10
to contend against *e* and to make no peace 260 9
and done what is *e* in your sight. 266 9
Do you reaffirm your renunciation of *e* 292 8
Will you persevere in resisting *e*, 293 23
Do you renounce the *e* powers of this world 302 10
Do you reaffirm your renunciation of *e*? 303 10
Will you persevere in resisting *e*, 304 26
but deliver us from *e*. 311 11
but deliver us from *e*. 336 27
to triumph over every *e*, 346 7
subject to *e* and death, 362 11
but deliver us from *e*. 364 11
In him, you have delivered us from *e*, 368 7
to triumph over every *e*, 379 3
but deliver us from *e*. 398 22
Do you reaffirm your renunciation of *e*? 415 9
Will you persevere in resisting *e*, 417 8
but deliver us from *e*. 428 18
I shall fear no *e*;* 443 8
May he deliver you from all *e*, 456 17
From all *e*, from all sin, from all tribulation, 463 3
from the power of *e*, 463 13
but deliver us from *e*. 464 14
from all *e*, and set him free from every bond; 464 17

from all *e*, and set him free from every bond; 466 17
The LORD shall preserve thee from all *e*; * 473 21
I will fear no *e*; * 476 9
I will fear no *e*; * 477 2
but deliver us from *e*. 486 4
but deliver us from *e*. 502 11
and *e* cannot dwell with you. 588 24
If I have repaid my friend with *e*, * 591 1
who conceive *e*, and give birth to a lie. 591 27
Break the power of the wicked and *e*; * 595 27
he does no *e* to his friend; * 599 9
Though they intend *e* against you 609 20
I shall fear no *e*; * 613 4
Whose hands are full of *e* plots, * 617 1
Keep your tongue from *e*-speaking * 628 19
Turn from *e* and do good; * 628 21
The face of the LORD is against those who do *e*, * 628 25
E shall slay the wicked, * 629 9
They pay me *e* in exchange for good; * 630 15
he does not abhor that which is *e*. 632 11
the one who succeeds in *e* schemes. 633 20
do not fret yourself; it leads only to *e*. 633 22
Turn from *e*, and do good, * 635 14
Those who repay *e* for good slander me, * 638 9
they do not resort to *e* spirits or turn to false gods. 640 10
and devise *e* against me. 642 14
Why should I be afraid in *e* days, * 652 13
You have loosed your lips for *e*, * 655 18
You are always speaking *e* of your brother * 655 20
and done what is *e* in your sight. 656 13
You love *e* more than good * 658 4
Render *e* to those who spy on me; * 659 26
For they have cast an *e* spell upon me * 660 11
their only thought is to do me *e*. 662 23
No; you devise *e* in your hearts, * 664 23
show no mercy to those who are faithless and *e*. 666 6
They hold fast to their *e* course; * 671 18
If I had found *e* in my heart, * 675 3
let those who seek to do me *e* be covered with scorn 684 5
and their *e* speech runs through the world. 687 18
There shall no *e* happen to you, * 720 5
To give them rest in *e* days, * 723 19
one which frames *e* into law? 724 6
The LORD loves those who hate *e*; * 727 17
yet punished them for their *e* deeds." 729 18
I hate the doers of *e* deeds; 730 13
I will not know *e*. 730 16
and their daughters to *e* spirits. 744 22
and went whoring in their *e* deeds. 745 2
They repay *e* for good, * 751 6
and to those who speak *e* against me. 752 14
They will not be afraid of any *e* rumors; * 755 17
I restrain my feet from every *e* way, * 771 21
The LORD shall preserve you from all *e*; * 779 13
so that the just shall not put their hands to *e*. 781 24
Who devise *e* in their hearts * 796 3
nor let their *e* plans prosper. 796 18
let the *e* of their lips overwhelm them. 796 20
and *e* shall hunt down the lawless. 796 24
let not my heart incline to any *e* thing. 797 9
from pride and arrogance, and from every *e* way. 820 6
power of *e*, sin, and death. 849 6

evildoer

from the clutches of the *e* and the oppressor. 683 8

evildoers

Depart from me, all *e*, * 590 14
Have they no knowledge, all those *e* * 598 21
and gangs of *e* circle around me; * 611 12
I have hated the company of *e*; * 616 16
When *e* came upon me to eat up my flesh, * 617 11
with the wicked or with the *e*, * 619 11
Do not fret yourself because of *e*; * 633 5
For *e* shall be cut off, * 634 1
Have they no knowledge, those *e* * 659 7
Rescue me from *e* * 665 20
from the mob of *e*. 671 13
all *e* are full of boasting. 723 2
who took my part against the *e*? 723 26
that I may root out all *e* from the city of the LORD. 730 27
the LORD will lead them away with the *e*; * 782 4
Deliver me, O LORD, from *e*; * 796 1
Let me not be occupied in wickedness with *e*, * 797 10
and from the traps of the *e*. 797 23

evils

all those *e* that we most justly have deserved; 155 9

evolved

What other sacramental rites *e* in the Church 860 7
Other sacramental rites which *e* in the Church 860 9

ewes

He brought him from following the *e*, * 700 21

exalt

the God of my people and I will *e* him. 85 6
praise him and highly *e* him for ever. 88 6
we will praise you and highly *e* you for ever. 90 8
and *e* us unto the same place 175 4
and *e* us to that place 226 16
and *e* us to everlasting life. 316 16
We will *e* you, O God our King; 393 2
May he *e* you, O Lord, in the midst of your people; 534 1
I will *e* you, O LORD, 621 3
let us *e* his Name together. 627 26
E yourself above the heavens, O God, * 664 8
E yourself above the heavens, O God, * 664 19
e him who rides upon the heavens; * 676 9
Let them *e* him in the congregation of the people * 748 19
E yourself above the heavens, O God, * 750 3
you are my God, and I will *e* you." 763 2
I will *e* you, O God my King, * 801 12

exaltation

Grant us who honor the *e* of her lowliness 189 13
Grant us who honor the *e* of her lowliness 240 21

exalted

praised and *e* above all for ever. 49 10
and hath *e* the humble and meek. 50 14
and hath *e* the humble and meek. 65 17
see that they remember that his Name is *e*. 86 10
O God, the King of glory, who hast *e* thine only Son 175 1
O God, the King of glory, you have *e* your only Son 226 13
thou art *e* as head above all. 344 11

e as head over all. [illegible]
I will be *e* among the nations, 472 5
and I will be *e* in the earth. 472 6
We praise you that you have highly *e* him, 545 4
how *e* is your Name in all the world! 592 8
E is the God of my salvation! 606 4
you *e* me above those who rose against me; * 606 8
Be *e*, O LORD, in your might; * 609 25
I will be *e* among the nations; 650 2
I will be *e* in the earth." 650 3
and he is highly *e*. 650 25
but the horns of the righteous shall be *e*. 691 25
and by your favor our might is *e*. 714 28
and have *e* one chosen out of the people. 715 5
You have *e* the right hand of his foes * 716 25
but you, O LORD, are *e* for evermore. 721 12
But my horn you have *e* like the horns of wild bulls; * 721 16
you are *e* far above all gods. 727 16
the right hand of the LORD is *e*! 762 2
for his Name only is *e*, 806 20
and you are *e* as head above all. 822 15

exalting
and for *e* him to be our great High Priest. 573 16

examination
observance of a holy Lent, by self-*e* and repentance; 265 11

examine
E your lives and conduct by the rule 317 1
e my heart and my mind. 616 11
e her strongholds; * 652 2
It is required that we should *e* our lives, 860 5

example
that all mankind should follow the *e* 168 4
follow the *e* of his patience, 168 6
both a sacrifice for sin and also an *e* of godly life: 180 20
for the *e* of the first martyr Stephen, 186 1
follow the *e* of her devotion to thy will; 189 14
follow the *e* of thy faithful servant Barnabas, 189 17
and after his *e* constantly speak the truth, 190 5
instructed by their teaching and *e*, 190 12
after his *e*, we may with ready wills 192 21
that after the *e* of thy servant James the Just, 193 18
who rejoice in her triumph may profit by her *e*; 196 4
following his *e* and the teaching of his holy life, 196 24
encouraged by the good *e* of thy servant 198 18
giving us the *e* of his great humility: 219 16
and also an *e* of godly life: 232 12
for the *e* of the first martyr Stephen, 237 14
to follow the *e* of her devotion to your will; 240 21
follow the *e* of your faithful servant Barnabas, 241 3
following his *e*, constantly speak the truth, 241 14
instructed by their teaching and *e*, 241 21
after his *e*, we may with ready wills 244 9
following the *e* of your servant 245 4
rejoice in her triumph may profit by her *e*; 247 16
following his *e* and the teaching of his holy life, 248 10
encouraged by the good *e* of your servant 250 2
giving us the *e* of his great humility: 272 10
an *e*, that you should do as I have done." 274 11
Will you proclaim by word and *e* the Good News 293 26
Will you proclaim by word and *e* the Good News 305 1
thy saints hast given us an *e* of righteousness, 348 4
your saints you have given us an *e* of righteousness, 380 21
Will you proclaim by word and *e* the Good News 417 11
following the *e* of our Lord and Savior, 443 29
gave us the *e* of obedience to your Father's will: 461 6
to follow the *e* of their steadfastness in thy faith, 487 15
a faithful pastor and wholesome *e* 517 11
an effective *e* in word and action, 523 6
may be a wholesome *e* to your people? 532 22
an effective *e* in word and action, 535 6
redemptive love known, by your word and *e*, 543 10
may be a wholesome *e* to all people? 544 10
an effective *e* in word and action, 547 2
an effective *e* in word and action, 564 6
fashion our lives according to the *e* of your Son, 817 15
following the *e* of our Savior 829 12
the truth of his Word and the *e* of his life; 836 13
Our Lord gave us the *e* of prayer 856 24

examples
good *e* of those who have served thee 202 4
following the good *e* of those who have served you 253 8
follow the good *e* of [________ and of] all thy saints, 330 5
thanks for the good *e* of all those thy servants, 488 5
encouraged by their *e*, aided by their prayers, 489 19
the good *e* of all your servants, 503 15
encouraged by their *e*, aided by their prayers, 504 17
follow their *e*, and offer our prayers 514 16

exceed
which *e* all that we can desire; 174 5
which *e* all that we can desire; 225 17

exceedingly
The LORD made his people *e* fruitful; * 740 1

excellent
into our hearts that most *e* gift of charity, 165 1
lovable and gracious, *e* and admirable, 443 28
Such knowledge is too wonderful and *e* for me; * 475 3
O LORD my God, how *e* is your greatness! 735 2
praise him for his *e* greatness. 808 2

except
e through the merits and mediation of Jesus 234 17
who is the Rock, *e* our God? 605 2

exchange
They pay me evil in *e* for good; * 630 15

exchanged
And so they *e* their Glory * 743 11

executed
you have *e* justice and righteousness in Jacob." 729 7

executes
The LORD *e* righteousness * 733 19

exercise
and *e* without reproach the high priesthood 521 9
to the *e* of this ministry? 526 6
to the *e* of this ministry? 538 6
grant wisdom and grace in the *e* of their duties. 821 21

exhorts
Saint Paul *e* all persons to prepare themselves 316 20
exile
no breaching of the walls, no going into *e*, * 801 8
exiles
he gathers the *e* of Israel. 804 5
exist
that we, who cannot *e* without thee, 180 15
that we, who cannot *e* without you, 232 7
existence
By everlasting life, we mean a new *e*, 862 26
expanse
At your command all things came to be: the vast *e* 370 8
expectancy
that with calm *e* I may make room for your power 461 2
expectation
in the joyful *e* of eternal life 481 12
and in the joyful *e* of eternal life 505 14
expense
"Do not let them rejoice at my *e*, * 638 1
exploit
make us rich, though we often *e* them. 839 2
exploitation
and our *e* of other people, 268 4
express
Who can *e* the noble acts of the LORD, * 478 13
Move us to *e* the wonder, 572 2
Confirmation is the rite in which we *e* 860 18
expression
give me readiness of thought and *e*; 563 7
extend
let his years *e* over many generations. 668 25
I shall make his dominion *e* * 715 16
extension
for the *e* of thy kingdom; 205 18
for the *e* of your kingdom; 256 15
extol
Therefore will I *e* you among the nations, O LORD, * 606 10
extortion
Put no trust in *e*; 670 5
extreme
If thou, LORD, wilt be *e* to mark what is done amiss, * 474 5
exult
so that those who love your Name may *e* in you. 589 20
"I will *e* and parcel out Shechem; 667 21
"I will *e* and parcel out Shechem; 750 8
exultation
There is a sound of *e* and victory * 761 26
exults
how greatly he *e* in your victory! 608 22
eye
Keep us, O Lord, as the apple of your *e*; 132 14
his piercing *e* weighs our worth. 596 18
Keep me as the apple of your *e*; * 601 14
For his wrath endures but the twinkling of an *e*, * 621 12
my *e* is consumed with sorrow, 623 4
I will guide you with my *e*. 625 19
Behold, the *e* of the LORD is upon those who fear him, * 627 11
and my *e* has seen the ruin of my foes. 660 4
he that formed the *e* does he not see? 723 12
eyelids
You will not let my *e* close; * 693 8
nor let my *e* slumber; 786 6
eyes
For mine *e* have seen thy salvation, * 51 25
and our *e* behold the vesper light, 64 5
For mine *e* have seen thy salvation, * 66 3
For these *e* of mine have seen the Savior, * 93 14
I lift up my *e* to the hills; * 104 13
and our *e* behold the vesper light, 112 5
and our *e* behold the vesper light, 118 5
For these *e* of mine have seen the Savior, * 120 3
Your *e* have only to behold * 130 13
For these *e* of mine have seen the Savior, * 135 3
and our *e* behold the vesper light, 139 5
For these *e* of mine have seen the Savior, * 140 9
Open, we pray thee, the *e* of our faith, 171 18
Open, we pray thee, the *e* of our faith, 173 6
Open the *e* of our faith, 223 11
Open the *e* of our faith, 224 20
Open, O Lord, the *e* of all people 329 22
Open our *e* to see your hand at work 372 3
Look upon him with the *e* of thy mercy; 458 4
whom I shall see for myself and mine *e* shall behold, 469 7
I will lift up mine *e* unto the hills; * 473 9
mine *e* from tears, and my feet from falling. 479 15
I myself shall see, and my *e* behold him 491 11
Spirit, open our *e*, our ears, and our hearts, 569 3
My *e* are wasted with grief * 590 12
His *e* behold the inhabited world; * 596 17
give light to my *e*, lest I sleep in death; 598 5
let your *e* be fixed on justice. 601 2
For all his judgments are before my *e*, * 604 7
but you will humble the haughty *e*. 604 19
and gives light to the *e*. 607 11
My *e* are ever looking to the LORD, * 615 18
For your love is before my *e*; * 616 12
"I have been cut off from the sight of your *e*." * 624 15
The *e* of the LORD are upon the righteous, * 628 23
"Aha! we saw it with our own *e*." 631 13
there is no fear of God before his *e*. 632 4
He flatters himself in his own *e* * 632 5
and the brightness of my *e* is gone from me. 637 17
I have put my case in order before your *e*. 655 25
My *e* are fixed on you, O my Strength; * 666 14
his *e* keep watch over the nations; * 674 7
my *e* have failed from looking for my God. 679 15

Let their *e* be darkened, that they may not see, * 681 10
they have not set you before their *e*. 711 3
Your *e* have only to behold * 720 1
My *e* also gloat over my enemies, * 721 18
I will set no worthless thing before my *e*; * 730 12
My *e* are upon the faithful in the land, 730 20
e have they, but they cannot see; 757 23
my *e* from tears, and my feet from stumbling. 759 17
and it is marvelous in our *e*. 762 18
Open my *e*, that I may see * 764 19
Turn my *e* from watching what is worthless; * 766 9
My *e* have failed from watching for your promise, * 770 5
My *e* have failed from watching for your salvation * 773 19
My *e* shed streams of tears, * 774 19
My *e* are open in the night watches, * 775 22
I lift up my *e* to the hills; * 779 1
To you I lift up my *e*, * 780 15
As the *e* of servants look to the hand of their masters, 780 17
and the *e* of a maid to the hand of her mistress, 780 18
So our *e* look to the LORD our God, * 780 19
I will not allow my *e* to sleep, * 786 5
e have they, but they cannot see. 789 8
Your *e* beheld my limbs, yet unfinished in the womb; 795 6
But my *e* are turned to you, Lord GOD; * 797 19
The *e* of all wait upon you, O LORD, * 802 17
the LORD opens the *e* of the blind; * 803 18
Open our *e* to behold thy gracious hand 814 2

F

face

for thou shalt go before the *f* of the Lord 51 12
which thou hast prepared before the *f* of all people, 51 26
and poureth them out upon the *f* of the earth: 62 4
which thou hast prepared before the *f* of all people, 66 4
The Spirit of the Lord renews the *f* of the earth: 81 8
the revelation of the glory of God in the *f* of Jesus 110 5
The Lord make his *f* to shine upon you 114 2
the revelation of the glory of God in the *f* of Jesus 139 15
where we may behold thy glory *f* to *f*; 162 16
and hid not his *f* from shame: 169 2
where we may see your glory *f* to *f*; 214 9
his body to be whipped and his *f* to be spit upon: 220 15
Hide your *f* from my sins * 266 20
For those who *f* temptation, doubt, and despair 279 8
knowledge of thy glory in the *f* of thy Son 346 3
knowledge of your glory in the *f* of your Son 378 16
May he gaze upon you, Lord, *f* to *f*, 466 1
My heart hath talked of thee, Seek ye my *f*. * 478 1
Thy *f*, LORD, will I seek. 478 2
O hide not thou thy *f* from me, * 478 3
the Lord make his *f* to shine upon him 485 13
surely, you will strike all my enemies across the *f*, 587 16
he hides his *f*; he will never notice." 595 17
and the just shall see his *f*. 596 26
how long will you hide your *f* from me? 597 22
But at my vindication I shall see your *f*; * 602 4
neither does he hide his *f* from them; * 612 2
of those who seek your *f*, O God of Jacob. 613 26
You speak in my heart and say, "Seek my *f*," * 618 12
Your *f*, LORD, will I seek. 618 13
Hide not your *f* from me, * 618 14
Then you hid your *f*, * 621 20
Make your *f* to shine upon your servant, * 623 25
The *f* of the LORD is against those who do evil, * 628 25
and shall set me before your *f* for ever. 642 25
my enemies mock me to my *f*; 644 6
and shame has covered my *f*; 646 16
Why have you hidden your *f* * 647 5
Hide your *f* from my sins * 656 24
and shame has covered my *f*. 680 2
"Hide not your *f* from your servant; * 680 25
and look upon the *f* of your Anointed. 708 9
why have you hidden your *f* from me? 713 7
love and truth go before your *f*. 714 22
hide not your *f* from me in the day of my trouble. 731 2
You hide your *f*, and they are terrified; * 737 11
and so you renew the *f* of the earth. 737 15
continually seek his *f*. 738 8
do not turn away the *f* of your Anointed. 786 18
do not hide your *f* from me 799 13
give them courage to *f* the perils which beset them; 823 5
that it may renew the *f* of the earth; 828 4

faces

and let not your *f* be ashamed. 628 4
Cover their *f* with shame, O LORD, * 707 9

fade

and *f* away suddenly like the grass. 472 20
and like the green grass *f* away. 633 8
we *f* away suddenly like the grass. 718 10

faded

I have *f* away like a shadow when it lengthens; * 752 20

fades

surrounding us, as daylight *f*, with the brightness 110 13
receive the crown of glory that never *f* away. 380 16

fadeth

receive the crown of glory that *f* not away. 347 22

fail

Who can *f* to do you homage, Lord, 94 14
for you never *f* to help and govern those 230 8
O Lord, your compassions never *f* 460 16
that my strength and courage may not *f*; 461 9
suffer not our trust in thee to *f*; 820 14

failed

My heart is pounding, my strength has *f* me; * 637 16
my eyes have *f* from looking for my God. 679 15
has his promise *f* for evermore? 693 17
My sight has *f* me because of trouble; * 712 20
My eyes have *f* from watching for your promise, * 770 5
My eyes have *f* from watching for your salvation * 773 19

failest

for thou never *f* to help and govern those 178 13

failing

where dwells the true and never-*f* Light, 110 21
comfort with thy presence those who are *f* and infirm, 151 26
O God, whose never-*f* providence ordereth all things 177 14

O God, your never-*f* providence sets in order all things 229 10
entrust this child to thy never-*f* care and love, 470 9
Grant us grace to entrust to thy never-*f* love; 481 17
us grace to entrust N. to your never-*f* care and love, 494 3
all who are dear to us to thy never-*f* care and love, 831 8

fails

Grant us, Lord, the lamp of charity which never *f*, 110 18
my strength *f* me because of affliction, 623 8
and my heart *f* me. 641 7
forsake me not when my strength *f*. 683 19
O LORD, make haste to answer me; my spirit *f* me; * 799 12

failure

our *f* to commend the faith that is in us, 268 13
take *f*, not as a measure of their worth, 829 18

failures

Support him in his successes and in his *f*, 444 21
We thank you also for those disappointments and *f* 836 10

fainted

I should utterly have *f*, * 478 5

faints

my soul thirsts for you, my flesh *f* for you, 670 13
I ponder, and my spirit *f*. 693 7
My spirit *f* within me; * 799 5

fair

to behold the *f* beauty of the LORD, 477 19
To behold the *f* beauty of the LORD * 617 22
enjoy a *f* portion of the riches of this land; 826 14
To be honest and *f* in our dealings; 848 12

fairest

You are the *f* of men; * 647 14

faith

That we may depart this life in thy *f* and fear, 68 18
to follow in *f* where thou hast led the way, 69 9
Regard not our sins, but the *f* of your Church, 107 19
That we may depart this life in your *f* and fear, 122 20
Grant to us your servants so to follow in *f* 123 7
Resist him, firm in your *f*. 132 10
Regard not our sins, but the *f* of your Church, 138 18
Lead us, who know thee now by *f*, to thy presence, 162 15
beholding by *f* the light of his countenance, 165 16
with penitent hearts and steadfast *f* to embrace 166 18
Open, we pray thee, the eyes of our *f*, 171 19
what they profess by their *f*; 172 5
what they profess by their *f*; 173 2
Open, we pray thee, the eyes of our *f*, 173 7
Mercifully give us *f* to perceive that, 174 10
by the confession of a true *f*, 176 2
that thou wouldest keep us steadfast in this *f* 176 5
the Church in thy steadfast *f* and love, 178 7
thy Church throughout the world may persevere with steadfast *f* 183 14
give unto us the increase of *f*, hope, and charity; 183 18
strengthen thine apostle Thomas with sure and certain *f* 185 15
that our *f* may never be found wanting 185 17
Keep thy Church steadfast upon the rock of this *f*, 187 3
that we, being mindful of their victory of *f*, may glorify 189 7
may by *f* behold the King in his beauty; 191 18
and courage to die for this *f*: 195 3
a like *f* and power of love, 196 3
and to others the word of *f*: 197 14
the author and perfecter of our *f*, 198 21
steadfast in the confession of this *f*, 199 15
that thy Church, being preserved in true *f* 204 12
Lead us, who know you now by *f*, to your presence, 214 9
beholding by *f* the light of his countenance, 217 9
with penitent hearts and steadfast *f* to embrace 218 9
Open the eyes of our *f*, 223 11
in their lives what they profess by their *f*; 223 18
in their lives what they profess by their *f*: 224 16
Open the eyes of our *f*, 224 20
Mercifully give us *f* to perceive that, 226 3
by the confession of a true *f*, 228 2
Keep us steadfast in this *f* and worship, 228 5
the Church in your steadfast *f* and love, 230 2
the world may persevere with steadfast *f* 235 6
increase in us the gifts of *f*, hope, and charity; 235 10
strengthened your apostle Thomas with firm and certain *f* 237 9
that our *f* may never be found wanting 237 11
Keep your Church steadfast upon the rock of this *f*, 238 16
mindful of their victory of *f*, may glorify 240 15
may by *f* behold the King in his beauty; 243 4
and courage to die for this *f*: 247 1
a like *f* and power of love, 247 15
and to others the word of *f*: 248 24
Christ, the pioneer and perfecter of our *f*, 250 6
steadfast in the confession of this *f*, 251 4
your Church, being preserved in true *f* 255 10
a time in which converts to the *f* were prepared 265 2
Christians continually have to renew their repentance and *f*. 265 9
commend the *f* that is in us, 268 14
That God will confirm his Church in *f*, 278 9
For those who have lost their *f* 279 22
and lead them to *f* and obedience. 279 29
and those whose *f* is known to God alone, 280 10
show forth in their lives what they profess by their *f*; 291 2
One Lord, one *F*, one Baptism; 299 9
brought up in the Christian *f* and life? 302 2
Keep them in the *f* and communion 305 21
we bring into his fellowship those who come to him in *f*, 307 1
Confess the *f* of Christ crucified, 308 12
Christ, dwelling in your hearts by *f*, 311 24
and living *f* we receive the holy Sacrament, 316 24
and the strengthening of your *f*. 317 16
with *f* in him, come boldly before the throne 317 21
departed this life in thy *f* and fear 330 2
Draw near with *f*, and make your humble confession 330 13
with hearty repentance and true *f* turn unto him, 332 3
and through *f* in his blood, 335 27
and feed on him in your hearts by *f*, 338 3
and feed on him in thy heart by *f*, with thanksgiving. 338 8
of many tongues in the confession of one *f*, 347 11
Therefore we proclaim the mystery of *f*: 363 6
and feed on him in your hearts by *f*, 365 2

guard its *f*, and preserve it in peace. 375 14
and those whose *f* is known to you alone; 375 19
of many tongues in the confession of one *f*, 380 5
That we may end our lives in *f* and hope, 385 7
and for those who have lost their *f*, 390 11
and those whose *f* is known to you alone, 391 16
Regard not our sins, but the *f* of your Church, 395 10
by *f*, may with joy behold thy Son at his coming 395 14
and feed on him in your hearts by *f*, 399 3
One Lord, one *f*, one Baptism; 413 9
receive your confession of sorrow and of *f*, 451 4
who in *f* and repentance receive this holy unction 455 12
the sense of his weakness may add strength to his *f* 460 2
So fill my heart with *f* in your love, 461 1
With *f* in Jesus Christ, we receive the body 466 12
and who walk as yet by *f*, 481 2
Give courage and *f* to those who are bereaved, 481 10
to follow the example of their steadfastness in thy *f*, 487 15
having finished their course in *f*, do now rest 488 6
departed in the true *f* of thy holy Name, 488 8
in the confidence of a certain *f*; 489 10
who have finished their course in thy *f* and fear; 489 16
Whoever has *f* in me shall have life, 491 2
and has committed himself to me in *f*, 491 5
Give us *f* to see in death the gate of eternal life, 493 20
proclaim our *f* and say, 496 2
let our *f* be our consolation, 497 23
Give us, we pray, the *f* to follow where you have led 498 5
having finished their course in *f*, now find rest 503 16
all who have died in the true *f* of your holy Name, 503 17
in the confidence of a certain *f*, 504 8
who have finished their course in your *f* and fear: 504 14
to follow in *f* where you have led the way, 504 22
Grant, O Lord, to all who are bereaved the spirit of *f* 505 10
You are called to guard the *f*, unity, and discipline 517 7
Your heritage is the *f* 517 14
Will you guard the *f*, unity, and discipline 518 19
chosen to be a guardian of the Church's *f*, 519 3
to lead us in confessing that *f*. 519 4
for those who have lost their *f*, 549 26
and those whose *f* is known to you alone, 550 21
There is one Lord, one *F*, one Baptism; 569 19
bring into his fellowship those who come to him in *f*, 570 16
For the *f* of those who have gone before us 579 7
For they had no *f* in God, * 696 20
and had no *f* in his wonderful works. 697 15
hold the *f* in unity of spirit, 815 5
a goodly fellowship of *f*. 817 11
one Lord, one *F*, one Baptism, 818 19
one holy bond of truth and peace, of *f* and charity, 818 22
Fill them with *f*, virtue, knowledge, temperance, 829 2
Give them strength to hold their *f* in you, 829 19
as their strength diminishes, increase their *f* 830 5
where there is doubt, *f*; 833 7
We thank you for the *f* we have inherited 839 12
to which a body of people responds in *f*. 846 22
the whole *F* to all people, to the end of time. 854 23
to guard the *f*, unity, and discipline 855 24
Christ given to his people, and received by *f*. 859 26
are sufficiently instructed in the Christian *F*, 860 25

faithful

God is *f* and just to forgive 38 11
thy *f* people is governed and sanctified: 57 20
who art the life of all who live, the light of the *f*, 70 4
God, who is *f* and just, will forgive our sins 76 10
your *f* people is governed and sanctified: 100 12
the life of all who live, the light of the *f*, 124 1
Know that the Lord does wonders for the *f*; * 128 14
O God the Holy Ghost, Sanctifier of the *f*, 148 5
grant to all the *f* departed eternal life and peace, 152 15
O God, who on this day didst teach the hearts of thy *f* 175 15
thy *f* people do unto thee true and laudable service: 184 2
thy *f* servant Matthias to be of the number of the Twelve: 188 2
may always be ordered and guided by *f* and true pastors; 188 4
thy *f* servant Barnabas, who, seeking not his own renown 189 18
for Simon and Jude; and we pray that, as they were *f* 194 3
Make us, we beseech thee, *f* stewards 194 18
and was *f* even unto death: 195 9
to be so *f* in our witness to thee in this world, 195 11
who was *f* in the care and nurture of thy flock; 196 23
who didst raise up thy *f* servant 197 4
we remember this day before thee thy *f* servant 202 9
thy *f* people is governed and sanctified: 206 2
f stewards of thy bounty; 208 13
who on this day taught the hearts of your *f* people 227 8
your *f* people offer you true and laudable service: 235 15
who in the place of Judas chose your *f* servant Matthias 239 11
be guided and governed by *f* and true pastors; 239 14
follow the example of your *f* servant Barnabas, 241 4
as they were *f* and zealous in their mission, 245 12
Make us, we pray, *f* stewards 246 3
and was *f* even to death: 247 7
f in our witness to you in this world, 247 9
who was *f* in the care and nurture of your flock; 248 9
who raised up your *f* servant 248 15
we remember before you today your *f* servant 253 13
your *f* people is governed and sanctified: 256 20
may be *f* stewards of your good gifts; 259 14
had been separated from the body of the *f* 265 4
your *f* people is governed and sanctified: 278 12
and by his blood delivered your *f* people. 287 5
God is *f* and just to forgive us our sins, 320 2
and be *f* stewards of thy bounty. 329 24
the blessed company of all *f* people; 339 8
Who dost bid thy *f* people cleanse their hearts, 346 9
and thy *f* servants bless thee, 348 8
for to thy *f* people, O Lord, life is changed, 349 8
God, who is *f* and just, will forgive our sins 352 3
as *f* witnesses of Christ our Lord. 366 11
You bid your *f* people cleanse their hearts, 379 5
and your *f* servants bless you, 381 2
For to your *f* people, O Lord, life is changed, 382 3
That they may be *f* ministers of your Word 387 7
that in *f* witness it may preach the Gospel 390 7
be *f* to him as long as you both shall live? 424 11
be *f* to her as long as you both shall live? 424 17
and, forsaking all others, to be *f* to her 433 7

and, forsaking all others, to be *f* to him 433 12
to the blessed company of your *f* people; 450 19
Grant to thy *f* people pardon and peace, 481 4
the souls of the *f*, after they are delivered 488 3
as into the hands of a *f* Creator 488 13
and with whom the souls of the *f* are in joy 503 13
and to be in all things a *f* pastor 517 11
Will you be *f* in prayer, 518 4
and be a *f* steward of his holy Word 521 20
We thank you for raising up among us *f* servants 523 4
Will you undertake to be a *f* pastor 532 14
Make him a *f* pastor, 534 4
We thank you for raising up among us *f* servants 535 4
Will you be *f* in prayer, 544 1
We thank you for raising up among us *f* servants 546 6
that in *f* witness it may preach the Gospel 549 21
We thank you for raising up among us *f* servants 564 4
restores us to the company of your *f* people, 579 2
Know that the LORD does wonders for the *f*; * 588 4
the *f* have vanished from among us. 597 2
With the *f* you show yourself *f*, O God; * 604 14
the LORD protects the *f*, 624 19
Therefore all the *f* will make their prayers to you 625 11
he does not forsake his *f* ones. 635 17
and whose spirit was not *f* to God. 695 19
and they were not *f* to his covenant. 697 25
So he shepherded them with a *f* and true heart * 700 24
and the flesh of your *f* ones to the beasts 701 6
for he is speaking peace to his *f* people 709 10
Keep watch over my life, for I am *f*; * 710 1
You spoke once in a vision and said to your *f* people: 715 3
My eyes are upon the *f* in the land, 730 20
let your *f* people sing with joy. 786 16
and her *f* people will rejoice and sing. 787 4
and your *f* servants bless you. 802 6
The LORD is *f* in all his words * 802 13
sing his praise in the congregation of the *f*. 807 3
Let the *f* rejoice in triumph; * 807 10
this is glory for all his *f* people. 807 19
Strengthen the *f*, arouse the careless, 817 20
that we may receive a *f* pastor, 818 11
by *f* administration and wise laws, 822 26
may be *f* stewards of thy bounty, 827 4
and *f* in adversity, 837 15
God required the chosen people to be *f*; 847 4

faithfully

which we have asked *f* according to thy will, 153 23
may have grace and power *f* to fulfill the same; 179 13
with all who have *f* served thee 202 12
that they may *f* serve before thee, to 205 9
may have grace and power *f* to accomplish them; 231 7
that, with all who have *f* served you 253 16
that they may *f* serve before you, 256 6
and promised to serve God *f* 292 6
Sanctify us also that we may *f* receive 363 15
and what we have asked *f*, grant 394 2
that you may *f* live together in this life, 431 12
that by your help she may live *f* 444 5
That he may *f* fulfill the duties 549 4
may *f* serve you and share in the fullness 552 10
and grant that I may *f* administer your holy Sacraments, 563 2
I have walked *f* with you. 616 13
to all who call upon him *f*. 802 24
f administered and *f* received. 817 14
that we may serve you *f* in our generation 822 14
that with steadfast purpose they may *f* serve 822 20
we have *f* asked according to thy will, 834 5

faithfulness

and his *f* endures from age to age. 83 9
his *f* shall be a shield and buckler. 130 5
in *f* and patience, in wisdom and true godliness, 431 5
All the paths of the LORD are love and *f* * 615 8
will the dust praise you or declare your *f*? 621 25
and your *f* to the clouds. 632 13
I have spoken of your *f* and your deliverance; * 640 27
I have not concealed your love and *f* 640 28
let your love and your *f* keep me safe for ever, 641 3
in your *f*, destroy them. 659 27
God will send forth his love and his *f*. 663 27
and your *f* reaches to the clouds. 664 18
bid love and *f* watch over him. 669 2
for your *f*, O my God; * 685 2
your *f* in the land of destruction? 712 26
from age to age my mouth will proclaim your *f*. 713 18
you have set your *f* firmly in the heavens. 713 20
and to your *f* in the assembly of the holy ones; 714 4
O mighty LORD, your *f* is all around you. 714 10
My *f* and love shall be with him, * 715 14
nor let my *f* prove false. 716 8
which you promised David in your *f*? 717 13
his *f* shall be a shield and buckler. 719 19
and of your *f* in the night season; 720 25
his mercy and *f* to the house of Israel, * 728 6
and his *f* endures from age to age. 730 6
and your *f* reaches to the clouds. 750 2
The works of his hands are *f* and justice; * 754 18
because of your love and because of your *f*. 757 15
and the *f* of the LORD endures for ever. 760 18
I have chosen the way of *f*; * 765 19
and that in *f* you have afflicted me. 769 15
Your *f* remains from one generation to another; * 770 22
with justice and in perfect *f*. 775 2
because of your love and *f*; 793 5
and in your *f* heed my supplications; * 798 19

faithless

Preserve us from *f* fears 165 8
Preserve us from *f* fears 217 1
Every one has proved *f*; 598 18
Every one has proved *f*; 659 4
show no mercy to those who are *f* and evil. 666 6
I look with loathing at the *f*, * 776 19
It sustains our life, though we have been *f* 839 13

fall

O come, let us worship and *f* down * 45 1
grant that this day we *f* into no sin, 57 10
because he is at my right hand, I shall not *f*. 61 12
that we may at length *f* asleep peacefully in thee, 69 9
For as rain and snow *f* from the heavens * 87 1
Glorify the Lord, every shower of rain and *f* of dew, * 88 13

All nations will draw near and *f* down before you, * 94 17
that we may not *f* into sin, nor be overcome 100 3
and he who watches over you will not *f* asleep. 104 18
because he is at my right hand, I shall not *f*. 115 12
that we may at length *f* asleep peacefully in you 123 8
I lie down in peace; at once I *f* asleep; * 129 6
A thousand shall *f* at your side 130 10
that we may not *f* into sin, nor be overcome 137 16
O come, let us worship and *f* down * 146 11
to raise up those who *f*; 152 13
whenever you *f* into sin, 293 24
whenever you *f* into sin, 304 27
whenever you *f* into sin, 417 9
through any pains of death, to *f* from thee. 484 17
that we may at length *f* asleep peacefully in you 504 23
I lie down in peace; at once I *f* asleep; * 588 15
let them *f*, because of their schemes. 589 14
and *f* into the hole that they have made. 592 2
the helpless *f* before their power. 595 15
because he is at my right hand I shall not *f*. 600 14
they *f* defeated at my feet. 605 17
They collapse and *f* down, * 608 17
he will not *f*. 609 11
all who go down to the dust *f* before him. 612 17
let those who plot my ruin *f* back and be dismayed. 629 21
let them *f* into the pit they dug. 630 7
If they stumble, they shall not *f* headlong, * 635 7
You have made us *f* back before our adversary, * 646 5
Let them *f* upon the edge of the sword, * 671 5
He let it *f* in the midst of their camp * 697 5
and *f* like any prince." 705 23
A thousand shall *f* at your side 719 24
and *f* down before his footstool; * 729 9
and he who watches over you will not *f* asleep. 779 6
let us *f* upon our knees before his footstool." 786 12
Let hot burning coals *f* upon them; * 796 21
Let the wicked *f* into their own nets, * 797 24
The LORD upholds all those who *f*; * 802 15
raise him up if he *f*; 830 16
though we often *f* short of them. 839 5

fallen

the first fruits of those who have *f* asleep. 83 22
It restores innocence to the *f*, 287 16
when we had *f* into sin and become subject to evil 362 10
The ungodly have *f* into the pit they dug, * 594 7
and my foes rejoice that I have *f*. 598 7
See how they are *f*, those who work wickedness! * 633 3
and the terrors of death have *f* upon me. 660 14
but have *f* into it themselves. 664 7
the scorn of those who scorn you has *f* upon me. 680 6
I had almost tripped and *f*; 687 4

falling

mine eyes from tears, and my feet from *f*. 479 15
Truly, I am on the verge of *f*, * 638 3
The peoples are *f* at your feet, * 647 23
it was like snow *f* in Zalmon. 677 9

falls

their violence *f* on their own scalp. 592 4
that *f* upon the hills of Zion. 787 16

false

will you worship dumb idols and run after *f* gods?" 128 13
From all *f* doctrine, heresy, and schism; 149 8
thy Church, being delivered from *f* apostles, 188 3
your Church, being delivered from *f* apostles, 239 13
For all *f* judgments, for uncharitable thoughts 268 20
Thou shalt not bear *f* witness against thy neighbor. 318 25
You shall not be a *f* witness. 350 19
will you worship dumb idols and run after *f* gods?" 588 3
for *f* witnesses have risen up against me, 618 24
they do not resort to evil spirits or turn to *f* gods. 640 10
their heart collects *f* rumors; 642 11
nor let my faithfulness prove *f*. 716 8
and delight in *f* gods! * 727 10
save us from all *f* choices, 832 10

falsehood

who have not pledged themselves to *f*, 613 21
all paths of *f* I abhor. 774 4
and whose right hand is raised in *f*. 800 18

falsely

Everyone speaks *f* with his neighbor; * 597 3

falter

and their footsteps shall not *f*. 635 25

faltered

I have trusted in the Lord and have not *f*. 616 9

familiar

my companion, my own *f* friend. 661 11

families

for our *f*, friends, and neighbors; 391 11
For our *f*, friends, and neighbors, 392 3
and all the *f* of the nations shall bow before him. 612 12
Ascribe to the LORD, you *f* of the peoples; * 726 5
and multiplied their *f* like flocks of sheep. 749 12
who settest the solitary in *f*: 828 23
For our daily food and drink, our homes and *f*, 837 9

family

From every *f*, language, people, and nation, * 94 3
we beseech thee graciously to behold this thy *f*, 169 15
who from the *f* of thy servant David didst raise up Joseph 188 8
we pray you graciously to behold this your *f*, 221 9
who from the *f* of your servant David raised up Joseph 239 17
we pray you graciously to behold this your *f*, 276 5
from whom every *f* in heaven and earth is named, 311 22
a joyous and solemn occasion in the life of a *f*. 440 2
this Christian *f*, for the gift of a child. 440 10
to be a member of their *f*. 440 14
have given to him our *f* name, 441 8
bestowed upon this *f* in giving them a child. 443 24
who has made the Church one *f*, 445 8
We thank you for giving him to us, his *f* 493 18
My brother, the Church is the *f* of God, 531 1
to build up the *f* of God? 532 17
of your *f*, or household, or community] 532 20
of your *f*, or household, or community] 544 8
For his *f* [the members of his household 549 12

Look with compassion on the whole human *f*; 815 15
hear our prayers for this parish *f*. 817 19
We thank you for the blessing of *f* and friends, 836 5
help our parents and *f*; 848 5
birth into God's *f* the Church, 858 19
The communion of saints is the whole *f* of God, 862 21

famine

from plague, pestilence, and *f*, 149 12
may be freed from poverty, *f*, and disaster, 390 23
may be freed from poverty, *f*, and disaster, 550 8
and to feed them in time of *f*. 627 14
and in days of *f* they shall have enough. 634 23
Then he called for a *f* in the land * 739 9

fanfare

sound a *f* with all your skill upon the trumpet. 626 6

fangs

pull the *f* of the young lions, O LORD. 665 6

far

Drive *f* from us all wrong desires, 56 20
to those who are *f* off and to those who are near: 58 3
Drive *f* from us all wrong desires, 99 15
to those who are *f* off and to those who are near: 100 19
Visit this place, O Lord, and drive *f* from it all snares 133 17
Visit this place, O Lord, and drive *f* from it all snares 140 13
ascended *f* above all heavens that he might fill 174 9
to those who are *f* off and to those who are near: 206 11
ascended *f* above all heavens that he might fill 226 2
to those who are *f* off and to those who are near: 257 7
When our disobedience took us *f* from you, 373 21
and I have wandered *f* in a land that is waste. 450 14
Why do you stand so *f* off, O LORD, * 594 19
your judgments are *f* above out of their sight; * 595 2
sweeter *f* than honey, 607 18
and are so *f* from my cry 610 2
Be not *f* from me, for trouble is near, * 610 23
Be not *f* away, O LORD; * 611 18
O LORD, be not *f* from me. 631 15
be not *f* from me, O my God. 638 12
I would flee to a *f*-off place * 660 19
and of the seas that are *f* away. 672 20
O God, be not *f* from me; * 684 1
You have put my friends *f* from me; 712 17
you are exalted *f* above all gods. 727 16
A crooked heart shall be *f* from me; * 730 15
As *f* as the east is from the west, * 734 5
so *f* has he removed our sins from us. 734 6
they are very *f* from your law. 776 4
Deliverance is *f* from the wicked, * 776 13
Put *f* from them, we beseech thee, 828 24

fashion

to *f* your life in accordance with its precepts. 531 9
f our lives according to the example of your Son, 817 15
and *f* into one united people the multitudes 820 7

fashioned

let me recite what I have *f* for the king; * 647 12
Your hands have made me and *f* me; * 769 9
they were *f* day by day, 795 8

fashions

He *f* all the hearts of them * 627 5

fast

hold *f* the unchangeable truth of thy Word, 166 19
hold *f* the blessed hope of everlasting life, 184 19
hold *f* the unchangeable truth of your Word, 218 10
to hold *f* to those that shall endure; 234 3
hold *f* the blessed hope of everlasting life, 236 11
My footsteps hold *f* to the ways of your law; * 601 7
he commanded, and it stood *f*. 626 18
But the LORD's will stands *f* for ever, * 626 21
In my integrity you hold me *f*, * 642 24
your right hand holds me *f*. 671 2
They hold *f* to their evil course; * 671 18
You make *f* the mountains by your power; * 672 21
I will make its pillars *f*. 691 9
My hand will hold him *f* * 715 8
It shall stand *f* for evermore like the moon, * 716 15
and their offspring shall stand *f* in your sight." 733 8
bound *f* in misery and iron; 747 2
They stand *f* for ever and ever, * 754 20
and their righteousness stands *f* for ever; 755 23
I hold *f* to your decrees; * 765 21
which cannot be moved, but stands *f* for ever. 781 18
and your right hand hold me *f*. 794 19
He made them stand *f* for ever and ever; * 806 5

fastened

"A deadly thing," they say, "has *f* on him; * 642 15

fasting

by thy Baptism, *F*, and Temptation, 149 19
prepare for them by a season of penitence and *f*. 265 1
by prayer, *f*, and self-denial; 265 12
and humbled myself by *f*; 630 18
I humbled myself with *f*, * 680 7
My knees are weak through *f*, * 752 23

fat

I will offer you sacrifices of *f* beasts 674 24
Their heart is gross and *f*, * 769 3
may our cattle be *f* and sleek. 801 7

father

I will arise and go to my *f*, and will say unto him, 38 17
"*F*, I have sinned against heaven, and before thee, 38 18
We give thanks unto the *F*, which hath made us meet 40 1
Grace be unto you, and peace, from God our *F*, 40 9
worship the *F* in spirit and in truth; 40 21
for the *F* seeketh such to worship him. 40 21
Almighty God our heavenly *F*, to render thanks 41 6
Almighty and most merciful *F*, we have erred 41 16
and grant, O most merciful *F*, for his sake, 42 8
Glory to the *F*, and to the Son, and to the Holy Spirit; 42 16
F, Son, and Holy Ghost, one God: 43 14
Glory to the *F*, and to the Son, and to the Holy Spirit: * 46 19
Let us bless the *F*, the Son, and the Holy Spirit; * 49 7
Blessed art thou, O *F*, Son, and Holy Spirit; * 49 22
Glory to the *F*, and to the Son, and to the Holy Spirit: * 50 20

Glory to the *F*, and to the Son, and to the Holy Spirit: * 51 21
Glory to the *F*, and to the Son, and to the Holy Spirit: * 52 1
O Lord God, heavenly King, God the *F* Almighty. 52 9
O Lord, God, Lamb of God, Son of the *F*, 52 11
Thou that sittest at the right hand of God the *F*, 52 16
art most high in the glory of God the *F*. 52 22
All the earth doth worship thee, the *F* everlasting. 52 24
acknowledge thee, the *F*, of an infinite majesty, 53 8
Thou art the everlasting Son of the *F*. 53 12
at the right hand of God, in the glory of the *F*. 53 17
I believe in God, the *F* almighty, 53 23
and sitteth on the right hand of God the *F* almighty. 54 3
Our *F*, who art in heaven, 54 14
O Lord, our heavenly *F*, almighty and everlasting God, 57 7
O heavenly *F*, in whom we live 57 14
Almighty God, *F* of all mercies 58 14
Grace be unto you, and peace, from God our *F*, 61 3
Almighty and most merciful *F*, we have erred 62 16
and grant, O most merciful *F*, for his sake, 63 11
Glory to the *F*, and to the Son, and to the Holy Spirit: 63 19
pure brightness of the everliving *F* in heaven, 64 2
F, Son, and Holy Spirit. 64 6
Glory to the *F*, and to the Son, and to the Holy Spirit: * 64 10
Glory to the *F*, and to the Son, and to the Holy Spirit: * 65 23
Glory to the *F*, and to the Son, and to the Holy Spirit: * 66 7
I believe in God, the *F* almighty, 66 9
and sitteth on the right hand of God the *F* almighty. 66 19
Our *F*, who art in heaven, 67 4
O God and *F* of all, whom the whole heavens adore: 70 15
Almighty God, *F* of all mercies, 71 10
I will arise and go to my *f*, and I will say to him, 76 16
"*F*, I have sinned against heaven and before you; 76 17
We give thanks to the *F*, who has made us worthy 77 22
Grace to you and peace from God our *F* 78 8
true worshipers will worship the *F* in spirit 78 20
for such the *F* seeks to worship him. 78 21
Almighty God our heavenly *F*, to set forth his praise, 79 2
Glory to the *F*, and to the Son, and to the Holy Spirit: 80 7
F, Son, and Holy Spirit, one God: 81 10
Glory to the *F*, and to the Son, and to the Holy Spirit: * 84 1
Glory to the *F*, and to the Son, and to the Holy Spirit: * 85 30
Glory to the *F*, and to the Son, and to the Holy Spirit; * 86 15
Glory to the *F*, and to the Son, and to the Holy Spirit: * 87 9
Glory to the *F*, and to the Son, and to the Holy Spirit: * 88 3
F, Son, and Holy Spirit; * 90 1
Glory to you, *F*, Son, and Holy Spirit; * 90 15
Glory to the *F*, and to the Son, and to the Holy Spirit: * 92 16
This was the oath he swore to our *f* Abraham, * 92 27
Glory to the *F*, and to the Son, and to the Holy Spirit: * 93 10
Glory to the *F*, and to the Son, and to the Holy Spirit: * 94 19
heavenly King, almighty God and *F*, 94 24
Lord Jesus Christ, only Son of the *F*, 95 3
you are seated at the right hand of the *F*: 95 7
in the glory of God the *F*. 95 14
You are the eternal *F*: 95 17
F, of majesty unbounded, 95 27
the eternal Son of the *F*. 96 2
I believe in God, the *F* almighty, 96 13
seated at the right hand of the *F*. 96 23
Our *F*, who art in heaven, 97 4
almighty and everlasting *F*, you have brought us 100 1
Heavenly *F*, in you we live 100 6
Almighty God, *F* of all mercies, 101 7
Glory to the *F*, and to the Son, and to the Holy Spirit: 103 3
Glory to the *F*, and to the Son, and to the Holy Spirit: * 105 18
Our *F*, who art in heaven, 106 14
Heavenly *F*, send your Holy Spirit into our hearts, 107 4
where with the *F* and the Holy Spirit you live 107 20
give glory to your *F* in heaven." 109 12
pure brightness of the everliving *F* in heaven, 112 2
F, Son, and Holy Spirit. 112 6
Grace to you and peace from God our *F* 115 3
Glory to the *F*, and to the Son, and to the Holy Spirit: 117 12
pure brightness of the everliving *F* in heaven, 118 2
F, Son, and Holy Spirit. 118 6
Glory to the *F*, and to the Son, and to the Holy Spirit: * 118 10
Glory to the *F*, and to the Son, and to the Holy Spirit: * 119 22
Glory to the *F*, and to the Son, and to the Holy Spirit: * 120 7
I believe in God, the *F* almighty, 120 9
and is seated at the right hand of the *F*. 120 19
Our *F*, who art in heaven, 121 4
O God and *F* of all, whom the whole heavens adore: 124 12
Almighty God, *F* of all mercies, 125 5
Almighty God, our heavenly *F*: 127 6
Glory to the *F*, and to the Son, and to the Holy Spirit: 128 5
Glory to the *F*, and to the Son, and to the Holy Spirit: * 131 10
Our *F*, who art in heaven, 132 19
Glory to the *F*, and to the Son, and to the Holy Spirit: * 135 7
The almighty and merciful Lord, *F*, Son, and Holy Spirit, 135 14
Glory to the *F*, and to the Son, and to the Holy Spirit: * 137 9
Blessed be the God and *F* of our Lord 137 11
almighty and everlasting *F*, you have brought us 137 14
where with the *F* and the Holy Spirit you live 138 19
pure brightness of the everliving *F* in heaven, 139 2
F, Son, and Holy Spirit. 139 6
The almighty and merciful Lord, *F*, Son, and Holy Spirit, 140 17
Glory to the *F*, and to the Son, * 141 1
Glory be to the *F*, and to the Son, * 141 5
O God the *F*, Creator of heaven and earth, 148 1
Our *F*, who art in heaven, 153 6

Glory be to the *F*, and to the Son, and to the Holy Ghost;	154	10
We humbly beseech thee, O *F*, mercifully to look	155	7
Eternal *F*, who didst give to thine incarnate Son	162	1
F in heaven, who at the baptism of Jesus	163	1
O most loving *F*, who willest us	165	6
Gracious *F*, whose blessed Son	167	10
Almighty *F*, whose dear Son,	169	7
Almighty *F*, who hast given	172	8
heavenly *F*, for that thou hast delivered us	172	14
see thee in thy one and eternal glory, O *F*;	176	7
where with thee, O *F*, and thee, O Holy Ghost,	184	13
Almighty *F*, who didst inspire Simon Peter,	187	1
F in heaven, by whose grace the virgin mother	189	11
who with thee, O *F*, and thee, O Holy Ghost,	191	19
We thank thee, heavenly *F*, for the witness	192	19
Almighty and gracious *F*, we give thee thanks	194	16
O heavenly *F*, Shepherd of thy people, we give	196	22
O God, our heavenly *F*, who didst raise up	197	4
F, Son, and Holy Spirit;	199	16
God our *F*, whose Son	201	1
Almighty and everlasting *F*, who hast given	204	8
Almighty *F*, whose blessed Son	204	17
Heavenly *F*, giver of life and health:	208	16
O Lord our heavenly *F*, whose blessed Son	209	9
Almighty God our heavenly *F*, who declarest	210	1
Eternal *F*, you gave to your incarnate Son	213	13
F in heaven, who at the baptism of Jesus	214	12
Most loving *F*, whose will it is for us to give thanks	216	20
Gracious *F*, whose blessed Son	219	1
Almighty *F*, whose dear Son,	221	1
Almighty *F*, who gave your only Son	224	1
heavenly *F*, that you have delivered us	224	7
see you in your one and eternal glory, O *F*;	228	6
Almighty *F*, who inspired Simon Peter,	238	14
F in heaven, by your grace the virgin mother	240	18
who with you, O *F*, and you, O Holy Spirit,	243	5
We thank you, heavenly *F*, for the witness	244	7
Almighty and gracious *F*, we give you thanks	246	1
Heavenly *F*, Shepherd of your people, we thank you	248	8
O God, our heavenly *F*, who raised	248	15
F, Son, and Holy Spirit;	251	5
God our *F*, whose Son our Lord	252	6
Almighty and everlasting *F*, you have given	255	6
Almighty *F*, whose blessed Son	255	15
Heavenly *F*, giver of life and health:	260	1
Heavenly *F*, whose blessed Son came	260	15
Almighty God our heavenly *F*, you declare	261	7
Most holy and merciful *F*:	267	12
Almighty God, the *F* of our Lord	269	3
Almighty *F*, whose dear Son,	274	1
Our heavenly *F* sent his Son	277	2
and glory; for with the *F* and the Holy Spirit	282	11
Holy *F*, accept our evening sacrifice,	287	23
God and *F* of all believers,	289	6
your promise to our *f* Abraham;	289	9
Do you believe in God the *F*?	292	11
I believe in God, the *F* almighty,	292	12
seated at the right hand of the *F*.	293	10
May Almighty God, the *F* of our Lord Jesus Christ,	294	4
F, Son, and Holy Spirit.	299	1
One God and *F* of all.	299	10
Do you believe in God the *F*?	304	1
I believe in God, the *F* almighty,	304	2
seated at the right hand of the *F*.	304	13
We thank you, *F*, for the water of Baptism.	306	20
baptizing them in the Name of the *F*,	307	2
Eternal *F*, whose blessed Son was anointed	307	9
I baptize you in the Name of the *F*,	307	14
Heavenly *F*, we thank you that by water	308	2
God, the *F*, Son, and Holy Spirit,	310	3
Our *F*, who art in heaven,	311	1
All praise and thanks to you, most merciful *F*,	311	15
Almighty God, the *F* of our Lord	311	21
I baptize you in the Name of the *F*,	313	2
Heavenly *F*, we thank you that by water	314	1
his Church renders to Almighty God our heavenly *F*	316	10
a kingdom of priests to serve his God and *F*,	317	19
Honor thy *f* and thy mother.	318	13
F, Son, and Holy Spirit	319	1
Almighty and most merciful *F*,	320	23
and grant, O most merciful *F*, for his sake,	321	11
Blessed be God: *F*, Son, and Holy Spirit.	323	1
O Lord God, heavenly King, God the *F* Almighty.	324	20
O Lord God, Lamb of God, Son of the *F*,	324	22
Thou that sittest at the right hand of God the *F*,	325	3
art most high in the glory of God the *F*.	325	9
We believe in one God, the *F*,	326	7
eternally begotten of the *F*,	326	12
of one Being with the *F*.	326	16
and is seated at the right hand of the *F*.	327	9
who proceeds from the *F* and the Son.	327	13
With the *F* and the Son he is worshiped and glorified.	327	14
I believe in one God, the *F* Almighty,	327	21
begotten of his *F* before all worlds,	327	26
being of one substance with the *F*;	327	30
and sitteth on the right hand of the *F*;	328	9
who proceedeth from the *F* and the Son;	328	14
who with the *F* and the Son together is worshiped	328	15
Give grace, O heavenly *F*, to all bishops	329	9
Grant these our prayers, O *F*, for Jesus	330	7
F of our Lord Jesus Christ,	331	2
have mercy upon us, most merciful *F*;	331	14
Almighty God, our heavenly *F*, who	332	1
If any man sin, we have an Advocate with the *F*,	332	15
holy *F*, almighty, everlasting God.	333	9
All glory be to thee, Almighty God, our heavenly *F*,	334	9
Wherefore, O Lord and heavenly *F*, according	335	8
And we most humbly beseech thee, O merciful *F*,	335	17
all honor and glory be unto thee, O *F* Almighty,	336	14
Our *F*, who art in heaven,	336	18
O heavenly *F*, so to assist us	339	10
God Almighty, the *F*, the Son, and the Holy Ghost,	339	18
The blessing of God Almighty, the *F*,	339	20
holy *F*, almighty, everlasting God.	341	3
Wherefore, O Lord and heavenly *F*, we	342	10
O merciful *F*, to hear us,	342	16
all honor and glory be unto thee, O *F* Almighty,	343	4
and we celebrate the one and equal glory of thee, O *F*,	347	15
Honor your *f* and your mother.	350	11
F, Son, and Holy Spirit.	351	1
F, Son, and Holy Spirit.	355	1
almighty God and *F*, we worship you,	356	4
Lord Jesus Christ, only Son of the *F*,	356	7

father

you are seated at the right hand of the *F*: 356 11
in the glory of God the *F*. 356 18
We believe in one God, the *F*, the Almighty, 358 4
eternally begotten of the *F*, 358 9
of one Being with the *F*. 358 13
and is seated at the right hand of the *F*. 358 25
who proceeds from the *F* and the Son. 359 4
With the *F* and the Son he is worshiped and glorified. 359 5
F Almighty, Creator of heaven and earth. 361 8
Holy and gracious *F*: 362 9
reconcile us to you, the God and *F* of all. 362 14
We celebrate the memorial of our redemption, O *F*, 363 10
glory is yours, Almighty *F*, now and for ever. 363 21
Our *F*, who art in heaven, 364 1
Eternal God, heavenly *F*, 365 9
And now, *F*, send us out 366 8
F Almighty, Creator of heaven and earth. 367 8
Therefore, according to his command, O *F*, 368 19
all honor and glory is yours, Almighty *F*, 369 16
And so, *F*, we who have been redeemed by him, 371 6
God and *F* of our Lord Jesus Christ: 372 2
Accept these prayers and praises, *F*, 372 10
It is truly right to glorify you, *F*, 373 1
F, you loved the world so much that 374 1
glorified by you, his heavenly *F*, 374 14
F, we now celebrate this memorial of our redemption. 374 24
Almighty God and *F*, in the unity 375 27
and we celebrate the one and equal glory of you, O *F*, 380 10
F, we pray for your holy Catholic Church; 387 1
all may be one as you and the *F* are one, 390 6
For yours is the majesty, O *F*, Son, and Holy Spirit; 391 23
Have mercy upon us, most merciful *F*; 393 9
Heavenly *F*, you have promised to hear what we ask 394 4
and to you we give glory, *F*, Son, and Holy Spirit, 395 6
where with the *F* and the Holy Spirit you live 395 11
Hasten, O *F*, the coming of thy kingdom; 395 13
By this my *F* is glorified, 397 10
As the *F* has loved me, so have I loved you; 397 11
Almighty *F*, whose dear Son, 397 13
Our *F*, who art in heaven, 398 12
Gracious *F*, we give you praise and thanks 399 7
And so, *F*, we bring you these gifts. 403 1
F, we now celebrate the memorial of your Son. 403 13
all honor and glory is yours, Almighty *F*, 403 20
all honor and glory is yours, Almighty *F*, 405 21
Glory be to the *F*, and to the Son,* 406 1
Hear us, O heavenly *F*, and with thy (your) Word 408 1
F, Son, and Holy Spirit. 413 1
One God and *F* of all. 413 10
Do you believe in God the *F*? 416 6
I believe in God, the *F* almighty, 416 7
and is seated at the right hand of the *F*. 416 18
God, the *F*, Son, and Holy Spirit, 418 19
in the Name of the *F*, and of the Son, and of the Holy Spirit 427 15
in the Name of the *F*, and of the Son, and of the Holy Spirit. 428 4
Our *F*, who art in heaven, 428 8
where, O *F*, with your Son and the Holy Spirit, 430 7
God the *F*, God the Son, God the Holy Spirit, bless, 431 9
heavenly *F*, the Lord of all life, 440 5
It has pleased God our heavenly *F* to answer 440 8
Do you take this man as your *f*? 441 3
May God, the *F* of all, bless our child 441 7
Glory to the *F*, and to the Son, and to the Holy Spirit:* 442 11
Glory to the *F*, and to the Son, and to the Holy Spirit:* 443 18
Grant, most merciful *F*, that by your help 444 4
O eternal God, you have promised to be a *f* 444 15
May God the *F*, who by Baptism adopts us 445 3
In the Name of the *F*, and of the Son, and of the Holy Spirit. 447 4
In the Name of the *F*, and of the Son, and of the Holy Spirit. 448 5
who offered himself to be sacrificed for us to the *F*, 448 8
If any man sin, we have an Advocate with the *F*, 450 1
Holy God, heavenly *F*, you formed me from the dust 450 8
who offered himself to be sacrificed for us to the *F*, 451 7
In the Name of the *F*, and of the Son, and of the Holy Spirit. 451 15
who offered himself to be sacrificed for us to the *F*, 452 2
O Lord, holy *F*, giver of health and salvation: 455 9
I lay my hands upon you in the Name of the *F*, 456 1
I anoint you with oil in the Name of the *F*, 456 11
so may our heavenly *F* grant you the inward anointing 456 14
Gracious *F*, we give you praise and thanks 457 5
O *F* of mercies and God of all comfort, 458 1
Heavenly *F*, watch with us over your child 458 22
Almighty God our heavenly *F*, graciously comfort 459 7
Heavenly *F*, giver of life and health: 459 17
May God the *F* bless you, 460 5
gave us the example of obedience to your *F*'s will: 461 7
O heavenly *F*, you give your children sleep 461 12
God the *F*, 462 5
Our *F*, who art in heaven, 464 4
where with the *F* and the Holy Spirit you live 464 19
In the Name of God the *F* Almighty who created you; 464 22
"Come, you blessed of my *F*." 465 22
Almighty God, our *F* in heaven, before whom live 466 7
where with the *F* and the Holy Spirit you live 466 19
saying, Come, O blessed of my *F*; 483 21
All that the *F* giveth me shall come to me; 484 18
Our *F*, who art in heaven, 485 20
F, grant that we, who now serve thee on earth, 486 13
F, inherit the kingdom prepared for you 487 20
Grant this, O *F*, for the sake of the same thy Son 487 21
Almighty God, our heavenly *F*, in whose hands 488 26
who with the *F* and the Holy Spirit livest 489 28
Almighty God, *F* of mercies and giver of all comfort: 489 30
I believe in God, the *F* almighty, 496 3
and is seated at the right hand of the *F*. 496 13
an occasion for us to renew our trust in your *F*'s love. 498 4
and where you live and reign with the *F* 498 6
F of all, we pray to you 498 8
saying, Come, O blessed of my *F*; 500 10
Everyone the *F* gives to me will come to me; 501 1
Our *F*, who art in heaven, 502 1
F of all, we pray to you for those we love, 504 26
Merciful God, *F* of our Lord 505 1
"Come, you blessed of my *F*, receive 505 6
Grant this, O merciful *F*, through Jesus 505 8
Almighty God, *F* of mercies and giver of comfort: 505 17
F, Son, and Holy Spirit. 512 1

In the Name of the *F*, and of the Son, and of the Holy Spirit,	513	7
We believe in one God, the *F*,	519	7
eternally begotten of the *F*,	519	12
of one Being with the *F*.	519	16
and is seated at the right hand of the *F*.	519	28
who proceeds from the *F* and the Son.	520	4
With the *F* and the Son he is worshiped and glorified.	520	5
God and *F* of our Lord Jesus Christ,	520	11
F of mercies and God of all comfort,	520	11
Therefore, *F*, make a bishop in your Church.	521	1
To you, O *F*, all hearts are open;	521	6
Almighty *F*, we thank you for feeding us	523	1
the *F*, the Son, and the Holy Spirit, be upon you,	523	16
F, Son, and Holy Spirit.	525	1
We believe in one God, the *F*,	529	10
eternally begotten of the *F*,	530	3
of one Being with the *F*.	530	7
and is seated at the right hand of the *F*.	530	19
who proceeds from the *F* and the Son.	530	23
With the *F* and the Son he is worshiped and glorified.	530	24
God and *F* of all, we praise you	533	1
Therefore, *F*, through Jesus Christ your Son, give	533	11
Almighty *F*, we thank you for feeding us	535	1
The blessing of God Almighty, the *F*,	535	11
F, Son, and Holy Spirit.	537	1
We believe in one God, the *F*,	541	10
eternally begotten of the *F*,	542	3
of one Being with the *F*.	542	7
and is seated at the right hand of the *F*.	542	19
who proceeds from the *F* and the Son.	542	23
With the *F* and the Son he is worshiped and glorified.	542	24
serving God the *F*, through the power of the Holy Spirit.	543	2
O God, most merciful *F*, we praise you	545	1
Therefore, *F*, through Jesus Christ your Son, give	545	9
Almighty *F*, we thank you for feeding us	546	3
God the *F*,	548	1
as you and the *F* are one,	549	18
Almighty *F*, we thank you for feeding us	564	1
In the Name of the *F*, and of the Son, and of the Holy Spirit.	568	3
Everliving *F*, watchful and caring,	568	7
committed into the *F*'s hands.	569	9
Now, O *F*, Son, and Holy Spirit,	569	10
F, we thank you that through the waters of Baptism	569	15
One God and *F* of all.	569	20
We dedicate this Font in the Name of the *F*,	569	21
We thank you, *F*, for the water of Baptism.	570	12
of the *F*, and of the Son, and of the Holy Spirit.	570	17
F, your eternal Word speaks to us	570	23
We dedicated this Lectern in the Name of the *F*,	571	7
F, in every age you have spoken through the voices	571	9
We dedicate this Pulpit in the Name of the *F*,	571	15
F, your people worship you with many voices	572	1
in the Name of the *F*, and of the Son, and of the Holy Spirit.	572	8
Blessed be your Name, *F*, Son, and Holy Spirit;	574	8
Though my *f* and my mother forsake me, *	618	19
forget your people and your *f*'s house.	648	12
F of orphans, defender of widows, *	676	11
He will say to me, "You are my *F*, *	715	18
As a *f* cares for his children, *	734	7
O heavenly *F*, who hast filled the world with beauty:	814	1
Peace, as children of one *F*;	815	26
Almighty God our heavenly *F*, guide the nations	816	1
O God, the *F* of all, whose Son commanded	816	5
Gracious *F*, we pray for thy holy Catholic Church.	816	10
O God the *F* of our Lord	818	14
one Baptism, one God and *F* of us all,	818	20
for you reign with the *F* and the Holy Spirit,	819	11
Almighty God our heavenly *F*, send	822	17
O God our *F*, whose Son forgave his enemies	823	8
Heavenly *F*, we remember before you those who suffer	824	11
Heavenly *F*, in your Word you have given us a vision	825	6
Grant this, *F*, for the love of your Son,	826	6
Look with pity, O heavenly *F*, upon the people	826	8
O gracious *F*, who openest thine hand	828	1
O God, heavenly *F*, who by thy Son	828	9
O God our heavenly *F*, you have blessed us	828	16
Almighty God, our heavenly *F*, who settest	828	22
Almighty God, heavenly *F*, you have blessed us	829	9
God our *F*, you see your children growing	829	14
Look with mercy, O God our *F*, on all	830	1
O God, our heavenly *F*, whose glory fills	831	1
O merciful *F*, who hast taught us	831	11
who live and reign with the *F* and the Holy Spirit,	834	10
who livest and reignest with the *F* and the Holy Spirit,	834	16
Give us grateful hearts, our *F*, for all thy mercies,	835	8
Let us give thanks to God our *F* for all his gifts	837	1
To him be praise and glory, with you, O *F*,	837	23
for Abraham, the *f* of believers,	838	10
Heavenly *F*, you sent your own Son into this world.	841	1
Almighty God and heavenly *F*, we give	841	7
Grant, O gracious *F*, that he,	841	10
We learn that there is one God, the *F* Almighty,	846	3
Jesus is the only perfect image of the *F*,	849	22
and is seated at the right hand of the *F*?	850	18
where he now reigns with the *F*	850	20
The Trinity is one God: *F*, Son, and Holy Spirit.	852	13
Christian prayer is response to God the *F*,	856	21
the person is baptized in the Name of the *F*,	858	14

fatherless

Let his children be *f*, *	751	14
and none to pity his *f* children.	751	21

fatherly

let your *f* hand ever be over these your servants;	310	8
And we earnestly desire thy *f* goodness	335	24
And we earnestly desire thy *f* goodness	342	21
let your *f* hand ever be over these your servants;	419	4
who mourn a sure confidence in thy *f* care,	481	7
we commend to thy *f* goodness	815	6
O God, whose *f* care reacheth to the uttermost parts	830	19

fathers

Blessed art thou, O Lord God of our *f*; *	49	9
Glory to you, Lord God of our *f*; *	90	5
The promise he made to our *f*, *	92	14
He promised to show mercy to our *f* *	92	25
Blessed are you, O Lord, the God of our *f*,	113	1
The promise he made to our *f*, *	119	20

When your *f* tempted me, * 146 19
we have heard with our ears, and our *f* have declared 154 5
when you brought our *f*, the children of Israel, 287 6
Lord God of our *F*; 372 1
The promise he made to our *f*,* 442 9
we may be gathered unto our *f*, 489 8
"In place of *f*, O king, you shall have sons; * 648 23
They turned away and were disloyal like their *f*; * 699 20
Let the wickedness of his *f* be remembered 751 24

fathom

it surpasses all that our minds can *f*. 91 4

fathomless

The *f* deep has overwhelmed them; * 85 12

fatness

My soul is content, as with marrow and *f*, * 670 21

fault

We have sinned against you, through our own *f*, 127 8
that we have sinned by our own *f* 267 16
and be found without *f* at the day 389 16
acknowledge their *f*, and to seek each other's forgiveness 429 15
I have sinned by my own *f* in thought, 447 6
and be found without *f* at the Day 548 12
not for any offense or *f* of mine, O Lord. 665 24
and find in them no *f*. 687 20
my Rock, in whom there is no *f*. 721 28

faults

spare thou those who confess their *f*, 42 4
spare thou those who confess their *f*, 63 7
spare thou those who confess their *f*, 321 7
cleanse me from my secret *f*. 607 23
and my *f* are not hidden from you. 679 21

favor

that the days to come may be spent in thy *f*; 56 4
for he has looked with *f* on his lowly servant. 91 29
that the week to come may be spent in your *f*; 98 22
for he has looked with *f* on his lowly servant. 119 6
thy *f* and goodness towards us; 339 6
all the saints who have found *f* 375 23
That our works may find *f* in your sight. 387 13
Almighty God, look with *f* upon this person 421 2
Look with *f* upon the world 429 3
the Lord mercifully with his *f* look upon you, 431 10
for he has looked with *f* on his lowly servant. 441 14
Remember me, O Lord, according to the *f* 478 17
to the *f* which thou bearest unto thy people. 481 19
Remember thy servant, O Lord, according to the *f* 488 21
in *f* with thee our God; 489 11
in *f* with you, our God, and in perfect charity 504 9
you will defend them with your *f* as with a shield. 589 22
his *f* for a lifetime. 621 13
You, Lord, with your *f*, made me as strong 621 18
Let those who *f* my cause sing out with joy 631 27
and your *f* to those who are true of heart. 632 25
the rich among the people seek your *f*." 648 16
Will he no more show his *f*? 693 15
and show *f* to the wicked? 705 12
Show me a sign of your *f*, 711 9
and by your *f* our might is exalted. 714 28
He will look with *f* on the prayer of the homeless; * 732 10
Remember me, O Lord, with the *f* 742 3
in those who await his gracious *f*. 804 25
a people mindful of thy *f* and glad to do thy will. 820 3
Look with *f*, we pray, on your servant 830 8
with thy most gracious *f*, 832 2
Grace is God's *f* towards us, 858 2

favorable

Be *f* and gracious to Zion, * 657 18

favorably

F with mercy hear our prayers; 155 1
F hear us, for your mercy is great. 268 28
Look *f* on your whole Church, 280 15
Look *f* on your whole Church, 291 12
Look *f* on your whole Church, 515 5
Look *f* on your whole Church, 528 3
Look *f* on your whole Church, 540 3

favored

because you *f* them. 645 17

fear

And his mercy is on them that *f* him * 50 9
might serve him without *f*, 51 8
may not *f* the power of any adversaries; 57 5
And his mercy is on them that *f* him * 65 12
That we may depart this life in thy faith and *f*, 68 18
defended from the *f* of all enemies, 69 20
All things quake with *f* at your presence; * 91 1
He has mercy on those who *f* him * 92 4
Free to worship him without *f*, * 92 29
may not *f* the power of any adversaries; 99 23
keep us from every evil, every sin, and every *f*; 113 7
he has mercy on those who *f* him * 119 10
That we may depart this life in your faith and *f*, 122 20
delivered from the *f* of all enemies, 123 19
give us a heart to love and *f* thee, 150 22
to have a perpetual *f* and love of thy holy Name, 178 12
to *f* nothing but the loss of you, 216 21
For those in loneliness, *f*, and anguish 279 7
departed this life in thy faith and *f* 330 2
we may without shame or *f* rejoice 345 11
we may without shame or *f* rejoice 378 7
For all who *f* God and believe in you, 390 4
For the victims of hunger, *f*, injustice, 392 8
He has mercy on those who *f* him * 441 18
I shall *f* no evil; * 443 8
a thousand generations of those who love and *f* you: 444 16
the residue of his life in thy *f*, and to thy glory; 458 8
Therefore will we not *f*, though the earth be moved, * 471 19
I will *f* no evil; * 476 9
I will *f* no evil; * 477 2
whom then shall I *f*? * 477 13
finished their course in thy faith and *f*; 489 16
finished their course in your faith and *f*: 504 14
For all who *f* God and believe in you, 549 16
Submit to the Lord with *f*, * 586 24
I do not *f* the multitudes of people * 587 13
my enemies shall be confounded and quake with *f*; * 590 18
Put *f* upon them, O Lord; * 594 17

See how they tremble with *f*, * 598 24
but he honors those who *f* the LORD. 599 12
The *f* of the LORD is clean 607 12
Praise the LORD, you that *f* him; * 611 26
I shall *f* no evil; * 613 4
Who are they who *f* the LORD? * 615 12
The LORD is a friend to those who *f* him * 615 16
whom then shall I *f*? * 617 8
and I was filled with *f*. 621 21
f is all around; * 623 17
which you have laid up for those who *f* you; * 624 5
Let all the earth *f* the LORD; * 626 15
Behold, the eye of the LORD is upon those who *f* 627 11
The angel of the LORD encompasses those who *f* 628 7
F the LORD, you that are his saints, * 628 11
for those who *f* him lack nothing. 628 12
I will teach you the *f* of the LORD. 628 16
there is no *f* of God before his eyes. 632 4
Therefore we will not *f*, though the earth be moved, * 649 3
F and trembling have come over me, * 660 15
they never change; they do not *f* God. 661 27
You have set up a banner for those who *f* you, * 667 16
the heritage of those who *f* your Name. 668 23
protect my life from *f* of the enemy. 671 11
Come and listen, all you who *f* God, * 674 27
Truly, his salvation is very near to those who *f* him, * 709 12
knit my heart to you that I may *f* your Name. 710 23
The nations shall *f* your Name, O LORD, * 732 6
so is his mercy great upon those who *f* him. 734 4
so does the LORD care for those who *f* him. 734 8
the LORD endures for ever on those who *f* him, * 734 16
He gives food to those who *f* him; * 754 14
The *f* of the LORD is the beginning of wisdom; * 755 1
Happy are they who *f* the LORD * 755 5
You who *f* the LORD, trust in the LORD; * 758 10
He will bless those who *f* the LORD, * 758 15
Let those who *f* the LORD now proclaim, * 761 3
The LORD is at my side, therefore I will not *f*; * 761 7
which you make to those who *f* you. 766 12
I am a companion of all who *f* you * 768 13
Those who *f* you will be glad when they see me, * 769 12
Let those who *f* you turn to me, * 769 23
Happy are they all who *f* the LORD, * 783 13
you who *f* the LORD, bless the LORD. 789 16
He fulfills the desire of those who *f* him; * 802 25
But the LORD has pleasure in those who *f* him, * 804 24
their calling to serve this people in thy *f*; 820 23
administer the law in the *f* of thee alone; 821 12

feared

therefore shalt thou be *f*. 474 8
For the LORD Most High is to be *f*; * 650 8
to him who is worthy to be *f*. 692 24
God is much to be *f* in the council of the holy ones, * 714 7
he is more to be *f* than all gods. 725 24
therefore you shall be *f*. 784 24

fearful

and *f* things at the Red Sea. 743 16

fearlessly

Grant us grace *f* to contend against evil 209 2
Grant us grace *f* to contend against evil 260 9

fears

Preserve us from faithless *f* and worldly anxieties, 165 9
Preserve us from faithless *f* and worldly anxieties, 217 2
who rightly *f* your indignation? 718 24
The man who *f* the LORD * 783 19
remove from them the *f* that beset them; 831 21
forgive our sins, banish our *f*, 835 4

feast

therefore let us keep the *f*, 46 3
therefore let us keep the *f*, 83 12
that we who celebrate with reverence the Paschal *f* 171 6
that we who celebrate with awe the Paschal *f* 222 23
grant that in this Paschal *f* we may so burn 285 10
at the *f* of the Passover paid for us the debt 287 4
Therefore let us keep the *f*. 337 2
prepare with joy for the Paschal *f*; 346 9
Therefore let us keep the *f*. 364 16
prepare with joy for the Paschal *f*; 379 6
bring them to that table where your saints *f* 430 23
They *f* upon the abundance of your house; * 632 20
and at the full moon, the day of our *f*. 704 6

feasts

and their sacred *f* a snare. 681 9
and the remnant of Hamath will keep your *f*. 692 21

feathers

whose *f* are like green gold. 677 7

fed

and you have *f* us with spiritual food 365 12
thou hast *f* us with the spiritual food 482 2
you have *f* us with the spiritual food 498 13
may be *f* and refreshed by his flesh and blood, 574 5
You have *f* them with the bread of tears; * 702 21

feed

and to *f* thy flock: 197 6
and to *f* your flock: 248 17
and *f* on him in your hearts by faith, 338 3
and *f* on him in thy heart by faith, 338 7
thank thee for that thou dost *f* us, 339 3
and *f* on him in your hearts by faith, 365 2
and *f* on him in your hearts by faith, 399 3
He shall *f* me in a green pasture, * 476 3
he may *f* and tend the flock of Christ, 521 9
F the flock of Christ committed to your charge, 521 18
and to *f* them in time of famine. 627 14
dwell in the land and *f* on its riches. 633 10
But Israel would I *f* with the finest wheat * 705 7

feeding

we thank you for *f* us with the spiritual food 366 2
we thank you for *f* us with the holy food 523 1
we thank you for *f* us with the holy food 535 1
we thank you for *f* us with the holy food 546 3
we thank you for *f* us with the holy food 564 1

feeds

for the image of an ox that *f* on grass. 743 12

feel

and make you know and *f* that the only Name 457 2
They have hands, but they cannot *f*; 758 1

feet

and to guide our *f* into the way of peace. 51 20
and guide our *f* into the way of peace; 56 21
and to guide our *f* into the way of peace. 93 9
and guide our *f* into the way of peace; 99 16
Your word is a lantern to my *f* * 103 6
trample the young lion and the serpent under your *f*. 130 25
and finally to beat down Satan under our *f*, 152 13
supped with his disciples and had washed their *f*, 274 9
mine eyes from tears, and my *f* from falling. 479 15
The Lord will guide our *f* into the way of peace, 483 18
The Lord will guide our *f* into the way of peace, 500 7
Your word is a lantern to our *f*, 571 13
you put all things under his *f*: 592 20
in your paths my *f* shall not stumble. 601 8
with a storm cloud under his *f*. 603 8
they fall defeated at my *f*. 605 17
they pierce my hands and my *f*; 611 13
for he shall pluck my *f* out of the net. 615 19
you have set my *f* in an open place. 623 2
he set my *f* upon a high cliff 640 4
The peoples are falling at your *f*, * 647 23
and the nations under our *f*. 650 11
rescued my soul from death and my *f* from stumbling, * 663 16
They have laid a net for my *f*, 664 4
they will bathe their *f* in the blood of the wicked. 665 14
and will not allow our *f* to slip. 674 12
and there is no firm ground for my *f*. 679 10
But as for me, my *f* had nearly slipped; * 687 3
and peace shall be a pathway for his *f*. 709 21
trample the young lion and the serpent under your *f*. 720 13
They bruised his *f* in fetters; * 739 13
He put their *f* on a straight path * 746 14
f, but they cannot walk; * 758 2
my eyes from tears, and my *f* from stumbling. 759 17
and turned my *f* toward your decrees. 768 6
I restrain my *f* from every evil way, * 771 21
Your word is a lantern to my *f* * 772 3
Now our *f* are standing * 779 20

felicity

That I may see the *f* of thy chosen, * 478 20
are in joy and *f*: 488 4
the souls of the faithful are in joy and *f*: 503 14
For you will give him everlasting *f* * 609 7

fell

my adversaries, who stumbled and *f*. 617 13
I *f* silent and did not open my mouth, * 639 13
Their priests *f* by the sword, * 700 7
They mounted up to the heavens and *f* 748 7
I was pressed so hard that I almost *f*, * 761 22

fellow

no more strangers and foreigners, but *f*-citizens 40 3
no longer strangers and sojourners, but *f* citizens 78 1
must shed light among your *f* men, 109 11
With your *f* bishops you will share in the leadership 517 13
Will you share with your *f* bishops in the government 518 22
will you sustain your *f* presbyters 518 24
together with your bishop and *f* presbyters, 531 6
with your *f* ministers to build 532 16
accept their responsibilities to their *f* citizens, 822 11
you made us *f* workers in your creation: 827 18

fellows

with the oil of gladness above your *f*. 648 5

fellowship

The goodly *f* of the prophets praise thee. 53 4
the *f* of the Holy Ghost, be with us all evermore. 59 23
the *f* of the Holy Ghost, be with us all evermore. 72 20
The noble *f* of prophets praise you. 95 24
the *f* of the Holy Spirit, be with us all evermore. 102 11
the *f* of the Holy Spirit, be with us all evermore. 126 11
in the *f* of [________ and] all the saints, 152 18
the *f* of the Holy Ghost, be with us all evermore. 154 2
reborn into the *f* of Christ's Body 172 3
reborn into the *f* of Christ's Body 172 22
communion and *f* in the mystical body 194 9
pilgrimage to abide in their *f*, 198 26
supported by this *f* of love and prayer, 199 7
We give thee thanks for the *f* 204 2
reborn into the *f* of Christ's Body 223 17
reborn into the *f* of Christ's Body 224 15
communion and *f* in the mystical body 245 17
during our earthly pilgrimage to abide in their *f*, 250 10
supported by this *f* of love and prayer, 250 16
We give you thanks for the *f* 254 20
and restored to the *f* of the Church. 265 6
reborn into the *f* of Christ's Body 291 1
Will you continue in the apostles' teaching and *f*, 293 20
Will you continue in the apostles' teaching and *f*, 304 23
into his *f* those who come to him in faith, 307 1
and we receive you into the *f* of this Communion. 310 2
that we may continue in that holy *f*, 339 11
rejoicing in their *f*, may run with patience 347 19
rejoice in their *f*, and run with endurance 380 14
Rejoicing in the *f* of [the ever-blessed Virgin Mary, 391 19
supported by this *f* of love and prayer, 395 20
and the *f* of the Holy Spirit 404 2
Will you continue in the apostles' teaching and *f*, 417 5
we receive you into the *f* of this Communion. 418 18
in the *f* of thy saints; 470 3
in one communion and *f*, in the mystical body 480 5
and strengthened by their *f*, 489 20
in the *f* of your saints; 493 12
give him *f* with all your saints. 497 17
and strengthened by their *f*, 504 18
through him in the *f* of your Holy Spirit. 523 3
through him in the *f* of your Holy Spirit. 535 3
through him in the *f* of your Holy Spirit. 546 5
Rejoicing in the *f* of [the ever-blessed Virgin Mary, 550 26
through him in the *f* of your Holy Spirit. 564 3
into his *f* those who come to him in faith, 570 15
For the *f* of [our patron, and of] 579 10
you have called us in this Diocese to a goodly *f* 817 11
and in the *f* of thy saints; 830 25
Enrich our lives by ever-widening circles of *f*, 840 3
who has called us into *f* with him. 848 21
in the teaching and *f* of the apostles 854 26

felt

While I *f* secure, 621 16

female
you have created us male and *f* in your image: 425 8

fence
as if you were a leaning *f*, a toppling wall? 669 11

fervent
f in prayer and in works of mercy, 346 9
f in prayer and in works of mercy, 379 6
O Lord our God, accept the *f* prayers of your people; 395 3
and so enkindle *f* charity among 829 6

festal
Happy are the people who know the *f* shout! * 714 23

fester
My wounds stink and *f* * 637 6

festival
the yearly *f* of the birth of your only Son 212 10
with pure minds we may attain to the *f* of everlasting light; 285 11

fetters
They bruised his feet in *f*; * 739 13

fever
the *f* of life is over, and our work is done. 833 16

few
When they were *f* in number, * 739 1
Let his days be *f*, * 751 12

fidelity
that with true *f* and steadfast love 425 10
Matrimony, may become one in heart and soul, live in *f* 432 5

field
even the wild beasts of the *f*, 592 22
He shall come down like rain upon the mown *f*, * 685 19
in the land of Egypt, in the *f* of Zoan. 695 27
and his omens in the *f* of Zoan. 698 14
to the beasts of the *f*. 701 7
and the beasts of the *f* have grazed upon it. 703 14
let the *f* be joyful and all that is therein. 726 16
we flourish like a flower of the *f*; 734 12
All the beasts of the *f* drink their fill from them, * 735 23

fields
and the creatures of the *f* are in my sight. 655 2
May the *f* of the wilderness be rich for grazing, * 673 13
the *f* of God as our possession." 707 2
They sowed *f*, and planted vineyards, * 749 3
we found it in the *f* of Jearim. 786 10
Bless those who work in the *f*; 824 8

fierce
in their *f* anger toward us; 781 6

fierceness
and let the *f* of your anger overtake them. 681 13

fiery
You will make them like a *f* furnace * 609 14

fig
He blasted their vines and their *f* trees * 740 19

fight
F those who *f* me, O Lord; * 629 13
for there are many who *f* me. 661 24
truly there are many who *f* against me, O Most High. 662 16
and *f* against me without a cause. 751 3
who trains my hands to *f* and my fingers to battle; 800 2

figures
which are the *f* of the true; 39 16

fill
May the God of hope *f* us with all joy and peace 60 1
May the God of hope *f* us with all joy and peace 73 1
May the God of hope *f* us with all joy and peace 102 12
May the God of hope *f* us with all joy and peace 126 12
ascended far above all heavens that he might *f* all things: 174 9
and so *f* them with the truth of thy doctrine 205 7
ascended far above all heavens that he might *f* all things: 226 2
and so *f* them with the truth of your doctrine 256 5
F them with your holy and life-giving Spirit. 305 19
you made all things and *f* them with your blessing; 373 5
and *f* you with all spiritual benediction 431 11
who sanctified a home at Nazareth, *f* you with love. 445 5
to uphold you and *f* you with his grace, 456 8
F his heart with confidence that, 459 9
So *f* my heart with faith in your love, 461 1
f, we pray, the heart of this your servant 521 6
your Holy Spirit to *f* him with grace and power, and 533 12
f him with grace and power, and make him a deacon 545 10
F my memory with the record of your mighty works; 562 12
Whose bellies you *f* with your treasure, * 602 1
"Open your mouth wide, and I will *f* it." 704 23
When many cares *f* my mind, * 724 3
All the beasts of the field drink their *f* from them, * 735 23
Which does not *f* the hand of the reaper, * 784 13
F it with all truth, 816 10
f our hearts with thankfulness, 820 13
F them with the love of truth and righteousness, 820 21
F them with faith, virtue, knowledge, temperance, 829 2
so *f* our imaginations, 832 25

filled
He hath *f* the hungry with good things, * 50 15
He hath *f* the hungry with good things, * 65 18
He has *f* the hungry with good things, * 92 10
Then was our mouth *f* with laughter, * 105 6
He has *f* the hungry with good things, * 119 16
find thee, and be *f* with thy joy and peace; 204 4
thy dominion may increase till the earth is *f* 207 11
find you, and be *f* with your joy and peace; 255 2
your dominion may increase until the earth is *f* 258 11
your dominion may increase, until the earth is *f* 279 1
you may be *f* with all the fullness of God. 311 24
be *f* with thy grace and heavenly benediction, 336 6
and be *f* with thy grace and heavenly benediction; 342 26
Church of God, that it may be *f* with truth 389 15
we who eat this bread and drink this cup may be *f* 405 17
He has *f* the hungry with good things, * 442 5

Church of God, that it may be *f* with truth 548 11
deacons, that they may be *f* with your love, 548 21
and I was *f* with fear. 621 21
My loins are *f* with searing pain; * 637 10
and if they are not *f*, they howl. 667 2
and may all the earth be *f* with his glory. 686 28
So they ate and were well *f*, * 697 7
it took root and *f* the land. 703 6
you open your hand, and they are *f* with good things. 737 10
I am *f* with a burning rage, * 767 19
Then was our mouth *f* with laughter, * 782 8
May our barns be *f* to overflowing 801 3
who hast *f* the world with beauty: 814 1
that they may be *f* with the strength of his presence; 819 4

fillest

who openest thine hand and *f* all things living 828 1

filleth

The Spirit of the Lord *f* the world: 43 12

fills

and his rage *f* them with terror. 586 11
the loving-kindness of the LORD *f* the whole earth. 626 10
and *f* the hungry with good things. 746 19
Father, whose glory *f* the whole creation, 831 1

finally

and *f* to beat down Satan under our feet, 152 13
temporal, that we *f* lose not the things eternal; 180 4
F, in your mercy, bring them to that table 430 22
and *f* partake of everlasting glory in the life to come; 444 6
that *f* he may dwell with thee in life everlasting; 458 9
F, we commend to thy fatherly goodness 815 6
And *f*, teach our people to rely on your strength 822 10
and *f*, by thy mercy, obtain everlasting life; 832 4

find

lest coming suddenly he *f* you sleeping. 37 3
may *f* it none other than the way of life 56 9
people everywhere may seek after thee and *f* thee; 58 4
lest he come suddenly and *f* you asleep. 75 3
may *f* it none other than the way of life 99 4
people everywhere may seek after you and *f* you; 100 20
and you shall *f* refuge under his wings; * 130 4
and you will *f* rest for your souls. 131 17
he may *f* in us a mansion 160 8
let each one *f* thee mighty to save; 166 12
may *f* it none other than the way of life 168 13
we pray that all who seek thee here may *f* thee, 204 4
people everywhere may seek after thee and *f* thee, 206 12
Christ, at his coming, may *f* in us a mansion 212 7
let each one *f* you mighty to save; 218 4
may *f* it none other than the way of life 220 4
we pray that all who seek you here may *f* you, 255 2
people everywhere may seek after you and *f* you, 257 8
may *f* it none other than the way of life 272 4
that they may *f* your mercy present with them 279 16
the Morning Star who knows no setting, *f* it ever burning 287 26
and *f* grace to help in time of need. 320 7
and *f* grace to help in time of need. 352 8
so that in seeking you we might *f* you. 373 23
And grant that we may *f* our inheritance 375 21
Pray that they may *f* and be found by him. 386 9
That our works may *f* favor in your sight. 387 13
f their lives strengthened 430 2
having finished their course in faith, now *f* rest 503 16
to *f* comfort and wisdom, 568 17
search out their wickedness until you *f* none. 595 28
melt me down; you will *f* no impurity in me. 601 4
by night as well, but I *f* no rest. 610 5
Will not God *f* it out? * 646 28
who will *f* out our crimes? * 671 21
for comforters, but I could *f* no one. 681 5
and *f* in them no fault. 687 20
Those who go through the desolate valley will *f* 708 1
and you shall *f* refuge under his wings; * 719 18
let me *f* grace through your law. 765 18
Until I *f* a place for the LORD, * 786 7
How deep I *f* your thoughts, O God! * 795 10
I look to my right hand and *f* no one who knows me; 798 7
that all may *f* suitable and fulfilling employment, 824 13
and those who learn may *f* you to be the source 824 19
f with one another the fulfillment of their humanity; 825 14
following in his steps, they may *f* fulfillment 829 24
and whose presence we *f* wherever we go: 831 2
Where may we *f* what Christians believe 851 18

finds

as one who *f* great spoils. 777 4

fine

more than much *f* gold, * 607 17
and set a crown of *f* gold upon his head. 609 2
It is like *f* oil upon the head * 787 11

finest

the *f* of those who bear armor have been drowned 85 10
But Israel would I feed with the *f* wheat * 705 7
he satisfies you with the *f* wheat. 805 6

fingers

When I consider your heavens, the work of your *f*, * 592 13
who trains my hands to fight and my *f* to battle; 800 2

finish

Help us, O Lord, to *f* the good work here begun. 839 16

finished

having *f* their course in faith, do now rest 488 5
have *f* their course in thy faith and fear; 489 15
having *f* their course in faith, now find rest 503 15
have *f* their course in your faith and fear: 504 13
As for the enemy, they are *f*, in perpetual ruin, * 593 11

fire

O ye *f* and heat, bless ye the Lord; 48 6
all winds and *f* and heat. 88 14
most merciful God, kindle within us the *f* 111 4
a pillar of cloud by day and a pillar of *f* by night: 111 9
from earthquake, *f*, and flood; 149 11
enkindled with the *f* of thy love, 198 10
Sanctify this new *f*, 285 9
a pillar of cloud by day and a pillar of *f* by night: 290 3
he makes his arrows shafts of *f*. 591 25
Upon the wicked he shall rain coals of *f* 596 21
and purified seven times in the *f*. 597 15

and a consuming f out of his mouth; *	603	5
burst hailstones and coals of f.	603	14
the words of the LORD are tried in the f; *	604	25
and f shall consume them.	609	17
The voice of the LORD splits the flames of f;	620	18
while I pondered, the f burst into flame; *	638	23
and burns the shields with f.	649	23
we went through f and water; *	674	18
as the wax melts at the f, so let the wicked perish	676	4
They set f to your holy place; *	689	21
and all the night through with a glow of f.	696	2
a f was kindled against Jacob,	696	18
The f consumed their young men; *	700	5
will your fury blaze like f for ever?	701	14
They burn it with f like rubbish; *	703	18
Like f that burns down a forest, *	707	5
how long will your anger burn like f?	717	7
A f goes before him *	727	1
and flames of f your servants.	735	10
and flames of f throughout their land.	740	18
and a f to give light in the night season.	741	4
F blazed up against their company, *	743	7
they blaze like a f of thorns; *	761	20
F and hail, snow and fog, *	806	9

firm

Resist him, f in your faith.	132	10
in unity by thy Spirit, may ever stand f	190	13
strengthened your apostle Thomas with f and certain faith	237	9
in unity by your Spirit, may ever stand f	241	22
and lets me stand f on the heights.	605	6
and made it f upon the rivers of the deep.	613	17
and there is no f ground for my feet.	679	10
and my covenant will stand f for him.	715	23
he has made the world so f that it cannot be moved;	726	12
it stands f in the heavens.	770	21

firmament

O ye waters that be above the f,	47	10
Blessed art thou in the f of heaven; *	49	20
In the f of his power, glorify the Lord, *	88	7
In the f of his power, glorify the Lord, *	90	3
and the f shows his handiwork.	606	16
praise him in the f of his power.	807	23

firmly

pray that we may be f grounded in its truth;	189	2
pray that we may be f grounded in its truth;	240	10
I f intend amendment of life,	447	9
My heart is f fixed, O God, my heart is fixed; *	664	10
you have set your faithfulness f in the heavens.	713	20
My heart is f fixed, O God, my heart is fixed; *	749	17

first

and become the f fruits of them that slept.	46	14
f he suffered pain, and entered not into glory	56	7
the f fruits of those who have fallen asleep.	83	22
f he suffered pain, and entered not into glory	99	2
f he suffered pain, and entered not into glory	168	11
the example of the f martyr Stephen,	186	2
didst inspire Simon Peter, f among the apostles,	187	1
apostle James, f among the Twelve to suffer	191	8
f he suffered pain, and entered not into glory	220	2
the example of the f martyr Stephen,	237	15
who inspired Simon Peter, f among the apostles,	238	14
apostle James, f among the Twelve to suffer	242	15
The f Christians observed with great devotion	264	10
f he suffered pain, and entered not into glory	272	2
This is the f and great commandment.	319	9
This is the f and great commandment.	324	3
f be reconciled to thy brother,	343	19
who on the f day of the week	345	1
"The f commandment is this:	351	7
his own f gift for those who believe,	374	11
f be reconciled to your brother,	376	15
who on the f day of the week overcame death	377	14
f miracle at a wedding in Cana of Galilee.	423	6
This is the f (or second, or third) time	437	4
But f, our friends wish us, here assembled, to witness	440	14
Teach us in all things to seek f your honor and glory.	818	4
on the f day of the week, you conquered sin,	835	2
Stephen, the f martyr, and all the martyrs	838	16
our Lord, the f-born of many from the dead.	838	20
How did God f help us?	845	17
God f helped us be revealing himself and his will,	845	18
This is the f and the great commandment.	851	13

firstborn

our Lord, the f of all creation,	369	12
f among many brethren, and the head of the Church.	533	4
He struck down all the f of Egypt, *	699	7
I will make him my f *	715	20
He struck down the f of their land, *	740	25
It was he who struck down the f of Egypt, *	788	17
the f both of man and beast.	788	18
Who struck down the f of Egypt, *	790	15

firstfruits

the f of all their strength.	740	26

fish

The birds of the air, the f of the sea, *	592	23
and caused their f to die.	740	12

fit

and f their arrows to the string, *	596	11

fitted

who must be f with bit and bridle,	625	21

fixed

Thou hast f all the boundaries of the earth;	61	8
You f all the boundaries of the earth;	115	8
so that our minds may be f on the doing of your will,	123	18
keep in perfect peace those whose minds are f on you;	138	10
our hearts may sure there be f where true joys	167	20
our hearts may surely there be f where true joys	219	10
promised to those whose minds are f on you;	461	15
let your eyes be f on justice.	601	2
For in you, O LORD, have I f my hope; *	637	27
My heart is firmly f, O God, my heart is f; *	664	10
My eyes are f on you, O my Strength; *	666	14
You f all the boundaries of the earth; *	690	18
My heart is firmly f, O God, my heart is f; *	749	17

flakes
drops of dew and *f* of snow. 88 18

flame
love, that by its cleansing *f* we may be purged 111 5
Stir up in us the *f* of that love 113 13
God, who didst enkindle the *f* of thy love 196 1
God, who kindled the *f* of your love 247 13
kindled with the *f* of your love, 249 19
All you who stand near this marvelous and holy *f*, 286 10
while I pondered, the fire burst into *f*; * 638 23
before him there is a consuming *f*, 654 7
like the *f* that sets mountains ablaze. 707 6

flames
The voice of the LORD splits the *f* of fire; 620 18
and *f* of fire your servants. 735 10
and *f* of fire throughout their land. 740 18
and *f* devoured the wicked. 743 8

flashed
your arrows *f* to and fro; 694 10

flashing
There he broke the *f* arrows, * 692 5

flask
I have become like a leather *f* in the smoke, * 770 7

flats
A fruitful land into salt *f*, * 748 23

flatter
they *f* with their tongue. 589 12

flattered
But they *f* him with their mouths * 697 22

flatters
He *f* himself in his own eyes * 632 5

fled
they retreated and *f* in terror. 651 11
At your rebuke they *f*; * 735 15
The sea beheld it and *f*; * 757 1
What ailed you, O sea, that you *f*? * 757 5

flee
I would *f* to a far-off place * 660 19
let those who hate him *f* before him. 676 2
where can I *f* from your presence? 794 13
I have no place to *f* to, and no one cares for me. 798 8
for I *f* to you for refuge. 799 20

fleeing
"Kings with their armies are *f* away; * 677 3

fleeth
My soul *f* unto the Lord before the morning watch; * 474 11

fleeting
Those of high degree are but a *f* breath, * 670 1

flesh
the Lord shall be revealed, and all *f* shall see it 37 6
The Word was made *f* and dwelt among us: 44 6
pour out thy Spirit upon all *f*; 58 5
the Lord shall be revealed, and all *f* shall see it 75 6
The Word was made *f* and dwelt among us: 82 1
pour out your Spirit upon all *f*; 100 21
deceits of the world, the *f*, and the devil, 149 6
to take upon him our *f*, and to suffer death 168 3
pour out thy Spirit upon all *f*, 206 13
pour out your Spirit upon all *f*, 257 9
Christ, who took upon himself our *f*, 316 13
so to eat the *f* of thy dear Son Jesus Christ, 337 14
Because in the mystery of the Word made *f*, 346 1
and above all in the Word made *f*, 368 4
perfect Man of the *f* of the Virgin Mary his mother; 378 11
Because in the mystery of the Word made *f*, 378 14
give for the life of the world is my *f*. 397 4
For my *f* is food indeed, and my blood is drink 397 4
Whoever eats my *f* and drinks my blood abides 397 5
make one *f* in Holy Matrimony. 429 6
my *f* also shall rest in hope. 485 5
the God of the spirits of all *f*, 486 7
after they are delivered from the burden of the *f*, 488 3
at this holy Table may be fed and refreshed by his *f* 574 5
When evildoers came upon me to eat up my *f*, * 617 11
There is no health in my *f*, 637 1
Do you think I eat the *f* of bulls, * 655 5
for what can *f* do to me? 662 21
my soul thirsts for you, my *f* faints for you, 670 13
To you that hear prayer shall all *f* come, * 672 9
Though my *f* and my heart should waste away, * 689 1
He rained down *f* upon them like dust * 697 3
For he remembered that they were but *f*, * 698 5
and the *f* of your faithful ones to the beasts 701 6
my heart and my *f* rejoice in the living God. 707 18
how frail you have made all *f*. 717 9
and my *f* is wasted and gaunt. 752 24
than to put any trust in *f*. 761 12
My *f* trembles with dread of you; * 773 13
let all *f* bless his holy Name for ever and ever. 803 2
who, in holy wedlock, have been made one *f*. 829 4

flew
He mounted on cherubim and *f*; * 603 9

flies
nor of the arrow that *f* by day; 130 7
He sent swarms of *f* among them, 698 17
nor of the arrow that *f* by day; 719 21

flight
How holy is this night, when wickedness is put to *f*, 287 17
you have put my enemies to *f*. 605 20
For you will put them to *f* * 609 23
my enemies will be put to *f*; * 663 9
you conquered sin, put death to *f*, 835 3

flint
and *f*-stone into a flowing spring. 757 12

flock
faithful in the care and nurture of thy *f*; 196 24
pastor in thy Church and to feed thy *f*: 197 6
faithful in the care and nurture of your *f*; 248 10
pastor in your Church and to feed your *f*: 248 17
be one *f* under one shepherd, Jesus 280 7
Through the great shepherd of thy *f*, Jesus 348 11

Through the great shepherd of your *f*, Jesus 381 5
a lamb of your own *f*, a sinner of your own redeeming. 465 3
a lamb of thine own *f*, a sinner of thine own redeeming. 483 8
a lamb of your own *f*, a sinner of your own redeeming. 499 15
wholesome example for the entire *f* of Christ. 517 12
he may feed and tend the *f* of Christ, 521 9
Feed the *f* of Christ committed to your charge, 521 18
Like a *f* of sheep they are destined to die; 653 8
You led your people like a *f* * 694 17
and guided them in the wilderness like a *f*. 699 10
Hear, O Shepherd of Israel, leading Joseph like a *f*; * 702 12

flocks

and all you *f* and herds. 89 15
May the meadows cover themselves with *f*, 673 15
You make grass grow for *f* and herds * 736 3
and multiplied their families like *f* of sheep. 749 12
may the *f* in our pastures increase by thousands 801 5
He provides food for *f* and herds * 804 20

flood

from earthquake, fire, and *f*; 149 12
and *f* my couch with tears. 590 11
The LORD sits enthroned above the *f*; * 620 25
They surround me all day long like a *f*; * 713 13

floods

O ye seas and *f*, bless ye the Lord; 48 22
all your rapids and *f* have gone over me. 643 22

flourish

how you destroyed nations and made your people *f*. 645 12
In his time shall the righteous *f*; * 685 21
may its fruit *f* like Lebanon, 686 19
and all the workers of iniquity *f*, 721 10
They *f* only to be destroyed for ever; * 721 11
The righteous shall *f* like a palm tree, * 721 21
shall *f* in the courts of our God; 721 24
we *f* like a flower of the field; 734 12
There will I make the horn of David *f*; * 787 5

flourishes

In the morning it is green and *f*; * 718 11

flourishing

f like a tree in full leaf. 636 7

flow

they *f* between the mountains. 735 22
he blows with his wind, and the waters *f*. 805 14

flowed

He opened the rock, and water *f*, * 741 7

flower

the *f* of manhood in the dwellings of Ham. 699 8
we flourish like a *f* of the field; 734 12

flowers

for the songs of birds and the loveliness of *f*. 840 9

flowing

you dried up ever-*f* rivers. 690 15
and flint-stone into a *f* spring. 757 12

flows

grace *f* from your lips, 647 15

fly

"*F* away like a bird to the hilltop; 596 9
I would *f* away and be at rest. 660 18

foam

Though its waters rage and *f*, * 649 6

foaming

full of spiced and *f* wine, which he pours out, * 691 19

foe

you saved me from my deadly *f*. 606 9
that he redeemed them from the hand of the *f*. 746 4

foes

and my *f* rejoice that I have fallen. 598 7
it was they, my *f* and my adversaries, 617 12
Do not let my treacherous *f* rejoice over me, * 631 6
and my eye has seen the ruin of my *f*. 660 4
my lying *f* who would destroy me are mighty. * 679 18
His *f* shall bow down before him, * 686 1
and turn my hand against their *f*. 705 4
I will crush his *f* before him * 715 12
You have exalted the right hand of his *f* * 716 25
and bring all my *f* to naught, * 799 26

fog

Fire and hail, snow and *f*, * 806 9

fold

bring the nations into thy *f*; 58 5
bring the nations into your *f*; 100 21
bring the nations into thy *f*, 206 13
bring the nations into your *f*, 257 9
bring home to your *f* those who have gone astray; 280 6
a sheep of your own *f*, a lamb of your own flock, 465 3
a sheep of thine own *f*, a lamb of thine own flock, 483 8
a sheep of your own *f*, a lamb of your own flock, 499 15
return seven-*f* into their bosoms. 702 8

follow

take up his cross, and *f* me." 38 25
to *f* in faith where thou hast led 69 8
take up his cross and *f* me." 76 24
we who *f* in their footsteps may be made worthy 111 13
to *f* in faith where you have led the way, 123 7
that all mankind should *f* the example 168 4
we may both *f* the example of his patience, 168 5
calleth us each by name, and *f* where he doth lead; 173 13
we may steadfastly *f* his steps 173 18
f the blessed steps of his most holy life; 181 1
that thy grace may always precede and *f* us, 183 7
grace to *f* him without delay, 185 10
proclaim the one truth and *f* the one Lord, 187 5
honor the exaltation of her lowliness to *f* the example 189 14
Grant, O God, that we may *f* the example 189 17
f his doctrine and holy life, that we may truly repent 190 4
take up our cross and *f* him; 192 17

obey the calling of our Lord to *f* him; 193 1
Grant us grace so to *f* thy blessed saints 194 10
courage, we beseech thee, to take up our cross and *f* 201 9
calls us each by name, and *f* where he leads; 225 5
that we may steadfastly *f* his steps 225 10
f daily in the blessed steps of his most holy life; 232 14
that your grace may always precede and *f* us, 234 21
grace to *f* him without delay, 237 4
we may proclaim the one truth and *f* 238 17
honor the exaltation of her lowliness to *f* the example 240 21
Grant, O God, that we may *f* the example 241 3
f his teaching and holy life, that we may truly repent 241 13
grace to take up our cross and *f* him; 244 5
obey the calling of our Lord to *f* him; 244 10
Give us grace so to *f* your blessed saints 245 18
Give us courage to take up our cross and *f* him; 252 14
f him in the way that leads to eternal life; 271 12
Do you promise to *f* and obey him 303 1
I do, and with God's grace I will *f* him 303 13
grant us grace so to *f* the good examples 330 4
I do, and with God's grace I will *f* him 415 12
reaffirmed his commitment to *f* Christ 421 3
Surely your goodness and mercy shall *f* me 443 15
Surely thy loving-kindness and mercy shall *f* me 476 16
Surely goodness and mercy shall *f* me 477 9
f the example of their steadfastness in thy faith, 487 15
Give us, we pray, the faith to *f* where you have led 498 5
f in faith where you have led the way, 504 22
Let us, therefore, *f* their examples, 514 15
Your joy will be to *f* him who came, 517 17
every Christian is called to *f* Jesus Christ, 543 1
grant that together they may *f* Jesus Christ, 560 8
Surely your goodness and mercy shall *f* me 613 11
because I *f* the course that is right. 638 10
after her the bridesmaids *f* in procession. 648 20
nor will their grandeur *f* them. 653 18
The singers go before, musicians *f* after, * 678 7
to *f* their own devices. 704 27
and all the true of heart will *f* it. 723 24
I will strive to *f* a blameless course; 730 9
and who *f* in his ways! 783 14
those whom you call to *f* you 819 8
The duty of all Christians is to *f* Christ; 856 13
to know Christ and be able to *f* him. 859 4

followed
we have *f* too much the devices and desires 41 18
we have *f* too much the devices and desires 62 18
we have *f* too much the devices and desires 320 25

followers
"Gather before me my loyal *f*, * 654 11

followeth
he that *f* me shall not walk in darkness, 62 9

following
by *f* his laws which he set before us. 76 21
by *f* the holy doctrine which he taught; 187 12
f his example and the teaching of his holy life, 196 24
f the good examples of those who have served thee 202 3
who, *f* in his steps, give themselves to the service 209 11
show ourselves thankful to you by *f* his holy teaching; 239 2
f his example, constantly speak the truth, 241 14
f the example of your servant James the Just, 245 4
f his example and the teaching of his holy life, 248 10
f the good examples of those who have served you 253 8
Bless all who, *f* in his steps, give themselves 260 16
lead a new life, *f* the commandments of God, 330 11
f the example of our Lord and Savior, 443 29
He brought him from *f* the ewes, * 700 21
whatever is just and true and good, *f* the example 829 12
f you is better than chasing after selfish goals. 829 16
f in his steps, they may find fulfillment in loving you 829 24

follows
whoever *f* me will not walk in darkness, 116 5

font
Wash him in the holy *f* of everlasting life, 465 17
We dedicate this *F* in the Name of the Father, 569 21

food
and be nourished by that spiritual *F*, 316 18
come to the banquet of that most heavenly *F*. 317 10
feed us, in these holy mysteries, with the spiritual *f* 339 4
the holy *f* and drink of new and unending life in him. 363 14
and you have fed us with spiritual *f* 365 12
we thank you for feeding us with the spiritual *f* 366 2
For my flesh is *f* indeed, 397 4
thou hast fed us with the spiritual *f* 482 2
you have fed us with the spiritual *f* 498 13
we thank you for feeding us with the holy *f* 523 2
we thank you for feeding us with the holy *f* 535 2
we thank you for feeding us with the holy *f* 546 4
we thank you for feeding us with the holy *f* 564 2
My tears have been my *f* day and night, * 643 5
They forage for *f*, * 667 1
and let them be *f* for jackals. 671 6
and gave him to the people of the desert for *f*. 690 13
demanding *f* for their craving. 696 10
he provided for them *f* enough. 696 27
though the *f* was still in their mouths. 697 10
They have given the bodies of your servants as *f* 701 4
That they may bring forth *f* from the earth, * 736 5
and seek their *f* from God. 736 20
to give them their *f* in due season. 737 8
They abhorred all manner of *f* * 747 17
He gives *f* to those who fear him; * 754 14
Who gives *f* to all creatures, * 791 19
and you give them their *f* in due season. 802 18
and *f* to those who hunger. 803 16
He provides *f* for flocks and herds * 804 20
our nation may give thanks to you for *f* and drink 825 21
give us *f* to sustain our lives 835 14
For our daily *f* and drink, our homes and families, 837 9

foods
nor eat of their choice *f*. 797 11

fool
The *f* has said in his heart, "There is no God." * 598 12
and do not make me the taunt of the *f*. 639 12
The *f* has said in his heart, "There is no God." * 658 21
nor does the *f* understand, * 721 8

foolish

how a *f* people despised your Name. 690 21

foolishly

Such is the way of those who *f* trust in themselves, * 653 6

foolishness

by reason of my *f*. 637 7
O God, you know my *f*, * 679 20

fools

remember how *f* revile you all day long. 690 29
when will you *f* understand? 723 10
Some were *f* and took to rebellious ways; * 747 15

foot

He will not let your *f* be moved * 104 17
lest you dash your *f* against a stone. 130 22
He will not suffer thy *f* to be moved, * 473 13
and in the snare they set is their own *f* caught. 594 8
My *f* stands on level ground; * 617 5
Let not the *f* of the proud come near me, * 633 1
those who gloat over me when my *f* slips." 638 2
and he shall tread our enemies under *f*. 668 11
so that they went through the water on *f*, * 674 4
That your *f* may be dipped in blood, * 678 3
lest you dash your *f* against a stone. 720 10
As often as I said, "My *f* has slipped," * 724 1
and he shall tread our enemies under *f*. 750 22
He will not let your *f* be moved * 779 5

footed

He makes me sure-*f* like a deer * 605 5

footing

he set my feet upon a high cliff and made my *f* sure. 640 4

footsteps

we who follow in their *f* may be worthy 111 14
My *f* hold fast to the ways of your law; * 601 7
and their *f* shall not falter. 635 25
nor did our *f* stray from your path; 646 23
they spy upon my *f*; 663 2
yet your *f* were not seen. 694 16
Steady my *f* in your word; * 774 13

footstool

and fall down before his *f*; * 729 9
until I make your enemies your *f*." 753 13
let us fall upon our knees before his *f*." 786 12

forage

They *f* for food, * 667 1

forasmuch

O God, *f* as without thee we are not able to please 182 1

forbearance

a zeal for justice and the strength of *f*, 207 4
a zeal for justice and the strength of *f*, 258 4
that a spirit of respect and *f* may grow 390 14
that a spirit of respect and *f* may grow 549 30
work together with mutual *f* and respect; 824 4

forces

all the spiritual *f* of wickedness that rebel against God? 302 7
keeping all the men and women of our armed *f* 823 2

forebears

a wayfarer, as all my *f* were. 639 24
They shall join the company of their *f*, * 653 21
as your *f* did in the wilderness, * 725 7
We have sinned as our *f* did; * 742 9

forefather

To perform the oath which he swore to our *f* Abraham, * 51 5

forefathers

as he promised to our *f*, 50 18
To perform the mercy promised to our *f*, * 51 3
as he promised to our *f*, 65 21
nor the offenses of our *f*; 148 10
Our *f* put their trust in you; * 610 8
our *f* have told us, * 645 7
and planted our *f* in the land; * 645 11
and what our *f* have told us, * 695 2
And not be like their *f*, 695 16
He worked marvels in the sight of their *f*, * 695 26

foreheads

and a crown upon their *f*. 430 19

foreign

The *f* peoples will lose heart; * 606 1
you shall not worship a *f* god. 704 20
from the hand of *f* peoples, 800 16
and deliver me from the hand of *f* peoples, 800 24

foreigners

Ye are no more strangers and *f*, but fellow-citizens 40 3

foresight

give courage, wisdom, and *f* to provide 822 3

forest

For all the beasts of the *f* are mine, * 654 23
The wild boar of the *f* has ravaged it, * 703 13
Like fire that burns down a *f*, * 707 5
in which all the beasts of the *f* prowl. 736 18

forests

and strips the *f* bare. 620 22

foretaste

hast given unto us a *f* of thy heavenly banquet. 482 4
have given us a *f* of your heavenly banquet. 498 14
the *f* of the heavenly banquet which is our nourishment 860 2

forgave

Then you *f* me the guilt of my sin. 625 10
But he was so merciful that he *f* their sins 698 1
you were a God who *f* them, 729 17
whose Son *f* his enemies while he was suffering 823 8

forget

we may not *f* thee, but may remember 57 17
we may not *f* you, but may remember 100 9

yet I do not *f* your law. 104 6
never *f* that our common life depends 134 14
But to do good and to distribute, *f* not; 344 3
Do not *f* the trust committed to you 534 12
he will not *f* the cry of the afflicted. 593 24
and also all the peoples that *f* God. 594 12
do not *f* the afflicted. 595 20
will you *f* me for ever? * 597 21
f your people and your father's house. 648 12
Consider this well, you who *f* God, * 655 26
Slay them, O God, lest my people *f*; * 666 18
never *f* the lives of your poor. 690 23
F not the clamor of your adversaries, * 691 1
and not *f* the deeds of God, 695 14
so that I *f* to eat my bread. 731 8
and *f* not all his benefits. 733 12
I will not *f* your word. 764 16
I do not *f* your law. 768 10
I will never *f* your commandments, * 771 5
yet I do not *f* your law. 772 12
because my enemies *f* your words. 775 4
yet I do not *f* your commandments. 775 8
for I do not *f* your law. 776 10
for I do not *f* your commandments. 778 9
If I *f* you, O Jerusalem, * 792 10
let my right hand *f* its skill. 792 11
neglected persons whom it would be easy for us to *f*: 826 3

forgive

God is faithful and just to *f* us our sins, 38 12
And *f* us our trespasses, 54 20
as we *f* those who trespass against us. 54 21
And *f* us our trespasses, 67 10
as we *f* those who trespass against us. 67 11
who is faithful and just, will *f* our sins 76 11
have mercy on us and *f* us; 79 19
Almighty God have mercy on you, *f* you all your sins 80 1
F me, Lord, *f* me. 91 17
And *f* us our trespasses, 97 10
as we *f* those 97 11
And *f* us our trespasses, 106 20
as we *f* those 106 21
have mercy on us and *f* us; 117 2
Almighty God have mercy on you, *f* you all your sins 117 6
And *f* us our trespasses, 121 10
as we *f* those 121 11
f us all our offenses; 127 12
And *f* us our trespasses, 133 2
as we *f* those 133 3
to *f* us all our sins, negligences, and ignorances; 152 3
That it may please thee to *f* our enemies, 152 8
And *f* us our trespasses, 153 12
as we *f* those who trespass against us. 153 13
Mercifully *f* the sins of thy people. 154 18
dost *f* the sins of all those who are penitent: 166 2
f the sins of all who are penitent: 217 15
f the sins of all who are penitent: 264 3
And *f* us our trespasses, 311 7
as we *f* those 311 8
ready to *f* those who have offended you, 317 7
God is faithful and just to *f* us our sins, 320 3
have mercy on us and *f* us; 320 19
f us all that is past; 331 16
have mercy on us and *f* us; 331 30
And *f* us our trespasses, 336 24
as we *f* those who trespass against us. 336 25
God, who is faithful and just, will *f* our sins 352 3
have mercy on us and *f* us; 352 19
Almighty God have mercy on you, *f* you all your sins 353 1
have mercy on us and *f* us; 360 11
Almighty God have mercy on you, *f* you all your sins 360 15
And *f* us our trespasses, 364 7
as we *f* those 364 8
in your compassion *f* us our sins, 393 10
have mercy on us and *f* us; 398 3
Almighty God have mercy on you, *f* you all your sins 398 7
And *f* us our trespasses, 398 18
as we *f* those 398 19
And *f* us our trespasses, 428 14
as we *f* those 428 15
of his great mercy *f* you all your offenses; 448 3
who conferred power on his Church to *f* sins, 448 9
Do you, then, *f* those who have sinned against you? 451 1
I *f* them. 451 2
who conferred power on his Church to *f* sins, 451 8
of his great mercy *f* you all your offenses; 451 13
have mercy on us and *f* us; 455 2
Almighty God have mercy on you, *f* you all your sins 455 6
Of his great mercy, may he *f* you your sins, 456 15
And *f* us our trespasses, 464 10
as we *f* those 464 11
And *f* us our trespasses, 486 1
as we *f* those who trespass against us. 486 2
And *f* us our trespasses, 502 7
as we *f* those 502 8
f my sin, for it is great. 615 11
and *f* me all my sin. 615 25
deliver us and *f* us our sins, 701 25
f us, and teach us to improve our justice. 826 21
f our sins, banish our fears, 835 4
F us. 839 3

forgiven

That we may be pardoned and *f* for our sins 68 12
That we may be pardoned and *f* for our sins 122 14
We have not *f* others, as we have been *f*. 267 21
in order that you yourselves may be *f*. 317 8
be *f* for their sins, united with one another, 574 6
Happy are they whose transgressions are *f*, * 624 23
You have *f* the iniquity of your people * 708 22

forgiveness

obtain *f* by his infinite goodness and mercy. 41 13
the *f* of sins, 54 8
obtain *f* by his infinite goodness and mercy. 62 13
the *f* of sins, 66 24
To the Lord our God belong mercy and *f*, 76 19
obtain *f* by his infinite goodness and mercy. 79 8
you have promised *f* to sinners, * 91 10
by the *f* of their sins. 93 4
the *f* of sins, 96 28
obtain *f* by his infinite goodness and mercy. 116 9
the *f* of sins, 120 24
May the Almighty God grant us *f* of all our sins, 128 1

perfect remission and *f*; 166 6
perfect remission and *f*; 217 19
perfect remission and *f*; 264 7
the faithful were reconciled by penitence and *f*, 265 5
the *f* of sins, 293 16
bestowed upon us the *f* of sins, 294 6
the *f* of sins, 304 19
bestowed upon these your servants the *f* of sin, 308 4
bestowed upon this your servant the *f* of sin 314 3
We acknowledge one baptism for the *f* of sins. 327 17
who of his great mercy hath promised *f* of sins 332 2
We acknowledge one baptism for the *f* of sins. 359 8
shed for you and for many for the *f* of sins. 363 4
shed for you and for many for the *f* of sins. 368 17
shed for you and for many for the *f* of sins. 371 17
shed for you and for many for the *f* of sins. 374 22
for the *f* of our sins, 391 7
We pray to you also for the *f* of our sins. 393 8
it may bring us *f* of our sins, 399 10
shed for you and for many for the *f* of sins. 403 11
shed for you and for many for the *f* of sins. 405 9
the *f* of sins, 417 1
seek each other's *f* and yours. 429 15
f heal guilt, and joy conquer despair. 429 19
I firmly intend amendment of life, and I humbly beg *f* 447 10
it may bring us *f* of our sins, 457 8
trust in the communion of saints, the *f* of sins, 481 15
the *f* of sins, 496 18
We acknowledge one baptism for the *f* of sins. 520 8
We acknowledge one baptism for the *f* of sins. 530 27
declare God's *f* to penitent sinners, 531 13
We acknowledge one baptism for the *f* of sins. 542 27
for the *f* of our sins, 550 16
to ask your *f*, to know your healing 568 10
For there is *f* with you; * 784 23
that all may know the power of his *f* 816 18
f of sins, and new life in the Holy Spirit. 858 19
The benefits we receive are the *f* of our sins, 859 29

forgivenesses

To the Lord our God belong mercies and *f*, 38 20

forgives

Bless the Lord who *f* all our sins. 109 5
Bless the Lord who *f* all our sins. 299 5
Bless the Lord who *f* all our sins. 351 5
Bless the Lord who *f* all our sins. 355 5
Bless the Lord who *f* all our sins. 413 5
f your sins by the grace of the Holy Spirit. 448 16
f your sins by the grace of the Holy Spirit. 452 2
Bless the Lord who *f* all our sins. 512 5
Bless the Lord who *f* all our sins. 525 5
Bless the Lord who *f* all our sins. 537 5
He *f* all your sins * 733 13
by grace God *f* our sins, 858 3

forgiveth

Bless the Lord who *f* all our sins. 319 6
Bless the Lord who *f* all our sins. 323 5

forgiving

f us those things whereof our conscience is afraid, 183 1
f us those things of which our conscience is afraid, 234 15
For you, O Lord, are good and *f*, * 710 7

forgot

They *f* what he had done, * 695 24
But they soon *f* his deeds * 742 24
They *f* God their Savior, * 743 13

forgotten

Let not the needy, O Lord, be *f*; 55 11
Let not the needy, O Lord, be *f*; 68 3
Let not the needy, O Lord, be *f*; 98 5
Let not the needy, O Lord, be *f*; 122 5
For the needy shall not always be *f*, * 594 13
They say in their heart, "God has *f*; * 595 16
I am *f* like a dead man, out of mind; * 623 14
"Why have you *f* me? * 644 2
yet we have not *f* you, 646 20
If we have *f* the Name of our God, * 646 26
and *f* our affliction and oppression? 647 6
Has God *f* to be gracious? * 693 18
righteousness in the country where all is *f*? 713 3
but I have not *f* your statutes. 770 8

form

Christ, who took on himself the *f* of a servant, 545 2
Their *f* shall waste away, * 653 11
f a procession with branches up to the horns 762 26
Renew the ties of mutual regard which *f* our civic life. 825 9

formed

You *f* us in your own image, 373 18
you *f* me from the dust in your image and likeness, 450 8
and we are mortal, *f* of the earth, 482 13
and we are mortal, *f* of the earth, 499 5
he that *f* the eye does he not see? 723 12

forsake

Let the wicked *f* their ways * 86 19
Do not *f* us, O Lord our God. 131 13
Do not *f* us, O Lord our God. 140 6
Give us grace to heed their warnings and *f* our sins, 159 11
so thou dost not *f* those who make their boast 181 19
Give us grace to heed their warnings and *f* our sins, 211 11
so you never *f* those who make their boast 233 11
for you never *f* those who seek you, O Lord. 593 20
do not *f* me, O God of my salvation. 618 18
Though my father and my mother *f* me, * 618 19
he does not *f* his faithful ones. 635 17
O Lord, do not *f* me; * 638 11
f me not when my strength fails. 683 19
O God, do not *f* me, * 684 17
Truly, those who *f* you will perish; * 689 3
"If his children *f* my law, * 716 1
nor will he *f* his own. 723 22
do not utterly *f* me. 763 20
because of the wicked who *f* your law. 767 20

forsaken

My God, my God, why have you *f* me? * 610 1
but never have I seen the righteous *f*, 635 10
They say, "God has *f* him; 683 22
but I have not *f* your commandments. 770 17

forsaking

and, *f* all others, be faithful to him 424 11
and, *f* all others, be faithful to her 424 17

and, *f* all others, to be faithful to her 433 7
and, *f* all others, to be faithful to him 433 12

forsook

He *f* the shrine at Shiloh, * 699 26

forth

to set *f* his most worthy praise, 41 7
And our mouth shall show *f* thy praise. 42 15
The Lord hath manifested *f* his glory: 43 4
reaching *f* our hands in love, 58 11
and that we show *f* thy praise, 59 4
Let my prayer be set *f* in thy sight as the incense, 61 1
Shed *f* thine unending day upon us who watch 69 12
Send *f* upon us the Spirit of love, 71 7
and that we show *f* thy praise, 72 1
Almighty God our heavenly Father, to set *f* his praise, 79 2
The Lord has shown *f* his glory: 81 1
You stretched *f* your right hand; * 85 19
Bringing *f* life and giving growth, * 87 3
So is my word that goes *f* from my mouth; * 87 5
and in me you will show *f* your goodness. 91 21
reaching *f* our hands in love, 101 4
truly thankful hearts we may show *f* your praise, 101 17
from this time *f* for evermore. 105 3
Let my prayer be set *f* in your sight as incense, 115 1
Shed *f* your unending day upon us who watch 123 11
Send *f* upon us the Spirit of love, 125 2
truly thankful hearts we may show *f* your praise, 125 15
from this time *f* for evermore. 138 4
set it *f*, and show it accordingly, 150 8
That it may please thee to send *f* laborers 150 12
and to bring *f* the fruits of the Spirit, 150 16
and to the setting *f* of thy glory; 153 25
the same light, enkindled in our hearts, may shine *f* 161 16
may show *f* in their lives what they profess 172 4
may show *f* in their lives what they profess 173 1
and bring *f* in us the fruit of good works: 181 14
may show *f* our thankfulness unto thee 187 11
physician to set *f* in the Gospel the love and healing 193 12
we also in our generation may show *f* thy praise, 196 18
and showest *f* thy handiwork in the heavens 210 2
that this light, enkindled in our hearts, may shine *f* 213 10
may show *f* in their lives what they profess 223 18
may show *f* in their lives what they profess 224 16
may show *f* your power among all peoples, 232 18
and bring *f* in us the fruit of good works; 233 5
physician to set *f* in the Gospel the love and healing 244 21
we also in our generation may show *f* your praise, 248 4
and show *f* your handiwork in the heavens 261 8
pardon and absolution set *f* in the Gospel 265 8
That we may show *f* your glory in the world. 268 30
Let us go *f* in peace. 271 17
O God, whose wonderful deeds of old shine *f* 289 12
may bring *f* abundant fruit in your glorious kingdom; 290 11
may show *f* in their lives what they profess 291 2
Send them *f* in the power of that Spirit 309 8
set *f* thy true and lively Word, 329 11
Let us go *f* in the name of Christ. 339 22
Let us go *f* into the world, rejoicing 340 3
to show *f* thy glory in all the world. 345 6
who after his resurrection sent *f* his apostles 348 12
Let us go *f* in the name of Christ. 366 14
Let us go *f* into the world, 366 18
From the primal elements you brought *f* the human race, 370 12
to show *f* your glory in all the world. 378 2
who after his resurrection sent *f* his apostles 381 6
and show *f* your glory in all that we do, 391 3
we show *f* the sacrifice of his death, 403 14
Send them *f* in the power of that Spirit 418 6
I know not what it will bring *f*, but make me ready, 461 20
for I went with the multitude, and brought them *f* 471 8
Before the mountains were brought *f*, 472 11
from this time *f* for evermore. 473 24
and lead me *f* beside the waters of comfort. 476 4
and bring me *f* in the paths of righteousness 476 6
or show *f* all his praise? 478 14
Let us go *f* in the name of Christ. 483 12
Let us go *f* in the name of Christ. 500 1
Let us go *f* in the name of Christ. 502 21
he chose and sent *f* his twelve apostles. 514 13
From this time *f* for evermore. 523 14
Let us go *f* into the world, rejoicing 523 18
Let us go *f* into the world, rejoicing 535 13
Let us go *f* into the world, 547 7
set *f* your true and living Word. 563 3
Let my vindication come *f* from your presence; * 601 1
hot burning coals blazed *f* from him. 603 6
it comes *f* like a bridegroom out of his chamber; 606 24
It goes *f* from the uttermost edge of the heavens 607 1
and do not go *f* with our armies. 646 4
and set *f* my riddle upon the harp. 652 12
My companion stretched *f* his hand against his comrade; * 661 28
God will send *f* his love and his faithfulness. 663 27
The earth has brought *f* her increase; * 675 20
God gives the solitary a home and brings *f* prisoners 676 13
O God, when you went *f* before your people, * 676 16
Send *f* your strength, O God; * 678 14
he sends *f* his voice, his mighty voice. 678 27
a breath that goes *f* and does not return. 698 6
and show *f* your praise from age to age. 702 11
shine *f*, you that are enthroned upon the cherubim. 702 13
Before the mountains were brought *f*, 718 1
That they may bring *f* food from the earth, * 736 5
Man goes *f* to his work * 736 23
You send *f* your Spirit, and they are created; * 737 14
So he led *f* his people with gladness, * 741 11
or show *f* all his praise? 741 22
He sent *f* his word and healed them * 747 21
from this time *f* for evermore. 756 5
from this time *f* for evermore. 758 26
You are good and you bring *f* good; * 768 23
When your word goes *f* it gives light; * 774 7
My lips shall pour *f* your praise, * 777 21
from this time *f* for evermore. 779 17
from this time *f* for evermore. 781 21
from this time *f* for evermore. 785 18
you stretch *f* your hand against the fury 793 17
Let my prayer be set *f* in your sight as incense, * 797 5
He sends *f* his word and melts them; * 805 13
show *f* thy praise among the nations of the earth. 820 12
let thy Spirit go *f*, that it may renew 828 4

and to the setting *f* of thy glory; 834 6
bring *f* in us the fruit of good living, 834 21
to set *f* the life and teachings of Jesus 853 16

forthright

with the *f* you show yourself *f*. 604 15

fortress

My help and my *f*, my stronghold and my deliverer, * 800 3

fortunate

more *f* than ourselves, 268 8

fortune

you have restored the good *f* of Jacob. 708 21

fortunes

When the LORD restored the *f* of Zion, * 105 4
Restore our *f*, O LORD, * 105 12
when the LORD restores the *f* of his people, 599 2
when God restores the *f* of his people 659 15
When the LORD restored the *f* of Zion, * 782 6
Restore our *f*, O LORD, * 782 14

forty

F years long was I grieved with this generation, 146 21
F years long I detested that generation 725 12

forward

to have and to hold from this day *f*, 427 2
to have and to hold from this day *f*, 427 6
to have and to hold from this day *f*, 436 2
to have and to hold from this day *f*, 436 7
come *f* now, and make it known. 527 5
come *f* now and make it known. 539 5
and marched *f* together. 651 9

found

Seek the Lord while he wills to be *f*; * 86 17
be fixed where true joys are to be *f*; 167 20
the Paschal feast may be *f* worthy to attain 171 6
that our faith may never be *f* wanting 185 17
be fixed where true joys are to be *f*; 219 10
the Paschal feast may be *f* worthy to attain 222 23
that our faith may never be *f* wanting 237 11
all the saints who have *f* favor 375 23
Pray that they may find and be *f* by him. 386 9
and be *f* without fault at the day of your coming, 389 16
for you were lost, and are *f*; 451 18
I *f* trouble and heaviness; 479 5
and be *f* without fault at the Day of your Coming, 548 12
that his hateful sin will not be *f* out. 632 6
nor let them be *f* guilty when brought to trial. 636 2
I searched for them, but they could not be *f*. 636 9
If I had *f* evil in my heart, * 675 3
Your people *f* their home in it; * 676 23
The sparrow has *f* her a house 707 19
I have *f* David my servant; * 715 6
they *f* no way to a city where they might dwell. 746 9
When he is judged, let him be *f* guilty, * 751 10
we *f* it in the fields of Jearim. 786 10
Where is this Old Covenant to be *f*? 847 6
The covenant with the Hebrew people is to be *f* 847 7
What Christians believe about Christ is *f* 851 20

foundation

govern those whom thou hast set upon the sure *f* 178 14
built thy Church upon the *f* of the apostles 178 19
stand firm upon the one *f*, 190 14
you have set upon the sure *f* of your loving-kindness; 230 9
built your Church upon the *f* of the apostles 230 13
may ever stand firm upon the one *f*, 241 22
from the *f* of the world." 487 21

foundations

When the *f* are being destroyed, * 596 13
and the *f* of the world laid bare, * 603 20
all the *f* of the earth are shaken. 705 19
you laid the *f* of the world and all that is in it. 714 16
Righteousness and justice are the *f* of your throne; * 714 21
righteousness and justice are the *f* of his throne. 726 26
In the beginning, O LORD, you laid the *f* 732 27
You have set the earth upon its *f*, * 735 11

founded

For it is he who *f* it upon the seas * 613 16
like the earth which he *f* for ever. 700 18
On the holy mountain stands the city he has *f*; * 711 12
and they *f* a city to dwell in. 749 2

founders

in whose Name the *f* of this country won liberty 190 17
in whose Name the *f* of this country won liberty 242 1

fountain

Almighty God, the *f* of all wisdom, 179 16
Almighty God, the *f* of all wisdom: 209 17
Almighty God, the *f* of all wisdom, 231 10
Almighty God, the *f* of all wisdom: 261 1
F of life and source of all goodness, 373 4
bless the LORD, you that are of the *f* of Israel. 678 10
O God, the *f* of wisdom, whose will is good 821 1

fourscore

though men be so strong that they come to *f* years, * 473 4

fowler

We have escaped like a bird from the snare of the *f*; * 781 13

fowls

O all ye *f* of the air, bless ye the Lord; * 48 25

fragile

and this *f* earth, our island home. 370 10

fragrant

All your garments are *f* with myrrh, aloes, and cassia, * 648 6

frail

how *f* you have made all flesh. 717 9

frames

one which *f* evil into law? 724 6

fraud

nor sworn by what is a *f*. 613 22

free

he has come to his people and set them *f*. 92 19
to set us *f* from the hands of our enemies, 92 28
F to worship him without fear, * 92 29

Lord, you now have set your servant *f* * 93 12
When you became man to set us *f* 96 3
Lord, you now have set your servant *f* * 120 1
you set me *f* when I am hard-pressed; 128 9
Lord, you now have set your servant *f* * 135 1
Lord, you now have set your servant *f* * 140 7
Set us *f*, O God, from the bondage of our sins 164 6
may with *f* hearts accomplish those things 177 5
Set us *f*, O God, from the bondage of our sins, 216 1
may accomplish with *f* hearts those things 229 1
and set him *f* from every bond; 464 17
and set him *f* from every bond; 466 17
Rise up, O LORD; set me *f*, O my God; * 587 15
you set me *f* when I am hard-pressed; 587 21
her streets are never *f* of oppression and deceit. 661 5
In your righteousness, deliver me and set me *f*; * 683 3
his hands were set *f* from bearing the load." 704 13
I am in prison and cannot get *f*. 712 19
and set *f* those condemned to die; 732 17
the ruler of the peoples set him *f*. 739 18
the LORD answered by setting me *f*. 761 6
The LORD sets the prisoners *f*; 803 17
It means that we are *f* to make choices: 845 5
Redemption is the act of God which sets us *f* 849 5
The Messiah is one sent by God to *f* us 849 12

freed

and enslaved by sin, may be *f* 185 4
and enslaved by sin, may be *f* 203 2
and enslaved by sin, may be *f* 236 17
and enslaved by sin, may be *f* 254 4
that the world may be *f* from poverty, 390 22
that being *f* from anxiety, 391 11
that the world may be *f* from poverty, 550 7
you have *f* me from my bonds. 760 7
in him we are *f* from the power of sin 850 9

freedom

whose service is perfect *f*: 57 3
and to serve you is perfect *f*: 99 21
Eternal God, who led your ancient people into *f* 111 8
bestow *f* upon all peoples, 151 3
lit the torch of *f* for nations then unborn: 190 19
to serve thee in *f* and peace: 207 2
that we may reverently use our *f*, 209 4
lit the torch of *f* for nations then unborn: 242 3
to serve you in *f* and in peace: 258 2
that we may reverently use our *f*, 260 10
to open for us the way of *f* and peace. 370 20
to prisoners, *f*; to the sorrowful, joy. 374 5
f of every person, we pray to you, O Lord. 390 18
For all who work for justice, *f*, and peace. 392 6
promote the dignity and *f* of every person, 550 3
and brings forth prisoners into *f*; * 676 14
who through addiction have lost their health and *f*. 831 20
benefits of true *f* and gladly accept its disciplines. 839 25
misused their *f* and made wrong choices. 845 11
Why do we not use our *f* as we should? 845 12
justice, *f*, and the necessities of life for all people; 848 13

freely

They have given *f* to the poor, * 755 22
for all his gifts so *f* bestowed upon us. 837 2

freewill

I will offer you a *f* sacrifice * 660 1

fresh

"All my *f* springs are in you." 711 25
I am anointed with *f* oil. 721 17

fret

Do not *f* yourself because of evildoers; * 633 5
Do not *f* yourself over the one who prospers, * 633 19
do not *f* yourself; it leads only to evil. 633 22

friend

who is my *f* and not a stranger. 491 12
You wept at the grave of Lazarus, your *f*; 497 7
If I have repaid my *f* with evil, * 591 1
he does no evil to his *f*; * 599 9
The LORD is a *f* to those who fear him * 615 16
as one would for a *f* or a brother; * 630 20
Even my best *f*, whom I trusted, 642 17
When you see a thief, you make him your *f*, * 655 16
my companion, my own familiar *f*. 661 11
My *f* and my neighbor you have put away from me, * 713 15

friendless

minister in his name to the suffering, the *f*, 209 13
minister in his Name to the suffering, the *f*, 260 19
For those who minister to the sick, the *f*, 392 10

friendly

Let the righteous smite me in *f* rebuke; 797 12

friends

Dear *f* in Christ, here in the presence of Almighty God, 62 11
Dear *f* in Christ, here in the presence of Almighty God, 116 7
Dear *f* in Christ: On this most holy night, 285 1
Through the Paschal mystery, dear *f*, we are buried 292 1
broke the bread, and gave it to his *f*, 371 11
for our families, *f*, and neighbors; 391 11
For our families, *f*, and neighbors, 392 3
broke the bread, and gave it to his *f*, 403 5
Dear *F*: The birth of a child 440 1
Dear *F*: It has pleased God 440 8
But first, our *f* wish us, here assembled, 440 14
Dear *F*: It was our Lord 465 9
for giving him to us, his family and *f*, 493 18
Dear *f* in Christ, you know the importance 527 1
Dear *f* in Christ, you know the importance 539 1
My *f* and companions draw back from my affliction; * 637 18
You have put my *f* far from me; 712 17
We thank you for the blessing of family and *f*, 836 5
and homes and families, and our *f*, 837 10

fro

They go to and *f* in the evening; * 666 7
your arrows flashed to and *f*; 694 10

frogs

and *f*, which destroyed them. 698 18
Their land was overrun by *f*, * 740 13

from

F the rising of the sun even unto the going down	38	5
and to cleanse us *f* all unrighteousness.	38	12
Grace be unto you, and peace, *f* God our Father,	40	9
f the Lord Jesus Christ.	40	10
we have erred and strayed *f* thy ways like lost sheep,	41	17
and his truth endureth *f* generation to generation.	45	22
Christ being raised *f* the dead dieth no more; *	46	7
Christ is risen *f* the dead, *	46	13
A Reading (Lesson) *f* ________.	47	1
For behold *f* henceforth *	50	5
He hath put down the mighty *f* their seat, *	50	13
That we should be saved *f* our enemies, *	51	1
and *f* the hand of all that hate us;	51	2
whereby the dayspring *f* on high hath visited us;	51	17
The third day he rose again *f* the dead.	54	1
F thence he shall come to judge	54	4
but deliver us *f* evil.	54	23
f all thy works and sanctify a day of rest	56	12
who dividest the day *f* the night	56	18
Drive far *f* us all wrong desires,	56	20
Glory to him *f* generation to generation	60	4
Grace be unto you, and peace, *f* God our Father,	61	3
f the Lord Jesus Christ.	61	4
we have erred and strayed *f* thy ways like lost sheep,	62	17
A Reading (Lesson) *f* ________.	64	12
For behold *f* henceforth *	65	8
He hath put down the mighty *f* their seat, *	65	16
The third day he rose again *f* the dead.	66	17
F thence he shall come to judge	66	20
but deliver us *f* evil.	67	13
O God, *f* whom all holy desires, all good counsels,	69	16
defended *f* the fear of all enemies,	69	20
great mercy defend us *f* all perils and dangers	70	2
Glory to him *f* generation to generation	73	4
F the rising of the sun to its setting	76	5
and cleanse us *f* all unrighteousness.	76	11
Grace to you and peace *f* God our Father	78	8
and his faithfulness endures *f* age to age.	83	9
Christ being raised *f* the dead will never die again; *	83	15
Christ has been raised *f* the dead, *	83	21
A Reading (Lesson) *f* ________.	84	3
f the springs of salvation.	86	6
For as rain and snow fall *f* the heavens *	87	1
So is my word that goes forth *f* my mouth; *	87	5
F this day all generations will call me blessed: *	92	1
He has cast down the mighty *f* their thrones, *	92	8
that he would save us *f* our enemies, *	92	23
f the hands of all who hate us.	92	24
to set us free *f* the hands of our enemies,	92	28
the dawn *f* on high shall break upon us,	93	6
F every family, language, people, and nation, *	94	3
Save us *f* the time of trial,	97	13
but deliver us *f* evil.	97	14
Lord, keep us *f* all sin today;	98	13
f all your works and sanctified a day of rest	99	7
whose light divides the day *f* the night	99	13
Drive far *f* us all wrong desires,	99	15
Glory to him *f* generation to generation	102	15
but I have not strayed *f* your commandments.	104	8
f where is my help to come?	104	14
My help comes *f* the LORD, *	104	15
The LORD shall preserve you *f* all evil; *	104	25
f this time forth for evermore.	105	3
All this is *f* God,	106	2
F the rising of the sun to its setting	106	6
Save us *f* the time of trial,	106	23
but deliver us *f* evil.	106	24
to defend us *f* all error,	107	6
great mercy defend us *f* all perils and dangers	111	2
keep us *f* every sin, every evil,	113	6
peace *f* God our Father and *f* the Lord	115	3
A Reading (Lesson) *f* ________.	118	12
F this day all generations will call me blessed: *	119	7
he has cast down the mighty *f* their thrones, *	119	14
Save us *f* the time of trial,	121	13
but deliver us *f* evil.	121	14
we, being delivered *f* the fear of all enemies,	123	19
defend us *f* all perils and dangers of this night;	123	22
Glory to him *f* generation to generation	126	15
He shall deliver you *f* the snare of the hunter *	130	1
and *f* the deadly pestilence.	130	2
Take my yoke upon you, and learn *f* me;	131	16
who brought again *f* the dead our Lord	132	1
Save us *f* the time of trial,	133	5
but deliver us *f* evil.	133	6
defend us *f* all perils and dangers of this night;	133	11
Look down, O Lord, *f* your heavenly throne,	133	17
Visit this place, O Lord, and drive far *f* it all snares	133	21
Cast me not away *f* your presence *	137	5
and take not your holy Spirit *f* me.	137	6
through the resurrection of Jesus Christ *f* the dead.	137	13
f this time forth for evermore.	138	4
F the rising of the sun to its going down *	138	5
Visit this place, O Lord, and drive far *f* it all snares	140	13
F all evil and wickedness;	148	15
f sin;	148	15
f the crafts and assaults of the devil;	148	15
and *f* everlasting damnation	148	16
F all blindness of heart; *f* pride,	149	1
f envy, hatred, and malice; and *f* all want	149	2
F all inordinate and sinful affections;	149	5
and *f* all the deceits	149	5
F all false doctrine, heresy, and schism;	149	8
f hardness of heart,	149	8
F lightning and tempest;	149	11
f earthquake, fire, and flood;	149	11
f plague, pestilence, and famine,	149	12
F all oppression, conspiracy, and rebellion;	149	14
f violence, battle, and murder;	149	14
and *f* dying suddenly	149	15
but deliver us *f* evil.	153	15
F our enemies defend us, O Christ;	154	15
turn *f* us all those evils	155	8
Set us free, O God, *f* the bondage of our sins	164	6
Preserve us *f* faithless	165	8
mortal life may hide *f* us the light of that love	165	10
and be changed into his likeness *f* glory to glory;	165	18
to all who have gone astray *f* thy ways,	166	17
that we may be defended *f* all adversities	167	5
and *f* all evil thoughts	167	6
Christ came down *f* heaven to be the true bread	167	11
the smiters and hid not his face *f* shame:	169	2

resurrection hast delivered us *f* the power	170	9
may be raised *f* the death of sin	171	1
thou hast delivered us *f* the dominion of sin	172	15
keep us, we beseech thee, *f* all things that may hurt	177	4
put away *f* us all hurtful things,	177	16
O God, *f* whom all good doth come:	178	1
thy Church, being delivered *f* false apostles,	188	3
O God, who *f* the family of thy servant David	188	8
delivered *f* the disquietude of this world,	191	18
Deliver us, we pray thee, *f* an inordinate love	198	2
Christ dost turn us *f* the old life of sin:	203	6
redeemed *f* the old life of sin by our baptism	203	13
we, who constantly receive good things *f* thy hand,	207	19
and serve thee *f* generation to generation;	209	20
f the service of self alone,	210	4
Set us free, O God, *f* the bondage of our sins,	216	1
Preserve us *f* faithless fears	217	1
this mortal life may hide *f* us the light	217	3
and be changed into his likeness *f* glory to glory;	217	11
to all who have gone astray *f* your ways,	218	8
that we may be defended *f* all adversities	218	15
and *f* all evil thoughts	218	16
Christ came down *f* heaven to be the true bread	219	2
resurrection delivered us *f* the power of our enemy:	222	3
may be raised *f* the death of sin	222	18
f the dominion of sin and death	224	8
f all things that may hurt us,	228	15
Put away *f* us, we entreat you,	229	11
O God, *f* whom all good proceeds:	229	15
your Church, being delivered *f* false apostles,	239	13
O God, who *f* the family of your servant David	239	17
we may be healed *f* all our infirmities	242	11
delivered *f* the disquietude of this world,	243	4
Deliver us *f* an inordinate love	249	12
you turn us *f* the old life of sin:	254	8
redeemed *f* the old life of sin by our baptism	254	14
receiving good things *f* your hand,	258	19
and serve you *f* generation to generation;	261	4
Deliver us in our various occupations *f* the service	261	9
had been separated *f* the body of the faithful	265	4
Wash me through and through *f* my wickedness *	266	4
and cleanse me *f* my sin.	266	5
Indeed, I have been wicked *f* my birth, *	266	12
a sinner *f* my mother's womb.	266	13
Purge me *f* my sin, and I shall be pure; *	266	16
Hide your face *f* my sins *	266	20
Cast me not away *f* your presence *	266	24
and take not your holy Spirit *f* me.	266	25
Deliver me *f* death, O God, *	267	3
contempt toward those who differ *f* us,	268	22
Restore us, good Lord, and let your anger depart *f* us;	268	27
turn *f* their wickedness and live,	269	5
might be delivered *f* the power of sin and death,	277	5
Lord Jesus passed over *f* death to life,	285	2
delivered *f* the gloom of sin,	287	10
and rose victorious *f* the grave.	287	13
arm your chosen people *f* slavery under Pharaoh,	289	14
resurrection delivered us *f* the power of your enemy:	295	3
A Reading (Lesson) *f* ________.	300	1
desires that draw you *f* the love of God?	302	14
Deliver them, O Lord, *f* the way of sin	305	14
f the bondage of sin into everlasting life.	306	19
that those who here are cleansed *f* sin	307	4
Save us *f* the time of trial	311	10
but deliver us *f* evil.	311	11
f whom every family in heaven and earth is named,	311	21
cleanse us *f* all unrighteousness.	320	3
we have erred and strayed *f* thy ways like lost sheep,	320	24
and *f* whom no secrets are hid:	323	8
A Reading (Lesson) *f* .	325	13
God *f* God, Light *f* Light,	326	13
true God *f* true God,	326	14
he came down *f* heaven:	326	19
he became incarnate *f* the Virgin Mary,	327	2
who proceeds *f* the Father and the Son.	327	13
came down *f* heaven,	328	2
who proceedeth *f* the Father and the Son;	328	14
walking *f* henceforth in his holy ways:	330	12
f time to time most grievously have committed,	331	6
pardon and deliver you *f* all your sins,	332	4
but deliver us *f* evil.	336	27
thou didst send thy beloved Son to redeem us *f*	345	7
that we might be delivered *f* the bondage of sin,	345	17
the Holy Ghost came down [on this day] *f* heaven,	347	7
who rose victorious *f* the dead,	349	6
cleanse us *f* all unrighteousness.	352	3
and *f* you no secrets are hid:	355	8
A Reading (Lesson) *f* .	357	4
God *f* God, Light *f* Light,	358	10
true God *f* true God,	358	11
he came down *f* heaven:	358	16
he became incarnate *f* the Virgin Mary,	358	18
who proceeds *f* the Father and the Son.	359	4
Save us *f* the time of trial,	364	10
but deliver us *f* evil.	364	11
you sent him to be incarnate *f* the Virgin Mary,	368	5
In him, you have delivered us *f* evil,	368	7
f your creation, this bread and this wine.	369	2
F the primal elements you brought forth the human race,	370	12
Deliver us *f* the presumption of coming to this Table	372	4
f generation to generation.	372	13
inaccessible *f* before time and for ever.	373	3
When our disobedience took us far *f* you,	373	21
and, rising *f* the grave, destroyed death,	374	7
and offering to you, *f* the gifts you have given us,	374	27
Because you sent your beloved Son to redeem us *f* sin	378	4
that we might be delivered *f* the bondage of sin,	378	12
the Holy Spirit came down [on this day] *f* heaven,	380	2
who rose victorious *f* the dead,	382	1
For the peace *f* above,	383	3
For deliverance *f* all danger,	385	1
Have compassion on those who suffer *f* any grief	387	14
That they may be delivered *f* their distress.	387	16
that the world may be freed *f* poverty,	390	22
that we may be delivered *f* hardness of heart,	391	2
that being freed *f* anxiety,	391	11
"I am the living bread which came down *f* heaven;	397	1
Save us *f* the time of trial,	398	21
but deliver us *f* evil.	398	22
A Reading (Lesson) *f* .	414	1
to have and to hold *f* this day forward,	427	2
to have and to hold *f* this day forward,	427	6
Save us *f* the time of trial,	428	17

but deliver us *f* evil.	428	18
Defend them *f* every enemy.	430	16
to have and to hold *f* this day forward,	436	2
F this day all generations will call me blessed:*	441	15
He has cast down the mighty *f* their thrones,*	442	3
I absolve you *f* all your sins:	448	4
Wash me through and through *f* my wickedness,	449	3
and cleanse me *f* my sin.	449	4
Holy God, heavenly Father, you formed me *f* the dust	450	8
and redeemed me *f* sin	450	9
Therefore, O Lord, *f* these and all other sins	450	16
I absolve you *f* all your sins:	451	14
release you *f* suffering,	456	16
May he deliver you *f* all evil,	456	17
preserve him *f* the temptations	458	5
you drive away *f* our bodies all sickness	458	17
guard him *f* all danger,	459	4
both relief *f* pain and hope of health	460	18
F all evil, *f* all sin, *f* all tribulation,	463	3
deliver the soul of your servant *f* the power	463	12
of evil, and *f* eternal death,	463	13
Save us *f* the time of trial,	464	13
but deliver us *f* evil.	464	14
Deliver your servant, O Sovereign Lord Christ, *f* all	464	16
and set him free *f* every bond;	464	17
that he may rest *f* his labors,	465	12
Deliver your servant, O Sovereign Lord Christ, *f* all	466	16
and set him free *f* every bond;	466	17
for they rest *f* their labors.	469	15
f one generation to another.	472	10
thou art God *f* everlasting, and world without end.	472	13
f whence cometh my help?	473	10
My help cometh even *f* the LORD, *	473	11
The LORD shall preserve thee *f* all evil; *	473	21
f this time forth for evermore.	473	24
he shall redeem Israel * *f* all his sins.	474	17
Whither shall I go then *f* thy Spirit? *	475	5
or whither shall I go then *f* thy presence?	475	6
O hide not thou thy face *f* me, *	478	3
And why? thou hast delivered my soul *f* death, *	479	14
mine eyes *f* tears, and my feet *f* falling.	479	15
be cleansed *f* all our sins,	481	5
go *f* strength to strength in the life of perfect service	481	21
Christ is risen *f* the dead,	483	14
through any pains of death, to fall *f* thee.	484	17
He that raised up Jesus *f* the dead	485	1
but deliver us *f* evil.	486	4
a voice *f* heaven didst proclaim,	486	8
who brought again *f* the dead our Lord	486	21
the kingdom prepared for you *f* the foundation	487	20
after they are delivered *f* the burden of the flesh,	488	3
finished their course in faith, do now rest *f*	488	6
he may go *f* strength to strength	488	23
Happy *f* now on are those who die	492	1
for they rest *f* their labors.	492	4
f whom can we seek help?	492	6
F you alone, O Lord,	492	7
turn us away *f* you at our last hour.	492	20
Christ is risen *f* the dead,	500	3
He who raised Jesus Christ *f* the dead	501	3
Save us *f* the time of trial,	502	10
but deliver us *f* evil.	502	11
who brought again *f* the dead our Lord	503	1
Raise us, we humbly pray, *f* the death of sin	505	2
receive the kingdom prepared for you *f* the beginning	505	7
and *f* you no secrets are hid:	512	8
A Reading (Lesson) *f*.	516	1
nourish them *f* the riches of God's grace,	518	14
God *f* God, Light *f* Light,	519	13
true God *f* true God,	519	14
he came down *f* heaven:	519	19
he became incarnate *f* the Virgin Mary,	519	21
who proceeds *f* the Father and the Son.	520	4
f the beginning you have gathered	520	14
f the creation you have graciously accepted the ministry	520	18
F this time forth for evermore.	523	14
and *f* you no secrets are hid:	525	8
A Reading (Lesson) *f*.	528	12
God *f* God, Light *f* Light,	530	4
true God *f* true God,	530	5
he came down *f* heaven:	530	10
he became incarnate *f* the Virgin Mary,	530	12
who proceeds *f* the Father and the Son.	530	23
nourish Christ's people *f* the riches of his grace,	531	18
and *f* you no secrets are hid:	537	8
A Reading (Lesson) *f*.	540	12
God *f* God, Light *f* Light,	542	4
true God *f* true God,	542	5
he came down *f* heaven:	542	10
he became incarnate *f* the Virgin Mary,	542	12
who proceeds *f* the Father and the Son.	542	23
Scriptures, to seek nourishment *f* them,	543	8
duties assigned to you *f* time to time.	543	16
that the world may be freed *f* poverty,	550	7
f the bondage of sin into everlasting life.	570	11
cleansed *f* sin and born again	570	19
We praise you for raising him *f* the dead,	573	16
"let us cast off their bonds *f* us."	586	7
and he answers me *f* his holy hill;	587	10
Depart *f* me, all evildoers, *	590	14
save and deliver me *f* all who pursue me;	590	21
see the misery I suffer *f* those who hate me,	594	2
O you who lift me up *f* the gate of death;	594	3
the ungodly shall perish *f* his land.	596	2
to shoot *f* ambush at the true of heart.	596	12
the faithful have vanished *f* among us.	597	2
with a smooth tongue they speak *f* a double heart.	597	4
like silver refined *f* ore	597	14
and save us *f* this generation for ever.	597	17
how long will you hide your face *f* me?	597	22
The LORD looks down *f* heaven upon us all, *	598	15
who speaks the truth *f* his heart.	599	7
listen to my prayer, which does not come *f* lying lips.	600	24
Let my vindication come forth *f* your presence; *	601	1
f those who rise up against them.	601	13
F the wicked who assault me, *	601	16
f my deadly enemies who surround me.	601	17
deliver me *f* the wicked by your sword.	601	26
f those whose portion in life is this world;	601	28
and so shall I be saved *f* my enemies.	602	13
He heard my voice *f* his heavenly dwelling; *	602	20
Smoke rose *f* his nostrils	603	4
hot burning coals blazed forth *f* him.	603	6

F the brightness of his presence, through the clouds, * 603 13
He reached down f on high and grasped me; * 603 23
He delivered me f my strong enemies 603 25
and f those who hated me; * 603 26
and his decrees I have not put away f me; 604 8
and have kept myself f iniquity; 604 10
You deliver me f the strife of the peoples; * 605 26
You rescued me f the fury of my enemies; 606 7
you saved me f my deadly foe. 606 9
It goes forth f the uttermost edge of the heavens 607 1
nothing is hidden f its burning heat. 607 3
cleanse me f my secret faults. 607 23
Above all, keep your servant f presumptuous sins; 607 24
Send you help f his holy place * 608 3
You will destroy their offspring f the land * 609 18
and their descendants f among the peoples 609 19
and are so far f my cry 610 2
and f the words of my distress? 610 3
Be not far f me, for trouble is near, * 610 23
Save me f the sword, * 611 20
my life f the power of the dog. 611 21
Save me f the lion's mouth, * 611 22
my wretched body f the horns of wild bulls. 611 23
neither does he hide his face f them; * 612 2
They shall receive a blessing f the LORD * 613 23
and a just reward f the God of their salvation." 613 24
for they are f everlasting. 614 25
Hide not your face f me, * 618 14
You brought me up, O LORD, f the dead; * 621 8
rescue me f the hand of my enemies, 623 23
and f those who persecute me. 623 24
You hide them in the covert of your presence f those 624 8
you keep them in your shelter f the strife of tongues. 624 10
"I have been cut off f the sight of your eyes." * 624 15
you preserve me f trouble; * 625 15
and the designs of his heart f age to age. 626 22
The LORD looks down f heaven, * 627 1
F where he sits enthroned he turns his gaze * 627 3
To pluck their lives f death, * 627 13
and saved me f all my troubles. 628 6
Keep your tongue f evil-speaking * 628 19
and your lips f lying words. 628 20
Turn f evil and do good; * 628 21
to root out the remembrance of them f the earth. 628 26
and delivers them f all their troubles. 629 2
You deliver the poor f those who are too strong 630 11
the poor and needy f those who rob them." 630 12
rescue me f the roaring beasts, 631 2
and my life f the young lions. 631 3
O LORD, be not far f me. 631 15
you give them drink f the river of your delights. 632 21
Refrain f anger, leave rage alone; * 633 21
Turn f evil, and do good, * 635 14
the deliverance of the righteous comes f the LORD; * 636 15
he will rescue them f the wicked and deliver them, 636 18
and my sighing is not hidden f you. 637 15
and the brightness of my eyes is gone f me. 637 17
My friends and companions draw back f my affliction; * 637 18
and f whose mouth comes no defense. 637 26
be not far f me, O my God. 638 12
I refrained f rash words; 638 20
Deliver me f all my transgressions * 639 11
Take your affliction f me; * 639 15
Turn your gaze f me, that I may be glad again, * 639 25
your love and faithfulness f the great congregation. 640 28
do not withhold your compassion f me; * 641 2
f age to age. 642 27
therefore I will remember you f the land of Jordan, 643 19
and f the peak of Mizar among the heights of Hermon. 643 20
deliver me f the deceitful and the wicked. 644 16
why have you put me f you? * 644 18
nor did our footsteps stray f your path; 646 23
grace flows f your lips, 647 15
music of strings f ivory palaces makes you glad. 648 7
f one generation to another; * 648 26
their dwelling places f generation to generation, * 653 2
he will snatch me f the grasp of death. 653 14
he has called the earth f the rising of the sun to 654 2
He calls the heavens and the earth f above * 654 9
I will take no bull-calf f your stalls, * 654 21
Wash me through and through f my wickedness * 656 8
and cleanse me f my sin. 656 9
Indeed, I have been wicked f my birth, * 656 16
a sinner f my mother's womb. 656 17
Purge me f my sin, and I shall be pure; * 656 20
Hide your face f my sins * 656 24
Cast me not away f your presence * 657 3
and take not your holy Spirit f me. 657 4
Deliver me f death, O God, * 657 9
topple you, and snatch you f your dwelling, 658 9
God looks down f heaven upon us all, * 659 1
For you have rescued me f every trouble, * 660 3
do not hide yourself f my petition. 660 6
f the stormy wind and tempest." 660 22
then I could have hidden f him. 661 9
He will bring me safely back f the battle 661 22
For you have rescued my soul f death and my feet 663 16
and my feet f stumbling, * 663 17
He will send f heaven and save me; 663 25
The wicked are perverse f the womb; * 664 25
liars go astray f their birth. 664 26
Rescue me f my enemies, O God; * 665 18
protect me f those who rise up against me. 665 19
Rescue me f evildoers * 665 20
and save me f those who thirst for my blood. 665 21
to be a refuge f the power of the bow. 667 17
God spoke f his holy place and said: * 667 20
I call upon you f the ends of the earth 668 14
f him comes my salvation. 669 6
They seek only to bring me down f my place 669 12
protect my life f fear of the enemy. 671 11
Hide me f the conspiracy of the wicked, * 671 12
f the mob of evildoers. 671 13
That they may shoot down the blameless f ambush; * 671 16
nor withheld his love f me. 675 8
the Lord comes in holiness f Sinai. 677 17
you have received gifts even f your enemies, * 677 19
The LORD has said, "I will bring them back f Bashan; 678 1
I will bring them back f the depths of the sea; 678 2
my eyes have failed f looking for my God. 679 15
and my faults are not hidden f you. 679 21
Save me f the mire; do not let me sink; * 680 17

let me be rescued *f* those who hate me 680 18
"Hide not your face *f* your servant; * 680 25
Deliver me, my God, *f* the hand of the wicked, * 683 7
f the clutches of the evildoer and the oppressor. 683 8
f my mother's womb you have been my strength; * 683 12
O God, be not far *f* me; * 684 1
and bring me up again *f* the deep places of the earth. 684 25
f one generation to another. 685 18
He shall rule *f* sea to sea, * 685 24
and *f* the River to the ends of the earth. 685 25
He shall redeem their lives *f* oppression 686 11
and may there be given to him gold *f* Arabia; * 686 14
Their iniquity comes *f* gross minds, * 687 13
come to an end, and perish *f* terror! 688 16
Yet God is my King *f* ancient times, * 690 8
For judgment is neither *f* the east nor *f* the west, * 691 14
nor yet *f* the wilderness or the mountains. 691 15
F heaven you pronounced judgment; * 692 16
we will not hide *f* their children. 695 3
and gave them drink as *f* the great deep. 696 4
and gave them grain *f* heaven. 696 25
in the day when he ransomed them *f* the enemy; 698 12
he did not spare their souls *f* death; * 699 5
Then the LORD woke as though *f* sleep, * 700 9
and took him away *f* the sheepfolds. 700 20
He brought him *f* following the ewes, * 700 21
and show forth your praise *f* age to age. 702 11
Turn now, O God of hosts, look down *f* heaven; 703 15
And so will we never turn away *f* you; * 703 22
"I eased his shoulder *f* the burden; 704 12
his hands were set free *f* bearing the load." 704 13
I answered you *f* the secret place of thunder 704 15
and satisfy him with honey *f* the rock. 705 8
deliver them *f* the power of the wicked. 705 16
They have said, "Come, let us wipe them out *f* among 706 9
They will climb *f* height to height, * 708 4
f those who walk with integrity. 708 17
and turned yourself *f* your wrathful indignation. 708 25
let your anger depart *f* us. 709 2
will you prolong your anger *f* age to age? 709 4
Truth shall spring up *f* the earth, * 709 16
and righteousness shall look down *f* heaven. 709 17
you have delivered me *f* the nethermost Pit. 710 27
for they are cut off *f* your hand. 712 12
You have put my friends far *f* me; 712 17
why have you hidden your face *f* me? 713 7
My friend and my neighbor you have put away *f* me, 713 15
f age to age my mouth will proclaim your faithfulness. 713 18
f the Great Sea to the River. 715 17
But I will not take my love *f* him, * 716 7
who can save himself *f* the power of the grave? 717 11
f one generation to another. 717 21
f age to age you are God. 718 3
He shall deliver you *f* the snare of the hunter * 719 15
and *f* the deadly pestilence. 719 16
you are *f* everlasting. 722 8
proclaim the good news of his salvation *f* day to day. 725 20
and delivers them *f* the hand of the wicked. 727 19
and his faithfulness endures *f* age to age. 730 6
A crooked heart shall be far *f* me; * 730 15
may root out all evildoers *f* the city of the LORD. 730 27
hide not your face *f* me in the day of my trouble. 731 2
and your Name *f* age to age. 731 24
For the LORD looked down *f* his holy place on high; * 732 14
f the heavens he beheld the earth; 732 15
He redeems your life *f* the grave * 733 15
As far as the east is *f* the west, * 734 5
so far has he removed our sins *f* us. 734 6
All the beasts of the field drink their fill *f* them, * 735 23
You water the mountains *f* your dwelling on high; * 736 1
That they may bring forth food *f* the earth, * 736 5
and seek their food *f* God. 736 20
Wandering *f* nation to nation * 739 3
and *f* one kingdom to another, 739 4
and he satisfied them with bread *f* heaven. 741 6
He saved them *f* the hand of those who hated them * 742 18
and redeemed them *f* the hand of the enemy. 742 19
to turn away his wrath *f* consuming them. 743 19
and gather us *f* among the nations, * 745 20
f everlasting and to everlasting; * 745 24
that he redeemed them *f* the hand of the foe. 746 4
f the east and *f* the west, 746 6
f the north and *f* the south. 746 7
and he delivered them *f* their distress. 746 13
and he delivered them *f* their distress. 747 8
and he delivered them *f* their distress. 747 20
and saved them *f* the grave. 747 22
and he delivered them *f* their distress. 748 12
God spoke *f* his holy place and said, * 750 7
let them be driven *f* the ruins of their homes. 751 17
but let him root out their names *f* the earth; 751 28
let it depart *f* him. 752 7
the recompense *f* the LORD to my accusers, * 752 14
to save his life *f* those who would condemn him. 753 11
Princely state has been yours *f* the day of your birth; * 753 16
like dew *f* the womb of the morning." 753 18
He will drink *f* the brook beside the road; * 754 3
f this time forth for evermore. 756 5
F the rising of the sun to its going down * 756 6
and lifts up the poor *f* the ashes. 756 13
the house of Jacob *f* a people of strange speech, 756 20
f this time forth for evermore. 758 26
For you have rescued my life *f* death, * 759 16
my eyes *f* tears, and my feet *f* stumbling. 759 17
you have freed me *f* my bonds. 760 7
we bless you *f* the house of the LORD. 762 24
let me not stray *f* your commandments. 764 4
do not hide your commandments *f* me. 764 22
cursed are they who stray *f* your commandments! 765 2
Turn *f* me shame and rebuke, * 765 3
Take *f* me the way of lying; * 765 17
Turn my eyes *f* watching what is worthless; * 766 9
but I have not turned *f* your law. 767 16
My eyes have failed *f* watching for your promise, * 770 5
Your faithfulness remains *f* one generation 770 22
I restrain my feet *f* every evil way, * 771 21
I do not shrink *f* your judgments, * 771 23
but I have not strayed *f* your commandments. 772 14
Away *f* me, you wicked! * 773 3
You spurn all who stray *f* your statutes; * 773 9
My eyes have failed *f* watching for your salvation * 773 19
Rescue me *f* those who oppress me, * 774 15
they are very far *f* your law. 776 4

Long have I known *f* your decrees * 776 7
Deliverance is far *f* the wicked, * 776 13
yet I have not swerved *f* your decrees. 776 18
Deliver me, O LORD, *f* lying lips * 778 12
and *f* the deceitful tongue. 778 13
f where is my help to come? 779 2
My help comes *f* the LORD, * 779 3
The LORD shall preserve you *f* all evil; * 779 13
f this time forth for evermore. 779 17
We have escaped like a bird *f* the snare of the fowler; * 781 13
f this time forth for evermore. 781 21
Children are a heritage *f* the LORD, * 783 6
The LORD bless you *f* Zion, * 783 21
and he shall redeem Israel *f* all their sins. 785 9
f this time forth for evermore. 785 18
He brings up rain clouds *f* the ends of the earth; * 788 14
your renown, O LORD, endures *f* age to age. 789 2
And brought out Israel *f* among them, * 790 17
And delivered us *f* our enemies, * 791 17
he perceives the haughty *f* afar. 793 15
you discern my thoughts *f* afar. 794 3
Where can I go then *f* your Spirit? * 794 12
where can I flee *f* your presence? 794 13
My body was not hidden *f* you, * 795 3
You that thirst for blood, depart *f* me. 795 17
Deliver me, O LORD, *f* evildoers; * 796 1
protect me *f* the violent. 796 2
Keep me, O LORD, *f* the hands of the wicked; * 796 7
protect me *f* the violent, 796 8
Protect me *f* the snare which they have laid for me * 797 22
and *f* the traps of the evildoers. 797 23
save me *f* those who pursue me, 798 13
do not hide your face *f* me 799 13
Deliver me *f* my enemies, O LORD, * 799 19
Stretch out your hand *f* on high; * 800 14
rescue me and deliver me *f* the great waters, 800 15
f the hand of foreign peoples, 800 16
Rescue me *f* the hurtful sword * 800 23
and deliver me *f* the hand of foreign peoples, 800 24
sons be like plants well nurtured *f* their youth, * 801 1
Praise the LORD *f* the heavens; * 805 21
Praise the LORD *f* the earth, * 806 7
Lead them and us *f* prejudice to truth; 816 6
deliver them and us *f* hatred, 816 7
f whom cometh every good and perfect gift: 817 3
hinder us *f* godly union and concord; 818 18
Save us *f* violence, discord, and confusion; 820 5
f pride and arrogance, and *f* every evil way. 820 6
f speaking in hate; 823 11
save them *f* bitterness; 823 12
want and anxiety *f* lack of work. 824 12
women *f* different cultures and with differing talents 825 13
honor the land and the water *f* which these good things come. 825 23
and save them *f* becoming brutal 826 23
that no one may suffer *f* our abuse of them, 827 20
save us *f* selfish use of what thou givest, 828 6
Put far *f* them, we beseech thee, every root 828 24
and bless those whom we love, now absent *f* us. 830 21
Defend them *f* all dangers of soul and body; 830 22
protect them *f* every danger; 831 4
remove *f* them the fears that beset them; 831 21
save us *f* all false choices, 832 10
f coldness of heart and wanderings of mind, 833 21
first-born of many *f* the dead. 838 20
It has drawn people *f* every nation, 839 9
have often hidden *f* its light. 839 10
show us your presence in those who differ most *f* us, 840 4
deliver *f* his sickness thy servant 841 9
Why then do we live apart *f* God 845 8
F the beginning, human beings have misused their freedom 845 10
learn about God as creator *f* the revelation to Israel? 846 1
What response did God require *f* the chosen people? 847 3
What do we learn *f* these commandments? 847 16
sets us free *f* the power of evil, 849 5
sent by God to free us *f* the power of sin, 849 12
incarnate *f* the Virgin Mary? 849 27
our human nature *f* the Virgin Mary, his mother. 849 29
are freed *f* the power of sin and reconciled to God. 850 9
God's Being draws praise *f* us. 857 6
How do they differ *f* the two sacraments 860 12
and receive strength *f* the Holy Spirit 860 19
We mean that God will raise us *f* death 862 17
shall separate us *f* the love of God 862 31

frost

O ye *f* and cold, bless ye the Lord; 48 10
F and cold, ice and sleet, glorify the Lord, * 88 19
and their sycamores with *f*. 698 22

frosts

O ye dews and *f*, bless ye the Lord; * 48 9

fruit

and bring forth in us the *f* of good works: 181 14
perceive within ourselves the *f* of his redemption; 201 5
bring forth in us the *f* of good works; 233 6
perceive within ourselves the *f* of his redemption; 252 9
bring forth abundant *f* in your glorious kingdom; 290 11
the *f* of lips that acknowledge his Name. 344 2
the *f* of lips that acknowledge his Name. 376 18
As the branch cannot bear *f* by itself, 397 8
that you bear much *f*, 397 11
bearing *f* in due season, 585 8
Before they bear *f*, let them be cut down 665 11
may its *f* flourish like Lebanon, 686 19
the *f* of their toil to the locust. 698 20
They shall still bear *f* in old age; * 721 25
the earth is fully satisfied by the *f* of your works. 736 2
and devoured the *f* of their soil. 740 24
and they took the *f* of others' toil. 741 14
and the *f* of the womb is a gift. 783 7
You shall eat the *f* of your labor; * 783 15
"A son, the *f* of your body * 786 21
f trees and all cedars; 806 12
that peace which is the *f* of righteousness, 816 3
that we may ever perceive within ourselves the *f* 834 15
bring forth in us the *f* of good living, 834 21

fruitful

The LORD made his people exceedingly *f*; * 740 1
A *f* land into salt flats, * 748 23

and brought in a *f* harvest. 749 4
Your wife shall be like a *f* vine 783 17
Almighty God, we thank you for making the earth *f*, 824 6

fruits

and become the first *f* of them that slept. 46 14
the first *f* of those who have fallen asleep. 83 22
to hear and receive thy Word, and to bring forth the *f* 150 16
the bountiful *f* of the earth, 151 10
for the *f* of the earth in their season 194 17
receive thankfully the *f* of his redeeming work, 232 13
for the *f* of the earth in their season 246 2
and for an abundance of the *f* 384 11
we may all share the *f* of the earth, 824 9
that we may receive the *f* of the earth, 828 13
increase of the ground and the gathering in of its *f*, 840 17

frustrate

and by thy great might *f* the designs of evil 186 16
your great might *f* the designs of evil tyrants 238 10

frustrates

but *f* the way of the wicked. 803 23

frustration

Our anger at our own *f*, and our envy 268 7

fulfill

F now, O Lord, the desires and petitions 59 16
F now, O Lord, the desires and petitions 72 13
F now, O Lord, our desires and petitions 102 5
I have applied my heart to *f* your statutes * 104 11
F now, O Lord, our desires and petitions 126 5
may have grace and power faithfully to *f* the same; 179 13
may *f* all the mind of him who loved it 204 13
may *f* all the mind of him who loved it 255 11
f your Law, to open for us the way of freedom 370 20
f your purpose he gave himself up to death; 374 6
Accept and *f* our petitions, 394 5
promise, with the help of God, to *f* the obligations 433 3
I will *f* my vows to the LORD* 442 23
Will you accept this call and *f* this trust 518 1
That he may faithfully *f* the duties of this ministry, 549 4
and day by day I will *f* my vows. 669 4
I will *f* my vows to the LORD * 760 1
I will *f* my vows to the LORD * 760 10
F your promise to your servant, * 766 11
I have applied my heart to *f* your statutes * 772 17
f our obligations in the community of nations. 822 4
and our nation be enabled to *f* your purposes; 822 27
and more surely *f* our role 827 15
and blessing of God to help them *f* their vows. 861 7

fulfilled

that your Church may rejoice to see *f* your promise 289 8
that your will for them may be *f*; 389 9
and I have *f* your commandments. 777 12

fulfilling

and in all we do, direct us to the *f* of your purpose; 100 4
and in all we do, direct us to the *f* of your purpose; 137 17
For the *f* of our desires and petitions 578 21
all may find suitable and *f* employment, 824 14

fulfillment

and to bring to *f* the sanctification of all. 374 12
In *f* of his true promise, 380 1
Give them such *f* of their mutual affection 429 23
f and bliss in your eternal and everlasting glory; 503 18
find with one another the *f* of their humanity; 825 14
f in loving you and their neighbors; 829 25
and anticipate its future *f*. 861 23

fulfills

He *f* the desire of those who fear him; * 802 25

full

The Lord is *f* of compassion and mercy: 43 6
Heaven and earth are *f* of the majesty of thy glory. 53 2
The Lord is *f* of compassion and mercy: 81 2
O Lord, you are *f* of compassion, * 91 5
heaven and earth are *f* of your glory. 95 22
in *f* assurance of the glory that shall be revealed; 169 3
into the *f* stature of Christ? 302 5
Almighty God, with *f* purpose of amendment of life, 317 5
Heaven and earth are *f* of thy glory. 334 5
a *f*, perfect, and sufficient sacrifice, 334 12
Heaven and earth are *f* of thy glory. 341 8
He made there a *f* and perfect sacrifice 341 16
heaven and earth are *f* of your glory. 362 5
heaven and earth are *f* of your glory. 367 14
heaven and earth are *f* of your glory. 371 2
heaven and earth are *f* of your glory. 373 13
heaven and earth are *f* of your glory. 402 10
heaven and earth are *f* of your glory. 404 12
our God is *f* of compassion. 442 18
Why art thou so *f* of heaviness, O my soul? * 471 12
and my cup shall be *f*. 476 15
Their mouth is *f* of cursing, deceit, and oppression; * 595 6
Whose hands are *f* of evil plots, * 617 1
and their right hand *f* of bribes. 617 2
in the *f* assembly I will bless the LORD. 617 6
but repays to the *f* those who act haughtily. 624 20
my soul is *f* of despair. 630 16
flourishing like a tree in *f* leaf. 636 7
Why are you so *f* of heaviness, O my soul? * 643 13
Why are you so *f* of heaviness, O my soul? * 644 9
Why are you so *f* of heaviness, O my soul? * 645 1
your right hand is *f* of justice. 651 22
the river of God is *f* of water. 673 6
Let my mouth be *f* of your praise * 683 16
f of spiced and foaming wine, which he pours out, * 691 19
When the LORD heard this, he was *f* of wrath; * 696 17
He gave *f* rein to his anger; 699 4
and at the *f* moon, the day of our feast. 704 6
But you, O LORD, are gracious and *f* of compassion, * 711 4
slow to anger, and *f* of kindness and truth. 711 5
For I am *f* of trouble; * 712 5
all evildoers are *f* of boasting. 723 2
The LORD is *f* of compassion and mercy, * 733 23
The trees of the LORD are *f* of sap, * 736 9
the earth is *f* of your creatures. 736 27
His work is *f* of majesty and splendor, * 754 10
the LORD is gracious and *f* of compassion. 754 13
the righteous are merciful and *f* of compassion. 755 12
our God is *f* of compassion. 759 11

The earth, O LORD, is *f* of your love; * 768 15
Happy is the man who has his quiver *f* of them! * 783 10
The LORD is gracious and *f* of compassion, * 802 1
that he may attain to that *f* stature 841 4

fullness
attain to the *f* of life everlasting; 186 10
into the stature of the *f* of our Lord 197 1
Grant us the *f* of your grace, 234 7
at length we may attain to the *f* of eternal life; 238 4
into the stature of the *f* of our Lord 248 12
into the *f* of the joy of our Lord, 280 12
will bring each of us to the *f* of redemption. 288 3
Bring them to the *f* of your peace and glory. 306 3
be filled with all the *f* of God. 311 25
they may come to the *f* of grace 346 11
In the *f* of time, 369 8
And in the *f* of time you sent your only Son, 370 19
in the *f* of time you sent your only Son 374 1
they may come to the *f* of grace 379 8
nor crying, but the *f* of joy with all thy saints; 482 7
in thy presence is the *f* of joy, 485 7
nor crying, but the *f* of joy with all your saints; 498 18
in your presence there is *f* of joy, 501 9
and share in the *f* of your life-giving Spirit; 552 10
Be with us in the *f* of your power as new members 569 5
in your presence there is *f* of joy, 600 20
and give us life in all its *f*. 851 3
to live with confidence in newness and *f* of life, 861 26
raise us from death in the *f* of our being, 862 18

fully
the earth is *f* satisfied by the fruit of your works. 736 2
that we should *f* keep them. 763 12
Since we do not *f* obey them, are they useful at all? 848 25
Since we do not *f* obey them, we see more clearly 848 26
in the joy of *f* knowing and loving God 862 27

furnace
You will make them like a fiery *f* * 609 14

furnished
and *f* it for the celebration of your holy mysteries. 573 3

furrows
You drench the *f* and smooth out the ridges; * 673 9
and made their *f* long. 784 6
As when a plowman turns over the earth in *f*, * 797 17

further
and *f* us with thy continual help; 832 2

fury
rise up against the *f* of my enemies. 591 7
You rescued me from the *f* of my enemies; 606 7
and are set against me in *f*. 660 12
f, indignation, and distress, 699 2
will your *f* blaze like fire for ever? 701 14
You have withdrawn all your *f* * 708 24
stretch forth your hand against the *f* of my enemies; 793 17

future
for there is a *f* for the peaceable. 636 12
the *f* of the wicked is cut off. 636 14
Let this be written for a *f* generation, * 732 12
and bring them hope for their *f*. 826 20
provision for its *f* in accordance with your will; 828 20
and anticipate its *f* fulfillment. 861 23

G

gain
He does not give his money in hope of *g*, * 599 15
and not to unjust *g*. 766 8
Through your commandments I *g* understanding; * 772 1

gains
let strangers plunder his *g*. 751 19

galaxies
g, suns, the planets in their courses, 370 9
all its marvelous order, its atoms, worlds, and *g*, 827 12

Galilee
first miracle at a wedding in Cana of *G*. 423 6

gall
They gave me *g* to eat, * 681 6

gallantly
And if I am to do nothing, let me do it *g*. 461 23

gangs
and *g* of evildoers circle around me; * 611 12

garden
in the *g*: 487 6
Son was laid in a sepulcher in the *g*: 503 8

garment
baptism you clothed me with the shining *g* 450 11
in his heavenly wedding *g*. 465 18
they all shall wear out like a *g*t; * 733 2
He put on cursing like a *g*, * 752 8

garments
Rend your heart, and not your *g*, 38 14
Rend your hearts and not your *g*. 76 13
spread their *g* and branches of palm along his way. 271 9
they divide my *g* among them; 611 16
All your *g* are fragrant with myrrh, 648 6

gasps
my soul *g* to you like a thirsty land. 799 11

gat
and the pains of hell *g* hold upon me. 479 4

gate
Christ hast overcome death and opened unto us the *g* 170 22
Christ overcame death and opened to us the *g* 222 16
that through the grave and *g* of death we may pass 480 10
Give us faith to see in death the *g* 493 20
O you who lift me up from the *g* of death; 594 3
Those who sit at the *g* murmur against me, * 680 11
"This is the *g* of the LORD; * 762 11
when he contends with his enemies in the *g*. 783 12

gates
O go your way into his *g* with thanksgiving 45 17
Enter his *g* with thanksgiving; 83 4

Your *g* will always be open; * 87 19
having opened to him the *g* of larger life, 202 10
having opened to him the *g* of larger life, 253 14
in the *g* of the city of Zion. 594 6
Lift up your heads, O *g*; 614 1
Lift up your heads, O *g*; 614 7
in the *g* of the city of Zion. 689 8
the LORD loves the *g* of Zion 711 13
Enter his *g* with thanksgiving; 730 1
Open for me the *g* of righteousness; * 762 8
within your *g*, O Jerusalem. 779 21
For he has strengthened the bars of your *g*; * 805 3

gather

prosper all who labor to *g* them, 207 18
prosper all who labor to *g* them, 258 18
to *g* in vigil and prayer. 285 3
We are not worthy so much as to *g* 337 11
G us by this Holy Communion into one body 403 17
Good Shepherd of the sheep, you *g* the lambs 459 1
let the assembly of the peoples *g* round you. 591 9
we heap up riches and cannot tell who will *g* them. 639 8
"*G* before me my loyal followers, * 654 11
how the mighty *g* together against me; * 665 23
You give it to them; they *g* it; * 737 9
and *g* us from among the nations, * 745 20
the righteous will *g* around me. 798 17

gathered

g together in his Name 59 15
g together in his Name 72 12
g together in his Name 102 4
g together in his Name 126 4
that thy Church, being *g* together in unity 181 6
that your Church, being *g* together in unity 232 17
we may be *g* unto our fathers, 489 8
we may be *g* to our ancestors, 504 6
g and prepared a people to be heirs of the covenant 520 15
we are now *g* to dedicate and consecrate 567 5
g together in your Name, 578 10
But when I stumbled, they were glad and *g* together; 630 23
they *g* against me; * 630 24
The nobles of the peoples have *g* together * 650 22
When the peoples are *g* together, * 732 20
He *g* them out of the lands; * 746 5
all peoples may be *g* under the banner 815 25
a community of love has been *g* together 838 5

gathering

for this *g*; and for all ministers and people. 385 18
increase of the ground and the *g* in of its fruits, 840 17

gathers

He *g* up the waters of the ocean as in a water-skin * 626 13
he *g* the exiles of Israel. 804 5

gaunt

and my flesh is wasted and *g*. 752 24

gave

and *g* us the ministry of reconciliation. 106 3
our Savior *g* his back to the smiters 169 1
g generously of his life and substance for the relief 189 19
him who loved it and *g* himself for it, 204 14
Father, you *g* to your incarnate Son the holy name 213 13
our Savior *g* his body to be whipped 220 14
who for our redemption *g* your only-begotten Son 222 1
Father, who *g* your only Son to die for our sins 224 1
God, who *g* such grace to your apostle Andrew 237 1
God, who *g* to your apostles Philip and James grace 240 13
g generously of his life and substance for the relief 241 5
God, who *g* to your apostle Bartholomew grace 243 14
God, who *g* to your servant N. boldness 246 8
God, you *g* to your servant N. special gifts 249 5
him who loved it and *g* himself for it, 255 12
that to redeem a slave, you *g* a Son. 287 16
who for our redemption *g* your only- begotten Son 295 1
that he *g* his only-begotten Son, 332 10
he brake it, and *g* it to his disciples, 334 18
and when he had given thanks, he *g* it to them, 335 4
he broke it, and *g* it to his disciples, 342 2
and when he had given thanks, he *g* it to them, 342 6
as Christ loved us and *g* himself for us, 343 12
who loveth her and *g* himself for her, 349 4
he broke it, and *g* it to his disciples, 362 20
and when he had given thanks, he *g* it to them, 363 2
g it to his disciples, 368 12
and when he had given thanks, he *g* it to them, 368 15
broke the bread, and *g* it to his friends, 371 11
After supper, he took the cup of wine, *g* thanks, 371 14
To fulfill your purpose he *g* himself up to death; 374 6
g it to his disciples, 374 17
and when he had given thanks, he *g* it to them, 374 20
as Christ loved us and *g* himself for us, 376 8
Because you *g* Jesus Christ, your only Son, to be born 378 9
who loves her and *g* himself for her, 381 19
God so loved the world that he *g* his only Son, 396 1
broke the bread, and *g* it to his friends, 403 5
After supper, he took the cup of wine, *g* thanks, 403 8
he broke it, and *g* it to his disciples, 405 3
and when he had given thanks, he *g* it to them, 405 7
and for which your Son *g* his life, 429 4
that he *g* his only-begotten Son, 449 15
g us the example of obedience to your Father's will: 461 6
He is the God who *g* me victory * 606 5
He asked you for life, and you *g* it to him: * 609 3
Surely, you *g* us victory over our adversaries * 645 25
The Lord *g* the word; * 677 1
They *g* me gall to eat, * 681 6
and when I was thirsty, they *g* me vinegar to drink. 681 7
and *g* him to the people of the desert for food. 690 13
He *g* his decrees to Jacob 695 7
and *g* them drink as from the great deep. 696 4
and *g* them grain from heaven. 696 25
for he *g* them what they craved. 697 8
He *g* their crops to the caterpillar, * 698 19
He *g* full rein to his anger; 699 4
He *g* his people to the sword * 700 3
So I *g* them over to the stubbornness of their hearts, * 704 26
kept his testimonies and the decree that he *g* them. 729 15
He *g* them hailstones instead of rain, * 740 17
He *g* his people the lands of the nations, * 741 13
He *g* them what they asked, * 743 1
He *g* them over to the hand of the heathen, * 745 6
He *g* their land to be an inheritance, * 788 26
And *g* away their lands for an inheritance, * 791 11

he *g* them a law which shall not pass away. 806 6
and *g* us the hope of everlasting life: 835 3
as you *g* to them, the hope of salvation 838 18
and *g* us the New Commandment. 851 8
Our Lord *g* us the example of prayer 856 24

gaze

May he *g* upon you, Lord, face to face, and taste the 466 1
From where he sits enthroned he turns his *g* * 627 3
Turn your *g* from me, that I may be glad again, * 639 25

gazed

Therefore I have *g* upon you in your holy place, * 670 15

Gebal

G, and Ammon, and Amalek; * 706 16

general

that at the day of the *g* resurrection, 487 17

generation

and his truth endureth from *g* to *g*. 45 22
Glory to him from *g* to *g* 60 5
Glory to him from *g* to *g* 73 5
who fear him * in every *g*. 92 5
Glory to him from *g* to *g* 102 16
of the world in every *g*: 111 13
who fear him * in every *g*. 119 11
Glory to him from *g* to *g* 126 16
Forty years long was I grieved with this *g*, 146 21
that we also in our *g* may show forth thy praise, 196 17
they may worship thee and serve thee from *g* to *g*; 209 20
that we also in our *g* may show forth your praise, 248 3
they may worship you and serve you from *g* to *g*; 261 4
those in every *g* who have looked to you in hope, 370 25
and worship, from *g* to *g*. 372 13
Praise God for those in every *g* in whom Christ 386 14
who fear him * in every *g*. 441 19
our refuge, * from one *g* to another. 472 10
when we shall have served thee in our *g*, 489 7
when we shall have served you in our *g*, 504 5
every *g* who have looked to God in hope. 517 16
and save us from this *g* for ever. 597 17
Such is the *g* of those who seek him, * 613 25
be remembered from one *g* to another; * 648 26
their dwelling places from *g* to *g*, * 653 2
till I make known your strength to this *g* 684 18
moon endure, * from one *g* to another. 685 18
I should have betrayed the *g* of your children. 688 8
a stubborn and rebellious *g*, * 695 17
a *g* whose heart was not steadfast, 695 18
our refuge * from one *g* to another. 717 21
Forty years long I detested that *g* and said, * 725 12
Let this be written for a future *g*, * 732 12
and his name be blotted out in the next *g*. 751 23
the *g* of the upright will be blessed. 755 8
Your faithfulness remains from one *g* to another; * 770 22
One *g* shall praise your works to another * 801 18
that we may serve you faithfully in our *g* 822 14

generations

all *g* shall call me blessed. 50 6
that fear him * throughout all *g*. 50 10
all *g* shall call me blessed. 65 9
that fear him * throughout all *g*. 65 13
From this day all *g* will call me blessed: * 92 1
From this day all *g* will call me blessed: * 119 7
and the lights of the world in their *g*. 348 3
and the lights of the world in their *g*. 380 19
From this day all *g* will call me blessed:* 441 15
a thousand *g* of those who love and fear you: 444 16
and the lights of the world in their several *g*; 487 14
let his years extend over many *g*. 668 25
We will recount to *g* to come 695 4
That the *g* to come might know, 695 10
and preserve your throne for all *g*.'" 714 2
your years endure throughout all *g*. 732 26
the promise he made for a thousand *g*: 738 16
throughout all *g* for ever. 744 10
your God, O Zion, throughout all *g*. 803 25
and that *g* yet to come may continue to praise you 827 20

generous

but the righteous are *g* in giving. 635 2
The righteous are always *g* in their lending, * 635 12
It is good for them to be *g* in lending * 755 13

generously

gave *g* of his life and substance for the relief 189 19
gave *g* of his life and substance for the relief 241 5

Gentiles

The *G* shall come to thy light, 38 1
I will give thee for a light to the *G*, 38 3
my Name shall be great among the *G*, 38 6
To be a light to lighten the *G*, * 51 27
To be a light to lighten the *G*, * 66 5
Paul to be an apostle to the *G*: 107 13

gentle

for I am *g* and lowly in heart, 131 17
offering of a pure, and *g*, 521 15

get

let them not *g* dominion over me; * 607 25
he has taken to his bed and will never *g* up again." 642 16
I am in prison and cannot *g* free. 712 19

Ghost

after that the Holy *G* is come upon you; 39 18
Father, Son, and Holy *G*, one God: 43 14
with the Holy *G*, art most high 52 21
also the Holy *G* the Comforter. 53 10
who was conceived by the Holy *G*, 53 26
I believe in the Holy *G*, 54 5
to whom, with thee and the Holy *G*, 59 10
the fellowship of the Holy *G*, be with us all evermore. 59 23
who was conceived by the Holy *G*, 66 12
I believe in the Holy *G*, 66 21
to whom, with thee and the Holy *G*, 72 7
the fellowship of the Holy *G*, be with us all evermore. 72 20
to the Son, * and to the Holy *G*: 141 6
O God the Holy *G*, Sanctifier of the faithful, 148 5
and by the Coming of the Holy *G*, 149 24
the fellowship of the Holy *G*, be with us all evermore. 154 2
to the Son, and to the Holy *G*; 154 11
who liveth and reigneth with thee and the Holy *G*, 159 7
with thee and the Holy *G*, be honor and glory, 160 5

who liveth and reigneth with thee and the Holy *G*, 160 16
Send thy Holy *G* and pour into our hearts 164 19
and the same Holy *G*, one God, now and for ever. 165 5
and the Holy *G* ever, one God, world without end. 169 18
and the Holy *G*, one God, world without end. 174 19
but send to us thine Holy *G* to comfort us, 175 4
and the same Holy *G*, one God, world without end. 175 6
where with thee, O Father, and thee, O Holy *G*, 184 13
who with thee, O Father, and thee, O Holy *G*, 191 20
with the Holy *G*, art most high 325 8
and was incarnate by the Holy *G* of the Virgin Mary, 328 3
And I believe in the Holy *G* the Lord, 328 13
and with whom, in the unity of the Holy *G* 336 13
Holy *G*, be all honor and glory, world without end. 339 14
God Almighty, the Father, the Son, and the Holy *G*, 339 18
Holy *G* all honor and glory be unto thee, 343 4
who, by the mighty power of the Holy *G*, 345 15
to whose true promise the Holy *G* came down 347 7
to the Son, * and to the Holy *G*: 406 2
with thee and the Holy *G* be all glory and honor, 840 23

Gideon

for Miriam and Joshua, Deborah and *G*, 838 12

gift

into our hearts that most excellent *g* of charity, 165 1
by the promised *g* of thy Holy Spirit: 175 9
Shed abroad this *g* throughout the world 175 10
merciful God, of whose only *g* it cometh 184 1
your greatest *g*, which is love, 216 15
by the promised *g* of your Holy Spirit: 227 2
Shed abroad this *g* throughout the world 227 3
it is only by your *g* that your faithful people offer 235 14
by your gracious *g* that we are given everlasting life; 265 19
Peace is my last *g* to you, 275 1
We thank you, Almighty God, for the *g* of water. 306 13
and the *g* of joy and wonder in all your works. 308 7
If thou bring thy *g* to the altar, 343 17
thy brother hath aught against thee, leave there thy *g* 343 18
and then come and offer thy *g*. 343 20
Spirit, his own first *g* for those who believe, 374 11
If you are offering your *g* at the altar, 376 13
that your brother has something against you, leave your *g* 376 14
reconciled to your brother, and then come and offer your *g*. 376 16
the *g* and heritage of children, 429 20
for the *g* of N. to be their son (daughter) 440 5
for the *g* of a child. 440 10
the *g* of a child, 441 10
Grant me this *g*, I pray; 461 13
We thank you, Almighty God, for the *g* of water. 570 5
The people of Tyre are here with a *g*; * 648 15
and the fruit of the womb is a *g*. 783 7
God, from whom cometh every good and perfect *g*: 817 4
Almighty God, giver of every good *g*: 818 8
Grant us the *g* of your Spirit, that we may know him 836 17

gifts

Give abundantly to all pastors the *g* of thy Holy Spirit, 197 6
We praise thy Name for the *g* of grace 197 14
may never be destitute of such *g*; 197 16
g of grace to understand and teach the truth as it is in 197 20
Almighty God, the giver of all good *g*, 205 4
increase in us the *g* of faith, hope, and charity; 235 9
Give abundantly to all pastors the *g* of your Holy Spirit, 248 17
We praise your Name for the *g* of grace 248 24
may never be destitute of such *g*; 249 2
Almighty God, you gave to your servant N. special *g* 249 5
Almighty God, the giver of all good *g*, 256 1
may be faithful stewards of your good *g*; 259 15
with these thy holy *g*, which we now offer unto thee, 335 11
these thy *g* and creatures of bread and wine; 335 19
The *g* of God for the People of God. 338 1
with these thy holy *g* which we now offer unto thee, 342 11
sanctify these *g* of bread and wine, 342 18
and ascension, we offer you these *g*. 363 12
The *g* of God for the People of God. 364 17
send your Holy Spirit upon these *g* 369 5
now bring before you these *g*. 371 8
the *g* you have given us, this bread and this cup, 374 28
Spirit may descend upon us, and upon these *g*, 375 5
and showing them to be holy *g* for your holy people, 375 6
The *g* of God for the People of God. 399 1
And so, Father, we bring you these *g*. 403 1
Send your Holy Spirit upon these *g*. 405 15
restore to him your *g* of gladness and strength, 459 4
your healing *g* through the skill of surgeons 459 14
support all baptized people in their *g* 518 13
offering the holy *g*, and wisely overseeing the life 521 13
having ascended into heaven, has poured his *g* 533 6
offering to you their *g* and talents; 560 9
We give you thanks, O God, for the *g* of your people, 573 1
you have received *g* even from your enemies, * 677 19
Kings shall bring *g* to you, * 678 16
and the kings of Arabia and Saba offer *g*. 686 4
let all around him bring *g* to him who is worthy 692 23
Bless, O Lord, thy *g* to our use and us to thy service; 835 11
Let us give thanks to God our Father for all his *g* 837 1
We praise you for these good *g*, 840 10
to rejoice in other people's *g* 848 19
according to the *g* given them, to carry on Christ's 855 17

Gilead

G is mine and Manasseh is mine; * 667 23
G is mine and Manasseh is mine; * 750 10

girded

You have *g* me with strength for the battle; * 605 18
they are *g* about with might. 672 22
and *g* himself with strength. 722 4

girds

It is God who *g* me about with strength * 605 3

give

I will *g* thee for a light to the Gentiles, 38 3
We *g* thanks unto the Father, 40 1
O *g* thanks unto the Lord, and call upon his Name; 40 7
sware to our forefather Abraham, * that he would *g* 51 6
To *g* knowledge of salvation unto his people * 51 14
To *g* light to them that sit in darkness 51 18
we *g* thanks to thee for thy great glory, 52 8
G us this day our daily bread. 54 19

G peace, O Lord, in all the world; 55 5
when the night cometh, rejoice to *g* thee thanks; 56 23
do *g* thee most humble and hearty thanks 58 16
g us that due sense of all thy mercies, 59 2
G us this day our daily bread. 67 9
G peace, O Lord, in all the world; 67 20
worship on the morrow may *g* thee glory; 69 15
G unto thy servants that peace 69 17
that peace which the world cannot *g*, 69 18
and *g* thine angels charge over those who sleep. 71 2
Tend the sick, Lord Christ; *g* rest to the weary, 71 3
do *g* thee most humble and hearty thanks 71 12
g us that due sense of all thy mercies, 71 21
I will *g* you as a light to the nations, 76 3
We *g* thanks to the Father, who has made us worthy 77 22
G thanks to the Lord, and call upon his Name; 78 6
g thanks to him and call upon his Name. 83 6
G thanks to the Lord and call upon his Name; 86 8
To *g* his people knowledge of salvation * 93 3
we worship you, we *g* you thanks, 95 1
G us this day our daily bread. 97 9
G peace, O Lord, in all the world; 97 22
G us this day such blessing 98 20
when night comes, rejoice to *g* you thanks; 99 18
we your unworthy servants *g* you humble thanks 101 8
And, we pray, *g* us such an awareness of your mercies, 101 16
G us this day our daily bread. 106 19
"Peace I *g* to you; 107 17
and *g* to us the peace and unity of that heavenly City, 107 19
g glory to your Father in heaven." 109 12
to *g* the light of revelation — 110 4
Almighty God, we *g* you thanks for surrounding us, 110 12
G us grace to behold you, present in your Word 113 11
and *g* you peace. 114 5
G us this day our daily bread. 121 9
G peace, O Lord, in all the world; 121 22
and our worship on the morrow *g* you glory; 123 13
G to us, your servants, that peace 123 16
that peace which the world cannot *g*, 123 17
and *g* your angels charge over those who sleep. 124 18
Tend the sick, Lord Christ; *g* rest to the weary, 124 19
we your unworthy servants *g* you humble thanks 125 6
And, we pray, *g* us such an awareness of your mercies, 125 14
For he shall *g* his angels charge over you, * 130 19
and I will *g* you rest. 131 16
G us this day our daily bread. 133 1
We *g* you thanks, O God, for revealing your Son 134 1
and *g* your angels charge over those who sleep. 134 7
Tend the sick, Lord Christ; *g* rest to the weary, 134 8
G me the joy of your saving help again * 137 7
G praise, you servants of the Lord; * 138 1
"Peace I *g* to you; 138 16
and *g* to us the peace and unity of that heavenly City, 138 18
to *g* the light of revelation— 139 13
That it may please thee to *g* to all people increase 150 15
That it may please thee to *g* us a heart to love 150 22
to *g* to all nations unity, peace, and concord; 151 2
That it may please thee to *g* and preserve 151 9
G us this day our daily bread. 153 11
Almighty God, *g* us grace that we may cast 159 1
G us grace to heed their warnings 159 11
Eternal Father, who didst *g* to thine incarnate Son 162 1
G us grace, O Lord, to answer readily the call 163 14
and *g* us, we beseech thee, the liberty 164 6
O most loving Father, who willest us to *g* thanks 165 6
Evermore *g* us this bread, that he may live in us, 167 12
didst *g* thine only-begotten Son 170 7
Mercifully *g* us faith to perceive that, 174 10
and to *g* us those things which are profitable for us; 177 16
mercifully *g* us for the worthiness of thy Son 179 20
G us grace that we may always most thankfully
receive 180 21
and art wont to *g* more than either 182 19
Almighty and everlasting God, *g* unto us the increase 183 17
didst *g* such grace to thine apostle Andrew 185 7
G unto us, who are called by thy Word, 185 9
We *g* thee thanks, O Lord of glory, 186 1
G us grace to imitate his uprightness of life 188 10
didst *g* to thine apostles Philip and James grace 189 5
who didst *g* to thine apostle Bartholomew grace 192 7
thy Church may *g* itself continually to prayer 193 20
Almighty and gracious Father, we *g* thee thanks 194 16
O Almighty God, who didst *g* to thy servant N. 195 1
may always be ready to *g* a reason for the hope 195 4
Shepherd of thy people, we *g* thee thanks 196 22
G abundantly to all pastors the gifts 197 6
who by thy Holy Spirit dost *g* to some the word 197 12
who didst *g* to thy servant N. special gifts of grace 197 19
G us grace to continue steadfast 199 14
G us courage, we beseech thee, to take up our cross 201 8
G, we beseech thee, to thy whole Church 202 1
We *g* thee thanks for the fellowship 204 2
G thy grace, we humbly beseech thee, to all 205 6
that thy gracious providence may *g* and preserve 207 16
good things from thy hand, may always *g* thee
thanks; 207 19
and *g* to us all a pride in what we do, 208 5
remembering the account that we must one day *g*, 208 12
and *g* thy power of healing to those who minister 208 17
g themselves to the service of others; 209 11
Almighty God, *g* us grace to cast away the works 211 1
G us grace to heed their warnings 211 11
G us grace, O Lord, to answer readily the call 215 7
and *g* us the liberty of that abundant life 216 1
g us the help of your grace, 216 8
Most loving Father, whose will it is for us to *g* thanks 216 20
Evermore *g* us this bread, that he may live in us, 219 3
G us grace to accept joyfully the sufferings 220 15
G us grace so to put away the leaven of malice 224 2
Mercifully *g* us faith to perceive that, 226 3
and *g* us those things which are profitable 229 12
and mercifully *g* us those things 231 12
G us grace to receive thankfully 232 12
and to *g* more than we either desire or deserve: 234 13
G us, who are called by your holy Word, 237 3
We *g* you thanks, O Lord of glory, for the example 237 14
G us grace to imitate his uprightness of life 239 19
your Church may *g* itself 245 5
G us grace so to follow your blessed saints 245 18
Almighty and gracious Father, we *g* you thanks 246 1
may always be ready to *g* a reason for the hope 247 2
G abundantly to all pastors the gifts 248 17
O God, by your Holy Spirit you *g* to some the word 248 22
G us grace to continue steadfast 251 3

G us courage to take up our cross and follow him; 252 13
G to your whole Church in paradise 253 6
We *g* you thanks for the fellowship 254 20
G your grace, we humbly pray, to all 256 3
G to the people of our country a zeal for justice 258 3
your gracious providence may *g* and preserve 258 16
may always *g* you thanks; 258 19
and *g* to us all a pride in what we do, 259 6
remembering the account that we must one day *g*, 259 14
and *g* your power of healing to those who minister 260 2
g themselves to the service of others; 260 16
that we may do the work you *g* us to do 261 10
G me the joy of your saving help again * 266 26
Let us *g* thanks to the Lord our God. 271 3
It is right to *g* him thanks and praise. 271 4
peace which the world cannot *g*, I *g* to you. 275 2
I *g* you a new commandment: 275 3
peace which the world cannot *g*, I *g* to you. 275 6
and *g* us, we pray, the strength to serve 279 17
G mercy and grace to the living; 282 8
Let us *g* thanks to the Lord our God. 286 19
It is right to *g* him thanks and praise. 286 20
G now the water of life to those who thirst for you, 290 9
Let us *g* thanks to the Lord our God. 306 11
It is right to *g* him thanks and praise. 306 12
G them an inquiring and discerning heart, 308 5
G us this day our daily bread. 311 6
we *g* thanks to thee for thy great glory, 324 19
and to *g* thanks for all men: 329 2
G grace, O heavenly Father, to all bishops 329 9
And to all thy people *g* thy heavenly grace, 329 13
Let us *g* thanks unto our Lord God. 333 5
at all times, and in all places, *g* thanks unto thee, 333 8
that thou, of thy tender mercy, didst *g* thine only Son 334 10
G us this day our daily bread. 336 23
Let us *g* thanks unto our Lord God. 340 13
at all times, and in all places, *g* thanks unto thee, 341 2
and, of thy tender mercy, didst *g* thine only Son 341 14
Because thou didst *g* Jesus Christ, thine only Son, 345 14
to *g* the knowledge of thy glory 346 2
we worship you, we *g* you thanks, 356 5
Let us *g* thanks to the Lord our God. 361 5
It is right to *g* him thanks and praise. 361 6
always and everywhere to *g* thanks to you, Father 361 8
G us this day our daily bread. 364 6
Let us *g* thanks to the Lord our God. 367 5
It is right to *g* him thanks and praise. 367 6
always and everywhere to *g* thanks to you, Father 367 8
We *g* thanks to you, O God, for the goodness 368 1
Let us *g* thanks to the Lord our God. 370 3
It is right to *g* him thanks and praise. 370 4
Let us *g* thanks to the Lord our God. 372 21
It is right to *g* him thanks and praise. 372 22
to glorify you, Father, and to *g* you thanks; 373 1
we *g* thanks to you, 375 2
and *g* you glory through your Son 375 25
to *g* the knowledge of your glory 378 15
G us grace to do your will in all that we undertake; 387 12
G to the departed eternal rest; 387 17
G us all a reverence for the earth 388 12
g them courage and hope in their troubles, 389 4
and to you we *g* glory, Father, 395 6
"Peace I *g* to you; 395 8
and *g* to us the peace and unity of that heavenly City, 395 10
the bread which I shall *g* for the life of the world 397 3
G us this day our daily bread. 398 17
Gracious Father, we *g* you praise and thanks 399 7
Let us *g* thanks to the Lord our God. 402 5
It is right to *g* him thanks and praise. 402 6
Let us *g* thanks to the Lord our God. 404 7
It is right to *g* him thanks and praise. 404 8
G him courage, patience, and vision; 421 4
I *g* you this ring as a symbol of my vow, 427 13
G us this day our daily bread. 428 13
G them wisdom and devotion in the ordering 429 7
G them grace, when they hurt each other, to recognize 429 14
G them such fulfillment of their mutual affection 429 23
we *g* you thanks for your tender love 430 10
We *g* you thanks for binding us together 432 2
and thereto I (plight) (*g*) thee my troth. 436 10
the gift of a child, let us now *g* thanks to him, 441 11
We *g* you thanks for the blessing 443 23
O gracious God, we *g* you humble and hearty thanks 444 1
and to *g* you that victory of life and peace 456 4
Gracious Father, we *g* you praise and thanks 457 5
and *g* him patience under his affliction. 458 6
perfect health which it is yours alone to *g*; 458 24
and *g* your power of healing to those who minister 459 18
the Holy Spirit *g* you strength. 460 6
We *g* you thanks for giving 460 17
O heavenly Father, you *g* your children sleep 461 12
and *g* me such a sense of your presence, 461 15
and *g* me the Spirit of Jesus. 461 24
That it may please you to *g* him joy and gladness 463 20
G him your peace. 463 28
G us this day our daily bread. 464 9
and I will *g* you rest." 465 11
and *g* them peace; 467 6
G us grace, we beseech thee, to entrust 470 8
O *g* thanks unto the LORD, for he is gracious, * 478 11
and *g* thanks with thine inheritance. 478 22
G courage and faith to those who are bereaved, 481 10
G rest, O Christ, to thy servant(s) with thy saints, 482 9
G rest, O Christ, to thy servant(s) with thy saints, 483 3
will also *g* life to our mortal bodies, 485 2
upon him and *g* him peace. 485 15
G us this day our daily bread. 485 25
most humbly beseeching thee to *g* us grace 487 14
We *g* thee hearty thanks 488 4
We *g* thee thanks for all thy servants 488 27
g us such a lively sense of thy righteous will, 488 30
G mercy and grace to the living, 489 25
G us faith to see in death the gate 493 20
G us grace to entrust 494 2
g to our brother (sister) eternal life. 497 10
g him fellowship with all your saints. 497 17
G us, we pray, the faith to follow where you have led 498 5
G rest, O Christ, to your servant(s) with your saints, 499 1
will also *g* new life to our mortal bodies 501 4
upon him and *g* him peace. 501 16
G us this day our daily bread. 502 6
We *g* you heartfelt thanks for the good examples 503 14
and to *g* his life a ransom for many. 517 18
We *g* you thanks that from the beginning 520 14

g you the grace and power to perform them. 532 31
g your Holy Spirit to N.; 533 11
g your Holy Spirit to N.; 545 9
g me readiness of thought and expression; 563 6
to rejoice and *g* thanks. 568 18
Let us *g* thanks to the Lord our God. 570 3
It is right to *g* him thanks and praise. 570 4
G us ears to hear and hearts to obey. 571 2
We *g* you thanks, O God, for the gifts of your people, 573 1
Ask of me, and I will *g* you the nations 586 17
G ear to my words, O LORD; * 588 17
and who will *g* you thanks in the grave? 590 8
G judgment for me according to my 591 12
who conceive evil, and *g* birth to a lie. 591 27
You *g* him mastery over the works of your hands; * 592 19
I will *g* thanks to you, O LORD, 593 1
To *g* justice to the orphan and oppressed, * 596 5
"and *g* them the help they long for." 597 12
g light to my eyes, lest I sleep in death; 598 5
He does not *g* his money in hope of gain, * 599 15
g heed to my cry; * 600 23
I *g* no offense with my mouth as others do; * 601 5
and my ankles do not *g* way. 605 13
O LORD, *g* victory to the king * 608 19
For you will *g* him everlasting felicity * 609 7
all you of Jacob's line, *g* glory. 611 28
G judgment for me, O LORD, 616 7
and *g* them their just deserts. 619 17
The LORD shall *g* strength to his people; * 621 1
the LORD shall *g* his people the blessing of peace. 621 2
g thanks for the remembrance of his holiness. 621 11
O LORD my God, I will *g* you thanks for ever. 622 6
I will *g* you thanks in the great congregation; * 631 4
G me justice, O LORD my God, 631 18
you *g* them drink from the river of your delights. 632 21
and he shall *g* you your heart's desire. 633 12
and *g* ear to my cry; * 639 21
for I will yet *g* thanks to him, 643 16
for I will yet *g* thanks to him, 644 12
G judgment for me, O God, 644 14
and on the harp I will *g* thanks to you, O God 644 26
for I will yet *g* thanks to him, 645 4
and my sword does not *g* me the victory. 645 24
G me the joy of your saving help again * 657 5
I will *g* you thanks for what you have done * 658 18
g ear to the words of my mouth. 659 20
my lips shall *g* you praise. 670 18
I will *g* you oxen and goats. 674 26
may God, our own God, *g* us his blessing. 675 21
May God *g* us his blessing, * 675 22
Must I then *g* back what I never stole? 679 19
and *g* them continual trembling in their loins. 681 11
G the King your justice, O God, * 685 9
We *g* you thanks, O God, we *g* you thanks, * 691 3
Truly, wrathful Edom will *g* you thanks, * 692 20
but is he able to *g* bread 696 15
we will *g* you thanks for ever 702 10
g us life, that we may call upon your Name. 703 23
he will *g* grace and glory; 708 15
Will you not *g* us life again, * 709 5
G ear, O LORD, to my prayer, * 710 9
g your strength to your servant; 711 7
will those who have died stand up and *g* you thanks? 712 24
For he shall *g* his angels charge over you, * 720 7
It is a good thing to *g* thanks to the LORD, * 720 22
g the arrogant their just deserts. 722 21
To *g* them rest in evil days, * 723 19
and *g* thanks to his holy Name. 727 23
g thanks to him and call upon his Name. 730 3
to *g* them their food in due season. 737 8
You *g* it to them; they gather it; * 737 9
G thanks to the LORD and call upon his Name; * 738 1
Saying, "To you will I *g* the land of Canaan * 738 21
and a fire to *g* light in the night season. 741 4
G thanks to the LORD, for he is good, * 741 19
that we may *g* thanks to your holy Name 745 21
G thanks to the LORD, for he is good, * 746 1
Let them *g* thanks to the LORD for his mercy * 746 16
Let them *g* thanks to the LORD for his mercy * 747 11
Let them *g* thanks to the LORD for his mercy * 748 17
I will *g* great thanks to the LORD with my mouth; * 753 8
I will *g* thanks to the LORD with my whole heart, * 754 6
G praise, you servants of the LORD; * 756 2
but to your Name *g* glory; * 757 14
G thanks to the LORD, for he is good; * 760 20
I will *g* thanks to you, for you answered me * 762 13
G thanks to the LORD, for he is good; * 763 3
and *g* attention to your ways. 764 14
g me life according to your word. 765 10
G me understanding, and I shall keep your law; * 766 3
g me life in your ways. 766 10
At midnight I will rise to *g* you thanks, * 768 11
g me understanding, that I may learn your 769 10
when will you *g* judgment against those who 770 10
because by them you *g* me life. 771 6
according to your judgments, *g* me life. 776 2
according to your promise, *g* me life. 776 12
g me understanding, according to your word. 777 18
g praise, you servants of the LORD, 788 3
G thanks to the LORD, for he is good, * 789 20
G thanks to the God of gods, * 789 22
G thanks to the Lord of lords, * 790 1
G thanks to the God of heaven, * 791 21
I will *g* thanks to you, O LORD, 793 1
Surely, the righteous will *g* thanks to your Name, * 797 1
Bring me out of prison, that I may *g* thanks 798 15
You *g* victory to kings * 800 21
and you *g* them their food in due season. 802 18
G us grace seriously to lay 818 15
and *g* unto them the spirit 821 10
G grace to your servants, O Lord. 821 23
g courage, wisdom, and foresight to provide 822 2
G grace to your servants, O Lord. 822 5
To the Judges and officers of our Courts *g* understanding 822 6
G grace to your servants, O Lord. 822 9
g them courage to face the perils which beset them; 823 4
g grace to respect their witness 823 13
g us seasonable weather; 824 8
g us times of refreshment and peace; 825 1
our nation may *g* thanks to you for food and drink 825 21
and *g* them hope for their future. 826 19
remembering the account which we must one day *g*, 827 4
G us wisdom and reverence so to use the resources 827 18

that our land may *g* her increase; 828 5
that men and women everywhere may *g* thee thanks; 828 7
and *g* us new insight into your purposes 828 18
G us calm strength and patient wisdom 829 10
g more life than the ways of the world, 829 16
G them strength to hold their faith in you, 829 19
g them understanding helpers, 830 3
lift up thy countenance upon him, and *g* him peace; 831 16
g patient understanding and persevering love. 831 23
G us grateful hearts, our Father, for all thy mercies, 835 8
g us food to sustain our lives 835 14
may *g* thanks to you in all things. 836 19
Let us *g* thanks to God our Father for all his gifts 837 1
Above all, we *g* you thanks for the great mercies 837 21
We *g* thanks to you, O Lord our God, for all 838 9
g us, as you gave to them, the hope of salvation 838 18
We *g* you thanks, most gracious God, for the beauty 840 7
g us a just sense of these great mercies, 840 20
we *g* thee humble thanks 841 7
and *g* us life in all its fullness. 851 3
and *g* for the spread of the kingdom 856 15

given

Almighty God, who hast *g* us grace at this time 59 12
who have this day *g* thanks for his resurrection, 69 3
Almighty God, who hast *g* us grace at this time 72 9
Almighty God, you have *g* us grace at this time 102 1
Holy Spirit that has been *g* to us. 105 21
Grant that we, who have this day *g* thanks 123 3
Almighty God, you have *g* us grace at this time 126 1
Almighty God, who has *g* us thy only-begotten Son 161 7
and *g* up into the hands of sinners, 169 16
that Spirit of adoption which is *g* to us in Baptism, 170 16
Almighty Father, who hast *g* thine only Son to die 172 8
Almighty and everlasting God, who hast *g* unto us 176 1
Almighty God, who hast *g* thy only Son 180 19
and make us continually to be *g* to all good 183 7
thou hast *g* us in our Savior 184 20
Mark the evangelist hast *g* to thy Church the Gospel 188 22
Father, who hast *g* the Holy Spirit 204 8
Almighty God, you have *g* your only-begotten Son 213 1
and *g* into the hands of sinners, 221 10
that Spirit of adoption which is *g* to us in Baptism, 222 10
Almighty and everlasting God, you have *g* to us 228 1
Almighty God, you have *g* your only Son 232 11
that we may continually be *g* to good works; 234 21
which you have *g* us in our Savior 236 12
Mark the evangelist you have *g* to your Church the Gospel 240 8
Father, you have *g* the Holy Spirit 255 6
your gracious gift that we are *g* everlasting life; 265 19
has *g* power and commandment to his ministers 269 5
of those mighty acts, whereby you have *g* us life 270 6
I have *g* you an example, 274 10
and *g* into the hands of sinners, 276 6
Christ, who has *g* us a new birth by water 294 5
that Spirit of adoption which is *g* to us in Baptism, 295 10
and when he had *g* thanks, he brake it, 334 18
"Take, eat, this is my Body, which is *g* for you. 335 1
and when he had *g* thanks, he gave it to them, 335 4
Body of our Lord Jesus Christ, which was *g* for thee, 338 5
and when he had *g* thanks to thee, he broke it, 342 2
"Take, eat, this is my Body, which is *g* for you. 342 4
and when he had *g* thanks, he gave it to them, 342 6
in the obedience of thy saints hast *g* us an example 348 4
g us the Holy Spirit to guide us into all truth. 348 22
thou hast *g* us an image of the heavenly Jerusalem, 349 1
and when he had *g* thanks to you, he broke it, 362 19
This is my Body, which is *g* for you. 362 21
and when he had *g* thanks, he gave it to them, 363 1
to do the work you have *g* us to do, 366 9
and when he had *g* thanks to you, he broke it, 368 11
"Take, eat: This is my Body, which is *g* for you. 368 13
and when he had *g* thanks, he gave it to them, 368 14
"Take, eat: This is my Body, which is *g* for you. 371 12
and when he had *g* thanks to you, he broke it, 374 16
"Take, eat: This is my Body, which is *g* for you. 374 18
and when he had *g* thanks, he gave it to them, 374 19
the gifts you have *g* us, this bread and this cup, 374 28
in the obedience of your saints you have *g* us an example 380 20
g us the Holy Spirit to guide us into all truth. 381 15
you have *g* us an image of the heavenly Jerusalem, 381 16
For the good earth which God has *g* us, 384 14
"Take, eat: This is my Body, which is *g* for you. 403 6
and when he had *g* thanks to you, he broke it, 405 2
"Take, eat: This is my Body, which is *g* for you. 405 4
and when he had *g* thanks, he gave it to them, 405 6
comfort *g* one another in prosperity and adversity; 423 11
have *g* themselves to each other by solemn vows, 428 1
have *g* to him our family name, 441 8
g for health and salvation is the Name of our Lord 457 3
g in the resurrection of your Son 462 3
and hast *g* unto us a foretaste 482 3
In the assurance of eternal life *g* at Baptism, 496 1
and have *g* us a foretaste 498 14
g that has been duly and lawfully elected 514 2
I will, by the grace *g* me. 518 27
May the Lord who has *g* you the will 532 30
Receive this Bible as a sign of the authority *g* you 534 10
The wicked shall be *g* over to the grave, * 594 11
You have *g* me your shield of victory; * 605 9
You have *g* him his heart's desire; * 608 23
You have *g* me a mere handful of days, 639 3
(you have *g* me ears to hear you); 640 17
you have *g* us wine that makes us stagger. 667 15
and may there be *g* to him gold from Arabia; * 686 14
They have *g* the bodies of your servants as food 701 4
you have *g* them bowls of tears to drink. 702 22
They have *g* freely to the poor, * 755 22
because you have *g* me hope. 767 12
he has not *g* us over to be a prey for their teeth. 781 12
Almighty God, who hast *g* us this good land 820 1
Heavenly Father, in your Word you have *g* us a vision 825 6
Almighty God, whose loving hand hath *g* us all 827 1
you have blessed us and *g* us dominion over all 828 16
promises *g* to us in Christ 837 22
The Old Covenant is the one *g* by God 846 24
The Ten Commandments are the laws *g* to Moses 847 14
To show respect for the life God has *g* us; 848 7
The Ten Commandments were *g* to define 848 23
g by Jesus Christ, the Messiah, to the apostles; 850 28
and, according to the gifts *g* them, to carry 855 17
and spiritual grace, *g* by Christ 857 27

The two great sacraments *g* by Christ to his Church 858 6
g and received according to Christ's command. 859 20
What is the inward and spiritual grace *g* in the Eucharist? 859 22
the Body and Blood of Christ *g* to his people, 859 25
by which God's grace is *g* for the healing of spirit, 861 15

giver

O Son of God, O *G* of life, 64 8
O Son of God, O *G* of life, 112 8
O Son of God, O *G* of life, 118 8
O Son of God, O *G* of life, 139 8
who art the author and *g* of all good things: 181 11
Almighty God, the *g* of all good gifts, 205 4
Heavenly Father, *g* of life and health: 208 16
the author and *g* of all good things: 233 3
Almighty God, the *g* of all good gifts, 256 1
Heavenly Father, *g* of life and health: 260 1
We believe in the Holy Spirit, the Lord, the *g* of life, 327 12
believe in the Holy Ghost the Lord, and *G* of Life, 328 13
We believe in the Holy Spirit, the Lord, the *g* of life, 359 3
author of salvation, and *g* of all grace: 429 3
O God, the *g* of all that is true 432 1
Almighty God, *g* of life and love, 444 8
O Lord, holy Father, *g* of health and salvation: 455 9
Heavenly Father, *g* of life and health: 459 17
G of life, that he will raise him to perfection 466 14
Father of mercies and *g* of all comfort: 489 30
Almighty God, Father of mercies and *g* of comfort: 505 17
We believe in the Holy Spirit, the Lord, the *g* of life, 520 3
We believe in the Holy Spirit, the Lord, the *g* of life, 530 22
We believe in the Holy Spirit, the Lord, the *g* of life, 542 22
Almighty God, *g* of every good gift: 818 8
Almighty God, *g* of all good things: 838 21
the *g* of life, the One who spoke 852 19

gives

Thanks be to God, who *g* us the victory 77 10
but on a lamp-stand where it *g* light for everyone 109 9
I will bless the Lord who *g* me counsel; 115 10
to be the true bread which *g* life to the world: 219 2
g us a pledge of eternal life; 221 5
g us a pledge of eternal life; 274 5
he who *g* his light to all 287 26
your Church *g* honor, glory, and worship, 372 12
g us a pledge of eternal life; 397 17
Who *g* (presents) this woman to be married 437 6
Everyone the Father *g* to me will come to me; 501 1
I will bless the LORD who *g* me counsel; * 600 11
and *g* wisdom to the innocent. 607 7
and *g* light to the eyes. 607 11
I know that the LORD *g* victory to his anointed: * 608 12
God *g* the solitary a home and brings forth prisoners 676 13
he *g* judgment in the midst of the gods: 705 10
He *g* food to those who fear him; * 754 14
that your promise *g* me life. 767 14
When your word goes forth it *g* light; * 774 7
it *g* understanding to the simple. 774 8
for he *g* to his beloved sleep. 783 5
For the LORD *g* his people justice * 789 3
Who *g* food to all creatures, * 791 19
Who *g* justice to those who are oppressed, * 803 15
He *g* snow like wool; * 805 9
Ordination is the rite in which God *g* authority 860 28

givest

to do the work which thou *g* us to do 151 14
may do the work which thou *g* us to do, 210 5
save us from selfish use of what thou *g*, 828 6

giveth

Thanks be to God, which *g* us the victory 39 11
I will bless the Lord who *g* me counsel; 61 10
to be the true bread which *g* life 167 11
g us a pledge of life eternal, 169 10
All that the Father *g* me shall come to me; 484 18

giving

by *g* up our selves to thy service, 59 6
by *g* up our selves to thy service, 72 3
Bringing forth life and *g* growth, * 87 3
by *g* up our selves to your service, 101 19
of the changes of day and night, *g* rest to the weary, 113 2
by *g* up our selves to your service, 125 17
raised from the death of sin by thy life-*g* Spirit; 171 2
and *g* us those good things which we are not worthy to ask, 183 2
g us the example of his great humility: 219 16
raised from the death of sin by your life-*g* Spirit; 222 19
g us those good things for which we are not worthy 234 16
g us the example of his great humility: 272 10
Fill them with your holy and life-*g* Spirit. 305 19
and *g* to thy Church the power 347 10
g voice to every creature under heaven, 373 10
g the whole world into our care, 373 19
and *g* to your Church the power 380 5
joining of hands and the *g* and receiving of a ring, 428 2
join N. [and N.] in *g* thanks to Almighty God 440 4
bestowed upon this family in *g* them a child. 443 24
Strengthen them by your life-*g* Spirit, 460 12
We give you thanks for *g* our brother (sister) N. both relief 460 17
and *g* life to those in the tomb. 483 15
The Sun of Righteousness is gloriously risen, *g* light 483 16
We thank you for *g* him to us, 493 17
and *g* life to those in the tomb. 500 4
The Sun of Righteousness is gloriously risen, *g* light 500 5
share in the fullness of your life-*g* Spirit; 552 11
but the righteous are generous in *g*. 635 2
g strength and power to his people! 679 5
in *g* them the lands of the nations. 754 17
g them patience under their sufferings, 815 10
life-*g* Spirit may so move every human heart 823 17
Almighty God, in *g* us dominion over things on earth, 827 17
For it is in *g* that we receive; 833 11

glad

we will rejoice and be *g* in it. 39 10
I was *g* when they said unto me, 40 11
and show ourselves *g* in him with psalms. 44 13
who makest us *g* with the weekly remembrance 56 1
we will rejoice and be *g* in it. 77 8
I was *g* when they said to me, 78 10
O God, you make us *g* with the weekly remembrance 98 19
and we are *g* indeed. 105 11

and show ourselves *g* in him with psalms. 146 4
who makest us *g* with the yearly remembrance 160 12
O God, you make us *g* by the yearly festival 212 10
Rejoice and be *g* now, Mother Church, 286 7
the streams whereof make *g* the city of God, * 471 23
Wherefore my heart is *g*, and my spirit rejoiceth; 485 4
My heart, therefore, is *g*, and my spirit rejoices; 501 6
But all who take refuge in you will be *g*; * 589 17
I will be *g* and rejoice in you; * 593 3
Jacob will rejoice and Israel be *g*. 599 3
My heart, therefore, is *g*, and my spirit rejoices; * 600 15
and will make him *g* with the joy of your presence. 609 8
I will rejoice and be *g* because of your mercy; * 622 22
Be *g*, you righteous, and rejoice in the LORD; * 625 25
But when I stumbled, they were *g* 630 23
who favor my cause sing out with joy and be *g*; * 631 27
Turn your gaze from me, that I may be *g* again, * 639 25
Let all who seek you rejoice in you and be *g*; * 641 16
music of strings from ivory palaces makes you *g*. 648 7
a river whose streams make *g* the city of God, * 649 10
Let Mount Zion be *g* 651 23
Jacob will rejoice and Israel be *g*. 659 16
The righteous will be *g* when they see 665 13
all those who swear by him will be *g*; * 671 8
Let the nations be *g* and sing for joy, * 675 15
But let the righteous be *g* and rejoice before God; * 676 6
The afflicted shall see and be *g*; * 682 1
Let all who seek you rejoice and be *g* in you; * 682 19
so shall we rejoice and be *g* all the days of our life. 719 2
Make us *g* by the measure of the days that you afflicted us * 719 3
For you have made me *g* by your acts, O LORD; * 721 3
Let the heavens rejoice, and let the earth be *g*; 726 14
let the multitude of the isles be *g*. 726 24
Zion hears and is *g*, and the cities of Judah rejoice, * 727 12
Egypt was *g* of their going, * 741 1
and be *g* with the gladness of your people, * 742 7
Then were they *g* because of the calm, * 748 15
we will rejoice and be *g* in it. 762 20
Those who fear you will be *g* when they see me, * 769 12
I am as *g* because of your promise * 777 3
I was *g* when they said to me, * 779 18
and we are *g* indeed. 782 13
mindful of thy favor and *g* to do thy will. 820 3
food to sustain our lives and make our hearts *g*; 835 14

gladden

G the soul of your servant, * 710 5
and wine to *g* our hearts, 736 6

gladly

that we may *g* suffer shame and loss 168 19
and to suffer *g* for the sake of the same our Lord 195 5
that we may *g* suffer shame and loss 220 10
and to suffer *g* for the sake of our Lord 247 3
true freedom and *g* accept its disciplines. 839 25

gladness

serve the Lord with *g* 45 12
serve the Lord with *g* 82 21
You have put *g* in my heart, * 129 4
Make me hear of joy and *g*, * 266 18
Let us with *g* present the offerings 344 12
with *g* and singleness of heart; 365 17
Let us with *g* present the offerings 377 10
restore to him your gifts of *g* and strength, 459 5
That it may please you to give him joy and *g* 463 20
an oblation with great *g*; * 477 26
and rejoice in the *g* of thy people, 478 21
You have put *g* in my heart, * 588 13
with sounds of great *g*; * 618 8
to the God of my joy and *g*; * 644 25
with the oil of *g* above your fellows. 648 5
With joy and *g* they are brought, * 648 21
Make me hear of joy and *g*, * 656 22
and joyful *g* for those who are truehearted. 727 21
serve the LORD with *g* 729 23
So he led forth his people with *g*, * 741 11
and be glad with the *g* of your people, * 742 7
we may learn to serve thee with *g*; 814 4

glimpses

and grant to them even now *g* of your beauty, 819 16

glistening

transfigured, in raiment white and *g*: 191 17
transfigured, in raiment white and *g*: 243 3

gloat

They stare and *g* over me; * 611 15
those who *g* over me when my foot slips." 638 2
and *g* over me be confounded, * 641 14
and *g* over me turn back, * 682 17
My eyes also *g* over my enemies, * 721 18

gloom

deep *g* enshrouds the peoples. 87 14
who believe in Christ are delivered from the *g* of sin, 287 10
Some sat in darkness and deep *g*, * 747 1
He led them out of darkness and deep *g* * 747 9

gloried

Every day we *g* in God, * 646 1

glorified

and to be *g* through all the worlds. 64 9
and to be *g* through all the worlds. 112 9
and to be *g* through all the worlds. 118 9
and to be *g* through all the worlds. 139 9
g thee by their martyrdom: 190 11
Almighty God, who willest to be *g* in thy saints, 196 15
Peter and Paul *g* you by their martyrdom: 241 19
Almighty God, whose will it is to be *g* in your saints, 248 1
With the Father and the Son he is worshiped and *g*. 327 14
together is worshiped and *g*; 328 16
thou art greatly *g* in the assembly of thy saints. 348 7
With the Father and the Son he is worshiped and *g*. 359 5
When the hour had come for him to be *g* by you, 374 13
you are greatly *g* in the assembly of your saints. 381 1
That your Name may be *g* by all people. 387 5
By this my Father is *g*, 397 10
promoted and your creation *g*; 460 14
With the Father and the Son he is worshiped and *g*. 520 5
With the Father and the Son he is worshiped and *g*. 530 24
and your Name *g* in all the world. 534 7
With the Father and the Son he is worshiped and *g*. 542 24
For you have *g* your Name * 793 6

glorify

we *g* thee,	52	7
G the Lord, all you works of the Lord, *	88	5
In the firmament of his power, *g* the Lord, *	88	7
G the Lord, you angels and all powers of the Lord, *	88	9
Sun and moon and stars of the sky, *g* the Lord, *	88	11
G the Lord, every shower of rain and fall of dew, *	88	13
Winter and summer, *g* the Lord, *	88	15
G the Lord, O chill and cold, *	88	17
Frost and cold, ice and sleet, *g* the Lord, *	88	19
G the Lord, O nights and days, *	89	1
Storm clouds and thunderbolts, *g* the Lord, *	89	3
Let the earth *g* the Lord, *	89	5
G the Lord, O mountains and hills,	89	7
G the Lord, O springs of water, seas, and streams, *	89	10
All birds of the air, *g* the Lord, *	89	12
G the Lord, O beasts of the wild, *	89	14
O men and women everywhere, *g* the Lord, *	89	16
Let the people of God *g* the Lord, *	89	18
G the Lord, O priests and servants of the Lord, *	89	20
G the Lord, O spirits and souls of the righteous, *	89	22
You that are holy and humble of heart, *g* the Lord, *	89	24
Let us *g* the Lord: Father, Son, and Holy Spirit; *	90	1
In the firmament of his power, *g* the Lord, *	90	3
night as by day your people may *g* your holy Name;	133	19
victory of faith, may *g* in life and death	189	7
victory of faith, may *g* in life and death	240	15
and *g* your holy resurrection;	281	2
we *g* thee,	324	18
It is truly right to *g* you, Father,	373	1
and *g* your Name, as we sing (say),	373	11
we may have grace to *g* Christ in our own day.	386	17
we praise and *g* your holy Name	504	12
and strengthen them to *g* God in this life	531	19
build up your Church, and *g* your Name,	549	5
worship you, O Lord, * and *g* your Name.	710	17
and *g* your Name for evermore.	710	25
with one mind and one mouth *g* thee;	818	23
by their life and worship may *g* your Name;	819	11
we may *g* thy holy Name,	832	3
in one united chorus, will *g* your holy Name.	839	20

glorious

The Lord is *g* in his saints:	44	8
Blessed art thou on the *g* throne of thy kingdom; *	49	18
The *g* company of the apostles praise thee.	53	3
the *g* resurrection of thy Son our Lord:	56	2
The Lord is *g* in his saints:	82	3
Your right hand, O Lord, is *g* in might; *	85	14
who is like you, *g* in holiness,	85	17
The *g* company of apostles praise you.	95	23
the *g* resurrection of your Son our Lord:	98	20
O holy, blessed, and *g* Trinity, one God,	148	7
by thy *g* Resurrection and Ascension;	149	23
he shall come again in his *g* majesty to judge	159	5
and by his *g* resurrection hast delivered us	170	9
O God, who by the *g* resurrection of thy Son	171	10
made like unto him in his eternal and *g* kingdom;	184	12
O God, we thank thee for the *g* company	194	1
Being of *g* majesty and perfect love as one God	199	13
he shall come again in his *g* majesty to judge	211	5
and by his *g* resurrection delivered us	222	2
O God, who by the *g* resurrection of your Son	223	4
made like him in his eternal and *g* kingdom;	236	6
O God, we thank you for the *g* company	245	10
Being of *g* majesty and perfect love as one God	251	2
bright with a *g* splendor,	286	5
bring forth abundant fruit in your *g* kingdom;	290	11
and by his *g* resurrection delivered us	295	2
we laud and magnify thy *g* Name;	334	2
his mighty resurrection and *g* ascension;	335	14
we laud and magnify thy *g* Name;	341	5
his mighty resurrection and *g* ascension;	342	14
and by his *g* resurrection opened to us the way	345	2
we bound to praise thee for the *g* resurrection	346	17
after his *g* resurrection manifestly appeared	347	2
and in their eternal joy a *g* pledge	348	5
We acclaim you, holy Lord, *g* in power.	373	17
and by his *g* resurrection opened to us the way	377	15
we bound to praise you for the *g* resurrection	379	14
After his *g* resurrection he openly appeared	379	21
and in their eternal joy a *g* pledge	380	21
thy Son at his coming in *g* majesty;	395	15
By your *g* Resurrection and Ascension,	463	8
into the *g* company of the saints in light.	465	6
and into the *g* company of the saints in light.	483	10
O God, who by the *g* resurrection of your Son	493	4
into the *g* company of the saints in light.	499	18
All *g* is the princess as she enters; *	648	17
And blessed be his *g* Name for ever! *	686	27
How *g* you are! *	692	7
G things are spoken of you, *	711	15
I will ponder the *g* splendor of your majesty *	801	20
and the *g* splendor of your kingdom.	802	10

gloriously

The Sun of Righteousness is *g* risen,	483	16
The Sun of Righteousness is *g* risen,	500	5

glory

The *g* of the Lord shall be revealed,	37	6
to the *g* of thy holy Name.	42	10
G to the Father, and to the Son,	42	16
The Lord hath manifested forth his *g*:	43	4
G to the Father, and to the Son,	46	19
G to the Father, and to the Son,	50	20
G to the Father, and to the Son,	51	21
and to be the *g* of thy people Israel.	51	28
G to the Father, and to the Son,	52	1
G be to God on high,	52	3
we give thanks to thee for thy great *g*,	52	8
art most high in the *g* of God the Father.	52	22
Heaven and earth are full of the majesty of thy *g*.	53	2
Thou art the King of *g*, O Christ.	53	11
the right hand of God, in the *g* of the Father.	53	17
with thy saints, in *g* everlasting.	53	22
For thine is the kingdom, and the power, and the *g*,	54	24
and entered not into *g* before he was crucified:	56	7
for the means of grace, and for the hope of *g*.	58	23
be all honor and *g*, world without end.	59	11
G to God whose power, working in us,	60	3
G to him from generation to generation	60	4
to the *g* of thy holy Name.	63	13
G to the Father, and to the Son,	63	19

G to the Father, and to the Son, 64 10
G to the Father, and to the Son, 65 23
and to be the *g* of thy people Israel. 66 6
G to the Father, and to the Son, 66 7
For thine is the kingdom, and the power, and the *g*, 67 14
our worship on the morrow may give thee *g*; 69 15
for the means of grace, and for the hope of *g*. 71 19
be all honor and *g*, world without end. 72 8
G to God whose power, working in us, 73 3
G to him from generation to generation 73 4
The *g* of the Lord shall be revealed, 75 6
to the *g* of your Name. 79 22
G to the Father, and to the Son, 80 7
The Lord has shown forth his *g*: 81 1
G to the Father, and to the Son, 84 1
G to the Father, and to the Son, 85 30
G to the Father, and to the Son, 86 15
G to the Father, and to the Son, 87 9
and the *g* of the Lord has dawned upon you. 87 12
and his *g* will appear upon you. 87 16
and your God will be your *g*. 88 2
G to the Father, and to the Son, 88 3
G to you, Lord God of our fathers; * 90 5
you are worthy of praise; *g* to you. 90 6
G to you for the radiance of your holy Name; * 90 7
G to you in the splendor of your temple; * 90 9
on the throne of your majesty, *g* to you. 90 10
G to you, seated between the Cherubim; * 90 11
G to you, beholding the depths; * 90 13
in the high vault of heaven, *g* to you. 90 14
G to you, Father, Son, and Holy Spirit; * 90 15
and yours is the *g* to ages of ages. 91 26
G to the Father, and to the Son, 92 16
G to the Father, and to the Son, 93 10
and the *g* of your people Israel. 93 17
G to the Father, and to the Son, 94 19
G to God in the highest, 94 21
we praise you for your *g*. 95 2
in the *g* of God the Father. 95 14
heaven and earth are full of your *g*. 95 22
You, Christ, are the king of *g*, 96 1
You are seated at God's right hand in *g*. 96 7
to *g* everlasting. 96 12
and the power, and the *g*, 97 16
and entered not into *g* before he was crucified: 99 2
for the means of grace, and for the hope of *g*. 101 15
be honor and *g* throughout all ages. 101 24
G to God whose power, working in us, 102 14
G to him from generation to generation 102 15
G to the Father, and to the Son, 103 3
G to the Father, and to the Son, 105 18
the world with the radiance of your *g*, 107 14
give *g* to your Father in heaven." 109 12
the revelation of the *g* of God in the face of Jesus 110 5
To you be *g* for endless ages. 113 8
to the *g* of your Name. 117 5
G to the Father, and to the Son, 117 12
G to the Father, and to the Son, 118 10
G to the Father, and to the Son, 119 22
and the *g* of your people Israel. 120 6
G to the Father, and to the Son, 120 7
and the power, and the *g*, 121 16
our worship on the morrow give you *g*; 123 14
for the means of grace, and for the hope of *g*. 125 13
be honor and *g* throughout all ages. 125 22
G to God whose power, working in us, 126 14
G to him from generation to generation 126 15
to the *g* of your Name. 127 15
G to the Father, and to the Son, 128 5
"You mortals, how long will you dishonor my *g*? * 128 11
G to the Father, and to the Son, 131 10
Christ, to whom be *g* for ever and ever. 132 5
sing your *g* at the close of this day, 134 3
and the *g* of your people Israel. 135 6
G to the Father, and to the Son, 135 7
G to the Father, and to the Son, 137 9
and his *g* above the heavens. 138 8
the revelation of the *g* of God 139 14
and the *g* of your people Israel. 140 12
G to the Father, and to the Son, * 141 1
G be to the Father, and to the Son, * 141 5
and to the setting forth of thy *g*; 153 25
G be to the Father, and to the Son, 154 10
for the *g* of thy Name, turn from us 155 8
and pureness of living, to thy honor and *g*; 155 12
the Holy Ghost, be honor and *g*, world without end. 160 5
one God, in *g* everlasting. 161 6
one God, in *g* everlasting. 162 5
where we may behold thy *g* face to face; 162 16
one God, in *g* everlasting. 163 6
may shine with the radiance of Christ's *g*, 163 10
perceive the *g* of his marvelous works; 163 17
didst reveal his *g* upon the holy mount: 165 15
changed into his likeness from *g* to *g*; 165 18
O God, whose *g* it is always to have mercy: 166 16
and entered not into *g* before he was crucified: 168 11
Grant us so to *g* in the cross of Christ, 168 19
assurance of the *g* that shall be revealed; 169 4
the *g* of the Lord's resurrection: 170 15
and rejoice in the hope of eternal *g*; 171 13
one God, in *g* everlasting. 174 14
O God, the King of *g*, who hast exalted thine only Son 175 1
acknowledge the *g* of the eternal Trinity, 176 3
bring us at last to see thee in thy one and eternal *g*, 176 6
to the *g* of thy Name; 181 7
Christ hast revealed thy *g* among the nations: 183 12
he shall appear again with power and great *g*, 184 11
We give thee thanks, O Lord of *g*, 186 1
the Holy Spirit, one God, in *g* everlasting. 186 5
and passion be brought unto the *g* of his resurrection; 188 18
may share with her the *g* of thine eternal kingdom; 192 3
grant that we, who *g* in the mystery 192 15
one God, in *g* everlasting. 192 18
to the praise and *g* of thy Name; 193 14
one God, in *g* everlasting. 194 15
to the *g* of thy Name; 194 20
to whose *g* we celebrate the dedication 204 1
the *g* of thy great Name 205 10
who hast made all peoples of the earth for thy *g*, 207 2
the *g* of thy holy Name; 209 6
our heavenly Father, who declarest thy *g* 210 1
the Holy Spirit, be honor and *g*, now and for ever. 212 5
one God, in *g* everlasting. 212 20

the same Spirit be honor and *g*, now and for ever. 213 6
one God, in *g* everlasting. 213 17
where we may see your *g* face to face; 214 9
one God, in *g* everlasting. 214 17
may shine with the radiance of Christ's *g*, 215 4
perceive the *g* of his marvelous works; 215 11
revealed his *g* upon the holy mountain: 217 8
changed into his likeness from *g* to *g*; 217 11
O God, whose *g* it is always to have mercy: 218 7
and entered not into *g* before he was crucified: 220 2
Grant us so to *g* in the cross of Christ, 220 10
confident of the *g* that shall be revealed; 220 17
shine with the *g* of the Lord's resurrection: 222 9
and rejoice in the hope of eternal *g*; 223 7
one God, in *g* everlasting. 226 6
O God, the King of *g*, you have exalted 226 13
one God, in *g* everlasting. 226 18
acknowledge the *g* of the eternal Trinity, 228 3
see you in your one and eternal *g*, O Father; 228 6
power among all peoples, to the *g* of your Name; 232 19
you have revealed your *g* among the nations: 235 4
with power and great *g*, we may be made like him 236 5
We give you thanks, O Lord of *g*, 237 14
one God, in *g* everlasting. 237 18
brought to the *g* of his resurrection; 240 4
may share with her the *g* of your eternal kingdom; 243 10
grant that we, who *g* in the mystery of 244 3
one God, in *g* everlasting. 244 6
to the praise and *g* of your Name; 245 1
one God, in *g* everlasting. 245 22
all who are in need, to the *g* of your Name; 246 5
God, to whose *g* we celebrate the dedication 254 19
to the *g* of your great Name 256 7
you have made all the peoples of the earth for your *g*, 258 2
to the *g* of your holy Name; 260 12
you declare your *g* and show forth your handiwork 261 7
That we may show forth your *g* in the world. 268 30
Peace in heaven and *g* in the highest. 270 2
reigns in *g* with you and the Holy Spirit, 271 13
and entered not into *g* before he was crucified: 272 2
We *g* in your cross, O Lord, 281 1
and to us sinners everlasting life and *g*; 282 11
for the *g* of your Name multiply, 289 6
shine with the *g* of the Lord's resurrection: 295 9
G to you, Lord Christ. 300 7
Bring them to the fullness of your peace and *g*. 306 3
and look for him to come again in *g*; 306 7
g, now and for ever. 307 8
and the power, and the *g*, 311 13
to him be *g* in the Church evermore. 317 19
to the *g* of thy Name. 320 22
to the *g* of thy holy Name. 321 13
G be to God on high, 324 14
we give thanks to thee for thy great *g*, 324 19
art most high in the *g* of God the Father. 325 9
G be to thee, O Lord. 326 3
He will come again in *g* to judge 327 10
and he shall come again, with *g*, 328 10
to the honor and *g* of thy Name; 331 19
to the *g* of thy Name. 331 33
Heaven and earth are full of thy *g*. 334 5
G be to thee, O Lord Most High. 334 6
All *g* be to thee, Almighty God, our heavenly Father, 334 9
all honor and *g* be unto thee, O Father Almighty, 336 14
For thine is the kingdom, and the power, and the *g*, 336 28
Holy Ghost, be all honor and *g*, world without end. 339 14
Heaven and earth are full of thy *g*. 341 8
G be to thee, O Lord Most High. 341 9
All *g* be to thee, O Lord our God, 341 12
for his coming again with power and great *g*. 342 15
Holy Ghost all honor and *g* be unto thee, 343 4
Worthy art thou, O Lord our God, to receive *g* 344 5
the greatness, and the power, and the *g*, 344 8
to show forth thy *g* in all the world. 345 6
of thy *g* in the face of thy Son 346 3
reign with him in *g*. 347 5
and we celebrate the one and equal *g* of thee, 347 15
may receive the crown of *g* 347 20
to the *g* of your Name. 352 22
G to God in the highest, 356 1
we praise you for your *g*. 356 6
in the *g* of God the Father. 356 18
G to you, Lord Christ. 357 10
He will come again in *g* to judge 359 1
to the *g* of your Name. 360 14
sing this hymn to proclaim the *g* of your Name: 362 3
heaven and earth are full of your *g*. 362 5
all honor and *g* is yours, 363 21
and the power, and the *g*, 364 13
be honor and *g*, now and for ever. 366 13
sing this hymn to proclaim the *g* of your Name: 367 12
heaven and earth are full of your *g*. 367 14
We await his coming in *g*; 368 22
Spirit all honor and *g* is yours, 369 16
you are worthy of *g* and praise. 370 6
G to you for ever and ever. 370 7
proclaim with them your *g*, in their unending hymn: 370 26
heaven and earth are full of your *g*. 371 2
Spirit, your Church gives honor, *g*, and worship, 372 12
beholding the *g* of your presence, 373 8
heaven and earth are full of your *g*. 373 13
awaiting his coming in *g*; 374 27
and give you *g* through your Son 375 25
all honor and *g* are yours, 375 27
O Lord our God, you are worthy to receive *g* 377 3
Yours, O Lord, is the greatness, the power, the *g*, 377 6
people in Jesus Christ our Lord, to show forth your *g* 378 2
knowledge of your *g* in the face of your Son 378 16
reign with him in *g*. 379 24
and we celebrate the one and equal *g* of you, 380 10
together with them, receive the crown of *g* 380 15
your *g* in the world. 388 4
and to your honor and *g*. 388 14
and show forth your *g* in all 391 3
yours is the kingdom and the power and the *g*, 391 24
to the honor and *g* of your Name; 393 15
to the *g* of thy Name; 394 3
lover of souls, and to you we give *g*, 395 6
to the *g* of your Name. 398 6
and the power, and the *g*, 398 24
proclaiming your *g*, as we sing (say), 402 8
heaven and earth are full of your *g*. 402 10
Spirit all honor and *g* is yours, 403 20
proclaiming your *g*, as we sing (say), 404 10

heaven and earth are full of your *g*. 404 12
we await his coming in *g*. 405 12
and *g* is yours, Almighty Father, 405 21
G be to the Father, and to the Son,* 406 1
G to you, Lord Christ. 414 7
G to you, Lord Christ. 426 3
and the power, and the *g*, 428 20
G to the Father, and to the Son, 442 11
G to the Father, and to the Son, 443 18
partake of everlasting *g* in the life to come; 444 6
to the *g* of your Name. 455 5
the residue of his life in thy fear, and to thy *g*; 458 8
G be to thee, O Lord. 479 22
bliss in thy eternal and everlasting *g*, 481 25
For thine is the kingdom, and the power, and the *g*, 486 5
to whom be *g* for ever and ever. 487 4
in thy eternal and everlasting *g*; 488 10
and to us sinners everlasting life and *g*; 489 28
and rejoice in his eternal *g*; 493 8
O God of grace and *g*, we remember 493 16
G to you, Lord Christ. 495 3
and the power, and the *g*, 502 13
to whom be *g* for ever and ever. 503 6
bliss in your eternal and everlasting *g*; 503 19
G to you, Lord Christ. 516 7
He will come again in *g* to judge 520 1
to the *g* and unceasing praise of your Name. 521 5
honor and power and *g* in the Church, 521 17
and always rejoice in your *g*; 523 8
G to you, Lord Christ. 529 6
He will come again in *g* to judge 530 20
your eternal and invisible *g*, 533 4
and always rejoice in your *g*; 535 8
G to you, Lord Christ. 541 6
He will come again in *g* to judge 542 20
Will you in all things seek not your *g* 544 12
the *g* of the Lord Christ? 544 13
and come to the unending *g* of him who, 545 17
and always rejoice in your *g*; 547 4
and always rejoice in your *g*; 564 8
to the praise and *g* of your Name; 567 12
all honor and *g*, now and for ever. 570 22
the power, and the *g* of your creation 572 3
offered to your honor and *g*. 578 6
the *g*, the victory, and the majesty; 579 14
you are my *g*, the one who lifts up my head. 587 8
"You mortals, how long will you dishonor my *g*; * 588 1
you adorn him with *g* and honor; 592 18
The heavens declare the *g* of God, * 606 15
all you of Jacob's line, give *g*. 611 28
and the King of *g* shall come in. 614 3
"Who is this King of *g*?" * 614 4
and the King of *g* shall come in. 614 9
"Who is he, this King of *g*?" * 614 10
he is the King of *g*." 614 12
and the place where your *g* abides. 616 23
ascribe to the LORD *g* and strength. 620 6
Ascribe to the LORD the *g* due his Name; * 620 7
the God of *g* thunders; * 620 10
all are crying, "*G*!" 620 24
I will *g* in the LORD; * 627 23
I will *g* in his victory. 630 9
the enemies of the LORD, like the *g* of the meadows, 634 25
God reveals himself in *g*. 654 5
and your *g* over all the earth. 664 9
that I might behold your power and your *g*. 670 16
and all who are true of heart will *g*. 672 6
sing the *g* of his Name; 673 19
sing the *g* of his praise. 673 20
and your *g* all the day long. 683 17
and may all the earth be filled with his *g*. 686 28
and afterwards receive me with *g*. 688 26
his *g* into the adversary's hand. 700 2
Help us, O God our Savior, for the *g* of your Name; * 701 24
he will give grace and *g*; 708 15
that his *g* may dwell in our land. 709 13
For you are the *g* of their strength, * 714 27
Declare his *g* among the nations * 725 21
and all the peoples see his *g*. 727 8
and all the kings of the earth your *g*. 732 7
and his *g* will appear. 732 9
May the *g* of the LORD endure for ever; * 737 16
G in his holy Name; * 738 5
that I may *g* with your inheritance. 742 8
And so they exchanged their *G* * 743 11
and *g* in your praise. 745 22
and your *g* over all the earth. 750 4
and his *g* above the heavens. 756 9
but to your Name give *g*; * 757 14
that great is the *g* of the LORD. 793 13
They make known the *g* of your kingdom * 802 7
this is *g* for all his faithful people. 807 19
dominion and *g*, now and for ever. 815 27
Teach us in all things to seek first your honor and *g*. 818 4
O Lord our Governor, whose *g* is in all the world: 820 16
to the *g* of thy Name and the welfare of this people; 821 6
which the nations of the world bring their *g*: 825 8
whose *g* fills the whole creation, 831 1
to thy *g* and the welfare of thy people; 833 3
and to the setting forth of thy *g*; 834 7
To him be praise and *g*, with you, O Father, 837 23
the *g* are yours for ever. 838 8
to the honor and *g* of your Name, now and for ever. 840 13
with thee and the Holy Ghost be all *g* and honor, 840 23
partaker of everlasting *g* in the life to come; 841 12
await the coming of Christ in *g*, 861 27
What do we mean by the coming of Christ in *g*? 862 1
By the coming of Christ in *g*, 862 2
We believe that Christ will come in *g* 862 14

glow
and all the night through with a *g* of fire. 696 2

glowing
along with hot *g* coals. 778 17

gnash
and *g* at them with their teeth. 634 8
they will *g* their teeth and pine away; * 755 26

gnashed
they *g* at me with their teeth. 630 28

gnats
and *g* within all their borders. 740 16

go
I will arise and g to my father, 38 17
"We will g into the house of the Lord." 40 11
O g your way into his gates with thanksgiving 45 17
for thou shalt g before the face of the Lord 51 12
I will arise and g to my father, 76 16
"Let us g to the house of the Lord." 78 10
g into his courts with praise; * 83 5
for you will g before the Lord to prepare his way, 93 2
to g in peace as you have promised; 93 13
Those who g out weeping, carrying the seed, * 105 16
to g in peace as you have promised; 120 2
to g in peace as you have promised; 135 2
to g in peace as you have promised; 140 8
Let us g forth in peace. 271 17
g and open your grief 317 12
Let us g forth in the name of Christ. 339 22
G in peace to love and serve the Lord. 340 1
Let us g forth into the world, 340 3
leave there thy gift before the altar, and g thy way; 343 19
Let us g forth in the name of Christ. 366 14
G in peace to love and serve the Lord. 366 16
Let us g forth into the world, 366 18
leave your gift there before the altar and g; 376 15
G (or abide) in peace, and pray for me, a sinner. 448 14
G (or abide) in peace. 451 19
Whither shall I g then from thy Spirit? * 475 5
or whither shall I g then from thy presence? 475 6
if I g down to hell, thou art there also. 475 8
g from strength to strength in the life 481 21
we g down to the dust; 483 1
Let us g forth in the name of Christ. 483 12
he may g from strength to strength 488 23
All of us g down to the dust; 499 7
Let us g forth in the name of Christ. 500 1
Let us g forth in the name of Christ. 502 21
Let us g forth into the world, 523 18
Let us g forth into the world, 535 13
Let us g forth into the world, 547 7
I lie down and g to sleep; * 587 11
g into your house; * 589 4
all who g down to the dust fall before him. 612 17
that I may g in procession round your altar, 616 19
I become like those who g down to the Pit. 619 7
if I g down to the Pit? * 621 24
teach you in the way that you should g; * 625 18
Their sword shall g through their own heart, * 634 14
I g about in mourning all the day long. 637 9
before I g my way and am no more. 639 26
they g outside and spread them. 642 12
why do I g so heavily while the enemy oppresses me?" 644 3
and do not g forth with our armies. 646 4
they g down straightway to the grave. 653 10
let them g down alive into the grave; * 661 15
liars g astray from their birth. 664 26
They g to and fro in the evening; * 666 7
g down into the depths of the earth; 671 4
and the hairy scalp of those who g on still 677 26
The singers g before, musicians follow after, * 678 7
g after him and seize him; * 683 23
they g about in darkness; * 705 18
Those who g through the desolate valley 708 1
Righteousness shall g before him, * 709 20
I am counted among those who g down to the Pit; * 712 7
love and truth g before your face. 714 22
"G back, O child of earth." 718 5
g into his courts with praise; * 730 2
to g to a city where they might dwell. 746 15
nor all those who g down into silence; 758 24
Make me g in the path of your commandments, * 766 5
"Let us g to the house of the LORD." 779 19
To which the tribes g up, 780 1
Those who g out weeping, carrying the seed, * 782 18
It is in vain that you rise so early and g to bed so late; * 783 3
So that those who g by say not as much as, 784 15
Where can I g then from your Spirit? * 794 12
or I shall be like those who g down to the Pit. 799 14
let thy Spirit g forth, 828 3
and whose presence we find wherever we g: 831 2

goals
better than chasing after selfish g. 829 17

goats
nor he-g out of your pens; 654 22
or drink the blood of g? 655 6
I will give you oxen and g. 674 26
The high hills are a refuge for the mountain g, * 736 13

GOD
Lord G of hosts; * 679 23
For you are my hope, O Lord G, * 683 9
I will begin with the mighty works of the Lord G; * 684 12
Blessed be the Lord G, the God of Israel, * 686 25
I have made the Lord G my refuge. 689 6
But you, O Lord my G, 752 16
O Lord G, the strength of my salvation, * 796 15
But my eyes are turned to you, Lord G; * 797 19

God
make straight in the desert a highway for our G. 37 5
Behold, the tabernacle of G is with men, 37 11
and G himself shall be with them, and be their G. 37 12
G is faithful and just to forgive us our sins, 38 11
and turn unto the Lord your G; 38 15
To the Lord our G belong mercies and forgivenesses, 38 20
neither have we obeyed the voice of the Lord our G, 38 22
Thanks be to G, which giveth us the victory 39 11
where Christ sitteth on the right hand of G. 39 14
to appear in the presence of G for us. 39 17
Holy, holy, holy, Lord G Almighty, 39 22
with the saints and of the household of G. 40 4
Grace be unto you, and peace, from G our Father, 40 9
Almighty G our heavenly Father, to render thanks 41 6
Let us humbly confess our sins unto Almighty G. 41 15
Father, Son, and Holy Ghost, one G: 43 14
For the Lord is a great G, * 44 14
For he is the Lord our G, * 45 3
Be ye sure that the Lord he is G; 45 14
but in that he liveth, he liveth unto G. 46 10
but alive unto G through Jesus 46 12
Thanks be to G. 47 3
O ye winds of G, bless ye the Lord; * 48 5

God

O ye people of G, bless ye the Lord; *	49	1
Blessed art thou, O Lord G of our fathers; *	49	9
and my spirit hath rejoiced in G my Savior.	50	2
Blessed be the Lord G of Israel, *	50	22
Through the tender mercy of our G, *	51	16
Glory be to G on high,	52	3
O Lord G, heavenly King, G the Father Almighty.	52	9
O Lord, G, Lamb of G, Son of the Father,	52	11
Thou that sittest at the right hand of G the Father,	52	16
art most high in the glory of G the Father.	52	22
We praise thee, O G;	52	23
Holy, holy, holy, Lord G of Sabaoth;	53	1
Thou sittest at the right hand of G,	53	17
I believe in G, the Father almighty,	53	23
and sitteth on the right hand of G the Father	54	3
Create in us clean hearts, O G;	55	13
O G, who makest us glad	56	1
Almighty G, whose most dear Son went not up to joy	56	6
Almighty G, who after the creation	56	11
O G, the King eternal, who dividest	56	18
O G, who art the author of peace	57	1
our heavenly Father, almighty and everlasting G,	57	7
Almighty and everlasting G, by whose Spirit	57	19
O G, who hast made of one blood	58	1
Almighty G, Father of all mercies	58	14
Almighty G, who hast given us grace	59	12
Thanks be to G.	59	21
The grace of our Lord Jesus Christ, and the love of G,	59	22
May the G of hope fill us with all joy and peace	60	1
Glory to G whose power, working in us,	60	3
Grace be unto you, and peace, from G our Father,	61	3
Thine is the day, O G, thine also the night;	61	7
here in the presence of Almighty G,	62	11
Let us humbly confess our sins unto Almighty G.	62	15
O G, make speed to save us.	63	17
we sing thy praises, O G:	64	6
O Son of G, O Giver of life,	64	8
Thanks be to G.	65	2
and my spirit hath rejoiced in G my Savior.	65	5
I believe in G, the Father almighty,	66	9
and sitteth on the right hand of G the Father	66	19
Create in us clean hearts, O G;	68	5
Lord G, whose Son our Savior Jesus Christ triumphed	69	1
O G, the source of eternal light:	69	12
O G, from whom all holy desires,	69	16
O G, who art the life of all who live,	70	4
O G and Father of all, whom the whole heavens	70	15
O G, who dost manifest	71	6
Almighty G, Father of all mercies,	71	10
Almighty G, who hast given us grace	72	9
Thanks be to G.	72	18
The grace of our Lord Jesus Christ, and the love of G,	72	19
May the G of hope fill us with all joy and peace	73	1
Glory to G whose power, working in us,	73	3
make straight in the desert a highway for our G.	75	5
Behold, the dwelling of G is with mankind.	75	11
and G himself will be with them, and be their G.	75	12
G, who is faithful and just, will forgive our sins	76	10
Return to the Lord your G,	76	14
To the Lord our G belong mercy and forgiveness,	76	19
have not obeyed the voice of the Lord our G	76	21
Thanks be to G, who gives us the victory	77	10
where Christ is, seated at the right hand of G.	77	13
the presence of G on our behalf.	77	16
Holy, holy, holy is the Lord G Almighty,	77	20
and members of the household of G.	78	3
Grace to you and peace from G our Father	78	8
Almighty G our heavenly Father, to set forth	79	2
Let us confess our sins against G and our neighbor.	79	9
Most merciful G,	79	10
Almighty G have mercy on you,	80	1
Father, Son, and Holy Spirit, one G:	81	10
For the Lord is a great G, *	82	9
For he is our G,	82	17
Know this: The Lord himself is G; *	83	1
but the life he lives, he lives to G.	83	18
and alive to G in Jesus Christ our Lord.	83	20
Thanks be to G.	84	5
This is my G and I will praise him, *	85	5
the G of my people and I will exalt him.	85	6
Surely, it is G who saves me; *	86	1
and to our G, for he will richly pardon.	86	22
and your G will be your glory.	88	2
Let the people of G glorify the Lord, *	89	18
Glory to you, Lord G of our fathers; *	90	5
G of Abraham, Isaac, and Jacob,	90	18
For you, O Lord, are the G of those who repent, *	91	20
my spirit rejoices in G my Savior; *	91	28
Blessed be the Lord, the G of Israel; *	92	18
In the tender compassion of our G *	93	5
are yours by right, O Lord our G,	93	21
for with your blood you have redeemed for G,	94	2
a kingdom of priests to serve our G.	94	4
O ruler of the universe, Lord G,	94	9
Glory to G in the highest,	94	21
Lord G, heavenly King,	94	23
almighty G and Father,	94	24
Lord G, Lamb of G,	95	4
in the glory of G the Father.	95	14
You are G: we praise you;	95	15
Holy, holy, holy Lord, G of power and might,	95	21
You are seated at G's right hand in glory.	96	7
I believe in G, the Father almighty,	96	13
Create in us clean hearts, O G;	98	7
O G, you make us glad with the weekly remembrance	98	19
Almighty G, whose most dear Son went not up to joy	99	1
Almighty G, who after the creation of the world rested	99	6
O G, the King eternal, whose light divides	99	13
O G, the author of peace and lover of concord,	99	20
Lord G, almighty and everlasting Father,	100	1
Almighty and everlasting G, by whose Spirit	100	11
O G, you have made of one blood	100	17
Almighty G, Father of all mercies,	101	7
Almighty G, you have given us grace	102	1
Thanks be to G.	102	9
The grace of our Lord Jesus Christ, and the love of G,	102	10
May the G of hope fill us with all joy and peace	102	12
Glory to G whose power, working in us,	102	14
O G, make speed to save us.	103	1
The love of G has been poured into our hearts	105	20
Thanks be to G.	105	22
All this is from G,	106	2
Thanks be to G.	106	5

Thanks be to G.	107	23
Thanks be to G.	109	2
For the same G who said,	110	3
the revelation of the glory of G in the face	110	5
Almighty G, we give you thanks for surrounding us,	110	12
O Lord G Almighty, as you have taught	110	23
we may know you to be the true G and eternal light,	110	27
Almighty and most merciful G, kindle	111	4
Eternal G, who led your ancient people into freedom	111	8
rejoice in the liberty of the children of G;	111	11
we sing your praises, O G:	112	6
O Son of G, O Giver of life,	112	8
Blessed are you, O Lord, the G of our fathers,	113	1
Almighty, everlasting G, let our prayer	113	9
Thanks be to G.	114	6
Grace to you and peace from G our Father	115	3
Yours is the day, O G, yours also the night;	115	7
here in the presence of Almighty G,	116	7
Let us confess our sins against G and our neighbor.	116	11
Most merciful G,	116	12
Almighty G have mercy on you,	117	6
O G, make speed to save us.	117	10
we sing your praises, O G:	118	6
O Son of G, O Giver of life,	118	8
Thanks be to G.	119	2
my spirit rejoices in G my Savior; *	119	5
I believe in G, the Father almighty,	120	9
Create in us clean hearts, O G;	122	7
Lord G, whose Son our Savior Jesus Christ triumphed	123	1
O G, the source of eternal light:	123	11
Most holy G, the source of all good desires,	123	15
O G, the life of all who live,	124	1
O G and Father of all, whom the whole heavens	124	12
O G, you manifest in your servants the signs	125	1
Almighty G, Father of all mercies,	125	5
Almighty G, you have given us grace	126	1
Thanks be to G.	126	9
The grace of our Lord Jesus Christ, and the love of G,	126	10
May the G of hope fill us with all joy and peace	126	12
Glory to G whose power, working in us,	126	14
Let us confess our sins to G.	127	5
Almighty G, our heavenly Father:	127	6
May the Almighty G grant us forgiveness	128	1
O G, make speed to save us.	128	3
Answer me when I call, O G, defender of my cause; *	128	8
O Lord, O G of truth.	129	20
my G in whom I put my trust."	129	25
Do not forsake us, O Lord our G.	131	13
Thanks be to G.	131	14
May the G of peace, who brought again	132	1
Thanks be to G.	132	7
For you have redeemed me, O Lord, O G of truth.	132	13
Be present, O merciful G, and protect	133	13
We give you thanks, O G, for revealing	134	1
O G, your unfailing providence sustains	134	11
Thanks be to G.	135	13
Create in me a clean heart, O G, *	137	3
Blessed be the G and Father of our Lord Jesus Christ!	137	11
Lord G, almighty and everlasting Father, you have brought	137	14
O G, you will keep in perfect peace	138	9
we sing your praise O G:	139	6
O Son of G, O Giver of life,	139	8
For the same G who said,	139	12
the revelation of the glory of G	139	14
Do not forsake us, O Lord our G.	140	6
For the Lord is a great G, *	146	5
For he is the Lord our G, *	146	13
O G the Father, Creator of heaven and earth,	148	1
O G the Son, Redeemer of the world,	148	3
O G the Holy Ghost, Sanctifier of the faithful,	148	5
O holy, blessed, and glorious Trinity, one G,	148	7
We sinners do beseech thee to hear us, O Lord G;	150	1
Son of G, we beseech thee to hear us.	152	22
O Lamb of G, that takest away the sins of the world,	152	24
Almighty G, who hast promised	153	19
The grace of our Lord Jesus Christ, and the love of G,	154	1
O G, we have heard with our ears,	154	5
Almighty G, give us grace	159	1
one G, now and for ever.	159	8
Merciful G, who didst send thy messengers	159	9
one G, now and for ever.	159	14
We beseech thee, Almighty G, to purify	160	6
one G, now and for ever.	160	10
O G, who makest us glad with the yearly	160	12
one G, world without end.	160	17
O G, who hast caused this holy night to shine	161	1
one G, in glory everlasting.	161	5
Almighty G, who has given us thy only-begotten Son	161	7
one G, world without end.	161	13
Almighty G, who hast poured upon us the new light	161	14
one G, now and for ever.	161	18
one G, in glory everlasting.	162	5
O G, who didst wonderfully create,	162	7
one G, for ever and ever.	162	12
O G, who by the leading of a star didst manifest	162	13
one G, now and for ever.	162	18
one G, in glory everlasting.	163	6
Almighty G, whose Son our Savior	163	7
one G, now and for ever.	163	13
one G, for ever and ever.	163	18
Almighty and everlasting G, who dost govern	164	1
one G, for ever and ever.	164	5
Set us free, O G, from the bondage	164	6
one G, now and for ever.	164	10
O G, the strength of all	164	11
one G, now and for ever.	165	5
O G, who before the passion	165	14
one G, for ever and ever.	165	20
Almighty and everlasting G, who hatest nothing	166	1
the G of all mercy,	166	5
one G, for ever and ever.	166	8
Almighty G, whose blessed Son was led by the Spirit	166	9
one G, now and for ever.	166	14
O G, whose glory it is always to have mercy:	166	16
one G, for ever and ever.	167	2
Almighty G, who seest that we have no power	167	3
one G, now and for ever.	167	14
O Almighty G, who alone canst order	167	15
one G, now and for ever.	167	22
Almighty and everlasting G, who,	168	1
one G, for ever and ever.	168	8
Almighty G, whose most dear Son went not up to joy	168	10
O G, who by the passion of thy blessed Son	168	17

O Lord G, whose blessed Son our Savior gave	169	1
one G, for ever and ever.	169	6
one G, world without end.	169	13
Almighty G, we beseech thee graciously to behold	169	14
O G, Creator of heaven and earth:	170	1
one G, for ever and ever.	170	6
O G, who for our redemption didst give	170	7
one G, now and for ever.	170	13
O G, who didst make this most holy night to shine	170	14
Almighty G, who through thine only-begotten Son	170	21
one G, world without end.	171	4
Grant, we beseech thee, Almighty G,	171	5
one G, now and for ever.	171	9
O G, who by the glorious resurrection	171	10
O G, whose blessed Son did manifest himself	171	17
everlasting G, who in the Paschal mystery	172	1
one G, for ever and ever.	172	6
one G, now and for ever.	172	13
everlasting G, who in the Paschal mystery	172	20
one G, for ever and ever.	173	3
O G, whose blessed Son did manifest himself	173	5
one G, now and for ever.	173	10
O G, whose Son Jesus is the good shepherd	173	11
G, whom truly to know is everlasting life:	173	16
O G, who hast prepared for those who love thee	174	1
one G, for ever and ever.	174	7
O Almighty G, whose blessed Son our Savior	174	8
one G, in glory everlasting.	174	13
Grant, we beseech thee, Almighty G,	174	15
one G, world without end.	174	19
O G, the King of glory, who hast exalted	175	1
one G, world without end.	175	6
Almighty G, who on this day didst open	175	8
one G, for ever and ever.	175	13
O G, who on this day didst teach	175	15
Almighty and everlasting G, who hast given	176	1
one G, for ever and ever.	176	8
one G, now and for ever.	177	2
O Almighty and most merciful G,	177	3
one G, for ever and ever.	177	13
O G, whose never-failing providence ordereth	177	14
O G, from whom all good doth come:	178	1
one G, for ever and ever.	178	5
one G, now and for ever.	178	11
O Almighty G, who hast built	178	18
one G, for ever and ever.	179	3
O G, who hast taught us to keep all thy commandments	179	4
Almighty G, the fountain of all wisdom,	179	16
one G, now and for ever.	179	22
O G, the protector of all that trust in thee,	180	1
one G, for ever and ever.	180	6
Almighty G, who hast given thy only Son	180	19
G, for ever and ever.	181	4
Grant, we beseech thee, merciful G,	181	5
one G, world without end.	181	9
one G, now and for ever.	181	22
O G, forasmuch as without thee we are not able	182	1
one G, now and for ever.	182	5
one G, for ever and ever.	182	10
O G, who declarest thy almighty power	182	12
Almighty and everlasting G, who art	182	18
one G, for ever and ever.	183	5
one G, now and for ever.	183	9
everlasting G, who in Christ hast revealed	183	11
Almighty and everlasting G, give	183	17
merciful G, of whose only gift it cometh	184	1
one G, now and for ever.	184	6
O G, whose blessed Son was manifested	184	7
the children of G and heirs of eternal life:	184	9
one G, world without end.	184	14
one G, for ever and ever.	184	21
Almighty and everlasting G, whose will	185	1
one G, now and for ever.	185	6
Almighty G, who didst give such grace	185	7
Everliving G, who didst strengthen	185	14
our Lord and our G,	185	17
one G, in glory everlasting.	186	5
one G, for ever and ever.	186	12
We remember this day, O G, the slaughter	186	13
to confess Jesus as Messiah and Son of the living G:	187	3
one G, now and for ever.	187	6
O G, who, by the preaching of thine apostle Paul,	187	8
Almighty and everliving G, we humbly beseech thee	187	16
O Almighty G, who into the place of Judas didst choose	188	1
one G, now and for ever.	188	6
O G, who from the family of thy servant David	188	8
one G, for ever and ever.	188	13
Almighty G, who by the hand of Mark the evangelist	188	21
the Gospel of Jesus Christ the Son of G:	189	1
one G, for ever and ever.	189	4
Almighty G, who didst give	189	5
one G, now and for ever.	189	9
Grant, O G, that we may follow the example	189	17
Almighty G, by whose providence	190	1
one G, for ever and ever.	190	9
Almighty G, whose blessed apostles Peter and Paul	190	10
Lord G Almighty, in whose Name the founders	190	17
Almighty G, whose blessed Son restored Mary Magdalene	191	1
one G, now and for ever.	191	6
O gracious G, we remember before thee this day	191	7
O G, who on the holy mount didst reveal	191	15
one G, world without end.	191	20
O G, who hast taken to thyself the blessed Virgin	192	1
one G, now and for ever.	192	6
O Almighty and everlasting G, who didst give	192	7
one G, for ever and ever.	192	12
Almighty G, whose Son our Savior	192	13
one G, in glory everlasting.	192	18
one G, now and for ever.	193	3
O everlasting G, who hast ordained and constituted	193	4
one G, for ever and ever.	193	9
Almighty G, who didst inspire thy servant Luke	193	11
Grant, we beseech thee, O G,	193	18
O G, we thank thee for the glorious company	194	1
one G, for ever and ever.	194	6
O Almighty G, who hast knit together thine elect	194	8
one G, in glory everlasting.	194	15
one G, now and for ever.	194	22
O Almighty G, who didst give	195	1
one G, for ever and ever.	195	7
O Almighty G, by whose grace and power	195	8

Almighty and everlasting G, who didst enkindle	196	1
one G, for ever and ever.	196	6
Almighty and everlasting G, we thank thee	196	7
one G, now and for ever.	196	13
Almighty G, who willest to be glorified in thy saints,	196	15
one G, for ever and ever.	197	3
O G, our heavenly Father, who didst raise	197	4
O G, who by thy Holy Spirit dost give	197	12
O Almighty G, who didst give	197	19
by this teaching we may know thee, the one true G,	197	22
O G, whose blessed Son became poor	198	1
one G, now and for ever.	198	7
O G, by whose grace thy servant N., enkindled	198	9
O Almighty G, who hast compassed	198	16
one G, for ever and ever.	198	22
O G, who hast brought	198	23
one G, now and for ever.	199	3
O Almighty G, who by thy Holy Spirit hast made	199	4
Almighty G, who hast revealed	199	12
Being of glorious majesty and perfect love as one G	199	13
one G, for ever and ever.	199	17
Almighty and most merciful G, grant,	200	1
one G, world without end.	200	5
O everlasting G, who hast ordained and constituted	200	6
one G, for ever and ever.	200	11
O G, who didst wonderfully create,	200	13
G our Father, whose Son our Lord	201	1
one G, for ever and ever.	201	6
Almighty G, whose beloved Son willingly endured	201	7
one G, now and for ever.	201	11
Grant, O Lord G, to all who have been baptized	201	12
O eternal Lord G, who holdest all souls in life:	202	1
one G, now and for ever.	202	7
Almighty G, we remember this day before thee	202	9
one G, for ever and ever.	202	15
Almighty and everlasting G, whose will	202	16
one G, now and for ever.	203	4
Almighty G, who by our baptism into the death	203	5
Grant, Almighty G, that we, who have been redeemed	203	12
O Almighty G, to whose glory we celebrate	204	1
one G, now and for ever.	204	6
one G, now and for ever.	205	3
Almighty G, the giver of all good gifts,	205	4
O G, who didst lead thy holy apostles to ordain	205	14
one G, for ever and ever.	205	21
Almighty and everlasting G, by whose Spirit	206	1
in the unity of the Holy Spirit, one G,	206	7
O G, who hast made of one blood	206	9
O G of all the nations of the earth:	206	17
one G, for ever and ever.	206	23
Lord G Almighty, who hast made all peoples	207	1
one G, for ever and ever.	207	6
O Almighty G, kindle, we beseech thee,	207	8
one G, now and for ever.	207	14
Almighty G, Lord of heaven and earth:	207	15
Almighty G, whose Son Jesus Christ in his earthly life	208	1
one G, now and for ever.	208	8
one G, for ever and ever.	208	15
Almighty G, who hast created us in thine own image:	209	1
one G, now and for ever.	209	7
one G, for ever and ever.	209	16
Almighty G, the fountain of all wisdom:	209	17
Almighty G our heavenly Father, who declarest	210	1
one G, for ever and ever.	210	8
Almighty G, who hast so linked	210	10
Almighty G, give us grace to cast away	211	1
one G, now and for ever.	211	7
Merciful G, who sent your messengers the prophets	211	9
Purify our conscience, Almighty G,	212	6
one G, now and for ever.	212	9
O G, you make us glad by the yearly festival	212	10
O G, you have caused this holy night to shine	212	16
one G, in glory everlasting.	212	20
Almighty G, you have given	213	1
Almighty G, you have poured	213	8
one G, now and for ever.	213	12
one G, in glory everlasting.	213	17
O G, who wonderfully created,	214	1
one G, for ever and ever.	214	5
O G, by the leading of a star you manifested	214	7
one G, now and for ever.	214	11
one G, in glory everlasting.	214	17
Almighty G, whose Son our Savior	215	1
one G, now and for ever.	215	6
one G, for ever and ever.	215	11
Almighty and everlasting G, you govern	215	12
Set us free, O G, from the bondage	216	1
one G, now and for ever.	216	4
O G, the strength of all who put their trust in you:	216	6
one G, for ever and ever.	216	11
one G, now and for ever.	217	6
O G, who before the passion	217	7
one G, for ever and ever.	217	12
Almighty and everlasting G, you hate nothing	217	14
the G of all mercy,	217	18
Almighty G, whose blessed Son was led	218	1
one G, now and for ever.	218	6
O G, whose glory it is always to have mercy:	218	7
one G, for ever and ever.	218	12
Almighty G, you know that we have no power	218	13
one G, now and for ever.	219	5
Almighty G, you alone can bring into order	219	6
Almighty and everliving G, in your tender love	219	13
one G, for ever and ever.	219	19
Almighty G, whose most dear Son went not up to joy	220	1
one G, for ever and ever.	220	6
O G, by the passion of your blessed Son you made	220	8
Lord G, whose blessed Son our Savior gave	220	14
one G, for ever and ever.	221	6
Almighty G, we pray you graciously to behold	221	8
O G, Creator of heaven and earth:	221	13
O G, who for our redemption gave	222	1
one G, now and for ever.	222	6
O G, who made this most holy night to shine	222	8
Almighty G, who through your only-begotten Son	222	15
Grant, we pray, Almighty G, that we who celebrate	222	22
one G, now and for ever.	223	2
O G, who by the glorious resurrection of your Son	223	4
O G, whose blessed Son made himself known	223	10
everlasting G, who in the Paschal mystery	223	15
one G, for ever and ever.	223	20
one G, now and for ever.	224	6
everlasting G, who in the Paschal mystery	224	13
one G, for ever and ever.	224	18

O *G*, whose blessed Son made himself known 224 19
one *G*, now and for ever. 225 1
O *G*, whose Son Jesus is the good shepherd 225 3
one *G*, for ever and ever. 225 6
Almighty *G*, whom truly to know is everlasting life: 225 8
Almighty *G*, whose blessed Son our Savior 226 1
one *G*, in glory everlasting. 226 6
Grant, we pray, Almighty *G*, 226 8
one *G*, for ever and ever. 226 12
O *G*, the King of glory, you have exalted 226 13
Almighty *G*, on this day you opened 227 1
one *G*, for ever and ever. 227 6
O *G*, who on this day taught 227 8
Almighty and everlasting *G*, you have given 228 1
one *G*, for ever and ever. 228 7
one *G*, now and for ever. 228 12
Almighty and merciful *G*, in your goodness keep us, 228 14
one *G*, now and for ever. 229 4
one *G*, for ever and ever. 229 9
O *G*, your never-failing providence sets 229 10
O *G*, from whom all good proceeds: 229 15
one *G*, now and for ever. 230 5
one *G*, for ever and ever. 230 11
Almighty *G*, you have built your Church 230 12
O *G*, you have taught 230 19
one *G*, for ever and ever. 231 3
one *G*, now and for ever. 231 9
Almighty *G*, the fountain of all wisdom, 231 10
O *G*, the protector of all who trust in you, 231 17
one *G*, for ever and ever. 232 5
Almighty *G*, you have given your only Son 232 11
one *G*, now and for ever. 232 16
Grant, O merciful *G*, that your Church, 232 17
one *G*, for ever and ever. 233 2
one *G*, now and for ever. 233 13
O *G*, because without you we are not able 233 14
one *G*, for ever and ever. 234 5
O *G*, you declare your almighty power 234 6
Almighty and everlasting *G*, you are always 234 12
one *G*, now and for ever. 235 2
everlasting *G*, in Christ you have revealed 235 3
one *G*, for ever and ever. 235 8
Almighty and everlasting *G*, increase 235 9
Almighty and merciful *G*, it is only by your gift 235 14
O *G*, whose blessed Son came into the world 236 1
and make us children of *G* 236 2
one *G*, for ever and ever. 236 7
Almighty and everlasting *G*, whose will 236 14
one *G*, now and for ever. 236 19
G, who gave such grace to your apostle Andrew 237 1
one *G*, now and for ever. 237 6
Everliving *G*, who strengthened your apostle Thomas 237 8
Lord and our *G*, that our faith may 237 11
one *G*, in glory everlasting. 237 18
one *G*, for ever and ever. 238 6
We remember today, O *G*, the slaughter 238 7
to confess Jesus as Messiah and Son of the living *G*: 238 15
one *G*, now and for ever. 238 19
O *G*, by the preaching of your apostle Paul 238 20
one *G*, now and for ever. 239 4
Almighty and everliving *G*, we humbly pray that, 239 6
Almighty *G*, who in the place of Judas chose 239 11
O *G*, who from the family of your servant David 239 17
one *G*, for ever and ever. 239 22
one *G*, now and for ever. 240 5
Almighty *G*, by the hand of Mark the evangelist 240 7
the Gospel of Jesus Christ the Son of *G*: 240 9
one *G*, for ever and ever. 240 11
Almighty *G*, who gave to your apostles Philip 240 13
one *G*, for ever and ever. 241 1
Grant, O *G*, that we may follow the example 241 3
Almighty *G*, by whose providence your servant John 241 10
Almighty *G*, whose blessed apostles Peter and Paul 241 19
one *G*, now and for ever. 241 24
Lord *G* Almighty, in whose Name the founders 242 1
one *G*, for ever and ever. 242 7
Almighty *G*, whose blessed Son restored Mary Magdalene 242 8
one *G*, now and for ever. 242 13
O gracious *G*, we remember before you today 242 14
O *G*, who on the holy mount revealed 243 1
one *G*, for ever and ever. 243 6
O *G*, you have taken to yourself the blessed Virgin 243 8
one *G*, now and for ever. 243 12
Almighty and everlasting *G*, who gave 243 14
Almighty *G*, whose Son our Savior 244 1
one *G*, in glory everlasting. 244 6
one *G*, now and for ever. 244 12
Everlasting *G*, you have ordained and constituted 244 13
one *G*, for ever and ever. 244 19
Almighty *G*, who inspired your servant Luke 244 20
one *G*, now and for ever. 245 3
Grant, O *G*, that, following the example 245 4
O *G*, we thank you for the glorious company 245 10
one *G*, for ever and ever. 245 15
Almighty *G*, you have knit together your elect 245 16
one *G*, in glory everlasting. 245 22
one *G*, now and for ever. 246 7
Almighty *G*, who gave to your servant N. boldness 246 8
one *G*, for ever and ever. 247 4
Almighty *G*, by whose grace and power 247 6
Almighty and everlasting *G*, who kindled 247 13
Almighty and everlasting *G*, we thank you 247 19
one *G*, now and for ever. 247 25
Almighty *G*, whose will it is to be glorified 248 1
one *G*, now and for ever. 248 6
one *G*, for ever and ever. 248 13
O *G*, our heavenly Father, who raised 248 15
O *G*, by your Holy Spirit you give 248 22
one *G*, for ever and ever. 249 4
Almighty *G*, you gave to your servant N. 249 5
by this teaching we may know you, the one true *G*, 249 8
O *G*, whose blessed Son became poor 249 11
one *G*, now and for ever. 249 17
O *G*, by whose grace your servant N., kindled 249 18
Almighty *G*, you have surrounded us 250 1
one *G*, for ever and ever. 250 7
O *G*, you have brought us near 250 8
one *G*, now and for ever. 250 13
Almighty *G*, by your Holy Spirit you have made 250 14
Almighty *G*, you have revealed to your Church 251 1
Being of glorious majesty and perfect love as one *G* 251 2
one *G*, now and for ever. 251 5
Almighty and most merciful *G*, grant 251 7

God

Everlasting G, you have ordained and constituted 251 12
one G, for ever and ever. 251 18
O G, who wonderfully created, 252 1
one G, for ever and ever. 252 5
G our Father, whose Son our Lord 252 6
Almighty G, whose beloved Son willingly endured 252 12
one G, now and for ever. 252 15
Grant, Lord G, to all who have been baptized 252 16
one G, now and for ever. 253 5
Eternal Lord G, you hold all souls in life: 253 6
Almighty G, we remember before you today 253 13
one G, for ever and ever. 253 19
Almighty and everlasting G, whose will it is to restore 254 1
one G, now and for ever. 254 6
Almighty G, by our baptism into the death 254 7
Grant, Almighty G, that we, who have been redeemed 254 13
Almighty G, to whose glory we celebrate 254 19
one G, now and for ever. 255 4
Almighty G, the giver of all good gifts, 256 1
one G, now and for ever. 256 9
O G, you led your holy apostles to ordain 256 11
one G, for ever and ever. 256 17
Almighty and everlasting G, by whose Spirit 256 19
one G, now and for ever. 257 4
O G, you have made of one blood 257 5
O G of all the nations of the earth: 257 13
one G, for ever and ever. 257 19
Lord G Almighty, you have made all the peoples 258 1
one G, for ever and ever. 258 7
Almighty G, kindle, we pray, 258 8
one G, now and for ever. 258 13
Almighty G, Lord of heaven and earth: 258 15
one G, for ever and ever. 259 2
Almighty G, whose Son Jesus Christ in his earthly life 259 3
one G, now and for ever. 259 9
one G, for ever and ever. 260 7
Almighty G, who created us in your own image: 260 8
one G, now and for ever. 260 14
Almighty G, the fountain of all wisdom: 261 1
one G, for ever and ever. 261 6
Almighty G our heavenly Father, you declare 261 7
Almighty G, you have so linked our lives 261 15
Almighty and everlasting G, you hate nothing 264 2
the G of all mercy, 264 6
one G, for ever and ever. 264 8
Dear People of G: 264 10
meditating on G's holy Word. 265 13
Almighty G, you have created us out of the dust 265 16
Have mercy on me, O G, 266 1
Create in me a clean heart, O G, * 266 22
Deliver me from death, O G, * 267 3
O G of my salvation. 267 5
The sacrifice of G is a troubled spirit; * 267 10
a broken and contrite heart, O G, you will not
despise. 267 11
Almighty G, the Father of our Lord 269 3
Assist us mercifully with your help, O Lord G 270 4
Let us give thanks to the Lord our G. 271 3
It is right to praise you, Almighty G, 271 5
Almighty G, whose most dear Son went not up to joy 272 1
Almighty and everliving G, in your tender love 272 7
one G, for ever and ever. 272 13
one G, for ever and ever. 274 6
Blessed by our G. 276 1
Almighty G, we pray you graciously to behold 276 4
one G, for ever and ever. 276 8
Dear People of G: 277 2
That G will confirm his Church in faith, 278 9
Almighty and everlasting G, by whose Spirit 278 11
That by G's help they may seek justice and truth, 278 23
Almighty G, kindle, we pray, 278 25
That G in his mercy will comfort and relieve them, 279 11
Gracious G, the comfort of all who sorrow, 279 14
That G will open their hearts to the truth, 279 28
Merciful G, Creator of all the peoples 280 1
Let us commit ourselves to our G, 280 8
and those whose faith is known to G alone, 280 11
O G of unchangeable power and eternal light: 280 14
one G, for ever and ever. 280 23
May G be merciful to us and bless us, 281 5
Let the peoples praise you, O G; 281 9
Lord Jesus Christ, Son of the living G, we pray 282 6
one G, now and for ever. 282 12
O G, Creator of heaven and earth: 283 1
one G, for ever and ever. 283 6
O G, through your Son you have bestowed 285 8
Thanks be to G. 285 14
pray with me to G the Almighty 286 11
one G, for ever and ever. 286 16
Let us give thanks to the Lord our G. 286 19
almighty, and eternal G, and your only-begotten Son, 287 2
How wonderful and beyond our knowing, O G, 287 14
and man is reconciled to G. 287 22
Let us hear the record of G's saving deeds in history, 288 1
and let us pray that our G 288 2
O G, who wonderfully created, 288 5
Almighty G, you have placed in the skies 289 1
G and Father of all believers, 289 6
O G, whose wonderful deeds of old shine forth 289 12
O G, you led your ancient people by a pillar of cloud 290 2
O G, you have created all things by the power 290 8
everlasting G, who in the Paschal mystery 290 14
Almighty G, by the Passover of your Son 291 5
O G of unchangeable power and eternal light: 291 11
and promised to serve G faithfully 292 6
Do you believe in G the Father? 292 11
I believe in G, the Father almighty, 292 12
Do you believe in Jesus Christ, the Son of G? 293 1
Do you believe in G the Holy Spirit? 293 12
I will, with G's help. 293 22
News of G in Christ? 293 27
I will, with G's help. 293 28
I will, with G's help. 294 3
May Almighty G, the Father of our Lord 294 4
Almighty G, who for our redemption gave 295 1
one G, now and for ever. 295 7
O G, who made this most holy night to shine 295 8
Blessed be G: 299 1
There is one hope in G's call to us; 299 8
One G and Father of all. 299 10
Thanks be to G. 300 3
I will, with G's help. 302 3
of wickedness that rebel against G? 302 8
which corrupt and destroy the creatures of G? 302 11

from the love of *G*?	302	14
and with *G*'s grace I will follow him	303	13
Do you believe in *G* the Father?	304	1
I believe in *G*, the Father almighty,	304	2
Do you believe in Jesus Christ, the Son of *G*?	304	4
Do you believe in *G* the Holy Spirit?	304	15
I will, with *G*'s help.	304	25
News of *G* in Christ?	305	2
I will, with *G*'s help.	305	3
Let us give thanks to the Lord our *G*.	306	11
We thank you, Almighty *G*, for the gift of water.	306	13
We receive you into the household of *G*.	308	12
Almighty *G*, we thank you that by the death	309	3
one *G*, now and for ever.	309	11
G, the Father, Son, and Holy Spirit,	310	3
Almighty and everliving *G*, let your fatherly hand	310	8
one *G*, for ever and ever.	311	20
Almighty *G*, the Father of our Lord Jesus Christ,	311	21
you may be filled with all the fullness of *G*.	311	25
Church renders to Almighty *G* our heavenly Father	316	10
might make us the children of *G*	316	15
conduct by the rule of *G*'s commandments,	317	1
Almighty *G*, with full purpose of amendment of life,	317	5
and made us a kingdom of priests to serve his *G*	317	18
[and humbly confess our sins to Almighty *G*].	317	23
G spake these words, and said:	317	24
I am the Lord thy *G* who brought	317	25
shalt not take the Name of the Lord thy *G* in vain.	318	7
Blessed be *G*:	319	1
Thou shalt love the Lord thy *G* with all thy heart,	319	9
G is faithful and just to forgive us our sins,	320	2
Jesus the Son of *G*, let us come boldly	320	6
Let us humbly confess our sins unto Almighty *G*.	320	9
Most merciful *G*,	320	10
Blessed be *G*:	323	1
Almighty *G*, unto whom all hearts are open,	323	7
Thou shalt love the Lord thy *G* with all thy heart,	324	2
Holy *G*,	324	10
Glory be to *G* on high,	324	14
O Lord *G*, heavenly King, *G* the Father Almighty.	324	20
O Lord *G*, Lamb of *G*, Son of the Father,	324	22
Thou that sittest at the right hand of *G* the Father,	325	3
art most high in the glory of *G* the Father.	325	9
Thanks be to *G*.	325	15
We believe in one *G*,	326	6
the only Son of *G*,	326	11
G from *G*, Light from Light,	326	13
true *G* from true *G*,	326	14
I believe in one *G*,	327	20
the only-begotten Son of *G*,	327	25
G of *G*, Light of Light,	327	27
very *G* of very *G*,	327	28
Almighty and everliving *G*, who in thy holy Word	329	1
lead a new life, following the commandments of *G*,	330	11
and make your humble confession to Almighty *G*,	330	13
Let us humbly confess our sins unto Almighty *G*.	330	15
Almighty *G*,	331	1
Most merciful *G*,	331	21
Almighty *G*, our heavenly Father,	332	1
Hear the Word of *G* to all who truly turn to him.	332	7
G so loved the world, that he gave	332	10
Let us give thanks unto our Lord *G*.	333	5
holy Father, almighty, everlasting *G*.	333	9
Holy, holy, holy, Lord *G* of Hosts:	334	4
All glory be to thee, Almighty *G*,	334	9
O Lamb of *G*, that takest away the sins of the world,	337	3
The Gifts of *G* for the People of *G*.	338	1
everliving *G*, we most heartily thank thee	339	2
The peace of *G*, which passeth all understanding,	339	15
in the knowledge and love of *G*,	339	16
G Almighty, the Father, the Son, and the Holy Ghost,	339	18
The blessing of *G* Almighty, the Father, the Son,	339	20
Thanks be to *G*.	339	23
Thanks be to *G*.	340	2
Let us give thanks unto our Lord *G*.	340	13
holy Father, almighty, everlasting *G*.	341	3
Holy, holy, holy, Lord *G* of Hosts:	341	7
All glory be to thee, O Lord our *G*,	341	12
Offer to *G* a sacrifice of thanksgiving,	343	8
offering and sacrifice to *G*.	343	13
I beseech you, brethren, by the mercies of *G*,	343	14
a living sacrifice, holy and acceptable to *G*,	343	15
Through Christ let us continually offer to *G*	344	1
for with such sacrifices *G* is well pleased.	344	4
Worthy art thou, O Lord our *G*, to receive glory	344	5
thy co-eternal Son and Holy Spirit, thou art one *G*,	347	13
Hear the commandments of *G* to his people:	350	1
I am the Lord your *G* who brought you out	350	2
not invoke with malice the Name of the Lord your *G*.	350	7
Blessed be *G*:	351	1
The Lord our *G* is the only Lord.	351	8
Love the Lord your *G* with all your heart,	351	9
G, who is faithful and just, will forgive our sins	352	2
passed through the heavens, Jesus, the Son of *G*,	352	6
Let us confess our sins against *G* and our neighbor.	352	9
Most merciful *G*,	352	10
Almighty *G* have mercy on you,	353	1
Blessed by *G*:	355	1
Almighty *G*, to you all hearts are open,	355	7
Glory to *G* in the highest,	356	1
Lord *G*, heavenly King,	356	3
almighty *G* and Father,	356	4
Lord *G*, Lamb of *G*,	356	8
in the glory of *G* the Father.	356	18
Holy *G*,	356	22
Thanks be to *G*.	357	6
We believe in one *G*,	358	3
the only Son of *G*,	358	8
G from *G*, Light from Light,	358	10
true *G* from true *G*,	358	11
Let us confess our sins against *G* and our neighbor.	360	1
Most merciful *G*,	360	2
Almighty *G* have mercy on you,	360	15
Let us give thanks to the Lord our *G*.	361	5
Holy, holy, holy Lord, *G* of power and might,	362	4
G and Father of all.	362	14
The Gifts of *G* for the People of *G*.	364	17
Eternal *G*, heavenly Father,	365	9
Almighty and everliving *G*,	366	1
Thanks be to *G*.	366	15
Let us give thanks to the Lord our *G*.	367	5
Holy, holy, holy Lord, *G* of power and might,	367	13
We give thanks to you, O *G*,	368	1
We pray you, gracious *G*, to send	369	4

Let us give thanks to the Lord our *G*. 370 3
G of all power, Ruler of the Universe, 370 5
Holy, holy, holy Lord, *G* of power and might, 371 1
Lord *G* of our Fathers; 372 1
G of Abraham, Isaac, and Jacob; 372 1
G and Father of our Lord Jesus Christ: 372 2
Let us give thanks to the Lord our *G*. 372 21
for you alone are *G*, living and true, 373 2
Holy, holy, holy Lord, *G* of power and might, 373 12
and we pray to you, Lord our *G*. 375 3
glory are yours, Almighty *G* and Father, 375 27
Offer to *G* a sacrifice of thanksgiving, 376 4
offering and sacrifice to *G*. 376 9
I appeal to you, brethren, by the mercies of *G*, 376 10
a living sacrifice, holy and acceptable to *G*, 376 11
Through Christ let us continually offer to *G* 376 17
for such sacrifices are pleasing to *G*. 377 2
O Lord our *G*, you are worthy to receive 377 3
you are one *G*, one Lord, in Trinity of Persons 380 9
for the loving-kindness of *G*, 383 3
for the welfare of the holy Church of *G*, 383 7
For the good earth which *G* has given us, 384 14
and all our life, to Christ our *G*. 385 15
To thee, O Lord our *G*. 385 16
I ask your prayers for *G*'s people 385 17
I ask your prayers for all who seek *G*, 386 7
Praise *G* for those in every generation 386 14
Grant, Almighty *G*, that all who confess 388 2
For the holy Church of *G*, that it may be filled 389 15
and for all the holy people of *G*, we pray to you, 390 3
For all who fear *G* and believe in you, 390 4
and all our life to Christ our *G*. 391 21
To you, O Lord our *G*. 391 22
In peace, we pray to you, Lord *G*. 392 1
For the peace and unity of the Church of *G*; 392 12
For all who serve *G* in his Church. 392 16
We will exalt you, O *G* our King; 393 2
Almighty and eternal *G*, ruler of all things 394 9
Almighty *G*, to whom our needs are known 394 12
O Lord our *G*, accept the fervent prayers 395 3
Almighty *G*, by your Holy Spirit you have made 395 17
G so loved the world that he gave his only Son, 396 1
Most merciful *G*, 397 19
Almighty *G* have mercy on you, 398 7
The Gifts of *G* for the People of *G*. 399 1
Thanks be to *G*. 399 14
Let us give thanks to the Lord our *G*. 402 5
Holy, holy, holy Lord, *G* of power and might, 402 9
love of *G* and the fellowship of the Holy Spirit 404 2
Let us give thanks to the Lord our *G*. 404 7
Holy, holy, holy Lord, *G* of power and might, 404 11
Lamb of *G*, you take away the sins of the world: 407 1
Blessed be *G*: 413 1
There is one hope in *G*'s call to us; 413 8
One *G* and Father of all. 413 10
Thanks be to *G*. 414 3
and with *G*'s grace I will follow him as my Savior 415 12
Do you believe in *G* the Father? 416 6
I believe in *G*, the Father almighty, 416 7
Do you believe in Jesus Christ, the Son of *G*? 416 9
Do you believe in *G* the Holy Spirit? 416 20
I will, with *G*'s help. 417 7
News of *G* in Christ? 417 12
Almighty *G*, we thank you that by the death 418 1
one *G*, now and for ever. 418 9
G, the Father, Son, and Holy Spirit, 418 19
Almighty and everliving *G*, let your fatherly hand 419 4
you may do *G*'s will in the service 420 2
Almighty *G*, look with favor upon this person 421 2
G to witness and bless the joining together 423 2
marriage was established by *G* in creation, 423 4
intended by *G* for their mutual joy; 423 10
when it is *G*'s will, for the procreation of children 423 12
purposes for which it was instituted by *G*. 423 16
here in the presence of *G*, 424 4
and in accordance with *G*'s Word, 424 6
O gracious and everliving *G*, you have created 425 7
one *G*, for ever and ever. 425 13
In the Name of *G*, I, N., take you, N., to be my wife, 427 1
In the Name of *G*, I, N., take you, N., to be my husband, 427 5
and of the Holy Spirit (or in the Name of *G*). 427 16
Those whom *G* has joined together let no one 428 6
Eternal *G*, creator and preserver of all life, 429 2
Most gracious *G*, we give you thanks 430 10
one *G*, for ever and ever. 430 25
O *G*, you have so consecrated 431 1
one *G*, now and for ever. 431 8
G the Father, *G* the Son, *G* the Holy Spirit, bless, 431 9
O *G*, the giver of all that is true and lovely 432 1
blessing of *G* and of his Church upon his marriage. 433 2
that you promise, with the help of *G*, to fulfill 433 3
Those whom *G* has joined together let no one 434 7
In the Name of *G*, I, N., take you, N., to be my 436 1
till death do us part, according to *G*'s holy ordinance; 436 9
in giving thanks to Almighty *G* 440 4
It has pleased *G* our heavenly Father 440 8
As *G* has made us his children by adoption and grace, 441 5
May *G*, the Father of all, bless our child 441 7
Since it has pleased *G* to bestow 441 10
my spirit rejoices in *G* my Savior;* 441 13
our *G* is full of compassion. 442 18
O *G*, you have taught us through your blessed Son 443 21
O gracious *G*, we give you humble and hearty thanks 444 1
Almighty *G*, giver of life and love, bless 444 8
O eternal *G*, you have promised to be a father 444 15
he may become the child of *G*; 444 19
Into your hands, O *G*, we place your child 444 20
May *G* the Father, who by Baptism adopts 445 3
May *G* the Son, who sanctified 445 5
May *G* the Holy Spirit, who has made the Church 445 7
I confess to Almighty *G*, 447 5
I pray *G* to have mercy on me. 447 9
and I humbly beg forgiveness of *G* 447 10
Thanks be to *G*. 448 13
Have mercy on me, O *G*, 449 1
Holy *G*, Holy and Mighty, Holy Immortal One, 449 7
May *G* in his love enlighten your heart, 449 10
Hear the Word of *G* to all who truly turn to him. 449 12
G so loved the world, that he gave 449 15
Almighty *G*, our Creator and our Redeemer. 450 7
Holy *G*, heavenly Father, you formed me 450 8
May Almighty *G* in mercy receive your confession 451 3
Thanks be to *G*. 451 21

God

Most merciful *G*,	454	1
Almighty *G* have mercy on you,	455	6
one *G*, for ever and ever.	455	14
Thanks be to *G*.	457	12
O Father of mercies and *G* of all comfort,	458	1
O *G*, the strength of the weak	458	11
O *G* of heavenly powers,	458	16
Almighty *G* our heavenly Father, graciously comfort	459	7
Strengthen your servant N., O *G*, to do	459	12
May *G* the Father bless you, *G* the Son heal you,	460	5
G the Holy Spirit give you strength.	460	6
May *G* the holy and undivided Trinity guard	460	6
O *G*, the source of all health:	461	1
you hold me in eternal life, my Lord and my *G*.	461	11
Almighty *G*, look on this your servant,	462	1
G the Father,	462	5
G the Son,	462	7
G the Holy Spirit,	462	9
Holy Trinity, one *G*,	463	1
Jesus, Lamb of *G*:	463	23
one *G*, for ever and ever.	464	19
In the Name of *G* the Father Almighty who created	464	22
and your dwelling place in the Paradise of *G*.	464	26
through the mercy of *G*, rest in peace.	465	8
G's eternal sabbath rest.	465	13
Almighty *G*, our Father in heaven,	466	7
the living *G*, and the *G* of those who live.	466	10
Let us pray with confidence to *G*,	466	13
one *G*, for ever and ever.	466	19
that they may cast their care on *G*,	467	2
Almighty *G*, look with pity upon the sorrows	467	3
though this body be destroyed, yet shall I see *G*;	469	6
O *G*, whose mercies cannot be numbered:	470	1
one *G*, now and for ever.	470	5
O *G*, whose beloved Son did take little children	470	7
so longeth my soul after thee, O *G*.	471	2
My soul is athirst for *G*, yea, even for the living *G*; *	471	3
when shall I come to appear before the presence of *G*?	471	4
Where now is thy *G*?	471	6
and brought them forth into the house of *G*;	471	9
O put thy trust in *G*; *	471	14
which is the help of my countenance, and my *G*.	471	16
G is our hope and strength, *	471	17
the streams whereof make glad the city of *G*, *	471	23
G is in the midst of her,	472	1
G shall help her, and that right early.	472	3
Be still then, and know that I am *G*; *	472	4
the *G* of Jacob is our refuge.	472	8
thou art *G* from everlasting, and world without end.	472	13
yea, our *G* is merciful.	479	9
Almighty *G*, who hast knit together thine elect	480	4
one *G*, for ever and ever.	481	29
Almighty *G*, we thank thee that in thy great love	482	1
Thanks be to *G*.	483	13
Yet, O Lord *G* most holy, O Lord most mighty,	484	8
but spare us, Lord most holy, O *G* most mighty,	484	13
we commend to Almighty *G* our brother	485	11
O Almighty *G*, the *G* of the spirits of all flesh,	486	7
through the mercy of *G*, rest in peace.	486	20
The *G* of peace, who brought again from the dead	486	21
O *G*, whose blessed Son was laid in a sepulcher	487	5
Almighty and everlasting *G*, we yield	487	10
Almighty *G*, with whom do live the spirits	488	1
Almighty *G*, our heavenly Father, in whose hands	488	26
O *G*, whose days are without end,	489	3
in favor with thee our *G*;	489	12
O *G*, the King of saints, we praise	489	14
O Lord Jesus Christ, Son of the living *G*, we pray	489	23
one *G*, now and for ever.	489	29
Almighty *G*, Father of mercies and giver	489	30
and in my body I shall see *G*.	491	10
Holy *G*, Holy and Mighty,	492	9
O *G*, who by the glorious resurrection of your Son	493	4
one *G*, for ever and ever.	493	9
O *G*, whose mercies cannot be numbered:	493	10
one *G*, now and for ever.	493	14
O *G* of grace and glory, we remember	493	16
O *G*, whose beloved Son took children	494	1
one *G*, now and for ever.	494	5
Most merciful *G*, whose wisdom is beyond	494	7
I believe in *G*, the Father almighty,	496	3
through the mercy of *G*, rest in peace.	498	11
Almighty *G*, we thank you that in your great love	498	12
Thanks be to *G*.	500	2
we commend to Almighty *G* our brother	501	13
through the mercy of *G*, rest in peace.	502	18
Thanks be to *G*.	502	22
The *G* of peace, who brought again from the dead	503	1
O *G*, whose blessed Son was laid in a sepulcher	503	7
Almighty *G*, with whom still live the spirits	503	12
O *G*, whose days are without end,	504	1
in favor with you, our *G*, and in perfect charity	504	9
O *G*, the King of saints, we praise and glorify	504	12
Merciful *G*, Father of our Lord	505	1
Almighty *G*, Father of mercies and giver	505	17
Blessed be *G*:	512	1
Almighty *G*, to you all hearts are open,	512	7
Bishop in the Church of *G*,	513	1
Testaments to be the Word of *G*,	513	10
bishop of the Church of *G* to serve	514	3
and offer our prayers to Almighty *G*	514	16
O *G* of unchangeable power and eternal light:	515	4
one *G*, for ever and ever.	515	13
Thanks be to *G*.	516	3
G's holy Church is called to be one	517	3
those of every generation who have looked to *G*	517	16
Are you persuaded that *G* has called you	517	19
nourish them from the riches of *G*'s grace,	518	14
I will, for the love of *G*.	518	21
you have committed yourself to *G*,	519	2
We believe in one *G*.	519	5
the only Son of *G*,	519	11
G from *G*, Light from Light,	519	13
true *G* from true *G*,	519	14
G and Father of our Lord Jesus Christ,	520	11
and *G* of all comfort, dwelling on high	520	12
one *G*, now and for ever.	523	10
The blessing, mercy, and grace of *G* Almighty,	523	15
Thanks be to *G*.	523	20
Blessed be *G*:	525	1
Almighty *G*, to you all hearts are open,	525	7
Bishop in the Church of *G*,	526	1
Testaments to be the Word of *G*,	526	16
O *G* of unchangeable power and eternal light:	528	2

one G, for ever and ever. 528 11
Thanks be to G. 529 2
We believe in one G, 529 9
the only Son of G, 530 2
G from G, Light from Light, 530 4
true G from true G, 530 5
My brother, the Church is the family of G, 531 1
declare G's forgiveness to penitent sinners, 531 13
to pronounce G's blessing, 531 14
and strengthen them to glorify G 531 19
do you believe that you are truly called by G 531 21
Will you endeavor so to minister the Word of G 532 9
build up the family of G? 532 17
asking G's grace, both for yourself and for others, 532 25
offering all your labors to G, 532 26
G and Father of all, we praise you 533 1
one G, for ever and ever. 534 9
preach the Word of G 534 11
priest of the Church of G. 534 13
one G, now and for ever. 535 10
The blessing of G Almighty, 535 11
Thanks be to G. 535 15
Blessed be G: 537 1
Almighty G, to you all hearts are open, 537 7
Bishop in the Church of G, 538 1
Testaments to be the Word of G, 538 16
O G of unchangeable power and eternal light: 540 2
one G, for ever and ever. 540 11
Thanks be to G. 541 2
We believe in one G, 541 9
the only Son of G, 542 2
G from G, Light from Light, 542 4
true G from true G, 542 5
serving G the Father, through the power 543 2
G now calls you to a special ministry 543 3
and in the ministration of G's Word 543 14
do you believe that you are truly called by G 543 19
O G, most merciful Father, we praise you 545 1
one G, for ever and ever. 545 18
the sign of your authority to proclaim G's Word 545 20
one G, now and for ever. 547 6
Thanks be to G. 547 9
G the Father, 548 1
G the Son, 548 3
G the Holy Spirit, 548 5
Holy Trinity, one G, 548 7
For the holy Church of G, that it may be filled 548 11
For all who fear G and believe in you, 549 16
and all our life to Christ our G. 550 28
To you, O Lord our G. 550 29
Everliving G, whose power is limitless, 552 6
Let us then offer our prayers to G for all his people, 560 1
Everliving G, strengthen and sustain 560 6
one G, for ever and ever. 560 10
O Lord my G, I am not worthy 562 9
one G, now and for ever. 564 10
Through the ages, Almighty G has moved 567 1
consecrate it in G's Name. 567 6
Almighty G, we thank you for making us 567 8
enjoy the liberty and splendor of the children of G. 569 18
One G and Father of all. 569 20
Let us give thanks to the Lord our G. 570 3
We thank you, Almighty G, for the gift of water. 570 5
Be acceptable to you, O Lord our G. 571 6
Almighty G, all times are your seasons, 572 9
We give you thanks, O G, for the gifts 573 1
We praise you, Almighty and eternal G, 573 8
Blessed be your Name, Lord G. 573 12
Lord G, hear us. 574 1
Let us thank G whom we worship 578 1
Eternal G, the heaven of heavens cannot contain you, 578 3
be still and know that you are G, 578 14
"There is no help for him in his G." 587 6
Rise up, O Lord; set me free, O my G; * 587 15
Answer me when I call, O G, defender of my cause; * 587 20
Hearken to my cry for help, my King and my G, * 588 19
For you are not a G who takes pleasure 588 23
Declare them guilty, O G; * 589 13
O Lord my G, I take refuge in you; * 590 20
O Lord my G, if I have done these things: * 590 24
Awake, O my G, decree justice; * 591 8
for you test the mind and heart, O righteous G. 591 17
G is my shield and defense; * 591 18
G is a righteous judge; * 591 20
G sits in judgment every day. 591 21
If they will not repent, G will whet his sword; * 591 22
and also all the peoples that forget G. 594 12
The wicked are so proud that they care not for G; * 594 25
their only thought is, "G does not matter." 594 26
They say in their heart, "G has forgotten; * 595 16
lift up your hand, O G; * 595 19
Why should the wicked revile G? * 595 21
Look upon me and answer me, O Lord my G; * 598 4
The fool has said in his heart, "There is no G." * 598 12
if there is one who seeks after G. 598 17
because G is in the company of the righteous. 598 25
Protect me, O G, for I take refuge in you; * 599 19
I call upon you, O G, for you will answer me; * 601 9
My G, my rock in whom I put my trust, * 602 9
and cried out to my G for help. 602 19
and have not offended against my G; 604 6
With the faithful you show yourself faithful, O G; * 604 14
my G, you make my darkness bright. 604 21
with the help of my G I will scale any wall. 604 23
As for G, his ways are perfect; 604 24
For who is G, but the Lord? * 605 1
who is the Rock, except our G? 605 2
It is G who girds me about with strength * 605 3
Exalted is the G of my salvation! 606 4
He is the G who gave me victory * 606 5
The heavens declare the glory of G, * 606 15
the Name of the G of Jacob defend you; 608 2
and triumph in the Name of our G; * 608 10
but we will call upon the Name of the Lord our G. 608 16
My G, my G, why have you forsaken me? * 610 1
O my G, I cry in the daytime, 610 4
you were my G when I was still in my 610 21
and a just reward from the G of their salvation." 613 24
of those who seek your face, O G of Jacob. 613 26
my G, I put my trust in you; * 614 14
for you are the G of my salvation; 614 22
Deliver Israel, O G, * 616 5
do not forsake me, O G of my salvation. 618 18
the G of glory thunders; * 620 10

O LORD my G, I cried out to you, *	621	6
O LORD my G, I will give you thanks for ever.	622	6
O LORD, O G of truth.	622	19
I have said, "You are my G.	623	21
Happy is the nation whose G is the LORD! *	626	23
to my defense, my G and my Lord!	631	17
Give me justice, O LORD my G,	631	18
there is no fear of G before his eyes.	632	4
How priceless is your love, O G! *	632	17
Those who are blessed by G shall possess the land, *	635	3
The law of their G is in their heart, *	635	24
you will answer me, O Lord my G.	637	28
be not far from me, O my G.	638	12
a song of praise to our G; *	640	6
Great things are they that you have done, O LORD my G!	640	11
"I love to do your will, O my G;	640	21
do not tarry, O my G.	641	22
Blessed be the LORD G of Israel, *	642	26
so longs my soul for you, O G.	643	2
My soul is athirst for G, athirst for the living G; *	643	3
when shall I come to appear before the presence of G?	643	4
"Where now is your G?"	643	7
house of G,	643	10
Put your trust in G; *	643	15
who is the help of my countenance, and my G.	643	17
a prayer to the G of my life.	643	25
I will say to the G of my strength,	644	1
and say to me, "Where now is your G?"	644	8
Put your trust in G; *	644	11
who is the help of my countenance, and my G.	644	13
Give judgment for me, O G,	644	14
For you are the G of my strength;	644	17
That I may go to the altar of G,	644	24
to the G of my joy and gladness; *	644	25
and on the harp I will give thanks to you, O G my G.	644	26
Put your trust in G; *	645	3
who is the help of my countenance, and my G.	645	5
We have heard with our ears, O G,	645	6
You are my King and my G; *	645	18
Every day we gloried in G, *	646	1
If we have forgotten the Name of our G, *	646	26
or stretched out our hands to some strange g,	646	27
Will not G find it out? *	646	28
because G has blessed you for ever.	647	16
Your throne, O G, endures for ever and ever, *	648	1
Therefore G, your G, has anointed you *	648	4
G is our refuge and strength, *	649	1
the G of Jacob is our stronghold.	649	9
whose streams make glad the city of G, *	649	10
G is in the midst of her;	649	12
G shall help her at the break of day.	649	14
G has spoken, and the earth shall melt away.	649	16
the G of Jacob is our stronghold.	649	18
"Be still, then, and know that I am G; *	650	1
the G of Jacob is our stronghold.	650	5
shout to G with a cry of joy.	650	7
G has gone up with a shout, *	650	14
Sing praises to G, sing praises; *	650	16
For G is King of all the earth; *	650	18
G reigns over the nations; *	650	20
G sits upon his holy throne.	650	21
with the people of the G of Abraham.	650	23
The rulers of the earth belong to G, *	650	24
in the city of our G is his holy hill.	651	2
G is in her citadels; *	651	6
in the city of the LORD of hosts, in the city of our G; *	651	16
G has established her for ever.	651	17
have waited in silence on your loving-kindness, O G, *	651	18
Your praise, like your Name, O G, reaches to	651	20
This G is our G for ever and ever; *	652	4
or deliver to G the price of our life;	652	18
But G will ransom my life; *	653	13
The LORD, the G of gods, has spoken; *	654	1
G reveals himself in glory.	654	5
Our G will come and will not keep silence; *	654	6
for G himself is judge.	654	15
for I am G, your G.	654	18
Offer to G a sacrifice of thanksgiving *	655	7
But to the wicked G says: *	655	11
Consider this well, you who forget G, *	655	26
the salvation of G."	656	4
Have mercy on me, O G, according to your	656	5
Create in me a clean heart, O G, *	657	1
Deliver me from death, O G, *	657	9
O G of my salvation.	657	11
The sacrifice of G is a troubled spirit; *	657	16
a broken and contrite heart, O G, you will not	657	17
Oh, that G would demolish you utterly, *	658	8
"This is the one who did not take G for a refuge, *	658	13
But I am like a green olive tree in the house of G; *	658	16
I trust in the mercy of G for ever and ever.	658	17
The fool has said in his heart, "There is no G." *	658	21
G looks down from heaven upon us all, *	659	1
if there is one who seeks after G.	659	3
and do not call upon G?	659	9
for G has scattered the bones of the enemy;	659	12
they are put to shame, because G has rejected them.	659	13
when G restores the fortunes of his people	659	15
Save me, O G, by your Name; *	659	17
Hear my prayer, O G; *	659	19
those who have no regard for G.	659	23
Behold, G is my helper; *	659	24
Hear my prayer, O G; *	660	5
and walked with the throng in the house of G.	661	13
But I will call upon G, *	661	17
G, who is enthroned of old, will hear me and	661	25
they never change; they do not fear G.	661	27
down to the pit of destruction, O G.	662	9
Have mercy on me, O G,	662	12
In G, whose word I praise,	662	19
in G I trust and will not be afraid, *	662	20
O G, in your anger, cast down the peoples.	663	5
this I know, for G is on my side.	663	10
In G the LORD, whose word I praise,	663	11
in G I trust and will not be afraid, *	663	12
I am bound by the vow I made to you, O G; *	663	14
that I may walk before G in the light of the living.	663	18
Be merciful to me, O G, be merciful,	663	19
I will call upon the Most High G, *	663	23
the G who maintains my cause.	663	24
G will send forth his love and his faithfulness.	663	27
Exalt yourself above the heavens, O G, *	664	8
My heart is firmly fixed, O G, my heart is fixed; *	664	10

Exalt yourself above the heavens, O G, * 664 19
O G, break their teeth in their mouths; * 665 5
surely, there is a G who rules in the earth." 665 17
Rescue me from my enemies, O G; * 665 18
for you, LORD G of hosts, are Israel's G. 666 4
for you, O G, are my stronghold. 666 15
My merciful G comes to meet me; * 666 16
G will let me look in triumph on my enemies. 666 17
Slay them, O G, lest my people forget; * 666 18
Let everyone know that G rules in Jacob, * 666 26
for you, O G, are my stronghold and my merciful G. 667 8
O G, you have cast us off and broken us; * 667 9
G spoke from his holy place and said: * 667 20
Have you not cast us off, O G? * 668 6
you no longer go out, O G, with our armies. 668 7
With G we will do valiant deeds, * 668 10
Hear my cry, O G, * 668 12
For you, O G, have heard my vows; * 668 21
Let him sit enthroned before G for ever; * 669 1
For G alone my soul in silence waits; * 669 5
For G alone my soul in silence waits; * 669 16
In G is my safety and my honor; * 669 20
G is my strong rock and my refuge. 669 21
pour out your hearts before him, for G is our refuge. 669 23
G has spoken once, twice have I heard it, * 670 8
that power belongs to G. 670 9
O G, you are my G; eagerly I seek you; * 670 12
But the king will rejoice in G; 671 7
Hear my voice, O G, when I complain; * 671 10
but G will loose an arrow at them, 671 24
Everyone will stand in awe and declare G's deeds; * 672 3
You are to be praised, O G, in Zion; * 672 7
O G of our salvation, * 672 18
the river of G is full of water. 673 6
Be joyful in G, all you lands; * 673 18
Say to G, "How awesome are your deeds! * 673 21
Come now and see the works of G, * 674 1
Bless our G, you peoples; * 674 9
For you, O G, have proved us; * 674 13
Come and listen, all you who fear G, * 674 27
But in truth G has heard me; * 675 5
Blessed be G, who has not rejected my prayer, * 675 7
May G be merciful to us and bless us, * 675 9
Let the peoples praise you, O G; * 675 13
Let the peoples praise you, O G; * 675 18
may G, our own G, give us his blessing. 675 21
May G give us his blessing, * 675 22
Let G arise, and let his enemies be scattered; * 676 1
the presence of G. 676 5
But let the righteous be glad and rejoice before G; * 676 6
Sing to G, sing praises to his Name; 676 8
G in his holy habitation! 676 12
G gives the solitary a home and brings forth prisoners 676 13
O G, when you went forth before your people, * 676 16
at the presence of G, the G of Sinai, * 676 19
at the presence of G, the G of Israel. 676 20
You sent a gracious rain, O G, 676 21
in your goodness, O G, you have made provision 676 24
at the hill which G chose for his resting place? * 677 13
The chariots of G are twenty thousand, 677 15
that the LORD G might dwell among them. 677 20
the G of our salvation, who bears our burdens. 677 22
He is our G, the G of our salvation; * 677 23
G is the LORD, by whom we escape death. 677 24
G shall crush the heads of his enemies, * 677 25
They see your procession, O G, * 678 5
procession into the sanctuary, my G and my King. 678 6
Bless G in the congregation; * 678 9
Send forth your strength, O G; * 678 14
establish, O G, what you have wrought for us. 678 15
let Ethiopia stretch out her hands to G. 678 23
Sing to G, O kingdoms of the earth; * 678 24
Ascribe power to G; * 679 1
How wonderful is G in his holy places! * 679 4
the G of Israel giving strength and power 679 5
Blessed be G! 679 6
Save me, O G, * 679 7
my eyes have failed from looking for my G. 679 15
O G, you know my foolishness, * 679 20
O G of Israel. 679 25
"In your great mercy, O G, * 680 15
your help, O G, will lift me up on high. 681 23
I will praise the Name of G in song; * 681 24
you who seek G, your heart shall live. 682 2
For G will save Zion and rebuild the cities of Judah; * 682 7
Be pleased, O G, to deliver me; * 682 11
come to me speedily, O G. 682 23
Deliver me, my G, from the hand of the wicked, * 683 7
They say, "G has forsaken him; 683 22
O G, be not far from me; * 684 1
come quickly to help me, O my G. 684 2
O G, you have taught me since I was young, * 684 14
And now that I am old and gray-headed, O G, 684 16
Your righteousness, O G, reaches to the heavens; * 684 20
who is like you, O G? 684 22
for your faithfulness, O my G; * 685 2
Give the King your justice, O G, * 685 9
Truly, G is good to Israel, * 687 1
They say, "How should G know? * 687 21
Until I entered the sanctuary of G * 688 11
G is the strength of my heart and my portion for ever. 689 2
But it is good for me to be near G; * 689 5
O G, why have you utterly cast us off? * 689 9
They burned down all the meeting-places of G 689 25
How long, O G, will the adversary scoff? * 690 4
Yet G is my King from ancient times, * 690 8
Arise, O G, maintain your cause; * 690 28
We give you thanks, O G, we give you thanks, * 691 3
"I will appoint a time," says G; * 691 6
It is G who judges; * 691 16
I will sing praises to the G of Jacob. 691 23
In Judah is G known; * 692 1
At your rebuke, O G of Jacob, * 692 12
When G rose up to judgment * 692 18
Make a vow to the LORD your G and keep it; * 692 22
I will cry aloud to G; * 693 1
I think of G, I am restless, * 693 6
Has G forgotten to be gracious? * 693 18
Your way, O G, is holy; * 693 26
who is so great a g as our G? 693 27
You are the G who works wonders * 694 1
The waters saw you, O G; 694 5
So that they might put their trust in G, * 695 13
and not forget the deeds of G, 695 14

and whose spirit was not faithful to *G*. 695 19
They did not keep the covenant of *G*, * 695 22
They tested *G* in their hearts, * 696 9
They railed against *G* and said, * 696 11
"Can *G* set a table in the wilderness? 696 12
For they had no faith in *G*, * 696 20
So *G*'s anger mounted against them; * 697 11
and repent, and diligently search for *G*. 697 19
They would remember that *G* was their rock, * 697 20
and the Most High *G* their redeemer. 697 21
Again and again they tempted *G* * 698 9
But they tested the Most High *G*, and defied him, * 699 18
When *G* heard this, he was angry * 699 24
O *G*, the heathen have come into your inheritance; 701 1
Help us, O *G* our Savior, 701 24
Why should the heathen say, "Where is their *G*?" * 702 1
Restore us, O *G* of hosts; * 702 16
O LORD *G* of hosts, * 702 18
Restore us, O *G* of hosts; * 703 1
Turn now, O *G* of hosts, look down from heaven; 703 15
Restore us, O LORD *G* of hosts; * 703 24
Sing with joy to *G* our strength * 704 1
and raise a loud shout to the *G* of Jacob. 704 2
a law of the *G* of Jacob. 704 8
There shall be no strange *g* among you; * 704 19
you shall not worship a foreign *g*. 704 20
I am the LORD your *G*, 704 21
G takes his stand in the council of heaven; * 705 9
Arise, O *G*, and rule the earth, * 706 1
O *G*, do not be silent; * 706 3
do not keep still nor hold your peace, O *G*; 706 4
the fields of *G* as our possession." 707 2
O my *G*, make them like whirling dust * 707 3
my heart and my flesh rejoice in the living *G*. 707 18
my King and my *G*. 707 22
and the *G* of gods will reveal himself in Zion. 708 5
LORD *G* of hosts, hear my prayer; * 708 6
hearken, O *G* of Jacob. 708 7
Behold our defender, O *G*; * 708 8
and to stand at the threshold of the house of my *G* 708 12
For the LORD *G* is both sun and shield; * 708 14
Restore us then, O *G* our Savior; * 709 1
I will listen to what the LORD *G* is saying, * 709 9
Be merciful to me, O LORD, for you are my *G*; * 710 3
and you alone are *G*. 710 20
I will thank you, O LORD my *G*, with all my heart, * 710 24
The arrogant rise up against me, O *G*, 711 1
O city of our *G*. 711 16
O LORD, my *G*, my Savior, * 712 1
G is much to be feared in the council 714 7
Who is like you, LORD *G* of hosts? * 714 9
my *G*, and the rock of my salvation.' 715 19
from age to age you are *G*. 718 3
the graciousness of the LORD our *G* be upon us; * 719 7
my *G* in whom I put my trust." 719 14
shall flourish in the courts of our *G*; 721 24
O LORD *G* of vengeance, * 722 18
O *G* of vengeance, show yourself. 722 19
the *G* of Jacob takes no notice." 723 8
and my *G* the rock of my trust. 724 10
the LORD our *G* will destroy them. 724 13
For the LORD is a great *G*, * 724 18
For he is our *G*, 725 3
seen the victory of our *G*. 728 9
Proclaim the greatness of the LORD our *G* 729 8
"O LORD our *G*, you answered them indeed; * 729 16
you were a *G* who forgave them, 729 17
Proclaim the greatness of the LORD our *G* 729 19
for the LORD our *G* is the Holy One. 729 21
Know this: The LORD himself is *G*; * 729 25
And I said, "O my *G*, 732 24
O LORD my *G*, how excellent is your greatness! 735 2
and seek their food from *G*. 736 20
I will praise my *G* while I have my being. 737 21
He is the LORD our *G*; * 738 13
For *G* remembered his holy word * 741 9
and they put *G* to the test in the desert. 742 27
They forgot *G* their Savior, * 743 13
Save us, O LORD our *G*, 745 19
Blessed be the LORD, the *G* of Israel, 745 23
Because they rebelled against the words of *G* * 747 3
My heart is firmly fixed, O *G*, my heart is fixed; * 749 17
Exalt yourself above the heavens, O *G*, * 750 3
G spoke from his holy place and said, * 750 7
Have you not cast us off, O *G*? * 750 17
you no longer go out, O *G*, with our armies. 750 18
With *G* we will do valiant deeds, * 750 21
Hold not your tongue, O *G* of my praise; * 750 23
Help me, O LORD my *G*; * 752 27
Who is like the LORD our *G*, who sits enthroned 756 10
Judah became *G*'s sanctuary * 756 21
at the presence of the *G* of Jacob, 757 10
"Where then is their *G*?" 757 17
Our *G* is in heaven; * 757 18
our *G* is full of compassion. 759 11
G is the LORD; he has shined upon us; * 762 25
"You are my *G*, and I will thank you; * 763 1
you are my *G*, and I will exalt you." 763 2
I will keep the commandments of my *G*. 773 4
Because of the house of the LORD our *G*, * 780 13
So our eyes look to the LORD our *G*, * 780 19
Let us go to *G*'s dwelling place; * 786 11
in the courts of the house of our *G*. 788 5
Give thanks to the *G* of gods, * 789 22
Give thanks to the *G* of heaven, * 791 21
How deep I find your thoughts, O *G*! * 795 10
Oh, that you would slay the wicked, O *G*! * 795 16
Search me out, O *G*, and know my heart; * 795 24
I have said to the LORD, "You are my *G*; * 796 13
Teach me to do what pleases you, for you are my *G*; * 799 21
O *G*, I will sing to you a new song; * 800 19
happy are the people whose *G* is the LORD! 801 11
I will exalt you, O *G* my King, * 801 12
I will sing praises to my *G* while I have my being. 803 6
Happy are they who have the *G* of Jacob 803 11
whose hope is in the LORD their *G*; 803 12
your *G*, O Zion, throughout all generations. 803 25
How good it is to sing praises to our *G*! * 804 2
make music to our *G* upon the harp. 804 15
praise your *G*, O Zion; 805 2
Let the praises of *G* be in their throat * 807 12
Praise *G* in his holy temple; * 807 22
O *G*, the creator and preserver of all mankind, 814 6
O *G*, you made us in your own image 815 13

Eternal G, in whose perfect kingdom no sword is drawn 815 22
Almighty G our heavenly Father, guide the nations 816 1
O G, the Father of all, whose Son commanded 816 5
Everliving G, whose will it is that all should come 816 16
one G, now and for ever. 817 2
Almighty and everlasting G, from whom cometh 817 3
O G, by your grace you have called us in this Diocese 817 10
Almighty and everliving G, ruler 817 18
Almighty and everliving G, source 818 1
Almighty G, giver of every good gift: 818 8
O G the Father of our Lord Jesus Christ, 818 14
one G and Father of us all, 818 20
O G, you prepared your disciples 819 1
one G, now and for ever. 819 12
O G, whom saints and angels delight 819 13
Almighty G, who hast given us this good land 820 1
one G, world without end. 820 25
O G, the fountain of wisdom, 821 1
Almighty G, who sittest in the throne judging right: 821 8
Almighty G our heavenly Father, 822 17
Almighty G, to whom we must account 822 23
Almighty G, we commend to your gracious care 823 1
O G our Father, whose Son forgave 823 8
Grant, O G, that your holy and life-giving Spirit 823 17
O G, you have bound us together in a common life. 824 1
G, we thank you for making the earth fruitful, 824 6
O Eternal G, bless all schools, colleges, 824 16
O G, in the course of this busy life, 825 1
you proclaimed the kingdom of G in villages, 825 17
Almighty and most merciful G, we remember 826 1
Almighty G, whose loving hand hath given 827 1
Almighty G, you proclaim your truth in every age 827 6
Almighty and everlasting G, you made the universe 827 11
Almighty G, in giving us dominion over things 827 17
O G, heavenly Father, who by thy Son 828 9
O G our heavenly Father, you have blessed 828 16
Almighty G, our heavenly Father, who settest 828 22
Almighty G, heavenly Father, you have blessed 829 9
G our Father, you see your children growing 829 14
Almighty G, whose Son had nowhere to lay his head: 829 22
Look with mercy, O G our Father, 830 1
O G, our times are in your hand: 830 8
O G, whose fatherly care reacheth 830 19
O G, our heavenly Father, whose glory fills 831 1
Almighty G, we entrust all who are dear to us 831 7
O G, by whom the meek are guided in judgment, 832 6
O G of peace, who hast taught 832 13
be still and know that thou art G; 832 17
Almighty and eternal G, so draw our hearts to thee, 832 24
O Almighty G, who pourest out on all who desire it 833 19
Almighty G, who hast promised to hear the petitions 834 1
one G, for ever and ever. 834 17
Grant, we beseech thee, Almighty G, 834 18
O G our King, by the resurrection 835 1
Blessed are you, O Lord G, King of the Universe, 835 13
G's holy Name be blessed 835 16
Let us give thanks to G our Father 837 1
Almighty G, you sent your Son 838 1
We give thanks to you, O Lord our G, 838 9
In your mercy, O Lord our G, 838 17
Almighty G, giver of all good things: 838 21
O G, who created all peoples in your image, 840 1
We give you thanks, most gracious G, 840 7
Most gracious G, by whose knowledge 840 14
Almighty G and heavenly Father, we give 841 7
We are part of G's creation, 845 2
made in the image of G. 845 3
What does it mean to be created in the image of G? 845 4
live in harmony with creation and with G. 845 7
Why then do we live apart from G 845 8
Because we rebel against G, 845 13
we put ourselves in the place of G. 845 14
Our help is in G. 845 16
How did G first help us? 845 17
G first helped us be revealing himself and his will, 845 18
What do we learn about G as creator 846 1
We learn that there is one G, the Father Almighty, 846 3
a single loving G who creates, sustains, and directs 846 8
in accordance with G's purposes. 846 12
because all are created in the image of G, 846 15
all can respond to the love of G. 846 16
community created by a covenant with G. 846 19
What is meant by a covenant with G? 846 20
A covenant is a relationship initiated by G, 846 21
The Old Covenant is the one given by G 846 24
What did G promise them? 846 26
G promised that they would be his people 847 1
What response did G require from the chosen people? 847 3
G required the chosen people to be faithful; 847 4
and to walk humbly with their G. 847 5
Where in the Old Testament is G's will 847 9
G's will for us is shown most clearly 847 11
our duty to G, and our duty to our neighbors. 847 17
What is our duty to G? 847 19
Our duty is to believe and trust in G; 847 20
To love and obey G and to bring 847 21
To put nothing in the place of G; 847 23
To show G respect in thought, word, and deed; 847 24
and the study of G's ways. 847 27
To show respect for the life G has given us; 848 7
to be kind to all the creatures of G; 848 10
To use all our bodily desires as G intended; 848 11
as ones who must answer for them to G; 848 15
and to do our duty for the love of G, 848 20
define our relationship with G and our neighbors. 848 24
seeking of our own will instead of the will of G, 848 30
thus distorting our relationship with G, 848 30
our relationship with G is distorted. 849 3
Redemption is the act of G which sets us free 849 5
How did G prepare us for redemption? 849 7
G sent the prophets to call us back to himself, to 849 8
The Messiah is one sent by G to free us 849 12
so that with the help of G we may live 849 13
in harmony with G, within ourselves, 849 14
the only Son of G. 849 18
and shows us the nature of G. 849 22
What is the nature of G revealed in Jesus? 849 23
G is love. 849 24
We mean that by G's own act, his divine Son received 849 28
might be adopted as children of G, 850 3
made heirs of G's kingdom. 850 4
freed from the power of sin and reconciled to G. 850 9
The New Covenant is the new relationship with G 850 27

Christ promised to bring us into the kingdom of *G* 851 2
You shall love the Lord your *G* with all your heart, 851 11
creeds are statements of our basic beliefs about *G*. 851 23
proclaiming the nature of the Incarnation and of *G* 852 10
The Trinity is one *G*: 852 13
G at work in the world 852 15
and harmony with *G*, with ourselves, 852 28
to show *G* at work in nature and history. 853 12
Why do we call the Holy Scriptures the Word of *G*? 853 23
We call them the Word of *G* 853 24
because *G* inspired their human authors 853 24
and because *G* still speaks to us 853 25
It is called the People of *G*, the New Israel, 854 8
and guides them to do *G*'s work. 854 19
unity with *G* and each other in Christ. 855 3
to proclaim the Word of *G*; 855 25
to bless and declare pardon in the name of *G*. 856 6
give for the spread of the kingdom of *G*. 856 16
Prayer is responding to *G*, 856 18
Christian prayer is response to *G* the Father, 856 21
the lifting up of the heart and mind to *G*, 857 2
asking nothing but to enjoy *G*'s presence. 857 3
Why do we praise *G*? 857 4
We praise *G*, not to obtain anything, 857 5
G's Being draws praise from us. 857 6
Thanksgiving is offered to *G* for all the blessings 857 8
whatever draws us closer to *G*. 857 10
in union with Christ, for the purposes of *G*. 857 16
Intercession brings before *G* the needs of others; 857 18
that *G*'s will may be done. 857 19
acknowledge the holiness of *G*, to hear *G*'s Word, 857 23
G is *G*'s favor towards us, 858 2
by grace *G* forgives our sins, 858 3
Holy Baptism is the sacrament by which *G* adopts us 858 9
and inheritors of the kingdom of *G*. 858 11
birth into *G*'s family the Church, 858 18
and redemption by *G*. 858 27
Ordination is the rite in which *G* gives authority 860 28
make their vows before *G* and the Church, 861 6
blessing of *G* to help them fulfill their vows. 861 7
confess them to *G* in the presence of a priest, 861 11
by which *G*'s grace is given 861 15
Is *G*'s activity limited to these rites? 861 17
G does not limit himself to these rites; 861 18
countless ways by which *G* uses material 861 19
and the completion of *G*'s purpose 861 27
we mean eternal life in our enjoyment of *G*; 862 6
by hell, we mean eternal death in our rejection of *G*. 862 7
and because we trust that in *G*'s presence 862 10
We mean that *G* will raise us from death 862 17
The communion of saints is the whole family of *G*, 862 21
united with all the people of *G*, 862 27
knowing and loving *G* and each other. 862 28
shall separate us from the love of *G* 862 31

godliness

in wisdom and true *g*, 431 5
knowledge, temperance, patience, *g*. 829 3

godly

hereafter live a *g*, righteous, and sober life, 42 9
ministry they may truly and *g* serve thee; 57 23
hereafter live a *g*, righteous, and sober life, 63 12
and also an example of *g* life: 180 20
saints in all virtuous and *g* living, 194 11
being preserved in true faith and *g* discipline, 204 12
ministry they may truly and *g* serve thee; 206 5
and also an example of *g* life: 232 12
in all virtuous and *g* living, 245 19
being preserved in true faith and *g* discipline, 255 10
live a *g*, righteous, and sober life, 321 12
live in unity and *g* love. 329 8
that they may serve you in a true and *g* life, 548 17
Help me, LORD, for there is no *g* one left; * 597 1
All my delight is upon the *g* that are in the land, * 600 1
The LORD cares for the lives of the *g*, * 634 20
against the *g* all day long? 657 24
in the presence of the *g*. 658 20
from *g* union and concord; 818 18
light riseth up in darkness for the *g*: 832 7

gods

and a great King above all *g*. 44 15
and a great King above all *g*. 82 10
compared with you, O Lord, among the *g*? * 85 16
and run after false *g*?" 128 13
and a great King above all *g*. 146 6
Thou shalt have none other *g* but me. 317 27
You shall have no other *g* but me. 350 3
and run after false *g*?" 588 3
But those who run after other *g* * 600 3
nor take the names of their *g* upon my lips. 600 6
Ascribe to the LORD, you *g*, * 620 5
they do not resort to evil spirits or turn to false *g*. 640 10
The LORD, the God of *g*, has spoken; * 654 1
he gives judgment in the midst of the *g*: 705 10
Now I say to you, "You are *g*, * 705 20
and the God of *g* will reveal himself in Zion. 708 5
Among the *g* there is none like you, O LORD, * 710 13
who is like the LORD among the *g*? 714 6
and a great King above all *g*. 724 19
he is more to be feared than all *g*. 725 24
As for all the *g* of the nations, they are but idols; * 726 1
and delight in false *g*! * 727 10
Bow down before him, all you *g*. 727 11
you are exalted far above all *g*. 727 16
and that our Lord is above all *g*. 788 11
Give thanks to the God of *g*, * 789 22
before the *g* I will sing your praise. 793 2

goes

So is my word that *g* forth from my mouth; * 87 5
It *g* forth from the uttermost edge of the heavens 607 1
a breath that *g* forth and does not return. 698 6
A fire *g* before him * 727 1
When the wind *g* over it, it is gone, * 734 13
Man *g* forth to his work * 736 23
When your word *g* forth it gives light; * 774 7

going

From the rising of the sun even unto the *g* down 38 5
The LORD shall watch over your *g* out 105 1
made the sun to know its *g* down: 110 25
From the rising of the sun to its *g* down * 138 5
The LORD shall preserve thy *g* out, 473 23

you restored my life as I was *g* down to the grave.	621	9
Egypt was glad of their *g*, *	741	1
From the rising of the sun to its *g* down *	756	6
The LORD shall watch over your *g* out and	779	15
no breaching of the walls, no *g* into exile, *	801	8

gold

More to be desired are they than *g*,	607	16
more than much fine *g*, *	607	17
and set a crown of fine *g* upon his head.	609	2
adorned with the *g* of Ophir.	648	10
her gown is cloth-of-*g*.	648	18
whose feathers are like green *g*.	677	7
and may there be given to him *g* from Arabia; *	686	14
He led out his people with silver and *g*; *	740	27
Their idols are silver and *g*, *	757	20
than thousands in *g* and silver.	769	8
more than *g* and precious stones.	774	2
The idols of the heathen are silver and *g*, *	789	5

gone

All we like sheep have *g* astray;	39	1
Their sound is *g* out into all lands;	40	5
All we like sheep have *g* astray;	76	25
Their sound has *g* out into all lands,	78	4
to all who have *g* astray from thy ways,	166	17
place whither our Savior Christ is *g* before;	175	5
to all who have *g* astray from your ways,	218	8
place where our Savior Christ has *g* before;	226	17
home to your fold those who have *g* astray;	280	6
For when thou art angry all our days are *g*; *	473	1
so soon passeth it away, and we are *g*.	473	6
we are reunited with those who have *g* before;	493	23
For the faith of those who have *g* before us	579	7
Their sound has *g* out into all lands, *	606	21
and the brightness of my eyes is *g* from me.	637	17
all your rapids and floods have *g* over me.	643	22
God has *g* up with a shout, *	650	14
until this time of trouble has *g* by.	663	22
You have *g* up on high and led captivity captive;	677	18
Had I *g* on speaking this way, *	688	7
nor change what has *g* out of my lips.	716	10
When you are angry, all our days are *g*: *	718	17
for they pass away quickly and we are *g*.	718	22
When the wind goes over it, it is *g*, *	734	13
I have *g* astray like a sheep that is lost; *	778	7
and the torrent *g* over us;	781	8
have *g* right over us.	781	10

good

Behold, I bring you *g* tidings of great joy,	37	8
be thankful unto him and speak *g* of his Name.	45	19
He hath filled the hungry with *g* things, *	50	15
and on earth peace, *g* will towards men.	52	4
He hath filled the hungry with *g* things, *	65	18
That this evening may be holy, *g*, and peaceful,	68	7
O God, from whom all holy desires, all *g* counsels,	69	16
Behold, I bring you *g* news of a great joy	75	8
For the Lord is *g*;	83	7
He has filled the hungry with *g* things, *	92	10
so that they may see the *g* you do, and	109	11
He has filled the hungry with *g* things, *	119	16
That this evening may be holy, *g*, and peaceful,	122	9
Most holy God, the source of all *g* desires,	123	15
equip you with everything *g* that you may do his will,	132	3
Spare us, *g* Lord, spare thy people,	148	11
Spare us, *g* Lord.	148	14
G Lord, deliver us.	148	17
We beseech thee to hear us, *g* Lord.	150	4
and for the common *g*,	151	15
We beseech thee to hear us, *g* Lord.	151	16
proclaim to all people the *G* News of his salvation,	163	15
we can do no *g* thing without thee,	164	13
O God, whose Son Jesus is the *g* shepherd	173	11
such *g* things as pass man's understanding:	174	2
O God, from whom all *g* doth come:	178	1
who art the author and giver of all *g* things:	181	12
and bring forth in us the fruit of *g* works:	181	14
and giving us those *g* things which we are not worthy	183	2
make us continually to be given to all *g* works;	183	7
Grant that we, encouraged by the *g* example	198	17
following the *g* examples of those who have served	202	4
Almighty God, the giver of all *g* gifts,	205	4
constantly receive *g* things from thy hand,	207	19
in truth and beauty and for the common *g*;	210	6
for *g* or ill, all other lives:	210	11
do it not for self alone, but for the common *g*;	210	13
proclaim to all people the *G* News	215	8
we can do nothing *g* without you,	216	8
O God, whose Son Jesus is the *g* shepherd	225	3
prepared for those who love you such *g* things	225	14
O God, from whom all *g* proceeds:	229	15
the author and giver of all *g* things:	233	3
and bring forth in us the fruit of *g* works;	233	6
giving us those *g* things for which we are not worthy	234	16
that we may continually be given to *g* works;	234	21
Grant that we, encouraged by the *g* example	250	2
and grant that we, following the *g* examples	253	8
Almighty God, the giver of all *g* gifts,	256	1
constantly receiving *g* things from your hand,	258	19
may be faithful stewards of your *g* gifts;	259	15
in truth and beauty and for the common *g*;	261	11
for *g* or ill, all other lives:	261	16
do it not for self alone, but for the common *g*;	261	18
Restore us, *g* Lord, and let your anger depart	268	27
For all who serve the common *g*	278	22
It is truly right and *g*, always and everywhere,	286	22
Will you proclaim by word and example the *G* News	293	26
Will you proclaim by word and example the *G* News	305	1
who has begun a *g* work in you,	310	5
and on earth peace, *g* will towards men.	324	15
and to grant us grace so to follow the *g* examples	330	4
all such *g* works as thou hast prepared for us	339	12
and make *g* thy vows unto the Most High.	343	8
But to do *g* and to distribute, forget not;	344	3
It is right, and a *g* and joyful thing,	361	7
It is right, and a *g* and joyful thing,	367	7
To the poor he proclaimed the *g* news	374	4
and make *g* your vows to the Most High.	376	4
But do not neglect to do *g* and to share	377	1
For the *g* earth which God has given us,	384	14
and serve the common *g*.	388	9
g things which we dare not,	395	1
Will you proclaim by word and example the *G* News	417	11
Spirit, who has begun a *g* work in you,	419	1

He has filled the hungry with *g* things,* 442 5
for all the *g* things he has done for me? 442 20
In thy *g* time, restore him to health, 458 7
Lord Jesus Christ, *G* Shepherd of the sheep, 459 1
Continue in him, we pray, the *g* work 460 19
G Lord, deliver him. 463 4
We beseech you to hear us, *g* Lord. 463 14
that the *g* work which thou didst begin 486 10
Make you perfect in every *g* work to do his will, 487 2
We give thee hearty thanks for the *g* examples 488 5
having the testimony of a *g* conscience; 489 9
Make you perfect in every *g* work to do his will, 503 4
We give you heartfelt thanks for the *g* examples 503 14
having the testimony of a *g* conscience, 504 6
work in them the *g* purpose of your perfect will; 504 29
through the high priest and *g* shepherd 552 11
there is none who does any *g*. 598 14
there is none who does *g*; no, not one. 598 20
my *g* above all other." 599 21
it is *g* for the just to sing praises. 626 2
Taste and see that the LORD is *g*; * 628 9
but those who seek the LORD lack nothing that is *g*. 628 14
Turn from evil and do *g*; * 628 21
They pay me evil in exchange for *g*; * 630 15
he has left off acting wisely and doing *g*. 632 8
and has set himself in no *g* way; * 632 10
Put your trust in the LORD and do *g*; * 633 9
Turn from evil, and do *g*, * 635 14
Those who repay evil for *g* slander me, * 638 9
and make *g* your vows to the Most High. 655 8
You love evil more than *g* * 658 4
there is none who does any *g*. 658 23
there is none who does *g*; no, not one. 659 6
and praise your Name, O LORD, for it is *g*. 660 2
Truly, God is *g* to Israel, * 687 1
But it is *g* for me to be near God; * 689 5
No *g* thing will the LORD withhold * 708 16
you have restored the *g* fortune of Jacob. 708 21
For you, O LORD, are *g* and forgiving, * 710 7
It is a *g* thing to give thanks to the LORD, * 720 22
proclaim the *g* news of his salvation from day to day. 725 20
For the LORD is *g*; 730 4
He satisfies you with *g* things, * 733 17
you open your hand, and they are filled with *g* things. 737 10
Give thanks to the LORD, for he is *g*, * 741 19
Give thanks to the LORD, for he is *g*, * 746 1
and fills the hungry with *g* things. 746 19
They repay evil for *g*, * 751 6
those who act accordingly have a *g* understanding; 755 2
It is *g* for them to be generous in lending * 755 13
for all the *g* things he has done for me? 759 24
Give thanks to the LORD, for he is *g*; * 760 20
Give thanks to the LORD, for he is *g*; * 763 3
because your judgments are *g*. 766 14
You are *g* and you bring forth *g*; * 768 23
It is *g* for me that I have been afflicted, * 769 5
Be surety for your servant's *g*; * 773 17
I will seek to do you *g*." 780 14
Show your *g*ness, O LORD, to those who are *g* * 782 1
Oh, how *g* and pleasant it is, * 787 9
Praise the LORD, for the LORD is *g*; * 788 6
Give thanks to the LORD, for he is *g*, * 789 20
The LORD will make *g* his purpose for me; * 793 19
let your *g* Spirit lead me on level ground. 799 22
How *g* it is to sing praises to our God! * 804 2
governed by thy *g* Spirit, 815 3
in your *g* time, all nations and races may serve you 815 19
in your *g* time enable us all to stand reconciled 816 8
from whom cometh every *g* and perfect gift: 817 4
Almighty God, giver of every *g* gift: 818 8
Almighty God, who hast given us this *g* land 820 1
O God, the fountain of wisdom, whose will is *g* 821 1
and the water from which these *g* things come. 825 24
whatever is just and true and *g*, 829 12
bring forth in us the fruit of *g* living, 834 21
Almighty God, giver of all *g* things: 838 21
Help us, O Lord, to finish the *g* work 839 16
We praise you for these *g* gifts, 840 10
This means that the universe is *g*, 846 7
and to proclaim the *G* News of the Kingdom 853 17

goodly

The *g* fellowship of the prophets praise thee. 53 4
indeed, I have a *g* heritage. 600 10
called us in this Diocese to a *g* fellowship 817 11

goodness

obtain forgiveness by his infinite *g* and mercy. 41 14
for all thy *g* and loving-kindness 58 17
obtain forgiveness by his infinite *g* and mercy. 62 14
for all thy *g* and loving-kindness 71 13
obtain forgiveness by his infinite *g* and mercy. 79 8
strengthen you in all *g*, 80 3
In your great *g*, Lord, 91 9
and make my appeal, sure of your gracious *g*. 91 13
and in me you will show forth your *g*. 91 21
for all your *g* and loving-kindness 101 9
obtain forgiveness by his infinite *g* and mercy. 116 10
strengthen you in all *g*, 117 8
for all your *g* and loving-kindness 125 7
of thy bountiful *g* keep us, 177 3
preserve it evermore by thy help and *g*; 180 11
nourish us with all *g*, 181 13
Almighty and merciful God, in your *g* keep us, 228 14
protect and govern it always by your *g*; 232 3
nourish us with all *g*; 233 5
And we most humbly beseech thee, of thy *g*, 329 26
and strengthen you in all *g*, 332 5
and, of thy almighty *g*, vouchsafe 335 18
And we earnestly desire thy fatherly *g* 335 24
assure us thereby of thy favor and *g* towards us; 339 6
And we earnestly desire thy fatherly *g* 342 21
strengthen you in all *g*, 353 3
strengthen you in all *g*, 360 17
We give thanks to you, O God, for the *g* 368 1
Fountain of life and source of all *g*, 373 4
Lord, we pray that in your *g* and mercy 375 4
strengthen you in all *g*, 398 9
be filled with your life and *g*. 405 18
Surely your *g* and mercy shall follow me 443 15
strengthen you in all *g*, 451 4
strengthen you in all *g*, 455 7
preserve you in all *g*, 456 18
comfort him with a sense of thy *g*; 458 5

Be present in your *g* with your servant 458 18
rejoicing in your *g*, 460 21
comfort them with a sense of your *g*; 467 6
Surely *g* and mercy shall follow me 477 9
but that I believe verily to see the *g* 478 6
but have confidence in your *g*, 494 11
remembrance of your great *g*, 505 14
the crowning of our years with your *g*, 579 5
Surely your *g* and mercy shall follow me 613 11
and for the sake of your *g*, O LORD. 615 3
that I should see the *g* of the LORD * 618 27
How great is your *g*, O LORD! 624 4
and declare the *g* of your Name 658 19
You crown the year with your *g*, * 673 11
in your *g*, O God, you have made provision 676 24
But the merciful *g* of the LORD endures for ever 734 15
Show your *g*, O LORD, to those who are good * 782 1
Of your *g*, destroy my enemies 799 25
shall publish the remembrance of your great *g*; * 801 24
we commend to thy fatherly *g* 815 7
rejoicing in your *g*; 824 10
opened to the *g* of your creation; 825 4
trust in your *g* all the days of his life; 830 11
comfort him with a sense of thy *g*, 831 16

goods

Our intemperate love of worldly *g* and comforts, 268 10
wickedness of those who put their trust in their *g*, * 652 15

goodwill

lead us in paths of peace and *g*, 68 10
lead us in paths of peace and *g*, 122 12
I ask your prayers for peace; for *g* among nations; 386 1

Gospel

by the preaching of the *G*, 175 11
caused the light of the *G* to shine 187 9
given to thy Church the *G* of Jesus 188 22
the relief of the poor and the spread of the *G*; 189 21
apostle and evangelist Matthew to the *G* 192 20
Luke the physician to set forth in the *G* 193 12
whom thou didst call to preach the *G* 196 8
by the preaching of the *G*, 227 4
caused the light of the *G* to shine 238 21
the evangelist you have given to your Church the *G* 240 8
the relief of the poor and the spread of the *G*; 241 7
and evangelist Matthew to the *G* 244 8
to set forth in the *G* the love and healing power 244 21
whom you called to preach the *G* 247 20
set forth in the *G* of our Savior, 265 8
and with sincere hearts believe his holy *G*. 269 9
Let us pray for all who have not received the *G* 279 20
let your *G* be preached 280 3
The Holy *G* of our Lord Jesus Christ 300 5
The *G* of the Lord. 300 8
The Holy *G* of our Lord Jesus Christ 326 1
The *G* of the Lord. 326 4
G command us to continue, a perpetual memory 334 15
G command us to continue, a perpetual memory 341 18
preach the *G* to all nations. 347 12
preach the *G* and to teach all nations; 348 13
The Holy *G* of our Lord Jesus Christ 357 8
The *G* of the Lord. 358 1
and to preach the *G* to all nations. 380 6
preach the *G* and to teach all nations; 381 7
preach the *G* to the ends of the earth, 390 8
that they may receive the light of the *G*, 390 11
For all who proclaim the *G*, 392 13
The Holy *G* of our Lord Jesus Christ 414 5
The *G* of the Lord 415 1
The Holy *G* of our Lord Jesus Christ 426 1
The *G* of the Lord. 426 4
The Holy *G* of our Lord Jesus Christ 479 20
The *G* of the Lord. 480 1
The Holy *G* of our Lord Jesus Christ 495 1
The *G* of the Lord. 495 4
The Holy *G* of our Lord Jesus Christ 516 5
The *G* of the Lord. 516 8
Christ's resurrection and interpreting the *G*, 517 4
Will you boldly proclaim and interpret the *G* 518 8
The Holy *G* of our Lord Jesus Christ 529 4
The *G* of the Lord. 529 7
proclaim by word and deed the *G* 531 9
boldly proclaim the *g* of salvation; 534 3
The Holy *G* of our Lord Jesus Christ 541 4
The *G* of the Lord. 541 7
preach the *G* to the ends of the earth, 549 22
that they may receive the light of the *G*, 549 26
preach the *G* to all nations. 838 4
proclaims the *G*, and promotes justice, 855 6
and proclaim the *G*; 856 5
in the proclamation of the *G* 856 11
What are the two great sacraments of the *G*? 858 5
the two sacraments of the *G*? 860 13

govern

G them and lift them up for ever. 55 16
We humbly pray thee so to guide and *g* us 57 15
G and uphold them, now and always. 98 10
We humbly pray you so to guide and *g* us 100 7
it may please thee to rule and *g* thy holy Church 150 2
Almighty and everlasting God, who dost *g* 164 1
g those whom thou hast set upon the sure foundation 178 14
Almighty and everlasting God, you *g* 215 12
for you never fail to help and *g* 230 8
protect and *g* it always by your goodness; 232 3
We pray for all who *g* and hold authority 387 9
The moon and the stars to *g* the night, * 790 13

governance

but that we, being ordered by thy *g*, 57 11
in the life, worship, and *g* 855 19

governed

body of thy faithful people is *g* and sanctified: 57 20
body of your faithful people is *g* and sanctified: 100 12
may be peaceably *g* by thy providence, 177 10
body of thy faithful people is *g* and sanctified: 206 2
may be peaceably *g* by your providence; 229 6
be guided and *g* by faithful and true pastors; 239 14
body of your faithful people is *g* and sanctified: 256 20
body of your faithful people is *g* and sanctified: 278 12
be so guided and *g* by thy good Spirit, 815 3

government

the authority of *g* in this and every land 329 19
bishops in the *g* of the whole Church; 518 23
we entrust the authority of *g*, 820 10

governor

O Lord our *G*, * 592 7
O Lord our *G*, * 592 25
O Lord our *G*, whose glory is in all the world: 820 16
the *G* of this State 820 19
O Lord our *G*, bless the leaders of our land, 821 15

governors

to *G* of States, 821 19

gown

her *g* is cloth-of-gold. 648 18

grace

G be unto you, and peace, from God our Father, 40 9
and the *g* and consolation of his Holy Spirit. 42 13
for the means of *g*, and for the hope of glory. 58 23
Almighty God, who hast given us *g* at this time 59 12
The *g* of our Lord Jesus Christ, 59 22
G be unto you, and peace, from God our Father, 61 3
and the *g* and consolation of his Holy Spirit. 63 16
thine abounding *g* may increase among us; 71 8
for the means of *g*, and for the hope of glory. 71 19
Almighty God, who hast given us *g* at this time 72 9
The *g* of our Lord Jesus Christ, 72 19
G to you and peace from God our Father 78 8
for the means of *g*, and for the hope of glory. 101 15
Almighty God, you have given us *g* at this time 102 1
The *g* of our Lord Jesus Christ, 102 10
Give us *g* to behold you, 113 11
G to you and peace from God our Father 115 3
your abounding *g* may increase among us; 125 3
for the means of *g*, and for the hope of glory. 125 13
Almighty God, you have given us *g* at this time 126 1
The *g* of our Lord Jesus Christ, 126 10
and the *g* and comfort of the Holy Spirit. 128 2
please thee to give to all people increase of *g* 150 15
endue us with the *g* of thy Holy Spirit 152 5
The *g* of our Lord Jesus Christ, 154 1
Almighty God, give us *g* that we may cast 159 1
Give us *g* to heed their warnings 159 11
let thy bountiful *g* and mercy speedily help 160 3
made thy children by adoption and *g*, 161 10
Give us *g*, O Lord, to answer readily the call 163 14
grant us the help of thy *g*, 164 14
Grant us *g* to take joyfully the sufferings 169 2
who hast given unto us thy servants *g*, 176 2
that by the help of thy *g* we may proclaim the truth 178 7
Grant us the *g* of thy Holy Spirit, 179 5
g and power faithfully to fulfill the same; 179 13
Give us *g* that we may always most thankfully receive 180 21
thy *g*, that we, running to obtain thy promises, 182 14
Lord, we pray thee that thy *g* may always precede 183 6
who didst give such *g* to thine apostle Andrew 185 7
g to follow him without delay, 185 10
Give us *g* to imitate his uprightness of life 188 10
We beseech thee, O Lord, pour thy *g* into our hearts, 188 15
who didst give to thine apostles Philip and James *g* 189 6
by whose *g* the virgin mother 189 11
that we and all the people of this land may have *g* 190 20
Mercifully grant that by thy *g* 191 3
didst give to thine apostle Bartholomew *g* 192 8
may have *g* to take up our cross 192 16
Grant us *g* so to follow thy blessed saints 194 10
by whose *g* and power thy holy martyr 195 8
we may by thy *g* grow into the stature 196 25
We praise thy Name for the gifts of *g* 197 14
gifts of *g* to understand and teach the truth 197 20
O God, by whose *g* thy servant N., enkindled 198 9
Give us *g* to continue steadfast 199 14
Bless, we beseech thee, with his *g* and presence, 204 10
Give thy *g*, we humbly beseech thee, 205 6
Grant us *g* fearlessly to contend against evil 209 2
Almighty God, give us *g* to cast away 211 1
Give us *g* to heed their warnings and forsake our sins, 211 11
let your bountiful *g* and mercy speedily help 212 3
made your children by adoption and *g*, 213 4
Give us *g*, O Lord, to answer readily the call 215 7
give us the help of your *g*, 216 9
Grant your people *g* to love what you command 219 7
Give us *g* to accept joyfully the sufferings 220 15
Give us *g* so to put away the leaven of malice 224 2
you have given to us your servants *g*, 228 2
that through your *g* we may proclaim your truth 230 2
Grant us the *g* of your Holy Spirit, 230 20
have *g* and power faithfully to accomplish them; 231 6
g to receive thankfully the fruits 232 13
Grant us the fullness of your *g*, 234 7
Lord, we pray that your *g* may always precede 234 20
God, who gave such *g* to your apostle Andrew 237 1
g to follow him without delay, 237 4
Give us *g* to imitate his uprightness of life 239 19
Pour your *g* into our hearts, O Lord, 240 1
who gave to your apostles Philip and James *g* 240 13
Father in heaven, by your *g* the virgin mother 240 18
all the people of this land may have *g* 242 4
by your *g* we may be healed from all our infirmities 242 10
who gave to your apostle Bartholomew *g* 243 15
may have *g* to take up our cross 244 4
Give us *g* so to follow your blessed saints 245 18
God, by whose *g* and power your holy martyr 247 6
we may by your *g* grow into the stature 248 11
We praise your Name for the gifts of *g* 248 24
g to understand and teach the truth 249 6
O God, by whose *g* your servant N., kindled 249 18
Give us *g* to continue steadfast 251 3
Bless, we pray, with his *g* and presence, 255 7
Give your *g*, we humbly pray, to all 256 3
Grant us *g* fearlessly to contend against evil 260 9
let your Gospel be preached with *g* 280 4
and pray for the *g* of a holy life, 280 8
Give mercy and *g* to the living; 282 9
for the *g* to sing the worthy praise 286 12
and are restored to *g* and holiness 287 10
multiply, by the *g* of the Paschal sacrament, 289 7
keep us in eternal life by his *g*, 294 7
Do you put your whole trust in his *g* and love? 302 19
I do, and with God's *g* I will follow him 303 13
Open their hearts to your *g* and truth. 305 17
raised them to the new life of *g*. 308 5

Defend, O Lord, your servant N. with your heavenly *g*, 309 15
raised him to the new life of *g*. 314 4
come boldly before the throne of *g* 317 22
come boldly unto the throne of *g*, 320 7
and find *g* to help in time of need. 320 7
and the *g* and consolation of his Holy Spirit. 321 16
Give *g*, O heavenly Father, to all bishops 329 9
And to all thy people give thy heavenly *g*, 329 13
and to grant us *g* so to follow 330 4
be filled with thy *g* and heavenly benediction, 336 6
so to assist us with thy *g*, 339 11
be filled with thy *g* and heavenly benediction; 342 27
by whose *g* we are able to triumph 346 5
they may come to the fullness of *g* 346 11
For the wonderful *g* and virtue declared 348 1
who have been the chosen vessels of thy *g*, 348 2
draw near to the throne of *g*, 352 7
find *g* to help in time of need. 352 8
Let the *g* of this Holy Communion make us one 372 6
By his *g* we are able to triumph 379 2
they may come to the fullness of *g* 379 8
For the wonderful *g* and virtue declared 380 17
who have been the chosen vessels of your *g*, 380 18
protect us, O Lord, by thy *g*. 385 11
Pray that we may have *g* to glorify Christ 386 17
Give us *g* to do your will in all that we undertake; 387 12
for the *g* of the Holy Spirit to amend our lives, 391 8
The *g* of our Lord Jesus Christ 404 1
I do, and with God's *g* I will follow him 415 12
Defend, O Lord, your servant N. with your heavenly *g*, 418 13
assist them with your *g*, 425 10
author of salvation, and giver of all *g*: 429 3
Give them *g*, when they hurt each other, 429 14
and the *g* to bring them up to know you, 429 21
may be so transformed by your *g*, 430 6
fill you with all spiritual benediction and *g*; 431 12
As God has made us his children by adoption and *g*, 441 5
As he grows in age, may he grow in *g*, 445 1
adopts us as his children, grant you *g*. 445 4
ministry by the *g* of the Holy Spirit, 448 9
forgives your sins by the *g* of the Holy Spirit. 448 16
ministry by the *g* of the Holy Spirit, 451 8
forgives your sins by the *g* of the Holy Spirit. 452 2
uphold you and fill you with his *g*, 456 9
sustain me by your *g*, 461 8
Give us *g*, we beseech thee, 470 8
Grant us *g* to entrust N. to thy never-failing love; 481 17
thanks for the wonderful *g* and virtue 487 11
who have been the choice vessels of thy *g*, 487 13
most humbly beseeching thee to give us *g* 487 14
g to the living, pardon and rest to the dead, 489 26
O God of *g* and glory, we remember 493 16
Give us *g* to entrust 494 2
nourish them from the riches of God's *g*, 518 15
I will, by the *g* given me. 518 27
The blessing, mercy, and *g* of God Almighty, 523 15
nourish Christ's people from the riches of his *g*, 531 19
asking God's *g*, both for yourself and for others, 532 25
give you the *g* and power to perform them. 532 31
fill him with *g* and power, 533 12
May the Lord by his *g* uphold you 544 15
fill him with *g* and power, 545 10
for the *g* of the Holy Spirit to amend our lives, 550 17
G be to this house, and to all who enter here: 568 2
as we grow in *g* through the years, 569 6
For making us your children by adoption and *g*, 578 16
For the knowledge of your will and the *g* to perform 578 19
g flows from your lips, 647 15
he will give *g* and glory; 708 15
let me find *g* through your law. 765 18
the healthful Spirit of thy *g*; 817 6
by your *g* you have called us in this Diocese 817 10
pursue it and the *g* to accomplish it; 818 6
Give us *g* seriously to lay to heart 818 15
grant wisdom and *g* in the exercise of their duties. 821 21
Give *g* to your servants, O Lord. 821 23
Give *g* to your servants, O Lord. 822 5
Defend them day by day with your heavenly *g*; 823 4
give *g* to respect their witness 823 13
Grant us *g* that we may honor thee 827 2
that he may grow in wisdom and *g*, 830 10
the *g* to ask what thou wouldest have us to do, 832 8
spirit of *g* and of supplication: 833 20
thy *g*, be so grafted inwardly in our hearts, 834 20
visible signs of inward and spiritual *g*, 857 27
means by which we receive that *g*. 857 28
What is *g*? 858 1
G is God's favor towards us, 858 2
by *g* God forgives our sins, 858 3
What is the inward and spiritual *g* in Baptism? 858 16
The inward and spiritual *g* in Baptism 858 17
What is the inward and spiritual *g* given 859 22
The inward and spiritual *g* in the Holy Communion 859 24
Although they are means of *g*, 860 14
the *g* of the Holy Spirit to those being made bishops, 860 29
and receive the *g* and blessing of God 861 6
assurance of pardon and the *g* of absolution. 861 12
by which God's *g* is given 861 15

gracefully

and *g* accept your healing; 461 3

graces

to rejoice in other people's gifts and *g*; 848 20

gracious

for he is *g* and merciful, 38 15
For the Lord is *g*; 45 20
O *g* Light, 64 1
for he is *g* and merciful, 76 14
and make my appeal, sure of your *g* goodness. 91 13
O *g* Light, 112 1
and be *g* to you. 114 3
O *g* Light, 118 1
O *g* Light, 139 1
Be *g* to all who have gone astray 166 16
G Father, whose blessed Son Jesus Christ came down 167 10
under his most *g* rule; 185 5
bring those near to us into his *g* presence; 185 11
O *g* God, we remember before thee this day 191 7
Almighty and *g* Father, we give thee thanks 194 16
under his most *g* rule; 203 3
in accordance with thy *g* will; 207 5

that thy *g* providence may give and preserve	207	16
Be *g* to all who have gone astray	218	7
G Father, whose blessed Son Jesus Christ came down	219	1
under his most *g* rule;	236	18
bring those near to us into his *g* presence;	237	5
O *g* God, we remember before you today	242	14
Almighty and *g* Father, we give you thanks	246	1
under his most *g* rule;	254	5
in accordance with your *g* will;	258	5
that your *g* providence may give and preserve	258	16
only by your *g* gift that we are given	265	19
G God, the comfort of all who sorrow,	279	14
the eyes of all people to behold thy *g* hand	329	22
Grant us therefore, *g* Lord,	337	14
Holy and *g* Father:	362	9
We pray you, *g* God, to send	369	4
for you are *g*, O lover of souls,	395	5
G Father, we give you praise and thanks	399	7
O *g* and everliving God, you have created	425	7
Most *g* God, we give you thanks	430	10
O God, the giver of all that is true and lovely and *g*:	432	1
G is the LORD and righteous;*	442	17
lovable and *g*, excellent and admirable,	443	28
O *g* God, we give you humble and hearty thanks	444	1
G Father, we give you praise and thanks	457	5
O give thanks unto the LORD, for he is *g*, *	478	11
G is the LORD, and righteous; *	479	8
and be *g* unto him, the Lord lift	485	14
and be *g* to him, the Lord lift	501	15
G and upright is the LORD; *	615	4
Be favorable and *g* to Zion, *	657	18
You sent a *g* rain, O God, upon your inheritance; *	676	21
Has God forgotten to be *g*? *	693	18
You have been *g* to your land, O LORD, *	708	20
But you, O LORD, are *g* and full of compassion, *	711	4
be *g* to your servants.	718	28
the LORD is *g* and full of compassion.	754	13
G is the LORD and righteous; *	759	10
The LORD is *g* and full of compassion, *	802	1
in those who await his *g* favor.	804	25
Open our eyes to behold thy *g* hand	814	2
G Father, we pray for thy holy Catholic Church.	816	10
whose will is good and *g*,	821	2
Almighty God, we commend to your *g* care	823	1
O *g* Father, who openest thine hand	828	1
in all our doings with thy most *g* favor,	832	1
defended by thy *g* and ready help;	832	22
For all that is *g* in the lives	837	6
We give you thanks, most *g* God,	840	7
Most *g* God, by whose knowledge	840	14
Grant, O *g* Father, that he,	841	10

graciously

G behold our afflictions.	154	16
G hear us, O Christ; *g* hear us, O Lord	155	4
Almighty God, we beseech thee *g* to behold	169	14
G continue in thy Church	193	13
Almighty God, we pray you *g* to behold	221	8
G continue in your Church this love	244	22
Almighty God, we pray you *g* to behold	276	4
you have *g* accepted us as living members	365	10
Almighty God our heavenly Father, *g* comfort	459	7
Deal *g*, we pray thee, with all those who mourn,	489	31
Deal *g* with NN. in their grief.	494	8
Deal *g*, we pray, with all who mourn;	505	18
from the creation you have *g* accepted the ministry	520	18
G receive our thanks for this place,	578	4
O LORD, you have dealt *g* with your servant, *	768	17
Look *g* on your Church,	818	8
We humbly beseech thee *g* to behold	830	20
thanks because thou hast been *g* pleased	841	8

graciousness

May the *g* of the LORD our God be upon us; *	719	7

graft

G in our hearts the love of thy Name,	181	12
G in our hearts the love of your Name;	233	4

grafted

be so *g* inwardly in our hearts,	834	20

grain

more than when *g* and wine and oil increase.	129	5
more than when *g* and wine and oil increase.	588	14
You prepare the *g*, *	673	7
and the valleys cloak themselves with *g*; *	673	16
May there be abundance of *g* on the earth,	686	17
and its *g* like grass upon the earth.	686	20
and gave them *g* from heaven.	696	25

grandeur

or when the *g* of their house increases;	653	16
nor will their *g* follow them.	653	18

grant

and *g*, O most merciful Father, for his sake,	42	8
The Almighty and merciful Lord *g* you absolution	42	11
And *g* us thy salvation.	55	2
G us this day such blessing	56	2
Mercifully *g* that we,	56	8
G that we, putting away all earthly anxieties,	56	13
and *g* that this day we fall into no sin,	57	9
G that people everywhere may seek after thee	58	3
and *g*, O most merciful Father, for his sake,	63	11
The Almighty and merciful Lord *g* you absolution	63	14
And *g* us thy salvation.	67	17
G that we, who have this day given thanks	69	3
G unto us thy servants so to follow	69	8
G this for the sake of thy love.	70	13
And *g* us your salvation.	97	19
Mercifully *g* that we,	99	3
G that we, putting away all earthly anxieties,	99	8
G that people everywhere may seek after you	100	19
G that all the peoples of the earth may look to you	107	9
G us, Lord, the lamp of charity which never fails,	110	18
G that we who walk in the light	111	9
G that we who follow in their footsteps	111	13
And *g* us your salvation.	121	19
G that we, who have this day given thanks	123	3
G to us your servants so to follow	123	7
G this for the sake of your love.	124	10
The Lord Almighty *g* us a peaceful night	127	1
and *g* that we may serve you	127	13
May the Almighty God *g* us forgiveness	128	1
G that as we sing your glory	134	2

and *g* that we may never forget	134	13
G that all the peoples of the earth may look to you	138	13
G this for the sake of your love.	139	19
g to all the faithful departed	152	15
to *g* that, in the fellowship	152	18
G us thy peace.	152	29
g that those things which we have asked	153	22
and *g* that in all our troubles	155	9
G that as we joyfully receive him	160	13
G us, we beseech thee,	161	2
G that we, being regenerate	161	9
G that the same light, enkindled	161	15
G that we may share the divine life	162	8
G that all who are baptized into his Name	163	3
G that thy people, illumined by thy Word	163	8
and in our time *g* us thy peace;	164	3
g us the help of thy grace,	164	14
G this for thine only Son	165	3
g that no clouds of this mortal life may hide	165	9
G unto us that we, beholding	165	15
G unto thy people that they may love	167	16
Mercifully *g* that we may both follow	168	5
Mercifully *g* that we,	168	12
G us so to glory in the cross of Christ,	168	19
G us grace to take joyfully the sufferings	169	2
Mercifully *g* that we may thankfully receive	169	9
G that, as the crucified body	170	1
G us so to die daily to sin,	170	10
G that we, who celebrate with joy	170	23
G, we beseech thee, Almighty God, that we who celebrate	171	5
G that we, who have been raised with him,	171	12
G that all who have been reborn	172	2
G us so to put away the leaven of malice	172	9
G that when we hear his voice we may know him	173	12
G us so perfectly to know thy Son	173	17
G, we beseech thee, Almighty God, that like as we do	174	15
G us by the same Spirit to have a right judgment	175	16
G, O Lord, we beseech thee, that the course of this world	177	9
G that by thy inspiration	178	1
G us so to be joined together	178	20
G us the grace of thy Holy Spirit,	179	5
and *g* that they may both perceive	179	11
G to us, Lord, we beseech thee, the spirit to think	180	14
G, we beseech thee, merciful God, that thy Church,	181	5
G us, O Lord, we pray thee, to trust	181	17
mercifully *g* that thy Holy Spirit may in all things	182	2
G us, O Lord, not to mind earthly things,	182	6
Mercifully *g* unto us such a measure	182	13
G, we beseech thee, that we may run without stumbling	184	3
G us, we beseech thee, that, having this hope,	184	9
G that we may in such wise hear them,	184	16
Mercifully *g* that the peoples of the earth,	185	3
G us so perfectly and without doubt to believe	185	15
G, we beseech thee, that we, having	187	10
G that thy Church, being delivered from false apostles,	188	3
G that we, being mindful of their victory	189	6
G us who honor the exaltation	189	13
G, O God, that we may follow the example	189	17
G that thy Church, instructed by their teaching	190	11
G, we beseech thee, that we and all the people	190	19
Mercifully *g* that by thy grace we may be healed	191	3
Mercifully *g* that we, being delivered	191	17
G that we, who have been redeemed by his blood,	192	2
G, we beseech thee, unto thy Church to love	192	9
Mercifully *g* that we, who glory in the mystery	192	15
g that, as thy holy angels always serve	193	6
G, we beseech thee, O God, that after the example	193	18
G us grace so to follow thy blessed saints	194	10
G that we may be always ready	195	3
G us, who now remember him with thanksgiving,	195	10
G to us, thy humble servants, a like faith	196	2
G, we beseech thee, that by this teaching	197	21
G that we also may be aflame with the spirit	198	11
G that we, encouraged by the good example	198	17
G us during our earthly pilgrimage to abide	198	25
G that in our earthly pilgrimage	199	5
g, we beseech thee, that be the indwelling	200	1
g that, as thy holy angels always serve	200	8
G that we may share the divine life	200	14
G us so to venerate the sacred mysteries	201	3
G, O Lord God, to all who have been baptized	201	12
and *g* that we, following the good examples	202	3
Mercifully *g* that the peoples of the earth,	203	1
G that we, being reborn to new life in him,	203	7
G, Almighty God, that we, who have been redeemed	203	12
G that thy Church, being bound together	204	19
G that thy Church, under the guidance	205	15
G that people everywhere may seek after thee	206	11
and *g* that, by the prayers and labors	206	20
G to the people of our country a zeal for justice	207	2
and *g* that we, remembering the account	208	11
G us grace fearlessly to contend against evil	209	2
G that we, who joyfully receive him	212	11
G that we, who have known the mystery of that Light	212	17
G that we, who have been born again	213	3
G that this light, enkindled	213	9
G that we may share the divine life	214	2
G that all who are baptized into his Name	214	14
G that your people, illumined by your Word	215	2
and in our time *g* us your peace;	215	15
G this for the sake of your only Son	216	17
G to us that we, beholding	217	8
G your people grace to love	219	7
Mercifully *g* that we may walk	219	16
Mercifully *g* that we,	220	3
G us so to glory in the cross of Christ,	220	10
Mercifully *g* that we may receive	221	3
G that, as the crucified body	221	13
G us so to die daily to sin,	222	3
G that we, who celebrate with joy	222	17
G, we pray, Almighty God, that we who celebrate	222	22
G that we, who have been raised with him,	223	6
G that all who have been reborn	223	16
G that all who have been reborn	224	14
G that when we hear his voice we may know him	225	4
G us so perfectly to know	225	8
G, we pray, Almighty God, that as we believe	226	8
G us by the same Spirit to have a right judgment	227	10
G, O Lord, that the course of this world	229	5
G that by your inspiration	229	15

G us so to be joined together 230 14
G us the grace of your Holy Spirit, 230 20
and *g* that they may know and understand 231 5
G to us, Lord, we pray, the spirit to think 232 6
G, O merciful God, that your Church, being gathered 232 17
G us, O Lord, to trust in you with all our hearts; 233 9
g that your Holy Spirit may in all things direct 233 15
G us, Lord, not to be anxious about earthly things, 234 1
G us the fullness of your grace, 234 7
G that we may run without stumbling 235 15
G that, having this hope, we may purify ourselves 236 3
G us so to hear them, 236 9
Mercifully *g* that the peoples of the earth, 236 16
G us so perfectly and without doubt to believe 237 9
G, we pray, that we, having his wonderful conversion 239 1
G that your Church, being delivered 239 12
G that we, being mindful of their victory of faith, 240 14
G us who honor the exaltation 240 20
G, O God, that we may follow the example 241 3
G that your Church, instructed 241 20
G that we and all the people of this land 242 3
Mercifully *g* that by your grace we may be healed 242 10
Mercifully *g* that we, being delivered 243 3
G that we, who have been redeemed by his blood, 243 9
G that your Church may love what he believed 243 16
Mercifully *g* that we, who glory in the mystery 244 3
Mercifully *g* that, as your holy angels always serve 244 15
G, O God, that, following the example 245 4
G that we may always be ready 247 1
G us, who now remember him in thanksgiving, 247 8
G to us, your humble servants, a like faith 247 14
G that by this teaching we may know you, 249 7
G that we also may be aflame with the spirit 249 20
G that we, encouraged by the good example 250 2
G us during our earthly pilgrimage to abide 250 9
G that in our earthly pilgrimage 250 15
g that by the indwelling 251 7
Mercifully *g* that, as your holy angels always serve 251 14
G that we may share the divine life 252 2
G us so to venerate the sacred mysteries 252 8
G, Lord God, to all who have been baptized 252 16
and *g* that we, following the good examples 253 8
Mercifully *g* that the peoples of the earth, 254 3
G that we, being reborn to new life in him, may live 254 9
G, Almighty God, that we, who have been redeemed 254 13
G that your Church, being bound together 255 17
G that your Church, under the guidance 256 12
G that people everywhere may seek after you 257 7
g that, by the prayers and labors of your holy Church, 257 16
and *g* that we, remembering the account 259 13
G us grace fearlessly to contend against evil 260 8
G that these ashes may be to us a sign 265 17
Therefore we beseech him to *g* us true repentance 269 10
g that we who bear them in his name may ever hail 271 10
Mercifully *g* that we, 272 3
Mercifully *g* that we may walk 272 10
Mercifully *g* that we may receive it thankfully 274 3
g them the knowledge of his love, 279 12
G that, as the crucified body 283 1
g that in this Paschal feast we may so burn 285 10
G that we may share the divine life 288 6
G that we, who are saved through water 289 2
G that all the peoples of the earth may be numbered 289 16
G that we, who serve you now on earth, may come 290 3
G that all who are reborn into the fellowship 290 15
G to those who are sealed by your Holy Spirit the will 291 7
G us so to die daily to sin, 295 3
G, O Lord, that all who are baptized into the death 306 5
g you to be strengthened with might 311 22
and *g*, O most merciful Father, for his sake, 321 11
The Almighty and merciful Lord *g* you absolution 321 14
and *g* that all those who do confess 329 6
beseeching thee to *g* them continual growth 330 3
and to *g* us grace so to follow the good 330 4
G these our prayers, O Father, for Jesus Christ's sake, 330 7
and *g* that we may ever hereafter 331 17
g that, by the merits and death of thy Son 335 26
g us thy peace. 337 8
G us therefore, gracious Lord, so to eat 337 13
G, we beseech thee, that all who partake 342 24
and *g* us strength and courage 365 15
G that all who share this bread and cup 375 9
And *g* that we may find our inheritance 375 21
G that every member of the Church may truly 387 3
G, Almighty God, that all who confess 388 2
and *g* that we may serve Christ in them, 388 17
g that we may obtain effectually, 394 2
g us for the sake of your Son 395 2
and *g* that we thy servants, who now live by faith, 395 13
G that in our earthly pilgrimage 395 18
Mercifully *g* that we may receive it thankfully 397 15
And *g* that we who eat this bread and drink this cup 405 16
g us peace. 407 6
G that their wills may be so knit together in your will, 429 11
G that all married persons who have witnessed 430 1
G that the bonds of our common humanity, 430 4
G that by your Holy Spirit, N. and N., now joined 432 4
G, most merciful Father, that by your help 444 4
G them wisdom and devotion 444 8
Baptism adopts us as his children, *g* you grace. 445 4
heavenly Father *g* you the inward anointing 456 14
and *g* that finally he may dwell with thee 458 8
and *g* to your servant N. the help of your power, 458 12
and *g* that he may be restored to that perfect health 458 22
and *g* that he may live with you in everlasting life; 460 3
G me this gift, I pray; 461 13
That it may please you to *g* him a place 463 17
and *g* him an entrance into the land of light 470 2
G, we beseech thee, to thy whole Church 480 6
G that all who have been baptized into Christ's death 480 8
G to us who are still in our pilgrimage, 481 1
G to thy faithful people pardon and peace, 481 4
G to all who mourn a sure confidence 481 7
G us grace to entrust to thy never-failing love; 481 17
G that, increasing in knowledge and love of thee, 481 20
G us, with all who have died 481 23
G that this Sacrament may be unto us a comfort 482 4
Father, *g* that we, who now serve thee on earth, 486 13
Rest eternal *g* to him, O Lord: 486 17
and *g* that he whose body is (is to be) buried 487 6
G this, O Father, for the sake of the same thy Son 487 21
and *g* that, increasing in knowledge and love of thee, 488 22
G to them thy mercy and the light of thy presence; 488 29
G that your servant N. being raised with him, 493 6

and *g* him an entrance into the land of light 493 11
g him a place at the table 497 19
G that his death may recall to us your victory 498 3
G to them eternal rest. 498 9
G that this Sacrament may be to us a comfort 498 15
Rest eternal *g* to him, O Lord; 502 15
and *g* that he whose body is (is to be) buried 503 8
G to us your servants so to follow in faith 504 22
G them your peace; 504 27
G this, O merciful Father, through Jesus 505 8
G, O Lord, to all who are bereaved the spirit 505 10
G that we, with him, may serve you now, 523 7
G that in all things he may serve without reproach, 534 5
G that we, with him, may serve you now, 535 7
G that we, with him, may serve you now, 547 3
G that N. who has been called to leadership 552 8
g that together they may follow Jesus 560 8
and *g* that I may faithfully administer 563 2
and *g* that, by the clearness and brightness 563 7
G that we, with him, may serve you now, 564 7
G through your Spirit that those baptized 569 16
G, by the power of your Holy Spirit, that those 570 18
and *g* that in these earthly things we may behold 573 4
G that all who eat and drink at this holy Table 574 4
G you your heart's desire * 608 7
may the LORD *g* all your requests. 608 11
G us your help against the enemy, * 668 8
and *g* us your salvation. 709 8
The LORD will indeed *g* prosperity, * 709 18
G us your help against the enemy, * 750 19
I am your servant; *g* me understanding, * 773 23
g me understanding, that I may live. 775 14
Do not *g* the desires of the wicked, O LORD, * 796 17
G this, O Lord, for the honor of our Advocate 817 8
G that your Word may be truly preached 817 12
and *g* that we may show the power of your love 817 16
G us all things necessary for our common life, 817 21
and *g* us both the courage to pursue it 818 5
and *g* to them even now glimpses of your beauty, 819 16
G to the President of the United States, 820 18
g wisdom and grace in the exercise 821 21
and *g* them a sense of your abiding presence 823 5
G, O God, that your holy and life-giving Spirit may 823 17
and *g* that we may all share the fruits 824 8
and *g* that those who teach and those who learn 824 19
and *g* that we may so use our leisure 825 2
G that your presence and power may be known 825 17
and *g* that all the people of our nation may give 825 20
G this, Father, for the love of your Son, 826 6
And *g* that every one of us may enjoy a fair portion 826 13
G us grace that we may honor thee 827 2
G that, as we probe the mysteries of your creation, 827 13
G that those who live alone may not be lonely 829 23
G that he may grow in wisdom and grace, 830 9
and *g* that both they and we, drawing nearer to thee, 830 22
G us, in all our doubts and uncertainties, 832 7
G that we may not so much seek to be consoled 833 9
Then in thy mercy, *g* us a safe lodging, 833 17
and *g* that those things which we have faithfully asked 834 4
G us, we beseech thee, so to venerate 834 13
G, we beseech thee, Almighty God, that the words 834 18
G us the gift of your Spirit, that we may know him 836 17
G that we may not rest 839 23
G that we may continue to grow 840 11
G, O gracious Father, that he, through thy help, 841 10

granted

you have *g* me the heritage of those who fear 668 22

granting

g us in this world knowledge of thy truth, 59 17
g us in this world knowledge of thy truth, 72 14
g us in this world knowledge of your truth, 102 6
g us in this world knowledge of your truth, 126 6

grants

The LORD *g* his loving-kindness in the daytime; * 643 23

grapes

so that all who pass by pluck off its *g*? 703 12

grasp

he will snatch me from the *g* of death. 653 14

grasped

He reached down from on high and *g* me; * 603 23

grass

and fade away suddenly like the *g*. 472 20
For they shall soon wither like the *g*, * 633 7
and like the green *g* fade away. 633 8
let them wither like trodden *g*. 665 8
and its grain like *g* upon the earth. 686 20
we fade away suddenly like the *g*. 718 10
My heart is smitten like *g* and withered, * 731 7
and I wither like the *g*. 731 22
Our days are like the *g*; * 734 11
You make *g* grow for flocks and herds * 736 3
for the image of an ox that feeds on *g*. 743 12
Let them be like *g* upon the housetops, * 784 11
He makes *g* to grow upon the mountains * 804 18

grateful

Give us *g* hearts, our Father, for all thy mercies, 835 8
we remember before you with *g* hearts 839 21
to grow in our *g* enjoyment of your abundant creation, 840 12

gratitude

in praises, heighten my love and *g*; 563 6
With *g* for the building 567 3

grave

and rose victorious from the *g*. 287 13
first day of the week overcame death and the *g*, 345 2
and, rising from the *g*, destroyed death, 374 7
first day of the week overcame death and the *g*, 377 15
that through the *g* and gate of death we may pass 480 10
yet even at the *g* we make our song: 483 1
Bless, we pray, this *g*, 487 6
You wept at the *g* of Lazarus, your friend; 497 7
yet even at the *g* we make our song: 499 8
Bless, we pray, this *g*, 503 8
Their throat is an open *g*; * 589 11
and who will give you thanks in the *g*? 590 8
The wicked shall be given over to the *g*, * 594 11
For you will not abandon me to the *g*, * 600 17
and you have laid me in the dust of the *g*. 611 10

you restored my life as I was going down to the *g*. 621 9
let them be silent in the *g*. 623 29
and never see the *g*. 652 22
they go down straightway to the *g*. 653 10
let them go down alive into the *g*; * 661 15
my life is at the brink of the *g*. 712 6
like the slain who lie in the *g*, 712 10
Will your loving-kindness be declared in the *g*? * 712 25
who can save himself from the power of the *g*? 717 11
He redeems your life from the *g* * 733 15
and saved them from the *g*. 747 22
the grip of the *g* took hold of me; * 759 6
if I make the *g* my bed, you are there also. 794 15
let their bones be scattered at the mouth of the *g*. 797 18

graven

Thou shalt not make to thyself any *g* image, 318 1

graves

Their *g* shall be their homes for ever, 653 1

gray

And now that I am old and *g*-headed, O God, 684 16

grazed

and the beasts of the field have *g* upon it. 703 14

grazing

May the fields of the wilderness be rich for *g*, * 673 13

great

Behold, I bring you good tidings of *g* joy, 37 8
my Name shall be *g* among the Gentiles, 38 6
for my Name shall be *g* among the heathen, 38 8
slow to anger and of *g* kindness, 38 16
thanks for the *g* benefits that we have received 41 7
For the Lord is a *g* God, * 44 14
and a *g* King above all gods. 44 15
we give thanks to thee for thy *g* glory, 52 8
not be condemned before the *g* judgment seat 68 19
g mercy defend us from all perils and dangers 70 2
Behold, I bring you good news of a *g* joy 75 8
my Name shall be *g* among the nations, 76 5
for my Name shall be *g* among the nations, 76 7
For the Lord is a *g* God, * 82 9
and a *g* King above all gods. 82 10
for he has done *g* things, * 86 11
for the *g* one in the midst of you 86 14
In your *g* goodness, Lord, 91 9
in accordance with your *g* mercy, * 91 23
the Almighty has done *g* things for me, 92 2
g deeds are they that you have done, * 94 10
"The LORD has done *g* things for them." 105 9
The LORD has done *g* things for us, * 105 10
my Name shall be *g* among the nations, 106 7
for my Name shall be *g* among the nations, 106 9
and we implore you of your *g* mercy 110 14
and by thy *g* mercy defend us from all perils 111 2
the Almighty has done *g* things for me, 119 8
and not be condemned before the *g* judgment seat 122 21
and in your *g* mercy defend us from all perils 123 21
Lord Jesus, the *g* shepherd of the sheep, 132 2
and in your *g* mercy defend us from all perils 133 10
By his *g* mercy we have been born anew 137 12
For the Lord is a *g* God, * 146 5
and a *g* King above all gods. 146 6
Christ came to visit us in *g* humility; 159 4
and with *g* might come among us; 160 1
follow the example of his *g* humility: 168 5
with *g* triumph unto thy kingdom in heaven: 175 2
when he shall appear again with power and *g* glory, 184 11
and by thy *g* might frustrate the designs of evil 186 16
faithful stewards of thy *g* bounty, 194 19
compassed us about with so *g* a cloud of witnesses: 198 16
to the glory of thy *g* Name 205 10
Christ came to visit us in *g* humility; 211 4
and with *g* might come among us; 212 1
giving us the example of his *g* humility: 219 16
Jesus Christ with *g* triumph to your kingdom 226 14
when he comes again with power and *g* glory, 236 5
by your *g* might frustrate the designs of evil tyrants 238 10
faithful stewards of your *g* bounty, 246 4
you have surrounded us with a *g* cloud of witnesses: 250 1
to the glory of your *g* Name 256 7
The first Christians observed with *g* devotion 264 10
in your *g* compassion blot out my offenses. 266 3
Favorably hear us, for your mercy is *g*. 268 28
giving us the example of his *g* humility: 272 10
to sing the worthy praise of this *g* light; 286 12
Having in mind, therefore, his *g* love for us, 316 8
For, as the benefit is *g*, if with penitent hearts 316 23
so is the danger *g*, if we receive it improperly, 316 24
This is the first and *g* commandment. 319 10
Seeing that we have a *g* high priest, 320 5
This is the first and *g* commandment. 324 3
we give thanks to thee for thy *g* glory, 324 19
who of his *g* mercy hath promised forgiveness 332 1
but in thy manifold and *g* mercies. 337 11
his coming again with power and *g* glory. 342 15
he shall come again in power and *g* triumph 345 10
hast compassed us about with so *g* a cloud 347 18
confessing before the rulers of this world the *g* Name 348 9
Through the *g* shepherd of thy flock, 348 11
Through Jesus Christ our *g* High Priest; 348 15
Since we have a *g* high priest who has passed 352 5
Christ our *g* High Priest, 372 11
when he shall come again in power and *g* triumph 378 6
surrounded us with a *g* cloud of witnesses, 380 13
the *g* Name of your only Son. 381 4
Through the *g* shepherd of your flock, 381 5
Through Jesus Christ our *g* High Priest; 381 9
For your mercy is *g*. 392 19
the Almighty has done *g* things for me, 441 16
his *g* mercy forgive you all your offenses; 448 3
in your *g* compassion blot out my offenses. 449 2
his *g* mercy forgive you all your offenses; 451 13
Of his *g* mercy, may he forgive you your sins, 456 15
look on this your servant, lying in *g* weakness, 462 1
an oblation with *g* gladness; * 477 26
in thy *g* love thou hast fed us with the spiritual food 482 1
Lord Jesus Christ, the *g* Shepherd of the sheep, 486 22
in your *g* love you have fed us with the spiritual food 498 12
Lord Jesus Christ, the *g* Shepherd of the sheep, 503 2
but in thankful remembrance of your *g* goodness, 505 13
that whoever would be *g* must be servant of all. 545 6
for exalting him to be our *g* High Priest. 573 17

he drew me out of *g* waters. 603 24
your loving care makes me *g*. 605 11
and in keeping them there is *g* reward. 607 21
and innocent of a *g* offense. 607 27
His honor is *g*, because of your victory; * 609 5
My praise is of him in the *g* assembly; * 612 4
forgive my sin, for it is *g*. 615 11
with sounds of *g* gladness; * 618 8
How *g* is your goodness, O LORD! 624 4
when the *g* waters overflow, 625 13
G are the tribulations of the wicked; * 625 23
a strong man is not delivered by his *g* strength. 627 8
I will give you thanks in the *g* congregation; * 631 4
let them say always, "*G* is the LORD, 631 28
your justice like the *g* deep; * 632 15
is better than *g* riches of the wicked. 634 17
G things are they that you have done, O LORD 640 11
how *g* your wonders and your plans for us! * 640 12
I proclaimed righteousness in the *g* congregation; * 640 23
and faithfulness from the *g* congregation. 640 29
"*G* is the LORD!" 641 18
he is the *g* King over all the earth. 650 9
G is the LORD, and highly to be praised; * 651 1
very center of the world and the city of the *g* King. 651 5
and boast of their *g* riches? 652 16
For the ransom of our life is so *g*, * 652 19
in your *g* compassion blot out my offenses. 656 7
but trusted in *g* wealth 658 14
because of your *g* strength your enemies 673 22
g was the company of women who bore the tidings: 677 2
"In your *g* mercy, O God, * 680 15
in your *g* compassion, turn to me." 680 24
"*G* is the LORD!" 682 21
you have done *g* things; 684 21
You have showed me *g* troubles and adversities, * 684 23
his Name is *g* in Israel. 692 2
who is so *g* a god as our God? 693 27
and your paths in the *g* waters, * 694 15
and gave them drink as from the *g* deep. 696 4
and by your *g* might spare those who are 702 5
and *g* is your love toward all who call upon you. 710 8
For you are *g*; 710 18
For *g* is your love toward me; * 710 26
and all your *g* waves overwhelm me. 712 16
g and terrible to all those round about him. 714 8
from the *G* Sea to the River. 715 17
LORD, how *g* are your works! * 721 5
For the LORD is a *g* God, * 724 18
and a *g* King above all gods. 724 19
The LORD is *g* in Zion; * 729 1
Let them confess his Name, which is *g* 729 3
slow to anger and of *g* kindness. 733 24
so is his mercy *g* upon those who fear him. 734 4
Yonder is the *g* and wide sea 737 1
creatures both small and *g*. 737 3
who had done *g* things in Egypt, 743 14
and relented in accordance with his *g* mercy. 745 16
I will give *g* thanks to the LORD with my mouth; * 753 8
G are the deeds of the LORD! * 754 8
and have *g* delight in his commandments! 755 6
both small and *g* together. 758 16
For his loving-kindness toward us is *g*, * 760 17
O LORD, I take *g* comfort. 767 18
G is your compassion, O LORD; * 776 15
as one who finds *g* spoils. 777 4
G peace have they who love your law; * 777 9
"The LORD has done *g* things for them." 782 11
The LORD has done *g* things for us, * 782 12
I do not occupy myself with *g* matters, * 785 12
For I know that the LORD is *g*, * 788 10
Who only does *g* wonders, * 790 3
Who created *g* lights, * 790 9
Who struck down *g* kings, * 791 3
that *g* is the glory of the LORD. 793 13
how *g* is the sum of them! 795 11
rescue me and deliver me from the *g* waters, 800 15
publish the remembrance of your *g* goodness; * 801 24
slow to anger and of *g* kindness. 802 2
G is our LORD and mighty in power; * 804 10
g dangers we are in by our unhappy divisions; 818 16
Be present, be present, O Jesus, our *g* High Priest, 834 8
your kingdom on the last *g* Day; 835 7
Above all, we give you thanks for the *g* mercies 837 21
We thank you for the *g* resources of this nation. 839 1
give us a just sense of these *g* mercies, 840 20
What is the *g* importance of Jesus' suffering 850 5
This is the first and the *g* commandment. 851 13
What are the two *g* sacraments of the Gospel? 858 5
The two *g* sacraments given by Christ to his Church 858 6
Liturgy, the Mass, and the *G* Offering. 859 17

greater

There is no other commandment *g* than these." 351 12
For your loving-kindness is *g* than the heavens, * 664 17
For your loving-kindness is *g* than the heavens, * 750 1
I have taken *g* delight in the way of your decrees * 764 11

greatest

pour into our hearts your *g* gift, which is love, 216 15

greatly

Because thou art *g* glorified in the assembly 348 7
Because you are *g* glorified in the assembly 381 1
how *g* he exults in your victory! 608 22
See how *g* they tremble, 659 10
so that I shall not be *g* shaken. 669 8
For great is the LORD and *g* to be praised; * 725 23
He blessed them, so that they increased *g*; * 749 5
"*G* have they oppressed me since my youth," * 784 1
Great is the LORD and *g* to be praised; * 801 16

greatness

My soul proclaims the *g* of the Lord, 91 27
My soul proclaims the *g* of the Lord, 119 4
Thine, O Lord, is the *g*, and the power, 344 8
Yours, O Lord, is the *g*, the power, 377 6
My soul proclaims the *g* of the Lord, 441 12
Yours, O Lord, is the *g*, the power, 579 13
But as for me, through the *g* of your mercy I will 589 3
Proclaim with me the *g* of the LORD; * 627 25
I will proclaim his *g* with thanksgiving. 681 25
Proclaim the *g* of the LORD our God 729 8
O LORD my God, how excellent is your *g*! 735 2

there is no end to his *g*. 801 17
and I will tell of your *g*. 801 23
praise him for his excellent *g*. 808 2

greed

To resist temptations to envy, *g*, and jealousy; 848 18

greedy

Like a lion, *g* for its prey, * 601 23

green

O all ye *g* things upon the earth, bless ye the Lord; * 48 19
He makes me lie down in *g* pastures* 443 3
In the morning it is *g*, and groweth up; * 472 21
He shall feed me in a *g* pasture, * 476 3
He maketh me to lie down in *g* pastures; * 476 21
He makes me lie down in *g* pastures * 612 25
and like the *g* grass fade away. 633 8
But I am like a *g* olive tree in the house of God; * 658 16
whose feathers are like *g* gold. 677 7
In the morning it is *g* and flourishes; * 718 11
they shall be *g* and succulent; 721 26
Which ate up all the *g* plants in their land * 740 23
and *g* plants to serve mankind. 804 19

greet

that we may *g* with joy the coming of Jesus 159 12
that we may *g* with joy the coming of Jesus 211 12
G your new Rector. 563 11

grew

He sent darkness, and it *g* dark; * 740 9

grief

open your *g* to a discreet and understanding priest, 317 12
Have compassion on those who suffer from any *g* 387 14
have rest in that place where there is no pain or *g*, 391 18
casting all their *g* on thee, they may know 481 8
Deal graciously with NN. in their *g*. 494 8
rest in that place where there is no pain or *g*, 550 23
My eyes are wasted with *g* * 590 12
and *g* in my heart, day after day? * 598 2
For my life is wasted with *g*, 623 6
And I said, "My *g* is this: * 693 20
I came to *g* and sorrow. 759 7

grieve

afflict or *g* the children of men: 831 12

grieved

Forty years long was I *g* with this generation, 146 21
We have *g* your Holy Spirit. 267 24
They *g* him with their hill-altars * 699 22

grieving

bowed down and *g*. 630 22

grievous

the remembrance of them is *g* unto us, 331 11

grievously

which we from time to time most *g* have committed, 331 6

grip

the *g* of the grave took hold of me; * 759 6

groan

I lie awake and *g*; * 731 13
That he might hear the *g* of the captive * 732 16

groaning

I grow weary because of my *g*; * 590 9
because of my *g* all day long. 625 4
I wail, because of the *g* of my heart. 637 13
Because of the voice of my *g* * 731 9

gross

Their iniquity comes from *g* minds, * 687 13
Their heart is *g* and fat, * 769 3

ground

and we commit his body to the *g*;* 485 11
and we commit his body to the *g*;* 501 13
trample my life into the *g*, 591 4
watching how they may cast me to the *g*, 601 22
My foot stands on level *g*; * 617 5
our body cleaves to the *g*. 647 8
with heavy rain you soften the *g* 673 10
and there is no firm *g* for my feet. 679 10
and razed it to the *g*. 689 23
You prepared the *g* for it; * 703 5
they became like dung upon the *g*. 706 23
defiled his crown, and hurled it to the *g*. 716 20
and cast his throne to the *g*. 717 2
and water-springs into thirsty *g*, 748 22
even to the *g*!" 792 18
he has crushed me to the *g*; * 799 2
let your good Spirit lead me on level *g*. 799 22
but casts the wicked to the *g*. 804 13
for the increase of the *g* 840 17
and the pillar and *g* of truth. 854 10

grounded

be firmly *g* in its truth; 189 2
be firmly *g* in its truth; 240 10

grove

men coming up with axes to a *g* of trees; * 689 18

grow

we may by thy grace *g* into the stature 196 25
we may by your grace *g* into the stature 248 11
by your prayers and witness help this child to *g* 302 4
forbearance may *g* among nations and peoples, 390 14
and their spirits in your Spirit, that they may *g* 429 12
As he grows in age, may he *g* in grace, 445 1
forbearance may *g* among nations and peoples, 549 30
may *g* closer to you through joy 569 4
as we *g* in grace through the years, 569 6
I *g* weary because of my groaning; * 590 9
that though the wicked *g* like weeds, 721 9
You make grass *g* for flocks and herds * 736 3
He makes grass to *g* upon the mountains * 804 18
that he may *g* in wisdom and grace, 830 10
to *g* in our grateful enjoyment 840 12
and enables us to *g* in the likeness of Christ. 852 22
those who have chosen to serve him will *g* in his love, 862 11

groweth

In the morning it is green, and *g* up; * 472 21

growing
g thick even on the hilltops; * 686 18
children g up in an unsteady and confusing world: 829 14

grown
and things which had g old are being made new, 280 19
and things which had g old are being made new, 291 16
and things which had g old are being made new, 515 9
and things which had g old are being made new, 528 7
and things which had g old are being made new, 540 7
I have g weary with my crying; 679 13

grows
and all that g upon the earth, * 89 8
As he g in age, may he grow in grace, 445 1

growth
Bringing forth life and giving g, * 87 3
grant them continual g in thy love 330 3

grumbled
They g in their tents * 743 22

guarantee
sponsors, who g that the infants will 859 2

guard
Guide us waking, O Lord, and g us sleeping; 134 16
Guide us waking, O Lord, and g us sleeping; 135 9
g its faith, and preserve it in peace. 375 14
g him from all danger, restore to him your gifts 459 4
undivided Trinity g your body, 460 7
You are called to g the faith, 517 7
Will you g the faith, 518 19
g and defend them in his truth, 521 19
and g the door of my lips; * 797 8
to g the faith, 855 24

guardian
raise up Joseph to be the g of thy incarnate Son 188 9
raised up Joseph to be the g of your incarnate Son 239 18
chosen to be a g of the Church's faith, 519 3

guidance
under the g of the Holy Spirit, 205 15
under the g of the Holy Spirit, 256 12
trusting in the g of the Holy Spirit, 513 2
under the g of the Holy Spirit? 860 8

guide
and to g our feet into the way of peace. 51 20
And g us in the way of justice and truth. 55 8
and g our feet into the way of peace; 56 21
We humbly pray thee so to g and govern us 57 15
And g us in the way of justice and truth. 67 23
and to g our feet into the way of peace. 93 9
and the Holy Spirit, advocate and g. 95 29
And g us in the way of justice and truth. 98 2
and g our feet into the way of peace; 99 16
We humbly pray you so to g and govern us 100 7
And g us in the way of justice and truth. 122 2
for the sake of your Name, lead me and g me. 129 15
G us waking, O Lord, and guard us sleeping; 134 16
G us waking, O Lord, and guard us sleeping; 135 9
that, thou being our ruler and g, we may so pass 180 3
and g with thy wisdom those who take counsel 207 9
So g us in the work we do, 210 11
that, with you as our ruler and g, 231 19
and g with your wisdom those who take counsel 258 9
So g us in the work we do, 261 16
and g with your wisdom those who take counsel 278 26
given us the Holy Spirit to g us into all truth. 348 22
given us the Holy Spirit to g us into all truth. 381 15
G the people of this land, and of all the nations, 388 7
May the Holy Spirit g and strengthen you, 420 1
The Lord will g our feet into the way of peace, 483 18
The Lord will g our feet into the way of peace, 500 7
will you g and strengthen the deacons 518 25
Be present always to g and to judge, 568 12
for the sake of your Name, lead me and g me. 622 14
I will g you with my eye. 625 19
he shall be our g for evermore. 652 5
and g all the nations upon earth. 675 17
You will g me by your counsel, * 688 25
g the nations of the world into the way of justice 816 1
G us to perceive what is right, 818 4
g the minds of those who shall choose a bishop 818 9
G and sanctify, we pray, 819 7
We beseech thee so to g and bless our Senators 821 2
G the people of the United States 822 24
G the people of this land 824 12
g him wherever he may be. 830 14
so g our minds, so fill our imaginations, 832 25

guided
ordered and g by faithful and true pastors; 188 4
be g and governed by faithful and true pastors; 239 14
Will you respect and be g by the pastoral direction 532 1
Will you be g by the pastoral direction 543 25
and g them in the wilderness like a flock. 699 10
and g them with the skillfulness of his hands. 700 25
that it may be so g and governed by thy good Spirit, 815 2
being g by thy Providence, 820 17
O God, by whom the meek are g in judgment, 832 6

guides
and g me along right pathways for his Name's sake. 443 6
and g me along right pathways for his Name's sake. 613 2
He g the humble in doing right * 615 6
who g the Church in the true interpretation 854 1
and g them to do God's work. 854 19

guiding
thy merciful g may perform the same; 178 3
your merciful g may do them; 229 17

guile
There is no g upon his tongue; 599 8
and in whose spirit there is no g! 625 2

guilt
forgiveness heal g, and joy conquer despair. 429 19
Happy are they to whom the LORD imputes no g, * 625 1
and did not conceal my g. 625 8
Then you forgave me the g of my sin. 625 10
Not because of any g of mine * 666 1
Lay to their charge g upon g, * 681 18

guilty

Declare them *g*, O God; * 589 13
nor let them be found *g* when brought to trial. 636 2
When he is judged, let him be found *g*, * 751 10
and bring the *g* to repentance 826 18

gullies

the waters gushed out, and the *g* overflowed; * 696 14

gushed

and the waters *g* out like rivers. 696 6
True, he struck the rock, the waters *g* out, 696 13

H

habitation

and the Most High your *h*, 130 16
the holy *h* of the Most High. 649 11
God in his holy *h*! 676 12
and the Most High your *h*, 720 4
he has desired her for his *h*: 786 27

habitations

all your saints in the eternal *h*; 464 18
all your saints in the eternal *h*; 466 18

had

And I said, "Oh, that I *h* wings like a dove! * 660 17
I was stupid and *h* no understanding; * 688 21
For they *h* no faith in God, * 696 20
and *h* no faith in his wonderful works. 697 15
for we have *h* more than enough of contempt 780 22
Almighty God, whose Son *h* nowhere to lay his head: 829 22

Hagarenes

the Moabites and the *H*; 706 15

hail

in his name may ever *h* him as our King, 271 11
He killed their vines with *h* * 698 21
He scatters his *h* like bread crumbs; * 805 11
Fire and *h*, snow and fog, * 806 9

hailstones

burst *h* and coals of fire. 603 14
He delivered their cattle to *h* * 698 23
He gave them *h* instead of rain, * 740 17

hairs

they are more in number than the *h* of my head, 641 6
hate me without a cause are more than the *h* of my head; 679 16

hairy

and the *h* scalp of those who go on still in their 677 26

half

They shall not live out *h* their days, * 662 10

Hallelujah

in the midst of you, O Jerusalem. *H*! 442 27
Bless the LORD, O my soul. * *H*! 737 27
and observe his laws. *H*! 741 17
H! Give thanks to the LORD, 741 19
let all the people say, "Amen!" *H*! 745 26
H! I will give thanks to the LORD 754 5
H! Happy are they who fear 755 4
H! Give praise, you servants 756 1
H! When Israel came out 756 18
for evermore. *H*! 758 27
O Jerusalem. *H*! 760 14
LORD endures for ever. *H*! 760 19
H! Praise the Name of the LORD; * 788 1
who dwells in Jerusalem. *H*! 789 19
H! Praise the LORD, 803 3
throughout all generations. *H*! 803 26
H! How good it is to sing praises 804 1
not revealed his judgments. *H*! 805 19
H! Praise the LORD 805 20
a people who are near him. *H*! 806 25
H! Sing to the LORD 807 1
glory for all his faithful people. *H*! 807 20
H! Praise God in his holy temple; 807 21
praise the LORD. *H*! 808 11

hallowed

h be thy Name, 54 15
h be thy Name, 67 5
h be thy Name, 97 5
h be thy Name, 106 15
h be thy Name, 121 5
h be thy Name, 132 20
h be thy Name, 153 7
shared our toil and *h* our labor: 208 2
shared our toil and *h* our labor: 259 4
h be thy Name, 311 2
h be thy Name, 336 19
h be thy Name, 364 2
h be thy Name, 398 13
h be thy Name, 428 9
by your patience in suffering you *h* earthly pain 461 5
h be thy Name, 464 5
h be thy Name, 485 21
h be thy Name, 502 2

Ham

the flower of manhood in the dwellings of *H*. 699 8
and Jacob became a sojourner in the land of *H*. 739 24
and portents in the land of *H*. 740 8
Wonderful deeds in the land of *H*, * 743 15

Hamath

and the remnant of *H* will keep your feasts. 692 21

hammers

all your carved work with hatchets and *h*. 689 20

hand

where Christ sitteth on the right *h* of God. 39 14
In his *h* are all the corners of the earth, * 44 16
and the sheep of his *h*. 45 5
and from the *h* of all that hate us; 51 2
That we being delivered out of the *h* of our enemies * 51 7
Thou that sittest at the right *h* of God the Father, 52 16
Thou sittest at the right *h* of God, 53 17
sitteth on the right *h* of God the Father almighty. 54 3
because he is at my right *h*, I shall not fall. 61 12
sitteth on the right *h* of God the Father almighty. 66 19
Lord Jesus, stay with us, for evening is at *h* 70 10

where Christ is, seated at the right *h* of God. 77 13
In his *h* are the caverns of the earth, * 82 11
the people of his pasture and the sheep of his *h*. * 82 18
Your right *h*, O Lord, is glorious in might; * 85 14
your right *h*, O Lord, has overthrown the enemy. 85 15
You stretched forth your right *h*; * 85 19
the sanctuary, O Lord, that your *h* has established. 85 27
You hold back your *h*; * 91 7
you are seated at the right *h* of the Father: 95 7
You are seated at God's right *h* in glory. 96 7
and is seated at the right *h* of the Father. 96 23
My life is always in my *h*, * 104 5
the LORD is your shade at your right *h*, 104 22
because he is at my right *h*, I shall not fall. 115 12
and is seated at the right *h* of the Father. 120 19
Lord Jesus, stay with us, for evening is at *h* 124 7
and ten thousand at your right *h*, * 130 11
Lord Jesus, stay with us, for evening is at *h* 139 16
In his *h* are all the corners of the earth, * 146 7
and the sheep of his *h*. 146 15
Christ, who standeth at thy right *h*; 186 4
who by the *h* of Mark the evangelist hast given 188 21
who constantly receive good things from thy *h*, 207 19
O merciful Creator, whose *h* is open wide 208 9
Christ, who stands at your right *h*; 237 17
by the *h* of Mark the evangelist you have given 240 7
are constantly receiving good things from your *h*, 258 19
O merciful Creator, your *h* is open wide 259 11
and is seated at the right *h* of the Father. 293 10
and is seated at the right *h* of the Father. 304 13
let your fatherly *h* ever be over these your servants; 310 8
Thou that sittest at the right *h* of God the Father, 325 3
and is seated at the right *h* of the Father. 327 9
and sitteth on the right *h* of the Father; 328 9
behold thy gracious *h* in all thy works, 329 23
you are seated at the right *h* of the Father: 356 11
and is seated at the right *h* of the Father. 358 25
to see your *h* at work in the world about us. 372 3
and ascension to your right *h*, 374 27
and is seated at the right *h* of the Father. 416 18
let your fatherly *h* ever be over these your servants; 419 4
the LORD is thy defense upon thy right *h*; 473 18
and laid thine *h* upon me. 475 2
Even there also shall thy *h* lead me, * 475 11
and thy right *h* shall hold me. 475 12
and at thy right *h* there is pleasure for evermore. 485 8
mystical body of thy Son, may be set on his right *h*, 487 18
and is seated at the right *h* of the Father. 496 13
and in your right *h* are pleasures for evermore. 501 10
and is seated at the right *h* of the Father. 519 28
and is seated at the right *h* of the Father. 530 19
and is seated at the right *h* of the Father. 542 19
O LORD, let not the ungodly have the upper *h*; * 594 15
lift up your *h*, O God; * 595 19
you see it and take it into your own *h*. 595 24
because he is at my right *h* I shall not fall. 600 14
and in your right *h* are pleasures for evermore. 600 21
O Savior of those who take refuge at your right *h* 601 12
Deliver me, O LORD, by your *h* * 601 27
your right *h* also sustains me; 605 10
with the victorious strength of his right *h*. 608 14
Your *h* will lay hold upon all your enemies; * 609 12
your right *h* will seize all those who hate you. 609 13
and their right *h* full of bribes. 617 2
Deliver me not into the *h* of my adversaries, * 618 23
My times are in your *h*; * 623 22
rescue me from the *h* of my enemies, 623 23
For your *h* was heavy upon me day and night; * 625 5
nor the *h* of the wicked push me aside. 633 2
for the LORD holds them by the *h*. 635 8
The LORD will not abandon them to their *h*, * 636 1
and your *h* presses hard upon me. 636 23
I am worn down by the blows of your *h*. 639 16
he does not *h* them over to the will of their enemies. 642 3
How with your *h* you drove the peoples out 645 10
but your right *h*, your arm, and the 645 15
Your right *h* will show you marvelous things; * 647 21
on your right *h* is the queen, 648 9
your right *h* is full of justice. 651 22
My companion stretched forth his *h* against his comrade; * 661 28
Save us by your right *h* and answer us, * 667 18
your right *h* holds me fast. 671 2
in the midst of maidens playing upon the *h*-drums. 678 8
Deliver me, my God, from the *h* of the wicked, * 683 7
you hold me by my right *h*. 688 24
Why do you draw back your *h*? * 690 6
why is your right *h* hidden in your bosom? 690 7
Do not *h* over the life of your dove to wild beasts; * 690 22
For in the LORD's *h* there is a cup, 691 18
none of the warriors can lift a *h*. 692 11
the right *h* of the Most High has lost its power." 693 21
by the *h* of Moses and Aaron. 694 18
the mountain his right *h* had won. 699 14
his glory into the adversary's *h*. 700 2
preserve what your right *h* has planted. 703 17
Let your *h* be upon the man of your right *h*, * 703 20
and turn my *h* against their foes. 705 4
for they are cut off from your *h*. 712 12
strong is your *h* and high is your right *h*. 714 20
My *h* will hold him fast * 715 8
You have exalted the right *h* of his foes * 716 25
and ten thousand at your right *h*, * 719 25
In his *h* are the caverns of the earth, * 724 20
the people of his pasture and the sheep of his *h*. * 725 4
and delivers them from the *h* of the wicked. 727 19
With his right *h* and his holy arm * 728 1
you open your *h*, and they are filled with good things. 737 10
He saved them from the *h* of those who hated them * 742 18
and redeemed them from the *h* of the enemy. 742 19
So he lifted his *h* against them, * 743 24
He gave them over to the *h* of the heathen, * 745 6
and they were humbled under their *h*. 745 9
that he redeemed them from the *h* of the foe. 746 4
save with your right *h* and answer me. 750 6
and let an accuser stand at his right *h*. 751 9
Let them know that this is your *h*, * 753 1
Because he stands at the right *h* of the needy, * 753 10
The LORD said to my Lord, "Sit at my right *h*, * 753 12
The Lord who is at your right *h* 753 21
"The right *h* of the LORD has triumphed! * 762 1
the right *h* of the LORD is exalted! 762 2
but he did not *h* me over to death. 762 7
My life is always in my *h*, * 772 11

You, O Lord, are near at *h*, * 776 5
Let your *h* be ready to help me, * 778 1
the Lord is your shade at your right *h*. 779 10
the eyes of servants look to the *h* of their masters, * 780 17
the eyes of a maid to the *h* of her mistress, 780 18
Like arrows in the *h* of a warrior * 783 8
Which does not fill the *h* of the reaper, * 784 13
With a mighty *h* and a stretched-out arm, * 790 19
let my right *h* forget its skill. 792 11
you stretch forth your *h* against the fury 793 17
your right *h* shall save me. 793 18
and lay your *h* upon me. 794 9
Even there your *h* will lead me * 794 18
and your right *h* hold me fast. 794 19
I look to my right *h* and find no one 798 7
Stretch out your *h* from on high; * 800 14
from the *h* of foreign peoples, 800 16
and whose right *h* is raised in falsehood. 800 18
and deliver me from the *h* of foreign peoples, 800 24
and whose right *h* is raised in falsehood. 800 26
You open wide your *h* * 802 19
and a two-edged sword in their *h*; 807 13
Open our eyes to behold thy gracious *h* 814 2
Almighty God, whose loving *h* hath given us all 827 1
O gracious Father, who openest thine *h* 828 1
O God, our times are in your *h*: 830 8
and is seated at the right *h* of the Father? 850 18

handed

On the night he was *h* over to suffering and death, 362 18
On the night he was *h* over to suffering and death, 405 1
How was this revelation *h* down to us? 846 17
This revelation was *h* down to us 846 18

handful

You have given me a mere *h* of days, 639 3

handiwork

and showest forth thy *h* in the heavens 210 2
and show forth your *h* in the heavens 261 8
and the firmament shows his *h*. 606 16
prosper our *h*. 719 9

handmaid

and save the child of your *h*. 711 8
I am your servant and the child of your *h*; 760 6

handmaiden

the lowliness of his *h*. 50 4
the lowliness of his *h*. 65 7

hands

Christ is not entered into the holy places made with *h*, 39 15
great benefits that we have received at his *h*, 41 7
and his *h* prepared the dry land. 44 19
reaching forth our *h* in love, 58 11
the lifting up of my *h* be an evening sacrifice. 61 2
Christ has entered, not into a sanctuary made with *h*, 77 14
and his *h* have molded the dry land. 82 14
from the *h* of all who hate us. 92 24
to set us free from the *h* of our enemies, 92 28
reaching forth our *h* in love, 101 4
the lifting up of our *h* as the evening sacrifice. 113 10
the lifting up of my *h* as the evening sacrifice. 115 2
Into your *h* I commend my spirit, * 129 18
They shall bear you in their *h*, * 130 21
Lift up your *h* in the holy place and bless the Lord; * 131 8
Into your *h*, O Lord, I commend my spirit; 132 12
Lift up your *h* in the holy place and bless the Lord; * 140 3
and his *h* prepared the dry land. 146 10
and given up into the *h* of sinners, 169 16
and given into the *h* of sinners, 221 10
and given into the *h* of sinners, 276 6
the joining of *h* and the giving and receiving of a ring, 428 2
Into your *h*, O God, we place your child 444 20
I lay my *h* upon you in the Name of the Father, 456 1
I lay my *h* upon you in the Name of our Lord 456 7
Into your *h*, O merciful Savior, we commend 465 1
Into your *h*, O Lord, 465 15
Into your *h*, O Lord, 466 3
Into thy *h*, O merciful Savior, we commend 483 6
Into thy *h*, O Lord, we commend 488 12
as into the *h* of a faithful Creator 488 13
in whose *h* are the living and the dead: 488 26
Into your *h*, O merciful Savior, we commend 499 13
We therefore ask you to lay your *h* upon him 513 4
Receive the work of our *h* in this place, 567 10
when we are committed into the Father's *h*. 569 9
for the work of many *h*, which have beautified 573 2
much less the walls of temples made with *h*. 578 4
and accept the work of our *h*, 578 6
if there is any wickedness in my *h*, 590 25
You give him mastery over the works of your *h*; * 592 19
the wicked are trapped in the works of their own *h*. 594 10
because my *h* were clean he rewarded me; 604 4
because of the cleanness of my *h* in his sight. 604 13
He trains my *h* for battle * 605 7
they pierce my *h* and my feet; 611 13
"Those who have clean *h* and a pure heart, * 613 20
I will wash my *h* in innocence, O Lord, * 616 18
Whose *h* are full of evil plots, * 617 1
when I lift up my *h* to your holy of holies. 619 9
According to the work of their *h* repay them, * 619 16
nor of the works of his *h*; * 619 19
Into your *h* I commend my spirit, * 622 17
or stretched out our *h* to some strange god, 646 27
Clap your *h*, all you peoples; * 650 6
and your *h* deal out violence in the land. 664 24
and lift up my *h* in your Name. 670 20
let Ethiopia stretch out her *h* to God. 678 23
and washed my *h* in innocence. 688 4
my *h* were stretched out by night and did not tire; 693 4
and guided them with the skillfulness of his *h*. 700 25
his *h* were set free from bearing the load." 704 13
I have stretched out my *h* to you. 712 22
prosper the work of our *h*; 719 8
They shall bear you in their *h*, * 720 9
and I shout for joy because of the works of your *h*. 721 4
and his *h* have molded the dry land. 724 23
Let the rivers clap their *h*, * 728 18
and the heavens are the work of your *h*; 732 29
The works of his *h* are faithfulness and justice; * 754 18
the work of human *h*. 757 21
They have *h*, but they cannot feel; 758 1
I will lift up my *h* to your commandments, * 767 9
Your *h* have made me and fashioned me; * 769 9

so that the just shall not put their *h* to evil. 781 24
Lift up your *h* in the holy place and bless the LORD; * 787 21
the work of human *h*. 789 6
do not abandon the works of your *h*. 793 21
Keep me, O LORD, from the *h* of the wicked; * 796 7
the lifting up of my *h* as the evening sacrifice. 797 6
I consider the works of your *h*. 799 9
I spread out my *h* to you; * 799 10
who trains my *h* to fight and my fingers to battle; 800 2
For minds to think, and hearts to love, and *h* to serve, 837 12
through prayer and the laying on of *h* 860 20
through prayer and the laying on of *h* by bishops. 861 2
or the laying on of *h*, 861 15

hang

h all the Law and the Prophets. 319 13
h all the Law and the Prophets. 324 6

Hannah

Samuel with *H* his mother; 838 13

happen

There shall no evil *h* to you, * 130 17
adversities which may *h* to the body, 167 6
adversities which may *h* to the body, 218 16
no harm shall *h* to me ever." 595 5
There shall no evil *h* to you, * 720 5

happens

to believe that what *h* to me here is of little account 461 10

happiness

h and prosperity shall be yours. 783 16

happy

Thou art worthy at all times to be praised by *h* voices, 64 7
You are worthy at all times to be praised by *h* voices, 112 7
You are worthy at all times to be praised by *h* voices, 118 7
You are worthy at all times to be praised by *h* voices, 139 7
H from now on are those who die 492 1
H are they who have not walked in the counsel 585 1
H are they all * 587 1
H are they whose transgressions are forgiven, * 624 23
H are they to whom the LORD imputes no guilt, * 625 1
H is the nation whose God is the LORD! * 626 23
h the people he has chosen to be his own! 626 24
h are they who trust in him! 628 10
H are they who trust in the LORD! * 640 9
H are they who consider the poor and needy! * 641 23
so that they may be *h* in the land; * 642 2
H are they whom you choose 672 13
H are they who dwell in your house! * 707 23
H are the people whose strength is in you! * 707 25
h are they who put their trust in you! 708 19
H are the people who know the festal shout! * 714 23
H are they whom you instruct, O Lord! * 723 17
H are those who act with justice * 742 1
H are they who fear the LORD * 755 5
H are those whose way is blameless, * 763 5
H are they who observe his decrees * 763 7
H is the man who has his quiver full of them! * 783 10
H are they all who fear the LORD, * 783 13
h the one who pays you back 792 20
H shall he be who takes your little ones, * 792 22
H are the people of whom this is so! * 801 10
h are the people whose God is the LORD! 801 11
H are they who have the God of Jacob 803 11
and a *h* issue out of all their afflictions. 815 11

harbor

and he brought them to the *h* they were bound for. 748 16

hard

on the *h* wood of the cross 58 9
on the *h* wood of the cross 101 2
you set me free when I am *h*-pressed; 128 9
you set me free when I am *h*-pressed; 587 21
They press me *h*, 601 20
and your hand presses *h* upon me. 636 23
it was too *h* for me; 688 10
He split the *h* rocks in the wilderness * 696 3
So he humbled their spirits with *h* labor; * 747 5
Who turned the *h* rock into a pool of water * 757 11
I was pressed so *h* that I almost fell, * 761 22
or with things that are too *h* for me. 785 13

harden

Today if ye will hear his voice, *h* not your hearts * 146 16
H not your hearts, 725 6

hardened

For those *h* by sin or indifference 279 23

hardness

from *h* of heart, 149 8
h of heart, and show forth your glory in all that we 391 3

hardship

You have made your people know *h*; * 667 14

hardships

and all the *h* he endured; 785 20

harm

For our enemies and those who wish us *h*; 391 5
no *h* shall happen to me ever." 595 5
and disgraced who sought to do me *h*. 685 8
and do my prophets no *h*." 739 8

harmony

serve you in *h* around your heavenly throne; 815 20
and to live in *h* with creation 845 6
and out of *h* with creation? 845 9
we may live in *h* with God, within ourselves, 849 14
brought into love and *h* with God, 852 28

harnessed

and *h* your tongue to a lie. 655 19

harp

Praise the LORD with the *h*; * 626 3
and on the *h* I will give thanks to you, 644 26
and set forth my riddle upon the *h*. 652 12
awake, lute and *h*; * 664 13
I will sing to you with the *h*, O Holy One of Israel. 685 3
the merry *h*, and the lyre. 704 4
and to the melody of the *h*. 721 2
Sing to the LORD with the *h*, * 728 12
with the *h* and the voice of song. 728 13
awake, lute and *h*; * 749 20

make music to our God upon the *h*. 804 15
let them sing praise to him with timbrel and *h*. 807 7
praise him with lyre and *h*. 808 4

harps

As for our *h*, we hung them up * 792 3

hart

Like as the *h* desireth the water-brooks, * 471 1

harvest

send forth laborers into thy *h*, 150 13
and for the labors of those who *h* them. 194 18
and for the labors of those who *h* them. 246 3
and brought in a fruitful *h*. 749 4
praise for the return of seedtime and *h*, 840 16

harvests

use the *h* of the land and of the seas, 207 17
use the *h* of the land and of the seas, 258 17
and multiply the *h* of the world; 828 3

has

also with the one who *h* a contrite and humble spirit, 78 24
death no longer *h* dominion over him. 83 16
He *h* mercy on those who fear him * 92 4
he *h* mercy on those who fear him * 119 10
that your brother *h* something against you, 376 14
who now *h* a new brother (sister)] in offering 440 11
He *h* mercy on those who fear him * 441 18
to do what he *h* to do 459 12
and bear what he *h* to bear; 459 13
Whoever *h* faith in me shall have life, 491 2
And everyone who *h* life, 491 4
For none of us *h* life in himself, 491 13
the Lord *h* them in derision. 586 9
The little that the righteous *h* * 634 16
and the oppressed who *h* no helper. 686 8
My soul *h* a desire and longing for the courts 707 16
I have become like one who *h* no strength; 712 8
he who teaches all the world, *h* he no knowledge? 723 14
and his kingship *h* dominion over all. 734 21
Let the creditor seize everything he *h*; * 751 18
but your commandment *h* no bounds. 771 12
Happy is the man who *h* his quiver full of them! * 783 10
he *h* no pleasure in the strength of a man; 804 23
But the LORD *h* pleasure in those who fear him, * 804 24
Let everything that *h* breath * 808 9
Sin *h* power over us because we lose our liberty 849 2

haste

O Lord, make *h* to help us. 63 18
O Lord, make *h* to help us. 103 2
O Lord, make *h* to help us. 117 11
O Lord, make *h* to help us. 128 4
make *h* to deliver me. 129 12
make *h* to deliver me. 622 11
Make *h* to help me, * 638 13
O LORD, make *h* to help me. 641 9
O LORD, make *h* to help me. 682 12
when I call, make *h* to answer me, 731 4
O LORD, make *h* to answer me; 799 12

hasten

h the coming of thy kingdom; 58 6
and *h* the coming of your kingdom; 100 22
h the coming of thy kingdom; through the same thy 206 14
and *h* the coming of your kingdom; 257 9
H, O Father, the coming of thy kingdom; 395 13
you are my strength, *h* to help me. 611 19
I would *h* to escape * 660 21
I *h* and do not tarry * 768 7
And *h* the day when all our people, 839 18

hastened

at the voice of your thunder they *h* away. 735 16

hatchets

they broke down all your carved work with *h* 689 19

hate

and from the hand of all that *h* us; 51 2
from the hands of all who *h* us. 92 24
God, you *h* nothing you have made 217 14
God, you *h* nothing you have made 264 2
you *h* all those who work wickedness. 588 26
see the misery I suffer from those who *h* me, 594 2
I destroy those who *h* me; 605 21
your right hand will seize all those who *h* you. 609 13
I *h* those who cling to worthless idols, * 622 20
and those who *h* the righteous will be punished. 629 10
nor let those who *h* me without a cause 631 7
and many in number are those who wrongfully *h* me. 638 8
and put those who *h* us to shame. 645 26
you love righteousness and *h* iniquity. 648 3
let those who *h* him flee before him. 676 2
Those who *h* me without a cause 679 16
let me be rescued from those who *h* me 680 18
Those who *h* the LORD would cringe before him, * 705 5
and those who *h* you have lifted up their heads. 706 6
so that those who *h* me may see it and be ashamed; * 711 10
and strike down those who *h* him. 715 13
The LORD loves those who *h* evil; * 727 17
I *h* the doers of evil deeds; 730 13
I will triumph over those who *h* me. 761 10
therefore I *h* every lying way. 772 2
I *h* those who have a divided heart, * 772 19
As for lies, I *h* and abhor them, * 777 5
Do I not *h* those, O LORD, who *h* you? * 795 20
I *h* them with a perfect hatred; * 795 22
save them from speaking in *h*; 823 11

hated

and from those who *h* me; * 603 26
I have *h* the company of evildoers; * 616 16
Whose heart he turned, so that they *h* his people, * 740 3
He saved them from the hand of those who *h* them * 742 18
and those who *h* them ruled over them. 745 7

hateful

that his *h* sin will not be found out. 632 6
they encompass me with *h* words 751 2
How *h* it is that I must lodge in Meshech * 778 18

hatest

God, who *h* nothing that thou hast made 166 1

hath
death *h* no more dominion over him. 46 8

hatred
from envy, *h*, and malice; 149 2
It casts out pride and *h*, 287 19
and they bear a violent *h* against me. 615 27
and *h* for my love. 751 7
I hate them with a perfect *h*; * 795 22
take away the arrogance and *h* 815 15
deliver them and us from *h*, cruelty, and revenge; 816 7
take away all *h* and prejudice, 818 17
to confront one another without *h* or bitterness, 824 3
Where there is *h*, let us sow love; 833 6
to bear no malice, prejudice, or *h* in our hearts; 848 9

hatreds
suspicions disappear, and *h* cease; 823 20

haughtily
h, disdainfully, and with contempt. 624 3
but repays to the full those who act *h*. 624 20

haughtiness
out of their *h* they plan oppression. 687 16

haughty
but you will humble the *h* eyes. 604 19
those who have a *h* look 730 18
I have no *h* looks. 785 11
he perceives the *h* from afar. 793 15

haunts
the dark places of the earth are *h* of violence. 690 25

have
If we say that we *h* no sin, 38 10
But thou, O Lord, *h* mercy upon us, 42 3
h mercy upon us. 52 13
O Lord, *h* mercy upon us, *h* mercy upon us. 55 20
in whom we live and move and *h* our being: 57 14
but shall *h* the light of life." 62 10
But thou, O Lord, *h* mercy upon us, 63 6
If we say we *h* no sin, we deceive ourselves, 76 9
h mercy on us and forgive us; 79 19
Almighty God *h* mercy on you, 80 1
and he will *h* compassion, * 86 21
they were created and *h* their being; 93 23
h mercy on us; 95 6
H mercy on us, Lord, *h* mercy. 98 14
in you we live and move and *h* our being: 100 6
Lord, *h* mercy. 106 11
Christ, *h* mercy. 106 12
that by its brightness we may *h* a vision 110 20
but will *h* the light of life." 116 6
h mercy on us and forgive us; 117 2
Almighty God *h* mercy on you, 117 6
h mercy on me and hear my prayer. 128 10
Your eyes *h* only to behold * 130 13
Lord, *h* mercy. 132 16
Christ, *h* mercy. 132 17
H mercy upon us. 148 2
That it may please thee to *h* mercy upon all mankind, 152 1
H mercy upon us. 152 25
Lord, *h* mercy upon us. 153 3
Christ, *h* mercy upon us. 153 4
O Son of David, *h* mercy upon us. 155 2
who seest that we *h* no power of ourselves 167 3
by the same Spirit to *h* a right judgment in all things, 175 17
we beseech thee, make us to *h* a perpetual fear 178 12
may *h* grace and power faithfully to fulfill the same; 179 13
H compassion, we beseech thee, 179 17
that we and all the people of this land may *h* grace 190 20
by which alone they may *h* true authority 191 11
may *h* grace to take up our cross 192 16
and *h* confidence in thy loving care; 208 20
O God, whose glory it is always to *h* mercy: 218 7
you know that we *h* no power in ourselves 218 13
Grant us by the same Spirit to *h* a right judgment 227 10
O Lord, make us *h* perpetual love 230 7
and also may *h* grace 231 6
H compassion on our weakness, 231 11
all the people of this land may *h* grace 242 4
service by which alone they may *h* true authority 242 18
may *h* grace to take up our cross 244 4
and *h* confidence in your loving care; 260 5
Christians continually *h* to renew their repentance 265 9
H mercy on me, O God, 266 1
H mercy on us, Lord. 267 22
H mercy on us, Lord. 267 26
h love for one another. 275 8
H compassion on all who do not know you 280 2
Thou shalt *h* none other gods but me. 317 26
Lord, *h* mercy upon us, 317 28
If we say that we *h* no sin, 320 1
Seeing that we *h* a great high priest, 320 5
h mercy on us and forgive us; 320 19
But thou, O Lord, *h* mercy upon us, 321 6
Lord, *h* mercy upon us. 324 7
Christ, *h* mercy upon us. 324 8
H mercy upon us. 324 13
h mercy upon us. 324 24
h mercy upon us. 325 4
and his kingdom will *h* no end. 327 11
whose kingdom shall *h* no end. 328 12
H mercy upon us, 331 13
h mercy upon us, most merciful Father; 331 14
h mercy on us and forgive us; 331 30
h mercy upon you, 332 3
h everlasting life. 332 12
If any man sin, we *h* an Advocate with the Father, 332 15
h mercy upon us. 337 4
whose property is always to *h* mercy. 337 13
they were created and *h* their being. 344 7
You shall *h* no other gods but me. 350 3
Lord *h* mercy. 350 4
If we say that we *h* no sin, 352 1
Since we *h* a great high priest 352 5
h mercy on us and forgive us; 352 19
Almighty God *h* mercy on you, 353 1
h mercy on us; 356 10
Lord, *h* mercy. 356 19
Christ, *h* mercy. 356 20
H mercy upon us. 356 25
and his kingdom will *h* no end. 359 2
h mercy on us and forgive us; 360 11

Almighty God *h* mercy on you,	360	15
By your will they were created and *h* their being.	370	11
H mercy, Lord, for we are sinners in your sight.	370	16
do not neglect to do good and to share what you *h*,	377	1
will they were created and *h* their being.	377	5
let us pray to the Lord, saying, "Lord, *h* mercy."	383	2
Lord, *h* mercy.	383	5
Lord, *h* mercy.	384	31
Pray that we may *h* grace to glorify Christ	386	17
H compassion on those who suffer from any grief	387	14
let us pray to the Lord, saying, "Lord, *h* mercy"	389	13
Lord, *h* mercy.	389	18
they may *h* rest in that place where there is no pain	391	17
We pray for all who *h* died, that they may *h* a place	393	4
H mercy upon us, most merciful Father;	393	9
but *h* eternal life.	396	2
h mercy on us and forgive us;	398	3
Almighty God *h* mercy on you,	398	7
h mercy on us.	407	2
will you *h* this man to be your husband;	424	8
will you *h* this woman to be your wife;	424	14
to *h* and to hold from this day forward,	427	2
with all that I am, and all that I *h*,	427	14
in the age to come *h* life everlasting.	431	13
to *h* and to hold from this day forward,	436	2
I pray God to *h* mercy on me.	447	9
H mercy on me, O God,	449	1
h mercy upon us.	449	8
h everlasting life.	449	17
If any man sin, we *h* an Advocate with the Father,	450	1
h mercy on us and forgive us;	455	2
Almighty God *h* mercy on you,	455	6
and *h* confidence in your loving care;	459	20
H mercy on your servant.	462	6
H mercy on him.	463	24
Lord, *h* mercy.	464	1
Christ, *h* mercy.	464	2
h mercy upon me, and hear me.	477	29
may *h* strength to meet the days ahead	481	11
to *h* our consummation and bliss	481	24
may *h* our perfect consummation and bliss,	488	8
Whoever has faith in me shall *h* life,	491	2
For if we *h* life, we are alive in the Lord,	491	15
but *h* confidence in your goodness,	494	10
h perfect fulfillment and bliss	503	17
that they may *h* strength to meet the days	505	11
that you may *h* the mind of Christ?	518	5
and defend those who *h* no helper?	518	29
and his kingdom will *h* no end.	520	2
and other ministers who may *h* authority over you	526	12
and his kingdom will *h* no end.	530	21
and other ministers who may *h* authority over you	538	12
and his kingdom will *h* no end.	542	21
H mercy on us.	548	2
they may *h* rest in that place where there is no pain	550	22
Lord, *h* mercy.	551	1
Christ, *h* mercy.	551	2
I am not worthy to *h* you come under my roof;	562	9
and will center in what you would *h* me do.	562	15
All that we are and all that we *h* is yours.	568	8
LORD, how many adversaries I *h*! *	587	3
h mercy on me and hear my prayer.	587	22
H pity on me, LORD, for I am weak; *	590	1
H pity on me, O LORD; *	594	1
O LORD, let not the ungodly *h* the upper hand; *	594	15
How long shall I *h* perplexity in my mind,	598	1
H they no knowledge, all those evildoers *	598	21
indeed, I *h* a goodly heritage.	600	10
Although they *h* no words or language, *	606	19
"Those who *h* clean hands and a pure heart, *	613	20
Turn to me and *h* pity on me, *	615	20
redeem me, O LORD and *h* pity on me.	617	4
h mercy on me and answer me.	618	11
They *h* no understanding of the LORD's doings,	619	18
Hear, O LORD, and *h* mercy upon me; *	622	1
H mercy on me, O LORD, for I am in trouble; *	623	3
which *h* no understanding; *	625	20
and in days of famine they shall *h* enough.	634	23
the Lord will *h* regard for me.	641	20
The king will *h* pleasure in your beauty; *	648	13
"In place of fathers, O king, you shall *h* sons; *	648	23
that we should never *h* enough to pay it,	652	20
Those who are honored, but *h* no understanding, *	653	23
H mercy on me, O God, according to your	656	5
H they no knowledge, those evildoers *	659	7
those who *h* no regard for God.	659	23
I *h* no peace, because of my cares.	660	8
H mercy on me, O God,	662	12
they shall live there and *h* it in possession.	682	8
He shall *h* pity on the lowy and poor; *	686	9
In the misfortunes of others they *h* no share; *	687	9
Whom *h* I in heaven but you? *	688	27
Turn to me and *h* mercy upon me; *	711	6
You *h* a mighty arm; *	714	19
Your eyes *h* only to behold *	720	1
Can a corrupt tribunal *h* any part with you, *	724	5
those who *h* a haughty look and a proud	730	18
You will arise and *h* compassion on Zion,	732	1
for it is time to *h* mercy upon her; *	732	2
I will praise my God while I *h* my being.	737	21
Remember me, O LORD, with the favor you *h*	742	3
those who act accordingly *h* a good understanding;	755	2
and *h* great delight in his commandments!	755	6
They *h* mouths, but they cannot speak; *	757	22
eyes *h* they, but they cannot see;	757	23
They *h* ears, but they cannot hear; *	757	24
They *h* hands, but they cannot feel;	758	1
Then shall I *h* a word for those who taunt me, *	766	19
I *h* more understanding than all my teachers, *	771	17
I hate those who *h* a divided heart, *	772	19
let no iniquity *h* dominion over me.	774	14
Great peace *h* they who love your law; *	777	9
H mercy upon us, O LORD, *h* mercy, *	780	21
I *h* no haughty looks.	785	11
They *h* mouths, but they cannot speak; *	789	7
eyes *h* they, but they cannot see.	789	8
They *h* ears, but they cannot hear; *	789	9
I *h* no place to flee to,	798	8
I will sing praises to my God while I *h* my being.	803	6
Happy are they who *h* the God of Jacob	803	11
H mercy upon all of us who live and work	825	19
and all who *h* none to care for them.	826	4
H mercy upon us. Help us to	826	10

the grace to ask what thou wouldest *h* us to do, 832 9
How does sin *h* power over us? 849 1

haven
that their home may be a *h* of blessing and peace; 431 6
O LORD my stronghold, my crag, and my *h*. 602 8

having
h done thy will with cheerfulness while it was day, 56 22
h done your will with cheerfulness during the day, 99 16
h this hope, we may purify ourselves 184 10
h his wonderful conversion in remembrance, 187 10
and we pray that, *h* opened to him the gates 202 10
Grant that, *h* this hope, 236 3
Grant, we pray, that we, *h* his wonderful conversion 239 1
and we pray that, *h* opened to him the gates 253 14
H in mind, therefore, his great love for us, 316 8
h in remembrance his blessed passion 335 13
h in remembrance his blessed passion 342 13
h loved his own who were in the world, 374 14
h taken away the sin of the world. 483 18
thy servants, who, *h* finished their course 488 5
h the testimony of a good conscience; 489 8
h taken away the sin of the world. 500 7
your servants, who, *h* finished their 503 15
h the testimony of a good conscience, in 504 6
dwelling on high but *h* regard for the lowly, 520 12
and, *h* ascended into heaven, 533 6
LORD, let me not be ashamed for *h* called upon you; * 623 27
and *h* you I desire nothing upon earth. 688 28

head
thou art exalted as *h* above all. 344 11
the *h* of the Church, and the author of our salvation. 369 13
exalted as *h* over all. 377 9
you have anointed my *h* with oil, 443 13
thou has anointed my *h* with oil, 476 14
thou anointest my *h* with oil; 477 7
And now shall he lift up mine *h* * 477 23
and the *h* of the Church. 533 4
you are my glory, the one who lifts up my *h*. 587 8
Their malice turns back upon their own *h*; * 592 3
you put me at the *h* of the nations. 605 27
and set a crown of fine gold upon his *h*. 609 2
you have anointed my *h* with oil, 613 9
Even now he lifts up my *h* * 618 5
they put their *h* together against me; 623 18
they are more in number than the hairs of my *h*, 641 6
There is Benjamin, least of the tribes, at the *h*; 678 11
are more than the hairs of my *h*; 679 17
therefore he will lift high his *h*. 754 4
they will hold up their *h* with honor. 755 24
It is like fine oil upon the *h* * 787 11
you have covered my *h* in the day of battle. 796 16
let not the oil of the unrighteous anoint my *h*; * 797 13
you are exalted as *h* above all. 822 16
Almighty God, whose Son had nowhere to lay his *h*: 829 22
the Body of which Jesus Christ is the *H* 854 7
because it is one Body, under one *H*, 854 16

headed
And now that I am old and gray-*h*, 684 16

headlong
If they stumble, they shall not fall *h*, * 635 7

heads
they curl their lips and wag their *h*, 610 15
Lift up your *h*, O gates; 614 1
and all who see them will shake their *h*. 672 2
You let enemies ride over our *h*; 674 17
God shall crush the *h* of his enemies, * 677 25
and shattered the *h* of the dragons upon the waters; 690 11
You crushed the *h* of Leviathan * 690 12
and those who hate you have lifted up their *h*. 706 6
they see and shake their *h*. 752 26
he will smash *h* over the wide earth. 754 2
Let not those who surround me lift up their *h*; * 796 19

heal
love and power to *h*, 193 14
love and power to *h*, 245 1
Comfort and *h* all those who suffer in body, 389 3
forgiveness *h* guilt, and joy conquer despair. 429 19
May God the Father bless you, God the Son *h* you, 460 5
h me according to your will; 461 9
h me, LORD, for my bones are racked. 590 2
h me, for I have sinned against you." 642 7
Help us to *h* those who are broken in body 826 4
h us. 838 24

healed
be *h* of all our infirmities 191 4
be *h* from all our infirmities 242 11
By his wounds, we are *h*. 370 22
anointed many that were sick and *h* them, 455 11
Reproach has broken my heart, and it cannot be *h*; * 681 3
He sent forth his word and *h* them * 747 21
divisions being *h*, we may live in justice and peace; 823 21

healer
and be among us as a *h* and reconciler. 561 6

healing
set forth in the Gospel the love and *h* power 193 12
and give thy power of *h* to those who minister 208 17
set forth in the Gospel the love and *h* power 244 21
and give your power of *h* to those who minister 260 2
that you may know the *h* power 456 9
accepting your *h* gifts through the skill 459 13
and give your power of *h* to those who minister 459 18
the study and practice of the arts of *h*, 460 11
and gracefully accept your *h*; 461 4
to ask your forgiveness, to know your *h* power, 568 10
grace is given for the *h* of spirit, mind, and body. 861 16

heals
and *h* all your infirmities; 733 14
He *h* the brokenhearted * 804 6

health
Thy saving *h* among all nations. 55 10
Thy saving *h* among all nations. 68 2
Your saving *h* among all nations. 98 4
Your saving *h* among all nations. 122 4
restored Mary Magdalene to *h* of body and mind, 191 2
Heavenly Father, giver of life and *h*: 208 16

restored Mary Magdalene to *h* of body and of mind, 242 9
Heavenly Father, giver of life and *h*: 260 1
your saving *h* among all nations. 281 8
they may live in joy, peace, and *h*, 391 12
honor and keep him, in sickness and in *h*; 424 10
honor and keep her, in sickness and in *h*; 424 16
for richer for poorer, in sickness and in *h*, 427 3
honor and keep her, in sickness and in *h*; 433 7
honor and keep him, in sickness and in *h*; 433 12
for richer for poorer, in sickness and in *h*, 436 4
for richer for poorer, in sickness and in *h*, 436 8
O Lord, holy Father, giver of *h* and salvation: 455 9
the only Name under heaven given for *h* and salvation 457 3
restore him to *h*, 458 7
that his sickness may be turned into *h*, 458 14
his *h* being renewed, he may bless 458 20
that he may be restored to that perfect *h* 458 23
Heavenly Father, giver of life and *h*: 459 17
that by their ministries the *h* of the community 460 13
both relief from pain and hope of *h* 460 18
O God, the source of all *h*: 461 1
and you restored me to *h*. 621 7
There is no *h* in my flesh, 637 1
there is no *h* in my body. 637 11
your saving *h* among all nations. 675 12
thy saving *h* unto all nations. 815 1
who through addiction have lost their *h* and freedom. 831 20

healthful

the *h* Spirit of thy grace; 817 6

heap

he does not *h* contempt upon his neighbor. 599 10
we *h* up riches and cannot tell who will gather them. 639 8
they have made Jerusalem a *h* of rubble. 701 3
He will *h* high the corpses; * 754 1

hear

his most worthy praise, to *h* his holy Word, 41 8
his praise, to *h* his holy Word, 79 3
Lord, *h* our prayer; 107 1
have mercy on me and *h* my prayer. 128 10
when I call upon the Lord, he will *h* me. 128 15
Lord, *h* our prayer; 133 7
Today if ye will *h* his voice, harden not your hearts 146 10
We sinners do beseech thee to *h* us, O Lord God; 150 1
We beseech thee to *h* us, good Lord. 150 4
to *h* and receive thy Word, 150 16
We beseech thee to *h* us, good Lord. 150 18
O Christ, *h* us. 153 1
Almighty God, who hast promised to *h* the petitions 153 19
Favorably with mercy *h* our prayers; 155 1
Both now and ever vouchsafe to *h* us, O Christ; 155 3
Graciously *h* us, O Christ; graciously *h* us, O Lord 155 4
Mercifully *h* the supplications 164 2
Grant that when we *h* his voice we may know him 173 12
who art always more ready to *h* than we to pray, 182 19
h them, read, mark, learn, and inwardly digest them; 184 17
Mercifully *h* the supplications 215 14
Grant that when we *h* his voice we may know him 225 4
you are always more ready to *h* than we are to pray, 234 13
Grant us so to *h* them, 236 9
Make me *h* of joy and gladness, * 266 18
Favorably *h* us, for your mercy is great. 268 28
Let us *h* the record of God's saving deeds in history, 288 1
Lord, *h* our prayer. 305 16
H what our Lord Jesus Christ saith: 319 8
H what our Lord Jesus Christ saith: 324 1
they may *h* and receive thy holy Word, 329 15
H the Word of God to all who truly turn to him. 332 7
beseech thee, O merciful Father, to *h* us; 335 18
beseech thee, O merciful Father, to *h* us, 342 17
H the commandments of God to his people: 350 1
"The first commandment is this: *H*, O Israel: 351 7
H our prayer. 388 6
H us, Lord; 392 18
Lord, *h* the prayers of thy people; 394 1
Heavenly Father, you have promised to *h* what we ask 394 4
H us, O heavenly Father, and with thy (your) Word 408 1
H the Word of God to all who truly turn to him. 449 12
H us, we pray, for your dear Name's sake. 459 6
We sinners beseech you to *h* us, Lord Christ: 463 11
We beseech you to *h* us, good Lord. 463 14
May he *h* your words of invitation, 465 21
Lord, *h* my voice. 474 2
have mercy upon me, and *h* me. 477 29
h that his most joyful voice: 487 19
H us, Lord. 497 6
Lord, *h* our prayer. 548 10
to *h* your Word, and to be nourished by the Body 568 11
Give us ears to *h* 571 2
Lord God, *h* us. 574 1
have mercy on me and *h* my prayer. 587 22
when I call upon the LORD, he will *h* me. 588 5
In the morning, LORD, you *h* my voice; * 588 21
The LORD will *h* the desire of the humble; * 596 3
H my plea of innocence, O LORD; 600 22
incline your ear to me and *h* my words. 601 10
no sooner shall they *h* than they shall obey me; * 605 29
lest, if you do not *h* me, 619 6
H the voice of my prayer when I cry out to you, * 619 8
H, O LORD, and have mercy upon me; * 622 1
let the humble *h* and rejoice. 627 24
But I am like the deaf who do not *h*, * 637 23
I have become like one who does not *h* * 637 25
H my prayer, O LORD, 639 20
(you have given me ears to *h* you); 640 17
"*H*, O daughter; consider and listen closely; * 648 11
H this, all you peoples; 652 6
H, O my people, and I will speak: 654 16
Make me *h* of joy and gladness, * 656 22
H my prayer, O God; * 659 19
H my prayer, O God; * 660 5
and he will *h* my voice. 661 21
God, who is enthroned of old, will *h* me 661 25
"For who," they say, "will *h* us?" 666 11
H my cry, O God, * 668 12
H my voice, O God, when I complain; * 671 10
To you that *h* prayer shall all flesh come, * 672 9
I will cry aloud, and he will *h* me. 693 2
H my teaching, O my people; * 694 19
H, O Shepherd of Israel, leading Joseph like a flock; * 702 12
H, O my people, and I will admonish you: * 704 17
And yet my people did not *h* my voice, * 704 24
LORD God of hosts, *h* my prayer; * 708 6

and my ears rejoice to *h* the doom of the wicked 721 19
He that planted the ear, does he not *h*? * 723 11
LORD, *h* my prayer, and let my cry come before you; * 731 1
That he might *h* the groan of the captive * 732 16
They have ears, but they cannot *h*; * 757 24
H my voice, O LORD, according to your loving-kindness; * 776 1
LORD, *h* my voice; * 784 19
They have ears, but they cannot *h*; * 789 9
h my voice when I cry to you. 797 4
LORD, *h* my prayer, 798 18
Let me *h* of your loving-kindness in the morning, 799 15
h our prayers for this parish family. 817 19
Almighty God, who hast promised to *h* the petitions 834 1
acknowledge the holiness of God, to *h* God's Word, 857 23

heard

Violence will no more be *h* in your land, * 87 23
O God, we have *h* with our ears, 154 5
For those who have never *h* the word of salvation 279 21
to those who have not *h* it; 280 5
because he has *h* the voice of my supplication; * 442 13
because he hath *h* the voice of my prayer; 478 24
you have *h* testimony 514 1
and your word only may be *h*. 571 12
for the LORD has *h* the sound of my weeping. 590 15
The LORD has *h* my supplication; * 590 16
He *h* my voice from his heavenly dwelling; * 602 20
and their voices are not *h*, 606 20
for he has *h* the voice of my prayer. 619 23
For I have *h* the whispering of the crowd; 623 16
Nevertheless, you *h* the sound of my entreaty 624 16
I called in my affliction and the LORD *h* me * 628 5
he stooped to me and *h* my cry. 640 2
We have *h* with our ears, O God, 645 6
As we have *h*, so have we seen, 651 15
For you, O God, have *h* my vows; * 668 21
God has spoken once, twice have I *h* it, * 670 8
make the voice of his praise to be *h*; 674 10
the Lord would not have *h* me; 675 4
But in truth God has *h* me; * 675 5
That which we have *h* and known, 695 1
When the LORD *h* this, he was full of wrath; * 696 17
When God *h* this, he was angry * 699 24
I *h* an unfamiliar voice saying, * 704 11
when he *h* their lamentation. 745 14
I love the LORD, because he has *h* the voice of 759 1
"The ark! We *h* it was in Ephratah; * 786 9
when they have *h* the words of your mouth. 793 11
may be truly preached and truly *h*, 817 13
we have *h* this day with our outward ears, 834 19

hearing

by *h* his Word and celebrating his Sacraments, 285 5

hearken

Oh, that today you would *h* to his voice! 82 19
H unto my voice, O LORD, when I cry unto thee; * 477 28
H to my cry for help, my King and my God, * 588 19
H to my voice, O LORD, when I call; * 618 10
h, all you who dwell in the world, * 652 7
h, O God of Jacob. 708 7
Oh, that today you would *h* to his voice! 725 5
and *h* to the voice of his word. 734 24

hears

but when they cry to him he *h* them. 612 3
The righteous cry, and the LORD *h* them * 629 1
Zion *h* and is glad, 727 12
he *h* their cry and helps them. 802 26

heart

Rend your *h*, and not your garments, 38 14
words of my mouth, and the meditation of my *h*, 40 13
and to revive the *h* of the contrite 41 3
prepare ourselves in *h* and mind to worship him, 41 11
O ye holy and humble men of *h*, 49 6
my *h* teacheth me, 61 10
words of my mouth and the meditation of my *h* 78 12
and to revive the *h* of the contrite." 78 25
prepare ourselves in *h* and mind to worship him, 79 5
We have not loved you with our whole *h*; 79 15
You that are holy and humble of *h*, 89 24
And now, O Lord, I bend the knee of my *h*, * 91 12
truly, they are the joy of my *h*. 104 10
I have applied my *h* to fulfill your statutes * 104 11
in the *h* of your Son as he bore his passion, 113 14
my *h* teaches me, night after night. 115 10
We have not loved you with our whole *h*; 116 17
speak to your *h* in silence upon your bed. 128 17
You have put gladness in my *h*, * 129 4
for I am gentle and lowly in *h*, 131 17
Create in me a clean *h*, O God, * 137 3
From all blindness of *h*; 149 1
from hardness of *h*, and contempt of thy Word 149 9
to give us a *h* to love and fear 150 22
with singleness of *h* as thy servants, 151 15
Plant in every *h*, we beseech thee, 162 3
so we may also in *h* and mind thither ascend, 174 17
that we may be devoted to thee with our whole *h*, 179 7
to trust in thee with all our *h*; 181 18
of thy love in the *h* of thy holy martyr N.: 196 2
we may serve thee with singleness of *h*, 198 4
O Almighty God, kindle, we beseech thee, in every *h* 207 8
Plant in every *h*, 213 14
so we may also in *h* and mind there ascend, 226 10
that we may be devoted to you with our whole *h*, 231 1
of your love in the *h* of your holy martyr N.: 247 14
may serve you with singleness of *h*, 249 14
Almighty God, kindle, we pray, in every *h* 258 8
Create in me a clean *h*, O God, * 266 22
a broken and contrite *h*, O God, 267 11
We have not loved you with our whole *h*, 267 19
Almighty God, kindle, we pray, in every *h* 278 25
with our whole *h* and mind and voice, 287 1
an inquiring and discerning *h*, 308 6
Thou shalt love the Lord thy God with all thy *h*, 319 9
We have not loved thee with our whole *h*; 320 15
Thou shalt love the Lord thy God with all thy *h*, 324 2
that, with meek *h* and 329 14
We have not loved thee with our whole *h*; 331 26
feed on him in thy *h* by faith, 338 8
Love the Lord your God with all your *h*, 351 9
We have not loved you with our whole *h*; 352 15

heart

We have not loved you with our whole *h*; 360 7
with gladness and singleness of *h*; 365 17
With all our *h* and with all our mind, 383 1
that we may be delivered from hardness of *h*, 391 3
We have not loved you with our whole *h*; 397 24
The union of husband and wife in *h*, body, and mind 423 9
Matrimony, may become one in *h* and soul, 432 5
The Lord be in your *h* and upon your lips 447 2
May God in his love enlighten your *h*, 449 10
confess your sins with a humble and obedient *h* 450 6
We have not loved you with our whole *h*; 454 6
Fill his *h* with confidence that, 459 9
in your world with a thankful *h*; 459 15
So fill my *h* with faith 461 1
Let his *h* and soul now ring 466 9
I pour out my *h* by myself; * 471 7
My *h* hath talked of thee, Seek ye my face. * 478 1
be strong, and he shall comfort thine *h*; 478 9
Wherefore my *h* is glad, and my spirit rejoiceth; 485 4
My *h*, therefore, is glad, and my spirit rejoices; 501 6
the *h* of this your servant whom you have chosen 521 6
my *h* and will center in what you would have me do. 562 15
and the meditation of our *h*, 571 5
speak to your *h* in silence upon your bed. 588 7
You have put gladness in my *h*, * 588 13
there is destruction in their *h*; 589 10
for you test the mind and *h*, O righteous God. 591 17
he is the savior of the true in *h*. 591 19
I will give thanks to you, O Lord, with my whole *h*; * 593 1
The wicked boast of their *h*'s desire; * 594 23
They say in their *h*, "I shall not be shaken; * 595 4
They say in their *h*, "God has forgotten; * 595 16
why should they say in their *h*, "You do not care"? 595 22
you will strengthen their *h* and your ears shall hear; 596 4
to shoot from ambush at the true of *h*. 596 12
with a smooth tongue they speak from a double *h*. 597 4
and grief in my *h*, day after day? * 598 2
my *h* is joyful because of your saving help. 598 9
The fool has said in his *h*, "There is no God." * 598 12
who speaks the truth from his *h*. 599 7
my *h* teaches me, night after night. 600 12
My *h*, therefore, is glad, and my spirit rejoices; * 600 15
Weigh my *h*, summon me by night, * 601 3
They have closed their *h* to pity, * 601 18
The foreign peoples will lose *h*; * 606 1
and rejoice the *h*; * 607 9
h be acceptable in your sight, * 607 29
Grant you your *h*'s desire * 608 7
You have given him his *h*'s desire; * 608 23
my *h* within my breast is melting wax. 611 7
"May your *h* live for ever!" 612 9
"Those who have clean hands and a pure *h*, * 613 20
The sorrows of my *h* have increased; * 615 22
examine my *h* and my mind. 616 11
yet my *h* shall not be afraid; 617 15
You speak in my *h* and say, "Seek my face," * 618 12
be strong, and he shall comfort your *h*; * 619 2
my *h* trusts in him, and I have been helped; 619 25
Therefore my *h* dances for joy, * 619 26
Therefore my *h* sings to you without ceasing; * 622 5
Be strong and let your *h* take courage, * 624 21
shout for joy, all who are true of *h*. 625 26
and the designs of his *h* from age to age. 626 22
Indeed, our *h* rejoices in him, * 627 17
I prayed with my whole *h*, 630 19
a voice of rebellion deep in the *h* of the wicked; * 632 3
and your favor to those who are true of *h*. 632 25
and he shall give you your *h*'s desire. 633 12
Their sword shall go through their own *h*, * 634 14
The law of their God is in their *h*, * 635 24
I wail, because of the groaning of my *h*. 637 13
My *h* is pounding, my strength has failed me; * 637 16
My *h* was hot within me; 638 22
your law is deep in my *h*.'" 640 22
Your righteousness have I not hidden in my *h*; 640 26
and my *h* fails me. 641 7
their *h* collects false rumors; 642 11
Our *h* never turned back, * 646 22
for he knows the secrets of the *h*. 646 29
My *h* is stirring with a noble song; 647 11
and the king's enemies are losing *h*. 647 24
and my *h* shall meditate on understanding. 652 10
Create in me a clean *h*, O God, * 657 1
a broken and contrite *h*, O God, you will not despise. 657 17
The fool has said in his *h*, "There is no God." * 658 21
My *h* quakes within me, * 660 13
There is corruption at her *h*; * 661 4
But it was you, a man after my own *h*, * 661 10
but war is in his *h*. 662 2
My *h* is firmly fixed, O God, my *h* is fixed; * 664 10
with heaviness in my *h*; * 668 15
though wealth increase, set not your *h* upon it. 670 7
The human mind and *h* are a mystery; * 671 23
and all who are true of *h* will glory. 672 6
If I had found evil in my *h*, * 675 3
Reproach has broken my *h*, and it cannot be healed; * 681 3
you who seek God, your *h* shall live. 682 2
to those who are pure in *h*. 687 2
In vain have I kept my *h* clean, * 688 3
I was sorely wounded in my *h*. 688 20
Though my flesh and my *h* should waste away, * 689 1
God is the strength of my *h* and my portion for ever. 689 2
The strong of *h* have been despoiled; 692 9
I commune with my *h* in the night; * 693 12
a generation whose *h* was not steadfast, 695 18
Their *h* was not steadfast toward him, * 697 24
So he shepherded them with a faithful and true *h* * 700 24
my *h* and my flesh rejoice in the living God. 707 18
knit my *h* to you that I may fear your Name. 710 23
I will thank you, O Lord my God, with all my *h*, * 710 24
and all the true of *h* will follow it. 723 24
I will walk with sincerity of *h* within my house. 730 11
A crooked *h* shall be far from me; * 730 15
and a proud *h* I cannot abide. 730 19
My *h* is smitten like grass and withered, * 731 7
and bread to strengthen the *h*. 736 8
Whose *h* he turned, so that they hated his people, * 740 3
My *h* is firmly fixed, O God, my *h* is fixed; * 749 17
and my *h* is wounded within me. 752 20
I will give thanks to the Lord with my whole *h*, * 754 6
their *h* is right; 755 18
Their *h* is established and will not shrink, * 755 20
I will thank you with an unfeigned *h*, * 763 17
With my whole *h* I seek you; * 764 3

I treasure your promise in my *h*, * 764 5
for you have set my *h* at liberty. 765 24
I shall keep it with all my *h*. 766 4
Incline my *h* to your decrees * 766 7
I entreat you with all my *h*, * 768 3
I will keep your commandments with my whole *h*. 769 2
Their *h* is gross and fat, * 769 3
Let my *h* be sound in your statutes, * 770 1
truly, they are the joy of my *h*. 772 16
I have applied my *h* to fulfill your statutes * 772 17
I hate those who have a divided *h*, * 772 19
therefore I obey them with all my *h*. 774 6
I call with my whole *h*; * 775 15
The *h* of your word is truth; * 776 23
but my *h* stands in awe of your word. 777 2
and to those who are true of *h*. 782 2
I will give thanks to you, O Lord, with my whole *h*; * 793 1
Search me out, O God, and know my *h*; * 795 24
let not my *h* incline to any evil thing. 797 9
my *h* within me is desolate. 799 6
be of one *h* and mind within your holy Church; 817 22
Give us grace seriously to lay to *h* 818 15
so we may all be of one *h* and of one soul, 818 21
move every human *h* 823 18
in making the *h* of this people wise, 827 9
and in his *h* may thy peace 830 16
from coldness of *h* and wanderings of mind, 833 21
You shall love the Lord your God with all your *h*, 851 11
Adoration is the lifting up of the *h* and mind to God, 857 2

hearted

comfort and help the weak-*h*; 152 12

heartfelt

in offering *h* thanks 440 12
We give you *h* thanks 503 14

heartily

let us *h* rejoice in the strength of our salvation. 44 11
let us *h* rejoice in the strength of our salvation. 146 2
and are *h* sorry for these our misdoings; 331 10
Almighty and everliving God, we most *h* thank thee 339 2

hearts

and with penitent and obedient *h* 41 12
the devices and desires of our own *h*, 41 19
the proud in the imagination of their *h*. 50 12
Create in us clean *h*, O God; 55 13
incline our *h* to keep thy law, 56 20
that our *h* may be unfeignedly thankful; 59 3
and with penitent and obedient *h* 62 12
devices and desires of our own *h*, 62 19
the proud in the imagination of their *h*. 65 15
Create in us clean *h*, O God; 68 5
that our *h* may be set to obey thy commandments, 69 18
be our companion in the way, kindle our *h*, 70 11
that our *h* may be unfeignedly thankful; 71 22
Rend your *h* and not your garments. 76 13
penitent and obedient *h* confess our sins, 79 7
Create in us clean *h*, O God; 98 7
incline our *h* to keep your law, 99 15
with truly thankful *h* we may show forth your praise, 101 17
The love of God has been poured into our *h* 105 20
Heavenly Father, send your Holy Spirit into our *h*, 107 4
so you would shine into our *h* 110 15
Dispel the darkness of our *h*, 110 26
and with penitent and obedient *h* 116 8
Create in us clean *h*, O God; 122 7
kindle our *h*, and awaken hope, 124 8
with truly thankful *h* we may show forth your praise, 125 15
kindle our *h*, and awaken hope, 139 17
Today if ye will hear his voice, harden not your *h* * 146 16
It is a people that do err in their *h*, 146 22
That it may please thee so to rule the *h* 150 25
and slanderers, and to turn their *h*, 152 9
With pity behold the sorrows of our *h*; 154 17
enkindled in our *h*, may shine forth in our lives; 161 16
into our *h* that most excellent gift of charity, 165 1
Create and make in us new and contrite *h*, 166 3
again with penitent *h* and steadfast faith 166 18
our *h* may surely there be fixed 167 19
Pour into our *h* such love toward thee, 174 3
O God, who on this day didst teach the *h* 175 15
h accomplish those things which belong to thy purpose; 177 6
Graft in our *h* the love of thy Name, 181 12
direct and rule our *h*; 182 3
presented unto thee with pure and clean *h* 187 19
We beseech thee, O Lord, pour thy grace into our *h*, 188 15
ready wills and *h* obey the calling of our Lord 193 1
Shine, we pray thee, in our *h*, 196 17
enkindled in our *h*, may shine forth in our lives; 213 10
pour into our *h* your greatest gift, which is love, 216 15
make in us new and contrite *h*, 217 16
again with penitent *h* and steadfast faith 218 9
our *h* may surely there be fixed 219 9
Pour into our *h* such love towards you, 225 15
O God, who on this day taught the *h* 227 8
may accomplish with free *h* 229 1
Graft in our *h* the love of your Name; 233 4
Grant us, O Lord, to trust in you with all our *h*; 233 9
direct and rule our *h*; 233 16
we may be presented to you with pure and clean *h* 239 8
Pour your grace into our *h*, O Lord, 240 1
and *h* obey the calling of our Lord to follow him; 244 10
Shine, we pray, in our *h*, 248 3
make in us new and contrite *h*, 264 4
repent, and with sincere *h* believe his holy Gospel. 269 9
That God will open their *h* to the truth, 279 28
turn the *h* of those who resist it; 280 5
Open their *h* to your grace and truth. 305 17
dwelling in your *h* by faith, 311 24
For, as the benefit is great, if with penitent *h* 316 23
and incline our *h* to keep this law. 317 29
and write all these thy laws in our *h*, 318 30
the devices and desires of our own *h*, 320 26
Almighty God, unto whom all *h* are open, 323 7
Cleanse the thoughts of our *h* 323 9
We beseech thee also so to rule the *h* 329 18
Lift up your *h*. 333 3
and feed on him in your *h* by faith, 338 3
keep your *h* and minds in the knowledge 339 16
Lift up your *h*. 340 11
caused a new light to shine in our *h*, 346 2
Who dost bid thy faithful people cleanse their *h*, 346 8

Almighty God, to you all *h* are open, 355 7
Cleanse the thoughts of our *h* 355 9
Lift up your *h*. 361 3
and feed on him in your *h* by faith, 365 2
Lift up your *h*. 367 3
Lift up your *h*. 370 1
Lift up your *h*. 372 19
caused a new light to shine in our *h*, 378 15
You bid your faithful people cleanse their *h*, 379 5
and feed on him in your *h* by faith, 399 3
Lift up your *h*. 402 3
Lift up your *h*. 404 5
Let their love for each other be a seal upon their *h*, 430 18
that we may apply our *h* unto wisdom. 473 8
Thou knowest, Lord, the secrets of our *h*; 484 11
Lord, you know the secrets of our *h*; 492 12
Almighty God, to you all *h* are open, 512 7
Cleanse the thoughts of our *h* 512 9
To you, O Father, all *h* are open; 521 6
Almighty God, to you all *h* are open, 525 7
Cleanse the thoughts of our *h* 525 9
Almighty God, to you all *h* are open, 537 7
Cleanse the thoughts of our *h* 537 9
Holy Spirit, open our eyes, our ears, and our *h*, 569 3
Give us ears to hear and *h* to obey. 571 3
while strife is in their *h*. 619 13
He fashions all the *h* of them * 627 5
Do not let them say in their *h*, 631 21
No; you devise evil in your *h*, * 664 23
but in their *h* they curse. 669 15
pour out your *h* before him, for God is our refuge. 669 23
and their *h* overflow with wicked thoughts. 687 14
They tested God in their *h*, * 696 9
So I gave them over to the stubbornness of their *h*, * 704 26
whose *h* are set on the pilgrims' way. 707 26
and to those who turn their *h* to him. 709 11
that we may apply our *h* to wisdom. 718 26
Harden not your *h*, 725 6
"This people are wayward in their *h*; 725 13
and wine to gladden our *h*, 736 6
let the *h* of those who seek the LORD rejoice. 738 6
their *h* melted because of their peril. 748 8
and seek him with all their *h*! 763 8
Who devise evil in their *h* * 796 3
hatred which infect our *h*; 815 16
the *h* and minds of your servants ready to receive 819 3
fill our *h* with thankfulness, 820 13
[and especially the *h* of the people of this land], 823 18
Turn the *h* of the parents to the children, 829 5
and the *h* of the children to the parents; 829 5
Almighty and eternal God, so draw our *h* to thee, 832 24
be so grafted inwardly in our *h*, 834 20
Give us grateful *h*, our Father, for all thy mercies, 835 8
give us food to sustain our lives and make our *h* glad; 835 14
For minds to think, and *h* to love, and hands to serve, 837 12
we remember before you with grateful *h* 839 22
prejudice, or hatred in our *h*; 848 9
stirs our *h*, and strengthens our wills. 858 4

hearty

do give thee most humble and *h* thanks 58 16
do give thee most humble and *h* thanks 71 12
h repentance and true faith turn unto him, 332 3
rendering unto thee most *h* thanks 335 15
O gracious God, we give you humble and *h* thanks 444 1
h thanks for the wonderful grace and virtue 487 11
We give thee *h* thanks 488 4
h thanks and praise for the return of seedtime 840 16

heat

O ye fire and *h*, bless ye the Lord; 48 6
all winds and fire and *h*. 88 14
nothing is hidden from its burning *h*. 607 3
my moisture was dried up as in the *h* of summer. 625 6

heathen

for my Name shall be great among the *h*, 38 8
O God, the *h* have come into your inheritance; 701 1
Pour out your wrath upon the *h* who have not 701 15
Why should the *h* say, 702 1
Let it be known among the *h* and in our sight 702 2
They intermingled with the *h* * 744 17
He gave them over to the hand of the *h*, * 745 6
Why should the *h* say, * 757 16
The idols of the *h* are silver and gold, * 789 5

heaven

"Father, I have sinned against *h*, and before thee, 38 18
but into *h* itself, 39 16
Christ the Lord ascendeth into *h*: 43 10
O ye stars of *h*, bless ye the Lord; 48 2
Blessed art thou in the firmament of *h*; * 49 20
h and earth are full of the majesty of thy glory. 53 2
thou didst open the kingdom of *h* to all believers. 53 16
maker of *h* and earth; 53 24
He ascended into *h*, 54 2
Our Father, who art in *h*, 54 14
on earth as it is in *h*. 54 18
eternal rest promised to thy people in *h*; 56 16
pure brightness of the everliving Father in *h*, 64 2
maker of *h* and earth; 66 10
He ascended into *h*, 66 18
Our Father, who art in *h*, 67 4
on earth as it is in *h*. 67 8
"Father, I have sinned against *h* and before you; 76 17
but into *h* itself, 77 15
Christ the Lord has ascended into *h*: 81 6
in the high vault of *h*, glory to you. 90 14
O Lord and Ruler of the hosts of *h*, * 90 17
For all the powers of *h* sing your praises, * 91 25
To you all angels, all the powers of *h*, 95 19
h and earth are full of your glory. 95 22
and opened the kingdom of *h* to all believers. 96 6
creator of *h* and earth. 96 14
He ascended into *h*, 96 22
Our Father, who art in *h*, 97 4
on earth as it is in *h*. 97 8
eternal rest promised to your people in *h*; 99 11
the maker of *h* and earth. 104 16
Our Father, who art in *h*, 106 14
on earth as it is in *h*. 106 18
give glory to your Father in *h*." 109 12
pure brightness of the everliving Father in *h*, 112 2
pure brightness of the everliving Father in *h*, 118 2
creator of *h* and earth. 120 10

He ascended into *h*, 120 18
Our Father, who art in *h*, 121 4
on earth as it is in *h*. 121 8
The maker of *h* and earth. 127 4
the Lord who made *h* and earth bless you 131 9
Our Father, who art in *h*, 132 19
on earth as it is in *h*. 132 23
pure brightness of the everliving Father in *h*, 139 2
the Lord who made *h* and earth bless you 140 4
O God the Father, Creator of *h* and earth, 148 1
Our Father, who art in *h*, 153 6
on earth as it is in *h*. 153 10
so may we also perfectly enjoy him in *h*; 161 4
Father in *h*, who at the baptism of Jesus 163 1
who dost govern all things in *h* and earth: 164 2
from *h* to be the true bread which giveth life 167 11
O God, Creator of *h* and earth: 170 1
with great triumph unto thy kingdom in *h*: 175 2
ordereth all things both in *h* and earth: 177 15
first martyr Stephen, who looked up to *h* and prayed 186 2
Father in *h*, by whose grace the virgin mother 189 11
as thy holy angels always serve and worship thee in *h*, 193 7
with thy saints in *h* and on earth: 199 5
as thy holy angels always serve and worship thee in *h*, 200 9
Almighty God, Lord of *h* and earth: 207 15
may also enjoy him perfectly in *h*; 212 19
Father in *h*, who at the baptism of Jesus 214 12
you govern all things both in *h* and on earth: 215 14
from *h* to be the true bread which gives life 219 2
O God, Creator of *h* and earth: 221 13
Christ to have ascended into *h*, 226 10
with great triumph to your kingdom in *h*: 226 14
sets in order all things both in *h* and earth: 229 11
first martyr Stephen, who looked up to *h* and prayed 237 15
Father in *h*, by your grace the virgin mother 240 18
angels always serve and worship you in *h*, 244 16
your saints in *h* and on earth: 250 15
angels always serve and worship you in *h*, 251 15
Almighty God, Lord of *h* and earth: 258 15
in *h* and on earth, 267 15
Peace in *h* and glory in the highest. 270 2
O God, Creator of *h* and earth: 283 1
when earth and *h* are joined 287 21
creator of *h* and earth. 292 13
he ascended into *h*, 293 9
creator of *h* and earth. 304 3
He ascended into *h*, 304 12
Our Father, who art in *h*, 311 1
on earth as it is in *h*. 311 5
whom every family in *h* and earth is named, 311 22
likeness of any thing that is in *h* above, 318 2
maker of *h* and earth, 326 8
he came down from *h*: 326 19
he ascended into *h* 327 8
maker of *h* and earth, 327 22
came down from *h*, 328 2
and ascended into *h*, 328 8
and with all the company of *h*, 334 2
H and earth are full of thy glory. 334 5
Our Father, who art in *h*, 336 18
on earth as it is in *h*. 336 22
The Body of Christ, the bread of *h*. 338 15
and with all the company of *h*, 341 5
H and earth are full of thy glory. 341 8
for that thou didst create *h* and earth, 341 13
For all that is in the *h* 344 9
and in their sight ascended into *h*, 347 3
Holy Ghost came down [on this day] from *h*, 347 8
maker of *h* and earth, 358 5
he came down from *h*: 358 16
he ascended into *h* 358 24
Creator of *h* and earth. 361 9
and with all the company of *h*, 362 2
h and earth are full of your glory. 362 5
Our Father, who art in *h*, 364 1
on earth as it is in *h*. 364 5
The Body of Christ, the bread of *h*. 365 6
Creator of *h* and earth. 367 9
and with all the company of *h*, 367 11
h and earth are full of your glory. 367 14
h and earth are full of your glory. 371 2
giving voice to every creature under *h*, 373 10
h and earth are full of your glory. 373 13
For everything in *h* and on earth 377 7
and in their sight ascended into *h*, 379 22
Holy Spirit came down [on this day] from *h*, 380 3
Almighty and eternal God, ruler of all things in *h* 394 9
with your saints in *h* and on earth: 395 18
the living bread which came down from *h*; 397 2
Our Father, who art in *h*, 398 12
on earth as it is in *h*. 398 16
h and earth are full of your glory. 402 10
h and earth are full of your glory. 404 12
creator of *h* and earth. 416 8
He ascended into *h*, 416 17
Our Father, who art in *h*, 428 8
on earth as it is in *h*. 428 12
be done on earth as it is in *h*; 430 7
Now there is rejoicing in *h*; 451 17
trust in him, to whom all things in *h*, 456 21
the only Name under *h* given for health 457 3
Our Father, who art in *h*, 464 4
on earth as it is in *h*. 464 8
Almighty God, our Father in *h*, 466 7
who hath made *h* and earth. 473 12
If I climb up into *h*, thou art there; * 475 7
Christ will open the kingdom of *h* to all 483 20
Our Father, who art in *h*, 485 20
on earth as it is in *h*. 485 24
voice from *h* didst proclaim, 486 8
creator of *h* and earth. 496 4
He ascended into *h*, 496 12
bring our brother (sister) to the joys of *h*. 497 14
Christ will open the kingdom of *h* to all 500 9
Our Father, who art in *h*, 502 1
on earth as it is in *h*. 502 5
maker of *h* and earth, 519 8
he came down from *h*: 519 19
he ascended into *h*, 519 27
The maker of *h* and earth. 523 12
maker of *h* and earth, 529 11
he came down from *h*: 530 10
he ascended into *h* 530 18
having ascended into *h*, has poured his gifts 533 6

maker of *h* and earth,	541	11
he came down from *h*:	542	10
he ascended into *h*	542	18
The maker of *h* and earth.	552	2
The maker of *h* and earth.	568	5
For everything in *h* and on earth is yours.	569	12
Eternal God, the *h* of heavens cannot contain you,	578	3
For everything in *h* and on earth is yours.	579	15
He whose throne is in *h* is laughing; *	586	8
the LORD's throne is in *h*.	596	16
The LORD looks down from *h* upon us all, *	598	15
The LORD thundered out of *h*; *	603	15
he will answer him out of his holy *h*,	608	13
The LORD looks down from *h*, *	627	1
God looks down from *h* upon us all, *	659	1
He will send from *h* and save me;	663	25
Whom have I in *h* but you? *	688	27
From *h* you pronounced judgment; *	692	16
and opened the doors of *h*.	696	23
and gave them grain from *h*.	696	25
He built his sanctuary like the heights of *h*, *	700	17
Turn now, O God of hosts, look down from *h*;	703	15
God takes his stand in the council of *h*; *	705	9
and righteousness shall look down from *h*.	709	17
and his throne as the days of *h*."	715	25
The LORD has set his throne in *h*, *	734	20
and he satisfied them with bread from *h*.	741	6
Our God is in *h*; *	757	18
the maker of *h* and earth.	758	20
The *h* of heavens is the LORD's, *	758	21
the maker of *h* and earth.	779	4
the maker of *h* and earth.	781	16
the LORD who made *h* and earth bless	787	22
The LORD does whatever pleases him, in *h* and	788	12
Give thanks to the God of *h*, *	791	21
If I climb up to *h*, you are there; *	794	14
Who made *h* and earth, the seas, and all	803	13
Praise him, *h* of heavens, *	806	1
his splendor is over earth and *h*.	806	21
ruler of all things in *h*	817	18
angels delight to worship in *h*:	819	14
creator of *h* and earth,	846	4
he ascended into *h*	850	18
Jesus took our human nature into *h*	850	20
What do we mean by *h* and hell?	862	5
By *h*, we mean eternal life in our enjoyment of God;	862	6

heavenly

Almighty God our *h* Father, to render thanks	41	6
O Lord God, *h* King, God the Father Almighty.	52	9
O Lord, our *h* Father, almighty and everlasting God,	57	7
O *h* Father, in whom we live	57	14
Almighty God our *h* Father, to set forth his praise,	79	2
Lord God, *h* King,	94	23
H Father, in you we live	100	6
H Father, send your Holy Spirit into our hearts,	107	4
unity of that *h* City,	107	20
h country where you live and reign	111	15
Almighty God, our *h* Father:	127	6
Look down, O Lord, from your *h* throne,	133	17
unity of that *h* City,	138	19
we may attain to thy *h* kingdom,	152	20
We thank thee, *h* Father,	172	14
but to love things *h*;	182	7
made partners of thy *h* treasure;	182	15
to obtain thy *h* promises;	184	4
We thank thee, *h* Father,	192	19
O *h* Father, Shepherd of thy people, we give	196	22
O God, our *h* Father, who didst raise	197	4
and in our *h* country	198	26
H Father, giver of life and health:	208	16
O Lord our *h* Father, whose blessed Son came	209	9
Almighty God our *h* Father, who declarest	210	1
We thank you, *h* Father,	224	7
but to love things *h*;	234	2
may become partakers of your *h* treasure;	234	9
to obtain your *h* promises;	235	16
We thank you, *h* Father,	244	7
H Father, Shepherd of your people,	248	8
O God, our *h* Father, who raised	248	15
in our *h* country to become partakers	250	11
H Father, giver of life and health:	260	1
H Father, whose blessed Son came	260	15
Almighty God our *h* Father, you declare	261	7
Our *h* Father sent his Son	277	2
in this Paschal feast we may so burn with *h* desires,	285	10
Rejoice now, *h* hosts and choirs of angels,	286	1
may come to the joy of that *h* Jerusalem,	290	4
H Father, we thank	308	2
Defend, O Lord, your servant N. with your *h* grace,	309	15
H Father, we thank	314	1
our *h* Father never-ending thanks	316	10
banquet of that most *h* Food.	317	10
O Lord God, *h* King, God the Father Almighty.	324	20
Give grace, O *h* Father, to all bishops	329	9
And to all thy people give thy *h* grace,	329	13
we may be partakers of thy *h* kingdom.	330	6
Almighty God, our *h* Father,	332	1
All glory be to thee, Almighty God, our *h* Father,	334	9
Wherefore, O Lord and *h* Father,	335	8
be filled with thy grace and *h* benediction,	336	6
O *h* Father, so to assist us	339	10
Wherefore, O Lord and *h* Father,	342	10
thy grace and *h* benediction;	342	27
an image of the *h* Jerusalem, adorned as a bride	349	2
Lord God, *h* King,	356	3
Eternal God, *h* Father,	365	9
that *h* country where,	369	10
joining with the *h* chorus,	370	23
his *h* Father, having loved his own	374	14
an image of the *h* Jerusalem, adorned as a bride	381	17
May we also come to share in your *h* kingdom.	387	20
H Father, you have promised	394	4
give to us the peace and unity of that *h* City,	395	11
Hear us, O *h* Father,	408	1
Defend, O Lord, your servant with your *h* grace,	418	13
saints feast for ever in your *h* home;	430	23
h Father, the Lord of all life,	440	5
It has pleased God our *h* Father	440	8
Holy God, *h* Father, you formed me	450	8
h Father grant you the inward anointing	456	14
O God of *h* powers, by the might	458	16
H Father, watch with us over your child	458	22
Almighty God our *h* Father, graciously comfort	459	7

H Father, giver of life and health: 459 17
safely to his *h* country; 460 8
O *h* Father, you give your children sleep 461 12
in his *h* wedding garment. 465 18
into the courts of your *h* dwelling place. 466 9
bring us all to thy *h* kingdom; 470 10
of perfect service in thy *h* kingdom. 481 22
foretaste of thy *h* banquet. 482 4
And of thy mercy, O *h* Father, 486 12
and may come to thy *h* kingdom; 487 8
of perfect service in thy *h* kingdom; 488 24
Almighty God, our *h* Father, in whose hands 488 26
and bring us all to your *h* kingdom; 494 3
at the table in your *h* kingdom. 497 20
foretaste of your *h* banquet. 498 15
and may come to your *h* kingdom; 503 10
the order and beauty of things *h*; 573 6
it be to us a sign of the *h* Altar 574 2
He heard my voice from his *h* dwelling; * 602 20
by the breath of his mouth all the *h* hosts. 626 12
O *h* Father, who hast filled the world with beauty: 814 1
harmony around your *h* throne; 815 20
Almighty God our *h* Father, guide 816 1
Almighty God our *h* Father, send 822 17
Defend them day by day with your *h* grace; 823 3
H Father, we remember 824 11
H Father, in your Word you have given 825 6
Look with pity, O *h* Father, upon the people 826 8
O God, *h* Father, who by thy Son 828 9
O God our *h* Father, you have blessed us 828 16
Almighty God, our *h* Father, who settest 828 22
Almighty God, *h* Father, you have blessed 829 9
O God, our *h* Father, whose glory fills 831 1
H Father, you sent 841 1
Almighty God and *h* Father, we give 841 7
foretaste of the *h* banquet 860 2

heavens

O ye *h*, bless ye the Lord; * 47 9
the *H* and all the Powers therein. 52 26
O God and Father of all, whom the whole *h* adore: 70 15
For as the *h* are higher than the earth, * 86 25
For as rain and snow fall from the *h* * 87 1
O *h* and all waters above the *h*. 88 10
You made the *h* and the earth, * 90 20
O God and Father of all, whom the whole *h* adore: 124 12
and his glory above the *h*. 138 8
ascended far above all *h* that he might fill all things: 174 9
ascended into the *h*, 174 17
and showest forth thy handiwork in the *h* 210 2
ascended far above all *h* that he might fill all things: 226 2
and show forth your handiwork in the *h* 261 8
that is passed into the *h*, 320 6
a dwelling place eternal in the *h*. 349 11
who has passed through the *h*, 352 6
prepared for us a dwelling place eternal in the *h*. 382 5
Eternal God, the heaven of *h* cannot contain you, 578 3
your majesty is praised above the *h*. 592 10
When I consider your *h*, the work of your fingers, * 592 13
He parted the *h* and came down * 603 7
The *h* declare the glory of God, * 606 15
It goes forth from the uttermost edge of the *h* 607 1
By the word of the LORD were the *h* made, * 626 11
Your love, O LORD, reaches to the *h*, * 632 12
He calls the *h* and the earth from above * 654 9
Let the *h* declare the rightness of his cause; * 654 14
Exalt yourself above the *h*, O God, * 664 8
For your loving-kindness is greater than the *h*, * 664 17
Exalt yourself above the *h*, O God, * 664 19
exalt him who rides upon the *h*; * 676 9
He rides in the *h*, the ancient *h*; * 678 26
Let the *h* and the earth praise him, * 682 5
Your righteousness, O God, reaches to the *h*; * 684 20
They set their mouths against the *h*, * 687 17
He caused the east wind to blow in the *h* * 697 1
you have set your faithfulness firmly in the *h*. 713 20
The *h* bear witness to your wonders, O LORD, * 714 3
Yours are the *h*; the earth also is yours; * 714 15
but it is the LORD who made the *h*. 726 2
Let the *h* rejoice, and let the earth be glad; 726 14
The *h* declare his righteousness, * 727 7
from the *h* he beheld the earth; 732 15
and the *h* are the work of your hands; 732 29
For as the *h* are high above the earth, * 734 3
and spread out the *h* like a curtain. 735 5
They mounted up to the *h* and fell back 748 7
For your loving-kindness is greater than the *h*, * 750 1
Exalt yourself above the *h*, O God, * 750 3
and his glory above the *h*. 756 9
but stoops to behold the *h* and the earth? 756 11
The heaven of *h* is the LORD's, * 758 21
it stands firm in the *h*. 770 21
to you enthroned in the *h*. 780 16
Who by wisdom made the *h*, * 790 5
Bow your *h*, O LORD, and come down; * 800 10
He covers the *h* with clouds * 804 16
Praise the LORD from the *h*; * 805 21
Praise him, heaven of *h*, * 806 1
and you waters above the *h*. 806 2

heavily

and why do I go so *h* while the enemy 644 3
Your anger weighs upon me *h*, * 712 15

heaviness

Why art thou so full of *h*, O my soul? * 471 12
I found trouble and *h*; 479 5
Why are you so full of *h*, O my soul? * 643 13
Why are you so full of *h*, O my soul? * 644 9
Why are you so full of *h*, O my soul? * 645 1
with *h* in my heart; * 668 15

heavy

Come to me, all who labor and are *h*-laden, 131 15
Come unto me, all ye that travail and are *h* laden, 332 8
Come unto me, all ye that travail and are *h* laden, 449 13
For your hand was *h* upon me day and night; * 625 5
like a *h* burden they are too much for me to bear. 637 5
My soul is *h* within me; * 643 18
with *h* rain you soften the ground 673 10
you laid *h* burdens upon our backs. 674 16

Hebrew

given by God to the *H* people. 846 25
The covenant with the *H* people 847 7

heed

Give us grace to *h* their warnings 159 11
Give us grace to *h* their warnings 211 11
give *h* to my cry; * 600 23
Which does not *h* the voice of the charmer, * 665 3
and in your faithfulness *h* my supplications; * 798 19

heeded

I have *h* the words of your lips. 601 6

heel

has lifted up his *h* and turned against me. 642 19

heels

when the wickedness of those at my *h* surrounds me, 652 14
which they hurled at the *h* of your anointed. 717 17

height

They will climb from *h* to *h*, * 708 4

heighten

h my love and gratitude; 563 6

heights

and the *h* of the hills are his also. 82 12
and lets me stand firm on the *h*. 605 6
and from the peak of Mizar among the *h* of Hermon. 643 20
He built his sanctuary like the *h* of heaven, * 700 17
and the *h* of the hills are his also. 724 21
praise him in the *h*. 805 22

heirs

make us the children of God and *h* of eternal life: 184 9
and make us children of God and *h* of eternal life: 236 3
become *h* with him of everlasting life. 277 6
and are also *h*, 339 8
and to make us *h* in him of everlasting life; 345 9
and *h* of your eternal kingdom. 366 7
and to make us *h* in him of everlasting life; 378 5
and prepared a people to be *h* of the covenant 520 15
made *h* of God's kingdom. 850 4

held

While I *h* my tongue, my bones withered away, * 625 3
So I *h* my tongue and said nothing; * 638 19
many times he *h* back his anger 698 3
by those who *h* them captive. 745 18
When any are *h* unjustly, bring them 826 20

hell

He descended into *h*. 53 30
He descended into *h*. 66 16
when Christ broke the bonds of death and *h*, 287 12
if I go down to *h*, thou art there also. 475 8
and the pains of *h* gat hold upon me. 479 4
The cords of *h* entangled me, * 602 16
What do we mean by heaven and *h*? 862 5
by *h*, we mean eternal death in our rejection of God. 862 7

helmet

Ephraim is my *h* and Judah my scepter. 667 24
Ephraim is my *h* and Judah my scepter. 750 11

help

We therefore pray thee, *h* thy servants, 53 19
O Lord, make haste to *h* us. 63 18
He has come to the *h* of his servant Israel, * 92 12
Come then, Lord, and *h* your people, 96 9
O Lord, make haste to *h* us. 103 2
from where is my *h* to come? 104 14
My *h* comes from the LORD, * 104 15
O Lord, make haste to *h* us. 117 11
He has come to the *h* of his servant Israel, * 119 18
Our *h* is in the Name of the Lord; 127 3
O Lord, make haste to *h* us. 128 4
Give me the joy of your saving *h* again * 137 7
That it may please thee to support, *h*, and comfort 151 28
comfort and *h* the weak-hearted; 152 12
O Lord, arise, *h* us; 154 3
let thy bountiful grace and mercy speedily *h* 160 3
grant us the *h* of thy grace, 164 14
Make speed to *h* thy servants 166 10
we have no power of ourselves to *h* ourselves: 167 4
that by the *h* of thy grace 178 7
for thou never failest to *h* 178 13
preserve it evermore by thy *h* 180 10
so by thy appointment they may *h* and defend us 193 7
so by thy appointment they may *h* and defend us 200 9
h us to employ it in the maintenance 209 4
let your bountiful grace and mercy speedily *h* 212 3
give us the *h* of your grace, 216 8
Come quickly to *h* us who are assaulted 218 2
we have no power in ourselves to *h* ourselves: 218 14
for you never fail to *h* and govern 230 8
it cannot continue in safety without your *h*, 232 3
h and defend us here on earth; 244 17
h and defend us here on earth; 251 16
h us to employ it in the maintenance of justice 260 11
Give me the joy of your saving *h* again * 266 26
Assist us mercifully with your *h*, 270 4
That by God's *h* they may seek justice 278 23
Save us and *h* us, we humbly beseech thee, O Lord. 282 5
I will, with God's *h*. 293 22
I will, with God's *h*. 302 3
Will you by your prayers and witness *h* this child 302 4
I will, with God's *h*. 304 25
And if, in your preparation, you need *h* and counsel, 317 11
h in time of need. 320 8
find grace to *h* in time of need. 352 8
you came to our *h*, 373 23
h us to ask only what accords with your will; 394 13
and all who turn to you for *h*; 395 5
I will, with God's *h*. 417 7
for the *h* and comfort given one another in prosperity 423 10
that you promise, with the *h* of God, to fulfill 433 3
He has come to the *h* of his servant Israel,* 442 7
that by your *h* she may live faithfully 444 5
Save us, and *h* us, we humbly beseech you, O Lord. 455 18
our only *h* in time of need: 458 1
the *h* of your power, that his sickness may be turned 458 13
and *h* me always to believe that what happens 461 9
h me to stand bravely. 461 21
h me to sit quietly. 461 22
h me to do it patiently. 461 22
which is the *h* of my countenance, 471 15
a very present *h* in trouble. 471 18
God shall *h* her, and that right early. 472 3
from whence cometh my *h*? 473 10

My *h* cometh even from the LORD, * 473 11
H us, we pray, in the midst of things 481 14
from whom can we seek *h*? 492 6
I will, for he is my *h*. 518 7
Our *h* is in the Name of the Lord; 523 11
h and serve those in need? 544 5
Our *h* is in the Name of the Lord; 552 1
and *h* me (*h* the bishop) baptize 561 3
Our *h* is in the Name of the Lord; 568 4
"There is no *h* for him in his God." 587 6
Hearken to my cry for *h*, my King and my God, * 588 19
H me, LORD, for there is no godly one left; * 597 1
"and give them the *h* they long for." 597 12
my heart is joyful because of your saving *h*. 598 9
and cried out to my God for *h*. 602 19
with the *h* of my God I will scale any wall. 604 23
they cry out, but there is none to *h* them; * 605 22
Send you *h* from his holy place * 608 3
and there is none to *h*. 610 24
you are my strength, hasten to *h* me. 611 19
he is our *h* and our shield. 627 16
and rise up to *h* me. 629 16
The LORD will *h* them and rescue them; * 636 17
Make haste to *h* me, * 638 13
O LORD, make haste to *h* me. 641 9
who is the *h* of my countenance, and my God. 643 17
who is the *h* of my countenance, and my God. 644 13
who is the *h* of my countenance, and my God. 645 5
Rise up, and *h* us, * 647 9
a very present *h* in trouble. 649 2
God shall *h* her at the break of day. 649 14
Give me the joy of your saving *h* again * 657 5
Grant us your *h* against the enemy, * 668 8
for vain is the *h* of man. 668 9
answer me with your unfailing *h*. 680 16
your *h*, O God, will lift me up on high. 681 23
O LORD, make haste to *h* me. 682 12
come quickly to *h* me, O my God. 684 2
H us, O God our Savior, for the glory 701 24
stir up your strength and come to *h* us. 702 15
and have come to *h* the people of Lot. 706 19
But as for me, O LORD, I cry to you for *h*; * 713 4
If the LORD had not come to my *h*, * 723 27
and visit me with your saving *h*; 742 5
they stumbled, and there was none to *h*. 747 6
Grant us your *h* against the enemy, * 750 19
for vain is the *h* of man. 750 20
H me, O LORD my God; * 752 27
he is their *h* and their shield. 758 7
The LORD is at my side to *h* me; * 761 9
but the LORD came to my *h*. 761 23
h me, for they persecute me with lies. 770 15
Let your hand be ready to *h* me, * 778 1
and let your judgments *h* me. 778 6
from where is my *h* to come? 779 2
My *h* comes from the LORD, * 779 3
Our *h* is in the Name of the LORD, * 781 15
Listen to my cry for *h*, 798 12
My *h* and my fortress, my stronghold 800 3
for there is no *h* in them. 803 8
they who have the God of Jacob for their *h*! * 803 11
H us, in the midst of our struggles 824 1
H us to heal 826 4
H us to eliminate our cruelty 826 10
H them to take failure, 829 17
and the willingness to accept help; 830 4
and further us with thy continual *h*; 832 2
defended by thy gracious and ready *h*; 832 22
H us, O Lord, to finish the good work here begun. 839 16
H us to remember that we are all your children, 841 3
through thy *h*, may live in this world 841 11
What *h* is there for us? 845 15
Our *h* is in God. 845 16
How did God first *h* us? 845 17
To love, honor, and *h* our parents 848 4
so that with the *h* of God we may live 849 13
We understand the meaning of the Bible by the *h* 853 28
and blessing of God to *h* them fulfill their vows. 861 7

helped

I was in misery, and he *h* me. 479 11
my heart trusts in him, and I have been *h*; 619 25
because you, O LORD, have *h* me and comforted me. 711 11
I was brought very low, and he *h* me. 759 13
God first *h* us be revealing himself and his will, 845 18

helper

defend those who have no *h*? 518 30
for you are the *h* of orphans. 595 26
You have been my *h*; 618 16
O LORD, be my *h*." 622 2
You are my *h* and my deliverer; * 641 21
Behold, God is my *h*; * 659 24
For you have been my *h*, * 670 25
You are my *h* and my deliverer; * 682 24
and the oppressed who has no *h*. 686 8

helpers

give them understanding *h*, 830 4

helpless

to show Christ's people that in serving the *h* 543 17
they spy out the *h*. 595 10
the *h* fall before their power. 595 15
The *h* commit themselves to you, * 595 25

helps

he hears their cry and *h* them. 802 26

hem

They *h* me in, they *h* me in on every side; * 761 17

hence

depart *h* in the Lord, 488 2

henceforth

For behold from *h* * 50 5
For behold from *h* * 65 8
walking from *h* in his holy ways: 330 12

heralds

h of thy kingdom, 196 11
h of your kingdom, 247 22

herd

a *h* of wild bulls with its calves. 678 19

herds

and all you flocks and *h*. 89 15
the *h* in their thousands upon the hills. 654 24
You make grass grow for flocks and *h* * 736 3
he did not let their *h* decrease. 749 6
He provides food for flocks and *h* * 804 20

hereafter

that we may *h* live a godly, righteous, and sober life, 42 9
that we may *h* live a godly, righteous, and sober life, 63 12
and that the rest of our life *h* may be pure 269 12
that we may *h* live a godly, righteous, and sober life, 321 12
and grant that we may ever *h* serve 331 17

heresy

From all false doctrine, *h*, and schism; 149 8

heritage

O Lord, save thy people, and bless thine *h*; 55 15
we may enter the everlasting *h* 369 11
the gift and *h* of children, 429 20
Your *h* is the faith of patriarchs, 517 14
indeed, I have a goodly *h*. 600 10
you have granted me the *h* of those 668 22
Children are a *h* from the LORD, * 783 6
hast given us this good land for our *h*: 820 2

Hermon

and Mount *H* like a young wild ox. 620 17
and from the peak of Mizar among the heights of *H*. 643 20
Tabor and *H* rejoice in your Name. 714 18
It is like the dew of *H* * 787 15

Herod

innocents of Bethlehem by the order of King *H*. 186 14
innocents of Bethlehem by King *H*. 238 8

hid

A city built on a hill cannot be *h*. 109 8
and *h* not his face from shame: 169 2
and from whom no secrets are *h*: 323 8
and from you no secrets are *h*: 355 8
and from you no secrets are *h*: 512 8
and from you no secrets are *h*: 525 8
and from you no secrets are *h*: 537 8
Then you *h* your face, * 621 20
let them be caught in the net they *h*; 630 6

hidden

nothing is *h* from its burning heat. 607 3
and my sighing is not *h* from you. 637 15
Your righteousness have I not *h* in my heart; 640 26
Why have you *h* your face * 647 5
then I could have *h* from him. 661 9
and my faults are not *h* from you. 679 21
why is your right hand *h* in your bosom? 690 7
why have you *h* your face from me? 713 7
My body was not *h* from you, * 795 3
The proud have *h* a snare for me 796 10
in the way wherein I walk they have *h* a trap for me. 798 6
have often *h* from its light. 839 10

hide

H us under the shadow of your wings. 132 15
mortal life may *h* from us the light 165 10
mortal life may *h* from us the light 217 3
H your face from my sins * 266 20
For in the time of trouble he shall *h* me 477 20
in the secret place of his dwelling shall he *h* me, 477 21
O *h* not thou thy face from me, * 478 3
and *h* yourself in time of trouble? 594 20
how long will you *h* your face from me? 597 22
h me under the shadow of your wings, 601 15
neither does he *h* his face from them; * 612 2
he shall *h* me in the secrecy of his dwelling 618 3
H not your face from me, * 618 14
You *h* them in the covert of your presence 624 8
H your face from my sins * 656 24
do not *h* yourself from my petition. 660 6
H me from the conspiracy of the wicked, * 671 12
they plan how they may *h* their snares. 671 19
"*H* not your face from your servant; * 680 25
we will not *h* from their children. 695 3
How long will you *h* yourself, O LORD? 717 5
will you *h* yourself for ever? * 717 6
h not your face from me in the day of my trouble. 731 2
You *h* your face, and they are terrified; * 737 11
do not *h* your commandments from me. 764 22
do not *h* your face from me 799 13

hides

he *h* his face; he will never notice." 595 17

hiding

You are my *h*-place; 625 14

high

Thus saith the *h* and lofty One 40 23
"I dwell in the *h* and holy place, 41 1
whereby the dayspring from on *h* hath visited us; 51 17
Glory be to God on *h*, 52 3
art most *h* in the glory of God the Father. 52 22
Thus says the *h* and lofty One 78 22
"I dwell in the *h* and holy place 78 23
in the *h* vault of heaven, glory to you. 90 14
shall be called the prophet of the Most *H*, * 93 1
the dawn from on *h* shall break upon us, 93 6
you alone are the Most *H*, 95 11
He who dwells in the shelter of the Most *H* * 129 21
and the Most *H* your habitation, 130 16
The Lord is *h* above all nations, * 138 7
h upon the cross that he might draw the whole world 192 14
h upon the cross that he might draw the whole world 244 2
Seeing that we have a great *h* priest, 320 5
Glory be to God on *h*, 324 14
art most *h* in the glory of God the Father. 325 9
Glory be to thee, O Lord Most *H*. 334 6
Glory be to thee, O Lord Most *H*. 341 9
vows unto the Most *H*. 343 9
who for our sins was lifted *h* upon the cross, 346 14
Through Jesus Christ our great *H* Priest; 348 15
Since we have a great *h* priest 352 5
you alone are the Most *H*, 356 15
Christ our great *H* Priest, 372 11
your vows to the Most *H*. 376 5
For our sins he was lifted *h* upon the cross, 379 11
Through Jesus Christ our great *H* Priest; 381 9
we yield unto thee most *h* praise 487 10

dwelling on *h* but having regard 520 12
and exercise without reproach the *h* priesthood 521 10
through the *h* priest and good shepherd 552 11
to be our great *H* Priest. 573 17
Be seated on your lofty throne, O Most *H*; * 591 10
and according to my innocence, O Most *H*. 591 14
I will praise the Name of the LORD Most *H*. 592 6
I will sing to your Name, O Most *H*. 593 4
I will praise the Name of the Lord Most *H*. 598 11
the Most *H* uttered his voice. 603 16
He reached down from on *h* and grasped me; * 603 23
because of the loving-kindness of the Most *H*, 609 10
lift them *h*, O everlasting doors; * 614 2
and set me *h* upon a rock. 618 4
he set my feet upon a *h* cliff 640 4
the holy habitation of the Most *H*. 649 11
For the LORD Most *H* is to be feared; * 650 8
you of *h* degree and low, rich and poor together. 652 8
and make good your vows to the Most *H*. 655 8
there are many who fight against me, O Most *H*. 662 16
I will call upon the Most *H* God, * 663 23
Those of *h* degree are but a fleeting breath, * 670 1
You have gone up on *h* and led captivity captive; 677 18
your help, O God, will lift me up on *h*. 681 23
is there knowledge in the Most *H*?" 687 22
Do not toss your horns so *h*, * 691 12
the right hand of the Most *H* has lost its power." 693 21
rebelling in the desert against the Most *H*. 696 8
and the Most *H* God their redeemer. 697 21
But they tested the Most *H* God, and defied him, * 699 18
and all of you children of the Most *H*; 705 21
you alone are the Most *H* over all the earth. 707 14
and the Most *H* himself shall sustain her." 711 21
strong is your hand and *h* is your right hand. 714 20
He who dwells in the shelter of the Most *H*, * 719 10
and the Most *H* your habitation, 720 4
and to sing praises to your Name, O Most *H*; 720 23
mightier is the LORD who dwells on *h*. 722 14
most *h* over all the earth; * 727 15
he is *h* above all peoples. 729 2
the LORD looked down from his holy place on *h*; * 732 14
For as the heavens are *h* above the earth, * 734 3
You water the mountains from your dwelling on *h*; * 736 1
The *h* hills are a refuge for the mountain goats, * 736 13
they defied the Most *H* at the Red Sea. 742 13
and despised the counsel of the Most *H*. 747 4
which tossed *h* the waves of the sea. 748 6
He will heap *h* the corpses; * 754 1
therefore he will lift *h* his head. 754 4
The LORD is *h* above all nations, * 756 8
like the LORD our God, who sits enthroned on *h*, * 756 10
Though the LORD be *h*, he cares for the lowly; * 793 14
it is so *h* that I cannot attain to it. 794 11
Stretch out your hand from on *h*; * 800 14
Be present, be present, O Jesus, our great *H* Priest, 834 8

higher

For as the heavens are *h* than the earth, * 86 25
so are my ways *h* than your ways, 86 26
set me upon the rock that is *h* than I. 668 16
and *h* than the kings of the earth. 715 21
the waters stood *h* than the mountains. 735 14

highest

shalt be called the prophet of the *H*, * 51 11
Glory to God in the *h*, 94 21
Peace in heaven and glory in the *h*. 270 2
Hosanna in the *h*. 271 16
Hosanna in the *h*. 334 8
Hosanna in the *h*. 341 11
Glory to God in the *h*, 356 1
Hosanna in the *h*. 362 6
Hosanna in the *h*. 367 15
Hosanna in the *h*. 371 3
Hosanna in the *h*. 373 14
Hosanna in the *h*. 402 11
Hosanna in the *h*. 404 13
the holy place of the tabernacle of the Most *H*. 471 24
if I do not set Jerusalem above my *h* joy. 792 14

highly

praise him and *h* exalt him for ever. 88 6
we will praise you and *h* exalt you for ever. 90 8
We praise you that you have *h* exalted him, 545 4
and that which is worthless is *h* prized by everyone. 597 19
and he is *h* exalted. 650 25
Great is the LORD, and *h* to be praised; * 651 1
Though they thought *h* of themselves 653 19

highway

make straight in the desert a *h* for our God. 37 5
make straight in the desert a *h* for our God. 75 5

hill

and bring me unto thy holy *h*, and to thy dwelling. 40 17
and bring me to your holy *h* and to your dwelling. 78 16
A city built on a *h* cannot be hid. 109 8
upon my holy *h* of Zion." 586 13
and he answers me from his holy *h*; 587 10
who may abide upon your holy *h*? 599 5
"Who can ascend the *h* of the LORD? * 613 18
and bring me to your holy *h* 644 22
in the city of our God is his holy *h*. 651 2
the joy of all the earth, is the *h* of Zion, * 651 4
O mighty mountain, O *h* of Bashan! * 677 10
O rugged mountain, O *h* of Bashan! 677 11
at the *h* which God chose for his resting place? * 677 13
They grieved him with their *h*-altars * 699 22
and worship him upon his holy *h*; * 729 20

hills

and the strength of the *h* is his also. 44 17
O ye mountains and *h*, bless ye the Lord; 48 18
and the heights of the *h* are his also. 82 12
Glorify the Lord, O mountains and *h*, 89 7
I lift up my eyes to the *h*; * 104 13
and the strength of the *h* is his also. 146 8
and though the *h* be carried into the midst of the sea; 471 20
I will lift up mine eyes unto the *h*; * 473 9
the herds in their thousands upon the *h*. 654 24
and the *h* be clothed with joy. 673 14
and the little *h* bring righteousness. 685 14
and the heights of the *h* are his also. 724 21
and let the *h* ring out with joy before the LORD, 728 19
They went up into the *h* and down to the valleys 735 17
The high *h* are a refuge for the mountain goats, * 736 13

and the little *h* like young sheep. 757 4
you little *h* like young sheep? 757 8
I lift up my eyes to the *h*; * 779 1
The *h* stand about Jerusalem; * 781 19
that falls upon the *h* of Zion. 787 16
Mountains and all *h*, * 806 11

hilltop

"Fly away like a bird to the *h*; 596 9

hilltops

growing thick even on the *h*; * 686 18

hinder

and whatever else may *h* us 818 17

hindered

because we are sorely *h* by our sins, 160 2
because we are sorely *h* by our sins, 212 2

history

Let us hear the record of God's saving deeds in *h*, 288 1
about your mighty acts and purposes in *h*, 570 25
through nature and *h*, 845 19
to show God at work in nature and *h*. 853 12

hither

brought *h* out of many kindreds and tongues. 820 8

hoarfrost

he scatters *h* like ashes. 805 10

hold

You *h* back your hand; * 91 7
h fast the unchangeable truth of thy Word, 166 19
and ever *h* fast the blessed hope of everlasting life, 184 19
h fast the unchangeable truth of your Word, 218 10
to *h* fast to those that shall 234 3
h fast the blessed hope of everlasting life, 236 11
Eternal Lord God, you *h* all souls in life: 253 6
We pray for all who govern and *h* authority 387 9
or else for ever *h* your peace. 424 3
to have and to *h* from this day forward, 427 2
to have and to *h* from this day forward, 436 2
you *h* me in eternal life, my Lord and my God. 461 11
and thy right hand shall *h* me. 475 12
and the pains of hell gat *h* upon me. 479 4
My footsteps *h* fast to the ways of your law; * 601 7
Your hand will lay *h* upon all your enemies; * 609 12
h not your peace at my tears. 639 22
In my integrity you *h* me fast, * 642 24
They *h* fast to their evil course; * 671 18
you *h* me by my right hand. 688 24
do not keep still nor *h* your peace, O God; 706 4
My hand will *h* him fast * 715 8
h not your tongue, O God of my praise; * 750 23
they will *h* up their head with honor. 755 24
the grip of the grave took *h* of me; * 759 6
I *h* fast to your decrees; * 765 21
H me up, and I shall be safe, * 773 7
I *h* all your commandments to be right for me; * 774 3
The scepter of the wicked shall not *h* sway 781 22
and your right hand *h* me fast. 794 19
h the faith in unity of spirit, 815 5
who *h* office in this State 822 18
Give them strength to *h* their faith in you, 829 19
We pray for them, because we still *h* them 862 9

holdest

O eternal Lord God, who *h* all souls in life: 202 1

holds

for the LORD *h* them by the hand. 635 8
your right hand *h* me fast. 671 2
Who *h* our souls in life, * 674 11
and your servant *h* it dear. 775 6

hole

and fall into the *h* that they have made. 592 2

holies

when I lift up my hands to your holy of *h*. 619 9

holiness

Worship the Lord in the beauty of *h*: 44 3
O worship the Lord in the beauty of *h*; * 45 6
Blessed art thou in the temple of thy *h*; * 49 13
In *h* and righteousness before him, * 51 9
in *h* and righteousness all our days; 59 8
O worship the Lord in the beauty of *h*; 61 5
in *h* and righteousness all our days; 72 5
Worship the Lord in the beauty of *h*: 81 12
who is like you, glorious in *h*, 85 17
in *h* and righteousness all our days; 101 21
Worship the Lord in the beauty of *h*; 115 5
in *h* and righteousness all our days; 125 19
and evermore serve thee in *h* 155 11
and live in righteousness and true *h*; 201 16
may live in righteousness and *h* all our days; 203 8
and live in righteousness and true *h*; 203 15
clothe them with *h* of life, 205 9
and live in righteousness and true *h*; 253 3
may live in righteousness and *h* all our days; 254 10
and live in righteousness and true *h*; 254 16
clothe them with *h* of life, 256 6
and are restored to grace and *h* 287 10
truly serving thee in *h* and righteousness 329 16
in *h* and righteousness all our days. 481 2
in *h* and righteousness all our days; 489 6
in *h* and righteousness all our days; 504 4
and in *h* of life. 523 7
and in *h* of life. 535 7
and in *h* of life. 547 3
and in *h* of life. 564 7
worship here in the beauty of *h*. 578 2
worship the LORD in the beauty of *h*. 620 8
give thanks for the remembrance of his *h*. 621 11
by the *h* of your temple. 672 16
the Lord comes in *h* from Sinai. 677 17
Once for all I have sworn by my *h*: * 716 11
and *h* adorns your house, O LORD, 722 16
Worship the LORD in the beauty of *h*; * 726 9
in the beauty of *h* have I begotten you, 753 17
acknowledge the *h* of God, to hear God's Word, 857 23

holpen

He remembering his mercy hath *h* his servant Israel, * 50 17
He remembering his mercy hath *h* his servant Israel, * 65 20

holy

not entered into the *h* places made with hands,	39	15
after that the *H* Ghost is come	39	18
H, *h*, *h*, Lord God Almighty, which was,	39	22
and bring me unto thy *h* hill,	40	17
The Lord is in his *h* temple;	40	18
whose name is *H*, "I dwell in the high and *h* place,	41	1
to hear his *h* Word, and to ask,	41	8
we have offended against thy *h* laws,	41	20
to the glory of thy *h* Name.	42	10
and the grace and consolation of his *H* Spirit.	42	13
to the Father, and to the Son, and to the *H* Spirit;	42	16
Father, Son, and *H* Ghost, one God:	43	14
to the Father, and to the Son, and to the *H* Spirit: *	46	19
O ye *h* and humble men of heart, bless ye the Lord;	49	6
Let us bless the Father, the Son, and the *H* Spirit; *	49	7
Blessed art thou, O Father, Son, and *H* Spirit; *	49	22
and *h* is his Name.	50	8
to the Father, and to the Son, and to the *H* Spirit: *	50	20
As he spake by the mouth of his *h* prophets, *	50	26
and to remember his *h* covenant;	51	4
to the Father, and to the Son, and to the *H* Spirit: *	51	21
to the Father, and to the Son, and to the *H* Spirit: *	52	1
For thou only art *h*,	52	18
with the *H* Ghost,	52	21
H, *h*, *h*, Lord God of Sabaoth;	53	1
The *h* Church throughout all the world	53	6
also the *H* Ghost the Comforter.	53	10
who was conceived by the *H* Ghost,	53	26
I believe in the *H* Ghost,	54	5
the *h* catholic Church,	54	6
And sustain us with thy *H* Spirit.	55	14
and govern us by thy *H* Spirit,	57	16
for all members of thy *h* Church,	57	22
with thee and the *H* Ghost,	59	10
the fellowship of the *H* Ghost,	59	23
believing through the power of the *H* Spirit.	60	2
we have offended against thy *h* laws,	63	1
to the glory of thy *h* Name.	63	13
and the grace and consolation of his *H* Spirit.	63	16
to the Father, and to the Son, and to the *H* Spirit:	63	19
O Jesus Christ, *h* and blessed!	64	3
Father, Son, and *H* Spirit.	64	6
to the Father, and to the Son, and to the *H* Spirit: *	64	10
and *h* is his Name.	65	11
to the Father, and to the Son, and to the *H* Spirit: *	65	23
to the Father, and to the Son, and to the *H* Spirit: *	66	7
who was conceived by the *H* Ghost,	66	12
I believe in the *H* Ghost,	66	21
the *h* catholic Church,	66	22
And sustain us with thy *H* Spirit.	68	6
That this evening may be *h*, good, and peaceful,	68	7
That thy *h* angels may lead us in paths of peace	68	9
That we may be bound together by thy *H* Spirit	68	22
O God, from whom all *h* desires, all good counsels,	69	16
with thee and the *H* Ghost,	72	7
the fellowship of the *H* Ghost,	72	20
believing through the power of the *H* Spirit.	73	2
You shall receive power when the *H* Spirit has come	77	17
H, *h*, *h* is the Lord God Almighty, who was,	77	20
and bring me to your *h* hill	78	16
The Lord is in his *h* temple;	78	17
whose name is *H*, "I dwell in the high and *h* place	78	23
hear his *h* Word, and to ask,	79	3
and by the power of the *H* Spirit keep you	80	3
to the Father, and to the Son, and to the *H* Spirit:	80	7
Father, Son, and *H* Spirit, one God:	81	10
to the Father, and to the Son, and to the *H* Spirit: *	84	1
you brought them in safety to your *h* dwelling.	85	23
to the Father, and to the Son, and to the *H* Spirit: *	85	30
for the great one in the midst of you is the *H* One	86	14
to the Father, and to the Son, and to the *H* Spirit; *	86	15
to the Father, and to the Son, and to the *H* Spirit: *	87	9
The Zion of the *H* One of Israel.	87	22
to the Father, and to the Son, and to the *H* Spirit: *	88	3
You that are *h* and humble of heart,	89	24
Father, Son, and *H* Spirit; *	90	1
Glory to you for the radiance of your *h* Name; *	90	7
Glory to you, Father, Son, and *H* Spirit; *	90	15
and *h* is his Name.	92	3
to the Father, and to the Son, and to the *H* Spirit: *	92	16
Through his *h* prophets he promised of old,	92	22
and to remember his *h* covenant.	92	26
h and righteous in his sight	92	30
to the Father, and to the Son, and to the *H* Spirit: *	93	10
for you only are the *H* One.	94	16
because your just and *h* works have been revealed.	94	18
to the Father, and to the Son, and to the *H* Spirit: *	94	19
For you alone are the *H* One,	95	9
with the *H* Spirit,	95	13
H, *h*, *h* Lord, God of power and might,	95	21
Throughout the world the *h* Church acclaims you;	95	26
and the *H* Spirit, advocate and guide.	95	29
He was conceived by the power of the *H* Spirit	96	16
I believe in the *H* Spirit,	96	25
the *h* catholic Church,	96	26
And sustain us with your *H* Spirit.	98	8
govern us by your *H* Spirit,	100	8
for all members of your *h* Church,	100	14
with you and the *H* Spirit,	101	23
the fellowship of the *H* Spirit,	102	11
believing through the power of the *H* Spirit.	102	13
to the Father, and to the Son, and to the *H* Spirit: as	103	3
to the Father, and to the Son, and to the *H* Spirit: *	105	18
H Spirit that has been given to us.	105	21
Heavenly Father, send your *H* Spirit into our hearts,	107	4
H Spirit you live and reign, now and for ever.	107	21
the brightness of your *h* Spirit;	110	16
we may have a vision of that *h* City,	110	20
O Jesus Christ, *h* and blessed!	112	3
Father, Son, and *H* Spirit.	112	6
and by the power of the *H* Spirit keep you	117	8
to the Father, and to the Son, and to the *H* Spirit: as	117	12
O Jesus Christ, *h* and blessed!	118	3
Father, Son, and *H* Spirit.	118	6
to the Father, and to the Son, and to the *H* Spirit: *	118	10
and *h* is his Name.	119	9
to the Father, and to the Son, and to the *H* Spirit: *	119	22
to the Father, and to the Son, and to the *H* Spirit: *	120	7
He was conceived by the power of the *H* Spirit	120	12
I believe in the *H* Spirit,	120	21
the *h* catholic Church,	120	22
And sustain us with your *H* Spirit.	122	8

That this evening may be *h*, good, and peaceful, 122 9
That your *h* angels may lead us in paths of peace 122 11
That we may be bound together by your *H* Spirit 122 24
Most *h* God, the source of all good desires, 123 15
with you and the *H* Spirit, 125 21
the fellowship of the *H* Spirit, 126 11
believing through the power of the *H* Spirit. 126 13
and the grace and comfort of the *H* Spirit. 128 2
to the Father, and to the Son, and to the *H* Spirit: 128 5
Lift up your hands in the *h* place 131 8
to the Father, and to the Son, and to the *H* Spirit: * 131 10
your people may glorify your *h* Name; 133 19
let your *h* angels dwell with us to preserve us 133 22
to the Father, and to the Son, and to the *H* Spirit: * 135 7
Father, Son, and *H* Spirit, 135 14
and take not your *h* Spirit from me. 137 6
to the Father, and to the Son, and to the *H* Spirit: * 137 9
H Spirit you live and reign, 138 20
O Jesus Christ, *h* and blessed! 139 3
Father, Son, and *H* Spirit. 139 6
Lift up your hands in the *h* place 140 3
let your *h* angels dwell with us to preserve us 140 14
Father, Son, and *H* Spirit, 140 17
and to the *H* Spirit: 141 2
and to the *H* Ghost: 141 6
O God the *H* Ghost, Sanctifier of the faithful, 148 5
O *h*, blessed, and glorious Trinity, one God, 148 7
By the mystery of thy *h* Incarnation; 149 18
by thy *h* Nativity and submission to the Law; 149 18
and by the Coming of the *H* Ghost, 149 24
it may please thee to rule and govern thy *h* Church 150 2
the grace of thy *h* Spirit to amend our lives 152 5
according to thy *h* Word, 152 6
the fellowship of the *H* Ghost, 154 2
to the Father, and to the Son, and to the *H* Ghost; 154 10
who liveth and reigneth with thee and the *H* Ghost, 159 7
who liveth and reigneth with thee and the *H* 159 13
with thee and the *H* Ghost, be honor and glory, 160 5
in the unity of the *H* Spirit, one God, 160 10
who liveth and reigneth with thee and the *H* Ghost, 160 16
O God, who hast caused this *h* night to shine 161 1
where with thee and the *H* Spirit he liveth 161 5
may daily be renewed by thy *H* Spirit; 161 11
the unity of the *H* Spirit, one God, 161 18
who didst give to thine incarnate Son the *h* name 162 1
who liveth and reigneth with thee and the *H* Spirit, 162 5
in the unity of the *H* Spirit, 162 11
who liveth and reigneth with thee and the *H* Spirit, 162 17
and anoint him with the *H* Spirit: 163 3
who with thee and the *H* Spirit liveth and reigneth, 163 12
reigneth with thee and the *H* Spirit, 163 18
who liveth and reigneth with thee and the *H* Spirit, 164 5
in the unity of the *H* Spirit, 164 9
who liveth and reigneth with thee and the *H* Spirit, 164 17
Send thy *H* Ghost and pour 164 19
and the same *H* Ghost, one God, 165 5
the unity of the *H* Spirit, one God, 165 13
didst reveal his glory upon the *h* mount: 165 15
who liveth and reigneth with thee and the *H* Spirit, 165 19
who liveth and reigneth with thee and the *H* Spirit, 166 7
who liveth and reigneth with thee and the *H* Spirit, 166 14
who with thee and the *H* Spirit liveth and reigneth, 167 1
H Spirit, one God, for ever and ever. 167 9
H Spirit, one God, now and for ever. 167 14
who liveth and reigneth with thee and the *H* Spirit, 168 8
who liveth and reigneth with thee and the *H* Spirit, 169 6
remembrance of him who in these *h* mysteries giveth 169 10
liveth and reigneth with thee and the *H* Spirit 169 12
and the *H* Ghost ever, one God, 169 18
rested on this *h* Sabbath, 170 3
liveth and reigneth with thee and the *H* Spirit, 170 5
O God, who didst make this most *h* night to shine 170 14
liveth and reigneth with thee and the *H* Spirit, 171 8
our Lord, to whom, with thee and the *H* Spirit, 171 15
in the unity of the *H* Spirit, one God, 171 21
liveth and reigneth with thee and the *H* Spirit, 172 6
in the unity of the *H* Spirit, one God, 172 19
liveth and reigneth with thee and the *H* Spirit, 173 3
in the unity of the *H* Spirit, one God, 173 9
with thee and the *H* Spirit, liveth and reigneth, 173 14
with thee, in the unity of the *H* Spirit, one God, 173 21
liveth and reigneth with thee and the *H* Spirit, 174 6
liveth and reigneth with thee and the *H* Ghost, 174 19
thine *H* Ghost to comfort us, 175 4
liveth and reigneth with thee and the same *H* Ghost, 175 6
by the promised gift of thy *H* Spirit; 175 9
by sending to them the light of thy *H* Spirit: 175 16
evermore to rejoice in his *h* comfort; 175 18
who with the Son and the *H* Spirit livest and reignest, 176 7
liveth and reigneth with thee and the *H* Spirit, 177 1
liveth and reigneth with thee and the *H* Spirit, 177 8
liveth and reigneth with thee and the *H* Spirit, 178 5
and love of thy *h* Name, 178 13
we may be made an *h* temple acceptable unto thee; 179 1
H Spirit, one God, for ever and ever. 179 3
H Spirit, that we may be devoted to thee 179 6
liveth and reigneth with thee and the *H* Spirit, 179 15
nothing is strong, nothing is *h*: 180 2
liveth and reigneth with thee and the *H* Spirit, 180 6
to follow the blessed steps of his most *h* life; 181 1
liveth and reigneth with thee and the *H* Spirit, 181 3
being gathered together in unity by thy *H* Spirit, 181 6
mercifully grant that thy *H* Spirit may in all things 182 2
liveth and reigneth with thee and the *H* Spirit, 182 10
liveth and reigneth with thee and the *H* Spirit, 183 5
liveth and reigneth with thee and the *H* Spirit, 184 5
where with thee, O Father, and thee, O *H* Ghost, 184 13
Blessed Lord, who hast caused all *h* Scriptures 184 15
by patience and comfort of thy *h* Word, 184 18
liveth and reigneth with thee and the *H* Spirit, 184 21
liveth and reigneth with thee and the *H* Spirit, 185 6
liveth and reigneth with thee and the *H* Spirit, 186 5
the slaughter of the *h* innocents of Bethlehem 186 13
in the unity of the *H* Spirit, one God, 186 19
liveth and reigneth with thee and the *H* Spirit, 187 6
by following the *h* doctrine 187 12
in the unity of the *H* Spirit, one God, 187 14
in the unity of the *H* Spirit, one God, 188 6
liveth and reigneth with thee and the *H* Spirit, 188 13
liveth and reigneth with thee and the *H* Spirit, 189 3
follow his doctrine and *h* life, 190 4
liveth and reigneth with thee and the *H* Spirit, 190 8
who with thee and the *H* Spirit liveth and reigneth, 191 5
liveth and reigneth with thee and the *H* Spirit, 191 13

O God, who on the *h* mount didst reveal 191 15
thee, O *H* Ghost, liveth and reigneth, one God, 191 20
in the unity of the *H* Spirit, one God, 192 6
liveth and reigneth with thee and the *H* Spirit, 192 12
liveth and reigneth with thee and the *H* Spirit, 193 3
as thy *h* angels always serve and worship thee 193 6
in the unity of the *H* Spirit, one God, 193 16
liveth and reigneth with thee and the *H* Spirit, 194 6
with thee and the *H* Spirit liveth and reigneth, 194 14
liveth and reigneth with thee and the *H* Spirit, 195 6
by whose grace and power thy *h* martyr N. triumphed 195 8
of thy love in the heart of thy *h* martyr N.: 196 2
liveth and reigneth with thee and the *H* Spirit, 196 6
and the teaching of his *h* life, 196 25
liveth and reigneth with thee and the *H* Spirit, 197 2
Give abundantly to all pastors the gifts of thy *H* Spirit, 197 7
O God, who by thy *H* Spirit dost give 197 12
in the unity of the *H* Spirit, one God, 198 7
in the unity of the *H* Spirit, liveth and reigneth, 198 14
liveth and reigneth with thee and the *H* Spirit, 198 22
liveth and reigneth with thee and the *H* Spirit, 199 2
O Almighty God, who by thy *H* Spirit hast made 199 4
Father, Son, and *H* Spirit; 199 16
indwelling of thy *H* Spirit we may be enlightened 200 2
as thy *h* angels always serve and worship thee 200 8
liveth and reigneth with thee and the *H* Spirit, 200 11
in the unity of the *H* Spirit, one God, 200 17
liveth and reigneth with thee and the *H* Spirit, 201 6
in the unity of the *H* Spirit, one God, 201 17
and reigneth with thee, in the unity of the *H* Spirit, 202 7
liveth and reigneth with thee and the *H* Spirit, 203 4
may be renewed in thy *H* Spirit, 203 15
in the unity of the *H* Spirit, one God, 204 6
who hast given the *H* Spirit to abide with us 204 8
and for the benefit of thy *h* Church; 205 10
in the unity of the *H* Spirit, one God, 205 12
who didst lead thy *h* apostles to ordain ministers 205 14
under the guidance of the *H* Spirit, may choose 205 16
for all members of thy *h* Church, 206 4
in the unity of the *H* Spirit, one God, 206 7
by the prayers and labors of thy *h* Church, 206 20
liveth and reigneth with thee and the *H* Spirit, 206 23
liveth and reigneth with thee and the *H* Spirit, 207 6
in the unity of the *H* Spirit, one God, 207 13
in the unity of the *H* Spirit, one God, 208 7
with thee and the *H* Spirit liveth and reigneth, 208 14
liveth and reigneth with thee and the *H* Spirit, 208 22
to the glory of thy *h* Name; 209 6
liveth and reigneth with thee and the *H* Spirit, 209 7
Enlighten by thy *H* Spirit those who teach 209 18
liveth and reigneth with thee and the *H* Spirit, 210 8
lives and reigns with you and the *H* Spirit, 211 7
with you and the *H* Spirit, be honor and glory, 212 5
in the unity of the *H* Spirit, one God, 212 9
lives and reigns with you and the *H* Spirit, 212 14
O God, you have caused this *h* night to shine 212 16
where with you and *H* Spirit he lives and reigns, 212 19
may daily be renewed by your *H* Spirit; 213 5
in the unity of the *H* Spirit, one God, 213 11
you gave to your incarnate Son the *h* name 213 13
who lives and reigns with you and the *H* Spirit, 213 16
in unity of the *H* Spirit, one God, 214 5
lives and reigns with you and the *H* Spirit, 214 11
and anointed him with the *H* Spirit: 214 14
who with you and the *H* Spirit lives and reigns, 214 16
the *H* Spirit lives and reigns, one God, 215 6
lives and reigns with you and the *H* Spirit, 215 12
in the unity of the *H* Spirit, one God, 216 4
lives and reigns with you and the *H* Spirit, 216 11
Send your *H* Spirit and pour 216 14
in the unity of the *H* Spirit, one God, 217 6
revealed his glory upon the *h* mountain: 217 8
lives and reigns with you and the *H* Spirit, 217 12
lives and reigns with you and the *H* Spirit, 218 6
who with you and the *H* Spirit lives and reigns, 218 11
lives and reigns with you and the *H* Spirit, 219 4
lives and reigns with you and the *H* Spirit, 220 6
who in these *h* mysteries gives us a pledge 221 4
lives and reigns with you and the *H* Spirit, 221 6
rested on this *h* Sabbath, 221 15
lives and reigns with you and the *H* Spirit, 222 6
who made this most *h* night to shine 222 8
in the unity of the *H* Spirit, one God, 222 13
lives and reigns with you and the *H* Spirit, 223 2
with you and the *H* Spirit, be dominion and praise 223 9
in the unity of the *H* Spirit, one God, 223 13
lives and reigns with you and the *H* Spirit, 224 6
in the unity of the *H* Spirit, one God, 224 11
in the unity of the *H* Spirit, one God, 225 1
with you and the *H* Spirit, lives and reigns, 225 6
lives and reigns with you and the *H* Spirit, 225 19
lives and reigns with you and the *H* Spirit, 226 6
Do not leave us comfortless, but send us your *H* Spirit 226 15
by the promised gift of your *H* Spirit: 227 2
in the unity of the *H* Spirit, one God, 227 6
by sending to them the light of your *H* Spirit: 227 9
and evermore to rejoice in his *h* comfort; 227 11
with the Son and the *H* Spirit live and reign, 228 7
lives and reigns with you and the *H* Spirit, 228 12
lives and reigns with you and the *H* Spirit, 229 3
lives and reigns with you and the *H* Spirit, 230 5
reverence for your *h* Name, 230 8
that we may be made a *h* temple 230 16
Grant us the grace of your *H* Spirit, 230 21
lives and reigns with you and the *H* Spirit, 231 3
nothing is strong, nothing is *h*: 231 18
lives and reigns with you and the *H* Spirit, 232 5
follow daily in the blessed steps of his most *h* life; 232 14
together in unity by your *H* Spirit, 232 18
lives and reigns with you and the *H* Spirit, 233 2
mercifully grant that your *H* Spirit may 233 15
lives and reigns with you and the *H* Spirit, 234 5
lives and reigns with you and the *H* Spirit, 235 2
lives and reigns with you and the *H* Spirit, 236 7
Lord, who caused all *h* Scriptures to be written 236 8
who are called by your *h* Word, 237 4
lives and reigns with you and the *H* Spirit, 237 6
lives and reigns with you and the *H* Spirit, 238 6
the slaughter of the *h* innocents of Bethlehem 238 7
in the unity of the *H* Spirit, one God, 238 13
by following his *h* teaching; 239 3
in the unity of the *H* Spirit, one God, 239 4
lives and reigns with you and the *H* Spirit, 239 10

in the unity of the *H* Spirit, one God, 240 5
lives and reigns with you and the *H* Spirit, 240 11
lives and reigns with you and the *H* Spirit, 241 1
follow his teaching and *h* life, 241 13
lives and reigns with you and the *H* Spirit, 241 17
in the unity of the *H* Spirit, one God, 241 24
lives and reigns with you and the *H* Spirit, 242 6
who with you and the *H* Spirit lives and reigns, 242 12
O God, who on the *h* mount revealed 243 1
O *H* Spirit, lives and reigns, 243 6
in the unity of the *H* Spirit, one God, 243 12
lives and reigns with you and the *H* Spirit, 243 18
lives and reigns with you and the *H* Spirit, 244 5
as your *h* angels always serve 244 15
in the unity of the *H* Spirit, one God, 245 3
lives and reigns with you and the *H* Spirit, 245 8
with you and the *H* Spirit lives and reigns, 245 21
lives and reigns with you and the *H* Spirit, 246 7
lives and reigns with you and the *H* Spirit, 247 4
by whose grace and power your *h* martyr 247 6
love in the heart of your *h* martyr N.: 247 14
lives and reigns with you and the *H* Spirit, 248 6
following his example and the teaching of his *h* life, 248 11
to all pastors the gifts of your *H* Spirit, 248 18
O God, by your *H* Spirit you give 248 22
with you and the *H* Spirit lives and reigns, 249 3
lives and reigns with you and the *H* Spirit, 249 9
in the unity of the *H* Spirit, 249 16
lives and reigns with you and the *H* Spirit, 250 6
by your *H* Spirit you have made us one 250 14
Father, Son, and *H* Spirit; 251 5
by the indwelling of your *H* Spirit we may be 251 8
in the unity of the *H* Spirit, 251 10
Mercifully grant that, as your *h* angels always serve 251 14
lives and reigns with you and the *H* Spirit, 251 17
in the unity of the *H* Spirit, one God, 252 5
lives and reigns with you and the *H* Spirit, 252 11
in the unity of the *H* Spirit, one God, 253 5
lives and reigns with you and the *H* Spirit, 254 6
may be renewed in your *H* Spirit, 254 16
in the unity of the *H* Spirit, one God, 255 4
you have given the *H* Spirit to abide with us 255 6
and for the benefit of your *h* Church; 256 7
in the unity of the *H* Spirit, one God, 256 9
O God, you led your *h* apostles to ordain ministers 256 11
under the guidance of the *H* Spirit, 256 12
lives and reigns with you and the *H* Spirit, 256 17
for all members of your *h* Church, 257 1
in the unity of the *H* Spirit, one God, 257 4
lives and reigns with you and the *H* Spirit, 257 11
by the prayers and labors of your *h* Church, 257 16
lives and reigns with you and the *H* Spirit, 258 6
in the unity of the *H* Spirit, one God, 258 13
lives and reigns with you and the *H* Spirit, 259 2
in the unity of the *H* Spirit, one God, 259 9
lives and reigns with you and the *H* Spirit, 260 7
to the glory of your *h* Name; 260 12
Enlighten by your *H* Spirit those who teach 261 2
lives and reigns with you and the *H* Spirit, 261 6
lives and reigns with you and the *H* Spirit, 264 8
converts to the faith were prepared for *H* Baptism. 265 2
observance of a *h* Lent, by self-examination 265 11
meditating on God's *h* Word. 265 13
and take not your *h* Spirit from me. 266 25
Most *h* and merciful Father: 267 12
We have grieved your *H* Spirit. 267 25
and with sincere hearts believe his *h* Gospel. 269 9
grant us true repentance and his *H* Spirit, 269 11
the rest of our life hereafter may be pure and *h*, 269 13
On this day he entered the *h* city of Jerusalem 271 7
lives and reigns in glory with you and the *H* Spirit, 271 13
lives and reigns with you and the *H* Spirit, 272 13
who in these *h* mysteries gives us a pledge 274 4
lives and reigns with you and the *H* Spirit, 274 6
lives and reigns with you and the *H* Spirit, 276 8
Let us pray for the *h* Catholic Church of Christ 278 1
for all members of your *h* Church, 278 14
pray for the grace of a *h* life, 280 9
in the unity of the *H* Spirit, one God, 280 23
and praise and glorify your *h* resurrection; 281 2
because by your *h* cross you have redeemed the world. 281 16
because by your *h* cross you have redeemed the world. 282 2
to your *h* Church peace and concord; 282 9
with the Father and the *H* Spirit you live and reign, 282 11
rested on this *h* Sabbath, 283 3
lives and reigns with you and the *H* Spirit, 283 5
On this most *h* night, 285 1
and let your *h* courts, in radiant light, 286 8
All you who stand near this marvelous and *h* flame, 286 10
in the unity of the *H* Spirit, one God, 286 15
How *h* is this night, when wickedness is put to flight, 287 17
H Father, accept our evening sacrifice, 287 23
Grant to those who are sealed by your *H* Spirit 291 7
renew the solemn promises and vows of *H* Baptism, 292 5
serve God faithfully in his *h* Catholic Church. 292 7
He was conceived by the power of the *H* Spirit 293 3
Do you believe in God the *H* Spirit? 293 12
I believe in the *H* Spirit, 293 13
the *h* catholic Church, 293 14
has given us a new birth by water and the *H* Spirit, 294 5
lives and reigns with you and the *H* Spirit, 295 6
O God, who made this most *h* night to shine 295 8
lives and reigns with you and the *H* Spirit, 295 13
Father, Son, and *H* Spirit. 299 1
The *H* Gospel of our Lord Jesus Christ 300 5
Candidate(s) for *H* Baptism will now be presented. 301 1
He was conceived by the power of the *H* Spirit 304 6
Do you believe in God the *H* Spirit? 304 15
I believe in the *H* Spirit, 304 16
the *h* catholic Church, 304 17
Fill them with your *h* and life-giving Spirit. 305 19
Keep them in the faith and communion of your *h* Church, 305 21
Over it the *H* Spirit moved in the beginning 306 14
baptism of John and was anointed by the *H* Spirit 306 17
Through it we are reborn by the *H* Spirit. 306 22
of the Father, and of the Son, and of the *H* Spirit. 307 2
by the power of your *H* Spirit, 307 4
To him, to you, and to the *H* Spirit, be all honor 307 7
Son was anointed by the *H* Spirit 307 10
lives and reigns with you and the *H* Spirit, 307 13
of the Father, and of the Son, and of the *H* Spirit. 307 15
we thank you that by water and the *H* Spirit 308 2
Sustain them, O Lord, in your *H* Spirit. 308 5

you are sealed by the *H* Spirit in Baptism	308	9
by the sealing of your *H* Spirit you have bound us	309	6
lives and reigns with you and the *H* Spirit,	309	11
Strengthen, O Lord, your servant N. with your *H* Spirit;	309	12
daily increase in your *H* Spirit more and more,	309	17
a member of the one *h* catholic and apostolic Church,	310	1
God, the Father, Son, and *H* Spirit,	310	3
may the *H* Spirit, who has begun a good work in you,	310	5
let your *H* Spirit ever be with them;	310	9
for incorporating us into your *h* Church,	311	17
lives and reigns with you and the *H* Spirit,	311	19
be strengthened with might by his *H* Spirit,	311	23
of the Father, and of the Son, and of the *H* Spirit.	313	2
we thank you that by water and the *H* Spirit	314	1
For in these *h* Mysteries we are made one with Christ,	316	5
make us the children of God by the power of the *H*	316	15
in the celebration of those *h* Mysteries,	316	17
remember the dignity of that *h* Sacrament.	316	19
faith we receive the *h* Sacrament,	316	24
Remember that thou keep *h* the Sabbath day.	318	10
Father, Son, and *H* Spirit	319	1
we have offended against thy *h* laws,	321	1
to the glory of thy *h* Name.	321	13
and the grace and consolation of his *H* Spirit.	321	16
Father, Son, and *H* Spirit.	323	1
by the inspiration of thy *H* Spirit,	323	9
and worthily magnify thy *h* Name;	323	11
H God,	324	10
H and Mighty,	324	11
H Immortal One,	324	12
For thou only art *h*;	325	5
with the *H* Ghost,	325	8
The *H* Gospel of our Lord Jesus Christ	326	1
by the power of the *H* Spirit	327	1
We believe in the *H* Spirit,	327	12
We believe in one *h* catholic and apostolic Church.	327	16
and was incarnate by the *H* Ghost	328	3
And I believe in the *H* Ghost the Lord,	328	13
And I believe one *h* Catholic and Apostolic Church;	328	18
who in thy *h* Word hast taught us to make prayers,	329	1
thy *h* Name may agree in the truth of thy *h* Word,	329	7
and rightly and duly administer thy *h* Sacraments.	329	12
they may hear and receive thy *h* Word,	329	15
And we also bless thy *h* Name for all thy servants	330	1
walking from henceforth in his *h* ways:	330	12
h Father, almighty, everlasting God.	333	9
H, *h*, *h*, Lord God of Hosts:	334	4
and in his *h* Gospel command us to continue,	334	14
with these thy *h* gifts, which we now offer	335	11
and sanctify, with thy Word and *H* Spirit,	335	19
thy Son our Savior Jesus Christ's *h* institution,	335	21
to be a reasonable, *h*, and living sacrifice unto thee;	336	2
who shall be partakers of this *H* Communion,	336	4
and with whom, in the unity of the *H* Ghost	336	13
for that thou dost feed us, in these *h* mysteries,	339	3
that we may continue in that *h* fellowship,	339	11
with thee and the *H* Ghost, be all honor and glory,	339	14
the Father, the Son, and the *H* Ghost,	339	18
the Father, the Son, and the *H* Spirit,	339	21
h Father, almighty, everlasting God.	341	3
H, *h*, *h*, Lord God of Hosts:	341	7
and in his *h* Gospel command us to continue,	341	18
celebrate and make, with these thy *h* gifts	342	11
and, with thy Word and *H* spirit, to bless	342	17
partake of this *H* Communion may worthily receive	342	25
in the unity of the *H* Ghost all honor and glory	343	4
a living sacrifice, *h* and acceptable to God,	343	15
Who by water and the *H* Spirit hast made us	345	5
by the mighty power of the *H* Ghost,	345	15
to whose true promise the *H* Ghost came down	347	7
For with thy co-eternal Son and *H* Spirit,	347	13
O Father, and of the Son, and of the *H* Spirit.	347	16
built up as living stones of a *h* temple,	348	16
a sacrifice of praise and prayer which is *h*	348	17
given us the *H* Spirit to guide us into all truth.	348	22
Remember the Sabbath day and keep it *h*.	350	9
Father, Son, and *H* Spirit.	351	1
and by the power of the *H* spirit keep	353	3
Father, Son, and *H* Spirit.	355	1
by the inspiration of your *H* Spirit,	355	9
and worthily magnify your *h* Name;	355	10
For you alone are the *H* One,	356	13
with the *H* Spirit,	356	17
H God,	356	22
H and Mighty,	356	23
H Immortal One,	356	24
The *H* Gospel of our Lord Jesus Christ	357	8
by the power of the *H* Spirit	358	17
We believe in the *H* Spirit, the Lord,	359	3
We believe in one *h* catholic and apostolic Church.	359	7
and by the power of the *H* Spirit keep	360	17
H, *h*, *h* Lord, God of power and might,	362	4
H and gracious Father:	362	9
Sanctify them by your *H* Spirit to be for your people	363	13
the *h* food and drink of new and unending life	363	14
receive this *h* Sacrament, and serve you in unity,	363	16
in the unity of the *H* Spirit all honor and glory	363	20
and for assuring us in these *h* mysteries	366	5
To him, to you, and to the *H* Spirit,	366	12
H, *h*, *h* Lord, God of power and might,	367	13
We pray you, gracious God, to send your *H* Spirit	369	4
being sanctified by the *H* Spirit.	369	8
in the unity of the *H* Spirit all honor and glory	369	15
H, *h*, *h* Lord, God of power and might,	371	1
Sanctify them by your *H* Spirit	371	8
Let the grace of this *H* Communion make	372	6
with you and the *H* Spirit, your Church gives honor,	372	12
H, *h*, *h* Lord, God of power and might,	373	12
We acclaim you, *h* Lord, glorious in power.	373	17
Incarnate by the *H* Spirit, born of the Virgin Mary,	374	3
who died and rose for us, he sent the *H* Spirit,	374	10
your *H* Spirit may descend upon us,	375	4
showing them to be *h* gifts for your *h* people,	375	6
your one *h* catholic and apostolic Church,	375	12
in the unity of the *H* Spirit,	375	28
a living sacrifice, *h* and acceptable to God,	376	11
For by water and the *H* Spirit you have made	378	1
by the mighty power of the *H* Spirit,	378	10
of his true promise, the *H* Spirit came down	380	2
For with your co-eternal Son and *H* Spirit,	380	8
O Father, and of the Son, and of the *H* Spirit.	380	11
built up as living stones of a *h* temple,	381	10
a sacrifice of praise and prayer which is *h*	381	11

given us the *H* Spirit to guide us into all truth. 381 15
for the welfare of the *h* Church 383 6
Father, we pray for your *h* Catholic Church; 387 1
For the *h* Church of God, that it may be filled 389 15
and for all the *h* people of God, 390 2
grace of the *H* Spirit to amend our lives, 391 8
O Father, Son, and *H* Spirit; 391 23
with the Father and the *H* Spirit, 395 7
with the Father and the *H* Spirit you live and reign, 395 12
by your *H* Spirit you have made 395 17
who in these *h* mysteries gives us a pledge 397 16
and by the power of the *H* Spirit keep 398 9
we give you praise and thanks for this *H* Communion 399 7
H, *h*, *h* Lord, God of power and might, 402 9
your *H* Spirit to be for your people 403 2
means of this *h* bread and cup, 403 14
Gather us by this *H* Communion into one body 403 17
in the unity of the *H* Spirit all honor and glory 403 19
the fellowship of the *H* Spirit be with you all. 404 2
H, *h*, *h* Lord, God of power and might, 404 11
Send your *H* Spirit upon these gifts. 405 15
in the unity of the *H* Spirit all honor and glory 405 20
and to the *H* Ghost: 406 2
H Spirit bless and sanctify this bread 408 2
Father, Son, and *H* Spirit. 413 1
The *H* Gospel of our Lord Jesus Christ 414 5
He was conceived by the power of the *H* Spirit 416 11
Do you believe in God the *H* Spirit? 416 20
I believe in the *H* Spirit, 416 21
the *h* catholic Church, 416 22
H Spirit you have bound us to your service. 418 4
lives and reigns with you and the *H* Spirit, 418 9
Strengthen, O Lord, your servant N. with your *H* 418 10
daily increase in your *H* Spirit more and more, 418 15
a member of the one *h* catholic and apostolic Church, 418 17
God, the Father, Son, and *H* Spirit, 418 19
may the *H* Spirit, who has begun a good work in you, 419 1
let your *H* Spirit ever be with them; 419 5
May the *H* Spirit guide and strengthen you, 420 1
this man and this woman in *H* Matrimony. 423 3
H Scripture commends it to be honored 423 8
Into this *h* union 424 1
in the unity of the *H* Spirit, one God, 425 13
The *H* Gospel of our Lord Jesus Christ 426 1
of the Father, and of the Son, and of the *H* Spirit 427 15
of the Father, and of the Son, and of the *H* Spirit. 428 5
make one flesh in *H* Matrimony. 429 6
O Father, with your Son and the *H* Spirit, 430 8
By the power of your *H* Spirit, 430 14
with you and the *H* Spirit lives and reigns, 430 24
lives and reigns with you and the *H* Spirit, 431 8
God the Father, God the Son, God the *H* Spirit, 431 9
thanks for binding us together in these *h* mysteries 432 2
Grant that by your *H* Spirit, 432 4
now joined in *H* Matrimony, 432 4
according to God's *h* ordinance; 436 9
they may not be joined together in *H* Matrimony, 437 3
and *h* is his Name. 441 17
to the Father, and to the Son, and to the *H* Spirit:* 442 11
to the Father, and to the Son, and to the *H* Spirit:* 443 18
May God the *H* Spirit, who has made 445 7
of the Father, and of the Son, and of the *H* Spirit. 447 4
of the Father, and of the Son, and of the *H* Spirit. 448 5
through my ministry by the grace of the *H* Spirit, 448 10
forgives your sins by the grace of the *H* Spirit. 448 17
H God, *H* and Mighty, *H* Immortal One, 449 7
H God, heavenly Father, you formed me 450 8
by the power of the *H* Spirit keep you in eternal life. 451 5
through my ministry by the grace of the *H* Spirit, 451 9
of the Father, and of the Son, and of the *H* Spirit. 451 15
forgives your sins by the grace of the *H* Spirit. 452 3
by the power of the *H* Spirit keep you in eternal life. 455 8
O Lord, *h* Father, giver of health and salvation: 455 9
Send your *H* Spirit to sanctify this oil; 455 10
that, as your *h* apostles anointed 455 10
who in faith and repentance receive this *h* unction 455 12
lives and reigns with you and the *H* Spirit, 455 14
of the Father, and of the Son, and of the *H* Spirit, 456 2
As you are outwardly anointed with this *h* oil, 456 13
grant you the inward anointing of the *H* Spirit. 456 14
we give you praise and thanks for this *H* Communion 457 5
he may bless your *h* Name; 458 20
God the *H* Spirit give you strength. 460 6
May God the *h* and undivided Trinity guard 460 6
God the *H* Spirit, 462 9
H Trinity, one God, 463 1
By your *h* Incarnation, by your Cross and Passion, 463 5
Coming of the *H* Spirit, 463 9
and the *H* Spirit you live and reign, 464 19
In the Name of the *H* Spirit who sanctifies you. 464 24
Wash him in the *h* font of everlasting life, 465 17
and the *H* Spirit you live and reign, 466 19
liveth and reigneth with thee and the *H* Spirit, 470 5
among such as keep *h*-day. 471 11
the *h* place of the tabernacle of the Most Highest. 471 24
The *H* Gospel of our Lord Jesus Christ 479 20
that thy *H* Spirit may lead us in holiness 481 2
in the comfort of a reasonable and *h* hope, 481 12
liveth and reigneth with thee and the *H* Spirit, 481 28
and bring thee into the *h* city Jerusalem. 484 2
Yet, O Lord God most *h*, O Lord most mighty, 484 8
O *h* and most merciful Savior, 484 9
Lord most *h*, O God most mighty, 484 13
O *h* and merciful Savior, 484 14
obedience to thy *h* commandments, 487 16
the true faith of thy *h* Name, 488 8
H Spirit lead us in holiness and righteousness 489 6
reasonable, religious, and *h* hope; 489 11
we praise and magnify thy *h* Name 489 14
for the *h* patriarchs, 489 16
to thy *h* Church peace and concord, 489 26
with the Father and the *H* Spirit livest and reignest, 489 28
H God, *H* and Mighty, 492 9
H and merciful Savior, 492 10
with you and the *H* Spirit lives and reigns, 493 8
lives and reigns with you and the *H* Spirit, 493 14
lives and reigns with you and the *H* Spirit, 494 5
The *H* Gospel of our Lord Jesus Christ 495 1
He was conceived by the power of the *H* Spirit 496 6
I believe in the *H* Spirit, 496 15
the *h* catholic Church, 496 16
washed in Baptism and anointed with the *H* Spirit; 497 17
reborn by water and the Spirit in *H* Baptism. 498 2
live and reign with the Father and the *H* Spirit, 498 7

and bring you into the *h* city Jerusalem. 500 13
all who have died in the true faith of your *h* Name, 503 17
and let your *H* Spirit lead us in holiness 504 3
in the comfort of a religious and *h* hope, 504 9
we praise and glorify your *h* Name 504 12
for the *h* patriarchs 504 14
Father, Son, and *H* Spirit. 512 1
by the inspiration of your *H* Spirit, 512 9
and worthily magnify your *h* Name; 512 10
trusting in the guidance of the *H* Spirit, 513 2
H Spirit to consecrate him a bishop 513 5
in the one, *h*, catholic, and apostolic Church. 513 5
of the Father, and of the Son, and of the *H* Spirit, 513 7
declare that I do believe the *H* Scriptures 513 9
for the work to which we trust the *H* Spirit 514 17
in the unity of the *H* Spirit, one God, 515 13
The *H* Gospel of our Lord Jesus Christ 516 5
God's *h* Church is called to be one with the apostles 517 3
and in the study of *H* Scripture, 518 5
by the power of the *H* Spirit 519 20
We believe in the *H* Spirit, the Lord, 520 3
We believe in one *h* catholic and apostolic Church. 520 7
offering the *h* gifts, 521 13
offering of a pure, and gentle, and *h* life; 521 15
with you and the *H* Spirit, be honor and power 521 16
Receive the *H* Scriptures. 521 18
and be a faithful steward of his *h* Word 521 20
we thank you for feeding us with the *h* food 523 1
through him in the fellowship of your *H* Spirit. 523 3
lives and reigns with you and the *H* Spirit, 523 10
the Father, the Son, and the *H* Spirit, 523 16
Father, Son, and *H* Spirit. 525 1
by the inspiration of your *H* Spirit, 525 9
and worthily magnify your *h* Name; 525 10
ordained a priest in Christ's *h* catholic Church. 526 3
do believe the *H* Scriptures 526 15
in the unity of the *H* Spirit, one God, 528 11
The *H* Gospel of our Lord Jesus Christ 529 4
by the power of the *H* Spirit 530 11
We believe in the *H* Spirit, the Lord, 530 22
We believe in one *h* catholic and apostolic Church. 530 26
and the temple of the *H* Spirit. 531 2
to share in the administration of *H* Baptism 531 14
the reading and study of the *H* Scriptures, 532 5
and in the sanctification of the *H* Spirit? 532 28
calling us to be a *h* people in the kingdom 533 2
give your *H* Spirit to N.; 533 12
with you and the *H* Spirit lives and reigns, 534 9
and to administer his *h* Sacraments. 534 11
we thank you for feeding us with the *h* food 535 1
through him in the fellowship of your *H* Spirit. 535 3
lives and reigns with you and the *H* Spirit, 535 10
the Father, the Son, and the *H* Spirit, 535 11
Father, Son, and *H* Spirit. 537 1
by the inspiration of your *H* Spirit, 537 9
and worthily magnify your *h* Name; 537 10
ordained a deacon in Christ's *h* catholic Church. 538 3
do believe the *H* Scriptures 538 15
in the unity of the *H* Spirit, one God, 540 11
The *H* Gospel of our Lord Jesus Christ 541 4
by the power of the *H* Spirit 542 11
We believe in the *H* Spirit, the Lord, 542 22
We believe in one *h* catholic and apostolic Church. 542 26
through the power of the *H* Spirit. 543 2
you are to study the *H* Scriptures, 543 7
and study of the *H* Scriptures? 544 2
give your *H* Spirit N.; 545 10
with you and the *H* Spirit, lives and reigns, 545 18
to assist in the ministration of his *h* Sacraments. 545 20
we thank you for feeding us with the *h* food 546 3
through him in the fellowship of your *H* Spirit. 546 5
lives and reigns with you and the *H* Spirit, 547 6
God the *H* Spirit, 548 5
H Trinity, one God, 548 7
For the *h* Church of God, 548 11
That by the indwelling of the *H* Spirit 549 8
grace of the *H* Spirit to amend our lives, 550 17
lives and reigns with you and the *H* Spirit, 560 10
with the light of your *H* Spirit; 562 14
may faithfully administer your *h* Sacraments, 563 3
clearness and brightness of your *h* Word, 563 8
we thank you for feeding us with the *h* food 564 1
through him in the fellowship of your *H* Spirit. 564 3
lives and reigns with you and the *H* Spirit, 564 10
the ministry of his *h* Word and Sacraments. 567 3
of the Father, and of the Son, and of the *H* Spirit. 568 3
H Spirit, open our eyes, our ears, and our hearts, 569 3
Now, O Father, Son, and *H* Spirit, 569 10
of the Father, and of the Son, and of the *H* Spirit. 569 22
the *H* Spirit moved in the beginning of creation. 570 6
and was anointed by the *H* Spirit as the Messiah, 570 9
Through it we are reborn by the *H* Spirit. 570 14
of the Father, and of the Son, and of the *H* Spirit. 570 17
Grant, by the power of your *H* Spirit, 570 18
To him, to you, and to the *H* Spirit, 570 21
speaks to us through the words of *H* Scripture. 570 24
of the Father, and of the Son, and of the *H* Spirit. 571 8
of the Father, and of the Son, and of the *H* Spirit. 572 8
for the celebration of your *h* mysteries. 573 3
for sending your *H* Spirit to make us *h*, 573 19
and to unite us in your *h* Church. 573 20
at this *h* Table may be fed and refreshed 574 5
Blessed be your Name, Father, Son, and *H* Spirit; 574 8
upon my *h* hill of Zion." 586 13
and he answers me from his *h* hill; 587 10
I will bow down toward your *h* temple in awe of you. 589 5
The LORD is in his *h* temple; * 596 15
who may abide upon your *h* hill? 599 5
nor let your *h* one see the Pit. 600 18
Send you help from his *h* place * 608 3
he will answer him out of his *h* heaven, 608 13
Yet you are the *H* One, * 610 6
and who can stand in his *h* place?" 613 19
when I lift up my hands to your *h* of holies. 619 9
for in his *h* Name we put our trust. 627 18
among those who keep *h*-day. 643 12
and bring me to your *h* hill 644 22
the *h* habitation of the Most High. 649 11
God sits upon his *h* throne. 650 21
in the city of our God is his *h* hill. 651 2
and take not your *h* Spirit from me. 657 4
God spoke from his *h* place and said: * 667 20
Therefore I have gazed upon you in your *h* place, * 670 15
God in his *h* habitation! 676 12

How wonderful is God in his *h* places! * 679 4
I will sing to you with the harp, O *H* One of Israel. 685 3
Your adversaries roared in your *h* place; * 689 16
They set fire to your *h* place; * 689 21
Your way, O God, is *h*; * 693 26
and provoked the *H* One of Israel. 698 10
He brought them to his *h* land, * 699 13
they have profaned your *h* temple; * 701 2
On the *h* mountain stands the city he has founded; * 711 12
in the assembly of the *h* ones; 714 4
in the council of the *h* ones, * 714 7
the *H* One of Israel is our King. 715 2
with my *h* oil have I anointed him. 715 7
and give thanks to his *h* Name. 727 23
With his right hand and his *h* arm * 728 1
he is the *H* One. 729 4
and worship him upon his *h* hill; * 729 20
for the LORD our God is the *H* One. 729 21
For the LORD looked down from his *h* place 732 14
and all that is within me, bless his *h* Name. 733 10
Glory in his *h* Name; * 738 5
For God remembered his *h* word * 741 9
and Aaron, the *h* one of the LORD. 743 4
that we may give thanks to your *h* Name 745 21
God spoke from his *h* place and said, * 750 7
h and awesome is his Name. 754 24
Lift up your hands in the *h* place and bless 787 21
I will bow down toward your *h* temple 793 3
let all flesh bless his *h* Name for ever and ever. 803 2
Praise God in his *h* temple; * 807 22
we pray for thy *h* Church universal; 815 2
we pray for thy *h* Catholic Church. 816 10
lives and reigns with you and the *H* Spirit, 817 2
be of one heart and mind within your *h* Church; 817 22
united in one *h* bond of truth 818 21
receive the blessing of the *H* Spirit, 819 4
reign with the Father and the *H* Spirit, 819 12
liveth and reigneth with thee and the *H* Spirit, 820 25
and honor your *h* Name. 822 14
Grant, O God, that your *h* and life-giving Spirit 823 17
that *h* City to which the nations of the world bring 825 7
All this we ask in your *h* Name. 825 24
who, in *h* wedlock, have been made one flesh. 829 4
by thy love in the communion of thy *H* Spirit, 830 24
O merciful Father, who hast taught us in thy *h* Word 831 11
thy *h* Name, and finally, by thy mercy, obtain 832 4
grant us a safe lodging, and a *h* rest, 833 17
live and reign with the Father and the *H* Spirit, 834 11
livest and reignest with the Father and the *H* Spirit, 834 17
God's *h* Name be blessed 835 16
with you, O Father, and the *H* Spirit, 837 24
glorify your *h* Name. 839 20
a humble, *h*, and obedient walking 840 21
with thee and the *H* Ghost be all glory and honor, 840 23
conceived by the power of the *H* Spirit 849 26
Father, Son, and *H* Spirit. 852 13
Who is the *H* Spirit? 852 14
The *H* Spirit is the Third Person 852 15
How is the *H* Spirit revealed in the Old Covenant? 852 17
The *H* Spirit is revealed in the Old Covenant 852 18
How is the *H* Spirit revealed in the New Covenant? 852 20
The *H* Spirit is revealed as the Lord 852 21
How do we recognize the presence of the *H* Spirit 852 24
We recognize the presence of the *H* Spirit 852 26
do we recognize the truths taught by the *H* Spirit? 853 1
recognize truths to be taught by the *H* Spirit 853 3
What are the *H* Scriptures? 853 5
The *H* Scriptures, commonly called the Bible, 853 6
under the inspiration of the *H* Spirit, 853 12
Why do we call the *H* Scriptures the Word of God? 853 23
the *H* Spirit, who guides the Church 854 1
a *h* nation, a royal priesthood, 854 9
The Church is described as one, *h*, catholic, 854 12
Why is the Church described as *h*? 854 17
The Church is *h*, because the *H* Spirit dwells in it, 854 18
in the power of the *H* Spirit. 856 22
are *H* Baptism and the *H* Eucharist. 858 7
What is *H* Baptism? 858 8
H Baptism is the sacrament by which God adopts us 858 9
of the Father, and of the Son, and of the *H* Spirit. 858 15
and new life in the *H* Spirit. 858 20
What is the *H* Eucharist? 859 5
The *H* Eucharist is the sacrament commanded 859 6
The *H* Eucharist is called the Lord's Supper, 859 15
called the Lord's Supper, and *H* Communion; 859 16
The inward and spiritual grace in the *H* Communion 859 24
under the guidance of the *H* Spirit? 860 8
include confirmation, ordination, *h* matrimony, 860 10
H Spirit through prayer and the laying on of hands 860 20
the grace of the *H* Spirit to those being made bishops, 860 29
What is *H* Matrimony? 861 3
H Matrimony is Christian marriage, 861 4

homage

Who can fail to do you *h*, Lord, 94 14

home

h to your fold those who have gone astray; 280 6
and this fragile earth, our island *h*. 370 10
saints feast for ever in your heavenly *h*; 430 23
that their *h* may be a haven of blessing and peace; 431 6
May God the Son, who sanctified a *h* at Nazareth, 445 5
and the land of the dead shall be their *h*. 653 12
God gives the solitary a *h* and brings forth prisoners 676 13
Your people found their *h* in it; * 676 23
the women at *h* are dividing the spoils." 677 4
that there may be justice and peace at *h*, 820 11
keeping all the men and women of our armed forces at *h* 823 2

homeless

the *h* and the hungry, 151 6
For the hungry and the *h*, 279 4
He will look with favor on the prayer of the *h*; * 732 10
the *h* and the destitute, 826 3

homes

and all whose *h* are broken or torn by strife, 151 22
Their graves shall be their *h* for ever, 653 1
let them be driven from the ruins of their *h*. 751 17
We commend to thy continual care the *h* 828 23
Provide for them *h* of dignity and peace; 830 3
For our daily food and drink, our *h* and families, 837 9

honest
Mark those who are *h*; 636 10
Send us *h* and able leaders. 825 10
To be *h* and fair in our dealings; 848 12

honey
sweeter far than *h*, 607 18
than *h* in the comb. 607 19
and satisfy him with *h* from the rock. 705 8
they are sweeter than *h* to my mouth. 771 26

honor
for the *h* of thy Name. 58 13
be all *h* and glory, world without end. 59 11
be all *h* and glory, world without end. 72 8
Splendor and *h* and kingly power * 93 20
the *h* of your Name. 101 6
be *h* and glory throughout all ages. 101 24
be *h* and glory throughout all ages. 125 22
I will rescue him and bring him to *h*. 131 3
to thy *h* and glory; 155 12
be *h* and glory, world without end. 160 5
Grant us who *h* the exaltation 189 13
be *h* and glory, now and for ever. 212 5
be *h* and glory, now and for ever. 213 6
Grant us who *h* the exaltation 240 20
the offering of this candle in your *h*. 287 24
be all *h* and glory, now and for ever. 307 7
H thy father and thy mother. 318 13
they may *h* thee with their substance, 329 24
to the *h* and glory of thy Name; 331 19
all *h* and glory be unto thee, 336 14
be all *h* and glory, world without end. 339 14
all *h* and glory be unto thee, 343 4
Ascribe to the Lord the *h* due his Name; 343 10
to receive glory and *h* and power; 344 5
H your father and your mother. 350 11
all *h* and glory is yours, 363 20
be *h* and glory, now and for ever. 366 13
all *h* and glory is yours, 369 16
your Church gives *h*, glory, and worship, 372 12
all *h* and glory are yours, 375 26
Ascribe to the Lord the *h* due his Name; 376 6
you are worthy to receive glory and *h* 377 3
that we may *h* one another 388 8
and to your *h* and glory. 388 14
to the *h* and glory of your Name; 393 15
all *h* and glory is yours, 403 20
all *h* and glory is yours, 405 20
h and keep him, in sickness and in health; 424 10
h and keep her, in sickness and in health; 424 16
they may *h* and keep the promises 425 11
and all that I have, I *h* you, 427 14
that they may so love, *h*, and cherish 431 4
love her, comfort her, *h* and keep her, 433 6
to love him, comfort him, *h* and keep him, 433 11
h and power and glory in the Church, 521 17
be all *h* and glory, now and for ever. 570 21
offered to your *h* and glory. 578 6
and lay my *h* in the dust. 591 5
you adorn him with glory and *h*; 592 18
His *h* is great, because of your victory; * 609 5
he is your master; therefore do him *h*. 648 14
I will deliver you, and you shall *h* me." 655 10
They seek only to bring me down from my place of *h*; 669 12
In God is my safety and my *h*; * 669 20
I will rescue him and bring him to *h*. 720 19
ascribe to the LORD *h* and power. 726 6
Ascribe to the LORD the *h* due his Name; * 726 7
they will hold up their head with *h*. 755 24
how pleasant it is to *h* him with praise! 804 3
Grant this, O Lord, for the *h* of our Advocate 817 8
Teach us in all things to seek first your *h* and glory. 818 4
and *h* your holy Name. 822 14
and *h* the land and the water 825 23
Grant us grace that we may *h* thee 827 2
to the *h* of Jesus Christ our Lord. 827 10
our comfort and to thy *h*; 828 14
to the *h* and praise of thy Name; 834 21
to the *h* and glory of your Name, 840 13
with thee and the Holy Ghost be all glory and *h*, 840 23
all people are worthy of respect and *h*, 846 15
To love, *h*, and help our parents 848 4
family; to *h* those in authority, 848 5

honorable
Bless our land with *h* industry, 820 4

honored
those in every generation in whom Christ has been *h* 386 15
Holy Scripture commends it to be *h* 423 8
Even though *h*, they cannot live for ever; * 653 4
Those who are *h*, but have no understanding, * 653 23

honors
but he *h* those who fear the LORD. 599 12
Whoever offers me the sacrifice of thanksgiving *h* me; * 656 2

hoofs
more than bullocks with horns and *h*. 681 27

hope
Nor the *h* of the poor be taken away. 55 12
for the means of grace, and for the *h* of glory. 58 23
May the God of *h* fill us with all joy 60 1
Nor the *h* of the poor be taken away. 68 4
awaken *h*, that we may know thee 70 12
for the means of grace, and for the *h* of glory. 71 19
May the God of *h* fill us with all joy 73 1
Nor the *h* of the poor be taken away. 98 6
In you, Lord, is our *h*; 98 17
And we shall never *h* in vain. 98 18
for the means of grace, and for the *h* of glory. 101 15
May the God of *h* fill us with all joy 102 12
Nor the *h* of the poor be taken away. 122 6
awaken *h*, that we may know you 124 9
for the means of grace, and for the *h* of glory. 125 13
May the God of *h* fill us with all joy 126 12
we have been born anew to a living *h* 137 12
awaken *h*, that we may know you 139 18
rejoice in the *h* of eternal glory; 171 13
faith, *h*, and charity; 183 18
having this *h*, we may purify ourselves 184 10
and ever hold fast the blessed *h* of everlasting life, 184 19
may always be ready to give a reason for the *h* 195 4

rejoice in the *h* of eternal glory; 223 7
faith, *h*, and charity; 235 10
Grant that, having this *h*, we may 236 3
hold fast the blessed *h* of everlasting life, 236 11
may always be ready to give a reason for the *h* 247 2
There is one *h* in God's call to us; 299 8
through *h*, of thy everlasting kingdom. 339 9
the *h* of our calling. 348 6
and doth comfort us with the blessed *h* 349 7
every generation who have looked to you in *h*, 370 25
and through the prophets you taught us to *h* 373 25
pledge of the *h* of our calling. 380 22
and comforts us with the blessed *h* 382 2
For all who have died in the *h* of the resurrection, 384 29
That we may end our lives in faith and *h*, 385 7
give them courage and *h* in their troubles, 389 4
There is one *h* in God's call to us; 413 8
both relief from pain and *h* of health 460 18
God is our *h* and strength, * 471 17
reasonable and holy *h*, 481 12
Grant us, with all who have died in the *h* of the 481 23
my flesh also shall rest in *h*. 485 5
In sure and certain *h* of the resurrection 485 9
reasonable, religious, and holy *h*; 489 11
and eternal life our *h*. 497 24
my body also shall rest in *h*. 501 7
In sure and certain *h* of the resurrection 501 11
holy *h*, in favor with you, our God, 504 9
without *h*, but in thankful remembrance 505 13
every generation who have looked to God in *h*. 517 16
and the *h* of the poor shall not perish for ever. 594 14
He does not give his money in *h* of gain, * 599 15
my body also shall rest in *h*. 600 16
for my *h* has been in you. 616 4
The horse is a vain *h* for deliverance; * 627 9
For in you, O LORD, have I fixed my *h*; * 637 27
And now, what is my *h*? * 639 9
O Lord, my *h* is in you. 639 10
truly, my *h* is in him. 669 17
O *H* of all the ends of the earth 672 19
Let not those who *h* in you be put to shame 679 22
For you are my *h*, O Lord GOD, * 683 9
for my *h* is in your judgments. 766 22
because you have given me *h*. 767 12
I have put my *h* in your word. 770 4
my *h* is in your word. 773 2
and let me not be disappointed in my *h*. 773 6
in his word is my *h*. 785 2
whose *h* is in the LORD their God; 803 12
know the power of his forgiveness and the *h* 816 18
and one Spirit, one *h* of our calling, 818 19
and give them *h* for their future. 826 20
where there is despair, *h*; 833 8
and gave us the *h* of everlasting life: 835 3
give us, as you gave to them, the *h* of salvation 838 18
How are the sacraments related to our Christian *h*? 861 21
Sacraments sustain our present *h* 861 22
What is the Christian *h*? 861 24
The Christian *h* is to live with confidence 861 25

hoped
I have *h* for your salvation, O LORD, * 777 11

hopes
interpret to the Church the needs, concerns, and *h* 543 12

Horeb
Israel made a bull-calf at *H* * 743 9

horn
my shield, the *h* of my salvation, and my refuge; 602 10
the LORD with the sound of the ram's-*h*. 650 15
Blow the ram's-*h* at the new moon, * 704 5
my *h* you have exalted like the *h*s of wild bulls; * 721 16
With trumpets and the sound of the *h* * 728 14
There will I make the *h* of David flourish; * 787 5
Praise him with the blast of the ram's-*h*; * 808 3

horns
my wretched body from the *h* of wild bulls. 611 23
more than bullocks with *h* and hoofs. 681 27
and to the wicked, "Do not toss your *h*; 691 11
Do not toss your *h* so high, * 691 12
He shall break off all the *h* of the wicked; * 691 24
but the *h* of the righteous shall be exalted. 691 25
my horn you have exalted like the *h* of wild bulls; * 721 16
with branches up to the *h* of the altar. 762 26

horror
and *h* overwhelms me. 660 16

horse
the *h* and its rider has he hurled into the sea. 85 2
Do not be like *h* or mule, which have no
understanding; * 625 20
The *h* is a vain hope for deliverance; * 627 9
both *h* and rider lie stunned. 692 13
He is not impressed by the might of a *h*; * 804 22

horses
Some put their trust in chariots and some in *h*, * 608 15

hosanna
H in the highest. 271 16
H in the highest. 334 8
H in the highest. 341 11
H in the highest. 362 6
H in the highest. 367 15
H in the highest. 371 3
H in the highest. 373 14
H in the highest. 402 11
H in the highest. 404 13
H, LORD, *h*! * 762 21

host
praise him, all his *h*. 805 24

hosts
saith the Lord of *h*. 38 9
among the nations, says the Lord of *h*. 76 8
O Lord and Ruler of the *h* of heaven, * 90 17
great among the nations, says the Lord of *H*. 106 9
Rejoice now, heavenly *h* and choirs of angels, 286 1
Holy, holy, holy, Lord God of *H*: 334 4

Holy, holy, holy, Lord God of *H*: 341 7
The Lord of *h* is with us; * 472 7
"The Lord of *h*, 614 11
by the breath of his mouth all the heavenly *h*. 626 12
The Lord of *h* is with us; * 649 8
The Lord of *h* is with us; * 650 4
in the city of the Lord of *h*, 651 16
for you, Lord God of *h*, are Israel's God. 666 4
Lord God of *h*; * 679 23
Restore us, O God of *h*; * 702 16
O Lord God of *h*, * 702 18
Restore us, O God of *h*; * 703 1
Turn now, O God of *h*, look down from heaven; 703 15
Restore us, O Lord God of *h*; * 703 24
How dear to me is your dwelling, O Lord of *h*! * 707 15
by the side of your altars, O Lord of *h*, 707 21
Lord God of *h*, hear my prayer; * 708 6
O Lord of *h*, * 708 18
Who is like you, Lord God of *h*? * 714 9
Bless the Lord, all you his *h*, * 734 25

hot

h burning coals blazed forth from him. 603 6
My heart was *h* within me; 638 22
why is your wrath so *h* against the sheep 689 10
and their livestock to *h* thunderbolts. 698 24
and my bones are *h* as burning coals. 731 6
along with *h* glowing coals. 778 17
Let *h* burning coals fall upon them; * 796 21

hound

They *h* me all the day long; * 662 15

hounding

for my enemies are *h* me; * 662 13

hour

The *h* cometh, and now is, 40 20
The *h* is coming, and now is, 78 19
Blessed Savior, at this *h* you hung upon the cross, 107 8
Blessed Savior, at this *h* you hung upon the cross, 138 12
the *h* of death, and in the day of judgment, 149 27
now and in the *h* of our death. 282 8
When the *h* had come for him to be glorified by you, 374 13
Suffer us not, at our last *h*, 484 16
now and in the *h* of our death. 489 25
turn us away from you at our last *h*. 492 20

hours

pray thee, in safety to the morning *h*; 70 8
Bring us in safety to the morning *h*; 124 5
and protect us through the *h* 133 13
that in the *h* of silence I may enjoy 461 16

house

ye know not when the master of the *h* cometh, 37 1
"We will go into the *h* of the Lord." 40 12
in the *h* of his servant David, 50 25
you do not know when the master of the *h* will come, 75 1
"Let us go to the *h* of the Lord." 78 10
born of the *h* of his servant David. 92 21
it gives light for everyone in the *h*. 109 10
you that stand by night in the *h* of the Lord. 131 7
you that stand by night in the *h* of the Lord. 140 2
celebrate the dedication of this *h* of prayer: 204 2
celebrate the dedication of this *h* of prayer: 254 20
out of the *h* of bondage. 317 26
In the courts of the Lord's *h*, * 442 25
and I will dwell in the *h* of the Lord for ever. 443 17
Peace be to this *h* (place), 453 1
the *h* of God; 471 9
and I will dwell in the *h* of the Lord for ever. 476 18
and I will dwell in the *h* of the Lord for ever. 477 11
even that I may dwell in the *h* of the Lord 477 17
called your servant to stand in your *h*, 562 11
Grace be to this *h*, and to all who enter here: 568 2
make this a temple of your presence and a *h* of prayer. 568 15
go into your *h*; * 589 4
and I will dwell in the *h* of the Lord for ever. 613 13
Lord, I love the *h* in which you dwell * 616 22
that I may dwell in the *h* of the Lord 617 20
They feast upon the abundance of your *h*; * 632 20
and led them into the *h* of God, 643 10
forget your people and your father's *h*. 648 12
or when the grandeur of their *h* increases; 653 16
But I am like a green olive tree in the *h* of God; * 658 16
and walked with the throng in the *h* of God. 661 13
I will dwell in your *h* for ever; * 668 19
they will be satisfied by the beauty of your *h*, 672 15
I will enter your *h* with burnt-offerings 674 20
Zeal for your *h* has eaten me up; * 680 5
The sparrow has found her a *h* 707 19
Happy are they who dwell in your *h*! * 707 23
and to stand at the threshold of the *h* of my God 708 12
Those who are planted in the *h* of the Lord * 721 23
and holiness adorns your *h*, O Lord, 722 16
the *h* of Israel, * 728 7
I will walk with sincerity of heart within my *h*. 730 11
Those who act deceitfully shall not dwell in my *h*, * 730 24
I am like a sparrow, lonely on a *h*-top. 731 14
Wealth and riches will be in their *h*, * 755 9
He makes the woman of a childless *h* * 756 16
the *h* of Jacob from a people of strange speech, 756 20
O *h* of Aaron, trust in the Lord, * 758 8
he will bless the *h* of Israel; 758 13
he will bless the *h* of Aaron; 758 14
In the courts of the Lord's *h*, * 760 12
Let the *h* of Aaron now proclaim, * 761 1
we bless you from the *h* of the Lord. 762 24
"Let us go to the *h* of the Lord." 779 19
the thrones of the *h* of David. 780 6
Because of the *h* of the Lord our God, * 780 13
Unless the Lord builds the *h*, * 782 20
like a fruitful vine within your *h*, * 783 17
"I will not come under the roof of my *h*, * 786 3
you that stand by night in the *h* of the Lord. 787 20
You who stand in the *h* of the Lord, * 788 4
in the courts of the *h* of our God. 788 5
Bless the Lord, O *h* of Israel; * 789 13
O *h* of Aaron, bless the Lord. 789 14
Bless the Lord, O *h* of Levi; * 789 15

household

with the saints and of the *h* of God. 40 4
citizens with the saints and members of the *h* 78 2
Keep, O Lord, we beseech thee, thy *h* the Church 178 6

Holy Spirit, that they may minister in thy *h* 197 7
Keep, O Lord, your *h* the Church 230 1
that they may minister in your *h* 248 18
We receive you into the *h* of God. 308 12
of your family, or *h*, or community] 532 20
of your family, or *h*, or community] 544 8
For his family [the members of his *h* or community], 549 12
as new memebers are added to your *h*, 569 6
He set him as a master over his *h*, * 739 19

houses

build *h* of prayer and praise, 567 2

housetops

Let them be like grass upon the *h*, * 784 11

how

"You mortals, *h* long will you dishonor my glory? * 128 11
h long will you worship dumb idols 128 12
H wonderful and beyond our knowing, 287 14
H holy is this night, 287 17
H blessed is this night, 287 21
h he saved his people in ages past; 288 1
you to consider *h* Saint Paul exhorts all persons 316 20
H shall I repay the LORD * 442 19
LORD, *h* many adversaries I have! * 587 3
h many there are who rise up against me! 587 4
H many there are who say of me, * 587 5
"You mortals, *h* long will you dishonor my glory; * 588 1
h long will you worship dumb idols 588 2
h long, O LORD, *h* long? 590 4
h exalted is your Name in all the world! 592 8
h then can you say to me, 596 8
For see *h* the wicked bend the bow 596 10
H long, O LORD? 597 20
h long will you hide your face from me? 597 22
H long shall I have perplexity in my mind, 598 1
h long shall my enemy triumph over me? 598 3
See *h* they tremble with fear, * 598 24
watching *h* they may cast me to the ground, 601 22
Who can tell *h* often he offends? * 607 22
h greatly he exults in your victory! 608 22
H great is your goodness, O LORD! 624 4
O Lord, *h* long will you look on? * 631 1
H priceless is your love, O God! * 632 17
See *h* they are fallen, those who work wickedness! * 633 3
so that I may know *h* short my life is. 639 2
h great your wonders and your plans for us! * 640 12
h I went with the multitude and led them into the 643 9
H with your hand you drove the peoples out 645 10
h you destroyed nations 645 12
See *h* greatly they tremble, 659 10
no matter *h* skillful his charming. 665 4
See *h* they lie in wait for my life, 665 22
h the mighty gather together against me; * 665 23
H long will you assail me to crush me, 669 9
they plan *h* they may hide their snares. 671 19
Say to God, "*H* awesome are your deeds! * 673 21
h wonderful he is in his doing toward all people. 674 2
H wonderful is God in his holy places! * 679 4
They say, "*H* should God know? * 687 21
Oh, *h* suddenly do they come to destruction, * 688 15
there is not one among us who knows *h* long. 690 3
H long, O God, will the adversary scoff? * 690 4
Remember, O LORD, *h* the enemy scoffed, * 690 20
h a foolish people despised your Name. 690 21
remember *h* fools revile you all day long. 690 29
H glorious you are! * 692 7
H often the people disobeyed him in the wilderness * 698 7
H he wrought his signs in Egypt * 698 13
H long will you be angry, O LORD? * 701 13
h long will you be angered 702 19
"*H* long will you judge unjustly, * 705 11
H dear to me is your dwelling, O LORD of hosts! * 707 15
H long will you hide yourself, O LORD? 717 5
h long will your anger burn like fire? 717 7
Remember, LORD, *h* short life is, * 717 8
h frail you have made all flesh. 717 9
Remember, Lord, *h* your servant is mocked, * 717 14
h I carry in my bosom the taunts of many peoples, 717 15
Return, O LORD; how long will you tarry? * 718 27
LORD, *h* great are your works! * 721 5
That they may show *h* upright the LORD is, * 721 27
H long shall the wicked, O LORD, * 722 22
h long shall the wicked triumph? 722 23
h like a puff of wind they are. 723 16
O LORD my God, *h* excellent is your greatness! 735 2
O LORD, *h* manifold are your works! * 736 25
H shall I repay the LORD * 759 23
H shall a young man cleanse his way? * 764 1
This is *h* it has been with me, * 767 25
H much longer must I wait? * 770 9
Oh, *h* I love your law! * 771 13
H sweet are your words to my taste! * 771 25
See *h* I love your commandments! * 776 21
H hateful it is that I must lodge in Meshech * 778 18
H he swore an oath to the LORD * 786 1
Oh, *h* good and pleasant it is, * 787 9
H shall we sing the LORD's song * 792 8
H deep I find your thoughts, O God! * 795 10
h great is the sum of them! 795 11
H good it is to sing praises to our God! * 804 2
h pleasant it is to honor him with praise! 804 3
H did God first help us? 845 17
H was this revelation handed down to us? 846 17
H does sin have power over us? 849 1
H did God prepare us for redemption? 849 7
H can we share in his victory over sin, 850 22
H many creeds does this Church use in its worship? 851 24
H is the Holy Spirit revealed in the Old Covenant? 852 17
H is the Holy Spirit revealed in the New Covenant? 852 20
H do we recognize the presence of the Holy Spirit 852 24
H do we recognize the truths taught 853 1
H do we understand the meaning of the Bible? 853 27
H is the Church described in the Bible? 854 5
H is the Church described in the creeds? 854 11
H does the Church pursue its mission? 855 4
H are the promises for infants made and carried out? 858 28
H do they differ from the two sacraments 860 12
H are the sacraments related to our Christian hope? 861 21

howl

and if they are not filled, they *h*. 667 2

human

surpassing *h* understanding. 94 11
wonderfully restore, the dignity of *h* nature: 162 8
wonderfully restore, the dignity of *h* nature: 200 14
wonderfully restored, the dignity of *h* nature: 214 2
for the *h* race you sent your Son 219 14
wonderfully restored, the dignity of *h* nature: 252 2
for our blindness to *h* need and suffering, 268 17
for the *h* race you sent your Son 272 8
wonderfully restored, the dignity of *h* nature: 288 6
and respect the dignity of every *h* being? 294 2
and respect the dignity of every *h* being? 305 8
to share our *h* nature, 362 12
primal elements you brought forth the *h* race, 370 12
For a blessing upon all *h* labor, 390 21
and respect the dignity of every *h* being? 417 18
to be born of a *h* mother, 430 12
shortness and uncertainty of *h* life; 504 3
For a blessing upon all *h* labor, 550 6
The *h* mind and heart are a mystery; * 671 23
The LORD knows our *h* thoughts; * 723 15
the work of *h* hands. 757 21
the work of *h* hands. 789 6
Look with compassion on the whole *h* family; 815 15
that *h* rights may be safeguarded 822 7
move every *h* heart 823 18
give us new insight into your purposes for the *h* race, 828 19
From the beginning, *h* beings have misused 845 10
What does this mean about *h* life? 846 13
our *h* nature from the Virgin Mary, 849 29
Why did he take our *h* nature? 850 1
The divine Son became *h*, 850 2
so that in him *h* beings might be adapted 850 2
We mean that Jesus took our *h* nature 850 19
God inspired their *h* authors 853 25

humane

keep them *h* and compassionate; 826 23

humanity

himself to share our *h*, 162 10
himself to share our *h*, 200 16
himself to share our *h*, 214 4
himself to share our *h*, 252 4
himself to share our *h*, 288 8
Grant that the bonds of our common *h*, 430 4
find with one another the fulfillment of their *h*; 825 14

humble

that is of a contrite and *h* spirit, 41 2
to revive the spirit of the *h*, 41 3
O ye holy and *h* men of heart, 49 6
and hath exalted the *h* and meek. 50 14
thou didst *h* thyself to be born of a Virgin. 53 14
Defend us, thy *h* servants, 57 3
do give thee most *h* and hearty thanks 58 16
and hath exalted the *h* and meek. 65 17
do give thee most *h* and hearty thanks 71 12
also with the one who has a contrite and *h* spirit, 78 24
revive the spirit of the *h* 78 25
You that are holy and *h* of heart, 89 24
your *h* servants, in all assaults of our enemies; 99 22
we your unworthy servants give you *h* thanks 101 8
we your unworthy servants give you *h* thanks 125 6
thy *h* servants, a like faith and power of love, 196 3
your *h* servants, a like faith and power of love, 247 15
and make your *h* confession to Almighty God, 330 13
we, thy *h* servants, do celebrate 335 10
O gracious God, we give you *h* and hearty thanks 444 1
confess your sins with a *h* and obedient heart 450 6
Make him, O Lord, modest and *h*, 545 12
The LORD will hear the desire of the *h*; * 596 3
but you will *h* the haughty eyes. 604 19
He guides the *h* in doing right * 615 6
let the *h* hear and rejoice. 627 24
defend the *h* and needy; 705 14
by a *h*, holy, and obedient walking 840 21
we give thee *h* thanks 841 7

humbled

the divine life of him who *h* himself 162 9
the divine life of him who *h* himself 200 15
the divine life of him who *h* himself 214 3
the divine life of him who *h* himself 252 3
the divine life of him who *h* himself 288 7
and *h* himself even to death on the cross, 316 14
and *h* himself, becoming obedient even to death 545 3
The innocent are broken and *h* before them; * 595 14
Let those who seek after my life be shamed and *h*; * 629 20
and *h* myself by fasting; 630 18
Nevertheless, you have rejected and *h* us * 646 3
I *h* myself with fasting, * 680 7
and they were *h* under their hand. 745 9
So he *h* their spirits with hard labor; * 747 5

humbly

Let us *h* confess our sins unto Almighty God. 41 15
We *h* pray thee so to guide 57 15
Let us *h* confess our sins unto Almighty God. 62 15
and *h* beseech thy merciful protection 70 6
We are truly sorry and we *h* repent. 79 17
We *h* pray you so to guide 100 7
We are truly sorry and we *h* repent. 116 19
and *h* ask for your protection 124 4
We *h* beseech thee, O Father, 155 7
We *h* beseech thee to put 177 15
Almighty and everliving God, we *h* beseech thee that, 187 16
Give thy grace, we *h* beseech thee, to all 205 6
We *h* pray that thy gracious providence 207 15
Almighty and everliving God, we *h* pray that, 239 6
Give your grace, we *h* pray, to all 256 3
We *h* pray that your gracious providence 258 15
Save us and help us, we *h* beseech thee, 282 5
[and *h* confess our sins to Almighty God] 317 22
Let us *h* confess our sins unto Almighty God. 320 9
We are truly sorry and we *h* repent. 320 17
And we most *h* beseech thee, 329 26
Let us *h* confess our sins unto Almighty God. 330 15
We are truly sorry and we *h* repent. 331 28
And we most *h* beseech thee, 335 17
And we most *h* beseech thee, 335 26
h beseeching thee to grant that, 336 3
h beseeching thee that we, 339 9
And we *h* beseech thee, 342 16
And we most *h* beseech thee, 352 17
We are truly sorry and we *h* repent.

We are truly sorry and we *h* repent. 360 9
may truly and *h* serve you; 387 4
We are truly sorry and we *h* repent. 398 1
truly and *h* confess your sins: 447 3
and I *h* beg forgiveness of God 447 10
We are truly sorry and we *h* repent. 454 8
Save us, and help us, we *h* beseech you, 455 18
We *h* beseech thee to behold, 458 2
Acknowledge, we *h* beseech you, a sheep 465 2
Acknowledge, we *h* beseech thee, a sheep 483 7
most *h* beseeching thee to give us grace 487 14
Acknowledge, we *h* beseech you, a sheep 499 14
Raise us, we *h* pray, 505 2
we *h* beseech thee for all sorts 814 6
We *h* beseech thee that we may always prove 820 2
We *h* beseech thee to bless 821 9
We *h* beseech thee graciously to behold 830 20
and to walk *h* with their God. 847 5

humiliated

let me not be *h*, 614 15

humiliation

My *h* is daily before me, * 646 15

humility

Christ came to visit us in great *h*; 159 4
follow the example of his great *h*: 168 5
Christ came to visit us in great *h*; 211 4
giving us the example of his great *h*: 219 16
giving us the example of his great *h*: 272 10

hung

at this hour you *h* upon the cross, 107 8
at this hour you *h* upon the cross, 138 12
As for our harps, we *h* them up * 792 3

hunger

For the victims of *h*, 392 8
whoever comes to me shall not *h*, 396 5
may *h* for truth, 548 21
The young lions lack and suffer *h*, * 628 13
and food to those who *h*. 803 16

hungry

He hath filled the *h* with good things, * 50 15
He hath filled the *h* with good things, * 65 18
He has filled the *h* with good things, * 92 10
He has filled the *h* with good things, * 119 16
the homeless and the *h*, 151 6
For the *h* and the homeless, 279 4
I ask your prayers for the poor, the sick, the *h*, 386 4
He has filled the *h* with good things,* 442 5
If I were *h*, I would not tell you, * 655 3
They were *h* and thirsty; * 746 10
and fills the *h* with good things. 746 19
He settled the *h* there, * 749 1

hunt

and evil shall *h* down the lawless. 796 24

hunter

He shall deliver you from the snare of the *h* * 130 1
He shall deliver you from the snare of the *h* * 719 15

hurl

H the lightning and scatter them; * 800 12

hurled

the horse and its rider has he *h* into the sea. 85 2
and his army has he *h* into the sea; * 85 9
he *h* thunderbolts and routed them. 603 18
defiled his crown, and *h* it to the ground. 716 20
The taunts your enemies have *h*, O LORD, * 717 16
which they *h* at the heels of your anointed. 717 17

hurt

thoughts which may assault and *h* the soul; 167 7
from all things that may *h* us, 177 4
thoughts which may assault and *h* the soul; 218 17
from all things that may *h* us, 228 15
Give them grace, when they *h* each other, 429 14
those who strive to *h* me speak of my ruin 637 21
You love all words that *h*, * 658 6
those whom we love and those whom we *h*, 862 23

hurtful

put away from us all *h* things, 177 16
Put away from us, we entreat you, all *h* things, 229 12
Rescue me from the *h* sword * 800 23

husband

Because in the love of wife and *h*, 349 1
Because in the love of wife and *h*, 381 16
The union of *h* and wife in heart, 423 9
will you have this man to be your *h*; 424 8
In the Name of God, I, N., take you, N., to be my *h*, 427 5
I pronounce that they are *h* and wife, 428 3
you have taken N. to be your *h*. 433 10
to be my (wife) (*h*), to have and to hold 436 2
to my wedded (wife) (*h*), to have and to hold 436 6

hushed

and the busy world is *h*, 833 16

hymn

sing this *h* to proclaim the glory of your Name: 362 3
sing this *h* to proclaim the glory of your Name: 367 12
proclaim with them your glory, in their unending *h*: 370 26

hypocrisy

from pride, vainglory, and *h*; 149 2
the pride, *h*, and impatience of our lives, 268 2

I

ice

O ye *i* and snow, bless ye the Lord; * 48 11
Frost and cold, *i* and sleet, glorify the Lord, * 88 19

idol

You shall not make for yourself any *i*. 350 5

idols

how long will you worship dumb *i* 128 12
how long will you worship dumb *i* 588 2
I hate those who cling to worthless *i*, * 622 20
and provoked his displeasure with their *i*. 699 23
As for all the gods of the nations, they are but *i*; * 726 1

So that they worshiped their *i*, * 744 19
which they offered to the *i* of Canaan, 744 25
Their *i* are silver and gold, * 757 20
The *i* of the heathen are silver and gold, * 789 5

if

I we say that we have no sin, we deceive ourselves, 38 10
but *i* we confess our sins, God is faithful 38 11
Behold and see *i* there be any sorrow 39 4
I ye then be risen with Christ, seek 39 13
I I say, "Surely the darkness will cover me, 62 5
I we say we have no sin, we deceive ourselves, 76 9
but *i* we confess our sins, God, who is faithful 76 10
Jesus said, "*I* anyone would come after me, 76 23
Look and see *i* there is any sorrow 77 3
I then you have been raised with Christ, seek 77 12
I anyone is in Christ he is a new creation; 106 1
I I say, "Surely the darkness will cover me, 110 7
I I say, "Surely the darkness will cover me, 116 1
Today *i* ye will hear his voice, harden not 146 16
I we have died with him, we shall also live 281 17
i we endure, we shall also reign with him. 281 18
I you are not already baptized, I baptize you 313 1
But *i* we are to share rightly in the celebration 316 17
For, as the benefit is great, *i* with penitent hearts 316 23
so is the danger great, *i* we receive it improperly, 316 24
And *i*, in your preparation, you need help 317 11
I we say that we have no sin, we deceive ourselves, 320 1
but *i* we confess our sins, God is faithful 320 2
I any man sin, we have an Advocate with the Father, 332 15
I thou bring thy gift to the altar, 343 17
I we say that we have no sin, we deceive ourselves, 352 1
But *i* we confess our sins, God, who is faithful 352 2
I you are offering your gift at the altar, 376 13
i anyone eats of this bread, he will live for ever; 397 2
I any of you can show just cause 424 2
that *i* either of you know any reason 424 5
Bestow on them, *i* it is your will, the gift 429 20
I any of you know just cause 437 2
I any man sin, we have an Advocate with the Father, 450 1
of little account *i* you hold me in eternal life, 461 10
I I am to stand up, help me 461 20
I I am to sit still, help me 461 21
I I am to lie low, help me 461 22
And *i* I am to do nothing, let me 461 23
For *i* we live, we live unto the Lord; 469 11
and *i* we die, we die unto the Lord. 469 12
I thou, LORD, wilt be extreme 474 5
I I climb up into heaven, thou art there; * 475 7
i I go down to hell, thou art there also. 475 8
I I take the wings of the morning, * 475 9
I I say, Peradventure the darkness shall cover me, * 475 13
For *i* we have life, we are alive in the Lord, 491 15
and *i* we die, we die in the Lord. 491 16
i any of you know any reason why 514 6
Therefore *i* any of you know any impediment 527 3
Therefore *i* any of you know any impediment 539 4
O LORD my God, *i* I have done these things: * 590 24
i there is any wickedness in my hands, 590 25
I I have repaid my friend with evil, * 591 1
I they will not repent, God will whet his sword; * 591 22
to see *i* there is any who is wise, 598 16
i there is one who seeks after God. 598 17
let him rescue him, *i* he delights in him." 610 17
What *i* I had not believed 618 26
lest, *i* you do not hear me, 619 6
i I go down to the Pit? * 621 24
I they stumble, they shall not fall headlong, * 635 7
i they come to see me, they speak empty words; * 642 10
I we have forgotten the Name of our God, * 646 26
I I were hungry, I would not tell you, * 655 3
to see *i* there is any who is wise, 659 2
i there is one who seeks after God. 659 3
and *i* they are not filled, they howl. 667 2
as *i* you were a leaning fence, a toppling wall? 669 11
I I had found evil in my heart, * 675 3
O Israel, *i* you would but listen to me! 704 18
"*I* his children forsake my law, * 716 1
I they break my statutes * 716 3
I the LORD had not come to my help, * 723 27
I my delight had not been in your law, * 771 3
I the LORD had not been on our side, * 781 1
I the LORD had not been on our side, * 781 3
I you, LORD, were to note what is done amiss, * 784 21
I your children keep my covenant 786 23
I I forget you, O Jerusalem, * 792 10
i I do not remember you, * 792 13
i I do not set Jerusalem above my highest joy. 792 14
I I climb up to heaven, you are there; * 794 14
i I make the grave my bed, you are there also. 794 15
I I take the wings of the morning * 794 16
I I say, "Surely the darkness will cover me, * 794 20
I I were to count them, they would be more in number 795 12
raise him up *i* he fall; 830 16

ignorance

and our *i* in asking: 179 17
and our *i* in asking: 231 11
not as we ask in our *i*, 394 6
Strengthen our efforts to blot our *i* and prejudice, 839 17

ignorances

forgive us all our sins, negligences, and *i*; 152 4

ill

that all we do affecteth, for good or *i*, 210 11
that all we do affects, for good or *i*, 261 16

illness

and ministers to them in their *i*. 642 5

illumination

i of the true Light: 161 2

illumine

We pray you to *i* the world 107 13
i this night with your celestial brightness; 133 18
That it may please thee to *i* all bishops, 150 5
to *i* and to bless your people. 568 13

illumined

Grant that thy people, *i* by thy Word 163 8
that we, being *i* by the teaching 186 7
Grant that your people, *i* by your Word 215 2
that we, being *i* by the teachings 238 2

image

multitudes who have been created in thine *i* 206 18
Almighty God, who hast created us in thine own *i*: 209 1
multitudes who have been created in your *i* 257 14
Almighty God, who created us in your own *i*: 260 8
Thou shalt not make to thyself any graven *i*, 318 1
and didst make us in thine own *i*; 341 14
who hast made us in thine *i*, 344 15
an *i* of the heavenly Jerusalem, 349 2
You formed us in your own *i*, 373 19
you made us in your *i*, 377 13
an *i* of the heavenly Jerusalem, 381 17
created us male and female in your *i*: 425 8
formed me from the dust in your *i* and likeness, 450 9
who is the *i* of your eternal 533 3
Almighty God, we thank you for making us in your *i*, 567 8
when you arise you will make their *i* vanish. 688 18
and worshiped a molten *i*; 743 10
for the *i* of an ox that feeds on grass. 743 12
O God, you made us in your own *i* and redeemed us 815 13
revealing the *i* of Christ, 837 7
O God, who created all peoples in your *i*, 840 1
made in the *i* of God. 845 2
What does it mean to be created in the *i* of God? 845 4
because all are created in the *i* of God, 846 15
We mean that Jesus is the only perfect *i* 849 21

images

Confounded be all who worship carved *i* 727 9

imagination

scattered the proud in the *i* of their hearts. 50 12
scattered the proud in the *i* of their hearts. 65 15

imaginations

so fill our *i*, 832 25

imagine

more than we can ask or *i*: 60 4
more than we can ask or *i*: 73 4
more than we can ask or *i*: 102 15
more than we can ask or *i*: 126 15

imitate

Give us grace to *i* his uprightness of life 188 10
Give us grace to *i* his uprightness of life 239 19

immaculate

i Lamb that was slain to take away the sins 488 16

immeasurable

but above all for your *i* love 101 13
but above all for your *i* love 125 11

immortal

we may rise to the life *i*; 159 6
the light of that love which is *i*, 165 11
we may rise to the life *i*; 211 6
hide from us the light of that love which is *i*, 217 3
Holy *I* One, 324 12
Holy *I* One, 356 24
Holy God, Holy and Mighty, Holy *I* One, 449 7
Thou only art *i*, the creator and maker of mankind; 482 12
You only are *i*, the creator and maker of mankind; 499 4

immortality

Christ didst destroy death and bring life and *i* 171 11
Christ destroyed death and brought life and *i* 223 5
whereby you have given us life and *i*; 270 7
Christ destroyed death, and brought life and *i* 493 5

impartially

i administer the law in the fear of thee alone; 821 12

imparts

and one night *i* knowledge to another. 606 18

impatience

pride, hypocrisy, and *i* of our lives, 268 2

impediment

if any of you know any *i* or crime 527 4
if any of you know any *i* or crime 539 4

implore

and we *i* you of your great mercy that, 110 14

importance

you know the *i* of this ministry, 527 1
you know the *i* of this ministry, 539 1
What is the great *i* of Jesus' suffering 850 5

impressed

He is not *i* by the might of a horse; * 804 22

imprisoned

when they are *i*, save them 823 12

improperly

so is the danger great, if we receive it *i*, 316 25

improve

forgive us, and teach us to *i* our justice. 826 21
constrain us to *i* their lot. All 826 25

impurity

melt me down; you will find no *i* in me. 601 4

imputes

Happy are they to whom the LORD *i* no guilt, * 625 1

inaccessible

i from before time and for ever. 373 3

inauguration

to witness the *i* of this new relationship. 440 15

incarnate

the new light of thine *i* Word: 161 15
who didst give to thine *i* Son 162 1
Joseph to be the guardian of thy *i* Son 188 9
thy *i* Son was blessed in bearing him, 189 12
mother of thy *i* Son: 192 2
the new light of your *i* Word: 213 9
you gave to your *i* Son 213 13
Joseph to be the guardian of your *i* Son 239 18
your *i* Son was blessed in bearing him, 240 19
mother of your *i* Son: 243 9
he became *i* from the Virgin Mary, 327 2
and was *i* by the Holy Ghost of the Virgin Mary, 328 3
he became *i* from the Virgin Mary, 358 18
For in these last days you sent him to be *i* 368 5

I by the Holy Spirit, 374 2
he became *i* from the Virgin Mary, 519 21
he became *i* from the Virgin Mary, 530 12
he became *i* from the Virgin Mary, 542 12
and became *i* from the Virgin Mary? 849 27

incarnation

By the mystery of thy holy *I*; 149 18
we who have known the *i* 188 16
we who have known the *i* 240 2
By your holy *I*, by your Cross and Passion, 463 5
proclaiming the nature of the *I* 852 10

incense

in every place *i* shall be offered unto my Name, 38 7
Let my prayer be set forth in thy sight as the *i*, 61 1
and in every place *i* shall be offered to my Name, 76 6
in every place *i* shall be offered to my Name, 106 7
let our prayer in your sight be as *i*, 113 10
Let my prayer be set forth in your sight as *i*, 115 1
Let my prayer be set forth in your sight as *i*, * 797 5

incline

i our hearts to keep thy law, 56 20
i our hearts to keep your law, 99 15
I your ear to me; * 129 11
i thine ear to us who have now made our prayers 153 21
and *i* our hearts to keep this law. 317 29
i your ear to me and hear my words. 601 10
I your ear to me; * 622 10
I will *i* my ear to a proverb * 652 11
i your ear to me and save me. 683 4
i your ears to the words of my mouth. 694 20
i your ear to my lamentation. 712 4
I your ear to me; * 731 3
I my heart to your decrees * 766 7
let not my heart *i* to any evil thing. 797 9
i thine ear to us who have now made our prayers 834 3

inclined

because he has *i* his ear to me 442 15
Because he hath *i* his ear unto me, * 479 1
because he has *i* his ear to me 759 3

include

i confirmation, ordination, holy matrimony, 860 10

included

are often *i* in the Bible. 853 8

incorporate

members *i* in the mystical body of thy Son, 339 7

incorporating

for *i* us into your holy Church, 311 16

increase

thine abounding grace may *i* among us; 71 9
your abounding grace may *i* among us; 125 4
more than when grain and wine and oil *i*. 129 5
That it may please thee to give to all people *i* 150 15
I and multiply 180 2
i in us true religion, 181 13
give unto us the *i* 183 17
thy dominion may *i* till the earth is filled 207 11
I and multiply 231 18
i in us true religion; 233 4
i in us the gifts of faith, 235 9
i until the earth is filled 258 11
confirm his Church in faith, *i* it in love, 278 9
i, until the earth is filled 279 1
and daily *i* in your Holy Spirit 309 16
and daily *i* in your Holy Spirit 418 14
more than when grain and wine and oil *i*. 588 14
though wealth *i*, set not your heart upon it. 670 7
you soften the ground and bless its *i*. 673 10
The earth has brought forth her *i*; * 675 20
always at ease, they *i* their wealth. 688 2
and our land will yield its *i*. 709 19
May the LORD *i* you more and more, * 758 17
may the flocks in our pastures *i* by thousands 801 5
that our land may give her *i*; 828 5
I our reverence before the mystery of life; 828 17
i their faith and their assurance 830 5
Watch over thy child, O Lord, as his days *i*; 830 13
for the *i* of the ground 840 17

increased

The sorrows of my heart have *i*; * 615 22
He blessed them, so that they *i* greatly; * 749 5
you *i* my strength within me. 793 9

increases

or when the grandeur of their house *i*; 653 16

increasing

that he, daily *i* in bodily strength, 460 20
Grant that, *i* in knowledge and love of thee, 481 20
grant that, *i* in knowledge and love of thee, 488 22
on all whose *i* years bring them weakness, 830 1

indeed

The Lord is risen *i*. 39 8
The Lord is risen *i*: 43 8
reckon ye also yourselves to be dead *i* unto sin, * 46 11
The Lord is risen *i*. 77 7
The Lord is risen *i*: 81 4
and we are glad *i*. 105 11
The Lord is risen *i*. 109 4
I, I have been wicked from my birth, * 266 12
wash me, and I shall be clean *i*. 266 17
The Lord is risen *i*. 294 9
The Lord is risen *i*. 299 4
The Lord is risen *i*. 319 5
The Lord is risen *i*. 323 4
The Lord is risen *i*. 351 4
The Lord is risen *i*. 355 4
For my flesh is food *i*, 397 4
my blood is drink *i*. 397 5
The Lord is risen *i*. 413 4
The Lord is risen *i*. 502 20
The Lord is risen *i*. 512 4
The Lord is risen *i*. 525 4
The Lord is risen *i*. 537 4
i, I have a goodly heritage. 600 10
I, our heart rejoices in him, * 627 17
I, for your sake we are killed all the day long; * 647 1
I, I have been wicked from my birth, * 656 16

wash me, and I shall be clean *i*. 656 21
Do you *i* decree righteousness, you rulers? * 664 21
The LORD will *i* grant prosperity, * 709 18
"O LORD our God, you answered them *i*; * 729 16
i, the appointed time has come. 732 3
and we are glad *i*. 782 13
shall thus *i* be blessed. 783 20
I, there is not a word on my lips, * 794 6

indifference

i to injustice and cruelty, 268 18
For those hardened by sin or *i* 279 23

indignation

provoking most justly thy wrath and *i* against us. 331 8
and are afraid at thy wrathful *i*. 472 24
because of your *i*; * 637 2
Pour out your *i* upon them, * 681 12
fury, *i*, and distress, 699 2
and turned yourself from your wrathful *i*. 708 25
we are afraid because of your wrathful *i*. 718 14
who rightly fears your *i*? 718 24
Because of your *i* and wrath * 731 19
My *i* has consumed me, * 775 3

indolent

Too much of the scorn of the *i* rich, * 780 23

indulgent

Our self-*i* appetites and ways, 268 4

industries

the *i* and commerce of this land 208 4
make those who carry on the *i* 259 5

industry

Bless our land with honorable *i*, 820 4

indwelling

that by the *i* of thy Holy Spirit 200 2
grant that by the *i* of your Holy Spirit 251 7
through his *i* Spirit. 501 5
That by the *i* of the Holy Spirit 549 8

ineffable

those *i* joys which thou hast prepared 194 12
those *i* joys that you have prepared 245 20

inestimable

but above all for thine *i* love 58 21
but above all for thine *i* love 71 17
thankfully receive that his *i* benefit, 180 22

infants

Out of the mouths of *i* and children * 592 9
Why then are *i* baptized? 858 24
Infants are baptized so that they can share citizenship 858 25
How are the promises for *i* made and carried out? 858 28
who guarantee that the *i* will be 859 2

infect

arrogance and hatred which *i* our hearts; 815 16

infinite

obtain forgiveness by his *i* goodness and mercy. 41 14
the Father, of an *i* majesty, 53 8
obtain forgiveness by his *i* goodness and mercy. 62 14
obtain forgiveness by his *i* goodness and mercy. 79 8
obtain forgiveness by his *i* goodness and mercy. 116 10
In your *i* love you made us 362 9
we praise you for your *i* love 533 1
the *i* complexity of living creatures: 827 13

infinitely

whose power, working in us, can do *i* more 60 3
whose power, working in us, can do *i* more 73 3
whose power, working in us, can do *i* more 102 14
whose power, working in us, can do *i* more 126 14

infirm

those who are failing and *i*, 151 26
For the aged and *i*, 384 20

infirmities

mercifully to look upon our *i*; 155 8
as thou knowest their several *i*, 166 12
we beseech thee, upon our *i*, 179 18
be healed of all our *i* 191 4
be healed from all our *i* 242 11
and heals all your *i*; 733 14

infirmity

drive away from our bodies all sickness and all *i*: 458 17

inflamed

my throat is *i*; * 679 14

inflict

To *i* on them the judgment decreed; * 807 18

inhabitants

Cry aloud, *i* of Zion, 86 13
Though the earth and all its *i* are quaking, * 691 8

inhabited

His eyes behold the *i* world; * 596 17

inhabiteth

Thus saith the high and lofty One that *i* eternity, 40 23

inhabits

Thus says the high and lofty One who *i* eternity, 78 22

inherit

i the kingdom prepared for you. 483 21
i the kingdom prepared for you 487 20
i the kingdom prepared for you. 500 10
and their offspring shall *i* the land. 615 15
The children of his servants will *i* it, * 682 9

inheritance

be partakers of the *i* of the saints in light. 40 2
share in the *i* of the saints in light. 77 23
Save your people, Lord, and bless your *i*; 98 9
Your decrees are my *i* for ever; * 104 9
rejoice in the *i* of Israel; 289 18
share in the *i* of the saints in light; 311 18
And grant that we may find our *i* 375 21
But I have squandered the *i* 450 13
and give thanks with thine *i*. 478 22
i in that kingdom where there is no death, 482 6
be partakers of the *i* of the saints in light; 486 14

be partakers of the *i* of the saints in light; 489 21
and a pledge of our *i* 498 16
be partakers of the *i* of the saints in light; 504 19
I will give you the nations for your *i* * 586 18
Save your people and bless your *i*; * 620 3
and their *i* shall last for ever. 634 21
He chooses our *i* for us, * 650 12
You sent a gracious rain, O God, upon your *i*; * 676 21
the tribe you redeemed to be your *i*, 689 12
and apportioned an *i* to them by lot; * 699 16
and was angered against his *i*. 700 4
and over Israel his *i*. 700 23
O God, the heathen have come into your *i*; 701 1
to be your allotted *i*." 738 22
that I may glory with your *i*. 742 8
and he abhorred his *i*. 745 5
Your decrees are my *i* for ever; * 772 15
He gave their land to be an *i*, * 788 26
an *i* for Israel his people. 788 27
And gave away their lands for an *i*, * 791 11
An *i* for Israel his servant, * 791 13

inherited

We thank you for the faith we have *i* 839 12

inheritors

and *i* of the kingdom of God. 858 11

iniquities

and blot out all my *i*. 266 21
For my *i* overwhelm me; * 637 4
and blot out all my *i*. 656 25
and their *i* with the lash; 716 6
Our *i* you have set before you, * 718 15

iniquity

and the Lord hath laid on him the *i* 39 2
and the Lord has laid on him the *i* 77 1
and have kept myself from *i*; 604 10
I will confess my *i* * 638 5
you love righteousness and hate *i*. 648 3
Their *i* comes from gross minds, * 687 13
You have forgiven the *i* of your people * 708 22
and all the workers of *i* flourish, 721 10
and all the workers of *i* shall be scattered. 721 15
and were brought down in their *i*. 745 12
let no *i* have dominion over me. 774 14

initiated

A covenant is a relationship *i* by God, 846 21

injured

whom we have *i* or offended, 391 6

injuries

ready to make restitution for all *i* 317 6

injury

where there is *i*, pardon; 833 6

injustice

indifference to *i* and cruelty, 268 18
For the victims of hunger, fear, *i*, and oppression. 392 8
who live with *i*, terror, disease, and death 826 9

inmost

For you yourself created my *i* parts; * 794 25

innocence

It restores *i* to the fallen, 287 18
and according to my *i*, O Most High. 591 14
Hear my plea of *i*, O LORD; 600 22
I will wash my hands in *i*, O LORD, * 616 18
and washed my hands in *i*. 688 4

innocent

into the arms of thy mercy all *i* victims; 186 15
into the arms of your mercy all innocent victims; 238 9
and in secret places they murder the *i*; * 595 9
The *i* are broken and humbled before them; * 595 14
nor does he take a bribe against the *i*. 599 16
and gives wisdom to the *i*. 607 7
and *i* of a great offense. 607 27
and condemn the *i* to death. 724 8
They shed *i* blood, 744 23
The LORD watches over the *i*; * 759 12

innocents

the slaughter of the holy *i* of Bethlehem 186 14
the slaughter of the holy *i* of Bethlehem 238 8

innumerable

who hast brought us near to an *i* company 198 23
you have brought us near to an *i* company 250 8
most hearty thanks for the *i* benefits 335 15
For *i* troubles have crowded upon me; 641 4

inordinate

From all *i* and sinful affections; 149 5
from an *i* love of this world, 198 3
from an *i* love of this world, 249 12

inquiring

an *i* and discerning heart, 308 6

insects

He spoke, and there came swarms of *i* * 740 15

insight

and give us new *i* into your purposes 828 18

insolence

They bluster in their *i*; * 723 1

insolent

You have rebuked the *i*; * 765 1

inspiration

Grant that by thy *i* we may think 178 2
Grant that by your *i* we may think 229 16
thoughts of our hearts by the *i* of thy Holy Spirit, 323 9
thoughts of our hearts by the *i* of your Holy Spirit, 355 9
thoughts of our hearts by the *i* of your Holy Spirit, 512 9
thoughts of our hearts by the *i* of your Holy Spirit, 525 9
thoughts of our hearts by the *i* of your Holy Spirit, 537 9
under the *i* of the Holy Spirit, 853 11

inspire

That it may please thee to *i* us, 151 13
Almighty Father, who didst *i* Simon Peter, 187 1
Almighty God, who didst *i* thy servant Luke 193 11

beseeching thee to *i* continually 329 4
What terror you *i*! * 692 14
I our witness to him, 816 17
I us. 839 7

inspired

i by the devotion of thy servant 198 3
Almighty Father, who *i* Simon Peter, 238 14
Almighty God, who *i* your servant Luke 244 20
that we, *i* by the devotion of your servant 249 13
I by the revelation of your Son, 571 1
We call them the Word of God because God *i* 853 24

instead

He chose *i* the tribe of Judah * 700 15
He gave them hailstones *i* of rain, * 740 17
Sin is the seeking of our own will *i* of the will 848 29

institute

did *i* the Sacrament of his Body and Blood: 169 8
and did *i*, and in his holy Gospel command 334 14
and did *i*, and in his holy Gospel command 341 17

instituted

i the Sacrament of his Body and Blood: 221 2
i the Sacrament of his Body and Blood: 274 2
i the Sacrament of his Body and Blood 316 2
i the Sacrament of his Body and Blood: 397 14
was *i* by God. 423 16

institution

i of thy dearly beloved Son 335 9
our Savior Jesus Christ's holy *i*, 335 21

institutions

Remember those who work in these *i*; 826 22

instruct

"I will *i* you and teach you in the way 625 17
Happy are they whom you *i*, O Lord! * 723 17
To *i* his princes according to his will * 739 21
i me in your statutes. 764 8
i me in your statutes. 765 12
i me in your statutes. 768 16

instructed

i by their teaching and example, 190 12
i by their teaching and example, 241 20
are sufficiently *i* in the Christian Faith, 860 24

instrument

make an *i* of shameful death to be unto us 168 18
made an *i* of shameful death to be for us 220 9
Make me an *i* of your salvation 563 1
We dedicate this (name of *i*) in the Name 572 7

instruments

Lord, make us *i* of your peace. 833 5

integrity

Let *i* and uprightness preserve me, * 616 3
for I have lived with *i*; * 616 8
As for me, I will live with *i*; * 617 3
In my *i* you hold me fast, * 642 24
from those who walk with *i*. 708 17
of our Courts give understanding and *i*, 822 7

intemperate

Our *i* love of worldly goods and comforts, 268 10

intend

and *i* to lead a new life, 330 10
I firmly *i* admendment of life, 447 9
Though they *i* evil against you 609 20

intended

i by God for their mutual joy; 423 10
i for him in your eternal kingdom; 841 5
To use all our bodily desires as God *i*; 848 11

intention

with the *i* to amend our lives. 857 13

interceded

Then Phinehas stood up and *i*, * 744 7

intercedes

reigns with the Father and *i* for us. 850 21

intercession

thanksgiving, penitence, oblation, *i*, 856 28
What are *i* and petition? 857 17
Intercession brings before God the needs of others; 857 18

intercessions

i are acceptable through the Spirit, 199 10
in whom all our *i* are acceptable 250 19
i are acceptable through the Spirit, 395 23
i offered in this place today 572 11

intermingled

They *i* with the heathen * 744 17

interpret

Will you boldly proclaim and *i* the Gospel 518 8
i to the Church the needs, concerns, and hopes 543 12

interpretation

i of the Scriptures. 854 2

interpreting

and *i* the Gospel, 517 4

interstellar

i space, galaxies, suns, the planets 370 9

intolerable

the burden of them is *i*. 331 12

invent

but *i* deceitful schemes against the quiet 631 10

invisible

to praise you, the *i*, almighty, and eternal God, 287 1
and of all things visible and *i*; 327 23
who is the image of your eternal and *i* glory, 533 3

invitation

May he hear your words of *i*, 465 21

invite

I *i* you, therefore, in the name of the Church, 265 10
and all occasions *i* your tender mercies: 572 10

invites

the Church *i* her members, 285 2

invoke
You shall not *i* with malice the Name of the Lord 350 7

inward
heavenly Father grant you the *i* anointing 456 14
visible signs of *i* and spiritual grace, 857 26
What is the *i* and spiritual grace in Baptism? 858 16
The *i* and spiritual grace in Baptism is union 858 17
What is the *i* and spiritual grace given 859 22
The *i* and spiritual grace in the Holy Communion 859 24

inwardly
outwardly in our bodies and *i* in our souls, 167 5
read, mark, learn, and *i* digest them; 184 17
i in our souls, that we may be defended 218 15
read, mark, learn, and *i* digest them, 236 10
be so grafted *i* in our hearts, 834 20

iron
You shall crush them with an *i* rod * 586 20
his neck they put in an *i* collar. 739 14
bound fast in misery and *i*; 747 2
and breaks in two the *i* bars. 747 14
and their nobles with links of *i*; 807 17

Isaac
God of Abraham, *I*, and Jacob, 90 18
God of Abraham, *I*, and Jacob; 372 1
the oath that he swore to *I*, 738 18

Isaiah
for *I* and all the prophets; 838 13

Ishmaelites
The tents of Edom and the *I*; * 706 14

island
and this fragile earth, our *i* home. 370 10

isles
The kings of Tarshish and of the *i* shall pay tribute, * 686 3
let the multitude of the *i* be glad. 726 24

isolation
years bring them weakness, distress, or *i*. 830 2

Israel
remembering his mercy hath holpen his servant *I*, * 50 17
Blessed be the Lord God of *I*, * 50 22
and to be the glory of thy people *I*. 51 28
remembering his mercy hath holpen his servant *I*, * 65 20
and to be the glory of thy people *I*. 66 6
in the midst of you is the Holy One of *I*. 86 14
The Zion of the Holy One of *I*. 87 22
He has come to the help of his servant *I*, * 92 12
Blessed be the Lord, the God of *I*; * 92 18
and the glory of your people *I*. 93 17
Behold, he who keeps watch over *I* * 104 19
He has come to the help of his servant *I*, * 119 18
and the glory of your people *I*. 120 6
and the glory of your people *I*. 135 6
and the glory of your people *I*. 140 12
the children of *I*, out of bondage in Egypt, 287 7
and rejoice in the inheritance of *I*; 289 18
Through it you led the children of *I* out 306 15
"The first commandment is this: Hear, O *I*: 351 7
in the calling of *I* to be your people; 368 3
He has come to the help of his servant *I*,* 442 7
Behold, he that keepeth *I* * 473 15
O *I*, trust in the LORD, 474 13
And he shall redeem *I* * 474 16
you led the children of *I* out of their bondage 570 7
Oh, that *I*'s deliverance would come out of Zion! * 599 1
Jacob will rejoice and *I* be glad. 599 3
enthroned upon the praises of *I*. 610 7
stand in awe of him, O offspring of *I*; 611 27
Deliver *I*, O God, * 616 5
Blessed be the LORD God of *I*, * 642 26
"O *I*, I will bear witness against you; * 654 17
Oh, that *I*'s deliverance would come out of Zion! * 659 14
Jacob will rejoice and *I* be glad. 659 16
for you, LORD God of hosts, are *I*'s God. 666 4
at the presence of God, the God of *I*. 676 20
bless the LORD, you that are of the fountain of *I*. 678 10
his majesty is over *I*; 679 2
the God of *I* giving strength and power to his people! 679 5
O God of *I*. 679 25
I will sing to you with the harp, O Holy One of *I*. 685 3
Blessed be the Lord GOD, the God of *I*, * 686 25
Truly, God is good to *I*, * 687 1
his Name is great in *I*. 692 2
and established a law for *I*, * 695 8
and his anger mounted against *I*; 696 19
and laid low the youth of *I*. 697 13
and provoked the Holy One of *I*. 698 10
he made the tribes of *I* to dwell in their tents. 699 17
and utterly rejected *I*. 699 25
and over *I* his inheritance. 700 23
Hear, O Shepherd of *I*, leading Joseph like a flock; * 702 12
For this is a statute for *I*, * 704 7
O *I*, if you would but listen to me! 704 18
and *I* would not obey me. 704 25
that *I* would walk in my ways! 705 2
But *I* would I feed with the finest wheat * 705 7
let the name of *I* be remembered no more." 706 11
the Holy One of *I* is our King. 715 2
the house of *I*, * 728 7
and his works to the children of *I*. 733 22
an everlasting covenant for *I*, 738 20
I came into Egypt, * 739 23
I made a bull-calf at Horeb * 743 9
Blessed be the LORD, the God of *I*, 745 23
When *I* came out of Egypt, * 756 19
and *I* his dominion. 756 22
O *I*, trust in the LORD; * 758 6
he will bless the house of *I*; 758 13
Let *I* now proclaim, * 760 22
Behold, he who keeps watch over *I* * 779 7
the assembly of *I*, 780 3
let *I* now say; 781 2
but peace be upon *I*. 782 5
may peace be upon *I*. 783 25
let *I* now say; 784 2
O *I*, wait for the LORD, * 785 6
and he shall redeem *I* from all their sins. 785 9
O *I*, wait upon the LORD, * 785 17
and *I* for his own possession. 788 9

an inheritance for *I* his people. 788 27
Bless the LORD, O house of *I*; * 789 13
And brought out *I* from among them, * 790 17
And made *I* to pass through the midst of it, * 790 23
An inheritance for *I* his servant, * 791 13
he gathers the exiles of *I*. 804 5
his statutes and his judgments to *I*. 805 16
the children of *I*, a people who are near him. 806 24
Let *I* rejoice in his Maker; * 807 4
and especially through the prophets of *I*. 845 20
from the revelation to *I*? 846 2
the laws given to Moses and the people of *I*. 847 15
It is called the People of God, the New *I*, 854 8

issue

and a happy *i* out of all their afflications. 815 11

issued

You have *i* your decrees * 775 1

ivory

and the music of strings from *i* palaces 648 7

J

Jabin

to Sisera, and to *J* at the river of Kishon: 706 21

jackals

and let them be food for *j*. 671 6

Jacob

God of Abraham, Isaac, and *J*, 90 18
God of Abraham, Isaac, and *J*; 372 2
the God of *J* is our refuge. 472 8
J will rejoice and Israel be glad. 599 3
the Name of the God of *J* defend you; 608 2
all you of *J*'s line, give glory. 611 28
of those who seek your face, O God of *J*. 613 26
you command victories for *J*. 645 19
the God of *J* is our stronghold. 649 9
the God of *J* is our stronghold. 649 18
the God of *J* is our stronghold. 650 5
the pride of *J* whom he loves. 650 13
J will rejoice and Israel be glad. 659 16
Let everyone know that God rules in *J*, * 666 26
I will sing praises to the God of *J*. 691 23
At your rebuke, O God of *J*, * 692 12
the children of *J* and Joseph. 694 4
He gave his decrees to *J* 695 7
a fire was kindled against *J*, 696 18
to be a shepherd over *J* his people 700 22
For they have devoured *J* * 701 19
and raise a loud shout to the God of *J*. 704 2
a law of the God of *J*. 704 8
hearken, O God of *J*. 708 7
you have restored the good fortune of *J*. 708 21
more than all the dwellings of *J*. 711 14
the God of *J* takes no notice." 723 8
you have executed justice and righteousness in *J*." 729 7
O children of *J* his chosen. 738 12
Which he established as a statute for *J*, * 738 19
and *J* became a sojourner in the land of Ham. 739 24
the house of *J* from a people of strange speech, 756 20
at the presence of the God of *J*, 757 10
and vowed a vow to the Mighty One of *J*: 786 2
a dwelling for the Mighty One of *J*." 786 8
For the LORD has chosen *J* for himself * 788 8
Happy are they who have the God of *J* for their help! * 803 11
He declares his word to *J*, * 805 15

jails

Visit our *j* and prisons with your pity and judgment. 826 17

James

give to thine apostles Philip and *J* grace 189 6
apostle *J*, first among the Twelve to suffer martyrdom 191 8
J the Just, brother of our Lord, thy Church may give 193 19
who gave to your apostles Philip and *J* grace 240 13
apostle *J*, first among the Twelve to suffer martyrdom 242 15
J the Just, brother of our Lord, your Church may give 245 5

jaws

They open wide their *j* at me, * 611 3

jealous

do not be *j* of those who do wrong. 633 6

jealousy

To resist temptations to envy, greed, and *j*; 848 19

Jearim

we found it in the fields of *J*. 786 10

Jerusalem

be witnesses unto me both in *J*, 39 20
prepared for us our place in the new *J*: 69 3
and you shall be my witnesses in *J*, 77 18
prepared for us our place in the new *J*: 123 3
On this day he entered the holy city of *J* 271 7
may come to the joy of that heavenly *J*, 290 4
an image of the heavenly *J*, adorned as a bride 349 2
an image of the heavenly *J*, adorned as a bride 381 17
in the midst of you, O *J*. 442 26
bring thee into the holy city *J*. 484 3
bring you into the holy city *J*. 500 14
and rebuild the walls of *J*. 657 19
to you shall vows be performed in *J*. 672 8
for your temple's sake at *J*. 678 17
they have made *J* a heap of rubble. 701 3
on every side of *J*, * 701 9
and his praise in *J*; 732 19
in the midst of you, O *J*. 760 13
within your gates, O *J*. 779 21
J is built as a city * 779 22
Pray for the peace of *J*: * 780 7
The hills stand about *J*; * 781 19
and may you see the prosperity of *J* 783 22
who dwells in *J*. 789 18
If I forget you, O *J*, * 792 10
if I do not set *J* above my highest joy. 792 14
Remember the day of *J*, O LORD, 792 15
The LORD rebuilds *J*; * 804 4
Worship the LORD, O *J*; * 805 1

Jesus

J said, "Whosoever will come after me, 38 24
giveth us the victory through our Lord *J* Christ. 39 12
from the Lord *J* Christ. 40 10
in Christ *J* our Lord; 42 7
through *J* Christ our Lord. 46 12
O Lord, the only-begotten Son, *J* Christ; 52 10
And in *J* Christ his only Son our Lord; 53 25
through the same *J* Christ our Lord. 56 4
through the same thy Son *J* Christ our Lord. 56 10
through *J* Christ our Lord. 56 16
the might of *J* Christ our Lord. 57 6
through *J* Christ our Lord. 57 12
through our Lord and Savior *J* Christ. 57 24
through the same thy Son *J* Christ our Lord. 58 7
Lord *J* Christ, who didst stretch out thine arms 58 8
in the redemption of the world by our Lord *J* Christ, 58 22
through *J* Christ our Lord, 59 9
The grace of our Lord *J* Christ, 59 22
in the Church, and in Christ *J* 60 5
from the Lord *J* Christ. 61 4
J said, "I am the light of the world; 62 9
in Christ *J* our Lord; 63 10
O *J* Christ, holy and blessed! 64 3
And in *J* Christ his only Son our Lord; 66 11
whose Son our Savior *J* Christ triumphed 69 1
O Lord *J* Christ, who by thy death 69 7
through *J* Christ our Lord. 69 15
through the merits of *J* Christ our Savior. 69 21
for the love of thy only Son, our Savior *J* Christ. 70 3
thy Son our Savior *J* Christ. 70 9
Lord *J*, stay with us, for evening is at hand 70 10
through *J* Christ our Lord. 70 18
through *J* Christ our Lord. 71 9
in the redemption of the world by our Lord *J* Christ, 71 18
through *J* Christ our Lord, 72 6
The grace of our Lord *J* Christ, 72 19
in the Church, and in Christ *J* 73 5
J said, "If anyone would come after me, 76 23
gives us the victory through our Lord *J* Christ. 77 11
peace from God our Father and the Lord *J* Christ. 78 9
For the sake of your Son *J* Christ, 79 18
through our Lord *J* Christ, strengthen you 80 2
alive to God in *J* Christ our Lord. 83 20
Lord *J* Christ, only Son of the Father, 95 3
you alone are the Most High, *J* Christ, 95 12
I believe in *J* Christ, his only Son, our Lord. 96 15
through *J* Christ our Lord. 98 22
through *J* Christ your Son our Lord. 99 5
through *J* Christ our Lord. 99 11
through the might of *J* Christ our Lord. 99 24
through *J* Christ our Lord. 100 5
through our Lord and Savior *J* Christ. 100 16
Lord *J* Christ, you stretched out your arms 101 1
in the redemption of the world by our Lord *J* Christ; 101 14
through *J* Christ our Lord, 101 22
The grace of our Lord *J* Christ, 102 10
in the Church, and in Christ *J* 102 16
through *J* Christ our Lord. 107 7
Lord *J* Christ, you said to your apostles, 107 17
Light and peace, in *J* Christ our Lord. 109 1
J said, "You are the light of the world. 109 7
J as Lord, and ourselves as your servants, for *J*' sake. 110 2
the glory of God in the face of *J* Christ. 110 6
through *J* Christ our Lord. 110 16
J Christ our Lord. 110 21
for the love of thy only Son, our Savior, *J* Christ. 111 3
through *J* Christ our Lord. 111 7
O *J* Christ, holy and blessed! 112 3
peace from God our Father and from the Lord *J* 115 4
J said, "I am the light of the world; 116 5
For the sake of your Son *J* Christ, 117 1
through our Lord *J* Christ, 117 7
O *J* Christ, holy and blessed! 118 3
I believe in *J* Christ, his only Son, our Lord. 120 11
whose Son our Savior *J* Christ triumphed 123 1
Lord *J* Christ, by your death you took away 123 6
through *J* Christ our Lord. 123 14
through the mercies of Christ *J* our Savior. 123 20
of your only Son, our Savior *J* Christ. 123 23
your Son our Savior *J* Christ. 124 6
Lord *J*, stay with us, for evening is at hand 124 7
through *J* Christ our Lord. 124 15
through *J* Christ our Lord. 125 4
in redemption of the world by our Lord *J* Christ; 125 12
The grace of our Lord *J* Christ, 126 10
in the Church, and in Christ *J* 126 16
For the sake of your Son our Lord *J* Christ, 127 11
Lord *J*, the great shepherd of the sheep, 132 2
through *J* Christ, to whom be glory 132 5
love of your only Son, our Savior *J* Christ. 133 12
through *J* Christ our Lord. 133 16
We give you thanks, O God, for revealing your Son *J* 134 1
through *J* Christ our Lord. 134 5
Blessed be the God and Father of our Lord *J* Christ! 137 11
through the resurrection of *J* Christ from the dead. 137 13
through *J* Christ our Lord. 137 18
Lord *J* Christ, you said to your apostles, 138 16
O *J* Christ, holy and blessed! 139 3
J as Lord, and ourselves as your servants, for *J*' sake. 139 11
glory of God in the face of *J* Christ. 139 15
Lord *J*, stay with us, for evening is at hand 139 16
through *J* Christ our Lord. 140 15
through *J* Christ our Lord. 153 25
The grace of our Lord *J* Christ, and the love of God, 154 1
J Christ our Lord. 155 13
this mortal life in which thy Son *J* Christ 159 3
that we may greet with joy the coming of *J* 159 12
through *J* Christ our Lord, 160 4
through the same *J* Christ our Lord, 160 9
the birth of thy only Son *J* Christ: 160 13
through the same our Lord *J* Christ, 161 11
through the same *J* Christ our Lord, 161 17
the holy name of *J* to be the sign of our salvation: 162 2
even our Lord *J* Christ; 162 4
to share our humanity, thy Son *J* Christ; 162 10
through the same *J* Christ our Lord, 162 16
who at the baptism of *J* in the River 163 1
whose Son our Savior *J* Christ is the light 163 7
through the same *J* Christ our Lord, 163 11
answer readily the call of our Savior *J* Christ 163 15
through *J* Christ our Lord, 164 3
manifested to us in thy Son our Savior *J* Christ; 164 8

through J Christ our Lord,	164	16
Grant this for thine only Son J Christ's sake,	165	4
manifested unto us in thy Son J Christ our Lord;	165	12
through the same J Christ our Lord,	165	18
through J Christ our Lord,	166	6
through J Christ thy Son our Lord,	166	13
hold fast the unchangeable truth of thy Word, J	166	19
through J Christ our Lord,	167	7
whose blessed Son J Christ came down	167	10
hast sent thy Son our Savior J Christ	168	2
through the same J Christ our Lord,	168	7
through the same thy Son J Christ our Lord,	168	14
and loss for the sake of thy Son our Savior J	168	20
through the same thy Son J Christ our Lord,	169	5
the same thy Son J Christ our Lord;	169	11
for which our Lord J Christ was contented	169	15
through the same J Christ our Lord,	170	18
who through thine only-begotten Son J	170	21
through the same J Christ our Lord,	171	2
who by the glorious resurrection of thy Son J	171	10
through the same thy Son J Christ our Lord,	171	20
through the same J Christ our Lord,	172	5
through the same thy Son J Christ our Lord,	172	12
through the same J Christ our Lord,	173	2
through the same thy Son J Christ our Lord,	173	8
whose Son J is the good shepherd of thy people:	173	11
Grant us so perfectly to know thy Son J Christ	173	17
through J Christ our Lord,	174	5
whose blessed Son our Savior J Christ ascended	174	8
through the same J Christ our Lord,	174	12
believe thy only-begotten Son our Lord J Christ	174	16
exalted thine only Son J Christ with great triumph	175	2
through J Christ our Lord,	175	12
through the merits of Christ J our Savior,	175	19
through J Christ our Lord,	176	11
through J Christ our Lord,	177	7
through J Christ our Lord,	178	3
for the sake of our Savior J Christ,	178	9
J Christ himself being the chief cornerstone:	178	19
through the same J Christ our Lord,	179	1
through J Christ our Lord,	179	8
for the worthiness of thy Son J Christ our Lord;	179	21
through J Christ our Lord,	180	5
through the same thy Son J Christ our Lord,	181	2
through J Christ our Lord,	181	8
through J Christ our Lord,	182	3
but through the merits and mediation of J	183	3
through J Christ our Lord,	183	8
through the same J Christ our Lord,	183	15
through J Christ our Lord,	184	4
thou hast given us in our Savior J Christ;	184	20
Andrew that he readily obeyed the call of thy Son J	185	8
so perfectly and without doubt to believe in J Christ,	185	16
for his persecutors to thy Son J Christ,	186	3
through J Christ our Lord,	186	10
Peter, first among the apostles, to confess J	187	2
follow the one Lord, our Savior J Christ;	187	5
through J Christ our Lord,	187	13
clean hearts by the same thy Son J Christ our Lord;	187	19
through J Christ our Lord,	188	5
through the same thy Son J Christ our Lord,	188	12
we who have known the incarnation of thy Son J	188	16
given to thy Church the Gospel of J Christ	188	22
through the same J Christ our Lord,	189	2
glorify in life and death the Name of our Lord J	189	8
through the same J Christ our Lord	189	15
through J Christ our Lord,	189	21
through the same thy Son J Christ our Lord,	190	7
which is J Christ our Lord;	190	14
through J Christ our Lord,	190	22
martyrdom for the Name of J Christ;	191	9
through the same J Christ our Lord,	191	12
through the same thy Son J Christ our Lord,	192	4
through J Christ our Lord,	192	10
whose Son our Savior J Christ was lifted	192	13
through J Christ our Lord,	193	2
through the same thy Son J Christ our Lord,	193	15
through the same our Lord J Christ,	193	22
love and mercy of our Lord and Savior J Christ;	194	5
through the same J Christ our Lord,	194	13
through J Christ our Lord,	194	21
confess the Name of our Savior J Christ	195	2
for the sake of the same our Lord J Christ;	195	6
through J Christ our Lord,	195	12
through J Christ our Lord,	196	5
unsearchable riches of our Savior J Christ;	196	12
the fullness of our Lord and Savior J	197	1
through the same J Christ our Lord,	197	9
through J Christ our Lord,	197	16
teach the truth as it is in Christ J:	197	21
and J Christ whom thou hast sent;	197	22
through the same thy Son J Christ our Lord,	198	6
through J Christ our Lord,	198	13
through J Christ, the author and perfecter	198	20
through J Christ our Lord,	199	1
We ask this for the sake of J Christ,	199	9
through J Christ our Lord,	200	3
to share our humanity, thy Son J Christ;	200	16
J Christ in a wonderful Sacrament hath left	201	1
death and resurrection of thy Son J Christ,	201	13
through the same J Christ our Lord,	201	16
through J Christ our Lord,	202	6
he may share in the eternal victory of J Christ	202	13
resurrection of thy Son J Christ dost turn	203	6
through the same thy Son J Christ our Lord,	203	9
resurrection of thy Son J Christ,	203	14
through the same J Christ our Lord,	203	16
through J Christ our Lord,	204	5
gave himself for it, thy Son J Christ our Saviour;	204	14
didst send, the same thy Son J Christ our Lord;	205	1
through J Christ our Lord,	205	11
Bishop of our souls, J Christ our Lord,	205	19
through our Lord and Savior J Christ,	206	6
through the same thy Son J Christ our Lord,	206	15
the redeeming work of our Savior J Christ;	206	19
through J Christ our Lord,	207	5
whose Son J Christ in his earthly life	208	1
through J Christ our Lord,	208	6
through J Christ our Lord,	209	6
the same thy Son our Saviour J Christ,	209	15
through J Christ our Lord,	209	21
thy Son J Christ our Lord,	210	7
through J Christ our Lord,	210	16
which your Son J Christ came to visit	211	3

greet with joy the coming of *J* Christ 211 12
through *J* Christ our Lord, 212 4
that your Son *J* Christ, at his coming, may find 212 7
of your only Son *J* Christ: 212 11
through our Lord *J* Christ, 213 5
the holy name of *J* to be the sign of our salvation: 213 14
our Lord *J* Christ; 213 16
your Son *J* Christ; 214 4
through *J* Christ our Lord, 214 10
who at the baptism of *J* in the River 214 12
whose Son our Savior *J* Christ is the light 215 1
through *J* Christ our Lord, 215 5
answer readily the call of our Savior *J* Christ 215 9
to us in your Son our Savior *J* Christ; 216 3
through *J* Christ our Lord, 216 10
Grant this for the sake of your only Son *J* Christ, 216 18
manifested to us in your Son *J* Christ 217 4
through *J* Christ our Lord, 217 11
through *J* Christ your Son our Lord, 218 5
J Christ your Son; 218 10
through *J* Christ our Lord, 218 17
whose blessed Son *J* Christ came down 219 1
through *J* Christ our Lord, 219 11
you sent your Son our Savior *J* Christ 219 14
through *J* Christ your Son our Lord, 220 5
for the sake of your Son our Savior *J* Christ; 220 12
through *J* Christ your Son our Lord, 220 17
in remembrance of *J* Christ our Lord, 221 4
for whom our Lord *J* Christ was willing to be betrayed, 221 9
through *J* Christ your Son our Lord, 222 5
through *J* Christ our Lord, 222 12
who through your only-begotten Son *J* 222 15
through *J* Christ our Lord, 223 1
who by the glorious resurrection of your Son *J* 223 4
through *J* Christ your Son our Lord, 224 4
through *J* Christ our Lord, 224 17
whose Son *J* is the good shepherd of your people: 225 3
to know your Son *J* Christ to be the way, 225 9
through *J* Christ your Son our Lord, 225 11
through *J* Christ our Lord, 225 18
whose blessed Son our Savior *J* Christ 226 1
through *J* Christ our Lord, 226 5
our Lord *J* Christ to have ascended 226 9
J Christ with great triumph to your kingdom 226 14
through *J* Christ our Lord, 227 5
through *J* Christ your Son our Lord, 227 12
through *J* Christ our Lord, 228 11
through *J* Christ our Lord, 229 2
for the sake of our Savior *J* Christ, 230 4
through *J* Christ our Lord, 230 10
J Christ himself being the chief cornerstone: 230 13
through *J* Christ our Lord, 231 2
through *J* Christ our Lord, 232 4
through *J* Christ our Lord, 233 1
through *J* Christ our Lord, 234 4
except through the merits and mediation of *J* 234 17
through *J* Christ our Lord, 235 1
given us in our Savior *J* Christ; 236 12
readily obeyed the call of your Son *J* Christ, 237 2
and without doubt to believe in *J* Christ, 237 10
to your Son *J* Christ, who stands 237 16
through *J* Christ our Lord, 238 5
to confess *J* as Messiah and Son of the living God: 238 15
the one Lord, our Savior *J* Christ; 238 18
through *J* Christ our Lord, 239 3
known the incarnation of your Son *J* Christ, 240 2
given to your Church the Gospel of *J* Christ 240 8
through *J* Christ our Lord, 240 10
glorify in life and death the Name of our Lord *J* 240 16
through *J* Christ our Lord, 241 7
through *J* Christ your Son our Lord, 241 16
which is *J* Christ our Lord; 241 23
through *J* Christ our Lord, 242 5
suffer martyrdom for the Name of *J* Christ; 242 16
through *J* Christ our Lord, 243 11
whose Son our Savior *J* Christ was lifted 244 1
through *J* Christ our Lord, 244 11
through *J* Christ our Lord, 245 1
and mercy of our Lord and Savior *J* Christ; 245 14
through *J* Christ our Lord, 246 6
confess the Name of our Savior *J* Christ 246 9
suffer gladly for the sake of our Lord *J* Christ; 247 3
through *J* Christ our Lord, 247 10
proclaim the unsearchable riches of our Savior *J* 247 24
through *J* Christ our Lord, 248 5
of the fullness of our Lord and Savior *J* Christ; 248 12
through *J* Christ our Lord, 249 2
and teach the truth as it is in Christ *J*: 249 6
and *J* Christ whom you have sent; 249 8
through *J* Christ, the pioneer and perfecter 250 5
through *J* Christ our Lord, 250 12
We ask this for the sake of *J* Christ, 250 19
through *J* Christ our Lord, 251 9
your Son *J* Christ; 252 4
J Christ in a wonderful Sacrament has left 252 6
death and resurrection of your Son *J* Christ, 253 1
through *J* Christ our Lord, 253 4
he may share in the eternal victory of *J* Christ 253 17
death and resurrection of your Son *J* Christ, 254 8
through *J* Christ our Lord, 254 10
through *J* Christ our Lord, 255 3
your Son *J* Christ our Savior; 255 12
your Son *J* Christ our Lord; 255 20
through *J* Christ our Lord, 256 8
and Bishop of our souls, *J* Christ our Lord, 256 16
through our Lord and Savior *J* Christ, 257 3
through *J* Christ our Lord, 257 10
known the redeeming work of our Savior *J* Christ; 257 15
through *J* Christ our Lord, 258 5
through *J* Christ our Lord, 259 1
whose Son *J* Christ in his earthly life 259 3
through *J* Christ our Lord, 260 6
your Son our Savior *J* Christ, 260 20
through *J* Christ our Lord, 261 5
your Son *J* Christ our Lord, 261 12
through *J* Christ our Lord, 264 7
through *J* Christ our Savior. 265 20
the Father of our Lord *J* Christ, 269 3
through *J* Christ our Lord. 269 14
through *J* Christ our Lord. 270 7
through your Son *J* Christ our Lord. 271 6
through *J* Christ our Lord. 272 5
you sent your Son our Savior *J* Christ 272 8

The Passion of our Lord J Christ according to	272	15
remembrance of J Christ our Lord,	274	4
The Lord J, after he had supped	274	8
for whom our Lord J Christ was willing to be betrayed,	276	5
The Passion of our Lord J Christ according to John.	277	1
through our Lord and Savior J Christ.	278	16
through J Christ our Lord.	279	2
your Son J Christ our Lord.	279	18
as you are revealed in your Son J Christ;	280	3
under one shepherd, J Christ our Lord.	280	7
your Son J Christ our Lord;	280	21
Lord J Christ, Son of the living God, we pray	282	6
Lord J passed over from death to life,	285	2
through J Christ our Lord.	285	12
through J Christ his Son our Lord,	286	13
J Christ our Lord;	287	3
your Son J Christ our Lord.	288	8
through J Christ our Lord.	289	4
through J Christ our Lord.	290	6
through J Christ our Lord.	291	3
your Son J Christ our Lord.	291	18
renew your commitment to J Christ?	292	9
Do you believe in J Christ,	293	1
I believe in J Christ,	293	2
the Father of our Lord J Christ,	294	4
in Christ J our Lord.	294	7
through J Christ your Son our Lord,	295	5
through J Christ our Lord,	295	12
The Holy Gospel of our Lord J Christ	300	5
Do you turn to J Christ and accept him	302	16
Do you renew you commitment to J Christ?	303	12
Do you believe in J Christ,	304	4
I believe in J Christ,	304	5
baptized into the death of J Christ	306	6
In it your Son J received the baptism of John	306	16
continue for ever in the risen life of J	307	5
share in the royal priesthood of J Christ;	307	12
death and resurrection of your Son J Christ	309	4
through J Christ your Son our Lord,	309	9
through J Christ our Lord.	310	12
through J Christ your Son our Lord,	311	18
the Father of our Lord J Christ,	311	21
Hear what our Lord J Christ saith:	319	8
J the Son of God, let us come boldly	320	6
For the sake of thy Son J Christ,	320	18
in Christ J our Lord;	321	10
Hear what our Lord J Christ saith:	324	1
O Lord, the only-begotten Son, J Christ;	324	21
The Holy Gospel of our Lord J Christ	326	1
We believe in one Lord, J Christ,	326	10
And in one Lord J Christ,	327	24
Grant these our prayers, O Father, for J Christ's sake,	330	7
Father of our Lord J Christ,	331	2
for thy Son our Lord J Christ's sake,	331	15
through J Christ our Lord.	331	20
For the sake of thy Son J Christ,	331	29
through J Christ our Lord.	332	6
that Christ J came into the world to save sinners.	332	14
J Christ the righteous;	332	15
didst give thine only Son J Christ to suffer death	334	10
institution of thy dearly beloved Son our Savior J	335	9
our Savior J Christ's holy institution,	335	21
death of thy Son J Christ,	335	27
receive the most precious Body and Blood of thy Son J	336	6
through J Christ our Lord;	336	12
so to eat the flesh of thy dear Son J Christ,	337	14
The Body of our Lord J Christ,	338	5
The Blood of our Lord J Christ,	338	9
The Body (Blood) of our Lord J Christ keep you	338	13
Body and Blood of thy Son our Savior J Christ;	339	5
through J Christ our Lord,	339	13
and of his Son J Christ our Lord;	339	17
J Christ to take our nature upon him,	341	15
Body and Blood of thy dearly-beloved Son J	342	19
Body and Blood of thy Son J Christ,	342	26
through the same J Christ the Lord;	343	1
and called us to new life in J Christ our Lord.	344	15
Through J Christ our Lord;	345	1
made us a new people in J Christ our Lord,	345	6
Because thou didst give J Christ,	345	14
in the face of thy Son J Christ our Lord.	346	3
Through J Christ our Lord;	346	4
resurrection of thy Son J Christ our Lord;	346	18
Through thy dearly beloved Son J Christ our Lord;	347	1
Through J Christ our Lord;	347	6
Through the great shepherd of thy flock, J	348	11
Through J Christ our great High Priest;	348	15
Because in J Christ our Lord thou hast received	348	20
thy Son J Christ our Lord;	349	3
Through J Christ our Lord;	349	6
J said, "The first commandment is this:	351	7
J, the Son of God, let us with confidence draw	352	6
For the sake of your Son J Christ,	352	18
through our Lord J Christ,	353	2
Lord J Christ, only Son of the Father,	356	7
you alone are the Most High, J Christ,	356	16
The Holy Gospel of our Lord J Christ	357	8
We believe in one Lord, J Christ,	358	7
For the sake of your Son J Christ,	360	10
through our Lord J Christ,	360	16
you, in your mercy, sent J	362	11
our Lord J Christ took bread;	362	19
All this we ask through your Son J Christ.	363	19
The Body (Blood) of our Lord J Christ keep you	365	4
of your Son our Savior J Christ,	365	11
of your Son our Savior J Christ;	366	4
in the Word made flesh, J, your Son.	368	4
our Lord J Christ took bread;	368	10
through J Christ our Lord,	369	12
Body and Blood of J Christ our Lord.	371	9
God and Father of our Lord J Christ:	372	2
through J Christ our great High Priest,	372	10
Body and Blood of your Son J Christ.	375	8
through your Son J Christ our Lord.	375	25
and called us to new life in J Christ our Lord.	377	13
Through J Christ our Lord;	377	14
made us a new people in J Christ our Lord,	378	2
Because you gave J Christ,	378	9
in the face of your Son J Christ	378	16
Through J Christ our Lord,	379	1
resurrection of your Son J Christ our Lord;	379	15
Through your dearly beloved Son J Christ our Lord.	379	20
Through J Christ our Lord.	380	1

Through the great shepherd of your flock, J	381	5
Through J Christ our great High Priest;	381	9
Because in J Christ our Lord you have received us	381	13
your Son J Christ our Lord;	381	18
Through J Christ our Lord;	382	1
through J Christ our Lord.	393	16
through J Christ our Lord.	394	3
but as you know and love us in your Son J	394	7
grant us for the sake of your Son J Christ our Lord.	395	2
Lord J Christ, you said to your apostles,	395	8
even J Christ, our only Mediator and Advocate.	395	15
ask this for the sake of J Christ,	395	22
J said, "I am the bread of life;	396	4
J said, "I am the living bread	397	1
J said, "Abide in me, as I in you.	397	7
remembrance of J Christ our Lord,	397	16
For the sake of your Son J Christ,	398	2
through our Lord J Christ,	398	8
The Body (Blood) of our Lord J Christ keep you	399	5
Body and Blood of your beloved Son J Christ,	399	9
through J Christ our Lord.	399	11
Body and Blood of J Christ our Lord.	403	3
Communion into one body in your Son J Christ.	403	18
The grace of our Lord J Christ	404	1
our Lord J Christ took bread;	405	2
All this we ask through your Son J Christ.	405	19
(your) Son J Christ our Lord,	408	4
The Holy Gospel of our Lord J Christ	414	5
Do you renew your commitment to J Christ?	415	11
Do you believe in J Christ,	416	9
I believe in J Christ,	416	10
death and resurrection of your Son J Christ	418	2
through J Christ your Son our Lord,	418	7
through J Christ our Lord.	419	8
through J Christ our Lord.	421	6
J Christ adorned this manner of life	423	5
through J Christ our Lord,	425	12
The Holy Gospel of our Lord J Christ	426	1
through J Christ our Lord.	427	12
in sending J Christ to come among us,	430	11
through J Christ our Lord,	430	23
through J Christ our Lord,	431	7
Body and Blood of your Son J Christ.	432	3
for the sake of J Christ our Lord.	432	7
through J Christ our Lord.	434	6
through J Christ our Lord.	441	9
the example of our Lord and Savior, J Christ.	443	29
through J Christ our Lord.	444	7
the knowledge of his Savior J Christ.	445	2
Our Lord J Christ,	448	1
J came into the world to save sinners.	449	19
we have an Advocate with the Father, J	450	1
death by the cross of your Son J Christ.	450	10
your Son our Savior J Christ.	450	21
Our Lord J Christ,	451	6
and are now alive in Christ J	451	18
Our Lord J Christ,	452	1
For the sake of your Son J Christ,	455	1
through our Lord J Christ,	455	7
through J Christ our Lord,	455	13
beseeching our Lord J Christ to sustain you	456	2
in the Name of our Lord and Savior J Christ,	456	8
through J Christ our Lord.	456	18
salvation is the Name of our Lord J Christ.	457	4
Body and Blood of your beloved Son J Christ,	457	7
through J Christ our Lord.	457	9
through J Christ our Lord.	458	10
Lord J Christ, Good Shepherd of the sheep,	459	1
through J Christ our Lord.	459	10
through J Christ our Lord.	460	4
through J Christ our Lord.	461	4
Lord J Christ, by your patience in suffering	461	5
and give me the Spirit of J.	461	25
given in the resurrection of your Son J	462	3
J, Lamb of God:	463	23
J, bearer of our sins:	463	25
J, redeemer of the world:	463	27
In the Name of J Christ who redeemed you;	464	23
It was our Lord J himself who said,	465	9
With faith in J Christ,	466	12
through J Christ our Lord.	467	7
through J Christ thy Son our Lord,	470	4
through the same thy Son J Christ our Lord,	470	11
The Holy Gospel of our Lord J Christ	479	20
share in the victory of thy Son J	481	27
Body and Blood of thy Son J Christ,	482	3
through J Christ our Savior.	482	8
He that raised up J from the dead	485	1
through our Lord J Christ,	485	10
in J the manifold blessings of thy love,	486	10
unto the day of J Christ.	486	12
for the sake of thy Son J Christ our Lord.	486	15
Lord J Christ, the great Shepherd of the sheep,	486	22
through J Christ,	487	3
thy Son J Christ our Lord.	487	9
of the same thy Son J Christ,	487	22
through J Christ our Lord.	488	10
through the merits of J Christ	488	20
through J Christ our Lord.	488	25
through J Christ thy Son our Lord.	489	2
through J Christ our Lord.	489	13
through the merits of thy Son J Christ our Lord.	489	22
O Lord J Christ, Son of the living God, we pray	489	23
who by the glorious resurrection of your Son J	493	4
through J Christ our Lord,	493	13
through J Christ our Lord,	494	4
through J Christ our Lord.	494	12
The Holy Gospel of our Lord J Christ	495	1
I believe in J Christ,	496	5
let us pray to our Lord J	497	1
J Christ, we commend to you our brother (sister)	498	1
Body and Blood of your Son J Christ,	498	14
through J Christ our Savior.	498	19
He who raised J Christ from the dead	501	3
through our Lord J Christ,	501	12
Lord J Christ, the great Shepherd of the sheep,	503	2
through J Christ, to whom be glory	503	5
through your Son J Christ our Lord.	503	11
through J Christ our Lord.	503	19
All this we ask through J Christ our Lord.	504	10
the merits of your Son J Christ our Lord.	504	20
Lord J Christ, by your death you took away	504	21
through J Christ our Lord.	504	29
Merciful God, Father of our Lord J Christ	505	1

through *J* Christ, our Mediator and Redeemer. 505 8
And this we ask in the Name of *J* Christ 505 15
through *J* Christ our Lord. 505 20
Brothers and sisters in Christ *J*, 514 1
your Son *J* Christ our Lord; 515 11
The Holy Gospel of our Lord *J* Christ 516 5
I will, for the sake of Christ *J*. 518 31
We believe in one Lord, *J* Christ, 519 10
God and Father of our Lord *J* Christ, 520 11
bestowed upon your beloved Son *J* Christ, 521 3
through *J* Christ your Son, 521 15
through *J* Christ your Son our Lord, 523 8
your Son *J* Christ our Lord; 528 9
The Holy Gospel of our Lord *J* Christ 529 4
We believe in one Lord, *J* Christ, 530 1
the Gospel of *J* Christ, 531 9
mediation of *J* Christ, 532 27
J our Lord, who is the image 533 3
through *J* Christ your Son, 533 11
this we ask through *J* Christ our Lord, 534 8
through *J* Christ your Son our Lord, 535 8
your Son *J* Christ our Lord; 540 9
The Holy Gospel of our Lord *J* Christ 541 4
We believe in one Lord, *J* Christ, 542 1
every Christian is called to follow *J* Christ, 543 1
In the name of *J* Christ, 543 4
praise you for sending your Son *J* Christ, 545 2
through *J* Christ your Son, 545 9
through *J* Christ your Son our Lord, 547 4
J Christ our Lord. 552 12
grant that together they may follow *J* Christ, 560 8
of your Son our Savior *J* Christ. 563 10
through *J* Christ your Son our Lord, 564 8
through *J* Christ our Lord. 567 12
Lord *J* Christ, make this a temple of your presence 568 14
In it your Son *J* received the baptism of John 570 8
in the risen life of *J* Christ our Savior. 570 20
through *J* Christ, our Mediator and Advocate. 572 12
through *J* Christ our Lord. 573 6
you sent your Son *J* Christ to be born 573 9
thy Son *J* Christ our Lord. 814 5
And this we beg for *J* Christ's sake. 815 12
through *J* your Son: 815 14
through *J* Christ our Lord. 815 20
become the kingdom of our Lord and Savior *J* Christ. 816 4
through *J* Christ our Lord. 816 9
of *J* Christ thy Son our Savior. 816 15
through your Son *J* Christ: 816 17
our Advocate and Mediator, *J* Christ. 817 9
through *J* Christ our Lord. 817 17
through *J* Christ our Lord. 818 6
O God the Father of our Lord *J* Christ, 818 14
through the teaching of your Son *J* Christ: 819 2
through *J* Christ our Lord. 819 5
O Lord *J* Christ, you became poor for our sake, 819 6
through *J* Christ our Lord. 820 15
through *J* Christ our Lord. 821 7
thy Son our Savior *J* Christ. 821 14
through *J* Christ our Lord. 822 21
through *J* Christ our Lord. 823 7
This we ask for the sake of *J* 823 15
through *J* Christ our Lord. 824 4
through *J* Christ our Lord. 825 5
J Christ our Lord. 826 7
Lord *J*, for our sake you were condemned 826 16
through *J* Christ our Lord. 827 5
to the honor of *J* Christ our Lord. 827 10
in the name of *J* Christ our Lord. 827 16
who by thy Son *J* Christ hast promised 828 9
through *J* Christ our Lord. 828 14
through *J* Christ our Lord. 829 8
following the example of our Savior *J* Christ. 829 13
This we ask in the name of *J* Christ 830 6
through *J* Christ our Lord. 830 11
through *J* Christ our Lord. 831 6
through *J* Christ our Lord. 832 5
through our Lord and Savior *J* Christ. 833 4
through *J* Christ our Lord. 833 23
through *J* Christ our Lord. 834 7
Be present, be present, O *J*, our great High Priest, 834 8
O Lord *J* Christ, who in a wonderful Sacrament 834 12
by the resurrection of your Son *J* Christ 835 1
through the same *J* Christ our Lord. 835 7
we thank you for your Son *J* Christ; 836 12
promises given to us in Christ *J* our Lord; 837 22
you sent your Son *J* Christ to reconcile 838 1
through *J* Christ our Lord, 838 19
we ask in the Name of *J* Christ our Lord. 839 26
through *J* Christ our Lord. 840 6
for the sake of your dear Son, *J* Christ our Lord. 841 6
through *J* Christ our Lord. 841 13
The Messiah, or Christ, is *J* of Nazareth, 849 17
What do we mean when we say that *J* is 849 19
We mean that *J* is the only perfect image 849 21
What is the nature of God revealed in *J*? 849 23
What do we mean when we say that *J* was 849 25
What is the great importance of *J*' suffering 850 5
By his obedience, even to suffering and death, *J* 850 7
What is the significance of *J*' resurrection? 850 10
By his resurrection, *J* overcame death 850 11
We mean that *J* took our human nature 850 19
given by *J* Christ, the Messiah, to the apostles; 850 28
confess *J* Christ as Lord 852 27
set forth the life and teachings of *J* 853 17
The Church is described as the Body of which *J* 854 6
our Lord *J* Christ. 854 16
through *J* Christ, in the power of the Holy Spirit. 856 22
and accept *J* as our Lord and Savior. 858 23
their confession of *J* Christ as Savior and Lord. 860 26
which is in Christ *J* our Lord. 862 32

John

teaching of thine apostle and evangelist *J*, 186 8
by whose providence thy servant *J* the Baptist 190 1
teaching of your apostle and evangelist *J*, 238 3
by whose providence your servant *J* the Baptist 241 10
The Passion of our Lord Jesus Christ according to *J*. 277 1
In it your Son Jesus received the baptism of *J* 306 17
Gospel of our Lord Jesus Christ according to *J*. 479 21
Gospel of our Lord Jesus Christ according to *J*. 495 2
In it your Son Jesus received the baptism of *J* 570 9

join

Let us *j* with those who are committing themselves 303 17
And so we *j* the saints and angels in proclaiming 402 7
And so we *j* the saints and angels in proclaiming 404 9
Let us *j* with those who are committing themselves 416 4
I bid you, therefore, to *j* 440 4
I bid you *j* with them 440 10
and to *j* in ordaining bishops; 440 10
They shall *j* the company of their forebears, * 653 21

joined

Grant us so to be *j* together 178 20
Grant us so to be *j* together 230 14
when earth and heaven are *j* 287 21
holy union N.N. and N.N. now come to be *j*. 424 1
Those whom God has *j* together let no one 428 6
now *j* in Holy Matrimony, 432 4
Those whom God has *j* together let no one put 434 7
they may not be *j* together in Holy Matrimony, 437 3
when we are *j* in marriage, 569 7
The Assyrians also have *j* them, * 706 18
They *j* themselves to Baal-Peor * 744 3

joining

j our voices with Angels and Archangels 362 1
j our voices with Angels and Archangels 367 10
j with the heavenly chorus, 370 23
Joining with them, and giving voice 373 9
bless the *j* together of this man and this woman 423 2
solemn vows, with the *j* of hands 428 2

joint

all my bones are out of *j*; * 611 6

Jordan

J didst proclaim him thy beloved Son 163 2
J proclaimed him your beloved Son 214 13
therefore I will remember you from the land of *J*, 643 19
J turned and went back. 757 2
O *J*, that you turned back? 757 6

Joseph

raise up *J* to be the guardian of thy incarnate Son 188 9
raised up *J* to be the guardian of your incarnate Son 239 18
the children of Jacob and *J*. 694 4
He rejected the tent of *J* * 700 13
Hear, O Shepherd of Israel, leading *J* like a flock; * 702 12
He laid it as a solemn charge upon *J*, * 704 9
J, who was sold as a slave. 739 12

Joshua

for Miriam and *J*, Deborah and Gideon, 838 12

journey

and bring them in safety to their *j*'s end; 831 5

journeys

You trace my *j* and my resting-places * 794 4

joy

I bring you good tidings of great *j*, 37 8
whose most dear Son went not up to *j* 56 6
May the God of hope fill us with all *j* and peace 60 1
May the God of hope fill us with all *j* and peace 73 1
I bring you good news of a great *j* 75 8
let us shout for *j* to the Rock of our salvation. 82 6
Cry aloud, inhabitants of Zion, ring out your *j*, * 86 13
Let your people sing with *j*. 97 21
whose most dear Son went not up to *j* 99 1
May the God of hope fill us with all *j* and peace 102 12
truly, they are the *j* of my heart. 104 10
and our tongue with shouts of *j*. 105 7
will reap with songs of *j*. 105 15
will come again with *j*, shouldering their sheaves. 105 17
Let your people sing with *j*. 121 21
May the God of hope fill us with all *j* and peace 126 12
our *j* may abound in the morning 134 3
Give me the *j* of your saving help again * 137 7
that we may greet with *j* the coming of Jesus Christ 159 12
whose most dear Son went not up to *j* 168 10
evermore live with him in the *j* of his resurrection; 170 11
Grant that we, who celebrate with *j* 170 23
with him attain to thine eternal *j*; 198 20
become partakers of their *j*; 199 1
enter with them into thine unending *j*; 202 6
and be filled with thy *j* and peace; 204 5
that we may greet with *j* the coming of Jesus Christ 211 12
whose most dear Son went not up to *j* 220 1
evermore live with him in the *j* of his resurrection; 222 4
Grant that we, who celebrate with *j* 222 17
attain to your eternal *j*; 250 5
become partakers of their *j*; 250 11
enter with them into your unending *j*; 253 10
and be filled with your *j* and peace; 255 3
Make me hear of *j* and gladness, * 266 18
Give me the *j* of your saving help again * 266 26
Bring us with all your saints to the *j* 269 2
so that at the last we may come to his eternal *j*; 269 13
that we may enter with *j* upon the contemplation 270 5
whose most dear Son went not up to *j* 272 1
into the fullness of the *j* of our Lord, 280 12
j has come to the whole world. 281 4
It restores innocence to the fallen, and *j* 287 18
may come to the *j* of that heavenly Jerusalem, 290 4
live with him in the *j* of his resurrection; 295 5
and the gift of *j* and wonder in all your works. 308 7
prepare with *j* for the Paschal feast; 346 9
and in their eternal *j* a glorious pledge 348 5
into the *j* of your eternal kingdom. 363 18
to the sorrowful, *j*. 374 5
the place of eternal *j* and light.] 375 20
prepare with *j* for the Paschal feast; 379 6
and in their eternal *j* a glorious pledge 380 21
We praise you for your saints who have entered into *j*; 387 19
bring them the *j* of your salvation. 389 5
they may live in *j*, peace, and health, we pray 391 12
may with *j* behold thy Son at his coming 395 14
intended by God for their mutual *j*; 423 10
and a companion in *j*. 429 10
forgiveness heal guilt, and *j* conquer despair. 429 19
Confirm their *j* by a lively sense of your presence 443 25
and a companion in *j*. 444 12
and our sorrow into *j*; 458 14
That it may please you to give him *j* and gladness 463 20
Let his heart and soul now ring out in *j* to you, 466 10
entrance into the land of light and *j*, 470 3
but the fullness of *j* with all thy saints; 482 7

in thy presence is the fullness of *j*, 485 7
are in *j* and felicity: 488 4
entrance into the land of light and *j*, 493 12
but the fullness of *j* with all your saints; 498 18
in your presence there is fullness of *j*, 501 9
are in *j* and felicity: 503 14
Your *j* will be to follow him who came, 517 16
may grow closer to you through *j* 569 4
in times of *j* and sorrow. 572 2
they will sing out their *j* for ever. 589 18
in your presence there is fullness of *j*, 600 20
We will shout for *j* at your victory 608 9
and will make him glad with the *j* of your presence. 609 8
Therefore my heart dances for *j*, * 619 26
but *j* comes in the morning. 621 15
you have put off my sack-cloth and clothed me with *j*. 622 4
shout for *j*, all who are true of heart. 625 26
Let those who favor my cause sing out with *j* 631 27
to the God of my *j* and gladness; * 644 25
With *j* and gladness they are brought, * 648 21
shout to God with a cry of *j*. 650 7
Beautiful and lofty, the *j* of all the earth, 651 3
Make me hear of *j* and gladness, * 656 22
Give me the *j* of your saving help again * 657 5
you make the dawn and the dusk to sing for *j*. 673 3
and the hills be clothed with *j*. 673 14
let them shout for *j* and sing. 673 17
Let the nations be glad and sing for *j*, * 675 15
My lips will sing with *j* when I play to you, * 685 4
Sing with *j* to God our strength * 704 1
and I shout for *j* because of the works of your hands. 721 4
let us shout for *j* to the Rock of our salvation. 724 15
Then shall all the trees of the wood shout for *j* 726 17
Shout with *j* to the LORD all you lands; * 728 10
shout with *j* before the King, the LORD. 728 15
and let the hills ring out with *j* before the LORD, 728 19
his chosen with shouts of *j*. 741 12
and tell of his acts with shouts of *j*. 747 26
truly, they are the *j* of my heart. 772 16
and our tongue with shouts of *j*. 782 9
will reap with songs of *j*. 782 17
will come again with *j*, shouldering their sheaves. 782 19
let your faithful people sing with *j*. 786 16
if I do not set Jerusalem above my highest *j*. 792 14
turn their sorrow into *j*. 826 6
blessed us with the *j* and care of children: 829 10
and to keep alive their *j* in your creation; 829 20
where there is sadness, *j*. 833 9
in the *j* of fully knowing and loving God 862 27

joyful

O be *j* in the Lord all ye lands; * 45 11
And make thy chosen people *j*. 55 4
And make thy chosen people *j*. 67 19
Be *j* in the Lord, all you lands; * 82 20
receive him more and more into thy *j* service, 202 12
receive him more and more into your *j* service, 253 16
Therefore in *j* obedience to your Son, 306 23
It is right, and a good and *j* thing, 361 7
It is right, and a good and *j* thing, 367 7
in offering heartfelt thanks for the *j* 440 12
to our *j* resurrection. 480 11
in the *j* expectation of eternal life 481 12
hear that his most *j* voice: 487 19
and in the *j* expectation of eternal life 505 14
j obedience to your Son, 570 15
my heart is *j* because of your saving help. 598 9
Then I will be *j* in the LORD; * 630 8
and my mouth praises you with *j* lips, 670 22
Be *j* in God, all you lands; * 673 18
let them also be merry and *j*. 676 7
let the field be *j* and all that is therein. 726 16
and *j* gladness for those who are truehearted. 727 21
Be *j* in the LORD, all you lands; * 729 22
to be a *j* mother of children. 756 17
let the children of Zion be *j* in their King. 807 5
let them be *j* on their beds. 807 11

joyfully

j receive him for our Redeemer, 160 14
to take *j* the sufferings of the present time, 169 3
may *j* serve thee in confidence and serenity; 177 11
j receive him as our Redeemer, 212 11
j the sufferings of the present time, 220 16
may *j* serve you in confidence and serenity; 229 7

joyous

shield the *j*; 71 5
shield the *j*; 124 21
shield the *j*; 134 10
The birth of a child is a *j* and solemn occasion 440 1

joys

be fixed where true *j* are to be found; 167 20
attain to everlasting *j*; 171 7
so by his love he may raise us to *j* eternal; 172 18
those ineffable *j* which thou hast prepared 194 12
be fixed where true *j* are to be found; 219 10
attain to everlasting *j*; 223 1
so by his love he may raise us to eternal *j*; 224 11
those ineffable *j* that you have prepared 245 20
in their *j* and in their sorrows; 430 21
and obtain those eternal *j* prepared for all 432 6
in his *j* and in his sorrows. 444 21
bring our brother (sister) to the *j* of heaven. 497 14

jubilant

they are *j* in your righteousness. 714 26

Judaea

and in all *J*, and in Samaria, 39 20

Judah

and the cities of *J* rejoice, * 651 24
Ephraim is my helmet and *J* my scepter. 667 24
the princes of *J* in a company; * 678 12
For God will save Zion and rebuild the cities of *J*; * 682 7
In *J* is God known; * 692 1
He chose instead the tribe of *J* * 700 15
Zion hears and is glad, and the cities of *J* rejoice, * 727 12
Ephraim is my helmet and *J* my scepter. 750 11
J became God's sanctuary * 756 21

Judas

who into the place of *J* didst choose 188 1
who in the place of *J* chose 239 11

Jude
and especially on this day for Simon and *J*; 194 2
and especially on this day for Simon and *J*; 245 11

Judea
and in all *J*, and Samaria, and to the ends 77 19

judge
For he cometh, for he cometh to *j* the earth, * 45 8
and with righteousness to *j* the world 45 9
We believe that thou shalt come to be our *j*. 53 18
he shall come to *j* the quick and the dead. 54 4
he shall come to *j* the quick and the dead. 66 20
We believe that you will come and be our *j*. 96 8
He will come again to *j* the living and the dead. 96 24
He will come again to *j* the living and the dead. 120 20
he shall come again in his glorious majesty to *j* 159 5
when he shall come to be our *J*; 160 15
to *j* both the living and the 211 5
behold him when he comes to be our *J*; 212 13
He will come again to *j* the living and the dead. 293 11
He will come again to *j* the living and the dead. 304 14
J yourselves, therefore, lest you be judged 316 26
to *j* the living and the dead, 327 10
to *j* both the quick and the dead; 328 11
maker of all things, *j* of all men: 331 3
and great triumph to *j* the world, 345 11
to *j* the living and the dead, 359 1
and great triumph to *j* the world, 378 7
He will come again to *j* the living and the dead. 416 19
thou most worthy *J* eternal. 484 15
O worthy and eternal *J*, 492 18
He will come again to *j* the living and the dead. 496 14
to *j* the living and the dead, 520 1
to *j* the living and the dead, 530 20
to *j* the living and the dead, 542 20
to *j*, to illumine and to bless your people. 568 13
O LORD, *j* the nations. 591 11
God is a righteous *j*; * 591 20
for God himself is *j*. 654 15
do you *j* the peoples with equity? 664 22
for you *j* the peoples with equity 675 16
"I will *j* with equity. 691 7
"How long will you *j* unjustly, * 705 11
Rise up, O *J* of the world; * 722 20
he will *j* the peoples with equity." 726 13
when he comes to *j* the earth. 726 19
He will *j* the world with righteousness * 726 20
when he comes to *j* the earth. 728 20
In righteousness shall he *j* the world * 728 21
through him who shall come to be our *J*, 821 13
Christ, our merciful and righteous *J*. 823 16
O *J* of the nations, we remember before you 839 21
in glory and *j* the living and the dead. 862 14

judged
Judge yourselves, therefore, lest you be *j* 316 26
let them be *j* before you. 594 16
When he is *j*, let him be found guilty, * 751 10

judgements
all right *j*, and all just works: 123 16

judges
he *j* the peoples with equity. 593 16
It is God who *j*; * 691 16
To the *J* and officers of our Courts give understanding 822 6

judging
you sit upon your throne *j* right. 593 8
who sittest in the throne *j* right: 821 8

judgment
not be condemned before the great *j* seat 68 19
not be condemned before the great *j* seat 122 21
and in the day of *j*, 149 27
to have a right *j* in all things, 175 17
to have a right *j* in all things, 227 10
and upright in your *j*. 266 11
between your *j* and our souls, 282 7
Blessed are they that alway keep *j*, * 478 15
between thy *j* and our souls, 489 24
the wicked shall not stand upright when *j* comes, * 585 13
Give *j* for me according to my righteousness, 591 12
God sits in *j* every day. 591 21
he has set up his throne for *j*. 593 14
Give *j* for me, O LORD, 616 7
Give *j* for me, O God, 644 14
to witness the *j* of his people. 654 10
and upright in your *j*. 656 15
For *j* is neither from the east nor from the west, * 691 14
From heaven you pronounced *j*; * 692 16
When God rose up to *j* * 692 18
he gives *j* in the midst of the gods: 705 10
For *j* will again be just, * 723 23
and *j* for all who are oppressed. 733 20
when will you give *j* against those who persecute me? 770 10
For there are the thrones of *j*, * 780 5
Enter not into *j* with your servant, * 798 21
To inflict on them the *j* decreed; * 807 18
Visit our jails and prisons with your pity and *j*. 826 17
by whom the meek are guided in *j*, 832 6
What do we mean by the last *j*? 862 13

judgments
to keep your righteous *j*. 103 9
and teach me your *j*. 104 4
For all false *j*, 268 20
your *j* are far above out of their sight; * 595 2
For all his *j* are before my eyes, * 604 7
the *j* of the LORD are true 607 14
because of your *j*. 651 25
and do not walk according to my *j*; 716 2
because of your *j*, O LORD. 727 13
his wonders and the *j* of his mouth, 738 10
his *j* prevail in all the world. 738 14
when I have learned your righteous *j*. 763 18
all the *j* of your mouth. 764 10
with longing for your *j*. 764 24
I have set your *j* before me. 765 20
because your *j* are good. 766 14
for my hope is in your *j*. 766 22
When I remember your *j* of old, * 767 17
because of your righteous *j*. 768 12
I know, O LORD, that your *j* are right * 769 14
I do not shrink from your *j*, * 771 23

to keep your righteous *j*. 772 6
and teach me your *j*. 772 10
I am afraid of your *j*. 773 14
and upright are your *j*. 774 22
according to your *j*, give me life. 776 2
preserve my life, according to your *j*. 776 16
all your righteous *j* endure for evermore. 776 24
because of your righteous *j*. 777 8
and let your *j* help me. 778 6
his statutes and his *j* to Israel. 805 16
to them he has not revealed his *j*. 805 18

just

God is faithful and *j* to forgive us our sins, 38 12
and all *j* works do proceed: 69 17
God, who is faithful and *j*, will forgive our sins 76 11
because your *j* and holy works have been revealed. 94 18
judgements, and all *j* works: 123 16
James the *J*, brother of our Lord, 193 19
and to the spirits of *j* men 198 24
and a *j* return for our labor; 208 5
James the *J*, brother of our Lord, 245 5
and to the spirits of *j* men made perfect: 250 9
and a *j* return for our labor; 259 7
God is faithful and *j* to forgive us our sins, 320 3
God, who is faithful and *j*, will forgive our sins 352 3
For the *j* and proper use of your creation; 392 7
If any of you can show *j* cause 424 2
If any of you know *j* cause 437 2
to love all that is true and noble, *j* and pure, 443 27
and the *j* shall see his face. 596 26
The statutes of the LORD are *j* 607 8
and a *j* reward from the God of their salvation." 613 24
and give them their *j* deserts. 619 17
it is good for the *j* to sing praises. 626 2
"Aha! *j* what we want!" * 631 22
and your *j* dealing as the noonday. 633 16
you have tried us *j* as silver is tried. 674 14
give the arrogant their *j* deserts. 722 21
For judgment will again be *j*, * 723 23
They conspire against the life of the *j* * 724 7
I have done what is *j* and right; * 773 15
land allotted to the *j*, * 781 23
so that the *j* shall not put their hands to evil. 781 24
and receive *j* payment for their labor; 824 14
whatever is *j* and true and good, 829 12
give us a *j* sense of these great mercies, 840 20
and to meet their *j* demands; 848 6

justice

And guide us in the way of *j* and truth. 55 8
And guide us in the way of *j* and truth. 67 23
And guide us in the way of *j* and truth. 98 2
And guide us in the way of *j* and truth. 122 2
that they may do *j*, and love mercy, 150 27
and minister thy *j* with compassion; 178 9
and establish thy rule of *j*, love, and peace; 186 17
the people of our country a zeal for *j* 207 3
j in our communities and among the nations, 209 5
and minister your *j* with compassion; 230 3
establish your rule of *j*, love, and peace; 238 11
Give to the people of our country a zeal for *j* 258 3
help us to employ it in the maintenance of *j* 260 11
That by God's help they may seek *j* and truth, 278 23
Will you strive for *j* and peace 294 1
Will you strive for *j* and peace 305 7
Pray for *j* and peace. 386 3
That there may be *j* and peace on the earth. 387 11
in the ways of *j* and peace; 388 8
that they may serve *j*, 390 17
For all who work for *j*, freedom, and peace. 392 6
Will you strive for *j* and peace 417 17
that they may serve *j* 550 2
Awake, O my God, decree *j*; * 591 8
The LORD is known by his acts of *j*; * 594 9
To give *j* to the orphan and oppressed, * 596 5
let your eyes be fixed on *j*. 601 2
He loves righteousness and *j*; * 626 9
Give me *j*, O LORD my God, 631 18
your *j* like the great deep; * 632 15
For the LORD loves *j*; * 635 16
and for the sake of *j*. 647 20
your right hand is full of *j*. 651 22
Give the King your *j*, O God, * 685 9
and the poor with *j*; 685 12
Righteousness and *j* are the foundations 714 21
righteousness and *j* are the foundations 726 26
"O mighty King, lover of *j*, 729 5
you have executed *j* and righteousness in Jacob." 729 7
I will sing of mercy and *j*; * 730 7
Happy are those who act with *j* * 742 1
The works of his hands are faithfulness and *j*; * 754 18
and to manage their affairs with *j*. 755 14
with *j* and in perfect faithfulness. 775 2
Your *j* is an everlasting *j* * 775 9
For the LORD gives his people *j* * 789 3
and render *j* to the needy. 796 26
Who gives *j* to those who are oppressed, * 803 15
into the way of *j* and truth, 816 2
that there may be *j* and peace at home, 820 10
humbly beseech thee to bless the courts of *j* 821 9
that human rights may be safeguarded and *j* served. 822 8
the spirit of wisdom, charity, and *j*; 822 19
we may live in *j* and peace; 823 21
in the midst of our struggles for *j* and truth, 824 2
with righteousness, and *j* with order, 825 12
and teach us to improve our *j*. 826 21
For all valiant seekers after truth, liberty, and *j*, 837 17
to love *j*, to do mercy, 847 5
j, freedom, and the necessities of life 848 13
proclaims the Gospel, and promotes *j*, 855 6

justification

and to rise again for our *j*: 172 9
and to rise for our *j*: 224 2

justified

And so you are *j* when you speak * 266 10
And so you are *j* when you speak * 656 14
for in your sight shall no one living be *j*. 798 22

justly

all those evils that we most *j* have deserved; 155 9
provoking most *j* thy wrath and indignation 331 8
who for our sins art *j* displeased? 484 7
who by our sins are *j* angered. 492 8

K

Kadesh
the LORD shakes the wilderness of *K*. 620 20

Kedar
and dwell among the tents of *K*! 778 19

keep
let all the earth *k* silence 40 18
therefore let us *k* the feast, 46 3
Lord, *k* this nation under thy care; 55 7
Vouchsafe, O Lord, to *k* us this day without sin; 55 19
incline our hearts to *k* thy law, 56 20
Lord, *k* this nation under thy care; 67 22
K watch, dear Lord, with those who work, 71 1
let all the earth *k* silence 78 17
and by the power of the Holy Spirit *k* you 80 3
therefore let us *k* the feast, 83 12
Lord, *k* this nation under your care; 98 1
Lord, *k* us from all sin today; 98 13
incline our hearts to *k* your law, 99 15
to *k* your righteous judgments. 103 9
it is he who shall *k* you safe. 104 26
k us from every sin, 113 6
The Lord bless you and *k* you. 114 1
and by the power of the Holy Spirit *k* you 117 8
Lord, *k* this nation under your care; 122 1
K watch, dear Lord, with those who work, 124 17
Be my strong rock, a castle to *k* me safe, 129 13
to *k* you in all your ways. 130 20
K us, O Lord, as the apple of your eye; 132 14
K watch, dear Lord, with those who work, 134 6
bless us and *k* us. 135 15
O God, you will *k* in perfect peace 138 9
bless us and *k* us. 140 18
That it may please thee to bless and *k* all thy people, 150 10
may *k* the covenant they have made, 163 4
K us both outwardly in our bodies 167 4
k us steadfast in this faith and worship, 176 5
k us, we beseech thee, from all things that may hurt 177 4
K, O Lord, we beseech thee, thy household 178 6
who hast taught us to *k* all thy commandments 179 4
K thy Church steadfast upon the rock of this faith, 187 3
may *k* the covenant they have made, 214 15
K us both outwardly in our bodies 218 14
K us steadfast in this faith and worship, 228 4
in your goodness *k* us, 228 14
K, O Lord, your household 230 1
you have taught us to *k* all your commandments 230 19
K your Church steadfast upon the rock of this faith, 238 16
k us in eternal life by his grace, 294 6
K them in the faith and communion 305 21
bless, preserve, and *k* you. 310 4
and *k* him safe for ever. 314 5
and incline our hearts to *k* this law. 317 29
Remember that thou *k* holy the Sabbath day. 318 10
Therefore let us *k* the feast. 337 2
The Body (Blood) of our Lord Jesus Christ *k* you 338 13
k your hearts and minds in the knowledge 339 15
Remember the Sabbath day and *k* it holy. 350 9
and by the power of the Holy spirit *k* you 353 3
and by the power of the Holy Spirit *k* you 360 17
Therefore let us *k* the feast. 364 16
The Body (Blood) of our Lord Jesus Christ *k* you 365 4
and by the power of the Holy Spirit *k* you 398 9
The Body (Blood) of our Lord Jesus Christ *k* you 399 5
bless, preserve, and *k* you. 418 20
comfort him, honor and *k* him, 424 10
comfort her, honor and *k* her, 424 16
honor and *k* the promises and vows they make; 425 11
bless, preserve, and *k* you; 431 10
love her, comfort her, honor and *k* her, 433 6
love him, comfort him, honor and *k* him, 433 11
k you in peace. 445 8
and by the power of the Holy Spirit *k* you 451 5
and by the power of the Holy Spirit *k* you 455 8
k me in that perfect peace 461 13
among such as *k* holy-day. 471 11
yea, it is even he that shall *k* thy soul. 473 22
Blessed are they that alway *k* judgment, * 478 15
bless him and *k* him, 485 13
K me as the apple of your eye; * 601 14
Above all, *k* your servant from presumptuous sins; 607 24
to those who *k* his covenant and his testimonies. 615 9
For in the day of trouble he shall *k* me safe 618 1
Be my strong rock, a castle to *k* me safe, 622 12
you *k* them in your shelter from the strife of tongues. 624 10
K your tongue from evil-speaking * 628 19
He will *k* safe all his bones; * 629 7
Wait upon the LORD and *k* his way; * 636 3
I said, "I will *k* watch upon my ways, * 638 15
let your love and your faithfulness *k* me safe for ever, 641 3
among those who *k* holy-day. 643 12
Our God will come and will not *k* silence; * 654 6
but to those who *k* in my way will I show 656 3
his eyes *k* watch over the nations; * 674 7
Be my strong rock, a castle to *k* me safe; * 683 5
and the remnant of Hamath will *k* your feasts. 692 21
Make a vow to the LORD your God and *k* it; * 692 22
but *k* his commandments; 695 15
They did not *k* the covenant of God, * 695 22
and did not *k* his commandments. 699 19
do not *k* still nor hold your peace, O God; 706 4
K watch over my life, for I am faithful; * 710 1
I will *k* my love for him for ever, * 715 22
and do not *k* my commandments; 716 4
to *k* you in all your ways. 720 8
nor will he *k* his anger for ever. 733 26
On those who *k* his covenant * 734 18
That they might *k* his statutes * 741 15
that we should fully *k* them. 763 12
that I might *k* your statutes! 763 14
I will *k* your statutes; * 763 19
that I may live and *k* your word. 764 18
and I shall *k* it to the end. 766 2
Give me understanding, and I shall *k* your law; * 766 3
I shall *k* it with all my heart. 766 4
I shall continue to *k* your law; * 767 1
I shall *k* it for ever and ever. 767 2
I have promised to *k* your words. 768 2
to *k* your commandments. 768 8
and of those who *k* your commandments. 768 14

but now I *k* your word. 768 22
but I will *k* your commandments 769 2
they do not *k* your law. 770 13
that I may *k* the decrees of your mouth. 770 19
that I may *k* your word. 771 22
to *k* your righteous judgments. 772 6
I will *k* the commandments of my God. 773 4
and I will *k* your commandments. 774 16
because people do not *k* your law. 774 20
answer me, O Lord, that I may *k* your statutes. 775 16
I will *k* your decrees. 775 19
it is he who shall *k* you safe. 779 14
If your children *k* my covenant 786 23
Though I walk in the midst of trouble, you *k* me safe; 793 16
K me, O Lord, from the hands of the wicked; * 796 7
Lord, *k* this nation under your care. 821 18
k them humane and compassionatac; 826 22
and to *k* alive their joy in your creation; 829 20
to believe in him and to *k* his commandments. 851 5

keeper

The Lord himself is thy *k*; * 473 17

keepeth

and he that *k* thee will not sleep. 473 14
Behold, he that *k* Israel * 473 15

keeping

that in *k* thy commandments we may please thee 164 14
but still more blessed in *k* thy word: 189 13
that in *k* your commandments we may please you 216 9
but still more blessed in *k* your word: 240 20
and in *k* them there is great reward. 607 21
By *k* to your words. 764 2
k all the men and women of our armed forces 823 2

keeps

Behold, he who *k* watch over Israel * 104 19
The Lord preserves them and *k* them alive, 642 1
Behold, he who *k* watch over Israel * 779 7
in vain the watchman *k* his vigil. 783 2
who *k* his promise for ever; 803 14

kept

For I have *k* the ways of the Lord * 604 5
and have *k* myself from iniquity; 604 10
and *k* me safe upon my mother's breast. 610 19
They shall be *k* safe for ever, * 635 18
These things you have done, and I *k* still, * 655 22
In vain have I *k* my heart clean, * 688 3
they *k* his testimonies and the decree 729 15
the righteous will be *k* in everlasting remembrance. 755 16
for I have *k* your decrees. 765 4
because I have *k* your commandments. 767 26
for they have not *k* your word. 776 20
I have *k* your decrees * 777 13
I have *k* your commandments and decrees, * 777 15

keys

receive these *k*, and let the doors of this place 562 1

kill

and seek occasion to *k* them. 635 27
and sought to *k* the brokenhearted. 752 3

killed

Indeed, for your sake we are *k* all the day long; * 647 1
He *k* their vines with hail * 698 21

kind

neither run into any *k* of danger; 57 10
in danger, sorrow, or any *k* of trouble; 392 9
Answer me, O Lord, for your love is *k*; * 680 23
k to all the creatures of God; 848 10

kindle

be our companion in the way, *k* our hearts, 70 11
k within us the fire 111 4
be our companion in the way, *k* our hearts, 124 8
be our companion in the way, *k* our hearts, 139 17
k, we beseech thee, in every heart 207 8
k, we pray, in every heart 258 8
k, we pray, in every heart 278 25

kindled

who *k* the flame of your love 247 13
k with the flame of your love, 249 18
for his wrath is quickly *k*. 586 27
a fire was *k* against Jacob, 696 18
Therefore the wrath of the Lord was *k* 745 3
that with steadfast thoughts and *k* affections 833 22

kindly

that we may evermore be *k* affectioned 829 7

kindness

slow to anger and of great *k*, 38 16
for all thy goodness and loving-*k* 58 17
for all thy goodness and loving-*k* 71 13
for all your goodness and loving-*k* 101 9
for all your goodness and loving-*k* 125 7
set upon the sure foundation of thy loving-*k*; 178 15
set upon the sure foundation of your loving-*k*; 230 9
according to your loving-*k*; * 266 2
O God, is your mercy and loving-*k* to us, 287 15
for the loving-*k* of God, 383 3
Lord, let your loving-*k* be upon them; 393 6
O God, according to your loving-*k*; 449 1
Surely thy loving-*k* and mercy shall follow me 476 16
Show me your marvelous loving-*k*, * 601 11
he shows loving-*k* to his anointed, 606 13
because of the loving-*k* of the Most High, 609 10
and in your loving-*k* save me." 623 26
the loving-*k* of the Lord fills the whole earth. 626 10
Let your loving-*k*, O Lord, be upon us, * 627 19
Continue your loving-*k* to those who know you, * 632 24
The Lord grants his loving-*k* in the daytime; * 643 23
We have waited in silence on your loving-*k*, 651 18
O God, according to your loving-*k*; * 656 6
For your loving-*k* is greater than the heavens, * 664 17
For your loving-*k* is better than life itself; * 670 17
Has his loving-*k* come to an end for ever? * 693 16
slow to anger, and full of *k* and truth. 711 5
Will your loving-*k* be declared in the grave? * 712 25
Satisfy us by your loving-*k* in the morning; * 719 1
To tell of your loving-*k* early in the morning * 720 24
and crowns you with mercy and loving-*k*; 733 16
slow to anger and of great *k*. 733 24

For your loving-*k* is greater than the heavens, * 750 1
Let there be no one to show him *k*, * 751 20
For his loving-*k* toward us is great, * 760 17
Let your loving-*k* come to me, O LORD, * 766 17
Let your loving-*k* be my comfort, * 769 16
In your loving-*k*, revive me, * 770 18
Deal with your servant according to your loving-*k* * 773 21
Hear my voice, O LORD, according to your loving-*k*; 776 1
Let me hear of your loving-*k* in the morning, 799 15
slow to anger and of great *k*. 802 2
show thy loving-*k*, 828 5

kindnesses

Where, Lord, are your loving-*k* of old, * 717 12

kindred

I have become a stranger to my own *k*, * 680 3

kindreds

brought hither out of many *k* and tongues. 820 8

kinds

What are the principal *k* of prayer? 856 26
The principal *k* of prayer are adoration, praise, 856 27

king

Our *K* and Savior draweth nigh: 43 1
and a great *K* above all gods. 44 15
O Lord God, heavenly *K*, God the Father Almighty. 52 9
Thou art the *K* of glory, O Christ. 53 11
O God, the *K* eternal, who dividest 56 18
Our *K* and Savior now draws near: 80 10
and a great *K* above all gods. 82 10
O *K* of all the ages. 94 13
Lord God, heavenly *K*, 94 23
You, Christ, are the *k* of glory, 96 1
O God, the *K* eternal, whose light divides 99 13
and a great *K* above all gods. 146 6
O God, the *K* of glory, who hast exalted 175 1
in thy well-beloved Son, the *K* of kings 185 2
by the order of *K* Herod. 186 14
behold the *K* in his beauty; 191 19
in thy well-beloved Son, the *K* of kings 202 17
O God, the *K* of glory, you have exalted 226 13
in your well-beloved Son, the *K* of kings 236 15
innocents of Bethlehem by *K* Herod. 238 8
behold the *K* in his beauty; 243 5
in your well-beloved Son, the *K* of kings 254 2
Blessed is the *K* who comes in the name of the Lord. 270 1
and was proclaimed as *K* of kings 271 8
in his name may ever hail him as our *K*, 271 11
for the victory of our mighty *K*. 286 3
for darkness has been vanquished by our eternal *K*. 286 6
O Lord God, heavenly *K*, God the Father Almighty. 324 20
Lord God, heavenly *K*, 356 3
We will exalt you, O God our *K*; 393 2
O God, the *K* of saints, we praise 489 14
O God, the *K* of saints, we praise 504 12
as Lord of lords and *K* of kings. 517 6
"I myself have set my *k* * 586 12
Hearken to my cry for help, my *K* and my God, * 588 19
The LORD is *K* for ever and ever; * 596 1
He multiplies the victories of his *k*; * 606 12
O LORD, give victory to the *k* * 608 19
The *k* rejoices in your strength, O LORD; * 608 21
For the *k* puts his trust in the LORD; * 609 9
and the *K* of glory shall come in. 614 3
"Who is this *K* of glory?" * 614 4
and the *K* of glory shall come in. 614 9
"Who is he, this *K* of glory?" * 614 10
he is the *K* of glory." 614 12
the LORD sits enthroned as *K* for evermore. 620 26
There is no *k* that can be saved by a mighty army; * 627 7
You are my *K* and my God; * 645 18
let me recite what I have fashioned for the *k*; * 647 12
and the *k*'s enemies are losing heart. 647 24
The *k* will have pleasure in your beauty; * 648 13
In embroidered apparel she is brought to the *k*; * 648 19
and enter into the palace of the *k*. 648 22
"In place of fathers, O *k*, you shall have sons; * 648 23
he is the great *K* over all the earth. 650 9
sing praises to our *K*, sing praises. 650 17
For God is *K* of all the earth; * 650 18
and the city of the great *K*. 651 5
Add length of days to the *k*'s life; * 668 24
But the *k* will rejoice in God; 671 7
procession into the sanctuary, my God and my *K*. 678 6
Give the *K* your justice, O God, * 685 9
and your righteousness to the *K*'s Son; 685 10
Yet God is my *K* from ancient times, * 690 8
my *K* and my God. 707 22
the Holy One of Israel is our *K*. 715 2
The LORD is *K*; 722 1
and a great *K* above all gods. 724 19
Tell it out among the nations: "The LORD is *K*! * 726 11
The LORD is *K*; 726 22
shout with joy before the *K*, the LORD. 728 15
The LORD is *K*; 728 23
"O mighty *K*, lover of justice, 729 5
The *k* sent and released him; * 739 17
Sihon, *k* of the Amorites, 788 23
and Og, the *k* of Bashan, * 788 24
Sihon, *k* of the Amorites, * 791 7
And Og, the *k* of Bashan, * 791 9
I will exalt you, O God my *K*, * 801 12
let the children of Zion be joyful in their *K*. 807 5
O God our *K*, by the resurrection 835 1
Blessed are you, O Lord God, *K* of the Universe, 835 13

kingdom

Blessed art thou on the glorious throne of thy *k*; * 49 18
thou didst open the *k* of heaven to all believers. 53 16
thy *k* come, 54 16
For thine is the *k*, and the power, and the glory, 54 24
hasten the coming of thy *k*; 58 6
thy *k* come, 67 6
For thine is the *k*, and the power, and the glory, 67 14
a *k* of priests to serve our God. 94 4
and opened the *k* of heaven to all believers. 96 6
thy *k* come, 97 6
For thine is the *k*, 97 15
and hasten the coming of your *k*; 100 22
thy *k* come, 106 16
thy *k* come, 121 6
For thine is the *k*, 121 15
thy *k* come, 132 21

and to draw all mankind into thy *k*, 150 13
attain to thy heavenly *k*, 152 20
thy *k* come, 153 8
into the *k* of thy Son; 172 16
with great triumph unto thy *k* in heaven: 175 2
unto him in his eternal and glorious *k*; 184 13
share with her the glory of thine eternal *k*; 192 4
evangelists and heralds of thy *k*, 196 11
their work for the extension of thy *k*; 205 18
hasten the coming of thy *k*; 206 14
brought us into the *k* of your Son; 224 9
with great triumph to your *k* in heaven: 226 14
in his eternal and glorious *k*; 236 6
share with her the glory of your eternal *k*; 243 11
evangelists and heralds of your *k*, 247 23
their work for the extension of your *k*; 256 15
hasten the coming of your *k*; 257 10
bring forth abundant fruit in your glorious *k*; 290 11
until he comes to your everlasting *k*. 309 18
uphold you in the service of Christ and his *k*. 310 7
thy *k* come, 311 3
For thine is the *k*, 311 12
and made us a *k* of priests to serve 317 18
And blessed be his *k*, now and for ever. 319 2
And blessed be his *k*, now and for ever. 323 2
and his *k* will have no end. 327 11
whose *k* shall have no end. 328 12
them we may be partakers of thy heavenly *k*. 330 6
thy *k* come, 336 20
For thine is the *k*, and the power, and the glory, 336 28
through hope, of thy everlasting *k*. 339 9
Thine is the *k*, O Lord, 344 10
made us citizens of thy *k*, 348 21
And blessed be his *k*, now and for ever. 351 2
And blessed be his *k*, now and for ever. 355 2
and his *k* will have no end. 359 2
into the joy of your eternal *k*. 363 18
thy *k* come, 364 3
For thine is the *k*, 364 12
and heirs of your eternal *k*. 366 7
Yours, O Lord, is the *k*, 377 8
made us citizens of your *k*, 381 14
May we also come to share in your heavenly *k*. 387 20
with all your saints in your eternal *k*. 389 10
yours is the *k* and the power and the glory, 391 24
your eternal *k*. 393 5
Hasten, O Father, the coming of thy *k*; 395 13
thy *k* come, 398 14
For thine is the *k*, 398 23
until he comes to your everlasting *k*. 418 16
uphold you in the service of Christ and his *k*. 419 3
in the service of the *k* of his Christ. 420 3
thy *k* come, 428 10
For thine is the *k*, 428 19
established me among your children in your *k*. 450 13
give him joy and gladness in your *k*, 463 21
thy *k* come, 464 6
bring us all to thy heavenly *k*; 470 10
thy heavenly *k*. 481 22
in that *k* where there is no death, 482 6
Christ will open the *k* of heaven to all who believe 483 20
inherit the *k* prepared for you. 483 22
thy *k* come, 485 22
For thine is the *k*, and the power, and the glory, 486 5
and may come to thy heavenly *k*; 487 8
Father, inherit the *k* prepared for you 487 20
in the life of perfect service in thy heavenly *k*; 488 24
bring us all to your heavenly *k*; 494 4
at the table in your heavenly *k*. 497 20
in that *k* where there is no death, 498 17
Christ will open the *k* of heaven to all 500 9
inherit the *k* prepared for you. 500 11
thy *k* come, 502 3
For thine is the *k*, 502 12
and may come to your heavenly *k*; 503 10
k prepared for you from the beginning of the world." 505 7
And blessed be his *k*, now and for ever. 512 2
and his *k* will have no end. 520 2
And blessed be his *k*, now and for ever. 525 2
and his *k* will have no end. 530 21
calling us to be a holy people in the *k* of your Son 533 2
and his *k* will have no end. 542 21
be drawn into your blessed *k*. 563 9
Yours, O Lord, is the *k*. 569 13
Yours, O Lord, is the *k*; 579 16
a scepter of righteousness is the scepter of your *k*; 648 2
and from one *k* to another, 739 4
They make known the glory of your *k* * 802 7
and the glorious splendor of your *k*. 802 10
Your *k* is an everlasting *k*; * 802 11
Eternal God, in whose perfect *k* no sword is drawn 815 22
may become the *k* of our Lord and Savior Jesus 816 4
For yours is the *k*, O Lord, and you are exalted 822 15
k of God in villages, towns, and lonely places: 825 17
hast promised to all those who seek thy *k* 828 10
to wait for the consummation of your *k* 835 6
in which we are raised to the life of your *k*. 836 16
for the *k* and the power and the glory 838 7
intended for him in your eternal *k*; 841 5
made heirs of God's *k*. 850 4
Christ promised to bring us into the *k* of God 851 2
and to proclaim the Good News of the *K* 853 17
and give for the spread of the *k* of God. 856 15
and inheritors of the *k* of God. 858 11

kingdoms

The nations make much ado, and the *k* are shaken; * 649 15
Sing to God, O *k* of the earth; * 678 24
and upon the *k* that have not called 701 17
and the *k* also, to serve the LORD. 732 21
and all the *k* of Canaan. 788 25

kingly

Splendor and honor and *k* power * 93 20

kings

and *k* to the brightness of thy rising. 38 1
and *k* to the brightness of your rising. 76 1
and *k* to the brightness of your dawning. 87 18
the King of *k* and Lord of lords: 185 2
the King of *k* and Lord of lords: 202 17
the King of *k* and Lord of lords: 236 15
the King of *k* and Lord of lords: 254 2
and was proclaimed as King of *k* 271 8
sovereignty as Lord of lords and King of *k*. 517 6

and have raised up prophets, *k*, and priests, 520 16
Why do the *k* of the earth rise up in revolt, 586 3
And now, you *k*, be wise; * 586 22
K' daughters stand among the ladies of the court; * 648 8
Behold, the *k* of the earth assembled * 651 8
"*K* with their armies are fleeing away; * 677 3
When the Almighty scattered *k*, * 677 8
K shall bring gifts to you, * 678 16
The *k* of Tarshish and of the isles shall pay tribute, * 686 3
and the *k* of Arabia and Saba offer gifts. 686 4
All *k* shall bow down before him, * 686 5
and strikes terror in the *k* of the earth. 692 26
and higher than the *k* of the earth. 715 21
and all the *k* of the earth your glory. 732 7
and rebuked *k* for their sake, 739 6
in the very chambers of their *k*. 740 14
will smite *k* in the day of his wrath; * 753 22
I will tell of your decrees before *k* * 767 5
and put mighty *k* to death: 788 22
Who struck down great *k*, * 791 3
And slew mighty *k*, * 791 5
All the *k* of the earth will praise you, O LORD, * 793 10
You give victory to *k* * 800 21
K of the earth and all peoples, * 806 15
To bind their *k* in chains * 807 16

kingship

For *k* belongs to the LORD; * 612 13
and his *k* has dominion over all. 734 21

Kishon

and to Jabin at the river of *K*: 706 21

kissed

righteousness and peace have *k* each other. 709 15

knee

Come, let us bow down, and bend the *k*, * 82 15
And now, O Lord, I bend the *k* of my heart, * 91 12
Come, let us bow down, and bend the *k*, * 725 1

kneel

k in silence, 41 12
and *k* before the Lord our Maker. 45 2
let us *k* in silence, 62 12
let us *k* in silence, and with 79 6
and *k* before the Lord our Maker. 82 16
let us *k* in silence, 116 8
and *k* before the Lord our Maker. 146 12
k before the Lord, our maker and redeemer. 265 15
and *k* before the LORD our Maker. 725 2

kneeling

confession to Almighty God, devoutly *k*. 330 14

knees

My *k* are weak through fasting, * 752 23
let us fall upon our *k* before his footstool." 786 12

knit

and *k* together in unity by thy Spirit, 190 12
O Almighty God, who hast *k* together thine elect 194 8
and *k* together in unity by your Spirit, 241 21
Almighty God, you have *k* together your elect 245 16
Grant that their wills may be so *k* together 429 11
And so *k* their wills together in your will 444 12
Almighty God, who hast *k* together thine elect 480 4
k my heart to you that I may fear your Name. 710 23
you *k* me together in my mother's womb. 794 26
K together in constant affection 829 3

know

Watch ye, for ye *k* not when the master 37 1
bring those who do not *k* thee to the knowledge 58 12
that we may *k* thee as thou art revealed 70 12
Watch, for you do not *k* when the master 75 1
K this: The Lord himself is God; * 83 1
and I *k* my wickedness only too well. 91 15
to *k* you is eternal life 99 20
bring those who do not *k* you to the knowledge 101 5
made the sun to *k* its going down: 110 25
that by your brightness we may *k* you 110 26
that we may *k* you as you are revealed 124 9
K that the Lord does wonders for the faithful; * 128 14
that we may *k* you as you are revealed 139 18
Lead us, who *k* thee now by faith, 162 14
Grant that when we hear his voice we may *k* him 173 12
whom truly to *k* is everlasting life: 173 16
Grant us so perfectly to *k* thy Son 173 17
perceive and *k* what things they ought to do, 179 12
be healed of all our infirmities and *k* thee 191 4
may *k* thee, the one true God, 197 22
and may *k* ourselves to be surrounded 199 7
they may be brought to *k* and worship thee 206 21
Lead us, who *k* you now by faith, 214 8
as you *k* the weaknesses of each of us, 218 3
you *k* that we have no power in ourselves 218 13
Grant that when we hear his voice we may *k* him 225 4
whom truly to *k* is everlasting life: 225 8
Grant us so perfectly to *k* your Son 225 9
and grant that they may *k* and understand 231 5
you *k* our necessities before we ask 231 10
be healed from all our infirmities and *k* you 242 11
Grant that by this teaching we may *k* you, 249 7
and *k* ourselves to be surrounded 250 17
they may be brought to *k* and worship you 257 17
For I *k* my transgressions, * 266 6
said to them, "Do you *k* what I, 274 9
By this shall the world *k* that you are my disciples: 275 7
Have compassion on all who do not *k* you 280 2
see and *k* that things which were cast down 280 18
see and *k* that things which were cast down 291 15
a spirit to *k* and to love you, 308 7
but as you *k* and love us in your Son 394 7
and *k* ourselves to be surrounded 395 20
that if either of you *k* any reason why 424 5
and the grace to bring them up to *k* you, 429 21
If any of you *k* just cause why 437 2
For I *k* my transgressions only too well, 449 5
that you may *k* the healing power of his love. 456 9
and make you *k* and feel that the only Name 457 2
I *k* now what it will bring 461 19
and *k* the consolation of his love. 467 2
I *k* that my Redeemer liveth, 469 4
Be still then, and *k* that I am God; * 472 4
they may *k* the consolation of thy love. 481 8
they may *k* the consolation of thy love; 489 32

As for me, I *k* that my Redeemer lives	491	7
Lord, you *k* the secrets of our hearts;	492	12
k the strength of his presence,	493	7
to *k* and to love as a companion	493	18
they may *k* the consolation of your love;	505	19
if any of you *k* any reason why	514	6
and *k* that things which were cast down	515	8
you *k* the importance of this ministry,	527	1
if any of you *k* any impediment or crime	527	4
and *k* that things which were cast down	528	6
you *k* the importance of this ministry,	539	1
if any of you *k* any impediment or crime	539	4
and *k* that things which were cast down	540	6
and that, through him, we *k*	545	5
many may come to *k* you and love you.	545	15
to ask your forgiveness, to *k* your healing	568	10
For this place where we may be still and *k*	578	13
K that the LORD does wonders for the faithful; *	588	4
Those who *k* your Name will put their trust in you, *	593	19
let the ungodly *k* they are but mortal.	594	18
Now I *k* that the LORD gives victory to his anointed: *	608	12
you *k* my distress.	622	24
they charge me with matters I *k* nothing about.	630	14
strangers whom I did not *k* tore me to pieces	630	25
Continue your loving-kindness to those who *k* you, *	632	24
O LORD, you *k* all my desires, *	637	14
LORD, let me *k* my end and the number of my days, *	639	1
so that I may *k* how short my life is.	639	2
and that, O LORD, you *k*.	640	25
By this I *k* you are pleased with me, *	642	22
'Be still, then, and *k* that I am God; *	650	1
I *k* every bird in the sky, *	655	1
For I *k* my transgressions, *	656	10
this I *k*, for God is on my side.	663	10
Let everyone *k* that God rules in Jacob, *	666	26
You have made your people *k* hardship; *	667	14
O God, you *k* my foolishness, *	679	20
You *k* my reproach, my shame, and my dishonor; *	681	1
though I cannot *k* the number of them.	684	11
They say, "How should God *k*? *	687	21
That the generations to come might *k*,	695	10
They do not *k*, neither do they understand;	705	17
Let them *k* that you, whose Name is YAHWEH, *	707	13
I count Egypt and Babylon among those who *k* me; *	711	17
Happy are the people who *k* the festal shout! *	714	23
The dullard does not *k*,	721	7
they do not *k* my ways."	725	14
K this: The LORD himself is God; *	729	25
I will not *k* evil.	730	16
and its place shall *k* it no more.	734	14
Let them *k* that this is your hand, *	753	1
I *k*, O LORD, that your judgments are right *	769	14
and also those who *k* your decrees.	769	24
that I may *k* your decrees.	773	24
For I *k* that the LORD is great, *	788	10
you *k* my sitting down and my rising up;	794	2
but you, O LORD, *k* it altogether.	794	7
your works are wonderful, and I *k* it well.	795	2
Search me out, O God, and *k* my heart; *	795	24
try me and *k* my restless thoughts.	795	25
I *k* that the LORD will maintain the cause	796	25
that they may *k* my words are true.	797	16
When my spirit languishes within me, you *k* my path; *	798	5
That the peoples may *k* of your power *	802	9
that all may *k* the power of his forgiveness	816	18
strength to *k* and to do thy will.	820	21
we may come to *k* you more truly,	827	14
where we may be still and *k* that thou art God;	832	16
Grant us the gift of your Spirit, that we may *k* him	836	17
to bring others to *k* him;	847	22
to *k* Christ and be able to follow him.	859	3

knowest

and, as thou *k* their several infirmities,	166	11
Almighty God, the fountain of all wisdom, who *k*	179	16
Thou *k* my down-sitting and mine up-rising;	474	19
but thou, O LORD, *k* it altogether.	474	24
Thou *k*, Lord, the secrets of our hearts;	484	11

knowing

How wonderful and beyond our *k*, O God,	287	14
for the lowly, *k* all things before they come to pass:	520	13
k that thou art doing for them better things	831	9
k and loving God and each other.	862	28

knowledge

To give *k* of salvation unto his people *	51	14
k of whom standeth our eternal life,	57	2
bring those who do not know thee to the *k*	58	12
granting us in this world *k* of thy truth,	59	18
granting us in this world *k* of thy truth,	72	15
To give his people *k* of salvation *	93	3
bring those who do not know you to the *k*	101	5
granting us in this world *k* of your truth,	102	6
granting us in this world *k* of your truth,	126	6
deacons, with true *k* and understanding	150	6
to others the word of *k*,	197	13
filled with the *k* of thy love;	207	12
rejoicing in the *k* of thy truth,	209	19
to others the word of *k*,	248	23
until the earth is filled with the *k*	258	11
rejoicing in the *k* of your truth,	261	3
until the earth is filled with the *k*	279	1
grant them the *k* of his love,	279	12
and so lead them in the *k* and obedience	310	10
keep your hearts and minds in the *k*	339	16
to give the *k* of thy glory	346	2
to give the *k* of your glory	378	16
or a deeper *k* of him.	386	8
and so lead them in the *k* and obedience	419	6
in the *k* and love of the Lord.	423	13
the *k* of his Savior Jesus Christ.	445	2
Such *k* is too wonderful and excellent for me; *	475	3
Grant that, increasing in *k* and love of thee,	481	20
increasing in *k* and love of thee,	488	23
Holy Scriptures, and in seeking the *k*	532	5
For the *k* of your will and the grace	578	19
Have they no *k*, all those evildoers *	598	21
and one night imparts *k* to another.	606	18
Have they no *k*, those evildoers *	659	7
is there *k* in the Most High?"	687	22
he who teaches all the world, has he no *k*?	723	14
Teach me discernment and *k*, *	768	19
Such *k* is too wonderful for me; *	794	10

Fill them with faith, virtue, *k*, 829 2
our *k* of your love is made perfect in our love 840 5
by whose *k* the depths are broken up 840 14

known

Let thy way be *k* upon earth; 55 9
Let thy way be *k* upon earth; 68 1
k his deeds among the peoples. 78 7
Make his deeds *k* among the peoples; * 86 9
and this is *k* in all the world. 86 12
Let your way be *k* upon earth; 98 3
Let your way be *k* upon earth; 122 3
for they have not *k* my ways; 146 23
as we have *k* the mystery of that Light upon earth, 161 3
that he may be *k*, worshiped, and obeyed 163 10
we who have *k* the incarnation of thy Son 188 16
so we may with ardent devotion make *k* 194 4
not *k* the redeeming work of our Savior 206 19
Grant that we, who have *k* 212 17
that he may be *k*, worshiped, and obeyed 215 4
that abundant life which you have made *k* 216 2
O God, whose blessed Son made himself *k* 223 10
O God, whose blessed Son made himself *k* 224 19
we who have *k* the incarnation of your Son 240 2
may with ardent devotion make *k* the love 245 13
have not *k* the redeeming work of our Savior 257 15
whose faith is *k* to God alone, 280 11
Let your ways be *k* upon earth, 281 7
all hearts are open, all desires *k*, 323 8
all hearts are open, all desires *k*, 355 7
which you have made *k* to us in creation; 368 2
Risen Lord, be *k* to us in the breaking of the Bread. 372 9
those whose faith is *k* to you alone; 375 19
those whose faith is *k* to you alone, 391 16
forgive us our sins, *k* and unknown, 393 11
to whom our needs are *k* before we ask: 394 12
O LORD, thou hast searched me out, and *k* me. * 474 18
thy righteous servants, *k* to us and unknown; 489 18
other righteous servants, *k* to us and unknown; 504 16
all hearts are open, all desires *k*, 512 7
let it now be made *k*. 514 7
all hearts are open, all desires *k*, 525 7
come forward now, and make it *k*. 527 6
are called to make Christ *k* as Savior and Lord, 531 3
reconciling love of Christ may be *k* 532 11
all hearts are open, all desires *k*, 537 7
come forward now and make it *k*. 539 6
redemptive love *k*, by your word and example, 543 10
those whose faith is *k* to you alone, 550 21
The LORD is *k* by his acts of justice; * 594 9
A people I have not *k* shall serve me; 605 28
they shall be *k* as the LORD's for ever. 612 20
They shall come and make *k* to a people yet unborn * 612 21
Oh, that I could make them *k* and tell them! * 640 14
he is *k* to be her sure refuge. 651 7
Let your ways be *k* upon earth, * 675 11
till I make *k* your strength to this generation 684 18
In Judah is God *k*; * 692 1
That which we have heard and *k*, 695 1
the heathen who have not *k* you * 701 16
Let it be *k* among the heathen and in our sight 702 2
Will your wonders be *k* in the dark? * 713 1
The LORD has made *k* his victory; * 728 3
He made his ways *k* to Moses * 733 21
make *k* his deeds among the peoples. 738 2
to make his power *k*. 742 15
Long have I *k* from your decrees * 776 7
LORD, you have searched me out and *k* me; * 794 1
They make *k* the glory of your kingdom * 802 7
wouldest be pleased to make thy ways *k* unto them, 814 8
no strength *k* but the strength of love: 815 23
that your presence and power may be *k* 825 18
and be *k* to us in the breaking of bread; 834 9
that we may know him and make him *k*; 836 18
the example of prayer *k* as the Lord's Prayer. 856 24
By what other names is this service *k*? 859 14
it is also *k* as the Divine Liturgy, 859 16

knows

I will protect him, because he *k* my Name. 130 28
May Christ, the Morning Star who *k* no setting, 287 25
For the LORD *k* the way of the righteous, * 585 15
for he *k* the secrets of the heart. 646 29
there is not one among us who *k* how long. 690 3
I will protect him, because he *k* my Name. 720 16
The LORD *k* our human thoughts; * 723 15
For he himself *k* whereof we are made; * 734 9
and the sun *k* the time of its setting. 736 16
I look to my right hand and find no one who *k* me; * 798 7

Kyrie

K eleison. 153 3
K eleison. 324 7
K eleison. 356 19
(or "*K* eleison"). 389 14
K eleison. 389 18

L

labor

the strength of those who *l*, 70 5
the strength of those who *l*, 124 2
Come to me, all who *l* and are heavy-laden, 131 15
in danger by reason of their *l* or their travel, 151 18
all who *l* to gather them, 207 18
shared our toil and hallowed our *l*: 208 2
and a just return for our *l*; 208 6
a proper return for our own *l*, 210 14
all who *l* to gather them, 258 18
shared our toil and hallowed our *l*: 259 4
and a just return for our *l*; 259 7
a proper return for our own *l*, 261 19
our life and *l* to the Lord. 344 13
our life and *l* to the Lord. 377 11
For a blessing upon all human *l*, 390 21
'Come to me, all you who *l* and are burdened, 465 10
yet is their strength then but *l* and sorrow, 473 5
For a blessing upon all human *l*, 550 6
Look at those who are in *l* with wickedness, * 591 26
yet the sum of them is but *l* and sorrow, 718 21
and to his *l* until the evening. 736 24
So he humbled their spirits with hard *l*; * 747 5
their *l* is in vain who build it. 782 21

You shall eat the fruit of your *l*; * 783 15
receive just payment for their *l*; 824 15
respect those who *l* to produce them, 825 22

laborers

That it may please thee to send forth *l* 150 12

laboring

whom you are called to serve, *l* together 532 15

labors

and for the *l* of those who harvest them. 194 17
by the prayers and *l* of thy holy Church, 206 20
and for the *l* of those who harvest them. 246 2
by the prayers and *l* of your holy Church, 257 16
that he may rest from his *l*, 465 12
for they rest from their *l*. 469 15
do now rest from their *l*. 488 6
for they rest from their *l*. 492 4
offering all your *l* to God, 532 26
gathered together by their prayers and *l*, 838 6
l, in union with Christ, for the purposes of God. 857 16

lack

and our *l* of concern for those who come after us, 268 24
therefore can I *l* nothing. 476 2
for those who fear him *l* nothing. 628 12
The young lions *l* and suffer hunger, * 628 13
but those who seek the LORD *l* nothing that is good. 628 14
want and anxiety from *l* of work. 824 12

laden

Come to me, all who labor and are heavy-*l*, 131 15
Come unto me, all ye that travail and are heavy *l*, 332 8
Come unto me, all ye that travail and are heavy *l*, 449 13

ladies

Kings' daughters stand among the *l* of the court; * 648 8

laid

and the Lord hath *l* on him the iniquity 39 2
and the Lord has *l* on him the iniquity 77 1
crucified body of thy dear Son was *l* in the tomb 170 2
for the love of him who *l* down his life for us, 209 14
crucified body of your dear Son was *l* in the tomb 221 14
who *l* down his life for us, 260 20
crucified body of your dear Son was *l* in the tomb 283 2
and *l* thine hand upon me. 475 2
O God, whose blessed Son was *l* in a sepulcher 487 5
who have *l* down their lives in the service 488 28
O God, whose blessed Son was *l* in a sepulcher 503 7
and the foundations of the world *l* bare, * 603 20
and you have *l* me in the dust of the grave. 611 10
which you have *l* up for those who fear you; * 624 5
They have *l* a net for my feet, 664 4
you *l* heavy burdens upon our backs. 674 16
the enemy has *l* waste everything in your sanctuary. 689 15
and *l* low the youth of Israel. 697 13
He *l* it as a solemn charge upon Joseph, * 704 9
You have *l* me in the depths of the Pit, * 712 13
you *l* the foundations of the world 714 16
and *l* his strongholds in ruins. 716 22
In the beginning, O LORD, you *l* the foundations 732 27
You *l* down your commandments, * 763 11
Protect me from the snare which they have *l* for me * 797 22

laity

the *l* here (or now, or soon to be) assembled 204 11
the bishops and the other clergy and the *l* 255 8
What is the ministry of the *l*? 855 14

lamb

O Lord, God, *L* of God, Son of the Father, 52 11
And yours, by right, O *L* that was slain, * 94 1
and to Christ the *L*, 94 6
Lord God, *L* of God, 95 4
O *L* of God, that takest away the sins of the world, 152 24
for he is the true Paschal *l*, 287 3
O Lord God, *L* of God, Son of the Father, 324 22
O *L* of God, that takest away the sins of the world, 337 3
for he is the very Paschal *L*, 346 19
Lord God, *L* of God, 356 8
for he is the true Paschal *L*, 379 16
L of God, you take away the sins of the world: 407 1
Jesus, *L* of God: 463 23
your own fold, a *l* of your own flock, 465 3
thine own fold, a *l* of thine own flock, 483 8
immaculate *L* that was slain to take away the sins 488 16
your own fold, a *l* of your own flock, 499 15

lambs

the *l* in your arms and carry them in your bosom: 459 2

lament

I will complain and *l*, * 661 20

lamentation

You have noted my *l*; 663 6
and their widows made no *l*. 700 8
incline your ear to my *l*. 712 4
when he heard their *l*. 745 14

lamenting

l our sins and acknowledging our wretchedness, 166 4
l our sins and acknowledging our wretchedness, 217 17
l our sins and acknowledging our wretchedness, 264 5

lamp

No one lights a *l* to put it under a bucket, 109 8
but on a *l*-stand where it gives light 109 9
And you, like the *l*, must shed light 109 10
Grant us, Lord, the *l* of charity which never fails, 110 18
You, O LORD, are my *l*; * 604 20
I have prepared a *l* for my Anointed. 787 6

land

and his hands prepared the dry *l*. 44 19
and his hands have molded the dry *l*. 82 14
For behold, darkness covers the *l*; * 87 13
Violence will no more be heard in your *l*, * 87 23
and his hands prepared the dry *l*. 146 10
that we and all the people of this *l* may have grace 190 20
Raise up, we beseech thee, in this and every *l* 196 10
use the harvests of the *l* and of the seas, 207 17
the industries and commerce of this *l* responsive 208 4
that we and all the people of this *l* may have grace 242 4
Raise up in this and every *l* evangelists 247 22
use the harvests of the *l* and of the seas, 258 17

the industries and commerce of this *l* responsive 259 6
and led them through the Red Sea on dry *l*. 287 8
out of their bondage in Egypt into the *l* of promise. 306 16
out of the *l* of Egypt, out of the house of bondage. 317 25
the authority of government in this and every *l* 329 19
For those who travel on *l*, on water, or in the air 384 17
Guide the people of this *l*, and of all the nations, 388 7
and I have wandered far in a *l* that is waste. 450 14
entrance into the *l* of light and joy, 470 3
the *l* of the living. 478 7
the *l* of the living. 479 17
entrance into the *l* of light and joy, 493 12
into the *l* of promise. 570 8
the ungodly shall perish from his *l*. 596 2
All my delight is upon the godly that are in the *l*, * 600 1
My boundaries enclose a pleasant *l*; * 600 9
You will destroy their offspring from the *l* * 609 18
and their offspring shall inherit the *l*. 615 15
in the *l* of the living! 618 28
invent deceitful schemes against the quiet in the *l*. 631 11
dwell in the *l* and feed on its riches. 633 10
but those who wait upon the LORD shall possess the *l*. 634 2
But the lowly shall possess the *l*; * 634 5
Those who are blessed by God shall possess the *l*, * 635 3
and dwell in the *l* for ever. 635 15
The righteous shall possess the *l* * 635 20
he will raise you up to possess the *l*, 636 4
so that they may be happy in the *l*; * 642 2
therefore I will remember you from the *l* of Jordan, 643 19
and planted our forefathers in the *l*; * 645 11
For they did not take the *l* by their sword, 645 13
and the *l* of the dead shall be their home. 653 12
and root you out of the *l* of the living! 658 10
and your hands deal out violence in the *l*. 664 24
as in a barren and dry *l* where there is no water. 670 14
He turned the sea into dry *l*, 674 3
you refreshed the *l* when it was weary. 676 22
the meeting-places of God in the *l*. 689 26
in the *l* of Egypt, in the field of Zoan. 695 27
He brought them to his holy *l*, * 699 13
it took root and filled the *l*. 703 6
when he came out of the *l* of Egypt. 704 10
who brought you out of the *l* of Egypt and said, * 704 22
You have been gracious to your *l*, O LORD, * 708 20
that his glory may dwell in our *l*. 709 13
and our *l* will yield its increase. 709 19
your faithfulness in the *l* of destruction? 712 26
or the *l* and the earth were born, * 718 2
I should soon have dwelt in the *l* of silence. 723 28
and his hands have molded the dry *l*. 724 23
My eyes are upon the faithful in the *l*, 730 20
I will soon destroy all the wicked in the *l*, * 730 26
Saying, "To you will I give the *l* of Canaan * 738 21
of little account, and sojourners in the *l*, 739 2
Then he called for a famine in the *l* * 739 9
and Jacob became a sojourner in the *l* of Ham. 739 24
and portents in the *l* of Ham. 740 8
Their *l* was overrun by frogs, * 740 13
and flames of fire throughout their *l*. 740 18
Which ate up all the green plants in their *l* * 740 23
He struck down the firstborn of their *l*, * 740 25
Wonderful deeds in the *l* of Ham, * 743 15
They refused the pleasant *l* * 743 20
and the *l* was defiled with blood. 744 26
A fruitful *l* into salt flats, * 748 23
and dry *l* into water-springs. 748 26
Their descendants will be mighty in the *l*; * 755 7
in the *l* of the living. 759 19
l allotted to the just, * 781 23
He gave their *l* to be an inheritance, * 788 26
on the trees in the midst of that *l*. 792 4
my portion in the *l* of the living." 798 11
my soul gasps to you like a thirsty *l*. 799 11
Almighty God, who hast given us this good *l* 820 1
Bless our *l* with honorable industry, 820 4
and the magistrates in all this *l*; 821 10
O Lord our Governor, bless the leaders of our *l*, 821 15
[and especially the hearts of the people of this *l*], 823 19
Guide the people of this *l* 824 13
power may be known throughout this *l*. 825 19
and honor the *l* and the water 825 23
upon the people in this *l* who live with injustice, 826 9
enjoy a fair portion of the riches of this *l*; 826 14
that our *l* may give her increase; 828 5
martyrs and saints in every age and in every *l*. 838 17
for the natural majesty and beauty of this *l*. 838 22
liberty which has been lit in this *l*. 839 9
until all the people of this *l* share 839 24

lands

Their sound is gone out into all *l*; 40 5
O be joyful in the Lord all ye *l*; * 45 11
Their sound has gone out into all *l*, 78 4
Be joyful in the Lord, all you *l*; * 82 20
Their sound has gone out into all *l*, * 606 21
though they call the *l* after their own names. 653 3
Be joyful in God, all you *l*; * 673 18
Shout with joy to the LORD all you *l*; * 728 10
the *l* and those who dwell therein. 728 17
Be joyful in the LORD, all you *l*; * 729 22
He gave his people the *l* of the nations, * 741 13
and to scatter them throughout the *l*. 744 2
He gathered them out of the *l*; * 746 5
in giving them the *l* of the nations. 754 17
And gave away their *l* for an inheritance, * 791 11
Bless the *l* and waters, 828 2

language

From every family, *l*, people, and nation, * 94 3
Although they have no words or *l*, * 606 19

languished

their spirits *l* within them. 746 11

languishes

When my spirit *l* within me, you know my path; * 798 5

lantern

Your word is a *l* to my feet * 103 6
Your word is a *l* to our feet, 571 13
Your word is a *l* to my feet * 772 3

larger

opened to him the gates of *l* life, 202 11
opened to him the gates of *l* life, 253 15

lash
and their iniquities with the *l*; 716 6

last
that in the *l* day, when he shall come again 159 4
at *l* to see thee in thy one and eternal glory, 176 6
may at the *l* enter with them into thine unending joy; 202 5
that in the *l* day, when he shall come again 211 4
at *l* to see you in your one and eternal glory, 228 5
at *l* we may with him attain to your eternal joy; 250 4
the *l* enter with them into your unending joy; 253 10
so that at the *l* we may come to his eternal joy; 269 13
Peace is my *l* gift to you, 275 1
and at the *l* day bring us with all your saints 363 17
For in these *l* days you sent him to be incarnate 368 5
Suffer us not, at our *l* hour, 484 16
may at *l*, together with them, be partakers 486 14
and that at the *l* he will stand upon the earth. 491 8
turn us away from you at our *l* hour. 492 20
and, at the *l*, when we are committed 569 8
and their inheritance shall *l* for ever. 634 21
and their punishment would *l* for ever. 705 6
and their righteousness will *l* for ever. 755 10
When they breathe their *l*, they return to earth, * 803 9
and peace at the *l*. 833 18
consummation of your kingdom on the *l* great Day; 835 6
What do we mean by the *l* judgment? 862 13

late
you rise so early and go to bed so *l*; * 783 3

latter
and that he shall stand at the *l* day upon the earth; 469 5

laud
we *l* and magnify thy glorious Name; 334 2
we *l* and magnify thy glorious Name; 341 5
l him, all you peoples. 760 16

laudable
faithful people do unto thee true and *l* service: 184 2
faithful people offer you true and *l* service: 235 15

laugh
All who see me *l* me to scorn; * 610 14
and they shall *l* at him, saying, 658 12
But you, O LORD, you *l* at them; * 666 12
you *l* all the ungodly to scorn. 666 13
and our enemies *l* us to scorn. 702 24

laughing
He whose throne is in heaven is *l*; * 586 8
a *l*-stock among the peoples. 646 14

laughs
The LORD *l* at the wicked, * 634 9

laughter
Then was our mouth filled with *l*, * 105 6
Then was our mouth filled with *l*, * 782 8

law
incline our hearts to keep thy *l*, 56 21
incline our hearts to keep your *l*, 99 16
yet I do not forget your *l*. 104 6
and submission to the *L*; 149 19
and incline our hearts to keep this *l*. 317 29
hang all the *L* and the Prophets. 319 13
hang all the *L* and the Prophets. 324 6
and sages you revealed your righteous *L*. 370 18
fulfill your *L*, to open for us the way of freedom 370 20
Their delight is in the *l* of the LORD, * 585 5
and they meditate on his *l* day and night. 585 6
My footsteps hold fast to the ways of your *l*; * 601 7
The *l* of the LORD is perfect 607 4
The *l* of their God is in their heart, * 635 24
your *l* is deep in my heart.'" 640 22
and established a *l* for Israel, * 695 8
and refused to walk in his *l*; 695 23
a *l* of the God of Jacob. 704 8
"If his children forsake my *l*, * 716 1
whom you teach out of your *l*; 723 18
one which frames evil into *l*? 724 6
who walk in the *l* of the LORD! 763 6
the wonders of your *l*. 764 20
let me find grace through your *l*. 765 18
Give me understanding, and I shall keep your *l*; * 766 3
I shall continue to keep your *l*; * 767 1
but I have not turned from your *l*. 767 16
because of the wicked who forsake your *l*. 767 20
and dwell upon your *l*. 767 24
I do not forget your *l*. 768 10
but my delight is in your *l*. 769 4
The *l* of your mouth is dearer to me * 769 7
for your *l* is my delight. 769 19
they do not keep your *l*. 770 13
If my delight had not been in your *l*, * 771 3
Oh, how I love your *l*! * 771 13
yet I do not forget your *l*. 772 12
but your *l* do I love. 772 20
for they have broken your *l*. 773 26
because people do not keep your *l*. 774 20
and your *l* is the truth. 775 10
they are very far from your *l*. 776 4
for I do not forget your *l*. 776 10
but your *l* is my love. 777 6
Great peace have they who love your *l*; * 777 9
and your *l* is my delight. 778 4
he gave them a *l* which shall not pass away. 806 6
and that, through obedience to thy *l*, 820 11
and whose *l* is truth: 821 2
administer the *l* in the fear of thee alone; 821 12
establishing equal protection of the *l* 826 12
Christ taught us the Summary of the *L* 851 8
What is the Summary of the *L*? 851 10

lawfully
just cause why they may not *l* be married, 424 2
reason why you may not be united in marriage *l*, 424 6
has been duly and *l* elected to be a bishop 514 2
prayerfully and *l* selected. 559 4

lawgiver
for Moses, the *l*, 838 11

lawless
and evil shall hunt down the *l*. 796 24

laws
the voice of the Lord our God, to walk in his *l* 38 22
we have offended against thy holy *l*, 41 20
we have offended against thy holy *l*, 63 1
of the Lord our God by following his *l* 76 21
and write all these thy *l* in our hearts, 318 30
we have offended against thy holy *l*, 321 1
and observe his *l*. 741 16
that they may enact such *l* as shall please thee, 821 5
l in States, Cities, and Towns, give courage, 822 2
that, by faithful administration and wise *l*, 822 26
The Ten Commandments are the *l* given to Moses 847 14

lay
I *l* my hands upon you in the Name of the Father, 456 1
I *l* my hands upon you in the Name of our Lord 456 7
We therefore ask you to *l* your hands upon him 513 4
and *l* my honor in the dust. 591 5
Your hand will *l* hold upon all your enemies; * 609 12
Those who seek after my life *l* snares for me; * 637 20
l to their charge guilt upon guilt, * 681 18
and the swallow a nest where she may *l* her young; * 707 20
You *l* the beams of your chambers in the waters 735 6
and *l* themselves down in their dens. 736 22
and *l* your hand upon me. 794 9
Give us grace seriously to *l* to heart 818 15
Almighty God, whose Son had nowhere to *l* his head: 829 22
The ministers of the Church are *l* persons, 855 12
The ministry of *l* persons is to represent Christ 855 15

laying
Holy Spirit through prayer and the *l* on of hands 860 20
through prayer and the *l* on of hands 861 1
l on of hands, by which God's grace is given 861 15

lays
nor of the sickness that *l* waste at mid-day. 130 9
he *l* upon you. 544 16
nor of the sickness that *l* waste at mid-day. 719 23

Lazarus
You wept at the grave of *L*, your friend; 497 7

lead
thy light and thy truth, that they may *l* me, 40 16
And *l* us not into temptation, 54 22
And *l* us not into temptation, 67 12
That thy holy angels may *l* us in paths of peace 68 9
your light and your truth, that they may *l* me, 78 15
And *l* us not into temptation, 97 13
And *l* us not into temptation, 106 23
and to *l* us into all truth; 107 6
And *l* us not into temptation, 121 13
That your holy angels may *l* us in paths of peace 122 11
for the sake of your Name, *l* me and guide me. 129 15
And *l* us not into temptation, 133 5
And *l* us not into temptation, 153 14
L us, who know thee now by faith, 162 14
and follow where he doth *l*; 173 13
who didst *l* thy holy apostles to ordain ministers 205 14
L us, who know you now 214 8
open their hearts to the truth, and *l* them 279 28
Spirit as the Messiah, the Christ, to *l* us, 306 18
and so *l* them in the knowledge 310 10
And *l* us not into temptation, 311 10
l a new life, following the commandments of God, 330 11
And *l* us not into temptation, 336 26
to teach them and to *l* them into all truth; 347 8
And *l* us not into temptation, 364 10
to teach them and to *l* them into all truth; 380 3
And *l* us not into temptation, 398 21
and so *l* them in the knowledge 419 6
And *l* us not into temptation, 428 17
L them into all peace. 430 16
restore him to health, and enable him to *l* 458 7
And *l* us not into temptation, 464 13
Even there also shall thy hand *l* me, * 475 11
and *l* me forth beside the waters of comfort. 476 4
that thy Holy Spirit may *l* us in holiness 481 2
Into paradise may the angels *l* thee; 484 1
And *l* us not into temptation, 486 3
l us in holiness and righteousness all our days; 489 6
Into paradise may the angels *l* you. 500 12
And *l* us not into temptation, 502 10
l us in holiness and righteousness all our days; 504 4
to *l* us in confessing that faith. 519 4
Spirit as the Messiah, the Christ, to *l* us, 570 10
L me, O LORD, in your righteousness, 589 6
L me in your truth and teach me, * 614 21
l me on a level path, because of my enemies. 618 22
for the sake of your Name, *l* me and guide me. 622 14
your light and your truth, that they may *l* me, * 644 21
Who will *l* me into the strong city? * 668 4
and only those who *l* a blameless life shall 730 22
Who will *l* me into the strong city? * 750 15
the LORD will *l* them away with the evildoers; * 782 4
Even there your hand will *l* me * 794 18
and *l* me in the way that is everlasting. 795 27
let your good Spirit *l* me on level ground. 799 22
L them and us from prejudice to truth; 816 6
l us to acknowledge our dependence on you alone. 836 11

leaders
pour out upon the *l* of thy Church that spirit 191 10
pour out upon the *l* of your Church that spirit 242 17
For our President, for the *l* of the nations, 384 4
Make their *l* like Oreb and Zeeb, * 706 24
O Lord our Governor, bless the *l* of our land, 821 15
elect trustworthy *l* and make wise decisions 822 12
Send us honest and able *l*. 825 10

leadership
With your fellow bishops you will share in the *l* 517 13
l of your bishop? 532 2
l of your bishop? 543 26
called to *l* in your Church, 552 9

leadeth
his steps in the way that *l* to eternal life; 173 19
he *l* me beside the still waters. 476 22
he *l* me in the paths of righteousness 476 24

leading

O God, who by the *l* of a star 162 13
O God, by the *l* of a star 214 7
Hear, O Shepherd of Israel, *l* Joseph like a flock; * 702 12
and for *l* us to accomplishments which satisfy 836 8

leads

and follow where he *l*; 225 5
steps in the way that *l* to eternal life; 225 11
and follow him in the way that *l* to eternal life; 271 12
and *l* me beside still waters. 443 4
Whoever *l* a blameless life and does what is right, * 599 6
and *l* me beside still waters. 612 26
do not fret yourself; it *l* only to evil. 633 22
The Holy Spirit is revealed as the Lord who *l* us 852 21

leaf

flourishing like a tree in full *l*. 636 7

leaning

as if you were a *l* fence, a toppling wall? 669 11

leanness

but sent *l* into their soul. 743 2

learn

Take my yoke upon you, and *l* from me; 131 16
read, mark, *l*, and inwardly digest them; 184 17
Holy Spirit those who teach and those who *l*, 209 18
read, mark, *l*, and inwardly digest them, 236 9
Holy Spirit those who teach and those who *l*, 261 2
that I might *l* your statutes. 769 6
give me understanding, that I may *l* 769 10
that, rejoicing in thy whole creation, we may *l* 814 3
and grant that those who teach and those who *l* 824 19
What do we *l* about God as creator 846 1
We *l* that there is one God, 846 3
What do we *l* from these commandments? 847 16
We *l* two things: 847 17

learned

and *l* their pagan ways, 744 18
when I have *l* your righteous judgments. 763 18

learning

Scriptures to be written for our *l*: 184 16
Scriptures to be written for our *l*: 236 9
Bless our land with honorable industry, sound *l*, 820 4
sound *l*, new discovery, and the pursuit of wisdom; 824 18

least

There is Benjamin, *l* of the tribes, at the head; 678 11

leather

I have become like a *l* flask in the smoke, * 770 7

leave

my own peace I *l* with you:" 107 18
my own peace I *l* with you:" 138 17
We beseech thee, *l* us not comfortless, 175 3
Do not *l* us comfortless, 226 15
my own peace I now *l* with you; 275 1
l there thy gift before the altar, 343 18
l your gift there before the altar and go; 376 14
my own peace I *l* with you:" 395 9
and *l* their wealth to their little ones. 602 3
Refrain from anger, *l* rage alone; * 633 21
and *l* their wealth to those who come after them. 652 25

leaven

Not with old *l*, 46 4
neither with the *l* of malice and wickedness, * 46 5
Not with the old *l*, the *l* of malice and evil, * 83 13
put away the *l* of malice and wickedness, 172 10
put away the *l* of malice and wickedness, 224 3

leaves

bearing fruit in due season, with *l* that do not withher; * 585 8

leaving

never *l* your temple untended. 520 17

Lebanon

the LORD breaks the cedars of *L*; 620 15
He makes *L* skip like a calf, * 620 16
may its fruit flourish like *L*, 686 19
and shall spread abroad like a cedar of *L*. 721 22
the cedars of *L* which he planted, 736 10

lectern

We dedicated this *L* in the Name of the Father, 571 7

led

follow in faith where thou hast *l* the way, 69 9
you *l* the people you redeemed; * 85 21
Eternal God, who *l* your ancient people into freedom 111 8
follow in faith where you have *l* the way, 123 8
Almighty God, whose blessed Son was *l* by the Spirit 166 9
Almighty God, whose blessed Son was *l* by the Spirit 218 1
O God, you *l* your holy apostles to ordain ministers 256 11
out of bondage in Egypt, and *l* them 287 7
O God, you *l* your ancient people by a pillar of cloud 290 2
you *l* the children of Israel out of their bondage 306 15
that they may be *l* to wise decisions 329 20
Give us, we pray, the faith to follow where you have *l* 498 5
follow in faith where you have *l* the way, 504 23
you *l* the children of Israel out of their bondage 570 7
how I went with the multitude and *l* them 643 9
You have gone up on high and *l* captivity captive; 677 18
You *l* your people like a flock * 694 17
He *l* them with a cloud by day, * 696 1
and *l* out the south wind by his might. 697 2
He *l* out his people like sheep * 699 9
He *l* them to safety, and they were not afraid; * 699 11
He *l* out his people with silver and gold; * 740 27
So he *l* forth his people with gladness, * 741 11
and he *l* them through the deep as through a desert. 742 17
He *l* them out of darkness and deep gloom * 747 9
Who *l* his people through the wilderness, * 791 1
For those who *l* us away captive asked us for a song, 792 5
Christians may be *l* into the way of truth, 815 4

left

we have *l* undone those things which we ought 41 21
we have *l* undone those things which we ought 63 2
and by what we have *l* undone. 79 14
and by what we have *l* undone. 116 16
and in what we have *l* undone. 127 10

wonderful Sacrament hath *l* unto us a memorial 201 2
wonderful Sacrament has *l* us a memorial 252 7
and by what we have *l* undone. 267 18
offended in what you have done or *l* undone, 317 3
and by what we have *l* undone. 320 14
we have *l* undone those things which we ought 321 2
and by what we have *l* undone. 331 25
and by what we have *l* undone. 352 14
and by what we have *l* undone. 360 6
things done and *l* undone; 393 12
and by what we have *l* undone. 397 23
things done and *l* undone; 447 7
Christ, who has *l* power to his Church 448 1
Christ, who has *l* power to his Church 451 11
and by what we have *l* undone. 454 5
Help me, LORD, for there is no godly one *l*; * 597 1
for I am *l* alone and in misery. 615 21
he has *l* off acting wisely and doing good. 632 8
there is no prophet *l*; * 690 2
not one of them was *l*. 742 21
wonderful Sacrament hast *l* unto us a memorial 834 12

legislature

assembled (or in the *L* of this State, 821 4

leisure

O tarry thou the LORD's *l*; * 478 8
l to rebuild our bodies and renew our minds, 825 3

lending

The righteous are always generous in their *l*, * 635 12
It is good for them to be generous in *l* * 755 13

length

that we may at *l* fall asleep peacefully in thee, 69 9
that we may at *l* fall asleep peacefully in you 123 8
may at *l* attain to the fullness of life everlasting; 186 9
until at *l*, through thy mercy, 198 19
at *l* we may attain to the fullness of eternal life; 238 4
that we may at *l* fall asleep peacefully in you 504 23
l of days, for ever and ever. 609 4
Add *l* of days to the king's life; * 668 24
and make them worthy at *l* to behold it unveiled 819 17

lengthen

You *l* my stride beneath me, * 605 12
until the shadows *l*, and the evening comes, 833 15

lengthens

I have faded away like a shadow when it *l*; * 752 21

Lent

This season of *L* provided 265 1
observance of a holy *L*, by self-examination 265 11

Lenten

L observance is ended, to renew the solemn promises 292 4

less

much *l* the walls of temples made with hands. 578 4

Lesson

A Reading (*L*) from ______. 47 1
Here endeth the *L* (Reading). 47 4
A Reading (*L*) from ______. 64 12
Here endeth the *L* (Reading). 65 3
A Reading (*L*) from ______. 84 3
Here ends the *L* (Reading). 84 6
A Reading (*L*) from ______. 118 12
Here ends the *L* (Reading). 119 3
A Reading (*L*) from ______. 300 1
A Reading (*L*) from ______. 325 13
A Reading (*L*) from ______. 357 4
A Reading (*L*) from ______. 414 1
A Reading (*L*) from ______. 516 1
A Reading (*L*) from ______. 528 12
A Reading (*L*) from ______. 540 12

lest

l coming suddenly he find you sleeping. 37 3
l he come suddenly and find you asleep. 75 3
l you dash your foot against a stone. 130 22
Judge yourselves, therefore, *l* you be judged 316 26
L he be angry and you perish; * 586 26
L like a lion they tear me in pieces * 590 22
give light to my eyes, *l* I sleep in death; 598 5
L my enemy say, "I have prevailed over him," * 598 6
l, if you do not hear me, 619 6
l I rend you and there be none to deliver you. 655 27
Slay them, O God, *l* my people forget; * 666 18
l you dash your foot against a stone. 720 10

let

"Whosoever will come after me, *l* him deny himself, 38 24
L the words of my mouth, 40 13
l all the earth keep silence 40 18
l us kneel in silence, 41 11
L us humbly confess our sins unto Almighty God. 41 15
O come, *l* us adore him. 43 1
O come, *l* us sing unto the Lord; * 44 10
l us heartily rejoice in the strength of our salvation. 44 11
L us come before his presence with thanksgiving, * 44 12
O come, *l* us worship and fall down * 45 1
l the whole earth stand in awe of him. 45 7
therefore *l* us keep the feast, 46 3
O *l* the earth bless the Lord; * 48 17
L us bless the Father, the Son, and the Holy Spirit; * 49 7
L us pray. 54 13
L thy way be known upon earth; 55 9
L not the needy, O Lord, be forgotten; 55 11
O Lord, *l* thy mercy be upon us; 55 21
L me never be confounded. 55 24
L us bless the Lord. 59 20
L my prayer be set forth in thy sight as the incense, 61 1
and *l* the lifting up of my hands 61 1
l the whole earth stand in awe of him. 61 5
l us kneel in silence, 62 12
L us humbly confess our sins unto Almighty God. 62 15
L us pray. 67 3
L thy way be known upon earth; 68 1
L not the needy, O Lord, be forgotten; 68 3
L the whole earth also worship thee, 70 16
L us bless the Lord. 72 17
"If anyone would come after me, *l* him deny himself 76 23
"*L* us go to the house of the Lord." 78 10
L the words of my mouth 78 12
l all the earth keep silence 78 17
l us kneel in silence, 79 6

L us confess our sins against God and our neighbor.	79	9
Come *l* us adore him.	80	10
Come, *l* us sing to the Lord; *	82	5
l us shout for joy to the Rock of our salvation.	82	6
L us come before his presence with thanksgiving *	82	7
Come, *l* us bow down, and bend the knee, *	82	15
therefore *l* us keep the feast,	83	12
L the wicked forsake their ways *	86	19
And *l* them turn to the Lord,	86	21
L the earth glorify the Lord, *	89	5
L the people of God glorify the Lord, *	89	18
L us glorify the Lord: Father, Son, and Holy Spirit; *	90	1
Do not *l* me perish in my sin, *	91	18
L us pray.	97	3
L your people sing with joy.	97	21
L your way be known upon earth;	98	3
L not the needy, O Lord, be forgotten;	98	5
L us bless the Lord.	102	8
He will not *l* your foot be moved *	104	17
And *l* our cry come to you.	107	2
L us pray.	107	3
L us bless the Lord.	107	22
"Out of darkness *l* light shine,"	110	3
L us pray.	110	11
l our prayer in your sight	113	9
as he bore his passion, and *l* it burn in us	113	14
L my prayer be set forth in your sight	115	1
L the whole earth tremble before him.	115	5
l us kneel in silence,	116	8
L us confess our sins against God and our neighbor.	116	11
L us pray.	121	3
L your people sing with joy.	121	21
L your way be known upon earth;	122	3
L not the needy, O Lord, be forgotten;	122	5
L the whole earth also worship you,	124	13
L us bless the Lord.	126	8
L us confess our sins to God.	127	5
l me never be put to shame: *	129	9
And *l* our cry come to you.	133	8
L us pray.	133	9
l your holy angels dwell with us	133	22
and *l* your blessing be upon us always;	133	23
L us bless the Lord.	135	12
L the Name of the Lord be blessed, *	138	3
l the Name of the Lord be praised.	138	6
"Out of darkness *l* light shine,"	139	12
l your holy angels dwell with us	140	14
and *l* your blessing be upon us always;	140	15
O come, *l* us sing unto the Lord; *	146	1
l us heartily rejoice in the strength of our salvation.	146	2
L us come before his presence with thanksgiving, *	146	3
O come, *l* us worship and fall down *	146	11
O Lord, *l* thy mercy be showed upon us;	153	16
L us pray.	153	18
L us pray.	155	6
l thy bountiful grace and mercy speedily help	160	3
l each one find thee mighty to save;	166	12
O Lord, we beseech thee, *l* thy continual pity cleanse	180	8
l your bountiful grace and mercy speedily help	212	3
l each one find you mighty to save;	218	4
L your continual mercy, O Lord, cleanse	232	1
L us pray.	264	1
l us now kneel before the Lord,	265	14
and *l* your anger depart from us;	268	27
L us pray.	270	3
L us give thanks to the Lord our God.	271	3
L these branches be for us signs of his victory,	271	10
L us go forth in peace.	271	17
L us pray.	272	6
L us pray.	276	3
L us pray for the holy Catholic Church of Christ	278	1
L us pray for all nations and peoples of the earth,	278	17
L us pray for all who suffer and are afflicted	279	3
L the cry of those in misery and need come	279	15
L us pray for all who have not received the Gospel	279	20
l your Gospel be preached	280	3
L us commit ourselves to our God,	280	8
l the whole world see	280	17
L your ways be known upon earth,	281	7
L the peoples praise you, O God;	281	9
l all the peoples praise you.	281	10
L us pray.	285	7
and *l* your trumpets shout Salvation	286	2
and *l* your holy courts, in radiant light,	286	8
L us give thanks to the Lord our God.	286	19
L us hear the record of God's saving deeds in history,	288	1
and *l* us pray that our God	288	2
L us pray.	288	4
l the whole world see	291	14
L us pray.	294	12
L us pray.	299	13
L us join with those who are committing themselves	303	17
L us now pray for these persons who are to receive	305	11
L us give thanks to the Lord our God.	306	11
L us pray.	308	1
L us welcome the newly baptized.	308	11
L us now pray for these persons who have renewed	309	1
God, *l* your fatherly hand ever be	310	8
l your Holy Spirit ever be	310	9
l us offer continually the sacrifice of praise,	317	20
God, *l* us come boldly unto the throne of grace,	320	6
L us humbly confess our sins unto Almighty God.	320	9
L us pray.	325	12
L us pray for the whole state of Christ's Church	328	22
L us humbly confess our sins unto Almighty God.	330	15
L us give thanks unto our Lord God.	333	5
Therefore *l* us keep the feast.	337	2
L us pray.	339	1
L us go forth in the name of Christ.	339	22
L us go forth into the world, rejoicing	340	3
L us bless the Lord.	340	6
L us give thanks unto our Lord God.	340	13
l us continually offer to God the sacrifice	344	1
L us with gladness present the offerings	344	12
l us with confidence draw near to the throne of grace,	352	6
L us confess our sins against God and our neighbor.	352	9
L us pray.	357	3
L us confess our sins against God and our neighbor.	360	1
L us give thanks to the Lord our God.	361	5
Therefore *l* us keep the feast.	364	16
L us pray.	365	8
L us go forth in the name of Christ.	366	14
L us go forth into the world,	366	18
L us bless the Lord.	366	21

L us give thanks to the Lord our God.	367	5
L us give thanks to the Lord our God.	370	3
L the grace of this Holy Communion make us one	372	6
L us give thanks to the Lord our God.	372	21
l us continually offer to God the sacrifice	376	17
L us with gladness present the offerings	377	10
l us pray to the Lord,	383	1
l us commend ourselves,	385	13
L light perpetual shine upon them.	387	18
L us pray for our own needs and those of others.	387	21
L us pray for the Church and for the world.	388	1
l us pray to the Lord,	389	13
l us commend ourselves,	391	20
Lord, *l* your loving-kindness be upon them;	393	6
L us pray in the words our Savior Christ has taught	398	11
L us bless the Lord.	399	13
L us give thanks to the Lord our God.	402	5
L us give thanks to the Lord our God.	404	7
L them be for us the Body and Blood	405	15
L us pray.	413	13
L us join with those who are committing themselves	416	4
L us now pray for these persons who have renewed	417	20
God, *l* your fatherly hand ever be	419	4
l your Holy Spirit ever be	419	5
L us pray.	421	1
L us pray.	425	6
has joined together *l* no one put asunder.	428	6
L us pray together in the words our Savior taught us.	428	7
L us pray.	429	1
L their love for each other be a seal	430	17
has joined together *l* no one put asunder.	434	7
L us say together:	440	7
L us now give thanks to him, and say together:	441	11
L us pray.	443	20
L us bless the Lord.	457	11
And if I am to do nothing, *l* me do it gallantly.	461	23
L us pray.	464	15
L us pray, then, for our brother (sister)	465	11
L his heart and soul now ring	466	9
L us pray with confidence to God,	466	13
L us also pray for all who mourn,	467	1
L us pray.	469	18
O *l* thine ears consider well *	474	3
In peace, *l* us pray to the Lord.	480	3
L us go forth in the name of Christ.	483	12
L us pray.	485	19
And *l* light perpetual shine upon him.	486	18
and *l* thy Holy Spirit lead us	489	5
do not *l* the pains of death	492	19
L us pray.	493	3
l us proclaim our faith and say,	496	1
l us pray to our Lord Jesus	497	1
l our faith be our consolation,	497	23
L light perpetual shine upon them.	498	9
L us go forth in the name of Christ.	500	1
L us pray.	501	20
And *l* light perpetual shine upon him.	502	16
L us go forth in the name of Christ.	502	21
and *l* your Holy Spirit lead us	504	3
l light perpetual shine upon them;	504	27
l it now be made known.	514	7
L us, therefore, follow their examples,	514	15
L us pray.	515	3
l the whole world see	515	7
L us go forth into the world,	523	18
In peace *l* us pray to the Lord.	527	11
L us pray.	528	1
l the whole world see	528	5
L us go forth into the world,	535	13
In peace *l* us pray to the Lord.	539	11
L us pray.	540	1
l the whole world see	540	5
L his life and teaching so reflect your commandments,	545	13
L us go forth into the world,	547	7
l us commend ourselves,	550	27
L us pray.	551	6
L us pray.	552	5
L us then offer our prayers to God for all his people,	560	1
L us pray.	560	5
and *l* the doors of this place be open	562	1
l all these be signs of the ministry	562	7
L us pray.	567	7
L the door(s) be opened.	568	1
L us pray.	568	6
L us give thanks to the Lord our God.	570	3
L us now pray for the setting apart of the Altar.	573	7
L it be to us a sign of the heavenly Altar	574	1
L us thank God whom we worship here	578	1
"*L* us break their yoke," they say; *	586	6
"*l* us cast off their bonds from us."	586	7
L me announce the decree of the LORD: *	586	14
l them fall, because of their schemes.	589	14
Then *l* my enemy pursue and overtake me, *	591	3
l the assembly of the peoples gather round you.	591	9
L the malice of the wicked come to an end,	591	15
O LORD, *l* not the ungodly have the upper hand; *	594	15
l them be judged before you.	594	16
l the ungodly know they are but mortal.	594	18
nor *l* your holy one see the Pit.	600	18
L my vindication come forth from your presence; *	601	1
l your eyes be fixed on justice.	601	2
l them not get dominion over me; *	607	25
L the words of my mouth and the meditation of my	607	28
"He trusted in the LORD; *l* him deliver him; *	610	16
l him rescue him, if he delights in him."	610	17
l me not be humiliated,	614	15
nor *l* my enemies triumph over me.	614	16
L none who look to you be put to shame; *	614	17
l the treacherous be disappointed in their schemes.	614	18
l me not be put to shame, for I have trusted in you.	616	2
L integrity and uprightness preserve me, *	616	3
and have not *l* my enemies triumph over me.	621	5
l me never be put to shame; *	622	8
l me not be ashamed for having called upon you; *	623	27
rather, *l* the wicked be put to shame;	623	28
l them be silent in the grave.	623	29
L the lying lips be silenced which speak against	624	1
Be strong and *l* your heart take courage, *	624	21
L all the earth fear the LORD; *	626	15
l all who dwell in the world stand in awe of him.	626	16
L your loving-kindness, O LORD, be upon us, *	627	19
l the humble hear and rejoice.	627	24
l us exalt his Name together.	627	26

and *l* not your faces be ashamed. 628 4
L those who seek after my life be shamed 629 20
l those who plot my ruin fall back and be dismayed. 629 21
L them be like chaff before the wind, * 629 22
and *l* the angel of the LORD drive them away. 629 23
L their way be dark and slippery, * 630 1
and *l* the angel of the LORD pursue them. 630 2
L ruin come upon them unawares; * 630 5
l them be caught in the net they hid; 630 6
l them fall into the pit they dug. 630 7
Do not *l* my treacherous foes rejoice over me, * 631 6
nor *l* those who hate me without a cause 631 7
do not *l* them triumph over me. 631 20
Do not *l* them say in their hearts, 631 21
Do not *l* them say, "We have swallowed him up." 631 23
L all who rejoice at my ruin be ashamed 631 24
l those who boast against me be clothed with 631 25
L those who favor my cause sing out with joy 631 27
l them say always, "Great is the LORD, 631 28
L not the foot of the proud come near me, * 633 1
nor *l* them be found guilty when brought to trial. 636 2
For I said, "Do not *l* them rejoice at my expense, * 638 1
LORD, *l* me know my end 639 1
l your love and your faithfulness keep me safe 641 3
L them be ashamed and altogether dismayed 641 10
l them draw back and be disgraced 641 12
L those who say "Aha!" and gloat over me 641 14
L all who seek you rejoice in you and be glad; * 641 16
l those who love your salvation continually say, 641 17
l me recite what I have fashioned for the king; * 647 12
L Mount Zion be glad 651 23
L the heavens declare the rightness of his cause; * 654 14
L death come upon them suddenly; 661 14
l them go down alive into the grave; * 661 15
he will never *l* the righteous stumble. 662 7
L them vanish like water that runs off; * 665 7
l them wither like trodden grass. 665 8
L them be like the snail that melts away, * 665 9
l them be cut down like a brier; * 665 11
like thorns and thistles *l* them be swept away. 665 12
God will *l* me look in triumph on my enemies. 666 17
l them be caught in their pride. 666 23
L everyone know that God rules in Jacob, * 666 26
l his years extend over many generations. 668 25
L him sit enthroned before God for ever; * 669 1
L them fall upon the edge of the sword, * 671 5
and *l* them be food for jackals. 671 6
l them shout for joy and sing. 673 17
l no rebel rise up against him. 674 8
You *l* enemies ride over our heads; 674 17
L your ways be known upon earth, * 675 11
L the peoples praise you, O God; * 675 13
l all the peoples praise you. 675 14
L the nations be glad and sing for joy, * 675 15
L the peoples praise you, O God; * 675 18
l all the peoples praise you. 675 19
L God arise, and *l* his enemies be scattered; * 676 1
l those who hate him flee before him. 676 2
L them vanish like smoke when the wind drives 676 3
so *l* the wicked perish 676 4
But *l* the righteous be glad and rejoice before God; * 676 6
l them also be merry and joyful. 676 7
L tribute be brought out of Egypt; * 678 22
l Ethiopia stretch out her hands to God. 678 23
L not those who hope in you be put to shame 679 22
l not those who seek you be disgraced because of me, 679 24
Save me from the mire; do not *l* me sink; * 680 17
l me be rescued from those who hate me 680 18
L not the torrent of waters wash over me, 680 20
neither *l* the deep swallow me up; * 680 21
do not *l* the Pit shut its mouth upon me. 680 22
L the table before them be a trap * 681 8
L their eyes be darkened, that they may not see, * 681 10
and *l* the fierceness of your anger overtake them. 681 13
L their camp be desolate, * 681 14
and *l* there be none to dwell in their tents. 681 15
and *l* them not receive your vindication. 681 19
L them be wiped out of the book of the living * 681 20
L the heavens and the earth praise him, * 682 5
L those who seek my life be ashamed 682 13
l those who take pleasure in my misfortune 682 15
L those who say to me "Aha!" and gloat over me 682 17
L all who seek you rejoice and be glad in you; * 682 19
l those who love your salvation say for ever, 682 20
l me never be ashamed. 683 2
L my mouth be full of your praise * 683 16
L those who set themselves against me 684 3
l those who seek to do me evil be covered with scorn 684 5
"*L* us destroy them altogether." * 689 24
L not the oppressed turn away ashamed; * 690 26
l the poor and needy praise your Name. 690 27
l all around him bring gifts to him who is worthy 692 23
You will not *l* my eyelids close; * 693 8
He split open the sea and *l* them pass through; * 695 28
He *l* it fall in the midst of their camp * 697 5
l your compassion be swift to meet us; * 701 22
L it be known among the heathen and in our sight 702 2
L the sorrowful sighing of the prisoners 702 4
at the rebuke of your countenance *l* them perish. 703 19
L your hand be upon the man of your right hand, * 703 20
They have said, "Come, *l* us wipe them out 706 9
l the name of Israel be remembered no more." 706 11
Who said, "*L* us take for ourselves * 707 1
L them be disgraced and terrified for ever; * 707 11
l them be put to confusion and perish. 707 12
L them know that you, whose Name is YAHWEH, * 707 13
l your anger depart from us. 709 2
L my prayer enter into your presence; * 712 3
nor *l* my faithfulness prove false. 716 8
Come, *l* us sing to the LORD; * 724 14
l us shout for joy to the Rock of our salvation. 724 15
L us come before his presence with thanksgiving * 724 16
Come, *l* us bow down, and bend the knee, * 725 1
l the whole earth tremble before him. 726 10
L the heavens rejoice, and *l* the earth be glad; 726 14
l the sea thunder and all that is in it; * 726 15
l the field be joyful and all that is therein. 726 16
l the earth rejoice; * 726 23
l the multitude of the isles be glad. 726 24
L the sea make a noise and all that is in it, * 728 16
L the rivers clap their hands, * 728 18
and *l* the hills ring out with joy before the LORD, 728 19
l the people tremble; * 728 24
l the earth shake. 728 26

libations

Their *l* of blood I will not offer, * 600 5

liberties

to maintain these *l* in righteousness and peace; 190 21
to maintain our *l* in righteousness and peace; 242 5
Defend our *l*, 820 7
ventured much for the *l* we now enjoy. 839 23

liberty

rejoice in the *l* of the children of God; 111 11
the *l* of that abundant life 164 7
country won *l* for themselves and for us, 190 18
that we may use our *l* 207 4
the *l* of that abundant life 216 2
country won *l* for themselves and for us, 242 2
that we may use our *l* 258 4
that those baptized here may enjoy the *l* 569 17
for you have set my heart at *l*. 765 24
I will walk at *l*, * 767 3
For all valiant seekers after truth, *l*, and justice, 837 17
We thank you for the torch of *l* which has been lit 839 8
Sin has power over us because we lose our *l* 849 2

lick

and his enemies *l* the dust. 686 2

lie

I *l* down in peace; at once I fall asleep; * 129 6
and when our mortal body doth *l* 349 9
He makes me *l* down in green pastures* 443 3
If I am to *l* low, help me to do it 461 22
He maketh me to *l* down in green pastures; * 476 21
I *l* down and go to sleep; * 587 11
I *l* down in peace; at once I fall asleep; * 588 15
because of those who *l* in wait for me; * 589 7
who conceive evil, and give birth to a *l*. 591 27
They *l* in wait, like a lion in a covert; 595 11
they *l* in wait to seize upon the lowly; * 595 12
He makes me *l* down in green pastures * 612 25
and harnessed your tongue to a *l*. 655 19
They band together; they *l* in wait; * 663 1
I *l* in the midst of lions that devour the people; * 664 1
See how they *l* in wait for my life, 665 22
and those who *l* in wait for my life 683 21
both horse and rider *l* stunned. 692 13
like the slain who *l* in the grave, 712 10
"I will not *l* to David. 716 12
I *l* awake and groan; * 731 13
Though the wicked *l* in wait for me to destroy me, * 771 9

lied

and *l* to him with their tongues. 697 23

lies

and when our mortal body *l* in death, 382 4
You destroy those who speak *l*; * 589 1
for the cursing and *l* that they utter, * 666 22
l are their chief delight. 669 13
for the mouth of those who speak *l* shall be stopped. 671 9
and those who tell *l* shall not continue in my sight. 730 25
The proud have smeared me with *l*, * 769 1
for they wrong me with *l*; * 769 21
help me, for they persecute me with *l*. 770 15
As for *l*, I hate and abhor them, * 777 5

life

necessary for our *l* and our salvation. 41 10
live a godly, righteous, and sober *l*, 42 9
amendment of *l*, 42 13
all the days of our *l*. 51 10
and the *l* everlasting. 54 10
may find it none other than the way of *l* 56 9
knowledge of whom standeth our eternal *l*, 57 2
that in all the cares and occupations of our *l* 57 16
and all the blessings of this *l*; 58 20
and in the world to come *l* everlasting. 59 18
but shall have the light of *l*." 62 10
live a godly, righteous, and sober *l*, 63 12
amendment of *l*, 63 16
O Son of God, O Giver of *l*, 64 8
and the *l* everlasting. 66 26
That we may depart this *l* in thy faith and fear, and 68 18
entrusting one another and all our *l* to Christ, 68 24
O God, who art the *l* of all who live, 70 4
and all the blessings of this *l*; 71 16
and in the world to come *l* everlasting. 72 15
those things that are necessary for our *l* 79 4
Spirit keep you in eternal *l*. 80 4
but the *l* he lives, he lives to God. 83 18
Bringing forth *l* and giving growth, * 87 3
praise you without ceasing all the days of my *l*. 91 24
all the days of our *l*. 92 31
and the *l* everlasting. 96 30
may find it none other than the way of *l* 99 4
to know you is eternal *l* 99 21
occupations of our *l* we may not forget you, 100 9
and all the blessings of this *l*; 101 12
and in the age to come *l* everlasting. 102 7
preserve my *l*, O LORD, according to your word. 104 2
My *l* is always in my hand, * 104 5
O Son of God, O Giver of *l*, 112 8
and the strength of our *l*. 113 8
to eternal *l* and to the ages of ages. 113 15
but will have the light of *l*." 116 6
Spirit keep you in eternal *l*. 117 9
O Son of God, O Giver of *l*, 118 8
and the *l* everlasting. Amen. 120 26
That we may depart this *l* in your faith and fear, 122 20
entrusting one another and all our *l* to Christ, 122 26
O God, the *l* of all who live, 124 1
and all the blessings of this *l*; 125 10
and in the age to come *l* everlasting. 126 7
in newness of *l*, 127 14
With long *l* will I satisfy him, * 131 4
this *l* may rest in your eternal changelessness; 133 15
sustains the world we live in and the *l* we live: 134 12
our common *l* depends upon each other's toil; 134 14
O Son of God, O Giver of *l*, 139 8
to all the faithful departed eternal *l* and peace, 152 16
in the time of this mortal *l* 159 3
we may rise to the *l* immortal; 159 6
that we may share the divine *l* of him 162 9
we beseech thee, the liberty of that abundant *l* 164 7
mortal *l* may hide from us the light of that love 165 10

the true bread which giveth *l*	167	11
may find it none other than the way of *l*	168	13
shameful death to be unto us the means of *l*:	168	18
mysteries giveth us a pledge of *l* eternal,	169	11
and rise with him to newness of *l*;	170	4
opened unto us the gate of everlasting *l*:	170	23
raised from the death of sin by thy *l*-giving Spirit;	171	2
Christ didst destroy death and bring *l*	171	11
death he hath recalled us to *l*,	172	17
whom truly to know is everlasting *l*:	173	16
the way, the truth, and the *l*,	173	18
his steps in the way that leadeth to eternal *l*;	173	19
l to every race and nation by the promised gift	175	9
and also an example of godly *l*:	180	20
follow the blessed steps of his most holy *l*;	181	1
make us the children of God and heirs of eternal *l*:	184	9
and ever hold fast the blessed hope of everlasting *l*,	184	19
attain to the fullness of *l* everlasting;	186	10
uprightness of *l* and his obedience to thy commands;	188	11
may glorify in *l* and death the Name of our Lord	189	8
gave generously of his *l*	189	19
follow his doctrine and holy *l*,	190	4
know thee in the power of his endless *l*;	191	5
may receive with him the crown of *l*;	195	12
and the teaching of his holy *l*,	196	25
that we may share the divine *l* of him	200	15
have put away the old *l* of sin,	201	14
who holdest all souls in *l*:	202	1
having opened to him the gates of larger *l*,	202	11
turn us from the old *l* of sin:	203	7
Grant that we, being reborn to new *l* in him,	203	7
from the old *l* of sin by our baptism	203	13
clothe them with holiness of *l*,	205	9
whose Son Jesus Christ in his earthly *l*	208	1
Heavenly Father, giver of *l* and health:	208	16
for the love of him who laid down his *l* for us,	209	14
mortal *l* in which your Son Jesus Christ came to visit	211	3
we may rise to the *l* immortal;	211	6
share the divine *l* of him who humbled himself	214	3
the liberty of that abundant *l*	216	2
that no clouds of this mortal *l* may hide from us	217	2
the true bread which gives *l* to the world:	219	2
may find it none other than the way of *l*	220	4
shameful death to be for us the means of *l*:	220	9
mysteries gives us a pledge of eternal *l*;	221	5
and rise with him to newness of *l*;	221	16
opened to us the gate of everlasting *l*:	222	17
raised from the death of sin by your *l*-giving Spirit;	222	19
Christ destroyed death and brought *l*	223	5
as by his death he has recalled us to *l*,	224	10
Almighty God, whom truly to know is everlasting *l*:	225	8
the way, the truth, and the *l*,	225	10
steps in the way that leads to eternal *l*;	225	11
on this day you opened the way of eternal *l*	227	1
and also an example of godly *l*:	232	12
follow daily in the blessed steps of his most holy *l*;	232	14
make us children of God and heirs of eternal *l*:	236	3
hold fast the blessed hope of everlasting *l*,	236	11
attain to the fullness of eternal *l*;	238	4
Give us grace to imitate his uprightness of *l*	239	20
may glorify in *l* and death the Name	240	15
l and substance for the relief of the poor	241	6
follow his teaching and holy *l*,	241	13
know you in the power of his unending *l*;	242	12
receive with him the crown of *l*;	247	10
following his example and the teaching of his holy *l*,	248	11
share the divine *l* of him who humbled himself	252	3
have put away the old *l* of sin,	253	2
you hold all souls in *l*:	253	6
opened to him the gates of larger *l*,	253	15
you turn us from the old *l* of sin:	254	8
Grant that we, being reborn to new *l* in him,	254	9
from the old *l* of sin by our baptism into the death	254	14
clothe them with holiness of *l*,	256	6
whose Son Jesus Christ in his earthly *l*	259	3
Heavenly Father, giver of *l* and health:	260	1
who laid down his *l* for us,	260	20
gracious gift that we are given everlasting *l*;	265	19
our dishonesty in daily *l* and work,	268	11
and that the rest of our *l* hereafter may be pure	269	12
whereby you have given us *l*	270	6
follow him in the way that leads to eternal *l*;	271	12
may find it none other than the way of *l*	272	4
mysteries gives us a pledge of eternal *l*;	274	5
become heirs with him of everlasting *l*.	277	6
pray for the grace of a holy *l*,	280	9
of *l* in the day of resurrection.	280	13
and to us sinners everlasting *l*	282	10
rise with him to newness of *l*;	283	5
Jesus passed over from death to *l*,	285	2
restored to grace and holiness of *l*.	287	11
share the divine *l* of him who humbled himself	288	7
Give now the water of *l* to those who thirst for you,	290	10
into righteousness and out of death into *l*:	291	6
and raised with him to newness of *l*.	292	3
and the *l* everlasting.	293	18
keep us in eternal *l* by his grace,	294	7
is brought up in the Christian faith and *l*?	302	2
support these persons in their *l* in Christ?	303	15
and the *l* everlasting.	304	21
Fill them with your holy and *l*-giving Spirit.	305	19
from the bondage of sin into everlasting *l*.	306	19
continue for ever in the risen *l* of Jesus	307	5
and have raised them to the new *l*	308	4
sustain him all the days of his *l*.	309	14
that they may serve you in this *l*,	310	11
with you in the *l* to come;	310	12
and have raised him to the new *l*	314	3
and for a spiritual sharing in his risen *l*.	316	5
and exalt us to everlasting *l*.	316	16
with full purpose of amendment of *l*,	317	5
live a godly, righteous, and sober *l*,	321	12
amendment of *l*,	321	16
in the Holy Spirit, the Lord, the giver of *l*,	327	12
and the *l* of the world to come.	327	19
in the Holy Ghost the Lord, and Giver of *l*,	328	13
and the *l* of the world to come.	328	21
their *l* and doctrine, set forth thy true	329	11
righteousness all the days of their *l*.	329	17
who, in this transitory *l*, are in trouble,	329	28
departed this *l* in thy faith and fear	330	2
lead a new *l*, following the commandments of God,	330	11
serve and please thee in newness of *l*,	331	18
and bring you to everlasting *l*;	332	6

have everlasting *l*.	332	12
preserve thy body and soul unto everlasting *l*.	338	6
Christ keep you in everlasting *l*.	338	14
our *l* and labor to the Lord.	344	13
Creator of the light and source of *l*,	344	14
and called us to new *l* in Jesus	344	15
resurrection opened to us the way of everlasting *l*.	345	3
and to make us heirs in him of everlasting *l*;	345	9
and by his rising to *l* again hath won	346	21
hath won for us everlasting *l*.	346	22
the blessed hope of everlasting *l*;	349	8
O Lord, *l* is changed, not ended;	349	8
Spirit keep you in eternal *l*.	353	4
the Holy Spirit, the Lord, the giver of *l*,	359	3
and the *l* of the world to come.	359	10
Spirit keep you in eternal *l*.	360	18
and unending *l* in him.	363	15
Christ keep you in everlasting *l*.	365	5
out of sin into righteousness, out of death into *l*.	368	9
Fountain of *l* and source of all goodness,	373	4
the bread of *l* and the cup of salvation,	375	7
our *l* and labor to the Lord.	377	11
For you are the source of light and *l*,	377	12
and called us to new *l* in Jesus Christ our Lord.	377	13
resurrection opened to us the way of everlasting *l*.	377	16
and to make us heirs in him of everlasting *l*;	378	5
and by his rising to *l* again he has won	379	18
he has won for us everlasting *l*.	379	19
comforts us with the blessed hope of everlasting *l*.	382	3
For to your faithful people, O Lord, *l* is changed,	382	3
commend ourselves, and one another, and all our *l*,	385	14
but *l* eternal, we pray to you, O Lord.	391	18
and all our *l* to Christ our God.	391	21
For all people in their daily *l* and work;	392	2
We thank you, Lord, for all the blessings of this *l*.	393	1
that we may live and serve you in newness of *l*,	393	14
but have eternal *l*.	396	3
Jesus said, "I am the bread of *l*;	396	4
the bread which I shall give for the *l* of the world	397	3
mysteries gives us a pledge of eternal *l*;	397	17
Spirit keep you in eternal *l*.	398	10
Christ keep you in everlasting *l*.	399	6
and drink this cup may be filled with your *l*	405	17
support these persons in their *l* in Christ?	416	2
and the *l* everlasting.	417	3
sustain him all the days of his *l*.	418	12
that they may serve you in this *l*,	419	7
dwell with you in the *l* to come;	419	8
Jesus Christ adorned this manner of *l* by his presence	423	5
Eternal God, creator and preserver of all *l*,	429	2
and for which your Son gave his *l*,	429	4
devotion in the ordering of their common *l*,	429	8
peace with you and one another all the days of their *l*.	429	13
Make their *l* together a sign of Christ's love	429	17
make the way of the cross to be the way of *l*.	430	13
in their *l* and in their death.	430	21
that you may faithfully live together in this *l*,	431	12
in the age to come have *l* everlasting.	431	13
occasion in the *l* of a family.	440	2
heavenly Father, the Lord of all *l*,	440	5
follow my all the days of my *l*,*	443	16
live faithfully according to your will in this *l*,	444	5
partake of everlasting glory in the *l* to come;	444	6
Almighty God, giver of *l* and love,	444	8
devotion in the ordering of their common *l*,	444	10
peace all the days of their *l*;	444	14
this child and preserve his *l*;	444	17
I firmly intend amendment of *l*,	447	10
not perish, but have everlasting *l*.	449	17
the power of the Holy Spirit keep you in eternal *l*.	451	5
the power of the Holy Spirit keep you in eternal *l*.	455	8
and to give you that victory of *l*	456	4
and bring you to everlasting *l*;	456	18
the residue of his *l* in thy fear,	458	8
that finally he may dwell with thee in *l* everlasting;	458	9
and raise him up to a *l* of service	459	5
Heavenly Father, giver of *l* and health:	459	17
he may live with you in everlasting *l*;	460	4
Strengthen them by your *l*-giving Spirit,	460	12
may so order his *l* and conduct	460	21
hold me in eternal *l*, my Lord and my God.	461	11
and comfort him with the promise of *l*	462	2
Wash him in the holy font of everlasting *l*,	465	17
Giver of *l*, that he will raise him to perfection	466	14
I am the resurrection and the *l*, saith the Lord;	469	1
follow me all the days of my *l*; *	476	17
follow me all the days of my *l*, *	477	10
the LORD is the strength of my *l*;	477	14
all the days of my *l*,	477	18
resurrection may die to sin and rise to newness of *l*,	480	9
l with those they love.	481	13
and the resurrection to *l* everlasting.	481	16
go from strength to strength in the *l* of perfect service	481	21
to receive the crown of *l*	481	26
neither sighing, but *l* everlasting.	482	11
neither sighing, but *l* everlasting.	483	5
and giving *l* to those in the tomb.	483	15
In the midst of *l* we are in death;	484	4
will also give *l* to our mortal bodies,	485	2
Thou shalt show me the path of *l*;	485	6
hope of the resurrection to eternal *l*	485	9
in the midst of this earthly *l* being purged	488	18
in the *l* of perfect service in thy heavenly kingdom;	488	24
sensible of the shortness and uncertainty of *l*;	489	5
and to us sinners everlasting *l*	489	27
I am Resurrection and I am *l*, says the Lord.	491	1
Whoever has faith in me shall have *l*,	491	2
And everyone who has *l*,	491	4
For none of us has *l* in himself,	491	13
For if we have *l*, we are alive in the Lord,	491	15
In the midst of *l* we are in death;	492	5
Christ destroyed death, and brought *l*	493	5
see in death the gate of eternal *l*,	493	21
In the assurance of eternal *l* given at Baptism,	496	1
and the *l* everlasting.	496	20
Christ who said, "I am Resurrection and I am *l*."	497	2
You raised the dead to *l*;	497	10
give to our brother (sister) eternal *l*.	497	11
and eternal *l* our hope.	497	23
neither sighing, but *l* everlasting.	499	3
and giving *l* to those in the tomb.	500	4
will also give new *l* to our mortal bodies	501	4
You will show me the path of *l*;	501	8
hope of the resurrection to eternal *l*	501	11

shortness and uncertainty of human *l*; 504 3
Christ who is the Resurrection and the *L*: 505 2
the death of sin to the *l* of righteousness; 505 3
when we depart this *l* we may rest in him, 505 4
and in the joyful expectation of eternal *l* 505 14
and to give his *l* a ransom for many. 517 18
in the Holy Spirit, the Lord, the giver of *l*, 520 3
and the *l* of the world to come. 520 10
and wisely overseeing the *l* and work 521 13
offering of a pure, and gentle, and holy *l*; 521 15
in love and patience, and in holiness of *l*. 523 7
And do you believe his manner of *l* to be suitable 526 5
in the Holy Spirit, the Lord, the giver of *l*, 530 22
and the *l* of the world to come. 530 29
fashion your *l* in accordance with its precepts. 531 9
glorify God in this *l* and in the *l* to come. 531 20
Will you do your best to pattern your *l* 532 19
and in holiness of *l*. 535 7
And do you believe his manner of *l* to be suitable 538 5
in the Holy Spirit, the Lord, the giver of *l*, 542 22
and the *l* of the world to come. 542 29
and to model your *l* upon them. 543 9
your *l* and teaching are to show Christ's people 543 16
and his Church to the *l* and work of a deacon? 543 20
Will you do your best to pattern your *l* 544 7
Let his *l* and teaching so reflect your commandments, 545 13
in love and patience, and in holiness of *l*. 547 3
that they may serve you in a true and godly *l*, 548 17
or grief, but *l* eternal, 550 23
and all our *l* to Christ our God. 550 28
share in the fullness of your *l*-giving Spirit; 552 11
and by my *l* and teaching set forth 563 3
in love and patience, and in holiness of *l*. 564 7
from the bondage of sin into everlasting *l*. 570 11
in the risen *l* of Jesus Christ our Savior. 570 20
We praise you for his *l* on earth, 573 13
refreshing us day by day with the bread of *l*. 578 17
trample my *l* into the ground, 591 4
Whoever leads a blameless *l* and does what is right, * 599 6
You will show me the path of *l*; * 600 19
from those whose portion in *l* is this world; 601 28
He asked you for *l*, and you gave it to him: * 609 3
my *l* from the power of the dog. 611 21
follow me all the days of my *l*, * 613 12
Protect my *l* and deliver me; * 616 1
nor my *l* with those who thirst for blood, 616 25
the LORD is the strength of my *l*; 617 9
all the days of my *l*; 617 21
you restored my *l* as I was going down to the grave. 621 9
For my *l* is wasted with grief, 623 6
They plot to take my *l*. 623 19
Who among you loves *l* * 628 17
and desires long *l* to enjoy prosperity? 628 18
The LORD ransoms the *l* of his servants, * 629 11
Let those who seek after my *l* be shamed 629 20
and my *l* from the young lions. 631 3
For with you is the well of *l*, * 632 22
Those who seek after my *l* lay snares for me; * 637 20
so that I may know how short my *l* is. 639 2
who seek after my *l* to destroy it; * 641 11
a prayer to the God of my *l*. 643 25
or deliver to God the price of our *l*; 652 18
For the ransom of our *l* is so great, * 652 19
But God will ransom my *l*; * 653 13
and the ruthless have sought my *l*, * 659 22
it is the Lord who sustains my *l*. 659 25
because they seek my *l*. 663 3
See how they lie in wait for my *l*, 665 22
Add length of days to the king's *l*; * 668 24
For your loving-kindness is better than *l* itself; * 670 17
May those who seek my *l* to destroy it * 671 3
protect my *l* from fear of the enemy. 671 11
Who holds our souls in *l*, * 674 11
Let those who seek my *l* be ashamed 682 13
and those who lie in wait for my *l* take counsel 683 21
but you will restore my *l* 684 24
Do not hand over the *l* of your dove to wild beasts; * 690 22
give us *l*, that we may call upon your Name. 703 23
Will you not give us *l* again, * 709 5
Keep watch over my *l*, for I am faithful; * 710 1
and a band of violent men seeks my *l*; * 711 2
my *l* is at the brink of the grave. 712 6
Remember, LORD, how short *l* is, * 717 8
The span of our *l* is seventy years, 718 19
so shall we rejoice and be glad all the days of our *l*. 719 2
With long *l* will I satisfy him, * 720 20
They conspire against the *l* of the just * 724 7
and only those who lead a blameless *l* shall 730 22
He redeems your *l* from the grave * 733 15
to save his *l* from those who would condemn him. 753 11
"O LORD, I pray you, save my *l*." 759 9
For you have rescued my *l* from death, * 759 16
give me *l* according to your word. 765 10
give me *l* in your ways. 766 10
in your righteousness preserve my *l*. 766 16
that your promise gives me *l*. 767 14
because by them you give me *l*. 771 6
preserve my *l*, O LORD, according to your word. 772 8
My *l* is always in my hand, * 772 11
according to your judgments, give me *l*. 776 2
according to your promise, give me *l*. 776 12
preserve my *l*, according to your judgments. 776 16
all the days of your *l*. 783 23
l for evermore. 787 18
to count them all, my *l* span would need to 795 14
do not strip me of my *l*. 797 21
For my enemy has sought my *l*; 799 1
and in righteousness of *l*. 815 6
Grant us all things necessary for our common *l*, 817 21
they may enrich your Church, and by their *l* 819 10
Grant, O God, that your holy and *l*-giving Spirit 823 17
O God, you have bound us together in a common *l*. 824 1
that it might produce what is needed for *l*: 824 7
O God, in the course of this busy *l*, 825 1
ties of mutual regard which form our civic *l*. 825 9
all other bodily necessities of *l*, 825 22
and amendment of *l* according to your will, 826 19
all things necessary to sustain their *l*: 828 11
Increase our reverence before the mystery of *l*; 828 18
and the pride of *l*. 829 2
give more *l* than the ways of the world, 829 16
trust in your goodness all the days of his *l*; 830 11
passeth understanding abide all the days of his *l*; 830 17
for this *l* and the *l* to come, 831 8

by thy mercy, obtain everlasting *l*; 832 5
changes and chances of this mortal *l*, 832 21
are born to eternal *l*. 833 13
and the fever of *l* is over, and our work is done. 833 16
and gave us the hope of everlasting *l*: 835 3
for the beauty of this world, for the wonder of *l*, 836 3
truth of his Word and the example of his *l*; 836 13
and for his rising to *l* again, 836 15
in which we are raised to the *l* of your kingdom. 836 16
and the promise of eternal *l*; 838 19
It sustains our *l*, though we have been faithless 839 13
thank you for the *l* of this child, 841 2
partaker of everlasting glory in the *l* to come; 841 12
What does this mean about human *l*? 846 13
To show respect for the *l* God has given us; 848 7
justice, freedom, and the necessities of *l* 848 13
for us the way of eternal *l*. 850 12
and give us *l* in all its fullness. 851 3
giver of *l*, the One who spoke through the prophets. 852 19
to set forth the *l* and teachings of Jesus 853 16
their place in the *l*, worship, and governance 855 19
for all the blessings of this *l*, 857 9
forgiveness of sins, and new *l* 858 19
for the continual remembrance of his *l*, 859 7
is our nourishment in eternal *l*. 860 3
woman and man enter into a *l*-long union, 861 5
live with confidence in newness and fullness of *l*, 861 26
we mean eternal *l* in our enjoyment of God; 862 6
What do we mean by everlasting *l*? 862 25
By everlasting *l*, we mean a new existence, 862 26

lifetime

his favor for a *l*. 621 13
and my *l* is as nothing in your sight; * 639 4

lift

Govern them and *l* them up for ever. 55 16
I *l* up my eyes to the hills; * 104 13
The Lord *l* upon his countenance upon you 114 4
L up the light of your countenance upon us, O Lord. 129 3
L up your hands in the holy place 131 8
L up your hands in the holy place 140 3
L up your hearts. 333 3
We *l* them up unto the Lord. 333 4
L up your hearts. 340 11
We *l* them up unto the Lord. 340 12
L up your hearts. 361 3
We *l* them up to the Lord. 361 4
L up your hearts. 367 3
We *l* them to the Lord. 367 4
L up your hearts. 370 1
We *l* them up to the Lord. 370 2
L up your hearts. 372 19
We *l* them to the Lord. 372 20
L up your hearts. 402 3
We *l* them to the Lord. 402 4
L up your hearts. 404 5
We *l* them to the Lord. 404 6
I will *l* up the cup of salvation* 442 21
l up your countenance upon them; 467 6
I will *l* up mine eyes unto the hills; * 473 9
And now shall he *l* up mine head * 477 23
the Lord *l* up his countenance upon him 485 14
the Lord *l* up his countenance upon him 501 15
L up the light of your countenance upon us, O LORD. 588 12
O you who *l* me up from the gate of death; 594 3
l up your hand, O God; * 595 19
L up your heads, O gates; 614 1
l them high, O everlasting doors; * 614 2
L up your heads, O gates; 614 7
l them high, O everlasting doors; * 614 8
To you, O LORD, I *l* up my soul; 614 13
when I *l* up my hands to your holy of holies. 619 9
and *l* up my hands in your Name. 670 20
your help, O God, will *l* me up on high. 681 23
none of the warriors can *l* a hand. 692 11
for to you, O LORD, I *l* up my soul. 710 6
l up your voice, rejoice, and sing. 728 11
therefore he will *l* high his head. 754 4
I will *l* up the cup of salvation * 759 25
I will *l* up my hands to your commandments, * 767 9
I *l* up my eyes to the hills; * 779 1
To you I *l* up my eyes, * 780 15
L up your hands in the holy place 787 21
Let not those who surround me *l* up their heads; * 796 19
for I *l* up my soul to you. 799 18
l up thy countenance upon him, 831 16
By the might of thy Spirit *l* us, 832 15

lifted

and has *l* up the lowly. 92 9
and has *l* up the lowly. 119 15
whose Son our Savior Jesus Christ was *l* 192 13
whose Son our Savior Jesus Christ was *l* 244 1
who for our sins was *l* 346 13
For our sins he was *l* 379 10
and has *l* up the lowly. 442 4
because you have *l* me up * 621 4
He *l* me out of the desolate pit, 640 3
has *l* up his heel and turned against me. 642 19
and those who hate you have *l* up their heads. 706 6
The waters have *l* up, O LORD, 722 9
the waters have *l* up their voice; * 722 10
the waters have *l* up their pounding waves. 722 11
you have *l* me up and thrown me away. 731 20
So he *l* his hand against them, * 743 24
He *l* up the poor out of misery * 749 11

lifting

the *l* up of my hands be an evening sacrifice. 61 2
the *l* up of our hands as the evening sacrifice. 113 10
the *l* up of my hands as the evening sacrifice. 115 1
the *l* up of my hands as the evening sacrifice. 797 6
Adoration is the *l* up of the heart and mind to God, 857 2

lifts

you are my glory, the one who *l* up my head. 587 8
Even now he *l* up my head * 618 5
he puts down one and *l* up another. 691 17
and *l* up the poor from the ashes. 756 13
he *l* up those who are bowed down. 802 16
the LORD *l* up those who are bowed down; 803 19
The LORD *l* up the lowly, * 804 12

light
The Gentiles shall come to thy *l*, 38 1
I will give thee for a *l* to the Gentiles, 38 3
be partakers of the inheritance of the saints in *l*. 40 2
O send out thy *l* and thy truth, 40 16
O ye *l* and darkness, bless ye the Lord; 48 14
To give *l* to them that sit in darkness 51 18
To be a *l* to lighten the Gentiles, * 51 27
and the *l* around me turn to night," 62 5
darkness and *l* to thee are both alike. 62 7
Jesus said, "I am the *l* of the world; 62 9
but shall have the *l* of life." 62 10
O gracious *L*, 64 1
and our eyes behold the vesper *l*, 64 5
To be a *l* to lighten the Gentiles, * 66 5
in that City of which he is the *l*; 69 5
O God, the source of eternal *l*: 69 12
who art the life of all who live, the *l* of the faithful, 70 4
Nations shall come to your *l*, 76 1
I will give you as a *l* to the nations, 76 3
share in the inheritance of the saints in *l*. 77 23
Send out your *l* and your truth, 78 15
Arise, shine, for your *l* has come, * 87 11
Nations will stream to your *l*, * 87 17
The sun will no more be your *l* by day; * 87 27
The Lord will be your everlasting *l*, * 88 1
O shining *l* and enfolding dark. 89 2
A *L* to enlighten the nations, * 93 16
O God, the King eternal, whose *l* divides the day 99 13
and a *l* upon my path. 103 7
L and peace, in Jesus Christ our Lord. 109 1
Jesus said, "You are the *l* of the world. 109 7
but on a lamp-stand where it gives *l* 109 9
And you, like the lamp, must shed *l* 109 10
God who said, "Out of darkness let *l* shine," 110 3
his *l* to shine within us, to give the *l* of revelation— 110 4
and the *l* around me turn to night," 110 7
darkness and *l* to you are both alike. 110 9
with the brightness of the vesper *l*; 110 13
the radiance of this *l*, 110 15
burn in us and shed its *l* on those around us, 110 19
where dwells the true and never-failing *L*, 110 21
the true God and eternal *l*, 110 27
we who walk in the *l* of your presence 111 10
O gracious *L*, 112 1
and our eyes behold the vesper *l*, 112 5
for you are our *l* and salvation, 113 7
and the *l* around me turn to night," 116 1
darkness and *l* to you are both alike. 116 3
Jesus said, "I am the *l* of the world; 116 5
but will have the *l* of life." 116 6
O gracious *L*, 118 1
and our eyes behold the vesper *l*, 118 5
A *L* to enlighten the nations, * 120 5
that City of which he is the *l*, 123 5
O God, the source of eternal *l*: 123 11
Be our *l* in the darkness, O Lord, 123 21
the life of all who live, the *l* of the faithful, 124 1
Lift up the *l* of your countenance upon us, O Lord. 129 3
For my yoke is easy, and my burden is *l*. 131 18
Be our *l* in the darkness, O Lord, 133 10
to us by the *l* of his resurrection: 134 2
A *L* to enlighten the nations, * 135 5
O gracious *L*, 139 1
and our eyes behold the vesper *l*, 139 5
God who said, "Out of darkness let *l* shine," 139 12
has caused his *l* to shine within us, 139 13
to give the *l* of revelation— 139 14
A *L* to enlighten the nations, * 140 11
and put upon us the armor of *l*, 159 2
illumination of the true *L*: 161 2
as we have known the mystery of that *L* upon earth, 161 3
who hast poured upon us the new *l* 161 14
Grant that the same *l*, enkindled in our hearts, 161 15
whose Son our Savior Jesus Christ is the *l* 163 7
mortal life may hide from us the *l* of that love 165 10
beholding by faith the *l* of his countenance, 165 16
brought life and immortality to *l*: 171 12
by sending to them the *l* of thy Holy Spirit: 175 16
O Lord, the brightness of thy *l*; 186 7
walk in the *l* of thy truth, 186 9
caused the *l* of the Gospel to shine 187 9
raise up thy servant N. to be a *l* to the world: 196 16
called us out of darkness into thy marvelous *l*; 196 19
became a burning and a shining *l* 198 10
walk before thee as children of *l*; 198 13
and on earth thy *l* and thy peace; 202 3
and put on the armor of *l*, 211 2
brightness of the true *L*: 212 17
the mystery of that *L* on earth, 212 18
you have poured upon us the new *l* 213 8
Grant that this *l*, enkindled in our hearts, 213 9
whose Son our Savior Jesus Christ is the *l* 215 1
hide from us the *l* of that love which is immortal, 217 3
beholding by faith the *l* of his countenance, 217 9
and brought life and immortality to *l*: 223 6
by sending to them the *l* of your Holy Spirit: 227 9
upon your Church, O Lord, the brightness of your *l*, 238 1
evangelist John, may so walk in the *l* of your truth, 238 3
the *l* of the Gospel to shine throughout the world: 238 21
raised up your servant N. to be a *l* in the world: 248 2
called us out of darkness into your marvelous *l*; 248 5
became a burning and a shining *l* 249 19
and walk before you as children of *l*; 249 21
and on earth your *l* and your peace; 253 7
O God of unchangeable power and eternal *l*: 280 14
show us the *l* of his countenance, and come to us. 281 6
bestowed upon your people the brightness of your *l*: 285 9
attain to the festival of everlasting *l*; 285 12
The *l* of Christ. 285 13
and let your holy courts, in radiant *l*, 286 8
to sing the worthy praise of this great *l*; 286 12
he who gives his *l* to all 287 26
O God of unchangeable power and eternal *l*: 291 11
share in the inheritance of the saints in *l*; 311 18
God from God, *L* from *L*, 326 13
God of God, *L* of *L*, 327 27
Creator of the *l* and source of life, 344 14
caused a new *l* to shine in our hearts, 346 2
God from God, *L* from *L*, 358 10
for you alone are God, living and true, dwelling in *l* 373 2
the place of eternal joy and *l*.] 375 20
For you are the source of *l* and life, 377 12

caused a new *l* to shine in our hearts, 378 15
Let *l* perpetual shine upon them. 387 18
that they may receive the *l* of the Gospel, 390 11
kingdom, with your saints in *l*, 463 21
glorious company of the saints in *l*. 465 6
and enter into the *l* of God's eternal sabbath rest. 465 12
entrance into the land of *l* and joy, 470 3
and our secret sins in the *l* of thy countenance. 472 26
the darkness and *l* to thee are both alike. 475 17
The LORD is my *l* and my salvation; 477 12
in paradise and on earth, thy *l* and thy peace. 480 7
into the glorious company of the saints in *l*. 483 11
The Sun of Righteousness is gloriously risen, giving *l* 483 16
inheritance of the saints in *l*; 486 15
And let *l* perpetual shine upon him. 486 18
Grant to them thy mercy and the *l* of thy presence; 488 29
partakers of the inheritance of the saints in *l*; 489 21
brought life and immortality to *l*: 493 6
entrance into the land of *l* and joy, 493 12
Let *l* perpetual shine upon them. 498 10
glorious company of the saints in *l*. 499 18
The Sun of Righteousness is gloriously risen, giving *l* 500 5
And let *l* perpetual shine upon him. 502 16
partakers of the inheritance of the saints in *l*; 504 19
let *l* perpetual shine upon them; 504 27
O God of unchangeable power and eternal *l*: 515 4
God from God, *L* from *L*, 519 13
O God of unchangeable power and eternal *l*: 528 2
God from God, *L* from *L*, 530 4
O God of unchangeable power and eternal *l*: 540 2
God from God, *L* from *L*, 542 4
that they may receive the *l* of the Gospel, 549 26
with the *l* of your Holy Spirit; 562 14
And a *l* upon our path. 571 14
Lift up the *l* of your countenance upon us, O LORD. 588 12
give *l* to my eyes, lest I sleep in death; 598 5
and gives *l* to the eyes. 607 11
The LORD is my *l* and my salvation; 617 7
and in your *l* we see *l*. 632 23
He will make your righteousness as clear as the *l* * 633 15
Send out your *l* and your truth, 644 21
l of your countenance, 645 16
who will never see the *l* again. 653 22
that I may walk before God in the *l* of the living. 663 18
show us the *l* of his countenance and come to us. 675 10
show the *l* of your countenance, 702 17
show the *l* of your countenance, 703 2
they walk, O LORD, in the *l* of your presence. 714 24
and our secret sins in the *l* of your countenance. 718 16
His lightnings *l* up the world; * 727 3
L has sprung up for the righteous, * 727 20
You wrap yourself with *l* as with a cloak * 735 4
and a fire to give *l* in the night season. 741 4
L shines in the darkness for the upright; * 755 11
and a *l* upon my path. 772 4
When your word goes forth it gives *l*; * 774 7
and the *l* around me turn to night," 794 21
darkness and *l* to you are both alike. 794 24
l riseth up in darkness for the godly: 832 7
and that in thy *l* we may see *l*, 832 10
where there is darkness, *l*; 833 8
have often hidden from its *l*. 839 10

lighten

To be a light to *l* the Gentiles, * 51 27
To be a light to *l* the Gentiles, * 66 5
L our darkness, we beseech thee, O Lord; 70 1
L our darkness, we beseech thee, O Lord; 111 1

lighter

On the scales they are *l* than a breath, * 670 3

lighting

l upon the disciples, to teach them 347 8
l upon the disciples, to teach them 380 3

lightly

not to be entered into unadvisedly or *l*, 423 14

lightning

From *l* and tempest; 149 11
he sends out *l* with the rain, 788 15
Hurl the *l* and scatter them; * 800 12

lightnings

O ye *l* and clouds, bless ye the Lord; * 48 15
your *l* lit up the world; * 694 12
His *l* light up the world; * 727 3

lights

No one *l* a lamp to put it under a bucket, 109 8
your saints have been the *l* of the world 111 12
and the *l* of the world in their generations. 348 2
and the *l* of the world in their generations. 380 18
and the *l* of the world in their several generations: 487 13
Who created great *l*, * 790 9

like

All we *l* sheep have gone astray; 39 1
there be any sorrow *l* unto my sorrow 39 5
strayed from thy ways *l* lost sheep, 41 17
strayed from thy ways *l* lost sheep, 62 17
All we *l* sheep have gone astray; 76 25
there is any sorrow *l* my sorrow 77 4
they sank into the depths *l* a stone. 85 13
who is *l* you, glorious in holiness, 85 17
then were we *l* those who dream. 105 5
l the watercourses of the Negev. 105 13
And you, *l* the lamp, must shed light 109 10
l a roaring lion, seeking someone to devour. 132 9
Grant, we beseech thee, Almighty God, that *l* 174 15
we may be made *l* unto him in his eternal 184 12
continue in thy Church the *l* loves and power to heal, 193 13
a *l* faith and power of love, 196 3
we may be made *l* him 236 5
a *l* faith and power of love, 247 15
And the second is *l* unto it: 319 11
strayed from thy ways *l* lost sheep, 320 24
And the second is *l* unto it: 324 4
L as the hart desireth the water-brooks, * 471 1
and fade away suddenly *l* the grass. 472 20
They are *l* trees planted by streams of water, 585 7
they are *l* chaff which the wind blows away. 585 11
and shatter them *l* a piece of pottery." 586 21
Lest *l* a lion they tear me in pieces * 590 22
They lie in wait, *l* a lion in a covert; 595 11
"Fly away *l* a bird to the hilltop; 596 9

l silver refined from ore	597	14
who eat up my people *l* bread	598	22
L a lion, greedy for its prey, *	601	23
and *l* a young lion lurking in secret places.	601	24
He makes me sure-footed *l* a deer *	605	5
I beat them *l* dust before the wind; *	605	24
I trample them *l* mud in the streets.	605	25
it comes forth *l* a bridegroom out of his chamber;	606	24
it rejoices *l* a champion to run its course.	606	25
You will make them *l* a fiery furnace *	609	14
l a ravening and a roaring lion.	611	4
I am poured out *l* water;	611	5
My mouth is dried out *l* a pot-sherd;	611	8
I become *l* those who go down to the Pit.	619	7
He makes Lebanon skip *l* a calf, *	620	16
and Mount Hermon *l* a young wild ox.	620	17
I am forgotten *l* a dead man, out of mind; *	623	14
Do not be *l* horse or mule,	625	20
Let them be *l* chaff before the wind, *	629	22
My very bones will say, "LORD, who is *l* you? *	630	10
I behaved *l* one who mourns for his mother,	630	21
Your righteousness is *l* the strong mountains,	632	14
your justice *l* the great deep; *	632	15
For they shall soon wither *l* the grass, *	633	7
and *l* the green grass fade away.	633	8
l the glory of the meadows,	634	25
they shall vanish *l* smoke.	634	27
flourishing *l* a tree in full leaf.	636	7
l a heavy burden they are too much for me to bear.	637	5
But I am *l* the deaf who do not hear, *	637	23
l those who are mute and do not open their mouth.	637	24
I have become *l* one who does not hear *	637	25
We walk about *l* a shadow,	639	6
l a moth you eat away all that is dear to us; *	639	18
You have made us *l* sheep to be eaten *	646	7
they writhed *l* a woman in childbirth,	651	13
l ships of the sea when the east wind shatters them.	651	14
Your praise, *l* your Name, O God, reaches to	651	20
l the dull and stupid they perish *	652	24
they are *l* the beasts that perish.	653	5
L a flock of sheep they are destined to die;	653	8
are *l* the beasts that perish.	653	24
and you thought that I am *l* you."	655	23
your tongue is *l* a sharpened razor, *	658	2
But I am *l* a green olive tree in the house of God; *	658	16
who eat up my people *l* bread	659	8
And I said, "Oh, that I had wings *l* a dove! *	660	17
they are *l* the deaf adder which stops its ears,	665	2
Let them vanish *l* water that runs off; *	665	7
let them wither *l* trodden grass.	665	8
Let them be *l* the snail that melts away, *	665	9
l a stillborn child that never sees the sun.	665	10
let them be cut down *l* a brier; *	665	11
l thorns and thistles let them be swept away.	665	12
they snarl *l* dogs and run about the city.	666	8
they snarl *l* dogs and run about the city.	666	29
They sharpen their tongue *l* a sword, *	671	14
and aim their bitter words *l* arrows,	671	15
Let them vanish *l* smoke when the wind drives	676	3
you shall be *l* a dove whose wings are covered	677	6
whose feathers are *l* green gold.	677	7
it was *l* snow falling in Zalmon.	677	9
who is *l* you, O God?	684	22
He shall come down *l* rain upon the mown field, *	685	19
l showers that water the earth.	685	20
may its fruit flourish *l* Lebanon,	686	19
and its grain *l* grass upon the earth.	686	20
Therefore they wear their pride *l* a necklace *	687	11
and wrap their violence about them *l* a cloak.	687	12
L a dream when one awakens, O Lord, *	688	17
I was *l* a brute beast in your presence.	688	22
They were *l* men coming up with axes to a grove	689	18
You led your people *l* a flock *	694	17
And not be *l* their forefathers,	695	16
he made the waters stand up *l* walls.	695	29
and the waters gushed out *l* rivers.	696	6
He rained down flesh upon them *l* dust *	697	3
and winged birds *l* the sand of the sea.	697	4
So he brought their days to an end *l* a breath *	697	16
He led out his people *l* sheep *	699	9
and guided them in the wilderness *l* a flock.	699	10
They turned away and were disloyal *l* their fathers; *	699	20
they were undependable *l* a warped bow.	699	21
l a warrior refreshed with wine.	700	10
He built his sanctuary *l* the heights of heaven, *	700	17
l the earth which he founded for ever.	700	18
They have shed their blood *l* water on every side	701	8
will your fury blaze *l* fire for ever?	701	14
Hear, O Shepherd of Israel, leading Joseph *l* a flock; *	702	12
They burn it with fire *l* rubbish; *	703	18
Nevertheless, you shall die *l* mortals, *	705	22
and fall *l* any prince.'"	705	23
they became *l* dung upon the ground.	706	23
Make their leaders *l* Oreb and Zeeb, *	706	24
and all their commanders *l* Zebah and Zalmunna,	706	25
O my God, make them *l* whirling dust *	707	3
and *l* chaff before the wind;	707	4
L fire that burns down a forest, *	707	5
l the flame that sets mountains ablaze.	707	6
Among the gods there is none *l* you, O LORD, *	710	13
nor anything *l* your works.	710	14
I have become *l* one who has no strength;	712	8
l the slain who lie in the grave,	712	10
They surround me all day long *l* a flood; *	713	13
who is *l* the LORD among the gods?	714	6
Who is *l* you, LORD God of hosts? *	714	9
It shall stand fast for evermore *l* the moon, *	716	15
how long will your anger burn *l* fire?	717	7
For a thousand years in your sight are *l* yesterday	718	6
and *l* a watch in the night.	718	8
You sweep us away *l* a dream; *	718	9
we fade away suddenly *l* the grass.	718	10
we bring our years to an end *l* a sigh.	718	18
that though the wicked grow *l* weeds,	721	9
my horn you have exalted *l* the horns of wild bulls; *	721	16
The righteous shall flourish *l* a palm tree, *	721	21
and shall spread abroad *l* a cedar of Lebanon.	721	22
how *l* a puff of wind they are.	723	16
The mountains melt *l* wax at the presence	727	5
For my days drift away *l* smoke, *	731	5
My heart is smitten *l* grass and withered, *	731	7
I have become *l* a vulture in the wilderness, *	731	11
l an owl among the ruins.	731	12
I am *l* a sparrow, lonely on a house-top.	731	14

My days pass away *l* a shadow, * 731 21
and I wither *l* the grass. 731 22
they all shall wear out *l* a garment; * 733 2
and your youth is renewed *l* an eagle's. 733 18
Our days are *l* the grass; * 734 11
we flourish *l* a flower of the field; 734 12
and spread out the heavens *l* a curtain. 735 5
They reeled and staggered *l* drunkards * 748 9
and multiplied their families *l* flocks of sheep. 749 12
He put on cursing *l* a garment, * 752 8
let it soak into his body *l* water 752 9
and into his bones *l* oil; 752 10
Let it be to him *l* the cloak which he 752 11
and *l* the belt that he wears continually. 752 13
I have faded away *l* a shadow when it lengthens; * 752 21
I am shaken off *l* a locust. 752 22
l dew from the womb of the morning." 753 18
Who is *l* the LORD our God, who sits enthroned 756 10
The mountains skipped *l* rams, * 757 3
and the little hills *l* young sheep. 757 4
You mountains, that you skipped *l* rams? * 757 7
you little hills *l* young sheep? 757 8
Those who make them are *l* them, * 758 4
They swarm about me *l* bees; 761 19
they blaze *l* a fire of thorns; * 761 20
Your statutes have been *l* songs to me * 767 21
I have become *l* a leather flask in the smoke, * 770 7
I have gone astray *l* a sheep that is lost; * 778 7
We have escaped *l* a bird from the snare 781 13
Those who trust in the LORD are *l* Mount Zion, * 781 17
then were we *l* those who dream. 782 7
l the watercourses of the Negev. 782 15
L arrows in the hand of a warrior * 783 8
Your wife shall be *l* a fruitful vine 783 17
your children *l* olive shoots round about your table. 783 18
Let them be *l* grass upon the housetops, * 784 11
l a child upon its mother's breast; * 785 15
It is *l* fine oil upon the head * 787 11
It is *l* the dew of Hermon * 787 15
Those who make them are *l* them, * 789 11
my life span would need to be *l* yours. 795 15
They have sharpened their tongues *l* a serpent; * 796 5
he has made me live in dark places *l* those 799 3
my soul gasps to you *l* a thirsty land. 799 11
or I shall be *l* those who go down to the Pit. 799 14
We are *l* a puff of wind; * 800 8
our days are *l* a passing shadow. 800 9
May our sons be *l* plants well nurtured 801 1
and our daughters *l* sculptured corners of a palace. 801 2
He gives snow *l* wool; * 805 9
he scatters hoarfrost *l* ashes. 805 10
He scatters his hail *l* bread crumbs; * 805 11
And the second is *l* it: 851 13

likeness

and awake up after thy *l*; 69 10
and wake up in your *l*; 123 9
changed into his *l* from glory to glory; 165 18
changed into his *l* from glory to glory; 217 11
l of any thing that is in heaven above, 318 2
your image and *l*, and redeemed me from sin 450 9
peacefully in you and wake up in your *l*; 504 24
I shall be satisfied, beholding your *l*. 602 6
and enables us to grow in the *l* 852 22

likewise

L reckon ye also yourselves to be dead 46 11
L, after supper, he took the cup; 335 3
L, after supper, he took the cup; 342 5
L, the apostles prayed before they appointed 514 14

limbs

Your eyes beheld my *l*, yet unfinished in the womb; 795 6

limit

there is no *l* to his wisdom. 804 11
God does not *l* himself to these rites; 861 18

limited

Is God's activity *l* to these rites? 861 17

limitless

Everliving God, whose power is *l*, 552 6

limits

You set the *l* that they should not pass; * 735 19

line

all you of Jacob's *l*, give glory. 611 28
"I will establish your *l* for ever, * 714 1
I will establish his *l* for ever * 715 24
His *l* shall endure for ever * 716 13

lingered

nor *l* in the way of sinners, 585 3
Though you *l* among the sheepfolds, * 677 5

linked

who hast so *l* our lives one with another 210 10
you have so *l* our lives one with another 261 15
Bless all whose lives are closely *l* with ours, 388 17

links

and their nobles with *l* of iron; 807 17

lion

You shall tread upon the *l* and adder; * 130 23
you shall trample the young *l* and the serpent 130 24
around like a roaring *l*, seeking someone to devour. 132 9
Lest like a *l* they tear me in pieces * 590 22
They lie in wait, like a *l* in a covert; 595 11
Like a *l*, greedy for its prey, * 601 23
and like a young *l* lurking in secret places. 601 24
like a ravening and a roaring *l*. 611 4
Save me from the *l*'s mouth, * 611 22
You shall tread upon the *l* and adder; * 720 11
you shall trample the young *l* and the serpent 720 12

lions

The young *l* lack and suffer hunger, * 628 13
and my life from the young *l*. 631 3
I lie in the midst of *l* that devour the people; * 664 1
pull the fangs of the young *l*, O LORD. 665 6
The *l* roar after their prey * 736 19

lips

O Lord, open thou our *l*. 42 14
not only with our *l*, but in our lives, 59 5
that our *l* may praise thee, 69 13

not only with our *l*, but in our lives, 72 2
Lord, open our *l*. 80 5
not only with our *l*, but in our lives, 101 18
Accept, O LORD, the willing tribute of my *l*, * 104 3
that our *l* may praise you, 123 12
not only with our *l*, but in our lives, 125 16
Open my *l*, O Lord, * 137 1
Open my *l*, O Lord, * 267 6
the fruit of *l* that acknowledge his Name. 344 2
the fruit of *l* that acknowledge his Name. 376 18
The Lord be in your heart and upon your *l* 447 2
Purify the lives and the *l* of those who speak here, 571 10
and close the *l* that utter proud boasts! 597 6
our *l* are our own; who is lord over us?" 597 8
nor take the names of their gods upon my *l*. 600 6
listen to my prayer, which does not come from lying *l*. 600 24
I have heeded the words of your *l*. 601 6
you have not denied him the request of his *l*. 608 24
they curl their *l* and wag their heads, saying, 610 15
Let the lying *l* be silenced 624 1
and your *l* from lying words. 628 20
behold, I did not restrain my *l*; 640 24
grace flows from your *l*, 647 15
and take my covenant upon your *l*; 655 13
You have loosed your *l* for evil, * 655 18
Open my *l*, O Lord, * 657 12
and taunts are on their *l*; * 666 10
For the sins of their mouths, for the words of their *l*, 666 21
They bless with their *l*, * 669 14
my *l* shall give you praise. 670 18
and my mouth praises you with joyful *l*, 670 22
which I promised with my *l* 674 22
My *l* will sing with joy when I play to you, * 685 4
nor change what has gone out of my *l*. 716 10
that he spoke rash words with his *l*. 744 14
With my *l* will I recite * 764 9
Accept, O LORD, the willing tribute of my *l*, * 772 9
My *l* shall pour forth your praise, * 777 21
Deliver me, O LORD, from lying *l* * 778 12
Indeed, there is not a word on my *l*, * 794 6
adder's poison is under their *l*. 796 6
let the evil of their *l* overwhelm them. 796 20
and guard the door of my *l*; * 797 8

listen

l to my prayer, which does not come from lying lips. 600 24
Come, children, and *l* to me; * 628 15
"Hear, O daughter; consider and *l* closely; * 648 11
L to me and answer me; * 660 7
and *l* to my prayer. 668 13
Come and *l*, all you who fear God, * 674 27
O Israel, if you would but *l* to me! 704 18
Oh, that my people would *l* to me! * 705 1
I will *l* to what the LORD God is saying, * 709 9
and would not *l* to the voice of the LORD. 743 23
l, O LORD, to my supplication. 796 14
L to my cry for help, 798 12
many *l* and write what many read; 827 8

listens

For the LORD *l* to the needy, * 682 3

lit

and *l* the torch of freedom 190 18
and *l* the torch of freedom 242 2
your lightnings *l* up the world; * 694 12
We thank you for the torch of liberty which has been *l* 839 8

little

whoever receives a *l* child in the name of Christ 443 22
to believe that what happens to me here is of *l* account 461 10
O God, whose beloved Son did take *l* children 470 7
You have made him but *l* lower than the angels; * 592 17
and leave their wealth to their *l* ones. 602 3
In a *l* while the wicked shall be no more; * 634 3
The *l* that the righteous has * 634 16
and the *l* hills bring righteousness. 685 14
of *l* account, and sojourners in the land, 739 2
and the *l* hills like young sheep. 757 4
you *l* hills like young sheep? 757 8
I am small and of *l* account, * 775 7
Happy shall he be who takes your *l* ones, * 792 22

liturgy

L, the Mass, and the Great Offering. 859 17

live

hereafter *l* a godly, righteous, and sober life, 42 9
For only in thee can we *l* in safety. 55 6
O heavenly Father, in whom we *l* and move 57 14
hereafter *l* a godly, righteous, and sober life, 63 12
For only in thee can we *l* in safety. 67 21
O God, who art the life of all who *l*, 70 4
For only in you can we *l* in safety. 97 23
Heavenly Father, in you we *l* and move 100 6
for you *l* and reign for ever and ever. 107 15
you *l* and reign, now and for ever. 107 21
where you *l* and reign for ever and ever. 111 15
For only in you can we *l* in safety. 121 23
may *l* in peace and quietness; 123 19
O God, the life of all who *l*, 124 1
sustains the world we *l* in and the life we *l*: 134 12
you *l* and reign, now and for ever. 138 20
and diligently to *l* after thy commandments, 150 23
Evermore give us this bread, that he may *l* in us, 167 12
l with him in the joy of his resurrection; 170 11
may by thee be enabled to *l* according to thy will; 180 16
and *l* in righteousness and true holiness; 201 15
l in righteousness and holiness all our days; 203 8
and *l* in righteousness and true holiness; 203 15
Evermore give us this bread, that he may *l* in us, 219 3
that we may evermore *l* with him in the joy 222 4
l and reign, one God, for ever and ever. 228 7
be enabled to *l* according to your will; 232 8
for you *l* and reign, one God, now and for ever. 251 5
and *l* in righteousness and true holiness; 253 3
may *l* in righteousness and holiness all our days; 254 9
and *l* in righteousness and true holiness; 254 16
turn from their wickedness and *l*, 269 5
and *l* in peace and concord. 278 23
If we have died with him, we shall also *l* with him; 281 17
you *l* and reign, one God, now and for ever. 282 12
that we may evermore *l* with him 295 4
of Jesus Christ your Son may *l* in the power 306 6

hereafter *l* a godly, righteous, and sober life, 321 12
l in unity and godly love. 329 8
and to *l* no longer unto ourselves, 346 6
to *l* and die as one of us, 362 13
And, that we might *l* no longer for ourselves, 374 9
and to *l* no longer for ourselves 379 3
and for those who *l* in them, 384 8
be united in your truth, *l* together in your love, 388 3
For all who *l* and work in this community 390 19
they may *l* in joy, peace, and health, 391 12
that we may *l* and serve you in newness of life, 393 14
you *l* and reign, now and for ever. 395 12
who now *l* by faith, may with joy behold 395 14
if anyone eats of this bread, he will *l* for ever; 397 2
to *l* together in the covenant of marriage? 424 8
as long as you both shall *l*? 424 12
you *l* and reign in perfect unity, 430 8
that you may faithfully *l* together in this life, 431 12
l in fidelity and peace, 432 5
as long as you both shall *l*? 433 8
that we may *l* together in love and affection; 441 8
l faithfully according to your will in this life, 444 5
that they may *l* together in love and peace 444 13
and grant that he may *l* with you in everlasting life; 460 3
you *l* and reign, one God, for ever and ever. 464 19
before whom *l* all who die in the Lord: 466 7
and the God of those who *l*. 466 11
you *l* and reign, one God, for ever and ever. 466 19
though he were dead, yet shall he *l*; 469 2
For if we *l*, we *l* unto the Lord; 469 11
Whether we *l*, therefore, or die, we are the Lord's. 469 13
therefore will I call upon him as long as I *l*. 479 2
with whom do *l* the spirits of those who depart 488 1
So, then, whether we *l* or die, 491 17
and where you *l* and reign with the Father 498 6
with whom still *l* the spirits of those who die 503 12
among whom you *l*, and work, and worship. 543 11
"May your heart *l* for ever!" 612 9
My soul shall *l* for him; 612 18
As for me, I will *l* with integrity; * 617 3
In order to *l* for ever and ever, * 652 21
Even though honored, they cannot *l* for ever; * 653 4
They shall not *l* out half their days, * 662 10
So will I bless you as long as I *l* * 670 19
but the rebels shall *l* in dry places. 676 15
you who seek God, your heart shall *l*. 682 2
they shall *l* there and have it in possession. 682 8
He shall *l* as long as the sun and moon endure, * 685 17
Long may he *l*! 686 13
Who can *l* and not see death? * 717 10
I will sing to the LORD as long as I *l*; * 737 20
I shall not die, but *l*, * 762 4
that I may *l* and keep your word. 764 18
Let your compassion come to me, that I may *l*, * 769 18
Sustain me according to your promise, that I may *l*, * 773 5
grant me understanding, that I may *l*. 775 14
Let me *l*, and I will praise you, * 778 5
Too long have I had to *l* * 778 20
May you *l* to see your children's children; * 783 24
when brethren *l* together in unity! 787 10
he has made me *l* in dark places like those who 799 3
I will praise the LORD as long as I *l*; 803 5
show the power of your love to all among whom we *l*; 817 17
we may *l* in justice and peace; 823 21
Have mercy upon all of us who *l* and work 825 19
who *l* with injustice, terror, disease, and death 826 9
Grant that those who *l* alone may not be lonely 829 23
who *l* and reign with the Father and the Holy Spirit, 834 10
may *l* in this world according to thy will, 841 11
and to *l* in harmony with creation 845 6
Why then do we *l* apart from God 845 8
so that with the help of God we may *l* 849 13
The Christian hope is to *l* with confidence 861 25
that we may *l* with Christ 862 18

lived

born of the Virgin Mary, he *l* as one of us, 374 3
for I have *l* with integrity; * 616 8
Though they thought highly of themselves while they *l*, * 653 19
the tabernacle where he had *l* among his people. 699 27
wherever I have *l* as a stranger. 767 22

lively

set forth thy true and *l* Word, 329 11
by a *l* sense of your patient wisdom 443 25
give us such a *l* sense of thy righteous will, 488 30
that they may be *l* centers for sound learning, 824 17

lives

not only with our lips, but in our *l*, 59 5
our *l* may bless thee, and our worship 69 14
not only with our lips, but in our *l*, 72 2
but the life he *l*, he *l* to God. 83 18
not only with our lips, but in our *l*, 101 18
and to recognize you in the *l* of those around us. 113 12
and where he *l* and reigns for ever and ever. 123 5
our *l* may bless you, and our worship 123 13
not only with our lips, but in our *l*, 125 16
with the grace of thy Holy Spirit to amend our *l* 152 5
may shine forth in our *l*; 161 16
may show forth in their *l* what they profess 172 4
may show forth in their *l* what they profess 173 1
who hast so linked our *l* one with another 210 10
that all we do affecteth, for good or ill, all other *l*: 210 11
through him who *l* and reigns with you 211 6
who *l* and reigns with you and the Holy Spirit, 211 13
who *l* and reigns with you, 212 8
who *l* and reigns with you and the Holy Spirit, 212 13
where with you and the Holy Spirit he *l* and reigns, 212 20
may shine forth in our *l*; 213 10
who *l* and reigns with you, 213 11
who *l* and reigns with you and the Holy Spirit, 213 16
who *l* and reigns with you, 214 4
who *l* and reigns with you and the Holy Spirit, 214 10
who with you and the Holy Spirit *l* and reigns, 214 17
who with you and the Holy Spirit *l* and reigns, 215 6
who *l* and reigns with you and the Holy Spirit, 215 11
who *l* and reigns with you, 216 3
who *l* and reigns with you and the Holy Spirit, 216 11
of all virtue, without which whoever *l* 216 16
who *l* and reigns with you and the Holy Spirit, 216 18
who *l* and reigns with you, 217 5
who *l* and reigns with you and the Holy Spirit, 217 12
who *l* and reigns with you and the Holy Spirit, 218 5

who with you and the Holy Spirit *l* and reigns, 218 11
who *l* and reigns with you and the Holy Spirit, 218 18
who *l* and reigns with you and the Holy Spirit, 219 4
who *l* and reigns with you and the Holy Spirit, 220 5
who now *l* and reigns with you and the Holy Spirit, 221 5
who *l* and reigns with you and the Holy Spirit, 222 6
who *l* and reigns with you, 222 12
who *l* and reigns with you and the Holy Spirit, 222 20
who *l* and reigns with you and the Holy Spirit, 223 1
who *l* and reigns with you, 223 12
show forth in their *l* what they profess 223 18
who *l* and reigns with you and the Holy Spirit, 224 5
who *l* and reigns with you, 224 11
show forth in their *l* what they profess 224 16
who, with you and the Holy Spirit, *l* and reigns, 225 6
who *l* and reigns with you, 225 12
who *l* and reigns with you and the Holy Spirit, 225 18
who *l* and reigns with you and the Holy Spirit, 226 5
who *l* and reigns with you, 227 5
who *l* and reigns with you and the Holy Spirit, 228 12
who *l* and reigns with you and the Holy Spirit, 229 3
who *l* and reigns with you and the Holy Spirit, 230 5
who *l* and reigns with you and the Holy Spirit, 231 2
who *l* and reigns with you and the Holy Spirit, 232 4
who *l* and reigns with you and the Holy Spirit, 233 1
who *l* and reigns with you and the Holy Spirit, 234 4
who *l* and reigns with you and the Holy Spirit, 235 1
where he *l* and reigns with you and the Holy Spirit, 236 6
who *l* and reigns with you and the Holy Spirit, 236 12
who *l* and reigns with you and the Holy Spirit, 237 5
who *l* and reigns with you and the Holy Spirit, 238 5
who *l* and reigns with you, 238 12
who *l* and reigns with you, 239 3
who *l* and reigns with you and the Holy Spirit, 239 9
who *l* and reigns with you, 240 4
who *l* and reigns with you and the Holy Spirit, 240 11
who *l* and reigns with you and the Holy Spirit, 241 1
who *l* and reigns with you, 241 23
who *l* and reigns with you and the Holy Spirit, 242 6
who with you and the Holy Spirit *l* and reigns, 242 13
O Holy Spirit, *l* and reigns, 243 6
who *l* and reigns with you, 243 11
who *l* and reigns with you and the Holy Spirit, 243 18
who *l* and reigns with you and the Holy Spirit, 244 5
who *l* and reigns with you, 245 2
who *l* and reigns with you and the Holy Spirit, 245 8
who with you and the Holy Spirit *l* and reigns, 245 22
who *l* and reigns with you and the Holy Spirit, 246 6
who *l* and reigns with you and the Holy Spirit, 247 4
who *l* and reigns with you and the Holy Spirit, 248 6
who with you and the Holy Spirit *l* and reigns, 249 3
who *l* and reigns with you and the Holy Spirit, 249 8
who *l* and reigns with you, 249 16
who *l* and reigns with you and the Holy Spirit, 250 6
and who *l* and reigns for ever and ever. 250 20
who *l* and reigns with you, 251 9
who *l* and reigns with you and the Holy Spirit, 251 17
who *l* and reigns with you, 252 4
who *l* and reigns with you and the Holy Spirit, 252 10
who *l* and reigns with you, 253 4
who *l* and reigns with you and the Holy Spirit, 254 5
who *l* and reigns with you, 255 3
who *l* and reigns with you, 256 8
who *l* and reigns with you and the Holy Spirit, 256 16
who *l* and reigns with you, 257 3
who *l* and reigns with you and the Holy Spirit, 257 11
who *l* and reigns with you and the Holy Spirit, 258 6
who *l* and reigns with you, 258 12
who *l* and reigns with you and the Holy Spirit, 259 1
who *l* and reigns with you, 259 8
who with you and the Holy Spirit *l* and reigns, 259 16
who *l* and reigns with you and the Holy Spirit, 260 6
who *l* and reigns with you and the Holy Spirit, 261 5
you have so linked our *l* one with another 261 15
that all we do affects, for good or ill, all other *l*: 261 16
who *l* and reigns with you and the Holy Spirit, 264 7
pride, hypocrisy, and impatience of our *l*, 268 2
who *l* and reigns in glory with you 271 12
who *l* and reigns with you and the Holy Spirit, 272 12
who now *l* and reigns with you and the Holy Spirit, 274 5
who now *l* and reigns with you and the Holy Spirit, 276 7
who *l* and reigns with you, 280 22
who now *l* and reigns with you and the Holy Spirit, 283 5
who *l* and reigns with him, 286 14
who *l* and reigns for ever and ever. 287 27
show forth in their *l* what they profess 291 2
who *l* and reigns with you and the Holy Spirit, 295 6
who *l* and reigns with you, 295 12
l and reigns now and for ever. 306 8
who *l* and reigns with you and the Holy Spirit, 307 12
who *l* and reigns with you and the Holy Spirit, 309 10
who *l* and reigns with you and the Holy Spirit, 311 19
Examine your *l* and conduct by the rule 317 1
That we may end our *l* in faith and hope, 385 7
Bless all whose *l* are closely linked with ours, 388 17
grace of the Holy Spirit to amend our *l*, 391 8
who *l* and reigns for ever and ever. 395 23
who *l* and reigns for ever and ever. 397 17
who *l* and reigns with you and the Holy Spirit, 418 8
who *l* and reigns with you 425 12
may find their *l* strengthened 430 2
who with you and the Holy Spirit *l* and reigns, 430 24
who *l* and reigns with you and the Holy Spirit, 431 7
who *l* and reigns with you and the Holy Spirit, 455 13
where he *l* and reigns for ever and ever. 460 8
who have laid down their *l* in the service 488 28
As for me, I know that my Redeemer *l* 491 7
who with you and the Holy Spirit *l* and reigns, 493 8
who *l* and reigns with you and the Holy Spirit, 493 13
who *l* and reigns with you and the Holy Spirit, 494 4
who *l* and reigns with you, 515 12
who *l* and reigns with you and the Holy Spirit, 523 9
who *l* and reigns with you, 528 10
who with you and the Holy Spirit *l* and reigns, 534 9
who *l* and reigns with you and the Holy Spirit, 535 9
who *l* and reigns with you, 540 10
who, with you and the Holy Spirit, *l* and reigns, 545 18
who *l* and reigns with you and the Holy Spirit, 547 5
grace of the Holy Spirit to amend our *l*, 550 17
who *l* and reigns with you and the Holy Spirit, 560 9
who *l* and reigns with you and the Holy Spirit, 564 9
so that our *l* are sustained and sanctified 569 1
Purify the *l* and the lips 571 10
The LORD *l*! Blessed is my Rock! * 606 3

To pluck their *l* from death, * 627 13
The LORD cares for the *l* of the godly, * 634 20
he shall preserve the *l* of the needy. 686 10
He shall redeem their *l* from oppression 686 11
never forget the *l* of your poor. 690 23
but delivered their *l* to the plague. 699 6
he preserves the *l* of his saints 727 18
who *l* and reigns with you and the Holy Spirit, 817 1
fashion our *l* according to the example 817 15
who spend their *l* establishing equal protection 826 12
give us food to sustain our *l* 835 14
For all that is gracious in the *l* of men and women, 837 6
Enrich our *l* by ever-widening circles of fellowship, 840 3
in our *l* by a humble, holy, and obedient walking 840 21
presence of the Holy Spirit in our *l*? 852 25
with the intention to amend our *l*. 857 13
Oblation is an offering of ourselves, our *l* 857 15
It is required that we should examine our *l*, 860 5

livest

who with the Son and the Holy Spirit *l* and reignest, 176 7
who *l* and reignest, 199 16
who with the Father and the Holy Spirit *l* 489 28
who *l* and reignest with the Father 834 16

livestock

and their *l* to hot thunderbolts. 698 24

liveth

but in that he *l*, he *l* unto God. 46 10
where he *l* and reigneth for ever and ever. 69 5
who *l* and reigneth with thee and the Holy Ghost, 159 7
who *l* and reigneth with thee, 160 9
who *l* and reigneth with thee and the Holy Ghost, 160 16
where with thee and the Holy Spirit he *l* and reigneth, 161 5
who *l* and reigneth with thee and the same Spirit ever, 161 12
who *l* and reigneth with thee, 161 17
who *l* and reigneth with thee and the Holy Spirit, 162 4
who *l* and reigneth with thee, 162 11
who with thee and the same Spirit *l* and reigneth, 163 6
who with thee and the Holy Spirit *l* and reigneth, 163 12
who *l* and reigneth with thee and the Holy Spirit, 164 4
who *l* and reigneth with thee, 164 9
virtues, without which whosoever *l* is counted dead 165 3
who *l* and reigneth with thee 165 4
who *l* and reigneth with thee, 165 12
who *l* and reigneth with thee and the Holy Spirit, 165 19
who *l* and reigneth with thee and the Holy Spirit, 166 7
who with thee and the Holy Spirit *l* and reigneth, 167 1
who *l* and reigneth with thee and the Holy Spirit, 167 8
who *l* and reigneth with thee and the Holy Spirit, 168 8
who *l* and reigneth with thee and the Holy Spirit, 169 5
who now *l* and reigneth with thee and the Holy Spirit 169 12
who now *l* and reigneth with thee 169 17
who now *l* and reigneth with thee 170 5
who *l* and reigneth with thee 170 19
who *l* and reigneth with thee and the same Spirit ever, 171 3
who *l* and reigneth with thee and the Holy Spirit, 171 8
who *l* and reigneth with thee, 171 20
who *l* and reigneth with thee and the Holy Spirit, 172 5
who *l* and reigneth with thee, 172 18
who *l* and reigneth with thee and the Holy Spirit, 173 2
who *l* and reigneth with thee, 173 8
who, with thee and the Holy Spirit, *l* and reigneth, 173 14
who *l* and reigneth with thee and the Holy Spirit, 174 6
who *l* and reigneth with thee 175 5
who *l* and reigneth with thee, 175 12
who *l* and reigneth with thee and the Holy Spirit, 177 1
who *l* and reigneth with thee and the Holy Spirit, 178 4
who *l* and reigneth with thee and the Holy Spirit, 179 2
who *l* and reigneth with thee and the Holy Spirit, 180 5
who *l* and reigneth with thee and the Holy Spirit, 181 3
who with thee and the same Spirit *l* and reigneth, 182 4
who *l* and reigneth with thee and the Holy Spirit, 182 9
who *l* and reigneth with thee and the Holy Spirit, 183 4
who *l* and reigneth with thee and the Holy Spirit, 184 5
he *l* and reigneth ever, 184 14
who *l* and reigneth with thee and the Holy Spirit, 185 5
where he *l* and reigneth with thee and the Holy Spirit, 186 4
who *l* and reigneth with thee and the Holy Spirit, 186 11
who *l* and reigneth with thee, 186 18
who *l* and reigneth with thee and the Holy Spirit, 187 5
who *l* and reigneth with thee, 187 13
who *l* and reigneth with thee, 188 5
who *l* and reigneth with thee and the Holy Spirit, 188 12
who *l* and reigneth with thee and the Holy Spirit, 189 3
who *l* and reigneth with thee and the Holy Spirit, 190 8
who *l* and reigneth with thee, 190 14
who with thee and the Holy Spirit *l* and reigneth, 191 5
who *l* and reigneth with thee and the Holy Spirit, 191 13
O Holy Ghost, *l* and reigneth, 191 20
who *l* and reigneth with thee, 192 5
who *l* and reigneth with thee and the Holy Spirit, 192 11
who *l* and reigneth with thee and the Holy Spirit, 193 2
who *l* and reigneth with thee, 193 15
who *l* and reigneth with thee and the Holy Spirit, 194 6
who with thee and the Holy Spirit *l* and reigneth, 194 14
who *l* and reigneth with thee and the Holy Spirit, 195 6
who *l* and reigneth with thee and the Holy Spirit, 196 5
who *l* and reigneth with thee and the Holy Spirit, 197 2
who with thee and the same Spirit *l* and reigneth, 197 17
who *l* and reigneth with thee, 198 6
in the unity of the Holy Spirit, *l* and reigneth, 198 14
who *l* and reigneth with thee and the Holy Spirit, 198 21
who *l* and reigneth with thee and the Holy Spirit, 199 2
who *l* and reigneth for ever and ever. 199 11
who *l* and reigneth with thee, 200 4
who *l* and reigneth with thee and the Holy Spirit, 200 10
who *l* and reigneth with thee and the Holy Spirit, 201 5
who *l* and reigneth with thee, 201 16
who *l* and reigneth with thee, 202 6
who *l* and reigneth with thee and the Holy Spirit, 203 3
who *l* and reigneth with thee, 204 5
who *l* and reigneth with thee, 205 2
who *l* and reigneth with thee and the same Spirit, 205 20
who *l* and reigneth with thee, 206 6
who *l* and reigneth with thee and the same Spirit, 206 15
who *l* and reigneth with thee and the Holy Spirit, 206 22
who *l* and reigneth with thee and the Holy Spirit, 207 6
who *l* and reigneth with thee, 207 13
who *l* and reigneth with thee, 208 7
who with thee and the Holy Spirit *l* and reigneth, 208 14
who *l* and reigneth with thee and the Holy Spirit, 208 21
who *l* and reigneth with thee and the Holy Spirit, 209 7
who *l* and reigneth with thee and the Holy Spirit, 210 7

and whosoever *l* and believeth in me shall never die. 469 3
I know that my Redeemer *l*, 469 4
For none of us *l* to himself, 469 9
who *l* and reigneth with thee and the Holy Spirit, 470 4
who *l* and reigneth with thee and the Holy Spirit, 481 28
who *l* and reigneth with thee and the Holy Spirit, 820 24

living

He will come again to judge the *l* and the dead. 96 24
l and reigning for ever and ever. 110 27
He will come again to judge the *l* and the dead. 120 20
we have been born anew to a *l* hope 137 12
and that both by their preaching and *l*, 150 7
serve thee in holiness and pureness of *l*, 155 12
serve thee in pureness of *l* and truth; 172 11
to confess Jesus as Messiah and Son of the *l* God: 187 2
saints in all virtuous and godly *l*, 194 11
needs of every *l* creature: 208 10
to judge both the *l* and the dead, 211 5
serve you in pureness of *l* and truth; 224 4
to confess Jesus as Messiah and Son of the *l* God: 238 15
in all virtuous and godly *l*, 245 19
needs of every *l* creature: 259 12
Lord Jesus Christ, Son of the *l* God, we pray 282 6
Give mercy and grace to the *l*; 282 9
covenant with all *l* things: 289 2
He will come again to judge the *l* and the dead. 293 11
He will come again to judge the *l* and the dead. 304 14
if with penitent hearts and *l* faith we receive 316 23
He will come again in glory to judge the *l* 327 10
to be a reasonable, holy, and *l* sacrifice unto thee; 336 2
a *l* sacrifice, holy and acceptable to God, 343 15
built up as *l* stones of a holy temple, 348 16
He will come again in glory to judge the *l* 359 1
you have graciously accepted us as *l* members 365 10
that we are *l* members of the Body of your Son, 366 6
for you alone are God, *l* and true, 373 2
a *l* sacrifice in Christ, 375 10
a *l* sacrifice, holy and acceptable to God, 376 11
built up as *l* stones of a holy temple, 381 10
Jesus said, "I am the *l* bread 397 1
Make us a *l* sacrifice of praise. 403 18
He will come again to judge the *l* and the dead. 416 19
and the *l* to the dead, 430 5
O Lord, the *l* God, 466 10
My soul is athirst for God, yea, even for the *l* God; * 471 3
in the land of the *l*. 478 7
in the land of the *l*. 479 17
in whose hands are the *l* and the dead: 488 27
O Lord Jesus Christ, Son of the *l* God, we pray 489 23
Give mercy and grace to the *l*, 489 26
He will come again to judge the *l* and the dead. 496 14
He will come again in glory to judge the *l* 520 1
He will come again in glory to judge the *l* 530 20
He will come again in glory to judge the *l* 542 20
set forth your true and *l* Word. 563 4
the building up of the *l*, 567 11
in the land of the *l*! 618 28
My soul is athirst for God, athirst for the *l* God; * 643 3
and root you out of the land of the *l*! 658 10
that I may walk before God in the light of the *l*. 663 18
Let them be wiped out of the book of the *l* * 681 20
my heart and my flesh rejoice in the *l* God. 707 18
with its *l* things too many to number, * 737 2
in the land of the *l*. 759 19
my portion in the land of the *l*." 798 11
for in your sight shall no one *l* be justified. 798 22
and satisfy the needs of every *l* creature. 802 20
the infinite complexity of *l* creatures: 827 13
fillest all things *l* with plenteousness: 828 2
bring forth in us the fruit of good *l*, 834 21
and become *l* members of Christ. 850 25
and judge the *l* and the dead. 862 15
the *l* and the dead, 862 22

lo

For *l*, there is not a word in my tongue, * 474 23
For *l*, your enemies, O Lord, 721 13
l, your enemies shall perish, * 721 14

load

his hands were set free from bearing the *l*." 704 13

loathe

and do I not *l* those who rise up against you? 795 21

loathing

I look with *l* at the faithless, * 776 19

locust

the fruit of their toil to the *l*. 698 20
He spoke, and the *l* came, * 740 21
I am shaken off like a *l*. 752 22

locusts

and young *l* without number, 740 22

lodge

How hateful it is that I must *l* in Meshech * 778 18

lodging

and make my *l* in the wilderness. 660 20
grant us a safe *l*, and a holy rest, 833 17

lofty

Thus saith the high and *l* One that inhabiteth eternity, 40 23
Thus says the high and *l* One who inhabits eternity, 78 22
I will sing to the Lord, for he is *l* and uplifted; * 85 1
Be seated on your *l* throne, O Most High; * 591 10
Beautiful and *l*, the joy of all the earth, is the 651 3

loins

My *l* are filled with searing pain; * 637 10
and give them continual trembling in their *l*. 681 11

loneliness

For those in *l*, fear, and anguish 279 7

lonely

That it may please thee to visit the *l*; 151 24
the sick, and the *l*. 543 6
I am like a sparrow, *l* on a house-top. 731 14
kingdom of God in villages, towns, and *l* places: 825 17
Grant that those who live alone may not be *l* 829 23

long

l-suffering, and abounding in mercy. 91 6
"You mortals, how *l* will you dishonor my glory? * 128 11

how *l* will you worship dumb idols 128 12
With *l* life will I satisfy him, * 131 4
Forty years *l* was I grieved with this generation, 146 21
be faithful to him as *l* as you both shall live? 424 11
be faithful to her as *l* as you both shall live? 424 17
to be faithful to her as *l* as you both shall live? 433 7
to be faithful to him as *l* as you both shall live? 433 13
thou understandest my thoughts *l* before. 474 20
therefore will I call upon him as *l* as I live. 479 2
"You mortals, how *l* will you dishonor my glory; * 588 1
how *l* will you worship dumb idols 588 2
how *l*, O LORD, how *l*? 590 4
"and give them the help they *l* for." 597 12
How *l*, O LORD? 597 20
how *l* will you hide your face from me? 597 22
How *l* shall I have perplexity in my mind, 598 1
how *l* shall my enemy triumph over me? 598 3
in you have I trusted all the day *l*. 614 23
because of my groaning all day *l*. 625 4
and desires *l* life to enjoy prosperity? 628 18
O Lord, how *l* will you look on? * 631 1
and of your praise all the day *l*. 632 2
I go about in mourning all the day *l*. 637 9
and plot treachery all the day *l*. 637 22
while all day *l* they say to me, 643 6
All day *l* they mock me * 644 7
Indeed, for your sake we are killed all the day *l*; * 647 1
against the godly all day *l*? 657 24
all day *l* they assault and oppress me. 662 14
They hound me all the day *l*; * 662 15
All day *l* they damage my cause; * 662 22
How *l* will you assail me to crush me, 669 9
So will I bless you as *l* as I live * 670 19
and your glory all the day *l*. 683 17
and saving deeds all day *l*; * 684 10
will proclaim your righteousness all day *l*, * 685 6
He shall live as *l* as the sun and moon endure, * 685 17
L may he live! 686 13
and may they bless him all the day *l*. 686 16
and be established as *l* as the sun endures; * 686 22
I have been afflicted all day *l*, * 688 5
Remember your congregation that you purchased *l* ago, * 689 11
there is not one among us who knows how *l*. 690 3
How *l*, O God, will the adversary scoff? * 690 4
remember how fools revile you all day *l*. 690 29
I remember the years *l* past; 693 11
How *l* will you be angry, O LORD? * 701 13
how *l* will you be angered 702 19
"How *l* will you judge unjustly, * 705 11
I call upon you all the day *l*. 710 4
They surround me all day *l* like a flood; * 713 13
How *l* will you hide yourself, O LORD? 717 5
how *l* will your anger burn like fire? 717 7
Return, O LORD; how *l* will you tarry? * 718 27
With *l* life will I satisfy him, * 720 20
How *l* shall the wicked, O LORD, * 722 22
how *l* shall the wicked triumph? 722 23
Forty years *l* I detested that generation and said, * 725 12
My enemies revile me all day *l*, * 731 15
I will sing to the LORD as *l* as I live; * 737 20
Behold, I *l* for your commandments; * 766 15
all the day *l* it is in my mind. 771 14
I *l* for your commandments. 774 10
L have I known from your decrees * 776 7
I *l* for your salvation, O LORD, * 778 3
Too *l* have I had to live * 778 20
and made their furrows *l*. 784 6
and stir up strife all day *l*. 796 4
like those who are *l* dead. 799 4
I will praise the LORD as *l* as I live; 803 5
O Lord, support us all the day *l*, 833 14
woman and man enter into a life-*l* union, 861 5

longed

My soul has *l* for your salvation; * 770 3

longer

no *l* worthy to be called your son." 76 18
You are no *l* strangers and sojourners, 78 1
death no *l* has dominion over him. 83 16
and to live no *l* unto ourselves, 346 6
And, that we might live no *l* for ourselves, 374 9
and to live no *l* for ourselves alone, 379 3
we love but see no *l*. 498 9
we love, but see no *l*: 504 27
you no *l* go out, O God, with our armies. 668 7
you no *l* go out, O God, with our armies. 750 18
How much *l* must I wait? * 770 9

longeth

so *l* my soul after thee, O God. 471 2

longing

My soul has a desire and *l* for the courts 707 16
with *l* for your judgments. 764 24

longs

As the deer *l* for the water-brooks, * 643 1
so *l* my soul for you, O God. 643 2

look

L and see if there is any sorrow 77 3
the earth may *l* to you and be saved; 107 10
L down, O Lord, from your heavenly throne, 133 17
the earth may *l* to you and be saved; 138 14
We humbly beseech thee, O Father, mercifully to *l* 155 7
For behold, you *l* for truth deep within me, * 266 14
L favorably on your whole Church, 280 14
L favorably on your whole Church, 291 11
l for him to come again in glory; 306 7
We *l* for the resurrection of the dead, 327 18
and I *l* for the resurrection of the dead, 328 20
We *l* for the resurrection of the dead, 359 9
l with compassion upon us 395 4
Almighty God, *l* with favor upon this person 421 2
L mercifully upon this man and this woman 425 8
L with favor upon the world you have made, 429 3
l upon you, and fill you with all spiritual benediction 431 11
L upon him with the eyes of thy mercy; 458 4
Almighty God, *l* on this your servant, 462 1
Almighty God, *l* with pity upon the sorrows 467 3
I *l* for the LORD; my soul doth wait for him; * 474 9
L favorably on your whole Church, 515 4
We *l* for the resurrection of the dead, 520 9
L favorably on your whole Church, 528 2

We *l* for the resurrection of the dead, 530 28
L favorably on your whole Church, 540 2
We *l* for the resurrection of the dead, 542 28
Will you *l* for Christ in all others, 544 4
L at those who are in labor with wickedness, * 591 26
L upon me and answer me, O LORD my God; * 598 4
Let none who *l* to you be put to shame; * 614 17
L upon my adversity and misery * 615 24
L upon my enemies, for they are many, * 615 26
L upon him and be radiant, * 628 3
O Lord, how long will you *l* on? * 631 1
Come now and *l* upon the works of the LORD, * 649 19
For behold, you *l* for truth deep within me, * 656 18
God will let me *l* in triumph on my enemies. 666 17
Why do you *l* with envy, O rugged mountain, 677 12
L upon your covenant; * 690 24
Turn now, O God of hosts, *l* down from heaven; 703 15
and *l* upon the face of your Anointed. 708 9
and righteousness shall *l* down from heaven. 709 17
those who have a haughty *l* and a proud 730 18
He will *l* with favor on the prayer of the homeless; * 732 10
All of them *l* to you * 737 7
I *l* with loathing at the faithless, * 776 19
As the eyes of servants *l* to the hand of their masters, * 780 17
So our eyes *l* to the LORD our God, * 780 19
L well whether there be any wickedness in me * 795 26
I *l* to my right hand and find no one 798 7
L with compassion on the whole human family; 815 14
L graciously on your Church, 818 8
L with pity, O heavenly Father, upon the people 826 8
L with mercy, O God our Father, on all 830 1
L with favor, we pray, 830 8
L with pity upon the sorrows of thy servant 831 13
L with compassion upon all who through addiction 831 18

looked

for he has *l* with favor on his lowly servant. 91 29
for he has *l* with favor on his lowly servant. 119 6
first martyr Stephen, who *l* up to heaven and prayed 186 2
first martyr Stephen, who *l* up to heaven and prayed 237 15
those in every generation who have *l* to you in hope, 370 25
for he has *l* with favor on his lowly servant. 441 14
those of every generation who have *l* to God in hope. 517 16
They *l* and were astounded; * 651 10
I *l* for sympathy, but there was none, 681 4
For the LORD *l* down from his holy place on high; * 732 14

looking

l for his coming again with power and great glory. 342 15
My eyes are ever *l* to the LORD, * 615 18
my eyes have failed from *l* for my God. 679 15

looks

The LORD *l* down from heaven upon us all, * 598 15
The LORD *l* down from heaven, * 627 1
God *l* down from heaven upon us all, * 659 1
He *l* at the earth and it trembles; * 737 18
I have no haughty *l*. 785 11

loose

but God will *l* an arrow at them, 671 24

loosed

He *l* his arrows and scattered them; * 603 17
You have *l* your lips for evil, * 655 18

LORD

preserve my life, O *L*, according to your word. 104 2
Accept, O *L*, the willing tribute of my lips, * 104 3
My help comes from the *L*, * 104 15
The *L* himself watches over you; * 104 21
the *L* is your shade at your right hand, 104 22
The *L* shall preserve you from all evil; * 104 25
The *L* shall watch over your going out 105 1
When the *L* restored the fortunes of Zion, * 105 4
"The *L* has done great things for them." 105 9
The *L* has done great things for us, * 105 10
Restore our fortunes, O *L*, * 105 12
I love the *L*, because he has heard the voice 442 13
Gracious is the *L* and righteous; * 442 17
How shall I repay the *L* * 442 19
and call upon the Name of the *L*, 442 22
I will fulfill my vows to the *L* * 442 23
In the courts of the *L*'s house, * 442 25
The *L* is my shepherd; * 443 1
and I will dwell in the house of the *L* for ever. 443 17
The *L* of hosts is with us; * 472 7
My help cometh even from the *L*, * 473 11
The *L* himself is thy keeper; * 473 17
the *L* is thy defense upon thy right hand; 473 18
The *L* shall preserve thee from all evil; * 473 21
The *L* shall preserve thy going out, 473 23
Out of the deep have I called unto thee, O *L*; * 474 1
If thou, *L*, wilt be extreme to mark what is done amiss, * 474 5
I look for the *L*; my soul doth wait for him; * 474 9
O Israel, trust in the *L*, 474 13
for with the *L* there is mercy, * 474 14
O *L*, thou hast searched me out, and known me. * 474 18
but thou, O *L*, knowest it altogether. 474 24
The *L* is my shepherd; * 476 1
and I will dwell in the house of the *L* for ever. 476 18
The *L* is my shepherd; * 476 19
and I will dwell in the house of the *L* for ever. 477 11
The *L* is my light and my salvation; 477 12
the *L* is the strength of my life; 477 14
One thing have I desired of the *L*, 477 16
even that I may dwell in the house of the *L* 477 17
to behold the fair beauty of the *L*, 477 19
I will sing and speak praises unto the *L*. 477 27
Hearken unto my voice, O *L*, when I cry unto thee; * 477 28
Thy face, *L*, will I seek. 478 2
I believe verily to see the goodness of the *L* 478 6
O tarry thou the *L*'s leisure; * 478 8
and put thou thy trust in the *L*. 478 10
O give thanks unto the *L*, for he is gracious, * 478 11
Who can express the noble acts of the *L*, * 478 13
Remember me, O *L*, according to the favor 478 17
My delight is in the *L*, * 478 23
then called I upon the Name of the *L*; * 479 6
O *L*, I beseech thee, deliver my soul. 479 7
Gracious is the *L*, and righteous; * 479 8
The *L* preserveth the simple; * 479 10
for the *L* hath rewarded thee. 479 13

I will walk before the *L* * 479 16
in the sight of the *L* is the death of his saints. 479 19
Their delight is in the law of the *L*, * 585 5
For the *L* knows the way of the righteous, * 585 15
against the *L* and against his Anointed? 586 5
Let me announce the decree of the *L*: * 586 14
Submit to the *L* with fear, * 586 24
L, how many adversaries I have! * 587 3
But you, O *L*, are a shield about me; * 587 7
I call aloud upon the *L*, * 587 9
I wake again, because the *L* sustains me. 587 12
Rise up, O *L*; set me free, O my God; * 587 15
Deliverance belongs to the *L*. * 587 18
Know that the *L* does wonders for the faithful; * 588 4
when I call upon the *L*, he will hear me. 588 5
and put your trust in the *L*. 588 9
Lift up the light of your countenance upon us, O *L*. 588 12
for only you, *L*, make me dwell in safety. 588 16
Give ear to my words, O *L*; * 588 17
In the morning, *L*, you hear my voice; * 588 21
the bloodthirsty and deceitful, O *L*, you abhor. 589 2
Lead me, O *L*, in your righteousness, 589 6
For you, O *L*, will bless the righteous; * 589 21
L, do not rebuke me in your anger; * 589 23
Have pity on me, *L*, for I am weak; * 590 1
heal me, *L*, for my bones are racked. 590 2
how long, O *L*, how long? 590 4
Turn, O *L*, and deliver me; * 590 5
for the *L* has heard the sound of my weeping. 590 15
The *L* has heard my supplication; * 590 16
the *L* accepts my prayer. 590 17
O *L* my God, I take refuge in you; * 590 20
O *L* my God, if I have done these things: * 590 24
Stand up, O *L*, in your wrath; * 591 6
O *L*, judge the nations. 591 11
according to my righteousness, O *L*, * 591 13
I will bear witness that the *L* is righteous; * 592 5
I will praise the Name of the *L* Most High. 592 6
O *L* our Governor, * 592 7
I will give thanks to you, O *L*, with my whole heart; * 593 1
But the *L* is enthroned for ever; * 593 13
The *L* will be a refuge for the oppressed, * 593 17
for you never forsake those who seek you, O *L*. 593 20
Sing praise to the *L* who dwells in Zion; * 593 21
Have pity on me, O *L*; * 594 1
The *L* is known by his acts of justice; * 594 9
Rise up, O *L*, let not the ungodly 594 15
Put fear upon them, O *L*; * 594 17
Why do you stand so far off, O *L*, * 594 19
the covetous curse and revile the *L*. 594 24
Rise up, O *L*; 595 18
The *L* is King for ever and ever; * 596 1
The *L* will hear the desire of the humble; * 596 3
In the *L* have I taken refuge; * 596 7
The *L* is in his holy temple; * 596 15
the *L*'s throne is in heaven. 596 16
The *L* weighs the righteous as well as the wicked, * 596 19
For the *L* is righteous; 596 24
Help me, *L*, for there is no godly one left; * 597 1
Oh, that the *L* would cut off all smooth tongues, * 597 5
I will rise up," says the *L* 597 11
The words of the *L* are pure words, * 597 13
O *L*, watch over us * 597 16
How long, O *L*? 597 20
Look upon me and answer me, O *L* my God; * 598 4
I will sing to the *L*, for he has dealt with me 598 10
The *L* looks down from heaven upon us all, * 598 15
and do not call upon the *L*? 598 23
but the *L* is their refuge. 598 27
when the *L* restores the fortunes of his people, 599 2
L, who may dwell in your tabernacle? * 599 4
but he honors those who fear the *L*. 599 12
I have said to the *L*, "You are my Lord, 599 20
O *L*, you are my portion and my cup; * 600 7
I will bless the *L* who gives me counsel; * 600 11
I have set the *L* always before me; * 600 13
Hear my plea of innocence, O *L*; 600 22
Arise, O *L*; confront them and bring them down; * 601 25
Deliver me, O *L*, by your hand * 601 27
I love you, O *L* my strength, * 602 7
O *L* my stronghold, my crag, and my haven. 602 8
I will call upon the *L*, * 602 12
I called upon the *L* in my distress * 602 18
The *L* thundered out of heaven; * 603 15
at your battle cry, O *L*, 603 21
but the *L* was my support. 603 29
The *L* rewarded me 604 3
For I have kept the ways of the *L* * 604 5
Therefore the *L* rewarded me according to my 604 11
You, O *L*, are my lamp; * 604 20
the words of the *L* are tried in the fire; * 604 25
For who is God, but the *L*? * 605 1
they cry to the *L*, but he does not answer. 605 23
The *L* lives! Blessed is my Rock! * 606 3
Therefore will I extol you among the nations, O *L*, * 606 10
The law of the *L* is perfect 607 4
the testimony of the *L* is sure 607 6
The statutes of the *L* are just 607 8
the commandment of the *L* is clear 607 10
The fear of the *L* is clean 607 12
the judgments of the *L* are true 607 14
O *L*, my strength and my redeemer. 607 30
May the *L* answer you in the day of trouble, * 608 1
may the *L* grant all your requests. 608 11
Now I know that the *L* gives victory to his anointed: * 608 12
but we will call upon the Name of the *L* our God. 608 16
O *L*, give victory to the king * 608 19
The king rejoices in your strength, O *L*; * 608 21
For the king puts his trust in the *L*; * 609 9
at the time of your appearing, O *L*; 609 15
Be exalted, O *L*, in your might; * 609 25
"He trusted in the *L*; let him deliver him; * 610 16
Be not far away, O *L*; * 611 18
Praise the *L*, you that fear him; * 611 26
and those who seek the *L* shall praise him: * 612 8
remember and turn to the *L*, * 612 11
For kingship belongs to the *L*; * 612 13
they shall be known as the *L*'s for ever. 612 20
The *L* is my shepherd; * 612 23
and I will dwell in the house of the *L* for ever. 613 13
The earth is the *L*'s and all that is in it, * 613 14
"Who can ascend the hill of the *L*? * 613 18
They shall receive a blessing from the *L* * 613 23
"The *L*, strong and mighty, 614 5

the *L*, mighty in battle."	614	6
"The *L* of hosts,	614	11
To you, O *L*, I lift up my soul;	614	13
Show me your ways, O *L*, *	614	19
Remember, O *L*, your compassion and love, *	614	24
and for the sake of your goodness, O *L*.	615	3
Gracious and upright is the *L*; *	615	4
All the paths of the *L* are love and faithfulness *	615	8
For your Name's sake, O *L*, *	615	10
Who are they who fear the *L*? *	615	12
The *L* is a friend to those who fear him *	615	16
My eyes are ever looking to the *L*, *	615	18
Give judgment for me, O *L*,	616	7
Test me, O *L*, and try me; *	616	10
I will wash my hands in innocence, O *L*, *	616	18
L, I love the house in which you dwell *	616	22
redeem me, O *L* and have pity on me.	617	4
in the full assembly I will bless the *L*.	617	6
The *L* is my light and my salvation;	617	7
the *L* is the strength of my life;	617	9
One thing have I asked of the *L*;	617	18
that I may dwell in the house of the *L*	617	20
To behold the fair beauty of the *L* *	617	22
I will sing and make music to the *L*.	618	9
Hearken to my voice, O *L*, when I call; *	618	10
Your face, *L*, will I seek.	618	13
the *L* will sustain me.	618	20
Show me your way, O *L*; *	618	21
that I should see the goodness of the *L* *	618	27
O tarry and await the *L*'s pleasure;	619	1
wait patiently for the *L*.	619	3
O *L*, I call to you;	619	4
They have no understanding of the *L*'s doings,	619	18
Blessed is the *L*! *	619	22
The *L* is my strength and my shield; *	619	24
The *L* is the strength of his people, *	620	1
Ascribe to the *L*, you gods, *	620	5
ascribe to the *L* glory and strength.	620	6
Ascribe to the *L* the glory due his Name; *	620	7
worship the *L* in the beauty of holiness.	620	8
The voice of the *L* is upon the waters;	620	9
the *L* is upon the mighty waters.	620	11
The voice of the *L* is a powerful voice; *	620	12
the voice of the *L* is a voice of splendor.	620	13
The voice of the *L* breaks the cedar trees; *	620	14
the *L* breaks the cedars of Lebanon;	620	15
The voice of the *L* splits the flames of fire;	620	18
the voice of the *L* shakes the wilderness; *	620	19
the *L* shakes the wilderness of Kadesh.	620	20
The voice of the *L* makes the oak trees writhe *	620	21
And in the temple of the *L* *	620	23
The *L* sits enthroned above the flood; *	620	25
the *L* sits enthroned as King for evermore.	620	26
The *L* shall give strength to his people; *	621	1
the *L* shall give his people the blessing of peace.	621	2
I will exalt you, O *L*,	621	3
O *L* my God, I cried out to you, *	621	6
You brought me up, O *L*, from the dead; *	621	8
Sing to the *L*, you servants of his; *	621	10
You, *L*, with your favor, made me as strong	621	18
I cried to you, O *L*; *	621	22
I pleaded with the *L*, saying,	621	23
Hear, O *L*, and have mercy upon me; *	622	1
O *L*, be my helper."	622	2
O *L* my God, I will give you thanks for ever.	622	6
In you, O *L*, have I taken refuge;	622	7
O *L*, O God of truth.	622	19
and I put my trust in the *L*.	622	21
Have mercy on me, O *L*, for I am in trouble; *	623	3
But as for me, I have trusted in you, O *L*. *	623	20
L, let me not be ashamed for having called	623	27
How great is your goodness, O *L*!	624	4
Blessed be the *L*! *	624	11
Love the *L*, all you who worship him; *	624	18
the *L* protects the faithful,	624	19
all you who wait for the *L*.	624	22
Happy are they to whom the *L* imputes no guilt, *	625	1
I said, "I will confess my transgressions to the *L*." *	625	9
but mercy embraces those who trust in the *L*.	625	24
Be glad, you righteous, and rejoice in the *L*; *	625	25
Rejoice in the *L*, you righteous; *	626	1
Praise the *L* with the harp; *	626	3
For the word of the *L* is right, *	626	7
the loving-kindness of the *L* fills the whole earth.	626	10
By the word of the *L* were the heavens made, *	626	11
Let all the earth fear the *L*; *	626	15
The *L* brings the will of the nations to naught; *	626	19
But the *L*'s will stands fast for ever, *	626	21
Happy is the nation whose God is the *L*! *	626	23
The *L* looks down from heaven, *	627	1
Behold, the eye of the *L* is upon those who fear him, *	627	11
Our soul waits for the *L*; *	627	15
Let your loving-kindness, O *L*, be upon us, *	627	19
I will bless the *L* at all times; *	627	21
I will glory in the *L*; *	627	23
Proclaim with me the greatness of the *L*; *	627	25
I sought the *L*, and he answered me *	628	1
I called in my affliction and the *L* heard me *	628	5
angel of the *L* encompasses those who fear him, *	628	7
Taste and see that the *L* is good; *	628	9
Fear the *L*, you that are his saints, *	628	11
but those who seek the *L* lack nothing that is good.	628	14
I will teach you the fear of the *L*.	628	16
The eyes of the *L* are upon the righteous, *	628	23
The face of the *L* is against those who do evil, *	628	25
The righteous cry, and the *L* hears them *	629	1
The *L* is near to the brokenhearted *	629	3
but the *L* will deliver him out of them all.	629	6
The *L* ransoms the life of his servants, *	629	11
Fight those who fight me, O *L*; *	629	13
and let the angel of the *L* drive them away.	629	23
and let the angel of the *L* pursue them.	630	2
Then I will be joyful in the *L*; *	630	8
My very bones will say, "*L*, who is like you? *	630	10
You saw it, O *L*; do not be silent; *	631	14
O *L*, be not far from me.	631	15
Give me justice, O *L* my God,	631	18
let them say always, "Great is the *L*,	631	28
Your love, O *L*, reaches to the heavens, *	632	12
you save both man and beast, O *L*.	632	16
Put your trust in the *L* and do good; *	633	9
Take delight in the *L*, *	633	11
Commit your way to the *L*	633	13

Be still before the *L* *	633	17
but those who wait upon the *L* shall possess the land.	634	2
The *L* laughs at the wicked, *	634	9
but the *L* upholds the righteous.	634	19
The *L* cares for the lives of the godly, *	634	20
and the enemies of the *L*, like the glory of	634	25
Our steps are directed by the *L*; *	635	5
for the *L* holds them by the hand.	635	8
For the *L* loves justice; *	635	16
The *L* will not abandon them to their hand, *	636	1
Wait upon the *L* and keep his way; *	636	3
deliverance of the righteous comes from the *L*; *	636	15
The *L* will help them and rescue them; *	636	17
O *L*, do not rebuke me in your anger; *	636	20
O *L*, you know all my desires, *	637	14
For in you, O *L*, have I fixed my hope; *	637	27
O *L*, do not forsake me; *	638	11
L, let me know my end and the number of my days, *	639	1
Hear my prayer, O *L*,	639	20
I waited patiently upon the *L*; *	640	1
and put their trust in the *L*.	640	8
Happy are they who trust in the *L*! *	640	9
Great things are they that you have done, O *L*	640	11
and that, O *L*, you know.	640	25
You are the *L*;	641	1
Be pleased, O *L*, to deliver me; *	641	8
O *L*, make haste to help me.	641	9
"Great is the *L*!"	641	18
the *L* will deliver them in the time of trouble.	641	24
The *L* preserves them and keeps them alive,	642	1
The *L* sustains them on their sickbed *	642	4
I said, "*L*, be merciful to me; *	642	6
But you, O *L*, be merciful to me and raise me up, *	642	20
Blessed be the *L* God of Israel, *	642	26
The *L* grants his loving-kindness in the daytime; *	643	23
The *L* of hosts is with us; *	649	8
Come now and look upon the works of the *L*, *	649	19
The *L* of hosts is with us; *	650	4
For the *L* Most High is to be feared; *	650	8
the *L* with the sound of the ram's-horn.	650	15
Great is the *L*, and highly to be praised; *	651	1
in the city of the *L* of hosts, in the city of our God; *	651	16
The *L*, the God of gods, has spoken; *	654	1
and praise your Name, O *L*, for it is good.	660	2
Swallow them up, O *L*;	660	23
and the *L* will deliver me.	661	18
Cast your burden upon the *L*,	662	5
In God the *L*, whose word I praise,	663	11
I will confess you among the peoples, O *L*; *	664	15
pull the fangs of the young lions, O *L*.	665	6
not for any offense or fault of mine, O *L*.	665	24
for you, *L* God of hosts, are Israel's God.	666	4
But you, O *L*, you laugh at them; *	666	12
The righteous will rejoice in the *L*	672	5
truly, the *L* will dwell there for ever.	677	14
that the *L* God might dwell among them.	677	20
God is the *L*, by whom we escape death.	677	24
The *L* has said, "I will bring them back	678	1
bless the *L*, you that are of the fountain of Israel.	678	10
at the time you have set, O *L*:	680	14
Answer me, O *L*, for your love is kind; *	680	23
This will please the *L* more than an offering	681	26
For the *L* listens to the needy, *	682	3
O *L*, make haste to help me.	682	12
"Great is the *L*!"	682	21
O *L*, do not tarry.	682	25
In you, O *L*, have I taken refuge; *	683	1
Remember, O *L*, how the enemy scoffed, *	690	20
For in the *L*'s hand there is a cup,	691	18
Make a vow to the *L* your God and keep it; *	692	22
I will remember the works of the *L*, *	693	22
the praiseworthy deeds and the power of the *L*, *	695	5
When the *L* heard this, he was full of wrath; *	696	17
Then the *L* woke as though from sleep, *	700	9
How long will you be angry, O *L*? *	701	13
O *L* God of hosts, *	702	18
Restore us, O *L* God of hosts; *	703	24
I am the *L* your God,	704	21
Those who hate the *L* would cringe before him, *	705	5
Cover their faces with shame, O *L*, *	707	9
How dear to me is your dwelling, O *L* of hosts! *	707	15
longing for the courts of the *L*;	707	17
by the side of your altars, O *L* of hosts,	707	21
L God of hosts, hear my prayer; *	708	6
For the *L* God is both sun and shield; *	708	14
No good thing will the *L* withhold *	708	16
O *L* of hosts, *	708	18
You have been gracious to your land, O *L*, *	708	20
Show us your mercy, O *L*, *	709	7
I will listen to what the *L* God is saying, *	709	9
The *L* will indeed grant prosperity, *	709	18
Bow down your ear, O *L*, and answer me, *	709	22
Be merciful to me, O *L*, for you are my God; *	710	3
for to you, O *L*, I lift up my soul.	710	6
For you, O *L*, are good and forgiving, *	710	7
Give ear, O *L*, to my prayer, *	710	9
Among the gods there is none like you, O *L*, *	710	13
worship you, O *L*, *	710	16
Teach me your way, O *L*,	710	21
I will thank you, O *L* my God, with all my heart, *	710	24
But you, O *L*, are gracious and full of compassion, *	711	4
because you, O *L*, have helped me and comforted me.	711	11
the *L* loves the gates of Zion	711	13
The *L* will record as he enrolls the peoples, *	711	22
O *L*, my God, my Savior, *	712	1
L, I have called upon you daily;	712	21
But as for me, O *L*, I cry to you for help; *	713	4
L, why have you rejected me? *	713	6
Your love, O *L*, for ever will I sing; *	713	17
The heavens bear witness to your wonders, O *L*, *	714	3
For who in the skies can be compared to the *L*? *	714	5
who is like the *L* among the gods?	714	6
Who is like you, *L* God of hosts? *	714	9
O mighty *L*, your faithfulness is all around you.	714	10
they walk, O *L*, in the light of your presence.	714	24
Truly, the *L* is our ruler; *	715	1
How long will you hide yourself, O *L*?	717	5
Remember, *L*, how short life is, *	717	8
The taunts your enemies have hurled, O *L*, *	717	16
Blessed be the *L* for evermore! *	717	18
Return, O *L*; how long will you tarry? *	718	27
May the graciousness of the *L* our God be upon us; *	719	7
He shall say to the *L*,	719	12
Because you have made the *L* your refuge, *	720	3

It is a good thing to give thanks to the _L_, *	720	22
For you have made me glad by your acts, O _L_; *	721	3
_L_, how great are your works! *	721	5
but you, O _L_, are exalted for evermore.	721	12
For lo, your enemies, O _L_,	721	13
Those who are planted in the house of the _L_ *	721	23
That they may show how upright the _L_ is, *	721	27
The _L_ is King;	722	1
the _L_ has put on his apparel	722	3
The waters have lifted up, O _L_,	722	9
mightier is the _L_ who dwells on high.	722	14
and holiness adorns your house, O _L_,	722	16
O _L_ God of vengeance, *	722	18
How long shall the wicked, O _L_, *	722	22
They crush your people, O _L_, *	723	3
Yet they say, "The _L_ does not see, *	723	7
The _L_ knows our human thoughts; *	723	15
For the _L_ will not abandon his people, *	723	21
If the _L_ had not come to my help, *	723	27
your love, O _L_, upheld me.	724	2
But the _L_ has become my stronghold, *	724	9
the _L_ our God will destroy them.	724	13
Come, let us sing to the _L_; *	724	14
For the _L_ is a great God, *	724	18
and kneel before the _L_ our Maker.	725	2
Sing to the _L_ a new song; *	725	17
sing to the _L_, all the whole earth.	725	18
Sing to the _L_ and bless his Name; *	725	19
For great is the _L_ and greatly to be praised; *	725	23
but it is the _L_ who made the heavens.	726	2
Ascribe to the _L_, you families of the peoples; *	726	5
ascribe to the _L_ honor and power.	726	6
Ascribe to the _L_ the honor due his Name; *	726	7
Worship the _L_ in the beauty of holiness; *	726	9
Tell it out among the nations: "The _L_ is King! *	726	11
before the _L_ when he comes, *	726	18
The _L_ is King;	726	22
mountains melt like wax at the presence of the _L_, *	727	5
because of your judgments, O _L_.	727	13
For you are the _L_,	727	14
The _L_ loves those who hate evil; *	727	17
Rejoice in the _L_, you righteous, *	727	22
Sing to the _L_ a new song, *	727	24
The _L_ has made known his victory; *	728	3
Shout with joy to the _L_ all you lands; *	728	10
Sing to the _L_ with the harp, *	728	12
shout with joy before the King, the _L_.	728	15
and let the hills ring out with joy before the _L_,	728	19
The _L_ is King;	728	23
The _L_ is great in Zion; *	729	1
Proclaim the greatness of the _L_ our God	729	8
they called upon the _L_, and he answered them.	729	13
"O _L_ our God, you answered them indeed; *	729	16
Proclaim the greatness of the _L_ our God	729	19
for the _L_ our God is the Holy One.	729	21
Be joyful in the _L_, all you lands; *	729	22
serve the _L_ with gladness	729	23
Know this: The _L_ himself is God; *	729	25
For the _L_ is good;	730	4
to you, O _L_, will I sing praises.	730	8
root out all evildoers from the city of the _L_.	730	27
_L_, hear my prayer, and let my cry come before you; *	731	1
But you, O _L_, endure for ever, *	731	23
The nations shall fear your Name, O _L_, *	732	6
For the _L_ will build up Zion, *	732	8
so that a people yet unborn may praise the _L_.	732	13
For the _L_ looked down from his holy place on high; *	732	14
That they may declare in Zion the Name of the _L_, *	732	18
and the kingdoms also, to serve the _L_.	732	21
In the beginning, O _L_, you laid the foundations	732	27
Bless the _L_, O my soul, *	733	9
Bless the _L_, O my soul, *	733	11
The _L_ executes righteousness *	733	19
The _L_ is full of compassion and mercy, *	733	23
so does the _L_ care for those who fear him.	734	8
But the merciful goodness of the _L_ endures for ever	734	15
The _L_ has set his throne in heaven, *	734	20
Bless the _L_, you angels of his,	734	22
Bless the _L_, all you his hosts, *	734	25
Bless the _L_, all you works of his,	734	27
bless the _L_, O my soul.	734	29
Bless the _L_, O my soul; *	735	1
O _L_ my God, how excellent is your greatness!	735	2
The trees of the _L_ are full of sap, *	736	9
O _L_, how manifold are your works! *	736	25
May the glory of the _L_ endure for ever; *	737	16
may the _L_ rejoice in all his works.	737	17
I will sing to the _L_ as long as I live; *	737	20
I will rejoice in the _L_.	737	23
Bless the _L_, O my soul. *	737	26
Give thanks to the _L_ and call upon his Name; *	738	1
let the hearts of those who seek the _L_ rejoice.	738	6
Search for the _L_ and his strength; *	738	7
He is the _L_ our God; *	738	13
the word of the _L_ tested him.	739	16
The _L_ made his people exceedingly fruitful; *	740	1
Give thanks to the _L_, for he is good, *	741	19
Who can declare the mighty acts of the _L_ *	741	21
Remember me, O _L_, with the favor you have	742	3
and Aaron, the holy one of the _L_.	743	4
and would not listen to the voice of the _L_.	743	23
as the _L_ had commanded them.	744	16
Therefore the wrath of the _L_ was kindled against	745	3
Save us, O _L_ our God,	745	19
Blessed be the _L_, the God of Israel,	745	23
Give thanks to the _L_, for he is good, *	746	1
Let all those whom the _L_ has redeemed proclaim *	746	3
Then they cried to the _L_ in their trouble, *	746	12
Let them give thanks to the _L_ for his mercy *	746	16
Then they cried to the _L_ in their trouble, *	747	7
Let them give thanks to the _L_ for his mercy *	747	11
Then they cried to the _L_ in their trouble, *	747	19
They beheld the works of the _L_ *	748	3
Then they cried to the _L_ in their trouble, *	748	11
Let them give thanks to the _L_ for his mercy *	748	17
The _L_ changed rivers into deserts, *	748	21
and consider well the mercies of the _L_.	749	16
I will confess you among the peoples, O _L_; *	749	22
be remembered before the _L_, *	751	25
Let their sin be always before the _L_; *	751	27
Let this be the recompense from the _L_	752	14
Help me, O _L_ my God; *	752	27
that you, O _L_, have done it.	753	2
I will give great thanks to the _L_ with my mouth; *	753	8

LORD

The _L_ said to my Lord, “Sit at my right hand, * 753 12
The _L_ will send the scepter of your power 753 14
The _L_ has sworn and he will not recant: * 753 19
I will give thanks to the _L_ with my whole heart, * 754 6
Great are the deeds of the _L_! * 754 8
the _L_ is gracious and full of compassion. 754 13
The fear of the _L_ is the beginning of wisdom; * 755 1
Happy are they who fear the _L_ * 755 5
Give praise, you servants of the _L_; * 756 2
praise the Name of the _L_. 756 3
Let the Name of the _L_ be blessed, * 756 4
let the Name of the _L_ be praised. 756 7
The _L_ is high above all nations, * 756 8
Who is like the _L_ our God, who sits enthroned 756 10
Not to us, O _L_, not to us, 757 13
O Israel, trust in the _L_; * 758 6
O house of Aaron, trust in the _L_, * 758 8
You who fear the _L_, trust in the _L_; * 758 10
The _L_ has been mindful of us, and he will bless us; * 758 12
He will bless those who fear the _L_, * 758 15
May the _L_ increase you more and more, * 758 17
May you be blessed by the _L_, * 758 19
The heaven of heavens is the _L_’s, * 758 21
The dead do not praise the _L_, * 758 23
But we will bless the _L_, * 758 25
I love the _L_, because he has heard the voice 759 1
Then I called upon the Name of the _L_: * 759 8
“O _L_, I pray you, save my life.” 759 9
Gracious is the _L_ and righteous; * 759 10
The _L_ watches over the innocent; * 759 12
for the _L_ has treated you well. 759 15
I will walk in the presence of the _L_ * 759 18
How shall I repay the _L_ * 759 23
and call upon the Name of the _L_. 759 26
I will fulfill my vows to the _L_ * 760 1
Precious in the sight of the _L_ * 760 3
O _L_, I am your servant; * 760 5
and call upon the Name of the _L_. 760 9
I will fulfill my vows to the _L_ * 760 10
In the courts of the _L_’s house, * 760 12
Praise the _L_, all you nations; * 760 15
and the faithfulness of the _L_ endures for ever. 760 18
Give thanks to the _L_, for he is good; * 760 20
Let those who fear the _L_ now proclaim, * 761 3
I called to the _L_ in my distress; * 761 5
the _L_ answered by setting me free. 761 6
The _L_ is at my side, therefore I will not fear; * 761 7
The _L_ is at my side to help me; * 761 9
It is better to rely on the _L_ * 761 11
in the name of the _L_ I will repel them. 761 16
but the _L_ came to my help. 761 23
The _L_ is my strength and my song, * 761 24
“The right hand of the _L_ has triumphed! * 762 1
the right hand of the _L_ is exalted! 762 2
the right hand of the _L_ has triumphed!” 762 3
and declare the works of the _L_. 762 5
The _L_ has punished me sorely, * 762 6
I will offer thanks to the _L_. 762 10
“This is the gate of the _L_; * 762 11
This is the _L_’s doing, * 762 17
On this day the _L_ has acted; * 762 19
Hosanna, _L_, hosanna! * 762 21
_L_, send us now success. 762 22
we bless you from the house of the _L_. 762 24
God is the _L_; he has shined upon us; * 762 25
Give thanks to the _L_, for he is good; * 763 3
who walk in the law of the _L_! 763 6
Blessed are you, O _L_; * 764 7
O _L_, let me not be put to shame. 765 22
Teach me, O _L_, the way of your statutes, * 766 1
Let your loving-kindness come to me, O _L_, * 766 17
O _L_, I take great comfort. 767 18
I remember your Name in the night, O _L_, * 767 23
You only are my portion, O _L_; * 768 1
The earth, O _L_, is full of your love; * 768 15
O _L_, you have dealt graciously with your servant, * 768 17
I know, O _L_, that your judgments are right * 769 14
O _L_, your word is everlasting; * 770 20
preserve my life, O _L_, according to your word. 772 8
Accept, O _L_, the willing tribute of my lips, * 772 9
It is time for you to act, O _L_, * 773 25
You are righteous, O _L_, * 774 21
answer me, O _L_, that I may keep your statutes. 775 16
Hear my voice, O _L_, 776 1
You, O _L_, are near at hand, * 776 5
Great is your compassion, O _L_; * 776 15
O _L_, in your mercy, preserve me. 776 22
I have hoped for your salvation, O _L_, * 777 11
Let my cry come before you, O _L_; * 777 17
I long for your salvation, O _L_, * 778 3
When I was in trouble, I called to the _L_; * 778 10
I called to the _L_, and he answered me. 778 11
Deliver me, O _L_, from lying lips * 778 12
My help comes from the _L_, * 779 3
The _L_ himself watches over you; * 779 9
the _L_ is your shade at your right hand. 779 10
The _L_ shall preserve you from all evil; * 779 13
The _L_ shall watch over your going out and 779 15
“Let us go to the house of the _L_.” 779 19
the tribes of the _L_, * 780 2
to praise the Name of the _L_. 780 4
Because of the house of the _L_ our God, * 780 13
So our eyes look to the _L_ our God, * 780 19
Have mercy upon us, O _L_, have mercy, * 780 21
If the _L_ had not been on our side, * 781 1
If the _L_ had not been on our side, * 781 3
Blessed be the _L_! * 781 11
Our help is in the Name of the _L_, * 781 15
Those who trust in the _L_ are like Mount Zion, * 781 17
so does the _L_ stand round about his people, 781 20
Show your goodness, O _L_, to those who are good * 782 1
the _L_ will lead them away with the evildoers; * 782 4
When the _L_ restored the fortunes of Zion, * 782 6
“The _L_ has done great things for them.” 782 11
The _L_ has done great things for us, * 782 12
Restore our fortunes, O _L_, * 782 14
Unless the _L_ builds the house, * 782 20
Unless the _L_ watches over the city, * 783 1
Children are a heritage from the _L_, * 783 6
Happy are they all who fear the _L_, * 783 13
The man who fears the _L_ * 783 19
The _L_ bless you from Zion, * 783 21
The _L_, the Righteous One, * 784 7
“The _L_ prosper you. * 784 16

We wish you well in the Name of the *L*." 784 17
Out of the depths have I called to you, O *L*; 784 18
L, hear my voice; * 784 19
If you, *L*, were to note what is done amiss, * 784 21
I wait for the *L*; my soul waits for him; * 785 1
My soul waits for the *L*, 785 3
O Israel, wait for the *L*, * 785 6
for with the *L* there is mercy; 785 7
O *L*, I am not proud; * 785 10
O Israel, wait upon the *L*, * 785 17
L, remember David, * 785 19
How he swore an oath to the *L* * 786 1
Until I find a place for the *L*, * 786 7
Arise, O *L*, into your resting-place, * 786 13
The *L* has sworn an oath to David; * 786 19
For the *L* has chosen Zion; * 786 26
For there the *L* has ordained the blessing: * 787 17
Behold now, bless the *L*, all you servants of the *L*, * 787 19
you that stand by night in the house of the *L*. 787 20
Lift up your hands in the holy place and bless the *L*; * 787 21
the *L* who made heaven and earth bless 787 22
Praise the Name of the *L*; * 788 2
give praise, you servants of the *L*, 788 3
You who stand in the house of the *L*, * 788 4
Praise the *L*, for the *L* is good; * 788 6
For the *L* has chosen Jacob for himself * 788 8
For I know that the *L* is great, * 788 10
The *L* does whatever pleases him, 788 12
O *L*, your Name is everlasting; * 789 1
your renown, O *L*, endures from age to age. 789 2
For the *L* gives his people justice * 789 3
Bless the *L*, O house of Israel; * 789 13
O house of Aaron, bless the *L*. 789 14
Bless the *L*, O house of Levi; * 789 15
you who fear the *L*, bless the *L*. 789 16
Blessed be the *L* out of Zion, * 789 17
Give thanks to the *L*, for he is good, * 789 20
How shall we sing the *L*'s song * 792 8
Remember the day of Jerusalem, O *L*, 792 15
I will give thanks to you, O *L*, with my whole heart; * 793 1
All the kings of the earth will praise you, O *L*, * 793 10
They will sing of the ways of the *L*, * 793 12
that great is the glory of the *L*. 793 13
Though the *L* be high, he cares for the lowly; * 793 14
The *L* will make good his purpose for me; * 793 19
O *L*, your love endures for ever; 793 20
L, you have searched me out and known me; * 794 1
but you, O *L*, know it altogether. 794 7
Do I not hate those, O *L*, who hate you? * 795 20
Deliver me, O *L*, from evildoers; * 796 1
Keep me, O *L*, from the hands of the wicked; * 796 7
I have said to the *L*, "You are my God; * 796 13
listen, O *L*, to my supplication. 796 14
Do not grant the desires of the wicked, O *L*, * 796 17
I know that the *L* will maintain the cause 796 25
O *L*, I call to you; come to me quickly; * 797 3
Set a watch before my mouth, O *L*, 797 7
I cry to the *L* with my voice; * 798 1
to the *L* I make loud supplication. 798 2
I cry out to you, O *L*; * 798 9
L, hear my prayer, 798 18
O *L*, make haste to answer me; my spirit fails me; * 799 12
Deliver me from my enemies, O *L*, * 799 19
Revive me, O *L*, for your Name's sake; * 799 23
Blessed be the *L* my rock! * 800 1
O *L*, what are we that you should care for us? * 800 6
Bow your heavens, O *L*, and come down; * 800 10
happy are the people whose God is the *L*! 801 11
Great is the *L* and greatly to be praised; * 801 16
The *L* is gracious and full of compassion, * 802 1
The *L* is loving to everyone * 802 3
All your works praise you, O *L*, * 802 5
The *L* is faithful in all his words * 802 13
The *L* upholds all those who fall; * 802 15
The eyes of all wait upon you, O *L*, * 802 17
The *L* is righteous in all his ways * 802 21
The *L* is near to those who call upon him, * 802 23
The *L* preserves all those who love him, * 802 27
My mouth shall speak the praise of the *L*; * 803 1
Praise the *L*, O my soul! * 803 4
I will praise the *L* as long as I live; 803 5
whose hope is in the *L* their God; 803 12
The *L* sets the prisoners free; 803 17
the *L* opens the eyes of the blind; * 803 18
the *L* lifts up those who are bowed down; 803 19
The *L* loves the righteous; 803 20
the *L* cares for the stranger; * 803 21
The *L* shall reign for ever, * 803 24
The *L* rebuilds Jerusalem; * 804 4
Great is our *L* and mighty in power; * 804 10
The *L* lifts up the lowly, * 804 12
Sing to the *L* with thanksgiving; * 804 14
But the *L* has pleasure in those who fear him, * 804 24
Worship the *L*, O Jerusalem; * 805 1
Praise the *L* from the heavens; * 805 21
Let them praise the Name of the *L*; * 806 3
Praise the *L* from the earth, * 806 7
Let them praise the Name of the *L*, * 806 19
Sing to the *L* a new song; * 807 2
For the *L* takes pleasure in his people * 807 8
praise the *L*. 808 10

Lord

Prepare ye the way of the *L*, 37 4
The glory of the *L* shall be revealed, 37 6
David a Savior, which is Christ the *L*. 37 10
saith the *L* of hosts. 38 9
turn unto the *L* your God; 38 15
To the *L* our God belong mercies and forgivenesses, 38 20
the voice of the *L* our God, 38 22
and the *L* hath laid on him the iniquity 39 2
wherewith the *L* hath afflicted me. 39 6
The *L* is risen indeed. 39 8
This is the day which the *L* hath made; 39 9
victory through our *L* Jesus Christ. 39 12
Holy, holy, holy, *L* God Almighty, 39 22
O give thanks unto the *L*, and call upon his Name; 40 7
from the *L* Jesus Christ. 40 10
"We will go into the house of the *L*." 40 12
be always acceptable in thy sight, O *L*, my strength 40 14
The *L* is in his holy temple; 40 18
But thou, O *L*, have mercy upon us, 42 3
declared unto mankind in Christ Jesus our *L*; 42 7
The Almighty and merciful *L* grant you absolution 42 11

O *L*, open thou our lips.	42	14
The *L* hath manifested forth his glory:	43	4
The *L* is full of compassion and mercy:	43	6
The *L* is risen indeed:	43	8
Christ the *L* ascendeth into heaven:	43	10
The Spirit of the *L* filleth the world:	43	12
The earth is the *L*'s for he made it:	44	1
Worship the *L* in the beauty of holiness:	44	3
The mercy of the *L* is everlasting:	44	5
The *L* is glorious in his saints:	44	8
O come, let us sing unto the *L*; *	44	10
For the *L* is a great God, *	44	14
and kneel before the *L* our Maker.	45	2
For he is the *L* our God, *	45	3
O worship the *L* in the beauty of holiness; *	45	6
O be joyful in the *L* all ye lands; *	45	11
serve the *L* with gladness	45	12
Be ye sure that the *L* he is God;	45	14
For the *L* is gracious;	45	20
but alive unto God through Jesus Christ our *L*.	46	12
The Word of the *L*.	47	2
O all ye works of the *L*, bless ye the *L*; *	47	5
O ye angels of the *L*, bless ye the *L*; *	47	7
O ye heavens, bless ye the *L*; *	47	9
waters that be above the firmament, bless ye the *L*;	47	10
O all ye powers of the *L*, bless ye the *L*; *	47	11
O ye sun and moon, bless ye the *L*; *	48	1
O ye stars of heaven, bless ye the *L*;	48	2
O ye showers and dew, bless ye the *L*; *	48	3
O ye winds of God, bless ye *L*; *	48	5
O ye fire and heat, bless ye the *L*;	48	6
O ye winter and summer, bless ye the *L*; *	48	7
O ye dews and frosts, bless ye the *L*; *	48	9
O ye frost and cold, bless ye the *L*;	48	10
O ye ice and snow, bless ye the *L*; *	48	11
O ye nights and days, bless ye the *L*; *	48	13
O ye light and darkness, bless ye the *L*;	48	14
O ye lightnings and clouds, bless ye the *L*; *	48	15
O let the earth bless the *L*; *	48	17
O ye mountains and hills, bless ye the *L*;	48	18
green things upon the earth, bless ye the *L*; *	48	19
O ye wells, bless ye the *L*; *	48	21
O ye seas and floods, bless ye the *L*;	48	22
and all that move in the waters, bless ye the *L*; *	48	23
O all ye fowls of the air, bless ye the *L*; *	48	25
O all ye beasts and cattle, bless ye the *L*;	48	26
O ye children of men, bless ye the *L*; *	48	27
O ye people of God, bless ye the *L*; *	49	1
O ye priests of the *L*, bless ye the *L*;	49	2
O ye servants of the *L*, bless ye the *L*; *	49	3
spirits and souls of the righteous, bless ye the *L*; *	49	5
O ye holy and humble men of heart, bless ye the *L*;	49	6
Blessed art thou, O *L* God of our fathers; *	49	9
My soul doth magnify the *L*,	50	1
Blessed be the *L* God of Israel, *	50	22
for thou shalt go before the face of the *L*	51	12
L, now lettest thou thy servant depart in peace, *	51	23
O *L* God, heavenly King, God the Father Almighty.	52	9
O *L*, the only-begotten Son, Jesus Christ;	52	10
O *L*, God, Lamb of God, Son of the Father,	52	11
thou only art the *L*,	52	19
we acknowledge thee to be the *L*.	52	23
Holy, holy, holy, *L* God of Sabaoth;	53	1
And in Jesus Christ his only Son our *L*;	53	25
The *L* be with you.	54	11
O *L*, show thy mercy upon us;	55	1
Give peace, O *L*, in all the world;	55	5
L, keep this nation under thy care;	55	7
Let not the needy, O *L*, be forgotten;	55	11
O *L*, save thy people, and bless thine heritage;	55	15
Vouchsafe, O *L*, to keep us this day without sin;	55	19
O *L*, have mercy upon us, have mercy upon us.	55	20
O *L*, let thy mercy be upon us;	55	21
O *L*, in thee have I trusted;	55	23
the glorious resurrection of thy Son our *L*:	56	2
through the same Jesus Christ our *L*.	56	5
through the same thy Son Jesus Christ our *L*.	56	10
the might of Jesus Christ our *L*.	57	6
O *L*, our heavenly Father, almighty and everlasting	57	7
through Jesus Christ our *L*.	57	13
through our *L* and Savior Jesus Christ.	57	24
through the same thy Son Jesus Christ our *L*.	58	7
L Jesus Christ, who didst stretch out thine arms	58	8
in the redemption of the world by our *L* Jesus Christ,	58	22
through Jesus Christ our *L*,	59	9
Fulfill now, O *L*, the desires and petitions	59	16
Let us bless the *L*.	59	20
The grace of our *L* Jesus Christ,	59	22
from the *L* Jesus Christ.	61	4
O worship the *L* in the beauty of holiness;	61	5
I will bless the *L* who giveth me counsel;	61	10
I have set the *L* always before me;	61	11
The *L* is his Name.	62	4
darkness is not dark to thee, O *L*;	62	6
But thou, O *L*, have mercy upon us,	63	6
in Christ Jesus our *L*;	63	10
The Almighty and merciful *L* grant you absolution	63	14
O *L*, make haste to help us.	63	18
The Word of the *L*.	65	1
My soul doth magnify the *L*, *	65	4
L, now lettest thou thy servant depart in peace, *	66	1
And in Jesus Christ his only Son our *L*;	66	11
The *L* be with you.	67	1
O *L*, show thy mercy upon us;	67	16
Give peace, O *L*, in all the world;	67	20
L, keep this nation under thy care;	67	22
Let not the needy, O *L*, be forgotten;	68	3
We entreat thee, O *L*.	68	8
L God, whose Son our Savior Jesus Christ triumphed	69	1
O *L* Jesus Christ, who by thy death didst	69	7
through Jesus Christ our *L*.	69	15
Lighten our darkness, we beseech thee, O *L*;	70	1
L Jesus, stay with us, for evening is at hand	70	10
through Jesus Christ our *L*.	70	19
Keep watch, dear *L*, with those who work,	71	1
Tend the sick, *L* Christ;	71	3
through Jesus Christ our *L*.	71	9
in the redemption of the world by our *L* Jesus Christ,	71	18
through Jesus Christ our *L*,	72	6
Fulfill now, O *L*, the desires and petitions	72	13
Let us bless the *L*.	72	17
The grace of our *L* Jesus Christ,	72	19
In the wilderness prepare the way of the *L*,	75	4
The glory of the *L* shall be revealed,	75	6

a Savior, who is Christ the *L*. 75 10
among the nations, says the *L* of hosts. 76 8
Return to the *L* your God, 76 13
To the *L* our God belong mercy and forgiveness, 76 19
of the *L* our God by following his laws 76 21
and the *L* has laid on him the iniquity 77 1
me, whom the *L* has afflicted. 77 5
The *L* is risen indeed. 77 7
On this day the *L* has acted; 77 8
who gives us the victory through our *L* 77 10
Holy, holy, holy is the *L* God Almighty, 77 20
Give thanks to the *L*, and call upon his Name; 78 6
peace from God our Father and the *L* 78 8
"Let us go to the house of the *L*." 78 11
be acceptable in your sight, O *L*, my strength 78 13
The *L* is in his holy temple; 78 17
through our *L* Jesus Christ, strengthen you 80 2
L, open our lips. 80 5
The *L* has shown forth his glory: 81 1
The *L* is full of compassion and mercy: 81 2
The *L* is risen indeed: 81 4
Christ the *L* has ascended into heaven: 81 6
The Spirit of the *L* renews the face of the earth: 81 8
The earth is the *L*'s for he made it: 81 11
Worship the *L* in the beauty of holiness: 81 12
The mercy of the *L* is everlasting: 81 14
The *L* is glorious in his saints: 82 3
Come, let us sing to the *L*; * 82 5
For the *L* is a great God, * 82 9
and kneel before the *L* our Maker. 82 16
Be joyful in the *L*, all you lands; * 82 20
serve the *L* with gladness 82 21
Know this: The *L* himself is God; * 83 1
For the *L* is good; 83 7
and alive to God in Jesus Christ our *L*. 83 20
The Word of the *L*. 84 4
I will sing to the *L*, for he is lofty and uplifted; * 85 1
The *L* is my strength and my refuge; * 85 3
the *L* has become my Savior. 85 4
The *L* is a mighty warrior; * 85 7
Your right hand, O *L*, is glorious in might; * 85 14
your right hand, O *L*, has overthrown the enemy. 85 15
Who can be compared with you, O *L*, 85 16
The resting-place you have made for yourself, O *L*, * 85 26
the sanctuary, O *L*, that your hand has established. 85 27
The *L* shall reign * 85 28
For the *L* is my stronghold and my sure defense, * 86 3
Give thanks to the *L* and call upon his Name; 86 8
Sing the praises of the *L*, 86 11
Seek the *L* while he wills to be found; * 86 17
And let them turn to the *L*, 86 21
nor your ways my ways, says the *L*. 86 24
and the glory of the *L* has dawned upon you. 87 12
But over you the *L* will rise, * 87 15
They will call you, The City of the *L*, * 87 21
The *L* will be your everlasting light, * 88 1
Glorify the *L*, all you works of the *L*, * 88 5
In the firmament of his power, glorify the *L*, * 88 7
Glorify the *L*, you angels and all powers of the *L*, * 88 9
Sun and moon and stars of the sky, glorify the *L*, * 88 11
Glorify the *L*, every shower of rain and fall of dew, * 88 13
Winter and summer, glorify the *L*, * 88 15
Glorify the *L*, O chill and cold, * 88 17
Frost and cold, ice and sleet, glorify the *L*, * 88 19
Glorify the *L*, O nights and days, * 89 1
Storm clouds and thunderbolts, glorify the *L*, * 89 3
Let the earth glorify the *L*, * 89 5
Glorify the *L*, O mountains and hills, 89 7
Glorify the *L*, O springs of water, seas, and streams, * 89 10
All birds of the air, glorify the *L*, * 89 12
Glorify the *L*, O beasts of the wild, * 89 14
O men and women everywhere, glorify the *L*, * 89 16
Let the people of God glorify the *L*, * 89 18
Glorify the *L*, O priests and servants of the *L*, * 89 20
Glorify the *L*, O spirits and souls of the righteous, * 89 22
holy and humble of heart, glorify the *L*, * 89 24
Let us glorify the *L*: Father, Son, and Holy Spirit; * 90 1
In the firmament of his power, glorify the *L*, * 90 3
Glory to you, *L* God of our fathers; * 90 5
O *L* and Ruler of the hosts of heaven, * 90 17
O *L*, you are full of compassion, * 91 5
In your great goodness, *L*, 91 9
And now, O *L*, I bend the knee of my heart, * 91 12
I have sinned, O *L*, I have sinned, * 91 14
Forgive me, *L*, forgive me. 91 17
For you, O *L*, are the God of those who repent, * 91 20
My soul proclaims the greatness of the *L*, 91 27
Blessed be the *L*, the God of Israel; * 92 18
for you will go before the *L* to prepare his way, 93 2
L, you now have set your servant free * 93 12
are yours by right, O *L* our God, 93 21
O ruler of the universe, *L* God, 94 9
Who can fail to do you homage, *L*, 94 14
L God, heavenly King, 94 23
L Jesus Christ, only Son of the Father, 95 3
L God, Lamb of God, 95 4
you alone are the *L*, 95 10
You are the *L*: we acclaim you; 95 16
Holy, holy, holy *L*, God of power and might, 95 21
Come then, *L*, and help your people, 96 9
I believe in Jesus Christ, his only Son, our *L*. 96 15
The *L* be with you. 97 1
Show us your mercy, O *L*; 97 18
Give peace, O *L*, in all the world; 97 22
L, keep this nation under your care; 98 1
Let not the needy, O *L*, be forgotten; 98 5
Save your people, *L*, and bless your inheritance; 98 9
L, keep us from all sin today; 98 13
Have mercy on us, *L*, have mercy. 98 14
L, show us your love and mercy; 98 15
In you, *L*, is our hope; 98 17
the glorious resurrection of your Son our *L*: 98 20
through Jesus Christ our *L*. 98 23
through Jesus Christ your Son our *L*. 99 5
through the might of Jesus Christ our *L*. 99 24
L God, almighty and everlasting Father, 100 1
your purpose; through Jesus Christ our *L*. 100 5
through our *L* and Savior Jesus Christ. 100 16
L Jesus Christ, you stretched out your arms of love 101 1
in the redemption of the world by our *L* Jesus Christ; 101 14
through Jesus Christ our *L*, 101 22
Fulfill now, O *L*, our desires and petitions 102 5
Let us bless the *L*. 102 8
The grace of our *L* Jesus Christ, 102 10

Lord

O *L*, make haste to help us.	103	2
great among the nations, says the *L* of Hosts.	106	9
L, have mercy.	106	11
L, hear our prayer;	107	1
through Jesus Christ our *L*.	107	7
L Jesus Christ, you said to your apostles,	107	17
Let us bless the *L*.	107	22
Light and peace, in Jesus Christ our *L*.	109	1
The *L* is risen indeed.	109	4
Bless the *L* who forgives all our sins.	109	5
we proclaim Christ Jesus as *L*,	110	2
darkness is not dark to you, O *L*;	110	9
through Jesus Christ our *L*.	110	17
Grant us, *L*, the lamp of charity which never fails,	110	18
Jesus Christ our *L*.	110	22
O *L* God Almighty, as you have taught us to call	110	23
Lighten our darkness, we beseech thee, O *L*;	111	1
through Jesus Christ our *L*.	111	7
L Christ, your saints have been the lights of the world	111	12
Blessed are you, O *L*, the God of our fathers,	113	1
The *L* bless you and keep you.	114	1
The *L* make his face to shine upon you	114	2
The *L* lift upon his countenance upon you	114	4
and from the *L* Jesus Christ.	115	4
Worship the *L* in the beauty of holiness;	115	5
I will bless the *L* who gives me counsel;	115	10
I have set the *L* always before me;	115	11
The *L* is his name.	115	16
darkness is not dark to you, O *L*;	116	3
through our *L* Jesus Christ, strengthen you	117	7
O *L*, make haste to help us.	117	11
The Word of the *L*.	119	1
My soul proclaims the greatness of the *L*,	119	4
L, you now have set your servant free *	120	1
I believe in Jesus Christ, his only Son, our *L*.	120	11
The *L* be with you.	121	1
Show us your mercy, O *L*;	121	18
Give peace, O *L*, in all the world;	121	22
L, keep this nation under your care;	122	1
Let not the needy, O *L*, be forgotten;	122	5
We entreat you, O *L*.	122	10
L God, whose Son our Savior Jesus Christ triumphed	123	1
L Jesus Christ, by your death you took away the sting	123	6
through Jesus Christ our *L*.	123	14
Be our light in the darkness, O *L*,	123	21
L Jesus, stay with us, for evening is at hand	124	7
through Jesus Christ our *L*.	124	16
Keep watch, dear *L*, with those who work,	124	17
Tend the sick, *L* Christ;	124	19
through Jesus Christ our *L*.	125	4
in redemption of the world by our *L* Jesus Christ;	125	12
Fulfill now, O *L*, our desires and petitions	126	5
Let us bless the *L*.	126	8
The grace of our *L* Jesus Christ,	126	10
The *L* Almighty grant us a peaceful night	127	1
Our help is in the Name of the *L*;	127	3
For the sake of your Son our *L* Jesus Christ,	127	11
O *L*, make haste to help us.	128	4
Know that the *L* does wonders for the faithful; *	128	14
when I call upon the *L*, he will hear me.	128	15
and put your trust in the *L*.	128	19
Lift up the light of your countenance upon us, O *L*.	129	3
for only you, *L*, make me dwell in safety.	129	7
In you, O *L*, have I taken refuge;	129	8
O *L*, O God of truth.	129	20
He shall say to the *L*,	129	23
Because you have made the *L* your refuge, *	130	15
Behold now, bless the *L*, all you servants of the *L*, *	131	6
you that stand by night in the house of the *L*.	131	7
Lift up your hands in the holy place and bless the *L*; *	131	8
the *L* who made heaven and earth bless you	131	9
L, you are in the midst of us,	131	12
Do not forsake us, O *L* our God.	131	13
L Jesus, the great shepherd of the sheep,	132	2
Into your hands, O *L*, I commend my spirit;	132	12
For you have redeemed me, O *L*, O God of truth.	132	13
Keep us, O *L*, as the apple of your eye;	132	14
L, have mercy.	132	16
L, hear our prayer;	133	7
Be our light in the darkness, O *L*,	133	10
through Jesus Christ our *L*.	133	16
Look down, O *L*, from your heavenly throne, and	133	17
Visit this place, O *L*, and drive far from it	133	21
through Jesus Christ our *L*.	134	5
Keep watch, dear *L*, with those who work,	134	6
Tend the sick, *L* Christ;	134	8
Guide us waking, O *L*, and guard us sleeping;	134	16
L, you now have set your servant free *	135	1
Guide us waking, O *L*, and guard us sleeping;	135	9
Let us bless the *L*.	135	12
The almighty and merciful *L*,	135	14
Open my lips, O *L*, *	137	1
Blessed be the God and Father of our *L* Jesus Christ!	137	11
L God, almighty and everlasting Father,	137	14
through Jesus Christ our *L*.	137	18
Give praise, you servants of the *L*; *	138	1
praise the Name of the *L*.	138	2
Let the Name of the *L* be blessed, *	138	3
let the Name of the *L* be praised.	138	6
The *L* is high above all nations, *	138	7
L Jesus Christ, you said to your apostles,	138	16
Jesus as *L*, and ourselves as your servants,	139	11
L Jesus, stay with us, for evening is at hand	139	16
Behold now, bless the *L*, all you servants of the *L*, *	140	1
you that stand by night in the house of the *L*.	140	2
Lift up your hands in the holy place and bless the *L*; *	140	3
the *L* who made heaven and earth bless you	140	4
L, you are in the midst of us	140	5
Do not forsake us, O *L* our God.	140	6
L, you now have set your servant free *	140	7
Visit this place, O *L*, and drive far from it	140	13
through Jesus Christ our *L*.	140	16
The almighty and merciful *L*,	140	17
O come, let us sing unto the *L*; *	146	1
For the *L* is a great God, *	146	5
and kneel before the *L* our Maker.	146	12
For he is the *L* our God, *	146	13
Remember not, *L* Christ, our offenses,	148	9
Spare us, good *L*, spare thy people,	148	11
Spare us, good *L*.	148	14
Good *L*, deliver us.	148	17
We sinners do beseech thee to hear us, O *L* God;	150	1
We beseech thee to hear us, good *L*.	150	4
L, have mercy upon us.	153	3

O *L*, let thy mercy be showed upon us; 153 16
through Jesus Christ our *L*. 153 25
The grace of our *L* Jesus Christ, 154 1
O *L*, arise, help us; 154 3
graciously hear us, O *L* 155 4
Jesus Christ our *L*. 155 13
Stir up thy power, O *L*, 160 1
through Jesus Christ our *L*, 160 4
that when thy Son our *L* cometh 160 7
through the same Jesus Christ our *L*, 160 9
through the same our *L* Jesus Christ, 161 11
through the same Jesus Christ our *L*, 161 17
even our *L* Jesus Christ; 162 4
through the same Jesus Christ our *L*, 162 16
confess him as *L* and Savior; 163 5
through the same Jesus Christ our *L*, 163 11
Give us grace, O *L*, to answer readily the call 163 14
through Jesus Christ our *L*, 164 4
O *L*, who has taught us 164 18
manifested unto us in thy Son Jesus Christ our *L*; 165 12
through the same Jesus Christ our *L*, 165 19
through Jesus Christ our *L*, 166 7
through Jesus Christ thy Son our *L*, 166 13
through Jesus Christ our *L*, 167 8
through the same Jesus Christ our *L*, 168 7
through the same thy Son Jesus Christ our *L*, 168 14
O *L* God, whose blessed Son our Savior gave 169 1
through the same thy Son Jesus Christ our *L*, 169 5
the same thy Son Jesus Christ our *L*; 169 11
for which our *L* Jesus Christ was contented 169 15
through the same thy Son Christ our *L*, 170 12
the glory of the *L*'s resurrection: 170 15
through the same Jesus Christ our *L*, 170 19
celebrate with joy the day of the *L*'s resurrection, 171 1
through the same Jesus Christ our *L*, 171 3
through Jesus Christ our *L*, 171 7
through the same Jesus Christ our *L*, 171 14
through the same thy Son Jesus Christ our *L*, 171 20
through the same Jesus Christ our *L*, 172 5
through the same thy Son Jesus Christ our *L*, 172 12
through the same Jesus Christ our *L*, 173 2
through the same thy Son Jesus Christ our *L*, 173 8
through Jesus Christ our *L*, 174 5
through the same Jesus Christ our *L*, 174 12
believe thy only-begotten Son our *L* Jesus Christ 174 16
through Jesus Christ our *L*, 175 12
Remember, O *L*, what thou hast wrought 176 9
through Jesus Christ our *L*, 177 1
Grant, O *L*, we beseech thee, that the course 177 9
through Jesus Christ our *L*, 178 4
Keep, O *L*, we beseech thee, thy household 178 6
O *L*, we beseech thee, make us 178 12
through the same Jesus Christ our *L*, 179 2
O *L*, we beseech thee mercifully to receive 179 10
for the worthiness of thy Son Jesus Christ our *L*; 179 21
through Jesus Christ our *L*, 180 5
O *L*, we beseech thee, let thy continual pity cleanse 180 8
through Jesus Christ our *L*, 180 11
Grant to us, *L*, we beseech thee, the spirit to think 180 14
through the same thy Son Jesus Christ our *L*, 181 2
through Jesus Christ our *L*, 181 8
L of all power and might, who art the author 181 11
Grant us, O *L*, we pray thee, to trust in thee 181 17
through Jesus Christ our *L*, 182 3
Grant us, O *L*, not to mind earthly things, 182 6
and mediation of Jesus Christ thy Son our *L*; 183 4
L, we pray thee that thy grace may always precede 183 6
through Jesus Christ our *L*, 183 8
through the same Jesus Christ our *L*, 183 15
through Jesus Christ our *L*, 184 5
Blessed *L*, who hast caused all holy Scriptures 184 15
the King of kings and *L* of lords: 185 2
Christ, our *L* and our God, 185 17
We give thee thanks, O *L* of glory, for the example 186 1
Shed upon thy Church, we beseech thee, O *L*, 186 6
through Jesus Christ our *L*, 186 10
follow the one *L*, our Savior Jesus Christ; 187 5
through Jesus Christ our *L*, 187 13
clean hearts by the same thy Son Jesus Christ our *L*; 187 19
through Jesus Christ our *L*, 188 5
through the same thy Son Jesus Christ our *L*, 188 12
We beseech thee, O *L*, pour thy grace into our hearts, 188 15
through the same Jesus Christ our *L*, 189 3
the Name of our *L* Jesus Christ; 189 8
through Jesus Christ our *L*, 189 21
through the same thy Son Jesus Christ our *L*, 190 8
which is Jesus Christ our *L*; 190 14
L God Almighty, in whose Name the founders 190 17
through Jesus Christ our *L*, 190 22
through the same Jesus Christ our *L*, 191 13
through the same thy Son Jesus Christ our *L*, 192 5
through Jesus Christ our *L*, 192 11
obey the calling of our *L* to follow 193 1
through Jesus Christ our *L*, 193 2
through the same thy Son Jesus Christ our *L*, 193 15
James the Just, brother of our *L*, 193 19
through the same our *L* Jesus Christ, 193 22
love and mercy of our *L* and Savior Jesus Christ; 194 5
the mystical body of thy Son Christ our *L*: 194 10
through the same Jesus Christ our *L*, 194 14
through Jesus Christ our *L*, 194 21
for the sake of the same our *L* 195 5
through Jesus Christ our *L*, 195 13
through Jesus Christ our *L*, 196 5
into the stature of the fullness of our *L* 197 1
through the same Jesus Christ our *L*, 197 9
through Jesus Christ our *L*, 197 17
through the same thy Son Jesus Christ our *L*, 198 6
through Jesus Christ our *L*, 198 13
through Jesus Christ our *L*, 199 1
through Jesus Christ our *L*, 200 4
God our Father, whose Son our *L* Jesus Christ 201 1
Grant, O *L* God, to all who have been baptized 201 12
through the same Jesus Christ our *L*, 201 16
O eternal *L* God, who holdest all souls in life: 202 1
through Jesus Christ our *L*, 202 6
victory of Jesus Christ our *L*; 202 14
the King of kings and *L* of lords: 202 17
through the same thy Son Jesus Christ our *L*, 203 9
through the same Jesus Christ our *L*, 203 16
through Jesus Christ our *L*, 204 5
didst send, the same thy Son Jesus Christ our *L*; 205 1
through Jesus Christ our *L*, 205 11
Shepherd and Bishop of our souls, Jesus Christ our *L*, 205 19

through our *L* and Savior Jesus Christ, 206 6
through the same thy Son Jesus Christ our *L*, 206 15
L God Almighty, who hast made all peoples 207 1
through Jesus Christ our *L*, 207 5
Almighty God, *L* of heaven and earth: 207 15
through Jesus Christ our *L*, 208 6
through Jesus Christ our *L*, 209 6
O *L* our heavenly Father, whose blessed Son came 209 9
one that serveth, thy Son Jesus Christ our *L*, 210 7
through Jesus Christ our *L*, 210 16
Stir up your power, O *L*, 212 1
through Jesus Christ our *L*, 212 4
through our *L* Jesus Christ, 213 5
our *L* Jesus Christ; 213 16
through Jesus Christ our *L*, 214 10
confess him as *L* and Savior; 214 16
through Jesus Christ our *L*, 215 5
Give us grace, O *L*, to answer readily the call 215 8
through Jesus Christ our *L*, 216 10
O *L*, you have taught us that without love 216 13
manifested to us in your Son Jesus Christ our *L*; 217 5
through Jesus Christ our *L*, 217 11
through Jesus Christ your Son our *L*, 218 5
through Jesus Christ our *L*, 219 11
through Jesus Christ your son our *L*, 220 5
L God, whose blessed Son our Savior gave his body 220 14
through Jesus Christ your Son our *L*, 220 18
in remembrance of Jesus Christ our *L*, 221 4
our *L* Jesus Christ was willing to be betrayed, 221 9
through Jesus Christ your Son our *L*, 222 5
shine with the glory of the *L*'s resurrection: 222 9
through Jesus Christ our *L*, 222 12
celebrate with joy the day of the *L*'s resurrection, 222 18
through Jesus Christ our *L*, 223 1
through Jesus Christ your Son our *L*, 224 5
through Jesus Christ your Son our *L*, 225 12
through Jesus Christ our *L*, 225 18
through Jesus Christ our *L*, 226 5
Son our *L* Jesus Christ to have ascended 226 9
through Jesus Christ our *L*, 227 5
through Jesus Christ your Son our *L*, 227 12
Remember, O *L*, what you have wrought in us 228 9
through Jesus Christ our *L*, 228 11
through Jesus Christ our *L*, 229 3
Grant, O *L*, that the course of this world 229 5
Keep, O *L*, your household the Church 230 1
O *L*, make us have perpetual love and reverence 230 7
through Jesus Christ our *L*, 230 10
through Jesus Christ our *L*, 231 2
O *L*, mercifully receive the prayers of your people 231 4
the worthiness of your Son Jesus Christ our *L*, 231 15
Let your continual mercy, O *L*, cleanse and defend 232 1
through Jesus Christ our *L*, 232 4
Grant to us, *L*, we pray, the spirit to think 232 6
through Jesus Christ our *L*, 233 1
L of all power and might, the author and giver 233 3
Grant us, O *L*, to trust in you with all our hearts; 233 9
Grant us, *L*, not to be anxious about earthly things, 234 1
through Jesus Christ our *L*, 234 4
L, we pray that your grace may always precede 234 20
through Jesus Christ our *L*, 235 1
Blessed *L*, who caused all holy Scriptures 236 8
the King of kings and *L* of lords: 236 15
believe in Jesus Christ, our *L* and our God, 237 11
We give you thanks, O *L* of glory, for the example 237 14
Shed upon your Church, O *L*, the brightness 238 1
through Jesus Christ our *L*, 238 5
follow the one *L*, our Savior Jesus Christ; 238 18
through Jesus Christ our *L*, 239 3
by Jesus Christ our *L*; 239 9
Pour your grace into our hearts, O *L*, 240 1
through Jesus Christ our *L*, 240 10
the Name of our *L* Jesus Christ; 240 16
through Jesus Christ our *L*, 241 7
through Jesus Christ your Son our *L*, 241 17
which is Jesus Christ our *L*; 241 23
L God Almighty, in whose Name the founders 242 1
through Jesus Christ our *L*, 242 6
through Jesus Christ our *L*, 243 11
obey the calling of our *L* to follow him; 244 10
through Jesus Christ our *L*, 244 11
through Jesus Christ our *L*, 245 2
James the Just, brother of our *L*, your Church may 245 5
mercy of our *L* and Savior Jesus Christ; 245 14
the mystical body of your Son Christ our *L*: 245 18
through Jesus Christ our *L*, 246 6
suffer gladly for the sake of our *L* Jesus Christ; 247 3
through Jesus Christ our *L*, 247 11
through Jesus Christ our *L*, 248 5
the fullness of our *L* and Savior Jesus Christ; 248 12
through Jesus Christ our *L*, 249 3
through Jesus Christ our *L*, 250 12
through Jesus Christ our *L*, 251 9
God our Father, whose Son our *L* Jesus Christ 252 6
Grant, *L* God, to all who have been baptized 252 16
through Jesus Christ our *L*, 253 4
Eternal *L* God, you hold all souls in life: 253 6
share in the eternal victory of Jesus Christ our *L*; 253 18
the King of kings and *L* of lords: 254 2
through Jesus Christ our *L*, 254 11
through Jesus Christ our *L*, 255 3
your Son Jesus Christ our *L*; 255 20
through Jesus Christ our *L*, 256 8
Bishop of our souls, Jesus Christ our *L*, 256 16
through our *L* and Savior Jesus Christ, 257 3
through Jesus Christ our *L*, 257 10
L God Almighty, you have made all the peoples 258 1
through Jesus Christ our *L*, 258 6
Almighty God, *L* of heaven and earth: 258 15
through Jesus Christ our *L*, 259 1
through Jesus Christ our *L*, 260 6
through Jesus Christ our *L*, 261 5
your Son Jesus Christ our *L*, 261 13
through Jesus Christ our *L*, 264 7
the days of our *L*'s passion and resurrection, 264 11
kneel before the *L*, our maker and redeemer. 265 15
Open my lips, O *L*, * 267 6
Have mercy on us, *L*. 267 22
We confess to you, *L*, all our past unfaithfulness: 268 1
We confess to you, *L*. 268 3
Accept our repentance, *L*, for the wrongs we have 268 16
Accept our repentance, *L*. 268 19
Restore us, good *L*, and let your anger depart 268 27
By the cross and passion of your Son our *L*, 269 1

Almighty God, the Father of our *L* Jesus Christ,	269	3
through Jesus Christ our *L*.	269	14
Blessed is the King who comes in the name of the *L*.	270	1
Assist us mercifully with your help, O *L* God	270	4
through Jesus Christ our *L*.	270	7
The *L* be with you.	271	1
Let us give thanks to the *L* our God.	271	3
through your Son Jesus Christ our *L*.	271	7
Blessed is he who comes in the name of the *L*.	271	15
through Jesus Christ our *L*.	272	5
The Passion of our *L* Jesus Christ according to	272	15
in remembrance of Jesus Christ our *L*,	274	4
The *L* Jesus, after he had supped with his disciples	274	8
what I, your *L* and Master, have done to you?	274	10
for whom our *L* Jesus Christ was willing to be betrayed,	276	5
The Passion of our *L* Jesus Christ according to John.	277	1
through our *L* and Savior Jesus Christ.	278	16
through Jesus Christ our *L*.	279	2
your Son Jesus Christ our *L*.	279	19
one flock under one shepherd, Jesus Christ our *L*.	280	7
into the fullness of the joy of our *L*,	280	12
your Son Jesus Christ our *L*;	280	22
We glory in your cross, O *L*,	281	1
Save us and help us, we humbly beseech thee, O *L*.	282	5
L Jesus Christ, Son of the living God, we pray	282	6
L Jesus passed over from death to life,	285	2
For this is the Passover of the *L*,	285	4
through Jesus Christ our *L*.	285	12
through Jesus Christ his Son our *L*,	286	13
The *L* be with you.	286	17
Let us give thanks to the *L* our God.	286	19
your only-begotten Son, Jesus Christ our *L*;	287	3
your Son Jesus Christ our *L*.	288	8
through Jesus Christ our *L*.	289	4
through Jesus Christ our *L*.	290	6
through Jesus Christ our *L*.	291	3
your Son Jesus Christ our *L*.	291	19
I believe in Jesus Christ, his only Son, our *L*.	293	2
repent and return to the *L*?	293	24
May Almighty God, the Father of our *L* Jesus Christ,	294	4
in Christ Jesus our *L*.	294	7
The *L* is risen indeed.	294	9
The *L* be with you.	294	10
through Jesus Christ your Son our *L*,	295	6
glory of the *L*'s resurrection:	295	9
through Jesus Christ our *L*,	295	12
The *L* is risen indeed.	299	4
Bless the *L* who forgives all our sins.	299	5
One *L*, one Faith, one Baptism;	299	9
The *L* be with you.	299	11
The Word of the *L*.	300	2
The Holy Gospel of our *L* Jesus Christ	300	5
Glory to you, *L* Christ.	300	7
The Gospel of the *L*.	300	8
Praise to you, *L* Christ.	300	9
obey him as your *L*?	303	2
follow him as my Savior and *L*.	303	14
I believe in Jesus Christ, his only Son, our *L*	304	5
repent and return to the *L*?	304	27
Deliver them, O *L*, from the way of sin	305	14
L, hear our prayer.	305	16
Grant, O *L*, that all who are baptized	306	5
The *L* be with you.	306	9
Let us give thanks to the *L* our God.	306	11
Sustain them, O *L*, in your Holy Spirit.	308	5
The peace of the *L* be always with you.	308	15
through Jesus Christ your Son our *L*,	309	10
Strengthen, O *L*, your servant	309	12
Defend, O *L*, your servant	309	15
through Jesus Christ our *L*.	310	12
The peace of the *L* be always with you.	310	13
through Jesus Christ your Son our *L*,	311	19
Almighty God, the Father of our *L* Jesus Christ,	311	21
Strengthen him, O *L*, with your presence,	314	4
Beloved in the *L*:	316	1
not recognizing the *L*'s Body.	316	25
lest you be judged by the *L*.	316	26
To Christ our *L* who loves us,	317	17
I am the *L* thy God who brought thee out of the land	317	25
L, have mercy upon us,	317	28
shalt not take the Name of the *L* thy God in vain.	318	7
L, have mercy upon us,	318	8
The *L* is risen indeed.	319	5
Bless the *L* who forgiveth all our sins.	319	6
Hear what our *L* Jesus Christ saith:	319	8
Thou shalt love the *L* thy God with all thy heart,	319	9
But thou, O *L*, have mercy upon us,	321	6
in Christ Jesus our *L*;	321	10
The Almighty and merciful *L* grant you absolution	321	14
The *L* is risen indeed.	323	4
Bless the *L* who forgiveth all our sins.	323	5
through Christ our *L*.	323	11
Hear what our *L* Jesus Christ saith:	324	1
Thou shalt love the *L* thy God with all thy heart,	324	2
L, have mercy upon us.	324	7
O *L* God, heavenly King, God the Father Almighty.	324	20
O *L*, the only-begotten Son, Jesus Christ;	324	21
O *L* God, Lamb of God, Son of the Father,	324	22
thou only art the *L*;	325	6
The *L* be with you.	325	10
The Word of the *L*	325	14
The Holy Gospel of our *L* Jesus Christ	326	1
Glory be to thee, O *L*.	326	3
The Gospel of the *L*.	326	4
We believe in one *L*, Jesus Christ,	326	10
We believe in the Holy Spirit, the *L*,	327	12
And in one *L* Jesus Christ,	327	24
And I believe in the Holy Ghost the *L*,	328	13
Open, O *L*, the eyes of all people to behold	329	22
humbly beseech thee, of thy goodness, O *L*,	329	26
Father of our *L* Jesus Christ,	331	2
for thy Son our *L* Jesus Christ's sake,	331	15
through Jesus Christ our *L*.	331	20
through Jesus Christ our *L*.	332	6
The peace of the *L* be always with you.	332	19
The *L* be with you.	333	1
We lift them up unto the *L*.	333	4
Let us give thanks unto our *L* God.	333	5
give thanks unto thee, O *L*,	333	8
Holy, holy, holy, *L* God of Hosts:	334	4
Glory be to thee, O *L* Most High.	334	6
Blessed is he that cometh in the name of the *L*.	334	7
Wherefore, O *L* and heavenly Father,	335	8

And here we offer and present unto thee, O *L*,	336	1
through Jesus Christ our *L*;	336	12
O merciful *L*, trusting in our own righteousness,	337	10
But thou art the same *L*	337	12
Grant us therefore, gracious *L*, so to eat	337	14
The Body of our *L* Jesus Christ,	338	5
The Blood of our *L* Jesus Christ,	338	9
The Body (Blood) of our *L* Jesus Christ keep you	338	13
through Jesus Christ our *L*,	339	13
and of his Son Jesus Christ our *L*;	339	17
Go in peace to love and serve the *L*.	340	1
Let us bless the *L*.	340	6
The *L* be with you.	340	9
We lift them up unto the *L*.	340	12
Let us give thanks unto our *L* God.	340	13
give thanks unto thee, O *L*,	341	2
Holy, holy, holy, *L* God of Hosts:	341	7
Glory be to thee, O *L* Most High.	341	9
Blessed is he that cometh in the name of the *L*.	341	10
All glory be to thee, O *L* our God,	341	12
Wherefore, O *L* and heavenly Father,	342	10
and present unto thee, O *L*, our selves,	342	23
through the same Jesus Christ our *L*;	343	2
Ascribe to the *L* the honor due his Name;	343	10
Worthy art thou, O *L* our God, to receive glory	344	5
Thine, O *L*, is the greatness, and the power,	344	8
Thine is the kingdom, O *L*,	344	10
our life and labor to the *L*.	344	13
new life in Jesus Christ our *L*.	344	16
Through Jesus Christ our *L*;	345	1
in Jesus Christ our *L*,	345	6
in the face of thy Son Jesus Christ our *L*.	346	3
Through Jesus Christ our *L*;	346	4
resurrection of thy Son Jesus Christ our *L*;	346	18
Through thy dearly beloved Son Jesus Christ our *L*;	347	1
Through Jesus Christ our *L*;	347	6
one *L*, in Trinity of Persons	347	14
Jesus Christ our *L*;	348	12
Because in Jesus Christ our *L* thou hast received	348	20
thy Son Jesus Christ our *L*;	349	3
Through Jesus Christ our *L*;	349	6
for to thy faithful people, O *L*, life	349	8
I am the *L* your God who brought you out	350	2
L have mercy.	350	4
invoke with malice the Name of the *L* your God.	350	7
The *L* is risen indeed.	351	4
Bless the *L* who forgives all our sins.	351	5
The *L* our God is the only *L*.	351	8
Love the *L* your God	351	8
through our *L* Jesus Christ,	353	2
The *L* is risen indeed.	355	4
Bless the *L* who forgives all our sins.	355	5
through Christ our *L*.	355	11
L God, heavenly King,	356	3
L Jesus Christ, only Son of the Father,	356	7
L God, Lamb of God,	356	8
you alone are the *L*,	356	14
L, have mercy.	356	19
The *L* be with you.	357	1
The Word of the *L*.	357	5
The Holy Gospel of our *L* Jesus Christ	357	8
Glory to you, *L* Christ.	357	10
The Gospel of the *L*.	358	1
Praise to you, *L* Christ.	358	2
We believe in one *L*, Jesus Christ,	358	7
We believe in the Holy Spirit, the *L*,	359	3
through our *L* Jesus Christ,	360	16
The peace of the *L* be always with you.	360	19
The *L* be with you.	361	1
We lift them up to the *L*.	361	4
Let us give thanks to the *L* our God.	361	5
Holy, holy, holy *L*, God of power and might,	362	4
Blessed is he who comes in the name of the *L*.	362	7
L Jesus Christ took bread;	362	19
The Body (Blood) of our *L* Jesus Christ keep	365	4
through Christ our *L*.	365	18
as faithful witnesses of Christ our *L*.	366	11
Go in peace to love and serve the *L*.	366	16
Let us bless the *L*.	366	21
The *L* be with you.	367	1
We lift them to the *L*.	367	4
Let us give thanks to the *L* our God.	367	5
Holy, holy, holy *L*, God of power and might,	367	13
Blessed is he who comes in the name of the *L*.	367	16
our *L* Jesus Christ took bread;	368	10
thanksgiving to you, O *L* of all;	369	2
through Jesus Christ our *L*,	369	12
The *L* be with you.	369	21
We lift them up to the *L*.	370	2
Let us give thanks to the *L* our God.	370	3
Have mercy, *L*, for we are sinners in your sight.	370	16
Holy, holy, holy *L*, God of power and might,	371	1
Blessed is he who comes in the name of the *L*.	371	4
Body and Blood of Jesus Christ our *L*.	371	9
L God of our Fathers;	372	1
God and Father of our *L* Jesus Christ:	372	2
Risen *L*, be known to us in the breaking of the Bread.	372	9
The *L* be with you.	372	17
We lift them to the *L*.	372	20
Let us give thanks to the *L* our God.	372	21
Holy, holy, holy *L*, God of power and might,	373	12
Blessed is he who comes in the name of the *L*.	373	15
We acclaim you, holy *L*, glorious in power.	373	17
and we pray to you, *L* our God.	375	3
L, we pray that in your goodness and mercy	375	4
Remember, *L*, your one holy catholic	375	12
through your Son Jesus Christ our *L*.	375	25
Ascribe to the *L* the honor due his Name;	376	6
O *L* our God, you are worthy to receive glory	377	3
Yours, O *L*, is the greatness, the power,	377	6
Yours, O *L*, is the kingdom,	377	8
our life and labor to the *L*.	377	11
and called us to new life in Jesus Christ our *L*.	377	13
Through Jesus Christ our *L*;	377	14
in Jesus Christ our *L*,	378	2
of your Son Jesus Christ our *L*.	378	17
Through Jesus Christ our *L*,	379	1
resurrection of your Son Jesus Christ our *L*;	379	15
Through your dearly beloved Son Jesus Christ our *L*.	379	20
Through Jesus Christ our *L*.	380	1
one *L*, in Trinity of Persons	380	9
Jesus Christ our *L*;	381	6
Because in Jesus Christ our *L* you have received	381	13
her bridegroom, your Son Jesus Christ our *L*;	381	18

Through Jesus Christ our *L*;	382	1
For to your faithful people, O *L*, life is changed,	382	3
pray to the *L*, saying, "*L*, have mercy."	383	2
let us pray to the *L*.	383	4
L, have mercy.	383	5
protect us, O *L*, by thy grace.	385	11
To thee, O *L* our God.	385	16
L, in your mercy	388	5
let us pray to the *L*, saying, "*L*, have mercy"	389	13
we pray to you, O *L*.	389	17
For all who fear God and believe in you, *L* Christ,	390	4
To you, O *L* our God.	391	22
In peace, we pray to you, *L* God.	392	1
Hear us, *L*;	392	18
We thank you, *L*, for all the blessings of this life.	393	1
L, let your loving-kindness be upon them;	393	6
through Jesus Christ our *L*.	393	16
L, hear the prayers of thy people;	394	1
through Jesus Christ our *L*.	394	3
love us in your Son Jesus Christ our *L*.	394	8
through Jesus Christ our *L*.	394	11
grant us for the sake of your Son Jesus Christ our *L*.	395	2
O *L* our God, accept the fervent prayers	395	3
L Jesus Christ, you said to your apostles,	395	8
in remembrance of Jesus Christ our *L*,	397	16
through our *L* Jesus Christ,	398	8
The Body (Blood) of our *L* Jesus Christ keep	399	5
through Jesus Christ our *L*.	399	12
Let us bless the *L*.	399	13
The *L* be with you.	402	1
We lift them to the *L*.	402	4
Let us give thanks to the *L* our God.	402	5
Holy, holy, holy *L*, God of power and might,	402	9
Blessed is he who comes in the name of the *L*.	402	12
of Jesus Christ our *L*.	403	3
The grace of our *L* Jesus Christ	404	1
We lift them to the *L*.	404	6
Let us give thanks to the *L* our God.	404	7
Holy, holy, holy *L*, God of power and might,	404	11
Blessed is he who comes in the name of the *L*.	404	14
L Jesus Christ took bread;	405	2
Accept, O *L*, our sacrifice of praise,	405	13
(your) Son Jesus Christ our *L*, who took bread	408	4
The *L* is risen indeed.	413	4
Bless the *L* who forgives all our sins.	413	5
One *L*, one Faith, one Baptism;	413	9
The *L* be with you.	413	11
The Word of the *L*.	414	2
The Holy Gospel of our *L* Jesus Christ	414	5
Glory to you, *L* Christ.	414	7
The Gospel of the *L*	415	1
Praise to you, *L* Christ.	415	2
follow him as my Savior and *L*.	415	13
I believe in Jesus Christ, his only Son, our *L*.	416	10
repent and return to the *L*?	417	9
through Jesus Christ your Son our *L*,	418	8
Strengthen, O *L*, your servant	418	10
Defend, O *L*, your servant	418	13
through Jesus Christ our *L*.	419	8
The peace of the *L* be always with you.	419	9
through Jesus Christ our *L*.	421	7
and our *L* Jesus Christ adorned	423	4
in the knowledge and love of the *L*.	423	13
The *L* be with you.	425	4
through Jesus Christ our *L*,	425	12
The Holy Gospel of our *L* Jesus Christ	426	1
Glory to you, *L* Christ.	426	3
The Gospel of the *L*.	426	4
Praise to you, *L* Christ.	426	5
Bless, O *L*, this ring to be a sign	427	10
through Jesus Christ our *L*.	427	12
through Jesus Christ our *L*,	430	24
through Jesus Christ our *L*,	431	7
the *L* mercifully with his favor	431	10
The peace of the *L* be always with you.	431	14
for the sake of Jesus Christ our *L*.	432	7
Bless, O *L*, this ring to be a sign	434	4
through Jesus Christ our *L*.	434	6
heavenly Father, the *L* of all life,	440	5
through Jesus Christ our *L*.	441	9
My soul proclaims the greatness of the *L*,	441	12
following the example of our *L* and Savior,	443	29
through Jesus Christ our *L*.	444	7
The *L* be in your heart and upon your lips	447	2
Our *L* Jesus Christ, who has left power	448	1
Our *L* Jesus Christ, who offered himself	448	7
The *L* has put away all your sins.	448	12
Therefore, O *L*, from these and all other sins	450	16
Will you turn again to Christ as your *L*?	450	22
Our *L* Jesus Christ, who offered himself	451	6
Our *L* Jesus Christ, who has left power	451	11
alive in Christ Jesus our *L*.	451	19
The *L* has put away all your sins.	451	19
Our *L* Jesus Christ, who offered himself	452	1
through our *L* Jesus Christ,	455	7
O *L*, holy Father, giver of health and salvation:	455	9
Save us, and help us, we humbly beseech you, O *L*.	455	18
beseeching our *L* Jesus Christ to sustain you	456	2
I lay my hands upon you in the Name of our *L*	456	7
through Jesus Christ our *L*.	456	19
The Almighty *L*, who is a strong tower	456	20
for health and salvation is the Name of our *L*	457	3
through Jesus Christ our *L*.	457	10
Let us bless the *L*.	457	11
through Jesus Christ our *L*.	458	10
L Jesus Christ, Good Shepherd of the sheep,	459	1
through Jesus Christ our *L*.	459	11
Sanctify, O *L*, the sickness of your servant	460	1
through Jesus Christ our *L*.	460	4
Sanctify, O *L*, those whom you have called	460	10
O *L*, your compassions never fail	460	16
through Jesus Christ our *L*.	461	4
L Jesus Christ, by your patience in suffering	461	5
you hold me in eternal life, my *L* and my God.	461	11
This is another day, O *L*.	461	19
but make me ready, *L*, for whatever it may be.	461	20
resurrection of your Son Jesus Christ our *L*.	462	4
Good *L*, deliver him.	463	4
We sinners beseech you to hear us, *L* Christ:	463	11
We beseech you to hear us, good *L*.	463	14
L, have mercy.	464	1
Deliver your servant, N., O Sovereign *L* Christ,	464	16
It was our *L* Jesus himself who said,	465	9
Receive, O *L*, your servant, for he returns to you.	465	14

Into your hands, O *L*, 465 15
May he gaze upon you, *L*, face to face, 466 1
Into your hands, O *L*, 466 3
before whom live all who die in the *L*: 466 8
out in joy to you, O *L*, the living God, 466 10
This we ask through Christ our *L*. 466 11
Deliver your servant, N., O Sovereign *L* Christ, 466 16
Remember them, *L*, in mercy; 467 4
through Jesus Christ our *L*. 467 7
I am the resurrection and the life, saith the *L*; 469 1
For if we live, we live unto the *L*; 469 11
and if we die, we die unto the *L*. 469 12
Whether we live, therefore, or die, we are the *L*'s. 469 13
Blessed are the dead who die in the *L*; 469 14
The *L* be with you. 469 16
through Jesus Christ thy Son our *L*, 470 4
through the same thy Son Jesus Christ our *L*, 470 11
L, thou hast been our refuge * 472 9
L, hear my voice. 474 2
O *L*, who may abide it? 474 6
My soul fleeth unto the *L* before the morning 474 11
The Holy Gospel of our *L* Jesus Christ 479 20
Glory be to thee, O *L*. 479 22
The Gospel of the *L*. 480 1
In peace, let us pray to the *L*. 480 3
in the mystical body of thy Son Christ our *L*: 480 6
The *L* will guide our feet into the way of peace, 483 18
but of thee, O *L*, 484 6
Yet, O *L* God most holy, O *L* most mighty, 484 8
Thou knowest, *L*, the secrets of our hearts; 484 11
but spare us, *L* most holy, O God most mighty, 484 13
through our *L* Jesus Christ, 485 10
The *L* bless him and keep him, 485 12
the *L* make his face to shine upon him 485 13
the *L* lift up his countenance upon him 485 14
The *L* be with you. 485 17
Blessed are the dead who die in the *L*: 486 9
for the sake of thy Son Jesus Christ our *L*. 486 16
Rest eternal grant to him, O *L*: 486 17
L Jesus Christ, the great Shepherd of the sheep, 486 22
thy son Jesus Christ our *L*. 487 9
depart hence in the *L*, 488 2
through Jesus Christ our *L*. 488 11
Into thy hands, O *L*, we commend thy servant 488 12
of Jesus Christ thine only Son our *L*. 488 20
Remember thy servant, O *L*, according to the favor 488 21
through Jesus Christ our *L*. 488 25
through Jesus Christ thy Son our *L*. 489 2
through Jesus Christ our *L*. 489 13
of thy Son Jesus Christ our *L*. 489 22
O *L* Jesus Christ, Son of the living God, we pray 489 23
I am Resurrection and I am Life, says the *L*. 491 1
For if we have life, we are alive in the *L*, 491 15
and if we die, we die in the *L*. 491 16
we are the *L*'s possession. 491 18
are those who die in the *L*! 492 2
From you alone, O *L*, 492 7
L, you know the secrets of our hearts; 492 12
but spare us, O *L*. 492 14
The *L* be with you. 493 1
through Jesus Christ our *L*, 493 13
through Jesus Christ our *L*, 494 4
The Holy Gospel of our *L* Jesus Christ 495 1
Glory to you, *L* Christ. 495 3
The Gospel of the *L*. 495 4
Praise to you, *L* Christ. 495 5
I believe in Jesus Christ, his only Son, our *L*. 496 5
let us pray to our *L* Jesus 497 1
L, you consoled Martha and Mary in their distress; 497 3
Hear us, *L*. 497 6
L Jesus Christ, we commend to you our brother 498 1
The *L* will guide our feet into the way of peace, 500 7
through our *L* Jesus Christ, 501 12
The *L* bless him and keep him, 501 14
the *L* lift up his countenance upon him 501 15
The *L* be with you. 501 18
Rest eternal grant to him, O *L*; 502 15
The *L* is risen indeed. 502 20
L Jesus Christ, the great Shepherd of the sheep, 503 2
your Son Jesus Christ our *L*. 503 11
the spirits of those who die in the *L*, 503 13
through Jesus Christ our *L*. 503 19
through Jesus Christ our *L*. 504 11
of your Son Jesus Christ our *L*. 504 20
L Jesus Christ, by your death you took away the sting 504 21
Merciful God, Father of our *L* Jesus Christ 505 1
Grant, O *L*, to all who are bereaved 505 10
through Jesus Christ our *L*. 505 20
The *L* is risen indeed. 512 4
Bless the *L* who forgives all our sins. 512 5
through Christ our *L*. 512 11
The *L* be with you 515 1
your Son Jesus Christ our *L*; 515 12
The Word of the *L*. 516 2
The Holy Gospel of our *L* Jesus Christ 516 5
Glory to you, *L* Christ. 516 7
The Gospel of the *L*. 516 8
Praise to you, *L* Christ. 516 9
testify to Christ's sovereignty as *L* of lords 517 5
We believe in one *L*, Jesus Christ, 519 10
We believe in the Holy Spirit, the *L*, 520 3
and Father of our *L* Jesus Christ, 520 11
The peace of the *L* be always with you. 522 1
through Jesus Christ your Son our *L*, 523 9
Our help is in the Name of the *L*; 523 11
Blessed be the Name of the *L*; 523 13
The *L* is risen indeed. 525 4
Bless the *L* who forgives all our sins. 525 5
through Christ our *L*. 525 11
In peace let us pray to the *L*. 527 11
The *L* be with you. 527 12
your Son Jesus Christ our *L*; 528 10
The Word of the *L*. 529 1
The Holy Gospel of our *L* Jesus Christ 529 4
Glory to you, *L* Christ. 529 6
The Gospel of the *L*. 529 7
Praise to you, *L* Christ. 529 8
We believe in one *L*, Jesus Christ, 530 1
We believe in the Holy Spirit, the *L*, 530 22
called to make Christ known as Savior and *L*, 531 3
May the *L* who has given you the will 532 30
Jesus our *L*, who is the image of your eternal 533 3
May he exalt you, O *L*, in the midst of your people; 534 1
through Jesus Christ our *L*, 534 8

The peace of the *L* be always with you. 534 14
through Jesus Christ your Son our *L*, 535 9
The *L* is risen indeed. 537 4
Bless the *L* who forgives all our sins. 537 5
through Christ our *L*. 537 11
In peace let us pray to the *L*. 539 11
The *L* be with you. 539 12
your Son Jesus Christ our *L*; 540 10
The Word of the *L*. 541 1
The Holy Gospel of our *L* Jesus Christ 541 4
Glory to you, *L* Christ. 541 6
The Gospel of the *L*. 541 7
Praise to you, *L* Christ. 541 8
We believe in one *L*, Jesus Christ, 542 1
We believe in the Holy Spirit, the *L*, 542 22
glory of the *L* Christ? 544 13
May the *L* by his grace uphold you 544 15
and made him *L* of all; 545 5
Make him, O *L*, modest and humble, 545 12
The peace of the *L* be always with you. 546 1
through Jesus Christ your Son our *L*, 547 5
We pray to you, *L* Christ. 548 9
L, hear our prayer. 548 10
we pray to you, O *L*. 548 14
For all who fear God and believe in you, *L* Christ, 549 16
To you, O *L* our God. 550 29
L, have mercy. 551 1
The *L* be with you. 551 4
Our help is in the Name of the *L*; 552 1
The *L* be with you. 552 3
Jesus Christ our *L*. 552 12
The *L* be with you. 560 3
obedience to our *L*. 561 4
O *L* my God, I am not worthy 562 9
The peace of the *L* be always with you. 563 12
through Jesus Christ your Son our *L*, 564 9
through Jesus Christ our *L*. 567 13
Our help is in the Name of the *L*; 568 4
L Jesus Christ, make this a temple 568 14
L Christ, that we are made one with you 568 19
Yours, O *L*, is the kingdom. 569 13
There is one *L*, one Faith, one Baptism; 569 19
The *L* be with you. 570 1
Let us give thanks to the *L* our God. 570 3
Be acceptable to you, O *L* our God. 571 6
through Jesus Christ our *L*. 573 6
Blessed be your Name, *L* God. 573 12
L God, hear us. 574 1
The peace of the *L* be always with you. 574 10
We thank you, *L*. 578 9
Yours, O *L*, is the greatness, the power, 579 13
Yours, O *L*, is the kingdom; 579 16
the *L* has them in derision. 586 9
I will praise the Name of the *L* Most High. 598 11
I have said to the *L*, "You are my *L*, 599 20
I have trusted in the *L* and have not faltered. 616 9
O *L*, how long will you look on? * 631 1
to my defense, my God and my *L*! 631 17
you will answer me, O *L* my God. 637 28
O *L* of my salvation. 638 14
O *L*, my hope is in you. 639 10
the *L* will have regard for me. 641 20
Awake, O *L*! why are you sleeping? * 647 3
Open my lips, O *L*, * 657 12
it is the *L* who sustains my life. 659 25
and put them down, O *L* our shield. 666 20
Steadfast love is yours, O *L*, * 670 10
the *L* would not have heard me; 675 4
The *L* gave the word; * 677 1
the *L* comes in holiness from Sinai. 677 17
Blessed be the *L* day by day, * 677 21
sing praises to the *L*. 678 25
L God of hosts; * 679 23
For you are my hope, O *L* God, * 683 9
I will begin with the mighty works of the *L* God; * 684 12
Blessed be the *L* God, the God of Israel, * 686 25
Like a dream when one awakens, O *L*, * 688 17
I have made the *L* God my refuge. 689 6
In the day of my trouble I sought the *L*; * 693 3
Will the *L* cast me off for ever? * 693 14
May the revilings with which they reviled you, O *L*, * 702 7
Where, *L*, are your loving-kindnesses of old, * 717 12
Remember, *L*, how your servant is mocked, * 717 14
L, you have been our refuge * 717 20
Happy are they whom you instruct, O *L*! * 723 17
at the presence of the *L* of the whole earth. 727 6
But you, O *L* my God, 752 16
The *L* said to my *L*, "Sit at my right hand, * 753 12
The *L* who is at your right hand 753 21
they put their trust in the *L*. 755 19
Tremble, O earth, at the presence of the *L*, * 757 9
Blessed is he who comes in the name of the *L*; * 762 23
O *L*, who could stand? 784 22
and that our *L* is above all gods. 788 11
Give thanks to the *L* of lords, * 790 1
O *L* God, the strength of my salvation, * 796 15
But my eyes are turned to you, *L* God; * 797 19
thy Son Jesus Christ our *L*. 814 5
through Jesus Christ our *L*. 815 21
become the kingdom of our *L* and Savior Jesus 816 4
through Jesus Christ our *L*. 816 9
Grant this, O *L*, for the honor 817 8
through Jesus Christ our *L*. 817 17
through Jesus Christ our *L*. 818 7
O God the Father of our *L* Jesus Christ, 818 14
one hope of our calling, one *L*, one Faith, 818 19
through Jesus Christ our *L*. 819 5
O *L* Jesus Christ, you became poor for our sake, 819 6
through Jesus Christ our *L*. 820 15
O *L* our Governor, whose glory is in all the world: 820 16
through Jesus Christ our *L*. 821 7
O *L* our Governor, bless the leaders of our land, 821 15
L, keep this nation under your care. 821 18
Give grace to your servants, O *L*. 821 23
For yours is the kingdom, O *L*, 822 15
through Jesus Christ our *L*. 822 22
through Jesus Christ our *L*. 823 7
through Jesus Christ our *L*. 824 5
through Jesus Christ our *L*. 825 5
L Christ, when you came among us, you proclaimed 825 16
Jesus Christ our *L*. 826 7
through Jesus Christ our *L*. 826 15
L Jesus, for our sake you were condemned 826 16
O *L*, we do for you, constrain us to improve their lot. 826 25

through Jesus Christ our *L*.	827	5
to the honor of Jesus Christ our *L*.	827	10
in the name of Jesus Christ our *L*.	827	16
through Jesus Christ our *L*.	827	22
through Christ our *L*.	828	8
through Jesus Christ our *L*.	828	15
through Jesus Christ our *L*.	829	8
in the name of Jesus Christ our *L*.	830	7
through Jesus Christ our *L*.	830	12
Watch over thy child, O *L*, as his days increase;	830	13
through Jesus Christ our *L*.	831	6
Remember him, O *L*, in mercy,	831	14
O blessed *L*, you ministered to all who came to you:	831	18
Direct us, O *L*, in all our doings	832	1
through Jesus Christ our *L*.	832	5
Assist us mercifully, O *L*, in these our supplications	832	18
through our *L* and Savior Jesus Christ.	833	3
L, make us instruments of your peace.	833	5
O *L*, support us all the day long,	833	14
through Jesus Christ our *L*.	833	24
through Jesus Christ our *L*.	834	7
O *L* Jesus Christ, who in a wonderful Sacrament	834	12
through the same Jesus Christ our *L*.	835	7
Bless, O *L*, thy gifts to our use	835	11
Blessed are you, O *L* God, King of the Universe,	835	13
through Jesus Christ our *L*.	835	15
Accept, O *L*, our thanks and praise	836	1
We thank you, *L*.	837	5
in Christ Jesus our *L*;	837	22
We give thanks to you, O *L* our God,	838	9
for Mary, the mother of our *L*;	838	14
In your mercy, O *L* our God,	838	17
through Jesus Christ our *L*, the	838	19
Help us, O *L*, to finish the good work here begun.	839	16
we ask in the Name of Jesus Christ our *L*.	839	26
through Jesus Christ our *L*.	840	6
your dear Son, Jesus Christ our *L*.	841	6
through Jesus Christ our *L*.	841	13
You shall love the *L* your God with all your heart,	851	11
The Holy Spirit is revealed as the *L* who leads	852	21
confess Jesus Christ as *L* and are brought into love	852	27
Head, our *L* Jesus Christ.	854	16
Our *L* gave us the example of prayer	856	24
prayer known as the *L*'s Prayer.	856	25
and accept Jesus as our *L* and Savior.	858	23
The Holy Eucharist is called the *L*'s Supper,	859	15
the benefits which we receive in the *L*'s Supper?	859	27
their confession of Jesus Christ as Savior and *L*.	860	26
the love of God which is in Christ Jesus our *L*.	862	32
lord		
our lips are our own; who is *l* over us?"	597	8
lords		
the King of kings and Lord of *l*:	185	3
the King of kings and Lord of *l*:	203	1
the King of kings and Lord of *l*:	236	16
the King of kings and Lord of *l*:	254	3
as Lord of *l* and King of kings.	517	5
Give thanks to the Lord of *l*, *	790	1
lose		
that we finally *l* not the things eternal;	180	4
that we *l* not the things eternal;	231	20
The foreign peoples will *l* heart; *	606	1
Sin has power over us because we *l* our liberty	849	2
losing		
and the king's enemies are *l* heart.	647	24
loss		
to dread nothing but the *l* of thee,	165	7
suffer shame and *l* for the sake of thy Son	168	20
to fear nothing but the *l* of you,	216	21
suffer shame and *l* for the sake of your Son	220	11
overwhelmed by their *l*, but have confidence	494	10
lost		
we have erred and strayed from thy ways like *l* sheep,	41	17
we have erred and strayed from thy ways like *l* sheep,	62	17
For those who have *l* their faith	279	22
we have erred and strayed from thy ways like *l* sheep,	320	24
and for those who have *l* their faith,	390	10
for you were *l*, and are found;	451	17
and for those who have *l* their faith,	549	25
the right hand of the Most High has *l* its power."	693	21
L among the dead, *	712	9
I have gone astray like a sheep that is *l*; *	778	7
all who through addiction have *l* their health	831	19
Lot		
and have come to help the people of *L*.	706	19
lot		
a scorching wind shall be their *l*.	596	23
it is you who uphold my *l*.	600	8
and you cast in your *l* with adulterers.	655	17
and apportioned an inheritance to them by *l*; *	699	16
constrain us to improve their *l*.	826	25
lots		
they cast *l* for my clothing.	611	17
loud		
and raise a *l* shout to him with psalms.	82	8
and raise a *l* shout to the God of Jacob.	704	2
and raise a *l* shout to him with psalms.	724	17
to the LORD I make *l* supplication.	798	2
praise him with *l*-clanging cymbals.	808	8
lovable		
pure, *l* and gracious, excellent and admirable,	443	28
love		
Christ, who didst stretch out thine arms of *l*	58	8
reaching forth our hands in *l*,	58	11
to the knowledge and *l* of thee;	58	12
but above all for thine inestimable *l*	58	21
The grace of our Lord Jesus Christ, and the *l* of God,	59	22
for the *l* of thy only Son,	70	3
Grant this for the sake of thy *l*.	70	14
l thee and serve thee in peace;	70	18
and all for thy *l*'s sake.	71	5
Send forth upon us the Spirit of *l*,	71	7
but above all for thine inestimable *l*	71	17
The grace of our Lord Jesus Christ, and the *l* of God,	72	19
abounding in steadfast *l*, and repents of evil.	76	15

With your constant *l* you led the people	85	21
Lord, show us your *l* and mercy;	98	15
Lord Jesus Christ, you stretched out your arms of *l*	101	1
that we, reaching forth our hands in *l*, may bring	101	4
to the knowledge and *l* of you;	101	5
but above all for your immeasurable *l*	101	13
The grace of our Lord Jesus Christ, and the *l* of God,	102	10
The *l* of God has been poured into our hearts	105	20
for the *l* of thy only Son, our Savior, Jesus Christ.	111	3
l, that by its cleansing flame we may be purged	111	5
Stir up in us the flame of that *l* which burned	113	13
for the *l* of your only Son,	123	22
Grant this for the sake of your *l*.	124	11
l you and serve you in peace;	124	15
and all for your *l*'s sake.	124	21
Send forth upon us the Spirit of *l*,	125	2
but above all for your immeasurable *l*	125	11
The grace of our Lord Jesus Christ, and the *l* of God,	126	10
Because he is bound to me in *l*,	130	26
l of your only Son, our Savior Jesus Christ.	133	12
and all for your *l*'s sake.	134	10
Grant this for the sake of your *l*.	139	20
That it may please thee to give us a heart to *l*	150	22
that they may do justice, and *l* mercy,	150	27
The grace of our Lord Jesus Christ, and the *l* of God,	154	1
we beseech thee, the *l* of him who is the Savior	162	3
mortal life may hide from us the light of that *l*	165	10
l the thing which thou commandest,	167	17
Almighty and everlasting God, who, of thy tender *l*	168	1
so by his *l* he may raise us	172	17
O God, who hast prepared for those who *l* thee	174	1
such *l* toward thee, that we, loving thee	174	3
thy steadfast faith and *l*,	178	7
and *l* of thy holy Name,	178	13
Graft in our hearts the *l* of thy Name,	181	12
not to mind earthly things, but to *l* things heavenly;	182	6
make us to *l* that which thou dost command;	183	19
establish thy rule of justice, *l*, and peace;	186	17
Grant, we beseech thee, unto thy Church to *l*	192	9
to set forth in the Gospel the *l* and healing	193	12
continue in thy Church the like *l* and power to heal,	193	14
l and mercy of our Lord and Savior Jesus Christ;	194	5
prepared for those who unfeignedly *l* thee;	194	13
of thy *l* in the heart of thy holy martyr N.:	196	2
a like faith and power of *l*,	196	3
inordinate *l* of this world, that, inspired	198	3
fire of thy *l*, became a burning and a shining light	198	10
of *l* and discipline, and may ever walk before thee	198	12
fellowship of *l* and prayer,	199	7
Being of glorious majesty and perfect *l* as one God	199	13
in *l* and obedience to thee,	204	20
true *l* of peace, and guide with thy wisdom	207	9
till the earth is filled with the knowledge of thy *l*;	207	12
for the *l* of him who laid down his life for us,	209	14
the *l* of him who is the Savior of the world,	213	15
O Lord, you have taught us that without *l*	216	13
your greatest gift, which is *l*, the true bond of peace	216	15
hide from us the light of that *l* which is immortal,	217	3
l what you command and desire what you promise;	219	8
Almighty and everliving God, in your tender *l*	219	13
so by his *l* he may raise us to eternal joys;	224	10
O God, you have prepared for those who *l* you	225	14
Pour into our hearts such *l* towards you,	225	16
the Church in your steadfast faith and *l*,	230	2
O Lord, make us have perpetual *l* and reverence	230	7
Graft in our hearts the *l* of your Name;	233	4
but to *l* things heavenly;	234	2
make us *l* what you command;	235	11
your rule of justice, *l*, and peace;	238	11
Grant that your Church may *l* what he believed	243	16
to set forth in the Gospel the *l* and healing power	244	21
Graciously continue in your Church this *l* and power	244	22
may with ardent devotion make known the *l*	245	13
joys that you have prepared for those who truly *l* you;	245	20
l in the heart of your holy martyr N.:	247	14
a like faith and power of *l*,	247	15
Deliver us from an inordinate *l* of this world,	249	12
flame of your *l*, became a burning and a shining light	249	19
aflame with the spirit of *l* and discipline,	249	21
supported by this fellowship of *l* and prayer,	250	17
Being of glorious majesty and perfect *l* as one God	251	2
Grant that your Church, being bound together in *l*	255	17
kindle, we pray, in every heart the true *l*	258	8
filled with the knowledge of your *l*;	258	12
for the *l* of him who laid down his life for us,	260	19
Our intemperate *l* of worldly goods and comforts,	268	10
Almighty God, for the acts of *l*	271	5
Almighty and everliving God, in your tender *l*	272	7
L one another as I have loved you.	275	3
you have *l* for one another.	275	8
confirm his Church in faith, increase it in *l*,	278	9
kindle, we pray, in every heart the true *l*	278	25
filled with the knowledge of your *l*;	279	2
grant them the knowledge of his *l*,	279	12
from the *l* of God?	302	14
Do you put your whole trust in his grace and *l*?	302	19
Teach them to *l* others in the power of the Spirit.	305	24
Send them into the world in witness to your *l*.	306	1
a spirit to know and to *l* you,	308	7
Blood as a sign and pledge of his *l*,	316	3
Having in mind, therefore, his great *l* for us,	316	8
for his *l* for all mankind,	316	12
Thou shalt *l* the Lord thy God with all thy heart,	319	9
l thy neighbor as thyself.	319	12
that we may perfectly *l* thee,	323	10
Thou shalt *l* the Lord thy God with all thy heart,	324	2
l thy neighbor as thyself.	324	5
live in unity and godly *l*.	329	8
to grant them continual growth in thy *l*	330	3
in *l* and charity with your neighbors,	330	10
in the knowledge and *l* of God,	339	16
Go in peace to *l* and serve the Lord.	340	1
Walk in *l*, as Christ loved us and gave himself for us,	343	12
thou hast prepared for those who *l* thee.	346	12
Because in the *l* of wife and husband,	349	1
L the Lord your God	351	8
L your neighbor as yourself.	351	10
perfectly *l* you, and worthily magnify	355	10
In your infinite *l* you made us for yourself;	362	9
to *l* and serve you	365	16
to *l* and serve you	366	10
Go in peace to *l* and serve the Lord.	366	16
We give thanks to you, O God, for the goodness and *l*	368	1
works reveal your wisdom and *l*.	373	18

Walk in *l*, as Christ loved us and gave himself for us, 376 8
prepared for those who *l* you. 379 9
Because in the *l* of wife and husband, 381 16
live together in your *l*, 388 3
that we may serve Christ in them, and *l* one another 388 18
filled with truth and *l*, 389 16
but as you know and *l* us in your Son Jesus 394 7
supported by this fellowship of *l* and prayer, 395 20
The grace of our Lord Jesus Christ and the *l* of God 404 1
in the knowledge and *l* of the Lord. 423 13
Will you *l* him, 424 9
Will you *l* her, 424 15
that with true fidelity and steadfast *l* 425 10
to *l* and to cherish, 427 3
that they may grow in *l* 429 12
Make their life together a sign of Christ's *l* 429 17
and the grace to bring them up to know you, to *l* you, 429 21
reach out in *l* and concern for others. 429 24
God, we give you thanks for your tender *l* 430 10
Let their *l* for each other be a seal 430 17
that they may so *l*, honor, and cherish each other 431 4
obtain those eternal joys prepared for all who *l* you; 432 7
l her, comfort her, honor and keep her, 433 6
l him, comfort him, honor and keep him, 433 11
to *l* and to cherish, 436 4
that we may live together in *l* and affection; 441 9
I *l* the LORD, because he has heard the voice 442 13
bring this child to *l* all that is true and noble, 443 26
Almighty God, giver of life and *l*, 444 8
that they may live together in *l* 444 13
a thousand generations of those who *l* and fear you: 444 16
fill you with *l*. 445 6
May God in his *l* enlighten your heart, 449 10
know the healing power of his *l*. 456 10
So fill my heart with faith in your *l*, 461 2
enjoy the blessed assurance of your *l*; 461 17
and know the consolation of his *l*. 467 2
entrust this child N. to thy never-failing care and *l*, 470 9
they may know the consolation of thy *l*. 481 9
expectation of eternal life with those they *l*. 481 13
Grant us grace to entrust N. to thy never-failing *l*; 481 17
Grant that, increasing in knowledge and *l* of thee, 481 20
Almighty God, we thank thee that in thy great *l* 482 1
in Jesus the manifold blessings of thy *l*, 486 10
increasing in knowledge and *l* of thee, 488 23
the consolation of thy *l*; 489 33
to know and to *l* as a companion 493 18
entrust N. to your never-failing care and *l*, 494 3
Surround them with your *l*, 494 9
renew our trust in your Father's *l*. 498 5
we *l* but see no longer. 498 9
Almighty God, we thank you that in your great *l* 498 12
Father of all, we pray to you for those we *l*, 504 26
expectation of eternal life with those they *l*. 505 15
the consolation of your *l*; 505 20
perfectly *l* you, and worthily magnify 512 10
I will, for the *l* of God. 518 21
with such *l* of you and of all the people, 521 8
example in word and action, in *l* and patience, 523 6
perfectly *l* you, and worthily magnify 525 10
You are to *l* and serve the people 531 10
that the reconciling *l* of Christ may be known 532 11
Father of all, we praise you for your infinite *l* 533 1
example in word and action, in *l* and patience, 535 6
perfectly *l* you, and worthily magnify 537 10
redemptive *l* known, by your word and example, 543 10
come to know you and *l* you. 545 15
example in word and action, in *l* and patience, 547 2
that it may be filled with truth and *l*, 548 12
that they may be filled with your *l*, 548 21
understanding he may *l* and care for your people; 560 7
in praises, heighten my *l* and gratitude; 563 6
example in word and action, in *l* and patience, 564 6
so that those who *l* your Name may exult in you. 589 20
I *l* you, O LORD my strength, * 602 7
Remember, O LORD, your compassion and *l*, * 614 24
remember me according to your *l*, 615 2
All the paths of the LORD are *l* and faithfulness * 615 8
For your *l* is before my eyes; * 616 12
LORD, I *l* the house in which you dwell * 616 22
for he has shown me the wonders of his *l* 624 12
L the LORD, all you who worship him; * 624 18
on those who wait upon his *l*, 627 12
Your *l*, O LORD, reaches to the heavens, * 632 12
How priceless is your *l*, O God! * 632 17
"I *l* to do your will, O my God; 640 21
I have not concealed your *l* and faithfulness 640 28
let your *l* and your faithfulness keep me safe for ever, 641 3
let those who *l* your salvation continually say, 641 17
and save us, for the sake of your steadfast *l*. 647 10
you *l* righteousness and hate iniquity. 648 3
You *l* evil more than good * 658 4
You *l* all words that hurt, * 658 6
God will send forth his *l* and his faithfulness. 663 27
I will celebrate your *l* in the morning; 667 4
bid *l* and faithfulness watch over him. 669 2
Steadfast *l* is yours, O Lord, * 670 10
nor withheld his *l* from me. 675 8
Answer me, O LORD, for your *l* is kind; * 680 23
and those who *l* his Name will dwell therein. 682 10
let those who *l* your salvation say for ever, 682 20
and great is your *l* toward all who call upon you. 710 8
For great is your *l* toward me; * 710 26
Your *l*, O LORD, for ever will I sing; * 713 17
persuaded that your *l* is established for ever; * 713 19
l and truth go before your face. 714 22
My faithfulness and *l* shall be with him, * 715 14
I will keep my *l* for him for ever, * 715 22
But I will not take my *l* from him, * 716 7
Because he is bound to me in *l*, 720 14
your *l*, O LORD, upheld me. 724 2
For your servants *l* her very rubble, * 732 4
nor remember the abundance of your *l*; * 742 12
Despite my *l*, they accuse me; * 751 4
and hatred for my love. 751 7
because of your *l* and because of your faithfulness. 757 15
I *l* the LORD, because he has heard the voice of 759 1
The earth, O LORD, is full of your *l*; * 768 15
Oh, how I *l* your law! * 771 13
but your law do I *l*. 772 20
therefore I *l* your decrees. 773 12
Truly, I *l* your commandments * 774 1
as you always do to those who *l* your Name. 774 12
See how I *l* your commandments! * 776 21

but your law is my *l*. 777 6
Great peace have they who *l* your law; * 777 9
"May they prosper who *l* you. 780 8
because of your *l* and faithfulness; 793 5
O Lord, your *l* endures for ever; 793 20
The Lord preserves all those who *l* him, * 802 27
unite us in bonds of *l*; 815 17
no strength known but the strength of *l*: 815 24
Father of all, whose Son commanded us to *l* 816 5
and grant that we may show the power of your *l* 817 16
l of truth and righteousness, 820 22
Grant this, Father, for the *l* of your Son, 826 6
that we may teach them to *l* 829 11
faith and their assurance of your *l*. 830 6
and bless those whom we *l*, 830 21
by thy *l* in the communion of thy Holy Spirit, 830 24
to thy never-failing care and *l*, 831 8
give patient understanding and persevering *l*. 831 24
Where there is hatred, let us sow *l*; 833 6
and for the mystery of *l*. 836 4
For minds to think, and hearts to *l*, 837 12
a community of *l* has been gathered together 838 5
our knowledge of your *l* is made perfect in our *l* 840 5
l and nurture him, that he may attain 841 4
It means that we are free to make choices: to *l*, 845 5
all can respond to the *l* of God. 846 16
the chosen people to be faithful; to *l* justice, 847 4
To *l* and obey God and to bring others to know him; 847 21
Our duty to our neighbors is to *l* them as ourselves, 848 2
To *l*, honor, and help our parents 848 4
and to do our duty for the *l* of God, 848 20
God is *l*. 849 24
You shall *l* the Lord your God with all your heart, 851 11
You shall *l* your neighbor as yourself. 851 14
The New Commandment is that we *l* one another 851 16
brought into *l* and harmony with God, 852 27
and promotes justice, peace, and *l*. 855 7
and be in *l* and charity with all people. 860 6
because we still hold them in our *l*, 862 10
who have chosen to serve him will grow in his *l*, 862 11
those whom we *l* and those whom we hurt, 862 22
shall separate us from the *l* of God 862 31

loved

We have not *l* you with our whole heart; 79 15
we have not *l* our neighbors as ourselves. 79 16
We have not *l* you with our whole heart; 116 17
we have not *l* our neighbors as ourselves. 116 18
may fulfill all the mind of him who *l* it 204 13
may fulfill all the mind of him who *l* it 255 11
We have not *l* you with our whole heart, 267 19
We have not *l* our neighbors as ourselves. 267 20
Love one another as I have *l* you. 275 4
We have not *l* thee with our whole heart; 320 15
we have not *l* our neighbors as ourselves. 320 16
We have not *l* thee with our whole heart; 331 26
we have not *l* our neighbors as ourselves. 331 27
God so *l* the world, that he gave his only-begotten 332 10
Walk in love, as Christ *l* us and gave himself for us, 343 12
We have not *l* you with our whole heart; 352 15
we have not *l* our neighbors as ourselves. 352 16
We have not *l* you with our whole heart; 360 7
we have not *l* our neighbors as ourseslves. 360 8
Father, you *l* the world so much 374 1
having *l* his own who were in the world, 374 14
he *l* them to the end; 374 15
Walk in love, as Christ *l* us and gave himself for us, 376 8
God so *l* the world that he gave his only Son, 396 1
As the Father has *l* me, so have I *l* you; 397 11
We have not *l* you with our whole heart; 397 24
we have not *l* our neighbors as ourselves. 397 25
God so *l* the world, that he gave his only-begotten 449 15
We have not *l* you with our whole heart; 454 6
we have not *l* our neighbors as ourselves. 454 7
and Mount Zion, which he *l*. 700 16
He *l* cursing, 752 4
which I have always *l*. 767 8
and I have *l* them deeply. 777 14
to be *l* as to love. 833 11
Christ *l* us. 851 17

loveliness

for the songs of birds and the *l* of flowers. 840 9

lovely

the giver of all that is true and *l* and gracious: 432 1
sing praises to his Name, for it is *l*. 788 7

lover

O God, who art the author of peace and *l* of concord, 57 1
O God, the author of peace and *l* of concord, 99 20
l of souls: 280 2
l of souls, 395 6
"O mighty King, *l* of justice, 729 5

loves

To Christ our Lord who *l* us, 317 17
who *l* her and gave himself for her, 381 18
love one another as he *l* us. 388 19
He *l* righteousness and justice; * 626 9
Who among you *l* life * 628 17
For the Lord *l* justice; * 635 16
the pride of Jacob whom he *l*. 650 13
the Lord *l* the gates of Zion 711 13
The Lord *l* those who hate evil; * 727 17
The Lord *l* the righteous; 803 20

loveth

who *l* her and gave himself for her, 349 3

loving

for all thy goodness and *l*-kindness 58 17
for all thy goodness and *l*-kindness 71 13
for all your goodness and *l*-kindness 101 9
stretching out your *l* arms: 107 9
for all your goodness and *l*-kindness 125 7
stretching out your *l* arms: 138 13
O most *l* Father, who willest us to give thanks 165 6
such love toward thee, that we, *l* thee 174 3
set upon the sure foundation of thy *l*-kindness; 178 15
by *l* thee and our neighbor: 179 5
ever thankful for thy *l* providence; 208 11
and have confidence in thy *l* care; 208 20
Most *l* Father, whose will it is for us to give thanks 216 20
love towards you, that we, *l* you in all things, 225 16
set upon the sure foundation of your *l*-kindness; 230 9

by *l* you and our neighbor: 230 20
thankful for your *l* providence; 259 13
and have confidence in your *l* care; 260 5
according to your *l*-kindness; * 266 2
your mercy and *l*-kindness to us, 287 15
l your neighbor as yourself? 293 29
l your neighbor as yourself? 305 4
For the peace from above, for the *l*-kindness of God, 383 3
Lord, let your *l*-kindness be upon them; 393 6
l your neighbor as yourself? 417 14
O God, according to your *l*-kindness; 449 1
commend to your *l* care this child 459 3
and have confidence in your *l* care; 459 20
Surely thy *l*-kindness and mercy shall follow me 476 16
and, in your *l* wisdom and almighty power, work 504 28
Show me your marvelous *l*-kindness, * 601 11
your *l* care makes me great. 605 11
he shows *l*-kindness to his anointed, 606 13
because of the *l*-kindness of the Most High, 609 10
and in your *l*-kindness save me." 623 26
the *l*-kindness of the LORD fills the whole earth. 626 10
Let your *l*-kindness, O LORD, be upon us, * 627 19
Continue your *l*-kindness to those who know you, * 632 24
The LORD grants his *l*-kindness in the daytime; * 643 23
waited in silence on your *l*-kindness, O God, * 651 18
according to your *l*-kindness; * 656 6
For your *l*-kindness is greater than the heavens, * 664 17
For your *l*-kindness is better than life itself; * 670 17
Has his *l*-kindness come to an end for ever? * 693 16
Will your *l*-kindness be declared in the grave? * 712 25
Where, Lord, are your *l*-kindnesses of old, * 717 12
Satisfy us by your *l*-kindness in the morning; * 719 1
To tell of your *l*-kindness early in the morning * 720 24
and crowns you with mercy and *l*-kindness; 733 16
For your *l*-kindness is greater than the heavens, * 750 1
For his *l*-kindness toward us is great, * 760 17
Let your *l*-kindness come to me, O LORD, * 766 17
Let your *l*-kindness be my comfort, * 769 16
In your *l*-kindness, revive me, * 770 18
Deal with your servant according to your *l*-kindness * 773 21
O LORD, according to your *l*-kindness; * 776 1
Let me hear of your *l*-kindness in the morning, 799 15
The LORD is *l* to everyone * 802 3
and *l* in all his works. 802 22
Almighty God, whose *l* hand hath given us all 827 1
l-kindness, that our land may give 828 5
fulfillment in *l* you and their neighbors; 829 25
surround them with your *l* care; 831 4
the *l* care which surrounds us on every side. 836 6
a single *l* God who creates, sustains, and directs it. 846 8
knowing and *l* God and each other. 862 28

low

If I am to lie *l*, help me to do it 461 22
of high degree and *l*, rich and poor together. 652 8
and I am bowed *l*; * 664 5
even those of *l* estate cannot be trusted. 670 2
and laid *l* the youth of Israel. 697 13
for we have been brought very *l*. 701 23
Yet when they were diminished and brought *l*, * 749 7
I was brought very *l*, and he helped me. 759 13
"I have been brought very *l*." * 759 21
Who remembered us in our *l* estate, * 791 15
for I have been brought very *l*; * 798 12

lower

You have made him but little *l* than the angels; * 592 17

lowliness

the *l* of his handmaiden. 50 4
the *l* of his handmaiden. 65 7
l to follow the example of her devotion to thy will; 189 14
l to follow the example of her devotion to your will; 240 21

lowly

for he has looked with favor on his *l* servant. 91 29
and has lifted up the *l*. 92 9
for he has looked with favor on his *l* servant. 119 6
and has lifted up the *l*. 119 15
for I am gentle and *l* in heart, 131 17
for he has looked with favor on his *l* servant. 441 14
and has lifted up the *l*. 442 4
for the *l*, knowing all things before they come to pass: 520 13
they lie in wait to seize upon the *l*; * 595 12
they seize the *l* and drag them away in their net. 595 13
You will save a *l* people, * 604 18
and teaches his way to the *l*. 615 7
But the *l* shall possess the land; * 634 5
He shall have pity on the *l* and poor; * 686 9
Though the LORD be high, he cares for the *l*; * 793 14
The LORD lifts up the *l*, * 804 12

loyal

Will you be *l* to the doctrine, discipline, and worship 526 9
Will you be *l* to the doctrine, discipline, and worship 538 9
"Gather before me my *l* followers, * 654 11
and praise for all his *l* servants, * 806 23

loyalties

may find their lives strengthened and their *l* 430 2

Luke

who didst inspire thy servant *L* the physician 193 11
who inspired your servant *L* the physician 244 20

lurk

They *l* in ambush in public squares 595 8

lurking

and like a young lion *l* in secret places. 601 24

lust

Trample down those who *l* after silver; * 678 20

lute

awake, *l* and harp; * 664 13
awake, *l* and harp; * 749 20

lying

look on this your servant, *l* in great weakness, 462 1
listen to my prayer, which does not come from *l* lips. 600 24
Let the *l* lips be silenced 624 1
and your lips from *l* words. 628 20
and *l* more than speaking the truth. 658 5
my *l* foes who would destroy me are mighty. * 679 18
They speak to me with a *l* tongue; * 751 1
Take from me the way of *l*; * 765 17

therefore I hate every *l* way. 772 2
Deliver me, O Lord, from *l* lips * 778 12

lyre

play to him upon the psaltery and *l*. 626 4
Therefore I will praise you upon the *l* 685 1
the merry harp, and the *l*. 704 4
On the psaltery, and on the *l*, * 721 1
I will play to you on a ten-stringed *l*. 800 20
praise him with *l* and harp. 808 4

M

made

This is the day which the Lord hath *m*; 39 9
not entered into the holy places *m* with hands, 39 15
which hath *m* us meet to be partakers 40 1
The earth is the Lord's for he *m* it: 44 1
The Word was *m* flesh and dwelt among us: 44 6
The sea is his and he *m* it, * 44 18
it is he that hath *m* us and not ourselves; * 45 15
even so in Christ shall all be *m* alive. 46 18
O God, who hast *m* of one blood all the peoples 58 1
thou hast *m* summer and winter. 61 9
Seek him that *m* the Pleiades and Orion, 62 1
entered, not into a sanctuary *m* with hands, 77 14
We give thanks to the Father, who has *m* us worthy 77 22
The earth is the Lord's for he *m* it: 81 11
The Word was *m* flesh and dwelt among us: 82 1
The sea is his, for he *m* it, * 82 13
he himself has *m* us, and we are his; 83 2
so also in Christ shall all be *m* alive. 83 26
The resting-place you have *m* for yourself, O Lord, * 85 26
You *m* the heavens and the earth, * 90 20
The promise he *m* to our fathers, * 92 14
O God, you have *m* of one blood all the peoples 100 17
to us and to all whom you have *m*. 101 10
m the sun to know its going down: 110 25
m worthy to worship you in spirit and in truth; 111 6
you *m* both summer and winter. 115 9
Seek him who *m* the Pleiades and Orion, 115 13
The promise he *m* to our fathers, * 119 20
to us and to all whom you have *m*. 125 8
Because you have *m* the Lord your refuge, * 130 15
the Lord who *m* heaven and earth bless you 131 9
the Lord who *m* heaven and earth bless you 140 4
The sea is his and he *m* it, * 146 9
to incline thine ear to us who have now *m* our prayers 153 21
m thy children by adoption and grace, 161 9
keep the covenant they have *m*, 163 4
who hatest nothing that thou hast *m* 166 2
and also be *m* partakers of his resurrection; 168 6
that we may be *m* an holy temple 178 21
m partners of thy heavenly treasure; 182 15
we may be *m* like unto him in his eternal 184 12
and to the spirits of just men *m* perfect: 198 24
God, who by thy Holy Spirit hast *m* us one 199 4
O God, who hast *m* of one blood all the peoples 206 9
Lord God Almighty, who hast *m* all peoples 207 1
m your children by adoption and grace, 213 3
keep the covenant they have *m*, 214 15
of that abundant life which you have *m* known 216 2
you hate nothing you have *m* 217 15
you *m* an instrument of shameful death 220 8
O God, who *m* this most holy night to shine 222 8
O God, whose blessed Son *m* himself known 223 10
O God, whose blessed Son *m* himself known 224 19
m a holy temple acceptable to you; 230 15
with power and great glory, we may be *m* like him 236 5
and to the spirits of just men *m* perfect: 250 9
Almighty God, by your Holy Spirit you have *m* us one 250 14
O God, you have *m* of one blood all the peoples 257 5
Lord God Almighty, you have *m* all the peoples 258 1
you hate nothing you have *m* 264 3
and things which had grown old are being *m* new, 280 19
by him through whom all things were *m*, 280 21
and things which had grown old are being *m* new, 291 16
by him through whom all things were *m*, 291 18
O God, who *m* this most holy night to shine 295 8
the covenant you *m* with them at their Baptism. 309 7
m one with Christ, and Christ with us; 316 6
and *m* us a kingdom of priests to serve his God 317 18
begotten, not *m*, 326 15
Through him all things were *m*. 326 17
and was *m* man. 327 3
begotten, not *m*, 327 29
by whom all things were *m*; 327 31
and was *m* man; 328 4
m there, by his one oblation of himself once offered, 334 12
and *m* one body with him, that he may dwell in us, 336 7
He *m* there a full and perfect sacrifice 341 16
thy whole Church may be *m* one body with him, 342 28
who hast *m* us in thine image, 344 14
Who by water and the Holy Spirit hast *m* us 345 5
was *m* very Man of the substance of the Virgin Mary 345 16
Because in the mystery of the Word *m* flesh, 346 1
m us citizens of thy kingdom, 348 21
begotten, not *m*, 358 12
Through him all things were *m*. 358 14
and was *m* man. 358 19
In your infinite love you *m* us for yourself; 362 9
which you have *m* known to us in creation; 368 2
and above all in the Word *m* flesh, 368 4
you have delivered us from evil, and *m* us worthy 368 7
You *m* us the rulers of creation. 370 13
m a new people by water and the Spirit, 371 7
Fountain of life and source of all goodness, you *m* all 373 4
destroyed death, and *m* the whole creation new. 374 7
you *m* us in your image, 377 12
you have *m* us a new people 378 1
mighty power of the Holy Spirit, was *m* perfect Man 378 10
Because in the mystery of the Word *m* flesh, 378 14
m us citizens of your kingdom, 381 14
Almighty God, by your Holy Spirit you have *m* us one 395 17
the covenant you *m* with them at their Baptism. 418 5
Look with favor upon the world you have *m*, 429 4
As God has *m* us his children by adoption and grace, 441 5
The promise he *m* to our fathers, * 442 9
May God the Holy Spirit, who has *m* the Church one 445 7
receive this holy unction be *m* whole; 455 13
and bless the means *m* use of for his cure. 459 8
or ever the earth and the world were *m*, * 472 12
who hath *m* heaven and earth. 473 12

didst begin in them may be *m* perfect 486 11
let it now be *m* known. 514 7
and things which had grown old are being *m* new, 515 9
by him through whom all things were *m*, 515 11
begotten, not *m*, 519 15
Through him all things were *m*. 519 17
and was *m* man. 519 22
and things which had grown old are being *m* new, 528 7
by him through whom all things were *m*, 528 9
begotten, not *m*, 530 6
Through him all things were *m*. 530 8
and was *m* man. 530 13
and things which had grown old are being *m* new, 540 7
by him through whom all things were *m*, 540 9
begotten, not *m*, 542 6
Through him all things were *m*. 542 8
and was *m* man. 542 13
and *m* him Lord of all; 545 5
Lord Christ, that we are *m* one with you 568 19
die to sin and are *m* new in Christ. 569 16
much less the walls of temples *m* with hands. 578 4
and fall into the hole that they have *m*. 592 2
You have *m* him but little lower than the angels; * 592 17
and the torrents of oblivion *m* me afraid. 602 15
he *m* dark waters and thick clouds his pavilion. 603 12
and *m* it firm upon the rivers of the deep. 613 17
You, LORD, with your favor, *m* me as strong as 621 18
By the word of the LORD were the heavens *m*, * 626 11
he set my feet upon a high cliff and *m* my footing 640 4
how you destroyed nations and *m* your people 645 12
You have *m* us fall back before our adversary, * 646 5
You have *m* us like sheep to be eaten * 646 7
You have *m* us the scorn of our neighbors, * 646 11
You have *m* us a byword among the nations, * 646 13
those who have *m* a covenant with me 654 12
"I have *m* my accusation; * 655 24
I am bound by the vow I *m* to you, O God; * 663 14
You have *m* your people know hardship; * 667 14
in your goodness, O God, you have *m* provision 676 24
may prayer be *m* for him always, 686 15
I have *m* the Lord GOD my refuge. 689 6
you *m* both summer and winter. 690 19
he *m* the waters stand up like walls. 695 29
he *m* the tribes of Israel to dwell in their tents. 699 17
and their widows *m* no lamentation. 700 8
they have *m* Jerusalem a heap of rubble. 701 3
and *m* his dwelling a ruin. 701 20
You have *m* us the derision of our neighbors, * 702 23
the son of man you have *m* so strong for yourself. 703 21
they have *m* an alliance against you: 706 13
All nations you have *m* will come and 710 15
you have *m* me to be abhorred by them; * 712 18
"I have *m* a covenant with my chosen one; * 713 21
You have *m* the north and the south; * 714 17
and *m* all his enemies rejoice. 716 26
how frail you have *m* all flesh. 717 9
Because you have *m* the LORD your refuge, * 720 3
For you have *m* me glad by your acts, O LORD; * 721 3
He has *m* the whole world so sure * 722 5
The sea is his, for he *m* it, * 724 22
but it is the LORD who *m* the heavens. 726 2
he has *m* the world so firm that it cannot be moved; 726 12
The LORD has *m* known his victory; * 728 3
he himself has *m* us, and we are his; 729 26
He *m* his ways known to Moses * 733 21
For he himself knows whereof we are *m*; * 734 9
in wisdom you have *m* them all; 736 26
which you have *m* for the sport of it. 737 6
the promise he *m* for a thousand generations: 738 16
The covenant he *m* with Abraham, * 738 17
The LORD *m* his people exceedingly fruitful; * 740 1
he *m* them stronger than their enemies; 740 2
Israel *m* a bull-calf at Horeb * 743 9
Oh, that my ways were *m* so direct * 763 13
Your hands have *m* me and fashioned me; * 769 9
They had almost *m* an end of me on earth, * 770 16
Your commandment has *m* me wiser 771 15
and *m* their furrows long. 784 6
the LORD who *m* heaven and earth bless 787 22
Who by wisdom *m* the heavens, * 790 5
And *m* Israel to pass through the midst of it, * 790 23
I will thank you because I am marvelously *m*; * 795 1
while I was being *m* in secret 795 4
he has *m* me live in dark places 799 3
Who *m* heaven and earth, the seas, and all 803 13
He *m* them stand fast for ever and ever; * 806 5
through whom all things were *m*, 814 5
O God, you *m* us in your own image and redeemed us 815 13
might be *m* rich through your poverty: 819 7
Almighty and everlasting God, you *m* the universe 827 11
you *m* us fellow workers in your creation: 827 18
who, in holy wedlock, have been *m* one flesh. 829 4
to incline thine ear to us who have now *m* our prayers 834 3
the men and women who have *m* this country strong. 839 4
our knowledge of your love is *m* perfect in our love 840 5
We are part of God's creation, *m* in the image 845 2
misused their freedom and *m* wrong choices. 845 11
made heirs of God's kingdom. 850 4
m the offering which we could not make; 850 8
How are the promises for infants *m* and carried out? 858 28
Promises are *m* for them by their parents 859 1
the way by which the sacrifice of Christ is *m* present, 859 12
the grace of the Holy Spirit to those being *m* bishops, 860 29

Magdalene

Almighty God, whose blessed Son restored Mary *M* 191 1
Almighty God, whose blessed Son restored Mary *M* 242 8
for Mary and Martha, and Mary *M*; 838 15

magistrates

bless the courts of justice and the *m* in all this land; 821 10

magnificence

Oh, the majesty and *m* of his presence! * 726 3

magnified

For he that is mighty hath *m* me, * 50 7
For he that is mighty hath *m* me, * 65 10

magnify

praise him and *m* him for ever. 47 6
My soul doth *m* the Lord, 50 1
Day by day we *m* thee; 55 17
My soul doth *m* the Lord, * 65 4
and worthily *m* thy holy Name; 323 10
we laud and *m* thy glorious Name; 334 2

we laud and *m* thy glorious Name; 341 5
and worthily *m* your holy Name; 355 10
the King of saints, we praise and *m* thy holy Name 489 14
and worthily *m* your holy Name; 512 10
and worthily *m* your holy Name; 525 10
and worthily *m* your holy Name; 537 10

maid

and the eyes of a *m* to the hand of her mistress, 780 18

maidens

in the midst of *m* playing upon the hand-drums. 678 8
there were no wedding songs for their *m*. 700 6
Young men and *m*, * 806 17

maintain

to *m* these liberties in righteousness and peace; 190 21
may have grace to *m* our liberties 242 4
Arise, O God, *m* your cause; * 690 28
I know that the LORD will *m* the cause of the poor * 796 25

maintained

For you have *m* my right and my cause; * 593 7

maintains

the God who *m* my cause. 663 24

maintenance

help us to employ it in the *m* of justice 209 4
help us to employ it in the *m* of justice 260 11

majesty

Blessed art thou for the Name of thy *M*; * 49 11
Heaven and earth are full of the *m* of thy glory. 53 2
the Father, of an infinite *m*, 53 8
on the throne of your *m*, glory to you. 90 10
Father, of *m* unbounded, 95 27
he shall come again in his glorious *m* to judge 159 5
of the Divine *m* to worship the Unity: 176 4
Being of glorious *m* and perfect love as one God 199 13
he shall come again in his glorious *m* to judge 211 5
power of your divine *M* to worship the Unity: 228 4
Being of glorious *m* and perfect love as one God 251 2
unto thy divine *M*, beseeching thee to inspire 329 4
by thought, word, and deed, against thy divine *M*, 331 7
thy divine *M*, with these thy holy gifts, 335 11
and the victory, and the *m*. 344 9
glory, the victory, and the *m*. 377 7
For yours is the *m*, O Father, Son, and Holy Spirit; 391 23
thy Son at his coming in glorious *m*; 395 15
the victory, and the *m*; 579 14
your *m* is praised above the heavens. 592 10
splendor and *m* have you bestowed upon him. 609 6
in your pride and in your *m*. 647 18
his *m* is over Israel; 679 2
Oh, the *m* and magnificence of his presence! * 726 3
you are clothed with *m* and splendor. 735 3
His work is full of *m* and splendor, * 754 10
I will ponder the glorious splendor of your *m* * 801 20
for the natural *m* and beauty of this land. 838 22

make

m straight in the desert a highway for our God. 37 4
M them to be numbered with thy saints, 53 21
And *m* thy chosen people joyful. 55 4
accord to *m* our common supplication unto thee, 59 13
O God, *m* speed to save us. 63 17
O Lord, *m* haste to help us. 63 18
And *m* thy chosen people joyful. 67 19
accord to *m* our common supplication unto thee, 72 10
m straight in the desert a highway for our God. 75 4
Give thanks to the Lord, and call upon his Name; *m* 78 6
M his deeds known among the peoples; * 86 9
and *m* my appeal, sure of your gracious goodness. 91 13
Therefore I *m* this prayer to you: * 91 16
O God, you *m* us glad with the weekly remembrance 98 19
accord to *m* our common supplication to you; 102 2
O God, *m* speed to save us. 103 1
O Lord, *m* haste to help us. 103 2
The Lord *m* his face to shine upon you 114 2
O God, *m* speed to save us. 117 10
O Lord, *m* haste to help us. 117 11
accord to *m* our common supplication to you; 126 2
O God, *m* speed to save us. 128 3
O Lord, *m* haste to help us. 128 4
for only you, Lord, *m* me dwell in safety. 129 7
m haste to deliver me. 129 12
That it may please thee to *m* wars to cease 151 1
Create and *m* in us new and contrite hearts, 166 3
M speed to help thy servants 166 10
Son didst *m* an instrument of shameful death 168 17
O God, who didst *m* this most holy night to shine 170 14
m us worthy of our calling; 176 11
we beseech thee, *m* us to have a perpetual fear 178 12
dost not forsake those who *m* their boast 181 20
and *m* us continually to be given to all good works; 183 7
m us to love that which thou dost command; 183 19
destroy the works of the devil and *m* us the children 184 8
M us so to follow his doctrine 190 3
so we may with ardent devotion *m* known the 194 4
M us, we beseech thee, faithful stewards 194 18
m those who carry on the industries 208 3
M us, we beseech thee, ever thankful 208 10
and to *m* no peace with oppression; 209 2
m us mindful of the rightful aspirations 210 14
you *m* us glad by the yearly festival of the birth 212 10
m in us new and contrite hearts, 217 16
m us worthy of our calling; 228 11
O Lord, *m* us have perpetual love and reverence 230 7
never forsake those who *m* their boast of your mercy; 233 11
m us love what you command; 235 11
destroy the works of the devil and *m* us children 236 2
M us so to follow his teaching and holy life, 241 12
may with ardent devotion *m* known the love 245 13
M us, we pray, faithful stewards 246 3
m those who carry on the industries 259 5
M us always thankful for your loving providence; 259 12
and to *m* no peace with oppression; 260 9
m us mindful of the rightful aspirations 261 19
m in us new and contrite hearts, 264 4
And, to *m* a right beginning of repentance, 265 13
and will *m* me understand wisdom secretly. 266 15
M me hear of joy and gladness, * 266 18
might *m* us the children of God by the power 316 15
ready to *m* restitution for all injuries and wrongs 317 6
Thou shalt not *m* to thyself any graven image, 318 1
taught us to *m* prayers, and supplications, 329 2

make

and *m* your humble confession to Almighty God, 330 13
we, thy humble servants, do celebrate and *m* here 335 10
the memorial thy Son hath commanded us to *m*; 335 13
and didst *m* us in thine own image; 341 13
celebrate and *m*, with these thy holy gifts 342 11
the memorial thy Son hath commanded us to *m*; 342 13
and *m* good thy vows unto the Most High. 343 8
and to *m* us heirs in him of everlasting life; 345 9
that he might *m* the whole creation new. 349 4
You shall not *m* for yourself any idol. 350 5
Let the grace of this Holy Communion *m* us one 372 6
and *m* good your vows to the Most High. 376 4
and to *m* us heirs in him of everlasting life; 378 5
that he might *m* the whole creation new. 381 19
M us a living sacrifice of praise. 403 18
honor and keep the promises and vows they *m*; 425 11
m one flesh in Holy Matrimony. 429 6
M their life together a sign of Christ's love 429 17
and to *m* the way of the cross 430 12
and *m* you know and feel that the only Name 457 2
I may *m* room for your power to possess me, 461 2
but *m* me ready, Lord, for whatever it may be. 461 20
M these words more than words, 461 24
the streams whereof *m* glad the city of God, * 471 23
yet even at the grave we *m* our song: 483 1
the Lord *m* his face to shine upon him 485 13
M you perfect in every good work to do his will, 487 1
M us, we beseech thee, deeply 489 4
yet even at the grave we *m* our song: 499 8
M you perfect in every good work to do his will, 503 3
M us, we pray, deeply aware 504 2
Therefore, Father, *m* N. a bishop in your Church. 521 1
come forward now, and *m* it known. 527 5
are called to *m* Christ known as Savior and Lord, 531 3
m you a stronger and more able minister 532 6
m him a priest in your Church. 533 13
M him a faithful pastor, 534 4
come forward now and *m* it known. 539 5
m Christ and his redemptive love known, 543 9
and *m* him a deacon in your Church. 545 10
M him, O Lord, modest and humble, 545 12
M me an instrument of your salvation 562 15
Lord Jesus Christ, *m* this a temple of your presence 568 14
in the music we *m* and in the songs we sing. 572 4
for sending your Holy Spirit to *m* us holy, 573 19
for only you, LORD, *m* me dwell in safety. 588 16
for I *m* my prayer to you. 588 20
early in the morning I *m* my appeal 588 22
m your way straight before me. 589 8
he will bend his bow and *m* it ready. 591 23
They dig a pit and *m* it deep * 592 1
my God, you *m* my darkness bright. 604 21
and will *m* him glad with the joy of your presence. 609 8
You will *m* them like a fiery furnace * 609 14
They shall come and *m* known to a people 612 21
I will sing and *m* music to the LORD. 618 9
m haste to deliver me. 622 11
M your face to shine upon your servant, * 623 25
Therefore all the faithful will *m* their prayers to you 625 11
He will *m* your righteousness as clear as the light * 633 15
M haste to help me, * 638 13
and do not *m* me the taunt of the fool. 639 12
Oh, that I could *m* them known and tell them! * 640 14
O LORD, *m* haste to help me. 641 9
you shall *m* them princes over all the earth. 648 24
I will *m* your name to be remembered 648 25
There is a river whose streams *m* glad the city of God, 649 10
The nations *m* much ado, 649 15
M the circuit of Zion; 651 26
and *m* good your vows to the Most High. 655 8
When you see a thief, you *m* him your friend, * 655 16
and will *m* me understand wisdom secretly. 656 19
M me hear of joy and gladness, * 656 22
and *m* my lodging in the wilderness. 660 20
Day and night the watchmen *m* their rounds 661 1
I will sing and *m* melody. 664 11
M an end of them in your wrath; * 666 24
m an end of them, and they shall be no more. 666 25
He will *m* them trip over their tongues, * 672 1
You *m* fast the mountains by your power; * 672 21
you *m* the dawn and the dusk to sing for joy. 673 3
you *m* it very plenteous; * 673 5
m the voice of his praise to be heard; 674 10
and the drunkards *m* songs about me. 680 12
O LORD, *m* haste to help me. 682 12
till I *m* known your strength to this generation 684 18
when you arise you will *m* their image vanish. 688 18
I will *m* its pillars fast. 691 9
M a vow to the LORD your God and keep it; * 692 22
M their leaders like Oreb and Zeeb, * 706 24
O my God, *m* them like whirling dust * 707 3
and my arm will *m* him strong. 715 9
I shall *m* his dominion extend * 715 16
I will *m* him my firstborn * 715 20
M us glad by the measure of the days 719 3
Let the sea *m* a noise and all that is in it, * 728 16
when I call, *m* haste to answer me, 731 4
you *m* the clouds your chariot; 735 7
You *m* the winds your messengers * 735 9
Beside them the birds of the air *m* their nests * 735 25
You *m* grass grow for flocks and herds * 736 3
Oil to *m* a cheerful countenance, * 736 7
You *m* darkness that it may be night, * 736 17
m known his deeds among the peoples. 738 2
to *m* his power known. 742 15
I will sing and *m* melody. 749 18
until I *m* your enemies your footstool." 753 13
they *m* no sound with their throat. 758 3
Those who *m* them are like them, * 758 4
M me understand the way of your commandments, * 765 13
M me go in the path of your commandments, * 766 5
which you *m* to those who fear you. 766 12
But I still my soul and *m* it quiet, 785 14
There will I *m* the horn of David flourish; * 787 5
Those who *m* them are like them, * 789 11
The LORD will *m* good his purpose for me; * 793 19
if I *m* the grave my bed, you are there also. 794 15
to the LORD I *m* loud supplication. 798 2
O LORD, *m* haste to answer me; my spirit fails me; * 799 12
They *m* known the glory of your kingdom * 802 7
m music to our God upon the harp. 804 15
wouldest be pleased to *m* thy ways known unto them, 814 8
M the hearts and minds of your servants ready 819 2
and *m* them worthy at length to behold it unveiled 819 17

and *m* them ever mindful of their calling 820 22
and those who *m* our laws 822 1
may elect trustworthy leaders and *m* wise decisions 822 12
Lord, *m* us instruments of your peace. 833 5
m us bold to praise you and to do your will; 835 5
m us mindful of the needs of others; 835 9
to sustain our lives and *m* our hearts glad; 835 14
that we may know him and *m* him known; 836 18
They *m* us rich, though we often exploit them. 839 2
It means that we are free to *m* choices: 845 5
made the offering which we could not *m*; 850 8
In penitence, we confess our sins and *m* restitution 857 12
m their vows before God and the Church, 861 5
and will *m* all things new. 862 3

maker

and kneel before the Lord our *M*. 45 2
m of heaven and earth; 53 24
m of heaven and earth; 66 10
and kneel before the Lord our *M*. 82 16
the *m* of heaven and earth. 104 16
The *m* of heaven and earth. 127 4
and kneel before the Lord our *M*. 146 12
kneel before the Lord, our *m* and redeemer. 265 15
m of heaven and earth, 326 8
m of heaven and earth, 327 22
m of all things, judge of all men: 331 3
m of heaven and earth, 358 5
immortal, the creator and *m* of mankind; 482 12
immortal, the creator and *m* of mankind; 499 4
m of heaven and earth, 519 8
The *m* of heaven and earth. 523 12
m of heaven and earth, 529 11
m of heaven and earth, 541 11
The *m* of heaven and earth. 552 2
The *m* of heaven and earth. 568 5
and kneel before the LORD our *M*. 725 2
the *m* of heaven and earth. 758 20
the *m* of heaven and earth. 779 4
the *m* of heaven and earth. 781 16
Let Israel rejoice in his *M*; * 807 4

makes

He *m* me lie down in green pastures * 443 3
he *m* his arrows shafts of fire. 591 25
and *m* my way secure. 605 4
He *m* me sure-footed like a deer * 605 5
your loving care *m* me great. 605 11
He *m* me lie down in green pastures * 612 25
He *m* Lebanon skip like a calf, * 620 16
The voice of the LORD *m* the oak trees writhe * 620 21
music of strings from ivory palaces *m* you glad. 648 7
It is he who *m* war to cease in all the world; * 649 21
you have given us wine that *m* us stagger. 667 15
and in whose tops the stork *m* his dwelling. 736 12
and *m* them wander in trackless wastes) 749 10
He *m* his marvelous works to be remembered; * 754 12
He *m* the woman of a childless house * 756 16
He *m* grass to grow upon the mountains * 804 18
and *m* us members of Christ's Body, 858 10

makest

O God, who *m* us glad with the weekly remembrance 56 1
O God, who *m* us glad with the yearly remembrance 160 12

maketh

He *m* me to lie down in green pastures; * 476 21

making

and for *m* us worthy to share 311 17
abundantly upon your people, *m* some apostles, 533 7
Almighty God, we thank you for *m* us in your image, 567 8
For *m* us your children by adoption and grace, 578 16
and are *m* no profit on the sale of them. 646 10
Almighty God, we thank you for *m* the earth fruitful, 824 6
in *m* the heart of this people wise, 827 9
m provision for its future 828 20

male

you have created us *m* and female 425 7

malice

neither with the leaven of *m* and wickedness, * 46 5
Not with the old leaven, the leaven of *m* and evil, * 83 13
from envy, hatred, and *m*; 149 2
the leaven of *m* and wickedness, 172 10
the leaven of *m* and wickedness, that we may always 224 3
You shall not invoke with *m* the Name of the Lord 350 7
Let the *m* of the wicked come to an end, 591 15
Their *m* turns back upon their own head; * 592 3
and also those who speak *m*. 618 25
and destroy them in their own *m*; * 724 12
They draw near who in *m* persecute me; * 776 3
to bear no *m*, 848 8

malicious

M witnesses rise up against me; * 630 13

maliciously

They scoff and speak *m*; * 687 15

man

For since by *m* came death, * 46 15
by *m* came also the resurrection of the dead. 46 16
When thou tookest upon thee to deliver *m*, 53 13
For since by a *m* came death, * 83 23
by a *m* has come also the resurrection of the dead. 83 24
When you became *m* to set us free 96 3
good things as pass *m*'s understanding: 174 2
and *m* is reconciled to God. 287 22
and was made *m*. 327 3
and was made *m*; 328 4
If any *m* sin, we have an Advocate with the Father, 332 15
was made very *M* of the substance of the Virgin Mary 345 16
and was made *m*. 358 19
perfect *M* of the flesh of the Virgin Mary his mother; 378 11
bless the joining together of this *m* and this woman 423 2
will you have this *m* to be your husband; 424 8
Look mercifully upon this *m* and this woman 425 8
this *m* and this woman have bound themselves 427 11
and especially upon this *m* and this woman 429 5
m and woman in his Name. 430 14
your blessing upon this *m* and this woman. 430 16
this *m* and this woman have bound themselves 434 5
(presents) this woman to be married to this *m*? 437 6

Who presents this woman and this *m* to be married	437	7
Do you take this *m* as your father?	441	3
If any *m* sin, we have an Advocate with the Father,	450	1
and no *m* dieth to himself.	469	10
Thou turnest *m* to destruction; *	472	14
and was made *m*.	519	22
and was made *m*.	530	13
and was made *m*.	542	13
receive this book, and be among us as a *m* of prayer.	561	5
What is *m* that you should be mindful of him? *	592	15
the son of *m* that you should seek him out?	592	16
But as for me, I am a worm and no *m*, *	610	12
I am forgotten like a dead *m*, out of mind; *	623	14
a strong *m* is not delivered by his great strength.	627	8
you save both *m* and beast, O LORD.	632	16
But it was you, a *m* after my own heart, *	661	10
for vain is the help of *m*.	668	9
Let your hand be upon the *m* of your right hand, *	703	20
the son of *m* you have made so strong for yourself.	703	21
nor any wicked *m* bring him down.	715	11
M goes forth to his work *	736	23
He sent a *m* before them, *	739	11
for vain is the help of *m*.	750	20
Set a wicked *m* against him, *	751	8
How shall a young *m* cleanse his way? *	764	1
Happy is the *m* who has his quiver full of them! *	783	10
The *m* who fears the LORD *	783	19
the firstborn both of *m* and beast.	788	18
he has no pleasure in the strength of a *m*;	804	23
woman and *m* enter into a life-long union,	861	5

manage

and to *m* their affairs with justice.	755	14

Manasseh

Gilead is mine and *M* is mine; *	667	23
In the presence of Ephraim, Benjamin, and *M*, *	702	14
Gilead is mine and *M* is mine; *	750	10

manhood

the flower of *m* in the dwellings of Ham.	699	8

manifest

O God, who dost *m* in thy servants the signs	71	6
O God, you *m* in your servants the signs	125	1
O God, who by the leading of a star didst *m*	162	13
O God, whose blessed Son did *m* himself	171	17
O God, whose blessed Son did *m* himself	173	5
may *m* thy power among all peoples,	181	7

manifested

The Lord hath *m* forth his glory:	43	4
hast *m* to us in thy Son our Savior Jesus Christ;	164	8
and which thou hast *m* unto us in thy Son	165	11
O God, whose blessed Son was *m*	184	7
the gifts of grace *m* in thy servant N.,	197	15
O God, by the leading of a star you *m* your only Son	214	7
and which you have *m* to us in your Son Jesus Christ	217	4
the gifts of grace *m* in your servant N.,	249	1

manifestly

after his glorious resurrection *m* appeared	347	2

manifold

help thy servants who are assaulted by *m* temptations;	166	11
among the sundry and *m* changes of the world,	167	19
We acknowledge and bewail our *m* sins	331	4
And although we are unworthy, through our *m* sins,	336	9
but in thy *m* and great mercies.	337	10
the *m* blessings of thy love,	486	10
O LORD, how *m* are your works! *	736	25

mankind

according to thy promises declared unto *m*	42	6
according to thy promises declared unto *m*	63	9
Behold, the dwelling of God is with *m*.	75	11
and to draw all *m* into thy kingdom,	150	13
That it may please thee to have mercy upon all *m*,	152	1
who, of thy tender love towards *m*, hast sent	168	2
that all *m* should follow the example	168	4
for his love for all *m*, and for the redemption	316	12
according to thy promises declared unto *m*	321	9
Thou only art immortal, the creator and maker of *m*;	482	12
You only are immortal, the creator and maker of *m*;	499	4
and plants to serve *m*;	736	4
and green plants to serve *m*.	804	19
O God, the creator and preserver of all *m*,	814	6

manna

He rained down *m* upon them to eat *	696	24

manner

Jesus Christ adorned this *m* of life by his presence	423	5
And do you believe his *m* of life to be suitable	526	5
And do you believe his *m* of life to be suitable	538	5
They abhorred all *m* of food *	747	17
than in all *m* of riches.	764	12
filled to overflowing with all *m* of crops; *	801	3

manners

sound learning, and pure *m*.	820	5

mansion

may find in us a *m* prepared for himself;	160	8
may find in us a *m* prepared for himself;	212	8

mantle

a *m* about their shoulders,	430	18
You covered it with the Deep as with a *m*; *	735	13

many

M are saying,	129	1
help us who are assaulted by *m* temptations;	218	3
for you, and for *m*, for the remission of sins.	335	6
for you, and for *m*, for the remission of sins.	342	8
uniting peoples of *m* tongues	347	9
for you and for *m* for the forgiveness of sins.	363	4
for you and for *m* for the forgiveness of sins.	368	17
for you and for *m* for the forgiveness of sins.	371	16
for you and for *m* for the forgiveness of sins.	374	22
uniting peoples of *m* tongues	380	4
for you and for *m* for the forgiveness of sins.	403	10
for you and for *m* for the forgiveness of sins.	405	9
anointed *m* that were sick and healed them,	455	11
and to give his life a ransom for *m*.	517	18
the firstborn among *m* brethren,	533	4
We praise you for the *m* ministries in your Church,	545	7

that through him *m* may come to know you 545 14
Father, your people worship you with *m* voices 572 1
for the work of *m* hands, which have beautified 573 2
LORD, how *m* adversaries I have! * 587 3
how *m* there are who rise up against me! 587 4
How *m* there are who say of me, * 587 5
M are saying, 588 10
Because of their *m* transgressions cast them out, * 589 15
M young bulls encircle me; * 611 1
Look upon my enemies, for they are *m*, * 615 26
M are the troubles of the righteous, * 629 5
and *m* in number are those who wrongfully hate me. 638 8
m shall see, and stand in awe, 640 7
for there are *m* who fight me. 661 24
truly there are *m* who fight against me, O Most High. 662 16
let his years extend over *m* generations. 668 25
I have become a portent to *m*; * 683 14
m times he held back his anger 698 3
how I carry in my bosom the taunts of *m* peoples, 717 15
Mightier than the sound of *m* waters, 722 12
When *m* cares fill my mind, * 724 3
with its living things too *m* to number, * 737 2
M a time did he deliver them, 745 10
There are *m* who persecute and oppress me, * 776 17
He overthrew *m* nations * 788 21
brought hither out of *m* kindreds and tongues. 820 8
you proclaim your truth in every age by *m* voices: 827 6
m listen and write what *m* read; 827 8
first-born of *m* from the dead. 838 20
all our people, with *m* voices in one united chorus, 839 19
through nature and history, through *m* seers 845 19
How *m* creeds does this Church use in its worship? 851 24

marched

and *m* forward together. 651 9
when you *m* through the wilderness, 676 17

Mark

who by the hand of *M* the evangelist hast given 188 21
by the hand of *M* the evangelist you have given 240 7

mark

hear them, read, *m*, learn, and inwardly digest them; 184 17
hear them, read, *m*, learn, and inwardly digest them, 236 9
and as a *m* of our mortal nature, 265 14
If thou, LORD, wilt be extreme to *m* what is done 474 5
M those who are honest; 636 10
You appointed the moon to *m* the seasons, * 736 15

marked

you are sealed by the Holy Spirit in Baptism and *m* 308 9

marriage

m was established by God in creation, 423 4
Therefore *m* is not to be entered into unadvisedly 423 13
why you may not be united in *m* lawfully, 424 6
together in the covenant of *m*? 424 9
power to uphold these two persons in their *m*? 425 2
O God, you have so consecrated the covenant of *m* 431 1
and of his Church upon his *m*. 433 2
the obligations which Christian *M* demands. 433 4
power to uphold these two persons in their *m*? 434 2
I publish the Banns of *M* between 437 1
when we are joined in *m*, when we turn to you 569 7
Holy Matrimony is Christian *m*, 861 4

married

just cause why they may not lawfully be *m*, 424 3
Grant that all *m* persons who have witnessed 430 1
Who gives (presents) this woman to be *m* to this man? 437 6
Who presents this woman and this man to be *m* to 437 7

marrow

My soul is content, as with *m* and fatness, * 670 21

Martha

Lord, you consoled *M* and Mary in their distress; 497 3
for Mary and *M*, and Mary Magdalene; 838 15

martyr

first *m* Stephen, who looked up to heaven and prayed 186 2
by whose grace and power thy holy *m* N. triumphed 195 8
of thy love in the heart of thy holy *m* N.: 196 2
first *m* Stephen, who looked up to heaven and prayed 237 15
by whose grace and power your holy *m* 247 6
love in the heart of your holy *m* N.: 247 14
Stephen, the first *m*, and all the martyrs and saints 838 16

martyrdom

glorified thee by their *m*: 190 11
m for the Name of Jesus Christ; 191 9
glorified you by their *m*: 241 20
and apostle James, first among the Twelve to suffer *m* 242 15

martyrs

The noble army of *m* praise thee. 53 5
The white-robed army of *m* praise you. 95 25
chorus, with prophets, apostles, and *m*, 370 24
Mary, with patriarchs, prophets, apostles, and *m*, 375 22
the *m* receive thee, and bring thee into the holy city 484 2
for the holy patriarchs, prophets, apostles, and *m*; 489 17
the *m* receive you, and bring you into the holy city 500 13
for the holy patriarchs, prophets, apostles, and *m*; 504 15
faith of patriarchs, prophets, apostles, and *m*, 517 15
Stephen, the first martyr, and all the *m* and saints 838 16

marvelous

perceive the glory of his *m* works; 163 17
called us out of darkness into thy *m* light; 196 19
perceive the glory of his *m* works; 215 11
called us out of darkness into your *m* light; 248 5
All you who stand near this *m* and holy flame, 286 10
I will tell of all your *m* works. 593 2
Show me your *m* loving-kindness, * 601 11
Your right hand will show you *m* things; * 647 21
the earth will tremble at your *m* signs; * 673 2
for he has done *m* things. 727 25
and speak of all his *m* works. 738 4
In Egypt they did not consider your *m* works, 742 11
He makes his *m* works to be remembered; * 754 12
and it is *m* in our eyes. 762 18
that I may meditate on your *m* works. 765 14
and all your *m* works. 801 21
all its *m* order, its atoms, worlds, and galaxies, 827 12

marvelously

I will thank you because I am *m* made; * 795 1

marvels

He worked *m* in the sight of their forefathers, * 695 26
Remember the *m* he has done, * 738 9

Mary

born of the Virgin *M*, 53 27
born of the Virgin *M*, 66 13
and born of the Virgin *M*. 96 17
and born of the Virgin *M*. 120 13
announced by an angel to the Virgin *M*, 188 17
whose blessed Son restored *M* Magdalene 191 1
God, who hast taken to thyself the blessed Virgin *M*, 192 1
announced by an angel to the Virgin *M*, 240 3
whose blessed Son restored *M* Magdalene 242 8
you have taken to yourself the blessed Virgin *M*, 243 8
and born of the Virgin *M*. 293 4
and born of the Virgin *M*. 304 7
he became incarnate from the Virgin *M*, 327 2
was incarnate by the Holy Ghost of the Virgin *M*, 328 3
was made very Man of the substance of the Virgin *M* 345 16
he became incarnate from the Virgin *M*, 358 18
sent him to be incarnate from the Virgin *M*, 368 6
Incarnate by the Holy Spirit, born of the Virgin *M*, 374 3
find our inheritance with [the Blessed Virgin *M*, 375 22
of the flesh of the Virgin *M* his mother; 378 11
the fellowship of [the ever-blessed Virgin *M*, 391 19
and born of the Virgin *M*. 416 12
for the blessed Virgin *M*; 489 16
and born of the Virgin *M*. 496 7
Lord, you consoled Martha and *M* in their distress; 497 3
for the blessed Virgin *M*; 504 14
he became incarnate from the Virgin *M*, 519 21
he became incarnate from the Virgin *M*, 530 12
he became incarnate from the Virgin *M*, 542 12
the fellowship of [the ever-blessed Virgin *M*, 550 26
for *M*, the mother of our Lord; 838 14
for *M* and Martha, and *M* Magdalene; 838 15
incarnate from the Virgin *M*? 849 27
our human nature from the Virgin *M*, his mother. 849 29

Mass

Liturgy, the *M*, and the Great Offering. 859 17

Massah

at Meribah, and on that day at *M*, 725 8

master

for ye know not when the *m* of the house cometh, 37 1
for you do not know when the *m* of the house will 75 1
I, your Lord and *M*, have done to you? 274 10
and none becomes his own *m* when he dies. 491 14
he is your *m*; therefore do him honor. 648 14
He set him as a *m* over his household, * 739 19

masters

As the eyes of servants look to the hand of their *m*, * 780 17

mastery

You give him *m* over the works of your hands; * 592 19

material

patterns of countless ways by which God uses *m* 861 19

matrimony

this man and this woman in Holy *M*. 423 3
make one flesh in Holy *M*. 429 6
M, may become one in heart and soul, 432 5
they may not be joined together in Holy *M*, 437 3
include confirmation, ordination, holy *m*, 860 10
What is Holy *M*? 861 3
Holy *M* is Christian marriage, 861 4

matter

their only thought is, "God does not *m*." 594 26
no *m* how skillful his charming. 665 4

matters

they charge me with *m* I know nothing about. 630 14
I do not occupy myself with great *m*, * 785 12

Matthew

apostle and evangelist *M* to the Gospel of thy Son 192 20
apostle and evangelist *M* to the Gospel of your Son 244 8

Matthias

faithful servant *M* to be of the number of the Twelve: 188 2
faithful servant *M* to be numbered among the Twelve: 239 12
they appointed *M* to be one of their number. 514 15

mature

Confirmation is the rite in which we express a *m* 860 18

mayors

to Governors of States, *M* of Cities, 821 20

meadows

the *m*, shall vanish; 634 26
May the *m* cover themselves with flocks, 673 15

mean

What does it *m* to be created in the image of God? 845 4
What does this *m*? 846 6
What does this *m* about our place in the universe? 846 9
What does this *m* about human life? 846 13
What do we *m* when we say that Jesus is 849 19
We *m* that Jesus is the only perfect image 849 21
What do we *m* when we say that Jesus was 849 25
We *m* that by God's own act, 849 28
What do we *m* when we say that he descended 850 13
We *m* that he went to the departed and offered 850 15
What do we *m* when we say that he ascended 850 17
We *m* that Jesus took our human nature 850 19
What do we *m* by the coming of Christ in glory? 862 1
By the coming of Christ in glory, we *m* that Christ 862 2
What do we *m* by heaven and hell? 862 5
By heaven, we *m* eternal life in our enjoyment of God; 862 6
by hell, we *m* eternal death in our rejection of God. 862 7
What do we *m* by the last judgment? 862 13
What do we *m* by the resurrection of the body? 862 16
We *m* that God will raise us from death in the 862 17
What do we *m* by everlasting life? 862 25
By everlasting life, we *m* a new existence, 862 26

meaning

How do we understand the *m* of the Bible? 853 27
We understand the *m* of the Bible by the help 853 28

means

for the *m* of grace, and for the hope of glory. 58 23
for the *m* of grace, and for the hope of glory. 71 19
for the *m* of grace, and for the hope of glory. 101 15
for the *m* of grace, and for the hope of glory. 125 13
of shameful death to be unto us the *m* of life: 168 18
of shameful death to be for us the *m* of life: 220 9
By *m* of this holy bread and cup, 403 14
and bless the *m* made use of for his cure. 459 8
It *m* that we are free to make choices: 845 5
This *m* that the universe is good, 846 7
It *m* that the world belongs to its creator; 846 10
It *m* that all people are worthy of respect 846 14
m by which we receive that grace. 857 28
Although they are *m* of grace, 860 14

meant

What is *m* by a covenant with God? 846 20
What is *m* by the Messiah? 849 11

measure

But your merciful promise is beyond all *m*; * 91 3
Mercifully grant unto us such a *m* 182 13
Make us glad by the *m* of the days 719 3
take failure, not as a *m* of their worth, 829 18

meat

My tears have been my *m* day and night, * 471 5
or to provide *m* for his people?" 696 16

mediation

but through the merits and *m* of Jesus 183 3
except through the merits and *m* of Jesus 234 17
through the *m* of Jesus Christ, 532 27

mediator

our only *M* and Advocate, 155 13
our only *M* and Advocate. 330 8
our only *M* and Advocate. 395 16
our only *M* and Advocate. 487 22
our *M* and Redeemer. 505 9
our *M* and Advocate. 572 12
for the honor of our Advocate and *M*, Jesus Christ. 817 9

meditate

and they *m* on his law day and night. 585 6
and my heart shall *m* on understanding. 652 10
and *m* on you in the night watches. 670 24
I will *m* on all your acts * 693 24
I will *m* on your commandments * 764 13
I will *m* on your statutes. 765 6
that I may *m* on your marvelous works. 765 14
and I will *m* on your statutes. 767 10
but I will *m* on your commandments. 769 22
that I may *m* upon your promise. 775 23

meditating

m on God's holy Word. 265 13

meditation

Let the words of my mouth, and the *m* of my heart, 40 13
Let the words of my mouth and the *m* of my heart 78 12
May the words of our mouth, and the *m* of our heart, 571 4
consider my *m*. 588 18
Let the words of my mouth and the *m* of my heart 607 28

meek

and hath exalted the humble and *m*. 50 14
and hath exalted the humble and *m*. 65 17
that, with *m* heart and due reverence, 329 14
O God, by whom the *m* are guided in judgment, 832 6

meet

which hath made us *m* to be partakers 40 1
It is *m* and right so to do. 333 6
It is very *m*, right, and our bounden duty, 333 7
It is *m* and right so to do. 340 14
It is very *m*, right, and our bounden duty, 341 1
may have strength to *m* the days ahead in the comfort 481 11
and strength to *m* the days to come; 494 11
that they may have strength to *m* the days to come 505 11
For you *m* him with blessings of prosperity, * 609 1
My merciful God comes to *m* me; * 666 16
let your compassion be swift to *m* us; * 701 22
those in authority, and to *m* their just demands; 848 5

meeting

They burned down all the *m*-places of God 689 25

Melchizedek

"You are a priest for ever after the order of *M*." 753 20

melody

I will sing and make *m*. 664 11
and to the *m* of the harp. 721 2
I will sing and make *m*. 749 18

melt

m me down; you will find no impurity in me. 601 4
God has spoken, and the earth shall *m* away. 649 16
The mountains *m* like wax at the presence 727 5

melted

their hearts *m* because of their peril. 748 8

melting

my heart within my breast is *m* wax. 611 7

melts

Let them be like the snail that *m* away, * 665 9
as the wax *m* at the fire, so let the wicked perish 676 4
My soul *m* away for sorrow; * 765 15
He sends forth his word and *m* them; * 805 13

member

we recognize you as a *m* of the one holy catholic 310 1
Grant that every *m* of the Church may truly 387 3
we recognize you as a *m* of the one holy catholic 418 17
m(s) of this Christian family, 440 9
to be a *m* of their family. 440 14

members

thee for all *m* of thy holy Church, 57 22
with the saints and *m* of the household 78 2
you for all *m* of your holy Church, 100 14
thee for all *m* of thy holy Church, 206 4
you for all *m* of your holy Church, 257 1
you for all *m* of your holy Church, 278 14
For the *M* and Representatives of the United Nations 278 21
her *m*, dispersed throughout the world, 285 3
and *m* one of another. 316 7

m incorporate in the mystical body of thy Son, 339 7
you have graciously accepted us as living *m* 365 10
that we are living *m* of the Body of your Son, 366 6
For all *m* of your Church in their vocation 548 16
For his family [the *m* of his household 549 12
Be with us in the fullness of your power as new *m* 569 5
To the President and *m* of the Cabinet, 821 19
and become living *m* of Christ. 850 25
all baptized persons are *m*. 854 8
consecrates its *m*, and guides them 854 19
through the ministry of all its *m*. 855 10
and makes us *m* of Christ's Body, 858 10

membership

m in Christ, and redemption 858 26

memorial

hath left unto us a *m* of his passion: 201 2
has left us a *m* of his passion: 252 7
the *m* thy Son hath commanded us to make; 335 12
the *m* thy Son hath commanded us to make; 342 12
We celebrate the *m* of our redemption, O Father, 363 10
Father, we now celebrate this *m* of our redemption. 374 24
Father, we now celebrate the *m* of your Son. 403 13
our sacrifice of praise, this *m* of our redemption. 405 13
hast left unto us a *m* of thy passion: 834 13

memory

a perpetual *m* of that his precious death and sacrifice, 334 15
a perpetual *m* of that his precious death and sacrifice, 341 19
and blessed us with *m*, reason, and skill. 370 13
Fill my *m* with the record of your mighty works; 562 12
their cities plowed under, the *m* of them perished; 593 12

men

Behold, the tabernacle of God is with *m*, 37 11
O ye children of *m*, bless ye the Lord; * 48 27
O ye holy and humble *m* of heart, bless ye the Lord; 49 6
and on earth peace, good will towards *m*. 52 4
loving-kindness to us and to all *m*. 58 18
m and women everywhere love thee and serve thee 70 17
loving-kindness to us and to all *m*. 71 14
O *m* and women everywhere, glorify the Lord, * 89 16
must shed light among your fellow *m*, 109 11
m and women everywhere love you 124 14
order the unruly wills and affections of sinful *m*: 167 16
ministries of angels and *m* in a wonderful order: 193 5
company of angels and to the spirits of just *m* 198 24
ministries of angels and *m* in a wonderful order: 200 7
company of angels, and to the spirits of just *m* 250 9
and on earth peace, good will towards *m*. 324 15
who for us *m* and for our salvation 328 1
and to give thanks for all *m*: 329 3
maker of all things, judge of all *m*: 331 3
and worthy of all *m* to be received, 332 13
and worthy of all *m* to be received, 449 18
again you sayest, Come again, ye children of *m*. 472 15
and though *m* be so strong that they come 473 4
You are the fairest of *m*; * 647 14
They were like *m* coming up with axes to a grove 689 18
he slew their strongest *m* 697 12
The fire consumed their young *m*; * 700 5
and a band of violent *m* seeks my life; * 711 2
Young *m* and maidens, * 806 17
beseech thee for all sorts and conditions of *m*; 814 7
keeping all the *m* and women of our armed forces 823 2
m and women everywhere may give thee thanks; 825 12
that *m* and women everywhere may give thee thanks 828 6
not willingly afflict or grieve the children of *m*: 831 12
For all that is gracious in the lives of *m* and women, 837 6
We thank you for the *m* and women who have made 839 4
the *m* and women of our country who in the day 839 22

mercies

To the Lord our God belong *m* and forgivenesses, 38 20
Almighty God, Father of all *m* 58 14
give us that due sense of all thy *m*, 59 2
thy tender *m*' sake. 69 11
Almighty God, Father of all *m*, 71 10
give us that due sense of all thy *m*, 71 21
Almighty God, Father of all *m*, 101 7
And, we pray, give us such an awareness of your *m*, 101 16
for your tender *m*' sake. 107 11
for your tender *m*' sake. 123 10
through the *m* of Christ Jesus our Savior. 123 20
Almighty God, Father of all *m*, 125 5
And, we pray, give us such an awareness of your *m*, 125 14
for your *m*' sake. 138 14
and great *m*. 337 11
I beseech you, brethren, by the *m* of God, 343 14
I appeal to you, brethren, by the *m* of God, 376 10
in the multitude of your *m*, 395 4
O Father of *m* and God of all comfort, 458 1
and your *m* are new every morning: 460 16
O God, whose *m* cannot be numbered: 470 1
and whose *m* cannot be numbered: 489 3
Almighty God, Father of *m* and giver of all comfort: 489 30
O God, whose *m* cannot be numbered: 493 10
and whose *m* cannot be numbered: 504 1
for your tender *m*' sake. 504 25
Almighty God, Father of *m* and giver of comfort: 505 17
Father of *m* and God of all comfort, 520 11
and all occasions invite your tender *m*: 572 10
and consider well the *m* of the LORD. 749 16
Give us grateful hearts, our Father, for all thy *m*, 835 8
For these and all his *m*, God's holy Name be blessed 835 16
Above all, we give you thanks for the great *m* 837 21
give us a just sense of these great *m*, 840 20

merciful

for he is gracious and *m*, 38 15
Almighty and most *m* Father, 41 16
and grant, O most *m* Father, for his sake, 42 8
The Almighty and *m* Lord grant you absolution 42 11
Almighty and most *m* Father, 62 16
and grant, O most *m* Father, for his sake, 63 11
The Almighty and *m* Lord grant you absolution 63 14
beseech thy *m* protection all the night. 70 7
for he is gracious and *m*, 76 14
Most *m* God, 79 10
But your *m* promise is beyond all measure; * 91 3
Almighty and most *m* God, kindle within us the fire 111 4
Most *m* God, 116 12
Be present, O *m* God, and protect us 133 13
The almighty and *m* Lord, Father, Son, 135 14

The almighty and *m* Lord, Father, Son, 140 17
M God, who didst send thy messengers the prophets 159 9
most *m* God, of thy bountiful goodness 177 3
thy *m* guiding may perform the same; 178 3
Grant, we beseech thee, *m* God, that thy Church, 181 5
Almighty and *m* God, of whose only gift it cometh 184 1
Almighty and most *m* God, grant, we beseech thee, 200 1
O *m* Creator, whose hand is open wide to satisfy 208 9
M God, who sent your messengers the prophets 211 9
Almighty and *m* God, in your goodness keep us, 228 14
your *m* guiding may do them; 229 17
Grant, O *m* God, that your Church, being gathered 232 17
Almighty and *m* God, it is only by your gift 235 14
Almighty and most *m* God, grant 251 7
O *m* Creator, your hand is open wide to satisfy 259 11
Most holy and *m* Father: 267 12
M God, Creator of all the peoples of the earth 280 1
May God be *m* to us and bless us, 281 5
All praise and thanks to you, most *m* Father, 311 15
Most *m* God, 320 10
Almighty and most *m* Father, 320 23
and grant, O most *m* Father, for his sake, 321 11
The Almighty and *m* Lord grant you absolution 321 14
have mercy upon us, most *m* Father; 331 14
Most *m* God, 331 21
And we most humbly beseech thee, O *m* Father, 335 17
not presume to come to this thy Table, O *m* Lord, 337 9
And we most humbly beseech thee, O *m* Father, 342 16
Most *m* God, 352 10
Most *m* God, 360 2
Have mercy upon us, most *m* Father; 393 9
Most *m* God, 397 19
Grant, most *m* Father, 444 4
Most *m* God, 454 1
Into your hands, O *m* Savior, we commend 465 1
yea, our God is *m*. 479 9
Into thy hands, O *m* Savior, we commend 483 6
O holy and most *m* Savior, 484 9
shut not thy *m* ears to our prayer; 484 12
O holy and *m* Savior, 484 14
a faithful Creator and most *m* Savior, 488 14
Holy and *m* Savior, 492 10
Most *m* God, whose wisdom is beyond 494 7
Into your hands, O *m* Savior, we commend 499 13
M God, Father of our Lord Jesus Christ who is 505 1
Grant this, O *m* Father, through Jesus Christ, 505 8
Will you be *m* to all, show compassion 518 28
O God, most *m* Father, we praise you for sending 545 1
I said, "Lord, be *m* to me; * 642 6
But you, O Lord, be *m* to me and raise me up, * 642 20
Be *m* to me, O God, be *m*, 663 19
My *m* God comes to meet me; * 666 16
for you, O God, are my stronghold and my *m* God. 667 8
May God be *m* to us and bless us, * 675 9
But he was so *m* that he forgave their sins 698 1
Be *m* to me, O Lord, for you are my God; * 710 3
But the *m* goodness of the Lord endures for ever 734 15
the righteous are *m* and full of compassion. 755 12
be *m* to me according to your promise. 768 4
and *m* in all his deeds. 802 14
commend this nation to thy *m* care, 820 17
Christ, our *m* and righteous Judge. 823 16
Almighty and most *m* God, we remember 826 1
O *m* Father, who hast taught us in thy holy Word 831 11
and for all the other blessings of thy *m* providence 840 18

mercifully

M grant that we, walking in the way of the cross, 56 8
M grant that we, walking in the way of the cross, 99 3
We beseech thee *m* to incline thine ear 153 20
M forgive the sins of thy people. 154 18
We humbly beseech thee, O Father, *m* to look 155 7
M hear the supplications 164 2
M accept our prayers; 164 12
M grant that we may both follow 168 5
M grant that we, walking in the way 168 12
M grant that we may thankfully receive 169 9
M give us faith to perceive that, 174 10
O Lord, we beseech thee *m* to receive the prayers 179 10
m give us for the worthiness 179 20
m grant that thy Holy Spirit may in all things 182 2
M grant unto us such a measure 182 13
M grant that the peoples of the earth, 185 3
M grant that by thy grace we may 191 3
M grant that we, being delivered 191 17
M grant that we, who glory 192 15
M grant that, as thy holy angels always serve 193 5
M grant that, as thy holy angels always serve 200 7
M grant that the peoples of the earth, 203 1
M hear the supplications 215 14
M accept our prayers; 216 7
M grant that we may walk in the way of his suffering, 219 16
M grant that we, walking in the way of the cross, 220 3
M grant that we may receive it thankfully 221 3
M give us faith to perceive that, 226 3
O Lord, *m* receive the prayers of your people 231 4
and *m* give us those things 231 12
m grant that your Holy Spirit may in all things direct 233 15
M grant that the peoples of the earth, 236 16
M grant that by your grace 242 10
M grant that we, being delivered 243 3
M grant that we, who glory 244 3
M grant that, as your holy angels always serve 244 15
M grant that, as your holy angels always serve 251 14
M grant that the peoples of the earth, 254 3
Assist us *m* with your help, O Lord God 270 4
M grant that we, walking in the way of the cross, 272 3
M grant that we may walk in the way of his suffering, 272 10
M grant that we may receive it thankfully 274 3
And we earnestly desire thy fatherly goodness *m* 335 24
M accept the prayers of your people, 394 10
M grant that we may receive it thankfully 397 15
Look *m* upon this man and this woman 425 8
the Lord *m* with his favor look upon you, 431 10
M accept our prayers, and grant 458 12
That it may please you *m* to pardon all his sins, 463 15
Assist us *m*, O Lord, in these our supplications 832 18
We beseech thee *m* to incline thine ear 834 2

mercy

obtain forgiveness by his infinite goodness and *m*. 41 14
But thou, O Lord, have *m* upon us, 42 3
The Lord is full of compassion and *m*: 43 6
The *m* of the Lord is everlasting: 44 5

his _m_ is everlasting; *	45	21
And his _m_ is on them that fear him *	50	9
He remembering his _m_ hath holpen his servant	50	17
To perform the _m_ promised to our forefathers, *	51	3
Through the tender _m_ of our God, *	51	16
have _m_ upon us.	52	13
O Lord, show thy _m_ upon us;	55	1
O Lord, have _m_ upon us, have _m_ upon us.	55	20
O Lord, let thy _m_ be upon us;	55	21
obtain forgiveness by his infinite goodness and _m_.	62	14
But thou, O Lord, have _m_ upon us,	63	6
And his _m_ is on them that fear him *	65	12
He remembering his _m_ hath holpen his servant	65	20
O Lord, show thy _m_ upon us;	67	16
by thy great _m_ defend us from all perils	70	2
To the Lord our God belong _m_ and forgiveness,	76	19
obtain forgiveness by his infinite goodness and _m_.	79	8
have _m_ on us and forgive us;	79	19
Almighty God have _m_ on you,	80	1
The Lord is full of compassion and _m_:	81	2
The _m_ of the Lord is everlasting:	81	14
his _m_ is everlasting; *	83	8
long-suffering, and abounding in _m_.	91	6
in accordance with your great _m_, *	91	23
He has _m_ on those who fear him *	92	4
for he has remembered his promise of _m_,	92	13
He promised to show _m_ to our fathers *	92	25
have _m_ on us;	95	6
Show us your _m_, O Lord;	97	18
Have _m_ on us, Lord, have _m_.	98	14
Lord, show us your love and _m_;	98	15
Lord, have _m_.	106	11
Christ, have _m_.	106	12
His _m_ endures for ever.	109	6
implore you of your great _m_ that,	110	14
great _m_ defend us from all perils and dangers	111	2
obtain forgiveness by his infinite goodness and _m_.	116	10
have _m_ on us and forgive us;	117	2
Almighty God have _m_ on you,	117	6
he has _m_ on those who fear him *	119	10
for he has remembered his promise of _m_,	119	19
Show us your _m_, O Lord;	121	18
in your great _m_ defend us from all perils	123	21
have _m_ on me and hear my prayer.	128	10
Lord, have _m_.	132	16
Christ, have _m_.	132	17
in your great _m_ defend us from all perils	133	10
By his great _m_ we have been born anew	137	12
Have _m_ upon us.	148	2
and by thy _m_ preserve us for ever.	148	12
that they may do justice, and love _m_,	150	27
That it may please thee to have _m_ upon all mankind,	152	1
Have _m_ upon us.	152	25
Lord, have _m_ upon us.	153	3
Christ, have _m_ upon us.	153	4
O Lord, let thy _m_ be showed upon us;	153	16
Favorably with _m_ hear our prayers;	155	1
O Son of David, have _m_ upon us.	155	2
put our whole trust and confidence in thy _m_,	155	11
let thy bountiful grace and _m_ speedily help	160	3
may obtain of thee, the God of all _m_,	166	5
O God, whose glory it is always to have _m_:	166	16
Increase and multiply upon us thy _m_,	180	3
not forsake those who make their boast of thy _m_;	181	20
power chiefly in showing _m_ and pity:	182	13
Pour down upon us the abundance of thy _m_,	183	1
Preserve the works of thy _m_,	183	13
we beseech thee, into the arms of thy _m_	186	15
devotion make known the love and _m_ of our Lord	194	5
through thy _m_, we may with him attain	198	19
surrounded by their witness to thy power and _m_.	199	8
let your bountiful grace and _m_ speedily help	212	3
may obtain of you, the God of all _m_,	217	18
O God, whose glory it is always to have _m_:	218	7
Increase and multiply upon us your _m_;	231	19
Let your continual _m_, O Lord, cleanse and defend	232	1
never forsake those who make their boast of your _m_;	233	12
power chiefly in showing _m_ and pity:	234	7
Pour upon us the abundance of your _m_,	234	14
Preserve the works of your _m_,	235	5
into the arms of your _m_ all innocent victims;	238	9
devotion make known the love and _m_ of our Lord	245	13
witness to your power and _m_.	250	18
may obtain of you, the God of all _m_,	264	6
Have _m_ on me, O God,	266	1
Have _m_ on us, Lord.	267	22
Favorably hear us, for your _m_ is great.	268	28
That God in his _m_ will comfort and relieve them,	279	11
that they may find your _m_ present with them	279	16
Give _m_ and grace to the living;	282	8
O God, is your _m_ and loving-kindness to us,	287	15
His _m_ endures for ever.	299	6
in the arms of your _m_, and keep him safe for ever.	314	5
Lord, have _m_ upon us,	317	28
His _m_ endureth for ever.	319	7
that we may obtain _m_, and find grace	320	7
have _m_ on us and forgive us;	320	19
But thou, O Lord, have _m_ upon us,	321	6
His _m_ endureth for ever.	323	6
Lord, have _m_ upon us.	324	7
Christ, have _m_ upon us.	324	8
Have _m_ upon us.	324	13
have _m_ upon us.	324	24
have _m_ upon us.	325	4
Have _m_ upon us,	331	13
have _m_ upon us, most merciful Father;	331	14
have _m_ on us and forgive us;	331	30
our heavenly Father, who of his great _m_	332	1
have _m_ upon you,	332	3
of thy tender _m_, didst give thine only Son	334	10
have _m_ upon us.	337	4
whose property is always to have _m_.	337	13
and, of thy tender _m_, didst give thine only Son	341	14
and in works of _m_, and renewed by thy Word	346	10
Lord have _m_.	350	4
His _m_ endures for ever.	351	6
that we may receive _m_ and find grace	352	7
have _m_ on us and forgive us;	352	19
Almighty God have _m_ on you,	353	1
His _m_ endures for ever.	355	6
have _m_ on us;	356	10
Lord, have _m_.	356	19
Christ, have _m_.	356	20
Have _m_ upon us.	356	25

have *m* on us and forgive us;	360	11
Almighty God have *m* on you,	360	15
you, in your *m*, sent Jesus	362	11
Have *m*, Lord, for we are sinners in your sight.	370	16
In your *m* you came to our help,	373	22
Lord, we pray that in your goodness and *m*	375	4
works of *m*, and renewed by your Word	379	7
Lord, saying, "Lord, have *m*."	383	2
Lord, have *m*.	383	5
Lord, in your *m*	388	5
We commend to your *m* all who have died,	389	8
Lord, in your *m*	389	11
let us pray to the Lord, saying, "Lord, have *m*"	389	13
Lord, have *m*.	389	18
For your *m* is great.	392	19
Have *m* upon us, most merciful Father;	393	9
surrounded by their witness to your power and *m*.	395	21
have *m* on us and forgive us;	398	3
Almighty God have *m* on you,	398	7
have *m* on us.	407	2
His *m* endures for ever.	413	6
Finally, in your *m*, bring them to that table	430	22
He has *m* on those who fear him*	441	18
for he has remembered his promise of *m*,	442	8
Surely your goodness and *m* shall follow me	443	15
I pray God to have *m* on me.	447	9
his great *m* forgive you all your offenses;	448	3
Have *m* on me, O God, according to your loving-	449	1
have *m* upon us.	449	8
remember in truth all your sins and his unfailing *m*.	449	11
Receive me again into the arms of your *m*,	450	18
May Almighty God in *m* receive your confession	451	3
his great *m* forgive you all your offenses;	451	13
have *m* on us and forgive us;	455	2
Almighty God have *m* on you,	455	6
Of his great *m*, may he forgive you	456	15
Look upon him with the eyes of thy *m*;	458	4
Have *m* on your servant.	462	6
Have *m* on him.	463	24
Lord, have *m*.	464	1
Christ, have *m*.	464	2
Receive him into the arms of your *m*,	465	4
through the *m* of God, rest in peace.	465	8
Remember them, Lord, in *m*;	467	4
For there is *m* with thee, *	474	7
for with the LORD there is *m*, *	474	14
Surely thy loving-kindness and *m* shall follow me	476	16
Surely goodness and *m* shall follow me	477	9
have *m* upon me, and hear me.	477	29
and his *m* endureth for ever.	478	12
receive him into the arms of thy *m*,	481	18
Receive him into the arms of thy *m*,	483	9
And of thy *m*, O heavenly Father, grant	486	12
through the *m* of God, rest in peace.	486	20
Grant to them thy *m* and the light of thy presence;	488	29
Give *m* and grace to the living,	489	25
through the *m* of God, rest in peace.	498	11
Receive him into the arms of your *m*,	499	16
through the *m* of God, rest in peace.	502	18
His *m* endures for ever.	512	6
The blessing, *m*, and grace of God Almighty,	523	15
His *m* endures for ever.	525	6
His *m* endures for ever.	537	6
Have *m* on us.	548	2
Lord, have *m*.	551	1
Christ, have *m*.	551	2
have *m* on me and hear my prayer.	587	22
through the greatness of your *m* I will	589	3
save me for your *m*'s sake.	590	6
But I put my trust in your *m*; *	598	8
Surely your goodness and *m* shall follow me	613	11
have *m* on me and answer me.	618	11
Hear, O LORD, and have *m* upon me; *	622	1
I will rejoice and be glad because of your *m*; *	622	22
Have *m* on me, O LORD, for I am in trouble; *	623	3
but *m* embraces those who trust in the LORD.	625	24
Have *m* on me, O God,	656	5
I trust in the *m* of God for ever and ever.	658	17
Have *m* on me, O God,	662	12
show no *m* to those who are faithless and evil.	666	6
"In your great *m*, O God, *	680	15
Show us your *m*, O LORD, *	709	7
M and truth have met together; *	709	14
Turn to me and have *m* upon me; *	711	6
He remembers his *m* and faithfulness	728	6
his *m* is everlasting; *	730	5
I will sing of *m* and justice; *	730	7
for it is time to have *m* upon her; *	732	2
and crowns you with *m* and loving-kindness;	733	16
The LORD is full of compassion and *m*, *	733	23
so is his *m* great upon those who fear him.	734	4
for his *m* endures for ever.	741	20
and relented in accordance with his great *m*.	745	16
and his *m* endures for ever.	746	2
Let them give thanks to the LORD for his *m* *	746	16
Let them give thanks to the LORD for his *m* *	747	11
Let them give thanks to the LORD for his *m* *	748	17
Because he did not remember to show *m*, *	752	1
for your tender *m*'s sake, deliver me.	752	18
save me for your *m*'s sake.	752	28
his *m* endures for ever.	760	21
"His *m* endures for ever."	760	23
"His *m* endures for ever."	761	2
his *m* endures for ever.	763	4
Turn to me in *m*, *	774	11
O LORD, in your *m*, preserve me.	776	22
until he show us his *m*.	780	20
Have *m* upon us, O LORD, have *m*, *	780	21
for with the LORD there is *m*;	785	7
for his *m* endures for ever.	789	21
Have *m* upon all of us who live and work	825	19
Have *m* upon us.	826	10
this we ask for your *m*'s sake.	826	26
Look with *m*, O God our Father, on all	830	1
Remember him, O Lord, in *m*,	831	14
the assurance of your unfailing *m*;	831	21
and finally, by thy *m*, obtain everlasting life;	832	4
Then in thy *m*, grant us a safe lodging,	833	17
In your *m*, O Lord our God, give us,	838	17
to do *m*, and to walk humbly with their God.	847	5

mere

so that *m* mortals may strike terror no more. 596 6
You have given me a *m* handful of days, 639 3
m mortals that you should think of us? 800 7

Meribah

and tested you at the waters of *M*. 704 16
at *M*, and on that day at Massah, 725 8
Again they provoked his anger at the waters of *M*, * 744 11

merits

through the *m* of Jesus Christ our Savior. 69 21
through the *m* of Christ Jesus our Savior, 175 18
but through the *m* and mediation of Jesus 183 3
except through the *m* and mediation of Jesus 234 17
by the *m* and death of thy Son 335 26
our bounded duty and service, not weighing our *m*, 336 11
through the *m* of Jesus Christ thine only Son 488 20
through the *m* of thy Son Jesus Christ our Lord. 489 22
through the *m* of your Son Jesus Christ our Lord. 504 20

merry

let them also be *m* and joyful. 676 7
the *m* harp, and the lyre. 704 4

Meshech

How hateful it is that I must lodge in *M* * 778 18

message

and their *m* to the ends of the world. 78 4
was put in mind of the *m* of pardon and absolution 265 7
and their *m* to the ends of the world. 606 22

messengers

Merciful God, who didst send thy *m* the prophets 159 9
Merciful God, who sent your *m* the prophets 211 9
You make the winds your *m* * 735 9

Messiah

to confess Jesus as *M* and Son of the living God: 187 2
to confess Jesus as *M* and Son of the living God: 238 15
as the *M*, the Christ, to lead us, 306 18
as the *M*, the Christ, to lead us, 570 10
announce the coming of the *M*. 849 10
What is meant by the *M*? 849 11
The *M* is one sent by God to free us 849 12
Who do we believe is the *M*? 849 16
The *M*, or Christ, is Jesus of Nazareth, 849 17
given by Jesus Christ, the *M*, to the apostles; 850 28
What did the *M* promise in the New Covenant? 851 1

met

Mercy and truth have *m* together; * 709 14

mid

nor of the sickness that lays waste at *m*-day. 130 9
nor of the sickness that lays waste at mid-day. 719 23

Midian

Do to them as you did to *M*, * 706 20

midnight

cometh, at even, or at *m*, or at the cock-crowing, 37 2
come, in the evening, or at *m*, or at cockcrow, 75 2
At *m* I will rise to give you thanks, * 768 11

midst

thou wilt be in the *m* of them: 59 16
thou wilt be in the *m* of them: 72 13
one in the *m* of you is the Holy One of Israel. 86 14
you will be in the *m* of them: 102 5
you will be in the *m* of them: 126 5
Lord, you are in the *m* of us, and we are called 131 12
Lord, you are in the *m* of us and we are called 140 5
in the *m* of you, O Jerusalem. 442 26
and though the hills be carried into the *m* of the sea; 471 20
God is in the *m* of her, 472 1
Help us, we pray, in the *m* of things 481 14
In the *m* of life we are in death; 484 4
in the *m* of this earthly life being purged 488 18
In the *m* of life we are in death; 492 5
May he exalt you, O Lord, in the *m* of your people; 534 1
in the *m* of the congregation I will praise you. 611 25
God is in the *m* of her; 649 12
in the *m* of your temple. 651 19
but trouble and misery are in the *m* of her. 661 3
for wickedness is in their dwellings, in their very *m*. 661 16
I lie in the *m* of lions that devour the people; * 664 1
in the *m* of maidens playing upon the hand-drums. 678 8
victorious in the *m* of the earth. 690 9
He let it fall in the *m* of their camp * 697 5
he gives judgment in the *m* of the gods: 705 10
do not take me away in the *m* of my days; * 732 25
in the *m* of the multitude will I praise him; 753 9
in the *m* of you, O Jerusalem. 760 13
signs and wonders into the *m* of you, O Egypt, * 788 19
And made Israel to pass through the *m* of it, * 790 23
on the trees in the *m* of that land. 792 4
Though I walk in the *m* of trouble, you keep me 793 16
in the *m* of our struggles for justice and truth, 824 2

might

the *m* of Jesus Christ our Lord. 57 6
Your right hand, O Lord, is glorious in *m*; * 85 14
with your *m* you brought them in safety 85 22
Holy, holy, holy Lord, God of power and *m*, 95 21
through the *m* of Jesus Christ our Lord. 99 24
Stir up thy power, O Lord, and with great *m* come 160 1
Lord of all power and *m*, who art the author 181 11
and by thy great *m* frustrate the designs of evil 186 16
Stir up your power, O Lord, and with great *m* come 212 1
Lord of all power and *m*, the author 233 3
by your great *m* frustrate the designs of evil 238 10
to be strengthened with *m* by his Holy Spirit, 311 23
Holy, holy, holy Lord, God of power and *m*, 362 4
Holy, holy, holy Lord, God of power and *m*, 367 13
Holy, holy, holy Lord, God of power and *m*, 371 1
Holy, holy, holy Lord, God of power and *m*, 373 12
Holy, holy, holy Lord, God of power and *m*, 402 9
Holy, holy, holy Lord, God of power and *m*, 404 11
heavenly powers, by the *m* of your command 458 16
Be exalted, O LORD, in your *m*; * 609 25
in your *m*, defend my cause. 659 18
send them reeling by your *m* 666 19
they are girded about with *m*. 672 22
In his *m* he rules for ever; 674 6
You divided the sea by your *m* * 690 10
and led out the south wind by his *m*. 697 2

and by your great *m* spare those who are 702 5
and by your favor our *m* is exalted. 714 28
They shall speak of the *m* of your wondrous acts, * 801 22
He is not impressed by the *m* of a horse; * 804 22
By the *m* of thy Spirit lift us, 832 15

mightier

M than the sound of many waters, 722 12
m than the breakers of the sea, * 722 13
m is the LORD who dwells on high. 722 14

mightily

So *m* spread abroad your Spirit, 815 24

mighty

For he that is *m* hath magnified me, * 50 7
He hath put down the *m* from their seat, * 50 13
And hath raised up a *m* salvation for us * 50 24
Defend us in the same with thy *m* power; 57 9
For he that is *m* hath magnified me, * 65 10
He hath put down the *m* from their seat, * 65 16
The Lord is a *m* warrior; * 85 7
He has cast down the *m* from their thrones, * 92 8
He has raised up for us a *m* savior, * 92 20
Preserve us with your *m* power, 100 3
he has cast down the *m* from their thrones, * 119 14
Preserve us with your *m* power, 137 15
let each one find thee *m* to save; 166 12
let each one find you *m* to save; 218 4
of those *m* acts, whereby you have given us life 270 6
for the victory of our *m* King. 286 3
you once delivered by the power of your *m* arm 289 13
Holy and *M*, 324 11
his *m* resurrection and glorious ascension; 335 14
his *m* resurrection and glorious ascension; 342 14
who, by the *m* power of the Holy Ghost, 345 15
Holy and *M*, 356 23
Your *m* works reveal your wisdom and love. 373 17
who, by the *m* power of the Holy Spirit, 378 10
He has cast down the *m* from their thrones,* 442 3
Holy God, Holy and *M*, Holy Immortal One, 449 7
Yet, O Lord God most holy, O Lord most *m*, 484 8
but spare us, Lord most holy, O God most *m*, 484 13
Holy God, Holy and *M*, 492 9
the record of your *m* works; 562 13
Here we read about your *m* acts 570 24
for they were too *m* for me. 603 27
"The LORD, strong and *m*, 614 5
the LORD, *m* in battle." 614 6
the LORD is upon the *m* waters. 620 11
There is no king that can be saved by a *m* army; * 627 7
I will praise you in the *m* throng. 631 5
Those who are my enemies without cause are *m*, * 638 7
Strap your sword upon your thigh, O *m* warrior, * 647 17
your arrows are very sharp, O *m* warrior. 647 22
how the *m* gather together against me; * 665 23
O *m* mountain, O hill of Bashan! * 677 10
he sends forth his voice, his *m* voice. 678 27
my lying foes who would destroy me are *m*. * 679 18
My mouth shall recount your *m* acts 684 9
I will begin with the *m* works of the Lord GOD; * 684 12
and ponder your *m* deeds. 693 25
O *m* LORD, your faithfulness is all around you. 714 10
you have scattered your enemies with your *m* arm. 714 14
You have a *m* arm; * 714 19
"O *m* King, lover of justice, 729 5
you *m* ones who do his bidding, * 734 23
Who can declare the *m* acts of the LORD * 741 21
Their descendants will be *m* in the land; * 755 7
and vowed a vow to the *M* One of Jacob: 786 2
a dwelling for the *M* One of Jacob." 786 8
and put *m* kings to death: 788 22
With a *m* hand and a stretched-out arm, * 790 19
And slew *m* kings, * 791 5
Great is our LORD and *m* in power; * 804 10
Praise him for his *m* acts; * 808 1

mind

prepare ourselves in heart and *m* to worship him, 41 11
may prepare ourselves in heart and *m* to worship him, 79 6
who suffer in *m*, body, and spirit; 151 25
being renewed both in body and *m*, may worship thee 170 17
so we may also in heart and *m* thither ascend, 174 17
Grant us, O Lord, not to *m* earthly things, 182 6
restored Mary Magdalene to health of body and *m*, 191 2
may fulfill all the *m* of him who loved it 204 13
being renewed both in body and *m*, may worship you 222 11
so we may also in heart and *m* there ascend, 226 10
that we, being ready both in *m* and body, 229 1
restored Mary Magdalene to health of body and of *m*, 242 9
may fulfill all the *m* of him who loved it 255 11
was put in *m* of the message of pardon 265 7
We have not loved you with our whole heart, and *m*, 267 19
We have not been true to the *m* of Christ. 267 24
who suffer and are afflicted in body or in *m*; 279 3
whole heart and *m* and voice, to praise you, 287 1
being renewed both in body and *m*, may worship you 295 11
Having in *m*, therefore, his great love for us, 316 8
with all thy soul, and with all thy *m*. 319 10
with all thy soul, and with all thy *m*. 324 3
with all your soul, with all your *m*, 351 10
With all our heart and with all our *m*, let us pray 383 1
Comfort and heal all those who suffer in body, *m*, 389 3
The union of husband and wife in heart, body, and *m* 423 9
and serve thee with a quiet *m*. 481 6
Holy Scripture, that you may have the *m* 518 5
for you test the *m* and heart, O righteous God. 591 17
How long shall I have perplexity in my *m*, 598 1
examine my heart and my *m*. 616 11
I am forgotten like a dead man, out of *m*; * 623 14
The human *m* and heart are a mystery; * 671 23
When my *m* became embittered, * 688 19
I ponder and search my *m*. 693 13
and call to *m* your wonders of old time. 693 23
I have borne your terrors with a troubled *m*. 713 10
When many cares fill my *m*, * 724 3
I will apply my *m* to your decrees. 771 10
all the day long it is in my *m*. 771 14
afflicted or distressed, in *m*, body, or estate; 815 8
to be of one heart and *m* within your holy Church; 817 22
of faith and charity, and may with one *m* 818 22
in making the heart of this people wise, its *m* sound, 827 9
from coldness of heart and wanderings of *m*, 833 21

with all your soul, and with all your *m*. 851 12
Adoration is the lifting up of the heart and *m* to God, 857 2
healing of spirit, *m*, and body. 861 16

mindful

that we, being *m* of their victory of faith, may glorify 189 7
make us *m* of the rightful aspirations 210 14
that we, being *m* of their victory of faith, may glorify 240 15
make us *m* of the rightful aspirations 261 19
What is man that you should be *m* of him? * 592 15
He has always been *m* of his covenant, * 738 15
he is ever *m* of his covenant. 754 15
The Lord has been *m* of us, and he will bless us; * 758 12
a people *m* of thy favor and glad to do thy will. 820 3
and make them ever *m* of their calling 820 22
make us *m* of the needs of others; 835 9

minds

it surpasses all that our *m* can fathom. 91 4
so that our *m* may be fixed on the doing of your will, 123 17
O God, you will keep in perfect peace those whose *m* 138 9
spirit of our *m*, and live in righteousness 201 15
spirit of our *m*, and live in righteousness 253 3
that with pure *m* we may attain to the festival 285 11
keep your hearts and *m* in the knowledge and love 339 16
promised to those whose *m* are fixed on you; 461 15
Christ, enlightening the *m* and stirring 518 9
Their iniquity comes from gross *m*, * 687 13
guide the *m* of those who shall choose a bishop 818 9
the hearts and *m* of your servants ready to receive 819 3
leisure to rebuild our bodies and renew our *m*, 825 3
so guide our *m*, so fill our imaginations, 832 25
For *m* to think, and hearts to love, 837 12
God forgives our sins, enlightens our *m*, 858 4

mingled

and *m* my drink with weeping. 731 18

minister

and *m* thy justice with compassion; 178 8
that they may *m* in thy household 197 7
power of healing to those who *m* to their needs, 208 18
Son came not to be ministered unto but to *m*: 209 10
they may *m* in his name to the suffering, 209 13
and *m* your justice with compassion; 230 3
that they may *m* in your household 248 18
those who *m* to their needs, 260 3
they may *m* in his Name to the suffering, 260 18
will and patience to *m* to their needs. 279 13
[Remember (NN. and) all who *m* in your Church.] 375 15
For those who *m* to the sick, 392 10
Now, in the presence of Christ, and of me, his *m*, 450 5
power of healing to those who *m* to his needs, 459 19
others who *m* in the Church? 518 26
a stronger and more able *m* of Christ? 532 7
Will you endeavor so to *m* the Word of God 532 9

ministered

Son came not to be *m* unto but to minister: 209 10
O blessed Lord, you *m* to all who came to you: 831 18

ministers

Endue thy *m* with righteousness; 55 3
Endue thy *m* with righteousness; 67 18
Clothe your *m* with righteousness; 97 20
Clothe your *m* with righteousness; 121 20
O God, who didst lead thy holy apostles to ordain *m* 205 14
O God, you led your holy apostles to ordain *m* 256 11
commandment to his *m* to declare and pronounce 269 6
For all bishops and other *m* 278 4
m [especially ________], that they may, 329 10
and for all *m* and people. 385 19
That they may be faithful *m* of your Word 387 7
for all bishops and other *m*, 390 2
for] all bishops and other *m*; 392 15
and other *m* who may have authority over you 526 12
with them and with your fellow *m* to build 532 16
and other *m* who may have authority over you 538 12
and *m* to them in their illness. 642 5
you *m* of his who do his will. 734 26
Who are the *m* of the Church? 855 11
The *m* of the Church are lay persons, bishops, 855 12

ministration

and in the *m* of God's Word 543 14
and to assist in the *m* of his holy Sacraments. 545 20

ministrations

and to perform the other *m* entrusted to you. 531 16

ministries

m of angels and men in a wonderful order: 193 5
m of angels and men in a wonderful order: 200 7
m of angels and mortals: 244 14
m of angels and mortals: 251 13
that by their *m* the health of the community 460 13
all baptized people in their gifts and *m*, 518 14
for the many *m* in your Church, 545 7
and equip us for our *m*; 818 12

ministry

and *m* they may truly and godly serve thee; 57 23
and *m* they may truly and devoutly serve you; 100 15
Christ reconciled us to himself and gave us the *m* 106 3
called to any office and *m* for thy people; 205 7
may choose suitable persons for the *m* 205 16
and *m* they may truly and godly serve thee; 206 5
called to any office and *m* for your people; 256 4
may choose suitable persons for the *m* 256 13
and *m* they may truly and devoutly serve you; 257 2
and *m* they may truly and devoutly serve you; 278 15
absolve you through my *m* by the grace 448 9
absolve you through my *m* by the grace 451 8
from the creation you have graciously accepted the *m* 520 18
serving before you day and night in the *m* 521 11
for raising up among us faithful servants for the *m* 523 4
to the exercise of this *m*? 526 6
you know the importance of this *m*, 527 2
Will you uphold him in this *m*? 527 9
equip the saints for the work of *m* 533 9
for raising up among us faithful servants for the *m* 535 4
to the exercise of this *m*? 538 6
you know the importance of this *m*, 539 2
Will you uphold him in this *m*? 539 9
God now calls you to a special *m* of servanthood 543 3
for raising up among us faithful servants for the *m* 546 6
and *m*, that they may serve you 548 17

That he may faithfully fulfill the duties of this *m*, 549 4
these tokens of your servant's *m* and dignity. 552 8
support and uphold N. in this *m*? 559 9
let all these be signs of the *m* which is mine 562 7
carrying out the duties of my *m*. 563 5
for raising up among us faithful servants for the *m* 564 4
the *m* of his holy Word and Sacraments. 567 3
The Church carries out its mission through the *m* 855 9
What is the *m* of the laity? 855 14
The *m* of lay persons is to represent Christ 855 15
What is the *m* of a bishop? 855 21
The *m* of a bishop is to represent Christ 855 22
ordain others to continue Christ's *m*. 855 28
What is the *m* of a priest or presbyter? 856 1
The *m* of a priest is to represent Christ 856 2
What is the *m* of a deacon? 856 7
The *m* of a deacon is to represent Christ 856 8

miracle

first *m* at a wedding in Cana of Galilee. 423 6

mire

out of the desolate pit, out of the *m* and clay; * 640 3
I am sinking in deep *m*, * 679 9
Save me from the *m*; do not let me sink; * 680 17
let them be cast into the *m*, never to rise up again." 796 22

Miriam

for *M* and Joshua, Deborah and Gideon, 838 12

mirth

and our oppressors called for *m*: * 792 6

mischief

under their tongue are *m* and wrong. 595 7

misdeeds

Thou hast set our *m* before thee, * 472 25

misdoings

and are heartily sorry for these our *m*; 331 10

misery

Let the cry of those in *m* and need come 279 15
I was in *m*, and he helped me. 479 11
see the *m* I suffer from those who hate me, 594 2
Surely, you behold trouble and *m*; * 595 23
and the poor cry out in *m*, * 597 10
for I am left alone and in *m*. 615 21
Look upon my adversity and *m* * 615 24
Though you thrust us down into a place of *m*, * 646 24
but trouble and *m* are in the midst of her. 661 3
for I am poor and in *m*. 709 23
bound fast in *m* and iron; 747 2
He lifted up the poor out of *m* * 749 11

misfortune

who take pleasure in my *m*. 641 13
let those who take pleasure in my *m* 682 15

misfortunes

In the *m* of others they have no share; * 687 9

mislead

To speak the truth, and not to *m* others 848 16

mission

as they were faithful and zealous in their *m*, 194 4
as they were faithful and zealous in their *m*, 245 12
For the *m* of the Church, 390 7
For the *m* of the Church, 549 21
for the renewal and *m* of your Church. 818 3
to carry out Christ's *m* to all people. 854 27
What is the *m* of the Church? 855 1
The *m* of the Church is to restore all people 855 2
How does the Church pursue its *m*? 855 4
The Church pursues its *m* as it prays 855 5
Through whom does the Church carry out its *m*? 855 8
The Church carries out its *m* through the ministry 855 9

mistress

and the eyes of a maid to the hand of her *m*, 780 18

misused

From the beginning, human beings have *m* 845 10

Mizar

peak of *M* among the heights of Hermon. 643 20

Moab

M is my wash-basin, 668 1
M is my washbasin, 750 12

Moabites

the *M* and the Hagarenes; 706 15

mob

from the *m* of evildoers. 671 13

mock

my enemies *m* me to my face; 644 6
All day long they *m* me * 644 7

mocked

They put me to the test and *m* me; * 630 27
Remember, Lord, how your servant is *m*, * 717 14

mockers

Because of the taunts of the *m* and blasphemers, * 646 17

mockery

a *m* and derision to those around us. 646 12

model

and to *m* your life upon them. 543 8

models

They are *m* for us, though we often fall 839 5

moderate

in this time of need, such *m* rain 828 12

modest

Make him, O Lord, *m* and humble, 545 12

moisture

my *m* was dried up as in the heat of summer. 625 6

molded

and his hands have *m* the dry land. 82 14
and his hands have *m* the dry land. 724 23

molten

and worshiped a *m* image; 743 10

money
He does not give his *m* in hope of gain, * 599 15
monsters
you sea-*m* and all deeps; 806 8
moon
O ye sun and *m*, bless ye the Lord; * 48 1
thou hast established the *m* and the sun. 61 8
by night you will not need the brightness of the *m*. 87 28
Sun and *m* and stars of the sky, glorify the Lord, * 88 11
nor the *m* by night. 104 24
night; you established the *m* and the sun. 115 8
neither the *m* by night. 473 20
the *m* and the stars you have set in their courses, 592 14
He shall live as long as the sun and *m* endure, * 685 17
there shall be abundance of peace till the *m* 685 22
you established the *m* and the sun. 690 17
Blow the ram's-horn at the new *m*, * 704 5
and at the full *m*, the day of our feast. 704 6
It shall stand fast for evermore like the *m*, * 716 15
You appointed the *m* to mark the seasons, * 736 15
nor the *m* by night. 779 12
The *m* and the stars to govern the night, * 790 13
Praise him, sun and *m*; * 805 25
more
am no *m* worthy to be called thy son." 38 19
Ye are no *m* strangers and foreigners, 40 3
Christ being raised from the dead dieth no *m*; * 46 7
death hath no *m* dominion over him. 46 8
m than we can ask or imagine: 60 4
m than we can ask or imagine: 73 4
Violence will no *m* be heard in your land, * 87 23
The sun will no *m* be your light by day; * 87 27
m than we can ask or imagine: 102 15
m than we can ask or imagine: 126 15
m than when grain and wine and oil increase. 129 5
wonderfully create, and yet *m* wonderfully restore, 162 7
everlasting God, who art always *m* ready 182 18
and art wont to give *m* than either 182 19
but still *m* blessed in keeping thy word: 189 12
wonderfully create, and yet *m* wonderfully restore, 200 13
thou wilt receive him *m* and *m* 202 11
wonderfully created, and yet *m* wonderfully restored, 214 1
you are always *m* ready to hear than we to pray, 234 12
and to give *m* than we either desire 234 13
but still *m* blessed in keeping your word: 240 19
wonderfully created, and yet *m* wonderfully restored, 252 1
you will receive him *m* and *m* 253 15
m fortunate than ourselves, 268 8
wonderfully created, and yet *m* wonderfully restored, 288 5
your Holy Spirit *m* and *m*, 309 17
your Holy Spirit *m* and *m*, 418 15
Make these words *m* than words, 461 24
where sorrow and pain are no *m*, 482 10
where sorrow and pain are no *m*, 483 4
where sorrow and pain are no *m*, 499 2
make you a stronger and *m* able minister 532 6
m than when grain and wine and oil increase. 588 14
so that mere mortals may strike terror no *m*. 596 6
M to be desired are they than gold, 607 16
m than much fine gold, * 607 17
In a little while the wicked shall be no *m*; * 634 3
before I go my way and am no *m*. 639 26
but they are *m* than I can count. 640 15
they are *m* in number than the hairs of my head, 641 6
You love evil *m* than good * 658 4
and lying *m* than speaking the truth. 658 5
make an end of them, and they shall be no *m*. 666 25
who hate me without a cause are *m* than the hairs 679 16
This will please the LORD *m* than an offering of oxen, 681 26
m than bullocks with horns and hoofs. 681 27
and shall praise you *m* and *m*. 684 8
You strengthen me *m* and *m*; * 684 26
peace till the moon shall be no *m*. 685 23
I will say to the boasters, 'Boast no *m*,' * 691 10
m splendid than the everlasting mountains! 692 8
Will he no *m* show his favor? 693 15
let the name of Israel be remembered no *m*." 706 11
m than all the dwellings of Jacob. 711 14
Whom you remember no *m*, * 712 11
he is *m* to be feared than all gods. 725 24
and its place shall know it no *m*. 734 14
and the wicked be no *m*. 737 25
May the LORD increase you *m* and *m*, * 758 17
I have *m* understanding than all my teachers, * 771 17
m than gold and precious stones. 774 2
What shall be done to you, and what *m* besides, * 778 14
for we have had *m* than enough of contempt. 780 22
m than watchmen for the morning, * 785 4
If I were to count them, they would be *m* in number 795 12
M especially we pray for thy holy Church universal; 815 1
you *m* truly, and *m* surely fulfill our role 827 15
give *m* life than the ways of the world, 829 16
Since we do not fully obey them, we see *m* clearly 848 26
morning
or at the cock-crowing, or in the *m*; 37 3
turnest the shadow of death into the *m*: 56 19
that turneth deep darkness into the *m*, 62 2
pray thee, in safety to the *m* hours; 70 8
at midnight, or at cockcrow, or in the *m*, 75 3
turns the shadow of death into the *m*: 99 14
evening, the *m*, and the noonday one day; 110 24
and turns deep darkness into the *m*, 115 14
Bring us in safety to the *m* hours; 124 5
in the *m* as we celebrate the Paschal mystery; 134 4
May Christ, the *M* Star who knows 287 25
and your mercies are new every *m*: 460 17
In the *m* it is green, and groweth up; * 472 21
My soul fleeth unto the Lord before the *m* watch; * 474 11
I say, before the *m* watch. 474 12
If I take the wings of the *m*, * 475 9
In the *m*, LORD, you hear my voice; * 588 21
early in the *m* I make my appeal and watch for you. 588 22
but joy comes in the *m*. 621 15
In the evening, in the *m*, and at noonday, 661 19
I will celebrate your love in the *m*; 667 4
and punished every *m*. 688 6
in the *m* my prayer comes before you. 713 5
In the *m* it is green and flourishes; * 718 11
Satisfy us by your loving-kindness in the *m*; * 719 1
To tell of your loving-kindness early in the *m* * 720 24
like dew from the womb of the *m*." 753 18

Early in the *m* I cry out to you, * 775 20
more than watchmen for the *m*, * 785 4
more than watchmen for the *m*. 785 5
If I take the wings of the *m* * 794 16
Let me hear of your loving-kindness in the *m*, 799 15

morrow

and our worship on the *m* may give thee glory; 69 14
and our worship on the *m* give you glory; 123 13

mortal

in the time of this *m* life in which thy Son 159 3
weakness of our *m* nature, we can do no good thing 164 13
m life may hide from us the light of that love 165 10
in the time of this *m* life in which your Son 211 3
that no clouds of this *m* life 217 2
and as a mark of our *m* nature, 265 14
For prisoners and captives, and those in *m* danger 279 10
and when our *m* body doth lie in death, 349 9
ended; and when our *m* body lies in death, there is 382 4
and we are *m*, formed of the earth, 482 13
will also give life to our *m* bodies, 485 2
and we are *m*, formed of the earth, 499 5
will also give new life to our *m* bodies 501 4
let the ungodly know they are but *m*. 594 18
changes and chances of this *m* life, 832 21

mortality

m and penitence, that we may remember 265 18

mortals

"You *m*, how long will you dishonor my glory? * 128 11
the ministries of angels and *m*: 244 14
the ministries of angels and *m*: 251 13
"You *m*, how long will you dishonor my glory; * 588 1
so that mere *m* may strike terror no more. 596 6
for what can *m* do to me? 663 13
So *m* ate the bread of angels; * 696 26
Nevertheless, you shall die like *m*, * 705 22
mere *m* that you should think of us? 800 7

Moses

by the hand of *M* and Aaron. 694 18
M and Aaron among his priests, 729 11
He made his ways known to *M* * 733 21
He sent *M* his servant, * 740 5
They envied *M* in the camp, * 743 3
had not *M* his chosen stood before him 743 18
so that he punished *M* because of them; 744 12
for *M*, the lawgiver, and Aaron, 838 11
The Ten Commandments are the laws given to *M* 847 14

most

his *m* worthy praise, to hear his holy Word, 41 8
Almighty and *m* merciful Father, 41 16
and grant, O *m* merciful Father, for his sake, 42 8
art *m* high in the glory of God the Father. 52 22
Almighty God, whose *m* dear Son went not up to joy 56 6
do give thee *m* humble and hearty thanks 58 16
Almighty and *m* merciful Father, 62 16
and grant, O *m* merciful Father, for his sake, 63 11
do give thee *m* humble and hearty thanks 71 12
M merciful God, 79 10
shall be called the prophet of the *M* High, * 93 1
you alone are the *M* High, 95 11
Almighty God, whose *m* dear Son went not up to joy 99 1
Almighty and *m* merciful God, kindle 111 4
M merciful God, 116 12
M holy God, the source of all good desires, 123 15
He who dwells in the shelter of the *M* High * 129 21
and the *M* High your habitation, 130 16
redeemed with thy *m* precious blood, 148 12
all those evils that we *m* justly have deserved; 155 9
into our hearts that *m* excellent gift of charity, 165 1
O *m* loving Father, who willest us to give thanks 165 6
Almighty God, whose *m* dear Son went not up to joy 168 10
O God, who didst make this *m* holy night to shine 170 14
O Almighty and *m* merciful God, 177 3
Give us grace that we may always *m* thankfully 180 21
follow the blessed steps of his *m* holy life; 181 1
under his *m* gracious rule; 185 5
Almighty and *m* merciful God, grant, 200 1
under his *m* gracious rule; 203 3
M loving Father, whose will it is for us to give thanks 216 20
Almighty God, whose *m* dear Son went not up to joy 220 1
O God, who made this *m* holy night to shine 222 8
follow daily in the blessed steps of his *m* holy life; 232 14
under his *m* gracious rule; 236 18
Almighty and *m* merciful God, grant 251 7
under his *m* gracious rule; 254 5
M holy and merciful Father: 267 12
Almighty God, whose *m* dear Son went not up to joy 272 1
On this *m* holy night, 285 1
O God, who made this *m* holy night to shine 295 8
All praise and thanks to you, *m* merciful Father, 311 15
banquet of that *m* heavenly Food. 317 10
M merciful God, 320 10
Almighty and *m* merciful Father, 320 23
and grant, O *m* merciful Father, for his sake, 321 11
art *m* high in the glory of God the Father. 325 9
And we *m* humbly beseech thee, of thy goodness, 329 26
from time to time *m* grievously have committed, 331 6
provoking *m* justly thy wrath and indignation 331 8
have mercy upon us, *m* merciful Father; 331 14
M merciful God, 331 21
Glory be to thee, O Lord *M* High. 334 6
rendering unto thee *m* hearty thanks 335 15
And we *m* humbly beseech thee, O merciful Father, 335 17
of his *m* blessed Body and Blood. 335 23
worthily receive the *m* precious Body and Blood 336 5
everliving God, we *m* heartily thank thee 339 2
spiritual food of the *m* precious Body and Blood 339 4
Glory be to thee, O Lord *M* High. 341 9
And we *m* humbly beseech thee, O merciful Father, 342 16
receive the *m* precious Body and Blood 342 25
vows unto the *M* High. 343 9
M merciful God, 352 10
you alone are the *M* High, 356 15
M merciful God, 360 2
of the *m* precious Body and Blood 366 3
your vows to the *M* High. 376 5
Have mercy upon us, *m* merciful Father; 393 9
M merciful God, 397 19
M gracious God, we give you thanks 430 10
Grant, *m* merciful Father, that by your help 444 4
M merciful God, 454 1

the holy place of the tabernacle of the *M* Highest. 471 24
Yet, O Lord God *m* holy, O Lord *m* mighty, 484 8
O holy and *m* merciful Savior, 484 9
but spare us, Lord *m* holy, O God *m* mighty, 484 13
thou *m* worthy Judge eternal. 484 15
everlasting God, we yield unto thee *m* high 487 10
m humbly beseeching thee to give us grace 487 14
hear that his *m* joyful voice: 487 19
as into the hands of a faithful Creator and *m* merciful 488 13
M merciful God, whose wisdom is beyond 494 7
O God, *m* merciful Father, we praise you 545 1
Be seated on your lofty throne, O *M* High; * 591 10
and according to my innocence, O *M* High. 591 14
I will praise the Name of the LORD *M* High. 592 6
I will sing to your Name, O *M* High. 593 4
I will praise the Name of the Lord *M* High. 598 11
the *M* High uttered his voice. 603 16
because of the loving-kindness of the *M* High, 609 10
the holy habitation of the *M* High. 649 11
For the LORD *M* High is to be feared; * 650 8
and make good your vows to the *M* High. 655 8
there are many who fight against me, O *M* High. 662 16
I will call upon the *M* High God, * 663 23
is there knowledge in the *M* High?" 687 22
the right hand of the *M* High has lost its power." 693 21
rebelling in the desert against the *M* High. 696 8
and the *M* High God their redeemer. 697 21
But they tested the *M* High God, and defied him, * 699 18
and all of you children of the *M* High; 705 21
you alone are the *M* High over all the earth. 707 14
and the *M* High himself shall sustain her." 711 21
He who dwells in the shelter of the *M* High, * 719 10
and the *M* High your habitation, 720 4
and to sing praises to your Name, O *M* High; 720 23
m high over all the earth; * 727 15
they defied the *M* High at the Red Sea. 742 13
and despised the counsel of the *M* High. 747 4
Almighty and *m* merciful God, we remember 826 1
in all our doings with thy *m* gracious favor, 832 1
show us your presence in those who differ *m* from us, 840 4
We give you thanks, *m* gracious God, 840 7
M gracious God, by whose knowledge 840 14
God's will for us shown *m* clearly? 847 10
God's will for us is shown *m* clearly 847 11

moth

like a *m* you eat away all that is dear to us; * 639 18

mother

spouse of his virgin *m*: 188 10
Father in heaven, by whose grace the virgin *m* 189 11
m of thy incarnate Son: 192 2
spouse of his virgin *m*: 239 19
Father in heaven, by your grace the virgin *m* 240 18
m of your incarnate Son: 243 9
a sinner from my *m*'s womb. 266 13
Rejoice and be glad now, *M* Church, 286 7
Honor thy father and thy *m*. 318 13
the substance of the Virgin Mary his *m*; 345 17
Honor your father and your *m*. 350 11
perfect Man of the flesh of the Virgin Mary his *m*; 378 11
to be born of a human *m*, 430 12
do you take this woman as your *m*? 441 1
and kept me safe upon my *m*'s breast. 610 19
when I was still in my *m*'s womb. 610 22
Though my father and my *m* forsake me, * 618 19
I behaved like one who mourns for his *m*, 630 21
and slandering your own *m*'s son. 655 21
a sinner from my *m*'s womb. 656 17
an alien to my *m*'s children. 680 4
from my *m*'s womb you have been my strength; * 683 12
and his *m*'s sin not be blotted out; 751 26
to be a joyful *m* of children. 756 17
like a child upon its *m*'s breast; * 785 15
you knit me together in my *m*'s womb. 794 26
Samuel with Hannah his *m*; 838 13
for Mary, the *m* of our Lord; 838 14
our human nature from the Virgin Mary, his *m*. 849 29

mount

on the *m* of your possession, 85 25
didst reveal his glory upon the holy *m*: 165 15
O God, who on the holy *m* didst reveal 191 15
O God, who on the holy *m* revealed 243 1
and *M* Hermon like a young wild ox. 620 17
Let *M* Zion be glad 651 23
and *M* Zion where you dwell. 689 13
and *M* Zion, which he loved. 700 16
Those who trust in the LORD are like *M* Zion, * 781 17

mountain

revealed his glory upon the holy *m*: 217 8
O mighty *m*, O hill of Bashan! * 677 10
O rugged *m*, O hill of Bashan! 677 11
Why do you look with envy, O rugged *m*, 677 12
the *m* his right hand had won. 699 14
On the holy *m* stands the city he has founded; * 711 12
The high hills are a refuge for the *m* goats, * 736 13

mountains

O ye *m* and hills, bless ye the Lord; 48 18
Glorify the Lord, O *m* and hills, 89 7
and though the *m* shake at the tempest of the same. 471 22
Before the *m* were brought forth, 472 11
the roots of the *m* shook; 603 2
made me as strong as the *m*." 621 19
Your righteousness is like the strong *m*, 632 14
and though the *m* be toppled 649 4
and though the *m* tremble at its tumult. 649 7
You make fast the *m* by your power; * 672 21
That the *m* may bring prosperity to the people, * 685 13
nor yet from the wilderness or the *m*. 691 15
more splendid than the everlasting *m*! 692 8
The *m* were covered by its shadow * 703 7
like the flame that sets *m* ablaze. 707 6
Before the *m* were brought forth, 718 1
The *m* melt like wax at the presence of the LORD, * 727 5
the waters stood higher than the *m*. 735 14
they flow between the *m*. 735 22
You water the *m* from your dwelling on high; * 736 1
he touches the *m* and they smoke. 737 19
The *m* skipped like rams, * 757 3
You *m*, that you skipped like rams? * 757 7
touch the *m*, and they shall smoke. 800 11
He makes grass to grow upon the *m* * 804 18

M and all hills, * 806 11
for the richness of *m*, plains, 840 8

mounted

He *m* on cherubim and flew; * 603 9
and his anger *m* against Israel; 696 19
So God's anger *m* against them; * 697 11
They *m* up to the heavens and fell back 748 7

mourn

and joy to those who *m*. 287 19
Let us also pray for all who *m*, 467 1
Grant to all who *m* a sure confidence 481 7
Deal graciously, we pray thee, with all those who *m*, 489 31
console us who *m*. 493 20
draw near to us who *m* for N., 497 4
graciously, we pray, with all who *m*; 505 18

mourning

I go about in *m* all the day long. 637 9

mourns

I behaved like one who *m* for his mother, 630 21

mouth

Let the words of my *m*, and the meditation 40 13
And our *m* shall slow forth thy praise. 42 15
As he spake by the *m* of his holy prophets, * 50 26
Let the words of my *m* and the meditation of my heart 78 12
And our *m* shall proclaim your praise. 80 6
So is my word that goes forth from my *m*; * 87 5
Then was our *m* filled with laughter, * 105 6
and my *m* shall proclaim your praise. 137 2
and my *m* shall proclaim your praise. 267 7
May the words of our *m*, and the meditation 571 4
For there is no truth in their *m*; * 589 9
Their *m* is full of cursing, deceit, and oppression; * 595 6
I give no offense with my *m* as others do; * 601 5
and their *m* speaks proud things. 601 19
and a consuming fire out of his *m*; * 603 5
Let the words of my *m* and the meditation of my heart 607 28
My *m* is dried out like a pot-sherd; 611 8
my tongue sticks to the roof of my *m*; * 611 9
Save me from the lion's *m*, * 611 22
by the breath of his *m* all the heavenly hosts. 626 12
his praise shall ever be in my *m*. 627 22
The words of his *m* are wicked and deceitful; * 632 7
The *m* of the righteous utters wisdom, * 635 22
like those who are mute and do not open their *m*. 637 24
and from whose *m* comes no defense. 637 26
I will put a muzzle on my *m* * 638 17
I fell silent and did not open my *m*, * 639 13
He put a new song in my *m*, 640 5
My *m* shall speak of wisdom, * 652 9
and my *m* shall proclaim your praise. 657 13
give ear to the words of my *m*. 659 20
and my *m* praises you with joyful lips, 670 22
for the *m* of those who speak lies shall be stopped. 671 9
and spoke with my *m* when I was in trouble. 674 23
I called out to him with my *m*, * 675 1
do not let the Pit shut its *m* upon me. 680 22
Let my *m* be full of your praise * 683 16
My *m* shall recount your mighty acts 684 9
incline your ears to the words of my *m*. 694 20
I will open my *m* in a parable; * 694 21
"Open your *m* wide, and I will fill it." 704 23
from age to age my *m* will proclaim your faithfulness. 713 18
his wonders and the judgments of his *m*, 738 10
but all wickedness will shut its *m*. 749 14
for the *m* of the wicked, 750 24
the *m* of the deceitful, is opened against me. 750 25
I will give great thanks to the LORD with my *m*; * 753 8
all the judgments of your *m*. 764 10
Do not take the word of truth out of my *m*, * 766 21
The law of your *m* is dearer to me * 769 7
that I may keep the decrees of your *m*. 770 19
they are sweeter than honey to my *m*. 771 26
I open my *m* and pant; * 774 9
Then was our *m* filled with laughter, * 782 8
neither is there any breath in their *m*. 789 10
Let my tongue cleave to the roof of my *m* 792 12
when they have heard the words of your *m*. 793 11
Set a watch before my *m*, O LORD, 797 7
let their bones be scattered at the *m* of the grave. 797 18
My *m* shall speak the praise of the LORD; * 803 1
with one mind and one *m* glorify thee; 818 23

mouths

Out of the *m* of infants and children * 592 9
They opened their *m* at me and said, * 631 12
O God, break their teeth in their *m*; * 665 5
Behold, they boast with their *m*, 666 9
For the sins of their *m*, for the words of their lips, 666 21
They set their *m* against the heavens, * 687 17
though the food was still in their *m*. 697 10
But they flattered him with their *m* * 697 22
They have *m*, but they cannot speak; * 757 22
They have *m*, but they cannot speak; * 789 7
Whose *m* speak deceitfully * 800 17

move

O ye whales and all that *m* in the waters, 48 23
O heavenly Father, in whom we live and *m* 57 14
O whales and all that *m* in the waters. 89 11
Heavenly Father, in you we live and *m* 100 6
M us to express the wonder, 572 2
so that it never shall *m* at any time. 735 12
There *m* the ships, 737 4
m every human heart 823 18

moved

He will not let your foot be *m* * 104 17
Over it the Holy Spirit *m* in the beginning 306 14
Therefore will we not fear, though the earth be *m*, * 471 19
He will not suffer thy foot to be *m*, * 473 13
Through the ages, Almighty God has *m* his people 567 1
the Holy Spirit *m* in the beginning of creation. 570 6
Therefore we will not fear, though the earth be *m*, * 649 3
that it cannot be *m*; 722 6
he has made the world so firm that it cannot be *m*; 726 12
and are *m* to pity even for her dust. 732 5
He will not let your foot be *m* * 779 5
which cannot be *m*, but stands fast for ever. 781 18

moves

the seas and all that *m* in them; 682 6

mown

He shall come down like rain upon the *m* field, * 685 19

much

we have followed too *m* the devices and desires 41 18
we have followed too *m* the devices and desires 62 18
we have followed too *m* the devices and desires 320 25
We are not worthy so *m* as to gather 337 11
Father, you loved the world so *m* that in the fullness 374 1
By this my Father is glorified, that you bear *m* fruit, 397 10
m less the walls of temples made with hands. 578 4
more than *m* fine gold, * 607 17
like a heavy burden they are too *m* for me to bear. 637 5
The nations make *m* ado, and the kingdoms 649 15
God is *m* to be feared in the council 714 7
How *m* longer must I wait? * 770 9
Too *m* of the scorn of the indolent rich, * 780 23
So that those who go by say not as *m* as, 784 15
Grant that we may not so *m* seek 833 9
decision ventured *m* for the liberties we now enjoy. 839 23

mud

I trample them like *m* in the streets. 605 25

mule

Do not be like horse or *m*, 625 20

multiplied

shall have their troubles *m*. 600 4
and *m* their families like flocks of sheep. 749 12

multiplies

He *m* the victories of his king; * 606 12

multiply

Increase and *m* 180 2
Increase and *m* 231 18
m, by the grace of the Paschal sacrament, the number 289 7
M, we beseech thee, to those who rest 486 9
and *m* the harvests of the world; 828 3

multitude

Who, in the *m* of thy saints, hast compassed us 347 17
For in the *m* of your saints you have surrounded us 380 12
the *m* of your mercies, look with compassion upon us 395 4
for I went with the *m*, and brought them forth 471 8
how I went with the *m* and led them 643 9
let the *m* of the isles be glad. 726 24
in the midst of the *m* will I praise him; 753 9

multitudes

m who have been created in thine image 206 18
m who have been created in your image 257 14
I do not fear the *m* of people * 587 13
and fashion into one united people the *m* 820 7

murder

from violence, battle, and *m*; 149 15
Thou shalt do no *m*. 318 16
You shall not commit *m*. 350 13
and in secret places they *m* the innocent; * 595 9
They *m* the widow and the stranger * 723 5

murmur

Those who sit at the gate *m* against me, * 680 11

muse

I *m* upon all your deeds; * 799 8

music

in the *m* we make and in the songs we sing. 572 4
I will sing and make *m* to the LORD. 618 9
m of strings from ivory palaces makes you glad. 648 7
make *m* to our God upon the harp. 804 15
art and *m* to perfect the praises offered by your people 819 15

musicians

The singers go before, *m* follow after, * 678 7

mute

like those who are *m* and do not open their mouth. 637 24

mutter

Why do the peoples *m* empty threats? 586 2

mutual

intended by God for their *m* joy; 423 10
Give them such fulfillment of their *m* affection 429 23
together with *m* forbearance and respect; 824 4
Renew the ties of *m* regard which form our civic life. 825 9

muzzle

I will put a *m* on my mouth * 638 17

myrrh

All your garments are fragrant with *m*, 648 6

mysteries

who in these holy *m* giveth us a pledge of life eternal, 169 10
servants of Christ and stewards of thy divine *m*; 197 8
Grant us so to venerate the sacred *m* 201 3
who in these holy *m* gives us a pledge of eternal life; 221 5
servants of Christ and stewards of your divine *m*; 248 19
Grant us so to venerate the sacred *m* 252 8
who in these holy *m* gives us a pledge of eternal life; 274 5
For in these holy *M* we are made one with Christ, 316 5
share rightly in the celebration of those holy *M*, 316 18
for that thou dost feed us, in these holy *m*, 339 3
and for assuring us in these holy *m* 366 5
who in these holy *m* gives us a pledge of eternal life; 397 17
m of the Body and Blood of your Son Jesus Christ. 432 3
celebration of the *m* of Christ's Body and Blood, 531 15
and furnished it for the celebration of your holy *m*. 573 3
I will declare the *m* of ancient times. 694 22
probe the *m* of your creation, 827 14
venerate the sacred *m* of thy Body and Blood, 834 14

mystery

in the morning as we celebrate the Paschal *m*; 134 4
By the *m* of thy holy Incarnation; 149 18
that as we have known the *m* of that Light 161 3
Almighty and everlasting God, who in the Paschal *m* 172 1
Mercifully grant that we, who glory in the *m* 192 15
Grant that we, who have known the *m* of that Light 212 18
Almighty and everlasting God, who in the Paschal *m* 223 15
Almighty and everlasting God, who in the Paschal *m* 224 13
Mercifully grant that we, who glory in the *m* 244 3
your whole Church, that wonderful and sacred *m*; 280 16
Almighty and everlasting God, who in the Paschal *m* 290 14
your whole Church, that wonderful and sacred *m*; 291 13
Through the Paschal *m*, dear friends, we are buried 292 1

Because in the *m* of the Word made flesh, 346 1
Therefore we proclaim the *m* of faith: 363 6
Because in the *m* of the Word made flesh, 378 14
the *m* of the union between Christ and his Church, 423 7
your whole Church, that wonderful and sacred *m*; 515 6
your whole Church, that wonderful and sacred *m*; 528 4
your whole Church, that wonderful and sacred *m*; 540 4
The human mind and heart are a *m*; * 671 23
Increase our reverence before the *m* of life; 828 18
and for the *m* of love. 836 4

mystical
fellowship in the *m* body of thy Son 194 9
fellowship in the *m* body of your Son 245 17
members incorporate in the *m* body of thy Son, 339 7
communion and fellowship, in the *m* body of thy Son 480 5
with all those who are of the *m* body of thy Son, 487 18

N

Name
N shall be great among the Gentiles, 38 6
incense shall be offered unto my *N*, 38 7
for my *N* shall be great among the heathen, 38 8
O give thanks unto the Lord, and call upon his *N*; 40 7
to the glory of thy holy *N*. 42 10
be thankful unto him and speak good of his *N*. 45 19
Blessed art thou for the *N* of thy Majesty; * 49 11
and holy is his *N*. 50 8
hallowed be thy *N*, 54 15
And we worship thy *N* ever, world without end. 55 18
for the honor of thy *N*. 58 13
are gathered together in his *N* 59 15
The Lord is his *N*. 62 4
to the glory of thy holy *N*. 63 13
and holy is his *N*. 65 11
hallowed be thy *N*, 67 5
are gathered together in his *N* 72 12
my *N* shall be great among the nations, 76 5
incense shall be offered to my *N*, 76 7
for my *N* shall be great among the nations, 76 7
Give thanks to the Lord, and call upon his *N*; 78 6
to the glory of your *N*. 79 22
give thanks to him and call upon his *N*. 83 6
Yahweh is his *N*. 85 8
Give thanks to the Lord and call upon his *N*; 86 8
see that they remember that his *N* is exalted. 86 10
Glory to you for the radiance of your holy *N*; * 90 7
and holy is his *N*. 92 3
and sing the praises of your *N*? * 94 15
hallowed be thy *N*, 97 5
We praise your *N* for ever. 98 12
the honor of your *N*. 101 6
are gathered together in his *N* 102 4
my *N* shall be great among the nations, 106 6
incense shall be offered to my *N*, 106 8
for my *N* shall be great among the nations, 106 8
hallowed be thy *N*, 106 15
to the glory of your *N*. 117 5
and holy is his *N*. 119 9
hallowed be thy *N*, hallowed be your *N*, 121 5
are gathered together in his *N* 126 4
Our help is in the *N* of the Lord; 127 3
to the glory of your *N*. 127 15
for the sake of your *N*, lead me and guide me. 129 15
I will protect him, because he knows my *N*. 130 28
and we are called by your *N*: 131 13
hallowed be thy *N*, 132 20
your people may glorify your holy *N*; 133 19
praise the *N* of the Lord. 138 2
Let the *N* of the Lord be blessed, * 138 3
let the *N* of the Lord be praised. 138 6
and we are called by your *N*: 140 6
hallowed be thy *N*, 153 7
those who ask in thy Son's *N*: 153 20
And deliver us for thy *N*'s sake. 154 4
and, for the glory of thy *N*, turn from us 155 8
Grant that all who are baptized into his *N* may keep 163 4
and love of thy holy *N*, 178 13
among all peoples, to the glory of thy *N*; 181 8
Graft in our hearts the love of thy *N*, 181 12
with steadfast faith in the confession of thy *N*; 183 14
the *N* of our Lord Jesus Christ; 189 8
Lord God Almighty, in whose *N* the founders 190 17
martyrdom for the *N* of Jesus Christ; 191 9
to the praise and glory of thy *N*; 193 14
to the glory of thy *N*; 194 20
confess the *N* of our Savior Jesus Christ 195 2
We praise thy *N* for the gifts of grace 197 14
assembled in thy *N*, 204 11
the glory of thy great *N* and for the benefit 205 10
to the glory of thy holy *N*; 209 6
Grant that all who are baptized into his *N* may keep 214 15
reverence for your holy *N*, 230 8
to the glory of your *N*; 232 19
Graft in our hearts the love of your *N*; 233 4
in the confession of your *N*; 235 7
the *N* of our Lord Jesus Christ; 240 16
Lord God Almighty, in whose *N* the founders 242 1
for the *N* of Jesus Christ; 242 16
to the praise and glory of your *N*; 245 1
to the glory of your *N*; 246 5
confess the *N* of our Savior Jesus Christ 246 9
We praise your *N* for the gifts of grace 248 24
assembled in your *N*, 255 9
to the glory of your great *N* and for the benefit of your holy 256 7
to the glory of your holy *N*; 260 13
they may minister in his *N* to the suffering, 260 18
for the glory of your *N* 289 6
baptizing them in the *N* of the Father, 307 2
I baptize you in the *N* of the Father, 307 14
hallowed be thy *N*, 311 2
I baptize you in the *N* of the Father, 313 2
I baptize you in the *N* of the Father, 313 3
shalt not take the *N* of the Lord thy God in vain. 318 7
to the glory of thy *N*. 320 22
to the glory of thy holy *N*. 321 13
and worthily magnify thy holy *N*; 323 11
thy holy *N* may agree in the truth of thy holy Word, 329 7
And we also bless thy holy *N* for all thy servants 330 1
to the honor and glory of thy *N*; 331 19

to the glory of thy *N*.	331	33
magnify thy glorious *N*;	334	3
hallowed by thy *N*,	336	19
magnify thy glorious *N*;	341	6
Ascribe to the Lord the honor due his *N*;	343	10
the fruit of lips that acknowledge his *N*.	344	2
confessing before the rulers of this world the great *N*	348	9
You shall not invoke with malice the *N* of the Lord	350	7
to the glory of your *N*.	352	22
and worthily magnify your holy *N*;	355	10
to the glory of your *N*.	360	14
sing this hymn to proclaim the glory of your *N*:	362	3
hallowed be thy *N*,	364	2
sing this hymn to proclaim the glory of your *N*:	367	12
and glorify your *N*,	373	11
to the praise of your *N*.	375	11
Ascribe to the Lord the honor due his *N*;	376	6
the fruit of lips that acknowledge his *N*.	376	18
the great *N* of your only Son.	381	4
That your *N* may be glorified by all people.	387	5
Grant, Almighty God, that all who confess your *N*	388	2
And praise your *N* for ever and ever.	393	3
to the honor and glory of your *N*;	393	15
to the glory of thy *N*;	394	3
hear what we ask in the *N* of your Son:	394	5
to the glory of your *N*.	398	6
hallowed be thy *N*,	398	13
In the *N* of God, I, N., take you, N., to be my wife,	427	1
In the *N* of God, I, N., take you, N., to be my husband,	427	5
I honor you, in the *N* of the Father,	427	14
(or in the *N* of God).	427	16
husband and wife, in the *N* of the Father,	428	4
hallowed be thy *N*,	428	9
man and woman in his *N*.	430	14
In the *N* of God, I, N., take you, N.,	436	1
and holy is his *N*.	441	17
and call upon the *N* of the LORD,	442	22
and guides me along right pathways for his *N*'s sake.	443	6
In the *N* of the Father,	447	3
In the *N* of the Father,	448	5
In the *N* of the Father,	451	15
to the glory of your *N*.	455	5
I lay my hands upon you in the *N* of the Father,	456	1
I lay my hands upon you in the *N* of our Lord	456	7
I anoint you with oil in the *N* of the Father,	456	11
and make you know and feel that the only *N*	457	2
for health and salvation is the *N* of our Lord	457	3
he may bless your holy *N*;	458	20
Hear us, we pray, for your dear *N*'s sake.	459	6
hallowed by thy *N*,	464	5
In the *N* of God the Father Almighty who created	464	22
In the *N* of Jesus Christ who redeemed you;	464	23
In the *N* of the Holy Spirit who sanctifies you.	464	24
for his *N*'s sake.	476	7
then called I upon the *N* of the LORD; *	479	6
heaven to all who believe in his *N*,	483	21
hallowed by thy *N*,	485	21
the true faith of thy holy *N*,	488	8
magnify thy holy *N*	489	15
heaven to all who believe in his *N*,	500	10
hallowed be thy *N*,	502	2
all who have died in the true faith of your holy *N*,	503	17
glorify your holy *N*	504	13
And this we ask in the *N* of Jesus Christ	505	15
and worthily magnify your holy *N*;	512	10
In the *N* of the Father,	513	7
to the glory and unceasing praise of your *N*.	521	5
declaring pardon in your *N*, offering the	521	12
Our help is in the *N* of the Lord;	523	11
Blessed be the *N* of the Lord;	523	13
and worthily magnify your holy *N*;	525	10
and your *N* glorified in all the world.	534	7
and worthily magnify your holy *N*;	537	10
and glorify your *N*,	549	5
Our help is in the *N* of the Lord;	552	1
consecrate it in God's *N*.	567	6
to the praise and glory of your *N*;	567	12
In the *N* of the Father,	568	3
Our help is in the *N* of the Lord;	568	4
we come to praise your *N*,	568	10
We dedicate this Font in the *N* of the Father,	569	21
baptizing them in the *N* of the Father,	570	16
We dedicate this Lectern in the *N* of the Father,	571	7
We dedicate this Pulpit in the *N* of the Father,	571	15
We dedicate this (name of instrument) in the *N*	572	7
Blessed be your *N*, Lord God.	573	12
Blessed be your *N*, Father, Son, and Holy Spirit;	574	8
gathered together in your *N*,	578	11
so that those who love your *N* may exult in you.	589	20
I will praise the *N* of the LORD Most High.	592	6
how exalted is your *N* in all the world!	592	8
how exalted is your *N* in all the world!	592	26
I will sing to your *N*, O Most High.	593	4
Those who know your *N* will put their trust in you, *	593	19
I will praise the *N* of the Lord Most High.	598	11
and sing praises to your *N*.	606	11
the *N* of the God of Jacob defend you;	608	2
and triumph in the *N* of our God; *	608	10
but we will call upon the *N* of the LORD our God.	608	16
I will declare your *N* to my brethren; *	611	24
and guides me along right pathways for his *N*'s sake.	613	2
For your *N*'s sake, O LORD, *	615	10
Ascribe to the LORD the glory due his *N*; *	620	7
for the sake of your *N*, lead me and guide me.	622	14
for in his holy *N* we put our trust.	627	18
let us exalt his *N* together.	627	26
through your *N* we trampled on those who	645	21
and we will praise your *N* for ever.	646	2
If we have forgotten the *N* of our God, *	646	26
Your praise, like your *N*, O God, reaches to	651	20
and declare the goodness of your *N* in the presence	658	19
Save me, O God, by your *N*; *	659	17
and praise your *N*, O LORD, for it is good.	660	2
who fear your *N*.	668	23
So will I always sing the praise of your *N*, *	669	3
and lift up my hands in your *N*.	670	20
sing the glory of his *N*;	673	19
sings to you, sings out your *N*."	673	25
Sing to God, sing praises to his *N*;	676	8
YAHWEH is his *N*, rejoice before him!	676	10
I will praise the *N* of God in song; *	681	24
and those who love his *N* will dwell therein.	682	10
May his *N* remain for ever,	686	21

And blessed be his glorious *N* for ever! * 686 27
they defiled the dwelling-place of your *N* 689 22
will the enemy blaspheme your *N* for ever? 690 5
how a foolish people despised your *N*. 690 21
let the poor and needy praise your *N*. 690 27
calling upon your *N* and declaring all your 691 4
his *N* is great in Israel. 692 2
the kingdoms that have not called upon your *N*. 701 18
Help us, O God our Savior, for the glory of your *N*; * 701 24
deliver us and forgive us our sins, for your *N*'s sake. 701 25
give us life, that we may call upon your *N*. 703 23
that they may seek your *N*. 707 10
Let them know that you, whose *N* is YAHWEH, * 707 13
and glorify your *N*. 710 17
knit my heart to you that I may fear your *N*. 710 23
and glorify your *N* for evermore. 710 25
Tabor and Hermon rejoice in your *N*. 714 18
They rejoice daily in your *N*; * 714 25
and he shall be victorious through my *N*. 715 15
I will protect him, because he knows my *N*. 720 16
and to sing praises to your *N*, O Most High; 720 23
Sing to the LORD and bless his *N*; * 725 19
Ascribe to the LORD the honor due his *N*; * 726 7
and give thanks to his holy *N*. 727 23
Let them confess his *N*, which is great and awesome; 729 3
and Samuel among those who call upon his *N*, * 729 12
give thanks to him and call upon his *N*. 730 3
and your *N* from age to age. 731 24
The nations shall fear your *N*, O LORD, * 732 6
That they may declare in Zion the *N* of the LORD, * 732 18
and all that is within me, bless his holy *N*. 733 10
Give thanks to the LORD and call upon his *N*; * 738 1
Glory in his holy *N*; * 738 5
But he saved them for his *N*'s sake, * 742 14
that we may give thanks to your holy *N* 745 21
oh, deal with me according to your *N*; * 752 17
holy and awesome is his *N*. 754 24
praise the *N* of the LORD. 756 3
Let the *N* of the LORD be blessed, * 756 4
let the *N* of the LORD be praised. 756 7
but to your *N* give glory; * 757 14
Then I called upon the *N* of the LORD: * 759 8
and call upon the *N* of the LORD. 759 26
and call upon the *N* of the LORD. 760 9
I remember your *N* in the night, O LORD, * 767 23
as you always do to those who love your *N*. 774 12
to praise the *N* of the LORD. 780 4
Our help is in the *N* of the LORD, * 781 15
We wish you well in the *N* of the LORD." 784 17
Praise the *N* of the LORD; * 788 2
sing praises to his *N*, for it is lovely. 788 7
O LORD, your *N* is everlasting; * 789 1
and praise your *N*, * 793 4
For you have glorified your *N* * 793 6
your enemies take your *N* in vain. 795 19
Surely, the righteous will give thanks to your *N*, * 797 1
that I may give thanks to your *N*; * 798 15
Revive me, O LORD, for your *N*'s sake; * 799 23
and bless your *N* for ever and ever. 801 13
and praise your *N* for ever and ever. 801 15
let all flesh bless his holy *N* for ever and ever. 803 2
Let them praise the *N* of the LORD; * 806 3
Let them praise the *N* of the LORD, * 806 19
for his *N* only is exalted, 806 20
Let them praise his *N* in the dance; * 807 6
may glorify your *N*; 819 11
those to whom in thy *N* we entrust 820 9
to the glory of thy *N* and the welfare of this people; 821 6
and honor your holy *N*. 822 14
All this we ask in your holy *N*. 825 24
we may glorify thy holy *N*, 832 4
those who ask in thy Son's *N*: 834 2
praise of thy *N*; 834 22
God's holy *N* be blessed 835 16
call upon your *N*; 838 7
glorify your holy *N*. 839 20
we ask in the *N* of Jesus Christ our Lord. 839 26
to the honor and glory of your *N*, 840 13
and praise thy *N*. 841 10
baptized in the *N* of the Father, 858 14

name

whose *n* is Holy, "I dwell in the high and holy place, 41 1
whose *n* is Holy, "I dwell in the high and holy place 78 23
The Lord is his *n*. 115 16
n of Jesus to be the sign of our salvation: 162 2
calleth us each by *n*, and follow where he doth lead; 173 13
minister in his *n* to the suffering, the friendless, 209 13
you gave to your incarnate Son the holy *n* 213 13
calls us each by *n*, and follow where he leads; 225 5
I invite you, therefore, in the *n* of the Church, 265 10
Blessed is the King who comes in the *n* of the Lord. 270 1
we who bear them in his *n* may ever hail him 271 11
Blessed is he who comes in the *n* of the Lord. 271 15
In the *n* of Christ. Amen. 271 18
For those who in the *n* of Christ have persecuted 279 27
Blessed is he that cometh in the *n* of the Lord. 334 7
Let us go forth in the *n* of Christ. 339 22
Blessed is he that cometh in the *n* of the Lord. 341 10
Blessed is he who comes in the *n* of the Lord. 362 7
Let us go forth in the *n* of Christ. 366 14
Blessed is he who comes in the *n* of the Lord. 367 16
Blessed is he who comes in the *n* of the Lord. 371 4
worthily serve the world in his *n*. 372 8
Blessed is he who comes in the *n* of the Lord. 373 15
Blessed is he who comes in the *n* of the Lord. 402 12
Blessed is he who comes in the *n* of the Lord. 404 14
In the *n* of this congregation I commend you 420 4
to follow Christ and to serve in his *n*. 421 4
have given to him our family *n*, 441 8
whoever receives a little child in the *n* of Christ 443 22
Let us go forth in the *n* of Christ. 483 12
Let us go forth in the *n* of Christ. 500 1
Let us go forth in the *n* of Christ. 502 21
I will obey Christ, and will serve in his *n*. 518 3
I will, in the *n* of Christ, the Shepherd and 518 17
In the *n* of Jesus Christ, you 543 4
chosen to serve as Rector of (*n* of church). 559 2
building (rebuilding, or adornment) of (*n* of church), 567 4
We dedicate this (*n* of instrument) in the Name of the 572 7
you have blotted out their *n* for ever and ever. 593 10
"When will he die, and his *n* perish?" 642 9
I will make your *n* to be remembered 648 25
let the *n* of Israel be remembered no more." 706 11

and his *n* be blotted out in the next generation. 751 23
in the *n* of the LORD I will repel them. 761 16
Blessed is he who comes in the *n* of the Lord; * 762 23
in the *n* of Jesus Christ our Lord. 827 16
This we ask in the *n* of Jesus Christ 830 6
to act in Christ's *n* for the reconciliation 855 26
to bless and declare pardon in the *n* of God. 856 6

named

whom every family in heaven and earth is *n*, 311 22

names

nor take the *n* of their gods upon my lips. 600 6
though they call the lands after their own *n*. 653 3
but let him root out their *n* from the earth; 751 28
and calls them all by their *n*. 804 9
By what other *n* is this service known? 859 14

Naphtali

and the princes of Zebulon and *N*. 678 13

nation

Lord, keep this *n* under thy care; 55 7
Lord, keep this *n* under thy care; 67 22
From every family, language, people, and *n*, * 94 3
Lord, keep this *n* under your care; 98 1
Lord, keep this *n* under your care; 122 1
the President of the United States (or of this *n*), 150 26
to every race and *n* by the promised gift 175 9
to every race and *n* by the promised gift 227 2
For this community, the *n*, and the world; 392 5
Happy is the *n* whose God is the LORD! * 626 23
and afflict your chosen *n*. 723 4
Wandering from *n* to *n* * 739 3
He has not done so to any other *n*; * 805 17
commend this *n* to thy merciful care, 820 17
Lord, keep this *n* under your care. 821 18
and our *n* be enabled to fulfill 822 27
people of our *n* may give thanks to you 825 21
We thank you for the great resources of this *n*. 839 1
It has drawn people from every *n*, 839 9
bestowed upon this *n* and people. 840 19
a holy *n*, a royal priesthood, 854 9

nations

Thy saving health among all *n*. 55 10
n into thy fold; 58 5
Thy saving health among all *n*. 68 2
all *n* obey thee, 70 16
N shall come to your light, 76 1
I will give you as a light to the *n*, 76 3
my Name shall be great among the *n*, 76 6
N will stream to your light, * 87 17
A Light to enlighten the *n*, * 93 16
All *n* will draw near and fall down before you, * 94 17
Your saving health among all *n*. 98 4
bring the *n* into your fold; 100 21
Then they said among the *n*, * 105 8
my Name shall be great among the *n*, 106 7
that all *n* may come and worship you; 107 14
A Light to enlighten the *n*, * 120 5
Your saving health among all *n*. 122 4
all *n* obey you, 124 13
A Light to enlighten the *n*, * 135 5
The Lord is high above all *n*, * 138 7
A Light to enlighten the *n*, * 140 11
to give to all *n* unity, peace, and concord; 151 2
revealed thy glory among the *n*: 183 12
torch of freedom for *n* then unborn: 190 19
bring the *n* into thy fold, 206 13
O God of all the *n* of the earth: 206 17
take counsel for the *n* of the earth, 207 10
justice in our communities and among the *n*, 209 5
revealed your glory among the *n*: 235 4
torch of freedom for *n* then unborn: 242 3
bring the *n* into your fold, 257 8
O God of all the *n* of the earth: 257 13
for the *n* of the earth, 258 10
justice in our communities and among the *n*, 260 12
Let us pray for all *n* and peoples of the earth, 278 17
For the Members and Representatives of the United *N* 278 21
those who take counsel for the *n* of the earth; 278 27
your saving health among all *n*. 281 8
to be a sign for us of the salvation of all *n* 289 15
preach the Gospel to all *n*. 347 12
preach the Gospel and to teach all *n*; 348 13
preach the Gospel to all *n*. 380 7
preach the Gospel and to teach all *n*; 381 7
For our President, for the leaders of the *n*, 384 4
for goodwill among *n*; 386 1
govern and hold authority in the *n* 387 9
Guide the people of this land, and of all the *n*, 388 7
forbearance may grow among *n* and peoples, 390 14
I will be exalted among the *n*, 472 5
forbearance may grow among *n* and peoples, 549 30
Why are the *n* in an uproar? * 586 1
Ask of me, and I will give you the *n* for 586 17
O LORD, judge the *n*. 591 11
you put me at the head of the *n*. 605 27
Therefore will I extol you among the *n*, O LORD, * 606 10
and all the families of the *n* shall bow before him. 612 12
he rules over the *n*. 612 14
The LORD brings the will of the *n* to naught; * 626 19
how you destroyed *n* and made your people flourish. 645 12
and have scattered us among the *n*. 646 8
You have made us a byword among the *n*, * 646 13
therefore *n* will praise you for ever and ever." 648 27
The *n* make much ado, and the kingdoms 649 15
I will be exalted among the *n*; 650 2
and the *n* under our feet. 650 11
God reigns over the *n*; * 650 20
I will sing praise to you among the *n*. 664 16
his eyes keep watch over the *n*; * 674 7
your saving health among all *n*. 675 12
Let the *n* be glad and sing for joy, * 675 15
and guide all the *n* upon earth. 675 17
and all the *n* do him service. 686 6
may all the *n* bless themselves in him and 686 23
you cast out the *n* and planted it. 703 4
for you shall take all *n* for your own. 706 2
wipe them out from among the *n*; * 706 10
All *n* you have made will come and 710 15
He who admonishes the *n*, will he not punish? * 723 13
Declare his glory among the *n* * 725 21
As for all the gods of the *n*, they are but idols; * 726 1
Tell it out among the *n*: "The LORD is King! * 726 11

the sight of the *n*. 728 5
The *n* shall fear your Name, O LORD, * 732 6
He gave his people the lands of the *n*, * 741 13
To cast out their seed among the *n*, * 744 1
and gather us from among the *n*, * 745 20
I will sing praises to you among the *n*. 749 23
he will rule over the *n*. 753 23
in giving them the lands of the *n*. 754 17
The LORD is high above all *n*, * 756 8
Praise the LORD, all you *n*; * 760 15
Then they said among the *n*, * 782 10
He overthrew many *n* * 788 21
To wreak vengeance on the *n* * 807 14
saving health unto all *n*. 815 1
all *n* and races may serve you 815 19
Almighty God our heavenly Father, guide the *n* 816 1
show forth thy praise among the *n* of the earth. 820 12
and a blessing to other *n* of the earth. 821 17
fulfill our obligations in the community of *n*. 822 4
that holy City to which the *n* of the world 825 7
preach the Gospel to all *n*. 838 4
O Judge of the *n*, we remember before you 839 21
bring all the *n* of the world to him. 847 2

Nativity

by thy holy N and submission to the Law; 149 18

natural

for the *n* majesty and beauty of this land. 838 22

nature

take our *n* upon him and as at this time to be born 161 8
wonderfully restore, the dignity of human *n*: 162 8
weakness of our mortal *n*, we can do no good thing 164 13
wonderfully restore, the dignity of human *n*: 200 14
take our *n* upon him, and to be born 213 2
wonderfully restored, the dignity of human *n*: 214 2
take upon him our *n*, and to suffer death 219 15
wonderfully restored, the dignity of human *n*: 252 2
and as a mark of our mortal *n*, 265 14
take upon him our *n*, and to suffer death 272 9
wonderfully restored, the dignity of human *n*: 288 6
to take our *n* upon him, and to suffer death 341 15
to share our human *n*, to live and die 362 13
and reverence so to use the resources of *n*, 827 19
What are we by *n*? 845 1
through *n* and history, 845 19
and shows us the *n* of God. 849 22
What is the *n* of God revealed in Jesus? 849 23
our human *n* from the Virgin Mary, his mother. 849 29
Why did he take our human *n*? 850 1
We mean that Jesus took our human *n* 850 19
proclaiming the *n* of the Incarnation and of God 852 10
to show God at work in *n* and history. 853 12

naught

The LORD brings the will of the nations to *n*; * 626 19
and bring all my foes to *n*, * 799 26

Nazareth

May God the Son, who sanctified a home at N, 445 5
The Messiah, or Christ, is Jesus of N, 849 17

near

who are far off and to those who are *n*: 58 3
Our King and Savior now draws *n*: 80 10
call upon him when he draws *n*. 86 18
All nations will draw *n* and fall down before you, * 94 17
who are far off and to those who are *n*: 100 19
but it shall not come *n* you. 130 12
neither shall any plague come *n* your dwelling. 130 18
and to bring those *n* to us into his gracious presence; 185 11
O God, who hast brought us *n* to an innumerable 198 23
who are far off and to those who are *n*: 206 11
bring those *n* to us into his gracious presence; 237 5
O God, you have brought us *n* to an innumerable 250 8
who are far off and to those who are *n*: 257 7
All you who stand *n* this marvelous and holy flame, 286 10
Draw *n* with faith, 330 12
draw *n* to the throne of grace, 352 7
Be *n* me in my time of weakness and pain; 461 7
draw *n* to us who mourn 497 4
Be always *n* us when we seek you 568 15
Be not far from me, for trouble is *n*, * 610 23
or else they will not stay *n* you." 625 22
The LORD is *n* to the brokenhearted * 629 3
Let not the foot of the proud come *n* me, * 633 1
Draw *n* to me and redeem me; * 680 27
But it is good for me to be *n* God; * 689 5
Truly, his salvation is very *n* to those who fear him, * 709 12
but it shall not come *n* you. 719 26
neither shall any plague come *n* your dwelling. 720 6
and drew *n* to death's door. 747 18
They draw *n* who in malice persecute me; * 776 3
You, O LORD, are *n* at hand, * 776 5
The LORD is *n* to those who call upon him, * 802 23
the children of Israel, a people who are *n* him. 806 24
Deliver us, when we draw *n* to thee, 833 21

nearer

and we, drawing *n* to thee, may be bound together 830 23

nearly

But as for me, my feet had *n* slipped; * 687 3

necessary

n for our life and our salvation. 41 10
n for our life and our salvation. 79 4
things *n* to salvation; 513 11
and to contain all things *n* 526 16
and to contain all things *n* 538 16
Grant us all things *n* for our common life, 817 21
all things *n* to sustain their life: 828 11
they are not *n* for all persons 860 15

necessities

who knowest our *n* before we ask 179 17
for the provision of our *n* 194 19
you know our *n* before we ask 231 11
for the provision of our *n* 246 4
according to their several *n*, 815 10
all other bodily *n* of life, 825 22
justice, freedom, and the *n* of life 848 13

necessity

comfort all who are in danger, *n*, and tribulation, 151 29
obtained effectually, to the relief of our *n*, 153 24
obtained, to the relief of our *n*, 834 6

neck

for the waters have risen up to my *n*. 679 8
nor speak with a proud *n*.'" 691 13
his *n* they put in an iron collar. 739 14

necklace

Therefore they wear their pride like a *n* * 687 11

need

by night you will not *n* the brightness of the moon. 87 28
the relief of all who are in *n*, 194 20
the relief of all who are in *n*, 246 5
the *n* which all Christians continually have to renew 265 8
for our blindness to human *n* and suffering, 268 17
Let the cry of those in misery and *n* come 279 15
And if, in your preparation, you *n* help and counsel, 317 11
help in time of *n*. 320 8
are in trouble, sorrow, *n*, sickness, 329 28
find grace to help in time of *n*. 352 8
Pray for those in any *n* or trouble. 386 6
that each may be to the other a strength in *n*, 429 8
that each may be to the other a strength in *n*, 444 10
time of *n*: 458 2
help and serve those in *n*? 544 5
when we turn to you in sickness or special *n*, 569 8
my life span would *n* to be like yours. 795 14
we entreat thee, in this time of *n*, such moderate rain 828 12
and our *n* for redemption. 848 27
show us our *n* for redemption, 849 9
particularly as a servant of those in *n*; 856 9

needed

that it might produce what is *n* for life: 824 7

needs

satisfy the *n* of every living creature: 208 10
healing to those who minister to their *n*, 208 18
satisfy the *n* of every living creature: 259 12
healing to those who minister to their *n*, 260 3
for people everywhere according to their *n*. 277 8
and patience to minister to their *n*. 279 13
Let us pray for our own *n* and those of others. 387 21
For the special *n* and concerns of this congregation. 392 17
God, to whom our *n* are known before we ask: 394 12
healing to those who minister to his *n*, 459 19
interpret to the Church the *n*, concerns, and hopes 543 12
satisfy the *n* of every living creature. 802 20
foresight to provide for the *n* of all our people, 822 3
make us mindful of the *n* of others; 835 9
Intercession brings before God the *n* of others; 857 18
we present our own *n*, that God's will 857 19

needy

Let not the *n*, O Lord, be forgotten; 55 11
Let not the *n*, O Lord, be forgotten; 68 3
Let not the *n*, O Lord, be forgotten; 98 5
Let not the *n*, O Lord, be forgotten; 122 5
to the suffering, the friendless, and the *n*; 209 14
to the suffering, the friendless, and the *n*; 260 19
to the sick, the friendless, and the *n*. 392 11
For the *n* shall not always be forgotten, * 594 13
"Because the *n* are oppressed, 597 9
the poor and *n* from those who rob them." 630 12
to strike down the poor and *n*, * 634 12
Happy are they who consider the poor and *n*! * 641 23
For the LORD listens to the *n*, * 682 3
But as for me, I am poor and *n*; * 682 22
He shall defend the *n* among the people; * 685 15
he shall preserve the lives of the *n*. 686 10
let the poor and *n* praise your Name. 690 27
defend the humble and *n*; 705 14
but persecuted the poor and *n* 752 2
For I am poor and *n*, * 752 19
Because he stands at the right hand of the *n*, * 753 10
and render justice to the *n*. 796 26

Negev

like the watercourses of the *N*. 105 13
like the watercourses of the *N*. 782 15

neglect

But do not *n* to do good and to share what you have, 377 1

neglected

we remember before you all poor and *n* persons 826 2

negligence

Our *n* in prayer and worship, 268 13

negligences

to forgive us all our sins, *n*, and ignorances; 152 4

neighbor

Let us confess our sins against God and our *n*. 79 9
Let us confess our sins against God and our *n*. 116 11
by loving thee and our *n*: 179 5
by loving you and our *n*: 230 20
loving your *n* as yourself? 293 30
loving your *n* as yourself? 305 5
Thou shalt not bear false witness against thy *n*. 318 25
love thy *n* as thyself. 319 12
love thy *n* as thyself. 324 5
You shall not covet anything that belongs to your *n*. 350 21
Love your *n* as yourself. 351 11
Let us confess our sins against God and our *n*. 352 9
Let us confess our sins against God and our *n*. 360 1
loving your *n* as yourself? 417 15
Everyone speaks falsely with his *n*; * 597 3
he does not heap contempt upon his *n*. 599 10
My friend and my *n* you have put away from me, * 713 15
You shall love your *n* as yourself. 851 14

neighbors

we have not loved our *n* as ourselves. 79 16
we have not loved our *n* as ourselves. 116 18
We have not loved our *n* as ourselves. 267 20
for uncharitable thoughts toward our *n*, 268 21
we have not loved our *n* as ourselves. 320 16
in love and charity with your *n*, 330 10
we have not loved our *n* as ourselves. 331 27
we have not loved our *n* as ourselves. 352 16
we have not loved our *n* as ourselves. 360 8
for our families, friends, and *n*; 391 11

For our families, friends, and *n*, 392 3
we have not loved our *n* as ourselves. 397 25
we have not loved our *n* as ourselves. 454 7
who speak peaceably with their *n*, 619 12
to all my enemies and even to my *n*, 623 11
my *n* stand afar off. 637 19
You have made us the scorn of our *n*, * 646 11
We have become a reproach to our *n*, * 701 11
You have made us the derision of our *n*, * 702 23
he has become the scorn of his *n*. 716 24
Those who in secret slander their *n* I will destroy; * 730 17
eliminate our cruelty to these our *n*. 826 11
fulfillment in loving you and their *n*; 829 25
our duty to God, and our duty to our *n*. 847 18
What is our duty to our *n*? 848 1
Our duty to our *n* is to love them as ourselves, 848 2
relationship with God and our *n*. 848 24
harmony with God, within ourselves, with our *n*, 849 14
with our *n*, and with all creation. 852 29

neither

n have we obeyed the voice of the Lord 38 21
n with the leaven of malice and wickedness, * 46 5
n run into any kind of danger; 57 10
shall *n* slumber nor sleep; 104 20
n shall any plague come near your dwelling. 130 18
n reward us according to our sins. 148 10
n can you, unless you abide in me. 397 8
shall *n* slumber nor sleep. 473 16
n the moon by night. 473 20
where there is no death, *n* sorrow nor crying, 482 6
n sighing, but life everlasting. 482 11
n sighing, but life everlasting. 483 5
where there is no death, *n* sorrow nor crying, 498 17
n sighing, but life everlasting. 499 3
n sighing, but life everlasting. 499 12
n does he hide his face from them; * 612 2
n let the deep swallow me up; * 680 21
For judgment is *n* from the east nor from the west, * 691 14
They do not know, *n* do they understand; 705 17
n shall any plague come near your dwelling. 720 6
shall *n* slumber nor sleep; 779 8
n is there any breath in their mouth. 789 10

nest

and the swallow a *n* where she may lay her young; * 707 20

nests

Beside them the birds of the air make their *n* * 735 25
In which the birds build their *n*, * 736 11

net

Take me out of the *n* that they have secretly set 129 16
they seize the lowly and drag them away in their *n*. 595 13
for he shall pluck my feet out of the *n*. 615 19
Take me out of the *n* that they have secretly set 622 15
For they have secretly spread a *n* for me 630 3
let them be caught in the *n* they hid; 630 6
They have laid a *n* for my feet, 664 4
and stretched out a *n* of cords; * 796 11

nethermost

you have delivered me from the *n* Pit. 710 27

nets

Let the wicked fall into their own *n*, * 797 24

never

Let me *n* be confounded. 55 24
Christ being raised from the dead will *n* die again; * 83 15
by day or night they will *n* be shut. 87 20
And we shall *n* hope in vain. 98 18
Grant us, Lord, the lamp of charity which *n* fails, 110 18
where dwells the true and *n*-failing Light, 110 21
let me *n* be put to shame: * 129 9
and grant that we may *n* forget 134 13
O God, whose *n*-failing providence ordereth 177 14
for thou *n* failest to help 178 13
that our faith may *n* be found wanting 185 17
may *n* be destitute of such gifts; 197 16
O God, your *n*-failing providence sets in order 229 10
for you *n* fail to help and govern 230 8
so you *n* forsake those who make their boast 233 11
that our faith may *n* be found wanting 237 11
may *n* be destitute of such gifts; 249 2
For those who have *n* heard the word of salvation 279 21
n-ending thanks for the creation of the world, 316 10
receive the crown of glory that *n* fades away. 380 16
and whoever believes in me shall *n* thirst." 396 5
O Lord, your compassions *n* fail 460 16
and whosoever liveth and believeth in me shall *n* die. 469 3
entrust this child N. to thy *n*-failing care and love, 470 9
Grant us grace to entrust to thy *n*-failing love; 481 17
Give us grace to entrust N. to your *n*-failing care 494 2
I will *n* turn away anyone who believes in me. 501 2
n leaving your temple untended. 520 17
for you *n* forsake those who seek you, O Lord. 593 20
he hides his face; he will *n* notice." 595 17
Whoever does these things shall *n* be overthrown. 599 18
"I shall *n* be disturbed. * 621 17
let me *n* be put to shame; * 622 8
but *n* have I seen the righteous forsaken, 635 10
he has taken to his bed and will *n* get up again." 642 16
Our heart *n* turned back, * 646 22
We can *n* ransom ourselves, * 652 17
that we should *n* have enough to pay it, 652 20
and *n* see the grave. 652 22
who will *n* see the light again. 653 22
such trembling as *n* was; * 659 11
her streets are *n* free of oppression and deceit. 661 5
they *n* change; they do not fear God. 661 27
he will *n* let the righteous stumble. 662 7
like a stillborn child that *n* sees the sun. 665 10
Must I then give back what I *n* stole? 679 19
let me *n* be ashamed. 683 2
n forget the lives of your poor. 690 23
And so will we *n* turn away from you; * 703 22
and your years will *n* end. 733 6
so that it *n* shall move at any time. 735 12
For they will *n* be shaken; * 755 15
Who *n* do any wrong, * 763 9
I will *n* forget your commandments, * 771 5
let them be cast into the mire, *n* to rise up again." 796 22
to thy *n*-failing care and love, 831 8

nevertheless

N, if any of you know 514 5
N, you heard the sound of my entreaty 624 16
N, you have rejected and humbled us * 646 3
N, you shall die like mortals, * 705 22
N, he saw their distress, * 745 13

new

prepared for us our place in the *n* Jerusalem: 69 3
brought us in safety to this *n* day: 100 2
If anyone is in Christ he is a *n* creation; 106 1
the old has passed away, behold the *n* has come. 106 2
prepared for us our place in the *n* Jerusalem: 123 2
brought us in safety to this *n* day: 137 15
Almighty God, who hast poured upon us the *n* light 161 14
Create and make in us *n* and contrite hearts, 166 3
hast established the *n* covenant of reconciliation: 172 2
Grant that we, being reborn to *n* life in him, 203 7
Almighty God, you have poured upon us the *n* light 213 8
make in us *n* and contrite hearts, 217 16
mystery established the *n* covenant of reconciliation: 223 16
mystery established the *n* covenant of reconciliation: 224 14
Grant that we, being reborn to *n* life in him, 254 9
make in us *n* and contrite hearts, 264 4
I give you a *n* commandment: 275 3
things which had grown old are being made *n*, 280 20
Sanctify this *n* fire, 285 9
established the *n* covenant of reconciliation: 290 15
things which had grown old are being made *n*, 291 17
has given us a *n* birth by water and the Holy Spirit, 294 5
receive the Sacrament of *n* birth 305 12
and have raised them to the *n* life 308 4
and have raised him to the *n* life 314 3
lead a *n* life, following the commandments of God, 330 11
for this is my Blood of the *N* Testament, 335 5
for this is my Blood of the *N* Covenant, 342 7
and called us to *n* life in Jesus Christ 344 15
by water and the Holy Spirit hast made us a *n* people 345 5
hast caused a *n* light to shine in our hearts, 346 2
that he might make the whole creation *n*. 349 5
This is my Blood of the *n* Covenant, 363 3
the holy food and drink of *n* and unending life 363 14
This is my Blood of the *n* Covenant, 368 16
and his Blood of the *n* Covenant. 369 6
made a *n* people by water and the Spirit, 371 7
This is my Blood of the *n* Covenant, 371 15
destroyed death, and made the whole creation *n*. 374 8
This is my Blood of the *n* Covenant, 374 21
and called us to *n* life in Jesus Christ 377 13
you have made us a *n* people 378 1
have caused a *n* light to shine in our hearts, 378 15
that he might make the whole creation *n*. 381 20
This is my Blood of the *n* Covenant, 403 9
This is my Blood of the *n* Covenant, 405 8
for a *n* brother (sister)]. 440 6
who now has a *n* brother (sister)] 440 11
to witness the inauguration of this *n* 440 15
your mercies are *n* every morning: 460 17
will also give *n* life to our mortal bodies 501 4
N Testaments to be the Word of God, 513 10
things which had grown old are being made *n*, 515 10
administration of the sacraments of the *N* Covenant; 517 9
N Testaments to be the Word of God, 526 15
things which had grown old are being made *n*, 528 8
and the sacraments of the *N* Covenant, 532 10
administer the sacraments of the *N* Covenant. 534 4
N Testaments to be the Word of God, 538 15
things which had grown old are being made *n*, 540 8
to this *n* trust and responsibility? 559 6
Will you who witness this *n* beginning support 559 8
Greet your *n* Rector. 563 11
Be with us in the fullness of your power as *n* members 569 5
die to sin and are made *n* in Christ. 569 16
Sing for him a *n* song; * 626 5
He put a *n* song in my mouth, 640 5
Blow the ram's-horn at the *n* moon, * 704 5
Sing to the LORD a *n* song; * 725 17
Sing to the LORD a *n* song, * 727 24
O God, I will sing to you a *n* song; * 800 19
Sing to the LORD a *n* song; * 807 2
n discovery, and the pursuit of wisdom; 824 18
and give us *n* insight into your purposes 828 18
and *n* wisdom and determination 828 19
but as a chance for a *n* start. 829 19
when we are baptized into the *N* Covenant 850 25
What is the *N* Covenant? 850 26
The *N* Covenant is the *n* relationship with God 850 27
What did the Messiah promise in the *N* Covenant? 851 1
and gave us the *N* Commandment. 851 9
What is the *N* Commandment? 851 15
The *N* Commandment is that we love one another 851 16
How is the Holy Spirit revealed in the *N* Covenant? 852 20
books of the Old and *N* Testaments; 853 7
What is the *N* Testament? 853 13
The *N* Testament consists of books written 853 14
books written by the people of the *N* Covenant, 853 15
The Church is the community of the *N* Covenant. 854 4
It is called the People of God, the *N* Israel, 854 8
forgiveness of sins, and *n* life in the Holy Spirit. 858 19
and will make all things *n*. 862 4
By everlasting life, we mean a *n* existence, 862 26

newly

Let us welcome the *n* baptized. 308 11

newness

grant that we may serve you in *n* of life, 127 14
and rise with him to *n* of life; 170 4
and rise with him to *n* of life; 221 16
and rise with him to *n* of life; 283 4
and raised to him with *n* of life. 292 3
serve and please thee in *n* of life, 331 18
that we may live and serve you in *n* of life, 393 14
may die to sin and rise to *n* of life, 480 9
to live with confidence in *n* and fullness of life, 861 25

news

Behold, I bring you good *n* of a great joy 75 8
proclaim to all people the Good *N* of his salvation, 163 16
proclaim to all people the Good *N* of his salvation, 215 9
the Good *N* of God in Christ? 293 27
the Good *N* of God in Christ? 305 2
To the poor he proclaimed the good *n* 374 4
the Good *N* of God in Christ? 417 12

proclaim the good *n* of his salvation from day to day. 725 20
proclaim the Good *N* of the Kingdom 853 17

next

and his name be blotted out in the *n* generation. 751 23

Nicene

The Apostles' Creed and the *N* Creed. 851 26
What is the *N* Creed? 852 5
The *N* Creed is the creed of the universal Church 852 6

nigh

Our King and Savior draweth *n*: 43 1

night

who dividest the day from the *n* 56 19
may, when the *n* cometh, rejoice to give thee thanks; 56 23
Thine is the day, O God, thine also the *n*; 61 7
my heart teacheth me, *n* after *n*. 61 11
and darkeneth the day into *n*; 62 2
and the light around me turn to *n*," 62 6
the *n* is as bright as the day; 62 7
defend us from all perils and dangers of this *n*; 70 3
beseech thy merciful protection all the *n*. 70 7
weep this *n*, and give thine angels charge 71 2
by day or *n* they will never be shut. 87 20
by *n* you will not need the brightness of the moon. 87 28
whose light divides the day from the *n* 99 14
when *n* comes, rejoice to give you thanks; 99 18
nor the moon by *n*. 104 24
and the light around me turn to *n*," 110 8
the *n* is as bright as the day; 110 9
defend us from all perils and dangers of this *n*; 111 3
a pillar of cloud by day and a pillar of fire by *n*: 111 9
creator of the changes of day and *n*, 113 2
so be with us in the coming *n*; 113 6
Yours is the day, O God, yours also the *n*; 115 7
my heart teaches me, *n* after *n*. 115 11
and darkens the day into *n*; 115 14
and the light around me turn to *n*," 116 2
the *n* is as bright as the day; 116 3
defend us from all perils and dangers of this *n*; 123 22
ask for your protection through the coming *n*. 124 4
weep this *n*, and give your angels charge 124 18
The Lord Almighty grant us a peaceful *n* 127 1
You shall not be afraid of any terror by *n*, * 130 6
you that stand by *n* in the house of the Lord. 131 7
defend us from all perils and dangers of this *n*; 133 11
protect us through the hours of this *n*, 133 14
illumine this *n* with your celestial brightness; 133 18
by *n* as by day your people may glorify 133 19
weep this *n*, and give your angels charge 134 7
Watch over those, both *n* and day, 134 12
you that stand by *n* in the house of the Lord. 140 2
O God, who hast caused this holy *n* to shine 161 1
whose dear Son, on the *n* before he suffered, 169 7
O God, who didst make this most holy *n* to shine 170 14
O God, you have caused this holy *n* to shine 212 16
whose dear Son, on the *n* before he suffered, 221 1
O God, who made this most holy *n* to shine 222 8
whose dear Son, on the *n* before he suffered, 274 1
On this most holy *n*, 285 1
This is the *n*, when you brought our fathers, 287 6
This is the *n*, when all who believe in Christ 287 9
This is the *n*, when Christ broke the bonds 287 12
How holy is this *n*, 287 17
How blessed is this *n*, 287 21
a pillar of cloud by day and a pillar of fire by *n*: 290 3
O God, who made this most holy *n* to shine 295 8
Our Savior Christ, on the *n* before he suffered, 316 1
For in the *n* in which he was betrayed, he took bread; 334 17
For in the *n* in which he was betrayed, he took bread; 342 1
On the *n* he was handed over to suffering and death, 362 18
On the *n* before he died for us, our Lord 368 10
On the *n* he was betrayed he took bread, said the 371 10
n and day; and, beholding the glory of your presence, 373 8
Almighty Father, whose dear Son, on the *n* before he 397 13
On the *n* he was betrayed he took bread, said the 403 4
On the *n* he was handed over to suffering and death, 405 1
My tears have been my meat day and *n*, * 471 5
and as a watch in the *n*. 472 18
neither the moon by *n*. 473 20
then shall my *n* be turned to day. 475 14
but the *n* is as clear as day; * 475 16
n in prayer before he chose and sent forth his twelve 514 13
called him, serving before you day and *n* 521 11
and they meditate on his law day and *n*. 585 6
every *n* I drench my bed 590 10
my heart teaches me, *n* after *n*. 600 12
Weigh my heart, summon me by *n*, * 601 3
and one *n* imparts knowledge to another. 606 18
by *n* as well, but I find no rest. 610 5
Weeping may spend the *n*, * 621 14
For your hand was heavy upon me day and *n*; * 625 5
My tears have been my food day and *n*, * 643 5
in the *n* season his song is with me, 643 24
Day and *n* the watchmen make their rounds 661 1
and meditate on you in the *n* watches. 670 24
Yours is the day, yours also the *n*; * 690 16
my hands were stretched out by *n* and did not tire; 693 4
I commune with my heart in the *n*; * 693 12
and all the *n* through with a glow of fire. 696 2
by day and *n* I cry to you. 712 2
and like a watch in the *n*. 718 8
You shall not be afraid of any terror by *n*, * 719 20
and of your faithfulness in the *n* season; 720 25
You make darkness that it may be *n*, * 736 17
and a fire to give light in the *n* season. 741 4
I remember your Name in the *n*, O LORD, * 767 23
My eyes are open in the *n* watches, * 775 22
nor the moon by *n*. 779 12
you that stand by *n* in the house of the LORD. 787 20
The moon and the stars to govern the *n*, * 790 13
and the light around me turn to *n*," 794 21
the *n* is as bright as the day; * 794 23

nights

O ye *n* and days, bless ye the Lord; * 48 13
Glorify the Lord, O *n* and days, * 89 1

no

If we say that we have *n* sin, we deceive ourselves, 38 10
am *n* more worthy to be called thy son." 38 19
Ye are *n* more strangers and foreigners, 40 3
Christ being raised from the dead dieth *n* more; * 46 7

death hath *n* more dominion over him.	46	8
this day we fall into *n* sin,	57	10
If we say we have *n* sin, we deceive ourselves,	76	9
I am *n* longer worthy to be called your son."	76	18
You are *n* longer strangers and sojourners,	78	1
death *n* longer has dominion over him.	83	16
Violence will *n* more be heard in your land, *	87	23
The sun will *n* more be your light by day; *	87	27
N one lights a lamp to put it under a bucket,	109	8
There shall *n* evil happen to you, *	130	17
we can do *n* good thing without thee,	164	13
and grant that *n* clouds of this mortal life	165	9
Almighty God, who seest that we have *n* power	167	3
and to make *n* peace with oppression;	209	3
n clouds of this mortal life	217	2
and to make *n* peace with oppression;	260	9
but you take *n* delight in burnt-offerings.	267	9
May Christ, the Morning Star who knows *n* setting,	287	25
Thou shalt do *n* murder.	318	16
If we say that we have *n* sin, we deceive ourselves,	320	1
and from whom *n* secrets are hid:	323	8
and his kingdom will have *n* end.	327	11
whose kingdom shall have *n* end.	328	12
and to live *n* longer unto ourselves,	346	6
You shall have *n* other gods but me.	350	3
There is *n* other commandment	351	11
If we say that we have *n* sin, we deceive ourselves,	352	1
and from you *n* secrets are hid:	355	8
and his kingdom will have *n* end.	359	2
And, that we might live *n* longer for ourselves,	374	9
and to live *n* longer for ourselves	379	3
they may have rest in that place where there is *n* pain	391	17
whom God has joined together let *n* one put asunder.	428	6
whom God has joined together let *n* one put asunder.	434	7
I shall fear *n* evil;*	443	8
and *n* man dieth to himself.	469	10
Yea, the darkness is *n* darkness with thee,	475	15
I will fear *n* evil; *	476	9
I will fear *n* evil; *	477	2
inheritance in that kingdom where there is *n* death,	482	6
where sorrow and pain are *n* more,	483	4
and him that cometh to me I will in *n* wise cast out.	484	19
and for all those whom we love but see *n* longer.	498	9
in that kingdom where there is *n* death,	498	17
where sorrow and pain are *n* more,	499	2
we pray to you for those we love, but see *n* longer:	504	26
and from you *n* secrets are hid:	512	8
and defend those who have *n* helper?	518	29
and his kingdom will have *n* end.	520	2
and from you *n* secrets are hid:	525	8
and his kingdom will have *n* end.	530	21
and from you *n* secrets are hid:	537	8
and his kingdom will have *n* end.	542	21
may have rest in that place where there is *n* pain	550	22
"There is *n* help for him in his God."	587	6
For there is *n* truth in their mouth; *	589	9
For in death *n* one remembers you; *	590	7
n harm shall happen to me ever."	595	5
so that mere mortals may strike terror *n* more.	596	6
Help me, LORD, for there is *n* godly one left; *	597	1
The fool has said in his heart, "There is *n* God." *	598	12
there is none who does good; *n*, not one.	598	20
Have they *n* knowledge, all those evildoers *	598	21
There is *n* guile upon his tongue;	599	8
he does *n* evil to his friend; *	599	9
He has sworn to do *n* wrong *	599	13
melt me down; you will find *n* impurity in me.	601	4
I give *n* offense with my mouth as others do; *	601	5
n sooner shall they hear than they shall obey me; *	605	29
Although they have *n* words or language, *	606	19
by night as well, but I find *n* rest.	610	5
But as for me, I am a worm and *n* man, *	610	12
I shall fear *n* evil; *	613	4
They have *n* understanding of the LORD's doings,	619	18
Happy are they to whom the LORD imputes *n* guilt, *	625	1
and in whose spirit there is *n* guile!	625	2
like horse or mule, which have *n* understanding; *	625	20
There is *n* king that can be saved by a mighty army; *	627	7
there is *n* fear of God before his eyes.	632	4
and has set himself in *n* good way; *	632	10
In a little while the wicked shall be *n* more; *	634	3
There is *n* health in my flesh,	637	1
there is *n* soundness in my body, because of my sin.	637	3
there is *n* health in my body.	637	11
and from whose mouth comes *n* defense.	637	26
before I go my way and am *n* more.	639	26
In a sacrifice and offering you take *n* pleasure *	640	16
and are making *n* profit on the sale of them.	646	10
I will take *n* bull-calf from your stalls, *	654	21
but you take *n* delight in burnt-offerings.	657	15
The fool has said in his heart, "There is *n* God." *	658	21
there is none who does good; *n*, not one.	659	6
Have they *n* knowledge, those evildoers *	659	7
those who have *n* regard for God.	659	23
I have *n* peace, because of my cares.	660	8
N; you devise evil in your hearts, *	664	23
n matter how skillful his charming.	665	4
show *n* mercy to those who are faithless and evil.	666	6
make an end of them, and they shall be *n* more.	666	25
you *n* longer go out, O God, with our armies.	668	7
Put *n* trust in extortion;	670	5
in robbery take *n* empty pride; *	670	6
as in a barren and dry land where there is *n* water.	670	14
let *n* rebel rise up against him.	674	8
and there is *n* firm ground for my feet.	679	10
for comforters, but I could find *n* one.	681	5
peace till the moon shall be *n* more.	685	23
and the oppressed who has *n* helper.	686	8
For they suffer *n* pain, *	687	7
In the misfortunes of others they have *n* share; *	687	9
and find in them *n* fault.	687	20
I was stupid and had *n* understanding; *	688	21
There are *n* signs for us to see;	690	1
there is *n* prophet left; *	690	2
I will say to the boasters, 'Boast *n* more,' *	691	10
Will he *n* more show his favor?	693	15
For they had *n* faith in God, *	696	20
and had *n* faith in his wonderful works.	697	15
there were *n* wedding songs for their maidens.	700	6
and their widows made *n* lamentation.	700	8
and there was *n* one to bury them.	701	10
There shall be *n* strange god among you; *	704	19
let the name of Israel be remembered *n* more."	706	11
N good thing will the LORD withhold *	708	16

I have become like one who has *n* strength;	712	8
Whom you remember *n* more, *	712	11
N enemy shall deceive him, *	715	10
There shall *n* evil happen to you, *	720	5
my Rock, in whom there is *n* fault.	721	28
the God of Jacob takes *n* notice."	723	8
he who teaches all the world, has he *n* knowledge?	723	14
I will set *n* worthless thing before my eyes; *	730	12
and the wicked be *n* more.	737	25
He let *n* one oppress them *	739	5
and do my prophets *n* harm."	739	8
they found *n* way to a city where they might dwell.	746	9
you *n* longer go out, O God, with our armies.	750	18
Let there be *n* one to show him kindness, *	751	20
he took *n* delight in blessing,	752	6
they make *n* sound with their throat.	758	3
In my distress I said, "*N* one can be trusted."	759	22
but your commandment has *n* bounds.	771	12
let *n* iniquity have dominion over me.	774	14
for them there is *n* stumbling block.	777	10
I have *n* haughty looks.	785	11
I look to my right hand and find *n* one	798	7
I have *n* place to flee to, and *n* one cares for me.	798	8
for in your sight shall *n* one living be justified.	798	22
n breaching of the walls, *n* going into exile, *	801	8
n wailing in the public squares.	801	9
there is *n* end to his greatness.	801	17
for there is *n* help in them.	803	8
there is *n* limit to his wisdom.	804	11
he has *n* pleasure in the strength of a man;	804	23
in whose perfect kingdom *n* sword is drawn	815	22
n strength known but the strength of love:	815	23
that *n* one may suffer from our abuse of them,	827	19
to bear *n* malice, prejudice, or hatred in our hearts;	848	8

noble

The *n* army of martyrs praise thee.	53	5
The *n* fellowship of prophets praise you.	95	24
the *n* works that thou didst in their days,	154	6
bring this child to love all that is true and *n*,	443	27
Who can express the *n* acts of the LORD, *	478	13
upon those who are *n* among the people.	600	2
My heart is stirring with a *n* song;	647	11

nobles

The *n* of the peoples have gathered together *	650	22
and their *n* with links of iron;	807	17

noise

One deep calls to another in the *n* of your cataracts; *	643	21
I am shaken by the *n* of the enemy *	660	9
Let the sea make a *n* and all that is in it, *	728	16

none

may find it *n* other than the way of life	56	9
may find it *n* other than the way of life	99	4
may find it *n* other than the way of life	168	13
may find it *n* other than the way of life	220	4
may find it *n* other than the way of life	272	4
Thou shalt have *n* other gods but me.	317	26
For *n* of us liveth to himself,	469	9
For *n* of us has life in himself,	491	13
and *n* becomes his own master when he dies.	491	14
and snatch me away with *n* to deliver me.	590	23
search out their wickedness until you find *n*.	595	28
there is *n* who does any good.	598	14
there is *n* who does good; no, not one.	598	20
they cry out, but there is *n* to help them; *	605	22
and there is *n* to help.	610	24
Let *n* who look to you be put to shame; *	614	17
and *n* will be punished who trust in him.	629	12
there is *n* who can be compared with you.	640	13
lest I rend you and there be *n* to deliver you.	655	27
there is *n* who does any good.	658	23
there is *n* who does good; no, not one.	659	6
I looked for sympathy, but there was *n*,	681	4
and let there be *n* to dwell in their tents.	681	15
because there is *n* who will save."	683	24
n of the warriors can lift a hand.	692	11
Among the gods there is *n* like you, O LORD, *	710	13
they stumbled, and there was *n* to help.	747	6
and *n* to pity his fatherless children.	751	21
when as yet there was *n* of them.	795	9
and all who have *n* to care for them.	826	4

noonday

who at *n* called your servant Saint Paul	107	12
call the evening, the morning, and the *n* one day;	110	24
and your just dealing as the *n*.	633	16
In the evening, in the morning, and at *n*,	661	19

north

You have made the *n* and the south; *	714	17
from the *n* and from the south.	746	7

noses

n, but they cannot smell;	757	25

nostrils

Smoke rose from his *n*	603	4
at the blast of the breath of your *n*.	603	22

note

If you, LORD, were to *n* what is done amiss, *	784	21

noted

You have *n* my lamentation;	663	6

nothing

Is it *n* to you, all ye that pass by?	39	4
Is it *n* to you, all you who pass by?	77	3
all our doings without charity are *n* worth:	164	19
to dread *n* but the loss of thee,	165	7
Almighty and everlasting God, who hatest *n*	166	1
n is strong, *n* is holy:	180	2
we can do *n* good without you,	216	8
whatever we do is worth *n*:	216	14
to fear *n* but the loss of you,	216	21
Almighty and everlasting God, you hate *n*	217	14
n is strong, *n* is holy:	231	18
Almighty and everlasting God, you hate *n*	264	2
And if I am to do *n*, let me do it gallantly.	461	23
therefore can I lack *n*.	476	2
n is hidden from its burning heat.	607	3
for those who fear him lack *n*.	628	12
but those who seek the LORD lack *n* that is good.	628	14
they charge me with matters I know *n* about.	630	14

So I held my tongue and said *n*; *	638	19
and my lifetime is as *n* in your sight; *	639	4
For they will carry *n* away at their death, *	653	17
and having you I desire *n* upon earth.	688	28
To put *n* in the place of God;	847	23
asking *n* but to enjoy God's presence.	857	3
Our assurance as Christians is that *n*,	862	30
notice		
he hides his face; he will never *n*."	595	17
the God of Jacob takes no *n*."	723	8
notorious		
because of *n* sins, had been separated	265	4
nourish		
n us with all goodness,	181	13
n us with all goodness;	233	5
n them with patience;	467	5
n them from the riches of God's grace,	518	14
In all that you do, you are to *n* Christ's people	531	18
n his soul with patience,	831	15
nourished		
and be *n* by that spiritual Food,	316	18
He was *n* with your Body and Blood;	497	19
and to be *n* by the Body and Blood of your Son.	568	11
nourishment		
to seek *n* from them,	543	8
our *n* in eternal life.	860	3
nowhere		
Almighty God, whose Son had *n* to lay his head:	829	22
numb		
I am utterly *n* and crushed; *	637	12
number		
faithful servant Matthias to be of the *n* of the Twelve:	188	2
multiply, by the grace of the Paschal sacrament, the *n*	289	7
So teach us to *n* our days, *	473	7
they appointed Matthias to be one of their *n*.	514	15
and many in *n* are those who wrongfully hate me.	638	8
LORD, let me know my end and the *n* of my days, *	639	1
they are more in *n* than the hairs of my head,	641	6
count the *n* of her towers.	651	28
though I cannot know the *n* of them.	684	11
So teach us to *n* our days *	718	25
he has shortened the *n* of my days;	732	23
with its living things too many to *n*, *	737	2
When they were few in *n*, *	739	1
and young locusts without *n*,	740	22
they would be more in *n* than the sand; *	795	12
He counts the *n* of the stars *	804	8
numbered		
Make them to be *n* with thy saints,	53	21
your faithful servant Matthias to be *n* among the Twelve:	239	12
n among the offspring of Abraham,	289	17
O God, whose mercies cannot be *n*:	470	1
and whose mercies cannot be *n*:	489	4
O God, whose mercies cannot be *n*:	493	10
and whose mercies cannot be *n*:	504	2
nurses		
gifts through the skill of surgeons and *n*,	459	14
nurture		
faithful in the care and *n* of thy flock;	196	24
who was faithful in the care and *n* of your flock;	248	9
for the procreation of children and their *n*	423	12
n him, that he may attain to that full stature	841	4
nurtured		
May our sons be like plants well *n* from their youth, *	801	1

O

oak		
The voice of the LORD makes the *o* trees writhe *	620	21
oath		
To perform the *o* which he swore	51	5
This was the *o* he swore	92	27
I have sworn an *o* to David my servant:	713	22
those who scoff at me have taken an *o* against me.	731	16
the *o* that he swore to Isaac,	738	18
How he swore an *o* to the LORD *	786	1
The LORD has sworn an *o* to David; *	786	19
obedience		
of life and his *o* to thy commands;	188	11
bound together in love and *o* to thee,	204	20
and his *o* to your commands;	239	20
bound together in love and *o* to you,	255	18
lead them to faith and *o*.	279	29
Therefore in joyful *o* to your Son, we bring	306	23
lead them in the knowledge and *o* of your Word,	310	10
o to his command, his Church renders	316	9
Who in the *o* of thy saints hast given	348	4
in *o* to your will, a perfect sacrifice	362	16
in *o* to you, our Creator, we might rule	373	20
Because in the *o* of your saints you have given	380	20
lead them in the knowledge and *o* of your Word,	419	6
gave us the example of *o* to your Father's will:	461	6
o to thy holy commandments,	487	16
fulfill this trust in *o* to Christ?	518	2
baptize in *o* to our Lord.	561	4
Therefore in joyful *o* to your Son, we bring	570	15
the vows of poverty, chastity, and *o*,	819	9
and that, through *o* to thy law,	820	11
his steadfast *o*, by which he overcame temptation;	836	14
By his *o*, even to suffering and death,	850	7
obedient		
and with penitent and *o* hearts confess	41	12
and with penitent and *o* hearts confess	62	12
and with penitent and *o* hearts confess	79	7
and with penitent and *o* hearts confess	116	8
confess your sins with a humble and *o* heart	450	6
and humbled himself, becoming *o* even to death	545	3
by a humble, holy, and *o* walking	840	21
obey		
that our hearts may be set to *o* thy commandments,	69	19
the whole earth also worship thee, all nations *o* thee,	70	16
the whole earth also worship you, all nations *o* you,	124	13

ready wills and hearts *o* the calling of our Lord 193 1
and hearts *o* the calling of our Lord to follow him; 244 10
Do you promise to follow and *o* him 303 1
the earth bow and *o*: 457 1
I will *o* Christ, and will serve in his name. 518 3
o your bishop and other ministers 526 11
o your bishop and other ministers 538 11
o these Canons, and be among us to share 562 3
Give us ears to hear and hearts to *o*. 571 3
no sooner shall they hear than they shall *o* me; * 605 29
and Israel would not *o* me. 704 25
therefore I *o* them with all my heart. 774 6
To love and *o* God and to bring others to know him; 847 21
Since we do not fully *o* them, are they useful at all? 848 25
Since we do not fully *o* them, we see more clearly 848 26

obeyed

neither have we *o* the voice of the Lord 38 21
and have not *o* the voice of the Lord 76 20
that he may be known, worshiped, and *o* 163 10
Andrew that he readily *o* the call 185 8
that he may be known, worshiped, and *o* 215 4
Andrew that he readily *o* the call 237 2

object

an *o* of scorn and derision to those around us. 701 12

oblation

by his one *o* of himself once offered, 334 12
and sufficient sacrifice, *o*, and satisfaction, 334 13
Therefore will I offer in his dwelling an *o* 477 25
Therefore I will offer in his dwelling an *o* 618 7
thanksgiving, penitence, *o*, intercession, 856 28
What is prayer of *o*? 857 14
O is an offering of ourselves, 857 15

oblations

Let us with gladness present the offerings and *o* 344 12
Let us with gladness present the offerings and *o* 377 10
with burnt-offerings and *o*; * 657 21

obligations

the *o* which Christian Marriage demands. 433 4
fulfill our *o* in the community of nations. 822 4

oblivion

and the torrents of *o* made me afraid. 602 15

observance

o of a holy Lent, by self-examination and repentance; 265 11
now that our Lenten *o* is ended, 292 4

observe

to *o* the discipline of Christ. 545 13
o the upright; * 636 11
and *o* his laws. 741 16
Happy are they who *o* his decrees * 763 7
because I *o* your commandments. 771 20

observed

The first Christians *o* with great devotion 264 10

obtain

confess our sins, that we may *o* forgiveness 41 13
confess our sins, so that we may *o* forgiveness 62 13
hearts confess our sins, that we may *o* forgiveness 79 8
confess our sins, so that we may *o* forgiveness 116 9
may *o* of thee, the God of all mercy, 166 5
and above all things, may *o* thy promises, 174 4
thy grace, that we, running to *o* thy promises, 182 14
and, that we may *o* that which thou dost promise, 183 18
run without stumbling to *o* thy heavenly promises; 184 4
may *o* of you, the God of all mercy, perfect remission 217 18
may *o* your promises, which exceed 225 17
running to *o* your promises, 234 8
and, that we may *o* what you promise, 235 10
run without stumbling to *o* your heavenly promises; 235 16
may *o* of you, the God of all mercy, perfect remission 264 6
that we may *o* mercy, and find grace 320 7
we, and all thy whole Church, may *o* remission 335 28
grant that we may *o* effectually, 394 2
and *o* those eternal joys prepared for all 432 6
and finally, by thy mercy, *o* everlasting life; 832 4
We praise God, not to *o* anything, 857 5

obtained

o effectually, to the relief of our necessity, 153 24
o, to the relief of our necessity, 834 6

occasion

The birth of a child is a joyous and solemn *o* 440 2
It is also an *o* for rejoicing 440 2
an *o* for us to renew our trust in your Father's love. 498 4
and seek *o* to kill them. 635 27

occasions

bestowing upon us *o* of song in the evening. 113 4
and all *o* invite your tender mercies: 572 9

occupations

that in all the cares and *o* of our life 57 16
that in all the cares and *o* of our life 100 8
Deliver us, we beseech thee, in our several *o* 210 3
Deliver us in our various *o* 261 9

occupied

Let me not be *o* in wickedness with evildoers, * 797 10

occupy

I do not *o* myself with great matters, * 785 12

ocean

He gathers up the waters of the *o* as in a water-skin * 626 13

off

peace to those who are far *o* and to those 58 3
peace to those who are far *o* and to those 100 19
peace to those who are far *o* and to those 206 11
peace to those who are far *o* and to those 257 7
"let us cast *o* their bonds from us." 586 7
Why do you stand so far *o*, O LORD, * 594 19
Oh, that the LORD would cut *o* all smooth tongues, * 597 5
you have put *o* my sack-cloth and clothed me 622 4
"I have been cut *o* from the sight of your eyes." * 624 15
he has left *o* acting wisely and doing good. 632 8
For evildoers shall be cut *o*, * 634 1
and when the wicked are cut *o*, you will see it. 636 5
the future of the wicked is cut *o*. 636 14
my neighbors stand afar *o*. 637 19
I would flee to a far-*o* place * 660 19
Let them vanish like water that runs *o*; * 665 7

O God, you have cast us _o_ and broken us; * 667 9
Have you not cast us _o_, O God? * 668 6
Do not cast me _o_ in my old age; * 683 18
O God, why have you utterly cast us _o_? * 689 9
He shall break _o_ all the horns of the wicked; * 691 24
Will the Lord cast me _o_ for ever? * 693 14
so that all who pass by pluck _o_ its grapes? 703 12
for they are cut _o_ from your hand. 712 12
But you have cast _o_ and rejected your anointed; * 716 17
Have you not cast us _o_, O God? * 750 17
I am shaken _o_ like a locust. 752 22

offend

so that I do not _o_ with my tongue. 638 16

offended

we have _o_ against thy holy laws, 41 20
we have _o_ against thy holy laws, 63 1
_o_ in what you have done or left undone, 317 3
forgive those who have _o_ you, 317 8
we have _o_ against thy holy laws, 321 1
for all whom we have injured or _o_, 391 6
and have not _o_ against my God; 604 6
and _o_ him in the desert! 698 8

offends

Who can tell how often he _o_? * 607 22

offense

I give no _o_ with my mouth as others do; * 601 5
and innocent of a great _o_. 607 27
not for any _o_ or fault of mine, O LORD. 665 24

offenses

and forgiven for our sins and _o_, 68 13
and forgiven for our sins and _o_, 122 15
forgive us all our _o_; 127 12
Remember not, Lord Christ, our _o_, 148 9
nor the _o_ of our forefathers; 148 9
in your great compassion blot out my _o_. 266 3
not weighing our merits, but pardoning our _o_, 336 12
For the absolution and remission of our sins and _o_, 385 4
his great mercy forgive you all your _o_; 448 3
in your great compassion blot out my _o_. 449 2
his great mercy forgive you all your _o_; 451 13
in your great compassion blot out my _o_. 656 7

offer

Receive our supplications and prayers which we _o_ 57 21
Receive our supplications and prayers which we _o_ 100 13
O the appointed sacrifices * 128 18
Receive our supplications and prayers, which we _o_ 206 3
faithful people _o_ you true and laudable service: 235 15
Receive our supplications and prayers, which we _o_ 256 21
Receive our supplications and prayers which we _o_ 278 13
may worthily _o_ to you our sacrifice of thanksgiving; 289 3
let us _o_ continually the sacrifice of praise, 317 20
Receive these our prayers which we _o_ 329 3
_o_ unto thee, the memorial thy Son hath commanded 335 12
And here we _o_ and present unto thee, O Lord, 336 1
to _o_ unto thee any sacrifice, yet we beseech thee 336 10
_o_ unto thee, the memorial thy Son hath commanded 342 12
whereby we _o_ and present unto thee, O Lord, 342 22
O to God a sacrifice of thanksgiving, 343 8
and then come and _o_ thy gift. 343 20
Through Christ let us continually _o_ to God 344 1
that we might _o_ before thee a sacrifice of praise 348 16
resurrection, and ascension, we _o_ you these gifts. 363 12
And we _o_ our sacrifice of praise and thanksgiving 369 1
they _o_ you unceasing praise. 373 9
O to God a sacrifice of thanksgiving, 376 4
and then come and _o_ your gift. 376 16
Through Christ let us continually _o_ to God 376 17
that we might _o_ before you a sacrifice of praise 381 10
who desires now to _o_ you her praises 444 3
Therefore will I _o_ in his dwelling an oblation 477 25
and _o_ our prayers to Almighty God 514 16
_o_ spiritual sacrifices acceptable to you; 534 1
Let us then _o_ our prayers to God for all his people, 560 1
O the appointed sacrifices * 588 8
Their libations of blood I will not _o_, * 600 5
Therefore I will _o_ in his dwelling an oblation 618 7
O to God a sacrifice of thanksgiving * 655 7
then shall they _o_ young bullocks upon your altar. 657 22
I will _o_ you a freewill sacrifice * 660 1
I will _o_ you sacrifices of fat beasts 674 24
and the kings of Arabia and Saba _o_ gifts. 686 4
Let them _o_ a sacrifice of thanksgiving * 747 25
I will _o_ you the sacrifice of thanksgiving * 760 8
I will _o_ thanks to the LORD. 762 10
For what do we _o_ thanksgiving? 857 7
to _o_ prayer, and to celebrate the sacraments. 857 24

offered

incense shall be _o_ unto my Name, 38 7
incense shall be _o_ to my Name, 76 6
incense shall be _o_ to my Name, 106 8
for whom our prayers are _o_ may be strengthened 208 19
for whom our prayers are _o_ may be strengthened 260 4
Had you desired it, I would have _o_ sacrifice; * 267 8
made there, by his one oblation of himself once _o_, 334 12
stretched out his arms upon the cross, and _o_ himself, 362 15
Our Lord Jesus Christ, who _o_ himself to be sacrificed 448 7
Our Lord Jesus Christ, who _o_ himself to be sacrificed 451 6
Our Lord Jesus Christ, who _o_ himself to be sacrificed 452 1
intercessions _o_ in this place today 572 11
through which he _o_ himself as a perfect sacrifice. 573 14
_o_ to your honor and glory. 578 6
Had you desired it, I would have _o_ sacrifice, * 657 14
and ate sacrifices _o_ to the dead. 744 4
which they _o_ to the idols of Canaan, 744 25
art and music to perfect the praises _o_ by your people 819 15
servant for whom our prayers are _o_. 831 14
We mean that he went to the departed and _o_ them 850 15
Thanksgiving is _o_ to God for all the blessings 857 8

offering

shall be offered unto my Name, and a pure _o_: 38 8
shall be offered to my Name, and a pure _o_; 76 7
shall be offered to my Name, and a pure _o_; 106 8
Holy Father, accept our evening sacrifice, the _o_ 287 23
and he is the perfect _o_ for our sins, 332 16
an _o_ and sacrifice to God. 343 13
and _o_ to you this sacrifice of thanksgiving, 371 19
and _o_ to you, from the gifts you have given us, 374 27
an _o_ and sacrifice to God. 376 9

If you are *o* your gift at the altar, 376 13
in *o* heartfelt thanks for the joyful and solemn 440 12
and he is the perfect *o* for our sins, 450 2
declaring pardon in your Name, *o* the holy gifts, 521 12
o of a pure, and gentle, and holy life; 521 15
o all your labors to God, 532 26
o to you their gifts and talents; 560 8
In a sacrifice and *o* you take no pleasure * 640 16
Burnt-*o* and sin-*o* you have not required, * 640 18
This will please the LORD more than an *o* of oxen, * 681 26
Jesus made the *o* which we could not make; 850 8
Oblation is an *o* of ourselves, 857 15
and in which he unites us to his one *o* 859 12
Liturgy, the Mass, and the Great O. 859 17

offerings

but you take no delight in burnt-*o*. 267 9
bring *o* and come into his courts. 343 10
Let us with gladness present the *o* and oblations 344 12
bring *o* and come into his courts. 376 7
Let us with gladness present the *o* and oblations 377 10
Remember all your *o* * 608 5
your *o* are always before me. 654 20
but you take no delight in burnt-*o*. 657 15
with burnt-*o* and oblations; * 657 21
I will present to you thank-*o*; 663 15
I will enter your house with burnt-*o* 674 20
bring *o* and come into his courts. 726 8

offers

Whoever *o* me the sacrifice of thanksgiving 656 1

office

called to any *o* and ministry for thy people; 205 7
called to any *o* and ministry for your people; 256 4
God has called you to the *o* of bishop? 517 19
to serve his Church in the *o* of bishop. 519 2
and let another take his *o*. 751 13
send down upon those who hold *o* in this State 822 18

officers

To the Judges and *o* of our Courts give understanding 822 6

offices

serve in their *o* to promote the well-being of all people; 822 21

officials

in the election of *o* and representatives; 822 25

offspring

and of all their righteous *o*: 90 19
numbered among the *o* of Abraham, 289 17
You will destroy their *o* from the land * 609 18
stand in awe of him, O *o* of Israel; 611 27
and their *o* shall inherit the land. 615 15
but the *o* of the wicked shall be destroyed. 635 19
and their *o* shall stand fast in your sight." 733 8
O *o* of Abraham his servant, * 738 11

oft

Do this, as *o* as ye shall drink it, 335 6
Do this, as *o* as ye shall drink it, 342 9

often

Who can tell how *o* he offends? * 607 22
How *o* the people disobeyed him in the wilderness * 698 7
As *o* as I said, "My foot has slipped," * 724 1
They restore us, though we *o* destroy them. 838 23
make us rich, though we *o* exploit them. 839 2
They are models for us, though we *o* fall 839 5
have *o* hidden from its light. 839 10
the Apocrypha, are *o* included in the Bible. 853 8

Og

and O, the king of Bashan, * 788 24
And O, the king of Bashan, * 791 9

oil

more than when grain and wine and *o* increase. 129 5
consecrate this *o*, that those who are sealed with it 307 11
you have anointed my head with *o*, 443 13
Send your Holy Spirit to sanctify this *o*; 455 10
I anoint you with *o* in the Name of the Father, 456 11
As you are outwardly anointed with this holy *o*, 456 13
thou has anointed my head with *o*, 476 14
thou anointest my head with *o*; 477 7
use this *o*, and be among us as a healer 561 6
more than when grain and wine and *o* increase. 588 14
you have anointed my head with *o*, 613 9
with the *o* of gladness above your fellows. 648 5
His words are smoother than *o*, * 662 3
with my holy *o* have I anointed him. 715 7
I am anointed with fresh *o*. 721 17
O to make a cheerful countenance, * 736 7
and into his bones like *o*; 752 10
It is like fine *o* upon the head * 787 11
let not the *o* of the unrighteous anoint my head; * 797 13
Unction is the rite of anointing the sick with *o*, 861 14

old

Not with *o* leaven, 46 4
Not with the *o* leaven, 83 13
Through his holy prophets he promised of *o*, 92 22
the *o* has passed away, behold the new has come. 106 1
and in the *o* time before them. 154 7
have put away the *o* life of sin, so we may be renewed 201 14
Christ dost turn us from the *o* life of sin: 203 6
from the *o* life of sin by our baptism into the death 203 13
have put away the *o* life of sin, so we may be renewed 253 2
you turn us from the *o* life of sin: 254 8
from the *o* life of sin by our baptism into the death 254 14
and things which had grown *o* are being made new, 280 19
O God, whose wonderful deeds of *o* shine forth 289 12
and things which had grown *o* are being made new, 291 16
believe the Holy Scriptures of the O and New 513 9
and things which had grown *o* are being made new, 515 9
believe the Holy Scriptures of the O and New 526 15
and things which had grown *o* are being made new, 528 7
caring alike for young and *o*, strong and weak, 531 12
believe the Holy Scriptures of the O and New 538 15
and things which had grown *o* are being made new, 540 7
I have been young and now I am *o*, * 635 9
in the days of *o*. 645 9
God, who is enthroned of *o*, will hear me 661 25
Do not cast me off in my *o* age; * 683 18
And now that I am *o* and gray-headed, 684 16

I consider the days of *o*; * 693 10
and call to mind your wonders of *o* time. 693 23
Where, Lord, are your loving-kindnesses of *o*, * 717 12
They shall still bear fruit in *o* age; * 721 25
When I remember your judgments of *o*, * 767 17
o and young together. 806 18
the homeless and the destitute, the *o* and the sick, 826 3
What is the O Covenant? 846 23
The O Covenant is the one given by God 846 24
Where is this O Covenant to be found? 847 6
the books which we call the O Testament. 847 8
Where in the O Testament is God's will for us shown 847 9
How is the Holy Spirit revealed in the O Covenant? 852 17
The Holy Spirit is revealed in the O Covenant 852 18
books of the O and New Testaments; 853 7
What is the O Testament? 853 9
The O Testament consists of books written 853 10
written by the people of the O Covenant, 853 11
written by people of the O Covenant, 853 21

olive

But I am like a green *o* tree in the house of God; * 658 16
your children like *o* shoots round about your table. 783 18

omens

and his *o* in the field of Zoan. 698 14

once

For in that he died, he died unto sin *o*; 46 9
The death that he died, he died to sin, *o* for all; * 83 17
I lie down in peace; at *o* I fall asleep; * 129 6
you *o* delivered by the power of your mighty arm 289 13
Holy Baptism, by which we *o* renounced Satan 292 5
by his one oblation of himself *o* offered, 334 12
I lie down in peace; at *o* I fall asleep; * 588 15
God has spoken *o*, twice have I heard it, * 670 8
You spoke *o* in a vision and said 715 3
O for all I have sworn by my holiness: * 716 11

one

we have turned every *o* to his own way; 39 1
saith the high and lofty O that inhabiteth eternity, 40 23
Father, Son, and Holy Ghost, *o* God: 43 14
O God, who hast made of *o* blood all the peoples 58 1
who hast given us grace at this time with *o* accord 59 12
entrusting *o* another and all our life to Christ, 68 24
in companionship with *o* another 71 8
who hast given us grace at this time with *o* accord 72 9
a copy of the true *o*, but into heaven itself, 77 15
Thus says the high and lofty O who inhabits eternity, 78 22
also with the *o* who has a contrite and humble spirit, 78 24
Father, Son, and Holy Spirit, *o* God: 81 10
for the great *o* in the midst of you is the Holy O 86 14
The Zion of the Holy O of Israel. 87 22
for you only are the Holy O. 94 16
For you alone are the Holy O, 95 9
O God, you have made of *o* blood all the peoples 100 17
you have given us grace at this time with *o* accord 102 1
No *o* lights a lamp to put it under a bucket, 109 8
evening, the morning, and the noonday *o* day; 110 24
entrusting *o* another and all our life to Christ, 122 26
in companionship with *o* another 125 3
you have given us grace at this time with *o* accord 126 1
O holy, blessed, and glorious Trinity, *o* God, 148 7
o God, now and for ever. 159 8
o God, now and for ever. 160 10
o God, world without end. 160 16
o God, in glory everlasting. 161 5
o God, world without end. 161 12
o God, now and for ever. 161 18
o God, in glory everlasting. 162 5
o God, for ever and ever. 162 12
o God, now and for ever. 162 17
o God, in glory everlasting. 163 6
o God, now and for ever. 163 12
o God, for ever and ever. 163 18
o God, for ever and ever. 164 5
o God, now and for ever. 164 10
o God, now and for ever. 165 5
o God, for ever and ever. 165 20
o God, for ever and ever. 166 8
let each *o* find thee mighty to save; 166 12
o God, now and for ever. 166 14
o God, for ever and ever. 167 2
o God, now and for ever. 167 14
o God, for ever and ever. 168 8
o God, for ever and ever. 169 6
o God, world without end. 169 13
o God, for ever and ever. 170 6
o God, now and for ever. 170 13
o God, world without end. 171 4
o God, now and for ever. 171 8
o God, for ever and ever. 172 6
o God, now and for ever. 172 13
o God, for ever and ever. 173 3
o God, now and for ever. 173 9
o God, for ever and ever. 174 6
o God, in glory everlasting. 174 13
o God, world without end. 174 19
o God, world without end. 175 6
o God, for ever and ever. 175 13
at last to see thee in thy *o* and eternal glory, 176 6
o God, for ever and ever. 176 8
o God, now and for ever. 177 2
o God, for ever and ever. 178 5
o God, now and for ever. 178 11
o God, for ever and ever. 179 3
and united to *o* another with pure affection; 179 7
o God, now and for ever. 179 22
o God, for ever and ever. 180 6
o God, now and for ever. 181 3
o God, world without end. 181 9
o God, for ever and ever. 181 16
o God, now and for ever. 182 4
o God, for ever and ever. 182 10
o God, for ever and ever. 183 5
o God, now and for ever. 183 9
o God, now and for ever. 184 6
o God, world without end. 184 14
o God, for ever and ever. 184 21
o God, now and for ever. 185 6
o God, in glory everlasting. 186 5
o God, now and for ever. 186 11
that in unity and peace we may proclaim the *o* truth 187 4
follow the *o* Lord, our Savior Jesus Christ; 187 5

o God, now and for ever. 187 6
o God, now and for ever. 188 6
o God, for ever and ever. 188 13
o God, for ever and ever. 189 4
o God, now and for ever. 189 9
o God, for ever and ever. 190 9
may ever stand firm upon the *o* foundation, 190 13
o God, for ever and ever. 190 15
o God, now and for ever. 191 6
o God, world without end. 191 20
o God, now and for ever. 192 6
o God, for ever and ever. 192 12
o God, in glory everlasting. 192 18
o God, now and for ever. 193 3
o God, for ever and ever. 193 9
o God, for ever and ever. 194 6
who hast knit together thine elect in *o* communion 194 8
o God, in glory everlasting. 194 15
o God, now and for ever. 194 22
o God, for ever and ever. 195 7
o God, for ever and ever. 196 6
o God, now and for ever. 196 13
o God, for ever and ever. 197 3
by this teaching we may know thee, the *o* true God, 197 22
o God, for ever and ever. 197 24
o God, now and for ever. 198 7
o God, for ever and ever. 198 22
o God, now and for ever. 199 2
who by thy Holy Spirit hast made us *o* with thy saints 199 4
Being of glorious majesty and perfect love as *o* God 199 13
o God, world without end. 200 5
o God, for ever and ever. 200 11
o God, for ever and ever. 201 6
o God, now and for ever. 201 11
o God, now and for ever. 202 7
o God, for ever and ever. 202 15
o God, now and for ever. 203 4
o God, now and for ever. 204 6
prayed for his disciples that they might be *o*, 204 18
even as thou and he are *o*: 204 19
may be united in *o* body by the *o* Spirit, 204 20
o God, now and for ever. 205 3
o God, for ever and ever. 205 20
o God, now and for ever. 206 7
O God, who hast made of *o* blood all the peoples 206 9
o God, for ever and ever. 206 23
o God, for ever and ever. 207 6
o God, now and for ever. 207 14
o God, now and for ever. 208 8
remembering the account that we must *o* day give, 208 12
o God, for ever and ever. 208 15
o God, now and for ever. 209 7
o God, for ever and ever. 209 16
o that serveth, thy Son Jesus Christ our Lord, 210 7
o God, for ever and ever. 210 8
who hast so linked our lives *o* with another 210 10
o God, now and for ever. 211 7
o God, now and for ever. 212 9
o God, in glory everlasting. 212 20
o God, now and for ever. 213 12
o God, in glory everlasting. 213 17
o God, for ever and ever. 214 5
o God, now and for ever. 214 11
o God, in glory everlasting. 214 17
o God, now and for ever. 215 6
o God, for ever and ever. 215 12
o God, now and for ever. 216 4
o God, for ever and ever. 216 11
o God, now and for ever. 217 6
o God, for ever and ever. 217 12
let each *o* find you mighty to save; 218 4
o God, now and for ever. 218 6
o God, for ever and ever. 218 12
o God, now and for ever. 219 4
o God, for ever and ever. 219 19
o God, for ever and ever. 220 6
o God, for ever and ever. 221 6
o God, now and for ever. 222 6
o God, now and for ever. 223 2
o God, for ever and ever. 223 20
o God, now and for ever. 224 6
o God, for ever and ever. 224 18
o God, now and for ever. 225 1
o God, for ever and ever. 225 6
o God, in glory everlasting. 226 6
o God, for ever and ever. 226 12
o God, for ever and ever. 227 6
see you in your *o* and eternal glory, O Father; 228 6
o God, for ever and ever. 228 7
o God, now and for ever. 228 12
o God, now and for ever. 229 4
o God, for ever and ever. 229 9
o God, now and for ever. 230 5
o God, for ever and ever. 230 11
and united to *o* another with pure affection; 231 1
o God, for ever and ever. 231 3
o God, now and for ever. 231 9
o God, for ever and ever. 232 5
o God, now and for ever. 232 16
o God, for ever and ever. 233 2
o God, now and for ever. 233 13
o God, for ever and ever. 234 5
o God, now and for ever. 235 2
o God, for ever and ever. 235 8
o God, for ever and ever. 236 7
o God, now and for ever. 236 19
o God, now and for ever. 237 6
o God, in glory everlasting. 237 18
o God, for ever and ever. 238 6
in unity and peace we may proclaim the *o* truth 238 17
follow the *o* Lord, our Savior Jesus Christ; 238 18
o God, now and for ever. 238 19
o God, now and for ever. 239 4
o God, for ever and ever. 239 22
o God, now and for ever. 240 5
o God, for ever and ever. 240 11
o God, for ever and ever. 241 1
may ever stand firm upon the *o* foundation, 241 22
o God, now and for ever. 241 24
o God, for ever and ever. 242 6
o God, now and for ever. 242 13
o God, for ever and ever. 243 6
o God, now and for ever. 243 12
o God, in glory everlasting. 244 6

o God, now and for ever. 244 12
o God, for ever and ever. 244 18
o God, now and for ever. 245 3
o God, for ever and ever. 245 15
you have knit together your elect in *o* communion 245 16
o God, in glory everlasting. 245 22
o God, now and for ever. 246 7
o God, for ever and ever. 247 4
o God, now and for ever. 247 25
o God, now and for ever. 248 6
o God, for ever and ever. 248 13
o God, for ever and ever. 249 3
by this teaching we may know you, the *o* true 249 7
o God, now and for ever. 249 16
o God, for ever and ever. 250 6
o God, now and for ever. 250 13
by your Holy Spirit you have made us *o* 250 14
Being of glorious majesty and perfect love as *o* God 251 2
o God, now and for ever. 251 5
o God, for ever and ever. 251 17
o God, for ever and ever. 252 5
o God, now and for ever. 252 15
o God, now and for ever. 253 5
o God, for ever and ever. 253 19
o God, now and for ever. 254 6
o God, now and for ever. 255 4
that they might be *o*, as you and he are *o*: 255 16
may be united in *o* body by the *o* Spirit, 255 18
o God, now and for ever. 256 9
o God, for ever and ever. 256 17
o God, now and for ever. 257 4
O God, you have made of *o* blood all the peoples 257 5
o God, for ever and ever. 257 19
o God, for ever and ever. 258 6
o God, now and for ever. 258 13
o God, for ever and ever. 259 2
o God, now and for ever. 259 9
remembering the account that we must *o* day give, 259 14
o God, for ever and ever. 260 7
o God, now and for ever. 260 14
o God, for ever and ever. 261 6
him who came among us as *o* who serves, your Son 261 12
you have so linked our lives *o* with another 261 15
o God, for ever and ever. 264 8
We confess to you and to *o* another, 267 13
o God, for ever and ever. 272 13
o God, for ever and ever. 274 6
Love *o* another as I have loved you. 275 3
you have love for *o* another. 275 8
o God, for ever and ever. 276 8
may be *o* flock under *o* shepherd, Jesus 280 7
o God, for ever and ever. 280 23
o God, now and for ever. 282 12
o God, for ever and ever. 283 6
o God, for ever and ever. 286 16
o God, now and for ever. 295 7
o God, now and for ever. 295 13
There is *o* Body and *o* Spirit; 299 7
There is *o* hope in God's call to us; 299 8
O Lord, *o* Faith, *o* Baptism; 299 9
O God and Father of all. 299 10
Holy Spirit, *o* God, now and for ever. 309 11
a member of the *o* holy catholic and apostolic 310 1
o God, for ever and ever. 311 20
we are made *o* with Christ, and Christ with us; 316 6
we are made *o* body in him, 316 6
and members *o* of another. 316 6
And then, being reconciled with *o* another, 317 9
Holy Immortal O, 324 12
We believe in *o* God, 326 6
We believe in *o* Lord, Jesus Christ, 326 10
of *o* Being with the Father. 326 16
We believe in *o* holy catholic and apostolic Church. 327 16
We acknowledge *o* baptism for the forgiveness of sins. 327 17
I believe in *o* God, 327 20
And in *o* Lord Jesus Christ, 327 24
being of *o* substance with the Father; 327 30
And I believe *o* holy Catholic and Apostolic Church; 328 18
I acknowledge *o* Baptism for the remission of sins; 328 19
made there, by his *o* oblation of himself once offered, 334 12
and made *o* body with him, that he may dwell in us, 336 7
thy whole Church may be made *o* body with him, 342 28
in the confession of *o* faith, 347 10
thou art *o* God, *o* Lord, in Trinity of Persons 347 13
and we celebrate the *o* and equal glory of thee, 347 15
For you alone are the Holy O, 356 13
Holy Immortal O, 356 24
We believe in *o* God, 358 3
We believe in *o* Lord, Jesus Christ, 358 7
of *o* Being with the Father. 358 13
We believe in *o* holy catholic and apostolic Church. 359 7
We acknowledge *o* baptism for the forgiveness of sins. 359 8
to live and die as *o* of us, to reconcile us to you, 362 13
and we turned against *o* another. 370 15
Communion make us *o* body, *o* spirit in Christ, 372 6
he lived as *o* of us, yet without sin. 374 3
may become *o* body and *o* spirit, 375 9
Remember, Lord, your *o* holy catholic and apostolic 375 12
in the confession of *o* faith, 380 5
you are *o* God, *o* Lord, in Trinity of Persons 380 8
we celebrate the *o* and equal glory of you, O Father, 380 10
commend ourselves, and *o* another, and all our life, 385 14
That we all may be *o*. 387 2
that we may honor *o* another 388 8
and love *o* another as he loves us. 388 18
that all may be *o* as you and the Father are *o*, 390 5
commend ourselves, and *o* another, and all our life 391 21
by your Holy Spirit you have made us *o* 395 17
Gather us by this Holy Communion into *o* body 403 17
There is *o* Body and *o* Spirit; 413 7
There is *o* hope in God's call to us; 413 8
O Lord, *o* Faith, *o* Baptism; 413 9
O God and Father of all. 413 10
o God, now and for ever. 418 9
a member of the *o* holy catholic and apostolic 418 17
given *o* another in prosperity and adversity; 423 11
o God, for ever and ever. 425 13
whom God has joined together let no *o* put asunder. 428 6
make *o* flesh in Holy Matrimony. 429 6
and peace with you and *o* another 429 13
your children are united *o* to another, 430 5
o God, for ever and ever. 430 25
o God, now and for ever. 431 8
Matrimony, may become *o* in heart and soul, 432 5

whom God has joined together let no *o* put asunder.	434	7
who has made the Church *o* family,	445	7
Holy God, Holy and Mighty, Holy Immortal O,	449	7
o God, for ever and ever.	455	14
Holy Trinity, *o* God,	463	1
o God, for ever and ever.	464	19
o God, for ever and ever.	466	19
o God, now and for ever.	470	5
from *o* generation to another.	472	10
O thing have I desired of the LORD,	477	16
who hast knit together thine elect in *o* communion	480	4
o God, for ever and ever.	481	29
o God, now and for ever.	489	29
o God, for ever and ever.	493	8
o God, now and for ever.	493	14
o God, now and for ever.	494	5
bishop in the *o*, holy, catholic, and apostolic Church.	513	5
they appointed Matthias to be *o* of their number.	514	15
o God, for ever and ever.	515	13
A bishop in God's holy Church is called to be *o*	517	3
We believe in *o* God.	519	5
We believe in *o* Lord, Jesus Christ,	519	10
of *o* Being with the Father.	519	16
We believe in *o* holy catholic and apostolic Church.	520	7
We acknowledge *o* baptism for the forgiveness of sins.	520	8
o God, now and for ever.	523	10
of the Holy Spirit, *o* God, for ever and ever.	528	11
We believe in *o* God,	529	9
We believe in *o* Lord, Jesus Christ,	530	1
of *o* Being with the Father.	530	7
We believe in *o* holy catholic and apostolic Church.	530	26
We acknowledge *o* baptism for the forgiveness of sins.	530	27
o God, for ever and ever.	534	9
o God, now and for ever.	535	10
o God, for ever and ever.	540	11
We believe in *o* God,	541	9
We believe in *o* Lord, Jesus Christ,	542	1
of *o* Being with the Father.	542	7
We believe in *o* holy catholic and apostolic Church.	542	26
We acknowledge *o* baptism for the forgiveness of sins.	542	27
o God, for ever and ever.	545	18
o God, now and for ever.	547	6
Holy Trinity, *o* God,	548	7
that all may be *o* as you and the Father are *o*,	549	17
commend ourselves, and *o* another, and all our life	550	28
o God, for ever and ever.	560	10
o who proclaims the Word.	561	2
o God, now and for ever.	564	10
that we are made *o* with you and with *o* another,	568	19
There is *o* Lord, *o* Faith, *o* Baptism;	569	19
O God and Father of all.	569	20
be forgiven for their sins, united with *o* another,	574	6
you are my glory, the *o* who lifts up my head.	587	8
For in death no *o* remembers you; *	590	7
Help me, LORD, for there is no godly *o* left; *	597	1
if there is *o* who seeks after God.	598	17
Every *o* has proved faithless;	598	18
there is none who does good; no, not *o*.	598	20
nor let your holy *o* see the Pit.	600	18
O day tells its tale to another, *	606	17
and *o* night imparts knowledge to another.	606	18
Yet you are the Holy O, *	610	6
O thing have I asked of the LORD;	617	18
o thing I seek; *	617	19
not *o* of them shall be broken.	629	8
as *o* would for a friend or a brother; *	630	20
I behaved like *o* who mourns for his mother,	630	21
Do not fret yourself over the *o* who prospers, *	633	19
the *o* who succeeds in evil schemes.	633	20
Transgressors shall be destroyed, *o* and all; *	636	13
I have become like *o* who does not hear *	637	25
O deep calls to another in the noise	643	21
from *o* generation to another; *	648	26
"This is the *o* who did not take God for a refuge, *	658	13
if there is *o* who seeks after God.	659	3
Every *o* has proved faithless;	659	4
there is none who does good; no, not *o*.	659	6
for comforters, but I could find no *o*.	681	5
I will sing to you with the harp, O Holy O of Israel.	685	3
from *o* generation to another.	685	18
Like a dream when *o* awakens, O Lord, *	688	17
there is not *o* among us who knows how long.	690	3
he puts down *o* and lifts up another.	691	17
and provoked the Holy O of Israel.	698	10
and there was no *o* to bury them.	701	10
For *o* day in your courts is better than	708	10
I have become like *o* who has no strength;	712	8
"I have made a covenant with my chosen *o*; *	713	21
the Holy O of Israel is our King.	715	2
and have exalted *o* chosen out of the people.	715	5
from *o* generation to another.	717	21
o which frames evil into law?	724	6
he is the Holy O.	729	4
for the LORD our God is the Holy O.	729	21
and from *o* kingdom to another,	739	4
He let no *o* oppress them *	739	5
in all their tribes there was not *o* that stumbled.	740	28
not *o* of them was left.	742	21
and Aaron, the holy *o* of the LORD.	743	4
Let there be no *o* to show him kindness, *	751	20
In my distress I said, "No *o* can be trusted."	759	22
faithfulness remains from *o* generation to another; *	770	22
as *o* who finds great spoils.	777	4
are the children of *o*'s youth.	783	9
The LORD, the Righteous O, *	784	7
and vowed a vow to the Mighty O of Jacob:	786	2
a dwelling for the Mighty O of Jacob."	786	8
"Sing us *o* of the songs of Zion."	792	7
happy the *o* who pays you back	792	20
I look to my right hand and find no *o*	798	7
I have no place to flee to, and no *o* cares for me.	798	8
for in your sight shall no *o* living be justified.	798	22
O generation shall praise your works to another *	801	18
Peace, as children of *o* Father;	815	26
o God, now and for ever.	817	2
us all to be of *o* heart and mind	817	22
as there is but *o* Body and *o* Spirit,	818	18
o hope of our calling, *o* Lord, *o* Faith,	818	19
o Baptism, *o* God and Father of us all,	818	20
of *o* heart and of *o* soul,	818	21
united in *o* holy bond of truth	818	21
and may with *o* mind and *o* mouth glorify thee;	818	22
o God, now and for ever.	819	12
and fashion into *o* united people the multitudes	820	7

o God, world without end. 820 25
confront *o* another without hatred or bitterness, 824 3
find with *o* another the fulfillment of their humanity; 825 14
And grant that every *o* of us may enjoy 826 13
remembering the account which we must *o* day give, 827 3
that no *o* may suffer 827 19
who, in holy wedlock, have been made *o* flesh. 829 4
may evermore be kindly affectioned *o* to another; 829 7
o God, for ever and ever. 834 17
with many voices in *o* united chorus, 839 19
We learn that there is *o* God, the Father Almighty, 846 3
The Old Covenant is the *o* given by God 846 24
The Messiah is *o* sent by God to free us 849 12
The New Commandment is that we love *o* another 851 16
The Trinity is *o* God: Father, Son, and Holy Spirit. 852 13
the O who spoke through the prophets. 852 19
The Church is described as *o*, holy, catholic, 854 12
Why is the Church described as *o*? 854 14
The Church is *o*, because it is *o* Body, under *o* Head, 854 15
and in which he unites us to his *o* offering 859 12
our union with Christ and *o* another, 860 1

ones

revive the heart of the contrite *o*." 41 4
and the evil *o* their thoughts; 86 20
and leave their wealth to their little *o*. 602 3
he does not forsake his faithful *o*. 635 17
and the flesh of your faithful *o* to the beasts 701 6
faithfulness in the assembly of the holy *o*; 714 4
feared in the council of the holy *o*, * 714 7
you mighty *o* who do his bidding, * 734 23
Happy shall he be who takes your little *o*, * 792 22
as *o* who must answer for them to God; 848 15

only

O Lord, the *o*-begotten Son, Jesus Christ; 52 10
For thou *o* art holy, 52 18
thou *o* art the Lord, 52 19
thou *o*, O Christ, 52 20
thine adorable, true, and *o* Son, 53 9
And in Jesus Christ his *o* Son our Lord; 53 25
For *o* in thee can we live in safety. 55 6
not *o* with our lips, but in our lives, 59 5
And in Jesus Christ his *o* Son our Lord; 66 11
For *o* in thee can we live in safety. 67 21
for the love of thy *o* Son, our Savior Jesus Christ. 70 3
not *o* with our lips, but in our lives, 72 2
and I know my wickedness *o* too well. 91 15
for you *o* are the Holy One. 94 16
Lord Jesus Christ, *o* Son of the Father, 95 3
your true and *o* Son, worthy of all worship, 95 28
I believe in Jesus Christ, his *o* Son, our Lord. 96 15
For *o* in you can we live in safety. 97 23
not *o* with our lips, but in our lives, 101 18
for the love of thy *o* Son, our Savior, Jesus Christ. 111 3
I believe in Jesus Christ, his *o* Son, our Lord. 120 11
For *o* in you can we live in safety. 121 23
of your *o* Son, our Savior Jesus Christ. 123 23
not *o* with our lips, but in our lives, 125 16
for *o* you, Lord, make me dwell in safety. 129 7
Your eyes have *o* to behold * 130 13
love of your *o* Son, our Savior Jesus Christ. 133 12
o Mediator and Advocate, Jesus Christ our Lord. 155 13
the birth of thy *o* Son Jesus Christ: 160 13
Almighty God, who has given us thy *o*-begotten Son 161 7
leading of a star didst manifest thy *o*-begotten Son 162 13
Grant this for thine *o* Son 165 3
O God, who before the passion of thy *o*-begotten Son 165 14
o-begotten Son to the death of the cross, 170 8
Almighty God, who through thine *o*-begotten Son 170 21
Almighty Father, who hast given thine *o* Son to die 172 8
believe thy *o*-begotten Son our Lord Jesus Christ 174 16
King of glory, who hast exalted thine *o* Son 175 1
Almighty God, who hast given thy *o* Son 180 19
merciful God, of whose *o* gift it cometh 184 1
as thy *o*-begotten Son was this day presented 187 17
festival of the birth of your *o* Son Jesus Christ: 212 11
Almighty God, you have given your *o*-begotten Son 213 1
by the leading of a star you manifested your *o* Son 214 7
Grant this for the sake of your *o* Son 216 17
who before the passion of your *o*-begotten Son 217 7
who for our redemption gave your *o*-begotten Son 222 1
Almighty God, who through your *o*-begotten Son 222 15
Almighty Father, who gave your *o* Son to die 224 1
o-begotten Son our Lord Jesus Christ to have ascended 226 9
King of glory, you have exalted your *o* Son 226 13
Almighty God, you have given your *o* Son 232 11
Almighty and merciful God, it is *o* by your gift 235 14
o-begotten Son was this day presented in the temple, 239 7
o by your gracious gift that we are given 265 19
Against you *o* have I sinned * 266 8
almighty, and eternal God, and your *o*-begotten Son, 287 2
I believe in Jesus Christ, his *o* Son, our Lord. 293 2
who for our redemption gave your *o*-begotten Son, 295 1
I believe in Jesus Christ, his *o* Son, our Lord 304 5
O Lord, the *o*-begotten Son, Jesus Christ; 324 21
For thou *o* art holy; 325 5
thou *o* art the Lord; 325 6
thou *o*, O Christ, 325 7
the *o* Son of God, 326 11
the *o*-begotten Son of God, 327 25
our *o* Mediator and Advocate. 330 8
that he gave his *o*-begotten Son, 332 10
and not for ours *o*, but for the sins 332 17
of thy tender mercy, didst give thine *o* Son 334 10
and, of thy tender mercy, didst give thine *o* Son 341 14
Because thou didst give Jesus Christ, thine *o* Son, 345 14
of thine *o* Son. 348 10
The Lord our God is the *o* Lord. 351 8
Lord Jesus Christ, *o* Son of the Father, 356 7
the *o* Son of God, 358 8
Christ, your *o* and eternal Son, 362 12
fullness of time you sent your *o* Son, 370 19
o, and not for strength; 372 5
for pardon *o*, and not for renewal. 372 5
time you sent your *o* Son to be our Savior. 374 2
Because you gave Jesus Christ, your *o* Son, to be born 378 9
the great Name of your *o* Son. 381 4
Help us to ask *o* what accords with your will; 394 13
our *o* Mediator and Advocate. 395 16
God so loved the world that he gave his *o* Son, 396 1
I believe in Jesus Christ, his *o* Son, our Lord. 416 10
For I know my transgressions *o* too well, 449 5

that he gave his *o*-begotten Son, 449 15
and not for ours *o*, but for the sins 450 3
and make you know and feel that the *o* Name 457 2
God of all comfort, our *o* help 458 1
Thou *o* art immortal, the creator and maker 482 12
thy Son Jesus Christ, our *o* Mediator 487 22
the merits of Jesus Christ thine *o* Son our Lord. 488 20
I believe in Jesus Christ, his *o* Son, our Lord. 496 5
You *o* are immortal, the creator and maker 499 4
the *o* Son of God, 519 11
the *o* Son of God, 530 2
the *o* Son of God, 542 2
that your word *o* may be proclaimed, 571 11
proclaimed, and your word *o* may be heard. 571 12
for *o* you, LORD, make me dwell in safety. 588 16
their *o* thought is, "God does not matter." 594 26
do not fret yourself; it leads *o* to evil. 633 22
Against you *o* have I sinned * 656 12
their *o* thought is to do me evil. 662 23
They seek *o* to bring me down 669 12
and darkness is my *o* companion. 713 16
Your eyes have *o* to behold * 720 1
They flourish *o* to be destroyed for ever; * 721 11
and *o* those who lead a blameless life shall 730 22
You *o* are my portion, O LORD; * 768 1
Who *o* does great wonders, * 790 3
for his Name *o* is exalted, 806 20
the Father of our Lord Jesus Christ, our *o* Savior, 818 14
Jesus of Nazareth, the *o* Son of God. 849 17
we say that Jesus is the *o* Son of God? 849 19
We mean that Jesus is the *o* perfect image 849 21

open

O Lord, *o* thou our lips. 42 14
thou didst *o* the kingdom of heaven to all believers. 53 16
Lord, *o* our lips. 80 5
Your gates will always be *o*; * 87 19
O my lips, O Lord, * 137 1
O, we pray thee, the eyes 171 18
O, we pray thee, the eyes 173 6
Almighty God, who on this day didst *o* the way 175 8
O merciful Creator, whose hand is *o* wide to satisfy 208 9
O the eyes of our faith, 223 11
O the eyes of our faith, 224 20
O merciful Creator, your hand is *o* wide to satisfy 259 11
O my lips, O Lord, * 267 6
That God will *o* their hearts to the truth, 279 28
O their hearts to your grace and truth. 305 17
o your grief to a discreet and understanding priest, 317 12
Almighty God, unto whom all hearts are *o*, 323 7
O, O Lord, the eyes of all people to behold 329 22
Almighty God, to you all hearts are *o*, 355 7
to *o* for us the way of freedom and peace. 370 20
O our eyes to see your hand at work 372 2
Christ will *o* the kingdom of heaven 483 20
Christ will *o* the kingdom of heaven 500 9
Almighty God, to you all hearts are *o*, 512 7
To you, O Father, all hearts are *o*; 521 6
Almighty God, to you all hearts are *o*, 525 7
Almighty God, to you all hearts are *o*, 537 7
and let the doors of this place be *o* 562 1
Holy Spirit, *o* our eyes, our ears, and our hearts, 569 3
Their throat is an *o* grave; * 589 11
He brought me out into an *o* place; * 604 1
They *o* wide their jaws at me, * 611 3
you have set my feet in an *o* place. 623 2
and his ears are *o* to their cry. 628 24
like those who are mute and do not *o* their mouth. 637 24
I fell silent and did not *o* my mouth, * 639 13
O my lips, O Lord, * 657 12
You have shaken the earth and split it *o*; * 667 12
You split *o* spring and torrent; * 690 14
I will *o* my mouth in a parable; * 694 21
He split *o* the sea and let them pass through; * 695 28
"O your mouth wide, and I will fill it." 704 23
you *o* your hand, and they are filled with good things. 737 10
O for me the gates of righteousness; * 762 8
O my eyes, that I may see * 764 19
I *o* my mouth and pant; * 774 9
My eyes are *o* in the night watches, * 775 22
You *o* wide your hand * 802 19
O our eyes to behold thy gracious hand 814 2

opened

and *o* the kingdom of heaven to all believers. 96 6
Christ hast overcome death and *o* unto us the gate 170 22
and we pray that, having *o* to him the gates 202 10
Christ overcame death and *o* to us the gate 222 16
Almighty God, on this day you *o* the way 227 1
and we pray that, having *o* to him the gates 253 14
resurrection *o* to us the way of everlasting life. 345 3
resurrection *o* to us the way of everlasting life. 377 16
Let the door(s) be *o*. 568 1
They *o* their mouths at me and said, * 631 12
and *o* the doors of heaven. 696 23
He *o* the rock, and water flowed, * 741 7
The earth *o* and swallowed Dathan * 743 5
the mouth of the deceitful, is *o* against me. 750 25
spirits may be *o* to the goodness of your creation; 825 4
Jesus overcame death and *o* for us 850 11

openest

O gracious Father, who *o* thine hand 828 1

openly

After his glorious resurrection he *o* appeared 379 21
his righteousness has he *o* shown 728 4

opens

the LORD *o* the eyes of the blind; * 803 18

Ophir

adorned with the gold of O. 648 10

opportunities

and equal *o* for all. 826 13

oppress

all day long they assault and *o* me. 662 14
He let no one *o* them * 739 5
let not the proud *o* me. 773 18
Rescue me from those who *o* me, * 774 15
There are many who persecute and *o* me, * 776 17

oppressed

hungry, and all who are desolate and *o*, 151 7
the destitute and the *o* 279 5

For the poor and the *o*, 384 25
the *o*, and those in prison. 386 5
The Lord will be a refuge for the *o*, * 593 17
To give justice to the orphan and *o*, * 596 5
"Because the needy are *o*, 597 9
and the *o* who has no helper. 686 8
Let not the *o* turn away ashamed; * 690 26
and to save all the *o* of the earth. 692 19
and judgment for all who are *o*. 733 20
Their enemies *o* them, * 745 8
"Greatly have they *o* me since my youth," * 784 1
Who gives justice to those who are *o*, * 803 15

oppresses

while the enemy *o* me? 644 4

oppression

From all *o*, conspiracy, and rebellion; 149 14
make no peace with *o*; and, 209 3
make no peace with *o*; 260 10
For deliverance from all danger, violence, *o*, 385 1
For the victims of hunger, fear, injustice, and *o*. 392 8
Their mouth is full of cursing, deceit, and *o*; * 595 6
and forgotten our affliction and *o*? 647 6
her streets are never free of *o* and deceit. 661 5
He shall redeem their lives from *o* and violence, * 686 11
out of their haughtiness they plan *o*. 687 16
to poverty, prejudice, and *o*, 825 11

oppressor

from the clutches of the evildoer and the *o*. 683 8
he shall rescue the poor and crush the *o*. 685 16

oppressors

The waters covered their *o*; * 742 20
do not deliver me to my *o*. 773 16
and our *o* called for mirth: * 792 6

ordain

O God, who didst lead thy holy apostles to *o* ministers 205 14
O God, you led your holy apostles to *o* ministers 256 11
For so thou didst *o* when thou createdst me, 482 14
For so did you *o* when you created me, 499 6
Is it your will that we *o* N. a bishop? 514 8
we *o* N. for the work to which we trust 514 17
to *o* priests and deacons 517 9
and to *o* others to continue Christ's ministry. 855 27

ordained

O everlasting God, who hast *o* and constituted 193 4
O everlasting God, who hast *o* and constituted 200 6
Everlasting God, you have *o* and constituted 244 13
Everlasting God, you have *o* and constituted 251 12
o a priest in Christ's holy catholic Church. 526 3
Is it your will that N. be *o* a priest? 527 7
o a deacon in Christ's holy catholic Church. 538 3
Is it your will that N. be *o* a deacon? 539 7
For there the Lord has *o* the blessing: * 787 17

ordaining

and to join in *o* bishops; 517 10

order

who alone canst *o* the unruly wills 167 15
innocents of Bethlehem by the *o* of King Herod. 186 14
ministries of angels and men in a wonderful *o*: 193 5
ministries of angels and men in a wonderful *o*: 200 7
you alone can bring into *o* the unruly wills 219 6
your never-failing providence sets in *o* all things 229 10
wonderful *o* the ministries of angels and mortals: 244 14
wonderful *o* the ministries of angels and mortals: 251 13
in *o* that you yourselves may be forgiven. 317 8
may so *o* his life and conduct 460 21
and we believe him to be qualified for this *o*. 526 8
and we believe him qualified for this *o*. 538 8
for ordination to the sacred *o* of deacons. 539 3
this your servant to the *o* of deacons. 545 8
earthly things we may behold the *o* and beauty 573 5
In *o* to live for ever and ever, * 652 21
I have put my case in *o* before your eyes. 655 25
"You are a priest for ever after the *o* of Melchizedek." 753 20
with righteousness, and justice with *o*, 825 12
all its marvelous *o*, its atoms, worlds, and galaxies, 827 12

ordered

but that we, being *o* by thy governance, 57 11
may always be *o* and guided by faithful and true pastors; 188 4

ordereth

O God, whose never-failing providence *o* all things 177 14

ordering

Give them wisdom and devotion in the *o* 429 7
Grant them wisdom and devotion in the *o* 444 9
share in the *o* of your world. 567 9

orders

providence hast appointed various *o* in thy Church: 205 5
providence you have appointed various *o* in your Church: 256 2

ordinance

according to God's holy *o*; 436 10

ordination

for *o* to the sacred priesthood. 527 3
for *o* to the sacred order of deacons. 539 3
include confirmation, *o*, holy matrimony, 860 10
What is O? 860 27
O is the rite in which God gives authority 860 28

ore

like silver refined from *o* 597 14

Oreb

Make their leaders like O and Zeeb, * 706 24

Orion

Seek him that made the Pleiades and O, 62 1
Seek him who made the Pleiades and O, 115 13

orphan

To give justice to the *o* and oppressed, * 596 5
Save the weak and the *o*; * 705 13
he sustains the *o* and widow, 803 22

orphans
women in childbirth, young children and *o*, 151 21
For the aged and infirm, for the widowed and *o*, 384 20
for you are the helper of *o*. 595 26
Father of *o*, defender of widows, * 676 11
and put the *o* to death. 723 6

other
may find it none *o* than the way of life 56 9
may find it none *o* than the way of life 99 4
our common life depends upon each *o*'s toil; 134 14
may find it none *o* than the way of life 168 13
the bishops and the *o* clergy 204 10
all we do affecteth, for good or ill, all *o* lives: 210 11
mindful of the rightful aspirations of *o* workers, 210 15
may find it none *o* than the way of life 220 4
the bishops and the *o* clergy 255 8
all we do affects, for good or ill, all *o* lives: 261 16
mindful of the rightful aspirations of *o* workers, 261 20
and our exploitation of *o* people, 268 5
may find it none *o* than the way of life 272 4
For all bishops and *o* ministers 278 4
The *o* Candidate(s) will now be presented. 303 4
Thou shalt have none *o* gods but me. 317 27
grace, O heavenly Father, to all bishops and *o* ministers 329 9
sickness, or any *o* adversity. 329 29
and all *o* benefits of his passion. 335 29
You shall have no *o* gods but me. 350 3
There is no *o* commandment greater than these." 351 11
for all bishops and *o* ministers, 390 2
for] all bishops and *o* ministers; 392 15
have bound themselves to each *o*; 427 12
Now that N. and N. have given themselves to each *o* 428 1
that each may be to the *o* a strength in need, 429 8
Give them grace, when they hurt each *o*, 429 14
and to seek each *o*'s forgiveness 429 15
Let their love for each *o* be a seal 430 17
that they may so love, honor, and cherish each *o* 431 4
have bound themselves to each *o*; 434 6
this woman and this man to be married to each *o*? 437 8
that each may be to the *o* a strength in need, 444 10
and all *o* sins which I cannot now remember, 447 8
Therefore, O Lord, from these and all *o* sins 450 16
and for all *o* thy righteous servants, 489 17
and for all your *o* righteous servants, 504 16
and *o* ministers who may have authority over you 526 12
and to perform the *o* ministrations 531 16
and *o* ministers who may have authority over you 538 12
and you are to carry out *o* duties assigned 543 15
my good above all *o*." 599 21
But those who run after *o* gods * 600 3
wink at each *o*. 631 8
righteousness and peace have kissed each *o*. 709 15
He has not done so to any *o* nation; * 805 17
Send down upon our bishops, and *o* clergy, 817 5
Bless our Bishop(s) N. [and N.], and *o* clergy, 817 12
a blessing to *o* nations of the earth. 821 17
all *o* bodily necessities of life, 825 22
and for all the *o* blessings of thy merciful providence 840 18
and to do to *o* people as we wish them to do to us; 848 3
to rejoice in *o* people's gifts 848 19
distorting our relationship with God, with *o* people, 848 30
o books, called the Apocrypha, are often included 853 7
unity with God and each *o* in Christ. 855 3
By what *o* names is this service known? 859 14
What *o* sacramental rites evolved in the Church 860 7
O sacramental rites which evolved in the Church 860 9
knowing and loving God and each *o*. 862 28

others
and to ask, for ourselves and on behalf of *o*, 41 9
and to ask, for ourselves and on behalf of *o*, 79 4
who work while *o* sleep, 134 13
o in authority, that they may do justice, 150 27
to *o* the word of knowledge, 197 13
and to *o* the word of faith: 197 13
give themselves to the service of *o*; 209 12
to *o* the word of knowledge, 248 23
and to *o* the word of faith: 248 23
give themselves to the service of *o*; 260 17
We have not forgiven *o*, as we have been forgiven. 267 21
who in the name of Christ have persecuted *o* 279 27
Teach them to love *o* in the power of the Spirit. 305 24
all injuries and wrongs done by you to *o*; 317 7
o who shall be partakers of this Holy Communion, 336 4
Let us pray for our own needs and those of *o*. 387 21
use its resources rightly in the service of *o* 388 13
and of service to *o*; 421 6
and, forsaking all *o*, be faithful to him 424 11
and, forsaking all *o*, be faithful to her 424 17
may reach out in love and concern for *o*. 429 24
and, forsaking all *o*, to be faithful to her 433 7
and, forsaking all *o*, to be faithful to him 433 12
deacons and all *o* who minister in the Church? 518 26
asking God's grace, both for yourself and for *o*, 532 26
Will you look for Christ in all *o*, 544 4
come with *o*, to find comfort and wisdom, 568 17
I give no offense with my mouth as *o* do; * 601 5
In the misfortunes of *o* they have no share; * 687 9
they are not afflicted as *o* are; 687 10
and they took the fruit of *o*' toil. 741 14
make us mindful of the needs of *o*; 835 9
To love and obey God and to bring *o* to 847 21
To speak the truth, and not to mislead *o* 848 16
and to ordain *o* to continue Christ's ministry. 855 27
Intercession brings before God the needs of *o*; 857 18
In corporate worship, we unite ourselves with *o* 857 22

ought
we have left undone those things which we *o* to 41 21
and we have done those things which we *o* not to 42 1
we have left undone those things which we *o* to 63 2
and we have done those things which we *o* not to 63 4
perceive and know what things they *o* to do, 179 12
what things they *o* to do, 231 6
we have left undone those things which we *o* to 321 2
and we have done those things which we *o* not to 321 4

outer
through *o* space], let us pray to the Lord. 384 18

outside
they go *o* and spread them. 642 12

outward

we have heard this day with our *o* ears,	834	19
The sacraments are *o* and visible signs	857	26
What is the *o* and visible sign in Baptism?	858	12
The *o* and visible sign in Baptism is water,	858	13
What is the *o* and visible sign in the Eucharist?	859	18
The *o* and visible sign in the Eucharist is bread	859	19

outwardly

Keep us both *o* in our bodies	167	4
Keep us both *o* in our bodies	218	14
As you are *o* anointed with this holy oil,	456	13

over

death hath no more dominion *o* him.	46	8
Christ triumphed *o* the powers of death	69	2
and give thine angels charge *o* those	71	2
death no longer has dominion *o* him.	83	16
But *o* you the Lord will rise, *	87	15
and he who watches *o* you will not fall asleep.	104	18
Behold, he who keeps watch *o* Israel *	104	19
The LORD himself watches *o* you; *	104	21
The LORD shall watch *o* your going out and	105	1
Christ triumphed *o* the powers of death	123	1
and give your angels charge *o* those	124	18
For he shall give his angels charge *o* you, *	130	19
and give your angels charge *o* those	134	7
Watch *o* those, both night and day,	134	12
N. triumphed *o* suffering and was faithful	195	9
N. triumphed *o* suffering and was faithful	247	7
Lord Jesus passed *o* from death to life,	285	2
in his victory *o* death.	285	6
O it the Holy Spirit moved in the beginning	306	14
hand ever be *o* these your servants;	310	9
for his continual providence *o* us,	316	11
able to triumph *o* every evil,	346	6
On the night he was handed *o* to suffering	362	18
exalted as head *o* all.	377	9
we are able to triumph *o* every evil,	379	3
On the night he was handed *o* to suffering	405	1
hand ever be *o* these your servants;	419	5
and my cup is running *o*.	443	14
Father, watch with us *o* your child	458	22
my cup runneth *o*.	477	8
may recall to us your victory *o* death,	498	3
and other ministers who may have authority *o* you	526	12
and other ministers who may have authority *o* you	538	12
O it the Holy Spirit moved in the beginning	570	5
You give him mastery *o* the works of your hands; *	592	19
The wicked shall be given *o* to the grave, *	594	11
our lips are our own; who is lord *o* us?"	597	8
O LORD, watch *o* us *	597	16
how long shall my enemy triumph *o* me?	598	3
Lest my enemy say, "I have prevailed *o* him," *	598	6
The breakers of death rolled *o* me, *	602	14
let them not get dominion *o* me; *	607	25
They stare and gloat *o* me; *	611	15
he rules *o* the nations.	612	14
and my cup is running *o*.	613	10
nor let my enemies triumph *o* me.	614	16
and have not let my enemies triumph *o* me.	621	5
Do not let my treacherous foes rejoice *o* me, *	631	6
do not let them triumph *o* me.	631	20
Do not fret yourself *o* the one who prospers, *	633	19
those who gloat *o* me when my foot slips."	638	2
Let those who say "Aha!" and gloat *o* me	641	14
he does not hand them *o* to the will of their enemies.	642	3
that my enemy does not triumph *o* me.	642	23
all your rapids and floods have gone *o* me.	643	22
Surely, you gave us victory *o* our adversaries *	645	25
and covered us *o* with deep darkness.	646	25
you shall make them princes *o* all the earth.	648	24
he is the great King *o* all the earth.	650	9
God reigns *o* the nations; *	650	20
Fear and trembling have come *o* me, *	660	15
and your glory *o* all the earth.	664	9
and *o* Philistia will I shout in triumph."	668	3
let his years extend *o* many generations.	668	25
bid love and faithfulness watch *o* him.	669	2
He will make them trip *o* their tongues, *	672	1
his eyes keep watch *o* the nations; *	674	7
You let enemies ride *o* our heads;	674	17
his majesty is *o* Israel;	679	2
and the torrent washes *o* me.	679	12
Let not the torrent of waters wash *o* me,	680	20
Let those who say to me "Aha!" and gloat *o* me	682	17
Do not hand *o* the life of your dove	690	22
to be a shepherd *o* Jacob his people	700	22
and *o* Israel his inheritance.	700	23
So I gave them *o* to the stubbornness	704	26
you alone are the Most High *o* all the earth.	707	14
Keep watch *o* my life, for I am faithful; *	710	1
Your blazing anger has swept *o* me; *	713	11
For he shall give his angels charge *o* you, *	720	7
My eyes also gloat *o* my enemies, *	721	18
most high *o* all the earth; *	727	15
When the wind goes *o* it, it is gone, *	734	13
and his kingship has dominion *o* all.	734	21
He set him as a master *o* his household, *	739	19
as a ruler *o* all his possessions,	739	20
He gave them *o* to the hand of the heathen, *	745	6
and those who hated them ruled *o* them.	745	7
and your glory *o* all the earth.	750	4
and *o* Philistia will I shout in triumph."	750	14
saying, "Rule *o* your enemies round about you.	753	15
he will rule *o* the nations.	753	23
he will smash heads *o* the wide earth.	754	2
The LORD watches *o* the innocent; *	759	12
I will triumph *o* those who hate me.	761	10
but he did not hand me *o* to death.	762	7
let no iniquity have dominion *o* me.	774	14
and he who watches *o* you will not fall asleep.	779	6
Behold, he who keeps watch *o* Israel *	779	7
The LORD himself watches *o* you; *	779	9
The LORD shall watch *o* your going out and	779	15
and the torrent gone *o* us;	781	8
raging waters * have gone right *o* us.	781	10
he has not given us *o* to be a prey for their teeth.	781	12
the wicked shall not hold sway *o* the land	781	22
Unless the LORD watches *o* the city, *	783	1
As when a plowman turns *o* the earth in furrows, *	797	17
and his compassion is *o* all his works.	802	4
his splendor is *o* earth and heaven.	806	21
in giving us dominion *o* things on earth,	827	17

and given us dominion *o* all the earth: 828 17
Watch *o* thy child, O Lord, as his days increase; 830 13
and the fever of life is *o*, 833 16
How does sin have power *o* us? 849 1
Sin has power *o* us because we lose 849 2
How can we share in his victory *o* sin, 850 22

overcame

You *o* the sting of death 96 5
Christ *o* death and opened to us the gate 222 16
on the first day of the week *o* death and the grave, 345 2
on the first day of the week *o* death and the grave, 377 15
obedience, by which he *o* temptation; 836 14
for his dying, through which he *o* death; 836 15
By his resurrection, Jesus *o* death 850 11

overcome

When thou hadst *o* the sharpness of death, 53 15
that we may not fall into sin, nor be *o* by adversity; 100 3
that we may not fall into sin, nor be *o* by adversity; 137 16
Christ hast *o* death and opened unto us the gate 170 22
resurrection of your Son Jesus Christ you have *o* sin 309 4
resurrection of your Son Jesus Christ you have *o* sin 418 2
that unity may *o* estrangement, 429 18
We thank you that by his death he has *o* death, 533 5

overflow

when the great waters *o*, they shall not reach them. 625 13
and your paths *o* with plenty. 673 12
and their hearts *o* with wicked thoughts. 687 14

overflowed

the waters gushed out, and the gullies *o*; * 696 14

overflowing

May our barns be filled to *o* 801 3

overrun

Their land was *o* by frogs, * 740 13

overseeing

and wisely *o* the life and work 521 13
with the bishop in the *o* of the Church; 856 4

overtake

Then let my enemy pursue and *o* me, * 591 3
I pursue my enemies and *o* them; * 605 14
and let the fierceness of your anger *o* them. 681 13

overtaken

my sins have *o* me, and I cannot see; * 641 5

overthrew

He *o* many nations * 788 21

overthrow

to *o* them in the wilderness, 743 25

overthrown

your right hand, O Lord, has *o* the enemy. 85 15
Whoever does these things shall never be *o*. 599 18
she shall not be *o*; * 649 13
Let their rulers be *o* in stony places, * 797 15

overwhelm

For my iniquities *o* me; * 637 4
and all your great waves *o* me. 712 16
let the evil of their lips *o* them. 796 20

overwhelmed

The fathomless deep has *o* them; * 85 12
o by their loss, but have confidence in your 494 10
but the sea *o* their enemies. 699 12
Then would the waters have *o* us * 781 7

overwhelms

and horror *o* me. 660 16

owl

like an *o* among the ruins. 731 12

own

we have turned every one to his *o* way; 39 2
too much the devices and desires of our *o* hearts, 62 19
we have turned every one to his *o* way; 77 1
bought with the price of your *o* blood, 96 10
my *o* peace I leave with you:" 107 18
We have sinned against you, through our *o* fault, 127 8
my *o* peace I leave with you:" 138 17
confide in their *o* strength, 181 19
Barnabas, who, seeking not his *o* renown 189 18
Almighty God, who hast created us in thine *o* image: 209 1
as we seek a proper return for our *o* labor, 210 14
resist the proud who confide in their *o* strength, 233 10
Barnabas, who, seeking not his *o* renown 241 4
Almighty God, who created us in your *o* image: 260 8
as we seek a proper return for our *o* labor, 261 19
that we have sinned by our *o* fault 267 16
Our anger at our *o* frustration, 268 7
Peace is my last gift to you, my *o* peace I now leave 275 1
deeds of old shine forth even to our *o* day, 289 13
and renew our *o* baptismal covenant. 303 18
as Christ's *o* for ever. 308 10
adopting us as your *o* children, 311 16
To Christ our Lord who loves us, 317 17
too much the devices and desires of our *o* hearts, 320 26
Lord, trusting in our *o* righteousness, 337 10
and didst make us in thine *o* image; 341 13
You formed us in your *o* image, 373 19
he sent the Holy Spirit, his *o* first gift 374 10
having loved his *o* who were in the world, 374 14
may have grace to glorify Christ in our *o* day. 386 17
Let us pray for our *o* needs and those of others. 387 21
Give us all a reverence for the earth as your *o* 388 12
For our Presiding Bishop, for our *o* Bishop(s), 390 1
my *o* peace I leave with you:" 395 9
to Christ and renew our *o* baptismal covenant. 416 5
do you take this child for your *o*? 440 17
you receive N. as your *o* son (daughter). 441 6
I have sinned by my *o* fault in thought, word, 447 6
a sheep of your *o* fold, a lamb of your *o* flock, 465 3
a sinner of your *o* redeeming. 465 4
a sheep of thine *o* fold, a lamb of thine *o* flock, 483 8
a sinner of thine *o* redeeming. 483 8
and none becomes his *o* master when he dies. 491 14
a sheep of your *o* fold, a lamb of your *o* flock, 499 15
a sinner of your *o* redeeming. 499 16

Their malice turns back upon their *o* head; * 592 3
their violence falls on their *o* scalp. 592 4
and in the snare they set is their *o* foot caught. 594 8
the wicked are trapped in the works of their *o* hands. 594 10
you see it and take it into your *o* hand. 595 24
our lips are our *o*; who is lord over us?" 597 8
happy the people he has chosen to be his *o*! 626 24
"Aha! we saw it with our *o* eyes." 631 13
He flatters himself in his *o* eyes * 632 5
Their sword shall go through their *o* heart, * 634 14
though they call the lands after their *o* names. 653 3
and the end of those who delight in their *o* words. 653 7
and slandering your *o* mother's son. 655 21
But it was you, a man after my *o* heart, * 661 10
my companion, my *o* familiar friend. 661 11
may God, our *o* God, give us his blessing. 675 21
I have become a stranger to my *o* kindred, * 680 3
to follow their *o* devices. 704 27
for you shall take all nations for your *o*. 706 2
a thousand in my *o* room, * 708 11
nor will he forsake his *o*. 723 22
and destroy them in their *o* malice; * 724 12
but they rebelled through their *o* devices, * 745 11
and Israel for his *o* possession. 788 9
they have become my *o* enemies. 795 23
Let the wicked fall into their *o* nets, * 797 24
O God, you made us in your *o* image 815 13
Heavenly Father, you sent your *o* Son into this world. 841 1
Sin is the seeking of our *o* will 848 29
We mean that by God's *o* act, his divine Son received 849 28
in petition, we present our *o* needs, 857 19

ox

and Mount Hermon like a young wild *o*. 620 17
for the image of an *o* that feeds on grass. 743 12

oxen

All sheep and *o*, * 592 21
I will give you *o* and goats. 674 26
will please the LORD more than an offering of *o*, * 681 26

P

packs

P of dogs close me in, 611 11

pagan

and learned their *p* ways, 744 18

paid

the feast of the Passover *p* for us the debt 287 4

pain

first he suffered *p*, and entered not into glory 56 7
first he suffered *p*, and entered not into glory 99 2
first he suffered *p*, and entered not into glory 168 11
first he suffered *p*, and entered not into glory 220 2
first he suffered *p*, and entered not into glory 272 2
they may have rest in that place where there is no *p* 391 17
preserved through the *p* and anxiety of child-birth 444 2
Relieve his *p*, guard him from all danger, 459 3
and to the prevention of disease and *p*. 460 12
brother (sister) N. both relief from *p* 460 18
by your patience in suffering you hallowed earthly *p* 461 6
Be near me in my time of weakness and *p*; 461 7
where sorrow and *p* are no more, 482 10
where sorrow and *p* are no more, 483 4
where sorrow and *p* are no more, 499 2
they may have rest in that place where there is no *p* 550 22
My loins are filled with searing *p*; * 637 10
and my *p* is always with me. 638 4
but my *p* became unbearable. 638 21
and add to the *p* of those whom you have pierced. 681 17
As for me, I am afflicted and in *p*; * 681 22
For they suffer no *p*, * 687 7

pains

and the *p* of hell gat hold upon me. 479 4
deliver us not into the bitter *p* of eternal death. 484 10
through any *p* of death, to fall from thee. 484 17
do not let the *p* of death 492 19

palace

and enter into the *p* of the king. 648 22
and our daughters like sculptured corners of a *p*. 801 2

palaces

and the music of strings from ivory *p* makes you glad. 648 7

palm

spread their garments and branches of *p* 271 9
The righteous shall flourish like a *p* tree, * 721 21

pant

I open my mouth and *p*; * 774 9

parable

I will open my mouth in a *p*; * 694 21

paradise

to thy whole Church in *p* and on earth 202 2
to your whole Church in *p* and on earth 253 7
and your dwelling place in the *P* of God. 464 26
to thy whole Church in *p* and on earth, 480 7
Into *p* may the angels lead thee; 484 1
buried here may dwell with Christ in *p*, 487 8
You promised *p* to the thief who repented; 497 13
Into *p* may the angels lead you. 500 12
buried here may dwell with Christ in *p*, 503 10

parcel

"I will exult and *p* out Shechem; 667 21
"I will exult and *p* out Shechem; 750 8

pardon

and to our God, for he will richly *p*. 86 22
was put in mind of the message of *p* and absolution 265 7
grace to the living; *p* and rest to the dead; 282 9
of scruple and doubt, the assurance of *p*, 317 15
p and deliver you from all your sins, 332 4
for *p* only, and not for renewal. 372 5
That it may please you mercifully to *p* all his sins, 463 15
Grant to thy faithful people *p* and peace, 481 4
grace to the living, *p* and rest to the dead, 489 26
reconciliation, declaring *p* in your Name, 521 12
For the *p* of our sins, which restores us 579 1
where there is injury, *p*; 833 6

to bless and declare *p* in the name of God. 856 6
assurance of *p* and the grace of absolution. 861 12

pardoned

That we may be *p* and forgiven for our sins 68 12
That we may be *p* and forgiven for our sins 122 14
it is in pardoning that we are *p*; 833 12

pardoning

not weighing our merits, but *p* our offenses, 336 12
it is in *p* that we are pardoned; 833 12

pardons

He *p* and absolves all those who truly repent, 269 8

parents

Turn the hearts of the *p* to the children, 829 5
and the hearts of the children to the *p*; 829 6
To love, honor, and help our *p* 848 4
Promises are made for them by their *p* 859 1

parish

hear our prayers for this *p* family. 817 19
a bishop for this Diocese (or, rector for this *p*), 818 10

part

and unto the uttermost *p* of the earth. 39 21
to love and to cherish, till death do us *p*, 436 9
For my *p*, I will sing of your strength; * 667 3
who took my *p* against the evildoers? 723 26
Can a corrupt tribunal have any *p* with you, * 724 5
do their *p* in making the heart of this people wise, 827 9
We are *p* of God's creation, 845 2

partake

Grant, we beseech thee, that all who *p* 342 24
p of everlasting glory in the life to come; 444 6

partaker

p of everlasting glory in the life to come; 841 12

partakers

be *p* of the inheritance of the saints in light. 40 2
and also be made *p* of his resurrection; 168 6
become *p* of their joy; 199 1
may become *p* of your heavenly treasure; 234 8
to become *p* of their joy; 250 11
we may be *p* of thy heavenly kingdom. 330 6
may be *p* of his most blessed Body and Blood. 335 22
others who shall be *p* of this Holy Communion, 336 4
be *p* of the inheritance of the saints in light; 486 14
be *p* of the inheritance of the saints in light; 489 21
be *p* of the inheritance of the saints in light; 504 19

parted

to love and to cherish, until we are *p* by death. 427 4
to love and to cherish, until we are *p* by death. 436 4
He *p* the heavens and came down * 603 7

particular

those who travel [in *p* ________]; surround 831 3

particularly

For those about to be baptized (*p* ________.) 278 8
are to serve all people, *p* the poor, 543 5
p as apostle, chief priest, and pastor 855 23
p as pastor to the people; 856 3
p as a servant of those in need; 856 9

partners

made *p* of thy heavenly treasure; 182 15

parts

and remain in the uttermost *p* of the sea; 475 10
and dwell in the uttermost *p* of the sea, 794 17
For you yourself created my inmost *p*; * 794 25
whose fatherly care reacheth to the uttermost *p* 830 19
We thank you that in all *p* of the earth 838 4

Paschal

in the morning as we celebrate the *P* mystery; 134 4
celebrate with reverence the *P* feast 171 6
Almighty and everlasting God, who in the *P* mystery 172 1
celebrate with awe the *P* feast 222 23
Almighty and everlasting God, who in the *P* mystery 223 15
Almighty and everlasting God, who in the *P* mystery 224 13
grant that in this *P* feast we may so burn 285 10
for he is the true *P* lamb, 287 3
multiply, by the grace of the *P* sacrament, the number 289 7
Almighty and everlasting God, who in the *P* mystery 290 14
Through the *P* mystery, dear friends, we are buried 292 1
prepare with joy for the *P* feast; 346 9
for he is the very *P* Lamb, who was sacrificed for us, 346 19
prepare with joy for the *P* feast; 379 6
for he is the true *P* Lamb, who was sacrificed for us, 379 16

pass

Is it nothing to you, all ye that *p* by? 39 4
may *p* our time in rest and quietness; 69 20
Is it nothing to you, all you who *p* by? 77 3
good things as *p* man's understanding: 174 2
we may so *p* through things temporal, 180 4
guide, we may so *p* through things temporal, 231 20
that through the grave and gate of death we may *p* 480 10
knowing all things before they come to *p*: 520 13
For he spoke, and it came to *p*; * 626 17
and he will bring it to *p*. 633 14
He split open the sea and let them *p* through; * 695 28
so that all who *p* by pluck off its grapes? 703 12
All who *p* by despoil him; * 716 23
for they *p* away quickly and we are gone. 718 22
My days *p* away like a shadow, * 731 21
You set the limits that they should not *p*; * 735 19
Until his prediction came to *p*, * 739 15
And made Israel to *p* through the midst of it, * 790 23
he gave them a law which shall not *p* away. 806 6

passed

the old has *p* away, behold the new has come. 106 1
Lord Jesus *p* over from death to life, 285 2
Seeing that we have a great high priest, that is *p* 320 5
Since we have a great high priest who has *p* 352 5

passeth

The peace of God, which *p* all understanding, 339 15
so soon *p* it away, and we are gone. 473 6
and in his heart may thy peace which *p* understanding 830 17

passing

placed among things that are *p* away, 182 8
placed among things that are *p* away, 234 3
our days are like a *p* shadow. 800 9

passion

heart of your Son as he bore his *p*, 113 14
by thy Cross and *P*; 149 22
O God, who before the *p* of thy only-begotten Son 165 14
O God, who by the *p* of thy blessed Son 168 17
p be brought unto the glory of his resurrection; 188 18
hath left unto us a memorial of his *p*: 201 3
whose blessed Son before his *p* prayed 204 17
O God, who before the *p* of your only-begotten Son 217 7
O God, by the *p* of your blessed Son 220 8
p be brought to the glory of his resurrection; 240 3
has left us a memorial of his *p*: 252 7
whose blessed Son before his *p* prayed 255 15
the days of our Lord's *p* and resurrection, 264 11
By the cross and *p* of your Son our Lord, 269 1
The *P* of our Lord Jesus Christ according to 272 15
The *P* of our Lord Jesus Christ according to John. 277 1
your *p*, cross, and death between your judgment 282 7
having in remembrance his blessed *p* 335 13
in remembrance of his death and *p*, 335 22
and all other benefits of his *p*. 335 29
having in remembrance his blessed *p* 342 13
By your holy Incarnation, by your Cross and *P*, 463 5
set thy *p*, cross, and death, between thy judgment 489 24
hast left unto us a memorial of thy *p*: 834 13

Passover

Christ our *P* is sacrificed for us, * 46 2
Christ our *P* has been sacrificed for us; * 83 11
For this is the *P* of the Lord, 285 4
the *P* paid for us the debt of Adam's sin, 287 4
Almighty God, by the *P* of your Son you have brought 291 5
Christ our *P* is sacrificed for us; 337 1
Christ our *P* is sacrificed for us; 364 15

past

for evening is at hand and the day is *p*; 70 11
protected us in the day that is *p*, 113 5
thank you for the blessings of the day that is *p*, 124 3
for evening is at hand and the day is *p*; 124 8
for evening is at hand and the day is *p*; 139 17
with all who have faithfully served thee in the *p*, 202 13
with all who have faithfully served you in the *p*, 253 17
We confess to you, Lord, all our *p* unfaithfulness: 268 1
he saved his people in ages *p*; 288 2
forgive us all that is *p*; 331 16
saints who have found favor with you in ages *p*. 375 24
are but as yesterday when it is *p*, * 472 17
I remember the years long *p*; 693 11
Remember not our *p* sins; 701 21
are like yesterday when it is *p* * 718 7
I remember the time *p*; 799 7
for all your servants and witnesses of time *p*: 838 10

pastor

to be a [bishop and] *p* in thy Church 197 5
to be a [bishop and] *p* in your Church 248 16
have chosen N. to be a bishop and chief *p*. 513 3
faithful *p* and wholesome example 517 11
As a chief priest and *p*, will you encourage 518 12
work as a *p*, priest, and teacher, 531 5
Will you undertake to be a faithful *p* 532 14
Make him a faithful *p*, 534 4
and be among us as a *p* and priest. 561 4
that we may receive a faithful *p*, who will care 818 11
particularly as apostle, chief priest, and *p* 855 23
particularly as *p* to the people; 856 3

pastoral

Will you respect and be guided by the *p* direction 532 1
Will you be guided by the *p* direction 543 25

pastors

be ordered and guided by faithful and true *p*; 188 4
Give abundantly to all *p* the gifts 197 6
be guided and governed by faithful and true *p*; 239 14
Give abundantly to all *p* the gifts 248 17
some evangelists, some *p* and teachers, 533 8
through the voices of prophets, *p*, and teachers. 571 10

pasture

and we are the people of his *p* 45 4
we are his people and the sheep of his *p*. 45 16
and we are the people of his *p* 82 18
we are his people and the sheep of his *p*. 83 3
and we are the people of his *p* 146 14
He shall feed me in a green *p*, * 476 3
why is your wrath so hot against the sheep of your *p*? 689 10
For we are your people and the sheep of your *p*; * 702 9
and we are the people of his *p* 725 4
we are his people and the sheep of his *p*. 729 27

pastures

He makes me lie down in green *p* * 443 3
He maketh me to lie down in green *p*; * 476 21
He makes me lie down in green *p* * 612 25
may the flocks in our *p* increase by thousands 801 5

path

and a light upon my *p*. 103 7
Thou art about my *p*, and about my bed, * 474 21
Thou shalt show me the *p* of life; 485 6
You will show me the *p* of life; 501 8
And a light upon our *p*. 571 14
You will show me the *p* of life; * 600 19
lead me on a level *p*, because of my enemies. 618 22
nor did our footsteps stray from your *p*; 646 23
He put their feet on a straight *p* * 746 14
Make me go in the *p* of your commandments, * 766 5
and a light upon my *p*. 772 4
they have set traps for me along the *p*. 796 12
spirit languishes within me, you know my *p*; * 798 5
and in thy straight *p* may not stumble; 832 11

paths

That thy holy angels may lead us in *p* of peace 68 9
That your holy angels may lead us in *p* of peace 122 11
and bring me forth in the *p* of righteousness 476 6
he leadeth me in the *p* of righteousness 476 24
and whatsoever walks in the *p* of the sea. 592 24
in your *p* my feet shall not stumble. 601 8
and teach me your *p*. 614 20

All the *p* of the LORD are love and faithfulness * 615 8
and your *p* overflow with plenty. 673 12
and your *p* in the great waters, * 694 15
all *p* of falsehood I abhor. 774 4

pathway
and peace shall be a *p* for his feet. 709 21

pathways
and guides me along right *p* for his Name's sake. 443 6
and guides me along right *p* for his Name's sake. 613 2

patience
follow the example of his *p*, 168 6
by *p* and comfort of thy holy Word, 184 18
that with wisdom, *p*, and courage, 209 12
that with wisdom, *p*, and courage, 260 18
stir up in us the will and *p* to minister to their needs. 279 13
may run with *p* the race that is set 347 19
Give him courage, *p*, and vision; 421 4
in faithfulness and *p*, in wisdom and true godliness, 431 5
and give him *p* under his affliction. 458 6
by your *p* in suffering you hallowed 461 5
nourish them with *p*; 467 5
come with steadfastness and *p*; 505 12
in word and action, in love and *p*, 523 6
in word and action, in love and *p*, 535 6
in word and action, in love and *p*, 547 2
that with *p* and understanding he may love 560 6
in word and action, in love and *p*, 564 6
But I shall always wait in *p*, * 684 7
giving them *p* under their sufferings, 815 10
knowledge, temperance, *p*, godliness. 829 3
nourish his soul with *p*, 831 15

patient
give them calm strength and *p* wisdom 443 26
Make him a faithful pastor, a *p* teacher, 534 4
Give us calm strength and *p* wisdom 829 10
give *p* understanding and persevering love. 831 23
For the brave and courageous, who are *p* in suffering 837 14

patiently
boldly rebuke vice, and *p* suffer 190 6
boldly rebuke vice, and *p* suffer 241 15
If I am to lie low, help me to do it *p*. 461 23
wait *p* for the LORD. 619 3
and wait *p* for him. 633 18
I waited *p* upon the LORD; * 640 1

patriarchs
with *p*, prophets, apostles, and martyrs, 375 22
holy *p*, prophets, apostles, and martyrs; 489 17
holy *p*, prophets, apostles, and martyrs; 504 15
of *p*, prophets, apostles, and martyrs, 517 15

patron
fellowship of [N., our *p*, and of] all your Saints, 579 10

pattern
Will you do your best to *p* your life 532 19
Will you do your best to *p* your life 544 7

patterns
they are *p* of countless ways by which God 861 19

Paul
P to be an apostle to the Gentiles: 107 13
O God, who, by the preaching of thine apostle *P*, 187 8
Almighty God, whose blessed apostles Peter and *P* 190 10
O God, by the preaching of your apostle *P* 238 20
Almighty God, whose blessed apostles Peter and *P* 241 19
consider how Saint *P* exhorts all persons 316 20
for Peter and *P* and all the apostles; 838 14

pavilion
he made dark waters and thick clouds his *p*. 603 12
In the deep has he set a *p* for the sun; * 606 23

pay
p my vows now in the presence of all his people; * 479 18
They *p* me evil in exchange for good; * 630 15
that we should never have enough to *p* it, 652 20
and will *p* you my vows, * 674 21
kings of Tarshish and of the isles shall *p* tribute, * 686 3

payment
and receive just *p* for their labor; 824 14

pays
happy the one who *p* you back 792 20

peace
Grace be unto you, and *p*, from God our Father, 40 9
and to guide our feet into the way of *p*. 51 20
Lord, now lettest thou thy servant depart in *p*, * 51 23
and on earth *p*, good will towards men. 52 4
Give *p*, O Lord, in all the world; 55 5
find it none other than the way of life and *p*; 56 10
and guide our feet into the way of *p*; 56 21
O God, who art the author of *p* and lover of concord, 57 1
and didst send thy blessed Son to preach *p* 58 2
May the God of hope fill us with all joy and *p* 60 1
Grace be unto you, and *p*, from God our Father, 61 3
Lord, now lettest thou thy servant depart in *p*, * 66 1
Give *p*, O Lord, in all the world; 67 20
That thy holy angels may lead us in paths of *p* 68 9
That there may be *p* to thy Church 68 15
Give unto thy servants that *p* 69 17
love thee and serve thee in *p*; 70 18
May the God of hope fill us with all joy and *p* 73 1
Grace to you and *p* from God our Father 78 8
and to guide our feet into the way of *p*. 93 9
to go in *p* as you have promised; 93 13
and *p* to his people on earth. 94 22
Give *p*, O Lord, in all the world; 97 22
find it none other than the way of life and *p*; 99 5
and guide our feet into the way of *p*; 99 16
O God, the author of *p* and lover of concord, 99 20
and sent your blessed Son to preach *p* 100 18
May the God of hope fill us with all joy and *p* 102 12
you said to your apostles, "*p* I give 107 17
my own *p* I leave with you:" 107 18
give to us the *p* and unity of that heavenly City, 107 19
Light and *p*, in Jesus Christ our Lord. 109 1
and give you *p*. 114 5
Grace to you and *p* from God our Father 115 3
to go in *p* as you have promised; 120 2
Give *p*, O Lord, in all the world; 121 22

That your holy angels may lead us in paths of *p* 122 11
That there may be *p* to your Church 122 17
Give to us, your servants, that *p* 123 17
may live in *p* and quietness; 123 19
love you and serve you in *p*; 124 15
May the God of hope fill us with all joy and *p* 126 12
I lie down in *p*; at once I fall asleep; * 129 6
May the God of *p*, who brought 132 1
let your holy angels dwell with us to preserve us in *p*; 133 23
and asleep we may rest in *p*. 134 17
to go in *p* as you have promised; 135 2
and asleep we may rest in *p*. 135 10
O God, you will keep in perfect *p* those whose minds 138 9
you said your apostles, "*P* I give 138 16
my own *p* I leave with you:" 138 17
and give to us the *p* and unity of that heavenly City, 138 18
to go in *p* as you have promised; 140 8
let your holy angels dwell with us to preserve us in *p*; 140 15
to give to all nations unity, *p*, and concord; 151 2
eternal life and *p*, 152 16
Grant us thy *p*. 152 29
and in our time grant us thy *p*; 164 3
bond of *p* and of all virtues, 165 2
may find it none other than the way of life and *p*; 168 14
and establish thy rule of justice, love, and *p*; 186 17
that in unity and *p* we may proclaim the one truth 187 4
to maintain these liberties in righteousness and *p*; 190 21
and on earth thy light and thy *p*; 202 3
and be filled with thy joy and *p*; 204 5
and didst send thy blessed Son to preach *p* 206 10
to serve thee in freedom and *p*: 207 2
in every heart the true love of *p*, 207 9
contend against evil and to make no *p* 209 3
and in our time grant us your *p*; 215 15
your greatest gift, which is love, the true bond of *p* 216 15
find it none other than the way of life and *p*; 220 5
your rule of justice, love, and *p*; 238 11
in unity and *p* we may proclaim the one truth 238 17
maintain our liberties in righteousness and *p*; 242 5
and on earth your light and your *p*; 253 8
and be filled with your joy and *p*; 255 3
and sent your blessed Son to preach *p* 257 6
to serve you in freedom and in *p*: 258 2
in every heart the true love of *p*, 258 9
contend against evil and to make no *p* 260 9
P in heaven and glory in the highest. 270 2
Let us go forth in *p*. 271 17
find it none other than the way of life and *p*; 272 5
P is my last gift to you, my own *p* I now leave 275 1
p which the world cannot give, I give to you. 275 2
and preserve it in *p*. 278 10
and live in *p* and concord. 278 24
in every heart the true love of *p*, 278 26
have died in the *p* of Christ, 280 10
to your holy Church *p* and concord; 282 10
It casts out pride and hatred, and brings *p* 287 20
Will you strive for justice and *p* among all people, 294 1
Will you strive for justice and *p* among all people, 305 7
Bring them to the fullness of your *p* and glory. 306 3
The *p* of the Lord be always with you. 308 15
The *p* of the Lord be always with you. 310 13
and on earth *p*, good will towards men. 324 15
actions for the welfare and *p* of the world. 329 21
The *p* of the Lord be always with you. 332 19
grant us thy *p*. 337 8
The *p* of God, which passeth all understanding, 339 15
Go in *p* to love and serve the Lord. 340 1
and *p* to his people on earth. 356 2
The *p* of the Lord be always with you. 360 19
serve you in unity, constancy, and *p*; 363 17
Send us now into the world in *p*, 365 14
Go in *p* to love and serve the Lord. 366 16
to open for us the way of freedom and *p*. 370 20
guard its faith, and preserve it in *p*. 375 14
[Remember all who have died in the *p* of Christ, 375 18
For the *p* from above, for the loving-kindness of God, 383 3
For the *p* of the world, 383 6
I ask your prayers for *p*; 386 1
Pray for justice and *p*. 386 3
That there may be justice and *p* on the earth. 387 11
in the ways of justice and *p*; 388 8
In *p*, let us pray to the Lord, 389 13
For the *p* of the world, 390 13
they may live in joy, *p*, and health, we pray 391 12
In *p*, we pray to you, Lord God. 392 1
For all who work for justice, freedom, and *p*. 392 6
For the *p* and unity of the Church of God; 392 12
you said to your apostles, "*P* I give 395 8
my own *p* I leave with you:" 395 9
give to us the *p* and unity of that heavenly City, 395 10
grant us *p*. 407 6
Will you strive for justice and *p* 417 17
The *p* of the Lord be always with you. 419 9
speak now; or else for ever hold your *p*. 424 3
p with you and one another all the days of their life. 429 13
Lead them into all *p*. 430 17
that their home may be a haven of blessing and *p*; 431 6
The *p* of the Lord be always with you. 431 14
live in fidelity and *p*, 432 6
p all the days of their life; 444 14
keep you in *p*. 445 8
and restore you in the perfect *p* 448 10
Go (or abide) in *p*, and pray for me, a sinner. 448 14
and restore you in the perfect *p* 451 9
Go (or abide) in *p*. 451 19
P be to this house (place), and to all who dwell in it. 453 1
and *p* which will enable you to serve him 456 5
in that perfect *p* which you have promised 461 14
Give him your *p*. 463 28
May your rest be this day in *p*, 464 25
into the blessed rest of everlasting *p*, 465 5
mercy of God, rest in *p*. 465 8
and saints welcome him in *p*. 466 5
and give them *p*; 467 7
In *p*, let us pray to the Lord. 480 3
in paradise and on earth, thy light and thy *p*. 480 7
Grant to thy faithful people pardon and *p*, 481 4
blessed rest of everlasting *p*, 483 10
The Lord will guide our feet into the way of *p*, 483 18
lift up his countenance upon him and give him *p*. 485 15
through the mercy of God, rest in *p*. 486 20
The God of *p*, who brought again from the dead 486 21
to thy holy Church *p* and concord, 489 27
through the mercy of God, rest in *p*. 498 11

into the blessed rest of everlasting *p*, 499 17
The Lord will guide our feet into the way of *p*, 500 7
lift up his countenance upon him and give him *p*. 501 16
through the mercy of God, rest in *p*. 502 18
The God of *p*, who brought again from the dead 503 1
Grant them your *p*; 504 27
The *p* of the Lord be always with you. 522 1
In *p* let us pray to the Lord. 527 11
The *p* of the Lord be always with you. 534 14
In *p* let us pray to the Lord. 539 11
The *p* of the Lord be always with you. 546 1
For the *p* of the world, 549 29
The *p* of the Lord be always with you. 563 12
The *p* of the Lord be always with you. 574 10
I lie down in *p*; at once I fall asleep; * 588 15
the LORD shall give his people the blessing of *p*. 621 2
seek *p* and pursue it. 628 22
For they do not plan for *p*, * 631 9
they will delight in abundance of *p*. 634 6
hold not your *p* at my tears. 639 22
I have no *p*, because of my cares. 660 8
there shall be abundance of *p* till the moon 685 22
do not keep still nor hold your *p*, O God; 706 4
for he is speaking *p* to his faithful people 709 10
righteousness and *p* have kissed each other. 709 15
and *p* shall be a pathway for his feet. 709 21
Great *p* have they who love your law; * 777 9
among the enemies of *p*. 778 21
I am on the side of *p*, * 778 22
Pray for the *p* of Jerusalem: * 780 7
P be within your walls * 780 9
but *p* be upon Israel. 782 5
may *p* be upon Israel. 783 25
He has established *p* on your borders; * 805 5
hold the faith in unity of spirit, in the bond of *p*, 815 5
P, as children of one Father; 815 26
that *p* which is the fruit of righteousness, 816 3
in all truth with all *p*. 816 11
Christ, our only Savior, the Prince of *P*: 818 15
united in one holy bond of truth and *p*, 818 22
that there may be justice and *p* at home, 820 11
by thy Providence, we may dwell secure in thy *p*. 820 18
may be a people at *p* among ourselves 821 16
we may live in justice and *p*; 823 21
give us times of refreshment and *p*; 825 2
that *p* may prevail with righteousness, 825 11
Provide for them homes of dignity and *p*; 830 3
and in his heart may thy *p* which passeth 830 16
lift up thy countenance upon him, and give him *p*; 831 17
O God of *p*, who hast taught us 832 13
Lord, make us instruments of your *p*. 833 5
and *p* at the last. 833 18
to work and pray for *p*; 848 8
and promotes justice, *p*, and love. 855 7

peaceable

for there is a future for the *p*. 636 12

peaceably

p governed by thy providence, 177 10
p governed by your providence; 229 6
who speak *p* with their neighbors, 619 12

peaceful

That this evening may be holy, good, and *p*, 68 7
That this evening may be holy, good, and *p*, 122 9
The Lord Almighty grant us a *p* night 127 1

peacefully

asleep *p* in thee, and awake up after thy likeness; 69 10
asleep *p* in you and wake up in your likeness; 123 9
asleep *p* in you and wake up in your likeness; 504 24

peak

the *p* of Mizar among the heights of Hermon. 643 20

pen

my tongue shall be the *p* of a skilled writer, 647 13

penance

Reconciliation of a Penitent, or *P*, is the rite 861 9

penitence

prepare for them by a season of *p* and fasting. 265 1
were reconciled by *p* and forgiveness, 265 5
a sign of our mortality and *p*, 265 18
thanksgiving, *p*, oblation, intercession, 856 28
What is *p*? 857 11
In *p*, we confess our sins and make restitution 857 12

penitent

and with *p* and obedient hearts confess our sins, 41 12
restore thou those who are *p*, 42 5
and with *p* and obedient hearts confess our sins, 62 12
restore thou those who are *p*, 63 8
and with *p* and obedient hearts confess our sins, 79 7
and with *p* and obedient hearts confess our sins, 116 8
forgive the sins of all those who are *p*: 166 3
with *p* hearts and steadfast faith to embrace 166 18
forgive the sins of all who are *p*: 217 15
with *p* hearts and steadfast faith to embrace 218 9
forgive the sins of all who are *p*: 264 3
pronounce to his people, being *p*, the absolution 269 7
For, as the benefit is great, if with *p* hearts 316 23
restore thou those who are *p*, 321 8
declare God's forgiveness to *p* sinners, 531 13
arouse the careless, and restore the *p*. 817 20
reconciliation of a *p*, and unction. 860 11
are *p* for their sins, and are ready to affirm 860 25
What is Reconciliation of a *P*? 861 8
Reconciliation of a *P*, or Penance, is the rite 861 9

pens

nor he-goats out of your *p*; 654 22

people

which shall be to all *p*. 37 9
and they shall be his *p*, 37 12
tell the *p* what things he hath done. 40 8
and we are the *p* of his pasture 45 4
we are his *p* and the sheep of his pasture. 45 16
O ye *p* of God, bless ye the Lord; * 49 1
for he hath visited and redeemed his *p*; 50 23
To give knowledge of salvation unto his *p* * 51 14
which thou hast prepared before the face of all *p*, 51 26
and to be the glory of thy *p* Israel. 51 28
And make thy chosen *p* joyful. 55 4
O Lord, save thy *p*, and bless thine heritage; 55 15

eternal rest promised to thy *p* in heaven; 56 16
body of thy faithful *p* is governed and sanctified: 57 20
Grant that *p* everywhere may seek after thee 58 3
which thou hast prepared before the face of all *p*, 66 4
and to be the glory of thy *p* Israel. 66 6
And make thy chosen *p* joyful. 67 19
which will come to all the *p*; 75 9
and they shall be his *p*, 75 12
and we are the *p* of his pasture 82 18
we are his *p* and the sheep of his pasture. 83 3
the God of my *p* and I will exalt him. 85 6
With your constant love you led the *p* 85 21
Let the *p* of God glorify the Lord, * 89 18
he has come to his *p* and set them free. 92 19
To give his *p* knowledge of salvation * 93 3
and the glory of your *p* Israel. 93 17
From every family, language, *p*, and nation, * 94 3
and peace to his *p* on earth. 94 22
Come then, Lord, and help your *p*, 96 9
Let your *p* sing with joy. 97 21
Save your *p*, Lord, and bless your inheritance; 98 9
eternal rest promised to your *p* in heaven; 99 11
body of your faithful *p* is governed and sanctified: 100 12
Grant that *p* everywhere may seek after you 100 19
Eternal God, who led your ancient *p* into freedom 111 8
and the glory of your *p* Israel. 120 6
Let your *p* sing with joy. 121 21
your *p* may glorify your holy Name; 133 19
and the glory of your *p* Israel. 135 6
and the glory of your *p* Israel. 140 12
and we are the *p* of his pasture 146 14
It is a *p* that do err in their hearts, 146 22
Spare us, good Lord, spare thy *p*, 148 11
That it may please thee to bless and keep all thy *p*, 150 10
That it may please thee to give to all *p* increase 150 15
Mercifully forgive the sins of thy *p*. 154 18
Grant that thy *p*, illumined by thy Word 163 8
and proclaim to all *p* the Good 163 15
Mercifully hear the supplications of thy *p*, 164 3
Grant unto thy *p* that they may love 167 16
whose Son Jesus is the good shepherd of thy *p*: 173 11
didst teach the hearts of thy faithful *p* 175 16
receive the prayers of thy *p* who call upon thee, 179 11
thy faithful *p* do unto thee true and laudable service: 184 2
that we and all the *p* of this land may have grace 190 20
they may have true authority among thy *p*; 191 12
p of ________ (or to the ________ *p*). 196 9
O heavenly Father, Shepherd of thy *p*, we give 196 22
called to any office and ministry for thy *p*; 205 7
body of thy faithful *p* is governed and sanctified: 206 2
Grant that *p* everywhere may seek after thee 206 11
Grant to the *p* of our country a zeal for justice 207 3
Be present with thy *p* where they work; 208 3
Grant that your *p*, illumined by your Word 215 2
and proclaim to all *p* the Good News 215 9
Mercifully hear the supplications of your *p*, 215 15
Grant your *p* grace to love what you command 219 7
whose Son Jesus is the good shepherd of your *p*: 225 3
taught the hearts of your *p* 227 9
O Lord, mercifully receive the prayers of your *p* 231 4
faithful *p* offer you true and laudable service: 235 15
all the *p* of this land may have grace to maintain 242 4
true authority among your *p*; 242 19
to the *p* of ________ (or to the ________ *p*). 247 21
Heavenly Father, Shepherd of your *p*, we thank you 248 8
called to any office and ministry for your *p*; 256 4
body of your faithful *p* is governed and sanctified: 256 20
Grant that *p* everywhere may seek after you 257 7
Give to the *p* of our country a zeal for justice 258 3
Be present with your *p* where they work; 259 5
Dear *P* of God: 264 10
and our exploitation of other *p*, 268 5
his *p*, being penitent, the absolution 269 7
Dear *P* of God: 277 2
We pray, therefore, for *p* everywhere 277 7
and the *p* whom they serve 278 5
For N., our Bishop, and all the *p* of this diocese 278 6
body of your faithful *p* is governed and sanctified: 278 12
p the brightness of your light: 285 9
resound with the praises of your *p*. 286 9
and by his blood delivered your faithful *p*. 287 5
he saved his *p* in ages past; 288 2
your chosen *p* from slavery under Pharaoh, 289 14
O God, you led your ancient *p* by a pillar of cloud 290 2
Will you strive for justice and peace among all *p*, 294 1
Will you strive for justice and peace among all *p*, 305 8
And to all thy *p* give thy heavenly grace, 329 13
Open, O Lord, the eyes of all *p* to behold 329 22
The Gifts of God for the *P* of God. 338 1
blessed company of all faithful *p*; 339 8
Wherefore, O Lord and heavenly Father, we thy *p* 342 10
by water and the Holy Spirit hast made us a new *p* 345 5
Who dost bid thy faithful *p* cleanse their hearts, 346 8
for to thy faithful *p*, O Lord, life is changed, 349 8
Hear the commandments of God to his *p*: 350 1
and peace to his *p* on earth. 356 2
Sanctify them by your Holy Spirit to be for your *p* 363 13
The Gifts of God for the *P* of God. 364 17
in the calling of Israel to be your *p*; 368 3
made a new *p* by water and the Spirit, 371 7
showing them to be holy gifts for your holy *p*, 375 6
[Remember all your *p*, and those who seek 375 16
a new *p* in Jesus Christ our Lord, 378 2
You bid your faithful *p* cleanse their hearts, 379 5
For to your faithful *p*, O Lord, life is changed, 382 3
and for all the clergy and *p*, let us pray 384 1
I ask your prayers for God's *p* throughout the world; 385 17
and for all ministers and *p*. 385 19
and for the well-being of all *p*. 386 2
That your Name may be glorified by all *p*. 387 5
Guide the *p* of this land, and of all the nations, 388 7
and for all the holy *p* of God, we pray to you, 390 2
For all *p* in their daily life and work; 392 2
Lord, hear the prayers of thy *p*; 394 1
Mercifully accept the prayers of your *p*, 394 10
O Lord our God, accept the fervent prayers of your *p*; 395 3
The Gifts of God for the *P* of God. 399 1
your Holy Spirit to be for your *p* the Body and Blood 403 2
Will you strive for justice and peace among all *p*, 417 18
Scripture commends it to be honored among all *p*. 423 8
in the presence of all his *p*, 442 24
to the blessed company of your faithful *p*; 450 19
favor that thou bearest unto thy *p*; * 478 18
and rejoice in the gladness of thy *p*, 478 21

I will pay my vows now in the presence of all his *p*; * 479 18
Grant to thy faithful *p* pardon and peace, 481 4
favor which thou bearest unto thy *p*. 481 19
favor which thou bearest unto thy *p*; 488 22
Bishop in the Church of God, the clergy and *p* 513 1
My brother, the *p* have chosen you 517 1
stirring up the conscience of your *p*? 518 10
support all baptized *p* in their gifts 518 13
gathered and prepared a *p* to be heirs of the covenant 520 15
with such love of you and of all the *p*, 521 8
on behalf of the clergy and *p* of the Diocese 526 2
All baptized *p* are called to make Christ known 531 2
serve the *p* among whom you work, 531 11
In all that you do, you are to nourish Christ's *p* 531 18
may be a wholesome example to your *p*? 532 22
calling us to be a holy *p* in the kingdom of your Son 533 2
poured his gifts abundantly upon your *p*, 533 7
May he exalt you, O Lord, in the midst of your *p*; 534 1
so that your *p* may be strengthened 534 6
on behalf of the clergy and *p* of the Diocese 538 2
serve all *p*, particularly the poor, 543 5
to show Christ's *p* that in serving the helpless 543 17
may be a wholesome example to all *p*? 544 10
Let us then offer our prayers to God for all his *p*, 560 1
and understanding he may love and care for your *p*; 560 7
let the doors of this place be open to all *p*. 562 2
an instrument of your salvation for the *p* 563 1
Through the ages, Almighty God has moved his *p* 567 1
to illumine and to bless your *p*. 568 13
Father, your *p* worship you with many voices 572 1
We give you thanks, O God, for the gifts of your *p*, 573 1
restores us to the company of your faithful *p*, 579 2
I do not fear the multitudes of *p* * 587 13
Your blessing be upon your *p*! 587 19
who eat up my *p* like bread 598 22
when the LORD restores the fortunes of his *p*, 599 2
upon those who are noble among the *p*. 600 2
You will save a lowly *p*, * 604 18
A *p* I have not known shall serve me; 605 28
scorned by all and despised by the *p*. 610 13
They shall come and make known to a *p* yet unborn * 612 21
The LORD is the strength of his *p*, * 620 1
Save your *p* and bless your inheritance; * 620 3
The LORD shall give strength to his *p*; * 621 1
the LORD shall give his *p* the blessing of peace. 621 2
happy the *p* he has chosen to be his own! 626 24
and beholds all the *p* in the world. 627 2
your *p* take refuge under the 632 18
and defend my cause against an ungodly *p*; * 644 15
how you destroyed nations and made your *p* flourish. 645 12
You are selling your *p* for a trifle * 646 9
forget your *p* and your father's house. 648 12
The *p* of Tyre are here with a gift; * 648 15
the rich among the *p* seek your favor." 648 16
with the *p* of the God of Abraham. 650 23
to witness the judgment of his *p*. 654 10
Hear, O my *p*, and I will speak: 654 16
who eat up my *p* like bread 659 8
when God restores the fortunes of his *p* 659 15
I lie in the midst of lions that devour the *p*; * 664 1
Slay them, O God, lest my *p* forget; * 666 18
You have made your *p* know hardship; * 667 14
Put your trust in him always, O *p*, * 669 22
how wonderful he is in his doing toward all *p*. 674 2
O God, when you went forth before your *p*, * 676 16
Your *p* found their home in it; * 676 23
the God of Israel giving strength and power to his *p*! 679 5
That he may rule your *p* righteously * 685 11
That the mountains may bring prosperity to the *p*, * 685 13
He shall defend the needy among the *p*; * 685 15
And so the *p* turn to them * 687 19
and gave him to the *p* of the desert for food. 690 13
how a foolish *p* despised your Name. 690 21
By your strength you have redeemed your *p*, * 694 3
You led your *p* like a flock * 694 17
Hear my teaching, O my *p*; * 694 19
The *p* of Ephraim, armed with the bow, * 695 20
or to provide meat for his *p*?" 696 16
How often the *p* disobeyed him in the wilderness * 698 7
He led out his *p* like sheep * 699 9
the tabernacle where he had lived among his *p*. 699 27
He gave his *p* to the sword * 700 3
to be a shepherd over Jacob his *p* 700 22
For we are your *p* and the sheep of your pasture; * 702 9
despite the prayers of your *p*? 702 20
Hear, O my *p*, and I will admonish you: * 704 17
And yet my *p* did not hear my voice, * 704 24
Oh, that my *p* would listen to me! * 705 1
They take secret counsel against your *p* * 706 7
and have come to help the *p* of Lot. 706 19
Happy are the *p* whose strength is in you! * 707 25
You have forgiven the iniquity of your *p* * 708 22
that your *p* may rejoice in you? 709 6
for he is speaking peace to his faithful *p* 709 10
Happy are the *p* who know the festal shout! * 714 23
spoke once in a vision and said to your faithful *p*: * 715 3
and have exalted one chosen out of the *p*. 715 5
They crush your *p*, O LORD, * 723 3
Consider well, you dullards among the *p*; * 723 9
For the LORD will not abandon his *p*, * 723 21
and we are the *p* of his pasture 725 4
"This *p* are wayward in their hearts; 725 13
The LORD is King; let the *p* tremble; * 728 24
we are his *p* and the sheep of his pasture. 729 27
so that a *p* yet unborn may praise the LORD. 732 13
The LORD made his *p* exceedingly fruitful; * 740 1
Whose heart he turned, so that they hated his *p*, * 740 3
He led out his *p* with silver and gold; * 740 27
So he led forth his *p* with gladness, * 741 11
He gave his *p* the lands of the nations, * 741 13
favor you have for your *p*, * 742 4
and be glad with the gladness of your *p*, * 742 7
the LORD was kindled against his *p* * 745 4
and let all the *p* say, "Amen!" 745 25
Let them exalt him in the congregation of the *p* * 748 19
He has shown his *p* the power of his works * 754 16
He sent redemption to his *p*; 754 22
with the princes of his *p*. 756 15
the house of Jacob from a *p* of strange speech, 756 20
in the presence of all his *p*. 760 2
because *p* do not keep your law. 774 20
so does the LORD stand round about his *p*, 781 20
let your faithful *p* sing with joy. 786 16
and her faithful *p* will rejoice and sing. 787 4

an inheritance for Israel his *p*. 788 27
For the LORD gives his *p* justice * 789 3
Who led his *p* through the wilderness, * 791 1
against the *p* of Edom, * 792 16
Happy are the *p* of whom this is so! * 801 10
happy are the *p* whose God is the LORD! 801 11
He has raised up strength for his *p* 806 22
the children of Israel, a *p* who are near him. 806 24
For the LORD takes pleasure in his *p* * 807 8
this is glory for all his faithful *p*. 807 19
and other clergy, and all our *p*. 817 12
care for your *p* and equip us for our ministries; 818 12
art and music to perfect the praises offered by your *p* 819 15
a *p* mindful of thy favor and glad to do thy will. 820 3
and fashion into one united *p* the multitudes 820 7
of their calling to serve this *p* in thy fear; 820 23
to the glory of thy Name and the welfare of this *p*; 821 6
a *p* at peace among ourselves and a blessing 821 16
to provide for the needs of all our *p*, 822 3
And finally, teach our *p* to rely on your strength 822 10
offices to promote the well-being of all *p*; 822 21
Guide the *p* of the United States 822 24
[and especially the hearts of the *p* of this land], 823 19
Guide the *p* of this land 824 12
and grant that all the *p* of our nation may give thanks 825 20
Look with pity, O heavenly Father, upon the *p* 826 8
in making the heart of this *p* wise, its mind sound, 827 9
the homes in which thy *p* dwell. 828 24
to thy glory and the welfare of thy *p*; 833 3
It has drawn *p* from every nation, 839 9
all our *p*, with many voices in one united chorus, 839 19
that we may not rest until all the *p* of this land share 839 24
bestowed upon this nation and *p*. 840 19
It means that all *p* are worthy of respect 846 14
to which a body of *p* responds in faith. 846 22
given by God to the Hebrew *p*. 846 25
God promised that they would be his *p* 847 1
What response did God require from the chosen *p*? 847 3
God required the chosen *p* to be faithful; 847 4
The covenant with the Hebrew *p* is to be found 847 7
given to Moses and the *p* of Israel. 847 15
and to do to other *p* as we wish them to do to us; 848 3
and the necessities of life for all *p*; 848 14
to rejoice in other *p*'s gifts 848 19
with God, with other *p*, and with all creation. 848 31
books written by the *p* of the Old Covenant, 853 11
books written by the *p* of the New Covenant, 853 15
Good News of the Kingdom for all *p*. 853 18
books written by *p* of the Old Covenant, 853 21
It is called the *P* of God, the New Israel, 854 8
Faith to all *p*, to the end of time. 854 23
to carry out Christ's mission to all *p*. 854 27
The mission of the Church is to restore all *p* 855 2
particularly as pastor to the *p*; 856 3
the Body and Blood of Christ given to his *p*, 859 25
and be in love and charity with all *p*. 860 6
are united with all the *p* of God, 862 27

peoples

and the *p* with his truth. 45 10
O God, who hast made of one blood all the *p* 58 1
make known his deeds among the *p*. 78 7
Make his deeds known among the *p*; * 86 9
deep gloom enshrouds the *p*. 87 14
O God, you have made of one blood all the *p* 100 17
Grant that all the *p* of the earth may look to you 107 9
Grant that all the *p* of the earth may look to you 138 13
bestow freedom upon all *p*, 151 3
begotten Son to the *p* of the earth: 162 14
manifest thy power among all *p*, 181 7
Mercifully grant that the *p* of the earth, 185 3
Mercifully grant that the *p* of the earth, 203 1
O God, who hast made of one blood all the *p* 206 9
Lord God Almighty, who hast made all *p* 207 1
manifested your only Son to the *p* of the earth: 214 8
power among all *p*, to the glory of your Name; 232 19
Mercifully grant that the *p* of the earth, 236 16
Mercifully grant that the *p* of the earth, 254 3
O God, you have made of one blood all the *p* 257 5
Lord God Almighty, you have made all the *p* 258 1
Let us pray for all nations and *p* of the earth, 278 17
Merciful God, Creator of all the *p* of the earth 280 1
Let the *p* praise you, O God; 281 9
let all the *p* praise you. 281 10
Grant that all the *p* of the earth 289 16
uniting *p* of many tongues 347 9
uniting *p* of many tongues 380 4
and for the unity of all *p*, let us pray 383 7
forbearance may grow among nations and *p*, 390 14
forbearance may grow among nations and *p*, 549 30
Why do the *p* mutter empty threats? 586 2
let the assembly of the *p* gather round you. 591 9
he judges the *p* with equity. 593 16
proclaim to the *p* the things he has done. 593 22
and also all the *p* that forget God. 594 12
You deliver me from the strife of the *p*; * 605 26
The foreign *p* will lose heart; * 606 1
and cast down the *p* beneath me. 606 6
and their descendants from among the *p* of the earth. 609 19
he thwarts the designs of the *p*. 626 20
How with your hand you drove the *p* out 645 10
a laughing-stock among the *p*. 646 14
The *p* are falling at your feet, * 647 23
Clap your hands, all you *p*; * 650 6
He subdues the *p* under us, * 650 10
The nobles of the *p* have gathered together * 650 22
Hear this, all you *p*; 652 6
O God, in your anger, cast down the *p*. 663 5
I will confess you among the *p*, O LORD; * 664 15
do you judge the *p* with equity? 664 22
and the clamor of the *p*. 672 25
Bless our God, you *p*; * 674 9
Let the *p* praise you, O God; * 675 13
let all the *p* praise you. 675 14
for you judge the *p* with equity 675 16
Let the *p* praise you, O God; * 675 18
let all the *p* praise you. 675 19
and the *p*, a herd of wild bulls with its calves. 678 19
scatter the *p* that delight in war. 678 21
and have declared your power among the *p*. 694 2
The LORD will record as he enrolls the *p*, * 711 22
how I carry in my bosom the taunts of many *p*, 717 15
and his wonders among all *p*. 725 22
Ascribe to the LORD, you families of the *p*; * 726 5

he will judge the *p* with equity." 726 13
and the *p* with his truth. 726 21
and all the *p* see his glory. 727 8
and the *p* with equity. 728 22
he is high above all *p*. 729 2
When the *p* are gathered together, * 732 20
make known his deeds among the *p*. 738 2
the ruler of the *p* set him free. 739 18
They did not destroy the *p* * 744 15
I will confess you among the *p*, O LORD; * 749 22
but he entrusted the earth to its *p*. 758 22
laud him, all you *p*. 760 16
who subdues the *p* under me. 800 5
from the hand of foreign *p*, 800 16
and deliver me from the hand of foreign *p*, 800 24
That the *p* may know of your power * 802 9
Kings of the earth and all *p*, * 806 15
and punishment on the *p*; 807 15
all *p* may be gathered under the banner 815 25
O God, who created all *p* in your image, 840 1

Peor

They joined themselves to Baal-*P* * 744 3

peradventure

If I say, *P* the darkness shall cover me, * 475 13

perceive

p the glory of his marvelous works; 163 17
Mercifully give us faith to *p* that, 174 10
p and know what things they ought to do, 179 12
that we may ever *p* within ourselves 201 4
that we and the whole world may *p* 215 10
Mercifully give us faith to *p* that, 226 3
that we may ever *p* within ourselves 252 9
that you may *p* wherein you have offended 317 2
p what is right, and grant us both the courage 818 5
that we may ever *p* within ourselves 834 15

perceives

he *p* the haughty from afar. 793 15

perfect

whose service is *p* freedom: 57 3
and to serve you is *p* freedom: 99 21
grant us a peaceful night and a *p* end. 127 1
O God, you will keep in *p* peace those whose minds 138 9
obtain of thee, the God of all mercy, *p* remission 166 6
spirits of just men made *p*: 198 25
Being of glorious majesty and *p* love as one God 199 13
obtain of you, the God of all mercy, *p* remission 217 18
and to the spirits of just men made *p*: 250 9
Being of glorious majesty and *p* love as one God 251 2
obtain of you, the God of all mercy, *p* remission 264 6
and he is the *p* offering 332 16
a full, *p*, and sufficient sacrifice, 334 13
a full and *p* sacrifice for the whole world; 341 17
a *p* sacrifice for the whole world. 362 16
p Man of the flesh of the Virgin Mary his mother; 378 11
you live and reign in *p* unity, 430 8
and restore you in the *p* peace 448 10
and he is the *p* offering 450 2
and restore you in the *p* peace 451 9
that he may be restored to that *p* health 458 23
in that *p* peace which you have promised 461 14
taste the blessedness of *p* rest. 466 2
go from strength to strength in the life of *p* service 481 21
work which thou didst begin in them may be made *p* 486 11
Make you *p* in every good work to do his will, 487 1
may have our *p* consummation and bliss, 488 8
in the life of *p* service in thy heavenly kingdom; 488 24
and in *p* charity with the world. 489 12
Make you *p* in every good work to do his will, 503 3
p fulfillment and bliss in your eternal 503 18
in favor with you, our God, and in *p* charity 504 9
in them the good purpose of your *p* will; 504 29
through which he offered himself as a *p* sacrifice. 573 14
As for God, his ways are *p*; 604 24
The law of the LORD is *p* 607 4
Out of Zion, *p* in its beauty, * 654 4
we have thought out a *p* plot." 671 22
with justice and in *p* faithfulness. 775 2
I hate them with a *p* hatred; * 795 22
in whose *p* kingdom no sword is drawn 815 22
from whom come every good and *p* gift: 817 4
art and music to *p* the praises 819 15
our knowledge of your love is made *p* in our love 840 5
We mean that Jesus is the only *p* image 849 21

perfected

which thou hast begun in them may be *p*; 489 1

perfecter

author and *p* of our faith, 198 21
the pioneer and *p* of our faith, 250 5

perfection

and that all things are being brought to their *p* 280 20
and that all things are being brought to their *p* 291 17
Giver of life, that he will raise him to *p* 466 14
and that all things are being brought to their *p* 515 10
and that all things are being brought to their *p* 528 8
and that all things are being brought to their *p* 540 8

perfectly

so may we also *p* enjoy him in heaven; 161 4
Grant us so *p* to know thy Son 173 17
Grant us so *p* and without doubt to believe 185 16
may also enjoy him *p* in heaven; 212 19
Grant us so *p* to know your Son 225 9
Grant us so *p* and without doubt to believe 237 10
that we may *p* love thee, 323 10
that we may *p* love you, 355 10
that we may *p* love you, 512 10
that we may *p* love you, 525 10
that we may *p* love you, 537 10

perform

To *p* the mercy promised to our forefathers, * 51 3
To *p* the oath which he swore to our forefather 51 5
thy merciful guiding may *p* the same; 178 3
p the service you set before them; 309 9
p the service you set before them; 418 7
and to *p* the other ministrations 531 16
give you the grace and power to *p* them. 532 31
For the knowledge of your will and the grace to *p* it, 578 19
I will *p* my vows in the presence 612 5

performed

to you shall vows be *p* in Jerusalem. 672 8

perhaps

p in strength even eighty; * 718 20

peril

their hearts melted because of their *p*. 748 8

perils

defend us from all *p* and dangers of this night; 70 2
defend us from all *p* and dangers of this night; 111 2
defend us from all *p* and dangers of this night; 123 22
defend us from all *p* and dangers of this night; 133 11
courage to face the *p* which beset them; 823 5

perish

Do not let me *p* in my sin, * 91 18
to the end that all that believe in him should not *p*, 332 11
whoever believes in him should not *p*, 396 2
to the end that all that believe in him should not *p*, 449 16
Lest he be angry and you *p*; * 586 26
they will stumble and *p* at your presence. 593 6
and the hope of the poor shall not *p* for ever. 594 14
the ungodly shall *p* from his land. 596 2
As for the wicked, they shall *p*, * 634 24
"When will he die, and his name *p*?" 642 9
like the dull and stupid they *p* * 652 24
they are like the beasts that *p*. 653 5
are like the beasts that *p*. 653 24
as the wax melts at the fire, so let the wicked *p* 676 4
come to an end, and *p* from terror! 688 16
Truly, those who forsake you will *p*; * 689 3
at the rebuke of your countenance let them *p*. 703 19
let them be put to confusion and *p*. 707 12
lo, your enemies shall *p*, * 721 14
They shall *p*, but you will endure; 733 1
the desires of the wicked will *p*. 755 27
and in that day their thoughts *p*. 803 10

perished

their cities plowed under, the memory of them *p*; 593 12
I should have *p* in my affliction. 771 4

permit

and did not *p* his wrath to be roused. 698 4

perpetual

O Lord, we beseech thee, make us to have a *p* fear 178 12
O Lord, make us have *p* love and reverence 230 7
command us to continue, a *p* memory 334 15
command us to continue, a *p* memory 341 18
Let light *p* shine upon them. 387 18
And let light *p* shine upon him. 486 18
Let light *p* shine upon them. 498 10
And let light *p* shine upon him. 502 16
let light *p* shine upon them; 504 27
As for the enemy, they are finished, in *p* ruin, * 593 11
and put them to *p* shame. 700 12

perplexity

a counselor in *p*, a comfort in sorrow, 429 9
a counselor in *p*, a comfort in sorrow, 444 11
How long shall I have *p* in my mind, 598 1

persecute

The wicked arrogantly *p* the poor, * 594 21
and from those who *p* me. 623 24
For they *p* him whom you have stricken * 681 16
judgment against those who *p* me? 770 11
help me, for they *p* me with lies. 770 15
They draw near who in malice *p* me; * 776 3
There are many who *p* and oppress me, * 776 17

persecuted

For those who in the name of Christ have *p* others 279 27
For the poor, the *p*, the sick, and all who suffer; 390 24
For the poor, the *p*, the sick, and all who suffer; 550 11
but *p* the poor and needy 752 2
Rulers have *p* me without a cause, * 777 1

persecutors

That it may please thee to forgive our enemies, *p*, 152 8
for his *p* to thy Son Jesus Christ, 186 3
for his *p* to your Son Jesus Christ, 237 16
p of his disciples 279 26

perseverance

encouragement by their *p*, 579 8

persevere

that thy Church throughout the world may *p* 183 13
may *p* in running the race that is set before us, 198 18
p with steadfast faith in the confession 235 6
p in running the race that is set before us, 250 3
Will you *p* in resisting evil, 293 23
Will you *p* in resisting evil, 304 26
the courage to will and to *p*, 308 7
Will you *p* in resisting evil, 417 8
Will you *p* in prayer, 532 24
and encouraged to *p* to the end, 549 9

persevering

give patient understanding and *p* love. 831 24

person

[and for those (this *p*) who have renewed 305 12
promote the dignity and freedom of every *p*, 390 18
Almighty God, look with favor upon this *p* 421 2
promote the dignity and freedom of every *p*, 550 3
The Holy Spirit is the Third *P* of the Trinity, 852 15
the *p* is baptized in the Name of the Father, 858 14

persons

as one God in Trinity of *P*: 199 14
may choose suitable *p* for the ministry 205 16
as one God in Trinity of *P*: 251 3
may choose suitable *p* for the ministry 256 13
Will you seek and serve Christ in all *p*, 293 29
I present these *p* for Confirmation. 303 5
I present these *p* to be received 303 6
I present these *p* who desire to reaffirm 303 8
support these *p* in their life in Christ? 303 15
Will you seek and serve Christ in all *p*, 305 4
Let us now pray for these *p* who are to receive 305 11
Let us now pray for these *p* who have renewed 309 1
consider how Saint Paul exhorts all *p* 316 20
one Lord, in Trinity of *P* and in Unity of Substance; 347 14
one Lord, in Trinity of *P* and in Unity of Being; 380 9

I present these *p* for Confirmation. 415 4
I present these *p* to be received 415 5
I present these *p* who desire to reaffirm 415 7
support these *p* in their life in Christ? 416 2
Will you seek and serve Christ in all *p*, 417 14
Let us now pray for these *p* who have renewed 417 20
uphold these two *p* in their marriage? 425 2
Grant that all married *p* who have witnessed 430 1
uphold these two *p* in their marriage? 434 2
all poor and neglected *p* whom it would be easy 826 2
Christ is the Head and of which all baptized *p* 854 7
The ministers of the Church are lay *p*, 855 12
The ministry of lay *p* is to represent Christ 855 15
they are not necessary for all *p* in the same way 860 15

persuaded

Are you *p* that God has called you 517 19
I am so *p*. 517 21
For I am *p* that your love is established for ever; * 713 19

perverse

The wicked are *p* from the womb; * 664 25

pestilence

and from the deadly *p*. 130 2
from plague, *p*, and famine, 149 12
and from the deadly *p*. 719 16

Peter

Almighty Father, who didst inspire Simon *P* 187 1
Almighty God, whose blessed apostles *P* and Paul 190 10
Almighty Father, who inspired Simon *P*, 238 14
Almighty God, whose blessed apostles *P* and Paul 241 19
for *P* and Paul and all the apostles; 838 14

petition

do not hide yourself from my *p*. 660 6
oblation, intercession, and *p*. 856 29
What are intercession and *p*? 857 17
in *p*, we present our own needs, 857 19

petitions

Fulfill now, O Lord, the desires and *p* 59 16
Fulfill now, O Lord, the desires and *p* 72 13
Fulfill now, O Lord, our desires and *p* 102 5
Fulfill now, O Lord, our desires and *p* 126 5
Almighty God, who hast promised to hear the *p* 153 19
Accept and fulfill our *p*, 394 5
For the fulfilling of our desires and *p* 578 21
Almighty God, who hast promised to hear the *p* 834 1

Pharaoh

The chariots of *P* and his army has he hurled 85 9
arm your chosen people from slavery under *P*, 289 14
against *P* and all his servants. 788 20
But swept *P* and his army into the Red Sea, * 790 25

Philip

God, who didst give to thine apostles *P* and James 189 5
God, who gave to your apostles *P* and James 240 13

Philistia

and over *P* will I shout in triumph." 668 3
behold *P*, Tyre, and Ethiopia: 711 18
and over *P* will I shout in triumph." 750 14

Philistines

the *P* and those who dwell in Tyre. 706 17

Phinehas

Then *P* stood up and interceded, * 744 7

physician

didst inspire thy servant Luke the *p* 193 12
who inspired your servant Luke the *p* 244 20

piece

and shatter them like a *p* of pottery." 586 21

pieces

Lest like a lion they tear me in *p* * 590 22
strangers whom I did not know tore me to *p* 630 25

pierce

they *p* my hands and my feet; 611 13

pierced

For your arrows have already *p* me, * 636 22
and add to the pain of those whom you have *p*. 681 17

piercing

his *p* eye weighs our worth. 596 18

Pilate

suffered under Pontius *P*, 53 28
suffered under Pontius *P*, 66 14
He suffered under Pontius *P*, 96 18
He suffered under Pontius *P*, 120 14
He suffered under Pontius *P*, 293 5
He suffered under Pontius *P*, 304 8
For our sake he was crucified under Pontius *P*; 327 4
and was crucified also for us under Pontius *P*; 328 5
For our sake he was crucified under Pontius *P*; 358 20
He suffered under Pontius *P*, 416 13
He suffered under Pontius *P*, 496 8
For our sake he was crucified under Pontius *P*; 519 23
For our sake he was crucified under Pontius *P*; 530 14
For our sake he was crucified under Pontius *P*; 542 14

pilgrimage

Grant us during our earthly *p* to abide 198 25
Grant that in our earthly *p* 199 6
Grant us during our earthly *p* to abide 250 10
Grant that in our earthly *p* 250 16
Grant that in our earthly *p* 395 19
Grant to us who are still in our *p*, 481 1
to love as a companion on our earthly *p*. 493 19

pilgrims

whose hearts are set on the *p*' way. 707 26

pillar

a *p* of cloud by day and a *p* of fire by night: 111 9
a *p* of cloud by day and a *p* of fire by night: 290 2
He spoke to them out of the *p* of cloud; * 729 14
and the *p* and ground of truth. 854 9

pillars

I will make its *p* fast. 691 9

pine

they will gnash their teeth and *p* away; * 755 26

pinions

He shall cover you with his *p*, 130 3
He shall cover you with his *p*, 719 17

pioneer

through Jesus Christ, the *p* and perfecter 250 5

pipe

Praise him with strings and *p*. 572 6
praise him with strings and *p*. 808 6

pit

They dig a *p* and make it deep * 592 1
The ungodly have fallen into the *p* they dug, * 594 7
nor let your holy one see the *P*. 600 18
I become like those who go down to the *P*. 619 7
if I go down to the *P*? * 621 24
without a cause they have dug a *p* to take me alive. 630 4
let them fall into the *p* they dug. 630 7
He lifted me out of the desolate *p*, 640 3
down to the *p* of destruction, O God. 662 9
they have dug a *p* before me, 664 6
do not let the *P* shut its mouth upon me. 680 22
you have delivered me from the nethermost *P*. 710 27
I am counted among those who go down to the *P*; * 712 7
You have laid me in the depths of the *P*, * 712 13
until a *p* is dug for the wicked. 723 20
or I shall be like those who go down to the *P*. 799 14

pitied

He caused them to be *p* * 745 17

pits

The proud have dug *p* for me; * 770 12

pity

soothe the suffering, *p* the afflicted, 71 4
soothe the suffering, *p* the afflicted, 124 20
soothe the suffering, *p* the afflicted, 134 9
it may please thee to show thy *p* upon all prisoners 151 5
With *p* behold the sorrows of our hearts; 154 17
O Lord, we beseech thee, let thy continual *p* cleanse 180 8
power chiefly in showing mercy and *p*: 182 13
power chiefly in showing mercy and *p*: 234 7
Almighty God, look with *p* upon the sorrows 467 3
Have *p* on me, LORD, for I am weak; * 590 1
Have *p* on me, O LORD; * 594 1
They have closed their heart to *p*, * 601 18
Turn to me and have *p* on me, * 615 20
redeem me, O LORD and have *p* on me. 617 4
He shall have *p* on the lowly and poor; * 686 9
and are moved to *p* even for her dust. 732 5
and none to *p* his fatherless children. 751 21
Look with *p*, O heavenly Father, upon the people 826 8
Visit our jails and prisons with your *p* and judgment. 826 17
Look with *p* upon the sorrows of thy servant 831 13

place

in every *p* incense shall be offered unto my Name, 38 7
"I dwell in the high and holy *p*, 41 1
and prepared for us our *p* in the new Jerusalem: 69 2
and in every *p* incense shall be offered to my Name, 76 6
"I dwell in the high and holy *p* 78 23
The resting-*p* you have made for yourself, O Lord, * 85 26
and in every *p* incense shall be offered to my Name, 106 7
prepared for us our *p* in the new Jerusalem: 123 2
Lift up your hands in the holy *p* and bless the Lord; * 131 8
Visit this *p*, O Lord, and drive 133 21
Lift up your hands in the holy *p* and bless the Lord; * 140 3
Visit this *p*, O Lord, and drive 140 13
exalt us unto the same *p* whither our Savior 175 5
God, who into the *p* of Judas didst choose 188 1
of those who have worshiped in this *p*; 204 3
apostles to ordain ministers in every *p*: 205 15
and exalt us to that *p* where our Savior 226 16
Almighty God, who in the *p* of Judas chose 239 11
of those who have worshiped in this *p*, 255 1
apostles to ordain ministers in every *p*: 256 12
to prepare a *p* for us; 347 4
there is prepared for us a dwelling *p* eternal 349 10
the *p* of eternal joy and light.] 375 20
to prepare a *p* for us; 379 23
prepared for us a dwelling *p* eternal 382 5
they may have rest in that *p* where there is no pain 391 17
We pray for all who have died, that they may have a *p* 393 4
Into your hands, O God, we *p* your child 444 20
Peace be to this house (*p*), 453 1
That it may please you to grant him a *p* 463 17
and your dwelling *p* in the Paradise of God. 464 26
into the courts of your heavenly dwelling *p*. 466 9
the holy *p* of the tabernacle of the Most Highest. 471 24
in the secret *p* of his dwelling shall he hide me, 477 21
*Or the deep, or the elements, or its resting *p*. 485 16
grant him a *p* at the table in your heavenly kingdom. 497 20
*Or the deep, or the elements, or its resting *p*. 501 17
your Church is built up in every *p*, 521 5
they may have rest in that *p* where there is no pain 550 22
Everliving God, whose power is limitless, we *p* 552 6
accept this Bible, and be among us (or be in this *p*) 561 1
and let the doors of this *p* be open 562 1
yours (the Bishop's and yours) in this *p*. 562 8
Receive the work of our hands in this *p*, 567 10
as we dedicate this *p* to which we come to praise 568 9
Be always near us when we seek you in this *p*. 568 16
sanctify this *p*; 569 11
intercessions offered in this *p* today 572 11
the work of many hands, which have beautified this *p* 573 2
receive our thanks for this *p*, and accept the work 578 5
For this *p* where we may be still 578 13
He brought me out into an open *p*; * 604 1
Send you help from his holy *p* * 608 3
and who can stand in his holy *p*?" 613 19
and the *p* where your glory abides. 616 23
you have set my feet in an open *p*. 623 2
You are my hiding-*p*; 625 14
you shall search out their *p*, 634 4
Though you thrust us down into a *p* of misery, * 646 24
"In *p* of fathers, O king, you shall have sons; * 648 23
I would flee to a far-off *p* * 660 19
God spoke from his holy *p* and said: * 667 20
They seek only to bring me down from my *p* 669 12
Therefore I have gazed upon you in your holy *p*, * 670 15
but you brought us out into a *p* of refreshment. 674 19
at the hill which God chose for his resting *p*? * 677 13
Your adversaries roared in your holy *p*; * 689 16
They set fire to your holy *p*; * 689 21

they defiled the dwelling-*p* of your Name 689 22
I answered you from the secret *p* of thunder 704 15
will find it a *p* of springs, * 708 2
For the LORD looked down from his holy *p* on high; * 732 14
and its *p* shall know it no more. 734 14
God spoke from his holy *p* and said, * 750 7
Until I find a *p* for the LORD, * 786 7
Let us go to God's dwelling *p*; * 786 11
Arise, O LORD, into your resting-*p*, * 786 13
"This shall be my resting-*p* for ever; * 786 28
Lift up your hands in the holy *p* and bless 787 21
I have no *p* to flee to, and no one cares for me. 798 8
and that in every *p* your servants 838 6
and we put ourselves in the *p* of God. 845 14
What does this mean about our *p* in the universe? 846 9
To put nothing in the *p* of God; 847 23
their *p* in the life, worship, and governance 855 19

placed

while we are *p* among things that are passing away, 182 7
while we are *p* among things that are passing away, 234 2
Almighty God, you have *p* in the skies the sign 289 1

places

Christ is not entered into the holy *p* made with hands, 39 15
at all times, and in all *p*, give thanks unto thee, 333 8
at all times, and in all *p*, give thanks unto thee, 341 2
build houses of prayer and praise, and to set apart *p* 567 2
and in secret *p* they murder the innocent; * 595 9
and like a young lion lurking in secret *p*. 601 24
their dwelling *p* from generation to generation, * 653 2
but the rebels shall live in dry *p*. 676 15
How wonderful is God in his holy *p*! * 679 4
and bring me up again from the deep *p* of the earth. 684 25
Surely, you set them in slippery *p*; * 688 13
They burned down all the meeting-*p* of God 689 25
the dark *p* of the earth are haunts of violence. 690 25
in dark *p*, and in the abyss. 712 14
in all *p* of his dominion; * 734 28
to the *p* you had appointed for them. 735 18
so the river ran in the dry *p*. 741 8
You trace my journeys and my resting-*p* * 794 4
Let their rulers be overthrown in stony *p*, * 797 15
he has made me live in dark *p* 799 3
kingdom of God in villages, towns, and lonely *p*: 825 17
in all *p*, may give thanks to you in all things. 836 19
For the communion of saints, in all times and *p*, 837 19

plague

Of the *p* that stalks in the darkness, * 130 8
neither shall any *p* come near your dwelling. 130 18
from *p*, pestilence, and famine, 149 12
but delivered their lives to the *p*. 699 6
Of the *p* that stalks in the darkness, * 719 22
neither shall any *p* come near your dwelling. 720 6
and a *p* broke out among them. 744 6
and the *p* came to an end. 744 8

plains

for the richness of mountains, *p*, and rivers; 840 8

plan

out in tranquillity the *p* of salvation; 280 17
out in tranquillity the *p* of salvation; 291 14
out in tranquillity the *p* of salvation; 515 7
out in tranquillity the *p* of salvation; 528 5
out in tranquillity the *p* of salvation; 540 5
For they do not *p* for peace, * 631 9
they *p* how they may hide their snares. 671 19
out of their haughtiness they *p* oppression. 687 16

planets

interstellar space, galaxies, suns, the *p* 370 9

plans

Their aim is to confound the *p* of the afflicted, * 598 26
and prosper all your *p*. 608 8
how great your wonders and your *p* for us! * 640 12
nor let their evil *p* prosper. 796 18

plant

You will bring them in and *p* them * 85 24
P in every heart, we beseech thee, the love 162 2
P in every heart, we beseech thee, the love 213 14

planted

They are like trees *p* by streams of water, 585 7
and *p* our forefathers in the land; * 645 11
you cast out the nations and *p* it. 703 4
preserve what your right hand has *p*. 703 17
Those who are *p* in the house of the LORD * 721 23
He that *p* the ear, does he not hear? * 723 11
the cedars of Lebanon which he *p*, 736 10
They sowed fields, and *p* vineyards, * 749 3

plants

and *p* to serve mankind; 736 4
Which ate up all the green *p* in their land * 740 23
May our sons be like *p* well nurtured 801 1
and green *p* to serve mankind. 804 19

play

p to him upon the psaltery and lyre. 626 4
My lips will sing with joy when I *p* to you, * 685 4
I will *p* to you on a ten-stringed lyre. 800 20

playing

in the midst of maidens *p* upon the hand-drums. 678 8

plea

Hear my *p* of innocence, O LORD; 600 22
he will not despise their *p*. 732 11

plead

P my cause and redeem me; * 776 11

pleaded

I *p* with the LORD, saying, 621 23

pleasant

My boundaries enclose a *p* land; * 600 9
They refused the *p* land * 743 20
Oh, how good and *p* it is, * 787 9
how *p* it is to honor him with praise! 804 3

please

that it may *p* thee to rule and govern thy holy Church 150 2
That it may *p* thee to illumine all bishops, 150 5
That it may *p* thee to bless and keep all thy people, 150 10
That it may *p* thee to send forth laborers 150 12

That it may *p* thee to give to all people increase 150 15
That it may *p* thee to bring into the way of truth 150 19
That it may *p* thee to give us a heart to love and fear 150 22
That it may *p* thee so to rule the hearts 150 25
That it may *p* thee to make wars to cease 151 1
That it may *p* thee to show thy pity upon all prisoners 151 5
That it may *p* thee to give and preserve to our use 151 9
That it may *p* thee to inspire us, 151 13
That it may *p* thee to preserve all who are in danger 151 17
That it may *p* thee to preserve, and provide for, 151 20
That it may *p* thee to visit the lonely; 151 24
That it may *p* thee to support, help, and comfort 151 28
That it may *p* thee to have mercy upon all mankind, 152 1
That it may *p* thee to give us true repentance; 152 3
That it may *p* thee to forgive our enemies, 152 8
That it may *p* thee to strengthen such as do stand; 152 11
That it may *p* thee to grant to all the faithful departed 152 15
That it may *p* thee to grant that, 152 18
we may *p* thee both in will and deed; 164 15
forasmuch as without thee we are not able to *p* 182 1
we may *p* you both in will and deed; 216 9
because without you we are not able to *p* you, 233 14
that those things may *p* him which we do 269 11
serve and *p* thee in newness of life, 331 18
that he may always think and do those things that *p* 460 22
That it may *p* you to deliver the soul 463 12
That it may *p* you mercifully to pardon all his sins, 463 15
That it may *p* you to grant him a place of refreshment 463 17
That it may *p* you to give him joy and gladness 463 20
This will *p* the LORD more than an offering of oxen, * 681 26
May these words of mine *p* him; * 737 22
that it may *p* thee to comfort and relieve 815 9
that they may truly *p* thee, 817 7
that they may enact such laws as shall *p* thee, 821 5

pleased

for with such sacrifices God is well *p*. 344 4
It has *p* God our heavenly Father 440 8
Since it has *p* God to bestow 441 10
Be *p*, O LORD, to deliver me; * 641 8
By this I know you are *p* with me, * 642 22
Then you will be *p* with the appointed sacrifices, 657 20
Be *p*, O God, to deliver me; * 682 11
wouldest be *p* to make thy ways known unto them, 814 8
because thou hast been graciously *p* to deliver 841 8

pleases

The LORD does whatever *p* him, in heaven 788 12
Teach me to do what *p* you, for you are my God; * 799 21

pleasing

do his will, working in you that which is *p* 132 4
holy and *p* in thy sight. 348 18
for such sacrifices are *p* to God. 377 2
holy and *p* in your sight. 381 12
that which is well *p* in his sight; 487 3
that which is well-*p* in his sight; 503 5

pleasure

and at thy right hand there is *p* for evermore. 485 8
For you are not a God who takes *p* in wickedness, * 588 23
O tarry and await the LORD's *p*; 619 1
In a sacrifice and offering you take no *p* * 640 16
who take *p* in my misfortune. 641 13
The king will have *p* in your beauty; * 648 13
let those who take *p* in my misfortune 682 15
he has no *p* in the strength of a man; 804 23
But the LORD has *p* in those who fear him, * 804 24
For the LORD takes *p* in his people * 807 8

pleasures

and in your right hand are *p* for evermore. 501 10
and in your right hand are *p* for evermore. 600 21

pledge

giveth us a *p* of life eternal, 169 11
gives us a *p* of eternal life; 221 5
gives us a *p* of eternal life; 274 5
as a sign and *p* of his love, 316 3
and in their eternal joy a glorious *p* 348 5
and in their eternal joy a glorious *p* 380 22
gives us a *p* of eternal life; 397 17
the *p* of our redemption; 399 9
and *p* you our prayers, encouragement, and support. 420 5
the *p* of our redemption; 457 7
a comfort in affliction, and a *p* of our inheritance 482 5
a comfort in affliction, and a *p* of our inheritance 498 16

pledged

who have not *p* themselves to falsehood, 613 21

Pleiades

Seek him that made the *P* and Orion, 62 1
Seek him who made the *P* and Orion, 115 13

plenteous

and with him is *p* redemption. 474 15
you make it very *p*; * 673 5
With him there is *p* redemption, * 785 8

plenteousness

fillest all things living with *p*: 828 2

plenty

and your paths overflow with *p*. 673 12

plied

and *p* their trade in deep waters; 748 2

plight

and thereto I (*p*) (give) thee my troth. 436 10

plot

and the princes *p* together, * 586 4
They *p* to take my life. 623 19
let those who *p* my ruin fall back and be dismayed. 629 21
The wicked *p* against the righteous * 634 7
and *p* treachery all the day long. 637 22
You *p* ruin; 658 1
we have thought out a perfect *p*." 671 22
and *p* against those whom you protect. 706 8
Even though rulers sit and *p* against me, * 765 5
and the princes *p* together, * 586 4
They *p* to take my life. 623 19
let those who *p* my ruin fall back and be dismayed. 629 21
The wicked *p* against the righteous * 634 7
and *p* treachery all the day long. 637 22
You *p* ruin; 658 1
we have thought out a perfect *p*." 671 22

and *p* against those whom you protect. 706 8
Even though rulers sit and *p* against me, * 765 5

plots
Whose hands are full of evil *p*, * 617 1

plowed
their cities *p* under, the memory of them perished; 593 12
The plowmen *p* upon my back * 784 5

plowman
As when a *p* turns over the earth in furrows, * 797 17

plowmen
The *p* plowed upon my back * 784 5

pluck
for he shall *p* my feet out of the net. 615 19
To *p* their lives from death, * 627 13
so that all who pass by *p* off its grapes? 703 12

plucked
which withers before it can be *p*; 784 12

plunder
let strangers *p* his gains. 751 19

plundered
or *p* him who without cause is my enemy; 591 2
and our enemies have *p* us. 646 6

point
I have been wretched and at the *p* of death; * 713 9

poison
adder's *p* is under their lips. 796 6

polluted
Thus they were *p* by their actions * 745 1

pollution
For our waste and *p* of your creation, 268 24

ponder
I *p*, and my spirit faints. 693 7
I *p* and search my mind. 693 13
and *p* your mighty deeds. 693 25
Whoever is wise will *p* these things, * 749 15
I will *p* the glorious splendor of your majesty * 801 20

pondered
while I *p*, the fire burst into flame; * 638 23

Pontius
suffered under *P* Pilate, 53 28
suffered under *P* Pilate, 66 14
He suffered under *P* Pilate, 96 18
He suffered under *P* Pilate, 120 14
He suffered under *P* Pilate, 293 5
He suffered under *P* Pilate, 304 8
For our sake he was crucified under *P* Pilate; 327 4
and was crucified also for us under *P* Pilate; 328 5
For our sake he was crucified under *P* Pilate; 358 20
He suffered under *P* Pilate, 416 13
He suffered under *P* Pilate, 496 8
For our sake he was crucified under *P* Pilate; 519 23
For our sake he was crucified under *P* Pilate; 530 14
For our sake he was crucified under *P* Pilate; 542 14

pool
Who turned the hard rock into a *p* of water * 757 11

pools
for the early rains have covered it with *p* of water. 708 3
He changed deserts into *p* of water * 748 25

poor
Nor the hope of the *p* be taken away. 55 12
Nor the hope of the *p* be taken away. 68 4
Nor the hope of the *p* be taken away. 98 6
Nor the hope of the *p* be taken away. 122 6
and substance for the relief of the *p* 189 20
O God, whose blessed Son became *p* 198 1
and substance for the relief of the *p* 241 6
O God, whose blessed Son became *p* 249 11
To the *p* he proclaimed the good news 374 4
For the *p* and the oppressed, 384 25
I ask your prayers for the *p*, 386 4
For the *p*, the persecuted, the sick, 390 24
show compassion to the *p* and strangers, 518 29
strong and weak, rich and *p*. 531 12
are to serve all people, particularly the *p*, 543 5
For the *p*, the persecuted, the sick, 550 11
and the hope of the *p* shall not perish for ever. 594 14
The wicked arrogantly persecute the *p*, * 594 21
and the *p* cry out in misery, * 597 10
For he does not despise nor abhor the *p* 612 1
The *p* shall eat and be satisfied, 612 7
You deliver the *p* from those who are too strong 630 11
the *p* and needy from those who rob them." 630 12
to strike down the *p* and needy, * 634 12
Though I am *p* and afflicted, * 641 19
Happy are they who consider the *p* and needy! * 641 23
you of high degree and low, rich and *p* together. 652 8
you have made provision for the *p*. 676 25
But as for me, I am *p* and needy; * 682 22
and the *p* with justice; 685 12
he shall rescue the *p* and crush the oppressor. 685 16
For he shall deliver the *p* who cries out in distress, * 686 7
He shall have pity on the lowly and *p*; * 686 9
never forget the lives of your *p*. 690 23
let the *p* and needy praise your Name. 690 27
Rescue the weak and the *p*; * 705 15
for I am *p* and in misery. 709 23
He lifted up the *p* out of misery * 749 11
but persecuted the *p* and needy 752 2
For I am *p* and needy, * 752 19
They have given freely to the *p*, * 755 22
and lifts up the *p* from the ashes. 756 13
and satisfy her *p* with bread. 787 2
the LORD will maintain the cause of the *p* * 796 25
and adorns the *p* with victory. 807 9
O Lord Jesus Christ, you became *p* for our sake, 819 6
remember before you all *p* and neglected persons 826 2
who for our sake became *p*, 826 7

poorer
for richer for *p*, in sickness and in health, 427 3
for richer for *p*, in sickness and in health, 436 3

portals
and all your *p*, Praise. 87 26

portent
I have become a *p* to many; * 683 14

portents
and *p* in the land of Ham. 740 8

portion
O LORD, you are my *p* and my cup; * 600 7
from those whose *p* in life is this world; 601 28
God is the strength of my heart and my *p* for ever. 689 2
You only are my *p*, O LORD; * 768 1
my *p* in the land of the living." 798 11
may enjoy a fair *p* of the riches of this land; 826 14

positions
For those in *p* of public trust 390 16
For those in *p* of public trust 550 1

possess
your power to *p* me, and gracefully accept 461 3
but those who wait upon the LORD shall *p* the land. 634 2
But the lowly shall *p* the land; * 634 5
Those who are blessed by God shall *p* the land, * 635 3
The righteous shall *p* the land * 635 20
he will raise you up to *p* the land, 636 4
hath given us all that we *p*: 827 2

possession
on the mount of your *p*, 85 25
we are the Lord's *p*. 491 18
and the ends of the earth for your *p*. 586 19
they shall live there and have it in *p*. 682 8
the fields of God as our *p*." 707 2
and Israel for his own *p*. 788 9

possessions
as a ruler over all his *p*, 739 20
and to use our talents and *p* 848 14

possible
where *p*, with the intention to amend our lives. 857 13

posterity
safeguard them for our *p*. 840 11

pot
My mouth is dried out like a *p*-sherd; 611 8
I am as useless as a broken *p*. 623 15

pottery
and shatter them like a piece of *p*." 586 21

pounding
My heart is *p*, my strength has failed me; * 637 16
the waters have lifted up their *p* waves. 722 11

pour
p out thy Spirit upon all flesh; 58 5
p out your Spirit upon all flesh; 100 21
Send thy Holy Ghost and *p* into our hearts 164 19
P into our hearts 174 2
P down upon us the abundance 182 20
We beseech thee, O Lord, *p* thy grace into our hearts, 188 15
thou wilt *p* out upon the leaders of thy Church 191 10
p out thy Spirit upon all flesh, 206 13
Send your Holy Spirit and *p* into our hearts 216 14
P into our hearts 225 15
P upon us the abundance of your mercy, 234 14
P your grace into our hearts, O Lord, 240 1
and we pray that you will *p* out upon the leaders 242 16
p out your Spirit upon all flesh, 257 9
p out the abundance of your blessing 430 15
Now when I think thereupon, I *p* out my heart 471 7
P out upon him the power 521 1
I *p* out my soul when I think on these things: * 643 8
p out your hearts before him, for God is our refuge. 669 23
P out your indignation upon them, * 681 12
P out your wrath upon the heathen who have not 701 15
My lips shall *p* forth your praise, * 777 21
I *p* out my complaint before him * 798 3
p upon them the continual dew 817 7

poured
The love of God has been *p* into our hearts 105 20
Almighty God, who hast *p* upon us the new light 161 14
Almighty God, you have *p* upon us the new light 213 8
and, having ascended into heaven, has *p* his gifts 533 6
I am *p* out like water; 611 5
The earth shook, and the skies *p* down rain, 676 18
The clouds *p* out water; 694 8
He *p* out upon them his blazing anger: * 699 1

pourest
O Almighty God, who *p* out on all who desire it 833 19

poureth
that calleth for the waters of the sea, and *p* them out 62 3

pours
who calls for the waters of the sea and *p* them out 115 15
full of spiced and foaming wine, which he *p* out, * 691 19
(He *p* contempt on princes * 749 9

poverty
that we through his *p* might be rich: 198 2
that we through his *p* might be rich: 249 12
freed from *p*, famine, and disaster, 390 23
freed from *p*, famine, and disaster, 550 8
does not despise nor abhor the poor in their *p*; 612 1
might be made rich through your *p*: 819 7
of *p*, chastity, and obedience, 819 9
eliminate *p*, prejudice, and oppression, 825 11
and to abolish *p* and crime. 839 18

power
Ye shall receive *p*, after that the Holy Ghost is come 39 18
For thine is the kingdom, and the *p*, and the glory, 54 24
may not fear the *p* of any adversaries; 57 5
Defend us in the same with thy mighty *p*; 57 9
believing through the *p* of the Holy Spirit. 60 2
Glory to God whose *p*, working in us, 60 3
For thine is the kingdom, and the *p*, and the glory, 67 14
believing through the *p* of the Holy Spirit. 73 2
Glory to God whose *p*, working in us, 73 3
You shall receive *p* when the Holy Spirit has come 77 17
and by the *p* of the Holy Spirit keep you 80 3
In the firmament of his *p*, glorify the Lord, * 88 7
In the firmament of his *p*, glorify the Lord, * 90 3
they tremble because of your *p*. 91 2
Splendor and honor and kingly *p* * 93 20

Holy, holy, holy Lord, God of *p* and might, 95 21
He was conceived by the *p* of the Holy Spirit 96 16
For the kingdom, the *p*, 97 15
and the *p*, and the glory, 97 16
we, surely trusting in your defense, may not fear the *p* 99 23
Preserve us with your mighty *p*, 100 3
believing through the *p* of the Holy Spirit. 102 13
Glory to God whose *p*, working in us, 102 14
and by the *p* of the Holy Spirit keep you 117 8
He was conceived by the *p* of the Holy Spirit 120 12
For the kingdom, the *p*, 121 15
and the *p*, and the glory, 121 16
believing through the *p* of the Holy Spirit. 126 13
Glory to God whose *p*, working in us, 126 14
Preserve us with your mighty *p*, 137 16
Stir up thy *p*, O Lord, and with great might come 160 1
Almighty God, who seest that we have no *p* 167 3
hast delivered us from the *p* of our enemy: 170 9
and in the *p* of the Divine Majesty to worship 176 3
may have grace and *p* faithfully to fulfill the same; 179 13
manifest thy *p* among all peoples, 181 7
Lord of all *p* and might, who art the author 181 11
O God, who declarest thy almighty *p* 182 12
when he shall appear again with *p* and great glory, 184 11
be healed of all our infirmities and know thee in the *p* 191 4
the love and healing *p* of thy Son: 193 13
thy Church the like love and *p* to heal, 193 14
God, by whose grace and *p* thy holy martyr 195 8
a like faith and *p* of love, 196 3
to be surrounded by their witness to thy *p* and mercy. 199 8
relieve thy sick servants, and give thy *p* of healing 208 17
Stir up your *p*, O Lord, and with great might come 212 1
Almighty God, you know that we have no *p* 218 13
delivered us from the *p* of our enemy: 222 3
and in the *p* of your divine Majesty to worship 228 4
may have grace and *p* faithfully to accomplish them; 231 7
may show forth your *p* among all peoples, 232 19
Lord of all *p* and might, the author 233 3
O God, you declare your almighty *p* 234 6
when he comes again with *p* and great glory, 236 5
know you in the *p* of his unending life; 242 12
to set forth in the Gospel the love and healing *p* 244 21
Graciously continue in your Church this love and *p* 244 22
God, by whose grace and *p* your holy martyr 247 6
a like faith and *p* of love, 247 15
witness to your *p* and mercy. 250 18
and give your *p* of healing to those who minister 260 2
has given *p* and commandment to his ministers 269 5
might be delivered from the *p* of sin and death, 277 5
Gospel be preached with grace and *p* 280 4
O God of unchangeable *p* and eternal light: 280 14
you once delivered by the *p* of your mighty arm 289 13
O God, you have created all things by the *p* 290 8
p to proclaim you to all the world; 291 8
O God of unchangeable *p* and eternal light: 291 11
He was conceived by the *p* of the Holy Spirit 293 3
delivered us from the *p* of your enemy: 295 3
p to support these persons in their life in Christ? 303 15
He was conceived by the *p* of the Holy Spirit 304 6
Teach them to love others in the *p* of the Spirit. 305 24
may live in the *p* of his resurrection 306 6
Now sanctify this water, we pray you, by the *p* 307 3
Send them forth in the *p* of that Spirit 309 8
For the kingdom, the *p*, 311 12
and the *p*, and the glory, 311 13
might make us the children of God by the *p* 316 15
by the *p* of the Holy Spirit 327 1
For thine is the kingdom, and the *p*, and the glory, 336 28
in the *p* of the Spirit. 340 4
looking for his coming again with *p* and great glory. 342 15
to receive glory and honor and *p*; 344 6
O Lord, is the greatness, and the *p*, and the glory, 344 8
that when he shall come again in *p* and great triumph 345 10
who, by the mighty *p* of the Holy Ghost, 345 15
and receive *p* to become thy children. 345 18
and giving to thy Church the *p* to serve thee 347 10
and by the *p* of the Holy spirit keep you 353 3
by the *p* of the Holy Spirit 358 17
and by the *p* of the Holy Spirit keep you 360 17
Holy, holy, holy Lord, God of *p* and might, 362 4
For the kingdom, the *p*, 364 12
and the *p*, and the glory, 364 13
rejoicing in the *p* of the Spirit. 366 19
Holy, holy, holy Lord, God of *p* and might, 367 13
God of all *p*, Ruler of the Universe, 370 5
Holy, holy, holy Lord, God of *p* and might, 371 1
Holy, holy, holy Lord, God of *p* and might, 373 12
We acclaim you, holy Lord, glorious in *p*. 373 17
you did not abandon us to the *p* of death. 373 22
you are worthy to receive glory and honor and *p*; 377 4
Yours, O Lord, is the greatness, the *p*, the glory, 377 6
when he shall come again in *p* and great triumph 378 6
who, by the mighty *p* of the Holy Spirit, 378 10
receive *p* to become your children. 378 13
and giving to your Church the *p* to serve you 380 5
yours is the kingdom and the *p* and the glory, 391 24
surrounded by their witness to your *p* and mercy. 395 21
and by the *p* of the Holy Spirit keep you 398 9
For the kingdom, the *p*, 398 23
and the *p*, and the glory, 398 24
Holy, holy, holy Lord, God of *p* and might, 402 9
Holy, holy, holy Lord, God of *p* and might, 404 11
Will you who witness these vows do all in your *p* 416 1
He was conceived by the *p* of the Holy Spirit 416 11
Send them forth in the *p* of that Spirit 418 6
p to uphold these two persons in their marriage? 425 2
For the kingdom, the *p*, 428 19
and the *p*, and the glory, 428 20
By the *p* of your Holy Spirit, 430 14
p to uphold these two persons in their marriage? 434 2
Our Lord Jesus Christ, who has left *p* to his Church 448 1
and who conferred *p* on his Church 448 8
the *p* of the Holy Spirit keep you in eternal life. 451 5
and who conferred *p* on his Church 451 7
Our Lord Jesus Christ, who has left *p* to his Church 451 11
and by the *p* of the Holy Spirit keep you 455 8
that you may know the healing *p* 456 9
the help of your *p*, that his sickness may be turned 458 13
and give your *p* of healing to those who minister 459 18
make room for your *p* to possess me, 461 3
deliver the soul of your servant from the *p* of evil, 463 12
For thine is the kingdom, and the *p*, and the glory, 486 5
He was conceived by the *p* of the Holy Spirit 496 6
For the kingdom, the *p*, 502 12

and the *p*, and the glory, 502 13
and, in your loving wisdom and almighty *p*, work 504 28
ask you to lay your hands upon him and in the *p* 513 4
O God of unchangeable *p* and eternal light: 515 4
I will, in the *p* of the Spirit. 518 11
by the *p* of the Holy Spirit 519 20
out upon him the *p* of your princely Spirit, 521 2
honor and *p* and glory in the Church, 521 17
rejoicing in the *p* of the Spirit. 523 19
O God of unchangeable *p* and eternal light: 528 2
by the *p* of the Holy Spirit 530 11
give you the grace and *p* to perform them. 532 31
to fill him with grace and *p*, 533 12
rejoicing in the *p* of the Spirit. 535 14
O God of unchangeable *p* and eternal light: 540 2
by the *p* of the Holy Spirit 542 11
through the *p* of the Holy Spirit. 543 2
fill him with grace and *p*, 545 10
rejoicing in the *p* of the Spirit. 547 8
Everliving God, whose *p* is limitless, 552 6
to know your healing *p*, to hear your Word, 568 11
Be with us in the fullness of your *p* as new members 569 5
Grant, by the *p* of your Holy Spirit, 570 18
the *p*, and the glory of your creation 572 3
Yours, O Lord, is the greatness, the *p*, 579 13
the helpless fall before their *p*. 595 15
Break the *p* of the wicked and evil; * 595 27
we will sing and praise your *p*. 609 26
my life from the *p* of the dog. 611 21
You have not shut me up in the *p* of the enemy; * 623 1
For the *p* of the wicked shall be broken, * 634 18
to be a refuge from the *p* of the bow. 667 17
that *p* belongs to God. 670 9
that I might behold your *p* and your glory. 670 16
You make fast the mountains by your *p*; * 672 21
Ascribe *p* to God; * 679 1
the God of Israel giving strength and *p* to his people! 679 5
and your *p* to all who are to come. 684 19
the right hand of the Most High has lost its *p*." 693 21
and have declared your *p* among the peoples. 694 2
the praiseworthy deeds and the *p* of the LORD, * 695 5
nor did they put their trust in his saving *p*. 696 21
They did not remember his *p* * 698 11
deliver them from the *p* of the wicked. 705 16
who can save himself from the *p* of the grave? 717 11
Who regards the *p* of your wrath? * 718 23
Oh, the *p* and the splendor of his sanctuary! 726 4
ascribe to the LORD honor and *p*. 726 6
to make his *p* known. 742 15
The LORD will send the scepter of your *p* 753 14
He has shown his people the *p* of his works * 754 16
and shall declare your *p*. 801 19
and speak of your *p*; 802 8
That the peoples may know of your *p* * 802 9
Great is our LORD and mighty in *p*; * 804 10
praise him in the firmament of his *p*. 807 23
that all may know the *p* of his forgiveness 816 18
Son, and grant that we may show the *p* of your love to 817 16
that your presence and *p* may be known throughout 825 18
whom you have sent in the *p* of the Spirit to preach 838 3
call upon your Name; for the kingdom and the *p* and 838 7
How does sin have *p* over us? 849 1
Sin has *p* over us because we lose our liberty when 849 2
free from the *p* of evil, sin, and death. 849 6
free us from the *p* of sin, 849 13
conceived by the *p* of the Holy Spirit 849 26
are freed from the *p* of sin and reconciled to God. 850 9
in the *p* of the Holy Spirit. 856 22
will come, not in weakness but in *p*, 862 3

powerful

The voice of the LORD is a *p* voice; * 620 12

powers

O all ye *p* of the Lord, bless ye the Lord; * 47 11
the Heavens and all the *P* therein. 52 26
over the *p* of death and prepared for us our place 69 2
Glorify the Lord, you angels and all *p* of the Lord, * 88 9
For all the *p* of heaven sing your praises, * 91 25
To you all angels, all the *p* of heaven, 95 19
over the *p* of death and prepared for us our place 123 2
Do you renounce the evil *p* of this world 302 10
O God of heavenly *p*, by the might of your command 458 16
God, to whom we must account for all our *p* 822 23

practice

and *p* of the arts of healing, 460 11

praise

to set forth his most worthy *p*, 41 8
And our mouth shall slow forth thy *p*. 42 15
and into his courts with *p*; * 45 18
p him and magnify him for ever. 47 6
We *p* thee, we bless thee, 52 5
We *p* thee, O God; we acknowledge thee 52 23
The glorious company of the apostles *p* thee. 53 3
The goodly fellowship of the prophets *p* thee. 53 4
The noble army of martyrs *p* thee. 53 5
and that we show forth thy *p*, 59 4
may *p* thee in that City of which he is the light; 69 4
that our lips may *p* thee, 69 13
and that we show forth thy *p*, 72 1
Almighty God our heavenly Father, to set forth his *p*, 79 2
And our mouth shall proclaim your *p*. 80 6
go into his courts with *p*; * 83 5
This is my God and I will *p* him, * 85 5
and all your portals, *P*. 87 26
p him and highly exalt him for ever. 88 6
you are worthy of *p*; glory to you. 90 6
we will *p* you and highly exalt you for ever. 90 8
and I will *p* you without ceasing all the days 91 24
Be worship and *p*, dominion and splendor, * 94 7
we *p* you for your glory. 95 2
You are God: we *p* you; 95 15
Cherubim and Seraphim, sing in endless *p*: 95 20
The glorious company of apostles *p* you. 95 23
The noble fellowship of prophets *p* you. 95 24
The white-robed army of martyrs *p* you. 95 25
We *p* your Name for ever. 98 12
with truly thankful hearts we may show forth your *p*, 101 17
may *p* you in that City of which he is the light, 123 4
that our lips may *p* you, 123 12
with truly thankful hearts we may show forth your *p*, 125 15
and my mouth shall proclaim your *p*. 137 2
Give *p*, you servants of the Lord; * 138 1

p the Name of the Lord. 138 2
be dominion and *p* for ever 171 15
to the *p* and glory of thy Name; 193 14
that we also in our generation may show forth thy *p*, 196 18
We *p* thy Name for the gifts of grace 197 14
be dominion and *p* for ever and ever. 223 9
to the *p* and glory of your Name; 245 1
that we also in our generation may show forth your *p*, 248 4
We *p* your Name for the gifts of grace 248 24
and my mouth shall proclaim your *p*. 267 7
It is right to give him thanks and *p*. 271 4
It is right to *p* you, 271 5
and *p* and glorify your holy resurrection; 281 2
Let the peoples *p* you, O God; 281 9
let all the peoples *p* you. 281 10
and *p* and glorify your holy resurrection; 281 12
for the grace to sing the worthy *p* of this great light; 286 12
It is right to give him thanks and *p*. 286 20
whole heart and mind and voice, to *p* you, 287 1
where your saints for ever sing your *p*; 290 6
P to you, Lord Christ. 300 9
It is right to give him thanks and *p*. 306 12
All *p* and thanks to you, most merciful Father, 311 15
let us offer continually the sacrifice of *p*, 317 20
We *p* thee, we bless thee, 324 16
P be to thee, O Christ. 326 5
accept this our sacrifice of *p* and thanksgiving; 335 25
accept this our sacrifice of *p* and thanksgiving, 342 22
p, that is, the fruit of lips that acknowledge his Name. 344 2
But chiefly are we bound to *p* thee 346 17
All thy creatures *p* thee, 348 8
a sacrifice of *p* and prayer which is holy 348 17
we *p* you for your glory. 356 6
P to you, Lord Christ. 358 2
It is right to give him thanks and *p*. 361 6
Therefore we *p* you, joining our voices 362 1
this sacrifice of *p* and thanksgiving. 363 11
It is right to give him thanks and *p*. 367 6
Therefore we *p* you, joining our voices 367 10
And we offer our sacrifice of *p* and thanksgiving 369 1
It is right to give him thanks and *p*. 370 4
you are worthy of glory and *p*. 370 6
And therefore we *p* you, joining 370 23
It is right to give him thanks and *p*. 372 22
they offer you unceasing *p*. 373 9
we *p* you and we bless you. 374 28
We *p* you, we bless you, 375 1
to the *p* of your Name. 375 10
We *p* you in union with them 375 24
p, that is, the fruit of lips that acknowledge his Name. 376 18
But chiefly are we bound to *p* you 379 14
All your creatures *p* you, 381 2
a sacrifice of *p* and prayer which is holy 381 11
P God for those in every generation in whom Christ 386 14
We *p* you for your saints who have entered into joy; 387 19
And *p* your Name for ever and ever. 393 3
Gracious Father, we give you *p* and thanks 399 7
It is right to give him thanks and *p*. 402 6
Make us a living sacrifice of *p*. 403 18
It is right to give him thanks and *p*. 404 8
Accept, O Lord, our sacrifice of *p*, 405 13
P to you, Lord Christ. 415 2
P to you, Lord Christ. 426 5
Gracious Father, we give you *p* and thanks 457 5
In the voice of *p* and thanksgiving, * 471 10
or show forth all his *p*? 478 14
P be to thee, O Christ. 480 2
p and hearty thanks for the wonderful grace 487 11
O God, the King of saints, we *p* and magnify 489 14
P to you, Lord Christ. 495 5
O God, the King of saints, we *p* and glorify 504 12
P to you, Lord Christ. 516 9
We *p* you also that from the creation 520 17
to the glory and unceasing *p* of your Name. 521 5
P to you, Lord Christ. 529 8
God and Father of all, we *p* you for your infinite love 533 1
P to you, Lord Christ. 541 8
O God, most merciful Father, we *p* you 545 1
We *p* you that you have highly exalted him, 545 4
We *p* you for the many ministries in your Church, 545 6
we place before you, with our *p* and thanks, 552 7
build houses of prayer and *p*, 567 2
to the *p* and glory of your Name; 567 12
as we dedicate this place to which we come to *p* 568 9
It is right to give him thanks and *p*. 570 4
P him with the sound of the trumpet; 572 5
P him with strings and pipe. 572 6
We *p* you, Almighty and eternal God, 573 8
We *p* you for his life on earth, 573 13
We *p* you for raising him from the dead, 573 16
We *p* you for sending your Holy Spirit 573 19
where your saints and angels *p* you for ever. 574 3
I will *p* the Name of the LORD Most High. 592 6
Sing *p* to the LORD who dwells in Zion; * 593 21
I will *p* the Name of the Lord Most High. 598 11
you are worthy of *p*. 602 11
we will sing and *p* your power. 609 26
in the midst of the congregation I will *p* you. 611 25
P the LORD, you that fear him; * 611 26
My *p* is of him in the great assembly; * 612 4
and those who seek the LORD shall *p* him: * 612 8
and in my song will I *p* him. 619 27
will the dust *p* you or declare your faithfulness? 621 25
P the LORD with the harp; * 626 3
his *p* shall ever be in my mouth. 627 22
I will *p* you in the mighty throng. 631 5
and of your *p* all the day long. 632 2
a song of *p* to our God; * 640 6
With the voice of *p* and thanksgiving, * 643 11
and we will *p* your Name for ever. 646 2
therefore nations will *p* you for ever and ever." 648 27
Your *p*, like your Name, O God, reaches to 651 20
and my mouth shall proclaim your *p*. 657 13
and *p* your Name, O LORD, for it is good. 660 2
In God, whose word I *p*, 662 19
In God the LORD, whose word I *p*, 663 11
I will sing *p* to you among the nations. 664 16
So will I always sing the *p* of your Name, * 669 3
my lips shall give you *p*. 670 18
sing the glory of his *p*. 673 20
make the voice of his *p* to be heard; 674 10
and his *p* was on my tongue. 675 2
Let the peoples *p* you, O God; * 675 13
let all the peoples *p* you. 675 14

Let the peoples *p* you, O God; * 675 18
let all the peoples *p* you. 675 19
I will *p* the Name of God in song; * 681 24
Let the heavens and the earth *p* him, * 682 5
my *p* shall be always of you. 683 13
Let my mouth be full of your *p* * 683 16
and shall *p* you more and more. 684 8
Therefore I will *p* you upon the lyre for your 685 1
let the poor and needy *p* your Name. 690 27
and show forth your *p* from age to age. 702 11
go into his courts with *p*; * 730 2
so that a people yet unborn may *p* the LORD. 732 13
and his *p* in Jerusalem; 732 19
I will *p* my God while I have my being. 737 21
or show forth all his *p*? 741 22
and sang him songs of *p*. 742 23
and glory in your *p*. 745 22
and *p* him in the council of the elders. 748 20
Hold not your tongue, O God of my *p*; * 750 23
in the midst of the multitude will I *p* him; 753 9
his *p* endures for ever. 755 3
Give *p*, you servants of the LORD; * 756 2
p the Name of the LORD. 756 3
The dead do not *p* the LORD, * 758 23
P the LORD, all you nations; * 760 15
Seven times a day do I *p* you, * 777 7
My lips shall pour forth your *p*, * 777 21
Let me live, and I will *p* you, * 778 5
to *p* the Name of the LORD. 780 4
P the Name of the LORD; * 788 2
give *p*, you servants of the LORD, 788 3
P the LORD, for the LORD is good; * 788 6
before the gods I will sing your *p*. 793 2
and *p* your Name, * 793 4
All the kings of the earth will *p* you, O LORD, * 793 10
and *p* your Name for ever and ever. 801 15
One generation shall *p* your works to another * 801 18
All your works *p* you, O LORD, * 802 5
My mouth shall speak the *p* of the LORD; * 803 1
P the LORD, O my soul! * 803 4
I will *p* the LORD as long as I live; 803 5
how pleasant it is to honor him with *p*! 804 3
p your God, O Zion; 805 2
P the LORD from the heavens; * 805 21
p him in the heights. 805 22
P him, all you angels of his; * 805 23
p him, all his host. 805 24
P him, sun and moon; * 805 25
p him, all you shining stars. 805 26
P him, heaven of heavens, * 806 1
Let them *p* the Name of the LORD; * 806 3
P the LORD from the earth, * 806 7
Let them *p* the Name of the LORD, * 806 19
and *p* for all his loyal servants, * 806 23
sing his *p* in the congregation of the faithful. 807 3
Let them *p* his Name in the dance; * 807 6
let them sing *p* to him with timbrel and harp. 807 7
P God in his holy temple; * 807 22
p him in the firmament of his power. 807 23
P him for his mighty acts; * 808 1
p him for his excellent greatness. 808 2
P him with the blast of the ram's-horn; * 808 3
p him with lyre and harp. 808 4
P him with timbrel and dance; * 808 5
p him with strings and pipe. 808 6
P him with resounding cymbals; * 808 7
p him with loud-clanging cymbals. 808 8
p the LORD. 808 10
may show forth thy *p* among the nations of the earth. 820 12
may continue to *p* you for your bounty; 827 21
to the honor and *p* of thy Name; 834 22
make us bold to *p* you and to do your will; 835 5
Accept, O Lord, our thanks and *p* 836 1
To him be *p* and glory, with you, O Father, 837 23
We *p* and bless you for those whom you have sent 838 2
We *p* you for these good gifts, 840 10
hearty thanks and *p* for the return of seedtime 840 16
in whose behalf we bless and *p* thy Name. 841 10
The principal kinds of prayer are adoration, *p*, 856 27
Why do we *p* God? 857 4
We *p* God, not to obtain anything, 857 5
God's Being draws *p* from us. 857 6
Because the Eucharist, the Church's sacrifice of *p* 859 10
by sacrament, prayer, and *p*. 862 24

praised

p and exalted above all for ever. 49 10
Thou art worthy at all times to be *p* by happy voices, 64 7
You are worthy at all times to be *p* by happy voices, 112 7
You are worthy at all times to be *p* by happy voices, 118 7
let the Name of the Lord be *p*. 138 6
You are worthy at all times to be *p* by happy voices, 139 7
your majesty is *p* above the heavens. 592 10
Great is the LORD, and highly to be *p*; * 651 1
and were *p* for their success, 653 20
You are to be *p*, O God, in Zion; * 672 7
For great is the LORD and greatly to be *p*; * 725 23
let the Name of the LORD be *p*. 756 7
Great is the LORD and greatly to be *p*; * 801 16
God's holy Name be blessed and *p*; 835 17

praises

we sing thy *p*, O God: 64 6
Sing the *p* of the Lord, 86 11
For all the powers of heaven sing your *p*, * 91 25
and sing the *p* of your Name? * 94 15
we sing your *p*, O God: 112 6
we sing your *p*, O God: 118 6
we sing your *p* O God: 139 6
resound with the *p* of your people. 286 9
Accept these prayers and *p*, Father, 372 10
who desires now to offer you her *p* 444 3
I will sing and speak *p* unto the LORD. 477 27
p, heighten my love and gratitude; 563 6
So that I may tell of all your *p* 594 4
and sing *p* to your Name. 606 11
enthroned upon the *p* of Israel. 610 7
it is good for the just to sing *p*. 626 2
Sing *p* to God, sing *p*; * 650 16
sing *p* to our King, sing *p*. 650 17
sing *p* with all your skill. 650 19
and my mouth *p* you with joyful lips, 670 22
Sing to God, sing *p* to his Name; 676 8
sing *p* to the Lord. 678 25

I will sing *p* to the God of Jacob. 691 23
and to sing *p* to your Name, O Most High; 720 23
to you, O Lord, will I sing *p*. 730 8
Sing to him, sing *p* to him, * 738 3
I will sing *p* to you among the nations. 749 23
sing *p* to his Name, for it is lovely. 788 7
I will sing *p* to my God while I have my being. 803 6
How good it is to sing *p* to our God! * 804 2
Let the *p* of God be in their throat * 807 12
art and music to perfect the *p* offered by your people 819 15

praiseworthy

the *p* deeds and the power of the Lord, * 695 5

praising

evermore *p* thee, and saying, 334 3
evermore *p* thee, and saying, 341 6
they will always be *p* you. 707 24

pray

We therefore *p* thee, help thy servants, 53 19
Let us *p*. 54 13
We humbly *p* thee so to guide and govern us 57 15
Let us *p*. 67 3
Bring us, we *p* thee, in safety to the morning hours; 70 8
Let us *p*. 97 3
We humbly *p* you so to guide and govern us 100 7
And, we *p*, give us such an awareness of your mercies, 101 16
Let us *p*. 107 3
We *p* you to illumine the world 107 13
Let us *p*. 110 11
Let us *p*. 121 3
And, we *p*, give us such an awareness of your mercies, 125 14
Let us *p*. 133 9
Let us *p*. 153 18
Let us *p*. 155 6
Open, we *p* thee, the eyes 171 18
and we *p* thee that, as by his death 172 16
Open, we *p* thee, the eyes 173 6
Grant us, O Lord, we *p* thee, to trust 181 17
who art always more ready to hear than we to *p*, 182 19
Lord, we *p* thee that thy grace may always precede 183 6
We thank thee for this witness, and *p* 189 1
and we *p* that thou wilt pour out upon the leaders 191 9
Savior; and we *p* that, after his example, 192 21
we *p* that, as they were faithful and zealous 194 3
we *p* thee, in our hearts, that we 196 17
and we *p* that, following his example 196 24
and we *p* that thy Church may never be destitute 197 15
Deliver us, we *p* thee, from an inordinate love 198 2
and we *p* that, having opened to him the gates 202 10
and we *p* that all who seek thee here 204 3
We humbly *p* that thy gracious providence may 207 15
Plant in every heart, we *p*, the love of him 213 15
Almighty God, we *p* you graciously to behold 221 8
Grant, we *p*, Almighty God, that we who celebrate 222 22
and we *p* that, as by his death 224 9
Grant, we *p*, Almighty God, that as we believe 226 8
keep us, we *p*, from all things that may hurt us, 228 15
Grant to us, Lord, we *p*, the spirit to think 232 6
you are always more ready to hear than we are to *p*, 234 13
we *p* that your grace may always precede 234 20
Receive, we *p*, into the arms of your mercy 238 8
Grant, we *p*, that we, having his wonderful conversion 239 1
Almighty and everliving God, we humbly *p* that, 239 6
We thank you for this witness, and *p* that we 240 9
and we *p* that you will pour out upon the leaders 242 16
we *p* that, after his example, we may with ready wills 244 9
and we *p* that, as they were faithful and zealous 245 11
Make us, we *p*, faithful stewards 246 3
Shine, we *p*, in our hearts, 248 3
and we *p* that, following his example 248 10
and we *p* that your Church may never be destitute 249 1
and we *p* that, having opened to him the gates 253 14
and we *p* that all who seek you here may find you, 255 1
Bless, we *p*, with his grace 255 7
Give your grace, we humbly *p*, to all 256 3
Almighty God, kindle, we *p*, in every heart 258 8
Lord of heaven and earth: We humbly *p* 258 15
Let us *p*. 264 1
Let us *p*. 270 3
Let us *p*. 272 6
Let us *p*. 276 3
Almighty God, we *p* you graciously to behold 276 4
We *p*, therefore, for people everywhere 277 7
Let us *p* for the holy Catholic Church of Christ 278 1
Let us *p* for all nations and peoples of the earth, 278 17
Almighty God, kindle, we *p*, in every heart 278 25
Let us *p* for all who suffer and are afflicted 279 3
and give us, we *p*, the strength to serve 279 17
Let us *p* for all who have not received the Gospel 279 20
Let us commit ourselves to our God, and *p* 280 8
we *p* you to set your passion, 282 6
Let us *p*. 285 7
p with me to God the Almighty 286 11
and let us *p* that our God 288 2
Let us *p*. 288 4
Let us *p*. 289 5
Let us *p*. 290 1
Let us *p*. 291 4
Let us *p*. 294 12
Let us *p*. 299 13
Let us now *p* for these persons who are to receive 305 11
Now sanctify this water, we *p* you, by the power 307 3
we *p* you to consecrate this oil, 307 10
Let us *p*. 308 1
Let us now *p* for these persons who have renewed 309 1
Let us *p*. 325 12
Let us *p* for the whole state of Christ's Church 328 22
Let us *p*. 339 1
Let us *p*. 357 3
we now *p*, 363 24
Let us *p*. 365 8
We *p* you, gracious God, to send your Holy Spirit 369 4
we now *p*, 369 20
we now *p*, 372 16
and we *p* to you, Lord our God. 375 3
we *p* that in your goodness and mercy 375 4
we now *p*, 376 3
let us *p* to the Lord, 383 1
P for the Church. 385 20
P for justice and peace. 386 3
P for those in any need or trouble. 386 6
P that they may find and be found by him. 386 9
P for those who have died. 386 11

P that we may have grace to glorify Christ 386 17
Father, we *p* for your holy Catholic Church; 387 1
We *p* for all bishops, priests, and deacons; 387 6
We *p* for all who govern and hold authority 387 9
Let us *p* for our own needs and those of others. 387 21
Let us *p* for the Church and for the world. 388 1
and we *p* that we may share with all your saints 389 9
In peace, let us *p* to the Lord, saying, 389 13
we *p* to you, O Lord. 389 17
In peace, we *p* to you, Lord God. 392 1
We *p* for all who have died, 393 4
We *p* to you also for the forgiveness of our sins. 393 8
we *p*, not as we ask in our ignorance, 394 6
Let us *p* in the words our Savior Christ has taught us. 398 11
and we *p* that it may bring us forgiveness of our sins, 399 9
Let us *p*. 413 13
Let us now *p* for these persons who have renewed 417 20
Let us *p*. 421 1
Let us *p*. 425 6
Let us *p* together in the words our Savior taught us. 428 7
Let us *p*. 429 1
Let us *p*. 443 20
I *p* God to have mercy on me. 447 9
Go (or abide) in peace, and *p* for me, a sinner. 448 14
P for me, a sinner. 449 9
and we *p* that it may bring us forgiveness of our sins, 457 7
Hear us, we *p*, for your dear Name's sake. 459 6
Continue in him, we *p*, the good work 460 19
Grant me this gift, I *p*; 461 13
Let us *p*. 464 15
Let us *p*, then, for our brother (sister) 465 11
Let us *p* with confidence to God, 466 13
Let us also *p* for all who mourn, 467 1
your servants for whom we *p*. 467 4
Let us *p*. 469 18
In peace, let us *p* to the Lord. 480 3
Help us, we *p*, in the midst of things 481 14
Let us *p*. 485 19
Bless, we *p*, this grave, 487 6
Wash him, we *p* thee, in the blood 488 15
we *p* thee to set thy passion, 489 23
Deal graciously, we *p* thee, with all those who mourn, 489 31
Let us *p*. 493 3
For our brother (sister) N., let us *p* to our Lord 497 1
Give us, we *p*, the faith to follow 498 5
Father of all, we *p* to you for N., 498 8
Let us *p*. 501 20
Bless, we *p*, this grave, 503 8
Make us, we *p*, deeply aware 504 2
p that, encouraged by their examples, 504 17
Father of all, we *p* to you for those we love, 504 26
Raise us, we humbly *p*, from the death of sin 505 2
graciously, we *p*, with all who mourn; 505 18
Let us *p*. 515 3
p for them without ceasing, 518 15
fill, we *p*, the heart of this your servant 521 6
We *p* that N. may be to us 523 5
In peace let us *p* to the Lord. 527 11
Let us *p*. 528 1
We *p* that N. may be to us 535 5
In peace let us *p* to the Lord. 539 11
Let us *p*. 540 1
We *p* that N. may be to us 547 1
We *p* to you, Lord Christ. 548 9
we *p* to you, O Lord. 548 14
Let us *p*. 551 6
Let us *p*. 552 5
Let us *p*. 560 5
We *p* that N. may be to us 564 5
Let us *p*. 567 7
Let us *p*. 568 6
Let us now *p* for the setting apart of the Altar. 573 7
but as for me, I *p* for them. 751 5
"O LORD, I *p* you, save my life." 759 9
P for the peace of Jerusalem: * 780 7
I *p* for your prosperity. 780 12
More especially we *p* for thy holy Church universal; 815 1
Gracious Father, we *p* for thy holy Catholic Church. 816 10
Guide and sanctify, we *p*, those whom you call 819 8
Behold and visit, we *p*, the cities 825 8
Direct, in our time, we *p*, those who speak 827 7
Look with favor, we *p*, on your servant 830 9
better things than we can desire or *p* for; 831 10
By the might of thy Spirit lift us, we *p* thee, 832 15
and then use us, we *p* thee, as thou wilt, 833 2
We praise you for these good gifts, and *p* 840 10
to work and *p* for peace; 848 8
to work, *p*, and give for the spread of the kingdom 856 15
Why do we *p* for the dead? 862 8
We *p* for them, because we still hold them 862 9

prayed

first martyr Stephen, who looked up to heaven and *p* 186 2
p for his disciples that they might be one, 204 18
first martyr Stephen, who looked up to heaven and *p* 237 15
whose blessed Son before his passion *p* 255 15
Likewise, the apostles *p* before they appointed 514 14
I *p* with my whole heart, 630 19

prayer

receive our *p*. 52 15
Let my *p* be set forth in thy sight as the incense, 61 1
Therefore I make this *p* to you: * 91 16
receive our *p*. 95 8
Lord, hear our *p*; 107 1
Almighty, everlasting God, let our *p* in your sight 113 9
Let my *p* be set forth in your sight as incense, 115 1
have mercy on me and hear my *p*. 128 10
Lord, hear our *p*; 133 7
give itself continually to *p* 193 20
supported by this fellowship of love and *p*, 199 7
the dedication of this house of *p*: 204 2
give itself continually to *p* 245 6
supported by this fellowship of love and *p*, 250 17
dedication of this house of *p* 254 20
by *p*, fasting, and self-denial; 265 12
Our negligence in *p* and worship, 268 13
to gather in vigil and *p*. 285 4
Lord, hear our *p*. 305 16
receive our *p*. 325 2
that, fervent in *p* and in works of mercy, 346 9
before thee a sacrifice of praise and *p* 348 17
receive our *p*. 356 12
that, fervent in *p* and in works of mercy, 379 6

before you a sacrifice of praise and *p* 381 11
Hear our *p*. 388 6
supported by this fellowship of love and *p*, 395 20
because he hath heard the voice of my *p*; 478 24
shut not thy merciful ears to our *p*; 484 12
Christ spent the whole night in *p* before he chose 514 13
Will you be faithful in *p*, 518 4
Will you persevere in *p*, 532 24
Will you be faithful in *p*, 544 1
Lord, hear our *p*. 548 10
receive this book, and be among us as a man of *p*. 561 5
In *p*, quicken my devotion; 563 5
build houses of *p* and praise, 567 2
make this a temple of your presence and a house of *p*. 568 15
have mercy on me and hear my *p*. 587 22
for I make my *p* to you. 588 20
the LORD accepts my *p*. 590 17
listen to my *p*, which does not come from lying lips. 600 24
Hear the voice of my *p* when I cry out to you, * 619 8
for he has heard the voice of my *p*. 619 23
Hear my *p*, O LORD, 639 20
a *p* to the God of my life. 643 25
Hear my *p*, O God; * 659 19
Hear my *p*, O God; * 660 5
and listen to my *p*. 668 13
To you that hear *p* shall all flesh come, * 672 9
he has attended to the voice of my *p*. 675 6
Blessed be God, who has not rejected my *p*, * 675 7
But as for me, this is my *p* to you, * 680 13
may *p* be made for him always, 686 15
LORD God of hosts, hear my *p*; * 708 6
Give ear, O LORD, to my *p*, * 710 9
Let my *p* enter into your presence; * 712 3
in the morning my *p* comes before you. 713 5
LORD, hear my *p*, and let my cry come before you; * 731 1
He will look with favor on the *p* of the homeless; * 732 10
Let my *p* be set forth in your sight as incense, * 797 5
for my *p* is continually against their wicked deeds. 797 14
LORD, hear my *p*, 798 18
by their *p* and service they may enrich your Church, 819 9
p, and the study of God's ways. 847 27
What is *p*? 856 17
P is responding to God, by thought and by deeds, 856 18
What is Christian *P*? 856 20
Christian *p* is response to God the Father, 856 21
What *p* did Christ teach us? 856 23
Our Lord gave us the example of *p* 856 24
known as the Lord's *P*. 856 24
What are the principal kinds of *p*? 856 26
The principal kinds of *p* are adoration, 856 27
What is *p* of oblation? 857 14
to offer *p*, and to celebrate the sacraments. 857 24
through *p* and the laying on of hands 860 20
through *p* and the laying on of hands 861 1
by sacrament, *p*, and praise. 862 24

prayerfully

p and lawfully selected. 559 4

prayers

Receive our supplications and *p* which we offer 57 21
Receive our supplications and *p* which we offer 100 13
to incline thine ear to us who have now made our *p* 153 21
Favorably with mercy hear our *p*; 155 1
Mercifully accept our *p*; 164 12
O Lord, we beseech thee mercifully to receive the *p* 179 10
Receive our supplications and *p*, which we offer 206 3
grant that, by the *p* and labors of thy holy Church, 206 20
for whom our *p* are offered may be strengthened 208 19
Mercifully accept our *p*; 216 7
O Lord, mercifully receive the *p* of your people 231 4
Receive our supplications and *p*, which we offer 256 21
grant that, by the *p* and labors of your holy Church, 257 16
for whom our *p* are offered may be strengthened 260 4
Receive our supplications and *p* which we offer 278 13
in the breaking of bread, and in the *p*? 293 21
Will you by your *p* and witness help this child 302 4
in the breaking of bread, and in the *p*? 304 24
taught us to make *p*, and supplications, 329 2
Receive these our *p* which we offer 329 3
Grant these our *p*, O Father, for Jesus Christ's sake, 330 7
Accept these *p* and praises, Father, 372 10
I ask your *p* for God's people throughout the world; 385 17
I ask your *p* for peace; 386 1
I ask your *p* for the poor, the sick, the hungry, 386 4
I ask your *p* for all who seek God, 386 7
I ask your *p* for the departed 386 10
I ask your *p* for ________. 386 12
For all who have commended themselves to our *p*; 391 10
Lord, hear the *p* of thy people; 394 1
Mercifully accept the *p* of your people, 394 10
O Lord our God, accept the fervent *p* of your people; 395 3
in the breaking of bread, and in the *p*? 417 6
and pledge you our *p*, encouragement, 420 5
answer the earnest *p* 440 9
for whom our *p* are desired. 458 3
Mercifully accept our *p*, 458 12
Accept our *p* on behalf of thy servant 470 2
aided by their *p*, 489 20
shut not your ears to our *p*, 492 13
Accept our *p* on behalf of your servant 493 11
aided by their *p*, 504 18
and offer our *p* to Almighty God 514 16
Let us then offer our *p* to God for all his people, 560 1
Accept our *p* and intercessions 572 10
Therefore all the faithful will make their *p* 625 11
despite the *p* of your people? 702 20
[especially those for whom our *p* are desired]; 815 8
hear our *p* for this parish family. 817 19
thy servant for whom our *p* are offered. 831 14
in these our supplications and *p*, 832 19
to incline thine ear to us who have now made our *p* 834 3
gathered together by their *p* and labors, 838 6

prays

The Church pursues its mission as it *p* 855 5

preach

and didst send thy blessed Son to *p* peace 58 2
and sent your blessed Son to *p* peace 100 18
p repentance and prepare the way for our salvation: 159 10
apostle Bartholomew grace truly to believe and to *p* 192 8
and to *p* what he taught; 192 10
whom thou didst call to *p* the Gospel 196 8

and didst send thy blessed Son to *p* peace 206 10
p repentance and prepare the way for our salvation: 211 10
Bartholomew grace truly to believe and to *p* 243 15
and *p* what he taught; 243 17
whom you called to *p* the Gospel 247 20
and sent your blessed Son to *p* peace 257 6
to serve thee as a royal priesthood, and to *p* 347 11
p the Gospel and to teach all nations; 348 13
to serve you as a royal priesthood, and to *p* 380 6
p the Gospel and to teach all nations; 381 7
p the Gospel to the ends of the earth, 390 8
You are to *p*, to declare God's forgiveness 531 12
p the Word of God and to administer 534 11
p the Gospel to the ends of the earth, 549 22
whom you have sent in the power of the Spirit to *p* 838 3

preached

let your Gospel be *p* with grace and power 280 4
may be truly *p* and truly heard, 817 13

preaching

and that both by their *p* and living, 150 7
by the *p* of the Gospel, 175 11
O God, who, by the *p* of thine apostle Paul, 187 8
prepare the way of thy Son our Savior by *p* 190 3
that we may truly repent according to his *p*; 190 5
by the *p* of the Gospel, 227 4
O God, by the *p* of your apostle Paul 238 20
prepare the way of your Son our Savior by *p* 241 12
that we may truly repent according to his *p*; 241 14
in *p*, give me readiness of thought and expression; 563 6

precede

Lord, we pray thee that thy grace may always *p* 183 6
Lord, we pray that your grace may always *p* 234 20

precepts

fashion your life in accordance with its *p*. 531 10

precious

whom thou hast redeemed with thy *p* blood. 53 20
whom thou hast redeemed with thy most *p* blood, 148 12
by thy *p* Death and Burial; 149 23
who by thy cross and *p* blood hast redeemed us: 282 4
a perpetual memory of that his *p* death and sacrifice, 334 16
having in remembrance his blessed passion and *p* 335 13
receive the most *p* Body and Blood 336 5
spiritual food of the most *p* Body and Blood 339 4
memory of that his *p* death and sacrifice, 341 19
in remembrance his blessed passion and *p* death, 342 13
receive the most *p* Body and Blood 342 25
of the most *p* Body and Blood 366 3
the Sacrament of the *p* Body (Blood) 408 3
by your cross and *p* blood 455 16
your *p* Death and Burial, 463 6
beseeching thee that he may be *p* in thy sight. 488 14
P in the sight of the LORD * 760 3
more than gold and *p* stones. 774 2

prediction

Until his *p* came to pass, * 739 15

prejudice

and for our *p* and contempt 268 21
Lead them and us from *p* to truth; 816 6
take away all hatred and *p*, 818 17
eliminate poverty, *p*, and oppression, 825 11
Strengthen our efforts to blot our ignorance and *p*, 839 17
to bear no malice, *p*, or hatred in our hearts; 848 9

preparation

that our rest here upon earth may be a *p* 56 15
that our rest here upon the earth may be a *p* 99 10
And if, in your *p*, you need help and counsel, 317 11

prepare

P ye the way of the Lord, 37 4
p ourselves in heart and mind to worship him, 41 11
to *p* his ways; 51 13
In the wilderness *p* the way of the Lord, 75 4
p ourselves in heart and mind to worship him, 79 5
for you will go before the Lord to *p* his way, 93 2
preach repentance and *p* the way for our salvation: 159 10
and sent to *p* the way of thy Son 190 2
and *p* the way for our salvation: 211 10
and sent to *p* the way of your Son 241 11
it became the custom of the Church to *p* for them 264 12
p themselves carefully before eating of that Bread 316 21
p with joy for the Paschal feast; 346 9
ascended into heaven, to *p* a place for us; 347 3
and *p* with joy for the Paschal feast; 379 5
ascended into heaven, to *p* a place for us; 379 22
Thou shalt *p* a table before me in the presence 476 12
they run and *p* themselves for battle. 666 2
You *p* the grain, * 673 7
How did God *p* us for redemption? 849 7

prepared

and his hands *p* the dry land. 44 19
which thou hast *p* before the face of all people, 51 26
may be duly *p* for the service of thy sanctuary, 56 14
which thou hast *p* before the face of all people, 66 4
over the powers of death and *p* for us our place 69 2
whom you have *p* for all the world to see: 93 15
may be duly *p* for the service of your sanctuary, 99 9
whom you have *p* for all the world to see: 120 4
the powers of death and *p* for us our place 123 2
whom you have *p* for all the world to see: 135 4
whom you have *p* for all the world to see: 140 10
and his hands *p* the dry land. 146 10
may find in us a mansion *p* for himself; 160 8
O God, who hast *p* for those who love thee 174 1
those ineffable joys which thou hast *p* 194 12
may find in us a mansion *p* for himself; 212 8
O God, you have *p* for those who love you 225 14
those ineffable joys that you have *p* for those 245 20
a time in which converts to the faith were *p* 265 2
all such good works as thou hast *p* for us to walk in; 339 12
thou hast *p* for those who love thee. 346 12
p for us a dwelling place eternal 349 10
p for those who love you. 379 9
p for us a dwelling place eternal 382 5
and obtain those eternal joys *p* for all 432 6
inherit the kingdom *p* for you. 483 22
Father, inherit the kingdom *p* for you 487 20

inherit the kingdom *p* for you. 500 11
receive the kingdom *p* for you 505 7
p a people to be heirs of the covenant 520 15
He has *p* his weapons of death; * 591 24
You *p* the ground for it; * 703 5
I have *p* a lamp for my Anointed. 787 6
O God, you *p* your disciples for the coming 819 1

prepares

and *p* rain for the earth; 804 17

preparest

Thou *p* a table before me in the presence 477 5

presbyter

What is the ministry of a priest or *p*? 856 1

presbyters

your fellow *p* and take counsel with them; 518 24
together with your bishop and fellow *p*, 531 6

presence

to appear in the *p* of God for us. 39 17
we have come together in the *p* of Almighty God 41 5
Let us come before his *p* with thanksgiving, * 44 12
and come before his *p* with a song. 45 13
here in the *p* of Almighty God, 62 11
manifest in thy servants the signs of thy *p*: 71 7
the *p* of God on our behalf. 77 16
we have come together in the *p* of Almighty God 79 1
Let us come before his *p* with thanksgiving * 82 7
and come before his *p* with a song. 82 22
All things quake with fear at your *p*; * 91 1
we who walk in the light of your *p* 111 10
here in the *p* of Almighty God, 116 7
manifest in your servants the signs of your *p*: 125 2
Cast me not away from your *p* * 137 5
Let us come before his *p* with thanksgiving, * 146 3
comfort with thy *p* those who are failing and infirm, 151 26
to thy *p*, where we may behold 162 15
abide in his *p* and rejoice in the hope of eternal glory; 171 13
bring those near to us into his gracious *p*; 185 11
Bless, we beseech thee, with his grace and *p*, 204 10
to your *p*, where we may see your glory 214 9
abide in his *p* and rejoice in the hope of eternal glory; 223 7
bring those near to us into his gracious *p*; 237 5
Bless, we pray, with his grace and *p*, 255 8
Cast me not away from your *p* * 266 24
Strengthen him, O Lord, with your *p*, 314 4
and, beholding the glory of your *p*, 373 8
We have come together in the *p* of God to 423 1
Christ adorned this manner of life by his *p* 423 5
I require and charge you both, here in the *p* of God, 424 4
in the *p* of all his people, 442 24
You spread a table before me in the *p* 443 11
by a lively sense of your *p* with them, 443 25
Now, in the *p* of Christ, and of me, his minister, 450 5
Christ to sustain you with his *p*, 456 3
and give me such a sense of your *p*, 461 16
when shall I come to appear before the *p* of God? 471 4
or whither shall I go then from thy *p*? 475 6
Thou shalt prepare a table before me in the *p* 476 12
Thou preparest a table before me in the *p* 477 5
I will pay my vows now in the *p* of all his people; * 479 18
in thy *p* is the fullness of joy, 485 7
Grant to them thy mercy and the light of thy *p*; 488 29
know the strength of his *p*, 493 7
in your *p* there is fullness of joy, 501 9
Do you now in the *p* of the Church commit 531 24
Do you now in the *p* of the Church commit 543 22
do you, in the *p* of this congregation, commit 559 5
Lord Jesus Christ, make this a temple of your *p* 568 14
For your *p* whenever two or three have gathered 578 10
they will stumble and perish at your *p*. 593 6
in your *p* there is fullness of joy, 600 20
Let my vindication come forth from your *p*; * 601 1
From the brightness of his *p*, through the clouds, * 603 13
and will make him glad with the joy of your *p*. 609 8
I will perform my vows in the *p* of those who 612 5
You spread a table before me in the *p* 613 7
You hide them in the covert of your *p* 624 8
while the wicked are in my *p*." 638 18
when shall I come to appear before the *p* of God? 643 4
Cast me not away from your *p* * 657 3
and declare the goodness of your Name in the *p* 658 19
let the wicked perish at the *p* of God. 676 5
at the *p* of God, the God of Sinai, * 676 19
at the *p* of God, the God of Israel. 676 20
I was like a brute beast in your *p*. 688 22
In the *p* of Ephraim, Benjamin, and Manasseh, * 702 14
Let my prayer enter into your *p*; * 712 3
they walk, O LORD, in the light of your *p*. 714 24
Let us come before his *p* with thanksgiving * 724 16
Oh, the majesty and magnificence of his *p*! * 726 3
The mountains melt like wax at the *p* of the LORD, * 727 5
at the *p* of the Lord of the whole earth. 727 6
and come before his *p* with a song. 729 24
Tremble, O earth, at the *p* of the Lord, * 757 9
at the *p* of the God of Jacob, 757 10
I will walk in the *p* of the LORD * 759 18
in the *p* of all his people. 760 2
in the *p* of all his people, 760 11
where can I flee from your *p*? 794 13
be filled with the strength of his *p*; 819 5
a sense of your abiding *p* wherever they may be; 823 6
your *p* and power may be known throughout 825 18
and whose *p* we find wherever we go: 831 2
to thy *p*, where we may be still 832 16
show us your *p* in those who differ most from us, 840 4
How do we recognize the *p* of the Holy Spirit 852 24
We recognize the *p* of the Holy Spirit 852 26
asking nothing but to enjoy God's *p*. 857 3
to God in the *p* of a priest, 861 11
and because we trust that in God's *p* 862 10

present

Give us grace to behold you, *p* in your Word 113 11
Be *p*, O merciful God, and protect us 133 13
to take joyfully the sufferings of the *p* time, 169 3
Be *p* with thy people where they work; 208 2
to accept joyfully the sufferings of the *p* time, 220 16
Be *p* with your people where they work; 259 4
that they may find your mercy *p* with them 279 16
I *p* N. to receive the Sacrament of Baptism. 301 2
Will you be responsible for seeing that the child you *p* 302 1
I *p* these persons for Confirmation. 303 5

I *p* these persons to be received 303 6
I *p* these persons who desire to reaffirm 303 8
to this congregation here *p*; 329 14
and *p* unto thee, O Lord, our selves, 336 1
and *p* unto thee, O Lord, our selves, 342 23
I beseech you, brethren, by the mercies of God, to *p* 343 14
Let us with gladness *p* the offerings 344 12
I appeal to you, brethren, by the mercies of God, to *p* 376 10
Let us with gladness *p* the offerings 377 10
For this congregation [for those who are *p*, 391 1
I *p* these persons for Confirmation. 415 4
I *p* these persons to be received 415 5
I *p* these persons who desire to reaffirm 415 7
Be *p* in your goodness with your servant 458 18
a very *p* help in trouble. 471 18
In all things may he *p* before you 521 14
we *p* to you N.N. to be ordained a priest 526 2
p to you N.N. to be ordained a deacon 538 2
Be *p* always to guide and to judge, 568 12
we seek your *p* purposes. 571 2
a very *p* help in trouble. 649 2
I will *p* to you thank-offerings; 663 15
be *p* with those who take counsel 818 2
Be ever *p* with your servants who seek 819 14
Be *p*, be *p*, O Jesus, our great High Priest, 834 8
as you were *p* with your disciples, 834 9
we *p* our own needs, that God's will 857 19
by which the sacrifice of Christ is made *p*, 859 12
Sacraments sustain our *p* hope and anticipate 861 22

presented

Son was this day *p* in the temple 187 17
so we may be *p* unto thee with pure and clean hearts 187 18
Son was this day *p* in the temple, 239 7
so we may be *p* to you with pure and clean hearts 239 8
The Candidate(s) for Holy Baptism will now be *p*. 301 1
The other Candidate(s) will now be *p*. 303 4
The Candidate(s) will now be *p*. 415 3
he may be *p* pure and without spot before thee; 488 19

presenting

p to you, from your creation, 369 2
and the weight of your responsibility in *p* 527 2
and the weight of your responsibility in *p* 539 2

presents

Who gives (*p*) this woman to be married to this man? 437 6
Who *p* this woman and this man to be married 437 7

preservation

We bless thee for our creation, *p*, 58 19
We bless thee for our creation, *p*, 71 15
We bless you for our creation, *p*, 101 11
We bless you for our creation, *p*, 125 9

preserve

P us with your mighty power, 100 2
p my life, O LORD, according to your word. 104 2
The LORD shall *p* you from all evil; * 104 25
let your holy angels dwell with us to *p* us 133 22
P us with your mighty power, 137 15
let your holy angels dwell with us to *p* us 140 14
and by thy mercy *p* us for ever. 148 13
That it may please thee to give and *p* to our use 151 9
That it may please thee to *p* all who are in danger 151 17
That it may please thee to *p*, and provide for, 151 20
P us from faithless fears and worldly anxieties, 165 8
p it evermore by thy help 180 10
P the works of thy mercy, 183 12
that thy gracious providence may give and *p* 207 16
P us from faithless fears and worldly anxieties, 217 1
P the works of your mercy, 235 4
that your gracious providence may give and *p* 258 16
and *p* it in peace. 278 10
bless, *p*, and keep you. 310 4
p thy body and soul unto everlasting life. 338 6
guard its faith, and *p* it in peace. 375 14
bless, *p*, and keep you. 418 20
bless, *p*, and keep you; 431 10
Bless this child and *p* his life; 444 17
deliver you from all evil, *p* you in all goodness, 456 17
p him from the temptations 458 5
The LORD shall *p* thee from all evil; * 473 21
The LORD shall *p* thy going out, and thy coming in, * 473 23
Let integrity and uprightness *p* me, * 616 3
you *p* me from trouble; * 625 15
he shall *p* the lives of the needy. 686 10
p what your right hand has planted. 703 17
and *p* your throne for all generations.'" 714 2
in your righteousness *p* my life. 766 16
p my life, O LORD, according to your word. 772 8
p my life, according to your judgments. 776 16
O LORD, in your mercy, *p* me. 776 22
The LORD shall *p* you from all evil; * 779 13
P those who travel 831 2

preserved

that thy Church, being *p* in true faith 204 12
your Church, being *p* in true faith 255 10
p through the pain and anxiety of child-birth 444 2

preserver

Eternal God, creator and *p* of all life, 429 2
O God, the creator and *p* of all mankind, 814 6

preserves

The LORD *p* them and keeps them alive, 642 1
he *p* the lives of his saints 727 18
The LORD *p* all those who love him, * 802 27

preserveth

The LORD *p* the simple; * 479 10

president

the *P* of the United States (or of this nation), 150 26
For N., the *P* of the United States 278 19
For our *P*, for the leaders of the nations, 384 4
to the *P* of the United States, 820 19
To the *P* and members of the Cabinet, 821 19

presiding

For our *P* Bishop, for our own Bishop(s), 390 1
For N., our *P* Bishop, and for all bishops, 548 20

press

They *p* me hard, 601 20
You *p* upon me behind and before * 794 8

pressed
you set me free when I am hard-*p*; 128 9
you set me free when I am hard-*p*; 587 21
I was *p* so hard that I almost fell, * 761 22

presses
and your hand *p* hard upon me. 636 23

pressure
and by the *p* of the wicked; 660 10

presume
We do not *p* to come to this thy Table, 337 9

presumption
the *p* of coming to this Table for solace 372 4

presumptuous
Above all, keep your servant from *p* sins; 607 24

prevail
Those who say, "With our tongue will we *p*; * 597 7
yet they shall not *p*. 609 22
his judgments *p* in all the world. 738 14
that peace may *p* with righteousness, 825 11

prevailed
Lest my enemy say, "I have *p* over him," * 598 6
but they have not *p* against me." 784 4

prevention
and to the *p* of disease and pain. 460 11

prey
Like a lion, greedy for its *p*, * 601 23
The lions roar after their *p* * 736 19
he has not given us over to be a *p* for their teeth. 781 12

price
bought with the *p* of your own blood, 96 10
or deliver to God the *p* of our life; 652 18

priceless
How *p* is your love, O God! * 632 17

pride
from *p*, vainglory, and hypocrisy; 149 1
and give to us all a *p* in what we do, 208 5
and give to us all a *p* in what we do, 259 7
the *p*, hypocrisy, and impatience of our lives, 268 2
It casts out *p* and hatred, 287 19
in your *p* and in your majesty. 647 18
the *p* of Jacob whom he loves. 650 13
let them be caught in their *p*. 666 23
in robbery take no empty *p*; * 670 6
Therefore they wear their *p* like a necklace * 687 11
from *p* and arrogance, and from every evil way. 820 6
the desire of vainglory, and the *p* of life. 829 1

priest
go and open your grief to a discreet and understanding *p*, 317 12
Seeing that we have a great high *p*, 320 5
Through Jesus Christ our great High *P*; 348 15
Since we have a great high *p* who has passed 352 5
Christ our great High *P*, 372 11
Through Jesus Christ our great High *P*; 381 9
As a chief *p* and pastor, will you encourage 518 12
ordained a *p* in Christ's holy catholic Church. 526 3
Is it your will that N. be ordained a *p*? 527 7
work as a pastor, *p*, and teacher, 531 5
As a *p*, it will be your task to proclaim 531 8
make him a *p* in your Church. 533 13
trust committed to you as a *p* of the Church of God. 534 13
For N., chosen bishop (*p*, deacon) in your Church, 549 1
through the high *p* and good shepherd 552 11
receive this stole, and be among us as a pastor and *p*. 561 4
him to be our great High *P*. 573 17
"You are a *p* for ever after the order of Melchizedek." 753 20
Be present, be present, O Jesus, our great High *P*, 834 8
for Moses, the lawgiver, and Aaron, the *p*; 838 12
particularly as apostle, chief *p*, and pastor 855 23
What is the ministry of a *p* or presbyter? 856 1
The ministry of a *p* is to represent Christ 856 2
to God in the presence of a *p*, 861 11

priesthood
share in the royal *p* of Jesus Christ; 307 12
share with us in his eternal *p*. 308 14
to serve thee as a royal *p*, 347 11
to serve you as a royal *p*, 380 6
and exercise without reproach the high *p* 521 10
for ordination to the sacred *p*. 527 3
and his Church to this *p*? 531 22
a holy nation, a royal *p*, 854 9

priests
O ye *p* of the Lord, bless ye the Lord; 49 2
Glorify the Lord, O *p* and servants of the Lord, * 89 20
a kingdom of *p* to serve our God. 94 4
That it may please thee to illumine all bishops, *p*, 150 5
and made us a kingdom of *p* to serve his God 317 18
We pray for all bishops, *p*, and deacons; 387 6
to ordain *p* and deacons 517 9
Abraham, and have raised up prophets, kings, and *p*, 520 16
You are to assist the bishop and *p* in public 543 13
For N., our Presiding Bishop, and for all bishops, *p*, 548 20
Their *p* fell by the sword, * 700 7
Moses and Aaron among his *p*, 729 11
Let your *p* be clothed with righteousness; * 786 15
I will clothe her *p* with salvation, * 787 3
lay persons, bishops, *p*, and deacons. 855 13
to assist bishops and *p* in the proclamation 856 10
to those being made bishops, *p*, and deacons, 861 1

primal
From the *p* elements you brought forth the human 370 12

prince
and fall like any *p*.'" 705 23
all peoples may be gathered under the banner of the *P* 815 25
Christ, our only Savior, the *P* of Peace: 818 15

princely
out upon him the power of your *p* Spirit, 521 2
P state has been yours from the day of your birth; * 753 16

princes
and the *p* plot together, * 586 4
you shall make them *p* over all the earth. 648 24
the *p* of Judah in a company; * 678 12

and the *p* of Zebulon and Naphtali. 678 13
He breaks the spirit of *p*, * 692 25
To instruct his *p* according to his will * 739 21
(He pours contempt on *p* * 749 9
He sets them with the *p*, * 756 14
with the *p* of his people. 756 15
p and all rulers of the world; 806 16

princess

All glorious is the *p* as she enters; * 648 17

principal

What are the *p* kinds of prayer? 856 26
The *p* kinds of prayer are adoration, praise, 856 27

prison

the oppressed, and those in *p*. 386 5
I am in *p* and cannot get free. 712 19
Bring me out of *p*, that I may give thanks 798 15
And since what we do for those in *p*, 826 24

prisoners

That it may please thee to show thy pity upon all *p* 151 5
For *p* and captives, and those in mortal danger 279 10
to *p*, freedom; to the sorrowful, joy. 374 5
for *p* and captives, 384 26
refugees, *p*, and all who are in danger; 390 25
refugees, *p*, and all who are in danger; 550 12
God gives the solitary a home and brings forth *p* 676 13
and his *p* he does not despise. 682 4
Let the sorrowful sighing of the *p* come before you, * 702 4
The LORD sets the *p* free; 803 17
Remember all *p*, and bring the guilty to repentance 826 18

prisons

Visit our jails and *p* with your pity and judgment. 826 17

private

Will you persevere in prayer, both in public and in *p*, 532 25
so to use our public and *p* wealth 824 13

privileges

account for all our powers and *p*: 822 24

prized

and that which is worthless is highly *p* by everyone. 597 19

probe

p the mysteries of your creation, 827 14

proceed

and all just works do *p*: 69 17
if any of you know any reason why we should not *p*, 514 6
of which we should not *p*, 527 5
of which we should not *p*, 539 5

proceedeth

who *p* from the Father and the Son; 328 14

proceeds

O God, from whom all good *p*: 229 15
who *p* from the Father and the Son. 327 13
who *p* from the Father and the Son. 359 4
who *p* from the Father and the Son. 520 4
who *p* from the Father and the Son. 530 23
who *p* from the Father and the Son. 542 23

procession

that I may go in *p* round your altar, 616 19
after her the bridesmaids follow in *p*. 648 20
They see your *p*, O God, * 678 5
your *p* into the sanctuary, my God and my King. 678 6
form a *p* with branches up to the horns of the altar. 762 26

proclaim

And our mouth shall *p* your praise. 80 6
It is not ourselves that we *p*; we *p* Christ 110 1
and my mouth shall *p* your praise. 137 2
It is not ourselves that we *p*; we *p* Christ 139 10
Jordan didst *p* him thy beloved Son and anoint him 163 2
and *p* to all people the Good News 163 15
may *p* thy truth with boldness, 178 8
that in unity and peace we may *p* the one truth 187 4
heralds of thy kingdom, that thy Church may *p* 196 11
and *p* to all people the Good News 215 9
that through your grace we may *p* 230 2
in unity and peace we may *p* the one truth 238 17
that your Church may *p* the unsearchable 247 23
and my mouth shall *p* your praise. 267 7
and power to *p* you to all the world; 291 8
Will you *p* by word and example the Good News 293 26
Will you *p* by word and example the Good News 305 1
of Christ crucified, *p* his resurrection, 308 13
sing this hymn to *p* the glory of your Name: 362 3
Therefore we *p* the mystery of faith: 363 6
sing this hymn to *p* the glory of your Name: 367 12
We *p* his resurrection, 368 21
p with them your glory, in their unending hymn: 370 26
For all who *p* the Gospel, and all who seek the Truth. 392 13
and *p* his resurrection, 403 15
Will you *p* by word and example the Good News 417 11
voice from heaven didst *p*, 486 8
p our faith and say, 496 2
Will you boldly *p* and interpret the Gospel 518 8
As a priest, it will be your task to *p* 531 8
boldly *p* the gospel of salvation; 534 2
Receive this Bible as the sign of your authority to *p* 545 19
p to the peoples the things he has done. 593 22
P with me the greatness of the LORD; * 627 25
and my mouth shall *p* your praise. 657 13
I will *p* his greatness with thanksgiving. 681 25
My tongue will *p* your righteousness all day long, * 685 6
from age to age my mouth will *p* your faithfulness. 713 18
p the good news of his salvation from day to day. 725 20
P the greatness of the LORD our God 729 8
Let all those whom the LORD has redeemed *p* * 746 3
Let Israel now *p*, * 760 22
Let the house of Aaron now *p*, * 761 1
Let those who fear the LORD now *p*, * 761 3
you *p* your truth in every age 827 6
to *p* the Good News of the Kingdom 853 17
to *p* the Word of God; 855 25
to *p* the Gospel; to administer the sacraments; 856 5

proclaimed

Jordan *p* him your beloved Son and anointed him 214 13
and was *p* as King of kings 271 8
To the poor he *p* the good news 374 4
that your word only may be *p*, 571 12

I *p* righteousness in the great congregation; * 640 23
Lord Christ, when you came among us, you *p* 825 16

proclaiming

p his resurrection and ascension 374 26
And so we join the saints and angels in *p* 402 7
And so we join the saints and angels in *p* 404 9
p Christ's resurrection and interpreting the Gospel, 517 4
p the nature of the Incarnation 852 10

proclaims

My soul *p* the greatness of the Lord, 91 27
My soul *p* the greatness of the Lord, 119 4
My soul *p* the greatness of the Lord, 441 12
one who *p* the Word. 561 2
The Church is catholic, because it *p* 854 22
worships, *p* the Gospel, and promotes justice, 855 6

proclamation

to assist bishops and priests in the *p* 856 10

procreation

for the *p* of children and their nurture 423 12

procured

benefits *p* unto us by the same. 335 16

produce

that it might *p* what is needed for life: 824 7
respect those who labor to *p* them, 825 23

profaned

they have *p* your holy temple; * 701 2

profess

may show forth in their lives what they *p* 172 4
may show forth in their lives what they *p* 173 1
may show forth in their lives what they *p* 223 18
may show forth in their lives what they *p* 224 16
may show forth in their lives what they *p* 291 2
all who *p* and call themselves Christians may be led 815 3

profit

who rejoice in her triumph may *p* by her example; 196 4
who rejoice in her triumph may *p* by her example; 247 16
"What *p* is there in my blood, 621 24
and are making no *p* on the sale of them. 646 10

profitable

give us those things which are *p* for us; 177 17
give us those things which are *p* for us; 229 12

prolong

will you *p* your anger from age to age? 709 4

promise

But your merciful *p* is beyond all measure; * 91 3
for he has remembered his *p* of mercy, 92 13
The *p* he made to our fathers, * 92 14
for he has remembered his *p* of mercy, 119 19
The *p* he made to our fathers, * 119 20
and desire that which thou dost *p*; 167 18
according to his *p*, he abideth 174 11
that we may obtain that which thou dost *p*, 183 19
love what you command and desire what you *p*; 219 8
according to his *p*, he abides 226 4
p, make us love what you command; 235 11
fulfilled your *p* to our father Abraham; 289 9
Do you *p* to follow and obey him 303 1
out of their bondage in Egypt into the land of *p*. 306 16
according to whose true *p* the Holy Ghost came 347 7
In fulfillment of his true *p*, the Holy Spirit came 380 2
that you *p*, with the help of God, to fulfill 433 3
Do you *p* to love her, 433 5
Do you *p* to love him, 433 10
for he has remembered his *p* of mercy, 442 8
The *p* he made to our fathers,* 442 9
and comfort him with the *p* of life 462 2
p to all who share in the victory of thy Son 481 27
out of their bondage in Egypt into the land of *p*. 570 8
has his *p* failed for evermore? 693 17
the *p* he made for a thousand generations: 738 16
and would not believe his *p*. 743 21
I treasure your *p* in my heart, * 764 5
Fulfill your *p* to your servant, * 766 11
and your salvation, according to your *p*. 766 18
that your *p* gives me life. 767 14
be merciful to me according to your *p*. 768 4
My eyes have failed from watching for your *p*, * 770 5
Sustain me according to your *p*, that I may live, * 773 5
and for your righteous *p*. 773 20
that I may meditate upon your *p*. 775 23
according to your *p*, give me life. 776 12
I am as glad because of your *p* * 777 3
deliver me, according to your *p*. 777 20
My tongue shall sing of your *p*, * 777 23
who keeps his *p* for ever; 803 14
the hope of salvation and the *p* of eternal life; 838 19
What did God *p* them? 846 26
What did the Messiah *p* in the New Covenant? 851 1

promised

as he *p* to our forefathers, 50 18
To perform the mercy *p* to our forefathers, * 51 3
eternal rest *p* to thy people in heaven; 56 16
hast *p* through thy well-beloved Son 59 14
as he *p* to our forefathers, 65 21
hast *p* through thy well-beloved Son 72 11
you have *p* forgiveness to sinners, * 91 10
Through his holy prophets he *p* of old, 92 22
He *p* to show mercy to our fathers * 92 25
to go in peace as you have *p*; 93 13
eternal rest *p* to your people in heaven; 99 11
have *p* through your well-beloved Son 102 3
to go in peace as you have *p*; 120 2
have *p* through your well-beloved Son 126 3
to go in peace as you have *p*; 135 2
to go in peace as you have *p*; 140 8
Almighty God, who hast *p* to hear the petitions 153 19
life to every race and nation by the *p* gift 175 9
life to every race and nation by the *p* gift 227 2
and *p* to serve God faithfully 292 6
hath *p* forgiveness of sins to all 332 2
and *p* to be with them always, 348 13
and *p* to be with them always, 381 7
Heavenly Father, you have *p* to hear what we ask 394 4
O eternal God, you have *p* to be a father 444 15
in that perfect peace which you have *p* 461 14

You *p* paradise to the thief who repented; 497 13
which I *p* with my lips 674 22
which you *p* David in your faithfulness? 717 13
I have *p* to keep your words. 768 2
as you have *p* to your servant. 769 17
hast *p* to all those who seek thy kingdom 828 10
Almighty God, who hast *p* to hear the petitions 834 1
God *p* that they would be his people 847 1
Christ *p* to bring us into the kingdom of God 851 2

promises

according to thy *p* declared unto mankind 42 6
according to thy *p* declared unto mankind 63 9
and above all things, may obtain thy *p*, 174 4
thy grace, that we, running to obtain thy *p*, 182 14
run without stumbling to obtain thy heavenly *p*; 184 4
may obtain your *p*, which exceed 225 17
running to obtain your *p*, 234 8
run without stumbling to obtain your heavenly *p*; 235 17
Lenten observance is ended, to renew the solemn *p* 292 4
according to thy *p* declared unto mankind 321 9
Will all of you witnessing these *p* do 425 1
they may honor and keep the *p* and vows they make; 425 11
Will you who have witnessed these *p* do 434 1
through these *p* you have committed yourself 519 1
p given to us in Christ Jesus our Lord; 837 22
How are the *p* for infants made and carried out? 858 28
P are made for them by their parents 859 1

promote

that they may serve justice, and *p* the dignity 390 17
that they may serve justice and *p* the dignity 550 2
offices to *p* the well-being of all people; 822 21

promoted

p and your creation glorified; 460 14

promotes

worships, proclaims the Gospel, and *p* justice, 855 6

pronounce

commandment to his ministers to declare and *p* 269 6
I *p* that they are husband and wife, 428 3
p: "Come, you blessed of my Father, 505 6
to *p* God's blessing, 531 13

pronounced

From heaven you *p* judgment; * 692 16

proper

and, as we seek a *p* return for our own labor, 210 13
and, as we seek a *p* return for our own labor, 261 18
For the just and *p* use of your creation; 392 7

property

whose *p* is always to have mercy. 337 13

prophet

And thou, child, shalt be called the *p* 51 11
You, my child, shall be called the *p* 93 1
there is no *p* left; * 690 2

prophets

As he spake by the mouth of his holy *p*, * 50 26
The goodly fellowship of the *p* praise thee. 53 4
Through his holy *p* he promised of old, 92 22
The noble fellowship of *p* praise you. 95 24
Merciful God, who didst send thy messengers the *p* 159 9
Church upon the foundation of the apostles and *p*, 178 19
Merciful God, who sent your messengers the *p* 211 9
Church upon the foundation of the apostles and *p*, 230 13
hang all the Law and the *P*. 319 13
hang all the Law and the *P*. 324 6
He has spoken through the *P*. 327 15
who spake by the *P*. 328 17
He has spoken through the *P*. 359 6
in your Word spoken through the *p*; 368 4
Through *p* and sages you revealed 370 17
with *p*, apostles, and martyrs, 370 24
and through the *p* you taught us to hope 373 25
with patriarchs, *p*, apostles, and martyrs, 375 22
holy patriarchs, *p*, apostles, and martyrs; 489 17
holy patriarchs, *p*, apostles, and martyrs; 504 15
of patriarchs, *p*, apostles, and martyrs, 517 15
He has spoken through the *P*. 520 6
and have raised up *p*, kings, and priests, 520 16
He has spoken through the *P*. 530 25
p, some evangelists, some pastors and teachers, 533 8
He has spoken through the *P*. 542 25
through the voices of *p*, pastors, and teachers. 571 10
and do my *p* no harm." 739 8
for Isaiah and all the *p*; 838 13
and especially through the *p* of Israel. 845 20
God sent the *p* to call us back to himself, 849 8
the One who spoke through the *p*. 852 19

prosper

and *p* in that for which I sent it. 87 8
and may *p* all who labor to gather them, 207 17
and may *p* all who labor to gather them, 258 17
everything they do shall *p*. 585 9
and *p* all your plans. 608 8
p the work of our hands; 719 8
p our handiwork. 719 9
"May they *p* who love you. 780 8
"The LORD *p* you. * 784 16
nor let their evil plans *p*. 796 18

prosperity

in all time of our *p*; 149 26
given one another in *p* and adversity; 423 11
For you meet him with blessings of *p*, * 609 1
They shall dwell in *p*, * 615 14
and desires long life to enjoy *p*? 628 18
who desires the *p* of his servant." 631 29
That the mountains may bring *p* to the people, * 685 13
and saw the *p* of the wicked: 687 6
The LORD will indeed grant *p*, * 709 18
That I may see the *p* of your elect 742 6
I pray for your *p*. 780 12
happiness and *p* shall be yours. 783 16
and may you see the *p* of Jerusalem 783 22
In the time of *p*, fill our hearts with thankfulness, 820 13

prospers

Do not fret yourself over the one who *p*, * 633 19

prostrate

I am utterly bowed down and *p*; * 637 8

protect

I will *p* him, because he knows my Name. 130 28
Be present, O merciful God, and *p* us 133 13
p and govern it always by your goodness; 232 3
Defend us, deliver us, and in thy compassion *p* us, 385 10
P me, O God, for I take refuge in you; * 599 19
P my life and deliver me; * 616 1
p me from those who rise up against me. 665 19
p my life from fear of the enemy. 671 11
and plot against those whom you *p*. 706 8
I will *p* him, because he knows my Name. 720 16
p me from the violent. 796 2
P me from the snare which they have laid for me * 797 22
p them from every danger; 831 4

protected

p us in the day that is past, 113 5
be relieved and *p*, 390 26
be relieved and *p*, 550 13
all may be *p* and our nation be enabled to fulfill 822 27

protection

beseech thy merciful *p* all the night. 70 7
humbly ask for your *p* through the coming night. 124 4
who spend their lives establishing equal *p* of the law 826 12

protector

O God, the *p* of all that trust in thee, 180 1
O God, the *p* of all who trust in you, 231 17

protects

the LORD *p* the faithful, 624 19

proud

he hath scattered the *p* in the imagination 50 12
he hath scattered the *p* in the imagination 65 15
he has scattered the *p* in their conceit. 92 7
he has scattered the *p* in their conceit. 119 13
seeing that, as thou dost alway resist the *p* 181 18
you always resist the *p* who confide 233 10
he has scattered the *p* in their conceit. 442 2
The wicked are so *p* that they care not for God; * 594 25
and close the lips that utter *p* boasts! 597 6
and their mouth speaks *p* things. 601 19
Let not the foot of the *p* come near me, * 633 1
Because I envied the *p* * 687 5
nor speak with a *p* neck.'" 691 13
those who have a haughty look and a *p* 730 18
The *p* have derided me cruelly, * 767 15
The *p* have smeared me with lies, * 769 1
The *p* have dug pits for me; * 770 12
let not the *p* oppress me. 773 18
and of the derision of the *p*. 780 24
O LORD, I am not *p*; * 785 10
The *p* have hidden a snare for me 796 10

prove

and so *p* to be my disciples. 397 11
nor let my faithfulness *p* false. 716 8
We humbly beseech thee that we may always *p* 820 2

proved

p me, and saw my works. 146 20
Every one has *p* faithless; 598 18
Every one has *p* faithless; 659 4
For you, O God, have *p* us; * 674 13

proverb

I will incline my ear to a *p* * 652 11

provide

That it may please thee to preserve, and *p* for, 151 20
to celebrate and to *p* for the administration 517 8
for so you *p* for the earth. 673 8
or to *p* meat for his people?" 696 16
where it is in want, *p* for it; 816 14
foresight to *p* for the needs of all our people, 822 3
P for them homes of dignity and peace; 830 2

provided

This season of Lent *p* a time in which converts 265 1
he *p* for them food enough. 696 27

providence

O God, your unfailing *p* sustains the world 134 11
may be peaceably governed by thy *p*, 177 10
O God, whose never-failing *p* ordereth 177 14
Almighty God, by whose *p* thy servant John 190 1
p hast appointed various orders in thy Church: 205 5
that thy gracious *p* may give and preserve 207 16
ever thankful for thy loving *p*; and grant that we, 208 11
peaceably governed by your *p*; 229 6
O God, your never-failing *p* sets in order 229 10
Almighty God, by whose *p* your servant John 241 10
in your divine *p* you have appointed 256 2
that your gracious *p* may give and preserve 258 16
Make us always thankful for your loving *p*; 259 13
by the effectual working of your *p*, 280 16
by the effectual working of your *p*, 291 13
for his continual *p* over us, 316 11
by the effectual working of your *p*, 515 6
by the effectual working of your *p*, 528 4
by the effectual working of your *p*, 540 4
by thy *P*, we may dwell secure in thy peace. 820 18
and for all the other blessings of thy merciful *p* 840 18

provides

He *p* food for flocks and herds * 804 20

provision

for the *p* of our necessities 194 19
for the *p* of our necessities 246 4
in your goodness, O God, you have made *p* 676 24
making *p* for its future in accordance with your will; 828 20

provisions

I will surely bless her *p*, * 787 1

provocation

as in the *p*, 146 17

provoked

and *p* the Holy One of Israel. 698 10
and *p* his displeasure with their idols. 699 23
They *p* him to anger with their actions, * 744 5
Again they *p* his anger at the waters of Meribah, * 744 11

provoking

p most justly thy wrath and indignation against us. 331 8

prowl

The wicked *p* on every side, * 597 18
in which all the beasts of the forest *p*. 736 18

prowls

Your adversary the devil *p* 132 8

psalms

and show ourselves glad in him with *p*. 44 13
and raise a loud shout to him with *p*. 82 8
and show ourselves glad in him with *p*. 146 4
and raise a loud shout to him with *p*. 724 17

psaltery

play to him upon the *p* and lyre. 626 4
On the *p*, and on the lyre, * 721 1

public

For those in positions of *p* trust 390 16
Will you persevere in prayer, both in *p* and in private, 532 24
You are to assist the bishop and priests in *p* 543 13
For those in positions of *p* trust 550 1
They lurk in ambush in *p* squares 595 8
no wailing in the *p* squares. 801 9
so to use our *p* and private wealth 824 13

publish

I *p* the Banns of Marriage 437 1
p the remembrance of your great goodness; * 801 24

puff

even those who stand erect are but a *p* of wind. 639 5
everyone is but a *p* of wind. 639 19
how like a *p* of wind they are. 723 16
We are like a *p* of wind; * 800 8

pull

p the fangs of the young lions, O LORD. 665 6

pulpit

We dedicate this *P* in the Name of the Father, 571 15

punish

you do not *p* as we deserve. 91 8
do not *p* me in your wrath. 589 24
do not *p* me in your wrath. 636 21
With rebukes for sin you *p* us; 639 17
Awake, and *p* all the ungodly; * 666 5
I will *p* their transgressions with a rod * 716 5
He who admonishes the nations, will he not *p*? * 723 13

punished

and those who hate the righteous will be *p*. 629 10
and none will be *p* who trust in him. 629 12
and *p* every morning. 688 6
yet *p* them for their evil deeds." 729 18
so that he *p* Moses because of them; 744 12
The LORD has *p* me sorely, * 762 6

punishment

and their *p* would last for ever. 705 6
and *p* on the peoples; 807 15

purchased

Remember your congregation that you *p* long ago, * 689 11

pure

offered unto my Name, and a *p* offering: 38 8
p brightness of the everliving Father in heaven, 64 2
offered to my Name, and a *p* offering; 76 7
offered to my Name, and a *p* offering; 106 8
p brightness of the everliving Father in heaven, 112 2
p brightness of the everliving Father in heaven, 118 2
p brightness of the everliving Father in heaven, 139 2
and as at this time to be born of a *p* virgin: 161 9
and united to one another with *p* affection; 179 7
we may purify ourselves even as he is *p*; 184 10
so we may be presented unto thee with *p* 187 18
and to be born [this day] of a *p* virgin: 213 2
and united to one another with *p* affection; 231 1
we may purify ourselves as he is *p*; 236 4
we may be presented to you with *p* and clean hearts 239 8
Purge me from my sin, and I shall be *p*; * 266 16
and that the rest of our life hereafter may be *p* 269 12
that with *p* minds we may attain to the festival 285 11
p, lovable and gracious, excellent and admirable, 443 28
he may be presented *p* and without spot before thee; 488 19
offering of a *p*, and gentle, and holy life; 521 15
The words of the LORD are *p* words, * 597 13
With the *p* you show yourself *p*, * 604 16
"Those who have clean hands and a *p* heart, * 613 20
Purge me from my sin, and I shall be *p*; * 656 20
to those who are *p* in heart. 687 2
sound learning, and *p* manners. 820 5

pureness

and *p* of living, to thy honor and glory; 155 12
serve thee in *p* of living and truth; 172 11
serve you in *p* of living and truth; 224 4

purge

P me from my sin, and I shall be pure; * 266 16
P me from my sin, and I shall be pure; * 656 20

purged

that by its cleansing flame we may be *p* 111 5
midst of this earthly life being *p* and done away, 488 18

purified

and *p* seven times in the fire. 597 15

purify

We beseech thee, Almighty God, to *p* our consciences 160 6
we may *p* ourselves even as he is pure; 184 10
P our conscience, Almighty God, 212 6
we may *p* ourselves as he is pure; 236 4
P the lives and the lips 571 10
Where it is corrupt, *p* it; 816 12

purpose

direct us to the fulfilling of your *p*; 100 5
direct us to the fulfilling of your *p*; 137 18
hearts accomplish those things which belong to thy *p*; 177 6
free hearts those things which belong to your *p*; 229 2
Almighty God, with full *p* of amendment of life, 317 5
To fulfill your *p* he gave himself up to death; 374 6
in them the good *p* of your perfect will; 504 29
The LORD will make good his *p* for me; * 793 19
that with steadfast *p* they may faithfully serve 822 20
fulfill our role in your eternal *p*; 827 16

What is the *p* of the Ten Commandments? 848 22
and the completion of God's *p* 861 27

purposed

But it will accomplish that which I have *p*, * 87 7

purposes

deliberately, and in accordance with the *p* 423 15
read about your mighty acts and *p* in history, 570 25
we seek your present *p*. 571 2
to accomplish your *p* on earth; 815 18
nation be enabled to fulfill your *p*; 822 28
and give us new insight into your *p* 828 18
to care for it in accordance with God's *p*. 846 12
in union with Christ, for the *p* of God. 857 16

pursue

save and deliver me from all who *p* me; 590 21
Then let my enemy *p* and overtake me, * 591 3
I *p* my enemies and overtake them; * 605 14
seek peace and *p* it. 628 22
bar the way against those who *p* me; * 629 18
and let the angel of the LORD *p* them. 630 2
save me from those who *p* me, 798 13
p it and the grace to accomplish it; 818 6
How does the Church *p* its mission? 855 4

pursues

The Church *p* its mission as it prays 855 5

pursuit

sound learning, new discovery, and the *p* of wisdom; 824 18

push

nor the hand of the wicked *p* me aside. 633 2

pushed

Through you we *p* back our adversaries; * 645 20

put

He hath *p* down the mighty from their seat, * 50 13
He hath *p* down the mighty from their seat, * 65 16
For we *p* our trust in you. 98 16
No one lights a lamp to *p* it under a bucket, 109 8
and *p* your trust in the Lord. 128 19
You have *p* gladness in my heart, * 129 4
let me never be *p* to shame: * 129 9
my God in whom I *p* my trust." 129 25
As we do *p* out trust in thee. 153 17
that in all our troubles we may *p* our whole trust 155 10
and *p* upon us the armor of light, 159 2
the strength of all those who *p* their trust in thee: 164 11
Grant us so to *p* away the leaven of malice 172 9
We humbly beseech thee to *p* away from us 177 15
we have *p* away the old life of sin, 201 14
and *p* on the armor of light, 211 2
the strength of all who *p* their trust in you: 216 6
Give us grace so to *p* away the leaven of malice 224 2
P away from us, we entreat you, all hurtful things, 229 11
we have *p* away the old life of sin, 253 2
p in mind of the message of pardon and absolution 265 7
holy is this night, when wickedness is *p* to flight, 287 17
Do you *p* your whole trust in his grace and love? 302 19
eternal salvation for all who *p* their trust in him. 346 16
p all things in subjection under your Christ, 369 9
eternal salvation for all who *p* their trust in him. 379 13
Who *p* their trust in you. 393 7
whom God has joined together let no one *p* asunder. 428 6
whom God has joined together let no one *p* asunder. 434 7
The Lord has *p* away all your sins. 448 12
The Lord has *p* away all your sins. 451 19
a strong tower to all who *p* their trust in him, 456 20
he yet may *p* his trust in you; 459 10
O *p* thy trust in God; * 471 14
and *p* thou thy trust in the LORD. 478 10
and *p* your trust in the LORD. 588 9
You have *p* gladness in my heart, * 588 13
they shall turn back and suddenly be *p* to shame. 590 19
you *p* all things under his feet: 592 20
who know your Name will *p* their trust in you, * 593 19
P fear upon them, O LORD; * 594 17
But I *p* my trust in your mercy; * 598 8
My God, my rock in whom I *p* my trust, * 602 9
and his decrees I have not *p* away from me; 604 8
you have *p* my enemies to flight. 605 20
you *p* me at the head of the nations. 605 27
Some *p* their trust in chariots and some in horses, * 608 15
For you will *p* them to flight * 609 23
Our forefathers *p* their trust in you; * 610 8
they trusted in you and were not *p* to shame. 610 11
my God, I *p* my trust in you; * 614 14
Let none who look to you be *p* to shame; * 614 17
let me not be *p* to shame, for I have trusted in you. 616 2
yet will I *p* my trust in him. 617 17
you have *p* off my sack-cloth and clothed me with joy. 622 4
let me never be *p* to shame; * 622 8
and I *p* my trust in the LORD. 622 21
they *p* their head together against me; 623 18
rather, let the wicked be *p* to shame; 623 28
for those who *p* their trust in you. 624 7
and whose sin is *p* away! 624 24
for in his holy Name we *p* our trust. 627 18
as we have *p* our trust in you. 627 20
They *p* me to the test and mocked me; * 630 27
P your trust in the LORD and do good; * 633 9
Commit your way to the LORD and *p* your trust 633 13
I will *p* a muzzle on my mouth * 638 17
He *p* a new song in my mouth, 640 5
and *p* their trust in the LORD. 640 8
P your trust in God; * 643 15
P your trust in God; * 644 11
why have you *p* me from you? * 644 18
P your trust in God; * 645 3
and *p* those who hate us to shame. 645 26
The wickedness of those who *p* their trust 652 15
I have *p* my case in order before your eyes. 655 25
they are *p* to shame, because God has rejected them. 659 13
but I will *p* my trust in you. 662 11
I will *p* my trust in you. 662 18
p my tears into your bottle; * 663 7
my enemies will be *p* to flight; * 663 9
and *p* them down, O Lord our shield. 666 20
P your trust in him always, O people, * 669 22
P no trust in extortion; 670 5
rejoice in the LORD and *p* their trust in him, * 672 5
Let not those who hope in you be *p* to shame 679 22
I *p* on sack-cloth also, * 680 9

who set themselves against me be *p* to shame 684 3
So that they might *p* their trust in God, * 695 13
nor did they *p* their trust in his saving power. 696 21
and *p* them to perpetual shame. 700 12
let them be *p* to confusion and perish. 707 12
happy are they who *p* their trust in you! 708 19
You have *p* my friends far from me; 712 17
My friend and my neighbor you have *p* away 713 15
You have *p* an end to his splendor * 717 1
my God in whom I *p* my trust." 719 14
he has *p* on splendid apparel; * 722 2
the LORD has *p* on his apparel 722 3
and *p* the orphans to death. 723 6
They *p* me to the test, * 725 10
his neck they *p* in an iron collar. 739 14
and they *p* God to the test in the desert. 742 27
He *p* their feet on a straight path * 746 14
He *p* on cursing like a garment, * 752 8
let those who rise up against me be *p* to shame, 753 4
they *p* their trust in the Lord. 755 19
and so are all who *p* their trust in them. 758 5
than to *p* any trust in flesh. 761 12
than to *p* any trust in rulers. 761 14
Then I should not be *p* to shame, * 763 15
O LORD, let me not be *p* to shame. 765 22
Let the arrogant be *p* to shame, for they wrong me 769 20
that I may not be *p* to shame. 770 2
I have *p* my hope in your word. 770 4
so that the just shall not *p* their hands to evil. 781 24
he shall not be *p* to shame 783 11
Let them be *p* to shame and thrown back, * 784 9
and *p* mighty kings to death: 788 22
and so are all who *p* their trust in them. 789 12
for I *p* my trust in you; * 799 16
P not your trust in rulers, nor in any child of earth, * 803 7
P far from them, we beseech thee, 828 24
you conquered sin, *p* death to flight, 835 2
and we *p* ourselves in the place of God. 845 13
To *p* nothing in the place of God; 847 23

puts
For the king *p* his trust in the LORD; * 609 9
he *p* down one and lifts up another. 691 17
save your servant who *p* his trust in you. 710 2

putting
Grant that we, *p* away all earthly anxieties, 56 13
Grant that we, *p* away all earthly anxieties, 99 8

Q

quails
They asked, and *q* appeared, * 741 5

quake
All things *q* with fear at your presence; * 91 1
my enemies shall be confounded and *q* with fear; * 590 18

quakes
My heart *q* within me, * 660 13

quaking
Though the earth and all its inhabitants are *q*, * 691 8

qualified
and we believe him to be *q* for this order. 526 8
and we believe him *q* for this order. 538 8
We believe that he is well *q*, 559 3

queen
on your right hand is the *q*, 648 9

quell
to *q* the enemy and the avenger. 592 12

quench
and the wild asses *q* their thirst. 735 24

quick
he shall come to judge the *q* and the dead. 54 4
he shall come to judge the *q* and the dead. 66 20
to judge both the *q* and the dead, 159 6
to judge both the *q* and the dead; 328 11

quicken
In prayer, *q* my devotion; 563 5

quickly
Come *q* to help us who are assaulted 218 2
for his wrath is *q* kindled. 586 27
come *q* to help me, O my God. 684 2
for they pass away *q* and we are gone. 718 22
O LORD, I call to you; come to me *q*; * 797 3

quiet
and serve thee with a *q* mind. 481 5
so that in *q* confidence we may continue 493 21
schemes against the *q* in the land. 631 11
But I still my soul and make it *q*, 785 14

quieted
and *q* the waves of the sea. 748 14
my soul is *q* within me. 785 16

quietly
If I am to sit still, help me to sit *q*. 461 22

quietness
may pass our time in rest and *q*; 69 21
may live in peace and *q*; 123 19
in *q* and trust shall be our strength. 138 11
and *q* within your towers. 780 10
in *q* and in confidence shall be our strength: 832 14

quiver
Happy is the man who has his *q* full of them! * 783 10

R

race
to every *r* and nation by the promised gift 175 9
may persevere in running the *r* 198 18
in your tender love for the human *r* you sent 219 14
to every *r* and nation by the promised gift 227 2
may persevere in running the *r* 250 3
in your tender love for the human *r* you sent 272 8

may run with patience the *r* 347 19
From the primal elements you brought forth the human *r*, 370 12
and run with endurance the *r* 380 14
new insight into your purposes for the human *r*, 828 19

races

all nations and *r* may serve you 815 19
the wonderful diversity of *r* and cultures in this world. 840 2

racked

heal me, LORD, for my bones are *r*. 590 2

radiance

Glory to you for the *r* of your holy Name; * 90 7
illumine the world with the *r* of your glory, 107 14
as you enfold us with the *r* of this light, 110 15
may shine with the *r* of Christ's glory, 163 9
may shine with the *r* of Christ's glory, 215 3
rejoice in the splendor of your *r*. 373 6

radiant

and let your holy courts, in *r* light, 286 8
Look upon him and be *r*, * 628 3

rage

Though the waters thereof *r* and swell, * 471 21
and his *r* fills them with terror. 586 11
Refrain from anger, leave *r* alone; * 633 21
Though its waters *r* and foam, * 649 6
I am filled with a burning *r*, * 767 19

raging

and round about him a *r* storm. 654 8
You rule the *r* of the sea * 714 11
Then would the *r* waters * 781 9

Rahab

You have crushed *R* of the deep 714 13

railed

They *r* against God and said, * 696 11

raiment

transfigured, in *r* white and glistening: 191 17
transfigured, in *r* white and glistening: 243 2

rain

For as *r* and snow fall from the heavens * 87 1
Glorify the Lord, every shower of *r* and fall of dew, * 88 13
Upon the wicked he shall *r* coals of fire 596 21
with heavy *r* you soften the ground 673 10
The earth shook, and the skies poured down *r*, 676 18
You sent a gracious *r*, O God, 676 21
He shall come down like *r* upon the mown field, * 685 19
He gave them hailstones instead of *r*, * 740 17
He brings up *r* clouds from the ends of the earth; * 788 14
he sends out lightning with the *r*, 788 15
and prepares *r* for the earth; 804 17
we entreat thee, in this time of need, such moderate *r* 828 12

rained

He *r* down manna upon them to eat * 696 24
He *r* down flesh upon them like dust * 697 3

rains

for the early *r* have covered it with pools of water. 708 3

raise

and *r* a loud shout to him with psalms. 82 8
to *r* up those who fall; 152 12
so by his love he may *r* us to joys eternal; 172 17
David didst *r* up Joseph 188 8
R up, we beseech thee, in this and every land 196 9
didst *r* up thy servant N. to be a light to the world: 196 16
who didst *r* up thy faithful servant N. 197 4
so by his love he may *r* us to eternal joys; 224 10
R up in this and every land 247 21
and *r* him up to a life of service 459 5
that he will *r* him to perfection 466 14
After my awaking, he will *r* me up; 491 9
R us, we humbly pray, from the death of sin 505 2
he will *r* you up to possess the land, 636 4
But you, O LORD, be merciful to me and *r* me up, * 642 20
and *r* a loud shout to the God of Jacob. 704 2
R a song and sound the timbrel, * 704 3
and *r* a loud shout to him with psalms. 724 17
r him up if he fall; 830 15
We mean that God will *r* us from death 862 17

raised

Christ being *r* from the dead dieth no more; * 46 7
And hath *r* up a mighty salvation for us * 50 24
If then you have been *r* with Christ, 77 12
Christ being *r* from the dead will never die again; * 83 15
Christ has been *r* from the dead, * 83 21
He has *r* up for us a mighty savior, * 92 20
may be *r* from the death of sin 171 1
Grant that we, who have been *r* with him, 171 12
may be *r* from the death of sin 222 18
Grant that we, who have been *r* with him, 223 6
David *r* up Joseph 239 17
who *r* up your servant N. to be a light in the world: 248 2
our heavenly Father, who *r* up your faithful servant 248 15
things which were cast down are being *r* up, 280 19
things which were cast down are being *r* up, 291 16
and *r* with him to newness of life. 292 2
and have *r* them to the new life 308 4
and have *r* him to the new life 314 3
He that *r* up Jesus from the dead 485 1
Grant that your servant N. being *r* with him, 493 6
You *r* the dead to life; 497 10
He who *r* Jesus Christ from the dead 501 3
things which were cast down are being *r* up, 515 9
and have *r* up prophets, kings, and priests, 520 16
things which were cast down are being *r* up, 528 7
things which were cast down are being *r* up, 540 7
and whose right hand is *r* in falsehood. 800 18
He has *r* up strength for his people 806 22
in which we are *r* to the life of your kingdom. 836 16

raising

r up among us faithful servants for the ministry 523 4
r up among us faithful servants for the ministry 535 4
r up among us faithful servants for the ministry 546 6
r up among us faithful servants for the ministry 564 4
We praise you for *r* him from the dead, 573 16

ram
the LORD with the sound of the r's-horn. 650 15
Blow the r's-horn at the new moon, * 704 5
Praise him with the blast of the r's-horn; * 808 3

rams
with the smoke of r; * 674 25
The mountains skipped like r, * 757 3
You mountains, that you skipped like r? * 757 7

ran
so the river r in the dry places. 741 8

ransom
and to give his life a r for many. 517 18
We can never r ourselves, * 652 17
For the r of our life is so great, * 652 19
But God will r my life; * 653 13

ransomed
in the day when he r them from the enemy; 698 12

ransoms
The LORD r the life of his servants, * 629 11

rapids
all your r and floods have gone over me. 643 22

rash
I refrained from r words; 638 20
that he spoke r words with his lips. 744 14

rather
but r that they may turn from their wickedness 269 4
r, let the wicked be put to shame; 623 28

ravaged
The wild boar of the forest has r it, * 703 13

ravening
like a r and a roaring lion. 611 4

ravens
and for the young r when they cry. 804 21

razed
and r it to the ground. 689 23

razor
your tongue is like a sharpened r, * 658 2

reach
within the r of thy saving embrace: 58 10
r to the end of the earth. 76 4
within the r of your saving embrace: 101 3
that it may r to the ends of the earth; 175 11
that it may r to the ends of the earth; 227 4
may r out in love and concern for others. 429 24
when the great waters overflow, they shall not r them. 625 13
things to r out to us. 861 20

reached
He r down from on high and grasped me; * 603 23

reaches
Your love, O LORD, r to the heavens, * 632 12
Your praise, like your Name, O God, r 651 20
and your faithfulness r to the clouds. 664 18
Your righteousness, O God, r to the heavens; * 684 20
and your faithfulness r to the clouds. 750 2

reacheth
O God, whose fatherly care r to the uttermost parts 830 19

reaching
that we, r forth our hands in love, 58 11
that we, r forth our hands in love, 101 4

read
r, mark, learn, and inwardly digest them; 184 17
r, mark, learn, and inwardly digest them, 236 9
Here we r about your mighty acts 570 24
many listen and write what many r; 827 8

readily
Give us grace, O Lord, to answer r the call 163 14
Andrew that he r obeyed the call 185 8
Give us grace, O Lord, to answer r the call 215 8
Andrew that he r obeyed the call 237 2

readiness
give me r of thought and expression; 563 7

reading
A R (Lesson) from ________. 47 1
Here endeth the Lesson (R). 47 4
A R (Lesson) from ________. 64 12
Here endeth the Lesson (R). 65 3
A R (Lesson) from ________. 84 3
Here ends the Lesson (R). 84 6
A R (Lesson) from ________. 118 12
Here ends the Lesson (R). 119 3
by prayer, fasting, and self-denial; and by r and 265 12
A R (Lesson) from________. 300 1
Here ends the R (Epistle). 300 4
A R (Lesson) from ________. 325 13
Here endeth the R (Epistle). 325 16
A R (Lesson) from ________. 357 4
Here ends the R (Epistle). 357 7
A R (Lesson) from ________. 414 1
Here ends the R (Epistle). 414 4
A R (Lesson) from ________. 516 1
Here ends the R (Epistle). 516 4
A R (Lesson) from ________. 528 12
Here ends the R (Epistle). 529 3
Will you be diligent in the r and study 532 4
A R (Lesson) from ________. 540 12
Here ends the R (Epistle). 541 3
Will you be faithful in prayer, and in the r 544 1

ready
that we, being r both in body and soul, 177 5
who art always more r to hear than we to pray, 182 18
r wills and hearts obey the calling of our Lord 193 1
may always be r to give a reason for the hope 195 4
that we, being r both in mind and body, 228 15
you are always more r to hear than we to pray, 234 12
r wills and hearts obey the calling of our Lord 244 9
may always be r to give a reason for the hope 247 2
r to make restitution for all injuries and wrongs 317 6
and also being r to forgive those 317 7
but make me r, Lord, for whatever it may be. 461 20

I am willing and *r* to do so; 526 14
I am willing and *r* to do so; 538 14
being *r* to help and serve those in need? 544 4
he will bend his bow and make it *r*. 591 23
Let your hand be *r* to help me, * 778 1
the hearts and minds of your servants *r* to receive 819 3
defended by thy gracious and *r* help; 832 22
are penitent for their sins, and are *r* to affirm 860 25

reaffirm

Do you *r* your renunciation of evil 292 8
these persons who desire to *r* their baptismal vows. 303 8
Do you *r* your renunciation of evil? 303 10
these persons who desire to *r* their baptismal vows. 415 7
Do you *r* your renunciation of evil? 415 9

reaffirmed

now *r* his commitment to follow Christ 421 3

reap

will *r* with songs of joy. 105 15
will *r* with songs of joy. 782 17

reaper

Which does not fill the hand of the *r*, * 784 13

reason

r of their labor or their travel, 151 18
may always be ready to give a *r* for the hope 195 4
may always be ready to give a *r* for the hope 247 2
and blessed us with memory, *r*, and skill. 370 13
any *r* why you may not be united in marriage 424 5
if any of you know any *r* why we should not proceed, 514 6
by *r* of my foolishness. 637 7
to *r*, and to live in harmony with creation 845 6

reasonable

to be a *r*, holy, and living sacrifice 336 2
the comfort of a *r* and holy hope, 481 12
the comfort of a *r*, religious, and holy hope; 489 11

rebel

of wickedness that *r* against God? 302 8
let no *r* rise up against him. 674 8
Because we *r* against God, 845 13

rebelled

though we have *r* against him; 38 21
we have *r* against him and have not obeyed 76 20
for they have *r* against you. 589 16
but the Egyptians *r* against his words. 740 10
but they *r* through their own devices, * 745 11
Because they *r* against the words of God * 747 3

rebelling

r in the desert against the Most High. 696 8

rebellion

From all oppression, conspiracy, and *r*; 149 14
There is a voice of *r* deep in the heart of the wicked; * 632 3

rebellious

a stubborn and *r* generation, * 695 17
Some were fools and took to *r* ways; * 747 15

rebels

but the *r* shall live in dry places. 676 15

reborn

Grant that all who have been *r* into the fellowship 172 3
Grant that we, being *r* to new life in him, 203 7
Grant that all who have been *r* into the fellowship 223 17
Grant that all who have been *r* into the fellowship 224 15
Grant that we, being *r* to new life in him, 254 9
Grant that all who are *r* into the fellowship 291 1
Through it we are *r* by the Holy Spirit. 306 22
our brother (sister) N., who was *r* by water 498 2
Through it we are *r* by the Holy Spirit. 570 14

rebuild

and *r* the walls of Jerusalem. 657 19
For God will save Zion and *r* the cities of Judah; * 682 7
to *r* our bodies and renew our minds, 825 3

rebuilding

for the building (*r*, or adornment) 567 4

rebuilds

The LORD *r* Jerusalem; * 804 4

rebuke

constantly speak the truth, boldly *r* vice, 190 6
constantly speak the truth, boldly *r* vice, 241 15
LORD, do not *r* me in your anger; * 589 23
O LORD, do not *r* me in your anger; * 636 20
R the wild beast of the reeds, * 678 18
At your *r*, O God of Jacob, * 692 12
at the *r* of your countenance let them perish. 703 19
At your *r* they fled; * 735 15
Turn from me shame and *r*, * 765 3
Let the righteous smite me in friendly *r*; 797 12

rebuked

You have *r* the ungodly and destroyed the wicked; * 593 9
and *r* kings for their sake, 739 6
He *r* the Red Sea, and it dried up, * 742 16
You have *r* the insolent; * 765 1

rebukes

With *r* for sin you punish us; 639 17

recall

Grant that his death may *r* to us your victory 498 3
I will *r* your righteousness, yours alone. 684 13
the Church's daily worship to *r* our Baptismal Covenant. 852 3

recalled

as by his death he hath *r* us to life, 172 17
as by his death he has *r* us to life, 224 10

recalling

R his death, resurrection, and ascension, 363 11
R Christ's death and his descent among the dead, 374 25
R now his suffering and death, 405 11
Accept here the continual *r* 574 3

recant

The LORD has sworn and he will not *r*: * 753 19

receive

Ye shall *r* power, after that the Holy Ghost is come 39 18
r our prayer. 52 15
R our supplications and prayers which we offer 57 21
You shall *r* power when the Holy Spirit has come 77 17
r our prayer. 95 8
R our supplications and prayers which we offer 100 13
to hear and *r* thy Word, 150 16
joyfully *r* him for our Redeemer, 160 14
Mercifully grant that we may thankfully *r* 169 9
O Lord, we beseech thee mercifully to *r* 179 10
Give us grace that we may always most thankfully *r* 180 21
R, we beseech thee, into the arms 186 14
r with him the crown of life; 195 12
thou wilt *r* him more and more 202 11
R our supplications and prayers, 206 3
that we, who constantly *r* good things from thy hand, 207 18
joyfully *r* him as our Redeemer, 212 12
Mercifully grant that we may *r* it thankfully 221 3
O Lord, mercifully *r* the prayers of your people 231 4
Give us grace to *r* thankfully 232 13
R, we pray, into the arms 238 8
r with him the crown of life; 247 10
you will *r* him more and more 253 15
R our supplications and prayers, 256 21
Mercifully grant that we may *r* it thankfully 274 3
R our supplications and prayers 278 13
and *r* the crown of life in the day of resurrection. 280 12
I present N. to *r* the Sacrament of Baptism. 301 2
Let us now pray for these persons who are to *r* 305 11
We *r* you into the household of God. 308 12
and we *r* you into the fellowship 310 2
faith we *r* the holy Sacrament, 316 24
if we *r* it improperly, not recognizing the Lord's Body. 316 25
confess your sins, that you may *r* the benefit 317 13
r our prayer. 325 2
R these our prayers which we offer 329 3
they may hear and *r* thy holy Word, 329 15
worthily *r* the most precious Body and Blood 336 5
partake of this Holy Communion may worthily *r* 342 25
Worthy art thou, O Lord our God, to *r* glory 344 5
and *r* power to become thy children. 345 18
together with them, may *r* the crown of glory 347 20
that we may *r* mercy and find grace 352 7
r our prayer. 356 12
r this holy Sacrament, and serve you in unity, 363 16
O Lord our God, you are worthy to *r* glory 377 3
r power to become your children. 378 13
together with them, *r* the crown of glory 380 15
that they may *r* the light of the Gospel, 390 11
Mercifully grant that we may *r* it thankfully 397 15
and we *r* you into the fellowship 418 18
r N. as your own son (daughter). 441 6
r him and enable him to *r* you, 444 17
R me again into the arms of your mercy, 450 18
May Almighty God in mercy *r* your confession 451 3
who in faith and repentance *r* this holy unction 455 12
R him into the arms of your mercy, 465 4
R, O Lord, your servant, for he returns to you. 465 14
R our brother N. into the courts 466 8
With faith in Jesus Christ, we *r* the body 466 12
r him into the arms of thy mercy, 481 17
to *r* the crown of life 481 26
R him into the arms of thy mercy, 483 9
and at thy coming may the martyrs *r* thee, 484 2
R him into the arms of your mercy, 499 16
At your coming may the martyrs *r* you, 500 13
r that blessing which your well-beloved Son 505 5
"Come, you blessed of my Father, *r* 505 6
R the Holy Scriptures. 521 18
R this Bible as a sign of the authority 534 10
R this Bible as the sign of your authority 545 19
that they may *r* the light of the Gospel, 549 26
r this stole, and be among us as a pastor and priest. 561 4
r this book, and be among us as a man of prayer. 561 5
r these keys, and let the doors of this place be open 562 1
R the work of our hands in this place, 567 9
r our thanks for this place, 578 5
They shall *r* a blessing from the LORD * 613 23
and let them not *r* your vindication. 681 19
and afterwards *r* me with glory. 688 26
that we may *r* a faithful pastor, 818 11
the hearts and minds of your servants ready to *r* 819 3
and *r* just payment 824 14
that we may *r* the fruits of the earth, 828 13
For it is in giving that we *r*; 833 11
means by which we *r* that grace. 857 28
What are the benefits which we *r* 859 27
The benefits we *r* are the forgiveness of our sins, 859 29
and *r* strength from the Holy Spirit 860 19
vows before God and the Church, and *r* the grace 861 6
and *r* the assurance of pardon 861 11

received

great benefits that we have *r* at his hands, 41 7
Let us pray for all who have not *r* the Gospel 279 20
I present these persons to be *r* into this 303 6
Jesus *r* the baptism of John and was anointed 306 17
This is a true saying, and worthy of all men to be *r*, 332 13
Because in Jesus Christ our Lord thou hast *r* us 348 20
Because in Jesus Christ our Lord you have *r* us 381 13
I present these persons to be *r* into this Communion. 415 5
This is a true saying, and worthy of all men to be *r*, 449 18
worship of Christ as this Church has *r* them? 526 10
love of Christ maybe known and *r*? 532 12
worship of Christ as this Church has *r* them? 538 10
In it your Son Jesus *r* the baptism of John 570 8
you have *r* gifts even from your enemies, * 677 19
faithfully administered and faithfully *r*. 817 14
We mean that by God's own act, his divine Son *r* 849 28
given and *r* according to Christ's command. 859 20
given to his people, and *r* by faith. 859 26

receives

whoever *r* a little child in the name of Christ *r* Christ 443 22

receiving

r good things from your hand, 258 19
that we, *r* them according to thy Son 335 20
the giving and *r* of a ring, 428 3

recite
let me *r* what I have fashioned for the king; * 647 12
"Why do you *r* my statutes, 655 12
With my lips will I *r* * 764 9

reckon
Likewise *r* ye also yourselves to be dead 46 11

reckoned
This was *r* to him as righteousness * 744 9

recognize
and to *r* you in the lives of those around us. 113 12
we *r* you as a member of the one holy catholic 310 1
we *r* you as a member of the one holy catholic 418 17
to *r* and acknowledge their fault, 429 14
they will *r* his works. 672 4
How do we *r* the presence of the Holy Spirit 852 24
We *r* the presence of the Holy Spirit 852 26
How do we *r* the truths taught by the Holy Spirit? 853 1
We *r* truths to be taught by the Holy Spirit 853 3

recognizing
we receive it improperly, not *r* the Lord's Body. 316 25

recompense
Let this be the *r* from the LORD to my accusers, * 752 14

reconcile
to live and die as one of us, to *r* us to you, 362 13
Almighty God, you sent your Son Jesus Christ to *r* 838 1

reconciled
Christ *r* us to himself and gave us the ministry 106 3
were *r* by penitence and forgiveness, 265 5
and man is *r* to God. 287 22
And then, being *r* with one another, come 317 9
first be *r* to thy brother, 343 19
By his blood, he *r* us. 370 21
first be *r* to your brother, 376 15
enable us all to stand *r* before you; 816 8
freed from the power of sin and *r* to God. 850 9

reconciler
use this oil, and be among us as a healer and *r*. 561 6

reconciliation
and gave us the ministry of *r*. 106 4
hast established the new covenant of *r*: 172 2
hast established the new covenant of *r*: 172 21
give itself continually to prayer and to the *r* 193 20
mystery established the new covenant of *r*: 223 16
mystery established the new covenant of *r*: 224 14
give itself continually to prayer and to the *r* 245 6
mystery established the new covenant of *r*: 290 15
r, declaring pardon in your Name, 521 12
Christ's work of *r* in the world; 855 18
in Christ's name for the *r* of the world 855 26
r of a penitent, and unction. 860 11
What is *R* of a Penitent? 861 8
R of a Penitent, or Penance, is the rite 861 9

reconciling
r love of Christ may be known 532 11

record
Let us hear the *r* of God's saving deeds in history, 288 1
the *r* of your mighty works; 562 13
The LORD will *r* as he enrolls the peoples, * 711 22

recorded
are they not *r* in your book? 663 8

recount
My mouth shall *r* your mighty acts 684 9
We will *r* to generations to come 695 4

recounting
and *r* all your wonderful deeds. 616 21

recovery
strengthen them in the work of their *r*; 831 22

rector
who has been chosen to serve as *R* of 559 2
for this congregation, and for N. their *R*. 560 2
Greet your new *R*. 563 11
choose a bishop for this Diocese (or, *r* 818 10

red
drowned in the *R* Sea. 85 11
and led them through the *R* Sea on dry land. 287 8
they defied the Most High at the *R* Sea. 742 13
He rebuked the *R* Sea, and it dried up, * 742 16
and fearful things at the *R* Sea. 743 16
Who divided the *R* Sea in two, * 790 21
But swept Pharaoh and his army into the *R* Sea, * 790 25

redeem
that to *r* a slave, you gave a Son. 287 15
Because thou didst send thy beloved Son to *r* us 345 8
Because you sent your beloved Son to *r* us 378 4
And he shall *r* Israel * 474 16
r me, O LORD and have pity on me. 617 4
Draw near to me and *r* me; * 680 27
He shall *r* their lives from oppression and violence, * 686 11
Plead my cause and *r* me; * 776 11
and he shall *r* Israel from all their sins. 785 9
R all our days by this victory; 835 3

redeemed
for he hath visited and *r* his people; 50 23
whom thou hast *r* with thy precious blood. 53 20
With your constant love you led the people you *r*; * 85 21
for with your blood you have *r* for God, 94 2
for you have *r* me, 129 19
For you have *r* me, O Lord, O God of truth. 132 13
r with thy most precious blood, 148 12
r by his blood, may share with her the glory 192 3
Grant, Almighty God, that we, who have been *r* 203 12
r by his blood, may share with her the glory 243 10
Grant, Almighty God, that we, who have been *r* 254 13
which you have *r* us through your Son 271 6
because by your holy cross you have *r* the world. 281 16
because by your holy cross you have *r* the world. 282 2
who by thy cross and precious blood hast *r* us: 282 4
And so, Father, we who have been *r* by him, 371 6
r by the blood of your Christ. 375 13
and *r* me from sin and death by the cross 450 9
in whom you have *r* the world, 450 20

by your cross and precious blood you have *r* us; 455 17
In the Name of Jesus Christ who *r* you; 464 23
for you have *r* me, 622 18
and so will my soul, which you have *r*. 685 5
the tribe you *r* to be your inheritance, 689 12
By your strength you have *r* your people, * 694 3
and *r* them from the hand of the enemy. 742 19
Let all those whom the LORD has *r* proclaim * 746 3
that he *r* them from the hand of the foe. 746 4
O God, you made us in your own image and *r* us 815 13

redeemer

O Lord, my strength and my *r*. 40 15
O Lord, my strength and my *r*. 78 14
O God the Son, *R* of the world, 148 3
greet with joy the coming of Jesus Christ our *R*; 159 13
joyfully receive him for our *R*, 160 14
greet with joy the coming of Jesus Christ our *R*; 211 13
joyfully receive him as our *R*, 212 12
kneel before the Lord, our maker and *r*. 265 15
the Virgin Mary, to be the Savior and *R* of the world. 368 6
Almighty God, our Creator and our *R*. 450 7
Jesus, *r* of the world: 463 27
I know that my *R* liveth, 469 4
As for me, I know that my *R* lives 491 7
through Jesus Christ, our Mediator and *R*. 505 9
O LORD, my strength and my *r*. 607 30
and the Most High God their *r*. 697 21

redeeming

that we may behold him in all his *r* work; 171 19
that we may behold him in all his *r* work; 173 7
not known the *r* work of our Savior Jesus Christ; 206 19
that we may behold him in all his *r* work; 223 12
that we may behold him in all his *r* work; 224 21
grace to receive thankfully the fruits of his *r* work, 232 13
known the *r* work of our Savior Jesus Christ; 257 15
a sinner of your own *r*. 465 4
a sinner of thine own *r*. 483 9
a sinner of your own *r*. 499 16

redeems

He *r* your life from the grave * 733 15

redemption

in the *r* of the world by our Lord Jesus Christ, 58 22
in the *r* of the world by our Lord Jesus Christ, 71 18
in the *r* of the world by our Lord Jesus Christ; 101 14
in *r* of the world by our Lord Jesus Christ; 125 12
O God, who for our *r* didst give 170 7
who glory in the mystery of our *r*, 192 16
perceive within ourselves the fruit of his *r*; 201 5
agony and shame of the cross for our *r*: 201 8
O God, who for our *r* gave 222 1
who glory in the mystery of our *r*, 244 4
perceive within ourselves the fruit of his *r*; 252 10
and shame of the cross for our *r*: 252 13
will bring each of us to the fullness of *r*. 288 3
Almighty God, who for our *r* gave 295 1
and for the *r* of the world 316 12
suffer death upon the cross for our *r*; 334 11
suffer death upon the cross for our *r*. 341 16
We celebrate the memorial of our *r*, 363 10
Remembering now his work of *r*, 371 19
Father, we now celebrate this memorial of our *r*. 374 24
Jesus Christ, the pledge of our *r*; 399 9
this memorial of our *r*. 405 14
Jesus Christ, the pledge of our *r*; 457 7
and with him is plenteous *r*. 474 15
with them the sacraments of our *r*? 518 16
He sent *r* to his people; 754 22
With him there is plenteous *r*, * 785 8
perceive within ourselves the fruit of thy *r*; 834 16
sin and our need for *r*. 848 27
What is *r*? 849 4
R is the act of God which sets us free 849 5
How did God prepare us for *r*? 849 7
show us our need for *r*, 849 9
also the benefits of *r*. 850 16
this life, for our *r*, and for whatever draws us 857 9
the Covenant, membership in Christ, and *r* 858 26

redemptive

r love known, by your word and example, 543 10

reeds

Rebuke the wild beast of the *r*, * 678 18

reeled

The earth *r* and rocked; * 603 1
they *r* because of his anger. 603 3
They *r* and staggered like drunkards * 748 9

reeling

send them *r* by your might 666 19

refined

like silver *r* from ore 597 14

reflect

Let his life and teaching so *r* your commandments, 545 14

reform

where it is in amiss, *r* it. 816 13

refrain

R from anger, leave rage alone; * 633 21

refrained

I *r* from rash words; 638 20

refresh

I will *r* you. 332 9
I will *r* you. 449 14

refreshed

at this holy Table may be fed and *r* 574 5
you *r* the land when it was weary. 676 22
like a warrior *r* with wine. 700 10

refreshing

sleep for the *r* of soul and body: 461 13
r us day by day with the bread of life. 578 17

refreshment

That it may please you to grant him a place of *r* 463 17
course in faith, now find rest and *r*. 503 16
but you brought us out into a place of *r*. 674 19
give us times of *r* and peace; 825 2

refuge
The Lord is my strength and my *r*; * 85 3
In you, O Lord, have I taken *r*; 129 8
"You are my *r* and my stronghold, * 129 24
and you shall find *r* under his wings; * 130 4
Because you have made the Lord your *r*, * 130 15
the God of Jacob is our *r*. 472 8
Lord, thou hast been our *r* * 472 9
who take *r* in him! 587 2
But all who take *r* in you will be glad; * 589 17
O LORD my God, I take *r* in you; * 590 20
The LORD will be a *r* for the oppressed, * 593 17
a *r* in time of trouble. 593 18
In the LORD have I taken *r*; * 596 7
but the LORD is their *r*. 598 27
Protect me, O God, for I take *r* in you; * 599 19
O Savior of those who take *r* at your right hand 601 12
my shield, the horn of my salvation, and my *r*; 602 10
a safe *r* for his anointed. 620 2
In you, O LORD, have I taken *r*; 622 7
your people take *r* under the shadow 632 18
because they seek *r* in him. 636 19
God is our *r* and strength, * 649 1
he is known to be her sure *r*. 651 7
"This is the one who did not take God for a *r*, * 658 13
for I have taken *r* in you; * 663 20
in the shadow of your wings will I take *r* 663 21
a *r* in the day of my trouble. 667 6
to be a *r* from the power of the bow. 667 17
For you have been my *r*, * 668 17
I will take *r* under the cover of your wings. 668 20
God is my strong rock and my *r*. 669 21
pour out your hearts before him, for God is our *r*. 669 23
In you, O LORD, have I taken *r*; * 683 1
but you are my *r* and my strength. 683 15
I have made the Lord GOD my *r*. 689 6
Lord, you have been our *r* * 717 20
"You are my *r* and my stronghold, * 719 13
and you shall find *r* under his wings; * 719 18
Because you have made the LORD your *r*, * 720 3
The high hills are a *r* for the mountain goats, * 736 13
You are my *r* and shield; * 773 1
in you I take *r*; 797 20
I say, "You are my *r*, 798 10
for I flee to you for *r*. 799 20

refugees
r, prisoners, and all who are in danger; 390 25
r, prisoners, and all who are in danger; 550 12

refuse
Since you *r* discipline, * 655 14

refused
I *r* to be comforted. 693 5
and *r* to walk in his law; 695 23
They *r* the pleasant land * 743 20

regard
my own peace I leave with you:" *R* not our sins, 107 18
my own peace I leave with you:" *R* not our sins, 138 17
my own peace I leave with you:" *R* not our sins, 395 9
dwelling on high but having *r* for the lowly, 520 12
the Lord will have *r* for me. 641 20
those who have no *r* for God. 659 23
when I *r* all your commandments. 763 16
Renew the ties of mutual *r* which form our civic life. 825 9

regarded
For he hath *r* * 50 3
For he hath *r* * 65 6

regards
Who *r* the power of your wrath? * 718 23

regenerate
Grant that we, being *r* and made thy children 161 9

regular
And to set aside *r* times for worship, 847 26

reign
The Lord shall *r* * 85 28
for you live and *r* for ever and ever. 107 15
you live and *r*, now and for ever. 107 21
you live and *r* for ever and ever. 111 15
you live and *r*, now and for ever. 138 20
live and *r*, one God, for ever and ever. 228 7
for you live and *r*, one God, now and for ever. 251 5
if we endure, we shall also *r* with him. 281 18
live and *r*, one God, now and for ever. 282 12
r with him in glory. 347 5
r with him in glory. 379 24
you live and *r*, now and for ever. 395 12
you live and *r* in perfect unity, 430 8
you live and *r*, one God, for ever and ever. 464 19
you live and *r*, one God, for ever and ever. 466 19
and where you live and *r* with the Father 498 6
The LORD shall *r* for ever, * 803 24
for you *r* with the Father 819 11
who live and *r* with the Father 834 10

reignest
livest and *r*, one God, for ever and ever. 176 8
who livest and *r*, one God, now and for ever. 199 16
livest and *r*, one God, now and for ever. 489 29
who livest and *r* with the Father 834 16

reigneth
and where he liveth and *r* for ever and ever. 69 5
him who liveth and *r* with thee 159 7
who liveth and *r* with thee 159 13
who liveth and *r* with thee, 160 9
liveth and *r*, one God, in glory everlasting. 161 5
liveth and *r* with thee and the same Spirit ever, 161 12
who liveth and *r* with thee, 161 17
who liveth and *r* with thee 162 5
liveth and *r*, one God, in glory everlasting. 163 6
liveth and *r*, one God, now and for ever. 163 12
who liveth and *r* with thee 163 18
who liveth and *r* with thee 164 4
who liveth and *r* with thee 165 4
who liveth and *r* with thee 166 7
liveth and *r*, one God, for ever and ever. 167 2
who liveth and *r* with thee 167 8
who liveth and *r* with thee 168 8
who liveth and *r* with thee 169 5

who now liveth and *r* with thee 169 12
who now liveth and *r* with thee 170 5
who liveth and *r* with thee 171 3
who liveth and *r* with thee 172 6
who liveth and *r* with thee 173 3
liveth and *r*, one God, for ever and ever. 173 14
who liveth and *r* with thee 174 6
who liveth and *r* with thee 175 6
who liveth and *r* with thee 177 1
who liveth and *r* with thee 178 4
who liveth and *r* with thee 179 2
who liveth and *r* with thee 180 6
who liveth and *r* with thee 181 3
liveth and *r*, one God, now and for ever. 182 4
who liveth and *r* with thee 182 10
who liveth and *r* with thee 183 4
who liveth and *r* with thee 184 5
he liveth and *r* ever, one God, world without end. 184 14
who liveth and *r* with thee 185 5
where he liveth and *r* with thee 186 4
who liveth and *r* with thee 186 11
who liveth and *r* with thee 187 6
who liveth and *r* with thee, 188 5
who liveth and *r* with thee 189 3
who liveth and *r* with thee 190 8
who liveth and *r*, one God, now and for ever. 191 6
who liveth and *r* with thee 191 13
O Holy Ghost, liveth and *r*, one God, 191 20
who liveth and *r* with thee, 192 5
who liveth and *r* with thee 193 2
who liveth and *r* with thee 194 6
who with thee and the Holy Spirit liveth and *r*, 194 14
who liveth and *r* with thee 195 6
who liveth and *r* with thee 196 5
who liveth and *r* with thee 197 2
who with thee and the same Spirit liveth and *r*, 197 17
who liveth and *r* with thee, 198 6
liveth and *r*, one God, now and for ever. 198 14
who liveth and *r* with thee 199 2
who liveth and *r* for ever and ever. 199 11
who liveth and *r* with thee, 200 4
who liveth and *r* with thee 201 5
who liveth and *r* with thee, 202 7
who liveth and *r* with thee 203 3
who liveth *r* with thee, 204 6
who liveth and *r* with thee, 205 2
who liveth and *r* with thee, 206 7
who liveth and *r* with thee 207 6
who liveth and *r* with thee, 208 7
who with thee and the Holy Spirit liveth and *r*, 208 14
who liveth and *r* with thee 209 7
who liveth and *r* with thee 210 8
who liveth and *r* with thee 470 5
who liveth and *r* with thee 481 28
who liveth and *r* with thee 820 24

reigning

living and *r* for ever and ever. 110 27

reigns

and where he lives and *r* for ever and ever. 123 5
who lives and *r* with you 211 7
who lives and *r* with you, 212 8
who lives and *r*, one God, in glory everlasting. 212 20
who lives and *r* with you, 213 11
who lives and *r* with you, 214 4
lives and *r*, one God, in glory everlasting. 214 17
lives and *r*, one God, now and for ever. 215 6
who lives and *r* with you 215 11
who lives and *r* with you, 216 3
who lives and *r* with you 217 5
who lives and *r* with you 218 5
who with you and the Holy Spirit lives and *r*, 218 11
who lives and *r* with you 219 4
who lives and *r* with you 220 6
who lives and *r* with you 221 6
who now lives and *r* with you 221 17
who lives and *r* with you 222 6
who lives and *r* with you 223 2
who lives and *r* with you 224 5
who lives and *r* with you, 225 1
lives and *r*, one God, for ever and ever. 225 6
who lives and *r* with you 226 6
who lives and *r* with you, 227 5
who lives and *r* with you 228 12
who lives and *r* with you 229 3
who lives and *r* with you 230 5
who lives and *r* with you 231 2
who lives and *r* with you 232 4
who lives and *r* with you 233 1
who lives and *r* with you 234 4
who lives and *r* with you 235 1
where he lives and *r* with you 236 6
who lives and *r* with you 236 12
who lives and *r* with you 237 6
where he lives and *r* with you 237 17
who lives and *r* with you 238 5
who lives and *r* with you, 239 4
who lives *r* with you, 240 5
who lives and *r* with you 241 1
who lives and *r* with you 242 6
who lives and *r*, one God, now and for ever. 242 13
lives and *r*, one God, for ever and ever. 243 6
who lives and *r* with you, 243 12
who lives and *r* with you 244 5
who lives and *r* with you, 245 2
lives and *r*, one God, in glory everlasting. 245 22
who lives and *r* with you 246 6
who lives and *r* with you 247 4
who lives and *r* with you 248 6
who with you and the Holy Spirit lives and *r*, 249 3
who lives and *r* with you 249 9
who lives and *r* with you 250 6
and who lives and *r* for ever and ever. 250 20
who lives and *r* with you, 251 10
who lives and *r* with you, 252 4
who lives and *r* with you, 253 4
who lives and *r* with you 254 5
who lives and *r* with you, 255 4
who lives and *r* with you, 256 8
who lives and *r* with you, 257 3
who lives and *r* with you 258 6
who lives and *r* with you 259 1
lives and *r*, one God, for ever and ever. 259 16

who lives and *r* with you	260	6
who lives and *r* with you	261	5
who lives and *r* with you	264	8
who lives and *r* in glory with you	271	13
who lives and *r* with you	272	13
who lives and *r* with you	274	6
who now lives and *r* with you	276	7
who lives and *r* with you,	280	22
who now lives and *r* with you	283	5
who lives and *r* with him,	286	14
who lives and *r* for ever and ever.	287	27
who lives and *r* with you	295	6
who lives and *r* now and for ever.	306	8
who lives and *r* with you	307	13
who lives and *r* with you	309	10
who lives and *r* with you	311	19
who lives and *r* for ever and ever.	395	24
who lives and *r* for ever and ever.	397	18
who lives and *r* with you	418	8
who lives and *r* with you	425	12
who lives and *r*, one God, for ever and ever.	430	25
who lives and *r* with you	431	7
who lives and *r* with you	455	14
where he lives and *r* for ever and ever.	460	8
who with you and the Holy Spirit lives and *r*,	493	8
who lives and *r* with you	493	14
who lives and *r* with you	494	5
who lives and *r* with you,	515	12
who lives and *r* with you	523	9
who lives and *r* with you,	528	10
lives and *r*, one God, for ever and ever.	534	9
who lives and *r* with you	535	9
who lives and *r* with you,	540	10
lives and *r*, one God, for ever and ever.	545	18
who lives and *r* with you	547	5
through him who lives and *r* with you	560	9
who lives and *r* with you	564	9
God *r* over the nations; *	650	20
who lives and *r* with you	817	1
where he now *r* with the Father	850	20

rein

He gave full *r* to his anger;	699	4

reject

Arise! do not *r* us for ever.	647	4

rejected

In his sight the wicked is *r*, *	599	11
Nevertheless, you have *r* and humbled us *	646	3
they are put to shame, because God has *r* them.	659	13
Blessed be God, who has not *r* my prayer, *	675	7
and utterly *r* Israel.	699	25
He *r* the tent of Joseph *	700	13
LORD, why have you *r* me? *	713	6
But you have cast off and *r* your anointed; *	716	17
The same stone which the builders *r* *	762	15
from speaking in hate; when they are *r*, save them	823	11

rejection

by hell, we mean eternal death in our *r* of God.	862	7

rejoice

we will *r* and be glad in it.	39	9
let us heartily *r* in the strength of our salvation.	44	11
may, when the night cometh, *r* to give thee thanks;	56	23
we will *r* and be glad in it.	77	8
when night comes, *r* to give you thanks;	99	18
r in the liberty of the children of God;	111	10
let us heartily *r* in the strength of our salvation.	146	2
abide in his presence and *r* in the hope	171	13
and evermore to *r* in his holy comfort;	175	18
r in her triumph may profit by her example;	196	4
abide in his presence and *r* in the hope	223	7
and evermore to *r* in his holy comfort;	227	11
r in her triumph may profit by her example;	247	16
that the body you have broken may *r*.	266	19
R now, heavenly hosts and choirs of angels,	286	1
R and sing now, all the round earth,	286	4
R and be glad now, Mother Church,	286	7
that your Church may *r* to see	289	8
and *r* in the inheritance of Israel;	289	17
we may without shame or fear *r*	345	11
r in the splendor of your radiance.	373	6
we may without shame or fear *r*	378	7
that we might *r* in their fellowship,	380	13
and *r* in the gladness of thy people,	478	21
and *r* in his eternal glory;	493	7
and always *r* in your glory;	523	8
and always *r* in your glory;	535	8
and always *r* in your glory;	547	4
and always *r* in your glory;	564	8
to *r* and give thanks.	568	18
I will be glad and *r* in you; *	593	3
and *r* in your salvation *	594	5
and my foes *r* that I have fallen.	598	7
Jacob will *r* and Israel be glad.	599	3
and *r* the heart; *	607	9
I will *r* and be glad because of your mercy; *	622	22
Be glad, you righteous, and *r* in the LORD; *	625	25
R in the LORD, you righteous; *	626	1
let the humble hear and *r*.	627	24
Do not let my treacherous foes *r* over me, *	631	6
Let all who *r* at my ruin be ashamed and disgraced; *	631	24
For I said, "Do not let them *r* at my expense, *	638	1
Let all who seek you *r* in you and be glad; *	641	16
and the cities of Judah *r*, *	651	24
that the body you have broken may *r*.	656	23
Jacob will *r* and Israel be glad.	659	16
and under the shadow of your wings I will *r*.	670	26
But the king will *r* in God;	671	7
The righteous will *r* in the LORD	672	5
But let the righteous be glad and *r* before God; *	676	6
YAHWEH is his Name, *r* before him!	676	10
Let all who seek you *r* and be glad in you; *	682	19
But I will *r* for ever; *	691	22
my heart and my flesh *r* in the living God.	707	18
that your people may *r* in you?	709	6
Tabor and Hermon *r* in your Name.	714	18
They *r* daily in your Name; *	714	25
and made all his enemies *r*.	716	26
so shall we *r* and be glad all the days of our life.	719	2
and my ears *r* to hear the doom of the wicked who	721	19

Let the heavens *r*, and let the earth be glad; 726 14
let the earth *r*; * 726 23
Zion hears and is glad, and the cities of Judah *r*, * 727 12
R in the LORD, you righteous, * 727 22
lift up your voice, *r*, and sing. 728 11
may the LORD *r* in all his works. 737 17
I will *r* in the LORD. 737 23
let the hearts of those who seek the LORD *r*. 738 6
The upright will see this and *r*, * 749 13
and your servant will *r*. 753 5
we will *r* and be glad in it. 762 20
and her faithful people will *r* and sing. 787 4
Let Israel *r* in his Maker; * 807 4
Let the faithful *r* in triumph; * 807 10
to *r* in other people's gifts 848 19

rejoiced

and my spirit hath *r* in God my Savior. 50 2
and my spirit hath *r* in God my Savior. 65 5
and there we *r* in him. 674 5

rejoices

my spirit *r* in God my Savior; * 91 28
my spirit *r* in God my Savior; * 119 5
my spirit *r* in God my Savior; * 441 13
My heart, therefore, is glad, and my spirit *r*; 501 6
My heart, therefore, is glad, and my spirit *r*; * 600 15
it *r* like a champion to run its course. 606 25
The king *r* in your strength, O LORD; * 608 21
Indeed, our heart *r* in him, * 627 17

rejoiceth

Wherefore my heart is glad, and my spirit *r*; 485 4

rejoicing

Therefore you shall draw water with *r* * 86 5
r in the knowledge of thy truth, 209 19
r in the knowledge of your truth, 261 3
that, *r* in thy whole creation, they may honor 329 23
Let us go forth into the world, *r* 340 3
that we, *r* in their fellowship, 347 18
r in the power of the Spirit. 366 19
R in the fellowship of [the ever-blessed Virgin Mary, 391 19
r in the Christian community. 440 3
Now there is *r* in heaven; 451 17
r in your goodness, may so order his life 460 21
Let us go forth into the world, *r* 523 18
Let us go forth into the world, *r* 535 13
r in the power of the Spirit. 547 8
R in the fellowship of [the ever-blessed Virgin Mary, 550 26
that, *r* in thy whole creation, we may learn 814 3
r in your goodness; 824 9

related

How are the sacraments *r* to our Christian hope? 861 21

relationship

witness the inauguration of this new *r*. 440 16
A covenant is a *r* initiated by God, 846 21
define our *r* with God and our neighbors. 848 24
thus distorting our *r* with God, 848 30
our *r* with God is distorted. 849 3
The New Covenant is the new *r* with God 850 27

release

r you from suffering, and restore you to wholeness 456 16
When any are held unjustly, bring them *r*; 826 21

released

The king sent and *r* him; * 739 17

relented

and *r* in accordance with his great mercy. 745 16

relied

and *r* upon wickedness." 658 15

relief

obtained effectually, to the *r* of our necessity, 153 24
and substance for the *r* of the poor 189 20
the *r* of all who are in need, 194 20
and substance for the *r* of the poor 241 6
the *r* of all who are in need, 246 5
both *r* from pain and hope of health 460 18
effectually be obtained, to the *r* of our necessity, 834 6

relieve

r thy sick servants, and give thy power of healing 208 17
r your sick servants, and give your power of healing 260 2
That God in his mercy will comfort and *r* them, 279 11
r thy sick servant N. for whom our prayers 458 3
R his pain, guard him from all danger, 459 3
r your sick servant N. and give your power of healing 459 18
that it may please thee to comfort and *r* 815 9

relieved

be *r* and protected, 390 26
be *r* and protected, 550 13

religion

increase in us true *r*, nourish us with all goodness, 181 13
increase in us true *r*; nourish us with all goodness; 233 5

religious

in the comfort of a reasonable, *r*, and holy hope; 489 11
in the comfort of a *r* and holy hope, 504 8

rely

For I do not *r* on my bow, * 645 23
It is better to *r* on the LORD * 761 11
And finally, teach our people to *r* on your strength 822 10

remain

be amongst you, and *r* with you always. 339 19
be upon you and *r* with you for ever. 339 21
and *r* in the uttermost parts of the sea; 475 10
and *r* with you for ever. 523 17
be among you, and *r* with you always. 535 12
May his Name *r* for ever, 686 21
they shall not *r* with me. 730 14

remains

Your faithfulness *r* from one generation to another; * 770 22

remember

and to *r* his holy covenant; 51 4
but may *r* that we are ever walking in thy sight; 57 17
see that they *r* that his Name is exalted. 86 10
and to *r* his holy covenant. 92 26
but may *r* that we are ever walking in your sight; 100 9

R not, Lord Christ, our offenses, 148 9
R, O Lord, what thou hast wrought 176 9
We *r* this day, O God, the slaughter 186 13
O gracious God, we *r* before thee this day 191 7
Grant us, who now *r* him with thanksgiving, 195 10
Almighty God, we *r* this day before thee 202 9
R the multitudes who have been created 206 17
R, O Lord, what you have wrought 228 9
We *r* today, O God, the slaughter 238 7
O gracious God, we *r* before you today 242 14
Grant us, who now *r* him in thanksgiving, 247 8
Almighty God, we *r* before you today 253 13
R the multitudes who have been created 257 13
that we may *r* that it is only by your gracious gift 265 18
R that you are dust, and to dust you shall return. 265 21
r the dignity of that holy Sacrament. 316 19
R that thou keep holy the Sabbath day. 318 10
R the Sabbath day and keep it holy. 350 9
We *r* his death, 368 20
R, Lord, your one holy catholic 375 12
[*R* (NN. and) all who minister in your Church.] 375 15
[*R* all your people, and those who seek your truth.] 375 16
[*R* ________.] 375 17
[*R* all who have died in the peace of Christ, 375 18
If you are offering your gift at the altar, and there *r* 376 13
and for all who *r* and care for them, 384 27
[especially ________ whom we *r* 386 15
and all other sins which I cannot now *r*, 447 8
r in truth all your sins and his unfailing mercy. 449 11
and all other sins I cannot now *r*, 450 17
R them, Lord, in mercy; 467 4
R me, O Lord, according to the favor 478 17
and *r* him according to the favor 481 18
R thy servant, O Lord, according to the favor 488 21
O God of grace and glory, we *r* before you 493 16
The Avenger of blood will *r* them; * 593 23
R all your offerings * 608 5
All the ends of the earth shall *r* 612 10
R, O Lord, your compassion and love, * 614 24
R not the sins of my youth and my transgressions; * 615 1
r me according to your love, 615 2
therefore I will *r* you from the land of Jordan, 643 19
When I *r* you upon my bed, * 670 23
R your congregation that you purchased long ago, * 689 11
R, O Lord, how the enemy scoffed, * 690 20
r how fools revile you all day long. 690 29
I *r* the years long past; 693 11
I will *r* the works of the Lord, * 693 22
They would *r* that God was their rock, * 697 20
They did not *r* his power * 698 11
R not our past sins; 701 21
Whom you *r* no more, * 712 11
R, Lord, how short life is, * 717 8
R, Lord, how your servant is mocked, * 717 14
and *r* his commandments and do them. 734 19
R the marvels he has done, * 738 9
R me, O Lord, with the favor you have 742 3
nor *r* the abundance of your love; * 742 12
Because he did not *r* to show mercy, * 752 1
R your word to your servant, * 767 11
When I *r* your judgments of old, * 767 17
I *r* your Name in the night, O Lord, * 767 23
Lord, *r* David, * 785 19
if I do not *r* you, * 792 13
R the day of Jerusalem, O Lord, 792 15
I *r* the time past; 799 7
Heavenly Father, we *r* before you those who suffer 824 11
Almighty and most merciful God, we *r* before you 826 1
R all prisoners, and bring the guilty to repentance 826 18
R those who work in these institutions; 826 22
R him, O Lord, in mercy, 831 14
O Judge of the nations, we *r* before you 839 21
Help us to *r* that we are all your children, 841 3

remembered

for he has *r* his promise of mercy, 92 13
for he has *r* his promise of mercy, 119 19
for he has *r* his promise of mercy, 442 8
I will make your name to be *r* 648 25
For he *r* that they were but flesh, * 698 5
let the name of Israel be *r* no more." 706 11
For God *r* his holy word * 741 9
He *r* his covenant with them * 745 15
Let the wickedness of his fathers be *r* 751 24
He makes his marvelous works to be *r*; * 754 12
Who *r* us in our low estate, * 791 15
when we *r* you, O Zion. 792 2

rememberest

If thou bring thy gift to the altar, and there *r* 343 17

remembering

He *r* his mercy hath holpen his servant Israel, * 50 17
He *r* his mercy hath holpen his servant Israel, * 65 20
r the account that we must one day give, 208 12
r the account that we must one day give, 259 13
R now his work of redemption, 371 19
r the account which we must one day give, 827 3

remembers

For in death no one *r* you; * 590 7
He *r* his mercy and faithfulness 728 6
he *r* that we are but dust. 734 10

remembrance

O God, who makest us glad with the weekly *r* 56 1
O God, you make us glad with the weekly *r* 98 19
O God, who makest us glad with the yearly *r* 160 12
in *r* of him who in these holy mysteries giveth 169 10
having his wonderful conversion in *r*, 187 11
receive it thankfully in *r* of Jesus 221 4
having his wonderful conversion in *r*, 239 2
receive it thankfully in *r* of Jesus 274 4
for the continual *r* of the sacrifice of his death, 316 4
the *r* of them is grievous unto us, 331 11
Do this in *r* of me." 335 2
ye shall drink it, in *r* of me." 335 7
having in *r* his blessed passion 335 13
in *r* of his death and passion, 335 22
Take them in *r* that Christ died 338 2
Take and eat this in *r* that Christ died for thee, 338 7
Drink this in *r* that Christ's Blood was shed for thee, 338 11
Do this in *r* of me." 342 4
drink it, in *r* of me." 342 9
having in *r* his blessed passion 342 13
Do this for the *r* of me." 362 22

do this for the *r* of me." 363 5
Take them in *r* that Christ died 365 1
Do this for the *r* of me." 368 13
do this for the *r* of me." 368 18
Do this for the *r* of me." 371 13
do this for the *r* of me." 371 18
Do this for the *r* of me." 374 18
do this for the *r* of me." 374 23
receive it thankfully in *r* of Jesus 397 16
Take them in *r* that Christ died 399 2
Do this for the *r* of me." 403 7
do this for the *r* of me." 403 12
Do this for the *r* of me." 405 5
do this for the *r* of me." 405 10
but in thankful *r* of your great goodness, 505 13
and the *r* of the dead, 567 11
give thanks for the *r* of his holiness. 621 11
to root out the *r* of them from the earth. 628 26
the righteous will be kept in everlasting *r*. 755 16
They shall publish the *r* of your great goodness; * 801 24
for the continual *r* of his life, 859 7

remission

grant you absolution and *r* of all your sins, 42 12
for the *r* of their sins, 51 15
grant you absolution and *r* of all your sins, 63 15
perfect *r* and forgiveness; 166 6
may obtain of you, the God of all mercy, perfect *r* 217 18
may obtain of you, the God of all mercy, perfect *r* 264 6
being penitent, the absolution and *r* 269 7
grant you absolution and *r* of all your sins, 321 15
I acknowledge one Baptism for the *r* of sins; 328 19
for you, and for many, for the *r* of sins. 335 6
we, and all thy whole Church, may obtain *r* 335 28
for you, and for many, for the *r* of sins. 342 8
For the absolution and *r* of our sins and offenses, 385 4

remnant

and the *r* of Hamath will keep your feasts. 692 21

removal

to the *r* of scruple and doubt, 317 14

remove

r from them the fears that beset them; 831 21

removed

therefore shall she not be *r*; * 472 2
so far has he *r* our sins from us. 734 6

rend

R your heart, and not your garments, 38 14
R your hearts and not your garments. 76 13
lest I *r* you and there be none to deliver you. 655 27

render

Almighty God our heavenly Father, to *r* thanks 41 6
R evil to those who spy on me; * 659 26
and *r* justice to the needy. 796 26

rendering

r unto thee most hearty thanks 335 15

renders

in obedience to his command, his Church *r* 316 9

renew

and *r* a right spirit within me. 137 4
Christians continually have to *r* their repentance 265 9
and *r* a right spirit within me. 266 23
and you *r* the earth by your Spirit: 290 9
to *r* the solemn promises and vows of Holy Baptism, 292 4
r your commitment to Jesus Christ? 292 9
Do you *r* you commitment to Jesus Christ? 303 12
and *r* our own baptismal covenant. 303 18
R in these your servants the covenant 309 6
Do you *r* your commitment to Jesus Christ? 415 11
and *r* our own baptismal covenant. 416 5
R in these your servants the covenant 418 4
and be an occasion for us to *r* our trust 498 4
and *r* a right spirit within me. 657 2
and so you *r* the face of the earth. 737 15
leisure to rebuild our bodies and *r* our minds, 825 3
R the ties of mutual regard which form our civic life. 825 9
that it may *r* the face of the earth; 828 4
R us. 839 15

renewal

for pardon only, and not for *r*. 372 6
for the *r* and mission of your Church. 818 3

renewed

may daily be *r* by thy Holy Spirit; 161 10
we, being *r* both in body and mind, may worship thee 170 17
so we may be *r* in the spirit of our minds, 201 14
may be *r* in thy Holy Spirit, 203 14
may daily be *r* by your Holy Spirit; 213 4
we, being *r* both in body and mind, may worship you 222 11
so we may be *r* in the spirit of our minds, 253 2
may be *r* in your Holy Spirit, 254 15
we, being *r* both in body and mind, may worship you 295 11
have *r* their commitment to Christ.] 305 13
Let us now pray for these persons who have *r* 309 1
and in works of mercy, and *r* by thy Word 346 10
works of mercy, and *r* by your Word 379 7
Let us now pray for these persons who have *r* 417 20
his health being *r*, he may bless your holy Name; 458 20
relief from pain and hope of health *r*. 460 19
and your youth is *r* like an eagle's. 733 18

renewing

r the strength of those who are spent, 113 3
share in the *r* of his world. 531 4

renews

The Spirit of the Lord *r* the face of the earth: 81 8

renounce

Do you *r* Satan and all the spiritual forces 302 7
I *r* them. 302 9
Do you *r* the evil powers of this world 302 10
I *r* them. 302 12
Do you *r* all sinful desires that draw you 302 13
I *r* them. 302 15
It is required that we *r* Satan, 858 22

renounced

by which we once *r* Satan 292 5

renown
awesome in *r*, and worker of wonders? 85 18
faithful servant Barnabas, who, seeking not his own *r* 189 18
faithful servant Barnabas, who, seeking not his own *r* 241 4
your *r*, O LORD, endures from age to age. 789 2

renunciation
Do you reaffirm your *r* of evil 292 8
Do you reaffirm your *r* of evil? 303 10
Do you reaffirm your *r* of evil? 415 9

repaid
If I have *r* my friend with evil, * 591 1

repair
r the cracks in it, for it totters. 667 13

repay
How shall I *r* the LORD * 442 19
R them according to their deeds, * 619 14
According to the work of their hands *r* them, * 619 16
The wicked borrow and do not *r*, * 635 1
Those who *r* evil for good slander me, * 638 9
and I shall *r* them. 642 21
for you *r* everyone according to his deeds. 670 11
They *r* evil for good, * 751 6
How shall I *r* the LORD * 759 23

repays
but *r* to the full those who act haughtily. 624 20

repel
in the name of the LORD I will *r* them. 761 16

repent
We are truly sorry and we humbly *r*. 79 17
that they may *r* of their sin and be saved. 91 11
For you, O Lord, are the God of those who *r*, * 91 20
We are truly sorry and we humbly *r*. 116 19
follow his doctrine and holy life, that we may truly *r* 190 4
follow his teaching and holy life, that we may truly *r* 241 13
r, and with sincere hearts believe his holy Gospel. 269 9
you fall into sin, *r* and return to the Lord? 293 24
you fall into sin, *r* and return to the Lord? 304 27
We are truly sorry and we humbly *r*. 320 17
Ye who do truly and earnestly *r* you of your sins, 330 9
We do earnestly *r*, 331 9
We are truly sorry and we humbly *r*. 331 28
We are truly sorry and we humbly *r*. 352 17
We are truly sorry and we humbly *r*. 360 9
We are truly sorry and we humbly *r*. 398 1
you fall into sin, *r* and return to the Lord? 417 9
absolve all sinners who truly *r* and believe in him, 448 2
absolve all sinners who truly *r* and believe in him, 451 12
We are truly sorry and we humbly *r*. 454 8
If they will not *r*, God will whet his sword; * 591 22
and *r*, and diligently search for God. 697 19
It is required that we renounce Satan, *r* of our sins, 858 22
examine our lives, *r* of our sins, 860 5
which those who *r* of their sins may confess them 861 10

repentance
remission of all your sins, true *r*, 42 12
remission of all your sins, true *r*, 63 15
That it may please thee to give us true *r*; 152 3
preach *r* and prepare the way for our salvation: 159 10
the way of thy Son our Savior by preaching *r*: 190 3
preach *r* and prepare the way for our salvation: 211 10
the way of your Son our Savior by preaching *r*: 241 12
Christians continually have to renew their *r* and faith. 265 9
a holy Lent, by self-examination and *r*; 265 11
And, to make a right beginning of *r*, 265 14
Accept our *r*, Lord, for the wrongs we have done: 268 16
Accept our *r*, Lord. 268 19
Therefore we beseech him to grant us true *r* 269 10
remission of all your sins, true *r*, 321 15
hearty *r* and true faith turn unto him, 332 3
now remember, I turn to you in sorrow and *r*. 450 17
who in faith and *r* receive this holy unction 455 12
and seriousness to his *r*; 460 3
Remember all prisoners, and bring the guilty to *r* 826 18

repented
You promised paradise to the thief who *r*; 497 13

repenteth
of great kindness, and *r* him of the evil. 38 16

repents
abounding in steadfast love, and *r* of evil. 76 15

repose
strength of those who labor, and the *r* of the dead: 70 5
strength of those who labor, and the *r* of the dead: 124 2

represent
The ministry of lay persons is to *r* Christ 855 15
The ministry of a bishop is to *r* Christ 855 22
The ministry of a priest is to *r* Christ 856 2
The ministry of a deacon is to *r* Christ 856 8

representatives
For the Members and *R* of the United Nations 278 21
and bless our Senators and *R* in Congress 821 3
To Senators and *R*, and those who make our laws 822 1
in the election of officials and *r*; 822 25

represented
that in it is *r* the spiritual unity between Christ 431 2

reproach
without suffering and without *r*, let us pray 385 8
exercise without *r* the high priesthood 521 10
serve without *r*, so that your people may 534 6
I have become a *r* to all my enemies 623 10
Surely, for your sake have I suffered *r*, * 680 1
but that was turned to my *r*. 680 8
You know my *r*, my shame, and my dishonor; * 681 1
R has broken my heart, and it cannot be healed; * 681 3
be covered with scorn and *r*. 684 6
We have become a *r* to our neighbors, * 701 11
I have become a *r* to them; * 752 25
Turn away the *r* which I dread, * 766 13

request
you have not denied him the *r* of his lips. 608 24

requests
may the LORD grant all your *r*. 608 11

require
I *r* and charge you both, here in the presence of God, 424 4
I *r*, therefore, that you promise, 433 2
One thing have I desired of the LORD, which I will *r*, * 477 16
What response did God *r* from the chosen people? 847 3
What response did Christ *r*? 851 4

required
Burnt-offering and sin-offering you have not *r*, * 640 18
God *r* the chosen people to be faithful; 847 4
What is *r* of us at Baptism? 858 21
It is *r* that we renounce Satan, 858 22
What is *r* of us when we come to the Eucharist? 860 4
It is *r* that we should examine our lives, 860 5
What is *r* of those to be confirmed? 860 22
It is *r* of those to be confirmed 860 23

requirements
We certify to you that he has satisfied the *r* 526 7
We certify to you that he has satisfied the *r* 538 7

rescue
I will *r* him and bring him to honor. 131 3
let him *r* him, if he delights in him." 610 17
r me from the hand of my enemies, 623 23
r me from the roaring beasts, 631 2
The LORD will help them and *r* them; * 636 17
he will *r* them from the wicked and deliver them, 636 18
R me from my enemies, O God; * 665 18
R me from evildoers * 665 20
he shall *r* the poor and crush the oppressor. 685 16
R the weak and the poor; * 705 15
I will *r* him and bring him to honor. 720 19
R me from those who oppress me, * 774 15
r me and deliver me from the great waters, 800 15
R me from the hurtful sword * 800 23

rescued
he *r* me because he delighted in me. 604 2
You *r* me from the fury of my enemies; 606 7
For you have *r* me from every trouble, * 660 3
For you have *r* my soul from death and my feet 663 16
let me be *r* from those who hate me 680 18
For you have *r* my life from death, * 759 16
and have *r* David your servant. 800 22

residue
the *r* of his life in thy fear, and to thy glory; 458 8

resist
R him, firm in your faith. 132 10
seeing that, as thou dost alway *r* the proud 181 18
you always *r* the proud who confide in their own 233 10
turn the hearts of those who *r* it; 280 5
To *r* temptations to envy, 848 18

resisting
Will you persevere in *r* evil, 293 23
Will you persevere in *r* evil, 304 26
Will you persevere in *r* evil, 417 8

resort
they do not *r* to evil spirits or turn to false gods. 640 10

resound
r with the praises of your people. 286 9

resounding
Praise him with *r* cymbals; * 808 7

resources
use its *r* rightly in the service of others 388 13
and reverence so to use the *r* of nature, 827 19
We thank you for the great *r* of this nation. 839 1

respect
and *r* the dignity of every human being? 294 2
and *r* the dignity of every human being? 305 8
For the peace of the world, that a spirit of *r* 390 13
and *r* the dignity of every human being? 417 18
Will you *r* and be guided by the pastoral direction 532 1
For the peace of the world, that a spirit of *r* 549 29
give grace to *r* their witness 823 13
together with mutual forbearance and *r*; 824 4
r those who labor to produce them, 825 22
It means that all people are worthy of *r* 846 14
To show God *r* in thought, word, and deed; 847 24
To show *r* for the life God has given us; 848 7

respond
all can *r* to the love of God. 846 16

responding
Prayer is *r* to God, by thought and by deeds, 856 18

responds
to which a body of people *r* in faith. 846 22

response
What *r* did God require from the chosen people? 847 3
What *r* did Christ require? 851 4
Christian prayer is *r* to God the Father, 856 21

responsibilities
accept their *r* to their fellow citizens, 822 11

responsibility
thanks for the joyful and solemn *r* 440 13
has approved him for this sacred *r*. 514 5
and the weight of your *r* in presenting 527 2
commit yourself to this trust and *r*? 531 25
and the weight of your *r* in presenting 539 2
commit yourself to this trust and *r*? 543 23
commit yourself to this new trust and *r*? 559 6

responsible
Will you be *r* for seeing that the child you present 302 1

responsive
industries and commerce of this land *r* to thy will; 208 4
industries and commerce of this land *r* to your will; 259 6

rest
who after the creation of the world didst *r* 56 11
and sanctify a day of *r* for all thy creatures: 56 12
that our *r* here upon earth may be a preparation 56 15
the eternal *r* promised to thy people in heaven; 56 16
may pass our time in *r* and quietness; 69 21
give *r* to the weary, bless the dying, 71 3
and sanctified a day of *r* for all your creatures: 99 7

that our r here upon the earth may be a preparation 99 10
the eternal r promised to your people in heaven; 99 11
giving r to the weary, 113 2
give r to the weary, bless the dying, 124 19
and I will give you r. 131 16
and you will find r for your souls. 131 17
this life may r in your eternal changelessness; 133 15
give r to the weary, bless the dying, 134 8
and asleep we may r in peace. 134 17
and asleep we may r in peace. 135 10
for in returning and r we shall be saved; 138 10
that they should not enter into my r. 146 25
those who have served thee here and are now at r, 202 5
those who have served you here and are now at r, 253 9
and that the r of our life hereafter may be pure 269 12
pardon and r to the dead; 282 9
Give to the departed eternal r; 387 17
they may have r in that place where there is no pain 391 17
that he may r with all your saints 464 17
May your r be this day in peace, 464 25
into the blessed r of everlasting peace, 465 5
mercy of God, r in peace. 465 8
and I will give you r." 465 11
that he may r from his labors, 465 12
God's eternal sabbath r. 465 13
and taste the blessedness of perfect r. 466 2
that he may r with all your saints 466 17
for they r from their labors. 469 15
Turn again then unto thy r, O my soul, * 479 12
Give r, O Christ, to thy servant(s) with thy saints, 482 9
Give r, O Christ, to thy servant(s) with thy saints, 483 3
into the blessed r of everlasting peace, 483 10
my flesh also shall r in hope. 485 5
Multiply, we beseech thee, to those who r 486 9
R eternal grant to him, O Lord: 486 17
through the mercy of God, r in peace. 486 20
do now r from their labors. 488 6
pardon and r to the dead, 489 26
for they r from their labors. 492 4
Grant to them eternal r. 498 9
departed, through the mercy of God, r in peace. 498 11
Give r, O Christ, to your servant(s) with your saints, 499 1
into the blessed r of everlasting peace, 499 17
my body also shall r in hope. 501 7
R eternal grant to him, O Lord; 502 15
through the mercy of God, r in peace. 502 18
now find r and refreshment. 503 16
when we depart this life we may r in him, 505 4
they may have r in that place where there is no pain 550 22
my body also shall r in hope. 600 16
by night as well, but I find no r. 610 5
I would fly away and be at r. 660 18
To give them r in evil days, * 723 19
"They shall not enter into my r." 725 16
Turn again to your r, O my soul, * 759 14
in returning and r we shall be saved, 832 14
grant us a safe lodging, and a holy r, 833 17
we may not r until all the people of this land share 839 24

rested

Almighty God, who after the creation of the world r 99 6
laid in the tomb and r on this holy Sabbath, 170 3
laid in the tomb and r on this holy Sabbath, 221 15
laid in the tomb and r on this holy Sabbath, 283 3

resting

The r-place you have made for yourself, O Lord, * 85 26
* Or the deep, or the elements, or its r place. 485 16
* Or the deep, or the elements, or its r place. 501 17
at the hill which God chose for his r place? * 677 13
Arise, O LORD, into your r-place, * 786 13
"This shall be my r-place for ever; * 786 28
You trace my journeys and my r-places * 794 4

restitution

ready to make r for all injuries and wrongs 317 6
In penitence, we confess our sins and make r 857 12

restless

I think of God, I am r, * 693 6
try me and know my r thoughts. 795 25

restore

r thou those who are penitent, 42 5
r thou those who are penitent, 63 8
R our fortunes, O LORD, * 105 12
wonderfully r, the dignity of human nature: 162 8
Almighty and everlasting God, whose will it is to r 185 1
wonderfully r, the dignity of human nature: 200 14
Almighty and everlasting God, whose will it is to r 202 16
Almighty and everlasting God, whose will it is to r 236 14
Almighty and everlasting God, whose will it is to r 254 1
R us, good Lord, and let your anger depart from us; 268 27
r thou those who are penitent, 321 8
and r you in the perfect peace 448 10
r me to the blessed company of your faithful people; 450 18
and r you in the perfect peace 451 9
release you from suffering, and r you to wholeness 456 16
In thy good time, r him to health, 458 7
r to him your gifts of gladness and strength, 459 4
but you will r my life 684 24
R us, O God of hosts; * 702 16
R us, O God of hosts; * 703 1
R us, O LORD God of hosts; * 703 24
R us then, O God our Savior; * 709 1
R our fortunes, O LORD, * 782 14
arouse the careless, and r the penitent. 817 20
R to them the assurance of your unfailing mercy; 831 20
They r us, though we often destroy them. 838 23
The mission of the Church is to r all people 855 2

restored

When the LORD r the fortunes of Zion, * 105 4
Almighty God, whose blessed Son r Mary Magdalene 191 1
wonderfully r, the dignity of human nature: 214 2
Almighty God, whose blessed Son r Mary Magdalene 242 8
wonderfully r, the dignity of human nature: 252 2
and r to the fellowship of the Church. 265 5
and are r to grace and holiness 287 10
wonderfully r, the dignity of human nature: 288 6
weakness may be banished and his strength r; 458 19
that he may be r to that perfect health 458 23
r to usefulness in your world with a thankful heart; 459 15
and you r me to health. 621 7

you *r* my life as I was going down to the grave. 621 9
you have *r* the good fortune of Jacob. 708 21
When the LORD *r* the fortunes of Zion, * 782 6

restores

It *r* innocence to the fallen, 287 18
For the pardon of our sins, which *r* us to the company 579 1
when the LORD *r* the fortunes of his people, 599 2
when God *r* the fortunes of his people 659 15

restoreth

He *r* my soul; * 476 23

restrain

behold, I did not *r* my lips; 640 24
I *r* my feet from every evil way, * 771 21

resurrection

by man came also the *r* of the dead. 46 16
the *r* of the body, 54 9
the glorious *r* of thy Son our Lord: 56 2
the *r* of the body, 66 25
who have this day given thanks for his *r*, 69 4
by a man has come also the *r* of the dead. 83 24
the *r* of the body, 96 29
the glorious *r* of your Son our Lord: 98 20
the *r* of the body, 120 25
who have this day given thanks for his *r*, 123 4
Christ to us by the light of his *r*: 134 2
through the *r* of Jesus Christ from the dead. 137 13
by thy glorious *R* and Ascension; 149 23
and also be made partakers of his *r*; 168 7
glorious *r* hast delivered us from the power 170 9
evermore live with him in the joy of his *r*; 170 11
shine with the glory of the Lord's *r*: 170 15
celebrate with joy the day of the Lord's *r*, 171 1
O God, who by the glorious *r* of thy Son 171 10
with sure and certain faith in thy Son's *r*: 185 15
and passion be brought unto the glory of his *r*; 188 18
and called her to be a witness of his *r*: 191 3
baptized into the death and *r* of thy Son 201 13
r of thy Son Jesus Christ dost turn us 203 6
r of thy Son Jesus Christ, may be renewed 203 14
and also share in his *r*; 219 18
and by his glorious *r* delivered us 222 2
live with him in the joy of his *r*; 222 5
shine with the glory of the Lord's *r*: 222 9
celebrate with joy the day of the Lord's *r*, 222 18
O God, who by the glorious *r* of your Son 223 4
firm and certain faith in your Son's *r*: 237 9
be brought to the glory of his *r*; 240 4
and called her to be a witness of his *r*: 242 10
baptized into the death and *r* of your Son 253 1
Almighty God, by our baptism into the death and *r* 254 7
by our baptism into the death and *r* 254 15
the days of our Lord's passion and *r*, 264 11
Bring us with all your saints to the joy of his *r*. 269 2
and also share in his *r*; 272 12
of life in the day of *r*. 280 13
and praise and glorify your holy *r*; 281 2
the *r* of the body, 293 17
his glorious *r* delivered us from the power 295 3
live with him in the joy of his *r*; 295 5
shine with the glory of the Lord's *r*: 295 9
the *r* of the body, 304 20
live in the power of his *r* 306 7
and *r*, from the bondage of sin 306 19
By it we share in his *r*. 306 22
proclaim his *r*, and share with us 308 13
r of your Son Jesus Christ you have overcome sin 309 4
We look for the *r* of the dead, 327 18
and I look for the *r* of the dead, 328 20
his mighty *r* and glorious ascension; 335 14
his mighty *r* and glorious ascension; 342 14
r opened to us the way of everlasting life. 345 3
praise thee for the glorious *r* of thy Son 346 18
after his glorious *r* manifestly appeared 347 2
who after his *r* sent forth his apostles 348 12
We look for the *r* of the dead, 359 9
r, and ascension, we offer you these gifts. 363 12
We proclaim his *r*, 368 21
We celebrate his death and *r*, 371 21
proclaiming his *r* and ascension 374 26
r opened to us the way of everlasting life. 377 16
praises you for the glorious *r* of your Son 379 15
After his glorious *r* he openly appeared 379 21
who after his *r* sent forth his apostles 381 6
For all who have died in the hope of the *r*, 384 29
and proclaim his *r*, 403 15
r and ascension, we await his coming in glory. 405 12
the *r* of the body, 417 2
r of your Son Jesus Christ you have overcome sin 418 2
given in the *r* of your Son 462 3
By your glorious *R* and Ascension, 463 8
I am the *r* and the life, saith the Lord; 469 1
r may die to sin and rise to newness of life, 480 9
we may pass with him to our joyful *r*. 480 11
and the *r* to life everlasting. 481 16
all who have died in the hope of the *r*, 481 24
In sure and certain hope of the *r* 485 9
at the day of the general *r*, 487 17
I am *R* and I am Life, says the Lord. 491 1
O God, who by the glorious *r* of your Son 493 4
the *r* of the body, 496 19
Christ who said, "I am *R* and I am Life." 497 2
In sure and certain hope of the *r* to eternal life 501 11
Christ who is the *R* and the Life: 505 2
and at the *r* receive that blessing 505 4
proclaiming Christ's *r* and interpreting the Gospel, 517 4
We look for the *r* of the dead, 520 9
We look for the *r* of the dead, 530 28
We look for the *r* of the dead, 542 28
r, from the bondage of sin into everlasting life. 570 11
By it we share in his *r*. 570 13
power of his forgiveness and the hope of his *r*; 817 1
O God our King, by the *r* of your Son 835 1
What is the significance of Jesus' *r*? 850 10
By his *r*, Jesus overcame death 850 11
union with Christ in his death and *r*, 858 18
and *r*, until his coming again. 859 8
What do we mean by the *r* of the body? 862 16

retreated

they *r* and fled in terror. 651 11

return

R to the Lord your God, 76 13
and *r* not again, but water the earth, 87 2
it will not *r* to me empty; 87 6
and a just *r* for our labor; 208 6
and, as we seek a proper *r* for our own labor, 210 13
and a just *r* for our labor; 259 7
and, as we seek a proper *r* for our own labor, 261 18
Remember that you are dust, and to dust you shall *r*. 265 21
and sinners shall *r* to you. 267 2
you fall into sin, repent and *r* to the Lord? 293 24
you fall into sin, repent and *r* to the Lord? 304 27
Again and again, you called us to *r*. 370 17
you fall into sin, repent and *r* to the Lord? 417 9
and unto earth shall we *r*. 482 14
"Dust thou art, and unto dust shalt thou *r*." 482 15
and to earth shall we *r*. 499 6
"You are dust, and to dust you shall *r*." 499 7
and sinners shall *r* to you. 657 8
a breath that goes forth and does not *r*. 698 6
r seven-fold into their bosoms. 702 8
R, O Lord; how long will you tarry? * 718 27
and they die and *r* to their dust. 737 13
When they breathe their last, they *r* to earth, * 803 9
thanks and praise for the *r* of seedtime and harvest, 840 16

returning

for in *r* and rest we shall be saved; 138 10
O God of peace, who hast taught us that in *r* 832 13

returns

Receive, O Lord, your servant, for he *r* to you. 465 14

reunite

where it is divided, *r* it; 816 14

reunited

we are *r* with those who have gone before; 493 22

reveal

didst *r* his glory upon the holy mount: 165 15
O God, who on the holy mount didst *r* 191 15
works *r* your wisdom and love. 373 18
R its unity, guard its faith, 375 13
and *r* your glory in the world. 388 3
and the God of gods will *r* himself in Zion. 708 5

revealed

The glory of the Lord shall be *r*, 37 6
that we may know thee as thou art *r* 70 12
The glory of the Lord shall be *r*, 75 6
because your just and holy works have been *r*. 94 18
awaken hope, that we may know you as you are *r* 124 9
awaken hope, that we may know you as you are *r* 139 18
assurance of the glory that shall be *r*; 169 4
Almighty and everlasting God, who in Christ hast *r* 183 11
Almighty God, who hast *r* to thy Church 199 12
worship thee as thou hast been *r* in thy Son; 206 22
r his glory upon the holy mountain: 217 8
confident of the glory that shall be *r*; 220 17
Almighty and everlasting God, in Christ you have *r* 235 3
O God, who on the holy mount *r* 243 1
Almighty God, you have *r* to your Church 251 1
worship you as you have been *r* in your Son; 257 18
as you are *r* in your Son Jesus Christ; 280 3
and sages you *r* your righteous Law. 370 18
to them he has not *r* his judgments. 805 18
What is the nature of God *r* in Jesus? 849 23
How is the Holy Spirit *r* in the Old Covenant? 852 17
The Holy Spirit is *r* in the Old Covenant 852 18
How is the Holy Spirit *r* in the New Covenant? 852 20
The Holy Spirit is *r* as the Lord who leads us 852 21

revealing

We give you thanks, O God, for *r* your Son 134 1
r the image of Christ, 837 7
God first helped us be *r* himself and his will, 845 18

reveals

God *r* himself in glory. 654 5

revelation

to give the light of *r*—the *r* of the glory 110 5
to give the light of *r*—the *r* of the glory 139 14
Inspired by the *r* of your Son, 571 1
God as creator from the *r* to Israel? 846 2
How was this *r* handed down to us? 846 17
This *r* was handed down to us through a community 846 18

revenge

deliver them and us from hatred, cruelty, and *r*; 816 7

reverence

celebrate with *r* the Paschal feast 171 6
O Lord, make us have perpetual love and *r* 230 7
with meek heart and due *r*, they may hear 329 15
Give us all a *r* for the earth as your own creation, 388 12
and *r* so to use the resources of nature, 827 19
Increase our *r* before the mystery of life; 828 17

reverently

and, that we may *r* use our freedom, 209 3
and, that we may *r* use our freedom, 260 10
not to be entered into unadvisedly or lightly, but *r*, 423 14

revile

the covetous curse and *r* the Lord. 594 24
Why should the wicked *r* God? * 595 21
remember how fools *r* you all day long. 690 29
My enemies *r* me all day long, * 731 15

reviled

May the revilings with which they *r* you, O Lord, * 702 7

revilings

May the *r* with which they reviled you, O Lord, * 702 7

revive

to *r* the spirit of the humble, 41 2
and to *r* the heart of the contrite 41 3
to *r* the spirit of the humble 78 25
In your loving-kindness, *r* me, * 770 18

revives

He *r* my soul * 443 5
and *r* the soul; * 607 5
He *r* my soul * 613 1

revolt

Why do the kings of the earth rise up in *r*, 586 3

reward

to see the *r* of the wicked. 130 14
neither *r* us according to our sins. 148 10
and in keeping them there is great *r*. 607 21
and a just *r* from the God of their salvation." 613 24
"Surely, there is a *r* for the righteous; * 665 16
to see the *r* of the wicked. 720 2

rewarded

for the LORD hath *r* thee. 479 13
The LORD *r* me because of my righteous dealing; * 604 3
because my hands were clean he *r* me; 604 4
Therefore the LORD *r* me according to my 604 11
nor *r* us according to our wickedness. 734 2

rich

and the *r* he hath sent empty away. 50 16
and the *r* he hath sent empty away. 65 19
and the *r* he has sent away empty. 92 11
and the *r* he has sent away empty. 119 17
that we through his poverty might be *r*: 198 2
that we through his poverty might be *r*: 249 12
and the *r* he has sent away empty. 442 6
strong and weak, *r* and poor. 531 12
the *r* among the people seek your favor." 648 16
you of high degree and low, *r* and poor together. 652 8
Do not be envious when some become *r*, * 653 15
May the fields of the wilderness be *r* for grazing, * 673 13
Too much of the scorn of the indolent *r*, * 780 23
might be made *r* through your poverty: 819 7
make us *r*, though we often exploit them. 839 2
for the faith we have inherited in all its *r* variety. 839 12

richer

for *r* for poorer, in sickness and in health, 427 3
for *r* for poorer, in sickness and in health, 436 3

riches

proclaim the unsearchable *r* of our Savior 196 12
and attain to the *r* of the age to come; 198 5
proclaim the unsearchable *r* of our Savior 247 24
and attain to the *r* of the age to come; 249 15
and for the right use of the *r* of creation, 390 22
nourish them from the *r* of God's grace, 518 14
nourish Christ's people from the *r* of his grace, 531 19
and for the right use of the *r* of creation, 550 7
dwell in the land and feed on its *r*. 633 10
is better than great *r* of the wicked. 634 17
we heap up *r* and cannot tell who will gather them. 639 8
and boast of their great *r*? 652 16
Wealth and *r* will be in their house, * 755 9
than in all manner of *r*. 764 12
enjoy a fair portion of the *r* of this land; 826 14

richly

and to our God, for he will *r* pardon. 86 22
I will sing to the LORD, for he has dealt with me *r*; * 598 10

richness

for the *r* of mountains, plains, and rivers; 840 8

riddle

and set forth my *r* upon the harp. 652 12

ride

R out and conquer in the cause of truth * 647 19
You let enemies *r* over our heads; 674 17
you *r* on the wings of the wind. 735 8

rider

the horse and its *r* has he hurled into the sea. 85 2
both horse and *r* lie stunned. 692 13

rides

exalt him who *r* upon the heavens; * 676 9
He *r* in the heavens, the ancient heavens; * 678 26

ridges

You drench the furrows and smooth out the *r*; * 673 9

right

where Christ sitteth on the *r* hand of God. 39 14
Thou that sittest at the *r* hand of God the Father, 52 16
Thou sittest at the *r* hand of God, 53 17
and sitteth on the *r* hand of God the Father almighty. 54 3
because he is at my *r* hand, I shall not fall. 61 12
and sitteth on the *r* hand of God the Father almighty. 66 19
where Christ is, seated at the *r* hand of God. 77 13
Your *r* hand, O Lord, is glorious in might; * 85 14
your *r* hand, O Lord, has overthrown the enemy. 85 15
You stretched forth your *r* hand; * 85 19
are yours by *r*, O Lord our God, 93 21
And yours, by *r*, O Lamb that was slain, * 94 1
you are seated at the *r* hand of the Father: 95 7
You are seated at God's *r* hand in glory. 96 7
and is seated at the *r* hand of the Father. 96 23
the LORD is your shade at your *r* hand, 104 22
because he is at my *r* hand, I shall not fall. 115 12
and is seated at the *r* hand of the Father. 120 19
the source of all good desires, all *r* judgments, 123 15
and ten thousand at your *r* hand, * 130 11
and renew a *r* spirit within me. 137 4
Universal in the *r* way, 150 3
Grant us by the same Spirit to have a *r* judgment 175 17
we may think those things that are *r*, 178 2
think and do always such things as are *r*, 180 15
Christ, who standeth at thy *r* hand; 186 4
Grant us by the same Spirit to have a *r* judgment 227 10
we may think those things that are *r*, 229 16
think and do always those things that are *r*, 232 7
Christ, who stands at your *r* hand; 237 17
And, to make a *r* beginning 265 13
and renew a *r* spirit within me. 266 23
It is *r* to give him thanks and praise. 271 4
It is *r* to praise you, Almighty God, 271 5
It is *r* to give him thanks and praise. 286 20
It is truly *r* and good, always and everywhere, 286 22
and is seated at the *r* hand of the Father. 293 10
and is seated at the *r* hand of the Father. 304 13
It is *r* to give him thanks and praise. 306 12
Thou that sittest at the *r* hand of God the Father, 325 3
and is seated at the *r* hand of the Father. 327 9
and sitteth on the *r* hand of the Father; 328 9
that they may be led to wise decisions and *r* actions 329 20
It is meet and *r* so to do. 333 6
It is very meet, *r*, and our bounden duty, 333 7
It is meet and *r* so to do. 340 14

It is very meet, *r*, and our bounden duty, 341 1
you are seated at the *r* hand of the Father: 356 11
and is seated at the *r* hand of the Father. 358 25
It is *r* to give him thanks and praise. 361 6
It is *r*, and a good and joyful thing, 361 7
It is *r* to give him thanks and praise. 367 6
It is *r*, and a good and joyful thing, 367 7
It is *r* to give him thanks and praise. 370 4
It is *r* to give him thanks and praise. 372 22
It is truly *r* to glorify you, Father, 373 1
and ascension to your *r* hand, 374 26
and for the *r* use of the riches of creation, 390 21
It is *r* to give him thanks and praise. 402 6
It is *r* to give him thanks and praise. 404 8
and is seated at the *r* hand of the Father. 416 18
and guides me along *r* pathways for his Name's sake. 443 6
God shall help her, and that *r* early. 472 3
the LORD is thy defense upon thy *r* hand; 473 18
and thy *r* hand shall hold me. 475 12
r dear in the sight of the LORD is the death 479 19
and at thy *r* hand there is pleasure for evermore. 485 8
mystical body of thy Son, may be set on his *r* hand, 487 18
and is seated at the *r* hand of the Father. 496 13
and in your *r* hand are pleasures for evermore. 501 10
and is seated at the *r* hand of the Father. 519 28
and is seated at the *r* hand of the Father. 530 19
and is seated at the *r* hand of the Father. 542 19
and for the *r* use of the riches of creation, 550 6
It is *r* to give him thanks and praise. 570 4
For you have maintained my *r* and my cause; * 593 7
you sit upon your throne judging *r*. 593 8
Whoever leads a blameless life and does what is *r*, * 599 6
because he is at my *r* hand I shall not fall. 600 14
and in your *r* hand are pleasures for evermore. 600 21
O Savior of those who take refuge at your *r* hand 601 12
your *r* hand also sustains me; 605 10
with the victorious strength of his *r* hand. 608 14
your *r* hand will seize all those who hate you. 609 13
and guides me along *r* pathways for his Name's sake. 613 2
He guides the humble in doing *r* * 615 6
and their *r* hand full of bribes. 617 2
For the word of the LORD is *r*, * 626 7
and their tongue speaks what is *r*. 635 23
because I follow the course that is *r*. 638 10
but your *r* hand, your arm, and the 645 15
Your *r* hand will show you marvelous things; * 647 21
on your *r* hand is the queen, 648 9
your *r* hand is full of justice. 651 22
and renew a *r* spirit within me. 657 2
Save us by your *r* hand and answer us, * 667 18
your *r* hand holds me fast. 671 2
you hold me by my *r* hand. 688 24
why is your *r* hand hidden in your bosom? 690 7
the *r* hand of the Most High has lost its power." 693 21
the mountain his *r* hand had won. 699 14
preserve what your *r* hand has planted. 703 17
Let your hand be upon the man of your *r* hand, * 703 20
strong is your hand and high is your *r* hand. 714 20
You have exalted the *r* hand of his foes * 716 25
and ten thousand at your *r* hand, * 719 25
With his *r* hand and his holy arm * 728 1
and always do what is *r*! 742 2
save with your *r* hand and answer me. 750 6
and let an accuser stand at his *r* hand. 751 9
Because he stands at the *r* hand of the needy, * 753 10
The LORD said to my Lord, "Sit at my *r* hand, * 753 12
The Lord who is at your *r* hand 753 21
their heart is *r*; 755 18
"The *r* hand of the LORD has triumphed! * 762 1
the *r* hand of the LORD is exalted! 762 2
the *r* hand of the LORD has triumphed!" 762 3
I know, O LORD, that your judgments are *r* * 769 14
I have done what is just and *r*; * 773 15
I hold all your commandments to be *r* for me; * 774 3
the LORD is your shade at your *r* hand. 779 10
have gone *r* over us. 781 10
let my *r* hand forget its skill. 792 11
your *r* hand shall save me. 793 18
and your *r* hand hold me fast. 794 19
I look to my *r* hand and find no one who knows me; * 798 7
and whose *r* hand is raised in falsehood. 800 18
Where it is *r*, strengthen it; 816 13
Guide us to perceive what is *r*, 818 5
Almighty God, who sittest in the throne judging *r*: 821 8
and is seated at the *r* hand of the Father? 850 18

righteous

that we may hereafter live a godly, *r*, and sober life, 42 9
O ye spirits and souls of the *r*, bless ye the Lord; * 49 5
do always what is *r* in thy sight; 57 12
that we may hereafter live a godly, *r*, and sober life, 63 12
Glorify the Lord, O spirits and souls of the *r*, * 89 22
and of all their *r* offspring: 90 19
holy and *r* in his sight 92 30
to keep your *r* judgments. 103 9
that we may hereafter live a godly, *r*, and sober life, 321 12
Christ the *r*; 332 16
and sages you revealed your *r* Law. 370 18
Gracious is the LORD and *r*; * 442 17
Christ the *r*; 450 2
Gracious is the LORD, and *r*; * 479 8
give us such a lively sense of thy *r* will, 488 30
thy *r* servants, known to us and unknown; 489 18
other *r* servants, known to us and unknown; 504 16
nor the sinner in the council of the *r*. 585 14
For the LORD knows the way of the *r*, * 585 15
For you, O LORD, will bless the *r*; * 589 21
but establish the *r*; * 591 16
for you test the mind and heart, O *r* God. 591 17
God is a *r* judge; * 591 20
I will bear witness that the LORD is *r*; * 592 5
what can the *r* do?" 596 14
The LORD weighs the *r* as well as the wicked, * 596 19
For the LORD is *r*; 596 24
he delights in *r* deeds; * 596 25
because God is in the company of the *r*. 598 25
The LORD rewarded me because of my *r* dealing; * 604 3
rewarded me according to my *r* dealing, * 604 12
judgments of the LORD are true and *r* altogether. 607 15
be silenced which speak against the *r*, * 624 2
Be glad, you *r*, and rejoice in the LORD; * 625 25
Rejoice in the LORD, you *r*; * 626 1
The eyes of the LORD are upon the *r*, * 628 23
The *r* cry, and the LORD hears them * 629 1

Many are the troubles of the *r*, * 629 5
and those who hate the *r* will be punished. 629 10
The wicked plot against the *r* * 634 7
The little that the *r* has * 634 16
but the LORD upholds the *r*. 634 19
but the *r* are generous in giving. 635 2
but never have I seen the *r* forsaken, 635 10
The *r* are always generous in their lending, * 635 12
The *r* shall possess the land * 635 20
The mouth of the *r* utters wisdom, * 635 22
The wicked spy on the *r* * 635 26
But the deliverance of the *r* comes from the LORD; * 636 15
The *r* shall see and tremble, * 658 11
he will never let the *r* stumble. 662 7
The *r* will be glad when they see the vengeance; * 665 13
"Surely, there is a reward for the *r*; * 665 16
The *r* will rejoice in the LORD 672 5
But let the *r* be glad and rejoice before God; * 676 6
and not be written among the *r*. 681 21
In his time shall the *r* flourish; * 685 21
but the horns of the *r* shall be exalted. 691 25
The *r* shall flourish like a palm tree, * 721 21
Light has sprung up for the *r*, * 727 20
Rejoice in the LORD, you *r*, * 727 22
the *r* are merciful and full of compassion. 755 12
the *r* will be kept in everlasting remembrance. 755 16
Gracious is the LORD and *r*; * 759 10
in the tents of the *r*: 761 27
he who is *r* may enter." 762 12
when I have learned your *r* judgments. 763 18
because of your *r* judgments. 768 12
to keep your *r* judgments. 772 6
and for your *r* promise. 773 20
You are *r*, O LORD, * 774 21
all your *r* judgments endure for evermore. 776 24
because of your *r* judgments. 777 8
for all your commandments are *r*. 777 24
The LORD, the *R* One, * 784 7
Surely, the *r* will give thanks to your Name, * 797 1
Let the *r* smite me in friendly rebuke; 797 12
the *r* will gather around me. 798 17
they shall sing of your *r* deeds. 801 25
The LORD is *r* in all his ways * 802 21
The LORD loves the *r*; 803 20
Christ, our merciful and *r* Judge. 823 16
its mind sound, and its will *r*; 827 10

righteously

That he may rule your people *r* * 685 11

righteousness

and with *r* to judge the world 45 9
In holiness and *r* before him, * 51 9
Endue thy ministers with *r*; 55 3
in holiness and *r* all our days; 59 8
Endue thy ministers with *r*; 67 18
in holiness and *r* all our days; 72 5
Your ways are ways of *r* and truth, * 94 12
Clothe your ministers with *r*; 97 20
in holiness and *r* all our days; 101 21
Clothe your ministers with *r*; 121 20
in holiness and *r* all our days; 125 19
deliver me in your *r*. 129 10
to maintain these liberties in *r* and peace; 190 21
and live in *r* and true holiness; 201 15
may live in *r* and holiness all our days; 203 8
and live in *r* and true holiness; 203 15
maintain our liberties in *r* and peace; 242 5
and live in *r* and true holiness; 253 3
may live in *r* and holiness all our days; 254 10
and live in *r* and true holiness; 254 16
and my tongue shall sing of your *r*, 267 4
out of sin into *r* and out of death into life: 291 6
truly serving thee in holiness and *r* 329 16
Lord, trusting in our own *r*, 337 10
thy saints hast given us an example of *r*, 348 5
out of sin into *r*, 368 9
you have given us an example of *r*, 380 21
clothed me with the shining garment of his *r*, 450 12
and bring me forth in the paths of *r* 476 6
he leadeth me in the paths of *r* 476 24
keep judgment, * and do *r*. 478 16
lead us in holiness and *r* all our days. 481 3
The Sun of *R* is gloriously risen, 483 16
Spirit lead us in holiness and *r* all our days; 489 6
The Sun of *R* is gloriously risen, 500 5
Spirit lead us in holiness and *r* all our days; 504 4
the death of sin to the life of *r*; 505 3
and may thirst after *r*, 548 22
Lead me, O LORD, in your *r*, 589 6
according to my *r*, O LORD, * 591 13
It is he who rules the world with *r*; * 593 15
deliver me in your *r*. 622 9
He loves *r* and justice; * 626 9
according to your *r*; * 631 19
And my tongue shall be talking of your *r* * 632 1
Your *r* is like the strong mountains, 632 14
He will make your *r* as clear as the light * 633 15
I proclaimed *r* in the great congregation; * 640 23
Your *r* have I not hidden in my heart; 640 26
a scepter of *r* is the scepter of your kingdom; 648 2
you love *r* and hate iniquity. 648 3
and my tongue shall sing of your *r*, 657 10
Do you indeed decree *r*, you rulers? * 664 21
Awesome things will you show us in your *r*, 672 17
In your *r*, deliver me and set me free; * 683 3
I will recall your *r*, yours alone. 684 13
Your *r*, O God, reaches to the heavens; * 684 20
My tongue will proclaim your *r* all day long, * 685 6
and your *r* to the King's Son; 685 10
and the little hills bring *r*. 685 14
r and peace have kissed each other. 709 15
and *r* shall look down from heaven. 709 17
r shall go before him, * 709 20
or your *r* in the country where all is forgotten? 713 2
R and justice are the foundations of your throne; * 714 21
they are jubilant in your *r*. 714 26
He will judge the world with *r* * 726 20
r and justice are the foundations of his throne. 726 26
The heavens declare his *r*, * 727 7
his *r* has he openly shown in 728 4
In *r* shall he judge the world * 728 21
you have executed justice and *r* in Jacob." 729 7
The LORD executes *r* * 733 19

and his *r* on children's children; 734 17
This was reckoned to him as *r* * 744 9
and his *r* endures for ever. 754 11
and their *r* will last for ever. 755 10
and their *r* stands fast for ever; 755 23
Open for me the gates of *r*; * 762 8
in your *r* preserve my life. 766 16
The *r* of your decrees is everlasting; * 775 13
Let your priests be clothed with *r*; * 786 15
answer me in your *r*. 798 20
for your *r*' sake, bring me out of trouble. 799 24
in the bond of peace, and in *r* of life. 815 6
no sword is drawn but the sword of *r*, 815 23
that peace which is the fruit of *r*, 816 3
Fill them with the love of truth and *r*, 820 22
that peace may prevail with *r*, 825 12
r all things necessary to sustain their life: 828 11

rightful

make us mindful of the *r* aspirations 210 14
make us mindful of the *r* aspirations 261 19

rightly

But if we are to share *r* in the celebration 316 17
and *r* and duly administer thy holy Sacraments. 329 12
that we may use its resources *r* in the service of others 388 13
and *r* administer the sacraments 534 3
who *r* fears your indignation? 718 24

rightness

Let the heavens declare the *r* of his cause; * 654 14

rights

that human *r* may be safeguarded 822 7
the *r* of all may be protected 822 26

ring

Cry aloud, inhabitants of Zion, *r* out your joy, * 86 13
Bless, O Lord, this *r* to be a sign of the vows 427 10
I give you this *r* as a symbol of my vow, 427 13
the giving and receiving of a *r*, 428 3
Bless, O Lord, this *r* to be a sign of the vows 434 4
Let his heart and soul now *r* 466 9
and let the hills *r* out with joy before the LORD, 728 19

rise

But over you the Lord will *r*, * 87 15
we may *r* to the life immortal; 159 6
and *r* with him to newness of life; 170 4
and to *r* again for our justification: 172 9
we may *r* to the life immortal; 211 6
and *r* with him to newness of life; 221 16
and to *r* for our justification: 224 2
and *r* with him to newness of life; 283 4
may die to sin and *r* to newness of life, 480 9
Why do the kings of the earth *r* up in revolt, 586 3
how many there are who *r* up against me! 587 4
R up, O LORD; set me free, O my God; * 587 15
r up against the fury of my enemies. 591 7
R up, O LORD, let not the ungodly 594 15
R up, O LORD; 595 18
I will *r* up," says the LORD 597 11
from those who *r* up against them. 601 13
I strike them down, and they cannot *r*; * 605 16
And though war should *r* up against me, * 617 16
and *r* up to help me. 629 16
Malicious witnesses *r* up against me; * 630 13
they are cast down and shall not be able to *r*. 633 4
R up, and help us, * 647 9
protect me from those who *r* up against me. 665 19
let no rebel *r* up against him. 674 8
the unending tumult of those who *r* up against you. 691 2
The arrogant *r* up against me, O God, 711 1
r up against me. 721 20
R up, O Judge of the world; * 722 20
let those who *r* up against me be put to shame, 753 4
At midnight I will *r* to give you thanks, * 768 11
It is in vain that you *r* so early and go to bed so late; * 783 3
and do I not loathe those who *r* up against you? 795 21
let them be cast into the mire, never to *r* up again." 796 22

risen

Christ is *r*. 39 7
The Lord is *r* indeed. 39 8
If ye then be *r* with Christ, seek 39 13
The Lord is *r* indeed: 43 8
Christ is *r* from the dead, * 46 13
Christ is *r* 77 6
The Lord is *r* indeed. 77 7
The Lord is *r* indeed: 81 4
Christ is *r*. 109 3
The Lord is *r* indeed. 109 4
Christ is *r*. 294 8
The Lord is *r* indeed. 294 9
Christ is *r*. 299 3
The Lord is *r* indeed. 299 4
may continue for ever in the *r* life of Jesus 307 5
and for a spiritual sharing in his *r* life. 316 5
Christ is *r*. 319 4
The Lord is *r* indeed. 319 5
Christ is *r*. 323 3
The Lord is *r* indeed. 323 4
Christ is *r*. 351 3
The Lord is *r* indeed. 351 4
Christ is *r*. 355 3
The Lord is *r* indeed. 355 4
Christ is *r*. 363 8
R Lord, be known to us in the breaking of the Bread. 372 9
Christ is *r*. 413 3
The Lord is *r* indeed. 413 4
Christ is *r* from the dead, 483 14
The Sun of Righteousness is gloriously *r*, 483 16
Christ is *r* from the dead, 500 3
The Sun of Righteousness is gloriously *r*, 500 5
Christ is *r*. 502 19
The Lord is *r* indeed. 502 20
Christ is *r*. 512 3
The Lord is *r* indeed. 512 4
Christ is *r*. 525 3
The Lord is *r* indeed. 525 4
Christ is *r*. 537 3
The Lord is *r* indeed. 537 4
may continue for ever in the *r* life of Jesus 570 20
for false witnesses have *r* up against me, 618 24
For the arrogant have *r* up against me, 659 21
for the waters have *r* up to my neck. 679 8

rises

The sun *r*, and they slip away * 736 21

riseth

light *r* up in darkness for the godly: 832 7

rising

and kings to the brightness of thy *r*. 38 2
From the *r* of the sun even unto the going down 38 5
and kings to the brightness of your *r*. 76 2
From the *r* of the sun to its setting 76 5
From the *r* of the sun to its setting 106 6
From the *r* of the sun to its going down * 138 5
and by his *r* to life again hath won 346 21
and, *r* from the grave, destroyed death, 374 6
and by his *r* to life again he has won 379 18
Thou knowest my down-sitting and mine up-*r*; 474 19
he has called the earth from the *r* of the sun 654 2
From the *r* of the sun to its going down * 756 6
you know my sitting down and my *r* up; 794 2
and for his *r* to life again, 836 15

rite

Confirmation is the *r* in which we express 860 18
Ordination is the *r* in which God gives authority 860 28
Reconciliation of a Penitent, or Penance, is the *r* 861 9
Unction is the *r* of anointing the sick with oil, 861 14

rites

What other sacramental *r* evolved in the Church 860 7
Other sacramental *r* which evolved in the Church 860 9
Is God's activity limited to these *r*? 861 17
God does not limit himself to these *r*; 861 18

river

Father in heaven, who at the baptism of Jesus in the *R* 163 1
Father in heaven, who at the baptism of Jesus in the *R* 214 12
There is a *r*, the streams whereof make glad 471 23
you give them drink from the *r* of your delights. 632 21
There is a *r* whose streams make glad 649 10
the *r* of God is full of water. 673 6
and from the *R* to the ends of the earth. 685 25
and its branches to the *R*. 703 10
and to Jabin at the *r* of Kishon: 706 21
from the Great Sea to the *R*. 715 17
so the *r* ran in the dry places. 741 8

rivers

and made it firm upon the *r* of the deep. 613 17
you dried up ever-flowing *r*. 690 15
and the waters gushed out like *r*. 696 6
He turned their *r* into blood, * 698 15
Let the *r* clap their hands, * 728 18
The LORD changed *r* into deserts, * 748 21
for the richness of mountains, plains, and *r*; 840 9

road

He will drink from the brook beside the *r*; * 754 3
show me the *r* that I must walk, 799 17

roar

The lions *r* after their prey * 736 19

roared

Your adversaries *r* in your holy place; * 689 16

roaring

around like a *r* lion, seeking someone to devour. 132 9
like a ravening and a *r* lion. 611 4
rescue me from the *r* beasts, 631 2
You still the *r* of the seas, * 672 23
the *r* of their waves, 672 24

rob

the poor and needy from those who *r* them." 630 12

robbery

in *r* take no empty pride; * 670 6

robe

and runs down upon the collar of his *r*. 787 14

robed

The white-*r* army of martyrs praise you. 95 25

rock

let us shout for joy to the *R* of our salvation. 82 6
Be my strong *r*, a castle to keep me safe, 129 13
Keep thy Church steadfast upon the *r* of this faith, 187 3
Keep your Church steadfast upon the *r* of this faith, 238 16
and set me up upon a *r* of stone. 477 22
My God, my *r* in whom I put my trust, * 602 9
who is the *R*, except our God? 605 2
The LORD lives! Blessed is my *R*! * 606 3
and set me high upon a *r*. 618 4
my *R*, do not be deaf to my cry; * 619 5
Be my strong *r*, a castle to keep me safe, 622 12
set me upon the *r* that is higher than I. 668 16
He alone is my *r* and my salvation, * 669 7
God is my strong *r* and my refuge. 669 21
Be my strong *r*, a castle to keep me safe; * 683 5
True, he struck the *r*, the waters gushed out, 696 13
They would remember that God was their *r*, * 697 20
and satisfy him with honey from the *r*. 705 8
my God, and the *r* of my salvation.' 715 19
my *R*, in whom there is no fault. 721 28
and my God the *r* of my trust. 724 10
let us shout for joy to the *R* of our salvation. 724 15
and the stony cliffs for the *r* badgers. 736 14
He opened the *r*, and water flowed, * 741 7
Who turned the hard *r* into a pool of water * 757 11
and dashes them against the *r*! 792 23
Blessed be the LORD my *r*! * 800 1

rocked

The earth reeled and *r*; * 603 1

rocks

He split the hard *r* in the wilderness * 696 3

rod

your *r* and your staff, they comfort me. 443 10
thy *r* and thy staff comfort me. 476 11
thy *r* and thy staff, they comfort me. 477 4
You shall crush them with an iron *r* * 586 20
your *r* and your staff, they comfort me. 613 6
I will punish their transgressions with a *r* * 716 5

role

surely fulfill our *r* in your eternal purpose; 827 15

roll
In the *r* of the book it is written concerning me: * 640 20

rolled
The breakers of death *r* over me, * 602 14

roof
I am not worthy to have you come under my *r*; 562 10
my tongue sticks to the *r* of my mouth; * 611 9
"I will not come under the *r* of my house, * 786 3
Let my tongue cleave to the *r* of my mouth 792 12

room
I may make *r* for your power to possess me, 461 2
a thousand in my own *r*, * 708 11

root
to *r* out the remembrance of them from the earth. 628 26
and *r* you out of the land of the living! 658 10
it took *r* and filled the land. 703 6
I may *r* out all evildoers from the city of the LORD. 730 27
but let him *r* out their names from the earth; 751 28
every *r* of bitterness, the desire of vainglory, 829 1

roots
the *r* of the mountains shook; 603 2

rose
The third day he *r* again from the dead. 54 1
The third day he *r* again from the dead. 66 17
died for us and *r* again, thy Son 70 9
On the third day he *r* again. 96 21
On the third day he *r* again. 120 17
died and *r* again for us, your Son 124 6
and *r* victorious from the grave. 287 13
On the third day he *r* again. 293 8
On the third day he *r* again. 304 11
On the third day he *r* again 327 6
and the third day he *r* again according to 328 7
but unto him who died for us and *r* again. 346 7
who *r* victorious from the dead, 349 6
On the third day he *r* again 358 22
but for him who died and *r* for us, 374 10
but for him who died for us and *r* again. 379 4
who *r* victorious from the dead, 382 1
On the third day he *r* again. 416 16
On the third day he *r* again. 496 11
On the third day he *r* again 519 25
On the third day he *r* again 530 16
On the third day he *r* again 542 16
Smoke *r* from his nostrils 603 4
you exalted me above those who *r* against me; * 606 8
trampled on those who *r* up against us. 645 22
When God *r* up to judgment * 692 18
Who *r* up for me against the wicked? * 723 25
when enemies *r* up against us; 781 4

round
Rejoice and sing now, all the *r* earth, 286 4
above mine enemies *r* about me. 477 24
The snares of death compassed me *r* about, * 479 3
let the assembly of the peoples gather *r* you. 591 9
that I may go in procession *r* your altar, 616 19
above my enemies *r* about me. 618 6
walk *r* about her; * 651 27
and *r* about him a raging storm. 654 8
and *r* about their dwellings. 697 6
great and terrible to all those *r* about him. 714 8
Clouds and darkness are *r* about him, * 726 25
saying, "Rule over your enemies *r* about you. 753 15
so does the LORD stand *r* about his people, 781 20
your children like olive shoots *r* about your table. 783 18

rounds
Day and night the watchmen make their *r* 661 1

rouse
R yourself, come to my side, and see; * 666 3

roused
and did not permit his wrath to be *r*. 698 4

rout
shoot out your arrows and *r* them. 800 13

routed
he hurled thunderbolts and *r* them. 603 18

royal
share in the *r* priesthood of Jesus Christ; 307 12
to serve thee as a *r* priesthood, 347 11
to serve you as a *r* priesthood, 380 6
a holy nation, a *r* priesthood, 854 9

rubbish
They burn it with fire like *r*; * 703 18

rubble
they have made Jerusalem a heap of *r*. 701 3
For your servants love her very *r*, * 732 4

rugged
O *r* mountain, O hill of Bashan! 677 11
Why do you look with envy, O *r* mountain, 677 12

ruin
r or destruction within your borders. 87 24
As for the enemy, they are finished, in perpetual *r*, * 593 11
let those who plot my *r* fall back and be dismayed. 629 21
Let *r* come upon them unawares; * 630 5
Let all who rejoice at my *r* be ashamed 631 24
those who strive to hurt me speak of my *r* 637 21
You plot *r*; 658 1
and my eye has seen the *r* of my foes. 660 4
you cast them down in *r*. 688 14
and made his dwelling a *r*. 701 20

ruins
Turn your steps toward the endless *r*; * 689 14
and laid his strongholds in *r*. 716 22
like an owl among the *r*. 731 12
let them be driven from the *r* of their homes. 751 17

rule
direct and *r* us according to your will, 107 5
it may please thee to *r* and govern thy holy Church 150 2
That it may please thee so to *r* the hearts 150 25
Spirit may in all things direct and *r* our hearts; 182 3
brought together under his most gracious *r*; 185 5
and establish thy *r* of justice, love, and peace; 186 17

brought together under his most gracious *r*; 203 3
Spirit may in all things direct and *r* our hearts; 233 16
brought together under his most gracious *r*; 236 18
and establish your *r* of justice, love, and peace; 238 11
brought together under his most gracious *r*; 254 5
Examine your lives and conduct by the *r* 317 1
We beseech thee also so to *r* the hearts 329 18
we might *r* and serve all your creatures. 373 20
That he may *r* your people righteously * 685 11
He shall *r* from sea to sea, * 685 24
Arise, O God, and *r* the earth, * 706 1
You *r* the raging of the sea * 714 11
saying, "*R* over your enemies round about you. 753 15
he will *r* over the nations. 753 23
The sun to *r* the day, * 790 11

ruled

and those who hated them *r* over them. 745 7

ruler

O Lord and *R* of the hosts of heaven, * 90 17
O *r* of the universe, Lord God, 94 9
that, thou being our *r* and guide, 180 3
that, with you as our *r* and guide, 231 19
God of all power, *R* of the Universe, 370 5
Almighty and eternal God, *r* of all things 394 9
Truly, the LORD is our *r*; * 715 1
the *r* of the peoples set him free. 739 18
as a *r* over all his possessions, 739 20
Almighty and everliving God, *r* of all things 817 18

rulers

Christ before the *r* of this world, 195 2
Christ before the *r* of this world, 246 9
confessing before the *r* of this world 348 9
You made us the *r* of creation. 370 14
confessing before the *r* of this world 381 3
be warned, you *r* of the earth. 586 23
The *r* of the earth belong to God, * 650 24
Do you indeed decree righteousness, you *r*? * 664 21
than to put any trust in *r*. 761 14
Even though *r* sit and plot against me, * 765 5
R have persecuted me without a cause, * 777 1
Let their *r* be overthrown in stony places, * 797 15
Put not your trust in *r*, nor in any child of earth, * 803 7
princes and all *r* of the world; 806 16

rules

It is he who *r* the world with righteousness; * 593 15
he *r* over the nations. 612 14
surely, there is a God who *r* in the earth." 665 17
Let everyone know that God *r* in Jacob, * 666 26
In his might he *r* for ever; 674 6

rumors

their heart collects false *r*; 642 11
They will not be afraid of any evil *r*; * 755 17

run

neither *r* into any kind of danger; 57 10
and *r* after false gods?" 128 13
Grant, we beseech thee, that we may *r* without stumbling 184 3
Grant that we may *r* without stumbling 235 16
may *r* with patience the race that is set 347 19
and *r* with endurance the race that is set 380 14
and *r* after false gods?" 588 3
But those who *r* after other gods * 600 3
it rejoices like a champion to *r* its course. 606 25
they *r* and prepare themselves for battle. 666 2
they snarl like dogs and *r* about the city. 666 8
I will *r* the way of your commandments, * 765 23

runneth

my cup *r* over. 477 8

running

r to obtain thy promises, may be made partakers 182 14
example of thy servant N., may persevere in *r* the race 198 18
r to obtain your promises, may become partakers 234 8
N., may persevere in *r* the race that is set 250 3
and my cup is *r* over. 443 14
and my cup is *r* over. 613 10

runs

and *r* about to the end of it again; * 607 2
Let them vanish like water that *r* off; * 665 7
and their evil speech *r* through the world. 687 18
that *r* down upon the beard, 787 12
and *r* down upon the collar of his robe. 787 14
and his word *r* very swiftly. 805 8

rural

Have mercy upon all of us who live and work in *r* areas 825 19

ruthless

and the *r* have sought my life, * 659 22

S

Saba

and the kings of Arabia and *S* offer gifts. 686 4

Sabaoth

Holy, holy, holy, Lord God of *S*; 53 1

sabbath

laid in the tomb and rested on this holy *S*, 170 3
laid in the tomb and rested on this holy *S*, 221 15
laid in the tomb and rested on this holy *S*, 283 3
Remember that thou keep holy the *S* day. 318 10
Remember the *S* day and keep it holy. 350 9
God's eternal *s* rest. 465 13

sack

you have put off my *s*-cloth and clothed me with joy. 622 4
But when they were sick I dressed in *s*-cloth * 630 17
I put on *s*-cloth also, * 680 9

sacrament

did institute the *S* of his Body and Blood: 169 8
wonderful *S* hath left unto us a memorial 201 2
persons for the ministry of Word and *S*, 205 17
instituted the *S* of his Body and Blood: 221 2
wonderful *S* has left us a memorial 252 7
persons for the ministry of Word and *S*, 256 14
instituted the *S* of his Body and Blood: 274 2

multiply, by the grace of the Paschal *s*, the number 289 7
I present N. to receive the *S* of Baptism. 301 2
the *S* of new birth [and for those (this person) 305 12
instituted the *S* of his Body and Blood 316 2
remember the dignity of that holy *S*. 316 19
and living faith we receive the holy *S*, 316 24
receive this holy *S*, and serve you in unity, 363 16
in the *S* of his Body and Blood. 365 13
that they may be the *S* of the Body of Christ 369 5
instituted the *S* of his Body and Blood: 397 14
may be the *S* of the precious Body (Blood) 408 3
that through the *S* of Baptism 444 18
Grant that this *S* may be unto us a comfort 482 4
Grant that this *S* may be to us a comfort 498 15
wonderful *S* hast left unto us a memorial 834 12
Holy Baptism is the *s* by which God adopts us 858 9
The Holy Eucharist is the *s* commanded 859 6
bound together in Christ by *s*, 862 23

sacramental

What other *s* rites evolved in the Church 860 7
Other *s* rites which evolved in the Church 860 9

sacraments

present in your Word and *S*, 113 12
illumined by thy Word and *S*, 163 9
illumined by your Word and *S*, 215 3
by hearing his Word and celebrating his *S*, 285 5
and rightly and duly administer thy holy *S*. 329 12
and renewed by thy Word and *S*, 346 11
and renewed by your Word and *S*, 379 7
faithful ministers of your Word and *S*. 387 8
administration of the *s* of the New Covenant; 517 9
with them the *s* of our redemption? 518 16
faithful steward of his holy Word and *S*. 521 21
servants for the ministry of your Word and *S*. 523 5
and the *s* of the New Covenant, 532 10
and rightly administer the *s* of the New Covenant. 534 3
to administer his holy *S*. 534 12
servants for the ministry of your Word and *S*. 535 5
ministration of God's Word and *S*, 543 15
assist in the ministration of his holy *S*. 545 21
servants for the ministry of your Word and *S*. 547 1
may faithfully administer your holy *S*, 563 3
servants for the ministry of your Word and *S*. 564 5
the ministry of his holy Word and *S*. 567 3
your *S* faithfully administered 817 13
to administer the *s*; 856 5
and the administration of the *s*. 856 11
to offer prayer, and to celebrate the *s*. 857 24
What are the *s*? 857 25
The *s* are outward and visible signs 857 26
What are the two great *s* of the Gospel? 858 5
The two great *s* given by Christ to his Church 858 6
How do they differ from the two *s* 860 12
How are the *s* related to our Christian hope? 861 21
S sustain our present hope 861 22

sacred

Grant us so to venerate the *s* mysteries 201 3
Grant us so to venerate the *s* mysteries 252 8
that wonderful and *s* mystery; 280 15
that wonderful and *s* mystery; 291 12
has approved him for this *s* responsibility. 514 5
that wonderful and *s* mystery; 515 5
for ordination to the *s* priesthood. 527 3
that wonderful and *s* mystery; 528 3
for ordination to the *s* order of deacons. 539 3
that wonderful and *s* mystery; 540 3
and their *s* feasts a snare. 681 9
so to venerate the *s* mysteries 834 14

sacrifice

the lifting up of my hands be an evening *s*. 61 2
the lifting up of our hands as the evening *s*. 113 10
the lifting up of my hands as the evening *s*. 115 2
both a *s* for sin and also an example of godly life: 180 20
Son to be for us a *s* for sin, 232 12
Had you desired it, I would have offered *s*; * 267 8
The *s* of God is a troubled spirit; * 267 10
Holy Father, accept our evening *s*, 287 23
offer to you our *s* of thanksgiving; 289 4
remembrance of the *s* of his death, 316 4
let us offer continually the *s* of praise, 317 20
and sufficient *s*, oblation, and satisfaction, 334 13
memory of that his precious death and *s*, 334 16
accept this our *s* of praise and thanksgiving; 335 25
a reasonable, holy, and living *s* unto thee; 336 3
to offer unto thee any *s*, 336 10
perfect *s* for the whole world; 341 17
memory of that his precious death and *s*, 341 19
our *s* of praise and thanksgiving, 342 22
Offer to God a *s* of thanksgiving, 343 8
an offering and *s* to God. 343 13
to present yourselves as a living *s*, 343 15
let us continually offer to God the *s* of praise, 344 1
before thee a *s* of praise and prayer which is holy 348 17
a perfect *s* for the whole world. 362 16
this *s* of praise and thanksgiving. 363 11
And we offer our *s* of praise and thanksgiving to you, 369 1
Unite us in your Son in his *s*, 369 7
and offering to you this *s* of thanksgiving, 371 20
a living *s* in Christ, 375 10
Offer to God a *s* of thanksgiving, 376 4
an offering and *s* to God. 376 9
to present yourselves as a living *s*, 376 11
let us continually offer to God the *s* of praise, 376 17
that we might offer before you a *s* of praise 381 11
we show forth the *s* of his death, 403 14
Make us a living *s* of praise. 403 18
Accept, O Lord, our *s* of praise, 405 13
through which he offered himself as a perfect *s*. 573 14
the continual recalling of the *s* of your Son. 574 4
and accept your burnt *s*; 608 6
In a *s* and offering you take no pleasure * 640 16
and sealed it with *s*." 654 13
Offer to God a *s* of thanksgiving * 655 7
Whoever offers me the *s* of thanksgiving 656 1
Had you desired it, I would have offered *s*, * 657 14
The *s* of God is a troubled spirit; * 657 16
I will offer you a freewill *s* * 660 1
Let them offer a *s* of thanksgiving * 747 25
I will offer you the *s* of thanksgiving * 760 8
the lifting up of my hands as the evening *s*. 797 6

Why is the Eucharist called a *s*? 859 9
Because the Eucharist, the Church's *s* of praise 859 10
the way by which the *s* of Christ is made present, 859 11

sacrificed

Christ our Passover is *s* for us, * 46 2
Christ our Passover has been *s* for us; * 83 11
Christ our Passover is *s* for us; 337 1
very Paschal Lamb, who was *s* for us, 346 19
Christ our Passover is *s* for us; 364 15
true Paschal Lamb, who was *s* for us, 379 16
Our Lord Jesus Christ, who offered himself to be *s* 448 7
Our Lord Jesus Christ, who offered himself to be *s* 451 6
Our Lord Jesus Christ, who offered himself to be *s* 452 1
They *s* their sons * 744 21

sacrifices

Offer the appointed *s* * 128 18
for with such *s* God is well pleased. 344 4
for such *s* are pleasing to God. 377 2
offer spiritual *s* acceptable to you; 534 2
Offer the appointed *s* * 588 8
I do not accuse you because of your *s*; * 654 19
Then you will be pleased with the appointed *s*, 657 20
I will offer you *s* of fat beasts 674 24
and ate *s* offered to the dead. 744 4

sadness

where there is *s*, joy. 833 9

safe

it is he who shall keep you *s*. 104 26
Be my strong rock, a castle to keep me *s*, 129 13
and keep him *s* for ever. 314 5
and kept me *s* upon my mother's breast. 610 19
For in the day of trouble he shall keep me *s* 618 1
a *s* refuge for his anointed. 620 2
Be my strong rock, a castle to keep me *s*, 622 12
He will keep *s* all his bones; * 629 7
They shall be kept *s* for ever, * 635 18
let your love and your faithfulness keep me *s* for ever, 641 3
Be my strong rock, a castle to keep me *s*; * 683 5
Hold me up, and I shall be *s*, * 773 7
it is he who shall keep you *s*. 779 14
in the midst of trouble, you keep me *s*; * 793 16
grant us a *s* lodging, and a holy rest, 833 17

safeguard

s them for our posterity. 840 11

safeguarded

that human rights may be *s* 822 7

safely

who hast *s* brought us to the beginning of this day: 57 8
and bring you *s* to his heavenly country; 460 8
He will bring me *s* back from the battle 661 22

safety

For only in thee can we live in *s*. 55 6
For only in thee can we live in *s*. 67 21
Bring us, we pray thee, in *s* to the morning hours; 70 8
with your might you brought them in *s* 85 22
For only in you can we live in *s*. 97 23
brought us in *s* to this new day: 100 2
For only in you can we live in *s*. 121 23
Bring us in *s* to the morning hours; 124 5
for only you, Lord, make me dwell in *s*. 129 7
you have brought us in *s* to this new day: 137 15
because it cannot continue in *s* without thy succor, 180 9
because it cannot continue in *s* without your help, 232 2
for only you, LORD, make me dwell in *s*. 588 16
In God is my *s* and my honor; * 669 20
He led them to *s*, and they were not afraid; * 699 11
and bring them in *s* to their journey's end; 831 5

sages

and *s* you revealed your righteous Law. 370 18

said

Jesus *s*, "Whosoever will come after me, 38 24
I was glad when they *s* unto me, "We will go 40 11
Jesus *s*, "I am the light of the world; 62 9
Jesus *s*, "If anyone would come after me, 76 23
I was glad when they *s* to me, "Let us go 78 10
Then they *s* among the nations, * 105 8
you *s* to your apostles, "Peace I give 107 17
Jesus *s*, "You are the light of the world. 109 7
For the same God who *s*, "Out of darkness 110 3
Jesus *s*, "I am the light of the world; 116 5
you *s* to your apostles, "Peace I give to 138 16
For the same God who *s*, "Out of darkness 139 12
I grieved with this generation, and *s*, * 146 21
washed their feet, *s* to them, "Do you know what I, 274 9
God spake these words, and *s*: 317 24
Jesus *s*, "The first commandment is this: 351 7
and gave it to his disciples, and *s*, "Take, eat: 362 20
he gave it to them, and *s*, "Drink this, 363 2
and gave it to his disciples, and *s*, "Take, eat: 368 12
he gave it to them, and *s*, "Drink this, 368 15
he took bread, *s* the blessing, 371 10
and gave it to his friends, and *s*, "Take, eat: 371 12
gave thanks, and *s*, "Drink this, 371 15
gave it to his disciples, and *s*, "Take, eat: 374 17
he gave it to them, and *s*, "Drink this, 374 20
Christ, you *s* to your apostles, "Peace I give 395 8
Jesus *s*, "I am the bread of life; 396 4
Jesus *s*, "I am the living bread 397 1
Jesus *s*, "Abide in me, as I in you. 397 7
he took bread, *s* the blessing, 403 4
and gave it to his friends, and *s*, "Take, eat: 403 6
gave thanks, and *s*, "Drink this, 403 9
and gave it to his disciples, and *s*, "Take, eat: 405 3
he gave it to them, and *s*, "Drink this, 405 7
and *s*, "This is my Body (Blood)." 408 5
It was our Lord Jesus himself who *s*, "Come to me, 465 9
Christ who *s*, "I am Resurrection and I am Life." 497 2
he *s* to me, "You are my Son; 586 15
The fool has *s* in his heart, "There is no God." * 598 12
I have *s* to the LORD, "You are my Lord, 599 20
While I felt secure, I *s*, 621 16
I have *s*, "You are my God. 623 21
Yet I *s* in my alarm, 624 14
I *s*, "I will confess my transgressions to the LORD." * 625 9
They opened their mouths at me and *s*, * 631 12
For I *s*, "Do not let them rejoice at my expense, * 638 1
I *s*, "I will keep watch upon my ways, * 638 15

So I held my tongue and *s* nothing; * 638 19
and so I *s*, "Behold, I come. 640 19
I *s*, "LORD, be merciful to me; * 642 6
The fool has *s* in his heart, "There is no God." * 658 21
And I *s*, "Oh, that I had wings like a dove! * 660 17
God spoke from his holy place and *s*: * 667 20
The LORD has *s*, "I will bring them back 678 1
They *s* to themselves, "Let us destroy them 689 24
And I *s*, "My grief is this: * 693 20
They railed against God and *s*, * 696 11
who brought you out of the land of Egypt and *s*, * 704 22
They have *s*, "Come, let us wipe them out 706 9
Who *s*, "Let us take for ourselves * 707 1
Of Zion it shall be *s*, "Everyone was born in her, * 711 20
spoke once in a vision and *s* to your faithful people: * 715 3
As often as I *s*, "My foot has slipped," * 724 1
Forty years long I detested that generation and *s*, * 725 12
And I *s*, "O my God, 732 24
God spoke from his holy place and *s*, * 750 7
The LORD *s* to my Lord, "Sit at my right hand, * 753 12
I believed, even when I *s*, 759 20
In my distress I *s*, "No one can be trusted." 759 22
I was glad when they *s* to me, * 779 18
Then they *s* among the nations, * 782 10
who *s*, "Down with it! down with it! 792 17
I have *s* to the LORD, "You are my God; * 796 13

saint

who at noonday called your servant *S* Paul 107 12
S Paul exhorts all persons to prepare themselves 316 20

saints

be partakers of the inheritance of the *s* in light. 40 2
with the *s* and of the household of God. 40 4
The Lord is glorious in his *s*: 44 8
Make them to be numbered with thy *s*, 53 21
the communion of *s*, 54 7
the communion of *s*, 66 23
the communion of [_________ and] all thy *s*, 68 23
share in the inheritance of the *s* in light. 77 23
citizens with the *s* and members of the household 78 2
The Lord is glorious in his *s*: 82 3
and bring us with your *s* 96 11
the communion of *s*, 96 27
Lord Christ, your *s* have been the lights of the world 111 12
the communion of *s*, 120 23
the communion of [_________ and] all your *s*, 122 25
in the fellowship of [_________ and] all the *s*, 152 19
Grant us grace so to follow thy blessed *s* 194 11
who willest to be glorified in thy *s*, 196 15
with thy *s* in heaven and on earth: 199 5
Give us grace so to follow your blessed *s* 245 18
whose will it is to be glorified in your *s*, 248 1
with your *s* in heaven and on earth: 250 15
and to the whole communion of *s* 267 14
Bring us with all your *s* to the joy of his resurrection. 269 2
and where your *s* for ever sing your praise; 290 5
the communion of *s*, 293 15
the communion of *s*, 304 18
share in the inheritance of the *s* in light; 311 18
the good examples of [_________ and of] all thy *s*, 330 5
Who, in the multitude of thy *s*, hast compassed us 347 17
wonderful grace and virtue declared in all thy *s*, 348 1
Who in the obedience of thy *s* hast given us 348 4
thou art greatly glorified in the assembly of thy *s*. 348 7
and at the last day bring us with all your *s* 363 17
with [_________ and] all your *s*, 369 11
all the *s* who have found favor 375 23
For in the multitude of your *s* you have surrounded us 380 12
wonderful grace and virtue declared in all your *s*, 380 17
Because in the obedience of your *s* you have given 380 20
glorified in the assembly of your *s*. 381 2
In the communion of [_________ and of all the] *s*, 385 13
We praise you for your *s* who have entered into joy; 387 19
with all your *s* in your eternal kingdom. 389 10
with all the *s*, they may have rest 391 17
(blessed _________) and] all the *s*, let us commend 391 20
with your *s* in heaven and on earth: 395 18
And so we join the *s* and angels in proclaiming 402 7
And so we join the *s* and angels in proclaiming 404 9
the communion of *s*, 416 23
s feast for ever in your heavenly home; 430 23
But I have squandered the inheritance of your *s*, 450 14
with your *s* in light, 463 21
all your *s* in the eternal habitations; 464 18
glorious company of the *s* in light. 465 6
May angels surround him, and *s* welcome him 466 5
perfection in the company of the *s*. 466 15
all your *s* in the eternal habitations; 466 18
in the fellowship of thy *s*; 470 4
dear in the sight of the LORD is the death of his *s*. 479 19
to believe and trust in the communion of *s*, 481 15
life which thou dost all thy *s*, 481 26
but the fullness of joy with all thy *s*; 482 7
Give rest, O Christ, to thy servant(s) with thy *s*, 482 9
Give rest, O Christ, to thy servant(s) with thy *s*, 483 3
into the glorious company of the *s* in light. 483 11
be partakers of the inheritance of the *s* in light; 486 15
grace and virtue declared in all thy *s*, 487 12
O God, the King of *s*, we praise and magnify 489 14
be partakers of the inheritance of the *s* in light; 489 21
in the fellowship of your *s*; 493 13
the communion of *s*, 496 17
give him fellowship with all your *s*. 497 17
but the fullness of joy with all your *s*; 498 18
Give rest, O Christ, to your servant(s) with your *s*, 499 1
into the glorious company of the *s* in light. 499 18
O God, the King of *s*, we praise and glorify 504 12
be partakers of the inheritance of the *s* in light; 504 19
equip the *s* for the work of ministry 533 9
with all the *s*, they may have rest 550 22
(blessed N.) and] all the *s*, let us commend ourselves, 550 27
a sign of the heavenly Altar where your *s* 574 2
of [N., our patron, and of] all your *S*, 579 11
Fear the LORD, you that are his *s*, * 628 11
he preserves the lives of his *s* 727 18
O God, whom *s* and angels delight to worship 819 13
and in the fellowship of thy *s*; 830 25
For the communion of *s*, in all times and places, 837 19
Stephen, the first martyr, and all the martyrs and *s* 838 16
through many seers and *s*, 845 20
communion of the *s*. 862 19
What is the communion of *s*? 862 20
The communion of *s* is the whole family of God, 862 21

saith

s the Lord of hosts.	38	9
Thus *s* the high and lofty One	40	23
Hear what our Lord Jesus Christ saith:	319	8
Hear what our Lord Jesus Christ *s*:	324	1
I am the resurrection and the life, *s* the Lord;	469	1
even so *s* the Spirit, for they rest from their labors.	469	15

sake

and grant, O most merciful Father, for his *s*,	42	8
and grant, O most merciful Father, for his *s*,	63	11
thy tender mercies' *s*.	69	11
Grant this for the *s* of thy love.	70	13
and all for thy love's *s*.	71	5
For the *s* of your Son Jesus Christ,	79	18
for your tender mercies' *s*.	107	11
and ourselves as your servants, for Jesus' *s*.	110	2
For the *s* of your Son Jesus Christ,	117	1
for your tender mercies' *s*.	123	10
Grant this for the *s* of your love.	124	10
and all for your love's *s*.	124	21
For the *s* of your Son our Lord Jesus Christ,	127	11
for the *s* of your Name, lead me and guide me.	129	15
and all for your love's *s*.	134	10
for your mercies' *s*.	138	15
and ourselves as your servants, for Jesus' *s*.	139	11
Grant this for the *s* of your love.	139	19
And deliver us for thy Name's *s*.	154	4
Grant this for thine only Son Jesus Christ's *s*,	165	4
suffer shame and loss for the *s* of thy Son	168	20
for the *s* of our Savior Jesus	178	9
and patiently suffer for the truth's *s*;	190	7
and to suffer gladly for the *s* of the same our Lord	195	5
We ask this for the *s* of Jesus Christ,	199	9
for the *s* of him who came among us	210	6
Grant this for the *s* of your only Son	216	17
suffer shame and loss for the *s* of your Son	220	11
for the *s* of our Savior Jesus Christ,	230	4
and patiently suffer for the truth's *s*;	241	16
and to suffer gladly for the *s* of our Lord	247	3
We ask this for the *s* of Jesus	250	18
for the *s* of him who came among us	261	11
for the *s* of him who suffered for us,	279	18
For the *s* of thy Son Jesus Christ,	320	18
and grant, O most merciful Father, for his *s*,	321	11
For our *s* he was crucified under Pontius Pilate;	327	4
our prayers, O Father, for Jesus Christ's *s*,	330	7
for thy Son our Lord Jesus Christ's *s*,	331	15
For the *s* of thy Son Jesus Christ,	331	29
For the *s* of your Son Jesus Christ,	352	18
For our *s* he was crucified under Pontius Pilate;	358	20
For the *s* of your Son Jesus Christ,	360	10
grant us for the *s* of your Son	395	2
ask this for the *s* of Jesus Christ,	395	22
For the *s* of your Son Jesus Christ,	398	2
for the *s* of Jesus Christ our Lord.	432	7
and guides me along right pathways for his Name's *s*.	443	6
For the *s* of your Son Jesus Christ,	455	1
Hear us, we pray, for your dear Name's *s*.	459	6
in the paths of righteousness for his Name's *s*.	476	7
for the *s* of thy Son Jesus Christ	486	15
Grant this, O Father, for the *s* of the same thy Son	487	21
for your tender mercies' *s*.	504	25
I will, for the *s* of Christ Jesus.	518	31
For our *s* he was crucified under Pontius Pilate;	519	23
For our *s* he was crucified under Pontius Pilate;	530	14
For our *s* he was crucified under Pontius Pilate;	542	14
All this I ask for the *s* of your Son	563	10
save me for your mercy's *s*.	590	6
and guides me along right pathways for his Name's *s*.	613	2
and for the *s* of your goodness, O LORD.	615	3
For your Name's *s*, O LORD, *	615	10
for the *s* of your Name, lead me and guide me.	622	14
Indeed, for your *s* we are killed all the day long; *	647	1
and save us, for the *s* of your steadfast love.	647	10
and for the *s* of justice.	647	20
for your temple's *s* at Jerusalem.	678	17
Surely, for your *s* have I suffered reproach, *	680	1
deliver us and forgive us our sins, for your Name's *s*.	701	25
and rebuked kings for their *s*,	739	6
But he saved them for his Name's *s*, *	742	14
for your tender mercy's *s*, deliver me.	752	18
save me for your mercy's *s*.	752	28
For my brethren and companions' *s*, *	780	11
For your servant David's *s*, *	786	17
Revive me, O LORD, for your Name's *s*; *	799	23
for your righteousness' *s*, bring me out of trouble.	799	24
for the *s* of him through whom all things were made,	814	4
And this we beg for Jesus Christ's *s*.	815	12
for the *s* of Jesus Christ thy Son	816	14
O Lord Jesus Christ, you became poor for our *s*,	819	6
Strengthen those who suffer for the *s* of conscience;	823	10
This we ask for the *s* of Jesus	823	15
Son, who for our *s* became poor,	826	7
Jesus, for our *s* you were condemned as a criminal:	826	16
this we ask for your mercy's *s*.	826	26
for Christ's *s*.	835	12
for the *s* of your dear Son,	841	5

sale

and are making no profit on the *s* of them.	646	10

Salem

At *S* is his tabernacle, *	692	3

salt

A fruitful land into *s* flats, *	748	23

salvation

my *s* unto the end of the earth.	38	4
necessary for our life and our *s*.	41	10
let us heartily rejoice in the strength of our *s*.	44	11
And hath raised up a mighty *s* for us *	50	24
To give knowledge of *s* unto his people *	51	14
For mine eyes have seen thy *s*, *	51	25
And grant us thy *s*.	55	2
For mine eyes have seen thy *s*, *	66	3
And grant us thy *s*.	67	17
that my *s* may reach to the end of the earth.	76	3
necessary for our life and our *s*.	79	5
let us shout for joy to the Rock of our *s*.	82	6
from the springs of *s*.	86	6
You will call your walls, *S*, *	87	25
To give his people knowledge of *s* *	93	3
And grant us your *s*.	97	19

for you are our light and *s*, 113 7
And grant us your *s*. 121 19
and show him my *s*. 131 5
let us heartily rejoice in the strength of our *s*. 146 2
preach repentance and prepare the way for our *s*: 159 10
name of Jesus to be the sign of our *s*: 162 2
proclaim to all people the Good News of his *s*, 163 16
preach repentance and prepare the way for our *s*: 211 10
name of Jesus to be the sign of our *s*: 213 14
proclaim to all people the Good News of his *s*, 215 10
O God of my *s*. 267 5
Accomplish in us the work of your *s*, 268 29
O Lord God of our *s*, 270 5
For those who have never heard the word of *s* 279 21
out in tranquillity the plan of *s*; 280 17
and let your trumpets shout *S* 286 2
sign for us of the *s* of all nations 289 15
out in tranquillity the plan of *s*; 291 14
For us and for our *s* 326 18
who for us men and for our *s* 328 1
The Blood of Christ, the cup of *s*. 338 16
eternal *s* for all who put their trust in him. 346 16
For us and for our *s* 358 15
The Blood of Christ, the cup of *s*. 365 7
and the author of our *s*. 369 14
and through the prophets you taught us to hope for *s*. 373 25
proclaimed the good news of *s*; 374 5
the bread of life and the cup of *s*, 375 7
eternal *s* for all who put their trust in him. 379 13
and for the *s* of our souls, 383 4
bring them the joy of your *s*. 389 5
strength in our weakness, and everlasting *s*; 399 11
author of *s*, and giver of all grace: 429 3
I will lift up the cup of *s* * 442 21
O Lord, holy Father, giver of health and *s*: 455 9
given for health and *s* is the Name of our Lord 457 3
strength in our weakness, and everlasting *s*; 457 9
The LORD is my light and my *s*; 477 12
O visit me with thy *s*; 478 19
and to contain all things necessary to *s*; 513 11
out in tranquillity the plan of *s*; 515 7
For us and for our *s* 519 18
and to contain all things necessary to *s*; 526 17
out in tranquillity the plan of *s*; 528 5
For us and for our *s* 530 9
boldly proclaim the gospel of *s*; 534 3
and to contain all things necessary to *s*; 538 17
out in tranquillity the plan of *s*; 540 5
For us and for our *s* 542 9
an instrument of your *s* for the people 563 1
that for us and for our *s*, you sent your Son 573 9
and rejoice in your *s* * 594 5
my shield, the horn of my *s*, and my refuge; 602 10
Exalted is the God of my *s*! 606 4
and a just reward from the God of their *s*." 613 24
for you are the God of my *s*; 614 22
The LORD is my light and my *s*; 617 7
do not forsake me, O God of my *s*. 618 18
say to my soul, "I am your *s*." 629 19
O Lord of my *s*. 638 14
let those who love your *s* continually say, 641 17
the *s* of God." 656 4
O God of my *s*. 657 11
from him comes my *s*. 669 6
He alone is my rock and my *s*, * 669 7
O God of our *s*, * 672 18
the God of our *s*, who bears our burdens. 677 22
He is our God, the God of our *s*; * 677 23
let those who love your *s* say for ever, 682 20
and grant us your *s*. 709 8
Truly, his *s* is very near to those who fear him, * 709 12
my God, and the rock of my *s*.' 715 19
and show him my *s*. 720 21
let us shout for joy to the Rock of our *s*. 724 15
proclaim the good news of his *s* from day to day. 725 20
I will lift up the cup of *s* * 759 25
and he has become my *s*. 761 25
and have become my *s*. 762 14
and your *s*, according to your promise. 766 18
My soul has longed for your *s*; * 770 3
My eyes have failed from watching for your *s* * 773 19
I have hoped for your *s*, O LORD, * 777 11
I long for your *s*, O LORD, * 778 3
I will clothe her priests with *s*, * 787 3
O Lord GOD, the strength of my *s*, * 796 15
towards the attainment of everlasting *s*; 832 20
give us, as you gave to them, the hope of *s* 838 18

Samaria

and in *S*, and unto the uttermost part of the earth. 39 20
and *S*, and to the ends of the earth. 77 19

same

rising of the sun even unto the going down of the *s* 38 6
through the *s* Jesus Christ our Lord. 56 4
through the *s* thy Son Jesus Christ our Lord. 56 10
Defend us in the *s* with thy mighty power; 57 9
through the *s* thy Son Jesus Christ our Lord. 58 6
For the *s* God who said, "Out of darkness 110 3
For the *s* God who said, "Out of darkness 139 12
through the *s* Jesus Christ our Lord, 160 9
through the *s* our Lord Jesus Christ, 161 11
liveth and reigneth with thee and the *s* Spirit ever, 161 12
Grant that the *s* light, enkindled 161 15
through the *s* Jesus Christ our Lord, 161 16
through the *s* Jesus Christ our Lord, 162 16
who with thee and the *s* Spirit liveth and reigneth, 163 5
through the *s* Jesus Christ our Lord, 163 11
liveth and reigneth with thee and the *s* Holy Ghost, 165 5
through the *s* Jesus Christ our Lord, 165 18
through the *s* Jesus Christ our Lord, 168 7
through the *s* thy Son Jesus Christ our Lord, 168 14
through the *s* thy Son Jesus Christ our Lord, 169 4
Mercifully grant that we may thankfully receive the *s* 169 9
the *s* thy Son Jesus Christ our Lord; 169 11
through the *s* thy Son Christ our Lord, 170 12
through the *s* Jesus Christ our Lord, 170 18
in the unity of the *s* Spirit, 170 20
through the *s* Jesus Christ our Lord, 171 2
liveth and reigneth with thee and the *s* Spirit ever, 171 3
through the *s* thy Son Jesus Christ our Lord, 171 20
through the *s* Jesus Christ our Lord, 172 5
through the *s* thy Son Jesus Christ our Lord, 172 11
through the *s* Jesus Christ our Lord, 173 2

through the *s* thy Son Jesus Christ our Lord, 173 8
through the *s* Jesus Christ our Lord, 174 12
and exalt us unto the *s* place 175 4
liveth and reigneth with thee and the *s* Holy Ghost, 175 6
in the unity of the *s* Spirit, 175 13
by the *s* Spirit to have a right judgment in all things, 175 17
in the unity of the *s* Spirit, 175 20
thy merciful guiding may perform the *s*; 178 3
through the *s* Jesus Christ our Lord, 179 1
liveth and reigneth with thee and the *s* Spirit, 179 9
may have grace and power faithfully to fulfill the *s*; 179 13
through the *s* thy Son Jesus Christ our Lord, 181 2
liveth and reigneth with thee and the *s* Spirit, 181 9
who with thee and the *s* Spirit liveth and reigneth, 182 4
through the *s* Jesus Christ our Lord, 183 15
show forth our thankfulness unto thee for the *s* 187 12
by the *s* thy Son Jesus Christ our Lord; 187 19
through the *s* thy Son Jesus Christ our Lord, 188 12
through the *s* Jesus Christ our Lord, 189 2
through the *s* thy Son Jesus Christ our Lord, 190 7
in the unity of the *s* Spirit, 190 15
through the *s* Jesus Christ our Lord, 191 12
through the *s* thy Son Jesus Christ our Lord, 192 4
through the *s* thy Son Jesus Christ our Lord, 193 15
through the *s* our Lord Jesus Christ, 193 21
through the *s* Jesus Christ our Lord, 194 13
for the sake of the *s* our Lord Jesus Christ; 195 5
through the *s* Jesus Christ our Lord, 197 9
liveth and reigneth with thee and the *s* Spirit, 197 10
who with thee and the *s* Spirit liveth and reigneth, 197 17
through the *s* thy Son Jesus Christ our Lord, 198 5
in the unity of the *s* Spirit ever, 200 5
through the *s* Jesus Christ our Lord, 201 16
through the *s* thy Son Jesus Christ our Lord, 203 9
through the *s* Jesus Christ our Lord, 203 16
in the unity of the *s* Spirit, 204 15
the *s* thy Son Jesus Christ our Lord; 205 1
in the unity of the *s* Spirit, 205 2
liveth and reigneth with thee and the *s* Spirit, 205 20
through the *s* thy Son Jesus Christ our Lord, 206 14
liveth and reigneth with thee and the *s* Spirit, 206 16
the *s* thy Son our Saviour Jesus Christ, 209 15
liveth and reigneth with thee and the *s* Spirit, 209 22
with you and the *s* Spirit be honor and glory, 213 6
Grant us by the *s* Spirit to have a right judgment 227 10
benefits procured unto us by the *s*. 335 16
But thou art the *s* Lord 337 12
through the *s* Jesus Christ our Lord; 343 1
through the *s* thy Son Jesus Christ our Lord, 470 10
the mountains shake at the tempest of the *s*. 471 22
for the sake of the *s* thy Son Jesus Christ, 487 22
But you are always the *s*, * 733 5
The *s* stone which the builders rejected * 762 15
through the *s* Jesus Christ our Lord. 835 7
not necessary for all persons in the *s* way 860 15

Samuel

and *S* among those who call upon his Name, * 729 12
and *S* with Hannah his mother; 838 13

sanctification

and to bring to fulfillment the *s* of all. 374 12
and in the *s* of the Holy Spirit? 532 27

sanctified

body of thy faithful people is governed and *s*: 57 20
and *s* a day of rest for all your creatures: 99 7
body of your faithful people is governed and *s*: 100 12
body of thy faithful people is governed and *s*: 206 2
body of your faithful people is governed and *s*: 256 20
body of your faithful people is governed and *s*: 278 12
being *s* by the Holy Spirit. 369 8
May God the Son, who *s* a home at Nazareth, 445 5
so that our lives are sustained and *s* 569 1

sanctifier

O God the Holy Ghost, *S* of the faithful, 148 5

sanctifies

In the Name of the Holy Spirit who *s* you. 464 24

sanctify

and *s* a day of rest for all thy creatures: 56 12
S this new fire, 285 9
Now *s* this water, we pray you, 307 3
and *s*, with thy Word and Holy Spirit, these thy gifts 335 19
s these gifts of bread and wine, 342 18
S them by your Holy Spirit to be for your people 363 13
S us also that we may faithfully receive 363 15
S them by your Holy Spirit 371 8
S them by your Holy Spirit 403 1
Holy Spirit bless and *s* this bread (wine) 408 2
Holy Spirit to *s* this oil; 455 10
S, O Lord, the sickness of your servant 460 1
S, O Lord, those whom you have called 460 10
s this place; 569 11
S this Table dedicated to you. 574 1
Guide and *s*, 819 7

sanctifying

Spirit may descend upon us, and upon these gifts, *s* 375 5

sanctuary

may be duly prepared for the service of thy *s*, 56 14
Christ has entered, not into a *s* made with hands, 77 14
the *s*, O Lord, that your hand has established. 85 27
may be duly prepared for the service of your *s*, 99 9
your procession into the *s*, my God and my King. 678 6
Until I entered the *s* of God * 688 11
the enemy has laid waste everything in your *s*. 689 15
He built his *s* like the heights of heaven, * 700 17
Oh, the power and the splendor of his *s*! 726 4
Judah became God's *s* * 756 21

sand

and winged birds like the *s* of the sea. 697 4
they would be more in number than the *s*; * 795 13

sandal

on Edom I throw down my *s* to claim it, * 668 2
on Edom I throw down my *s* to claim it, * 750 13

sang

and *s* him songs of praise. 742 23

sank

they *s* into the depths like a stone. 85 13

sap

The trees of the LORD are full of *s*, * 736 9

Sarah

for Abraham, the father of believers, and *S* his wife; 838 11

sat

those who *s* in darkness and in the shadow of death. 483 17
those who *s* in darkness and in the shadow of death. 500 6
nor *s* in the seats of the scornful! 585 4
I have not *s* with the worthless, * 616 14
Some *s* in darkness and deep gloom, * 747 1
By the waters of Babylon we *s* down and wept, * 792 1

Satan

and finally to beat down *S* under our feet, 152 13
Son was led by the Spirit to be tempted of *S*: 166 10
Son was led by the Spirit to be tempted by *S*: 218 2
by which we once renounced *S* and all his works, 292 6
Do you renounce *S* and all the spiritual forces 302 7
It is required that we renounce *S*, 858 22

satisfaction

and sufficient sacrifice, oblation, and *s*, 334 13

satisfied

We certify to you that he has *s* the requirements 526 7
We certify to you that he has *s* the requirements 538 7
when I awake, I shall be *s*, 602 5
The poor shall eat and be *s*, 612 7
they will be *s* by the beauty of your house, 672 15
the earth is fully *s* by the fruit of your works. 736 2
and he *s* them with bread from heaven. 741 6

satisfies

He *s* you with good things, * 733 17
For he *s* the thirsty * 746 18
he *s* you with the finest wheat. 805 6

satisfy

With long life will I *s* him, * 131 4
O merciful Creator, whose hand is open wide to *s* 208 9
O merciful Creator, your hand is open wide to *s* 259 11
and *s* him with honey from the rock. 705 8
S us by your loving-kindness in the morning; * 719 1
With long life will I *s* him, * 720 20
and *s* her poor with bread. 787 2
and *s* the needs of every living creature. 802 20
and for leading us to accomplishments which *s* 836 8

save

O Lord, *s* thy people, and bless thine heritage; 55 15
O God, make speed to *s* us. 63 17
Unworthy as I am, you will *s* me, 91 22
that he would *s* us from our enemies, * 92 23
S us from the time of trial, 97 13
S your people, Lord, and bless your inheritance; 98 9
O God, make speed to *s* us. 103 1
S us from the time of trial, 106 23
O God, make speed to *s* us. 117 10
S us from the time of trial, 121 13
O God, make speed to *s* us. 128 3
S us from the time of trial, 133 5
let each one find thee mighty to *s*; 166 12
let each one find you mighty to *s*; 218 4
S us and help us, we humbly beseech thee, O Lord. 282 5
S us from the time of trial 311 10
Jesus came into the world to *s* sinners. 332 14
S us from the time of trial, 364 10
S us from the time of trial, 398 21
S us from the time of trial, 428 17
Jesus came into the world to *s* sinners. 449 19
S us, and help us, we humbly beseech you, O Lord. 455 18
undivided Trinity guard your body, *s* your soul, 460 7
S us from the time of trial, 464 13
S us from the time of trial, 502 10
s me for your mercy's sake. 590 6
s and deliver me from all who pursue me; 590 21
and *s* us from this generation for ever. 597 17
You will *s* a lowly people, * 604 18
S me from the sword, * 611 20
S me from the lion's mouth, * 611 22
S your people and bless your inheritance; * 620 3
and in your loving-kindness *s* me." 623 26
for all its strength it cannot *s*. 627 10
and will *s* those whose spirits are crushed. 629 4
you *s* both man and beast, O LORD. 632 16
and *s* us, for the sake of your steadfast love. 647 10
S me, O God, by your Name; * 659 17
He will send from heaven and *s* me; 663 25
and *s* me from those who thirst for my blood. 665 21
S us by your right hand and answer us, * 667 18
S me, O God, * 679 7
S me from the mire; do not let me sink; * 680 17
For God will *s* Zion and rebuild the cities of Judah; * 682 7
incline your ear to me and *s* me. 683 4
because there is none who will *s*." 683 24
and to *s* all the oppressed of the earth. 692 19
S the weak and the orphan; * 705 13
s your servant who puts his trust in you. 710 2
and *s* the child of your handmaid. 711 8
who can *s* himself from the power of the grave? 717 11
S us, O LORD our God, 745 19
s with your right hand and answer me. 750 6
s me for your mercy's sake. 752 28
to *s* his life from those who would condemn him. 753 11
"O LORD, I pray you, *s* my life." 759 9
I am yours; oh, that you would *s* me! * 771 7
oh, that you would *s* me! * 775 18
your right hand shall *s* me. 793 18
s me from those who pursue me, 798 13
S us from violence, discord, and confusion; 820 5
when they are accused, *s* them from speaking in hate; 823 10
when they are rejected, *s* them from bitterness; 823 11
when they are imprisoned, *s* them from despair; 823 12
and *s* them from becoming brutal or callous. 826 23
s us from selfish use of what thou givest, 828 6
the Spirit of wisdom may *s* us from all false choices, 832 9

saved

That we should be *s* from our enemies, * 51 1
that they may repent of their sin and be *s*. 91 11
the earth may look to you and be *s*; 107 10
for in returning and rest we shall be *s*; 138 10

the earth may look to you and be *s*; 138 14
but that the world through him might be *s*; 277 4
how he *s* his people in ages past; 288 2
Grant that we, who are *s* 289 2
and so shall I be *s* from my enemies. 602 13
you *s* me from my deadly foe. 606 9
There is no king that can be *s* by a mighty army; * 627 7
and *s* me from all my troubles. 628 6
show the light of your countenance, and we shall be *s*. 702 17
show the light of your countenance, and we shall be *s*. 703 2
You called on me in trouble, and I *s* you; * 704 14
But he *s* them for his Name's sake, * 742 14
He *s* them from the hand of those who hated them * 742 18
and *s* them from the grave. 747 22
in returning and rest we shall be *s*, 832 14

saves

Surely, it is God who *s* me; * 86 1

saving

Thy *s* health among all nations. 55 10
within the reach of thy *s* embrace: 58 10
Thy *s* health among all nations. 68 2
Your *s* health among all nations. 98 4
the reach of your *s* embrace: 101 3
Your *s* health among all nations. 122 4
Give me the joy of your *s* help again * 137 7
Give me the joy of your *s* help again * 266 26
your *s* health among all nations. 281 8
Let us hear the record of God's *s* deeds in history, 288 1
my heart is joyful because of your *s* help. 598 9
the *s* deeds that he has done. 612 22
Give me the joy of your *s* help again * 657 5
your *s* health among all nations. 675 12
and *s* deeds all day long; * 684 10
nor did they put their trust in his *s* power. 696 21
and visit me with your *s* help; 742 5
thy *s* health unto all nations. 815 1

savior

David a *S*, which is Christ the Lord. 37 10
Our King and *S* draweth nigh: 43 1
and my spirit hath rejoiced in God my *S*. 50 2
through our Lord and *S* Jesus Christ. 57 24
and my spirit hath rejoiced in God my *S*. 65 5
Lord God, whose Son our *S* Jesus Christ triumphed 69 1
through the merits of Jesus Christ our *S*. 69 22
for the love of thy only Son, our *S* Jesus Christ. 70 3
thy Son our *S* Jesus Christ. 70 9
David, a *S*, who is Christ the Lord. 75 10
Our King and *S* now draws near: 80 10
the Lord has become my *S*. 85 4
and he will be my *S*. 86 4
my spirit rejoices in God my *S*; * 91 28
He has raised up for us a mighty *s*, * 92 20
For these eyes of mine have seen the *S*, * 93 14
through our Lord and *S* Jesus Christ. 100 16
Blessed *S*, at this hour you hung upon the cross, 107 8
Almighty *S*, who at noonday called 107 12
for the love of thy only Son, our *S*, Jesus Christ. 111 3
my spirit rejoices in God my *S*; * 119 5
For these eyes of mine have seen the *S*, * 120 3
Lord God, whose Son our *S* Jesus Christ triumphed 123 1
through the mercies of Christ Jesus our *S*. 123 20
of your only Son, our *S* Jesus Christ. 123 23
your Son our *S* Jesus Christ. 124 6
your only Son, our *S* Jesus Christ. 133 12
For these eyes of mine have seen the *S*, * 135 3
Blessed *S*, at this hour you hung upon the cross, 138 12
For these eyes of mine have seen the *S*, * 140 9
the love of him who is the *S* of 162 3
confess him as Lord and *S*; 163 5
whose Son our *S* Jesus Christ is the light 163 7
to answer readily the call of our *S* Jesus Christ 163 15
hast manifested to us in thy Son our *S* Jesus Christ; 164 8
hast sent thy Son our *S* Jesus Christ 168 2
suffer shame and loss for the sake of thy Son our *S* 168 20
O Lord God, whose blessed Son our *S* gave his back 169 1
O Almighty God, whose blessed Son our *S* Jesus 174 8
whither our *S* Christ is gone before; 175 5
through the merits of Christ Jesus our *S*, 175 19
for the sake of our *S* Jesus Christ, 178 9
hast given us in our *S* Jesus Christ; 184 20
follow the one Lord, our *S* Jesus Christ; 187 5
thy Son our *S* by preaching repentance: 190 3
whose Son our *S* Jesus Christ was lifted 192 13
to the Gospel of thy Son our *S*; 192 21
love and mercy of our Lord and *S* Jesus Christ; 194 5
confess the Name of our *S* Jesus Christ 195 2
unsearchable riches of our *S* Jesus Christ; 196 12
into the stature of the fullness of our Lord and *S* 197 1
thy Son Jesus Christ our *S*; 204 14
through our Lord and *S* Jesus Christ, 206 6
the redeeming work of our *S* Jesus Christ; 206 19
the same thy Son our *S* Jesus Christ, 209 15
the love of him who is the *S* of the world, 213 15
confess him as Lord and *S*; 214 16
whose Son our *S* Jesus Christ is the light 215 1
to answer readily the call of our *S* Jesus Christ 215 9
known to us in your Son our *S* Jesus Christ; 216 3
you sent your Son our *S* Jesus Christ 219 14
suffer shame and loss for the sake of your Son our *S* 220 11
whose blessed Son our *S* gave his body 220 14
whose blessed Son our *S* Jesus Christ 226 1
exalt us to that place where our *S* Christ has gone 226 16
for the sake of our *S* Jesus Christ, 230 4
the merits and mediation of Jesus Christ our *S*; 234 18
which you have given us in our *S* Jesus Christ; 236 12
the one Lord, our *S* Jesus Christ; 238 18
prepare the way of your Son our *S* 241 12
whose Son our *S* Jesus Christ was lifted 244 1
Matthew to the Gospel of your Son our *S*; 244 8
the love and mercy of our Lord and *S* Jesus Christ; 245 14
confess the Name of our *S* Jesus Christ 246 9
proclaim the unsearchable riches of our *S* Jesus 247 24
of the fullness of our Lord and *S* Jesus Christ; 248 12
your Son Jesus Christ our *S*; 255 12
through our Lord and *S* Jesus Christ, 257 3
known the redeeming work of our *S* Jesus Christ; 257 15
who laid down his life for us, your Son our *S* 260 20
set forth in the Gospel of our *S*, 265 8
through Jesus Christ our *S*. 265 20
you sent your Son our *S* Jesus Christ 272 8
through our Lord and *S* Jesus Christ. 278 16
O *S* of the world, 282 3

and accept him as your *S*? 302 17
I do, and with God's grace I will follow him as my *S* 303 13
in the risen life of Jesus Christ our *S*. 307 6
Holy Spirit to be the *S* and servant of all, 307 10
Our *S* Christ, on the night before he suffered, 316 1
by our *S* Christ, who took upon himself our flesh, 316 13
of thy dearly beloved Son our *S* Jesus Christ, 335 9
thy Son our *S* Jesus Christ's holy institution, 335 21
And now, as our *S* Christ hath taught us, 336 16
Body and Blood of thy Son our *S* Jesus Christ; 339 5
And now, as our *S* Christ hath taught us, 343 6
And now, as our *S* 363 22
of your Son our *S* Jesus Christ, 365 11
of your Son our *S* Jesus Christ; 366 4
to be the *S* and Redeemer of the world. 368 6
And now, as our *S* 369 18
And now, as our *S* 372 14
you sent your only Son to be our *S*. 374 2
And now, as our *S* 376 1
Let us pray in the words our *S* Christ has taught us. 398 11
I do, and with God's grace I will follow him as my *S* 415 12
Let us pray together in the words our *S* taught us. 428 7
my spirit rejoices in God my *S*;* 441 13
following the example of our Lord and *S*, 443 29
the knowledge of his *S* Jesus Christ. 445 2
your Son our *S* Jesus Christ. 450 20
S of the world, by your cross and precious blood 455 16
S Jesus Christ, beseeching him to uphold you 456 8
through Jesus Christ our *S*. 461 18
Into your hands, O merciful *S*, we commend 465 1
through Jesus Christ our *S*. 482 8
Into thy hands, O merciful *S*, we commend 483 6
O holy and most merciful *S*, 484 9
O holy and merciful *S*, 484 14
a faithful Creator and most merciful *S*, 488 14
Holy and merciful *S*, 492 10
through Jesus Christ our *S*. 498 19
Into your hands, O merciful *S*, we commend 499 13
in the Name of Jesus Christ our *S*. 505 16
The Scriptures tell us that our *S* Christ spent 514 12
are called to make Christ known as *S* and Lord, 531 3
for the sake of your Son our *S* Jesus Christ. 563 10
in the risen life of Jesus Christ our *S*. 570 20
he is the *S* of the true in heart. 591 19
O *S* of those who take refuge at your right hand 601 12
Help us, O God our *S*, for the glory of your Name; * 701 24
Restore us then, O God our *S*; * 709 1
O LORD, my God, my *S*, * 712 1
They forgot God their *S*, * 743 13
the kingdom of our Lord and *S* Jesus Christ. 816 4
of Jesus Christ thy Son our *S*. 816 15
the Father of our Lord Jesus Christ, our only *S*, 818 14
thy Son our *S* Jesus Christ. 821 14
our *S* Jesus Christ. 829 13
and *S* Jesus Christ. 833 4
and accept Jesus as our Lord and *S*. 858 23
their confession of Jesus Christ as *S* and Lord. 860 26

saw

proved me, and *s* my works. 146 20
"Aha! we *s* it with our own eyes." 631 13
You *s* it, O LORD; do not be silent; * 631 14
and *s* the prosperity of the wicked: 687 6
The waters *s* you, O God; 694 5
the waters *s* you and trembled; * 694 6
Nevertheless, he *s* their distress, * 745 13

say

If we *s* that we have no sin, we deceive ourselves, 38 10
I will arise and go to my father, and will *s* unto him, 38 17
If I *s*, "Surely the darkness will cover me, 62 5
If we *s* we have no sin, we deceive ourselves, 76 9
I will arise and go to my father, and I will *s* to him, 76 16
And on that day you shall *s*, * 86 7
If I *s*, "Surely the darkness will cover me, 110 7
If I *s*, "Surely the darkness will cover me, 116 1
He shall *s* to the Lord, 129 23
If we *s* that we have no sin, we deceive ourselves, 320 1
we are bold to *s*, 336 17
we are bold to *s*, 343 7
If we *s* that we have no sin, we deceive ourselves, 352 1
we are bold to *s*, 363 24
we are bold to *s*, 369 20
we are bold to *s*, 372 16
and glorify your Name, as we sing (*s*), 373 11
we are bold to *s*, 376 3
glory, as we sing (*s*), 402 8
glory, as we sing (*s*), 404 10
Let us *s* together: 440 7
let us now give thanks to him, and *s* together: 441 11
while they daily *s* unto me, Where now is thy God? 471 6
I *s*, before the morning watch. 474 12
If I *s*, Peradventure the darkness shall cover me, * 475 13
proclaim our faith and *s*, 496 2
"Let us break their yoke," they *s*; * 586 6
How many there are who *s* of me, * 587 5
They *s* in their heart, "I shall not be shaken; * 595 4
They *s* in their heart, "God has forgotten; * 595 16
why should they *s* in their heart, "You do not care"? 595 22
how then can you *s* to me, 596 8
Those who *s*, "With our tongue will we prevail; * 597 7
Lest my enemy *s*, "I have prevailed over him," * 598 6
You speak in my heart and *s*, "Seek my face," * 618 12
s to my soul, "I am your salvation." 629 19
My very bones will *s*, "LORD, who is like you? * 630 10
Do not let them *s* in their hearts, 631 21
Do not let them *s*, "We have swallowed him up." 631 23
let them *s* always, "Great is the LORD, 631 28
Let those who *s* "Aha!" and gloat over me 641 14
let those who love your salvation continually *s*, 641 17
"A deadly thing," they *s*, "has fastened on him; * 642 15
while all day long they *s* to me, 643 6
I will *s* to the God of my strength, 644 1
and *s* to me, "Where now is your God?" 644 8
And they will *s*, 665 15
"For who," they *s*, "will hear us?" 666 11
They *s*, "Who will see us? 671 20
S to God, "How awesome are your deeds! * 673 21
Let those who *s* to me "Aha!" and gloat over me 682 17
let those who love your salvation *s* for ever, 682 20
They *s*, "God has forsaken him; 683 22
They *s*, "How should God know? * 687 21
I will *s* to the boasters, 'Boast no more,' * 691 10
Why should the heathen *s*, "Where is their God?" * 702 1

Now I *s* to you, "You are gods, * 705 20
The singers and the dancers will *s*, * 711 24
He will *s* to me, "You are my Father, * 715 18
Amen, I *s*, Amen. 717 19
You turn us back to the dust and *s*, * 718 4
He shall *s* to the LORD, 719 12
Yet they *s*, "The LORD does not see, * 723 7
and let all the people *s*, "Amen!" 745 25
Why should the heathen *s*, * 757 16
and I *s*, "When will you comfort me?" 770 6
let Israel now *s*; 781 2
let Israel now *s*; 784 2
So that those who go by *s* not as much as, 784 15
If I *s*, "Surely the darkness will cover me, * 794 20
I *s*, "You are my refuge, 798 10
What do we mean when we *s* that Jesus 849 19
What do we mean when we *s* that Jesus 849 25
What do we mean when we *s* that he descended 850 13
What do we mean when we *s* that he ascended 850 17

sayest

again you *s*, Come again, ye children of men. 472 15

saying

Many are *s*, 129 1
This is a true *s*, and worthy of all men to be received, 332 13
evermore praising thee, and *s*, 334 3
and gave it to his disciples, *s*, "Take, eat, 335 1
he gave it to them, *s*, "Drink ye all of this; 335 4
evermore praising thee, and *s*, 341 6
and gave it to his disciples, *s*, "Take, eat, 342 3
he gave it to them, *s*, "Drink this, 342 6
s, "Lord, have mercy." 383 2
let us pray to the Lord, *s*, "Lord, have mercy" 389 13
This is a true *s*, and worthy of all men to be received, 449 18
s, "Dust thou art, and unto dust shalt thou return." 482 15
s, Come, O blessed of my Father; 483 21
For so did you ordain when you created me, *s*, 499 6
s, Come, O blessed of my Father; 500 10
Many are *s*, 588 10
they curl their lips and wag their heads, *s*, 610 15
I pleaded with the LORD, *s*, 621 23
My enemies are *s* wicked things about me: * 642 8
and they shall laugh at him, *s*, 658 12
I heard an unfamiliar voice *s*, * 704 11
I will listen to what the LORD God is *s*, * 709 9
S, "To you will I give the land of Canaan * 738 21
S, "Do not touch my anointed * 739 7
s, "Rule over your enemies round about you. 753 15

says

among the nations, *s* the Lord of hosts. 76 8
Thus *s* the high and lofty One who inhabits eternity, 78 22
nor your ways my ways, *s* the Lord. 86 24
great among the nations, *s* the Lord of Hosts. 106 9
I am Resurrection and I am Life, *s* the Lord. 491 1
So it is, *s* the Spirit, 492 3
I will rise up," *s* the LORD 597 11
But to the wicked God *s*: * 655 11
"I will appoint a time," *s* God; * 691 6

scale

with the help of my God I will *s* any wall. 604 23

scales

On the *s* they are lighter than a breath, * 670 3

scalp

their violence falls on their own *s*. 592 4
and the hairy *s* of those who go on still 677 26

scatter

s the peoples that delight in war. 678 21
and to *s* them throughout the lands. 744 2
Hurl the lightning and *s* them; * 800 12

scattered

he hath *s* the proud in the imagination of their hearts. 50 12
he hath *s* the proud in the imagination of their hearts. 65 15
he has *s* the proud in their conceit. 92 7
he has *s* the proud in their conceit. 119 13
he has *s* the proud in their conceit. 442 2
He loosed his arrows and *s* them; * 603 17
and have *s* us among the nations. 646 8
for God has *s* the bones of the enemy; 659 12
Let God arise, and let his enemies be *s*; * 676 1
When the Almighty *s* kings, * 677 8
you have *s* your enemies with your mighty arm. 714 14
and all the workers of iniquity shall be *s*. 721 15
let their bones be *s* at the mouth of the grave. 797 18

scatterest

As soon as thou *s* them they are even as a sleep, * 472 19

scatters

he *s* hoarfrost like ashes. 805 10
He *s* his hail like bread crumbs; * 805 11

scepter

a *s* of righteousness is the *s* of your kingdom; 648 2
Ephraim is my helmet and Judah my *s*. 667 24
Ephraim is my helmet and Judah my *s*. 750 11
The LORD will send the *s* of your power 753 14
The *s* of the wicked shall not hold sway over the 781 22

schemes

let them fall, because of their *s*. 589 14
but they are trapped in the *s* they have devised. 594 22
and devise wicked *s*, * 609 21
let the treacherous be disappointed in their *s*. 614 18
but invent deceitful *s* against the 631 10
the one who succeeds in evil *s*. 633 20

schism

From all false doctrine, heresy, and *s*; 149 8

schools

O Eternal God, bless all *s*, colleges, and universities 824 16

scoff

They *s* and speak maliciously; * 687 15
How long, O God, will the adversary *s*? * 690 4
and those who *s* at me have taken an oath against me. 731 16

scoffed

Remember, O LORD, how the enemy *s*, * 690 20

scorching

a *s* wind shall be their lot. 596 23

scorn

All who see me laugh me to *s*; * 610 14
You have made us the *s* of our neighbors, * 646 11
you laugh all the ungodly to *s*. 666 13
the *s* of those who *s* you has fallen upon me. 680 6
let those who seek to do me evil be covered with *s* 684 5
an object of *s* and derision to those around us. 701 12
and our enemies laugh us to *s*. 702 24
he has become the *s* of his neighbors. 716 24
Too much of the *s* of the indolent rich, * 780 23

scorned

s by all and despised by the people. 610 13

scornful

For the contemptuous and the *s* 279 24
nor sat in the seats of the *s*! 585 4

Scripture

revealed in *S* and the breaking of bread. 70 13
revealed in *S* and the breaking of bread. 124 10
revealed in *S* and the breaking of bread. 139 19
Holy *S* commends it to be honored among all people. 423 8
and in the study of Holy *S*, 518 5
speaks to us through the words of Holy *S*. 570 24

Scriptures

who hast caused all holy *S* to be written 184 15
who caused all holy *S* to be written 236 8
in accordance with the *S*; 327 7
and the third day he rose again according to the *S*, 328 7
in accordance with the *S*; 358 23
declare that I do believe the Holy *S* 513 9
The *S* tell us that our Savior Christ spent 514 12
in accordance with the *S*; 519 26
Receive the Holy *S*. 521 18
declare that I do believe the Holy *S* 526 15
in accordance with the *S*; 530 17
in the reading and study of the Holy *S*, 532 5
declare that I do believe the Holy *S* 538 15
in accordance with the *S*; 542 17
you are to study the Holy *S*, 543 8
and study of the Holy *S*? 544 2
found in the *S* and summed up in the creeds. 851 21
when they are in accord with the *S*. 853 4
What are the Holy *S*? 853 5
The Holy *S*, commonly called the Bible, 853 6
Why do we call the Holy *S* the Word of God? 853 23
in the true interpretation of the *S*. 854 2

scruple

to the removal of *s* and doubt, 317 15

sculptured

and our daughters like *s* corners of a palace. 801 2

sea

The *s* is his and he made it, * 44 18
that calleth for the waters of the *s*, 62 3
The *s* is his, for he made it, * 82 13
the horse and its rider has he hurled into the *S*. 85 2
and his army has he hurled into the *s*; * 85 9
drowned in the Red *s*. 85 11
who calls for the waters of the *s* 115 15
The *s* is his and he made it, * 146 9
and led them through the Red *S* on dry land. 287 8
and though the hills be carried into the midst of the *s*; 471 20
and remain in the uttermost parts of the *s*; 475 10
The birds of the air, the fish of the *s*, * 592 23
and whatsoever walks in the paths of the *s*. 592 24
and stores up the depths of the *s*. 626 14
toppled into the depths of the *s*; 649 5
like ships of the *s* when the east wind shatters them. 651 14
He turned the *s* into dry land, 674 3
I will bring them back from the depths of the *s*; 678 2
He shall rule from *s* to *s*, * 685 24
You divided the *s* by your might * 690 10
Your way was in the *s*, 694 14
He split open the *s* and let them pass through; * 695 28
and winged birds like the sand of the *s*. 697 4
but the *s* overwhelmed their enemies. 699 12
You stretched out its tendrils to the *S* * 703 9
You rule the raging of the *s* * 714 11
from the Great *S* to the River. 715 17
mightier than the breakers of the *s*, * 722 13
The *s* is his, for he made it, * 724 22
let the *s* thunder and all that is in it; * 726 15
Let the *s* make a noise and all that is in it, * 728 16
Yonder is the great and wide *s* 737 1
they defied the Most High at the Red *S*. 742 13
He rebuked the Red *S*, and it dried up, * 742 16
and fearful things at the Red *S*. 743 16
Some went down to the *s* in ships * 748 1
which tossed high the waves of the *s*. 748 6
and quieted the waves of the *s*. 748 14
The *s* beheld it and fled; * 757 1
What ailed you, O *s*, that you fled? * 757 5
Who divided the Red *S* in two, * 790 21
But swept Pharaoh and his army into the Red *S*, * 790 25
and dwell in the uttermost parts of the *s*, 794 17
you *s*-monsters and all deeps; 806 8
in earth and sky and *s*, 837 4
for the beauty of earth and sky and *s*; 840 8

seal

Let their love for each other be a *s* 430 17

sealed

Grant to those who are *s* by your Holy Spirit the will 291 7
consecrate this oil, that those who are *s* 307 11
you are *s* by the Holy Spirit in Baptism 308 9
and *s* it with sacrifice." 654 13

sealing

and that by the *s* of your Holy Spirit 309 5
and that by the *s* of your Holy Spirit 418 3

search

s out their wickedness until you find none. 595 28
you shall *s* out their place, but they will not be there. 634 4
I ponder and *s* my mind. 693 13
and repent, and diligently *s* for God. 697 19
S for the LORD and his strength; * 738 7
s for your servant, 778 8
S me out, O God, and know my heart; * 795 24

searched

O Lord, thou hast *s* me out, and known me. * 474 18
I *s* for them, but they could not be found. 636 9
Lord, you have *s* me out and known me; * 794 1

searing

My loins are filled with *s* pain; * 637 10

seas

O ye *s* and floods, bless ye the Lord; 48 22
Glorify the Lord, O springs of water, *s*, 89 10
use the harvests of the land and of the *s*, 207 17
use the harvests of the land and of the *s*, 258 17
The beds of the *s* were uncovered, 603 19
For it is he who founded it upon the *s* * 613 16
and of the *s* that are far away. 672 20
You still the roaring of the *s*, * 672 23
the *s* and all that moves in them; 682 6
in the *s* and all the deeps. 788 13
Who made heaven and earth, the *s*, 803 13

season

fruits of the earth in their *s* 194 17
fruits of the earth in their *s* 246 2
prepare for them by a *s* of penitence and fasting. 265 1
This *s* of Lent provided a time 265 1
bearing fruit in due *s*, 585 8
in the night *s* his song is with me, 643 24
and of your faithfulness in the night *s*; 720 25
to give them their food in due *s*. 737 8
and a fire to give light in the night *s*. 741 4
and you give them their food in due *s*. 802 18

seasonable

For *s* weather, and for an abundance of the fruits 384 11
give us *s* weather; 824 8

seasons

Almighty God, all times are your *s*, 572 9
You appointed the moon to mark the *s*, * 736 15

seat

He hath put down the mighty from their *s*, * 50 13
He hath put down the mighty from their *s*, * 65 16
not be condemned before the great judgment *s* 68 19
and not be condemned before the great judgment *s* 122 21

seated

where Christ is, *s* at the right hand of God. 77 13
Glory to you, *s* between the Cherubim; * 90 11
you are *s* at the right hand of the Father: 95 7
You are *s* at God's right hand in glory. 96 7
and is *s* at the right hand of the Father. 96 23
and is *s* at the right hand of the Father. 120 19
and is *s* at the right hand of the Father. 293 10
and is *s* at the right hand of the Father. 304 13
and is *s* at the right hand of the Father. 327 9
you are *s* at the right hand of the Father: 356 11
and is *s* at the right hand of the Father. 358 25
and is *s* at the right hand of the Father. 416 18
and is *s* at the right hand of the Father. 496 13
and is *s* at the right hand of the Father. 519 28
and is *s* at the right hand of the Father. 530 19
and is *s* at the right hand of the Father. 542 19
Be *s* on your lofty throne, O Most High; * 591 10
and is *s* at the right hand of the Father? 850 18

seats

nor sat in the *s* of the scornful! 585 4

second

And the *s* is like unto it: 319 11
And the *s* is like unto it: 324 4
The *s* is this: 351 10
This is the first (or *s*, or third) time 437 4
And the *s* is like it: 851 13

secrecy

he shall hide me in the *s* of his dwelling 618 3

secret

and our *s* sins in the light of thy countenance. 472 26
yea, in the *s* place of his dwelling shall he hide me, 477 21
and in *s* places they murder the innocent; * 595 9
and like a young lion lurking in *s* places. 601 24
cleanse me from my *s* faults. 607 23
I answered you from the *s* place of thunder 704 15
They take *s* counsel against your people * 706 7
and our *s* sins in the light of your countenance. 718 16
who in *s* slander their neighbors I will destroy; * 730 17
while I was being made in *s* 795 4

secretly

Take me out of the net that they have *s* set for me, * 129 16
and will make me understand wisdom *s*. 266 15
Take me out of the net that they have *s* set for me, * 622 15
For they have *s* spread a net for me without a cause; * 630 3
and will make me understand wisdom *s*. 656 19

secrets

and from whom no *s* are hid: 323 8
and from you no *s* are hid: 355 8
Thou knowest, Lord, the *s* of our hearts; 484 11
Lord, you know the *s* of our hearts; 492 12
and from you no *s* are hid: 512 8
and from you no *s* are hid: 525 8
and from you no *s* are hid: 537 8
for he knows the *s* of the heart. 646 29

secure

and makes my way *s*. 605 4
While I felt *s*, I said, 621 16
by thy Providence, we may dwell *s* in thy peace. 820 18

see

and all flesh shall *s* it together. 37 6
Behold and *s* if there be any sorrow 39 4
and all flesh shall *s* it together. 75 6
Look and *s* if there is any sorrow 77 3
s that they remember that his Name is exalted. 86 10
whom you have prepared for all the world to *s*: 93 15
so that they may *s* the good you do, 109 11
whom you have prepared for all the world to *s*: 120 4
"Oh, that we might *s* better times!" * 129 2
to *s* the reward of the wicked. 130 14
whom you have prepared for all the world to *s*: 135 4
whom you have prepared for all the world to *s*: 140 10
and bring us at last to *s* thee 176 6
to your presence, where we may *s* your glory 214 9

s you in your one and eternal glory, O Father; 228 6
s and know that things which were cast down 280 18
that your Church may rejoice to *s* fulfilled 289 8
s and know that things which were cast down 291 15
s your hand at work in the world about us. 372 3
and though this body be destroyed, yet shall I *s* God; 469 6
whom I shall *s* for myself and mine eyes shall behold, 469 7
but that I believe verily to *s* the goodness of the LORD 478 6
That I may *s* the felicity of thy chosen, * 478 20
and in my body I shall *s* God. 491 10
I myself shall *s*, and my eyes behold him 491 11
Give us faith to *s* in death the gate 493 20
for all those whom we love but *s* no longer. 498 9
for those we love, but *s* no longer: 504 26
s and know that things which were cast down 515 8
s and know that things which were cast down 528 6
s and know that things which were cast down 540 6
petitions as you *s* best for us, 578 21
"Oh, that we might *s* better times!" * 588 11
s the misery I suffer from those who hate me, 594 2
you *s* it and take it into your own hand. 595 24
For *s* how the wicked bend the bow 596 10
and the just shall *s* his face. 596 26
to *s* if there is any who is wise, 598 16
S how they tremble with fear, * 598 24
nor let your holy one *s* the Pit. 600 18
But at my vindication I shall *s* your face; * 602 4
All who *s* me laugh me to scorn; * 610 14
that I should *s* the goodness of the LORD * 618 27
when they *s* me in the street they avoid me. 623 13
Taste and *s* that the LORD is good; * 628 9
and in your light we *s* light. 632 23
S how they are fallen, those who work wickedness! * 633 3
and when the wicked are cut off, you will *s* it. 636 5
many shall *s*, and stand in awe, 640 7
my sins have overtaken me, and I cannot *s*; * 641 5
Even if they come to *s* me, they speak empty words; * 642 10
and never *s* the grave. 652 22
For we *s* that the wise die also; 652 23
who will never *s* the light again. 653 22
When you *s* a thief, you make him your friend, * 655 16
The righteous shall *s* and tremble, * 658 11
to *s* if there is any who is wise, 659 2
S how greatly they tremble, 659 10
righteous will be glad when they *s* the vengeance; * 665 13
S how they lie in wait for my life, 665 22
Rouse yourself, come to my side, and *s*; * 666 3
They say, "Who will *s* us? 671 20
and all who *s* them will shake their heads. 672 2
Come now and *s* the works of God, * 674 1
They *s* your procession, O God, * 678 5
Let their eyes be darkened, that they may not *s*, * 681 10
The afflicted shall *s* and be glad; * 682 1
There are no signs for us to *s*; 690 1
so that those who hate me may *s* it and be ashamed; * 711 10
Who can live and not *s* death? * 717 10
to *s* the reward of the wicked. 720 2
Yet they say, "The LORD does not *s*, * 723 7
he that formed the eye does he not *s*? 723 12
and all the peoples *s* his glory. 727 8
That I may *s* the prosperity of your elect 742 6
The upright will *s* this and rejoice, * 749 13
they *s* and shake their heads. 752 26
until they *s* their desire upon their enemies. 755 21
The wicked will *s* it and be angry; 755 25
eyes have they, but they cannot *s*; 757 23
Open my eyes, that I may *s* * 764 19
Those who fear you will be glad when they *s* me, * 769 12
I *s* that all things come to an end, * 771 11
S how I love your commandments! * 776 21
and may you *s* the prosperity of Jerusalem all the days 783 22
May you live to *s* your children's children; * 783 24
eyes have they, but they cannot *s*. 789 8
God our Father, you *s* your children growing up 829 14
and that in thy light we may *s* light, 832 10
Since we do not fully obey them, we *s* more clearly 848 26
they *s* him as he is. 862 12

seed

Abraham and his *s* for ever. 50 19
Abraham and his *s* for ever. 65 22
s for sowing and bread for eating, 87 4
Those who go out weeping, carrying the *s*, * 105 16
To cast out their *s* among the nations, * 744 1
Those who go out weeping, carrying the *s*, * 782 18

seedtime

hearty thanks and praise for the return of *s* and harvest, 840 16

seeing

s that, as thou dost alway resist the proud 181 18
Will you be responsible for *s* that the child 302 1
s that we have a great high priest, 320 5

seek

s those things which are above, 39 13
may *s* after thee and find thee; 58 4
S him that made the Pleiades and Orion, 62 1
s the things that are above, 77 12
S the Lord while he wills to be found; * 86 17
may *s* after you and find you; 100 20
S him who made the Pleiades and Orion, 115 13
all who *s* thee here may find thee, 204 4
may *s* after thee and find thee, 206 12
and, as we *s* a proper return 210 13
all who *s* you here may find you, 255 2
may *s* after you and find you, 257 8
and, as we *s* a proper return 261 18
That by God's help they may *s* justice and truth, 278 23
Will you *s* and serve Christ in all persons, 293 29
Will you *s* and serve Christ in all persons, 305 4
all your people, and those who *s* your truth.] 375 16
I ask your prayers for all who *s* God, 386 7
who proclaim the Gospel, and all who *s* the Truth. 392 13
Will you *s* and serve Christ in all persons, 417 14
and to *s* each other's forgiveness 429 15
you have come here today to *s* the blessing 433 1
give them calm strength and patient wisdom as they *s* 443 26
My heart hath talked of thee, *S* ye my face. * 478 1
Thy face, LORD, will I *s*. 478 2
of whom may we *s* for succor, 484 5
from whom can we *s* help? 492 6
to *s* nourishment from them, 543 8
Will you in all things *s* not your glory 544 12

Be always near us when we *s* you 568 15
we *s* your present purposes. 571 2
the son of man that you should *s* him out? 592 16
for you never forsake those who *s* you, O LORD. 593 20
and those who *s* the LORD shall praise him: * 612 8
Such is the generation of those who *s* him, * 613 25
of those who *s* your face, O God of Jacob. 613 26
one thing I *s*; * 617 19
and to *s* him in his temple. 617 23
You speak in my heart and say, "*S* my face," * 618 12
Your face, LORD, will I *s*. 618 13
but those who *s* the LORD lack nothing that is good. 628 14
s peace and pursue it. 628 22
Let those who *s* after my life be shamed 629 20
and *s* occasion to kill them. 635 27
because they *s* refuge in him. 636 19
Those who *s* after my life lay snares for me; * 637 20
who *s* after my life to destroy it; * 641 11
Let all who *s* you rejoice in you and be glad; * 641 16
the rich among the people *s* your favor." 648 16
because they *s* my life. 663 3
They *s* only to bring me down from my place 669 12
O God, you are my God; eagerly I *s* you; * 670 12
May those who *s* my life to destroy it * 671 3
let not those who *s* you be disgraced because of me, 679 24
you who *s* God, your heart shall live. 682 2
Let those who *s* my life be ashamed 682 13
Let all who *s* you rejoice and be glad in you; * 682 19
let those who *s* to do me evil be covered with scorn 684 5
Whenever he slew them, they would *s* him, * 697 18
that they may *s* your Name. 707 10
and *s* their food from God. 736 20
let the hearts of those who *s* the LORD rejoice. 738 6
continually *s* his face. 738 8
and *s* him with all their hearts! 763 8
With my whole heart I *s* you; * 764 3
I will *s* to do you good." 780 14
Teach us in all things to *s* first your honor and glory. 818 4
heaven: Be ever present with your servants who *s* 819 14
hast promised to all those who *s* thy kingdom 828 10
Grant that we may not so much *s* 833 9
to *s* justice, freedom, and the necessities of life 848 12

seekers

For all valiant *s* after truth, liberty, and justice, 837 17

seeketh

s such to worship him. 40 22

seeking

around like a roaring lion, *s* someone to devour. 132 9
faithful servant Barnabas, who, *s* not his own renown 189 18
faithful servant Barnabas, who, *s* not his own renown 241 4
so that in *s* you we might find 373 23
who come to you *s* your blessing, 425 9
and in *s* the knowledge of such things 532 5
Sin is the *s* of our own will 848 29

seeks

Father *s* to worship him. 78 21
if there is one who *s* after God. 598 17
if there is one who *s* after God. 659 3
and a band of violent men *s* my life; * 711 2

seen

For mine eyes have *s* thy salvation, * 51 25
For mine eyes have *s* thy salvation, * 66 3
For these eyes of mine have *s* the Savior, * 93 14
For these eyes of mine have *s* the Savior, * 120 3
For these eyes of mine have *s* the Savior, * 135 3
For these eyes of mine have *s* the Savior, * 140 9
of all that is, *s* and unseen. 326 9
of all that is, *s* and unseen. 358 6
of all that is, *s* and unseen. 519 9
of all that is, *s* and unseen. 529 12
of all that is, *s* and unseen. 541 12
for you have *s* my affliction; 622 23
but never have I *s* the righteous forsaken, 635 10
I have *s* the wicked in their arrogance, * 636 6
As we have heard, so have we *s*, 651 15
and my eye has *s* the ruin of my foes. 660 4
for I have *s* violence and strife in the city. 660 25
yet your footsteps were not *s*. 694 16
though they had *s* my works. 725 11
and all the ends of the earth have *s* the victory 728 8
of all that is, *s* and unseen. 846 4

seers

through many *s* and saints, 845 19

sees

because he *s* that their day will come. 634 10
like a stillborn child that never *s* the sun. 665 10
the earth *s* it and is afraid. 727 4

seest

Almighty God, who *s* that we have no power 167 3

seize

they lie in wait to *s* upon the lowly; * 595 12
they *s* the lowly and drag them away in their net. 595 13
your right hand will *s* all those who hate you. 609 13
go after him and *s* him; * 683 23
Let the creditor *s* everything he has; * 751 18

seized

Trembling *s* them there; * 651 12
A craving *s* them in the wilderness, * 742 26

selected

Has he been *s* in accordance with the canons 526 4
Has he been *s* in accordance with the canons 538 4
prayerfully and lawfully *s*. 559 4

self

of *s*-denying service by which alone 191 11
from the service of *s* alone, 210 4
that we may do it not for *s* alone, 210 12
leaders of your Church that spirit of *s*-denying service 242 17
from the service of *s* alone, 261 10
that we may do it not for *s* alone, 261 17
a holy Lent, by *s*-examination and repentance; 265 11
by prayer, fasting, and *s*-denial; 265 12
Our *s*-indulgent appetites and ways, 268 4

selfish

save us from *s* use of what thou givest, 828 6
better than chasing after *s* goals. 829 17

selling
You are *s* your people for a trifle * 646 9

selves
by giving up our *s* to thy service, 59 6
by giving up our *s* to thy service, 72 3
by giving up our *s* to your service, 101 19
by giving up our *s* to your service, 125 17
we offer and present unto thee, O Lord, our *s*, 336 1
we offer and present unto thee, O Lord, our *s*, 342 23

senators
and bless our *S* and Representatives in Congress 821 3
To *S* and Representatives, 822 1

send
O *s* out thy light and thy truth, 40 16
and didst *s* thy blessed Son to preach peace 58 2
S forth upon us the Spirit of love, 71 7
S out your light and your truth, 78 15
Heavenly Father, *s* your Holy Spirit into our hearts, 107 4
S forth upon us the Spirit of love, 125 2
That it may please thee to *s* forth laborers 150 12
Merciful God, who didst *s* thy messengers 159 9
S thy Holy Ghost and pour 164 19
leave us not comfortless, but *s* to us thine Holy Ghost 175 3
believe in him whom thou didst *s*, 205 1
and didst *s* thy blessed Son to preach peace 206 10
S your Holy Spirit and pour 216 14
Do not leave us comfortless, but *s* us your Holy Spirit 226 15
S them into the world in witness to your love. 306 1
S them forth in the power of that Spirit 309 8
Because thou didst *s* thy beloved Son to redeem us 345 8
S us now into the world in peace, 365 14
And now, Father, *s* us out 366 8
We pray you, gracious God, to *s* your Holy Spirit 369 4
S your Holy Spirit upon these gifts. 405 15
S them forth in the power of that Spirit 418 6
S therefore your blessing upon these your servants, 431 3
S your Holy Spirit to sanctify this oil; 455 9
S you help from his holy place * 608 3
S out your light and your truth, 644 21
He will *s* from heaven and save me; 663 25
God will *s* forth his love and his faithfulness. 663 27
s them reeling by your might 666 19
S forth your strength, O God; * 678 14
You *s* the springs into the valleys; * 735 21
You *s* forth your Spirit, and they are created; * 737 14
The LORD will *s* the scepter of your power 753 14
LORD, *s* us now success. 762 22
S down upon our bishops, 817 4
heavenly Father, *s* down upon those who hold office 822 17
S us honest and able leaders. 825 10
S us, we entreat thee, in this time of need, 828 11

sending
by *s* to them the light of thy Holy Spirit: 175 16
by *s* to them the light of your Holy Spirit: 227 9
in *s* Jesus Christ to come among us, 430 11
Father, we praise you for *s* your Son 545 1
We praise you for *s* your Holy Spirit to make us holy, 573 19

sends
he *s* forth his voice, his mighty voice. 678 27
he *s* out lightning with the rain, 788 15
He *s* out his command to the earth, * 805 7
He *s* forth his word and melts them; * 805 13

sense
give us that due *s* of all thy mercies, 59 2
give us that due *s* of all thy mercies, 71 21
by a lively *s* of your presence with them, 443 25
comfort him with a *s* of thy goodness; 458 5
the *s* of his weakness may add strength to his faith 460 2
and give me such a *s* of your presence, 461 15
comfort them with a *s* of your goodness; 467 5
give us such a lively *s* of thy righteous will, 488 30
and grant them a *s* of your abiding presence 823 6
comfort him with a *s* of thy goodness, 831 15
give us a just *s* of these great mercies, 840 20

sensible
s of the shortness and uncertainty of life; 489 5

sent
and the rich he hath *s* empty away. 50 16
and the rich he hath *s* empty away. 65 19
and prosper in that for which I *s* it. 87 8
and the rich he has *s* away empty. 92 11
and *s* your blessed Son to preach peace 100 18
and the rich he has *s* away empty. 119 17
hast *s* thy Son our Savior Jesus Christ 168 2
and *s* to prepare the way of thy Son 190 2
and Jesus Christ whom thou hast *s*; 197 23
Merciful God, who *s* your messengers the prophets 211 9
you *s* your Son our Savior Jesus Christ 219 14
and *s* to prepare the way of your Son 241 11
and Jesus Christ whom you have *s*; 249 8
that the world may believe in him whom you have *s*, 255 19
and *s* your blessed Son to preach peace 257 6
you *s* your Son our Savior Jesus Christ 272 8
Our heavenly Father *s* his Son 277 2
who after his resurrection *s* forth his apostles 348 12
you, in your mercy, *s* Jesus 362 11
For in these last days you *s* him to be incarnate 368 5
you *s* your only Son, born of a woman, 370 19
you *s* your only Son to be our Savior. 374 2
who died and rose for us, he *s* the Holy Spirit, 374 10
Because you *s* your beloved Son to redeem us from sin 378 4
who after his resurrection *s* forth his apostles 381 6
and the rich he has *s* away empty. 442 6
before he chose and *s* forth his twelve 514 13
you *s* your Son Jesus Christ to be born 573 9
You *s* a gracious rain, O God, 676 21
He *s* swarms of flies among them, 698 17
He *s* a man before them, * 739 11
The king *s* and released him; * 739 17
He *s* Moses his servant, * 740 5
He *s* darkness, and it grew dark; * 740 9
but *s* leanness into their soul. 743 2
He *s* forth his word and healed them * 747 21
He *s* redemption to his people; 754 22
He *s* signs and wonders into the midst of you, 788 19
you *s* your Son Jesus Christ to reconcile 838 1
whom you have *s* in the power of the Spirit 838 3

you *s* your own Son into this world. 841 1
God *s* the prophets to call us back to himself, 849 8
The Messiah is one *s* by God to free us 849 12
s to carry out Christ's mission to all people. 854 26

separate

break down the walls that *s* us; 815 16
not even death, shall *s* us 862 31

separated

had been *s* from the body of the faithful 265 4

sepulcher

O God, whose blessed Son was laid in a *s* 487 5
O God, whose blessed Son was laid in a *s* 503 7

seraphim

To thee Cherubim and *S* continually do cry: 52 27
Cherubim and *S*, sing in endless praise: 95 20

serenity

Church may joyfully serve thee in confidence and *s*; 177 11
Church may joyfully serve you in confidence and *s*; 229 7

seriously

Give us grace *s* to lay to heart 818 15

seriousness

his faith and *s* to his repentance; 460 3

serpent

you shall trample the young lion and the *s* 130 24
They are as venomous as a *s*, * 665 1
you shall trample the young lion and the *s* 720 12
They have sharpened their tongues like a *s*; * 796 5

servant

He remembering his mercy hath holpen his *s* Israel, * 50 17
in the house of his *s* David, 50 25
Lord, now lettest thou thy *s* depart in peace, * 51 23
He remembering his mercy hath holpen his *s* Israel, * 65 20
Lord, now lettest thou thy *s* depart in peace, * 66 1
for he has looked with favor on his lowly *s*. 91 29
He has come to the help of his *s* Israel, * 92 12
born of the house of his *s* David. 92 21
Lord, you now have set your *s* free * 93 12
who at noonday called your *s* Saint Paul 107 12
for he has looked with favor on his lowly *s*. 119 6
He has come to the help of his *s* Israel, * 119 18
Lord, you now have set your *s* free * 120 1
Lord, you now have set your *s* free * 135 1
Lord, you now have set your *s* free * 140 7
faithful *s* Matthias to be of the number of the Twelve: 188 2
O God, who from the family of thy *s* David 188 8
faithful *s* Barnabas, who, seeking not his own renown 189 18
by whose providence thy *s* John the Baptist 190 1
s and apostle James, first among the Twelve to suffer 191 8
who didst inspire thy *s* Luke the physician 193 11
s James the Just, brother of our Lord, 193 19
O Almighty God, who didst give to thy *s* N. boldness 195 1
s N., whom thou didst call to preach the Gospel 196 8
didst raise up thy *s* N. to be a light to the world: 196 16
s N., who was faithful in the care 196 23
s N. to be a [bishop and] pastor in thy Church 197 5
manifested in thy *s* N., and we pray that thy Church 197 15
who didst give to thy *s* N. special gifts of grace 197 19
inspired by the devotion of thy *s* N., we may serve 198 4
O God, by whose grace thy *s* N., enkindled 198 9
s N., may persevere in running the race 198 18
we remember this day before thee thy faithful *s* N.,: 202 10
s Matthias to be numbered among the Twelve: 239 12
O God, who from the family of your *s* David raised 239 17
faithful *s* Barnabas, who, seeking not his own renown 241 4
by whose providence your *s* John the Baptist 241 10
remember before you today your *s* and apostle James, 242 14
who inspired your *s* Luke the physician 244 20
following the example of your *s* James the Just, 245 4
Almighty God, who gave to your *s* N. boldness 246 8
s N., whom you called to preach the Gospel 247 20
and who raised up your *s* N. to be a light 248 2
your *s* N., who was faithful in the care and nurture 248 9
s N., to be a [bishop and] pastor in your Church 248 16
manifested in your *s* N., and we pray 249 1
Almighty God, you gave to your *s* N. special gifts 249 5
inspired by the devotion of your *s* N., 249 13
O God, by whose grace your *s* N., kindled 249 18
your *s* N., may persevere in running the race 250 3
we remember before you today your faithful *s* N.; 253 14
Holy Spirit to be the Savior and *s* of all, 307 10
Strengthen, O Lord, your *s* N. with your Holy Spirit; 309 12
Defend, O Lord, your *s* N. with your heavenly grace, 309 15
Spirit you have bestowed upon this your *s* 314 2
Strengthen, O Lord, your *s* N. with your Holy Spirit; 418 10
Defend, O Lord, your *s* N. with your heavenly grace, 418 13
for he has looked with favor on his lowly *s*. 441 14
He has come to the help of his *s* Israel,* 442 7
your *s* N. who desires now to offer you her praises 444 3
relieve thy sick *s* N. for whom our prayers are desired. 458 3
Mercifully accept our prayers, and grant to your *s* N. 458 12
Be present in your goodness with your *s* N. 458 18
graciously comfort your *s* N. in his suffering, 459 8
Strengthen your *s* N., O God, to do what he has to do 459 12
Comfort and relieve your sick *s* N., 459 18
Sanctify, O Lord, the sickness of your *s* N., 460 1
Almighty God, look on this your *s*, 462 1
Have mercy on your *s*. 462 6
deliver the soul of your *s* from the power 463 12
Deliver your *s*, N., O Sovereign Lord Christ, 464 16
we commend your *s* N. 465 2
Receive, O Lord, your *s*, for he returns to you. 465 14
Deliver your *s*, N., O Sovereign Lord Christ, 466 16
prayers on behalf of thy *s* N. and grant him 470 2
nor cast thy *s* away in displeasure. 478 4
Give rest, O Christ, to thy *s*(s) with thy saints, 482 9
Give rest, O Christ, to thy *s*(s) with thy saints, 483 3
Into thy hands, O merciful Savior, we commend thy *s* 483 6
Into thy hands, O Lord, we commend thy *s* N., 488 12
Remember thy *s*, O Lord, according to the favor 488 21
Grant that your *s* N., being raised with him, 493 6
Accept our prayers on behalf of your *s* N., 493 11
Give rest, O Christ, to your *s*(s) with your saints, 499 1
we commend your *s* N. 499 14
of this your *s* whom you have chosen to be a bishop 521 7
who took on himself the form of a *s*, 545 2
that whoever would be great must be *s* of all. 545 6
this your *s* to the order of deacons. 545 8
these tokens of your *s*'s ministry and dignity. 552 8

yet you have called your *s* to stand 562 10
By them also is your *s* enlightened, * 607 20
Above all, keep your *s* from presumptuous sins; 607 24
nor turn away your *s* in displeasure. 618 15
Make your face to shine upon your *s*, * 623 25
who desires the prosperity of his *s*." 631 29
"Hide not your face from your *s*; * 680 25
He chose David his *s*, * 700 19
save your *s* who puts his trust in you. 710 2
Gladden the soul of your *s*, * 710 5
give your strength to your *s*; 711 7
I have sworn an oath to David my *s*: 713 22
I have found David my *s*; * 715 6
You have broken your covenant with your *s*, * 716 19
Remember, Lord, how your *s* is mocked, * 717 14
O offspring of Abraham his *s*, * 738 11
He sent Moses his *s*, * 740 5
and Abraham his *s*. 741 10
and your *s* will rejoice. 753 5
O Lord, I am your *s*; * 760 5
I am your *s* and the child of your handmaid; 760 6
Deal bountifully with your *s*, * 764 17
Fulfill your promise to your *s*, * 766 11
Remember your word to your *s*, * 767 11
O Lord, you have dealt graciously with your *s*, * 768 17
as you have promised to your *s*. 769 17
Be surety for your *s*'s good; * 773 17
Deal with your *s* according to your loving-kindness * 773 21
I am your *s*; grant me understanding, * 773 23
Let your countenance shine upon your *s* * 774 17
and your *s* holds it dear. 775 6
search for your *s*, 778 8
For your *s* David's sake, * 786 17
An inheritance for Israel his *s*, * 791 13
Enter not into judgment with your *s*, * 798 21
for truly I am your *s*. 799 27
and have rescued David your *s*. 800 22
on your *s* N. as he begins another year. 830 9
Look with pity upon the sorrows of thy *s* 831 13
deliver from his sickness thy *s* N., 841 9
particularly as a *s* of those in need; 856 9

servanthood

God now calls you to a special ministry of *s* 543 3

servants

O ye *s* of the Lord, bless ye the Lord; * 49 3
We therefore pray thee, help thy *s*, 53 19
Defend us, thy humble *s*, 57 3
we thine unworthy *s* do give 58 15
petitions of thy *s* as may be best for us; 59 17
Grant unto us thy *s* so to follow in faith 69 8
Give unto thy *s* that peace 69 17
O God, who dost manifest in thy *s* the signs 71 6
we thine unworthy *s* do give 71 11
petitions of thy *s* as may be best for us; 72 14
Glorify the Lord, O priests and *s* of the Lord, * 89 20
us, your humble *s*, in all assaults of our enemies; 99 22
we your unworthy *s* give you humble thanks 101 8
Jesus as Lord, and ourselves as your *s*, 110 2
Grant to us your *s* so to follow in faith 123 7
Give to us, your *s*, that peace 123 16
O God, you manifest in your *s* the signs 125 1
we your unworthy *s* give you humble thanks 125 6
Behold now, bless the Lord, all you *s* of the Lord, * 131 6
Give praise, you *s* of the Lord; * 138 1
Jesus as Lord, and ourselves as your *s*, 139 11
Behold now, bless the Lord, all you *s* of the Lord, * 140 1
That it may please thee so to rule the hearts of thy *s*, 150 25
as thy *s*, and for the common good, 151 15
Make speed to help thy *s* 166 10
thy *s* grace, by the confession of a true faith, 176 2
thy humble *s*, a like faith and power of love, 196 3
s of Christ and stewards of thy divine mysteries; 197 8
Comfort and relieve thy sick *s*, 208 17
your *s* grace, by the confession of a true faith, 228 2
your humble *s*, a like faith and power of love, 247 15
true *s* of Christ and stewards of your divine mysteries; 248 19
Comfort and relieve your sick *s*, 260 2
Spirit you have bestowed upon these your *s* 308 3
these your *s* the covenant you made with them 309 7
hand ever be over these your *s*; 310 9
And we also bless thy holy Name for all thy *s* 330 1
we, thy humble *s*, do celebrate 335 10
and thy faithful *s* bless thee, 348 8
and your faithful *s* bless you, 381 3
we thy *s*, who now live by faith, may with joy behold 395 14
these your *s* the covenant you made with them 418 5
hand ever be over these your *s*; 419 5
Send therefore your blessing upon these your *s*, 431 4
the sorrows of your *s* for whom we pray. 467 4
good examples of all those thy *s*, 488 5
We give thee thanks for all thy *s* 488 27
for all thy *s* who have finished their course 489 15
thy righteous *s*, known to us and unknown; 489 18
of all your *s*, who, having finished their course 503 15
for all your *s* who have finished their course 504 13
other righteous *s*, known to us and unknown; 504 16
Grant to us your *s* so to follow in faith 504 22
raising up among us faithful *s* for the ministry 523 4
raising up among us faithful *s* for the ministry 535 4
raising up among us faithful *s* for the ministry 546 6
raising up among us faithful *s* for the ministry 564 4
Sing to the Lord, you *s* of his; * 621 10
The Lord ransoms the life of his *s*, * 629 11
The children of his *s* will inherit it, * 682 9
They have given the bodies of your *s* as food for the 701 4
that you avenge the shedding of your *s*' blood. 702 3
be gracious to your *s*. 718 28
Show your *s* your works * 719 5
lead a blameless life shall be my *s*. 730 23
For your *s* love her very rubble, * 732 4
The children of your *s* shall continue, * 733 7
and flames of fire your *s*. 735 10
and dealt unjustly with his *s*. 740 4
Give praise, you *s* of the Lord; * 756 2
is the death of his *s*. 760 4
for all things are your *s*. 771 2
As the eyes of *s* look to the hand of their masters, * 780 17
Behold now, bless the Lord, all you *s* of the Lord, * 787 19
give praise, you *s* of the Lord, 788 3
against Pharaoh and all his *s*. 788 20
and shows compassion to his *s*. 789 4
and your faithful *s* bless you. 802 6

and praise for all his loyal *s*, * 806 23
the hearts and minds of your *s* ready to receive 819 3
Be ever present with your *s* who seek 819 14
Give grace to your *s*, O Lord. 821 23
and to us your *s*, give grace 823 13
and dispose the way of thy *s* towards the attainment 832 19
that in every place your *s* call upon your Name; 838 6
We give thanks to you, O Lord our God, for all your *s* 838 9

serve

s the Lord with gladness 45 12
might *s* him without fear, 51 8
and ministry they may truly and godly *s* thee; 57 23
where love thee and *s* thee in peace; 70 18
s the Lord with gladness 82 21
a kingdom of priests to *s* our God. 94 4
and to *s* you is perfect freedom: 99 21
and ministry they may truly and devoutly *s* you; 100 15
love you and *s* you in peace; 124 15
and grant that we may *s* you 127 13
and evermore *s* thee in holiness 155 11
s thee in pureness of living and truth; 172 11
may joyfully *s* thee in confidence and serenity; 177 11
as thy holy angels always *s* and worship thee 193 6
we may *s* thee with singleness of heart, 198 4
as thy holy angels always *s* and worship thee 200 8
that they may faithfully *s* before thee, 205 9
and ministry they may truly and godly *s* thee; 206 5
to *s* thee in freedom and peace: 207 2
and *s* thee from generation to generation; 209 20
s you in pureness of living and truth; 224 4
may joyfully *s* you in confidence and serenity; 229 7
Mercifully grant that, as your holy angels always *s* 244 15
may *s* you with singleness of heart, 249 14
Mercifully grant that, as your holy angels always *s* 251 14
that they may faithfully *s* before you, 256 6
and ministry they may truly and devoutly *s* you; 257 2
to *s* you in freedom and in peace: 258 2
Son came not to be *sd* but to *s*: 260 16
and *s* you from generation to generation; 261 4
We have been deaf to your call to *s*, 267 23
and the people whom they *s* 278 5
and ministry they may truly and devoutly *s* you; 278 15
For all who *s* the common good 278 22
and give us, we pray, the strength to *s* 279 17
Grant that we, who *s* you 290 3
and promised to *s* God faithfully 292 6
Will you seek and *s* Christ in all persons, 293 29
Will you seek and *s* Christ in all persons, 305 4
that they may *s* you in this life, 310 11
and made us a kingdom of priests to *s* his God 317 18
s and please thee in newness of life, 331 18
Go in peace to love and *s* the Lord. 340 1
to *s* thee as a royal priesthood, 347 11
receive this holy Sacrament, and *s* you in unity, 363 16
to love and *s* you 365 16
to love and *s* you 366 10
Go in peace to love and *s* the Lord. 366 16
that we may worthily *s* the world in his name. 372 7
Countless throngs of angels stand before you to *s* you 373 7
we might rule and *s* all your creatures. 373 20
to *s* you as a royal priesthood, 380 6
may truly and humbly *s* you; 387 4
and *s* the common good. 388 9
that we may *s* Christ in them, 388 18
that they may *s* justice, 390 17
For all who *s* God in his Church. 392 16
that we may live and *s* you in newness of life, 393 14
Will you seek and *s* Christ in all persons, 417 14
that they may *s* you in this life, 419 7
to follow Christ and to *s* in his name. 421 3
to love you, and to *s* you. 429 22
and peace which will enable you to *s* him 456 5
and *s* thee with a quiet mind. 481 5
Father, grant that we, who now *s* thee on earth, 486 13
bishop of the Church of God to *s* in the Diocese 514 3
to *s*, and to give his life a ransom for many. 517 18
I will obey Christ, and will *s* in his name. 518 3
to *s* his Church in the office of bishop. 519 2
Grant that we, with him, may *s* you now, 523 7
You are to love and *s* the people 531 10
pastor to all whom you are called to *s*, 532 15
Grant that in all things he may *s* without reproach, 534 6
Grant that we, with him, may *s* you now, 535 7
s all people, particularly the poor, 543 5
help and *s* those in need? 544 5
As your Son came not to be served but to *s*, 545 16
Grant that we, with him, may *s* you now, 547 3
that they may *s* you in a true and godly life, 548 17
that they may *s* justice 550 2
may faithfully *s* you and share in the fullness 552 10
who has been chosen to *s* as Rector 559 2
and to *s* at your altar. 562 11
Grant that we, with him, may *s* you now, 564 7
A people I have not known shall *s* me; 605 28
my descendants shall *s* him; * 612 19
s the LORD with gladness 729 23
and the kingdoms also, to *s* the LORD. 732 21
and plants to *s* mankind; 736 4
and green plants to *s* mankind. 804 19
rejoicing in thy whole creation, we may learn to *s* 814 3
all nations and races may *s* you 815 19
of their calling to *s* this people in thy fear; 820 23
that we may *s* you faithfully in our generation 822 13
they may faithfully *s* in their offices 822 20
and hearts to love, and hands to *s*, 837 12
those who have chosen to *s* him will grow in his love, 862 11

served

good examples of those who have *s* thee here 202 4
that, with all who have faithfully *s* thee 202 12
those who have *s* you here and are now at rest, 253 9
that, with all who have faithfully *s* you 253 16
whose blessed Son came not to be *s* but to serve: 260 15
We have been deaf to your call to serve, as Christ *s* us. 267 23
when we shall have *s* thee in our generation, 489 7
when we shall have *s* you in our generation, 504 5
who came, not to be *s*, but to serve, 517 17
As your Son came not to be *s* but to serve, 545 16
rights may be safeguarded and justice *s*. 822 8

serves

who came among us as one who *s*, 261 12

serveth

who came among us as one that *s*, 210 7

service

may be duly prepared for the *s* of thy sanctuary, 56 14
whose *s* is perfect freedom: 57 2
by giving up our selves to thy *s*, 59 6
by giving up our selves to thy *s*, 72 3
may be duly prepared for the *s* of your sanctuary, 99 9
by giving up our selves to your *s*, 101 19
by giving up our selves to your *s*, 125 17
and, as thou hast called us to thy *s*, 176 10
thy faithful people do unto thee true and laudable *s*: 184 2
that spirit of self-denying *s* 191 11
and strengthened for thy *s*; 200 3
receive him more and more into thy joyful *s*, 202 12
who, following in his steps, give themselves to the *s* 209 11
from the *s* of self alone, 210 4
and, as you have called us to your *s*, 228 10
faithful people offer you true and laudable *s*: 235 15
that spirit of self-denying *s* 242 18
and strengthened for your *s*; 251 9
receive him more and more into your joyful *s*, 253 16
give themselves to the *s* of others; 260 17
from the *s* of self alone, 261 9
For its unity in witness and *s* 278 3
Holy Spirit you have bound us to your *s*. 309 6
perform the *s* you set before them; 309 9
empower him for your *s*; 309 13
direct and uphold you in the *s* of Christ 310 6
praise, which is our bounden duty and *s*, 317 21
grant them continual growth in thy love and *s*; 330 4
to accept this our bounden duty and *s*, 336 11
use its resources rightly in the *s* of others 388 13
Holy Spirit you have bound us to your *s*. 418 4
perform the *s* you set before them; 418 7
empower him for your *s*; 418 11
direct and uphold you in the *s* of Christ 419 2
do God's will in the *s* of the kingdom of his Christ. 420 2
of witness to the world, and of *s* to others; 421 6
and raise him up to a life of *s* 459 5
go from strength to strength in the life of perfect *s* 481 21
go from strength to strength in the life of perfect *s* 488 24
who have laid down their lives in the *s* of our country. 488 28
May the Lord by his grace uphold you in the *s* 544 15
may this deacon share in Christ's *s*, 545 16
To you and to your *s* I devote myself, 562 11
sustained and sanctified for your *s*. 569 2
and strengthened for your *s*. 574 7
and all the nations do him *s*. 686 6
by their prayer and *s* they may enrich your Church, 819 10
Bless, O Lord, thy gifts to our use and us to thy *s*; 835 11
By what other names is this *s* known? 859 14

serving

truly *s* thee in holiness and righteousness 329 16
s before you day and night in the ministry 521 11
s God the Father, through the power 543 2
to show Christ's people that in *s* the helpless 543 17
they are *s* Christ himself. 543 18

set

to walk in his laws which he *s* before us. 38 23
to *s* forth his most worthy praise, 41 7
Let my prayer be *s* forth in thy sight as the incense, 61 1
I have *s* the Lord always before me; 61 11
that our hearts may be *s* to obey thy commandments, 69 18
by following his laws which he *s* before us. 76 21
God our heavenly Father, to *s* forth his praise, 79 2
he has come to his people and *s* them free. 92 19
to *s* us free from the hands of our enemies, 92 28
Lord, you now have *s* your servant free * 93 12
When you became man to *s* us free 96 3
The wicked have *s* a trap for me, * 104 7
Let my prayer be *s* forth in your sight as incense, 115 1
I have *s* the Lord always before me; 115 11
Lord, you now have *s* your servant free * 120 1
you *s* me free when I am hard-pressed; 128 9
Take me out of the net that they have secretly *s* 129 16
Lord, you now have *s* your servant free * 135 1
Lord, you now have *s* your servant free * 140 7
s it forth, and show it accordingly, 150 8
S us free, O God, from the bondage of our sins 164 6
govern those whom thou hast *s* upon the sure foundation 178 14
to *s* forth in the Gospel the love and healing 193 12
may persevere in running the race that is *s* before us, 198 19
S us free, O God, from the bondage of our sins, 216 1
s upon the sure foundation of your loving-kindness; 230 9
to *s* forth in the Gospel the love and healing 244 21
may persevere in running the race that is *s* before us, 250 3
pardon and absolution *s* forth in the Gospel 265 7
we pray you to *s* your passion, 282 6
perform the service you *s* before them; 309 9
s forth thy true and lively Word, 329 11
may run with patience the race that is *s* before us; 347 19
and run with endurance the race that is *s* before us; 380 14
perform the service you *s* before them; 418 7
and *s* him free from every bond; 464 17
and *s* him free from every bond; 466 17
Thou hast *s* our misdeeds before thee, * 472 25
and *s* me up upon a rock of stone. 477 22
may be *s* on his right hand, 487 18
we pray thee to *s* thy passion, 489 24
s forth your true and living Word. 563 3
and to *s* apart places for the ministry 567 2
now to be *s* apart for your worship, 567 10
"I myself have *s* my king * 586 12
who *s* themselves against me all around. 587 14
Rise up, O LORD; *s* me free, O my God; * 587 15
you *s* me free when I am hard-pressed; 587 21
You have *s* up a stronghold 592 11
the moon and the stars you have *s* in their courses, 592 14
he has *s* up his throne for judgment. 593 14
and in the snare they *s* is their own foot caught. 594 8
I have *s* the LORD always before me; * 600 13
and the snares of death were *s* for me. 602 17
In the deep has he *s* a pavilion for the sun; * 606 23
and *s* a crown of fine gold upon his head. 609 2
and *s* me high upon a rock. 618 4
Take me out of the net that they have secretly *s* 622 15
you have *s* my feet in an open place. 623 2

and has *s* himself in no good way; * 632 10
he *s* my feet upon a high cliff 640 4
and shall *s* me before your face for ever. 642 25
and *s* forth my riddle upon the harp. 652 12
and are *s* against me in fury. 660 12
You have *s* up a banner for those who fear you, * 667 16
s me upon the rock that is higher than I. 668 16
though wealth increase, *s* not your heart upon it. 670 7
at the time you have *s*, O LORD: 680 14
In your righteousness, deliver me and *s* me free; * 683 3
who *s* themselves against me be put to shame 684 3
They *s* their mouths against the heavens, * 687 17
Surely, you *s* them in slippery places; * 688 13
they *s* up their banners as tokens of victory. 689 17
They *s* fire to your holy place; * 689 21
"Can God *s* a table in the wilderness? 696 12
his hands were *s* free from bearing the load." 704 13
whose hearts are *s* on the pilgrims' way. 707 26
they have not *s* you before their eyes. 711 3
you have *s* your faithfulness firmly in the heavens. 713 20
"I have *s* the crown upon a warrior 715 4
Our iniquities you have *s* before you, * 718 15
I will *s* no worthless thing before my eyes; * 730 12
and *s* free those condemned to die; 732 17
The LORD has *s* his throne in heaven, * 734 20
You have *s* the earth upon its foundations, * 735 11
You *s* the limits that they should not pass; * 735 19
the ruler of the peoples *s* him free. 739 18
He *s* him as a master over his household, * 739 19
S a wicked man against him, * 751 8
I have *s* your judgments before me. 765 20
for you have *s* my heart at liberty. 765 24
The wicked have *s* a trap for me, * 772 13
will I *s* upon your throne. 786 22
if I do not *s* Jerusalem above my highest joy. 792 14
they have *s* traps for me along the path. 796 12
Let my prayer be *s* forth in your sight as incense, * 797 5
S a watch before my mouth, O LORD, 797 7
And to *s* aside regular times for worship, 847 26
to *s* forth the life and teachings of Jesus 853 16

sets

your never-failing providence *s* in order all things 229 10
like the flame that *s* mountains ablaze. 707 6
He *s* them with the princes, * 756 14
The LORD *s* the prisoners free; 803 17
Redemption is the act of God which *s* us free 849 5

settest

Father, who *s* the solitary in families: 828 22

setting

Now as we come to the *s* of the sun, 64 4
From the rising of the sun to its *s* 76 5
From the rising of the sun to its *s* 106 6
Now as we come to the *s* of the sun, 112 4
Now as we come to the *s* of the sun, 118 4
Now as we come to the *s* of the sun, 139 4
and to the *s* forth of thy glory; 153 25
he who gives his light to all *s*, 287 26
Let us now pray for the *s* apart of the Altar. 573 7
from the rising of the sun to its *s*. 654 3
and the sun knows the time of its *s*. 736 16
the LORD answered by *s* me free. 761 6
and to the *s* forth of thy glory; 834 6
We thank you for *s* us at tasks which demand our best 836 7

settled

He *s* the hungry there, * 749 1

seven

and purified *s* times in the fire. 597 15
return *s*-fold into their bosoms. 702 8
S times a day do I praise you, * 777 7

seventy

The span of our life is *s* years, 718 19

several

to inspire us, in our *s* callings, 151 13
and, as thou knowest their *s* infirmities, 166 12
Deliver us, we beseech thee, in our *s* occupations 210 3
and the lights of the world in their *s* generations; 487 13
relieve them according to their *s* necessities, 815 10

shade

the LORD is your *s* at your right hand, 104 22
the LORD is your *s* at your right hand. 779 10

shadow

that sit in darkness and in the *s* of death, * 51 19
and turnest the *s* of death into the morning: 56 19
who dwell in darkness and the *s* of death, * 93 8
and turns the *s* of death into the morning: 99 14
abides under the *s* of the Almighty. 129 22
Hide us under the *s* of your wings. 132 15
Though I walk through the valley of the *s* of death, 443 7
though I walk through the valley of the *s* of death, 476 8
though I walk through the valley of the *s* of death, 477 1
those who sat in darkness and in the *s* of death. 483 17
those who sat in darkness and in the *s* of death. 500 6
hide me under the *s* of your wings, 601 15
Though I walk through the valley of the *s* of death, 613 3
take refuge under the *s* of your wings. 632 19
We walk about like a *s*, 639 6
in the *s* of your wings will I take refuge 663 21
and under the *s* of your wings I will rejoice. 670 26
The mountains were covered by its *s* * 703 7
abides under the *s* of the Almighty. 719 11
My days pass away like a *s*, * 731 21
I have faded away like a *s* when it lengthens; * 752 21
our days are like a passing *s*. 800 9

shadows

support us all the day long, until the *s* lengthen, 833 14

shafts

he makes his arrows *s* of fire. 591 25

shake

though the mountains *s* at the tempest of the same. 471 22
and all who see them will *s* their heads. 672 2
let the earth *s*. 728 26
they see and *s* their heads. 752 26

shaken

They say in their heart, "I shall not be *s*; * 595 4
nations make much ado, and the kingdoms are *s*; * 649 15
I am *s* by the noise of the enemy * 660 9

You have *s* the earth and split it open; * 667 12
my stronghold, so that I shall not be greatly *s*. 669 8
my stronghold, so that I shall not be *s*. 669 19
the very depths were *s*. 694 7
all the foundations of the earth are *s*. 705 19
I am *s* off like a locust. 752 22
For they will never be *s*; * 755 15

shakes

My spirit *s* with terror; * 590 3
the voice of the LORD *s* the wilderness; * 620 19
the LORD *s* the wilderness of Kadesh. 620 20

shame

let me never be put to *s*: * 129 9
suffer *s* and loss for the sake of thy Son 168 20
the smiters and hid not his face from *s*: 169 2
agony and *s* of the cross for our redemption: 201 8
suffer *s* and loss for the sake of your Son 220 11
agony and *s* of the cross for our redemption: 252 13
we may without *s* or fear rejoice 345 11
we may without *s* or fear rejoice 378 7
they shall turn back and suddenly be put to *s*. 590 19
they trusted in you and were not put to *s*. 610 11
Let none who look to you be put to *s*; * 614 17
let me not be put to *s*, for I have trusted in you. 616 2
let me never be put to *s*; * 622 8
rather, let the wicked be put to *s*; 623 28
be clothed with dismay and *s*. 631 26
and put those who hate us to *s*. 645 26
and *s* has covered my face; 646 16
they are put to *s*, because God has rejected them. 659 13
Let not those who hope in you be put to *s* 679 22
and *s* has covered my face. 680 2
You know my reproach, my *s*, and my dishonor; * 681 1
Let those who set themselves against me be put to *s* 684 3
and put them to perpetual *s*. 700 12
Cover their faces with *s*, O LORD, * 707 9
and have covered him with *s*. 717 4
let those who rise up against me be put to *s*, 753 4
and wrap themselves in their *s* as in a cloak. 753 7
Then I should not be put to *s*, * 763 15
Turn from me *s* and rebuke, * 765 3
O LORD, let me not be put to *s*. 765 22
Let the arrogant be put to *s*, for they wrong me 769 20
that I may not be put to *s*. 770 2
he shall not be put to *s* 783 11
Let them be put to *s* and thrown back, * 784 9
As for his enemies, I will clothe them with *s*; * 787 7
while he was suffering *s* and death: 823 9

shamed

Let those who seek after my life be *s* and humbled; * 629 20

shameful

s death to be unto us the means of life: 168 18
s death to be for us the means of life: 220 9

share

s in the inheritance of the saints in light. 77 23
that we may *s* the divine life of him 162 9
him who humbled himself to *s* our humanity, 162 10
may *s* with her the glory of thine eternal kingdom; 192 3
that we may *s* the divine life of him 200 15
him who humbled himself to *s* our humanity, 200 16
he may *s* in the eternal victory of Jesus 202 13
Grant that we may *s* the divine life of him 214 3
who humbled himself to *s* our humanity, 214 3
and also *s* in his resurrection; 219 17
may *s* with her the glory of your eternal kingdom; 243 10
Grant that we may *s* the divine life of him 252 3
who humbled himself to *s* our humanity, 252 3
he may *s* in the eternal victory of Jesus 253 17
and also *s* in his resurrection; 272 11
we *s* in his victory over death. 285 5
Grant that we may *s* the divine life of him 288 7
who humbled himself to *s* our humanity, 288 7
By it we *s* in his resurrection. 306 21
s in the royal priesthood of Jesus Christ; 307 12
and *s* with us in his eternal priesthood. 308 13
and for making us worthy to *s* in the inheritance 311 17
But if we are to *s* rightly in the celebration 316 17
to *s* our human nature, 362 12
that all who *s* this bread and cup may become one 375 9
But do not neglect to do good and to *s* what you have, 377 1
May we also come to *s* in your heavenly kingdom. 387 20
and we pray that we may *s* with all your saints 389 9
to all who *s* in the victory of thy Son 481 27
With your fellow bishops you will *s* in the leadership 517 13
Will you *s* with your fellow bishops 518 22
s in the renewing of his world. 531 4
and to take your *s* in the councils of the Church. 531 6
to *s* in the administration of Holy Baptism 531 14
may this deacon *s* in Christ's service, 545 16
may faithfully serve you and *s* in the fullness 552 10
and be among us to *s* in the councils of this diocese. 562 3
to *s* in the ordering of your world. 567 9
By it we *s* in his resurrection. 570 13
In the misfortunes of others they have no *s*; * 687 9
we may all *s* the fruits of the earth, 824 9
that we may not rest until all the people of this land *s* 839 24
How can we *s* in his victory over sin, 850 22
We *s* in his victory when we are baptized 850 24
to *s* with the bishop in the overseeing of the Church; 856 3
Infants are baptized so that they can *s* citizenship 858 25

shared

s our toil and hallowed our labor: 208 2
s our toil and hallowed our labor: 259 4

sharing

and for a spiritual *s* in his risen life. 316 5

sharp

your arrows are very *s*, O mighty warrior. 647 22
their tongue a *s* sword. 664 3

sharpen

They *s* their tongue like a sword, * 671 14

sharpened

your tongue is like a *s* razor, * 658 2
The *s* arrows of a warrior, * 778 16
They have *s* their tongues like a serpent; * 796 5

sharpness

When thou hadst overcome the *s* of death, 53 15

shatter

and *s* them like a piece of pottery." 586 21

shattered

and *s* the heads of the dragons upon the waters; 690 11
and *s* every tree in their country. 740 20

shatters

he breaks the bow, and *s* the spear, 649 22
like ships of the sea when the east wind *s* them. 651 14
For he *s* the doors of bronze * 747 13

sheaves

will come again with joy, shouldering their *s*. 105 17
will come again with joy, shouldering their *s*. 782 19
nor the bosom of him who binds the *s*; 784 14

Shechem

"I will exult and parcel out *S*; 667 21
"I will exult and parcel out *S*; 750 8

shed

S forth thine unending day upon us 69 12
And you, like the lamp, must *s* light 109 10
may burn in us and *s* its light on those around us, 110 19
S forth your unending day upon us 123 11
S abroad this gift throughout the world 175 10
S upon thy Church, we beseech thee, O Lord, 186 6
S abroad this gift throughout the world 227 3
S upon your Church, O Lord, the brightness 238 1
my Blood of the New Testament, which is *s* for you, 335 5
The Blood of our Lord Jesus Christ, which was *s* 338 9
remembrance that Christ's Blood was *s* for thee, 338 11
my Blood of the New Covenant, which is *s* for you, 342 7
my Blood of the new Covenant, which is *s* for you 363 3
my Blood of the new Covenant, which is *s* for you 368 16
my Blood of the new Covenant, which is *s* for you 371 16
my Blood of the new Covenant, which is *s* for you 374 21
my Blood of the new Covenant, which is *s* for you 403 10
my Blood of the new Covenant, which is *s* for you 405 8
They have *s* their blood like water on every side 701 8
They *s* innocent blood, 744 23
My eyes *s* streams of tears, * 774 19

shedding

that you avenge the *s* of your servants' blood. 702 3

sheep

All we like *s* have gone astray; 39 1
we have erred and strayed from thy ways like lost *s*, 41 17
and the *s* of his hand. 45 5
we are his people and the *s* of his pasture. 45 16
we have erred and strayed from thy ways like lost *s*, 62 17
All we like *s* have gone astray; 76 25
the people of his pasture and the *s* of his hand. * 82 18
we are his people and the *s* of his pasture. 83 3
Lord Jesus, the great shepherd of the *s*, 132 2
and the *s* of his hand. 146 15
we have erred and strayed from thy ways like lost *s*, 320 24
Lord Jesus Christ, Good Shepherd of the *s*, 459 1
Acknowledge, we humbly beseech you, a *s* 465 2
Acknowledge, we humbly beseech thee, a *s* 483 7
Lord Jesus Christ, the great Shepherd of the *s*, 486 22
Acknowledge, we humbly beseech you, a *s* 499 14
Lord Jesus Christ, the great Shepherd of the *s*, 503 2
All *s* and oxen, * 592 21
You have made us like *s* to be eaten * 646 7
we are accounted as *s* for the slaughter. 647 2
Like a flock of *s* they are destined to die; 653 8
why is your wrath so hot against the *s* 689 10
He led out his people like *s* * 699 9
For we are your people and the *s* of your pasture; * 702 9
the people of his pasture and the *s* of his hand. * 725 4
we are his people and the *s* of his pasture. 729 27
and multiplied their families like flocks of *s*. 749 12
and the little hills like young *s*. 757 4
you little hills like young *s*? 757 8
I have gone astray like a *s* that is lost; * 778 7

sheepfolds

Though you lingered among the *s*, * 677 5
and took him away from the *s*. 700 20

shelter

He who dwells in the *s* of the Most High * 129 21
You will *s* them, * 589 19
he shall keep me safe in his *s*; * 618 2
you keep them in your *s* from the strife of tongues. 624 10
He who dwells in the *s* of the Most High, * 719 10

shepherd

Lord Jesus, the great *s* of the sheep, 132 2
O God, whose Son Jesus is the good *s* of thy people: 173 11
O heavenly Father, *S* of thy people, 196 22
through him who is the *S* and Bishop of our souls, 205 19
O God, whose Son Jesus is the good *s* of your people: 225 3
Heavenly Father, *S* of your people, we thank you 248 8
through him who is the *S* and Bishop of our souls, 256 15
may be one flock under one *s*, 280 7
Through the great *s* of thy flock, 348 11
Through the great *s* of your flock, 381 5
The LORD is my *s*;* 443 1
Lord Jesus Christ, Good *S* of the sheep, 459 1
The LORD is my *s*; * 476 1
Lord Jesus Christ, the great *S* of the sheep, 486 22
Lord Jesus Christ, the great *S* of the sheep, 503 2
Christ, the *S* and Bishops of our souls. 518 17
through the high priest and good *s* 552 11
The LORD is my *s*; * 612 23
s them and carry them for ever. 620 4
Death is their *s*; * 653 9
to be a *s* over Jacob his people 700 22
Hear, O *S* of Israel, leading Joseph like a flock; * 702 12

shepherded

So he *s* them with a faithful and true heart * 700 24

sherd

My mouth is dried out like a pot-*s*; 611 8

shield

pity the afflicted, *s* the joyous; 71 4
pity the afflicted, *s* the joyous; 124 20
his faithfulness shall be a *s* and buckler. 130 5
pity the afflicted, *s* the joyous; 134 9
But you, O LORD, are a *s* about me; * 587 7
you will defend them with your favor as with a *s*. 589 22
God is my *s* and defense; * 591 18

my *s*, the horn of my salvation, and my refuge; 602 10
he is a *s* to all who trust in him. 604 26
You have given me your *s* of victory; * 605 9
The LORD is my strength and my *s*; * 619 24
he is our help and our *s*. 627 16
Take up *s* and armor * 629 15
and put them down, O Lord our *s*. 666 20
the *s*, the sword, and the weapons of battle. 692 6
For the LORD God is both sun and *s*; * 708 14
his faithfulness shall be a *s* and buckler. 719 19
he is their help and their *s*. 758 7
he is their help and their *s*. 758 9
You are my refuge and *s*; * 773 1
my *s* in whom I trust, 800 4

shields

and burns the *s* with fire. 649 23

Shiloh

He forsook the shrine at *S*, * 699 26

shine

Arise, *s*, for your light has come, * 87 11
To *s* on those who dwell in darkness 93 7
"Out of darkness let light *s*," 110 3
has caused his light to *s* within us, 110 4
so you would *s* into our hearts 110 15
The Lord make his face to *s* upon you 114 2
"Out of darkness let light *s*," 139 13
has caused his light to *s* within us, 139 13
O God, who hast caused this holy night to *s* 161 1
may *s* forth in our lives; 161 16
may *s* with the radiance of Christ's glory, 163 9
O God, who didst make this most holy night to *s* 170 14
the light of the Gospel to *s* throughout the world: 187 9
S, we pray thee, in our hearts, 196 16
O God, you have caused this holy night to *s* 212 16
may *s* forth in our lives; 213 10
may *s* with the radiance of Christ's glory, 215 3
O God, who made this most holy night to *s* 222 8
the light of the Gospel to *s* throughout the world: 238 21
S, we pray, in our hearts, 248 3
May it *s* continually to drive away all darkness. 287 24
O God, whose wonderful deeds of old *s* forth 289 12
O God, who made this most holy night to *s* 295 8
thou hast caused a new light to *s* in our hearts, 346 2
you have caused a new light to *s* in our hearts, 378 15
Let light perpetual *s* upon them. 387 18
the Lord make his face to *s* upon him 485 13
And let light perpetual *s* upon him. 486 18
Let light perpetual *s* upon them. 498 10
And let light perpetual *s* upon him. 502 16
let light perpetual *s* upon them; 504 27
Make your face to *s* upon your servant, * 623 25
s forth, you that are enthroned upon the cherubim. 702 13
Let your countenance *s* upon your servant * 774 17
but as for him, his crown will *s*." 787 8

shined

God is the LORD; he has *s* upon us; * 762 25

shines

Light *s* in the darkness for the upright; * 755 11

shining

O *s* light and enfolding dark. 89 2
became a burning and a *s* light 198 10
became a burning and a *s* light 249 19
you clothed me with the *s* garment 450 11
praise him, all you *s* stars. 805 26

ships

like *s* of the sea when the east wind shatters them. 651 14
There move the *s*, 737 4
Some went down to the sea in *s* * 748 1

shook

the roots of the mountains *s*; 603 2
The earth *s*, and the skies poured down rain, 676 18
the earth trembled and *s*. 694 13

shoot

to *s* from ambush at the true of heart. 596 12
That they may *s* down the blameless from ambush; * 671 16
they *s* without warning and are not afraid. 671 17
s out your arrows and rout them. 800 13

shoots

your children like olive *s* round about your table. 783 18

short

so that I may know how *s* my life is. 639 2
You have cut *s* the days of his youth * 717 3
Remember, LORD, how *s* life is, * 717 8
though we often fall *s* of them. 839 6

shortened

he has *s* the number of my days; 732 23

shortness

sensible of the *s* and uncertainty of life; 489 5
aware of the *s* and uncertainty of human life; 504 3

shoulder

"I eased his *s* from the burden; 704 12

shouldering

will come again with joy, *s* their sheaves. 105 17
will come again with joy, *s* their sheaves. 782 19

shoulders

a mantle about their *s*, 430 18

shout

let us *s* for joy to the Rock of our salvation. 82 6
and raise a loud *s* to him with psalms. 82 8
and let your trumpets *s* Salvation 286 2
We will *s* for joy at your victory 608 9
s for joy, all who are true of heart. 625 26
s to God with a cry of joy. 650 7
God has gone up with a *s*, * 650 14
and over Philistia will I *s* in triumph." 668 3
let them *s* for joy and sing. 673 17
and raise a loud *s* to the God of Jacob. 704 2
Happy are the people who know the festal *s*! * 714 23
and I *s* for joy because of the works of your hands. 721 4
let us *s* for joy to the Rock of our salvation. 724 15
and raise a loud *s* to him with psalms. 724 17
Then shall all the trees of the wood *s* for joy 726 17

S with joy to the LORD all you lands; * 728 10
s with joy before the King, the LORD. 728 15
and over Philistia will I *s* in triumph." 750 14

shouts

and our tongue with *s* of joy. 105 7
you surround me with *s* of deliverance. 625 16
his chosen with *s* of joy. 741 12
and tell of his acts with *s* of joy. 747 26
and our tongue with *s* of joy. 782 9

show

and *s* ourselves glad in him with psalms. 44 13
O Lord, *s* thy mercy upon us; 55 1
and that we *s* forth thy praise, 59 4
O Lord, *s* thy mercy upon us; 67 16
and that we *s* forth thy praise, 72 1
and in me you will *s* forth your goodness. 91 21
He promised to *s* mercy to our fathers * 92 25
S us your mercy, O Lord; 97 18
Lord, *s* us your love and mercy; 98 15
with truly thankful hearts we may *s* forth your praise, 101 17
S us your mercy, O Lord; 121 18
with truly thankful hearts we may *s* forth your praise, 125 15
and *s* him my salvation. 131 5
and *s* ourselves glad in him with psalms. 146 4
set it forth, and *s* it accordingly, 150 8
That it may please thee to *s* thy pity upon all 151 5
s forth in their lives what they profess 172 4
s forth in their lives what they profess 173 1
s forth our thankfulness unto thee 187 11
we also in our generation may *s* forth thy praise, 196 18
s forth in their lives what they profess 223 18
s forth in their lives what they profess 224 16
s forth your power among all peoples, 232 18
may *s* ourselves thankful to you 239 2
we also in our generation may *s* forth your praise, 248 4
and *s* forth your handiwork in the heavens 261 8
That we may *s* forth your glory in the world. 268 30
s us the light of his countenance, 281 6
may *s* forth in their lives 291 1
to *s* forth thy glory in all the world. 345 6
to *s* forth your glory in all the world. 378 2
and *s* forth your glory in all that we do, 391 3
we *s* forth the sacrifice of his death, 403 14
If any of you can *s* just cause 424 2
or *s* forth all his praise? 478 14
Thou shalt *s* me the path of life; 485 6
You will *s* me the path of life; 501 8
s compassion to the poor and strangers, 518 28
to *s* Christ's people that in serving the helpless 543 17
You will *s* me the path of life; * 600 19
S me your marvelous loving-kindness, * 601 11
With the faithful you *s* yourself faithful, O God; * 604 14
with the forthright you *s* yourself forthright. 604 15
With the pure you *s* yourself pure, * 604 16
S me your ways, O LORD, * 614 19
and will *s* them his covenant. 615 17
S me your way, O LORD; * 618 21
Your right hand will *s* you marvelous things; * 647 21
but to those who keep in my way will I *s* 656 3
s no mercy to those who are faithless and evil. 666 6
Awesome things will you *s* us in your righteousness, 672 17
s us the light of his countenance and come to us. 675 10
Will he no more *s* his favor? 693 15
and *s* forth your praise from age to age. 702 11
s the light of your countenance, 702 17
s the light of your countenance, 703 2
and *s* favor to the wicked? 705 12
S us your mercy, O LORD, * 709 7
S me a sign of your favor, 711 9
S your servants your works * 719 5
and *s* him my salvation. 720 21
That they may *s* how upright the LORD is, * 721 27
O God of vengeance, *s* yourself. 722 19
or *s* forth all his praise? 741 22
Let there be no one to *s* him kindness, * 751 20
Because he did not remember to *s* mercy, * 752 1
until he *s* us his mercy. 780 20
S your goodness, O LORD, to those who are good * 782 1
s me the road that I must walk, 799 17
and grant that we may *s* the power of your love 817 16
s forth thy praise among the nations of the earth. 820 12
s thy loving-kindness, 828 4
S them that your ways give more life 829 15
s us your presence in those who differ most from us, 840 4
To *s* God respect in thought, word, 847 24
To *s* respect for the life God has given us; 848 7
s us our need for redemption, 849 9
to *s* God at work in nature and history. 853 12

showed

He hath *s* strength with his arm; * 50 11
he hath *s* strength with his arm; * 65 14
O Lord, let thy mercy be *s* upon us; 153 16
You have *s* me great troubles and adversities, * 684 23

shower

Glorify the Lord, every *s* of rain and fall of dew, * 88 13

showers

O ye *s* and dew, bless ye the Lord; * 48 3
like *s* that water the earth. 685 20
such moderate rain and *s*, 828 13

showest

and *s* forth thy handiwork in the heavens 210 2

showing

O God, who declarest thy almighty power chiefly in *s* 182 12
O God, you declare your almighty power chiefly in *s* 234 6
and *s* them to be holy gifts for your holy people, 375 6

shown

The Lord has *s* forth his glory: 81 1
He has *s* the strength of his arm, * 92 6
He has *s* the strength of his arm, * 119 12
He has *s* the strength of his arm,* 442 1
for he has *s* me the wonders of his love 624 12
and the wonders he had *s* them. 695 25
his righteousness has he openly *s* 728 4
He has *s* his people the power of his works * 754 16
Where in the Old Testament is God's will for us *s* 847 9
God's will for us is *s* most clearly 847 11

shows
he *s* loving-kindness to his anointed, 606 13
and the firmament *s* his handiwork. 606 16
and *s* compassion to his servants. 789 4
and *s* us the nature of God. 849 22

shrine
He forsook the *s* at Shiloh, * 699 26

shrink
Their heart is established and will not *s*, * 755 20
I do not *s* from your judgments, * 771 23

shun
you did not *s* the Virgin's womb. 96 4

shut
by day or night they will never be *s*. 87 20
s not thy merciful ears to our prayer; 484 12
s not your ears to our prayers, 492 13
You have not *s* me up in the power of the enemy; * 623 1
do not let the Pit *s* its mouth upon me. 680 22
but all wickedness will *s* its mouth. 749 14

sick
Tend the *s*, Lord Christ; 71 3
Tend the *s*, Lord Christ; 124 19
Tend the *s*, Lord Christ; 134 8
relieve thy *s* servants, and give thy power of healing 208 17
relieve your *s* servants, and give your power of healing 260 2
For the *s*, the wounded, and the crippled 279 6
for the *s* and the suffering, let us pray to the Lord. 384 21
I ask your prayers for the poor, the *s*, the hungry, 386 4
For the poor, the persecuted, the *s*, 390 24
For those who minister to the *s*, the friendless, 392 10
anointed many that were *s* and healed them, 455 11
relieve thy *s* servant N. for whom our prayers 458 3
relieve your *s* servant N. and give your power 459 18
particularly the poor, the weak, the *s*, and the lonely. 543 6
For the poor, the persecuted, the *s*, 550 11
But when they were *s* I dressed in sack-cloth * 630 17
the homeless and the destitute, the old and the *s*, 826 3
What is Unction of the *S*? 861 13
Unction is the rite of anointing the *s* with oil, 861 14

sickbed
The LORD sustains them on their *s* * 642 4

sickness
nor of the *s* that lays waste at mid-day. 130 9
are in trouble, sorrow, need, *s*, 329 28
honor and keep him, in *s* and in health; 424 10
honor and keep her, in *s* and in health; 424 16
for richer for poorer, in *s* and in health, 427 3
honor and keep her, in *s* and in health; 433 6
honor and keep him, in *s* and in health; 433 11
for richer for poorer, in *s* and in health, 436 3
for richer for poorer, in *s* and in health, 436 8
to drive away all *s* of body and spirit, 456 4
that his *s* may be turned into health, 458 13
drive away from our bodies all *s* and all infirmity: 458 17
Sanctify, O Lord, the *s* of your servant 460 1
when we turn to you in *s* or special need, 569 8
nor of the *s* that lays waste at mid-day. 719 23
deliver from his *s* thy servant 841 9

side
A thousand shall fall at your *s* 130 10
The wicked prowl on every *s*, * 597 18
this I know, for God is on my *s*. 663 10
Rouse yourself, come to my *s*, and see; * 666 3
They have shed their blood like water on every *s* 701 8
by the *s* of your altars, O LORD of hosts, 707 21
they encompass me on every *s*. 713 14
A thousand shall fall at your *s* 719 24
and burns up his enemies on every *s*. 727 2
The LORD is at my *s*, therefore I will not fear; * 761 7
The LORD is at my *s* to help me; * 761 9
They hem me in, they hem me in on every *s*; * 761 17
I am on the *s* of peace, * 778 22
If the LORD had not been on our *s*, * 781 1
the loving care which surrounds us on every *s*. 836 6

sigh
we bring our years to an end like a *s*. 718 18

sighing
neither *s*, but life everlasting. 482 11
neither *s*, but life everlasting. 483 5
neither *s*, but life everlasting. 499 3
and my years with *s*; * 623 7
and my *s* is not hidden from you. 637 15
Let the sorrowful *s* of the prisoners come before you, * 702 4

sight
be always acceptable in thy *s*, O Lord, 40 14
do always what is righteous in thy *s*; 57 12
remember that we are ever walking in thy *s*; 57 18
Let my prayer be set forth in thy *s* as the incense, 61 1
be acceptable in your *s*, O Lord, 78 13
holy and righteous in his *s* 92 30
remember that we are ever walking in your *s*; 100 10
let our prayer in your *s* be as incense, 113 9
Let my prayer be set forth in your *s* as incense, 115 1
working in you that which is pleasing in his *s*; 132 5
that our faith may never be found wanting in thy *s*; 185 18
that our faith may never be found wanting in your *s*; 237 12
and done what is evil in your *s*. 266 9
and in their *s* ascended into heaven, 347 3
holy and pleasing in thy *s*. 348 18
Have mercy, Lord, for we are sinners in your *s*. 370 16
and in their *s* ascended into heaven, 379 22
holy and pleasing in your *s*. 381 12
That our works may find favor in your *s*. 387 13
For a thousand years in thy *s* are but as yesterday 472 16
dear in the *s* of the LORD is the death of his saints. 479 19
working in you that which is well pleasing in his *s*; 487 3
that he may be precious in thy *s*. 488 15
working in you that which is well-pleasing in his *s*; 503 5
Braggarts cannot stand in your *s*; * 588 25
your judgments are far above out of their *s*; * 595 2
In his *s* the wicked is rejected, * 599 11
because of the cleanness of my hands in his *s*. 604 13
heart be acceptable in your *s*, * 607 29
which you have done in the *s* of all 624 6

"I have been cut off from the *s* of your eyes." * 624 15
and my lifetime is as nothing in your *s*; * 639 4
and the creatures of the fields are in my *s*. 655 2
and done what is evil in your *s*. 656 13
my adversaries are all in your *s*." 681 2
and dear shall their blood be in his *s*. 686 12
He worked marvels in the *s* of their forefathers, * 695 26
Let it be known among the heathen and in our *s* 702 2
My *s* has failed me because of trouble; * 712 20
For a thousand years in your *s* are like yesterday 718 6
the *s* of the nations. 728 5
and those who tell lies shall not continue in my *s*. 730 25
and their offspring shall stand fast in your *s*." 733 8
Precious in the *s* of the LORD * 760 3
In your *s* all the wicked of the earth are but dross; * 773 11
and the upright shall continue in your *s*. 797 2
Let my prayer be set forth in your *s* as incense, * 797 5
for in your *s* shall no one living be justified. 798 22

sign

the holy name of Jesus to be the *s* of our salvation: 162 2
the holy name of Jesus to be the *s* of our salvation: 213 14
Grant that these ashes may be to us a *s* 265 17
you have placed in the skies the *s* 289 1
to be a *s* for us of the salvation 289 15
as a *s* and pledge of his love, 316 3
Bless, O Lord, this ring to be a *s* of the vows 427 10
Make their life together a *s* of Christ's love 429 17
Bless, O Lord, this ring to be a *s* of the vows 434 4
Receive this Bible as a *s* of the authority 534 10
Receive this Bible as the *s* of your authority 545 19
be to us a *s* of the heavenly Altar 574 2
Show me a *s* of your favor, 711 9
What is the outward and visible *s* in Baptism? 858 12
The outward and visible *s* in Baptism is water, 858 13
What is the outward and visible *s* in the Eucharist? 859 18
The outward and visible *s* in the Eucharist is bread 859 19

significance

What is the *s* of Jesus' resurrection? 850 10

signifies

It *s* to us the mystery of the union 423 6

signs

O God, who dost manifest in thy servants the *s* 71 6
O God, you manifest in your servants the *s* 125 1
Let these branches be for us *s* of his victory, 271 10
leadership in your Church, and bears these *s*, 552 9
let all these be *s* of the ministry which is mine 562 7
the earth will tremble at your marvelous *s*; * 673 2
There are no *s* for us to see; 690 1
How he wrought his *s* in Egypt * 698 13
They worked his *s* among them, * 740 7
He sent *s* and wonders into the midst of you, 788 19
The sacraments are outward and visible *s* 857 26

Sihon

S, king of the Amorites, 788 23
S, king of the Amorites, * 791 7

silence

let all the earth keep *s* 40 18
kneel in *s*, and with penitent and obedient hearts 41 12
kneel in *s*, and with penitent and obedient hearts 62 12
let all the earth keep *s* 78 17
kneel in *s*, and with penitent and obedient hearts 79 6
kneel in *s*, and with penitent and obedient hearts 116 8
speak to your heart in *s* upon your bed. 128 17
that in the hours of *s* I may enjoy 461 16
speak to your heart in *s* upon your bed. 588 7
We have waited in *s* on your loving-kindness, 651 18
Our God will come and will not keep *s*; * 654 6
For God alone my soul in *s* waits; * 669 5
I should soon have dwelt in the land of *s*. 723 28
nor all those who go down into *s*; 758 24
and not to mislead others by our *s*; 848 17

silenced

Let the lying lips be *s* 624 1

silent

let them be *s* in the grave. 623 29
You saw it, O LORD; do not be *s*; * 631 14
I fell *s* and did not open my mouth, * 639 13
O God, do not be *s*; * 706 3

silver

like *s* refined from ore 597 14
you have tried us just as *s* is tried. 674 14
like a dove whose wings are covered with *s*, 677 6
Trample down those who lust after *s*; * 678 20
He led out his people with *s* and gold; * 740 27
Their idols are *s* and gold, * 757 20
than thousands in gold and *s*. 769 8
The idols of the heathen are *s* and gold, * 789 5

Simon

Almighty Father, who didst inspire *S* Peter, 187 1
and especially on this day for *S* and Jude; 194 2
Almighty Father, who inspired *S* Peter, 238 14
and especially on this day for *S* and Jude; 245 11

simple

The LORD preserveth the *s*; * 479 10
it gives understanding to the *s*. 774 8

sin

If we say that we have no *s*, we deceive ourselves, 38 10
For in that he died, he died unto *s* once; 46 9
reckon ye also yourselves to be dead indeed unto *s*, * 46 11
Vouchsafe, O Lord, to keep us this day without *s*; 55 19
this day we fall into no *s*, 57 10
If we say we have no *s*, we deceive ourselves, 76 9
The death that he died, he died to *s*, once for all; * 83 17
So also consider yourselves dead to *s*, * 83 19
that they may repent of their *s* and be saved. 91 11
Do not let me perish in my *s*, * 91 18
you take away the *s* of the world: 95 5
who *s* against us. 97 12
Lord, keep us from all *s* today; 98 13
that we may not fall into *s*, 100 3
who *s* against us. 106 22
keep us from every *s*, every evil, 113 6
who *s* against us. 121 12
Tremble, then, and do not *s*; * 128 16
who *s* against us. 133 4
that we may not fall into *s*, 137 16

From all evil and wickedness; from *s*; 148 15
Grant us so to die daily to *s*, 170 10
raised from the death of *s* by thy life-giving Spirit; 171 2
from the dominion of *s* and death 172 15
both a sacrifice for *s* and also an example 180 20
and enslaved by *s*, may be freed and brought together 185 4
have put away the old life of *s*, 201 14
and enslaved by *s*, may be freed and brought together 203 2
turn us from the old life of *s*: 203 7
redeemed from the old life of *s* by our baptism 203 13
Grant us so to die daily to *s*, 222 4
raised from the death of *s* by your life-giving Spirit; 222 19
from the dominion of *s* and death 224 8
to be for us a sacrifice for *s*, and also an example 232 12
and enslaved by *s*, may be freed and brought together 236 17
have put away the old life of *s*, 253 2
and enslaved by *s*, may be freed and brought together 254 4
you turn us from the old life of *s*: 254 8
redeemed from the old life of *s* by our baptism 254 14
and cleanse me from my *s*. 266 5
and my *s* is ever before me. 266 7
Purge me from my *s*, and I shall be pure; * 266 16
might be delivered from the power of *s* and death, 277 5
For those hardened by *s* or indifference 279 23
paid for us the debt of Adam's *s*, 287 4
delivered from the gloom of *s*, and are restored 287 10
wickedness is put to flight, and *s* is washed away. 287 18
you have brought us out of *s* into righteousness 291 6
whenever you fall into *s*, repent 293 24
Grant us so to die daily to *s*, 295 4
whenever you fall into *s*, repent 304 27
Deliver them, O Lord, from the way of *s* 305 14
from the bondage of *s* into everlasting life. 306 19
that those who here are cleansed from *s* 307 4
the forgiveness of *s*, and have raised them 308 4
you have overcome *s* and brought us to yourself, 309 4
who *s* against us. 311 9
the forgiveness of *s* and have raised him 314 3
If we say that we have no *s*, we deceive ourselves, 320 1
If any man *s*, we have an Advocate with the Father, 332 15
Son to redeem us from *s* and death, 345 9
that we might be delivered from the bondage of *s*, 345 17
tempted as we are, yet did not *s*; 346 5
taken away the *s* of the world; 346 20
If we say that we have no *s*, we deceive ourselves, 352 1
you take away the *s* of the world: 356 9
and, when we had fallen into *s* 362 10
who *s* against us. 364 9
out of *s* into righteousness, 368 9
he lived as one of us, yet without *s*. 374 4
you sent your beloved Son to redeem us from *s* 378 4
that we might be delivered from the bondage of *s*, 378 12
tempted in every way as we are, yet did not *s*. 379 2
and has taken away the *s* of the world. 379 17
who *s* against us. 398 20
whenever you fall into *s*, repent 417 9
you have overcome *s* and brought us to yourself, 418 2
who *s* against us. 428 16
and cleanse me from my *s*. 449 4
and my *s* is ever before me. 449 6
If any man *s*, we have an Advocate with the Father, 450 1
and redeemed me from *s* and death 450 9
From all evil, from all *s*, from all tribulation, 463 3
who *s* against us. 464 12
may die to *s* and rise to newness of life, 480 9
taken away the *s* of the world. 483 19
taken away the *s* of the world. 500 8
who *s* against us. 502 9
the death of *s* to the life of righteousness; 505 3
die to *s* and are made new in Christ. 569 16
from the bondage of *s* into everlasting life. 570 11
are cleansed from *s* and born again 570 19
Tremble, then, and do not *s*; * 588 6
forgive my *s*, for it is great. 615 11
and forgive me all my *s*. 615 25
and whose *s* is put away! 624 24
Then I acknowledged my *s* to you, * 625 7
Then you forgave me the guilt of my *s*. 625 10
that his hateful *s* will not be found out. 632 6
there is no soundness in my body, because of my *s*. 637 3
and be sorry for my *s*. 638 6
With rebukes for *s* you punish us; 639 17
and *s*-offering you have not required, * 640 18
and cleanse me from my *s*. 656 9
and my *s* is ever before me. 656 11
Purge me from my *s*, and I shall be pure; * 656 20
and his mother's *s* not be blotted out; 751 26
Let their *s* be always before the LORD; * 751 27
that I may not *s* against you. 764 6
on the first day of the week, you conquered *s*, 835 2
s and our need for redemption. 848 27
What is *s*? 848 28
S is the seeking of our own will 848 29
How does *s* have power over us? 849 1
S has power over us because we lose our liberty 849 2
power of evil, *s*, and death. 849 6
power of *s*, so that with the help of God 849 13
are freed from the power of *s* and reconciled to God. 850 9
How can we share in his victory over *s*, 850 22

Sinai

at the presence of God, the God of *S*, * 676 19
the Lord comes in holiness from *S*. 677 17

since

For *s* by man came death, * 46 15
which have been *s* the world began: 50 27
For *s* by a man came death, * 83 23
S we have a great high priest who has passed 352 5
S it has pleased God to bestow 441 10
I have been entrusted to you ever *s* I was born; * 610 20
S you refuse discipline, * 655 14
my confidence *s* I was young. 683 10
I have been sustained by you ever *s* I was born; 683 11
O God, you have taught me *s* I was young, * 684 14
Ever *s* my youth, I have been wretched 713 8
Ever *s* the world began, your throne 722 7
"Greatly have they oppressed me *s* my youth," * 784 1
And *s* what we do for those in prison, 826 24
S we do not fully obey them, are they useful at all? 848 25
S we do not fully obey them, we see more clearly 848 26

sincere

and with *s* hearts believe his holy Gospel. 269 9

sincerity
but with the unleavened bread of *s* and truth. 46 6
but with the unleavened bread of *s* and truth. 83 14
may worship thee in *s* and truth; 170 18
may worship you in *s* and truth; 222 12
may worship you in *s* and truth; 295 12
I will walk with *s* of heart within my house. 730 11

sinful
From all inordinate and *s* affections; 149 5
the unruly wills and affections of *s* men: 167 16
Do you renounce all *s* desires that draw you 302 13
a sign of Christ's love to this *s* and broken world, 429 17

sinfulness
nor as we deserve in our *s*, 394 7

sing
O come, let us *s* unto the Lord; * 44 10
we *s* thy praises, O God: 64 6
Come, let us *s* to the Lord; * 82 5
I will *s* to the Lord, for he is lofty and uplifted; * 85 1
S the praises of the Lord, 86 11
For all the powers of heaven *s* your praises, * 91 25
and *s* the praises of your Name? * 94 15
Cherubim and Seraphim, *s* in endless praise: 95 20
Let your people *s* with joy. 97 21
we *s* your praises, O God: 112 6
we *s* your praises, O God: 118 6
Let your people *s* with joy. 121 21
s your glory at the close of this day, 134 3
we *s* your praises O God: 139 6
O come, let us *s* unto the Lord; * 146 1
and my tongue shall *s* of your righteousness, 267 4
Rejoice and *s* now, all the round earth, 286 4
for the grace to *s* the worthy praise 286 12
where your saints for ever *s* your praise; 290 6
s this hymn to proclaim the glory of your Name: 362 3
s this hymn to proclaim the glory of your Name: 367 12
and glorify your Name, as we *s* (say), 373 11
proclaiming your glory, as we *s* (say), 402 8
proclaiming your glory, as we *s* (say), 404 10
I will *s* and speak praises unto the LORD. 477 27
in the music we make and in the songs we *s*. 572 4
they will *s* out their joy for ever. 589 18
I will *s* to your Name, O Most High. 593 4
S praise to the LORD who dwells in Zion; * 593 21
I will *s* to the LORD, 598 10
and *s* praises to your Name. 606 11
we will *s* and praise your power. 609 26
I will *s* and make music to the LORD. 618 9
S to the LORD, you servants of his; * 621 10
it is good for the just to *s* praises. 626 2
S for him a new song; * 626 5
Let those who favor my cause *s* out with joy 631 27
S praises to God, *s* praises; * 650 16
s praises to our King, *s* praises. 650 17
s praises with all your skill. 650 19
and my tongue shall *s* of your righteousness, 657 10
I will *s* and make melody. 664 11
I will *s* praise to you among the nations. 664 16
For my part, I will *s* of your strength; * 667 3
To you, O my Strength, will I *s*; * 667 7
So will I always *s* the praise of your Name, * 669 3
you make the dawn and the dusk to *s* for joy. 673 3
let them shout for joy and *s*. 673 17
s the glory of his Name; 673 19
s the glory of his praise. 673 20
Let the nations be glad and *s* for joy, * 675 15
S to God, *s* praises to his Name; 676 8
S to God, O kingdoms of the earth; * 678 24
s praises to the Lord. 678 25
I will *s* to you with the harp, O Holy One of Israel. 685 3
My lips will *s* with joy when I play to you, * 685 4
I will *s* praises to the God of Jacob. 691 23
S with joy to God our strength * 704 1
Your love, O LORD, for ever will I *s*; * 713 17
and to *s* praises to your Name, O Most High; 720 23
Come, let us *s* to the LORD; * 724 14
S to the LORD a new song; * 725 17
s to the LORD, all the whole earth. 725 18
S to the LORD and bless his Name; * 725 19
S to the LORD a new song, * 727 24
lift up your voice, rejoice, and *s*. 728 11
S to the LORD with the harp, * 728 12
I will *s* of mercy and justice; * 730 7
to you, O LORD, will I *s* praises. 730 8
and *s* among the branches. 735 26
I will *s* to the LORD as long as I live; * 737 20
S to him, *s* praises to him, * 738 3
I will *s* and make melody. 749 18
I will *s* praises to you among the nations. 749 23
My tongue shall *s* of your promise, * 777 23
let your faithful people *s* with joy. 786 16
and her faithful people will rejoice and *s*. 787 4
s praises to his Name, for it is lovely. 788 7
"*S* us one of the songs of Zion." 792 7
How shall we *s* the LORD's song * 792 8
before the gods I will *s* your praise. 793 2
They will *s* of the ways of the LORD, * 793 12
O God, I will *s* to you a new song; * 800 19
they shall *s* of your righteous deeds. 801 25
I will *s* praises to my God while I have my being. 803 6
How good it is to *s* praises to our God! * 804 2
S to the LORD with thanksgiving; * 804 14
S to the LORD a new song; * 807 2
s his praise in the congregation of the faithful. 807 3
let them *s* praise to him with timbrel and harp. 807 7

singers
The *s* go before, musicians follow after, * 678 7
The *s* and the dancers will say, * 711 24

singing
S aloud a song of thanksgiving * 616 20

single
a *s* loving God who creates, sustains, and directs it. 846 8

singleness
givest us to do with *s* of heart 151 14
we may serve thee with *s* of heart, 198 4
may serve you with *s* of heart, 249 14
with gladness and *s* of heart; 365 17

sings

Therefore my heart *s* to you without ceasing; * 622 5
s to you, *s* out your Name." 673 25

sink

We *s* down into the dust; * 647 7
Save me from the mire; do not let me *s*; * 680 17
they *s* into sleep; * 692 10

sinking

I am *s* in deep mire, * 679 9

sinned

"Father, I have *s* against heaven, and before thee, 38 18
"Father, I have *s* against heaven and before you; 76 17
we confess that we have *s* against you 79 11
I have *s*, O Lord, I have *s*, * 91 14
we confess that we have *s* against you 116 13
We have *s* against you, 127 7
Against you only have I *s* * 266 8
that we have *s* by our own fault 267 16
we confess that we have *s* against thee 320 11
we confess that we have *s* against thee 331 22
we confess that we have *s* against you 352 11
we confess that we have *s* against you 360 3
we confess that we have *s* against you 397 20
Bless me, for I have *s*. 447 1
I have *s* by my own fault in thought, word, and deed, 447 6
Do you, then, forgive those who have *s* against you? 451 1
we confess that we have *s* against you 454 2
heal me, for I have *s* against you." 642 7
Against you only have I *s* * 656 12
We have *s* as our forebears did; * 742 9

sinner

a *s* from my mother's womb. 266 13
Go (or abide) in peace, and pray for me, a *s*. 448 14
Pray for me, a *s*. 449 9
a *s* of your own redeeming. 465 3
a *s* of thine own redeeming. 483 8
a lamb of your own flock, a *s* of your own redeeming. 499 15
nor the *s* in the council of the righteous. 585 14
a *s* from my mother's womb. 656 17

sinners

you have promised forgiveness to *s*, * 91 10
We *s* do beseech thee to hear us, O Lord God; 150 1
betrayed, and given up into the hands of *s*, 169 16
wills and affections of *s*: 219 7
betrayed, and given into the hands of *s*, 221 10
and *s* shall return to you. 267 2
desires not the death of *s*, 269 4
betrayed, and given into the hands of *s*, 276 6
and to us *s* everlasting life 282 10
that Christ Jesus came into the world to save *s*. 332 14
Have mercy, Lord, for we are *s* in your sight. 370 16
absolve all *s* who truly repent and believe in him, 448 2
that Christ Jesus came into the world to save *s*. 449 19
absolve all *s* who truly repent and believe in him, 451 12
We *s* beseech you to hear us, Lord Christ: 463 11
and to us *s* everlasting life 489 27
declare God's forgiveness to penitent *s*, 531 13
nor lingered in the way of *s*, 585 3
therefore he teaches *s* in his way. 615 5
Do not sweep me away with *s*, * 616 24
and *s* shall return to you. 657 8
Let *s* be consumed out of the earth, * 737 24

sinning

But they went on *s* against him, * 696 7
In spite of all this, they went on *s* * 697 14

sins

but if we confess our *s*, God is faithful 38 11
and just to forgive us our *s*, and to cleanse us 38 12
confess our *s*, that we may obtain forgiveness 41 13
Let us humbly confess our *s* unto Almighty God. 41 15
remission of all your *s*, true repentance, 42 12
for the remission of their *s*, 51 15
that takest away the *s* of the world, 52 12
Thou that takest away the *s* of the world, 52 14
the forgiveness of *s*, 54 8
confess our *s*, so that we may obtain forgiveness 62 13
Let us humbly confess our *s* unto Almighty God. 62 15
remission of all your *s*, true repentance, 63 15
the forgiveness of *s*, 66 24
That we may be pardoned and forgiven for our *s* 68 12
but if we confess our *s*, God, who is faithful 76 10
and just, will forgive our *s* and cleanse us 76 11
and with penitent and obedient hearts confess our *s*, 79 7
Let us confess our *s* against God and our neighbor. 79 9
God have mercy on you, forgive you all your *s* 80 1
by the forgiveness of their *s*. 93 4
the forgiveness of *s*, 96 28
Forgive us our *s* 97 10
Forgive us our *s* 106 20
Regard not our *s*, 107 18
Bless the Lord who forgives all our *s*. 109 5
purged of all our *s* and made worthy to worship 111 6
confess our *s*, so that we may obtain forgiveness 116 9
Let us confess our *s* against God and our neighbor. 116 11
forgive you all your *s* through our Lord 117 7
the forgiveness of *s*, 120 24
Forgive us our *s* 121 10
That we may be pardoned and forgiven for our *s* 122 14
Let us confess our *s* to God. 127 5
Almighty God grant us forgiveness of all our *s*, 128 1
Forgive us our *s* 133 2
Regard not our *s*, 138 17
neither reward us according to our *s*. 148 10
forgive us all our *s*, negligences, and ignorances; 152 4
O Lamb of God, that takest away the *s* of the world, 152 24
Mercifully forgive the *s* of thy people. 154 18
grace to heed their warnings and forsake our *s*, 159 11
and, because we are sorely hindered by our *s*, 160 2
Set us free, O God, from the bondage of our *s* 164 6
and dost forgive the *s* of all those who are penitent: 166 2
worthily lamenting our *s* and acknowledging 166 4
Son to die for our *s* and to rise again 172 9
grace to heed their warnings and forsake our *s*, 211 11
and, because we are sorely hindered by our *s*, 212 2
Set us free, O God, from the bondage of our *s*, 216 1
and forgive the *s* of all who are penitent: 217 15
lamenting our *s* and acknowledging 217 17
Son to die for our *s* and to rise for our justification: 224 1

and forgive the *s* of all who are penitent:	264	3
lamenting our *s* and acknowledging	264	5
who, because of notorious *s*, had been separated	265	4
Hide your face from my *s* *	266	20
the absolution and remission of their *s*.	269	8
the forgiveness of *s*,	293	16
bestowed upon us the forgiveness of *s*,	294	6
Bless the Lord who forgives all our *s*.	299	5
the forgiveness of *s*,	304	19
Forgive us our *s*	311	7
And acknowledge your *s* before Almighty God,	317	4
and confess your *s*, that you may receive	317	13
[and humbly confess our *s* to Almighty God].	317	23
Bless the Lord who forgiveth all our *s*.	319	6
but if we confess our *s*, God is faithful	320	2
and just to forgive us our *s*, and to cleanse us	320	3
Let us humbly confess our *s* unto Almighty God.	320	9
remission of all your *s*, true repentance,	321	15
Bless the Lord who forgiveth all our *s*.	323	5
that takest away the *s* of the world,	324	23
Thou that takest away the *s* of the world,	325	1
We acknowledge one baptism for the forgiveness of *s*.	327	17
I acknowledge one Baptism for the remission of *s*;	328	19
Ye who do truly and earnestly repent you of your *s*,	330	9
Let us humbly confess our *s* unto Almighty God.	330	15
We acknowledge and bewail our manifold *s*	331	4
hath promised forgiveness of *s* to all those	332	2
pardon and deliver you from all your *s*,	332	4
he is the perfect offering for our *s*,	332	17
but for the *s* of the whole world.	332	17
for the *s* of the whole world;	334	14
shed for you, and for many, for the remission of *s*.	335	6
may obtain remission of our *s*,	335	29
although we are unworthy, through our manifold *s*,	336	9
O Lamb of God, that takest away the *s* of the world,	337	3
shed for you, and for many, for the remission of *s*.	342	8
who for our *s* was lifted high upon the cross,	346	13
Bless the Lord who forgives all our *s*.	351	5
But if we confess our *s*, God, who is faithful	352	2
will forgive our *s* and cleanse us	352	3
Let us confess our *s* against God and our neighbor.	352	9
God have mercy on you, forgive you all your *s*	353	1
Bless the Lord who forgives all our *s*.	355	5
We acknowledge one baptism for the forgiveness of *s*.	359	8
Let us confess our *s* against God and our neighbor.	360	1
God have mercy on you, forgive you all your *s*	360	15
shed for you and for many for the forgiveness of *s*.	363	4
Forgive us our *s*	364	7
shed for you and for many for the forgiveness of *s*.	368	17
shed for you and for many for the forgiveness of *s*.	371	17
shed for you and for many for the forgiveness of *s*.	374	22
For our *s* he was lifted high upon the cross,	379	10
For the absolution and remission of our *s*	385	4
for the forgiveness of our *s*,	391	7
We pray to you also for the forgiveness of our *s*.	393	8
in your compassion forgive us our *s*,	393	10
Regard not our *s*,	395	9
God have mercy on you, forgive you all your *s*	398	7
Forgive us our *s*	398	18
it may bring us forgiveness of our *s*,	399	10
shed for you and for many for the forgiveness of *s*.	403	11
shed for you and for many for the forgiveness of *s*.	405	9
Lamb of God, you take away the *s* of the world:	407	1
Bless the Lord who forgives all our *s*.	413	5
the forgiveness of *s*,	417	1
Forgive us our *s*	428	14
truly and humbly confess your *s*:	447	3
and all other *s* which I cannot now remember,	447	8
I absolve you from all your *s*:	448	4
conferred power on his Church to forgive *s*,	448	9
The Lord has put away all your *s*.	448	12
forgives your *s* by the grace of the Holy Spirit.	448	16
remember in truth all your *s* and his unfailing mercy.	449	11
he is the perfect offering for our *s*,	450	3
but for the *s* of the whole world.	450	3
confess your *s* with a humble and obedient heart	450	6
Therefore, O Lord, from these and all other *s*	450	16
who conferred power on his Church to forgive *s*,	451	8
I absolve you from all your *s*:	451	14
The Lord has put away all your *s*.	451	20
forgives your *s* by the grace of the Holy Spirit.	452	2
God have mercy on you, forgive you all your *s*	455	6
Of his great mercy, may he forgive you your *s*,	456	15
pray that it may bring us forgiveness of our *s*,	457	8
That it may please you mercifully to pardon all his *s*,	463	15
Jesus, bearer of our *s*:	463	25
Forgive us our *s*	464	10
and our secret *s* in the light of thy countenance.	472	26
And he shall redeem Israel * from all his *s*.	474	17
that we may be cleansed from all our *s*,	481	5
the forgiveness of *s*, and the resurrection	481	16
who for our *s* art justly displeased?	484	7
immaculate Lamb that was slain to take away the *s*	488	16
who by our *s* are justly angered.	492	8
the forgiveness of *s*,	496	18
Forgive us our *s*	502	7
Bless the Lord who forgives all our *s*.	512	5
We acknowledge one baptism for the forgiveness of *s*.	520	8
Bless the Lord who forgives all our *s*.	525	5
We acknowledge one baptism for the forgiveness of *s*.	530	27
Bless the Lord who forgives all our *s*.	537	5
We acknowledge one baptism for the forgiveness of *s*.	542	27
for the forgiveness of our *s*,	550	16
be forgiven for their *s*, united with one another,	574	6
For the pardon of our *s*, which restores us	579	1
Above all, keep your servant from presumptuous *s*;	607	24
Remember not the *s* of my youth	615	1
my *s* have overtaken me, and I cannot see; *	641	5
Hide your face from my *s* *	656	24
For the *s* of their mouths, for the words of their lips,	666	21
Our *s* are stronger than we are, *	672	11
But he was so merciful that he forgave their *s*	698	1
Remember not our past *s*;	701	21
deliver us and forgive us our *s*, for your Name's sake.	701	25
and blotted out all their *s*.	708	23
and our secret *s* in the light of your countenance.	718	16
He forgives all your *s* *	733	13
He has not dealt with us according to our *s*, *	734	1
so far has he removed our *s* from us.	734	6
they were afflicted because of their *s*.	747	16
and he shall redeem Israel from all their *s*.	785	9
forgive our *s*, banish our fears,	835	4
In penitence, we confess our *s* and make restitution	857	12
by grace God forgives our *s*,	858	3

forgiveness of *s*, and new life	858	19
It is required that we renounce Satan, repent of our *s*,	858	22
The benefits we receive are the forgiveness of our *s*,	859	29
repent of our *s*, and be in love and charity	860	6
are penitent for their *s*, and are ready to affirm	860	25
which those who repent of their *s* may confess them	861	10

Sisera

to *S*, and to Jabin at the river of Kishon:	706	21

sister

for a new brother (*s*)].	440	7
who now has a new brother (*s*)]	440	12
brother (*s*) N. both relief from pain	460	18
Let us pray, then, for our brother (*s*)	465	11
we commend our brother (*s*) N.	465	16
receive the body of our brother (*s*) for burial.	466	13
we remember before you this day our brother (*s*) N.	493	17
For our brother (*s*) N., let us pray	497	1
give to our brother (*s*) eternal life.	497	10
bring our brother (*s*) to the joys of heaven.	497	14
Our brother (*s*) was washed in Baptism	497	16
our sorrows at the death of our brother (*s*);	497	23
we commend to you our brother (*s*) N.,	498	1

sisters

Brothers and *s* in Christ Jesus,	514	1

sit

To give light to them that *s* in darkness	51	18
If I am to *s* still,	461	21
help me to *s* quietly.	461	22
you *s* upon your throne judging right.	593	8
I will not *s* down with the wicked.	616	17
Let him *s* enthroned before God for ever; *	669	1
Those who *s* at the gate murmur against me, *	680	11
The LORD said to my Lord, "*S* at my right hand, *	753	12
Even though rulers *s* and plot against me, *	765	5
their children will *s* upon your throne for evermore."	786	25

sits

And so, to him who *s* upon the throne, *	94	5
God *s* in judgment every day.	591	21
The LORD *s* enthroned above the flood; *	620	25
the LORD *s* enthroned as King for evermore.	620	26
From where he *s* enthroned he turns his gaze *	627	3
God *s* upon his holy throne.	650	21
Who is like the LORD our God, who *s* enthroned	756	10

sittest

Thou that *s* at the right hand of God the Father,	52	16
Thou *s* at the right hand of God,	53	17
Thou that *s* at the right hand of God the Father,	325	3
Almighty God, who *s* in the throne judging right:	821	8

sitteth

where Christ *s* on the right hand of God.	39	14
and *s* on the right hand of God the Father almighty.	54	3
and *s* on the right hand of God the Father almighty.	66	19
and *s* on the right hand of the Father;	328	9

sitting

Thou knowest my down-*s* and mine up-rising;	474	19
you know my *s* down and my rising up;	794	2

skies

Almighty God, you have placed in the *s* the sign	289	1
The earth shook, and the *s* poured down rain,	676	18
his strength is in the *s*.	679	3
the *s* thundered; *	694	9
For who in the *s* can be compared to the LORD? *	714	5

skill

and blessed us with memory, reason, and *s*.	370	13
gifts through the *s* of surgeons and nurses,	459	14
sound a fanfare with all your *s* upon the trumpet.	626	6
sing praises with all your *s*.	650	19
let my right hand forget its *s*.	792	11

skilled

my tongue shall be the pen of a *s* writer,	647	13

skillful

no matter how *s* his charming.	665	4

skillfulness

and guided them with the *s* of his hands.	700	25

skin

gathers up the waters of the ocean as in a water-*s* *	626	13
I am but *s* and bones.	731	10

skip

He makes Lebanon *s* like a calf, *	620	16

skipped

The mountains *s* like rams, *	757	3
You mountains, that you *s* like rams? *	757	7

sky

Sun and moon and stars of the *s*, glorify the Lord, *	88	11
I know every bird in the *s*, *	655	1
the abiding witness in the *s*."	716	16
in earth and *s* and sea,	837	4
for the beauty of earth and *s* and sea;	840	8

slain

And yours, by right, O Lamb that was *s*, *	94	1
immaculate Lamb that was *s* to take away the sins	488	16
like the *s* who lie in the grave,	712	10

slander

from those who *s* them; *	624	9
Those who repay evil for good *s* me, *	638	9
Those who in secret *s* their neighbors I will destroy; *	730	17

slanderer

A *s* shall not be established on the earth, *	796	23

slanderers

forgive our enemies, persecutors, and *s*,	152	9

slandering

and *s* your own mother's son.	655	21

slaughter

We remember this day, O God, the *s*	186	13
We remember today, O God, the *s*	238	7
to *s* those who are upright in their ways.	634	13
we are accounted as sheep for the *s*.	647	2

slave
that to redeem a *s*, you gave a Son. 287 15
Joseph, who was sold as a *s*. 739 12

slavery
arm your chosen people from *s* under Pharaoh, 289 14

slay
Evil shall *s* the wicked, * 629 9
S them, O God, lest my people forget; * 666 18
Oh, that you would *s* the wicked, O God! * 795 16

sleek
and their bodies are *s* and sound; 687 8
may our cattle be fat and *s*. 801 7

sleep
give thine angels charge over those who *s*. 71 3
shall neither slumber nor *s*; 104 20
give your angels charge over those who *s*. 124 19
give your angels charge over those who *s*. 134 8
who work while others *s*, 134 13
O heavenly Father, you give your children *s* 461 12
As soon as thou scatterest them they are even as a *s*, * 472 19
and he that keepeth thee will not *s*. 473 14
shall neither slumber nor *s*. 473 16
I lie down and go to *s*; * 587 11
give light to my eyes, lest I *s* in death; 598 5
To him alone all who *s* in the earth bow down 612 15
they sink into *s*; * 692 10
Then the LORD woke as though from *s*, * 700 9
shall neither slumber nor *s*; 779 8
for he gives to his beloved *s*. 783 5
I will not allow my eyes to *s*, * 786 5

sleeping
lest coming suddenly he find you *s*. 37 3
Guide us waking, O Lord, and guard us *s*; 134 16
Guide us waking, O Lord, and guard us *s*; 135 9
in their *s* and in their waking; 430 20
Awake, O Lord! why are you *s*? * 647 3

sleet
Frost and cold, ice and *s*, glorify the Lord, * 88 19

slept
and become the first fruits of them that *s*. 46 14

slew
he *s* their strongest men 697 12
Whenever he *s* them, they would seek him, * 697 18
And *s* mighty kings, * 791 5

slip
and will not allow our feet to *s*. 674 12
The sun rises, and they *s* away * 736 21

slipped
But as for me, my feet had nearly *s*; * 687 3
As often as I said, "My foot has *s*," * 724 1

slippery
Let their way be dark and *s*, * 630 1
Surely, you set them in *s* places; * 688 13

slips
those who gloat over me when my foot *s*." 638 2

slow
s to anger and of great kindness, 38 15
And our mouth shall *s* forth thy praise. 42 15
s to anger and abounding in steadfast love, 76 14
s to anger, and full of kindness and truth. 711 5
s to anger and of great kindness. 733 24
s to anger and of great kindness. 802 2

slumber
shall neither *s* nor sleep; 104 20
shall neither *s* nor sleep. 473 16
shall neither *s* nor sleep; 779 8
nor let my eyelids *s*; 786 6

small
creatures both *s* and great. 737 3
both *s* and great together. 758 16
I am *s* and of little account, * 775 7

smash
he will *s* heads over the wide earth. 754 2

smeared
The proud have *s* me with lies, * 769 1

smell
noses, but they cannot *s*; 757 25

smite
will *s* kings in the day of his wrath; * 753 22
Let the righteous *s* me in friendly rebuke; 797 12

smiters
our Savior gave his back to the *s* 169 2

smitten
My heart is *s* like grass and withered, * 731 7

smoke
S rose from his nostrils 603 4
they shall vanish like *s*. 634 27
with the *s* of rams; * 674 25
Let them vanish like *s* when the wind drives it away; * 676 3
For my days drift away like *s*, * 731 5
he touches the mountains and they *s*. 737 19
I have become like a leather flask in the *s*, * 770 7
touch the mountains, and they shall *s*. 800 11

smooth
with a *s* tongue they speak from a double heart. 597 4
Oh, that the LORD would cut off all *s* tongues, * 597 5
You drench the furrows and *s* out the ridges; * 673 9

smoother
His words are *s* than oil, * 662 3

snail
Let them be like the *s* that melts away, * 665 9

snare
He shall deliver you from the *s* of the hunter * 130 1
and in the *s* they set is their own foot caught. 594 8
You brought us into the *s*; * 674 15
and their sacred feasts a *s*. 681 9

He shall deliver you from the *s* of the hunter * 719 15
which became a *s* to them. 744 20
We have escaped like a bird from the *s* of the fowler; * 781 13
the *s* is broken, and we have escaped. 781 14
The proud have hidden a *s* for me 796 10
Protect me from the *s* which they have laid for me * 797 22

snares
Visit this place, O Lord, and drive far from it all *s* 133 21
Visit this place, O Lord, and drive far from it all *s* 140 13
The *s* of death compassed me round about, * 479 3
and the *s* of death were set for me. 602 17
Those who seek after my life lay *s* for me; * 637 20
they plan how they may hide their *s*. 671 19

snarl
they *s* like dogs and run about the city. 666 8

snatch
and *s* me away with none to deliver me. 590 23
Do not *s* me away with the wicked 619 10
he will *s* me from the grasp of death. 653 14
topple you, and *s* you from your dwelling, 658 9

snow
O ye ice and *s*, bless ye the Lord; * 48 11
For as rain and *s* fall from the heavens * 87 1
drops of dew and flakes of *s*. 88 18
it was like *s* falling in Zalmon. 677 9
He gives *s* like wool; * 805 9
Fire and hail, *s* and fog, * 806 9

soak
let it *s* into his body like water 752 9

sober
hereafter live a godly, righteous, and *s* life, 42 9
hereafter live a godly, righteous, and *s* life, 63 12
Be *s*, be watchful. 132 8
hereafter live a godly, righteous, and *s* life, 321 12

society
make wise decisions for the well-being of our *s*; 822 13
that our *s* may be cleansed 823 14

soften
with heavy rain you *s* the ground 673 10

softer
His speech is *s* than butter, * 662 1

soil
and devoured the fruit of their *s*. 740 24
sing the LORD's song * upon an alien *s*? 792 9

sojourner
For I am but a *s* with you, * 639 23
and Jacob became a *s* in the land of Ham. 739 24

sojourners
You are no longer strangers and *s*, 78 1
of little account, and *s* in the land, 739 2

solace
from the presumption of coming to this Table for *s* 372 4

sold
Joseph, who was *s* as a slave. 739 12

solemn
to renew the *s* promises and vows of Holy Baptism 292 4
This is my *s* vow. 427 4
This is my *s* vow. 427 9
given themselves to each other by *s* vows, 428 2
This is my *s* vow. 436 5
The birth of a child is a joyous and *s* occasion 440 1
heartfelt thanks for the joyful and *s* responsibility 440 12
He laid it as a *s* charge upon Joseph, * 704 9

solemnly
Bishop of the Church in N., *s* declare 513 8
and I do *s* engage to conform to the doctrine, 513 11
and I *s* declare that I do believe 526 14
and I do *s* engage to conform to the doctrine, 526 17
and I *s* declare that I do believe 538 14
and I do *s* engage to conform to the doctrine, 538 17

solitary
God gives the *s* a home 676 13
Father, who settest the *s* in families: 828 22

solitude
those who live alone may not be lonely in their *s*, 829 24

some
who by thy Holy Spirit dost give to *s* the word 197 12
O God, by your Holy Spirit you give to *s* the word 248 22
making *s* apostles, *s* prophets, 533 7
s evangelists, *s* pastors and teachers, 533 8
S put their trust in chariots and *s* in horses, * 608 15
or stretched out our hands to *s* strange god, 646 27
Do not be envious when *s* become rich, * 653 15
S wandered in desert wastes; * 746 8
S sat in darkness and deep gloom, * 747 1
S were fools and took to rebellious ways; * 747 15
S went down to the sea in ships * 748 1

someone
around like a roaring lion, seeking *s* to devour. 132 9

something
that your brother has *s* against you, 376 14

son
am no more worthy to be called thy *s*." 38 19
Glory to the Father, and to the *S*, 42 16
Father, *S*, and Holy Ghost, one God: 43 14
Glory to the Father, and to the *S*, 46 19
Let us bless the Father, the *S*, and the Holy Spirit; * 49 7
Blessed art thou, O Father, *S*, and Holy Spirit; * 49 22
Glory to the Father, and to the *S*, 50 20
Glory to the Father, and to the *S*, 51 21
Glory to the Father, and to the *S*, 52 1
O Lord, the only-begotten *S*, Jesus Christ; 52 10
O Lord, God, Lamb of God, *S* of the Father, 52 11
thine adorable, true, and only *S*, 53 9
Thou art the everlasting *S* of the Father. 53 12
And in Jesus Christ his only *S* our Lord; 53 25
the glorious resurrection of thy *S* our Lord: 56 2
Almighty God, whose most dear *S* went not up to joy 56 6
through the same thy *S* Jesus Christ our Lord. 56 10

and didst send thy blessed *S* to preach peace	58	2
through the same thy *S* Jesus Christ our Lord.	58	7
hast promised through thy well-beloved *S*	59	14
Glory to the Father, and to the *S*,	63	19
Father, *S*, and Holy Spirit.	64	6
O *S* of God, O Giver of life,	64	8
Glory to the Father, and to the *S*,	64	10
Glory to the Father, and to the *S*,	65	23
Glory to the Father, and to the *S*,	66	7
And in Jesus Christ his only *S* our Lord;	66	11
whose *S* our Savior Jesus Christ triumphed	69	1
for the love of thy only *S*,	70	3
and rose again, thy *S* our Savior Jesus Christ.	70	9
hast promised through thy well-beloved *S*	72	11
no longer worthy to be called your *s*."	76	18
For the sake of your *S* Jesus Christ,	79	18
Glory to the Father, and to the *S*,	80	7
Father, *S*, and Holy Spirit, one God:	81	10
Glory to the Father, and to the *S*,	84	1
Glory to the Father, and to the *S*,	85	30
Glory to the Father, and to the *S*,	86	15
Glory to the Father, and to the *S*,	87	9
Glory to the Father, and to the *S*,	88	3
Father, *S*, and Holy Spirit; *	90	1
Glory to you, Father, *S*, and Holy Spirit; *	90	15
Glory to the Father, and to the *S*,	92	16
Glory to the Father, and to the *S*,	93	10
Glory to the Father, and to the *S*,	94	19
Lord Jesus Christ, only *S* of the Father,	95	3
your true and only *S*, worthy of all worship,	95	28
the eternal *S* of the Father.	96	2
I believe in Jesus Christ, his only *S*, our Lord.	96	15
the glorious resurrection of your *S* our Lord:	98	20
Almighty God, whose most dear *S* went not up to joy	99	1
through Jesus Christ your *S* our Lord.	99	5
and sent your blessed *S* to preach peace	100	18
have promised through your well-beloved *S*	102	3
Glory to the Father, and to the *S*,	103	3
Glory to the Father, and to the *S*,	105	18
for the love of thy only *S*, our Savior, Jesus Christ.	111	3
Father, *S*, and Holy Spirit.	112	6
O *S* of God, O Giver of life,	112	8
heart of your *S* as he bore his passion,	113	14
For the sake of your *S* Jesus Christ,	117	1
Glory to the Father, and to the *S*,	117	12
Father, *S*, and Holy Spirit.	118	6
O *S* of God, O Giver of life,	118	8
Glory to the Father, and to the *S*,	118	10
Glory to the Father, and to the *S*,	119	22
Glory to the Father, and to the *S*,	120	7
I believe in Jesus Christ, his only *S*, our Lord.	120	11
whose *S* our Savior Jesus Christ triumphed	123	1
of your only *S*, our Savior Jesus Christ.	123	23
and rose again for us, your *S* our Savior Jesus Christ.	124	6
have promised through your well-beloved *S*	126	3
For the sake of your *S* our Lord Jesus Christ,	127	11
Glory to the Father, and to the *S*,	128	5
Glory to the Father, and to the *S*,	131	10
love of your only *S*, our Savior Jesus Christ.	133	12
We give you thanks, O God, for revealing your *S* Jesus	134	1
Glory to the Father, and to the *S*,	135	7
The almighty and merciful Lord, Father, *S*,	135	14
Glory to the Father, and to the *S*,	137	9
Father, *S*, and Holy Spirit.	139	6
O *S* of God, O Giver of life,	139	8
The almighty and merciful Lord, Father, *S*,	140	17
Glory to the Father, and to the *S*, *	141	1
Glory be to the Father, and to the *S*, *	141	5
O God the *S*, Redeemer of the world,	148	3
S of God, we beseech thee to hear us.	152	22
those who ask in thy *S*'s Name:	153	20
Glory be to the Father, and to the *S*,	154	10
O *S* of David, have mercy upon us.	155	2
in the time of this mortal life in which thy *S*	159	3
that when thy *S* our Lord cometh he may find	160	7
the birth of thy only *S* Jesus Christ:	160	13
Almighty God, who has given us thy only-begotten *S*	161	7
Eternal Father, who didst give to thine incarnate *S*	162	1
to share our humanity, thy *S* Jesus Christ;	162	10
thy only-begotten *S* to the peoples of the earth:	162	14
Jordan didst proclaim him thy beloved *S*	163	2
whose *S* our Savior Jesus Christ is the light	163	7
hast manifested to us in thy *S* our Savior Jesus Christ;	164	8
Grant this for thine only *S* Jesus Christ's sake,	165	4
and which thou hast manifested unto us in thy *S*	165	11
who before the passion of thy only-begotten *S*	165	14
Almighty God, whose blessed *S* was led by the Spirit	166	9
through Jesus Christ thy *S* our Lord,	166	13
truth of thy Word, Jesus Christ thy *S*;	167	1
whose blessed *S* Jesus Christ came down	167	10
hast sent thy *S* our Savior Jesus Christ	168	2
whose most dear *S* went not up to joy	168	10
through the same thy *S* Jesus Christ our Lord,	168	14
who by the passion of thy blessed *S* didst make	168	17
suffer shame and loss for the sake of thy *S*	168	20
whose blessed *S* our Savior gave his back	169	1
through the same thy *S* Jesus Christ our Lord,	169	5
Almighty Father, whose dear *S*, on the night	169	7
the same thy *S* Jesus Christ our Lord;	169	11
crucified body of thy dear *S* was laid in the tomb	170	2
only-begotten *S* to the death of the cross,	170	8
the same thy *S* Christ our Lord,	170	12
who through thine only-begotten *S*	170	21
who by the glorious resurrection of thy *S*	171	10
whose blessed *S* did manifest himself to his disciples	171	17
through the same thy *S* Jesus Christ our Lord,	171	20
who hast given thine only *S* to die	172	8
through the same thy *S* Jesus Christ our Lord,	172	12
hast brought us into the kingdom of thy *S*;	172	16
whose blessed *S* did manifest himself to his disciples	173	5
through the same thy *S* Jesus Christ our Lord,	173	8
whose *S* Jesus is the good shepherd of thy people:	173	11
Grant us so perfectly to know thy *S* Jesus Christ	173	17
through the same thy *S* Jesus Christ our Lord,	173	20
O Almighty God, whose blessed *S* our Savior Jesus	174	8
believe thy only-begotten *S* our Lord Jesus Christ	174	16
the King of glory, who hast exalted thine only *S*	175	1
who with the *S* and the Holy Spirit livest	176	7
for the worthiness of thy *S* Jesus Christ our Lord;	179	21
who hast given thy only *S* to be unto us	180	19
through the same thy *S* Jesus Christ our Lord,	181	2
mediation of Jesus Christ thy *S* our Lord;	183	4
O God, whose blessed *S* was manifested	184	7
in thy well-beloved *S*, the King of kings	185	2

Andrew that he readily obeyed the call of thy *S*	185	8
with sure and certain faith in thy *S*'s resurrection:	185	15
for his persecutors to thy *S* Jesus Christ,	186	3
to confess Jesus as Messiah and *S*	187	2
as thy only-begotten *S* was this day presented	187	17
by the same thy *S* Jesus Christ our Lord;	187	19
Joseph to be the guardian of thy incarnate *S*	188	9
through the same thy *S* Jesus Christ our Lord,	188	12
we who have known the incarnation of thy *S*	188	16
the Gospel of Jesus Christ the *S* of God:	188	22
incarnate *S* was blessed in bearing him,	189	12
thy *S* our Savior by preaching repentance:	190	3
through the same thy *S* Jesus Christ our Lord,	190	7
whose blessed *S* restored Mary Magdalene	191	1
thy well-beloved *S*, wonderfully transfigured,	191	16
the blessed Virgin Mary, mother of thy incarnate *S*:	192	2
through the same thy *S* Jesus Christ our Lord,	192	4
whose *S* our Savior Jesus Christ was lifted	192	13
evangelist Matthew to the Gospel of thy *S* our Savior;	192	20
the love and healing power of thy *S*:	193	13
through the same thy *S* Jesus Christ our Lord,	193	15
fellowship in the mystical body of thy *S*	194	9
O God, whose blessed *S* became poor	198	1
through the same thy *S* Jesus Christ our Lord,	198	6
Father, *S*, and Holy Spirit;	199	16
to share our humanity, thy *S* Jesus Christ;	200	16
God our Father, whose *S* our Lord Jesus Christ	201	1
Almighty God, whose beloved *S* willingly endured	201	7
death and resurrection of thy *S* Jesus Christ,	201	13
in thy well-beloved *S*, the King of kings	202	17
resurrection of thy *S* Jesus Christ dost turn us	203	6
the same thy *S* Jesus Christ our Lord,	203	9
resurrection of thy *S* Jesus Christ,	203	14
gave himself for it, thy *S* Jesus Christ our Saviour;	204	14
Almighty Father, whose blessed *S* before his passion	204	17
didst send, the same thy *S* Jesus Christ our Lord;	205	1
didst send thy blessed *S* to preach peace	206	10
through the same thy *S* Jesus Christ our Lord,	206	15
thou hast been revealed in thy *S*;	206	22
whose *S* Jesus Christ in his earthly life	208	1
O Lord our heavenly Father, whose blessed *S* came	209	9
the same thy *S* our Saviour Jesus Christ,	209	15
one that serveth, thy *S* Jesus Christ our Lord,	210	7
this mortal life in which your *S* Jesus Christ came	211	3
that your *S* Jesus Christ, at his coming,	212	7
festival of the birth of your only *S* Jesus Christ:	212	11
Almighty God, you have given your only-begotten *S*	213	1
Eternal Father, you gave to your incarnate *S*	213	13
share our humanity, your *S* Jesus Christ;	214	4
by the leading of a star you manifested your only *S*	214	7
Jordan proclaimed him your beloved *S*	214	13
whose *S* our Savior Jesus Christ is the light	215	1
made known to us in your *S* our Savior Jesus Christ;	216	3
Grant this for the sake of your only *S*	216	17
and which you have manifested to us in your *S*	217	4
who before the passion of your only-begotten *S*	217	7
Almighty God, whose blessed *S* was led by the Spirit	218	1
through Jesus Christ your *S* our Lord,	218	5
truth of your Word, Jesus Christ your *S*;	218	11
Gracious Father, whose blessed *S* Jesus Christ came	219	1
you sent your *S* our Savior Jesus Christ	219	14
Almighty God, whose most dear *S* went not up to joy	220	1

through Jesus Christ your *S* our Lord,	220	5
by the passion of your blessed *S* you made	220	8
suffer shame and loss for the sake of your *S*	220	11
Lord God, whose blessed *S* our Savior gave his body	220	14
through Jesus Christ your *S* our Lord,	220	17
Almighty Father, whose dear *S*, on the night	221	1
crucified body of your dear *S* was laid in the tomb	221	14
gave your only-begotten *S* to the death of the cross,	222	2
through Jesus Christ your *S* our Lord,	222	5
Almighty God, who through your only-begotten *S*	222	15
O God, who by the glorious resurrection of your *S*	223	4
O God, whose blessed *S* made himself known	223	10
who gave your only *S* to die for our sins	224	1
through Jesus Christ your *S* our Lord,	224	5
brought us into the kingdom of your *S*;	224	9
O God, whose blessed *S* made himself known	224	19
O God, whose *S* Jesus is the good shepherd	225	3
to know your *S* Jesus Christ to be the way,	225	9
through Jesus Christ your *S* our Lord,	225	12
Almighty God, whose blessed *S* our Savior Jesus	226	1
S our Lord Jesus Christ to have ascended	226	9
King of glory, you have exalted your only *S*	226	13
through Jesus Christ your *S* our Lord,	227	12
who with the *S* and the Holy Spirit live and reign,	228	7
through the worthiness of your *S*	231	14
you have given your only *S* to be for us a sacrifice	232	11
through Jesus Christ your *S* our Lord,	232	15
O God, whose blessed *S* came into the world	236	1
in your well-beloved *S*, the King of kings	236	15
that he readily obeyed the call of your *S* Jesus Christ,	237	2
and certain faith in your *S*'s resurrection:	237	9
for his persecutors to your *S* Jesus Christ,	237	16
to confess Jesus as Messiah and *S* of the living God:	238	15
your only-begotten *S* was this day presented	239	7
Joseph to be the guardian of your incarnate *S*	239	18
known the incarnation of your *S* Jesus Christ,	240	2
given to your Church the Gospel of Jesus Christ the *S*	240	8
the virgin mother of your incarnate *S* was blessed	240	19
your *S* our Savior by preaching repentance:	241	12
through Jesus Christ your *S* our Lord,	241	16
whose blessed *S* restored Mary Magdalene	242	8
your well-beloved *S*, wonderfully transfigured,	243	2
the blessed Virgin Mary, mother of your incarnate *S*:	243	9
whose *S* our Savior Jesus Christ was lifted	244	1
Matthew to the Gospel of your *S* our Savior;	244	8
the love and healing power of your *S*:	244	22
fellowship in the mystical body of your *S*	245	17
O God, whose blessed *S* became poor	249	11
Father, *S*, and Holy Spirit;	251	5
to share our humanity, your *S* Jesus Christ;	252	4
God our Father, whose *S* our Lord Jesus Christ	252	6
whose beloved *S* willingly endured the agony	252	12
death and resurrection of your *S* Jesus Christ,	253	1
in your well-beloved *S*, the King of kings	254	2
the death and resurrection of your *S* Jesus Christ,	254	8
resurrection of your *S* Jesus Christ,	254	15
your *S* Jesus Christ our Savior;	255	12
whose blessed *S* before his passion prayed	255	15
your *S* Jesus Christ our Lord;	255	20
and sent your blessed *S* to preach peace	257	6
as you have been revealed in your *S*;	257	18
whose *S* Jesus Christ in his earthly life	259	3

whose blessed *S* came not to be served but to serve:	260	15
who laid down his life for us, your *S*	260	20
your *S* Jesus Christ our Lord,	261	12
By the cross and passion of your *S* our Lord,	269	1
which you have redeemed us through your *S* Jesus	271	6
whose most dear *S* went not up to joy	272	1
you sent your *S* our Savior Jesus Christ	272	8
Almighty Father, whose dear *S*, on the night	274	1
Our heavenly Father sent his *S* into the world,	277	2
for the sake of him who suffered for us, your *S*	279	18
as you are revealed in your *S* Jesus Christ;	280	3
through whom all things were made, your *S*	280	21
S of the living God, we pray you to set	282	6
crucified body of your dear *S* was laid in the tomb	283	2
O God, through your *S* you have bestowed	285	8
through Jesus Christ his *S* our Lord,	286	13
almighty, and eternal God, and your only-begotten *S*,	287	2
to redeem a slave, you gave a *S*.	287	16
your *S* Jesus Christ our Lord.	288	8
by the Passover of your *S* you have brought	291	5
by him through whom all things were made, your *S*	291	18
Do you believe in Jesus Christ, the *S* of God?	293	1
I believe in Jesus Christ, his only *S*, our Lord.	293	2
begotten *S* to the death of the cross,	295	2
through Jesus Christ your *S* our Lord,	295	5
Father, *S*, and Holy Spirit.	299	1
Do you believe in Jesus Christ, the *S* of God?	304	4
I believe in Jesus Christ, his only *S*, our Lord	304	5
of Jesus Christ your *S* may live in the power	306	6
In it your *S* Jesus received the baptism	306	16
Therefore in joyful obedience to your *S*,	306	23
in the Name of the Father, and of the *S*,	307	2
Eternal Father, whose blessed *S* was anointed	307	9
in the Name of the Father, and of the *S*,	307	14
your *S* Jesus Christ you have overcome sin	309	4
through Jesus Christ your *S* our Lord,	309	10
God, the Father, *S*, and Holy Spirit,	310	3
through Jesus Christ your *S* our Lord,	311	19
in the Name of the Father, and of the *S*,	313	2
in the Name of the Father, and of the *S*,	313	3
Father, *S*, and Holy Spirit	319	1
Jesus the *S* of God, let us come boldly	320	6
For the sake of thy *S* Jesus Christ,	320	18
Father, *S*, and Holy Spirit.	323	1
O Lord, the only-begotten *S*, Jesus Christ;	324	21
O Lord God, Lamb of God, *S* of the Father,	324	22
the only *S* of God,	326	11
who proceeds from the Father and the *S*.	327	13
With the Father and the *S* he is worshiped	327	14
the only-begotten *S* of God,	327	25
who proceedeth from the Father and the *S*;	328	14
who with the Father and the *S* together is worshiped	328	15
for thy *S* our Lord Jesus Christ's sake,	331	15
For the sake of thy *S* Jesus Christ,	331	29
that he gave his only-begotten *S*,	332	10
of thy tender mercy, didst give thine only *S*	334	10
institution of thy dearly beloved *S* our Savior	335	9
offer unto thee, the memorial thy *S* hath commanded	335	12
thy *S* our Savior Jesus Christ's holy institution,	335	21
by the merits and death of thy *S* Jesus Christ,	335	27
receive the most precious Body and Blood of thy *S*	336	5
so to eat the flesh of thy dear *S* Jesus Christ,	337	14
Body and Blood of thy *S* our Savior Jesus Christ;	339	5
incorporate in the mystical body of thy *S*,	339	7
and of his *S* Jesus Christ our Lord;	339	17
the Father, the *S*, and the Holy Ghost,	339	18
The blessing of God Almighty, the Father, the *S*,	339	20
and, of thy tender mercy, didst give thine only *S*	341	14
offer unto thee, the memorial thy *S* hath commanded	342	12
Body and Blood of thy dearly-beloved *S* Jesus Christ.	342	19
Body and Blood of thy *S* Jesus Christ,	342	26
Because thou didst send thy beloved *S* to redeem us	345	8
Because thou didst give Jesus Christ, thine only *S*,	345	14
in the face of thy *S* Jesus Christ our Lord.	346	3
resurrection of thy *S* Jesus Christ our Lord;	346	18
Through thy dearly beloved *S* Jesus Christ our Lord;	347	1
For with thy co-eternal *S* and Holy Spirit,	347	13
and of the *S*, and of the Holy Spirit.	347	16
the great Name of thine only *S*.	348	10
her bridegroom, thy *S* Jesus Christ our Lord;	349	3
Father, *S*, and Holy Spirit.	351	1
passed through the heavens, Jesus, the *S* of God,	352	6
For the sake of your *S* Jesus Christ,	352	18
Father, *S*, and Holy Spirit.	355	1
Lord Jesus Christ, only *S* of the Father,	356	7
Jesus Christ, the only *S* of God,	358	8
who proceeds from the Father and the *S*.	359	4
With the Father and the *S* he is worshiped	359	5
For the sake of your *S* Jesus Christ,	360	10
Christ, your only and eternal *S*, to share	362	12
the Body and Blood of your *S*,	363	14
All this we ask through your *S* Jesus Christ.	363	19
of your *S* our Savior Jesus Christ,	365	11
of your *S* our Savior Jesus Christ;	366	4
that we are living members of the Body of your *S*,	366	6
the Word made flesh, Jesus, your *S*.	368	5
Unite us to your *S* in his sacrifice,	369	7
you sent your only *S*, born of a woman,	370	19
you sent your only *S* to be our Savior.	374	2
the Body and Blood of your *S* Jesus Christ.	375	8
give you glory through your *S* Jesus Christ our Lord.	375	25
Because you sent your beloved *S* to redeem us	378	4
Because you gave Jesus Christ, your only *S*, to be born	378	9
knowledge of your glory in the face of your *S*	378	16
resurrection of your *S* Jesus Christ our Lord;	379	15
Through your dearly beloved *S* Jesus Christ our Lord.	379	20
For with your co-eternal *S* and Holy Spirit,	380	8
and of the *S*, and of the Holy Spirit.	380	11
the great Name of your only *S*.	381	4
her bridegroom, your *S* Jesus Christ our Lord;	381	18
For yours is the majesty, O Father, *S*, and Holy Spirit;	391	23
hear what we ask in the Name of your *S*:	394	5
but as you know and love us in your *S*	394	7
grant us for the sake of your *S* Jesus Christ our Lord.	395	2
and to you we give glory, Father, *S*,	395	6
thy *S* at his coming in glorious majesty;	395	15
God so loved the world that he gave his only *S*,	396	1
Almighty Father, whose dear *S*, on the night	397	13
For the sake of your *S* Jesus Christ,	398	2
Communion of the Body and Blood of your beloved *S*	399	8
Father, we now celebrate the memorial of your *S*.	403	13
Communion into one body in your *S* Jesus Christ.	403	18
the Body and Blood of your *S*.	405	16
All this we ask through your *S* Jesus Christ.	405	19

Glory be to the Father, and to the *S*,*	406	1
(your) *S* Jesus Christ our Lord,	408	4
Father, *S*, and Holy Spirit.	413	1
Do you believe in Jesus Christ, the *S* of God?	416	9
I believe in Jesus Christ, his only *S*, our Lord.	416	10
your *S* Jesus Christ you have overcome sin	418	2
through Jesus Christ your *S* our Lord,	418	8
God, the Father, *S*, and Holy Spirit,	418	19
in the Name of the Father, and of the *S*,	427	15
in the Name of the Father, and of the *S*,	428	4
and for which your *S* gave his life,	429	4
O Father, with your *S* and the Holy Spirit,	430	8
God the Father, God the *S*, God the Holy Spirit,	431	9
the Body and Blood of your *S* Jesus Christ.	432	3
for the gift of N. to be their *s* (daughter)	440	6
you receive N. as your own *s* (daughter).	441	6
Glory to the Father, and to the *S*,	442	11
Glory to the Father, and to the *S*,	443	18
O God, you have taught us through your blessed *S*	443	21
May God the *S*, who sanctified a home at Nazareth,	445	5
In the Name of the Father, and of the *S*,	447	4
In the Name of the Father, and of the *S*,	448	5
that he gave his only-begotten *S*,	449	15
death by the cross of your *S* Jesus Christ.	450	10
in whom you have redeemed the world, your *S*	450	20
In the Name of the Father, and of the *S*,	451	15
For the sake of your *S* Jesus Christ,	455	1
in the Name of the Father, and of the *S*,	456	2
the Body and Blood of your beloved *S*	457	6
May God the Father bless you, God the *S* heal you,	460	5
given in the resurrection of your *S* Jesus	462	3
God the *S*,	462	7
through Jesus Christ thy *S* our Lord,	470	4
O God, whose beloved *S* did take little children	470	7
through the same thy *S* Jesus Christ our Lord,	470	11
in the mystical body of thy *S*	480	5
promise to all who share in the victory of thy *S*	481	27
the Body and Blood of thy *S* Jesus Christ,	482	3
for the sake of thy *S* Jesus Christ our Lord.	486	15
O God, whose blessed *S* was laid in a sepulcher	487	5
through thy *S* Jesus Christ our Lord.	487	9
all those who are of the mystical body of thy *S*,	487	18
for the sake of the same thy *S* Jesus Christ,	487	22
through the merits of Jesus Christ thine only *S*	488	20
through Jesus Christ thy *S* our Lord.	489	2
through the merits of thy *S* Jesus Christ our Lord.	489	22
O Lord Jesus Christ, *S* of the living God, we pray	489	23
O God, who by the glorious resurrection of your *S*	493	4
O God, whose beloved *S* took children into his arms	494	1
I believe in Jesus Christ, his only *S*, our Lord.	496	5
the Body and Blood of your *S* Jesus Christ,	498	14
O God, whose blessed *S* was laid in a sepulcher	503	7
through your *S* Jesus Christ our Lord.	503	11
the merits of your *S* Jesus Christ our Lord.	504	20
receive that blessing which your well-beloved *S*	505	5
Father, *S*, and Holy Spirit.	512	1
In the Name of the Father, and of the *S*,	513	7
your *S* Jesus Christ our Lord;	515	11
the only *S* of God,	519	11
who proceeds from the Father and the *S*.	520	4
With the Father and the *S* he is worshiped	520	5
bestowed upon your beloved *S* Jesus Christ,	521	3
Spirit, be Christ your *S*, to whom,	521	16
of the Body and Blood of your *S*,	523	2
through Jesus Christ your *S* our Lord,	523	9
the Father, the *S*, and the Holy Spirit,	523	16
Father, *S*, and Holy Spirit.	525	1
your *S* Jesus Christ our Lord;	528	9
the only *S* of God,	530	2
who proceeds from the Father and the *S*.	530	23
With the Father and the *S* he is worshiped	530	24
to be a holy people in the kingdom of your *S*	533	2
Therefore, Father, through Jesus Christ your *S*,	533	11
of the Body and Blood of your *S*,	535	2
through Jesus Christ your *S* our Lord,	535	9
the Father, the *S*, and the Holy Spirit,	535	11
Father, *S*, and Holy Spirit.	537	1
your *S* Jesus Christ our Lord;	540	9
the only *S* of God,	542	2
who proceeds from the Father and the *S*.	542	23
With the Father and the *S* he is worshiped	542	24
we praise you for sending your *S* Jesus Christ,	545	2
Therefore, Father, through Jesus Christ your *S*,	545	9
As your *S* came not to be served	545	15
of the Body and Blood of your *S*,	546	4
through Jesus Christ your *S* our Lord,	547	5
God the *S*,	548	3
for the sake of your *S* our Savior Jesus Christ.	563	10
of the Body and Blood of your *S*,	564	2
through Jesus Christ your *S* our Lord,	564	9
In the Name of the Father, and of the *S*,	568	3
the Body and Blood of your *S*.	568	12
Now, O Father, *S*, and Holy Spirit,	569	10
in the Name of the Father, and of the *S*,	569	22
In it your *S* Jesus received the baptism of John	570	8
Therefore in joyful obedience to your *S*,	570	15
in the Name of the Father, and of the *S*,	570	17
Inspired by the revelation of your *S*,	571	1
in the Name of the Father, and of the *S*,	571	8
in the Name of the Father, and of the *S*,	572	8
you sent your *S* Jesus Christ to be born	573	9
of the sacrifice of your *S*.	574	4
Blessed be your Name, Father, *S*, and Holy Spirit;	574	8
he said to me, "You are my *S*;	586	15
the *s* of man that you should seek him out?	592	16
and slandering your own mother's *s*.	655	21
and your righteousness to the King's *S*;	685	10
the *s* of man you have made so strong for yourself.	703	21
"A *s*, the fruit of your body *	786	21
thy *S* Jesus Christ our Lord.	814	5
and redeemed us through Jesus your *S*:	815	14
the Father of all, whose *S* commanded us to love	816	5
of Jesus Christ thy *S* our Savior.	816	15
through your *S* Jesus Christ:	816	17
according to the example of your *S*,	817	16
through the teaching of your *S* Jesus Christ:	819	2
through him who shall come to be our Judge, thy *S*	821	13
O God our Father, whose *S* forgave his enemies	823	8
Grant this, Father, for the love of your *S*, who for	826	6
O God, heavenly Father, who by thy *S* Jesus Christ	828	9
Almighty God, whose *S* had nowhere to lay his head:	829	22
those who ask in thy *S*'s Name:	834	2
by the resurrection of your *S* Jesus Christ	835	1
Above all, we thank you for your *S* Jesus Christ;	836	12

you sent your *S* Jesus Christ to reconcile 838 1
you sent your own *S* into this world. 841 1
your dear *S*, Jesus Christ our Lord. 841 6
Jesus of Nazareth, the only *S* of God. 849 18
Jesus is the only *S* of God? 849 20
his divine *S* received our human nature 849 28
The divine *S* became human, 850 2
Father, *S*, and Holy Spirit. 852 13
in the Name of the Father, and of the *S*, 858 15

song

and come before his presence with a *s*. 45 13
and come before his presence with a *s*. 82 22
occasions of *s* in the evening. 113 4
yet even at the grave we make our *s*: 483 2
yet even at the grave we make our *s*: 499 8
Singing aloud a *s* of thanksgiving * 616 20
and in my *s* will I praise him. 619 27
Sing for him a new *s*; * 626 5
He put a new *s* in my mouth, 640 5
a *s* of praise to our God; * 640 6
in the night season his *s* is with me, 643 24
My heart is stirring with a noble *s*; 647 11
I will praise the Name of God in *s*; * 681 24
Raise a *s* and sound the timbrel, * 704 3
Sing to the LORD a new *s*; * 725 17
Sing to the LORD a new *s*, * 727 24
with the harp and the voice of *s*. 728 13
and come before his presence with a *s*. 729 24
The LORD is my strength and my *s*, * 761 24
For those who led us away captive asked us for a *s*, 792 5
How shall we sing the LORD's *s* * 792 8
O God, I will sing to you a new *s*; * 800 19
Sing to the LORD a new *s*; * 807 2

songs

will reap with *s* of joy. 105 15
music we make and in the *s* we sing. 572 4
and the drunkards make *s* about me. 680 12
there were no wedding *s* for their maidens. 700 6
and sang him *s* of praise. 742 23
Your statutes have been like *s* to me * 767 21
will reap with *s* of joy. 782 17
"Sing us one of the *s* of Zion." 792 7
for the *s* of birds and the loveliness of flowers. 840 9

sons

received us as thy *s* and daughters, 348 21
enter the everlasting heritage of your *s* and daughters; 369 11
received us as your *s* and daughters, 381 14
through him we might become your *s* and daughters. 573 10
"In place of fathers, O king, you shall have *s*; * 648 23
They sacrificed their *s* * 744 21
the blood of their *s* and daughters, * 744 24
May our *s* be like plants well nurtured 801 1

soon

the laity here (or now, or *s* to be) assembled 204 11
the laity here (or now, or *s* to be) assembled 255 9
As *s* as thou scatterest them they are even as a sleep, * 472 19
so *s* passeth it away, and we are gone. 473 6
For they shall *s* wither like the grass, * 633 7
I should *s* subdue their enemies * 705 3
I should *s* have dwelt in the land of silence. 723 28
I will *s* destroy all the wicked in the land, * 730 26
But they *s* forgot his deeds * 742 24

sooner

no *s* shall they hear than they shall obey me; * 605 29

soothe

s the suffering, pity the afflicted, 71 4
s the suffering, pity the afflicted, 124 20
s the suffering, pity the afflicted, 134 9

sorely

and, because we are *s* hindered by our sins, 160 2
and, because we are *s* hindered by our sins, 212 2
I was *s* wounded in my heart. 688 20
The LORD has punished me *s*, * 762 6

sorrow

any *s* like unto my *s* which is done 39 5
any *s* like my *s* which was brought 77 4
Gracious God, the comfort of all who *s*, 279 14
are in trouble, *s*, need, sickness, 329 28
are in danger, *s*, or any kind of trouble; 392 9
a counselor in perplexity, a comfort in *s*, 429 9
a counselor in perplexity, a comfort in *s*, 444 11
now remember, I turn to you in *s* and repentance. 450 17
receive your confession of *s* and of faith, 451 4
and our *s* into joy; 458 14
yet is their strength then but labor and *s*, 473 5
neither *s* nor crying, but the fullness of joy 482 7
where *s* and pain are no more, 482 10
where *s* and pain are no more, 483 4
comfort us in our *s*. 497 8
neither *s* nor crying, but the fullness of joy 498 17
where *s* and pain are no more, 499 2
in times of joy and *s*. 572 2
my eye is consumed with *s*, 623 4
yet the sum of them is but labor and *s*, 718 21
through stress of adversity and *s*, 749 8
I came to grief and *s*. 759 7
My soul melts away for *s*; * 765 15
and to turn their *s* into joy. 826 5

sorrowful

For the *s* and bereaved 279 9
to prisoners, freedom; to the *s*, joy. 374 5
Let the *s* sighing of the prisoners come before you, * 702 4
comfort him when discouraged or *s*; 830 15

sorrowing

not *s* as those without hope, 505 12

sorrows

With pity behold the *s* of our hearts; 154 17
in their joys and in their *s*; 430 21
in his joys and in his *s*. 445 1
Almighty God, look with pity upon the *s* 467 3
Comfort us in our *s* at the death 497 22
The *s* of my heart have increased; * 615 22
Look with pity upon the *s* of thy servant 831 13

sorry

We are truly *s* and we humbly repent. 79 17
We are truly *s* and we humbly repent. 116 19

We are truly *s* and we humbly repent.	320	17
and are heartily *s* for these our misdoings;	331	10
We are truly *s* and we humbly repent.	331	28
We are truly *s* and we humbly repent.	352	17
We are truly *s* and we humbly repent.	360	9
We are truly *s* and we humbly repent.	398	1
I am truly *s*.	447	9
We are truly *s* and we humbly repent.	454	8
and be *s* for my sin.	638	6

sorts

beseech thee for all *s* and conditions of men;	814	7

sought

I *s* the LORD, and he answered me *	628	1
and the ruthless have *s* my life, *	659	22
for they are ashamed and disgraced who *s*	685	7
In the day of my trouble I *s* the Lord; *	693	3
and *s* to kill the brokenhearted.	752	3
For my enemy has *s* my life;	799	1

soul

My *s* doth magnify the Lord,	50	1
My *s* doth magnify the Lord, *	65	4
My *s* proclaims the greatness of the Lord,	91	27
My *s* proclaims the greatness of the Lord,	119	4
thoughts which may assault and hurt the *s*;	167	7
being ready both in body and *s*,	177	5
thoughts which may assault and hurt the *s*;	218	17
with all thy *s*, and with all thy mind.	319	10
with all thy *s*, and with all thy mind.	324	3
preserve thy body and *s* unto everlasting life.	338	6
with all your heart, with all your *s*,	351	9
Matrimony, may become one in heart and *s*,	432	5
My *s* proclaims the greatness of the Lord,	441	12
He revives my *s**	443	5
undivided Trinity guard your body, save your *s*,	460	7
for the refreshing of *s* and body:	461	13
deliver the *s* of your servant from the power	463	12
Depart, O Christian *s*, out of this world;	464	21
May his *s* and the souls of all the departed,	465	7
Let his heart and *s* now ring	466	9
so longeth my *s* after thee, O God.	471	2
My *s* is athirst for God,	471	3
Why art thou so full of heaviness, O my *s*? *	471	12
yea, it is even he that shall keep thy *s*.	473	22
I look for the LORD; my *s* doth wait for him; *	474	9
My *s* fleeth unto the Lord before the morning	474	11
He shall convert my *s*, *	476	5
He restoreth my *s*; *	476	23
O LORD, I beseech thee, deliver my *s*.	479	7
Turn again then unto thy rest, O my *s*, *	479	12
And why? thou hast delivered my *s* from death, *	479	14
May his *s*, and the souls of all the departed,	486	19
consummation and bliss, both in body and *s*,	488	9
May his *s* and the souls of all the departed,	498	10
May his *s*, and the souls of all the departed,	502	17
I devote myself, body, *s*, and spirit.	562	12
and revives the *s*; *	607	5
My *s* shall live for him;	612	18
He revives my *s* *	613	1
To you, O LORD, I lift up my *s*;	614	13
Our *s* waits for the LORD; *	627	15
say to my *s*, "I am your salvation."	629	19
my *s* is full of despair.	630	16
so longs my *s* for you, O God.	643	2
My *s* is athirst for God, athirst for the living God; *	643	3
I pour out my *s* when I think on these things: *	643	8
Why are you so full of heaviness, O my *s*? *	643	13
My *s* is heavy within me; *	643	18
Why are you so full of heaviness, O my *s*? *	644	9
Why are you so full of heaviness, O my *s*? *	645	1
For you have rescued my *s* from death and my feet	663	16
For God alone my *s* in silence waits; *	669	5
my *s* thirsts for you, my flesh faints for you,	670	13
My *s* is content, as with marrow and fatness, *	670	21
My *s* clings to you; *	671	1
and so will my *s*, which you have redeemed.	685	5
My *s* has a desire and longing for the courts	707	16
Gladden the *s* of your servant, *	710	5
for to you, O LORD, I lift up my *s*.	710	6
your consolations cheer my *s*.	724	4
Bless the LORD, O my *s*, *	733	9
bless the LORD, O my *s*.	734	29
Bless the LORD, O my *s*; *	735	1
Bless the LORD, O my *s*. *	737	26
but sent leanness into their *s*.	743	2
Turn again to your rest, O my *s*, *	759	14
My *s* is consumed at all times *	764	23
My *s* cleaves to the dust; *	765	9
My *s* melts away for sorrow; *	765	15
My *s* has longed for your salvation; *	770	3
I wait for the LORD; my *s* waits for him; *	785	1
My *s* waits for the LORD,	785	3
But I still my *s* and make it quiet,	785	14
my *s* is quieted within me.	785	16
my *s* gasps to you like a thirsty land.	799	11
for I lift up my *s* to you.	799	18
Praise the LORD, O my *s*! *	803	4
of one heart and of one *s*, united	818	21
from all dangers of *s* and body;	830	22
nourish his *s* with patience,	831	15
with all your *s*, and with all your mind.	851	12

souls

O ye spirits and *s* of the righteous,	49	5
Glorify the Lord, O spirits and *s* of the righteous, *	89	22
and you will find rest for your *s*.	131	18
outwardly in our bodies and inwardly in our *s*,	167	5
O eternal Lord God, who holdest all *s* in life:	202	1
Shepherd and Bishop of our *s*, Jesus Christ our Lord,	205	19
outwardly in our bodies and inwardly in our *s*,	218	15
Eternal Lord God, you hold all *s* in life:	253	6
Shepherd and Bishop of our *s*, Jesus Christ our Lord,	256	16
Creator of all the peoples of the earth and lover of *s*:	280	2
between your judgment and our *s*,	282	8
our selves, our *s* and bodies,	336	2
present unto thee, O Lord, our selves, our *s*	342	23
and for the salvation of our *s*,	383	4
for you are gracious, O lover of *s*,	395	6
May his soul and the *s* of all the departed,	465	7
May his soul, and the *s* of all the departed,	486	19
and with whom the *s* of the faithful,	488	2
between thy judgment and our *s*,	489	25
May his soul and the *s* of all the departed,	498	10

May his soul, and the *s* of all the departed, 502 17
and with whom the *s* of the faithful 503 13
Bishop of our *s*. 518 18
Who holds our *s* in life, * 674 11
he did not spare their *s* from death; * 699 5

sound

Their *s* is gone out into all lands; 40 5
Their *s* has gone out into all lands, 78 4
Praise him with the *s* of the trumpet; 572 5
for the LORD has heard the *s* of my weeping. 590 15
Their *s* has gone out into all lands, * 606 21
then shall I be whole and *s*, 607 26
Nevertheless, you heard the *s* of my entreaty 624 16
s a fanfare with all your skill upon the trumpet. 626 6
the LORD with the *s* of the ram's-horn. 650 15
and their bodies are sleek and *s*; 687 8
The *s* of your thunder was in the whirlwind; 694 11
Raise a song and *s* the timbrel, * 704 3
Mightier than the *s* of many waters, 722 12
With trumpets and the *s* of the horn * 728 14
they make no *s* with their throat. 758 3
There is a *s* of exultation and victory * 761 26
Let my heart be *s* in your statutes, * 770 1
Bless our land with honorable industry, *s* learning, 820 4
s learning, new discovery, and the pursuit of wisdom; 824 18
in making the heart of this people wise, its mind *s*, 827 9

soundness

there is no *s* in my body, because of my sin. 637 3

sounds

worship you with many voices and *s*, 572 2
with *s* of great gladness; * 618 8

source

O God, the *s* of eternal light: 69 12
O God, the *s* of eternal light: 123 11
Most holy God, the *s* of all good desires, 123 15
Creator of the light and *s* of life, 344 14
Fountain of life and *s* of all goodness, 373 4
For you are the *s* of light and life, 377 12
s of eternal salvation for all who put their trust 379 13
O God, the *s* of all health: 461 1
Everliving Father, watchful and caring, our *s* 568 7
Almighty and everliving God, *s* of all wisdom 818 1
to be the *s* of all truth; 824 20

south

and led out the *s* wind by his might. 697 2
You have made the north and the *s*; * 714 17
from the north and from the *s*. 746 7

sovereign

Deliver your servant, N., O *S* Lord Christ, 464 16
Deliver your servant, N., O *S* Lord Christ, 466 16

sovereignty

and to testify to Christ's *S* as Lord of lords 517 5

sow

Where there is hatred, let us *s* love; 833 6

sowed

Those who *s* with tears * 105 14
They *s* fields, and planted vineyards, * 749 3
Those who *s* with tears * 782 16

sowing

seed for *s* and bread for eating, 87 4

space

the vast expanse of interstellar *s*, galaxies, suns, 370 9
or in the air [or through outer *s*], 384 18

spake

As he *s* by the mouth of his holy prophets, * 50 26
God *s* these words, and said: 317 24
who *s* by the Prophets. 328 17

span

The *s* of our life is seventy years, 718 19
to count them all, my life *s* would need 795 14

spare

s thou those who confess their faults, 42 4
s thou those who confess their faults, 63 7
S us, good Lord, *s* thy people, 148 11
S us, good Lord. 148 14
s thou those who confess their faults, 321 7
but *s* us, Lord most holy, O God most mighty, 484 13
but *s* us, O Lord. 492 14
he did not *s* their souls from death; * 699 5
and by your great might *s* those 702 5

sparrow

The *s* has found her a house 707 19
I am like a *s*, lonely on a house-top. 731 14

speak

be thankful unto him and *s* good of his Name. 45 19
s to your heart in silence upon your bed. 128 17
s the truth, boldly rebuke vice, 190 6
constantly *s* the truth, boldly rebuke vice, 241 15
And so you are justified when you *s* * 266 10
s now; or else for ever hold your peace. 424 3
I will sing and *s* praises unto the LORD. 477 27
Purify the lives and the lips of those who *s* here, 571 11
s to your heart in silence upon your bed. 588 7
You destroy those who *s* lies; * 589 1
with a smooth tongue they *s* from a double heart. 597 4
You *s* in my heart and say, "Seek my face," * 618 12
and also those who *s* malice. 618 25
who *s* peaceably with their neighbors, 619 12
Let the lying lips be silenced which *s* 624 1
those who strive to hurt me *s* of my ruin 637 21
Even if they come to see me, they *s* empty words; * 642 10
My mouth shall *s* of wisdom, * 652 9
Hear, O my people, and I will *s*: 654 16
And so you are justified when you *s* * 656 14
for the mouth of those who *s* lies shall be stopped. 671 9
They scoff and *s* maliciously; * 687 15
I will *s* of all your works * 689 7
nor *s* with a proud neck.'" 691 13
I am troubled and I cannot *s*. 693 9
and *s* of all his marvelous works. 738 4
They *s* to me with a lying tongue; * 751 1

and to those who *s* evil against me. 752 15
They have mouths, but they cannot *s*; * 757 22
but when I *s* of it, they are for war. 778 23
They have mouths, but they cannot *s*; * 789 7
They *s* despitefully against you; * 795 18
Whose mouths *s* deceitfully * 800 17
Whose mouths *s* deceitfully * 800 25
They shall *s* of the might of your wondrous acts, * 801 22
and *s* of your power; 802 8
My mouth shall *s* the praise of the LORD; * 803 1
Direct, in our time, we pray, those who *s* 827 7
To *s* the truth, and not to mislead others 848 16

speaking

Keep your tongue from evil-*s* * 628 19
You are always *s* evil of your brother * 655 20
and lying more than *s* the truth. 658 5
Had I gone on *s* this way, * 688 7
for he is *s* peace to his faithful people 709 10
save them from *s* in hate; 823 11

speaks

Father, your eternal Word *s* to us 570 23
Then he *s* to them in his wrath, * 586 10
Everyone *s* falsely with his neighbor; * 597 3
who *s* the truth from his heart. 599 7
and their mouth *s* proud things. 601 19
and their tongue *s* what is right. 635 23
and because God still *s* to us 853 25

spear

he breaks the bow, and shatters the *s*, 649 22

spears

their teeth are *s* and arrows, 664 2

special

who didst give to thy servant N. *s* gifts 197 19
you gave to your servant N. *s* gifts 249 5
For the *s* needs and concerns of this congregation. 392 17
God now calls you to a *s* ministry of servanthood 543 3
when we turn to you in sickness or *s* need, 569 8

speech

confound their *s*; * 660 24
His *s* is softer than butter, * 662 1
and their evil *s* runs through the world. 687 18
the house of Jacob from a people of strange *s*, 756 20

speed

O God, make *s* to save us. 63 17
O God, make *s* to save us. 103 1
O God, make *s* to save us. 117 10
O God, make *s* to save us. 128 3
Make *s* to help thy servants 166 10

speedily

let thy bountiful grace and mercy *s* help 160 3
let your bountiful grace and mercy *s* help 212 3
come to me *s*, O God. 682 23

spell

For they have cast an evil *s* upon me * 660 11

spend

Weeping may *s* the night, * 621 14
who *s* their lives establishing equal protection 826 12

spent

that the days to come may be *s* in thy favor; 56 4
that the week to come may be *s* in your favor; 98 22
renewing the strength of those who are *s*, 113 3
The Scriptures tell us that our Savior Christ *s* 514 12

spiced

full of *s* and foaming wine, which he pours out, * 691 19

spirit

worship the Father in *s* and in truth; 40 21
that is of a contrite and humble *s*, 41 2
to revive the *s* of the humble, 41 3
and the grace and consolation of his Holy *S*. 42 13
and to the Son, and to the Holy *S*; 42 16
The *S* of the Lord filleth the world: 43 12
and to the Son, and to the Holy *S*: * 46 19
Let us bless the Father, the Son, and the Holy *S*; * 49 7
Blessed art thou, O Father, Son, and Holy *S*; * 49 22
and my *s* hath rejoiced in God my Savior. 50 2
and to the Son, and to the Holy *S*: * 50 20
and to the Son, and to the Holy *S*: * 51 21
and to the Son, and to the Holy *S*: * 52 1
And with thy *s*. 54 12
And sustain us with thy Holy *S*. 55 14
govern us by thy Holy *S*, 57 16
God, by whose *S* the whole body 57 19
pour out thy *S* upon all flesh; 58 5
So clothe us in thy *S* that we, reaching 58 11
through the power of the Holy *S*. 60 2
and the grace and consolation of his Holy *S*. 63 16
and to the Son, and to the Holy *S*: as 63 19
Father, Son, and Holy *S*. 64 6
and to the Son, and to the Holy *S*: * 64 10
and my *s* hath rejoiced in God my Savior. 65 5
and to the Son, and to the Holy *S*: * 65 23
and to the Son, and to the Holy *S*: * 66 7
And with thy *s*. 67 2
And sustain us with thy Holy *S*. 68 6
That we may be bound together by thy Holy *S* 68 22
Send forth upon us the *S* of love, 71 7
believing through the power of the Holy *S*. 73 2
You shall receive power when the Holy *S* has come 77 17
will worship the Father in *s* and truth, 78 20
with the one who has a contrite and humble *s*, 78 24
to revive the *s* of the humble 78 25
and by the power of the Holy *S* keep you 80 3
and to the Son, and to the Holy *S*: 80 7
The *S* of the Lord renews the face of the earth: 81 8
Father, Son, and Holy *S*, one God: 81 10
and to the Son, and to the Holy *S*: * 84 1
and to the Son, and to the Holy *S*: * 85 30
and to the Son, and to the Holy *S*; * 86 15
and to the Son, and to the Holy *S*: * 87 9
and to the Son, and to the Holy *S*: * 88 3
Father, Son, and Holy *S*; * 90 1
Glory to you, Father, Son, and Holy *S*; * 90 15
my *s* rejoices in God my Savior; * 91 28
and to the Son, and to the Holy *S*: * 92 16

and to the Son, and to the Holy *S*: *	93	10
and to the Son, and to the Holy *S*: *	94	19
with the Holy *S*,	95	13
and the Holy *S*, advocate and guide.	95	29
He was conceived by the power of the Holy *S*	96	16
I believe in the Holy *S*,	96	25
And sustain us with your Holy *S*.	98	8
and govern us by your Holy *S*,	100	8
by whose *S* the whole body	100	11
pour out your *S* upon all flesh;	100	21
So clothe us in your *S*	101	3
to whom, with you and the Holy *S*,	101	23
the fellowship of the Holy *S*, be with us	102	11
believing through the power of the Holy *S*.	102	13
and to the Son, and to the Holy *S*:	103	3
and to the Son, and to the Holy *S*: *	105	18
Holy *S* that has been given to us.	105	21
send your Holy *S* into our hearts,	107	4
Holy *S* you live and reign, now and for ever.	107	21
the brightness of your holy *S*;	110	16
to worship you in *s* and in truth;	111	6
Father, Son, and Holy *S*.	112	6
and by the power of the Holy *S* keep you	117	8
and to the Son, and to the Holy *S*:	117	12
Father, Son, and Holy *S*.	118	6
and to the Son, and to the Holy *S*: *	118	10
my *s* rejoices in God my Savior; *	119	5
and to the Son, and to the Holy *S*: *	119	22
and to the Son, and to the Holy *S*: *	120	7
He was conceived by the power of the Holy *S*	120	12
I believe in the Holy *S*,	120	21
And sustain us with your Holy *S*.	122	8
That we may be bound together by your Holy *S*	122	24
Send forth upon us the *S* of love,	125	2
to whom, with you and the Holy *S*,	125	21
the fellowship of the Holy *S*, be with us	126	11
believing through the power of the Holy *S*.	126	13
and the grace and comfort of the Holy *S*.	128	2
and to the Son, and to the Holy *S*:	128	5
Into your hands I commend my *s*, *	129	18
and to the Son, and to the Holy *S*: *	131	10
Into your hands, O Lord, I commend my *s*;	132	12
and to the Son, and to the Holy *S*: *	135	7
merciful Lord, Father, Son, and Holy *S*,	135	14
and renew a right *s* within me.	137	4
and take not your holy *S* from me.	137	6
and sustain me with your bountiful *S*.	137	8
and to the Son, and to the Holy *S*: *	137	9
Holy *S* you live and reign, now and for ever.	138	20
Father, Son, and Holy *S*.	139	6
merciful Lord, Father, Son, and Holy *S*,	140	17
and to the Holy *S*:	141	2
bring forth the fruits of the *S*,	150	17
who suffer in mind, body, and *s*;	151	25
with the grace of thy Holy *S* to amend our lives	152	5
Holy *S*, one God, now and for ever.	159	14
in the unity of the Holy *S*, one God,	160	10
and the Holy *S* he liveth and reigneth,	161	5
may daily be renewed by thy Holy *S*;	161	11
with thee and the same *S* ever, one God,	161	12
the unity of the Holy *S*, one God,	161	18
liveth and reigneth with thee and the Holy *S*,	162	5
in the unity of the Holy *S*,	162	11
who liveth and reigneth with thee and the Holy *S*,	162	17
and anoint him with the Holy *S*:	163	3
who with thee and the same *S* liveth and reigneth,	163	6
who with thee and the Holy *S* liveth and reigneth,	163	12
liveth and reigneth with thee and the Holy *S*,	163	18
liveth and reigneth with thee and the Holy *S*,	164	5
in the unity of the Holy *S*,	164	9
liveth and reigneth with thee and the Holy *S*,	164	17
in the unity of the Holy *S*,	165	13
liveth and reigneth with thee and the Holy *S*,	165	20
liveth and reigneth with thee and the Holy *S*,	166	7
whose blessed Son was led by the *S*	166	9
liveth and reigneth with thee and the Holy *S*,	166	14
who with thee and the Holy *S* liveth and reigneth,	167	1
liveth and reigneth with thee and the Holy *S*,	167	9
liveth and reigneth with thee and the Holy *S*,	168	8
liveth and reigneth with thee and the Holy *S*,	169	6
liveth and reigneth with thee and the Holy *S*,	170	5
that *S* of adoption which is given to us in Baptism,	170	16
in the unity of the same *S*,	170	20
from the death of sin by thy life-giving *S*;	171	2
liveth and reigneth with thee and the same *S* ever,	171	4
liveth and reigneth with thee and the Holy *S*,	171	8
to whom, with thee and the Holy *S*,	171	15
in the unity of the Holy *S*,	171	21
liveth and reigneth with thee and the Holy *S*,	172	6
in the unity of the Holy *S*,	172	19
liveth and reigneth with thee and the Holy *S*,	173	3
in the unity of the Holy *S*,	173	9
with thee and the Holy *S*, liveth and reigneth,	173	14
in the unity of the Holy *S*,	173	21
liveth and reigneth with thee and the Holy *S*,	174	6
by the promised gift of thy Holy *S*:	175	10
in the unity of the same *S*,	175	13
by sending to them the light of thy Holy *S*:	175	16
by the same *S* to have a right judgment	175	17
in the unity of the same *S*,	175	20
who with the Son and the Holy *S* livest and reignest,	176	7
liveth and reigneth with thee and the Holy *S*,	177	1
liveth and reigneth with thee and the Holy *S*,	178	5
in unity of *s* by their doctrine,	178	21
liveth and reigneth with thee and the Holy *S*,	179	3
Grant us the grace of thy Holy *S*,	179	6
liveth and reigneth with thee and the same *S*,	179	9
liveth and reigneth with thee and the Holy *S*,	180	6
Grant to us, Lord, we beseech thee, the *s* to think	180	14
liveth and reigneth with thee and the Holy *S*,	181	3
being gathered together in unity by thy Holy *S*,	181	6
liveth and reigneth with thee and the same *S*,	181	9
mercifully grant that thy Holy *S* may in all things	182	2
who with thee and the same *S* liveth and reigneth,	182	4
liveth and reigneth with thee and the Holy *S*,	182	10
liveth and reigneth with thee and the Holy *S*,	183	5
liveth and reigneth with thee and the Holy *S*,	184	5
liveth and reigneth with thee and the Holy *S*,	185	6
liveth and reigneth with thee and the Holy *S*,	186	5
in the unity of the Holy *S*,	186	19
liveth and reigneth with thee and the Holy *S*,	187	6
in the unity of the Holy *S*,	187	14
in the unity of the Holy *S*,	188	6
liveth and reigneth with thee and the Holy *S*,	188	13

liveth and reigneth with thee and the Holy *S*,	189	4
liveth and reigneth with thee and the Holy *S*,	190	8
and knit together in unity by thy *S*,	190	13
in the unity of the same *S*,	190	15
who with thee and the Holy *S* liveth and reigneth,	191	5
pour out upon the leaders of thy Church that *s*	191	10
liveth and reigneth with thee and the Holy *S*,	191	14
in the unity of the Holy *S*,	192	6
liveth and reigneth with thee and the Holy *S*,	193	3
in the unity of the Holy *S*,	193	16
liveth and reigneth with thee and the Holy *S*,	194	6
who with thee and the Holy *S* liveth and reigneth,	194	14
liveth and reigneth with thee and the Holy *S*,	195	7
liveth and reigneth with thee and the Holy *S*,	196	6
liveth and reigneth with thee and the Holy *S*,	197	3
to all pastors the gifts of thy Holy *S*,	197	7
liveth and reigneth with thee and the same *S*,	197	10
who by thy Holy *S* dost give to some the word	197	12
who with thee and the same *S* liveth and reigneth,	197	17
in the unity of the Holy *S*,	198	7
Grant that we also may be aflame with the *S*	198	11
liveth and reigneth with thee and the Holy *s*,	198	22
liveth and reigneth with thee and the Holy *S*,	199	2
who by thy Holy *S* hast made us one	199	4
intercessions are acceptable through the *S*,	199	10
Father, Son, and Holy *S*;	199	16
that by the indwelling of thy Holy *S*	200	2
in the unity of the same *S* ever,	200	5
liveth and reigneth with thee and the Holy *S*,	200	11
in the unity of the Holy *S*,	200	17
liveth and reigneth with thee and the Holy *S*,	201	6
so we may be renewed in the *s* of our minds,	201	15
in the unity of the Holy *S*,	201	17
in the unity of the Holy *S*,	202	7
liveth and reigneth with thee and the Holy *S*,	203	4
may be renewed in thy Holy *S*,	203	15
in the unity of the Holy *S*,	204	6
who hast given the Holy *S* to abide with us for ever:	204	9
in the unity of the same *S*,	204	15
may be united in one body by the one *S*,	204	21
in the unity of the same *S*,	205	2
in the unity of the Holy *S*,	205	12
under the guidance of the Holy *S*,	205	16
liveth and reigneth with thee and the same *S*,	205	20
by whose *S* the whole body	206	1
in the unity of the Holy *S*,	206	7
pour out thy *S* upon all flesh,	206	13
liveth and reigneth with thee and the same *S*,	206	16
liveth and reigneth with thee and the Holy *S*,	206	23
liveth and reigneth with thee and the Holy *S*,	207	6
in the unity of the Holy *S*,	207	13
in the unity of the Holy *S*,	208	7
who with thee and the Holy *S* liveth and reigneth,	208	14
liveth and reigneth with thee and the Holy *S*,	208	22
liveth and reigneth with thee and the Holy *S*,	209	7
Enlighten by thy Holy *S* those who teach	209	18
liveth and reigneth with thee and the same *S*,	209	22
liveth and reigneth with thee and the Holy *S*,	210	8
lives and reigns with you and the Holy *S*,	211	7
with you and the Holy *S*, be honor and glory,	212	5
in the unity of the Holy *S*,	212	9
lives and reigns with you and the Holy *S*,	212	14
where with you and Holy *S* he lives and reigns,	212	19
may daily be renewed by your Holy *S*;	213	5
with you and the same *S* be honor and glory,	213	6
in the unity of the Holy *S*,	213	12
lives and reigns with you and the Holy *S*,	213	17
in unity of the Holy *S*,	214	5
lives and reigns with you and the Holy *S*,	214	11
and anointed him with the Holy *S*	[illegible]	14
who with you and the Holy *S* lives and reigns,	214	17
who with you and the Holy *S* lives and reigns,	215	6
lives and reigns with you and the Holy *S*,	215	12
in the unity of the Holy *S*,	216	4
lives and reigns with you and the Holy *S*,	216	11
Send your Holy *S* and pour	216	14
lives and reigns with you and the Holy *S*,	216	19
in the unity of the Holy *S*,	217	6
lives and reigns with you and the Holy *S*,	217	12
whose blessed Son was led by the *S*	218	1
lives and reigns with you and the Holy *S*,	218	6
who with you and the Holy *S* lives and reigns,	218	11
lives and reigns with you and the Holy *S*,	219	4
lives and reigns with you and the Holy *S*,	220	6
lives and reigns with you and the Holy *S*,	221	6
lives and reigns with you and the Holy *S*,	222	6
S of adoption which is given to us in Baptism,	222	10
in the unity of the Holy *S*,	222	13
of sin by your life-giving *S*;	222	19
lives and reigns with you and the Holy *S*,	222	20
lives and reigns with you and the Holy *S*,	223	2
with you and the Holy *S*, be dominion and praise	223	9
in the unity of the Holy *S*,	223	13
lives and reigns with you and the Holy *S*,	224	6
in the unity of the Holy *S*,	224	12
in the unity of the Holy *S*,	225	1
who, with you and the Holy *S*, lives and reigns,	225	6
lives and reigns with you and the Holy *S*,	225	19
lives and reigns with you and the Holy *S*,	226	6
Do not leave us comfortless, but send us your Holy *S*	226	15
by the promised gift of your Holy *S*:	227	3
in the unity of the Holy *S*,	227	6
by sending to them the light of your Holy *S*:	227	9
Grant us by the same *S* to have a right judgment	227	10
who with the Son and the Holy *S* live and reign,	228	7
lives and reigns with you and the Holy *S*,	228	12
lives and reigns with you and the Holy *S*,	229	4
lives and reigns with you and the Holy *S*,	230	5
in unity of *s* by their teaching,	230	15
Grant us the grace of your Holy *S*,	230	21
lives and reigns with you and the Holy *S*,	231	3
lives and reigns with you and the Holy *S*,	232	5
Grant to us, Lord, we pray, the *s* to think	232	6
being gathered together in unity by your Holy *S*,	232	18
lives and reigns with you and the Holy *S*,	233	2
grant that your Holy *S* may in all things direct	233	15
lives and reigns with you and the Holy *S*,	234	5
lives and reigns with you and the Holy *S*,	235	2
lives and reigns with you and the Holy *S*,	236	7
lives and reigns with you and the Holy *S*,	237	6
lives and reigns with you and the Holy *S*,	238	6
in the unity of the Holy *S*,	238	13
lives and reigns with you and the Holy *S*,	238	19
in the unity of the Holy *S*,	239	4

lives and reigns with you and the Holy *S*, 239 10
in the unity of the Holy *S*, 240 5
lives and reigns with you and the Holy *S*, 240 11
lives and reigns with you and the Holy *S*, 241 1
and knit together in unity by your *S*, 241 22
in the unity of the Holy *S*, 241 24
lives and reigns with you and the Holy *S*, 242 6
who with you and the Holy *S* lives and reigns, 242 12
pour out upon the leaders of your Church that *s* 242 17
you, O Holy *S*, lives and reigns, 243 6
in the unity of the Holy *S*, 243 12
lives and reigns with you and the Holy *S*, 243 18
lives and reigns with you and the Holy *S*, 244 6
in the unity of the Holy *S*, 245 3
lives and reigns with you and the Holy *S*, 245 8
who with you and the Holy *S* lives and reigns, 245 22
lives and reigns with you and the Holy *S*, 246 7
lives and reigns with you and the Holy *S*, 247 4
who lives and reigns with you and the Holy *S*, 248 6
to all pastors the gifts of your Holy *S*, 248 18
by your Holy *S* you give to some the word 248 22
who with you and the Holy *S* lives and reigns, 249 3
lives and reigns with you and the Holy *S*, 249 9
in the unity of the Holy *S*, 249 16
Grant that we also may be aflame with the *s* 249 20
in the unity of the Holy *S*, 249 23
lives and reigns with you and the Holy *S*, 250 6
by your Holy *S* you have made us one 250 14
our intercessions are acceptable through the *S*, 250 20
Father, Son, and Holy *S*; 251 5
by the indwelling of your Holy *S* we may be enlightened 251 8
in the unity of the Holy *S*, 251 10
lives and reigns with you and the Holy *S*, 251 17
in the unity of the Holy *S*, 252 5
lives and reigns with you and the Holy *S*, 252 11
so we may be renewed in the *s* of our minds, 253 3
in the unity of the Holy *S*, 253 5
lives and reigns with you and the Holy *S*, 254 6
may be renewed in your Holy *S*, 254 16
in the unity of the Holy *S*, 255 4
you have given the Holy *S* to abide with us for ever: 255 7
may be united in one body by the one *S*, 255 18
in the unity of the Holy *S*, 256 9
under the guidance of the Holy *S*, 256 13
lives and reigns with you and the Holy *S*, 256 17
by whose *S* the whole body 256 19
in the unity of the Holy *S*, 257 4
pour out your *S* upon all flesh, 257 9
lives and reigns with you and the Holy *S*, 257 11
lives and reigns with you and the Holy *S*, 258 6
in the unity of the Holy *S*, 258 13
lives and reigns with you and the Holy *S*, 259 2
in the unity of the Holy *S*, 259 9
who with you and the Holy *S* lives and reigns, 259 16
lives and reigns with you and the Holy *S*, 260 7
Enlighten by your Holy *S* those who teach 261 2
lives and reigns with you and the Holy *S*, 261 6
lives and reigns with you and the Holy *S*, 264 8
and renew a right *s* within me. 266 23
and take not your holy *S* from me. 266 25
and sustain me with your bountiful *S*. 266 27
The sacrifice of God is a troubled *s*; * 267 10
We have grieved your Holy *S*. 267 25
grant us true repentance and his Holy *S*, 269 11
lives and reigns in glory with you and the Holy *S*, 271 13
lives and reigns with you and the Holy *S*, 272 13
lives and reigns with you and the Holy *S*, 274 6
lives and reigns with you and the Holy *S*, 276 8
by whose *S* the whole body 278 11
in the unity of the Holy *S*, 280 23
for with the Father and the Holy *S* you live and reign, 282 11
lives and reigns with you and the Holy *S*, 283 5
in the unity of the Holy *S*, 286 15
who are saved through water and the *S*, 289 3
and you renew the earth by your *S*: 290 9
Grant to those who are sealed by your Holy *S* the will 291 7
He was conceived by the power of the Holy *S* 293 3
Do you believe in God the Holy *S*? 293 12
I believe in the Holy *S*, 293 13
has given us a new birth by water and the Holy *S*, 294 5
lives and reigns with you and the Holy *S*, 295 6
that *S* of adoption which is given to us in Baptism, 295 10
lives and reigns with you and the Holy *S*, 295 13
Father, Son, and Holy *S*. 299 1
There is one Body and one *S*; 299 7
He was conceived by the power of the Holy *S* 304 6
Do you believe in God the Holy *S*? 304 15
I believe in the Holy *S*, 304 16
Fill them with your holy and life-giving *S*. 305 19
Teach them to love others in the power of the *S*. 305 24
Over it the Holy *S* moved in the beginning 306 14
anointed by the Holy *S* as the Messiah, 306 18
Through it we are reborn by the Holy *S*. 306 22
and of the Son, and of the Holy *S*. 307 2
by the power of your Holy *S*, 307 4
To him, to you, and to the Holy *S*, be all honor 307 7
anointed by the Holy *S* to be the Savior 307 10
lives and reigns with you and the Holy *S*, 307 13
and of the Son, and of the Holy *S*. 307 15
by water and the Holy *S* you have bestowed 308 3
Sustain them, O Lord, in your Holy *S*. 308 5
a *s* to know and to love you, 308 7
you are sealed by the Holy *S* in Baptism 308 9
by the sealing of your Holy *S* 309 6
Send them forth in the power of that *S* 309 8
lives and reigns with you and the Holy *S*, 309 11
Strengthen, O Lord, your servant N. with your Holy *S*; 309 12
increase in your Holy *S* more and more, 309 17
God, the Father, Son, and Holy *S*, 310 3
may the Holy *S*, who has begun a good work in you, 310 5
let your Holy *S* ever be with them; 310 9
lives and reigns with you and the Holy *S*, 311 20
to be strengthened with might by his Holy *S*, 311 23
and of the Son, and of the Holy *S*. 313 2
by water and the Holy *S* you have bestowed 314 2
children of God by the power of the Holy *S*, 316 16
Father, Son, and Holy *S* 319 1
and the grace and consolation of his Holy *S*. 321 16
Father, Son, and Holy *S*. 323 1
by the inspiration of thy Holy *S*, 323 9
And with thy *s*. 325 11
by the power of the Holy *S* 327 1

We believe in the Holy *S*, the Lord,	327	12
the Universal Church with the *s* of truth,	329	5
And with thy *s*.	332	20
And with thy *s*.	333	2
sanctify, with thy Word and Holy *S*, these thy gifts	335	19
the Father, the Son, and the Holy *S*,	339	21
rejoicing in the power of the *S*.	340	4
And with thy *s*.	340	10
and, with thy Word and Holy *s*, to bless	342	17
Who by water and the Holy *S* hast made us	345	5
For with thy co-eternal Son and Holy *S*,	347	13
and of the Son, and of the Holy *S*.	347	16
given us the Holy *S* to guide us into all truth.	348	22
Father, Son, and Holy *S*.	351	1
and by the power of the Holy *s* keep you	353	3
Father, Son, and Holy *S*.	355	1
by the inspiration of your Holy *S*,	355	9
with the Holy *S*,	356	17
by the power of the Holy *S*	358	17
We believe in the Holy *S*, the Lord,	359	3
and by the power of the Holy *S* keep you	360	17
Sanctify them by your Holy *S*	363	13
in the unity of the Holy *S* all honor	363	20
To him, to you, and to the Holy *S*,	366	12
rejoicing in the power of the *S*.	366	19
We pray you, gracious God, to send your Holy *S*	369	4
being sanctified by the Holy *S*.	369	8
in the unity of the Holy *S* all honor	369	16
made a new people by water and the *S*,	371	7
Sanctify them by your Holy *S*	371	8
one *s* in Christ,	372	7
with you and the Holy *S*, your Church gives honor,	372	12
Incarnate by the Holy *S*, born of the Virgin Mary,	374	3
who died and rose for us, he sent the Holy *S*,	374	10
your Holy *S* may descend upon us,	375	5
become one body and one *s*, a living sacrifice	375	10
in the unity of the Holy *S*,	375	28
For by water and the Holy *S* you have made	378	1
who, by the mighty power of the Holy *S*,	378	10
the Holy *S* came down [on this day]	380	2
For with your co-eternal Son and Holy *S*,	380	8
and of the Son, and of the Holy *S*.	380	11
given us the Holy *S* to guide us into all truth.	381	15
who suffer in body, mind, or *s*;	389	4
For the peace of the world, that a *s* of respect	390	13
grace of the Holy *S* to amend our lives,	391	8
O Father, Son, and Holy *S*;	391	23
and so uphold us by your *S*	393	13
Father, Son, and Holy *S*,	395	7
where with the Father and the Holy *S* you live	395	12
by your Holy *S* you have made us one	395	17
intercessions are acceptable through the *S*,	395	23
and by the power of the Holy *S* keep you	398	9
Sanctify them by your Holy *S*	403	2
in the unity of the Holy *S* all honor	403	20
the fellowship of the Holy *S* be with you all.	404	2
Send your Holy *S* upon these gifts.	405	15
in the unity of the Holy *S* all honor	405	20
Holy *S* bless and sanctify this bread (wine)	408	2
Father, Son, and Holy *S*.	413	1
There is one Body and one *S*;	413	7
He was conceived by the power of the Holy *S*	416	11
Do you believe in God the Holy *S*?	416	20
I believe in the Holy *S*,	416	21
by the sealing of your Holy *S* you have bound	418	4
Send them forth in the power of that *S*	418	6
lives and reigns with you and the Holy *S*,	418	9
Strengthen, O Lord, your servant N. with your Holy *S*;	418	10
and daily increase in your Holy *S* more and more,	418	15
God, the Father, Son, and Holy *S*,	418	19
may the Holy *S*, who has begun a good work in you,	419	1
let your Holy *S* ever be with them;	419	5
May the Holy *S* guide and strengthen you,	420	1
in the unity of the Holy *S*,	425	13
and of the Son, and of the Holy *S*	427	15
and of the Son, and of the Holy *S*.	428	5
and their spirits in your *S*,	429	12
O Father, with your Son and the Holy *S*,	430	8
By the power of your Holy *S*, pour	430	15
who with you and the Holy *S* lives and reigns,	430	24
God the Father, God the Son, God the Holy *S*, bless,	431	9
Grant that by your Holy *S*,	432	4
my *s* rejoices in God my Savior;*	441	13
and to the Son, and to the Holy *S*:*	442	11
and to the Son, and to the Holy *S*:*	443	18
and their spirits in your *S*,	444	13
May God the Holy *S*, who has made the Church one	445	7
and of the Son, and of the Holy *S*.	447	4
and of the Son, and of the Holy *S*.	448	6
through my ministry by the grace of the Holy *S*,	448	10
forgives your sins by the grace of the Holy *S*.	448	17
the power of the Holy *S* keep you in eternal life.	451	5
through my ministry by the grace of the Holy *S*,	451	9
and of the Son, and of the Holy *S*.	451	16
forgives your sins by the grace of the Holy *S*.	452	3
by the power of the Holy *S* keep you	455	8
Send your Holy *S* to sanctify this oil;	455	10
lives and reigns with you and the Holy *S*,	455	14
and of the Son, and of the Holy *S*,	456	2
to drive away all sickness of body and *s*,	456	4
grant you the inward anointing of the Holy *S*.	456	15
God the Holy *S* give you strength.	460	6
Strengthen them by your life-giving *S*,	460	12
these words more than words, and give me the *S*	461	24
God the Holy *S*,	462	9
Coming of the Holy *S*,	463	9
where with the Father and the Holy *S* you live	464	19
In the Name of the Holy *S* who sanctifies you.	464	24
where with the Father and the Holy *S* you live	466	19
even so saith the *S*, for they rest from their labors.	469	15
And with thy *s*.	469	17
liveth and reigneth with thee and the Holy *S*,	470	5
Whither shall I go then from thy *S*? *	475	5
that thy Holy *S* may lead us in holiness	481	2
liveth and reigneth with thee and the Holy *S*,	481	29
by his *S* that dwelleth in us.	485	3
Wherefore my heart is glad, and my *s* rejoiceth;	485	4
And with thy *s*.	485	18
and let thy Holy *S* lead us in holiness	489	6
who with the Father and the Holy *S* livest	489	28
So it is, says the *S*,	492	3
who with you and the Holy *S* lives and reigns,	493	8
lives and reigns with you and the Holy *S*,	493	14

lives and reigns with you and the Holy *S*, 494 5
He was conceived by the power of the Holy *S* 496 6
I believe in the Holy *S*, 496 15
washed in Baptism and anointed with the Holy *S*; 497 17
who was reborn by water and the *S* in Holy Baptism. 498 2
live and reign with the Father and the Holy *S*, 498 7
through his indwelling *S*. 501 5
My heart, therefore, is glad, and my *s* rejoices; 501 6
S lead us in holiness and righteousness all our days; 504 4
Grant, O Lord, to all who are bereaved the *s* of faith 505 10
Father, Son, and Holy *S*. 512 1
by the inspiration of your Holy *S*, 512 9
trusting in the guidance of the Holy *S*, 513 2
in the power of the Holy *S* to consecrate him a bishop 513 5
and of the Son, and of the Holy *S*, 513 8
ordain N. for the work to which we trust the Holy *S* 514 17
in the unity of the Holy *S*, 515 13
I will, in the power of the *S*. 518 11
by the power of the Holy *S* 519 20
We believe in the Holy *S*, the Lord, the giver of life, 520 3
out upon him the power of your princely *S*, 521 2
to whom, with you and the Holy *S*, be honor 521 16
through him in the fellowship of your Holy *S*. 523 3
lives and reigns with you and the Holy *S*, 523 10
the Father, the Son, and the Holy *S*, 523 16
rejoicing in the power of the *S*. 523 19
Father, Son, and Holy *S*. 525 1
by the inspiration of your Holy *S*, 525 9
in the unity of the Holy *S*, 528 11
by the power of the Holy *S* 530 11
We believe in the Holy *S*, the Lord, the giver of life, 530 22
the body of Christ, and the temple of the Holy *S*. 531 2
and in the sanctification of the Holy *S*? 532 28
give your Holy *S* to N.; 533 12
who with you and the Holy *S* lives and reigns, 534 9
through him in the fellowship of your Holy *S*. 535 3
lives and reigns with you and the Holy *S*, 535 10
the Father, the Son, and the Holy *S*, 535 12
rejoicing in the power of the *S*. 535 14
Father, Son, and Holy *S*. 537 1
by the inspiration of your Holy *S*, 537 9
in the unity of the Holy *S*, 540 11
by the power of the Holy *S* 542 11
We believe in the Holy *S*, the Lord, the giver of life, 542 22
serving God the Father, through the power of the
Holy *S*. 543 2
give your Holy *S* to N.; 545 10
with you and the Holy *S*, lives and reigns, 545 18
through him in the fellowship of your Holy *S*. 546 5
lives and reigns with you and the Holy *S*, 547 6
rejoicing in the power of the *S*. 547 8
God the Holy *S*, 548 5
That by the indwelling of the Holy *S* 549 8
that a *s* of respect and forbearance may grow 549 29
for the grace of the Holy *S* to amend our lives, 550 17
share in the fullness of your life-giving *S*; 552 11
lives and reigns with you and the Holy *S*, 560 10
I devote myself, body, soul, and *s*. 562 12
with the light of your Holy *S*; 562 14
through him in the fellowship of your Holy *S*. 564 3
lives and reigns with you and the Holy *S*, 564 10
and of the Son, and of the Holy *S*. 568 3
Holy *S*, open our eyes, our ears, and our hearts, 569 3
Now, O Father, Son, and Holy *S*, 569 10
Grant through your *S* that those baptized 569 17
and of the Son, and of the Holy *S*. 569 22
the Holy *S* moved in the beginning of creation. 570 6
and was anointed by the Holy *S* as the Messiah, 570 9
Through it we are reborn by the Holy *S*. 570 14
and of the Son, and of the Holy *S*. 570 17
Grant, by the power of your Holy *S*, 570 18
To him, to you, and to the Holy *S*, be all honor 570 21
and of the Son, and of the Holy *S*. 571 8
and of the Son, and of the Holy *S*. 572 8
We praise you for sending your Holy *S* 573 19
Blessed be your Name, Father, Son, and Holy *S*; 574 8
My *s* shakes with terror; * 590 3
My heart, therefore, is glad, and my *s* rejoices; * 600 15
Into your hands I commend my *s*, * 622 17
and in whose *s* there is no guile! 625 2
and renew a right *s* within me. 657 2
and take not your holy *S* from me. 657 4
and sustain me with your bountiful *S*. 657 6
The sacrifice of God is a troubled *s*; * 657 16
Wake up, my *s*, 664 12
He breaks the *s* of princes, * 692 25
I ponder, and my *s* faints. 693 7
and whose *s* was not faithful to God. 695 19
You send forth your *S*, and they are created; * 737 14
For they so embittered his *s* * 744 13
Wake up, my *s*; 749 19
Where can I go then from your *S*? * 794 12
When my *s* languishes within me, you know 798 5
My *s* faints within me; * 799 5
O Lord, make haste to answer me; my *s* fails me; * 799 12
let your good *S* lead me on level ground. 799 22
be so guided and governed by thy good *S*, 815 3
hold the faith in unity of *s*, 815 5
So mightily spread abroad your *S*, 815 24
lives and reigns with you and the Holy *S*, 817 2
the healthful *S* of thy grace; 817 6
By your *S*, fashion our lives 817 15
as there is but one Body and one *S*, 818 19
the coming of the *S* through the teaching 819 2
receive the blessing of the Holy *S*, 819 4
for you reign with the Father and the Holy *S*, 819 12
Endue with the *s* of wisdom 820 9
liveth and reigneth with thee and the Holy *S*, 820 25
and give unto them the *s* of wisdom 821 10
the *s* of wisdom, charity, and justice; 822 19
Grant, O God, that your holy and life-giving *S* 823 17
who are broken in body or *s*, 826 5
let thy *S* go forth, 828 3
by thy love in the communion of thy Holy *S*, 830 24
that the *S* of wisdom may save us 832 9
By the might of thy *S* lift us, we pray thee, 832 15
the *s* of grace and of supplication: 833 20
worship thee in *s* and in truth; 833 23
live and reign with the Father and the Holy *S*, 834 11
livest and reignest with the Father and the Holy *S*, 834 17
Grant us the gift of your *S*, 836 17
with you, O Father, and the Holy *S*, 837 24
whom you have sent in the power of the *S* to preach 838 3
conceived by the power of the Holy *S* 849 26

Father, Son, and Holy *S.* 852 13
Who is the Holy *S*? 852 14
The Holy *S* is the Third Person of the Trinity, 852 15
How is the Holy *S* revealed in the Old Covenant? 852 17
The Holy *S* is revealed in the Old Covenant 852 18
How is the Holy *S* revealed in the New Covenant? 852 20
The Holy *S* is revealed as the Lord who leads us 852 21
How do we recognize the presence of the Holy *S* 852 24
We recognize the presence of the Holy *S* 852 26
the truths taught by the Holy *S*? 853 2
We recognize truths to be taught by the Holy *S* 853 3
under the inspiration of the Holy *S*, 853 12
by the help of the Holy *S*, 854 1
The Church is holy, because the Holy *S* dwells in it, 854 18
in the power of the Holy *S*. 856 22
and of the Son, and of the Holy *S*. 858 15
and new life in the Holy *S*. 858 20
under the guidance of the Holy *S*? 860 8
receive strength from the Holy *S* through prayer 860 20
the grace of the Holy *S* to those being made bishops, 860 29
healing of *s*, mind, and body. 861 16

spirits
O ye *s* and souls of the righteous, bless ye the Lord; * 49 5
Glorify the Lord, O *s* and souls of the righteous, * 89 22
and to the *s* of just men made perfect: 198 24
and to the *s* of just men made perfect: 250 9
and their *s* in your Spirit, 429 12
and their *s* in your Spirit, 444 13
O Almighty God, the God of the *s* of all flesh, 486 7
Almighty God, with whom do live the *s* 488 1
Almighty God, with whom still live the *s* 503 12
and will save those whose *s* are crushed. 629 4
they do not resort to evil *s* or turn to false gods. 640 10
and their daughters to evil *s*. 744 22
their *s* languished within them. 746 11
So he humbled their *s* with hard labor; * 747 5
s may be opened to the goodness of your creation; 825 4

spiritual
Do you renounce Satan and all the *s* forces 302 7
and for a *s* sharing in his risen life. 316 4
and be nourished by that *s* Food, 316 18
and *s* counsel and advice; 317 14
the *s* food of the most precious Body and Blood 339 4
which is your *s* worship. 343 16
and you have fed us with *s* food 365 12
we thank you for feeding us with the *s* food 366 2
which is your *s* worship. 376 12
the *s* unity between Christ and his Church: 431 2
and fill you with all *s* benediction 431 11
fed us with the *s* food and drink 482 2
fed us with the *s* food and drink 498 13
s sacrifices acceptable to you; 534 2
and visible signs of inward and *s* grace, 857 27
What is the inward and *s* grace in Baptism? 858 16
The inward and *s* grace in Baptism is union 858 17
What is the inward and *s* grace given 859 22
The inward and *s* grace in the Holy Communion 859 24

spit
whipped and his face to be *s* upon: 220 15

spite
In *s* of all this, they went on sinning * 697 14

splendid
more *s* than the everlasting mountains! 692 8
he has put on *s* apparel; * 722 2

splendor
Glory to you in the *s* of your temple; * 90 9
S and honor and kingly power * 93 20
Be worship and praise, dominion and *s*, * 94 7
bright with a glorious *s*, 286 5
rejoice in the *s* of your radiance. 373 6
s of the children of God. 569 18
s and majesty have you bestowed upon him. 609 6
the voice of the LORD is a voice of *s*. 620 13
You have put an end to his *s* * 717 1
and your *s* to their children. 719 6
Oh, the power and the *s* of his sanctuary! 726 4
you are clothed with majesty and *s*. 735 3
His work is full of majesty and *s*, * 754 10
I will ponder the glorious *s* of your majesty * 801 20
and the glorious *s* of your kingdom. 802 10
his *s* is over earth and heaven. 806 21
We thank you for the *s* of the whole creation, 836 2

split
You have shaken the earth and *s* it open; * 667 12
You *s* open spring and torrent; * 690 14
He *s* open the sea and let them pass through; * 695 28
He *s* the hard rocks in the wilderness * 696 3

splits
The voice of the LORD *s* the flames of fire; 620 18

spoils
the women at home are dividing the *s*." 677 4
as one who finds great *s*. 777 4

spoke
For he *s*, and it came to pass; * 626 17
I *s* out with my tongue: 638 24
God *s* from his holy place and said: * 667 20
and *s* with my mouth when I was in trouble. 674 23
You *s* once in a vision and said 715 3
He *s* to them out of the pillar of cloud; * 729 14
He *s*, and there came swarms of insects * 740 15
He *s*, and the locust came, * 740 21
that he *s* rash words with his lips. 744 14
Then he *s*, and a stormy wind arose, * 748 5
God *s* from his holy place and said, * 750 7
giver of life, the One who *s* through the prophets. 852 19

spoken
He has *s* through the Prophets. 327 15
He has *s* through the Prophets. 359 6
in your Word *s* through the prophets; 368 3
He has *s* through the Prophets. 520 6
He has *s* through the Prophets. 530 25
He has *s* through the Prophets. 542 25
Father, in every age you have *s* through the voices of 571 9
I have *s* of your faithfulness and your deliverance; * 640 27
God has *s*, and the earth shall melt away. 649 16

The LORD, the God of gods, has *s*; * 654 1
God has *s* once, twice have I heard it, * 670 8
Glorious things are *s* of you, * 711 15

sponsors
Promises are made for them by their parents and *s*, 859 2

sport
which you have made for the *s* of it. 737 6

spot
he may be presented pure and without *s* before thee; 488 19

spouse
and the *s* of his virgin mother: 188 10
and the *s* of his virgin mother: 239 19

spread
for the relief of the poor and the *s* of the Gospel; 189 20
for the relief of the poor and the *s* of the Gospel; 241 6
s their garments and branches of palm along his way. 271 9
You *s* a table before me in the presence 443 11
You *s* a table before me in the presence 613 7
For they have secretly *s* a net for me 630 3
they go outside and *s* them. 642 12
and shall *s* abroad like a cedar of Lebanon. 721 22
and *s* out the heavens like a curtain. 735 5
He *s* out a cloud for a covering * 741 3
Who *s* out the earth upon the waters, * 790 7
I *s* out my hands to you; * 799 10
So mightily *s* abroad your Spirit, 815 24
work, pray, and give for the *s* of the kingdom 856 15

spring
You split open *s* and torrent; * 690 14
Truth shall *s* up from the earth, * 709 16
and flint-stone into a flowing *s*. 757 12

springs
from the *s* of salvation. 86 6
Glorify the Lord, O *s* of water, seas, and streams, * 89 10
find it a place of *s*, * 708 2
"All my fresh *s* are in you." 711 25
You send the *s* into the valleys; * 735 21
and water-*s* into thirsty ground, 748 22
and dry land into water-*s*. 748 26

sprung
Light has *s* up for the righteous, * 727 20

spurn
You *s* all who stray from your statutes; * 773 9

spy
they *s* out the helpless. 595 10
The wicked *s* on the righteous * 635 26
Render evil to those who *s* on me; * 659 26
they *s* upon my footsteps; 663 2

squandered
But I have *s* the inheritance 450 13

squares
They lurk in ambush in public *s* 595 8
no wailing in the public *s*. 801 9

staff
your rod and your *s*, they comfort me. 443 10
thy rod and thy *s* comfort me. 476 11
thy rod and thy *s*, they comfort me. 477 4
your rod and your *s*, they comfort me. 613 6

stagger
you have given us wine that makes us *s*. 667 15

staggered
They reeled and *s* like drunkards * 748 9

stalks
Of the plague that *s* in the darkness, * 130 8
Of the plague that *s* in the darkness, * 719 22

stalls
I will take no bull-calf from your *s*, * 654 21

stand
let the whole earth *s* in awe of him. 45 7
let the whole earth *s* in awe of him. 61 6
but on a lamp-*s* where it gives light for everyone 109 9
you that *s* by night in the house of the Lord. 131 7
you that *s* by night in the house of the Lord. 140 2
That it may please thee to strengthen such as do *s*; 152 11
may ever *s* firm upon the one foundation, 190 13
may ever *s* firm upon the one foundation, 241 22
All you who *s* near this marvelous and holy flame, 286 10
and made us worthy to *s* before you. 368 8
Countless throngs of angels *s* before you to serve you 373 7
If I am to *s* up, help me to *s* bravely. 461 21
and that he shall *s* at the latter day upon the earth; 469 5
and that at the last he will *s* upon the earth. 491 8
yet you have called your servant to *s* 562 10
Therefore the wicked shall not *s* upright 585 12
Braggarts cannot *s* in your sight; * 588 25
S up, O LORD, in your wrath; * 591 6
Why do you *s* so far off, O LORD, * 594 19
and lets me *s* firm on the heights. 605 6
but we will arise and *s* upright. 608 18
s in awe of him, O offspring of Israel; 611 27
and who can *s* in his holy place?" 613 19
let all who dwell in the world *s* in awe of him. 626 16
my neighbors *s* afar off. 637 19
truly, even those who *s* erect are but a puff of wind. 639 5
many shall see, and *s* in awe, 640 7
Kings' daughters *s* among the ladies of the court; * 648 8
Everyone will *s* in awe and declare God's deeds; * 672 3
and may all the ends of the earth *s* in awe of him. 675 23
who can *s* before you when you are angry? 692 15
he made the waters *s* up like walls. 695 29
God takes his *s* in the council of heaven; * 705 9
and to *s* at the threshold of the house of my God 708 12
will those who have died *s* up and give you thanks? 712 24
and my covenant will *s* firm for him. 715 23
It shall *s* fast for evermore like the moon, * 716 15
and their offspring shall *s* fast in your sight." 733 8
and let an accuser *s* at his right hand. 751 9
They *s* fast for ever and ever, * 754 20
The hills *s* about Jerusalem; * 781 19
so does the LORD *s* round about his people, 781 20
O Lord, who could *s*? 784 22

you that *s* by night in the house of the LORD. 787 20
You who *s* in the house of the LORD, * 788 4
who can *s* against his cold? 805 12
He made them *s* fast for ever and ever; * 806 5
enable us all to *s* reconciled before you; 816 8

standeth

knowledge of whom *s* our eternal life, 57 2
Christ, who *s* at thy right hand; 186 3

standing

Now our feet are *s* * 779 20

stands

Christ, who *s* at your right hand; 237 16
My foot *s* on level ground; * 617 5
But the LORD's will *s* fast for ever, * 626 21
On the holy mountain *s* the city he has founded; * 711 12
Because he *s* at the right hand of the needy, * 753 10
and their righteousness *s* fast for ever; 755 23
it *s* firm in the heavens. 770 21
but my heart *s* in awe of your word. 777 2
which cannot be moved, but *s* fast for ever. 781 18
Strengthen him when he *s*; 830 15

star

O God, who by the leading of a *s* didst manifest 162 13
O God, by the leading of a *s* you manifested 214 7
May Christ, the Morning *S* who knows no setting, 287 25

stare

They *s* and gloat over me; * 611 15

stars

O ye *s* of heaven, bless ye the Lord; 48 2
Sun and moon and *s* of the sky, glorify the Lord, * 88 11
the moon and the *s* you have set in their courses, 592 14
The moon and the *s* to govern the night, * 790 13
He counts the number of the *s* * 804 8
praise him, all you shining *s*. 805 26

start

but as a chance for a new *s*. 829 19

state

Let us pray for the whole *s* of Christ's Church 328 22
Princely *s* has been yours from the day 753 16
the Governor of this *S* (or Commonwealth), 820 20
(or in the Legislature of this *S*, or Commonwealth), 821 4
who hold office in this *S* (Commonwealth, City, County, 822 18

statements

The creeds are *s* of our basic beliefs about God. 851 23

states

the President of the United *S* (or of this nation), 150 26
For N., the President of the United *S* 278 19
Grant to the President of the United *S*, 820 19
to Governors of *S*, Mayors of Cities, 821 20
and those who make our laws in *S*, 822 2
Guide the people of the United *S* 822 24

stature

into the *s* of the fullness of our Lord 197 1
into the *s* of the fullness of our Lord 248 12
into the full *s* of Christ? 302 5
love and nurture him, that he may attain to that full *s* 841 4

statute

For this is a *s* for Israel, * 704 7
Which he established as a *s* for Jacob, * 738 19

statutes

I have applied my heart to fulfill your *s* * 104 11
The *s* of the LORD are just 607 8
"Why do you recite my *s*, 655 12
If they break my *s* * 716 3
That they might keep his *s* * 741 15
that I might keep your *s*! 763 14
I will keep your *s*; * 763 19
instruct me in your *s*. 764 8
My delight is in your *s*; * 764 15
I will meditate on your *s*. 765 6
instruct me in your *s*. 765 12
Teach me, O LORD, the way of your *s*, * 766 1
and I will meditate on your *s*. 767 10
Your *s* have been like songs to me * 767 21
instruct me in your *s*. 768 16
that I might learn your *s*. 769 6
Let my heart be sound in your *s*, * 770 1
but I have not forgotten your *s*. 770 8
I have applied my heart to fulfill your *s* * 772 17
and my delight shall be ever in your *s*. 773 8
You spurn all who stray from your *s*; * 773 9
and teach me your *s*. 773 22
and teach me your *s*. 774 18
answer me, O LORD, that I may keep your *s*. 775 16
for they do not study your *s*. 776 14
when you teach me your *s*. 777 22
his *s* and his judgments to Israel. 805 16

stay

Lord Jesus, *s* with us, for evening is at hand 70 10
Lord Jesus, *s* with us, for evening is at hand 124 7
Lord Jesus, *s* with us, for evening is at hand 139 16
or else they will not *s* near you." 625 22

steadfast

abounding in *s* love, and repents of evil. 76 15
again with penitent hearts and *s* faith 166 18
keep us *s* in this faith and worship, 176 5
the Church in thy *s* faith and love, 178 7
with *s* faith in the confession of thy Name; 183 14
Keep thy Church *s* upon the rock of this faith, 187 3
Give us grace to continue *s* 199 14
again with penitent hearts and *s* faith 218 9
Keep us *s* in this faith and worship, 228 5
the Church in your *s* faith and love, 230 1
persevere with *s* faith in the confession 235 6
Keep your Church *s* upon the rock of this faith, 238 16
Give us grace to continue *s* 251 3
that with true fidelity and *s* love 425 10
and save us, for the sake of your *s* love. 647 10
s love is yours, O Lord, * 670 10
a generation whose heart was not *s*, 695 18
Their heart was not *s* toward him, * 697 24

that with *s* purpose they may faithfully serve 822 20
that with *s* thoughts and kindled affections 833 22
for his *s* obedience, 836 13

steadfastly

that we may *s* follow his steps 173 18
that we may *s* follow his steps 225 10

steadfastness

to follow the example of their *s* in thy faith, 487 15
come with *s* and patience; 505 12

steady

S my footsteps in your word; * 774 13

steal

Thou shalt not *s*. 318 22
You shall not *s*. 350 17

steel

and *s* us to wait for the consummation 835 5

Stephen

first martyr *S*, who looked up to heaven and prayed 186 2
first martyr *S*, who looked up to heaven and prayed 237 15
for *S*, the first martyr, and all the martyrs and saints 838 16

steps

follow his *s* in the way that leadeth to eternal life; 173 19
follow the blessed *s* of his most holy life; 181 1
who, following in his *s*, give themselves to the service 209 11
follow his *s* in the way that leads to eternal life; 225 11
follow daily in the blessed *s* of his most holy life; 232 14
Bless all who, following in his *s*, give 260 16
Our *s* are directed by the LORD; * 635 5
Turn your *s* toward the endless ruins; * 689 14
but that, following in his *s*, they may find 829 24

steward

and be a faithful *s* of his holy Word 521 20

stewards

Make us, we beseech thee, faithful *s* 194 18
servants of Christ and *s* of thy divine mysteries; 197 8
faithful *s* of thy bounty; 208 13
Make us, we pray, faithful *s* 246 3
servants of Christ and *s* of your divine mysteries; 248 19
may be faithful *s* of your good gifts; 259 14
and be faithful *s* of thy bounty. 329 25
may be faithful *s* of thy bounty, 827 4

sticks

my tongue *s* to the roof of my mouth; * 611 9

still

but *s* more blessed in keeping thy word: 189 12
but *s* more blessed in keeping your word: 240 19
and leads me beside *s* waters. 443 4
If I am to sit *s*, help me to sit quietly. 461 21
Be *s* then, and know that I am God; * 472 4
he leadeth me beside the *s* waters. 476 22
Grant to us who are *s* in our pilgrimage, 481 1
Almighty God, with whom *s* live the spirits 503 12
For this place where we may be *s* 578 13
you were my God when I was *s* in my mother's womb. 610 21
and leads me beside *s* waters. 612 26
Be *s* before the LORD * 633 17
"Be *s*, then, and know that I am God; * 650 1
These things you have done, and I kept *s*, * 655 22
You *s* the roaring of the seas, * 672 23
and the hairy scalp of those who go on *s* 677 26
the earth was afraid and was *s*; 692 17
though the food was *s* in their mouths. 697 10
do not keep *s* nor hold your peace, O God; 706 4
and *s* the surging of its waves. 714 12
They shall *s* bear fruit in old age; * 721 25
But I *s* my soul and make it quiet, 785 14
where we may be *s* and know that thou art God; 832 16
and because God *s* speaks to us 853 25
because we *s* hold them in our love, 862 9

stillborn

like a *s* child that never sees the sun. 665 10

stilled

He *s* the storm to a whisper * 748 13

sting

who by thy death didst take away the *s* of death: 69 8
You overcame the *s* of death 96 5
by your death you took away the *s* of death: 123 6
by your death you took away the *s* of death: 504 21

stink

My wounds *s* and fester * 637 6

stir

S up in us the flame of that love which burned 113 13
S up thy power, O Lord, and with great might come 160 1
S up in thy Church that Spirit of adoption 170 15
S up your power, O Lord, and with great might come 212 1
S up in your Church that Spirit of adoption 222 9
and *s* up in us the will and patience 279 12
S up in your Church that Spirit of adoption 295 9
s up your strength and come to help us. 702 15
and *s* up strife all day long. 796 4

stirring

enlightening the minds and *s* up 518 9
My heart is *s* with a noble song; 647 11

stirs

s our hearts, and strengthens our wills. 858 4

stock

a laughing-*s* among the peoples. 646 14

stole

receive this *s*, and be among us as a pastor and priest. 561 4
Must I then give back what I never *s*? 679 19

stone

they sank into the depths like a *s*. 85 13
lest you dash your foot against a *s*. 130 22
and set me up upon a rock of *s*. 477 22
lest you dash your foot against a *s*. 720 10
and flint-*s* into a flowing spring. 757 12
The same *s* which the builders rejected * 762 15

stones
built up as living *s* of a holy temple, 348 16
built up as living *s* of a holy temple, 381 10
more than gold and precious *s*. 774 2

stony
and the *s* cliffs for the rock badgers. 736 14
Let their rulers be overthrown in *s* places, * 797 15

stood
he commanded, and it *s* fast. 626 18
the waters *s* higher than the mountains. 735 14
had not Moses his chosen *s* before him in the breach, * 743 18
Then Phinehas *s* up and interceded, * 744 7

stooped
he *s* to me and heard my cry. 640 2

stoops
but *s* to behold the heavens and the earth? 756 11

stop
tore me to pieces and would not *s*. 630 26
But they did not *s* their craving, * 697 9

stopped
for the mouth of those who speak lies shall be *s*. 671 9

stops
they are like the deaf adder which *s* its ears, 665 2

storehouse
and brings the winds out of his *s*. 788 16

stores
and *s* up the depths of the sea. 626 14

stork
and in whose tops the *s* makes his dwelling. 736 12

storm
S clouds and thunderbolts, glorify the Lord, * 89 3
with a *s* cloud under his feet. 603 8
and round about him a raging *s*. 654 8
and terrify them with your *s*; 707 8
He stilled the *s* to a whisper * 748 13

stormy
from the *s* wind and tempest." 660 22
Then he spoke, and a *s* wind arose, * 748 5

straight
make *s* in the desert a highway for our God. 37 4
make *s* in the desert a highway for our God. 75 4
make your way *s* before me. 589 8
He put their feet on a *s* path * 746 14
and in thy *s* path may not stumble; 832 11

straightway
they go down *s* to the grave. 653 10

strange
or stretched out our hands to some *s* god, 646 27
There shall be no *s* god among you; * 704 19
the house of Jacob from a people of *s* speech, 756 20

stranger
and not as a *s*. 469 8
who is my friend and not a *s*. 491 12
I have become a *s* to my own kindred, * 680 3
They murder the widow and the *s* * 723 5
I am a *s* here on earth; * 764 21
wherever I have lived as a *s*. 767 22
the LORD cares for the *s*; * 803 21

strangers
Ye are no more *s* and foreigners, 40 3
You are no longer *s* and sojourners, 78 1
show compassion to the poor and *s*, 518 29
s will cringe before me. 605 30
s whom I did not know tore me to pieces 630 25
let *s* plunder his gains. 751 19

strap
S your sword upon your thigh, O mighty warrior, * 647 17

stray
nor did our footsteps *s* from your path; 646 23
let me not *s* from your commandments. 764 4
cursed are they who *s* from your commandments! 765 2
You spurn all who *s* from your statutes; * 773 9

strayed
we have erred and *s* from thy ways like lost sheep, 41 17
we have erred and *s* from thy ways like lost sheep, 62 17
but I have not *s* from your commandments. 104 8
we have erred and *s* from thy ways like lost sheep, 320 24
but I have not *s* from your commandments. 772 14

stream
Nations will *s* to your light, * 87 17

streams
Glorify the Lord, O springs of water, seas, and *s*, * 89 10
the *s* whereof make glad the city of God, * 471 23
They are like trees planted by *s* of water, 585 7
There is a river whose *s* make glad the city of God, * 649 10
He brought *s* out of the cliff, * 696 5
so that they could not drink of their *s*. 698 16
My eyes shed *s* of tears, * 774 19

street
when they see me in the *s* they avoid me. 623 13

streets
I trample them like mud in the *s*. 605 25
her *s* are never free of oppression and deceit. 661 5

strength
O Lord, my *s* and my redeemer. 40 14
let us heartily rejoice in the *s* of our salvation. 44 11
and the *s* of the hills is his also. 44 17
He hath showed *s* with his arm; * 50 11
he hath showed *s* with his arm; * 65 14
the *s* of those who labor, and the repose of the dead: 70 5
O Lord, my *s* and my redeemer. 78 13
The Lord is my *s* and my refuge; * 85 3
He has shown the *s* of his arm, * 92 6
renewing the *s* of those who are spent, 113 3
you are our light and salvation, and the *s* of our life. 113 7
He has shown the *s* of his arm, * 119 12

the _s_ of those who labor,	124	2
for you are my tower of _s_.	129	17
quietness and trust shall be our _s_.	138	11
let us heartily rejoice in the _s_ of our salvation.	146	2
and the _s_ of the hills is his also.	146	8
O God, the _s_ of all those who put their trust in thee:	164	11
resist the proud who confide in their own strength,	181	19
give to thine apostles Philip and James grace and _s_	189	6
a zeal for justice and the _s_ of forbearance,	207	3
O God, the _s_ of all who put their trust in you:	216	6
resist the proud who confide in their own _s_,	233	10
gave to your apostles Philip and James grace and _s_	240	14
we may use our liberty in _s_ of forbearance,	258	4
with our whole heart, and mind, and _s_.	267	20
the _s_ of all who suffer:	279	14
and give us, we pray, the _s_ to serve	279	17
with all your mind, and with all your _s_.	351	10
and grant us _s_ and courage	365	15
for solace only, and not for _s_;	372	5
forgiveness of our sins, _s_ in our weakness,	399	10
that each may be to the other a _s_ in need,	429	8
He has shown the _s_ of his arm, *	442	1
give them calm _s_ and patient wisdom	443	26
that each may be to the other a _s_ in need,	444	10
and restore you to wholeness and _s_.	456	17
forgiveness of our sins, _s_ in our weakness,	457	8
the _s_ of the weak and the comfort of sufferers:	458	11
his weakness may be banished and his _s_ restored;	458	19
restore to him your gifts of gladness and _s_,	459	5
the sense of his weakness may add _s_ to his faith	460	2
the Holy Spirit give you _s_.	460	6
that he, daily increasing in bodily _s_,	460	20
that my _s_ and courage may not fail;	461	8
God is our hope and _s_, *	471	17
yet is their _s_ then but labor and sorrow,	473	5
the LORD is the _s_ of my life;	477	14
may have _s_ to meet the days ahead	481	11
go from _s_ to _s_ in the life of perfect service	481	21
go from _s_ to _s_ in the life of perfect service	488	23
know the _s_ of his presence,	493	7
and _s_ to meet the days to come;	494	11
that they may have _s_ to meet the days	505	11
I love you, O LORD my _s_, *	602	7
It is God who girds me about with _s_ *	605	3
You have girded me with _s_ for the battle; *	605	18
O LORD, my _s_ and my redeemer.	607	30
with the victorious _s_ of his right hand.	608	14
The king rejoices in your _s_, O LORD; *	608	21
you are my _s_, hasten to help me.	611	19
the LORD is the _s_ of my life;	617	9
The LORD is my _s_ and my shield; *	619	24
The LORD is the _s_ of his people, *	620	1
ascribe to the LORD glory and _s_.	620	6
The LORD shall give _s_ to his people; *	621	1
for you are my tower of _s_.	622	16
my _s_ fails me because of affliction,	623	8
a strong man is not delivered by his great _s_.	627	8
for all its _s_ it cannot save.	627	10
My heart is pounding, my _s_ has failed me; *	637	16
I will say to the God of my _s_,	644	1
For you are the God of my _s_;	644	17
God is our refuge and _s_, *	649	1
My eyes are fixed on you, O my _S_; *	666	14
For my part, I will sing of your _s_; *	667	3
To you, O my _S_, will I sing; *	667	7
because of your great _s_ your enemies	673	22
Send forth your _s_, O God; *	678	14
his _s_ is in the skies.	679	3
the God of Israel giving _s_ and power to his people!	679	5
from my mother's womb you have been my _s_; *	683	12
but you are my refuge and my _s_.	683	15
forsake me not when my _s_ fails.	683	19
till I make known your _s_ to this generation	684	18
God is the _s_ of my heart and my portion for ever.	689	2
By your _s_ you have redeemed your people, *	694	3
stir up your _s_ and come to help us.	702	15
Sing with joy to God our _s_ *	704	1
Happy are the people whose _s_ is in you! *	707	25
give your _s_ to your servant;	711	7
I have become like one who has no _s_;	712	8
For you are the glory of their _s_, *	714	27
perhaps in _s_ even eighty; *	718	20
and girded himself with _s_.	722	4
He has brought down my _s_ before my time; *	732	22
Search for the LORD and his _s_; *	738	7
the firstfruits of all their _s_.	740	26
The LORD is my _s_ and my song, *	761	24
you and the ark of your _s_.	786	14
you increased my _s_ within me.	793	9
O Lord GOD, the _s_ of my salvation, *	796	15
he has no pleasure in the _s_ of a man;	804	23
He has raised up _s_ for his people	806	22
no _s_ known but the _s_ of love:	815	23
filled with the _s_ of his presence;	819	5
and _s_ to know and to do thy will.	820	21
And finally, teach our people to rely on your _s_	822	10
Give us calm _s_ and patient wisdom	829	10
Give them _s_ to hold their faith in you,	829	19
as their _s_ diminishes, increase their faith	830	5
and in confidence shall be our _s_:	832	15
and receive _s_ from the Holy Spirit	860	19

strengthen

_s_ you in all goodness,	80	2
_s_ you in all goodness,	117	7
to _s_ all who suffer in mind, body, and spirit;	151	24
That it may please thee to _s_ such as do stand;	152	11
who didst _s_ thine apostle Thomas	185	14
_s_ us, and exalt us to that place	226	16
_S_, O Lord, your servant N. with your Holy Spirit;	309	12
_S_ him, O Lord, with your presence,	314	4
and _s_ you in all goodness,	332	5
_s_ you in all goodness,	353	2
_s_ you in all goodness,	360	16
_s_ us to do your will;	394	11
_s_ you in all goodness,	398	8
_S_, O Lord, your servant N. with your Holy Spirit;	418	10
May the Holy Spirit guide and _s_ you,	420	1
_s_ us all in our Christian vocation of witness	421	5
_s_ you in all goodness,	451	4
_s_ you in all goodness,	455	7
_S_ your servant N., O God, to do what he has to do	459	12
_S_ them by your life-giving Spirit,	460	12
will you guide and _s_ the deacons	518	25

and *s* them to glorify God 531 19
s and sustain N., that with patience 560 6
you will *s* their heart and your ears shall hear; 596 4
and *s* you out of Zion; 608 4
You *s* me more and more; * 684 26
and bread to *s* the heart. 736 8
s me according to your word. 765 16
Where it is right, *s* it; 816 13
S the faithful, arouse the careless, 817 19
s them in their trials and temptations; 823 4
S those who suffer for the sake of conscience; 823 9
S those who spend their lives establishing 826 11
and *s* his trust in your goodness 830 10
S him when he stands; 830 14
s them in the work of their recovery; 831 22
S our efforts to blot our ignorance and prejudice, 839 17

strengthened

be *s* to bear our cross, 165 17
and *s* for thy service; 200 3
for whom our prayers are offered may be *s* 208 19
be *s* to bear our cross, 217 10
who *s* your apostle Thomas 237 8
we may be enlightened and *s* 251 8
for whom our prayers are offered may be *s* 260 4
to be *s* with might by his Holy Spirit, 311 23
vows may find their lives *s* 430 2
that he may be *s* in his weakness 459 19
and *s* by their fellowship, 489 20
and *s* by their fellowship, 504 18
so that your people may be *s* 534 7
to be supported and *s*, 568 18
and *s* for your service. 574 7
For he has *s* the bars of your gates; * 805 3
our society may be cleansed and *s*. 823 15

strengthening

and the *s* of your faith. 317 16
the *s* of our union with Christ 860 1

strengthens

he *s* those in whose way he delights. 635 6
stirs our hearts, and *s* our wills. 858 4

stress

through *s* of adversity and sorrow, 749 8

stretch

Christ, who didst *s* out thine arms of love 58 8
let Ethiopia *s* out her hands to God. 678 23
you *s* forth your hand against the fury of my enemies; 793 17
S out your hand from on high; * 800 14

stretched

You *s* forth your right hand; * 85 19
Christ, you *s* out your arms of love 101 1
He *s* out his arms upon the cross, 362 15
or *s* out our hands to some strange god, 646 27
companion *s* forth his hand against his comrade; * 661 28
my hands were *s* out by night and did not tire; 693 4
You *s* out its tendrils to the Sea * 703 9
I have *s* out my hands to you. 712 22
With a mighty hand and a *s*-out arm, * 790 19
and *s* out a net of cords; * 796 11

stretching

s out your loving arms: 107 9
s out your loving arms: 138 13

stricken

For they persecute him whom you have *s* * 681 16

stride

You lengthen my *s* beneath me, * 605 12

strife

and all whose homes are broken or torn by *s*, 151 22
You deliver me from the *s* of the peoples; * 605 26
while *s* is in their hearts. 619 13
you keep them in your shelter from the *s* of tongues. 624 10
for I have seen violence and *s* in the city. 660 25
and stir up *s* all day long. 796 4

strike

So that the sun shall not *s* you by day, * 104 23
surely, you will *s* all my enemies across the face, 587 16
so that mere mortals may *s* terror no more. 596 6
I *s* them down, and they cannot rise; * 605 16
to *s* down the poor and needy, * 634 12
and *s* down those who hate him. 715 13
So that the sun shall not *s* you by day, * 779 11

strikes

and *s* terror in the kings of the earth. 692 26

string

and fit their arrows to the *s*, * 596 11

stringed

I will play to you on a ten-*s* lyre. 800 20

strings

Praise him with *s* and pipe. 572 6
and the music of *s* from ivory palaces makes you glad. 648 7
praise him with *s* and pipe. 808 6

strip

do not *s* me of my life. 797 21

strips

and *s* the forests bare. 620 22

strive

Will you *s* for justice and peace among all people, 294 1
Will you *s* for justice and peace among all 305 7
Will you *s* for justice and peace among all 417 17
those who *s* to hurt me speak of my ruin 637 21
I will *s* to follow a blameless course; 730 9

strong

Be my *s* rock, a castle to keep me safe, 129 13
nothing is *s*, nothing is holy: 180 2
nothing is *s*, nothing is holy: 231 18
The Almighty Lord, who is a *s* tower to all 456 20
and though men be so *s* that they come to fourscore 473 4
be *s*, and he shall comfort thine heart; 478 9
for young and old, *s* and weak, rich and poor. 531 12
Make him, O Lord, modest and humble, *s* 545 12
He delivered me from my *s* enemies 603 25
s bulls of Bashan surround me. 611 2
"The Lord, *s* and mighty, 614 5

be *s*, and he shall comfort your heart; * 619 2
You, LORD, with your favor, made me as *s* as 621 18
Be my *s* rock, a castle to keep me safe, 622 12
Be *s* and let your heart take courage, * 624 21
a *s* man is not delivered by his great strength. 627 8
You deliver the poor from those who are too *s* 630 11
Your righteousness is like the *s* mountains, 632 14
Who will lead me into the *s* city? * 668 4
a *s* tower against the enemy. 668 18
God is my *s* rock and my refuge. 669 21
Be my *s* rock, a castle to keep me safe; * 683 5
The *s* of heart have been despoiled; 692 9
the son of man you have made so *s* for yourself. 703 21
s is your hand and high is your right hand. 714 20
and my arm will make him *s*. 715 9
Who will lead me into the *s* city? * 750 15
for they are too *s* for me. 798 14
men and women who have made this country *s*. 839 5

stronger

a *s* and more able minister of Christ? 532 6
Our sins are *s* than we are, * 672 11
he made them *s* than their enemies; 740 2

strongest

he slew their *s* men 697 12

stronghold

For the Lord is my *s* and my sure defense, * 86 3
for you are my crag and my *s*; * 129 14
"You are my refuge and may *s*, * 129 24
You have set up a *s* against your adversaries, * 592 11
O LORD my *s*, my crag, and my haven. 602 8
for you are my crag and my *s*; * 622 13
he is their *s* in time of trouble. 636 16
the God of Jacob is our *s*. 649 9
the God of Jacob is our *s*. 650 5
for you, O God, are my *s*. 666 15
For you have become my *s*, * 667 5
for you, O God, are my *s* and my merciful God. 667 8
my *s*, so that I shall not be greatly shaken. 669 8
my *s*, so that I shall not be shaken. 669 19
you are my crag and my *s*. 683 6
"You are my refuge and my *s*, * 719 13
But the LORD has become my *s*, * 724 9
My help and my fortress, my *s* and my deliverer, * 800 3

strongholds

they shall come trembling out of their *s*. 606 2
examine her *s*; * 652 2
and laid his *s* in ruins. 716 22

struck

True, he *s* the rock, the waters gushed out, 696 13
He *s* down all the firstborn of Egypt, * 699 7
He *s* his enemies on the backside * 700 11
He *s* down the firstborn of their land, * 740 25
It was he who *s* down the firstborn of Egypt, * 788 17
Who *s* down the firstborn of Egypt, * 790 15
Who *s* down great kings, * 791 3

struggle

and work through our *s* and confusion 815 17

struggles

in the midst of our *s* for justice and truth, 824 2

stubborn

a *s* and rebellious generation, * 695 17

stubbornness

So I gave them over to the *s* of their hearts, * 704 26

studied

they are *s* by all who delight in them. 754 9

study

Sanctify, O Lord, those whom you have called to the *s* 460 10
Will you be faithful in prayer, and in the *s* 518 4
Will you be diligent in the reading and *s* 532 4
As a deacon in the Church, you are to *s* 543 7
and *s* of the Holy Scriptures? 544 2
because I *s* your commandments. 767 4
for I *s* your commandments. 771 8
for your decrees are my *s*. 771 18
for they do not *s* your statutes. 776 14
prayer, and the *s* of God's ways. 847 27

stumble

they will *s* and perish at your presence. 593 6
in your paths my feet shall not *s*. 601 8
If they *s*, they shall not fall headlong, * 635 7
he will never let the righteous *s*. 662 7
and in thy straight path may not *s*; 832 11

stumbled

my adversaries, who *s* and fell. 617 13
But when I *s*, they were glad and gathered together; 630 23
in all their tribes there was not one that *s*. 740 28
they *s*, and there was none to help. 747 6

stumbling

Grant, we beseech thee, that we may run without *s* 184 3
Grant that we may run without *s* 235 16
and my feet from *s*, * 663 17
and my feet from *s*. 759 17
for them there is no *s* block. 777 10

stunned

both horse and rider lie *s*. 692 13

stupid

like the dull and *s* they perish * 652 24
I was *s* and had no understanding; * 688 21

subdue

I should soon *s* their enemies * 705 3

subdues

He *s* the peoples under us, * 650 10
who *s* the peoples under me. 800 5

subject

and become *s* to evil and death, 362 11

subjection

put all things in *s* under your Christ, 369 9

submission

by thy holy Nativity and *s* to the Law; 149 19

submit

S to the Lord with fear, * 586 24

substance

and *s* for the relief of the poor 189 20
and *s* for the relief of the poor 241 6
being of one *s* with the Father; 327 30
they may honor thee with their *s*, 329 24
was made very Man of the *s* of the Virgin Mary 345 16
in Trinity of Persons and in Unity of *s*; 347 14
that we may honor thee with our *s*, 827 3

succeeds

the one who *s* in evil schemes. 633 20

success

and were praised for their *s*, 653 20
Lord, send us now *s*. 762 22

successes

in his *s* and in his failures, 444 21

succor

because it cannot continue in safety without thy *s*, 180 10
to comfort and *s* [__________ and] all those who, 329 27
of whom may we seek for *s*, 484 5

Succoth

I will divide the valley of *S*. 667 22
I will divide the valley of *S*. 750 9

succulent

they shall be green and *s*; 721 26

such

for the Father seeketh *s* to worship him. 40 22
s blessing through our worship of thee, 56 3
for *s* the Father seeks to worship him. 78 20
s blessing through our worship of you, 98 21
And, we pray, give us *s* an awareness of your mercies, 101 16
And, we pray, give us *s* an awareness of your mercies, 125 14
bring into the way of truth all *s* as have erred, 150 19
That it may please thee to strengthen *s* as do stand; 152 11
prepared for those who love thee *s* good things 174 1
Pour into our hearts *s* love toward thee, 174 3
and do always *s* things as are right, 180 15
Mercifully grant unto us *s* a measure 182 13
Grant that we may in *s* wise hear them, 184 16
who didst give *s* grace to thine apostle Andrew 185 7
may never be destitute of *s* gifts; 197 16
prepared for those who love you *s* good things 225 14
Pour into our hearts *s* love towards you, 225 15
who gave *s* grace to your apostle Andrew 237 1
may never be destitute of *s* gifts; 249 2
all *s* good works as thou hast prepared for us 339 12
for with *s* sacrifices God is well pleased. 344 3
for *s* sacrifices are pleasing to God. 377 2
Give them *s* fulfillment of their mutual affection 429 23
and give me *s* a sense of your presence, 461 15
among *s* as keep holy-day. 471 11
S knowledge is too wonderful and excellent for me; * 475 3
give us *s* a lively sense of thy righteous will, 488 30
with *s* love of you and of all the people, 521 8
s things as may make you a stronger 532 6
S is the generation of those who seek him, * 613 25
S is the way of those who foolishly trust 653 6
s trembling as never was; * 659 11
S knowledge is too wonderful for me; * 794 10
that they may enact *s* laws as shall please thee, 821 5
we entreat thee, in this time of need, *s* moderate rain 828 12
a just sense of these great mercies, *s* as may appear 840 20

sudden

and their years in *s* terror. 697 17

suddenly

lest coming *s* he find you sleeping. 37 3
lest he come *s* and find you asleep. 75 3
and from dying *s* and unprepared, 149 15
and fade away *s* like the grass. 472 20
they shall turn back and *s* be put to shame. 590 19
Let death come upon them *s*; 661 14
and *s* they will be wounded. 671 25
Oh, how *s* do they come to destruction, * 688 15
we fade away *s* like the grass. 718 10

suffer

who *s* in mind, body, and spirit; 151 25
and to *s* death upon the cross, 168 3
s shame and loss for the sake of thy Son 168 20
and to *s* death upon the cross; 169 16
and patiently *s* for the truth's sake; 190 6
apostle James, first among the Twelve to *s* 191 8
to *s* gladly for the sake of the same our Lord 195 5
and to *s* death upon the cross, 219 15
s shame and loss for the sake of your Son 220 11
and to *s* death upon the cross; 221 10
s for the truth's sake; 241 16
and apostle James, first among the Twelve to *s* 242 15
and to *s* gladly for the sake of our Lord 247 3
and to *s* death upon the cross, 272 9
and to *s* death upon the cross; 276 6
Let us pray for all who *s* and are afflicted 279 3
the strength of all who *s*: 279 15
Christ to *s* death upon the cross for our redemption; 334 11
and to *s* death upon the cross 341 15
Have compassion on those who *s* from any grief 387 14
Comfort and heal all those who *s* 389 3
For the poor, the persecuted, the sick, and all who *s*; 390 24
He will not *s* thy foot to be moved, * 473 13
S us not, at our last hour, 484 16
For the poor, the persecuted, the sick, and all who *s*; 550 11
see the misery I *s* from those who hate me, 594 2
The young lions lack and *s* hunger, * 628 13
For they *s* no pain, * 687 7
s not our trust in thee to fail; 820 14
Strengthen those who *s* for the sake of conscience; 823 9
Father, we remember before you those who *s* 824 11
that no one may *s* from our abuse of them, 827 20

suffered

s under Pontius Pilate, 53 28
first he *s* pain, and entered not into glory 56 7
s under Pontius Pilate, 66 14
He *s* under Pontius Pilate, 96 18
first he *s* pain, and entered not into glory 99 2
He *s* under Pontius Pilate, 120 14
first he *s* pain, and entered not into glory 168 11

Son, on the night before he *s*, 169 8
first he *s* pain, and entered not into glory 220 2
Son, on the night before he *s*, 221 2
first he *s* pain, and entered not into glory 272 2
Son, on the night before he *s*, 274 2
for the sake of him who *s* for us, 279 18
He *s* under Pontius Pilate, 293 5
He *s* under Pontius Pilate, 304 8
Christ, on the night before he *s*, 316 2
he *s* death and was buried. 327 5
he *s* and was buried; 328 6
he *s* death and was buried. 358 21
Son, on the nilght before he *s*, 397 14
He *s* under Pontius Pilate, 416 13
He *s* under Pontius Pilate, 496 8
he *s* death and was buried. 519 24
he *s* death and was buried. 530 15
he *s* death and was buried. 542 15
Surely, for your sake have I *s* reproach, * 680 1
and the years in which we *s* adversity. 719 4

sufferers

and the comfort of *s*: 458 11

suffering

soothe the *s*, pity the afflicted, 71 4
long-*s*, and abounding in mercy. 91 6
soothe the *s*, pity the afflicted, 124 20
soothe the *s*, pity the afflicted, 134 9
N. triumphed over *s* and was faithful 195 9
minister in his name to the *s*, 209 13
that we may walk in the way of his *s*, 219 17
N. triumphed over *s* and was faithful 247 7
to the *s*, the friendless, and the needy; 260 19
for our blindness to human need and *s*, 268 17
that we may walk in the way of his *s*, 272 11
who by his *s* and death became the author 346 15
On the night he was handed over to *s* and death, 362 18
and, by his *s* and death, he became 379 12
for the sick and the *s*, 384 21
without *s* and without reproach, 385 8
On the night he was handed over to *s* and death, 405 1
Recalling now his *s* and death, 405 11
release you from *s*, 456 16
servant in his *s*, 459 8
Christ, by your patience in *s* you hallowed 461 5
grow closer to you through joy and through *s*. 569 4
while he was *s* shame and death: 823 9
For the brave and courageous, who are patient in *s* 837 14
What is the great importance of Jesus' *s* 850 5
By his obedience, even to *s* and death, Jesus 850 7
How can we share in his victory over sin, *s*, 850 22

sufferings

to take joyfully the *s* of the present time, 169 3
to accept joyfully the *s* of the present time, 220 16
giving them patience under their *s*, 815 11

sufficient

and *s* sacrifice, oblation, and satisfaction, 334 13

sufficiently

are *s* instructed in the Christian Faith, 860 24

suitability

You have been assured of his *s* 514 4

suitable

may choose *s* persons for the ministry 205 16
may choose *s* persons for the ministry 256 13
And do you believe his manner of life to be *s* 526 5
And do you believe his manner of life to be *s* 538 5
that all may find *s* and fulfilling employment, 824 14

sulphur

he shall rain coals of fire and burning *s*; * 596 22

sum

yet the *s* of them is but labor and sorrow, 718 21
how great is the *s* of them! 795 11

summary

Christ taught us the *S* of the Law 851 8
What is the *S* of the Law? 851 10

summed

found in the Scriptures and *s* up in the creeds. 851 21

summer

O ye winter and *s*, bless ye the Lord; * 48 7
thou hast made *s* and winter. 61 9
Winter and *s*, glorify the Lord, * 88 15
you made both *s* and winter. 115 9
my moisture was dried up as in the heat of *s*. 625 6
you made both *s* and winter. 690 19

summon

Weigh my heart, *s* me by night, * 601 3

sun

From the rising of the *s* even unto the going down 38 5
O ye *s* and moon, bless ye the Lord; * 48 1
thou hast established the moon and the *s*. 61 8
Now as we come to the setting of the *s*, 64 4
From the rising of the *s* to its setting 76 5
The *s* will no more be your light by day; * 87 27
S and moon and stars of the sky, glorify the Lord, * 88 11
So that the *s* shall not strike you by day, * 104 23
From the rising of the *s* to its setting 106 6
made the *s* to know its going down: 110 25
Now as we come to the setting of the *s*, 112 4
you established the moon and the *s*. 115 8
Now as we come to the setting of the *s*, 118 4
From the rising of the *s* to its going down * 138 5
Now as we come to the setting of the *s*, 139 4
So that the *s* shall not burn thee by day, * 473 19
The *S* of Righteousness is gloriously risen, 483 16
The *S* of Righteousness is gloriously risen, 500 5
In the deep has he set a pavilion for the *s*; * 606 23
he has called the earth from the rising of the *s* 654 2
like a stillborn child that never sees the *s*. 665 10
He shall live as long as the *s* and moon endure, * 685 17
and be established as long as the *s* endures; * 686 22
you established the moon and the *s*. 690 17
For the LORD God is both *s* and shield; * 708 14
and his throne as the *s* before me; 716 14
and the *s* knows the time of its setting. 736 16
The *s* rises, and they slip away * 736 21
From the rising of the *s* to its going down * 756 6
So that the *s* shall not strike you by day, * 779 11

The *s* to rule the day, * 790 11
Praise him, *s* and moon; * 805 25

sundry
that so, among the *s* and manifold changes 167 18

suns
galaxies, *s*, the planets in their courses, 370 9

supped
The Lord Jesus, after he had *s* with his disciples 274 8

supper
Likewise, after *s*, he took the cup; 335 3
Likewise, after *s*, he took the cup; 342 5
After *s* he took the cup of wine; 363 1
After *s* he took the cup of wine; 368 14
After *s*, he took the cup of wine, 371 14
at *s* with them he took bread, 374 15
After *s* he took the cup of wine; 374 19
After *s*, he took the cup of wine, 403 8
After *s* he took the cup of wine; 405 6
The Holy Eucharist is called the Lord's *S*, 859 15
which we receive in the Lord's *S*? 859 28

supplication
accord to make our common *s* unto thee, 59 13
accord to make our common *s* unto thee, 72 10
accord to make our common *s* to you; 102 2
accord to make our common *s* to you; 126 2
because he has heard the voice of my *s*,* 442 14
The LORD has heard my *s*; * 590 16
because he has heard the voice of my *s*, * 759 2
Let my *s* come before you; * 777 19
let your ears consider well the voice of my *s*. 784 20
listen, O LORD, to my *s*. 796 14
to the LORD I make loud *s*. 798 2
the spirit of grace and of *s*: 833 20

supplications
Receive our *s* and prayers which we offer 57 21
Receive our *s* and prayers which we offer 100 13
made our prayers and *s* unto thee; 153 22
Mercifully hear the *s* of thy people, 164 2
Receive our *s* and prayers, 206 3
Mercifully hear the *s* of your people, 215 14
Receive our *s* and prayers, 256 21
Receive our *s* and prayers 278 13
taught us to make prayers, and *s*, 329 2
and attend to the voice of my *s*. 710 10
and in your faithfulness heed my *s*; * 798 19
Assist us mercifully, O Lord, in these our *s* 832 18
made our prayers and *s* unto thee; 834 4

supplied
who are well *s* with children 602 2

supply
and destroyed the *s* of bread. 739 10

support
That it may please thee to *s*, help, and comfort 151 28
s these persons in their life in Christ? 303 15
s these persons in their life in Christ? 416 2
pledge you our prayers, encouragement, and *s*. 420 6
S him in his successes and in his failures, 444 20
s all baptized people in their gifts 518 13
Will you who witness this new beginning *s* 559 8
but the LORD was my *s*. 603 29
O Lord, *s* us all the day long, 833 14

supported
we may ever be *s* by this fellowship 199 6
we may always be *s* by this fellowship 250 16
we may always be *s* by this fellowship 395 19
to be *s* and strengthened, 568 17

supreme
For the Congress and the *S* Court 278 20

sure
Be ye *s* that the Lord he is God; 45 14
For the Lord is my stronghold and my *s* defense, * 86 3
and make my appeal, *s* of your gracious goodness. 91 13
so we may with *s* confidence behold him 160 14
whom thou hast set upon the *s* foundation 178 14
with *s* and certain faith in thy Son's resurrection: 185 15
may with *s* confidence behold him 212 12
whom you have set upon the *s* foundation 230 9
Grant to all who mourn a *s* confidence 481 7
In *s* and certain hope of the resurrection 485 9
In *s* and certain hope of the resurrection 501 11
He makes me *s*-footed like a deer * 605 5
the testimony of the LORD is *s* 607 6
and all his works are *s*. 626 8
set my feet upon a high cliff and made my footing *s*. 640 4
he is known to be her *s* refuge. 651 7
He has made the whole world so *s* * 722 5
Your testimonies are very *s*, * 722 15
all his commandments are *s*. 754 19
given by Christ as *s* and certain means 857 27

surely
that we, *s* trusting in thy defense, 57 4
If I say, "*S* the darkness will cover me, 62 5
S, it is God who saves me; * 86 1
we, *s* trusting in your defense, may not fear 99 23
If I say, "*S* the darkness will cover me, 110 7
If I say, "*S* the darkness will cover me, 116 1
our hearts may *s* there be fixed 167 19
our hearts may *s* there be fixed 219 10
S your goodness and mercy shall follow me 443 15
S thy loving-kindness and mercy shall follow me 476 16
S goodness and mercy shall follow me 477 9
s, you will strike all my enemies across the face, 587 16
S, you behold trouble and misery; * 595 23
S your goodness and mercy shall follow me 613 11
for *s* it was you that did it. 639 14
S, you gave us victory over our adversaries * 645 25
"*S*, there is a reward for the righteous; * 665 16
s, there is a God who rules in the earth." 665 17
S, for your sake have I suffered reproach, * 680 1
S, you set them in slippery places; * 688 13
I will *s* bless her provisions, * 787 1
If I say, "*S* the darkness will cover me, * 794 20
S, the righteous will give thanks to your Name, * 797 1
and more *s* fulfill our role 827 15

surety

Be *s* for your servant's good; * 773 17

surface

pours them out upon the *s* of the earth: 115 16

surgeons

through the skill of surgeons and nurses, 459 14

surging

and still the *s* of its waves. 714 12

surpass

such good things as *s* our understanding: 225 15

surpasses

it *s* all that our minds can fathom. 91 4

surpassing

s human understanding. 94 11

surround

May angels *s* him, and saints welcome him in peace. 466 5
S them with your love, 494 9
from my deadly enemies who *s* me. 601 17
now they *s* me, * 601 21
strong bulls of Bashan *s* me. 611 2
you *s* me with shouts of deliverance. 625 16
They *s* me all day long like a flood; * 713 13
Let not those who *s* me lift up their heads; * 796 19
s them with your loving care; 831 3

surrounded

to be *s* by their witness to thy power and mercy. 199 8
Almighty God, you have *s* us with a great cloud 250 1
and know ourselves to be *s* by their witness 250 17
For in the multitude of your saints you have *s* us 380 12
s by their witness to your power and mercy. 395 21

surrounding

Almighty God, we give you thanks for *s* us, 110 12

surrounds

when the wickedness of those at my heels *s* me, 652 14
the loving care which *s* us on every side. 836 6

suspicions

s disappear, and hatreds cease; 823 20

sustain

And *s* us with thy Holy Spirit. 55 14
And *s* us with thy Holy Spirit. 68 6
And *s* us with your Holy Spirit. 98 8
And *s* us with your Holy Spirit. 122 8
and *s* me with your bountiful Spirit. 137 8
and *s* me with your bountiful Spirit. 266 27
S them, O Lord, in your Holy Spirit. 308 5
and *s* him all the days of his life. 309 13
and *s* him all the days of his life. 418 11
Christ to *s* you with his presence, 456 3
s me by your grace, 461 8
will you *s* your fellow presbyters 518 23
Everliving God, strengthen and *s* N., 560 6
the LORD will *s* me. 618 20
and *s* me with your bountiful Spirit. 657 6
and he will *s* you; * 662 6
and the Most High himself shall *s* her." 711 21
S me according to your promise, that I may live, * 773 5
all things necessary to *s* their life: 828 11
give us food to *s* our lives and make our hearts glad; 835 14
Sacraments *s* our present hope 861 22

sustained

That by the indwelling of the Holy Spirit he may be *s* 549 8
so that our lives are *s* and sanctified 569 1
I have been *s* by you ever since I was born; 683 11
and have not *s* him in battle. 716 28

sustains

O God, your unfailing providence *s* the world 134 11
I wake again, because the LORD *s* me. 587 12
your right hand also *s* me; 605 10
The LORD *s* them on their sickbed * 642 4
it is the Lord who *s* my life. 659 25
he *s* the orphan and widow, 803 22
It *s* our life, though we have been faithless 839 13
a single loving God who creates, *s*, and directs it. 846 8

swallow

You will *s* them up in your wrath, * 609 16
S them up, O LORD; 660 23
neither let the deep *s* me up; * 680 21
and the *s* a nest where she may lay her young; * 707 20

swallowed

the earth *s* them up. 85 20
Do not let them say, "We have *s* him up." 631 23
The earth opened and *s* Dathan * 743 5
Then would they have *s* us up alive * 781 5

sware

Unto whom I *s* in my wrath, * 146 24

swarm

They *s* about me like bees; 761 19

swarms

He sent *s* of flies among them, which ate them up, * 698 17
He spoke, and there came *s* of insects * 740 15

sway

The scepter of the wicked shall not hold *s* 781 22

swear

all those who *s* by him will be glad; * 671 8

sweat

By thine Agony and Bloody *S*; 149 22

sweep

Do not *s* me away with sinners, * 616 24
You *s* us away like a dream; * 718 9

sweet

We took *s* counsel together, * 661 12
How *s* are your words to my taste! * 771 25

sweeter

s far than honey, 607 18
they are *s* than honey to my mouth. 771 26

swell

Though the waters thereof rage and *s*, * 471 21

swept
like thorns and thistles let them be *s* away. 665 12
Your blazing anger has *s* over me; * 713 11
But *s* Pharaoh and his army into the Red Sea, * 790 25

swerved
yet I have not *s* from your decrees. 776 18

swift
among the *s* and varied changes of the world, 219 9
be *s* and answer me, for I am in distress. 680 26
let your compassion be *s* to meet us; * 701 22

swiftly
and his word runs very *s*. 805 8

swooped
he *s* on the wings of the wind. 603 10

sword
If they will not repent, God will whet his *s*; * 591 22
deliver me from the wicked by your *s*. 601 26
Save me from the *s*, * 611 20
Draw the *s* and bar the way 629 17
The wicked draw their *s* and bend their bow 634 11
Their *s* shall go through their own heart, * 634 14
For they did not take the land by their *s*, 645 13
and my *s* does not give me the victory. 645 24
Strap your *s* upon your thigh, O mighty warrior, * 647 17
their tongue a sharp *s*. 664 3
Let them fall upon the edge of the *s*, * 671 5
They sharpen their tongue like a *s*, * 671 14
the shield, the *s*, and the weapons of battle. 692 6
He gave his people to the *s* * 700 3
Their priests fell by the *s*, * 700 7
You have turned back the edge of his *s* * 716 27
Rescue me from the hurtful *s* * 800 23
and a two-edged *s* in their hand; 807 13
in whose perfect kingdom no *s* is drawn 815 22
but the *s* of righteousness, 815 23

swords
but they are drawn *s*. 662 4

swore
the oath which he *s* to our forefather Abraham, * 51 5
This was the oath he *s* to our father Abraham, * 92 27
So I *s* in my wrath, * 725 15
the oath that he *s* to Isaac, 738 18
How he *s* an oath to the LORD * 786 1

sworn
I have *s* and am determined * 103 8
He has *s* to do no wrong * 599 13
nor *s* by what is a fraud. 613 22
I have *s* an oath to David my servant: 713 22
Once for all I have *s* by my holiness: * 716 11
The LORD has *s* and he will not recant: * 753 19
I have *s* and am determined * 772 5
The LORD has *s* an oath to David; * 786 19

sycamores
and their *s* with frost. 698 22

symbol
I give you this ring as a *s* of my vow, 427 13
these visible buildings are the *s*, 578 8

sympathy
I looked for *s*, but there was none, 681 4

T

tabernacle
Behold, the *t* of God is with men, 37 11
the holy place of the *t* of the Most Highest. 471 24
For in the time of trouble he shall hide me in his *t*; * 477 20
LORD, who may dwell in your *t*? * 599 4
At Salem is his *t*, * 692 3
the *t* where he had lived among his people. 699 27

table
We do not presume to come to this thy *T*, 337 9
gather up the crumbs under thy *T*. 337 12
the presumption of coming to this *T* for solace 372 4
Finally, in your mercy, bring them to that *t* 430 22
You spread a *t* before me in the presence 443 11
Thou shalt prepare a *t* before me in the presence 476 12
Thou preparest a *t* before me in the presence 477 5
grant him a place at the *t* in your heavenly kingdom. 497 20
Sanctify this *T* dedicated to you. 574 1
Grant that all who eat and drink at this holy *T* 574 5
You spread a *t* before me in the presence 613 7
Let the *t* before them be a trap * 681 8
"Can God set a *t* in the wilderness? 696 12
your children like olive shoots round about your *t*. 783 18

Tabor
T and Hermon rejoice in your Name. 714 18

take
and *t* up his cross, and follow me." 38 25
who by thy death didst *t* away the sting of death: 69 7
and *t* up his cross and follow me." 76 24
you *t* away the sin of the world: 95 5
T me out of the net that they have secretly set 129 16
T my yoke upon you, and learn from me; 131 16
and *t* not your holy Spirit from me. 137 6
t our nature upon him and as at this time to be born 161 8
to *t* upon him our flesh, and to suffer death 168 3
to *t* joyfully the sufferings of the present time, 169 3
may have grace to *t* up our cross and follow him; 192 16
to *t* up our cross and follow him; 201 9
t counsel for the nations of the earth, 207 10
t our nature upon him, and to be born 213 2
t upon him our nature, and to suffer death 219 15
may have grace to *t* up our cross and follow him; 244 4
to *t* up our cross and follow him; 252 14
and guide with your wisdom those who *t* counsel 258 9
and *t* not your holy Spirit from me. 266 25
but you *t* no delight in burnt-offerings. 267 9
to *t* upon him our nature, 272 8
and guide with your wisdom those who *t* counsel 278 26
shalt not *t* the Name of the Lord thy God in vain. 318 7
"*T*, eat, this is my Body, 335 1
T them in remembrance that Christ died 338 2

T and eat this in remembrance that 338 6
to *t* our nature upon him, and to suffer death 341 15
"*T*, eat, this is my Body, 342 3
you *t* away the sin of the world: 356 9
"*T*, eat: This is my Body, 362 20
T them in remembrance that Christ died for 365 1
"*T*, eat: This is my Body, 368 12
"*T*, eat: This is my Body, 371 12
"*T*, eat: This is my Body, 374 17
T them in remembrance that Christ died 399 2
"*T*, eat: This is my Body, 403 6
"*T*, eat: This is my Body, 405 4
Lamb of God, you *t* away the sins of the world: 407 1
Lamb of God, you *t* away the sins of the world: 407 3
In the Name of God, I, N., *t* you, N., to be my wife, 427 1
In the Name of God, I, N., *t* you, N., to be my (wife) (husband), 436 1
I, N., *t* thee N., to be my wedded (wife) (husband), 436 6
do you *t* this child for your own? 440 17
do you *t* this woman as your mother? 441 1
Do you *t* this man as your father? 441 3
O God, whose beloved Son did *t* little children 470 7
If I *t* the wings of the morning, * 475 9
immaculate Lamb that was slain to *t* away the sins 488 16
your fellow presbyters and *t* counsel with them; 518 24
and to *t* your share in the councils of the Church. 531 6
t this water, and help me (help the bishop) baptize 561 3
t this bread and wine, and be among us to break 562 5
who *t* refuge in him! 587 2
But all who *t* refuge in you will be glad; * 589 17
O Lord my God, I *t* refuge in you; * 590 20
you see it and *t* it into your own hand. 595 24
and does not *t* back his word. 599 14
nor does he *t* a bribe against the innocent. 599 16
Protect me, O God, for I *t* refuge in you; * 599 19
nor *t* the names of their gods upon my lips. 600 6
O Savior of those who *t* refuge at your right hand 601 12
T me out of the net that they have secretly set 622 15
They plot to *t* my life. 623 19
Be strong and let your heart *t* courage, * 624 21
T up shield and armor * 629 15
without a cause they have dug a pit to *t* me alive. 630 4
your people *t* refuge under the 632 18
T delight in the Lord, * 633 11
T your affliction from me; * 639 15
In a sacrifice and offering you *t* no pleasure * 640 16
who *t* pleasure in my misfortune. 641 13
For they did not *t* the land by their sword, 645 13
I will *t* no bull-calf from your stalls, * 654 21
and *t* my covenant upon your lips; 655 13
and *t* not your holy Spirit from me. 657 4
but you *t* no delight in burnt-offerings. 657 15
"This is the one who did not *t* God for a refuge, * 658 13
in the shadow of your wings will I *t* refuge 663 21
oh, *t* us back to you again. 667 11
I will *t* refuge under the cover of your wings. 668 20
in robbery *t* no empty pride; * 670 6
let those who *t* pleasure in my misfortune 682 15
and those who lie in wait for my life *t* counsel 683 21
for you shall *t* all nations for your own. 706 2
They *t* secret counsel against your people * 706 7
Who said, "Let us *t* for ourselves * 707 1
But I will not *t* my love from him, * 716 7
do not *t* me away in the midst of my days; * 732 25
you *t* away their breath, 737 12
and let another *t* his office. 751 13
T from me the way of lying; * 765 17
Do not *t* the word of truth out of my mouth, * 766 21
O Lord, I *t* great comfort. 767 18
If I *t* the wings of the morning * 794 16
your enemies *t* your Name in vain. 795 19
in you I *t* refuge; 797 20
t away the arrogance and hatred 815 15
be present with those who *t* counsel 818 2
t away all hatred and prejudice, 818 16
t failure, not as a measure of their worth, 829 18
Why did he *t* our human nature? 850 1
and to *t* their place in the life, 855 18

taken

Nor the hope of the poor be *t* away. 55 12
Nor the hope of the poor be *t* away. 68 4
Nor the hope of the poor be *t* away. 98 6
Nor the hope of the poor be *t* away. 122 6
In you, O Lord, have I *t* refuge; 129 8
O God, who hast *t* to thyself the blessed Virgin Mary, 192 1
O God, you have *t* to yourself the blessed Virgin 243 8
t away the sin of the world; 346 20
t away the sin of the world. 379 16
you have *t* N. to be your wife. 433 5
you have *t* N. to be your husband. 433 10
t away the sin of the world. 483 19
t away the sin of the world. 500 8
In the Lord have I *t* refuge; * 596 7
In you, O Lord, have I *t* refuge; 622 7
he has *t* to his bed and will never get up again." 642 16
for I have *t* refuge in you; * 663 20
In you, O Lord, have I *t* refuge; * 683 1
and those who scoff at me have *t* an oath against me. 731 16
I have *t* greater delight in the way of your decrees * 764 11

takes

For you are not a God who *t* pleasure in wickedness, * 588 23
God *t* his stand in the council of heaven; * 705 9
the God of Jacob *t* no notice." 723 8
He *t* up the weak out of the dust * 756 12
Happy shall he be who *t* your little ones, * 792 22
For the Lord *t* pleasure in his people * 807 8

takest

that *t* away the sins of the world, 52 12
Thou that *t* away the sins of the world, 52 14
O Lamb of God, that *t* away the sins of the world, 152 24
that *t* away the sins of the world, 324 23
Thou that *t* away the sins of the world, 325 1
O Lamb of God, that *t* away the sins of the world, 337 3

tale

our years to an end, as it were a *t* that is told. 473 2
One day tells its *t* to another, * 606 17

talents

offering to you their gifts and *t*; 560 9
women from different cultures and with differing *t* 825 13
and to use our *t* and possessions 848 14

talked

My heart hath *t* of thee, Seek ye my face. * 478 1

talking

And my tongue shall be *t* of your righteousness * 632 1
For my enemies are *t* against me, * 683 20

tarry

O *t* thou the LORD's leisure; * 478 8
O *t* and await the LORD's pleasure; 619 1
do not *t*, O my God. 641 22
O LORD, do not *t*. 682 25
Return, O LORD; how long will you *t*? * 718 27
I hasten and do not *t* * 768 7

Tarshish

The kings of *T* and of the isles shall pay tribute, * 686 3

task

As a priest, it will be your *t* to proclaim 531 8

tasks

We thank you for setting us at *t* which demand 836 7

taste

and *t* the blessedness of perfect rest. 466 1
T and see that the LORD is good; * 628 9
How sweet are your words to my *t*! * 771 25

taught

as you have *t* us to call the evening, 110 23
who has *t* us that all our doings 164 18
who hast *t* us to keep all thy commandments 179 4
by following the holy doctrine which he *t*; 187 13
to love what he believed and to preach what he *t*; 192 10
you have *t* us that without love 216 13
who on this day *t* the hearts of your faithful people 227 8
you have *t* us to keep all your commandments 230 19
love what he believed and preach what he *t*; 243 17
in thy holy Word hast *t* us to make prayers, 329 2
And now, as our Savior Christ hath *t* us, 336 16
And now, as our Savior Christ hath *t* us, 343 6
Christ has *t* us, 363 23
Christ has *t* us, 369 19
Christ has *t* us, 372 15
and through the prophets you *t* us to hope 373 25
Christ has *t* us, 376 2
Let us pray in the words our Savior Christ has *t* us. 398 11
Let us pray together in the words our Savior *t* us. 428 7
O God, you have *t* us through your blessed Son 443 21
O God, you have *t* me since I was young, * 684 14
because you yourself have *t* me. 771 24
who hast *t* us in thy holy Word 831 11
who hast *t* us that in returning 832 13
What are the commandments *t* by Christ? 851 7
Christ *t* us the Summary of the Law 851 8
How do we recognize the truths *t* by the Holy Spirit? 853 1
We recognize truths to be *t* by the Holy Spirit 853 3

taunt

and do not make me the *t* of the fool. 639 12
Then shall I have a word for those who *t* me, * 766 19

taunted

For had it been an adversary who *t* me, 661 6

taunts

Because of the *t* of the mockers and blasphemers, * 646 17
and *t* are on their lips; * 666 10
how I carry in my bosom the *t* of many peoples, 717 15
The *t* your enemies have hurled, O LORD, * 717 16

teach

and *t* me your judgments. 104 4
this day didst *t* the hearts of thy faithful people 175 15
grace to understand and *t* the truth 197 20
Holy Spirit those who *t* and those who learn, 209 18
grace to understand and *t* the truth 249 6
Holy Spirit those who *t* and those who learn, 261 2
I shall *t* your ways to the wicked, * 267 1
T them to love others in the power of the Spirit. 305 24
lighting upon the disciples, to *t* them and to lead 347 8
preach the Gospel and to *t* all nations; 348 13
lighting upon the disciples, to *t* them and to lead 380 3
preach the Gospel and to *t* all nations; 381 7
So *t* us to number our days, * 473 7
and *t* me your paths. 614 20
Lead me in your truth and *t* me, * 614 21
he will *t* them the way that they should choose. 615 13
"I will instruct you and *t* you in the way that you 625 17
I will *t* you the fear of the LORD. 628 16
I shall *t* your ways to the wicked, * 657 7
which he commanded them to *t* their children; 695 9
T me your way, O LORD, 710 21
So *t* us to number our days * 718 25
whom you *t* out of your law; 723 18
and to *t* his elders wisdom. 739 22
T me, O LORD, the way of your statutes, * 766 1
T me discernment and knowledge, * 768 19
and *t* me your judgments. 772 10
and *t* me your statutes. 773 22
and *t* me your statutes. 774 18
when you *t* me your statutes. 777 22
and my testimonies that I shall *t* them, * 786 24
T me to do what pleases you, for you are my God; * 799 21
T us in all things to seek first your honor and glory. 818 4
And finally, *t* our people to rely on your strength 822 10
and grant that those who *t* and those who learn 824 19
forgive us, and *t* us to improve our justice. 826 21
that we may *t* them to love whatever is just 829 11
What prayer did Christ *t* us? 856 23

teacher

work as a pastor, priest, and *t*, 531 5
Make him a faithful pastor, a patient *t*, 534 5

teachers

some pastors and *t*, to equip the saints 533 8
prophets, pastors, and *t*. Purify the lives and the lips 571 10
I have more understanding than all my *t*, * 771 17

teaches

my heart *t* me, night after night. 115 10
my heart *t* me, night after night. 600 12
therefore he *t* sinners in his way. 615 5
and *t* his way to the lowly. 615 7
he who *t* all the world, has he no knowledge? 723 14

teacheth

my heart *t* me, night after night. 61 11

teaching

the *t* of thine apostle and evangelist John, 186 8
instructed by their *t* and example, 190 12
and the *t* of his holy life, we may by thy grace grow 196 25
we beseech thee, that by this *t* we may know thee, 197 21
joined together in unity of spirit by their *t*, 230 15
thankful to you by following his holy *t*; 239 3
Make us so to follow his *t* and holy life, 241 13
instructed by their *t* and example, 241 21
and the *t* of his holy life, we may by your grace grow 248 11
Grant that by this *t* we may know you, 249 7
Will you continue in the apostles' *t* 293 19
Will you continue in the apostles' *t* 304 22
Will you continue in the apostles' *t* 417 4
At all times, your life and *t* are to show 543 16
Let his life and *t* so reflect your commandments, 545 13
by my life and *t* set forth your true and living Word. 563 3
Hear my *t*, O my people; * 694 19
the coming of the Spirit through the *t* of your Son 819 2
continues in the *t* and fellowship of the apostles 854 26

teachings

illumined by the *t* of your apostle and evangelist 238 2
in accordance with the *t* of Christ, 532 21
in accordance with the *t* of Christ, 544 9
to set forth the life and *t* of Jesus 853 16

tear

Lest like a lion they *t* me in pieces * 590 22

tears

Those who sowed with *t* * 105 14
where all *t* are wiped away 290 5
My *t* have been my meat day and night, * 471 5
mine eyes from *t*, and my feet from falling. 479 15
and dry the *t* of those who weep. 497 4
and flood my couch with *t*. 590 11
hold not your peace at my *t*. 639 22
My *t* have been my food day and night, * 643 5
put my *t* into your bottle; * 663 7
You have fed them with the bread of *t*; * 702 21
you have given them bowls of *t* to drink. 702 22
my eyes from *t*, and my feet from stumbling. 759 17
My eyes shed streams of *t*, * 774 19
Those who sowed with *t* * 782 16

teeth

you will break the *t* of the wicked. 587 17
they gnashed at me with their *t*. 630 28
and gnash at them with their *t*. 634 8
their *t* are spears and arrows, 664 2
O God, break their *t* in their mouths; * 665 5
they will gnash their *t* and pine away; * 755 26
he has not given us over to be a prey for their *t*. 781 12

tell

t the people what things he hath done. 40 7
The Scriptures *t* us that our Savior Christ spent 514 12
I will *t* of all your marvelous works. 593 2
So that I may *t* of all your praises 594 4
Who can *t* how often he offends? * 607 22
we heap up riches and cannot *t* who will gather them. 639 8
Oh, that I could make them known and *t* them! * 640 14
that you may *t* those who come after. 652 3
If I were hungry, I would not *t* you, * 655 3
and I will *t* you what he has done for me. 674 28
and to this day I *t* of your wonderful works. 684 15
that they in their turn might *t* it to their children; 695 12
To *t* of your loving-kindness early in the morning * 720 24
T it out among the nations: "The LORD is King! * 726 11
and those who *t* lies shall not continue in my sight. 730 25
and *t* of his acts with shouts of joy. 747 26
I will *t* of your decrees before kings * 767 5
and *t* him all my trouble. 798 4
and I will *t* of your greatness. 801 23

tells

One day *t* its tale to another, * 606 17

temperance

Fill them with faith, virtue, knowledge, *t*, 829 2

tempest

From lightning and *t*; 149 11
and though the mountains shake at the *t* of the same. 471 22
from the stormy wind and *t*." 660 22
Drive them with your *t* * 707 7

tempestuous

t wind, doing his will; 806 10

temple

The Lord is in his holy *t*; 40 18
Blessed art thou in the *t* of thy holiness; * 49 13
The Lord is in his holy *t*; 78 17
Glory to you in the splendor of your *t*; * 90 9
that we may be made an holy *t* acceptable unto thee; 179 1
Son was this day presented in the *t*, 187 18
that we may be made a holy *t* acceptable to you; 230 16
Son was this day presented in the *t*, 239 7
built up as living stones of a holy *t*, 348 16
built up as living stones of a holy *t*, 381 10
behold the fair beauty of the LORD, and to visit his *t*. 477 19
never leaving your *t* untended. 520 17
Christ, and the *t* of the Holy Spirit. 531 2
Christ, make this a *t* of your presence 568 14
I will bow down toward your holy *t* in awe of you. 589 5
The LORD is in his holy *t*; * 596 15
and to seek him in his *t*. 617 23
And in the *t* of the LORD * 620 23
in the midst of your *t*. 651 19
by the holiness of your *t*. 672 16
for your *t*'s sake at Jerusalem. 678 17
they have profaned your holy *t*; * 701 2
I will bow down toward your holy *t* 793 3
Praise God in his holy *t*; * 807 22

temples

much less the walls of *t* made with hands. 578 4

temporal

may so pass through things *t*, 180 4
may so pass through things *t*, 231 20

temptation
And lead us not into *t*, 54 22
And lead us not into *t*, 67 12
And lead us not into *t*, 97 13
And lead us not into *t*, 106 23
And lead us not into *t*, 121 13
And lead us not into *t*, 133 5
and as in the day of *t* in the wilderness; 146 18
by thy Baptism, Fasting, and *T*, 149 20
And lead us not into *t*, 153 14
For those who face *t*, doubt, and despair 279 8
And lead us not into *t*, 311 10
And lead us not into *t*, 336 26
And lead us not into *t*, 364 10
And lead us not into *t*, 398 21
And lead us not into *t*, 428 17
And lead us not into *t*, 464 13
And lead us not into *t*, 486 3
And lead us not into *t*, 502 10
obedience, by which he overcame *t*; 836 14

temptations
servants who are assaulted by manifold *t*; 166 11
help us who are asssaulted by many *t*; 218 3
preserve him from the *t* of the enemy; 458 5
strengthen them in their trials and *t*; 823 4
To resist *t* to envy, greed, and jealousy; 848 18

tempted
When your fathers *t* me, * 146 19
Son was led by the Spirit to be *t* of Satan: 166 10
Son was led by the Spirit to be *t* by Satan: 218 2
t as we are, yet did not sin; 346 5
Through Jesus Christ our Lord, who was *t* 379 1
Again and again they *t* God * 698 9
that day at Massah, when they *t* me. 725 9

ten
and *t* thousand at your right hand, * 130 11
The days of our age are threescore years and *t*; 473 3
and *t* thousand at your right hand, * 719 25
I will play to you on a *t*-stringed lyre. 800 20
God's will for us is shown most clearly in the *T* 847 11
What are the *T* Commandments? 847 13
The *T* Commandments are the laws given to Moses 847 14
What is the purpose of the *T* Commandments? 848 22
The *T* Commandments were given to define 848 23

tend
T the sick, Lord Christ; 71 3
T the sick, Lord Christ; 124 19
T the sick, Lord Christ; 134 8
he may feed and *t* the flock of Christ, 521 9
behold and *t* this vine; * 703 16

tender
Through the *t* mercy of our God, * 51 16
thy *t* mercies' sake. 69 11
In the *t* compassion of our God * 93 5
for your *t* mercies' sake. 107 10
for your *t* mercies' sake. 123 10
God, who, of thy *t* love towards mankind, 168 1
God, in your *t* love for the human race 219 13
God, in your *t* love for the human race 272 7
that thou, of thy *t* mercy, didst give thine only Son 334 10
and, of thy *t* mercy, didst give thine only Son 341 14
gracious God, we give you thanks for your *t* love 430 10
for your *t* mercies' sake. 504 25
and all occasions invite your *t* mercies: 572 10
for your *t* mercy's sake, deliver me. 752 18

tendrils
You stretched out its *t* to the Sea * 703 9

tens
pastures increase by thousands and *t* of thousands; 801 6

tent
He rejected the *t* of Joseph * 700 13

tents
and let there be none to dwell in their *t*. 681 15
he made the tribes of Israel to dwell in their *t*. 699 17
The *t* of Edom and the Ishmaelites; * 706 14
than to dwell in the *t* of the wicked. 708 13
They grumbled in their *t* * 743 22
in the *t* of the righteous: 761 27
and dwell among the *t* of Kedar! 778 19

terrible
great and *t* to all those round about him. 714 8

terrified
Let them be disgraced and *t* for ever; * 707 11
You hide your face, and they are *t*; * 737 11

terrify
and *t* them with your storm; 707 8

terror
You shall not be afraid of any *t* by night, * 130 6
and his rage fills them with *t*. 586 11
My spirit shakes with *t*; * 590 3
so that mere mortals may strike *t* no more. 596 6
and delivered me out of all my *t*. 628 2
they retreated and fled in *t*. 651 11
come to an end, and perish from *t*! 688 16
What *t* you inspire! * 692 14
and strikes *t* in the kings of the earth. 692 26
and their years in sudden *t*. 697 17
You shall not be afraid of any *t* by night, * 719 20
who live with injustice, *t*, disease, and death 826 9

terrors
and the *t* of death have fallen upon me. 660 14
I have borne your *t* with a troubled mind. 713 10
your *t* have destroyed me; 713 12

test
for you *t* the mind and heart, O righteous God. 591 17
T me, O Lord, and try me; * 616 10
They put me to the *t* and mocked me; * 630 27
They put me to the *t*, * 725 10
and they put God to the *t* in the desert. 742 27

Testament
for this is my Blood of the New *T*, 335 5
the books which we call the Old *T*. 847 8
Where in the Old *T* is God's will for us shown 847 9

What is the Old *T*? 853 9
The Old *T* consists of books written 853 10
What is the New *T*? 853 13
The New *T* consists of books written 853 14

Testaments

the Old and New *T* to be the Word of God, 513 10
the Old and New *T* to be the Word of God, 526 15
the Old and New *T* to be the Word of God, 538 15
the books of the Old and New *T*; 853 7

tested

They *t* God in their hearts, * 696 9
But they *t* the Most High God, and defied him, * 699 18
and *t* you at the waters of Meribah. 704 16
the word of the LORD *t* him. 739 16
Your word has been *t* to the uttermost, * 775 5

testify

and to *t* to Christ's sovereignty as Lord of lords 517 5

testimonies

to those who keep his covenant and his *t*. 615 9
Your *t* are very sure, * 722 15
they kept his *t* and the decree that he gave them. 729 15
and my *t* that I shall teach them, * 786 24

testimony

having the *t* of a good conscience; 489 8
having the *t* of a good conscience, 504 6
you have heard *t* given 514 1
the *t* of the LORD is sure 607 6

thank

We *t* thee for the timely blessings of the day, 70 6
t you for the blessings of the day that is past, 124 3
We *t* thee, heavenly Father, for that thou hast delivered 172 14
We *t* thee for this witness, and pray 189 1
We *t* thee, heavenly Father, for the witness 192 19
O God, we *t* thee for the glorious company 194 1
God, we *t* thee for thy servant 196 7
We *t* you, heavenly Father, that you have delivered 224 7
We *t* you for this witness, and pray 240 9
We *t* you, heavenly Father, for the witness 244 7
O God, we *t* you for the glorious company 245 10
God, we *t* you for your servant 247 19
Shepherd of your people, we *t* you for your servant 248 8
We *t* you, Almighty God, for the gift of water. 306 13
We *t* you, Father, for the water of Baptism. 306 20
Heavenly Father, we *t* you that by water 308 2
Almighty God, we *t* you that by the death 309 3
Heavenly Father, we *t* you that by water 314 1
we most heartily *t* thee for that thou dost feed us, 339 2
we *t* you for feeding us with the spiritual food 366 2
We *t* you, Lord, for all the blessings of this life. 393 1
Almighty God, we *t* you that by the death 418 1
We *t* you, also, for consecrating the union 430 13
for I will yet *t* him, which is the help 471 15
Almighty God, we *t* thee that in thy great love 482 1
We *t* you for giving him to us, 493 17
Almighty God, we *t* you that in your great love 498 12
Almighty Father, we *t* you for feeding us 523 1
We *t* you for raising up among us faithful servants 523 3
We *t* you that by his death he has overcome 533 5
Almighty Father, we *t* you for feeding us 535 1
We *t* you for raising up among us faithful servants 535 3
Almighty Father, we *t* you for feeding us 546 3
We *t* you for raising up among us faithful servants 546 5
Almighty Father, we *t* you for feeding us 564 1
We *t* you for raising up among us faithful servants 564 3
Almighty God, we *t* you for making us in your image, 567 8
Father, we *t* you that through the waters of Baptism 569 15
We *t* you, Almighty God, for the gift of water. 570 5
We *t* you, Father, for the water of Baptism. 570 12
Let us *t* God whom we worship here in the beauty 578 1
We *t* you, Lord. 578 9
I will present to you *t*-offerings; 663 15
I will *t* you, O LORD my God, with all my heart, * 710 24
"You are my God, and I will *t* you; * 763 1
I will *t* you with an unfeigned heart, * 763 17
I will *t* you because I am marvelously made; * 795 1
Almighty God, we *t* you for making the earth fruitful, 824 6
We *t* you for the splendor of the whole 836 2
We *t* you for the blessing of family and friends, 836 5
We *t* you for setting us at tasks which demand 836 7
We *t* you also for those disappointments and failures 836 10
Above all, we *t* you for your Son Jesus Christ; 836 12
We *t* you, Lord. 837 5
We *t* you that in all parts 838 4
We *t* you for the natural majesty and beauty 838 22
We *t* you for the great resources of this nation. 839 1
We *t* you for the men and women who have made 839 4
We *t* you for the torch of liberty which has been lit 839 8
We *t* you for the faith we have inherited 839 12
we *t* you for the wonderful diversity of races 840 1
t you for the life of this child, 841 2

thankful

be *t* unto him and speak good of his Name. 45 19
that our hearts may be unfeignedly *t*; 59 3
that our hearts may be unfeignedly *t*; 71 22
that with truly *t* hearts we may show forth 101 17
that with truly *t* hearts we may show forth 125 15
ever *t* for thy loving providence; 208 11
show ourselves *t* to you by following 239 2
Make us always *t* for your loving providence; 259 12
Christ's Blood was shed for thee, and be *t*. 338 12
restored to usefulness in your world with a *t* heart; 459 15
but in *t* remembrance of your great goodness, 505 13

thankfully

Mercifully grant that we may *t* receive the same 169 9
Give us grace that we may always most *t* receive 180 21
Mercifully grant that we may receive it *t* 221 3
grace to receive *t* the fruits of his redeeming work, 232 13
Mercifully grant that we may receive it *t* 274 3
Mercifully grant that we may receive it *t* 397 15

thankfulness

may show forth our *t* unto thee 187 11
In the time of prosperity, fill our hearts with *t*, 820 13

thanks

T be to God, which giveth us the victory 39 11
We give *t* unto the Father, which hath made us 40 1
O give *t* unto the Lord, and call upon his Name; 40 7

Almighty God our heavenly Father, to render *t*	41	6
T be to God.	47	3
we give *t* to thee for thy great glory,	52	8
may, when the night cometh, rejoice to give thee *t*;	56	23
do give thee most humble and hearty *t*	58	16
T be to God.	59	21
T be to God.	65	2
t for his resurrection, may praise thee	69	4
do give thee most humble and hearty *t*	71	12
T be to God.	72	18
T be to God, who gives us the victory	77	10
We give *t* to the Father, who has made us	77	22
Give *t* to the Lord, and call upon his Name;	78	6
give *t* to him and call upon his Name.	83	6
T be to God.	84	5
Give *t* to the Lord and call upon his Name;	86	8
we worship you, we give you *t*,	95	1
when night comes, rejoice to give you *t*;	99	18
we your unworthy servants give you humble *t*	101	8
T be to God.	102	9
T be to God.	105	22
T be to God.	106	5
T be to God.	107	23
T be to God.	109	2
Almighty God, we give you *t* for surrounding us,	110	12
T be to God.	114	6
T be to God.	114	7
T be to God.	119	2
Grant that we, who have this day given *t*	123	3
we your unworthy servants give you humble *t*	125	6
T be to God.	126	9
T be to God.	131	14
T be to God.	132	7
We give you *t*, O God, for revealing your Son	134	1
T be to God.	135	13
O most loving Father, who willest us to give *t*	165	6
We give thee *t*, O Lord of glory, for the example	186	1
we give thee *t* for the fruits of the earth	194	16
we give thee *t* for thy servant	196	23
We give thee *t* for the fellowship	204	2
may always give thee *t*;	207	19
Most loving Father, whose will it is for us to give *t*	216	20
We give you *t*, O Lord of glory, for the example	237	14
Father, we give you *t* for the fruits of the earth	246	1
We give you *t* for the fellowship	254	20
may always give you *t*;	259	1
Let us give *t* to the Lord our God.	271	3
It is right to give him *t* and praise.	271	4
T be to God.	285	14
Let us give *t* to the Lord our God.	286	19
It is right to give him *t* and praise.	286	20
T be to God.	300	3
Let us give *t* to the Lord our God.	306	11
It is right to give him *t* and praise.	306	12
All praise and *t* to you, most merciful Father,	311	15
God our heavenly Father never-ending *t*	316	10
we give *t* to thee for thy great glory,	324	19
T be to God.	325	15
and to give *t* for all men:	329	3
Let us give *t* unto our Lord God.	333	5
and in all places, give *t* unto thee, O Lord,	333	8
and when he had given *t*, he brake it,	334	18
and when he had given *t*, he gave it to them,	335	4
rendering unto thee most hearty *t*	335	15
T be to God.	339	23
Let us give *t* unto our Lord God.	340	13
and in all places, give *t* unto thee, O Lord,	341	2
and when he had given *t* to thee, he broke it,	342	2
and when he had given *t*, he gave it to them,	342	6
we worship you, we give you *t*,	356	5
T be to God.	357	6
Let us give *t* to the Lord our God.	361	5
It is right to give him *t* and praise.	361	6
where to give *t* to you, Father Almighty,	361	8
and when he had given *t* to you, he broke it,	362	19
when he had given *t*, he gave it to them,	363	2
T be to God.	366	15
Let us give *t* to the Lord our God.	367	5
It is right to give him *t* and praise.	367	6
where to give *t* to you, Father Almighty,	367	8
We give *t* to you, O God, for the goodness and love	368	1
and when he had given *t* to you, he broke it,	368	11
and when he had given *t*, he gave it to them,	368	15
Let us give *t* to the Lord our God.	370	3
It is right to give him *t* and praise.	370	4
After supper, he took the cup of wine, gave *t*,	371	14
Let us give *t* to the Lord our God.	372	21
It is right to give him *t* and praise.	372	22
glorify you, Father, and to give you *t*;	373	1
and when he had given *t* to you, he broke it,	374	16
and when he had given *t*, he gave it to them,	374	20
we give *t* to you,	375	2
Gracious Father, we give you praise and *t*	399	7
T be to God.	399	14
Let us give *t* to the Lord our God.	402	5
It is right to give him *t* and praise.	402	6
After supper, he took the cup of wine, gave *t*,	403	8
Let us give *t* to the Lord our God.	404	7
It is right to give him *t* and praise.	404	8
and when he had given *t* to you, he broke it,	405	2
and when he had given *t*, he gave it to them,	405	7
T be to God.	414	3
Most gracious God, we give you *t* for your tender love	430	10
We give you *t* for binding us together	432	2
in giving *t* to Almighty God	440	4
in offering heartfelt *t* for the joyful	440	12
let us now give *t* to him, and say together:	441	11
We give you *t* for the blessing	443	23
O gracious God, we give you humble and hearty *t*	444	1
T be to God.	448	13
T be to God.	451	21
Gracious Father, we give you praise and *t*	457	5
T be to God.	457	12
We give you *t* for giving	460	17
O give *t* unto the LORD, for he is gracious, *	478	11
and give *t* with thine inheritance.	478	22
T be to God.	483	13
praise and hearty *t* for the wonderful grace	487	11
We give thee hearty *t* for the good examples	488	4
We give thee *t* for all thy servants	488	27
T be to God.	500	2
T be to God.	502	22
We give you heartfelt *t* for the good examples	503	14
T be to God.	516	3

We give you *t* that from the beginning you have 520 14
T be to God. 523 20
T be to God. 529 2
T be to God. 535 15
T be to God. 541 2
T be to God. 547 9
with our praise and *t*, these tokens 552 7
and strengthened, to rejoice and give *t*. 568 18
Let us give *t* to the Lord our God. 570 3
It is right to give him *t* and praise. 570 4
We give you *t*, O God, for the gifts of your people, 573 1
receive our *t* for this place, and accept the work 578 5
and who will give you *t* in the grave? 590 8
I will give *t* to you, O LORD, with my whole heart; * 593 1
give *t* for the remembrance of his holiness. 621 11
O LORD my God, I will give you *t* for ever. 622 6
I will give you *t* in the great congregation; * 631 4
for I will yet give *t* to him, 643 16
for I will yet give *t* to him, 644 12
and on the harp I will give *t* to you, O God my God. 644 26
for I will yet give *t* to him, 645 4
I will give you *t* for what you have done * 658 18
We give you *t*, O God, we give you *t*, * 691 3
Truly, wrathful Edom will give you *t*, * 692 20
we will give you *t* for ever 702 10
will those who have died stand up and give you *t*? 712 24
It is a good thing to give *t* to the LORD, * 720 22
and give *t* to his holy Name. 727 23
give *t* to him and call upon his Name. 730 3
Give *t* to the LORD and call upon his Name; * 738 1
Give *t* to the LORD, for he is good, * 741 19
that we may give *t* to your holy Name 745 21
Give *t* to the LORD, for he is good, * 746 1
Let them give *t* to the LORD for his mercy * 746 16
Let them give *t* to the LORD for his mercy * 747 11
Let them give *t* to the LORD for his mercy * 748 17
I will give great *t* to the LORD with my mouth; * 753 8
I will give *t* to the LORD with my whole heart, * 754 6
Give *t* to the LORD, for he is good; * 760 20
I will offer *t* to the LORD. 762 10
I will give *t* to you, for you answered me * 762 13
Give *t* to the LORD, for he is good; * 763 3
At midnight I will rise to give you *t*, * 768 11
Give *t* to the LORD, for he is good, * 789 20
Give *t* to the God of gods, * 789 22
Give *t* to the Lord of lords, * 790 1
Give *t* to the God of heaven, * 791 21
I will give *t* to you, O LORD, with my whole heart; * 793 1
Surely, the righteous will give *t* to your Name, * 797 1
Bring me out of prison, that I may give *t* 798 15
may give *t* to you for food and drink 825 21
that men and women everywhere may give thee *t*; 828 7
Accept, O Lord, our *t* and praise for all 836 1
may give *t* to you in all things. 836 19
Let us give *t* to God our Father for all his gifts 837 1
Above all, we give you *t* for the great mercies 837 21
We give *t* to you, O Lord our God, for all 838 9
We give you *t*, most gracious God, for the beauty 840 7
t and praise for the return of seedtime and harvest, 840 16
t because thou hast been graciously pleased 841 8

thanksgiving

Let us come before his presence with *t*, * 44 12
O go your way into his gates with *t* 45 17
Let us come before his presence with *t* * 82 7
Enter his gates with *t*; 83 4
Let us come before his presence with *t*, * 146 3
death: Grant us, who now remember him with *t*, 195 10
Grant us, who now remember him in *t*, 247 8
offer to you our sacrifice of *t*; 289 4
accept this our sacrifice of praise and *t*; 335 25
your hearts by faith, with *t*. 338 4
in thy heart by faith, with *t*. 338 8
our sacrifice of praise and *t*, 342 22
Offer to God a sacrifice of *t*, 343 8
this sacrifice of praise and *t*. 363 11
your hearts by faith, with *t*. 365 3
And we offer our sacrifice of praise and *t* 369 1
and offering to you this sacrifice of *t*, 371 20
Offer to God a sacrifice of *t*, 376 4
I ask your *t* for ________. 386 13
your hearts by faith, with *t*. 399 4
In the voice of praise and *t*, * 471 10
Singing aloud a song of *t* * 616 20
With the voice of praise and *t*, * 643 11
Offer to God a sacrifice of *t* * 655 7
Whoever offers me the sacrifice of *t* 656 1
I will proclaim his greatness with *t*. 681 25
Let us come before his presence with *t* * 724 16
Enter his gates with *t*; 730 1
Let them offer a sacrifice of *t* * 747 25
I will offer you the sacrifice of *t* * 760 8
Sing to the LORD with *t*; * 804 14
t, penitence, oblation, intercession, 856 28
For what do we offer *t*? 857 7
T is offered to God for all the blessings 857 8
the Church's sacrifice of praise and *t*, 859 11

thanksgivings

desires now to offer you her praises and *t*. 444 4

thence

From *t* he shall come to judge the quick and the dead. 54 4
From *t* he shall come to judge the quick and the dead. 66 20

thereby

T, the whole congregation was put in mind 265 6
and dost assure us *t* of thy favor 339 5

therein

the Heavens and all the Powers *t*. 52 26
the world and all who dwell *t*. 613 15
and those who love his Name will dwell *t*. 682 10
let the field be joyful and all that is *t*. 726 16
the lands and those who dwell *t*. 728 17

thereof

Though the waters *t* rage and swell, * 471 21

thereto

and *t* I (plight) (give) thee my troth. 436 10

thereupon

Now when I think *t*, I pour out my heart by myself; * 471 7

thick

he made dark waters and *t* clouds his pavilion. 603 12
growing *t* even on the hilltops; * 686 18

thief

You promised paradise to the *t* who repented; 497 13
When you see a *t*, you make him your friend, * 655 16

thigh

Strap your sword upon your *t*, O mighty warrior, * 647 17

thine

t adorable, true, and only Son, 53 9
For *t* is the kingdom, and the power, and the glory, 54 24
O Lord, save thy people, and bless *t* heritage; 55 15
Christ, who didst stretch out *t* arms of love 58 8
Father of all mercies, we *t* unworthy servants 58 15
but above all for *t* inestimable love 58 21
T is the day, O God, *t* also the night; 61 7
For *t* is the kingdom, and the power, and the glory, 67 14
Shed forth *t* unending day upon us 69 12
and give *t* angels charge over those who sleep. 71 2
companionship with one another *t* abounding grace 71 8
Father of all mercies, we *t* unworthy servants 71 11
but above all for *t* inestimable love 71 17
For *t* is the kingdom, 97 15
For *t* is the kingdom, 121 15
By *t* Agony and Bloody Sweat; 149 22
to incline *t* ear to us who have now made our prayers 153 21
the new light of *t* incarnate Word: 161 15
Eternal Father, who didst give to *t* incarnate Son 162 1
Grant this for *t* only Son Jesus Christ's 165 3
who for our redemption didst give *t* only-begotten 170 7
Almighty God, who through *t* only-begotten Son 170 21
Almighty Father, who hast given *t* only Son 172 8
King of glory, who hast exalted *t* only Son 175 1
but send to us *t* Holy Ghost to comfort us, 175 4
who didst give such grace to *t* apostle Andrew 185 7
God, who didst strengthen *t* apostle Thomas 185 14
teaching of *t* apostle and evangelist John, 186 8
O God, who, by the preaching of *t* apostle Paul, 187 8
who didst give to *t* apostles Philip and James 189 5
may share with her the glory of *t* eternal kingdom; 192 3
who didst give to *t* apostle Bartholomew grace 192 7
for the witness of *t* apostle and evangelist Matthew 192 19
O Almighty God, who hast knit together *t* elect 194 8
we may with him attain to *t* eternal joy; 198 20
who hast revealed to thy Church *t* eternal Being 199 12
may at the last enter with them into *t* unending joy; 202 5
multitudes who have been created in *t* image 206 18
Almighty God, who hast created us in *t* own image: 209 1
For *t* is the kingdom, 311 12
that thou, of thy tender mercy, didst give *t* only Son 334 10
For *t* is the kingdom, and the power, and the glory, 336 28
and didst make us in *t* own image; 341 13
and, of thy tender mercy, didst give *t* only Son 341 14
T, O Lord, is the greatness, and the power, 344 8
For all that is in the heaven and in the earth is *t*. 344 10
T is the kingdom, O Lord, and thou art exalted 344 10
who hast made us in *t* image, 344 15
Because thou didst give Jesus Christ, *t* only Son, 345 14
the great Name of *t* only Son. 348 10
For *t* is the kingdom, 364 12
For *t* is the kingdom, 398 23
For *t* is the kingdom, 428 19
O let *t* ears consider well * 474 3
and laid *t* hand upon me. 475 2
be strong, and he shall comfort *t* heart; 478 9
and give thanks with *t* inheritance. 478 22
Almighty God, who hast knit together *t* elect 480 4
we humbly beseech thee, a sheep of *t* own fold, 483 7
a lamb of *t* own flock, a sinner of *t* own redeeming. 483 8
For *t* is the kingdom, and the power, and the glory, 486 5
through the merits of Jesus Christ *t* only Son 488 20
For *t* is the kingdom, 502 12
O gracious Father, who openest *t* hand and fillest 828 1
that we may be wholly *t*, 833 1
to incline *t* ear to us who have now made our prayers 834 3

thing

we can do no good *t* without thee, 164 13
love the *t* which thou commandest, 167 17
likeness of any *t* that is in heaven above, 318 2
It is right, and a good and joyful *t*, 361 7
It is right, and a good and joyful *t*, 367 7
One *t* have I desired of the LORD, 477 16
One *t* have I asked of the LORD; 617 18
one *t* I seek; * 617 19
"A deadly *t*," they say, "has fastened on him; * 642 15
No good *t* will the LORD withhold * 708 16
It is a good *t* to give thanks to the LORD, * 720 22
I will set no worthless *t* before my eyes; * 730 12
let not my heart incline to any evil *t*. 797 9
where in any *t* it is amiss, reform it. 816 12

things

seek those *t* which are above, 39 13
tell the people what *t* he hath done. 40 8
those *t* that are necessary for our life 41 9
left undone those *t* which we ought to have done, 41 21
done those *t* which we ought not to have done. 42 1
O all ye green *t* upon the earth, bless ye the Lord; * 48 19
He hath filled the hungry with good *t*, * 50 15
left undone those *t* which we ought to have done, 63 2
done those *t* which we ought not to have done. 63 4
He hath filled the hungry with good *t*, * 65 18
seek the *t* that are above, 77 12
those *t* that are necessary for our life 79 4
praises of the Lord, for he has done great *t*, * 86 11
All *t* quake with fear at your presence; * 91 1
the Almighty has done great *t* for me, 92 2
He has filled the hungry with good *t*, * 92 10
"The LORD has done great *t* for them." 105 9
The LORD has done great *t* for us, * 105 10
the Almighty has done great *t* for me, 119 8
He has filled the hungry with good *t*, * 119 16
and grant that those *t* which we have asked 153 22
who dost govern all *t* in heaven and earth: 164 1
who willest us to give thanks for all *t*, 165 7
loving thee in all good *t* as pass man's understanding: 174 2
loving thee in all *t* and above all *t*, 174 4
ascended far above all heavens that he might fill all *t*: 174 9
the same Spirit to have a right judgment in all *t*, 175 17
keep us, we beseech thee, from all *t* that may hurt us, 177 4
accomplish those *t* which belong to thy purpose; 177 6

O God, whose never-failing providence ordereth all *t*	177	14
put away from us all hurtful *t*,	177	16
give us those *t* which are profitable for us;	177	16
we may think those *t* that are right,	178	2
perceive and know what *t* they ought to do,	179	12
t which for our unworthiness we dare not,	179	19
we may so pass through *t* temporal,	180	4
that we finally lose not the *t* eternal;	180	5
the spirit to think and do always such *t* as are right,	180	15
who art the author and giver of all good *t*:	181	12
thy Holy Spirit may in all *t* direct and rule our hearts;	182	2
Grant us, O Lord, not to mind earthly *t*,	182	6
not to mind earthly things, but to love *t* heavenly;	182	7
while we are placed among *t* that are passing away,	182	8
forgiving us those *t* whereof our conscience is afraid,	183	1
those good *t* which we are not worthy to ask,	183	2
restore all *t* in thy well-beloved Son,	185	2
restore all *t* in thy well-beloved Son,	202	17
that we, who constantly receive good *t* from thy hand,	207	19
Almighty and everlasting God, you govern all *t*	215	13
whose will it is for us to give thanks for all *t*,	216	21
such good *t* as surpass our understanding:	225	15
loving you in all *t*, and above all *t*,	225	16
ascended far above all heavens that he might fill all *t*:	226	2
by the same Spirit to have a right judgment in all *t*,	227	11
from all *t* that may hurt us,	228	15
those *t* which belong to your purpose;	229	2
your never-failing providence sets in order all *t*	229	10
Put away from us, we entreat you, all hurtful *t*,	229	12
and give us those *t* which are profitable for us;	229	12
we may think those *t* that are right,	229	16
understand what *t* they ought to do,	231	6
those *t* which for our unworthiness we dare not,	231	13
pass through *t* temporal,	231	20
that we lose not the *t* eternal;	231	20
think and do always those *t* that are right,	232	7
the author and giver of all good *t*:	233	4
Holy Spirit may in all *t* direct and rule our hearts;	233	15
Grant us, Lord, not to be anxious about earthly *t*,	234	1
love *t* heavenly;	234	2
while we are placed among *t* that are passing away,	234	3
forgiving us those *t* of which our conscience is afraid,	234	15
giving us those good *t* for which we are not worthy	234	16
restore all *t* in your well-beloved Son,	236	15
restore all *t* in your well-beloved Son,	254	2
receiving good *t* from your hand,	258	19
that those *t* may please him which we do	269	11
t which were cast down are being raised up,	280	18
and *t* which had grown old are being made new,	280	19
and that all *t* are being brought to their perfection	280	20
by him through whom all *t* were made,	280	21
the sign of your covenant with all living *t*:	289	2
O God, you have created all *t* by the power	290	8
t which were cast down are being raised up,	291	15
and *t* which had grown old are being made new,	291	16
and that all *t* are being brought to their perfection	291	17
by him through whom all *t* were made,	291	18
left undone those *t* which we ought to have done,	321	2
done those *t* which we ought not to have done.	321	4
Through him all *t* were made.	326	17
and of all *t* visible and invisible;	327	23
by whom all *t* were made;	327	31
maker of all *t*, judge of all men:	331	3
for thou hast created all *t*,	344	6
Through him all *t* were made.	358	14
put all *t* in subjection under your Christ,	369	9
At your command all *t* came to be:	370	8
you made all *t* and fill them with your blessing;	373	5
because you have created all *t*,	377	4
t done and left undone;	393	12
Almighty and eternal God, ruler of all *t*	394	9
and those good *t* which we dare not,	395	1
that in this, and in all *t*, you may do God's will	420	2
the Almighty has done great *t* for me,	441	16
He has filled the hungry with good *t*,*	442	5
for all the good *t* he has done for me?	442	20
t done and left undone;	447	7
trust in him, to whom all *t* in heaven,	456	21
think and do those *t* that please you;	460	22
in the midst of *t* we cannot understand,	481	14
contain all *t* necessary to salvation;	513	11
t which were cast down are being raised up,	515	8
t which had grown old are being made new,	515	9
and that all *t* are being brought to their perfection	515	10
by him through whom all *t* were made,	515	11
and to be in all *t* a faithful pastor	517	11
Through him all *t* were made.	519	17
knowing all *t* before they come to pass:	520	13
In all *t* may he present before you	521	14
and to contain all *t* necessary	526	16
t which were cast down are being raised up,	528	6
and *t* which had grown old are being made new,	528	7
and that all *t* are being brought to their perfection	528	8
by him through whom all *t* were made,	528	9
Through him all *t* were made.	530	8
t as may make you a stronger and more able minister	532	6
t give you the grace and power to perform them.	532	31
Grant that in all *t* he may serve without reproach,	534	5
and to contain all *t* necessary	538	16
t which were cast down are being raised up,	540	6
and *t* which had grown old are being made new,	540	7
and that all *t* are being brought to their perfection	540	8
by him through whom all *t* were made,	540	9
Through him all *t* were made.	542	8
Will you in all *t* seek not your glory	544	12
in these earthly *t* we may behold	573	5
the order and beauty of *t* heavenly;	573	5
O LORD my God, if I have done these *t*: *	590	24
you put all *t* under his feet:	592	20
proclaim to the peoples the *t* he has done.	593	22
Whoever does these *t* *	599	17
and their mouth speaks proud *t*.	601	19
Great *t* are they that you have done, O LORD my God!	640	11
My enemies are saying wicked *t* about me: *	642	8
I pour out my soul when I think on these *t*: *	643	8
Your right hand will show you marvelous *t*; *	647	21
what awesome *t* he has done on earth.	649	20
These *t* you have done, and I kept still, *	655	22
Awesome *t* will you show us in your righteousness,	672	17
you have done great *t*;	684	21
When I tried to understand these *t*, *	688	9
you do wondrous *t*; *	710	19
Glorious *t* are spoken of you, *	711	15
for he has done marvelous *t*.	727	25

He satisfies you with good *t*, * 733 17
with its living *t* too many to number, * 737 2
you open your hand, and they are filled with good *t*. 737 10
who had done great *t* in Egypt, 743 14
and fearful *t* at the Red Sea. 743 16
and fills the hungry with good *t*. 746 19
Whoever is wise will ponder these *t*, * 749 15
for all the good *t* he has done for me? 759 24
for all *t* are your servants. 771 2
I see that all *t* come to an end, * 771 11
"The LORD has done great *t* for them." 782 11
The LORD has done great *t* for us, * 782 12
or with *t* that are too hard for me. 785 13
and your word above all *t*. 793 7
creeping *t* and winged birds; 806 14
for the sake of him through whom all *t* were made, 814 5
Almighty and everliving God, ruler of all *t* 817 18
Grant us all *t* necessary for our common life, 817 21
Teach us in all *t* to seek first your honor and glory. 818 4
from which these good *t* come. 825 24
in giving us dominion over *t* on earth, 827 17
fillest all *t* living with plenteousness: 828 2
all *t* necessary to sustain their life: 828 11
knowing that thou art doing for them better *t* than we 831 9
grant that those *t* which we have faithfully asked 834 4
may give thanks to you in all *t*. 836 19
Almighty God, giver of all good *t*: 838 21
We learn two *t*: 847 17
God uses material *t* to reach out to us. 861 20
and will make all things new. 862 4

think

we may *t* those things that are right, 178 2
Grant to us, Lord, we beseech thee, the spirit to *t* 180 14
we may *t* those things that are right, 229 16
Grant to us, Lord, we pray, the spirit to *t* 232 6
that he may always *t* and do those things 460 22
Now when I *t* thereupon, I pour out my heart 471 7
I pour out my soul when I *t* on these things: * 643 8
Do you *t* I eat the flesh of bulls, * 655 5
I *t* of God, I am restless, * 693 6
mere mortals that you should *t* of us? 800 7
For minds to *t*, and hearts to love, and hands to serve, 837 12

thinks

He *t* up wickedness upon his bed 632 9

third

The *t* day he rose again from the dead. 54 1
The *t* day he rose again from the dead. 66 17
On the *t* day he rose again. 96 21
On the *t* day he rose again. 120 17
coming of the *t* day, and rise with him 170 4
coming of the *t* day, and rise with him 221 16
coming of the *t* day, and rise with him 283 4
On the *t* day he rose again. 293 8
On the *t* day he rose again. 304 11
On the *t* day he rose again 327 6
t day he rose again according to the Scriptures, 328 7
On the *t* day he rose again 358 22
On the *t* day he rose again. 416 16
This is the first (or second, or *t*) time 437 4
On the *t* day he rose again. 496 11
On the *t* day he rose again 519 25
On the *t* day he rose again 530 16
On the *t* day he rose again 542 16
The Holy Spirit is the *T* Person of the Trinity, 852 15

thirst

water of life to those who *t* for you, 290 10
and whoever believes in me shall never *t*." 396 5
and may *t* after righteousness, 548 22
nor my life with those who *t* for blood, 616 25
and save me from those who *t* for my blood. 665 21
and the wild asses quench their *t*. 735 24
You that *t* for blood, depart from me. 795 17

thirsts

my soul *t* for you, my flesh faints for you, 670 13

thirsty

and when I was *t*, they gave me vinegar to drink. 681 7
They were hungry and *t*; * 746 10
For he satisfies the *t* * 746 18
and water-springs into *t* ground, 748 22
my soul gasps to you like a *t* land. 799 11

thistles

like thorns and *t* let them be swept away. 665 12

thither

t ascend, and with him continually dwell; 174 18

Thomas

Everliving God, who didst strengthen thine apostle *T* 185 14
Everliving God, who strengthened your apostle *T* 237 8

thorns

like *t* and thistles let them be swept away. 665 12
they blaze like a fire of *t*; * 761 20

though

t we have rebelled against him; 38 21
T I walk through the valley of the shadow of death, 443 7
t at times he may be afraid, 459 9
t he were dead, yet shall he live; 469 2
and *t* this body be destroyed, yet shall I see God; 469 6
Therefore will we not fear, *t* the earth be moved, * 471 19
and *t* the hills be carried into the midst of the sea; 471 20
T the waters thereof rage and swell, * 471 21
and *t* the mountains shake at the tempest of the same. 471 22
t men be so strong that they come to fourscore years, 473 4
t I walk through the valley of the shadow of death, 476 8
t I walk through the valley of the shadow of death, 477 1
even *t* he die. 491 3
T they intend evil against you 609 20
T I walk through the valley of the shadow of death, 613 3
T an army should encamp against me, * 617 14
And *t* war should rise up against me, * 617 16
T my father and my mother forsake me, * 618 19
T I am poor and afflicted, * 641 19
T you thrust us down into a place of misery, * 646 24
Therefore we will not fear, *t* the earth be moved, * 649 3
and *t* the mountains be toppled into the 649 4
T its waters rage and foam, * 649 6
and *t* the mountains tremble at its tumult. 649 7
t they call the lands after their own names. 653 3
Even *t* honored, they cannot live for ever; * 653 4

T they thought highly of themselves 653 19
t wealth increase, set not your heart upon it. 670 7
T you lingered among the sheepfolds, * 677 5
t I cannot know the number of them. 684 11
T my flesh and my heart should waste away, * 689 1
T the earth and all its inhabitants are quaking, * 691 8
t the food was still in their mouths. 697 10
Then the LORD woke as *t* from sleep, * 700 9
that *t* the wicked grow like weeds, 721 9
t they had seen my works. 725 11
Even *t* rulers sit and plot against me, * 765 5
T the cords of the wicked entangle me, * 768 9
T the wicked lie in wait for me to destroy me, * 771 9
T the LORD be high, he cares for the lowly; * 793 14
T I walk in the midst of trouble, you keep me safe; * 793 16
They restore us, *t* we often destroy them. 838 23
t we often exploit them. 839 2
They are models for us, *t* we often fall short of them. 839 5
t we have often hidden from its light. 839 9
It sustains our life, *t* we have been faithless 839 13

thought

in *t*, word, and deed, 79 12
in *t*, word, and deed, 116 14
in *t*, and word, and deed, 127 9
in *t*, word, and deed; 267 17
in *t*, word, or deed. 317 4
in *t*, word, and deed, 320 12
by *t*, word, and deed, 331 7
in *t*, word, and deed, 331 23
in *t*, word, and deed, 352 12
in *t*, word, and deed, 360 4
in *t*, word, and deed, 397 21
I have sinned by my own fault in *t*, word, and deed, 447 6
in *t*, word, and deed, 454 3
readiness of *t* and expression; 563 7
their only *t* is, "God does not matter." 594 26
Though they *t* highly of themselves 653 19
and you *t* that I am like you." 655 23
their only *t* is to do me evil. 662 23
we have *t* out a perfect plot." 671 22
To show God respect in *t*, word, and deed; 847 24
Prayer is responding to God, by *t* and by deeds, 856 18

thoughts

and the evil ones their *t*; 86 20
For my *t* are not your *t*, * 86 23
and my *t* than your *t*. 86 27
t which may assault and hurt the soul; 167 7
t which may assault and hurt the soul; 218 17
For all false judgments, for uncharitable *t* 268 20
t of our hearts by the inspiration of thy Holy Spirit, 323 9
Cleanse the *t* of our hearts 355 8
thou understandest my *t* long before. 474 20
Cleanse the *t* of our hearts 512 8
Cleanse the *t* of our hearts 525 8
Cleanse the *t* of our hearts 537 8
and their hearts overflow with wicked *t*. 687 14
your *t* are very deep. 721 6
The LORD knows our human *t*; * 723 15
you discern my *t* from afar. 794 3
How deep I find your *t*, O God! * 795 10
try me and know my restless *t*. 795 25
and in that day their *t* perish. 803 10
that with steadfast *t* and kindled affections 833 22

thousand

A *t* shall fall at your side 130 10
and ten *t* at your right hand, * 130 11
a *t* generations of those who love and fear you: 444 16
For a *t* years in thy sight are but as yesterday 472 16
The chariots of God are twenty *t*, 677 15
a *t* in my own room, * 708 11
For a *t* years in your sight are like yesterday 718 6
A *t* shall fall at your side 719 24
and ten *t* at your right hand, * 719 25
the promise he made for a *t* generations: 738 16

thousands

the herds in their *t* upon the hills. 654 24
even *t* of *t*; * 677 16
than *t* in gold and silver. 769 8
may the flocks in our pastures increase by *t* 801 5
and tens of *t*; 801 6

threats

Why do the peoples mutter empty *t*? 586 2

three

t are gathered together in his Name 59 15
t are gathered together in his Name 72 12
t are gathered together in his Name 102 4
t are gathered together in his Name 126 4
t have gathered together in your Name, 578 10

threescore

The days of our age are *t* years and ten; 473 3

threshold

and to stand at the *t* of the house of my God 708 12

throat

Their *t* is an open grave; * 589 11
and also my *t* and my belly. 623 5
my *t* is inflamed; * 679 14
they make no sound with their *t*. 758 3
Let the praises of God be in their *t* * 807 12

throne

Blessed art thou on the glorious *t* of thy kingdom; * 49 18
on the *t* of your majesty, glory to you. 90 10
And so, to him who sits upon the *t*, * 94 5
Look down, O Lord, from your heavenly *t*, and 133 17
boldly before the *t* of grace 317 22
let us come boldly unto the *t* of grace, 320 7
let us with confidence draw near to the *t* of grace, 352 7
He whose *t* is in heaven is laughing; * 586 8
Be seated on your lofty *t*, O Most High; * 591 10
you sit upon your *t* judging right. 593 8
he has set up his *t* for judgment. 593 14
the LORD's *t* is in heaven. 596 16
Your *t*, O God, endures for ever and ever, * 648 1
God sits upon his holy *t*. 650 21
and preserve your *t* for all generations.'" 714 2
the foundations of your *t*; * 714 21
and his *t* as the days of heaven." 715 25
and his *t* as the sun before me; 716 14

and cast his *t* to the ground. 717 2
your *t* has been established; * 722 7
the foundations of his *t*. 726 26
The LORD has set his *t* in heaven, * 734 20
will I set upon your *t*. 786 22
their children will sit upon your *t* for evermore." 786 25
harmony around your heavenly *t*; 815 20
Almighty God, who sittest in the *t* judging right: 821 8

thrones
He has cast down the mighty from their *t*, * 92 8
he has cast down the mighty from their *t*, * 119 14
He has cast down the mighty from their *t*,* 442 3
For there are the *t* of judgment, * 780 5
the *t* of the house of David. 780 6

throng
I will praise you in the mighty *t*. 631 5
and walked with the *t* in the house of God. 661 13

throngs
Countless *t* of angels stand before you to serve you 373 7

through
which giveth us the victory *t* our Lord 39 11
but alive unto God *t* Jesus Christ our Lord. 46 12
T the tender mercy of our God, * 51 16
such blessing *t* our worship of thee, 56 3
t the same Jesus Christ out Lord. 56 4
t the same thy Son Jesus Christ our Lord. 56 10
t Jesus Christ our Lord. 56 16
t the might of Jesus 57 5
t Jesus Christ our Lord. 57 12
t our Lord and Savior Jesus Christ. 57 24
t the same thy Son Jesus 58 6
t Jesus Christ our Lord, 59 9
hast promised *t* thy well-beloved Son 59 14
believing *t* the power of the Holy Spirit. 60 2
and to be glorified *t* all the worlds. 64 9
t Jesus Christ our Lord. 69 15
t the merits of Jesus 69 21
t him who died for us and rose again, 70 8
t Jesus Christ our Lord. 70 18
t Jesus Christ our Lord. 71 9
t Jesus Christ our Lord, 72 6
hast promised *t* thy well-beloved Son 72 11
believing *t* the power of the Holy Spirit. 73 2
who gives us the victory *t* our Lord 77 10
t our Lord Jesus Christ, 80 2
T his holy prophets he promised of old, 92 22
such blessing *t* our worship of you, 98 21
t Jesus Christ our Lord. 98 22
t Jesus Christ your Son our Lord. 99 5
t the might of Jesus Christ our Lord. 99 24
t Jesus Christ our Lord. 100 5
t our Lord and Savior Jesus Christ. 100 16
t Jesus Christ our Lord, 101 22
have promised *t* your well-beloved Son 102 3
believing *t* the power of the Holy Spirit. 102 13
poured into our hearts *t* the Holky Spirit 105 20
who *t* Christ reconciled us to himself 106 3
t Jesus Christ our Lord. 107 7
t Jesus Christ our Lord. 110 16
t Jesus Christ our Lord. 111 7
and to be glorified *t* all the worlds. 112 9
t our Lord Jesus Christ, 117 7
and to be glorified *t* all the worlds. 118 9
t Jesus Christ our Lord. 123 14
t the mercies of Christ Jesus our Savior. 123 20
ask for your protection *t* the coming night. 124 4
t him who died and rose again for us, 124 5
t Jesus Christ our Lord. 124 15
t Jesus Christ our Lord. 125 4
have promised *t* your well-beloved Son 126 3
believing *t* the power of the Holy Spirit. 126 13
t our own fault, 127 8
t Jesus Christ, to whom be glory 132 5
and protect us *t* the hours 133 13
t Jesus Christ our Lord. 133 16
t Jesus Christ our Lord. 134 4
t the resurrection of Jesus Christ from the dead. 137 13
t Jesus Christ our Lord. 137 18
and to be glorified *t* all the worlds. 139 9
t Jesus Christ our Lord. 140 15
t Jesus Christ our Lord. 153 25
t our only Mediator and Advocate, Jesus 155 12
t him who liveth and reigneth 159 6
t Jesus Christ our Lord, 160 4
t the same Jesus Christ our Lord, 160 8
t the same our Lord Jesus Christ, 161 11
t the same Jesus Christ our Lord, 161 16
t the same Jesus Christ our Lord, 162 16
t the same Jesus Christ our Lord, 163 11
t Jesus Christ our Lord, 164 3
t the weakness of our mortal nature, 164 12
t the same Jesus Christ our Lord, 165 18
t Jesus Christ our Lord, 166 6
t Jesus Christ thy Son our Lord, 166 13
t Jesus Christ our Lord, 167 7
t the same Jesus Christ our Lord, 168 7
t the same thy Son Jesus Christ our Lord, 168 14
t the same thy Son Jesus Christ our Lord, 169 4
t the same thy Son Christ our Lord, 170 11
t the same Jesus Christ our Lord, 170 18
who *t* thine only-begotten Son Jesus 170 21
t the same Jesus Christ our Lord, 171 2
t Jesus Christ our Lord, 171 7
t the same thy Son Jesus Christ our Lord, 171 20
t the same Jesus Christ our Lord, 172 5
t the same thy Son Jesus Christ our Lord, 172 11
t the same Jesus Christ our Lord, 173 2
t the same thy Son Jesus Christ our Lord, 173 8
t Jesus Christ our Lord, 174 5
t the same Jesus Christ our Lord, 174 12
t Jesus Christ our Lord, 175 12
t the merits of Christ Jesus our Savior, 175 18
t Jesus Christ our Lord, 176 11
t Jesus Christ our Lord, 177 7
t Jesus Christ our Lord, 178 3
t the same Jesus Christ our Lord, 179 1
t Jesus Christ our Lord, 179 8
we may so pass *t* things temporal, 180 4
t Jesus Christ our Lord, 180 5
t the same thy Son Jesus Christ our Lord, 181 2
t Jesus Christ our Lord, 181 8

t Jesus Christ our Lord,	181	13
t Jesus Christ our Lord,	182	3
but *t* the merits and mediation of Jesus	183	3
t Jesus Christ our Lord,	183	8
t the same Jesus Christ our Lord,	183	14
t Jesus Christ our Lord,	184	4
t him who liveth and reigneth with thee	185	18
t Jesus Christ our Lord,	186	10
t Jesus Christ our Lord,	187	13
t Jesus Christ our Lord,	188	5
t the same thy Son Jesus Christ our Lord,	188	12
t the same Jesus Christ our Lord,	189	2
t Jesus Christ our Lord,	189	21
t the same thy Son Jesus Christ our Lord,	190	7
t Jesus Christ our Lord,	190	22
t the same Jesus Christ our Lord,	191	12
t the same thy Son Jesus Christ our Lord,	192	4
t Jesus Christ our Lord,	192	10
t Jesus Christ our Lord,	193	2
t the same thy Son Jesus Christ our Lord,	193	15
t the same our Lord Jesus Christ,	193	21
t the same Jesus Christ our Lord,	194	13
t Jesus Christ our Lord,	194	21
t Jesus Christ our Lord,	195	12
t Jesus Christ our Lord,	196	5
t the same Jesus Christ our Lord,	197	9
t Jesus Christ our Lord,	197	16
poor that we *t* his poverty might be rich:	198	1
t the same thy Son Jesus Christ our Lord,	198	5
t Jesus Christ our Lord,	198	13
t thy mercy, we may with him attain	198	19
t Jesus Christ, the author and perfecter	198	20
t Jesus Christ our Lord,	199	1
intercessions are acceptable *t* the Spirit,	199	10
t Jesus Christ our Lord,	200	3
t the same Jesus Christ our Lord,	201	16
t Jesus Christ our Lord,	202	6
t the same thy Son Jesus Christ our Lord,	203	8
t the same Jesus Christ our Lord,	203	16
t Jesus Christ our Lord,	204	5
t Jesus Christ our Lord,	205	11
t him who is the Shepherd and Bishop	205	18
t our Lord and Savior Jesus Christ,	206	6
t the same thy Son Jesus Christ our Lord,	206	14
t Jesus Christ our Lord,	207	5
t Jesus Christ our Lord,	208	6
t Jesus Christ our Lord,	209	6
t Jesus Christ our Lord,	210	16
t him who lives and reigns with you	211	6
t Jesus Christ our Lord,	212	4
t our Lord Jesus Christ,	213	5
t Jesus Christ our Lord,	213	10
t Jesus Christ our Lord,	214	10
t Jesus Christ our Lord,	215	5
t Jesus Christ our Lord,	216	10
t Jesus Christ our Lord,	217	11
t Jesus Christ your Son our Lord,	218	4
t Jesus Christ our Lord,	218	17
t Jesus Christ our Lord,	219	11
t Jesus Christ your Son our Lord,	220	5
t Jesus Christ your Son our Lord,	222	5
t Jesus Christ our Lord,	222	12
who *t* your only-begotten Son Jesus	222	15
t Jesus Christ our Lord,	223	1
t Jesus Christ your Son our Lord,	224	4
t Jesus Christ our Lord,	224	17
t Jesus Christ your Son our Lord,	225	11
t Jesus Christ our Lord,	225	18
t Jesus Christ our Lord,	226	5
t Jesus Christ our Lord,	227	5
t Jesus Christ your Son our Lord,	227	11
t Jesus Christ our Lord,	228	11
t Jesus Christ our Lord,	229	2
that *t* your grace we may proclaim	230	2
t Jesus Christ our Lord,	230	10
t Jesus Christ our Lord,	231	1
t the worthiness of your Son	231	14
we may so pass *t* things temporal,	231	20
t Jesus Christ our Lord,	232	4
t Jesus Christ your Son our Lord,	232	15
t Jesus Christ our Lord,	233	1
t Jesus Christ our Lord,	234	4
except *t* the merits and mediation of Jesus	234	17
t Jesus Christ our Lord,	235	1
t him who lives and reigns with you	237	12
t Jesus Christ our Lord,	238	4
t Jesus Christ our Lord,	239	3
t Jesus Christ our Lord,	240	10
t Jesus Christ our Lord,	241	7
t Jesus Christ your Son our Lord,	241	16
t Jesus Christ our Lord,	242	5
t Jesus Christ our Lord,	243	11
t Jesus Christ our Lord,	244	11
t Jesus Christ our Lord,	245	1
t Jesus Christ our Lord,	246	6
t Jesus Christ our Lord,	247	10
t Jesus Christ our Lord,	248	5
t Jesus Christ our Lord,	249	2
poor that we *t* his poverty might be rich:	249	11
t Jesus Christ, the pioneer and perfecter	250	5
t Jesus Christ our Lord,	250	12
intercessions are acceptable *t* the Spirit,	250	20
t Jesus Christ our Lord,	251	9
t Jesus Christ our Lord,	253	4
t Jesus Christ our Lord,	254	10
t Jesus Christ our Lord,	255	3
t Jesus Christ our Lord,	256	8
t him who is the Shepherd and Bishop	256	15
t our Lord and Savior Jesus Christ,	257	2
t Jesus Christ our Lord,	257	10
t Jesus Christ our Lord,	258	5
t Jesus Christ our Lord,	259	1
t Jesus Christ our Lord,	260	6
t Jesus Christ our Lord,	261	4
t Jesus Christ our Lord,	264	7
t Jesus Christ our Savior.	265	20
Wash me *t* and *t* from my wickedness *	266	4
t Jesus Christ our Lord.	269	14
t Jesus Christ our Lord.	270	7
which you have redeemed us *t* your Son Jesus	271	6
t Jesus Christ our Lord.	272	5
the world *t* him might be saved;	277	4
t our Lord and Savior Jesus Christ.	278	16
t Jesus Christ our Lord.	279	2

by him *t* whom all things were made, 280 21
O God, *t* your Son you have bestowed 285 8
t Jesus Christ our Lord. 285 12
t Jesus Christ his Son our Lord, 286 13
and led them *t* the Red Sea on dry land. 287 7
who are saved *t* water and the Spirit, 289 3
t Jesus Christ our Lord. 289 4
t Jesus Christ our Lord. 290 6
t Jesus Christ our Lord. 291 2
t whom all things were made, 291 18
T the Paschal mystery, dear friends, 292 1
t Jesus Christ your Son our Lord, 295 5
t Jesus Christ our Lord, 295 12
T it you led the children of Israel 306 15
the Christ, to lead us, *t* his death 306 18
T it we are reborn by the Holy Spirit. 306 22
t Jesus Christ your Son our Lord, 309 9
t Jesus Christ our Lord. 310 12
t Jesus Christ your Son our Lord, 311 18
T him let us offer continually the sacrifice 317 19
t Christ our Lord. 323 11
T him all things were made. 326 17
He has spoken *t* the Prophets. 327 15
t Jesus Christ our Lord. 331 20
t Jesus Christ our Lord. 332 6
and *t* faith in his blood, 335 27
we are unworthy, *t* our manifold sins, 336 9
t Jesus Christ our Lord; 336 12
heirs, *t* hope, of thy everlasting kingdom. 339 9
t Jesus Christ our Lord, 339 13
t the same Jesus Christ our Lord; 343 1
T Christ let us continually offer 344 1
T Jesus Christ our Lord; 345 1
T Jesus Christ our Lord; 346 4
T Jesus Christ our Lord; 346 13
T thy dearly beloved Son Jesus Christ our Lord; 347 1
T Jesus Christ our Lord; 347 6
T the great shepherd of thy flock, 348 11
T Jesus Christ our great High Priest; 348 15
T Jesus Christ our Lord; 349 6
a great high priest who has passed *t* the heavens, 352 5
t our Lord Jesus Christ, 353 2
t Christ our Lord. 355 11
T him all things were made. 358 14
He has spoken *t* the Prophets. 359 6
t our Lord Jesus Christ, 360 16
All this we ask *t* your Son Jesus Christ. 363 19
t Christ our Lord. 365 18
in your Word spoken *t* the prophets; 368 3
that we may be acceptable *t* him, 369 7
t Jesus Christ our Lord, 369 12
T prophets and sages you revealed 370 17
t Jesus Christ our great High Priest, 372 10
and *t* the prophets you taught us to hope 373 25
and give you glory *t* your Son Jesus 375 25
T Christ, and with Christ, and in Christ, 375 26
T Christ let us continually offer to God 376 17
T Jesus Christ our Lord; 377 14
T Jesus Christ our Lord, 379 1
T your dearly beloved Son Jesus Christ our Lord. 379 20
T Jesus Christ our Lord. 380 1
T the great shepherd of your flock, 381 5
T Jesus Christ our great High Priest; 381 9
T Jesus Christ our Lord; 382 1
[or *t* outer space], 384 18
t Jesus Christ our Lord. 393 16
t Jesus Christ our Lord. 394 3
intercessions are acceptable *t* the Spirit, 395 23
t our Lord Jesus Christ, 398 8
t Jesus Christ our Lord. 399 11
All this we ask *t* your Son Jesus Christ. 405 19
t Jesus Christ your Son our Lord, 418 7
t Jesus Christ our Lord. 419 8
t Jesus Christ our Lord. 421 6
t Jesus Christ our Lord, 425 12
t Jesus Christ our Lord. 427 12
t Jesus Christ our Lord, 430 23
t Jesus Christ our Lord, 431 7
t Jesus Christ our Lord. 434 6
t Jesus Christ our Lord. 441 9
Though I walk *t* the valley of the shadow 443 7
you have taught us *t* your blessed Son 443 21
you have preserved *t* the pain and anxiety 444 2
t Jesus Christ our Lord. 444 7
that *t* the Sacrament of Baptism 444 18
absolve you *t* my ministry by the grace 448 9
Wash me *t* and *t* from my wickedness, 449 3
T the water of baptism you clothed me 450 10
t him in whom you have redeemed the world, 450 19
absolve you *t* my ministry by the grace 451 8
t our Lord Jesus Christ, 455 7
t Jesus Christ our Lord, 455 13
t Jesus Christ our Lord. 456 18
t Jesus Christ our Lord. 457 9
t Jesus Christ our Lord. 458 9
t Jesus Christ our Lord. 459 10
t the skill of surgeons and nurses, 459 14
t Jesus Christ our Lord. 460 4
t Jesus Christ our Lord. 461 4
t the mercy of God, rest in peace. 465 7
This we ask *t* Christ our Lord. 466 11
t Jesus Christ our Lord. 467 7
t Jesus Christ thy Son our Lord, 470 4
t the same thy Son Jesus Christ our Lord, 470 10
Yea, though I walk *t* the valley of the shadow 476 8
Yea, though I walk *t* the valley of the shadow 477 1
t the grave and gate of death we may pass 480 10
t Jesus Christ our Savior. 482 8
t any pains of death, to fall from thee. 484 17
t our Lord Jesus Christ, 485 10
t the mercy of God, rest in peace. 486 20
t the blood of the everlasting covenant: 486 22
t Jesus Christ, to whom be glory 487 3
t thy Son Jesus Christ our Lord. 487 8
t Jesus Christ our Lord. 488 10
t the merits of Jesus Christ thine only Son 488 20
t Jesus Christ thy Son our Lord. 489 1
t Jesus Christ our Lord. 489 13
t the merits of thy Son Jesus Christ our Lord. 489 22
t Jesus Christ our Lord, 493 13
t Jesus Christ our Lord, 494 4
t the mercy of God, rest in peace. 498 11
t Jesus Christ our Savior. 498 18
t his indwelling Spirit. 501 5

t our Lord Jesus Christ,	501	12
t the mercy of God, rest in peace.	502	18
t the blood of the everlasting covenant:	503	2
t Jesus Christ, to whom be glory	503	5
t your Son Jesus Christ our Lord.	503	10
t Jesus Christ our Lord.	503	19
All this we ask *t* Jesus Christ our Lord.	504	10
t the merits of your Son Jesus Christ our Lord.	504	19
t Jesus Christ our Lord.	504	29
Grant this, O merciful Father, *t* Jesus Christ,	505	8
t Jesus Christ our Lord.	505	20
t Christ our Lord.	512	11
t whom all things were made,	515	11
t these promises you have committed yourself	519	1
T him all things were made.	519	17
He has spoken *t* the Prophets.	520	6
t Jesus Christ your Son,	521	15
t him in the fellowship of your Holy Spirit.	523	3
t Jesus Christ your Son our Lord,	523	8
t Christ our Lord.	525	11
t whom all things were made,	528	9
T him all things were made.	530	8
He has spoken *t* the Prophets.	530	25
t the mediation of Jesus Christ,	532	26
t Jesus Christ your Son,	533	11
this we ask *t* Jesus Christ our Lord,	534	8
t him in the fellowship of your Holy Spirit.	535	3
t Jesus Christ your Son our Lord,	535	8
t Christ our Lord.	537	11
t whom all things were made,	540	9
T him all things were made.	542	8
He has spoken *t* the Prophets.	542	25
t the power of the Holy Spirit.	543	2
and that, *t* him, we know	545	5
t Jesus Christ your Son,	545	9
that *t* him many may come to know you	545	14
t him in the fellowship of your Holy Spirit.	546	5
t Jesus Christ your Son our Lord,	547	4
t the high priest and good shepherd	552	11
t him who lives and reigns with you	560	9
t him in the fellowship of your Holy Spirit.	564	3
t Jesus Christ your Son our Lord,	564	8
T the ages, Almighty God has moved	567	1
t Jesus Christ our Lord.	567	12
grow closer to you *t* joy and *t* suffering.	569	4
as we grow in grace *t* the years,	569	6
we thank you that *t* the waters of Baptism	569	15
Grant *t* your Spirit that those baptized	569	16
T it you led the children of Israel	570	6
the Christ, to lead us, *t* his death	570	10
T it we are reborn by the Holy Spirit.	570	14
your eternal Word speaks to us *t* the words	570	23
in every age you have spoken *t* the voices	571	9
t Jesus Christ, our Mediator and Advocate.	572	12
t Jesus Christ our Lord.	573	6
t him we might become your sons and daughters.	573	10
t which he offered himself as a perfect sacrifice.	573	14
t the greatness of your mercy I will go	589	3
From the brightness of his presence, *t* the clouds, *	603	13
Though I walk *t* the valley of the shadow of death,	613	3
Their sword shall go *t* their own heart, *	634	14
T you we pushed back our adversaries; *	645	20
t your Name we trampled on those who	645	21
Wash me *t* and *t* from my wickedness *	656	8
so that they went *t* the water on foot, *	674	4
we went *t* fire and water; *	674	18
when you marched *t* the wilderness,	676	17
those who hope in you be put to shame *t* me,	679	22
and their evil speech runs *t* the world.	687	18
He split open the sea and let them pass *t*; *	695	28
and all the night *t* with a glow of fire.	696	2
Those who go *t* the desolate valley will find	708	1
and he shall be victorious *t* my Name.	715	15
and he led them *t* the deep as *t* a desert.	742	17
but they rebelled *t* their own devices, *	745	11
t stress of adversity and sorrow,	749	8
My knees are weak *t* fasting, *	752	23
let me find grace *t* your law.	765	18
T your commandments I gain understanding; *	772	1
And made Israel to pass *t* the midst of it, *	790	23
Who led his people *t* the wilderness, *	791	1
for the sake of him *t* whom all things	814	4
redeemed us *t* Jesus your Son:	815	14
and work *t* our struggle and confusion	815	17
t Jesus Christ our Lord.	815	20
t Jesus Christ our Lord.	816	9
t your Son Jesus Christ:	816	17
t Jesus Christ our Lord.	817	17
t Jesus Christ our Lord.	818	6
t the teaching of your Son Jesus Christ:	819	2
t Jesus Christ our Lord.	819	5
might be made rich *t* your poverty:	819	7
seek *t* art and music to perfect the praises	819	14
t Jesus Christ our Lord.	819	18
t obedience to thy law, we may show	820	11
t Jesus Christ our Lord.	820	15
t Jesus Christ our Lord.	821	7
t him who shall come to be our Judge,	821	13
t Jesus Christ our Lord.	822	21
t Jesus Christ our Lord.	822	28
t Jesus Christ our Lord.	823	7
t Jesus Christ our Lord.	824	4
t Jesus Christ our Lord.	825	5
t Jesus Christ our Lord.	826	14
t Jesus Christ our Lord.	827	4
t Christ our Lord.	828	7
t Jesus Christ our Lord.	828	14
t Jesus Christ our Lord.	829	8
t Jesus Christ our Lord.	830	11
t Jesus Christ our Lord.	831	5
compassion upon all who *t* addiction have lost	831	19
t Jesus Christ our Lord.	832	5
t our Lord and Savior Jesus Christ.	833	3
t Jesus Christ our Lord.	833	23
t Jesus Christ our Lord.	834	7
t thy grace, be so grafted	834	19
t the same Jesus Christ our Lord.	835	7
t Jesus Christ our Lord.	835	9
t which he overcame death;	836	15
and *t* him, at all times and in all places,	836	18
t Jesus Christ our Lord,	838	19
t Jesus Christ our Lord.	840	6
t thy help, may live in this world	841	11
t Jesus Christ our Lord.	841	13

t nature and history, 845 19
t many seers and saints, 845 19
and especially *t* the prophets of Israel. 845 20
handed down to us *t* a community 846 18
t them, to all who believe in him. 850 29
the One who spoke *t* the prophets. 852 19
God still speaks to us *t* the Bible. 853 26
T whom does the Church carry out its mission? 855 8
carries out its mission *t* the ministry 855 9
response to God the Father, *t* Jesus Christ, 856 21
Spirit *t* prayer and the laying on of hands 860 20
t prayer and the laying on of hands 861 1

throughout

t all generations. 50 10
The holy Church *t* all the world 53 6
t all generations. 65 13
T the world the holy Church acclaims you; 95 26
be honor and glory *t* all ages. 101 24
be honor and glory *t* all ages. 125 22
Shed abroad this gift *t* the world 175 10
that thy Church *t* the world may persevere 183 13
the light of the Gospel to shine *t* the world: 187 9
Shed abroad this gift *t* the world 227 3
that your Church *t* the world may persevere 235 5
the light of the Gospel to shine *t* the world: 238 21
Church of Christ *t* the world; 278 2
her members, dispersed *t* the world, 285 3
I ask your prayers for God's people *t* the world; 385 17
the Church *t* the world. 517 14
your years endure *t* all generations. 732 26
and flames of fire *t* their land. 740 18
and to scatter them *t* the lands. 744 2
t all generations for ever. 744 10
your dominion endures *t* all ages. 802 12
your God, O Zion, *t* all generations. 803 25
that your presence and power may be known *t* 825 18

throw

on Edom I *t* down my sandal to claim it, * 668 2
on Edom I *t* down my sandal to claim it, * 750 13

thrown

you have lifted me up and *t* me away. 731 20
Let them be put to shame and *t* back, * 784 9

thrust

Though you *t* us down into a place of misery, * 646 24

thunder

The sound of your *t* was in the whirlwind; 694 11
I answered you from the secret place of *t* 704 15
let the sea *t* and all that is in it; * 726 15
at the voice of your *t* they hastened away. 735 16

thunderbolts

Storm clouds and *t*, glorify the Lord, * 89 3
he hurled *t* and routed them. 603 18
and their livestock to hot *t*. 698 24

thundered

The LORD *t* out of heaven; * 603 15
the skies *t*; * 694 9

thunders

the God of glory *t*; * 620 10

thus

T saith the high and lofty One that inhabiteth 40 23
T says the high and lofty One who inhabits eternity, 78 22
T they were polluted by their actions * 745 1
shall *t* indeed be blessed. 783 20
t distorting our relationship with God, 848 30

thwarts

he *t* the designs of the peoples. 626 20

tidings

Behold, I bring you good *t* of great joy, 37 8
great was the company of women who bore the *t*: 677 2

ties

Renew the *t* of mutual regard which form our civic 825 9

till

thy dominion may increase *t* the earth is filled 207 11
t death do us part, 436 9
I will not turn back *t* I have destroyed them. 605 15
t I make known your strength to this generation 684 18
there shall be abundance of peace *t* the moon 685 22

timbrel

Raise a song and sound the *t*, * 704 3
let them sing praise to him with *t* and harp. 807 7
Praise him with *t* and dance; * 808 5

time

who hast given us grace at this *t* 59 12
may pass our *t* in rest and quietness; 69 20
who hast given us grace at this *t* 72 9
Save us from the *t* of trial, 97 13
you have given us grace at this *t* 102 1
from this *t* forth for evermore. 105 3
Save us from the *t* of trial, 106 23
Save us from the *t* of trial, 121 13
you have given us grace at this *t* 126 1
Save us from the *t* of trial, 133 5
from this *t* forth for evermore. 138 4
In all *t* of our tribulation; 149 26
in all *t* of our prosperity; 149 26
so that in due *t* all may enjoy them, 151 10
and in the old *t* before them. 154 7
in the *t* of this mortal life 159 3
take our nature upon him and as at this *t* to be born 161 8
and in our *t* grant us thy peace; 164 3
to take joyfully the sufferings of the present *t*, 169 3
in the *t* of this mortal life 211 2
and in our *t* grant us your peace; 215 15
accept joyfully the sufferings of the present *t*, 220 16
a *t* in which converts to the faith were prepared 265 2
It was also a *t* when those who, 265 3
Save us from the *t* of trial 311 10

and find grace to help in *t* of need. 320 8
which we from *t* to *t* most grievously have committed, 331 6
and find grace to help in *t* of need. 352 8
Save us from the *t* of trial, 364 10
In the fullness of *t*, 369 8
And in the fullness of *t* you sent your only Son, 370 19
inaccessible from before *t* and for ever. 373 3
in the fullness of *t* you sent your only Son 374 2
Save us from the *t* of trial, 398 21
Save us from the *t* of trial, 428 17
This is the first (or second, or third) *t* 437 4
our only help in *t* of need: 458 2
In thy good *t*, restore him to health, 458 7
Be near me in my *t* of weakness and pain; 461 7
Save us from the *t* of trial, 464 13
from this *t* forth for evermore. 473 24
For in the *t* of trouble he shall hide me 477 20
Save us from the *t* of trial, 502 10
From this *t* forth for evermore. 523 14
other duties assigned to you from *t* to *t* 543 16
a refuge in *t* of trouble. 593 18
and hide yourself in *t* of trouble? 594 20
at the *t* of your appearing, O LORD; 609 15
t of trouble; * 625 12
and to feed them in *t* of famine. 627 14
he is their stronghold in *t* of trouble. 636 16
the LORD will deliver them in the *t* of trouble. 641 24
until this *t* of trouble has gone by. 663 22
at the *t* you have set, O LORD: 680 14
In his *t* shall the righteous flourish; * 685 21
"I will appoint a *t*," says God; * 691 6
and call to mind your wonders of old *t*. 693 23
In the *t* of my trouble I will call upon you, * 710 11
for it is *t* to have mercy upon her; * 732 2
indeed, the appointed *t* has come. 732 3
He has brought down my strength before my *t*; * 732 22
so that it never shall move at any *t*. 735 12
and the sun knows the *t* of its setting. 736 16
Many a *t* did he deliver them, 745 10
from this *t* forth for evermore. 756 5
from this *t* forth for evermore. 758 26
It is *t* for you to act, O LORD, * 773 25
from this *t* forth for evermore. 779 17
from this *t* forth for evermore. 781 21
from this *t* forth for evermore. 785 18
I remember the *t* past; 799 7
in your good *t*, all nations and races may serve you 815 19
in your good *t* enable us all to stand reconciled 816 8
In the *t* of prosperity, 820 13
Direct, in our *t*, we pray, those who speak 827 7
we entreat thee, in this *t* of need, such moderate rain 828 12
for all your servants and witnesses of *t* past: 838 10
Faith to all people, to the end of *t*. 854 23

timely

We thank thee for the *t* blessings of the day, 70 6

times

Thou art worthy at all *t* to be praised by happy voices, 64 7
You are worthy at all *t* to be praised by happy voices, 112 7
You are worthy at all *t* to be praised by happy voices, 118 7
"Oh, that we might see better *t*!" * 129 2
You are worthy at all *t* to be praised by happy voices, 139 7
at all *t*, and in all places, give thanks unto thee, 333 8
at all *t*, and in all places, give thanks unto thee, 341 2
Fill his heart with confidence that, though at *t* 459 9
At all *t*, your life and teaching are to show 543 16
in *t* of joy and sorrow. 572 2
Almighty God, all *t* are your seasons, 572 9
"Oh, that we might see better *t*!" * 588 11
Their ways are devious at all *t*; 595 1
and purified seven *t* in the fire. 597 15
My *t* are in your hand; * 623 22
I will bless the LORD at all *t*; * 627 21
They shall not be ashamed in bad *t*, * 634 22
Yet God is my King from ancient *t*, * 690 8
I will declare the mysteries of ancient *t*. 694 22
many *t* he held back his anger 698 3
My soul is consumed at all *t* * 764 23
Seven *t* a day do I praise you, * 777 7
give us *t* of refreshment and peace; 825 1
O God, our *t* are in your hand: 830 8
and through him, at all *t* and in all places, 836 18
For the communion of saints, in all *t* and places, 837 19
And to set aside regular *t* for worship, 847 26

tire

my hands were stretched out by night and did not *t*; 693 4

today

Oh, that *t* you would hearken to his voice! 82 19
Give us *t* our daily bread. 97 9
Lord, keep us from all sin *t*; 98 13
Give us *t* our daily bread. 106 19
Give us *t* our daily bread. 121 9
Give us *t* our daily bread. 133 1
T if ye will hear his voice, harden not your hearts * 146 16
We remember *t*, O God, the slaughter 238 7
we remember before you *t* your servant 242 14
we remember before you *t* your faithful servant 253 13
Give us *t* our daily bread. 311 6
Give us *t* our daily bread. 364 6
[especially ________ whom we remember *t*]. 386 16
Give us *t* our daily bread. 398 17
Give us *t* our daily bread. 428 13
you have come here *t* to seek the blessing 433 1
Give us *t* our daily bread. 464 9
Give us *t* our daily bread. 502 6
Bishop N., we have come together *t* to welcome 559 1
intercessions offered in this place *t* 572 11
Oh, that *t* you would hearken to his voice! 725 5

together

and all flesh shall see it *t*. 37 7
Dearly beloved, we have come *t* 41 5
three are gathered *t* in his Name 59 15
That we may be bound *t* by thy Holy Spirit 68 22
three are gathered *t* in his Name 72 12
and all flesh shall see it *t*. 75 7
Dearly beloved, we have come *t* 79 1
three are gathered *t* in his Name 102 4
That we may be bound *t* by your Holy Spirit 122 24
three are gathered *t* in his Name 126 4
Grant us so to be joined *t* 178 20

being gathered *t* in unity by thy Holy Spirit,	181	6
may be freed and brought *t*	185	4
and knit *t* in unity by thy Spirit,	190	12
O Almighty God, who hast knit *t* thine elect	194	8
may be freed and brought *t*	203	2
Grant that thy Church, being bound *t*	204	19
Grant us so to be joined *t*	230	14
being gathered *t* in unity by your Holy Spirit,	232	18
may be freed and brought *t*	236	17
and knit *t* in unity by your	241	21
Almighty God, you have knit *t* your elect	245	16
may be freed and brought *t*	254	4
Grant that your Church, being bound *t*	255	17
who with the Father and the Son *t* is worshiped	328	15
t with them, may receive the crown of glory	347	20
t with them, receive the crown of glory	380	15
be united in your truth, live *t* in your love,	388	3
Dearly beloved: We have come *t*	423	1
God to witness and bless the joining *t*	423	2
to live *t* in the covenant of marriage?	424	9
Those whom God has joined *t* let no one	428	6
Let us pray *t* in the words our Savior taught us.	428	7
Grant that their wills may be so knit *t* in your will,	429	11
Make their life *t* a sign of Christ's love	429	17
that you may faithfully live *t* in this life,	431	12
We give you thanks for binding us *t*	432	2
Those whom God has joined *t* let no one	434	7
they may not be joined *t* in Holy Matrimony,	437	3
Let us say *t*:	440	7
that we may live *t* in love and affection;	441	8
let us now give thanks to him, and say *t*:	441	11
And so knit their wills *t* in your will	444	12
that they may live *t* in love and peace	444	13
Almighty God, who hast knit *t* thine elect	480	4
t with them, be partakers of the inheritance	486	14
t with your bishop and fellow presbyters,	531	5
whom you are called to serve, laboring *t*	532	15
Bishop N., we have come *t* today to welcome	559	1
grant that *t* they may follow Jesus Christ,	560	8
three have gathered *t* in your Name,	578	11
and the princes plot *t*, *	586	4
they put their head *t* against me;	623	18
let us exalt his Name *t*.	627	26
But when I stumbled, they were glad and gathered *t*;	630	23
All my enemies whisper *t* about me *	642	13
The nobles of the peoples have gathered *t* *	650	22
and marched forward *t*.	651	9
you of high degree and low, rich and poor *t*.	652	8
We took sweet counsel *t*, *	661	12
They band *t*; they lie in wait; *	663	1
how the mighty gather *t* against me; *	665	23
all of you *t*, *	669	10
all of them *t*.	670	4
and those who lie in wait for my life take counsel *t*.	683	21
They have conspired *t*; *	706	12
Mercy and truth have met *t*; *	709	14
When the peoples are gathered *t*, *	732	20
both small and great *t*.	758	16
when brethren live *t* in unity!	787	10
you knit me *t* in my mother's womb.	794	26
old and young *t*.	806	18
O God, you have bound us *t* in a common life.	824	1
t with mutual forbearance and respect;	824	4
Knit *t* in constant affection	829	3
drawing nearer to thee, may be bound *t*	830	23
a community of love has been gathered *t*	838	5
t week by week for corporate worship;	856	14
bound *t* in Christ by sacrament,	862	23

toil

our common life depends upon each other's *t*;	134	14
shared our *t* and hallowed our labor:	208	2
shared our *t* and hallowed our labor:	259	4
the fruit of their *t* to the locust.	698	20
and they took the fruit of others' *t*.	741	14
vain, too, to eat the bread of *t*,	783	4

tokens

these *t* of your servant's ministry and dignity.	552	7
they set up their banners as *t* of victory.	689	17

told

as it were a tale that is *t*.	473	2
our forefathers have *t* us, *	645	7
and what our forefathers have *t* us, *	695	2

tomb

the crucified body of thy dear Son was laid in the *t*	170	2
the crucified body of your dear Son was laid in the *t*	221	14
the crucified body of your dear Son was laid in the *t*	283	2
and giving life to those in the *t*.	483	15
and giving life to those in the *t*.	500	4

tongue

and our *t* with shouts of joy.	105	7
and my *t* shall sing of your righteousness,	267	4
For lo, there is not a word in my *t*, *	474	23
they flatter with their *t*.	589	12
under their *t* are mischief and wrong.	595	7
with a smooth *t* they speak from a double heart.	597	4
Those who say, "With our *t* will we prevail; *	597	7
There is no guile upon his *t*;	599	8
my *t* sticks to the roof of my mouth; *	611	9
While I held my *t*, my bones withered away, *	625	3
Keep your *t* from evil-speaking *	628	19
And my *t* shall be talking of your righteousness *	632	1
and their *t* speaks what is right.	635	23
so that I do not offend with my *t*.	638	16
So I held my *t* and said nothing; *	638	19
I spoke out with my *t*:	638	24
my *t* shall be the pen of a skilled writer,	647	13
and harnessed your *t* to a lie.	655	19
and my *t* shall sing of your righteousness,	657	10
your *t* is like a sharpened razor, *	658	2
O you deceitful *t*.	658	7
their *t* a sharp sword.	664	3
They sharpen their *t* like a sword, *	671	14
and his praise was on my *t*.	675	2
My *t* will proclaim your righteousness all day long, *	685	6
Hold not your *t*, O God of my praise; *	750	23
They speak to me with a lying *t*; *	751	1
My *t* shall sing of your promise, *	777	23
and from the deceitful *t*.	778	13
O you deceitful *t*?	778	15
and our *t* with shouts of joy.	782	9
Let my *t* cleave to the roof of my mouth	792	12

tongues

all *t* confess and bless thee, 70 17
all *t* confess and bless you, 124 14
uniting peoples of many *t* 347 9
uniting peoples of many *t* 380 4
Oh, that the LORD would cut off all smooth *t*, * 597 5
you keep them in your shelter from the strife of *t*. 624 10
He will make them trip over their *t*, * 672 1
the *t* of your dogs in the blood of your enemies." 678 4
and lied to him with their *t*. 697 23
They have sharpened their *t* like a serpent; * 796 5
brought hither out of many kindreds and *t*. 820 8

too

we have followed *t* much the devices and desires 41 18
we have followed *t* much the devices and desires 62 18
and I know my wickedness only *t* well. 91 15
we have followed *t* much the devices and desires 320 25
For I know my transgressions only *t* well, 449 5
Such knowledge is *t* wonderful and excellent 475 3
for they were *t* mighty for me. 603 27
You deliver the poor from those who are *t* strong 630 11
like a heavy burden they are *t* much for me to bear. 637 5
it was *t* hard for me; 688 10
with its living things *t* many to number, * 737 2
T long have I had to live * 778 20
T much of the scorn of the indolent rich, * 780 23
vain, *t*, to eat the bread of toil, 783 4
or with things that are *t* hard for me. 785 13
Such knowledge is *t* wonderful for me; * 794 10
for they are *t* strong for me. 798 14

took

by your death you *t* away the sting of death: 123 6
who *t* upon himself our flesh, 316 13
For in the night in which he was betrayed, he *t* bread; 334 17
Likewise, after supper, he *t* the cup; 335 3
For in the night in which he was betrayed, he *t* bread; 342 1
Likewise, after supper, he *t* the cup; 342 5
Lord Jesus Christ *t* bread; 362 19
After supper he *t* the cup of wine; 363 1
our Lord Jesus Christ *t* bread; 368 10
After supper he *t* the cup of wine; 368 14
On the night he was betrayed he *t* bread, 371 10
After supper, he *t* the cup of wine, 371 14
When our disobedience *t* us far from you, 373 21
at supper with them he *t* bread, 374 15
After supper he *t* the cup of wine; 374 19
On the night he was betrayed he *t* bread, 403 4
After supper, he *t* the cup of wine, 403 8
Lord Jesus Christ *t* bread; 405 2
After supper he *t* the cup of wine; 405 6
who *t* bread (the cup) 408 4
O God, whose beloved Son *t* children into his arms 494 1
by your death you *t* away the sting of death: 504 21
who *t* on himself the form of a servant, 545 2
Yet you are he who *t* me out of the womb, * 610 18
We *t* sweet counsel together, * 661 12
and *t* him away from the sheepfolds. 700 20
it *t* root and filled the land. 703 6
who *t* my part against the evildoers? 723 26
and they *t* the fruit of others' toil. 741 14
Some were fools and *t* to rebellious ways; * 747 15
he *t* no delight in blessing, 752 6
the grip of the grave *t* hold of me; * 759 6
We mean that Jesus *t* our human nature 850 19

tookest

When thou *t* upon thee to deliver man, 53 13

top

I am like a sparrow, lonely on a house-*t*. 731 14

topple

t you, and snatch you from your dwelling, 658 9

toppled

and though the mountains be *t* 649 4

toppling

as if you were a leaning fence, a *t* wall? 669 11

tops

and in whose *t* the stork makes his dwelling. 736 12

torch

lit the *t* of freedom for nations then unborn: 190 19
lit the *t* of freedom for nations then unborn: 242 3
We thank you for the *t* of liberty 839 8

tore

strangers whom I did not know *t* me to pieces 630 25

torn

and all whose homes are broken or *t* by strife, 151 22

torrent

and the *t* washes over me. 679 12
Let not the *t* of waters wash over me, 680 20
You split open spring and *t*; * 690 14
and the *t* gone over us; 781 8

torrents

and the *t* of oblivion made me afraid. 602 15

toss

and *t* my words behind your back? 655 15
and to the wicked, "Do not *t* your horns; 691 11
Do not *t* your horns so high, * 691 12

tossed

which *t* high the waves of the sea. 748 6

totters

repair the cracks in it, for it *t*. 667 13

touch

Saying, "Do not *t* my anointed * 739 7
t the mountains, and they shall smoke. 800 11

touches

he *t* the mountains and they smoke. 737 19

toward

such love *t* thee, that we, loving thee 174 3
for uncharitable thoughts *t* our neighbors, 268 20
contempt *t* those who differ from us, 268 21
I will bow down *t* your holy temple in awe of you. 589 5
how wonderful he is in his doing *t* all people. 674 2
Turn your steps *t* the endless ruins; * 689 14

Their heart was not steadfast *t* him, * 697 24
and great is your love *t* all who call upon you. 710 8
For great is your love *t* me; * 710 26
For his loving-kindness *t* us is great, * 760 17
and turned my feet *t* your decrees. 768 6
in their fierce anger *t* us; 781 6
I will bow down *t* your holy temple 793 3

towards

and on earth peace, good will *t* men. 52 4
of thy tender love *t* mankind, 168 2
Pour into our hearts such love *t* you, 225 16
and on earth peace, good will *t* men. 324 15
thy favor and goodness *t* us; 339 6
the way of thy servants *t* the attainment 832 19
Grace is God's favor *t* us, 858 2

tower

for you are my *t* of strength. 129 17
The Almighty Lord, who is a strong *t* to all 456 20
for you are my *t* of strength. 622 16
a strong *t* against the enemy. 668 18

towering

and the *t* cedar trees by its boughs. 703 8

towers

count the number of her *t*. 651 28
and quietness within your *t*. 780 10

town

For this city (*t*, village, __________), 384 7
in this State (Commonwealth, City, County, *T*, 822 19

towns

laws in States, Cities, and *T*, 822 2
in villages, *t*, and lonely places: 825 17

trace

You *t* my journeys and my resting-places * 794 4

trackless

and makes them wander in *t* wastes) 749 10

trade

and plied their *t* in deep waters; 748 2

trains

He *t* my hands for battle * 605 7
who *t* my hands to fight and my fingers to battle; 800 2

trample

you shall *t* the young lion and the serpent 130 24
t my life into the ground, 591 4
I *t* them like mud in the streets. 605 25
he will confound those who *t* upon me; * 663 26
T down those who lust after silver; * 678 20
you shall *t* the young lion and the serpent 720 12

trampled

through your Name we *t* on those who 645 21

trampling

Christ is risen from the dead, *t* down death by death, 483 14
Christ is risen from the dead, *t* down death by death, 500 3

tranquillity

that in *t* thy dominion may increase 207 10
that in *t* your dominion may increase 258 10
that in *t* your dominion may increase, 278 27
carry out in *t* the plan of salvation; 280 17
carry out in *t* the plan of salvation; 291 14
carry out in *t* the plan of salvation; 515 7
carry out in *t* the plan of salvation; 528 5
carry out in *t* the plan of salvation; 540 5

transfigured

witnesses thy well-beloved Son, wonderfully *t*, 191 16
witnesses your well-beloved Son, wonderfully *t*, 243 2

transformed

may be so *t* by your grace, 430 6

transgressions

For I know my *t*, * 266 6
For I know my *t* only too well, 449 5
Because of their many *t* cast them out, * 589 15
Remember not the sins of my youth and my *t*; * 615 1
Happy are they whose *t* are forgiven, * 624 23
I said, "I will confess my *t* to the LORD." * 625 9
Deliver me from all my *t* * 639 11
For I know my *t*, * 656 10
because of their *t*. 672 10
I will punish their *t* with a rod * 716 5

transgressors

T shall be destroyed, one and all; * 636 13

transitory

in this *t* life, are in trouble, 329 28

trap

The wicked have set a *t* for me, * 104 7
Let the table before them be a *t* * 681 8
The wicked have set a *t* for me, * 772 13
in the way wherein I walk they have hidden a *t* for me. 798 6

trapped

the wicked are *t* in the works of their own hands. 594 10
but they are *t* in the schemes they have devised. 594 22

traps

they have set *t* for me along the path. 796 12
and from the *t* of the evildoers. 797 23

travail

Come unto me, all ye that *t* and are heavy laden, 332 8
Come unto me, all ye that *t* and are heavy laden, 449 13

travel

reason of their labor or their *t*, 151 18
For those who *t* on land, on water, or in the air 384 17
Preserve those who *t* 831 3

treacherous

let the *t* be disappointed in their schemes. 614 18
Do not let my *t* foes rejoice over me, * 631 6

treachery

and plot *t* all the day long. 637 22

tread
You shall *t* upon the lion and adder; * 130 23
and he shall *t* our enemies under foot. 668 11
You shall *t* upon the lion and adder; * 720 11
and he shall *t* our enemies under foot. 750 22

treasure
made partners of thy heavenly *t*; 182 15
may become partakers of your heavenly *t*; 234 9
Whose bellies you fill with your *t*, * 602 1
I *t* your promise in my heart, * 764 5

treated
for the LORD has *t* you well. 759 15

tree
flourishing like a *t* in full leaf. 636 7
But I am like a green olive *t* in the house of God; * 658 16
The righteous shall flourish like a palm *t*, * 721 21
and shattered every *t* in their country. 740 20

trees
They are like *t* planted by streams of water, 585 7
The voice of the LORD breaks the cedar *t*; * 620 14
The voice of the LORD makes the oak *t* writhe * 620 21
like men coming up with axes to a grove of *t*; * 689 18
and the towering cedar *t* by its boughs. 703 8
Then shall all the *t* of the wood shout for joy 726 17
The *t* of the LORD are full of sap, * 736 9
He blasted their vines and their fig *t* * 740 19
on the *t* in the midst of that land. 792 4
fruit *t* and all cedars; 806 12

tremble
they *t* because of your power. 91 2
let the whole earth *t* before him. 115 6
T, then, and do not sin; * 128 16
T, then, and do not sin; * 588 6
See how they *t* with fear, * 598 24
and though the mountains *t* at its tumult. 649 7
The righteous shall see and *t*, * 658 11
See how greatly they *t*, 659 10
Those who dwell at the ends of the earth will *t* 673 1
let the whole earth *t* before him. 726 10
let the people *t*; * 728 24
T, O earth, at the presence of the Lord, * 757 9

trembled
the waters saw you and *t*; * 694 6
the earth *t* and shook. 694 13

trembles
He looks at the earth and it *t*; * 737 18
My flesh *t* with dread of you; * 773 13

trembling
and with *t* bow before him; 586 25
they shall come *t* out of their strongholds. 606 2
T seized them there; * 651 12
such *t* as never was; * 659 11
Fear and *t* have come over me, * 660 15
and give them continual *t* in their loins. 681 11

trespass
as we forgive those who *t* against us. 54 21
as we forgive those who *t* against us. 67 11
who *t* against us. 97 12
who *t* against us. 106 22
who *t* against us. 121 12
who *t* against us. 133 4
as we forgive those who *t* against us. 153 13
who *t* against us. 311 9
as we forgive those who *t* against us. 336 25
who *t* against us. 364 9
who *t* against us. 398 20
who *t* against us. 428 16
who *t* against us. 464 12
as we forgive those who *t* against us. 486 2
who *t* against us. 502 9

trespasses
And forgive us our *t*, 54 20
And forgive us our *t*, 67 10
And forgive us our *t*, 97 10
And forgive us our *t*, 106 20
And forgive us our *t*, 121 10
And forgive us our *t*, 133 2
And forgive us our *t*, 153 12
And forgive us our *t*, 311 7
And forgive us our *t*, 336 24
And forgive us our *t*, 364 7
And forgive us our *t*, 398 18
And forgive us our *t*, 428 14
And forgive us our *t*, 464 10
And forgive us our *t*, 486 1
And forgive us our *t*, 502 7

trial
Save us from the time of *t*, 97 13
Save us from the time of *t*, 106 23
Save us from the time of *t*, 121 13
Save us from the time of *t*, 133 5
Save us from the time of *t* 311 10
Save us from the time of *t*, 364 10
Save us from the time of *t*, 398 21
Save us from the time of *t*, 428 17
Save us from the time of *t*, 464 13
Save us from the time of *t*, 502 10
nor let them be found guilty when brought to *t*. 636 2

trials
strengthen them in their *t* and temptations; 823 4

tribe
the *t* you redeemed to be your inheritance, 689 12
and did not choose the *t* of Ephraim; 700 14
He chose instead the *t* of Judah * 700 15

tribes
There is Benjamin, least of the *t*, at the head; 678 11
he made the *t* of Israel to dwell in their tents. 699 17
in all their *t* there was not one that stumbled. 740 28
To which the *t* go up, 780 1
the *t* of the LORD, * 780 2

tribulation

In all time of our *t*; 149 26
are in danger, necessity, and *t*, 151 29
From all evil, from all sin, from all *t*, 463 3

tribulations

Great are the *t* of the wicked; * 625 23

tribunal

Can a corrupt *t* have any part with you, * 724 5

tribute

Accept, O LORD, the willing *t* of my lips, * 104 3
Let *t* be brought out of Egypt; * 678 22
The kings of Tarshish and of the isles shall pay *t*, * 686 3
Accept, O LORD, the willing *t* of my lips, * 772 9

tried

the words of the LORD are *t* in the fire; * 604 25
you have *t* us just as silver is *t*. 674 14
When I *t* to understand these things, * 688 9

trifle

You are selling your people for a *t* * 646 9

Trinity

O holy, blessed, and glorious *T*, one God, 148 7
acknowledge the glory of the eternal *T*, 176 3
as one God in *T* of Persons: 199 14
acknowledge the glory of the eternal *T*, 228 3
as one God in *T* of Persons: 251 3
in *T* of Persons and in Unity of Substance; 347 14
in *T* of Persons and in Unity of Being; 380 9
undivided *T* guard your body, 460 7
Holy *T*, one God, 463 1
Holy *T*, one God, 548 7
and of God as *T*. 852 11
What is the *T*? 852 12
The *T* is one God: 852 13
The Holy Spirit is the Third Person of the *T*, 852 15

trip

He will make them *t* over their tongues, * 672 1
who are determined to *t* me up. 796 9

tripped

I had almost *t* and fallen; 687 4

triumph

with great *t* unto thy kingdom in heaven: 175 2
rejoice in her *t* may profit by her example; 196 4
with great *t* to your kingdom in heaven: 226 14
rejoice in her *t* may profit by her example; 247 16
he entered the holy city of Jerusalem in *t*, 271 8
he shall come again in power and great *t* 345 10
by whose grace we are able to *t* over every evil, 346 6
he shall come again in power and great *t* 378 6
By his grace we are able to *t* over every evil, 379 3
how long shall my enemy *t* over me? 598 3
and *t* in the Name of our God; * 608 10
nor let my enemies *t* over me. 614 16
and have not let my enemies *t* over me. 621 5
do not let them *t* over me. 631 20
that my enemy does not *t* over me. 642 23
God will let me look in *t* on my enemies. 666 17
and over Philistia will I shout in *t*." 668 3
how long shall the wicked *t*? 722 23
and over Philistia will I shout in *t*." 750 14
I will *t* over those who hate me. 761 10
Let the faithful rejoice in *t*; * 807 10

triumphed

Lord God, whose Son our Savior Jesus Christ *t* 69 1
Lord God, whose Son our Savior Jesus Christ *t* 123 1
N. *t* over suffering and was faithful even unto death: 195 9
N. *t* over suffering and was faithful even to death: 247 7
"The right hand of the LORD has *t*! * 762 1

trodden

let them wither like *t* grass. 665 8

troop

a *t* of destroying angels. 699 3

troth

and thereto I (plight) (give) thee my *t*. 436 10

trouble

I am with him in *t*; 131 2
in *t*, sorrow, need, sickness, or any other adversity. 329 28
Pray for those in any need or *t*. 386 6
who suffer from any grief or *t*; 387 15
For all who are in danger, sorrow, or any kind of *t*; 392 9
in the presence of those who *t* me; * 443 12
a very present help in *t*. 471 18
in the presence of them that *t* me; * 476 13
For in the time of *t* he shall hide me 477 20
I found *t* and heaviness; 479 5
a refuge in time of *t*. 593 18
and hide yourself in time of *t*? 594 20
Surely, you behold *t* and misery; * 595 23
May the LORD answer you in the day of *t*, * 608 1
Be not far from me, for *t* is near, * 610 23
in the presence of those who *t* me; * 613 8
For in the day of *t* he shall keep me safe 618 1
Have mercy on me, O LORD, for I am in *t*; * 623 3
make their prayers to you in time of *t*; * 625 12
you preserve me from *t*; * 625 15
he is their stronghold in time of *t*. 636 16
the LORD will deliver them in the time of *t*. 641 24
a very present help in *t*. 649 2
Call upon me in the day of *t*; * 655 9
For you have rescued me from every *t*, * 660 3
but *t* and misery are in the midst of her. 661 3
until this time of *t* has gone by. 663 22
a refuge in the day of my *t*. 667 6
and spoke with my mouth when I was in *t*. 674 23
In the day of my *t* I sought the Lord; * 693 3
You called on me in *t*, and I saved you; * 704 14
In the time of my *t* I will call upon you, * 710 11
For I am full of *t*; * 712 5
My sight has failed me because of *t*; * 712 20
I am with him in *t*; 720 18
hide not your face from me in the day of my *t*. 731 2
Then they cried to the LORD in their *t*, * 746 12
Then they cried to the LORD in their *t*, * 747 7
Then they cried to the LORD in their *t*, * 748 11
This is my comfort in my *t*, * 767 13
T and distress have come upon me, * 775 11

When I was in *t*, I called to the LORD; * 778 10
Though I walk in the midst of *t*, you keep me safe; * 793 16
and tell him all my *t*. 798 4
for your righteousness' sake, bring me out of *t*. 799 24
and in the day of *t*, suffer not our trust 820 14

troubled

I am deeply *t*; * 104 1
The sacrifice of God is a *t* spirit; * 267 10
The sacrifice of God is a *t* spirit; * 657 16
I am *t* and I cannot speak. 693 9
I have borne your terrors with a *t* mind. 713 10
I am deeply *t*; * 772 7

troubles

that in all our *t* we may put our whole trust 155 10
give them courage and hope in their *t*, 389 4
shall have their *t* multiplied. 600 4
bring me out of my *t*. 615 23
out of all his *t*. 616 6
and saved me from all my *t*. 628 6
and delivers them from all their *t*. 629 2
Many are the *t* of the righteous, * 629 5
For innumerable *t* have crowded upon me; 641 4
You have showed me great *t* and adversities, * 684 23

true

which are the figures of the *t*; 39 16
when the *t* worshipers shall worship the Father 40 20
remission of all your sins, *t* repentance, 42 12
thine adorable, *t*, and only Son, 53 9
remission of all your sins, *t* repentance, 63 15
a copy of the *t* one, but into heaven itself, 77 15
when the *t* worshipers will worship the Father 78 19
your *t* and only Son, worthy of all worship, 95 28
where dwells the *t* and never-failing Light, 110 21
know you to be the *t* God and eternal light, 110 27
with *t* knowledge and understanding 150 6
That it may please thee to give us *t* repentance; 152 3
shine with the illumination of the *t* Light: 161 2
from heaven to be the *t* bread which giveth life 167 11
be fixed where *t* joys are to be found; 167 20
by the confession of a *t* faith, 176 2
increase in us *t* religion, nourish us with all goodness, 181 13
faithful people do unto thee *t* and laudable service: 184 2
be ordered and guided by faithful and *t* pastors; 188 4
by which alone they may have *t* authority 191 11
that they may minister in thy household as *t* servants 197 7
by this teaching we may know thee, the one *t* God, 197 22
and live in righteousness and *t* holiness; 201 15
and live in righteousness and *t* holiness; 203 15
thy Church, being preserved in *t* faith 204 12
in every heart the *t* love of peace, 207 9
shine with the brightness of the *t* Light: 212 17
your greatest gift, which is love, the *t* bond of peace 216 15
the *t* bread which gives life to the world: 219 2
there be fixed where *t* joys are to be found; 219 10
by the confession of a *t* faith, 228 2
increase in us *t* religion; 233 5
faithful people offer you *t* and laudable service: 235 15
be guided and governed by faithful and *t* pastors; 239 14
service by which alone they may have *t* authority 242 18
t servants of Christ and stewards 248 19
by this teaching we may know you, the one *t* God, 249 7
and live in righteousness and *t* holiness; 253 3
and live in righteousness and *t* holiness; 254 16
your Church, being preserved in *t* faith 255 10
kindle, we pray, in every heart the *t* love of peace, 258 8
We have not been *t* to the mind of Christ. 267 24
Therefore we beseech him to grant us *t* repentance 269 10
kindle, we pray, in every heart the *t* love of peace, 278 25
for he is the *t* Paschal lamb, 287 3
remission of all your sins, *t* repentance, 321 15
t God from *t* God, 326 14
set forth thy *t* and lively Word, 329 11
hearty repentance and *t* faith turn unto him, 332 3
This is a *t* saying, and worthy of all men 332 13
according to whose *t* promise 347 6
t God from *t* God, 358 11
for you alone are God, living and *t*, 373 2
for he is the *t* Paschal Lamb, 379 16
In fulfillment of his *t* promise, 380 1
that with *t* fidelity and steadfast love 425 10
in wisdom and *t* godliness, 431 5
O God, the giver of all that is *t* and lovely 432 1
bring this child to love all that is *t* and noble, 443 27
This is a *t* saying, and worthy of all men 449 18
the *t* faith of thy holy Name, 488 8
all who have died in the *t* faith of your holy Name, 503 17
t God from *t* God, 519 14
t God from *t* God, 530 5
t God from *t* God, 542 5
that they may serve you in a *t* and godly life, 548 17
set forth your *t* and living Word. 563 4
he is the savior of the *t* in heart. 591 19
to shoot from ambush at the *t* of heart. 596 12
the judgments of the LORD are *t* 607 14
shout for joy, all who are *t* of heart. 625 26
and your favor to those who are *t* of heart. 632 25
and all who are *t* of heart will glory. 672 6
T, he struck the rock, the waters gushed out, and the 696 13
So he shepherded them with a faithful and *t* heart * 700 24
and all the *t* of heart will follow it. 723 24
All your commandments are *t*; * 770 14
and all your commandments are *t*. 776 6
and to those who are *t* of heart. 782 2
that they may know my words are *t*. 797 16
whatever is just and *t* and good, 829 12
benefits of *t* freedom and gladly accept its disciplines. 839 25
who guides the Church in the *t* interpretation of the Scriptures. 854 1

truehearted

and joyful gladness for those who are *t*. 727 21

truly

they may *t* and godly serve thee; 57 23
We are *t* sorry and we humbly repent. 79 17
they may *t* and devoutly serve you; 100 15
with *t* thankful hearts we may show forth your praise, 101 17
t, they are the joy of my heart. 104 10
We are *t* sorry and we humbly repent. 116 19
with *t* thankful hearts we may show forth your praise, 125 15
whom *t* to know is everlasting life: 173 16
that we may *t* repent according to his preaching; 190 4

grace *t* to believe and to preach thy Word: 192 8
they may *t* and godly serve thee; 206 5
whom *t* to know is everlasting life: 225 8
that we may *t* repent according to his preaching; 241 13
grace *t* to believe and to preach your Word: 243 15
prepared for those who *t* love you; 245 20
they may *t* and devoutly serve you; 257 2
absolves all those who *t* repent, 269 8
they may *t* and devoutly serve you; 278 15
It is *t* right and good, always and everywhere, 286 22
We are *t* sorry and we humbly repent. 320 17
t serving thee in holiness and righteousness 329 16
Ye who do *t* and earnestly repent you of your sins, 330 9
We are *t* sorry and we humbly repent. 331 28
Hear the Word of God to all who *t* turn to him. 332 7
We are *t* sorry and we humbly repent. 352 17
We are *t* sorry and we humbly repent. 360 9
It is *t* right to glorify you, Father, 373 1
may *t* and humbly serve you; 387 3
We are *t* sorry and we humbly repent. 398 1
t and humbly confess your sins: 447 3
sins which I cannot now remember, I am *t* sorry. 447 8
absolve all sinners who *t* repent and believe in him, 448 2
Hear the Word of God to all who *t* turn to him. 449 12
absolve all sinners who *t* repent and believe in him, 451 12
We are *t* sorry and we humbly repent. 454 8
My brother, do you believe that you are *t* called 531 21
My brother, do you believe that you are *t* called 543 19
T, I am on the verge of falling, * 638 3
t, even those who stand erect are but a puff of wind. 639 5
t, everyone is but a puff of wind. 639 19
t there are many who fight against me, O Most High. 662 16
t, my hope is in him. 669 17
t, the LORD will dwell there for ever. 677 14
T, God is good to Israel, * 687 1
T, those who forsake you will perish; * 689 3
T, wrathful Edom will give you thanks, * 692 20
T, his salvation is very near to those who fear him, * 709 12
T, the LORD is our ruler; * 715 1
t, they are the joy of my heart. 772 16
T, I love your commandments * 774 1
for *t* I am your servant. 799 27
t please thee, pour upon them the continual dew 817 7
your Word may be *t* preached and *t* heard, 817 13
we may come to know you more *t*, 827 15

trumpet

Praise him with the sound of the *t*; 572 5
sound a fanfare with all your skill upon the *t*. 626 6

trumpets

and let your *t* shout Salvation 286 2
With *t* and the sound of the horn * 728 14

trust

As our *t* in thee. 55 22
I will *t* in him and not be afraid. 86 2
For we put our *t* in you. 98 16
and put your *t* in the Lord. 128 19
my God in whom I put my *t*." 129 25
quietness and *t* shall be our strength. 138 11
As we do put out *t* in thee. 153 17
in all our troubles we may put our whole *t* 155 10
the strength of all those who put their *t* in thee: 164 11
the protector of all that *t* in thee, 180 1
Grant us, O Lord, we pray thee, to *t* in thee 181 17
the strength of all who put their *t* in you: 216 6
the protector of all who *t* in you, 231 17
Grant us, O Lord, to *t* in you with all our hearts; 233 9
Do you put your whole *t* in his grace and love? 302 19
eternal salvation for all who put their *t* in him. 346 16
and betrayed your *t*; 370 15
eternal salvation for all who put their *t* in him. 379 13
For those in positions of public *t* [especially ________], 390 16
Who put their *t* in you. 393 7
a strong tower to all who put their *t* in him, 456 21
he yet may put his *t* in you; 459 10
O put thy *t* in God; * 471 14
in his word is my *t*. 474 10
O Israel, *t* in the LORD, 474 13
and put thou thy *t* in the LORD. 478 10
to believe and *t* in the communion of saints, 481 15
and be an occasion for us to renew our *t* 498 4
the work to which we *t* the Holy Spirit 514 17
their *t* in you by acclaiming your election. 517 2
Will you accept this call and fulfill this *t* 518 1
commit yourself to this *t* and responsibility? 531 25
Do not forget the *t* committed to you 534 12
commit yourself to this *t* and responsibility? 543 23
For those in positions of public *t* 550 1
commit yourself to this new *t* and responsibility? 559 6
and put your *t* in the LORD. 588 9
Those who know your Name will put their *t* in you, * 593 19
But I put my *t* in your mercy; * 598 8
My God, my rock in whom I put my *t*, * 602 9
he is a shield to all who *t* in him. 604 26
Some put their *t* in chariots and some in horses, * 608 15
For the king puts his *t* in the LORD; * 609 9
Our forefathers put their *t* in you; * 610 8
my God, I put my *t* in you; * 614 14
yet will I put my *t* in him. 617 17
and I put my *t* in the LORD. 622 21
for those who put their *t* in you. 624 7
but mercy embraces those who *t* in the LORD. 625 24
for in his holy Name we put our *t*. 627 18
as we have put our *t* in you. 627 20
happy are they who *t* in him! 628 10
and none will be punished who *t* in him. 629 12
Put your *t* in the LORD and do good; * 633 9
Commit your way to the LORD and put your *t* in him, * 633 13
and put their *t* in the LORD. 640 8
Happy are they who *t* in the LORD! * 640 9
Put your *t* in God; * 643 15
Put your *t* in God; * 644 11
Put your *t* in God; * 645 3
those who put their *t* in their goods, * 652 15
those who foolishly *t* in themselves, * 653 6
I *t* in the mercy of God for ever and ever. 658 17
but I will put my *t* in you. 662 11
I will put my *t* in you. 662 18
in God I *t* and will not be afraid, * 662 20
in God I *t* and will not be afraid, * 663 12
Put your *t* in him always, O people, * 669 22

Put no *t* in extortion; 670 5
rejoice in the LORD and put their *t* in him, * 672 5
So that they might put their *t* in God, * 695 13
nor did they put their *t* in his saving power. 696 21
happy are they who put their *t* in you! 708 19
save your servant who puts his *t* in you. 710 2
my God in whom I put my *t*." 719 14
and my God the rock of my *t*. 724 10
they put their *t* in the Lord. 755 19
and so are all who put their *t* in them. 758 5
O Israel, *t* in the LORD; * 758 6
O house of Aaron, *t* in the LORD, * 758 8
You who fear the LORD, *t* in the LORD; * 758 10
than to put any *t* in flesh. 761 12
than to put any *t* in rulers. 761 14
because I *t* in your words. 766 20
because I *t* in your word. 769 13
for in your word is my *t*. 775 21
Those who *t* in the LORD are like Mount Zion, * 781 17
and so are all who put their *t* in them. 789 12
for I put my *t* in you; * 799 16
my shield in whom I *t*, 800 4
Put not your *t* in rulers, nor in any child of earth, * 803 7
suffer not our *t* in thee to fail; 820 14
t in your goodness all the days of his life; 830 11
Our duty is to believe and *t* in God; 847 20
and because we *t* that in God's presence 862 10

trusted

O Lord, in thee have I *t*; 55 23
they *t*, and you delivered them. 610 9
they *t* in you and were not put to shame. 610 11
"He *t* in the LORD; let him deliver him; * 610 16
in you have I *t* all the day long. 614 23
let me not be put to shame, for I have *t* in you. 616 2
I have *t* in the Lord and have not faltered. 616 9
But as for me, I have *t* in you, O LORD. * 623 20
Even my best friend, whom I *t*, 642 17
but *t* in great wealth 658 14
even those of low estate cannot be *t*. 670 2
In my distress I said, "No one can be *t*." 759 22

trusting

that we, surely *t* in thy defense, 57 4
that we, surely *t* in your defense, 99 23
Lord, *t* in our own righteousness, 337 10
t in the guidance of the Holy Spirit, 513 2

trusts

my heart *t* in him, and I have been helped; 619 25

trustworthy

may elect *t* leaders and make wise decisions for 822 12

truth

we deceive ourselves, and the *t* is not in us; 38 11
O send out thy light and thy *t*, 40 16
shall worship the Father in spirit and in *t*; 40 21
and the peoples with his *t*. 45 10
and his *t* endureth from generation to generation. 45 22
but with the unleavened bread of sincerity and *t*. 46 6
And guide us in the way of justice and *t*. 55 8
granting us in this world knowledge of thy *t*, 59 18
And guide us in the way of justice and *t*. 67 23
granting us in this world knowledge of thy *t*, 72 15
we deceive ourselves, and the *t* is not in us, 76 9
Send out your light and your *t*, that they may lead me, 78 15
worship the Father in spirit and *t*, 78 20
but with the unleavened bread of sincerity and *t*. 83 14
Your ways are ways of righteousness and *t*, * 94 12
And guide us in the way of justice and *t*. 98 2
granting us in this world knowledge of your *t*, 102 7
to defend us from all error, and to lead us into all *t*; 107 7
made worthy to worship you in spirit and in *t*; 111 6
And guide us in the way of justice and *t*. 122 2
granting us in this world knowledge of your *t*, 126 7
O Lord, O God of *t*. 129 20
For you have redeemed me, O Lord, O God of *t*. 132 13
That it may please thee to bring into the way of *t* 150 19
and walk in the ways of *t*, 150 28
hold fast the unchangeable *t* of thy Word, 166 19
may worship thee in sincerity and *t*; 170 18
serve thee in pureness of living and *t*; 172 11
Christ to be the way, the *t*, and the life, 173 18
may proclaim thy *t* with boldness, 178 8
may so walk in the light of thy *t*, 186 9
in unity and peace we may proclaim the one *t* 187 4
be firmly grounded in its *t*; 189 2
grace and strength to bear witness to the *t*: 189 6
speak the *t*, boldly rebuke vice, 190 6
patiently suffer for the *t*'s sake; 190 7
gifts of grace to understand and teach the *t* 197 20
fill them with the *t* of thy doctrine 205 8
rejoicing in the knowledge of thy *t*, 209 19
which thou givest us to do, in *t* and beauty 210 5
hold fast the unchangeable *t* of your Word, 218 10
may worship you in sincerity and *t*; 222 12
serve you in pureness of living and *t*; 224 4
Christ to be the way, the *t*, and the life, 225 10
proclaim your *t* with boldness, 230 3
may so walk in the light of your *t*, 238 3
in unity and peace we may proclaim the one *t* 238 17
pray that we may be firmly grounded in its *t*; 240 10
and strength to bear witness to the *t*: 240 14
constantly speak the *t*, boldly rebuke vice, 241 15
and patiently suffer for the *t*'s sake; 241 16
grace to understand and teach the *t* 249 6
fill them with the *t* of your doctrine 256 5
rejoicing in the knowledge of your *t*, 261 3
in *t* and beauty and for the common good; 261 11
For behold, you look for *t* deep within me, * 266 14
That by God's help they may seek justice and *t*, 278 23
That God will open their hearts to the *t*, 279 28
may worship you in sincerity and *t*; 295 12
Open their hearts to your grace and *t*. 305 17
we deceive ourselves, and the *t* is not in us; 320 2
the Universal Church with the spirit of *t*, 329 5
thy holy Name may agree in the *t* of thy holy Word, 329 7
to teach them and to lead them into all *t*; 347 9
given us the Holy Spirit to guide us into all *t*. 348 22
we deceive ourselves, and the *t* is not in us. 352 2
you have brought us out of error into *t*, 368 9
all your people, and those who seek your *t*.] 375 16
to teach them and to lead them into all *t*; 380 4
given us the Holy Spirit to guide us into all *t*. 381 15
all who confess your Name may be united in your *t*, 388 3

that it may be filled with *t* and love, 389 15
all who proclaim the Gospel, and all who seek the *T.* 392 13
remember in *t* all your sins and his unfailing mercy. 449 11
guard and defend them in his *t*, 521 20
that it may be filled with *t* and love, 548 11
may hunger for *t*, and may thirst after righteousness, 548 22
For there is no *t* in their mouth; * 589 9
who speaks the *t* from his heart. 599 7
Lead me in your *t* and teach me, * 614 21
O LORD, O God of *t*. 622 19
Send out your light and your *t*, 644 21
Ride out and conquer in the cause of *t* * 647 19
For behold, you look for *t* deep within me, * 656 18
and lying more than speaking the *t*. 658 5
But in *t* God has heard me; * 675 5
Mercy and *t* have met together; * 709 14
T shall spring up from the earth, * 709 16
and I will walk in your *t*; * 710 22
slow to anger, and full of kindness and *t*. 711 5
love and *t* go before your face. 714 22
and the peoples with his *t*. 726 21
because they are done in *t* and equity. 754 21
Do not take the word of *t* out of my mouth, * 766 21
and your law is the *t*. 775 10
The heart of your word is *t*; * 776 23
in *t*, he will not break it: 786 20
Christians may be led into the way of *t*, 815 4
the world into the way of justice and *t*, 816 2
Lead them and us from prejudice to *t*; 816 6
Fill it with all *t*, in all *t* with all peace. 816 11
united in one holy bond of *t* 818 21
Fill them with the love of *t* and righteousness, 820 22
whose will is good and gracious, and whose law is *t*: 821 2
that they may discern the *t*, 821 11
to respect their witness and to discern the *t*, 823 14
in the midst of our struggles for justice and *t*, 824 2
find you to be the source of all *t*; 824 20
Almighty God, you proclaim your *t* in every age 827 6
worship thee in spirit and in *t*; 833 23
for the *t* of his Word and the example of his life; 836 13
For all valiant seekers after *t*, liberty, and justice, 837 17
To speak the *t*, and not to mislead others 848 16
the Lord who leads us into all *t* 852 22
and the pillar and ground of *t*. 854 10

truths

How do we recognize the *t* taught by the Holy Spirit? 853 1
We recognize *t* to be taught by the Holy Spirit 853 3

try

Test me, O LORD, and *t* me; * 616 10
t me and know my restless thoughts. 795 25

tumult

and though the mountains tremble at its *t*. 649 7
the unending *t* of those who rise up against you. 691 2
For your enemies are in *t*, * 706 5

turmoil

and in vain we are in *t*; * 639 7

turn

and *t* unto the Lord your God; 38 14
and the light around me *t* to night," 62 6
And let them *t* to the Lord, 86 21
and the light around me *t* to night," 110 8
and the light around me *t* to night," 116 2
and slanderers, and to *t* their hearts, 152 9
t from us all those evils 155 8
t us from the old life of sin: 203 6
you *t* us from the old life of sin: 254 8
but rather that they may *t* from their wickedness 269 4
t the hearts of those who resist it; 280 5
Do you *t* to Jesus Christ and accept him as your 302 16
with hearty repentance and true faith *t* unto him, 332 3
Hear the Word of God to all who truly *t* to him. 332 7
and all who *t* to you for help; 395 5
Hear the Word of God to all who truly *t* to him. 449 12
I *t* to you in sorrow and repentance. 450 17
Will you *t* again to Christ as your Lord? 450 22
T again then unto thy rest, O my soul, * 479 12
t us away from you at our last hour. 492 20
I will never *t* away anyone who believes in me. 501 2
when we *t* to you in sickness or special need, 569 7
T, O LORD, and deliver me; * 590 5
they shall *t* back and suddenly be put to shame. 590 19
I will not *t* back till I have destroyed them. 605 15
All the ends of the earth shall remember and *t* to 612 10
T to me and have pity on me, * 615 20
nor *t* away your servant in displeasure. 618 15
T from evil and do good; * 628 21
T from evil, and do good, * 635 14
T your gaze from me, that I may be glad again, * 639 25
they do not resort to evil spirits or *t* to false gods. 640 10
in your great compassion, *t* to me." 680 24
say to me "Aha!" and gloat over me *t* back, * 682 17
And so the people *t* to them * 687 19
T your steps toward the endless ruins; * 689 14
Let not the oppressed *t* away ashamed; * 690 26
that they in their *t* might tell it to their children; 695 12
T now, O God of hosts, look down from heaven; 703 15
And so will we never *t* away from you; * 703 22
and *t* my hand against their foes. 705 4
and to those who *t* their hearts to him. 709 11
T to me and have mercy upon me; * 711 6
You *t* us back to the dust and say, * 718 4
He will *t* their wickedness back upon them 724 11
to *t* away his wrath from consuming them. 743 19
T again to your rest, O my soul, * 759 14
T from me shame and rebuke, * 765 3
T my eyes from watching what is worthless; * 766 9
T away the reproach which I dread, * 766 13
Let those who fear you *t* to me, * 769 23
T to me in mercy, * 774 11
As for those who *t* aside to crooked ways, 782 3
do not *t* away the face of your Anointed. 786 18
and the light around me *t* to night," 794 21
and to *t* their sorrow into joy. 826 5
T the hearts of the parents to the children, 829 4

turned

we have *t* every one to his own way; 39 1
we have *t* every one to his own way; 76 25
But we *t* against you, and betrayed your trust; 370 14
and we *t* against one another. 370 15
that his sickness may be *t* into health, 458 13

then shall my night be *t* to day. 475 14
all alike have *t* bad; * 598 19
You have *t* my wailing into dancing; * 622 3
has lifted up his heel and *t* against me. 642 19
Our heart never *t* back, * 646 22
all alike have *t* bad; * 659 5
He *t* the sea into dry land, 674 3
but that was *t* to my reproach. 680 8
t back in the day of battle; 695 21
He *t* their rivers into blood, * 698 15
They *t* away and were disloyal like their fathers; * 699 20
and *t* yourself from your wrathful indignation. 708 25
You have *t* back the edge of his sword * 716 27
Whose heart he *t*, so that they hated his people, * 740 3
He *t* their waters into blood * 740 11
Jordan *t* and went back. 757 2
O Jordan, that you *t* back? 757 6
Who *t* the hard rock into a pool of water * 757 11
but I have not *t* from your law. 767 16
and *t* my feet toward your decrees. 768 6
But my eyes are *t* to you, Lord GOD; * 797 19

turnest

and *t* the shadow of death into the morning: 56 19
Thou *t* man to destruction; * 472 14

turneth

that *t* deep darkness into the morning, 62 1

turns

and *t* the shadow of death into the morning: 99 14
and *t* deep darkness into the morning, 115 13
Their malice *t* back upon their own head; * 592 3
From where he sits enthroned he *t* his gaze * 627 3
As when a plowman *t* over the earth in furrows, * 797 17

twelve

faithful servant Matthias to be of the number of the *T*: 188 2
apostle James, first among the *T* to suffer martyrdom 191 8
faithful servant Matthias to be numbered among the *T*: 239 12
apostle James, first among the *T* to suffer martyrdom 242 15
night in prayer before he chose and sent forth his *t* 514 13

twenty

The chariots of God are *t* thousand, 677 15

twice

God has spoken once, *t* have I heard it, * 670 8

twinkling

For his wrath endures but the *t* of an eye, * 621 12

two

when *t* or three are gathered together 59 14
when *t* or three are gathered together 72 11
when *t* or three are gathered together 102 3
when *t* or three are gathered together 126 3
On these *t* commandments hang all the Law 319 12
On these *t* commandments hang all the Law 324 5
uphold these *t* persons in their marriage? 425 2
uphold these *t* persons in their marriage? 434 2
whenever *t* or three have gathered together 578 10
and breaks in *t* the iron bars. 747 14
Who divided the Red Sea in *t*, * 790 21
and a *t*-edged sword in their hand; 807 13
We learn *t* things: 847 17
This Church uses *t* creeds: 851 25
What are the *t* great sacraments of the Gospel? 858 5
The *t* great sacraments given by Christ 858 6
How do they differ from the *t* sacraments 860 12

tyrant

You *t*, why do you boast of wickedness * 657 23

tyrants

frustrate the designs of evil *t* 186 17
frustrate the designs of evil *t* 238 10

Tyre

The people of *T* are here with a gift; * 648 15
the Philistines and those who dwell in *T*. 706 17
behold Philistia, *T*, and Ethiopia: 711 18

U

unadvisedly

not to be entered into *u* or lightly, but reverently, 423 14

unawares

Let ruin come upon them *u*; * 630 5

unbearable

but my pain became *u*. 638 21

unborn

torch of freedom for nations then *u*: 190 19
torch of freedom for nations then *u*: 242 3
They shall come and make known to a people yet *u* * 612 21
and the children yet *u*; * 695 11
so that a people yet *u* may praise the LORD. 732 13

unbounded

Father, of majesty *u*, 95 27

unceasing

they offer you *u* praise. 373 9
to the glory and *u* praise of your Name. 521 5

uncertainties

Grant us, in all our doubts and *u*, 832 8

uncertainty

sensible of the shortness and *u* of life; 489 5
aware of the shortness and *u* of human life; 504 3

unchangeabale

hold fast the *u* truth of thy Word, 166 19
hold fast the *u* truth of your Word, 218 10
O God of *u* power and eternal light: 280 14
O God of *u* power and eternal light: 291 11
O God of *u* power and eternal light: 515 4
O God of *u* power and eternal light: 528 2
O God of *u* power and eternal light: 540 2

uncharitable

For all false judgments, for *u* thoughts 268 20

uncovered

The beds of the seas were *u*, 603 19

unction
who in faith and repentance receive this holy *u* 455 12
reconciliation of a penitent, and *u*. 860 11
What is *U* of the Sick? 861 13
U is the rite of anointing the sick with oil, 861 14

undependable
they were *u* like a warped bow. 699 21

under
suffered *u* Pontius Pilate, 53 28
Lord, keep this nation *u* thy care; 55 7
suffered *u* Pontius Pilate, 66 14
Lord, keep this nation *u* thy care; 67 22
He suffered *u* Pontius Pilate, 96 18
Lord, keep this nation *u* your care; 98 1
No one lights a lamp to put it *u* a bucket, 109 8
He suffered *u* Pontius Pilate, 120 14
Lord, keep this nation *u* your care; 122 1
abides *u* the shadow of the Almighty. 129 22
and you shall find refuge *u* his wings; * 130 4
and the serpent *u* your feet. 130 25
Hide us *u* the shadow of your wings. 132 15
and finally to beat down Satan *u* our feet, 152 13
brought together *u* his most gracious rule; 185 5
brought together *u* his most gracious rule; 203 3
u the guidance of the Holy Spirit, 205 15
brought together *u* his most gracious rule; 236 18
brought together *u* his most gracious rule; 254 5
u the guidance of the Holy Spirit, 256 12
may be one flock *u* one shepherd, Jesus 280 7
your chosen people from slavery *u* Pharaoh, 289 14
He suffered *u* Pontius Pilate, 293 5
He suffered *u* Pontius Pilate, 304 8
or in the water *u* the earth; 318 3
For our sake he was crucified *u* Pontius Pilate; 327 4
and was crucified also for us *u* Pontius Pilate; 328 5
gather up the crumbs *u* thy Table. 337 12
For our sake he was crucified *u* Pontius Pilate; 358 20
put all things in subjection *u* your Christ, 369 9
giving voice to every creature *u* heaven, 373 10
He suffered *u* Pontius Pilate, 416 13
all things in heaven, on earth, and *u* the earth 456 21
know and feel that the only Name *u* heaven 457 2
and give him patience *u* his affliction. 458 6
He suffered *u* Pontius Pilate, 496 8
For our sake he was crucified *u* Pontius Pilate; 519 23
For our sake he was crucified *u* Pontius Pilate; 530 14
For our sake he was crucified *u* Pontius Pilate; 542 14
ministry of servanthood directly *u* your bishop. 543 4
I am not worthy to have you come *u* my roof; 562 9
you put all things *u* his feet: 592 20
their cities plowed *u*, the memory of them perished; 593 12
u their tongue are mischief and wrong. 595 7
hide me *u* the shadow of your wings, 601 15
with a storm cloud *u* his feet. 603 8
your people take refuge *u* the 632 18
He subdues the peoples *u* us, * 650 10
and the nations *u* our feet. 650 11
and he shall tread our enemies *u* foot. 668 11
I will take refuge *u* the cover of your wings. 668 20
and *u* the shadow of your wings I will rejoice. 670 26
abides *u* the shadow of the Almighty. 719 11
and you shall find refuge *u* his wings; * 719 18
and the serpent *u* your feet. 720 13
and they were humbled *u* their hand. 745 9
and he shall tread our enemies *u* foot. 750 22
"I will not come *u* the roof of my house, * 786 3
adder's poison is *u* their lips. 796 6
who subdues the peoples *u* me. 800 5
giving them patience *u* their sufferings, 815 11
all peoples may be gathered *u* the banner 815 25
those whom you call to follow you *u* the vows 819 8
Lord, keep this nation *u* your care. 821 18
u the inspiration of the Holy Spirit, 853 11
because it is one Body, *u* one Head, 854 15
u the guidance of the Holy Spirit? 860 8

understand
gifts of grace to *u* and teach the truth 197 20
and grant that they may know and *u* 231 5
gifts of grace to *u* and teach the truth 249 6
and will make me *u* wisdom secretly. 266 15
Help us, we pray, in the midst of things we cannot *u*, 481 14
and will make me *u* wisdom secretly. 656 19
When I tried to *u* these things, * 688 9
They do not know, neither do they *u*; 705 17
nor does the fool *u*, * 721 8
when will you fools *u*? 723 10
Make me *u* the way of your commandments, * 765 13
to be understood as to *u*; 833 10
How do we *u* the meaning of the Bible? 853 27
We *u* the meaning of the Bible by the help 853 28

understandest
thou *u* my thoughts long before. 474 20

understanding
surpassing human *u*. 94 11
with true knowledge and *u* of thy Word; 150 6
such good things as pass man's *u*: 174 2
such good things as surpass our *u*: 225 15
open your grief to a discreet and *u* priest, 317 12
The peace of God, which passeth all *u*, 339 15
whose wisdom is beyond our *u*: 494 8
and *u* he may love and care for your people; 560 7
enlighten my *u* with the light 562 13
They have no *u* of the LORD's doings, 619 18
Do not be like horse or mule, which have no *u*; * 625 20
and my heart shall meditate on *u*. 652 10
Those who are honored, but have no *u*, * 653 23
I was stupid and had no *u*; * 688 21
those who act accordingly have a good *u*; 755 2
Give me *u*, and I shall keep your law; * 766 3
give me *u*, that I may learn your 769 10
I have more *u* than all my teachers, * 771 17
Through your commandments I gain *u*; * 772 1
I am your servant; grant me *u*, * 773 23
it gives *u* to the simple. 774 8
grant me *u*, that I may live. 775 14
give me *u*, according to your word. 777 18
source of all wisdom and *u*, 818 2
give unto them the spirit of wisdom and *u*, 821 11
To the Judges and officers of our Courts give *u* 822 6

give them *u* helpers, 830 3
thy peace which passeth *u* 830 17
give patient *u* and 831 23

understands

and *u* all their works. 627 6

understood

to be *u* as to understand; 833 10

undertake

Give us grace to do your will in all that we *u*; 387 12
Will you *u* to be a faithful pastor 532 14

undeserved

God's favor towards us, unearned and *u*; 858 3

undivided

May God the holy and *u* Trinity guard 460 7

undone

we have left *u* those things 41 21
we have left *u* those things 63 2
and by what we have left *u*. 79 14
and by what we have left *u*. 116 16
and in what we have left *u*. 127 10
and by what we have left *u*. 267 18
offended in what you have done or left *u*, 317 3
and by what we have left *u*. 320 14
we have left *u* those things 321 2
and by what we have left *u*. 331 25
and by what we have left *u*. 352 14
and by what we have left *u*. 360 6
things done and left *u*; 393 12
and by what we have left *u*. 397 23
things done and left *u*; 447 7
and by what we have left *u*. 454 5

unearned

Grace is God's favor towards us, *u* 858 2

unemployed

for the *u* and the destitute, 384 25

unending

Shed forth thine *u* day upon us 69 12
Shed forth your *u* day upon us 123 11
enter with them into thine *u* joy; 202 6
know you in the power of his *u* life; 242 12
enter with them into your *u* joy; 253 10
of new and *u* life in him. 363 15
proclaim with them your glory, in their *u* hymn: 370 26
and come to the *u* glory of him who, 545 17
the *u* tumult of those who rise up against you. 691 2

unfailing

O God, your *u* providence sustains the world 134 11
remember in truth all your sins and his *u* mercy. 449 11
answer me with your *u* help. 680 16
Restore to them the assurance of your *u* mercy; 831 21

unfaithful

you destroy all who are *u*. 689 4

unfaithfulness

We confess to you, Lord, all our past *u*: 268 1

unfamiliar

I heard an *u* voice saying, * 704 11

unfeigned

I will thank you with an *u* heart, * 763 17

unfeignedly

that our hearts may be *u* thankful; 59 3
that our hearts may be *u* thankful; 71 22
prepared for those who *u* love thee; 194 13

unfinished

Your eyes beheld my limbs, yet *u* in the womb; 795 6

ungodly

You have rebuked the *u* and destroyed the wicked; * 593 9
The *u* have fallen into the pit they dug, * 594 7
Rise up, O Lord, let not the *u* have the upper hand; * 594 15
let the *u* know they are but mortal. 594 18
the *u* shall perish from his land. 596 2
and defend my cause against an *u* people; * 644 15
Awake, and punish all the *u*; * 666 5
you laugh all the *u* to scorn. 666 13
All the *u* encompass me; * 761 15

unhappy

great dangers we are in by our *u* divisions; 818 16

union

We praise you in *u* with them 375 24
the mystery of the *u* between Christ and his Church, 423 7
The *u* of husband and wife in heart, body, and mind 423 9
Into this holy *u* N.N. and N.N. now come 424 1
We thank you, also, for consecrating the *u* 430 13
hinder us from godly *u* and concord; 818 18
where there is discord, *u*; where there is doubt, faith; 833 7
in *u* with Christ, for the purposes of God. 857 16
The inward and spiritual grace in Baptism is *u* 858 17
the strengthening of our *u* with Christ 860 1
woman and man enter into a life-long *u*, 861 5

unite

U us to your Son in his sacrifice, 369 6
and to *u* us in your holy Church. 573 20
u us in bonds of love; 815 17
In corporate worship, we *u* ourselves with others 857 22

united

the President of the *U* States (or of this nation), 150 26
and *u* to one another with pure affection; 179 7
may be *u* in one body by the one Spirit, 204 20
and *u* to one another with pure affection; 231 1
may be *u* in one body by the one Spirit, 255 18
For N., the President of the *U* States 278 19
and Representatives of the *U* Nations 278 21
be *u* in your truth, live together in your love, 388 3
why you may not be *u* in marriage lawfully, 424 6
your children are *u* one to another, 430 5
u with one another, 574 6
u in one holy bond of truth 818 21
and fashion into one *u* people the multitudes 820 7
Grant to the President of the *U* States, 820 19
Guide the people of the *U* States 822 24
with many voices in one *u* chorus, 839 19
are *u* with all the people of God, 862 27

unites

and in which he *u* us to his one offering 859 12

uniting

u peoples of many tongues 347 9
u peoples of many tongues 380 4
and for *u* us through him and the fellowship 523 2
and for *u* us through him and the fellowship 535 2
and for *u* us through him and the fellowship 546 4
and for *u* us through him and the fellowship 564 2

unity

give to us the peace and *u* of that heavenly City, 107 20
give to us the peace and *u* of that heavenly City, 138 19
to give to all nations *u*, peace, and concord; 151 2
in the *u* of the Holy Spirit, 160 10
in the *u* of the Holy Spirit, 161 18
in the *u* of the Holy Spirit, 162 11
in the *u* of the Holy Spirit, 164 9
in the *u* of the Holy Spirit, 165 13
in the *u* of the same Spirit, 170 19
in the *u* of the Holy Spirit, 171 21
in the *u* of the Holy Spirit, 172 19
in the *u* of the Holy Spirit, 173 9
in the *u* of the same Spirit, 175 13
in the *u* of the same Spirit, 175 20
of the Divine Majesty to worship the *U*: 176 4
in *u* of spirit by their doctrine, 178 21
being gathered together in *u* by thy Holy Spirit, 181 6
in the *u* of the Holy Spirit, 186 19
that in *u* and peace we may proclaim the one truth 187 4
in the *u* of the Holy Spirit, 187 14
in the *u* of the Holy Spirit, 188 6
and knit together in *u* by thy Spirit, 190 13
in the *u* of the same Spirit, 190 15
in the *u* of the Holy spirit, 192 5
in the *u* of the Holy Spirit, 193 16
in the *u* of the Holy Spirit, 198 7
in the *u* of the same Spirit 200 4
in the *u* of the Holy Spirit, 201 17
in the *u* of the Holy Spirit, 202 7
in the *u* of the Holy Spirit, 204 6
in the *u* of the same Spirit, 204 15
in the *u* of the same Spirit, 205 2
in the *u* of the Holy Spirit, 205 12
in the *u* of the Holy Spirit, 206 7
in the *u* of the Holy Spirit, 207 13
in the *u* of the Holy Spirit, 208 7
in the *u* of the Holy Spirit, 212 9
in the *u* of the Holy 213 11
in *u* of the Holy Spirit, 214 5
in the *u* of the Holy Spirit, 216 4
in the *u* of the Holy Spirit, 217 5
in the *u* of the Holy Spirit, 222 13
in the *u* of the Holy Spirit, 223 13
in the *u* of the Holy Spirit, 224 11
in the *u* of the Holy Spirit, 225 1
in the *u* of the Holy Spirit, 227 6
power of your divine Majesty to worship the *U*: 228 4
in *u* of spirit by their teaching, 230 15
together in *u* by your Holy Spirit, 232 18
in the *u* of the Holy Spirit, 238 12
in *u* and peace we may proclaim the one truth 238 17
in the *u* of the Holy Spirit, 239 4
in the *u* of the Holy Spirit, 240 5
and knit together in *u* by your Spirit, 241 21
in the *u* of the Holy Spirit, 241 24
in the *u* of the Holy Spirit, 243 12
in the *u* of the Holy Spirit, 245 2
in the *u* of the Holy Spirit, 249 16
in the *u* of the Holy Spirit, 251 10
in the *u* of the Holy Spirit, 252 5
in the *u* of the Holy Spirit, 253 5
in the *u* of the Holy Spirit, 255 4
in the *u* of the Holy Spirit, 256 9
in the *u* of the Holy Spirit, 257 4
in the *u* of the Holy Spirit, 258 13
in the *u* of the Holy Spirit, 259 9
For its *u* in witness and service 278 3
in the *u* of the Holy Spirit, 280 22
in the *u* of the Holy Spirit, 286 15
with the spirit of truth, *u*, and concord; 329 6
live in *u* and godly love. 329 8
in the *u* of the Holy Ghost 336 13
in the *u* of the Holy Ghost all honor 343 3
in Trinity of Persons and in *U* of Substance; 347 14
and serve you in *u*, constancy, and peace; 363 16
in the *u* of the Holy Spirit 363 20
in the *u* of the Holy Spirit 369 15
Reveal its *u*, guard its faith, 375 14
in the *u* of the Holy Spirit, 375 27
in Trinity of Persons and in *U* of Being; 380 9
and for the *u* of all peoples, 383 7
For the peace and *u* of the Church of God; 392 12
give to us the peace and *u* of that heavenly City, 395 11
in the *u* of the Holy Spirit 403 19
in the *u* of the Holy Spirit 405 20
in the *u* of the Holy Spirit, 425 13
that *u* may overcome estrangement, 429 18
you live and reign in perfect *u*, 430 8
that in it is represented the spiritual *u* 431 2
in the *u* of the Holy Spirit, 515 12
You are called to guard the faith, *u*, and discipline 517 7
Will you guard the faith, *u*, and discipline 518 19
in the *u* of the Holy Spirit, 528 10
in the *u* of the Holy Spirit, 540 10
that is at *u* with itself; 779 23
when brethren live together in *u*! 787 10
hold the faith in *u* of spirit, 815 5
u with God and each other in Christ. 855 3
to guard the faith, *u*, and discipline 855 24

universal

govern thy holy Church *U* in the right way, 150 3
the *U* Church with the spirit of truth, 329 5
For the Church *u*, of which these visible buildings 578 7
we pray for thy holy Church *u*; 815 2
The Nicene Creed is the creed of the *u* Church 852 6

universe

O ruler of the *u*, Lord God, 94 9
God of all power, Ruler of the *U*, 370 5
Almighty and everlasting God, you made the *u* 827 11

Blessed are you, O Lord God, King of the *U*, 835 13
This means that the *u* is good, 846 7
What does this mean about our place in the *u*? 846 9

universities

O Eternal God, bless all schools, colleges, and *u* 824 16

unjust

and not to *u* gain. 766 8

unjustly

"How long will you judge *u*, * 705 11
and dealt *u* with his servants. 740 4
When any are held *u*, bring them release; 826 20

unknown

forgive us our sins, known and *u*, 393 11
thy righteous servants, known to us and *u*; 489 18
other righteous servants, known to us and *u*; 504 16

unleavened

but with the *u* bread of sincerity and truth. 46 6
but with the *u* bread of sincerity and truth. 83 14

unless

cannot bear fruit by itself, *u* it abides in the vine, 397 8
neither can you, *u* you abide in me. 397 9
U the LORD builds the house, * 782 20
U the LORD watches over the city, * 783 1

unprepared

and from dying suddenly and *u*, 149 16

unrighteous

let not the oil of the *u* anoint my head; * 797 13

unrighteousness

cleanse us from all *u*. 38 13
cleanse us from all *u*. 76 12
cleanse us from all *u*. 320 4
cleanse us from all *u*. 352 4

unruly

O Almighty God, who alone canst order the *u* wills 167 15
God, you alone can bring into order the *u* wills 219 6

unsearchable

proclaim the *u* riches of our Savior 196 12
proclaim the *u* riches of our Savior 247 23

unseen

of all that is, seen and *u*. 326 9
of all that is, seen and *u*. 358 6
of all that is, seen and *u*. 519 9
of all that is, seen and *u*. 529 12
of all that is, seen and *u*. 541 12
of all that is, seen and *u*. 846 5

unsteady

growing up in an *u* and confusing world: 829 15

untended

never leaving your temple *u*. 520 17

unveiled

and make them worthy at length to behold it *u* 819 17

unworthiness

things which for our *u* we dare not, 179 19
things which for our *u* we dare not, 231 13

unworthy

we thine *u* servants 58 15
we thine *u* servants 71 11
U as I am, you will save me, 91 22
we your *u* servants give you humble thanks 101 8
we your *u* servants give you humble thanks 125 6
And although we are *u*, through our manifold sins, 336 9

up

and take *u* his cross, and follow me." 38 25
And hath raised *u* a mighty salvation for us * 50 24
Govern them and lift them *u* for ever. 55 16
whose most dear Son went not *u* to joy 56 6
by giving *u* our selves to thy service, 59 6
the lifting *u* of my hands be an evening sacrifice. 61 2
and awake *u* after thy likeness; 69 10
by giving *u* our selves to thy service, 72 3
and take *u* his cross and follow me." 76 24
the earth swallowed them *u*. 85 20
and has lifted *u* the lowly. 92 9
He has raised *u* for us a mighty savior, * 92 20
whose most dear Son went not *u* to joy 99 1
by giving *u* our selves to your service, 101 19
I lift *u* my eyes to the hills; * 104 13
the lifting *u* of our hands as the evening sacrifice. 113 10
Stir *u* in us the flame of that love which burned 113 13
the lifting *u* of my hands as the evening sacrifice. 115 2
and has lifted *u* the lowly. 119 15
asleep peacefully in you and wake *u* in your likeness; 123 9
by giving *u* our selves to your service, 125 17
Lift *u* the light of your countenance upon us, O Lord. 129 3
Lift *u* your hands in the holy place 131 8
Lift *u* your hands in the holy place 140 3
to raise *u* those who fall; 152 12
Stir *u* thy power, O Lord, and with great might come 160 1
whose most dear Son went not *u* to joy 168 10
and given *u* into the hands of sinners, 169 16
Stir *u* in thy Church that Spirit of adoption 170 15
first martyr Stephen, who looked *u* to heaven 186 2
David didst raise *u* Joseph to be the guardian 188 9
may have grace to take *u* our cross 192 16
Raise *u*, we beseech thee, in this and every land 196 10
and didst raise *u* thy servant N. to be a light 196 16
who didst raise *u* thy faithful servant 197 4
courage, we beseech thee, to take *u* our cross 201 9
Stir *u* your power, O Lord, and with great might come 212 1
whose most dear Son went not *u* to joy 220 1
Stir *u* in your Church that Spirit of adoption 222 9
first martyr Stephen, who looked *u* to heaven 237 15
David raised *u* Joseph to be the guardian 239 18
may have grace to take *u* our cross 244 4
Raise *u* in this and every land 247 22
and who raised *u* your servant N. to be a light 248 2
who raised *u* your faithful servant 248 15
courage to take *u* our cross and follow him; 252 14
whose most dear Son went not *u* to joy 272 1
and stir *u* in us the will and patience 279 12
things which were cast down are being raised *u*, 280 19

things which were cast down are being raised *u*, 291 16
Stir *u* in your Church that Spirit of adoption 295 9
brought *u* in the Christian faith and life? 302 2
Lift *u* your hearts. 333 3
We lift them *u* unto the Lord. 333 4
as to gather *u* the crumbs under thy Table. 337 12
Lift *u* your hearts. 340 11
We lift them *u* unto the Lord. 340 12
built *u* as living stones of a holy temple, 348 16
Lift *u* your hearts. 361 3
We lift them *u* to the Lord. 361 4
Lift *u* your hearts. 367 3
Lift *u* your hearts. 370 1
We lift them *u* to the Lord. 370 2
Lift *u* your hearts. 372 19
fulfill your purpose he gave himself *u* to death; 374 6
built *u* as living stones of a holy temple, 381 10
Lift *u* your hearts. 402 3
Lift *u* your hearts. 404 5
and the grace to bring them *u* to know you, 429 21
and has lifted *u* the lowly. 442 4
I will lift *u* the cup of salvation * 442 21
and raise him *u* to a life of service 459 5
If I am to stand *u*, help me to stand bravely. 461 21
lift *u* your countenance upon them; 467 6
In the morning it is green, and groweth *u*; * 472 21
but in the evening it is cut down, dried *u*, 472 22
I will lift *u* mine eyes unto the hills; * 473 9
Thou knowest my down-sitting and mine *u*-rising; 474 19
If I climb *u* into heaven, thou art there; * 475 7
and set me *u* upon a rock of stone. 477 22
And now shall he lift *u* mine head * 477 23
He that raised *u* Jesus from the dead 485 1
the Lord lift *u* his countenance 485 14
After my awaking, he will raise me *u*; 491 9
the Lord lift *u* his countenance upon him 501 15
and wake *u* in your likeness; 504 24
things which were cast down are being raised *u*, 515 9
enlightening the minds and stirring *u* the conscience 518 9
and have raised *u* prophets, kings, and priests, 520 16
and by whom your Church is built *u* 521 4
for raising *u* among us faithful servants 523 4
things which were cast down are being raised *u*, 528 7
to build *u* the family of God? 532 17
the work of ministry and the building *u* of his body. 533 9
We thank you for raising *u* among us faithful servants 535 4
things which were cast down are being raised *u*, 540 7
We thank you for raising *u* among us faithful servants 546 6
build *u* your Church, and glorify your Name, 549 5
We thank you for raising *u* among us faithful servants 564 4
building *u* of the living, 567 11
Why do the kings of the earth rise *u* in revolt, 586 3
how many there are who rise *u* against me! 587 4
you are my glory, the one who lifts *u* my head. 587 8
Rise *u*, O LORD; set me free, O my God; * 587 15
Lift *u* the light of your countenance upon us, 588 12
Stand *u*, O LORD, in your wrath; * 591 6
rise *u* against the fury of my enemies. 591 7
You have set *u* a stronghold 592 11
he has set *u* his throne for judgment. 593 14
O you who lift me *u* from the gate of death; 594 3
Rise *u*, O LORD, let not the ungodly 594 15
Rise *u*, O LORD; 595 18
lift *u* your hand, O God; * 595 19
I will rise *u*," says the LORD 597 11
who eat *u* my people like bread 598 22
from those who rise *u* against them. 601 13
You will swallow them *u* in your wrath, * 609 16
Lift *u* your heads, O gates; 614 1
To you, O LORD, I lift *u* my soul; 614 13
When evildoers came upon me to eat *u* my flesh, * 617 11
And though war should rise *u* against me, * 617 16
Even now he lifts *u* my head * 618 5
for false witnesses have risen *u* against me, 618 24
when I lift *u* my hands to your holy of holies. 619 9
break them down and not build them *u*. 619 21
because you have lifted me *u* * 621 4
You brought me *u*, O LORD, from the dead; * 621 8
You have not shut me *u* in the power of the enemy; * 623 1
which you have laid *u* for those who fear you; * 624 5
my moisture was dried *u* as in the heat of summer. 625 6
He gathers *u* the waters of the ocean 626 13
and stores *u* the depths of the sea. 626 14
Take *u* shield and armor * 629 15
and rise *u* to help me. 629 16
Malicious witnesses rise *u* against me; * 630 13
Do not let them say, "We have swallowed him *u*." 631 23
He thinks *u* wickedness upon his bed 632 9
he will raise you *u* to possess the land, 636 4
we heap *u* riches and cannot tell who will gather 639 8
taken to his bed and will never get *u* again." 642 16
has lifted *u* his heel and turned against me. 642 19
be merciful to me and raise me *u*, * 642 20
rose *u* against us. 645 22
Rise *u*, and help us, * 647 9
God has gone *u* with a shout, * 650 14
who eat *u* my people like bread 659 8
For the arrogant have risen *u* against me, 659 21
Swallow them *u*, O LORD; 660 23
Wake *u*, my spirit, 664 12
protect me from those who rise *u* against me. 665 19
You have set *u* a banner for those who fear you, * 667 16
and lift *u* my hands in your Name. 670 20
let no rebel rise *u* against him. 674 8
You have gone *u* on high and led captivity captive; 677 18
for the waters have risen *u* to my neck. 679 8
Zeal for your house has eaten me *u*; * 680 5
neither let the deep swallow me *u*; * 680 21
your help, O God, will lift me *u* on high. 681 23
bring me *u* again from the deep places of the earth. 684 25
they set *u* their banners as tokens of victory. 689 17
like men coming *u* with axes to a grove of trees; * 689 18
you dried *u* ever-flowing rivers. 690 15
the unending tumult of those who rise *u* against you. 691 2
he puts down one and lifts *u* another. 691 17
When God rose *u* to judgment * 692 18
your lightnings lit *u* the world; * 694 12
he made the waters stand *u* like walls. 695 29
swarms of flies among them, which ate them *u*, * 698 17
stir *u* your strength and come to help us. 702 15
and those who hate you have lifted *u* their heads. 706 6
Truth shall spring *u* from the earth, * 709 16
for to you, O LORD, I lift *u* my soul. 710 6
The arrogant rise *u* against me, O God, 711 1

those who have died stand *u* and give you thanks? 712 24
in the evening it is dried *u* and withered. 718 12
rise *u* against me. 721 20
The waters have lifted *u*, O LORD, 722 9
the waters have lifted *u* their voice; * 722 10
the waters have lifted *u* their pounding waves. 722 11
Rise *u*, O Judge of the world; * 722 20
Who rose *u* for me against the wicked? * 723 25
and burns *u* his enemies on every side. 727 2
His lightnings light *u* the world; * 727 3
Light has sprung *u* for the righteous, * 727 20
lift *u* your voice, rejoice, and sing. 728 11
you have lifted me *u* and thrown me away. 731 20
For the LORD will build *u* Zion, * 732 8
They went *u* into the hills and down to the valleys 735 17
Which ate *u* all the green plants in their land * 740 23
He rebuked the Red Sea, and it dried *u*, * 742 16
Fire blazed *u* against their company, * 743 7
Then Phinehas stood *u* and interceded, * 744 7
They mounted *u* to the heavens and fell back 748 7
He lifted *u* the poor out of misery * 749 11
Wake *u*, my spirit; 749 19
let those who rise *u* against me be put to shame, 753 4
they will hold *u* their head with honor. 755 24
He takes *u* the weak out of the dust * 756 12
and lifts *u* the poor from the ashes. 756 13
I will lift *u* the cup of salvation * 759 25
with branches *u* to the horns of the altar. 762 26
I will lift *u* my hands to your commandments, * 767 9
Hold me *u*, and I shall be safe, * 773 7
I lift *u* my eyes to the hills; * 779 1
To which the tribes go *u*, 780 1
To you I lift *u* my eyes, * 780 15
when enemies rose *u* against us; 781 4
Then would they have swallowed us *u* alive * 781 5
nor climb *u* into my bed; 786 4
Lift *u* your hands in the holy place 787 21
He brings *u* rain clouds from the ends 788 14
As for our harps, we hung them *u* * 792 3
you know my sitting down and my rising *u*; 794 2
If I climb *u* to heaven, you are there; * 794 14
and do I not loathe those who rise *u* against you? 795 21
and stir *u* strife all day long. 796 4
who are determined to trip me *u*. 796 9
Let not those who surround me lift *u* their heads; * 796 19
cast into the mire, never to rise *u* again." 796 22
the lifting *u* of my hands as the evening sacrifice. 797 6
for I lift *u* my soul to you. 799 18
he lifts *u* those who are bowed down. 802 16
the LORD lifts *u* those who are bowed down; 803 19
and binds *u* their wounds. 804 7
The LORD lifts *u* the lowly, * 804 12
He has raised *u* strength for his people 806 22
wisdom as we bring them *u*, 829 11
you see your children growing *u* 829 14
raise him *u* if he fall; 830 16
lift *u* thy countenance upon him, 831 16
light riseth *u* in darkness for the godly: 832 7
broken *u* and the clouds drop down the dew: 840 15
Scriptures and summed *u* in the creeds. 851 21
and the building *u* of the Church; 855 27
Adoration is the lifting *u* of the heart 857 2
infants will be brought *u* within the Church, 859 3

upheld

your love, O LORD, *u* me. 724 2

uphold

Govern and *u* them, now and always. 98 10
and may *u* them in their work 205 17
and may *u* them in their work 256 14
direct and *u* you in the service of Christ 310 6
and so *u* us by your Spirit 393 13
direct and *u* you in the service of Christ 419 2
power to *u* these two persons in their marriage? 425 2
power to *u* these two persons in their marriage? 434 2
Christ, beseeching him to *u* you 456 8
Will you *u* N. as bishop? 514 10
Will you *u* him in this ministry? 527 9
Will you *u* him in this ministry? 539 9
May the Lord by his grace *u* you in the service 544 15
who witness this new beginning support and *u* 559 8
it is you who *u* my lot. 600 8

upholds

but the LORD *u* the righteous. 634 19
The LORD *u* all those who fall; * 802 15

uplifted

I will sing to the Lord, for he is lofty and *u*; * 85 1

upper

O LORD, let not the ungodly have the *u* hand; * 594 15

upright

and *u* in your judgment. 266 11
Therefore the wicked shall not stand *u* 585 12
but we will arise and stand *u*. 608 18
Gracious and *u* is the LORD; * 615 4
to slaughter those who are *u* in their ways. 634 13
observe the *u*; * 636 11
and *u* in your judgment. 656 15
That they may show how *u* the LORD is, * 721 27
The *u* will see this and rejoice, * 749 13
in the assembly of the *u*, in the congregation. 754 7
the generation of the *u* will be blessed. 755 8
Light shines in the darkness for the *u*; * 755 11
and *u* are your judgments. 774 22
and the *u* shall continue in your sight. 797 2

uprightness

u of life and his obedience to thy commands; 188 11
u of life and his obedience to your commands; 239 20
Let integrity and *u* preserve me, * 616 3

uproar

Why are the nations in an *u*? * 586 1

use

preserve to our *u* the bountiful fruits of the earth, 151 9
that we may *u* our liberty 207 4
u the harvests of the land and of the seas, 207 17
that we may reverently *u* our freedom, 209 3
that we may *u* our liberty 258 4
u the harvests of the land and of the seas, 258 17
that we may reverently *u* our freedom, 260 10

that we may *u* its resources rightly 388 13
and for the right *u* of the riches of creation, 390 21
For the just and proper *u* of your creation; 392 7
and bless the means made *u* of for his cure. 459 8
and for the right *u* of the riches of creation, 550 6
u this oil, and be among us as a healer and reconciler. 561 6
u our public and private wealth that all may find 824 13
and grant that we may so *u* our leisure 825 2
reverence so to *u* the resources of nature, 827 19
save us from selfish *u* of what thou givest, 828 6
and then *u* us, we pray thee, as thou wilt, 833 2
Bless, O Lord, thy gifts to our *u* and us to thy service; 835 11
Why do we not *u* our freedom as we should? 845 12
To *u* all our bodily desires as God intended; 848 11
and to *u* our talents and possessions 848 14
How many creeds does this Church *u* in its worship? 851 24

used

u in the Church's daily worship to recall 852 3
and is *u* at the Eucharist. 852 7
and *u* in the Christian Church. 853 21

useful

Since we do not fully obey them, are they *u* at all? 848 25

usefulness

restored to *u* in your world with a thankful heart; 459 15

useless

I am as *u* as a broken pot. 623 15

uses

This Church *u* two creeds: 851 25
patterns of countless ways by which God *u* material 861 19

utter

and close the lips that *u* proud boasts! 597 6
for the cursing and lies that they *u*, * 666 22

uttered

the Most High *u* his voice. 603 16

utterly

I should *u* have fainted, * 478 5
I am *u* bowed down and prostrate; * 637 8
I am *u* numb and crushed; * 637 12
Oh, that God would demolish you *u*, * 658 8
O God, why have you *u* cast us off? * 689 9
and *u* rejected Israel. 699 25
do not *u* forsake me. 763 20
that we may be wholly thine, *u* dedicated 833 1

uttermost

u part of the earth. 39 21
and remain in the *u* parts of the sea; 475 10
It goes forth from the *u* edge of the heavens 607 1
Your word has been tested to the *u*, * 775 5
and dwell in the *u* parts of the sea, 794 17
O God, whose fatherly care reacheth to the *u* parts 830 19

utters

The mouth of the righteous *u* wisdom, * 635 22

V

vain

And we shall never hope in *v*. 98 18
shalt not take the Name of the Lord thy God in *v*. 318 7
The horse is a *v* hope for deliverance; * 627 9
and in *v* we are in turmoil; * 639 7
for *v* is the help of man. 668 9
In *v* have I kept my heart clean, * 688 3
for *v* is the help of man. 750 20
and let his appeal be in *v*. 751 11
their deceitfulness is in *v*. 773 10
their labor is in *v* who build it. 782 21
in *v* the watchman keeps his vigil. 783 2
It is in *v* that you rise so early and go to bed so late; * 783 3
v, too, to eat the bread of toil, 783 4
your enemies take your Name in *v*. 795 19

vainglory

from pride, *v*, and hypocrisy; 149 1
every root of bitterness, the desire of *v*, 829 1

valiant

With God we will do *v* deeds, * 668 10
With God we will do *v* deeds, * 750 21
For all *v* seekers after truth, liberty, and justice, 837 17

valley

Though I walk through the *v* of the shadow of death, 443 7
though I walk through the *v* of the shadow of death, 476 8
though I walk through the *v* of the shadow of death, 477 1
Though I walk through the *v* of the shadow of death, 613 3
I will divide the *v* of Succoth. 667 22
Those who go through the desolate *v* will find 708 1
I will divide the *v* of Succoth. 750 9

valleys

and the *v* cloak themselves with grain; * 673 16
into the hills and down to the *v* beneath, * 735 17
You send the springs into the *v*; * 735 21

vanish

like the glory of the meadows, shall *v*; 634 26
they shall *v* like smoke. 634 27
Let them *v* like water that runs off; * 665 7
Let them *v* like smoke when the wind drives it away; * 676 3
when you arise you will make their image *v*. 688 18

vanished

the faithful have *v* from among us. 597 2

vanquished

for darkness has been *v* by our eternal King. 286 6

variance

all who are at *v* and enmity; 193 21
all who are at *v* and enmity; 245 7

varied

among the swift and *v* changes of the world, 219 9

variety

inherited in all its rich *v*. 839 13

various

providence hast appointed *v* orders in thy Church:	205	5
you have appointed *v* orders in your Church:	256	2
Deliver us in our *v* occupations from the service	261	9

vast

with all their *v* array.	90	21
the *v* expanse of interstellar space,	370	8

vault

in the high *v* of heaven, glory to you.	90	14

vaunted

or had it been an enemy who *v* himself against me,	661	8

venerate

Grant us so to *v* the sacred mysteries	201	3
Grant us so to *v* the sacred mysteries	252	8
so to *v* the sacred mysteries	834	14

vengeance

The righteous will be glad when they see the *v*; *	665	13
O LORD God of *v*, *	722	18
O God of *v*, show yourself.	722	19
To wreak *v* on the nations *	807	14

venomous

They are as *v* as a serpent, *	665	1

ventured

v much for the liberties we now enjoy.	839	23

verge

Truly, I am on the *v* of falling, *	638	3

verily

but that I believe *v* to see the goodness of the LORD	478	6

very

the *v* bond of peace and of all virtues,	165	1
v God of *v* God,	327	28
It is *v* meet, right, and our bounden duty,	333	7
and that we are *v* members incorporate	339	6
It is *v* meet, right, and our bounden duty,	341	1
was made *v* Man of the substance of the Virgin Mary	345	16
for he is the *v* Paschal Lamb, who was sacrificed	346	19
a *v* present help in trouble.	471	18
My *v* bones will say, "LORD, who is like you? *	630	10
your arrows are *v* sharp, O mighty warrior.	647	22
a *v* present help in trouble.	649	2
the *v* center of the world and the city	651	5
wickedness is in their dwellings, in their *v* midst.	661	16
you make it *v* plenteous; *	673	5
the *v* depths were shaken.	694	7
for we have been brought *v* low.	701	23
his salvation is *v* near to those who fear him, *	709	12
your thoughts are *v* deep.	721	6
Your testimonies are *v* sure, *	722	15
For your servants love her *v* rubble, *	732	4
in the *v* chambers of their kings.	740	14
I was brought *v* low, and he helped me.	759	13
"I have been brought *v* low." *	759	21
they are *v* far from your law.	776	4
for I have been brought *v* low; *	798	12
and his word runs *v* swiftly.	805	8

vesper

and our eyes behold the *v* light,	64	5
with the brightness of the *v* light;	110	13
and our eyes behold the *v* light,	112	5
and our eyes behold the *v* light,	118	5
and our eyes behold the *v* light,	139	5

vessels

who have been the chosen *v* of thy grace,	348	2
who have been the chosen *v* of your grace,	380	18
who have been the choice *v* of thy grace,	487	12

vice

speak the truth, boldly rebuke *v*, and patiently suffer	190	6
speak the truth, boldly rebuke *v*, and patiently suffer	241	15

victims

into the arms of thy mercy all innocent *v*;	186	16
into the arms of your mercy all innocent *v*;	238	9
For the *v* of hunger, fear, injustice, and oppression.	392	8

victories

He multiplies the *v* of his king; *	606	12
you command *v* for Jacob.	645	19

victorious

and rose *v* from the grave.	287	13
who rose *v* from the dead,	349	6
who rose *v* from the dead,	382	1
with the *v* strength of his right hand.	608	14
v in the midst of the earth.	690	9
and he shall be *v* through my Name.	715	15

victory

Thanks be to God, which giveth us the *v*	39	11
Thanks be to God, who gives us the *v*	77	10
that we, being mindful of their *v* of faith, may glorify	189	7
he may share in the eternal *v* of Jesus	202	13
that we, being mindful of their *v* of faith, may glorify	240	15
he may share in the eternal *v* of Jesus	253	17
Let these branches be for us signs of his *v*,	271	10
in his *v* over death.	285	6
for the *v* of our mighty King.	286	3
and the *v*, and the majesty.	344	9
glory, the *v*, and the majesty.	377	7
and to give you that *v* of life	456	4
promise to all who share in the *v* of thy Son	481	27
his death may recall to us your *v* over death,	498	3
the *v*, and the majesty;	579	14
You have given me your shield of *v*; *	605	9
He is the God who gave me *v* *	606	5
We will shout for joy at your *v*	608	9
Now I know that the LORD gives *v* to his anointed: *	608	12
O LORD, give *v* to the king *	608	19
how greatly he exults in your *v*!	608	22
His honor is great, because of your *v*; *	609	5
I will glory in his *v*.	630	9
nor did their arm win the *v* for them; *	645	14
and my sword does not give me the *v*.	645	24
Surely, you gave us *v* over our adversaries *	645	25
they set up their banners as tokens of *v*.	689	17
has he won for himself the *v*.	728	2
The LORD has made known his *v*; *	728	3
have seen the *v* of our God.	728	9

There is a sound of exultation and *v* * 761 26
You give *v* to kings * 800 21
and adorns the poor with *v*. 807 9
Redeem all our days by this *v*; 835 4
How can we share in his *v* over sin, 850 22
We share in his *v* when we are baptized 850 24

vigil

to gather in *v* and prayer. 285 4
in vain the watchman keeps his *v*. 783 2

village

For this city (town, *v*, ________), 384 7

villages

kingdom of God in *v*, towns, and lonely places: 825 17

vindication

Let my *v* come forth from your presence; * 601 1
But at my *v* I shall see your face; * 602 4
and let them not receive your *v*. 681 19

vine

cannot bear fruit by itself, unless it abides in the *v*, 397 8
I am the *v*, you are the branches. 397 9
You have brought a *v* out of Egypt; * 703 3
behold and tend this *v*; * 703 16
Your wife shall be like a fruitful *v* 783 17

vinegar

and when I was thirsty, they gave me *v* to drink. 681 7

vines

He killed their *v* with hail * 698 21
He blasted their *v* and their fig trees * 740 19

vineyards

They sowed fields, and planted *v*, * 749 3

violence

V will no more be heard in your land, * 87 23
from *v*, battle, and murder; 149 15
For deliverance from all danger, *v*, 385 1
their *v* falls on their own scalp. 592 4
but those who delight in *v* he abhors. 596 20
for I have seen *v* and strife in the city. 660 25
and your hands deal out *v* in the land. 664 24
He shall redeem their lives from oppression and *v*, * 686 11
and wrap their *v* about them like a cloak. 687 12
the dark places of the earth are haunts of *v*. 690 25
Save us from *v*, discord, and confusion; 820 5

violent

and they bear a *v* hatred against me. 615 27
and a band of *v* men seeks my life; * 711 2
protect me from the *v*. 796 2

virgin

thou didst humble thyself to be born of a *V*. 53 14
born of the *V* Mary, 53 27
born of the *V* Mary, 66 13
you did not shun the *V*'s womb. 96 4
and born of the *V* Mary. 96 17
and born of the *V* Mary. 120 13
and as at this time to be born of a pure *v*: 161 9
and the spouse of his *v* mother: 188 10
announced by an angel to the *V* Mary, 188 17
Father in heaven, by whose grace the *v* mother 189 11
O God, who hast taken to thyself the blessed *V* Mary, 192 1
and to be born [this day] of a pure *v*: 213 3
and the spouse of his *v* mother: 239 19
announced by an angel to the *V* Mary, 240 3
Father in heaven, by your grace the *v* mother 240 18
you have taken to yourself the blessed *V* Mary, 243 8
and born of the *V* Mary. 293 4
and born of the *V* Mary. 304 7
he became incarnate from the *V* Mary, 327 2
and was incarnate by the Holy Ghost of the *V* Mary, 328 3
was made very Man of the substance of the *V* Mary 345 16
he became incarnate from the *V* Mary, 358 18
to be incarnate from the *V* Mary, 368 6
Incarnate by the Holy Spirit, born of the *V* Mary, 374 3
find our inheritance with [the Blessed *V* Mary, 375 22
made perfect Man of the flesh of the *V* Mary 378 11
Rejoicing in the fellowship of [the ever-blessed *V* 391 19
and born of the *V* Mary. 416 12
for the blessed *V* Mary; 489 16
and born of the *V* Mary. 496 7
for the blessed *V* Mary; 504 14
he became incarnate from the *V* Mary, 519 21
he became incarnate from the *V* Mary, 530 12
he became incarnate from the *V* Mary, 542 12
Rejoicing in the fellowship of [the ever-blessed *V* 550 26
incarnate from the *V* Mary? 849 27
our human nature from the *V* Mary, his mother. 849 29

virtue

and of all *v*, without which whoever lives is 216 16
for by *v* of your cross 281 3
for by *v* of your cross 281 13
the wonderful grace and *v* declared in all thy saints, 348 1
the wonderful grace and *v* declared in all your saints, 380 17
the wonderful grace and *v* declared in all thy saints, 487 11
Fill them with faith, *v*, knowledge, temperance. 829 2

virtues

the very bond of peace and of all *v*, 165 2
that they may be adorned with all Christian *v*, 549 13

virtuous

thy blessed saints in all *v* and godly living, 194 11
your blessed saints in all *v* and godly living, 245 19

visible

and of all things *v* and invisible; 327 23
For the Church universal, of which these *v* buildings 578 7
The sacraments are outward and *v* signs 857 26
What is the outward and *v* sign in Baptism? 858 12
The outward and *v* sign in Baptism is water, in 858 13
What is the outward and *v* sign in the Eucharist? 859 18
The outward and *v* sign in the Eucharist is bread 859 19

vision

by its brightness we may have a *v* of that holy City, 110 20
Give him courage, patience, and *v*; 421 4
spoke once in a *v* and said to your faithful people: * 715 3
Heavenly Father, in your Word you have given us a *v* 825 6

visit

V this place, O Lord, and drive far from it all snares 133 21
V this place, O Lord, and drive far from it all snares 140 13
That it may please thee to *v* the lonely; 151 24
came to *v* us in great humility; 159 4
mortal life in which your Son Jesus Christ came to *v* 211 3
behold, *v*, and relieve thy sick servant 458 2
the Lord, and to *v* his temple. 477 19
O *v* me with thy salvation; 478 19
You *v* the earth and water it abundantly; 673 4
and *v* me with your saving help; 742 5
Behold and *v*, we pray, the cities of the earth. 825 8
V our jails and prisons with your pity and judgment. 826 17

visitation

to purify our consciences by thy daily *v*, 160 7
Purify our conscience, Almighty God, by your daily *v*, 212 6

visited

for he hath *v* and redeemed his people; 50 23
whereby the dayspring from on high hath *v* us; 51 17

vocation

v and ministry they may truly and godly serve thee; 57 23
v and ministry they may truly and devoutly serve you; 100 15
v and ministry they may truly and godly serve thee; 206 5
v and ministry they may truly and devoutly serve you; 257 1
v and ministry they may truly and devoutly serve you; 278 15
strengthen us all in our Christian *v* of witness 421 5
For all members of your Church in their *v* 548 16

voice

neither have we obeyed the *v* of the Lord our God, 38 22
have not obeyed the *v* of the Lord our God 76 20
Oh, that today you would hearken to his *v*! 82 19
Today if ye will hear his *v*, harden not your hearts * 146 16
Grant that when we hear his *v* we may know him 173 12
Grant that when we hear his *v* we may know him 225 4
whole heart and mind and *v*, to praise you, 287 1
giving *v* to every creature under heaven, 373 10
I love the Lord, because he has heard the *v* 442 13
In the *v* of praise and thanksgiving, * 471 10
Lord, hear my *v*. 474 2
the *v* of my complaint. 474 4
Hearken unto my *v*, O Lord, when I cry unto thee; * 477 28
because he hath heard the *v* of my prayer; 478 24
v from heaven didst proclaim, Blessed are the dead 486 8
hear that his most joyful *v*: "Come, ye blessed of my 487 19
In the morning, Lord, you hear my *v*; * 588 21
He heard my *v* from his heavenly dwelling; * 602 20
the Most High uttered his *v*. 603 16
Hearken to my *v*, O Lord, when I call; * 618 10
Hear the *v* of my prayer when I cry out to you, * 619 8
for he has heard the *v* of my prayer. 619 23
The *v* of the Lord is upon the waters; 620 9
The *v* of the Lord is a powerful *v*; * 620 12
the *v* of the Lord is a *v* of splendor. 620 13
The *v* of the Lord breaks the cedar trees; * 620 14
The *v* of the Lord splits the flames of fire; 620 18
the *v* of the Lord shakes the wilderness; * 620 19
The *v* of the Lord makes the oak trees writhe * 620 21
a *v* of rebellion deep in the heart of the wicked; * 632 3
With the *v* of praise and thanksgiving, * 643 11
and he will hear my *v*. 661 21
Which does not heed the *v* of the charmer, * 665 3
Hear my *v*, O God, when I complain; * 671 10
make the *v* of his praise to be heard; 674 10
he has attended to the *v* of my prayer. 675 6
he sends forth his *v*, his mighty *v*. 678 27
I heard an unfamiliar *v* saying, * 704 11
And yet my people did not hear my *v*, * 704 24
and attend to the *v* of my supplications. 710 10
the waters have lifted up their *v*; * 722 10
Oh, that today you would hearken to his *v*! 725 5
lift up your *v*, rejoice, and sing. 728 11
with the harp and the *v* of song. 728 13
Because of the *v* of my groaning * 731 9
and hearken to the *v* of his word. 734 24
at the *v* of your thunder they hastened away. 735 16
and would not listen to the *v* of the Lord. 743 23
I love the Lord, because he has heard the *v* of 759 1
Hear my *v*, O Lord, according to your loving- 776 1
Lord, hear my *v*; * 784 19
let your ears consider well the *v* of my supplication. 784 20
hear my *v* when I cry to you. 797 4
I cry to the Lord with my *v*; * 798 1

voices

Thou art worthy at all times to be praised by happy *v*, 64 7
You are worthy at all times to be praised by happy *v*, 112 7
You are worthy at all times to be praised by happy *v*, 118 7
You are worthy at all times to be praised by happy *v*, 139 7
Therefore we praise you, joining our *v* with Angels 362 1
Therefore we praise you, joining our *v* with Angels 367 10
Father, in every age you have spoken through the *v* 571 9
Father, your people worship you with many *v* 572 1
and their *v* are not heard, 606 20
proclaim your truth in every age by many *v*: 827 7
all our people, with many *v* in one united chorus, 839 19

vouchsafe

V, O Lord, to keep us this day without sin; 55 19
Both now and ever *v* to hear us, O Christ; 155 3
and, of thy almighty goodness, *v* to bless 335 18

vow

This is my solemn *v*. 427 4
This is my solemn *v*. 427 9
I give you this ring as a symbol of my *v*, 427 13
This is my solemn *v*. 436 5
I am bound by the *v* I made to you, O God; * 663 14
Make a *v* to the Lord your God and keep it; * 692 22
and vowed a *v* to the Mighty One of Jacob: 786 2

vowed

and *v* a vow to the Mighty One of Jacob: 786 2

vows

to renew the solemn promises and *v* of Holy Baptism, 292 5
to reaffirm their baptismal *v*. 303 9
Will you who witness these *v* do all in your power 303 14
and make good thy *v* unto the Most High. 343 9
and make good your *v* to the Most High. 376 5
to reaffirm their baptismal *v*. 415 8
Will you who witness these *v* do all in your power 416 1
they may honor and keep the promises and *v* 425 11
Bless, O Lord, this ring to be a sign of the *v* 427 10

have given themselves to each other by solemn *v*, 428 2
witnessed these *v* may find their lives strengthened 430 2
Bless, O Lord, this ring to be a sign of the *v* 434 4
I will fulfill my *v* to the LORD * 442 23
I will pay my *v* now in the presence of all his people; * 479 18
For the blessing of our *v* and the crowning 579 4
I will perform my *v* in the presence of those who 612 5
and make good your *v* to the Most High. 655 8
For you, O God, have heard my *v*; * 668 21
and day by day I will fulfill my *v*. 669 4
to you shall *v* be performed in Jerusalem. 672 8
and will pay you my *v*, * 674 21
I will fulfill my *v* to the LORD * 760 1
I will fulfill my *v* to the LORD * 760 10
those whom you call to follow you under the *v* 819 8
make their *v* before God and the Church, 861 6
and blessing of God to help them fulfill their *v*. 861 7

vulture

I have become like a *v* in the wilderness, * 731 11

W

wag

they curl their lips and *w* their heads, 610 15

waged

from the battle *w* against me; * 661 23

waifs

Let his children be *w* and beggars; * 751 16

wail

I *w*, because of the groaning of my heart. 637 13

wailing

You have turned my *w* into dancing; * 622 3
no *w* in the public squares. 801 9

wait

I look for the LORD; my soul doth *w* for him; * 474 9
because of those who lie in *w* for me; * 589 7
They lie in *w*, like a lion in a covert; 595 11
they lie in *w* to seize upon the lowly; * 595 12
w patiently for the LORD. 619 3
all you who *w* for the LORD. 624 22
on those who *w* upon his love, 627 12
and *w* patiently for him. 633 18
but those who *w* upon the LORD shall possess 634 2
W upon the LORD and keep his way; * 636 3
They band together; they lie in *w*; * 663 1
See how they lie in *w* for my life, 665 22
and those who lie in *w* for my life take counsel 683 21
But I shall always *w* in patience, * 684 7
and did not *w* for his counsel. 742 25
How much longer must I *w*? * 770 9
Though the wicked lie in *w* for me to destroy me, * 771 9
I *w* for the LORD; my soul waits for him; * 785 1
O Israel, *w* for the LORD, * 785 6
O Israel, *w* upon the LORD, * 785 17
The eyes of all *w* upon you, O LORD, * 802 17
to *w* for the consummation of your kingdom 835 6

waited

I *w* patiently upon the LORD; * 640 1
We have *w* in silence on your loving-kindness, 651 18

waits

Our soul *w* for the LORD; * 627 15
For God alone my soul in silence *w*; * 669 5
For God alone my soul in silence *w*; * 669 16
I wait for the LORD; my soul *w* for him; * 785 1
My soul *w* for the LORD, 785 3

wake

and *w* up in your likeness; 123 9
and *w* up in your likeness; 504 24
I *w* again, because the LORD sustains me. 587 12
W up, my spirit, 664 12
W up, my spirit; 749 19

waken

I myself will *w* the dawn. 664 14
I myself will *w* the dawn. 749 21

waking

Guide us *w*, O Lord, and guard us sleeping; 134 16
Guide us *w*, O Lord, and guard us sleeping; 135 9
in their sleeping and in their *w*; 430 20

walk

to *w* in his laws which he set before us. 38 22
he that followeth me shall not *w* in darkness, 62 10
and *w* in your ways, 79 21
we who *w* in the light of your presence may rejoice 111 10
whoever follows me will not *w* in darkness, 116 6
and *w* in your ways, 117 4
and *w* in the ways of truth, 150 28
may so *w* in the light of thy truth, 186 8
and may ever *w* before thee as children of light; 198 12
that we may *w* in the way of his suffering, 219 17
may so *w* in the light of your truth, 238 3
and *w* before you as children of light; 249 21
that we may *w* in the way of his suffering, 272 11
and *w* in thy ways, 320 21
and *w* in thy ways, 331 32
good works as thou hast prepared for us to *w* in; 339 12
W in love, as Christ loved us and gave himself for us, 343 12
and *w* in your ways, 352 21
and *w* in your ways, 360 13
W in love, as Christ loved us and gave himself for us, 376 8
and *w* in your ways, 398 5
Though I *w* through the valley of the shadow 443 7
and *w* in your ways, 455 4
though I *w* through the valley of the shadow of death, 476 8
though I *w* through the valley of the shadow of death, 477 1
I will *w* before the LORD * 479 16
and who *w* as yet by faith, 481 1
Though I *w* through the valley of the shadow 613 3
We *w* about like a shadow, 639 6
w round about her; * 651 27
that I may *w* before God in the light of the living. 663 18
and refused to *w* in his law; 695 23
that Israel would *w* in my ways! 705 2
from those who *w* with integrity. 708 17

and I will *w* in your truth; * 710 22
they *w*, O LORD, in the light of your presence. 714 24
and do not *w* according to my judgments; 716 2
I will *w* with sincerity of heart within my house. 730 11
feet, but they cannot *w*; * 758 2
I will *w* in the presence of the LORD * 759 18
who *w* in the law of the LORD! 763 6
but always *w* in his ways. 763 10
I will *w* at liberty, * 767 3
Though I *w* in the midst of trouble, 793 16
in the way wherein I *w* they have hidden a trap 798 6
show me the road that I must *w*, 799 17
and to *w* humbly with their God. 847 5

walked

Happy are they who have not *w* in the counsel 585 1
I have *w* faithfully with you. 616 13
and *w* with the throng in the house of God. 661 13

walking

w in the way of the cross, 56 8
we are ever *w* in thy sight; 57 18
and by *w* before thee 59 7
and by *w* before thee 72 4
w in the way of the cross, 99 3
we are ever *w* in your sight; 100 10
and by *w* before you 101 20
and by *w* before you 125 18
w in the way of the cross, 168 12
w in the way of the cross, 220 3
w in the way of the cross, 272 3
w from henceforth in his holy ways: 330 12
and obedient *w* before thee all our days; 840 21

walks

and whatsoever *w* in the paths of the sea. 592 24

wall

with the help of my God I will scale any *w*. 604 23
as if you were a leaning fence, a toppling *w*? 669 11
Why have you broken down its *w*, * 703 11

walls

You will call your *w*, Salvation, * 87 25
much less the *w* of temples made with hands. 578 4
and rebuild the *w* of Jerusalem. 657 19
the watchmen make their rounds upon her *w*, * 661 2
he made the waters stand up like *w*. 695 29
You have breached all his *w* * 716 21
Peace be within your *w* * 780 9
May there be no breaching of the *w*, 801 8
infect our hearts; break down the *w* that separate us; 815 16

wander

and makes them *w* in trackless wastes) 749 10

wandered

and I have *w* far in a land that is waste. 450 14
Some *w* in desert wastes; * 746 8

wandering

W from nation to nation * 739 3

wanderings

from coldness of heart and *w* of mind, 833 21

want

and from all *w* of charity, 149 2
I shall not be in *w*. 443 2
I shall not *w*. 476 20
I shall not be in *w*. 612 24
"Aha! just what we *w*!" * 631 22
where it is in *w*, provide for it; 816 14
those who suffer *w* and anxiety from lack of work. 824 12

wanting

that our faith may never be found *w* 185 17
that our faith may never be found *w* 237 11

war

And though *w* should rise up against me, * 617 16
It is he who makes *w* to cease in all the world; * 649 21
but *w* is in his heart. 662 2
scatter the peoples that delight in *w*. 678 21
but when I speak of it, they are for *w*. 778 23

warned

be *w*, you rulers of the earth. 586 23

warning

they shoot without *w* and are not afraid. 671 17

warnings

Give us grace to heed their *w* and forsake our sins, 159 11
Give us grace to heed their *w* and forsake our sins, 211 11

warped

they were undependable like a *w* bow. 699 21

warrior

The Lord is a mighty *w*; * 85 7
Strap your sword upon your thigh, O mighty *w*, * 647 17
your arrows are very sharp, O mighty *w*. 647 22
like a *w* refreshed with wine. 700 10
"I have set the crown upon a *w* 715 4
The sharpened arrows of a *w*, * 778 16
Like arrows in the hand of a *w* * 783 8

warriors

none of the *w* can lift a hand. 692 11

wars

That it may please thee to make *w* to cease 151 1

wash

W me through and through from my wickedness * 266 4
w me, and I shall be clean indeed. 266 17
W me through and through from my wickedness, 449 3
W him in the holy font of everlasting life, and clothe 465 17
W him, we pray thee, in the blood 488 15
I will *w* my hands in innocence, O LORD, * 616 18
W me through and through from my wickedness * 656 8
w me, and I shall be clean indeed. 656 21
Moab is my *w*-basin, 668 1
Let not the torrent of waters *w* over me, 680 20

washbasin

Moab is my *w*, 750 12

washed

had *w* their feet, said to them, 274 9
when wickedness is put to flight, and sin is *w* away. 287 18

and *w* us in his own blood, 317 17
Our brother (sister) was *w* in Baptism 497 16
and *w* my hands in innocence. 688 4

washes

and the torrent *w* over me. 679 12

waste

nor of the sickness that lays *w* at mid-day. 130 9
For our *w* and pollution of your creation, 268 24
and I have wandered far in a land that is *w*. 450 14
Their form shall *w* away, * 653 11
Though my flesh and my heart should *w* away, * 689 1
the enemy has laid *w* everything in your sanctuary. 689 15
nor of the sickness that lays *w* at mid-day. 719 23

wasted

My eyes are *w* with grief * 590 12
For my life is *w* with grief, 623 6
and my flesh is *w* and gaunt. 752 24

wastes

Some wandered in desert *w*; * 746 8
and makes them wander in trackless *w*) 749 10

watch

W ye, for ye know not when the master 37 1
Shed forth thine unending day upon us who *w* for thee, 69 13
Keep *w*, dear Lord, with those who work, or *w*, 71 1
W, for you do not know when the master 75 1
Behold, he who keeps *w* over Israel * 104 19
The LORD shall *w* over your going out and 105 1
Shed forth your unending day upon us who *w* 123 12
Keep *w*, dear Lord, with those who work, or *w*, 124 17
Keep *w*, dear Lord, with those who work, or *w*, 134 6
W over those, both night and day, 134 12
that awake we may *w* with Christ, 134 17
that awake we may *w* with Christ, 135 10
Heavenly Father, *w* with us over your child 458 22
and as a *w* in the night. 472 18
My soul fleeth unto the Lord before the morning *w*; * 474 11
I say, before the morning *w*. 474 12
early in the morning I make my appeal and *w* for you. 588 22
O LORD, *w* over us * 597 16
I said, "I will keep *w* upon my ways, * 638 15
bid love and faithfulness *w* over him. 669 2
his eyes keep *w* over the nations; * 674 7
Keep *w* over my life, for I am faithful; * 710 1
and like a *w* in the night. 718 8
Behold, he who keeps *w* over Israel * 779 7
The LORD shall *w* over your going out and 779 15
Set a *w* before my mouth, O LORD, 797 7
W over thy child, O Lord, as his days increase; 830 13

watches

and he who *w* over you will not fall asleep. 104 18
The LORD himself *w* over you; * 104 21
and meditate on you in the night *w*. 670 24
The LORD *w* over the innocent; * 759 12
My eyes are open in the night *w*, * 775 22
and he who *w* over you will not fall asleep. 779 6
The LORD himself *w* over you; * 779 9
Unless the LORD *w* over the city, * 783 1

watchful

Be sober, be *w*. 132 8
Everliving Father, *w* and caring, 568 7

watching

w how they may cast me to the ground, 601 22
Turn my eyes from *w* what is worthless; * 766 9
My eyes have failed from *w* for your promise, * 770 5
My eyes have failed from *w* for your salvation * 773 19

watchman

in vain the *w* keeps his vigil. 783 2

watchmen

Day and night the *w* make their rounds 661 1
more than *w* for the morning, * 785 4

water

Therefore you shall draw *w* with rejoicing * 86 5
and return not again, but *w* the earth, 87 2
Glorify the Lord, O springs of *w*, seas, and streams, * 89 10
who are saved through *w* and the Spirit, 289 3
salvation of all nations by the *w* of Baptism: 289 15
Give now the *w* of life to those who thirst for you, 290 10
has given us a new birth by *w* and the Holy Spirit, 294 5
We thank you, Almighty God, for the gift of *w*. 306 13
We thank you, Father, for the *w* of Baptism. 306 20
Now sanctify this *w*, we pray you, by the power 307 3
we thank you that by *w* and the Holy Spirit 308 2
we thank you that by *w* and the Holy Spirit 314 1
or in the earth beneath, or in the *w* under the earth; 318 3
Who by *w* and the Holy Spirit hast made us 345 5
made a new people by *w* and the Spirit, 371 7
For by *w* and the Holy Spirit you have made us 378 1
For those who travel on land, on *w*, or in the air 384 17
Through the *w* of baptism you clothed me 450 11
Like as the hart desireth the *w*-brooks, * 471 1
who was reborn by *w* and the Spirit in Holy Baptism. 498 2
take this *w*, and help me (help the bishop) baptize 561 3
We thank you, Almighty God, for the gift of *w*. 570 5
We thank you, Father, for the *w* of Baptism. 570 12
They are like trees planted by streams of *w*, 585 7
I am poured out like *w*; 611 5
He gathers up the waters of the ocean as in a *w*-skin * 626 13
As the deer longs for the *w*-brooks, * 643 1
Let them vanish like *w* that runs off; * 665 7
as in a barren and dry land where there is no *w*. 670 14
You visit the earth and *w* it abundantly; 673 4
the river of God is full of *w*. 673 6
so that they went through the *w* on foot, * 674 4
we went through fire and *w*; * 674 18
like showers that *w* the earth. 685 20
The clouds poured out *w*; 694 8
They have shed their blood like *w* on every side 701 8
for the early rains have covered it with pools of *w*. 708 3
You *w* the mountains from your dwelling on high; * 736 1
He opened the rock, and *w* flowed, * 741 7
and *w*-springs into thirsty ground, 748 22
He changed deserts into pools of *w* * 748 25
and dry land into *w*-springs. 748 26
let it soak into his body like *w* 752 9

Who turned the hard rock into a pool of *w* * 757 11
and honor the land and the *w* 825 23
The outward and visible sign in Baptism is *w*, 858 13

watercourses

like the *w* of the Negev. 105 13
like the *w* of the Negev. 782 15

waters

O ye *w* that be above the firmament, 47 10
O ye whales and all that move in the *w*, 48 23
that calleth for the *w* of the sea, 62 3
O heavens and all *w* above the heavens. 88 10
O whales and all that move in the *w*. 89 11
who calls for the *w* of the sea 115 15
and leads me beside still *w*. 443 4
Though the *w* thereof rage and swell, * 471 21
and lead me forth beside the *w* of comfort. 476 4
he leadeth me beside the still *w*. 476 22
Father, we thank you that through the *w* of Baptism 569 15
he made dark *w* and thick clouds his pavilion. 603 12
he drew me out of great *w*. 603 24
and leads me beside still *w*. 612 26
The voice of the LORD is upon the *w*; 620 9
the LORD is upon the mighty *w*. 620 11
when the great *w* overflow, they shall not reach them. 625 13
He gathers up the *w* of the ocean as in a water-skin * 626 13
Though its *w* rage and foam, * 649 6
for the *w* have risen up to my neck. 679 8
I have come into deep *w*, * 679 11
and out of the deep *w*. 680 19
Let not the torrent of *w* wash over me, 680 20
and shattered the heads of the dragons upon the *w*; 690 11
The *w* saw you, O God; 694 5
the *w* saw you and trembled; * 694 6
and your paths in the great *w*, * 694 15
he made the *w* stand up like walls. 695 29
and the *w* gushed out like rivers. 696 6
True, he struck the rock, the *w* gushed out, 696 13
and tested you at the *w* of Meribah. 704 16
The *w* have lifted up, O LORD, 722 9
the *w* have lifted up their voice; * 722 10
the *w* have lifted up their pounding waves. 722 11
Mightier than the sound of many *w*, 722 12
You lay the beams of your chambers in the *w* above; * 735 6
the *w* stood higher than the mountains. 735 14
He turned their *w* into blood * 740 11
The *w* covered their oppressors; * 742 20
Again they provoked his anger at the *w* of Meribah, * 744 11
and plied their trade in deep *w*; 748 2
Then would the *w* have overwhelmed us * 781 7
Then would the raging *w* * 781 9
Who spread out the earth upon the *w*, * 790 7
By the *w* of Babylon we sat down and wept, * 792 1
rescue me and deliver me from the great *w*, 800 15
he blows with his wind, and the *w* flow. 805 14
and you *w* above the heavens. 806 2
Bless the lands and *w*, 828 2

waves

the roaring of their *w*, 672 24
and all your great *w* overwhelm me. 712 16
and still the surging of its *w*. 714 12
the waters have lifted up their pounding *w*. 722 11
which tossed high the *w* of the sea. 748 6
and quieted the *w* of the sea. 748 14

wax

my heart within my breast is melting *w*. 611 7
as the *w* melts at the fire, so let the wicked perish 676 4
The mountains melt like *w* at the presence 727 5

way

Prepare ye the *w* of the Lord, 37 4
we have turned every one to his own *w*; 39 2
O go your *w* into his gates with thanksgiving 45 17
and to guide our feet into the *w* of peace. 51 20
And guide us in the *w* of justice and truth. 55 8
Let thy *w* be known upon earth; 55 9
walking in the *w* of the cross, 56 8
may find it none other than the *w* of life 56 9
and guide our feet into the *w* of peace; 56 21
And guide us in the *w* of justice and truth. 67 23
Let thy *w* be known upon earth; 68 1
follow in faith where thou hast led the *w*, 69 9
be our companion in the *w*, kindle our hearts, 70 11
In the wilderness prepare the *w* of the Lord, 75 4
we have turned every one to his own *w*; 77 1
for you will go before the Lord to prepare his *w*, 93 2
and to guide our feet into the *w* of peace. 93 9
And guide us in the *w* of justice and truth. 98 2
Let your *w* be known upon earth; 98 3
walking in the *w* of the cross, 99 3
may find it none other than the *w* of life 99 4
and guide our feet into the *w* of peace; 99 16
And guide us in the *w* of justice and truth. 122 2
Let your *w* be known upon earth; 122 3
follow in faith where you have led the *w*, 123 8
be our companion in the *w*, kindle our hearts, 124 8
be our companion in the *w*, kindle our hearts, 139 17
govern thy holy Church Universal in the right *w*, 150 3
That it may please thee to bring into the *w* of truth 150 19
preach repentance and prepare the *w* 159 10
walking in the *w* of the cross, 168 12
may find it none other than the *w* of life 168 13
Christ to be the *w*, the truth, and the life, 173 18
folllow his steps in the *w* that leadeth to eternal life; 173 19
who on this day didst open the *w* of eternal life 175 8
and sent to prepare the *w* of thy Son 190 2
and prepare the *w* for our salvation: 211 10
that we may walk in the *w* of his suffering, 219 17
walking in the *w* of the cross, 220 3
may find it none other than the *w* of life 220 4
to know your Son Jesus Christ to be the *w*, 225 9
steps in the *w* that leads to eternal life; 225 11
on this day you opened the *w* of eternal life 227 1
and sent to prepare the *w* of your Son 241 11
garments and branches of palm along his *w*. 271 9
and follow him in the *w* that leads to eternal life; 271 12
walking in the *w* of the cross, 272 3
may find it none other than the *w* of life 272 4
that we may walk in the *w* of his suffering, 272 11
Deliver them, O Lord, from the *w* of sin 305 14
before the altar, and go thy *w*; 343 19
resurrection opened to us the *w* of everlasting life. 345 3

who was in every *w* tempted as we are,	346	4
to open for us the *w* of freedom and peace.	370	20
resurrection opened to us the *w* of everlasting life.	377	16
was tempted in every *w* as we are, yet did not sin.	379	2
the *w* of the cross to be the way of life.	430	12
The Lord will guide our feet into the *w* of peace,	483	18
follow where you have led the *w*;	498	6
The Lord will guide our feet into the *w* of peace,	500	7
follow in faith where you have led the *w*,	504	23
nor lingered in the *w* of sinners,	585	3
For the LORD knows the *w* of the righteous, *	585	15
but the *w* of the wicked is doomed.	585	16
make your *w* straight before me.	589	8
and makes my *w* secure.	605	4
and my ankles do not give *w*.	605	13
therefore he teaches sinners in his *w*.	615	5
and teaches his *w* to the lowly.	615	7
he will teach them the *w* that they should choose.	615	13
Show me your *w*, O LORD; *	618	21
"I will instruct you and teach you in the *w* that you	625	17
Draw the sword and bar the *w* against those	629	17
Let their *w* be dark and slippery, *	630	1
and has set himself in no good *w*; *	632	10
Commit your *w* to the LORD	633	13
he strengthens those in whose *w* he delights.	635	6
Wait upon the LORD and keep his *w*; *	636	3
before I go my *w* and am no more.	639	26
Such is the *w* of those who foolishly trust	653	6
but to those who keep in my *w* will I show	656	3
Had I gone on speaking this *w*, *	688	7
Your *w*, O God, is holy; *	693	26
Your *w* was in the sea,	694	14
whose hearts are set on the pilgrims' *w*.	707	26
Teach me your *w*, O LORD,	710	21
they found no *w* to a city where they might dwell.	746	9
Happy are those whose *w* is blameless, *	763	5
How shall a young man cleanse his *w*? *	764	1
I have taken greater delight in the *w* of your decrees *	764	11
Make me understand the *w* of your commandments,	765	13
Take from me the *w* of lying; *	765	17
I have chosen the *w* of faithfulness; *	765	19
I will run the *w* of your commandments, *	765	23
Teach me, O LORD, the *w* of your statutes, *	766	1
I restrain my feet from every evil *w*, *	771	21
therefore I hate every lying *w*.	772	2
and lead me in the *w* that is everlasting.	795	27
in the *w* wherein I walk they have hidden a trap	798	6
but frustrates the *w* of the wicked.	803	23
Christians may be led into the *w* of truth,	815	4
guide the nations of the world into the *w* of justice	816	2
from pride and arrogance, and from every evil *w*.	820	6
dispose the *w* of thy servants towards the attainment	832	19
opened for us the *w* of eternal life.	850	12
is the *w* by which the sacrifice of Christ	859	11
necessary for all persons in the same *w*	860	15

wayfarer

a *w*, as all my forebears were.	639	24

ways

we have erred and strayed from thy *w* like lost sheep,	41	17
to prepare his *w*;	51	13
we have erred and strayed from thy *w* like lost sheep,	62	17
and walk in your *w*,	79	21
Let the wicked forsake their *w* *	86	19
nor your *w* my *w*, says the Lord.	86	24
so are my *w* higher than your *w*,	86	26
Your *w* are *w* of righteousness and truth, *	94	12
and walk in your *w*,	117	4
to keep you in all your *w*.	130	20
for they have not known my *w*;	146	23
and walk in the *w* of truth,	150	28
to all who have gone astray from thy *w*,	166	17
to all who have gone astray from your *w*,	218	8
I shall teach your *w* to the wicked, *	267	1
Our self-indulgent appetites and *w*,	268	4
Let your *w* be known upon earth,	281	7
and walk in thy *w*,	320	21
we have erred and strayed from thy *w* like lost sheep,	320	24
walking from henceforth in his holy *w*:	330	12
and walk in thy *w*,	331	32
and walk in your *w*,	352	21
and walk in your *w*,	360	13
in the *w* of justice and peace;	388	8
and walk in your *w*,	398	5
and walk in your *w*,	455	4
and art acquainted with all my *w*.	474	22
Their *w* are devious at all times;	595	1
My footsteps hold fast to the *w* of your law; *	601	7
For I have kept the *w* of the LORD *	604	5
As for God, his *w* are perfect;	604	24
Show me your *w*, O LORD, *	614	19
to slaughter those who are upright in their *w*.	634	13
I said, "I will keep watch upon my *w*, *	638	15
I shall teach your *w* to the wicked, *	657	7
Let your *w* be known upon earth, *	675	11
that Israel would walk in my *w*!	705	2
to keep you in all your *w*.	720	8
they do not know my *w*."	725	14
He made his *w* known to Moses *	733	21
and learned their pagan *w*,	744	18
Some were fools and took to rebellious *w*; *	747	15
but always walk in his *w*.	763	10
Oh, that my *w* were made so direct *	763	13
and give attention to your *w*.	764	14
I have confessed my *w*, and you answered me; *	765	11
give me life in your *w*.	766	10
I have considered my *w* *	768	5
for all my *w* are before you.	777	16
As for those who turn aside to crooked *w*,	782	3
and who follow in his *w*!	783	14
They will sing of the *w* of the LORD, *	793	12
and are acquainted with all my *w*.	794	5
The LORD is righteous in all his *w* *	802	21
be pleased to make thy *w* known unto them,	814	8
all those who are in any *w* afflicted or distressed,	815	7
Show them that your *w* give more life	829	15
give more life than the *w* of the world,	829	16
and the study of God's *w*.	847	27
patterns of countless *w* by which God uses material	861	19

wayward

"This people are *w* in their hearts;	725	13

weak

comfort and help the *w*-hearted; 152 12
the strength of the *w* and the comfort of sufferers: 458 11
strong and *w*, rich and poor. 531 12
serve all people, particularly the poor, the *w*, 543 5
Have pity on me, LORD, for I am *w*; * 590 1
Save the *w* and the orphan; * 705 13
Rescue the *w* and the poor; * 705 15
My knees are *w* through fasting, * 752 23
He takes up the *w* out of the dust * 756 12

weakness

through the *w* of our mortal nature, 164 13
strengthened in their *w* and have confidence 208 20
and because in our *w* we can do nothing good 216 7
Have compassion on our *w*, 231 12
strengthened in their *w* and have confidence 260 5
strength in our *w*, and everlasting salvation; 399 11
strength in our *w*, and everlasting salvation; 457 9
w may be banished and his strength restored; 458 19
may be strengthened in his *w* and have confidence 459 20
the sense of his *w* may add strength 460 2
Be near me in my time of *w* and pain; 461 7
lying in great *w*, and comfort him 462 2
bring them *w*, distress, or isolation. 830 2
will come, not in *w* but in power, 862 3

wealth

and leave their *w* to their little ones. 602 3
and leave their *w* to those who come after them. 652 25
but trusted in great *w* 658 14
though *w* increase, set not your heart upon it. 670 7
always at ease, they increase their *w*. 688 2
W and riches will be in their house, * 755 9
use our public and private *w* that all may find 824 13

weapons

He has prepared his *w* of death; * 591 24
the shield, the sword, and the *w* of battle. 692 6

wear

Therefore they *w* their pride like a necklace * 687 11
they all shall *w* out like a garment; * 733 2

wearied

so that we who are *w* by the changes 133 14

wears

and like the belt that he *w* continually. 752 13

weary

Tend the sick, Lord Christ; give rest to the *w*, 71 3
the changes of day and night, giving rest to the *w*, 113 2
Tend the sick, Lord Christ; give rest to the *w*, 124 19
Tend the sick, Lord Christ; give rest to the *w*, 134 8
I grow *w* because of my groaning; * 590 9
you refreshed the land when it was *w*. 676 22
I have grown *w* with my crying; 679 13

weather

For seasonable *w*, and for an abundance of the fruits 384 11
give us seasonable *w*; 824 8

wedded

to my *w* (wife) (husband), to have and to hold 436 6

wedding

first miracle at a *w* in Cana of Galilee. 423 6
him in his heavenly *w* garment. 465 18
there were no *w* songs for their maidens. 700 6

wedlock

who, in holy *w*, have been made one flesh. 829 4

weeds

that though the wicked grow like *w*, 721 9

week

that the *w* to come may be spent in your favor; 98 21
who on the first day of the *w* overcame death 345 2
who on the first day of the *w* overcame death 377 15
on the first day of the *w*, you conquered sin, 835 2
together *w* by *w* for corporate worship; 856 14

weekly

O God, who makest us glad with the *w* remembrance 56 1
O God, you make us glad with the *w* remembrance 98 19

weep

w this night, and give thine angels charge 71 2
w this night, and give your angels charge 124 18
w this night, and give your angels charge 134 7
dry the tears of those who *w*. 497 5

weeping

Those who go out *w*, carrying the seed, * 105 16
for the LORD has heard the sound of my *w*. 590 15
W may spend the night, * 621 14
and mingled my drink with *w*. 731 18
Those who go out *w*, carrying the seed, * 782 18

weigh

W my heart, summon me by night, * 601 3

weighing

this our bounded duty and service, not *w* our merits, 336 11

weighs

his piercing eye *w* our worth. 596 18
The LORD *w* the righteous as well as the wicked, * 596 19
Your anger *w* upon me heavily, * 712 15

weight

and the *w* of your responsibility in presenting 527 2
and the *w* of your responsibility in presenting 539 2

welcome

Let us *w* the newly baptized. 308 11
May angels surround him, and saints *w* him in peace. 466 5
Bishop N., we have come together today to *w* 559 1

welfare

actions for the *w* and peace of the world. 329 21
for the *w* of the holy Church 383 6
to the glory of thy Name and the *w* of this people; 821 6
to thy glory and the *w* of thy people; 833 3

well

hast promised through thy *w*-beloved Son 59 14
hast promised through thy *w*-beloved Son 72 11
and I know my wickedness only too *w*. 91 15
have promised through your *w*-beloved Son 102 3
have promised through your *w*-beloved Son 126 3

things in thy *w*-beloved Son, the King of kings 185 2
but the *w*-being of thy Church, 189 19
witnesses thy *w*-beloved Son, 191 16
things in thy *w*-beloved Son, the King of kings 202 17
things in your *w*-beloved Son, the King of kings 236 15
but the *w*-being of your Church, 241 5
your *w*-beloved Son, wonderfully transfigured, 243 2
things in your *w*-beloved Son, the King of kings 254 2
for with such sacrifices God is *w* pleased. 344 4
and for the *w*-being of all people. 386 2
For I know my transgressions only too *w*, 449 5
O let thine ears consider *w* * 474 3
working in you that which is *w* pleasing in his sight; 487 3
working in you that which is *w*-pleasing in his sight; 503 5
receive that blessing which your *w*-beloved Son 505 5
We believe that he is *w* qualified, 559 3
The LORD weighs the righteous as *w* as the wicked, * 596 19
who are *w* supplied with children 602 2
by night as *w*, but I find no rest. 610 5
For with you is the *w* of life, * 632 22
Consider *w* her bulwarks; 652 1
Consider this *w*, you who forget God, * 655 26
So they ate and were *w* filled, * 697 7
Consider *w*, you dullards among the people; * 723 9
and consider *w* the mercies of the LORD. 749 16
for the LORD has treated you *w*. 759 15
We wish you *w* in the Name of the LORD." 784 17
let your ears consider *w* the voice of my supplication. 784 20
your works are wonderful, and I know it *w*. 795 2
Look *w* whether there be any wickedness in me * 795 26
May our sons be like plants *w* nurtured 801 1
make wise decisions for the *w*-being of our society; 822 13
offices to promote the *w*-being of all people; 822 21

wells

O ye *w*, bless ye the Lord; * 48 21

went

Almighty God, whose most dear Son *w* not up to joy 56 6
Almighty God, whose most dear Son *w* not up to joy 99 1
Almighty God, whose most dear Son *w* not up to joy 168 10
Almighty God, whose most dear Son *w* not up to joy 220 1
Almighty God, whose most dear Son *w* not up to joy 272 1
for I *w* with the multitude, and brought them forth 471 8
I *w* by, and behold, they were not there; * 636 8
how I *w* with the multitude and led them 643 9
so that they *w* through the water on foot, * 674 4
we *w* through fire and water; * 674 18
O God, when you *w* forth before your people, * 676 16
But they *w* on sinning against him, * 696 7
In spite of all this, they *w* on sinning * 697 14
They *w* up into the hills and down to the valleys 735 17
and *w* whoring in their evil deeds. 745 2
Some *w* down to the sea in ships * 748 1
Jordan turned and *w* back. 757 2
Before I was afflicted I *w* astray, * 768 21
We mean that he *w* to the departed 850 15

wept

You *w* at the grave of Lazarus, your friend; 497 7
By the waters of Babylon we sat down and *w*, * 792 1

west

judgment is neither from the east nor from the *w*, * 691 14
As far as the east is from the *w*, * 734 5
from the east and from the *w*, 746 6

whales

O ye *w* and all that move in the waters, 48 23
O *w* and all that move in the waters. 89 11

whatever

without love *w* we do is worth nothing: 216 13
but make me ready, Lord, for *w* it may be. 461 20
w he wills to do he does. 757 19
The LORD does *w* pleases him, 788 12
and *w* else may hinder us 818 17
w is just and true and good, 829 12
and for *w* draws us closer to God. 857 9

whatsoever

that, *w* defilements he may have contracted 488 17
and *w* walks in the paths of the sea. 592 24

wheat

But Israel would I feed with the finest *w* * 705 7
he satisfies you with the finest *w*. 805 6

whet

If they will not repent, God will *w* his sword; * 591 22

whether

w in thought, word, or deed. 317 3
W we live, therefore, or die, we are the Lord's. 469 13
So, then, *w* we live or die, 491 17
Look well *w* there be any wickedness in me * 795 26

whipped

w and his face to be spit upon: 220 15

whirling

O my God, make them like *w* dust * 707 3

whirlwind

The sound of your thunder was in the *w*; 694 11

whisper

All my enemies *w* together about me * 642 13
He stilled the storm to a *w* * 748 13

whispering

For I have heard the *w* of the crowd; 623 16

white

The *w*-robed army of martyrs praise you. 95 25
transfigured, in raiment *w* and glistening: 191 17
transfigured, in raiment *w* and glistening: 243 3

whither

unto the same place *w* our Savior Christ is gone before; 175 5
W shall I go then from thy Spirit? * 475 5
or *w* shall I go then from thy presence? 475 6

whoever

w follows me will not walk in darkness, 116 5
and of all virtue, without which *w* lives 216 16
w believes in him should not perish, 396 2
w comes to me shall not hunger, 396 4

and *w* believes in me shall never thirst." 396 5
w eats my flesh and drinks my blood abides 397 5
w receives a little child in the name of Christ receives 443 22
W has faith in me shall have life, 491 2
that *w* would be great must be servant of all. 545 6
W leads a blameless life and does what is right, * 599 6
W does these things * 599 17
W offers me the sacrifice of thanksgiving 656 1
W is wise will ponder these things, * 749 15

whole

let the *w* earth stand in awe of him. 45 7
by whose Spirit the *w* body of thy faithful people 57 19
let the *w* earth stand in awe of him. 61 5
peace to thy Church and to the *w* world, 68 15
O God and Father of all, whom the *w* heavens adore: 70 15
Let the *w* earth also worship thee, 70 16
We have not loved you with our *w* heart; 79 15
by whose Spirit the *w* body of your faithful people 100 11
let the *w* earth tremble before him. 115 5
We have not loved you with our *w* heart; 116 17
peace to your Church and to the *w* world, 122 17
O God and Father of all, whom the *w* heavens adore: 124 12
Let the *w* earth also worship you, 124 13
put our *w* trust and confidence in thy mercy, 155 10
that we and all the *w* world may perceive 163 16
that we may be devoted to thee with our *w* heart, 179 6
that he might draw the *w* world unto himself: 192 14
to thy *w* Church in paradise and on earth 202 2
by whose Spirit the *w* body of thy faithful people 206 1
that we and the *w* world may perceive 215 10
that we may be devoted to you with our *w* heart, 230 21
that he might draw the *w* world to himself: 244 2
Give to your *w* Church in paradise and on earth 253 7
by whose Spirit the *w* body of your faithful people 256 19
Thereby, the *w* congregation was put in mind 265 6
and to the *w* communion of saints 267 14
We have not loved you with our *w* heart, 267 19
by whose Spirit the *w* body of your faithful people 278 11
Look favorably on your *w* Church, 280 15
let the *w* world see and know 280 17
joy has come to the *w* world. 281 4
with our *w* heart and mind and voice, 287 1
Look favorably on your *w* Church, 291 12
let the *w* world see and know 291 14
Do you put your *w* trust in his grace and love? 302 19
We have not loved thee with our *w* heart; 320 15
Let us pray for the *w* state of Christ's Church 328 22
that, rejoicing in thy *w* creation, 329 23
We have not loved thee with our *w* heart; 331 26
but for the sins of the *w* world. 332 17
for the sins of the *w* world; 334 14
we, and all thy *w* Church, may obtain remission 335 28
perfect sacrifice for the *w* world; 341 17
thy *w* Church may be made one body with him, 342 28
that he might draw the *w* world to himself; 346 14
that he might make the *w* creation new. 349 4
We have not loved you with our *w* heart; 352 15
We have not loved you with our *w* heart; 360 7
a perfect sacrifice for the *w* world. 362 16
giving the *w* world into our care, 373 19
and made the *w* creation new. 374 7
that he might draw the *w* world to himself; 379 11
that he might make the *w* creation new. 381 19
We have not loved you with our *w* heart; 397 24
but for the sins of the *w* world. 450 3
We have not loved you with our *w* heart; 454 6
receive this holy unction be made *w*; 455 13
Grant, we beseech thee, to thy *w* 480 6
Christ spent the *w* night in prayer 514 12
Look favorably on your *w* Church, 515 5
let the *w* world see and know 515 7
in the government of the *w* Church; 518 23
Look favorably on your *w* Church, 528 3
let the *w* world see and know 528 5
Look favorably on your *w* Church, 540 3
let the *w* world see and know 540 5
I will give thanks to you, O LORD, with my *w* heart; * 593 1
then shall I be *w* and sound, 607 26
the loving-kindness of the LORD fills the *w* earth. 626 10
I prayed with my *w* heart, 630 19
for the *w* world is mine and all that is in it. 655 4
He has made the *w* world so sure * 722 5
sing to the LORD, all the *w* earth. 725 18
let the *w* earth tremble before him. 726 10
at the presence of the Lord of the *w* earth. 727 6
I will give thanks to the LORD with my *w* heart, * 754 6
With my *w* heart I seek you; * 764 3
but I will keep your commandments with my *w* heart. 769 2
I call with my *w* heart; * 775 15
I will give thanks to you, O LORD, with my *w* heart; * 793 1
that, rejoicing in thy *w* creation, we may learn 814 3
Look with compassion on the *w* human family; 815 14
whose glory fills the *w* creation, 831 1
We thank you for the splendor of the *w* creation, 836 2
because it proclaims the *w* Faith 854 22
and discipline of the *w* Church; 855 25
The communion of saints is the *w* family of God, 862 21

wholeness

and restore you to *w* and strength. 456 16

wholesome

and *w* example for the entire flock of Christ. 517 11
may be a *w* example to your people? 532 22
may be a *w* example to all people? 544 10

wholly

that we may be *w* thine, utterly dedicated 833 1

whoring

and went *w* in their evil deeds. 745 2

whosoever

Jesus said, "*W* will come after me, 38 24
without which *w* liveth is counted dead 165 2
and *w* liveth and believeth in me shall never die. 469 3

why

If any of you can show just cause *w* 424 2
that if either of you know any reason *w* 424 5
If any of you know just cause *w* 437 2
W art thou so full of heaviness, O my soul? * 471 12
and *w* art thou so disquieted within me? 471 13
And *w*? thou hast delivered my soul from death, * 479 14
if any of you know any reason *w* we should not 514 6

W are the nations in an uproar? * 586 1
W do the peoples mutter empty threats? 586 2
W do the kings of the earth rise up in revolt, 586 3
W do you stand so far off, O LORD, * 594 19
W should the wicked revile God? * 595 21
w should they say in their heart, "You do not care"? 595 22
My God, my God, *w* have you forsaken me? * 610 1
W are you so full of heaviness, O my soul? * 643 13
and *w* are you so disquieted within me? 643 14
"*W* have you forgotten me? * 644 2
and *w* do I go so heavily while the enemy 644 3
W are you so full of heaviness, O my soul? * 644 9
and *w* are you so disquieted within me? 644 10
w have you put me from you? * 644 18
and *w* do I go so heavily while the enemy 644 19
W are you so full of heaviness, O my soul? * 645 1
and *w* are you so disquieted within me? 645 2
Awake, O Lord! *w* are you sleeping? * 647 3
W have you hidden your face * 647 5
W should I be afraid in evil days, * 652 13
"*W* do you recite my statutes, 655 12
You tyrant, *w* do you boast of wickedness * 657 23
W do you look with envy, O rugged mountain, 677 12
O God, *w* have you utterly cast us off? * 689 9
w is your wrath so hot against the sheep 689 10
W do you draw back your hand? * 690 6
w is your right hand hidden in your bosom? 690 7
W should the heathen say, "Where is their God?" * 702 1
W have you broken down its wall, * 703 11
LORD, *w* have you rejected me? * 713 6
w have you hidden your face from me? 713 7
W should the heathen say, * 757 16
W then do we live apart from God and out of 845 8
W do we not use our freedom as we should? 845 12
W did he take our human nature? 850 1
W do we call the Holy Scriptures the Word of God? 853 23
W is the Church described as one? 854 14
W is the Church described as holy? 854 17
W is the Church described as catholic? 854 21
W is the Church described as apostolic? 854 24
W do we praise God? 857 4
W then are infants baptized? 858 24
W is the Eucharist called a sacrifice? 859 9
W do we pray for the dead? 862 8

wicked

Let the *w* forsake their ways * 86 19
The *w* have set a trap for me, * 104 7
to see the reward of the *w*. 130 14
Indeed, I have been *w* from my birth, * 266 12
I shall teach your ways to the *w*, * 267 1
in the counsel of the *w*, * 585 2
It is not so with the *w*; * 585 10
Therefore the *w* shall not stand upright when 585 12
but the way of the *w* is doomed. 585 16
you will break the teeth of the *w*. 587 17
Let the malice of the *w* come to an end, 591 15
You have rebuked the ungodly and destroyed the *w*; * 593 9
the *w* are trapped in the works of their own hands. 594 10
The *w* shall be given over to the grave, * 594 11
The *w* arrogantly persecute the poor, * 594 21
The *w* boast of their heart's desire; * 594 23
The *w* are so proud that they care not for God; * 594 25
Why should the *w* revile God? * 595 21
Break the power of the *w* and evil; * 595 27
For see how the *w* bend the bow 596 10
The LORD weighs the righteous as well as the *w*, * 596 19
Upon the *w* he shall rain coals of fire and 596 21
The *w* prowl on every side, * 597 18
In his sight the *w* is rejected, * 599 11
From the *w* who assault me, * 601 16
deliver me from the *w* by your sword. 601 26
and devise *w* schemes, * 609 21
I will not sit down with the *w*. 616 17
Do not snatch me away with the *w* or with the 619 10
rather, let the *w* be put to shame; 623 28
Great are the tribulations of the *w*; * 625 23
Evil shall slay the *w*, * 629 9
a voice of rebellion deep in the heart of the *w*; * 632 3
The words of his mouth are *w* and deceitful; * 632 7
nor the hand of the *w* push me aside. 633 2
In a little while the *w* shall be no more; * 634 3
The *w* plot against the righteous * 634 7
The LORD laughs at the *w*, * 634 9
The *w* draw their sword and bend their bow 634 11
is better than great riches of the *w*. 634 17
For the power of the *w* shall be broken, * 634 18
As for the *w*, they shall perish, * 634 24
The *w* borrow and do not repay, * 635 1
but the offspring of the *w* shall be destroyed. 635 19
The *w* spy on the righteous * 635 26
and when the *w* are cut off, you will see it. 636 5
I have seen the *w* in their arrogance, * 636 6
the future of the *w* is cut off. 636 14
he will rescue them from the *w* and deliver them, 636 18
while the *w* are in my presence." 638 18
My enemies are saying *w* things about me: * 642 8
deliver me from the deceitful and the *w*. 644 16
But to the *w* God says: * 655 11
Indeed, I have been *w* from my birth, * 656 16
I shall teach your ways to the *w*, * 657 7
and by the pressure of the *w*; 660 10
The *w* are perverse from the womb; * 664 25
they will bathe their feet in the blood of the *w*. 665 14
Hide me from the conspiracy of the *w*, * 671 12
as the wax melts at the fire, so let the *w* perish at 676 4
Deliver me, my God, from the hand of the *w*, * 683 7
and saw the prosperity of the *w*: 687 6
and their hearts overflow with *w* thoughts. 687 14
So then, these are the *w*; * 688 1
and discerned the end of the *w*. 688 12
and to the *w*, "Do not toss your horns; 691 11
and all the *w* of the earth shall drink and 691 20
He shall break off all the horns of the *w*; * 691 24
and show favor to the *w*? 705 12
deliver them from the power of the *w*. 705 16
than to dwell in the tents of the *w*. 708 13
nor any *w* man bring him down. 715 11
to see the reward of the *w*. 720 2
that though the *w* grow like weeds, 721 9
and my ears rejoice to hear the doom of the *w* who 721 19
How long shall the *w*, O LORD, * 722 22
how long shall the *w* triumph? 722 23
until a pit is dug for the *w*. 723 20

Who rose up for me against the *w*? * 723 25
and delivers them from the hand of the *w*. 727 19
I will soon destroy all the *w* in the land, * 730 26
and the *w* be no more. 737 25
and flames devoured the *w*. 743 8
for the mouth of the *w*, 750 24
Set a *w* man against him, * 751 8
The *w* will see it and be angry; 755 25
the desires of the *w* will perish. 755 27
because of the *w* who forsake your law. 767 20
Though the cords of the *w* entangle me, * 768 9
Though the *w* lie in wait for me to destroy me, * 771 9
The *w* have set a trap for me, * 772 13
Away from me, you *w*! * 773 3
In your sight all the *w* of the earth are but dross; * 773 11
Deliverance is far from the *w*, * 776 13
The scepter of the *w* shall not hold sway over the 781 22
has cut the cords of the *w*. 784 8
Oh, that you would slay the *w*, O God! * 795 16
Keep me, O LORD, from the hands of the *w*; * 796 7
Do not grant the desires of the *w*, O LORD, * 796 17
for my prayer is continually against their *w* deeds. 797 14
Let the *w* fall into their own nets, * 797 24
but he destroys all the *w*. 802 28
but frustrates the way of the *w*. 803 23
but casts the *w* to the ground. 804 13

wickedly

we have done wrong and dealt *w*. 742 10

wickedness

neither with the leaven of malice and *w*, * 46 5
and I know my *w* only too well. 91 15
From all evil and *w*; from sin; 148 15
put away the leaven of malice and *w*, 172 10
put away the leaven of malice and *w*, 224 3
Wash me through and through from my *w* * 266 4
turn from their *w* and live, 269 5
How holy is this night, when *w* is put to flight, 287 17
forces of *w* that rebel against God? 302 8
bewail our manifold sins and *w*, 331 5
Wash me through and through from my *w*, 449 3
For you are not a God who takes pleasure in *w*, * 588 23
you hate all those who work *w*. 588 26
if there is any *w* in my hands, 590 25
Look at those who are in labor with *w*, * 591 26
search out their *w* until you find none. 595 28
and according to the *w* of their actions. 619 15
He thinks up *w* upon his bed 632 9
See how they are fallen, those who work *w*! * 633 3
when the *w* of those at my heels surrounds me, 652 14
The *w* of those who put their trust in their goods, * 652 15
Wash me through and through from my *w* * 656 8
You tyrant, why do you boast of *w* * 657 23
and relied upon *w*." 658 15
for *w* is in their dwellings, in their very midst. 661 16
Shall they escape despite their *w*? * 663 4
those who go on still in their *w*. 677 27
He will turn their *w* back upon them 724 11
nor rewarded us according to our *w*. 734 2
because of the *w* of those who dwell there. 748 24
but all *w* will shut its mouth. 749 14
Let the *w* of his fathers be remembered 751 24
Look well whether there be any *w* in me * 795 26
Let me not be occupied in *w* with evildoers, * 797 10

wide

O merciful Creator, whose hand is open *w* to satisfy 208 9
O merciful Creator, your hand is open *w* to satisfy 259 11
They open *w* their jaws at me, * 611 3
"Open your mouth *w*, and I will fill it." 704 23
Yonder is the great and *w* sea 737 1
he will smash heads over the *w* earth. 754 2
You open *w* your hand * 802 19

widening

Enrich our lives by ever-*w* circles of fellowship, 840 3

widow

They murder the *w* and the stranger * 723 5
and his wife become a *w*. 751 15
he sustains the orphan and *w*, 803 22

widowed

the *w*, and all whose homes are broken 151 22
For the aged and infirm, for the *w* and orphans, 384 20

widows

Father of orphans, defender of *w*, * 676 11
and their *w* made no lamentation. 700 8

wife

Because in the love of *w* and husband, 349 1
Because in the love of *w* and husband, 381 16
The union of husband and *w* in heart, body, 423 9
will you have this woman to be your *w*; 424 14
In the Name of God, I, N., take you, N., to be my *w*, 427 1
I pronounce that they are husband and *w*, 428 4
N., you have taken N. to be your *w*. 433 5
I, N., take you, N., to be my (*w*) (husband), 436 2
I, N., take thee, N., to my wedded (*w*) (husband), 436 6
and his *w* become a widow. 751 15
Your *w* shall be like a fruitful vine 783 17
for Abraham, the father of believers, and Sarah his *w*; 838 11

wild

Glorify the Lord, O beasts of the *w*, * 89 14
even the *w* beasts of the field, 592 22
my wretched body from the horns of *w* bulls. 611 23
and Mount Hermon like a young *w* ox. 620 17
Rebuke the *w* beast of the reeds, * 678 18
and the peoples, a herd of *w* bulls with its calves. 678 19
Do not hand over the life of your dove to *w* beasts; * 690 22
The *w* boar of the forest has ravaged it, * 703 13
my horn you have exalted like the horns of *w* bulls; * 721 16
and the *w* asses quench their thirst. 735 24
W beasts and all cattle, * 806 13

wilderness

In the *w* prepare the way of the Lord, 75 4
and as in the day of temptation in the *w*; 146 18
the voice of the LORD shakes the *w*; * 620 19
the LORD shakes the *w* of Kadesh. 620 20
and make my lodging in the *w*. 660 20
May the fields of the *w* be rich for grazing, * 673 13
when you marched through the *w*, 676 17
nor yet from the *w* or the mountains. 691 15

He split the hard rocks in the *w* * 696 3
"Can God set a table in the *w*? 696 12
How often the people disobeyed him in the *w* * 698 7
and guided them in the *w* like a flock. 699 10
as your forebears did in the *w*, * 725 7
I have become like a vulture in the *w*, * 731 11
A craving seized them in the *w*, * 742 26
to overthrow them in the *w*, 743 25
Who led his people through the *w*, * 791 1

will

and on earth peace, good *w* towards men. 52 4
thy *w* be done, 54 17
having done thy *w* with cheerfulness while it was day, 56 22
thy *w* be done, 67 7
that we may delight in your *w*, 79 20
and by your *w* they were created and have their being; 93 23
thy *w* be done, 97 7
having done your *w* with cheerfulness during the day, 99 17
thy *w* be done, 106 17
direct and rule us according to your *w*, 107 5
that we may delight in your *w*, 117 3
thy *w* be done, 121 7
fixed on the doing of your *w*, 123 18
that you may do his *w*, 132 4
thy *w* be done, 132 22
thy *w* be done, 153 9
which we have asked faithfully according to thy *w*, 153 23
we may please thee both in *w* and deed; 164 15
to live according to thy *w*; 180 17
whose *w* it is to restore all things 185 1
to follow the example of her devotion to thy *w*; 189 14
whose *w* it is to restore all things 202 16
in accordance with thy gracious *w*; 207 5
commerce of this land responsive to thy *w*; 208 5
we may please you both in *w* and deed; 216 10
Most loving Father, whose *w* it is for us to give thanks 216 20
may by you be enabled to live according to your *w*; 232 8
whose *w* it is to restore all things 236 14
the example of her devotion to your *w*: 240 22
whose *w* it is to be glorified in your saints, 248 1
whose *w* it is to restore all things 254 1
in accordance with your gracious *w*; 258 5
and commerce of this land responsive to your *w*; 259 6
the *w* and patience to minister to their needs. 279 13
the *w* and the power to proclaim you 291 7
the courage to *w* and to persevere, 308 6
thy *w* be done, 311 4
that we may delight in thy *w*, 320 20
and on earth peace, good *w* towards men. 324 15
that we may delight in thy *w*, 331 31
thy *w* be done, 336 21
and by thy *w* they were created 344 6
that we may delight in your *w*, 352 20
that we may delight in your *w*, 360 12
in obedience to your *w*, 362 16
thy *w* be done, 364 4
By your *w* they were created and have their being. 370 11
and by your *w* they were created 377 5
and for the wisdom and *w* to conserve it, 384 15
Give us grace to do your *w* in all that we undertake; 387 12
that your *w* for them may be fulfilled; 389 8
strengthen us to do your *w*; 394 11
Help us to ask only what accords with your *w*; 394 13
that we may delight in your *w*, 398 4
thy *w* be done, 398 15
you may do God's *w* in the service 420 2
and, when it is God's *w*, for the procreation 423 12
thy *w* be done, 428 11
that their wills may be so knit together in your *w*, 429 11
Bestow on them, if it is your *w*, the gift 429 20
that your *w* may be done on earth 430 6
live faithfully according to your *w* in this life, 444 5
And so knit their wills together in your *w* 444 12
that we may delight in your *w*, 455 3
the example of obedience to your Father's *w*: 461 7
heal me according to your *w*; 461 9
thy *w* be done, 464 7
thy *w* be done, 485 23
in every good work to do his *w*, 487 2
give us such a lively sense of thy righteous *w*, 488 30
thy *w* be done, 502 4
every good work to do his *w*, 503 4
in them the good purpose of your perfect *w*; 504 29
Is it your *w* that we ordain N. a bishop? 514 8
That is our *w*. 514 9
Is it your *w* that N. be ordained a priest? 527 7
May the Lord who has given you the *w* to do 532 30
Is it your *w* that be ordained a deacon? 539 7
whom you chose as the agents of your *w*. 571 1
For the knowledge of your *w* 578 19
The LORD brings the *w* of the nations to naught; * 626 19
But the LORD's *w* stands fast for ever, * 626 21
"I love to do your *w*, O my God; 640 21
he does not hand them over to the *w* of their enemies. 642 3
you ministers of his who do his *w*. 734 26
To instruct his princes according to his *w* * 739 21
tempestuous wind, doing his *w*; 806 10
whose *w* it is that all should come to you 816 16
a people mindful of thy favor and glad to do thy *w*. 820 3
and strength to know and to do thy *w*. 820 21
O God, the fountain of wisdom, whose *w* is good 821 1
and amendment of life according to your *w*, 826 19
its mind sound, and its *w* righteous; 827 10
provision for its future in accordance with your *w*; 828 20
have faithfully asked according to thy *w*, 834 5
make us bold to praise you and to do your *w*; 835 5
may live in this world according to thy *w*, 841 11
God first helped us be revealing himself and his *w*, 845 18
Where in the Old Testament is God's *w* for us shown 847 9
God's *w* for us is shown most clearly 847 11
Sin is the seeking of our own *w* 848 29
instead of the *w* of God, 848 29
we present our own needs, that God's *w* may be done. 857 19

willest

O most loving Father, who *w* us to give thanks 165 6
Almighty God, who *w* to be glorified in thy saints, 196 15

willing

Accept, O LORD, the *w* tribute of my lips, * 104 3
our Lord Jesus Christ was *w* to be betrayed, 221 9
our Lord Jesus Christ was *w* to be betrayed, 276 5

I am *w* and ready to do so; 526 14
I am *w* and ready to do so; 538 14
Accept, O LORD, the *w* tribute of my lips, * 772 9

willingly

whose beloved Son *w* endured the agony 201 7
whose beloved Son *w* endured the agony 252 12
thou dost not *w* afflict or grieve the children of men: 831 12

willingness

and the *w* to accept help; 830 4

wills

Seek the Lord while he *w* to be found; * 86 17
who alone canst order the unruly *w* 167 15
ready *w* and hearts obey the calling of our Lord 193 1
the unruly *w* and affections of sinners: 219 7
ready *w* and hearts obey the calling of our Lord 244 9
Grant that their *w* may be so knit together 429 11
And so knit their *w* together in your will 444 12
whatever he *w* to do he does. 757 19
so control our *w*, that we may be wholly thine, 833 1
stirs our hearts, and strengthens our *w*. 858 4

wilt

thou *w* be in the midst of them: 59 15
thou *w* be in the midst of them: 72 12
thou *w* pour out upon the leaders of thy Church 191 10
thou *w* receive him more and more 202 11
If thou, LORD, *w* be extreme to mark what is done 474 5
and then use us, we pray thee, as thou *w*, 833 2

wily

but with the crooked you are *w*. 604 17

win

nor did their arm *w* the victory for them; * 645 14

wind

they are like chaff which the *w* blows away. 585 11
a scorching *w* shall be their lot. 596 23
he swooped on the wings of the *w*. 603 10
I beat them like dust before the *w*; * 605 24
Let them be like chaff before the *w*, * 629 22
truly, even those who stand erect are but a puff of *w*. 639 5
truly, everyone is but a puff of *w*. 639 19
like ships of the sea when the east *w* shatters them. 651 14
from the stormy *w* and tempest." 660 22
vanish like smoke when the *w* drives it away; * 676 3
He caused the east *w* to blow in the heavens * 697 1
and led out the south *w* by his might. 697 2
and like chaff before the *w*; 707 4
how like a puff of *w* they are. 723 16
When the *w* goes over it, it is gone, * 734 13
you ride on the wings of the *w*. 735 8
Then he spoke, and a stormy *w* arose, * 748 5
We are like a puff of *w*; * 800 8
he blows with his *w*, and the waters flow. 805 14
tempestuous *w*, doing his will; 806 10

winds

O ye *w* of God, bless ye Lord; * 48 5
all *w* and fire and heat. 88 14
You make the *w* your messengers * 735 9
and brings the *w* out of his storehouse. 788 16

wine

more than when grain and *w* and oil increase. 129 5
these thy gifts and creatures of bread and *w*; 335 20
sanctify these gifts of bread and *w*, 342 18
After supper he took the cup of *w*; 363 1
After supper he took the cup of *w*; 368 14
from your creation, this bread and this *w*. 369 3
After supper, he took the cup of *w*, 371 14
After supper he took the cup of *w*; 374 19
After supper, he took the cup of *w*, 403 8
After supper he took the cup of *w*; 405 6
Holy Spirit bless and sanctify this bread (*w*) that it, 408 2
take this bread and *w*, and be among us 562 5
more than when grain and *w* and oil increase. 588 14
you have given us *w* that makes us stagger. 667 15
full of spiced and foaming *w*, which he pours out, * 691 19
like a warrior refreshed with *w*. 700 10
and *w* to gladden our hearts, 736 6
and *w*, given and received according to Christ's 859 20

wingèd

and *w* birds like the sand of the sea. 697 4
creeping things and *w* birds; 806 14

wings

and you shall find refuge under his *w*; * 130 4
Hide us under the shadow of your *w*. 132 15
If I take the *w* of the morning, * 475 9
hide me under the shadow of your *w*, 601 15
he swooped on the *w* of the wind. 603 10
refuge under the shadow of your *w*. 632 19
And I said, "Oh, that I had *w* like a dove! * 660 17
in the shadow of your *w* will I take refuge 663 21
I will take refuge under the cover of your *w*. 668 20
and under the shadow of your *w* I will rejoice. 670 26
like a dove whose *w* are covered with silver, 677 6
and you shall find refuge under his *w*; * 719 18
you ride on the *w* of the wind. 735 8
If I take the *w* of the morning * 794 16

wink

w at each other. 631 8

winter

O ye *w* and summer, bless ye the Lord; * 48 7
thou hast made summer and *w*. 61 9
W and summer, glorify the Lord, * 88 15
you made both summer and *w*. 115 9
you made both summer and *w*. 690 19

wipe

They have said, "Come, let us *w* them out 706 9

wiped

where all tears are *w* away 290 5
Let them be *w* out of the book of the living * 681 20

wisdom

Almighty God, the fountain of all *w*, 179 16
Spirit dost give to some the word of *w*, 197 13
and guide with thy *w* those who take counsel 207 9
that with *w*, patience, and courage, 209 12
Almighty God, the fountain of all *w*: 209 17
Almighty God, the fountain of all *w*, 231 10

Spirit you give to some the word of *w*, 248 23
and guide with your *w* those who take counsel 258 9
that with *w*, patience, and courage, 260 17
Almighty God, the fountain of all *w*: 261 1
and will make me understand *w* secretly. 266 15
and guide with your *w* those who take counsel 278 26
works reveal your *w* and love. 373 18
and for the *w* and will to conserve it, 384 15
Give them *w* and devotion in the ordering 429 7
in *w* and true godliness, 431 5
give them calm strength and patient *w* as they seek 443 26
Grant them *w* and devotion in the ordering 444 9
that we may apply our hearts unto *w*. 473 8
God, whose *w* is beyond our understanding: 494 7
and, in your loving *w* and almighty power, work 504 28
come with others, to find comfort and *w*, 568 17
and gives *w* to the innocent. 607 7
The mouth of the righteous utters *w*, * 635 22
My mouth shall speak of *w*, * 652 9
and will make me understand *w* secretly. 656 19
that we may apply our hearts to *w*. 718 26
in *w* you have made them all; 736 26
and to teach his elders *w*. 739 22
The fear of the LORD is the beginning of *w*; * 755 1
Who by *w* made the heavens, * 790 5
there is no limit to his *w*. 804 11
Almighty and everliving God, source of all *w* 818 1
with the spirit of *w* those to whom in thy Name 820 9
and to all in authority, *w* and strength to know 820 20
O God, the fountain of *w*, 821 1
and give unto them the spirit of *w* and understanding, 821 11
grant *w* and grace in the exercise of their duties. 821 21
give courage, *w*, and foresight 822 2
the spirit of *w*, charity, and justice; 822 19
sound learning, new discovery, and the pursuit of *w*; 824 18
Give us *w* and reverence so to use the resources 827 18
and new *w* and determination in making provision 828 19
Give us calm strength and patient *w* 829 11
that he may grow in *w* and grace, 830 10
that the Spirit of *w* may save us from all false choices, 832 9

wise

Grant that we may in such *w* hear them, 184 16
that they may be led to *w* decisions 329 20
and him that cometh to me I will in no *w* cast out. 484 19
a patient, teacher, and a *w* councilor. 534 5
And now, you kings, be *w*; * 586 22
to see if there is any who is *w*, 598 16
For we see that the *w* die also; 652 23
to see if there is any who is *w*, 659 2
Whoever is *w* will ponder these things, * 749 15
may elect trustworthy leaders and make *w* decisions 822 12
that, by faithful administration and *w* laws, 822 26
part in making the heart of this people *w*, 827 9

wisely

and *w* overseeing the life and work 521 13
he has left off acting *w* and doing good. 632 8

wiser

Your commandment has made me *w* 771 15
I am *w* than the elders, * 771 19

wish

For our enemies and those who *w* us harm; 391 5
But first, our friends *w* us, 440 14
We *w* you well in the Name of the LORD." 784 17
and to do to other people as we *w* them to do to us; 848 3

withdrawn

You have *w* all your fury * 708 24

wither

fruit in due season, with leaves that do not *w*; * 585 8
For they shall soon *w* like the grass, * 633 7
let them *w* like trodden grass. 665 8
and I *w* like the grass. 731 22

withered

but in the evening it is cut down, dried up, and *w*. 472 22
While I held my tongue, my bones *w* away, * 625 3
in the evening it is dried up and *w*. 718 12
My heart is smitten like grass and *w*, * 731 7

withers

which *w* before it can be plucked; 784 12

withheld

nor *w* his love from me. 675 8
has he, in his anger, *w* his compassion? 693 19

withhold

do not *w* your compassion from me; * 641 2
No good thing will the LORD *w* * 708 16

within

w the reach of thy saving embrace: 58 10
ruin or destruction *w* your borders. 87 24
that everyone might come *w* the reach 101 2
has caused his light to shine *w* us, 110 4
Almighty and most merciful God, kindle *w* us the fire 111 4
and renew a right spirit *w* me. 137 4
has caused his light to shine *w* us, 139 13
that we may ever perceive *w* ourselves 201 4
that we may ever perceive *w* ourselves 252 9
For behold, you look for truth deep *w* me, * 266 14
and renew a right spirit *w* me. 266 23
and why art thou so disquieted *w* me? 471 13
my heart *w* my breast is melting wax. 611 7
My heart was hot *w* me; 638 22
and why are you so disquieted *w* me? 643 14
My soul is heavy *w* me; * 643 18
and why are you so disquieted *w* me? 644 10
and why are you so disquieted *w* me? 645 2
For behold, you look for truth deep *w* me, * 656 18
and renew a right spirit *w* me. 657 2
My heart quakes *w* me, * 660 13
I will walk with sincerity of heart *w* my house. 730 11
and all that is *w* me, bless his holy Name. 733 10
and gnats *w* all their borders. 740 16
their spirits languished *w* them. 746 11
and my heart is wounded *w* me. 752 20
w your gates, O Jerusalem. 779 21
Peace be *w* your walls * 780 9
and quietness *w* your towers. 780 10
Your wife shall be like a fruitful vine *w* your house, * 783 17
my soul is quieted *w* me. 785 16

you increased my strength *w* me. 793 9
When my spirit languishes *w* me, 798 5
My spirit faints *w* me; * 799 5
my heart *w* me is desolate. 799 6
he has blessed your children *w* you. 805 4
of one heart and mind *w* your holy Church; 817 22
that we may ever perceive *w* ourselves 834 15
harmony with God, *w* ourselves, 849 14
brought up *w* the Church, to know Christ 859 3

without

might serve him *w* fear, 51 8
And we worship thy Name ever, world *w* end. 55 18
Vouchsafe, O Lord, to keep us this day *w* sin; 55 19
be all honor and glory, world *w* end. 59 11
be all honor and glory, world *w* end. 72 8
and I will praise you *w* ceasing 91 24
Free to worship him *w* fear, * 92 29
world *w* end. 141 8
world *w* end. 154 12
be honor and glory, world *w* end. 160 5
one God, world *w* end. 160 17
one God, world *w* end. 161 13
we can do no good thing *w* thee, 164 14
all our doings *w* charity are nothing worth: 164 18
w which whosoever liveth is counted dead 165 2
one God, world *w* end. 169 13
one God, world *w* end. 169 18
one God, world *w* end. 171 4
one God, world *w* end. 174 20
one God, world *w* end. 175 7
one God, world *w* end. 175 20
w whom nothing is strong, nothing is holy: 180 1
it cannot continue in safety *w* thy succor, 180 10
that we, who cannot exist *w* thee, 180 16
one God, world *w* end. 181 10
O God, forasmuch as *w* thee we are not able 182 1
Grant, we beseech thee, that we may run *w* stumbling 184 3
one God, world *w* end. 184 14
grace to follow him *w* delay, 185 10
so perfectly and *w* doubt to believe in Jesus 185 16
one God, world *w* end. 191 21
one God, world *w* end. 200 5
we can do nothing good *w* you, 216 8
O Lord, you have taught us that *w* love 216 13
w which whoever lives is accounted dead before you. 216 16
w whom nothing is strong, nothing is holy: 231 17
because it cannot continue in safety *w* your help, 232 2
that we, who cannot exist *w* your help, 232 7
O God, because *w* you we are not able 233 14
Grant that we may run *w* stumbling 235 16
grace to follow him *w* delay, 237 4
so perfectly and *w* doubt to believe in Jesus 237 10
O Father Almighty, world *w* end. 336 15
be all honor and glory, world *w* end. 339 14
O Father Almighty, world *w* end. 343 5
we may *w* shame or fear rejoice 345 11
he lived as one of us, yet *w* sin. 374 4
we may *w* shame or fear rejoice 378 7
w suffering and *w* reproach, 385 7
and be found *w* fault at the day 389 16
world *w* end. 406 4
thou art God from everlasting, and world *w* end. 472 13
he may be presented pure and *w* spot before thee; 488 19
O God, whose days are *w* end, 489 3
O God, whose days are *w* end, 504 1
w hope, but in thankful remembrance 505 13
pray for them *w* ceasing, 518 15
and exercise *w* reproach the high priesthood 521 10
Grant that in all things he may serve *w* reproach, 534 6
and be found *w* fault at the Day of your Coming, 548 12
or plundered him who *w* cause is my enemy; 591 2
Therefore my heart sings to you *w* ceasing; * 622 5
For they have secretly spread a net for me *w* a cause; * 630 3
w a cause they have dug a pit to take me alive. 630 4
nor let those who hate me *w* a cause 631 7
Those who are my enemies *w* cause are mighty, * 638 7
they shoot *w* warning and are not afraid. 671 17
Those who hate me *w* a cause are more than the hairs 679 16
and young locusts *w* number, 740 22
and fight against me *w* a cause. 751 3
Rulers have persecuted me *w* a cause, * 777 1
one God, world *w* end. 820 25
confront one another *w* hatred or bitterness, 824 3
be all glory and honor, world *w* end. 840 24
with or *w* words. 856 19

witness

We thank thee for this *w*, 189 1
James grace and strength to bear *w* to the truth: 189 6
and called her to be a *w* of his resurrection: 191 2
We thank thee, heavenly Father, for the *w* 192 19
to be so faithful in our *w* to thee in this world, 195 11
to be surrounded by their *w* to thy power and mercy. 199 8
We thank you for this *w*, 240 9
and strength to bear *w* to the truth: 240 14
and called her to be a *w* of his resurrection: 242 9
for the *w* of your apostle and evangelist Matthew 244 7
to be so faithful in our *w* to you in this world, 247 9
surrounded by their *w* to your power and mercy. 250 18
For its unity in *w* and service 278 3
Will you by your prayers and *w* help this child 302 4
Will you who *w* these vows do all in your power 303 14
Send them into the world in *w* to your love. 306 1
Thou shalt not bear false *w* against thy neighbor. 318 25
You shall not be a false *w*. 350 19
that in faithful *w* it may preach the Gospel 390 7
surrounded by their *w* to your power and mercy. 395 21
Will you who *w* these vows do all in your power 416 1
strengthen us all in our Christian vocation of *w* 421 5
to *w* and bless the joining together 423 2
to *w* the inauguration of this new relationship. 440 15
that in faithful *w* it may preach the Gospel 549 21
Will you who *w* this new beginning support 559 8
I will bear *w* that the LORD is righteous; * 592 5
to *w* the judgment of his people. 654 10
"O Israel, I will bear *w* against you; * 654 17
The heavens bear *w* to your wonders, O LORD, * 714 3
the abiding *w* in the sky.'" 716 16
Inspire our *w* to him, 816 17
respect their *w* and to discern the truth, 823 14
to bear *w* to him wherever they may be; 855 16

witnessed
Grant that all married persons who have *w* 430 1
Will you who have *w* these promises do all 434 1

witnesses
and ye shall be *w* unto me both 39 19
and you shall be my *w* in Jerusalem, 77 18
who on the holy mount didst reveal to chosen *w* 191 16
with so great a cloud of *w*: 198 17
who on the holy mount revealed to chosen *w* 243 1
surrounded us with a great cloud of *w*: 250 2
us about with so great a cloud of *w*, 347 18
as faithful *w* of Christ our Lord. 366 11
surrounded us with a great cloud of *w*, 380 13
for false *w* have risen up against me, 618 24
Malicious *w* rise up against me; * 630 13
for all your servants and *w* of time past: 838 10

witnessing
Will all of you *w* these promises do all 425 1

wits
and were at their *w*' end. 748 10

woke
Then the LORD *w* as though from sleep, * 700 9

woman
you sent your only Son, born of a *w*, 370 19
of this man and this *w* in Holy Matrimony. 423 3
will you have this *w* to be your wife; 424 14
this man and this *w* who come to you seeking 425 9
this man and this *w* have bound themselves 427 11
and especially upon this man and this *w* 429 5
for consecrating the union of man and *w* 430 14
of your blessing upon this man and this *w*. 430 16
this man and this *w* have bound themselves 434 5
gives (presents) this *w* to be married to this man? 437 6
Who presents this *w* and this man to be married 437 7
do you take this *w* as your mother? 441 1
they writhed like a *w* in childbirth, 651 13
He makes the *w* of a childless house * 756 16
w and man enter into a life-long union, 861 5

womb
you did not shun the Virgin's *w*. 96 4
a sinner from my mother's *w*. 266 13
Yet you are he who took me out of the *w*, * 610 18
when I was still in my mother's *w*. 610 22
a sinner from my mother's *w*. 656 17
The wicked are perverse from the *w*; * 664 25
from my mother's *w* you have been my strength; * 683 12
like dew from the *w* of the morning." 753 18
and the fruit of the *w* is a gift. 783 7
you knit me together in my mother's *w*. 794 26
Your eyes beheld my limbs, yet unfinished in the *w*; 795 6

women
and men and *w* everywhere love thee 70 17
O men and *w* everywhere, glorify the Lord, * 89 16
and men and *w* everywhere love you 124 14
all *w* in childbirth, young children and orphans, 151 21
great was the company of *w* who bore the tidings: 677 2
the *w* at home are dividing the spoils." 677 4
all the men and *w* of our armed forces at home 823 2
and that men and *w* from different cultures 825 13
that men and *w* everywhere may give thee thanks; 828 7
For all that is gracious in the lives of men and *w*, 837 6
We thank you for the men and *w* who have made 839 4
the men and *w* of our country who in the day 839 22

won
w liberty for themselves and for us, 190 18
w liberty for themselves and for us, 242 2
and by his rising to life again hath *w* 346 21
and by his rising to life again he has *w* 379 18
the mountain his right hand had *w*. 699 14
has he *w* for himself the victory. 728 2

wonder
and *w* in all your works. 308 8
the *w*, the power, and the glory of your creation 572 3
for the beauty of this world, for the *w* of life, 836 3
For the beauty and *w* of your creation, 837 3

wonderful
having his *w* conversion in remembrance, 187 10
ministries of angels and men in a *w* order: 193 5
ministries of angels and men in a *w* order: 200 7
a *w* Sacrament hath left unto us a memorial 201 2
Grant, we pray, that we, having his *w* conversion 239 1
w order the ministries of angels and mortals: 244 14
w order the ministries of angels and mortals: 251 13
a *w* Sacrament has left us a memorial 252 7
that *w* and sacred mystery; 280 15
How *w* and beyond our knowing, O God, 287 14
O God, whose *w* deeds of old shine forth 289 12
that *w* and sacred mystery; 291 12
For the *w* grace and virtue declared in all thy saints, 348 1
For the *w* grace and virtue declared in all your saints, 380 17
Such knowledge is too *w* and excellent for me; * 475 3
praise and hearty thanks for the *w* grace 487 11
that *w* and sacred mystery; 515 5
that *w* and sacred mystery; 528 3
that *w* and sacred mystery; 540 3
and recounting all your *w* deeds. 616 21
how *w* he is in his doing toward all people. 674 2
How *w* is God in his holy places! * 679 4
and to this day I tell of your *w* works. 684 15
declaring all your *w* deeds. 691 5
and the *w* works he has done. 695 6
and had no faith in his *w* works. 697 15
W deeds in the land of Ham, * 743 15
Your decrees are *w*; * 774 5
Such knowledge is too *w* for me; * 794 10
your works are *w*, and I know it well. 795 2
who in a *w* Sacrament hast left unto us a memorial 834 12
for the *w* diversity of races and cultures 840 2

wonderfully
O God, who didst *w* create, 162 7
w restore, the dignity of human nature: 162 8
thy servant John the Baptist was *w* born, 190 2
thy well-beloved Son, *w* transfigured, 191 16
O God, who didst *w* create, 200 13
w restore, the dignity of human nature: 200 14
O God, who *w* created, and yet more *w* restored, 214 1

your servant John the Baptist was *w* born, 241 11
your well-beloved Son, *w* transfigured, 243 2
O God, who *w* created, and yet more *w* restored, 252 1
O God, who *w* created, and yet more *w* restored, 288 5

wonders

awesome in renown, and worker of *w*? 85 18
Know that the Lord does *w* for the faithful; * 128 14
Know that the LORD does *w* for the faithful; * 588 4
for he has shown me the *w* of his love in a 624 12
how great your *w* and your plans for us! * 640 12
and call to mind your *w* of old time. 693 23
You are the God who works *w* * 694 1
and the *w* he had shown them. 695 25
Do you work *w* for the dead? * 712 23
Will your *w* be known in the dark? * 713 1
The heavens bear witness to your *w*, O LORD, * 714 3
and his *w* among all peoples. 725 22
his *w* and the judgments of his mouth, 738 10
and the *w* he does for his children. 746 17
and the *w* he does for his children. 747 12
and the *w* he does for his children. 747 24
and his *w* in the deep. 748 4
and the *w* he does for his children. 748 18
the *w* of your law. 764 20
He sent signs and *w* into the midst of you, O Egypt, * 788 19
Who only does great *w*, * 790 3

wondrous

who alone does *w* deeds! 686 26
you do *w* things; * 710 19
They shall speak of the might of your *w* acts, * 801 22

wont

art *w* to give more than either we desire or deserve: 182 19

wood

on the hard *w* of the cross that everyone might 58 9
on the hard *w* of the cross that everyone might 101 2
Then shall all the trees of the *w* shout for joy 726 17

wool

He gives snow like *w*; * 805 9

word

to hear his holy *W*, and to ask, 41 8
The *W* was made flesh and dwelt among us: 44 6
The *W* of the Lord. 47 2
according to thy *w*; 51 24
The *W* of the Lord. 65 1
according to thy *w*; 66 2
to hear his holy *W*, and to ask, 79 3
in thought, *w*, and deed, 79 12
The *W* was made flesh and dwelt among us: 82 1
The *W* of the Lord. 84 4
So is my *w* that goes forth from my mouth; * 87 5
Your *w* is a lantern to my feet * 103 6
preserve my life, O LORD, according to your *w*. 104 2
present in your *W* and Sacraments, 113 11
in thought, *w*, and deed, 116 14
The *W* of the Lord. 119 1
in thought, and *w*, and deed, 127 9
and contempt of thy *W* and commandment, 149 9
with true knowledge and understanding of thy *W*; 150 7
to hear and receive thy *W*, 150 16
according to thy holy *W*, 152 6
poured upon us the new light of thine incarnate *W*: 161 15
Grant that thy people, illumined by thy *W* 163 8
hold fast the unchangeable truth of thy *W*, 166 19
by patience and comfort of thy holy *W*, 184 18
Give unto us, who are called by thy *W*, 185 10
but still more blessed in keeping thy *w*: 189 13
to believe and to preach thy *W*: 192 9
dost give to some the *w* of wisdom, 197 12
to others the *w* of knowledge, 197 13
and to others the *w* of faith: 197 14
for the ministry of *W* and Sacrament, 205 17
poured upon us the new light of your incarnate *W*: 213 9
illumined by your *W* and Sacraments, 215 2
hold fast the unchangeable truth of your *W*, 218 10
who are called by your holy *W*, 237 4
but still more blessed in keeping your *w*: 240 20
to believe and to preach your *W*: 243 16
you give to some the *w* of wisdom, 248 22
to others the *w* of knowledge, 248 23
and to others the *w* of faith: 248 24
for the ministry of *W* and Sacrament, 256 13
meditating on God's holy *W*. 265 13
in thought, *w*, and deed; 267 17
For those who have never heard the *w* of salvation 279 21
by hearing his *W* and celebrating his Sacraments, 285 5
you have created all things by the power of your *W*, 290 9
Will you proclaim by *w* and example the Good News 293 26
The *W* of the Lord. 300 2
Will you proclaim by *w* and example the Good News 305 1
in the knowledge and obedience of your *W*, 310 11
in thought, *w*, or deed. 317 4
in thought, *w*, and deed, 320 12
The *W* of the Lord 325 14
who in thy holy *W* hast taught us to make prayers, 329 1
may agree in the truth of thy holy *W*, 329 7
set forth thy true and lively *W*, 329 11
they may hear and receive thy holy *W*, 329 15
by thought, *w*, and deed, 331 7
Hear the *W* of God to all who truly turn to him. 332 7
and sanctify, with thy *W* and Holy Spirit, 335 19
hear us, and, with thy *W* and Holy spirit, 342 17
Because in the mystery of the *W* made flesh, 346 1
and renewed by thy *W* and Sacraments, 346 10
in thought, *w*, and deed, 352 12
The *W* of the Lord. 357 5
in thought, *w*, and deed, 360 4
in your *W* spoken through the prophets; 368 3
and above all in the *W* made flesh, 368 4
Because in the mystery of the *W* made flesh, 378 14
and renewed by your *W* and Sacraments, 379 7
That they may be faithful ministers of your *W* 387 7
in thought, *w*, and deed, 397 21
and with thy (your) *W* and Holy Spirit bless 408 1
The *W* of the Lord. 414 2
Will you proclaim by *w* and example the Good News 417 11
in the knowledge and obedience of your *W*, 419 7
in accordance with God's *W*, you do now confess it. 424 7
sinned by my own fault in thought, *w*, and deed, 447 6
Hear the *W* of God to all who truly turn to him. 449 12
in thought, *w*, and deed, 454 3

in his *w* is my trust. 474 10
For lo, there is not a *w* in my tongue, * 474 23
the Old and New Testaments to be the *W* of God, 513 10
The *W* of the Lord. 516 2
a faithful steward of his holy *W* and Sacraments. 521 20
for the ministry of your *W* and Sacraments. 523 5
an effective example in *w* and action, 523 6
the Old and New Testaments to be the *W* of God, 526 16
The *W* of the Lord. 529 1
it will be your task to proclaim by *w* and deed 531 8
Will you endeavor so to minister the *W* of God 532 9
preach the *W* of God and to administer 534 11
for the ministry of your *W* and Sacraments. 535 5
an effective example in *w* and action, 535 6
the Old and New Testaments to be the *W* of God, 538 16
The *W* of the Lord. 541 1
redemptive love known, by your *w* and example, 543 10
and in the ministration of God's *W* and Sacraments, 543 14
proclaim God's *W* and to assist in the ministration 545 20
for the ministry of your *W* and Sacraments. 547 1
an effective example in *w* and action, 547 2
one who proclaims the *W*. 561 2
set forth your true and living *W*. 563 4
by the clearness and brightness of your holy *W*, 563 8
for the ministry of your *W* and Sacraments. 564 5
an effective example in *w* and action, 564 6
the ministry of his holy *W* and Sacraments. 567 3
to hear your *W*, and to be nourished 568 11
Father, your eternal *W* speaks to us 570 23
that your *w* only may be proclaimed, 571 11
and your *w* only may be heard. 571 12
Your *w* is a lantern to our feet, 571 13
and does not take back his *w*. 599 14
For the *w* of the LORD is right, * 626 7
By the *w* of the LORD were the heavens made, * 626 11
In God, whose *w* I praise, 662 19
In God the LORD, whose *w* I praise, 663 11
The Lord gave the *w*; * 677 1
and hearken to the voice of his *w*. 734 24
the *w* of the LORD tested him. 739 16
For God remembered his holy *w* * 741 9
He sent forth his *w* and healed them * 747 21
I will not forget your *w*. 764 16
that I may live and keep your *w*. 764 18
give me life according to your *w*. 765 10
strengthen me according to your *w*. 765 16
Then shall I have a *w* for those who taunt me, * 766 19
Do not take the *w* of truth out of my mouth, * 766 21
Remember your *w* to your servant, * 767 11
according to your *w*. 768 18
but now I keep your *w*. 768 22
because I trust in your *w*. 769 13
I have put my hope in your *w*. 770 4
O LORD, your *w* is everlasting; * 770 20
that I may keep your *w*. 771 22
Your *w* is a lantern to my feet * 772 3
preserve my life, O LORD, according to your *w*. 772 8
my hope is in your *w*. 773 2
When your *w* goes forth it gives light; * 774 7
Steady my footsteps in your *w*; * 774 13
Your *w* has been tested to the uttermost, * 775 5
for in your *w* is my trust. 775 21
for they have not kept your *w*. 776 20
The heart of your *w* is truth; * 776 23
but my heart stands in awe of your *w*. 777 2
give me understanding, according to your *w*. 777 18
in his *w* is my hope. 785 2
and your *w* above all things. 793 7
Indeed, there is not a *w* on my lips, * 794 6
and his *w* runs very swiftly. 805 8
He sends forth his *w* and melts them; * 805 13
He declares his *w* to Jacob, * 805 15
Grant that your *W* may be truly preached 817 12
in your *W* you have given us a vision 825 6
who hast taught us in thy holy *W* 831 11
the truth of his *W* and the example of his life; 836 13
To show God respect in thought, *w*, and deed. 847 24
Why do we call the Holy Scriptures the *W* of God? 853 23
We call them the *W* of God because God inspired 853 24
to proclaim the *W* of God; 855 25
acknowledge the holiness of God, to hear God's *W*, 857 23

words

and their *w* into the ends of the world. 40 5
Let the *w* of my mouth, and the meditation 40 13
Let the *w* of my mouth and the meditation 78 12
God spake these *w*, and said: 317 24
Let us pray in the *w* our Savior Christ has taught us. 398 11
Let us pray together in the *w* our Savior taught us. 428 7
Make these *w* more than *w*, and give me the Spirit 461 24
May he hear your *w* of invitation, 465 21
speaks to us through the *w* of Holy Scripture. 570 23
May the *w* of our mouth, 571 4
Give ear to my *w*, O LORD; * 588 17
The *w* of the LORD are pure *w*, * 597 13
I have heeded the *w* of your lips. 601 6
incline your ear to me and hear my *w*. 601 10
the *w* of the LORD are tried in the fire; * 604 25
Although they have no *w* or language, * 606 19
Let the *w* of my mouth and the meditation of my 607 28
and from the *w* of my distress? 610 3
and your lips from lying *w*. 628 20
The *w* of his mouth are wicked and deceitful; * 632 7
I refrained from rash *w*; 638 20
Even if they come to see me, they speak empty *w*; * 642 10
and the end of those who delight in their own *w*. 653 7
and toss my *w* behind your back? 655 15
You love all *w* that hurt, * 658 6
give ear to the *w* of my mouth. 659 20
His *w* are smoother than oil, * 662 3
For the sins of their mouths, for the *w* of their lips, 666 21
and aim their bitter *w* like arrows, 671 15
incline your ears to the *w* of my mouth. 694 20
May these *w* of mine please him; * 737 22
but the Egyptians rebelled against his *w*. 740 10
Then they believed his *w* * 742 22
that he spoke rash *w* with his lips. 744 14
Because they rebelled against the *w* of God * 747 3
they encompass me with hateful *w* 751 2
By keeping to your *w*. 764 2
because I trust in your *w*. 766 20
I have promised to keep your *w*. 768 2
How sweet are your *w* to my taste! * 771 25
because my enemies forget your *w*. 775 4

when they have heard the *w* of your mouth. 793 11
that they may know my *w* are true. 797 16
The LORD is faithful in all his *w* * 802 13
that the *w* which we have heard this day 834 18
with or without *w*. 856 19

work

Keep watch, dear Lord, with those who *w*, 71 1
Keep watch, dear Lord, with those who *w*, 124 17
Keep watch, dear Lord, with those who *w*, 134 6
who *w* while others sleep, 134 13
to do the *w* which thou givest us to do 151 14
that we may behold him in all his redeeming *w*; 171 19
that we may behold him in all his redeeming *w*; 173 7
and may uphold them in their *w* 205 17
have not known the redeeming *w* of our Savior 206 19
Be present with thy people where they *w*; 208 3
do the *w* which thou givest us to do, 210 4
So guide us in the *w* we do, 210 12
arouse our concern for those who are out of *w*; 210 16
that we may behold him in all his redeeming *w*; 223 12
that we may behold him in all his redeeming *w*; 224 21
receive thankfully the fruits of his redeeming *w*, 232 13
in their *w* for the extension of your kingdom; 256 14
have not known the redeeming *w* of our Savior 257 15
Be present with your people where they *w*; 259 5
that we may do the *w* you give us to do 261 10
So guide us in the *w* we do, 261 17
arouse our concern for those who are out of *w*; 261 21
our dishonesty in daily life and *w*, 268 11
Accomplish in us the *w* of your salvation, 268 29
may the Holy Spirit, who has begun a good *w* in you, 310 5
to do the *w* you have given us to do, 366 9
Remembering now his *w* of redemption, 371 19
eyes to see your hand at *w* in the world about us. 372 3
to complete his *w* in the world, 374 11
For all who live and *w* in this community 390 19
For all people in their daily life and *w*; 392 2
For all who *w* for justice, freedom, and peace. 392 6
may the Holy Spirit, who has begun a good *w* in you, 419 1
I commend you to this *w*, 420 5
Bless them in their *w* and in their companionship; 430 19
Continue in him, we pray, the good *w* 460 19
w which thou didst begin in them may be 486 11
Make you perfect in every good *w* to do his will, 487 2
w which thou hast begun in them may be perfected; 488 30
Make you perfect in every good *w* to do his will, 503 4
w in them the good purpose of your perfect will; 504 28
we ordain N. for the *w* to which we trust 514 17
wisely overseeing the life and *w* of the Church. 521 13
authority over you and your *w*? 526 13
w as a pastor, priest, and teacher, 531 5
serve the people among whom you *w*, 531 11
equip the saints for the *w* of ministry 533 9
authority over you and your *w*? 538 13
among whom you live, and *w*, and worship. 543 11
and his Church to the life and *w* of a deacon? 543 20
Receive the *w* of our hands in this place, 567 9
for the *w* of many hands, 573 2
and accept the *w* of our hands, 578 5
you hate all those who *w* wickedness. 588 26
consider your heavens, the *w* of your fingers, * 592 13
According to the *w* of their hands repay them, * 619 16
See how they are fallen, those who *w* wickedness! * 633 3
they broke down all your carved *w* with hatchets 689 19
Do you *w* wonders for the dead? * 712 23
prosper the *w* of our hands; 719 8
and the heavens are the *w* of your hands; 732 29
Man goes forth to his *w* * 736 23
His *w* is full of majesty and splendor, * 754 10
the *w* of human hands. 757 21
the *w* of human hands. 789 6
and *w* through our struggle and confusion 815 17
and to *w* together with mutual forbearance 824 3
Bless those who *w* in the fields; 824 8
those who suffer want and anxiety from lack of *w*. 824 12
Have mercy upon all of us who live and *w* 825 19
Remember those who *w* in these institutions; 826 22
strengthen them in the *w* of their recovery; 831 22
and the fever of life is over, and our *w* is done. 833 16
Help us, O Lord, to finish the good *w* here begun. 839 16
that it is the *w* of a single loving God 846 7
to *w* and pray for peace; 848 8
God at *w* in the world and in the Church even now. 852 16
to show God at *w* in nature and history. 853 12
and guides them to do God's *w*. 854 20
Christ's *w* of reconciliation in the world; 855 18
w, pray, and give for the spread of the kingdom 856 15

worked

He *w* marvels in the sight of their forefathers, * 695 26
They *w* his signs among them, * 740 7

worker

awesome in renown, and *w* of wonders? 85 18
O *w* of deception. 658 3

workers

mindful of the rightful aspirations of other *w*, 210 15
mindful of the rightful aspirations of other *w*, 261 20
and all the *w* of iniquity flourish, 721 10
and all the *w* of iniquity shall be scattered. 721 15
you made us fellow *w* in your creation: 827 18

working

Glory to God whose power, *w* in us, 60 3
Glory to God whose power, *w* in us, 73 3
Glory to God whose power, *w* in us, 102 14
Glory to God whose power, *w* in us, 126 14
may do his will, *w* in you that which is pleasing 132 4
by the effectual *w* of your providence, 280 16
by the effectual *w* of your providence, 291 13
w in you that which is well pleasing in his sight; 487 2
w in you that which is well-pleasing in his sight; 503 4
by the effectual *w* of your providence, 515 6
by the effectual *w* of your providence, 528 4
by the effectual *w* of your providence, 540 4

works

O all ye *w* of the Lord, bless ye the Lord; * 47 5
from all thy *w* and sanctify a day of rest 56 12
all just *w* do proceed: 69 17
Glorify the Lord, all you *w* of the Lord, * 88 5
because your just and holy *w* have been revealed. 94 18
rested from all your *w* and sanctified 99 7
all right judgments, and all just *w*: 123 16

proved me, and saw my *w*. 146 20
the noble *w* that thou didst in their days, 154 6
that we may cast away the *w* of darkness, 159 2
perceive the glory of his marvelous *w*; 163 17
and bring forth in us the fruit of good *w*: 181 14
make us continually to be given to all good *w*; 183 8
Preserve the *w* of thy mercy, 183 12
destroy the *w* of the devil 184 8
give us grace to cast away the *w* of darkness, 211 1
perceive the glory of his marvelous *w*; 215 11
and bring forth in us the fruit of good *w*; 233 6
that we may continually be given to good *w*; 234 21
Preserve the *w* of your mercy, 235 4
destroy the *w* of the devil 236 2
renounced Satan and all his *w*, 292 6
and wonder in all your *w*. 308 8
behold thy gracious hand in all thy *w*, 329 23
all such good *w* as thou hast prepared for us 339 12
fervent in prayer and in *w* of mercy, 346 10
Your mighty *w* reveal your wisdom and love. 373 18
fervent in prayer and in *w* of mercy, 379 7
That our *w* may find favor in your sight. 387 13
the record of your mighty *w*; 562 13
You give him mastery over the *w* of your hands; * 592 19
I will tell of all your marvelous *w*. 593 2
the wicked are trapped in the *w* of their own hands. 594 10
nor of the *w* of his hands; * 619 19
and all his *w* are sure. 626 8
and understands all their *w*. 627 6
Come now and look upon the *w* of the LORD, * 649 19
they will recognize his *w*. 672 4
Come now and see the *w* of God, * 674 1
I will begin with the mighty *w* of the Lord GOD; * 684 12
and to this day I tell of your wonderful *w*. 684 15
I will speak of all your *w* * 689 7
I will remember the *w* of the LORD, * 693 22
You are the God who *w* wonders * 694 1
and the wonderful *w* he has done. 695 6
and had no faith in his wonderful *w*. 697 15
nor anything like your *w*. 710 14
Show your servants your *w* * 719 5
and I shout for joy because of the *w* of your hands. 721 4
LORD, how great are your *w*! * 721 5
though they had seen my *w*. 725 11
and his *w* to the children of Israel. 733 22
Bless the LORD, all you *w* of his, 734 27
the earth is fully satisfied by the fruit of your *w*. 736 2
O LORD, how manifold are your *w*! * 736 25
may the LORD rejoice in all his *w*. 737 17
and speak of all his marvelous *w*. 738 4
In Egypt they did not consider your marvelous *w*, 742 11
They beheld the *w* of the LORD * 748 3
He makes his marvelous *w* to be remembered; * 754 12
He has shown his people the power of his *w* * 754 16
The *w* of his hands are faithfulness and justice; * 754 18
and declare the *w* of the LORD. 762 5
that I may meditate on your marvelous *w*. 765 14
do not abandon the *w* of your hands. 793 21
your *w* are wonderful, and I know it well. 795 2
I consider the *w* of your hands. 799 9
One generation shall praise your *w* to another * 801 18
and all your marvelous *w*. 801 21
and his compassion is over all his *w*. 802 4
All your *w* praise you, O LORD, * 802 5
and loving in all his *w*. 802 22
behold thy gracious hand in all thy *w*; 814 2
w begun, continued, and ended in thee, 832 3

world

the ends of the *w*. 40 6
The Spirit of the Lord filleth the *w*: 43 12
and with righteousness to judge the *w* 45 9
which have been since the *w* began: 50 27
that takest away the sins of the *w*, 52 12
Thou that takest away the sins of the *w*, 52 14
The holy Church throughout all the *w* 53 6
Give peace, O Lord, in all the *w*; 55 5
And we worship thy Name ever, *w* without end. 55 18
who after the creation of the *w* didst rest 56 11
in the redemption of the *w* by our Lord Jesus Christ, 58 22
be all honor and glory, *w* without end. 59 11
granting us in this *w* knowledge of thy truth, 59 18
and in the *w* to come life everlasting. 59 18
Jesus said, "I am the light of the *w*; 62 9
Give peace, O Lord, in all the *w*; 67 20
to thy Church and to the whole *w*, 68 16
that peace which the *w* cannot give, 69 18
in the redemption of the *w* by our Lord Jesus Christ, 71 18
be all honor and glory, *w* without end. 72 8
granting us in this *w* knowledge of thy truth, 72 15
and in the *w* to come life everlasting. 72 15
the ends of the *w*. 78 5
and this is known in all the *w*. 86 12
whom you have prepared for all the *w* to see: 93 15
you take away the sin of the *w*: 95 5
Throughout the *w* the holy Church acclaims you; 95 26
Give peace, O Lord, in all the *w*; 97 22
who after the creation of the *w* rested 99 6
in the redemption of the *w* by our Lord Jesus Christ; 101 14
granting us in this *w* knowledge 102 6
illumine the *w* with the radiance of your glory, 107 14
Jesus said, "You are the light of the *w*. 109 7
your saints have been the lights of the *w* 111 12
Jesus said, "I am the light of the *w*; 116 5
whom you have prepared for all the *w* to see: 120 4
Give peace, O Lord, in all the *w*; 121 22
to your Church and to the whole *w*, 122 18
that peace which the *w* cannot give, 123 17
in redemption of the *w* by our Lord Jesus Christ; 125 12
granting us in this *w* knowledge 126 6
O God, your unfailing providence sustains the *w* 134 11
whom you have prepared for all the *w* to see: 135 4
whom you have prepared for all the *w* to see: 140 10
w without end. 141 8
O God the Son, Redeemer of the *w*, 148 3
deceits of the *w*, the flesh, and the devil, 149 6
to make wars to cease in all the *w*; 151 1
O Lamb of God, that takest away the sins of the *w*, 152 24
w without end. 154 12
be honor and glory, *w* without end. 160 5
one God, *w* without end. 160 17
one God, *w* without end. 161 13
the love of him who is the Savior of the *w*, 162 4
Christ is the light of the *w*: 163 8

that we and all the whole *w* may perceive 163 16
which giveth life to the *w*: 167 12
among the sundry and manifold changes of the *w*, 167 19
one God, *w* without end. 169 13
one God, *w* without end. 171 4
one God, *w* without end. 174 19
one *w* without end. 175 7
Shed abroad this gift throughout the *w* 175 10
that the course of this *w* may be peaceably governed 177 9
one God, *w* without end. 181 9
that thy Church throughout the *w* may persevere 183 13
one God, *w* without end. 184 14
the light of the Gospel to shine throughout the *w*: 187 9
delivered from the disquietude of this *w*, 191 18
one God, *w* without end. 191 20
that he might draw the whole *w* unto himself: 192 14
Christ before the rulers of this *w*, 195 3
to be so faithful in our witness to thee in this *w*, 195 11
didst raise up thy servant N. to be a light to the *w*: 196 16
from an inordinate love of this *w*, 198 3
one God, *w* without end. 200 5
that the *w* may believe in him 204 21
the love of him who is the Savior of the *w*, 213 15
Christ is the light of the *w*: 215 2
that we and the whole *w* may perceive 215 10
to be the true bread which gives life to the *w*: 219 2
among the swift and varied changes of the *w*, 219 9
Shed abroad this gift throughout the *w* 227 3
that the course of this *w* may be peaceably governed 229 5
that your Church throughout the *w* may persevere 235 5
whose blessed Son came into the *w* 236 1
the light of the Gospel to shine throughout the *w*: 238 21
being delivered from the disquietude of this *w*, 243 4
that he might draw the whole *w* to himself: 244 2
before the rulers of this *w*, 247 1
faithful in our witness to you in this *w*, 247 9
who raised up your servant N. to be a light in the *w*: 248 2
Deliver us from an inordinate love of this *w*, 249 13
that the *w* may believe in him whom you have sent, 255 19
That we may show forth your glory in the *w*. 268 30
peace which the *w* cannot give, I give to you. 275 2
peace which the *w* cannot give, I give to you. 275 6
By this shall the *w* know that you are my disciples: 275 7
Our heavenly Father sent his Son into the *w*, 277 3
not to condemn the *w*, but that the *w* through him 277 3
Church of Christ throughout the *w*; 278 2
that, with all who have departed this *w* 280 9
let the whole *w* see and know 280 17
joy has come to the whole *w*. 281 4
joy has come to the whole *w*. 281 14
because by your holy cross you have redeemed the *w*. 281 16
because by your holy cross you have redeemed the *w*. 282 2
O Savior of the *w*, 282 3
her members, dispersed throughout the *w*, 285 3
and power to proclaim you to all the *w*; 291 8
let the whole *w* see and know that things 291 14
Do you renounce the evil powers of this *w* 302 10
Send them into the *w* in witness to your love. 306 1
thanks for the creation of the *w*, 316 11
redemption of the *w* by our Savior Christ, 316 13
that takest away the sins of the *w*, 324 23
Thou that takest away the sins of the *w*, 325 1
and the life of the *w* to come. 327 19
and the life of the *w* to come. 328 21
the whole state of Christ's Church and the *w*. 328 23
actions for the welfare and peace of the *w*. 329 21
God so loved the *w*, that he gave his only-begotten 332 10
that Christ Jesus came into the *w* to save sinners. 332 14
but for the sins of the whole *w*. 332 18
for the sins of the whole *w*; 334 14
O Father Almighty, *w* without end. 336 14
O Lamb of God, that takest away the sins of the *w*, 337 3
be all honor and glory, *w* without end. 339 14
Let us go forth into the *w*, rejoicing 340 3
a full and perfect sacrifice for the whole *w*; 341 17
Almighty, *w* without end. 343 5
to show forth thy glory in all the *w*. 345 7
in power and great triumph to judge the *w*, 345 11
that he might draw the whole *w* to himself; 346 14
and hath taken away the sin of the *w*; 346 20
and the lights of the *w* in their generations. 348 3
confessing before the rulers of this *w* 348 9
you take away the sin of the *w*: 356 9
and the life of the *w* to come. 359 10
a perfect sacrifice for the whole *w*. 362 17
Send us now into the *w* in peace, 365 14
Let us go forth into the *w*, 366 18
to be the Savior and Redeemer of the *w*. 368 6
eyes to see your hand at work in the *w* about us. 372 3
serve the *w* in his name. 372 8
giving the whole *w* into our care, 373 19
Father, you loved the *w* so much that in the fullness 374 1
to complete his work in the *w*, 374 12
having loved his own who were in the *w*, 374 15
to show forth your glory in all the *w*. 378 3
in power and great triumph to judge the *w*, 378 7
that he might draw the whole *w* to himself; 379 11
and has taken away the sin of the *w*. 379 17
of the *w* in their generations. 380 19
confessing before the rulers of this *w* 381 3
For the peace of the *w*, 383 6
I ask your prayers for God's people throughout the *w*; 385 17
hold authority in the nations of the *w*; 387 10
Let us pray for the Church and for the *w*. 388 1
and reveal your glory in the *w*. 388 4
For the peace of the *w*, 390 13
that the *w* may be freed from poverty, 390 22
For this community, the nation, and the *w*; 392 5
God so loved the *w* that he gave his only Son, 396 1
the bread which I shall give for the life of the *w* 397 3
w without end. 406 4
Lamb of God, you take away the sins of the *w*: 407 1
our Christian vocation of witness to the *w*, 421 6
Look with favor upon the *w* you have made, 429 4
Christ's love to this sinful and broken *w*, 429 18
God so loved the *w*, that he gave his only-begotten 449 15
that Christ Jesus came into the *w* to save sinners. 449 19
but for the sins of the whole *w*. 450 4
in whom you have redeemed the *w*, 450 20
Savior of the *w*, by your cross and precious blood 455 16
restored to usefulness in your *w* 459 15
Jesus, redeemer of the *w*: 463 27
Depart, O Christian soul, out of this *w*; 464 21
or ever the earth and the *w* were made, * 472 12

thou art God from everlasting, and *w* without end. 472 13
taken away the sin of the *w*. 483 19
and the lights of the *w* in their several generations; 487 13
from the foundation of the *w*." 487 21
to take away the sins of the *w*; 488 17
and in perfect charity with the *w*. 489 12
taken away the sin of the *w*. 500 8
and in perfect charity with the *w*. 504 10
prepared for you from the beginning of the *w*." 505 7
let the whole *w* see and know 515 7
the leadership of the Church throughout the *w*. 517 14
and the life of the *w* to come. 520 10
Let us go forth into the *w*, rejoicing 523 18
let the whole *w* see and know 528 5
and the life of the *w* to come. 530 29
share in the renewing of his *w*. 531 4
and your Name glorified in all the *w*. 534 7
Let us go forth into the *w*, rejoicing 535 13
let the whole *w* see and know 540 5
and the life of the *w* to come. 542 29
the needs, concerns, and hopes of the *w*. 543 13
Let us go forth into the *w*, 547 7
For the peace of the *w*, 549 29
that the *w* may be freed from poverty, 550 7
all the *w* may be drawn 563 8
share in the ordering of your *w*. 567 9
how exalted is your Name in all the *w*! 592 8
It is he who rules the *w* with righteousness; * 593 15
His eyes behold the inhabited *w*; * 596 17
from those whose portion in life is this *w*; 601 28
and the foundations of the *w* laid bare, * 603 20
and their message to the ends of the *w*. 606 22
the *w* and all who dwell therein. 613 15
let all who dwell in the *w* stand in awe of him. 626 16
and beholds all the people in the *w*. 627 2
It is he who makes war to cease in all the *w*; * 649 21
the very center of the *w* and the city 651 5
O God, reaches to the *w*'s end; * 651 21
hearken, all you who dwell in the *w*, * 652 7
for the whole *w* is mine and all that is in it. 655 4
and their evil speech runs through the *w*. 687 18
your lightnings lit up the *w*; * 694 12
you laid the foundations of the *w* and all that is in it. 714 16
He has made the whole *w* so sure * 722 5
Ever since the *w* began, 722 7
Rise up, O Judge of the *w*; * 722 20
he who teaches all the *w*, has he no knowledge? 723 14
he has made the *w* so firm that it cannot be moved; 726 12
He will judge the *w* with righteousness * 726 20
His lightnings light up the *w*; * 727 3
In righteousness shall he judge the *w* * 728 21
his judgments prevail in all the *w*. 738 14
princes and all rulers of the *w*; 806 16
who hast filled the *w* with beauty: 814 1
guide the nations of the *w* into the way of justice 816 2
O Lord our Governor, whose glory is in all the *w*: 820 16
one God, *w* without end. 820 25
that holy City to which the nations of the *w* 825 7
and multiply the harvests of the *w*; 828 3
growing up in an unsteady and confusing *w*: 829 15
give more life than the ways of the *w*, 829 16
and the evening comes, and the busy *w* is hushed, 833 15
for the beauty of this *w*, for the wonder of life, 836 3
Christ to reconcile the *w* to yourself: 838 2
wonderful diversity of races and cultures in this *w*. 840 2
be all glory and honor, *w* without end. 840 23
Heavenly Father, you sent your own Son into this *w*. 841 1
may live in this *w* according to thy will, 841 11
It means that the *w* belongs to its creator; 846 10
all the nations of the *w* to him. 847 2
work in the *w* and in the Church even now. 852 16
Christ's work of reconciliation in the *w*; 855 18
in Christ's name for the reconciliation of the *w* 855 26
God's purpose for the *w*. 861 28

worldly

Preserve us from faithless fears and *w* anxieties, 165 9
Preserve us from faithless fears and *w* anxieties, 217 2
Our intemperate love of *w* goods and comforts, 268 10

worlds

and to be glorified through all the *w*. 64 9
and to be glorified through all the *w*. 112 9
and to be glorified through all the *w*. 118 9
and to be glorified through all the *w*. 139 9
begotten of his Father before all *w*, 327 26
all its marvelous order, its atoms, *w*, and galaxies, 827 12

worm

But as for me, I am a *w* and no man, * 610 12

worn

and *w* away because of all my enemies. 590 13
I am *w* down by the blows of your hand. 639 16

worse

for better for *w*, for richer for poorer, 427 2
for better for *w*, for richer for poorer, 427 7
for better for *w*, for richer for poorer, 436 3
for better for *w*, for richer for poorer, 436 7

worship

shall *w* the Father in spirit and in truth; 40 21
for the Father seeketh such to *w* him. 40 22
prepare ourselves in heart and mind to *w* him, 41 11
W the Lord in the beauty of holiness: 44 3
O come, let us *w* and fall down * 45 1
O *w* the Lord in the beauty of holiness; * 45 6
we *w* thee, 52 6
All the earth doth *w* thee, 52 24
And we *w* thy Name ever, world without end. 55 18
such blessing through our *w* of thee, 56 3
O *w* the Lord in the beauty of holiness; 61 5
and our *w* on the morrow may give thee glory; 69 14
Let the whole earth also *w* thee, 70 16
will *w* the Father in spirit and truth, 78 20
for such the Father seeks to *w* him. 78 21
prepare ourselves in heart and mind to *w* him, 79 6
W the Lord in the beauty of holiness: 81 12
Free to *w* him without fear, * 92 29
Be *w* and praise, dominion and splendor, * 94 7
we *w* you, we give you thanks, 95 1
your true and only Son, worthy of all *w*, 95 28
such blessing through our *w* of you, 98 21
that all nations may come and *w* you; 107 15
and made worthy to *w* you in spirit and in truth; 111 6

W the Lord in the beauty of holiness; 115 5
and our *w* on the morrow give you glory; 123 13
Let the whole earth also *w* you, 124 13
how long will you *w* dumb idols 128 12
O come, let us *w* and fall down * 146 11
being renewed both in body and mind, may *w* thee 170 17
of the Divine Majesty to *w* the Unity: 176 4
wouldest keep us steadfast in this faith and *w*, 176 5
as thy holy angels always serve and *w* thee 193 6
and constant in our *w* of thee, 199 15
as thy holy angels always serve and *w* thee 200 8
they may be brought to know and *w* thee 206 21
they may *w* thee and serve thee 209 19
may *w* you in sincerity and truth; 222 11
power of your divine Majesty to *w* the Unity: 228 4
steadfast in this faith and *w*, 228 5
angels always serve and *w* you in heaven, 244 16
and constant in our *w* of you, 251 4
angels always serve and *w* you in heaven, 251 15
they may be brought to know and *w* you 257 17
they may *w* you and serve you 261 3
Our negligence in prayer and *w*, 268 13
may *w* you in sincerity and truth; 295 11
thou shalt not bow down to them, nor *w* them. 318 4
we *w* thee, 324 17
which is your spiritual *w*. 343 16
we *w* you, we give you thanks, 356 5
your Church gives honor, glory, and *w*, 372 12
which is your spiritual *w*. 376 12
conform to the doctrine, discipline, and *w* 513 12
Will you be loyal to the doctrine, discipline, and *w* 526 9
and *w* of The Episcopal Church. 526 18
Will you be loyal to the doctrine, discipline, and *w* 538 9
and *w* of The Episcopal Church. 538 18
among whom you live, and work, and *w*. 543 11
assist the bishop and priests in public *w* 543 14
now to be set apart for your *w*, 567 10
Father, your people *w* you with many voices 572 1
Let us thank God whom we *w* here 578 1
how long will you *w* dumb idols 588 2
in the presence of those who *w* him. 612 6
all who sleep in the earth bow down in *w*; * 612 16
w the LORD in the beauty of holiness. 620 8
Love the LORD, all you who *w* him; * 624 18
you shall not *w* a foreign god. 704 20
come and *w* you, O LORD, * 710 16
W the LORD in the beauty of holiness; * 726 9
Confounded be all who *w* carved images 727 9
and *w* him upon his holy hill; * 729 20
W the LORD, O Jerusalem; * 805 1
by their life and *w* may glorify your Name; 819 11
O God, whom saints and angels delight to *w* 819 13
w thee in spirit and in truth; 833 23
And to set aside regular times for *w*, 847 26
How many creeds does this Church use in its *w*? 851 24
used in the Church's daily *w* to recall 852 3
their place in the life, *w*, and governance 855 19
together week by week for corporate *w*; 856 14
What is corporate *w*? 857 21
In corporate *w*, we unite ourselves with others 857 22

worshiped

that he may be known, *w*, and obeyed 163 10
of those who have *w* in this place; 204 3
that he may be known, *w*, and obeyed 215 4
of those who have *w* in this place, 255 1
With the Father and the Son he is *w* and glorified. 327 14
who with the Father and the Son together is *w* 328 15
With the Father and the Son he is *w* and glorified. 359 5
With the Father and the Son he is *w* and glorified. 520 5
With the Father and the Son he is *w* and glorified. 530 24
With the Father and the Son he is *w* and glorified. 542 24
and *w* a molten image; 743 10
So that they *w* their idols, * 744 19

worshipers

The hour cometh, and now is, when the true *w* 40 20
The hour is coming, and now is, when the true *w* 78 19

worships

All creation *w* you. 95 18
w, proclaims the Gospel, and promotes justice, 855 6

worth

all our doings without charity are nothing *w*: 164 19
without love whatever we do is *w* nothing: 216 14
his piercing eye weighs our *w*. 596 18
take failure, not as a measure of their *w*, 829 18

worthily

we, *w* lamenting our sins 166 4
we, *w* lamenting our sins 217 16
we, *w* lamenting our sins 264 4
may *w* offer to you our sacrifice 289 3
and *w* magnify thy holy Name; 323 10
w receive the most precious Body and Blood 336 5
w receive the most precious Body and Blood 342 25
and *w* magnify your holy Name; 355 10
that we may *w* serve the world 372 7
and *w* magnify your holy Name; 512 10
and *w* magnify your holy Name; 525 10
and *w* magnify your holy Name; 537 10

worthiness

mercifully give us for the *w* of thy Son 179 20
through the *w* of your Son 231 14

worthless

and that which is *w* is highly prized by everyone. 597 19
I have not sat with the *w*, * 616 14
I hate those who cling to *w* idols, * 622 20
I will set no *w* thing before my eyes; * 730 12
Turn my eyes from watching what is *w*; * 766 9

worthy

am no more *w* to be called thy son." 38 19
his most *w* praise, to hear his holy Word, 41 8
Thou art *w* at all times to be praised 64 7
no longer *w* to be called your son." 76 18
We give thanks to the Father, who has made us *w* 77 22
you are *w* of praise; glory to you. 90 6
your true and only Son, *w* of all worship, 95 28
and made *w* to worship you in spirit and in truth; 111 6
may be *w* to enter with them 111 14
You are *w* at all times to be praised 112 7

You are *w* at all times to be praised 118 7
You are *w* at all times to be praised 139 7
may be found *w* to attain 171 6
make us *w* of our calling; 176 11
those good things which we are not *w* to ask, 183 3
may be found *w* to attain 222 23
make us *w* of our calling; 228 11
those good things for which we are not *w* 234 16
we may be accounted *w* to enter 280 11
to sing the *w* praise of this great light; 286 12
and for making us *w* to share in the inheritance 311 17
and *w* of all men to be received, 332 13
We are not *w* so much as to gather 337 11
W art thou, O Lord our God, to receive glory 344 5
you have delivered us from evil, and made us *w* 368 7
God of all power, Ruler of the Universe, you are *w* 370 5
O Lord our God, you are *w* to receive glory 377 3
This is a true saying, and *w* of all men to be received, 449 18
thou most *w* Judge eternal. 484 15
O *w* and eternal Judge, 492 18
O Lord my God, I am not *w* to have you 562 9
you are *w* of praise. 602 11
let all around him bring gifts to him who is *w* 692 23
and make them *w* at length to behold it unveiled 819 17
It means that all people are *w* of respect 846 14

wound

crushed Rahab of the deep with a deadly *w*; * 714 13

wounded

For the sick, the *w*, and the crippled 279 6
and suddenly they will be *w*. 671 25
I was sorely *w* in my heart. 688 20
and my heart is *w* within me. 752 20

wounds

By his *w*, we are healed. 370 22
My *w* stink and fester * 637 6
and binds up their *w*. 804 7

woven

and *w* in the depths of the earth. 795 5

wrap

and *w* their violence about them like a cloak. 687 12
You *w* yourself with light as with a cloak * 735 4
and *w* themselves in their shame as in a cloak. 753 7

wrapped

He *w* darkness about him; * 603 11

wraps

the cloak which he *w* around himself, * 752 12

wrath

Unto whom I sware in my *w*, * 146 24
provoking most justly thy *w* and indignation 331 8
Then he speaks to them in his *w*, * 586 10
for his *w* is quickly kindled. 586 27
do not punish me in your *w*. 589 24
Stand up, O LORD, in your *w*; * 591 6
You will swallow them up in your *w*, * 609 16
For his *w* endures but the twinkling of an eye, * 621 12
do not punish me in your *w*. 636 21
Make an end of them in your *w*; * 666 24
why is your *w* so hot against the sheep 689 10
When the LORD heard this, he was full of *w*; * 696 17
and did not permit his *w* to be roused. 698 4
Pour out your *w* upon the heathen 701 15
Who regards the power of your *w*? * 718 23
So I swore in my *w*, * 725 15
Because of your indignation and *w* * 731 19
to turn away his *w* from consuming them. 743 19
Therefore the *w* of the LORD was kindled 745 3
will smite kings in the day of his *w*; * 753 22

wrathful

and are afraid at thy *w* indignation. 472 24
Truly, *w* Edom will give you thanks, * 692 20
and turned yourself from your *w* indignation. 708 25
we are afraid because of your *w* indignation. 718 14

wreak

To *w* vengeance on the nations * 807 14

wretched

my *w* body from the horns of wild bulls. 611 23
Ever since my youth, I have been *w* 713 8

wretchedness

lamenting our sins and acknowledging our *w*, 166 5
lamenting our sins and acknowledging our *w*, 217 17
lamenting our sins and acknowledging our *w*, 264 5

write

and *w* all these thy laws in our hearts, 318 30
many listen and *w* what many read; 827 8

writer

my tongue shall be the pen of a skilled *w*, 647 13

writhe

The voice of the LORD makes the oak trees *w* * 620 21

writhed

they *w* like a woman in childbirth, 651 13

written

Scriptures to be *w* for our learning: 184 16
Scriptures to be *w* for our learning: 236 8
In the roll of the book it is *w* concerning me: * 640 20
and not be *w* among the righteous. 681 21
Let this be *w* for a future generation, * 732 12
all of them were *w* in your book; * 795 7
The Old Testament consists of books *w* 853 10
The New Testament consists of books *w* 853 14
w by people of the Old Covenant, 853 21

wrong

Drive far from us all *w* desires, 56 20
Drive far from us all *w* desires, 99 15
under their tongue are mischief and *w*. 595 7
He has sworn to do no *w* * 599 13
do not be jealous of those who do *w*. 633 6
we have done *w* and dealt wickedly. 742 10
Who never do any *w*, * 763 9
Let the arrogant be put to shame, for they *w* me 769 20
freedom and made *w* choices. 845 11

wrongfully

and many in number are those who *w* hate me. 638 8

wrongs

Accept our repentance, Lord, for the *w* we have done: 268 16
ready to make restitution for all injuries and *w* 317 6

wrought

Remember, O Lord, what thou hast *w* in us 176 9
Remember, O Lord, what you have *w* in us 228 9
establish, O God, what you have *w* for us. 678 15
How he *w* his signs in Egypt * 698 13

X

Y

Yahweh (small caps)

Y is his Name, rejoice before him! 676 10
Let them know that you, whose Name is *Y*, * 707 13

Yahweh

Y is his Name. 85 8

yea

y, even for the living God; * 471 3
y, it is even he that shall keep thy soul. 473 22
Y, the darkness is no darkness with thee, 475 15
Y, though I walk through the valley 476 8
Y, though I walk through the valley 477 1
y, in the secret place of his dwelling 477 21
y, our God is merciful. 479 9

year

You crown the *y* with your goodness, * 673 11
on your servant N. as he begins another *y*. Grant 830 9

yearly

O God, who makest us glad with the *y* remembrance 160 12
O God, you make us glad by the *y* festival 212 10

years

Forty *y* long was I grieved with this generation, 146 21
For a thousand *y* in thy sight are but as yesterday 472 16
we bring our *y* to an end, 473 2
The days of our age are threescore *y* and ten; 473 3
men be so strong that they come to fourscore *y*, * 473 4
as we grow in grace through the *y*, 569 7
blessing of our vows and the crowning of our *y* 579 4
and my *y* with sighing; * 623 7
let his *y* extend over many generations. 668 25
I remember the *y* long past; 693 11
and their *y* in sudden terror. 697 17
For a thousand *y* in your sight are like yesterday 718 6
we bring our *y* to an end like a sigh. 718 18
The span of our life is seventy *y*, 718 19
and the *y* in which we suffered adversity. 719 4
Forty *y* long I detested that generation and said, * 725 12
your *y* endure throughout all generations. 732 26
and your *y* will never end. 733 6
y bring them weakness, distress, or isolation. 830 2

yesterday

For a thousand years in thy sight are but as *y* 472 16
For a thousand years in your sight are like *y* 718 6

yet

y I do not forget your law. 104 6
create, and *y* more wonderfully restore, 162 7
create, and *y* more wonderfully restore, 200 13
created, and *y* more wonderfully restored, 214 1
created, and *y* more wonderfully restored, 252 1
created, and *y* more wonderfully restored, 288 5
y we beseech thee to accept this our bounden duty 336 10
tempted as we are, *y* did not sin; 346 5
he lived as one of us, *y* without sin. 374 4
tempted in every way as we are, *y* did not sin. 379 2
For those who do not *y* believe, 390 10
he *y* may put his trust in you; 459 10
though he were dead, *y* shall he live; 469 2
and though this body be destroyed, *y* shall I see God; 469 6
for I will *y* thank him, 471 15
y is their strength then but labor and sorrow, 473 5
and who walk as *y* by faith, 481 2
y even at the grave we make our song: 483 1
Y, O Lord God most holy, O Lord most mighty, 484 8
y even at the grave we make our song: 499 8
For those who do not *y* believe, 549 25
y you have called your servant to stand 562 10
y they shall not prevail. 609 22
Y you are the Holy One, * 610 6
Y you are he who took me out of the womb, * 610 18
shall come and make known to a people *y* unborn * 612 21
y my heart shall not be afraid; 617 15
y will I put my trust in him. 617 17
Y I said in my alarm, 624 14
for I will *y* give thanks to him, 643 16
for I will *y* give thanks to him, 644 12
for I will *y* give thanks to him, 645 4
y we have not forgotten you, 646 20
Y I am always with you; * 688 23
Y God is my King from ancient times, * 690 8
nor *y* from the wilderness or the mountains. 691 15
y your footsteps were not seen. 694 16
and the children *y* unborn; * 695 11
And *y* my people did not hear my voice, * 704 24
y the sum of them is but labor and sorrow, 718 21
Y they say, "The LORD does not see, * 723 7
y punished them for their evil deeds." 729 18
so that a people *y* unborn may praise the LORD. 732 13
Y when they were diminished and brought low, * 749 7
y I do not forget your law. 772 12
y I do not forget your commandments. 775 8
y your commandments are my delight. 775 12
y I have not swerved from your decrees. 776 18
Your eyes beheld my limbs, *y* unfinished in the womb; 795 6
when as *y* there was none of them. 795 9
generations *y* to come may continue to praise 827 20

yield

Almighty and everlasting God, we *y* unto thee 487 10
and our land will *y* its increase. 709 19
We *y* thee hearty thanks and praise 840 15

yoke

Take my *y* upon you, and learn from me; 131 16
For my *y* is easy, and my burden is light. 131 18
"Let us break their *y*," they say; * 586 6

yonder

Y is the great and wide sea 737 1

young

you shall trample the *y* lion and the serpent 130 24
women in childbirth, *y* children and orphans, 151 21
caring alike for *y* and old, 531 11
and like a *y* lion lurking in secret places. 601 24
Many *y* bulls encircle me; * 611 1
and Mount Hermon like a *y* wild ox. 620 17
The *y* lions lack and suffer hunger, * 628 13
and my life from the *y* lions. 631 3
I have been *y* and now I am old, * 635 9
then shall they offer *y* bullocks upon your altar. 657 22
pull the fangs of the *y* lions, O LORD. 665 6
my confidence since I was *y*. 683 10
O God, you have taught me since I was *y*, * 684 14
The fire consumed their *y* men; * 700 5
and the swallow a nest where she may lay her *y*; * 707 20
you shall trample the *y* lion and the serpent 720 12
and *y* locusts without number, 740 22
and the little hills like *y* sheep. 757 4
you little hills like *y* sheep? 757 8
How shall a *y* man cleanse his way? * 764 1
and for the *y* ravens when they cry. 804 21
Y men and maidens, * 806 17
old and *y* together. 806 18

youth

Remember not the sins of my *y* 615 1
and laid low the *y* of Israel. 697 13
Ever since my *y*, I have been wretched 713 8
You have cut short the days of his *y* * 717 3
and your *y* is renewed like an eagle's. 733 18
are the children of one's *y*. 783 9
"Greatly have they oppressed me since my *y*," * 784 1
sons be like plants well nurtured from their *y*, * 801 1

Z

Zalmon

it was like snow falling in Z. 677 9

Zalmunna

and all their commanders like Zebah and Z, 706 25

zeal

Grant to the people of our country a *z* for justice 207 3
Give to the people of our country a *z* for justice 258 3
Z for your house has eaten me up; * 680 5

zealous

we pray that, as they were faithful and *z* 194 3
we pray that, as they were faithful and *z* 245 12

Zebah

and all their commanders like Z and Zalmunna, 706 25

Zebulon

and the princes of Z and Naphtali. 678 13

Zeëb

Make their leaders like Oreb and Z, * 706 24

Zion

Cry aloud, inhabitants of Z, ring out your joy, * 86 13
The Z of the Holy One of Israel. 87 22
When the LORD restored the fortunes of Z, * 105 4
who made heaven and earth bless you out of Z. 131 9
who made heaven and earth bless you out of Z. 140 4
upon my holy hill of Z." 586 13
Sing praise to the LORD who dwells in Z; * 593 21
in the gates of the city of Z. 594 6
Oh, that Israel's deliverance would come out of Z! * 599 1
and strengthen you out of Z; 608 4
the joy of all the earth, is the hill of Z, * 651 4
Let Mount Z be glad 651 23
Make the circuit of Z; 651 26
Out of Z, perfect in its beauty, * 654 4
Be favorable and gracious to Z, * 657 18
Oh, that Israel's deliverance would come out of Z! * 659 14
You are to be praised, O God, in Z; * 672 7
For God will save Z and rebuild the cities of Judah; * 682 7
in the gates of the city of Z. 689 8
and Mount Z where you dwell. 689 13
and his dwelling is in Z. 692 4
and Mount Z, which he loved. 700 16
and the God of gods will reveal himself in Z. 708 5
the LORD loves the gates of Z 711 13
in Z were they born. 711 19
Of Z it shall be said, "Everyone was born in her, * 711 20
Z hears and is glad, and the cities of Judah rejoice, * 727 12
The LORD is great in Z; * 729 1
You will arise and have compassion on Z, 732 1
For the LORD will build up Z, * 732 8
That they may declare in Z the Name of the LORD, * 732 18
LORD will send the scepter of your power out of Z, * 753 14
Those who trust in the LORD are like Mount Z, * 781 17
When the LORD restored the fortunes of Z, * 782 6
The LORD bless you from Z, * 783 21
all those who are enemies of Z. 784 10
For the LORD has chosen Z; * 786 26
that falls upon the hills of Z. 787 16
who made heaven and earth bless you out of Z. 787 23
Blessed be the LORD out of Z, * 789 17
when we remembered you, O Z. 792 2
"Sing us one of the songs of Z." 792 7
your God, O Z, throughout all generations. 803 25
praise your God, O Z; 805 2
let the children of Z be joyful in their King. 807 5

Zoan

in the land of Egypt, in the field of Z. 695 27
and his omens in the field of Z. 698 14

Section Two

Rubrics, Notes, Historical Documents

A

ability

give alms to the poor, according to his *a*. 876 16

able

The candidates who are *a* to answer for themselves 301 —
not neglecting, if they are *a*, to leave bequests 445 11
will be *a* to separate us from the love of God 507 8
and be more *a* to exhort others 866 11

abolish

Church hath authority to ordain, change, and *a*, 874 31

above

the dated days listed *a*, only the following feasts, 16 3
In place of the *a*, 109 —
In place of the *a*, 299 —
If on any one of the *a*-named days the ministry 312 8
If on the four days listed *a* there are no candidates 312 15
In place of the *a*, 319 —
In place of the *a*, 323 —
In place of the *a*, 351 —
In place of the *a*, 355 —
In the absence of a priest, all that is described *a*, 407 5
In place of the *a*, 413 —
In place of the *a*, 512 —
The Bishop-elect then signs the *a* Declaration 513 —
In place of the *a*, 525 —
The Ordinand then signs the *a* Declaration 527 —
In place of the *a*, 537 —
The Ordinand then signs the *a* Declaration 539 —
Works besides, over and *a*, God's Commandments, 870 19
While the *a* form of the Quadrilateral was adopted 877 26

Abraham

A's sacrifice of Isaac 289 2

abridged

by common consent and authority, may be altered, *a*, 9 7

absence

In the *a* of a bishop or priest, 269 —
In the *a* of a bishop or priest, 272 —
In the *a* of a bishop or priest, 282 —
In the *a* of a bishop, 284 16
In the *a* of a bishop or priest, 284 23
In the *a* of candidates for Baptism or Confirmation, 292 —
In the *a* of a bishop, 298 13
In the *a* of a deacon or priest, 316 —
In the *a* of a deacon, 322 13
In the *a* of a deacon, 354 13
In the *a* of a priest, 407 5
In the *a* of sufficient deacons and priests, 408 6
In the bishop's *a*, 558 9
In the *a* of the bishop, 561 —
The Bishop, or in the Bishop's *a* a Priest 563 —

absent

not required for the Communion of the *a*, 555 5
52. For the *A* 812 3
52. For the *A* 830 —

absolute

The secrecy of a confession is morally *a* 446 27

absolution

Celebrant concludes with an *a* or a suitable Collect. 393 —
the Church and its ministers declaring *a*. 446 6
The *a* in these services may be pronounced 446 11
but it must be made clear to the penitent that *a* 446 13
face to face for a spiritual conference leading to *a* 446 18
and encouragement as are needed and pronounces *a*. 446 22
Before giving *a*, the priest may assign 446 23
The Priest then pronounces this *a* 448 —

absorb

4. That this Church does not seek to *a* other Communions, 877 1

abstain

of single life, or to *a* from marriage: 874 13

academic

distinctive of ecclesiastical or *a* rank or order. 511 17
distinctive of ecclesiastical or *a* rank or order. 524 8
distinctive of ecclesiastical or *a* rank or office. 536 8

acceptable

no power to do good works pleasant and *a* to God, 869 36
yet are they pleasing and *a* to God in Christ, 870 9

accepting

this ministry, *a* its privileges and responsibilities 557 8

access

See also the Prayer of Humble *A* on page 337. 834 —

acclamation

The Clergy and People offer their *a* and applause. 522 —

accord

following the holy fathers, we all with one *a* teach 864 4

accordance

The festival of a saint is observed in *a* with the rules 195 —
The festival of a saint is observed in *a* with the rules 246 —
or in *a* with the directions 328 —
In *a* with ancient custom, 511 3
Now, in *a* with the Canons, you have been selected 557 5
or in *a* with the directions 560 —

according

"*a* to the various exigency of times 9 9
to do that which, *a* to her best understanding, 10 9
a to her judgment, there be not any thing 10 14
a to the discretion of the officiant. 141 4
Eucharist *a* to their order. 284 19
administer Baptism *a* to the following form. 313 23
Intercession is offered *a* to the following form, 328 —
a to the canon may administer the Chalice. 408 8
The Holy Eucharist may be celebrated either *a* 436 14
Rite One or Rite Two in this Book, or *a* to the Order 436 15
Prayers may be offered *a* to the occasion. 454 14
The new bishop is now vested *a* to the order 521 —
The new priest is now vested *a* to the order of priests. 534 —
The new deacon is now vested *a* to the order 545 —
The celebration of the Holy Eucharist may be *a* 552 3
Alterations in the service are then made *a* 558 6

and deacons assist *a* to their order. 558 12
he be diligent to frame his life *a* to that Law, 871 26
Sacraments be duly ministered *a* to Christ's ordinance, 871 31
and may be changed *a* to the diversity of countries, 874 23
whosoever are consecrated or ordered *a* to said Form, 875 24
ordered *a* to the Rites of that Book, 875 31
liberally to give alms to the poor, *a* to his ability. 876 15
done *a* to the Prophet's teaching in justice, 876 21

accordingly
and we find *a*, that, seeking 9 25
A, a Commission for a review was issued 10 20
A, the manner of ordaining in this Church 510 29
be called *a* to God's purpose by his Spirit 871 6

account
and shall give *a* for their own works. 865 35
a them Canonical. 869 5
branches of Christendom, we *a* the following, to wit: 877 13

accounted
We are *a* righteous before God, 870 2

accursed
They also are to be had *a* that presume to say, 871 25

accused
Ministers, and that they be *a* by those 873 11

accustomed
celebrant standing in the *a* place. 468 25
celebrant standing in the *a* place. 490 25

acknowledge
we all with one accord teach men to *a* 864 4
compelled by the Christian verity to *a* every Person 865 5

acknowledged
indifferent, and alterable, and so *a*; 9 17

acknowledging
a briefly the purpose of their gathering, 492 —

across
should face the people *a* the font, 313 4

act
Eucharist, the principal *a* of Christian worship 13 3
Lay persons may *a* as readers, 312 24
in consultation with the celebrant, the *A* of Commitment, 420 —
makes the *A* of Commitment. 420 —
the Celebrant may begin with the *A* of Thanksgiving, 439 11
A of Thanksgiving 441 —
as a sign of penitence and *a* of thanksgiving. 446 25
Council of Chalcedon, 451 A.D., *A* V 864 3

action
When this *a* has been completed for all candidates, 308 —
Or this *a* may be done immediately after 308 —
and the formula and *a* which follow. 312 11
a clear view of the *a*. 313 6
incorporated in a general plan referred for study and *a* 877 27

actions
and perform other *a* as indicated in the rubrics. 558 15

active
and other persons, to take *a* parts in the service. 284 11

activities
social purposes, or for other suitable *a*. 566 12

activity
or as the prelude to an evening meal or other *a*. 108 6
Or, it may be followed by a meal or other *a*, 112 —

acts
The following days are observed by special *a* 17 21

Acts
A 1:8 39 —
A 1:8 77 —
or *A* 6:2–7 540 —

actual
also for *a* sins of men. 868 8
the sins of the whole world, both original and *a*; 874 7

Adam
Original sin standeth not in the following of *A*, 869 23
engendered of the offspring of *A*; 869 25
The condition of Man after the fall of *A* is such, 869 34

adaptations
A or insertions suitable to the occasion may be made. 383 —

adapted
prayers in contemporary language may be *a* 108 22
the indented petitions may be *a* 277 —
may be added to, omitted, or *a*, as appropriate 561 —
Portions of the service may be used, or *a* 566 3
the service may be *a* to the circumstances. 576 30
and that the service be *a*. 577 3
prayer may be said, or *a* to the circumstances; 577 11
4. The Historic Episcopate, locally *a* in the methods 877 18
(d) The Historic Episcopate, locally *a* in the methods 878 4

adapting
Provisions for *a* the rite to special circumstances 566 7

adapts
Incorporates or *a* the Proper Preface of the Day, 402 —
Incorporates or *a* the Proper Preface of the Day, 404 —

add
Except in Lent, *a* 80 —
Except in Lent, *a* 103 —
Except in Lent, *a* 117 —
Except in Lent, *a* 128 —
In Easter Season, *a* 134 —
In Easter Season, *a* 135 —
The Officiant may *a* other Prayers, 154 —
and may *a* 338 —
and may *a* 365 —
The People may *a* their own petitions. 388 —
The People may *a* their own petitions 392 —
The People may *a* their own thanksgivings 393 —
The People may *a* their own petitions 393 —
and may *a* 399 —

to *a* a little water to the wine.	407	16
The Celebrant may *a* one or more of the following	444	—
The Priest may *a*	456	—
The Celebrant may *a* the following prayer	494	—
The witnesses *a* their signatures.	513	—

added

may be *a*.	42	—
A citation giving chapter and verse may be *a*.	47	—
one of these prayers for mission is *a*	57	—
be *a* to the preceding versicle and response.	59	—
may be *a*.	63	—
A citation giving chapter and verse may be *a*.	64	—
one of these prayers for mission is *a*	70	—
be *a* to the preceding versicle and response.	72	—
A citation giving chapter and verse may be *a*.	84	—
one of these prayers for mission is *a*	100	—
be *a* to the preceding versicle and response.	102	—
A citation giving chapter and verse may be *a*.	118	—
one of these prayers for mission is *a*	124	—
be *a* to the preceding versicle and response.	126	—
One of the following prayers may be *a*	134	—
No blessing or dismissal is *a*.	282	—
A citation giving chapter and verse may be *a*.	300	—
received and presented, and other prayers may be *a*,	311	—
Other prayers, such as the following, may be *a*.	314	2
A citation giving chapter and verse may be *a*.	325	—
Here may be *a*	334	—
may be *a* to any of the dismissals.	340	—
Here may be *a*	341	—
A citation giving chapter and verse may be *a*.	357	—
may be *a* to any of the dismissals.	366	—
A citation giving chapter and verse may be *a*.	414	—
work in which the person will be engaged may be *a*.	421	—
Other prayers may be *a*.	502	—
A citation giving chapter and verse may be *a*.	516	—
be *a* to the dismissal and to the response.	523	—
A citation giving chapter and verse may be *a*.	528	—
be *a* to the dismissal and to the response.	535	—
A citation giving chapter and verse may be *a*.	540	—
be *a* to the dismissal and to the response.	547	—
the presentations that follow may be *a* to,	561	—
that have been *a*, altered, or renovated.	566	5

addiction

56. For the Victims of *A*	812	7
56. For the Victims of *A*	831	10

adding

A Dismissal may be used (*a* "Alleluia, alleluia"	114	—

addition

In *a* to these services and the other rites	13	7
in *a* to its observance of the fixed date.	15	22
In *a* to the dated days listed above,	16	2
is used as a substitute for, or as an *a* to,	18	14
a or omission, as appropriate, at the discretion	277	—
sung or said, in *a* to, or in place of, the preceding,	324	—
In place of, or in *a* to, the preceding,	364	—
in *a* to, the Gospel in English.	406	24
In place of this prayer, or in *a* to it, the Celebrant	486	—
in *a* to saying the prayer over the font as given,	575	25
in *a* to the Eucharist, the Lessons at the Office	888	13

additional

A Directions are on page 141.	36	10
A Directions are on page 141.	74	9
A Directions are on page 142.	108	25
A Directions	141	1
If an *a* hymn is desired, it may be sung	143	29
A Directions are on page 312.	298	28
(See *A* Directions, page 312.)	300	—
A Directions	312	1
A Directions are on page 406.	322	22
A petitions and thanksgivings may be included here.	330	—
the Celebrant consecrates *a* bread and wine,	338	—
A Directions are on page 406.	354	22
the Celebrant consecrates *a* bread and wine,	365	—
A Directions	406	1
a chalices may be filled after the Breaking	407	20
A Directions are on page 437.	422	23
A Directions	437	—
the *A* Prayers.	486	—
A Prayers	487	—
A Prayers	503	—
A Directions are on page 552.	511	26
A Directions are on page 552.	524	20
and *a* presenters if desired,	526	—
A Directions are on page 552.	536	20
and *a* presenters if desired,	538	—
A Directions	552	—
A Directions are on page 564.	558	25
A Directions	564	13
but *a*, or other, persons may do this when desired.	565	5
A Directions	575	1

additions

a, or new furnishings in a church or chapel.	577	10

address

after which the Celebrant may *a* the people	285	—
The Celebrant may first *a* the people	292	—
the Celebrant may *a* the congregation,	492	—
or an *a* about the work of the congregation	565	17
speak in response to the *a* or sermon.	565	20
Sermon or *A*	572	—
If there is an *a* instead of a sermon,	576	11
The sermon or *a* may be followed by an appropriate	576	15
5. Liturgy of the Word, with sermon or *a*	578	1

addressed

"The peace of the Lord be always with you," is *a*	407	7
The following questions are then *a* to the bishop-elect	517	—

addresses

the Celebrant *a* the congregation,	303	—
the Bishop *a* the congregation, saying	416	—
a the congregation and says	423	—
The Celebrant then *a* the congregation, saying	425	—
Celebrant, who *a* them in these or similar words	433	—
The Celebrant then *a* the husband, saying	433	—
The Celebrant then *a* the wife, saying	433	—
The Celebrant then *a* the congregation, saying	434	—
The Celebrant *a* the congregation in these	440	—
The Celebrant *a* the congregation in these	440	—
Presiding Bishop *a* the bishop-elect	517	—

The Bishop *a* the ordinand as follows 531 —
The Bishop *a* the ordinand as follows 543 —
The Bishop then *a* the congregation 559 —

adds

The Celebrant *a* a concluding Collect. 385 —
The Celebrant *a* a concluding Collect. 387 —
The Celebrant *a* a concluding Collect. 388 —
The Celebrant *a* a concluding Collect. 389 —
The Celebrant *a* a concluding Collect, 391 —
the Priest *a* this blessing 431 —
The Priest *a* 448 —

administer

Where it is desired to *a* Holy Communion 275 —
a Easter Communion from the Sacrament 284 29
any baptized person may *a* Baptism 313 22
customary for the celebrant to *a* the consecrated Bread 408 4
some may *a* the Bread and others the Wine. 408 6
the bishop according to the canon may *a* the Chalice. 408 8
it is suitable to *a* the Sacrament in one kind only. 457 —
others *a* Holy Communion. 554 30

administered

In places where Holy Communion is to be *a* 282 —
be *a* here or after the Gospel. 292 —
Confirmation may also be *a*. 292 —
Holy Baptism is appropriately *a* 298 5
These omitted portions of the rite may be *a* 312 12
The Sacrament is *a* with the following 399 —
Reaffirmation of Baptismal Vows are *a* 412 12
If Communion is to be *a* from the reserved Sacrament, 457 —
If Holy Baptism is not to be *a*, 575 25
If Baptism is to be *a*, the following order is used: 575 28

administering

the Word of God and *a* his holy Sacraments. 510 12

administers

presides at Baptism and *a* Confirmation, 284 13
The person who *a* emergency Baptism 314 3

administration

and *A* of the Sacraments, and other Rites 8 8
Eucharist with the *a* of Easter Communion. 284 9
may be done immediately after the *a* of the water 308 —
and at the *a* of Baptism, 313 3
except the *a* of the water. 314 9
may take place at the time of the *a* of the Sacrament 407 10
a of Communion by a deacon to a congregation 409 2
When necessary, the *a* may take place 553 12
followed, if possible, by the *a* of Holy Baptism. 577 16
adapted in the methods of its *a* to the varying needs 877 18
adapted in the methods of its *a* to the varying needs 878 4

admitted

called by God to the ordained ministry are *a* 510 17

admitting

and too much easiness in *a* variations 9 26

Adonai

A ('Lord') and the personal name YHWH. 583 16
A was substituted for it. 583 20
Name was provided with the vowels of the word *A*. 583 23
from "Lord" as a translation of *A*, 583 29
From time to time, the Hebrew text has *A* and YHWH 583 31

adopted

A by the House of Bishops 876 23
While the above form of the Quadrilateral was *a* 877 26

adoption

A Thanksgiving for the Birth or *A* of a Child 439 2
after receiving a child by *a*, the parents, 439 4
For an *A* 440 —
such as Thanksgiving for the Birth or *A* of a Child, 576 16
they be made sons of God by *a*: 871 8
and of our *a* to be the sons of God 873 17

adoration

concerning Purgatory, Pardons, Worshipping and *A*, 872 12

adult

At the Burial of an *A* 470 —
At the Burial of an *A* 493 —

adults

Sponsors of *a* and older children present 298 18
A and Older Children 301 —
Those baptized as *a*, unless baptized with laying 412 7

advance

prepare in *a*, in consultation with the celebrant, 420 —

advancement

and for a great *a* of godliness: 866 7

Advent

But the Sundays of *A* are always the four Sundays 15 10
seasons of *A*, Lent, and Easter. 16 10
A 37 —
In *A* 43 —
A 75 —
In *A* 80 —
Isaiah 60:19–20 (*A*) 108 16
Luke 12:35–37 (*A*) 108 17
A 111 —
Collect for the First Sunday of *A* 111 —
During *A*, the lighting of an *A* Wreath may take place 143 14
First Sunday of *A* 159 —
Preface of *A* 159 —
Second Sunday of *A* 159 —
Preface of *A* 159 —
Third Sunday of *A* 160 —
Preface of *A* 160 —
Fourth Sunday of *A* 160 —
Preface of *A* 160 —
Preface of *A* 190 —
First Sunday of *A* 211 —
Preface of *A* 211 —
Second Sunday of *A* 211 —
Preface of *A* 211 —
Third Sunday of *A* 212 —
Preface of *A* 212 —

Fourth Sunday of *A* 212 —
Preface of *A* 212 —
Preface of *A* 241 —
A 345 —
A 378 —
the Sundays or ordinary weekdays of *A* or Lent. 406 16
in this sort the book of Isaiah was begun in *A*, 866 20
Year A always begins on the First Sunday of *A* 888 3
Year A, therefore, begins on *A* Sunday of that year.) 888 5
Year One begins on the First Sunday of *A* 934 3
Year Two begins on the First Sunday of *A* 934 4
(Thus, on the First Sunday of *A*, 1976, the Lectionary 934 5
(except in the weeks from 4 *A* to 1 Epiphany, 934 22

adversaries

and to confute them that were *a* to the truth. 866 12

advisedly

admitting varations in things once *a* established, 10 1

affect

by the sad divisions which *a* the Christian Church 877 20

affecting

in the clearest, plainest, most *a* and majestic manner, 11 21

affection

some the *a*, some the desire, of the flesh), 869 30

affirm

we do hereby *a* that the Christian unity 877 5

affirmation

make a mature public *a* of their faith 412 4
are also expected to make a public *a* of their faith 412 8

affirmed

It is also recognized and *a* that the threefold ministry 510 26

affliction

2 Corinthians 1:3–5 (God comforts us in *a*) 453 15

afore

And in this Trinity none is *a*, or after other; 865 14
Though it be appointed in the *a* written preface, 867 23

aforesaid

So that in all things, as is *a*, the Unity in Trinity 865 16

after

use from and *a* the First Day of October, 8 12
Easter Day is always the first Sunday *a* the full moon 15 7
the full moon that falls on or *a* March 21. 15 8
It cannot occur before March 22 or *a* April 25. 15 8
the Ascension on a Thursday forty days *a* Easter Day. 15 13
but not from the Last Sunday *a* Pentecost 16 16
through the First Sunday *a* the Epiphany, 16 16
or from the Last Sunday *a* the Epiphany 16 17
Saturdays *a* the First Sunday in Lent, 18 6
A each Lesson the Reader may say 47 —
Silence may be kept *a* each Reading. 47 —
is sung or said *a* each Reading. 47 —
read *a* the second Canticle. 47 —
A each Lesson the Reader may say 65 —
Silence may be kept *a* each Reading. 65 —
is sung or said *a* each Reading. 65 —
a the second Canticle. 65 —
A each Lesson the Reader may say 84 —
Silence may be kept *a* each Reading. 84 —
is sung or said *a* each Reading. 84 —
read *a* the second Canticle. 84 —
Collect for the First Sunday *a* Christmas 111 —
A each Lesson the Reader may say 119 —
Silence may be kept *a* each Reading. 119 —
is sung or said *a* each Reading. 119 —
a the second Canticle. 119 —
This devotion may be used before or *a* the evening meal. 139 —
and may be used *a* the Invitatory Psalm 141 12
a each Psalm, and *a* each section of Psalm 119. 141 13
and of the Canticles *a* the Readings, 141 21
A sermon may be preached *a* the Office; 142 11
or, within the Office, *a* the Readings 142 11
or at the time of the hymn or anthem *a* the Collects. 142 12
may take place *a* the Prayer for Light. 143 14
it is appropriate *a* the candles have been lighted 143 19
or *a* the Collects of Morning or Evening Prayer; 148 —
The Proper to be used on each of the Sundays *a* Pentecost 158 10
the Proper for the Sunday *a* Trinity Sunday 158 12
(the Second Sunday *a* Pentecost) 158 13
or is closest to it, whether before or *a*. 158 15
if the Sunday *a* Trinity Sunday is May 26, 158 16
If the Sunday *a* Trinity Sunday is June 13, 158 18
and the First Sunday *a* Christmas Day. 161 7
First Sunday *a* Christmas Day 161 —
Second Sunday *a* Christmas Day 162 —
those for the Second Sunday *a* Christmas Day, 162 —
First Sunday *a* the Epiphany: 163 —
Second Sunday *a* the Epiphany 163 —
Third Sunday *a* the Epiphany 163 —
Fourth Sunday *a* the Epiphany 164 —
Fifth Sunday *a* the Epiphany 164 —
Sixth Sunday *a* the Epiphany 164 —
Seventh Sunday *a* the Epiphany 164 —
Eighth Sunday *a* the Epiphany 165 —
Last Sunday *a* the Epiphany 165 —
The Sunday *a* Ascension Day 175 —
First Sunday *a* Pentecost: 176 —
The Season *a* Pentecost 176 —
The Wednesday, Friday, and Saturday *a* September 14 182 —
and the First Sunday *a* Christmas Day. 213 —
First Sunday *a* Christmas Day 213 —
Second Sunday *a* Christmas Day 214 —
those for the Second Sunday *a* Christmas, 214 —
First Sunday *a* the Epiphany: 214 —
Second Sunday *a* the Epiphany 215 —
Third Sunday *a* the Epiphany 215 —
Fourth Sunday *a* the Epiphany 215 —
Fifth Sunday *a* the Epiphany 216 —
Sixth Sunday *a* the Epiphany 216 —
Seventh Sunday *a* the Epiphany 216 —
Eighth Sunday *a* the Epiphany 216 —
Last Sunday *a* the Epiphany 217 —
The Sunday *a* Ascension Day 226 —
First Sunday *a* Pentecost: 228 —
The Season *a* Pentecost 228 —
The Wednesday, Friday, and Saturday *a* September 14 233 —

A the Sermon, all stand, and the Celebrant	264	—
or *a* the prayer of blessing.	270	—
The customary responses before and *a* the Gospel	272	—
a which the Celebrant stands	276	—
The customary responses before and *a* the Gospel	277	—
A the Gospel (and homily),	283	—
a which the Celebrant may address the people	285	—
A each Lesson, the Psalm or Canticle listed,	288	—
A homily may be preached *a* any of the preceding	292	—
be administered here or *a* the Gospel.	292	—
or *a* the Gospel.	292	—
A each Reading, the Reader may say	300	—
A the Gospel, the Reader says	300	—
Or the Sermon may be preached *a* the Peace.	301	—
A all have been presented, the Celebrant addresses	303	—
Or this action may be done immediately *a*	308	—
on All Saints' Day or the Sunday *a*	312	3
(the First Sunday *a* the Epiphany).	312	5
sung immediately *a* the opening versicles	312	18
A the Baptism, a candle	313	7
A each Reading, the Reader may say	325	—
A the Gospel, the Reader says	326	—
A each paragraph of this prayer,	328	—
A Communion, the Celebrant says	339	—
A each Reading, the Reader may say	357	—
A the Gospel, the Reader says	358	—
A Communion, the Celebrant says	365	—
In the course of the silence *a* each bidding,	385	—
Here and *a* every petition the People respond	389	—
A the Reading, the Celebrant may comment	397	—
a all have received, any of the Sacrament	401	13
(before or *a* the sentence of Invitation).	407	11
made before the service, *a* the Creed,	407	12
may be filled *a* the Breaking of the Bread.	407	20
communicate, and *a* them the people.	407	24
1. *A* the Liturgy of the Word	408	20
drink it, either *a* the Communion of the people	409	4
or *a* the Dismissal.	409	5
A hymn may be sung before or *a* the postcommunion prayer.	409	6
sung immediately *a* the opening versicles	412	13
A each Reading the Reader may say	414	—
A the Gospel, the Reader says	415	—
A all have been presented, the Bishop addresses	416	—
A this, the Celebrant says these	420	—
A the Gospel, the Reader says	426	—
a which greetings may be exchanged	431	—
receive Communion first, *a* the ministers.	432	—
A the Gospel (and homily),	433	—
A the Declaration of Consent,	437	8
Creed may be recited *a* the Lessons, or *a* the homily,	437	20
a the birth of a child, or *a* receiving a child	439	3
A any Reading, the Celebrant may comment	454	13
a which the Celebrant says	466	—
a which the Celebrant says	467	—
A the Old Testament Lesson,	470	—
A the New Testament Lesson,	475	—
a which the Celebrant says one of the following	493	—
At the end of the litany, *a* the Kyries,	515	—
A each Reading, the Reader may say	516	—
A the Gospel, the Reader says	516	—
A the Sermon, the Congregation sings a hymn.	516	—
A this other symbols of office may be given.	521	—
A Communion	522	—
At the end of the litany, *a* the Kyries,	527	—
A each Reading, the Reader may say	529	—
A the Gospel, the Reader says	529	—
A Communion	535	—
A receiving Holy Communion, the new deacon assists	536	14
At the end of the litany, *a* the Kyries,	539	—
A each Reading, the Reader may say	541	—
A the Gospel, the Reader says	541	—
A Communion	546	—
a which the new Deacon dismisses	547	—
the Prayers of the People *a* the Creed,	552	6
A the pontifical blessing and the dismissal,	553	14
a the entire Prayer of Consecration is completed,	553	22
a the entire Prayer of Consecration is completed,	554	13
A laying hands upon all the ordinands,	554	23
A participating in the Peace, the deacons go	554	28
A the Sermon, and any responses to it,	560	—
A Communion	564	3
a the building is ready for regular use	566	10
a the Epistle the Bishop proceeds	572	—
A a period of silence, the Bishop concludes	572	—
A the postcommunion prayer, the Bishop blesses	574	—
A a brief silence, the Celebrant concludes	579	—
singing a refrain *a* each verse or group of verses.	582	21
a the invention of vowel points,	583	22
67. *A* Receiving Communion	812	22
68. *A* Worship	812	23
For use *a* the Collects of Morning or Evening Prayer	814	—
67. *A* Receiving Communion	834	—
68. *A* Worship	834	—
or at any time *a* the Collects at Morning	836	—
And in this Trinity none is afore, or *a* other;	865	14
A a like sort were other books of holy Scripture used.	866	21
The condition of Man *a* the fall of Adam is such,	869	34
which are the fruits of Faith, and follow *a* Justification,	870	7
XVI. Of Sin *a* Baptism.	870	31
Not every deadly sin willingly committed *a* Baptism	870	32
denied to such as fall into sin *a* Baptism.	870	34
A we have received the Holy Ghost,	870	34
only *a* an heavenly and spiritual manner.	873	31
be used as refrains *a* each verse or group of verses.	935	11

afternoon

on suitable occasions in the late *a* or evening.	108	3

afterwards

A, other instruments or symbols of office	553	23

again

saying *a* the words of the Eucharistic Prayer,	408	13
rose *a* the third day from the dead.	865	32
At whose coming all men shall rise *a*	865	35
Christ did truly rise *a* from death, and took *a* his body,	868	13
and born *a* in Christ, yet offend in many things;	870	29
and by the grace of God we may arise *a*,	870	35

against
seek occasion, of cavil or quarrel *a* her Liturgy. 10 13
A Collect for Aid *a* Perils 70 —
A Collect for Aid *a* Perils 123 —
committed after Baptism is sin *a* the Holy Ghost, 870 32
ought not to decree any thing *a* the same, 871 41
so that nothing be ordained *a* God's Word. 874 24
as he that offendeth *a* the common order 874 28
2 *A* Peril of Idolatry. 875 3
5 *A* Gluttony and Drunkenness. 875 7
6 *A* Excess of Apparel. 875 8
20 *A* Idleness. 875 12
21 *A* Rebellion. 875 13

Agape
When a common meal or *A* is a part of the celebration, 401 15

age
those baptized at an early *a* are expected, 412 3

aged
49. For the *A* 811 32
49. For the *A* 830 —

ages
begotten of the Father before the *a*, 864 9
undivided Catholic Church during the first *a* 877 7

agreeable
much *a* to the mind and purpose of the old fathers, 866 43
a with the institution of Christ. 873 21

agriculture
29. For *A* 811 8
29. For *A* 824 —

aid
A Collect for *A* against Perils 70 —
A Collect for *A* against Perils 123 —

aim
Her general *a* in these different reviews 10 8

alb
The bishop-elect is vested in a rochet or *a*, 511 16
The ordinand is to be vested in surplice or *a*, 524 7
The ordinand is to be vested in a surplice or *a*, 536 7

albeit
A that Good Works, which are the fruits of Faith, 870 7

Alexandria
A, and Antioch, have erred; 871 33

alike
To be used on Sundays and weekdays *a*, 345 —
To be used on Sundays and weekdays *a*, 378 —
Care *a* for young and old, strong and weak, 557 11
ministered to all Christian men *a*. 874 4

all
received as such by *a* the members of the same: 8 11
equity ought to be allowed to *a* human writings; 10 18
the proper end of *a* such prayers, namely, 10 36
lead quiet and peaceable lives, in *a* godliness 11 2
unnecessary to enumerate *a* the different alterations 11 9
In *a* services, the entire Christian assembly participates 13 16
The sequence of *a* Sundays of the Church Year depends 15 9
A Saints' Day, November 1 15 16
A Saints' Day may always be observed 15 20
A Sundays of the year are feasts of our Lord 16 2
A other Feasts of our Lord, 16 11
have precedence over *a* other days of commemoration 16 24
A feasts of Apostles 17 2
A feasts of Evangelists 17 3
Saint Michael and *A* Angels 17 3
the Epiphany, and *A* Saints' Day. 17 19
Good Friday and *a* other Fridays of the year, 17 25
Prayer may be used in place of *a* that precedes 36 9
A Saints and other Major Saints' Days 40 —
Officiant and People together, *a* kneeling 41 —
A stand 42 —
On *A* Saints and other Major Saints' Days 44 —
Officiant and People together, *a* standing 53 —
Officiant and People together, *a* kneeling 62 —
A stand 63 —
Officiant and People together, *a* standing 66 —
Prayer may be used in place of *a* that precedes 74 8
A Saints and other Major Saints' Days 77 —
Officiant and People together, *a* kneeling 79 —
A stand 80 —
On *A* Saints and other Major Saints' Days 82 —
A stand, and the Officiant greets the people 109 —
Officiant and People together, *a* kneeling 116 —
A stand 117 —
Officiant and People together, *a* standing 120 —
is sung or said by *a* 134 —
A repeat the Antiphon 135 —
On *a* other occasions, the Officiant and People say 153 —
As necessary, the observance of one, two, or *a* three 161 —
Preface of *A* Saints 189 —
Preface of *A* Saints 191 —
Saint Michael and *A* Angels September 29 193 —
Preface of *A* Saints 193 —
A Saints' Day November 1 194 —
Preface of *A* Saints 194 —
7. For *A* Baptized Christians 201 —
III. For *a* Christians in their vocation 206 —
As necessary, the observance of one, two, or *a* three 213 —
Preface of *A* Saints 240 —
Preface of *A* Saints 242 —
Saint Michael and *A* Angels September 29 244 —
Preface of *A* Saints 245 —
A Saints' Day November 1 245 —
Preface of *A* Saints 245 —
7. For *a* Baptized Christians 252 —
III. For *a* Christians in their vocation 256 —
After the Sermon, *a* stand, 264 —
Silence is then kept for a time, *a* kneeling. 265 —
The Celebrant and People together, *a* kneeling 267 —
a that precedes may be led by a deacon 269 —
so that *a* may go into the church in procession. 270 —
During the procession, *a* hold branches 271 —
or anthems are sung, such as the hymn "*A* glory, laud, 271 —
Mark 15:22, Luke 23:33) *a* stand. 273 —
A then kneel for silent prayer, 276 —

arrival at Golgotha (John 19:17) *a* stand.	277	—
A standing, the Deacon, or other person appointed,	277	—
devotions may follow, which may include any or *a*	281	—
a that precedes may be led by a deacon	282	—
It is customary for *a* the ordained ministers present,	284	10
customary that the Paschal Candle burn at *a* services	287	—
Salvation offered freely to *a*	290	—
the people in these or similar words, *a* standing	292	—
Then, *a* standing, the Deacon or a Priest reads	300	—
When *a* have been presented the Celebrant asks	302	—
After *a* have been presented, the Celebrant addresses	303	—
When this action has been completed for *a* candidates,	308	—
When *a* have been baptized, the Celebrant says	308	—
on *A* Saints' Day or the Sunday after *A* Saints' Day,	312	3
At *a* celebrations of the Liturgy, it is fitting	322	4
Prayer may be used in place of *a* that precedes	322	18
or in place of, the preceding, *a* standing	324	—
Then, *a* standing, the Deacon or a Priest reads	326	—
and other Major Feasts there follows, *a* standing	326	—
A stand. The Celebrant says to the people	332	—
Here a Proper Preface is sung or said on *a* Sundays,	334	—
Here a Proper Preface is sung or said on *a* Sundays,	341	—
A Saints	347	—
At *a* celebrations of the Liturgy, it is fitting	354	4
Prayer may be used in place of *a* that precedes	354	18
sung or said, *a* standing	356	—
Then, *a* standing, the Deacon or a Priest reads	357	—
and other Major Feasts there follows, *a* standing	358	—
The Nation and *a* in authority	359	—
A stand.	360	—
Here a Proper Preface is sung or said on *a* Sundays,	361	—
Here a Proper Preface is sung or said on *a* Sundays,	367	—
A Saints	380	—
The Nation and *a* in authority	383	—
or elsewhere in the service, *a* greet one another	401	2
after *a* have received,	401	13
The Celebrant then prays that *a* may receive	405	—
on *a* the days of Easter Week,	406	14
If there is no Communion, *a* that is appointed	406	25
In the absence of a priest, *a* that is described above,	407	5
In *a* such cases, the priest is required to notify	409	24
Then, *a* standing, the Deacon or a Priest reads	414	—
After *a* have been presented, the Bishop addresses	416	—
passage from the Gospel is to be read, *a* stand,	426	—
A standing, the Celebrant says	428	—
It is appropriate that *a* remain standing	437	17
for the wedding party, so that *a* may	437	18
and of *a* persons to make wills,	445	—
The Reconciliation of a Penitent is available for *a*	446	7
When the penitent has confessed *a* serious sins	446	20
Psalm 103 (He forgives *a* your sins)	454	3
Psalm 145:14–22 (The eyes of *a* wait upon you,	454	11
Celebrant is to assure that person that *a* the benefits	457	—
If necessary, or if desired, *a* or part of the service	468	10
A stand while one or more of the following anthems	469	—
Isaiah 61:1–3 (To comfort *a* that mourn)	470	—
Revelation 21:2–7 (Behold, I make *a* things new)	475	—
Then, *a* standing, the Deacon or Minister appointed	479	—
(*A* that the Father giveth me shall come to me)	480	—
The Apostles' Creed may be said, *a* standing.	480	—
or if desired, *a* or part of the service	490	10
A stand while one or more of the following anthems	491	—
When *a* are in place, the Celebrant may address	492	—
Revelation 21:2–7 (Behold, I make *a* things new)	495	—
Then, *a* standing, the Deacon or Minister appointed	495	—
(*A* that the Father gives me will come to me)	495	—
The Apostles' Creed may then be said, *a* standing.	496	—
It finds *a* its meaning in the resurrection.	507	2
nor anything else in *a* creation,	507	8
assist bishops and priests in *a* of this work.	510	13
so that *a* may see and hear what is done.	511	13
signs the above Declaration in the sight of *a*	513	—
A stand.	513	—
A kneel, and the Person appointed leads the Litany	515	—
Then, *a* standing, a Deacon or a Priest reads	516	—
A now sit, except the bishop-elect, who stands	517	—
A stand.	519	—
Then *a* sing or say together	519	—
A continue to stand, except the bishop-elect,	520	—
and facing them, so that *a* may	524	5
signs the above Declaration in the sight of *a* present.	527	—
A stand.	527	—
A kneel, and the Person appointed leads	527	—
Then, *a* standing, the Deacon or,	529	—
A are seated except the ordinand,	531	—
A now stand except the ordinand,	533	—
and facing them, so that *a* may see	536	5
signs the above Declaration in the sight of *a* present.	539	—
A stand.	539	—
A kneel, and the Person appointed leads	539	—
Then, *a* standing, the Deacon or,	541	—
A are seated except the ordinand,	543	—
A now stand except the ordinand,	544	—
At *a* Ordinations	552	2
When they have laid their hands upon *a*	554	2
A the newly ordained take part in the exchange	554	7
Similarly, *a* the new priests break	554	9
upon *a* the ordinands, the bishop continues,	554	24
should be large enough to be visible to *a*	565	21
It is desirable that *a* members of the congregation,	566	16
When *a* are ready, the Bishop says the following	567	5
A then stand for the Gospel,	572	—
2. For *a* Sorts and Conditions of Men	810	7
and *a* in Civil Authority	810	28
2. For *A* Sorts and Conditions of Men	814	—
and *a* in Civil Authority	820	—
we *a* with one accord teach men to acknowledge one	864	4
like us in *a* respects, apart from sin;	864	8
before *a* things it is necessary that he hold	864	22
is *a* one, the Glory	864	28
So that in *a* things, as is aforesaid,	865	15
At whose coming *a* men shall rise again	865	34
For they so ordered the matter, that *a* the whole Bible	866	8
a the rest were unread.	866	19
that *a* things shall be done in order,	866	36
now from henceforth, *a* the whole realm	867	10
because that *a* things must be read	867	11
to appease *a* such diversity (if any arise),	867	17
resolution of *a* doubts, concerning the manner	867	18
that *a* things shall be read and sung	867	23
and Preserver of *a* things both visible	867	36
with flesh, bones, and *a* things appertaining	868	13
until he return to judge *a* Men at the last day.	868	15

Holy Scripture containeth *a* things necessary 868 20
A the Books of the New Testament, 869 4
When ye have done *a* that are commanded to you, 870 23
truth of our nature was made like unto us in *a* things, 870 25
But *a* we the rest, although baptized, 870 28
a those things that of necessity are requisite 871 32
whereof *a* be not governed with the Spirit and Word 872 7
ought to be ministered to *a* 874 3
for *a* the sins of the whole world, 874 7
lawful for them, as for *a* other Christian men, 874 13
Traditions and Ceremonies be in *a* places one, 874 22
for at *a* times they have been divers, 874 23
so that *a* things be done to edifying. 874 32
But *a* references to the constitution 875 15
doth contain *a* things necessary to such 875 22
decree *a* such to be rightly, 875 25
Power of the Civil Magistrate extendeth to *a* men, 875 35
a men who are professors of the Gospel, 875 37
Government of *a* Estates of this Realm, 875 41
in *a* causes doth appertain, 875 41
given always to *a* godly Princes in holy Scriptures 876 3
that they should rule *a* estates 876 4
do hereby solemnly declare to *a* 876 26
"That we *a* may be one," 876 29
2. That we believe that *a* who have been duly baptized 876 31
3. That in *a* things of human ordering 876 33
humility to forego *a* preferences of her own; 876 35
return of *a* Christian communions to the principles 877 6
common and equal benefit of *a* men. 877 11
enter into brotherly conference with *a* or any 877 22
"containing *a* things necessary to salvation," 877 33
for use at *a* public services on such days, 888 7
if the Office is read only once in the day, *a* three 934 9

alleluia

From Easter Day through the Day of Pentecost "*A, a*" 59 —
From Easter Day through the Day of Pentecost "*A, a*" 72 —
From Easter Day through the Day of Pentecost "*A, a*" 102 —
A Dismissal may be used (adding "*A, a*" in Easter 114 —
From Easter Day through the Day of Pentecost "*A, a*" 126 —
"*A*" may be sung and repeated. 295 6
In Lent, *A* is omitted, and may be omitted 337 —
through the Day of Pentecost "*A, a*" 340 —
In Lent, *A* is omitted, and may be omitted 364 —
through the Day of Pentecost "*A, a*" 366 —
From Easter Day through the Day of Pentecost "*A, a*," 523 —
From Easter Day through the Day of Pentecost "*A, a*," 535 —
From Easter Day through the Day of Pentecost, "*A, a*" 547 —
rather than the Latin form "*A*," 584 6

alleluias

The *A* in the following Antiphons are used 44 —
The *A* in the following Antiphons are used 82 —

allow

the priest shall *a* those who are penitent to come 409 22

allowed

usages may without offence be *a*, 9 4
if *a* such just and favourable construction 10 17
common equity ought to be *a* to all human writings; 10 18
No persons are *a* to exercise the offices 510 21
partly are states of life *a* in the Scriptures; 872 35

allowing

not *a* such persons to receive Communion 409 14

almighties

And yet they are not three *A*, but one Almighty. 864 39

almighty

and to give thanks to *A* God. 439 6
So likewise the Father is *A*, 864 38
the Son *A*, 864 38
and the Holy Ghost *A*. 864 38
And yet they are not three Almighties, but one *A*. 864 39
he sitteth on the right hand of the Father, God *A*, 865 33

almost

forasmuch as nothing can, *a*, be so plainly set forth, 867 16

alms

A may be received and presented, 311 —
11 Of *A*-doing. 875 2
liberally to give *a* to the poor, 876 15

alone

The priest *a* stands and says 42 —
The Priest *a* stands and says 63 —
The Priest *a* stands and says 80 —
The Priest *a* stands and says 117 —
The Priest *a* says 398 2
because such ministers *a* have the function 422 8
The Priest *a* says 455 —
the bishop *a* says over each ordinand 553 32
48. For Those Who Live *A* 811 31
The Son is of the Father *a*, 865 9
48. For Those Who Live *A* 829 —
XV. Of Christ *a* without Sin. 870 24
there is none other satisfaction for sin, but that *a*. 874 8

aloud

prayers, either silently or *a*. 385 —

already

yet upon the principles *a* laid down, 10 19
For a child *a* baptized 444 —
or have *a* received such ordination 510 23
If the Apostles' Creed has not *a* been said, 572 —

also

the reasons of them *a*, 11 11
In which it will *a* appear that this Church 11 12
A, subject to the direction of the bishop, 13 8
authorize a deacon to preside at other rites *a*, 14 1
date of Easter *a* determines the beginning of Lent 15 12
It may *a* be used daily until the Day of Pentecost. 45 —
It may *a* be used daily until the Day of Pentecost. 83 —
It is appropriate *a* for use in private houses. 108 6
any one of the following is *a* appropriate, 108 15
It may *a* be omitted at one of the Offices 142 3
The Proper appointed for the Sunday is *a* used 158 7
See *a* the Table on pages 884–885. 158 21
the corresponding Psalm and Lessons, *a* serves 217 —
A deacon may *a*, when the services of a priest cannot 284 27
except for those at the Altar, may *a* be lighted. 286 —
Confirmation may *a* be administered. 292 —

and *a* take vows on behalf of their candidates. 298 22
The petitions (page 305) may *a* be led 312 25
Deacons should *a* serve at the Lord's Table, 322 11
Deacons should *a* serve at the Lord's Table, 354 11
are *a* expected to make a public affirmation 412 8
It may *a* be used prior to cremation. 468 12
It may *a* be used prior to cremation. 490 12
It is *a* a special responsibility of deacons 510 13
It is *a* recognized and affirmed that the threefold 510 26
The new Bishop *a* greets other members of the clergy, 522 —
Priests who are present *a* laying on their hands. 533 —
are *a* to be said to each one. 554 27
It may *a* be used for the installation of deans 558 3
if any, who serve in the same congregation *a* stand 558 11
the family of the new minister may *a* be presented 563 —
Hymns and anthems may *a* be sung. 568 6
tools used in its construction may *a* be carried 575 18
If the place of public worship is *a* to serve 576 29
If the church is *a* to be used for regular worship 577 1
blessing of an Altar is *a* reserved for a bishop, 577 18
This Litany may *a* be used on the anniversary 579 —
It was *a* a traditional manner of chanting 582 24
but *a* to regain for our liturgy a form 584 7
See *a* Various Occasions no. 18. 815 —
See *a* the prayers for the Mission of the Church 816 —
See *a* Various Occasions no. 13. 818 —
See *a* Various Occasions no. 14, 818 —
See *a* Various Occasions no. 17. 820 —
See *a* Various Occasions no. 21. 823 —
See *a* Various Occasions no. 19. 824 —
See *a* Various Occasions no. 19. 827 —
See *a* Various Occasions no. 20. 831 —
See *a* the Prayer of Humble Access on page 337. 834 —
See *a* The General Thanksgiving on pages 58 837 —
See *a* the prayer "O God, the King of Saints," 838 —
See *a* the Thanksgiving for a Child on page 439. 841 —
It may *a* be used to form a simple service; 844 9
consisting *a* of a reasonable soul and body; 864 6
As *a* there are not three incomprehensibles, 864 36
necessary to everlasting salvation that he *a* believe 865 19
It is *a* more commodious, both for the shortness 867 4
a for actual sins of men. 868 8
so *a* is it to be believed, that he went down 868 10
They *a* are to be had accursed that presume to say, 871 25
so *a* the Church of Rome hath erred, 871 33
but *a* in matters of Faith. 871 34
and *a* Invocation of Saints, is a fond thing, 872 13
but *a* strengthen and confirm our Faith in him. 872 28
but it is *a* a sign of Regeneration or New-Birth, 873 15
which *a* suspends the order for the reading 875 17
the which thing the Injunctions *a* lately set forth 876 1

altar

The candles at the *A* are now lighted, 112 —
For the lighting of the candles at the *A* and elsewhere, 143 10
placed on or near the *A*, 143 13
except for those at the *A*, may also be lighted. 286 —
The candles at the *A* may now be lighted 294 —
stand with the celebrant at the *A*, 322 8
while the offerings are presented and placed on the *A*. 333 —
stand with the celebrant at the *A*, 354 8
while the offerings are presented and placed on the *A*. 361 —
that there be only one chalice on the *A*, 407 19
consecrated Sacrament on the *A*, 408 22
They may approach the *A*, either for the exchange 437 15
of the family to present themselves before the *A*. 439 18
inside the *a* rails or in a place set aside 446 16
brought to the *A* by the family or friends 511 22
brought to the *A* by the family or friends 524 13
stand at the *A* with the bishop, 524 15
brought to the *A* by the family or friends 536 13
at the *A* as fellow ministers of the Sacrament. 553 10
priests at the *A* for the Great Thanksgiving. 554 8
participating in the Peace, the deacons go to the *A* 554 28
remove the vessels from the *A*, 555 6
stand with the chief celebrant at the *A*, 558 12
assist the celebrant at the *A*, 558 21
Members of the congregation vest the *A*, 574 —
For the covering and decoration of the *A*, 576 22
The blessing of an *A* is also reserved for a bishop, 577 18

alterable

being things in their own nature indifferent, and *a*, 9 16

alterations

such changes and *a* should be made therein, 9 19
a and amendments in her Forms of Public Worship; 9 24
make such *a* in some particulars, 10 4
Her general aim in these different reviews and *a* 10 8
a would in time be found expedient. 10 20
a in the Liturgy which became necessary 10 33
But while these *a* were in review 11 3
to establish such other *a* and amendments 11 7
It seems unnecessary to enumerate all the different *a* 11 9
A in the service are then made 558 6
used by the bishop or a priest for blessing *a*, 577 9

altered

consent and authority, may be *a*, abridged, enlarged, 9 7
Its wording may be *a* by the bishop 565 1
that have been added, *a*, or renovated. 566 5
a, broken, and neglected, by planting 866 17

alternate

The *a* recitation concludes 582 15
the Old Testament Reading for the *a* year is used 934 13

alternating

the minister *a* with the congregation, 582 28

alternation

Antiphonal recitation is the verse-by-verse *a* 582 13

alternative

A Ending 311 —
An *a* form will be found on page 340. 333 —
A Form 340 —
A forms will be found on page 367 and following. 361 —
A Forms 367 —
When an *a* Lesson is cited, 888 23
and *a* Psalmody provided. 935 4

alternatives

use the bracketed Psalms rather than the *a*. 935 6

although

a, according to her judgment, there be not any thing 10 14
a quatrains are usually distributed 583 11
Who *a* he be God and Man, yet he is not two, 865 28
A the Law given from God by Moses, 869 10
And *a* there is no condemnation for them that believe 869 31
But all we the rest, *a* baptized, 870 28
Wherefore, *a* the Church be a witness and a keeper 871 40
A in the visible Church the evil be ever mingled 873 2
a they be ministered by evil men. 873 9
a they do carnally and visibly press 873 37

altogether

One *a*; not by confusion of Substance, 865 29

always

Easter Day is *a* the first Sunday after the full moon 15 7
But the Sundays of Advent are *a* the four Sundays 15 10
may *a* be observed on the Sunday following November 1, 15 21
Gloria Patri is *a* sung or said at the conclusion 141 11
the Gospel is *a* included. 142 21
This Proper is *a* used on the Sunday 165 —
This Proper is *a* used on the Sunday 217 —
of which one is *a* the Lesson from Exodus. 288 —
provided that a lesson from the Gospel is *a* included, 322 19
provided that a lesson from the Gospel is *a* included, 354 19
A reading from the Gospel is *a* included. 400 11
The greeting, "The peace of the Lord be *a* with you," 407 7
Opportunity is *a* to be given to every communicant 407 25
a passage from the Gospel *a* concludes 426 —
one of which is *a* from Holy Scripture, 435 15
a Reading from the Gospel is *a* included. 435 17
The Lord's Prayer is *a* included. 453 5
Part One of this service may *a* be led by a deacon 453 6
a passage from the Gospel *a* concludes the Readings. 470 —
a passage from the Gospel *a* concludes the Readings. 494 —
Opportunity is *a* given to the people 511 24
Opportunity is *a* given to the people 524 18
Opportunity is *a* given to the people 536 18
the bishop *a* stands for the salutation 565 7
blessing of a new font or baptistry should *a* be done 577 15
The blessing of an Altar is also reserved for a bishop, 577 18
a resort to the Bishop of the Diocese, 867 20
so that the flesh lusteth *a* contrary to the Spirit; 869 26
given *a* to all godly Princes in holy Scriptures by God 876 3
Year A *a* begins on the First Sunday of Advent 888 3
the first is *a* from the Old Testament 934 15

amend

the grace of God we may arise again, and *a* our lives. 870 35

amended

a, or otherwise disposed of, as may seem most convenient 9 8

amendment

has given clear proof of repentance and *a* of life. 409 11

amendments

alterations and *a* in her Forms of Public Worship; 9 24
to establish such other alterations and *a* 11 7
all the different alterations and *a*. 11 10

America

Church in the United States of *A*, in Convention, 8 4
Church in the United States of *A*, in Convention, 867 32
Church in the United States of *A*, in Council 876 25

American

these *A* States became independent 10 24

among

The priests who are present share *a* them the reading 284 14
It is fitting that parents be included *a* the godparents 298 24
James 5:14–16 (Is any *a* you sick?) 454 6
5. For Peace *A* the Nations 810 10
5. For Peace *A* the Nations 816 —
as, *a* other things, it may plainly appear 866 4
the love that Christians ought to have *a* themselves 873 23
a the divided branches of Christendom, we account 877 13

Amos

A 5:8 62 —
A 5:8 115 —

Anabaptists

as certain *A* do falsely boast. 876 14

ancient

The Holy Scriptures and *a* Christian writers make 510 2
In accordance with *a* custom, it is desirable, 511 3
this is by no means certain, because from very *a* times 583 18
The *a* praise-shout, "Hallelujah," has been restored, 584 4
if a man would search out by the *a* fathers, 866 6
this godly and decent order of the *a* fathers 866 16
the *a* fathers had divided the Psalms 866 27

Andrew

Saint *A* November 30 185 —
Saint *A* November 30 237 —

angels

Saint Michael and All *A* 17 3
Saint Michael and All *A* September 29 193 —
3. Of the Holy *A* 200 4
Saint Michael and All *A* September 29 244 —
3. Of the Holy *A* 251 10
Psalm 91 (He will give his *a* charge over you) 453 16
"neither death, nor life, nor *a*, nor principalities, 507 6

annexed

and Chapels to the same *a*, shall serve the congregation. 867 28

anniversary

12. On the *A* of the Dedication of a Church 204 —
12. On the *A* of the Dedication of a Church 254 —
This Litany may also be used on the *a* 579 —

announced

The Passion Gospel is *a* in the following manner 272 —
The Passion Gospel is *a* in the following manner 276 —

announcement

and should be read without *a* or conclusion. 143 8

announcements

Necessary *a* may be made before the service, 407 12
Necessary *a* may now be made. 567 —

annulled

distinction of natures being in no way *a* by the union, 864 13

Annunciation

The *A* 16 29
except the feast of the *A*. 17 24
The *A* March 25 188 —
The *A* March 25 240 —

anointed

Psalm 23 (You have *a* my head with oil) 454 7
Mark 6:7, 12–13 (They *a* with oil many that were sick) 454 8
If the person is to be *a*, the Priest dips 456 —

anointing

When the Laying on of Hands or *A* takes place 453 7
When *A* is to follow 454 5
Part II. Laying on of Hands and *A* 455 —
If oil for the *A* of the Sick is to be blessed, 455 —
a deacon or lay person may perform the *a*, 456 —

another

Then the Ministers and People may greet one *a* 332 —
Then the Ministers and People may greet one *a* 360 —
or elsewhere in the service, all greet one *a* 401 2
When the celebrant is assisted by a deacon or *a* priest, 408 3
1 John 4:7-16 (Let us love one *a* for love is of God) 426 —
John 15:9–12 (Love one *a* as I have loved you) 426 —
A Christian may be asked to hear a confession, 446 12
The People greet one *a*. 522 —
The Clergy and People greet one *a*. 534 —
The Clergy and People greet one *a*. 546 —
The People greet one *a*. 563 —
or *a* prayer suitable to the occasion, 565 8
dedicating a chapel or an oratory within *a* building. 566 6
the bishop and other clergy and the people greet one *a*. 574 —
as the ministers move from one part of the church to *a*. 576 5
a donor, or a lay reader, or *a* suitable person. 576 10
of the Father, *a* of the Son, and *a* of the Holy Ghost. 864 27
none is greater, or less than *a*; 865 14
breaking one piece thereof from *a*. 866 37
that it be repugnant to *a*. 871 40
ought to have among themselves one to *a*; 873 24

answer

A 47 —
A 65 —
A 84 —
A 119 —
A 286 —
The candidates who are able to *a* for themselves 301 —
Then the candidates unable to *a* for themselves 301 —
A 302 —
A 303 —
To either question, the appropriate *a* is, "I do." 437 11
Then if the child is old enough to *a*, 441 —
A 517 —
A 518 —
A 526 —
A 531 —
A 532 —
A 538 —
A 543 —
A 544 —
traditional question and *a* form for ease of reference. 844 6

answering

65. For the *A* of Prayer 812 20
65. For the *A* of Prayers 834 —

answers

or of a series of questions and *a*, 420 —
The Woman *a* 424 —
The Man *a* 424 —
The Husband *a* 433 —
The Wife *a* 433 —

anthem

music may be substituted for a hymn or *a*. 14 10
Here may be sung a hymn or *a*. 58 —
Here may be sung a hymn or *a*. 71 —
Here may be sung a hymn or *a*. 101 —
an appropriate *a* or psalm may be sung, 112 —
Here may be sung a hymn or *a*. 125 —
or at the time of the hymn or *a* after the Collects. 142 12
The following or some other suitable *a* is sung 270 —
The following or some other suitable *a* may then be sung 271 —
concluded here with the singing of a hymn or *a*, 280 —
A 1 281 —
A 2 281 —
A 3 282 —
A "In the midst of life" (page 484 or 492) is sung 283 —
A hymn, psalm, or *a* may be sung. 299 —
A Psalm, hymn, or *a* may follow each Reading. 300 —
as Psalm 42, or a hymn or *a*, may be sung. 312 32
a hymn or *a*, may be sung during the procession. 313 12
A hymn, psalm, or *a* may be sung. 319 —
A hymn, psalm, or *a* may be sung. 323 —
A Psalm, hymn, or *a* may follow each Reading. 326 —
a hymn, psalm, or *a* may be sung. 333 —
The following or some other suitable *a* may be sung 337 —
A hymn, psalm, or *a* may be sung. 351 —
A hymn, psalm, or *a* may be sung. 355 —
A Psalm, hymn, or *a* may follow each Reading. 357 —
a hymn, psalm, or *a* may be sung. 361 —
some other suitable *a* may be used. 364 10
A hymn or *a* may then be sung, 407 1
The following *a* may be used at the Breaking 407 21
A hymn, psalm, or *a* may be sung. 413 —
A Psalm, hymn, or *a* may follow each Reading. 414 —
a hymn, psalm, or *a* may be sung, 423 —
A hymn, psalm, or *a* may follow. 425 —
a Psalm, hymn, or *a* may be sung 426 —
A hymn, psalm, or *a* may be sung, 431 —
a hymn, psalm, or *a* may be sung; 432 —
The following *a* is said 455 —

a suitable psalm or *a* may be sung 467 —
This *a*, or some other suitable *a*, or a hymn, 482 —
The following *a* is sung or said 484 —
A hymn, psalm, or some other suitable *a* may be sung 491 —
Or else this *a* 492 1
This *a*, or some other suitable *a*, or a hymn, 499 —
The following *a* or one of those on pages 491–492 501 —
A hymn, psalm, or *a* may be sung. 525 —
A hymn, psalm, or *a* may be sung. 537 —
A hymn, psalm, or *a* may be sung. 559 —
music is now played, or a hymn or *a* sung. 572 —

anthems

The words of *a* are to be from Holy Scripture, 14 7
appropriate hymns, psalms, or *a* are sung, 271 —
the following or other suitable *a* may be sung 274 —
the following, or other suitable *a*. 281 —
hymns, psalms, or *a* may be sung. 338 —
hymns, psalms, or *a* may be sung. 365 —
The *a* at the beginning of the service are sung 468 23
All stand while one or more of the following *a* is sung 469 —
one or more of these *a* may be sung or said 483 —
The *a* at the beginning of the service are sung 490 23
All stand while one or more of the following *a* is sung 491 —
one or more of these *a* may be sung or said 500 —
A from Holy Scripture or psalms may be sung 506 7
a may follow the readings. 506 11
Hymns, psalms, and *a* may be sung 512 —
Hymns and *a* may also be sung. 568 —
familiar from its use in many well-known *a*. 584 8
For this cause be cut off *A*, 866 37

Antioch

Church of Jerusalem, Alexandria, and *A*, have erred; 871 33

antiphon

concludes with the Song of Simeon with this *A*, 134 —
All repeat the *A* 135 2
or with a refrain (called the *a*) recited 582 16

antiphonal

A recitation is the verse-by-verse alternation 582 13

antiphonally

may be sung or said three times, or *a*. 406 11

antiphons

One of the following *A* may be sung or said 43 —
The Alleluias in the following *A* are used 44 —
One of the following *A* may be sung or said 80 —
The Alleluias in the following *A* are used 82 —
proper *a* on pages 43–44 and 80–82 may be used 141 6
A drawn from the Psalms themselves, 141 8
Invitatory *A* for the Venite makes possible 582 23
A drawn from the Pslams themselves, 935 7
The *a* may be sung or said 935 9

antique

Name was written in *a* and obsolete letters; 583 21

anxiety

especially in times of war, or of national *a*, 154 —

any

there be not *a* thing in it contrary 10 14
proper to revive it by *a* new Commission. 10 23
unrestrained by *a* worldly authority 11 5
in *a* essential point of doctrine, 11 13
In *a* of the Proper Liturgies for Special Days, 14 3
feasts take precedence of *a* other day or observance. 15 20
may be observed on *a* open day 17 17
and *a* Feasts of our Lord which occur on a Friday. 17 27
the Eucharist for *a* such occasion 18 11
At *a* Time 40 —
At *a* Time 78 —
A part or parts of this service may be led 108 7
a one of the following is also appropriate, 108 14
A of the prayers in contemporary language 108 22
using *a* one of the following 110 —
continue in *a* of the following ways: 112 —
or *a* of the Collects appointed in the Daily Offices, 136 —
A of the opening sentences of Scripture, 141 3
may be used at *a* time according 141 4
The Short Lessons may be read from *a* version 143 6
Thus, in *a* year, the Proper 158 12
The Collect appointed for *a* Sunday 158 22
The Collect immediately preceding and *a* of the sets 161 —
Lessons for Christmas Day serve for *a* weekdays 161 —
and as appropriate, *a* of the following Collects, 195 —
A of the Collects appointed for use at the Burial 202 —
and *a* of the sets of Proper Lessons 213 —
Lessons for Christmas Day serve for *a* weekdays 213 —
and as appropriate, *a* of the following Collects, 246 —
A of the Collects appointed for use at the Burial 253 —
which may include *a* or all of the following, 281 —
may be preached after *a* of the preceding Readings. 292 —
If on *a* one of the above-named days the ministry 312 8
a baptized person may administer Baptism 313 22
and *a* other vessel containing wine 334 —
may be added to *a* of the dismissals. 340 —
and *a* other vessel containing wine 342 —
Those who suffer and those in *a* trouble 359 —
and *a* other vessel containing wine 362 —
may be added to *a* of the dismissals. 366 15
and *a* other vessel containing wine 368 —
and *a* other vessel containing wine 371 —
and *a* other vessel containing wine 374 —
Those who suffer and those in *a* trouble 383 —
A of the forms which follow may be used. 383 —
A of the forms may be conformed to the language 383 —
a of the Sacrament that remains is then consumed. 401 14
and *a* other vessel containing wine 403 —
and *a* other vessel containing wine 405 —
a appropriate words of greeting may be used. 407 9
If *a* of the consecrated Bread or Wine remain, 408 28
apart from *a* which may be required 408 28
may be used with *a* authorized liturgy 437 5
James 5:14–16 (Is *a* among you sick?) 454 6
After *a* Reading, the Celebrant may comment 454 13
the Celebrant may use *a* of the Additional Prayers. 486 —
A of the authorized eucharistic prayers 506 22
Other priests, if *a*, who serve in the same congregation 558 11
After the Sermon, and *a* responses to it, 560 —

A of the presentations that follow 561 —
A of the Readings, including the Gospel, 565 10
a of the authorized eucharistic prayers may be used. 565 27
to dedicate and consecrate a church at *a* time 566 9
A of the usual forms of the Prayers of the People 576 18
or at *a* time after the Collects at Morning 836 —
There was never *a* thing by the wit of man 866 3
when *a* book of the Bible was begun, 866 18
And if *a* would judge this way more painful, 867 11
to appease all such diversity (if *a* arise), 867 17
the parties that so doubt, or diversely take *a* thing, 867 19
so that the same order be not contrary to *a* thing 867 21
in *a* language that they themselves do understand. 867 26
Neither that *a* man shall be bound 867 26
thereby, is not to be required of *a* man, 868 21
of whose authority was never *a* doubt in the Church. 868 24
but yet doth it not apply them to establish *a* doctrine; 868 35
ought of necessity to be received in *a* commonwealth; 869 12
yet it is not lawful for the Church to ordain *a* thing 871 38
ought not to decree *a* thing against the same, 871 41
a thing to be believed for necessity of Salvation. 871 42
It is not lawful for *a* man to take upon him the office 872 16
for that they have not *a* visible sign or ceremony 872 36
The Baptism of young Children is in *a* wise 873 20
neither hath it *a* thing that, of itself, 875 23
neither hath it *a* thing, 875 29
nor ought to be, subject to *a* foreign Jurisdiction. 875 42
so soon as there shall be *a* authorized response 877 21
to enter into brotherly conference with all or *a* 877 22
A Reading may be lengthened at discretion. 888 29
A Reading may be lengthened at discretion. 934 20
a of the Psalms appointed for a given day may be used 934 28
Likewise, Psalms appointed for *a* day may be used 934 29
on *a* other day in the same week, 934 30

anything

nor powers, nor height, nor depth, nor *a* else 507 7

anytime

Confessions may be heard *a* and anywhere. 446 8

anywhere

Confessions may be heard anytime and *a*. 446 9

apart

gather at a place *a* from the church, 270 —
a from any which may be required 408 28
grave is in a place that has not previously been set *a* 487 —
grave is in a place that has not previously been set *a* 503 —
place *a* from the church or chapel. 567 —
like us in all respects, *a* from sin; 864 8

Apocrypha

the Old Testament (or the *A*). 934 16

apostle

yet the *A* doth confess, 869 32
Christ, and James his *A*, so we judge, 876 19

apostles

All feasts of *A* 17 2
The *A'* Creed 53 —
The *A'* Creed 66 —
The *A'* Creed 96 —
The *A'* Creed 120 —
the *A'* Creed may be said. 137 —
The *A'* Creed is omitted from the Office 142 2
the Nicene Creed may take the place of the *A'* Creed, 142 18
Preface of *A* 185 —
Preface of *A* 187 —
Preface of *A* 188 —
Preface of *A* 189 —
Preface of *A* 190 —
Preface of *A* 191 —
Preface of *A* 192 —
Preface of *A* 193 —
Preface of *A* 194 —
Preface of *A* 205 —
Preface of *A* 237 —
Preface of *A* 238 —
Preface of *A* 239 —
Preface of *A* 240 —
Preface of *A* 241 —
Preface of *A* 242 —
Preface of *A* 243 —
Preface of *A* 244 —
Preface of *A* 245 —
Preface of *A* 256 —
A and Ordinations 348 —
A and Ordinations 381 —
The *A'* Creed may be recited after the Lessons, 437 20
The *A'* Creed may be said, all standing. 480 —
The *A'* Creed may then be said, all standing. 496 —
and the *A'* Creed may be recited. 506 13
from the *a'* time, there have been different 510 3
feasts of *a* or evangelists. 511 5
the Preface may be that for *A* and Ordinations. 564 1
If the *A'* Creed has not already been said, 572 —
and that which is commonly called the *A'* Creed, 869 16
and that which is commonly called the *A'* Creed..." 869 21
grown partly of the corrupt following of the *A*, 872 34
A to the Church unto the end of the world, 877 9
(b) The *A'* Creed, as the Baptismal Symbol; 877 35

apostolic

the order of bishops who carry on the *a* work 510 6

apparel

6 Against Excess of *A*. 875 8

appear

They will *a*, and it is to be hoped, 11 10
In which it will also *a* that this Church is far 11 12
appointed Psalms and Lessons, which *a* in tables 158 5
where the words elder, elders, and fellow elder, *a* 528 —
a by the common prayers in the Church, 866 5

appears

the Divine Name be spelled out, and it *a* as YAHWEH. 584 2

appease

to *a* all such diversity (if any arise), 867 17

appeasing

take order for the quieting and *a* of the same; 867 21

appertain

doth *a*, and is not, nor ought to be, subject 875 42

appertaineth

Nevertheless, it *a* to the discipline of the Church, 873 10

appertaining

things *a* to the perfection of Man's nature; 868 14

applause

The Clergy and People offer their acclamation and *a*. 522 —
A is appropriate. 563 —

apply

This provision does not *a* to Christmas 17 18
but yet doth it not *a* them to establish any doctrine; 868 35

appointed

Forms of Divine Worship, and the Rites and Ceremonies *a* 9 15
the regular services *a* for public worship 13 5
a by civil or Church authority, 13 12
in the form *a* at the Eucharist. 13 24
only the following feasts, *a* on fixed days, 16 3
and all other Major Feasts *a* on fixed days 16 11
Lessons *a* for the Feast may be substituted 16 15
Feasts *a* on fixed days in the Calendar 17 10
and other Major Feasts *a* on fixed days, 17 16
that none of the Propers *a* for Various Occasions 18 13
Proper *a* for the Principal Feasts. 18 15
The Psalm or Psalms *A* 46 —
One or two Lessons, as *a*, are read, 47 —
continuing with the *a* Psalmody; 61 —
The Psalm or Psalms *A* 64 —
One or two Lessons, as *a*, are read, 64 —
The Psalm of Psalms *A* 84 —
One or two Lessons, as *a*, are read, 84 —
continuing with the *a* Psalmody; 115 —
The Psalm or Psalms *A* 118 —
One or two Lessons, as *a*, are read, 118 —
or any of the Collects *a* in the Daily Offices, 136 —
The Psalms and Readings may be replaced by those *a* 136 —
Proper of the Church Year includes the *a* Collects; 158 3
and the *a* Psalms and Lessons, which appear in tables 158 5
The Proper *a* for the Sunday is also used 158 7
The Collect *a* for any Sunday or other Feast 158 22
weekdays which follow, except as otherwise *a*. 166 —
except as otherwise *a*. 174 —
more of the *a* Lessons are read before the Gospel, 175 —
Any of the Collects *a* for use at the Burial 202 —
one of the forms *a* for the Burial 202 —
the weekdays which follow, except as otherwise *a*. 217 —
except as otherwise *a*. 226 —
more of the *a* Lessons are read before the Gospel, 227 —
Any of the Collects *a* for use at the Burial 253 —
For the Prayers of the People, one of the forms *a* 253 —
and the Celebrant or Minister *a* invites 264 —
the prayer for forgiveness *a* at Morning Prayer. 269 —
Here a Deacon or other person *a* reads 270 —
All standing, the Deacon, or other person *a*, says 277 —
The biddings may be read by a Deacon or other person *a*. 277 —
Then the Deacon, or other person *a*, standing 286 —
One or two Lessons, as *a*, are read, 300 —
A Person *a* leads the following petitions 305 —
Lay persons *a* by the celebrant should normally 322 15
When *a*, the following hymn or some other song 324 —
One or two Lessons, as *a*, are read, 325 —
The Deacon or other person *a* says 328 —
and on other occasions as *a*. 334 —
and on other occasions as *a*. 341 —
To be used on Sundays as *a*, 344 —
a for Holy Days and Various Occasions 345 —
Lay persons *a* by the celebrant should normally 354 15
When *a*, the following hymn or some other song 356 —
One or two Lessons, as *a*, are read, 357 —
and on other occasions as *a*. 361 —
and on other occasions as *a*. 367 —
To be used on Sundays as *a*, 377 —
a for Holy Days and Various Occasions 378 —
one of those *a* for Various Occasions. 396 —
a reader *a* by the celebrant may read 406 22
all that is *a* through the Prayers of the People 406 25
One or two Lessons, as *a*, are read, 414 —
At the time *a*, the persons to be married, 423 —
and the Deacon or Minister *a* says 426 —
The Deacon or other person *a* reads 429 —
and Lessons *a* in the Marriage service. 433 —
such as those *a* for the Vigil 467 —
Then, all standing, the Deacon or Minister *a* reads 479 —
Then, all standing, the Deacon or Minister *a* reads 495 —
ordination and consecration are *a*. 510 21
a bishop *a* by the Presiding Bishop, presides 511 7
The people standing, the Bishop *a* says 512 —
All kneel, and the Person *a* leads the Litany 515 —
All kneel, and the Person *a* leads the Litany 527 —
All kneel, and the Person *a* leads the Litany 539 —
The Bishop says the *a* Collect. 551 —
One, *a* by the bishop, is to say 554 30
when desired, deacons may be *a* to carry the Sacrament 555 1
but, if necessary, a deputy may be *a*. 558 8
led by a person *a*. 560 —
On the day *a*, the clergy and people gather 567 3
The bishop, or a priest *a*, is the chief celebrant. 574 —
Though it be *a* in the afore written preface, 867 23
The Psalms and Lessons *a* for the Sundays 888 6
those *a* in the Office Lectionary; 888 16
a for the same day in the Daily Office Lectionary. 888 24
any of the Psalms *a* for a given day may be used 934 28
Likewise, Psalms *a* for any day may be used 934 29

approach

They may *a* the Altar, either for the exchange of vows, 437 15
a may be by God's blessing made towards Home Reunion: 877 32

approaches

As the procession *a* the door of the church, 567 —

appropriate

On occasion, and as *a*, instrumental music 14 9
It is *a* that other persons be assigned to read 36 5
It is *a* that other persons be assigned to read 74 4
It is *a* also for use in private houses. 108 6
This order is not *a* for use on Monday, 108 11
following is also *a*, especially for the seasons 108 15
a to the occasion or to the season, 109 —

During the candle-lighting, an *a* anthem or psalm	112	—
For convenience, *a* Psalms, Readings, and Collects	136	—
It is *a* that prayers of thanksgiving	140	—
A musical prelude or processional is not *a*.	142	27
it is *a* after the candles have been lighted	143	19
Psalms generally *a* to the evening	143	23
At the discretion of the Celebrant, and as *a*,	195	—
At the discretion of the Celebrant, and as *a*,	246	—
by an *a* invitation and a penitential psalm.	269	—
and *a* hymns, psalms, or anthems are sung,	271	—
other *a* Collect is said	271	—
addition or omission, as *a*, at the discretion	277	—
A devotions may follow,	281	—
Holy Baptism is especially *a* at the Easter Vigil,	312	2
and it is *a* for sponsors to be assigned	312	24
inform the priest of the *a* parish,	314	4
It is *a* that the other priests present stand	322	7
the People may make an *a* response,	328	—
or some other *a* sentence of Scripture,	343	—
It is *a* that the other priests present stand	354	7
(with commemoration of a saint when *a*)	359	—
or some other *a* sentence of Scripture,	376	—
(with commemoration of a saint when *a*)	383	—
(a) a Collect *a* to the season	394	—
a to the day or occasion,	396	—
Recalls before God, when *a*, the particular occasion	402	—
Recalls before God, when *a*, the particular occasion	404	—
read from a book or books of *a* size and dignity.	406	20
any *a* words of greeting may be used.	407	9
it is *a* that there be only one chalice	407	18
It is *a* that the oblations of bread and wine	412	16
The Celebrant then says this or some other *a* prayer	421	—
assemble in the church or some other *a* place.	423	—
A Psalms are 67, 127, and 128	426	—
it is *a* that the newly married couple	432	—
To either question, the *a* answer is, "I do."	437	11
It is *a* that all remain standing	437	17
Luke 18:15–17 is *a*.	439	14
say one or more of these or other *a* verses	449	—
the following service are used, as *a*;	453	—
It is *a* that the family and friends come together	465	—
A devotions, such as those appointed	467	—
It is *a* that it be covered with a pall	468	9
It is *a* that the bishop,	468	13
It is *a* that it be covered with a pall	490	9
It is *a* that the bishop,	490	13
The following Psalms are *a*:	494	—
The following Psalms are *a*:	495	—
this Book is deemed *a*, the following form is used.	506	3
assigned *a* duties in the service.	511	10
Thereafter, it is *a* to refer to him	511	19
At the Offertory, it is *a* that the bread and wine	511	21
Thereafter, it is *a* to refer to him	524	10
At the Offertory, it is *a* that the bread and wine	524	12
Thereafter, it is *a* to refer to him	536	10
At the Offertory, it is *a* that the bread and wine	536	12
During the Eucharistic Prayer, it is *a*	553	8
it is *a* for the deacons to remove the vessels	555	5
read one of the Lessons and assist where *a*.	558	24
The Litany for Ordinations, or some other *a* litany,	560	—
may be added to, omitted, or adapted, as *a*	561	—
When *a*, the family of the new minister may also	563	—
Applause is *a*.	563	—
The Letter of Institution is *a* for the induction	564	17
A selections may be found	565	13
The priest's prayer on page 562 is *a* only for rectors	565	24
may be assigned *a* parts in the service.	566	15
instrumental music are *a*.	567	—
or some other *a* psalm is sung.	568	—
the Bishop proceeds to an *a* place, and says	572	—
it is *a* that it remain silent until dedicated.	575	11
carried by *a* persons.	575	19
address may be followed by an *a* Pastoral	576	15
If incense is to be used, it is *a* at this time.	576	24
or one *a* to the name of the church.	576	26
it is *a* that their representatives take part	577	2
a prayer may be said, or adapted	577	11
a when a congregation attains recognition	577	24
It is particularly *a* for the psalm	582	9
the Latin form "Alleluia," as being more *a*	584	6
version is particularly *a* for use at the Office,	888	20
throughout the year, except for *a* variations	934	24
appropriately		
a concludes the Office with a blessing.	36	7
a concludes the Office with a blessing.	74	6
the ceremony of the washing of feet *a*	274	—
Holy Baptism is *a* administered within the Eucharist	298	5
Ministers of other Churches may *a* be invited	558	19
approval		
The Congregation expresses its *a*.	563	—
approved		
in a manner *a* by the bishop.	408	1
or some other *a* litany.	515	—
or some other *a* litany.	527	—
or some other *a* litany.	539	—
ordained and *a* by common authority,	874	27
April		
It cannot occur before March 22 or after *A* 25.	15	8
Saint Mark *A* 25	188	—
Saint Mark *A* 25	240	—
archbishops		
"The Book of Consecration of *A* and Bishops,	875	27
architect		
a, builders, musicians, artists, benefactors,	566	18
areas		
When possible, the *a* or furnishings should be put	577	13
34. For Towns and Rural *A*	811	13
34. For Towns and Rural *A*	825	—
arise		
be so plainly set forth, but doubts may *a*	867	16
to appease all such diversity (if any *a*),	867	17
we may *a* again, and amend our lives.	870	35
armed		
25. For those in the *A* Forces of our Country	811	3
25. For those in the *A* Forces of our Country	823	—
arms		
Bishop goes to the Table and, with *a* extended, says	573	—

around
may go *a* the building(s) to be dedicated 575 8

arrange
desirable that the priest *a* to celebrate the Eucharist 396 —

arranged
since the matter is *a* under headings, 844 9
The Lectionary for Sundays is *a* in a three-year cycle, 888 2
The Daily Office Lectionary is *a* in a two-year cycle. 934 2
the Psalms are *a* in a seven-week pattern 934 23

arrangements
and *a* for the funeral should be made 468 3
and *a* for the funeral should be made 490 3

arranging
make wills, while they are in health, 445 —

arrival
verse which mentions the *a* at Golgotha 273 —
verse which mentions the *a* at Golgotha 277 —

arrogancy
Supererogation, cannot be taught without *a* 870 —

art
instrumental music, other *a* forms, silence. 400 10

article
signed, as directed by *A* VIII of the Constitution 552 10
believed as an *a* of the Faith, or be thought requisite 868 22
The original *A* given Royal assent in 1571 869 19
The original 1571, 1662 text of this *A*, omitted 872 4
the several titles whereof we have joined under this *A*, 874 35
[This *A* is received in this Church, 875 14
The original 1571, 1662 text of this *A* reads as follows: 875 26
The original 1571, 1662 text of this *A* reads as follows: 875 39

articles
hath not only in her Preface, but likewise in her *A* 9 22
A of Religion 867 29
[The Twenty-first of the former *A* is omitted; 872 2
as to the remaining parts of it, in other *A*.] 872 3
the following *A* supply a basis 877 31

artificial
there should be as little *a* light as possible 142 26

artisans
benefactors, donors, artists, *a*, and others. 576 21

artists
builders, musicians, *a*, benefactors, and friends. 566 18
benefactors, donors, *a*, artisans, and others. 576 21
17. For Church Musicians and *A* 810 24
17. For Church Musicians and *A* 819 —

ascended
He *a* into heaven, he sitteth on the right hand 865 33
wherewith he *a* into Heaven, 868 14

Ascension
and the feast of the *A* on a Thursday 15 13
A Day 15 17
Wednesday before *A* Day 18 9
Easter Season, including *A* Day 39 —
From Easter Day until the *A* 43 —
From *A* Day until the Day of Pentecost 43 —
Easter Season, including *A* Day 77 —
From Easter Day until the *A* 81 —
From *A* Day until the Day of Pentecost 81 —
Psalm 36:5–9 (*A*) 108 17
A Day 174 —
Preface of the *A* 174 —
A Day, serves for the following weekdays, 174 —
Seventh Sunday of Easter: The Sunday after *A* Day 175 —
Preface of the *A* 175 —
Preface of the *A*, or of Baptism 203 —
A Day 226 —
Preface of the *A* 226 —
A Day, serves for the following weekdays, 226 —
Seventh Sunday of Easter: The Sunday after *A* Day 226 —
Preface of the *A* 226 —
Preface of the *A*, or of Baptism 254 —
A 347 —
A 379 —
and on *A* Day; 406 15

ascertained
of matrimony, and their free consent, is publicly *a*. 435 14

ash
determines the beginning of Lent on *A* Wednesday, 15 12
A Wednesday 17 9
A Wednesday. 17 15
A Wednesday and the other weekdays of Lent 17 23
occasion on *A* Wednesday, Maundy Thursday, 18 12
always used on the Sunday before *A* Wednesday. 165 —
A Wednesday 166 1
always used on the Sunday before *A* Wednesday 217 4
A Wednesday 217 —
A Wednesday 264 —

ashes
If *a* are to be imposed, the Celebrant says 265 —
The *a* are imposed with the following words 265 —

aside
or in a place set *a* to give greater privacy, 446 16

ask
Members of the congregation may *a* the prayers 386 —
a for the Declaration of Consent, 422 12
The Priest may *a* God's blessing on a ring or rings 427 —

asked
Another Christian may be *a* to hear a confession, 446 12

asks
The Celebrant *a* each candidate when presented 301 —
When all have been presented the Celebrant *a* the parents 302 —
Then the Celebrant *a* the following questions 302 —
The Bishop *a* the candidates 303 —
The Bishop *a* the candidates 415 —
presentation, the Celebrant *a*, 437 9
The Celebrant *a* the parent or parents 440 13
if the child is old enough to answer, the Celebrant *a* 441 —

Bishop then says the following, or similar words, and *a* 513 —
The Bishop then *a* the new priest to bless the people. 535 —

assemble

in its customary place before the people *a*; 143 4
a in the church or some other appropriate place. 423 —
and friends *a* in the church 435 9
When the clergy and people *a* before the service, 575 5
the congregation may *a* inside the church; 575 13

assembled

prayer of Christians *a* for public worship, 446 4
a as Bishops in the Church of God, 876 26

assembles

in place before the congregation *a*. 506 6

assembly

In all services, the entire Christian *a* participates 13 16
The leader of worship in a Christian *a* 13 20
addressed to the entire *a*. 407 8
exchanged throughout the *a*. 436 12
or a Priest if no deacon is present, dismisses the *a*. 564 12
(forasmuch as they be an *a* of men, 872 6

assent

The original Article given Royal *a* in 1571 869 19

assign

the priest may *a* to the penitent a psalm, 446 23

assigned

It is appropriate that other persons be *a* to read 36 5
other parts of the service not *a* to the officiant. 36 6
It is appropriate that other persons be *a* to read 74 4
other parts of the service not *a* to the officiant. 74 5
Specific roles may be *a* to different persons, 273 —
Specific roles may be *a* to different persons, 277 —
A lay person may be *a* to chant the Exsultet. 284 21
for sponsors to be *a* this function. 312 25
persons appointed by the celebrant should normally be *a* 322 15
persons appointed by the celebrant should normally be *a* 354 15
a appropriate duties in the service. 511 10
may be *a* appropriate parts in the service. 566 15
a the task of pouring the water. 575 24
a to a given Office has been bracketed, 935 4

assist

follow each Lesson, and *a* at Baptism and the Eucharist. 284 15
Deacons likewise *a* at Baptism 284 18
read the Lessons, and the Epistle, and *a* 284 20
Thirdly, there are deacons who *a* bishops 510 12
If there are many deacons, some *a* in the Offertory 554 29
and deacons *a* according to their order. 558 12
elements at the Offertory, *a* the celebrant at the Altar, 558 21
and *a* where appropriate. 558 24
to *a* in rendering them into contemporary speech. 814 —

assistant

and the *a* the Chalice. 408 5
including vicars of missions and *a* ministers. 558 5

assisted

whether bishop or priest, be *a* by other priests, 322 5
whether bishop or priest, be *a* by other priests, 354 5
The deacon may be *a* by other ministers. 407 16
When the celebrant is *a* by a deacon or another priest, 408 3
The newly ordained bishop, *a* by other ministers, 553 11

assisting

or to an *a* priest or deacon, 307 —
and *a* in the ministration of the Sacrament 322 12
these duties may be performed by an *a* priest. 322 14
and *a* in the ministration of the Sacrament 354 12
these duties may be performed by an *a* priest. 354 14
A deacon, or an *a* priest, may deliver the charge, 422 12
and perform other *a* functions at the Eucharist. 422 13

assists

After receiving Holy Communion, the new deacon *a* 536 14

associated

a with them are the presbyters, or ordained elders, 510 8

associates

Altar with the bishop, as *a* and fellow ministers 524 15

assure

the Celebrant is to *a* that person that all the benefits 457 —

asterisk

An *a* divides each verse into two parts for reading 583 13
a distinct pause should be made at the *a*. 583 14

Athanasius

The Creed of Saint *A* 864 21
"The Three Creeds, Nicene Creed, *A*'s Creed, 869 20

attain

a to everlasting felicity. 871 10

attains

a congregation *a* recognition as a parish. 577 25

attendants

a will enter in procession through the principal door. 575 14

attends

when the same congregation *a* two or more services. 888 8

attention

The *a* of this Church was in the first place drawn 10 32

attested

the ceremony be *a* by at least two witnesses; 422 5

attribute

Where we *a* to the King's Majesty the chief government, 875 43

attributed

62. A Prayer *a* to St. Francis 812 13
62. A Prayer *a* to St. Francis 833 —

August

Proper 13 The Sunday closest to *A* 3 180 —
Proper 14 The Sunday closest to *A* 10 180 —
Proper 15 The Sunday closest to *A* 17 180 —
Proper 16 The Sunday closest to *A* 24 181 —
Proper 17 The Sunday closest to *A* 31 181 —

The Transfiguration *A* 6 191 —
Saint Mary the Virgin *A* 15 192 —
Saint Bartholomew *A* 24 192 —
Proper 13 The Sunday closest to *A* 3 232 —
Proper 14 The Sunday closest to *A* 10 232 —
Proper 15 The Sunday closest to *A* 17 232 —
Proper 16 The Sunday closest to *A* 24 232 —
Proper 17 The Sunday closest to *A* 31 233 —
The Transfiguration *A* 6 243 —
Saint Mary the Virgin *A* 15 243 —
Saint Bartholomew *A* 24 243 —

Augustine

press with their teeth (as Saint *A* saith) 873 38

authority

by common consent and *a*, may be altered, 9 7
those that are in place of *A* should, 9 20
and the Civil *A* has not since thought 10 22
unrestrained by any worldly *a* whatsoever) 11 6
other forms set forth by *a* within this Church 13 8
appointed by civil or Church *a*, 13 13
The Nation and all in *a* 359 —
The Nation and all in *a* 383 —
and the *a* being conferred. 565 —
the President of the United States and all in Civil *A* 810 28
the President of the United States and all in Civil *A* 820 —
of whose *a* was never any doubt in the Church. 868 24
XX. Of the *A* of the Church. 871 36
and *a* in Controversies of Faith: 871 37
XXI. Of the *A* of General Councils. 872 1
necessary to salvation have neither strength nor *a*, 872 9
have public *a* given unto them in the Congregation, 872 19
have chief *a* in the Ministration of the Word 873 3
and do minister by his commission and *a*, 873 5
by a Judge that hath *a* thereunto. 874 20
ordained and approved by common *a*, 874 27
hurteth the *a* of the Magistrate, 874 29
Every particular or national Church hath *a* to ordain, 874 31
Rites of the Church ordained only by man's *a*, 874 32
and confirmed at the same time by *a* of Parliament, 875 28
but hath no *a* in things purely spiritual. 875 36
to pay respectful obedience to the Civil *A*, 875 37

authorization

with the *a* of the bishop, officiate at public Baptism; 284 28

authorize

the bishop may, at discretion, *a* a deacon to preside 13 26
the bishop may specially *a* a deacon to preside. 312 9
the bishop may, at discretion, *a* a deacon to distribute 408 18

authorized

understood as those *a* by this Church. 14 7
previously *a* liturgical texts may be used 14 13
and Lessons duly *a* by this Church: 18 2
A intercessions and thanksgivings may follow. 58 —
A intercessions and thanksgivings may follow. 71 —
A intercessions and thanksgivings may follow. 101 —
A intercessions and thanksgivings may follow. 125 —
a for public worship in this Church, 143 7
a liturgy for the Holy Eucharist. 437 6
Any of the *a* eucharistic prayers may be used. 506 22
a sign that you are fully empowered and *a* 557 7
any of the *a* eucharistic prayers 565 27
a response to this Declaration, 877 22

authors

or (as the School-*a* say) deserve grace of congruity: 870 15

autumnal

traditional *a* Ember Days. 182 —
traditional *a* Ember Days. 233 —

available

celebration of the Communion, or if a priest is not *a*, 330 —
celebration of the Communion, or if a priest is not *a*, 359 —
when no priest is *a*, the celebrant or deacon, 409 3
and no priest or bishop is *a*, a deacon may 422 16
and when no priest or bishop is *a*, a deacon may 435 5
Reconciliation of a Penitent is *a* for all who desire it. 446 7

avoid

secure continuity or *a* repetition. 934 19

avoided

XXXIII. Of excommunicate Persons, how they are to be *a*. 874 16

away

Revelation 7:9–17 (God shall wipe *a* all tears) 475 —
Revelation 7:9–17 (God will wipe *a* every tear) 495 —
put *a* our sins, and endure the severity 870 8
sacrifice of himself once made, should take *a* the sins 870 27
Neither is the effect of Christ's ordinance taken *a* 873 6

B

badges

Sacraments ordained of Christ be not only *b* 872 26

Bangor

some the use of *B*, some of York, 867 10

Banns

If *B* are to be published, the following form is used 437 2

baptism

From the Epiphany through the *B* of Christ, 43 —
From the Epiphany through the *B* of Christ, 81 —
The *B* of our Lord 163 —
Holy *B* or Confirmation 175 —
Preface of *B* 201 —
Preface of the Ascension, or of *B* 203 —
10. At *B* 203 —
Preface of *B* 203 —
Preface of *B*, or of Pentecost 203 —
Preface of *B*, or of Trinity Sunday 205 —
Preface of *B*, or of the Season 206 —
The *B* of our Lord 214 —
Holy *B* or Confirmation 227 —
Preface of the Lord's Day, or of *B* 236 —
Preface of *B* 253 —
Preface of the Ascension, or of *B* 254 —
10. At *B* 254 —
Preface of *B* 254 —
Preface of *B*, or of Pentecost 254 —
Preface of *B*, or of Trinity Sunday 255 —

Preface of *B*, or of the Season	257	—
the chief celebrant, presides at *B*	284	12
and assist at *B* and the Eucharist.	284	15
Deacons likewise assist at *B* and the Eucharist	284	18
authorization of the bishop, officiate at public *B*;	284	28
Holy *b* (beginning with the Presentation	292	—
In the absence of candidates for *B* or Confirmation,	292	—
Holy *B*	297	—
Holy *B* is full initiation by water and the Holy Spirit	298	2
The bond which God establishes in *B*	298	3
Holy *B* is appropriately administered	298	5
and preside at *B* and the Eucharist.	298	8
At *B*, the bishop officiates at the Presentation	298	8
Each candidate for Holy *B* is to be sponsored	298	16
instructed in the meaning of *B*,	298	26
Holy *B*	299	—
they are selected from "At *B*."	300	—
The *B*	307	—
the Proper Preface of *B* may be used.	310	—
Holy *B* is especially appropriate at the Easter Vigil,	312	2
and on the Feast of the *B* of our Lord	312	4
subsequent occasion of public *b* at which a bishop	312	13
four days listed above there are no candidates for *B*,	312	15
the Lessons provided for use at *B*	312	22
and at the administration of *B*,	313	4
After the *B*, a candle (which may be lighted	313	7
Conditional *B*	313	15
(which are the essential parts of *B*),	313	18
Emergency *B*	313	21
emergency, any baptized person may administer *B*	313	22
The person who administers emergency *B*	314	3
baptized person recovers, the *B* should be recognized	314	5
B	348	—
B	381	—
commitment to the responsibilities of their *B*	412	5
When there is no *B*, the rites of Confirmation,	412	11
The Bishop may consecrate oil of Chrism for use at *B*,	419	—
If no *B* is to take place [water may be poured	570	—
If Holy *B* is not to be administered,	575	24
as in the service of Holy *B*,	575	26
If *B* is to be administered, the following order	575	28
the Gospel from "At *B*," page 928;	575	29
then the service of Holy *B*,	575	29
Holy *B*.	577	17
Holy *B*	858	—
XVI. Of Sin after *B*.	870	31
Not every deadly sin willingly committed after *B*	870	32
such as fall into sin after *B*.	870	34
that is to say, *B*, and the Supper of the Lord.	872	31
but yet have not like nature of Sacraments with *B*,	872	35
XXVII. Of *B*.	873	13
B is not only a sign of profession,	873	14
they that receive *B* rightly are grafted	873	16
The *B* of young Children is in any wise to be retained	873	20
3. The two Sacraments,—*B* and the Supper	877	16
Sacraments ordained by Christ Himself—*B*	878	1

baptismal

B Vows, page 292, follows the Sermon.	175	—
B Vows, page 292, follows the Sermon.	227	—
3. Christian Initiation, or the Renewal of *B* Vows.	284	8
first two parts of the service, the Renewal of *B* Vows,	284	24
Celebrant leads the people in the Renewal of *B* Vows,	292	—
The Renewal of *B* Vows	292	—
Baptism, Confirmation, or the Renewal of *B* Vows	295	—
The *B* Covenant	304	—
If Confirmation, Reception, or the Reaffirmation of *B*	308	—
the Renewal of *B* Vows, page 292, may take the place	312	16
The oblations of bread and wine at the *b* Eucharist	313	13
Reaffirmation of *B* Vows are administered	412	12
the Reaffirmation of *B* Vows	413	—
The *B* Covenant	416	—
reaffirmation of *b* promises.	420	—
6. Renewal of *B* Vows	578	2
about to be Baptized or to renew their *B* Covenant	810	21
to renew their *B* Covenant	819	—
(b) The Apostles' Creed, as the *B* Symbol;	877	35

baptisms

B be reserved for these occasions or when a bishop	312	6

Baptist

Saint John the *B*	16	27
The Nativity of Saint John the *B* June 24	190	—
The Nativity of Saint John the *B* June 24	241	—

baptistry

The blessing of a new font or *b* should always be done	577	15

baptized

7. For All *B* Christians	201	—
7. For all *B* Christians	252	—
and concluding with the reception of the newly *b*)	292	—
If a priest uses Chrism in signing the newly *b*,	298	14
sponsored by one or more *b* persons.	298	17
When all have been *b*, the Celebrant says	308	—
given to each of the newly *b* or to a godparent.	313	8
presented by the newly *b* or their godparents.	313	14
reasonable doubt that a person has been *b* with water,	313	16
the person is *b* in the usual manner,	313	18
emergency, any *b* person may administer Baptism	313	22
Using the given name of the one to be *b* (if known),	313	24
b person recovers, the Baptism should be recognized	314	5
and the person *b* under emergency conditions,	314	7
those *b* at an early age are expected,	412	2
Those *b* as adults, unless *b* with laying on hands	412	7
one, at least, of the parties must be a *b* Christian;	422	4
For a child not yet *b*	444	—
For a child already *b*	444	—
B Christians are properly buried from the church.	468	5
B Christians are properly buried from the church.	490	5
If there are persons to be *b*, water is now poured	569	—
reception of the newly *b*.	575	31
15. For those about to be *B*	810	21
15. For those about to be *B*	819	—
no condemnation for them that believe and are *b*;	869	31
But all we the rest, although *b*,	870	28
2. That we believe that all who have been duly *b*	876	31

bar

A *b* in the margin indicates petitions	383	—

Barnabas

Saint *B* June 11 189 —
Saint *B* June 11 241 —

Bartholomew

Saint *B* August 24 192 —
Saint *B* August 24 243 —

Baruch

The Book of Judith, *B* the Prophet, 868 40

based

Hebrew versification, which is not *b* on meter 583 2

basic

devotions follow the *b* structure of the Daily Office 136 —

basis

from time to time on a regular *b*, 396 —
with them on the *b* of a common Faith and Order, 877 2
the following Articles supply a *b* on which approach 877 31

battle

The hymn "Sing, my tongue, the glorious *b*," 282 —

bearer

and for our salvation, of Mary the Virgin, the God-*b* 864 10

bearing

(the Celebrant if there is no deacon) *b* the Candle, 285 —
the congregation *b* the lighted Paschal Candle 467 —

Beatitudes

Matthew 5:1–10 (The *B*) 426 —

beauty

8. For the *B* of the Earth 813 11
8. For the *B* of the Earth 840 —

became

b independent with respect to civil government, 10 25
alterations in the Liturgy which *b* necessary 10 33

become

(A man cleaves to his wife and they *b* one flesh) 426 —

been

have still *b* continued firm and unshaken. 10 7
aim in these different reviews and alterations hath *b*, 10 8
no service or prayer has *b* provided in this Book, 13 14
it is appropriate after the candles have *b* 143 —
If candles have *b* distributed to members 286 —
it must have *b* previously consecrated by the bishop. 298 15
When all have *b* presented the Celebrant asks the parents 302 —
After all have *b* presented, the Celebrant addresses 303 —
When this action has *b* completed for all candidates, 308 —
When all have *b* baptized, the Celebrant says 308 —
doubt that a person has *b* baptized with water, 313 16
said here if it has not *b* said earlier. 330 —
said here if it has not *b* said earlier. 359 —
when they are ready and have *b* duly prepared, 412 3
After all have *b* presented, the Bishop addresses 416 —
canons of this Church having *b* complied with, 435 7
reconciliation, which has *b* committed by Christ 446 2
grave is in a place that has not previously *b* set apart 487 —
grave is in a place that has not previously *b* set apart 503 —
service has *b* held, or at the graveside. 506 20
there have *b* different ministries within the Church. 510 3
orders of ordained ministers have *b* characteristic 510 5
It has *b*, and is, the intention and purpose 510 19
such as has *b*, and is, most generally recognized 510 30
Presbyter of the Church of God, you have *b* called 557 2
with the Canons, you have *b* selected to serve 557 5
furnishings, that have *b* added, 566 4
If the Apostles' Creed has not already *b* said, 572 —
When buildings have *b* used for public worship 577 21
period of time without having *b* consecrated, 577 22
the method which has *b* most frequently used 582 27
because from very ancient times it has *b* considered 583 18
a hybrid form which has *b* transliterated "Jehovah." 583 24
b carried over into the classical English versions, 583 26
ancient praise-shout, "Hallelujah," has *b* restored, 584 4
The Hebrew form has *b* used, 584 5
composed in traditional idiom have not *b* modernized; 814 —
pronouns and verbs have *b* put in italics 814 —
in continuance of time hath not *b* corrupted: 866 4
decent order of the ancient fathers hath *b* so altered, 866 16
hath *b* read in Latin to the people, 866 24
hearts, spirit, and mind, have not *b* edified thereby. 866 26
now of late time a few of them have *b* daily said 866 28
great charge for books, as in time past they have *b*. 867 7
there hath *b* great diversity in saying and singing 867 8
for at all times they have *b* divers, 874 23
we see to have *b* given always to all godly Princes 876 3
2. That we believe that all who have *b* duly baptized 876 31
or surrender by those who have *b* ordained 877 10
assigned to a given Office has *b* bracketed, 935 4

before

these alterations were in review *b* the Convention, 11 3
lighted candles may be carried *b* them, 143 1
Recalls *b* God, when appropriate, 402 —
Recalls *b* God, when appropriate, 404 —
and, standing *b* the congregation, makes 420 —
the husband and wife stand *b* the Celebrant, 433 —
They may then remain *b* the Lord's Table 438 2
the family to present themselves *b* the Altar. 439 18
customary that the celebrant meet the body and go *b* 468 21
customary that the celebrant meet the body and go *b* 490 21
and Lay Persons, standing *b* the Presiding Bishop, 513 —
who kneels *b* the Presiding Bishop. 520 —
standing *b* the bishop, present the ordinand, 526 —
seated except the ordinand, who stands *b* the Bishop. 531 —
standing *b* the bishop, present the ordinand, 538 —
seated except the ordinand, who stands *b* the Bishop. 543 —
standing *b* the bishop with the new minister, 559 —
b the bishop with the new minister. 561 —
We are accounted righteous *b* God, only for the merit 870 2
to have continually *b* their eyes the sentence 871 17

began

and *b* as follows, "The Three Creeds, 869 20

begin

dark, or partially so, when the service is to *b*.	109	—
to *b* the service by its light.	143	5
The Celebrant may *b* the Offertory with one	333	—
The Celebrant may *b* the Offertory with one	361	—
the priest may *b* the celebration at the Offertory,	396	—
the Celebrant may *b* with the Act of Thanksgiving,	439	11
The Priest and Penitent *b* as follows	449	—

beginning

Easter also determines the *b* of Lent	15	12
For the Short Lesson at the *b* of the service,	108	14
With Evening Prayer, *b* with the Psalms;	112	—
the Holy Eucharist, *b* with the Salutation	112	—
or candles carried in at the *b* of the service	143	12
which appear in tables *b* on page 889.	158	6
(*b* with the Presentation of the Candidates),	175	—
(*b* with the Presentation of the Candidates),	227	—
(*b* with the Presentation of the Candidates,	292	—
For use at the *b* of the Liturgy,	319	—
When this Order is used at the *b* of the Liturgy,	321	—
For use at the *b* of the Liturgy,	351	—
When this Order is used at the *b* of the Liturgy,	353	—
See the forms *b* on page 383.	359	—
b with the words which follow	408	14
b with the [Peace and] Lord's Prayer	457	—
Thanksgiving for a *B* of Recovery	460	8
The anthems at the *b* of the service are sung or said	468	23
The anthems at the *b* of the service are sung or said	490	23
From the *b* of the service until the Offertory,	511	12
From the *b* of the service until the Offertory,	524	4
From the *b* of the service until the Offertory,	536	4
or in the Bishop's absence a Priest *b* a new ministry,	563	13
b with the Presentation of the Candidates,	575	29
9. The Eucharist, *b* with the Offertory	578	5
numbered Collects *b* on pages 199 and 251.	813	18
sung or said at the *b* and end of each Psalm	935	10

begins

The Officiant *b* the service with one or more	37	—
The Officiant *b* the service with one or more	61	—
The Officiant *b* the service with one or more	75	—
b with the Invocation and concludes	88	—
The Officiant then *b* the Prayers	106	—
The Officiant *b* the service with one or more	115	—
The Officiant *b*	127	—
and the Eucharist *b* with the Salutation	153	—
the sequence *b* with Proper 3	158	17
the sequence *b* with Proper 6	158	19
it *b* with the Service of Light,	175	—
it *b* with the Service of Light,	227	—
the Celebrant *b* the liturgy with the Salutation	264	—
the celebration *b* with the Salutation	272	—
The Eucharist *b* in the usual manner,	274	—
b the liturgy with the Collect of the Day.	276	—
the Celebrant *b* with the Collect of the Day	283	—
and the Eucharist *b* with the Salutation	406	4
service *b* with the Penitential Order.)	407	1
The Rite *b* as prescribed for celebrations	433	—
and the Eucharist *b* with the Offertory.	437	7
The Penitent *b*	447	—
The Celebrant *b* the service with the following	453	11
the Priest *b* with the [Peace and]	457	—
it precedes the commendation, and *b* with the Peace	506	21
The Presiding Bishop then *b* this Prayer	520	—
The Bishop goes to the Table and *b*	546	—
the Bishop *b* the Prayer for the Consecration	568	—
Year A always *b* on the First Sunday of Advent	888	3
Year A, therefore, *b* on Advent Sunday	888	5
Year One *b* on the First Sunday of Advent	934	3
Year Two *b* on the First Sunday of Advent	934	4

begotten

b of the Father before the ages,	864	9
but yet as regards his manhood *b*,	864	10
one and the same Christ, Son, Lord, Only-*b*,	864	11
but one and the same Son and Only-*b* God the Word,	864	15
The Father is made of none, neither created, nor *b*.	865	8
not made, nor created, but *b*,	865	9
of the Substance of the Father, *b* before the worlds;	865	23
b from everlasting of the Father,	868	2
they be made like the image of his only-*b* Son	871	8

begun

when any book of the Bible was *b*,	866	19
in this sort the book of Isaiah was *b* in Advent,	866	20
but they were only *b*, and never read through.	866	21
the Lectionary for Year One is *b*.)	934	6

behalf

and also take vows on *b* of their candidates.	298	22
on *b* of the infants and younger children	302	—

behold

Revelation 21:2–7 (*B*, I make all things new)	475	—
Revelation 21:2–7 (*B*, I make all things new)	495	7

being

b things in their own nature indifferent,	9	16
this important work *b* brought to a conclusion,	11	16
lighted and while the hymn Phos hilaron is *b* sung.	143	20
(Propers 1 and 2 *b* used on the weekdays	158	17
and Propers 4 and 5 *b* used in Pentecost	158	20
conformed to the language of the Rite *b* used.	383	—
appropriate to the season or occasion *b* celebrated;	394	—
the particular occasion *b* celebrated;	402	—
the particular occasion *b* celebrated;	404	—
provision for the well-*b* of their families,	445	—
A homily may be preached, the people *b* seated.	480	—
recognized by the Church as *b* called by God	510	16
and while the new bishop is *b* clothed	553	2
This order is for use when a priest is *b* instituted	558	2
In the bishop's absence, a priest *b* inducted	558	9
A lay person *b* instituted should read	558	23
and the authority *b* conferred.	565	3
When a new church is *b* consecrated,	575	15
the Latin form "Alleluia," as *b* more appropriate	584	6
natures *b* in no way annulled by the union,	864	13
each nature *b* preserved and coming together to form	864	14
b both God and Man.	869	9
b such as have grown partly of the corrupt	872	34
finally, *b* found guilty, by just judgment be deposed.	873	12
and as *b* the rule and ultimate standard of faith.	877	34

Bel
Of *B* and the Dragon, 869 3

belief
but is not meant to be a complete statement of *b* 844 4

believe
the Declaration "I do *b* the Holy Scriptures..." 552 8
that he also *b* rightly the Incarnation 865 19
For the right Faith is, that we *b* and confess, 865 21
which except a man *b* faithfully, 865 39
no condemnation for them that *b* and are baptized; 869 31
2. That we *b* that all who have been duly baptized 876 31
which principles we *b* to be the substantial deposit 877 7

believed
so also is it to be *b*, that he went down into Hell. 868 10
it should be *b* as an article of the Faith, 868 22
ought thoroughly to be received and *b*: 869 17
any thing to be *b* for necessity of Salvation. 871 42

believes
John 5:24–27 (He who *b* has everlasting life) 495 —

believeth
John 5:24–27 (He that *b* hath everlasting life) 480 —

bells
B may now be rung and music played. 574 —

belong
b to Doctrine must be referred to Discipline; 9 6

below
and the final prayer *b*. 282 —

benefactors
architect, builders, musicians, artists, *b*, and friends. 566 18
b, donors, artists, artisans, and others. 576 21
7. Intercessions, including commemoration of *b* 578 3

benefit
be endued with so excellent a *b* of God, 871 6
common and equal *b* of all men. 877 11

benefits
prays that all may receive the *b* of Christ's work, 405 —
all the *b* of Communion are received, 457 —

bequests
not neglecting, if they are able, to leave *b* 445 —

bereaved
prayers for the deceased and the *b*. 492 —
3. Prayer may be offered for the *b*. 506 9

bereavement
55. For a Person in Trouble or *B* 812 6
55. For a Person in Trouble or *B* 831 —

besides
Voluntary Works *b*, over and above, God's Commandments, 870 19
so *b* the same ought it not to enforce 871 41

best
according to her *b* understanding, 10 10

better
as they shall judge the same to serve *b* to godliness. 874 14

between
keep the happy mean *b* too much stiffness in refusing, 9 25
with silence or singing *b* them. 143 26
serve for any weekdays *b* Holy Innocents' Day 161 —
serve for any weekdays *b* Holy Innocents' Day 213 —
b the Epiphany and the following Sunday. 214 —
celebrated at a convenient time *b* sunset 284 3
In the exchange *b* individuals 407 8
When the priest sees that there is hatred *b* members 409 17
a solemn and public covenant *b* a man and a woman 422 2
B the Readings, a Psalm, hymn, or anthem 426 —
sung responsively *b* a bishop and the congregation, 552 15
suggested in the lectionary for use *b* the Lessons 582 10
recitation is the verse-by-verse alternation *b* groups 582 13
e.g., *b* choir and congregation, 582 14
or *b* one side of the congregation and the other. 582 14
of chanting the psalms *b* the Lessons at the Eucharist, 582 25
who is the only Mediator *b* God and Man, 869 8
when the Psalm is sung *b* the Lessons 888 21

Bible
numeration of the Revised Standard Version of the *B*. 14 17
B Reading. 113 —
Tobit 8:5b–8 (New English *B*) 426 —
A *B* is presented with these words 521 —
The Bishop then gives a *B* to the newly ordained, 534 —
The Bishop gives a *B* to the newly ordained, 545 —
Following the presentation of the *B*, 553 5
and immediately before the *B* is presented. 553 23
A *B* is to be given to each new priest, 554 5
"Receive this *B*..." are to be said to each one. 554 6
and immediately before the *B* is given. 554 14
A *B* is to be given to each new deacon, 554 26
"Receive this *B*..." are also to be said to each one. 554 27
Representatives of the congregation present a *B*, 561 8
the *B* is brought forward and put 576 9
and *B* readings related to the particular occasion 577 12
that all the whole *B* (or the greatest part thereof) 866 8
when any book of the *B* was begun, 866 19
for their public service, but this book and the *B*: 867 6

Bibles
in printed *B*, after the invention of vowel points, 583 22

biblical
used with the Psalms and *b* Canticles. 141 10
non-*b* Christian literature may follow the *b* Readings. 142 14
be used with the Psalms and *b* Canticles. 935 9

bidding
either at the *b*, or in the course of the prayer; 142 9
or this *b* 344 4
or this *b* 377 4
In the course of the silence after each *b*, 385 —
and *b* their prayers 492 —

biddings
In the *b* which follow, the indented petitions 277 —
The *b* may be read by a Deacon or other person 277 —

bind

as touching Ceremonies and Rites, do not *b* Christian	869	11

binds

(Love which *b* everything together in harmony)	426	—

birth

A Thanksgiving for the *B*	439	1
As soon as convenient after the *b* of a child,	439	3
For the *B* of a Child	440	—
such as Thanksgiving for the *B* or Adoption	576	16
IX. Of Original or *B*-Sin.	869	22
a sign of Regeneration or New-*B*,	873	16

birthday

50. For a *B*	812	1
51. For a *B*	812	2
50. For a *B*	830	—
51. For a *B*	830	—

bishop

subject to the direction of the *b*,	13	9
the *b* may set forth such forms	13	14
worship in a Christian assembly is normally a *b*	13	20
(when a *b* or priest is not present)	13	23
the *b* may, at discretion, authorize a deacon to preside	13	26
With the express permission of the *b*,	16	19
The *b*, when present, appropriately concludes	36	6
The *b*, when present, appropriately concludes	74	5
The *b*, when present, should give	108	9
A *b* or priest may use the following	114	—
The *B*, if present, or the Priest, stands and,	269	—
In the absence of a *b* or priest,	269	—
In the absence of a *b* or priest,	272	—
In the absence of a *b* or priest,	282	—
The *b*, when present, is the chief celebrant,	284	12
In the absence of a *b*, a priest presides at the service.	284	16
In the absence of a *b* or priest, a deacon	284	23
with the authorization of the *b*, officiate	284	28
The *b*, when present, is the celebrant;	298	7
At Baptism, the *b* officiates at the Presentation	298	8
In the absence of a *b*, a priest is the celebrant	298	13
been previously consecrated by the *b*.	298	15
When there are others to be presented, the *B* says	303	—
The *B* asks the candidates	303	—
B	303	—
The *B* may then consecrate oil of Chrism,	307	—
the *B* or Priest, at a place in full sight	308	—
Then the *B* or Priest places a hand	308	—
The *B* says to the congregation	309	—
Then the *B* says	309	—
The *B* lays hands upon each one and says	309	—
Then the *B* says	310	—
B	310	—
Offertory of the Eucharist, at which the *B*,	310	—
reserved for these occasions or when a *b* is present.	312	6
on any one of the above-named days the ministry of a *b*	312	8
cannot be obtained, the *b* may specially authorize a	312	9
subsequent occasion of public baptism at which a *b*	312	13
When a *b* is present, or on other occasions	312	20
at a public celebration of the Sacrament with a *b*	314	6
The *B* when present, or the Priest, stands and says	321	—
It is the *b*'s prerogative, when present,	322	2
whether *b* or priest, be assisted by other priests,	322	5
The *B* when present, or the Priest, stands and says	332	—
The Celebrant, whether *b* or priest,	333	—
The *B* when present, or the Priest, gives the blessing	339	—
The Celebrant, whether *b* or priest,	340	—
The *B* when present, or the Priest, stands and says	353	—
It is the *b*'s prerogative, when present,	354	2
whether *b* or priest, be assisted by other priests,	354	5
The *B* when present, or the Priest, stands and says	360	—
The Celebrant, whether *b* or priest,	361	—
The *B* when present, or the Priest, may bless	366	—
The Celebrant, whether *b* or priest,	367	—
The Celebrant, whether *b* or priest, faces them	369	—
The Celebrant, whether *b* or priest,	372	—
in a manner approved by the *b*.	408	2
lay persons licensed by the *b*	408	7
services of a priest cannot be obtained, the *b* may,	408	17
the priest is required to notify the *b*,	409	24
receive the laying on of hands by the *b*.	412	6
laying on of hands by a *b*,	412	8
of a *b* and to receive the laying on of hands.	412	10
The people standing, the *B* says	413	—
B	413	—
The *B* then continues	413	—
B	413	—
B	413	—
B	413	—
At the discretion of the *b*,	414	—
The *B* says	415	—
The *B* asks the candidates	415	—
B	415	—
the *B* addresses the congregation, saying	416	—
The *B* then says these or similar words	416	—
B	416	—
B	417	—
The *B* then says to the congregation	417	—
Then the *B* says	418	—
The *B* lays hands upon each one and says	418	—
The *B* concludes with this prayer	419	—
B	419	—
at which the *B* should be the principal celebrant.	419	—
and such other devotions as the *B* may direct.	419	—
The *B* may consecrate oil of Chrism	419	—
A priest or a *b* normally presides at the Celebration	422	7
When both a *b* and a priest are present and officiating,	422	10
the *b* should pronounce the blessing	422	10
and no priest or *b* is available, a deacon may use	422	16
Normally, the celebrant is a priest or *b*.	435	4
when no priest or *b* is available, a deacon may	435	5
7. A priest or *b* pronounces a solemn blessing	436	9
may be pronounced only by a *b* or priest.	446	12
using oil blessed by a *b* or priest.	456	—
It is appropriate that the *b*,	468	13
The Celebrant, or the *B* if present, may then bless	483	—
It is appropriate that the *b*,	490	13
The Celebrant, or the *B* if present, may then bless	500	—
exercise the offices of *b*, priest, or deacon	510	22
suitable for the conferring of the sacred orders of *b*,	510	31
Ordination of a *B*	511	2
When a *b* is to be ordained,	511	6

bishop

the Presiding *B* of the Church,	511	6
or a *b* appointed by the Presiding *B*, presides	511	7
for which the new *b* is to be consecrated,	511	10
The *b*-elect is vested in a rochet or alb,	511	16
When the *b*-elect is presented, his full name	511	18
The Ordination of a *B*	512	—
The people standing, the *B* appointed says	512	—
B	512	—
The *B* then says	512	—
standing before the Presiding *B*, present	513	—
present the *b*-elect, saying	513	—
The Presiding *B* then directs that testimonials	513	—
the Presiding *B* requires	513	—
the following promise from the *B*-elect	513	—
The *B*-elect then signs the above Declaration	513	—
The Presiding *B* then says the following,	513	—
If no objection is made, the Presiding *B* continues	514	—
Presiding *B*	514	—
The Presiding *B* then says	514	—
Presiding *B* stands and reads the Collect for the Day,	515	—
B may select Readings from the Proper of the Day.	515	—
All now sit, except the *b*-elect, who stands	517	—
Presiding *B* addresses the *b*-elect	517	—
questions are then addressed to the *b*-elect	517	—
B	518	—
The Presiding *B* then says	519	—
B-elect	519	—
The Consecration of the *B*	520	—
All continue to stand, except the *b*-elect, who kneels	520	—
who kneels before the Presiding *B*.	520	—
stand to the right and left of the Presiding *B*.	520	—
The Presiding *B* then begins this Prayer	520	—
The Presiding *B* and other *B*s now lay their hands	521	—
upon the head of the *b*-elect, and say together	521	—
The Presiding *B* continues	521	—
The new *b* is now vested according to the order	521	—
The Presiding *B* presents to the people their new *b*.	522	—
The new *B* then says	522	—
The Presiding *B* and other Bishops greet the new *b*.	522	—
The new *B* also greets other members of the clergy,	522	—
The new *B*, if the *B* of the Diocese, may now	522	—
Then the new *B* goes to the Lord's Table	522	—
The new *B* blesses the people, first saying	523	—
New *B*	523	—
When a *b* is to confer Holy Orders,	524	2
the service until the Offertory, the *b* presides	524	4
Altar with the *b*, as associates and fellow ministers	524	15
and communicate with the *b*.	524	16
The people standing, the *B* says	525	—
B	525	—
The *b* and people sit.	526	—
presenters if desired, standing before the *b*, present	526	—
B	526	—
The *B* says to the ordinand	526	—
The *B* says to the people	527	—
If no objection is made, the *B* continues	527	—
B	527	—
The *B* then calls the people to prayer	527	—
B stands and reads the Collect for the Day,	527	—
or on a Sunday, the *B* may select Readings	528	—
seated except the ordinand, who stands before the *B*.	531	—
The *B* addresses the ordinand as follows	531	—
B	531	—
B	532	—
stand except the ordinand, who kneels facing the *B*	533	—
presbyters who stand to the right and left of the *B*.	533	—
The *B* then says this Prayer of Consecration.	533	—
Here the *B* lays hands upon the head of the ordinand,	533	—
At the same time the *B* prays	533	—
The *B* then continues	534	—
The *B* then gives a Bible to the newly ordained,	534	—
The *B* greets the newly ordained.	534	—
Standing at the Lord's Table, with the *B*	535	—
The *B* then asks the new priest to bless the people.	535	—
When a *b* is to confer Holy Orders,	536	2
the service until the Offertory, the *b* presides	536	4
The people standing, the *B* says	537	—
B	537	—
The *b* and people sit.	538	—
presenters if desired, standing before the *b*, present	538	—
B	538	—
The *B* says to the ordinand	538	—
The *B* says to the people	539	—
If no objection is made, the *B* continues	539	—
B	539	—
The *B* then calls the people to prayer	539	—
B stands and reads the Collect for the Day,	539	—
or on a Sunday, the *B* may select Readings	540	—
seated except the ordinand, who stands before the *B*.	543	—
The *B* addresses the ordinand as follows	543	—
B	543	—
B	544	—
stand except the ordinand, who kneels facing the *b*.	544	—
The *B* then says this Prayer of Consecration	545	—
Here the *B* lays hands upon the head of the ordinand,	545	—
The *B* then continues	545	—
The *B* gives a Bible to the newly ordained, saying	545	—
The *B* then says to the congregation	546	—
The *B* and the Clergy present now greet	546	—
The *B* goes to the Table and begins	546	—
The *B* blesses the people,	547	—
At ordinations, the *B* who is presiding stands and says	551	—
B	551	—
The *B* says the appointed Collect.	551	—
sung responsively between a *b* and the congregation,	552	15
At the Ordination of a *B*	553	1
and while the new *b* is being clothed	553	2
with the new *b* at the Altar as fellow ministers	553	10
The newly ordained *b*, assisted by other ministers,	553	11
or in succession, as the *b* may direct.	553	26
Consecration, the *b* and priests lay their hands	553	30
the *b* alone says over each ordinand	553	32
the *b* continues "May they exalt you, O Lord,	554	3
the *b* and other priests at the Altar	554	8
or in succession, as the *b* may direct.	554	16
During the Prayer of Consecration the *B* is to lay hands	554	20
the *b* continues, "Make them, O Lord,	554	24
One, appointed by the *b*, is to say the dismissal.	554	30
together with your *B* and fellow-Presbyters	557	3
a priest of this Diocese, in communion with your *B*.	557	9
B of __________.	557	21
The chief minister is normally the *b*;	558	7
The *b*, when present, is the chief celebrant	558	8

In the *b*'s absence, a priest being inducted	558	9
Wardens, standing before the *b* with the new minister,	559	—
The *B* may read the Letter of Institution,	559	—
The *B* then says	559	—
The *B* then addresses the congregation	559	—
The *B*, standing, says	560	—
At the end of the litany, the *B*, standing, says	560	—
B	560	—
before the *b* with the new minister.	561	—
In the absence of the *b*, the deputy substitutes	561	—
The *B* presents a vessel of water, saying	561	—
The *B* then says	562	—
The *B* then presents the new minister	563	—
The *B* greets the new minister.	563	—
The *B*, or in the *B*'s absence a Priest	563	—
the *B* leads the people in the following prayer;	564	5
A newly inducted Priest may, at the *b*'s request,	564	10
b and other ministers may be clearly seen and heard	564	16
Its wording may be altered by the *b*	565	1
the *b* may state briefly the nature	565	2
The new minister is normally presented to the *b*	565	4
but the *b* always stands for the salutation	565	6
The sermon may be preached by the *b*,	565	16
the *b*, or other persons present, may speak	565	19
The *b* presides.	566	13
the clergy and people gather with the *b*	567	—
When all are ready, the *B* says the following	567	—
Standing at the door of the church, the *B* says	568	—
With the pastoral staff the *B* marks	568	—
The congregation standing, the *B* begins the Prayer	568	—
B	568	—
The *B* concludes	569	—
B	569	—
The *B* moves to the Font, lays a hand upon it,	569	—
the *B* says	570	—
B	570	—
Facing the Font, the *B* says	570	—
The *B* proceeds to the Lectern, lays a hand upon it,	570	—
The *B* goes to the Pulpit, lays a hand upon it,	571	—
B proceeds to an appropriate place, and says	572	—
After a period of silence, the *B* concludes	572	—
The *B* then says	573	—
The *B* goes to the Table and, with arms extended,	573	—
The *B* lays a hand upon the Table, and continues	573	—
The *B* says to the people	574	—
Then the *b* and other clergy and the people greet	574	—
The *b*, or a priest appointed, is the chief celebrant.	574	—
After the postcommunion prayer, the *B* blesses	574	—
but the *b*, other clergy, and attendants will enter	575	13
The cross signed on the threshold by the *b*	575	20
the *b* may consecrate oil of Chrism,	575	26
The *b* may respond, indicating the place	576	13
Suitable portions of this service may be used by the *b*,	577	4
with the *b*'s permission, for dedicating	577	5
used by the *b* or a priest for blessing alterations,	577	9
should always be done by a *b*,	577	16
The blessing of an Altar is also reserved for a *b*,	577	18
13. For the Election of a *B* or other Minister	810	19
13. For the Election of a *B* or other Minister	818	—
always resort to the *B* of the Diocese,	867	20
The *B* of Rome hath no jurisdiction in this Realm	876	7

bishops

By the *B*, the Clergy, and the Laity	8	3
each order within the Church, lay persons, *b*,	13	17
The *b*, priests, and deacons at the Holy Table	407	23
First, there is the order of *b* who carry	510	6
Together with the *b*, they take part	510	9
assist *b* and priests in all of this work.	510	13
by *b* who are themselves duly qualified to confer	510	24
the *b* be ordained on Sundays and other feasts	511	4
At least two other *b* serve as co-consecrators.	511	8
The other *b*, or a convenient number of them,	511	14
during the entrance of the *b* and other ministers.	512	—
The *b* and people sit.	513	—
except the bishop-elect, who stands facing the *b*.	517	—
by one or more of the other *b*	517	—
The other *b* stand to the right and left	520	—
The Presiding Bishop and other *B* now lay their hands	521	—
new bishop is now vested according to the order of *b*.	521	—
and other *B* greet the new bishop.	522	—
joined by other *b* and presbyters, proceeds	522	—
one of the *b* leads the people in the following	522	—
it is appropriate that some of the consecrating *b*,	553	9
The *b* who are present are not to depart without signing	553	16
As established by the *B*, the Clergy, and the Laity	867	30
B, Priests, and Deacons, are not commanded	874	12
XXXVI. Of Consecration of *B* and Ministers.	875	20
The Book of Consecration of *B*,	875	21
Archbishops and *B*, and Ordering of Priests	875	27
Adopted by the House of *B*	876	23
We, *B* of the Protestant Episcopal Church	876	25
assembled as *B* in the Church of God, do hereby	876	26
the Quadrilateral was adopted by the House of *B*,	877	26

blasphemous

pain or guilt, were *b* fables, and dangerous deceits.	874	10

bless

The Bishop when present, or the Priest, may *b*	366	—
The Celebrant may then *b* the family	445	—
or the Bishop if present, may then *b* the people,	483	—
or the Bishop if present, may then *b* the people,	500	—
The Bishop then asks the new priest to *b* the people.	535	—

blessed

It is a most invaluable part of that *b* "liberty	9	2
for the sake of Jesus Christ, our *b* Lord and Saviour.	11	22
If a ring or rings are to be *b*, the wife extends	434	—
If oil for the Anointing of the Sick is to be *b*,	455	—
using oil *b* by a bishop or priest.	456	—
took Man's nature in the womb of the *b* Virgin,	868	4

blesses

The Celebrant *b* the water, first saying	306	—
The new Bishop *b* the people, first saying	523	—
The Bishop *b* the people,	547	—
the Bishop *b* the people;	574	—

blessing

appropriately concludes the Office with a *b*.	36	7
appropriately concludes the Office with a *b*.	74	6
and the *B* or Dismissal at the end.	108	9
The bishop, when present, should give the *B*.	108	10

followed by the Lord's Prayer and a grace or *b*; 112 —
B or Dismissal, or both. 113 —
may precede the *B* or Dismissal. 113 —
priest may use the following or some other *b* 114 —
A deacon or lay person using the preceding *b* 114 —
sung immediately before the *B* or Dismissal. 143 30
When a meal is to follow, a *b* over food may serve 143 31
or after the prayer of *b*. 270 —
The Celebrant then says the following *b* 271 —
No *b* or dismissal is added. 282 —
and the Grace or a *b*. 321 —
The Bishop when present, or the Priest, gives the *b* 339 —
and the Grace or a *b*. 353 —
The service concludes with a *b* or with a dismissal 399 —
and with either the Grace or a *b*, 407 3
except for the *b*, may be said by a deacon, 407 6
a bishop normally presides at the Celebration and *B* 422 7
the function of pronouncing the nuptial *b*, 422 9
pronounce the *b* and preside at the Eucharist. 422 11
omitting the nuptial *b* which follows The Prayers. 422 17
B of a Marriage 423 —
The Priest may ask God's *b* on a ring or rings 427 —
The *B* of the Marriage 430 —
husband and wife still kneeling, the Priest adds this *b* 431 —
The *B* 433 —
but does not pronounce a nuptial *b*. 435 6
7. A priest or bishop pronounces a solemn *b* 436 9
The Celebration and *B* of a Marriage may be used 437 5
or for the *B* of the Marriage. 437 16
The service concludes with a *b* or with a dismissal 457 —
the service continues with the [*b* and] 482 —
the service continues with the [*b* and] 499 —
such *b* is to take place at some convenient time 552 17
After the pontifical *b* and the dismissal, 553 14
at the bishop's request, pronounce a *b*. 564 11
Christian Service, or *B* of Oil for the Sick. 576 17
used by the bishop or a priest for *b* alterations, 577 9
The *b* of a new font or baptistry should always be done 577 15
The *b* of an Altar is also reserved for a bishop, 577 18
and likewise the Cup of *B* is a partaking 873 26
a *b* might happily be brought to pass. 877 24
may be by God's *b* made towards Home Reunion: 877 32

blessings

prayers of thanksgiving for the *b* of the day, 140 —

blood

The Body and *B* of the Lord are shared 401 13
partaking of the *B* of Christ. 873 27
the Sacrament of the Body and *B* of Christ; 873 38
Body and *B* of Christ. 875 7

blueprint

Such things as the deed for the property and the *b* 575 17

boast

as certain Anabaptists do falsely *b*. 876 14

bodies

for regular worship by other Christian *b*, 577 2
At whose coming all men shall rise again with their *b* 865 35
Christian *B* seeking the restoration of the organic unity 877 23

body

yet so as that the main *b* and essential parts 10 5
the Holy Spirit into Christ's *B* the Church. 298 3
The *B* and Blood of the Lord are shared 401 13
For Health of *B* and Soul 460 —
Reception of the *B* 466 —
form may be used at whatever time the *b* is brought 466 —
The Celebrant meets the *b* at the door of the church 466 —
the *b* is then brought into the church, 467 —
It is customary that the celebrant meet the *b* 468 21
sung or said as the *b* is borne into the church, 468 23
If the *b* is not present, the service continues 482 —
and other ministers take their places at the *b*. 482 —
The Celebrant, facing the *b*, says 483 —
As the *b* is borne from the church, 483 —
It is customary that the celebrant meet the *b* 490 21
sung or said as the *b* is borne into the church, 490 23
(The imperishable *b*) 495 —
If the *b* is not present, the service continues 499 —
and other ministers take their places at the *b*. 499 —
The Celebrant, facing the *b*, says 499 —
As the *b* is borne from the church, 500 —
1. The *b* is received. 506 4
The celebrant may meet the *b* and conduct it 506 4
and the *b* is committed to its resting place. 506 18
The Psalter is a *b* of liturgical poetry. 582 2
consisting also of a reasonable soul and *b*; 864 6
everlasting, without *b*, parts, or passions; 867 35
did truly rise again from death, and took again his *b*, 868 13
which we break is a partaking of the *B* of Christ; 873 26
The *B* of Christ is given, taken, and eaten, 873 31
And the mean whereby the *B* of Christ is received 873 32
XXIX. Of the Wicked, which eat not the *B* of Christ 873 36
the Sacrament of the *B* and Blood of Christ; 873 38
B and Blood of Christ. 875 7
to heal the wounds of the *B* of Christ, 877 3

bond

The *b* which God establishes in Baptism 298 3

bones

The valley of dry *b* 291 —
and took again his body, with flesh, *b*, 868 13

bonus

73 Quam *b* Israel! 687 —

book

The *B* of Common Prayer (1789) 8 2
set forth A *B* of Common Prayer, 8 7
do hereby establish the said *B*: 8 9
And this *B* shall be in use 8 11
in the Preface of her *B* of Common Prayer, 9 14
upon a comparison of this with the *B* of Common 11 11
set forth in this *B*, are the regular services 13 5
these services and the other rites contained in the *B*, 13 7
special devotions taken from this *B*, 13 10
no service or prayer has been provided in this *B*, 13 14
and in other services contained in this *B* 14 4
Hymns referred to in the rubrics of this *B* 14 6
or from this *B*, or from texts congruent with them. 14 8
of the corresponding texts in this *B*. 14 15
Scriptural citations in this *B*, except for the Psalms, 14 16

for which no Proper is provided in this *B* 195 —
for which no Proper is provided in this *B* 246 —
read from a *b* or books of appropriate size 406 20
as provided on page 423 of this *B*, 435 3
Rite One or Rite Two in this *B*, 436 15
neither of the burial rites in this *B* 506 2
Others present a *b* of prayers or other symbol, saying 561 —
the classical English versions, the Prayer *B* 583 26
B One 585 —
B Two 643 —
B Three 687 —
B Four 717 —
B Five 746 —
for an inquiring stranger who picks up a Prayer *B*. 844 8
The First *B* of Common Prayer (1549) 866 2
that commonly when any *b* of the Bible was begun, 866 18
in this sort the *b* of Isaiah was begun in Advent, 866 20
and the *b* of Genesis in Septuagesima; 866 20
that to turn the *B* only, was so hard 866 31
for their public service, but this *b* and the Bible: 867 6
because that all things must be read upon the *b*, 867 12
which daily they shall obtain by reading upon the *b*, 867 14
the things contained in this *b*: 867 19
not contrary to any thing contained in this *b*. 867 22
The First *B* of Samuel, 868 26
The *B* of Esther, 868 26
The Second *B* of Samuel, 868 27
The *B* of Job, 868 27
The First *B* of Kings, 868 28
The Second *B* of Kings, 868 29
The First *B* of Chronicles, 868 30
The Second *B* of Chronicles, 868 31
The First *B* of Esdras, 868 32
The Second *B* of Esdras, 868 33
The Third *B* of Esdras, 868 37
The rest of the *B* of Esther, 868 37
The Fourth *B* of Esdras, 868 38
The *B* of Wisdom, 868 38
The *B* of Tobias, 868 39
The *B* of Judith, 868 40
The First *B* of Maccabees, 869 2
The Second *B* of Maccabees. 869 3
The Second *B* of Homilies, 874 35
as doth the former *B* of Homilies, 874 37
The *B* of Consecration of Bishops, and Ordering 875 21
"The *B* of Consecration of Archbishops and Bishops, 875 26
ordered according to the Rites of that *B*, 875 31

books

read from a book or *b* of appropriate size and dignity. 406 20
other *b* of holy Scripture used. 866 22
need none other *b* for their public service, 867 6
the people shall not be at so great charge for *b*, 867 7
those canonical *B* of the Old and New Testament, 868 23
Of the Names and Number of the Canonical *B*. 868 25
And the other *B* (as Hierome saith) the Church 868 34
All the *B* of the New Testament, 869 4
so far as it declares the *B* of Homilies to be an explication 875 14

born

of the Substance of his Mother, *b* in the world; 865 23
and therefore in every person *b* into this world, 869 27
and *b* again in Christ, yet offend in many things; 870 29

borne

sung or said as the body is *b* into the church, 468 24
As the body is *b* from the church, 483 —
sung or said as the body is *b* into the church, 490 24
As the body is *b* from the church, 500 —

both

Before the close of the Office one or *b* 58 —
Before the close of the Office one or *b* 71 —
Before the close of the Office one or *b* 101 —
Silence, or a suitable Collect, or *b*, 113 —
Blessing or Dismissal, or *b*. 113 —
Before the close of the Office one or *b* 125 —
The ministers receive the Sacrament in *b* kinds, 338 —
The ministers receive the Sacrament in *b* kinds, 365 —
the celebrant receives the Sacrament in *b* kinds. 407 23
Sacrament may be received in *b* kinds simultaneously, 408 1
consecrate more of either or *b*, by saying 408 11
or else the celebrant may consecrate more of *b* kinds, 408 13
When *b* a bishop and a priest are present 422 10
Then one or *b* parents say these or similar words 441 —
Representatives of the diocese, *b* Priests and Lay 513 —
or the following Collect, or *b*, first saying 515 —
or *b*, first saying 527 —
either the Bread or the Wine, or *b*. 536 16
or *b*, first saying 539 —
If one reading stand is to serve as *b* lectern and pulpit, 576 6
himself to be *b* God and Lord, 865 6
for the understanding, *b* of the readers and hearers. 867 3
more commodious, *b* for the shortness thereof, 867 4
Preserver of all things *b* visible and invisible. 867 36
b in the Old and New Testament everlasting life is offered 869 7
being *b* God and Man. 869 9
clearly void, *b* in his flesh, and in his spirit. 870 26
use their Ministry, *b* in hearing the Word of God, 873 5
XXX. Of *b* Kinds. 874 1
for *b* the parts of the Lord's Sacrament, 874 2
the sins of the whole world, *b* original and actual; 874 7
If two Readings are desired at *b* Offices, 934 12

bound

man shall be *b* to the saying of them, 867 27
not only render unto God as much as they are *b* to do, 870 21

bounden

they do more for his sake, than of *b* duty is required: 870 22

bracketed

Psalter assigned to a given Office has been *b*, 935 4
use the *b* Psalms rather than the alternatives. 935 6

brackets

B and parentheses are used 935 1
(*b* in the case of whole Psalms, 935 1

branches

The *b* of palm or of other trees or shrubs 270 —
During the procession, all hold *b* in their hands, 271 —
among the divided *b* of Christendom, 877 13

bread

The oblations of *b* and wine at the baptismal 313 13
in the consecration of the gifts, in breaking the *B*, 322 8
placing on it the offerings of *b* and wine, 322 12
the congregation bring the people's offerings of *b* 333 —
At the following words concerning the *b*, 334 —
The Breaking of the *B* 337 —
The Celebrant breaks the consecrated *B*. 337 —
The *B* and the Cup are given to the communicants 338 —
the Celebrant consecrates additional *b* and wine, 338 —
At the following words concerning the *b*, 342 —
in the consecration of the gifts, in breaking the *B*, 354 8
placing on it the offerings of *b* and wine, 354 12
the congregation bring the people's offerings of *b* 361 —
At the following words concerning the *b*, 362 —
The Breaking of the *B* 364 —
The Celebrant breaks the consecrated *B*. 364 —
The *B* and the Cup are given to the communicants 365 —
the Celebrant consecrates additional *b* and wine, 365 —
At the following words concerning the *b*, 368 —
At the following words concerning the *b*, 371 —
At the following words concerning the *b*, 374 —
the *b*, the cup of wine, and other offerings, 401 5
Break the *B* 401 11
At the following words concerning the *b*, 403 —
At the following words concerning the *b*, 405 —
preparing and placing upon it the *b* and cup of wine. 407 —
chalices may be filled after the Breaking of the *B*. 407 20
anthem may be used at the Breaking of the *B*: 407 21
receive the consecrated *B* and Wine separately. 407 26
the celebrant to administer the consecrated *B* 408 4
may administer the *B* and others the Wine. 408 6
If the consecrated *B* or Wine does not suffice 408 9
3. And then, omitting the breaking of the *B*, 408 25
If any of the consecrated *B* or Wine remain, 408 28
It is appropriate that the oblations of *b* and wine 412 16
couple may present the offerings of *b* and wine. 432 —
At the Offertory, it is desirable that the *b* and wine 438 1
John 6:47–51 (I am the *b* of life) 454 12
sick person cannot receive either the consecrated *B* 457 —
physical disability, is unable to eat and drink the *B* 457 —
At the Offertory, it is appropriate that the *b* 511 21
At the Offertory, it is appropriate that the *b* 524 12
in the Breaking of the *B*. 535 —
At the Offertory, it is appropriate that the *b* 536 12
ministering either the *B* or the Wine, 536 15
The newly ordained Deacon prepares the *b*, 546 —
Similarly, all the new priests break the consecrated *B* 554 9
Other Representatives of the congregation present *b* 562 —
b and wine may be used in the Eucharist 565 23
worthily, and with faith, receive the same, the *B* 873 25
Transubstantiation (or the change of the substance of *B* 873 28

break

B the Bread 401 11
all the new priests *b* the consecrated Bread 554 9
as did *b* the continual course of the reading 866 38
which we *b* is a partaking of the Body of Christ; 873 26
willingly and purposely, doth openly *b* the Traditions 874 25

breaking

join in the consecration of the gifts, in *b* the Bread, 322 8
The *B* of the Bread 337 —
join in the consecration of the gifts, in *b* the Bread, 354 8
The *B* of the Bread 364 —
chalices may be filled after the *B* of the Bread. 407 20
anthem may be used at the *B* of the Bread: 407 21
3. And then, omitting the *b* of the Bread, 408 25
and in the *B* of the Bread. 535 —
b one piece thereof from another. 866 37

breaks

The Celebrant *b* the consecrated Bread. 337 —
The Celebrant *b* the consecrated Bread. 364 —

brethren

woundeth the consciences of the weak *b*. 874 30

brief

or a *b* silence, may follow the Reading. 113 —
After a *b* silence, the Celebrant concludes 579 —
use of this catechism is to provide a *b* summary 844 7

briefer

When desired, a *b* form of this service may be used, 439 10

briefly

After the Reading, the Celebrant may comment on it *b*. 397 —
formularies and canons of this Church, is *b* stated. 435 12
After any Reading, the Celebrant may comment on it *b*. 454 13
acknowledging *b* the purpose of their gathering, 492 —
bishop may state *b* the nature of the person's office 565 2

bring

the congregation *b* the people's offerings 333 —
the congregation *b* the people's offerings 361 —
or other lay persons, *b* them forward 576 23
and to *b* them by Christ to everlasting salvation, 871 4

brings

b deep sorrow when we are parted 507 11

broken

and must under no circumstances be *b*. 446 28
b, and neglected, by planting in uncertain stories, 866 17

brotherly

to enter into *b* conference with all 877 22

brought

this important work being *b* to a conclusion, 11 16
a wooden cross may now be *b* into the church 281 —
form may be used at whatever time the body is *b* 466 —
the body is then *b* into the church, 467 —
it is appropriate that the bread and wine be *b* 511 21
it is appropriate that the bread and wine be *b* 524 12
it is appropriate that the bread and wine be *b* 536 12
dedication of the lectern, the Bible is *b* forward 576 9
a blessing might happily be *b* to pass. 877 25

builders

b, musicians, artists, benefactors, and friends. 566 18

building

When a confession is heard in a church *b*, 446 15
for dedicating parts of a *b*, or furnishings, 566 4
dedicating a chapel or an oratory within another *b*. 566 6
the *b* is ready for regular use as a place of worship. 566 10
The service does not preclude the use of the *b* 566 11
place of worship, or in some other *b*. 575 7
may go around the *b*(s) to be dedicated 575 8
and decorations be carried into the *b* 575 16
the *b*(s), the keys, and tools used in its construction 575 18

buildings

When *b* have been used for public worship 577 21

built

(Like a wise man who *b* his house upon the rock) 426 —

burial

the Collects appointed for use at the *B* of the Dead 202 —
the forms appointed for the *B* of the Dead 202 —
the Collects appointed for use at the *B* of the Dead 253 —
the forms appointed for the *B* of the Dead 253 —
(such as those in the *B* service) may be used. 465 —
If the *B* service is not to follow immediately, 467 —
When the order for the *B* of the Dead follows 467 —
At the *b* of a child, the passages from Lamentations, 468 19
The *B* of the Dead: 469 —
At the *B* of an Adult 470 —
At the *B* of a Child 470 —
not previously been set apart for Christian *b*, 487 —
At the *b* of a child, the passages from Lamentations, 490 19
The *B* of the Dead: 491 —
At the *B* of an Adult 493 —
At the *B* of a Child 494 —
not previously been set apart for Christian *b*, 503 —
An Order for *B* 506 1
neither of the *b* rites in this Book 506 2

buried

Baptized Christians are properly *b* from the church. 468 5
Baptized Christians are properly *b* from the church. 490 5
suffered, was crucified, dead, and *b*, 868 7
As Christ died for us, and was *b*; 868 10

burn

It is customary that the Paschal Candle *b* 287 —

burning

the Paschal Candle, if used, should be *b* 143 3

business

there was more *b* to find out 866 31

C

calendar

The *C* 15 1
Feasts appointed on fixed days in the *C*, 16 12
Feasts appointed on fixed days in the *C* 17 10
Commemorations listed in the *C* 18 3
determined by the *c* date of that Sunday. 158 11
the *c* date of which falls on that Sunday, 158 14
precedence set forth in the C of the Church Year. 195 —
a) at the commemoration of a saint listed in the C 195 —
a saint not listed in the C. 195 —
set forth in the C of the Church Year. 199 —
precedence set forth in the C of the Church Year. 246 —
a) at the commemoration of a saint listed in the C 246 —
a saint not listed in the C. 246 —
set forth in the C of the Church Year. 251 —

call

which they *c* Works of Supererogation, 870 19
to *c* and send Ministers into the Lord's vineyard. 872 19

called

commonly *c* godparents, present their candidates, 298 21
c by God to the ordained ministry 510 17
Presbyter of the Church of God, you have been *c* 557 2
or with a refrain (*c* the antiphon) recited 582 16
commonly *c* the Catechism 845 —
commonly *c* The Creed of Saint Athanasius 864 20
prayers in the Church, commonly *c* Divine Service: 866 5
whereof every one was *c* a nocturn, 866 28
hardness of the Rules *c* the Pie, 866 30
the Commandments which are *c* Moral. 869 14
and that which is commonly *c* the Apostles' Creed, 869 16
and that which is commonly *c* the Apostles' Creed 869 21
the lust of the flesh, *c* in Greek 869 29
be *c* accordingly to God's purpose 871 6
before he be lawfully *c*, and sent to execute 872 17
And those we ought to judge lawfully *c* and sent, 872 18
Those five commonly *c* Sacraments, that is to say, 872 32
and peoples *c* of God into the unity of His Church. 877 19
and peoples *c* of God into the Unity of His Church. 878 5

calling

strength and good works, to faith, and *c* upon God. 869 35
they through Grace obey the *c*: 871 7

calls

The Bishop then *c* the people to prayer 527 —
The Bishop then *c* the people to prayer 539 —

came

He *c* to be the Lamb without spot, 870 26

candid

and every sincere Christian, with a meek, *c*, 11 18

candidate

Each *c* for Holy Baptism is to be sponsored 298 16
The Celebrant asks each *c* when presented 301 —
C 301 —
C 303 —
Each *c* is presented by name to the Celebrant, 307 —
or pours water upon, the *c*, saying 307 —
C 415 —

candidates

(beginning with the Presentation of the C), 175 —
(beginning with the Presentation of the C), 227 —
(beginning with the Presentation of the C, 292 —
In the absence of *c* for Baptism or Confirmation, 292 —
the Presentation and Examination of the C; 298 9

Sponsors of adults and older children present their *c*	298	18
thereby signify their endorsement of the *c*	298	19
commonly called godparents, present their *c*,	298	21
take vows on behalf of their *c*.	298	23
Presentation and Examination of the C	301	—
The *c* who are able to answer for themselves	301	—
Then the *c* unable to answer for themselves	301	—
the Celebrant asks the following questions of the *c*	302	—
The Bishop asks the *c*	303	—
Prayers for the C	305	—
When this action has been completed for all *c*,	308	—
the deacon omits the prayer over the *c*,	312	11
listed above there are no *c* for Baptism,	312	15
Presentation of the C does not take place at the font,	312	28
the ministers, *c*, and sponsors go to the font	312	29
Presentation and Examination of the C	415	—
The Bishop asks the *c*	415	—
Prayers for the C	417	—
beginning with the Presentation of the C,	575	30

candle

Lighting of the Paschal C.	108	13
During the *c*-lighting, an appropriate anthem	112	—
the Paschal C, if used, should be burning	143	3
the flame may be taken from the Paschal C.	143	11
the *c* or candles carried in at the beginning	143	12
a deacon to carry the Paschal C to its place,	284	17
The Lighting of the Paschal C	285	—
Paschal C is then lighted from the newly kindled fire,	285	—
(the Celebrant if there is no deacon) bearing the C,	285	—
lighted from the Paschal C at this time.	286	—
The Paschal C is placed in its stand.	286	—
Deacon, or other person appointed, standing near the C,	286	—
It is customary that the Paschal C burn at all services	287	—
may now be lighted from the Paschal C.	294	—
a *c* (which may be lighted from the Paschal C)	313	7
the congregation bearing the lighted Paschal C	467	—

candles

The *c* at the Altar are now lighted, as are other *c* and lamps	112	—
one or two lighted *c* may be carried before them,	142	28
For the lighting of the *c* at the Altar and elsewhere,	143	10
the candle or *c* carried in at the beginning	143	12
and other *c* may be lighted from them.	143	13
On special occasions, lighted *c* may be distributed	143	15
c may be lighted at the dining table,	143	17
it is appropriate after the *c* have been lighted	143	19
If *c* have been distributed to members	286	—
Other *c* and lamps in the church,	286	—
The *c* at the Altar may now be lighted	294	—
place the vessels on it, and light the *c*.	574	—
members of the congregation with flowers, *c*,	576	2

canon

according to the *c* may administer the Chalice.	408	8

canonical

and other priests having similar *c* charge.	565	26
we do understand those *c* Books	868	23
Of the Names and Number of the C Books.	868	25
we do receive, and account them C.	869	5

canons

to the laws of the State and the *c* of this Church.	422	6
The laws of the State and the *c* of this Church	435	7
declared in the formularies and *c* of this Church,	435	12
in accordance with the C, you have been selected	557	5
installation of deans and *c* of cathedrals,	558	4
clergy of the diocese present the Constitution and C	562	—

canticle

read after the second C.	47	—
This C may be shortened by omitting section II or III	47	—
read after the second C.	65	—
read after the second C.	84	—
One or more sections of this C may be used.	88	—
C.	113	—
The Magnificat or other *c*, or some other hymn	113	—
read after the second C.	119	—
A hymn or *c* may be used;	137	—
and may be used after the Invitatory Psalm or the C	141	12
in place of a C, a hymn may be sung.	142	1
followed by a Psalm, C, or hymn.	175	—
followed by a Psalm, C, or hymn.	227	—
After each Lesson, the Psalm or C listed,	288	—
some other suitable psalm, *c*, or hymn may be sung.	288	—
C 8, The Song of Moses	289	—
C 9, The First Song of Isaiah, or Psalm 42:1–7	290	—
Psalm 42:1–7, or C 9, The First Song of Isaiah	290	—
C the Celebrant may say to the people	294	—
After the Old Testament Lesson, a suitable *c*	470	—
After the New Testament Lesson, a suitable *c*	475	—
A suitable psalm, hymn, or *c* may follow.	494	—
A suitable psalm, hymn, or *c* may follow.	495	—
A Psalm, *c*, or hymn follows each Reading.	516	—
A Psalm, *c*, or hymn follows each Reading.	529	—
A Psalm, *c*, or hymn follows each Reading.	541	—
construction occurs in the C, "The Song of Moses."	584	3
at the beginning and end of each Psalm or C,	935	10

canticles

One of the following C,	47	—
or one of those on pages 85–95 (C 8–21),	47	—
One of the following C,	65	—
One of the following C,	84	—
or one of those on pages 47–52 (C 1–7),	84	—
One of the following C,	119	—
used with the Psalms and biblical C.	141	10
the conclusion of certain C may be omitted	141	14
and of the C after the Readings,	141	21
One of the following C is then sung.	294	—
The C	294	—
or one of these C	484	—
or one of these C,	500	—
used with the Psalms and biblical C.	935	9

capital

YHWH is represented in *c* and small *c* letters:	583	29

care

continuance of nursing *c* and protection,	9	13
And the principal *c* herein was to make	10	34
exercised through the *c* each Christian has	446	3

C alike for young and old, strong and weak, 557 11
46. For the C of Children 811 29
46. For the C of Children 829 —

careful

This rite requires *c* preparation by the Priest 400 3

carnal

So, for curious and *c* persons, 871 16

carnally

although they do *c* and visibly press with their teeth 873 37

carried

one or two lighted candles may be *c* 142 28
the candle or candles *c* in at the beginning 143 12
branches of palm or of other trees or shrubs to be *c* 270 —
and decorations be *c* into the building 575 16
c by appropriate persons. 575 19
been *c* over into the classical English versions, 583 26
ordained of Christ to be gazed upon, or to be *c* about, 872 37
was not by Christ's ordinance reserved, *c* about, 873 34

carry

a deacon to *c* the Paschal Candle to its place, 284 17
First, there is the order of bishops who *c* on 510 6
deacons may be appointed to *c* the Sacrament 555 1

carrying

in the *c* out of its missionary 510 10

case

in which *c* Phos hilaron may be followed 112 —
In that *c*, the deacon omits the prayer 312 10
In *c* of emergency, any baptized person may 313 22
(in the *c* of Eucharistic Prayer C, 408 15
in which *c* the Celebrant may begin with the Act 439 —
In *c* of illness, the Minister of the Congregation 453 2
In either *c*, the rubrics of the service of ordination 552 4
In each such *c*, the appropriate prayer 577 10
(brackets in the *c* of whole Psalms, 935 1
parentheses in the *c* of verses) 935 2

cases

In all such *c*, the priest is required to notify 409 24
In *c* of necessity, a deacon or lay person may perform 456 —
In other *c*, the bishop may state briefly 565 2
Dedication of Churches and Chapels in Special C 576 28

cast

Then, while earth is *c* upon the coffin, 485 —
Then, while earth is *c* upon the coffin, 501 —
and it is *c* in the traditional question 844 5

catechism

Concerning the C 844 1
This *c* is primarily intended for use by parish priests, 844 2
The second use of this *c* is to provide a brief summary 844 7
commonly called the C 845 —

catechists

and lay *c*, to give an outline for instruction. 844 3

cathedral

the dean of a *c*, and others having similar tenure 564 18
in C and Collegiate Churches, 867 27

cathedrals

the installation of deans and canons of *c*, 558 4

catholic

characteristic of Christ's holy *c* Church. 510 5
property of this portion of Christ's *c* Church, 510 27
it is necessary that he hold the C Faith. 864 22
And the C Faith is this: 864 25
So are we forbidden by the C Religion, to say, 865 7
This is the C Faith, 865 39
are members of the Holy C Church; 876 32
C Church during the first ages of its existence; 877 7

cause

intended for use with those who for reasonable *c* 396 —
weighty *c* could not be present at the celebration, 409 1
sickness or other grave *c*, could not be present 555 3
and the manifold changings of the service, was the *c*, 866 30
For this *c* be cut off Anthems, 866 37
Magistrate requireth, in a *c* of faith and charity, 876 20

causes

in all *c* doth appertain, and is not, 875 42

cavil

seek occasion, of *c* or quarrel against her Liturgy. 10 13

celebrant

At the discretion of the C, and as appropriate, 195 —
At the discretion of the C, and as appropriate, 246 —
On this day, the C begins the liturgy 264 —
After the Sermon, all stand, and the C or Minister 264 —
If ashes are to be imposed, the C says 265 —
The C and People together, all kneeling 267 —
The C continues 267 —
C 270 —
The C then says the following blessing 271 —
C 271 —
kneel for silent prayer, after which the C stands 276 —
Immediately before the Collect, the C may say 276 —
omission, as appropriate, at the discretion of the C. 277 —
The C says the Collects. 277 —
When there is a Liturgy of the Word, the C begins 283 —
The bishop, when present, is the chief *c*, 284 12
after which the C may address the people 285 —
The C may say the following prayer 285 —
(the C if there is no deacon) bearing the Candle, 285 —
The C may introduce the Scripture readings 288 —
the C leads the people in the Renewal 292 —
The C may first address the people 292 —
C 292 —
C 293 —
C 294 —
The *c* concludes the Renewal of Vows as follows 294 —
before the Canticle the C may say to the people 294 —
The C then says 294 —
The C says one of the following Collects 295 —
The bishop, when present, is the *c*; 298 7
In the absence of a bishop, a priest is the *c* 298 13
The people standing, the C says 299 —
C 299 —
The C then continues 299 —
The C says 301 —

The C asks each candidate when presented	301	—
When all have been presented the C asks the parents	302	—
C	302	—
Then the C asks the following questions	302	—
After all have been presented, the C addresses	303	—
The C then says these or similar words	303	—
C	304	—
C	305	—
The C then says to the congregation	305	—
The C says	306	—
The C blesses the water, first saying	306	—
C	306	—
At the following words, the C touches the water	307	—
Each candidate is presented by name to the C,	307	—
When all have been baptized, the C says	308	11
C and People	308	—
C	308	—
should be the principal C.	310	—
The C then says	311	—
the *c*, whenever possible, should face the people	313	4
The people standing, the C says	319	—
C	319	—
The C may read one of the following sentences	319	—
The Deacon or C then says	320	—
when present, to be the principal *c*	322	2
the Liturgy, it is fitting that the principal *c*,	322	4
the other priests present stand with the *c*	322	7
Lay persons appointed by the *c* should normally	322	15
The people standing, the C may say	323	—
C	323	—
The C says	323	—
The C says to the people	325	—
C	325	—
The C says the Collect.	325	—
The Deacon or C says the following,	330	—
The C says to the people	332	—
The C may begin the Offertory with one	333	—
and money or other gifts, to the deacon or *c*.	333	—
The C, whether bishop or priest,	333	—
C	333	—
Then, facing the Holy Table, the C proceeds	333	—
C and People	334	—
Then the C continues	334	—
concerning the bread, the C is to hold it,	334	—
People and C	336	—
The C breaks the consecrated Bread.	337	—
the C may say the following Invitation	338	—
the C consecrates additional bread and wine,	338	—
After Communion, the C says	339	—
The Deacon, or the C, may dismiss the people	339	—
The C, whether bishop or priest,	340	—
C	340	—
Then, facing the Holy Table, the C proceeds	341	—
C and People	341	—
Then the C continues	341	—
concerning the bread, the C is to hold it,	342	—
The people standing, the C says	351	—
C	351	—
The C may read one of the following sentences	351	—
The Deacon or C then says	352	—
when present, to be the principal *c*	354	2
the Liturgy, it is fitting that the principal *c*,	354	4
the other priests present stand with the *c*	354	7
Lay persons appointed by the *c* should normally	354	15
The people standing, the C says	355	—
C	355	—
The C may say	355	—
The C says to the people	357	—
C	357	—
The C says the Collect	357	—
The Deacon or C says	360	—
The C says to the people	360	—
The C may begin the Offertory with one of	361	—
and money or other gifts, to the deacon or *c*.	361	—
The C, whether bishop or priest,	361	—
C	361	—
Then, facing the Holy Table, the C proceeds	361	—
C and People	362	—
Then the C continues	362	—
concerning the bread, the C is to hold it,	362	—
C and People	363	—
The C continues	363	—
People and C	364	—
The C breaks the consecrated Bread.	364	—
Facing the people, the C says the following Invitation	364	—
the C consecrates additional bread and wine,	365	—
After Communion, the C says	365	—
C and People	365	—
The Deacon, or the C, dismisses them	366	—
The C, whether bishop or priest,	367	—
C	367	—
Then, facing the Holy Table, the C proceeds	367	—
C and People	367	—
Then the C continues	368	—
concerning the bread, the C is to hold it,	368	—
C and People	368	—
The C continues	369	—
The C, whether bishop or priest, faces them	369	—
Then, facing the Holy Table, the C proceeds	370	—
C and People	371	—
The C continues	371	—
concerning the bread, the C is to hold it,	371	—
The C, whether bishop or priest,	372	—
C	372	—
Then, facing the Holy Table, the C proceeds	373	—
C and People	373	—
Then the C continues	373	—
concerning the bread, the C is to hold it,	374	—
C and People	375	—
The C continues	375	—
The C may introduce the Prayers with a sentence	383	—
The C adds a concluding Collect.	385	—
The C adds a concluding Collect.	387	—
The C adds a concluding Collect.	388	—
The C adds a concluding Collect.	389	—
The C adds a concluding Collect,	391	—
The C concludes with an absolution	393	—
For the concluding Collect, the C selects	394	—
The C, whether priest or deacon, reads	396	—
After the Reading, the C may comment on it briefly.	397	—
The Lord's Prayer is said, the C first saying	398	—
The C may say the following Invitation	399	—
In making Eucharist, the C uses one	402	—
C	402	—

The *C* gives thanks to God the Father for his work	402	—
C and People	402	—
The *C* now praises God for the salvation	403	—
concerning the bread, the *C* is to hold it,	403	—
C	404	—
The *C* gives thanks to God the Father for his work	404	—
C and People	404	—
The *C* now praises God for the salvation	404	—
concerning the bread, the *C* is to hold it,	405	—
The *C* then prays that all may receive the benefits	405	—
other than English, a reader appointed by the *c*	406	22
c receives the Sacrament in both kinds.	407	23
When the *c* is assisted by a deacon or another priest,	408	3
customary for the *c* to administer the consecrated	408	4
the *c* is to return to the Holy Table,	408	10
or else the *c* may consecrate more of both kinds,	408	13
the *c* or deacon, and other communicants,	409	3
at which the Bishop should be the principal *c*.	419	—
prepare in advance, in consultation with the *c*,	420	—
comes forward at the invitation of the *c*,	420	—
After this, the *C* says these or similar words	420	—
The *C* then says this or some other appropriate prayer	421	—
Then the *C*, facing the people	423	—
Then the *C* says to the persons to be married	424	—
The *C* says to the woman	424	—
The *C* says to the man	424	—
The *C* then addresses the congregation, saying	425	—
The *C* then says to the people	425	—
Then the *C* joins the right hands of husband and wife	428	—
All standing, the *C* says	428	—
People and *C*	428	—
The *C* may say to the people	431	—
the husband and wife stand before the *C*,	433	—
The *C* then addresses the husband, saying	433	—
The *C* then addresses the wife, saying	433	—
The *C* then addresses the congregation, saying	434	—
The *C* joins the right hands of the husband and wife	434	—
Normally, the *c* is a priest or bishop.	435	4
a deacon may function as *c*,	435	6
5. The *C* declares the union of the man and woman	436	4
or presentation, the *C* asks,	437	9
the *C* may begin with the Act of Thanksgiving,	439	11
At the proper time, the *C* invites the parents	439	17
The *C* addresses the congregation	440	—
The *C* asks the parent or parents	440	—
Then if the child is old enough to answer, the *C* asks	441	—
C	441	—
Then the *C*, holding or taking the child by the hand,	441	—
The *C* says	441	—
The *C* then says this prayer	443	—
The *C* may add one or more of the following prayers	444	—
The *C* may then bless the family	445	—
The *C* begins the service with the following	453	11
After any Reading, the *C* may comment on it briefly.	454	13
the *C* is to assure that person that all the benefits	457	—
The *C* meets the body at the door of the church	466	—
after which the *C* says	466	—
after which the *C* says	467	—
It is customary that the *c* meet the body	468	21
or by the *c* standing in the accustomed place.	468	25
The *C* says one of the following Collects,	469	—
C	469	—
The *C* and other ministers take their places	482	—
The *C*, facing the body, says	483	—
The *C*, or the Bishop if present, may then bless	483	—
Then, while earth is cast upon the coffin, the *C* says	485	—
The *C* says	485	—
C and People	485	—
Then the *C* may say	486	—
this prayer, or in addition to it, the *C* may use	486	—
The *C* dismisses the people with these words	486	—
It is customary that the *c* meet the body	490	21
or by the *c* standing in the accustomed place.	490	25
the *C* may address the congregation,	492	—
The *C* then says	493	—
C	493	—
after which the *C* says one of the following	493	—
The *C* may add the following prayer	494	—
Here there may be a homily by the *C*,	495	—
The *C* may introduce the Creed	496	—
C and People	496	—
The *C* concludes with one of the following	497	—
The *C* and other ministers take their places	499	—
The *C*, facing the body, says	499	—
The *C*, or the Bishop if present, may then bless	500	—
while earth is cast upon the coffin, the *C* says	501	—
The *C* says	501	—
C	501	—
C and People	502	—
The *C* dismisses the people with these words	502	—
C	502	—
The *c* may meet the body and conduct it	506	4
new Bishop goes to the Lord's Table as chief *C* and,	522	—
The bishop, when present, is the chief *c*	558	8
a priest being inducted is the chief *c*.	558	10
stand with the chief *c* at the Altar,	558	12
assist the *c* at the Altar,	558	21
standing at the Lord's Table as chief *c*,	563	—
The bishop, or a priest appointed, is the chief *c*.	574	—
After a brief silence, the *C* concludes	579	—
C	579	—

celebrate

desirable that the priest arrange to *c* the Eucharist	396	—
If it is desired to *c* a marriage otherwise	435	2

celebrated

c in the context of a Rite One service,	14	4
It is *c* at a convenient time	284	3
When the Vigil is not *c*, the Service of Light	284	30
Collect appropriate to the season or occasion being *c*;	394	—
the particular occasion being *c*;	402	—
the particular occasion being *c*;	404	—
The Holy Eucharist may be *c* either according	436	14
If the Eucharist is to be *c*, the Priest begins	457	—

celebrating

An Order for *C*	400	1
and of *c* the Holy Eucharist.	422	9

celebration

Provided, that there is no *c* of the Eucharist	18	11
With the *c* of the Holy Eucharist,	112	—
At services on this day other than the principal *c*,	272	—
c begins with the Salutation and Collect of the Day	272	—

There is no *c* of the Eucharist on this day. 283 —
The *c* continues with the Prayers of the People. 295 —
If there is no *c* of the Eucharist, 311 —
at a public *c* of the Sacrament with a bishop or priest 314 6
C of the Holy Communion 315 —
Concerning the C 322 1
If there is no *c* of the Communion, 330 —
Concerning the C 354 1
If there is no *c* of the Communion, 359 —
present at a public *c* of the Eucharist. 396 —
the priest may begin the *c* at the Offertory, 396 —
for use at the principal Sunday or weekly *c* 400 4
When a common meal or Agape is a part of the *c*, 401 15
spread with a clean white cloth during the *c*. 406 2
deacon to make ready the Table for the *c*, 407 14
weighty cause could not be present at the *c*, 409 1
If there is no *c* of the Eucharist, 419 —
A priest or a bishop normally presides at the C 422 7
The C and Blessing of a Marriage 423 —
The C and Blessing of a Marriage may be used 437 5
Anointing takes place at a public *c* of the Eucharist, 453 8
At the C of the Eucharist 522 —
proceeds with the *c* of the Eucharist. 522 —
At the C of the Eucharist 535 —
Priest joins in the *c* of the Holy Eucharist 535 —
At the C of the Eucharist 546 —
The *c* of the Holy Eucharist may be according 552 3
in this *c* as an expression of the collegiality 558 17
C of a New Ministry 559 —
have some individual or collective part in the *c*, 566 17
followed by the *c* of the Holy Eucharist. 577 19

celebrations

At *c* of the Holy Eucharist, 36 8
At *c* of the Holy Eucharist, 74 7
The Proper appointed for the Sunday is also used at *c* 158 7
At all *c* of the Liturgy, 322 4
At all *c* of the Liturgy, 354 4
The Rite begins as prescribed for *c* 433 —

ceremonies

C of the Church, do hereby establish the said Book: 8 9
Divine Worship, and the Rites and C appointed 9 15
and the *c* that follow it. 313 11
as touching C and Rites, do not bind Christian men, 869 11
erred, not only in their living and manner of C, 871 34
The Church hath power to decree Rites or C, 871 37
It is not necessary that Traditions and C 874 22
and C of the Church, which be not repugnant 874 26
C or Rites of the Church ordained only by man's authority, 874 32

ceremony

When observed, the *c* of the washing of feet 274 —
During the *c*, the following or other suitable anthems 274 —
that the *c* be attested by at least two witnesses; 422 5
for that they have not any visible sign or *c* 872 36

certain

The Gloria printed at the conclusion of *c* Canticles 141 14
this is by no means *c*, because from very ancient times 583 18
but, except in *c* classical prayers which do not lend 814 —
c rules are here set forth, which, as they be few 866 41
for they may be proved by most *c* warrants 869 17
but rather they be *c* sure witnesses, 872 27
as *c* Anabaptists do falsely boast. 876 14

certainty

liturgy, therefore, is characterized by joy, in the *c* 507 5

chair

presides from a *c* placed close to the people, 511 13
may now be escorted to the episcopal *c*. 522 —
from a *c* placed close to the people, and facing them, 524 5
from a *c* placed close to the people, and facing them, 536 5

Chalcedon

Council of C, 451 A.D., Act V 864 3

chalice

one *c* on the Altar, and, if need be, a flagon of wine 407 19
and the assistant the C. 408 5
according to the canon may administer the C. 408 8
(and a little water) into the *c*, 546 —

chalices

additional *c* may be filled after the Breaking 407 20

chancel

procession to the *c*, pausing three times and singing 285 —
occur at the entrance of the *c*, or in some other place 564 15

change

without confusion, without *c*, without division, 864 12
Transubstantiation (or the *c* of the substance 873 28
Church hath authority to ordain, *c*, and abolish, 874 31

changed

c to the plural where necessary. 553 28
c to the plural where necessary. 554 18
and may be *c* according to the diversity of countries, 874 23

changes

such *c* and alterations should be made therein, 9 19

changing

by *c* the pronouns and the corresponding verbs. 108 23

changings

and the manifold *c* of the service, was the cause, 866 30

chant

and to *c* the Exsultet. 284 18
A lay person may be assigned to *c* the Exsultet. 284 21

chanted

The Passion Gospel may be read or *c* by lay persons. 273 —
The Passion Gospel may be read or *c* by lay persons. 277 —

chanting

Direct recitation denotes the reading or *c* 582 8
found a satisfactory method of *c* them. 582 12
of *c* the psalms between the Lessons at the Eucharist, 582 25
divides each verse into two parts for reading or *c*. 583 13

chapel

and conduct it into the church or *c*, 506 5
used for dedicating a *c* or an oratory 566 6
For a church or *c* long in use, 566 19
place apart from the church or *c*. 567 4
a Church is to be used at the opening of a church or *c*. 575 3

for dedicating a private *c* or oratory. 577 5
or Parts of a Church or C 577 7
additions, or new furnishings in a church or *c*. 577 10
For a Church or C Long in Use 577 20

chapels

Dedication of Churches and C in Special Cases 576 28
parish Churches, and C to the same annexed, 867 28

chaplains

vicars of missions, hospital *c*, and other priests 565 25

chapter

A citation giving *c* and verse may be added. 47 —
A citation giving *c* and verse may be added. 64 —
A citation giving *c* and verse may be added. 84 —
A citation giving *c* and verse may be added. 118 —
A citation giving *c* and verse may be added. 300 —
A citation giving *c* and verse may be added. 325 —
A citation giving *c* and verse may be added. 357 —
A citation giving *c* and verse may be added. 414 —
A citation giving *c* and verse may be added. 516 —
A citation giving *c* and verse may be added. 528 —
A citation giving *c* and verse may be added. 540 —

chapters

before three or four C were read out, 866 19

characteristic

c of Christ's holy catholic Church. 510 5

characteristics

but rather the *c* of each nature being preserved 864 13

characterized

The liturgy, therefore, is *c* by joy, 507 5

charge

A deacon, or an assisting priest, may deliver the *c*, 422 12
Psalm 91 (He will give his angels *c* over you) 453 16
and other priests having similar canonical *c*. 565 26
The rector or minister in *c* takes part 566 13
The Rector or Minister in *c* continues 569 1
the people shall not be at so great *c* for books, 867 7
rule all estates and degrees committed to their *c* 876 4

charitable

with a meek, candid, and *c* frame of mind; 11 18
religious and *c* uses. 445 —

charity

the Magistrate requireth, in a cause of faith and *c*, 876 20
promote the *c* which is the chief of Christian graces 877 3

Chicago

The C-Lambeth Quadrilateral 1886, 1888 876 22
C, 1886 876 24

chief

The bishop, when present, is the *c* celebrant, 284 12
c service on a Sunday or other feast. 298 6
Presiding Bishop, presides and serves as *c* consecrator. 511 7
the *c* consecrator presides from a chair 511 12
sit to the right and left of the *c* consecrator. 511 15
Bishop goes to the Lord's Table as *c* Celebrant and, 522 —
The *c* minister is normally the bishop; 558 7
The bishop, when present, is the *c* celebrant 558 8
a priest being inducted is the *c* celebrant. 558 10
also stand with the *c* celebrant at the Altar, 558 12
standing at the Lord's Table as *c* celebrant, 563 —
bishop, or a priest appointed, is the *c* celebrant. 574 —
c authority in the Ministration of the Word 873 3
hath the *c* power in this Realm of England, 875 40
the *c* Government of all Estates of this Realm, 875 40
attribute to the King's Majesty the *c* government, 875 43
the charity which is the *c* of Christian graces 877 3

chiefest

(as well in the *c* materials, as in the frame 10 6

child

the Birth or Adoption of a C 439 2
As soon as convenient after the birth of a *c*, 439 3
or after receiving a *c* by adoption, 439 3
For the Birth of a C 440 —
Then if the *c* is old enough to answer, 441 —
C 441 —
the Celebrant, holding or taking the *c* by the hand, 441 —
gives the *c* to the mother or father, saying 441 —
For a *c* not yet baptized 444 —
For a *c* already baptized 444 —
For a Sick C 458 —
At the burial of a *c*, 468 19
At the Burial of a C 470 —
At the burial of a *c*, 490 19
At the Burial of a C 494 —
such as Thanksgiving for the Birth or Adoption of a C, 576 16
10. For the Gift of a C 813 14
10. For the Gift of a C 841 —
See also the Thanksgiving for a C on page 439. 841 —

children

Sponsors of adults and older *c* present 298 18
among the godparents of their own *c*. 298 25
Adults and Older C 301 —
Infants and Younger C 301 —
on behalf of the infants and younger *c* 302 —
At the dedication of the font, *c* or other lay persons 575 23
46. For the Care of C 811 29
46. For the Care of C 829 —
The Song of the Three C, The Prayer of Manasses, 869 1
The Baptism of young C is in any wise to be retained 873 20

choice

II. For the *c* of fit persons for the ministry 205 —
II. For the *c* of fit persons for the ministry 256 —
3. That in all things of human ordering or human *c*, 876 33

choir

e.g., between *c* and congregation, 582 14
with the *c* and congregation singing a refrain 582 20

chosen

The persons who are *c* and recognized by the Church 510 16
the trust of those who have *c* you. 557 11
those whom he hath *c* in Christ out of mankind, 871 4
which be *c* and called to this work 872 18

chrism

[consecrates the C;] 298 10
If a priest uses C in signing the newly baptized, 298 14
Consecration of the C 307 —
The Bishop may then consecrate oil of C, 307 —
the sign of the cross [using C if desired] 308 —
Bishop may consecrate oil of C for use at Baptism, 419 —
the bishop may consecrate oil of C, 575 26

Christ

invaluable part of that blessed "liberty wherewith C 9 2
and majestic manner, for the sake of Jesus C, 11 22
All Sundays of the year are feasts of our Lord Jesus C. 16 2
From the Epiphany through the Baptism of C, 43 —
C our Passover 46 —
A Collect for the Presence of C 70 —
From the Epiphany through the Baptism of C, 81 —
C our Passover 83 —
A Collect for the Presence of C 124 —
"C our Passover," after each Psalm, 141 13
9. Of the Reign of C 202 —
9. Of the Reign of C 254 —
the Holy Spirit into C's Body the Church. 298 3
Jesus C our Lord. 403 —
Jesus C our Lord. 404 —
that all may receive the benefits of C's work, 405 5
the words our Savior C hath (has) taught us." 408 24
commitment to the service of C in the world, 420 4
Ephesians 5:1–2, 21–33 (Walk in love, as C loved us) 426 —
reconciliation, which has been committed by C 446 2
C our Passover, Pascha nostrum 484 —
C our Passover, Pascha nostrum 500 —
promises of God in C about eternal life. 506 17
will be able to separate us from the love of God in C 507 8
The very love we have for each other in C 507 11
characteristic of C's holy catholic Church. 510 5
deacons to minister in C's name to the poor, 510 14
property of this portion of C's catholic Church, 510 27
says over each ordinand "Father, through Jesus C 553 32
C your Son, give your Holy Spirit to N.; 554 22
Love and serve C's people. 557 13
and Human Natures in the Person of C 864 2
and the same Son, our Lord Jesus C, at once complete 864 5
one and the same C, Son, Lord, Only-begotten, 864 11
and Only-begotten God the Word, Lord Jesus C; 864 16
and our Lord Jesus C himself taught us, 864 17
Incarnation of our Lord Jesus C. 865 20
that we believe and confess, that our Lord Jesus C, 865 21
he be God and Man, yet he is not two, but one C; 865 28
soul and flesh is one man, so God and Man is one C; 865 31
whereof is one C, very God, and very Man; 868 6
III. Of the going down of C into Hell. 868 9
As C died for us, and was buried; 868 10
IV. Of the Resurrection of C. 868 12
C did truly rise again from death, 868 13
everlasting life is offered to Mankind by C, 869 8
the grace of God by C preventing us, 869 37
C by Faith, and not for our own works or deservings. 870 3
acceptable to God in C, and do spring out necessarily 870 9
Works done before the grace of C, 870 13
forasmuch as they spring not of faith in Jesus C; 870 14
whereas C saith plainly, 870 22
XV. Of C alone without Sin. 870 24
C in the truth of our nature was made like unto us 870 25
and born again in C, yet offend in many things; 870 29
those whom he hath chosen in C out of mankind, 871 4
bring them by C to everlasting salvation, 871 5
the image of his only-begotten Son Jesus C: 871 9
Predestination, and our Election in C, 871 11
working of the Spirit of C, mortifying the works 871 13
faith of eternal Salvation to be enjoyed through C, 871 15
lacking the Spirit of C, to have continually 871 17
obtaining eternal Salvation only by the Name of C. 871 24
the Name of Jesus C, whereby men must be saved. 871 28
The visible Church of C is a congregation 871 30
be duly ministered according to C's ordinance, 871 31
Sacraments ordained of C be not only badges 872 26
two Sacraments ordained of C our Lord 872 30
The Sacraments were not ordained of C to be gazed 872 37
they do not the same in their own name, but in C's, 873 4
Neither is the effect of C's ordinance taken away 873 6
which be effectual, because of C's institution 873 8
agreeable with the institution of C. 873 21
it is a Sacrament of our Redemption by C's death: 873 24
which we break is a partaking of the Body of C; 873 26
partaking of the Blood of C. 873 27
The Body of C is given, taken, and eaten, 873 31
And the mean whereby the Body of C is received 873 32
the Lord's Supper was not by C's ordinance reserved, 873 34
eat not the Body of C in the use of the Lord's Supper. 873 36
the Sacrament of the Body and Blood of C; 873 38
yet in no wise are they partakers of C: 873 39
Sacrament, by C's ordinance 874 3
XXXI. Of the one Oblation of C finished 874 5
Offering of C once made is that perfect redemption, 874 6
that the Priest did offer C for the quick and the dead, 874 9
12 Of the Nativity of C. 875 3
13 Of the Passion of C. 875 4
14 Of the Resurrection of C. 875 5
Body and Blood of C. 875 7
C, and James his Apostle, so we judge, 876 19
have contended for the religion of C: 876 28
to heal the wounds of the Body of C, 877 3
and the visible manifestation of C to the world; 877 4
deposit of Christian Faith and Order committed by C 877 8
unfailing use of C's words of institution 877 17
(c) The two Sacraments ordained by C Himself— 878 1
with unfailing use of C's words of Institution, 878 2

Christendom

unity among the divided branches of C, 877 13

christened

discerned from others that be not *c*, 873 15

Christian

and every sincere C, with a meek, candid, 11 18
The Holy Eucharist, the principal act of C worship 13 3
In all services, the entire C assembly participates 13 16
The leader of worship in a C assembly 13 20
A sermon or homily, a passage from C literature, 113 —
non-biblical C literature may follow 142 14
3. C Initiation, or the Renewal of Baptismal Vows. 284 8
support them by prayer and example in their C life. 298 20
In the course of their C development, 412 2

A Form of Commitment to C Service 420 —
C marriage is a solemn and public covenant 422 2
one, at least, of the parties must be a baptized C; 422 4
Subsequently, only their C names are used. 422 21
for the C community, and for the world. 436 8
about the duty of C parents to make prudent 445 —
exercised through the care each C has for others, 446 3
Another C may be asked to hear a confession, 446 12
not previously been set apart for C burial, 487 —
not previously been set apart for C burial, 503 —
those who mourn, and for the C community, 506 16
Scriptures and ancient C writers make it clear 510 2
most generally recognized by C people 510 30
the C name by which he wishes to be known. 511 20
the C name by which he wishes to be known. 524 11
the C name by which he wishes to be known. 536 11
Commitment to C Service, or Blessing of Oil 576 17
used for regular worship by other C bodies, 577 1
The C Hope 861 —
For like as we are compelled by the C verity 865 5
as touching Ceremonies and Rites, do not bind C 869 11
no C man whatsoever is free from the obedience 869 13
be not only badges or tokens of C men's profession, 872 26
whereby C men are discerned from others 873 14
ministered to all C men alike. 874 4
C men, to marry at their own discretion, 874 14
explication of C doctrine, and instructive in piety 875 15
Laws of the Realm may punish C men with death, 876 8
It is lawful for C men, at the commandment 876 10
Of C Men's Goods, which are not common. 876 12
XXXIX. Of a C Man's Oath. 876 17
vain and rash Swearing is forbidden C men 876 18
so we judge, that C Religion doth not prohibit, 876 19
promote the charity which is the chief of C graces 877 3
But furthermore, we do hereby affirm that the C unity 877 5
the return of all C communions to the principles 877 6
to be the substantial deposit of C Faith and Order 877 8
as the sufficient statement of the C Faith. 877 15
the sad divisions which affect the C Church 877 20
C Bodies seeking the restoration of the organic unity 877 23
to a newly created Joint Commission on C Reunion. 877 28
as the sufficient statement of the C faith. 877 36

Christianity

what C is, and what the truths of the Gospel are; 11 20

Christians

denominations of C in these States were left 10 27
7. For All Baptized C 201 —
III. For all C in their vocation 206 —
7. For all Baptized C 252 —
III. For all C in their vocation 256 —
their duties to help the new C grow in the knowledge 298 26
through the common prayer of C assembled 446 4
Baptized C are properly buried from the church. 468 5
Baptized C are properly buried from the church. 490 5
a sign of the love that C ought to have 873 23
The Riches and Goods of C are not common, 876 13
concern, and especially to our fellow-C 876 27

Christmas

our Lord's Nativity or C Day. 15 6
before C Day, whether it occurs on a Sunday 15 11
C Day, December 25 15 17
This provision does not apply to C 17 18
except for Fridays in the C and Easter 17 26
C 37 —
On the Twelve Days of C 43 —
C 75 —
On the Twelve Days of C 80 —
John 1:1–5 (C) 108 18
C, Epiphany, and other Feasts of the Incarnation 111 —
Collect for the First Sunday after C 111 —
C Day December 25 160 —
Proper Lessons for C Day serve for any weekdays 161 —
and the First Sunday after C Day. 161 —
First Sunday after C Day 161 —
the three Holy Days which follow C Day. 161 —
Second Sunday after C Day 162 —
those for the Second Sunday after C Day, 162 —
The Nativity of Our Lord: C Day December 25 212 —
Proper Lessons for C Day serve for any weekdays 213 —
and the First Sunday after C Day. 213 —
First Sunday after C Day 213 —
the three Holy Days which follow C Day. 213 —
Second Sunday after C Day 214 —
or those for the Second Sunday after C, 214 8
C Day through the Feast of the Epiphany; 406 13

Chronicles

1 C 29:11 344 —
1 C 29:11 377 —
The First Book of C, Ecclesiastes or Preacher, 868 30
The Second Book of C, Cantica, or Songs of Solomon, 868 31

Chrysostom

A Prayer of St. C 59 —
A Prayer of St. C 72 —
A Prayer of St. C 102 —
A Prayer of St. C 126 —

church

Episcopal C in the United States of America, 8 4
and Ceremonies of the C, do hereby establish 8 9
they declare it to be the Liturgy of this C: 8 10
in every C, what cannot be clearly determined 9 5
C of England, to which the Protestant Episcopal C 9 11
The same C hath not only in her Preface, 9 22
and unity in the C; 10 11
The attention of this C was in the first place drawn 10 32
Book of Common Prayer of the C of England. 11 12
In which it will also appear that this C 11 12
from intending to depart from the C of England 11 13
examined by every true member of our C, 11 18
Concerning the Service of the C 13 2
appointed for public worship in this C. 13 6
forms set forth by authority within this C may be used. 13 8
appointed by civil or C authority, 13 12
that the members of each order within the C, 13 17
understood as those authorized by this C. 14 7
The Calendar of the C Year 15 2
The C Year consists of two cycles of feasts 15 3
The sequence of all Sundays of the C Year depends 15 9
The Principal Feasts observed in this C 15 15

The feast of the Dedication of a C, 16 8
and Lessons duly authorized by this C: 18 2
The *c* is dark, or partially so, 109 —
the Daily Office of the C. 136 —
daily selections for the C Year. 136 —
as little artificial light as possible in the *c*. 142 27
authorized for public worship in this C, 143 7
The Collects for the C Year 157 —
Concerning the Proper of the C Year 158 2
The Proper of the C Year includes the appointed 158 3
precedence set forth in the Calendar of the C Year. 195 —
set forth in the Calendar of the C Year. 199 —
12. On the Anniversary of the Dedication of a C 204 —
The Litany of Thanksgiving for a C, 204 —
Preface of the Dedication of a C 204 —
13. For a C Convention 204 —
14. For the Unity of the C 204 —
16. For the Mission of the C 206 —
precedence set forth in the Calendar of the C Year. 246 —
Calendar of the C Year. 251 —
12. On the Anniversary of the Dedication of a C 254 —
The Litany of Thanksgiving for a C, 255 —
Preface of the Dedication of a C 255 —
13. For a C Convention 255 —
14. For the Unity of the C 255 —
16. For the Mission of the C 257 —
apart from the *c*, so that all may go into the *c* 270 —
a wooden cross may now be brought into the *c* 281 —
Other candles and lamps in the *c*, 286 —
the Holy Spirit into Christ's Body the C. 298 3
and in their responsibilities as members of his C. 298 27
found desirable to return to the front of the *c* 313 9
Dedication of a C 348 —
The Universal C, its members, and its mission 359 —
Dedication of a C 381 —
The Universal C, its members, and its mission 383 —
(c) a Collect for the mission of the C; 394 —
Pray for the World and the C 400 12
In the Episcopal C it is required 422 3
the laws of the State and the canons of this C. 422 6
assemble in the *c* or some other appropriate place. 423 —
the wedding party leaves the *c*. 431 —
As the wedding party leaves the *c*, 432 —
The laws of the State and the canons of this C 435 7
and friends assemble in the *c* 435 9
1. The teaching of the C concerning Holy Matrimony, 435 11
declared in the formularies and canons of this C, 435 12
to the *c* to be welcomed by the congregation 439 5
committed by Christ to his C, 446 3
and through the priesthood of the C and its ministers 446 5
When a confession is heard in a *c* building, 446 15
that the ministrations of the C may be provided. 462 —
the body is brought to the *c*. 466 —
The Celebrant meets the body at the door of the *c* 466 —
the body is then brought into the *c*, 467 —
lead the procession into the *c*. 467 —
The death of a member of the C should be reported 468 2
Baptized Christians are properly buried from the *c*. 468 5
Committal may be said in the *c*. 468 11
before the service in the *c*. 468 12
into the *c* or towards the grave. 468 22
as the body is borne into the *c*, 468 24
Unless the Committal follows immediately in the *c*, 482 —
As the body is borne from the *c*, 483 —
The death of a member of the C should be reported 490 2
Baptized Christians are properly buried from the *c*. 490 5
Committal may be said in the *c*. 490 11
before the service in the *c*. 490 12
into the *c* or towards the grave. 490 22
as the body is borne into the *c*, 490 24
Unless the Committal follows immediately in the *c*, 499 —
As the body is borne from the *c*, 500 —
conduct it into the *c* or chapel, 506 5
there have been different ministries within the C. 510 3
characteristic of Christ's holy catholic C. 510 6
work of leading, supervising, and uniting the C. 510 7
part in the governance of the C, 510 10
The persons who are chosen and recognized by the C 510 16
the intention and purpose of this C to maintain 510 19
the offices of bishop, priest, or deacon in this C 510 22
property of this portion of Christ's catholic C, 510 27
Accordingly, the manner of ordaining in this C 510 29
to be ordained, the Presiding Bishop of the C, 511 6
directed by Article VIII of the Constitution of this C 552 10
at several conveniently separated places in the *c*. 553 13
and make him a priest in your C." 554 2
and make him a deacon in your C." 554 23
N.N., Presbyter of the C of God, you have been called 557 2
and to take your share in the councils of the C. 557 4
serve God in ________ C [of] ________. 557 6
present the keys of the *c*, saying 562 —
and Canons of this C, saying 562 —
kneel in the midst of the *c*, and say 562 —
provides for the dedication and consecration of a *c* 566 2
service may be used to dedicate and consecrate a *c* 566 9
For a *c* or chapel long in use, a special order 566 19
Consecration of a C 567 —
place apart from the *c* or chapel. 567 —
As the procession approaches the door of the *c*, 567 —
Standing at the door of the *c*, the Bishop says 568 —
As the procession moves into the *c*, 568 —
Consecration of the C 568 —
The Preface of the Dedication of a C may be used. 574 —
a C is to be used at the opening of a *c* or chapel. 575 3
the congregation may assemble inside the *c*; 575 13
When a new *c* is being consecrated, 575 15
for subsequent use in this *c*. 575 27
As the furnishings in the *c* are dedicated, 576 1
the ministers move from one part of the *c* to another. 576 5
or one appropriate to the name of the *c*. 576 26
If the *c* is also to be used for regular worship 577 1
or Parts of a C or Chapel 577 7
C may be used by the bishop or a priest for blessing 577 9
additions, or new furnishings in a *c* or chapel. 577 10
For a C or Chapel Long in Use 577 20
3. Litany of Thanksgiving for a C, 577 28
A Litany of Thanksgiving for a C 578 6
consecration of a *c*, or on other suitable occasions. 579 —
Prayers for the C 810 12
7. For the C 810 13
8. For the Mission of the C 810 14
12. For a C Convention or Meeting 810 18
14. For the Unity of the C 810 20
17. For C Musicians and Artists 810 24

Thanksgivings for the C	813	2
3. For the Mission of the C	813	3
Prayers for the C	816	—
7. For the C	816	—
8. For the Mission of the C	816	—
See also the prayers for the Mission of the C	816	—
12. For a C Convention or Meeting	818	—
14. For the Unity of the C	818	—
17. For C Musicians and Artists	819	—
Thanksgivings for the C	838	—
3. For the Mission of the C	838	—
C's teaching for an inquiring stranger who picks up	844	8
The C	854	—
Historical Documents of the C	863	—
appear by the common prayers in the C,	866	5
(by daily hearing of holy Scripture read in the C)	866	13
language spoken to the people in the C,	866	23
hearing the same, the Service in the C of England	866	24
read and sung in the *c* in the English tongue,	867	24
of the Protestant Episcopal C in the United States	867	31
of whose authority was never any doubt in the C.	868	24
other Books (as Hierome saith) the C doth read	868	34
XIX. Of the C.	871	29
The visible C of Christ is a congregation	871	30
As the C of Jerusalem, Alexandria, and Antioch,	871	33
so also the C of Rome hath erred,	871	33
XX. Of the Authority of the C.	871	36
The C hath power to decree Rites or Ceremonies,	871	37
and yet it is not lawful for the C to ordain any thing	871	38
Wherefore, although the C be a witness and a keeper	871	40
Word of God, and the custom of the Primitive C,	872	22
to have public Prayer in the C,	872	23
Although in the visible C the evil be ever mingled	873	2
it appertaineth to the discipline of the C,	873	10
Baptism rightly are grafted into the C;	873	17
young Children is in any wise to be retained in the C,	873	20
That person which by open denunciation of the C	874	17
cut off from the unity of the C,	874	18
received into the C by a Judge that hath authority	874	20
XXXIV. Of the Traditions of the C.	874	21
the Traditions and Ceremonies of the C,	874	26
he that offendeth against the common order of the C,	874	28
Every particular or national C hath authority	874	31
Ceremonies or Rites of the C ordained	874	32
1 Of the right Use of the C.	875	2
[This Article is received in this C,	875	14
inapplicable to the circumstances of this C	875	17
the General Convention of this C in 1792,	875	22
We, Bishops of the Protestant Episcopal C	876	25
assembled as Bishops in the C of God,	876	26
are members of the Holy Catholic C;	876	32
this C is ready in the spirit of love	876	34
4. That this C does not seek to absorb other Communions,	877	1
Catholic C during the first ages of its existence;	877	7
Apostles to the C unto the end of the world,	877	9
peoples called of God into the unity of His C.	877	19
the sad divisions which affect the Christian C	877	20
seeking the restoration of the organic unity of the C,	877	23
and peoples called of God into the Unity of His C.	878	5

churches

liberty to model and organize their respective C,	10	28
Ministers of other C may appropriately be invited	558	19
For the Dedication of C	576	27
most frequently used in Episcopal *c*,	582	28
hath been great diversity in saying and singing in *c*	867	8
C, parish C, and Chapels to the same annexed,	867	28
we judge them to be read in C by the Ministers,	874	38
3 Of repairing and keeping clean of C.	875	5
the order for the reading of said Homilies in *c*,	875	17

circumstances

or further than local *c* require.	11	15
Under exceptional *c*, when the services of a priest	13	25
In special *c*, in place of a Canticle,	142	1
When *c* permit, the congregation may gather	270	2
Special C	396	—
and must under no *c* be broken.	446	28
the form for Communion under Special C is used,	457	—
Alterations in the service are then made according to *c*.	558	6
wording may be altered by the bishop when *c* require.	565	1
passages suitable to the *c* may be substituted.	565	13
Provisions for adapting the rite to special *c* are given	566	7
or other *c* make it necessary,	575	12
the service may be adapted to the *c*.	576	31
appropriate prayer may be said, or adapted to the *c*;	577	11
laws of England are considered as inapplicable to the *c*	875	16

citation

A *c* giving chapter and verse may be added.	47	—
A *c* giving chapter and verse may be added.	64	—
A *c* giving chapter and verse may be added.	84	—
A *c* giving chapter and verse may be added.	118	—
A *c* giving chapter and verse may be added.	300	—
A *c* giving chapter and verse may be added.	325	—
A *c* giving chapter and verse may be added.	357	—
A *c* giving chapter and verse may be added.	414	—
A *c* giving chapter and verse may be added.	516	—
A *c* giving chapter and verse may be added.	528	—
A *c* giving chapter and verse may be added.	540	—
In the *c* of the Psalms,	934	26

citations

Scriptural *c* in this Book, except for the Psalms,	14	16

cited

or from the passages *c* in the service.	565	12
c in the selected Sunday Proper may be used instead.	888	17
the selections from the Psalter are frequently *c*	888	18
When an alternative Lesson is *c*,	888	23

cities

33. For C	811	12
33. For C	825	—

city

Given under my hand and seal, in the C of ________,	557	17

civil

and the C Authority has not since thought	10	22
became independent with respect to *c* government,	10	25

C Rulers, in consequence of the Revolution. 10 34
appointed by *c* or Church authority, 13 12
Where it is permitted by *c* law that deacons 422 15
The Blessing of a C Marriage 433 —
Where permitted by *c* law, 435 4
President of the United States and all in C Authority 810 28
President of the United States and all in C Authority 820 —
do not bind Christian men, nor the C precepts 869 11
because it is partly of a local and *c* nature 872 2
XXXVII. Of the Power of the C Magistrates. 875 34
The Power of the C Magistrate extendeth to all men, 875 35
to pay respectful obedience to the C Authority, 875 37
whether they be Ecclesiastical or C, 875 41
and restrain with the *c* sword the stubborn 876 5

classical

been carried over into the *c* English versions, 583 26
but, except in certain *c* prayers 814 —

clause

(omitting the final *c*) 528 —

clauses

but on parallelism of *c*, a symmetry of form and sense. 583 —

clean

the font is to be filled with *c* water immediately 313 1
The Holy Table is spread with a *c* white cloth 406 2
3 Of repairing and keeping *c* of Churches. 875 4

cleanse

consume the remaining Elements, and *c* the vessels 555 6

clear

a *c* view of the action. 313 6
has given *c* proof of repentance and amendment 409 11
but it must be made *c* to the penitent that absolution 446 13
Scriptures and ancient Christian writers make it *c* 510 2
when the referent is not otherwise *c*, 888 27

clearest

for promulgating them to mankind in the *c*, 11 21

clearing

may be conveniently made, for the *c* of them, 875 18

clearly

and that, in every Church, what cannot be *c* determined 9 5
bishop and other ministers may be *c* seen and heard 564 16
he was *c* void, both in his flesh, and in his spirit. 870 26

cleaves

(A man *c* to his wife and they become one flesh) 426 —

clergy

By the Bishops, the C, and the Laity 8 3
The C and People offer their acclamation and applause. 522 —
The new Bishop also greets other members of the *c*, 522 —
The C and People greet one another. 534 —
The Bishop and the C present now greet 546 —
The C and People greet one another. 546 —
Other *c* of the diocese participate 558 16
Representatives of the congregation and of the *c* 561 —
Representative *c* of the diocese present 562 —
The new Minister then greets other members of the *c*, 563 —
and joined by the other *c*, proceeds 563 —
On the day appointed, the *c* and people gather 567 —
Then the bishop and other *c* and the people greet 574 —
When the *c* and people assemble before the service, 575 5
but the bishop, other *c*, and attendants 575 13
9. For C and People 810 15
9. For C and People 817 —
once in the year, intending thereby, that the C, 866 9
As established by the Bishops, the C, and the Laity 867 30
Magistrate extendeth to all men, as well C as Laity, 875 35

clerical

c or lay, who leads the Office. 36 4
c or lay, who leads the Office. 74 3

close

Before the *c* of the Office one or both of the following 58 —
Before the *c* of the Office one or both of the following 71 —
Before the *c* of the Office one or both of the following 101 —
Before the *c* of the Office one or both of the following 125 —
At the C of Day 140 —
the officiant then goes to a place *c* by it 143 4
take place before the *c* of the Office. 439 9
presides from a chair placed *c* to the people, 511 13
from a chair placed *c* to the people, 524 5
from a chair placed *c* to the people, 536 5

closed

The coffin is to be *c* before the service, 468 8
and it remains *c* thereafter. 468 8
The coffin is to be *c* before the service, 490 8
and it remains *c* thereafter. 490 8

closely

most *c* to the date of Pentecost in that year is used. 176 —
most *c* to the date of Trinity Sunday in that year 176 —
most *c* to the date of Pentecost in that year is used. 227 —
most *c* to the date of Trinity Sunday in that year 228 —

closest

date of which falls on that Sunday, or is *c* 158 14
Proper 1 Week of the Sunday *c* to May 11 176 —
Proper 2 Week of the Sunday *c* to May 18 177 —
Proper 3 The Sunday *c* to May 25 177 —
Proper 4 The Sunday *c* to June 1 177 —
Proper 5 The Sunday *c* to June 8 178 —
Proper 6 The Sunday *c* to June 15 178 —
Proper 7 The Sunday *c* to June 22 178 —
Proper 8 The Sunday *c* to June 29 178 —
Proper 9 The Sunday *c* to July 6 179 —
Proper 10 The Sunday *c* to July 13 179 —
Proper 11 The Sunday *c* to July 20 179 —
Proper 12 The Sunday *c* to July 27 180 —
Proper 13 The Sunday *c* to August 3 180 —
Proper 14 The Sunday *c* to August 10 180 —
Proper 15 The Sunday *c* to August 17 180 —
Proper 16 The Sunday *c* to August 24 181 —
Proper 17 The Sunday *c* to August 31 181 —
Proper 18 The Sunday *c* to September 7 181 —
Proper 19 The Sunday *c* to September 14 182 —
Proper 20 The Sunday *c* to September 21 182 —
Proper 21 The Sunday *c* to September 28 182 —

Proper 22 The Sunday *c* to October 5	182	—
Proper 23 The Sunday *c* to October 12	183	—
Proper 24 The Sunday *c* to October 19	183	—
Proper 25 The Sunday *c* to October 26	183	—
Proper 26 The Sunday *c* to November 2	184	—
Proper 27 The Sunday *c* to November 9	184	—
Proper 28 The Sunday *c* to November 16	184	—
Proper 29 The Sunday *c* to November 23	185	—
Proper 1 Week of the Sunday *c* to May 11	228	—
Proper 2 Week of the Sunday *c* to May 18	228	—
Proper 3 The Sunday *c* to May 25	229	—
Proper 4 The Sunday *c* to June 1	229	—
Proper 5 The Sunday *c* to June 8	229	—
Proper 6 The Sunday *c* to June 15	230	—
Proper 7 The Sunday *c* to June 22	230	—
Proper 8 The Sunday *c* to June 29	230	—
Proper 9 The Sunday *c* to July 6	230	—
Proper 10 The Sunday *c* to July 13	231	—
Proper 11 The Sunday *c* to July 20	231	—
Proper 12 The Sunday *c* to July 27	231	—
Proper 13 The Sunday *c* to August 3	232	—
Proper 14 The Sunday *c* to August 10	232	—
Proper 15 The Sunday *c* to August 17	232	—
Proper 16 The Sunday *c* to August 24	232	—
Proper 17 The Sunday *c* to August 31	233	—
Proper 18 The Sunday *c* to September 7	233	—
Proper 19 The Sunday *c* to September 14	233	—
Proper 20 The Sunday *c* to September 21	234	—
Proper 21 The Sunday *c* to September 28	234	—
Proper 22 The Sunday *c* to October 5	234	—
Proper 23 The Sunday *c* to October 12	234	—
Proper 24 The Sunday *c* to October 19	235	—
Proper 25 The Sunday *c* to October 26	235	—
Proper 26 The Sunday *c* to November 2	235	—
Proper 27 The Sunday *c* to November 9	236	—
Proper 28 The Sunday *c* to November 16	236	—
Proper 29 The Sunday *c* to November 23	236	—

cloth

The Holy Table is spread with a clean white *c*	406	2

clothed

c with the vesture of the episcopate,	553	3

coffin

The *c* is to be closed before the service,	468	8
Then, while earth is cast upon the *c*,	485	—
The *c* is to be closed before the service,	490	8
Then, while earth is cast upon the *c*,	501	—

Collect

the C, Preface, and one or more of the Lessons	16	14
The C of the Day	55	—
A C for Sundays	56	—
A C for Fridays	56	—
A C for Saturdays	56	—
A C for the Renewal of Life	56	—
A C for Peace	57	—
A C for Grace	57	—
A C for Guidance	57	—
The C of the Day	68	—
A C for Sundays	69	—
A C for Fridays	69	—
A C for Saturdays	69	—
A C for Peace	69	—
A C for Aid against Perils	70	—
A C for Protection	70	—
A C for the Presence of Christ	70	—
The C of the Day	98	—
A C for Sundays	98	—
A C for Fridays	99	—
A C for Saturdays	99	—
A C for the Renewal of Life	99	—
A C for Peace	99	—
A C for Grace	100	—
A C for Guidance	100	—
C of the Day may be used.	107	—
C for the First Sunday of Advent	111	—
C for the First Sunday after Christmas	111	—
and C of the Day;	112	—
Silence, or a suitable C, or both,	113	—
other days of special significance, the C of the Day,	113	—
The C of the Day	122	—
C for Sundays	123	—
A C for Fridays	123	—
A C for Saturdays	123	—
A C for Peace	123	—
A C for Aid against Perils	123	—
A C for Protection	124	—
A C for the Presence of Christ	124	—
A C for Saturdays	134	—
one person is present, the Reading and the C	136	—
When desired, however, the C of the Day,	136	—
The C	137	—
The C	138	—
The C	139	—
The C	140	—
and its response, to the C of the Day.	142	20
the C of the Day.	153	—
Officiant concludes with the following or some other C	153	—
For use in the Litany in place of the Versicle and C	154	—
The C appointed for any Sunday or other Feast	158	22
The C immediately preceding and any of the sets	161	—
The preceding C, with the Psalm and Lessons	162	—
This C, with the corresponding Psalm and Lessons,	166	—
and continues with the Salutation and C of the Day.	175	—
The C "For the Nation," page 207, may be used	190	—
The C for Independence Day may be used instead.	207	—
The C immediately preceding and any of the sets	213	—
The preceding C, with the Psalm and Lessons	214	—
This C, with the corresponding Psalm and Lessons,	217	—
and continues with the Salutation and C of the Day.	227	—
The C "For the Nation," page 258, may be used	242	—
The C for Independence Day may be used instead.	258	—
C of the Day.	264	—
other appropriate C is said	271	—
celebration begins with the Salutation and C	272	—
begins in the usual manner, using the following C,	274	—
begins the liturgy with the C of the Day.	276	—
Immediately before the C, the Celebrant may say	276	—
C of the Day.	283	—
and the C provided, or some other suitable C,	288	—
The C of the Day	300	—
the principal service on a Sunday or other feast, the C	300	—

C (page 203 or 254) and one or more of the Lessons	312	21
The C of the Day	325	—
The Celebrant says the C.	325	—
The C of the Day	357	—
The Celebrant says the C	357	—
The Celebrant adds a concluding C.	385	—
The Celebrant adds a concluding C.	387	—
The Celebrant adds a concluding C.	388	—
The Celebrant adds a concluding C.	389	—
The Celebrant adds a concluding C,	391	—
concludes with an absolution or a suitable C.	393	—
The C at the Prayers	394	—
For the concluding C, the Celebrant selects	394	—
(a) a C appropriate to the season or occasion	394	—
(b) a C expressive of some special need	394	—
(c) a C for the mission of the Church;	394	—
(d) a general C such as the following:	394	—
with the following or some other C	397	—
Salutation and the C of the Day.	406	5
The C of the Day	414	—
the principal service on a Sunday or other feast, the C	414	—
C (page 203 or 254) and one or more of the Lessons	414	—
the C and Lessons appointed in the Marriage service.	433	—
until the conclusion of the C.	437	18
The Officiant says this C	464	—
Presiding Bishop stands and reads the C for the Day,	515	—
following C, or both, first saying	515	—
Bishop stands and reads the C for the Day,	527	—
or the following C,	527	—
Bishop stands and reads the C for the Day,	539	—
or the following C,	539	—
The Bishop says the appointed C.	551	—
the Officiant concludes with a suitable C.	551	—
or some other C, first saying	560	—
stands for the salutation and C at the end of it.	565	7
The C of the Day, or a C of the season,	565	7
See also Various Occasions no. 14, and C no. 6	818	—

collective

have some individual or *c* part in the celebration,	566	17

Collects

the following may be observed with the C,	18	1
Officiant then says one or more of the following C	55	—
Officiant then says one or more of the following C	68	—
Officiant then says one or more of the following C	98	—
The Officiant then says one of the following C.	107	—
either of the following, or one of the C	113	—
Officiant then says one or more of the following C	122	—
The Officiant then says one of the following C	133	—
convenience, appropriate Psalms, Readings, and C	136	—
or any of the C appointed in the Daily Offices,	136	—
or at the time of the hymn or anthem after the C.	142	12
or after the C of Morning or Evening Prayer;	148	—
The C	157	—
The Proper of the Church Year includes the appointed C;	158	3
C: Traditional	159	—
Either of the preceding C,	174	—
and of the following C,	195	—
Any of the C appointed for use at the Burial	202	—
C: Contemporary	211	—
Either of the preceding C,	226	—
any of the following C,	246	—
Any of the C appointed for use at the Burial	253	—
The Solemn C	277	—
Celebrant says the C.	277	—
share among them the reading of the C	284	14
The Celebrant says one of the following C	295	—
Suitable Psalms, Lessons, and C	465	—
The Celebrant says one of the following C,	469	—
C	493	—
numbered C beginning on pages 199 and 251.	813	18
For use after the C of Morning or Evening Prayer	814	—
People at the Eucharist, or at any time after the C	836	—

colleges

31. For Schools and C	811	10
31. For Schools and C	824	—

collegiality

as an expression of the *c* of the ministry	558	17

collegiate

from time to time, in Cathedral and C Churches,	867	27

Colossians

C 3:1	39	—
C 1:12	40	—
C 3:1	77	—
C 1:12	77	—
C 1:9, 11–14 (Saints' Days)	108	19
C 3:12–17 (Love which binds everything together	426	—

combined

follows suit, rendering the *c* title	583	33

combining

re-ordered by lengthening, *c*, or omitting some	934	18

come

intends to *c* to Communion, the priest shall speak	409	9
and tell him that he may not *c* to the Holy Table	409	10
the priest shall allow those who are penitent to *c*	409	22
parents, with other members of the family, should *c*	439	4
c together to join in the Litany.	462	—
It is appropriate that the family and friends *c*	465	—
(All that the Father giveth me shall *c* to me)	480	—
(All that the Father gives me will *c* to me)	495	—
nor things to *c*, nor powers, nor height, nor depth,	507	7
God in this life and in the life to *c*.	557	14
whence he shall *c* to judge the quick and the dead.	865	34

comes

the person *c* forward at the invitation	420	—

comfort

Here the Priest may offer counsel, direction, and *c*.	447	—
The Priest may then offer words of *c* and counsel.	450	—
Isaiah 61:1–3 (To *c* all that mourn)	470	—
Isaiah 6:1–3 (To *c* those who mourn)	494	—
a most wholesome Doctrine, and very full of *c*,	870	4
and unspeakable *c* to godly persons,	871	12

comforts

2 Corinthians 1:3–5 (God *c* us in affliction)	453	15

coming

While the people are *c* forward to receive 407 22
and *c* together to form one person and subsistence, 864 14
At whose *c* all men shall rise again with their bodies 865 35

commanded

not done as God hath willed and *c* them to be done, 870 16
When ye have done all that are *c* to you, say, 870 23
are not *c* by God's Law, either to vow the estate 874 12

commandment

Councils may not be gathered together without the *c* 872 5
Sacrament, by Christ's ordinance and *c*, 874 3
men, at the *c* of the Magistrate, to wear weapons, 876 10

commandments

Then the Ten C (page 317) may be said, 324 —
The Ten C 847 —
man whatsoever is free from the obedience of the C 869 13
Voluntary Works besides, over and above, God's C, 870 19

commemoration

have precedence over all other days of *c* 16 24
Good Friday and all other Fridays of the year, in *c* 17 25
a) at the *c* of a saint listed in the Calendar 195 —
b) at the patronal festival or *c* of a saint 195 —
Preface of the C of the Dead 202 —
a) at the *c* of a saint listed in the Calendar 246 —
b) at the patronal festival or *c* of a saint 246 —
Preface of the C of the Dead 253 —
C of the Dead 349 —
The departed (with *c* of a saint when appropriate) 359 —
C of the Dead 382 —
The departed (with *c* of a saint when appropriate) 383 —
Preface of the C of the Dead 482 —
Preface of the C of the Dead 498 —
and with *c* of benefactors, 576 20
7. Intercessions, including *c* of benefactors 578 3

commemorations

C listed in the Calendar 18 3
Other C, using the Common of Saints 18 4
vain repetitions, C, and Synodals, 866 18

commendation

A C at the Time of Death 464 —
preside at the Eucharist and pronounce the C. 468 14
C, or with the Committal. 481 —
C is used. 482 —
The C 482 —
preside at the Eucharist and pronounce the C. 490 14
C, or with the Committal. 498 —
C is used. 499 —
The C 499 —
8. If there is a Communion, it precedes the *c*, 506 21

commendatory

A C Prayer 465 —

commended

7. The deceased is *c* to God, 506 18

comment

After the Reading, the Celebrant may *c* on it briefly. 397 —
After any Reading, the Celebrant may *c* on it briefly. 454 13

commentary

It is a *c* on the creeds, 844 3

commerce

II. For *c* and industry 208 —
II. For *c* and industry 259 —

commission

Accordingly, a C for a review was issued 10 20
proper to revive it by any new C. 10 23
own name, but in Christ's, and do minister by his *c* 873 4
to a newly created Joint C on Christian Reunion. 877 28

commitment

make a mature public affirmation of their faith and *c* 412 4
and *c* to the responsibilities of their Baptism 412 9
A Form of C 420 1
c to the service of Christ in the world, 420 —
essential that the person seeking to make or renew a *c* 420 —
C, which may be in the form either of a statement 420 —
makes the Act of C. 420 —
C to Christian Service, or Blessing of Oil for the Sick. 576 17
an opportunity for the congregation to reaffirm its *c* 577 23

committal

or if desired, all or part of the service of C 468 10
If preferred, the C service may take place 468 11
continues with the Commendation, or with the C. 481 —
Unless the C follows immediately in the church, 482 —
The C 484 —
the service of C or at some other convenient time 487 —
or if desired, all or part of the service of C 490 10
If preferred, the C service may take place 490 11
continues with the Commendation, or with the C. 498 —
Unless the C follows immediately in the church, 499 —
The C 501 —
the service of C or at some other convenient time 503 —
The *c* may take place either where the preceding 506 19

committed

The ministry of reconciliation, which has been *c* 446 2
deceased is commended to God, and the body is *c* 506 18
Having *c* yourself to this work, do not forget 557 10
Not every deadly sin willingly *c* after Baptism 870 32
rule all estates and degrees *c* to their charge 876 4
deposit of Christian Faith and Order *c* by Christ 877 8

commodious

more profitable and *c*, than that which of late was used. 866 44
It is also more *c*, both for the shortness thereof, 867 4

common

The Book of C Prayer (1789) 8 2
set forth A Book of C Prayer, 8 8
c consent and authority, may be altered, abridged, 9 7
Book of C Prayer, laid it down as a rule, 9 14
c equity ought to be allowed to all human writings; 10 18
upon a comparison of this with the Book of C Prayer 11 11
Other Commemorations, using the C of Saints 18 4
Lectionary for Sundays, Holy Days, the C of Saints, 136 —
Directions concerning the C of Saints and services 158 24
The C of Saints 195 1
The C of Saints 246 6

When a *c* meal or Agape is a part of the celebration, 401 15
through the *c* prayer of Christians assembled 446 4
The most *c* verse is a couplet, 583 10
The First Book of C Prayer (1549) 866 2
appear by the *c* prayers in the Church, 866 5
ordained and approved by *c* authority, 874 27
as he that offendeth against the *c* order 874 28
9 That C Prayers and Sacraments 875 11
Of Christian Men's Goods, which are not *c*. 876 12
The Riches and Goods of Christians are not *c*, 876 13
with them on the basis of a *c* Faith and Order, 877 2
c and equal benefit of all men. 877 11

commonly

c called godparents, present their candidates, 298 21
c called the Catechism 845 —
c called The Creed of Saint Athanasius 864 20
c called Divine Service: 866 5
c when any book of the Bible was begun, 866 18
Books of the New Testament, as they are *c* received, 869 4
and that which is *c* called the Apostles' Creed, 869 16
and that which is *c* called the Apostles' Creed..." 869 21
Those five *c* called Sacraments, that is to say, 872 32
it was *c* said, that the Priest did offer Christ 874 9

commonwealth

thereof ought of necessity to be received in any *c*; 869 12

communicant

Opportunity is always to be given to every *c* to receive 407 25

communicants

The Bread and the Cup are given to the *c* 338 —
The Bread and the Cup are given to the *c* 365 —
does not suffice for the number of *c*, 408 10
available, the celebrant or deacon, and other *c*, 409 3
minister Holy Communion to those *c* who, 555 2

communicate

when possible, to *c* with them. 396 —
deacons at the Holy Table then *c*, and after them 407 24
Opportunity is always given to the people to *c*. 511 25
and *c* with the bishop. 524 16
Opportunity is always given to the people to *c*. 524 19
Opportunity is always given to the people to *c*. 536 19

communicated

or when desired, such persons may be *c* 396 —

communion

When there is a C 142 16
When C follows, the service continues 269 —
Where it is desired to administer Holy C 275 —
In places where Holy C is to be administered 282 —
The C 282 —
Holy Eucharist with the administration of Easter C. 284 9
administer Easter C from the Sacrament 284 29
Celebration of the Holy C 315 —
and in distributing C. 322 9
If there is no celebration of the C, 330 —
The Holy C 333 —
During the ministration of C, 338 —
After C, the Celebrant says 339 —
and in distributing C. 354 9
If there is no celebration of the C, 359 —
The Holy C 361 —
During the ministration of C, 365 —
After C, the Celebrant says 365 —
C under Special Circumstances 396 —
If there is no C, all that is appointed 406 25
While the people are coming forward to receive C, 407 22
authorize a deacon to distribute Holy C 408 18
during which time a *c* hymn may be sung. 408 22
may be required for the C of the sick, 408 29
administration of C by a deacon to a congregation 409 2
either after the C of the people or after the Dismissal. 409 4
intends to come to C, the priest shall speak 409 9
not allowing such persons to receive C 409 14
they may not receive C until they have forgiven 409 19
those who are penitent to come to C, 409 23
giving the reasons for refusing C. 409 25
If there is to be a C, 426 —
If C is to follow, 428 —
If there is not to be a C, 429 —
When C is not to follow, 431 —
At the C, it is appropriate that the newly married 432 —
receive C first, after the ministers. 432 —
If there is to be a C, 435 16
8. If there is no C, the service concludes 436 10
9. If there is to be a C, the service continues 436 13
and receive Holy C before other members 438 3
precede the distribution of Holy C, 453 9
When C is to follow 454 9
If C is not to follow, 456 —
Part III. Holy C 457 —
If C is to be administered from the reserved 457 —
form for C under Special Circumstances is used, 457 —
the benefits of C are received, 457 —
If there is to be a C, 470 —
If there is not to be a C, 480 —
When there is a C, the following serves 480 —
When there is no C, the service continues 481 —
If there is to be a C, 494 —
If there is not to be a C, 496 —
When there is a C, 496 —
When there is no C, the service continues 498 —
If there is to be a C, 506 11
8. If there is a C, it precedes 506 21
The family of the newly ordained may receive C 511 23
After C 522 —
The family of the newly ordained may receive C 524 17
After C 535 —
After receiving Holy C, the new deacon assists 536 14
The family of the newly ordained may receive C 536 17
After C 546 —
distributes Holy C to the people. 553 12
and receive Holy C. 554 10
others administer Holy C. 554 30
minister Holy C to those communicants who, 555 2
If the remaining Elements are not required for the C 555 4
priest of this Diocese, in *c* with your Bishop. 557 9
After C 564 —
in place of the usual postcommunion prayer, 564 —
66. Before Receiving C 812 21

67. After Receiving C 812 22
66. Before Receiving C 834 —
67. After Receiving C 834 —

communions

fellow-Christians of the different C in this land, 876 27
4. That this Church does not seek to absorb other C, 877 1
return of all Christian *c* to the principles of unity 877 6

community

The concerns of the local *c* 359 —
The concerns of the local *c* 383 —
the Christian *c*, and for the world. 436 8
for those who mourn, and for the Christian *c*, 506 16
Representatives of the congregation or of the *c*, 565 19
for the distinctive nature of the *c*, 576 20

comparison

upon a *c* of this with the Book of Common Prayer 11 11

compelled

For like as we are *c* by the Christian verity 865 5

compiling

since the first *c* of her Liturgy in the time of Edward 10 2

complete

a *c* rite in place of Evening Prayer, 108 4
Or, it may continue as a *c* evening Office 112 —
When this service continues as a *c* Office, 143 21
The *c* form of the service for the Dedication 575 2
but is not meant to be a *c* statement of belief 844 4
at once *c* in Godhead and *c* in manhood, 864 5

completed

When this action has been *c* for all candidates, 308 —
after the entire Prayer of Consecration is *c*, 553 23
after the entire Prayer of Consecration is *c*, 554 14

complied

c with, the man and the woman, together 435 8

Compline

Prayer or from C, may be so used 113 —
An Order for C 127 —

composed

When it is desired to use music *c* for them, 14 13
When a portion of the congregation is *c* of persons 406 21
other form may be *c* for the occasion, 576 19
Prayers originally *c* in traditional idiom 814 —

composers

increasingly favored by modern *c*. 582 26

compromise

and therefore incapable of *c* 877 9

concern

declare to all whom it may *c*, 876 27

concerning

C the Service 13 1
ordered in the preceding rules *c* Sundays, 16 23
C the Service 36 2
C the Service 74 1
C the Service 108 1
C the Proper 158 1
Directions *c* the Common of Saints and services 158 24
C the Vigil 284 1
C the Service 298 1
C the Celebration 322 1
At the following words *c* the bread, 334 —
and at the words *c* the cup, 334 —
At the following words *c* the bread, 342 —
and at the words *c* the cup, 342 —
C the Celebration 354 1
At the following words *c* the bread, 362 —
and at the words *c* the cup, 362 —
At the following words *c* the bread, 368 —
and at the words *c* the cup, 368 —
At the following words *c* the bread, 371 —
and at the words *c* the cup, 371 —
At the following words *c* the bread, 374 —
and at the words *c* the cup, 374 —
At the following words *c* the bread, 403 —
and at the words *c* the cup, 403 —
At the following words *c* the bread, 405 —
and at the words *c* the cup, 405 —
C the Service 412 1
C the Service 422 1
1. The teaching of the Church *c* Holy Matrimony, 435 11
C the Rite 446 1
C the Service 468 1
C the Service 490 1
C the Ordination of a Bishop 511 1
C the Service 524 1
C the Service 536 1
C the Service 558 1
C the Service 566 1
C the Psalter 582 1
C the Catechism 844 1
c the manner how to understand, do, and execute, 867 18
The Romish Doctrine *c* Purgatory, 872 12
C the Lectionary 888 1
C the Daily Office Lectionary 934 1

concerns

The *c* of the local community 359 —
The *c* of the local community 383 —

conclude

The Officiant may then *c* with one of the following 59 —
The Officiant may then *c* with one of the following 72 —
The Officiant may then *c* with one of the following 102 —
The Officiant may then *c* with one of the following 126 —
The service may then *c* with the Lord's Prayer; 407 3

concluded

The service may be *c* here with the singing of a hymn 280 —
The service may be *c* here with the Lord's Prayer 282 —
the service is *c* as directed on page 406. 330 —
the service is *c* as directed on page 406. 359 —
When a psalm is used, it may be *c* with Gloria Patri. 406 7

concludes

appropriately *c* the Office with a blessing. 36 7
appropriately *c* the Office with a blessing. 74 6
begins with the Invocation and *c* with the Doxology. 88 —
The service *c* as follows 107 —

The service *c* with the Song of Simeon	134	—
The Officiant *c*	135	—
the Litany *c* here, and the Eucharist begins	153	—
The Officiant *c* with the following	153	—
The Officiant *c*	155	—
The service *c* with the following prayer.	282	—
The service then *c* with the Lord's Prayer	283	—
The celebrant *c* the Renewal of Vows as follows	294	—
When used separately, it *c* with suitable prayers,	321	—
When used separately, it *c* with suitable prayers,	353	—
The Celebrant *c* with an absolution	393	—
The service *c* with a blessing or with a dismissal	399	—
The Prayer *c* with these or similar words	405	—
the Litany *c* with the Kyries,	406	4
The Bishop *c* with this prayer	419	—
a passage from the Gospel always *c* the Readings.	426	—
the service *c* with the Peace,	436	—
The Priest *c*	448	—
The Priest *c*	451	—
The Priest *c*	456	—
The service *c* with a blessing or with a dismissal	457	—
The Officiant *c*	466	—
a passage from the Gospel always *c* the Readings.	470	—
a passage from the Gospel always *c* the Readings.	494	—
The Celebrant *c* with one of the following	497	4
the Officiant *c* with a suitable Collect.	551	—
The Bishop *c*	569	—
After a period of silence, the Bishop *c*	572	—
After a brief silence, the Celebrant *c*	579	—
The alternate recitation *c*	582	15

concluding

c with the Prayers of the People,	284	25
and *c* with the reception of the newly baptized)	292	—
c with this prayer	311	—
The Celebrant adds a *c* Collect.	385	—
The Celebrant adds a *c* Collect.	387	—
The Celebrant adds a *c* Collect.	388	—
The Celebrant adds a *c* Collect.	389	—
The Celebrant adds a *c* Collect,	391	—
For the *c* Collect, the Celebrant selects	394	—
Suitable prayers may be offered, *c* with the following	397	—
and *c* with the reception	575	30

conclusion

And now, this important work being brought to a *c*,	11	16
Gloria Patri is always sung or said at the *c*	141	11
The Gloria printed at the *c* of certain Canticles	141	14
and should be read without announcement or *c*.	143	8
the *c* of this form of service.	143	30
It is appropriate that all remain standing until the *c*	437	17

concupiscence

that *c* and lust hath of itself the nature of sin.	869	32

condemnation

And although there is no *c* for them that believe	869	31
but rather, to their *c*, do eat	873	39

condemned

they are to be *c*, which say, they can no more sin	870	36

condition

The *c* of Man after the fall of Adam is such,	869	34

conditional

C Baptism	313	15

conditions

and the person baptized under emergency *c*,	314	7
2. For all Sorts and C of Men	810	7
2. For All Sorts and C of Men	814	—
study of the *c* under which so priceless a blessing	877	24

conduct

The celebrant may meet the body and *c* it	506	4

confer

by bishops who are themselves duly qualified to *c*	510	24
When a bishop is to *c* Holy Orders,	524	2
When a bishop is to *c* Holy Orders,	536	2

conference

face to face for a spiritual *c* leading to absolution	446	18
to enter into brotherly *c* with all	877	22
Lambeth C of 1888	877	29
That, in the opinion of this C, the following Articles	877	31

conferred

and the authority being *c*.	565	3

conferring

suitable for the *c* of the sacred orders of bishop,	510	31

confess

For the right Faith is, that we believe and *c*,	865	21
yet the Apostle doth *c*, that concupiscence and lust	869	32
As we *c* that vain and rash Swearing is forbidden	876	18

confessed

When the penitent has *c* all serious sins	446	20

confesses

Here the Penitent *c* particular sins.	450	—

confession

The following C of Sin may then be said;	41	—
C of Sin	41	—
The following C of Sin may then be said;	62	—
C of Sin	62	—
The following C of Sin may then be said;	79	—
C of Sin	79	—
The following C of Sin may then be said;	116	—
C of Sin	116	—
C of Saint Peter January 18	187	—
C of Saint Peter January 18	238	—
C of Sin may be omitted at this service.	273	—
A C of Sin	282	—
C of Sin	330	—
A C of Sin is said here if it has not been said earlier.	330	—
the C may be omitted.	330	—
C of Sin	359	—
A C of Sin is said here if it has not been said earlier.	359	—
the C may be omitted.	359	—
A C of Sin may follow.	397	—
(If it is desired to include a C of Sin,	406	26
Another Christian may be asked to hear a *c*,	446	12
When a *c* is heard in a church building,	446	15
The content of a *c* is not normally a matter	446	26
The secrecy of a *c* is morally absolute	446	27

The Priest may suggest the making of a special *c*, 454 15
Or else the following general *c* may be said 454 18
after the Creed, the General C, 552 6

confessions

C may be heard anytime 446 8

confessor

the *c* may sit inside the altar rails 446 15
If preferred, the *c* and penitent may sit 446 17
a confession is morally absolute for the *c*, 446 28

confidence

For Strength and C 459 —
59. For Quiet C 812 —
59. For Quiet C 832 —

confirm

establish and *c* their faith of eternal Salvation 871 15
strengthen and *c* our Faith in him. 872 29

confirmation

Holy Baptism or C 175 —
11. At C 203 —
Holy Baptism or C 227 —
11. At C 254 —
administers C, and normally preaches 284 13
C may also be administered. 292 —
In the absence of candidates for Baptism or C, 292 —
Holy Baptism, C, or the Renewal of Baptismal Vows 295 —
If C, Reception, or the Reaffirmation 308 —
At C, Reception, or Reaffirmation 309 —
For C 309 —
When there is no Baptism, the rites of C, 412 11
C 413 —
provided "At C" (page 929) may be substituted. 414 6
For C 418 —
five commonly called Sacraments, that is to say, C, 872 32

confirmed

presented by persons newly *c*. 412 17
Faith is *c*, and Grace increased by virtue 873 18
and *c* at the same time by authority of Parliament, 875 28

conflict

28. In Times of C 811 7
28. In Times of C 824 —

conform

The Intercessions on such occasions are to *c* 142 22
and that the intercessions *c* to the directions 322 20
and that the intercessions *c* to the directions 354 20
c to the laws of the State and the canons 422 6

conformable

herein was to make them *c* to what ought to be 10 35

conformed

the contemporary idiom may be *c* to traditional language. 14 5
Any of the forms may be *c* to the language of the Rite 383 —

confounding

neither *c* the Persons, nor dividing the Substance. 864 26

confusion

natures, without *c*, without change, without division, 864 12
not by *c* of Substance, but by unity of Person. 865 30

confute

and to *c* them that were adversaries to the truth. 866 12

congregation

the needs of the *c* so require. 13 11
members of the *c* to express intentions or objects 142 8
distributed to members of the *c*. 143 16
When circumstances permit, the *c* may gather 270 —
the *c* taking the part of the crowd. 273 —
The *c* may be seated for the first part of the Passion. 273 —
the *c* taking the part of the crowd. 277 —
The *c* may be seated for the first part of the Passion. 277 —
the *c* reads the parts in italics. 281 —
If candles have been distributed to members of the *c*, 286 —
have been presented, the Celebrant addresses the *c*, 303 —
The Celebrant then says to the *c* 305 —
at a place in full sight of the *c*, prays over them, 308 —
The Bishop says to the *c* 309 —
Representatives of the *c* bring the people's offerings 333 —
Representatives of the *c* bring the people's offerings 361 —
Members of the *c* may ask the prayers 386 —
in the life of the local *c*; 394 —
or from the midst of the *c*. 406 19
When a portion of the *c* is composed of persons 406 21
to the *c* from the reserved Sacrament 408 19
administration of Communion by a deacon to a *c* 409 2
a scandal to the other members of the *c*, 409 14
hatred between members of the *c*, 409 18
the Bishop addresses the *c*, saying 416 —
The Bishop then says to the *c* 417 —
and, standing before the *c*, makes 420 —
addresses the *c* and says 423 —
The Celebrant then addresses the *c*, saying 425 —
may be exchanged throughout the *c*. 431 —
The Celebrant then addresses the *c*, saying 434 —
The C responds 434 —
before other members of the *c*. 438 4
to be welcomed by the *c* and to give thanks 439 5
The Celebrant addresses the *c* 440 —
The Celebrant addresses the *c* 440 —
The Minister of the C is directed to instruct 445 —
the Minister of the C is to be notified. 453 2
When a person is near death, the Minister of the C 462 —
A member of the *c* bearing the lighted Paschal Candle 467 —
in consultation with, the Minister of the C. 468 4
should be held at a time when the *c* has opportunity 468 6
in consultation with, the Minister of the C. 490 4
should be held at a time when the *c* has opportunity 490 6
the Celebrant may address the *c*, 492 —
or chapel, or it may be in place before the *c* 506 5
before other members of the *c*. 511 24
After the Sermon, the C sings a hymn. 516 —
family members, and the *c*. 522 —
before other members of the *c*. 524 18
The C then says or sings the Nicene Creed 529 —
The new Priest then says to the *c* 534 —
before other members of the *c*. 536 18
The C then says or sings the Nicene Creed. 541 —

The Bishop then says to the *c*	546	2
sung responsively between a bishop and the *c*,	552	15
Other priests, if any, who serve in the same *c*	558	11
Lay persons from the *c* read the Old Testament	558	14
and dismiss the *c*.	558	22
The Bishop then addresses the *c*	559	—
and any responses to it, the *c* sings a hymn.	560	—
Representatives of the *c* and of the clergy	561	—
Representatives of the *c* present a Bible, saying	561	—
Other Representatives of the *c* present bread	562	—
The Bishop then presents the new minister to the *c*,	563	—
The C expresses its approval.	563	—
family members, and the *c*.	563	—
or an address about the work of the *c*	565	17
Representatives of the *c*	565	18
remain in the sight of the *c* during the Induction.	565	22
It is desirable that all members of the *c*,	566	16
The *c* standing, the Bishop begins the Prayer	568	—
A Warden or other representative of the *c* continues	568	—
The Deacon or a member of the *c* leads the Prayers	572	—
Members of the *c* vest the Altar,	574	—
the *c* may assemble inside the church;	575	12
members of the *c* with flowers, candles, hangings,	576	2
lay person outline the plans of the *c* for witness	576	12
bishop may respond, indicating the place of this *c*	576	13
an opportunity for the *c* to reaffirm its commitment	577	23
c attains recognition as a parish.	577	25
e.g., between choir and *c*,	582	14
or between one side of the *c* and the other.	582	15
c singing a refrain after each verse	582	21
the minister alternating with the *c*,	582	28
especially such as were Ministers of the *c*,	866	10
to the end that the *c* may be thereby edified:	867	24
and Chapels to the same annexed, shall serve the *c*.	867	28
The visible Church of Christ is a *c* of faithful men,	871	30
XXIII. Of Ministering in the C.	872	15
or ministering the Sacraments in the C,	872	17
have public authority given unto them in the C,	872	19
XXIV. Of Speaking in the C in such a Tongue	872	21
when the same *c* attends two or more services.	888	8
c is present for Morning or Evening Prayer,	888	12

congregational

c use, whether by singing or reading.	582	3

congress

20. For C or a State Legislature	810	29
20. For C or a State Legislature	821	—

congruent

or from this Book, or from texts *c* with them.	14	8

congruity

or (as the School-authors say) deserve grace of *c*:	870	15

conjunction

the Hebrew text has Adonai and YHWH in *c*.	583	32

conjunctions

c which refer only to what has preceded,	888	26

conscience

with a good *c* use and submit unto,	10	16
penitent has confessed all serious sins troubling the *c*	446	20
if the sick person's *c* is troubled,	454	16
26. For those who Suffer for the sake of C	811	4
26. For those who suffer for the sake of C	823	—

consciences

and woundeth the *c* of the weak	874	29

consecrate

The Bishop may then *c* oil of Chrism,	307	—
c more of either or both, by saying	408	11
or else the celebrant may *c* more of both kinds,	408	13
The Bishop may *c* oil of Chrism for use at Baptism,	419	—
This service may be used to dedicate and *c* a church	566	9
the bishop may *c* oil of Chrism,	575	26

consecrated

the Sacrament for that purpose is *c* at this service.	275	4
Easter Communion from the Sacrament previously *c*.	284	29
been previously *c* by the bishop.	298	15
containing wine to be *c*.	334	—
The Celebrant breaks the *c* Bread.	337	—
containing wine to be *c*.	342	—
containing wine to be *c*.	362	—
The Celebrant breaks the *c* Bread.	364	—
containing wine to be *c*.	368	—
containing wine to be *c*.	371	—
containing wine to be *c*.	374	—
containing wine to be *c*.	403	—
containing wine to be *c*.	405	—
the *c* Bread and Wine separately.	407	26
customary for the celebrant to administer the *c* Bread	408	4
If the *c* Bread or Wine does not suffice	408	9
the deacon reverently places the *c* Sacrament	408	21
If any of the *c* Bread or Wine remain,	408	28
If the sick person cannot receive either the *c* Bread	457	—
for which the new bishop is to be *c*,	511	10
Similarly, all the new priests break the *c* Bread	554	9
When a new church is being *c*,	575	15
period of time without having been *c*,	577	22
And, therefore, whosoever are *c* or ordered	875	24
rightly, orderly, and lawfully *c* and ordered.	875	25
And therefore whosoever are *c*	875	30
or hereafter shall be *c* or ordered to the same Rites;	875	32
rightly, orderly, and lawfully *c* and ordered."	875	33

consecrates

[*c* the Chrism;]	298	10
When necessary, the Celebrant *c* additional bread	338	—
When necessary, the Celebrant *c* additional bread	365	—

consecrating

c bishops, and representative presbyters of the diocese,	553	9

consecration

C of the Chrism	307	—
and join in the *c* of the gifts,	322	8
and join in the *c* of the gifts,	354	8
The C of a Grave	487	—
The C of a Grave	503	—
ordination and *c* are appointed.	510	21
The C of the Bishop	520	—
The Presiding Bishop then begins this Prayer of C	520	—
The C of the Priest	533	—

The Bishop then says this Prayer of C. 533 —
The C of the Deacon 544 —
The Bishop then says this Prayer of C 545 —
The hymn to the Holy Spirit before the Prayer of C 552 14
Following the C Prayer, 553 2
without signing the Letters of C. 553 17
placed upon the new priest after the entire Prayer of C 553 22
During the Prayer of C, the bishop and priests lay 553 30
after the entire Prayer of C is completed, 554 14
During the Prayer of C the Bishop is to lay hands 554 20
the ________ year of my *c*. 557 19
This service provides for the dedication and *c* 566 2
C of a Church 567 —
C of the Church 568 —
complete form of the service for the Dedication and C 575 2
portions of the service for the Dedication and C 577 8
c of a church, or on other suitable occasions. 579 —
XXXVI. Of C of Bishops and Ministers. 875 20
The Book of C of Bishops, and Ordering of Priests 875 21
all things necessary to such C and Ordering; 875 23
"The Book of C of Archbishops and Bishops, 875 26
contain all things necessary to such C and Ordering: 875 29

consecrator

presides and serves as chief *c*. 511 8
c presides from a chair placed close to the people, 511 13
sit to the right and left of the chief *c*. 511 15

consecrators

At least two other bishops serve as co-*c*. 511 8

consecutively

the Propers are used *c*. 158 16

consent

common *c* and authority, may be altered, abridged, 9 7
Declaration of C, read the Gospel, and perform 422 13
The Declaration of C 424 —
and their free *c*, is publicly ascertained. 435 14
After the Declaration of C, 437 8

consequence

Civil Rulers, in *c* of the Revolution. 10 34

conservation

41. For the C of Natural Resources 811 23
41. For the C of Natural Resources 827 —

consideration

c of the great profit that shall ensue thereof. 867 15
As the godly *c* of Predestination, and our Election 871 11

considerations

important *c*, according to the various exigency 9 18
upon just and weighty *c* her thereunto moving, 10 3
When, for pastoral *c*, neither of the burial rites 506 2

considered

c too sacred to be pronounced; 583 19
These inconveniences therefore *c*, here is set forth 866 33
laws of England are *c* as inapplicable 875 16

considering

seriously *c* what Christianity is, 11 19

consistently

c with the constitution and laws of their country. 10 30

consisting

c also of a reasonable soul and body; 864 6

consists

Church Year *c* of two cycles of feasts and holy days: 15 3
The service normally *c* of four parts: 284 5

constantly

he hath *c* decreed by his counsel secret to us, 871 3

constituted

regularly and legitimately *c*. 875 38

constitution

consistently with the *c* and laws of their country. 10 30
as directed by Article VIII of the C of this Church 552 10
Representative clergy of the diocese present the C 562 5
c and laws of England are considered as inapplicable 875 16

construction

if allowed such just and favourable *c* 10 17
the building(s), the keys, and tools used in its *c* 575 18
c occurs in the Canticle, "The Song of Moses." 584 3

consultation

prepare in advance, in *c* with the celebrant, 420 —
in *c* with, the Minister of the Congregation. 468 4
in *c* with, the Minister of the Congregation. 490 4

consume

c the remaining Elements, and cleanse the vessels 555 6

consumed

any of the Sacrament that remains is then *c*. 401 14

contain

doth *c* a godly and wholesome Doctrine, 874 36
doth *c* all things necessary to such Consecration 875 22

contained

to these services and the other rites *c* in the Book, 13 7
c in this Book celebrated in the context of a Rite 14 4
the things *c* in this book: 867 19
contrary to any thing *c* in this book. 867 22

containeth

Holy Scripture *c* all things necessary to salvation: 868 20

containing

hand upon the cup and any other vessel *c* wine 334 —
hand upon the cup and any other vessel *c* wine 342 —
hand upon the cup and any other vessel *c* wine 362 —
hand upon the cup and any other vessel *c* wine 368 —
hand upon the cup and any other vessel *c* wine 371 —
hand upon the cup and any other vessel *c* wine 374 —
hand upon the cup and any other vessel *c* wine 403 —
hand upon the cup and any other vessel *c* wine 405 —
as "*c* all things necessary to salvation," 877 33

contemporary

the *c* idiom may be conformed to traditional 14 5
Any of the prayers in *c* language may be adapted 108 22
Collects: C 211 —

The Decalogue: *C* 350 —
to assist in rendering them into *c* speech. 814 —

contended
have *c* for the religion of Christ: 876 28

content
The *c* of a confession is not normally a matter 446 26

context
this Book celebrated in the *c* of a Rite One service, 14 4
the *c* requires that the Divine Name 584 1
as being more appropriate to this *c*; 584 7

continual
as did break the *c* course of the reading 866 38

continually
c profit more and more in the knowledge of God, 866 14
to have *c* before their eyes the sentence 871 17

continuance
c of nursing care and protection, 9 13
in *c* of time hath not been corrupted: 866 4

continue
c at once with "O Lord, open thou our lips." 41 —
c at once with "O God, make speed to save us." 62 —
c at once with "Lord, open our lips." 79 —
The service may then *c* in any of the following ways: 112 —
Or, it may *c* as a complete evening Office 112 —
c at once with "O God, make speed to save us." 116 —
C with the Lord's Prayer, page 336. 343 —
C with the Lord's Prayer on page 364. 369 —
C with the Lord's Prayer on page 364. 372 —
C with the Lord's Prayer on page 364. 376 —
to maintain and *c* these three orders; 510 20
All *c* to stand, except the bishop-elect, 520 —

continued
have still been *c* firm and unshaken. 10 7

continues
The service then *c* with the [Peace and] Offertory. 142 24
When this service *c* as a complete Office, 143 21
and *c* with the Salutation and Collect of the Day. 175 —
and *c* with the Salutation and Collect of the Day. 227 —
The Celebrant *c* 267 —
the service *c* with the Offertory. 269 —
The service *c* with the Prayers of the People. 275 —
The celebration *c* with the Prayers of the People. 295 —
The Celebrant then *c* 299 —
The service then *c* with the Prayers of the People 310 —
the service *c* with the Lord's Prayer 311 2
c with the Kyrie eleison, the Trisagion, 321 —
Then the Celebrant *c* 334 —
Then the Celebrant *c* 341 —
c with the Gloria in excelsis, the Kyrie eleison, 353 —
Then the Celebrant *c* 362 —
The Celebrant *c* 363 —
Then the Celebrant *c* 368 —
The Celebrant *c* 369 —
The Celebrant *c* 371 —
Then the Celebrant *c* 373 —
The Celebrant *c* 375 —
The Prayer *c* with these words 403 —
The Bishop then *c* 413 —
The service then *c* with the Prayers of the People 419 —
the service *c* with the Lord's Prayer 419 —
The service then *c* with the exchange of the Peace 421 —
The liturgy *c* with the Offertory, 432 —
The service *c* with The Prayers on page 428. 434 —
the service *c* with the Peace 436 13
The service *c* with the Magnificat 440 —
The Priest then *c* 450 —
the service *c* on page 469 or 491. 467 —
the service *c* with the following prayer 480 —
the service *c* with the Commendation, 481 —
The service *c* with the Peace and the Offertory. 482 —
the service *c* with the [blessing and] 482 —
the service *c* with the Prayers of the People, 496 —
the service *c* with the Commendation, 498 —
The service *c* with the Peace and the Offertory. 498 —
the service *c* with the [blessing and] 499 —
If no objection is made, the Presiding Bishop *c* 514 —
The Presiding Bishop *c* 521 —
The liturgy *c* with the Offertory. 522 —
If no objection is made, the Bishop *c* 527 —
The Bishop then *c* 534 —
The liturgy *c* with the Offertory. 535 —
If no objection is made, the Bishop *c* 539 —
The Bishop then *c* 545 —
The liturgy *c* with the Offertory. 546 —
the bishop *c* "May they exalt you, 554 3
the bishop *c*, "Make them, 554 24
The service *c* with the Offertory. 563 —
Warden or other representative of the congregation *c* 568 —
The Rector or Minister in charge *c* 569 —
and the service *c* as directed on page 575. 569 —
The Bishop lays a hand upon the Table, and *c* 573 —
The service *c* with the Offertory. 574 —

continuing
and *c* with the appointed Psalmody; 61 —
and *c* with the appointed Psalmody; 115 —

continuity
secure *c* or avoid repetition. 934 19

contrary
there be not any thing in it *c* 10 14
so that the same order be not *c* 867 21
The Old Testament is not *c* to the New: 869 7
so that the flesh lusteth always *c* to the Spirit; 869 26
not lawful for the Church to ordain any thing that is *c* 871 38

contrast
or of *c* (The Lord knows 583 6

contrition
and has given evidence of due *c*, 446 21

controversies
to decree Rites or Ceremonies, and authority in *C* 871 37

convenience
For *c*, appropriate Psalms, Readings, and Collects 136 —

convenient

or otherwise disposed of, as may seem most *c* 9 8
in their respective times were thought *c*; 10 5
c for their future prosperity; 10 30
transferred to the first *c* open day within the week. 16 13
candles and lamps as may be *c*. 112 2
or in some other *c* manner. 136 —
dining table, or at some other *c* place. 143 18
It is celebrated at a *c* time 284 3
a *c* time before the Liturgy on Easter Day. 284 31
or at the end of the service, as *c*. 407 13
assemble in the church or in some other *c* place. 435 9
As soon as *c* after the birth of a child, 439 3
the service of Committal or at some other *c* time 487 —
the service of Committal or at some other *c* time 503 —
The other bishops, or a *c* number of them, 511 14
members and others, as may be *c*. 534 —
members and others, as may be *c*. 546 —
or in some other *c* manner. 552 16
take place at some *c* time prior to the service. 552 18
cleanse the vessels in some *c* place. 555 7
When *c*, the procession may go 575 7

conveniently

remain where they may *c* hear the reading 437 14
place at several *c* separated places in the church. 553 13
until a revision of them may be *c* made, 875 18

convention

Episcopal Church in the United States of America, in C, 8 4
This C having, in their present session, 8 7
while these alterations were in review before the C, 11 3
13. For a Church C 204 —
13. For a Church C 255 —
12. For a Church C or Meeting 810 18
12. For a Church C or Meeting 818 1
Episcopal Church in the United States of America, in C, 867 32
the General C of this Church in 1792, 875 22

conversion

C of Saint Paul January 25 187 4
C of Saint Paul January 25 238 10
One, not by *c* of the Godhead into flesh, 865 29

copy

each is to be presented with a separate *c* 552 12

Corinthians

1 C 15:57 39 —
1 C 5:7–8; 46 —
1 C 15:20–22 46 —
2 C 13:14 59 —
2 C 13:14 72 —
1 C 15:57 77 —
1 C 5:7–8; 83 —
1 C 15:20–22 83 —
2 C 13:14 102 —
2 C 5:17–18 106 —
2 C 4:5–6 110 —
2 C 13:14 126 —
2 C 4:5–6 139 —
2 C 5:2ob–6:10 264 —
1 C 11:23–26 (27–32) 274 —
1 C 13:1–13 (Love is patient and kind) 426 —
2 C 1:3–5 (God comforts us in affliction) 453 —
1 C 15:20–26, 35–38, 42–44, 53–58 475 —
2 C 4:16–5:9 475 —
1 C 15:20–26, 35–38, 42–44, 53–38 495 —
2 C 4:16–5:9 495 —
or 2 C 3:4–9 515 —
2 C 4:1–6, 540 —
or 1 C 3:1–11, 16–17, 571 —

correctional

37. For Prisons and C Institutions 811 16
37. For Prisons and C Institutions 826 —

correspond

lines *c* to Hebrew versification, 583 2

corresponding

liturgical texts may be used in place of the *c* texts 14 14
by changing the pronouns and the *c* verbs. 108 23
This Collect, with the *c* Psalm and Lessons, 166 —
with one of the *c* sets of Psalms and Lessons, 195 —
This Collect, with the *c* Psalm and Lessons, 217 —
with one of the *c* sets of Psalms and Lessons, 246 —

corresponds

the numbered Proper which *c* 176 —
the numbered Proper which *c* 176 —
the numbered Proper which *c* 227 —
the numbered Proper which *c* 228 —

corrupt

have grown partly of the *c* following of the Apostles, 872 34

corrupted

in continuance of time hath not been *c*: 866 4

corruption

it is the fault and *c* of the Nature of every man, 869 24

cosmic

II The C Order 47 —
I The C Order 88 —

council

C of Chalcedon, 451 A.D., Act V 864 3
Episcopal Church in the United States of America, in C 876 25

councils

and to take your share in the *c* of the Church. 557 4
XXI. Of the Authority of General C. 872 1
"General C may not be gathered together 872 5

counsel

evidence of due contrition, the priest gives such *c* 446 21
Here the Priest may offer *c*, direction, and comfort. 447 —
The Priest may then offer words of comfort and *c*. 450 —
he hath constantly decreed by his *c* secret to us, 871 3

counted

are not to be *c* for Sacraments of the Gospel, 872 33

countries

and may be changed according to the diversity of *c*, 874 23

country

and laws of their *c*.	10	31
18. For our C	810	27
25. For those in the Armed Forces of our C	811	3
18. For our C	820	—
25. For those in the Armed Forces of our C	823	—

couple

The newly married *c* then greet each other,	431	—
c may present the offerings of bread and wine.	432	—
it is appropriate that the newly married *c*	432	—
or bishop pronounces a solemn blessing upon the *c*.	436	9

couplet

The most common verse is a *c*,	583	10

course

But when in the *c* of Divine Providence,	10	24
either at the bidding, or in the *c* of the prayer;	142	9
In the *c* of the silence after each bidding,	385	—
In the *c* of their Christian development,	412	2
as did break the continual *c* of the reading	866	—

courts

21. For C of Justice	810	30
21. For C of Justice	821	—

covenant

The Baptismal C	304	—
The Baptismal C	416	—
Christian marriage is a solemn and public *c*	422	2
to renew their Baptismal C	810	22
to renew their Baptismal C	819	—
The Old C	846	—
The New C	850	—

covered

It is appropriate that it be *c* with a pall	468	9
It is appropriate that it be *c* with a pall	490	9

covering

that it be covered with a pall or other suitable *c*.	468	9
that it be covered with a pall or other suitable *c*.	490	9
For the *c* and decoration of the Altar,	576	22

created

Genesis 1:26–28 (Male and female he *c* them)	426	—
The Father is made of none, neither *c*, but begotten.	865	8
neither made, nor *c*, nor begotten,	865	9
to a newly *c* Joint Commission on Christian Reunion.	877	28

creation

1 A Song of C	47	—
12 A Song of C	88	—
III. For stewardship of *c*	208	—
III. For stewardship of *c*	259	—
The story of C	288	—
gives thanks to God the Father for his work in *c*	402	11
gives thanks to God the Father for his work in *c*	404	—
nor anything else in all *c*,	507	8
1. For Joy in God's C	810	6
40. For Knowledge of God's C	811	22
1. For Joy in God's C	814	—
40. For Knowledge of God's C	827	—

creator

The hymn, Veni C Spiritus,	520	—
The hymn, Veni C Spiritus,	533	—
The hymn, Veni C Spiritus,	544	—

creatures

III The Earth and its C	48	—
II The Earth and its C	89	—

creed

The Apostles' C	53	—
The text of the C on page 96 may be used instead.	54	—
The Apostles' C	66	—
The text of the C on page 120 may be used instead.	66	—
The Apostles' C	96	—
The Apostles' C	120	—
the Apostles' C may be said.	137	—
The Apostles' C is omitted from the Office	142	2
the Eucharist with its own C is to follow.	142	3
the Nicene C may take the place of the Apostles' C,	142	18
the Nicene C and the Confession of Sin	273	—
The Nicene C is not used at this service.	295	—
take the place of the Nicene C at the Eucharist.	312	17
The Nicene C is not used at this service.	312	27
The Nicene C	326	—
The Nicene C	358	—
the C may be omitted.	406	6
after the C, before the Offertory, or at the end	407	13
The Nicene C is not used at this service.	412	15
The Apostles' C may be recited after the Lessons,	437	20
The Apostles' C may be said, all standing.	480	—
The Apostles' C may then be said, all standing.	496	—
introduce the C with these or similar words	496	—
and the Apostles' C may be recited.	506	13
The Congregation then says or sings the Nicene C	529	—
The Congregation then says or sings the Nicene C.	541	—
the Prayers of the People after the C,	552	6
If the Apostles' C has not already been said,	572	—
the Nicene C is now said or sung.	572	—
and the *c* of the Fathers has handed down to us.	864	17
The C of Saint Athanasius	864	21
The Nicene C, and that which is	869	16
commonly called the Apostles' C,	869	16
"The Three Creeds, Nicene C, Athanasius's C,	869	20
and that which is commonly called the Apostles' C	869	21
2. The Nicene C as the sufficient statement	877	15
(b) The Apostles' C, as the Baptismal Symbol;	877	35
and the Nicene C, as the sufficient statement	877	35

creeds

It is a commentary on the *c*,	844	4
The C	851	—
VIII. Of the C.	869	15
entitled "Of the Three C;	869	20
"The Three C, Nicene Creed, Athanasius's Creed,	869	20

cremation

It may also be used prior to *c*.	468	12
It may also be used prior to *c*.	490	12

cross

Holy C Day	16	29
Holy C Day, and December 13	18	7

the transfiguration and Holy *C*	43	—
the Transfiguration and Holy *C*	81	—
Holy *C* Day September 14	192	—
6. Of the Holy *C*	201	—
Holy *C* Day September 14	244	—
6. Of the Holy *C*	252	—
If desired, a wooden *c* may now be brought	281	—
extolling the glory of the *c*, is then sung.	282	—
the sign of the *c* [using Chrism if desired]	308	—
makes the sign of the *c* on the sick person's forehead,	456	7
with the sign of the *c* saying	568	—
The *c* signed on the threshold by the bishop	575	20
processional *c* may be used for the signing.	575	22
Of the one Oblation of Christ finished upon the *C*.	874	5

crowd

taking the part of the *c*.	273	—
taking the part of the *c*.	277	—

crucified

who truly suffered, was *c*, dead,	868	6

crucifixion

in commemoration of the Lord's *c*,	17	26

cultures

7. For the Diversity of Races and *C*	813	9
7. For the Diversity of Races and *C*	840	—

cup

and at the words concerning the *c*,	334	8
place a hand upon the *c* and any other vessel	334	9
The Bread and the *C* are given to the communicants	338	5
and at the words concerning the *c*,	342	2
place a hand upon the *c* and any other vessel	342	3
and at the words concerning the *c*,	362	5
place a hand upon the *c* and any other vessel	362	6
The Bread and the *C* are given to the communicants	365	4
and at the words concerning the *c*,	368	4
place a hand upon the *c* and any other vessel	368	5
and at the words concerning the *c*,	371	4
place a hand upon the *c* and any other vessel	371	5
and at the words concerning the *c*,	374	2
place a hand upon the *c* and any other vessel	374	3
the bread, the *c* of wine, and other offerings,	401	5
and at the words concerning the *c*,	403	5
place a hand upon the *c* and any other vessel	403	6
and at the words concerning the *c*,	405	2
place a hand upon the *c* and any other vessel	405	3
preparing and placing upon it the bread and *c*	407	15
and likewise the *C* of Blessing is a partaking	873	26
C of the Lord is not to be denied to the Lay-people:	874	2

curates

by this order the *c* shall need none other books	867	5

curious

So, for *c* and carnal persons,	871	16

curse

to deliver from *c* and damnation those	871	4

custom

In accordance with ancient *c*, it is desirable,	511	3
Then, the Hebrew *c* is to substitute Elohim	583	32
and the *c* of the Primitive Church,	872	22

customary

Candle, if used, should be burning in its *c* place	143	3
c responses before and after the Gospel are omitted.	272	14
c responses before and after the Gospel are omitted.	277	1
It is *c* for all the ordained ministers present,	284	10
It is *c* that the Paschal Candle burn at all services	287	2
It is *c* to add a little water to the wine.	407	15
it is *c* for the celebrant to administer	408	4
It is *c* that the celebrant meet the body	468	21
It is *c* that the celebrant meet the body	490	21

customs

or to traditional *c*, this Church is ready in the spirit	876	34

cut

For this cause be *c* off Anthems,	866	37
by open denunciation of the Church is rightly *c* off	874	17

cutting

and, finally, the *c* off occasion,	10	12

cycle

The Lectionary for Sundays is arranged in a three-year *c*,	888	2
of the other years of the three-year Sunday *c*,	888	14
Daily Office Lectionary is arranged in a two-year *c*.	934	2

cycles

The Church Year consists of two *c* of feasts and holy	15	3

D

daily

major Feasts, and *D* Morning and Evening Prayer,	13	4
whether in the form provided in the *D* Offices,	13	23
The *D* Office	35	—
In the *D* Office, the term "Officiant" is used to denote	36	—
D Morning Prayer:	37	—
It may also be used *d* until the Day of Pentecost.	45	—
D Evening Prayer:	61	—
In the *D* Office, the term "Officiant" is used to denote	74	2
D Morning Prayer:	75	—
It may also be used *d* until the Day of Pentecost.	83	—
D Evening Prayer:	115	—
D Devotions for Individuals and Families	136	—
devotions follow the basic structure of the *D* Office	136	—
or any of the Collects appointed in the *D* Offices,	136	—
b) the *D* Office Lectionary, page 934	136	—
manual of devotion which provides *d* selections	136	—
24. For Vocation in *D* Work	210	—
24. For Vocation in *D* Work	261	—
or the *D* Office, or it may be used separately.	548	—
reciting the psalms in the *D* Office.	582	—
this form of sacred song in the *D* Office.	582	24
(by *d* hearing of holy Scripture read in the Church)	866	13
now of late time a few of them have been *d* said	866	28
which *d* they shall obtain by reading upon the book,	867	14
or that of the *D* Office.	888	11

Lectionary for the *D* Office. 888 15
appointed for the same day in the *D* Office Lectionary. 888 24
Concerning the *D* Office Lectionary 934 1
The *D* Office Lectionary is arranged in a two-year 934 2

damnation

it deserveth God's wrath and *d*. 869 27
and *d* those whom he hath chosen in Christ 871 4
purchase to themselves *d*, as Saint Paul saith. 872 40

dance

and response may include readings, song, talk, *d*, 400 9

dangerous

Predestination, is a most *d* downfall, 871 18
or guilt, were blasphemous fables, and *d* deceits. 874 10

Daniel

D 9:9,10 38 —
D 9:9,10 76 —

dark

The church is *d*, or partially so, when the service 109 —

darkness

In the *d*, fire is kindled; 285 —

date

dependent upon the movable *d* of the Sunday 15 4
the other, upon the fixed *d* of December 25, 15 5
depends upon the *d* of Easter Day. 15 9
The *d* of Easter also determines the beginning of Lent 15 12
in addition to its observance of the fixed *d*. 15 22
determined by the calendar *d* of that Sunday. 158 11
the calendar *d* of which falls on that Sunday, 158 14
to the *d* of Pentecost in that year is used. 176 —
to the *d* of Trinity Sunday in that year is used. 176 —
to the *d* of Pentecost in that year is used. 227 —
to the *d* of Trinity Sunday in that year is used. 228 —

dated

the *d* days listed above, only the following feasts, 16 3

day

this Sixteenth *D* of October, in the Year of Our Lord 8 5
in use from and after the First *D* of October, 8 12
on the Lord's *D* and other major Feasts, 13 4
the Sunday of the Resurrection or Easter *D*; 15 5
our Lord's Nativity or Christmas *D*. 15 6
Easter *D* is always the first Sunday after the full moon 15 7
depends upon the date of Easter *D*. 15 10
always the four Sundays before Christmas *D*, 15 11
Ascension on a Thursday forty days after Easter *D*. 15 13
Easter *D* 15 16
All Saints' *D*, November 1 15 16
Ascension *D* 15 17
Christmas *D*, December 25 15 17
The *D* of Pentecost 15 18
These feasts take precedence of any other *d* or observance. 15 20
All Saints' *D* may always be observed on the Sunday 15 21
transferred to the first convenient open *d* 16 13
Holy Cross *D* 16 29
Independence *D* 17 5
Thanksgiving *D* 17 6
observed on any open *d* within the week. 17 18
Christmas *D*, the Epiphany, and All Saints' *D*. 17 19
the First Sunday in Lent, the *D* of Pentecost, 18 6
Holy Cross *D*, and December 13 18 7
Wednesday before Ascension *D* 18 9
Easter Season, including Ascension *D* 39 —
and the *D* of Pentecost 39 —
From Easter *D* until the Ascension 43 —
From Ascension *D* until the *D* of Pentecost 43 —
On the *D* of Pentecost 43 —
It may also be used daily until the *D* of Pentecost. 45 —
The Collect of the *D* 55 —
From Easter *D* through the *D* of Pentecost 59 —
The Collect of the *D* 68 —
From Easter *D* through the *D* of Pentecost 72 —
Easter Season, including Ascension *D* 77 —
and the *D* of Pentecost 77 —
From Easter *D* until the Ascension 81 —
From Ascension *D* until the *D* of Pentecost 81 —
On the *D* of Pentecost 81 —
It may also be used daily until the *D* of Pentecost. 83 —
The Collect of the *D* 98 —
From Easter *D* through the *D* of Pentecost 102 —
An Order of Service for Noonday 103 —
Collect of the *D* may be used. 107 —
from Easter *D* through the *D* of Pentecost 109 —
and Collect of the *D*; 112 —
days of special significance, the Collect of the *D*, 113 —
The Collect of the *D* 122 —
From Easter *D* through the *D* of Pentecost 126 —
When desired, however, the Collect of the *D*, 136 —
At the Close of *D* 140 —
prayers of thanksgiving for the blessings of the *d*, 140 —
and its response, to the Collect of the *D*. 142 20
From Easter *D* through the *D* of Pentecost, 143 2
from the Office Lectionary or the Proper of the *D*, 143 24
the Collect of the *D*. 153 —
evening service of the *d* before. 158 23
Christmas *D* December 25 160 —
for Christmas *D* serve for any weekdays 161 —
between Holy Innocents' *D* 161 —
and the First Sunday after Christmas *D*. 161 —
First Sunday after Christmas *D* 161 —
Holy Days which follow Christmas *D*. 161 —
is postponed one *d*. 161 —
Second Sunday after Christmas *D* 162 —
those for the Second Sunday after Christmas *D*, 162 —
Preface of the Epiphany, or of the Lord's *D* 163 —
Preface of the Epiphany, or of the Lord's *D* 164 —
Preface of the Epiphany, or of the Lord's *D* 165 —
The Proper Liturgy for this *d* is on page 264. 166 —
The Proper Liturgy for this *d* is on page 270. 168 —
The Proper Liturgy for this *d* is on page 274. 169 —
The Proper Liturgy for this *d* is on page 276. 169 —
The Proper Liturgy for this *d* is on page 283. 170 —
Easter *D* 170 —
Ascension *D* 174 —
Ascension *D*, serves for the following weekdays, 174 —
The Sunday after Ascension *D* 175 —
The *D* of Pentecost: Whitsunday 175 —
continues with the Salutation and Collect of the *D*. 175 —

Preface of the Lord's *D*	177	—
Independence *D* July 4	190	—
Holy Cross *D* September 14	192	—
All Saints' *D* November 1	194	—
Thanksgiving *D*	194	—
The Collect for Independence *D* may be used instead.	207	—
25. For Labor *D*	210	—
Christmas *D* December 25	212	—
for Christmas *D* serve for any weekdays	213	—
between Holy Innocents' *D*	213	—
and the First Sunday after Christmas *D*.	213	—
First Sunday after Christmas *D*	213	—
Holy Days which follow Christmas *D*.	213	—
is postponed one *d*.	213	—
Second Sunday after Christmas *D*	214	—
Preface of the Epiphany, or of the Lord's *D*	215	—
Preface of the Epiphany, or of the Lord's *D*	216	—
Preface of the Epiphany, or of the Lord's *D*	217	—
The Proper Liturgy for this *d* is on page 264.	217	—
The Proper Liturgy for this *d* is on page 270.	219	—
The Proper Liturgy for this *d* is on page 274.	221	—
The Proper Liturgy for this *d* is on page 276.	221	—
The Proper Liturgy for this *d* is on page 283.	221	—
Easter *D*	222	—
Ascension *D*	226	—
Ascension *D*, serves for the following weekdays,	226	—
The Sunday after Ascension *D*	226	—
The *D* of Pentecost: Whitsunday	227	—
continues with the Salutation and Collect of the *D*.	227	—
Preface of the Lord's *D*	229	—
Preface of the Lord's *D*, or of Baptism	236	—
Independence *D* July 4	242	—
Holy Cross *D* September 14	244	—
All Saints' *D* November 1	245	—
Thanksgiving *D*	246	—
The Collect for Independence *D* may be used instead.	258	—
25. For Labor *D*	261	—
On this *d*, the Celebrant begins the liturgy	264	—
Collect of the *D*.	264	—
At services on this *d* other than the principal	272	—
begins with the Salutation and Collect of the *D*	272	—
On this *d* the ministers enter in silence.	276	—
begins the liturgy with the Collect of the *D*.	276	—
There is no celebration of the Eucharist on this *d*.	283	—
Collect of the *D*.	283	—
when observed, is the first service of Easter *D*.	284	2
convenient time before the Liturgy on Easter *D*.	284	31
Easter *D* through the *D* of Pentecost.	287	—
from Easter *D* through the *D* of Pentecost	299	—
The Collect of the *D*	300	—
Lessons are properly those of the *D*.	300	—
on the *D* of Pentecost, on All Saints' *D*	312	3
or the Sunday after All Saints' *D*,	312	4
for the Proper of the *D*.	312	23
from Easter *D* through the *D* of Pentecost	319	—
from Easter *D* through the *D* of Pentecost	323	—
The Collect of the *D*	325	—
From the Easter Vigil through the *D* of Pentecost	340	—
Preface of the Lord's *D*	344	—
from Easter *D* through the *D* of Pentecost	351	—
from Easter *D* through the *D* of Pentecost	355	—
The Collect of the *D*	357	—
From the Easter Vigil through the *D* of Pentecost	366	—
Preface of the Lord's *D*	377	—
or the season, or the Proper of the *D*.	383	—
on a regular basis, using either the Proper of the *D*	396	—
appropriate to the *d* or occasion,	396	—
Incorporates or adapts the Proper Preface of the *D*,	402	—
Incorporates or adapts the Proper Preface of the *D*,	404	—
Salutation and the Collect of the *D*.	406	5
Christmas *D* through the Feast of the Epiphany;	406	13
Easter *D* through the *D* of Pentecost,	406	14
and on Ascension *D*;	406	15
from Easter *D* through the *D* of Pentecost	413	—
The Collect of the *D*	414	—
Lessons are properly those of the *D*.	414	—
from Easter *D* through the *D* of Pentecost	512	—
Bishop stands and reads the Collect for the *D*,	515	—
Bishop may select Readings from the Proper of the *D*.	515	—
From Easter *D* through the *D* of Pentecost	523	—
from Easter *D* through the *D* of Pentecost	525	—
Bishop stands and reads the Collect for the *D*,	527	—
select Readings from the Proper of the *D*.	528	—
From Easter *D* through the *D* of Pentecost	535	—
from Easter *D* through the *D* of Pentecost	537	—
Bishop stands and reads the Collect for the *D*,	539	—
select Readings from the Proper of the *D*.	540	—
From Easter *D* through the *D* of Pentecost,	547	—
on the ________ *d* of ________, 19________,	557	18
The Collect of the *D*,	565	8
selected from the Proper of the *D*,	565	12
On the *d* appointed, the clergy and people gather	567	—
selections may be made from the Proper of the *D*.	571	—
First *D*: Morning Prayer	585	—
First *D*: Evening Prayer	589	—
Second *D*: Morning Prayer	593	—
Second *D*: Evening Prayer	597	—
Third *D*: Morning Prayer	599	—
Third *D*: Evening Prayer	602	—
Fourth *D*: Morning Prayer	606	—
Fourth *D*: Evening Prayer	610	—
Fifth *D*: Morning Prayer	613	—
Fifth *D*: Evening Prayer	617	—
Sixth *D*: Morning Prayer	621	—
Sixth *D*: Evening Prayer	624	—
Seventh *D*: Morning Prayer	629	—
Seventh *D*: Evening Prayer	633	—
Eighth *D*: Morning Prayer	636	—
Eighth *D*: Evening Prayer	641	—
Ninth *D*: Morning Prayer	645	—
Ninth *D*: Evening Prayer	650	—
Tenth *D*: Morning Prayer	654	—
Tenth *D*: Evening Prayer	658	—
Eleventh *D*: Morning Prayer	662	—
Eleventh *D*: Evening Prayer	665	—
Twelfth *D*: Morning Prayer	669	—
Twelfth *D*: Evening Prayer	672	—
Thirteenth *D*: Morning Prayer	676	—
Thirteenth *D*: Evening Prayer	679	—
Fourteenth *D*: Morning Prayer	683	—
Fourteenth *D*: Evening Prayer	687	—
Fifteenth *D*: Morning Prayer	691	—
Fifteenth *D*: Evening Prayer	694	—
Sixteenth *D*: Morning Prayer	701	—

Sixteenth *D*: Evening Prayer 705 —
Seventeenth *D*: Morning Prayer 709 —
Seventeenth *D*: Evening Prayer 713 —
Eighteenth *D*: Morning Prayer 717 —
Eighteenth *D*: Evening Prayer 722 —
Nineteenth *D*: Morning Prayer 724 —
Nineteenth *D*: Evening Prayer 727 —
Twentieth *D*: Morning Prayer 731 —
Twentieth *D*: Evening Prayer 735 —
Twenty-first *D*: Morning Prayer 738 —
Twenty-first *D*: Evening Prayer 741 —
Twenty-second *D*: Morning Prayer 746 —
Twenty-second *D*: Evening Prayer 749 —
Twenty-third *D*: Morning Prayer 753 —
Twenty-third *D*: Evening Prayer 756 —
Twenty-fourth *D*: Morning Prayer 759 —
Twenty-fourth *D*: Evening Prayer 763 —
Twenty-fifth *D*: Morning Prayer 766 —
Twenty-fifth *D*: Evening Prayer 769 —
Twenty-sixth *D*: Morning Prayer 772 —
Twenty-sixth *D*: Evening Prayer 775 —
Twenty-seventh *D*: Morning Prayer 778 —
Twenty-seventh *D*: Evening Prayer 782 —
Twenty-eighth *D*: Morning Prayer 785 —
Twenty-eighth *D*: Evening Prayer 789 —
Twenty-ninth *D*: Morning Prayer 794 —
Twenty-ninth *D*: Evening Prayer 797 —
Thirtieth *D*: Morning Prayer 800 —
Thirtieth *D*: Evening Prayer 804 —
For optional use on Thanksgiving *D*, 836 —
rose again the third *d* from the dead. 865 32
on the twelfth *d* of September, 867 33
until he return to judge all Men at the last *d*. 868 15
for the same *d* in the Daily Office Lectionary. 888 24
or, if the Office is read only once in the *d*, 934 9
When the Office is read twice in the *d*, 934 10
any of the Psalms appointed for a given *d* may 934 28
Likewise, Psalms appointed for any *d* may be used 934 29
other *d* in the same week, except on major Holy Days. 934 30

days

For special *d* of fasting or thanksgiving, 13 12
In any of the Proper Liturgies for Special *D*, 14 3
consists of two cycles of feasts and holy *d*: 15 3
Ascension on a Thursday forty *d* after Easter Day. 15 13
the dated *d* listed above, only the following feasts, 16 3
appointed on fixed *d*, take precedence of a Sunday: 16 4
other Major Feasts appointed on fixed *d* in the Calendar, 16 12
3. Holy *D* 16 21
The following Holy *D* are regularly observed 16 22
have precedence over all other *d* of commemoration 16 24
Feasts appointed on fixed *d* in the Calendar 17 10
observed on the *d* of Holy Week or of Easter Week. 17 11
Feasts appointed on fixed *d* in the Calendar 17 14
and other Major Feasts appointed on fixed *d*, 17 16
4. *D* of Special Devotion 17 20
The following *d* are observed by special acts 17 21
5. *D* of Optional Observance 17 28
and Holy *D*, the following may be observed 18 1
The Ember *D*, traditionally observed 18 5
The Rogation *D*, traditionally observed on Monday, 18 8
All Saints and other Major Saints' *D* 40 —
On the Twelve *D* of Christmas 43 —
On All Saints and other Major Saints' *D* 44 —
All Saints and other Major Saints' *D* 77 —
On the Twelve *D* of Christmas 80 —
On All Saints and other Major Saints' *D* 82 —
Colossians 1:9, 11–14 (Saints' *D*) 108 19
1 Peter 2:9 (Saints' *D*) 108 20
Revelation 22:1,4–5 (Saints' *D*) 108 21
On feasts or other *d* of special significance, 113 —
On other *d*, either of the following, 113 —
a) the Lectionary for Sundays, Holy *D*, 136 —
specific seasons or *d*, may be used 141 4
especially in Lent and on Rogation *d*. 148 —
for Holy *D* and Various Occasions. 158 9
the traditional winter Ember *D*. 160 —
This Sunday takes precedence over the three Holy *D* 161 —
the traditional spring Ember *D*. 166 —
the traditional Rogation *D*. 174 —
the traditional summer Ember *D*. 176 —
the traditional autumnal Ember *D*. 182 —
Holy *D* 185 —
15. For the Ministry (Ember *D*) 205 —
For use on the traditional *d* or at other times 205 —
19. For Rogation *D* 207 —
For use on the traditional *d* or at other times 207 —
the traditional winter Ember *D*. 212 —
This Sunday takes precedence over the three Holy *D* 213 —
the traditional spring Ember *D*. 218 —
the traditional Rogation *D*. 225 —
the traditional summer Ember *D*. 227 —
the traditional autumnal Ember *D*. 233 —
Holy *D* 237 —
15. For the Ministry (Ember *D*) 256 —
For use on the traditional *d* or at other times 256 —
19. For Rogation *D* 258 —
For use on the traditional *d* or at other times 258 —
If on any one of the above-named *d* the ministry 312 8
If on the four *d* listed above there are no candidates 312 15
appointed for Holy *D* and Various Occasions 345 —
appointed for Holy *D* and Various Occasions 378 —
on all the *d* of Easter Week, 406 14
fourteen *d* at the most, giving the reasons 409 25
On Ember *D* or other occasions, 548 —
17 For the Rogation-*d*. 875 9
Sundays and for other major Holy *D* are intended 888 7
for use at all public services on such *d*, 888 7
in the same week, except on major Holy *D*. 934 30

deacon

the bishop may, at discretion, authorize a *d* to preside 13 26
A *d* or lay person using the preceding form remains 42 —
A *d* or lay person using the preceding form remains 63 —
A *d* or lay person using the preceding form remains 80 —
d, when presiding, should read the Prayer for Light, 108 8
A *d* or lay person using the preceding blessing 114 —
A *d* or lay person using the preceding form remains 117 —
A *d* or lay reader leading the service remains 269 —
a *d* or lay reader. 269 —
Here a *D* or other person appointed reads 270 —
D 271 —
a *d* or lay reader. 272 —

All standing, the *D*, or other person appointed, 277 —
The biddings may be read by a *D* or other person 277 —
a *d* or lay reader. 282 —
It is the prerogative of a *d* to carry 284 17
In the absence of a bishop or priest, a *d* 284 23
A *d* may also, when the services of a priest 284 27
D (the Celebrant if there is no *d*) bearing 285 —
Then the *D*, or other person appointed, standing 286 —
D 286 —
Then, all standing, the *D* or a Priest reads 300 —
priest or *d*, who then immerses, or pours water upon, 307 —
may specially authorize a *d* to preside. 312 10
In that case, the *d* omits the prayer 312 10
In the absence of a *d* or priest, 316 —
The *D* or Celebrant then says 320 —
A *d* or lay person using the preceding form 321 —
A *d* should read the Gospel and may lead 322 10
In the absence of a *d*, these duties may 322 13
Then, all standing, the *D* or a Priest reads the Gospel, 326 —
The *D* or other person appointed says 328 —
The *D* or Celebrant says the following, 330 —
and money or other gifts, to the *d* or celebrant. 333 —
The *D*, or the Celebrant, may dismiss the people 339 —
D 340 —
The *D* or Celebrant then says 352 —
A *d* or lay person using the preceding form substitutes 353 —
A *d* should read the Gospel and may lead 354 10
In the absence of a *d*, these duties may 354 13
Then, all standing, the *D* or a Priest reads the Gospel, 357 —
The *D* or Celebrant says 360 —
and money or other gifts, to the *d* or celebrant. 361 —
The *D*, or the Celebrant, dismisses them 366 —
D 366 —
D or other leader 383 —
D or other leader 388 —
D or other leader 389 —
The Celebrant, whether priest or *d*, reads a passage 396 —
A *d* using the preceding form substitutes "us" 398 —
blessing, may be said by a *d*, or, if there is no *d*, 407 6
It is the function of a *d* to make ready the Table 407 14
The *d* may be assisted by other ministers. 407 16
When the celebrant is assisted by a *d* 408 3
authorize a *d* to distribute Holy Communion 408 18
the *d* reverently places the consecrated Sacrament 408 21
2. The Lord's Prayer is then said, the *d* first saying, 408 23
omitting the breaking of the Bread, the *d* proceeds 408 25
administration of Communion by a *d* 409 2
the celebrant or *d*, and other communicants, 409 3
Then, all standing, the *D* or a Priest reads the Gospel, 414 —
A *d*, or an assisting priest, may deliver the charge, 422 12
or bishop is available, a *d* may use the service 422 16
all stand, and the *D* or Minister appointed says 426 —
The *D* or other person appointed reads 429 —
a *d* may function as celebrant, 435 5
to be used by a *D* or Lay Person 448 —
to be used by a *D* or Lay Person 452 —
this service may always be led by a *d* or lay person. 453 6
A *d* or lay person using the preceding form substitutes 455 —
In cases of necessity, a *d* or lay person may perform 456 —
a *d* or lay reader may preside at the service. 468 17
Then, all standing, the *D* or Minister appointed reads 479 —
The *D* or other leader says 480 —
D or other Minister may dismiss them, saying 483 —
a *d* or lay reader may preside at the service. 490 17
Then, all standing, the *D* or Minister appointed reads 495 —
D or other Minister may dismiss them, saying 500 —
exercise the offices of bishop, priest, or *d* 510 22
the sacred orders of bishop, priest, and *d*. 510 32
Then, all standing, a *D* or a Priest reads 516 —
A *D* dismisses the people 523 —
Then, all standing, the *D* or, if no *d* is present, 529 —
A *D*, or a Priest if no *d* is present, dismisses 535 —
After receiving Holy Communion, the new *d* assists 536 14
The Ordination of a *D* 537 —
Then, all standing, the *D* or, if no *d* is present, 541 —
The Consecration of the *D* 544 —
The new *d* is now vested according to the order 545 —
The new *D* then exchanges greetings with family 546 —
The newly ordained *D* prepares the bread, 546 —
after which the new *D* dismisses 547 —
At the Ordination of a *D* 554 11
or other insignia of the office of *d*, 554 13
is placed upon the new *d* after the entire Prayer 554 13
and make him a *d* in your Church." 554 23
A Bible is to be given to each new *d*, 554 26
A *d* or priest reads the Gospel. 558 16
The new minister, if a *d*, should read the Gospel, 558 20
At the Induction of a priest or *d*, 564 4
A *D*, or a Priest if no *d* is present, dismisses 564 12
found in the service for the Ordination of a *D* 565 14
The *D* (or a Priest) reads the Gospel. 571 —
The *D* or a member of the congregation leads 572 —
D or Priest dismisses them. 574 —

deacons

and *d*, fulfill the functions proper 13 18
D by virtue of their order do not exercise 13 21
D likewise assist at Baptism 284 18
be assisted by other priests, and by *d* 322 5
D should also serve at the Lord's Table, 322 11
be assisted by other priests, and by *d* 354 5
D should also serve at the Lord's Table, 354 11
d at the Holy Table then communicate, 407 24
When several *d* or priests are present, 408 5
In the absence of sufficient *d* and priests, 408 7
Where it is permitted by civil law that *d* may perform 422 15
Thirdly, there are *d* who assist 510 12
d to minister in Christ's name to the poor, 510 14
D prepare the Table. 522 —
D prepare the Table. 535 —
new deacon is now vested according to the order of *d*. 545 —
participating in the Peace, the *d* go to the Altar 554 28
If there are many *d*, some assist 554 29
When desired, *d* may be appointed to carry 555 1
it is appropriate for the *d* to remove the vessels 555 5
the chief celebrant at the Altar, and *d* assist 558 12
primarily intended for use by parish priests, *d*, 844 2
and *D*, are not commanded by God's Law, 874 12
and Ordering of Priests and *D*, 875 21
and Ordering of Priests and *D*, lately set forth 875 27

dead

the Collects appointed for use at the Burial of the *D* 202 —
Burial of the *D* may be used. 202 —

Preface of the Commemoration of the *D* 202 —
Collects appointed for use at the Burial of the *D* 253 —
Burial of the *D* may be used. 253 —
Preface of the Commemoration of the *D* 253 —
Commemoration of the *D* 349 —
Commemoration of the *D* 382 —
When the order for the Burial of the *D* follows 467 —
The Burial of the *D*: 469 —
Preface of the Commemoration of the *D* 482 —
The Burial of the *D*: 491 —
Preface of the Commemoration of the *D* 498 —
The liturgy for the *d* is an Easter liturgy. 507 2
Because Jesus was raised from the *d*, 507 3
Prayers for the *d* are on pages 202, 253, 812 16
rose again the third day from the *d*. 865 32
whence he shall come to judge the quick and the *d*. 865 34
who truly suffered, was crucified, *d*, 868 6
the Priest did offer Christ for the quick and the *d*, 874 9

deadly

Not every *d* sin willingly committed after Baptism 870 32

deal

and a great *d* more profitable and commodious, 866 43

dean

the *d* of a cathedral, and others having similar tenure 564 18

deans

It may also be used for the installation of *d* 558 3

death

Time of *D* 462 2
When a person is near *d*, the Minister 462 3
A Prayer for a Person near *D* 462 5
Litany at the Time of *D* 462 7
A Commendation at the Time of *D* 464 5
The Litany at the Time of *D* 465 —
The *d* of a member of the Church should be reported 468 —
Isaiah 25:6–9 (He will swallow up *d* in victory) 470 —
The *d* of a member of the Church should be reported 490 2
Isaiah 25:6–9 (He will swallow up *d* for ever) 494 —
"neither *d*, nor life, nor angels, nor principalities, 507 6
when we are parted by *d*. 507 12
Christ did truly rise again from *d*, 868 13
our Redemption by Christ's *d*: 873 25
Laws of the Realm may punish Christian men with *d*, 876 8

debt

does not require that the premises be *d*-free or owned. 575 4

Decalogue

The *D*: Traditional 317 —
The *D*, page 317, may be said, the people kneeling. 319 —
The *D*: Contemporary 350 —
The *D* may be said, the people kneeling. 351 —

deceased

prayers for the *d* and the bereaved. 492 —
including the Lord's Prayer, is offered for the *d*, 506 15
7. The *d* is commended to God, 506 18

deceits

were blasphemous fables, and dangerous *d*. 874 10

deceive

we *d* ourselves, and the truth is not in us. 870 30

December

the other, upon the fixed date of *D* 25, 15 5
Christmas Day, *D* 25 15 17
Holy Cross Day, and *D* 13 18 7
Christmas Day *D* 25 160 —
Saint Thomas *D* 21 185 —
Saint Stephen *D* 26 186 —
Saint John *D* 27 186 —
The Holy Innocents *D* 28 186 —
Christmas Day *D* 25 212 —
Saint Thomas *D* 21 237 —
Saint Stephen *D* 26 237 —
Saint John *D* 27 238 —
The Holy Innocents *D* 28 238 —

decent

this godly and *d* order of the ancient fathers 866 16

declaration

ask for the *D* of Consent, 422 13
The *D* of Consent 424 —
After the *D* of Consent, if there is to be a giving 437 8
instead, a *d* of forgiveness is provided. 446 14
a *d* of forgiveness. 446 19
D of Forgiveness 448 8
D of Forgiveness 452 —
The Bishop-elect then signs the above *D* 513 —
The Ordinand then signs the above *D* 527 —
The Ordinand then signs the above *D* 539 —
At the Presentation of the Ordinand, the *D* 552 8
authorized response to this *D*, 877 22

declare

they *d* it to be the Liturgy of this Church: 8 10
for by them men do *d*, 870 21
do hereby solemnly *d* to all whom it may concern, 876 26
we hereby *d* our desire and readiness, 877 21

declared

d the necessity and expediency of occasional alterations 9 23
persons to be married are *d*. 422 21
d in the formularies and canons of this Church, 435 12
expressly *d* unto us in the Word of God. 871 23
have neither strength nor authority, unless it may be *d* 872 9

declares

she further *d* in her said Preface, 10 9
5. The Celebrant *d* the union of the man and woman 436 4
so far as it *d* the Books of Homilies 875 14

declaring

and its ministers *d* absolution. 446 5

decorated

they may be *d* by members 576 1

decoration

For the covering and *d* of the Altar, 576 22

decorations

and *d* be carried into the building 575 16

decree

The Church hath power to *d* Rites or Ceremonies, 871 37
ought not to *d* any thing against the same, 871 41
d all such to be rightly, orderly, 875 25
we *d* all such to be rightly, orderly, 875 33

decreed

he hath constantly *d* by his counsel secret to us, 871 3

dedicate

This service may be used to *d* and consecrate a church 566 9

dedicated

If vestments or other symbols of office are to be *d*, 552 17
When an instrument of music is to be *d*, 572 —
may go around the building(s) to be *d* 575 8
appropriate that it remain silent until *d*. 575 11
As the furnishings in the church are *d*, 576 1

dedicating

for *d* parts of a building, or furnishings, 566 4
used for *d* a chapel or an oratory 566 6
for *d* a private chapel or oratory. 577 5

dedication

The feast of the *D* of a Church, 16 8
12. On the Anniversary of the *D* of a Church 204 —
Preface of the *D* of a Church 204 —
12. On the Anniversary of the *D* of a Church 254 —
Preface of the *D* of a Church 255 —
D of a Church 348 —
D of a Church 381 —
This service provides for the *d* and consecration 566 2
The *D* and Consecration of a Church 567 —
The Preface of the *D* of a Church may be used. 574 —
The complete form of the service for the *D* 575 2
At the *d* of the font, 575 23
followed by the words of *d*. 576 8
At the *d* of the lectern, the Bible is brought forward 576 9
For the *D* of Churches 576 27
For the *D* of Furnishings, 577 6
Relevant portions of the service for the *D* 577 8
Litany may also be used on the anniversary of the *d* 579 —
61. A Prayer of Self-*D* 812 12
61. A Prayer of Self-*D* 832 —

deed

Such things as the *d* for the property 575 17

deemed

as might be *d* expedient. 11 8
is *d* appropriate, the following form is used. 506 3

deep

brings *d* sorrow when we are parted 507 11

deepest

into its *d* and truest sense, be speedily fulfilled; 876 30

deeply

D grieved by the sad divisions which affect 877 20

defensible

d, if allowed such just and favourable construction 10 17

definition

D of the Union of the Divine 864 1

degrees

that they should rule all estates and *d* committed 876 4

deliver

d it to the people. 338 —
d it to the people. 365 —
A deacon, or an assisting priest, may *d* the charge, 422 12
to *d* from curse and damnation 871 3

deliverance

Israel's *d* at the Red Sea 289 —

delivery

For a safe *d* 444 —

denial

special acts of discipline and self-*d*: 17 22

denied

Wherefore the grant of repentance is not to be *d* 870 33
The Cup of the Lord is not to be *d* to the Lay-people: 874 2

denominations

d of Christians in these States were left at full 10 27

denote

In the Daily Office, the term "Officiant" is used to *d* 36 3
In the Daily Office, the term "Officiant" is used to *d* 74 2

denotes

Direct recitation *d* the reading or chanting 582 8

denunciation

That person which by open *d* of the Church 874 17

deny

or *d* the place of forgiveness to such as truly repent. 870 37

depart

from intending to *d* from the Church of England 11 13
bishops who are present are not to *d* without signing 553 16
we may *d* from grace given, 870 34

departed

8. For the *D* 202 —
8. For the *D* 253 —
The *d* (with commemoration of a saint 359 —
The *d* (with commemoration of a saint 383 —
4. For the Saints and Faithful *D* 813 4
Thanksgivings for the *d* 813 16
4. For the Saints and Faithful *D* 838 —
Thanksgivings for the *d* 841 —

departure

rather, it is a point of *d* for the teacher, 844 5

dependent

d upon the movable date of the Sunday 15 4

depends

all Sundays of the Church Year *d* upon the date 15 9

deposed
finally, being found guilty, by just judgment be *d*. 873 12

deposit
to be the substantial *d* of Christian Faith and Order 877 8
As inherent parts of this sacred *d*, 877 12

depth
nor things to come, nor powers, nor height, nor *d*, 507 7

deputies
enacted by the House of *D*, 877 27

deputy
but, if necessary, a *d* may be appointed. 558 7
the *d* substitutes the words given 561 —

descended
Who suffered for our salvation, *d* into hell, 865 32

described
subject to the limitations *d* in the directions 14 1
In the absence of a priest, all that is *d* above, 407 5

deserve
or (as the School-authors say) *d* grace of congruity: 870 15

deserveth
it *d* God's wrath and damnation. 869 27

deservings
and not for our own works or *d*. 870 3

designated
his full name (*d* by the symbol N.N.) 511 18
his full name (*d* by the symbol N.N.) 524 9
his full name (*d* by the symbol N.N.) 536 9

designed
It is *d* for vocal, congregational use, 582 2

desirable
It is *d* that each Lesson be read 284 21
It may be found *d* to return to the front 313 9
d that the priest arrange to celebrate the Eucharist 396 —
d that a passage from the Gospel first be read. 396 —
It is *d* that fellow parishioners, relatives, 396 —
It is *d* that the Lessons be read from a lectern 406 17
It is *d* that the Lessons and Gospel be read 406 19
It is *d* that the Lessons from the Old Testament 422 18
At the Offertory, it is *d* that the bread and wine 438 1
It is *d* that this take place at a Sunday service. 439 6
it is *d* that it precede the distribution 453 8
When possible, it is *d* that members of the family 462 —
It is *d* that the Lesson from the Old Testament, 468 15
It is *d* that the Lesson from the Old Testament, 490 15
In accordance with ancient custom, it is *d*, 511 3
It is *d* that all members of the congregation, 566 16
When a new church is being consecrated, it is *d* 575 15

desire
d and promise to make up for their faults, 409 21
a Penitent is available for all who *d* it. 446 7
some the affection, some the *d*, of the flesh), 869 30
1. Our earnest *d* that the Saviour's prayer, 876 29
we hereby declare our *d* and readiness, 877 21
Those who *d* to recite the Psalter in its entirety 935 5

desired
When it is *d* to use music composed for them, 14 13
When *d*, however, the Collect, Preface, 16 14
If *d*, the Collect of the Day may be used. 107 —
When *d*, however, the Collect of the Day, 136 —
certain Canticles may be omitted when *d*. 141 15
When *d*, more than one Lesson may be read, 143 27
If an additional hymn is *d*, it may be sung 143 29
(substituting, if *d*, the Gloria in excelsis 175 —
For optional use, when *d*, subject to the rules 199 —
(substituting, if *d*, the Gloria in excelsis 227 —
For optional use, when *d*, subject to the rules 251 —
Where it is *d* to administer Holy Communion 275 —
If *d*, a wooden cross may now be brought 281 —
the sign of the cross [using Chrism if *d*] 308 —
If *d*, the hymn Gloria in excelsis may be sung 312 18
At other times, or when *d*, such persons may 396 —
or adapts the Proper Preface of the Day, if *d*. 402 —
or adapts the Proper Preface of the Day, if *d*. 404 —
and at other times as *d*; 406 15
(If it is *d* to include a Confession of Sin, 406 26
If *d*, the hymn Gloria in excelsis may be sung 412 13
If it is *d* to celebrate a marriage otherwise 435 2
When *d*, some other suitable symbol of the vows 437 22
When *d*, a briefer form of this service may be used, 439 10
If necessary, or if *d*, all or part of the service 468 10
If necessary, or if *d*, all or part of the service 490 10
and may be lengthened if *d*. 515 —
and additional presenters if *d*, standing 526 —
and may be lengthened if *d*. 528 —
and additional presenters if *d*, standing 538 —
and may be lengthened if *d*. 540 —
On Ember Days or other occasions, if *d*, 548 —
When *d*, deacons may be appointed to carry 555 1
but additional, or other, persons may do this when *d*. 565 5
The word may, if *d*, be omitted 584 9
but, when *d*, the Psalm cited 888 16
If two Readings are *d* at both Offices, 934 12

desires
If a person *d* to receive the Sacrament, 457 —

desperation
into *d*, or into wretchlessness of most unclean living, 871 19
no less perilous than *d*. 871 20

determined
and that, in every Church, what cannot be clearly *d* 9 5
d by the calendar date of that Sunday. 158 11

determines
also *d* the beginning of Lent on Ash Wednesday, 15 12

Deum
7 We Praise Thee Te *D* laudamus 52 —
21 You are God Te *D* Laudamus 95 —
Te *D* laudamus 294 —
4. Te *D* 577 29

Deus
4 The Song of Zechariah Benedictus Dominus *D* 50 —
9 The First Song of Isaiah Ecce, *D* 86 —

16 The Song of Zechariah Benedictus Dominus *D* 92 —
Psalm 51 Miserere mei, *D* 266 —
Psalm 46 *D* noster refugium 471 —

Deuteronomy

D, The First Book of Chronicles, Ecclesiastes 868 30

development

In the course of their Christian *d*, those baptized 412 2

devil

dangerous downfall, whereby the *D* doth thrust them 871 18

devised

There was never any thing by the wit of man so well *d*, 866 3

devotion

and *d* in the worship of God; 10 12
4. Days of Special *D* 17 20
or with some other Office or *D*; 112 —
c) some other manual of *d* which provides daily 136 17
This *d* may be used before or after the evening meal. 139 —
or as a separate *d*; 154 —

devotions

special *d* taken from this Book, 13 9
A litany, or other suitable *d*, 113 —
Daily *D* for Individuals and Families 136 1
These *d* follow the basic structure of the Daily Office 136 3
Appropriate *d* may follow, 281 —
and such other *d* as the Bishop may direct. 419 —
Appropriate *d*, such as those appointed 467 —

diaconate

Representatives of the presbyterate, *d*, and laity 511 9

died

As Christ *d* for us, and was buried; 868 10

difference

Baptism is not only a sign of profession, and mark of *d*, 873 14

different

that in his worship *d* forms and usages 9 3
Her general aim in these *d* reviews and alterations 10 8
and the *d* religious denominations 10 26
unnecessary to enumerate all the *d* alterations 11 9
may be assigned to *d* persons, 273 —
may be assigned to *d* persons, 277 —
Lesson be read by a *d* reader. 284 22
there have been *d* ministries within the Church. 510 3
fellow-Christians of the *d* Communions in this land, 876 27

dignity

read from a book or books of appropriate size and *d*. 406 20

diligent

which he professeth, so that he be *d* to frame his life 871 26

diligently

read in Churches by the Ministers, *d* and distinctly, 874 38

diminished

nor the grace of God's gifts *d* from such as by faith, 873 7

dimittis

5 The Song of Simeon Nunc *d* 51 —
The Song of Simeon Nunc *d* 66 —
17 The Song of Simeon Nunc *d* 93 —
The Song of Simeon Nunc *d* 120 —
The Song of Simeon, Nunc *d* 484 —
The Song of Simeon, Nunc *d* 500 —

dining

at the *d* table, or at some other convenient place. 143 18

diocesan

inauguration of other ministries, *d* or parochial, 558 4

diocese

the presbyterate, diaconate, and laity of the *d* 511 9
Representatives of the *d*, 513 —
The new Bishop, if the Bishop of the *D*, 522 —
bishops, and representative presbyters of the *d*, stand 553 9
a priest of this *D*, in communion with your Bishop. 557 9
Other clergy of the *d* participate 558 16
the congregation and of the clergy of the *d* stand 561 —
clergy of the *d* present the Constitution 562 —
within the life of the *D*. 576 14
10. For the *D* 810 16
10. For the *D* 817 —
always resort to the Bishop of the *D*, 867 20

dips

the Priest *d* a thumb in the holy oil, 456 —

direct

and such other devotions as the Bishop may *d*. 419 —
as the bishop may *d*. 553 27
as the bishop may *d*. 554 17
D recitation denotes the reading or chanting 582 8

directed

The people may be *d* to stand or kneel. 277 —
make an appropriate response, as *d*. 328 —
the service is concluded as *d* on page 406. 330 —
the service is concluded as *d* on page 406. 359 —
The Minister of the Congregation is *d* to instruct 445 —
For use at Ordinations as *d*. 548 —
signed, as *d* by Article VIII of the Constitution 552 10
and the service continues as *d* on page 575. 569 —

direction

subject to the *d* of the bishop, 13 9
Here the Priest may offer counsel, *d*, and comfort. 447 —

directions

as set forth in the rubrical *d* for each service. 13 19
subject to the limitations described in the *d* 14 1
Additional *D* are on page 141. 36 10
Additional *D* are on page 141. 74 9
Additional *D* are on page 142. 108 25
Additional *D* 141 1
are to conform to the *d* on page 383. 142 22
Proper Prefaces, *d* for which are to be found 158 4
D concerning the Common of Saints and services 158 24
D for the use of the Propers which follow 176 —
D for the use of the Propers which follow 228 —
Additional *D* are on page 312. 298 28
(See Additional *D*, page 312.) 300 —

Additional *D* 312 1
and that the intercessions conform to the *d* given 322 20
Additional *D* are on page 406. 322 22
with the *d* on page 383. 328 4
and that the intercessions conform to the *d* given 354 20
Additional *D* are on page 406. 354 22
Additional *D* 406 1
Additional *D* are on page 437. 422 23
Additional *D* 437 1
Additional *D* are on page 552. 511 26
Additional *D* are on page 552. 524 20
Additional *D* are on page 552. 536 20
Additional *D* 552 1
Additional *D* are on page 564. 558 25
the *d* on page 565. 560 —
Additional *D* 564 13
Additional *D* 575 1

directs

The Presiding Bishop then *d* that testimonials 513 —

disability

by reason of extreme sickness or physical *d*, 457 —

disaster

of national anxiety, or of *d*. 154 —

discerned

evidently known as a tree *d* by the fruit. 870 10
d from others that be not christened, 873 15

disciplinary

D Rubrics 409 7

discipline

belong to Doctrine must be referred to *D*; 9 6
and *d*, in such manner as they might judge 10 29
point of doctrine, *d*, or worship; 11 14
The following days are observed by special acts of *d* 17 21
Nevertheless, it appertaineth to the *d* of the Church, 873 10
relating to modes of worship and *d*, 876 34

discountenance

on the basis of a common Faith and Order, to *d* schism, 877 2

discretion

the bishop may, at *d*, authorize a deacon to preside 13 26
according to the *d* of the officiant. 141 5
On occasion, at the *d* of the Minister, 142 13
At the *d* of the Celebrant, and as appropriate, 195 —
At the *d* of the Celebrant, and as appropriate, 246 —
as appropriate, at the *d* of the Celebrant. 277 —
the bishop may, at *d*, authorize a deacon 408 18
At the *d* of the bishop, 414 —
Bishop of the Diocese, who by his *d* shall take order 867 20
to marry at their own *d*, as they shall judge 874 14
may be further lengthened or shortened at *d*. 888 22
Any Reading may be lengthened at *d*. 888 29
Any Reading may be lengthened at *d*. 934 20
At the *d* of the officiant, however, 934 27

discussion

not normally a matter of subsequent *d*. 446 27

dismiss

The Deacon, or the Celebrant, may *d* the people 339 —
Deacon or other Minister may *d* them, saying 483 —
Deacon or other Minister may *d* them, saying 500 —
and *d* the congregation. 558 22

dismissal

Blessing or *D* at the end. 108 9
Blessing or *D*, or both. 113 —
proper to the season, may precede the Blessing or *D*. 113 —
A *D* may be used 114 —
before the Blessing or *D*. 143 30
No blessing or *d* is added. 282 —
the Lord's Prayer, and the *D*. 284 26
The service concludes with a blessing or with a *d* 399 —
or after the *D*. 409 5
The service concludes with a blessing or with a *d* 457 —
continues with the [blessing and] *d*. 482 —
continues with the (blessing and) *d*. 499 —
be added to the *d* and to the response. 523 —
be added to the *d* and to the response. 535 —
be added to the *d* and to the response. 547 —
After the pontifical blessing and the *d*, 553 14
to say the *d*. 554 31

dismissals

may be added to any of the *d*. 340 —
may be added to any of the *d*. 366 —

dismisses

The Deacon, or the Celebrant, *d* them 366 —
and then *d* the people. 408 27
The Celebrant *d* the people with these words 486 —
The Celebrant *d* the people with these words 502 —
A Deacon *d* the people 523 —
or a Priest if no deacon is present, *d* the people. 535 —
after which the new Deacon *d* them 547 —
or a Priest if no deacon is present, *d* the assembly. 564 12
a Deacon or Priest *d* them. 574 —

disposal

arranging for the *d* of their temporal goods, 445 —

disposed

or otherwise *d* of, as may seem most convenient 9 8

distinct

three *d* orders of ordained ministers 510 4
a *d* pause should be made at the asterisk. 583 14

distinction

d of natures being in no way annulled by the union, 864 13

distinctive

d of ecclesiastical or academic rank or order. 511 17
d of ecclesiastical or academic rank or order. 524 8
d of ecclesiastical or academic rank or office. 536 8
due regard for the *d* nature of the community, 576 20

distinctly

read in Churches by the Ministers, diligently and *d*, 874 38

distinguish

In order to *d* it, however, from "Lord" 583 28

distribute
authorize a deacon to *d* Holy Communion 408 18
distributed
d to members of the congregation. 143 16
d to the people before the service, 270 —
If candles have been *d* to members 286 —
although quatrains are usually *d* 583 11
distributes
newly ordained bishop, assisted by other ministers, *d* 553 11
distributing
and in *d* Communion. 322 9
and in *d* Communion. 354 9
distribution
it is desirable that it precede the *d* 453 8
deacon assists in the *d* of the Sacrament, 536 15
divers
for at all times they have been *d*, 874 23
diversely
the parties that so doubt, or *d* take any thing, 867 19
diversity
7. For the *D* of Races and Cultures 813 9
7. For the *D* of Races and Cultures 840 —
where heretofore, there hath been great *d* in saying 867 8
to appease all such *d* (if any arise), 867 17
and may be changed according to the *d* of countries, 874 23
divided
ancient fathers had *d* the Psalms into seven portions, 866 27
were joined together in one Person, never to be *d*, 868 5
among the *d* branches of Christendom, 877 13
(For example, 1977 *d* by 3 is 659 with no remainder. 888 4
divides
An asterisk *d* each verse into two parts 583 13
dividing
neither confounding the Persons, nor *d* the Substance. 864 26
divine
Forms of *D* Worship, and the Rites and Ceremonies 9 15
But when in the course of *D* Providence, 10 24
In the oldest manuscripts, the *D* Name was written 583 20
context requires that the *D* Name be spelled out, 584 2
Definition of the Union of the *D* 864 1
prayers in the Church, commonly called *D* Service: 866 5
divisible
in years evenly *d* by three. 888 4
division
without change, without *d*, without separation; 864 12
divisions
Deeply grieved by the sad *d* which affect 877 20
doctors
For *D* and Nurses 460 —
doctrine
belong to *D* must be referred to Discipline; 9 6
to the Word of God, or to sound *d*, 10 15
point of *d*, discipline, or worship; 11 14
exhort others by wholesome *d*, and to confute them 866 12
but yet doth it not apply them to establish any *d*; 868 35
a most wholesome *D*, and very full of comfort, 870 4
The Romish *D* concerning Purgatory, 872 12
doth contain a godly and wholesome *D*, 874 36
explication of Christian *d*, and instructive in piety 875 15
document
to be provided as a separate *d* 552 9
documents
Historical *D* of the Church 863 2
doers
restrain with the civil sword the stubborn and evil-*d*. 876 6
doing
11 Of Alms-*d*. 875 2
doings
and, in our *d*, that Will of God is to be followed, 871 22
Domine
13 A Song of Praise Benedictus es, *D* 90 —
Psalm 31 In te, *D*, speravi 129 —
Psalm 90 *D*, refugium 472 —
Psalm 139 *D*, probasti 474 —
Domini
1 A Song of Creation Benedicite, omnia opera *D* 47 —
2 A Song of Praise Benedictus es, *D* 49 —
12 A Song of Creation Benedicite, omnia opera *D* 88 —
dominions
power in this Realm of England, and other his *D*, 875 40
Domino
8 The Song of Moses Cantemus *D* 85 —
Psalm 106 Confitemini *D* 478 —
Dominum
10 The Second Song of Isaiah Quaerite *D* 86 —
Dominus
4 The Song of Zechariah Benedictus *D* Deus 50 —
16 The Song of Zechariah Benedictus *D* Deus 92 —
Psalm 23 *D* regit me 476 —
Psalm 27 *D* illuminatio 477 —
done
Or this action may be *d* immediately after 308 —
those who have *d* wrong to their neighbors 409 12
they have made restitution for the wrong they have *d*, 409 15
or hymn to be said, or something to be *d*, as a sign 446 24
see and hear what is *d*. 511 14
see and hear what is *d*. 524 6
see and hear what is *d*. 536 6
blessing of a new font or baptistry should always be *d* 577 15
And they that have *d* good shall go 865 37
and they that have *d* evil 865 37
so set forth, that all things shall be *d* in order, 866 36
Works *d* before the grace of Christ, 870 13
not *d* as God hath willed 870 16
and commanded them to be *d*, 870 16
When ye have *d* all that are commanded to you, say, 870 23
so that all things be *d* to edifying. 874 33
d according to the Prophet's teaching in justice, 876 21

donor

place by a *d*, or a lay reader, 576 10

donors

benefactors, *d*, artists, artisans, and others. 576 21
and decoration of the Altar, it is suitable that the *d* 576 22

doomed

but the way of the wicked is *d*. 583 7

door

The Celebrant meets the body at the *d* of the church 466 —
As the procession approaches the *d* of the church, 567 —
Standing at the *d* of the church, the Bishop says 568 —
The *d* is opened. 568 —
and then go to the principal *d*. 575 9
enter in procession through the principal *d*. 575 14

doors

out of *d*, in the parish house, 575 6

doth

other Books (as Hierome saith) the Church *d* read 868 34
but yet *d* it not apply them to establish any doctrine; 868 35
And this infection of nature *d* remain, 869 28
Apostle *d* confess, that concupiscence and lust 869 32
as well because it *d* greatly establish 871 14
because it *d* fervently kindle their love towards God: 871 16
whereby the Devil *d* thrust them 871 18
For Holy Scripture *d* set out unto us 871 27
by the which he *d* work invisibly in us, 872 28
and *d* not only quicken, 872 28
purposely, *d* openly break the Traditions 874 25
d contain a godly and wholesome Doctrine, 874 36
as *d* the former book of Homilies, 874 36
d contain all things necessary to such Consecration 875 22
d contain all things necessary 875 28
d appertain, and is not, nor ought to be, subject 875 42
so we judge, that Christian Religion *d* not prohibit, 876 19

doubt

If there is reasonable *d* that a person 313 16
without *d* he shall perish 864 23
the parties that so *d*, or diversely take any thing, 867 19
of whose authority was never any *d* in the Church. 868 24
we *d* not but they have the nature of sin. 870 16

doubts

but *d* may arise in the use and practicing of the same: 867 16
and for the resolution of all *d*, 867 18

down

Book of Common Prayer, laid it *d* as a rule, 9 14
principles already laid *d*, it cannot but be supposed 10 19
and the creed of the Fathers has handed *d* 864 17
III. Of the going *d* of Christ into Hell. 868 9
it to be believed, that he went *d* into Hell. 868 10

downfall

Predestination, is a most dangerous *d*, 871 18

Doxology

it begins with the Invocation and concludes
with the *D*. 88 —
D 90 —
adds a concluding Collect, or the following *D* 391 —
the Celebrant concludes with the following *D* 579 —

dragon

Of Bel and the *D*, 869 3

drawing

and *d* up their mind to high and heavenly things, 871 14

drawn

The attention of this Church was in the first place *d* 10 32
Antiphons *d* from the Psalms themselves, 141 8
a readiness in this matter, here is *d* out a Kalendar 866 34
Antiphons *d* from the Psalms themselves, 935 7

drink

reverently eat and *d* it, either after the Communion 409 4
unable to eat and *d* the Bread and Wine, 457 —
d the sign or Sacrament of so great a thing. 873 40

drunkenness

5 Against Gluttony and *D*. 875 7

dry

The valley of *d* bones 291 —

due

and has given evidence of *d* contrition, 446 21
having *d* regard for the distinctive nature 576 19
by his Spirit working in *d* season: 871 7

duly

and Lessons *d* authorized by this Church: 18 2
when they are ready and have been *d* prepared, 412 3
by bishops who are themselves *d* qualified to confer 510 24
and the Sacraments be *d* ministered according 871 31
but that we should *d* use them. 872 38
believe that all who have been *d* baptized with water, 876 31

during

D the candle-lighting, an appropriate anthem 112 —
D Advent, the lighting of an Advent Wreath 143 14
D the procession, all hold branches in their hands, 271 —
D the ceremony, the following or other 274 —
before or *d* the petitions (page 305), 312 29
a hymn or anthem, may be sung *d* the procession. 313 12
either *d* the Liturgy or at other times. 316 —
D the Offertory, a hymn, psalm, or anthem may 333 —
except *d* Easter Season. 337 —
D the ministration of Communion, 338 —
D the Offertory, a hymn, psalm, or anthem may 361 —
except *d* Easter Season. 364 —
D the ministration of Communion, 365 —
spread with a clean white cloth *d* the celebration. 406 2
D the Great Thanksgiving, 407 18
d which time a communion hymn may be sung. 408 22
D their entrance, a hymn, psalm, or anthem may 423 —
D the prayers, some parents may wish to express 439 15
d which time a suitable psalm or anthem 467 —
or *d* the entrance of the ministers, 468 24
or *d* the entrance of the ministers, 490 24
psalms, and anthems may be sung *d* the entrance 512 —
D the Eucharistic Prayer, 553 8
D the Prayer of Consecration, 553 30
D the laying on of hands, 553 31

D the Prayer of Consecration the Bishop is to lay 554 20
in the sight of the congregation *d* the Induction. 565 22
be omitted *d* the season of Lent. 584 9
Church *d* the first ages of its existence; 877 7

duties

in their *d* to help the new Christians grow 298 26
In the absence of a deacon, these *d* may be performed 322 13
In the absence of a deacon, these *d* may be performed 354 13
assigned appropriate *d* in the service. 511 11

duty

about the *d* of Christian parents to make prudent 445 —
do more for his sake, than of bounden *d* is required: 870 22
And we hold it to be the *d* of all men 875 36

dying

Prayers for the *d* are on pages 462–465. 812 15

E

each

e order within the Church, lay persons, bishops, 13 17
as set forth in the rubrical directions for *e* service. 13 19
directions for *e* service. 14 2
After *e* Lesson the Reader may say 47 —
Silence may be kept after *e* Reading. 47 —
sung or said after *e* Reading. 47 —
After *e* Lesson the Reader may say 65 —
Silence may be kept after *e* Reading. 65 —
sung or said after *e* Reading. 65 —
After *e* Lesson the Reader may say 84 —
Silence may be kept after *e* Reading. 84 —
sung or said after *e* Reading. 84 —
After *e* Lesson the Reader may say 119 —
Silence may be kept after *e* Reading. 119 —
sung or said after *e* Reading. 119 —
and Collects are provided in *e* service. 136 —
after *e* Psalm, and after *e* section of Psalm 119. 141 13
The Proper to be used on *e* of the Sundays 158 10
e followed by a Psalm, 175 —
e followed by a Psalm, 227 —
the Collects which follow *e* Lesson, 284 15
It is desirable that *e* Lesson be read 284 21
After *e* Lesson, the Psalm or Canticle listed, 288 —
E candidate for Holy Baptism is to be sponsored 298 16
After *e* Reading, the Reader may say 300 —
A Psalm, hymn, or anthem may follow *e* Reading. 300 —
The Celebrant asks *e* candidate when presented 301 —
E candidate is presented by name to the Celebrant, 307 —
and saying to *e* one 308 —
The Bishop lays hands upon *e* one and says 309 —
may be given to *e* of the newly baptized 313 8
After *e* Reading, the Reader may say 325 —
A Psalm, hymn, or anthem may follow *e* Reading. 326 —
After *e* paragraph of this prayer, 328 —
After *e* Reading, the Reader may say 357 —
A Psalm, hymn, or anthem may follow *e* Reading. 357 —
In the course of the silence after *e* bidding, 385 —
he shall speak privately to *e* of them, 409 18
receive Communion until they have forgiven *e* other. 409 19
After *e* Reading the Reader may say 414 —
A Psalm, hymn, or anthem may follow *e* Reading. 414 —
The Bishop lays hands upon *e* one and says 418 —
The newly married couple then greet *e* other, 431 —
husband and wife first greeting *e* other. 436 11
exercised through the care *e* Christian has 446 3
The very love we have for *e* other in Christ 507 11
After *e* Reading, the Reader may say 516 —
A Psalm, canticle, or hymn follows *e* Reading. 516 —
After *e* Reading, the Reader may say 529 —
A Psalm, canticle, or hymn follows *e* Reading. 529 —
After *e* Reading, the Reader may say 541 —
A Psalm, canticle, or hymn follows *e* Reading. 541 —
by the rubrics in *e* of the ordination rites. 552 11
e is to be presented with a separate copy 552 12
e is to have his own presenters. 553 25
upon the head of *e* ordinand. 553 31
the bishop alone says over *e* ordinand 553 32
A Bible is to be given to *e* new priest, 554 5
are to be said to *e* one. 554 6
e is to have his own presenters. 554 15
the head of *e* ordinand, and say over *e* one 554 21
A Bible is to be given to *e* new deacon, 554 26
are also to be said to *e* one. 554 27
In *e* such case, the appropriate prayer 577 10
e of which can be elaborate or simple, 582 6
singing a refrain after *e* verse or group of verses. 582 21
An asterisk divides *e* verse into two parts 583 13
of *e* nature being preserved and coming together 864 14
Three Readings are provided for *e* Sunday 934 7
and weekday in *e* of the two years. 934 7
in *e* instance, use the bracketed Psalms 935 6
sung or said at the beginning and end of *e* Psalm 935 10
be used as refrains after *e* verse or group of verses. 935 11

earlier

If a sermon or homily was not preached *e*, 295 —
said here if it has not been said *e*. 330 —
said here if it has not been said *e*. 359 —

earliest

even as the prophets from *e* times spoke of him, 864 16

early

In the *E* Evening 139 —
those baptized at an *e* age 412 2

earnest

1. Our *e* desire that the Saviour's prayer, 876 29
the *e* study of the conditions under which so priceless 877 24

earnestly

and *e* beseeching Almighty God to accompany 11 20

ears

so that they have heard with their *e* 866 25

earth

III The *E* and its Creatures 48 —
II The *E* and its Creatures 89 —
Then, while *e* is cast upon the coffin, 485 —
Then, while *e* is cast upon the coffin, 501 —
8. For the Beauty of the *E* 813 11
8. For the Beauty of the *E* 840 —

earthly

mortifying the works of the flesh, and their *e* members, 871 13

ease

question and answer form for *e* of reference. 844 6

easiness

and too much *e* in admitting variations 9 26

Easter

Sunday of the Resurrection or *E* Day; 15 5
E Day is always the first Sunday after the full moon 15 7
depends upon the date of *E* Day. 15 10
The date of *E* also determines the beginning 15 12
the Ascension on a Thursday forty days after *E* Day. 15 13
E Day 15 16
seasons of Advent, Lent, and *E*. 16 10
days of Holy Week or of *E* Week. 17 11
the week following the Second Sunday of *E*, 17 12
except for Fridays in the Christmas and *E* 17 26
E Season, including Ascension Day 39 —
From *E* Day until the Ascension 43 —
in the following Antiphons are used only in *E* Season. 44 —
In *E* Week, in place of an Invitatory Psalm, 45 —
From *E* Day through the Day of Pentecost 59 —
From *E* Day through the Day of Pentecost 72 —
E Season, including Ascension Day 77 —
From *E* Day until the Ascension 81 —
in the following Antiphons are used only in *E* Season. 82 —
In *E* Week, in place of an Invitatory Psalm, 83 —
Especially suitable for use in *E* Season 85 —
From *E* Day through the Day of Pentecost 102 —
E Eve has its own form 108 12
Revelation 21:10, 22–24 (*E*) 108 16
from *E* Day through the Day of Pentecost 109 —
E Season 111 —
(adding "Alleluia, alleluia" in *E* Season) 114 —
In *E* Season the People respond 114 —
From *E* Day through the Day of Pentecost 126 —
In *E* Season, add 134 —
In *E* Season, add 135 —
From *E* Day through the Day of Pentecost, 143 2
in *E* Season the flame may be taken 143 10
E Day 170 —
The Liturgy of the *E* Vigil is on page 285. 170 —
Preface of *E* 171 —
Monday in *E* Week 171 —
Preface of *E* 171 —
Tuesday in *E* Week 171 —
Preface of *E* 171 —
Wednesday in *E* Week 171 —
Preface of *E* 171 —
Thursday in *E* Week 172 —
Preface of *E* 172 —
Friday in *E* Week 172 —
Preface of *E* 172 —
Saturday in *E* Week 172 —
Preface of *E* 172 —
Second Sunday of *E* 172 —
Preface of *E* 173 —
Third Sunday of *E* 173 —
Preface of *E* 173 —
Fourth Sunday of *E* 173 —
Preface of *E* 173 —
Fifth Sunday of *E* 173 —
Preface of *E* 173 —
Sixth Sunday of *E* 174 —
Preface of *E* 174 —
Seventh Sunday of *E*: 175 —
E Day 222 —
The Liturgy of the *E* Vigil is on page 285. 222 —
Preface of *E* 222 —
Monday in *E* Week 222 —
Preface of *E* 223 —
Tuesday in *E* Week 223 —
Preface of *E* 223 —
Wednesday in *E* Week 223 —
Preface of *E* 223 —
Thursday in *E* Week 223 —
Preface of *E* 223 —
Friday in *E* Week 224 —
Preface of *E* 224 —
Saturday in *E* Week 224 —
Preface of *E* 224 —
Second Sunday of *E* 224 —
Preface of *E* 224 —
Third Sunday of *E* 224 —
Preface of *E* 225 —
Fourth Sunday of *E* 225 —
Preface of *E* 225 —
Fifth Sunday of *E* 225 —
Preface of *E* 225 —
Sixth Sunday of *E* 225 —
Preface of *E* 225 —
Seventh Sunday of *E*: 226 —
when observed, is the first service of *E* Day. 284 2
sunrise on *E* Morning. 284 4
Eucharist with the administration of *E* Communion. 284 9
E Communion from the Sacrament previously consecrated. 284 29
convenient time before the Liturgy on *E* Day. 284 31
The Great Vigil of *E* 285 —
E Day through the Day of Pentecost. 287 —
from *E* Day through the Day of Pentecost 299 —
Holy Baptism is especially appropriate at the *E* Vigil, 312 2
from *E* Day through the Day of Pentecost 319 —
from *E* Day through the Day of Pentecost 323 —
at other times except during *E* Season. 337 —
From the *E* Vigil through the Day of Pentecost 340 —
E 346 —
from *E* Day through the Day of Pentecost 351 —
from *E* Day through the Day of Pentecost 355 —
at other times except during *E* Season. 364 —
From the *E* Vigil through the Day of Pentecost 366 —
E 379 —
E Day through the Day of Pentecost, 406 14
on all the days of *E* Week, 406 14
from *E* Day through the Day of Pentecost 413 —
The liturgy for the dead is an *E* liturgy. 507 2
from *E* Day through the Day of Pentecost 512 —
From *E* Day through the Day of Pentecost 523 —
from *E* Day through the Day of Pentecost 525 —
From *E* Day through the Day of Pentecost 535 —
from *E* Day through the Day of Pentecost 537 —

From *E* Day through the Day of Pentecost, 547 —
and Palm Sunday to 2 *E*), 934 23
variations in Lent and *E* Season. 934 25

easy

which is plain and *e* to be understood, 866 35
so they be plain and *e* to be understood. 866 41
order as is most *e* and plain for the understanding, 867 3
the order, and for that the rules be few and *e*. 867 5

eat

reverently *e* and drink it, either after the Communion 409 4
unable to *e* and drink the Bread and Wine 457 14
which *e* not the Body of Christ in the use 873 36
but rather, to their condemnation, do *e* and drink the sign 873 39

eaten

The Body of Christ is given, taken, and *e*, 873 31
mean whereby the Body of Christ is received and *e* 873 32

Ecclesiastes

The First Book of Chronicles, *E* or Preacher, 868 30

ecclesiastical

their *e* independence was necessarily included; 10 25
vesture distinctive of *e* or academic rank or order. 511 17
vesture distinctive of *e* or academic rank or order. 524 8
vesture distinctive of *e* or academic rank or office. 536 8
Estates of this Realm, whether they be *E* or Civil, 875 41
whether they be *E* or Temporal, and restrain 876 5

Ecclesiasticus

Old Testament Jeremiah 1:4–9, or *E* 39:1–8 540 —

edification

e of the people, "according to the various exigency 9 9

edified

hearts, spirit, and mind, have not been *e* thereby. 866 26
to the end that the congregation may be thereby *e*: 867 24

edifying

so that all things be done to *e*. 874 33

education

23. For *E* 209 —
23. For *E* 261 —
For *E*, see Various Occasions no. 23. 825 —

educational

service does not preclude the use of the building for *e* 566 11

Edward

compiling of her Liturgy in the time of *E* the Sixth, 10 2
which were set forth in the time of *E* the Sixth; and 874 37
lately set forth in the time of *E* the Sixth, 875 28
the forenamed King *E* unto this time, 875 32

effect

they have a wholesome *e* or operation: 872 39
which hinders not the *e* of the Sacraments. 873 1
Neither is the *e* of Christ's ordinance taken away 873 6

effectual

they be certain sure witnesses, and *e* signs of grace, 872 27
which be *e*, because of Christ's institution 873 8

eighteenth

E Day: Morning Prayer 717 —
E Day: Evening Prayer 722 —

eighth

E Sunday after the Epiphany 165 —
E Sunday after the Epiphany 216 —
E Day: Morning Prayer 636 —
E Day: Evening Prayer 641 —
Twenty-*e* Day: Morning Prayer 785 —
Twenty-*e* Day: Evening Prayer 789 —

eighty

One Thousand Seven Hundred and *E*-Nine. 8 6

either

seem *e* necessary or expedient." 9 20
e of the following, or one of the Collects 113 —
with *e* of the Invitatory Psalms. 141 7
e at the bidding, or in the course of the prayer; 142 9
E of the preceding Collects, with the proper Psalm 174 —
E of the preceding Collects, with the proper Psalm 226 —
Baptismal Vows, *e* here or after the Gospel. 292 —
e during the Liturgy or at other times. 316 —
prayers, *e* silently or aloud. 385 —
on a regular basis, using *e* the Proper of the Day 396 —
E here or elsewhere in the service, 401 2
Gospel in the language of the people, *e* in place of, 406 23
and with *e* the Grace or a blessing, 407 3
consecrate more of *e* or both, by saying 408 11
e after the Communion of the people 409 4
service of Christ in the world, *e* in general terms, 420 —
which may be in the form *e* of a statement of intention 420 —
The Holy Eucharist may be celebrated *e* according 436 14
To *e* question, the appropriate answer is, "I do." 437 11
approach the Altar, *e* for the exchange of vows, 437 15
E Luke 2:41–51, or Luke 18:15–17, 439 13
the sick person cannot receive *e* the consecrated Bread 457 —
following prayer, *e* before the service of Committal 487 —
following prayer, *e* before the service of Committal 503 —
may take place *e* where the preceding service 506 19
ministering *e* the Bread or the Wine, 536 15
In *e* case, the rubrics of the service of ordination 552 4
e with the Gloria Patri, or with a refrain 582 16
Devil doth thrust them *e* into desperation, 871 18
e to vow the estate of single life, 874 12
ministering *e* of God's Word, or of the Sacraments, 876 1

elaborate

methods, each of which can be *e* or simple, 582 6

elder

where the words *e*, elders, and fellow *e*, appear 528 —

elders

with them are the presbyters, or ordained *e*, 510 8
*It is to be noted that where the words elder, *e*, 528 —

elect

The bishop-*e* is vested in a rochet or alb, 511 16
When the bishop-*e* is presented, 511 18
present the bishop-*e*, saying 513 —
requires the following promise from the Bishop-*e* 513 —

The Bishop-*e* then signs the above Declaration 513 —
All now sit, except the bishop-*e*, who stands 517 —
Presiding Bishop addresses the bishop-*e* 517 —
questions are then addressed to the bishop-*e* 517 —
Bishop-*e* 519 —
All continue to stand, except the bishop-*e*, 520 —
upon the head of the bishop-*e*, and say together 521 —

election

Bishop then directs that testimonials of the *e* 513 —
13. For the *E* of a Bishop or other Minister 810 19
24. For an *E* 811 2
13. For the *E* of a Bishop or other Minister 818 —
24. For an *E* 822 —
XVII. Of Predestination and *E*. 871 1
consideration of Predestination, and our *E* in Christ, 871 11

eleison

continues with the Kyrie *e*, the Trisagion, 321 —
continues with the Gloria in excelsis, the Kyrie *e*, 353 —
Kyrie *e* (or "Lord, have mercy") may be sung or said 406 9

elements

with the following *e*: 112 —
If the remaining *E* are not required 555 4
consume the remaining *E*, and cleanse the vessels 555 6
prepare the *e* at the Offertory, 558 21
words of institution and of the *e* ordained by Him. 877 17
words of Institution, and of the *e* ordained by Him. 878 2

eleventh

E Day: Morning Prayer 662 —
E Day: Evening Prayer 665 —

Elizabeth

set forth by *E* our Queen do most plainly testify; 876 2

Elohim

E ("God"), Adonai ("Lord") 583 15
Then, the Hebrew custom is to substitute *E* 583 32

else

Celebrant says the following, or *e* the Exhortation 330 —
to the day or occasion, or *e* one of the following 396 —
or *e* the celebrant may consecrate more of both kinds, 408 13
Or *e* the following general confession may be said 454 18
Or *e* this anthem 492 —
People is used, or *e* the form on page 465 or 480. 496 —
nor powers, nor height, nor depth, nor anything *e* 507 7
may read the Letter of Institution, or *e* may state 559 —
not otherwise clear, or *e* prefix to the Reading 888 27

elsewhere

For the lighting of the candles at the Altar and *e*, 143 10
Either here or *e* in the service, 401 2

ember

The *E* Days, traditionally observed 18 5
the traditional winter *E* Days. 160 —
the traditional spring *E* Days. 166 —
the traditional summer *E* Days. 176 —
the traditional autumnal *E* Days. 182 —
15. For the Ministry (*E* Days) 205 —
the traditional winter *E* Days. 212 —
the traditional spring *E* Days. 218 —
the traditional summer *E* Days. 227 —
the traditional autumnal *E* Days. 233 —
15. For the Ministry (*E* Days) 256 —
On *E* Days or other occasions, 548 —

embrace

with gratitude to God, *e* the happy occasion 11 4

emergency

E Baptism 313 21
In case of *e*, any baptized person may administer 313 22
The person who administers *e* Baptism should inform 314 3
and the person baptized under *e* conditions, 314 7

empowered

This letter is a sign that you are fully *e* 557 7

enacted

e by the House of Deputies, but rather incorporated 877 27

encouragement

and *e* as are needed and pronounces absolution. 446 22

end

the proper *e* of all such prayers, 10 36
At the *e* of the Psalms is sung or said 46 —
At the *e* of the Psalms is sung or said 64 —
At the *e* of the Psalms is sung or said 84 —
At the *e* of the Psalms is sung or said 105 —
the Blessing or Dismissal at the *e*. 108 9
At the *e* of the Psalms is sung or said 118 —
At the *e* of the Psalms is sung or said 131 —
add other Prayers, and *e* the Litany, saying 154 —
or at the *e* of Morning of Evening Prayer; 154 —
or at the *e* of the service, as convenient. 407 13
as far as the *e* of the postcommunion prayer, 408 26
At the *e* of the Gospel, the Reader says 480 —
At the *e* of the Gospel, the Reader says 495 —
At the *e* of the litany, after the Kyries, 515 —
At the *e* of the litany, after the Kyries, 527 —
At the *e* of the litany, after the Kyries, 539 —
At the *e* of the litany, the Bishop, standing, says 560 —
stands for the salutation and Collect at the *e* of it. 565 7
to the *e* that the congregation may be thereby edified: 867 24
Apostles to the Church unto the *e* of the world, 877 9
at the beginning and *e* of each Psalm or Canticle, 935 10

ended

When the reading of the testimonials is *e*, 513 —

ending

Alternative *E* 311 1
and *e* with the Invocation 408 15
e with the narrative of the Institution). 408 16

endorsement

thereby signify their *e* of the candidates 298 19

endued

be *e* with so excellent a benefit of God, 871 6

endure

put away our sins, and *e* the severity of God's judgment; 870 8

enemies

6. For our *E* 810 11
6. For our *E* 816 —

enforce

so besides the same ought it not to *e* any thing 871 41

engaged

for the special work in which the person will be *e* 421 —

engendered

the Nature of every man, that naturally is *e* 869 24

England

Church of *E*, to which the Protestant Episcopal 9 11
Book of Common Prayer of the Church of *E*. 11 12
from intending to depart from the Church of *E* 11 13
hearing the same, the Service in the Church of *E* 866 24
the constitution and laws of *E* are considered 875 16
power in this Realm of *E*, and other his Dominions, 875 40
Rome hath no jurisdiction in this Realm of *E*. 876 7

English

whose native tongue is other than *E*, 406 22
or in addition to, the Gospel in *E*. 406 24
Tobit 8:5b–8 (New *E* Bible) 426 —
been carried over into the classical *E* versions, 583 26
and our *E* tradition follows suit, 583 33
its *E* equivalent, "Praise the Lord." 584 5
and sung in the church in the *E* tongue, 867 24

enjoyed

faith of eternal Salvation to be *e* through Christ, 871 15

enlarged

consent and authority, may be altered, abridged, *e*, 9 7

enough

Then if the child is old *e* to answer, 441 —
The symbols presented should be large *e* to be visible 565 21

ensue

the great profit that shall *e* thereof. 867 15

enter

When the ministers *e*, 142 28
On this day the ministers *e* in silence. 276 —
2. The intention of the man and the woman to *e* 435 13
e in procession through the principal door. 575 14
to *e* into brotherly conference with all 877 22

entered

e into the nearer presence of our Lord, 507 13

entire

provided the substance of the Faith be kept *e*; 9 5
In all services, the *e* Christian assembly participates 13 16
always sung or said at the conclusion of the *e* portion 141 11
addressed to the *e* assembly. 407 8
upon the new priest after the *e* Prayer of Consecration 553 22
upon the new deacon after the *e* Prayer 554 13
In some instances, the *e* portion of the Psalter 935 3

entirety

Those who desire to recite the Psalter in its *e* should, 935 5

entitled

Royal assent in 1571 and reaffirmed in 1662, was *e* 869 19

entrance

During their *e*, a hymn, psalm, or anthem may be sung, 423 —
or during the *e* of the ministers, 468 24
or during the *e* of the ministers, 490 24
psalms, and anthems may be sung during the *e* 512 —
occur at the *e* of the chancel, or in some other place 564 15

enumerate

It seems unnecessary to *e* all the different alterations 11 9

Ephesians

E 2:19 40 —
E 3:20,21 60 —
E 3:20, 21 73 —
E 2:19 78 —
E 3:20, 21 102 —
E 3:20,21 126 —
E 5:2 343 —
E 5:2 376 —
E 3:14–19 (The Father from whom every family 426 —
E 5:1–2, 21–33 (Walk in love, as Christ loved us) 426 —
or *E* 4:7, 11–16, 528 —
or *E* 4:7, 11–16 560 —

Epiphany

The *E*, January 6 15 18
through the First Sunday after the *E*, 16 17
or from the Last Sunday after the *E* 16 17
the *E*, and All Saints' Day. 17 19
E 38 —
From the *E* through the Baptism of Christ, 43 —
E 76 —
From the *E* through the Baptism of Christ, 81 —
Isaiah 60:1–3 (*E*) 108 19
Christmas, *E*, and other Feasts of the Incarnation 111 —
The *E* January 6 162 —
Preface of the *E* 162 —
with the Psalm and Lessons for the *E*, 162 —
The Preface of the *E* is used. 162 —
First Sunday after the *E*: 163 —
Preface of the *E* 163 —
Second Sunday after the *E* 163 —
Preface of the *E*, or of the Lord's Day 163 —
Third Sunday after the *E* 163 —
Preface of the *E*, or of the Lord's Day 163 —
Fourth Sunday after the *E* 164 —
Preface of the *E*, or of the Lord's Day 164 —
Fifth Sunday after the *E* 164 —
Preface of the *E*, or of the Lord's Day 164 —
Sixth Sunday after the *E* 164 —
Preface of the *E*, or of the Lord's Day 164 —
Seventh Sunday after the *E* 164 —
Preface of the *E*, or of the Lord's Day 165 —
Eighth Sunday after the *E* 165 —
Preface of the *E*, or of the Lord's Day 165 —
Last Sunday after the *E* 165 —
Preface of the *E* 165 —
Preface of the *E* 187 —
Preface of the *E* 188 —

Preface of the *E* 189 —
Preface of the *E* 191 —
Preface of the *E* 200 —
Preface of the *E* 201 —
The *E* January 6 214 —
Preface of the *E* 214 —
with the Psalm and Lessons for the *E*, 214 —
between the *E* and the following Sunday. 214 —
The Preface of the *E* is used. 214 —
First Sunday after the *E*: 214 —
Preface of the *E* 214 —
Second Sunday after the *E* 215 —
Preface of the *E*, or of the Lord's Day 215 —
Third Sunday after the *E* 215 —
Preface of the *E*, or of the Lord's Day 215 —
Fourth Sunday after the *E* 215 —
Preface of the *E*, or of the Lord's Day 215 —
Fifth Sunday after the *E* 216 —
Preface of the *E*, or of the Lord's Day 216 —
Sixth Sunday after the *E* 216 —
Preface of the *E*, or of the Lord's Day 216 —
Seventh Sunday after the *E* 216 —
Preface of the *E*, or of the Lord's Day 216 —
Eighth Sunday after the *E* 216 —
Preface of the *E*, or of the Lord's Day 217 —
Last Sunday after the *E* 217 —
Preface of the *E* 217 —
Preface of the *E* 239 —
Preface of the *E* 240 —
Preface of the *E* 241 —
Preface of the *E* 243 —
Preface of the *E* 252 —
(the First Sunday after the *E*). 312 5
E 346 —
E 378 —
Christmas Day through the Feast of the *E*; 406 13
(except in the weeks from 4 Advent to 1 *E*, 934 22

episcopal

and the Laity of the Protestant *E* Church 8 3
to which the Protestant *E* Church in these States 9 11
In the *E* Church it is required 422 3
E Services 509 —
orders by solemn prayer and the laying on of *e* hands. 510 18
escorted to the *e* chair. 522 —
most frequently used in *E* churches, 582 28
of the Protestant *E* Church in the United States 867 31
We, Bishops of the Protestant *E* Church 876 25

episcopate

clothed with the vesture of the *e*, 553 3
4. The Historic *E*, locally adapted in the methods 877 18
(d) The Historic *E*, locally adapted in the methods 878 4

Epistle

E 2 Corinthians 5:20b–6:10 264 —
E Philippians 2:5–11 272 —
E 1 Corinthians 11:23–26 (27–32) 274 —
E Hebrews 10:1–25 276 —
E 1 Peter 4:1–8 283 —
Lay persons read the Lessons, and the *E*, 284 20
E Romans 6:3–11 295 —
the Lesson from the Old Testament, and the *E*, 468 15
the Lesson from the Old Testament, and the *E*, 490 15
read the Old Testament Lesson and the *E*. 515 9
E Hebrews 5:1–10, or 1 Timothy 3:1–7, 515 —
read the Old Testament Lesson and the *E*. 528 —
E 1 Peter 5:1–4,* or Ephesians 4:7, 11–16, 528 —
read the Old Testament Lesson and the *E*. 540 —
E 2 Corinthians 4:1–6, or 1 Timothy 3:8–13, 540 —
read the Old Testament Lesson and the *E*, 558 15
E Romans 12:1–18, or Ephesians 4:7, 11–16 560 —
read the Old Testament Lesson and the *E*. 571 —
E Revelation 21:2–7, or 1 Corinthians 3:1–11, 16–17, 571 —
an instrument of music is to be dedicated, after the *E* 572 —

Epistles

and the *E* be read by lay persons. 422 18

equal

left at full and *e* liberty 10 27
the Glory *e*, the Majesty co-eternal. 864 29
three Persons are co-eternal together and co-*e*. 865 15
E to the Father, as touching his Godhead; 865 26
common and *e* benefit of all men. 877 11

equity

common *e* ought to be allowed to all human writings; 10 18

equivalent

Two *e* forms of service are provided here 446 10
its English *e*, "Praise the Lord." 584 5

err

they may *e*, and sometimes have erred, 872 7

erred

Jerusalem, Alexandria, and Antioch, have *e*; 871 33
Rome hath *e*, not only in their living and manner 871 34
sometimes have *e*, even in things pertaining to God. 872 8

escorted

new Bishop, if the Bishop of the Diocese, may now be *e* 522 —

Esdras

The First Book of *E*, 868 32
The Second Book of *E*, 868 33
The Third Book of *E*, 868 37
The Fourth Book of *E*, 868 38

especially

E suitable for use in Easter Season 85 —
E suitable in Lent, and on other penitential occasions 90 —
e for the seasons suggested: 108 15
e in Lent and on Rogation days. 148 —
e in times of war, or of national anxiety, 154 —
E suitable for Thursdays 201 —
E suitable for Fridays 201 —
E suitable for Saturdays 201 —
E suitable for Thursdays 252 —
E suitable for Fridays 252 —
E suitable for Saturdays 252 —
Holy Baptism is *e* appropriate at the Easter Vigil, 312 2
e in the hospital or at home; 439 10
(*e* suitable for use in the evening) 560 —
e such as were Ministers of the congregation, 866 10
e to our fellow-Christians 876 27

essential

yet so as that the main body and *e* parts 10 5
the Church of England in any *e* point of doctrine, 11 13
(which are the *e* parts of Baptism), 313 18
It is *e* that the person seeking to make or renew 420 —
and therefore as *e* to the restoration of unity 877 12

establish

do hereby *e* the said Book: 8 9
to *e* such other alterations and amendments 11 7
but yet doth it not apply them to *e* any doctrine; 868 35
e and confirm their faith of eternal Salvation 871 15

established

things once advisedly *e*, she hath, 10 1
by the wit of man so well devised, or so sure *e*, 866 3
As *e* by the Bishops, the Clergy, and the Laity 867 30

establishes

The bond which God *e* in Baptism 298 3

estate

either to vow the *e* of single life, 874 12

estates

of all *E* of this Realm, whether they be Ecclesiastical 875 41
rule all *e* and degrees committed to their charge 876 4

Esther

The Book of *E*, 868 26
The rest of the Book of *E*, 868 37

estimation

10 Of the reverend *E* of God's Word. 875 13

eternal

(That you may know that you have *e* life) 454 —
(Things which are not seen are *e*) 475 —
2 Corinthians 4:16–5:9 (Things that are unseen are *e*) 495 —
promises of God in Christ about *e* life. 506 17
the Glory equal, the Majesty co-*e*. 864 29
The Father *e*, the Son *e*, and the Holy Ghost *e*. 864 34
And yet they are not three eternals, but one *e*. 864 35
three Persons are co-*e* together and co-equal. 865 15
and *e* God, and of one substance with the Father, 868 3
with the Father and the Son, very and *e* God. 868 18
faith of *e* Salvation to be enjoyed through Christ, 871 15
Of obtaining *e* Salvation only by the Name of Christ. 871 24

eternals

And yet they are not three *e*, but one eternal. 864 35

eternity

of one substance, power, and *e*; 867 38

Eucharist

The Holy *E*, the principal act of Christian worship 13 3
in the form appointed at the *E*. 13 24
Provided, that there is no celebration of the *E* 18 11
At celebrations of the Holy *E*, 36 8
Then, unless the *E* or a form of general intercession 57 —
Then, unless the *E* or a form of general intercession 70 —
At celebrations of the Holy *E*, 74 7
Then, unless the *E* or a form of general intercession 100 —
With the celebration of the Holy *E*, 112 —
Then, unless the *E* or a form of general intercession 124 —
Creed is omitted from the Office when the *E* 142 2
the *E* is to follow immediately. 142 6
used as the Liturgy of the Word at the *E*, 142 18
before the *E* or after the Collects 148 —
the Litany is sung or said immediately before the *E*, 153 —
and the *E* begins with the Salutation 153 —
the *E* on the weekdays following, 158 8
5. Of the Holy *E* 201 —
5. Of the Holy *E* 252 —
At the *E* 272 —
the Liturgy of the Psalms immediately precedes the *E*, 272 —
The *E* begins in the usual manner, 274 —
There is no celebration of the *E* on this day. 283 —
4. The Holy *E* with the administration 284 9
follow each Lesson, and assist at Baptism and the *E*. 284 15
the *E* according to their order. 284 19
Ministry of the Word of the Vigil *E*, 284 25
At the *E* 294 —
Baptism is appropriately administered within the *E* 298 5
and preside at Baptism and the *E*. 298 8
At the *E* 310 —
Offertory of the *E*, at which the Bishop, when present, 310 —
If there is no celebration of the *E*, 311 —
Nicene Creed at the *E*. 312 17
The oblations of bread and wine at the baptismal *E* 313 13
The Holy *E* 315 —
The Holy *E*: Rite One 323 —
The Holy *E*: Rite Two 355 —
be present at a public celebration of the *E*. 396 —
desirable that the priest arrange to celebrate the *E* 396 —
An Order for Celebrating the Holy *E* 400 2
weekly celebration of the Holy *E*. 400 5
Make *E* 401 7
In making *E*, the Celebrant uses 402 —
Great Litany is sung or said immediately before the *E*, 406 3
Litany concludes with the Kyries, and the *E* begins 406 4
the Offertory of the *E*, at which the Bishop 419 —
If there is no celebration of the *E*, 419 —
Before the Offertory of the *E*, 420 —
the nuptial blessing, and of celebrating the Holy *E*. 422 9
should pronounce the blessing and preside at the *E*. 422 11
assisting functions at the *E*. 422 14
At the *E* 432 —
begins as prescribed for celebrations of the Holy *E*, 433 —
The Holy *E* may be celebrated 436 14
authorized liturgy for the Holy *E*. 437 6
and the *E* begins with the Offertory. 437 7
In the *E* it may follow the Prayers 439 7
at a public celebration of the *E*, 453 8
If the *E* is to be celebrated, 457 —
preside at the *E* and pronounce the Commendation. 468 14
At the *E* 482 —
preside at the *E* and pronounce the Commendation. 490 14
At the *E*. 498 —
with the Peace and Offertory of the *E*. 506 22
At the Celebration of the *E* 522 —
proceeds with the celebration of the *E*. 522 —
At the Celebration of the *E* 535 —
Priest joins in the celebration of the Holy *E* 535 —
At the Celebration of the *E* 546 —
at the *E* or the Daily Office, 548 —

The celebration of the Holy *E* 552 3
the chief celebrant of the *E*. 558 9
At the *E* 563 —
the Great Thanksgiving of the *E*. 563 —
bread and wine may be used in the *E* which follows. 565 23
At the *E* 574 —
followed by the celebration of the Holy *E*. 577 19
9. The *E*, beginning with the Offertory 578 5
for use between the Lessons at the *E*, 582 11
of chanting the psalms between the Lessons at the *E*, 582 25
at the *E*, or at any time after the Collects 836 —
The Holy *E* 859 —
Liturgy of the Word takes the form given in the Holy *E*, 888 10
in addition to the *E*, the Lessons at the Office 888 13
when the Psalm is sung between the Lessons at the *E*. 888 21

eucharistic

E Prayer I 333 —
E Prayer II 340 —
E Prayer A 361 —
E Prayer B 367 —
E Prayer C 369 —
E Prayer D 372 —
the Celebrant uses one of the *E* Prayers 402 —
saying again the words of the *E* Prayer, 408 17
(in the case of *E* Prayer C, 408 15
During the *E* Prayer, it is appropriate 553 8

evangelists

All feasts of *E* 17 3
feasts of apostles or *e*. 511 5

eve

Easter *E* has its own form 108 12

even

e though the Sacrament is not received 457 —
of Advent preceding *e*-numbered years. 934 4
e as the prophets from earliest times spoke of him, 864 16
sometimes have erred, *e* in things pertaining to God. 872 8

evening

other major Feasts, and Daily Morning and *E* Prayer, 13 4
the Order for Morning or *E* Prayer 36 8
Daily *E* Prayer: 61 —
the Order for Morning or *E* Prayer 74 7
This Order provides a form of *e* service or vespers 108 2
on suitable occasions in the late afternoon or *e*. 108 3
complete rite in place of *E* Prayer, 108 4
E Prayer or some other service, 108 5
or as the prelude to an *e* meal 108 5
An Order of Worship for the *E* 109 —
With *E* Prayer, beginning with the Psalms; 112 —
Or, it may continue as a complete *e* Office 112 —
or one of the Collects from *E* Prayer 113 —
Daily *E* Prayer: 115 —
A hymn suitable for the *e* may be sung. 132 —
In the Early *E* 139 —
This devotion may be used before or after the *e* meal. 139 —
The Order of Worship for the *E*, 139 —
Morning and *E* Prayer 141 2
In Rite One services of Morning Prayer and *E* Prayer, 141 18
When Morning or *E* Prayer is used as the Liturgy 142 17
Order of Worship for the *E* 142 25
Psalms generally appropriate to the *e* include: 143 23
or after the Collects of Morning or *E* Prayer; 148 3
or at the end of Morning of *E* Prayer; 154 —
the *e* service of the day before. 158 23
Morning or *E* Prayer may be used 322 18
Morning or *E* Prayer may be used 354 18
At Morning or *E* Prayer it may take place 439 8
(especially suitable for use in the *e*) 560 —
First Day: *E* Prayer 589 —
Second Day: *E* Prayer 597 —
Third Day: *E* Prayer 602 —
Fourth Day: *E* Prayer 610 —
Fifth Day: *E* Prayer 617 —
Sixth Day: *E* Prayer 624 —
Seventh Day: *E* Prayer 633 —
Eighth Day: *E* Prayer 641 —
Ninth Day: *E* Prayer 650 —
Tenth Day: *E* Prayer 658 —
Eleventh Day: *E* Prayer 665 —
Twelfth Day: *E* Prayer 672 —
Thirteenth Day: *E* Prayer 679 —
Fourteenth Day: *E* Prayer 687 —
Fifteenth Day: *E* Prayer 694 —
Sixteenth Day: *E* Prayer 705 —
Seventeenth Day: *E* Prayer 713 —
Eighteenth Day: *E* Prayer 722 —
Nineteenth Day: *E* Prayer 727 —
Twentieth Day: *E* Prayer 735 —
Twenty-first Day: *E* Prayer 741 —
Twenty-second Day: *E* Prayer 749 —
Twenty-third Day: *E* Prayer 756 —
Twenty-fourth Day: *E* Prayer 763 —
Twenty-fifth Day: *E* Prayer 769 —
Twenty-sixth Day: *E* Prayer 775 —
Twenty-seventh Day: *E* Prayer 782 —
Twenty-eighth Day: *E* Prayer 789 —
Twenty-ninth Day: *E* Prayer 797 —
Thirtieth Day: *E* Prayer 804 —
63. In the *E* 812 18
and for morning and *e*, 812 27
For use after the Collects of Morning or *E* Prayer 814 —
and for morning and *e*, 833 —
63. In the *E* 833 —
E Prayer, or separately. 836 —
When the same congregation is present for Morning or *E* Prayer, 888 12
used in the morning and one in the *e*; 934 9
the Gospel Reading be used in the *e* in Year One, 934 11
First Reading at *E* Prayer. 934 14
and then those for the *e*. 934 27
used in the morning or in the *e*. 934 29

evenly

Advent in years *e* divisible by three. 888 3

Evensong

but when men say Matins and *E* privately, 867 25

ever

Isaiah 25:6–9 (He will swallow up death for *e*) 494 —
Although in the visible Church the evil be *e* mingled 873 2

everlasting

John 5:24–27 (He that believeth hath *e* life) 480 —
John 5:24–27 (He who believes has *e* life) 495 —
it is necessary to *e* salvation that he also believe 865 19
And they that have done good shall go into life *e*; 865 37
and they that have done evil into *e* fire. 865 38
There is but one living and true God, *e*, without body, 867 35
the Word of the Father, begotten from *e* of the Father, 868 2
e life is offered to Mankind by Christ, 869 8
Predestination to Life is the *e* purpose of God, 871 2
and to bring them by Christ to *e* salvation, 871 5
they attain to *e* felicity. 871 10

everlastingly

without doubt he shall perish *e*. 864 24

every

in *e* Church, what cannot be clearly determined 9 5
will be received and examined by *e* true member 11 17
and *e* sincere Christian, with a meek, candid, 11 18
Here and after *e* petition the People respond 389 —
Opportunity is always to be given to *e* communicant 407 —
(The Father from whom *e* family is named) 426 —
The People respond to *e* petition with Amen. 480 —
Revelation 7:9–17 (God will wipe away *e* tear) 495 —
the Christian verity to acknowledge *e* Person 865 5
whereof *e* one was called a nocturn, 866 28
the fault and corruption of the Nature of *e* man, 869 24
therefore in *e* person born into this world, 869 27
Not *e* deadly sin willingly committed after Baptism 870 32
That *e* man shall be saved by the Law 871 25
E particular or national Church hath authority 874 31
Notwithstanding, *e* man ought, 876 14

everyone

Which Faith except *e* do keep whole and undefiled, 864 23

everything

with the sponsors or godparents, taking part in *e* 314 8
(Love which binds *e* together in harmony) 426 —

everywhere

and the proclamation of his Gospel *e*. 510 29

evidence

and has given *e* of due contrition, 446 21

evidently

or that which is *e* grounded upon the same; 867 2
a lively Faith may be as *e* known as a tree 870 10

evil

a person who is living a notoriously *e* life 409 8
and they that have done *e* into everlasting fire. 865 37
and is of his own nature inclined to *e*, 869 26
Although in the visible Church the *e* be ever mingled 873 2
the *e* have chief authority in the Ministration 873 3
although they be ministered by *e* men. 873 9
that inquiry be made of *e* Ministers, 873 10
the stubborn and *e*-doers. 876 6

exalt

the bishop continues "May they *e* you, O Lord, 554 3

examination

officiates at the Presentation and *E* of the Candidates; 298 9
Presentation and *E* 301 —
Presentation and *E* 415 —
The *E* 517 —
The *E* 531 —
The *E* 543 —

examined

the whole will be received and *e* by every true member 11 17
The ordinands are *e* together. 553 28
The ordinands are *e* together. 554 18

example

For *e*, if the Sunday after Trinity Sunday is May 26, 158 16
support them by prayer and *e* in their Christian life. 298 20
(as Hierome saith) the Church doth read for *e* of life 868 34
(For *e*, 1977 divided by 3 is 659 888 4

excellent

be endued with so *e* a benefit of God, 871 6

excelsis

Gloria in *e* 52 —
Gloria in *e* 94 —
(substituting, if desired, the Gloria in *e* 175 —
(substituting, if desired, the Gloria in *e* 227 —
Gloria in *e* 294 —
If desired, the hymn Gloria in *e* may be sung 312 18
the Kyrie eleison, the Trisagion, or the Gloria in *e*. 321 —
the Gloria in *e*, the Kyrie eleison, or the Trisagion. 353 —
Gloria in *e*, or the hymn used in place of it, 406 12
If desired, the hymn Gloria in *e* may be sung 412 13
The Summary of the Law, the Gloria in *e*, 552 5

except

Scriptural citations in this Book, *e* for the Psalms, 14 16
e in the seasons of Advent, 16 9
e the feast of the Annunciation. 17 24
e for Fridays in the Christmas and Easter 17 26
E in Lent, may be added. 42 —
E in Lent, may be added. 63 —
E in Lent, add 80 —
E in Lent, add 103 —
E in Lent, add 117 —
E in Lent, add 128 —
(*e* for Trinity Sunday) 158 10
weekdays which follow, *e* as otherwise appointed. 166 —
e as otherwise appointed. 174 —
e as otherwise appointed. 217 —
e as otherwise appointed. 226 —
e for those at the Altar, may also be lighted. 286 —
E on Principal Feasts, 310 —
e the administration of the water. 314 9
omitted at other times *e* during Easter Season. 337 —
e as otherwise appointed for Holy Days 345 —
omitted at other times *e* during Easter Season. 364 —
e as otherwise appointed for Holy Days 378 —
all that is described above, *e* for the blessing, 407 5
All now sit, *e* the bishop-elect, who stands 517 —
All continue to stand, *e* the bishop-elect, who kneels 520 —
All are seated *e* the ordinand, who stands 531 —
All now stand *e* the ordinand, who kneels 533 —

All are seated *e* the ordinand, who stands 543 —
All now stand *e* the ordinand, who kneels 544 —
E on Major Feasts, 564 1
but, *e* in certain classical prayers 814 —
Which Faith *e* everyone do keep whole and undefiled, 864 23
which *e* a man believe faithfully, he cannot be saved. 865 39
nature was made like unto us in all things, sin only *e*, 870 25
e when the same congregation attends 888 7
(*e* in the weeks from 4 Advent to 1 Epiphany, 934 22
e for appropriate variations in Lent 934 24
e on major Holy Days. 934 30

exceptional

Under *e* circumstances, when the services 13 25

excess

6 Against *E* of Apparel. 875 8

exchange

E the Peace 401 1
or with the *e* of the Peace. 407 4
In the *e* between individuals 407 8
e of the Peace may take place at the time 407 10
The service then continues with the *e* of the Peace 421 —
may precede the *e* of vows. 435 16
may approach the Altar, either for the *e* of vows, 437 15
before the *e* of the Peace. 453 10
All the newly ordained take part in the *e* of the Peace, 554 7

exchanged

The Peace may then be *e*. 113 —
The Peace is then *e*. 269 —
the Peace is now *e* 308 —
The Peace is then *e* 310 —
The Peace may then be *e*. 398 —
The Peace is then *e* 419 —
greetings may be *e* throughout the congregation. 431 —
4. The vows of the man and woman are *e*, 435 18
The Peace may be *e* 436 11
The Peace may be *e*. 445 —

exchanges

The new Deacon then *e* greetings with family members 546 —

exciting

the procuring of reverence, and the *e* of piety 10 11

exclusive

e property of this portion of Christ's catholic Church, 510 27
The *e* use of a single method 582 4

excommunicate

XXXIII. Of *e* Persons, how they are to be avoided. 874 16

excommunicated

and *e*, ought to be taken of the whole multitude 874 18

execute

understanding to *e* justice, and to maintain truth;" 11 1
concerning the manner how to understand, do, and *e*, 867 18
before he be lawfully called, and sent to *e* the same. 872 17

exemplified

unity *e* by the undivided Catholic Church 877 6

exercise

Deacons by virtue of their order do not *e* 13 21
e the offices of bishop, priest, or deacon 510 22
e this ministry, accepting its privileges 557 8

exercised

e through the care each Christian has for others, 446 3

exhort

and be more able to *e* others by wholesome doctrine, 866 11

exhortation

An *E* 316 —
This *E* may be used, in whole or in part, 316 —
E may be read by a lay person. 316 —
When used as a separate service, the *E*, 319 —
Deacon or Celebrant says the following, or else the *E* 330 —
When used as a separate service, the *E*, 351 —
In the opening *e* (at the symbol of N.N.), 422 20

exigency

"according to the various *e* of times 9 9

existence

Catholic Church during the first ages of its *e*; 877 7

Exodus

E 15:1–6, 11–13, 17–18 85 —
Old Testament *E* 12:1–14a 274 —
the Lesson from *E*. 288 —
E 14:10—15:1 289 —
E, 868 27

expansion

or of logical *e* (Our eyes look to the Lord our God, 583 8

expected

and is *e* to preach the Word 298 7
e, when they are ready and have been duly prepared, 412 3
are also *e* to make a public affirmation of their faith 412 8

expediency

declared the necessity and *e* of occasional alterations 9 23

expedient

seem either necessary or *e*." 9 21
alterations would in time be found *e*. 10 20
as might be deemed *e*. 11 8

explication

an *e* of Christian doctrine, 875 15

expound

(which some do *e* the wisdom, 869 29
neither may it so *e* one place of Scripture, 871 39

express

With the *e* permission of the bishop, 16 19
the congregation to *e* intentions or objects of prayer 142 8
During the prayers, some parents may wish to *e* thanks 439 15

expressed

e in the Homily of Justification. 870 5

expresses

The Congregation *e* its approval. 563 —

expression

as an *e* of the collegiality of the ministry 558 17

expressive

(b) a Collect *e* of some special need in the life 394 —

expressly

e declared unto us in the Word of God. 871 23

Exsultet

and to chant the *E*. 284 18
A lay person may be assigned to chant the *E*. 284 21
sings or says the *E*, as follows 286 —

extended

When persons are unable to be present for *e* periods, 396 —
The Bishop goes to the Table and, with arms *e*, says 573 —
public worship for an *e* period of time 577 21

extendeth

The Power of the Civil Magistrate *e* to all men, 875 35

extends

If a ring or rings are to be blessed, the wife *e* her hand 434 —
the husband *e* his hand) toward the Priest, who says 434 —
(or *e* a hand over the penitent), 451 5

extolling

e the glory of the cross, is then sung. 282 —

extreme

receive the Sacrament, but, by reason of *e* sickness 457 —
and *E* Unction, are not to be counted for Sacraments 872 33

eyes

Psalm 145:14–22 (The *e* of all wait upon you, 454 11
(Our *e* look to the Lord our God, 583 8
to have continually before their *e* the sentence 871 17

Ezekiel

E 36:24–28 290 —
E 37:1–14 291 —

F

fables

were blasphemous *f*, and dangerous deceits. 874 10

face

the celebrant, whenever possible, should *f* the people 313 4
f to *f* for a spiritual conference leading to absolution 446 18

faces

f them and sings or says 333 —
f them and sings or says 340 —
f them and sings or says 361 —
f them and sings or says 367 —
f them and sings or says 369 —
f them and sings or says 372 —

facing

or the Priest, stands and, *f* the people, says 269 —
Then, *f* the Holy Table, the Celebrant proceeds 333 —
F the people, the Celebrant may say 338 —
Then, *f* the Holy Table, the Celebrant proceeds 341 —
Then, *f* the Holy Table, the Celebrant proceeds 361 —
F the people, the Celebrant says 364 —
Then, *f* the Holy Table, the Celebrant proceeds 367 —
Then, *f* the Holy Table, the Celebrant proceeds 370 —
Then, *f* the Holy Table, the Celebrant proceeds 373 —
Then the Celebrant, *f* the people 423 —
The Man, *f* the woman and taking her right hand 427 —
the Woman, still *f* the man, 427 —
The Celebrant, *f* the body, says 483 —
The Celebrant, *f* the body, says 499 —
except the bishop-elect, who stands *f* the bishops. 517 —
from a chair placed close to the people, and *f* them, 524 5
stand except the ordinand, who kneels *f* the Bishop 533 —
from a chair placed close to the people, and *f* them, 536 5
except the ordinand, who kneels *f* the bishop. 544 —
F the Font, the Bishop says 570 —

fact

so that the *f* can be properly registered. 314 4

fairly

or which is not *f* defensible, 10 16

faith

provided the substance of the *F* be kept 9 4
mature public affirmation of their *f* and commitment 412 4
expected to make a public affirmation of their *f* 412 8
Luke 17:11–19 (Your *f* has made you well) 453 17
(Looking to Jesus, the perfecter of our *f*) 454 2
An Outline of the *F* 843 —
An Outline of the *F* 845 —
it is necessary that he hold the Catholic *F*. 864 22
Which *F* except everyone do keep whole 864 23
And the Catholic *F* is this: 864 25
For the right *F* is, that we believe and confess, 865 21
This is the Catholic *F*, which except a man believe 865 39
I. Of *F* in the Holy Trinity. 867 34
believed as an article of the *F*, or be thought requisite 868 22
by his own natural strength and good works, to *f*, 869 35
by *F*, and not for our own works or deservings. 870 3
by *F* only, is a most wholesome Doctrine, 870 4
Good Works, which are the fruits of *F*, 870 7
and do spring out necessarily of a true and lively *F*; 870 9
a lively *F* may be as evidently known as a tree 870 10
forasmuch as they spring not of *f* in Jesus Christ; 870 14
establish and confirm their *f* of eternal Salvation 871 15
but also in matters of *F*. 871 35
and authority in Controversies of *F*: 871 38
strengthen and confirm our *F* in him. 872 29
grace of God's gifts diminished from such as by *f*, 873 7
F is confirmed, 873 18
insomuch that to such as rightly, worthily, and with *f*, 873 25
and eaten in the Supper, is *F*. 873 33
The Wicked, and such as be void of a lively *f*, 873 37
the Magistrate requireth, in a cause of *f* and charity, 876 20
with them on the basis of a common *F* and Order, 877 2
to be the substantial deposit of Christian *F* and Order 877 8
the sufficient statement of the Christian *F*. 877 15
and as being the rule and ultimate standard of *f*. 877 34
statement of the Christian *f*. 877 36

faithful

4. For the Saints and *F* Departed 813 4
4. For the Saints and *F* Departed 838 —
The visible Church of Christ is a congregation of *f* 871 30
ought to be taken of the whole multitude of the *f*, 874 18

faithfully

Catholic Faith, which except a man believe *f*, 865 39

fall

which *f* upon or are transferred to a weekday, 17 17
The condition of Man after the *f* of Adam is such, 869 34
repentance is not to be denied to such as *f* into sin 870 33
we may depart from grace given, and *f* 870 35

falling

Major Feasts *f* in these weeks 17 11

falls

after the full moon that *f* on or after March 21. 15 7
the calendar date of which *f* on that Sunday, 158 14

falsely

as certain Anabaptists do *f* boast. 876 14

familiar

f from its use in many well-known anthems. 584 8

families

Individuals and *F* 136 —
f, and friends assemble in the church 435 9
provision for the well-being of their *f*, 445 —
45. For *F* 811 28
45. For *F* 828 —

family

(The Father from whom every *f* is named) 426 —
parents, with other members of the *f*, should come 439 4
the *f* to present themselves before the Altar. 439 18
The Celebrant may then bless the *f* 445 —
When possible, it is desirable that members of the *f* 462 —
It is appropriate that the *f* and friends come together 465 —
a homily by the Celebrant, or a member of the *f*, 495 —
the Altar by the *f* or friends of the newly ordained. 511 22
The *f* of the newly ordained may receive Communion 511 23
greets other members of the clergy, *f* members, 522 —
the Altar by the *f* or friends of the newly ordained. 524 13
The *f* of the newly ordained may receive Communion 524 17
who then greets *f* members and others, 534 —
the Altar by the *f* or friends of the newly ordained. 536 13
The *f* of the newly ordained may receive Communion 536 17
The new Deacon then exchanges greetings with *f* 546 —
the *f* of the new minister may also be presented 563 —
greets other members of the clergy, *f* members, 563 —
3. For the Human *F* 810 8
Prayers for *F* and Personal Life 811 27
Thanksgivings for *F* and Personal Life 813 13
3. For the Human *F* 815 —
Prayers for *F* and Personal Life 828 —
Thanksgivings for *F* and Personal Life 841 —

far

this Church is *f* from intending to depart 11 12
It is recommended that, as *f* as possible, 312 5
with what follows in the liturgy as *f* as the end 408 26
man is very *f* gone from original righteousness, 869 25
so *f* as it declares the Books of Homilies 875 14

fasting

For special days of *f* or thanksgiving, 13 12
4 Of good Works: first of *F*. 875 6

fasts

F 17 8

father

"Heavenly *F*, we thank you that by water 298 11
"Heavenly *F*, we thank you that by water 313 10
"In the Name of the *F*, and of the Son, 313 17
1. Of God the *F* 344 —
1. Of God the *F* 377 —
The Celebrant gives thanks to God the *F* 402 11
The Celebrant gives thanks to God the *F* 404 —
(The *F* from whom every family is named) 426 —
in the Name of the *F*, and of the Son, 436 5
child to the mother or *f*, saying 441 —
(All that the *F* giveth me shall come to me) 480 —
(In my *F*'s house are many mansions) 480 —
(All that the *F* gives me will come to me) 495 —
(In my *F*'s house are many rooms) 495 —
bishop alone says over each ordinand "*F*, 553 32
and say over each one "*F*, 554 21
God the *F* 846 —
(homoousios) with the *F* as regards his Godhead, 864 7
begotten of the *F* before the ages, 864 9
For there is one Person of the *F*, 864 27
But the Godhead of the *F*, of the Son, 864 28
Such as the *F* is, such is the Son, 864 30
The *F* uncreate, the Son uncreate, 864 31
The *F* incomprehensible, the Son incomprehensible, 864 32
The *F* eternal, the Son eternal, 864 34
So likewise the *F* is Almighty, the Son Almighty, 864 38
So the *F* is God, the Son is God, 865 1
So likewise the *F* is Lord, the Son Lord, 865 3
The *F* is made of none, neither created, but begotten. 865 8
The Son is of the *F* alone, 865 9
The Holy Ghost is of the *F* and of the Son, 865 10
So there is one *F*, not three *F*s; 865 12
of the Substance of the *F*, begotten before the worlds; 865 23
Equal to the *F*, as touching his Godhead; 865 26
and inferior to the *F*, as touching his Manhood. 865 26
he sitteth on the right hand of the *F*, God Almighty, 865 33
the *F*, the Son, and the Holy Ghost. 867 38
The Son, which is the Word of the *F*, 868 2
begotten from everlasting of the *F*, 868 2
and of one substance with the *F*, 868 3
and buried, to reconcile his *F* to us, 868 7
The Holy Ghost, proceeding from the *F* and the Son, 868 17
with the *F* and the Son, very and eternal God. 868 18
in the name of the *F*, and of the Son, 876 32

fathers

following the holy *f*, we all with one accord 864 4
and the creed of the *F* has handed down to us. 864 17
So there is one Father, not three *F*; 865 12
if a man would search out by the ancient *f*, 866 6
this godly and decent order of the ancient *f* 866 16

the ancient *f* had divided the Psalms	866	27
much agreeable to the mind and purpose of the old *f*,	866	43
the old *F* did look only for transitory promises.	869	10

fault

it is the *f* and corruption of the Nature of every man,	869	24

faults

desire and promise to make up for their *f*,	409	21

favored

increasingly *f* by modern composers.	582	26

favourable

if allowed such just and *f* construction	10	17

fear

(that others may *f* to do the like,)	874	28

feast

the *F* of our Lord's Nativity	15	5
and the *f* of the Ascension on a Thursday	15	13
The *f* of the Dedication of a Church,	16	8
and the *f* of its patron	16	8
the Lessons appointed for the *F* may be substituted	16	15
except the *f* of the Annunciation.	17	24
The Collect appointed for any Sunday or other *F*	158	22
chief service on a Sunday or other *f*.	298	6
At the principal service on a Sunday or other *f*,	300	—
and on the *F* of the Baptism of our Lord	312	4
Christmas Day through the *F* of the Epiphany;	406	13
At the principal service on a Sunday or other *f*,	414	—
On a Major *F* or on a Sunday,	515	—
On a Major *F*, or on a Sunday,	528	—
On a Major *F*, or on a Sunday,	540	—
but on a Major *F*, Sunday,	571	—
selections may be made from the Proper of the Day.	571	—
When a Major *F* interrupts the sequence of Readings,	934	17

feasts

the Lord's Day and other major *F*,	13	4
Year consists of two cycles of *f* and holy days:	15	3
1. Principal *F*	15	14
The Principal *F* observed in this Church	15	15
These *f* take precedence of any other day	15	20
All Sundays of the year are *f* of our Lord Jesus Christ.	16	2
the dated days listed above, only the following *f*,	16	3
All other *F* of our Lord, and all other Major *F*	16	11
Other *F* of our Lord	16	26
Other Major *F*	17	1
All *f* of Apostles	17	2
All *f* of Evangelists	17	3
F appointed on fixed days in the Calendar	17	10
Major *F* falling in these weeks	17	11
F appointed on fixed days in the Calendar	17	14
F of our Lord and other Major *F* appointed	17	16
and any *F* of our Lord which occur on a Friday.	17	27
the rules of precedence governing Principal *F*,	17	29
Proper appointed for the Principal *F*.	18	15
on the *F* of the Transfiguration and Holy Cross	43	—
On *F* of the Incarnation	44	—
on the *F* of the Transfiguration and Holy Cross	81	—
On *F* of the Incarnation	82	—
Christmas, Epiphany, and other *F* of the Incarnation	111	—
On *f* or other days of special significance, the Collect	113	—
Except on Principal *F*, the Proper Preface of Baptism	310	—
On Sundays and other Major *F* there follows,	326	—
On Sundays and other Major *F* there follows,	358	—
bishops be ordained on Sundays and other *f* of our Lord	511	4
f of apostles or evangelists.	511	5
Except on Major *F*, the Preface may be that	564	1

February

The Presentation *F* 2	187	—
Saint Matthias *F* 24	188	—
The Presentation *F* 2	239	—
Saint Matthias *F* 24	239	—

feel

and such as *f* in themselves the working	871	12

feet

When observed, the ceremony of the washing of *f*	274	—

feign

which *f* that the old Fathers did look	869	9

felicity

attain to everlasting *f*.	871	10

fellow

It is desirable that *f* parishioners,	396	—
as associates and *f* ministers of the Sacrament,	524	15
where the words elder, elders, and *f* elder, appear	528	—
and *f* presbyter, are to be substituted.	528	—
bishop at the Altar as *f* ministers of the Sacrament.	553	10
with your Bishop and *f*-Presbyters as a pastor,	557	3
to our *f*-Christians of the different Communions	876	27

female

Genesis 1:26–28 (Male and *f* he created them)	426	—

fervently

because it doth *f* kindle their love towards God:	871	16

festival

The *f* of a saint is observed in accordance	195	—
b) at the patronal *f* or commemoration of a saint	195	—
The *f* of a saint is observed in accordance	246	—
b) at the patronal *f* or commemoration of a saint	246	—

festivals

F of Saints	111	—

few

now of late time a *f* of them have been daily said	866	28
here set forth, which, as they be *f* in number;	866	41
and for that the rules be *f* and easy.	867	5

fifteenth

F Day: Morning Prayer	691	—
F Day: Evening Prayer	694	—

fifth

F Sunday after the Epiphany	164	—
F Sunday in Lent	167	—
F Sunday of Easter	173	—
F Sunday after the Epiphany	216	—
F Sunday in Lent	219	—
F Sunday of Easter	225	—

F Day: Morning Prayer	613	—
F Day: Evening Prayer	617	—
Twenty-*f* Day: Morning Prayer	766	—
Twenty-*f* Day: Evening Prayer	769	—

fill

f him with grace and power,	554	1

filled

Where practicable, the font is to be *f* with clean water	313	1
additional chalices may be *f*	407	20

final

and the *f* prayer on page 282.	280	—
and the *f* prayer below.	282	—
(omitting the *f* clause)	528	—

finally

and, *f*, the cutting off occasion,	10	12
f, being found guilty, by just judgment be deposed.	873	12

find

and we *f* accordingly, that, seeking	9	24
search out by the ancient fathers, he shall *f*,	866	6
to *f* out what should be read, than to read it	866	32

finds

It *f* all its meaning in the resurrection.	507	2

finger

The giver places the ring on the ring-*f*	427	—

finished

Of the one Oblation of Christ *f* upon the Cross.	874	5

fire

In the darkness, *f* is kindled;	285	—
Candle is then lighted from the newly kindled *f*,	285	—
and they that have done evil into everlasting *f*.	865	38

firm

have still been continued *f* and unshaken.	10	7

first

use from and after the *F* Day of October,	8	12
indebted, under God, for her *f* foundation	9	12
since the *f* compiling of her Liturgy	10	2
The attention of this Church was in the *f* place drawn	10	32
Easter Day is always the *f* Sunday after the full moon	15	7
transferred to the *f* convenient open day	16	13
through the *F* Sunday after the Epiphany,	16	16
after the *F* Sunday in Lent, the Day of Pentecost,	18	6
as appointed, are read, the Reader *f* saying	47	—
as appointed, are read, the Reader *f* saying	64	—
as appointed, are read, the Reader *f* saying	84	—
9 The *F* Song of Isaiah Ecce, Deus	86	—
following or some other suitable prayer, *f* saying	110	—
Collect for the *F* Sunday of Advent	111	—
Collect for the *F* Sunday after Christmas	111	—
as appointed, are read, the Reader *f* saying	118	—
F Sunday of Advent	159	—
and the *F* Sunday after Christmas Day.	161	—
F Sunday after Christmas Day	161	—
F Sunday after the Epiphany: The Baptism	163	—
F Sunday in Lent	166	—
F Sunday after Pentecost: Trinity Sunday	176	—
F Sunday of Advent	211	—
and the *F* Sunday after Christmas Day.	213	—
F Sunday after Christmas Day	213	—
F Sunday after the Epiphany: The Baptism	214	—
F Sunday in Lent	218	—
F Sunday after Pentecost: Trinity Sunday	228	—
The congregation may be seated for the *f* part	273	—
The congregation may be seated for the *f* part	277	—
when observed, is the *f* service of Easter Day.	284	2
f two parts of the service,	284	24
The *F* Song of Isaiah,	290	—
The Celebrant may *f* address the people	292	—
the Reader *f* saying	300	—
a Priest reads the Gospel, *f* saying	300	—
The Celebrant blesses the water, *f* saying	306	—
(the *F* Sunday after the Epiphany).	312	4
the Reader *f* saying	325	—
the Deacon or a Priest reads the Gospel, *f* saying	326	—
one or more of the following sentences, *f* saying	332	—
the Reader *f* saying	357	—
the Deacon or a Priest reads the Gospel, *f* saying	357	—
desirable that a passage from the Gospel *f* be read.	396	—
The Lord's Prayer is said, the Celebrant *f* saying	398	—
The Lord's Prayer is then said, the deacon *f* saying,	408	23
the Reader *f* saying	414	—
the Deacon or a Priest reads the Gospel, *f* saying	414	—
receive Communion *f*, after the ministers.	432	—
husband and wife *f* greeting each other.	436	11
passage from Scripture may *f* be read.	439	13
verses of Scripture, *f* saying	449	—
says one of the following Collects, *f* saying	469	—
f saying	479	—
f saying	495	—
F, there is the order of bishops who carry	510	6
the following Collect, or both, *f* saying	515	—
The Reader *f* says	516	—
a Deacon or a Priest reads the Gospel, *f* saying	516	—
The new Bishop blesses the people, *f* saying	523	—
or both, *f* saying	527	—
The Reader *f* says	528	—
the Gospel, *f* saying	529	—
or both, *f* saying	539	—
The Reader *f* says	540	—
the Gospel, *f* saying	541	—
the following or some other Collect, *f* saying	560	—
F Day: Morning Prayer	585	—
F Day: Evening Prayer	589	—
Twenty-*f* Day: Morning Prayer	738	—
Twenty-*f* Day: Evening Prayer	741	—
The *F* Book of Common Prayer (1549)	866	2
the *f* original and ground whereof,	866	5
The *F* Book of Samuel,	868	26
The *F* Book of Kings,	868	28
The *F* Book of Chronicles,	868	30
The *F* Book of Esdras,	868	32
The *F* Book of Maccabees,	869	2
[The Twenty-*f* of the former Articles is omitted;	872	2
4 Of good Works: *f* of Fasting.	875	6
Catholic Church during the *f* ages of its existence;	877	7
Year A always begins on the *F* Sunday of Advent	888	3
begins on the *F* Sunday of Advent	934	3
Year Two begins on the *F* Sunday of Advent	934	4

(Thus, on the *F* Sunday of Advent, 1976, 934 5
F Reading at Evening Prayer. 934 14
the *f* is always from the Old Testament 934 15
the Psalms, those for the morning are given *f*, 934 26

fit

II. For the choice of *f* persons for the ministry 205 —
II. For the choice of *f* persons for the ministry 256 —

fitting

such forms as are *f* to the occasion. 13 15
It is *f* that parents be included among the godparents 298 24
it is *f* that the principal celebrant, 322 4
it is *f* that the principal celebrant, 354 4
it is *f* that the man and woman to be married 437 13

five

Book *F* 746 1
Those *f* commonly called Sacraments, that is to say, 872 32

fixed

the other, upon the *f* date of December 25, 15 5
in addition to its observance of the *f* date. 15 22
only the following feasts, appointed on *f* days, 16 3
Major Feasts appointed on *f* days in the Calendar, 16 12
Feasts appointed on *f* days in the Calendar 17 10
and other Major Feasts appointed on *f* days, 17 16

flagon

one chalice on the Altar, and, if need be, a *f* of wine 407 19

flame

the *f* may be taken from the Paschal Candle. 143 11

flesh

(A man cleaves to his wife and they become one *f*) 426 —
a reasonable soul and human *f* subsisting; 865 25
One, not by conversion of the Godhead into *f*, 865 29
For as the reasonable soul and *f* is one man, 865 31
and took again his body, with *f*, 868 13
so that the *f* lusteth always contrary to the Spirit; 869 26
whereby the lust of the *f*, called in Greek 869 29
some the affection, some the desire, of the *f*), 869 30
clearly void, both in his *f*, and in his spirit. 870 26
the Spirit of Christ, mortifying the works of the *f*, 871 13

flood

The *F* 288 —

flowers

members of the congregation with *f*, candles, 576 2

folks

understand the minds of some slanderous *f* to be offended; 875 44

follow

except for the Psalms, *f* the numeration 14 16
or a form of general intercession is to *f*, 57 —
Authorized intercessions and thanksgivings may *f*. 58 —
or a form of general intercession is to *f*, 70 —
Authorized intercessions and thanksgivings may *f*. 71 —
or a form of general intercession is to *f*, 100 —
Authorized intercessions and thanksgivings may *f*. 101 —
A meditation, silent or spoken, may *f*. 106 —
f the Psalmody. 113 —
or a brief silence, may *f* the Reading. 113 —
or a form of general intercession is to *f*, 124 —
Authorized intercessions and thanksgivings may *f*. 125 —
These devotions *f* the basic structure 136 —
A period of silence may *f*. 137 —
Prayers for ourselves and others may *f*. 140 —
its own Creed is to *f*. 142 3
the Eucharist is to *f* immediately. 142 6
Christian literature may *f* the biblical Readings. 142 14
When a meal is to *f*, a blessing over food may serve 143 31
takes precedence over the three Holy Days which *f* 161 —
serves for the weekdays which *f*, 166 —
On the weekdays which *f*, the numbered Proper 176 —
Directions for the use of the Propers which *f* 176 —
takes precedence over the three Holy Days which *f* 213 —
also serves for the weekdays which *f*, 217 —
On the weekdays which *f*, the numbered Proper 227 —
On the weekdays which *f*, the numbered Proper 228 —
Directions for the use of the Propers which *f* 228 —
In the biddings which *f*, the indented petitions 277 —
Appropriate devotions may *f*, which may include 281 —
the Collects which *f* each Lesson, 284 15
Silence may *f*. 300 —
A Psalm, hymn, or anthem may *f* each Reading. 300 —
Reaffirmation of Baptismal Vows is not to *f*, 308 —
and the formula and action which *f*. 312 11
and the ceremonies that *f* it. 313 11
Silence may *f*. 326 —
A Psalm, hymn, or anthem may *f* each Reading. 326 —
Silence may *f*. 357 —
A Psalm, hymn, or anthem may *f* each Reading. 357 —
Any of the forms which *f* may be used. 383 —
A Confession of Sin may *f*. 397 —
exchange between individuals which may *f*, 407 9
beginning with the words which *f* the Sanctus, 408 14
The priest shall *f* the same procedure 409 12
Silence may *f*. 414 —
A Psalm, hymn, or anthem may *f* each Reading. 414 —
A hymn, psalm, or anthem may *f*. 425 —
A homily or other response to the Readings may *f*. 426 —
If Communion is to *f*, the Lord's Prayer 428 —
When Communion is not to *f*, the wedding party 431 —
it may *f* the Prayers of the People preceding 439 7
When Anointing is to *f* 454 5
When Communion is to *f* 454 9
If Communion is not to *f*, the Lord's Prayer 456 —
If the Burial service is not to *f* immediately, 467 —
the Vigil on page 465, may *f*. 467 —
A suitable psalm, hymn, or canticle may *f*. 494 —
A suitable psalm, hymn, or canticle may *f*. 495 —
anthems may *f* the readings. 506 11
5. A homily may *f* the Readings, 506 13
Silence may *f*. 516 —
Silence may *f*. 529 —
Silence may *f*. 541 —
Any of the presentations that *f* may be added to, 561 —
Other Pastoral Offices may *f*. 572 10
the fruits of Faith, and *f* after Justification, 870 7

followed

Or, it may be *f* by a meal or other activity, 112 —
may be *f* by the Lord's Prayer and a grace or blessing; 112 —

each *f* by a Psalm, Canticle, or hymn.	175	—
each *f* by a Psalm, Canticle, or hymn.	227	—
rubrics of the service of ordination are *f*.	552	5
are used, *f* by the words of dedication.	576	7
The sermon or address may be *f*	576	15
and should be *f*, if possible, by the administration	577	16
f by the celebration of the Holy Eucharist.	577	19
and, in our doings, that Will of God is to be *f*,	871	22

following

Principal Feasts observed in this Church are the *f*:	15	15
may always be observed on the Sunday *f* November 1,	15	21
the dated days listed above, only the *f* feasts,	16	3
The *f* Holy Days are regularly observed	16	22
transferred to the week *f* the Second Sunday of Easter,	17	12
The *f* days are observed by special acts of discipline	17	21
the *f* may be observed with the Collects,	18	1
The *f* Confession of Sin may then be said;	41	—
One of the *f* Antiphons may be sung or said	43	—
The Alleluias in the *f* Antiphons are used	44	—
in place of an Invitatory Psalm, the *f* is sung	45	—
One of the *f* Canticles,	47	—
The Officiant then says one or more of the *f* Collects	55	—
or the *f*	57	—
one or both of the *f* may be used	58	—
The Officiant may then conclude with one of the *f*	59	—
Officiant begins the service with one or more of the *f*	61	—
The *f* Confession of Sin may then be said;	62	—
The *f*, or some other suitable hymn,	64	—
One of the *f* Canticles,	65	—
The Officiant then says one or more of the *f* Collects	68	—
or the *f*	70	—
one or both of the *f* may be used	71	—
The Officiant may then conclude with one of the *f*	72	—
The *f* Confession of Sin may then be said;	79	—
One of the *f* Antiphons may be sung or said	80	—
The Alleluias in the *f* Antiphons are used	82	—
in place of an Invitatory Psalm, the *f* is sung	83	—
One of the *f* Canticles,	84	—
The Officiant then says one or more of the *f* Collects	98	—
or the *f*	100	—
one or both of the *f* may be used	101	—
The Officiant may then conclude with one of the *f*	102	—
One or more of the *f* Psalms is sung or said.	103	—
One of the *f*, or some other suitable passage	105	—
or the *f*	105	—
The Officiant then says one of the *f* Collects.	107	—
any one of the *f* is also appropriate,	108	15
One of the *f*, or some other Short Lesson of Scripture	109	—
the *f* or some other suitable prayer,	110	—
The *f* hymn, or a metrical version of it,	112	—
The service may then continue in any of the *f* ways:	112	—
continue as a complete evening Office with the *f*	112	—
either of the *f*, or one of the Collects	113	—
A bishop or priest may use the *f*	114	—
begins the service with one or more of the *f*	115	—
The *f* Confession of Sin may then be said;	116	—
The *f*, or some other suitable hymn,	117	—
One of the *f* Canticles,	119	—
Officiant then says one or more of the *f* Collects	122	—
or the *f*	124	—
one or both of the *f* may be used	125	—
The Officiant may then conclude with one of the *f*	126	—
One or more of the *f* Psalms are sung or said.	128	—
One of the *f*, or some other suitable passage	131	—
or the *f*	131	—
The Officiant then says one of the *f* Collects	133	—
One of the *f* prayers may be added	134	—
The *f* may be said	140	—
The *f* pointing of the Gloria may be used:	141	16
the *f* form of the Gloria may be used:	141	18
The Officiant concludes with the *f*	153	—
to be found in the pages *f*;	158	5
the Eucharist on the weekdays *f*,	158	8
or the *f*	160	—
serves for the *f* weekdays,	174	—
any of the *f* Collects,	195	—
or the *f*	195	—
between the Epiphany and the *f* Sunday.	214	—
serves for the *f* weekdays,	226	—
any of the *f* Collects,	246	—
or the *f*	247	—
the Celebrant says the *f* prayer	265	—
The ashes are imposed with the *f* words	265	—
The *f* Psalm is then sung or said	265	—
The *f* or some other suitable anthem is sung	270	—
Deacon or other person appointed reads one of the *f*	270	—
The Celebrant then says the *f* blessing	271	—
The *f* or some other suitable anthem may then	271	—
the procession may halt while the *f*	271	—
The Passion Gospel is announced in the *f* manner	272	—
in the usual manner, using the *f* Collect,	274	—
the *f* or other suitable anthems	274	—
The Passion Gospel is announced in the *f* manner	276	—
the *f*, or other suitable anthems.	281	—
the reserved Sacrament, the *f* order is observed	282	—
The service concludes with the *f* prayer.	282	—
The Celebrant may say the *f* prayer	285	—
At least two of the *f* Lessons are read,	288	—
One of the *f* Canticles is then sung.	294	—
The Celebrant says one of the *f* Collects	295	—
Then the Celebrant asks the *f* questions	302	—
A Person appointed leads the *f* petitions	305	—
At the *f* words, the Celebrant touches the water	307	—
according to the *f* form.	313	23
Other prayers, such as the *f*, may be added.	314	2
The Celebrant may read one of the *f* sentences	319	—
Ten Commandments (page 317) may be said, or the *f*	324	—
When appointed, the *f* hymn or some other song	324	—
Intercession is offered according to the *f* form,	328	—
The Deacon or Celebrant says the *f*,	330	—
A Minister may then say one or more of the *f*	332	—
At the *f* words concerning the bread,	334	—
The *f* or some other suitable anthem may be sung	337	—
The *f* prayer may be said.	337	—
the Celebrant may say the *f* Invitation	338	—
or the *f*	339	—
At the *f* words concerning the bread,	342	—
One of the *f*, or some other appropriate sentence	343	—
or the *f*	344	—
The Celebrant may read one of the *f* sentences	351	—
When appointed, the *f* hymn or some other song	356	—
On other occasions the *f* is used	356	—
Alternative forms will be found on page 367 and *f*.	361	—

At the *f* words concerning the bread,	362	—
the Celebrant says the *f* Invitation	364	—
or the *f*	365	—
At the *f* words concerning the bread,	368	—
At the *f* words concerning the bread,	371	—
At the *f* words concerning the bread,	374	—
One of the *f*, or some other appropriate sentence	376	—
or the *f*	377	—
adds a concluding Collect, or the *f* Doxology	391	—
(d) a general Collect such as the *f*:	394	—
from the reserved Sacrament, using the *f* form.	396	—
to the day or occasion, or else one of the *f*	396	—
Suitable prayers may be offered, concluding with the *f*	397	—
The *f* or some other form is used	397	—
The Celebrant may say the *f* Invitation	399	—
The Sacrament is administered with the *f*	399	—
usual postcommunion prayers is then said, or the *f*	399	—
from Rite One or Rite Two, or one of the *f* forms	402	3
At the *f* words concerning the bread,	403	—
At the *f* words concerning the bread,	405	—
The Prayers of the People *f*	406	5
the *f* form of the Gloria may be used:	406	8
f anthem may be used at the Breaking of the Bread:	407	21
from the reserved Sacrament in the *f* manner:	408	19
Baptismal Vows are administered in the *f* form.	412	12
more of the *f* passages from Holy Scripture is read.	426	—
Deacon or other person appointed reads the *f* prayers,	429	—
the Priest says one of the *f* prayers	430	—
the usual postcommunion prayer, the *f* is said	432	—
The vows of the man and woman are exchanged, using the *f*	435	18
If Banns are to be published, the *f* form is used	437	2
or the *f*	437	10
The Celebrant may add one or more of the *f* prayers	444	—
saying one of the *f*	451	—
one or more parts of the *f* service are used,	453	3
The Celebrant begins the service with the *f*	453	11
One or more of the *f* or other passages of Scripture	453	13
Or else the *f* general confession may be said	454	18
The *f* anthem is said	455	—
and says one of the *f*	455	—
the usual postcommunion prayers is said, or the *f*	457	—
may be said, or the *f*	465	—
The *f* form may be used at whatever time the body	466	—
All stand while one or more of the *f* anthems is sung	469	—
The Celebrant says one of the *f* Collects, first saying	469	—
One or more of the *f* passages from Holy Scriptures	470	—
the *f* Psalms may be sung or said	470	—
the *f* Psalms may be sung or said.	475	—
service continues with the *f* prayer of intercession,	480	—
When there is a Communion, the *f* serves	480	—
the usual postcommunion prayer, the *f* is said	482	—
the *f* Commendation is used.	482	—
The *f* anthem is sung or said	484	—
Christian burial, the Priest may use the *f* prayer,	487	—
All stand while one or more of the *f* anthems is sung	491	—
after which the Celebrant says one of the *f*	493	—
The Celebrant may add the *f* prayer	494	—
One or more of the *f* passages from Holy Scripture	494	—
The *f* Psalms are appropriate:	494	—
The *f* Psalms are appropriate:	495	—
When there is a Communion, the *f* form	496	—
The Celebrant concludes with one of the *f*	497	—
the usual postcommunion prayer, the *f* is said	498	—
the *f* Commendation is used.	499	—
The *f* anthem or one of those on pages 491–492	501	—
or with the *f*	502	—
for Christian burial, the Priest may use the *f* prayer,	503	—
is deemed appropriate, the *f* form is used.	506	3
requires the *f* promise from the Bishop-elect	513	—
The Presiding Bishop then says the *f*,	513	—
the *f* Collect, or both, first saying	515	—
The Readings are ordinarily selected from the *f* list	515	—
The *f* questions are then addressed to the bishop-elect	517	—
the bishop leads the people in the *f*	522	—
and reads the Collect for the Day, or the *f* Collect,	527	—
The Readings are ordinarily selected from the *f* list	528	—
the usual postcommunion prayer, the *f* is said	535	—
and reads the Collect for the Day, or the *f* Collect,	539	—
The Readings are ordinarily selected from the *f* list	540	—
the usual postcommunion prayer, the *f* is said	546	—
The *f* form may be used	552	19
F the Consecration Prayer, and while the new bishop	553	2
F the presentation of the Bible, and the formula	553	5
says the *f* or some other Collect, first saying	560	—
The Readings are selected from the *f* list,	560	—
the Bishop leads the people in the *f* prayer;	564	5
the Bishop says the *f* or similar words	567	5
Selections are ordinarily made from the *f* list;	571	—
All then stand for the Gospel, which may be the *f*	572	—
the Bishop concludes with the *f* prayers	572	—
If Baptism is to be administered, the *f* order is used:	575	28
the *f* order may provide an opportunity	577	22
the Celebrant concludes with the *f* Doxology	579	—
are the *f*:	582	7
The term "Various Occasions" in the *f* pages refers	813	17
Therefore, *f* the holy fathers, we all with one accord	864	4
some *f* Salisbury use, some Hereford use,	867	9
such are these *f*:	868	36
Original sin standeth not in the *f* of Adam,	869	23
have grown partly of the corrupt *f* of the Apostles,	872	34
branches of Christendom, we account the *f*, to wit:	877	13
the *f* Articles supply a basis	877	31

follows

Then *f* one of the Invitatory Psalms,	42	—
Then *f*	46	—
Then *f* one of these Suffrages	55	—
Then *f*	64	—
Then *f* one of these sets of Suffrages	67	—
Then *f* one of the Invitatory Psalms,	80	—
Then *f*	84	—
Then *f* one of these sets of Suffrages	97	—
The service concludes as *f*	107	—
Then *f*	118	—
Then *f* one of these sets of Suffrages	121	—
Then *f*	132	—
the Litany in place of the Versicle and Collect which *f*	154	—
Baptismal Vows, page 292, *f* the Sermon.	175	—
Baptismal Vows, page 292, *f* the Sermon.	227	—
When Communion *f*, the service continues	269	—
f the Gospel and homily.	274	—
The Sermon *f*.	277	—
as *f* (the indicated sections may be omitted)	286	—

The celebrant concludes the Renewal of Vows as *f* 294 —
sermon or homily was not preached earlier, it *f* here. 295 —
and officiates at what *f*. 298 12
individually by their Sponsors, as *f* 301 —
individually by their Parents and Godparents, as *f* 301 —
On Sundays and other Major Feasts there *f*, 326 —
On Sundays and other Major Feasts there *f*, 358 —
or Agape is a part of the celebration, it *f* here. 401 15
with what *f* in the liturgy as far as the end 408 26
A period of silence *f*. 417 —
a deacon may use the service which *f*, 422 17
omitting the nuptial blessing which *f* The Prayers. 422 17
Priest may ask God's blessing on a ring or rings as *f* 427 —
The Priest and Penitent begin as *f* 449 —
When the order for the Burial of the Dead *f* 467 —
Unless the Committal *f* immediately in the church, 482 —
Unless the Committal *f* immediately in the church, 499 —
A Psalm, canticle, or hymn *f* each Reading. 516 —
A period of silent prayer *f*, the people still standing. 520 —
A Psalm, canticle, or hymn *f* each Reading. 529 —
The Bishop addresses the ordinand as *f* 531 —
A period of silent prayer *f*, the people still standing. 533 —
A Psalm, canticle, or hymn *f* each Reading. 541 —
The Bishop addresses the ordinand as *f* 543 —
A period of silent prayer *f*, the people still standing. 544 —
bread and wine may be used in the Eucharist which *f*. 565 23
the Psalms which *f* is set out in lines of poetry. 583 1
and our English tradition *f* suit, 583 33
and began as *f*, "The Three Creeds, 869 20
the version of 1801, reads as *f*: 872 5
The original 1571, 1662 text of this Article reads as *f*: 875 26
The original 1571, 1662 text of this Article reads as *f*: 875 39

fond

Invocation of Saints, is a *f* thing, vainly invented, 872 13

font

the Candidates does not take place at the *f*, 312 28
go to the *f* for the Thanksgiving over the Water. 312 30
If the movement to the *f* is a formal procession, 312 31
Where practicable, the *f* is to be filled 313 1
face the people across the *f*, 313 5
The Bishop moves to the *F*, lays a hand upon it, 569 —
water is now poured into the *F*, 569 —
[water may be poured into the *F*, and] 570 —
Facing the *F*, the Bishop says 570 —
At the dedication of the *f*, 575 23
in addition to saying the prayer over the *f* as given, 575 25
The blessing of a new *f* or baptistry should always 577 15

food

When a meal is to follow, a blessing over *f* may serve 143 31

foot

the *f* of a processional cross 575 21

forasmuch

And *f* as nothing can, almost, be so plainly set forth, 867 16
f as they spring not of faith in Jesus Christ; 870 14
(*f* as they be an assembly of men, 872 6
yet *f* as they do not the same in their own name, 873 3

forbidden

So are we *f* by the Catholic Religion, to say, 865 7
vain and rash Swearing is *f* Christian men 876 18

forces

25. For those in the Armed *F* of our Country 811 3
25. For those in the Armed *F* of our Country 823 —

forego

humility to *f* all preferences of her own; 876 35

forehead

marking on the *f* the sign of the cross 308 —
and makes the sign of the cross on the sick person's *f*, 456 —

foreign

nor ought to be, subject to any *f* Jurisdiction. 875 42

forenamed

since the second year of the *f* King 875 31

forget

committed yourself to this work, do not *f* the trust 557 10

forgive

the person or persons on one side truly *f* the others 409 20
refuse to *f*, the priest shall allow 409 22

forgiven

not receive Communion until they have *f* each other. 409 19
Matthew 9:2–8 (Your sins are *f*) 454 4

forgiveness

the prayer for *f* appointed at Morning Prayer. 269 —
instead, a declaration of *f* is provided. 446 14
or a declaration of *f*. 446 19
Declaration of *F* 448 —
Declaration of *F* 452 —
or deny the place of *f* to such as truly repent. 870 37
the promises of the *f* of sin, 873 17

forgives

Psalm 103 (He *f* all your sins) 454 3

form

whether in the *f* provided in the Daily Offices, 13 23
in the *f* appointed at the Eucharist. 13 24
A deacon or lay person using the preceding *f* remains 42 —
unless the Eucharist or a *f* of general intercession 57 —
A deacon or lay person using the preceding *f* remains 63 —
unless the Eucharist or a *f* of general intercession 70 —
A deacon or lay person using the preceding *f* remains 80 —
unless the Eucharist or a *f* of general intercession 100 —
This Order provides a *f* of evening service 108 2
Easter Eve has its own *f* 108 12
A deacon or lay person using the preceding *f* remains 117 —
unless the Eucharist or a *f* of general intercession 124 —
the following *f* of the Gloria may be used: 141 19
the conclusion of this *f* of service. 143 32
in the usual manner, but this *f* of words is used 313 19
according to the following *f*. 313 23
lay person using the preceding *f* substitutes 321 —
Intercession is offered according to the following *f*, 328 —
An alternative *f* will be found on page 340. 333 —
using the *f* on page 408. 338 —
Alternative *F* 340 —

lay person using the preceding *f* substitutes	353	—
using the *f* on page 408.	365	—
F I	383	—
F II	385	—
F III	387	—
F IV	388	—
F V	389	—
F VI	392	—
This *f* is intended for use with those	396	—
from the reserved Sacrament, using the following *f*.	396	—
The following or some other *f* is used	397	—
A deacon using the preceding *f* substitutes	398	—
F 1	402	—
F 2	404	—
the following *f* of the Gloria may be used:	406	8
threefold, sixfold, or ninefold *f*.	406	10
Baptismal Vows are administered in the following *f*.	412	12
A *F* of Commitment	420	—
This *f* may be used when a person wishes to make	420	—
which may be in the *f* either of a statement	420	—
using the following *f*	435	19
If Banns are to be published, the following *f* is used	437	2
When desired, a briefer *f* of this service may be used,	439	10
F One	447	—
F Two	449	—
and use the *f* for the Reconciliation	454	16
lay person using the preceding *f* substitutes	455	—
the *f* for Communion under Special Circumstances	457	—
following *f* may be used at whatever time the body	466	—
When there is a Communion, the following *f*	496	—
or else the *f* on page 465 or 480.	496	—
is deemed appropriate, the following *f* is used.	506	3
The following *f* may be used	552	19
The complete *f* of the service for the Dedication	575	2
marked in lasting *f* (incised, painted, inlaid).	575	21
other *f* may be composed for the occasion,	576	19
this *f* of sacred song in the Daily Office.	582	24
on parallelism of clauses, a symmetry of *f* and sense.	583	3
parallelism can take the *f* of similarity	583	4
a hybrid *f* which has been transliterated "Jehovah."	583	24
The Hebrew *f* has been used,	584	5
rather than the Latin *f* "Alleluia,"	584	6
but also to regain for our liturgy a *f* of the word	584	7
question and answer *f* for ease of reference.	844	6
It may also be used to *f* a simple service;	844	9
and coming together to *f* one person and subsistence,	864	14
consecrated or ordered according to said *F*,	875	24
While the above *f* of the Quadrilateral was adopted	877	26
the Word takes the *f* given in the Holy Eucharist,	888	10

formal

If the movement to the font is a *f* procession,	312	31

former

in the parish house, in a *f* or neighboring place	575	6
[The Twenty-first of the *f* Articles is omitted;	872	2
as doth the *f* Book of Homilies,	874	37

forms

that in his worship different *f* and usages may	9	3
"The particular *F* of Divine Worship,	9	15
and amendments in her *F* of Public Worship;	9	24
and *f* of worship, and discipline,	10	28
other *f* set forth by authority within this Church	13	8
the bishop may set forth such *f* as are fitting	13	14
For the Prayers of the People, one of the *f* appointed	202	—
For the Prayers of the People, one of the *f* appointed	253	—
See the *f* beginning on page 383.	359	—
Alternative *f* will be found on page 367	361	—
Alternative *F*	367	—
Any of the *f* which follow may be used.	383	—
Any of the *f* may be conformed to the language	383	—
instrumental music, other art *f*, silence.	400	10
from Rite One or Rite Two, or one of the following *f*	402	3
Confirmation with *f* for Reception	413	—
Two equivalent *f* of service are provided here	446	10
Any of the usual *f* of the Prayers of the People	576	18

formula

and the *f* and action which follow.	312	11
Following the presentation of the Bible, and the *f*	553	5

formularies

declared in the *f* and canons of this Church,	435	12

forth

set *f* A Book of Common Prayer,	8	7
as set *f* in this Book, are the regular services	13	5
other forms set *f* by authority within this Church	13	8
the bishop may set *f* such forms as are fitting	13	14
as set *f* in the rubrical directions for each service.	13	19
precedence set *f* in the Calendar of the Church Year.	195	—
subject to the rules set *f* in the Calendar	199	—
precedence set *f* in the Calendar of the Church Year.	246	—
subject to the rules set *f* in the Calendar	251	—
therefore considered, here is set *f* such an order,	866	33
the reading of holy Scripture is so set *f*,	866	36
certain rules are here set *f*,	866	41
forasmuch as nothing can, almost, be so plainly set *f*,	867	16
God's promises in such wise, as they be generally set *f*	871	21
which were set *f* in the time of Edward the Sixth;	874	37
as set *f* by the General Convention	875	21
and Ordering of Priests and Deacons, lately set *f*	875	27
lately set *f* by Elizabeth our Queen do most	876	2

forty

the Ascension on a Thursday *f* days after Easter Day.	15	13

forward

While the people are coming *f* to receive	407	22
the Offertory of the Eucharist, the person comes *f*	420	—
the dedication of the lectern, the Bible is brought *f*	576	9
these furnishings, or other lay persons, bring them *f*	576	23

found

alterations would in time be *f* expedient.	10	20
Proper Prefaces, directions for which are to be *f*	158	4
It may be *f* desirable to return to the front	313	9
An alternative form will be *f* on page 340.	333	—
Alternative forms will be *f* on page 367	361	—
f in the service for the Ordination of a Deacon	565	14
f a satisfactory method of chanting them.	582	12
than to read it when it was *f* out.	866	32
finally, being *f* guilty, by just judgment be deposed.	873	12

foundation

these States is indebted, under God, for her first *f*	9	12

foundations
(before the *f* of the world were laid) 871 2

four
But the Sundays of Advent are always the *f* Sundays 15 10
The service normally consists of *f* parts: 284 5
If on the *f* days listed above there are no candidates 312 15
The "*F*-letter Name" (Tetragrammaton) 583 16
Book *F* 717 —
before three or *f* Chapters were read out, 866 19
F Prophets the greater, 868 32

fourteen
f days at the most, giving the reasons for refusing 409 25

fourteenth
F Day: Morning Prayer 683 —
F Day: Evening Prayer 687 —

fourth
F Sunday of Advent 160 —
F Sunday after the Epiphany 164 —
F Sunday in Lent 167 —
F Sunday of Easter 173 —
F Sunday of Advent 212 —
F Sunday after the Epiphany 215 —
F Sunday in Lent 219 —
F Sunday of Easter 225 —
F Day: Morning Prayer 606 —
F Day: Evening Prayer 610 —
Twenty-*f* Day: Morning Prayer 759 —
Twenty-*f* Day: Evening Prayer 763 —
The *F* Book of Esdras, 868 38

frame
(as well in the chiefest materials, as in the *f* and order 10 6
and charitable *f* of mind; 11 19
so that he be diligent to *f* his life 871 26

Francis
62. A Prayer attributed to St. *F* 812 13
62. A Prayer attributed to St. *F* 833 —

free
"liberty wherewith Christ hath made us *f*," 9 3
F intercessions may be offered. 107 —
Silence may be kept, and *f* intercessions 134 —
and their *f* consent, is publicly ascertained. 435 14
does not require that the premises be debt-*f* 575 4
f from the obedience of the Commandments 869 13
X. Of *F*-Will. 869 33

freely
Salvation offered *f* to all 290 —
they be justified *f*: 871 7

frequent
but triplets are very *f*, 583 10

frequently
recitation is the method which has been most *f* used 582 27
the selections from the Psalter are *f* cited 888 18

Friday
Good *F* 17 9
Good *F* and all other Fridays of the year, 17 25
and any Feasts of our Lord which occur on a *F*. 17 27
on Ash Wednesday, Maundy Thursday, Good *F*, 18 12
or Wednesday in Holy Week, or on Good *F*. 108 12
F, and Saturday of this week are the traditional winter 160 —
F, and Saturday of this week are the traditional spring 166 —
Good *F* 169 —
F in Easter Week 172 —
F, and Saturday of this week are the traditional 176 —
The Wednesday, *F*, and Saturday after September 14 182 —
F, and Saturday of this week are the traditional winter 212 —
F, and Saturday of this week are the traditional spring 218 —
Good *F* 221 —
F in Easter Week 224 —
F, and Saturday of this week are the traditional 227 —
The Wednesday, *F*, and Saturday after September 14 233 —
from the reserved Sacrament on Good *F*, 275 —
Good *F* 276 —
Prayers for *F*, Saturday, and Sunday, 812 26
Prayers for *F*, Saturday, and Sunday, 833 —

Fridays
Good Friday and all other *F* of the year, 17 25
except for *F* in the Christmas and Easter seasons, 17 26
traditionally observed on the Wednesdays, *F*, 18 5
A Collect for *F* 56 —
A Collect for *F* 69 —
A Collect for *F* 99 —
A Collect for *F* 123 —
Especially suitable for *F* 201 —
Especially suitable for *F* 252 —

friend
a member of the family, or a *f*. 495 22
Jesus himself wept at the grave of his *f*. 507 12

friends
desirable that fellow parishioners, relatives, and *f* 396 —
f assemble in the church or in some other convenient 435 9
it is desirable that members of the family and *f* 462 —
It is appropriate that the family and *f* come together 465 —
by the family or *f* of the newly ordained. 511 22
by the family or *f* of the newly ordained. 524 13
by the family or *f* of the newly ordained. 536 13
builders, musicians, artists, benefactors, and *f*. 566 18

from
use *f* and after the First Day of October, 8 12
in place of Authority should, *f* time to time, seem 9 20
f them that seek occasion, of cavil or quarrel 10 13
f intending to depart *f* the Church of England 11 13
special devotions taken *f* this Book, 13 9
or *f* Holy Scripture, may be used when the needs 13 10
The words of anthems are to be *f* Holy Scripture, 14 7
or *f* this Book, or *f* texts congruent with them. 14 8
or *f* the Last Sunday after the Epiphany 16 17
F the Epiphany through the Baptism of Christ, 43 —
F Easter Day until the Ascension 43 —
F Ascension Day until the Day of Pentecost 43 —
the Lesson *f* the Gospel is read 47 —
F Easter Day through the Day of Pentecost 59 —
the Lesson *f* the Gospel is read 65 —
F Easter Day through the Day of Pentecost 72 —
F the Epiphany through the Baptism of Christ, 81 —

from

F Easter Day until the Ascension	81	—
F Ascension Day until the Day of Pentecost	81	—
the Lesson *f* the Gospel is read	84	—
F Easter Day through the Day of Pentecost	102	—
selection *f* Psalms 120 through 133.	103	—
f Easter Day through the Day of Pentecost	109	—
Selection *f* the Psalter.	113	—
or homily, a passage *f* Christian literature,	113	—
or one of the Collects *f* Evening Prayer	113	—
or *f* Compline, may be so used	113	—
the Lesson *f* the Gospel is read	119	—
F Easter Day through the Day of Pentecost	126	—
F Psalm 51	137	—
F Psalm 113	138	—
Antiphons drawn *f* the Psalms themselves,	141	8
or *f* the opening sentences	141	8
or *f* other passages of Scripture may be used	141	9
The Apostles' Creed is omitted *f* the Office	142	2
The Lord's Prayer may be omitted *f* the Office	142	5
a reading *f* non-biblical Christian literature	142	13
the officiant may pass at once *f* the salutation	142	19
A Lesson *f* the Gospel	142	20
F Easter Day through the Day of Pentecost,	143	2
The Short Lessons may be read *f* any version	143	6
the flame may be taken *f* the Paschal Candle.	143	11
and other candles may be lighted *f* them.	143	13
f the Office Lectionary or the Proper of the Day,	143	22
apart *f* the church, so that all may go into the church	270	—
Holy Communion *f* the reserved Sacrament	275	—
to be administered *f* the reserved Sacrament,	282	—
administer Easter Communion *f* the Sacrament	284	29
Candle is then lighted *f* the newly kindled fire,	285	—
lighted *f* the Paschal Candle at this time.	286	—
Candle burn at all services *f* Easter Day	287	—
always the Lesson *f* Exodus.	288	—
may now be lighted *f* the Paschal Candle.	294	—
f Easter Day through the Day of Pentecost	299	—
they are selected *f* "At Baptism."	300	—
a candle (which may be lighted *f* the Paschal	313	7
f Easter Day through the Day of Pentecost	319	—
a lesson *f* the Gospel is always included,	322	19
f Easter Day through the Day of Pentecost	323	—
F the Easter Vigil through the Day of Pentecost	340	—
f Easter Day through the Day of Pentecost	351	—
a lesson *f* the Gospel is always included,	354	19
f Easter Day through the Day of Pentecost	355	—
One of the sentences *f* the Penitential Order	359	—
F the Easter Vigil through the Day of Pentecost	366	—
f time to time on a regular basis,	396	—
a passage *f* the Gospel first be read.	396	—
f the reserved Sacrament, using the following form.	396	—
A reading *f* the Gospel is always included.	400	10
f Rite One or Rite Two,	402	—
is sung or said *f* Christmas Day	406	12
on Sundays *f* Easter Day	406	13
that the Lessons be read *f* a lectern or pulpit,	406	17
f the same lectern, or *f* the pulpit, or *f* the midst	406	18
read *f* a book or books of appropriate size	406	20
a flagon of wine *f* which additional chalices	407	19
f the reserved Sacrament in the following manner:	408	19
apart *f* any which may bes required	408	28
f Easter Day through the Day of Pentecost	413	—
It is desirable that the Lessons *f* the Old Testament	422	18
the following passages *f* Holy Scripture is read.	426	—
a passage *f* the Gospel always concludes	426	—
(The Father *f* whom every family is named)	426	—
When a passage *f* the Gospel is to be read,	426	—
one of which is always *f* Holy Scripture,	435	15
a Reading *f* the Gospel is always included.	435	17
passage *f* Scripture may first be read.	439	13
instruct the people, *f* time to time,	445	—
to be administered *f* the reserved Sacrament,	457	—
For Recovery *f* Sickness	458	—
Baptized Christians are properly buried *f* the church.	468	5
It is desirable that the Lesson *f* the Old Testament,	468	15
At the burial of a child, the passages *f* Lamentations,	468	19
or more of the following passages *f* Holy Scriptures	470	—
a passage *f* the Gospel always concludes	470	—
F the Old Testament	470	—
F the New Testament	475	—
As the body is borne *f* the church,	483	—
Baptized Christians are properly buried *f* the church.	490	5
It is desirable that the Lesson *f* the Old Testament,	490	15
At the burial of a child, the passages *f* Lamentations,	490	19
or more of the following passages *f* Holy Scripture	494	—
a passage *f* the Gospel always concludes	494	—
F the Old Testament	494	—
F the New Testament	495	—
As the body is borne *f* the church,	500	—
2. Anthems *f* Holy Scripture or psalms	506	7
Reading is *f* the Gospel.	506	12
Because Jesus was raised *f* the dead,	507	3
able to separate us *f* the love of God in Christ	507	8
writers make it clear that *f* the apostles' time,	510	2
f God for the nurture of his people	510	28
F the beginning of the service until the Offertory,	511	12
presides *f* a chair placed close to the people,	511	13
f Easter Day through the Day of Pentecost	512	—
requires the following promise *f* the Bishop-elect	513	—
The Readings are ordinarily selected *f* the following	515	—
Bishop may select Readings *f* the Proper of the Day.	515	—
F Easter Day through the Day of Pentecost	523	—
F the beginning of the service until the Offertory,	524	4
f a chair placed close to the people,	524	5
f Easter Day through the Day of Pentecost	525	—
The Readings are ordinarily selected *f* the following	528	—
select Readings *f* the Proper of the Day.	528	—
F Easter Day through the Day of Pentecost	535	—
F the beginning of the service until the Offertory,	536	4
f a chair placed close to the people,	536	5
f Easter Day through the Day of Pentecost	537	—
The Readings are ordinarily selected *f* the following	540	—
select Readings *f* the Proper of the Day.	540	—
F Easter Day through the Day of Pentecost,	547	—
the deacons to remove the vessels *f* the Altar,	555	5
f the congregation read the Old Testament Lesson	558	14
The Readings are selected *f* the following list,	560	—
there may be one or two Readings *f* Scripture.	565	10
including the Gospel, may be selected *f* the Proper	565	11
or *f* the passages cited in the service.	565	12
a place apart *f* the church or chapel.	567	—
ordinarily made *f* the following list;	571	—
selections may be made *f* the Proper of the Day.	571	—
the Gospel *f* "At Baptism," page 928;	575	29

move *f* one part of the church to another. 576 5
because *f* very ancient times it has been 583 18
In order to distinguish it, however, *f* "Lord" 583 28
F time to time, the Hebrew text has Adonai 583 31
familiar *f* its use in many well-known anthems. 584 8
like us in all respects, apart *f* sin; 864 8
even as the prophets *f* earliest times spoke of him, 864 16
rose again the third day *f* the dead. 865 32
f whence he shall come to judge 865 33
breaking one piece thereof *f* another. 866 37
now *f* henceforth, all the whole realm 867 10
the saying of them, but such as *f* time to time, 867 27
begotten *f* everlasting of the Father, 868 2
Christ did truly rise again *f* death, 868 13
The Holy Ghost, proceeding *f* the Father and the Son, 868 17
Although the Law given *f* God 869 10
free *f* the obedience of the Commandments 869 13
whereby man is very far gone *f* original righteousness, 869 25
sin only except, *f* which he was clearly void, 870 25
we may depart *f* grace given, 870 34
to deliver *f* curse and damnation 871 3
God's gifts diminished *f* such as by faith, 873 7
discerned *f* others that be not christened, 873 15
of single life, or to abstain *f* marriage: 874 13
rightly cut off *f* the unity of the Church, 874 17
for the clearing of them, as well *f* obsolete words 875 18
as *f* the local references.] 875 19
f one of the other years of the three-year Sunday 888 14
the selections *f* the Psalter are frequently cited 888 18
longer and shorter version, usually *f* the same Psalm. 888 19
the first is always *f* the Old Testament 934 15
(except in the weeks *f* 4 Advent to 1 Epiphany, 934 22
Antiphons drawn *f* the Pslams themselves, 935 7
or *f* the opening sentences 935 7
or *f* other passages of Scripture, 935 8

front

It may be found desirable to return to the *f* 313 9

fruit

known as a tree discerned by the *f*. 870 11

fruitful

I. For *f* seasons 207 —
I. For *f* seasons 258 —

fruits

Albeit that Good Works, which are the *f* of Faith, 870 7

fulfill

f the functions proper to their respective orders, 13 18

fulfilled

in its deepest and truest sense, be speedily *f*; 876 30

full

Christians in these States were left at *f* 10 27
always the first Sunday after the *f* moon 15 7
Holy Baptism is *f* initiation by water 298 2
at a place in *f* sight of the congregation, 308 —
the *f* names of the persons to be married 422 20
When the bishop-elect is presented, his *f* name 511 18
When the ordinand is presented, his *f* name 524 9
When the ordinand is presented, his *f* name 536 9

a most wholesome Doctrine, and very *f* of comfort, 870 4
and our Election in Christ, is *f* of sweet, 871 11

fully

This letter is a sign that you are *f* empowered 557 7

function

do not exercise a presiding *f*; 13 22
for sponsors to be assigned this *f*. 312 25
It is the *f* of a deacon to make ready the Table 407 14
because such ministers alone have the *f* 422 8
a deacon may *f* as celebrant, 435 5

functions

fulfill the *f* proper to their respective orders, 13 18
assisting *f* at the Eucharist. 422 14

funeral

come together for prayers prior to the *f*. 465 —
arrangements for the *f* should be made in consultation 468 3
arrangements for the *f* should be made in consultation 490 3

furnishings

consecration of a church and its *f*. 566 3
for dedicating parts of a building, or *f*, 566 4
As the *f* in the church are dedicated, 576 1
it is suitable that the donors of these *f*, 576 23
For the Dedication of *F*, 577 6
or new *f* in a church or chapel. 577 10
the areas or *f* should be put into use 577 13

further

she *f* declares in her said Preface, 10 9
it cannot but be supposed that *f* alterations 10 19
to take a *f* review of the Public Service, 11 6
or *f* than local circumstances require. 11 14
and provided *f*, that none of the Propers appointed 18 13
And *f*, that the people (by daily hearing 866 13
may be *f* lengthened or shortened at discretion. 888 22

furthermore

F, it is necessary to everlasting salvation 865 19
And *f*, notwithstanding that the ancient fathers 866 26
F, by this order the curates shall need none 867 5
F, we must receive God's promises in such wise, 871 21
But *f*, we do hereby affirm that the Christian unity... 877 5
F, Deeply grieved by the sad divisions 877 20

future

convenient for their *f* prosperity; 10 30
44. For the *F* of the Human Race 811 26
44. For the *F* of the Human Race 828 —

G

gather

When circumstances permit, the congregation may *g* 270 —
G in the Lord's Name 400 —
On the day appointed, the clergy and people *g* 567 3
people assemble before the service, they may *g* 575 5

gathered

"General Councils may not be *g* together 872 5
And when they be *g* together, 872 6

gathering

The *g* of God's people 291 —
said by the Priest in the name of the *g*, 401 8
acknowledging briefly the purpose of their *g*, 492 —

gazed

Sacraments were not ordained of Christ to be *g* upon, 872 37

general

Her *g* aim in these different reviews and alterations 10 8
Eucharist or a form of *g* intercession is to follow, 57 —
The *G* Thanksgiving 58 —
Eucharist or a form of *g* intercession is to follow, 70 —
The *G* Thanksgiving 71 —
Eucharist or a form of *g* intercession is to follow, 100 —
The *G* Thanksgiving 101 —
Eucharist or a form of *g* intercession is to follow, 124 —
The *G* Thanksgiving 125 —
(d) a *g* Collect such as the following: 394 —
the service of Christ in the world, either in *g* terms, 420 —
G 453 —
Or else the following *g* confession may be said 454 18
the *G* Confession, 552 6
G Thanksgivings 812 29
1. A *G* Thanksgiving 812 30
The *G* Thanksgiving is on pages 58 and 101. 813 1
G Thanksgivings 836 —
1. A *G* Thanksgiving 836 —
See also The *G* Thanksgiving on pages 58 and 101. 837 —
XXI. Of the Authority of *G* Councils. 872 1
"*G* Councils may not be gathered together 872 5
the *G* Convention of this Church in 1792, 875 22
but rather incorporated in a *g* plan referred for study 877 27

generally

Psalms *g* appropriate to the evening 143 23
elders, in subsequent times *g* known as priests. 510 9
most *g* recognized by Christian people 510 30
God's promises in such wise, as they be *g* set forth 871 21

Genesis

Old Testament Isaiah 52:13–53:12, or *G* 22:1–18, 276 —
G 1:1–2:2 288 —
G 7:1–5, 11–18; 8:6–18; 9:8–13 288 —
G 22:1–18 289 —
G 1:26–28 (Male and female he created them) 426 —
G 2:4–9, 15–24 (A man cleaves to his wife 426 —
and the book of *G* in Septuagesima; 866 20
G, 868 26

Ghost

another of the Son, and another of the Holy *G*. 864 27
Godhead of the Father, of the Son, and of the Holy *G*, 864 28
such is the Son, and such is the Holy *G*. 864 30
the Son uncreate, and the Holy *G* uncreate. 864 31
the Son incomprehensible, and the Holy *G* incomprehensible. 864 32
the Son eternal, and the Holy *G* eternal. 864 34
the Son Almighty, and the Holy *G* Almighty. 864 38
the Son is God, and the Holy *G* is God. 865 1
the Son Lord, and the Holy *G* Lord. 865 3
The Holy *G* is of the Father and of the Son, 865 10
one Holy *G*, not three Holy Ghosts. 865 12
the Father, the Son, and the Holy *G*. 867 38
V. Of the Holy *G*. 868 16
The Holy *G*, proceeding from the Father and the Son, 868 17
committed after Baptism is sin against the Holy *G*, 870 32
After we have received the Holy *G*, 870 34
adoption to be the sons of God by the Holy *G*, 873 18
16 Of the Gifts of the Holy *G*. 875 8
of the Father, and of the Son, and of the Holy *G*, 876 32

Ghosts

one Holy Ghost, not three Holy *G*. 865 13

gift

but is a *g* from God for the nurture 510 27
10. For the *G* of a Child 813 14
10. For the *G* of a Child 841 —

gifts

and join in the consecration of the *g*, 322 8
and money or other *g*, to the deacon or celebrant. 333 —
and join in the consecration of the *g*, 354 8
and money or other *g*, to the deacon or celebrant. 361 —
Share the *G* of God 401 12
38. For the Right Use of God's *G* 811 17
38. For the Right Use of God's *G* 827 —
nor the grace of God's *g* diminished from such 873 7
16 Of the *G* of the Holy Ghost. 875 8

give

The bishop, when present, should *g* the Blessing. 108 9
to be welcomed by the congregation and to *g* thanks 439 5
or in a place set aside to *g* greater privacy, 446 16
Psalm 91 (He will *g* his angels charge over you) 453 16
g your Holy Spirit to N.; 554 1
g you the grace and power to perform them. 557 15
and lay catechists, to *g* an outline for instruction. 844 3
rise again with their bodies and shall *g* account 865 35
we *g* not our Princes the ministering 875 44
as he possesseth, liberally to *g* alms to the poor, 876 15

given

the opening sentences *g* in the Offices, 141 9
opportunity may be *g* for the members 142 7
opportunity may be *g* for silent prayer. 142 10
may be *g* to each of the newly baptized 313 8
Using the *g* name of the one to be baptized 313 24
and that the intercessions conform to the directions *g* 322 20
The Bread and the Cup are *g* to the communicants 338 —
and that the intercessions conform to the directions *g* 354 20
The Bread and the Cup are *g* to the communicants 365 —
Opportunity is always to be *g* to every communicant 407 25
has *g* clear proof of repentance and amendment 409 11
and has *g* evidence of due contrition, 446 21
Opportunity is always *g* to the people 511 24
After this other symbols of office may be *g*. 521 —
Opportunity is always *g* to the people 524 18
Opportunity is always *g* to the people 536 18
Reasonable opportunity is to be *g* for the priests 553 19
other instruments or symbols of office may be *g*. 553 24
A Bible is to be *g* to each new priest, 554 5

and immediately before the Bible is *g*. 554 14
A Bible is to be *g* to each new deacon, 554 26
May the Lord, who has *g* you the will to do 557 15
G under my hand and seal, in the city of ________, 557 17
the deputy substitutes the words *g* 561 —
for adapting the rite to special circumstances are *g* 566 7
in addition to saying the prayer over the font as *g*, 575 25
recitation is the name *g* to a method of psalmody 582 19
Although the Law *g* from God by Moses, 869 10
The original Article *g* Royal assent in 1571 869 19
received the Holy Ghost, we may depart from grace *g*, 870 34
public authority *g* unto them in the Congregation, 872 19
and hath *g* occasion to many superstitions. 873 30
The Body of Christ is *g*, taken, and eaten, 873 31
we see to have been *g* always to all godly Princes 876 3
the Word takes the form *g* in the Holy Eucharist, 888 10
those for the morning are *g* first, 934 26
any of the Psalms appointed for a *g* day may be used 934 28
assigned to a *g* Office has been bracketed, 935 4
or from the opening sentences *g* in the Offices, 935 8

giver

The *g* places the ring on the ring-finger 427 —

gives

Bishop when present, or the Priest, *g* the blessing 339 —
The Celebrant *g* thanks to God the Father 402 —
The Celebrant *g* thanks to God the Father 404 —
Celebrant, holding or taking the child by the hand, *g* 441 —
the priest *g* such counsel 446 21
(All that the Father *g* me will come to me) 495 —
The Bishop then *g* a Bible to the newly ordained, 534 —
The Bishop *g* a Bible to the newly ordained, 545 —

giveth

(All that the Father *g* me shall come to me) 480 —

giving

A citation *g* chapter and verse may be added. 47 —
A citation *g* chapter and verse may be added. 64 —
A citation *g* chapter and verse may be added. 84 —
A citation *g* chapter and verse may be added. 118 —
A citation *g* chapter and verse may be added. 300 —
A citation *g* chapter and verse may be added. 325 —
A citation *g* chapter and verse may be added. 357 —
g the reasons for refusing Communion. 409 25
A citation *g* chapter and verse may be added. 414 —
If there is to be a presentation or a *g* in marriage, 425 —
if there is to be a *g* in marriage, 437 8
Before *g* absolution, the priest may assign 446 23
A citation *g* chapter and verse may be added. 516 —
A citation *g* chapter and verse may be added. 528 —
A citation *g* chapter and verse may be added. 540 —

Gloria

G in excelsis 52 —
G in excelsis 94 —
G Patri is always sung or said at the conclusion 141 11
The *G* printed at the conclusion of certain Canticles 141 14
The following pointing of the *G* may be used: 141 16
the following form of the *G* may be used: 141 19
(substituting, if desired, the *G* in excelsis 175 —
(substituting, if desired, the *G* in excelsis 227 —
G in excelsis 294 —
If desired, the hymn *G* in excelsis may be sung 312 18
the Trisagion, or the *G* in excelsis. 321 —
continues with the *G* in excelsis, the Kyrie eleison, 353 —
When a psalm is used, it may be concluded with *G* 406 7
the following form of the *G* may be used: 406 8
G in excelsis, or the hymn used in place of it, is sung 406 12
If desired, the hymn *G* in excelsis may be sung 412 13
The Summary of the Law, the *G* in excelsis, 552 5
either with the *G* Patri, or with a refrain 582 16

glorify

Nourish them, and strengthen them to *g* God 557 13

glorious

The hymn "Sing, my tongue, the *g* battle," 282 —

glory

6 *G* be to God 52 —
20 *G* to God 94 —
or anthems are sung, such as the hymn "All *g*, laud, 271 —
extolling the *g* of the cross, is then sung. 282 —
(The *g* that shall be revealed) 475 —
(The *g* that shall be revealed) 495 —
is all one, the *G* equal, 864 28
and *g*, with the Father and the Son, 868 18

gluttony

5 Against *G* and Drunkenness. 875 7

go

so that all may *g* into the church in procession. 270 —
sponsors *g* to the font for the Thanksgiving 312 30
that the celebrant meet the body and *g* before it 468 21
that the celebrant meet the body and *g* before it 490 21
participating in the Peace, the deacons *g* to the Altar 554 28
may *g* around the building(s) to be dedicated 575 8
and then *g* to the principal door. 575 8
they that have done good shall *g* into life everlasting; 865 36

GOD

the combined title as "Lord *G*." 583 34

God

indebted, under *G*, for her first foundation 9 12
and devotion in the worship of *G*; 10 12
to the Word of *G*, or to sound doctrine, 10 15
could not but, with gratitude to *G*, embrace 11 4
IV The People of *G* 49 —
6 Glory be to *G* 52 —
or with the versicle "O *G*, make speed to save us" 61 —
continue at once with "O *G*, make speed to save us." 62 —
III The People of *G* 89 —
20 Glory to *G* 94 —
21 You are *G* 95 —
or with the versicle "O *G*, make speed to save us" 115 —
continue at once with "O *G*, make speed to save us." 116 —
G's Presence in a renewed Israel 290 —
The gathering of *G*'s people 291 —
The bond which *G* establishes in Baptism 298 3
Christians grow in the knowledge and love of *G*, 298 27
Proclamation of the Word of *G* 315 —
The Word of *G* 323 —
1. Of *G* the Father 344 —
2. Of *G* the Son 345 —

3. Of *G* the Holy Spirit	345	—
The Word of *G*	355	—
1. Of *G* the Father	377	—
2. Of *G* the Son	377	—
3. Of *G* the Holy Spirit	378	—
Proclaim and Respond to the Word of *G*	400	8
Share the Gifts of *G*	401	12
The Celebrant gives thanks to *G* the Father	402	—
Recalls before *G*, when appropriate, the particular	402	—
The Celebrant now praises *G* for the salvation	403	—
The Celebrant gives thanks to *G* the Father	404	—
Recalls before *G*, when appropriate, the particular	404	—
The Celebrant now praises *G* for the salvation	404	—
The Trisagion, "Holy *G*," may be sung	406	10
a man and a woman in the presence of *G*.	422	3
(Let us love one another for love is of *G*)	426	—
The Priest may ask *G*'s blessing on a ring or rings	427	—
and to give thanks to Almighty *G*.	439	6
or with the prayer "O *G*, you have taught us."	439	12
(*G* comforts us in affliction)	453	15
For Trust in *G*	461	—
(The souls of the righteous are in the hands of *G*)	470	—
Revelation 7:9–17 (*G* shall wipe away all tears)	475	—
(The souls of the righteous are in the hands of *G*)	494	—
Revelation 7:9–17 (*G* will wipe away every tear)	495	—
promises of *G* in Christ about eternal life.	506	17
7. The deceased is commended to *G*,	506	18
will be able to separate us from the love of *G*	507	8
and in the preaching of the Word of *G*	510	11
called by *G* to the ordained ministry are admitted	510	17
from *G* for the nurture of his people	510	28
Presbyter of the Church of *G*, you have been called	557	2
serve *G* in __________ Church [of] __________.	557	6
glorify *G* in this life and in the life to come.	557	14
(Our eyes look to the Lord our *G*,	583	8
Three terms are used in the Psalms with reference to *G*:	583	15
Elohim ("*G*"), Adonai ("Lord") and the personal name	583	16
reverence and reticence with regard to the Name of *G*	583	25
1. For Joy in *G*'s Creation	810	6
38. For the Right Use of *G*'s Gifts	811	17
40. For Knowledge of *G*'s Creation	811	22
1. For Joy in *G*'s Creation	814	—
38. For the Right Use of *G*'s Gifts	827	—
40. For Knowledge of *G*'s Creation	827	—
See also the prayer "O *G*, the King of Saints,"	838	—
G the Father	846	—
G the Son	849	—
truly *G* and truly man, consisting	864	6
for our salvation, of Mary the Virgin, the *G*-bearer	864	10
and Only-begotten *G* the Word, Lord Jesus Christ;	864	16
we worship one *G* in Trinity, and Trinity in Unity,	864	25
So the Father is *G*,	865	1
the Son is *G*,	865	1
and the Holy Ghost is *G*.	865	1
And yet they are not three *G*s, but one *G*.	865	2
himself to be both *G* and Lord,	865	6
the Son of *G*, is *G* and Man;	865	22
G, of the Substance of the Father,	865	23
Perfect *G* and perfect Man, of a reasonable soul	865	25
Who although he be *G* and Man, yet he is not two,	865	28
but by taking of the Manhood into *G*;	865	29
so *G* and Man is one Christ;	865	31
he sitteth on the right hand of the Father, *G* Almighty,	865	33
and meditation of *G*'s word)	866	11
profit more and more in the knowledge of *G*,	866	14
nothing to be read, but the very pure word of *G*,	867	1
There is but one living and true *G*, everlasting,	867	35
Of the Word or Son of *G*, which was made very Man.	868	1
and eternal *G*, and of one substance with the Father,	868	3
whereof is one Christ, very *G*, and very Man;	868	6
with the Father and the Son, very and eternal *G*.	868	18
who is the only Mediator between *G* and Man,	869	8
being both *G* and Man.	869	9
Although the Law given from *G* by Moses,	869	10
it deserveth *G*'s wrath and damnation.	869	27
not subject to the Law of *G*.	869	31
good works, to faith, and calling upon *G*.	869	35
no power to do good works pleasant and acceptable to *G*,	869	36
the grace of *G* by Christ preventing us,	869	37
We are accounted righteous before *G*,	870	2
and endure the severity of *G*'s judgment;	870	8
acceptable to *G* in Christ, and do spring out	870	9
are not pleasant to *G*,	870	14
that they are not done as *G* hath willed	870	16
Works besides, over and above, *G*'s Commandments,	870	19
only render unto *G* as much as they are bound to do,	870	21
and by the grace of *G* we may arise again,	870	35
Predestination to Life is the everlasting purpose of *G*,	871	2
be endued with so excellent a benefit of *G*,	871	6
be called accordingly to *G*'s purpose	871	6
they be made sons of *G* by adoption:	871	8
in good works, and at length, by *G*'s mercy,	871	9
because it doth fervently kindle their love towards *G*:	871	16
before their eyes the sentence of *G*'s Predestination,	871	17
we must receive *G*'s promises in such wise,	871	21
and, in our doings, that Will of *G* is to be followed,	871	22
expressly declared unto us in the Word of *G*.	871	23
G is preached, and the Sacraments be duly ministered	871	31
ordain any thing that is contrary to *G*'s Word written,	871	38
all be not governed with the Spirit and Word of *G*,)	872	7
sometimes have erred, even in things pertaining to *G*.	872	8
but rather repugnant to the Word of *G*.	872	14
It is a thing plainly repugnant to the Word of *G*,	872	22
and effectual signs of grace, and *G*'s good will	872	27
have not any visible sign or ceremony ordained of *G*.	872	36
use their Ministry, both in hearing the Word of *G*,	873	5
nor the grace of *G*'s gifts diminished from such	873	7
adoption to be the sons of *G*	873	18
increased by virtue of prayer unto *G*.	873	19
and Deacons, are not commanded by *G*'s Law,	874	12
so that nothing be ordained against *G*'s Word.	874	24
which be not repugnant to the Word of *G*,	874	26
10 Of the reverend Estimation of *G*'s Word.	875	13
ministering either of *G*'s Word, or of the Sacraments,	876	1
to all Godly Princes in holy Scriptures by *G*	876	3
and degrees committed to their charge by *G*,	876	5
assembled as Bishops in the Church of *G*,	876	26
Old and New Testament as the revealed Word of *G*.	877	14
varying needs of the nations and peoples called of *G*	877	19
may be by *G*'s blessing made towards Home Reunion:	877	32
varying needs of the nations and peoples called of *G*	878	5

Godhead
at once complete in G and complete in manhood, 864 5
(homoousios) with the Father as regards his G, 864 7
as regards his G, begotten of the Father 864 9
But the G of the Father, of the Son, 864 28
Equal to the Father, as touching his G; 865 26
One, not by conversion of the G into flesh, 865 29
And in unity of this G there be three Persons, 867 37
the G and Manhood, were joined together in one 868 5

godliness
quiet and peaceable lives, in all g and honesty." 11 2
and for a great advancement of g: 866 8
be stirred up to g themselves, 866 11
to serve better to g. 874 15

godly
or which a g man may not with a good conscience 10 15
But these many years passed, this g and decent order 866 16
As the g consideration of Predestination, 871 11
pleasant, and unspeakable comfort to g persons, 871 12
doth contain a g and wholesome Doctrine, 874 36
we see to have been given always to all g Princes 876 3

godparent
may be given to each of the newly baptized or to a g. 313 8

godparents
commonly called g, present their candidates, 298 21
It is fitting that parents be included among the g 298 24
Parents and g are to be instructed in the meaning 298 25
individually by their Parents and G, as follows 301 —
Parents and G 301 —
the Celebrant asks the parents and g 302 —
Parents and G 302 —
Parents and G 302 —
and of the parents and g who speak 302 —
presented by the newly baptized or their g. 313 14
together with the sponsors or g, taking part 314 8

Gods
And yet they are not three G, but one God. 865 2
to say, There be three G, or three Lords. 865 7

goes
the officiant then g to a place close by it 143 4
Then the new Bishop g to the Lord's Table 522 —
The Bishop g to the Table and begins 546 —
The Bishop g to the Pulpit, lays a hand upon it, 571 —
The Bishop g to the Table and, with arms extended, 573 —

going
III. Of the g down of Christ into Hell. 868 9

Golgotha
verse which mentions the arrival at G 273 —
verse which mentions the arrival at G 277 —

gone
man is very far g from original righteousness, 869 25

good
with a g conscience use and submit unto, 10 16
but this great and g work 10 21
G Friday 17 9
G Friday and all other Fridays of the year, 17 25
on Ash Wednesday, Maundy Thursday, G Friday, 18 12
in Holy Week, or on G Friday. 108 12
G Friday 169 —
G Friday 221 —
from the reserved Sacrament on G Friday, 275 —
G Friday 276 —
(The Lord is g unto them that wait for him) 470 —
John 10:11–16 (I am the g shepherd) 480 —
(The Lord is g to those who wait for him) 494 —
John 10:11–16 (I am the g shepherd) 495 —
32. For the G Use of Leisure 811 11
32. For the G Use of Leisure 825 —
they that have done g shall go into life everlasting; 865 37
that the same was not ordained, but of a g purpose, 866 7
by his own natural strength and g works, to faith, 869 35
Wherefore we have no power to do g works pleasant 869 36
by Christ preventing us, that we may have a g will, 869 37
when we have that g will. 869 38
XII. Of G Works. 870 6
Albeit that G Works, which are the fruits of Faith, 870 7
they walk religiously in g works, and at length, 871 9
and effectual signs of grace, and God's g will 872 27
the evil be ever mingled with the g, 873 2
4 Of g Works: first of Fasting. 875 6

goodness
infinite power, wisdom, and g; 867 36

goods
temporal g, not neglecting, if they are able, to leave 445 —
Of Christian Men's G, which are not common. 876 12
The Riches and G of Christians are not common, 876 13

Gospel
what Christianity is, and what the truths of the G 11 20
If three Lessons are used, the Lesson from the G 47 —
If three Lessons are used, the Lesson from the G 65 —
If three Lessons are used, the Lesson from the G 84 —
If three Lessons are used, the Lesson from the G 119 —
the G is always included. 142 21
or more of the appointed Lessons are read before the G, 175 —
or more of the appointed Lessons are read before the G, 227 —
G Matthew 6:1–6, 16–21 264 —
The Passion G is announced in the following manner 272 —
The customary responses before and after the G 272 —
The Passion G may be read or chanted by lay persons. 273 —
G John 13:1–15, or Luke 22:14–30 274 —
follows the G and homily. 274 —
The Passion G is announced in the following manner 276 —
The customary responses before and after the G 277 —
The Passion G may be read or chanted by lay persons. 277 —
G Matthew 27:57–66, or John 19:38–42 283 —
After the G (and homily), in place of the Prayers 283 —
be administered here or after the G. 292 —
either here or after the G. 292 —
G Matthew 28:1–10 295 —
the Deacon or a Priest reads the G, 300 —
After the G, the Reader says 300 —
at the Lord's Table, and to preach the G. 322 3
A deacon should read the G and may lead the Prayers 322 10

reading of the Lessons which precede the *G*, 322 16
provided that a lesson from the *G* is always included, 322 19
the Deacon or a Priest reads the *G*, 326 —
After the *G*, the Reader says 326 —
at the Lord's Table, and to preach the *G*. 354 3
A deacon should read the *G* and may lead the Prayers 354 10
reading of the Lessons which precede the *G*, 354 16
provided that a lesson from the *G* is always included, 354 19
the Deacon or a Priest reads the *G*, 357 —
After the *G*, the Reader says 358 —
it is desirable that a passage from the *G* first be read. 396 —
A reading from the *G* is always included. 400 10
and that the *G* be read from the same lectern, 406 18
It is desirable that the Lessons and *G* be read 406 19
read the *G* in the language of the people, 406 23
or in addition to, the *G* in English. 406 24
the Deacon or a Priest reads the *G*, 414 —
After the *G*, the Reader says 415 —
Declaration of Consent, read the *G*, and perform 422 13
a passage from the *G* always concludes 426 —
When a passage from the *G* is to be read, all stand, 426 —
After the *G*, the Reader says 426 —
After the *G* (and homily), the husband and wife stand 433 —
a Reading from the *G* is always included. 435 17
a passage from the *G* always concludes 470 —
The *G* 479 —
the Deacon or Minister appointed reads the *G*, 479 —
At the end of the *G*, the Reader says 480 —
a passage from the *G* always concludes 494 —
The *G* 495 —
the Deacon or Minister appointed reads the *G*, 495 —
At the end of the *G*, the Reader says 495 —
Reading is from the *G*. 506 12
and the proclamation of his *G* everywhere. 510 29
Then, all standing, a Deacon or a Priest reads the *G*, 516 —
After the *G*, the Reader says 516 —
a Priest reads the *G*, first saying 529 —
After the *G*, the Reader says 529 —
a Priest reads the *G*, first saying 541 —
After the *G*, the Reader says 541 —
By your words, and in your life, proclaim the *G*. 557 12
A deacon or priest reads the *G*. 558 16
The new minister, if a deacon, should read the *G*, 558 20
G John 15:9–16, or Luke 10:1–2, or John 14:11–15 560 —
Before the *G*, there may be one or two Readings 565 10
including the *G*, may be selected from the Proper 565 11
The Deacon (or a Priest) reads the *G*. 571 —
All then stand for the *G*, which may be the following 572 —
the *G* from "At Baptism," 575 28
for witness to the *G*. 576 13
two Sacraments ordained of Christ our Lord in the *G*, 872 30
are not to be counted for Sacraments of the *G*, 872 33
all men who are professors of the *G*, 875 37
the *G* Reading be used in the evening in Year One, 934 11

governance
take part in the *g* of the Church, 510 10

governed
whereof all be not *g* with the Spirit and Word 872 7

governing
Subject to the rules of precedence *g* Principal Feasts, 17 29

government
became independent with respect to civil *g*, 10 25
22. For Sound *G* 810 31
23. For Local *G* 811 1
22. For Sound *G* 821 —
23. For Local *G* 822 —
G of all Estates of this Realm, 875 41
Where we attribute to the King's Majesty the chief *g*, 875 43

grace
all such prayers, namely, that "Rulers may have *g*, 10 36
A Collect for *G* 57 —
A Collect for *G* 100 —
followed by the Lord's Prayer and a *g* or blessing; 112 —
may use the following or some other blessing or *g* 114 —
concludes with the Lord's Prayer and the *G*. 283 —
it concludes with suitable prayers, and the *G* 321 —
it concludes with suitable prayers, and the *G* 353 —
and with either the *G* or a blessing, 407 3
fill him with *g* and power, 554 1
give you the *g* and power to perform them. 557 16
70. *G* at Meals 812 25
70. *G* at Meals 835 —
the *g* of God by Christ preventing us, 869 37
Works done before the *g* of Christ, 870 13
to receive *g*, or (as the School-authors say) deserve *g* 870 15
received the Holy Ghost, we may depart from *g* given, 870 34
and by the *g* of God we may arise again, 870 35
they through *G* obey the calling: 871 7
and effectual signs of *g*, and God's good will 872 27
nor the *g* of God's gifts diminished 873 7
Faith is confirmed, and *G* increased by virtue 873 18

graces
charity which is the chief of Christian *g* 877 4

gracious
O *G* Light Phos hilaron 64 —
O *G* Light Phos hilaron 112 —
O *G* Light Phos hilaron 118 —

grafted
they that receive Baptism rightly are *g* 873 16

grant
Wherefore the *g* of repentance is not to be denied 870 33

gratitude
could not but, with *g* to God, embrace 11 4

grave
into the church or towards the *g*. 468 22
The Consecration of a *G* 487 —
If the *g* is in a place that has not previously 487 —
into the church or towards the *g*. 490 22
The Consecration of a *G* 503 —
If the *g* is in a place that has not previously 503 —
Jesus himself wept at the *g* of his friend. 507 12
or other *g* cause, could not be present 555 3

graveside
service has been held, or at the *g*. 506 20

great
but this *g* and good work 10 21
The *G* Litany 147 —
The *G* Litany 148 —
The *G* Vigil, when observed, is the first service 284 2
The *G* Vigil of Easter 285 —
The *G* Thanksgiving 333 —
Alternative Form of the *G* Thanksgiving 340 —
The *G* Thanksgiving 361 —
Alternative Forms of the *G* Thanksgiving 367 —
The *G* Thanksgiving is said by the Priest 401 8
At the *G* Thanksgiving 402 1
When the *G* Litany is sung or said 406 3
During the *G* Thanksgiving, 407 18
At the *G* Thanksgiving, the new priest 524 14
goes to the Table and begins the *G* Thanksgiving. 546 —
other priests at the Altar for the *G* Thanksgiving. 554 8
proceeds with the *G* Thanksgiving 563 —
For the *G* Thanksgiving, 565 27
but of a good purpose, and for a *g* advancement 866 7
and purpose of the old fathers, and a *g* deal 866 43
the people shall not be at so *g* charge for books, 867 7
And where heretofore, there hath been *g* diversity 867 8
the *g* profit that shall ensue thereof. 867 15
drink the sign or Sacrament of so *g* a thing. 873 40

greater
or in a place set aside to give *g* privacy, 446 16
none is *g*, or less than another; 865 14
Four Prophets the *g*, 868 32

greatest
that all the whole Bible (or the *g* part 866 8

greatly
as well because it doth *g* establish 871 14

Greek
the original *G* terms presbyter, presbyters, 528 —
whereby the lust of the flesh, called in *G*, 869 29

greet
Then the Ministers and People may *g* one another 332 —
Then the Ministers and People may *g* one another 360 —
or elsewhere in the service, all *g* one another 401 2
The newly married couple then *g* each other, 431 —
Presiding Bishop and other Bishops *g* the new bishop. 522 —
The People *g* one another. 522 —
The Presbyters present *g* the newly ordained; 534 —
The Clergy and People *g* one another. 534 —
and the Clergy present now *g* the newly ordained. 546 —
The Clergy and People *g* one another. 546 —
The People *g* one another. 563 —
and other clergy and the people *g* one another. 574 —

greeting
The *g*, "The peace of the Lord be always with you," 407 7
any appropriate words of *g* may be used. 407 9
husband and wife first *g* each other. 436 11
begins the service with the following or some other *g* 453 11

greetings
after which *g* may be exchanged 431 —
The new Deacon then exchanges *g* with family 546 —

greets
and the Officiant *g* the people with these words 109 —
The new Bishop also *g* other members of the clergy, 522 —
The Bishop *g* the newly ordained. 534 —
who then *g* family members and others, 534 —
The Bishop *g* the new minister. 563 —
The new Minister then *g* other members of the clergy, 563 —

grief
joy, however, does not make human *g* unchristian. 507 10

grieved
Furthermore, Deeply *g* by the sad divisions 877 20

grievous
men with death, for heinous and *g* offences. 876 8

ground
the first original and *g* whereof, 866 6

grounded
or that which is evidently *g* upon the same; 867 2
g upon no warranty of Scripture, 872 14

group
singing a refrain after each verse or *g* of verses. 582 21
be used as refrains after each verse or *g* of verses. 935 11

grouped
and the sponsors should be so *g* that the people 313 5

groups
recitation is the verse-by-verse alternation between *g* 582 13

grow
to help the new Christians *g* in the knowledge 298 26
(That she and I may *g* old together) 426 —

grown
being such as have *g* partly of the corrupt 872 34

guidance
A Collect for *G* 57 —
A Collect for *G* 100 —
57. For *G* 812 8
58. For *G* 812 9
57. For *G* 832 —
58. For *G* 832 —

guilt
and to be a sacrifice, not only for original *g*, 868 7
of pain or *g*, were blasphemous fables, 874 10

guilty
finally, being found *g*, by just judgment be deposed. 873 12

H

Habakkuk
H 2:20 40 —
H 2:20 78 —

habitat
Psalm 91 Qui *h* 129 —

hall

worship is also to serve as a school or parish *h*, 576 29

hallelujah

The ancient praise-shout, "*H*," has been restored, 584 4

halt

At a suitable place, the procession may *h* 271 —

hand

placing a *h* on the vessel of oil, 307 —
the Bishop or Priest places a *h* on the person's head, 308 —
or lay a *h* upon it; 334 —
to hold or place a *h* upon the cup 334 —
or lay a *h* upon it; 342 —
to hold or place a *h* upon the cup 342 —
or lay a *h* upon it; 362 —
to hold or place a *h* upon the cup 362 —
or lay a *h* upon it; 368 —
to hold or place a *h* upon the cup 368 —
or lay a *h* upon it; 371 —
to hold or place a *h* upon the cup 371 —
or lay a *h* upon it; 374 —
to hold or place a *h* upon the cup 374 —
or lay a *h* upon it; 403 —
to hold or place a *h* upon the cup 403 —
or lay a *h* upon it; 405 —
to hold or place a *h* upon the cup 405 —
The Man, facing the woman and taking her right *h* 427 —
takes his right *h* in hers, and says 427 —
places the ring on the ring-finger of the other's *h* 427 —
ring or rings are to be blessed, the wife extends her *h* 434 —
(and the husband extends his *h*) 434 —
the Celebrant, holding or taking the child by the *h*, 441 —
The Priest then lays a *h* upon the penitent's head 451 —
(or extends a *h* over the penitent), 451 —
Given under my *h* and seal, in the city of ________, 557 17
The Bishop moves to the Font, lays a *h* upon it, 569 —
The Bishop proceeds to the Lectern, lays a *h* upon it, 570 —
The Bishop goes to the Pulpit, lays a *h* upon it, 571 —
The Bishop lays a *h* upon the Table, and continues 573 —
he sitteth on the right *h* of the Father, 865 33

handed

and the creed of the Fathers has *h* down 864 17

hands

During the procession, all hold branches in their *h*, 271 —
The Bishop lays *h* upon each one and says 309 —
their Baptism and to receive the laying on of *h* 412 5
baptized as adults, unless baptized with laying on *h* 412 7
of a bishop and to receive the laying on of *h*. 412 10
The Bishop lays *h* upon each one and says 418 —
Then they loose their *h*, 427 —
They loose their *h*. 427 —
Then the Celebrant joins the right *h* 428 —
The Celebrant joins the right *h* 434 —
When the Laying on of *H* or Anointing takes place 453 7
Part II. Laying on of *H* and Anointing 455 —
The Priest then lays *h* upon the sick person, 455 —
(The souls of the righteous are in the *h* of God) 470 —
(The souls of the righteous are in the *h* of God) 494 —
by solemn prayer and the laying on of episcopal *h*. 510 18
the laying on of *h* by bishops 510 24
Presiding Bishop and other Bishops now lay their *h* 521 —
Bishop lays *h* upon the head of the ordinand, 533 —
Priests who are present also laying on their *h*. 533 —
Bishop lays *h* upon the head of the ordinand, 545 —
to join in the laying on of *h*. 553 20
Consecration, the bishop and priests lay their *h* 553 30
During the laying on of *h*, 553 31
When they have laid their *h* upon all 554 2
During the Prayer of Consecration the Bishop is to lay *h* 554 20
After laying *h* upon all the ordinands, 554 23

hangings

members of the congregation with flowers, candles, *h*, 576 2

happily

a blessing might *h* be brought to pass. 877 24

happy

accordingly, that, seeking to keep the *h* mean 9 25
but, with gratitude to God, embrace the *h* occasion 11 4

hard

to turn the Book only, was so *h* and intricate a matter, 866 31

hardness

the number and *h* of the Rules called the Pie, 866 29

harmony

(Love which binds everything together in *h*) 426 —

harvest

42. For the *H* of Lands and Waters 811 24
9. For the *H* 813 12
42. For the *H* of Lands and Waters 828 —
9. For the *H* 840 —

has

Easter Eve *h* its own form 108 12
through the care each Christian *h* for others, 446 3
at a time when the congregation *h* opportunity 468 6
at a time when the congregation *h* opportunity 490 6
John 5:24–27 (He who believes *h* everlasting life) 495 —
From time to time, the Hebrew text *h* Adonai 583 31

hath

John 5:24–27 (He that believeth *h* everlasting life) 480 —
concupiscence and lust *h* of itself the nature of sin. 869 32
The Church *h* power to decree Rites or Ceremonies, 871 37
Church by a Judge that *h* authority thereunto. 874 20
Every particular or national Church *h* authority 874 31
neither *h* it any thing that, of itself, 875 23
neither *h* it any thing, 875 29
but *h* no authority in things purely spiritual. 875 36
"The King's Majesty *h* the chief power 875 39
The Bishop of Rome *h* no jurisdiction in this Realm 876 7

hatred

When the priest sees that there is *h* between members 409 17

have

namely, that "Rulers may *h* grace, wisdom, 10 36
h precedence over all other days of commemoration 16 24
it is appropriate after the candles *h* been lighted 143 19

because such ministers alone *h* the function 422 8
(That you may know that you *h* eternal life) 454 10
The very love we *h* for each other in Christ 507 11
each is to *h* his own presenters. 553 25
each is to *h* his own presenters. 554 15
young and old, *h* some individual or collective part 566 17
might understand, and *h* profit by hearing the same, 866 23
So that here you *h* an order for prayer 866 42
the whole realm shall *h* but one use. 867 11
Wherefore we *h* no power to do good works 869 36
by Christ preventing us, that we may *h* a good will, 869 37
when we *h* that good will. 869 38
but they *h* the nature of sin. 870 17
and if we say we *h* no sin, 870 29
to *h* continually before their eyes the sentence 871 17
salvation *h* neither strength nor authority, 872 9
this work by men who *h* public authority 872 19
to *h* public Prayer in the Church, 872 23
but yet *h* not like nature of Sacraments with Baptism, 872 35
for that they *h* not any visible sign or ceremony 872 36
they *h* a wholesome effect or operation: 872 38
h chief authority in the Ministration of the Word 873 3
accused by those that *h* knowledge of their offences; 873 11
not only a sign of the love that Christians ought to *h* 873 23
for the quick and the dead, to *h* remission 874 9

having

This Convention *h*, in their present session, 8 7
the canons of this Church *h* been complied with, 435 7
h committed yourself to this work, 557 10
and others *h* similar tenure of office. 564 18
and other priests *h* similar canonical charge. 565 25
h due regard for the distinctive nature 576 19
period of time without *h* been consecrated, 577 22

head

the Bishop or Priest places a hand on the person's *h*, 308 —
The Priest then lays a hand upon the penitent's *h* 451 —
Psalm 23 (You have anointed my *h* with oil) 454 7
upon the *h* of the bishop-elect, and say together 521 —
Bishop lays hands upon the *h* of the ordinand, 533 —
Bishop lays hands upon the *h* of the ordinand, 545 —
lay their hands upon the *h* of each ordinand. 553 31
lay hands upon the *h* of each ordinand, 554 21

headings

since the matter is arranged under *h*, 844 10

heal

to *h* the wounds of the Body of Christ, 877 2

health

to make wills, while they are in *h*, 445 —
For *H* of Body and Soul 460 —
11. For the Restoration of *H* 813 15
11. For the Restoration of *H* 841 —

hear

remain where they may conveniently *h* the reading 437 14
Another Christian may be asked to *h* a confession, 446 12
see and *h* what is done. 511 14
see and *h* what is done. 524 6
see and *h* what is done. 536 6

heard

Confessions may be *h* anytime 446 8
When a confession is *h* in a church building, 446 15
ministers may be clearly seen and *h* by the people. 564 16
so that they have *h* with their ears 866 25
Wherefore they are not to be *h*, 869 9

hearers

both of the readers and *h*. 867 4

hearing

(by daily *h* of holy Scripture read in the Church) 866 13
and have profit by *h* the same, 866 24
both in *h* the Word of God, 873 5

heart

A new *h* and a new spirit 290 —
they could say many things by *h*: 867 13

hearts

and their *h*, spirit, and mind, have not been edified 866 26

heathen

as an *H* and Publican, until he be openly reconciled 874 19

heaven

He ascended into *h*, he sitteth on the right hand 865 33
wherewith he ascended into *H*, 868 14

heavenly

"*H* Father, we thank you that by water 298 11
"*H* Father, we thank you that by water 313 10
and drawing up their mind to high and *h* things, 871 14
in the Supper, only after an *h* and spiritual manner. 873 31

Hebrew

lines correspond to *H* versification, 583 2
The *H* reverence and reticence with regard 583 25
the *H* text has Adonai and YHWH 583 31
Then, the *H* custom is to substitute Elohim 583 32
The *H* form has been used, 584 5

Hebrews

H 9:24 39 —
H 9:24 77 —
H 13:20–21 132 —
Epistle *H* 10:1–25 276 —
H 4:14, 16 320 —
H 13:15, 16 344 —
H 4:14, 16 352 —
H 13:15, 16 377 —
H 12:1–2 (Looking to Jesus, the perfecter of our faith) 454 2
Epistle *H* 5:1–10, 515 —

height

nor things to come, nor powers, nor *h*, nor depth, 507 7

heinous

death, for *h* and grievous offences. 876 8

held

service should be *h* at a time when the congregation 468 6
service should be *h* at a time when the congregation 490 6
service has been *h*, or at the graveside. 506 20

hell

descended into *h*, rose again the third day 865 32
III. Of the going down of Christ into *H*. 868 9
that he went down into *H*. 868 11

help

in their duties to *h* the new Christians grow 298 26

helpless

the sick, the suffering, and the *h*. 510 15

henceforth

now from *h*, all the whole realm 867 10

hereafter

or *h* shall be consecrated or ordered to the same 875 32

hereby

do *h* establish the said Book: 8 9
in the Church of God, do *h* solemnly declare to all 876 26
we do *h* affirm that the Christian unity... 877 5
we *h* declare our desire and readiness, 877 21

Hereford

some following Salisbury use, some *H* use, 867 9

herein

h was to make them conformable to what ought to be 10 35

heretofore

And where *h*, there hath been great diversity 867 8

heroic

6. For *H* Service 813 7
6. For *H* Service 839 —

Hierome

other Books (as *H* saith) the Church doth read 868 34

high

and drawing up their mind to *h* and heavenly things, 871 14

hinders

which *h* not the effect of the Sacraments. 873 1

historic

4. The *H* Episcopate, locally adapted in the methods 877 18
(d) The *H* Episcopate, locally adapted in the methods 878 4

historical

H Documents of the Church 863 —

hold

During the procession, all *h* branches in their hands, 271 —
words concerning the bread, the Celebrant is to *h* it, 334 —
to *h* or place a hand upon the cup 334 —
words concerning the bread, the Celebrant is to *h* it, 342 —
to *h* or place a hand upon the cup 342 —
words concerning the bread, the Celebrant is to *h* it, 362 —
to *h* or place a hand upon the cup 362 —
words concerning the bread, the Celebrant is to *h* it, 368 —
to *h* or place a hand upon the cup 368 —
words concerning the bread, the Celebrant is to *h* it, 371 —
to *h* or place a hand upon the cup 371 —
words concerning the bread, the Celebrant is to *h* it, 374 —
to *h* or place a hand upon the cup 374 —
words concerning the bread, the Celebrant is to *h* it, 403 —
to *h* or place a hand upon the cup 403 —
words concerning the bread, the Celebrant is to *h* it, 405 —
to *h* or place a hand upon the cup 405 —
it is necessary that he *h* the Catholic Faith. 864 22
And we *h* it to be the duty 875 36

holding

Celebrant, *h* or taking the child by the hand, 441 —

holy

H Eucharist, the principal act of Christian worship 13 3
or from *H* Scripture, may be used when the needs 13 10
from *H* Scripture, or from this Book, 14 8
Year consists of two cycles of feasts and *h* days: 15 3
The *H* Name 16 5
3. *H* Days 16 21
The following *H* Days are regularly observed 16 22
The *H* Name 16 27
H Cross Day 16 29
The *H* Innocents 17 5
the days of *H* Week or of Easter Week. 17 11
and the other weekdays of Lent and of *H* Week, 17 23
and *H* Days, the following may be observed 18 1
the Day of Pentecost, *H* Cross Day, 18 6
Maundy Thursday, Good Friday, and *H* Saturday; 18 12
At celebrations of the *H* Eucharist, 36 8
H Week 39 1
the transfiguration and *H* Cross 43 —
At celebrations of the *H* Eucharist, 74 7
H Week 76 —
the Transfiguration and *H* Cross 81 —
in *H* Week, or on Good Friday. 108 12
With the celebration of the *H* Eucharist, 112 —
a) the Lectionary for Sundays, *H* Days, 136 —
unless otherwise ordered for *H* Days 158 8
serve for any weekdays between *H* Innocents' Day 161 —
takes precedence over the three *H* Days which follow 161 —
The *H* Name January 1 162 —
Preface of *H* Week 168 —
Monday in *H* Week 168 —
Preface of *H* Week 168 —
Tuesday in *H* Week 168 —
Preface of *H* Week 168 —
Wednesday in *H* Week 169 —
Preface of *H* Week 169 —
Preface of *H* Week 169 —
H Saturday 170 —
H Baptism or Confirmation 175 —
H Days 185 —
The *H* Innocents December 28 186 —
H Cross Day September 14 192 —
Preface of *H* Week 192 —
1. Of the *H* Trinity 199 —
2. Of the *H* Spirit 200 —
3. Of the *H* Angels 200 —
5. Of the *H* Eucharist 201 —
6. Of the *H* Cross 201 —
Preface of *H* Week 201 —
serve for any weekdays between *H* Innocents' Day 213 —
takes precedence over the three *H* Days which follow 213 —
The *H* Name January 1 213 —
Preface of *H* Week 219 —

Monday in *H* Week	220	—
Preface of *H* Week	220	—
Tuesday in *H* Week	220	—
Preface of *H* Week	220	—
Wednesday in *H* Week	220	—
Preface of *H* Week	220	—
Preface of *H* Week	221	—
H Saturday	221	—
H Baptism or Confirmation	227	—
H Days	237	1
The *H* Innocents December 28	238	—
H Cross Day September 14	244	—
Preface of *H* Week	244	—
1. Of the *H* Trinity	251	—
2. Of the *H* Spirit	251	—
3. Of the *H* Angels	251	—
5. Of the *H* Eucharist	252	—
6. Of the *H* Cross	252	—
Preface of *H* Week	252	—
invites the people to the observance of a *h* Lent,	264	—
Preface of *H* Week	273	—
Where it is desired to administer *H* Communion	275	—
Preface of *H* Week	275	—
In places where *H* Communion is to be administered	282	—
H Saturday	283	—
a convenient time between sunset on *H* Saturday	284	3
4. The *H* Eucharist with the administration	284	9
H baptism (beginning with the Presentation	292	—
H Baptism, Confirmation, or the Renewal	295	—
H Baptism	297	—
H Baptism is full initiation by water and the *H* Spirit	298	2
H Baptism is appropriately administered	298	5
we thank you that by water and the *H* Spirit;"	298	11
Each candidate for *H* Baptism is to be sponsored	298	16
H Baptism	299	—
H Baptism is especially appropriate at the Easter	312	2
we thank you that by water and the *H* Spirit,"	313	10
and of the Son, and of the *H* Spirit"	313	17
The *H* Eucharist	315	—
Celebration of the *H* Communion	315	—
The *H* Eucharist: Rite One	323	—
The *H* Communion	333	—
Then, facing the *H* Table, the Celebrant proceeds	333	—
Then, facing the *H* Table, the Celebrant proceeds	341	—
3. Of God the *H* Spirit	345	—
appointed for *H* Days and Various Occasions	345	—
H Week	346	—
The *H* Eucharist: Rite Two	355	—
The *H* Communion	361	—
Then, facing the *H* Table, the Celebrant proceeds	361	—
Then, facing the *H* Table, the Celebrant proceeds	367	—
Then, facing the *H* Table, the Celebrant proceeds	370	—
Then, facing the *H* Table, the Celebrant proceeds	373	—
3. Of God the *H* Spirit	378	—
appointed for *H* Days and Various Occasions	378	—
H Week	379	—
the *H* Eucharist	400	2
the *H* Eucharist.	400	5
and the renewal of the *H* Spirit.	405	—
The *H* Table is spread with a clean white cloth	406	2
The Trisagion, "*H* God," may be sung	406	10
deacons at the *H* Table then communicate,	407	24
the celebrant is to return to the *H* Table,	408	10
authorize a deacon to distribute *H* Communion	408	18
and tell him that he may not come to the *H* Table	409	10
and of celebrating the *H* Eucharist.	422	9
the following passages from *H* Scripture is read.	426	—
as prescribed for celebrations of the *H* Eucharist,	433	—
teaching of the Church concerning *H* Matrimony,	435	11
one of which is always from *H* Scripture,	435	15
and of the Son, and of the *H* Spirit.	436	5
The *H* Eucharist may be celebrated	436	14
authorized liturgy for the *H* Eucharist.	437	6
and receive *H* Communion before other members	438	3
precede the distribution of *H* Communion,	453	9
the Priest dips a thumb in the *h* oil,	456	—
Part III. *H* Communion	457	—
the following passages from *H* Scripture is read.	470	—
the following passages from *H* Scripture is read.	494	—
2. Anthems from *H* Scripture or psalms may be sung	506	7
4. One or more passages of *H* Scripture are read.	506	10
The *H* Scriptures and ancient Christian writers make	510	2
characteristic of Christ's *h* catholic Church.	510	5
and administering his *h* Sacraments.	510	12
duly qualified to confer *H* Orders.	510	24
When a bishop is to confer *H* Orders,	524	2
Priest joins in the celebration of the *H* Eucharist	535	—
When a bishop is to confer *H* Orders,	536	2
After receiving *H* Communion, the new deacon	536	14
The celebration of the *H* Eucharist may be according	552	3
"I do believe the *H* Scriptures..."	552	9
The hymn to the *H* Spirit before the Prayer	552	14
"Receive the *H* Scriptures..."	553	6
distributes *H* Communion to the people.	553	11
give your *H* Spirit to N.;	554	1
and receive *H* Communion.	554	10
Christ your Son, give your *H* Spirit to N.;	554	22
others administer *H* Communion.	554	30
minister *H* Communion to those communicants who,	555	2
If *H* Baptism is not to be administered,	575	24
as in the service of *H* Baptism,	575	26
then the service of *H* Baptism, beginning	575	29
by the administration of *H* Baptism.	577	17
followed by the celebration of the *H* Eucharist.	577	19
The *H* Spirit	852	—
The *H* Scriptures	853	—
H Baptism	858	—
The *H* Eucharist	859	—
Therefore, following the *h* fathers,	864	4
another of the Son, and another of the *H* Ghost.	864	27
of the Father, of the Son, and of the *H* Ghost,	864	28
such is the Son, and such is the *H* Ghost.	864	30
the Son uncreate, and the *H* Ghost uncreate.	864	31
and the *H* Ghost incomprehensible.	864	32
the Son eternal, and the *H* Ghost eternal.	864	34
the Son Almighty, and the *H* Ghost Almighty.	864	38
the Son is God, and the *H* Ghost is God.	865	1
the Son Lord, and the *H* Ghost Lord.	865	3
The *H* Ghost is of the Father and of the Son,	865	10
one *H* Ghost, not three *H* Ghosts.	865	12
(by daily hearing of *h* Scripture read in the Church)	866	13
other books of *h* Scripture used.	866	22
the reading of *h* Scripture is so set forth,	866	36
(as touching the reading of the *h* Scripture),	866	43

but the very pure word of God, the *h* Scriptures, 867 2
I. Of Faith in the *H* Trinity. 867 34
the Father, the Son, and the *H* Ghost. 867 38
V. Of the *H* Ghost. 868 16
H Ghost, proceeding from the Father and the Son, 868 17
VI. Of the Sufficiency of the *H* Scriptures 868 19
H Scripture containeth all things necessary 868 20
name of the *H* Scripture we do understand 868 23
by most certain warrents of *H* Scripture. 869 18
committed after Baptism is sin against the *H* Ghost, 870 32
After we have received the *H* Ghost, 870 34
set forth to us in *H* Scripture: 871 22
For *H* Scripture doth set out unto us 871 27
the Church be a witness and a keeper of *H* Writ, 871 40
that they be taken out of *h* Scripture." 872 10
to be the sons of God by the *H* Ghost, 873 18
cannot be proved by *H* Writ; 873 29
16 Of the Gifts of the *H* Ghost. 875 8
given always to all godly Princes in *h* Scriptures 876 3
of the Father, and of the Son, and of the *H* Ghost, 876 32
are members of the *H* Catholic Church; 876 32
1. The *H* Scriptures of the Old and New Testament 877 14
(a) The *H* Scriptures of the Old and New Testaments, 877 33
H Days are intended for use at all public services 888 7
the Word takes the form given in the *H* Eucharist, 888 10
any other day in the same week, except on major *H* Days. 934 30

home

used, especially in the hospital or at *h*; 439 11
may be by God's blessing made towards *H* Reunion: 877 32

homilies

but likewise in her Articles and *H*, declared 9 23
XXXV. Of the *H*. 874 34
The Second Book of *H*, 874 35
the former Book of *H*, which were set forth 874 37
Of the Names of the *H* 875 1
so far as it declares the Books of *H* 875 14
the order for the reading of said *H* in churches, 875 17

homily

A sermon or *h*, a passage from Christian literature, 113 —
follows the Gospel and *h*. 274 —
After the Gospel (and *h*), 283 —
A *h* may be preached after any of the preceding 292 —
If a sermon or *h* was not preached earlier, 295 —
read, or a *h* preached. 319 —
read, or a *h* preached. 351 —
A *h* or other response to the Readings may follow. 426 —
After the Gospel (and *h*), the husband and wife stand 433 —
be seated for the Lessons and the *h*. 437 19
may be recited after the Lessons, or after the *h*, 437 20
A *h* may be preached, the people being seated. 480 —
Here there may be a *h* by the Celebrant, 495 —
5. A *h* may follow the Readings, 506 13
expressed in the *h* of Justification. 870 5

homoousios

(*h*) with the Father as regards his Godhead, 864 7

honesty

quiet and peaceable lives, in all godliness and *h*." 11 2

honor

"All glory, laud, and *h*" 271 —

honour

to everlasting salvation, as vessels made to *h*. 871 5

hope

The Christian *H* 861 —

hoped

They will appear, and it is to be *h*, the reasons 11 10
important work being brought to a conclusion, it is *h* 11 16

hospital

used, especially in the *h* or at home; 439 11
vicars of missions, *h* chaplains, and other priests 565 25

house

(Like a wise man who built his *h* upon the rock) 426 —
John 14:1–6 (In my Father's *h* are many mansions) 480 —
John 14:1–6 (In my Father's *h* are many rooms) 495 —
out of doors, in the parish *h*, 575 6
Adopted by the *H* of Bishops 876 23
the Quadrilateral was adopted by the *H* of Bishops, 877 26
enacted by the *H* of Deputies, but rather incorporated 877 27

houses

It is appropriate also for use in private *h*. 108 6
When this service is used in private *h*, 143 17

how

concerning the manner *h* to understand, do, 867 18
Of excommunicate Persons, *h* they are to be avoided. 874 16

however

h, the Collect, Preface, and one or more 16 14
When desired, *h*, the Collect of the Day, 136 —
h, the Collect (page 203 or 254) and one or more 414 —
This joy, *h*, does not make human grief unchristian. 507 10
In order to distinguish it, *h*, from "Lord" 583 28
At the discretion of the officiant, *h*, 934 27

human

common equity ought to be allowed to all *h* writings; 10 18
This joy, however, does not make *h* grief unchristian. 507 10
3. For the *H* Family 810 8
44. For the Future of the *H* Race 811 26
3. For the *H* Family 815 —
44. For the Future of the *H* Race 828 —
H Nature 845 —
and *H* Natures in the Person of Christ 864 2
of a reasonable soul and *h* flesh subsisting; 865 25
3. That in all things of *h* ordering or *h* choice, 876 33

humble

"Make them, O Lord, modest and *h*. . ." 554 25
See also the Prayer of *H* Access on page 337. 834 —

humility

and *h* to forego all preferences of her own; 876 35

hundred

in the Year of Our Lord One Thousand Seven *H* 8 5
one thousand seven *h* and ninety. 8 13

hurteth

and *h* the authority of the Magistrate, 874 29

husband

Celebrant joins the right hands of *h* and wife	428	—
The *h* and wife kneel,	430	—
The *h* and wife still kneeling,	431	—
After the Gospel (and homily), the *h* and wife stand	433	—
The Celebrant then addresses the *h*, saying	433	—
The *h* answers	433	—
(and the *h* extends his hand) toward the Priest,	434	—
The Celebrant joins the right hands of the *h* and wife	434	—
the union of the man and woman as *h* and wife,	436	—
6. Prayers are offered for the *h* and wife,	436	—
the *h* and wife first greeting each other.	436	—

hybrid

a *h* form which has been transliterated "Jehovah."	583	24

hymn

may be substituted for a *h* or anthem.	14	10
Here may be sung a *h* or anthem.	58	—
The following, or some other suitable *h*,	64	—
Here may be sung a *h* or anthem.	71	—
Here may be sung a *h* or anthem.	101	—
A suitable *h* may be sung.	103	—
The following *h*, or a metrical version of it,	112	—
or some other *h*, is then sung	112	—
or some other *h* of praise.	113	—
The following, or some other suitable *h*,	117	—
Here may be sung a *h* or anthem.	125	—
A *h* suitable for the evening may be sung.	132	—
A *h* or canticle may be used;	137	—
in place of a Canticle, a *h* may be sung.	142	1
or at the time of the *h* or anthem after the Collects.	142	12
and while the *h* Phos hilaron is being sung.	143	20
If an additional *h* is desired,	143	27
followed by a Psalm, Canticle, or *h*.	175	—
followed by a Psalm, Canticle, or *h*.	227	—
such as the *h* "All glory, laud,	271	—
A *h* may then be sung.	277	—
be concluded here with the singing of a *h* or anthem,	280	—
The *h* "Sing, my tongue, the glorious battle,"	282	—
or some other *h*	282	—
some other suitable psalm, canticle, or *h* may	288	—
or some other suitable psalm or a *h* may be sung.	295	—
A *h*, psalm, or anthem may be sung.	299	—
A Psalm, *h*, or anthem may follow each Reading.	300	—
If desired, the *h* Gloria in excelsis may be sung	312	18
or a *h* or anthem, may be sung.	312	32
a *h* or anthem, may be sung during the procession.	313	12
A *h*, psalm, or anthem may be sung.	319	—
A *h*, psalm, or anthem may be sung.	323	—
When appointed, the following *h* or some other song	324	—
A Psalm, *h*, or anthem may follow each Reading.	326	—
a *h*, psalm, or anthem may be sung.	333	—
A *h*, psalm, or anthem may be sung.	351	—
A *h*, psalm, or anthem may be sung.	355	—
When appointed, the following *h* or some other song	356	—
A Psalm, *h*, or anthem may follow each Reading.	357	—
a *h*, psalm, or anthem may be sung.	361	—
Gloria in excelsis, or the *h* used in place of it,	406	12
A *h* or anthem may then be sung,	407	1
during which time a communion *h* may be sung.	408	22
A *h* may be sung before or after	409	6
If desired, the *h* Gloria in excelsis may be sung	412	13
A *h*, psalm, or anthem may be sung.	413	—
A Psalm, *h*, or anthem may follow each Reading.	414	—
a *h*, psalm, or anthem may be sung,	423	—
A *h*, psalm, or anthem may follow.	425	—
a Psalm, *h*, or anthem may be sung or said.	426	—
A *h*, psalm, or anthem may be sung,	431	—
As the wedding party leaves the church, a *h*,	432	—
or *h* to be said, or something to be done,	446	24
the New Testament Lesson, a suitable canticle or *h*,	475	—
This anthem, or some other suitable anthem, or a *h*,	482	—
As the body is borne from the church, a *h*,	483	—
A *h*, psalm, or some other suitable anthem may	491	—
A suitable psalm, *h*, or canticle may follow.	494	—
A suitable psalm, *h*, or canticle may follow.	495	—
This anthem, or some other suitable anthem, or a *h*,	499	—
As the body is borne from the church, a *h*,	500	—
or a *h* may be sung.	506	8
A Psalm, canticle, or *h* follows each Reading.	516	—
After the Sermon, the Congregation sings a *h*.	516	—
The *h*, Veni Creator Spiritus,	520	—
or the *h*, Veni Sancte Spiritus,	520	—
A *h*, psalm, or anthem may be sung.	525	—
A Psalm, canticle, or *h* follows each Reading.	529	—
The *h*, Veni Creator Spiritus,	533	—
or the *h*, Veni Sancte Spiritus,	533	—
A *h*, psalm, or anthem may be sung.	537	—
A Psalm, canticle, or *h* follows each Reading.	541	—
The *h*, Veni Creator Spiritus,	544	—
or the *h*, Veni Sancte Spiritus,	544	—
The *h* to the Holy Spirit before the Prayer	552	14
pontifical blessing and the dismissal, a *h* of praise	553	14
A *h*, psalm, or anthem may be sung.	559	—
and any responses to it, the congregation sings a *h*.	560	—
music is now played, or a *h* or anthem sung.	572	—

hymns

H referred to in the rubrics of this Book	14	6
h, psalms, or anthems are sung,	271	—
During the ministration of Communion, *h*,	338	—
During the ministration of Communion, *h*,	365	—
Psalms, *h*, or anthems may follow the readings.	506	10
H, psalms, and anthems may be sung	512	—
H and anthems may also be sung.	568	—
H or psalms may be used in procession.	575	9
Selected verses of psalms and *h*,	576	4
introduce prayers and *h* as needed.	844	11

I

identical

When an alternative Lesson is cited, it is sometimes *i*	888	23

idiom

i may be conformed to traditional language.	14	5
Prayers originally composed in traditional *i*	814	—

idleness

20 Against *I*.	875	12

idolatry

2 Against Peril of *I*.	875	3

if

i allowed such just and favourable construction	10	17
I three Lessons are used,	47	—
I three Lessons are used,	65	—
I three Lessons are used,	84	—
I desired, the Collect of the Day may be used.	107	—
I three Lessons are used,	119	—
the Paschal Candle, *i* used, should be burning	143	3
I incense is to be used,	143	19
I an additional hymn is desired,	143	27
i the Sunday after Trinity Sunday is May 26,	158	16
I the Sunday after Trinity Sunday is June 13,	158	18
(substituting, *i* desired, the Gloria	175	—
(substituting, *i* desired, the Gloria	227	—
I ashes are to be imposed,	265	—
The Bishop, *i* present, or the Priest, stands and,	269	—
I desired, a wooden cross may now be brought	281	—
I the texts are recited rather than sung,	281	—
(the Celebrant *i* there is no deacon)	285	—
I candles have been distributed to members	286	—
I a sermon or homily was not preached earlier,	295	—
I a priest uses Chrism in signing the newly baptized,	298	14
the sign of the cross [using Chrism *i* desired]	308	—
I Confirmation, Reception, or the Reaffirmation	308	—
I there is no celebration of the Eucharist,	311	—
I on any one of the above-named days the ministry	312	8
I on the four days listed above there are no candidates	312	15
I desired, the hymn Gloria in excelsis may be sung	312	18
I the Presentation of the Candidates does not	312	28
I the movement to the font is a formal procession,	312	31
I there is reasonable doubt that a person	313	—
the given name of the one to be baptized (*i* known),	313	—
I the baptized person recovers,	314	—
I there is no celebration of the Communion,	330	—
or *i* a priest is not available,	330	—
A Confession of Sin is said here *i* it has not been said	330	—
I there is no celebration of the Communion,	359	—
or *i* a priest is not available,	359	—
A Confession of Sin is said here *i* it has not been said	359	—
I it is necessary to shorten the service,	396	8
or adapts the Proper Preface of the Day, *i* desired.	402	—
I the Sanctus is to be included,	402	—
or adapts the Proper Preface of the Day, *i* desired.	404	—
I the Sanctus is to be included,	404	—
I there is no Communion,	406	25
(*I* it is desired to include a Confession of Sin,	406	26
a deacon, or, *i* there is no deacon, by a lay reader.	407	6
I preferred, the exchange of the Peace	407	9
one chalice on the Altar, and, *i* need be, a flagon	407	19
I the consecrated Bread or Wine does not suffice	408	9
I any of the consecrated Bread or Wine remain,	408	28
I the priest knows that a person who is living	409	8
And *i* the person or persons on one side truly forgive	409	20
I desired, the hymn Gloria in excelsis may be sung	412	13
I there is no celebration of the Eucharist,	419	11
I there is to be a presentation or a giving in marriage,	425	—
I there is to be a Communion,	426	—
I Communion is to follow,	428	—
I there is not to be a Communion,	429	—
I a ring or rings are to be blessed,	434	—
I it is desired to celebrate a marriage otherwise	435	2
I there is to be a Communion,	435	16
8. *I* there is no Communion,	436	—
9. *I* there is to be a Communion,	436	—
I Banns are to be published, the following form	437	2
i there is to be a giving in marriage,	437	—
I more than one person responds,	437	—
or after the homily, *i* there is one.	437	—
Then *i* the child is old enough to answer,	441	—
not neglecting, *i* they are able, to leave bequests	445	—
I preferred, the confessor and penitent may sit	446	17
i the sick person's conscience is troubled,	454	—
I oil for the Anointing of the Sick is to be blessed,	455	—
I the person is to be anointed,	456	—
I Communion is not to follow,	456	—
I the Eucharist is to be celebrated,	457	—
I Communion is to be administered from the reserved	457	—
I the sick person cannot receive	457	—
I a person desires to receive the Sacrament,	457	—
I the Burial service is not to follow immediately,	467	—
I necessary, or *i* desired, all or part of the service	468	10
I preferred, the Committal service may take place	468	11
I there is to be a Communion,	470	—
I there is not to be a Communion,	480	—
I the body is not present,	482	5
Celebrant, or the Bishop *i* present, may then bless	483	—
I the grave is in a place that has not previously	487	—
I necessary, or *i* desired, all or part of the service	490	10
I preferred, the Committal service may take place	490	11
I there is to be a Communion,	494	—
I there is not to be a Communion,	496	—
I the body is not present,	499	—
Celebrant, or the Bishop *i* present, may then bless	500	—
I the grave is in a place that has not previously	503	—
I there is to be a Communion,	506	11
8. *I* there is a Communion,	506	21
with ancient custom, it is desirable, *i* possible,	511	3
I no objection is made, the Presiding Bishop continues	514	—
and may be lengthened *i* desired.	515	—
The new Bishop, *i* the Bishop of the Diocese,	522	—
presenters *i* desired, standing before the bishop,	526	—
I no objection is made, the Bishop continues	527	—
and may be lengthened *i* desired.	528	—
the Deacon or, *i* no deacon is present, a Priest reads	529	—
or a Priest *i* no deacon is present, dismisses	535	—
presenters *i* desired, standing before the bishop,	538	—
I no objection is made, the Bishop continues	539	—
and may be lengthened *i* desired.	540	—
the Deacon or, *i* no deacon is present, a Priest reads	541	—
On Ember Days or other occasions, *i* desired,	548	—
I vestments or other symbols of office are to be dedicated,	552	17
I two or more are ordained together,	553	25
I two or more are ordained together,	554	15
I there are many deacons, some assist	554	29
I the remaining Elements are not required	555	4
but, *i* necessary, a deputy may be appointed.	558	7
Other priests, *i* any, who serve	558	11
The new minister, *i* a deacon, should read	558	20
I the new minister is the rector or vicar of the parish,	562	—
The new Minister, *i* a priest, may then kneel	562	—
but *i* the new minister is a lay person,	564	—

A Deacon, or a Priest *i* no deacon is present, 564 —
I there are persons to be baptized, 569 —
I no Baptism is to take place 570 —
I the Apostles' Creed has not already been said, 572 —
I there is an organ, 575 10
I Holy Baptism is not to be administered, 575 24
I Baptism is to be administered, 575 28
I one reading stand is to serve as both lectern 576 6
I there is an address instead of a sermon, 576 11
I incense is to be used, 576 24
I the place of public worship is also to serve 576 29
I the church is also to be used for regular worship 577 1
and should be followed, *i* possible, by the administration 577 16
The word may, *i* desired, be omitted 584 8
i a man would search out by the ancient fathers, 866 6
And *i* any would judge this way more painful, 867 11
i those men will weigh their labor with the profit 867 13
to appease all such diversity (*i* any arise), 867 17
and *i* we say we have no sin, 870 29
or, *i* the Office is read only once in the day, 934 9
I two Readings are desired at both 934 12

illness
In case of *i*, the Minister of the Congregation 453 2
For the Sanctification of *I* 460 —

image
they be made like the *i* of his only-begotten Son 871 8

images
as well of *I* as of Relics, 872 13

immediately
the Eucharist is to follow *i*. 142 6
it may be sung *i* before the Blessing 143 27
When the Litany is sung or said *i* before the Eucharist, 153 —
The Collect *i* preceding and any of the sets 161 —
The Collect *i* preceding and any of the sets 213 —
When the Liturgy of the Palms *i* precedes the Eucharist, 272 —
I before the Collect, the Celebrant may say 276 —
I before the Canticle the Celebrant may say 294 —
Or this action may be done *i* after the administration 308 —
may be sung *i* after the opening versicles 312 18
the font is to be filled with clean water *i* 313 1
and then *i* deliver it to the people. 338 —
and then *i* deliver it to the people. 365 —
Great Litany is sung or said *i* before the Eucharist, 406 3
may be sung *i* after the opening versicles 412 13
and it is recommended that it take place *i* 453 9
If the Burial service is not to follow *i*, 467 —
When the order for the Burial of the Dead follows *i*, 467 —
Unless the Committal follows *i* in the church, 482 —
Unless the Committal follows *i* in the church, 499 —
and *i* before the Bible is presented. 553 23
and *i* before the Bible is given. 554 14

immerses
priest or deacon, who then *i*, or pours water upon, 307 —

imperishable
(The *i* body) 495 —

impiety
cannot be taught without arrogancy and *i*: 870 20

important
i considerations, according to the various exigency 9 18
And now, this *i* work being brought to a conclusion, 11 16

imposed
If ashes are to be *i*, the Celebrant says 265 —
The ashes are *i* with the following words 265 —

inapplicable
constitution and laws of England are considered as *i* 875 16

inauguration
or the *i* of other ministries, 558 4

incapable
the end of the world, and therefore *i* of compromise 877 9

incarnation
On Feasts of the *I* 44 —
On Feasts of the *I* 82 —
Christmas, Epiphany, and other Feasts of the *I* 111 —
Preface of the *I* 161 —
Preface of the *I* 162 3
Preface of the *I* 186 3
Preface of the *I* 192 3
4. Of the *I* 200 7
Preface of the *I* 213 3
Preface of the *I* 214 3
Preface of the *I* 237 10
Preface of the *I* 238 3
Preface of the *I* 243 —
4. Of the *I* 252 —
I 345 —
I 378 —
I of our Lord Jesus Christ. 865 20

incense
If *i* is to be used, it is appropriate after the candles 143 19
If *i* is to be used, it is appropriate at this time. 576 24

incised
marked in lasting form (*i*, painted, inlaid). 575 21

inclement
When the weather is *i*, 575 12

inclined
and is of his own nature *i* to evil, 869 26

include
understood to *i* "or sung," and vice versa. 14 12
selections *i* Psalms 19, 67, one or more sections 103 —
Psalms generally appropriate to the evening *i*: 143 24
Appropriate devotions may follow, which may *i* 281 —
The proclamation and response may *i* readings, 400 9
(If it is desired to *i* a Confession of Sin, 406 26
but which should *i* a reaffirmation 420 —

included
their ecclesiastical independence was necessarily *i*; 10 26
and penitence for our sins, be *i*. 140 —
the Gospel is always *i*. 142 21
It is fitting that parents be *i* among the godparents 298 24

a lesson from the Gospel is always *i*, 322 20
Additional petitions and thanksgivings may be *i* here. 330 —
a lesson from the Gospel is always *i*, 354 20
A reading from the Gospel is always *i*. 400 11
If the Sanctus is to be *i*, 402 —
If the Sanctus is to be *i*, 404 —
a Reading from the Gospel is always *i*. 435 17
The Lord's Prayer is always *i*. 453 5

includes

Proper of the Church Year *i* the appointed Collects; 158 3

including

Easter Season, *i* Ascension Day 39 —
Easter Season, *i* Ascension Day 77 —
or other suitable devotions, *i* the Lord's Prayer. 113 —
the opening sentences of Scripture, *i* those listed 141 3
6. Prayer, *i* the Lord's Prayer, 506 15
i vicars of missions and assistant ministers. 558 5
the Readings, *i* the Gospel, may be selected 565 11
7. Intercessions, *i* commemoration of benefactors 578 3

incomprehensible

The Father *i*, the Son *i*, and the Holy Ghost *i*. 864 32
but one uncreated, and one *i*. 864 37

incomprehensibles

As also there are not three *i*, 864 36

inconveniences

These *i* therefore considered, 866 33

incorporated

but rather *i* in a general plan referred for study 877 27

incorporates

I or adapts the Proper Preface of the Day, if desired. 402 —
i or adapts the Proper Preface of the Day, if desired. 404 —

incorruption

(Raised in *i*) 475 —

increased

i by virtue of prayer unto God. 873 19

increasingly

i favored by modern composers. 582 26

indebted

i, under God, for her first foundation 9 12

indented

biddings which follow, the *i* petitions may be adapted 277 —

independence

their ecclesiastical *i* was necessarily included; 10 26
I Day 17 5
I Day July 4 190 —
The Collect for *I* Day may be used instead. 207 —
I Day July 4 242 —
The Collect for *I* Day may be used instead. 258 —

independent

became *i* with respect to civil government, 10 25

indicate

When rubrics *i* that a part of a service is to be "said," 14 11
to *i* Psalms and verses of Psalms 935 2

indicated

(the *i* sections may be omitted) 286 —
they are used in the order *i*. 453 —
and perform other actions as *i* in the rubrics. 558 15
minister in charge takes part as *i*. 566 —

indicates

A bar in the margin *i* petitions which may be omitted. 383 —

indicating

The bishop may respond, *i* the place 576 13

indifferent

used therein, being things in their own nature *i*, 9 16

indissoluble

The bond which God establishes in Baptism is *i*. 298 4

individual

have some *i* or collective part in the celebration, 566 17

individually

i by their Sponsors, as follows 301 —
i by their Parents and Godparents, as follows 301 —

individuals

I and Families 136 —
In the exchange between *i* 407 8

inducted

for use when a priest is being instituted and *i* 558 2
In the bishop's absence, a priest being *i* 558 9
A newly *i* Priest may, at the bishop's request, 564 10

induction

The *I* 561 —
At the *I* of a priest or deacon, 564 4
The Institution, the Ministry of the Word, and the *I* 564 14
The Letter of Institution is appropriate for the *i* 564 17
remain in the sight of the congregation during the *I*. 565 22

industry

II. For commerce and *i* 208 —
II. For commerce and *i* 259 —
Prayers for *I* and Labor are on pages 208, 210, 811 19
For prayers for *I* and Labor, 824 —

infants

Sponsors of *i*, commonly called godparents, present 298 21
I and Younger Children 301 —
on behalf of the *i* and younger children 302 —

infection

And this *i* of nature doth remain, yea in them 869 28

inferior

and *i* to the Father, as touching his Manhood. 865 26

infinite

of *i* power, wisdom, and goodness; 867 36

inflamed

more in the knowledge of God, and be the more *i* 866 14

influence

39. For those who *I* Public Opinion 811 18
39. For those who *I* Public Opinion 827 —

inform
administers emergency Baptism should *i* the priest 314 3

inherent
As *i* parts of this sacred deposit, 877 12

initial
the Reader should omit *i* conjunctions 888 25

initiation
3. Christian *I*, or the Renewal of Baptismal Vows. 284 8
Holy Baptism is full *i* by water and the Holy Spirit 298 2

injunctions
or of the Sacraments, the which thing the *I* 876 1

inlaid
marked in lasting form (incised, painted, *i*). 575 21

innocents
The Holy *I* 17 5
serve for any weekdays between Holy *I'* Day 161 —
The Holy *I* December 28 186 —
serve for any weekdays between Holy *I'* Day 213 —
The Holy *I* December 28 238 —

inquiring
teaching for an *i* stranger who picks up a Prayer Book. 844 8

inquiry
the discipline of the Church, that *i* be made of evil 873 10

insertions
Adaptations or *i* suitable to the occasion may 383 —

inside
i the altar rails or in a place set aside 446 16
the congregation may assemble *i* the church; 575 13

insignia
i of office may be presented. 553 7
or other *i* of the office of priest, 553 21
or other *i* of the office of deacon, 554 12

insomuch
i that by them a lively Faith may be as evidently known 870 10
i that to such as rightly, worthily, and with faith, 873 25

inspiration
and the *I* of his Spirit, are not pleasant 870 13

installation
It may also be used for the *i* of deans 558 3

instance
in each *i*, use the bracketed Psalms 935 6

instances
In some *i*, the entire portion of the Psalter 935 3

instead
The text of the Creed on page 96 may be used *i*. 54 —
The text of the Creed on page 120 may be used *i*. 66 —
in the Daily Offices, may be used *i*. 136 12
Worship for the Evening, page 109, may be used *i*. 139 —
Collect "For the Nation," page 207, may be used *i*. 190 —
the Burial of the Dead may be used *i*. 202 —
The Collect for Independence Day may be used *i*. 207 —
Collect "For the Nation," page 258, may be used *i*. 242 —
the Burial of the Dead may be used *i*. 253 —
The Collect for Independence Day may be used *i*. 258 —
i, a declaration of forgiveness is provided. 446 14
or some other suitable anthem may be sung *i*. 491 —
prayer suitable to the occasion, may be used *i*. 565 9
If there is an address *i* of a sermon, 576 11
I of the Proper Preface suggested, 576 25
in the selected Sunday Proper may be used *i*. 888 17

instituted
This order is for use when a priest is being *i* 558 2
A lay person being *i* should read one of the Lessons 558 23

institution
Prayer C, ending with the narrative of the *I*). 408 16
Letter of *I* of a Minister 557 1
The *I* 559 —
The Bishop may read the Letter of *I*, 559 —
The *I*, the Ministry of the Word, 564 14
The Letter of *I* is appropriate for the induction 564 17
which be effectual, because of Christ's *i* 873 8
agreeable with the *i* of Christ. 873 21
unfailing use of Christ's words of *i* 877 17
—ministered with unfailing use of Christ's words of *I*, 878 2

institutions
37. For Prisons and Correctional *I* 811 16
37. For Prisons and Correctional *I* 826 —

instruct
the Congregation is directed to *i* the people, 445 —

instructed
Parents and godparents are to be *i* in the meaning 298 25

instruction
and lay catechists, to give an outline for *i*. 844 3
for example of life and *i* of manners; 868 35

instructive
and *i* in piety and morals. 875 15

instrument
When an *i* of music is to be dedicated, 572 1
whereby, as by an *i*, they that receive Baptism rightly 873 16

instrumental
On occasion, and as appropriate, *i* music 14 9
i music, other art forms, silence. 400 10
or *i* music may be played. 423 —
A hymn, psalm, or anthem may be sung, or *i* music 431 —
or *i* music may be played. 432 —
i music may be played. 553 3
singing and *i* music are appropriate. 567 —
I music is now played, or a hymn or anthem sung. 572 —
or *i* music may be used 576 4

instruments
other *i* or symbols of office may be given. 553 24
The use of portable musical *i* is suitable. 575 10

intended

This form is *i* for use with those 396 —
It is not *i* for use at the principal Sunday 400 4
This catechism is primarily *i* for use 844 2
Holy Days are *i* for use at all public services 888 7

intending

from *i* to depart from the Church of England 11 13
read over once in the year, *i* thereby, that the Clergy, 866 9

intends

i to come to Communion, the priest shall speak 409 9

intention

signify their endorsement of the candidates and their *i* 298 19
which may be in the form either of a statement of *i* 420 —
2. The *i* of the man and the woman to enter the state 435 13
and is, the *i* and purpose of this Church to maintain 510 19

intentions

the congregation to express *i* or objects of prayer 142 8

intercession

the Eucharist or a form of general *i* is to follow, 57 —
the Eucharist or a form of general *i* is to follow, 70 —
the Eucharist or a form of general *i* is to follow, 100 —
the Eucharist or a form of general *i* is to follow, 124 —
I is offered according to the following form, 328 —
Prayer is offered with *i* 359 —
Prayer is offered with *i* 383 —
the service continues with the following prayer of *i*, 480 —

intercessions

Authorized *i* and thanksgivings may follow. 58 —
Authorized *i* and thanksgivings may follow. 71 —
Authorized *i* and thanksgivings may follow. 101 —
Free *i* may be offered. 107 —
Authorized *i* and thanksgivings may follow. 125 —
Silence may be kept, and free *i* 134 —
In the *I* and Thanksgivings, 142 —
The *I* on such occasions are to conform 142 —
included, and that the *i* conform 322 20
included, and that the *i* conform 354 20
7. *I*, including commemoration of benefactors 578 3

interrupts

When a Major Feast *i* the sequence of Readings, 934 17

intricate

the Book only, was so hard and *i* a matter, 866 31

introduce

The Celebrant may *i* the Scripture readings 288 —
The Celebrant may *i* the Prayers with a sentence 383 —
i the Creed with these or similar words 496 —
i prayers and hymns as needed. 844 11

introduced

If the Sanctus is to be included, it is *i* with these 402 —
If the Sanctus is to be included, it is *i* with these 404 —

introduction

complete rite in place of Evening Prayer, or as the *i* 108 4
Reading some such *i* as, "N. said (to N.)." 888 28

invaluable

It is a most *i* part of that blessed "liberty 9 2

invented

Invocation of Saints, is a fond thing, vainly *i*, 872 13

invention

and in printed Bibles, after the *i* of vowel points, 583 22

invisible

of all things both visible and *i*. 867 37

invisibly

by the which he doth work *i* in us, 872 28

invitation

by an appropriate *i* and a penitential psalm. 269 —
the Celebrant may say the following *I* 338 —
the Celebrant says the following *I* 364 —
introduce the Prayers with a sentence of *i* 383 —
The Celebrant may say the following *I* 399 —
(before or after the sentence of *I*). 407 11
the person comes forward at the *i* of the celebrant, 420 —

invitatories

I, and such like things, as did break 866 38

invited

Churches may appropriately be *i* to participate. 558 19
Neighboring ministers should be *i* to participate, 566 14

invites

i the people to the observance of a holy Lent, saying 264 —
At the proper time, the Celebrant *i* the parents 439 17

invocation

I *I* 47 —
it begins with the *I* and concludes with the Doxology. 88 —
I 88 —
and ending with the *I* 408 15
I of Saints, is a fond thing, vainly invented, 872 13

Isaac

Abraham's sacrifice of *I* 289 —

Isaiah

I 40:3 37 —
I 40:5 37 —
I 60:3 38 —
I 49:6b 38 —
I 54:6 39 —
I 57:15 41 —
I 40:3 75 —
I 40:5 75 —
I 60:3 76 —
I 40:6b 76 —
I 53:6 77 —
I 57:15 78 —
9 The First Song of *I* Ecce, Deus 86 —
I 12:2–6 86 —
10 The Second Song of *I* Quaerite Dominum 86 —
I 55:6–11 86 —
11 The Third Song of *I* Surge, illuminare 87 —
I 60:1–3, 11a, 14c, 18–19 87 —
I 60:19–20 (Advent) 108 16
I 60:1–3 (Epiphany) 108 19

I 26:3; 30:15 138 —
Old Testament Joel 2:1–2, 12–17, or *I* 58:1–12 264 —
Old Testament *I* 45:21–25, or *I* 52:13–53:12 272 —
Old Testament *I* 52:13–53:12, or Genesis 22:1–18, 276 —
I 4:2–6 290 —
I 55:1–11 290 —
Canticle 9, The First Song of *I*, or Psalm 42:1–7 290 —
Psalm 42:1–7, or Canticle 9, The First Song of *I* 290 —
I 25:6–9 (He will swallow up death in victory) 470 —
I 61:1–3 (To comfort all that mourn) 470 —
I 25:6–9 (He will swallow up death for ever) 494 —
I 6:1–3 (To comfort those who mourn) 494 —
Old Testament *I* 61:1–8, or *I* 42:1–9 515 —
Old Testament *I* 6:1–8, or Numbers 11:16–17, 24–25 528 —
in this sort the book of *I* was begun in Advent, 866 20

Israel

I's deliverance at the Red Sea 289 —
God's Presence in a renewed *I* 290 —

issued

for a review was *i* in the year 1689: 10 21

italics

the congregation reads the parts in *i*. 281 —
the lines in *i* are spoken by the People. 369 —
pronouns and verbs have been put in *i* 814 —
The responses in *i* may be omitted 821 6

J

James

Saint *J* of Jerusalem 17 4
Saint Philip and Saint *J* May 1 189 —
Saint *J* July 25 191 —
Saint *J* of Jerusalem October 23 193 —
Saint Philip and Saint *J* May 1 240 —
Saint *J* July 25 242 —
Saint *J* of Jerusalem October 23 245 —
J 5:14–16 (Is any among you sick?) 454 6
Psalm 23 King *J* Version 476 —
and the King *J* Old Testament, 583 27
Christ, and *J* his Apostle, so we judge, 876 19

January

The Epiphany, *J* 6 15 18
The Holy Name *J* 1 162 —
The Epiphany *J* 6 162 —
Confession of Saint Peter *J* 18 187 —
Conversion of Saint Paul *J* 25 187 —
The Holy Name *J* 1 213 —
The Epiphany *J* 6 214 —
Confession of Saint Peter *J* 18 238 —
Conversion of Saint Paul *J* 25 238 —

Jehovah

a hybrid form which has been transliterated "*J*." 583 24

Jeremiah

J 14:9,22 131 —
J 14:9,22 140 —
Old Testament *J* 1:4–9, or Ecclesiasticus 39:1–8 540 —

Jerusalem

Saint James of *J* 17 4
Saint James of *J* October 23 193 —
Saint James of *J* October 23 245 —
Church of *J*, Alexandria, and Antioch, have erred; 871 33

Jesus

and majestic manner, for the sake of *J* Christ, 11 22
All Sundays of the year are feasts of our Lord *J* Christ. 16 2
J Christ our Lord. 403 —
J Christ our Lord. 404 —
Hebrews 12:1–2 (Looking to *J*, the perfecter 454 2
Because *J* was raised from the dead, 507 3
the love of God in Christ *J* our Lord." 507 9
J himself wept at the grave of his friend. 507 12
says over each ordinand "Father, through *J* Christ 553 32
and say over each one "Father, through *J* Christ 554 21
our Lord *J* Christ, at once complete in Godhead 864 5
God the Word, Lord *J* Christ; 864 16
and our Lord *J* Christ himself taught us, 864 17
Incarnation of our Lord *J* Christ. 865 20
that we believe and confess, that our Lord *J* Christ, 865 21
The Book of Tobias, *J* the Son of Sirach 868 39
only for the merit of our Lord and Saviour *J* Christ 870 2
forasmuch as they spring not of faith in *J* Christ; 870 14
the image of his only-begotten Son *J* Christ: 871 9
the Name of *J* Christ, whereby men must be saved. 871 28
forbidden Christian men by our Lord *J* Christ 876 18

Job

Old Testament *J* 14:1–14 283 —
J 19:21–27a (I know that my Redeemer liveth) 470 —
J 19:21–27a (I know that my Redeemer lives) 494 —
The Book of *J*, 868 27

Joel

J 2:13 38 —
J 2:13 76 —
J 2:28–30 (Whitsunday) 108 18
Old Testament *J* 2:1–2, 12–17, or Isaiah 58:1–12 264 —

John

Saint *J* the Baptist 16 27
1 *J* 1:8, 9 38 —
J 4:23 40 —
J 8:12 62 —
1 *J* 1:8, 9 76 —
J 4:23 78 —
J 1:1–5 (Christmas) 108 18
1 *J* 1:5–7 (Lent) 108 20
J 12:35–36a (Lent) 108 21
J 8:12 116 —
Saint *J* December 27 186 —
The Nativity of Saint *J* the Baptist June 24 190 —
Saint *J* December 27 238 —
The Nativity of Saint *J* the Baptist June 24 241 —
Gospel *J* 13:1–15, or Luke 22:14–30 274 —
J 18:1–19:37 or 19:1–37 277 —
the arrival at Golgotha (*J* 19:17) all stand. 277 —
Gospel Matthew 27:57–66, or *J* 19:38–42 283 —
1 *J* 1:8, 9 320 —
J 3:16 332 —
1 *J* 2:1–2 332 —

1 *J* 1:8, 9 352 —
J 3:16 396 —
J 6:35 396 —
J 6:51, 55–56 397 —
J 15: 4–5a, 8-9 397 —
1 *J* 4:7–16 (Let us love one another 426 —
J 15:9–12 (Love one another 426 —
J 3:16 449 —
1 *J* 2:1–2 450 —
1 *J* 5:13–15 (That you may know 454 10
J 6:47–51 (I am the bread of life) 454 12
the passages from Lamentations, 1 *J*, 468 19
J 6, together with Psalm 23, are recommended. 468 20
1 *J* 3:1–2 (We shall be like him) 475 —
J 5:24–27 (He that believeth hath everlasting life) 480 —
J 6:37–40 (All that the Father giveth me 480 —
J 10:11–16 (I am the good shepherd) 480 —
J 11:21–27 (I am the resurrection and the life) 480 —
J 14:1–6 (In my Father's house are many mansions) 480 —
the passages from Lamentations, 1 *J*, 490 19
J 6, together with Psalm 23, are recommended. 490 20
1 *J* 3:1–2 (We shall be like him) 495 —
J 5:24–27 (He who believes has everlasting life) 495 —
J 6:37–40 (All that the Father gives me 495 —
J 10:11–16 (I am the good shepherd) 495 —
J 11:21–27 (I am the resurrection and the life) 495 —
J 14:1–6 (In my Father's house are many rooms) 495 —
J 20:19–23, or *J* 17:1–9, 18–21, 516 —
Matthew 9:35–38, or *J* 10:11–18, or *J* 6:35–38 529 —
Gospel *J* 15:9–16, or Luke 10:1–2, or *J* 14:11–15 560 —
and sin (as Saint *J* saith) was not in him. 870 28

join

and *j* in the consecration of the gifts, 322 8
The People may *j* in saying 337 —
The People may *j* in saying this prayer 339 —
and *j* in the consecration of the gifts, 354 8
come together to *j* in the Litany. 462 —
to be given for the priests present to *j* 553 19
take part in the exchange of the Peace, and *j* 554 7

joined

j by other bishops and presbyters, 522 —
and *j* by the other clergy, 563 —
j together in one Person, never to be divided, 868 5
several titles whereof we have *j* under this Article, 874 35

joins

the Celebrant *j* the right hands of husband and wife 428 —
Celebrant *j* the right hands of the husband and wife 434 —
Priest *j* in the celebration of the Holy Eucharist 535 —

joint

to a newly created *J* Commission on Christian Reunion. 877 28

Joseph

Saint *J* 17 6
Saint *J* March 19 188 —
Saint *J* March 19 239 —

Joshua

Old Testament *J* 1:7–9, or Numbers 11:16–17, 24–25a 560 —
J, 868 31

joy

The liturgy, therefore, is characterized by *j*, 507 5
j, however, does not make human grief unchristian. 507 10
1. For *J* in God's Creation 810 6
1. For *J* in God's Creation 814 —

Jubilate

follows one of the Invitatory Psalms, Venite or *J*. 42 —
J Psalm 100 45 —
follows one of the Invitatory Psalms, Venite or *J*. 80 —
J Psalm 100 82 —

Jude

Saint Simon and Saint *J* October 28 194 —
Saint Simon and Saint *J* October 28 245 —

judge

in such manner as they might *j* 10 29
whence he shall come to *j* the quick and the dead. 865 34
And if any would *j* this way more painful, 867 11
until he return to *j* all Men at the last day. 868 15
And those we ought to *j* lawfully called and sent, 872 18
as they shall *j* the same to serve better 874 14
by a *J* that hath authority thereunto. 874 20
we *j* them to be read in Churches by the Ministers, 874 38
so we *j*, that Christian Religion doth not prohibit, 876 19

Judges

J, The First Book of Esdras, 868 32

judgment

although, according to her *j*, there be not any thing 10 14
put away our sins, and endure the severity of God's *j*; 870 8
finally, being found guilty, by just *j* be deposed. 873 12
through his private *j*, willingly and purposely, 874 25
to the Prophet's teaching in justice, *j*, and truth. 876 21

Judith

The Book of *J*, 868 40

July

Proper 9 The Sunday closest to *J* 6 179 —
Proper 10 The Sunday closest to *J* 13 179 —
Proper 11 The Sunday closest to *J* 20 179 —
Proper 12 The Sunday closest to *J* 27 180 —
Independence Day *J* 4 190 —
Saint Mary Magdalene *J* 22 191 —
Saint James *J* 25 191 —
Proper 9 The Sunday closest to *J* 6 230 —
Proper 10 The Sunday closest to *J* 13 231 —
Proper 11 The Sunday closest to *J* 20 231 —
Proper 12 The Sunday closest to *J* 27 231 —
Independence Day *J* 4 242 —
Saint Mary Magdalene *J* 22 242 —
Saint James *J* 25 242 —

June

Sunday is *J* 13, the sequence begins with Proper 6 158 19
Proper 4 The Sunday closest to *J* 1 177 —
Proper 5 The Sunday closest to *J* 8 178 —
Proper 6 The Sunday closest to *J* 15 178 —
Proper 7 The Sunday closest to *J* 22 178 —
Proper 8 The Sunday closest to *J* 29 178 —
Saint Barnabas *J* 11 189 —
The Nativity of Saint John the Baptist *J* 24 190 —

Saint Peter and Saint Paul *J* 29 190 —
Proper 4 The Sunday closest to *J* 1 229 —
Proper 5 The Sunday closest to *J* 8 229 —
Proper 6 The Sunday closest to *J* 15 230 —
Proper 7 The Sunday closest to *J* 22 230 —
Proper 8 The Sunday closest to *J* 29 230 —
Saint Barnabas *J* 11 241 —
The Nativity of Saint John the Baptist *J* 24 241 —
Saint Peter and Saint Paul *J* 29 241 —

jurisdiction

and is not, nor ought to be, subject to any foreign *J*. 875 42
The Bishop of Rome hath no *j* in this Realm 876 7

just

upon *j* and weighty considerations her thereunto moving, 10 3
if allowed such *j* and favourable construction 10 17
finally, being found guilty, by *j* judgment be deposed. 873 12

justice

and understanding to execute *j*, 11 1
21. For Social *J* 209 —
21. For Social *J* 260 —
21. For Courts of *J* 810 30
27. For Social *J* 811 6
21. For Courts of *J* 821 —
27. For Social *J* 823 —
Prophet's teaching in *j*, judgment, and truth. 876 21

justification

XI. Of the *J* of Man. 870 1
expressed in the Homily of *J*. 870 5
which are the fruits of Faith, and follow after *J*, 870 7
XIII. Of Works before *J*. 870 12

justified

Wherefore, that we are *j* by Faith only, 870 3
they be *j* freely: 871 7

K

kalendar

a readiness in this matter, here is drawn out a *K* 866 34

keep

accordingly, that, seeking to *k* the happy mean 9 25
Which Faith except everyone do *k* whole 864 23

keeper

although the Church be a witness and a *k* of Holy Writ, 871 40

keeping

3 Of repairing and *k* clean of Churches. 875 4

kept

provided the substance of the Faith be *k* 9 4
Silence may be *k*. 41 —
Silence may be *k* after each Reading. 47 —
Silence may be *k*. 62 —
Silence may be *k* after each Reading. 65 —
Silence may be *k*. 79 —
Silence may be *k* after each Reading. 84 —
sung, or silence *k*. 112 —
Silence may be *k*. 116 —
Silence may be *k* after each Reading. 119 —
Silence may be *k*. 127 —
Silence may be *k*, 134 —
Silence is then *k* for a time, all kneeling. 265 —
silence may be *k*; 288 —
Silence may be *k*. 309 —
Silence may be *k*. 320 —
Silence may be *k*. 330 —
A period of silence is *k*. 337 —
Silence may be *k*. 352 —
Silence may be *k*. 360 —
A period of silence is *k*. 364 —
Silence may be *k*. 393 —
Silence may be *k*; 466 —
Silence may be *k*; 467 —
Silence may be *k*; 493 —
Silence may be *k*. 497 —

keys

present the *k* of the church, saying 562 —
the *k*, and tools used in its construction 575 18

kind

1 Corinthians 13:1–13 (Love is patient and *k*) 426 —
suitable to administer the Sacrament in one *k* only. 457 —

kindle

because it doth fervently *k* their love towards God: 871 16

kindled

In the darkness, fire is *k*; 285 —
Paschal Candle is then lighted from the newly *k* fire, 285 —

kinds

The ministers receive the Sacrament in both *k*, 338 —
The ministers receive the Sacrament in both *k*, 365 —
celebrant receives the Sacrament in both *k*. 407 23
received in both *k* simultaneously, 408 1
or else the celebrant may consecrate more of both *k*, 408 13
XXX. Of both *K*. 874 1

king

Psalm 23 *K* James Version 476 2
Psalter and the *K* James Old Testament, 583 27
See also the prayer "O God, the *K* of Saints," 838 —
since the second year of the forenamed *K* 875 31
"The *K*'s Majesty hath the chief power 875 39
attribute to the *K*'s Majesty the chief government, 875 43

kings

Old Testament 1 *K* 8:22–23, 27b–30, 571 —
The First Book of *K*, 868 28
The Second Book of *K*, 868 29

kneel

The people stand or *k* 54 —
The people stand or *k* 67 —
The people stand or *k* 97 —
The people stand or *k* 121 —
All then *k* for silent prayer, 276 —
The people may be directed to stand or *k*. 277 —
The people *k* or stand. 334 —
The people *k* or stand. 341 —

The people stand or *k*. 362 —
The people stand or *k*. 368 —
The people stand or *k*. 373 —
The husband and wife *k*, 430 —
All *k*, and the Person appointed leads the Litany 515 —
All *k*, and the Person appointed leads the Litany 527 —
All *k*, and the Person appointed leads the Litany 539 —
The new Minister, if a priest, may then *k* 562 —

kneeling

Officiant and People together, all *k* 41 —
using the preceding form remains *k*, 42 —
Officiant and People together, all *k* 62 —
using the preceding form remains *k*, 63 —
Officiant and People together, all *k* 79 —
using the preceding form remains *k*, 80 —
Officiant and People together, all *k* 116 —
using the preceding form remains *k*, 117 —
To be said or sung, *k*, standing, or in procession; 148 —
Silence is then kept for a time, all *k*. 265 —
The Celebrant and People together, all *k* 267 —
A deacon or lay reader leading the service remains *k* 269 —
The Decalogue, page 317, may be said, the people *k*. 319 —
The Decalogue may be said, the people *k*. 351 —
The husband and wife still *k*, the Priest adds 431 —
The Litany may be sung or said standing or *k*, 565 6

kneels

and the penitent *k* nearby. 446 17
All continue to stand, except the bishop-elect, who *k* 520 —
All now stand except the ordinand, who *k* 533 —
All now stand except the ordinand, who *k* 544 —

know

(That you may *k* that you have eternal life) 454 10
Job 19:21–27a (I *k* that my Redeemer liveth) 470 —
Job 19:21–27a (I *k* that my Redeemer lives) 494 —

knowledge

duties to help the new Christians grow in the *k* 298 26
40. For *K* of God's Creation 811 22
40. For *K* of God's Creation 827 —
continually profit more and more in the *k* of God, 866 14
men will weigh their labor with the profit in *k*, 867 13
accused by those that have *k* of their offences; 873 11

known

Using the given name of the one to be baptized (if *k*), 313 24
times generally *k* as priests. 510 9
the Christian name by which he wishes to be *k*. 511 20
Christian name by which he wishes to be *k*. 524 11
Christian name by which he wishes to be *k*. 536 11
familiar from its use in many well-*k* anthems. 584 8
a lively Faith may be as evidently *k* as a tree 870 10
ought to be ministered in a *k* tongue. 875 12

knows

If the priest *k* that a person who is living 409 8
(The Lord *k* the ways of the righteous; 583 6

Kyrie

14 A Song of Penitence *K* Pantokrator 90 4
continues with the *K* eleison, the Trisagion, 321 —
continues with the Gloria in excelsis, the *K* eleison, 353 —
The *K* eleison (or "Lord, have mercy") may be sung 406 9

Kyries

the Litany concludes with the *K*, 406 4
At the end of the litany, after the *K*, 515 —
At the end of the litany, after the *K*, 527 —
At the end of the litany, after the *K*, 539 —

L

labor

25. For *L* Day 210 —
25. For *L* Day 261 —
Prayers for Industry and *L* 811 19
For prayers for Industry and *L*, 824 —
if those men will weigh their *l* with the profit 867 13

lacking

carnal persons, *l* the Spirit of Christ, 871 17

laid

Book of Common Prayer, *l* it down as a rule, 9 14
yet upon the principles already *l* down, 10 19
When they have *l* their hands upon all 554 2
(before the foundations of the world were *l*) 871 3

laity

By the Bishops, the Clergy, and the *L* 8 3
the presbyterate, diaconate, and *l* of the diocese 511 9
As established by the Bishops, the Clergy, and the *L* 867 30
Magistrate extendeth to all men, as well Clergy as *L*, 875 35

lamb

18 A Song to the *L* Dignus es 93 —
He came to be the *L* 870 26

Lambeth

The Chicago-*L* Quadrilateral 1886, 1888 876 22
L Conference of 1888 877 29

Lamentations

L 1:12 39 —
L 1:12 77 —
At the burial of a child, the passages from *L*, 468 19
L 3:22–26, 31–33 (The Lord is good unto them 470 —
At the burial of a child, the passages from *L*, 490 19
L 3:22–26, 31–33 (The Lord is good to those 494 —

lamps

now lighted, as are other candles and *l* 112 —
Other candles and *l* in the church, 286 —

land

Christians of the different Communions in this *l*, 876 27
in our own *l*, we hereby declare our desire 877 21

lands

42. For the Harvest of *L* and Waters 811 24
42. For the Harvest of *L* and Waters 828 —

language

idiom may be conformed to traditional *l*. 14 5
Any of the prayers in contemporary *l* may be adapted 108 22
traditional *l* by changing the pronouns 108 23

Any of the forms may be conformed to the *l* 383 —
read the Gospel in the *l* of the people, 406 23
l spoken to the people in the Church, 866 23
l and order as is most easy and plain 867 3
same in any *l* that they themselves do understand. 867 26

large

symbols presented should be *l* enough to be visible 565 21

largely

and very full of comfort, as more *l* is expressed 870 4

last

but not from the *L* Sunday after Pentecost 16 16
or from the *L* Sunday after the Epiphany 16 17
L Sunday after the Epiphany 165 —
L Sunday after the Epiphany 217 —
If there is to be a Communion, the *l* Reading 506 11
until he return to judge all Men at the *l* day. 868 15

lasting

the threshold by the bishop may be marked in *l* form 575 20

late

on suitable occasions in the *l* afternoon or evening. 108 3
now of *l* time a few of them have been daily said 866 28
commodious, than that which of *l* was used. 866 44

lately

and Ordering of Priests and Deacons, *l* set forth 875 27
l set forth by Elizabeth our Queen do 876 2

later

Lessons are to be read *l* in the service, 143 9

Latin

rather than the *L* form "Alleluia," 584 6
read in *L* to the people, which they understood not; 866 25

laud

sung, such as the hymn "All glory, *l*, 271 —

law

by civil *l* that deacons may perform marriages, 422 15
Where permitted by civil *l*, 435 5
The Summary of the *L*, the Gloria in excelsis, 552 5
Although the *L* given from God by Moses, 869 10
not subject to the *L* of God. 869 30
saved by the *L* or Sect which he professeth, 871 26
to frame his life according to that *L*, 871 27
and Deacons, are not commanded by God's *L*, 874 12

lawful

and yet it is not *l* for the Church to ordain 871 38
It is not *l* for any man to take upon him the office 872 16
therefore it is *l* for them, 874 13
It is *l* for Christian men, at the commandment 876 10

lawfully

before he be *l* called, and sent to execute 872 17
And those we ought to judge *l* called and sent, 872 18
be rightly, orderly, and *l* consecrated and ordered. 875 25
be rightly, orderly, and *l* consecrated and ordered." 875 33

laws

and *l* of their country. 10 31
conform to the *l* of the State and the canons 422 6
The *l* of the State and the canons of this Church 435 7
the constitution and *l* of England are considered 875 16
The *L* of the Realm may punish Christian men 876 8

lay

members of each order within the Church, *l* persons, 13 17
but, like *l* persons, may officiate 13 22
clerical or *l*, who leads the Office. 36 4
A deacon or *l* person using the preceding form 42 —
A deacon or *l* person using the preceding form 63 —
clerical or *l*, who leads the Office. 74 3
A deacon or *l* person using the preceding form 80 —
parts of this service may be led by *l* persons. 108 7
A deacon or *l* person using the preceding blessing 114 —
A deacon or *l* person using the preceding form 117 —
A deacon or *l* reader leading the service remains 269 —
led by a deacon or *l* reader. 269 —
led by a deacon or *l* reader. 272 —
The Passion Gospel may be read or chanted by *l* 273 —
The Passion Gospel may be read or chanted by *l* 277 —
led by a deacon or *l* reader. 282 —
ordained ministers present, together with *l* readers, 284 10
L persons read the Lessons, and the Epistle, 284 20
l person may be assigned to chant the Exsultet. 284 21
a bishop or priest, a deacon or *l* reader may lead 284 23
L persons may act as readers, 312 24
Exhortation may be read by a *l* person. 316 —
A deacon or *l* person using the preceding form 321 —
and by deacons and *l* persons. 322 6
L persons appointed by the celebrant 322 15
or *l* a hand upon it; 334 —
or *l* a hand upon it; 342 —
A deacon or *l* person using the preceding form 353 —
and by deacons and *l* persons. 354 6
L persons appointed by the celebrant 354 15
or *l* a hand upon it; 362 —
or *l* a hand upon it; 368 —
or *l* a hand upon it; 371 —
or *l* a hand upon it; 374 —
or *l* a hand upon it; 403 —
or *l* a hand upon it; 405 —
or, if there is no deacon, by a *l* reader. 407 6
l persons licensed by the bishop 408 7
and the Epistles be read by *l* persons. 422 19
to be used by a Deacon or *L* Person 448 —
to be used by a Deacon or *L* Person 452 —
service may always be led by a deacon or *l* person. 453 6
A deacon or *l* person using the preceding form 455 —
a deacon or *l* person may perform the anointing, 456 —
be read by *l* persons. 468 16
a deacon or *l* reader may preside at the service. 468 17
be read by *l* persons. 490 16
a deacon or *l* reader may preside at the service. 490 17
L Persons, standing before the Presiding Bishop, 513 —
L persons read the Old Testament Lesson 515 —
Presiding Bishop and other Bishops now *l* their hands 521 —
A Priest and a *L* Person, 526 —
L persons read the Old Testament Lesson 528 —
A Priest and a *L* Person, 538 —
L persons read the Old Testament Lesson 540 —
the bishop and priests *l* their hands 553 30
the Prayer of Consecration the Bishop is to *l* hands 554 20

L persons from the congregation read 558 14
A *l* person being instituted should read 558 23
but if the new minister is a *l* person, 564 6
L persons read the Old Testament Lesson 571 —
dedication of the font, children or other *l* persons 575 23
by a donor, or a *l* reader, or another suitable person. 576 10
or other *l* person outline the plans 576 12
or other *l* persons, bring them forward 576 23
and *l* catechists, to give an outline for instruction. 844 3
Cup of the Lord is not to be denied to the *L*-people: 874 2

laying

of their Baptism and to receive the *l* on of hands 412 5
baptized as adults, unless baptized with *l* on hands 412 7
of a bishop and to receive the *l* on of hands. 412 10
When the *L* on of Hands or Anointing takes place 453 7
Part II. *L* on of Hands and Anointing 455 —
by solemn prayer and the *l* on of episcopal hands. 510 18
such ordination with the *l* on of hands 510 23
Priests who are present also *l* on their hands. 533 —
to join in the *l* on of hands. 553 20
During the *l* on of hands, 553 31
After *l* hands upon all the ordinands, 554 23

lays

The Bishop *l* hands upon each one and says 309 —
The Bishop *l* hands upon each one and says 418 —
The Priest then *l* a hand upon the penitent's head 451 —
The Priest then *l* hands upon the sick person, 455 —
Bishop *l* hands upon the head of the ordinand, 533 —
Bishop *l* hands upon the head of the ordinand, 545 —
The Bishop moves to the Font, *l* a hand upon it, 569 —
The Bishop proceeds to the Lectern, *l* a hand upon it, 570 —
The Bishop goes to the Pulpit, *l* a hand upon it, 571 —
The Bishop *l* a hand upon the Table, and continues 573 —

lead

"may *l* quiet and peaceable lives, in all godliness 11 2
to *l* other parts of the service not assigned 36 6
to *l* other parts of the service not assigned 74 5
a deacon or lay reader may *l* the first two parts 284 23
and may *l* the Prayers of the People. 322 10
and may *l* the Prayers of the People. 322 16
and may *l* the Prayers of the People. 354 10
and may *l* the Prayers of the People. 354 16
l the procession into the church. 467 —

leader

The *l* of worship in a Christian assembly 13 20
L 305 10
L 306 —
Deacon or other *l* 383 —
The *L* and People pray responsively 387 —
Deacon or other *l* 388 —
Deacon or other *l* 389 —
The *L* and People pray responsively 392 —
L and People 393 —
The Deacon or other *l* says 480 —
and the *l* may introduce prayers 844 10

leading

A deacon or lay reader *l* the service remains kneeling 269 —
face to face for a spiritual conference *l* to absolution 446 18
work of *l*, supervising, and uniting the Church. 510 7

leads

clerical or lay, who *l* the Office. 36 4
clerical or lay, who *l* the Office. 74 3
l the procession to the chancel, 285 —
Celebrant *l* the people in the Renewal of Baptismal 292 —
A Person appointed *l* the following petitions 305 —
Person appointed *l* the Litany for Ordinations, 515 —
one of the bishops *l* the people in the following 522 —
Person appointed *l* the Litany for Ordinations, 527 —
Person appointed *l* the Litany for Ordinations, 539 —
the Bishop *l* the people in the following prayer; 564 5
of the congregation *l* the Prayers of the People. 572 —

least

At *l* two of the following Lessons are read, 288 —
or have at *l* promised to do so. 409 15
one, at *l*, of the parties must be a baptized Christian; 422 4
ceremony be attested by at *l* two witnesses; 422 5
At *l* two other bishops serve as co-consecrators. 511 8
at *l* two presbyters must be present. 524 2
at *l* two presbyters must be present. 536 2

leave

not neglecting, if they are able, to *l* bequests 445 —

leaves

the wedding party *l* the church. 431 —
As the wedding party *l* the church, 432 —

lectern

It is desirable that the Lessons be read from a *l* 406 17
and that the Gospel be read from the same *l*, 406 18
The Bishop proceeds to the *L*, 570 —
If one reading stand is to serve as both *l* and pulpit, 576 6
At the dedication of the *l*, 576 9

lectionary

a) the *L* for Sundays, 136 —
b) the Daily Office *L*, 136 —
from the Office *L* or the Proper of the Day, 143 —
the service for the Ordination of a Deacon or in the *L* 565 14
verses suggested in the *l* for use 582 10
Concerning the *L* 888 1
The *L* for Sundays is arranged in a three-year cycle, 888 2
L for the Daily Office. 888 15
those appointed in the Office *L*; 888 16
In this *L*, the selections from the Psalter 888 18
appointed for the same day in the Daily Office *L*. 888 24
Concerning the Daily Office *L* 934 1
The Daily Office *L* is arranged in a two-year cycle. 934 2
(Thus, on the First Sunday of Advent, 1976, the *L* 934 5
In this *L* (except in the weeks 934 22

led

or parts of this service may be *l* by lay persons. 108 7
all that precedes may be *l* by a deacon 269 —
the preceding service may be *l* by a deacon 272 —
all that precedes may be *l* by a deacon 282 —
may also be *l* by one of the sponsors. 312 25
Part One of this service may always be *l* by a deacon 453 6
appropriate litany, is *l* by a person appointed. 560 —

left

denominations of Christians in these States were *l* 10 27
with the woman to the right and the man to the *l*, 423 —
sit to the right and *l* of the chief consecrator. 511 15
The other bishops stand to the right and *l* 520 —
the presbyters who stand to the right and *l* 533 —
The stole worn over the *l* shoulder, 554 12
l out many things, whereof some be untrue, 866 45

legends

by planting in uncertain stories, *L*, Responds, Verses, 866 17

legislature

20. For Congress or a State *L* 810 29
20. For Congress or a State *L* 821 —

legitimately

regularly and *l* constituted. 875 38

leisure

32. For the Good Use of *L* 811 11
32. For the Good Use of *L* 825 —

lend

prayers which do not *l* themselves to modernization, 814 —

length

religiously in good works, and at *l*, by God's mercy, 871 9

lengthened

and may be *l* if desired. 515 —
and may be *l* if desired. 528 —
and may be *l* if desired. 540 —
The selections may be further *l* or shortened 888 22
Any Reading may be *l* at discretion. 888 29
Any Reading may be *l* at discretion. 934 20

lengthening

re-ordered by *l*, combining, or omitting 934 18

lengthenings

Suggested *l* are shown in parentheses. 888 29
Suggested *l* are shown in parentheses. 934 20

Lent

also determines the beginning of *L* on Ash Wednesday, 15 12
seasons of Advent, *L*, and Easter. 16 10
and the other weekdays of *L* and of Holy Week, 17 23
Saturdays after the First Sunday in *L*, 18 6
L 38 —
Except in *L*, Alleluia may be added. 42 —
In *L* 43 —
Except in *L*, Alleluia may be added. 63 —
L 76 —
Except in *L*, add 80 —
In *L* 81 —
Especially suitable in *L*, 90 —
Except in *L*, add 103 —
1 John 1:5–7 (*L*) 108 20
John 12:35–36a (*L*) 108 21
In *L* and on other penitential occasions 109 —
L and other times of penitence 111 —
Except in *L*, add 117 —
Except in *L*, add 128 —
especially in *L* and on Rogation days. 148 —
Preface of *L* 166 —
First Sunday in *L* 166 —
Second Sunday in *L* 166 —
Preface of *L* 167 —
Third Sunday in *L* 167 —
Fourth Sunday in *L* 167 —
Fifth Sunday in *L* 167 —
Preface of *L* 217 —
First Sunday in *L* 218 —
Preface of *L* 218 —
Second Sunday in *L* 218 —
Third Sunday in *L* 218 —
Fourth Sunday in *L* 219 —
Preface of *L* 219 —
Fifth Sunday in *L* 219 —
invites the people to the observance of a holy *L*, 264 —
Preface of *L* 269 —
In *L* and on other penitential occasions 299 —
In *L* and on other penitential occasions 319 —
In *L* and on other penitential occasions 323 —
In *L*, Alleluia is omitted, 337 —
L 346 —
In *L* and on other penitential occasions 351 —
In *L* and on other penitential occasions 355 —
In *L*, Alleluia is omitted, 364 —
L 379 —
the Sundays or ordinary weekdays of Advent or *L*. 406 16
In *L* and on other penitential occasions 413 —
In *L* and on other penitential occasions 512 —
In *L* and on other penitential occasions 525 —
In *L* and on other penitential occasions 537 —
be omitted during the season of *L*. 584 9
variations in *L* and Easter Season. 934 25

less

none is greater, or *l* than another; 865 14
Twelve Prophets the *l*. 868 33
no *l* perilous than desperation. 871 19

lesson

After each *L* the Reader may say 47 —
the *L* from the Gospel is read 47 —
After each *L* the Reader may say 65 —
the *L* from the Gospel is read 65 —
After each *L* the Reader may say 84 —
the *L* from the Gospel is read 84 —
For the Short *L* at the beginning of the service, 108 14
One of the following, or some other Short *L* 109 —
After each *L* the Reader may say 119 —
the *L* from the Gospel is read 119 —
A *L* from the Gospel is always included. 142 20
the opening Short *L* and the Prayer for Light. 143 2
the Short *L* may be omitted. 143 9
When desired, more than one *L* may be read, 143 25
the reading of the Collects which follow each *L*, 284 15
each *L* be read by a different reader. 284 22
of which one is always the *L* from Exodus. 288 —
After each *L*, the Psalm or Canticle listed, 288 —
provided that a *l* from the Gospel is always included, 322 19
provided that a *l* from the Gospel is always included, 354 19
It is desirable that the *L* from the Old Testament, 468 15

After the Old Testament *L*,	470	—
After the New Testament *L*,	475	—
It is desirable that the *L* from the Old Testament,	490	15
Lay persons read the Old Testament *L*	515	—
Lay persons read the Old Testament *L*	528	—
Lay persons read the Old Testament *L*	540	—
persons from the congregation read the Old Testament *L*	558	14
Lay persons read the Old Testament *L*	571	—
When an alternative *L* is cited,	888	23
L appointed for the same day in the Daily Office	888	24

lessons

and one or more of the *L* appointed	16	14
and *L* duly authorized by this Church:	18	2
that other persons be assigned to read the *L*,	36	5
The *L*	47	—
One or two *L*, as appointed, are read,	47	—
If three *L* are used,	47	—
The *L*	64	—
One or two *L*, as appointed, are read,	64	—
If three *L* are used,	65	—
that other persons be assigned to read the *L*,	74	4
The *L*	84	—
One or two *L*, as appointed, are read,	84	—
If three *L* are used,	84	—
The *L*	118	—
One or two *L*, as appointed, are read,	118	—
If three *L* are used,	119	—
The Short *L* may be read from any version	143	6
When one or more Scripture *L* are to be read later	143	8
service continues as a complete Office, Psalms and *L*	143	21
and the appointed Psalms and *L*,	158	5
immediately preceding and any of the sets of Proper *L*	161	—
with the Psalm and *L* for the Epiphany,	162	—
This Collect, with the corresponding Psalm and *L*,	166	—
the preceding Collects, with the proper Psalm and *L*	174	—
or more of the appointed *L* are read	175	—
sets of Psalms and *L*, may be used	195	—
immediately preceding and any of the sets of Proper *L*	213	—
with the Psalm and *L* for the Epiphany,	214	—
This Collect, with the corresponding Psalm and *L*,	217	—
the preceding Collects, with the proper Psalm and *L*	226	—
or more of the appointed *L* are read	227	—
sets of Psalms and *L*, may be used	246	—
using the following Collect, Psalm, and *L*	274	—
2. The Service of *L*.	284	7
Lay persons read the *L*, and the Epistle,	284	20
At least two of the following *L* are read,	288	—
L are properly those of the Day.	300	—
The *L*	300	—
One or two *L*, as appointed, are read,	300	—
and one or more of the *L* provided	312	21
reading of the *L* which precede the Gospel,	322	16
The *L*	325	—
One or two *L*, as appointed, are read,	325	—
reading of the *L* which precede the Gospel,	354	16
The *L*	357	—
One or two *L*, as appointed, are read,	357	—
It is desirable that the *L* be read from a lectern	406	17
It is desirable that the *L* and Gospel be read	406	19
L are properly those of the Day.	414	—
Collect (page 203 or 254) and one or more of the *L*	414	—
The *L*	414	—
One or two *L*, as appointed, are read,	414	—
It is desirable that the *L* from the Old Testament	422	18
the Collect and *L* appointed in the Marriage service.	433	—
be seated for the *L* and the homily.	437	19
The Apostles' Creed may be recited after the *L*,	437	20
Suitable Psalms, *L*, and Collects	465	—
Three *L* are read.	515	—
Three *L* are read.	528	—
Three *L* are read.	540	—
A lay person being instituted should read one of the *L*	558	23
Three *L* are read.	571	—
suggested in the lectionary for use between the *L*	582	10
of chanting the psalms between the *L*	582	25
The Psalms and *L* appointed for the Sundays	888	6
L are to be read at the principal morning service,	888	9
the *L* at the Office may be selected	888	13
when the Psalm is sung between the *L*	888	21
In the opening verses of *L*,	888	25

let

L us pray.	291	—
the deacon first saying, "*L* us pray	408	23
(*L* us love one another for love is of God)	426	—
(You are the light...*L* your light so shine)	426	—

letter

L of Institution of a Minister	557	1
This *l* is a sign that you are fully empowered	557	7
The Bishop may read the *L* of Institution,	559	—
The *L* of Institution is appropriate	564	17
The "Four-*l* Name" (Tetragrammaton) is probably	583	17

letters

are not to depart without signing the *L*	553	16
Name was written in antique and obsolete *l*;	583	21
YHWH is represented in capital and small capital *l*:	583	29

Leviticus

L, The First Book of Kings,	868	28

liberally

as he possesseth, *l* to give alms to the poor,	876	15

liberty

It is a most invaluable part of that blessed "*l*	9	2
l to model and organize their respective Churches,	10	28

licensed

lay persons *l* by the bishop	408	7

life

A Collect for the Renewal of *L*	56	—
A Collect for the Renewal of *L*	99	—
the Anthem "In the midst of *l*"	283	—
by prayer and example in their Christian *l*.	298	20
(b) a Collect expressive of some special need in the *l*	394	—
that a person who is living a notoriously evil *l*	409	8
given clear proof of repentance and amendment of *l*.	409	11
for the husband and wife, for their *l* together,	436	7
(That you may know that you have eternal *l*)	454	10
(I am the bread of *l*)	454	12
(He that believeth hath everlasting *l*)	480	—
(I am the resurrection and the *l*)	480	—

(He who believes has everlasting *l*) 495 —
(I am the resurrection and the *l*) 495 —
promises of God in Christ about eternal *l*. 506 17
"neither death, nor *l*, nor angels, nor principalities, 507 6
By your words, and in your *l*, proclaim the Gospel. 557 12
God in this *l* and in the *l* to come. 557 14
within the *l* of the Diocese. 576 14
Prayers for National *L* 810 26
Prayers for Family and Personal *L* 811 27
Thanksgivings for National *L* 813 5
Thanksgivings for Family and Personal *L* 813 13
Prayers for National *L* 820 —
Prayers for Family and Personal *L* 828 —
Thanksgivings for National *L* 838 —
Thanksgivings for Family and Personal *L* 841 —
they that have done good shall go into *l* everlasting; 865 37
the Church doth read for example of *l* 868 34
everlasting *l* is offered to Mankind by Christ, 869 8
Predestination to *L* is the everlasting purpose of God, 871 2
so that he be diligent to frame his *l* 871 26
states of *l* allowed in the Scriptures; 872 35
of single *l*, or to abstain from marriage: 874 13

lifted

take the form of similarity (The waters have *l* up, 583 4
the waters have *l* up their voice; 583 5
the waters have *l* up their pounding waves. 583 5
carried about, *l* up, or worshipped. 873 35

light

or with the Service of *L* on pages 109–112, 61 —
O Gracious *L* 64 3
deacon, when presiding, should read the Prayer for *L*, 108 8
The Officiant then says the Prayer for *L*, 110 —
O Gracious *L* 112 —
or with the Service of *L* on pages 109–112, 115 —
O Gracious *L* 118 —
there should be as little artificial *l* as possible 142 26
and used to provide *l* for reading the opening 143 1
the opening Short Lesson and the Prayer for *L*. 143 2
by it to begin the service by its *l*. 143 5
take place after the Prayer for *L*. 143 15
it begins with the Service of *L*, 175 —
it begins with the Service of *L*, 227 —
1. The Service of *L*. 284 6
the Service of *L* may take place 284 30
(You are the *l*. . . Let your *l* so shine) 426 —
place the vessels on it, and *l* the candles. 574 —
according to that Law, and the *l* of Nature 871 27

lighted

The candles at the Altar are now *l*, 112 —
one or two *l* candles may be carried 142 28
and other candles may be *l* from them. 143 13
On special occasions, *l* candles may be distributed 143 15
in private houses, candles may be *l* 143 17
after the candles have been *l* 143 20
Candle is then *l* from the newly kindled fire, 285 —
l from the Paschal Candle at this time. 286 —
except for those at the Altar, may also be *l*. 286 —
The candles at the Altar may now be *l* 294 —
(which may be *l* from the Paschal Candle) 313 7
the congregation bearing the *l* Paschal Candle 467 —

lighting

L of the Paschal Candle. 108 13
During the candle-*l*, 112 —
For the *l* of the candles at the Altar 143 10
During Advent, the *l* of an Advent Wreath 143 14
The *L* of the Paschal Candle 285 —

like

but, *l* lay persons, may officiate 13 22
(*L* a wise man who built his house upon the rock) 426 —
1 John 3:1–2 (We shall be *l* him) 475 —
1 John 3:1–2 (We shall be *l* him) 495 —
l us in all respects, apart from sin; 864 8
For *l* as we are compelled by the Christian verity 865 5
After a *l* sort were other books 866 21
and such *l* things, as did break 866 38
truth of our nature was made *l* unto us in all things, 870 25
they be made *l* the image of his only-begotten Son 871 8
but yet have not *l* nature of Sacraments with Baptism, 872 35
and Ceremonies be in all places one, or utterly *l*; 874 22
(that others may fear to do the *l*,) 874 28

likewise

in her Preface, but *l* in her Articles 9 22
Deacons *l* assist at Baptism 284 18
L, suitable parts of this rite 566 5
So *l* the Father is Almighty, 864 38
So *l* the Father is Lord, 865 3
and *l* the Cup of Blessing is a partaking 873 26
L, Psalms appointed for any day may be used 934 29

limitations

subject to the *l* described in the directions 14 1

Lincoln

the use of Bangor, some of York, and some of *L*: 867 10

lines

In this prayer, the *l* in italics are spoken 369 —
the Psalms which follows is set out in *l* of poetry. 583 1
l correspond to Hebrew versification, 583 2

lips

or with the versicle "O Lord, open thou our *l*" 37 —
continue at once with "O Lord, open thou our *l*." 41 —
or with the versicle "Lord, open our *l*" 75 —
continue at once with "Lord, open our *l*." 79 —

list

Readings are ordinarily selected from the following *l* 515 —
Readings are ordinarily selected from the following *l* 528 —
Readings are ordinarily selected from the following *l* 540 —
Readings are selected from the following *l*, 560 —
ordinarily made from the following *l*; 571 —

listed

In addition to the dated days *l* above, 16 3
Commemorations *l* in the Calendar 18 3
including those *l* for specific seasons or days, 141 3
a) at the commemoration of a saint *l* in the Calendar 195 —
patronal festival or commemoration of a saint not *l* 195 —
a) at the commemoration of a saint *l* in the Calendar 246 —
patronal festival or commemoration of a saint not *l* 246 —
After each Lesson, the Psalm or Canticle *l*, 288 —
If on the four days *l* above there are no candidates 312 15

litany

A *l*, or other suitable devotions, 113 —
may be omitted from the Office when the *L* 142 5
The Great *L* 147 —
The Great *L* 148 —
When the *L* is sung or said immediately before 153 —
the *L* concludes here, and the Eucharist begins 153 —
Officiant may add other Prayers, and end the *L*, 154 —
For use in the *L* in place of the Versicle 154 —
For the Prayers of the People, the *L* of Thanksgiving 194 —
The *L* of Thanksgiving for a Church, 204 —
For the Prayers of the People, the *L* of Thanksgiving 246 —
The *L* of Thanksgiving for a Church, 255 —
L of Penitence 267 —
The *L* of Penitence may be used at other times, 269 —
When the Great *L* is sung or said immediately before 406 3
the *L* concludes with the Kyries, 406 4
L at the Time of Death 462 —
come together to join in the *L*. 462 —
The *L* at the Time of Death may be said, 465 —
All kneel, and the Person appointed leads the *L* 515 —
or some other approved *l*. 515 —
At the end of the *l*, after the Kyries, 515 —
All kneel, and the Person appointed leads the *L* 527 —
or some other approved *l*. 527 —
At the end of the *l*, after the Kyries, 527 —
All kneel, and the Person appointed leads the *L* 539 —
or some other approved *l*. 539 —
At the end of the *l*, after the Kyries, 539 —
The *L* for Ordinations 548 —
this *L* may be used for the Prayers of the People 548 —
When this *L* is used on other occasions, 551 —
The *L* for Ordinations, or some other appropriate *l*, 560 —
At the end of the *l*, the Bishop, standing, 560 —
The *L* may be sung or said standing or kneeling, 565 6
3. *L* of Thanksgiving for a Church, 577 28
A *L* of Thanksgiving for a Church 578 6
This *L* may also be used on the anniversary 579 6
2. A *L* of Thanksgiving 812 31
2. A *L* of Thanksgiving 836 —

literature

A sermon or homily, a passage from Christian *l*, 113 —
non-biblical Christian *l* may follow 142 14

little

there should be as *l* artificial light as possible 142 26
to add a *l* water to the wine. 407 16
(and a *l* water) into the chalice, 546 —

liturgical

l texts may be used in place of the corresponding texts 14 14
The Psalter is a body of *l* poetry. 582 2

liturgies

In any of the Proper *L* for Special Days, 14 3

liturgy

they declare it to be the *L* of this Church: 8 10
since the first compiling of her *L* 10 2
seek occasion, of cavil or quarrel against her *L*. 10 13
alterations in the *L* which became necessary 10 33
like lay persons, may officiate at the *L* of the Word, 13 22
or Evening Prayer is used as the *L* of the Word 142 17
The Proper *L* for this day is on page 264. 166 —
The Proper *L* for this day is on page 270. 168 —
The Proper *L* for this day is on page 274. 169 —
The Proper *L* for this day is on page 276. 169 —
The Proper *L* for this day is on page 283. 170 —
The *L* of the Easter Vigil is on page 285. 170 —
The Proper *L* for this day is on page 264. 217 —
The Proper *L* for this day is on page 270. 219 —
The Proper *L* for this day is on page 274. 221 —
The Proper *L* for this day is on page 276. 221 —
The Proper *L* for this day is on page 283. 221 —
The *L* of the Easter Vigil is on page 285. 222 —
On this day, the Celebrant begins the *l* 264 —
The *L* of the Palms 270 —
When the *L* of the Palms immediately precedes 272 —
When the *L* of the Palms has preceded, 273 —
begins the *l* with the Collect of the Day. 276 —
When there is a *L* of the Word, 283 —
convenient time before the *L* on Easter Day. 284 31
The *L* of the Word 288 —
The *L* for the Proclamation of the Word 315 —
during the *L* or at other times. 316 —
For use at the beginning of the *L*, 319 —
When this Order is used at the beginning of the *L*, 321 —
At all celebrations of the *L*, 322 4
For use at the beginning of the *L*, 351 —
When this Order is used at the beginning of the *L*, 353 —
At all celebrations of the *L*, 354 4
1. After the *L* of the Word 408 20
proceeds with what follows in the *l* as far as the end 408 26
The *l* continues with the Offertory, 432 —
with any authorized *l* for the Holy Eucharist. 437 —
The *L* of the Word 494 —
The *l* for the dead is an Easter *l*. 507 2
The *l*, therefore, is characterized by joy, 507 5
The *l* continues with the Offertory. 522 —
The *l* continues with the Offertory. 535 —
The *l* continues with the Offertory. 546 —
At the *L* of the Word 560 —
At the *L* of the Word 571 —
5. *L* of the Word, with sermon or address 578 1
but also to regain for our *l* a form of the word 584 7
the *L* of the Word takes the form given 888 10

live

48. For Those Who *L* Alone 811 31
48. For Those Who *L* Alone 829 —
they can no more sin as long as they *l* 870 36

lively

and do spring out necessarily of a true and *l* Faith; 870 9
that by them a *l* Faith may be as evidently known 870 10
The Wicked, and such as be void of a *l* faith, 873 37

lives

"may lead quiet and peaceable *l*, in all godliness 11 2
Job 19:21–27a (I know that my Redeemer *l*) 494 —
grace of God we may arise again, and amend our *l*. 870 35

liveth

Job 19:21–27a (I know that my Redeemer *l*) 470 —

living

If the priest knows that a person who is *l* 409 8
There is but one *l* and true God, 867 35
or into wretchlessness of most unclean *l*, 871 19
erred, not only in their *l* and manner of Ceremonies, 871 34

local

or further than *l* circumstances require. 11 14
The concerns of the *l* community 359 —
The concerns of the *l* community 383 —
special need in the life of the *l* congregation; 394 4
23. For *L* Government 811 1
23. For *L* Government 822 —
because it is partly of a *l* and civil nature, 872 2
obsolete words and phrases, as from the *l* references.] 875 19

locally

4. The Historic Episcopate, *l* adapted in the methods 877 18
(d) The Historic Episcopate, *l* adapted in the methods 878 4

logical

or of *l* expansion (Our eyes look to the Lord our God, 583 8

long

and a *l* continuance of nursing care and protection, 9 12
For a church or chapel *l* in use, 566 19
For a Church or Chapel *L* in Use 577 20
they can no more sin as *l* as they live 870 36

longer

Mark 10:6–9, 13–16 (They are no *l* two but one) 426 —
cited in a *l* and shorter version, 888 19
The *l* version is particularly appropriate 888 19

look

or of logical expansion (Our eyes *l* to the Lord 583 8
the old Fathers did *l* only for transitory promises. 869 10

looking

Hebrews 12:1–2 (*L* to Jesus, the perfecter 454 2

loose

Then they *l* their hands, 427 —
They *l* their hands. 427 —

Lord (small capitals)

represented in capital and small capital letters: *L*. 583 30

Lord

in the Year of Our *L* One Thousand Seven Hundred 8 5
in the Year of our *L* one thousand seven hundred 8 12
our blessed *L* and Saviour. 11 24
the principal act of Christian worship on the *L*'s Day 13 3
our *L*'s Nativity or Christmas Day. 15 6
of the year are feasts of our *L* Jesus Christ. 16 2
All other Feasts of our *L*, 16 11
Other Feasts of our *L* 16 26
Feasts of our *L* and other Major Feasts 17 16
in commemoration of the *L*'s crucifixion, 17 26
and any Feasts of our *L* which occur on a Friday. 17 27
or with the versicle "O *L*, open thou our lips" 37 —
continue at once with "O *L*, open thou our lips." 41 —
or with the versicle "*L*, open our lips" 75 —
continue at once with "*L*, open our lips." 79 —
followed by the *L*'s Prayer and a grace or blessing; 112 —
suitable devotions, including the *L*'s Prayer. 113 —
The *L*'s Prayer 137 —
The *L*'s Prayer 138 —
The *L*'s Prayer 139 —
The *L*'s Prayer 140 —
The *L*'s Prayer may be omitted from the Office 142 5
pass at once from the salutation "The *L* be with you," 142 19
and Collect which follows the *L*'s Prayer; 154 —
The Nativity of Our *L*: 160 —
The Baptism of our *L* 163 —
Preface of the Epiphany, or of the *L*'s Day 163 —
Preface of the Epiphany, or of the *L*'s Day 164 —
Preface of the Epiphany, or of the *L*'s Day 165 —
Preface of the *L*'s Day 177 —
Preface of the *L*'s Day 178 —
Preface of the *L*'s Day 179 —
Preface of the *L*'s Day 180 —
Preface of the *L*'s Day 181 —
Preface of the *L*'s Day 182 —
Preface of the *L*'s Day 183 —
Preface of the *L*'s Day 184 —
Preface of the *L*'s Day 185 —
The Nativity of Our *L*: 212 —
The Baptism of our *L* 214 —
Preface of the Epiphany, or of the *L*'s Day 215 —
Preface of the Epiphany, or of the *L*'s Day 216 —
Preface of the Epiphany, or of the *L*'s Day 217 —
Preface of the *L*'s Day 229 —
Preface of the *L*'s Day 230 —
Preface of the *L*'s Day 231 —
Preface of the *L*'s Day 232 —
Preface of the *L*'s Day 233 —
Preface of the *L*'s Day 234 —
Preface of the *L*'s Day 235 —
Preface of the *L*'s Day 236 —
Preface of the *L*'s Day, or of Baptism 236 —
the *L*'s Prayer, and the final prayer on page 282. 280 —
The service may be concluded here with the *L*'s Prayer 282 —
The *L*'s Prayer 282 —
The service then concludes with the *L*'s Prayer and the Grace. 283 —
the *L*'s Prayer, and the Dismissal. 284 26
the service continues with the *L*'s Prayer 311 —
and on the Feast of the Baptism of our *L* 312 4
and before the salutation "The *L* be with you." 312 19
The *L*'s Prayer is then said. 314 1
celebrant at the *L*'s Table, and to preach the Gospel. 322 3
Deacons should also serve at the *L*'s Table, 322 11
greet one another in the name of the *L*. 332 —
Continue with the *L*'s Prayer, page 336. 343 —
Preface of the *L*'s Day 344 —
celebrant at the *L*'s Table, and to preach the Gospel. 354 3
Deacons should also serve at the *L*'s Table, 354 11
in the name of the *L*. 360 —
Continue with the *L*'s Prayer on page 364. 369 —
Continue with the *L*'s Prayer on page 364. 372 —
Continue with the *L*'s Prayer on page 364. 376 —
Preface of the *L*'s Day 377 —
The *L*'s Prayer is said, the Celebrant first saying 398 —
Gather in the *L*'s Name 400 7
in the name of the *L*. 401 3
The Body and Blood of the *L* are shared 401 13

through Jesus Christ our *L*.	403	—
through Jesus Christ our *L*.	404	—
The Kyrie eleison (or "*L*, have mercy") may be sung	406	9
conclude with the *L*'s Prayer;	407	3
The greeting, "The peace of the *L* be always	407	7
2. The *L*'s Prayer is then said,	408	23
and before the salutation "The *L* be with you."	412	14
the *L*'s Prayer and such other devotions	419	—
the *L*'s Prayer may be omitted here.	428	—
They may then remain before the *L*'s Table	438	3
The *L*'s Prayer is always included.	453	5
(The eyes of all wait upon you, O *L*)	454	11
the *L*'s Prayer is now said.	456	—
with the [Peace and] *L*'s Prayer on page 398.	457	—
Lamentations 3:22–26, 31–33 (The *L* is good	470	—
the *L*'s Prayer is said here,	480	—
Lamentations 3:22–26, 31–33 (The *L* is good	494	—
the *L*'s Prayer is said here,	496	—
6. Prayer, including the *L*'s Prayer,	506	15
the love of God in Christ Jesus our *L*."	507	9
entered into the nearer presence of our *L*,	507	13
ordained on Sundays and other feasts of our *L*	511	4
Then the new Bishop goes to the *L*'s Table	522	—
Standing at the *L*'s Table, with the Bishop	535	—
and places the vessels on the *L*'s Table.	546	—
the bishop continues "May they exalt you, O *L*,	554	3
the bishop continues, "Make them, O *L*,	554	24
May the *L*, who has given you the will to do	557	15
standing at the *L*'s Table as chief celebrant,	563	—
(The waters have lifted up, O *L*	583	5
(The *L* knows the ways of the righteous;	583	6
(Our eyes look to the *L* our God,	583	8
Adonai ("*L*") and the personal name YHWH.	583	16
where it is regularly rendered "*L*."	583	28
distinguish it, however, from "*L*" as a translation	583	28
rendering the combined title as "*L* God."	583	34
its English equivalent, "Praise the *L*."	584	5
same Son, our *L* Jesus Christ, at once complete	864	5
one and the same Christ, Son, *L*, Only-begotten,	864	11
and Only-begotten God the Word, *L* Jesus Christ;	864	16
and our *L* Jesus Christ himself taught us,	864	17
So likewise the Father is *L*, the Son *L*,	865	3
and the Holy Ghost *L*.	865	3
And yet not three *L*s, but one *L*.	865	4
by himself to be both God and *L*,	865	6
Incarnation of our *L* Jesus Christ.	865	20
we believe and confess, that our *L* Jesus Christ,	865	21
in the Year of our *L*, 1801.	867	33
righteous before God, only for the merit of our *L*	870	2
and send Ministers into the *L*'s vineyard.	872	20
Sacraments ordained of Christ our *L* in the Gospel,	872	30
that is to say, Baptism, and the Supper of the *L*.	872	31
the *L*'s Supper, for that they have not any visible sign	872	36
XXVIII. Of the *L*'s Supper.	873	22
The Supper of the *L* is not only a sign of the love	873	23
in the Supper of the *L*,	873	29
The Sacrament of the *L*'s Supper was not	873	34
the Body of Christ in the use of the *L*'s Supper.	873	36
Cup of the *L* is not to be denied to the Lay-people:	874	2
for both the parts of the *L*'s Sacrament,	874	2
forbidden Christian men by our *L* Jesus Christ,	876	18
two Sacraments,—Baptism and the Supper of the *L*,	877	16
by Christ Himself—Baptism and the Supper of the *L*	878	1

Lords

And yet not three *L*, but one Lord.	865	4
to say, There be three Gods, or three *L*.	865	7

loud

The People in a *l* voice respond	521	—
The People in a *l* voice respond	534	—
The People in a *l* voice respond	545	—

love

grow in the knowledge and *l* of God,	298	27
(Many waters cannot quench *l*)	426	—
(*L* is patient and kind)	426	—
(Walk in *l*, as Christ loved us)	426	—
(*L* which binds everything together in harmony)	426	—
(Let us *l* one another for *l* is of God)	426	—
(*L* one another as I have loved you)	426	—
will be able to separate us from the *l* of God	507	8
The very *l* we have for each other in Christ	507	10
one we *l* has entered into the nearer presence	507	13
L and serve Christ's people.	557	12
54. For those we *L*	812	5
54. For those we *L*	831	—
the *l* of his true religion.	866	15
because it doth fervently kindle their *l* towards God:	871	16
The Supper of the Lord is not only a sign of the *l*	873	23
this Church is ready in the spirit of *l*	876	34

loved

(Walk in love, as Christ *l* us)	426	—
(Love one another as I have *l* you)	426	—

Luke

L 2:10,11	37	—
L 15:18,19	38	—
L 1:46–55	50	—
L 1:68–79	50	—
L 2:29–32	51	—
L 1:46–55	65	—
L 2:29–32	66	—
L 2:10,11	75	—
L 15:18,19	76	—
28 *L* 1:46–55	91	—
L 1:68–794	92	—
L 2:29–324	93	—
L 12:35–37 (Advent)	108	17
L 1:46–55	119	—
L 2:29–32	120	—
Saint *L* October 18	193	—
Saint *L* October 18	244	—
Year C *L* 19:29–40	271	—
Year C *L* 22:39—23:49(50–56) or 23:1–49(50–56)	273	—
Mark 15:22, *L* 23:33) all stand.	273	—
Gospel John 13:1–15, or *L* 22:14–30	274	—
Either *L* 2:41–51, or *L* 18:15–17, is appropriate.	439	13
L 17:11–19 (Your faith has made you well)	453	17
John 20:19–23, or John 17:1–9, 18–21, or *L* 24:44–49a	516	—
L 12:35–38, or *L* 22:24–27	541	—
Gospel John 15:9–16, or *L* 10:1–2, or John 14:11–15	560	—

lust

whereby the *l* of the flesh, 869 28
and *l* hath of itself the nature of sin. 869 32

lusteth

so that the flesh *l* always contrary to the Spirit; 869 26

M

Maccabees

The First Book of *M*, 869 2
The Second Book of *M*. 869 3

made

"liberty wherewith Christ hath *m* us free," 9 3
such changes and alterations should be *m* therein, 9 19
or insertions suitable to the occasion may be *m*. 383 —
announcements may be *m* before the service, 407 12
they have *m* restitution for the wrong they have done, 409 15
but it must be *m* clear to the penitent that absolution 446 13
Luke 17:11–19 (Your faith has *m* you well) 453 17
arrangements for the funeral should be *m* 468 3
arrangements for the funeral should be *m* 490 3
If no objection is *m*, the Presiding Bishop continues 514 —
If no objection is *m*, the Bishop continues 527 —
If no objection is *m*, the Bishop continues 539 —
Alterations in the service are then *m* 558 6
and of the new minister may be *m*. 565 18
Necessary announcements may now be *m*. 567 7
ordinarily *m* from the following list; 571 —
selections may be *m* from the Proper of the Day. 571 —
a distinct pause should be *m* at the asterisk. 583 14
Father is *m* of none, neither created, but begotten. 865 8
not *m*, nor created, nor begotten, 865 9
neither *m*, nor created, nor begotten, 865 10
Of the Word or Son of God, which was *m* very Man. 868 1
our nature was *m* like unto us in all things, 870 25
without spot, who, by sacrifice of himself once *m*, 870 27
to everlasting salvation, as vessels *m* to honour. 871 5
they be *m* sons of God by adoption: 871 8
they be *m* like the image of his only-begotten Son 871 8
that inquiry be *m* of evil Ministers, 873 10
Offering of Christ once *m* is that perfect redemption, 874 6
until a revision of them may be conveniently *m*, 875 18
by God's blessing *m* towards Home Reunion: 877 32

Magdalene

Saint Mary *M* 17 7
Saint Mary *M* July 22 191 —
Saint Mary *M* July 22 242 —

magistrate

hurteth the authority of the *M*, 874 29
The Power of the Civil *M* extendeth to all men, 875 35
at the commandment of the *M*, to wear weapons, 876 10
that a man may swear when the *M* requireth, 876 20

magistrates

XXXVII. Of the Power of the Civil *M*. 875 34

Magnificat

3 The Song of Mary *M* 50 —
The Song of Mary *M* 65 —
15 The Song of Mary *M* 91 —
The *M* or other canticle, 113 —
The Song of Mary *M* 119 —
service continues with the *M* or one of the Psalms 440 —

main

yet so as that the *m* body and essential parts 10 5

maintain

understanding to execute justice, and to *m* truth;" 11 1
to *m* and continue these three orders; 510 19

majestic

and *m* manner, for the sake of Jesus Christ, 11 22

majesty

the Glory equal, the *M* co-eternal. 864 29
is of one substance, *m*, and glory, 868 17
"The King's *M* hath the chief power 875 39
we attribute to the King's *M* the chief government, 875 43

major

worship on the Lord's Day and other *m* Feasts, 13 4
All other Feasts of our Lord, and all other *M* Feasts 16 11
Other *M* Feasts 17 1
M Feasts falling in these weeks 17 11
Feasts of our Lord and other *M* Feasts 17 16
All Saints and other *M* Saints' Days 40 —
On All Saints and other *M* Saints' Days 44 —
All Saints and other *M* Saints' Days 77 —
On All Saints and other *M* Saints' Days 82 —
On Sundays and other *M* Feasts there follows, 326 —
On Sundays and other *M* Feasts there follows, 358 —
On a *M* Feast or on a Sunday, 515 —
On a *M* Feast, or on a Sunday, 528 —
On a *M* Feast, or on a Sunday, 540 —
Except on *M* Feasts, the Preface may be 564 —
but on a *M* Feast, Sunday, or Patronal Feast, 571 —
appointed for the Sundays and for other *m* Holy Days 888 6
When a *M* Feast interrupts the sequence of Readings, 934 17
day in the same week, except on *m* Holy Days. 934 30

make

m such alterations in some particulars, 10 4
m them conformable to what ought to be the proper 10 35
"O God, *m* speed to save us" 61 —
"O God, *m* speed to save us." 62 —
"O God, *m* speed to save us" 115 —
"O God, *m* speed to save us." 116 —
m promises in their own names, 298 21
the People may *m* an appropriate response, 328 —
M Eucharist 401 7
It is the function of a deacon to *m* ready the Table 407 14
desire and promise to *m* up for their faults, 409 21
m a mature public affirmation of their faith 412 4
are also expected to *m* a public affirmation 412 8
a person wishes to *m* or renew a commitment 420 —
the person seeking to *m* or renew a commitment 420 —
about the duty of Christian parents to *m* prudent 445 —
and of all persons to *m* provision 445 —
Revelation 21:2–7 (Behold, I *m* all things new) 475 —
Revelation 21:2–7 (Behold, I *m* all things new) 495 —
joy, however, does not *m* human grief unchristian. 507 10
and ancient Christian writers *m* it clear 510 2

and *m* him a priest in your Church." 554 1
and *m* him a deacon in your Church." 554 23
the bishop continues, "*M* them, O Lord, 554 24
or other circumstances *m* it necessary, 575 12
neither do they *m* men meet to receive grace, 870 14

Maker

the *M*, and Preserver of all things 867 36

makes

before the congregation, *m* the Act of Commitment. 420 —
m the sign of the cross on the sick person's forehead, 456 —
m the recitation of the Psalter needlessly monotonous. 582 5
Antiphons for the Venite *m* possible a recovery 582 23

making

In *m* Eucharist, the Celebrant uses one 402 —
The Priest may suggest the *m* of a special confession, 454 15

Malachi

M 1:11 38 —
M 1:11 76 4
M 1:11 106 —

male

Genesis 1:26–28 (*M* and female he created them) 426 —

man

a godly *m* may not with a good conscience use 10 15
public covenant between a *m* and a woman 422 2
with the woman to the right and the *m* to the left, 423 —
The Celebrant says to the *m* 424 —
The *M* answers 424 —
(A *m* cleaves to his wife and they become one flesh) 426 —
(Like a wise *m* who built his house upon the rock) 426 —
The *M*, facing the woman and taking her right hand 427 —
and the Woman, still facing the *m*, takes 427 —
the *m* and the woman, together with their witnesses, 435 8
2. The intention of the *m* and the woman to enter 435 13
4. The vows of the *m* and woman are exchanged, 435 18
the union of the *m* and woman as husband and wife, 436 4
fitting that the *m* and woman to be married remain 437 13
complete in manhood, truly God and truly *m*, 864 6
the Son of God, is God and *M*; 865 22
and *M*, of the Substance of his Mother, 865 23
Perfect God and perfect *M*, of a reasonable soul 865 25
Who although he be God and *M*, yet he is not two, 865 28
For as the reasonable soul and flesh is one *m*, 865 31
so God and *M* is one Christ; 865 31
except a *m* believe faithfully, he cannot be saved. 865 39
was never any thing by the wit of *m* so well devised, 866 3
if a *m* would search out by the ancient fathers, 866 6
Neither that any *m* shall be bound 867 26
Of the Word or Son of God, which was made very *M*. 868 1
took *M*'s nature in the womb of the Blessed Virgin, 868 3
whereof is one Christ, very God, and very *M*; 868 6
things appertaining to the perfection of *M*'s nature; 868 14
may be proved thereby, is not to be required of any *m*, 868 21
between God and *M*, being both God and *M*. 869 9
no Christian *m* whatsoever is free from the obedience 869 13
is the fault and corruption of the Nature of every *m*, 869 24
m is very far gone from original righteousness, 869 25
The condition of *M* after the fall of Adam is such, 869 34
XI. Of the Justification of *M*. 870 1
That every *m* shall be saved by the Law 871 25
It is not lawful for any *m* to take upon him the office 872 16
Rites of the Church ordained only by *m*'s authority, 874 32
every *m* ought, of such things as he possesseth, 876 15
XXXIX. Of a Christian *M*'s Oath. 876 17
that a *m* may swear when the Magistrate requireth, 876 20

Manasseh

Prayer of *M*, 1–2, 4, 6–7, 11–15 90 —

Manasses

The Prayer of *M*, 869 1

manhood

at once complete in Godhead and complete in *m*, 864 6
one substance with us as regards his *m*; 864 8
but yet as regards his *m* begotten, 864 9
and inferior to the Father, as touching his *M*. 865 27
but by taking of the *M* into God; 865 29
Godhead and *M*, were joined together in one Person, 868 5

manifestation

and the visible *m* of Christ to the world; 877 4

manifold

and the *m* changings of the service, was the cause, 866 30

mankind

for promulgating them to *m* in the clearest, 11 21
everlasting life is offered to *M* by Christ, 869 8
those whom he hath chosen in Christ out of *m*, 871 4

manner

in such *m* as they might judge most convenient 10 29
most affecting and majestic *m*, 11 23
in unison, or in some other convenient *m*. 136 —
The Passion Gospel is announced in the following *m* 272 —
The Eucharist begins in the usual *m*, 274 —
The Passion Gospel is announced in the following *m* 276 —
the person is baptized in the usual *m*, 313 19
and Blood of the Lord are shared in a reverent *m*; 401 13
in a *m* approved by the bishop. 408 1
from the reserved Sacrament in the following *m*: 408 19
Accordingly, the *m* of ordaining in this Church 510 29
or in some other convenient *m*. 552 16
It was also a traditional *m* of chanting the psalms 582 24
of all doubts, concerning the *m* how to understand, 867 18
erred, not only in their living and *m* of Ceremonies, 871 34
in the Supper, only after an heavenly and spiritual *m*. 873 32

manners

read for example of life and instruction of *m*; 868 35
the diversity of countries, times, and men's *m*, 874 24

mansions

John 14:1–6 (In my Father's house are many *m*) 480 —

manual

c) some other *m* of devotion which provides 136 —

manuscripts

In the oldest *m*, the Divine Name was written 583 20
in more recent *m* and in printed Bibles, 583 22

many

(*M* waters cannot quench love) 426 —
(They anointed with oil *m* that were sick) 454 8
(In my Father's house are *m* mansions) 480 —
(In my Father's house are *m* rooms) 495 —
If there are *m* deacons, some assist in the Offertory 554 29
familiar from its use in *m* well-known anthems. 584 8
But these *m* years passed, this godly and decent order 866 16
the Service in the Church of England (these *m* years) 866 24
was so hard and intricate a matter, that *m* times, 866 31
because here are left out *m* things, 866 45
they could say *m* things by heart: 867 13
and born again in Christ, yet offend in *m* things; 870 29
and hath given occasion to *m* superstitions. 873 30

March

after the full moon that falls on or after *M* 21. 15 8
It cannot occur before *M* 22 or after April 25. 15 8
Saint Joseph *M* 19 188 —
The Annunciation *M* 25 188 —
Saint Joseph *M* 19 239 —
The Annunciation *M* 25 240 —

margin

A bar in the *m* indicates petitions which may be omitted. 383 —

Mark

M 13:35, 36 37 —
M 8:34 38 —
M 13:35, 36 75 —
M 8:34 76 —
Saint *M* April 25 188 —
Saint *M* April 25 240 —
Year B *M* 11:1–11a 271 —
Year B *M* 14:32—15:39(40–47) or 15:1–39(40–47) 273 —
M 15:22, Luke 23:33) all stand. 273 —
M 12:29–31 351 —
M 10:6–9, 13–16 (They are no longer two but one) 426 —
M 6:7, 12–13 (They anointed with oil 454 8

mark

not only a sign of profession, and *m* of difference, 873 14

marked

cross signed on the threshold by the bishop may be *m* 575 20

marking

m on the forehead the sign of the cross 308 —

marks

With the pastoral staff the Bishop *m* the threshold 568 —

marriage

M 349 —
M 381 —
Christian *m* is a solemn and public covenant 422 2
and that the *m* conform to the laws of the State 422 5
the Celebration and Blessing of a *M*, 422 8
Blessing of a *M* 423 —
If there is to be a presentation or a giving in *m*, 425 —
The *M* 427 —
The Blessing of the *M* 430 —
Preface of *M* 432 —
The Blessing of a Civil *M* 433 —
the Collect and Lessons appointed in the *M* service. 433 —
An Order for *M* 435 1
desired to celebrate a *m* otherwise than as provided 435 2
The Celebration and Blessing of a *M* may be used 437 5
if there is to be a giving in *m*, 437 8
or for the Blessing of the *M*. 437 16
XXXII. Of the *M* of Priests. 874 11
vow the estate of single life, or to abstain from *m*: 874 13

marriages

permitted by civil law that deacons may perform *m*, 422 15

married

the full names of the persons to be *m* are declared. 422 21
At the time appointed, the persons to be *m*, 423 —
facing the people and the persons to be *m*, 423 —
Then the Celebrant says to the persons to be *m* 424 —
The newly *m* couple then greet each other, 431 —
at which the newly *m* couple may present 432 —
that the newly *m* couple receive Communion first, 432 —
fitting that the man and woman to be *m* remain 437 —
to the ministers by the newly *m* persons. 438 2

marry

Christian men, to *m* at their own discretion, 874 14

martyr

Of a *M* 195 —
Of a *M* 246 —

Mary

Saint *M* the Virgin 17 2
Saint *M* Magdalene 17 7
3 The Song of *M* Magnificat 50 —
The Song of *M* Magnificat 65 —
15 The Song of *M* Magnificat 91 —
The Song of *M* Magnificat 119 —
Saint *M* Magdalene July 22 191 —
Saint *M* the Virgin August 15 192 —
Saint *M* Magdalene July 22 242 —
Saint *M* the Virgin August 15 243 —
The Song of *M* 441 —
for us men and for our salvation, of *M* the Virgin, 864 10

masses

Wherefore the sacrifices of *M*, 874 8

materials

(as well in the chiefest *m*, as in the frame and order 10 6

Matins

when men say *M* and Evensong privately, they may 867 25

matrimony

1. The teaching of the Church concerning Holy *M*, 435 11
the man and the woman to enter the state of *m*, 435 14
M, and Extreme Unction, are not to be counted 872 33
18 Of the State of *M*. 875 10

matter

The content of a confession is not normally a *m* 446 26
since the *m* is arranged under headings, 844 9
For they so ordered the *m*, that all the whole Bible 866 8
to turn the Book only, was so hard and intricate a *m*, 866 31
And for a readiness in this *m*, here is drawn 866 34

matters

and manner of Ceremonies, but also in *m* of Faith. 871 34

Matthew

M 5:14–16 109 —
M 11:28–30 131 —
Saint *M* September 21 192 —
Saint *M* September 21 244 —
Gospel *M* 6:1–6, 16–21 264 —
Year A *M* 21:1–11 271 —
Year A *M* 26:36—27:54(55–66) or 27:1–54(55–66) 273 —
verse which mentions the arrival at Golgotha (*M* 27:33, 273 —
Gospel *M* 27:57–66, or John 19:38–42 283 —
Gospel *M* 28:1–10 295 —
M 22:37–40 319 —
M 11:28 332 —
M 5:23, 24 343 —
M 5:23, 24 376 —
M 5:1–10 (The Beatitudes) 426 —
M 5:13–16 (You are the light... Let your light so shine) 426 —
M 7:21, 24–29 (Like a wise man who built his house 426 —
M 11:28 449 —
M 9:2–8 (Your sins are forgiven) 454 4
M 9:35–38, or John 10:11–18, or John 6:35–38 529 —
M 7:13–14, 24–25, or *M* 21:10–14 572 —

Matthias

Saint *M* February 24 188 —
Saint *M* February 24 239 —

mature

make a *m* public affirmation of their faith and commitment 412 4

Maundy

occasion on Ash Wednesday, *M* Thursday, 18 12
M Thursday 169 —
M Thursday 221 —
M Thursday 274 —

May

if the Sunday after Trinity Sunday is *M* 26, 158 16
Proper 1 Week of the Sunday closest to *M* 11 176 12
Proper 2 Week of the Sunday closest to *M* 18 177 3
Proper 3 The Sunday closest to *M* 25 177 6
Saint Philip and Saint James *M* 1 189 3
The Visitation *M* 31 189 6
Proper 1 Week of the Sunday closest to *M* 11 228 8
Proper 2 Week of the Sunday closest to *M* 18 228 11
Proper 3 The Sunday closest to *M* 25 229 3
Saint Philip and Saint James *M* 1 240 7
The Visitation *M* 31 240 10

meal

the prelude to an evening *m* or other activity. 108 6
Or, it may be followed by a *m* or other activity, 112 —
This devotion may be used before or after the evening *m*. 139 —
When a *m* is to follow, a blessing over food may serve 143 29
When a common *m* or Agape is a part 401 15

meals

70. Grace at *M* 812 25
70. Grace at *M* 835 —

mean

find accordingly, that, seeking to keep the happy *m* 9 25
And the *m* whereby the Body of Christ is received 873 32

meaning

godparents are to be instructed in the *m* of Baptism, 298 25
It finds all its *m* in the resurrection. 507 2

means

but this is by no *m* certain, 583 18
by the *m* whereof, the people shall not 867 6

meant

but is not *m* to be a complete statement of belief 844 4
yet it is not *m*, but when men say Matins 867 25

mediator

Christ, who is the only *M* between God and Man, 869 8

meditation

A *m*, silent or spoken, may follow. 106 —
(by often reading, and *m* of God's word) 866 11

meek

with a *m*, candid, and charitable frame of mind; 11 18

meet

forms of service are provided here to *m* the needs 446 10
It is customary that the celebrant *m* the body 468 21
It is customary that the celebrant *m* the body 490 21
The celebrant may *m* the body and conduct it 506 4
neither do they make men *m* to receive grace, 870 14

meeting

12. For a Church Convention or *M* 810 18
12. For a Church Convention or *M* 818 —

meets

The Celebrant *m* the body at the door of the church 466 —

member

whole will be received and examined by every true *m* 11 17
A *m* of the congregation bearing 467 9
The death of a *m* of the Church should be reported 468 2
The death of a *m* of the Church should be reported 490 2
a homily by the Celebrant, or a *m* of the family, 495 —
The Deacon or a *m* of the congregation leads 572 —

members

received as such by all the *m* of the same: 8 11
that the *m* of each order within the Church, 13 17
m of the congregation to express intentions or objects 142 8
distributed to *m* of the congregation. 143 16
If candles have been distributed to *m* 286 —
and in their responsibilities as *m* of his Church. 298 27
The Universal Church, its *m*, and its mission 359 —
The Universal Church, its *m*, and its mission 383 —
M of the congregation may ask the prayers 386 —
to their neighbors and are a scandal to the other *m* 409 13
When the priest sees that there is hatred between *m* 409 17
and receive Holy Communion before other *m* 438 3
the parents, with other *m* of the family, should come 439 4

the Celebrant invites the parents and other *m* 439 17
When possible, it is desirable that *m* of the family 462 —
receive Communion before other *m* 511 24
The new Bishop also greets other *m* of the clergy, 522 —
family *m*, and the congregation. 522 —
receive Communion before other *m* 524 18
who then greets family *m* and others, 534 —
receive Communion before other *m* 536 18
The new Deacon then exchanges greetings with family *m* 546 —
The new Minister then greets other *m* of the clergy, 563 —
family *m*, and the congregation. 563 —
It is desirable that all *m* of the congregation, 566 16
M of the congregation vest the Altar, 574 2
they may be decorated by *m* of the congregation 576 2
mortifying the works of the flesh, and their earthly *m*, 871 13
are *m* of the Holy Catholic Church; 876 32

men

Song of the Three Young *M*, 35–65 47 —
Song of the Three Young *M*, 29–34 49 —
Song of the Three Young *M*, 35–65 88 —
Song of the Three Young *M*, 29–34 90 —
2. For all Sorts and Conditions of *M* 810 7
2. For All Sorts and Conditions of *M* 814 —
we all with one accord teach *m* to acknowledge 864 4
for us *m* and for our salvation, of Mary the Virgin, 864 10
At whose coming all *m* shall rise again 865 35
if those *m* will weigh their labor with the profit 867 13
but when *m* say Matins and Evensong privately, 867 25
but also for actual sins of *m*. 868 8
until he return to judge all *M* at the last day. 868 15
touching Ceremonies and Rites, do not bind Christian *m*, 869 11
neither do they make *m* meet to receive grace, 870 14
for by them *m* do declare, 870 20
the Name of Jesus Christ, whereby *m* must be saved. 871 28
Church of Christ is a congregation of faithful *m*, 871 30
(forasmuch as they be an assembly of *m*, 872 7
called to this work by *m* who have public authority 872 19
only badges or tokens of Christian *m*'s profession, 872 26
although they be ministered by evil *m*. 873 9
whereby Christian *m* are discerned from others 873 14
ought to be ministered to all Christian *m* alike. 874 4
Christian *m*, to marry at their own discretion, 874 14
the diversity of countries, times, and *m*'s manners, 874 24
The Power of the Civil Magistrate extendeth to all *m*, 875 35
the duty of all *m* who are professors of the Gospel, 875 37
The Laws of the Realm may punish Christian *m* 876 8
It is lawful for Christian *m*, at the commandment 876 10
Of Christian *M*'s Goods, which are not common. 876 12
that vain and rash Swearing is forbidden Christian *m* 876 18
trustees for the common and equal benefit of all *m*. 877 11

mentions

At the verse which *m* the arrival at Golgotha 273 —
At the verse which *m* the arrival at Golgotha 277 —

mercy

The Kyrie eleison (or "Lord, have *m*") may be sung 406 9
until he show us his *m*. 583 9
religiously in good works, and at length, by God's *m*, 871 9

merit

righteous before God, only for the *m* of our Lord 870 2

meter

Hebrew versification, which is not based on *m* 583 2

method

The exclusive use of a single *m* 582 4
found a satisfactory *m* of chanting them. 582 12
This is probably the most satisfying *m* for reciting 582 17
recitation is the name given to a *m* of psalmody 582 19
This was the traditional *m* of singing the Venite, 582 22
recitation is the *m* which has been most frequently 582 27

methods

There are several traditional *m* of psalmody. 582 4
The traditional *m*, each of which can be elaborate 582 6
locally adapted in the *m* of its administration 877 18
locally adapted in the *m* of its administration 878 4

metrical

The following hymn, or a *m* version of it, 112 —
M versions of the Invitatory Psalms, 141 21

Michael

Saint *M* and All Angels 17 3
Saint *M* and All Angels September 29 193 —
Saint *M* and All Angels September 29 244 —

midst

the Anthem "In the *m* of life" 283 —
or from the *m* of the congregation. 406 19
"May they exalt you, O Lord, in the *m*..." 554 4
The new Minister, if a priest, may then kneel in the *m* 562 —

mind

a meek, candid, and charitable frame of *m*; 11 19
and their hearts, spirit, and *m*, have not been edified 866 26
agreeable to the *m* and purpose of the old fathers, 866 43
and drawing up their *m* to high and heavenly things, 871 14

minds

the *m* of some slanderous folks to be offended; 875 44

mingled

in the visible Church the evil be ever *m* with the good, 873 2

minister

On occasion, at the discretion of the *M*, 142 13
all stand, and the Celebrant or *M* appointed 264 —
M and People 320 —
M and People 331 —
A *M* may then say one or more of the following 332 —
M and People 352 —
M and People 360 —
and the Deacon or *M* appointed says 426 —
The *M* of the Congregation is directed to instruct 445 —
the *M* of the Congregation is to be notified. 453 2
the *M* of the Congregation should be notified, 462 —
in consultation with, the *M* of the Congregation. 468 4
the Deacon or *M* appointed reads the Gospel, 479 —
a Deacon or other *M* may dismiss them, saying 483 —
in consultation with, the *M* of the Congregation. 490 4
the Deacon or *M* appointed reads the Gospel, 495 —
a Deacon or other *M* may dismiss them, saying 500 —

deacons to *m* in Christ's name to the poor, 510 14
and *m* Holy Communion to those communicants 555 2
Letter of Institution of a *M* 557 1
The chief *m* is normally the bishop; 558 7
The new *m*, if a deacon, should read the Gospel, 558 20
Wardens, standing before the bishop with the new *m*, 559 5
New *m* 559 —
stand before the bishop with the new *m*. 561 —
nature of the new ministry, and to the order of the *m*. 561 —
If the new *m* is the rector or vicar of the parish, 562 —
The new *M*, if a priest, may then kneel 562 —
The Bishop then presents the new *m* 563 —
the family of the new *m* may also be presented 563 —
The Bishop greets the new *m*. 563 —
The new *M* then says to the people 563 —
The new *M* then greets other members of the clergy, 563 —
but if the new *m* is a lay person, 564 6
The new *m* is normally presented to the bishop 565 4
sermon may be preached by the bishop, the new *m*, 565 16
and of the new *m* may be made. 565 18
The rector or *m* in charge takes part as indicated. 566 13
The Rector or *M* in charge continues 569 —
the *m* alternating with the congregation, 582 28
13. For the Election of a Bishop or other *M* 810 19
13. For the Election of a Bishop or other *M* 818 —
or to *m* the Sacraments, in a tongue not understanded 872 23
and do *m* by his commission and authority, 873 4

ministered

Sacraments be duly *m* according to Christ's 871 31
do receive the Sacraments *m* unto them; 873 8
although they be *m* by evil men. 873 9
ordinance and commandment, ought to be *m* to all 874 3
Sacraments ought to be *m* in a known tongue. 875 12
m with unfailing use of Christ's words of institution 877 16
m with unfailing use of Christ's words of Institution, 878 2

ministering

m either the Bread or the Wine, 536 15
XXIII. Of *M* in the Congregation. 872 15
or *m* the Sacraments in the Congregation, 872 16
m either of God's Word, or of the Sacraments, 876 1

ministers

When the *m* enter, one or two lighted candles 142 28
On this day the *m* enter in silence. 276 —
It is customary for all the ordained *m* present, 284 10
the *m*, candidates, and sponsors go to the font 312 29
Then the *M* and People may greet one another 332 —
The *m* receive the Sacrament in both kinds, 338 —
Then the *M* and People may greet one another 360 —
The *m* receive the Sacrament in both kinds, 365 —
The deacon may be assisted by other *m*. 407 17
because such *m* alone have the function 422 8
married couple receive Communion first, after the *m*. 432 —
presented to the *m* by the newly married persons. 438 —
the Church and its *m* declaring absolution. 446 5
or during the entrance of the *m*, 468 —
and other *m* take their places at the body. 482 —
or during the entrance of the *m*, 490 24
and other *m* take their places at the body. 499 —
three distinct orders of ordained *m* 510 5
the entrance of the bishops and other *m*. 512 —
as associates and fellow *m* of the Sacrament, 524 15
at the Altar as fellow *m* of the Sacrament. 553 10
The newly ordained bishop, assisted by other *m*, 553 11
including vicars of missions and assistant *m*. 558 5
M of other Churches may appropriately be invited 558 19
the bishop and other *m* may be clearly seen and heard 564 16
Neighboring *m* should be invited to participate, 566 14
as the *m* move from one part of the church to another. 576 5
especially such as were *M* of the congregation, 866 10
and send *M* into the Lord's vineyard. 872 20
XXVI. Of the Unworthiness of the *M*, 873 1
that inquiry be made of evil *M*, 873 11
we judge them to be read in Churches by the *M*, 874 38
XXXVI. Of Consecration of Bishops and *M*. 875 20

ministration

and assisting in the *m* of the Sacrament 322 12
During the *m* of Communion, 338 —
and assisting in the *m* of the Sacrament 354 12
During the *m* of Communion, 365 —
M to the Sick 453 1
At the *M*, one or more parts of the following service 453 3
M at the Time of Death 462 —
chief authority in the *M* of the Word and Sacraments, 873 3

ministrations

in order that the *m* of tne Church may be provided. 462 —

ministries

there have been different *m* within the Church. 510 3
or the inauguration of other *m*, 558 4

ministry

15. For the *M* (Ember Days) 205 —
II. For the choice of fit persons for the *m* 205 —
15. For the *M* (Ember Days) 256 —
II. For the choice of fit persons for the *m* 256 —
and the *M* of the Word of the Vigil Eucharist, 284 25
If on any one of the above-named days the *m* 312 8
The *M* of the Word 425 —
This service then replaces the *M* of the Word, 437 7
For the *M* of the Word it is fitting 437 13
The *m* of reconciliation, which has been committed 446 2
Part I. *M* of the Word 453 12
as being called by God to the ordained *m* 510 17
It is also recognized and affirmed that the threefold *m* 510 26
The *M* of the Word 515 —
The *M* of the Word 528 —
The *M* of the Word 540 —
fully empowered and authorized to exercise this *m*, 557 8
as an expression of the collegiality of the *m* 558 17
Celebration of a New *M* 559 —
or else may state the purpose of the new *m*. 559 —
as appropriate to the nature of the new *m*, 561 —
in the Bishop's absence a Priest beginning a new *m*, 563 —
The Institution, the *M* of the Word, 564 14
to reaffirm its commitment to its mission and *m*, 577 24
Prayers for the Ordained *M* are on pages 205 and 810 25
The *M* 855 —
we may use their *M*, both in hearing the Word 873 5

miscarried

but this great and good work *m* at that time; 10 22

Miserere

Psalm 51 *M* mei, Deus	266	—

mission

one of these prayers for *m* is added	57	—
one of these prayers for *m* is added	70	—
one of these prayers for *m* is added	100	—
one of these prayers for *m* is added	124	—
16. For the *M* of the Church	206	—
16. For the *M* of the Church	257	—
The Universal Church, its members, and its *m*	359	—
The Universal Church, its members, and its *m*	383	—
(c) a Collect for the *m* of the Church;	394	—
to reaffirm its commitment to its *m* and ministry,	577	24
8. For the *M* of the Church	810	14
3. For the *M* of the Church	813	3
8. For the *M* of the Church	816	—
See also the prayers for the *M* of the Church	816	—
3. For the *M* of the Church	838	—

missionary

Of a *M*	196	3
Of a *M*	247	7
in the carrying out of its *m* and pastoral work,	510	10

missions

including vicars of *m* and assistant ministers.	558	5
vicars of *m*, hospital chaplains, and other priests	565	25

mitre

a ring, staff, and *m*, or other suitable insignia	553	6

model

to *m* and organize their respective Churches,	10	28

modern

and it is increasingly favored by *m* composers.	582	26

modernization

classical prayers which do not lend themselves to *m*,	814	—

modernized

composed in traditional idiom have not been *m*;	814	—

modes

relating to *m* of worship and discipline,	876	33

modest

"Make them, O Lord, *m* and humble..."	554	25

monastic

Of a *M*	198	—
Of a *M*	249	—
16. For *M* Orders and Vocations	810	23
16. For *M* Orders and Vocations	819	—

Monday

The Rogation Days, traditionally observed on *M*,	18	8
This order is not appropriate for use on *M*,	108	11
M in Holy Week	168	—
M in Easter Week	171	—
M, Tuesday, and Wednesday of this week	174	—
M in Holy Week	220	—
M in Easter Week	222	—
M, Tuesday, and Wednesday of this week	225	—

money

and *m* or other gifts, to the deacon or celebrant.	333	—
and *m* or other gifts, to the deacon or celebrant.	361	—

monotonous

makes the recitation of the Psalter needlessly *m*.	582	5

moon

Easter Day is always the first Sunday after the full *m*	15	7

moral

the Commandments which are called *M*.	869	14

morally

The secrecy of a confession is *m* absolute	446	27

morals

of Christian doctrine, and instructive in piety and *m*.	875	15

more

the Collect, Preface, and one or *m* of the Lessons	16	14
begins the service with one or *m* of these sentences	37	—
then says one or *m* of the following Collects	55	—
begins the service with one or *m* of the following	61	—
then says one or *m* of the following Collects	68	—
begins the service with one or *m* of these sentences	75	—
One or *m* sections of this Canticle may be used.	88	—
then says one or *m* of the following Collects	98	—
One or *m* of the following Psalms is sung or said.	103	—
one or *m* sections of Psalm 119,	103	—
begins the service with one or *m* of the following	115	—
then says one or *m* of the following Collects	122	—
One or *m* of the following Psalms are sung or said.	128	—
When *m* than one person is present,	136	—
When one or *m* Scripture Lessons are to be read later	143	8
When desired, *m* than one Lesson may be read,	143	25
Three or *m* of the appointed Lessons are read	175	—
Three or *m* of the appointed Lessons are read	227	—
Baptism is to be sponsored by one or *m* baptized persons.	298	16
and one or *m* of the Lessons provided	312	21
may then say one or *m* of the following sentences,	332	—
consecrate *m* of either or both, by saying	408	11
or else the celebrant may consecrate *m* of both kinds,	408	13
and one or *m* of the Lessons	414	—
Then one or *m* of the following passages	426	—
one or *m* of the prayers may be omitted.	429	—
3. One or *m* Readings, one of which is always	435	15
If *m* than one person responds,	437	11
The Celebrant may add one or *m* of the following	444	—
The Priest may then say one or *m* of these	449	—
one or *m* parts of the following service are used,	453	3
but when two or *m* are used together,	453	4
One or *m* of the following or other passages	453	13
All stand while one or *m* of the following anthems	469	—
One or *m* of the following passages	470	—
or with one or *m* suitable prayers	480	—
or one or *m* of these anthems may be sung	483	—
All stand while one or *m* of the following anthems	491	—
One or *m* of the following passages	494	—
or with one or *m* suitable prayers	496	—
or one or *m* of these anthems may be sung	500	—
4. One or *m* passages of Holy Scripture are read.	506	10
by one or *m* of the other bishops	517	—

(When there are *m* ordinands than one, 552 11
If two or *m* are ordained together, 553 25
If two or *m* are ordained together, 554 15
in *m* recent manuscripts and in printed Bibles, 583 21
as being *m* appropriate to this context; 584 6
and be *m* able to exhort others 866 11
continually profit *m* and *m* in the knowledge of God, 866 14
the *m* inflamed with the love of his true religion. 866 14
there was *m* business to find out what should be read, 866 31
and a great deal *m* profitable and commodious, 866 44
It is *m* profitable, because here are left out 866 44
It is also *m* commodious, both for the shortness 867 4
And if any would judge this way *m* painful, 867 11
as *m* largely is expressed in the Homily 870 4
do *m* for his sake, than of bounden duty is required: 870 22
which say, they can no *m* sin as long as they live 870 36
when the same congregation attends two or *m* services. 888 8
When *m* than one Reading is used at an Office, 934 15

moreover

And *m*, whereas St. Paul would have such language 866 22
M, the number and hardness of the Rules called the Pie, 866 29

morning

other major Feasts, and Daily *M* and Evening Prayer, 13 4
the Order for *M* or Evening Prayer may be used 36 8
Daily *M* Prayer: 37 —
the Order for *M* or Evening Prayer may be used 74 7
Daily *M* Prayer: 75 —
In the *M* 137 —
M and Evening Prayer 141 2
In Rite One services of *M* Prayer and Evening Prayer, 141 18
When *M* or Evening Prayer is used as the Liturgy 142 17
or after the Collects of *M* of Evening Prayer; 148 —
or at the end of *M* or Evening Prayer; 154 —
the prayer for forgiveness appointed at *M* Prayer. 269 —
sunrise on Easter *M*. 284 4
M or Evening Prayer may be used 322 18
M or Evening Prayer may be used 354 18
At *M* or Evening Prayer it may take place 439 8
In the *M* 461 —
First Day: *M* Prayer 585 —
Second Day: *M* Prayer 593 —
Third Day: *M* Prayer 599 —
Fourth Day: *M* Prayer 606 —
Fifth Day: *M* Prayer 613 —
Sixth Day: *M* Prayer 621 —
Seventh Day: *M* Prayer 629 —
Eighth Day: *M* Prayer 636 —
Ninth Day: *M* Prayer 645 —
Tenth Day: *M* Prayer 654 —
Eleventh Day: *M* Prayer 662 —
Twelfth Day: *M* Prayer 669 —
Thirteenth Day: *M* Prayer 676 —
Fourteenth Day: *M* Prayer 683 —
Fifteenth Day: *M* Prayer 691 —
Sixteenth Day: *M* Prayer 701 —
Seventeenth Day: *M* Prayer 709 —
Eighteenth Day: *M* Prayer 717 —
Nineteenth Day: *M* Prayer 724 —
Twentieth Day: *M* Prayer 731 —
Twenty-first Day: *M* Prayer 738 —
Twenty-second Day: *M* Prayer 746 —
Twenty-third Day: *M* Prayer 753 —
Twenty-fourth Day: *M* Prayer 759 —
Twenty-fifth Day: *M* Prayer 766 —
Twenty-sixth Day: *M* Prayer 772 —
Twenty-seventh Day: *M* Prayer 778 —
Twenty-eighth Day: *M* Prayer 785 —
Twenty-ninth Day: *M* Prayer 794 —
Thirtieth Day: *M* Prayer 800 —
Prayers for Friday, Saturday, and Sunday, and for *m* 812 26
For use after the Collects of *M* or Evening Prayer 814 —
Prayers for Friday, Saturday, and Sunday, and for *m* 833 —
or at any time after the Collects at *M* 836 —
Lessons are to be read at the principal *m* service, 888 9
same congregation is present for *M* or Evening Prayer, 888 12
Two of the Readings may be used in the *m* 934 8
and in the *m* in Year Two. 934 12
those for the *m* are given first, 934 26
appointed for a given day may be used in the *m* 934 28

mortifying

the Spirit of Christ, *m* the works of the flesh, 871 13

Moses

8 The Song of *M* Cantemus Domino 85 —
Canticle 8, The Song of *M* 289 —
construction occurs in the Canticle, "The Song of *M*." 584 3
Although the Law given from God by *M*, 869 11

most

It is a *m* invaluable part of that blessed "liberty 9 2
or otherwise disposed of, as may seem *m* convenient 9 8
might *m* tend to the preservation of peace 10 10
in such manner as they might judge *m* convenient 10 29
in the clearest, plainest, *m* affecting and majestic 11 21
m closely to the date of Pentecost in that year 176 —
m closely to the date of Trinity Sunday in that year 176 —
m closely to the date of Pentecost in that year 227 —
m closely to the date of Trinity Sunday in that year 228 —
notify the bishop, within fourteen days at the *m*, 409 25
and is, *m* generally recognized by Christian people 510 30
This is probably the *m* satisfying method for reciting 582 17
the method which has been *m* frequently used 582 27
The *m* common verse is a couplet, 583 10
order as is *m* easy and plain for the understanding, 867 3
for they may be proved by *m* certain warrants 869 17
a *m* wholesome Doctrine, and very full of comfort, 870 4
Predestination, is a *m* dangerous downfall, 871 18
or into wretchlessness of *m* unclean living, 871 19
as *m* agreeable with the institution of Christ. 873 20
by Elizabeth our Queen do *m* plainly testify; 876 2

mother

gives the child to the *m* or father, saying 441 —
of the Substance of his *M*, born in the world; 865 24

mourn

Isaiah 61:1–3 (To comfort all that *m*) 470 —
Isaiah 6:1–3 (To comfort those who *m*) 494 —
for those who *m*, and for the Christian community, 506 16
we sorrow in sympathy with those who *m*. 507 14

mouth
the Sacrament is not received with the *m*. 457 —

movable
upon the *m* date of the Sunday of the Resurrection 15 4

move
as the ministers *m* from one part of the church to another. 576 5

movement
If the *m* to the font is a formal procession, 312 31

moves
As the procession *m* into the church, 568 —
The Bishop *m* to the Font, lays a hand upon it, 569 —

moving
upon just and weighty considerations her thereunto *m*, 10 3

much
happy mean between too *m* stiffness in refusing, 9 25
and too *m* easiness in admitting variations 9 26
wherein (so *m* as may be) the reading 866 35
m agreeable to the mind and purpose of the old fathers, 866 43
not only render unto God as *m* as they are bound 870 21

multitude
ought to be taken of the whole *m* of the faithful, 874 18

music
instrumental *m* may be substituted 14 9
When it is desired to use *m* composed for them, 14 13
instrumental *m*, other art forms, silence. 400 10
or instrumental *m* may be played. 423 —
or instrumental *m* may be played. 431 —
or instrumental *m* may be played. 432 —
instrumental *m* may be played. 553 3
singing and instrumental *m* are appropriate. 567 —
When an instrument of *m* is to be dedicated, 572 —
Instrumental *m* is now played, or a hymn or anthem 572 —
Bells may now be rung and *m* played. 574 —
or instrumental *m* may be used 576 4

musical
A *m* prelude or processional is not appropriate. 142 27
The use of portable *m* instruments is suitable. 575 10

musicians
builders, *m*, artists, benefactors, and friends. 566 18
17. For Church *M* and Artists 810 24
17. For Church *M* and Artists 819 —

must
to belong to Doctrine *m* be referred to Discipline; 9 6
it *m* be understood to include "or sung," 14 11
at least, of the parties *m* be a baptized Christian; 422 4
but it *m* be made clear to the penitent that absolution 446 13
and *m* under no circumstances be broken. 446 28
at least two presbyters *m* be present. 524 2
at least two presbyters *m* be present. 536 2
He therefore that will be saved *m* thus think 865 18
but that of necessity there *m* be some rules: 866 40
all things *m* be read upon the book, 867 12
we *m* receive God's promises in such wise, 871 21
the Name of Jesus Christ, whereby men *m* be saved. 871 28

N

Name
The Holy *N* 16 5
The Holy *N* January 1 162 —
The Holy *N* January 1 213 —
"In the *N* of the Father, and of the Son, 313 17
Gather in the Lord's *N* 400 7
and wife, in the *N* of the Father, and of the Son, 436 5
The "Four-letter *N*" (Tetragrammaton) 583 17
Divine *N* was written in antique and obsolete letters; 583 21
N was provided with the vowels of the word Adonai. 583 23
reverence and reticence with regard to the *N* of God 583 25
that the Divine *N* be spelled out, 584 2
obtaining eternal Salvation only by the *N* of Christ. 871 24
doth set out unto us only the *N* of Jesus Christ, 871 27

name
Each candidate is presented by *n* to the Celebrant, 307 —
Using the given *n* of the one to be baptized 313 24
greet one another in the *n* of the Lord. 332 —
greet one another in the *n* of the Lord. 360 —
all greet one another in the *n* of the Lord. 401 2
said by the Priest in the *n* of the gathering, 401 8
deacons to minister in Christ's *n* to the poor, 510 14
When the bishop-elect is presented, his full *n* 511 18
the Christian *n* by which he wishes to be known. 511 20
When the ordinand is presented, his full *n* 524 9
the Christian *n* by which he wishes to be known. 524 11
When the ordinand is presented, his full *n* 536 9
the Christian *n* by which he wishes to be known. 536 11
or one appropriate to the *n* of the church. 576 26
Responsorial recitation is the *n* given to a method 582 19
Adonai ("Lord") and the personal *n* YHWH. 583 16
In the *n* of the Holy Scripture we do understand 868 23
they do not the same in their own *n*, but in Christ's, 873 4
in the *n* of the Father, and of the Son, 876 31

named
If on any one of the above-*n* days the ministry 312 8
(The Father from whom every family is *n*) 426 —

namely
all such prayers, *n*, that "Rulers may have grace, 10 36

names
make promises in their own *n*, 298 22
the full *n* of the persons to be married 422 20
only their Christian *n* are used. 422 22
Of the *N* and Number of the Canonical Books. 868 25
Of the *N* of the Homilies 875 1

narrative
Prayer C, ending with the *n* of the Institution). 408 16

nation
The Collect "For the *N*," page 207, may be used 190 —
17. For the *N* 207 —
The Collect "For the *N*," page 258, may be used 242 —
17. For the *N* 258 —

The *N* and all in authority 359 —
The *N* and all in authority 383 —
5. For the *N* 813 6
5. For the *N* 838 —

national

especially in times of war, or of *n* anxiety, 154 —
Prayers for *N* Life 810 26
Thanksgivings for *N* Life 813 5
Prayers for *N* Life 820 —
Thanksgivings for *N* Life 838 —
or *n* Church hath authority to ordain, 874 31

nations

5. For Peace among the *N* 810 10
5. For Peace Among the *N* 816 —
varying needs of the *n* and peoples called of God 877 19
varying needs of the *n* and peoples called of God 878 5

native

persons whose *n* tongue is other than English, 406 21

nativity

our Lord's *N* or Christmas Day. 15 6
The *N* of Our Lord: Christmas Day December 25 160 —
The *N* of Saint John the Baptist June 24 190 —
The *N* of Our Lord: Christmas Day December 25 212 —
The *N* of Saint John the Baptist June 24 241 —
12 Of the *N* of Christ. 875 3

natural

Prayers for the *N* Order 811 21
41. For the Conservation of *N* Resources 811 23
Thanksgivings for the *N* Order 813 10
Prayers for the *N* Order 827 —
41. For the Conservation of *N* Resources 827 —
Thanksgivings for the *N* Order 840 —
by his own *n* strength and good works, 869 35

naturally

that *n* is engendered of the offspring of Adam; 869 24

nature

being things in their own *n* indifferent, and alterable, 9 16
as appropriate to the *n* of the new ministry, 561 —
bishop may state briefly the *n* of the person's office 565 2
for the distinctive *n* of the community, 576 20
Human *N* 845 —
of each *n* being preserved and coming together 864 14
took Man's *n* in the womb of the blessed Virgin, 868 3
things appertaining to the perfection of Man's *n*; 868 14
it is the fault and corruption of the *N* of every man, 869 24
and is of his own *n* inclined to evil, 869 26
And this infection of *n* doth remain, 869 28
concupiscence and lust hath of itself the *n* of sin. 869 32
but they have the *n* of sin. 870 17
Christ in the truth of our *n* was made like unto us 870 25
according to that Law, and the light of *N*. 871 27
because it is partly of a local and civil *n*, 872 3
but yet have not like *n* of Sacraments with Baptism, 872 35
overthroweth the *n* of a Sacrament, 873 30

natures

Divine and Human *N* in the Person of Christ 864 2
recognized in two *n*, without confusion, 864 12
the distinction of *n* being in no way annulled 864 13
so that two whole and perfect *N*, 868 4

near

placed on or *n* the Altar, 143 13
or other person appointed, standing *n* the Candle, 286 —
When a person is *n* death, the Minister 462 3
A Prayer for a Person *n* Death 462 5

nearby

and the penitent kneels *n*. 446 17

nearer

love has entered into the *n* presence of our Lord, 507 13

necessarily

their ecclesiastical independence was *n* included; 10 26
and do spring out *n* of a true and lively Faith; 870 9

necessary

seem either *n* or expedient." 9 21
alterations in the Liturgy which became *n* 10 33
As *n*, the observance of one, two, or all three 161 —
As *n*, the observance of one, two, or all three 213 —
When *n*, the Celebrant consecrates additional bread 338 —
When *n*, the Celebrant consecrates additional bread 365 —
If it is *n* to shorten the service, 396 —
N announcements may be made before the service, 407 12
If *n*, or if desired, all or part of the service 468 10
If *n*, or if desired, all or part of the service 490 10
When *n*, the administration may take place 553 12
changed to the plural where *n*. 553 28
changed to the plural where *n*. 554 18
but, if *n*, a deputy may be appointed. 558 7
n, for dedicating parts of a building, or furnishings, 566 4
N announcements may now be made. 567 7
or other circumstances make it *n*, 575 12
it is *n* that he hold the Catholic Faith. 864 22
Furthermore, it is *n* to everlasting salvation 865 19
Holy Scripture containeth all things *n* to salvation: 868 20
or be thought requisite or *n* to salvation. 868 22
n to salvation have neither strength nor authority, 872 9
It is not *n* that Traditions and Ceremonies 874 22
wholesome Doctrine, and *n* for these times, 874 36
doth contain all things *n* to such Consecration 875 22
"containing all things *n* to salvation," 877 34

necessity

n and expediency of occasional alterations 9 23
In cases of *n*, a deacon or lay person may perform 456 —
no remedy, but that of *n* there must be some rules: 866 40
ought of *n* to be received in any commonwealth; 869 12
all those things that of *n* are requisite to the same. 871 32
any thing to be believed for *n* of Salvation. 871 42

neck

The stole worn about the *n*, or other insignia 553 21

need

(b) a Collect expressive of some special *n* in the life 394 —
and, if *n* be, a flagon of wine 407 19
n none other books for their public service, 867 6

needed

counsel and encouragement as are *n* 446 22
introduce prayers and hymns as *n*. 844 11

needlessly

makes the recitation of the Psalter *n* monotonous. 582 5

needs

used when the *n* of the congregation so require. 13 10
provided here to meet the *n* of penitents. 446 10
varying *n* of the nations and peoples called of God 877 19
varying *n* of the nations and peoples called of God 878 5

neglected

35. For the Poor and *N* 811 14
35. For the Poor and the *N* 826 —
broken, and *n*, by planting in uncertain stories, 866 17

neglecting

not *n*, if they are able, to leave bequests 445 —

neighboring

N ministers should be invited to participate, 566 14
in the parish house, in a former or *n* place 575 6

neighbors

have done wrong to their *n* and are a scandal 409 13

neither

for pastoral considerations, *n* of the burial rites 506 2
"*n* death, nor life, nor angels, nor principalities, 507 6
n confounding the Persons, nor dividing 864 26
The Father is made of none, *n* created, but begotten. 865 8
n made, nor created, nor begotten, 865 10
N that any man shall be bound 867 26
n do they make men meet to receive grace, 870 14
n may it so expound one place of Scripture, 871 39
as necessary to salvation have *n* strength 872 9
N is the effect of Christ's ordinance taken away 873 6
n hath it any thing that, of itself, is superstitious 875 23
n hath it any thing, 875 29

never

There was *n* any thing by the wit of man 866 3
but they were only begun, and *n* read through. 866 21
were joined together in one Person, *n* to be divided, 868 5
of whose authority was *n* any doubt in the Church. 868 24

nevertheless

N, it appertaineth to the discipline of the Church, 873 10

new

proper to revive it by any *n* Commission. 10 23
A *n* heart and a *n* spirit 290 —
duties to help the *n* Christians grow in the knowledge 298 26
Tobit 8:5b–8 (*N* English Bible) 426 —
From the *N* Testament 475 —
Revelation 21:2–7 (Behold, I make all things *n*) 475 —
After the *N* Testament Lesson, a suitable canticle 475 —
From the *N* Testament 495 —
Revelation 21:2–7 (Behold, I make all things *n*) 495 —
In particular, since the time of the *N* Testament, 510 4
for which the *n* bishop is to be consecrated, 511 10
The *n* bishop is now vested according to the order 521 —
presents to the people their *n* bishop. 522 —
The *n* Bishop then says 522 —
and other Bishops greet the *n* bishop. 522 —
The *n* Bishop also greets other members of the clergy, 522 —
The *n* Bishop, if the Bishop of the Diocese, 522 —
Then the *n* Bishop goes to the Lord's Table as chief 522 —
The *n* Bishop blesses the people, first saying 523 —
N Bishop 523 —
the *n* priest and other priests stand 524 14
The *n* priest is now vested according to the order 534 —
The *n* Priest then says to the congregation 534 —
The Bishop then asks the *n* priest to bless the people. 535 —
The *n* Priest says 535 —
the *n* deacon assists in the distribution 536 14
The *n* deacon is now vested according to the order 545 —
The *n* Deacon then exchanges greetings with family 546 —
after which the *n* Deacon dismisses them 547 —
and while the *n* bishop is being clothed 553 2
with the *n* bishop at the Altar as fellow ministers 553 10
placed upon the *n* priest after the entire Prayer 553 22
A Bible is to be given to each *n* priest, 554 5
all the *n* priests break the consecrated Bread 554 9
placed upon the *n* deacon after the entire Prayer 554 13
A Bible is to be given to each *n* deacon, 554 26
The *n* minister, if a deacon, should read the Gospel, 558 20
N Ministry 559 —
standing before the bishop with the *n* minister, 559 —
state the purpose of the *n* ministry. 559 —
N minister 559 —
stand before the bishop with the *n* minister. 561 3
as appropriate to the nature of the *n* ministry, 561 —
If the *n* minister is the rector or vicar of the parish, 562 —
The *n* Minister, if a priest, may then kneel 562 —
then presents the *n* minister to the congregation, 563 —
the family of the *n* minister may also be presented 563 —
The Bishop greets the *n* minister. 563 —
The *n* Minister then says to the people 563 —
n Minister then greets other members of the clergy, 563 —
a Priest beginning a *n* ministry, 563 —
but if the *n* minister is a lay person, 564 6
The *n* minister is normally presented to the bishop 565 4
may be preached by the bishop, the *n* minister, 565 16
and of the *n* minister may be made. 565 18
When a *n* church is being consecrated, 575 15
additions, or *n* furnishings in a church or chapel. 577 10
The blessing of a *n* font or baptistry should always 577 15
The *N* Covenant 850 —
those canonical Books of the Old and *N* Testament, 868 23
All the Books of the *N* Testament, 869 4
The Old Testament is not contrary to the *N*: 869 7
for both in the Old and *N* Testament 869 7
a sign of Regeneration or *N*-Birth, 873 16
1. The Holy Scriptures of the Old and *N* Testament 877 14
(a) The Holy Scriptures of the Old and *N* Testaments, 877 33

newly

then lighted from the *n* kindled fire, 285 —
and concluding with the reception of the *n* baptized) 292 —
If a priest uses Chrism in signing the *n* baptized, 298 14
given to each of the *n* baptized or to a godparent. 313 8
presented by the *n* baptized or their godparents. 313 14
presented by persons *n* confirmed. 412 17
The *n* married couple then greet each other, 431 —

at which the *n* married couple may present 432 —
the *n* married couple receive Communion first, 432 —
presented to the ministers by the *n* married persons. 438 2
by the family or friends of the *n* ordained. 511 22
family of the *n* ordained may receive Communion 511 23
by the family or friends of the *n* ordained. 524 13
family of the *n* ordained may receive Communion 524 17
The Bishop then gives a Bible to the *n* ordained, 534 —
The Bishop greets the *n* ordained. 534 —
The Presbyters present greet the *n* ordained; 534 —
the *n* ordained Priest joins in the celebration 535 —
by the family or friends of the *n* ordained. 536 13
family of the *n* ordained may receive Communion 536 17
The Bishop gives a Bible to the *n* ordained, saying 545 —
and the Clergy present now greet the *n* ordained. 546 —
The *n* ordained Deacon prepares the bread, 546 —
The *n* ordained bishop, assisted by other ministers, 553 11
All the *n* ordained take part in the exchange 554 7
A *n* inducted Priest may, at the bishop's request, 564 10
the reception of the *n* baptized. 575 31
to a *n* created Joint Commission on Christian Reunion. 877 28

Nicene

N Creed may take the place of the Apostles' Creed, 142 18
When the Liturgy of the Palms has preceded, the *N* Creed 273 —
The *N* Creed is not used at this service. 295 —
take the place of the *N* Creed at the Eucharist. 312 17
The *N* Creed is not used at this service. 312 27
The *N* Creed 326 —
The *N* Creed 358 —
The *N* Creed is not used at this service. 412 15
The Congregation then says or sings the *N* Creed 529 —
The Congregation then says or sings the *N* Creed. 541 —
the *N* Creed is now said or sung. 572 —
The *N* Creed, and that which is commonly called 869 16
"The Three Creeds, *N* Creed, Athanasius's Creed, 869 20
2. The *N* Creed as the sufficient statement 877 15
and the *N* Creed, as the sufficient statement 877 35

nine

One Thousand Seven Hundred and Eighty-*N*. 8 6

ninefold

said in threefold, sixfold, or *n* form. 406 10

nineteenth

N Day: Morning Prayer 724 —
N Day: Evening Prayer 727 —

ninety

one thousand seven hundred and *n*. 8 13

ninth

N Day: Morning Prayer 645 —
N Day: Evening Prayer 650 —
Twenty-*n* Day: Morning Prayer 794 —
Twenty-*n* Day: Evening Prayer 797 —

no

for which *n* service or prayer has been provided 13 13
Provided, that there is *n* celebration of the Eucharist 18 11
N Proper Preface is used. 177 —
for which *n* Proper is provided 195 —
N Proper Preface is used. 228 —
N Proper Preface is used. 229 —
for which *n* Proper is provided 246 —
N blessing or dismissal is added. 282 —
There is *n* celebration of the Eucharist on this day. 283 —
the Deacon (the Celebrant if there is *n* deacon) 285 —
If there is *n* celebration of the Eucharist, 311 —
If on the four days listed above there are *n* candidates 312 15
If there is *n* celebration of the Communion, 330 —
If there is *n* celebration of the Communion, 359 —
If there is *n* Communion, all that is appointed 406 25
a deacon, or, if there is *n* deacon, by a lay reader. 407 6
to a congregation when *n* priest is available. 409 2
When there is *n* Baptism, the rites of Confirmation, 412 11
If there is *n* celebration of the Eucharist, 419 —
and *n* priest or bishop is available, 422 16
Mark 10:6–9, 13–16 (They are *n* longer two but one) 426 —
and when *n* priest or bishop is available, 435 5
8. If there is *n* Communion, the service concludes 436 10
and must under *n* circumstances be broken. 446 28
When there is *n* Communion, the service continues 481 —
When there is *n* Communion, the service continues 498 —
N persons are allowed to exercise the offices 510 21
If *n* objection is made, the Presiding Bishop continues 514 —
If *n* objection is made, the Bishop continues 527 —
the Deacon or, if *n* deacon is present, a Priest reads 529 —
a Priest if *n* deacon is present, dismisses the people. 535 —
If *n* objection is made, the Bishop continues 539 —
the Deacon or, if *n* deacon is present, a Priest reads 541 —
a Priest if *n* deacon is present, dismisses the assembly. 564 12
If *n* Baptism is to take place 570 —
but this is by *n* means certain, 583 18
distinction of natures being in *n* way annulled 864 13
Yet because there is *n* remedy, but that of necessity 866 40
n Christian man whatsoever is free 869 12
n condemnation for them that believe 869 31
Wherefore we have *n* power to do good works 869 36
and if we say we have *n* sin, 870 29
which say, they can *n* more sin as long as they live 870 36
unclean living, *n* less perilous than desperation. 871 19
and grounded upon *n* warranty of Scripture, 872 14
yet in *n* wise are they partakers of Christ: 873 39
but hath *n* authority in things purely spiritual. 875 36
Rome hath *n* jurisdiction in this Realm of England. 876 7
(For example, 1977 divided by 3 is 659 with *n* remainder. 888 4

nocturn

whereof every one was called a *n*, 866 28

none

and provided further, that *n* of the Propers appointed 18 13
The Father is made of *n*, neither created, 865 8
And in this Trinity *n* is afore, or after other; 865 14
n is greater, or less than another; 865 14
shall need *n* other books for their public service, 867 6
and there is *n* other satisfaction for sin. 874 7

noon

At *N* 138 1

noonday

An Order of Service for *N* 103 2

normally

worship in a Christian assembly is *n* a bishop 13 20
when they occur on a Sunday, are *n* transferred 16 12
The service *n* consists of four parts: 284 5
administers Confirmation, and *n* preaches 284 13
the celebrant should *n* be assigned 322 15
the celebrant should *n* be assigned 354 15
A priest or a bishop *n* presides at the Celebration 422 7
N, the celebrant is a priest or bishop. 435 4
confession is not *n* a matter of subsequent discussion. 446 26
A priest *n* presides at the service. 468 13
A priest *n* presides at the service. 490 13
The chief minister is *n* the bishop; 558 7
The new minister is *n* presented to the bishop 565 4
The Psalms at such Offices are *n* those appointed 888 15

note

N: The liturgy for the dead is an Easter liturgy. 507 1
N: While the above form of the Quadrilateral 877 26

noted

*It is to be *n* that where the words elder, 528 —

nothing

and is ordained *n* to be read, 867 1
forasmuch as *n* can, almost, be so plainly set forth, 867 16
so that *n* be ordained against God's Word. 874 24

notified

illness, the Minister of the Congregation is to be *n*. 453 2
n, in order that the ministrations of the Church 462 4

notify

the priest is required to *n* the bishop, 409 24

notoriously

priest knows that a person who is living a *n* evil life 409 8

notwithstanding

n that the ancient fathers had divided the Psalms 866 27
yet *n*, no Christian man whatsoever is free 869 12
N, every man ought, of such things 876 14

nouns

substitute *n* for pronouns 888 26

nourish

N them, and strengthen them to glorify God 557 13

November

All Saints' Day, *N* 1 15 16
may always be observed on the Sunday following *N* 1, 15 21
Proper 26 The Sunday closest to *N* 2 184 —
Proper 27 The Sunday closest to *N* 9 184 —
Proper 28 The Sunday closest to *N* 16 184 —
Proper 29 The Sunday closest to *N* 23 185 —
Saint Andrew *N* 30 185 —
All Saints' Day *N* 1 194 —
Proper 26 The Sunday closest to *N* 2 235 —
Proper 27 The Sunday closest to *N* 9 236 —
Proper 28 The Sunday closest to *N* 16 236 —
Proper 29 The Sunday closest to *N* 23 236 —
Saint Andrew *N* 30 237 —
All Saints' Day *N* 1 245 —

number

the numbered Proper (*n* 3 through *n* 8), 158 13
does not suffice for the *n* of communicants, 408 9
The other bishops, or a convenient *n* of them, 511 15
the *n* and hardness of the Rules called the Pie, 866 29
rules are here set forth, which, as they be few in *n*; 866 41
Of the Names and *N* of the Canonical Books. 868 25

numbered

the *n* Proper (number 3 through 158 13
the *n* Proper which corresponds 176 —
the *n* Proper which corresponds 176 —
the *n* Proper which corresponds 227 —
the *n* Proper which corresponds 228 —
the *n* Collects beginning on pages 199 and 251. 813 18
on the First Sunday of Advent preceding odd-*n* years, 934 3
on the First Sunday of Advent preceding even-*n* years. 934 4

Numbers

Old Testament Isaiah 6:1–8, or *N* 11:16–17, 24–25 528 —
Old Testament Joshua 1:7–9, or *N* 11:16–17, 24–25a 560 —
N, 868 29

numeration

the *n* of the Revised Standard Version of the Bible. 14 17

nuptial

the function of pronouncing the *n* blessing, 422 9
omitting the *n* blessing which follows The Prayers. 422 17
but does not pronounce a *n* blessing. 435 6

nurses

For Doctors and *N* 460 —

nursing

and a long continuance of *n* care and protection, 9 13

nurture

but is a gift from God for the *n* of his people 510 28

O

oath

XXXIX. Of a Christian Man's O. 876 17

obedience

whatsoever is free from the *o* of the Commandments 869 13
to pay respectful *o* to the Civil Authority, 875 37

obey

they through Grace *o* the calling: 871 7

objection

If no *o* is made, the Presiding Bishop continues 514 —
If no *o* is made, the Bishop continues 527 —
If no *o* is made, the Bishop continues 539 —

objects

the congregation to express intentions or *o* of prayer 142 8

oblation

Of the one O of Christ finished upon the Cross. 874 5

oblations

The *o* of bread and wine at the baptismal Eucharist 313 13
It is appropriate that the *o* of bread and wine be presented 412 16

observance

These feasts take precedence of any other day or *o*. 15 20
in addition to its *o* of the fixed date. 15 22
days of commemoration or of special *o*: 16 25
5. Days of Optional O 17 28
the *o* of one, two, or all three of them, 161 —
the *o* of one, two, or all three of them, 213 —
invites the people to the *o* of a holy Lent, saying 264 —

observed

Principal Feasts *o* in this Church are the following: 15 15
All Saints' Day may always be *o* on the Sunday 15 21
may be *o* on, or be transferred to, a Sunday, 16 9
some other special occasion may be *o* on a Sunday. 16 20
Holy Days are regularly *o* throughout the year. 16 22
are not *o* on the days of Holy Week 17 10
may be *o* on any open day within the week. 17 17
The following days are *o* by special acts of discipline 17 21
the following may be *o* with the Collects, 18 1
The Ember Days, traditionally *o* on the Wednesdays, 18 5
The Rogation Days, traditionally *o* on Monday, 18 8
When a Vigil of Pentecost is *o*, it begins 175 —
The festival of a saint is *o* in accordance 195 —
When a Vigil of Pentecost is *o*, it begins 227 —
The festival of a saint is *o* in accordance 246 —
When *o*, the ceremony of the washing of feet 274 —
from the reserved Sacrament, the following order is *o* 282 —
The Great Vigil, when *o*, is the first service 284 2

obsolete

the Divine Name was written in antique and *o* letters; 583 21
as well from *o* words and phrases, 875 19

obtain

which daily they shall *o* by reading upon the book, 867 14

obtained

when the services of a priest cannot be *o*, 13 26
when the services of a priest cannot be *o*, 284 27
or priest cannot be *o*, 312 9
When the services of a priest cannot be *o*, 408 17
When the services of a priest cannot be *o*, 468 17
When the services of a priest cannot be *o*, 490 17

obtaining

Of *o* eternal Salvation only by the Name of Christ. 871 24

occasion

and, finally, the cutting off *o*, 10 12
from them that seek *o*, of cavil or quarrel 10 13
but, with gratitude to God, embrace the happy *o* 11 4
such forms as are fitting to the *o*. 13 15
On *o*, and as appropriate, instrumental music 14 9
some other special *o* may be observed on a Sunday. 16 20
the Eucharist for any such *o* on Ash Wednesday, 18 12
appropriate to the *o* or to the season, 109 —
On *o*, at the discretion of the Minister, a reading 142 13
suitable to the season or the *o*, may be used. 143 23
on some subsequent *o* of public baptism 312 13
On *o*, the Confession may be omitted. 330 —
On *o*, the Confession may be omitted. 359 —
Adaptations or insertions suitable to the *o* 383 —
related to the *o*, or the season, 383 —
(a) a Collect appropriate to the season or *o* 394 —
appropriate to the day or *o*, 396 —
the particular *o* being celebrated; 402 —
the particular *o* being celebrated; 404 —
Prayers may be offered according to the *o*. 454 14
or another prayer suitable to the *o*, 565 9
or some other form may be composed for the *o*, 576 19
prayers and Bible readings related to the particular *o* 577 12
and hath given *o* to many superstitions. 873 30

occasional

declared the necessity and expediency of *o* alterations 9 23

occasions

the various exigency of times and *o*." 9 10
and for other special *o* for which no service or prayer 13 13
Various O 18 10
Various O is used as a substitute for, 18 14
O of Thanksgiving 40 —
O of Thanksgiving 78 —
Especially suitable in Lent, and on other penitential *o* 90 —
on suitable *o* in the late afternoon or evening. 108 3
In Lent and on other penitential *o* 109 —
Various O, page 888 136 —
The Intercessions on such *o* are to conform 142 22
On special *o*, lighted candles may be distributed 143 15
On all other *o*, the Officiant and People say 153 —
for Holy Days and Various O. 158 9
Various O are on pages 195, 199, 246 and 251. 158 25
Various O 199 —
Various O 251 —
In Lent and on other penitential *o* 299 —
On other *o* they are selected 300 —
reserved for these *o* or when a bishop is present. 312 6
When a bishop is present, or on other *o* 312 20
In Lent and on other penitential *o* 319 —
In Lent and on other penitential *o* 323 —
and on other *o* as appointed. 334 —
and on other *o* as appointed. 341 —
appointed for Holy Days and Various O 345 —
Prefaces for Other O 347 —
In Lent and on other penitential *o* 351 —
In Lent and on other penitential *o* 355 —
On other *o* the following is used 356 —
and on other *o* as appointed. 361 —
and on other *o* as appointed. 367 —
appointed for Holy Days and Various O 378 —
Prefaces for Other O 380 —
one of those appointed for Various O. 396 —
In Lent and on other penitential *o* 413 —
In Lent and on other penitential *o* 512 —
In Lent and on other penitential *o* 525 —
In Lent and on other penitential *o* 537 —
On Ember Days or other *o*, 548 —
When this Litany is used on other *o*, 551 —
in the Lectionary for Various O. 565 15

consecration of a church, or on other suitable *o*. 579 —
The term "Various O" in the following pages refers 813 17
See also Various O no. 18. 815 —
101, and Various O no. 16. 816 —
See also Various O no. 13. 818 —
See also Various O no. 14, 818 —
For those to be ordained, see Various O no. 15. 819 —
See also Various O no. 17. 820 —
See also Various O no. 21. 823 —
See also Various O no. 19. 824 —
For prayers for Industry and Labor, see Various O 824 —
For Education, see Various O no. 23. 825 —
For Social Service, see Various O no. 22. 827 —
See also Various O no. 19. 827 —
See also Various O no. 20. 831 —
On Special O, the officiant may select 935 12

occur

It cannot *o* before March 22 or after April 25. 15 8
fixed days in the Calendar, when they *o* on a Sunday, 16 12
and any Feasts of our Lord which *o* on a Friday. 17 27
the Induction should *o* at the entrance of the chancel, 564 13

occurred

and, whenever it *o*, Adonai was substituted for it. 583 19

occurrence

in the order of their *o*. 17 13

occurs

Christmas Day, whether it *o* on a Sunday or a weekday. 15 11
construction *o* in the Canticle, "The Song of Moses." 584 3

October

in Convention, this Sixteenth Day of O, 8 5
use from and after the First Day of O, 8 12
Philadelphia, O, 1789. 11 24
Proper 22 The Sunday closest to O 5 182 —
Proper 23 The Sunday closest to O 12 183 —
Proper 24 The Sunday closest to O 19 183 —
Proper 25 The Sunday closest to O 26 183 —
Saint Luke O 18 193 —
Saint James of Jerusalem O 23 193 —
Saint Simon and Saint Jude O 28 194 —
Proper 22 The Sunday closest to O 5 234 —
Proper 23 The Sunday closest to O 12 234 —
Proper 24 The Sunday closest to O 19 235 —
Proper 25 The Sunday closest to O 26 235 —
Saint Luke O 18 244 —
Saint James of Jerusalem O 23 245 —
Saint Simon and Saint Jude O 28 245 —

odd

begins on the First Sunday of Advent preceding *o*-numbered years, 934 3

off

and, finally, the cutting *o* occasion, 10 12
For this cause be cut *o* Anthems, Responds, 866 37
by open denunciation of the Church is rightly cut *o* 874 17

offence

and usages may without *o* be allowed, 9 4

offences

accused by those that have knowledge of their *o*; 873 11
death, for heinous and grievous *o*. 876 9

offend

and born again in Christ, yet *o* in many things; 870 29

offended

understand the minds of some slanderous folks to be *o*; 875 44

offendeth

as he that *o* against the common order of the Church, 874 28

offer

the People *o* their own prayers, 385 —
Here the Priest may *o* counsel, direction, 447 —
The Priest may then *o* words of comfort and counsel. 450 —
The Clergy and People *o* their acclamation 522 —
the Priest did *o* Christ for the quick and the dead, 874 9

offered

the happy occasion which was *o* to them 11 5
Free intercessions may be *o*. 107 —
and thanksgivings may be *o*. 134 —
Prayers may be *o* for ourselves and others. 137 —
Prayers may be *o* for ourselves and others. 138 —
Prayers may be *o* for ourselves and others. 139 —
Salvation *o* freely to all 290 —
Intercession is *o* according to the following form, 328 —
Prayer is *o* with intercession for 359 —
Prayer is *o* with intercession for 383 —
Suitable prayers may be *o*, 397 —
6. Prayers are *o* for the husband and wife, 436 7
Prayers may be *o* according to the occasion. 454 14
3. Prayer may be *o* for the bereaved. 506 9
including the Lord's Prayer, is *o* for the deceased, 506 15
everlasting life is *o* to Mankind by Christ, 869 8

offering

An *o* may be received and presented at the Office. 142 15
(and the receiving of the people's *o*), 408 21
O of Christ once made is that perfect redemption, 874 6

offerings

and placing on it the *o* of bread and wine, 322 12
Representatives of the congregation bring the people's *o* 333 —
the *o* are presented and placed on the Altar. 333 —
and placing on it the *o* of bread and wine, 354 12
Representatives of the congregation bring the people's *o* 361 —
the *o* are presented and placed on the Altar. 361 —
and other *o*, are placed upon it. 401 6
and the *o* of the people received. 407 2
couple may present the *o* of bread and wine. 432 —

Offertory

Prayer may be used in place of all that precedes the O. 36 9
Prayer may be used in place of all that precedes the O. 74 8
The service then continues with the [Peace and] O. 142 24
the service continues with the O. 269 —
O of the Eucharist, at which the Bishop, 310 —
all that precedes the Peace and the O, 322 19
The Celebrant may begin the O with one 333 —

During the O, a hymn, psalm, or anthem may 333 —
O Sentences 343 —
all that precedes the Peace and the O, 354 19
The Celebrant may begin the O with one 361 2
During the O, a hymn, psalm, or anthem may 361 —
O Sentences 376 —
the priest may begin the celebration at the O, 396 —
before the O, or at the end of the service, 407 13
O of the Eucharist, at which the bishop 419 —
Before the O of the Eucharist, the person comes forward 420 —
the exchange of the Peace and the O. 421 —
The liturgy continues with the O, 432 —
with the Peace and the O. 436 14
and the Eucharist begins with the O. 437 7
At the O, it is desirable that the bread and wine 438 1
the Prayers of the People preceding the O. 439 8
the Priest begins with the [Peace and] O. 457 —
The service continues with the Peace and the O. 482 —
The service continues with the Peace and the O. 498 —
begins with the Peace and O of the Eucharist. 506 22
From the beginning of the service until the O, 511 12
At the O, it is appropriate that the bread and wine 511 21
The liturgy continues with the O. 522 —
From the beginning of the service until the O, 524 4
At the O, it is appropriate that the bread and wine 524 12
The liturgy continues with the O. 535 —
From the beginning of the service until the O, 536 4
At the O, it is appropriate that the bread and wine 536 12
The liturgy continues with the O. 546 —
the deacons go to the Altar for the O. 554 29
If there are many deacons, some assist in the O 554 29
prepare the elements at the O, 558 21
The service continues with the O. 563 —
The service continues with the O. 574 —
9. The Eucharist, beginning with the O 578 5

office

The Daily O 35 1
In the Daily O, the term "Officiant" is used 36 3
the person, clerical or lay, who leads the O. 36 4
appropriately concludes the O with a blessing. 36 7
or the O may continue at once 41 —
Before the close of the O one or both of the following 58 —
or the O may continue at once 62 —
Before the close of the O one or both of the following 71 —
In the Daily O, the term "Officiant" is used 74 2
the person, clerical or lay, who leads the O. 74 3
appropriately concludes the O with a blessing. 74 6
or the O may continue at once 79 —
Before the close of the O one or both of the following 101 —
or with some other O or Devotion; 112 —
Or, it may continue as a complete evening O 112 —
or the O may continue at once 116 —
Before the close of the O one or both of the following 125 —
devotions follow the basic structure of the Daily O 136 —
b) the Daily O Lectionary, 136 —
The Apostles' Creed is omitted from the O 142 2
The Lord's Prayer may be omitted from the O 142 5
A sermon may be preached after the O; 142 11
or, within the O, after the Readings 142 11
An offering may be received and presented at the O. 142 15
When this service continues as a complete O, 143 21
from the O Lectionary or the Proper of the Day, 143 22
take place before the close of the O. 439 9
After this other symbols of *o* may be given. 521 —
distinctive of ecclesiastical or academic rank or *o*. 536 8
or the Daily O, or it may be used separately. 548 —
If vestments or other symbols of *o* are to be dedicated, 552 17
insignia of *o* may be presented. 553 7
or other insignia of the *o* of priest, 553 21
other instruments or symbols of *o* may be given. 553 24
or other insignia of the *o* of deacon, 554 12
and others having similar tenure of *o*. 564 18
bishop may state briefly the nature of the person's *o* 565 2
O, such as Thanksgiving for the Birth or Adoption 576 16
for reciting the psalms in the Daily O. 582 18
this form of sacred song in the Daily O. 582 24
for any man to take upon him the *o* of public preaching, 872 16
or that of the Daily O. 888 11
the Lessons at the O may be selected 888 13
or from the Lectionary for the Daily O. 888 15
those appointed in the O Lectionary; 888 16
version is particularly appropriate for use at the O, 888 20
appointed for the same day in the Daily O Lectionary. 888 24
Concerning the Daily O Lectionary 934 1
Daily O Lectionary is arranged in a two-year cycle. 934 2
or, if the O is read only once in the day, 934 9
When the O is read twice in the day, 934 10
When more than one Reading is used at an O, 934 15
the Psalter assigned to a given O has been bracketed, 935 4

offices

whether in the form provided in the Daily O, 13 23
or any of the Collects appointed in the Daily O, 136 —
or from the opening sentences given in the O, 141 9
It may also be omitted at one of the O 142 3
Pastoral O 411 —
exercise the *o* of bishop, priest, or deacon 510 22
Other Pastoral O may follow. 572 —
The Psalms at such O are normally those appointed 888 15
If two Readings are desired at both O, 934 13
or from the opening sentences given in the O, 935 8

officiant

the term "O" is used to denote the person, 36 3
lead other parts of the service not assigned to the *o*. 36 6
The O begins the service with one or more 37 3
The O says to the people 41 —
O and People together, all kneeling 41 —
O 42 —
O and People 42 —
O and People together, all standing 53 —
O 54 —
O and People 54 —
O then says one or more of the following Collects 55 —
O and People 58 —
The O may then conclude with one of the following 59 —
The O begins the service with one or more 61 —
The O says to the people 62 —
O and People together, all kneeling 62 —
O 63 —

O and People 63 —
O and People together, all standing 66 —
O 67 —
O and People 67 —
O then says one or more of the following Collects 68 —
O and People 71 —
The O may then conclude with one of the following 72 —
the term "O" is used to denote the person, 74 2
lead other parts of the service not assigned to the *o*. 74 5
The O begins the service with one or more 75 —
The O says to the people 79 —
O and People together, all kneeling 79 —
O 80 —
O and People 80 —
O and People together, standing 96 —
O 97 —
O and People 97 —
O then says one or more of the following Collects 98 —
O and People 101 —
The O may then conclude with one of the following 102 —
O 103 —
O and People 103 —
The O then begins the Prayers 106 —
O and People 106 —
O 107 —
The O then says one of the following Collects. 107 —
O 107 —
All stand, and the O greets the people 109 —
O 109 —
The O then says the Prayer for Light, 110 —
The O begins the service with one or more 115 —
The O says to the people 116 —
O and People together, all kneeling 116 —
O 117 —
O and People 117 —
O and People together, all standing 120 —
O 121 —
O and People 121 —
O then says one or more of the following Collects 122 —
O and People 125 —
The O may then conclude with one of the following 126 —
The O begins 127 —
O 127 —
The O may then say 127 —
O and People 127 —
O 128 —
The O then says 128 —
O and People 128 —
O and People 132 —
O 133 —
The O then says one of the following Collects 133 —
O Let us bless the Lord. 135 —
The O concludes 135 —
according to the discretion of the *o*. 141 5
and the *o* may pass at once from the salutation 142 19
the *o* then goes to a place close by 143 4
On all other occasions, the O and People say together 153 —
The O concludes with the following 153 —
The O may add other Prayers, and end the Litany, 154 —
The O concludes 155 —
O and People 464 —
The O says this Collect 464 —
The O concludes 466 —
Litany is used on other occasions, the O concludes 551 —
At the discretion of the *o*, however, 934 27
Special Occasions, the *o* may select suitable Psalms 935 12

officiate

like lay persons, may *o* at the Liturgy of the Word, 13 22
authorization of the bishop, *o* at public Baptism; 284 28

officiates

o at the Presentation and Examination of the Candidates; 298 9
and *o* at what follows. 298 12

officiating

When both a bishop and a priest are present and *o*, 422 10

offspring

engendered of the *o* of Adam; 869 25

oft

(and *o* repeated), and the rest utterly omitted. 866 29

often

o be found a satisfactory method of chanting them. 582 11
(by *o* reading, and meditation of God's word) 866 10
whereas before, by reason of so *o* repetition, 867 12

oil

The Bishop may then consecrate *o* of Chrism, 307 —
placing a hand on the vessel of *o*, and saying 307 —
The Bishop may consecrate *o* of Chrism 419 —
Psalm 23 (You have anointed my head with *o*) 454 7
(They anointed with *o* many that were sick) 454 8
If *o* for the Anointing of the Sick is to be blessed, 455 —
anointed, the Priest dips a thumb in the holy *o*, 456 —
using *o* blessed by a bishop or priest. 456 —
Others present olive *o* or some other symbol, saying 561 —
the bishop may consecrate *o* of Chrism, 575 26
or Blessing of O for the Sick. 576 17

old

O Testament Joel 2:1–2, 12–17, or Isaiah 58:1–12 264 —
O Testament Isaiah 45:21–25, or Isaiah 52:13—53:12 272 —
O Testament Exodus 12:1–14a 274 —
O Testament Isaiah 52:13—53:12, 276 —
O Testament Job 14:1–14 283 —
It is desirable that the Lessons from the O Testament 422 18
(That she and I may grow *o* together) 426 —
Then if the child is *o* enough to answer, 441 —
It is desirable that the Lesson from the O Testament, 468 15
From the O Testament 470 —
After the O Testament Lesson, 470 —
It is desirable that the Lesson from the O Testament, 490 15
From the O Testament 494 —
Lay persons read the O Testament Lesson 515 —
O Testament Isaiah 61:1–8, or Isaiah 42:1–9 515 —
Lay persons read the O Testament Lesson 528 —
O Testament Isaiah 6:1–8, or Numbers 11:16–17, 528 —
Lay persons read the O Testament Lesson 540 —
O Testament Jeremiah 1:4–9, or Ecclesiasticus 540 —
Care alike for young and *o*, strong and weak, 557 11
Lay persons from the congregation read the O Testament Lesson 558 14
O Testament Joshua 1:7–9, or Numbers 11:16–17, 560 —

all members of the congregation, young and *o*, 566 16
Lay persons read the O Testament Lesson 571 —
O Testament 1 Kings 8:22–23, 27b–30, 571 —
King James O Testament, where it is regularly rendered 583 27
The O Covenant 846 —
agreeable to the mind and purpose of the *o* fathers, 866 43
those canonical Books of the O and New Testament, 868 23
VII. Of the O Testament. 869 6
The O Testament is not contrary to the New: 869 7
for both in the O and New Testament 869 7
the *o* Fathers did look only for transitory promises. 869 10
1. The Holy Scriptures of the O and New Testament 877 14
The Holy Scriptures of the O and New Testaments, 877 33
the O Testament Reading for the alternate year 934 13
the O Testament (or the Apocrypha). 934 16

older

Sponsors of adults and *o* children present 298 18
Adults and O Children 301 —

oldest

In the *o* manuscripts, the Divine Name 583 20

olive

Others present *o* oil or some other symbol, saying 561 —

omission

petitions may be adapted by addition or *o*, 277 —

omit

the Reader should *o* initial conjunctions 888 25

omits

In that case, the deacon *o* the prayer 312 10

omitted

the conclusion of certain Canticles may be *o* 141 14
The Apostles' Creed is *o* from the Office 142 2
It may also be *o* at one of the Offices 142 3
The Lord's Prayer may be *o* from the Office 142 5
the Short Lesson may be *o*. 143 9
(Propers 1 through 3 being *o* that year, 158 20
responses before and after the Gospel are *o*. 272 —
Confession of Sin may be *o* at this service. 273 —
responses before and after the Gospel are *o*. 277 —
(the indicated sections may be *o*) 286 —
These *o* portions of the rite may be administered 312 12
On occasion, the Confession may be *o*. 330 —
In Lent, Alleluia is *o*, and may be *o* at other times 337 —
On occasion, the Confession may be *o*. 359 —
In Lent, Alleluia is *o*, and may be *o* at other times 364 —
bar in the margin indicates petitions which may be *o*. 383 13
the Creed may be *o*. 406 6
the Lord's Prayer may be *o* here. 428 —
one or more of the prayers may be *o*. 429 —
may be added to, *o*, or adapted, as appropriate 561 —
be *o* during the season of Lent. 584 9
The responses in italics may be *o* 821 —
(and oft repeated), and the rest utterly *o*. 866 29
[The Twenty-first of the former Articles is *o*; 872 2
1662 text of this Article, *o* in the version of 1801, 872 4
and verses of Psalms which may be *o*. 935 3

omitting

This Canticle may be shortened by *o* section II or III 47 —
3. And then, *o* the breaking of the Bread, 408 25
o the nuptial blessing which follows The Prayers. 422 17
(*o* the final clause) 528 —
by lengthening, combining, or *o* some of them, 934 18

once

things *o* advisedly established, she hath, 10 1
continue at *o* with "O Lord, open thou our lips." 41 —
continue at *o* with "O God, make speed to save us." 62 —
continue at *o* with "Lord, open our lips." 79 —
continue at *o* with "O God, make speed to save us." 116 —
and the officiant may pass at *o* from the salutation 142 19
at *o* complete in Godhead and complete in manhood, 864 5
should be read over *o* in the year, intending thereby, 866 9
who, by sacrifice of himself *o* made, should take away 870 27
Offering of Christ *o* made is that perfect redemption, 874 6
or, if the Office is read only *o* in the day, 934 9

one

in the Year of Our Lord O Thousand Seven Hundred 8 5
in the Year of our Lord *o* thousand seven hundred 8 12
celebrated in the context of a Rite O service, 14 4
o is dependent upon the movable date 15 3
and *o* or more of the Lessons 16 14
Rite O 37 —
The Officiant begins the service with *o* or more 37 —
Then follows *o* of the Invitatory Psalms, 42 —
O of the following Antiphons may be sung or said 43 —
O or two Lessons, as appointed, are read, 47 —
O of the following Canticles, 47 —
or *o* of those on pages 85–95 (Canticles 8–21), 47 —
Then follows *o* of these Suffrages 55 —
The Officiant then says *o* or more of the following 55 —
o of these prayers for mission is added 57 —
Before the close of the Office *o* or both 58 —
The Officiant may then conclude with *o* 59 —
Rite O 61 —
The Officiant begins the service with *o* or more 61 —
O or two Lessons, as appointed, are read, 64 —
O of the following Canticles, 65 —
or *o* of those on pages 47–52, or 85–95, is sung 65 —
Then follows *o* of these sets of Suffrages 67 —
The Officiant then says *o* or more of the following 68 —
o of these prayers for mission is added 70 —
Before the close of the Office *o* or both 71 —
The Officiant may then conclude with *o* 72 —
The Officiant begins the service with *o* or more 75 —
Then follows *o* of the Invitatory Psalms, 80 —
O of the following Antiphons may be sung or said 80 —
O or two Lessons, as appointed, are read, 84 —
O of the following Canticles, 84 —
or *o* of those on pages 47–52 (Canticles 1–7), is sung 84 —
O or more sections of this Canticle may be used. 88 —
Then follows *o* of these sets of Suffrages 97 —
The Officiant then says *o* or more of the following 98 —
o of these prayers for mission is added 100 —
Before the close of the Office *o* or both 101 —
Officiant may then conclude with *o* of the following 102 —
O or more of the following Psalms is sung or said. 103 —
o or more sections of Psalm 119, 103 —

O of the following, or some other suitable passage	105	—
The Officiant then says *o* of the following Collects.	107	—
any *o* of the following is also appropriate,	108	14
O of the following, or some other Short Lesson	109	—
says the Prayer for Light, using any *o* of the following	110	—
or *o* proper to the season, may precede the Blessing	113	—
or *o* of the Collects from Evening Prayer	113	—
The Officiant begins the service with *o* or more	115	—
O or two Lessons, as appointed, are read,	118	—
O of the following Canticles,	119	—
or *o* of those on pages 47–52, or 85–95, is sung	119	—
Then follows *o* of these sets of Suffrages	121	—
The Officiant then says *o* or more of the following	122	—
o of these prayers for mission is added	124	—
Before the close of the Office *o* or both	125	—
Officiant may then conclude with *o* of the following	126	—
O or more of the following Psalms are sung or said.	128	—
O of the following, or some other suitable passage	131	—
The Officiant then says *o* of the following Collects	133	—
O of the following prayers may be added	134	—
When more than *o* person is present, the Reading	136	—
the Collect should be read by *o* person,	136	—
In Rite O services of Morning Prayer and Evening	141	18
It may also be omitted at *o* of the Offices	142	3
When the ministers enter, *o* or two lighted candles	142	28
When *o* or more Scripture Lessons are to be read	143	8
When desired, more than *o* Lesson may be read,	143	25
As necessary, the observance of *o*, two, or all three	161	—
of them, is postponed *o* day.	161	—
with *o* of the corresponding sets of Psalms	195	—
For the Prayers of the People, *o* of the forms	202	—
As necessary, the observance of *o*, two, or all three	213	—
of them, is postponed *o* day.	213	—
with *o* of the corresponding sets of Psalms	246	—
For the Prayers of the People, *o* of the forms	253	—
Here a Deacon or other person appointed reads *o*	270	—
of which *o* is always the Lesson from Exodus.	288	—
O of the following Canticles is then sung.	294	—
The Celebrant says *o* of the following Collects	295	—
Each candidate for Holy Baptism is to be sponsored by *o*	298	16
O or two Lessons, as appointed, are read,	300	—
and saying to each *o*	308	—
The Bishop lays hands upon each *o* and says	309	—
If on any *o* of the above-named days the ministry	312	8
and *o* or more of the Lessons provided	312	21
The petitions (page 305) may also be led by *o*	312	25
Using the given name of the *o* to be baptized	313	24
A Penitential Order: Rite O	319	—
The Celebrant may read *o* of the following sentences	319	—
The Holy Eucharist: Rite O	323	—
O or two Lessons, as appointed, are read,	325	—
A Minister may then say *o* or more of the following	332	—
Then the Ministers and People may greet *o* another	332	—
The Celebrant may begin the Offertory with *o*	333	—
O of the following, or some other appropriate	343	—
The Celebrant may read *o* of the following sentences	351	—
O or two Lessons, as appointed, are read,	357	—
O of the sentences from the Penitential Order	359	—
Then the Ministers and People may greet *o* another	360	—
The Celebrant may begin the Offertory with *o*	361	—
O of the following, or some other appropriate	376	—
o of those appointed for Various Occasions.	396	—
or else *o* of the following	396	—
O of the usual postcommunion prayers is then said,	399	—
or elsewhere in the service, all greet *o* another	401	2
using *o* of the eucharistic prayers provided.	401	9
the Celebrant uses *o* of the Eucharistic Prayers	402	—
from Rite O or Rite Two, or *o* of the following forms	402	—
Rite O services, the following form of the Gloria	406	8
o chalice on the Altar, and, if need be, a flagon	407	19
And if the person or persons on *o* side truly forgive	409	20
and *o* or more of the Lessons	414	—
O or two Lessons, as appointed, are read,	414	—
The Bishop lays hands upon each *o* and says	418	—
o, at least, of the parties must be a baptized Christian;	422	4
Then *o* or more of the following passages	426	—
(A man cleaves to his wife and they become *o* flesh)	426	—
(Let us love *o* another for love is of God)	426	—
(They are no longer two but *o*)	426	—
(Love *o* another as I have loved you)	426	—
o or more of the prayers may be omitted.	429	—
says *o* of the following prayers	430	—
3. O or more Readings, *o* of which is always	435	15
according to Rite O or Rite Two in this Book,	436	15
If more than *o* person responds,	437	11
the homily, if there is *o*.	437	21
continues with the Magnificat or *o* of the Psalms	440	—
Then *o* or both parents say these or similar words	441	—
The Celebrant may add *o* or more of the following	444	—
Form O	447	—
The Priest may then say *o* or more of these	449	—
over the penitent), saying *o* of the following	451	—
o or more parts of the following service are used,	453	3
Part O of this service may always be led by a deacon	453	6
O or more of the following or other passages	453	13
upon the sick person, and says *o* of the following	455	—
suitable to administer the Sacrament in *o* kind only.	457	—
O of the usual postcommunion prayers is said,	457	—
Rite O	469	—
All stand while *o* or more of the following anthems	469	—
The Celebrant says *o* of the following Collects,	469	—
O or more of the following passages	470	—
a suitable canticle or *o* of the following Psalms	470	—
canticle or hymn, or *o* of the following Psalms	475	—
or with *o* or more suitable prayers	480	—
or *o* or more of these anthems may be sung or said	483	—
or *o* of these Canticles	484	—
All stand while *o* or more of the following anthems	491	—
after which the Celebrant says *o* of the following	493	—
O or more of the following passages	494	—
or with *o* or more suitable prayers	496	—
The Celebrant concludes with *o* of the following	497	—
or *o* or more of these anthems may be sung or said	500	—
or *o* of these Canticles,	500	—
following anthem or *o* of those on pages 491–492	501	—
4. O or more passages of Holy Scripture are read.	506	10
o we love has entered into the nearer presence	507	13
by *o* or more of the other bishops	517	—
The People greet *o* another.	522	—
o of the bishops leads the people in the following	522	—
The Clergy and People greet *o* another.	534	—
The Clergy and People greet *o* another.	546	—

the Holy Eucharist may be according to Rite O 552 3
(When there are more ordinands than *o*, 552 12
are to be said to each *o*. 554 6
upon the head of each ordinand, and say over each *o* 554 21
are also to be said to each *o*. 554 27
O, appointed by the bishop, is to say the dismissal. 554 30
A lay person being instituted should read *o* of the Lessons 558 23
The People greet *o* another. 563 —
there may be *o* or two Readings from Scripture. 565 10
and other clergy and the people greet *o* another. 574 7
ministers move from *o* part of the church to another. 576 5
If *o* reading stand is to serve as both lectern 576 6
only *o* of the prayers, 576 6
and *o* of the versicles and responses, 576 6
or *o* appropriate to the name of the church. 576 26
or between *o* side of the congregation and the other. 582 14
Book O 585 2
we all with *o* accord teach men to acknowledge 864 4
o and the same Son, our Lord 864 4
of *o* substance (homoousios) with the Father 864 6
o substance with us as regards his manhood; 864 8
o and the same Christ, Son, Lord, Only-begotten, 864 11
coming together to form *o* person and subsistence, 864 14
but *o* and the same Son and Only-begotten God 864 15
That we worship *o* God in Trinity, 864 25
For there is *o* Person of the Father, 864 27
and of the Holy Ghost, is all *o*, 864 28
And yet they are not three eternals, but *o* eternal. 864 35
nor three uncreated, but *o* uncreated, 864 36
and *o* incomprehensible. 864 37
they are not three Almighties, but *o* Almighty. 864 39
And yet they are not three Gods, but *o* God. 865 2
And yet not three Lords, but *o* Lord. 865 4
So there is *o* Father, not three Fathers; 865 12
o Son, not three Sons; 865 12
o Holy Ghost, not three Holy Ghosts. 865 12
he be God and Man, yet he is not two, but *o* Christ; 865 28
O, not by conversion of the Godhead into flesh, 865 29
O altogether; 865 30
For as the reasonable soul and flesh is *o* man, 865 31
so God and Man is *o* Christ; 865 31
whereof every *o* was called a nocturn, 866 28
breaking *o* piece thereof from another. 866 37
all the whole realm shall have but *o* use. 867 11
There is but *o* living and true God, 867 35
this Godhead there be three Persons, of *o* substance, 867 37
and eternal God, and of *o* substance with the Father, 868 3
were joined together in *o* Person, never to be divided, 868 5
whereof is *o* Christ, very God, and very Man; 868 6
of *o* substance, majesty, and glory, 868 17
neither may it so expound *o* place of Scripture, 871 39
to have among themselves *o* to another; 873 24
Of the *o* Oblation of Christ finished upon the Cross. 874 5
and Ceremonies be in all places *o*, or utterly like; 874 22
that the Saviour's prayer, "That we all may be *o*," 876 29
o of the other years of the three-year Sunday cycle, 888 14
Year O begins on the First Sunday 934 2
the Lectionary for Year O is begun.) 934 6
used in the morning and *o* in the evening; 934 8
the Gospel Reading be used in the evening in Year O, 934 11
When more than *o* Reading is used at an Office, 934 15

ones

or *o* suitable to the season 143 22

only

The same Church hath not *o* in her Preface, 9 22
o the following feasts, appointed on fixed days 16 3
the following Antiphons are used *o* in Easter Season. 44 —
the following Antiphons are used *o* in Easter Season. 82 —
it is appropriate that there be *o* one chalice 407 18
Subsequently, *o* their Christian names are used. 422 21
these services may be pronounced *o* by a bishop 446 11
suitable to administer the Sacrament in one kind *o*. 457 —
refer to him *o* by the Christian name 511 19
refer to him *o* by the Christian name 524 10
refer to him *o* by the Christian name 536 10
appropriate *o* for rectors of parishes, 565 24
o one of the prayers 576 6
one and the same Christ, Son, Lord, O-begotten, 864 11
but one and the same Son and O-begotten God 864 15
but they were *o* begun, and never read through. 866 21
heard with their ears *o*; 866 26
that to turn the Book *o*, was so hard 866 31
and to be a sacrifice, not *o* for original guilt, 868 7
Christ, who is the *o* Mediator between God 869 8
the old Fathers did look *o* for transitory promises. 869 10
righteous before God, *o* for the merit of our Lord 870 2
justified by Faith *o*, is a most wholesome Doctrine, 870 4
not *o* render unto God as much as they are bound 870 21
like unto us in all things, sin *o* except, 870 25
they be made like the image of his *o*-begotten Son 871 8
obtaining eternal Salvation *o* by the Name of Christ. 871 24
For Holy Scripture doth set out unto us *o* the Name 871 27
erred, not *o* in their living and manner 871 34
Sacraments ordained of Christ be not *o* badges 872 26
he doth work invisibly in us, and doth not *o* quicken, 872 28
And in such *o* as worthily receive the same, 872 38
Baptism is not *o* a sign of profession, 873 14
The Supper of the Lord is not *o* a sign of the love 873 23
Supper, *o* after an heavenly and spiritual manner. 873 31
Rites of the Church ordained *o* by man's authority, 874 32
but that *o* prerogative, 876 2
restored *o* by the return of all Christian communions 877 5
conjunctions which refer *o* to what has preceded, 888 26
or, if the Office is read *o* once in the day, 934 9

open

transferred to the first convenient *o* day 16 13
observed on any *o* day within the week. 17 18
or with the versicle "O Lord, *o* thou our lips" 37 —
continue at once with "O Lord, *o* thou our lips." 41 —
or with the versicle "Lord, *o* our lips" 75 —
continue at once with "Lord, *o* our lips." 79 —
That person which by *o* denunciation of the Church 874 17

opened

The door is *o*. 568 —

opening

Any of the *o* sentences of Scripture, 141 3
from the Psalms themselves, or from the *o* sentences 141 8
provide light for reading the *o* Short Lesson 143 1
the *o* versicles and before the salutation 312 19
the *o* versicles and before the salutation 412 14

In the *o* exhortation (at the symbol of N.N.), 422 20
to be used at the *o* of a church or chapel. 575 3
In the *o* verses of Lessons, 888 25
from the Psalms themselves, or from the *o* sentences 935 7

openly

until he be *o* reconciled by penance, 874 19
doth *o* break the Traditions 874 25
by common authority, ought to be rebuked *o*, 874 27

operating

not seek to absorb other Communions, but rather, co-*o* 877 1

operation

Before an O 459 4
they have a wholesome effect or *o*: 872 39

opinion

39. For those who Influence Public O 811 18
39. For those who Influence Public O 827 —
in the *o* of this Conference, the following Articles 877 31

opportunity

In the Intercessions and Thanksgivings, *o* may be given 142 7
o may be given for silent prayer. 142 10
O is always to be given to every communicant 407 25
when the congregation has *o* to be present. 468 6
when the congregation has *o* to be present. 490 6
O is always given to the people 511 24
O is always given to the people 524 18
O is always given to the people 536 18
Reasonable *o* is to be given for the priests present 553 19
provide an *o* for the congregation to reaffirm 577 23

oppressed

36. For the O 811 15
36. For the O 826 —

optional

5. Days of O Observance 17 28
For *o* use, when desired, subject to the rules 199 —
For *o* use, when desired, subject to the rules 251 —
For *o* use on Thanksgiving Day, 836 —

oratory

dedicating a chapel or an *o* within another building. 566 6
for dedicating a private chapel or *o*. 577 5

ordain

and yet it is not lawful for the Church to *o* any thing 871 38
or national Church hath authority to *o*, 874 31

ordained

I. For those to be *o* 205 —
I. For those to be *o* 256 —
It is customary for all the *o* ministers present, 284 10
o ministers have been characteristic 510 5
associated with them are the presbyters, or *o* elders, 510 8
called by God to the *o* ministry are admitted 510 17
unless they are so *o*, or have already received 510 23
that bishops be *o* on Sundays and other feasts 511 4
When a bishop is to be *o*, the Presiding Bishop 511 6
by the family or friends of the newly *o*. 511 22
The family of the newly *o* may receive Communion 511 23
by the family or friends of the newly *o*. 524 13
The family of the newly *o* may receive Communion 524 17
The Bishop then gives a Bible to the newly *o*, saying 534 —
The Bishop greets the newly *o*. 534 —
The Presbyters present greet the newly *o*; 534 —
the newly *o* Priest joins in the celebration 535 —
by the family or friends of the newly *o*. 536 13
The family of the newly *o* may receive Communion 536 17
The Bishop gives a Bible to the newly *o*, saying 545 —
and the Clergy present now greet the newly *o*. 546 —
The newly *o* Deacon prepares the bread, 546 —
The newly *o* bishop, assisted by other ministers, 553 11
If two or more are *o* together, 553 25
All the newly *o* take part in the exchange of the Peace, 554 7
If two or more are *o* together, 554 15
Prayers for the O Ministry are on pages 205 and 206. 810 25
For those to be *o*, see Various Occasions no. 15. 819 —
that the same was not *o*, but of a good purpose, 866 7
and is *o* nothing to be read, 867 1
Wherefore things *o* by them as necessary to salvation 872 8
Sacraments *o* of Christ be not only badges 872 26
There are two Sacraments *o* of Christ our Lord 872 30
they have not any visible sign or ceremony *o* of God. 872 36
Sacraments were not *o* of Christ to be gazed upon, 872 37
so that nothing be *o* against God's Word. 874 24
o and approved by common authority, 874 27
or Rites of the Church *o* only by man's authority, 874 32
surrender by those who have been *o* to be its stewards 877 10
words of institution and of the elements *o* by Him. 877 17
(c) The two Sacraments *o* by Christ Himself 878 1
and of the elements *o* by Him. 878 3

ordaining

Accordingly, the manner of *o* in this Church 510 29

order

in the chiefest materials, as in the frame and *o* 10 6
that the members of each *o* within the Church, 13 17
Deacons by virtue of their *o* do not exercise 13 21
in the *o* of their occurrence. 17 13
the O for Morning or Evening Prayer 36 8
II The Cosmic O 47 —
the O for Morning or Evening Prayer 74 7
I The Cosmic O 88 —
An O of Service 103 —
This O provides a form of evening service or vespers 108 2
This *o* is not appropriate for use on Monday, 108 11
An O of Worship 109 —
An O for Compline 127 —
The O of Worship for the Evening, 139 —
O of Worship for the Evening 142 25
reserved Sacrament, the following *o* is observed 282 —
the Eucharist according to their *o*. 284 19
A Penitential O: Rite One 319 —
When this O is used at the beginning of the Liturgy, 321 —
A Penitential O: Rite Two 351 —
When this O is used at the beginning of the Liturgy, 353 —
One of the sentences from the Penitential O 359 —
An O for Celebrating 400 1
the service begins with the Penitential O.) 407 1
An O for Marriage 435 1
this O is used. 435 3

or according to the *O* on page 401. 436 15
they are used in the *o* indicated. 453 5
in *o* that the ministrations of the Church 462 —
When the *o* for the Burial of the Dead follows 467 —
An *O* for Burial 506 1
First, there is the *o* of bishops who carry on 510 6
distinctive of ecclesiastical or academic rank or *o*. 511 17
bishop is now vested according to the *o* of bishops. 521 —
distinctive of ecclesiastical or academic rank or *o*. 524 8
priest is now vested according to the *o* of priests. 534 —
deacon is now vested according to the *o* of deacons. 545 —
This *o* is for use when a priest is being instituted 558 2
deacons assist according to their *o*. 558 13
of the new ministry, and to the *o* of the minister. 561 —
a special *o* is provided on page 577. 566 19
Baptism is to be administered, the following *o* is used: 575 28
the following *o* may provide an opportunity 577 22
In *o* to distinguish it, however, from "Lord" 583 28
Prayers for the Social *O* 811 5
Prayers for the Natural *O* 811 21
Thanksgiving for the Social *O* 813 8
Thanksgivings for the Natural *O* 813 10
Prayers for the Social *O* 823 —
Prayers for the Natural *O* 827 —
Thanksgiving for the Social *O* 840 —
Thanksgivings for the Natural *O* 840 —
this godly and decent *o* of the ancient fathers 866 16
therefore considered, here is set forth such an *o*, 866 33
set forth, that all things shall be done in *o*, 866 36
So that here you have an *o* for prayer 866 42
o as is most easy and plain for the understanding, 867 3
and for the plainness of the *o*, 867 5
Furthermore, by this *o* the curates shall need none 867 5
who by his discretion shall take *o* for the quieting 867 20
so that the same *o* be not contrary to any thing 867 21
that offendeth against the common *o* of the Church, 874 28
which also suspends the *o* for the reading 875 17
with them on the basis of a common Faith and *O*, 877 2
to be the substantial deposit of Christian Faith and *O* 877 8

ordered

Unless otherwise *o* in the preceding rules 16 23
unless otherwise *o* for Holy Days 158 8
For they so *o* the matter, that all the whole Bible 866 8
whosoever are consecrated or *o* according to said Form, 875 24
rightly, orderly, and lawfully consecrated and *o*. 875 25
o according to the Rites of that Book, 875 31
hereafter shall be consecrated or *o* to the same Rites; 875 32
rightly, orderly, and lawfully consecrated and *o*." 875 33
re-*o* by lengthening, combining, or omitting some 934 18

ordering

Consecration of Bishops, and *O* of Priests 875 21
all things necessary to such Consecration and *O*; 875 23
and *O* of Priests and Deacons, lately set forth 875 27
all things necessary to such Consecration and *O*: 875 29
3. That in all things of human *o* or human choice, 876 33

orderly

rightly, *o*, and lawfully consecrated and ordered. 875 25

orders

o, as set forth in the rubrical directions 13 19
since the time of the New Testament, three distinct *o* 510 4
admitted to these *o* by solemn prayer 510 18
maintain and continue these three *o*; 510 20
duly qualified to confer Holy *O*. 510 25
suitable for the conferring of the sacred *o* of bishop, 510 31
When a bishop is to confer Holy *O*, 524 2
When a bishop is to confer Holy *O*, 536 2
16. For Monastic *O* and Vocations 810 23
16. For Monastic *O* and Vocations 819 —
Sacraments, that is to say, Confirmation, Penance, *O*, 872 32

ordinance

Sacraments be duly ministered according to Christ's *o*, 871 31
Neither is the effect of Christ's *o* taken away 873 6
the Lord's Supper was not by Christ's *o* reserved, 873 34
by Christ's *o* and commandment, ought to be ministered 874 3

ordinand

The *o* is to be vested in surplice or alb, 524 7
When the *o* is presented, his full name 524 9
standing before the bishop, present the *o*, 526 —
The Bishop says to the *o* 526 —
The *O* then signs the above Declaration 527 —
All are seated except the *o*, who stands 531 —
The Bishop addresses the *o* as follows 531 —
All now stand except the *o*, who kneels 533 —
Here the Bishop lays hands upon the head of the *o*, 533 —
The *o* is to be vested in a surplice or alb, 536 7
When the *o* is presented, 536 9
standing before the bishop, present the *o*, 538 —
The Bishop says to the *o* 538 —
The *O* then signs the above Declaration 539 —
All are seated except the *o*, who stands 543 —
The Bishop addresses the *o* as follows 543 —
All now stand except the *o*, who kneels 544 —
Here the Bishop lays hands upon the head of the *o*, 545 —
At the Presentation of the *O*, 552 8
Thereafter, references to the *o* in the singular 553 27
priests lay their hands upon the head of each *o*. 553 31
the bishop alone says over each *o* 553 32
Thereafter, references to the *o* in the singular 554 17
to lay hands upon the head of each *o*, 554 21

ordinands

(When there are more *o* than one, 552 12
The *o* may be presented together, or in succession, 553 26
The *o* are examined together. 553 28
laid their hands upon all the *o*, 554 3
The *o* may be presented together, or in succession, 554 16
The *o* are examined together. 554 18
After laying hands upon all the *o*, 554 24

ordinarily

The Readings are *o* selected from the following list 515 —
The Readings are *o* selected from the following list 528 —
The Readings are *o* selected from the following list 540 —
Selections are *o* made from the following list; 571 —

ordinary

the Sundays or *o* weekdays of Advent or Lent. 406 16

ordination

Preface to the O Rites 510 1
these services of *o* and consecration are appointed. 510 21
are so ordained, or have already received such *o* 510 23
O of a Bishop 511 2
The O of a Bishop 512 —
The O of a Priest 525 —
The O of a Deacon 537 —
In either case, the rubrics of the service of *o* 552 4
by the rubrics in each of the *o* rites. 552 11
At the O of a Bishop 553 1
At the O of a Priest 553 18
At the O of a Deacon 554 11
or other grave cause, could not be present at the *o*. 555 3
service for the O of a Deacon or in the Lectionary 565 14

ordinations

Apostles and O 348 4
Apostles and O 381 2
and the Person appointed leads the Litany for O, 515 —
and the Person appointed leads the Litany for O, 527 —
and the Person appointed leads the Litany for O, 539 —
The Litany for O 548 —
For use at O as directed. 548 —
At *o*, the Bishop who is presiding stands and says 551 —
At all O 552 2
The Litany for O, or some other appropriate litany, 560 —
the Preface may be that for Apostles and O. 564 2

organ

If there is an *o*, 575 10

organic

seeking the restoration of the *o* unity of the Church, 877 23

organize

liberty to model and *o* their respective Churches, 10 28

original

the *o* Greek terms presbyter, presbyters, 528 —
the first *o* and ground whereof, if a man would search 866 6
and to be a sacrifice, not only for *o* guilt, 868 7
The *o* Article given Royal assent in 1571 869 19
IX. Of O or Birth-Sin. 869 22
O sin standeth not in the following of Adam, 869 23
whereby man is very far gone from *o* righteousness, 869 25
The *o* 1571, 1662 text of this Article, 872 4
all the sins of the whole world, both *o* and actual; 874 7
The *o* 1571, 1662 text of this Article reads as follows: 875 26

originally

Prayers *o* composed in traditional idiom 814 —

ornaments

that sacred vessels, *o*, and decorations be carried 575 16
flowers, candles, hangings, or other *o*. 576 3

other

and Administration of the Sacraments, and *o* Rites 8 8
to establish such *o* alterations and amendments 11 7
worship on the Lord's Day and *o* major Feasts, 13 4
services and the *o* rites contained in this Book, 13 7
o forms set forth by authority within this Church 13 8
and for *o* special occasions for which no service 13 13
at *o* rites also, subject to the limitations described 14 1
Proper Liturgies for Special Days, and in *o* services 14 3
the *o*, upon the fixed date of December 25, 15 5
These feasts take precedence of any *o* day 15 20
All *o* Feasts of our Lord, 16 11
and all *o* Major Feasts appointed on fixed days 16 11
some *o* special occasion may be observed 16 20
have precedence over all *o* days of commemoration 16 24
O Feasts of our Lord 16 26
O Major Feasts 17 1
and *o* Major Feasts appointed on fixed days, 17 16
Ash Wednesday and the *o* weekdays of Lent 17 23
Good Friday and all *o* Fridays of the year, 17 25
O Commemorations, using the Common of Saints 18 4
It is appropriate that *o* persons be assigned to read 36 5
to lead *o* parts of the service not assigned 36 6
All Saints and *o* Major Saints' Days 40 —
On *o* Sundays and Weekdays 44 —
On All Saints and *o* Major Saints' Days 44 —
The following, or some *o* suitable hymn, 64 —
It is appropriate that *o* persons be assigned to read 74 4
to lead *o* parts of the service not assigned 74 5
All Saints and *o* Major Saints' Days 77 —
On *o* Sundays and weekdays 81 —
On All Saints and *o* Major Saints' Days 82 —
suitable in Lent, and on *o* penitential occasions 90 —
O suitable selections include Psalms 103 —
or some *o* suitable passage of Scripture, is read 105 —
Evening Prayer or some *o* service, 108 5
prelude to an evening meal or *o* activity. 108 6
In Lent and on *o* penitential occasions 109 —
the following, or some *o* Short Lesson of Scripture 109 —
the following or some *o* suitable prayer, first saying 110 —
Christmas, Epiphany, and *o* Feasts of the Incarnation 111 —
Lent and *o* times of penitence 111 —
are now lighted, as are *o* candles and lamps 112 —
a metrical version of it, or some *o* hymn, is then sung, 112 —
or with some *o* Office or Devotion; 112 —
Or, it may be followed by a meal or *o* activity, 112 —
or *o* canticle, or some *o* hymn of praise. 113 —
A litany, or *o* suitable devotions, 113 —
On feasts or *o* days of special significance, 113 —
On *o* days, either of the following, 113 —
use the following or some *o* blessing or grace 114 —
The following, or some *o* suitable hymn, 117 —
O suitable selections may be substituted. 128 —
or some *o* suitable passage of Scripture, is read 131 —
read by one person, and the *o* parts said in unison, 136 —
some *o* convenient manner. 136 —
c) some *o* manual of devotion which provides daily 136 —
or from *o* passages of Scripture may be used 141 9
At *o* times, the candle or candles 143 11
and *o* candles may be lighted from them. 143 13
at the dining table, or at some *o* convenient place. 143 18
On all *o* occasions, the Officiant and People say 153 —
concludes with the following or some *o* Collect 153 —
The Officiant may add *o* Prayers, and end the Litany, 154 —
The Collect appointed for any Sunday or *o* Feast 158 22
For use on the traditional days or at *o* times 205 —
For use on the traditional days or at *o* times 207 —

For use on the traditional days or at *o* times	256	—
For use on the traditional days or at *o* times	258	—
The Litany of Penitence may be used at *o* times,	269	—
The branches of palm or of *o* trees or shrubs	270	—
The following or some *o* suitable anthem is sung	270	—
Here a Deacon or *o* person appointed reads	270	—
The following or some *o* suitable anthem	271	—
or some *o* appropriate Collect is said	271	—
on this day *o* than the principal celebration,	272	—
the following or *o* suitable anthems may be sung	274	—
All standing, the Deacon, or *o* person appointed,	277	—
may be read by a Deacon or *o* person appointed.	277	—
any or all of the following, or *o* suitable anthems.	281	—
or some *o* hymn extolling the glory of the cross,	282	—
and *o* persons, to take active parts in the service.	284	11
the Lessons, and the Epistle, and assist in *o* ways.	284	20
O candles and lamps in the church,	286	—
Then the Deacon, or *o* person appointed,	286	—
some *o* suitable psalm, canticle, or hymn may	288	—
or some *o* suitable Collect, may be said.	288	—
or some *o* suitable psalm or a hymn may be sung.	295	—
the chief service on a Sunday or *o* feast.	298	6
In Lent and on *o* penitential occasions	299	—
At the principal service on a Sunday or *o* feast,	300	—
On *o* occasions they are selected	300	—
and *o* prayers may be added,	311	—
or on *o* occasions for sufficient reason,	312	20
O prayers, such as the following, may be added.	314	2
either during the Liturgy or at *o* times.	316	—
In Lent and on *o* penitential occasions	319	—
be assisted by *o* priests, and by deacons	322	5
It is appropriate that the *o* priests present stand	322	7
In Lent and on *o* penitential occasions	323	—
the following hymn or some *o* song of praise is sung	324	—
On Sundays and *o* Major Feasts there follows,	326	—
The Deacon or *o* person appointed says	328	—
or with some *o* sentence of Scripture.	333	—
and wine, and money or *o* gifts, to the deacon	333	—
on all Sundays, and on *o* occasions as appointed.	334	—
any *o* vessel containing wine to be consecrated.	334	—
Alleluia is omitted, and may be omitted at *o* times	337	—
following or some *o* suitable anthem may be sung	337	—
on all Sundays, and on *o* occasions as appointed.	341	—
any *o* vessel containing wine to be consecrated.	342	—
or some *o* appropriate sentence of Scripture,	343	—
Prefaces for O Occasions	347	—
In Lent and on *o* penitential occasions	351	—
be assisted by *o* priests, and by deacons	354	5
It is appropriate that the *o* priests present stand	354	7
In Lent and on *o* penitential occasions	355	10
the following hymn or some *o* song of praise is sung	356	—
On *o* occasions the following is used	356	—
On Sundays and *o* Major Feasts there follows,	358	—
or with some *o* sentence of Scripture.	361	—
and wine, and money or *o* gifts, to the deacon	361	—
on all Sundays, and on *o* occasions as appointed.	361	—
any *o* vessel containing wine to be consecrated.	362	—
Alleluia is omitted, and may be omitted at *o* times	364	—
some *o* suitable anthem may be used.	364	—
on all Sundays, and on *o* occasions as appointed.	367	—
any *o* vessel containing wine to be consecrated.	368	—
any *o* vessel containing wine to be consecrated.	371	—
any *o* vessel containing wine to be consecrated.	374	—
or some *o* appropriate sentence of Scripture,	376	—
Prefaces for O Occasions	380	—
Deacon or *o* leader	383	—
Deacon or *o* leader	388	—
Deacon or *o* leader	389	—
At *o* times, or when desired, such persons	396	—
concluding with the following or some *o* Collect	397	—
The following or some *o* form is used	397	—
administered with the following or *o* words	399	—
preparation by the Priest and *o* participants.	400	3
instrumental music, *o* art forms, silence.	400	10
o offerings, are placed upon it.	401	6
any *o* vessel containing wine to be consecrated.	403	—
any *o* vessel containing wine to be consecrated.	405	—
and at *o* times as desired;	406	15
persons whose native tongue is *o* than English,	406	22
The deacon may be assisted by *o* ministers.	407	16
the celebrant or deacon, and *o* communicants,	409	3
to their neighbors and are a scandal to the *o* members	409	13
receive Communion until they have forgiven each *o*.	409	19
but those on the *o* side refuse to forgive,	409	21
In Lent and on *o* penitential occasions	413	—
At the principal service on a Sunday or *o* feast,	414	—
and such *o* devotions as the Bishop may direct.	419	—
Celebrant then says this or some *o* appropriate prayer	421	—
and perform *o* assisting functions at the Eucharist.	422	13
assemble in the church or some *o* appropriate place.	423	—
A homily or *o* response to the Readings may follow.	426	—
places the ring on the ring-finger of the *o*'s hand	427	—
The Deacon or *o* person appointed reads	429	—
The newly married couple then greet each *o*,	431	—
assemble in the church or in some *o* convenient place.	435	9
husband and wife first greeting each *o*.	436	11
some *o* suitable symbol of the vows may be used	437	22
and receive Holy Communion before *o* members	438	3
the parents, with *o* members of the family, should come	439	4
the Celebrant invites the parents and *o* members	439	17
say one or more of these or *o* appropriate verses	449	—
the service with the following or some *o* greeting	453	11
the following or *o* passages of Scripture are read	453	13
covered with a pall or *o* suitable covering.	468	9
The Deacon or *o* leader says	480	—
and *o* ministers take their places at the body.	482	—
This anthem, or some *o* suitable anthem, or a hymn,	482	—
Deacon or *o* Minister may dismiss them, saying	483	—
Committal or at some *o* convenient time	487	—
covered with a pall or *o* suitable covering.	490	9
A hymn, psalm, or some *o* suitable anthem may	491	—
concludes with one of the following or some *o* prayer	497	—
and *o* ministers take their places at the body.	499	—
This anthem, or some *o* suitable anthem, or a hymn,	499	—
a Deacon or *o* Minister may dismiss them, saying	500	—
O prayers may be added.	502	—
Committal or at some *o* convenient time	503	—
The very love we have for each *o* in Christ	507	11
bishops be ordained on Sundays and *o* feasts	511	4
At least two *o* bishops serve as co-consecrators.	511	8
The *o* bishops, or a convenient number of them,	511	14
o vesture distinctive of ecclesiastical or academic rank	511	17
may receive Communion before *o* members	511	23

bishops and *o* ministers. 512 —
In Lent and on *o* penitential occasions 512 —
The People respond in these or *o* words 514 —
or some *o* approved litany. 515 —
or more of the *o* bishops 517 —
The *o* bishops stand to the right and left 520 —
Presiding Bishop and *o* Bishops now lay their hands 521 —
After this *o* symbols of office may be given. 521 —
and *o* Bishops greet the new bishop. 522 —
The new Bishop also greets *o* members of the clergy, 522 —
joined by *o* bishops and presbyters, proceeds 522 —
o vesture distinctive of ecclesiastical or academic rank 524 8
the new priest and *o* priests stand at the Altar 524 14
may receive Communion before *o* members 524 17
In Lent and on *o* penitential occasions 525 —
The People respond in these or *o* words 527 —
or some *o* approved litany. 527 —
with the Bishop and *o* presbyters, 535 —
without tippet or *o* vesture 536 7
may receive Communion before *o* members 536 17
In Lent and on *o* penitential occasions 537 —
The People respond in these or *o* words 539 —
or some *o* approved litany. 539 —
On Ember Days or *o* occasions, 548 —
When this Litany is used on *o* occasions, 551 —
or in some *o* convenient manner. 552 16
If vestments or *o* symbols of office are to be dedicated, 552 17
a ring, staff, and mitre, or *o* suitable insignia 553 6
The newly ordained bishop, assisted by *o* ministers, 553 11
The stole worn about the neck, or *o* insignia 553 21
o instruments or symbols of office may be given. 553 24
the bishop and *o* priests at the Altar 554 8
The stole worn over the left shoulder, or *o* insignia 554 12
sickness or *o* grave cause, could not be present 555 3
or the inauguration of *o* ministries, 558 4
O priests, if any, who serve 558 11
and perform *o* actions as indicated in the rubrics. 558 15
O clergy of the diocese participate 558 16
Ministers of *o* Churches may appropriately 558 19
Ordinations, or some *o* appropriate litany, is led 560 —
the following or some *o* Collect, first saying 560 —
Others present a stole or *o* symbol, saying 561 —
Others present a book of prayers or *o* symbol, saying 561 —
Others present olive oil or some *o* symbol, saying 561 —
O Representatives of the congregation present 562 —
new Minister then greets *o* members of the clergy, 563 —
and joined by the *o* clergy, proceeds 563 —
at the entrance of the chancel, or in some *o* place 564 15
bishop and *o* ministers may be clearly seen and heard 564 16
In *o* cases, the bishop may state briefly the nature 565 2
but additional, or *o*, persons may do this 565 5
O passages suitable to the circumstances 565 12
the new minister, or some *o* person; 565 17
the bishop, or *o* persons present, may speak 565 19
vicars of missions, hospital chaplains, and *o* priests 565 25
social purposes, or for *o* suitable activities. 566 12
or some *o* appropriate psalm is sung. 568 —
A Warden or *o* representative of the congregation 568 —
O Pastoral Offices may follow. 572 —
Then the bishop and *o* clergy and the people greet 574 —
neighboring place of worship, or in some *o* building. 575 7
or *o* circumstances make it necessary, 575 12
but the bishop, *o* clergy, and attendants will enter 575 13
dedication of the font, children or *o* lay persons 575 23
flowers, candles, hangings, or *o* ornaments. 576 2
o lay person outline the plans of the congregation 576 12
or some *o* form may be composed for the occasion, 576 19
or *o* lay persons, bring them forward 576 23
or for some *o* suitable purpose, the service 576 30
used for regular worship by *o* Christian bodies, 577 1
consecration of a church, or on *o* suitable occasions. 579 —
one side of the congregation and the *o*. 582 15
13. For the Election of a Bishop or *o* Minister 810 19
O Prayers 812 17
13. For the Election of a Bishop or *o* Minister 818 —
O Prayers 833 —
O Sacramental Rites 860 —
And in this Trinity none is afore, or after *o*; 865 14
as, among *o* things, it may plainly appear 866 4
o books of holy Scripture used. 866 22
need none *o* books for their public service, 867 6
And the *o* Books (as Hierome saith) the Church 868 34
as to the remaining parts of it, in *o* Articles.] 872 3
and there is none *o* satisfaction for sin, 874 7
it is lawful for them, as for all *o* Christian men, 874 13
in this Realm of England, and *o* his Dominions, 875 40
this Church does not seek to absorb *o* Communions, 877 1
appointed for the Sundays and for *o* major Holy Days 888 6
from one of the *o* years of the three-year Sunday cycle, 888 14
any *o* day in the same week, except on major Holy Days. 934 30
given in the Offices, or from *o* passages of Scripture, 935 8

others

Prayers may be offered for ourselves and *o*. 137 —
Prayers may be offered for ourselves and *o*. 138 —
Prayers may be offered for ourselves and *o*. 139 —
Prayers for ourselves and *o* may follow. 140 —
When there are *o* to be presented, the Bishop says 303 —
may administer the Bread and *o* the Wine. 408 6
required for the Communion of the sick, or of *o* 408 29
the person or persons on one side truly forgive the *o* 409 20
exercised through the care each Christian has for *o*, 446 3
family members and *o*, as may be convenient. 534 —
and *o*, as may be convenient. 546 —
and *o* administer Holy Communion. 554 30
O present a stole or other symbol, saying 561 —
O present a book of prayers or other symbol, saying 561 —
O present olive oil or some other symbol, saying 561 —
and *o* having similar tenure of office. 564 18
benefactors, donors, artists, artisans, and *o*. 576 21
to exhort *o* by wholesome doctrine, 866 12
discerned from *o* that be not christened, 873 15
(that *o* may fear to do the like,) 874 27

otherwise

or *o* disposed of, as may seem most convenient 9 8
Unless *o* ordered in the preceding rules 16 23
weekdays following, unless *o* ordered for Holy Days 158 8
weekdays which follow, except as *o* appointed. 166 —
the following weekdays, except as *o* appointed. 174 —
the weekdays which follow, except as *o* appointed. 217 —

the following weekdays, except as *o* appointed. 226 —
and weekdays alike, except as *o* appointed 345 —
and weekdays alike, except as *o* appointed 378 —
desired to celebrate a marriage *o* than as provided 435 2
pronouns when the referent is not *o* clear, 888 27

ought

equity *o* to be allowed to all human writings; 10 18
conformable to what *o* to be the proper end 10 35
o of necessity to be received in any commonwealth; 869 12
o thoroughly to be received and believed: 869 16
o not to decree any thing against the same, 871 41
so besides the same *o* it not to enforce 871 41
And those we *o* to judge lawfully called and sent, 872 18
not only a sign of the love that Christians *o* to have 873 23
commandment, *o* to be ministered to all 874 3
o to be taken of the whole multitude of the faithful, 874 18
approved by common authority, *o* to be rebuked 874 27
Sacraments *o* to be ministered in a known tongue. 875 12
nor *o* to be, subject to any foreign Jurisdiction. 875 42
o, of such things as he possesseth, liberally to give 876 15

out

in the carrying *o* of its missionary and pastoral work, 510 10
they may gather *o* of doors, in the parish house, 575 6
The version of the Psalms which follows is set *o* 583 1
context requires that the Divine Name be spelled *o*, 584 2
if a man would search *o* by the ancient fathers, 866 6
before three or four Chapters were read *o*, 866 19
to find *o* what should be read, 866 32
than to read it when it was found *o*. 866 32
a readiness in this matter, here is drawn *o* a Kalendar 866 34
here are left *o* many things, whereof some be untrue, 866 45
and do spring *o* necessarily of a true and lively Faith; 870 9
those whom he hath chosen in Christ *o* of mankind, 871 4
For Holy Scripture doth set *o* unto us only the Name 871 27
that they be taken *o* of holy Scripture." 872 10

outline

or other lay person *o* the plans of the congregation 576 12
An O of the Faith 843 —
and lay catechists, to give an *o* for instruction. 844 3
An O of the Faith 845 —

over

they have precedence *o* all other days 16 23
When a meal is to follow, a blessing *o* food may serve 143 29
This Sunday takes precedence *o* the three Holy Days 161 —
This Sunday takes precedence *o* the three Holy Days 213 —
says the Thanksgiving *o* the Water; 298 10
Thanksgiving *o* the Water 306 —
in full sight of the congregation, prays *o* them, saying 308 —
the deacon omits the prayer *o* the candidates, 312 10
go to the font for the Thanksgiving *o* the Water. 312 30
before the Thanksgiving *o* the Water. 313 —
At the Thanksgiving *o* the Water, 313 —
(or extends a hand *o* the penitent), 451 —
Psalm 91 (He will give his angels charge *o* you) 453 —
the bishop alone says *o* each ordinand 553 32
The stole worn *o* the left shoulder, 554 12
upon the head of each ordinand, and say *o* each one 554 21
in addition to saying the prayer *o* the font as given, 575 25
usually distributed *o* two verses. 583 12
been carried *o* into the classical English versions, 583 26
should be read *o* once in the year, 866 9
Voluntary Works besides, *o* and above, God's Commandments, 870 19

overthroweth

o the nature of a Sacrament, 873 30

own

being things in their *o* nature indifferent, 9 16
Easter Eve has its *o* form 108 12
the Eucharist with its *o* Creed is to follow. 142 3
make promises in their *o* names, and also take vows 298 22
included among the godparents of their *o* children. 298 24
the People offer their *o* prayers, 385 —
The People may add their *o* petitions. 388 —
The People may add their *o* petitions 392 —
The People may add their *o* thanksgivings 393 —
The People may add their *o* petitions 393 —
express thanks in their *o* words. 439 16
ordained together, each is to have his *o* presenters. 553 25
ordained together, each is to have his *o* presenters. 554 15
and shall give account for their *o* works. 865 36
and is of his *o* nature inclined to evil, 869 26
by his *o* natural strength and good works, 869 35
and not for our *o* works or deservings. 870 3
they do not the same in their *o* name, but in Christ's, 873 4
Christian men, to marry at their *o* discretion, 874 14
humility to forego all preferences of her *o*; 876 35
in our *o* land, we hereby declare our desire 877 21

owned

does not require that the premises be debt-free or *o*. 575 4

P

page

Additional Directions are on *p* 141. 36 9
the versicle "O Lord, open thou our lips" on *p* 42. 37 —
or Psalm 95, *p* 146. 45 —
The text of the Creed on *p* 96 may be used instead. 54 —
the versicle "O God, make speed to save us" on *p* 63. 61 —
The text of the Creed on *p* 120 may be used instead. 66 —
Additional Directions are on *p* 141. 74 9
or with the versicle "Lord, open our lips" on *p* 80. 75 —
or Psalm 95, *p* 724. 82 —
Additional Directions are on *p* 142. 108 25
the versicle "O God, make speed to save us" on *p* 117 115 —
Psalms, see *p* 582.) 136 —
Various Occasions, *p* 888 136 —
b) the Daily Office Lectionary, *p* 934 136 —
The Order of Worship for the Evening, *p* 109, 139 —
to conform to the directions on *p* 383. 142 23
in tables beginning on *p* 889. 158 6
The Proper Liturgy for this day is on *p* 264. 166 —
The Proper Liturgy for this day is on *p* 270. 168 —
The Proper Liturgy for this day is on *p* 274. 169 —
The Proper Liturgy for this day is on *p* 276. 169 —
The Proper Liturgy for this day is on *p* 283. 170 —
The Liturgy of the Easter Vigil is on *p* 285. 170 —
it begins with the Service of Light, *p* 109 175 —
Baptismal Vows, *p* 292, follows the Sermon. 175 —

See *p* 158.	176	—
the use of the Propers which follow are on *p* 158.	176	—
The Collect "For the Nation," *p* 207,	190	—
the Litany of Thanksgiving on *p* 836	194	—
The postcommunion prayer on *p* 482 may be used.	202	10
The Litany of Thanksgiving for a Church, *p* 578,	204	3
The postcommunion prayer on *p* 457 may be used.	208	—
The Proper Liturgy for this day is on *p* 264.	217	—
The Proper Liturgy for this day is on *p* 270.	219	—
The Proper Liturgy for this day is on *p* 274.	221	—
The Proper Liturgy for this day is on *p* 276.	221	—
The Proper Liturgy for this day is on *p* 283.	221	—
The Liturgy of the Easter Vigil is on *p* 285.	222	—
it begins with the Service of Light, *p* 109	227	—
Baptismal Vows, *p* 292, follows the Sermon.	227	—
See *p* 158.	227	—
the use of the Propers which follow are on *p* 158.	228	—
The Collect "For the Nation," *p* 258,	242	—
the Litany of Thanksgiving on *p* 836	246	—
The postcommunion prayer on *p* 498 may be used.	253	—
The Litany of Thanksgiving for a Church, *p* 578,	255	—
The postcommunion prayer on *p* 457 may be used.	260	—
the Lord's Prayer, and the final prayer on *p* 282.	280	—
"In the midst of life" (*p* 484 or 492) is sung or said.	283	—
the Presentation of the Candidates, *p* 301,	292	—
Additional Directions are on *p* 312.	298	28
(See Additional Directions, *p* 312.)	300	—
the prayer over the candidates, *p* 308,	312	11
the Renewal of Baptismal Vows, *p* 292,	312	16
the Collect (*p* 203 or 254)	312	21
for use at Baptism (*p* 928)	312	22
The petitions (*p* 305) may also be led	312	25
before or during the petitions (*p* 305),	312	29
used as a separate service, the Exhortation, *p* 316,	319	—
The Decalogue, *p* 317, may be said,	319	—
Additional Directions are on *p* 406.	322	22
Then the Ten Commandments (*p* 317) may be said,	324	—
with the directions on *p* 383.	328	—
the service is concluded as directed on *p* 406.	330	—
or else the Exhortation on *p* 316	330	—
An alternative form will be found on *p* 340.	333	—
using the form on *p* 408.	338	—
Continue with the Lord's Prayer, *p* 336.	343	—
used as a separate service, the Exhortation, *p* 316,	351	—
Additional Directions are on *p* 406.	354	22
See the forms beginning on *p* 383.	359	—
the service is concluded as directed on *p* 406.	359	—
from the Penitential Order on *p* 351 may be said.	359	—
with one of the sentences on *p* 376,	361	—
Alternative forms will be found on *p* 367	361	—
using the form on *p* 408.	365	—
Continue with the Lord's Prayer on *p* 364.	369	—
Continue with the Lord's Prayer on *p* 364.	372	—
Continue with the Lord's Prayer on *p* 364.	376	—
however, the Collect (*p* 203 or 254)	414	—
"At Confirmation" (*p* 929) may be substituted.	414	—
using the prayer on *p* 307.	419	—
Additional Directions are on *p* 437.	422	23
See *p* 437.	425	—
The service continues with The Prayers on *p* 428.	434	—
otherwise than as provided on *p* 423 of this Book,	435	2
or according to the Order on *p* 401.	436	15
with the [Peace and] Lord's Prayer on *p* 398.	457	—
the Vigil on *p* 465, may follow.	467	—
service continues on *p* 469 or 491.	467	—
People is used, or else the form on *p* 465 or 480.	496	—
Additional Directions are on *p* 552.	511	26
Additional Directions are on *p* 552.	524	20
Additional Directions are on *p* 552.	536	20
Additional Directions are on *p* 564.	558	25
the directions on *p* 565.	560	—
The priest's prayer on *p* 562 is appropriate	565	24
special circumstances are given on *p* 576.	566	8
a special order is provided on *p* 577.	566	19
and the service continues as directed on *p* 575.	569	11
from "At Baptism," *p* 928;	575	29
3. Litany of Thanksgiving for a Church, *p* 578	577	28
Various Occasions no. 14, and Collect no. 6 (*p* 395).	818	—
A prayer for parents is on *p* 444.	829	—
See also the Prayer of Humble Access on *p* 337.	834	—
prayer "O God, the King of Saints," *p* 489 and 504.	838	—
See also the Thanksgiving for a Child on *p* 439.	841	—
See *p* 364.	856	—

pages

or one of those on *p* 85–95 (Canticles 8–21),	47	—
sentences of Scripture, or of those on *p* 37–40;	61	—
or with the Service of Light on *p* 109–112,	61	—
or one of those on *p* 47–52, or 85–95,	65	—
or one of those on *p* 47–52 (Canticles 1–7),	84	—
sentences of Scripture, or of those on *p* 75–78;	115	—
or with the Service of Light on *p* 109–112,	115	—
or one of those on *p* 47–52, or 85–95,	119	—
antiphons on *p* 43–44 and 80–82 may be used	141	6
which are to be found in the *p* following;	158	4
See also the Table on *p* 884–885.	158	21
Occasions are on *p* 195, 199, 246 and 251.	158	25
with one of the sentences on *p* 343–344,	333	—
The petitions on *p* 305–306 may be used.	417	—
or one of the Psalms on *p* 441–443.	440	—
more suitable prayers (see *p* 487–489).	480	—
more suitable prayers (see *p* 503–505).	496	—
The following anthem or one of those on *p* 491–492	501	—
for the Ordained Ministry are on *p* 205 and 206.	810	25
Prayers for Industry and Labor are on *p* 208, 210,	811	19
Prayers for the sick are on *p* 458–461.	812	14
Prayers for the dying are on *p* 462–465.	812	15
Prayers for the dead are on *p* 202, 253, 487, and 503.	812	16
are on *p* 56, 69, 98, and 123.	812	27
The General Thanksgiving is on *p* 58 and 101.	813	1
for the departed are on *p* 487–489 and 503–504.	813	16
The term "Various Occasions" in the following *p*	813	17
numbered Collects beginning on *p* 199 and 251.	813	18
the Mission of the Church on *p* 58, 100 and 101,	816	—
Prayers for the sick are on *p* 458–461.	831	—
are on *p* 56, 69, 98, and 123.	833	—
See also The General Thanksgiving on *p* 58 and 101.	837	—
for the departed are on *p* 487–489 and 503–504.	841	—
See *p* 317 and 350.	847	—
See *p* 53, 96, 326, 327, and 864.	851	—

pain

In *P* 461 —
they will not refuse the *p*, 867 14
remission of *p* or guilt, were blasphemous fables, 874 10

painful

And if any would judge this way more *p*, 867 11

painted

marked in lasting form (incised, *p*, inlaid). 575 21

pall

It is appropriate that it be covered with a *p* 468 9
It is appropriate that it be covered with a *p* 490 9

palm

Sunday of the Passion: *P* Sunday 168 —
Sunday of the Passion: *P* Sunday 219 —
The branches of *p* or of other trees or shrubs 270 —
and *P* Sunday to 2 Easter), 934 23

palms

The Liturgy of the *P* 270 —
When the Liturgy of the *P* immediately precedes 272 —
When the Liturgy of the *P* has preceded, 273 —

Pantokrator

14 A Song of Penitence Kyrie *P* 90 —

paragraph

After each *p* of this prayer, 328 —

parallelism

but on *p* of clauses, a symmetry of form and sense. 583 3
p can take the form of similarity 583 4

pardons

The Romish Doctrine concerning Purgatory, *P*, 872 12

parent

The Celebrant asks the *p* or parents 440 —

parentheses

the deputy substitutes the words given in *p*. 561 —
Suggested lengthenings are shown in *p*. 888 30
Suggested lengthenings are shown in *p*. 934 21
Brackets and *p* are used 935 1
p in the case of verses) 935 2

parents

It is fitting that *p* be included 298 24
P and godparents are to be instructed 298 25
presented individually by their *P* and Godparents, 301 —
P and Godparents 301 —
the Celebrant asks the *p* and godparents 302 —
P and Godparents 302 —
and of the *p* and godparents who speak 302 —
or after receiving a child by adoption, the *p*, 439 4
some *p* may wish to express thanks 439 15
At the proper time, the Celebrant invites the *p* 439 17
The Celebrant asks the parent or *p* 440 —
P 440 —
Then one or both *p* say these or similar words 441 —
For the *p* 444 —
the duty of Christian *p* to make prudent provision 445 —
A prayer for *p* is on page 444. 829 —

parish

inform the priest of the appropriate *p*, 314 4
and inducted as the rector of a *p*. 558 3
If the new minister is the rector or vicar of the *p*, 562 —
the induction of a rector of a *p*, 564 18
by the wardens of the *p*, 565 5
out of doors, in the *p* house, 575 6
public worship is also to serve as a school or *p* hall, 576 29
congregation attains recognition as a *p*. 577 25
11. For the *P* 810 17
11. For the *P* 817 —
catechism is primarily intended for use by *p* priests, 844 2
p Churches, and Chapels to the same annexed, 867 28

parishes

appropriate only for rectors of *p*, 565 24

parishioners

It is desirable that fellow *p*, 396 —

Parliament

and confirmed at the same time by authority of *P*, 875 28

parochial

or *p*, including vicars of missions 558 5

part

It is a most invaluable *p* of that blessed "liberty 9 2
When rubrics indicate that a *p* of a service 14 11
Any *p* or parts of this service may be led 108 7
the congregation taking the *p* of the crowd. 273 —
The congregation may be seated for the first *p* 273 —
the congregation taking the *p* of the crowd. 277 —
The congregation may be seated for the first *p* 277 —
taking *p* in everything except the administration 314 8
This Exhortation may be used, in whole or in *p*, 316 —
When a common meal or Agape is a *p* 401 15
P One of this service may always be led by a deacon 453 6
P I. Ministry of the Word 453 12
P II. Laying on of Hands and Anointing 455 —
P III. Holy Communion 457 —
If necessary, or if desired, all or *p* of the service 468 10
If necessary, or if desired, all or *p* of the service 490 10
they take *p* in the governance of the Church, 510 10
All the newly ordained take *p* in the exchange 554 7
The rector or minister in charge takes *p* 566 13
some individual or collective *p* in the celebration, 566 17
ministers move from one *p* of the church to another. 576 5
their representatives take *p* in the service, 577 2
P 1 Diligam te, Domine 602 —
Psalm 18: *P* II Et retribuet mihi 604 —
P I Noli oemulari 633 5
Psalm 37: *P* II Novit Dominus 634 —
P 1 Attendite, popule 694 —
Psalm 78: *P* 2 Quoties exacerbaverunt 698 —
P 1 Misericordias Domini 713 —
Psalm 89: *P* II Tunc locutus es 715 —
P I Confitemini Domino 738 —
Psalm 105: *P* II Et intravit Israel 739 —
P I Confitemini Domino 741 —
Psalm 106: *P* II Et fecerunt vitulum 743 —
P I Confitemini Domino 746 —
Psalm 107: *P* II Posuit flumina 748 —
the whole Bible (or the greatest *p* thereof) 866 8

partakers

yet in no wise are they *p* of Christ: 873 39

partaking

the Bread which we break is a *p* 873 26
the Cup of Blessing is a *p* 873 27

parted

brings deep sorrow when we are *p* 507 11
not as *p* or separated into two persons, 864 15

partially

The church is dark, or *p* so, when the service 109 3

participants

requires careful preparation by the Priest and other *p*. 400 3

participate

Other clergy of the diocese *p* 558 16
other Churches may appropriately be invited to *p*. 558 19
Neighboring ministers should be invited to *p*, 566 14

participates

In all services, the entire Christian assembly *p* 13 16

participating

After *p* in the Peace, the deacons go to the Altar 554 28

particular

"The *p* Forms of Divine Worship, 9 14
the *p* occasion being celebrated; 402 —
the *p* occasion being celebrated; 404 —
Here the Penitent confesses *p* sins. 450 —
In *p*, since the time of the New Testament, 510 4
and Bible readings related to the *p* occasion 577 12
Every *p* or national Church hath authority to ordain, 874 31

particularly

and it will be *p* appropriate 577 24
It is *p* appropriate for the psalm 582 9
version is *p* appropriate for use at the Office, 888 20

particulars

make such alterations in some *p*, 10 4

parties

one, at least, of the *p* must be a baptized Christian; 422 4
the *p* that so doubt, or diversely take any thing, 867 19

partly

because it is *p* of a local and civil nature 872 2
grown *p* of the corrupt following of the Apostles, 872 34
p are states of life allowed in the Scriptures; 872 34

parts

yet so as that the main body and essential *p* 10 5
p of the service not assigned to the officiant. 36 6
p of the service not assigned to the officiant. 74 5
Any part or *p* of this service may be led 108 7
read by one person, and the other *p* said in unison, 136 —
the congregation reads the *p* in italics. 281 —
The service normally consists of four *p*: 284 5
to take active *p* in the service. 284 11
first two *p* of the service, the Renewal 284 24
(which are the essential *p* of Baptism), 313 18
one or more *p* of the following service are used, 453 3
for dedicating *p* of a building, or furnishings, 566 4
Likewise, suitable *p* of this rite may be used 566 5
and may be assigned appropriate *p* in the service. 566 15
or *P* of a Church or Chapel 577 7
An asterisk divides each verse into two *p* 583 13
everlasting, without body, *p*, or passions; 867 35
as to the remaining *p* of it, in other Articles.] 872 3
for both the *p* of the Lord's Sacrament, 874 2
As inherent *p* of this sacred deposit, 877 12

party

the wedding *p* leaves the church. 431 —
As the wedding *p* leaves the church, 432 —
Seating may be provided for the wedding *p*, 437 18

Pascha

Christ our Passover *P* nostrum 46 —
Christ our Passover *P* nostrum 83 —
P nostrum 294 —
Christ our Passover, *P* nostrum 484 —
Christ our Passover, *P* nostrum 500 —

Paschal

the Lighting of the *P* Candle. 108 13
the *P* Candle, if used, should be burning 143 3
the flame may be taken from the *P* Candle. 143 11
It is the prerogative of a deacon to carry the *P* Candle 284 17
The Lighting of the *P* Candle 285 —
The *P* Candle is then lighted 285 —
lighted from the *P* Candle at this time. 286 —
The *P* Candle is placed in its stand. 286 —
It is customary that the *P* Candle burn 287 —
at the Altar may now be lighted from the *P* Candle. 294 —
a candle (which may be lighted from the *P* candle) 313 7
the congregation bearing the lighted *P* Candle 467 —

pass

and the officiant may *p* at once from the salutation 142 19
blessing might happily be brought to *p*. 877 25

passage

or some other suitable *p* of Scripture, is read 105 —
A sermon or homily, a *p* from Christian literature, 113 —
or some other suitable *p* of Scripture, is read 131 —
desirable that a *p* from the Gospel first be read. 396 —
whether priest or deacon, reads a *p* of Scripture 396 —
a *p* from the Gospel always concludes the Readings. 426 —
When a *p* from the Gospel is to be read, all stand, 426 —
A *p* from Scripture may first be read. 439 13
a *p* from the Gospel always concludes the Readings. 470 —
a *p* from the Gospel always concludes the Readings. 494 —

passages

or from other *p* of Scripture may be 141 9
Then one or more of the following *p* 426 —
One or more of the following or other *p* of Scripture 453 13
At the burial of a child, the *p* from Lamentations, 468 19
One or more of the following *p* from Holy Scripture 470 —
At the burial of a child, the *p* from Lamentations, 490 19
One or more of the following *p* from Holy Scripture 494 —
4. One or more *p* of Holy Scripture are read. 506 10
or from the *p* cited in the service. 565 12
Other *p* suitable to the circumstances 565 12
In two *p* (Psalm 68:4 and Psalm 83:18), 584 1
given in the Offices, or from other *p* of Scripture, 935 8

passed

But these many years *p*, this godly and decent order 866 16

Passion

Sunday of the *P*: Palm Sunday 168 —
Sunday of the *P*: Palm Sunday 219 —
The *P* Gospel is announced in the following manner 272 —
The *P* Gospel may be read or chanted by lay persons. 273 —
The congregation may be seated for the first part of the *P*. 273 —
The *P* Gospel is announced in the following manner 276 —
The *P* Gospel may be read or chanted by lay persons. 277 —
The congregation may be seated for the first part of the *P*. 277 —
13 Of the *P* of Christ. 875 4

passions

and true God, everlasting, without body, parts, or *p*; 867 35

Passover

Christ our *P* Pascha nostrum 46 —
Christ our *P* Pascha nostrum 83 —
"Christ our *P*," after each Psalm, 141 13
Christ our *P*, Pascha nostrum 484 —
Christ our *P*, Pascha nostrum 500 —

past

charge for books, as in time *p* they have been. 867 7

pastor

Of a *P* 196 —
Of a *P* 248 —
with your Bishop and fellow-Presbyters as a *p*, 557 3

pastoral

P Offices 411 —
When, for *p* considerations, neither of the burial rites 506 2
and *p* work, and in the preaching of the Word of God 510 11
With the *p* staff the Bishop marks the threshold 568 2
Other *P* Offices may follow. 572 —
In place of a *p* staff, 575 21
may be followed by an appropriate *P* Office, 576 15

patient

1 Corinthians 13:1–13 (Love is *p* and kind) 426 —

Patri

Gloria *P* is always sung or said at the conclusion 141 11
psalm is used, it may be concluded with Gloria *P*. 406 7
either with the Gloria *P*, or with a refrain 582 16

patron

the Dedication of a Church, and the feast of its *p* 16 8

patronal

b) at the *p* festival or commemoration of a saint 195 —
b) at the *p* festival or commemoration of a saint 246 —
or *P* Feast, selections may be made from the Proper 571 —

pattern

in a seven-week *p* which recurs throughout the year, 934 24

Paul

Conversion of Saint *P* January 25 187 —
Saint Peter and Saint *P* June 29 190 —
Conversion of Saint *P* January 25 238 —
Saint Peter and Saint *P* June 29 241 —
whereas St. *P* would have such language spoken 866 22
purchase to themselves damnation, as Saint *P* saith. 872 40

pause

a distinct *p* should be made at the asterisk. 583 14

pausing

p three times and singing or saying 285 9

pay

to *p* respectful obedience to the Civil Authority, 875 37

peace

might most tend to the preservation of *p* 10 10
A Collect for *P* 57 —
A Collect for *P* 69 —
A Collect for *P* 99 —
The *P* may then be exchanged. 113 —
A Collect for *P* 123 —
The service then continues with the [*P* and] Offertory. 142 24
18. For *P* 207 —
18. For *P* 258 —
The *P* is then exchanged. 269 —
Or the Sermon may be preached after the *P*. 301 —
the *P* is now exchanged 308 —
The *P* is then exchanged 310 —
all that precedes the *P* and the Offertory, 322 19
The *P* 332 —
all that precedes the *P* and the Offertory, 354 19
The *P* 360 —
The *P* may then be exchanged. 398 —
Exchange the *P* 401 1
or with the exchange of the *P*. 407 4
The greeting, "The *p* of the Lord be always with you," 407 7
exchange of the *P* may take place at the time 407 10
The *P* is then exchanged 419 —
The service then continues with the exchange of the *P* 421 —
The *P* 431 —
the service concludes with the *P*, 436 10
The *P* may be exchanged 436 11
the service continues with the *P* 436 13
The *P* may be exchanged. 445 —
before the exchange of the *P*. 453 10
the Priest begins with the [*P* and] Offertory. 457 —
beginning with the [*P* and] Lord's Prayer on page 398. 457 —
The service continues with the *P* and the Offertory. 482 —
The service continues with the *P* and the Offertory. 498 —
begins with the *P* and Offertory of the Eucharist. 506 22
The *P* 522 —
The *P* 534 —
The *P* 546 —
the newly ordained take part in the exchange of the *P*, 554 7
After participating in the *P*, the deacons go 554 28
The *P* 574 —
8. The *P* 578 4
4. For *P* 810 9
5. For *P* among the Nations 810 10
4. For *P* 815 —
5. For *P* Among the Nations 816 —

peaceable

"may lead quiet and *p* lives, in all godliness	11	2

Pelagians

(as the *P* do vainly talk;)	869	23

penance

Sacraments, that is to say, Confirmation, *P*,	872	32
until he be openly reconciled by *p*, and received	874	19

penitence

14 A Song of *P* Kyrie Pantokrator	90	—
Lent and other times of *p*	111	—
the blessings of the day, and *p* for our sins	140	—
Litany of *P*	267	—
The Litany of *P* may be used at other times,	269	—
or something to be done, as a sign of *p*	446	24
P	454	1

penitent

the priest shall allow those who are *p* to come	409	22
The Reconciliation of a *p* is available for all	446	7
but it must be made clear to the *p* that absolution	446	13
and the *p* kneels nearby.	446	17
If preferred, the confessor and *p* may sit	446	17
When the *p* has confessed all serious sins	446	20
the priest may assign to the *p* a psalm,	446	23
The Reconciliation of a *P*	447	—
The *P* begins	447	—
P	447	—
P	448	—
The Priest and *P* begin as follows	449	—
P	449	—
The *P* says	450	—
Here the *P* confesses particular sins.	450	—
P	450	—
P	451	—
The Priest then lays a hand upon the *p*'s head	451	—
(or extends a hand over the *p*),	451	—
P	451	—
The Reconcilation of a *P*.	454	—

penitential

Especially suitable in Lent, and on other *p* occasions	90	—
In Lent and on other *p* occasions	109	—
by an appropriate invitation and a *p* psalm.	269	—
In Lent and on other *p* occasions	299	—
A *P* Order: Rite One	319	—
In Lent and on other *p* occasions	319	—
In Lent and on other *p* occasions	323	—
A *P* Order: Rite Two	351	—
In Lent and on other *p* occasions	351	—
In Lent and on other *p* occasions	355	—
One of the sentences from the *P* Order	359	—
the service begins with the *P* Order.)	407	1
In Lent and on other *p* occasions	413	—
In Lent and on other *p* occasions	512	—
In Lent and on other *p* occasions	525	—
In Lent and on other *p* occasions	537	—

penitents

to meet the needs of *p*.	446	11

Pentecost

The Day of *P*	15	18
but not from the Last Sunday after *P*	16	16
Saturdays after the First Sunday in Lent, the Day of *P*,	18	6
P	39	—
From Ascension Day until the Day of *P*	43	—
On the Day of *P*	43	—
It may also be used daily until the Day of *P*.	45	—
From Easter Day through the Day of *P*	59	—
From Easter Day through the Day of *P*	72	—
including Ascension Day and the Day of *P*	77	—
From Ascension Day until the Day of *P*	81	—
On the Day of *P*	81	—
It may also be used daily until the Day of *P*.	83	—
From Easter Day through the Day of *P*	102	—
from Easter Day through the Day of *P*	109	—
From Easter Day through the Day of *P*	126	—
From Easter Day through the Day of *P*,	143	3
The Proper to be used on each of the Sundays after *P*	158	10
(the Second Sunday after *P*) is the numbered Proper	158	13
on the weekdays of *P* and Trinity weeks).	158	18
and Propers 4 and 5 being used in *P*	158	20
The Day of *P*: Whitsunday	175	—
When a Vigil of *P* is observed,	175	—
Preface of *P*	175	—
most closely to the date of *P* in that year is used.	176	—
First Sunday after *P*: Trinity Sunday	176	—
The Season after *P*	176	—
Preface of *P*	196	—
Preface of *P*	200	—
Preface of Baptism, or of *P*	203	—
Preface of *P*, or of the Season	204	—
Preface of the Season, or of *P*	206	—
The Day of *P*: Whitsunday	227	—
When a Vigil of *P* is observed,	227	—
Preface of *P*	227	—
most closely to the date of *P* in that year is used.	227	—
First Sunday after *P*: Trinity Sunday	228	—
The Season after *P*	228	—
Preface of *P*	248	—
Preface of *P*	251	—
Preface of Baptism, or of *P*	254	—
Preface of *P*, or of the Season	255	—
Preface of the Season, or of *P*	257	—
Easter Day through the Day of *P*.	287	—
from Easter Day through the Day of *P*	299	—
on the Day of *P*, on All Saints' Day	312	3
from Easter Day through the Day of *P*	319	—
from Easter Day through the Day of *P*	323	—
From the Easter Vigil through the Day of *P*	340	—
P	347	—
from Easter Day through the Day of *P*	351	—
from Easter Day through the Day of *P*	355	—
From the Easter Vigil through the Day of *P*	366	—
P	380	—
from Easter Day through the Day of *P*,	406	14
from Easter Day through the Day of *P*	413	—
from Easter Day through the Day of *P*	512	—
From Easter Day through the Day of *P*	523	—
from Easter Day through the Day of *P*	525	—

From Easter Day through the Day of *P*	535	—
from Easter Day through the Day of *P*	537	—
From Easter Day through the Day of *P*,	547	—

people

for the edification of the *p*,	9	9
the *p* "may lead quiet and peaceable lives,	11	2
The Officiant says to the *p*	41	—
Officiant and *P* together, all kneeling	41	—
P	42	—
Officiant and *P*	42	—
IV The *P* of God	49	—
Officiant and *P* together, all standing	53	—
The *p* stand or kneel	54	—
P	54	—
Officiant and *P*	54	—
The Officiant says to the *p*	62	—
Officiant and *P* together, all kneeling	62	—
P	63	—
Officiant and *P*	63	—
Officiant and *P* together, all standing	66	—
The *p* stand or kneel	67	—
P	67	—
Officiant and *P*	67	—
Officiant and *P*	71	—
The Officiant says to the *p*	79	—
Officiant and *P* together, all kneeling	79	—
P	80	—
Officiant and *P*	80	—
III The *P* of God	89	—
Officiant and *P* together, standing	96	—
The *p* stand or kneel	97	—
P	97	—
Officiant and *P*	97	—
Officiant and *P*	101	—
P	103	—
Officiant and *P*	103	—
P	105	—
P	106	—
Officiant and *P*	106	—
P	107	—
All stand, and the Officiant greets the *p*	109	—
P	109	—
The *P* respond	114	—
In Easter Season the *P* respond	114	—
The Officiant says to the *p*	116	—
Officiant and *P* together, all kneeling	116	—
P	117	—
Officiant and *P*	117	—
Officiant and *P* together, all standing	120	—
The *p* stand or kneel	121	—
P	121	—
Officiant and *P*	121	—
Officiant and *P*	125	—
P	127	—
Officiant and *P*	127	—
P	128	—
Officiant and *P*	128	—
P	131	—
P	132	—
Officiant and *P*	132	—
P	133	—
P	135	—
in its customary place before the *p* assemble;	143	4
the Officiant and *P* say together	153	—
For the Prayers of the *P*, the Litany of Thanksgiving	194	—
For the Prayers of the *P*, one of the forms appointed	202	—
may be used for the Prayers of the *P*.	204	—
For the Prayers of the *P*, the Litany of Thanksgiving	246	—
For the Prayers of the *P*, one of the forms appointed	253	—
may be used for the Prayers of the *P*.	255	—
invites the *p* to the observance of a holy Lent, saying	264	—
The Celebrant and *P* together, all kneeling	267	—
or the Priest, stands and, facing the *p*, says	269	—
may be distributed to the *p* before the service,	270	—
suitable anthem is sung or said, the *p* standing	270	—
P	271	—
The service continues with the Prayers of the *P*.	275	—
P	276	—
the Deacon, or other person appointed, says to the *p*	277	—
The *p* may be directed to stand or kneel.	277	—
placed in the sight of the *p*.	281	—
(and homily), in place of the Prayers of the *P*,	283	—
concluding with the Prayers of the *P*,	284	26
address the *p* in these or similar words	285	—
P	285	—
The gathering of God's *p*	291	—
Celebrant leads the *p* in the Renewal of Baptismal	292	—
address the *p* in these or similar words,	292	—
P	292	—
P	293	—
P	294	—
Canticle the Celebrant may say to the *p*	294	—
The celebration continues with the Prayers of the *P*.	295	—
The *p* standing, the Celebrant says	299	—
P	299	—
P	300	—
The *p* sit.	300	—
P	300	—
P	303	—
P	304	—
P	305	—
P	306	—
Celebrant and *P*	308	—
P	308	—
P	310	—
The service then continues with the Prayers of the *P*	310	—
the celebrant, whenever possible, should face the *p*	313	4
so grouped that the *p* may have a clear view	313	5
The *p* stand or sit.	316	—
The *p* standing, the Celebrant says	319	—
P	319	—
The Decalogue, page 317, may be said, the *p* kneeling.	319	—
Minister and *P*	320	—
read the Gospel and may lead the Prayers of the *P*.	322	10
ministration of the Sacrament to the *p*.	322	13
and may lead the Prayers of the *P*.	322	17
directions given for the Prayers of the *P*.	322	21
The *p* standing, the Celebrant may say	323	—
P	323	—
The Celebrant says to the *p*	325	—
P	325	—
The *p* sit.	325	—
P	326	—

The Prayers of the *P*	328	—
the *P* may make an appropriate response,	328	—
Minister and *P*	331	—
The Celebrant says to the *p*	332	—
P	332	—
Then the Ministers and *P* may greet one another	332	—
the congregation bring the *p*'s offerings	333	—
The *p* stand while the offerings are presented	333	—
The *p* remain standing.	333	—
P	333	—
Celebrant and *P*	334	—
The *p* kneel or stand.	334	—
P and Celebrant	336	—
The *P* may join in saying	337	—
Facing the *p*, the Celebrant may say the following	338	—
deliver it to the *p*.	338	—
The *P* may join in saying this prayer	339	—
or the Celebrant, may dismiss the *p* with these words	339	—
P	339	—
P	340	—
The *P* respond	340	—
The *p* remain standing.	340	—
Celebrant and *P*	341	—
The *p* kneel or stand.	341	—
The *p* standing, the Celebrant says	351	—
P	351	—
The Decalogue may be said, the *p* kneeling.	351	—
Minister and *P*	352	—
read the Gospel and may lead the Prayers of the *P*.	354	10
ministration of the Sacrament to the *p*.	354	13
and may lead the Prayers of the *P*.	354	17
directions given for the Prayers of the *P*.	354	21
The *p* standing, the Celebrant says	355	—
P	355	—
The Celebrant says to the *p*	357	—
P	357	—
The *p* sit.	357	—
P	358	—
The Prayers of the *P*	359	—
Minister and *P*	360	—
The Celebrant says to the *p*	360	—
P	360	—
Then the Ministers and *P* may greet one another	360	—
the congregation bring the *p*'s offerings of bread	361	—
p stand while the offerings are presented	361	—
The *p* remain standing.	361	—
P	361	—
Celebrant and *P*	362	—
The *p* stand or kneel.	362	—
Celebrant and *P*	363	—
P and Celebrant	364	—
Facing the *p*, the Celebrant says the following	364	—
deliver it to the *p*.	365	—
Celebrant and *P*	365	—
or the Priest, may bless the *p*.	366	—
P	366	—
The *P* respond	366	—
The *p* remain standing.	367	—
P	367	—
Celebrant and *P*	367	—
The *p* stand or kneel.	368	—
Celebrant and *P*	368	—
the lines in italics are spoken by the *P*.	369	—
Celebrant and *P*	371	—
The *p* remain standing.	372	—
P	372	—
Celebrant and *P*	373	—
The *p* stand or kneel.	373	—
Celebrant and *P*	375	—
The Prayers of the *P*	383	—
the *P* offer their own prayers,	385	—
The Leader and *P* pray responsively	387	—
The *P* may add their own petitions.	388	—
Here and after every petition the *P* respond	389	—
The Leader and *P* pray responsively	392	—
The *P* may add their own petitions	392	—
The *P* may add their own thanksgivings	393	—
The *P* may add their own petitions	393	—
Leader and *P*	393	—
The *P* and Priest	400	6
The *p* respond—Amen!	401	10
P	402	—
and his revelation of himself to his *p*;	402	—
Celebrant and *P*	402	—
P	404	—
and his revelation of himself to his *p*;	404	—
Celebrant and *P*	404	—
The Prayers of the *P* following the Creed	406	5
read the Gospel in the language of the *p*,	406	23
the Prayers of the *P* may be said.	406	26
and the offerings of the *p* received.	407	2
While the *p* are coming forward to receive	407	22
then communicate, and after them the *p*.	407	24
(and the receiving of the *p*'s offering),	408	20
and then dismisses the *p*.	408	27
either after the Communion of the *p*	409	4
The *p* standing, the Bishop says	413	—
P	413	—
P	414	—
The *p* sit.	414	—
P	415	—
P	416	—
P	417	—
P	419	—
The service then continues with the Prayers of the *P*	419	—
facing the *p* and the persons to be married,	423	—
P	425	—
The Celebrant then says to the *p*	425	—
P	426	—
P	428	—
P and Celebrant	428	—
to which the *P* respond, saying, Amen.	429	—
The *p* remain standing.	430	—
The Celebrant may say to the *p*	431	—
P	431	—
P	434	—
In the Eucharist it may follow the Prayers of the *P*	439	7
the Congregation is directed to instruct the *p*,	445	7
Officiant and *P*	464	—
P	469	—
The *p* sit.	470	—
P	479	—
P	480	—
A homily may be preached, the *p* being seated.	480	—

the following serves for the Prayers of the *P*.	480	—
The *P* respond to every petition with Amen.	480	—
or the Bishop if present, may then bless the *p*,	483	—
P	485	—
Celebrant and *P*	485	—
The Celebrant dismisses the *p* with these words	486	—
P	493	—
The *p* sit.	494	—
P	495	—
Celebrant and *P*	496	—
service continues with the Prayers of the *P*,	496	—
following form of the Prayers of the *P* is used,	496	—
or the Bishop if present, may then bless the *p*,	500	—
P	501	—
Celebrant and *P*	502	—
The Celebrant dismisses the *p* with these words	502	—
P	502	—
from God for the nurture of his *p*	510	28
most generally recognized by Christian *p*	510	31
presides from a chair placed close to the *p*,	511	13
Opportunity is always given to the *p*	511	24
The *p* standing, the Bishop appointed says	512	—
P	512	—
The bishops and *p* sit.	513	—
the response of the *p*	513	—
The *P* respond in these or other words	514	—
P	515	—
P	516	—
A period of silent prayer follows, the *p* still standing.	520	—
The *P* in a loud voice respond	521	—
The Presiding Bishop presents to the *p* their new bishop.	522	—
Clergy and *P* offer their acclamation and applause.	522	—
P	522	—
The *P* greet one another.	522	—
one of the bishops leads the *p* in the following	522	—
The new Bishop blesses the *p*, first saying	523	—
P	523	—
A Deacon dismisses the *p*	523	—
from a chair placed close to the *p*, and facing them,	524	5
Opportunity is always given to the *p*	524	18
The *p* standing, the Bishop says	525	3
P	525	—
The bishop and *p* sit.	526	—
The Bishop says to the *p*	527	—
The *P* respond in these or other words	527	—
The Bishop then calls the *p* to prayer	527	—
P	527	—
P	529	—
A period of silent prayer follows, the *p* still standing.	533	—
The *P* in a loud voice respond	534	—
P	534	—
The Clergy and *P* greet one another	534	—
The Bishop then asks the new priest to bless the *p*.	535	—
or a Priest if no deacon is present, dismisses the *p*.	535	—
P	535	—
from a chair placed close to the *p*, and facing them,	536	5
Opportunity is always given to the *p*	536	18
The *p* standing, the Bishop says	537	—
P	537	—
The bishop and *p* sit.	538	—
The Bishop says to the *p*	539	—
The *P* respond in these or other words	539	—
The Bishop then calls the *p* to prayer	539	—
P	539	—
P	541	—
A period of silent prayer follows, the *p* still standing.	544	—
The *P* in a loud voice respond	545	—
P	546	—
The Clergy and *P* greet one another.	546	—
The Bishop blesses the *p*,	547	—
P	547	—
this Litany may be used for the Prayers of the *P*	548	—
P	551	—
the Prayers of the *P* after the Creed,	552	6
distributes Holy Communion to the *p*.	553	12
Love and serve Christ's *p*.	557	13
P	559	—
P	560	—
P	561	—
P	562	—
The new Minister then says to the *p*	563	—
P	563	—
The *P* greet one another.	563	—
the Bishop leads the *p* in the following prayer;	564	5
ministers may be clearly seen and heard by the *p*.	564	16
the clergy and *p* gather with the bishop	567	3
P	568	—
P	569	—
P	570	—
the congregation leads the Prayers of the *P*.	572	—
The Bishop says to the *p*	574	—
P	574	—
and other clergy and the *p* greet one another.	574	—
the Bishop blesses the *p*;	574	—
When the clergy and *p* assemble before the service,	575	5
the usual forms of the Prayers of the *P* may be used;	576	18
P	579	—
9. For Clergy and *P*	810	15
9. For Clergy and *P*	817	—
in place of the Prayers of the *P* at the Eucharist,	836	—
that the *p* (by daily hearing of holy Scripture read	866	13
such language spoken to the *p* in the Church,	866	23
hath been read in Latin to the *p*,	866	25
the *p* shall not be at so great charge for books,	867	7
in such a Tongue as the *p* understandeth.	872	21
in a tongue not understanded of the *p*.	872	24
The Cup of the Lord is not to be denied to the Lay-*p*:	874	2
that they may be understanded of the *p*.	874	39

peoples

varying needs of the nations and *p* called of God	877	19
varying needs of the nations and *p* called of God	878	5

perfect

P God and *p* Man, of a reasonable soul and human	865	25
so that two whole and *p* Natures,	868	4
Offering of Christ once made is that *p* redemption,	874	6

perfecter

Hebrews 12:1–2 (Looking to Jesus, the *p* of our faith)	454	2

perfection

things appertaining to the *p* of Man's nature;	868	14

perform

and *p* other assisting functions at the Eucharist. 422 13
permitted by civil law that deacons may *p* marriages, 422 15
a deacon or lay person may *p* the anointing, 456 —
the grace and power to *p* them. 557 16
and *p* other actions as indicated in the rubrics. 558 15

performed

p by an assisting priest. 322 14
p by an assisting priest. 354 14

peril

2 Against *P* of Idolatry. 875 3

perilous

unclean living, no less *p* than desperation. 871 19

perils

A Collect for Aid against *P* 70 —
A Collect for Aid against *P* 123 —

period

A *p* of silence may follow. 137 —
A *p* of silence may be kept. 288 6
A *p* of silence is kept. 337 —
A *p* of silence is kept. 364 —
A *p* of silence follows. 417 —
A *p* of silent prayer follows, 520 —
A *p* of silent prayer follows, 533 —
A *p* of silent prayer follows, 544 —
After a *p* of silence, the Bishop concludes 572 —
extended *p* of time without having been consecrated, 577 22

periods

When persons are unable to be present for extended *p*, 396 —

perish

keep whole and undefiled, without doubt he shall *p* 864 23

permission

With the express *p* of the bishop, 16 19
with the bishop's *p*, for dedicating a private chapel 577 5

permit

When circumstances *p*, the congregation may gather 270 —

permitted

Where it is *p* by civil law that deacons may perform 422 15
Where *p* by civil law, 435 4

person

the term "Officiant" is used to denote the *p*, 36 3
A deacon or lay *p* using the preceding form remains 42 —
A deacon or lay *p* using the preceding form remains 63 —
the term "Officiant" is used to denote the *p*, 74 2
A deacon or lay *p* using the preceding form remains 80 —
A deacon or lay *p* using the preceding blessing 114 —
A deacon or lay *p* using the preceding form remains 117 —
When more than one *p* is present, 136 —
the Collect should be read by one *p*, 136 —
Here a Deacon or other *p* appointed reads 270 —
All standing, the Deacon, or other *p* appointed, 277 —
The biddings may be read by a Deacon or other *p* 277 —
A lay *p* may be assigned to chant the Exsultet. 284 21
Then the Deacon, or other *p* appointed, 286 —
A *P* appointed leads the following petitions 305 —
the Bishop or Priest places a hand on the *p*'s head, 308 —
If there is reasonable doubt that a *p* has been baptized 313 16
the *p* is baptized in the usual manner, 313 18
any baptized *p* may administer Baptism 313 22
The *p* who administers emergency Baptism 314 3
If the baptized *p* recovers, 314 5
and the *p* baptized under emergency conditions, 314 7
Exhortation may be read by a lay *p*. 316 —
A deacon or lay *p* using the preceding form 321 —
The Deacon or other *p* appointed says 328 —
A deacon or lay *p* using the preceding form 353 —
If the priest knows that a *p* who is living 409 8
the priest shall speak to that *p* 409 9
And if the *p* or persons on one side truly forgive 409 20
form may be used when a *p* wishes to make or renew 420 —
It is essential that the *p* seeking to make or renew 420 —
the Offertory of the Eucharist, the *p* comes forward 420 —
for the special work in which the *p* will be engaged 421 —
or other *p* appointed reads the following prayers, 429 —
If more than one *p* responds, 437 12
to be used by a Deacon or Lay *P* 448 —
to be used by a Deacon or Lay *P* 452 —
of this service may always be led by a deacon or lay *p*. 453 6
if the sick *p*'s conscience is troubled, 454 16
A deacon or lay *p* using the preceding form 455 —
The Priest then lays hands upon the sick *p*, 455 —
If the *p* is to be anointed, the Priest dips 456 —
makes the sign of the cross on the sick *p*'s forehead, 456 —
a deacon or lay *p* may perform the anointing, 456 —
If the sick *p* cannot receive either the consecrated 457 —
If a *p* desires to receive the Sacrament, 457 —
the Celebrant is to assure that *p* that all the benefits 457 —
For a Sick *P* 458 —
Prayers for use by a Sick *P* 461 —
When a *p* is near death, 462 —
A Prayer for a *P* near Death 462 —
and the *P* appointed leads the Litany for Ordinations, 515 —
A Priest and a Lay *P*, 526 —
and the *P* appointed leads the Litany for Ordinations, 527 —
A Priest and a Lay *P*, 538 —
and the *P* appointed leads the Litany for Ordinations, 539 —
A lay *p* being instituted should read one 558 23
led by a *p* appointed. 560 —
but if the new minister is a lay *p*, 564 6
bishop may state briefly the nature of the *p*'s office 565 2
bishop, the new minister, or some other *p*; 565 17
by a donor, or a lay reader, or another suitable *p*. 576 10
lay *p* outline the plans of the congregation for witness 576 12
55. For a *P* in Trouble or Bereavement 812 6
55. For a *P* in Trouble or Bereavement 831 —
and Human Natures in the *P* of Christ 864 2
and coming together to form one *p* and subsistence, 864 14
For there is one *P* of the Father, 864 27
by the Christian verity to acknowledge every *P* 865 5
not by confusion of Substance, but by unity of *P*. 865 30
were joined together in one *P*, 868 5
therefore in every *p* born into this world, 869 27
That *p* which by open denunciation of the Church 874 17

personal

Adonai ("Lord") and the *p* name YHWH. 583 16
Prayers for Family and *P* Life 811 27
Thanksgivings for Family and *P* Life 813 13
Prayers for Family and *P* Life 828 —
Thanksgivings for Family and *P* Life 841 —

persons

the members of each order within the Church, lay *p*, 13 17
but, like lay *p*, may officiate at the Liturgy 13 22
It is appropriate that other *p* be assigned to read 36 5
It is appropriate that other *p* be assigned to read 74 4
Any part or parts of this service may be led by lay *p*. 108 7
II. For the choice of fit *p* for the ministry 205 —
II. For the choice of fit *p* for the ministry 256 —
The Passion Gospel may be read or chanted by lay *p*. 273 —
Specific roles may be assigned to different *p*, 273 —
The Passion Gospel may be read or chanted by lay *p*. 277 —
Specific roles may be assigned to different *p*, 277 —
and other *p*, to take active parts in the service. 284 11
Lay *p* read the Lessons, and the Epistle, and assist 284 20
sponsored by one or more baptized *p*. 298 17
Lay *p* may act as readers, 312 24
and by deacons and lay *p*. 322 6
Lay *p* appointed by the celebrant should normally 322 15
and by deacons and lay *p*. 354 6
Lay *p* appointed by the celebrant should normally 354 —
When *p* are unable to be present for extended 396 —
such *p* may be communicated 396 —
When a portion of the congregation is composed of *p* 406 21
lay *p* licensed by the bishop 408 7
not allowing such *p* to receive Communion 409 14
And if the person or *p* on one side truly forgive 409 20
presented by *p* newly confirmed. 412 17
the Epistles be read by lay *p*. 422 19
the *p* to be married are declared. 422 21
At the time appointed, the *p* to be married, 423 —
facing the people and the *p* to be married, 423 —
Then the Celebrant says to the *p* to be married 424 —
the ministers by the newly married *p*. 438 2
for the well-being of their families, and of all *p* 445 —
be read by lay *p*. 468 16
be read by lay *p*. 490 16
The *p* who are chosen and recognized by the Church 510 16
No *p* are allowed to exercise the office 510 21
Lay *P*, standing before the Presiding Bishop, present 513 —
Lay *p* read the Old Testament Lesson 515 —
Lay *p* read the Old Testament Lesson 528 —
Lay *p* read the Old Testament Lesson 540 —
Lay *p* from the congregation read the Old Testament 558 14
but additional, or other, *p* may do this when desired. 565 5
the bishop, or other *p* present, may speak in response 565 19
If there are *p* to be baptized, 569 10
Lay *p* read the Old Testament Lesson 571 —
may also be carried by appropriate *p*. 575 19
At the dedication of the font, children or other lay *p* 575 23
or other lay *p*, bring them forward 576 23
47. For Young *P* 811 30
47. For Young *P* 829 —
not as parted or separated into two *p*, but one 864 15
neither confounding the *P*, nor dividing 864 26
But the whole three *P* are co-eternal together 865 15
And in unity of this Godhead there be three *P*, 867 37
and unspeakable comfort to godly *p*, 871 12
So, for curious and carnal *p*, 871 16
Of excommunicate *P*, how they are to be avoided. 874 16

pertaining

sometimes have erred, even in things *p* to God. 872 8

Peter

1 *P* 2:9 (Saints' Days) 108 20
1 *P* 5:8–9a 132 —
1 *P* 1:3 137 —
Confession of Saint *P* January 18 187 —
Saint *P* and Saint Paul June 29 190 —
Confession of Saint *P* January 18 238 —
Saint *P* and Saint Paul June 29 241 —
Epistle 1 *P* 4:1–8 283 —
Epistle 1 *P* 5:1–4,* or Ephesians 4:7, 11–16, 528 —
in translations of 1 *P* 5:1, the original Greek terms 528 —
or 1 *P* 2:1–9 571 —

petition

Here and after every *p* the People respond 389 —
The People respond to every *p* with Amen. 480 —

petitions

the indented *p* may be adapted 277 —
A Person appointed leads the following *p* 305 —
The *p* (page 305) may also be led by one 312 25
before or during the *p* (page 305), 312 29
Additional *p* and thanksgivings may be included here. 330 —
A bar in the margin indicates *p* which may be omitted. 383 —
The People may add their own *p*. 388 —
The People may add their own *p* 392 —
The People may add their own *p* 393 —
The *p* on pages 305–306 may be used. 417 —

Philadelphia

P, October, 1789. 11 24

Philip

Saint *P* and Saint James May 1 189 —
Saint *P* and Saint James May 1 240 —

Philippians

P 1:2 40 —
P 1:2 61 —
P 1:2 78 —
P 1:2 115 —
Epistle *P* 2:5–11 272 —
or Ephesians 4:7, 11–16, or *P* 4:4–9 528 —

phrases

obsolete words and *p*, as from the local references.] 875 19

physical

sickness or *p* disability, is unable to eat and drink 457 14

picks

for an inquiring stranger who *p* up a Prayer Book. 844 8

Pie

the number and hardness of the Rules called the *P*, 866 30

piece

without breaking one *p* thereof from another. 866 37

piety

the procuring of reverence, and the exciting of *p* 10 11
Christian doctrine, and instructive in *p* and morals. 875 15

place

those that are in *p* of Authority should, 9 20
The attention of this Church was in the first *p* drawn 10 32
texts may be used in *p* of the corresponding texts 14 14
Prayer may be used in *p* of all that precedes 36 9
In Easter Week, in *p* of an Invitatory Psalm, 45 —
Prayer may be used in *p* of all that precedes 74 8
In Easter Week, in *p* of an Invitatory Psalm, 83 —
complete rite in *p* of Evening Prayer, 108 4
In *p* of the above, from Easter Day through 109 —
In special circumstances, in *p* of a Canticle, 142 1
Nicene Creed may take the *p* of the Apostles' Creed, 142 18
in its customary *p* before the people assemble; 143 4
the officiant then goes to a *p* close by it 143 4
the lighting of an Advent Wreath may take *p* 143 14
dining table, or at some other convenient *p*. 143 18
For use in the Litany in *p* of the Versicle 154 —
the congregation may gather at a *p* apart 270 —
At a suitable *p*, the procession may halt 271 —
in *p* of the Prayers of the People, 283 —
a deacon to carry the Paschal Candle to its *p*, 284 17
the Service of Light may take *p* at a convenient time 284 30
Baptismal Vows may take *p* here. 295 —
In *p* of the above, from Easter Day 299 —
at a *p* in full sight of the congregation, 308 —
may take the *p* of the Nicene Creed 312 16
Presentation of the Candidates does not take *p* 312 28
In *p* of the above, from Easter Day 319 —
Morning or Evening Prayer may be used in *p* 322 18
In *p* of the above, from Easter Day 323 —
sung or said, in addition to, or in *p* of, 324 —
p a hand upon the cup and any other vessel 334 —
p a hand upon the cup and any other vessel 342 —
In *p* of the above, from Easter Day 351 —
Morning or Evening Prayer may be used in *p* 354 18
In *p* of the above, from Easter Day 355 —
p a hand upon the cup and any other vessel 362 —
In *p* of, or in addition to, the preceding, 364 —
p a hand upon the cup and any other vessel 368 —
p a hand upon the cup and any other vessel 371 —
p a hand upon the cup and any other vessel 374 —
p a hand upon the cup and any other vessel 403 —
p a hand upon the cup and any other vessel 405 —
Gloria in excelsis, or the hymn used in *p* of it, 406 12
in the language of the people, either in *p* of, 406 23
Peace may take *p* at the time of the administration 407 10
In *p* of the above, from Easter Day 413 —
assemble in the church or some other appropriate *p*. 423 —
it takes *p* at this time. 425 —
In *p* of the usual postcommunion prayer, 432 —
or in some other convenient *p*. 435 10
vows may be used in *p* of the ring. 437 23
It is desirable that this take *p* at a Sunday service. 439 6
At Morning or Evening Prayer it may take *p* 439 8
inside the altar rails or in a *p* set aside 446 16
When the Laying on of Hands or Anointing takes *p* 453 7
and it is recommended that it take *p* immediately 453 9
If preferred, the Committal service may take *p* 468 11
celebrant standing in the accustomed *p*. 468 25
In *p* of the usual postcommunion prayer, 482 —
In *p* of this prayer, or in addition to it, 486 —
If the grave is in a *p* that has not previously been set 487 —
If preferred, the Committal service may take *p* 490 11
celebrant standing in the accustomed *p*. 490 25
When all are in *p*, the Celebrant may address 492 —
In *p* of the usual postcommunion prayer, 498 —
If the grave is in a *p* that has not previously been set 503 —
or it may be in *p* before the congregation 506 5
the body is committed to its resting *p*. 506 19
The committal may take *p* either where 506 19
In *p* of the above, from Easter Day 512 —
In *p* of the usual postcommunion prayer, 522 —
In *p* of the above, from Easter Day 525 —
In *p* of the usual postcommunion prayer, 535 —
In *p* of the above, from Easter Day 537 —
In *p* of the usual postcommunion prayer, 546 —
take *p* at some convenient time prior to the service. 552 18
take *p* at several conveniently separated places 553 13
and cleanse the vessels in some convenient *p*. 555 7
in *p* of the usual postcommunion prayer, 564 4
or in some other *p* where the bishop 564 15
building is ready for regular use as a *p* of worship. 566 10
in a *p* apart from the church or chapel. 567 4
If no Baptism is to take *p* 570 —
Bishop proceeds to an appropriate *p*, and says 572 —
p the vessels on it, and light the candles. 574 —
in the parish house, in a former or neighboring *p* 575 6
In *p* of a pastoral staff, 575 21
and put into *p* by a donor, or a lay reader, 576 10
respond, indicating the *p* of this congregation 576 13
bring them forward and put them in *p*. 576 24
If the *p* of public worship is also to serve as a school 576 29
restored, in *p* of its English equivalent, 584 4
in *p* of the Prayers of the People at the Eucharist, 836 —
or deny the *p* of forgiveness to such as truly repent. 870 37
neither may it so expound one *p* of Scripture, 871 39
8 Of the Time and *P* of Prayer. 875 10

placed

service may be *p* on or near the Altar, 143 13
p in the sight of the people. 281 —
The Paschal Candle is *p* in its stand. 286 —
while the offerings are presented and *p* on the Altar. 333 —
while the offerings are presented and *p* on the Altar. 361 —
other offerings, are *p* upon it. 401 6
presides from a chair *p* close to the people, 511 13
from a chair *p* close to the people, and facing them, 524 5
from a chair *p* close to the people, and facing them, 536 5
p upon the new priest after the entire Prayer 553 22
p upon the new deacon after the entire Prayer 554 13

places

In *p* where Holy Communion is to be administered 282 —
the Bishop or Priest *p* a hand on the person's head, 308 —
the deacon reverently *p* the consecrated Sacrament 408 21
The giver *p* the ring on the ring-finger 427 —
and other ministers take their *p* at the body. 482 —

and other ministers take their *p* at the body. 499 —
and *p* the vessels on the Lord's Table. 546 —
at several conveniently separated *p* in the church. 553 13
that Traditions and Ceremonies be in all *p* one, 874 22

placing
p a hand on the vessel of oil, 307 —
preparing and *p* on it the offerings 322 11
preparing and *p* on it the offerings 354 11
preparing and *p* upon it the bread and cup of wine. 407 15

plain
that purpose, which is *p* and easy to be understood, 866 35
so they be *p* and easy to be understood. 866 41
order as is most easy and *p* for the understanding, 867 3
but is repugnant to the *p* words of Scripture, 873 29

plainest
for promulgating them to mankind in the clearest, *p*, 11 21

plainly
as, among other things, it may *p* appear 866 4
forasmuch as nothing can, almost, be so *p* set forth, 867 16
whereas Christ saith *p*, 870 22
It is a thing *p* repugnant to the Word of God, 872 22
set forth by Elizabeth our Queen do most *p* testify; 876 2

plainness
for the shortness thereof, and for the *p* of the order, 867 4

plan
in a general *p* referred for study and action 877 27

plans
outline the *p* of the congregation for witness 576 12

planting
by *p* in uncertain stories, Legends, Responds, Verses, 866 17

played
or instrumental music may be *p*. 423 —
or instrumental music may be *p*. 431 —
or instrumental music may be *p*. 432 —
instrumental music may be *p*. 553 4
Instrumental music is now *p*, or a hymn or anthem 572 —
Bells may now be rung and music *p*. 574 2

pleasant
Wherefore we have no power to do good works *p* 869 36
and the Inspiration of his Spirit, are not *p* to God, 870 13
p, and unspeakable comfort to godly persons, 871 12

pleasing
yet are they *p* and acceptable to God in Christ, 870 8

plural
changed to the *p* where necessary. 553 28
changed to the *p* where necessary. 554 18

poetry
The Psalter is a body of liturgical *p*. 582 2
the Psalms which follows is set out in lines of *p*. 583 1

point
p of doctrine, discipline, or worship; 11 14
rather, it is a *p* of departure for the teacher, 844 5

pointing
The following *p* of the Gloria may be used: 141 16

points
and in printed Bibles, after the invention of vowel *p*, 583 22

pontifical
After the *p* blessing and the dismissal, 553 14

poor
deacons to minister in Christ's name to the *p*, 510 14
strong and weak, rich and *p*. 557 12
35. For the *P* and Neglected 811 14
35. For the *P* and the Neglected 826 —
as he possesseth, liberally to give alms to the *p*, 876 15

portable
The use of *p* musical instruments is suitable. 575 10

portion
always sung or said at the conclusion of the entire *p* 141 11
When a *p* of the congregation is composed 406 21
property of this *p* of Christ's catholic Church, 510 27
or *p* of a psalm, in unison. 582 9
In some instances, the entire *p* of the Psalter 935 3

portions
p of the preceding may be used. 272 —
These omitted *p* of the rite may be administered 312 12
P of the service may be used, 566 3
Suitable *p* of this service may be used by the bishop, 577 4
Relevant *p* of the service for the Dedication 577 8
ancient fathers had divided the Psalms into seven *p*, 866 27

possesseth
man ought, of such things as he *p*, liberally to give 876 15

possession
the right, title, and *p* of the same; 876 14

possible
there should be as little artificial light as *p* 142 26
It is recommended that, as far as *p*, 312 5
the celebrant, whenever *p*, should face the people 313 4
be present, when *p*, to communicate with them. 396 —
When *p*, it is desirable that members of the family 462 —
reported as soon as *p* to, 468 3
reported as soon as *p* to, 490 3
accordance with ancient custom, it is desirable, if *p*, 511 3
When *p*, the areas or furnishings should be put 577 13
and should be followed, if *p*, by the administration 577 16
Invitatory Antiphons for the Venite makes *p* 582 23

postcommunion
The *p* prayer on page 482 may be used. 202 —
The *p* prayer on page 457 may be used. 208 —
The *p* prayer on page 498 may be used. 253 —
The *p* prayer on page 457 may be used. 260 —
One of the usual *p* prayers is then said, 399 —
in the liturgy as far as the end of the *p* prayer, 408 26
A hymn may be sung before or after the *p* prayer. 409 6
In place of the usual *p* prayer, the following is said 432 —
One of the usual *p* prayers is said, or the following 457 —
In place of the usual *p* prayer, the following is said 482 —
In place of the usual *p* prayer, the following is said 498 —

In place of the usual *p* prayer, one of the bishops 522 —
In place of the usual *p* prayer, the following is said 535 —
In place of the usual *p* prayer, the following is said 546 —
and the usual *p* prayer are not used. 552 7
in place of the usual *p* prayer, 564 4
the usual *p* prayer is used. 564 6
After the *p* prayer, the Bishop blesses the people; 574 —

postponed
or all three of them, is *p* one day. 161 —
or all three of them, is *p* one day. 213 —

pounding
their *p* waves. 583 6

pour
p water on him or her, saying 313 24

poured
persons to be baptized, water is now *p* into the Font, 569 —
[water may be *p* into the Font, and] 570 —

pouring
assigned the task of *p* the water. 575 24

pours
immerses, or *p* water upon, the candidate, saying 307 —
Deacon prepares the bread, *p* sufficient wine 546 —

power
fill him with grace and *p*, 554 1
fill him with grace and *p*, 554 23
give you the grace and *p* to perform them. 557 16
of infinite *p*, wisdom, and goodness; 867 36
three Persons, of one substance, *p*, and eternity; 867 37
Wherefore we have no *p* to do good works pleasant 869 36
The Church hath *p* to decree Rites or Ceremonies, 871 37
XXXVII. Of the *P* of the Civil Magistrates. 875 34
The *P* of the Civil Magistrate extendeth to all men, 875 35
the chief *p* in this Realm of England, 875 40

powers
nor *p*, nor height, nor depth, nor anything else 507 7

practicable
Where *p*, the font is to be filled with clean water 313 1

practice
a complete statement of belief and *p*; 844 5

practicing
doubts may arise in the use and *p* of the same: 867 17

praise
2 A Song of *P* Benedictus es, Domini 49 —
7 We *P* Thee Te Deum laudamus 52 —
13 A Song of *P* Benedictus es, Domine 90 —
or other canticle, or some other hymn of *p*. 113 —
the following hymn or some other song of *p* is sung 324 —
the following hymn or some other song of *p* is sung 356 —
a hymn of *p* may be sung. 553 14
The ancient *p*-shout, "Hallelujah," has been restored, 584 4
its English equivalent, "*P* the Lord." 584 5

praises
The Celebrant now *p* God for the salvation 403 —
The Celebrant now *p* God for the salvation 404 —

pray
Let us *p*. 291 —
The Leader and People *p* responsively 387 —
The Leader and People *p* responsively 392 —
P for the World and the Church 400 12
"Let us *p* in the words our Savior hath (has) taught 408 23

prayer
The Book of Common *P* (1789) 8 2
set forth A Book of Common *P*, 8 8
in the Preface of her Book of Common *P*, 9 14
in the *p* for our Civil Rulers, 10 33
upon a comparison of this with the Book of Common *P* 11 11
major Feasts, and Daily Morning and Evening *P*, 13 4
for other special occasions for which no service or *p* 13 13
the Order for Morning or Evening *P* may be used 36 9
Daily Morning *P*: 37 —
A *P* of St. Chrysostom 59 —
Daily Evening *P*: 61 —
A *P* of St. Chrysostom 72 —
the Order for Morning or Evening *P* may be used 74 8
Daily Morning *P*: 75 —
P of Manasseh, 1–2, 4, 6–7, 11–15 90 —
A *P* of St. Chrysostom 102 —
a complete rite in place of Evening *P*, 108 4
Evening *P* or some other service, 108 5
deacon, when presiding, should read the *P* for Light, 108 8
The Officiant then says the *P* for Light, 110 —
the following or some other suitable *p*, first saying 110 —
With Evening *P*, beginning with the Psalms; 112 —
followed by the Lord's *P* and a grace or blessing; 112 —
or other suitable devotions, including the Lord's *P*. 113 —
or one of the Collects from Evening *P* 113 —
Daily Evening *P*: 115 —
A *P* of St. Chrysostom 126 —
The Lord's *P* 137 —
The Lord's *P* 138 —
The Lord's *P* 139 —
The Lord's *P* 140 —
Morning and Evening *P* 141 2
In Rite One services of Morning *P* and Evening *P*, 141 18
The Lord's *P* may be omitted from the Office 142 5
to express intentions or objects of *p* 142 8
either at the bidding, or in the course of the *p*; 142 9
opportunity may be given for silent *p*. 142 10
When Morning or Evening *P* is used as the Liturgy 142 17
the opening Short Lesson and the *P* for Light. 143 2
take place after the *P* for Light. 143 15
or after the Collects of Morning or Evening *P*; 148 —
and Collect which follows the Lord's *P*; 154 —
or at the end of Morning or Evening *P*; 154 —
The postcommunion *p* on page 482 may be used. 202 —
The postcommunion *p* on page 457 may be used. 208 —
The postcommunion *p* on page 498 may be used. 253 —
The postcommunion *p* on page 457 may be used. 260 —
imposed, the Celebrant says the following *p* 265 —
the *p* for forgiveness appointed at Morning *P*. 269 —
or after the *p* of blessing. 270 —
All then kneel for silent *p*, 276 —
the Lord's *P*, and the final *p* on page 282. 280 —
The service may be concluded here with the Lord's *P* 282 —

and the final *p* below.	282	—
The Lord's *P*	282	—
The service concludes with the following *p*.	282	—
The service then concludes with the Lord's *P*	283	—
the Lord's *P*, and the Dismissal.	284	26
The Celebrant may say the following *p*	285	—
reads the *p*, "Heavenly Father,	298	11
support them by *p* and example in their Christian life.	298	20
and before the preceding *p*.	308	—
the service continues with the Lord's *P*	311	—
concluding with this *p*	311	—
In that case, the deacon omits the *p*	312	10
for the *p*, "Heavenly Father,	313	10
The Lord's *P* is then said.	314	1
Morning or Evening *P* may be used	322	18
After each paragraph of this *p*,	328	—
Eucharistic *P* I	333	—
The following *p* may be said.	337	—
The People may join in saying this *p*	337	—
The People may join in saying this *p*	339	—
Eucharistic *P* II	340	—
Continue with the Lord's *P*, page 336.	343	—
Morning or Evening *P* may be used	354	18
P is offered with intercession for	359	—
Eucharistic *P* A	361	—
Eucharistic *P* B	367	—
Continue with the Lord's *P* on page 364.	369	—
Eucharistic *P* C	369	—
In this *p*, the lines in italics are spoken	369	—
Continue with the Lord's *P* on page 364.	372	—
Eucharistic *P* D	372	—
Continue with the Lord's *P* on page 364.	376	—
P is offered with intercession for	383	—
The Lord's *P* is said, the Celebrant first saying	398	—
The *P* continues with these words	403	—
The *P* concludes with these or similar words	405	—
conclude with the Lord's *P*;	407	3
saying again the words of the Eucharistic *P*,	408	14
(in the case of Eucharistic *P* C,	408	16
2. The Lord's *P* is then said,	408	23
as far as the end of the postcommunion *p*,	408	27
A hymn may be sung before or after the postcommunion *p*.	409	6
The Bishop concludes with this *p*	419	—
the service continues with the Lord's *P*	419	—
using the *p* on page 307.	419	—
Celebrant then says this or some other appropriate *p*	421	—
A *p* for the special work in which the person	421	—
If Communion is to follow, the Lord's *P* may	428	—
In place of the usual postcommunion *p*,	432	—
At Morning or Evening *P* it may take place	439	8
or with the *p* "O God, you have taught us."	439	12
The Celebrant then says this *p*	443	—
common *p* of Christians assembled for public worship,	446	4
the priest may assign to the penitent a psalm, *p*,	446	23
The Lord's *P* is always included.	453	5
If Communion is not to follow, the Lord's *P* is	456	—
with the [Peace and] Lord's *P* on page 398.	457	—
A *P* for a Person near Death	462	—
A Commendatory *P*	465	—
not to be a Communion, the Lord's *P* is said here,	480	—
service continues with the following *p* of intercession,	480	—
In place of the usual postcommunion *p*,	482	—
In place of this *p*, or in addition to it,	486	—
Christian burial, the Priest may use the following *p*,	487	—
The Celebrant may add the following *p*	494	—
not to be a Communion, the Lord's *P* is said here,	496	—
concludes with one of the following or some other *p*	497	—
In place of the usual postcommunion *p*,	498	—
Christian burial, the Priest may use the following *p*,	503	—
3. *P* may be offered for the bereaved.	506	9
6. *P*, including the Lord's *P*, is offered	506	15
by solemn *p* and the laying on of episcopal hands.	510	18
A period of silent *p* follows,	520	—
Presiding Bishop then begins this *P* of Consecration	520	—
In place of the usual postcommunion *p*,	522	—
The Bishop then calls the people to *p*	527	—
A period of silent *p* follows,	533	—
The Bishop then says this *P* of Consecration.	533	—
In place of the usual postcommunion *p*,	535	—
The Bishop then calls the people to *p*	539	—
A period of silent *p* follows,	544	—
The Bishop then says this *P* of Consecration	545	—
In place of the usual postcommunion *p*,	546	—
and the usual postcommunion *p* are not used.	552	7
hymn to the Holy Spirit before the *P* of Consecration	552	14
Following the Consecration *P*,	553	2
During the Eucharistic *P*,	553	8
upon the new priest after the entire *P* of Consecration	553	22
During the *P* of Consecration,	553	30
after the entire *P* of Consecration is completed,	554	13
During the *P* of Consecration the Bishop is to lay hands	554	20
in place of the usual postcommunion *p*,	564	5
the Bishop leads the people in the following *p*;	564	5
the usual postcommunion *p* is used.	564	6
or another *p* suitable to the occasion,	565	8
The priest's *p* on page 562 is appropriate only	565	24
the *P* for the Consecration of the Church	568	7
After the postcommunion *p*, the Bishop blesses	574	—
in addition to saying the *p* over the font as given,	575	25
the appropriate *p* may be said, or adapted	577	11
the classical English versions, the *P* Book Psalter	583	26
First Day: Morning *P*	585	—
First Day: Evening *P*	589	—
Second Day: Morning *P*	593	—
Second Day: Evening *P*	597	—
Third Day: Morning *P*	599	—
Third Day: Evening *P*	602	—
Fourth Day: Morning *P*	606	—
Fourth Day: Evening *P*	610	—
Fifth Day: Morning *P*	613	—
Fifth Day: Evening *P*	617	—
Sixth Day: Morning *P*	621	—
Sixth Day: Evening *P*	624	—
Seventh Day: Morning *P*	629	—
Seventh Day: Evening *P*	633	—
Eighth Day: Morning *P*	636	—
Eighth Day: Evening *P*	641	—
Ninth Day: Morning *P*	645	—
Ninth Day: Evening *P*	650	—
Tenth Day: Morning *P*	654	—
Tenth Day: Evening *P*	658	—

Eleventh Day: Morning *P*	662	—
Eleventh Day: Evening *P*	665	—
Twelfth Day: Morning *P*	669	—
Twelfth Day: Evening *P*	672	—
Thirteenth Day: Morning *P*	676	—
Thirteenth Day: Evening *P*	679	—
Fourteenth Day: Morning *P*	683	—
Fourteenth Day: Evening *P*	687	—
Fifteenth Day: Morning *P*	691	—
Fifteenth Day: Evening *P*	694	—
Sixteenth Day: Morning *P*	701	—
Sixteenth Day: Evening *P*	705	—
Seventeenth Day: Morning *P*	709	—
Seventeenth Day: Evening *P*	713	—
Eighteenth Day: Morning *P*	717	—
Eighteenth Day: Evening *P*	722	—
Nineteenth Day: Morning *P*	724	—
Nineteenth Day: Evening *P*	727	—
Twentieth Day: Morning *P*	731	—
Twentieth Day: Evening *P*	735	—
Twenty-first Day: Morning *P*	738	—
Twenty-first Day: Evening *P*	741	—
Twenty-second Day: Morning *P*	746	—
Twenty-second Day: Evening *P*	749	—
Twenty-third Day: Morning *P*	753	—
Twenty-third Day: Evening *P*	756	—
Twenty-fourth Day: Morning *P*	759	—
Twenty-fourth Day: Evening *P*	763	—
Twenty-fifth Day: Morning *P*	766	—
Twenty-fifth Day: Evening *P*	769	—
Twenty-sixth Day: Morning *P*	772	—
Twenty-sixth Day: Evening *P*	775	—
Twenty-seventh Day: Morning *P*	778	—
Twenty-seventh Day: Evening *P*	782	—
Twenty-eighth Day: Morning *P*	785	—
Twenty-eighth Day: Evening *P*	789	—
Twenty-ninth Day: Morning *P*	794	—
Twenty-ninth Day: Evening *P*	797	—
Thirtieth Day: Morning *P*	800	—
Thirtieth Day: Evening *P*	804	—
61. A *P* of Self-Dedication	812	12
62. A *P* attributed to St. Francis	812	13
65. For the Answering of *P*	812	20
the Collects of Morning or Evening *P* or separately.	814	—
A *p* for parents is on page 444.	829	—
61. A *P* of Self-Dedication	832	—
62. A *P* attributed to St. Francis	833	—
See also the *P* of Humble Access on page 337.	834	—
the Collects at Morning or Evening *P*, or separately.	836	—
See also the *p* "O God, the King of Saints,"	838	—
for an inquiring stranger who picks up a *P* Book.	844	8
P and Worship	856	—
The First Book of Common *P* (1549)	866	2
So that here you have an order for *p*	866	42
The *P* of Manasses,	869	1
to have public *P* in the Church,	872	23
increased by virtue of *p* unto God.	873	19
7 Of *P*.	875	9
8 Of the Time and Place of *P*.	875	10
1. Our earnest desire that the Saviour's *p*,	876	29
congregation is present for Morning or Evening *P*,	888	12
First Reading at Evening *P*.	934	14

prayers

the proper end of all such *p*,	10	36
The *P*	54	—
one of these *p* for mission is added	57	—
The *P*	67	—
one of these *p* for mission is added	70	—
The *P*	97	—
one of these *p* for mission is added	100	—
The Officiant then begins the *P*	106	—
p in contemporary language may be adapted	108	22
P.	113	—
The *P*	121	—
one of these *p* for mission is added	124	—
One of the following *p* may be added	134	—
P may be offered for ourselves and others.	137	—
P may be offered for ourselves and others.	138	—
P may be offered for ourselves and others.	139	—
P for ourselves and others may follow.	140	—
p of thanksgiving for the blessings of the day,	140	—
The Officiant may add other *P*,	154	—
For the *P* of the People, the Litany of Thanksgiving	194	—
For the *P* of the People, one of the forms appointed	202	—
may be used for the *P* of the People.	204	—
For the *P* of the People, the Litany of Thanksgiving	246	—
For the *P* of the People, one of the forms appointed	253	—
may be used for the *P* of the People.	255	—
The service continues with the *P* of the People.	275	—
in place of the *P* of the People,	283	—
concluding with the *P* of the People,	284	25
The celebration continues with the *P* of the People.	295	—
P for the Candidates	305	—
The service then continues with the *P* of the People	310	—
be received and presented, and other *p* may be added,	311	—
Other *p*, such as the following, may be added.	314	2
When used separately, it concludes with suitable *p*,	321	—
read the Gospel and may lead the *P* of the People.	322	10
and may lead the *P* of the People.	322	17
the directions given for the *P* of the People.	322	21
The *P* of the People	328	—
it concludes with suitable *p*,	353	—
read the Gospel and may lead the *P* of the People.	354	10
and may lead the *P* of the People.	354	17
the directions given for the *P* of the People.	354	21
The *P* of the People	359	—
The *P* of the People	383	—
introduce the *P* with a sentence of invitation	383	—
their own *p*, either silently or aloud.	385	—
Members of the congregation may ask the *p*	386	—
The Collect at the *P*	394	—
Suitable *p* may be offered,	397	—
One of the usual postcommunion *p* is then said,	399	—
using one of the eucharistic *p* provided.	401	9
the Celebrant uses one of the Eucharistic *P*	402	—
The *P* of the People following the Creed	406	5
the *P* of the People may be said.	406	25
P for the Candidates	417	—
The service then continues with the *P* of the People	419	—
omitting the nuptial blessing which follows The *P*.	422	17
The *P*	428	—
or other person appointed reads the following *p*,	429	—

If there is not to be a Communion, one or more of the *p*	429	—
says one of the following *p*	430	—
The service continues with The *P* on page 428.	434	—
6. *P* are offered for the husband and wife,	436	7
it may follow the *P* of the People	439	7
During the *p*, some parents may wish	439	15
P	444	—
Celebrant may add one or more of the following *p*	444	—
P may be offered according to the occasion.	454	14
One of the usual postcommunion *p* is said,	457	—
P for the Sick	458	—
P for use by a Sick Person	461	—
P for a Vigil	465	—
the family and friends come together for *p*	465	—
or more suitable *p* (see pages 487–489).	480	—
the following serves for the *P* of the People.	480	—
use any of the Additional *P*.	486	—
Additional *P*	487	—
p for the deceased and the bereaved.	492	—
the service continues with the *P* of the People,	496	—
or more suitable *p* (see pages 503–505).	496	—
the following form of the *P* of the People is used,	496	—
Other *p* may be added.	502	—
Additional *P*	503	—
eucharistic *p* may be used.	506	23
this Litany may be used for the *P* of the People	548	—
the *P* of the People after the Creed,	552	5
Others present a book of *p* or other symbol, saying	561	—
any of the authorized eucharistic *p*	565	27
the congregation leads the *P* of the People.	572	—
the Bishop concludes with the following *p*	572	—
only one of the *p*, and one of the versicles	576	7
Any of the usual forms of the *P* of the People	576	18
p and Bible readings related to the particular occasion	577	12
P and Thanksgivings	809	—
P and Thanksgivings	810	3
P	810	4
P for the World	810	5
P for the Church	810	12
P for the Ordained Ministry are on pages 205	810	25
P for National Life	810	26
P for the Social Order	811	5
P for Industry and Labor are on pages 208, 210,	811	19
P for the Natural Order	811	21
P for Family and Personal Life	811	27
P for the sick are on pages 458–461.	812	14
P for the dying are on pages 462–465.	812	15
P for the dead are on pages 202, 253, 487, and 503.	812	16
Other *P*	812	17
P for Friday, Saturday, and Sunday,	812	26
P and Thanksgivings	814	—
P	814	—
P originally composed in traditional idiom	814	—
but, except in certain classical *p* which do not lend	814	—
P for the World	814	—
P for the Church	816	—
See also the *p* for the Mission of the Church	816	—
P for National Life	820	—
P for the Social Order	823	—
For *p* for Industry and Labor,	824	—
P for the Natural Order	827	—
P for Family and Personal Life	828	—
P for the sick are on pages 458–461.	831	—
Other *P*	833	—
P for Friday, Saturday, and Sunday,	833	—
65. For the Answering of *P*	834	—
in place of the *P* of the People at the Eucharist,	836	—
introduce *p* and hymns as needed.	844	11
plainly appear by the common *p* in the Church,	866	5
9 That Common *P* and Sacraments	875	11

prays

in full sight of the congregation, *p* over them,	308	—
The Celebrant then *p* that all may receive	405	5
At the same time the Bishop *p*	533	—
lays hands upon the head of the ordinand, and *p*	545	—

preach

and is expected to *p* the Word	298	7
celebrant at the Lord's Table, and to *p* the Gospel.	322	3
celebrant at the Lord's Table, and to *p* the Gospel.	354	3

preached

A sermon may be *p* after the Office;	142	11
A homily may be *p* after any of the preceding	292	—
If a sermon or homily was not *p* earlier,	295	—
Or the Sermon may be *p* after the Peace.	301	—
may be read, or a homily *p*.	319	—
may be read, or a homily *p*.	351	—
A homily may be *p*, the people being seated.	480	—
The sermon may be *p* by the bishop,	565	16
in which the pure Word of God is *p*,	871	31

Preacher

Ecclesiastes or *P*,	868	30

preaches

administers Confirmation, and normally *p*	284	13

preaching

and in the *p* of the Word of God	510	11
for any man to take upon him the office of public *p*,	872	16

precede

may *p* the Blessing or Dismissal.	113	—
the reading of the Lessons which *p* the Gospel,	322	16
the reading of the Lessons which *p* the Gospel,	354	16
may *p* the exchange of vows.	435	16
it is desirable that it *p* the distribution	453	8

preceded

and may be *p* by an appropriate invitation	269	—
When the Liturgy of the Palms has *p*,	273	—
conjunctions which refer only to what has *p*,	888	26

precedence

These feasts take *p* of any other day or observance.	15	20
on fixed days, take *p* of a Sunday:	16	4
have *p* over all other days of commemoration	16	24
on fixed days in the Calendar do not take *p*	17	14
Subject to the rules of *p* governing Principal Feasts,	17	29
This Sunday takes *p* over the three Holy Days	161	—
p set forth in the Calendar of the Church Year.	195	—
This Sunday takes *p* over the three Holy Days	213	—
p set forth in the Calendar of the Church Year.	246	—

precedes
Prayer may be used in place of all that *p* 36 9
Prayer may be used in place of all that *p* 74 8
absence of a bishop or priest, all that *p* may be led 269 —
Liturgy of the Palms immediately *p* the Eucharist, 272 —
absence of a bishop or priest, all that *p* may be led 282 —
Evening Prayer may be used in place of all that *p* 322 18
Evening Prayer may be used in place of all that *p* 354 18
8. If there is a Communion, it *p* the commendation, 506 21

preceding
otherwise ordered in the *p* rules concerning Sundays, 16 23
or lay person using the *p* form remains kneeling, 42 —
be added to the *p* versicle and response. 59 —
or lay person using the *p* form remains kneeling, 63 —
be added to the *p* versicle and response. 72 —
or lay person using the *p* form remains kneeling, 80 —
be added to the *p* versicle and response. 102 —
A deacon or lay person using the *p* blessing 114 —
or lay person using the *p* form remains kneeling, 117 —
added to the *p* versicle and response. 126 —
The Collect immediately *p* and any of the sets 161 —
The *p* Collect, with the Psalm and Lessons 162 —
Either of the *p* Collects, with the proper Psalm 174 —
The Collect immediately *p* and any of the sets 213 —
The *p* Collect, with the Psalm and Lessons 214 —
Either of the *p* Collects, with the proper Psalm 226 —
absence of a bishop or priest, the *p* service may be led 272 —
portions of the *p* may be used. 272 —
A homily may be preached after any of the *p* 292 —
and before the *p* prayer. 308 —
A deacon or lay person using the *p* form 321 —
sung or said, in addition to, or in place of, the *p*, 324 —
A deacon or lay person using the *p* form 353 —
In place of, or in addition to, the *p*, 364 —
A deacon using the *p* form substitutes "us" for "you" 398 —
the Prayers of the People *p* the Offertory. 439 7
A deacon or lay person using the *p* form 455 4
where the *p* service has been held, 506 19
on the First Sunday of Advent *p* odd-numbered years, 934 3
on the First Sunday of Advent *p* even-numbered years. 934 4

precepts
do not bind Christian men, nor the Civil *p* 869 11

preclude
The service does not *p* the use of the building 566 11

predestination
XVII. Of *P* and Election. 871 1
P to Life is the everlasting purpose of God, 871 2
As the godly consideration of *P*, 871 11
P, is a most dangerous downfall, 871 18

preface
P 9 1
in the *P* of her Book of Common Prayer, 9 13
The same Church hath not only in her *P*, 9 22
she further declares in her said *P*, 10 9
the Collect, *P*, and one or more of the Lessons 16 14
P of Advent 159 —
P of Advent 160 —
P of the Incarnation 161 —
P of the Incarnation 162 —
P of the Epiphany 162 —
The *P* of the Epiphany is used. 162 —
P of the Epiphany 163 —
P of the Epiphany, or of the Lord's Day 163 —
P of the Epiphany, or of the Lord's Day 164 —
P of the Epiphany, or of the Lord's Day 165 —
P of the Epiphany 165 —
P of Lent 166 —
P of Lent 167 —
P of Holy Week 168 —
P of Holy Week 169 —
P of Easter 171 —
P of Easter 172 —
P of Easter 173 —
P of Easter 174 —
P of the Ascension 174 —
P of the Ascension 175 —
P of Pentecost 175 —
P of Trinity Sunday 176 —
No Proper *P* is used. 177 —
P of the Lord's Day 177 —
P of the Lord's Day 178 —
P of the Lord's Day 179 —
P of the Lord's Day 180 —
P of the Lord's Day 181 —
P of the Lord's Day 182 —
P of the Lord's Day 183 —
P of the Lord's Day 184 —
P of the Lord's Day 185 —
P of Apostles 185 —
P of the Incarnation 186 —
P of Apostles 187 —
P of the Epiphany 187 —
P of Apostles 188 —
P of the Epiphany 188 —
P of All Saints 189 —
P of Apostles 189 —
P of the Epiphany 189 —
P of Advent 190 —
P of Apostles 190 —
P of Trinity Sunday 190 —
P of All Saints 191 —
P of Apostles 191 —
P of the Epiphany 191 —
P of the Incarnation 192 —
P of Apostles 192 —
P of Holy Week 192 —
P of Apostles 193 —
P of Trinity Sunday 193 —
P of All Saints 193 —
P of Apostles 194 —
P of All Saints 194 —
P of Trinity Sunday 194 —
P of a Saint 196 —
P of Pentecost 196 —
P of a Saint 197 —
P of a Saint, or of Trinity Sunday 197 —
P of a Saint 198 —
P of a Saint 199 —
P of Trinity Sunday 199 —
P of Pentecost 200 —

P of Trinity Sunday	200	—
P of the Epiphany	200	—
P of the Epiphany	201	—
P of Holy Week	201	—
P of Baptism	201	—
P of the Commemoration of the Dead	202	—
P of the Ascension, or of Baptism	203	—
P of Baptism	203	—
P of Baptism, or of Pentecost	203	—
P of the Dedication of a Church	204	—
P of Pentecost, or of the Season	204	—
P of Baptism, or of Trinity Sunday	205	—
P of Apostles	205	—
P of the Season	205	—
P of Baptism, or of the Season	206	—
P of the Season, or of Pentecost	206	—
P of Trinity Sunday	207	—
P of the Season	207	—
P of the Season	208	—
P of the Season	209	—
P of the Season	210	—
P of Advent	211	—
P of Advent	212	—
P of the Incarnation	213	—
P of the Incarnation	214	—
P of the Epiphany	214	—
The *P* of the Epiphany is used.	214	—
P of the Epiphany, or of the Lord's Day	215	—
P of the Epiphany, or of the Lord's Day	216	—
P of the Epiphany, or of the Lord's Day	217	—
P of the Epiphany	217	—
P of Lent	217	—
P of Lent	218	—
P of Lent	219	—
P of Holy Week	219	—
P of Holy Week	220	—
P of Holy Week	221	—
P of Easter	222	—
P of Easter	223	—
P of Easter	224	—
P of Easter	225	—
P of the Ascension	226	—
P of Pentecost	227	—
P of Trinity Sunday	228	—
No Proper *P* is used.	228	—
No Proper *P* is used.	229	—
P of the Lord's Day	229	—
P of the Lord's Day	230	—
P of the Lord's Day	231	—
P of the Lord's Day	232	—
P of the Lord's Day	233	—
P of the Lord's Day	234	—
P of the Lord's Day	235	—
P of the Lord's Day	236	—
P of the Lord's Day, or of Baptism	236	—
P of Apostles	237	—
P of the Incarnation	237	—
P of the Incarnation	238	—
P of Apostles	238	—
P of Apostles	239	—
P of the Epiphany	239	—
P of the Epiphany	240	—
P of All Saints	240	—
P of Apostles	240	—
P of the Epiphany	241	—
P of Apostles	241	—
P of Advent	241	—
P of Trinity Sunday	242	—
P of All Saints	242	—
P of Apostles	242	—
P of the Epiphany	243	—
P of the Incarnation	243	—
P of Apostles	243	—
P of Holy Week	244	—
P of Apostles	244	—
P of Trinity Sunday	244	—
P of All Saints	245	—
P of Apostles	245	—
P of All Saints	245	—
P of Trinity Sunday	246	—
P of a Saint	247	—
P of Pentecost	248	—
P of a Saint	248	—
P of a Saint, or of Trinity Sunday	249	—
P of a Saint	249	—
P of a Saint	250	—
P of Trinity Sunday	251	—
P of Pentecost	251	—
P of the Epiphany	252	—
P of Holy Week	252	—
P of Baptism	253	—
P of the Commemoration of the Dead	253	—
P of the Ascension, or of Baptism	254	—
P of Baptism	254	—
P of Baptism, or of Pentecost	254	—
P of the Dedication of a Church	255	—
P of Pentecost, or of the Season	255	—
P of Baptism, or of Trinity Sunday	255	—
P of Apostles	256	—
P of the Season	256	—
P of Baptism, or of the Season	257	—
P of the Season, or of Pentecost	257	—
P of Trinity Sunday	258	—
P of the Season	258	—
P of the Season	259	—
P of the Season	260	—
P of the Season	261	—
P of Lent	269	—
P of Holy Week	273	—
P of Holy Week	275	—
the Proper *P* of Baptism may be used.	310	—
Here a Proper *P* is sung or said on all Sundays,	334	—
Here a Proper *P* is sung or said on all Sundays,	341	—
P of the Lord's Day	344	—
Here a Proper *P* is sung or said on all Sundays,	361	—
Here a Proper *P* is sung or said on all Sundays,	367	—
P of the Lord's Day	377	—
Incorporates or adapts the Proper *P* of the Day,	402	—
Incorporates or adapts the Proper *P* of the Day,	404	—
P of Marriage	432	—
P of the Commemoration of the Dead	482	—
P of the Commemoration of the Dead	498	—
P to the Ordination Rites	510	1
the *P* may be that for Apostles and Ordinations.	564	1

The *P* of the Dedication of a Church may be used. 574 —
Instead of the Proper *P* suggested, 576 25
P 866 1
Though it be appointed in the afore written *p*, 867 23

prefaces
Proper *P*, directions for which are to be found 158 4
Proper *P* 344 —
P for Seasons 345 —
P for Other Occasions 347 —
Proper *P* 377 —
P for Seasons 378 —
P for Other Occasions 380 —

preferences
humility to forego all *p* of her own; 876 35

preferred
If *p*, the exchange of the Peace 407 9
If *p*, the confessor and penitent may sit 446 17
If *p*, the Committal service may take place 468 11
If *p*, the Committal service may take place 490 11

prefix
or else *p* to the Reading some such introduction as, 888 27

prejudice
without *p* or prepossessions; 11 19

prelude
or as the *p* to an evening meal 108 5
A musical *p* or processional is not appropriate. 142 27

premises
does not require that the *p* be debt-free or owned. 575 4

preparation
This rite requires careful *p* by the Priest 400 3

prepare
P the Table 401 4
Some of those present *p* the table; 401 5
p in advance, in consultation with the celebrant, 420 —
Deacons *p* the Table. 522 —
Deacons *p* the Table. 535 —
p the elements at the Offertory, 558 20
The condition of Man after the fall of Adam is such, that he cannot turn and *p* 869 34

prepared
when they are ready and have been duly *p*, 412 3

prepares
The newly ordained Deacon *p* the bread, 546 —

preparing
p and placing on it the offerings of bread and wine, 322 11
p and placing on it the offerings of bread and wine, 354 11
p and placing upon it the bread and cup of wine. 407 15

prepossessions
without prejudice or *p*; 11 19

prerogative
It is the *p* of a deacon to carry the Paschal Candle 284 17
It is the bishop's *p*, when present, 322 2
It is the bishop's *p*, when present, 354 2
but that only *p*, which we see 876 2

presbyter
the original Greek terms *p*, presbyters, and fellow *p*, 528 —
P of the Church of God, you have been called to work 557 2

presbyterate
Representatives of the *p*, diaconate, and laity 511 9

presbyters
associated with them are the *p*, or ordained elders, 510 8
joined by other bishops and *p*, 522 —
at least two *p* must be present. 524 2
the original Greek terms presbyter, *p*, 528 —
the *p* who stand to the right and left of the Bishop. 533 —
The *P* present greet the newly ordained; 534 —
at the Lord's Table, with the Bishop and other *p*, 535 3
at least two *p* must be present. 536 2
and representative *p* of the diocese, stand 553 9
together with your Bishop and fellow-*P* as a pastor, 557 3

prescribed
The Rite begins as *p* for celebrations 433 —

presence
A Collect for the *P* of Christ 70 —
A Collect for the *P* of Christ 124 —
God's *P* in a renewed Israel 290 —
their Baptism in the *p* of a bishop 412 9
covenant between a man and a woman in the *p* 422 3
we love has entered into the nearer *p* of our Lord, 507 13

present
This Convention having, in their *p* session, set 8 7
(when a bishop or priest is not *p*) 13 24
The bishop, when *p*, appropriately concludes 36 7
The bishop, when *p*, appropriately concludes 74 6
The bishop, when *p*, should give 108 9
When more than one person is *p*, 136 —
The Bishop, if *p*, or the Priest, stands and, 269 —
It is customary for all the ordained ministers *p*, 284 10
The bishop, when *p*, is the chief celebrant, 284 12
The priests who are *p* share among them the reading 284 14
The bishop, when *p*, is the celebrant; 298 7
of adults and older children *p* their candidates 298 18
commonly called godparents, *p* their candidates, 298 21
the Eucharist, at which the Bishop, when *p*, 310 —
or when a bishop is *p*. 312 7
When a bishop is *p*, or on other occasions 312 20
The Bishop when *p*, or the Priest, stands and says 321 —
It is the bishop's prerogative, when *p*, to be 322 2
It is appropriate that the other priests *p* stand 322 7
The Bishop when *p*, or the Priest, stands and says 332 —
The Bishop when *p*, or the Priest, gives the blessing 339 —
The Bishop when *p*, or the Priest, stands and says 353 —
It is the bishop's prerogative, when *p*, to be 354 2
It is appropriate that the other priests *p* stand 354 7
The Bishop when *p*, or the Priest, stands and says 360 —
The Bishop when *p*, or the Priest, may bless 366 —
or the thanksgivings of those *p* 386 —
be *p* at a public celebration of the Eucharist. 396 —
When persons are unable to be *p* for extended 396 —
that fellow parishioners, relatives, and friends be *p*, 396 —

Some of those *p* prepare the table; 401 5
When several deacons or priests are *p*, 408 5
weighty cause could not be *p* at the celebration, 409 1
When both a bishop and a priest are *p* 422 10
couple may *p* the offerings of bread and wine. 432 —
family to *p* themselves before the Altar. 439 18
the congregation has opportunity to be *p*. 468 7
It is appropriate that the bishop, when *p*, preside 468 14
If the body is not *p*, the service continues 482 —
The Celebrant, or the Bishop if *p*, may then bless 483 —
the congregation has opportunity to be *p*. 490 7
It is appropriate that the bishop, when *p*, preside 490 14
If the body is not *p*, the service continues 499 —
The Celebrant, or the Bishop if *p*, may then bless 500 1
nor life, nor angels, nor principalities, nor things *p*, 507 6
Lay Persons, standing before the Presiding Bishop, *p* 513 —
Declaration in the sight of all *p*. 513 —
at least two presbyters must be *p*. 524 3
standing before the bishop, *p* the ordinand, 526 —
signs the above Declaration in the sight of all *p*. 527 —
the Deacon or, if no deacon is *p*, a Priest reads 529 —
Priests who are *p* also laying on their hands. 533 —
The Presbyters *p* greet the newly ordained; 534 —
or a Priest if no deacon is *p*, dismisses the people. 535 —
at least two presbyters must be *p*. 536 3
standing before the bishop, *p* the ordinand, 538 —
signs the above Declaration in the sight of all *p*. 539 —
the Deacon or, if no deacon is *p*, a Priest reads 541 —
and the Clergy *p* now greet the newly ordained. 546 —
bishops who are *p* are not to depart without signing 553 16
the priests *p* to join in the laying on of hands. 553 19
other grave cause, could not be *p* at the ordination. 555 3
The bishop, when *p*, is the chief celebrant 558 8
Representatives of the congregation *p* a Bible, saying 561 —
Others *p* a stole or other symbol, saying 561 —
Others *p* a book of prayers or other symbol, saying 561 —
Others *p* olive oil or some other symbol, saying 561 —
p the keys of the church, saying 562 —
clergy of the diocese *p* the Constitution 562 —
Representatives of the congregation *p* bread and wine, 562 —
or a Priest if no deacon is *p*, dismisses the assembly. 564 12
the bishop, or other persons *p*, may speak in response 565 19
congregation is *p* for Morning or Evening Prayer, 888 12

presentation

The *P* 16 6
The *P* 16 28
(beginning with the *P* of the Candidates), 175 —
The *P* February 2 187 —
(beginning with the *P* of the Candidates), 227 —
The *P* February 2 239 —
(beginning with the *P* of the Candidates, 292 —
officiates at the *P* and Examination 298 9
P and Examination 301 —
If the *P* of the Candidates does not take place 312 28
P and Examination 415 —
If there is to be a *p* or a giving in marriage, 425 —
or *p*, the Celebrant asks, 437 9
The *P* 513 —
The *P* 526 —
The *P* 538 —
At the *P* of the Ordinand, 552 8
Following the *p* of the Bible, 553 5
with the *P* of the Candidates, 575 30

presentations

Any of the *p* that follow may be added to, 561 —

presented

An offering may be received and *p* at the Office. 142 15
candidates who are able to answer for themselves are *p* 301 —
The Celebrant asks each candidate when *p* 301 —
the candidates unable to answer for themselves are *p* 301 —
When all have been *p* the Celebrant asks the parents 302 —
When there are others to be *p*, the Bishop says 303 —
After all have been *p*, the Celebrant addresses 303 —
Each candidate is *p* by name to the Celebrant, 307 —
Alms may be received and *p*, 311 —
p by the newly baptized or their godparents. 313 14
while the offerings are *p* and placed on the Altar. 333 —
while the offerings are *p* and placed on the Altar. 361 —
appropriate that the oblations of bread and wine be *p* 412 16
After all have been *p*, the Bishop addresses 416 —
it is desirable that the bread and wine be *p* 438 1
When the bishop-elect is *p*, his full name 511 18
A Bible is *p* with these words 521 —
When the ordinand is *p*, his full name 524 9
When the ordinand is *p*, his full name 536 9
each is to be *p* with a separate copy 552 12
suitable insignia of office may be *p*. 553 7
and immediately before the Bible is *p*. 553 23
The ordinands may be *p* together, 553 26
The ordinands may be *p* together, 554 16
the family of the new minister may also be *p* 563 —
The new minister is normally *p* to the bishop 565 4
The symbols *p* should be large enough to be visible 565 21

presenters

P 303 —
P 415 —
p if desired, standing before the bishop, present 526 —
P 526 —
p if desired, standing before the bishop, present 538 —
P 538 —
more are ordained together, each is to have his own *p*. 553 25
more are ordained together, each is to have his own *p*. 554 15

presents

Presiding Bishop *p* to the people their new bishop. 522 —
The Bishop *p* a vessel of water, saying 561 11
The Bishop then *p* the new minister 563 —

preservation

might most tend to the *p* of peace 10 10

preserved

each nature being *p* and coming together to form one 864 14

preserver

the Maker, and *P* of all things 867 36

preside

the bishop may, at discretion, authorize a deacon to *p* 13 26
preach the Word and *p* at Baptism and the Eucharist. 298 8
the bishop may specially authorize a deacon to *p*. 312 10
should pronounce the blessing and *p* at the Eucharist. 422 11

p at the Eucharist and pronounce 468 14
a deacon or lay reader may p at the service. 468 18
p at the Eucharist and pronounce 490 14
a deacon or lay reader may p at the service. 490 18

president
19. For the P of the United States 810 —
19. For the P of the United States 820 —

presides
when present, is the chief celebrant, p at Baptism 284 12
In the absence of a bishop, a priest p at the service. 284 16
a priest is the celebrant and p at the service. 298 13
public baptism at which a bishop or priest p. 312 14
A priest or a bishop normally p at the Celebration 422 7
A priest normally p at the service. 468 13
A priest normally p at the service. 490 13
p and serves as chief consecrator. 511 7
consecrator p from a chair placed close to the people, 511 13
until the Offertory, the bishop p 524 4
until the Offertory, the bishop p 536 4
The bishop p. 566 13

presiding
by virtue of their order do not exercise a p function; 13 21
deacon, when p, should read the Prayer for Light, 108 8
Sacrament with a bishop or priest p, 314 7
bishop is to be ordained, the P Bishop of the Church, 511 6
bishop appointed by the P Bishop, presides 511 7
Lay Persons, standing before the P Bishop, present 513 —
The P Bishop then directs that testimonials 513 —
the P Bishop requires the following promise 513 —
The P Bishop then says the following, 513 —
If no objection is made, the P Bishop continues 514 —
P Bishop 514 —
The P Bishop then says 514 —
P Bishop stands and reads the Collect for the Day, 515 —
the P Bishop may select Readings 515 —
P Bishop addresses the bishop-elect 517 —
The P Bishop then says 519 —
who kneels before the P Bishop. 520 —
stand to the right and left of the P Bishop. 520 —
The P Bishop then begins this Prayer of Consecration 520 —
The P Bishop and other Bishops now lay their hands 521 —
The P Bishop continues 521 —
The P Bishop presents to the people their new bishop. 522 —
P Bishop and other Bishops greet the new bishop. 522 —
At ordinations, the Bishop who is p stands and says 551 —

press
they do carnally and visibly p with their teeth 873 37

presume
They also are to be had accursed that p to say, 871 25

preventing
the grace of God by Christ p us, 869 37

previously
to use music composed for them, p authorized 14 13
Communion from the Sacrament p consecrated. 284 29
it must have been p consecrated by the bishop. 298 15
If the grave is in a place that has not p been set 487 —
If the grave is in a place that has not p been set 503 —

priceless
study of the conditions under which so p a blessing 877 24

priest
normally a bishop or p. 13 21
(when a bishop or p is not present) 13 24
when the services of a p cannot be obtained, 13 25
The p alone stands and says 42 —
The P alone stands and says 63 —
The P alone stands and says 80 —
A p or deacon, when presiding, should read 108 7
A bishop or p may use the following 114 —
The P alone stands and says 117 —
The Bishop, if present, or the P, stands and, 269 —
In the absence of a bishop or p, 269 —
In the absence of a bishop or p, 272 —
In the absence of a bishop or p, 282 —
a p presides at the service. 284 16
In the absence of a bishop or p, 284 23
when the services of a p cannot be obtained, 284 27
a p is the celebrant and presides 298 13
If a p uses Chrism in signing the newly baptized, 298 14
all standing, the Deacon or a P reads the Gospel, 300 —
p or deacon, who then immerses, or pours water 307 —
P, at a place in full sight of the congregation, 308 —
Bishop or P places a hand on the person's head, 308 —
or p cannot be obtained, 312 9
public baptism at which a bishop or p presides. 312 13
who administers emergency Baptism should inform the p 314 3
celebration of the Sacrament with a bishop or p 314 6
In the absence of a deacon or p, 316 —
The Bishop when present, or the P, stands and says 321 —
whether bishop or p, be assisted by other priests, 322 5
these duties may be performed by an assisting p. 322 14
all standing, the Deacon or a P reads the Gospel, 326 —
or if a p is not available, 330 —
The Bishop when present, or the P, stands and says 332 —
The Celebrant, whether bishop or p, 333 —
The Bishop when present, or the P, gives the blessing 339 —
The Celebrant, whether bishop or p, 340 —
The Bishop when present, or the P, stands and says 353 —
whether bishop or p, be assisted by other priests, 354 5
these duties may be performed by an assisting p. 354 14
all standing, the Deacon or a P reads the Gospel, 357 —
or if a p is not available, 359 —
The Bishop when present, or the P, stands and says 360 —
The Celebrant, whether bishop or p, 361 —
The Bishop when present, or the P, may bless 366 —
The Celebrant, whether bishop or p, 367 —
The Celebrant, whether bishop or p, faces them 369 —
The Celebrant, whether bishop or p, 372 —
desirable that the p arrange to celebrate the Eucharist 396 —
the p may begin the celebration at the Offertory, 396 —
The Celebrant, whether p or deacon, reads 396 —
The P alone says 398 —
This rite requires careful preparation by the P 400 3
The People and P 400 6
The Great Thanksgiving is said by the P 401 8
In the absence of a p, 407 5
the celebrant is assisted by a deacon or another p, 408 3
When the services of a p cannot be obtained, 408 17

when no *p* is available, the celebrant or deacon,	409	3
If the *p* knows that a person who is living	409	8
the *p* shall speak to that person	409	9
The *p* shall follow the same procedure with those	409	12
When the *p* sees that there is hatred between members	409	17
the *p* shall allow those who are penitent to come	409	22
the *p* is required to notify the bishop,	409	24
the Deacon or a *P* reads the Gospel,	414	—
A *p* or a bishop normally presides at the Celebration	422	7
When both a bishop and a *p* are present	422	10
A deacon, or an assisting *p*, may deliver the charge,	422	12
and no *p* or bishop is available, a deacon may use	422	16
The *P* may ask God's blessing on a ring or rings	427	—
The husband and wife kneel, and the *P* says	430	—
the *P* adds this blessing	431	—
toward the *P*, who says	434	—
Normally, the celebrant is a *p* or bishop.	435	4
and when no *p* or bishop is available,	435	5
7. A *p* or bishop pronounces a solemn blessing	436	9
pronounced only by a bishop or *p*.	446	12
evidence of due contrition, the *p* gives such counsel	446	21
the *p* may assign to the penitent a psalm,	446	23
The *P* says	447	—
Here the *P* may offer counsel, direction, and comfort.	447	—
The *P* then pronounces this absolution	448	—
The *P* adds	448	—
The *P* concludes	448	—
The *P* and Penitent begin as follows	449	—
P	449	—
The *P* may then say one or more of these	449	—
The *P* then continues	450	—
The *P* may then offer words of comfort and counsel.	450	—
P	450	—
P	451	—
The *P* then lays a hand upon the penitent's head	451	—
The *P* concludes	451	—
P may suggest the making of a special confession,	454	15
The *P* alone says	455	—
the Anointing of the Sick is to be blessed, the *P* says	455	—
The *P* then lays hands upon the sick person,	455	—
the *P* dips a thumb in the holy oil,	456	—
The *P* may add	456	—
using oil blessed by a bishop or *p*.	456	—
The *P* concludes	456	—
the *P* begins with the [Peace and]	457	—
A *p* normally presides at the service.	468	13
When the services of a *p* cannot be obtained,	468	17
the *P* may use the following prayer,	487	—
A *p* normally presides at the service.	490	13
When the services of a *p* cannot be obtained,	490	17
the *P* may use the following prayer,	503	—
exercise the offices of bishop, *p*, or deacon	510	22
for the conferring of the sacred orders of bishop, *p*,	510	31
Then, all standing, a Deacon or a *P* reads the Gospel,	516	—
the new *p* and other priests stand	524	14
The Ordination of a *P*	525	—
A *P* and a Lay Person, and additional presenters	526	—
the Deacon or, if no deacon is present, a *P* reads	529	—
The Consecration of the *P*	533	—
The new *p* is now vested according to the order	534	—
The new *P* then says to the congregation	534	—
the newly ordained *P* joins in the celebration	535	—
The Bishop then asks the new *p* to bless the people.	535	—
The new *P* says	535	—
A Deacon, or a *P* if no deacon is present, dismisses	535	—
A *P* and a Lay Person, and additional presenters	538	—
the Deacon or, if no deacon is present, a *P* reads	541	—
At the Ordination of a *P*	553	18
or other insignia of the office of *p*,	553	21
placed upon the new *p* after the entire Prayer	553	22
and make him a *p* in your Church."	554	2
A Bible is to be given to each new *p*,	554	5
with your Bishop and fellow-Presbyters as a pastor, *p*,	557	3
responsibilities as a *p* of this Diocese,	557	9
This order is for use when a *p* is being instituted	558	2
In the bishop's absence, a *p* being inducted	558	9
A deacon or *p* reads the Gospel.	558	16
The new Minister, if a *p*, may then kneel	562	—
The Bishop, or in the Bishop's absence a *P*	563	—
At the Induction of a *p* or deacon,	564	4
A newly inducted *P* may, at the bishop's request,	564	10
A Deacon, or a *P* if no deacon is present, dismisses	564	12
The *p*'s prayer on page 562 is appropriate	565	24
The Deacon (or a *P*) reads the Gospel.	571	—
The bishop, or a *p* appointed, is the chief celebrant.	574	—
a Deacon or *P* dismisses them.	574	—
this service may be used by the bishop, or by a *p*	577	4
used by the bishop or a *p* for blessing alterations,	577	9
that the *P* did offer Christ for the quick and the dead,	874	9

priesthood

and through the *p* of the Church and its ministers	446	5

priests

p, and deacons, fulfill the functions proper	13	18
The *p* who are present share among them the reading	284	14
whether bishop or priest, be assisted by other *p*,	322	5
It is appropriate that the other *p* present stand	322	7
whether bishop or priest, be assisted by other *p*,	354	5
It is appropriate that the other *p* present stand	354	7
The bishops, *p*, and deacons at the Holy Table	407	23
When several deacons or *p* are present,	408	5
In the absence of sufficient deacons and *p*,	408	7
elders, in subsequent times generally known as *p*.	510	9
assist bishops and *p* in all of this work.	510	13
Representatives of the diocese, both *P* and Lay	513	—
the new priest and other *p* stand	524	14
the *P* who are present also laying on their hands.	533	—
new priest is now vested according to the order of *p*.	534	—
Reasonable opportunity is to be given for the *p*	553	19
the bishop and *p* lay their hands	553	30
and other *p* at the Altar for the Great Thanksgiving.	554	8
all the new *p* break the consecrated Bread and receive	554	9
Other *p*, if any, who serve in the same congregation	558	11
and other *p* having similar canonical charge.	565	25
catechism is primarily intended for use by parish *p*,	844	2
XXXII. Of the Marriage of *P*.	874	11
P, and Deacons, are not commanded by God's Law,	874	12
Consecration of Bishops, and Ordering of *P*	875	21
Archbishops and Bishops, and Ordering of *P*	875	27

primarily

This catechism is *p* intended for use by parish priests,	844	2

primitive
and the custom of the *P* Church, 872 22

princes
established, she hath, in the reign of several *P*, 10 1
without the commandment and will of *P*. 872 6
we give not our *P* the ministering 875 44
given always to all godly *P* in holy Scriptures by God 876 3

principal
And the *p* care herein was to make them conformable 10 34
The Holy Eucharist, the *p* act of Christian worship 13 3
1. *P* Feasts 15 14
The *P* Feasts observed in this Church are 15 15
Subject to the rules of precedence governing *P* Feasts, 17 29
Proper appointed for the *P* Feasts. 18 15
At services on this day other than the *p* celebration, 272 —
At the *p* service on a Sunday or other feast, 300 —
the Bishop, when present, should be the *p* Celebrant. 310 —
Except on *P* Feasts, the Proper Preface of Baptism 310 —
when present, to be the *p* celebrant 322 2
it is fitting that the *p* celebrant, 322 4
when present, to be the *p* celebrant 354 2
it is fitting that the *p* celebrant, 354 4
It is not intended for use at the *p* Sunday 400 4
At the *p* service on a Sunday or other feast, 414 —
at which the Bishop should be the *p* celebrant. 419 —
and then go to the *p* door. 575 9
enter in procession through the *p* door. 575 14
Lessons are to be read at the *p* morning service, 888 9

principalities
"neither death, nor life, nor angels, nor *p*, 507 6

principles
yet upon the *p* already laid down, 10 19
return of all Christian communions to the *p* of unity 877 6
which *p* we believe to be the substantial deposit 877 7

printed
The Gloria *p* at the conclusion of certain Canticles 141 14
in more recent manuscripts and in *p* Bibles, 583 22

prior
come together for prayers *p* to the funeral. 465 7
It may also be used *p* to cremation. 468 12
It may also be used *p* to cremation. 490 12
take place at some convenient time *p* to the service. 552 18

prisons
37. For *P* and Correctional Institutions 811 16
37. For *P* and Correctional Institutions 826 —

privacy
or in a place set aside to give greater *p*, 446 16

private
It is appropriate also for use in *p* houses. 108 6
When this service is used in *p* houses, 143 17
for dedicating a *p* chapel or oratory. 577 5
through his *p* judgment, willingly and purposely, 874 25

privately
the priest shall speak to that person *p*, 409 10
he shall speak *p* to each of them, 409 18
but when men say Matins and Evensong *p*, 867 25

privileges
this ministry, accepting its *p* and responsibilities 557 8

probably
This is *p* the most satisfying method for reciting 582 17
(Tetragrammaton) is *p* to be vocalized Yahweh; 583 17

procedure
The priest shall follow the same *p* 409 12

proceeding
neither made, nor created, nor begotten, but *p*, 865 11
The Holy Ghost, *p* from the Father and the Son, 868 17

proceeds
Then, facing the Holy Table, the Celebrant *p* 333 —
Then, facing the Holy Table, the Celebrant *p* 341 —
Then, facing the Holy Table, the Celebrant *p* 361 —
Then, facing the Holy Table, the Celebrant *p* 367 —
Then, facing the Holy Table, the Celebrant *p* 370 —
Then, facing the Holy Table, the Celebrant *p* 373 —
omitting the breaking of the Bread, the deacon *p* 408 25
other bishops and presbyters, *p* with the celebration 522 —
p with the Great Thanksgiving of the Eucharist. 563 —
The Bishop *p* to the Lectern, 570 —
the Bishop *p* to an appropriate place, and says 572 —

procession
To be said or sung, kneeling, standing, or in *p*; 148 —
so that all may go into the church in *p*. 270 —
shrubs to be carried in the *p* may be distributed 270 —
The *P* 271 —
During the *p*, all hold branches in their hands, 271 —
At a suitable place, the *p* may halt 271 —
leads the *p* to the chancel, pausing three times 285 —
If the movement to the font is a formal *p*, 312 31
or a hymn or anthem, may be sung during the *p*. 313 12
lead the *p* into the church. 467 —
As the *p* approaches the door of the church, 567 8
As the *p* moves into the church, 568 5
When convenient, the *p* may go around 575 7
Hymns or psalms may be used in *p*. 575 9
enter in *p* through the principal door. 575 14
carried into the building in the *p*. 575 17
1. *P* 577 26

processional
A musical prelude or *p* is not appropriate. 142 27
the foot of a *p* cross may be used for the signing. 575 22

proclaim
P and Respond to the Word of God 400 8
By your words, and in your life, *p* the Gospel. 557 12

proclamation
P of the Word of God 315 3
The *p* and response may include readings, 400 9
and the *p* of his Gospel everywhere. 510 28

procuring
the *p* of reverence, and the exciting of piety 10 11

produced
This *p* a hybrid form 583 23

professeth
saved by the Law or Sect which he *p*, 871 26

profession
be not only badges or tokens of Christian men's *p*, 872 26
Baptism is not only a sign of *p*, 873 14

professors
all men who are *p* of the Gospel, 875 37

profit
continually *p* more and more in the knowledge 866 14
as they might understand, and have *p* by hearing 866 23
men will weigh their labor with the *p* in knowledge, 867 13
consideration of the great *p* that shall ensue thereof. 867 15

profitable
and a great deal more *p* and commodious, 866 44
It is more *p*, because here are left out many things, 866 44

profundis
Psalm 130 De *p* 474 —

prohibit
so we judge, that Christian Religion doth not *p*, 876 19

promise
desire and *p* to make up for their faults, 409 21
requires the following *p* from the Bishop-elect 513 —
because of Christ's institution and *p*, 873 9

promised
or have at least *p* to do so. 409 16

promises
make *p* in their own names, and also take vows 298 22
reaffirmation of baptismal *p*. 420 —
p of God in Christ about eternal life. 506 17
the old Fathers did look only for transitory *p*. 869 10
Furthermore, we must receive God's *p* in such wise, 871 21
the *p* of the forgiveness of sin, 873 17

promote
p the charity which is the chief of Christian graces 877 3

promulgating
for *p* them to mankind in the clearest, 11 21

pronounce
should *p* the blessing and preside at the Eucharist. 422 11
but does not *p* a nuptial blessing. 435 6
preside at the Eucharist and *p* the Commendation. 468 14
preside at the Eucharist and *p* the Commendation. 490 14
newly inducted Priest may, at the bishop's request, *p* 564 10

pronounced
The absolution in these services may be *p* 446 11
absolution will not be *p*; 446 14
it has been considered too sacred to be *p*; 583 19

pronounces
7. A priest or bishop *p* a solemn blessing 436 9
and encouragement as are needed and *p* absolution. 446 22
The Priest then *p* this absolution 448 —

pronouncing
ministers alone have the function of *p* the nuptial blessing, 422 9

pronouns
adapted to traditional language by changing the *p* 108 23
p and verbs have been put in italics 814 —
substitute nouns for *p* when the referent 888 27

proof
has given clear *p* of repentance and amendment 409 11

proper
p to revive it by any new Commission. 10 23
to what ought to be the *p* end of all such prayers, 10 35
fulfill the functions *p* to their respective orders, 13 18
In any of the *P* Liturgies for Special Days, 14 3
P appointed for the Principal Feasts. 18 15
or one *p* to the season, may precede the Blessing 113 —
p antiphons on pages 43–44 and 80–82 may be used 141 6
from the Office Lectionary or the *P* of the Day, 143 22
Concerning the *P* 158 1
The *P* of the Church Year includes 158 3
P Prefaces, directions for which are to be found 158 4
The *P* appointed for the Sunday is also used 158 7
The *P* to be used on each of the Sundays 158 10
the *P* for the Sunday after Trinity Sunday 158 12
is the numbered *P* 158 13
the sequence begins with *P* 3 158 17
the sequence begins with *P* 6 158 19
preceding and any of the sets of *P* Lessons 161 —
This *P* is always used on the Sunday before 165 —
The *P* Liturgy for this day is on page 264. 166 —
The *P* Liturgy for this day is on page 270. 168 —
The *P* Liturgy for this day is on page 274. 169 —
The *P* Liturgy for this day is on page 276. 169 —
The *P* Liturgy for this day is on page 283. 170 —
the preceding Collects, with the *p* Psalm and Lessons 174 —
On the weekdays which follow, the numbered *P* 176 —
On the weekdays which follow, the numbered *P* 176 —
P 1 Week of the Sunday closest to May 11 176 —
No *P* Preface is used. 177 —
P 2 Week of the Sunday closest to May 18 177 —
No *P* Preface is used. 177 —
P 3 The Sunday closest to May 25 177 —
P 4 The Sunday closest to June 1 177 —
P 5 The Sunday closest to June 8 178 —
P 6 The Sunday closest to June 15 178 —
P 7 The Sunday closest to June 22 178 —
P 8 The Sunday closest to June 29 178 —
P 9 The Sunday closest to July 6 179 —
P 10 The Sunday closest to July 13 179 —
P 11 The Sunday closest to July 20 179 —
P 12 The Sunday closest to July 27 180 —
P 13 The Sunday closest to August 3 180 —
P 14 The Sunday closest to August 10 180 —
P 15 The Sunday closest to August 17 180 —
P 16 The Sunday closest to August 24 181 —

P 17 The Sunday closest to August 31 181 —
P 18 The Sunday closest to September 7 181 —
P 19 The Sunday closest to September 14 182 —
P 20 The Sunday closest to September 21 182 —
P 21 The Sunday closest to September 28 182 —
P 22 The Sunday closest to October 5 182 —
P 23 The Sunday closest to October 12 183 —
P 24 The Sunday closest to October 19 183 —
P 25 The Sunday closest to October 26 183 —
P 26 The Sunday closest to November 2 184 —
P 27 The Sunday closest to November 9 184 —
P 28 The Sunday closest to November 16 184 —
P 29 The Sunday closest to November 23 185 —
no P is provided in this Book 195 —
preceding and any of the sets of P Lessons 213 —
This P is always used on the Sunday before 217 —
The P Liturgy for this day is on page 264. 217 —
The P Liturgy for this day is on page 270. 219 —
The P Liturgy for this day is on page 274. 221 —
The P Liturgy for this day is on page 276. 221 —
The P Liturgy for this day is on page 283. 221 —
the preceding Collects, with the p Psalm and Lessons 226 —
On the weekdays which follow, the numbered P 227 —
On the weekdays which follow, the numbered P 228 —
P 1 Week of the Sunday closest to May 11 228 —
No P Preface is used. 228 —
P 2 Week of the Sunday closest to May 18 228 —
No P Preface is used. 229 —
P 3 The Sunday closest to May 25 229 —
P 4 The Sunday closest to June 1 229 —
P 5 The Sunday closest to June 8 229 —
P 6 The Sunday closest to June 15 230 —
P 7 The Sunday closest to June 22 230 —
P 8 The Sunday closest to June 29 230 —
P 9 The Sunday closest to July 6 230 —
P 10 The Sunday closest to July 13 231 —
P 11 The Sunday closest to July 20 231 —
P 12 The Sunday closest to July 27 231 —
P 13 The Sunday closest to August 3 232 —
P 14 The Sunday closest to August 10 232 —
P 15 The Sunday closest to August 17 232 —
P 16 The Sunday closest to August 24 232 —
P 17 The Sunday closest to August 31 233 —
P 18 The Sunday closest to September 7 233 —
P 19 The Sunday closest to September 14 233 —
P 20 The Sunday closest to September 21 234 —
P 21 The Sunday closest to September 28 234 —
P 22 The Sunday closest to October 5 234 —
P 23 The Sunday closest to October 12 234 —
P 24 The Sunday closest to October 19 235 —
P 25 The Sunday closest to October 26 235 —
P 26 The Sunday closest to November 2 235 —
P 27 The Sunday closest to November 9 236 —
P 28 The Sunday closest to November 16 236 —
P 29 The Sunday closest to November 23 236 —
no P is provided in this Book 246 —
the P Preface of Baptism may be used. 310 —
may be substituted for the P of the Day. 312 22
Here a P Preface is sung or said on all Sundays, 334 —
Here a P Preface is sung or said on all Sundays, 341 —
P Prefaces 344 —
Here a P Preface is sung or said on all Sundays, 361 —
Here a P Preface is sung or said on all Sundays, 367 —
P Prefaces 377 —
to the occasion, or the season, or the P of the Day. 383 —
on a regular basis, using either the P of the Day 396 —
Incorporates or adapts the P Preface of the Day, 402 15
Incorporates or adapts the P Preface of the Day, 404 —
At the p time, the Celebrant invites the parents 439 17
Bishop may select Readings from the P of the Day. 515 —
select Readings from the P of the Day. 528 —
select Readings from the P of the Day. 540 —
may be selected from the P of the Day, 565 11
selections may be made from the P of the Day. 571 —
Instead of the P Preface suggested, 576 25
the selected Sunday P may be used instead. 888 17

properly

Lessons are p those of the Day. 300 —
so that the fact can be p registered. 314 4
Lessons are p those of the Day. 414 4
Baptized Christians are p buried from the church. 468 5
Baptized Christians are p buried from the church. 490 5

Propers

none of the P appointed for Various Occasions is used 18 13
Thereafter, the P are used 158 15
(P 1 and 2 being used on the weekdays 158 17
(P 1 through 3 being omitted that year, 158 19
and P 4 and 5 being used in Pentecost 158 20
Directions for the use of the P which follow 176 —
Directions for the use of the P which follow 228 —

property

not the exclusive p of this portion 510 27
Such things as the deed for the p and the blueprint 575 17

prophet

Baruch the P, 868 40
done according to the P's teaching in justice, 876 21

prophets

even as the p from earliest times spoke of him, 864 16
Four P the greater, 868 32
Twelve P the less. 868 33

propitiation

that perfect redemption, p, and satisfaction, 874 6

prosperity

convenient for their future p; 10 30

protection

continuance of nursing care and p, 9 13
A Collect for P 70 —
A Collect for P 124 —
60. For P 812 11
60. For P 832 —

Protestant

and the Laity of the P Episcopal Church 8 3
the P Episcopal Church in these States is indebted, 9 11
of the P Episcopal Church in the United States 867 31
We, Bishops of the P Episcopal Church 876 25

proved

nor may be *p* thereby, is not to be required 868 21
for they may be *p* by most certain warrants 869 17
cannot be *p* by Holy Writ; 873 29

Proverbs

The *P*, 868 29

provide

and used to *p* light for reading 143 1
p an opportunity for the congregation to reaffirm 577 23
second use of this catechism is to *p* a brief summary 844 7

provided

p the substance of the Faith be kept 9 4
no service or prayer has been *p* in this Book, 13 14
whether in the form *p* in the Daily Offices, 13 23
P, that there is no celebration of the Eucharist 18 11
and *p* further, that none of the Propers appointed 18 13
and Collects are *p* in each service. 136 —
no Proper is *p* in this Book 195 —
no Proper is *p* in this Book 246 —
and the Collect *p*, or some other suitable Collect, 288 —
and one or more of the Lessons *p* 312 21
p that a lesson from the Gospel is always included, 322 19
p that a lesson from the Gospel is always included, 354 19
using one of the eucharistic prayers *p*. 401 9
p "At Confirmation" (page 929) may be substituted. 414 —
desired to celebrate a marriage otherwise than as *p* 435 2
Seating may be *p* for the wedding party, 437 18
Two equivalent forms of service are *p* here 446 10
instead, a declaration of forgiveness is *p*. 446 14
that the ministrations of the Church may be *p*. 462 —
to be *p* as a separate document 552 9
a special order is *p* on page 577. 566 19
Name was *p* with the vowels of the word Adonai. 583 23
and is *p* for, as to the remaining parts of it, 872 3
Three Readings are *p* for each Sunday and weekday 934 7
and alternative Psalmody *p*. 935 5

providence

But when in the course of Divine *P*, 10 24

provides

This Order *p* a form of evening service or vespers 108 2
manual of devotion which *p* daily selections 136 —
This service *p* for the dedication and consecration 566 2

provision

This *p* does not apply to Christmas 17 18
p for the well-being of their families, 445 —

provisions

P for adapting the rite to special circumstances 566 7

prudent

about the duty of Christian parents to make *p* provision 445 —

psalm

P 118:24 39 —
P 19:4 40 —
P 105:1 40 —
P 122:1 40 —
P 19:14 40 —
P 43:3 40 —
P 43 —
Venite *P* 95:1–7; 96:9,13 44 —
or *P* 95, page 146. 45 —
Jubilate *P* 100 45 —
In Easter Week, in place of an Invitatory *P*, 45 —
The *P* or Psalms Appointed 46 —
P 141:2 61 —
P 96:9 61 —
P 74:15,16 61 —
P 16:7,8 61 —
P 139:10,11 62 —
or some other suitable hymn, or an Invitatory *P*, 64 —
The *P* or Psalms Appointed 64 —
P 118:24 77 —
P 19:4 78 —
P 105:1 78 —
P 122:1 78 —
P 19:14 78 —
P 43:3 78 —
P 80 —
Venite *P* 95:1–7 82 —
or *P* 95, page 724. 82 —
Jubilate *P* 100 82 —
In Easter Week, in place of an Invitatory *P*, 83 —
The *P* of Psalms Appointed 84 —
one or more sections of *P* 119, 103 —
P 119 Lucerna pedibus meis 103 —
P 121 Levavi oculos 104 —
P 126 In convertendo 105 —
P 36:5–9 (Ascension) 108 17
P 139:10–11 110 —
an appropriate anthem or *p* may be sung, 112 —
P 141:2 115 —
P 96:9 115 —
P 74:15,16 115 —
P 16:7,8 115 —
P 139:10,11 116 —
or some other suitable hymn, or an Invitatory *P*, 117 —
The *P* or Psalms Appointed 118 —
P 4 Cum invocarem 128 —
P 31 In te, Domine, speravi 129 —
P 91 Qui habitat 129 —
P 134 Ecce nunc 131 —
From *P* 51 137 —
From *P* 113 138 —
P 134 140 —
and may be used after the Invitatory *P* 141 12
"Christ our Passover," after each *P*, 141 13
and after each section of *P* 119. 141 13
P 95: Traditional Venite, exultemus 146 —
with the *P* and Lessons for the Epiphany, 162 —
This Collect, with the corresponding *P* and Lessons, 166 —
Either of the preceding Collects, with the proper *P* 174 —
followed by a *P*, Canticle, or hymn. 175 —
with the *P* and Lessons for the Epiphany, 214 —
This Collect, with the corresponding *P* and Lessons, 217 —
Either of the preceding Collects, with the proper *P* 226 —
followed by a *P*, Canticle, or hymn. 227 —
P 103, or 103:8–14 264 —
The following *P* is then sung or said 265 —
P 51 Miserere mei, Deus 266 —

an appropriate invitation and a penitential *p*.	269	—
and *P* 118:19–29.	271	—
P 22:1–21, or 22:1–11	272	—
P, and Lessons	274	—
P 78:14–20, 23–25	274	—
P 22:1–11 (12–21), or 40:1–14, or 69:1–23	276	—
P 130, or 31:1–5	283	—
After each Lesson, the *P* or Canticle listed,	288	—
some other suitable *p*, canticle, or hymn may be sung.	288	—
P 33:1–11, or *P* 36:5–10	288	—
P 46	288	—
P 33:12–22, or *P* 16	289	—
P 122	290	—
Canticle 9, The First Song of Isaiah, or *P* 42:1–7	290	—
P 42:1–7, or Canticle 9, The First Song of Isaiah	290	—
P 30, or *P* 143	291	—
P 98, or *P* 126	291	—
P 114, or some other suitable *p* or a hymn may	295	—
A hymn, *p*, or anthem may be sung.	299	—
A *P*, hymn, or anthem may follow each Reading.	300	14
a formal procession, a suitable *p*,	312	31
as *P* 42, or a hymn or anthem, may be sung.	312	32
A suitable *p*, such as *P* 23,	313	11
A hymn, *p*, or anthem may be sung.	319	—
A hymn, *p*, or anthem may be sung.	323	—
A *P*, hymn, or anthem may follow each Reading.	326	—
During the Offertory, a hymn, *p*, or anthem may	333	—
P 50:14	343	—
P 96:8	343	—
A hymn, *p*, or anthem may be sung.	351	—
A hymn, *p*, or anthem may be sung.	355	—
A *P*, hymn, or anthem may follow each Reading.	357	—
During the Offertory, a hymn, *p*, or anthem may	361	—
P 50:14	376	—
P 96:8	376	—
When a *p* is used, it may be concluded with Gloria	406	7
A hymn, *p*, or anthem may be sung.	413	—
A *P*, hymn, or anthem may follow each Reading.	414	—
During their entrance, a hymn, *p*, or anthem may	423	—
A hymn, *p*, or anthem may follow.	425	—
a *P*, hymn, or anthem may be sung or said.	426	—
A hymn, *p*, or anthem may be sung,	431	—
a hymn, *p*, or anthem may be sung;	432	—
P 116	442	—
P 23	443	—
the priest may assign to the penitent a *p*,	446	23
P 91 (He will give his angels charge over you)	453	16
P 103 (He forgives all your sins)	454	3
P 23 (You have anointed my head with oil)	454	7
P 145:14–22 (The eyes of all wait upon you, O Lord)	454	11
during which time a suitable *p* or anthem may	467	—
John 6, together with *P* 23, are recommended.	468	20
P 42 Quaemadmodum	471	—
P 46 Deus noster refugium	471	—
P 90 Domine, refugium	472	—
P 121 Levavi oculos	473	—
P 130 De profundis	474	—
P 139 Domine, probasti	474	—
P 23 Dominus regit me	476	—
P 23 King James Version	476	—
P 27 Dominus illuminatio	477	—
P 106 Confitemini Domino	478	—
P 116 Dilexi, quoniam	478	—
John 6, together with *P* 23, are recommended.	490	20
A hymn, *p*, or some other suitable anthem may	491	—
A suitable *p*, hymn, or canticle may follow.	494	—
A suitable *p*, hymn, or canticle may follow.	495	—
P 99, or 40:1–14, or 100	515	—
A *P*, canticle, or hymn follows each Reading.	516	—
A hymn, *p*, or anthem may be sung.	525	—
P 43, or 132:8–19	528	—
A *P*, canticle, or hymn follows each Reading.	529	—
A hymn, *p*, or anthem may be sung.	537	—
P 84, or 119:33–40	540	—
A *P*, canticle, or hymn follows each Reading.	541	—
A hymn, *p*, or anthem may be sung.	559	—
P 43, or 132:1–9, or 146, or 133 and 134	560	—
As the procession moves into the church, *P* 122	568	5
or some other appropriate *p* is sung.	568	6
P 84, or 48	571	—
denotes the reading or chanting of a whole *p*,	582	8
or portion of a *p*, in unison.	582	9
It is particularly appropriate for the *p* verses	582	9
the verses of a *p* are sung by a solo voice,	582	20
their pounding waves. *P* 93:4),	583	6
but the way of the wicked is doomed. *P* 1:6),	583	7
show us his mercy. *P* 123:3).	583	9
In two passages (*P* 68:4 and *P* 83:18),	584	1
but, when desired, the *P* cited	888	16
a longer and shorter version, usually from the same *P*.	888	19
when the *P* is sung between the Lessons	888	21
said at the beginning and end of each *P* or Canticle,	935	10

psalmody

appointed *P*;	61	—
follow the *P*.	113	—
appointed *P*;	115	—
traditional methods of *p*.	582	4
recitation is the name given to a method of *p*	582	19
and alternative *P* provided.	935	4

psalms

Scriptural citations in this Book, except for the *P*,	14	16
the following may be observed with the Collects, *P*,	18	1
Then follows one of the Invitatory *P*,	42	—
The Psalm or *P* Appointed	46	—
At the end of the *P* is sung or said	46	—
The Psalm or *P* Appointed	64	—
At the end of the *P* is sung or said	64	—
Then follows one of the Invitatory *P*,	80	—
The Psalm of *P* Appointed	84	—
At the end of the *P* is sung or said	84	—
One or more of the following *P* is sung or said.	103	—
selections include *P* 19, 67,	103	—
selection from *P* 120 through 133.	103	—
At the end of the *P* is sung or said	105	—
With Evening Prayer, beginning with the *P*;	112	—
The Psalm or *P* Appointed	118	—
At the end of the *P* is sung or said	118	—
One or more of the following *P* are sung or said.	128	—
At the end of the *P* is sung or said	131	—
P, see page 582.)	136	—
For convenience, appropriate *P*, Readings,	136	—
The *P* and Readings may be replaced	136	—

with either of the Invitatory *P*. 141 7
Antiphons drawn from the *P* themselves, 141 8
used with the *P* and biblical Canticles. 141 10
Metrical versions of the Invitatory *P*, 141 21
service continues as a complete Office, *P* and Lessons 143 21
P generally appropriate to the evening include: 143 23
and the appointed *P* and Lessons, 158 5
with one of the corresponding sets of *P* 195 —
with one of the corresponding sets of *P* 246 —
hymns, *p*, or anthems are sung, 271 —
During the ministration of Communion, hymns, *p*, 338 —
During the ministration of Communion, hymns, *p*, 365 —
Appropriate *P* are 67, 127, and 128 426 —
service continues with the Magnificat or one of the *P* 440 —
Suitable *P*, Lessons, and Collects 465 —
the following *P* may be sung or said 470 —
the following *P* may be sung or said. 475 —
The following *P* are appropriate: 494 —
The following *P* are appropriate: 495 —
Anthems from Holy Scripture or *p* may be sung 506 7
P, hymns, or anthems may follow the readings. 506 10
Hymns, *p*, and anthems may be sung 512 —
Hymns or *p* may be used in procession. 575 9
Selected verses of *p* and hymns, 576 4
reciting the *p* in the Daily Office. 582 18
of chanting the *p* between the Lessons 582 25
The version of the *P* which follows is set out in lines 583 1
Three terms are used in the *P* with reference to God: 583 15
ancient fathers had divided the *P* into seven portions, 866 27
The *P*, 868 28
The *P* and Lessons appointed for the Sundays 888 6
The *P* at such Offices are normally those appointed 888 15
the *P* are arranged in a seven-week pattern 934 23
In the citation of the *P*, 934 26
any of the *P* appointed for a given day may be used 934 28
Likewise, *P* appointed for any day may be used 934 29
(brackets in the case of whole *P*, 935 1
to indicate *P* and verses of *P* 935 2
use the bracketed *P* rather than the alternatives. 935 6
Antiphons drawn from the *P* themselves, 935 7
may be used with the *P* and biblical Canticles. 935 9
Special Occasions, the officiant may select suitable *P* 935 12

Psalter
The Invitatory and *P* 42 —
The Invitatory and *P* 63 —
The Invitatory and *P* 80 —
Selection from the *P*. 113 —
The Invitatory and *P* 117 —
the conclusion of the entire portion of the *P*; 141 12
The *P* 581 —
Concerning the *P* 582 1
The *P* is a body of liturgical poetry. 582 2
the recitation of the *P* needlessly monotonous. 582 5
the Prayer Book *P* and the King James Old Testament, 583 27
The *P* 585 1
the selections from the *P* are frequently cited 888 18
In some instances, the entire portion of the *P* assigned 935 3
Those who desire to recite the *P* in its entirety should, 935 5

public
amendments in her Forms of *P* Worship; 9 24
to take a further review of the *P* Service, 11 6
the regular services appointed for *p* worship 13 5
authorized for *p* worship in this Church, 143 7
authorization of the bishop, officiate at *p* Baptism; 284 28
on some subsequent occasion of *p* baptism 312 13
at a *p* celebration of the Sacrament 314 6
be present at a *p* celebration of the Eucharist. 396 —
make a mature *p* affirmation of their faith 412 4
also expected to make a *p* affirmation of their faith 412 8
Christian marriage is a solemn and *p* covenant 422 2
prayer of Christians assembled for *p* worship, 446 4
Anointing takes place at a *p* celebration 453 7
If the place of *p* worship is also to serve as a school 576 29
When buildings have been used for *p* worship 577 21
39. For those who Influence *P* Opinion 811 18
39. For those who Influence *P* Opinion 827 —
need none other books for their *p* service, 867 6
for any man to take upon him the office of *p* preaching, 872 16
this work by men who have *p* authority 872 19
to have *p* Prayer in the Church, 872 23
intended for use at all *p* services on such days, 888 7

publican
as an Heathen and *P*, until he be openly reconciled 874 19

publicly
of matrimony, and their free consent, is *p* ascertained. 435 14

published
If Banns are to be *p*, the following form is used 437 2

pulpit
desirable that the Lessons be read from a lectern or *p*, 406 17
Gospel be read from the same lectern, or from the *p*, 406 18
The Bishop goes to the *P*, lays a hand upon it, 571 —
If one reading stand is to serve as both lectern and *p*, 576 6

punish
Laws of the Realm may *p* Christian men with death, 876 8

purchase
p to themselves damnation, 872 39

pure
nothing to be read, but the very *p* word of God, 867 1
in which the *p* Word of God is preached, 871 30

purely
but hath no authority in things *p* spiritual. 875 36

purgatory
XXII. Of *P*. 872 11
The Romish Doctrine concerning *P*, 872 12

purpose
the Sacrament for that *p* is consecrated at this service. 275 —
acknowledging briefly the *p* of their gathering, 492 —
and is, the intention and *p* of this Church to maintain 510 19
and for this *p* these services of ordination 510 20
state the *p* of the new ministry. 559 —
or for some other suitable *p*, 576 30
that the same was not ordained, but of a good *p*, 866 7

that *p*, which is plain and easy to be understood, 866 35
much agreeable to the mind and *p* of the old fathers, 866 43
Predestination to Life is the everlasting *p* of God, 871 2
be called accordingly to God's *p* by his Spirit 871 6

purposely
willingly and *p*, doth openly break the Traditions 874 25

purposes
social *p*, or for other suitable activities. 566 12

put
the Bible is brought forward and *p* into place 576 9
bring them forward and *p* them in place. 576 23
the areas or furnishings should be *p* into use 577 13
pronouns and verbs have been *p* in italics 814 —
p away our sins, and endure the severity 870 8

Q

Quadrilateral
The Chicago-Lambeth *Q* 1886, 1888 876 22
While the above form of the *Q* was adopted 877 26

qualified
who are themselves duly *q* to confer Holy Orders. 510 24

quarrel
seek occasion, of cavil or *q* against her Liturgy. 10 13

quatrains
and *q* are not unknown; 583 11
although *q* are usually distributed over two verses. 583 11

queen
by Elizabeth our *Q* do most plainly testify; 876 2

quench
(Many waters cannot *q* love) 426 —

question
Q 302 —
Q 303 —
To either *q*, the appropriate answer is, "I do." 437 11
the traditional *q* and answer form for ease 844 6

questions
Then the Celebrant asks the following *q* 302 —
or of a series of *q* and answers, 420 —
The following *q* are then addressed 517 —

quick
whence he shall come to judge the *q* and the dead. 865 34
the Priest did offer Christ for the *q* and the dead, 874 9

quicken
he doth work invisibly in us, and doth not only *q*, 872 28

quiet
"may lead *q* and peaceable lives, in all godliness 11 2
59. For *Q* Confidence 812 10
59. For *Q* Confidence 832 —

quieting
for the *q* and appeasing of the same; 867 21

R

race
44. For the Future of the Human *R* 811 26
44. For the Future of the Human *R* 828 —

races
7. For the Diversity of *R* and Cultures 813 9
7. For the Diversity of *R* and Cultures 840 —

rails
inside the altar *r* or in a place set aside 446 16

rain
43. For *R* 811 25
43. For *R* 828 —

raised
(*R* in incorruption) 475 —
Because Jesus was *r* from the dead, 507 3
we, too, shall be *r*. 507 4

rank
distinctive of ecclesiastical or academic *r* or order. 511 17
distinctive of ecclesiastical or academic *r* or order. 524 8
distinctive of ecclesiastical or academic *r* or office. 536 8

rash
As we confess that vain and *r* Swearing is forbidden 876 18

rather
If the texts are recited *r* than sung, 281 —
when the verses are recited *r* than sung, 582 11
r than the Latin form "Alleluia," 584 6
r, it is a point of departure for the teacher, 844 5
but *r* the characteristics of each nature 864 13
yea *r*, for that they are not done 870 15
but *r* repugnant to the Word of God. 872 14
but *r* they be certain sure witnesses, 872 27
but *r* it is a Sacrament of our Redemption 873 24
but *r*, to their condemnation, do eat and drink 873 39
but *r*, co-operating with them 877 1
but *r* incorporated in a general plan referred for study 877 27
use the bracketed Psalms *r* than the alternatives. 935 6

ratification
The *R* of The Book of Common Prayer (1789) 8 1

read
other persons be assigned to *r* the Lessons, 36 5
One or two Lessons, as appointed, are *r*, 47 —
the Gospel is *r* after the second Canticle. 47 —
One or two Lessons, as appointed, are *r*, 64 —
the Gospel is *r* after the second Canticle. 65 —
other persons be assigned to *r* the Lessons, 74 4
One or two Lessons, as appointed, are *r*, 84 —
the Gospel is *r* after the second Canticle. 84 —
or some other suitable passage of Scripture, is *r* 105 —
when presiding, should *r* the Prayer for Light, 108 8
to the occasion or to the season, may then be *r* 109 —
One or two Lessons, as appointed, are *r*, 118 —
the Gospel is *r* after the second Canticle. 119 —
or some other suitable passage of Scripture, is *r* 131 —
the Collect should be *r* by one person, 136 —

The Short Lessons may be *r* from any version 143 6
and should be *r* without announcement 143 7
to be *r* later in the service, 143 9
When desired, more than one Lesson may be *r*, 143 25
the appointed Lessons are *r* before the Gospel, 175 —
the appointed Lessons are *r* before the Gospel, 227 —
The Passion Gospel may be *r* or chanted 273 —
The Passion Gospel may be *r* or chanted 277 —
The biddings may be *r* by a Deacon or other person 277 —
Lay persons *r* the Lessons, and the Epistle, 284 20
each Lesson be *r* by a different reader. 284 22
At least two of the following Lessons are *r*, 288 —
One or two Lessons, as appointed, are *r*, 300 —
this Exhortation may be *r* by a lay person. 316 —
the Exhortation, page 316, may be *r*, 319 —
The Celebrant may *r* one of the following sentences 319 —
A deacon should *r* the Gospel and may lead 322 10
One or two Lessons, as appointed, are *r*, 325 —
the Exhortation, page 316, may be *r*, 351 —
The Celebrant may *r* one of the following sentences 351 —
A deacon should *r* the Gospel and may lead 354 10
One or two Lessons, as appointed, are *r*, 357 —
desirable that a passage from the Gospel first be *r*. 396 —
It is desirable that the Lessons be *r* from a lectern 406 17
and that the Gospel be *r* from the same lectern, 406 18
r from a book or books of appropriate size 406 20
r the Gospel in the language of the people, 406 23
One or two Lessons, as appointed, are *r*, 414 —
r the Gospel, and perform other assisting functions 422 13
and the Epistles be *r* by lay persons. 422 19
the following passages from Holy Scripture is *r*. 426 —
When a passage from the Gospel is to be *r*, 426 —
A passage from Scripture may first be *r*. 439 13
the following or other passages of Scripture are *r* 453 13
and the Epistle, be *r* by lay persons. 468 16
the following passages from Holy Scriptures is *r*. 470 —
and the Epistle, be *r* by lay persons. 490 16
the following passages from Holy Scripture is *r*. 494 —
4. One or more passages of Holy Scripture are *r*. 506 10
that testimonials of the election be *r*. 513 —
Three Lessons are *r*. 515 —
Lay persons *r* the Old Testament Lesson 515 —
Three Lessons are *r*. 528 —
Lay persons *r* the Old Testament Lesson 528 —
Three Lessons are *r*. 540 —
Lay persons *r* the Old Testament Lesson 540 —
Lay persons from the congregation *r* the Old 558 14
The new minister, if a deacon, should *r* the Gospel, 558 20
A lay person being instituted should *r* 558 23
The Bishop may *r* the Letter of Institution, 559 —
Three Lessons are *r*. 571 —
Lay persons *r* the Old Testament Lesson 571 —
should be *r* over once in the year, 866 9
(by daily hearing of holy Scripture *r* in the Church) 866 13
before three or four Chapters were *r* out, 866 19
but they were only begun, and never *r* through. 866 21
hath been *r* in Latin to the people, 866 24
more business to find out what should be *r*, 866 32
than to *r* it when it was found out. 866 32
and is ordained nothing to be *r*, 867 1
all things must be *r* upon the book, 867 12
that all things shall be *r* and sung 867 23
so that whatsoever is not *r* therein, 868 20
the Church doth *r* for example of life 868 34
we judge them to be *r* in Churches by the Ministers, 874 38
to be *r* at the principal morning service, 888 9
or, if the Office is *r* only once in the day, 934 9
When the Office is *r* twice in the day, 934 10

reader

the *R* first saying 47 —
After each Lesson the *R* may say 47 —
Or the *R* may say 47 —
the *R* first saying 64 —
After each Lesson the *R* may say 65 —
Or the *R* may say 65 —
the *R* first saying 84 —
After each Lesson the *R* may say 84 —
Or the *R* may say 84 —
the *R* first saying 118 —
After each Lesson the *R* may say 119 —
Or the *R* may say 119 —
A deacon or lay *r* leading the service remains kneeling 269 —
led by a deacon or lay *r*. 269 —
led by a deacon or lay *r*. 272 —
led by a deacon or lay *r*. 282 —
each Lesson be read by a different *r*. 284 22
a deacon or lay *r* may lead 284 23
the *R* first saying 300 —
After each Reading, the *R* may say 300 —
or the *R* may say 300 —
After the Gospel, the *R* says 300 —
the *R* first saying 325 —
After each Reading, the *R* may say 325 —
or the *R* may say 325 —
After the Gospel, the *R* says 326 —
the *R* first saying 357 —
After each Reading, the *R* may say 357 —
or the *R* may say 357 —
After the Gospel, the *R* says 358 —
a *r* appointed by the celebrant may read 406 22
or, if there is no deacon, by a lay *r*. 407 6
the *R* first saying 414 —
After each Reading the *R* may say 414 —
or the *R* may say 414 —
After the Gospel, the *R* says 415 —
After the Gospel, the *R* says 426 —
a deacon or lay *r* may preside at the service. 468 17
At the end of the Gospel, the *R* says 480 —
a deacon or lay *r* may preside at the service. 490 17
At the end of the Gospel, the *R* says 495 —
The *R* first says 516 —
After each Reading, the *R* may say 516 —
or the *R* may say 516 —
After the Gospel, the *R* says 516 —
The *R* first says 528 —
After each Reading, the *R* may say 529 —
or the *R* may say 529 —
After the Gospel, the *R* says 529 —
The *R* first says 540 —
After each Reading, the *R* may say 541 —
or the *R* may say 541 —
After the Gospel, the *R* says 541 —

or a lay *r*, or another suitable person.	576	10
the *R* should omit initial conjunctions	888	25

readers

together with lay *r*, singers, and other persons,	284	11
Lay persons may act as *r*,	312	24
alternation between groups of singers or *r*;	582	14
for the understanding, both of the *r* and hearers.	867	3

readiness

And for a *r* in this matter, here is drawn out	866	34
in our own land, we hereby declare our desire and *r*,	877	21

reading

Silence may be kept after each *R*.	47	—
is sung or said after each *R*.	47	—
Silence may be kept after each *R*.	65	—
is sung or said after each *R*.	65	—
Silence may be kept after each *R*.	84	—
is sung or said after each *R*.	84	—
Bible *R*.	113	—
or a brief silence, may follow the *R*.	113	—
Silence may be kept after each *R*.	119	—
is sung or said after each *R*.	119	—
the *R* and the Collect should be read	136	—
(For suggestions about *r* the Psalms,	136	—
A *R*	137	—
A *R*	138	—
A *R*	139	—
A *R*	140	—
a *r* from non-biblical Christian literature	142	13
and used to provide light for *r* the opening	143	1
share among them the *r* of the Collects	284	14
After each *R*, the Reader may say	300	—
A Psalm, hymn, or anthem may follow each *R*.	300	—
the *r* of the Lessons which precede the Gospel,	322	16
After each *R*, the Reader may say	325	—
A Psalm, hymn, or anthem may follow each *R*.	326	—
the *r* of the Lessons which precede the Gospel,	354	16
After each *R*, the Reader may say	357	—
A Psalm, hymn, or anthem may follow each *R*.	357	—
After the *R*, the Celebrant may comment on it briefly.	397	—
A *r* from the Gospel is always included.	400	10
After each *R* the Reader may say	414	—
A Psalm, hymn, or anthem may follow each *R*.	414	—
a *R* from the Gospel is always included.	435	17
remain where they may conveniently hear the *r*	437	14
After any *R*, the Celebrant may comment on it	454	13
the last *R* is from the Gospel.	506	12
When the *r* of the testimonials is ended,	513	—
After each *R*, the Reader may say	516	—
A Psalm, canticle, or hymn follows each *R*.	516	—
After each *R*, the Reader may say	529	—
A Psalm, canticle, or hymn follows each *R*.	529	—
After each *R*, the Reader may say	541	—
A Psalm, canticle, or hymn follows each *R*.	541	—
If one *r* stand is to serve as both lectern	576	6
congregational use, whether by singing or *r*.	582	3
Direct recitation denotes the *r* or chanting	582	8
each verse into two parts for *r* or chanting.	583	13
In *r*, a distinct pause should be made at the asterisk.	583	14
(by often *r*, and meditation of God's word)	866	10
the *r* of holy Scripture is so set forth,	866	36
as did break the continual course of the *r*	866	38
(as touching the *r* of the holy Scripture),	866	42
which daily they shall obtain by *r* upon the book,	867	14
suspends the order for the *r* of said Homilies	875	17
R some such introduction as,	888	28
Any *R* may be lengthened at discretion.	888	29
the Gospel *R* be used in the evening in Year One,	934	11
the Old Testament *R* for the alternate year is used	934	13
First *R* at Evening Prayer.	934	14
When more than one *R* is used at an Office,	934	15
Any *R* may be lengthened at discretion.	934	20

readings

For convenience, appropriate Psalms, *R*, and Collects	136	—
R may be replaced by those appointed	136	—
the *R*, may be used.	141	22
after the *R* or at the time of the hymn	142	12
Christian literature may follow the biblical *R*.	142	14
The Celebrant may introduce the Scripture *r*	288	—
homily may be preached after any of the preceding *R*.	292	—
The proclamation and response may include *r*,	400	9
the Gospel always concludes the *R*.	426	—
Between the *R*, a Psalm, hymn, or anthem may	426	—
A homily or other response to the *R* may follow.	426	—
3. One or more *R*,	435	15
the Gospel always concludes the *R*.	470	—
the Gospel always concludes the *R*.	494	—
anthems may follow the *r*.	506	11
5. A homily may follow the *R*,	506	13
The *R* are ordinarily selected	515	—
Bishop may select *R* from the Proper of the Day.	515	—
The *R* are ordinarily selected	528	—
select *R* from the Proper of the Day.	528	—
The *R* are ordinarily selected	540	5
select *R* from the Proper of the Day.	540	—
The *R* are selected from the following list,	560	—
there may be one or two *R* from Scripture.	565	10
Any of the *R*, including the Gospel,	565	11
prayers and Bible *r* related to the particular occasion	577	12
Three *R* are provided for each Sunday and weekday	934	7
Two of the *R* may be used in the morning	934	8
all three *R* may be used.	934	10
If two *R* are desired at both Offices,	934	12
When a Major Feast interrupts the sequence of *R*,	934	17
the officiant may select suitable Psalms and *R*.	935	13

reads

Here a Deacon or other person appointed *r*	270	—
the congregation *r* the parts in italics.	281	—
r the prayer, "Heavenly Father,	298	10
the Deacon or a Priest *r* the Gospel, first saying	300	—
the Deacon or a Priest *r* the Gospel, first saying	326	—
the Deacon or a Priest *r* the Gospel, first saying	357	—
The Celebrant, whether priest or deacon, *r*	396	—
the Deacon or a Priest *r* the Gospel, first saying	414	—
The Deacon or other person appointed *r*	429	—
the Deacon or Minister appointed *r* the Gospel,	479	—
the Deacon or Minister appointed *r* the Gospel,	495	—
Presiding Bishop stands and *r* the Collect	515	—
a Deacon or a Priest *r* the Gospel, first saying	516	—
the Bishop stands and *r* the Collect for the Day,	527	—
a Priest *r* the Gospel, first saying	529	—

the Bishop stands and *r* the Collect for the Day, 539 —
if no deacon is present, a Priest *r* 541 —
A deacon or priest *r* the Gospel. 558 16
The Deacon (or a Priest) *r* the Gospel. 571 —
omitted in the version of 1801, *r* as follows: 872 4
1662 text of this Article *r* as follows: 875 26
1662 text of this Article *r* as follows: 875 39

ready

It is the function of a deacon to make *r* the Table 407 14
when they are *r* and have been duly prepared, 412 3
building is *r* for regular use as a place of worship. 566 10
When all are *r*, the Bishop says the following 567 5
this Church is *r* in the spirit of love 876 34

reaffirm

opportunity for the congregation to *r* its commitment 577 23

reaffirmation

If Confirmation, Reception, or the *R* 308 —
At Confirmation, Reception, or *R* 309 —
For *R* 310 —
R of Baptismal Vows are administered 412 12
the *R* of Baptismal Vows 413 —
For *R* 419 —
a *r* of baptismal promises. 420 —

reaffirmed

Article given Royal assent in 1571 and *r* in 1662, 869 19

realm

and singing in churches within this *r*: 867 9
all the whole *r* shall have but one use. 867 10
the chief power in this *R* of England, 875 40
Government of all Estates of this *R*, 875 41
Rome hath no jurisdiction in this *R* of England. 876 7
The Laws of the *R* may punish Christian men 876 8

reason

and for urgent and sufficient *r*, 16 20
or on other occasions for sufficient *r*, 312 20
by *r* of extreme sickness or physical disability, 457 —
whereas before, by *r* of so often repetition, 867 12

reasonable

it is but *r* that upon weighty and important considerations, 9 17
If there is *r* doubt that a person has been baptized 313 16
form is intended for use with those who for *r* cause 396 —
R opportunity is to be given for the priests present 553 19
consisting also of a *r* soul and body; 864 6
of a *r* soul and human flesh subsisting; 865 25
For as the *r* soul and flesh is one man, 865 31

reasons

They will appear, and it is to be hoped, the *r* of them 11 10
giving the *r* for refusing Communion. 409 25

rebellion

21 Against *R*. 875 13

rebuked

approved by common authority, ought to be *r* openly, 874 27

recalls

R before God, when appropriate, 402 —
R before God, when appropriate, 404 —

receive

The ministers *r* the Sacrament in both kinds, 338 —
The ministers *r* the Sacrament in both kinds, 365 —
The Celebrant then prays that all may *r* the benefits 405 5
While the people are coming forward to *r* 407 22
always to be given to every communicant to *r* 407 25
not allowing such persons to *r* Communion 409 14
they may not *r* Communion until they have forgiven 409 19
and to *r* the laying on of hands by the bishop. 412 5
and to *r* the laying on of hands. 412 10
the newly married couple *r* Communion first, 432 —
and *r* Holy Communion before other members 438 3
If the sick person cannot *r* 457 —
If a person desires to *r* the Sacrament, 457 —
The family of the newly ordained may *r* Communion 511 23
The family of the newly ordained may *r* Communion 524 17
The family of the newly ordained may *r* Communion 536 17
and the formula "*R* the Holy Scriptures..." 553 5
and the words "*R* this Bible..." 554 5
break the consecrated Bread and *r* Holy Communion. 554 9
and the words "*R* this Bible..." 554 26
as they are commonly received, we do *r*, 869 4
r grace, or (as the School-authors say) deserve grace 870 15
Furthermore, we must *r* God's promises in such wise, 871 21
And in such only as worthily *r* the same, 872 38
but they that *r* them unworthily, 872 39
do *r* the Sacraments ministered unto them; 873 7
they that *r* Baptism rightly are grafted 873 16
such as rightly, worthily, and with faith, *r* the same, 873 25

received

r as such by all the members of the same: 8 11
whole will be *r* and examined by every true member 11 17
An offering may be *r* and presented at the Office. 142 15
Alms may be *r* and presented, 311 —
after all have *r*, any of the Sacrament 401 14
and the offerings of the people *r*. 407 2
r in both kinds simultaneously, 408 1
all the benefits of Communion are *r*, 457 —
even though the Sacrament is not *r* 457 —
1. The body is *r*. 506 4
or have already *r* such ordination 510 23
as they are commonly *r*, we do receive, 869 4
ought of necessity to be *r* in any commonwealth; 869 12
ought thoroughly to be *r* and believed: 869 17
After we have *r* the Holy Ghost, 870 34
And the mean whereby the Body of Christ is *r* 873 32
and *r* into the Church by a Judge 874 19
[This Article is *r* in this Church, 875 14

receives

the celebrant *r* the Sacrament in both kinds. 407 23

receiving

(and the *r* of the people's offering), 408 20
or after *r* a child by adoption, 439 3
After *r* Holy Communion, 536 14
66. Before *R* Communion 812 21
67. After *R* Communion 812 22

66. Before *R* Communion 834 —
67. After *R* Communion 834 —
in hearing the Word of God, and in *r* the Sacraments. 873 5
15 Of the worthy *r* of the Sacrament 875 6

recent

in more *r* manuscripts and in printed Bibles, 583 21

reception

and concluding with the *r* of the newly baptized) 292 —
If Confirmation, *R*, or the Reaffirmation 308 —
At Confirmation, *R*, or Reaffirmation 309 —
For *R* 310 —
When there is no Baptism, the rites of Confirmation, *R*, 412 11
with forms for *R* 413 —
For *R* 418 —
R of the Body 466 —
r of the newly baptized. 575 31

recitation

makes the *r* of the Psalter needlessly monotonous. 582 5
Direct *r* denotes the reading or chanting 582 8
Antiphonal *r* is the verse-by-verse alternation 582 13
The alternate *r* concludes 582 15
Responsorial *r* is the name given to a method 582 19
Responsive *r* is the method which has been 582 27

recite

Those who desire to *r* the Psalter in its entirety 935 5

recited

If the texts are *r* rather than sung, 281 —
The Apostles' Creed may be *r* after the Lessons, 437 20
the Apostles' Creed may be *r*. 506 14
when the verses are *r* rather than sung, 582 11
or with a refrain (called the antiphon) *r* in unison. 582 16

reciting

This is probably the most satisfying method for *r* 582 17

recognition

when a congregation attains *r* as a parish. 577 25

recognized

the Baptism should be *r* 314 5
The persons who are chosen and *r* by the Church 510 16
It is also *r* and affirmed that the threefold ministry 510 26
and is, most generally *r* by Christian people 510 30
Son, Lord, Only-begotten, *r* in two natures, 864 11

recommended

It is *r* that, as far as possible, 312 5
and it is *r* that it take place immediately 453 9
John 6, together with Psalm 23, are *r*. 468 20
John 6, together with Psalm 23, are *r*. 490 20

reconcile

to *r* his Father to us, and to be a sacrifice, 868 7

reconciled

until he be openly *r* by penance, and received 874 19

reconciliation

ministry of *r*, which has been committed by Christ 446 2
The *R* of a Penitent is available for all who desire it. 446 7

The *R* 447 1
and use the form for the *R* 454 16

recovers

If the baptized person *r*, 314 5

recovery

For *R* from Sickness 458 —
Thanksgiving for a Beginning of *R* 460 —
Invitatory Antiphons for the Venite makes possible a *r* 582 23

rector

and inducted as the *r* of a parish. 558 3
If the new minister is the *r* or vicar of the parish, 562 —
appropriate for the induction of a *r* of a parish, 564 17
The *r* or minister in charge takes part 566 13
The *R* or Minister in charge continues 569 —

rectors

priest's prayer on page 562 is appropriate only for *r* 565 24

recurs

a seven-week pattern which *r* throughout the year, 934 24

red

Israel's deliverance at the *R* Sea 289 —

redeemed

19 The Song of the *R* Magna et mirabilia 94 —

redeemer

Job 19:21–27a (I know that my *R* liveth) 470 —
Job 19:21–27a (I know that my *R* lives) 494 —

redemption

Sin and *R* 848 —
but rather it is a Sacrament of our *R* 873 24
The Offering of Christ once made is that perfect *r*, 874 6

redressed

whereby the same shall be *r*. 866 34

refer

Thereafter, it is appropriate to *r* to him 511 19
Thereafter, it is appropriate to *r* to him 524 10
Thereafter, it is appropriate to *r* to him 536 10
conjunctions which *r* only to what has preceded, 888 26

reference

Three terms are used in the Psalms with *r* to God: 583 15
traditional question and answer form for ease of *r*. 844 6

references

r to the ordinand in the singular are changed 553 27
r to the ordinand in the singular are changed 554 17
But all *r* to the constitution and laws 875 15
obsolete words and phrases, as from the local *r*.] 875 19

referent

pronouns when the *r* is not otherwise clear, 888 27

referred

belong to Doctrine must be *r* to Discipline; 9 6
Hymns *r* to in the rubrics of this Book 14 6
but rather incorporated in a general plan *r* for study 877 27

refers

"Various Occasions" in the following pages *r* 813 17

refrain
or with a *r* (called the antiphon) recited 582 16
singing a *r* after each verse or group of verses. 582 21

refrains
antiphons on pages 43–44 and 80–82 may be used as *r* 141 6
be used as *r* after each verse or group of verses. 935 11

refugium
Psalm 46 Deus noster *r* 471 —
Psalm 90 Domine, *r* 472 —

refuse
but those on the other side *r* to forgive, 409 22
by reading upon the book, they will not *r* the pain, 867 14

refusing
mean between too much stiffness in *r*, 9 26
giving the reasons for *r* Communion. 409 25

regain
but also to *r* for our liturgy a form of the word 584 7

regard
having due *r* for the distinctive nature 576 19
Hebrew reverence and reticence with *r* to the Name 583 25

regards
(homoousios) with the Father as *r* his Godhead, 864 7
one substance with us as *r* his manhood; 864 8
as *r* his Godhead, 864 9
but yet as *r* his manhood 864 9

regenerated
infection of nature doth remain, yea in them that are *r*; 869 28

regeneration
that be not christened, but it is also a sign of *R* 873 15

registered
appropriate parish, so that the fact can be properly *r*. 314 4

regular
the *r* services appointed for public worship 13 5
from time to time on a *r* basis, 396 —
the building is ready for *r* use as a place of worship. 566 10
If the church is also to be used for *r* worship 577 1

regularly
The following Holy Days are *r* observed throughout 16 22
where it is *r* rendered "Lord". 583 27
r and legitimately constituted. 875 38

reign
she hath, in the *r* of several Princes, 10 1
9. Of the *R* of Christ 202 —
9. Of the *R* of Christ 254 —

rejoice
r that one we love has entered into the nearer presence 507 13

related
r to the occasion, or the season, 383 —
and Bible readings *r* to the particular occasion 577 12

relating
or human choice, *r* to modes of worship 876 33

relatives
It is desirable that fellow parishioners, *r*, 396 —

relevant
R portions of the service for the Dedication 577 8

relics
of Images as of *R*, and also Invocation of Saints, 872 13

religion
So are we forbidden by the Catholic *R*, to say, 865 7
the love of his true *r*. 866 15
Articles of *R* 867 29
so we judge, that Christian *R* doth not prohibit, 876 19
several spheres, have contended for the *r* of Christ: 876 28

religious
and the different *r* denominations 10 26
to leave bequests for *r* and charitable uses. 445 —

religiously
they walk *r* in good works, 871 9

remain
The people *r* standing. 333 —
The people *r* standing. 340 —
The people *r* standing. 361 —
The people *r* standing. 367 —
The people *r* standing. 372 —
If any of the consecrated Bread or Wine *r*, 408 28
The people *r* standing. 430 —
r where they may conveniently hear the reading 437 14
It is appropriate that all *r* standing 437 17
They may then *r* before the Lord's Table 438 2
and should *r* in the sight of the congregation 565 22
it is appropriate that it *r* silent until dedicated. 575 11
And this infection of nature doth *r*, 869 28

remainder
1977 divided by 3 is 659 with no *r*. 888 5

remaining
If the *r* Elements are not required for the Communion 555 4
consume the *r* Elements, and cleanse the vessels 555 6
as to the *r* parts of it, in other Articles.] 872 3

remains
lay person using the preceding form *r* kneeling, 42 —
lay person using the preceding form *r* kneeling, 63 —
lay person using the preceding form *r* kneeling, 80 —
lay person using the preceding form *r* kneeling, 117 —
lay reader leading the service *r* kneeling and 269 —
any of the Sacrament that *r* is then consumed. 401 14
and it *r* closed thereafter. 468 8
and it *r* closed thereafter. 490 8

remedy
Yet because there is no *r*, but that of necessity 866 40

remembering
the Christian community, *r* the promises of God 506 16

remission
the quick and the dead, to have *r* of pain or guilt, 874 9

remove
it is appropriate for the deacons to *r* the vessels 555 5

render
do not only *r* unto God as much as they are bound 870 21

rendered
where it is regularly *r* "Lord". 583 27

rendering
English tradition follows suit, *r* the combined title 583 33
to assist in *r* them into contemporary speech. 814 7

renew
may be used when a person wishes to make or *r* 420 —
It is essential that the person seeking to make or *r* 420 —
15. For those about to be Baptized or to *r* 810 21
to *r* their Baptismal Covenant 819 2

renewal
A Collect for the *R* of Life 56 —
A Collect for the *R* of Life 99 —
or the *R* of Baptismal Vows, 175 —
or the *R* of Baptismal Vows, 227 —
3. Christian Initiation, or the *R* of Baptismal Vows. 284 8
two parts of the service, the *R* of Baptismal Vows, 284 24
Celebrant leads the people in the *R* of Baptismal 292 —
The *R* of Baptismal Vows 292 —
The celebrant concludes the *R* of Vows as follows 294 —
Confirmation, or the *R* of Baptismal Vows 295 —
R of Baptismal Vows, page 292, may take the place 312 16
and the *r* of the Holy Spirit. 405 6
6. *R* of Baptismal Vows 578 2

renewed
God's Presence in a *r* Israel 290 —

renovated
have been added, altered, or *r*. 566 5

repairing
3 Of *r* and keeping clean of Churches. 875 4

repeat
All *r* the Antiphon 135 —

repeated
"Alleluia" may be sung and *r*. 295 —
(and oft *r*), and the rest utterly omitted. 866 29

repent
or deny the place of forgiveness to such as truly *r*. 870 37

repentance
has given clear proof of *r* and amendment of life. 409 11
Wherefore the grant of *r* is not to be denied 870 33
19 Of *R*. 875 11

repetition
whereas before, by reason of so often *r*, 867 12
secure continuity or avoid *r*. 934 19

repetitions
vain *r*, Commemorations, and Synodals, 866 18

replaced
and Readings may be *r* by those appointed 136 —

replaces
This service then *r* the Ministry of the Word, 437 6

reported
The death of a member of the Church should be *r* 468 2
The death of a member of the Church should be *r* 490 2

representative
and *r* presbyters of the diocese, stand 553 9
R clergy of the diocese present the Constitution 562 —
A Warden or other *r* of the congregation continues 568 11

representatives
R of the congregation bring the people's offerings 333 —
R of the congregation bring the people's offerings 361 —
R of the presbyterate, diaconate, and laity 511 9
R of the diocese, both Priests and Lay Persons, 513 —
R of the congregation and of the clergy 561 —
R of the congregation present a Bible, saying 561 —
Other *R* of the congregation present bread and wine, 562 —
R of the congregation or of the community, 565 18
appropriate that their *r* take part in the service, 577 2

represented
YHWH is *r* in capital and small capital letters: 583 29

repugnant
that it be *r* to another. 871 39
but rather *r* to the Word of God. 872 14
It is a thing plainly *r* to the Word of God, 872 22
but is *r* to the plain words of Scripture, 873 29
which be not *r* to the Word of God, 874 26

request
A newly inducted Priest may, at the bishop's *r*, 564 10

require
And *r* that it be received as such 8 10
or further than local circumstances *r*. 11 15
when the needs of the congregation so *r*. 13 11
may be altered by the bishop when circumstances *r*. 565 1
does not *r* that the premises be debt-free or owned. 575 4

required
may be *r* for the Communion of the sick, 408 29
In all such cases, the priest is *r* to notify the bishop, 409 24
In the Episcopal Church it is *r* 422 3
If the remaining Elements are not *r* 555 4
nor may be proved thereby, is not to be *r* of any man, 868 21
they do more for his sake, than of bounden duty is *r*: 870 22

requires
This rite *r* careful preparation by the Priest 400 3
r the following promise from the Bishop-elect 513 —
passages (Psalm 68:4 and Psalm 83:18), the context *r* 584 1

requireth
that a man may swear when the Magistrate *r*, 876 20

requisite
or be thought *r* or necessary to salvation. 868 22
all those things that of necessity are *r* to the same. 871 32

reserved
Holy Communion from the *r* Sacrament 275 —
from the *r* Sacrament, the following order is observed 282 —

Baptisms be *r* for these occasions 312 6
from the *r* Sacrament, using the following form. 396 —
from the *r* Sacrament in the following manner: 408 19
Communion is to be administered from the *r* 457 —
The blessing of an Altar is also *r* for a bishop, 577 18
the Lord's Supper was not by Christ's ordinance *r*, 873 34

resolution

r of all doubts, concerning the manner 867 18
R 11 877 30

resort

always *r* to the Bishop of the Diocese, 867 20

resources

41. For the Conservation of Natural *R* 811 23
41. For the Conservation of Natural *R* 827 —

respect

became independent with *r* to civil government, 10 25

respectful

to pay *r* obedience to the Civil Authority, 875 37

respective

alterations in some particulars, as in their *r* times 10 4
liberty to model and organize their *r* Churches, 10 28
fulfill the functions proper to their *r* orders, 13 18

respects

like us in all *r*, apart from sin; 864 8

respond

The People *r* 114 —
In Easter Season the People *r* 114 —
The People *r* 340 —
The People *r* 366 —
Here and after every petition the People *r* 389 —
Proclaim and *R* to the Word of God 400 8
The people *r*—Amen! 401 10
to which the People *r*, saying, Amen. 429 —
The People *r* to every petition with Amen. 480 —
The People *r* in these or other words 514 —
The People in a loud voice *r* 521 —
The People *r* in these or other words 527 —
The People in a loud voice *r* 534 —
The People *r* in these or other words 539 —
The People in a loud voice *r* 545 —
The bishop may *r*, indicating the place 576 13

responds

The Congregation *r* 434 7
If more than one person *r*, they do so together. 437 12
by planting in uncertain stories, Legends, *R*, 866 17
For this cause be cut off Anthems, *R*, 866 37

response

be added to the preceding versicle and *r*. 59 —
be added to the preceding versicle and *r*. 72 —
be added to the preceding versicle and *r*. 102 —
be added to the preceding versicle and *r*. 126 —
and its *r*, to the Collect of the Day. 142 20
make an appropriate *r*, as directed. 328 —
The proclamation and *r* may include readings, 400 9
A homily or other *r* to the Readings may follow. 426 —
the *r* of the people 513 —
be added to the dismissal and to the *r*. 523 —
be added to the dismissal and to the *r*. 535 —
be added to the dismissal and to the *r*. 547 —
the bishop, or other persons present, may speak in *r* 565 19
any authorized *r* to this Declaration, 877 22

responses

The customary *r* before and after the Gospel 272 —
The customary *r* before and after the Gospel 277 —
After the Sermon, and any *r* to it, 560 —
and one of the versicles and *r*, are used, 576 7
The *r* in italics may be omitted 821 6

responsibilities

and in their *r* as members of his Church. 298 27
commitment to the *r* of their Baptism 412 5
exercise this ministry, accepting its privileges and *r* 557 8

responsibility

or upon undertaking some special *r*. 420 —
It is also a special *r* of deacons 510 13

responsive

R recitation is the method which has been 582 27

responsively

The Leader and People pray *r* 387 —
The Leader and People pray *r* 392 —
sung *r* between a bishop and the congregation, 552 15

responsorial

R recitation is the name given to a method 582 19

rest

four Chapters were read out, all the *r* were unread. 866 19
(and oft repeated, and the *r* utterly omitted. 866 29
The *r* of the Book of Esther, 868 37
But all we the *r*, although baptized, 870 28

resting

the body is committed to its *r* place. 506 19

restitution

they have made *r* for the wrong they have done, 409 15

restoration

and the *r* of Invitatory Antiphons 582 22
11. For the *R* of Health 813 15
11. For the *R* of Health 841 —
and therefore as essential to the *r* of unity 877 12
Christian Bodies seeking the *r* of the organic unity 877 23

restored

The ancient praise-shout, "Hallelujah," has been *r*, 584 4
Christian unity...can be *r* only by the return 877 5

restrain

and *r* with the civil sword the stubborn 876 5

restricted

It is not *r* to times of sickness. 446 8

resurrection

dependent upon the movable date of the Sunday of the *R* 15 4
John 11:21–27 (I am the *r* and the life) 480 —
John 11:21–27 (I am the *r* and the life) 495 —

It finds all its meaning in the *r*. 507 3
IV. Of the *R* of Christ. 868 12
14 Of the *R* of Christ. 875 5

retained
The Baptism of young Children is in any wise to be *r* 873 20

reticence
The Hebrew reverence and *r* with regard to the Name 583 25

return
It may be found desirable to *r* to the front 313 9
the celebrant is to *r* to the Holy Table, 408 10
until he *r* to judge all Men at the last day. 868 15
the *r* of all Christian communions to the principles 877 6

reunion
to a newly created Joint Commission on Christian *R*. 877 28
by God's blessing made towards Home *R*: 877 32

revealed
(The glory that shall be *r*) 475 —
(The glory that shall be *r*) 495 —
the Old and New Testament as the *r* Word of God. 877 14

revelation
R 21:3 37 —
R 4:8 39 —
R 21:3 75 —
R 4:8 77 —
R 4:11; 5:9–10, 13 93 —
R 15:3–4 94 —
R 21:10, 22–24 (Easter) 108 16
R 22:1,4–5 (Saints' Days) 108 21
R 4:11 344 —
R 4:11 377 —
and his *r* of himself to his people; 402 —
and his *r* of himself to his people; 404 —
R 7:9–17 (God shall wipe away all tears) 475 —
R 21:2–7 (Behold, I make all things new) 475 —
R 7:9–17 (God will wipe away every tear) 495 —
R 21:2–7 (Behold, I make all things new) 495 —
Epistle *R* 21:2–7, or 1 Corinthians 3:1–11, 16–17, 571 —

reverence
the procuring of *r*, and the exciting of piety 10 11
The Hebrew *r* and reticence with regard to the Name 583 25

reverend
10 Of the *r* Estimation of God's Word. 875 13

reverent
Body and Blood of the Lord are shared in a *r* manner; 401 13

reverently
the deacon *r* places the consecrated Sacrament 408 21
r eat and drink it, 409 4

review
for a *r* was issued in the year 1689: 10 21
But while these alterations were in *r* 11 3
to take a further *r* of the Public Service, 11 6

reviews
Her general aim in these different *r* and alterations 10 8

revised
numeration of the *R* Standard Version of the Bible. 14 17

revision
until a *r* of them may be conveniently made, 875 18

revive
proper to *r* it by any new Commission. 10 23

revolution
Civil Rulers, in consequence of the *R*. 10 34

rhyme
which is not based on meter or *r*, 583 3

rich
strong and weak, *r* and poor. 557 12

riches
The *R* and Goods of Christians are not common, 876 13

right
with the woman to the *r* and the man to the left, 423 —
facing the woman and taking her *r* hand in his, 427 —
takes his *r* hand in hers, and says 427 —
Then the Celebrant joins the *r* hands 428 1
The Celebrant joins the *r* hands 434 —
sit to the *r* and left of the chief consecrator. 511 15
The other bishops stand to the *r* and left 520 —
the presbyters who stand to the *r* and left 533 —
38. For the *R* Use of God's Gifts 811 17
38. For the *R* Use of God's Gifts 827 —
For the *r* Faith is, that we believe and confess, 865 21
he sitteth on the *r* hand of the Father, 865 33
1 Of the *r* Use of the Church. 875 2
as touching the *r*, title, and possession of the same; 876 13

righteous
(The souls of the *r* are in the hands of God) 470 —
(The souls of the *r* are in the hands of God) 494 —
(The Lord knows the ways of the *r*; 583 7
We are accounted *r* before God, 870 2

righteousness
whereby man is very far gone from original *r*, 869 25

rightly
to everlasting salvation that he also believe *r* 865 19
diminished from such as by faith, and *r*, do receive 873 7
they that receive Baptism *r* are grafted 873 16
insomuch that to such as *r*, worthily, and with faith, 873 25
denunciation of the Church is *r* cut off from the unity 874 17
all such to be *r*, orderly, and lawfully consecrated 875 25

ring
The Priest may ask God's blessing on a *r* or rings 427 —
The giver places the *r* on the *r*-finger 427 —
If a *r* or rings are to be blessed, the wife extends 434 —
vows may be used in place of the *r*. 437 23
a *r*, staff, and mitre, or other suitable insignia 553 6

rings
The Priest may ask God's blessing on a ring or *r* 427 —
If a ring or *r* are to be blessed, the wife extends 434 —

rise

At whose coming all men shall *r* again 865 35
Christ did truly *r* again from death, 868 13

rite

celebrated in the context of a *R* One service, 14 4
R One 37 —
R One 61 —
R Two 75 —
a complete *r* in place of Evening Prayer, 108 4
R Two 115 —
In *R* One services of Morning Prayer 141 18
These omitted portions of the *r* may be administered 312 12
A Penitential Order: *R* One 319 —
The Holy Eucharist: *R* One 323 —
A Penitential Order: *R* Two 351 —
The Holy Eucharist: *R* Two 355 —
the forms may be conformed to the language of the *R* 383 —
This *r* requires careful preparation by the Priest 400 3
from *R* One or *R* Two, or one of the following forms 402 —
In *R* One services, the following form 406 8
The *R* begins as prescribed for celebrations 433 —
according to *R* One or *R* Two in this Book, 436 15
Concerning the *R* 446 1
R One 469 —
R Two 491 —
according to *R* One or *R* Two. 552 3
Likewise, suitable parts of this *r* may be used 566 5
Provisions for adapting the *r* to special circumstances 566 7

rites

and Administration of the Sacraments, and other *R* 8 8
and the *R* and Ceremonies appointed to be used 9 15
In addition to these services and the other *r* 13 7
a deacon to preside at other *r* also, 14 1
When there is no Baptism, the *r* of Confirmation, 412 11
for pastoral considerations, neither of the burial *r* 506 2
Preface to the Ordination *R* 510 1
by the rubrics in each of the ordination *r*. 552 11
Other Sacramental *R* 860 —
Moses, as touching Ceremonies and *R*, do not bind 869 11
The Church hath power to decree *R* or Ceremonies, 871 37
Ceremonies or *R* of the Church ordained 874 32
ordered according to the *R* of that Book, 875 31
ordered according to the same *R*; 875 33

rochet

The bishop-elect is vested in a *r* or alb, 511 16

rock

(Like a wise man who built his house upon the *r*) 426 21

Rogation

The *R* Days, traditionally observed on Monday, 18 8
especially in Lent and on *R* days. 148 —
week are the traditional *R* Days. 174 —
19. For *R* Days 207 —
week are the traditional *R* Days. 225 —
19. For *R* Days 258 —
17 For the *R*-days. 875 9

roles

Specific *r* may be assigned 273 —
Specific *r* may be assigned 277 —

Romans

1 Corinthians 5:7–8; *R* 6:9–11; 46 —
R 15:13 60 —
3 *R* 15:13 73 —
1 Corinthians 5:7–8; *R* 6:9–11; 83 —
15 *R* 15:13 102 —
R 5:54 105 —
R 15:13 126 —
Epistle *R* 6:3–11 295 —
R 12:1 343 —
R 12:1 376 —
R 8:14–19, 34–35, 37–39 475 —
R 8:14–19, 34–35, 37–39 495 —
Epistle *R* 12:1–18, or Ephesians 4:7, 11–16 560 —

Rome

R hath erred, not only in their living 871 34
The Bishop of *R* hath no jurisdiction in this Realm 876 7

Romish

The *R* Doctrine concerning Purgatory, 872 12

rooms

John 14:1–6 (In my Father's house are many *r*) 495 —

rose

r again the third day from the dead. 865 32

royal

The original Article given *R* assent in 1571 869 19

rubrical

as set forth in the *r* directions for each service. 13 19

rubrics

Hymns referred to in the *r* of this Book 14 6
When *r* indicate that a part of a service 14 11
Disciplinary *R* 409 7
In either case, the *r* of the service of ordination 552 4
by the *r* in each of the ordination rites. 552 11
and perform other actions as indicated in the *r*. 558 15

rule

her Book of Common Prayer, laid it down as a *r*, 9 14
that is, that they should *r* all estates 876 4
and as being the *r* and ultimate standard of faith. 877 34

rulers

necessary in the prayers for our Civil *R*, 10 34
namely, that "*R* may have grace, wisdom, 10 36

rules

Unless otherwise ordered in the preceding *r* 16 23
Subject to the *r* of precedence 17 29
a saint is observed in accordance with the *r* 195 —
For optional use, when desired, subject to the *r* 199 —
a saint is observed in accordance with the *r* 246 —
For optional use, when desired, subject to the *r* 251 —
hardness of the *R* called the Pie, 866 30
but that of necessity there must be some *r*: 866 40
certain *r* are here set forth, 866 41
and for that the *r* be few and easy. 867 5

rung

Bells may now be *r* and music played. 574 2

rural

34. For Towns and *R* Areas 811 13
34. For Towns and *R* Areas 825 —

Ruth

R, The Second Book of Esdras, 868 33

S

sacrament

Communion from the reserved *S* on Good Friday, 275 —
S for that purpose is consecrated 275 —
from the reserved *S*, the following order 282 —
Communion from the *S* previously consecrated. 284 29
Baptism should be recognized at a public celebration of the *S* 314 6
assisting in the ministration of the *S* 322 13
The ministers receive the *S* in both kinds, 338 —
assisting in the ministration of the *S* 354 13
The ministers receive the *S* in both kinds, 365 —
may be communicated from the reserved *S*, 396 —
The *S* is administered with the following 399 —
S that remains is then consumed. 401 14
at the time of the administration of the *S* 407 11
The celebrant receives the *S* in both kinds. 407 23
the *S* may be received in both kinds 407 26
to the congregation from the reserved *S* 408 19
deacon reverently places the consecrated *S* 408 21
from the reserved *S*, the form for Communion 457 —
it is suitable to administer the *S* 457 —
If a person desires to receive the *S*, 457 —
even though the *S* is not received 457 —
associates and fellow ministers of the *S*, 524 16
deacon assists in the distribution of the *S*, 536 15
as fellow ministers of the *S*. 553 10
deacons may be appointed to carry the *S* 555 1
but rather it is a *S* of our Redemption 873 24
overthroweth the nature of a *S*, 873 30
The *S* of the Lord's Supper was not 873 34
(as Saint Augustine saith) the *S* 873 38
do eat and drink the sign or *S* 873 40
for both the parts of the Lord's *S*, 874 3
15 Of the worthy receiving of the *S* 875 6

sacramental

Other *S* Rites 860 —

sacraments

and Administration of the *S*, 8 8
administering his holy *S*. 510 12
The *S* 857 —
God is preached, and the *S* be duly ministered 871 31
or ministering the *S* in the Congregation, 872 17
or to minister the *S*, in a tongue not understanded 872 23
XXV. Of the *S*. 872 25
S ordained of Christ be not only badges 872 26
There are two *S* ordained of Christ 872 30
Those five commonly called *S*, 872 32
are not to be counted for *S* of the Gospel, 872 33
have not like nature of *S* with Baptism, 872 35
The *S* were not ordained of Christ 872 37
hinders not the effect of the *S*. 873 1
authority in the Ministration of the Word and *S*, 873 3
and in receiving the *S*. 873 6
rightly, do receive the *S* ministered unto them; 873 8
9 That Common Prayers and *S* 875 11
ministering either of God's Word, or of the *S*, 876 1
3. The two *S*,—Baptism and the Supper 877 16
(c) The two *S* ordained by Christ Himself 878 1

sacred

are admitted to these *s* orders 510 17
suitable for the conferring of the *s* orders 510 31
it is desirable that *s* vessels 575 15
form of *s* song in the Daily Office. 582 24
considered too *s* to be pronounced; 583 19
As inherent parts of this *s* deposit, 877 12

sacrifice

Abraham's *s* of Isaac 289 2
reconcile his Father to us, and to be a *s*, 868 7
who, by *s* of himself once made, 870 27

sacrifices

Wherefore the *s* of Masses, 874 8

sad

Deeply grieved by the *s* divisions 877 20

safe

For a *s* delivery 444 —

said

do hereby establish the *s* Book: 8 9
she further declares in her *s* Preface, 10 9
that a part of a service is to be "*s*," 14 11
Confession of Sin may then be *s*; 41 —
Antiphons may be sung or *s* 43 —
the following is sung or *s*. 45 4
At the end of the Psalms is sung or *s* 46 —
is sung or *s* after each Reading. 47 —
Then may be *s* 59 —
Confession of Sin may then be *s*; 62 —
an Invitatory Psalm, may be sung or *s* 64 —
At the end of the Psalms is sung or *s* 64 —
is sung or *s* after each Reading. 65 —
Then may be *s* 72 —
Confession of Sin may then be *s*; 79 —
Antiphons may be sung or *s* 80 —
the following is sung or *s*. 83 —
At the end of the Psalms is sung or *s* 84 —
is sung or *s* after each Reading. 84 —
Then may be *s* 102 —
following Psalms is sung or *s*. 103 —
At the end of the Psalms is sung or *s* 105 —
The following Confession of Sin may then be *s*; 116 —
an Invitatory Psalm, may be sung or *s* 117 —
At the end of the Psalms is sung or *s* 118 —
is sung or *s* after each Reading. 119 —
Then may be *s* 126 —
One or more of the following Psalms are sung or *s*. 128 —
At the end of the Psalms is sung or *s* 131 —
Antiphon, which is sung or *s* by all 134 —
and the other parts *s* in unison, 136 —
the Apostles' Creed may be *s*. 137 —

The following may be *s*	140	—
Gloria Patri is always sung or *s*	141	11
To be *s* or sung, kneeling, standing,	148	—
When the Litany is sung or *s*	153	—
The following Psalm is then sung or *s*	265	—
or some other suitable anthem is sung or *s*,	270	—
or some other suitable anthem may then be sung or *s*	271	—
other appropriate Collect is *s*	271	—
or other suitable anthems may be sung or *s*	274	—
(page 484 or 492) is sung or *s*.	283	—
or some other suitable Collect, may be *s*.	288	—
The Lord's Prayer is then *s*.	314	1
The Decalogue, page 317, may be *s*,	319	—
Ten Commandments (page 317) may be *s*,	324	—
Here is sung or *s*	324	—
song of praise is sung or *s*,	324	—
A Confession of Sin is *s* here	330	—
Here a Proper Preface is sung or *s*	334	—
Then may be sung or *s*	337	—
or some other suitable anthem may be sung or *s*	337	—
The following prayer may be *s*.	337	—
Here a Proper Preface is sung or *s*	341	—
The Decalogue may be *s*,	351	—
song of praise is sung or *s*,	356	—
A Confession of Sin is *s* here	359	—
Penitential Order on page 351 may be *s*.	359	—
Here a Proper Preface is sung or *s*	361	—
Then may be sung or *s*	364	—
Here a Proper Preface is sung or *s*	367	—
The Lord's Prayer is *s*,	398	—
postcommunion prayers is then *s*,	399	—
The Great Thanksgiving is *s* by the Priest	401	8
When the Great Litany is sung or *s*	406	3
(or "Lord, have mercy") may be sung or *s*	406	9
"Holy God," may be sung or *s* three times,	406	11
hymn used in place of it, is sung or *s*	406	12
Prayers of the People may be *s*.	406	26
blessing, may be *s* by a deacon,	407	6
The Lord's Prayer is then *s*,	408	23
Psalm, hymn, or anthem may be sung or *s*.	426	—
the following is *s*	432	—
psalm, prayer, or hymn to be *s*,	446	24
following general confession may be *s*	454	18
The following anthem is *s*	455	—
the Lord's Prayer is now *s*.	456	—
One of the usual postcommunion prayers is *s*,	457	—
Time of Death may be *s*,	465	—
a suitable psalm or anthem may be sung or *s*.	467	—
Committal may be *s* in the church.	468	11
are sung or *s* as the body	468	23
following anthems is sung or *s*.	469	—
following Psalms may be sung or *s*	470	—
the following Psalms may be sung or *s*.	475	—
The Apostles' Creed may be *s*,	480	—
the Lord's Prayer is *s* here,	480	—
prayer, the following is *s*	482	—
or a hymn, may be sung or *s*	482	—
anthems may be sung or *s*	483	—
The following anthem is sung or *s*	484	—
Then may be *s*	486	—
Committal may be *s* in the church.	490	11
are sung or *s* as the body	490	23
following anthems is sung or *s*.	491	—
The Apostles' Creed may then be *s*,	496	—
the Lord's Prayer is *s* here,	496	—
prayer, the following is *s*	498	—
or a hymn, may be sung or *s*	499	—
anthems may be sung or *s*	500	—
on pages 491–492 is sung or *s*	501	—
Then may be *s*	502	—
Scripture or psalms may be sung or *s*,	506	7
prayer, the following is *s*	535	—
prayer, the following is *s*	546	—
words "Receive this Bible . . ." are to be *s*	554	6
words "Receive this Bible . . ." are also to be *s*	554	27
The Litany may be sung or *s* standing	565	6
If the Apostles' Creed has not already been *s*,	572	—
Nicene Creed is now *s* or sung.	572	—
the appropriate prayer may be *s*,	577	11
have been daily *s* (and oft repeated)	866	28
commonly *s*, that the Priest did offer Christ	874	9
suspends the order for the reading of *s* Homilies	875	17
consecrated or ordered according to *s* Form,	875	24
such introduction as, "N. *s* (to N.)."	888	28
antiphons may be sung or *s*	935	10

saint

S John the Baptist	16	27
S Mary the Virgin	17	2
S Michael and All Angels	17	3
S Stephen	17	4
S James of Jerusalem	17	4
S Joseph	17	6
S Mary Magdalene	17	7
S Andrew November 30	185	—
S Thomas December 21	185	—
S Stephen December 26	186	—
S John December 27	186	—
Confession of *S* Peter January 18	187	—
Conversion of *S* Paul January 25	187	—
S Matthias February 24	188	—
S Joseph March 19	188	—
S Mark April 25	188	—
S Philip and *S* James May 1	189	—
S Barnabas June 11	189	—
The Nativity of *S* John the Baptist June 24	190	—
S Peter and *S* Paul June 29	190	—
S Mary Magdalene July 22	191	—
S James July 25	191	—
S Mary the Virgin August 15	192	—
S Bartholomew August 24	192	—
S Matthew September 21	192	—
S Michael and All Angels September 29	193	—
S Luke October 18	193	—
S James of Jerusalem October 23	193	—
S Simon and *S* Jude October 28	194	—
The festival of a *s* is observed	195	—
a) at the commemoration of a *s*	195	—
patronal festival or commemoration of a *s*	195	—
Preface of a *S*	196	—
Preface of a *S*	197	—
Preface of a *S*, or of Trinity Sunday	197	—
Preface of a *S*	198	—
Of a *S*	198	—

Preface of a *S*	199	—
S Andrew November 30	237	—
S Thomas December 21	237	—
S Stephen December 26	237	—
S John December 27	238	—
Confession of *S* Peter January 18	238	—
Conversion of *S* Paul January 25	238	—
S Matthias February 24	239	—
S Joseph March 19	239	—
S Mark April 25	240	—
S Philip and *S* James May 1	240	—
S Barnabas June 11	241	—
The Nativity of *S* John the Baptist June 24	241	—
S Peter and *S* Paul June 29	241	—
S Mary Magdalene July 22	242	—
S James July 25	242	—
S Mary the Virgin August 15	243	—
S Bartholomew August 24	243	—
S Matthew September 21	244	—
S Michael and All Angels September 29	244	—
S Luke October 18	244	—
S James of Jerusalem October 23	245	—
S Simon and *S* Jude October 28	245	—
The festival of a *s* is observed	246	—
a) at the commemoration of a *s*	246	—
patronal festival or commemoration of a *s*	246	—
Preface of a *S*	247	—
Preface of a *S*	248	—
Preface of a *S*, or of Trinity Sunday	249	—
Preface of a *S*	249	—
Of a *S*	250	—
Preface of a *S*	250	—
A *S*	348	—
(with commemoration of a *s* when appropriate)	359	—
A *S*	380	—
(with commemoration of a *s* when appropriate)	383	—
The Creed of *S* Athanasius	864	21
and sin (as *S* John saith) was not in him.	870	28
damnation, as *S* Paul saith.	872	40
with their teeth (as *S* Augustine saith)	873	38

saints

All *S'* Day, November 1	15	16
All *S'* Day may always be observed	15	20
the Epiphany, and All *S'* Day.	17	19
Other Commemorations, using the Common of *S*	18	4
All *S* and other Major *S'* Days	40	1
On All *S* and other Major *S'* Days	44	—
All *S* and other Major *S'* Days	77	—
On All *S* and other Major *S'* Days	82	—
Colossians 1:9, 11–14 (*S'* Days)	108	19
1 Peter 2:9 (*S'* Days)	108	20
Revelation 22:1,4–5 (*S'* Days)	108	21
Festivals of *S*	111	10
for Sundays, Holy Days, the Common of *S*,	136	—
Directions concerning the Common of *S*	158	24
Preface of All *S*	189	—
Preface of All *S*	191	—
Preface of All *S*	193	—
All *S'* Day November 1	194	—
Preface of All *S*	194	—
The Common of *S*	195	—
Preface of All *S*	240	—
Preface of All *S*	242	—
Preface of All *S*	245	—
All *S'* Day November 1	245	—
Preface of All *S*	245	—
The Common of *S*	246	—
on All *S'* Day or the Sunday after All *S'* Day,	312	3
All *S*	347	—
All *S*	380	—
4. For the *S* and Faithful Departed	813	4
4. For the *S* and Faithful Departed	838	—
the prayer "O God, the King of *S*,"	838	—
also Invocation of *S*, is a fond thing,	872	13

saith

other Books (as Hierome *s*) the Church doth read	868	34
whereas Christ *s* plainly,	870	22
and sin (as Saint John *s*) was not in him.	870	28
damnation, as Saint Paul *s*.	872	40
with their teeth (as Saint Augustine *s*) the Sacrament	873	38

sake

majestic manner, for the *s* of Jesus Christ,	11	22
who Suffer for the *s* of Conscience	811	4
who suffer for the *s* of Conscience	823	—
they do more for his *s*, than of bounden duty	870	22

Salisbury

some following *S* use,	867	9

salutation

Eucharist, beginning with the *S*	112	—
may pass at once from the *s*	142	19
the Eucharist begins with the *S*	153	—
and continues with the *S*	175	—
and continues with the *S*	227	—
Celebrant begins the liturgy with the *S*	264	—
celebration begins with the *S*	272	—
opening versicles and before the *s*	312	19
Eucharist begins with the *S*	406	5
opening versicles and before the *s*	412	14
bishop always stands for the *s*	565	7

salvation

S offered freely to all	290	6
Celebrant now praises God for the *s*	403	—
Celebrant now praises God for the *s*	404	—
begotten, for us men and for our *s*,	864	10
it is necessary to everlasting *s*	865	19
Who suffered for our *s*,	865	32
Sufficiency of the Holy Scriptures for *S*.	868	19
Scripture containeth all things necessary to *s*:	868	20
be thought requisite or necessary to *s*.	868	22
bring them by Christ to everlasting *s*,	871	5
confirm their faith of eternal *S*	871	15
XVIII. Of obtaining eternal *S*	871	24
any thing to be believed for necessity of *S*.	871	42
things ordained by them as necessary to *s*	872	9
necessary to *s*," and as being the rule	877	34

same

received as such by all the members of the *s*:	8	11
The *s* Church hath not only in her Preface,	9	22
body and essential parts of the *s*	10	6

Gospel be read from the *s* lectern, 406 18
The priest shall follow the *s* procedure 409 12
At the *s* time the Bishop prays 533 —
priests, if any, who serve in the *s* congregation 558 11
the *s* Son, our Lord Jesus Christ, 864 5
and at the *s* time of one substance with us 864 7
one and the *s* Christ, Son, Lord, 864 11
but one and the *s* Son and Only-begotten 864 15
the *s* was not ordained, but of a good purpose, 866 7
and have profit by hearing the *s*, 866 24
order, whereby the *s* shall be redressed. 866 34
Scriptures, or that which is evidently grounded upon the *s*; 867 2
may arise in the use and practicing of the *s*: 867 17
for the quieting and appeasing of the *s*; 867 21
so that the *s* order be not contrary 867 21
they may say the *s* in any language 867 26
parish Churches, and Chapels to the *s* annexed, 867 28
things that of necessity are requisite to the *s*. 871 32
ought not to decree any thing against the *s*, 871 41
besides the *s* ought it not to enforce 871 41
and sent to execute the *s*. 872 18
And in such only as worthily receive the *s*, 872 38
they do not the *s* in their own name, 873 4
worthily, and with faith, receive the *s*, 873 25
as they shall judge the *s* to serve better 874 14
Edward the Sixth, and confirmed at the *s* time 875 28
hereafter shall be consecrated or ordered to the *s* 875 32
title, and possession of the *s*; 876 14
when the *s* congregation attends two or more 888 8
the *s* Lessons are to be read 888 9
When the *s* congregation is present for 888 12
longer and shorter version, usually from the *s* Psalm. 888 19
identical with a Lesson appointed for the *s* day 888 24
may be used on any other day in the *s* week, 934 30

Samuel

or 2 *S* 6:12–15, 17–19 571 —
The First Book of *S*, 868 26
The Second Book of *S*, 868 27

sanctification

For the *S* of Illness 460 —

Sanctus

If the *S* is to be included, it is introduced 402 —
If the *S* is to be included, it is introduced 404 —
words which follow the *S*, and ending 408 15

satisfaction

perfect redemption, propitiation, and *s*, 874 6
there is none other *s* for sin, 874 8

satisfactory

found a *s* method of chanting them. 582 12

satisfying

This is probably the most *s* method for reciting 582 17

Saturday

Good Friday, and Holy *S*; 18 13
and *S* of this week are the traditional winter 160 —
and *S* of this week are the traditional spring 166 —
Holy *S* 170 —
S in Easter Week 172 —
and *S* of this week are the traditional summer 176 —
and *S* after September 14 are 182 —
and *S* of this week are the traditional winter 212 —
and *S* of this week are the traditional spring 218 —
Holy *S* 221 —
S in Easter Week 224 —
and *S* of this week are the traditional summer 227 —
and *S* after September 14 are 233 —
Holy *S* 283 —
a convenient time between sunset on Holy *S* 284 3
Prayers for Friday, *S*, and Sunday, 812 26
Prayers for Friday, *S*, and Sunday, 833 —

Saturdays

S after the First Sunday in Lent, 18 6
A Collect for *S* 56 —
A Collect for *S* 69 —
A Collect for *S* 99 —
A Collect for *S* 123 —
A Collect for *S* 134 —
Especially suitable for *S* 201 —
Especially suitable for *S* 252 —

save

with the versicle "O God, make speed to *s* us" 61 —
continue at once with "O God, make speed to *s* us." 62 —
with the versicle "O God, make speed to *s* us" 115 —
continue at once with "O God, make speed to *s* us." 116 —

saved

Whosoever will be *s*, before all things 864 22
He therefore that will be *s* must thus think 865 18
except a man believe faithfully, he cannot be *s*. 865 39
accursed that presume to say, That every man shall be *s* 871 25
Jesus Christ, whereby men must be *s*. 871 28

Savior

the words our *S* Christ hath (has) taught us." 408 24

Saviour

Jesus Christ, our blessed Lord and *S*. 11 23
only for the merit of our Lord and *S* 870 2
1. Our earnest desire that the *S*'s prayer, 876 29

say

After each Lesson the Reader may *s* 47 —
Or the Reader may *s* 47 —
After each Lesson the Reader may *s* 65 —
Or the Reader may *s* 65 —
After each Lesson the Reader may *s* 84 —
Or the Reader may *s* 84 —
After each Lesson the Reader may *s* 119 —
Or the Reader may *s* 119 —
The Officiant may then *s* 127 —
the Officiant and People *s* together 153 —
Immediately before the Collect, the Celebrant may *s* 276 —
The Celebrant may *s* the following prayer 285 —
the Celebrant may *s* to the people 294 —
After each Reading, the Reader may *s* 300 —
or the Reader may *s* 300 —
The people standing, the Celebrant may *s* 323 —
After each Reading, the Reader may *s* 325 —

or the Reader may *s*	325	—
A Minister may then *s* one or more of the following	332	—
the Celebrant may *s* the following Invitation	338	—
The Celebrant may *s*	355	—
After each Reading, the Reader may *s*	357	—
or the Reader may *s*	357	—
The Celebrant may *s* the following Invitation	399	—
After each Reading the Reader may *s*	414	—
or the Reader may *s*	414	—
The Celebrant may *s* to the people	431	—
Then one or both parents *s* these or similar words	441	—
The Priest may then *s* one or more of these	449	—
Then the Celebrant may *s*	486	—
After each Reading, the Reader may *s*	516	—
or the Reader may *s*	516	—
Then all sing or *s* together	519	—
hands upon the head of the bishop-elect, and *s*	521	—
After each Reading, the Reader may *s*	529	—
or the Reader may *s*	529	—
After each Reading, the Reader may *s*	541	—
or the Reader may *s*	541	—
hands upon the head of each ordinand, and *s*	554	21
One, appointed by the bishop, is to *s*	554	31
standing before the bishop with the new minister, *s*	559	—
kneel in the midst of the church, and *s*	562	—
So are we forbidden by the Catholic Religion, to *s*,	865	7
repetition, they could *s* many things by heart:	867	13
but when men *s* Matins and Evensong privately,	867	25
they may *s* the same in any language	867	25
two whole and perfect Natures, that is to *s*,	868	4
(as the School-authors *s*) deserve grace of congruity:	870	15
s, We are unprofitable servants.	870	23
and if we *s* we have no sin,	870	29
condemned, which *s*, they can no more sin	870	36
accursed that presume to *s*, That every man	871	25
that is to *s*, Baptism,	872	30
Those five commonly called Sacraments, that is to *s*,	872	32

saying

are read, the Reader first *s*	47	—
are read, the Reader first *s*	64	—
are read, the Reader first *s*	84	—
or some other suitable prayer, first *s*	110	—
are read, the Reader first *s*	118	—
may add other Prayers, and end the Litany, *s*	154	—
invites the people to the observance of a holy Lent, *s*	264	—
pausing three times and singing or *s*	285	—
the Reader first *s*	300	—
Deacon or a Priest reads the Gospel, first *s*	300	—
Celebrant addresses the congregation, *s*	303	—
The Celebrant blesses the water, first *s*	306	—
placing hand on the vessel of oil, and *s*	307	—
pours water upon, the candidate, *s*	307	—
full sight of the congregation, prays over them, *s*	308	—
sign of the cross [using Chrism if desired] and *s*	308	—
pour water on him or her, *s*	313	25
are read, the Reader first *s*	325	—
Deacon or a Priest reads the Gospel, first *s*	326	—
one or more of the following sentences, first *s*	332	—
The People may join in *s* this prayer	337	—
The People may join in *s* this prayer	339	—
the Reader first *s*	357	—
Deacon or a Priest reads the Gospel, first *s*	357	—
The Lord's Prayer is said, the Celebrant first *s*	398	—
consecrate more of either or both, by *s*	408	11
consecrate more of both kinds, *s* again	408	13
2. The Lord's Prayer is then said, the deacon first *s*,	408	23
the Reader first *s*	414	—
Deacon or a Priest reads the Gospel, first *s*	414	—
the Bishop addresses the congregation, *s*	416	—
The Celebrant then addresses the congregation, *s*	425	—
to which the People respond, *s*, Amen.	429	—
The Celebrant then addresses the husband, *s*	433	—
The Celebrant then addresses the wife, *s*	433	—
The Celebrant then addresses the congregation, *s*	434	—
gives the child to the mother or father, *s*	441	—
appropriate verses of Scripture, first *s*	449	—
extends a hand over the penitent), *s*	451	—
sign of the cross on the sick person's forehead, *s*	456	—
the following Collects, first *s*	469	—
reads the Gospel, first *s*	479	—
Deacon or other Minister may dismiss them, *s*	483	—
reads the Gospel, first *s*	495	—
Deacon or other Minister may dismiss them, *s*	500	—
present the bishop-elect, *s*	513	—
or the following Collect, or both, first *s*	515	—
Deacon or a Priest reads the Gospel, first *s*	516	—
The new Bishop blesses the people, first *s*	523	—
present the ordinand, *s*	526	—
or the following Collect, or both, first *s*	527	—
a Priest reads the Gospel, first *s*	529	—
gives a Bible to the newly ordained, *s*	534	—
present the ordinand, *s*	538	—
or the following Collect, or both, first *s*	539	—
a Priest reads the Gospel, first *s*	541	—
gives a Bible to the newly ordained, *s*	545	—
or some other Collect, first *s*	560	—
Representatives of the congregation present a Bible, *s*	561	—
The Bishop presents a vessel of water, *s*	561	—
Others present a stole or other symbol, *s*	561	—
Others present a book of prayers or other symbol, *s*	561	—
Others present olive oil or some other symbol, *s*	561	—
Warden may now present the keys of the church, *s*	562	—
Canons of this Church, *s*	562	—
present bread and wine, *s*	562	—
the new minister to the congregation, *s*	563	—
threshold with the sign of the cross *s*	568	—
in addition to *s* the prayer over the font	575	25
there hath been great diversity in *s* and singing	867	8
Neither that any man shall be bound to the *s* of them,	867	27

says

The Officiant *s* to the people	41	—
The priest alone stands and *s*	42	—
The Officiant then *s* one or more of the following	55	—
The Officiant *s* to the people	62	—
The Priest alone stands and *s*	63	—
The Officiant then *s* one or more of the following	68	—
The Officiant *s* to the people	79	—
The Priest alone stands and *s*	80	—
The Officiant then *s* one or more of the following	98	—
The Officiant then *s* one of the following Collects.	107	—
The Officiant then *s* the Prayer for Light,	110	—
The Officiant *s* to the people	116	—

The Priest alone stands and *s*	117	—
The Officiant then *s* one or more of the following	122	—
The Officiant then *s*	128	—
The Officiant then *s* one of the following Collects	133	—
If ashes are to be imposed, the Celebrant *s*	265	—
or the Priest, stands and, facing the people, *s*	269	—
The Celebrant then *s* the following blessing	271	—
or other person appointed, *s* to the people	277	—
Celebrant *s* the Collects.	277	—
sings or *s* the Exsultet, as follows	286	—
The Celebrant then *s*	294	—
The Celebrant *s* one of the following Collects	295	—
s the Thanksgiving over the Water;	298	10
The people standing, the Celebrant *s*	299	—
After the Gospel, the Reader *s*	300	—
The Celebrant *s*	301	—
When there are others to be presented, the Bishop *s*	303	—
The Celebrant then *s* these or similar words	303	—
The Celebrant then *s* to the congregation	305	—
The Celebrant *s*	306	—
When all have been baptized, the Celebrant *s*	308	—
The Bishop *s* to the congregation	309	—
Then the Bishop *s*	309	—
The Bishop lays hands upon each one and *s*	309	—
Then the Bishop *s*	310	—
The Celebrant then *s*	311	—
The people standing, the Celebrant *s*	319	—
The Deacon or Celebrant then *s*	320	—
The Bishop when present, or the Priest, stands and *s*	321	—
The Celebrant *s*	323	—
The Celebrant *s* to the people	325	—
The Celebrant *s* the Collect.	325	—
After the Gospel, the Reader *s*	326	—
The Deacon or other person appointed *s*	328	—
The Deacon or Celebrant *s* the following,	330	—
or the Priest, stands and *s*	332	—
The Celebrant *s* to the people	332	—
bishop or priest, faces them and sings or *s*	333	—
After Communion, the Celebrant *s*	339	—
bishop or priest, faces them and sings or *s*	340	—
The people standing, the Celebrant *s*	351	—
The Deacon or Celebrant then *s*	352	—
The Bishop when present, or the Priest, stands and *s*	353	—
The people standing, the Celebrant *s*	355	—
The Celebrant *s* to the people	357	—
The Celebrant *s* the Collect	357	—
After the Gospel, the Reader *s*	358	—
The Deacon or Celebrant *s*	360	—
The Bishop when present, or the Priest, stands and *s*	360	—
The Celebrant *s* to the people	360	—
bishop or priest, faces them and sings or *s*	361	—
Facing the people, the Celebrant *s* the following	364	—
After Communion, the Celebrant *s*	365	—
bishop or priest, faces them and sings or *s*	367	—
bishop or priest, faces them and sings or *s*	369	—
bishop or priest, faces them and sings or *s*	372	—
The Priest alone *s*	398	—
The people standing, the Bishop *s*	413	—
After the Gospel, the Reader *s*	415	—
The Bishop *s*	415	—
The Bishop then *s* these or similar words	416	—
The Bishop then *s* to the congregation	417	—
Then the Bishop *s*	418	—
The Bishop lays hands upon each one and *s*	418	—
After this, the Celebrant *s* these or similar words	420	—
The Celebrant then *s* this or some other	421	—
addresses the congregation and *s*	423	—
Then the Celebrant *s* to the persons to be married	424	—
The Celebrant *s* to the woman	424	—
The Celebrant *s* to the man	424	—
The Celebrant then *s* to the people	425	—
the Deacon or Minister appointed *s*	426	—
After the Gospel, the Reader *s*	426	—
and taking her right hand in his, *s*	427	—
takes his right hand in hers, and *s*	427	—
ring-finger of the other's hand and *s*	427	—
joins the right hands of husband and wife and *s*	428	—
All standing, the Celebrant *s*	428	—
the Priest *s* one of the following prayers	430	—
husband extends his hand) toward the Priest, who *s*	434	—
joins the right hands of the husband and wife and *s*	434	—
The Celebrant *s*	441	—
The Celebrant then *s* this prayer	443	—
The Priest *s*	447	—
The Penitent *s*	450	—
The Priest alone *s*	455	—
Anointing of the Sick is to be blessed, the Priest *s*	455	—
Priest then lays hands upon the sick person, and *s*	455	—
The Officiant *s* this Collect	464	—
meets the body at the door of the church and *s*	466	—
Silence may be kept; after which the Celebrant *s*	466	—
Silence may be kept; after which the Celebrant *s*	467	—
The Celebrant *s* one of the following Collects,	469	—
At the end of the Gospel, the Reader *s*	480	—
The Deacon or other leader *s*	480	—
The Celebrant, facing the body, *s*	483	—
Then, while earth is cast upon the coffin, the Celebrant *s*	485	—
The Celebrant *s*	485	—
The Celebrant then *s*	493	—
Silence may be kept; after which the Celebrant *s*	493	—
At the end of the Gospel, the Reader *s*	495	—
The Celebrant, facing the body, *s*	499	—
Then, while earth is cast upon the coffin, the Celebrant *s*	501	—
The Celebrant *s*	501	—
The people standing, the Bishop appointed *s*	512	—
The Bishop then *s*	512	—
The Presiding Bishop then *s* the following,	513	—
The Presiding Bishop then *s*	514	—
The Reader first *s*	516	—
After the Gospel, the Reader *s*	516	—
The Presiding Bishop then *s*	519	—
The new Bishop then *s*	522	—
The people standing, the Bishop *s*	525	—
The Bishop *s* to the ordinand	526	—
The Bishop *s* to the people	527	—
The Reader first *s*	528	—
After the Gospel, the Reader *s*	529	—
The Congregation then *s* or sings the Nicene Creed	529	—
The Bishop then *s* this Prayer of Consecration.	533	—
The new Priest then *s* to the congregation	534	—
The new Priest *s*	535	—
The people standing, the Bishop *s*	537	—

The Bishop *s* to the ordinand 538 —
All stand. The Bishop *s* to the people 539 —
The Reader first *s* 540 —
After the Gospel, the Reader *s* 541 —
The Congregation then *s* or sings the Nicene Creed. 541 —
The Bishop then *s* this Prayer of Consecration 545 —
The Bishop then *s* to the congregation 546 —
the Bishop who is presiding stands and *s* 551 —
The Bishop *s* the appointed Collect. 551 —
bishop alone *s* over each ordinand 553 32
The Bishop then *s* 559 —
The Bishop, standing, *s* 560 —
At the end of the litany, the Bishop, standing, *s* 560 —
The Bishop then *s* 562 —
The new Minister then *s* to the people 563 —
When all are ready, the Bishop *s* the following 567 5
Standing at the door of the church, the Bishop *s* 568 —
Bishop moves to the Font, lays a hand upon it, and *s* 569 —
the Bishop *s* 570 —
Facing the Font, the Bishop *s* 570 —
proceeds to the Lectern, lays a hand upon it, and *s* 570 —
Bishop goes to the Pulpit, lays a hand upon it, and *s* 571 —
Bishop proceeds to an appropriate place, and *s* 572 —
The Bishop then *s* 573 —
The Bishop goes to the Table and, with arms extended, *s* 573 —
The Bishop *s* to the people 574 —

scandal

have done wrong to their neighbors and are a *s* 409 13

schism

to discountenance *s*, to heal 877 2

school

If the place of public worship is also to serve as a *s* 576 29
(as the *S*-authors say) deserve grace of congruity: 870 15

schools

31. For *S* and Colleges 811 10
31. For *S* and Colleges 824 —

scriptural

S citations in this Book, except for the Psalms, 14 16

scripture

or from Holy *S*, may be used when the needs 13 10
Holy *S*, or from this Book, or from texts congruent 14 8
S, or with the versicle "O Lord, 37 —
one or more of the following sentences of *S*, 61 —
S, or with the versicle "Lord, open 75 —
or some other suitable passage of *S*, is read 105 —
or some other Short Lesson of *S* 109 —
one or more of the following sentences of *S*, 115 —
or some other suitable passage of *S*, is read 131 —
Any of the opening sentences of *S*, 141 3
or from other passages of *S* may be used 141 9
When one or more *S* Lessons are to be read 143 8
The Celebrant may introduce the *S* readings 288 —
or with some other sentence of *S*. 333 —
or some other appropriate sentence of *S*, 343 —
or with some other sentence of *S*. 361 —
or some other appropriate sentence of *S*, 376 —
priest or deacon, reads a passage of *S* 396 —
the following passages from Holy *S* is read. 426 —
one of which is always from Holy *S*, 435 15
may conveniently hear the reading of *S*. 437 15
A passage from *S* may first be read. 439 13
or other appropriate verses of *S*, 449 —
or other passages of *S* are read 453 13
of the following passages from Holy *S* is read. 494 —
2. Anthems from Holy *S* or psalms 506 7
4. One or more passages of Holy *S* are read. 506 10
there may be one or two Readings from *S*. 565 10
(by daily hearing of holy *S* read in the Church) 866 13
After a like sort were other books of holy *S* used. 866 22
the reading of holy *S* is so set forth, 866 36
continual course of the reading of the *S*. 866 39
(as touching the reading of the holy *S*), 866 43
Holy *S* containeth all things necessary to salvation: 868 20
In the name of the Holy *S* 868 23
by most certain warrants of Holy *S*. 869 18
generally set forth to us in Holy *S*: 871 22
For Holy *S* doth set out unto us 871 27
neither may it so expound one place of *S*, 871 39
may be declared that they be taken out of holy *S*." 872 10
grounded upon no warranty of *S*, 872 14
but is repugnant to the plain words of *S*, 873 29
or from other passages of *S*, 935 8

scriptures

may be read from any version of the *S* 143 6
following passages from Holy *S* is read. 470 —
The Holy *S* and ancient Christian writers 510 2
Declaration "I do believe the Holy *S*..." 552 9
formula "Receive the Holy *S*..." 553 6
The Holy *S* 853 —
very pure word of God, the holy *S*, 867 2
Of the Sufficiency of the Holy *S* 868 19
are states of life allowed in the *S*; 872 35
given always to all godly Princes in holy *S* 876 3
1. The Holy *S* of the Old and New Testament 877 14
(a) The Holy *S* of the Old and New Testaments, 877 33

sea

Israel's deliverance at the Red *S* 289 7

seal

Given under my hand and *s*, in the city of 557 17

sealed

are visibly signed and *s*; 873 18

search

if a man would *s* out by the ancient fathers, 866 6

season

Easter *S*, including Ascension Day 39 —
following Antiphons are used only in Easter *S*. 44 —
Easter *S*, including Ascension Day 77 —
following Antiphons are used only in Easter *S*. 82 —
Especially suitable for use in Easter *S* 85 —
appropriate to the occasion or to the *s*, 109 —
Easter *S* 111 —
one proper to the *s*, may precede the Blessing 113 —
(adding "Alleluia, alleluia" in Easter *S*) 114 —
In Easter *S* the People respond 114 —
In Easter *S*, add 134 —

In Easter *S*, add 135 —
in Easter *S* the flame may be taken 143 11
ones suitable to the *s* or the occasion, may be used. 143 23
The *S* after Pentecost 176 —
Preface of Pentecost, or of the *S* 204 —
Preface of the *S* 205 —
Preface of Baptism, or of the *S* 206 —
Preface of the *S*, or of Pentecost 206 —
Preface of the *S* 207 —
Preface of the *S* 208 —
Preface of the *S* 209 —
Preface of the *S* 210 —
The *S* after Pentecost 228 —
Preface of Pentecost, or of the *S* 255 —
Preface of the *S* 256 —
Preface of Baptism, or of the *S* 257 —
Preface of the *S*, or of Pentecost 257 —
Preface of the *S* 258 —
Preface of the *S* 259 —
Preface of the *S* 260 —
Preface of the *S* 261 —
at other times except during Easter *S*. 337 —
at other times except during Easter *S*. 364 —
related to the occasion, or the *s*, 383 —
(a) a Collect appropriate to the *s* 394 —
or a Collect of the *s*, or another prayer 565 8
that of the *s* may be used, 576 25
be omitted during the *s* of Lent. 584 9
God's purpose by his Spirit working in due *s*: 871 7
appropriate variations in Lent and Easter *S*. 934 25

seasons

except in the *s* of Advent, Lent, and Easter. 16 10
Fridays in the Christmas and Easter *s*, 17 27
is also appropriate, especially for the *s* suggested: 108 15
including those listed for specific *s* or days, 141 4
I. For fruitful *s* 207 —
I. For fruitful *s* 258 —
Prefaces for *S* 345 —
Prefaces for *S* 378 —

seated

The congregation may be *s* for the first part 273 —
The congregation may be *s* for the first part 277 —
be *s* for the Lessons and the homily. 437 19
A homily may be preached, the people being *s*. 480 —
All are *s* except the ordinand, 531 —
All are *s* except the ordinand, 543 —

seating

S may be provided for the wedding party, 437 18

second

transferred to the week following the *S* Sunday 17 12
Gospel is read after the *s* Canticle. 47 —
Gospel is read after the *s* Canticle. 65 —
Gospel is read after the *s* Canticle. 84 —
10 The *S* Song of Isaiah Quaerite Dominum 86 —
Gospel is read after the *s* Canticle. 119 —
Trinity Sunday (the *S* Sunday after Pentecost) 158 12
S Sunday of Advent 159 —
S Sunday after Christmas Day 162 —
or those for the *S* Sunday after Christmas Day, 162 —
S Sunday after the Epiphany 163 —
S Sunday in Lent 166 —
S Sunday of Easter 172 —
S Sunday of Advent 211 —
S Sunday after Christmas Day 214 —
or those for the *S* Sunday after Christmas, 214 —
S Sunday after the Epiphany 215 —
S Sunday in Lent 218 —
S Sunday of Easter 224 —
S Day: Morning Prayer 593 —
S Day: Evening Prayer 597 —
Twenty-*s* Day: Morning Prayer 746 —
Twenty-*s* Day: Evening Prayer 749 —
The *s* use of this catechism is to provide 844 7
The *S* Book of Samuel, 868 27
The *S* Book of Kings, 868 29
The *S* Book of Chronicles, 868 31
The *S* Book of Esdras, 868 33
The *S* Book of Maccabees. 869 3
The *S* Book of Homilies, the several titles whereof 874 35
since the *s* year of the forenamed King Edward 875 31

secondly

S, associated with them are the presbyters, 510 7

secrecy

The *s* of a confession is morally absolute 446 27

secret

he hath constantly decreed by his counsel *s* to us, 871 3

sect

saved by the Law or *S* which he professeth, 871 26

section

This Canticle may be shortened by omitting *s* 47 —
after each Psalm, and after each *s* of Psalm 119. 141 13

sections

One or more *s* of this Canticle may be used. 88 —
include Psalms 19, 67, one or more *s* of Psalm 119, 103 —
(the indicated *s* may be omitted) 286 —

secure

omitting some of them, to *s* continuity 934 19

see

reading the Psalms, *s* page 582.) 136 8
S also the Table on pages 884–885. 158 21
Pentecost in that year is used. *S* page 158. 176 —
Pentecost in that year is used. *S* page 158. 227 —
from "At Baptism." (*S* Additional Directions, 300 —
S the forms beginning on page 383. 359 —
it takes place at this time. *S* page 437. 425 —
more suitable prayers (*s* pages 487–489). 480 —
more suitable prayers (*s* pages 503–505). 496 —
so that all may *s* and hear what is done. 511 14
so that all may *s* and hear what is done. 524 6
so that all may *s* and hear what is done. 536 6
S also Various Occasions no. 18. 815 —
S also the prayers for the Mission of the Church 816 —
S also Various Occasions no. 13. 818 —
S also Various Occasions no. 14, 818 —
For those to be ordained, *s* Various Occasions no. 15. 819 —
S also Various Occasions no. 17. 820 —

S also Various Occasions no. 21. 823 —
S also Various Occasions no. 19. 824 —
For prayers for Industry and Labor, *s* Various Occasions no. 19, 824 —
For Education, *s* Various Occasions no. 23. 825 —
For Social Service, *s* Various Occasions no. 22. 827 —
S also Various Occasions no. 19. 827 —
S also Various Occasions no. 20. 831 —
S also the Prayer of Humble Access on page 337. 834 —
S also The General Thanksgiving on pages 58 837 —
S also the prayer "O God, the King of Saints," 838 —
S also the Thanksgiving for a Child on page 439. 841 —
S pages 317 and 350. 847 —
S pages 53, 96, 326, 327, and 864. 851 —
S page 364. 856 —
we *s* to have been given always to all godly Princes 876 3

seek

them that *s* occasion, of cavil or quarrel 10 13
this Church does not *s* to absorb other Communions, 877 1

seeking

that, *s* to keep the happy mean 9 25
It is essential that the person *s* to make or renew 420 —
Christian Bodies *s* the restoration of the organic unity 877 23

seem

disposed of, as may *s* most convenient 9 8
from time to time, *s* either necessary or expedient." 9 20

seems

It *s* unnecessary to enumerate all the different alterations 11 9

seen

(Things which are not *s* are eternal) 475 —
other ministers may be clearly *s* and heard 564 —

sees

When the priest *s* that there is hatred 409 17

select

Bishop may *s* Readings from the Proper 515 —
Bishop may *s* Readings from the Proper 528 —
Bishop may *s* Readings from the Proper 540 —
On Special Occasions, the officiant may *s* 935 12

selected

On other occasions they are *s* 300 —
The Readings are ordinarily *s* from 515 —
The Readings are ordinarily *s* from 528 —
The Readings are ordinarily *s* from 540 —
in accordance with the Canons, you have been *s* 557 5
The Readings are *s* from the following list, 560 —
Gospel, may be *s* from the Proper 565 11
S verses of psalms and hymns, or instrumental music 576 4
particular occasion may be *s*. 577 13
the Lessons at the Office may be *s* 888 13
the Psalm cited in the *s* Sunday Proper 888 17

selection

Whatever the *s*, it begins 88 —
or a *s* from Psalms 120 through 133. 103 —
S from the Psalter. 113 —

selections

s include Psalms 19, 67, 103 —
Other suitable *s* may be substituted. 128 —
manual of devotion which provides daily *s* 136 —
Appropriate *s* may be found 565 13
S are ordinarily made 571 10
s may be made from the Proper of the Day. 571 12
the *s* from the Psalter are frequently cited 888 18
The *s* may be further lengthened 888 21

selective

it is suitable for *s* use, 844 10

selects

For the concluding Collect, the Celebrant *s* 394 —

self

special acts of discipline and *s*-denial: 17 22
61. A Prayer of *S*-Dedication 812 12
61. A Prayer of *S*-Dedication 832 —

send

and *s* Ministers into the Lord's vineyard. 872 20

sense

parallelism of clauses, a symmetry of form and *s*. 583 3
may, in its deepest and truest *s*, 876 30

sensuality

some *s*, some the affection, some the desire, 869 30

sent

before he be lawfully called, and *s* 872 17
And those we ought to judge lawfully called and *s*, 872 18

sentence

or with some other *s* of Scripture. 333 —
or some other appropriate *s* of Scripture, 343 —
or with some other *s* of Scripture. 361 —
or some other appropriate *s* of Scripture, 376 —
The Celebrant may introduce the Prayers with a *s* 383 —
(before or after the *s* of Invitation). 407 11
continually before their eyes the *s* of God's 871 17

sentences

begins the service with one or more of these *s* 37 —
one or more of the following *s* 61 —
begins the service with one or more of these *s* 75 —
one or more of the following *s* 115 —
Any of the opening *s* of Scripture, 141 3
opening *s* given in the Offices, 141 9
The Celebrant may read one of the following *s* 319 —
Minister may then say one or more of the following *s*, 332 —
may begin the Offertory with one of the *s* 333 —
Offertory *S* 343 —
The Celebrant may read one of the following *s* 351 —
One of the *s* from the Penitential Order 359 —
may begin the Offertory with one of the *s* 361 —
Offertory *S* 376 —
opening *s* given in the Offices, 935 8

separate

s devotion; especially in times of war, 154 —
at the beginning of the Liturgy, or as a *s* service. 319 —
When used as a *s* service, the Exhortation, 319 —

at the beginning of the Liturgy, or as a *s* service. 351 —
When used as a *s* service, the Exhortation, 351 —
will be able to *s* us from the love of God 507 8
Scriptures..." is to be provided as a *s* document 552 9
each is to be presented with a *s* copy 552 12

separated

several conveniently *s* places in the church. 553 13
not as parted or *s* into two persons, 864 15

separately

or *s*; especially in Lent 148 4
When used *s*, it concludes with suitable prayers, 321 —
When used *s*, it concludes with suitable prayers, 353 —
receive the consecrated Bread and Wine *s*. 407 26
or it may be used *s*. 548 —
the Collects of Morning or Evening Prayer or *s*. 814 —
the Collects at Morning or Evening Prayer, or *s*. 836 —

separation

without change, without division, without *s*; 864 12

September

Proper 18 The Sunday closest to *S* 7 181 —
Proper 19 The Sunday closest to *S* 14 182 —
The Wednesday, Friday, and Saturday after *S* 14 182 —
Proper 20 The Sunday closest to *S* 21 182 —
Proper 21 The Sunday closest to *S* 28 182 —
Holy Cross Day *S* 14 192 —
Saint Matthew *S* 21 192 —
Saint Michael and All Angels *S* 29 193 —
Proper 18 The Sunday closest to *S* 7 233 —
Proper 19 The Sunday closest to *S* 14 233 —
The Wednesday, Friday, and Saturday after *S* 14 233 —
Proper 20 The Sunday closest to *S* 21 234 —
Proper 21 The Sunday closest to *S* 28 234 —
Holy Cross Day *S* 14 244 —
Saint Matthew *S* 21 244 —
Saint Michael and All Angels *S* 29 244 —
twelfth day of *S*, in the Year of our Lord, 1801. 867 33

sequence

The *s* of all Sundays of the Church Year 15 9
the *s* begins with Proper 3 158 17
the *s* begins with Proper 6 158 19
When a Major Feast interrupts the *s* of Readings, 934 17

series

statement of intention or of a *s* of questions 420 —

serious

When the penitent has confessed all *s* sins 446 20

seriously

without prejudice or prepossessions; *s* considering 11 19

sermon

A *s* or homily, a passage from Christian literature, 113 —
A *s* may be preached after the Office; 142 11
Baptismal Vows, page 292, follows the *S*. 175 —
Baptismal Vows, page 292, follows the *S*. 227 —
After the *S*, all stand, 264 —
The *S* follows. 277 —
and normally preaches the *s*. 284 13
If a *s* or homily was not preached earlier, 295 —
The *S* 301 —
Or the *S* may be preached after the Peace. 301 —
The *S* 326 —
The *S* 358 —
The *S* 415 —
The *S* 516 —
After the *S*, the Congregation sings a hymn. 516 —
The *S* 529 —
The *S* 541 —
The *S* 560 —
After the *S*, and any responses to it, 560 —
The *s* may be preached by the bishop, 565 16
speak in response to the address or *s*. 565 20
S or Address 572 —
If there is an address instead of a *s*, 576 11
The *s* or address may be followed 576 15
5. Liturgy of the Word, with *s* or address 578 1

servants

say, We are unprofitable *s*. 870 23

serve

a blessing over food may *s* as the conclusion 143 29
Proper Lessons for Christmas Day *s* for any weekdays 161 —
Proper Lessons for Christmas Day *s* for any weekdays 213 —
Deacons should also *s* at the Lord's Table, 322 11
Deacons should also *s* at the Lord's Table, 354 11
At least two other bishops *s* as co-consecrators. 511 8
you have been selected to *s* 557 5
Love and *s* Christ's people. 557 13
Other priests, if any, who *s* in the same congregation 558 11
If one reading stand is to *s* as both lectern and pulpit, 576 6
If the place of public worship is also to *s* as a school 576 29
and Chapels to the same annexed, shall *s* the congregation. 867 28
judge the same to *s* better to godliness. 874 14
to wear weapons, and *s* in the wars." 876 11

serves

s for weekdays between the Epiphany 162 —
s for the weekdays which follow, 166 —
s for the following weekdays, 174 —
s for weekdays between the Epiphany 214 —
also *s* for the weekdays which follow, 217 —
s for the following weekdays, 226 —
the following *s* for the Prayers of the People 480 —
bishop appointed by the Presiding Bishop, presides and *s* 511 7

service

to take a further review of the Public *S*, 11 6
Concerning the *S* 13 1
and for other special occasions for which no *s* 13 13
as set forth in the rubrical directions for each *s*. 13 19
limitations described in the directions for each *s*. 14 2
celebrated in the context of a Rite One *s*, 14 4
When rubrics indicate that a part of a *s* is to be "said," 14 11
Concerning the *S* 36 2
lead other parts of the *s* not assigned to the officiant. 36 6
The Officiant begins the *s* 37 —
The Officiant begins the *s* 61 —
or with the *S* of Light on pages 109–112, 61 —
Concerning the *S* 74 1

lead other parts of the *s* not assigned to the officiant.	74	5
The Officiant begins the *s*	75	—
An Order of *S*	103	—
The *s* concludes as follows	107	—
Concerning the *S*	108	1
This Order provides a form of evening *s*	108	2
Evening Prayer or some other *s*,	108	5
Any part or parts of this *s* may be led	108	7
For the Short Lesson at the beginning of the *s*,	108	14
church is dark, or partially so, when the *s* is to begin.	109	—
The *s* may then continue in any	112	—
The Officiant begins the *s*	115	—
or with the *S* of Light on pages 109–112,	115	—
The *s* concludes with the Song of Simeon	134	—
and Collects are provided in each *s*.	136	—
The *s* then continues with the [Peace	142	24
Before this *s*, there should be as little artificial light	142	26
to begin the *s* by its light.	143	5
Lessons are to be read later in the *s*,	143	9
candles carried in at the beginning of the *s*	143	12
When this *s* is used in private houses,	143	17
When this *s* continues as a complete Office,	143	21
serve as the conclusion of this form of *s*.	143	30
may be used at the evening *s*	158	23
it begins with the *S* of Light,	175	—
22. For Social *S*	209	—
it begins with the *S* of Light,	227	—
22. For Social *S*	260	—
A deacon or lay reader leading the *s*	269	—
When Communion follows, the *s* continues	269	—
may be distributed to the people before the *s*,	270	—
In the absence of a bishop or priest, the preceding *s*	272	—
Confession of Sin may be omitted at this *s*.	273	—
The *s* continues with the Prayers of the People.	275	—
for that purpose is consecrated at this *s*.	275	—
s may be concluded here with the singing	280	—
s may be concluded here with the Lord's Prayer	282	—
The *s* concludes with the following prayer.	282	—
The *s* then concludes with the Lord's Prayer	283	—
The Great Vigil, when observed, is the first *s*	284	2
The *s* normally consists of four parts:	284	5
1. The *S* of Light.	284	6
2. The *S* of Lessons.	284	7
to take active parts in the *s*.	284	11
a priest presides at the *s*.	284	16
may lead the first two parts of the *s*,	284	24
When the Vigil is not celebrated, the *S* of Light	284	30
The Nicene Creed is not used at this *s*.	295	—
Concerning the *S*	298	1
Eucharist as the chief *s* on a Sunday	298	6
and presides at the *s*.	298	14
At the principal *s* on a Sunday or other feast,	300	—
The *s* then continues with the Prayers	310	—
If there is no celebration of the Eucharist, the *s*	311	—
The Nicene Creed is not used at this *s*.	312	27
beginning of the Liturgy, or as a separate *s*.	319	—
When used as a separate *s*, the Exhortation,	319	—
the *s* continues with the Kyrie eleison,	321	—
the *s* is concluded as directed on page 406.	330	—
beginning of the Liturgy, or as a separate *s*.	351	—
When used as a separate *s*, the Exhortation,	351	—
the *s* continues with the Gloria	353	—
the *s* is concluded as directed on page 406.	359	—
If it is necessary to shorten the *s*,	396	—
The *s* concludes with a blessing	399	—
Either here or elsewhere in the *s*, all greet	401	2
s begins with the Penitential Order.)	407	1
The *s* may then conclude with the Lord's Prayer;	407	2
announcements may be made before the *s*,	407	12
or at the end of the *s*, as convenient.	407	13
Concerning the *S*	412	1
The Nicene Creed is not used at this *s*.	412	15
At the principal *s* on a Sunday	414	—
The *s* then continues with the Prayers	419	—
If there is no celebration of the Eucharist, the *s*	419	—
to Christian *S*	420	—
commitment to the *s* of Christ in the world,	420	—
The *s* then continues with the exchange of the Peace	421	—
Concerning the *S*	422	1
a deacon may use the *s* which follows,	422	16
Lessons appointed in the Marriage *s*.	433	—
The *s* continues with The Prayers on page 428.	434	—
8. If there is no Communion, the *s* concludes	436	10
9. If there is to be a Communion, the *s* continues	436	13
This *s* then replaces the Ministry of the Word,	437	—
It is desirable that this take place at a Sunday *s*.	439	6
When desired, a briefer form of this *s*	439	10
The *s* continues with the Magnificat	440	—
Two equivalent forms of *s* are provided	446	10
one or more parts of the following *s* are used,	453	3
Part One of this *s* may always be led by a deacon	453	6
The Celebrant begins the *s* with the following	453	11
The *s* concludes with a blessing	457	—
Collects (such as those in the Burial *s*)	465	—
If the Burial *s* is not to follow immediately,	467	—
s continues on page 469 or 491.	467	—
Concerning the *S*	468	1
The *s* should be held at a time	468	5
The coffin is to be closed before the *s*,	468	8
all or part of the *s* of Committal may be said	468	10
If preferred, the Committal *s* may	468	11
take place before the *s* in the church.	468	12
A priest normally presides at the *s*.	468	13
lay reader may preside at the *s*.	468	18
The anthems at the beginning of the *s*	468	23
s continues with the following	480	—
When there is no Communion, the *s* continues	481	—
The *s* continues with the Peace	482	—
If the body is not present, the *s* continues	482	—
either before the *s* of Committal or	487	—
Concerning the *S*	490	1
The *s* should be held at a time	490	5
The coffin is to be closed before the *s*,	490	8
all or part of the *s* of Committal may be said	490	10
If preferred, the Committal *s* may	490	11
take place before the *s* in the church.	490	12
A priest normally presides at the *s*.	490	13
lay reader may preside at the *s*.	490	18
The anthems at the beginning of the *s*	490	23
s continues with the Prayers of the People,	496	—
When there is no Communion, the *s* continues	498	—
The *s* continues with the Peace	498	—
If the body is not present, the *s* continues	499	—
either before the *s* of Committal or	503	—

the preceding *s* has been held, or at the graveside. 506 20
are assigned appropriate duties in the *s*. 511 11
From the beginning of the *s* until the Offertory, 511 12
Concerning the *S* 524 1
From the beginning of the *s* until the Offertory, 524 4
Concerning the *S* 536 1
From the beginning of the *s* until the Offertory, 536 4
rubrics of the *s* of ordination are followed. 552 4
take place at some convenient time prior to the *s*. 552 18
Concerning the *S* 558 1
Alterations in the *s* are then made 558 6
The *s* continues with the Offertory. 563 —
from the passages cited in the *s*. 565 12
found in the *s* for the Ordination of a Deacon 565 14
Concerning the *S* 566 1
This *s* provides for the dedication and 566 2
Portions of the *s* may be used, or adapted 566 3
This *s* may be used to dedicate 566 9
The *s* does not preclude the use of the building 566 11
may be assigned appropriate parts in the *s*. 566 15
the *s* continues as directed on page 575. 569 —
The *s* continues with the Offertory. 574 —
The complete form of the *s* for the Dedication 575 2
This *s* does not require 575 3
When the clergy and people assemble before the *s*, 575 5
as in the *s* of Holy Baptism, 575 26
then the *s* of Holy Baptism, 575 29
Commitment to Christian *S*, 576 17
the *s* may be adapted 576 30
their representatives take part in the *s*, 577 2
and that the *s* be adapted. 577 3
Suitable portions of this *s* may be used 577 4
Relevant portions of the *s* for the Dedication 577 8
6. For Heroic *S* 813 7
For Social *S*, see Various Occasions no. 22. 827 —
6. For Heroic *S* 839 —
It may also be used to form a simple *s*; 844 9
prayers in the Church, commonly called Divine *S*: 866 5
the *S* in the Church of England (these many years) 866 24
and the manifold changings of the *s*, 866 30
need none other books for their public *s*, 867 6
Lessons are to be read at the principal morning *s*, 888 9

services

are the regular *s* appointed for public 13 5
In addition to these *s* and the other rites 13 7
In all *s*, the entire Christian assembly 13 16
when the *s* of a priest cannot be obtained, 13 25
and in other *s* contained in this Book 14 3
In Rite One *s* of Morning Prayer and 141 18
concerning the Common of Saints and *s* 158 24
At *s* on this day other than the principal 272 —
when the *s* of a priest cannot be obtained, 284 27
customary that the Paschal Candle burn at all *s* 287 —
In Rite One *s*, the following form 406 8
When the *s* of a priest cannot be obtained, 408 17
The absolution in these *s* may be pronounced 446 11
When the *s* of a priest cannot be obtained, 468 17
When the *s* of a priest cannot be obtained, 490 17
Episcopal *S* 509 1
and for this purpose these *s* of ordination 510 20
intended for use at all public *s* on such days, 888 7
when the same congregation attends two or more *s*. 888 8

session

This Convention having, in their present *s*, 8 7

set

in their present session, *s* forth A Book 8 7
as *s* forth in this Book, are the regular services 13 5
other forms *s* forth by authority 13 8
the bishop may *s* forth such forms 13 14
as *s* forth in the rubrical directions 13 19
precedence *s* forth in the Calendar 195 —
subject to the rules *s* forth in the Calendar 199 —
precedence *s* forth in the Calendar 246 —
subject to the rules *s* forth in the Calendar 251 —
or in a place *s* aside to give greater privacy, 446 16
a place that has not previously been *s* apart 487 —
a place that has not previously been *s* apart 503 —
The version of the Psalms which follows is *s* out 583 1
here is *s* forth such an order, 866 33
reading of holy Scripture is so *s* forth, 866 36
certain rules are here *s* forth, 866 41
nothing can, almost, be so plainly *s* forth, 867 16
as they be generally *s* forth to us in Holy Scripture: 871 21
For Holy Scripture doth *s* out unto us 871 27
which were *s* forth in the time of Edward the Sixth; 874 37
as *s* forth by the General Convention 875 21
lately *s* forth in the time of Edward the Sixth, 875 27
lately *s* forth by Elizabeth our Queen 876 2

sets

Then follows one of these *s* of Suffrages 67 —
Then follows one of these *s* of Suffrages 97 —
Then follows one of these *s* of Suffrages 121 —
and any of the *s* of Proper Lessons 161 —
with one of the corresponding *s* of Psalms 195 —
preceding and any of the *s* of Proper Lessons 213 —
with one of the corresponding *s* of Psalms 246 —

seven

Year of Our Lord One Thousand *S* Hundred 8 5
Year of our Lord one thousand *s* hundred 8 13
had divided the Psalms into *s* portions, 866 27
the Psalms are arranged in a *s*-week pattern 934 23

seventeenth

S Day: Morning Prayer 709 —
S Day: Evening Prayer 713 —

seventh

S Sunday after the Epiphany 164 —
S Sunday of Easter: The Sunday after Ascension Day 175 —
S Sunday after the Epiphany 216 —
S Sunday of Easter: The Sunday after Ascension Day 226 —
S Day: Morning Prayer 629 —
S Day: Evening Prayer 633 —
Twenty-*s* Day: Morning Prayer 778 —
Twenty-*s* Day: Evening Prayer 782 —

several

she hath, in the reign of *s* Princes, 10 1
When *s* deacons or priests are present, 408 5
place at *s* conveniently separated places 553 13

There are *s* traditional methods 582 3
The Second Book of Homilies, the *s* titles whereof 874 35
who, in their *s* spheres, have contended 876 28

severity
and endure the *s* of God's judgment; 870 8

share
The priests who are present *s* among them 284 14
S the Gifts of God 401 12
and to take your *s* in the councils of the Church. 557 4
the ministry in which they *s*. 558 18

shared
The Body and Blood of the Lord are *s* 401 13

shepherd
(I am the good *s*) 480 —
(I am the good *s*) 495 —

shine
(You are the light... Let your light so *s*) 426 —

short
For the *S* Lesson at the beginning 108 14
or some other *S* Lesson of Scripture 109 —
to provide light for reading the opening *S* Lesson 143 1
The *S* Lessons may be read from any version 143 6
the *S* Lesson may be omitted. 143 9

shorten
If it is necessary to *s* the service, 396 —

shortened
This Canticle may be *s* 47 —
may be further lengthened or *s* at discretion. 888 22

shorter
cited in a longer and *s* version, 888 19
the *s* version when the Psalm is sung 888 20

shortness
It is also more commodious, both for the *s* thereof, 867 4

shoulder
The stole worn over the left *s*, or other insignia 554 12

shout
The ancient praise-*s*, "Hallelujah," has been restored, 584 4

show
until he *s* us his mercy. Psalm 123:3). 583 9

shown
s in parentheses. 888 30
s in parentheses. 934 21

shrubs
The branches of palm or of other trees or *s* 270 —

sick
20. For the *S* 208 —
20. For the *S* 260 —
may be required for the Communion of the *s*, 408 29
Ministration to the *S* 453 1
(Is any among you *s*?) 454 6
(They anointed with oil many that were *s*) 454 8
if the *s* person's conscience is troubled, 454 15
If oil for the Anointing of the *S* is to be blessed, 455 —
The Priest then lays hands upon the *s* person, 455 —
sign of the cross on the *s* person's forehead, 456 —
If the *s* person cannot receive either the consecrated 457 —
Prayers for the *S* 458 —
For a *S* Person 458 —
For a *S* Child 458 —
Prayers for use by a *S* Person 461 —
to minister in Christ's name to the poor, the *s*, 510 14
or Blessing of Oil for the *S*. 576 17
Prayers for the *s* are on pages 458–461. 812 14
Prayers for the *s* are on pages 458–461. 831 —

sickness
It is not restricted to times of *s*. 446 8
reason of extreme *s* or physical disability, is unable 457 —
For Recovery from *S* 458 —
because of *s* or other grave cause, could not 555 3

side
And if the person or persons on one *s* truly forgive 409 20
but those on the other *s* refuse to forgive, 409 21
between one *s* of the congregation and the other. 582 15

sight
placed in the *s* of the people. 281 —
Priest, at a place in full *s* of the congregation, 308 —
signs the above Declaration in the *s* of all 513 —
then signs the above Declaration in the *s* of all 527 —
then signs the above Declaration in the *s* of all 539 —
and should remain in the *s* of the congregation 565 22

sign
marking on the forehead the *s* of the cross 308 —
or something to be done, as a *s* of penitence 446 24
makes the *s* of the cross on the sick person's forehead, 456 —
This letter is a *s* that you are fully empowered 557 7
marks the threshold with the *s* of the cross saying 568 3
they have not any visible *s* or ceremony ordained 872 36
Baptism is not only a *s* of profession, 873 14
christened, but it is also a *s* of Regeneration 873 15
The Supper of the Lord is not only a *s* of the love 873 23
and drink the *s* or Sacrament of so great a thing. 873 40

signature
with a separate copy for *s*.) 552 13

signatures
The witnesses add their *s*. 513 —

signed
s, as directed by Article VIII of the Constitution 552 10
(*S*) ________ 557 20
The cross *s* on the threshold by the bishop 575 20
God by the Holy Ghost, are visibly *s* and sealed; 873 18

significance
On feasts or other days of special *s*, 113 —

signify
thereby *s* their endorsement of the candidates 298 19

signing

If a priest uses Chrism in *s* the newly baptized,	298	14
are not to depart without *s* the Letters	553	16
foot of a processional cross may be used for the *s*.	575	22
2. *S* of threshold	577	27

signs

The Bishop-elect then *s* the above Declaration	513	—
The Ordinand then *s* the above Declaration	527	—
The Ordinand then *s* the above Declaration	539	—
they be certain sure witnesses, and effectual *s*	872	27

silence

S may be kept.	41	7
S may be kept after each Reading.	47	—
S may be kept.	62	—
S may be kept after each Reading.	65	—
S may be kept.	79	—
S may be kept after each Reading.	84	—
psalm may be sung, or *s* kept.	112	—
S, or a suitable Collect, or both,	113	—
or a brief *s*, may follow the Reading.	113	—
S may be kept.	116	—
S may be kept after each Reading.	119	—
S may be kept.	127	—
S may be kept, and free intercessions	134	—
A period of *s* may follow.	137	—
more than one Lesson may be read, with *s*	143	25
S is then kept for a time, all kneeling.	265	—
On this day the ministers enter in *s*.	276	—
S	278	—
S	279	—
S	280	—
s may be kept;	288	—
(*S*)	288	—
(*S*)	289	—
(*S*)	290	—
(*S*)	291	—
S may follow.	300	—
S may be kept.	309	—
S may be kept.	320	—
S may follow.	326	—
S may be kept.	330	—
A period of *s* is kept.	337	—
S may be kept.	352	—
S may follow.	357	—
S may be kept.	360	—
A period of *s* is kept.	364	—
S	385	—
In the course of the *s* after each bidding,	385	—
S	385	—
S	386	—
S	387	—
S	388	—
S	389	—
S	391	—
S	392	—
S	393	—
S may be kept.	393	—
instrumental music, other art forms, *s*.	400	10
S may follow.	414	—
A period of *s* follows.	417	—
S may be kept; after which the Celebrant says	466	—
S may be kept; after which the Celebrant says	467	—
S may be kept; after which the Celebrant says	493	—
S may be kept.	497	—
S may follow.	516	—
S may follow.	529	—
S may follow.	541	—
After a period of *s*, the Bishop concludes	572	—
After a brief *s*, the Celebrant concludes	579	—

silent

A meditation, *s* or spoken, may follow.	106	—
opportunity may be given for *s* prayer.	142	10
All then kneel for *s* prayer,	276	—
A period of *s* prayer follows, the people still standing.	520	—
A period of *s* prayer follows, the people still standing.	533	—
A period of *s* prayer follows, the people still standing.	544	—
it is appropriate that it remain *s* until dedicated.	575	11

silently

People offer their own prayers, either *s* or aloud.	385	6

Simeon

5 The Song of *S* Nunc dimittis	51	—
The Song of *S* Nunc dimittis	66	—
17 The Song of *S* Nunc dimittis	93	—
The Song of *S* Nunc dimittis	120	—
The service concludes with the Song of *S*	134	—
The Song of *S*, Nunc dimittis	484	—
The Song of *S*, Nunc dimittis	500	—

similar

Celebrant may address the people in these or *s* words	285	4
introduce the Scripture readings in these or *s* words	288	—
may first address the people in these or *s* words,	292	—
The Celebrant then says these or *s* words	303	—
it is introduced with these or *s* words	402	—
it is introduced with these or *s* words	404	—
The Prayer concludes with these or *s* words	405	—
The Bishop then says these or *s* words	416	—
After this, the Celebrant says these or *s* words	420	—
Celebrant, who addresses them in these or *s* words	433	—
addresses the congregation in these or *s* words	440	—
Then one or both parents say these or *s* words	441	—
may introduce the Creed with these or *s* words	496	—
Presiding Bishop then says the following, or *s* words,	513	—
calls the people to prayer with these or *s* words	527	—
calls the people to prayer with these or *s* words	539	—
say these or *s* words	559	—
and others having *s* tenure of office.	564	18
and other priests having *s* canonical charge	565	25
the Bishop says the following or *s* words	567	5
A *s* construction occurs in the Canticle,	584	2

similarity

parallelism can take the form of *s*	583	4

similarly

S, all the new priests break the consecrated Bread	554	9

Simon

Saint *S* and Saint Jude October 28	194	—
Saint *S* and Saint Jude October 28	245	—

simple

methods, each of which can be elaborate or *s*, 582 6
It may also be used to form a *s* service; 844 9

simultaneously

Sacrament may be received in both kinds *s*, 408 1

sin

The following Confession of *S* may then be said; 41 —
Confession of *S* 41 —
The following Confession of *S* may then be said; 62 —
Confession of *S* 62 —
The following Confession of *S* may then be said; 79 —
Confession of *S* 79 —
The following Confession of *S* may then be said; 116 —
Confession of *S* 116 —
Confession of *S* may be omitted at this service. 273 —
A Confession of *S* 282 —
Confession of *S* 330 —
A Confession of *S* is said here 330 —
Confession of *S* 359 —
A Confession of *S* is said here 359 —
A Confession of *S* may follow. 397 —
(If it is desired to include a Confession of *S*, 406 26
S and Redemption 848 —
like us in all respects, apart from *s*; 864 8
IX. Of Original or Birth-*S*. 869 22
Original *s* standeth not in the following of Adam, 869 23
concupiscence and lust hath of itself the nature of *s*. 869 32
but they have the nature of *s*. 870 17
XV. Of Christ alone without *S*. 870 24
was made like unto us in all things, *s* only except, 870 25
and *s* (as Saint John saith) was not in him. 870 28
and if we say we have no *s*, we deceive ourselves 870 29
XVI. Of *S* after Baptism. 870 31
Not every deadly *s* willingly committed 870 32
is *s* against the Holy Ghost, 870 32
repentance is not to be denied to such as fall into *s* 870 33
we may depart from grace given, and fall into *s*, 870 35
they can no more *s* as long as they live here, 870 36
the promises of the forgiveness of *s*, 873 17
there is none other satisfaction for *s*, but that alone. 874 8

since

s the first compiling of her Liturgy 10 2
and the Civil Authority has not *s* thought 10 22
In particular, *s* the time of the New Testament, 510 4
s the matter is arranged under headings, 844 9
s the second year of the forenamed King Edward 875 31

sincere

member of our Church, and every *s* Christian, 11 18

sing

The hymn "*S*, my tongue, the glorious battle," 282 —
Then all *s* or say together 519 —

singers

together with lay readers, *s*, and other persons, 284 11
alternation between groups of *s* or readers; 582 14

singing

may be read, with silence or *s* between them. 143 26
service may be concluded here with the *s* of a hymn 280 —
pausing three times and *s* or saying 285 —
s and instrumental music are appropriate. 567 —
congregational use, whether by *s* or reading. 582 3
choir and congregation *s* a refrain 582 21
This was the traditional method of *s* the Venite, 582 22
there hath been great diversity in saying and *s* 867 8

single

The exclusive use of a *s* method makes the recitation 582 4
to vow the estate of *s* life, or to abstain 874 13

sings

s or says the Exsultet, 286 —
bishop or priest, faces them and *s* or says 333 —
bishop or priest, faces them and *s* or says 340 —
bishop or priest, faces them and *s* or says 361 —
bishop of priest, faces them and *s* or says 367 —
bishop or priest, faces them and *s* or says 369 —
bishop or priest, faces them and *s* or says 372 —
After the Sermon, the Congregation *s* a hymn. 516 —
The Congregation then says or *s* the Nicene Creed 529 —
The Congregation then says or *s* the Nicene Creed. 541 —
and any responses to it, the congregation *s* a hymn. 560 —

singular

Thereafter, references to the ordinand in the *s* 553 27
Thereafter, references to the ordinand in the *s* 554 17

sins

and penitence for our *s*, be included. 140 8
When the penitent has confessed all serious *s* 446 20
Here the Penitent confesses particular *s*. 450 —
Psalm 103 (He forgives all your *s*) 454 3
Matthew 9:2–8 (Your *s* are forgiven) 454 4
but also for actual *s* of men. 868 8
after Justification, cannot put away our *s*, 870 8
should take away the *s* of the world; 870 27
and satisfaction, for all the *s* of the whole world, 874 7

Sirach

Jesus the Son of *S* 868 39

sit

The people *s*. 300 —
The people stand or *s*. 316 —
The people *s*. 325 —
The people *s*. 357 —
The people *s*. 414 —
the confessor may *s* inside the altar rails 446 15
the confessor and penitent may *s* face to face 446 17
The people *s*. 470 —
The people *s*. 494 —
s to the right and left of the chief consecrator. 511 15
The bishops and people *s*. 513 —
All now *s*, except the bishop-elect, 517 —
The bishop and people *s*. 526 —
The bishop and people *s*. 538 —

sitteth

he *s* on the right hand of the Father, 865 33
and there *s*, until he return to judge 868 15

sixfold

or said in threefold, *s*, or ninefold form. 406 10

sixteenth

in Convention, this *S* Day of October, 8 4
S Day: Morning Prayer 701 —
S Day: Evening Prayer 705 —

sixth

compiling of her Liturgy in the time of Edward the *S*, 10 2
S Sunday after the Epiphany 164 —
S Sunday of Easter 174 —
S Sunday after the Epiphany 216 —
S Sunday of Easter 225 —
S Day: Morning Prayer 621 —
S Day: Evening Prayer 624 —
Twenty-*s* Day: Morning Prayer 772 —
Twenty-*s* Day: Evening Prayer 775 —
which were set forth in the time of Edward the *S*; 874 37
lately set forth in the time of Edward the *S*, 875 28

size

a book or books of appropriate *s* and dignity. 406 20

slanderous

we understand the minds of some *s* folks to be offended; 875 44

sleep

For *S* 461 —

small

YHWH is represented in capital and *s* capital letters: 583 29

social

21. For *S* Justice 209 —
22. For *S* Service 209 —
21. For *S* Justice 260 —
22. For *S* Service 260 —
use of the building for educational or *s* purposes, 566 12
Prayers for the *S* Order 811 5
27. For *S* Justice 811 6
Thanksgiving for the *S* Order 813 8
Prayers for the *S* Order 823 —
27. For *S* Justice 823 —
For *S* Service, see Various Occasions no. 22. 827 —
Thanksgiving for the *S* Order 840 —

solemn

The *S* Collects 277 10
Christian marriage is a *s* and public covenant 422 2
7. A priest or bishop pronounces a *s* blessing 436 9
by *s* prayer and the laying on of episcopal hands. 510 18

solemnly

do hereby *s* declare to all 876 26

Solomon

Song of *S* 2:10–13; 8:6–7 426 —
Cantica, or Songs of *S*, 868 31

some

make such alterations in *s* particulars, 10 4
s other special occasion may be observed 16 20
The following, or *s* other suitable hymn, 64 —
One of the following, or *s* other suitable passage 105 —
Evening Prayer or *s* other service, 108 5
One of the following, or *s* other Short Lesson 109 —
following or *s* other suitable prayer, 110 —
or a metrical version of it, or *s* other hymn, 112 —
or with *s* other Office or Devotion; 112 —
other canticle, or *s* other hymn of praise. 113 —
may use the following or *s* other blessing 114 —
The following, or *s* other suitable hymn, 117 —
One of the following, or *s* other suitable passage 131 —
unison, or in *s* other convenient manner. 136 —
c) *s* other manual of devotion 136 —
dining table, or at *s* other convenient place. 143 18
concludes with the following or *s* other Collect 153 —
The following or *s* other suitable anthem 270 —
The following or *s* other suitable anthem 271 —
the procession may halt while the following or *s* 271 —
"Sing, my tongue, the glorious battle," or *s* other 282 —
s other suitable psalm, canticle, or hymn may 288 —
the Collect provided, or *s* other suitable 288 —
Psalm 114, or *s* other suitable 295 —
s subsequent occasion of public baptism 312 12
following hymn or *s* other song of praise 324 —
or with *s* other sentence of Scripture. 333 —
The following or *s* other suitable anthem 337 —
One of the following, or *s* other appropriate sentence 343 —
following hymn or *s* other song of praise 356 —
or with *s* other sentence of Scripture. 361 —
s other suitable anthem may be used. 364 —
One of the following, or *s* other appropriate sentence 376 —
(b) a Collect expressive of *s* special need 394 —
concluding with the following or *s* other Collect 397 —
The following or *s* other form is used 397 —
S of those present prepare the table; 401 5
s may administer the Bread 408 5
or upon undertaking *s* special responsibility. 420 —
then says this or *s* other appropriate prayer 421 —
assemble in the church or *s* other appropriate place. 423 —
assemble in the church or in *s* other convenient place. 435 9
When desired, *s* other suitable symbol of the vows 437 22
During the prayers, *s* parents may wish to express 439 15
begins the service with the following or *s* other greeting 453 11
This anthem, or *s* other suitable anthem, 482 —
service of Committal or at *s* other convenient time 487 —
A hymn, psalm, or *s* other suitable anthem 491 —
concludes with one of the following or *s* other prayer 497 —
This anthem, or *s* other suitable anthem, 499 —
the service of Committal or at *s* other convenient time 503 —
Litany for Ordinations, or *s* other approved litany. 515 —
Litany for Ordinations, or *s* other approved litany. 527 —
Litany for Ordinations, or *s* other approved litany. 539 —
or in *s* other convenient manner. 552 15
take place at *s* convenient time prior to the service. 552 18
it is appropriate that *s* of the consecrating bishops, 553 8
If there are many deacons, *s* assist in the Offertory 554 29
and cleanse the vessels in *s* convenient place. 555 6
The Litany for Ordinations, or *s* other 560 —
following or *s* other Collect, 560 —
Others present olive oil or *s* other symbol, 561 —
at the entrance of the chancel, or in *s* other place 564 15
the new minister, or *s* other person; 565 16
have *s* individual or collective part in the celebration, 566 17
Psalm 122 or *s* other appropriate psalm 568 —
place of worship, or in *s* other building. 575 7

or *s* other form may be composed 576 18
for *s* other suitable purpose, the service may 576 30
but that of necessity there must be *s* rules: 866 40
here are left out many things, whereof *s* be untrue, 866 45
s uncertain, *s* vain 866 45
s following Salisbury use, 867 9
s Hereford use, *s* the use of Bangor, 867 9
s of York, and *s* of Lincoln: 867 10
(which *s* do expound the wisdom, *s* sensuality, 869 29
s the affection, *s* the desire, of the flesh), 869 30
understand the minds of *s* slanderous folks to be offended; 875 44
Reading *s* such introduction as, "N. said (to N.)." 888 28
by lengthening, combining, or omitting *s* of them, 934 18
In *s* instances, the entire portion of the Psalter 935 3

something

or *s* to be done, as a sign of penitence 446 24

sometimes

they may err, and *s* have erred, 872 8
and *s* the evil have chief authority 873 2
When an alternative Lesson is cited, it is *s* identical 888 23

Son

"In the Name of the Father, and of the *S*, 313 17
2. Of God the *S* 345 1
2. Of God the *S* 377 10
in the Name of the Father, and of the *S*, 436 5
through Jesus Christ your *S*, give your Holy Spirit 554 1
God the *S* 849 —
and the same *S*, our Lord Jesus Christ, 864 5
one and the same Christ, *S*, Lord, 864 11
but one and the same *S* and Only-begotten 864 15
For there is one Person of the Father, another of the *S*, 864 27
But the Godhead of the Father, of the *S*, 864 28
Such as the Father is, such is the *S*, 864 30
The Father uncreate, the *S* uncreate, 864 31
Father incomprehensible, the *S* incomprehensible, 864 32
The Father eternal, the *S* eternal, 864 34
So likewise the Father is Almighty, the *S* Almighty, 864 38
So the Father is God, the *S* is God, 865 1
So likewise the Father is Lord, the *S* Lord, 865 3
The *S* is of the Father alone, 865 9
The Holy Ghost is of the Father and of the *S*, 865 10
one *S*, not three Sons; 865 12
the *S* of God, is God and Man; 865 21
the Father, the *S*, and the Holy Ghost. 867 38
Of the Word or *S* of God, which was made very Man. 868 1
The *S*, which is the Word of the Father, 868 2
Holy Ghost, proceeding from the Father and the *S*, 868 17
with the Father and the *S*, very and eternal God. 868 18
Jesus the *S* of Sirach 868 39
image of his only-begotten *S* Jesus Christ: 871 9
Father, and of the *S*, and of the Holy Ghost, 876 32

song

1 A *S* of Creation Benedicite, omnia opera Domini 47 —
S of the Three Young Men, 35–65 47 —
2 A *S* of Praise Benedictus es, Domini 49 —
S of the Three Young Men, 29–34 49 —
3 The *S* of Mary Magnificat 50 —
4 The *S* of Zechariah Benedictus Dominus Deus 50 —
5 The *S* of Simeon Nunc dimittis 51 —
The *S* of Mary Magnificat 65 —
The *S* of Simeon Nunc dimittis 66 —
8 The *S* of Moses Cantemus Domino 85 —
9 The First *S* of Isaiah Ecce, Deus 86 —
10 The Second *S* of Isaiah Quaerite Dominum 86 —
11 The Third *S* of Isaiah Surge, illuminare 87 —
12 A *S* of Creation Benedicite, omnia opera Domini 88 —
S of the Three Young Men, 35–65 88 —
13 A *S* of Praise Benedictus es, Domine 90 —
S of the Three Young Men, 29–34 90 —
14 A *S* of Penitence Kyrie Pantokrator 90 —
15 The *S* of Mary Magnificat 91 —
16 The *S* of Zechariah Benedictus Dominus Deus 92 —
17 The *S* of Simeon Nunc dimittis 93 —
18 A *S* to the Lamb Dignus es 93 —
19 The *S* of the Redeemed Magna et mirabilia 94 —
The *S* of Mary Magnificat 119 —
The *S* of Simeon Nunc dimittis 120 —
The service concludes with the *S* of Simeon 134 —
Canticle 8, The *S* of Moses 289 —
Canticle 9, The First *S* of Isaiah, or Psalm 42:1–7 290 —
Psalm 42:1–7, or Canticle 9, The First *S* of Isaiah 290 —
the following hymn or some other *s* of praise 324 —
the following hymn or some other *s* of praise 356 —
and response may include readings, *s*, 400 9
S of Solomon 2:10–13; 8:6–7 426 —
The *S* of Mary 441 —
The *S* of Zechariah, Benedictus 484 —
The *S* of Simeon, Nunc dimittis 484 —
The *S* of Zechariah, Benedictus 500 —
The *S* of Simeon, Nunc dimittis 500 —
recovery of this form of sacred *s* in the Daily Office. 582 24
construction occurs in the Canticle, "The *S* 584 3
The *S* of the Three Children, 869 1

songs

or *S* of Solomon, 868 31

sons

one Son, not three *S*; 865 12
they be made *s* of God by adoption: 871 8
and of our adoption to be the *s* 873 17

soon

As *s* as convenient after the birth of a child, 439 3
The death of a member of the Church should be reported as *s* 468 2
The death of a member of the Church should be reported as *s* 490 2
so *s* as there shall be any authorized response 877 21

sorrow

brings deep *s* when we are parted 507 11
we *s* in sympathy with those who mourn. 507 14

sort

in this *s* the book of Isaiah was begun in Advent, 866 20
After a like *s* were other books of holy Scripture used. 866 21

sorts

2. For all *S* and Conditions of Men 810 7
2. For All *S* and Conditions of Men 814 —

soul

For Health of Body and *S*	460	—
consisting also of a reasonable *s* and body;	864	6
Perfect God and perfect Man, of a reasonable *s*	865	25
For as the reasonable *s* and flesh is one man,	865	31

souls

(The *s* of the righteous are in the hands of God)	470	—
(The *s* of the righteous are in the hands of God)	494	—

sound

to the Word of God, or to *s* doctrine,	10	15
22. For *S* Government	810	31
22. For *S* Government	821	—

speak

candidates who can *s* for themselves,	302	—
the priest shall *s* to that person	409	9
he shall *s* privately to each of them,	409	18
other persons present, may *s* in response	565	19

speaking

Of *S* in the Congregation in such a Tongue	872	21

special

subject to the direction of the bishop, *s* devotions	13	9
For *s* days of fasting or thanksgiving,	13	12
and for other *s* occasions for which no service	13	13
In any of the Proper Liturgies for *S* Days,	14	3
some other *s* occasion may be observed on a Sunday.	16	20
of commemoration or of *s* observance:	16	24
4. Days of *S* Devotion	17	20
The following days are observed by *s* acts	17	21
On feasts or other days of *s* significance,	113	—
In *s* circumstances, in place of a Canticle,	142	1
On *s* occasions, lighted candles may be	143	15
(b) a Collect expressive of some *s* need	394	—
S Circumstances	396	—
or upon undertaking some *s* responsibility.	420	—
A prayer for the *s* work	421	—
Priest may suggest the making of a *s* confession,	454	15
form for Communion under *S* Circumstances is used,	457	—
It is also a *s* responsibility of deacons	510	13
Provisions for adapting the rite to *s* circumstances	566	7
a *s* order is provided on page 577.	566	19
and Chapels in *S* Cases	576	28
On *S* Occasions, the officiant may select	935	12

specially

the bishop may *s* authorize a deacon	312	9

specific

those listed for *s* seasons or days,	141	4
S roles may be assigned to different persons,	273	—
S roles may be assigned to different persons,	277	—

speech

to assist in rendering them into contemporary *s*.	814	—

speed

or with the versicle "O God, make *s* to save us"	61	—
continue at once with "O God, make *s* to save us."	62	—
or with the versicle "O God, make *s* to save us"	115	—
continue at once with "O God, make *s* to save us."	116	—

speedily

in its deepest and truest sense, be *s* fulfilled;	876	30

spelled

context requires that the Divine Name be *s* out,	584	2

spheres

who, in their several *s*, have contended	876	28

spirit

2. Of the Holy *S*	200	—
2. Of the Holy *S*	251	—
A new heart and a new *s*	290	—
Baptism is full initiation by water and the Holy *S*	298	2
by water and the Holy *S*;"	298	12
by water and the Holy *S*,"	313	10
and of the Son, and of the Holy *S*"	313	17
3. Of God the Holy *S*	345	—
3. Of God the Holy *S*	378	—
Christ's work, and the renewal of the Holy *S*.	405	6
and of the Son, and of the Holy *S*.	436	—
The hymn to the Holy *S* before the Prayer	552	14
give your Holy *S* to N.;	554	1
The Holy *S*	852	—
and their hearts, *s*, and mind, have not been edified	866	26
the flesh lusteth always contrary to the *S*;	869	26
and the Inspiration of his *S*,	870	13
void, both in his flesh, and in his *s*.	870	26
by his *S* working in due season:	871	7
in themselves the working of the *S* of Christ,	871	13
carnal persons, lacking the *S* of Christ,	871	17
whereof all be not governed with the *S* and Word	872	7
this Church is ready in the *s* of love	876	34

spiritual

a *s* conference leading to absolution	446	18
only after an heavenly and *s* manner.	873	32
but hath no authority in things purely *s*.	875	36

spoke

even as the prophets from earliest times *s* of him,	864	16

spoken

A meditation, silent or *s*, may follow.	106	6
In this prayer, the lines in italics are *s* by the People.	369	—
language *s* to the people in the Church,	866	23

sponsor

S	301	—

sponsored

Each candidate for Holy Baptism is to be *s*	298	16

sponsors

S of adults and older children present	298	18
S of infants,	298	20
presented individually by their *S*,	301	—
it is appropriate for *s* to be assigned	312	24
may also be led by one of the *s*.	312	26
s go to the font for the Thanksgiving	312	30
and the *s* should be so grouped that the people	313	5
together with the *s* or godparents,	314	8

spot

without *s*, who, by sacrifice of himself once made,	870	27

spread

The Holy Table is *s* with a clean white cloth	406	2

spring

are the traditional *s* Ember Days.	166	—
are the traditional *s* Ember Days.	218	—
and do *s* out necessarily of a true and lively Faith;	870	9
forasmuch as they *s* not of faith in Jesus Christ;	870	14

staff

a ring, *s*, and mitre, or other suitable	553	6
With the pastoral *s* the Bishop marks the	568	—
In place of a pastoral *s*,	575	21

stand

All *s*	42	—
The people *s* or kneel	54	—
All *s*	63	—
The people *s* or kneel	67	—
All *s*	80	—
The people *s* or kneel	97	—
All *s*, and the Officiant greets the people	109	—
All *s*	117	—
The people *s* or kneel	121	—
After the Sermon, all *s*, and the Celebrant	264	—
all *s*.	273	—
arrival at Golgotha (John 19:17) all *s*.	277	—
The people may be directed to *s* or kneel.	277	—
The Paschal Candle is placed in its *s*.	286	—
The people *s* or sit.	316	—
It is appropriate that the other priests present *s*	322	7
All *s*.	332	—
people *s* while the offerings are presented	333	—
The people kneel or *s*.	334	—
The people kneel or *s*.	341	—
It is appropriate that the other priests present *s*	354	7
All *s*.	360	—
people *s* while the offerings are presented	361	—
The people *s* or kneel.	362	—
The people *s* or kneel.	368	—
The people *s* or kneel.	373	—
When a passage from the Gospel is to be read, all *s*,	426	—
After the Gospel (and homily), the husband and wife *s*	433	—
All *s* while one or more of the following anthems	469	—
All *s* while one or more of the following anthems	491	—
All *s*.	513	—
All *s*.	519	—
All continue to *s*, except the bishop-elect,	520	—
The other bishops *s* to the right and left	520	—
the new priest and other priests *s*	524	14
All *s*.	527	—
All now *s* except the ordinand,	533	—
the presbyters who *s* to the right and left	533	—
All *s*.	539	—
All now *s* except the ordinand,	544	—
and representative presbyters of the diocese, *s*	553	9
who serve in the same congregation also *s*	558	11
and of the clergy of the diocese *s*	561	2
All then *s* for the Gospel,	572	—
If one reading *s* is to serve as both lectern and pulpit,	576	6

standard

numeration of the Revised *S* Version of the Bible.	14	17
and as being the rule and ultimate *s* of faith.	877	34

standeth

Original sin *s* not in the following of Adam,	869	23

standing

Officiant and People together, all *s*	53	—
Officiant and People together, all *s*	66	—
Officiant and People together, *s*	96	—
Officiant and People together, all *s*	120	—
To be said or sung, kneeling, *s*, or in procession;	148	—
sung or said, the people *s*	270	—
All *s*, the Deacon, or other person appointed,	277	—
or other person appointed, *s* near the Candle,	286	—
these or similar words, all *s*	292	—
The people *s*, the Celebrant says	299	—
Then, all *s*, the Deacon or a Priest reads	300	—
The people *s*, the Celebrant says	319	—
The people *s*, the Celebrant may say	323	—
or in place of, the preceding, all *s*	324	—
Then, all *s*, the Deacon or a Priest reads	326	—
and other Major Feasts there follows, all *s*	326	—
The people remain *s*.	333	—
The people remain *s*.	340	—
The people *s*, the Celebrant says	351	—
The people *s*, the Celebrant says	355	—
sung or said, all *s*	356	—
Then, all *s*, the Deacon or a Priest reads	357	—
and other Major Feasts there follows, all *s*	358	—
The people remain *s*.	361	—
The people remain *s*.	367	—
The people remain *s*.	372	—
The people *s*, the Bishop says	413	—
Then, all *s*, the Deacon or a Priest reads	414	—
and, *s* before the congregation,	420	—
All *s*, the Celebrant says	428	—
The people remain *s*.	430	—
It is appropriate that all remain *s* until the conclusion	437	17
celebrant *s* in the accustomed place.	468	25
Then, all *s*, the Deacon or Minister appointed	479	—
The Apostles' Creed may be said, all *s*.	480	—
celebrant *s* in the accustomed place.	490	25
Then, all *s*, the Deacon or Minister appointed	495	—
The Apostles' Creed may then be said, all *s*.	496	—
The people *s*, the Bishop appointed says	512	—
and Lay Persons, *s* before the Presiding Bishop,	513	—
Then, all *s*, a Deacon or a Priest reads	516	—
silent prayer follows, the people still *s*.	520	—
The people *s*, the Bishop says	525	—
presenters if desired, *s* before the bishop,	526	—
Then, all *s*, the Deacon or,	529	—
silent prayer follows, the people still *s*.	533	—
S at the Lord's Table, with the Bishop	535	—
The people *s*, the Bishop says	537	—
presenters if desired, *s* before the bishop,	538	—
Then, all *s*, the Deacon or,	541	—
silent prayer follows, the people still *s*.	544	—
The Wardens, *s* before the bishop	559	—
The Bishop, *s*, says	560	—
At the end of the litany, the Bishop, *s*,	560	—

s at the Lord's Table as chief celebrant, 563 —
The Litany may be sung or said *s* or kneeling, 565 6
S at the door of the church, the Bishop says 568 —
The congregation *s*, the Bishop begins the Prayer 568 —

stands

The priest alone *s* and says 42 —
The Priest alone *s* and says 63 —
The Priest alone *s* and says 80 —
The Priest alone *s* and says 117 —
The Bishop, if present, or the Priest, *s* 269 —
silent prayer, after which the Celebrant *s* 276 —
The Bishop when present, or the Priest, *s* 321 —
The Bishop when present, or the Priest, *s* 332 —
The Bishop when present, or the Priest, *s* 353 —
The Bishop when present, or the Priest, *s* 360 —
Presiding Bishop *s* and reads the Collect for the Day, 515 —
except the bishop-elect, who *s* facing the bishops. 517 —
Bishop *s* and reads the Collect for the Day, 527 —
except the ordinand, who *s* before the Bishop. 531 —
Bishop *s* and reads the Collect for the Day, 539 —
except the ordinand, who *s* before the Bishop. 543 —
At ordinations, the Bishop who is presiding *s* 551 —
the bishop always *s* for the salutation 565 7

state

conform to the laws of the *S* and the canons 422 6
The laws of the *S* and the canons of this Church 435 7
to enter the *s* of matrimony 435 13
The Bishop may read the Letter of Institution, or else may *s* 559 —
bishop may *s* briefly the nature of the person's office 565 2
20. For Congress or a *S* Legislature 810 29
20. For Congress or a *S* Legislature 821 —
18 Of the *S* of Matrimony. 875 10

stated

and canons of this Church, is briefly *s*. 435 12

statement

Commitment, which may be in the form either of a *s* 420 —
but is not meant to be a complete *s* of belief 844 4
2. The Nicene Creed as the sufficient *s* 877 15
Nicene Creed, as the sufficient *s* 877 36

states

Church in the United *S* of America, in Convention, 8 4
Church in these *S* is indebted, under God, 9 12
Providence, these American *S* became independent 10 24
Christians in these *S* were left at full and equal 10 27
19. For the President of the United *S* and all 810 28
19. For the President of the United *S* and all 820 —
Protestant Episcopal Church in the United *S* 867 31
partly are *s* of life allowed in the Scriptures; 872 34
Bishops of the Protestant Episcopal Church in the United *S* 876 25

Stephen

Saint *S* 17 4
Saint *S* December 26 186 1
Saint *S* December 26 237 —

stewards

have been ordained to be its *s* 877 10

stewardship

III. For *s* of creation 208 —
III. For *s* of creation 259 —

stiffness

mean between too much *s* in refusing, 9 26

still

have *s* been continued firm and unshaken. 10 7
and the Woman, *s* facing the man, 427 —
The husband and wife *s* kneeling, the Priest adds 431 —
prayer follows, the people *s* standing. 520 —
prayer follows, the people *s* standing. 533 —
prayer follows, the people *s* standing. 544 —

stirred

be *s* up to godliness themselves, 866 11

stole

bishop-elect is vested in a rochet or alb, without *s*, 511 16
ordinand is to be vested in surplice or alb, without *s*, 524 7
The *s* worn about the neck, or other insignia 553 21
The *s* worn over the left shoulder, or other insignia 554 12
Others present a *s* or other symbol, saying 561 —

stories

neglected, by planting in uncertain *s*, 866 17

story

The *s* of Creation 288 —
The *S* of Susanna, 869 2

stranger

Church's teaching for an inquiring *s* 844 8

strength strength to strength 481

For *S* and Confidence 459 —
himself, by his own natural *s* and good works, 869 35
as necessary to salvation have neither *s* 872 9

strengthen

Nourish them, and *s* them to glorify 557 13
s and confirm our Faith in him. 872 29

strong

Care alike for young and old, *s* and weak, 557 11

structure

These devotions follow the basic *s* of the Daily Office 136 —

stubborn

come to Communion, but not those who are *s*. 409 23
restrain with the civil sword the *s* 876 6

study

the earnest *s* of the conditions under which so priceless 877 24
a general plan referred for *s* and action 877 27

subject

s to the direction of the bishop, special devotions 13 9
s to the limitations described in the directions 14 1
S to the rules of precedence governing Principal 17 29
For optional use, when desired, *s* to the rules 199 —
For optional use, when desired, *s* to the rules 251 —
is not *s* to the Law of God. 869 30
nor ought to be, *s* to any foreign Jurisdiction. 875 42

submit

may not with a good conscience use and *s* unto,	10	16

subsequent

on some *s* occasion of public baptism	312	13
confession is not normally a matter of *s* discussion.	446	26
in *s* times generally known as priests.	510	8
for *s* use in this church.	575	27

subsequently

S, only their Christian names are used.	422	21

subsistence

coming together to form one person and *s*,	864	14

subsisting

of a reasonable soul and human flesh *s*;	865	25

substance

provided the *s* of the Faith be kept entire;	9	4
of one *s* (homoousios) with the Father	864	7
of one *s* with us as regards his manhood;	864	8
neither confounding the Persons, nor dividing the *S*.	864	26
God, of the *S* of the Father, begotten before	865	23
and Man, of the *S* of his Mother,	865	23
not by confusion of *S*, but by unity of Person.	865	30
there be three Persons, of one *s*,	867	37
eternal God, and of one *s* with the Father,	868	3
in the womb of the blessed Virgin, of her *s*:	868	4
is of one *s*, majesty, and glory,	868	17
Transubstantiation (or the change of the *s*	873	28

substantial

to be the *s* deposit of Christian Faith	877	8

substitute

s for, or as an addition to, the Proper	18	14
Then, the Hebrew custom is to *s* Elohim	583	32
s nouns for pronouns when the referent	888	26

substituted

as appropriate, instrumental music may be *s*	14	9
Lessons appointed for the Feast may be *s*	16	15
Other suitable selections may be *s*.	128	—
may be *s* for the Proper	312	22
"At Confirmation" (page 929) may be *s*.	414	—
presbyters, and fellow presbyter, are to be *s*.	528	—
passages suitable to the circumstances may be *s*.	565	13
whenever it occurred, Adonai was *s* for it.	583	20

substitutes

s "us" for "you" and "our" for "your."	42	—
s "us" for "you" and "our" for "your."	63	—
s "us" for "you" and "our" for "your."	80	—
or lay person using the preceding blessing *s* "us"	114	—
s "us" for "You" and "our" for "your."	117	—
s the prayer for forgiveness appointed	269	—
or lay person using the preceding form *s* "us"	321	—
or lay person using the preceding form *s* "us"	353	—
A deacon using the preceding form *s* "us"	398	—
or lay person using the preceding form *s* "us"	455	—
in the absence of the bishop, the deputy *s*	561	—

substituting

(*s*, if desired, the Gloria in excelsis	175	—
(*s*, if desired, the Gloria in excelsis	227	—

succeeding

as appointed, but not on the *s* weekdays	344	—
as appointed, but not on the *s* weekdays	377	—

succession

The ordinands may be presented together, or in *s*,	553	26
The ordinands may be presented together, or in *s*,	554	16

such

And require that it be received as *s* by all	8	11
s changes and alterations should be made therein,	9	19
yielded to make *s* alterations	10	4
if allowed *s* just and favourable construction	10	17
in *s* manner as they might judge most convenient	10	29
the proper end of all *s* prayers,	10	36
to establish *s* other alterations and amendments	11	7
the bishop may set forth *s* forms	13	14
Christian assembly participates in *s* a way	13	16
no celebration of the Eucharist for any *s* occasion	18	11
The Intercessions on *s* occasions are to conform	142	22
s as the hymn "All glory, laud,	271	—
a suitable psalm, *s* as Psalm 42,	312	31
A suitable psalm, *s* as Psalm 23,	313	11
Other prayers, *s* as the following,	314	2
(d) a general Collect *s* as the following:	394	—
or when desired, *s* persons may be communicated	396	—
not allowing *s* persons to receive Communion	409	14
In all *s* cases, the priest is required	409	24
and *s* other devotions as the Bishop may direct.	419	—
because *s* ministers alone have the function	422	8
the priest gives *s* counsel	446	21
Psalms, Lessons, and Collects (*s* as those	465	—
Appropriate devotions, *s* as those appointed	467	—
or have already received *s* ordination	510	23
ordaining in this Church is to be *s* as has been,	510	30
s blessing is to take place at some convenient time	552	17
S things as the deed for the property	575	17
s as Thanksgiving for the Birth or Adoption	576	16
In each *s* case, the appropriate prayer	577	10
S as the Father is, *s* is the Son,	864	30
and *s* is the Holy Ghost.	864	30
especially *s* as were Ministers of the congregation,	866	10
whereas St. Paul would have *s* language spoken	866	22
here is set forth *s* an order, whereby	866	33
Invitatories, and *s* like things,	866	38
and that in *s* a language and order	867	2
to appease all *s* diversity (if any arise),	867	17
but *s* as from time to time, in Cathedral	867	27
s are these following:	868	35
The condition of Man after the fall of Adam is *s*,	869	34
repentance is not to be denied to *s* as fall	870	33
deny the place of forgiveness to *s* as truly repent.	870	37
s as feel in themselves the working of the Spirit	871	12
we must receive God's promises in *s* wise,	871	21
Of Speaking in the Congregation in *s* a Tongue	872	21
being *s* as have grown partly of the corrupt following	872	34
And in *s* only as worthily receive the same,	872	38
nor the grace of God's gifts diminished from *s*	873	7
that to *s* as rightly, worthily, and with faith,	873	25

The Wicked, and *s* as be void of a lively faith, 873 37
all things necessary to *s* Consecration 875 22
we decree all *s* to be rightly, orderly, and lawfully 875 25
all things necessary to *s* Consecration 875 29
we decree all *s* to be rightly, orderly, and lawfully 875 33
of *s* things as he possesseth, liberally to give 876 15
are intended for use at all public services on *s* days, 888 7
The Psalms at *s* Offices are normally 888 15
Reading some *s* introduction as, "N. said (to N.)." 888 28

suffer

Those who *s* and those in any trouble 359 —
Those who *s* and those in any trouble 383 —
26. For those who *S* for the sake of Conscience 811 —
26. For those who *s* for the sake of Conscience 823 —

suffered

Who *s* for our salvation, 865 32
who truly *s*, was crucified, 868 6

suffering

minister in Christ's name to the poor, the sick, the *s*, 510 14

suffice

If the consecrated Bread or Wine does not *s* 408 9

sufficiency

VI. Of the *S* of the Holy Scriptures for Salvation. 868 19

sufficient

and for urgent and *s* reason 16 19
or on other occasions for *s* reason, 312 20
In the absence of *s* deacons 408 7
Deacon prepares the bread, pours *s* wine 546 —
2. The Nicene Creed as the *s* statement 877 15
the Nicene Creed, as the *s* statement 877 35

suffrages

Then follows one of these *S* 55 —
Then follows one of these sets of *S* 67 —
Then follows one of these sets of *S* 97 —
Then follows one of these sets of *S* 121 —

suggest

The Priest may *s* the making of a special confession, 454 —

suggested

also appropriate, especially for the seasons *s*: 108 15
Instead of the Proper Preface *s*, that of the season 576 25
verses *s* in the lectionary 582 10
S lengthenings are shown 888 29
it is *s* that the Gospel Reading be used 934 11
S lengthenings are shown 934 20

suggestions

(For *s* about reading the Psalms, 136 7

suit

YHWH, and our English tradition follows *s*, 583 33

suitable

The following, or some other *s* hymn, 64 —
Especially *s* for use in Easter Season 85 —
Especially *s* in Lent, 90 —
A *s* hymn may be sung. 103 —
Other *s* selections include 103 —
One of the following, or some other *s* passage 105 —
on *s* occasions in the late afternoon or evening. 108 3
the following or some other *s* prayer, 110 —
Silence, or a *s* Collect, or both, 113 —
A litany, or other *s* devotions, 113 —
The following, or some other *s* hymn, 117 —
Other *s* selections may be substituted. 128 8
One of the following, or some other *s* passage 131 —
A hymn *s* for the evening may be sung. 132 —
or ones *s* to the season or the occasion, 143 22
Especially *s* for Thursdays 201 —
Especially *s* for Fridays 201 —
Especially *s* for Saturdays 201 —
Especially *s* for Thursdays 252 —
Especially *s* for Fridays 252 —
Especially *s* for Saturdays 252 —
The following or some other *s* anthem 270 —
The following or some other *s* anthem 271 —
At a *s* place, the procession may halt 271 —
s portions of the preceding may be used. 272 —
the following or other *s* anthems 274 —
or other *s* anthems. 281 —
some other *s* psalm, canticle, or hymn 288 —
or some other *s* Collect, 288 —
some other *s* psalm or a hymn 295 —
a *s* psalm, such as Psalm 42, 312 31
A *s* psalm, such as Psalm 23, 313 11
When used separately, it concludes with *s* prayers, 321 —
The following or some other *s* anthem 337 —
When used separately, it concludes with *s* prayers, 353 —
some other *s* anthem may be used. 364 —
Adaptations or insertions *s* to the occasion 383 —
concludes with an absolution or a *s* Collect. 393 —
S prayers may be offered, 397 —
When desired, some other *s* symbol of the vows 437 22
it is *s* to administer the Sacrament in one kind 457 —
S Psalms, Lessons, and Collects 465 7
during which time a *s* psalm or anthem 467 4
covered with a pall or other *s* covering. 468 9
After the Old Testament Lesson, a *s* canticle 470 —
After the New Testament Lesson, a *s* canticle 475 —
one or more *s* prayers 480 —
This anthem, or some other *s* anthem, 482 —
covered with a pall or other *s* covering. 490 9
A hymn, psalm, or some other *s* anthem 491 —
A *s* psalm, hymn, or canticle 494 —
A *s* psalm, hymn, or canticle 495 —
one or more *s* prayers 496 —
This anthem, or some other *s* anthem, 499 —
s for the conferring of the sacred orders 510 31
Officiant concludes with a *s* Collect. 551 —
or other *s* insignia of office 553 6
(especially *s* for use in the evening) 560 —
or another prayer *s* to the occasion, 565 8
Other passages *s* to the circumstances 565 12
s parts of this rite may be used for dedicating 566 5
social purposes, or for other *s* activities. 566 12
The use of portable musical instruments is *s*. 575 10
or a lay reader, or another *s* person. 576 10
it is *s* that a warden or other lay person 576 11
it is *s* that the donors of these furnishings, 576 22
for some other *s* purpose, the service may be adapted 576 30

S portions of this service may be used by the bishop, 577 4
consecration of a church, or on other *s* occasions. 579 —
it is *s* for selective use, 844 10
On Special Occasions, the officiant may select *s* 935 12

summary
The *S* of the Law, the Gloria in excelsis, 552 5
second use of this catechism is to provide a brief *s* 844 7

summer
are the traditional *s* Ember Days. 176 —
are the traditional *s* Ember Days. 227 —

Sunday
the movable date of the *S* of the Resurrection 15 4
Easter Day is always the first *S* after the full moon 15 7
Christmas Day, whether it occurs on a *S* 15 11
Trinity *S* 15 19
always be observed on the *S* following November 1, 15 21
take precedence of a *S*: 16 4
may be observed on, or be transferred to, a *S*, 16 9
fixed days in the Calendar, when they occur on a *S*, 16 12
may be substituted for those of the *S* 16 15
but not from the Last *S* after Pentecost 16 16
or from the Last *S* after the Epiphany through 16 17
Trinity *S*. 16 18
some other special occasion may be observed on a *S*. 16 20
the week following the Second *S* of Easter, 17 12
Saturdays after the First *S* in Lent, 18 6
Trinity *S* 39 —
On Trinity *S* 43 —
Trinity *S* 77 —
On Trinity *S* 81 —
Collect for the First *S* of Advent 111 —
Collect for the First *S* after Christmas 111 —
The Proper appointed for the *S* is also used 158 7
(except for Trinity *S*) 158 11
is determined by the calendar date of that *S*. 158 11
the Proper for the *S* after Trinity *S* 158 12
(the Second *S* after Pentecost) 158 13
the calendar date of which falls on that *S*, 158 14
if the *S* after Trinity *S* is May 26, 158 16
If the *S* after Trinity *S* is June 13, 158 18
The Collect appointed for any *S* or other Feast 158 22
First *S* of Advent 159 —
Second *S* of Advent 159 —
Third *S* of Advent 160 —
Fourth *S* of Advent 160 —
and the First *S* after Christmas Day. 161 —
First *S* after Christmas Day 161 —
This *S* takes precedence over the three Holy Days 161 —
Second *S* after Christmas Day 162 —
or those for the Second *S* after Christmas Day, 162 —
First *S* after the Epiphany: 163 —
Second *S* after the Epiphany 163 —
Third *S* after the Epiphany 163 —
Fourth *S* after the Epiphany 164 —
Fifth *S* after the Epiphany 164 —
Sixth *S* after the Epiphany 164 —
Seventh *S* after the Epiphany 164 —
Eighth *S* after the Epiphany 165 —
Last *S* after the Epiphany 165 —
This Proper is always used on the *S* before Ash Wednesday. 165 —
First *S* in Lent 166 —
Second *S* in Lent 166 —
Third *S* in Lent 167 —
Fourth *S* in Lent 167 —
Fifth *S* in Lent 167 —
S of the Passion: Palm *S* 168 —
Second *S* of Easter 172 —
Third *S* of Easter 173 —
Fourth *S* of Easter 173 —
Fifth *S* of Easter 173 —
Sixth *S* of Easter 174 —
Seventh *S* of Easter: 175 —
The *S* after Ascension Day 175 —
First *S* after Pentecost: Trinity *S* 176 —
Preface of Trinity *S* 176 —
most closely to the date of Trinity *S* in that year 176 —
Proper 1 Week of the *S* closest to May 11 176 —
Proper 2 Week of the *S* closest to May 18 177 —
Proper 3 The *S* closest to May 25 177 —
Proper 4 The *S* closest to June 1 177 —
Proper 5 The *S* closest to June 8 178 —
Proper 6 The *S* closest to June 15 178 —
Proper 7 The *S* closest to June 22 178 —
Proper 8 The *S* closest to June 29 178 —
Proper 9 The *S* closest to July 6 179 —
Proper 10 The *S* closest to July 13 179 —
Proper 11 The *S* closest to July 20 179 —
Proper 12 The *S* closest to July 27 180 —
Proper 13 The *S* closest to August 3 180 —
Proper 14 The *S* closest to August 10 180 —
Proper 15 The *S* closest to August 17 180 —
Proper 16 The *S* closest to August 24 181 —
Proper 17 The *S* closest to August 31 181 —
Proper 18 The *S* closest to September 7 181 —
Proper 19 The *S* closest to September 14 182 —
Proper 20 The *S* closest to September 21 182 —
Proper 21 The *S* closest to September 28 182 —
Proper 22 The *S* closest to October 5 182 —
Proper 23 The *S* closest to October 12 183 —
Proper 24 The *S* closest to October 19 183 —
Proper 25 The *S* closest to October 26 183 —
Proper 26 The *S* closest to November 2 184 —
Proper 27 The *S* closest to November 9 184 —
Proper 28 The *S* closest to November 16 184 —
Proper 29 The *S* closest to November 23 185 —
Preface of Trinity *S* 190 —
Preface of Trinity *S* 193 —
Preface of Trinity *S* 194 —
Preface of a Saint, or of Trinity *S* 197 —
Preface of Trinity *S* 199 —
Preface of Trinity *S* 200 —
Preface of Baptism, or of Trinity *S* 205 —
Preface of Trinity *S* 207 —
First *S* of Advent 211 —
Second *S* of Advent 211 —
Third *S* of Advent 212 —
Fourth *S* of Advent 212 —
and the First *S* after Christmas Day. 213 —
First *S* after Christmas Day 213 —
This *S* takes precedence over the three Holy Days 213 —

Second *S* after Christmas Day	214	—
or those for the Second *S* after Christmas,	214	—
between the Epiphany and the following *S*.	214	—
First *S* after the Epiphany:	214	—
Second *S* after the Epiphany	215	—
Third *S* after the Epiphany	215	—
Fourth *S* after the Epiphany	215	—
Fifth *S* after the Epiphany	216	—
Sixth *S* after the Epiphany	216	—
Seventh *S* after the Epiphany	216	—
Eighth *S* after the Epiphany	216	—
Last *S* after the Epiphany	217	—
This Proper is always used on the *S* before Ash Wednesday	217	—
First *S* in Lent	218	—
Second *S* in Lent	218	—
Third *S* in Lent	218	—
Fourth *S* in Lent	219	—
Fifth *S* in Lent	219	—
S of the Passion: Palm *S*	219	—
Second *S* of Easter	224	—
Third *S* of Easter	224	—
Fourth *S* of Easter	225	—
Fifth *S* of Easter	225	—
Sixth *S* of Easter	225	—
Seventh *S* of Easter:	226	—
The *S* after Ascension Day	226	—
First *S* after Pentecost: Trinity *S*	228	—
Preface of Trinity *S*	228	—
corresponds most closely to the date of Trinity *S*	228	—
Proper 1 Week of the *S* closest to May 11	228	—
Proper 2 Week of the *S* closest to May 18	228	—
Proper 3 The *S* closest to May 25	229	—
Proper 4 The *S* closest to June 1	229	—
Proper 5 The *S* closest to June 8	229	—
Proper 6 The *S* closest to June 15	230	—
Proper 7 The *S* closest to June 22	230	—
Proper 8 The *S* closest to June 29	230	—
Proper 9 The *S* closest to July 6	230	—
Proper 10 The *S* closest to July 13	231	—
Proper 11 The *S* closest to July 20	231	—
Proper 12 The *S* closest to July 27	231	—
Proper 13 The *S* closest to August 3	232	—
Proper 14 The *S* closest to August 10	232	—
Proper 15 The *S* closest to August 17	232	—
Proper 16 The *S* closest to August 24	232	—
Proper 17 The *S* closest to August 31	233	—
Proper 18 The *S* closest to September 7	233	—
Proper 19 The *S* closest to September 14	233	—
Proper 20 The *S* closest to September 21	234	—
Proper 21 The *S* closest to September 28	234	—
Proper 22 The *S* closest to October 5	234	—
Proper 23 The *S* closest to October 12	234	—
Proper 24 The *S* closest to October 19	235	—
Proper 25 The *S* closest to October 26	235	—
Proper 26 The *S* closest to November 2	235	—
Proper 27 The *S* closest to November 9	236	—
Proper 28 The *S* closest to November 16	236	—
Proper 29 The *S* closest to November 23	236	—
Preface of Trinity *S*	242	—
Preface of Trinity *S*	244	—
Preface of Trinity *S*	246	—
Preface of a Saint, or of Trinity *S*	249	—
Preface of Trinity *S*	251	—
Preface of Baptism, or of Trinity *S*	255	—
Preface of Trinity *S*	258	—
chief service on a *S* or other feast.	298	6
At the principal service on a *S* or other feast,	300	—
on All Saints' Day or the *S* after All Saints'	312	3
on the Feast of the Baptism of our Lord (the First *S*	312	4
Trinity *S*	347	—
Trinity *S*	380	—
It is not intended for use at the principal *S*	400	4
At the principal service on a *S* or other feast,	414	—
It is desirable that this take place at a *S* service.	439	6
On a Major Feast or on a *S*, the Presiding Bishop	515	—
On a Major Feast, or on a *S*, the Bishop	528	—
On a Major Feast, or on a *S*, the Bishop	540	—
on a Major Feast, *S*, or Patronal Feast, selections	571	—
69. On *S*	812	24
Prayers for Friday, Saturday, and *S*,	812	26
Prayers for Friday, Saturday, and *S*,	833	—
69. On *S*	835	1
Year A always begins on the First *S* of Advent	888	3
Year A, therefore, begins on Advent *S*	888	5
from one of the other years of the three-year *S* cycle,	888	14
Psalm cited in the selected *S* Proper may be used	888	17
Year One begins on the First *S* of Advent	934	3
Year Two begins on the First *S* of Advent	934	4
(Thus, on the First *S* of Advent, 1976,	934	5
Three Readings are provided for each *S*	934	7
and Palm *S* to 2 Easter),	934	23

Sundays

sequence of all *S* of the Church Year depends	15	9
But the *S* of Advent are always	15	10
the four *S* before Christmas Day,	15	10
2. *S*	16	1
All *S* of the year are feasts of our Lord	16	2
ordered in the preceding rules concerning *S*,	16	23
rules of precedence governing Principal Feasts, *S*,	17	29
On other *S* and Weekdays	44	—
A Collect for *S*	56	—
A Collect for *S*	69	—
On other *S* and weekdays	81	—
A Collect for *S*	98	—
Collect for *S*	123	—
a) the Lectionary for *S*,	136	—
The Proper to be used on each of the *S*	158	10
On *S* and other Major Feasts there follows,	326	—
Here a Proper Preface is sung or said on all *S*,	334	—
Here a Proper Preface is sung or said on all *S*,	341	—
To be used on *S* as appointed,	344	—
To be used on *S* and weekdays alike,	345	—
On *S* and other Major Feasts there follows,	358	—
Here a Proper Preface is sung or said on all *S*,	361	—
Here a Proper Preface is sung or said on all *S*,	367	—
To be used on *S* as appointed,	377	—
To be used on *S* and weekdays alike,	378	—
on *S* from Easter Day	406	13
the *S* or ordinary weekdays of Advent or Lent.	406	16
that bishops be ordained on *S*	511	4
Lectionary for *S* is arranged in a three-year cycle,	888	2
The Psalms and Lessons appointed for the *S*	888	6

sung

"said," it must be understood to include "or *s*,"	14	12
One of the following Antiphons may be *s*	43	—
in place of an Invitatory Psalm, the following is *s*	45	—
At the end of the Psalms is *s* or said	46	—
one of those on pages 85–95 (Canticles 8–21), is *s*	47	—
Here may be *s* a hymn or anthem.	58	—
an Invitatory Psalm, may be *s*	64	—
At the end of the Psalms is *s* or said	64	—
one of those on pages 47–52, or 85–95, is *s*	65	—
Here may be *s* a hymn or anthem.	71	—
One of the following Antiphons may be *s*	80	—
in place of an Invitatory Psalm, the following is *s*	83	—
At the end of the Psalms is *s* or said	84	—
one of those on pages 47–52 (Canticles 1–7), is *s*	84	—
Here may be *s* a hymn or anthem.	101	—
A suitable hymn may be *s*.	103	—
One or more of the following Psalms is *s* or said.	103	—
At the end of the Psalms is *s* or said	105	—
psalm may be *s*, or silence kept.	112	—
or some other hymn, is then *s*	112	—
an Invitatory Psalm, may be *s*	117	—
At the end of the Psalms is *s* or said	118	—
one of those on pages 47–52, or 85–95, is *s*	119	—
Here may be *s* a hymn or anthem.	125	—
One or more of the following Psalms are *s* or said.	128	—
At the end of the Psalms is *s* or said	131	—
A hymn suitable for the evening may be *s*.	132	—
Song of Simeon with this Antiphon, which is *s*	134	—
Gloria Patri is always *s* or said	141	11
in place of a Canticle, a hymn may be *s*.	142	1
while the hymn Phos hilaron is being *s*.	143	20
If an additional hymn is desired, it may be *s*	143	27
To be said or *s*, kneeling, standing, or in procession;	148	—
When the Litany is *s* or said	153	—
The following Psalm is then *s* or said	265	—
following or some other suitable anthem is *s* or said,	270	—
or some other suitable anthem may then be *s*	271	—
hymns, psalms, or anthems are *s*,	271	—
suitable anthems may be *s* or said	274	—
A hymn may then be *s*.	277	—
If the texts are recited rather than *s*,	281	—
hymn extolling the glory of the cross, is then *s*.	282	—
Anthem "In the midst of life" (page 484 or 492) is *s*	283	—
suitable psalm, canticle, or hymn may be *s*.	288	—
One of the following Canticles is then *s*.	294	—
'Alleluia" may be *s* and repeated.	295	—
suitable psalm or a hymn may be *s*.	295	—
A hymn, psalm, or anthem may be *s*.	299	—
If desired, the hymn Gloria in excelsis may be *s*	312	18
Psalm 42, or a hymn or anthem, may be *s*.	312	32
hymn or anthem, may be *s* during the procession.	313	12
A hymn, psalm, or anthem may be *s*.	319	—
A hymn, psalm, or anthem may be *s*.	323	—
Here is *s* or said	324	—
hymn or some other song of praise is *s*	324	—
During the Offertory, a hymn, psalm, or anthem may be *s*.	333	—
Here a Proper Preface is *s* or said	334	—
Then may be *s* or said	337	—
or some other suitable anthem may be *s*	337	—
hymns, psalms, or anthems may be *s*.	338	—
Here a Proper Preface is *s* or said	341	—
A hymn, psalm, or anthem may be *s*.	351	—
A hymn, psalm, or anthem may be *s*.	355	—
hymn or some other song of praise is *s*	356	—
During the Offertory, a hymn, psalm, or anthem may be *s*.	361	—
Here a Proper Preface is *s* or said	361	—
Then may be *s* or said	364	—
hymns, psalms, or anthems may be *s*.	365	—
Here a Proper Preface is *s* or said	367	—
When the Great Litany is *s* or said	406	3
Kyrie eleison (or "Lord, have mercy") may be *s*	406	9
The Trisagion, "Holy God," may be *s*	406	11
Gloria in excelsis, or the hymn used in place of it, is *s*	406	12
A hymn or anthem may then be *s*,	407	2
during which time a communion hymn may be *s*.	408	22
may be *s* before or after the postcommunion prayer.	409	6
If desired, the hymn Gloria in excelsis may be *s*	412	13
A hymn, psalm, or anthem may be *s*.	413	—
a hymn, psalm, or anthem may be *s*,	423	—
a Psalm, hymn, or anthem may be *s*	426	—
A hymn, psalm, or anthem may be *s*,	431	—
a hymn, psalm, or anthem may be *s*;	432	—
suitable psalm or anthem may be *s* or said.	467	—
The anthems at the beginning of the service are *s*	468	23
one or more of the following anthems is *s*	469	—
the following Psalms may be *s* or said	470	—
the following Psalms may be *s* or said	475	—
some other suitable anthem, or a hymn, may be *s*	482	—
one or more of these anthems may be *s*	483	—
The following anthem is *s* or said	484	—
The anthems at the beginning of the service are *s*	490	23
one or more of the following anthems is *s*	491	—
some other suitable anthem may be *s*	491	—
some other suitable anthem, or a hymn, may be *s*	499	—
one or more of these anthems may be *s*	500	—
or one of those on pages 491–492 is *s*	501	—
2. Anthems from Holy Scripture or psalms may be *s*	506	7
or a hymn may be *s*.	506	8
and anthems may be *s* during the entrance	512	—
or the hymn, Veni Sancte Spiritus, is *s*.	520	—
A hymn, psalm, or anthem may be *s*.	525	—
or the hymn, Veni Sancte Spiritus, is *s*.	533	—
A hymn, psalm, or anthem may be *s*.	537	—
or the hymn, Veni Sancte Spiritus, is *s*.	544	—
Prayer of Consecration may be *s* responsively	552	15
a hymn of praise may be *s*.	553	15
A hymn, psalm, or anthem may be *s*.	559	—
The Litany may be *s* or said standing	565	6
or some other appropriate psalm is *s*.	568	—
Hymns and anthems may also be *s*.	568	—
music is now played, or a hymn or anthem *s*.	572	—
the Nicene Creed is now said or *s*.	572	—
when the verses are recited rather than *s*,	582	11
the verses of a psalm are *s* by a solo voice,	582	20
shall be read and *s* in the English tongue,	867	23
when the Psalm is *s* between the Lessons	888	21
may be *s* or said at the beginning and end	935	10

sunrise

sunset on Holy Saturday and *s* on Easter	284	4

sunset
s on Holy Saturday and sunrise on Easter 284 3

supererogation
XIV. Of Works of *S*. 870 18
which they call Works of *S*, 870 20

superstitions
hath given occasion to many *s*. 873 30

superstitious
some uncertain, some vain and *s*: 867 1
neither hath it any thing that, of itself, is *s* 875 23
neither hath it any thing, that of itself is *s* 875 30

supervising
work of leading, *s*, and uniting the Church. 510 7

supper
Baptism, and the *S* of the Lord. 872 31
the Lord's *S*, for that they have not any visible sign 872 36
XXVIII. Of the Lord's *S*. 873 22
The *S* of the Lord is not only a sign of the love 873 23
change of the substance of Bread and Wine) in the *S* 873 28
Body of Christ is given, taken, and eaten, in the *S*, 873 31
is received and eaten in the *S*, is Faith. 873 33
The Sacrament of the Lord's *S* was not by Christ's 873 34
eat not the Body of Christ in the use of the Lord's *S*. 873 36
3. The two Sacraments,—Baptism and the *S* 877 16
ordained by Christ Himself—Baptism and the *S* 878 1

supplication
The *S* 154 —

supply
the following Articles *s* a basis 877 31

support
s them by prayer and example in their Christian life. 298 20

supposed
it cannot but be *s* that further alterations 10 19

sure
by the wit of man so well devised, or so *s* established, 866 3
but rather they be certain *s* witnesses, 872 27

surplice
The ordinand is to be vested in *s* 524 7
The ordinand is to be vested in a *s* 536 7

surrender
therefore incapable of compromise or *s* by those 877 10

Susanna
The Story of *S*, 869 2

suspends
which also *s* the order for the reading of said 875 17

swallow
(He will *s* up death in victory) 470 —
(He will *s* up death for ever) 494 —

swear
that a man may *s* when the Magistrate requireth, 876 20

swearing
As we confess that vain and rash *S* is forbidden 876 18

sweet
and our Election in Christ, is full of *s*, 871 11

sword
and restrain with the civil *s* the stubborn 876 5

symbol
(at the *s* of N.N.), the full names 422 20
some other suitable *s* of the vows 437 22
(designated by the *s* N.N.) 511 19
(designated by the *s* N.N.) 524 9
(designated by the *s* N.N.) 536 9
Others present a stole or other *s*, 561 —
Others present a book of prayers or other *s*, 561 —
Others present olive oil or some other *s*, 561 —
(b) The Apostles' Creed, as the Baptismal *S*; 877 35

symbols
After this other *s* of office may be given. 521 —
If vestments or other *s* of office are to be dedicated, 552 17
other instruments or *s* of office may be given. 553 24
The *s* presented should be large enough 565 21

symmetry
but on parallelism of clauses, a *s* of form and sense. 583 3

sympathy
we sorrow in *s* with those who mourn. 507 14

synodals
vain repetitions, Commemorations, and *S*, 866 18

T

table
candles may be lighted at the dining *t*, 143 18
See also the *T* on pages 884–885. 158 21
to be the principal celebrant at the Lord's *T*, 322 3
Deacons should also serve at the Lord's *T*, 322 11
Then, facing the Holy *T*, the Celebrant proceeds 333 —
Then, facing the Holy *T*, the Celebrant proceeds 341 —
to be the principal celebrant at the Lord's *T*, 354 3
Deacons should also serve at the Lord's *T*, 354 11
Then, facing the Holy *T*, the Celebrant proceeds 361 —
Then, facing the Holy *T*, the Celebrant proceeds 367 —
Then, facing the Holy *T*, the Celebrant proceeds 370 —
Then, facing the Holy *T*, the Celebrant proceeds 373 —
Prepare the *T* 401 4
Some of those present prepare the *t*; 401 5
The Holy *T* is spread with a clean white cloth 406 2
the function of a deacon to make ready the *T* 407 14
deacons at the Holy *T* then communicate, 407 24
the celebrant is to return to the Holy *T*, 408 10
and tell him that he may not come to the Holy *T* until 409 10
They may then remain before the Lord's *T* 438 3
Deacons prepare the *T*. 522 —
Then the new Bishop goes to the Lord's *T* 522 —
Deacons prepare the *T*. 535 —
Standing at the Lord's *T*, with the Bishop 535 —
places the vessels on the Lord's *T*. 546 —

The Bishop goes to the *T* and begins	546	—
standing at the Lord's *T* as chief celebrant,	563	—
The Bishop goes to the *T* and, with arms extended,	573	3
The Bishop lays a hand upon the *T*, and continues	573	4

tables

appointed Psalms and Lessons, which appear in *t*	158	5

take

to *t* a further review of the Public Service,	11	6
These feasts *t* precedence of any other day	15	20
feasts, appointed on fixed days, *t* precedence	16	4
fixed days in the Calendar do not *t* precedence	17	14
the Nicene Creed may *t* the place of the Apostles'	142	18
the lighting of an Advent Wreath may *t* place after	143	14
and other persons, to *t* active parts in the service.	284	11
the Service of Light may *t* place	284	30
Baptismal Vows may *t* place here.	295	—
also *t* vows on behalf of their candidates.	298	22
Baptismal Vows, page 292, may *t* the place of	312	16
If the Presentation of the Candidates does not *t* place	312	28
exchange of the Peace may *t* place	407	10
It is desirable that this *t* place at a Sunday	439	6
At Morning or Evening Prayer it may *t* place before	439	8
it is recommended that it *t* place immediately	453	9
If preferred, the Committal service may *t* place	468	11
The Celebrant and other ministers *t* their places	482	—
If preferred, the Committal service may *t* place	490	11
The Celebrant and other ministers *t* their places	499	—
The committal may *t* place either where	506	19
they *t* part in the governance	510	9
blessing is to *t* place at some convenient time	552	18
the administration may *t* place at several	553	12
All the newly ordained *t* part in the exchange	554	7
and to *t* your share in the councils of the Church.	557	4
If no Baptism is to *t* place	570	—
appropriate that their representatives *t* part	577	2
parallelism can *t* the form of similarity	583	4
the parties that so doubt, or diversely *t* any thing,	867	19
by his discretion shall *t* order	867	20
should *t* away the sins of the world	870	27
It is not lawful for any man to *t* upon him	872	16

taken

special devotions *t* from this Book,	13	9
the flame may be *t* from the Paschal Candle.	143	11
that they be *t* out of holy Scripture."	872	10
Neither is the effect of Christ's ordinance *t* away	873	6
The Body of Christ is given, *t*, and eaten,	873	31
ought to be *t* of the whole multitude	874	18

takes

This Sunday *t* precedence	161	—
This Sunday *t* precedence	213	—
or a giving in marriage, it *t* place at this time.	425	—
Woman, still facing the man, *t* his right hand in hers,	427	—
When the Laying on of Hands or Anointing *t* place	453	7
The rector or minister in charge *t* part	566	13
Liturgy of the Word *t* the form given	888	10

taking

the congregation *t* the part of the crowd.	273	—
the congregation *t* the part of the crowd.	277	—
t part in everything except the administration	314	—
The Man, facing the woman and *t* her right hand	427	—
Then the Celebrant, holding or *t* the child	441	—
but by *t* of the Manhood into God;	865	29

talk

and response may include readings, song, *t*,	400	9
(as the Pelagians do vainly *t*;)	869	23

task

assigned the *t* of pouring the water.	575	24

taught

words our Savior Christ hath (has) *t* us."	408	24
or with the prayer "O God, you have *t* us."	439	12
and our Lord Jesus Christ himself *t* us,	864	17
Supererogation, cannot be *t* without arrogancy	870	20

teach

we all with one accord *t* men to acknowledge	864	4

teacher

Of a Theologian and *T*	197	—
Of a Theologian and *T*	248	—
pastor, priest, and *t*,	557	4
rather, it is a point of departure for the *t*,	844	5

teaching

t of the Church concerning Holy Matrimony,	435	11
provide a brief summary of the Church's *t*	844	8
done according to the Prophet's *t* in justice,	876	21

tear

(God will wipe away every *t*)	495	6

tears

(God shall wipe away all *t*)	475	6

teeth

do carnally and visibly press with their *t*	873	38

tell

and *t* him that he may not come to the Holy Table	409	10

telling

t them that they may not receive Communion	409	18

temporal

arranging for the disposal of their *t* goods,	445	—
Clergy as Laity, in all things *t*;	875	36
whether they be Ecclesiastical or *T*,	876	5

ten

Then the *T* Commandments (page 317) may be said,	324	—
The *T* Commandments	847	—

tend

might most *t* to the preservation of peace	10	10

tenth

T Day: Morning Prayer	654	—
T Day: Evening Prayer	658	—

tenure

and others having similar *t* of office.	564	18

term

In the Daily Office, the *t* "Officiant" 36 3
In the Daily Office, the *t* "Officiant" 74 2
The *t* "Various Occasions" in the following pages 813 17

terms

service of Christ in the world, either in general *t*, 420 —
the original Greek *t* presbyter, presbyters, 528 —
Three *t* are used in the Psalms with reference to God: 583 15

Testament

Old *T* Joel 2:1–2, 12–17, 264 —
Old *T* Isaiah 45:21–25, 272 —
Old *T* Exodus 12:1–14a 274 —
Old *T* Isaiah 52:13–53:12, 276 —
Old *T* Job 14:1–14 283 —
It is desirable that the Lessons from the Old *T* 422 18
It is desirable that the Lesson from the Old *T*, 468 15
From the Old *T* 470 —
After the Old *T* Lesson, a suitable canticle 470 —
From the New *T* 475 —
After the New *T* Lesson, a suitable canticle 475 —
It is desirable that the Lesson from the Old *T*, 490 15
From the Old *T* 494 —
From the New *T* 495 —
In particular, since the time of the New *T*, 510 4
Lay persons read the Old *T* Lesson 515 —
Old *T* Isaiah 61:1–8, 515 13
Lay persons read the Old *T* Lesson 528 —
Old *T* Isaiah 6:1–8, 528 —
Lay persons read the Old *T* Lesson 540 —
Old *T* Jeremiah 540 —
Lay persons from the congregation read the Old *T* 558 14
Old *T* Joshua 1:7–9, 560 —
Lay persons read the Old *T* Lesson 571 —
Old *T* 1 Kings 8:22–23, 27b–30, 571 —
Prayer Book Psalter and the King James Old *T*, 583 27
canonical books of the Old and New *T*, 868 24
All the Books of the New *T*, 869 4
VII. Of the Old *T*. 869 6
The Old *T* is not contrary to the New: 869 7
for both in the Old and New *T* 869 7
1. The Holy Scriptures of the Old and New *T* 877 14
the Old *T* Reading for the alternate year is used 934 13
first is always from the Old *T* (or the Apocrypha). 934 16

Testaments

The Holy Scriptures of the Old and New *T*, 877 33

testify

set forth by Elizabeth our Queen do most plainly *t*; 876 2

testimonials

The Presiding Bishop then directs that *t* 513 —
When the reading of the *t* is ended, 513 —

Tetragrammaton

(*T*) is probably to be vocalized Yahweh; 583 17

text

The *t* of the Creed on page 96 may be used 54 —
The *t* of the Creed on page 120 may be used 66 —
From time to time, the Hebrew *t* has Adonai 583 31
The original 1571, 1662 *t* of this Article, 872 4
The original 1571, 1662 *t* of this Article 875 26
The original 1571, 1662 *t* of this Article 875 39

texts

or from this Book, or from *t* congruent with them. 14 8
previously authorized liturgical *t* may be used 14 14
in place of the corresponding *t* 14 14
If the *t* are recited rather than sung 281 —

thank

"Heavenly Father, we *t* you that by water 298 11
"Heavenly Father, we *t* you that by water 313 10

thanks

The Celebrant gives *t* to God the Father 402 —
The Celebrant gives *t* to God the Father 404 —
to be welcomed by the congregation and to give *t* 439 5
some parents may wish to express *t* 439 15

thanksgiving

For special days of fasting or *t*, 13 12
T Day 17 6
Occasions of *T* 40 —
The General *T* 58 —
The General *T* 71 —
Occasions of *T* 78 —
The General *T* 101 —
The General *T* 125 —
prayers of *t* for the blessings of the day, 140 —
or objects of prayer and *t*, 142 9
T Day 194 —
the Litany of *T* on page 836 may be used. 194 —
The Litany of *T* for a Church, page 578, 204 —
T Day 246 —
the Litany of *T* on page 836 may be used. 246 —
The Litany of *T* for a Church, page 578, 255 —
says the *T* over the Water; 298 10
T over the Water 306 —
sponsors go to the font for the *T* over the Water. 312 30
before the *T* over the Water. 313 2
At the *T* over the Water, 313 3
The Great *T* 333 —
Alternative Form of the Great *T* 340 —
The Great *T* 361 —
Alternative Forms of the Great *T* 367 —
The Great *T* is said by the Priest 401 8
At the Great *T* 402 —
During the Great *T*, it is appropriate that there be 407 18
A *T* for the Birth 439 1
Celebrant may begin with the act of *T*, 439 12
Act of *T* 441 —
sign of penitence and act of *t*. 446 25
T for a Beginning of Recovery 460 —
At the Great *T*, the new priest 524 14
Bishop goes to the Table and begins the Great *T*. 546 —
and other priests at the Altar for the Great *T*. 554 8
proceeds with the Great *T* 563 —
For the Great *T*, any of the authorized 565 27
such as *T* for the Birth or Adoption 576 16
3. Litany of *T* for a Church, 577 28
A Litany of *T* for a Church 578 6
1. A General *T* 812 30
2. A Litany of *T* 812 31

The General *T* is on pages 58 and 101. 813 1
T for the Social Order 813 8
1. A General *T* 836 —
2. A Litany of *T* 836 —
For optional use on *T* Day, 836 6
See also The General *T* on pages 58 and 101. 837 —
T for the Social Order 840 —
See also the *T* for a Child on page 439. 841 —

thanksgivings

Authorized intercessions and *t* may follow. 58 —
Authorized intercessions and *t* may follow. 71 —
Authorized intercessions and *t* may follow. 101 —
Authorized intercessions and *t* may follow. 125 —
and free intercessions and *t* may be offered 134 —
In the Intercessions and *T*, opportunity may be given 142 7
Additional petitions and *t* may be included 330 —
ask the prayers or the *t* of those present 386 —
The People may add their own *t* 393 —
T 809 —
Prayers and *T* 810 3
T 812 28
General *T* 812 29
T for the Church 813 2
T for National Life 813 5
T for the Natural Order 813 10
T for Family and Personal Life 813 13
T for the departed are on pages 487–489 813 16
Prayers and *T* 814 —
T 836 —
General *T* 836 —
T for the Church 838 —
T for National Life 838 —
T for the Natural Order 840 —
T for Family and Personal Life 841 —
T for the departed are on pages 487–489 841 —

theologian

Of a *T* and Teacher 197 —
Of a *T* and Teacher 248 —

Theotokos

Mary the Virgin, the God-bearer (*T*); 864 11

thereafter

T, the Propers are used 158 15
and it remains closed *t*. 468 8
and it remains closed *t*. 490 8
T, it is appropriate to refer to him only by 511 19
T, it is appropriate to refer to him only by 524 10
T, it is appropriate to refer to him only by 536 10
T, references to the ordinand in the singular 553 27
T, references to the ordinand in the singular 554 17

thereby

t signify their endorsement of the candidates 298 19
intending *t*, that the Clergy, 866 9
and mind, have not been edified *t*. 866 26
to the end that the congregation may be *t* edified: 867 24
is not read therein, nor may be proved *t*, 868 21

therefore

and *t*, by common consent and authority 9 6
The liturgy, *t*, is characterized by joy, 507 5
T, following the holy fathers, 864 4
He *t* that will be saved must thus think 865 18
These inconveniences *t* considered, 866 33
t certain rules are here set forth 866 40
t in every person born into this world, 869 27
t they are to be condemned, which say, 870 36
t it is lawful for them, as for all other 874 13
t we judge them to be read in Churches 874 38
t, whosoever are consecrated 875 24
t whosoever are consecrated 875 30
and *t* incapable of compromise 877 9
t as essential to the restoration of unity 877 12
Year A, *t*, begins on Advent Sunday 888 5

therein

Ceremonies appointed to be used *t*, 9 16
such changes and alterations should be made *t*, 9 19
to establish such other alterations and amendments *t* 11 7
so that whatsoever is not read *t*, 868 21

thereof

as in the frame and order *t*) 10 7
(or the greatest part *t*) 866 9
without breaking one piece *t* from another. 866 37
It is also more commodious, both for the shortness *t*, 867 4
the great profit that shall ensue *t*. 867 15
nor the Civil precepts *t* ought of necessity 869 12

thereunto

upon just and weighty considerations her *t* moving, 10 3
received into the Church by a Judge that hath authority *t*. 874 20

thing

there be not any *t* in it contrary 10 14
never any *t* by the wit of man so well devised, 866 3
the parties that so doubt, or diversely take any *t*, 867 19
that the same order be not contrary to any *t* 867 21
it is not lawful for the Church to ordain any *t* that is contrary 871 38
ought not to decree any *t* against the same, 871 41
ought it not to enforce any *t* to be believed 871 42
and also Invocation of Saints, is a fond *t*, 872 13
It is a *t* plainly repugnant to the Word of God, 872 22
drink the sign or Sacrament of so great a *t*. 873 40
neither hath it any *t* that, of itself, is superstitious 875 23
neither hath it any *t*, that of itself is superstitious 875 29
the which *t* the Injunctions also 876 1

things

being *t* in their own nature indifferent, 9 16
variations in *t* once advisedly established, 10 1
(*T* which are not seen are eternal) 475 —
(Behold, I make all *t* new) 475 —
(*T* that are unseen are eternal) 495 —
(Behold, I make all *t* new) 495 —
nor principalities, nor *t* present, 507 6
nor *t* to come, nor powers, nor height, 507 7
who has given you the will to do these *t*, 557 15
Such *t* as the deed for the property 575 17
Whosoever will be saved, before all *t* it is necessary 864 22
So that in all *t*, as is aforesaid, the Unity 865 16
as, among other *t*, it may plainly appear 866 4
that all *t* shall be done in order, 866 36

and such like *t*, as did break the continual course 866 38
because here are left out many *t*, 866 45
all *t* must be read upon the book, 867 11
they could say many *t* by heart: 867 13
execute, the *t* contained in this book: 867 19
that all *t* shall be read and sung 867 23
the Maker, and Preserver of all *t* 867 36
t appertaining to the perfection of Man's nature; 868 14
Holy Scripture containeth all *t* necessary 868 20
was made like unto us in all *t*, 870 25
born again in Christ, yet offend in many *t*; 870 29
drawing up their mind to high and heavenly *t*, 871 14
all those *t* that of necessity are requisite 871 32
sometimes have erred, even in *t* pertaining to God. 872 8
Wherefore *t* ordained by them as necessary 872 8
so that all *t* be done to edifying. 874 32
doth contain all *t* necessary to such Consecration 875 22
as well Clergy as Laity, in all *t* temporal; 875 35
but hath no authority in *t* purely spiritual. 875 36
of such *t* as he possesseth, liberally to give 876 15
3. That in all *t* of human ordering 876 33
"containing all *t* necessary to salvation," 877 33

think

He therefore that will be saved must thus *t* of the Trinity. 865 18

third

11 The *T* Song of Isaiah 87 —
T Sunday of Advent 160 —
T Sunday after the Epiphany 163 —
T Sunday in Lent 167 —
T Sunday of Easter 173 —
T Sunday of Advent 212 —
T Sunday after the Epiphany 215 —
T Sunday in Lent 218 —
T Sunday of Easter 224 —
T Day: Morning Prayer 599 —
T Day: Evening Prayer 602 —
Twenty-*t* Day: Morning Prayer 753 —
Twenty-*t* Day: Evening Prayer 756 —
rose again the *t* day from the dead. 865 32
The *T* Book of Esdras, 868 37

thirdly

T, there are deacons who assist 510 12

thirteenth

T Day: Morning Prayer 676 —
T Day: Evening Prayer 679 —

thirtieth

T Day: Morning Prayer 800 —
T Day: Evening Prayer 804 —

Thomas

Saint *T* December 21 185 —
Saint *T* December 21 237 —

thoroughly

ought *t* to be received and believed: 869 17

though

even *t* the Sacrament is not received 457 —
T it be appointed in the afore written preface, 867 23

thought

in their respective times were *t* convenient; 10 5
and the Civil Authority has not since *t* 10 22
or be *t* requisite or necessary to salvation. 868 22

thousand

Year of Our Lord One *T* Seven Hundred and 8 5
Year of our Lord one *t* seven hundred and ninety. 8 13

three

If *t* Lessons are used, the Lesson from the Gospel 47 —
Song of the *T* Young Men, 47 —
Song of the *T* Young Men, 49 —
If *t* Lessons are used, the Lesson from the Gospel 65 —
If *t* Lessons are used, the Lesson from the Gospel 84 —
Song of the *T* Young Men, 88 —
Song of the *T* Young Men, 90 —
If *t* Lessons are used, the Lesson from the Gospel 119 —
takes precedence over the *t* Holy Days 161 —
the observance of one, two, or all *t* 161 —
T or more of the appointed Lessons 175 —
takes precedence over the *t* Holy Days 213 —
the observance of one, two, or all *t* 213 —
T or more of the appointed Lessons 227 —
pausing *t* times and singing or saying 285 —
may be sung or said *t* times, 406 11
t distinct orders of ordained ministers 510 4
to maintain and continue these *t* orders; 510 20
T Lessons are read. 515 —
T Lessons are read. 528 —
T Lessons are read. 540 —
T Lessons are read. 571 —
T terms are used in the Psalms with reference to God: 583 15
Book *T* 687 —
And yet they are not *t* eternals, 864 35
As also there are not *t* incomprehensibles, 864 36
nor *t* uncreated, but one uncreated, 864 36
And yet they are not *t* Almighties, 864 39
And yet they are not *t* Gods, 865 2
And yet not *t* Lords, 865 4
to say, There be *t* Gods, or *t* Lords. 865 7
So there is one Father, not *t* Fathers; 865 12
one Son, not *t* Sons; 865 12
one Holy Ghost, not *t* 865 12
But the whole *t* Persons are co-eternal 865 15
before *t* or four Chapters were read out, 866 19
And in unity of this Godhead there be *t* Persons, 867 37
The Song of the *T* Children, 869 1
"Of the *T* Creeds; 869 20
and began as follows, "The *T* Creeds, 869 20
Lectionary for Sundays is arranged in a *t*-year cycle, 888 2
divisible by *t*. 888 4
one of the other years of the *t*-year Sunday cycle, 888 14
T Readings are provided for each Sunday 934 7
all *t* Readings may be used. 934 9

threefold

said in *t*, sixfold, or ninefold form. 406 10
the *t* ministry is not the exclusive property 510 26

threshold

Bishop marks the *t* with the sign of the cross	568	—
The cross signed on the *t* by the bishop	575	20
2. Signing of *t*	577	27

through

the Last Sunday after the Epiphany *t* Trinity Sunday.	16	17
From the Epiphany *t* the Baptism of Christ,	43	—
From Easter Day *t* the Day of Pentecost	59	—
From Easter Day *t* the Day of Pentecost	72	—
From the Epiphany *t* the Baptism of Christ,	81	—
From Easter Day *t* the Day of Pentecost	102	—
a selection from Psalms 120 *t* 133.	103	—
from Easter Day *t* the Day of Pentecost	109	—
From Easter Day *t* the Day of Pentecost	126	—
From Easter Day *t* the Day of Pentecost	143	—
the numbered Proper (number 3 *t* number 8),	158	13
(Propers 1 *t* 3 being ommitted that year,	158	19
Easter Day *t* the Day of Pentecost.	287	—
from Easter Day *t* the Day of Pentecost	299	—
from Easter Day *t* the Day of Pentecost	319	—
from Easter Day *t* the Day of Pentecost	323	—
From the Easter Vigil *t* the Day of Pentecost	340	—
from Easter Day *t* the Day of Pentecost	351	—
from Easter Day *t* the Day of Pentecost	355	—
From the Easter Vigil *t* the Day of Pentecost	366	—
the salvation of the world *t* Jesus	403	—
the salvation of the world *t* Jesus	404	—
Christmas Day *t* the Feast of the Epiphany;	406	13
Easter Day *t* the Day of Pentecost,	406	14
all that is appointed *t* the Prayers	406	25
from Easter Day *t* the Day of Pentecost	413	—
exercised *t* the care each Christian has	446	3
t the common prayer of Christians assembled	446	4
and *t* the priesthood of the Church	446	5
from Easter Day *t* the Day of Pentecost	512	—
From Easter Day *t* the Day of Pentecost	523	—
from Easter Day *t* the Day of Pentecost	525	—
From Easter Day *t* the Day of Pentecost	535	—
from Easter Day *t* the Day of Pentecost	537	—
From Easter Day *t* the Day of Pentecost,	547	—
"Father, *t* Jesus Christ your Son,	553	32
"Father, *t* Jesus Christ your Son,	554	21
enter in procession *t* the principal door.	575	14
but they were only begun, and never read *t*.	866	21
they *t* Grace obey the calling:	871	7
eternal Salvation to be enjoyed *t* Christ,	871	15
t his private judgment, willingly and purposely,	874	25

throughout

following Holy Days are regularly observed *t* the year.	16	22
greetings may be exchanged *t* the congregation.	431	9
Peace may be exchanged *t* the assembly.	436	—
seven-week pattern which recurs *t* the year,	934	24

thrust

whereby the Devil doth *t* them	871	18

thumb

Priest dips a *t* in the holy oil,	456	—

Thursday

Ascension on a *T* forty days after Easter Day.	15	13
Ash Wednesday, Maundy *T*, Good Friday,	18	12
Maundy *T*	169	—
T in Easter Week	172	—
Maundy *T*	221	—
T in Easter Week	223	—
Maundy *T*	274	—

Thursdays

Especially suitable for *T*	201	—
Especially suitable for *T*	252	—

thus

T, in any year, the Proper	158	11
He therefore that will be saved must *t* think	865	18
T, the same Lessons are to be read	888	8
(*T*, on the First Sunday of Advent,	934	5

time

in place of Authority should, from *t* to *t*,	9	20
compiling of her Liturgy in the *t* of Edward	10	2
alterations would in *t* be found expedient.	10	20
good work miscarried at that *t*;	10	22
At any *T*	40	—
At any *T*	78	—
may be used at any *t* according	141	4
or at the *t* of the hymn or anthem	142	12
Silence is then kept for a *t*,	265	—
It is celebrated at a convenient *t*	284	3
at a convenient *t* before the Liturgy on Easter Day.	284	31
lighted from the Paschal Candle at this *t*.	286	—
from *t* to *t* on a regular basis,	396	—
Peace may take place at the *t* of the administration	407	10
during which *t* a communion hymn may be sung.	408	22
At the *t* appointed, the persons to be married,	423	—
giving in marriage, it takes place at this *t*.	425	—
At the proper *t*, the Celebrant invites the parents	439	17
instruct the people, from *t* to *t*,	445	—
T of Death	462	—
Litany at the *T* of Death	462	—
A Commendation at the *T* of Death	464	—
The Litany at the *T* of Death may	465	—
whatever *t* the body is brought to the church.	466	—
during which *t* a suitable psalm or anthem	467	—
held at a *t* when the congregation has opportunity	468	6
or at some other convenient *t*	487	—
held at a *t* when the congregation has opportunity	490	6
or at some other convenient *t*	503	—
writers make it clear that from the apostles' *t*,	510	3
In particular, since the *t* of the New Testament,	510	4
At the same *t* the Bishop prays	533	—
at some convenient *t* prior to the service.	552	18
may also be presented at this *t*.	563	—
and consecrate a church at any *t*	566	9
If incense is to be used, it is appropriate at this *t*.	576	24
should be put into use at this *t*.	577	14
public worship for an extended period of *t*	577	22
From *t* to *t*, the Hebrew text has Adonai	583	31
or at any *t* after the Collects	836	—
at the same *t* of one substance with us	864	7
which in continuance of *t* hath not been corrupted:	866	4
of late *t* a few of them have been daily said	866	28

so great charge for books, as in *t* past they have been. 867 7
such as from *t* to *t*, in Cathedral 867 27
Homilies, which were set forth in the *t* of Edward 874 37
8 Of the *T* and Place of Prayer. 875 10
lately set forth in the *t* of Edward 875 27
confirmed at the same *t* by authority of Parliament, 875 28
second year of the forenamed King Edward unto this *t*, 875 32

times

"according to the various exigency of *t* 9 9
as in their respective *t* were thought convenient; 10 4
Lent and other *t* of penitence 111 —
At other *t*, the candle or candles 143 11
especially in *t* of war, or of national anxiety, 154 —
For use on the traditional days or at other *t* 205 —
For use on the traditional days or at other *t* 207 —
For use on the traditional days or at other *t* 256 —
For use on the traditional days or at other *t* 258 —
The Litany of Penitence may be used at other *t*, 269 —
pausing three *t* and singing or saying 285 —
during the Liturgy or at other *t*. 316 —
and may be omitted at other *t* 337 —
and may be omitted at other *t* 364 —
At other *t*, or when desired, such persons may be communicated 396 —
"Holy God," may be sung or said three *t*, 406 11
on Ascension Day; and at other *t* as desired; 406 15
It is not restricted to *t* of sickness. 446 8
in subsequent *t* generally known as priests. 510 9
from very ancient *t* it has been considered 583 18
28. In *T* of Conflict 811 7
28. In *T* of Conflict 824 —
as the prophets from earliest *t* spoke of him, 864 16
was so hard and intricate a matter, that many *t*, 866 31
at all *t* they have been divers, and may be changed 874 23
the diversity of countries, *t*, and men's manners, 874 24
wholesome Doctrine, and necessary for these *t*, 874 36

Timothy

1 *T* 1:15 332 —
1 *T* 1:15 449 —
Hebrews 5:1–10, or 1 *T* 3:1–7, 515 —
2 Corinthians 4:1–6, or 1 *T* 3:8–13, or Acts 6:2–7 540 —

tippet

vested in a rochet or alb, without stole, *t*, 511 16
vested in surplice or alb, without stole, *t*, 524 7
vested in a surplice or alb, without *t* 536 7

title

the feast of its patron or *t*, 16 9
rendering the combined *t* as "Lord God." 583 34
are not common, as touching the right, *t*, 876 13

titles

Homilies, the several *t* whereof we have joined 874 35
by which *T* we understand the minds of some 875 43

Tobias

The Book of *T*, 868 39

Tobit

T 8:5b–8 (New English Bible) 426 —

together

Officiant and People *t*, all kneeling 41 —
Officiant and People *t*, all standing 53 —
Officiant and People *t*, all kneeling 62 —
Officiant and People *t*, all standing 66 —
Officiant and People *t*, all kneeling 79 —
Officiant and People *t*, standing 96 —
Officiant and People *t*, all kneeling 116 —
Officiant and People *t*, all standing 120 —
On all other occasions, the Officiant and People say *t* 153 —
The Celebrant and People *t*, all kneeling 267 —
all the ordained ministers present, *t* with lay readers, 284 10
t with the sponsors or godparents, taking part 314 8
(That she and I may grow old *t*) 426 —
(Love which binds everything *t* 426 —
the man and the woman, *t* with their witnesses, 435 8
for the husband and wife, for their life *t*, 436 7
than one person responds, they do so *t*. 437 12
but when two or more are used *t*, they are used 453 4
and friends come *t* to join in the Litany. 462 —
family and friends come *t* for prayers 465 —
t with Psalm 23, are recommended. 468 20
t with Psalm 23, are recommended. 490 20
T with the bishops, they take part 510 9
Then all sing or say *t* 519 —
upon the head of the bishop-elect, and say *t* 521 —
If two or more are ordained *t*, 553 25
The ordinands may be presented *t*, 553 26
The ordinands are examined *t*. 553 29
If two or more are ordained *t*, 554 15
The ordinands may be presented *t*, 554 16
Thes ordinands are examined *t*. 554 19
t with your Bishop and fellow-Presbyters 557 3
and coming *t* to form one person 864 14
But the whole three Persons are co-eternal *t* 865 15
Godhead and Manhood, were joined *t* in one Person, 868 5
"General Councils may not be gathered *t* without 872 5
And when they be gathered *t*, 872 6

tokens

Sacraments ordained of Christ be not only badges or *t* 872 26

tongue

The hymn "Sing, my *t*, the glorious battle," 282 2
persons whose native *t* is other than English, 406 22
read and sung in the church in the English *t*, 867 24
such a *T* as the people understandeth. 872 21
in a *t* not understanded of the people. 872 23
Sacraments ought to be ministered in a known *t*. 875 12

too

the happy mean between *t* much stiffness in refusing, 9 25
and *t* much easiness in admitting variations 9 26
Because Jesus was raised from the dead, we, *t*, 507 3
it has been considered *t* sacred to be pronounced; 583 19

took

t Man's nature in the womb 868 3
and *t* again his body, 868 13

tools

the keys, and *t* used in its construction may also 575 18

touches

the Celebrant *t* the water 307 —

touching

Equal to the Father, as *t* his Godhead; 865 26
inferior to the Father, as *t* his Manhood. 865 26
(as *t* the reading of the holy Scripture) 866 42
as *t* Ceremonies and Rites, 869 11
Goods of Christians are not common, as *t* the right, 876 13

toward

husband extends his hand) *t* the Priest, 434 —

towards

into the church or *t* the grave. 468 22
into the church or *t* the grave. 490 22
doth fervently kindle their love *t* God: 871 16
and God's good will *t* us, 872 28
may be by God's blessing made *t* Home Reunion: 877 32

towns

34. For *T* and Rural Areas 811 13
34. For *T* and Rural Areas 825 —

tradition

and our English *t* follows suit, 583 33

traditional

idiom may be conformed to *t* language. 14 5
may be adapted to *t* language 108 23
Psalm 95: *T* 146 —
Collects: *T* 159 —
are the *t* winter Ember Days. 160 —
are the *t* spring Ember Days. 166 —
are the *t* Rogation Days. 174 —
are the *t* summer Ember Days. 176 —
are the *t* autumnal Ember Days. 182 —
For use on the *t* days or at other times 205 —
For use on the *t* days or at other times 207 —
are the *t* winter Ember Days. 212 —
are the *t* spring Ember Days. 218 —
are the *t* Rogation Days. 225 —
are the *t* summer Ember Days. 227 —
are the *t* autumnal Ember Days. 233 —
For use on the *t* days or at other times 256 —
For use on the *t* days or at other times 258 —
The Decalogue: *T* 317 —
There are several *t* methods of psalmody. 582 4
The *t* methods, each of which 582 6
was the *t* method of singing the Venite, 582 22
It was also a *t* manner of chanting 582 24
Prayers originally composed in *t* idiom 814 —
cast in the *t* question and answer form 844 6
modes of worship and discipline, or to *t* customs, 876 34

traditionally

The Ember Days, *t* observed on 18 5
The Rogation Days, *t* observed on 18 8

traditions

XXXIV. Of the *T* of the Church. 874 21
It is not necessary that *T* and Ceremonies 874 22
doth openly break the *T* and Ceremonies 874 25

transferred

may be observed on, or be *t* to, a Sunday, 16 9
t to the first convenient open day 16 13
t to the week following the Second Sunday of Easter, 17 12
which fall upon or are *t* to a weekday, 17 17

transfiguration

The *T* 16 7
The *T* 16 28
the *T* and Holy Cross 43 —
the *T* and Holy Cross 81 —
The *T* August 6 191 —
The *T* August 6 243 —

transitory

the old Fathers did look only for *t* promises. 869 10

translation

to distinguish it, however, from "Lord" as a *t* 583 28

translations

fellow elder, appear in *t* of 1 Peter 5:1, 528 13

transliterated

hybrid form which has been *t* "Jehovah." 583 24

Transubstantiation

T (or the change of the substance of Bread and Wine) 873 28

travelers

53. For *T* 812 4
53. For *T* 831 —

tree

a lively Faith may be as evidently known as a *t* 870 10

trees

The branches of palm or of other *t* 270 4

Trinity

T Sunday 15 19
T Sunday. 16 18
T Sunday 39 —
On *T* Sunday 43 —
T Sunday 77 —
On *T* Sunday 81 —
after Pentecost (except for *T* Sunday) 158 11
the Proper for the Sunday after *T* Sunday 158 12
if the Sunday after *T* Sunday is May 26, 158 16
weekdays of Pentecost and *T* weeks). 158 18
If the Sunday after *T* Sunday is June 13, 158 18
being used in Pentecost and *T* weeks). 158 21
First Sunday after Pentecost: *T* Sunday 176 —
Preface of *T* Sunday 176 —
which corresponds most closely to the date of *T* 176 —
Preface of *T* Sunday 190 —
Preface of *T* Sunday 193 —
Preface of *T* Sunday 194 —
Preface of a Saint, or of *T* Sunday 197 —
1. Of the Holy *T* 199 —
Preface of *T* Sunday 199 —
Preface of *T* Sunday 200 —
Preface of Baptism, or of *T* Sunday 205 —
Preface of *T* Sunday 207 —
First Sunday after Pentecost: *T* Sunday 228 —
Preface of *T* Sunday 228 —
which corresponds most closely to the date of *T* 228 —
Preface of *T* Sunday 242 —
Preface of *T* Sunday 244 —
Preface of *T* Sunday 246 —
Preface of a Saint, or of *T* Sunday 249 —

1. Of the Holy *T* 251 —
Preface of *T* Sunday 251 —
Preface of *T* Sunday 251 —
Preface of Baptism, or of *T* Sunday 255 —
Preface of *T* Sunday 258 —
T Sunday 347 —
T Sunday 380 —
That we worship one God in *T*, 864 25
and *T* in Unity, 864 25
And in this *T* none is afore, or after other; 865 14
the Unity in *T* and the *T* in Unity 865 16
that will be saved must thus think of the *T*. 865 18
I. Of Faith in the Holy *T*. 867 34

triplets

common verse is a couplet, but *t* are very frequent, 583 10

Trisagion

the *T*, or the Gloria in excelsis. 321 —
the Kyrie eleison, or the *T*. 353 —
The *T*, "Holy God," 406 10

trouble

Those who suffer and those in any *t* 359 —
Those who suffer and those in any *t* 383 —
55. For a Person in *T* or Bereavement 812 —
55. For a Person in *T* or Bereavement 831 —

troubled

if the sick person's conscience is *t*, 454 16

troubling

When the penitent has confessed all serious sins *t* 446 20

true

will be received and examined by every *t* member 11 17
inflamed with the love of his *t* religion. 866 15
There is but one living and *t* God, 867 35
and do spring out necessarily of a *t* and lively Faith; 870 9

truest

in its deepest and *t* sense, be speedily fulfilled; 876 30

truly

And if the person or persons on one side *t* forgive 409 20
t God and *t* man, 864 6
who *t* suffered, was crucified, dead, 868 6
Christ did *t* rise again from death, 868 13
or deny the place of forgiveness to such as *t* repent. 870 37

trust

For *T* in God 461 —
do not forget the *t* of those 557 10

trustees

who have been ordained to be its stewards and *t* 877 10

truth

to execute justice, and to maintain *t*;" 11 1
to confute them that were adversaries to the *t*. 866 12
Christ in the *t* of our nature was made 870 25
we deceive ourselves, and the *t* is not in us. 870 30
according to the Prophet's teaching in justice, judgment, and *t*. 876 21

truths

and what the *t* of the Gospel are; 11 20

Tuesday

Rogation Days, traditionally observed on Monday, *T*, 18 8
This order is not appropriate for use on Monday, *T*, 108 11
T in Holy Week 168 —
T in Easter Week 171 —
T, and Wednesday of this week are the traditional 174 —
T in Holy Week 220 —
T in Easter Week 223 —
T, and Wednesday of this week are the traditional 225 —

turn

that to *t* the Book only, was so hard 866 30
that he cannot *t* and prepare himself 869 34

twelfth

T Day: Morning Prayer 669 —
T Day: Evening Prayer 672 —
in Convention, on the *t* day of September, 867 32

twelve

On the *T* Days of Christmas 43 —
On the *T* Days of Christmas 80 —
T Prophets the less. 868 33

twentieth

T Day: Morning Prayer 731 —
T Day: Evening Prayer 735 —

twenty

T-first Day: Morning Prayer 738 —
T-first Day: Evening Prayer 741 —
T-second Day: Morning Prayer 746 —
T-second Day: Evening Prayer 749 —
T-third Day: Morning Prayer 753 —
T-third Day: Evening Prayer 756 —
T-fourth Day: Morning Prayer 759 —
T-fourth Day: Evening Prayer 763 —
T-fifth Day: Morning Prayer 766 —
T-fifth Day: Evening Prayer 769 —
T-sixth Day: Morning Prayer 772 —
T-sixth Day: Evening Prayer 775 —
T-seventh Day: Morning Prayer 778 —
T-seventh Day: Evening Prayer 782 —
T-eighth Day: Morning Prayer 785 —
T-eighth Day: Evening Prayer 789 —
T-ninth Day: Morning Prayer 794 —
T-ninth Day: Evening Prayer 797 —
[The *T*-first of the former Articles is omitted; 872 2

twice

When the Office is read *t* in the day, 934 10

two

The Church Year consists of *t* cycles of feasts and 15 3
One or *t* Lessons, as appointed, are read, 47 —
One or *t* Lessons, as appointed, are read, 64 —
Rite *T* 75 —
One or *t* Lessons, as appointed, are read, 84 —
Rite *T* 115 —
One or *t* Lessons, as appointed, are read, 118 —
When the ministers enter, one or *t* lighted candles 142 28
As necessary, the observance of one, *t*, or all three 161 —
As necessary, the observance of one, *t*, or all three 213 —
lay reader may lead the first *t* parts of the service, 284 24

At least *t* of the following Lessons are read, 288 —
One or *t* Lessons, as appointed, are read, 300 —
One or *t* Lessons, as appointed, are read, 325 —
A Penitential Order: Rite *T* 351 —
The Holy Eucharist: Rite *T* 355 —
One or *t* Lessons, as appointed, are read, 357 —
Eucharistic Prayers from Rite One or Rite *T*, 402 3
One or *t* Lessons, as appointed, are read, 414 —
ceremony be attested by at least *t* witnesses; 422 5
Mark 10:6–9, 13–16 (They are no longer *t* but one) 426 —
either according to Rite One or Rite *T* 436 15
T equivalent forms of service are provided 446 10
Form *T* 449 —
but when *t* or more are used together, 453 4
Rite *T* 491 —
At least *t* other bishops serve as co-consecrators. 511 8
When a bishop is to confer Holy Orders, at least *t* presbyters 524 2
When a bishop is to confer Holy Orders, at least *t* presbyters 536 2
according to Rite One or Rite *T*. 552 4
If *t* or more are ordained together, 553 25
If *t* or more are ordained together, 554 15
Before the Gospel, there may be one or *t* Readings 565 10
quatrains are usually distributed over *t* verses. 583 12
An asterisk divides each verse into *t* parts 583 13
In *t* passages (Psalm 68:4 and Psalm 83:18), the context requires 584 1
Book *T* 643 1
Only-begotten, recognized in *t* natures, 864 11
not as parted or separated into *t* persons, 864 15
yet he is not *t*, but one Christ; 865 28
so that *t* whole and perfect Natures, 868 4
There are *t* Sacraments ordained of Christ our Lord 872 30
3. The *t* Sacraments,—Baptism and the Supper 877 16
(c) The *t* Sacraments ordained by Christ Himself 878 1
when the same congregation attends *t* or more 888 8
Office Lectionary is arranged in a *t*-year cycle. 934 2
Year *T* begins on the First Sunday of Advent 934 4
Sunday and weekday in each of the *t* years. 934 8
T of the Readings may be used in the morning 934 8
and in the morning in Year *T*. 934 12
If *t* Readings are desired at both 934 12

U

ultimate

as being the rule and *u* standard of faith. 877 34

unable

Then the candidates *u* to answer for themselves 301 —
When persons are *u* to be present 396 —
is *u* to eat and drink the Bread and Wine, 457 —

uncertain

by planting in *u* stories, Legends, Responds, 866 17
whereof some be untrue, some *u*, 866 45

unchristian

This joy, however, does not make human grief *u*. 507 10

unclean

or into wretchlessness of most *u* living, 871 19

uncreate

The Father *u*, the Son *u*, 864 31
and the Holy Ghost *u*. 864 31

uncreated

there are not three incomprehensibles, nor three *u*, 864 36
but one *u*, 864 36

unction

U, are not to be counted for Sacraments of the Gospel, 872 33

undefiled

Which Faith except everyone do keep whole and *u*, 864 23

under

these States is indebted, *u* God, 9 12
U exceptional circumstances, 13 24
and the person baptized *u* emergency conditions, 314 7
Communion *u* Special Circumstances 396 —
confessor, and must *u* no circumstances be broken. 446 28
the form for Communion *u* Special Circumstances is used, 457 —
Given *u* my hand and seal, in the city of ________, 557 17
since the matter is arranged *u* headings, 844 10
the several titles whereof we have joined *u* this Article, 874 35
study of the conditions *u* which so priceless a blessing 877 24

understand

language spoken to the people in the Church, as they might *u*, 866 23
resolution of all doubts, concerning the manner how to *u*, 867 18
same in any language that they themselves do *u*. 867 26
we do *u* those canonical Books of the Old and New 868 23
u the minds of some slanderous folks to be offended; 875 44

understanded

in a tongue not *u* of the people. 872 24
that they may be *u* of the people. 874 39

understandeth

in such a Tongue as the people *u*. 872 21

understanding

do that which, according to her best *u* 10 10
and *u* to execute justice, and to maintain truth;" 11 1
order as is most easy and plain for the *u*, 867 3

understood

Hymns referred to in the rubrics of this Book are to be *u* as 14 6
u to include "or sung," and vice versa. 14 12
read in Latin to the people, which they *u* not; 866 25
for that purpose, which is plain and easy to be *u*, 866 35
they be plain and easy to be *u*. 866 42

undertaking

or upon *u* some special responsibility. 420 —

undivided

unity exemplified by the *u* Catholic Church 877 7

unemployed
30. For the *U* 811 9
30. For the *U* 824 —

unfailing
ministered with *u* use of Christ's words 877 17
—ministered with *u* use of Christ's words 878 2

ungodly
of itself, is superstitious and *u*. 875 24

uninfluenced
(*u* and unrestrained by any worldly authority 11 5

union
Celebrant declares the *u* of the man and woman 436 4
Definition of the *U* of the Divine 864 1
distinction of natures being in no way annulled by the *u*, 864 13

unison
read by one person, and the other parts said in *u*, 136 —
or portion of a psalm, in *u*. 582 9
refrain (called the antiphon) recited in *u*. 582 17

united
Church in the *U* States of America, in Convention, 8 4
19. For the President of the *U* States 810 28
19. For the President of the *U* States 820 —
of the Protestant Episcopal Church in the *U* States 867 31
We, Bishops of the Protestant Episcopal Church in the *U* States 876 25

uniting
work of leading, supervising, and *u* the Church. 510 7

unity
peace and *u* in the Church; 10 11
14. For the *U* of the Church 204 —
14. For the *U* of the Church 255 —
14. For the *U* of the Church 810 20
14. For the *U* of the Church 818 —
we worship one God in Trinity, and Trinity in *U*, 864 25
the *U* in Trinity and the Trinity in *U* 865 16
not by confusion of Substance, but by *u* of Person. 865 30
And in *u* of this Godhead there be three Persons, 867 37
the Church is rightly cut off from the *u* 874 17
the Christian *u*...can be restored only by 877 5
return of all Christian communions to the principles of *u* 877 6
therefore as essential to the restoration of *u* 877 12
nations and peoples called of God into the *u* 877 19
Bodies seeking the restoration of the organic *u* 877 23
nations and peoples called of God into the *U* 878 5

universal
The *U* Church, its members, and its mission 359 —
The *U* Church, its members, and its mission 383 —

unknown
quatrains are not *u*; 583 11

unless
U otherwise ordered in the preceding rules 16 23
u the Eucharist or a form of general intercession 57 —
u the Eucharist or a form of general intercession 70 —
u the Eucharist or a form of general intercession 100 —
u the Eucharist or a form of general intercession 124 —
u otherwise ordered for Holy Days 158 8
Those baptized as adults, *u* baptized with laying on 412 7
U the Committal follows immediately 482 —
U the Committal follows immediately 499 —
or deacon in this Church *u* they are so ordained, 510 22
u it may be declared that they be taken 872 9

unnecessary
It seems *u* to enumerate all the different alterations 11 9

unpardonable
sin against the Holy Ghost, and *u*. 870 33

unprofitable
say, We are *u* servants. 870 23

unread
or four Chapters were read out, all the rest were *u*. 866 19

unrestrained
(uninfluenced and *u* by any worldly authority 11 5

unseen
(Things that are *u* are eternal) 495 —

unshaken
have still been continued firm and *u*. 10 7

unspeakable
pleasant, and *u* comfort to godly persons, 871 12

untrue
here are left out many things, whereof some be *u*, 866 45

unworthily
but they that receive them *u*, purchase to themselves 872 39

unworthiness
XXVI. Of the *U* of the Ministers, 873 1

up
and promise to make *u* for their faults, 409 21
Isaiah 25:6–9 (He will swallow *u* death in victory) 470 —
Isaiah 25:6–9 (He will swallow *u* death for ever) 494 —
the form of similarity (The waters have lifted *u*, 583 4
the waters have lifted *u* their voice; 583 5
the waters have lifted *u* their pounding waves. 583 5
for an inquiring stranger who picks *u* a Prayer Book. 844 8
be stirred *u* to godliness themselves, 866 11
drawing *u* their mind to high and heavenly things, 871 14
lifted *u*, or worshipped. 873 35

urgent
With the express permission of the bishop, and for *u* 16 18

usages
in his worship different forms and *u* may 9 3

use
And this Book shall be in *u* from and after 8 12
with a good conscience *u* and submit unto, 10 16
When it is desired to *u* music composed for them, 14 13
Especially suitable for *u* in Easter Season 85 —
or vespers for *u* on suitable occasions 108 2
It is appropriate also for *u* in private houses. 108 6
This order is not appropriate for *u* on Monday, 108 11

A bishop or priest may *u* the following 114 —
For *u* in the Litany in place of the Versicle 154 —
Directions for the *u* of the Propers which follow 176 —
For optional *u*, when desired, subject to the rules 199 —
Any of the Collects appointed for *u* at the Burial 202 —
For *u* on the traditional days or at other times 205 —
For *u* on the traditional days or at other times 207 —
Directions for the *u* of the Propers which follow 228 —
For optional *u*, when desired, subject to the rules 251 —
Any of the Collects appointed for *u* at the Burial 253 —
For *u* on the traditional days or at other times 256 —
For *u* on the traditional days or at other times 258 —
Lessons provided for *u* at Baptism 312 22
For *u* at the beginning of the Liturgy, 319 —
For *u* at the beginning of the Liturgy, 351 —
for *u* with those who for reasonable cause cannot 396 —
It is not intended for *u* at the principal Sunday 400 4
Bishop may consecrate oil of Chrism for *u* 419 —
a deacon may *u* the service 422 16
and *u* the form for the Reconciliation 454 16
Prayers for *u* by a Sick Person 461 —
Celebrant may *u* any of the Additional Prayers. 486 4
the Priest may *u* the following prayer, 487 —
the Priest may *u* the following prayer, 503 —
For *u* at Ordinations as directed. 548 —
This order is for *u* when a priest is being instituted 558 2
for *u* in the evening) 560 —
after the building is ready for regular *u* 566 10
does not preclude the *u* of the building 566 11
For a church or chapel long in *u*, a special order 566 19
The *u* of portable musical instruments is suitable. 575 9
for subsequent *u* in this church. 575 27
the areas or furnishings should be put into *u* 577 13
For a Church or Chapel Long in *U* 577 20
congregational *u*, whether by singing or reading. 582 3
The exclusive *u* of a single method 582 4
suggested in the lectionary for *u* between the Lessons 582 10
familiar from its *u* in many well-known anthems. 584 8
32. For the Good *U* of Leisure 811 11
38. For the Right *U* of God's Gifts 811 17
For *u* after the Collects of Morning or Evening Prayer 814 3
32. For the Good *U* of Leisure 825 —
38. For the Right *U* of God's Gifts 827 —
For optional *u* on Thanksgiving Day, 836 —
catechism is primarily intended for *u* by parish 844 2
The second *u* of this catechism is to provide 844 7
it is suitable for selective *u*, 844 10
some following Salisbury *u*, 867 9
some Hereford *u*, 867 9
some the *u* of Bangor, 867 9
whole realm shall have but one *u*. 867 11
doubts may arise in the *u* and practicing 867 17
but that we should duly *u* them. 872 38
we may *u* their Ministry, both in hearing 873 5
Body of Christ in the *u* of the Lord's Supper. 873 36
1 Of the right *U* of the Church. 875 2
unfailing *u* of Christ's words of institution 877 17
unfailing *u* of Christ's words of Institution, 878 2
intended for *u* at all public services on such days, 888 7
version is particularly appropriate for *u* at the Office, 888 20
u the bracketed Psalms rather than 935 6

used

Ceremonies appointed to be *u* therein, 9 16
forms set forth by authority within this Church may be *u*. 13 8
from Holy Scripture, may be *u* when the needs 13 10
previously authorized liturgical texts may be *u* 14 14
Various Occasions is *u* as a substitute for, 18 14
the term "Officiant" is *u* to denote 36 2
or Evening Prayer may be *u* in place of all 36 8
Antiphons are *u* only in Easter Season. 44 —
may also be *u* daily until the Day of Pentecost. 45 —
If three Lessons are *u*, 47 —
the Creed on page 96 may be *u* instead. 54 —
one or both of the following may be *u* 58 —
If three Lessons are *u*, 65 —
the Creed on page 120 may be *u* instead. 66 —
one or both of the following may be *u* 71 —
the term "Officiant" is *u* to denote 74 2
or Evening Prayer may be *u* in place of all 74 8
Antiphons are *u* only in Easter Season. 82 —
may also be *u* daily until the Day of Pentecost. 83 —
If three Lessons are *u*, 84 —
One or more sections of this Canticle may be *u*. 88 —
one or both of the following may be *u* 101 —
Collect of the Day may be *u*. 107 —
It may be *u* as a complete rite 108 3
or from Compline, may be so *u* 113 —
A Dismissal may be *u* (adding "Alleluia, 114 —
If three Lessons are *u*, 119 —
one or both of the following may be *u* 125 —
Collects appointed in the Daily Offices, may be *u* 136 —
A hymn or canticle may be *u*; 137 —
This devotion may be *u* before or after 139 —
Worship for the Evening, page 109, may be *u* instead. 139 —
may be *u* at any time according to the discretion 141 4
may be *u* as refrains with either 141 6
u with the Psalms and biblical Canticles. 141 10
may be *u* after the Invitatory Psalm 141 12
following pointing of the Gloria may be *u*: 141 16
following form of the Gloria may be *u*: 141 19
after the Readings, may be *u*. 141 22
or Evening Prayer is *u* as the Liturgy 142 17
and *u* to provide light for reading 143 1
the Paschal Candle, if *u*, should be burning 143 3
When this service is *u* in private houses, 143 17
If incense is to be *u*, it is appropriate 143 19
suitable to the season or the occasion, may be *u*. 143 23
Proper appointed for the Sunday is also *u* 158 7
The Proper to be *u* on each of the Sundays 158 10
Thereafter, the Propers are *u* consecutively. 158 15
(Propers 1 and 2 being *u* on the weekdays 158 17
and Propers 4 and 5 being *u* in Pentecost 158 20
Collect appointed for any Sunday or other Feast may be *u* 158 22
The Preface of the Epiphany is *u*. 162 —
Proper is always *u* on the Sunday before Ash Wednesday. 165 —
closely to the date of Pentecost in that year is *u*. 176 —
closely to the date of Trinity Sunday in that year is *u*. 176 —
No Proper Preface is *u*. 177 —
Collect "For the Nation," page 207, may be *u* instead. 190 —

Thanksgiving on page 836 may be *u*.	194	—
set of Psalms and Lessons, may be *u*	195	—
Burial of the Dead may be *u* instead.	202	—
Burial of the Dead may be *u*.	202	—
postcommunion prayer on page 482 may be *u*.	202	—
Litany of Thanksgiving for a Church, page 578, may be *u*	204	—
The Collect for Independence Day may be *u* instead.	207	—
The postcommunion prayer on page 457 may be *u*.	208	—
The Preface of the Epiphany is *u*.	214	—
Proper is always *u* on the Sunday before Ash	217	—
closely to the date of Pentecost in that year is *u*.	227	—
closely to the date of Trinity Sunday in that year is *u*.	228	—
No Proper Preface is *u*.	228	—
No Proper Preface is *u*.	229	—
The Collect "For the Nation," page 258, may be *u*	242	—
Thanksgiving on page 836 may be *u*.	246	—
set of Psalms and Lessons, may be *u*	246	—
Burial of the Dead may be *u* instead.	253	—
Burial of the Dead may be *u*.	253	—
postcommunion prayer on page 498 may be *u*.	253	—
Thanksgiving for a Church, page 578, may be *u*	255	—
The Collect for Independence Day may be *u* instead.	258	—
postcommunion prayer on page 457 may be *u*.	260	—
Litany of Penitence may be *u* at other times,	269	—
portions of the preceding may be *u*.	272	—
The Nicene Creed is not *u* at this service.	295	—
the Proper Preface of Baptism may be *u*.	310	—
The Nicene Creed is not *u* at this service.	312	27
but this form of words is *u*	313	19
This Exhortation may be *u*, in whole or in part,	316	—
When *u* as a separate service, the Exhortation,	319	—
When this Order is *u* at the beginning of the Liturgy,	321	—
When *u* separately, it concludes with suitable prayers,	321	—
or Evening Prayer may be *u* in place of all	322	18
sentence of Scripture, may be *u*	343	—
To be *u* on Sundays as appointed,	344	—
To be *u* on Sundays and weekdays alike,	345	—
When *u* as a separate service, the Exhortation,	351	—
When this Order is *u* at the beginning of the Liturgy,	353	—
When *u* separately, it concludes with suitable prayers,	353	—
or Evening Prayer may be *u* in place of all	354	18
On other occasions the following is *u*	356	—
other suitable anthem may be *u*.	364	—
sentence of Scripture, may be *u*	376	—
To be *u* on Sundays as appointed,	377	—
To be *u* on Sundays and weekdays alike,	378	—
Any of the forms which follow may be *u*.	383	—
conformed to the language of the Rite being *u*.	383	—
or some other form is *u*	397	—
When a psalm is *u*, it may be concluded	406	7
the following form of the Gloria may be *u*:	406	8
Gloria in excelsis, or the hymn *u* in place of it,	406	12
but it is not *u* on the Sundays	406	15
any appropriate words of greeting may be *u*.	407	9
anthem may be *u* at the Breaking of the Bread:	407	21
The Nicene Creed is not *u* at this service.	412	15
The petitions on pages 305–306 may be *u*.	417	—
This form may be *u* when a person wishes to make or	420	—
only their Christian names are *u*.	422	22
on page 423 of this Book, this Order is *u*.	435	3
If Banns are to be published, the following form is *u*	437	2
The Celebration and Blessing of a Marriage may be *u*	437	5
some other suitable symbol of the vows may be *u*	437	22
a briefer form of this service may be *u*,	439	10
to be *u* by a Deacon or Lay Person	448	—
to be *u* by a Deacon or Lay Person	452	—
one or more parts of the following service are *u*,	453	3
but when two or more are *u* together,	453	4
they are *u* in the order indicated.	453	4
Communion under Special Circumstances is *u*,	457	—
those in the Burial service) may be *u*.	465	—
The following form may be *u* at whatever time	466	—
It may also be *u* prior to cremation.	468	12
the following Commendation is *u*.	482	—
It may also be *u* prior to cremation.	490	12
the Prayers of the People is *u*,	496	—
the following Commendation is *u*.	499	—
is deemed appropriate, the following form is *u*.	506	3
eucharistic prayers may be *u*.	506	23
(designated by the symbol N.N.) is *u*.	511	19
(designated by the symbol N.N.) is *u*.	524	10
(designated by the symbol N.N.) is *u*.	536	10
this Litany may be *u* for the Prayers of the People	548	—
or the Daily Office, or it may be *u* separately.	548	—
When this Litany is *u* on other occasions,	551	—
usual postcommunion prayer are not *u*.	552	7
following form may be *u*	552	19
It may also be *u* for the installation of deans	558	3
usual postcommunion prayer is *u*.	564	—
prayer suitable to the occasion, may be *u* instead.	565	9
and bread and wine may be *u* in the Eucharist	565	23
authorized eucharistic prayers may be *u*.	565	28
Portions of the service may be *u*, or adapted	566	3
u for dedicating a chapel or an oratory	566	6
This service may be *u* to dedicate and consecrate	566	9
The Preface of the Dedication of a Church may be *u*.	574	11
is to be *u* at the opening of a church or chapel.	575	3
Hymns or psalms may be *u* in procession.	575	9
the keys, and tools *u* in its construction may also	575	18
processional cross may be *u* for the signing.	575	22
If Baptism is to be administered, the following order is *u*:	575	28
psalms and hymns, or instrumental music may be *u*	576	4
and one of the versicles and responses, are *u*,	576	7
the usual forms of the Prayers of the People may be *u*;	576	18
If incense is to be *u*, it is appropriate	576	24
that of the season may be *u*,	576	25
If the church is also to be *u* for regular worship	577	1
portions of this service may be *u* by the bishop,	577	4
may be *u* by the bishop or a priest for blessing	577	9
When buildings have been *u* for public worship	577	21
This Litany may also be *u* on the anniversary	579	6
the method which has been most frequently *u*	582	27
terms are *u* in the Psalms with reference to God:	583	15
The Hebrew form has been *u*,	584	5
It may also be *u* to form a simple service;	844	9
were other books of holy Scripture *u*.	866	22
and commodious, than that which of late was *u*.	866	44
cited in the selected Sunday Proper may be *u* instead.	888	17
Two of the Readings may be *u* in the morning	934	8
all three Readings may be *u*.	934	10
suggested that the Gospel Reading be *u* in the evening	934	11
Old Testament Reading for the alternate year is *u*	934	13

When more than one Reading is *u* at an Office, 934 15
Psalms appointed for a given day may be *u* 934 28
Psalms appointed for any day may be *u* 934 29
Brackets and parentheses are *u* 935 1
may be *u* with the Psalms 935 9
may be *u* as refrains after each verse 935 11

uses

If a priest *u* Chrism in signing the newly baptized, 298 14
the Celebrant *u* one of the Eucharistic Prayers 402 —
bequests for religious and charitable *u*. 445 12

using

Other Commemorations, *u* the Common of Saints 18 4
A deacon or lay person *u* the preceding form 42 —
A deacon or lay person *u* the preceding form 63 —
A deacon or lay person *u* the preceding form 80 —
Officiant then says the Prayer for Light, *u* 110 —
A deacon or lay person *u* the preceding blessing 114 —
A deacon or lay person *u* the preceding form 117 —
Eucharist begins in the usual manner, *u* 274 —
the sign of the cross [*u* Chrism if desired] 308 —
U the given name of the one to be baptized 313 24
A deacon or lay person *u* the preceding form 321 —
u the form on page 408. 338 —
A deacon or lay person *u* the preceding form 353 —
u the form on page 408. 365 —
on a regular basis, *u* either the Proper 396 —
from the reserved Sacrament, *u* the following form. 396 —
A deacon *u* the preceding form substitutes 398 —
u one of the eucharistic prayers provided. 401 9
oil of Chrism for use at Baptism, *u* 419 —
u the Collect and Lessons appointed 433 —
4. The vows of the man and woman are exchanged, *u* 435 18
A deacon or lay person *u* the preceding form 455 —
u oil blessed by a bishop or priest. 456 —

usual

The Eucharist begins in the *u* manner, 274 —
person is baptized in the *u* manner, 313 19
One of the *u* postcommunion prayers is then said, 399 —
In place of the *u* postcommunion prayer, 432 —
One of the *u* postcommunion prayers is said, 457 —
In place of the *u* postcommunion prayer, 482 —
In place of the *u* postcommunion prayer, 498 —
In place of the *u* postcommunion prayer, 522 —
In place of the *u* postcommunion prayer, 535 —
In place of the *u* postcommunion prayer, 546 —
Confession, and the *u* postcommunion prayer 552 6
in place of the *u* postcommunion prayer, 564 4
the *u* postcommunion prayer is used. 564 6
Any of the *u* forms of the Prayers of the People 576 18

usually

although quatrains are *u* distributed 583 11
and shorter version, *u* from the same Psalm. 888 19

utterly

(and oft repeated), and the rest *u* omitted. 866 29
Ceremonies be in all places one, or *u* like; 874 22

V

vain

v repetitions, Commemorations, and Synodals, 866 18
some be untrue, some uncertain, some *v* 866 45
As we confess that *v* and rash Swearing is forbidden 876 18

vainly

(as the Pelagians do *v* talk;) 869 23
also Invocation of Saints, is a fond thing, *v* invented, 872 13

valley

The *v* of dry bones 291 —

variations

too much easiness in admitting variations 9 26
appropriate *v* in Lent and Easter Season. 934 25

various

"according to the *v* exigency of times 9 9
V Occasions 18 10
V Occasions is used as a substitute for, 18 14
V Occasions, page 888 136 —
Holy Days and *V* Occasions. 158 9
and services for *V* Occasions 158 24
V Occasions 199 —
V Occasions 251 —
appointed for Holy Days and *V* Occasions 345 —
appointed for Holy Days and *V* Occasions 378 —
one of those appointed for *V* Occasions. 396 —
the Lectionary for *V* Occasions. 565 15
The term "*V* Occasions" in the following pages 813 17
See also *V* Occasions no. 18. 815 —
101, and *V* Occasions no. 16. 816 —
See also *V* Occasions no. 13. 818 —
See also *V* Occasions no. 14, 818 —
For those to be ordained, see *V* Occasions no. 15. 819 —
See also *V* Occasions no. 17. 820 —
See also *V* Occasions no. 21. 823 —
See also *V* Occasions no. 19. 824 —
prayers for Industry and Labor, see *V* Occasions 824 —
For Education, see *V* Occasions no. 23. 825 —
For Social Service, see *V* Occasions no. 22. 827 —
See also *V* Occasions no. 19. 827 —
See also *V* Occasions no. 20. 831 —

varying

v needs of the nations and peoples 877 19
v needs of the nations and peoples 878 5

veni

The hymn, *V* Creator Spiritus, 520 —
or the hymn, *V* Sancte Spiritus, 520 —
The hymn, *V* Creator Spiritus, 533 —
or the hymn, *V* Sancte Spiritus, 533 —
The hymn, *V* Creator Spiritus, 544 —
or the hymn, *V* Sancte Spiritus, 544 —

Venite

Then follows one of the Invitatory Psalms, *V* 42 —
V Psalm 95:1–7; 96:9,13 44 —
Then follows one of the Invitatory Psalms, *V* 80 —
V Psalm 95:1–7 82 —

Psalm 95: Traditional *V*, 146 —
was the traditional method of singing the *V*, 582 22
restoration of Invitatory Antiphons for the *V* 582 23

verbs

and the corresponding *v*. 108 24
pronouns and *v* have been put in italics 814 —

verity

as we are compelled by the Christian *v* 865 5

versa

understood to include "or sung," and vice *v*. 14 12

verse

A citation giving chapter and *v* may be added. 47 —
A citation giving chapter and *v* may be added. 64 —
A citation giving chapter and *v* may be added. 84 —
A citation giving chapter and *v* may be added. 118 —
v which mentions the arrival at Golgotha 273 —
v which mentions the arrival at Golgotha 277 —
A citation giving chapter and *v* may be added. 300 —
A citation giving chapter and *v* may be added. 325 —
A citation giving chapter and *v* may be added. 357 —
A citation giving chapter and *v* may be added. 414 —
A citation giving chapter and *v* may be added. 516 —
A citation giving chapter and *v* may be added. 528 —
A citation giving chapter and *v* may be added. 540 —
Antiphonal recitation is the *v*-by-*v* alternation 582 13
singing a refrain after each *v* or group of verses. 582 21
alternating with the congregation *v* by *v*. 582 29
The most common *v* is a couplet, 583 10
An asterisk divides each *v* into two parts 583 13
used as refrains after each *v* or group of verses. 935 11

verses

one or more of these or other appropriate *v* 449 —
Selected *v* of psalms and hymns, 576 4
appropriate for the psalm *v* suggested 582 10
when the *v* are recited rather than sung, 582 11
v of a psalm are sung by a solo voice, 582 20
refrain after each verse or group of *v*. 582 21
quatrains are usually distributed over two *v*. 583 12
uncertain stories, Legends, Responds, *V*, 866 17
In the opening *v* of Lessons, 888 25
parentheses in the case of *v*) 935 2
to indicate Psalms and *v* of Psalms 935 2
refrains after each verse or group of *v*. 935 11

versicle

or with the *v* "O Lord, open thou our lips" 37 —
added to the preceding *v* and response. 59 —
or with the *v* "O God, make speed to save us" 61 —
added to the preceding *v* and response. 72 —
or with the *v* "Lord, open our lips" 75 —
added to the preceding *v* and response. 102 —
or with the *v* "O God, make speed to save us" 115 —
added to the preceding *v* and response. 126 —
For use in the Litany in place of the *V* 154 —

versicles

after the opening *v* and before the salutation 312 19
after the opening *v* and before the salutation 412 14
and one of the *v* and responses, are used, 576 7

versification

lines correspond to Hebrew *v*, 583 2

version

numeration of the Revised Standard *V* of the Bible. 14 17
The following hymn, or a metrical *v* of it, 112 —
Lessons may be read from any *v* of the Scriptures 143 6
Psalm 23 King James *V* 476 —
The *v* of the Psalms which follows is set out 583 1
1662 text of this Article, omitted in the *v* of 1801, 872 4
and shorter *v*, usually from the same Psalm. 888 19
The longer *v* is particularly appropriate 888 20
shorter *v* when the Psalm is sung 888 20

versions

Metrical *v* of the Invitatory Psalms, 141 21
carried over into the classical English *v*, 583 26

very

The *v* love we have for each other 507 10
but triplets are *v* frequent, 583 10
by no means certain, because from *v* ancient times 583 18
nothing to be read, but the *v* pure word of God, 867 1
Son of God, which was made *v* Man. 868 1
the *v* and eternal God, 868 2
whereof is one Christ, *v* God, and *v* Man; 868 6
with the Father and the Son, *v* and eternal God. 868 18
man is *v* far gone from original righteousness, 869 25
a most wholesome Doctrine, and *v* full of comfort, 870 4

vespers

Order provides a form of evening service or *v* 108 2

vessel

placing a hand on the *v* of oil, 307 5
place a hand upon the cup and any other *v* 334 —
place a hand upon the cup and any other *v* 342 —
place a hand upon the cup and any other *v* 362 —
place a hand upon the cup and any other *v* 368 —
place a hand upon the cup and any other *v* 371 —
place a hand upon the cup and any other *v* 374 —
place a hand upon the cup and any other *v* 403 —
place a hand upon the cup and any other *v* 405 —
The Bishop presents a *v* of water, saying 561 —

vessels

places the *v* on the Lord's Table. 546 —
it is appropriate for the deacons to remove the *v* 555 5
and cleanse the *v* in some convenient place. 555 6
vest the Altar, place the *v* on it, 574 3
it is desirable that sacred *v*, ornaments, 575 16
to everlasting salvation, as *v* made to honour. 871 5

vest

v the Altar, place the vessels on it, 574 —

vested

The bishop-elect is *v* in a rochet or alb, 511 16
The new bishop is now *v* according to the order 521 —
The ordinand is to be *v* in surplice or alb, 524 7
The new priest is now *v* according to the order 534 —
The ordinand is to be *v* in a surplice or alb, 536 7
The new deacon is now *v* according to the order 545 —

vestments

If *v* or other symbols of office are to be dedicated, 552 17
v and bread and wine may be used in the Eucharist 565 23

vesture

other *v* distinctive of ecclesiastical 511 17
other *v* distinctive of ecclesiastical 524 8
other *v* distinctive of ecclesiastical 536 8
clothed with the *v* of the episcopate, 553 3

vicar

If the new minister is the rector or *v* of the parish, 562 1

vicars

including *v* of missions and assistant ministers. 558 5
v of missions, hospital chaplains, and other priests 565 25

vice

understood to include "or sung," and *v* versa. 14 12

victims

56. For the *V* of Addiction 812 7
56. For the *V* of Addiction 831 —

victory

(He will swallow up death in *v*) 470 —

view

people may have a clear *v* of the action. 313 6
with a *v* to the earnest study 877 23

Vigil

The Liturgy of the Easter *V* is on page 285. 170 —
When a *V* of Pentecost is observed, 175 —
The Liturgy of the Easter *V* is on page 285. 222 —
When a *V* of Pentecost is observed, 227 —
Concerning the *V* 284 1
The Great *V*, when observed, is the first service 284 2
Ministry of the Word of the *V* Eucharist, 284 25
When the *V* is not celebrated, the Service of Light 284 30
The Great *V* of Easter 285 —
Baptism is especially appropriate at the Easter *V*, 312 2
From the Easter *V* through the Day of Pentecost 340 —
From the Easter *V* through the Day of Pentecost 366 —
Prayers for a *V* 465 —
the *V* on page 465, may follow. 467 —

vineyard

and send Ministers into the Lord's *v*. 872 20

virgin

Saint Mary the *V* 17 2
Saint Mary the *V* August 15 192 —
Saint Mary the *V* August 15 243 —
for us men and for our salvation, of Mary the *V*, 864 10
Man's nature in the womb of the blessed *V*, 868 4

virtue

Deacons by *v* of their order do not exercise 13 21
increased by *v* of prayer unto God. 873 19

visible

symbols presented should be large enough to be *v* 565 21
Preserver of all things both *v* 867 36
The *v* Church of Christ is a congregation 871 30
have not any *v* sign or ceremony ordained of God. 872 36
Although in the *v* Church the evil be ever mingled 873 2
and the *v* manifestation of Christ to the world; 877 4

visibly

God by the Holy Ghost, are *v* signed and sealed; 873 18
and *v* press with their teeth 873 37

visitation

The *V* 16 30
The *V* May 31 189 —
The *V* May 31 240 —

vocal

It is designed for *v*, congregational use, 582 2

vocalized

(Tetragrammaton) is probably to be *v* Yahweh; 583 17

vocation

III. For all Christians in their *v* 206 —
24. For *V* in Daily Work 210 —
III. For all Christians in their *v* 256 —
24. For *V* in Daily Work 261 —

vocations

16. For Monastic Orders and *V* 810 23
16. For Monastic Orders and *V* 819 —

voice

The People in a loud *v* respond 521 —
The People in a loud *v* respond 534 —
The People in a loud *v* respond 545 —
the verses of a psalm are sung by a solo *v*, 582 20
the waters have lifted up their *v*; 583 5

void

from which he was clearly *v*, 870 26
and such as be *v* of a lively faith, 873 37

voluntary

V Works besides, over and above, 870 19

vow

not commanded by God's Law, either to *v* 874 12

vowel

in printed Bibles, after the invention of *v* points, 583 22

vowels

provided with the *v* of the word Adonai. 583 23

vows

Baptismal *V*, page 292, follows the Sermon. 175 —
Baptismal *V*, page 292, follows the Sermon. 227 —
Christian Initiation, or the Renewal of Baptismal *V*. 284 8
first two parts of the service, the Renewal of Baptismal *V*, 284 24
Celebrant leads the people in the Renewal of Baptismal *V*, 292 —
The Renewal of Baptismal *V* 292 —
The celebrant concludes the Renewal of *V* as follows 294 —
Confirmation, or the Renewal of Baptismal *V* 295 —
promises in their own names, and also take *v* 298 22
If Confirmation, Reception, or the Reaffirmation of Baptismal *V* 308 —
Renewal of Baptismal *V*, page 292, may 312 16
Reaffirmation of Baptismal *V* are administered 412 12

the Reaffirmation of Baptismal *V* 413 —
may precede the exchange of *v*. 435 16
4. The *v* of the man and woman are exchanged, 435 18
may approach the Altar, either for the exchange of *v*, 437 15
some other suitable symbol of the *v* may be used 437 22
6. Renewal of Baptismal *V* 578 2

W

wait

(The eyes of all *w* upon you, O Lord) 454 11
(The Lord is good unto them that *w* 470 —
(The Lord is good to those who *w* 494 —

walk

(*W* in love, as Christ loved us) 426 —
they *w* religiously in good works, 871 9

war

especially in times of *w*, or of national anxiety, 154 —

warden

a *W* may now present the keys 562 —
W or other representative of the congregation continues 568 11
it is suitable that a *w* or other 576 11

wardens

The *W*, standing before the bishop 559 —
minister is normally presented to the bishop by the *w* 565 4

warrants

for they may be proved by most certain *w* 869 17

warranty

grounded upon no *w* of Scripture, 872 14

wars

to wear weapons, and serve in the *w*." 876 11

washing

When observed, the ceremony of the *w* of feet 274 —

water

Holy Baptism is full initiation by *w* 298 2
says the Thanksgiving over the *W*; 298 10
"Heavenly Father, we thank you that by *w* 298 11
Thanksgiving over the *W* 306 —
The Celebrant blesses the *w*, first saying 306 —
the Celebrant touches the *w* 307 —
who then immerses, or pours *w* upon, 307 —
after the administration of the *w* 308 —
go to the font for the Thanksgiving over the *W*. 312 30
the font is to be filled with clean *w* 313 1
before the Thanksgiving over the *W*. 313 2
At the Thanksgiving over the *W*, 313 3
'Heavenly Father, we thank you that by *w* 313 10
doubt that a person has been baptized with *w*, 313 16
pour *w* on him or her, saying 313 24
except the administration of the *w*. 314 9
customary to add a little *w* to the wine. 407 16
pours sufficient wine (and a little *w*) 546 —
The Bishop presents a vessel of *w*, saying 561 —
w is now poured into the Font, 569 —
[*w* may be poured into the Font, and] 570 —
assigned the task of pouring the *w*. 575 24
believe that all who have been duly baptized with *w*, 876 31

waters

(Many *w* cannot quench love) 426 —
(The *w* have lifted up, O Lord 583 4
the *w* have lifted up their voice; 583 5
the *w* have lifted up their pounding waves. 583 5
42. For the Harvest of Lands and *W* 811 24
42. For the Harvest of Lands and *W* 828 —

waves

the waters have lifted up their pounding *w*. 583 6

way

entire Christian assembly participates in such a *w* 13 16
but the *w* of the wicked is doomed. 583 7
distinction of natures being in no *w* annulled 864 13
And if any would judge this *w* more painful, 867 11

ways

continue in any of the following *w*: 112 8
and the Epistle, and assist in other *w*. 284 20
(The Lord knows the *w* of the righteous; 583 7

weak

Care alike for young and old, strong and *w*, 557 11
woundeth the consciences of the *w* 874 29

weapons

at the commandment of the Magistrate, to wear *w*, 876 10

wear

commandment of the Magistrate, to *w* weapons, 876 10

weather

When the *w* is inclement, 575 11

wedding

the *w* party leaves the church. 431 —
As the *w* party leaves the church, 432 —
Seating may be provided for the *w* party, 437 18

Wednesday

determines the beginning of Lent on Ash *W*, 15 12
Ash *W* 17 9
take precedence of Ash *W*. 17 15
Ash *W* and the other weekdays of Lent 17 23
W before Ascension Day 18 9
on Ash *W*, Maundy Thursday, 18 12
not appropriate for use on Monday, Tuesday, or *W* 108 11
W, Friday, and Saturday of this week are 160 —
Proper is always used on the Sunday before Ash *W*. 165 —
Ash *W* 166 —
W, Friday, and Saturday of this week are 166 —
W in Holy Week 169 —
W in Easter Week 171 —
and *W* of this week are the traditional 174 —
W, Friday, and Saturday of this week are 176 —
The *W*, Friday, and Saturday after September 14 182 —
W, Friday, and Saturday of this week are 212 —
Proper is always used on the Sunday before Ash *W* 217 —
Ash *W* 217 —
W, Friday, and Saturday of this week are 218 —
W in Holy Week 220 —

W in Easter Week 223 —
and *W* of this week are the traditional 225 —
W, Friday, and Saturday of this week are 227 —
The *W*, Friday, and Saturday after September 14 233 —
Ash *W* 264 —

Wednesdays

The Ember Days, traditionally observed on the *W*, 18 —

week

first convenient open day within the *w*. 16 13
on the days of Holy *W* or of Easter *W*. 17 11
transferred to the *w* following the Second Sunday 17 12
on any open day within the *w*. 17 18
other weekdays of Lent and of Holy *W*, 17 23
Holy *W* 39 —
In Easter *W*, in place of an Invitatory Psalm, 45 —
Holy *W* 76 —
In Easter *W*, in place of an Invitatory Psalm, 83 —
in Holy *W*, or on Good Friday. 108 12
Wednesday, Friday, and Saturday of this *w* 160 —
Wednesday, Friday, and Saturday of this *w* 166 —
Preface of Holy *W* 168 —
Monday in Holy *W* 168 —
Preface of Holy *W* 168 —
Tuesday in Holy *W* 168 —
Preface of Holy *W* 168 —
Wednesday in Holy *W* 169 —
Preface of Holy *W* 169 —
Preface of Holy *W* 169 —
Monday in Easter *W* 171 —
Tuesday in Easter *W* 171 —
Wednesday in Easter *W* 171 —
Thursday in Easter *W* 172 —
Friday in Easter *W* 172 —
Saturday in Easter *W* 172 —
Monday, Tuesday, and Wednesday of this *w* 174 —
Wednesday, Friday, and Saturday of this *w* 176 —
Proper 1 *W* of the Sunday closest to May 11 176 —
Proper 2 *W* of the Sunday closest to May 18 177 —
Preface of Holy *W* 192 —
Preface of Holy *W* 201 —
Wednesday, Friday, and Saturday of this *w* 212 —
Wednesday, Friday, and Saturday of this *w* 218 —
Preface of Holy *W* 219 —
Monday in Holy *W* 220 —
Preface of Holy *W* 220 —
Tuesday in Holy *W* 220 —
Preface of Holy *W* 220 —
Wednesday in Holy *W* 220 —
Preface of Holy *W* 220 —
Preface of Holy *W* 221 —
Monday in Easter *W* 222 —
Tuesday in Easter *W* 223 —
Wednesday in Easter *W* 223 —
Thursday in Easter *W* 223 —
Friday in Easter *W* 224 —
Saturday in Easter *W* 224 —
Monday, Tuesday, and Wednesday of this *w* 225 —
Wednesday, Friday, and Saturday of this *w* 227 —
Proper 1 *W* of the Sunday closest to May 11 228 —
Proper 2 *W* of the Sunday closest to May 18 228 —
Preface of Holy *W* 244 —
Preface of Holy *W* 252 —
Preface of Holy *W* 273 —
Preface of Holy *W*. 275 —
Holy *W* 346 —
Holy *W* 379 —
on all the days of Easter *W*, 406 14
the Psalms are arranged in a seven-*w* pattern 934 23
on any other day in the same *w*, 934 30

weekday

whether it occurs on a Sunday or a *w*. 15 11
which fall upon or are transferred to a *w*, 17 17
Three Readings are provided for each Sunday and *w* 934 7

weekdays

Ash Wednesday and the other *w* of Lent 17 23
On other Sundays and *W* 44 —
On other Sundays and *w* 81 —
at one of the Offices on *w*. 142 4
of the Eucharist on the *w* following, 158 8
w of Pentecost and Trinity weeks). 158 18
serve for any *w* between Holy Innocents' Day 161 —
serves for *w* between the Epiphany 162 —
serves for the *w* which follow, 166 —
serves for the following *w*, 174 —
On the *w* which follow, the numbered Proper 176 —
serve for any *w* between Holy Innocents' Day 213 —
serves for *w* between the Epiphany 214 —
also serves for the *w* which follow, 217 —
serves for the following *w*, 226 —
On the *w* which follow, the numbered Proper 227 —
On the *w* which follow, the numbered Proper 228 —
but not on the succeeding *w* 344 —
To be used on Sundays and *w* alike, 345 —
but not on the succeeding *w* 377 —
To be used on Sundays and *w* alike, 378 —
the Sundays or ordinary *w* of Advent or Lent. 406 16

weekly

at the principal Sunday or *w* celebration 400 4

weeks

Major Feasts falling in these *w* 17 11
weekdays of Pentecost and Trinity *w*). 158 18
used in Pentecost and Trinity *w*). 158 21
(except in the *w* from 4 Advent to 1 Epiphany, 934 22

weigh

if those men will *w* their labor 867 13

weighty

it is but reasonable that upon *w* and important 9 17
upon just and *w* considerations her thereunto 10 3
who for *w* cause could not be present 409 1

welcomed

to be *w* by the congregation 439 5

welfare

The *w* of the world 359 —
The *w* of the world 383 —

well

(as *w* in the chiefest materials, as in the frame 10 6

provision for the *w*-being of their families, 445 —
(Your faith has made you *w*) 453 17
collective part in the celebration, as *w* as 566 17
familiar from its use in many *w*-known anthems. 584 8
never any thing by the wit of man so *w* devised, 866 3
to high and heavenly things, as *w* because 871 14
as *w* of Images as of Relics, 872 12
clearing of them, as *w* from obsolete words 875 18
Magistrate extendeth to all men, as *w* Clergy as Laity, 875 35

went

to be believed, that he *w* down into Hell. 868 10

wept

Jesus himself *w* at the grave of his friend. 507 12

whatever

W the selection, it begins 88 —
form may be used at *w* time the body is brought 466 —

whatsoever

and unrestrained by any worldly authority *w*) 11 6
so that *w* is not read therein, 868 20
no Christian man *w* is free from the obedience 869 13

whether

w in the form provided in the Daily Offices, 13 23
w it occurs on a Sunday or a weekday. 15 11
w before or after. 158 15
celebrant, *w* bishop or priest, be assisted 322 5
The Celebrant, *w* bishop or priest, 333 —
The Celebrant, *w* bishop or priest, 340 —
w bishop or priest, be assisted 354 5
The Celebrant, *w* bishop or priest, 361 11
The Celebrant, *w* bishop or priest, 367 —
The Celebrant, *w* bishop or priest, 369 —
The Celebrant, *w* bishop or priest, 372 —
The Celebrant, *w* priest or deacon, 396 —
congregational use, *w* by singing or reading. 582 —
w they be Ecclesiastical or Civil, 875 41
w they be Ecclesiastical or Temporal, 876 5
w the Liturgy of the Word takes the form 888 9

white

The Holy Table is spread with a clean *w* cloth 406 2

Whitsunday

Joel 2:28–30 (*W*) 108 18
The Day of Pentecost: *W* 175 —
The Day of Pentecost: *W* 227 —

whole

the *w* will be received and examined by every true member 11 17
This Exhortation may be used, in *w* or in part, 316 —
denotes the reading or chanting of a *w* psalm, 582 8
Which Faith except everyone do keep *w* 864 23
But the *w* three Persons are co-eternal together 865 15
For they so ordered the matter, that all the *w* Bible 866 8
all the *w* realm shall have but one use. 867 10
of her substance: so that two *w* and perfect Natures, 868 4
for all the sins of the *w* world, both original and 874 7
ought to be taken of the *w* multitude of the faithful, 874 18
(brackets in the case of *w* Psalms, 935 1

wholesome

exhort others by *w* doctrine, 866 12
is a most *w* Doctrine, and very full of comfort, 870 4
they have a *w* effect or operation: 872 39
doth contain a godly and *w* Doctrine, 874 36

whosoever

W will be saved, before all things it is necessary 864 22
W, through his private judgment, 874 24
And, therefore, *w* are consecrated or ordered 875 24
And therefore *w* are consecrated or ordered 875 30

wicked

but the way of the *w* is doomed. 583 7
XXIX. Of the *W*, which eat not the Body of Christ 873 36
The *W*, and such as be void of a lively faith, 873 37

wickedness

Neither is the effect of Christ's ordinance taken away by their *W*, 873 6

wife

(A man cleaves to his *w* and they become one flesh) 426 —
Celebrant joins the right hands of husband and *w* 428 —
The husband and *w* kneel, 430 —
The husband and *w* still kneeling, the Priest adds 431 —
After the Gospel (and homily), the husband and *w* 433 —
The Celebrant then addresses the *w*, saying 433 —
The *W* answers 433 —
If a ring or rings are to be blessed, the *w* extends her hand 434 —
Celebrant joins the right hands of the husband and *w* 434 —
husband and *w*, in the Name of the Father, 436 5
6. Prayers are offered for the husband and *w*, 436 7
the husband and *w* first greeting each other. 436 11

will

May the Lord, who has given you the *w* 557 15
X. Of Free-*W*. 869 33
that we may have a good *w*, 869 37
when we have that good *w*. 869 38
and, in our doings, that *W* of God is to be followed, 871 22
without the commandment and *w* of Princes. 872 6
effectual signs of grace, and God's good *w* 872 27

willed

not done as God hath *w* and commanded them 870 16

willingly

Not every deadly sin *w* committed after Baptism 870 32
w and purposely, doth openly break the Traditions 874 25

wills

w, while they are in health, arranging for the disposal 445 —

wine

oblations of bread and *w* at the baptismal Eucharist 313 13
placing on it the offerings of bread and *w*, 322 12
people's offerings of bread and *w*, 333 —
hand upon the cup and any other vessel containing *w* 334 —
the Celebrant consecrates additional bread and *w*, 338 —
hand upon the cup and any other vessel containing *w* 342 —
placing on it the offerings of bread and *w*, 354 12
people's offerings of bread and *w*, 361 —
hand upon the cup and any other vessel containing *w* 362 —

the Celebrant consecrates additional bread and *w*, 365 —
hand upon the cup and any other vessel containing *w* 368 —
hand upon the cup and any other vessel containing *w* 371 —
hand upon the cup and any other vessel containing *w* 374 —
prepare the table; the bread, the cup of *w*, 401 5
hand upon the cup and any other vessel containing *w* 403 —
hand upon the cup and any other vessel containing *w* 405 —
placing upon it the bread and cup of *w*. 407 15
customary to add a little water to the *w*. 407 16
chalice on the Altar, and, if need be, a flagon of *w* 407 19
receive the consecrated Bread and *W* separately. 407 26
may administer the Bread and others the *W*. 408 6
If the consecrated Bread or *W* does not suffice 408 9
If any of the consecrated Bread or *W* remain, 408 28
It is appropriate that the oblations of bread and *w* 412 16
couple may present the offerings of bread and *w*. 432 —
it is desirable that the bread and *w* be presented 438 1
or the *W*, it is suitable to administer the Sacrament 457 —
unable to eat and drink the Bread and *W*, 457 —
it is appropriate that the bread and *w* be brought 511 21
it is appropriate that the bread and *w* be brought 524 12
it is appropriate that the bread and *w* be brought 536 12
ministering either the Bread or the *W*, 536 15
Deacon prepares the bread, pours sufficient *w* 546 —
Representatives of the congregation present bread and *w*, 562 —
vestments and bread and *w* may be used 565 23
(or the change of the substance of Bread and *W*) 873 28

winter

and Saturday of this week are the traditional *w* 160 —
and Saturday of this week are the traditional *w* 212 —

wipe

(God shall *w* away all tears) 475 —
(God will *w* away every tear) 495 —

wisdom

that "Rulers may have grace, *w*, 10 36
or *W* 2:1, 12–24 276 9
W 3:1–5, 9 (The souls of the righteous 470 —
W 3:1–5, 9 (The souls of the righteous 494 —
infinite power, *w*, and goodness; 867 36
The Book of *W*, 868 38
(which some do expound the *w*, 869 29

wise

(Like a *w* man who built his house upon the rock) 426 —
we must receive God's promises in such *w*, 871 21
The Baptism of young Children is in any *w* 873 20
yet in no *w* are they partakers of Christ: 873 39

wish

some parents may *w* to express thanks 439 15

wishes

form may be used when a person *w* to make or renew 420 —
Christian name by which he *w* to be known. 511 20
Christian name by which he *w* to be known. 524 11
Christian name by which he *w* to be known. 536 11

wit

never any thing by the *w* of man so well devised, 866 3
we account the following, to *w*: 877 13

within

other forms set forth by authority *w* this Church may 13 8
that the members of each order *w* the Church, 13 17
to the first convenient open day *w* the week. 16 13
on any open day *w* the week. 17 18
after the Office; or, *w* the Office, 142 11
Baptism is appropriately administered *w* the Eucharist 298 5
notify the bishop, *w* fourteen days 409 24
there have been different ministries *w* the Church. 510 3
dedicating a chapel or an oratory *w* another building. 566 6
w the life of the Diocese. 576 14
saying and singing in churches *w* this realm: 867 9

without

may *w* offence be allowed, 9 4
w prejudice or prepossessions; 11 19
and should be read *w* announcement 143 7
w stole, tippet, or other vesture 511 16
w stole, tippet, or other vesture 524 7
w tippet or other vesture 536 7
not to depart *w* signing the Letters 553 16
period of time *w* having been consecrated, 577 22
w confusion, *w* change, *w* division, *w* separation; 864 12
w doubt he shall perish 864 23
w breaking one piece thereof from another. 866 36
w body, parts, or passions; 867 35
w the grace of God 869 36
cannot be taught *w* arrogancy and impiety: 870 20
XV. Of Christ alone *w* Sin. 870 24
He came to be the Lamb *w* spot, 870 27
"General Councils may not be gathered together *w* 872 5

witness

outline the plans of the congregation for *w* 576 12
although the Church be a *w* and a keeper 871 40

witnesses

ceremony be attested by at least two *w*; 422 5
the persons to be married, with their *w*, 423 —
man and the woman, together with their *w*, 435 8
The *w* add their signatures. 513 —
but rather they be certain sure *w*, and effectual signs 872 27

woman

covenant between a man and a *w* 422 3
with the *w* to the right and the man to the left, 423 —
The Celebrant says to the *w* 424 —
The *W* answers 424 —
The Man, facing the *w* and taking her right hand 427 —
Then they loose their hands, and the *W*, 427 —
the man and the *w*, together with their witnesses, 435 8
intention of the man and the *w* to enter the state 435 13
4. The vows of the man and *w* are exchanged, 435 18
The Celebrant declares the union of the man and *w* 436 4
it is fitting that the man and *w* to be married 437 13

womb

took Man's nature in the *w* of the blessed Virgin, 868 3

wooden

a *w* cross may now be brought into the church 281 —

word

not any thing in it contrary to the *W* of God,	10	15
like lay persons, may officiate at the Liturgy of the *W*,	13	22
or Evening Prayer is used as the Liturgy of the *W*	142	17
When there is a Liturgy of the *W*, the Celebrant	283	—
Ministry of the *W* of the Vigil Eucharist,	284	25
The Liturgy of the *W*	288	—
expected to preach the *W*	298	8
Proclamation of the *W* of God	315	—
The *W* of God	323	—
The *W* of God	355	—
Proclaim and Respond to the *W* of God	400	8
1. After the Liturgy of the *W*	408	20
The Ministry of the *W*	425	—
replaces the Ministry of the *W*,	437	7
For the Ministry of the *W* it is fitting	437	13
Part I. Ministry of the *W*	453	12
The Liturgy of the *W*	494	—
and in the preaching of the *W* of God	510	11
The Ministry of the *W*	515	—
The Ministry of the *W*	528	—
The Ministry of the *W*	540	—
At the Liturgy of the *W*	560	—
The Institution, the Ministry of the *W*,	564	14
At the Liturgy of the *W*	571	—
5. Liturgy of the *W*, with sermon or address	578	1
provided with the vowels of the *w* Adonai.	583	23
a form of the *w* that is familiar	584	7
The *w* may, if desired, be omitted	584	8
God the *W*, Lord Jesus Christ;	864	16
(by often reading, and meditation of God's *w*)	866	11
nothing to be read, but the very pure *w* of God,	867	1
II. Of the *W* or Son of God,	868	1
The Son, which is the *W* of the Father,	868	2
expressly declared unto us in the *W* of God.	871	23
a congregation of faithful men, in which the pure *W*	871	30
that is contrary to God's *W* written,	871	39
whereof all be not governed with the Spirit and *W*	872	7
but rather repugnant to the *W* of God.	872	14
It is a thing plainly repugnant to the *W* of God,	872	22
chief authority in the Ministration of the *W*	873	3
we may use their Ministry, both in hearing the *W*	873	5
so that nothing be ordained against God's *W*.	874	24
which be not repugnant to the *W* of God,	874	26
10 Of the reverend Estimation of God's *W*.	875	13
ministering either of God's *W*, or of the Sacraments,	876	1
and New Testament as the revealed *W* of God.	877	14
Liturgy of the *W* takes the form given	888	10

wording

Its *w* may be altered by the bishop	565	1

words

The *w* of anthems are to be from	14	7
Officiant greets the people with these *w*	109	—
ashes are imposed with the following *w*	265	—
address the people in these or similar *w*	285	4
readings in these or similar *w*	288	—
address the people in these or similar *w*,	292	—
The Celebrant then says these or similar *w*	303	—
At the following *w*, the Celebrant touches	307	—
but this form of *w* is used	313	19
At the following *w* concerning the bread,	334	—
and at the *w* concerning the cup,	334	—
given to the communicants with these *w*	338	—
or with these *w*	338	—
dismiss the people with these *w*	339	—
At the following *w* concerning the bread,	342	—
and at the *w* concerning the cup,	342	—
At the following *w* concerning the bread,	362	—
and at the *w* concerning the cup,	362	—
given to the communicants with these *w*	365	—
or with these *w*	365	—
dismisses them with these *w*	366	—
At the following *w* concerning the bread,	368	—
and at the *w* concerning the cup,	368	—
At the following *w* concerning the bread,	371	—
and at the *w* concerning the cup,	371	—
At the following *w* concerning the bread,	374	—
and at the *w* concerning the cup,	374	—
Sacrament is administered with the following or other *w*	399	—
introduced with these or similar *w*	402	—
The Prayer continues with these *w*	403	—
At the following *w* concerning the bread,	403	—
and at the *w* concerning the cup,	403	—
introduced with these or similar *w*	404	—
At the following *w* concerning the bread,	405	—
and at the *w* concerning the cup,	405	—
The Prayer concludes with these or similar *w*	405	—
any appropriate *w* of greeting may be used.	407	9
saying again the *w* of the Eucharistic Prayer,	408	14
beginning with the *w* which follow	408	14
the *w* our Savior Christ hath (has) taught us."	408	24
The Bishop then says these or similar *w*	416	—
the Celebrant says these or similar *w*	420	—
who addresses them in these or similar *w*	433	—
express thanks in their own *w*.	439	16
addresses the congregation in these or similar *w*	440	—
one or both parents say these or similar *w*	441	—
The Priest may then offer *w* of comfort	450	—
the Celebrant says these *w*	485	—
Celebrant dismisses the people with these *w*	486	—
introduce the Creed with these or similar *w*	496	—
the Celebrant says these *w*	501	—
Celebrant dismisses the people with these *w*	502	—
Presiding Bishop then says the following, or similar *w*,	513	—
The People respond in these or other *w*	514	—
The People respond in these or other *w*	514	—
A Bible is presented with these *w*	521	—
The People respond in these or other *w*	527	—
calls the people to prayer with these or similar *w*	527	—
*It is to be noted that where the *w* elder, elders,	528	—
The People respond in these or other *w*	539	—
calls the people to prayer with these or similar *w*	539	—
to each new priest, and the *w* "Receive this	554	5
to each new deacon, and the *w* "Receive this	554	26
By your *w*, and in your life, proclaim the Gospel.	557	12
say these or similar *w*	559	—
the deputy substitutes the *w* given	561	—
Bishop says the following or similar *w*	567	—
followed by the *w* of dedication.	576	8
but is repugnant to the plain *w* of Scripture,	873	29

as well from obsolete *w* and phrases, 875 19
unfailing use of Christ's *w* of institution 877 17
unfailing use of Christ's *w* of Institution, 878 2

work

but this great and good *w* miscarried 10 21
this important *w* being brought to a conclusion, 11 16
24. For Vocation in Daily *W* 210 —
24. For Vocation in Daily *W* 261 —
gives thanks to God the Father for his *w* in creation 402 —
gives thanks to God the Father for his *w* in creation 404 —
that all may receive the benefits of Christ's *w*, 405 —
A prayer for the special *w* 421 —
who carry on the apostolic *w* of leading, 510 7
carrying out of its missionary and pastoral *w*, 510 11
assist bishops and priests in all of this *w*. 510 13
Presbyter of the Church of God, you have been called to *w* 557 —
Having committed yourself to this *w*, do not forget 557 —
or an address about the *w* of the congregation 565 17
which be chosen and called to this *w* 872 19
by the which he doth *w* invisibly in us, 872 28

working

w with us, when we have that good will. 869 37
God's purpose by his Spirit *w* in due season: 871 7
feel in themselves the *w* of the Spirit 871 13

works

shall give account for their own *w*. 865 36
by his own natural strength and good *w*, to faith, 869 35
we have no power to do good *w* pleasant 869 36
and not for our own *w* or deservings. 870 3
XII. Of Good *W*. 870 6
Albeit that Good *W*, which are the fruits of Faith, 870 7
XIII. Of *W* before Justification. 870 12
W done before the grace of Christ, 870 13
XIV. Of *W* of Supererogation. 870 18
Voluntary *W* besides, over and above, God's Commandments, 870 19
they walk religiously in good *w*, 871 9
mortifying the *w* of the flesh, 871 13
4 Of good *W*: first of Fasting. 875 6

world

The welfare of the *w* 359 —
The welfare of the *w* 383 —
Pray for the *W* and the Church 400 12
praises God for the salvation of the *w* 403 —
praises God for the salvation of the *w* 404 —
commitment to the service of Christ in the *w*, 420 —
for the Christian community, and for the *w*. 436 8
Prayers for the *W* 810 5
Prayers for the *W* 814 —
of his Mother, born in the *w*; 865 24
therefore in every person born into this *w*, 869 27
should take away the sins of the *w*; 870 28
(before the foundations of the *w* were laid) 871 3
satisfaction, for all the sins of the whole *w*, 874 7
and the visible manifestation of Christ to the *w*; 877 4
to the Church unto the end of the *w*, 877 9

worldly

unrestrained by any *w* authority whatsoever) 11 5

worlds

of the Substance of the Father, begotten before the *w*; 865 23

worn

The stole *w* about the neck, or other insignia 553 21
The stole *w* over the left shoulder, or other insignia 554 12

worship

that in his *w* different forms and usages may 9 3
"The particular Forms of Divine *W*, 9 15
amendments in her Forms of Public *W*; 9 24
exciting of piety and devotion in the *w* of God; 10 12
and forms of *w*, and discipline, 10 29
in any essential point of doctrine, discipline, or *w*; 11 14
the principal act of Christian *w* 13 3
regular services appointed for public *w* 13 6
The leader of *w* in a Christian assembly is normally 13 20
An Order of *W* 109 —
The Order of *W* for the Evening, 139 —
Order of *W* for the Evening 142 25
Scriptures authorized for public *w* in this Church, 143 7
prayer of Christians assembled for public *w*, 446 4
building is ready for regular use as a place of *w*. 566 10
neighboring place of *w*, or in some other building. 575 7
If the place of public *w* is also to serve as a school 576 29
used for regular *w* by other Christian bodies, 577 1
When buildings have been used for public *w* 577 21
64. Before *W* 812 19
68. After *W* 812 23
64. Before *W* 833 —
68. After *W* 834 —
Prayer and *W* 856 —
And the Catholic Faith is this: That we *w* one God 864 25
relating to modes of *w* and discipline, 876 33

worshipped

the Trinity in Unity is to be *w*. 865 17
carried about, lifted up, or *w*. 873 35

worshipping

Romish Doctrine concerning Purgatory, Pardons, *W* 872 12

worthily

And in such only as *w* receive the same, 872 38
to such as rightly, *w*, and with faith, receive the same, 873 25

worthy

15 Of the *w* receiving of the Sacrament 875 6

woundeth

and *w* the consciences of the weak 874 29

wounds

to heal the *w* of the Body of Christ, 877 3

wrath

it deserveth God's *w* and damnation. 869 27

wreath

the lighting of an Advent *W* may take place 143 14

wretchlessness

into desperation, or into *w* of most unclean living, 871 19

writ

the Church be a witness and a keeper of Holy *W*, 871 40
cannot be proved by Holy *W*; but is repugnant 873 29

writers

ancient Christian *w* make it clear 510 2

writings

common equity ought to be allowed to all human *w*; 10 18

written

Divine Name was *w* in antique and obsolete letters; 583 21
Though it be appointed in the afore *w* preface, 867 23
any thing that is contrary to God's Word *w*, 871 39

wrong

those who have done *w* to their neighbors 409 13
until they have made restitution for the *w* 409 15

X

Y

YAHWEH

the Divine Name be spelled out, and it appears as *Y*. 584 2

Yahweh

(Tetragrammaton) is probably to be vocalized *Y*; 583 17

yea

infection of nature doth remain, *y* in them 869 28
y rather, for that they are not done as God 870 15

year

in the *Y* of Our Lord One Thousand Seven Hundred 8 5
in the *Y* of our Lord one thousand seven hundred 8 12
Commission for a review was issued in the *y* 1689: 10 21
The Calendar of the Church *Y* 15 2
The Church *Y* consists of two cycles of feasts 15 3
The sequence of all Sundays of the Church *Y* depends 15 9
All Sundays of the *y* are feasts of our Lord 16 2
Holy Days are regularly observed throughout the *y*. 16 22
Fridays of the *y*, in commemoration of the Lord's crucifixion, 17 25
provides daily selections for the Church *Y*. 136 —
The Collects for the Church *Y* 157 3
Concerning the Proper of the Church *Y* 158 2
The Proper of the Church *Y* includes 158 3
in any *y*, the Proper for the Sunday after Trinity 158 12
(Propers 1 through 3 being omitted that *y*, 158 20
closely to the date of Pentecost in that *y* is used. 176 —
closely to the date of Trinity Sunday in that *y* is used. 176 —
precedence set forth in the Calendar of the Church *Y*. 195 —
rules set forth in the Calendar of the Church *Y*. 199 —
closely to the date of Pentecost in that *y* is used. 227 —
closely to the date of Trinity Sunday in that *y* is used. 228 —
precedence set forth in the Calendar of the Church *Y*. 246 —
rules set forth in the Calendar of the Church *Y*. 251 —
Y A Matthew 21:1–11 271 —
Y B Mark 11:1–11a 271 —
Y C Luke 19:29–40 271 —
Y A Matthew 26:36–27:54(55–66) or 273 —
Y B Mark 14:32–15:39(40–47) or 15:1–39(40–47) 273 —
Y C Luke 22:39–23:49(50–56) or 23:1–49(50–56) 273 —
the ________ *y* of my consecration. 557 19
should be read over once in the *y*, 866 9
in the *Y* of our Lord, 1801. 867 33
since the second *y* of the forenamed King Edward 875 31
Lectionary for Sundays is arranged in a three-*y* cycle, 888 2
Y A always begins on the First Sunday of Advent 888 3
Y A, therefore, begins on Advent Sunday 888 5
one of the other years of the three-*y* Sunday cycle, 888 14
Daily Office Lectionary is arranged in a two-*y* cycle. 934 2
Y Two begins on the First Sunday of Advent 934 4
the Lectionary for *Y* One is begun.) 934 6
the Gospel Reading be used in the evening in *Y* One, 934 11
and in the morning in *Y* Two. 934 12
Old Testament Reading for the alternate *y* is used 934 13
seven-week pattern which recurs throughout the *y*, 934 24

years

But these many *y* passed, this godly and decent order 866 16
the Service in the Church of England (these many *y*) 866 24
First Sunday of Advent in *y* evenly 888 3
one of the other *y* of the three-year Sunday cycle, 888 14
First Sunday of Advent preceding odd-numbered *y*, 934 3
First Sunday of Advent preceding even-numbered *y*. 934 5
each Sunday and weekday in each of the two *y*. 934 8

yet

y so as that the main body and essential parts 10 5
y upon the principles already laid down, 10 18
For a child not *y* baptized 444 —
but *y* as regards his manhood begotten; 864 9
And *y* they are not three eternals, but one eternal. 864 35
And *y* they are not three Almighties, but one 864 39
And *y* they are not three Gods, but one God. 865 2
And *y* not three Lords, but one Lord. 865 4
y he is not two, but one Christ; 865 28
Y because there is no remedy, but that of necessity 866 40
y it is not meant, but when men say Matins 867 25
but *y* doth it not apply them to establish 868 35
y notwithstanding, no Christian man whatsoever 869 12
y the Apostle doth confess, tht concupiscence 869 31
y are they pleasing and acceptable to God 870 8
born again in Christ, *y* offend in many things; 870 29
and *y* it is not lawful for the Church to ordain 871 38
y, as it ought not to decree any thing against 871 40
y have not like nature of Sacraments with Baptism, 872 35
y forasmuch as they do not the same 873 3
y in no wise are they partakers of Christ: 873 39

YHWH

Adonai ("Lord") and the personal name *Y*. 583 16
Y is represented in capital and small capital letters: 583 29
the Hebrew text has Adonai and *Y* in conjunction. 583 31
Hebrew custom is to substitute Elohim for *Y*, 583 33

yielded

y to make such alterations in some particulars, 10 3

York

some of *Y*, and some of Lincoln: 867 10

young

Song of the Three *Y* Men, 35–65 47 —

Song of the Three *Y* Men, 29–34	49	—
Song of the Three *Y* Men, 35–65	88	—
Song of the Three *Y* Men, 29–34	90	—
Care alike for *y* and old, strong and weak,	557	11
all members of the congregation, *y* and old,	566	16
47. For *Y* Persons	811	30
47. For *Y* Persons	829	—
Baptism of *y* Children is in any wise to be retained	873	20

younger

Infants and *Y* Children	301	—
on behalf of the infants and *y* children	302	—

Z

Zechariah

4 The Song of *Z*	50	—
16 The Song of *Z*	92	—
The Song of *Z*, Benedictus	484	—
The Song of *Z*, Benedictus	500	—

Zephaniah

Z 3:12–20	291	—

Glossary

Glossary

There are 6,423 separate and distinct words which appear at least once in *The Book of Common Prayer,* 1979. The following Glossary lists all of these words and the number of their occurrences in the Prayer Book as defined by the two sections of this Concordance.

Out of a total of 6,423 possible key word listings in the Concordance, 121 words were not indexed in Section One and 350 words were not indexed in Section 2. The following explanation points to the classes of words which were excluded in either Section One or Two or from both Sections entirely.

Most parts of speech are included in the Concordance; however, not all are necessary or useful in research. All personal, possessive, and reflexive pronouns, as well as intensive, relative, interrogative, and demonstrative pronouns have been left out. Indefinite pronouns have been retained. Prepositions not dealing with action, direction, or time have been cut. All coordinating conjunctions have been deleted. The first half of the construction of correlative conjunctions has been retained, and some subordinating conjunctions have been left for semantic interest. All articles, infinitives, interjections and most auxiliary verbs have been cut. Other usages of these auxiliary verbs have been retained (such as, "thy will be done").

In Section Two only all Latin incipits have been excluded, but not their references in the text of the rubrics or in the various Offices and Special Liturgies.

The Glossary uses an asterisk (*) to indicate those words which have been deleted. For a complete list of these words, see the Table of Deletions and Retentions at the end of the Glossary.

Key Word	Occurrences Section One	Occurrences Section Two
a	*756	*915
Aaron	10	
abandon	5	
abhor	5	
abhorred	3	
abhors	1	
abide	16	
abides	7	
abideth	1	
abiding	2	
abiit		*1
ability		1
Abiram	1	
ablaze	1	
able	9	4
abolish	1	1
abominable	2	
abound	1	
abounding	4	
about	*44	*9
above	56	19
Abraham	17	1
abroad	5	
abridged		1
absence		15
absent	2	3
absolute		1
absolution	9	8
absolve	6	
absolves	1	
absorb		1
abstain		1
abundance	9	
abundant	4	
abundantly	3	

Key Word	Occurrences Section One	Occurrences Section Two
abuse	1	
abyss	1	
academic		3
accept	36	
acceptable	14	2
accepted	2	
accepting	1	1
accepts	1	
access		1
acclaim	3	
acclaiming	1	
acclaims	1	
acclamation		1
accomplish	7	
accomplishments	1	
accord	6	1
accordance	20	6
according	78	25
accordingly	2	4
accords	1	
account	7	3
accounted	3	1
accursed		1
accusation	1	
accuse	3	
accused	2	1
accuser	1	
accusers	2	
accustomed		2
acknowledge	20	2
acknowledged	1	1
acknowledging	3	1
acquaintance	1	
acquainted	2	
across	1	1

Key Word	Occurrences Section One	Occurrences Section Two
act	8	8
acted	2	
acting	1	
action	4	5
actions	4	1
active		1
activities		1
activity	1	2
Acts		3
acts	14	1
actual		2
ad		*6
Adam	3	3
adaptations		1
adapted		9
adapting		1
adapts		2
add	3	19
added	1	36
adder	4	
addiction	1	2
adding		1
addition		11
additional	1	30
additions		1
address		9
addressed		2
addresses		14
adds		7
adhaesit		*1
adjutorium		*1
administer	6	8
administered	1	10
administering		1
administers		2

Key Word	Occurrences Section One	Occurrences Section Two
administration	4	11
administrative	1	
admirable	1	
admitted		1
admitting		1
admonish	1	
admonishes	1	
ado	1	
Adonai		5
adopted	1	2
adopting	1	
adoption	7	6
adopts	2	
adorable	1	
adoration	3	1
adore	30	
adorn	1	
adorned	5	
adornment	1	
adorns	2	
adult		2
adulterers	1	
adultery	2	
adults		3
advance		1
advancement		1
Advent		40
adversaries	12	1
adversary	5	
adversities	3	
adversity	8	
advice	1	
advisedly		1
advocate	9	
aeternum		*1

Key Word	Occurrences Section One	Occurrences Section Two
afar	3	
affairs	1	
affect		1
affecteth	1	
affecting		1
affection	5	1
affectioned	1	
affections	4	
affects	1	
afferte		*1
affirm	1	1
affirmation		2
affirmed	1	1
afflict	2	
afflicted	20	
affliction	11	1
afflictions	4	
aflame	2	
afore		2
aforesaid		1
afraid	23	
after	58	183
afternoon		1
afterwards	1	1
again	*88	7
against	151	12
Agape		1
age	32	1
aged	1	2
agents	1	
ages	19	2
ago	1	
agony	3	
agree	1	
agreeable		2

Key Word	Occurrences Section One	Occurrences Section Two
agriculture		2
aha	4	
ahead	1	
aid		2
aided	2	
ailed	1	
aim	3	1
air	6	
alarm	1	
alb		3
albeit		1
Aleph		*1
Alexandria		1
alien	2	
alike	8	4
alive	11	
all	1307	229
alleluia	87	24
alleluias		2
alliance	1	
allotted	2	
allow	2	1
allowed		5
allowing		1
Almighties		1
almighty	352	6
almost	3	1
alms		3
aloes	1	
alone	38	13
along	5	
aloud	6	1
already	*2	4
also	*116	67
altar	11	27

Key Word	Occurrences Section One	Occurrences Section Two
altars	2	
alterable		1
alterations		11
altered		4
alternate		2
alternating		1
alternation		1
alternative		7
alternatives		1
although	3	10
altogether	6	1
alway	2	
always	90	31
am	*97	*5
Amalek	1	
ambush	3	
AMEN	*8	
Amen	*34	*825
amend	4	1
amended		1
amendment	6	1
amendments		3
America		3
American		1
amiss	3	
Ammon	1	
among	130	8
amongst	1	
Amorites	2	
Amos		2
an	*89	*59
Anabaptists		1
ancestors	1	
ancient	7	7
and	*7217	*1331

Key Word	Occurrences Section One	Occurrences Section Two
Andrew	2	2
anew	1	
angel	5	
angels	41	7
anger	28	
angered	3	
angry	8	
anguish	2	
anima		*3
ankles	1	
annexed		1
anniversary		3
announce	2	
announced	2	2
announcement		1
announcements		2
annulled		1
Annunciation		4
anoint	3	
anointed	23	3
anointest	1	
anointing	2	5
another	43	22
answer	29	44
answered	9	
answering		2
answers	1	5
anthem		51
anthems		18
anticipate	1	
Antioch		1
antiphon		3
antiphonal		1
antiphonally		1
antiphons		9

Key Word	Occurrences Section One	Occurrences Section Two
antique		1
anxieties	4	
anxiety	3	1
anxious	1	
any	55	93
anyone	5	
anything	3	1
anytime		1
anywhere		1
apart	4	6
Apocrypha	3	1
apostle	16	2
apostles	41	49
apostolic	13	1
apparel	3	1
appeal	4	
appear	8	5
appeared	3	
appearing	3	
appears		1
appease		1
appeasing		1
appertain		1
appertaineth		1
appertaining		1
appetites	1	
applause		2
apple	2	
applied	2	
apply	3	2
appoint	1	
appointed	9	91
appointment	4	
apportioned	1	
approach		2

Key Word	Occurrences Section One	Occurrences Section Two
approaches		1
appropinquet		*1
appropriate		89
appropriately		5
approval		1
approved	1	5
April		3
Arabia	2	
archangels	4	
archbishops		1
architect		1
ardent	2	
are	*781	*259
areas	1	3
arise	16	3
ark	3	
arm	13	
armed	2	2
armies	4	
armor	4	
arms	17	1
army	6	
arose	1	
around	17	1
arouse	3	
arrange		1
arranged		4
arrangements		2
arranging		1
array	1	
arrival		2
arrogance	3	
arrogancy		1
arrogant	4	
arrogantly	1	

Key Word	Occurrences Section One	Occurrences Section Two
arrow	3	
arrows	13	
art	58	1
article		8
articles		5
artificial		1
artisans		1
artists		4
arts	1	
as	*506	*257
ascend	3	
ascended	23	2
ascendeth	1	
ascension	7	25
ascribe	9	
ascertained		1
ash		10
ashamed	13	
ashes	8	2
aside	3	1
ask	49	3
asked	8	1
asking	5	
asks		10
asleep	11	
aspirations	2	
assail	1	
assault	4	
assaulted	2	
assaults	3	
assemble		5
assembled	5	2
assembles		1
assembly	8	6
assent		1

Key Word	Occurrences Section One	Occurrences Section Two
asses	1	
assign		1
assigned	1	14
assist	7	9
assistant		2
assisted		5
assisting		7
assists		1
associated		1
associates		1
assurance	9	
assure	1	1
assured	1	
assuring	1	
Assyrians	1	
asterisk		2
astounded	1	
astray	8	
asunder	3	
at	*218	*296
ate	5	
Athanasian	2	
Athanasius		2
athirst	3	
atoms	1	
attack	1	
attacking	1	
attain	13	1
attainment	1	
attains		1
attend	1	
attendants		1
attended	1	
attendite		*1
attends		1

Key Word	Occurrences Section One	Occurrences Section Two
attention	1	1
attested		1
attribute		1
attributed		2
audite		*1
aught	1	
August		16
Augustine		1
auribus		*2
author	8	
authority	18	27
authorization		1
authorize		3
authorized		13
authors	1	1
autumnal		2
available		6
avenge	1	
avenger	3	
avoid	1	1
avoided		1
await	9	
awaiting	1	
awake	11	
awaken	3	
awakens	1	
awaking	1	
aware	1	
awareness	2	
away	119	5
awe	10	
awesome	6	
axes	1	
Ayin		*1
Baal	1	

Key Word	Occurrences Section One	Occurrences Section Two
Babylon	3	
back	35	
backs	1	
backside	1	
bad	3	
badgers	1	
badges		1
band	2	
Bangor		1
banish	1	
banished	1	
banner	2	
banners	1	
Banns	1	1
banquet	4	
baptism	52	78
baptismal	5	19
baptisms		1
Baptist	2	3
baptistry		1
baptize	4	
baptized	19	29
baptizing	2	
bar	1	1
bare	2	
Barnabas	2	2
barns	1	
barren	1	
barriers	1	
bars	2	
Bartholomew	2	2
Baruch		1
based		1
Bashan	6	
basic	1	1

Key Word	Occurrences Section One	Occurrences Section Two
basin	1	
basis		3
bathe	1	
battle	12	1
be	*1203	*751
beams	1	
bear	23	
beard	2	
bearer	1	1
bearest	3	
bearing	4	2
bears	2	
beast	4	
beasts	14	
beat	2	
beati		*3
Beatitudes		1
beatus		*3
beautified	1	
beautiful	1	
beauty	25	2
became	24	2
because	*141	*11
become	35	1
becomes	1	
becoming	2	
bed	10	
beds	2	
been	*89	50
bees	1	
before	205	89
beg	2	
began	2	1
beggars	1	
begging	1	

Key Word	Occurrences Section One	Occurrences Section Two
begin	2	7
beginning	46	27
begins	1	32
begotten	34	10
begun	6	4
behalf	8	2
behaved	1	
beheld	4	
behind	3	
behold	68	2
beholdest	1	
beholding	5	
beholds	1	
being	89	26
beings	2	
Bel		1
belief		1
beliefs	1	
believe	102	7
believed	6	4
believers	4	
believes	3	1
believeth	2	1
believing	4	
bellies	1	
bells		1
belly	1	
belong	5	1
belongs	5	
beloved	31	
below		1
belt	1	
bend	6	
bending	1	
beneath	5	

Key Word	Occurrences Section One	Occurrences Section Two
benedic		*2
benedicam		*1
benedicite		*2
benediction	3	
benedictus		*7
benedixisti		*1
benefactors		3
benefit	5	2
benefits	8	2
Benjamin	2	
bequests		1
bereaved	3	2
bereavement		2
beseech	111	
beseeching	8	
beset	3	
beside	6	
besides	1	2
besieged	1	
best	9	1
bestow	3	
bestowed	9	
bestowing	1	
Beth		*1
Bethlehem	2	
betrayed	10	
better	13	1
between	8	18
bewail	1	
beyond	3	
Bible	9	19
Bibles		1
biblical		4
bid	5	
bidden	1	

Key Word	Occurrences Section One	Occurrences Section Two
bidding	1	5
biddings		2
bind	1	1
binding	1	
binds	2	1
bird	3	
birds	8	
birth	12	6
birthday		4
bishop	41	321
bishops	17	31
bit	1	
bitter	2	
bitterness	6	
blameless	6	
blaspheme	1	
blasphemers	1	
blasphemous	1	1
blast	2	
blasted	1	
blaze	2	
blazed	2	
blazing	2	
bless	176	5
blessed	165	6
blessedness	2	
blesses		4
blessing	35	46
blessings	11	1
blind	1	
blindness	5	
bliss	3	
block	1	
blood	94	4
bloodthirsty	2	

Key Word	Occurrences Section One	Occurrences Section Two
bloody	1	
blot	7	
blotted	4	
blow	2	
blows	3	
blueprint		1
bluster	1	
boar	1	
boast	8	1
boasters	1	
boasting	1	
boasts	1	
bodies	10	3
bodily	3	
body	142	35
bold	7	
boldly	8	
boldness	4	
bond	7	1
bondage	11	
bonds	6	
bones	13	2
bonitatem		*1
bonum		*2
bonus		*1
book	5	62
books	6	9
borders	3	
bore	2	
born	36	3
borne	2	4
borrow	1	
bosom	4	
bosoms	1	
both	48	32

Key Word	Occurrences Section One	Occurrences Section Two
bottle	1	
boughs	1	
bought	1	
bound	18	2
boundaries	4	
bounden	4	1
boundless	1	
bounds	1	
bountiful	7	
bountifully	2	
bounty	6	
bow	24	
bowed	5	
bowls	1	
bows	1	
bracketed		2
brackets		2
braggarts	1	
brake	1	
branch	1	
branches	6	3
brave	1	
bravely	1	
breach	1	
breached	1	
breaching	1	
bread	90	51
break	14	5
breakers	2	
breaking	12	9
breaks	5	2
breast	3	
breath	9	
breathe	1	
brethren	6	1

Key Word	Occurrences Section One	Occurrences Section Two
bribe	1	
bribes	1	
bride	2	
bridegroom	3	
bridesmaids	1	
bridle	1	
brief		3
briefer		1
briefly		5
brier	1	
bright	7	
brightness	19	
bring	97	4
bringing	1	
brings	6	1
brink	1	
broke	13	
broken	21	2
brokenhearted	3	
bronze	2	
brook	1	
brooks	2	
brother	35	
brotherly		1
brothers	1	
brought	69	9
bruised	1	
brutal	1	
brute	1	
bucket	1	
buckler	2	
build	7	
builders	1	1
building	4	9
buildings	1	1

Key Word	Occurrences Section One	Occurrences Section Two
builds	1	
built	8	1
bull	2	
bullocks	2	
bulls	6	
bulwarks	1	
burden	6	
burdened	1	
burdens	2	
burial	3	19
buried	19	4
burn	6	1
burned	2	
burning	9	1
burns	3	
burnt	6	
burst	2	
bury	1	
business		1
busy	2	
but	*312	*92
butter	1	
by	*660	*230
byword	2	
Cabinet	1	
calendar		15
calf	3	
call	75	2
called	67	20
calleth	2	
calling	12	2
callings	1	
callous	1	
calls	6	2
calm	3	

Key Word	Occurrences Section One	Occurrences Section Two
calves	1	
came	42	1
camp	3	
can	*55	*7
Cana	1	
Canaan	3	
Canaanites	1	
candid		1
candidate	3	9
candidates		24
candle	1	17
candles		14
cannot	*48	*17
canon		1
canonical		4
canons	7	6
canst	1	
Cantate		*3
Cantemus		*1
Cantica		*1
canticle		28
canticles		14
capital		2
captive	4	
captives	3	
captivity	2	
care	42	6
careful		1
carefully	1	
careless	1	
cares	9	
carest	1	
caring	2	
carnal		1
carnally		1

Key Word	Occurrences Section One	Occurrences Section Two
carried	2	8
carries	1	
carry	15	3
carrying	3	1
carved	2	
case	2	10
cases		4
cassia	1	
cast	42	3
casting	3	
castle	3	
casts	2	
cataracts	1	
Catechism		4
catechists		1
caterpillar	1	
Cathedral		2
cathedrals		1
catholic	29	8
cattle	4	
caught	3	
cause	24	6
caused	13	
causes		1
caverns	2	
cavil		1
cease	5	
ceasing	3	
cedar	3	
cedars	3	
celebrant		293
celebrate	19	2
celebrated		8
celebrating	2	2
celebration	3	35

Key Word	Occurrences Section One	Occurrences Section Two
celebrations		6
celestial		1
center	2	
centers	1	
ceremonies		9
ceremony		4
certain	7	7
certainty		1
certify	2	
chaff	3	
chains	1	
chair		4
Chalcedon		1
chalice		4
chalices		1
chamber	1	
chambers	2	
champion	1	
chance	1	
chancel		2
chances	2	
change	3	3
changed	7	3
changelessness	1	
changes	5	1
changing		1
changings		1
chant		2
chanted		2
chanting		4
chapel		9
chapels		2
chaplains		1
chapter		11
chapters		1

Key Word	Occurrences Section One	Occurrences Section Two
characteristic		1
characteristics		1
characterized		1
charge	11	7
chariot	1	
chariots	3	
charitable		2
charity	13	2
charmer	1	
charming	1	
chasing	1	
chastity	1	
cheer	1	
cheerful	1	
cheerfulness	2	
cherish	5	
cherubim	7	
Chicago		2
chief	7	17
chiefest		1
chiefly	4	
child	29	20
childbirth	2	
childless	1	
children	83	10
chill	1	
choice	2	3
choices	3	
choir		2
choirs	1	
choose	7	
chooses	1	
chorus	2	
chose	6	
chosen	30	4

Key Word	Occurrences Section One	Occurrences Section Two
chrism		7
Christ	1116	98
Christe	3	
Christendom		1
christened		1
Christian	16	51
Christianity		1
Christians	10	12
Christmas		27
Chronicles		4
Chrysostom		4
church	255	208
churches		10
circle	1	
circles	1	
circuit	1	
circumstances		15
citadels	1	
citation		12
citations		1
cited		4
cities	7	2
citizens	5	
citizenship	1	
city	39	1
civic	1	
civil		16
claim	2	
clamavi		*2
clamor	2	
clanging	1	
clap	2	
classical		2
clause		1
clauses		1

Key Word	Occurrences Section One	Occurrences Section Two
clay	1	
clean	15	3
cleanness	1	
cleanse	18	1
cleansed	4	
cleansing	1	
clear	3	5
clearest		1
clearing		1
clearly	3	3
clearness	1	
cleave	2	
cleaves	2	1
clergy	8	20
clerical		2
cliff	2	
cliffs	1	
climb	4	
cling	1	
clings	1	
cloak	5	
close	4	10
closed	1	4
closely	2	4
closer	2	
closest		59
cloth	4	1
clothe	9	
clothed	7	1
clothing	2	
cloud	10	
clouds	16	
clutches	1	
coals	6	
cock	1	

Key Word	Occurrences Section One	Occurrences Section Two
cockcrow	1	
coeli		*1
coffin		4
cold	4	
coldness	1	
collapse	1	
collar	2	
Collect		112
collection	1	
collective		1
Collects	1	32
colleges	1	2
collegiality		1
collegiate		1
Colossians		6
comb	1	
combined		1
combining		1
come	276	11
comes	32	1
cometh	13	
comfort	57	6
comforted	2	
comforter	1	
comforters	1	
comfortless	2	
comforts	2	1
coming	41	3
command	12	
commanded	11	3
commanders	1	
commandest	1	
commandment	14	3
commandments	69	4
commands	2	

Key Word	Occurrences Section One	Occurrences Section Two
commemoration		16
commemorations		3
commend	25	
commendation		10
commendatory		1
commended	1	1
commends	1	
comment		2
commentary		1
commerce	2	2
commission		4
commit	13	
commitment	8	9
committal		13
committed	9	6
committing	2	
commodious		2
common	18	23
commonly	1	10
commonwealth	2	1
commune	1	
communicant		1
communicants		5
communicate		6
communicated		1
communion	38	77
communions		3
communities	2	
community	14	6
companion	10	
companions	3	
companionship	3	
company	24	
compared	3	
comparison		1

Key Word	Occurrences Section One	Occurrences Section Two
compassed	3	
compassion	38	
compassionate	1	
compassions	1	
compelled		1
compiling		1
complain	2	
complaint	2	
complete	1	7
completed		3
completion	1	
complexity	1	
complied		1
Compline		2
composed		4
composers		1
compromise		1
comrade	1	
conceal	1	
concealed	1	
conceit	3	
conceive	1	
conceived	9	
concern	4	1
concerning	1	44
concerns	2	2
conclude		5
concluded		5
concludes		34
concluding		11
conclusion		6
concord	9	
concupiscence		1
condemn	4	
condemnation		2

Key Word	Occurrences Section One	Occurrences Section Two
condemned	5	1
condition		1
conditional		1
conditions	1	4
conduct	2	1
confer		3
conference		4
conferred	2	1
conferring		1
confess	61	3
confessed	1	1
confesses		1
confessing	3	
confession	11	27
confessions		1
confessor		3
confide	2	
confidence	19	3
confident	1	
confido		*1
confidunt		*1
confirm	3	2
confirmation	5	16
confirmed	3	3
confitebimur		*1
confitebor		*3
confitemini		*6
confiteri		*1
conflict		2
conform	3	4
conformable		1
conformed		2
confound	3	
confounded	4	
confounding		1

Key Word	Occurrences Section One	Occurrences Section Two
confront	2	
confronted	1	
confusing	1	
confusion	3	2
confute		1
congregation	16	95
congregational		1
congregations	1	
Congress	2	2
congruent		1
congruity		1
conjunction		1
conjunctions		1
conquer	2	
conquered	1	
conscience	7	5
consciences	1	1
consecrate	3	6
consecrated	1	28
consecrates	1	3
consecrating	1	1
consecration		31
consecrator		3
consecrators		1
consecutively		1
consent		5
consequence		1
conserva		*1
conservation		2
conserve	1	
consider	15	
consideration		2
considerations		3
considered	1	3

Key Word	Occurrences Section One	Occurrences Section Two
considering		1
consistently		1
consisting		1
consists	2	2
consolation	8	
consolations	1	
console	2	
consoled	2	
consort	1	
conspiracy	2	
conspire	1	
conspired	1	
constancy	1	
constant	6	
constantly	4	1
constituted	4	1
constitution		4
constrain	1	
construction		3
consultation		3
consume	3	1
consumed	6	1
consuming	3	
consummation	3	
contain	4	3
contained		4
containeth		1
containing		9
contemplation	1	
contemporary		5
contempt	6	
contemptuous	1	
contend	2	
contended		1
contends	1	

Key Word	Occurrences Section One	Occurrences Section Two
content	1	1
contented	1	
context		3
continual	11	1
continually	17	2
continuance		2
continue	27	12
continued	1	1
continues	1	58
continuing		2
continuity		1
contracted	1	
contrary		5
contrast		1
contrite	9	
contrition		1
control	1	
controversies		1
convenience		1
convenient		21
conveniently		3
convention		9
conversion	2	3
convert	1	
convertendo		*2
converts	1	
copy	1	1
cor		*2
corde		*1
cords	5	
Corinthians		24
corners	3	
cornerstone	3	
corporate	3	
corpses	1	

Key Word	Occurrences Section One	Occurrences Section Two
correctional		2
correspond		1
corresponding		6
corresponds		4
corrigit		*1
corrupt	5	1
corrupted		1
corruption	1	1
cosmic		2
couch	1	
could	*8	*4
council	4	2
councilor	1	
councils	2	3
counsel	18	4
counselor	2	
counselors	1	
counsels	1	
count	6	
counted	2	1
countenance	24	
countless	2	
countries		1
country	14	5
counts	1	
county	1	
couple		4
couplet		1
courage	17	
courageous	1	
course	12	5
courses	2	
court	2	
courts	17	2
covenant	75	7

Key Word	Occurrences Section One	Occurrences Section Two
cover	11	
covered	12	2
covering	1	3
covers	2	
covert	2	
covet	2	
covetous	1	
cracks	1	
crafts	1	
crag	4	
craved	1	
craving	3	
create	14	
created	28	5
createdst	1	
creates	1	
creation	44	12
creator	27	3
creature	4	
creatures	13	2
creditor	1	
creed	10	40
creeds	6	5
creeping	1	
cremation		2
cried	9	
cries	1	
crime	3	
crimes	1	
criminal	1	
cringe	3	
crippled	1	
crooked	3	
crops	2	
cross	58	16

Key Word	Occurrences Section One	Occurrences Section Two
crowd	1	2
crowded	1	
crowing	1	
crown	12	
crowning	1	
crowns	1	
crucified	23	1
crucifixion		1
cruelly	1	
cruelty	3	
crumble	1	
crumbs	2	
crush	6	
crushed	5	
cry	39	
crying	4	
cultures	2	2
Cum		*2
cup	26	22
curates		1
cure	1	
curious		1
curl	1	
curse	3	1
cursed	2	
cursing	4	
curtain	1	
custodiam		*1
custom	1	3
customary		9
customs		1
cut	10	2
cutting		1
cycle		3
cycles		1

Key Word	Occurrences Section One	Occurrences Section Two
cymbals	2	
daily	45	29
Daleth		*1
damage	1	
damnation	1	3
dance	2	1
dancers	1	
dances	1	
dancing	1	
danger	11	
dangerous		2
dangers	6	
Daniel		2
dare	3	
dark	12	1
darkened	1	
darkeneth	1	
darkens	1	
darkness	54	1
dash	2	
dashes	1	
date		11
dated		1
Dathan	1	
daughter	4	
daughters	8	
David	19	
dawn	4	
dawned	1	
dawning	1	
day	224	326
daylight	1	
days	69	68
dayspring	1	
daytime	2	

Key Word	Occurrences Section One	Occurrences Section Two
de		*3
deacon	9	116
deacons	9	25
dead	79	20
deadly	6	1
deaf	4	
deal	7	1
dealing	3	
dealings	1	
dealt	6	
dean		1
deans		1
dear	38	
dearer	1	
dearly	7	
death	195	15
Deborah	1	
debt	1	1
Decalogue		4
deceased		3
deceit	2	
deceitful	10	
deceitfully	3	
deceitfulness	1	
deceits	1	1
deceive	5	1
deceived	1	
December		13
decent		1
deception	1	
decet		*1
decision	1	
decisions	2	
declaration		12
declare	23	4

Key Word	Occurrences Section One	Occurrences Section Two
declared	9	5
declares	1	3
declarest	2	
declaring	2	1
decorated		1
decoration		1
decorations		1
decrease	1	
decree	5	4
decreed	1	1
decrees	26	
dedicate	5	1
dedicated	3	5
dedicating		3
dedication	2	20
deed	17	1
deeds	33	
deemed		1
deep	32	1
deeper	1	
deepest		1
deeply	5	1
deeps	2	
deer	2	
defeated	1	
deficit		*1
defend	30	
defended	4	
defender	4	
defense	8	
defensible		1
defied	2	
defiled	3	
defilements	1	
define	1	

Key Word	Occurrences Section One	Occurrences Section Two
definition		1
defy	1	
degradation	1	
degree	2	
degrees		1
delay	2	
deliberately	1	
delight	36	
delighted	1	
delights	4	
deliver	112	4
deliverance	9	1
delivered	38	
deliverer	3	
delivers	2	
delivery		1
demand	1	
demanding	1	
demands	2	
demolish	1	
denial	1	1
denied	1	2
denominations		1
denote		2
denotes		1
dens	1	
denunciation		1
deny	2	1
denying	2	
Deo		*4
Deorum		*1
depart	12	3
departed	12	8
departure		1
dependence	1	

Key Word	Occurrences Section One	Occurrences Section Two
dependent		1
depends	1	1
deposed		1
deposit		2
deprecatio		*1
depth		1
depths	14	
deputies		1
deputy		2
derided	1	
derision	5	
descend	1	
descendants	5	
descended	9	1
descent	1	
described	8	2
desert	8	
deserts	4	
deserve	6	1
deserved	1	
deserveth		1
deservings		1
designated		3
designed		1
designs	4	
desirable		17
desire	24	6
desired	7	37
desires	28	1
desireth	1	
desolate	5	
despair	5	
desperation		2
despise	5	
despised	3	

Key Word	Occurrences Section One	Occurrences Section Two
despite	3	
despitefully	1	
despoil	1	
despoiled	1	
destined	1	
destitute	5	
destroy	22	
destroyed	20	
destroying	1	
destroys	1	
destruction	7	
determination	1	
determined	3	1
determines		1
detested	1	
Deum		4
Deus		34
Deuteronomy		1
development		1
devices	5	
devil	5	1
devious	1	
devise	4	
devised	1	1
devote	1	
devoted	2	
devotion	10	6
devotions		7
devour	2	
devoured	3	
devoutly	4	
dew	7	
dews	1	
diaconate		1
did	*50	*4

Key Word	Occurrences Section One	Occurrences Section Two
didst	*47	
die	36	
died	33	1
dies	1	
dieth	2	
differ	3	
difference		1
different	1	9
differing	1	
dig	1	
digest	2	
dignity	13	1
dignus		*1
dilecta		*1
dilexi		*3
diligam		*1
diligent	1	1
diligently	2	1
diminished	1	1
diminishes	1	
dimittis		6
dining		1
diocesan		1
diocese	9	12
dipped	1	
dips		1
direct	11	4
directed	1	8
direction	3	2
directions		30
directly	1	
directs	1	1
disability		1
disappear	1	
disappointed	2	

Key Word	Occurrences Section One	Occurrences Section Two
disappointments	1	
disaster	3	1
discern	3	
discerned	1	2
discerning	1	
discernment	1	
disciples	22	
disciplinary		1
discipline	14	6
disciplines	1	
discord	2	
discountenance		1
discouraged	1	
discovery	1	
discreet	1	
discretion		14
discussion		1
disdainfully	1	
disease	2	
disgrace	1	
disgraced	7	
dishonesty	1	
dishonor	3	
disloyal	1	
dismay	2	
dismayed	3	
dismiss		4
dismissal		17
dismissals		2
dismisses		9
disobedience	1	
disobeyed	1	
dispel	1	
dispersed	1	
displeased	2	

Key Word	Occurrences Section One	Occurrences Section Two
displeasure	5	
disposal		1
dispose	1	
disposed		1
disquieted	4	
disquietude	2	
distinct		2
distinction		1
distinctive		4
distinctly		1
distinguish		1
distorted	1	
distorting	1	
distress	17	
distressed	1	
distribute	1	1
distributed		4
distributes		1
distributing		2
distribution		2
disturbed	1	
divers		1
diversely		1
diversity	1	5
divide	4	
divided	8	4
divides	1	1
dividest	1	
dividing	1	1
divine	17	6
division		1
divisions	4	1
dixi		*1
dixit		*4
do	*350	*37

Key Word	Occurrences Section One	Occurrences Section Two
doctors		1
doctrine	12	9
document	1	1
documents		1
doers	1	1
does	*52	*8
dog	1	
dogs	4	
doing	7	1
doings	3	1
Domine		38
Domini		5
dominion	20	
dominions		1
Domino		11
Dominum		9
Dominus		17
done	*97	17
donor		1
donors		2
doom	1	
doomed	2	1
door	3	6
doors	5	1
dost	*15	
doth	*9	17
double	1	
doubt	5	5
doubts	1	2
dove	3	
down	141	5
downfall		1
Doxology		4
drag	1	
dragon		1

Key Word	Occurrences Section One	Occurrences Section Two
dragons	1	
drain	1	
draw	23	
draweth	1	
drawing	1	1
drawn	4	4
draws	4	
dread	3	
dream	4	
dregs	1	
drench	2	
dressed	1	
drew	2	
dried	6	
drift	1	
drink	36	3
drinking	1	
drinks	1	
drive	9	
driven	2	
drives	1	
drop	1	
drops	1	
dross	1	
drove	2	
drowned	1	
drums	1	
drunkards	2	
drunkenness		1
dry	11	1
due	11	3
dug	6	
dull	1	
dullard	1	
dullards	1	

Key Word	Occurrences Section One	Occurrences Section Two
duly	7	6
dumb	2	
dung	1	
during	3	29
dusk	1	
dust	29	
duties	4	4
duty	13	3
dwell	63	
dwellest	1	
dwelleth	1	
dwelling	29	
dwellings	4	
dwells	7	
dwelt	3	
dying	6	1
each	21	75
eagerly	1	
eagle	1	
ear	18	
earlier		3
earliest		1
early	6	2
earnest	1	2
earnestly	4	1
ears	18	1
earth	341	6
earthly	15	1
earthquake	1	
ease	1	1
eased	1	
easiness	5	1
Easter		116
easy	2	4
eat	24	4

Key Word	Occurrences Section One	Occurrences Section Two
eaten	3	2
eating	2	
eats	2	
ecce		*4
Ecclesiastes		1
ecclesiastical		6
Ecclesiasticus		1
edge	3	
edged	1	
edification		1
edified		2
edifying		1
Edom	7	
education		3
educational		1
Edward		4
effect		3
effective	4	
effectual	5	2
effectually	3	
efforts	2	
Egypt	20	
Egyptians	1	
eighteenth		2
eighth		6
eighty	1	1
either	3	31
ejus		*1
elaborate		1
elder		2
elders	3	2
elect	5	11
elected	1	
election	2	7
eleison	11	3

Key Word	Occurrences Section One	Occurrences Section Two
elements	3	6
eleventh		2
Elizabeth		1
eliminate	2	
Elohim		2
else	3	8
elsewhere		2
ember		12
embittered	2	
embrace	6	1
embraces	1	
embroidered	1	
emergency		4
employ	2	
employment	1	
empower	2	
empowered		1
empty	9	
enable	5	
enabled	3	
enables	1	
enact	1	
enacted		1
enarrant		*1
encamp	1	
encircle	1	
enclose	1	
enclosure	1	
encompass	3	
encompasses	1	
encourage	1	
encouraged	5	
encouragement	2	1
end	71	22
endeavor	2	

Key Word	Occurrences Section One	Occurrences Section Two
ended	4	1
endeth	3	
ending	1	3
endless	5	
Endor	1	
endorsement		1
endowed	1	
ends	28	
endue	4	
endued		1
endurance	1	
endure	9	1
endured	3	
endures	54	
endureth	4	
enemies	90	2
enemy	33	
enfold	3	
enfolding	1	
enforce		1
engage	3	
engaged		1
engendered		1
England		7
English		7
enjoy	10	
enjoyed		1
enjoyment	2	
enkindle	2	
enkindled	3	
enlarged		1
enlighten	9	
enlightened	3	
enlightening	1	
enlightens	1	

Key Word	Occurrences Section One	Occurrences Section Two
enmity	2	
enough	4	2
enraged	1	
enrich	2	
enrolls	1	
enshrouds	1	
enslaved	4	
ensue		1
entangle	1	
entangled	2	
enter	19	5
entered	11	1
enters	1	
enthroned	11	
entire	1	7
entirety		1
entitled		1
entrance	2	5
entreat	15	
entreaty	1	
entrust	5	
entrusted	5	
entrusting	2	
enumerate		1
envied	2	
envious	1	
envy	4	
Ephesians		12
Ephraim	5	
Ephratah	1	
Epiphany		74
episcopal	3	9
episcopate		3
Epistle	7	20
Epistles		1

Key Word	Occurrences Section One	Occurrences Section Two
equal	4	5
equip	3	
equity	8	1
equivalent		2
erect	1	
Eripe		*2
err	1	1
erred	4	3
error	3	
Eructavit		*1
es		*5
escape	4	
escaped	2	
escorted		1
Esdras		4
especially	20	16
essential		3
est		*3
establish	7	4
established	23	3
establishes		1
establishing	1	
estate	3	1
estates		2
Esther		2
estimation		1
esto		*1
estrangement	1	
et		*6
eternal	134	14
eternally	5	
eternals		1
eternity	2	1
Ethiopia	2	

Key Word	Occurrences Section One	Occurrences Section Two
Eucharist	12	86
eucharistic		13
evangelist	6	
evangelists	3	2
eve		1
even	50	4
evening	20	72
evenly		1
Evensong		1
ever	894	2
everlasting	170	11
everlastingly		1
everliving	22	
evermore	46	
every	88	16
everyone	13	1
everything	9	2
everywhere	9	1
evidence		1
evidently		2
evil	116	8
evildoer	1	
evildoers	18	
evils	1	
evolved	2	
ewes	1	
exacerbaverunt		*1
exalt	34	1
exaltabo		*2
exaltation	2	
exalted	35	
exalting	1	
examination	1	6
examine	4	
examined		3

Key Word	Occurrences Section One	Occurrences Section Two
example	47	4
examples	8	
exaudi		*6
exaudiat		*1
exceed	2	
exceedingly	1	
excellent	5	1
excelsis		11
except	2	38
exceptional		1
excess		1
exchange	1	9
exchanged	1	10
exchanges		1
exciting		1
exclusive		2
excommunicate		1
excommunicated		1
execute		3
executed	1	
executes	1	
exemplified		1
exercise	4	3
exercised		1
exhort		1
exhortation		7
exhorts	1	
exigency		2
exile	1	
exiles	1	
exist	2	
existence	1	1
exitu		*1
Exodus		5
expanse	1	

Key Word	Occurrences Section One	Occurrences Section Two
expansion		1
expectancy	1	
Expectans		*1
expectation	2	
expectavi		*1
expected		3
expediency		1
expedient		3
expense	1	
explication		1
exploit	1	
exploitation	1	
expound		2
express	3	3
expressed		1
expresses		1
expression	1	1
expressive		1
expressly		1
expugnaverunt		*1
Exsultet		3
exsurgat		*1
extend	2	
extended		3
extendeth		1
extends		3
extension	2	
extol	1	
extolling		1
extortion	1	
extreme	2	2
exult	3	
Exultate		*2
exultation	1	
exultemus		*2

Key Word	Occurrences Section One	Occurrences Section Two
exults	1	
eye	9	
eyelids	2	
eyes	70	3
Ezekiel		2
fables		1
fac		*2
face	55	3
faces	2	6
facing		20
fact		1
fade	3	
faded	1	
fades	2	
fadeth	1	
fail	5	
failed	6	
failest	1	
failing	8	
fails	5	
failure	2	
failures	2	
fainted	1	
faints	3	
fair	4	
fairest	1	
fairly		1
faith	141	36
faithful	102	4
faithfully	22	1
faithfulness	36	
faithless	7	
fall	46	4
fallen	10	
falling	4	1

Key Word	Occurrences Section One	Occurrences Section Two
falls	2	2
false	14	
falsehood	4	
falsely	1	1
falter	1	
faltered	1	
familiar	1	1
families	7	5
family	25	24
famine	6	
fanfare	1	
fangs	1	
far	31	5
fashion	3	
fashioned	3	
fashions	1	
fast	23	
fastened	1	
fasting	6	2
fasts		1
fat	3	
father	467	44
fatherless	2	
fatherly	7	
fathers	15	8
fathom	1	
fathomless	1	
fatness	1	
fault	9	1
faults	5	1
favor	33	
favorable	1	
favorably	7	
favored	1	1
favourable		1

Key Word	Occurrences Section One	Occurrences Section Two
fear	86	1
feared	6	
fearful	1	
fearlessly	2	
fears	6	
feast	13	18
feasts	2	33
feathers	1	
February		4
fecerunt		*2
feci		*1
fecisti		*1
fed	5	
feed	13	
feeding	5	
feeds	1	
feel	2	1
feet	38	1
feign		1
felicity	4	1
fell	5	
fellow	10	7
fellows	1	
fellowship	52	
felt	1	
female	1	1
fence	1	
fervent	4	
fervently		1
festal	1	
fester	1	
festival	2	4
festivals		1
fetters	1	
fever	1	

Key Word	Occurrences Section One	Occurrences Section Two
few	2	3
fidelity	2	
field	9	
fields	6	
fierce	1	
fierceness	1	
fiery	1	
fifteenth		2
fifth		10
fig	1	
fight	6	
figures	1	
fill	29	2
filled	30	2
fillest	1	
filleth	1	
fills	4	
final		3
finally	8	2
find	49	3
finds	1	1
fine	3	
finest	3	
finger		1
fingers	2	
finish	1	
finished	5	1
fire	35	3
firm	10	1
firmament	6	
firmly	6	
first	32	89
firstborn	8	
firstfruits	1	
fish	2	

Key Word	Occurrences Section One	Occurrences Section Two
fit	1	2
fitted	1	
fitting		5
five		2
fixed	15	7
flakes	1	
flagon		1
flame	9	1
flames	4	
flashed	1	
flashing	1	
flask	1	
flats	1	
flatter	1	
flattered	1	
flatters	1	
fled	4	
flee	5	
fleeing	1	
fleeth	1	
fleeting	1	
flesh	41	10
flew	1	
flies	3	
flight	5	
flint	1	
flock	17	
flocks	6	
flood	4	1
floods	2	
flourish	9	
flourishes	1	
flourishing	1	
flow	2	
flowed	1	

Key Word	Occurrences Section One	Occurrences Section Two
flower	2	
flowers	1	1
flowing	2	
flows	1	
flumina		*2
fly	2	
foam	1	
foaming	1	
foe	2	
foes	10	
fog	1	
fold	9	
folks		1
follow	61	68
followed	3	10
followers	1	
followeth	1	
following	17	216
follows	1	51
fond		1
font	2	12
food	33	1
foods	1	
fool	4	
foolish	1	
foolishly	1	
foolishness	2	
fools	3	
foot	14	1
footed	1	
footing	1	
footsteps	7	
footstool	3	
for	*2371	*705
forage	1	

Key Word	Occurrences Section One	Occurrences Section Two
forasmuch	1	4
forbearance	5	
forbidden		2
forces	2	2
forebears	4	
forefather	1	
forefathers	10	
forego		1
forehead		2
foreheads	1	
foreign	4	1
foreigners	1	
forenamed		1
foresight	1	
forest	4	
forests	1	
foretaste	3	
forgave	4	
forget	29	1
forgive	93	2
forgiven	8	2
forgiveness	50	7
forgivenesses	1	
forgives	12	1
forgiveth	2	
forgiving	3	
forgot	3	
forgotten	14	
form	4	70
formal		1
formed	5	
former		3
forms		18
formula		2

Key Word	Occurrences Section One	Occurrences Section Two
formularies		1
forsake	19	
forsaken	4	
forsaking	4	
forsook	1	
forth	118	18
forthright	2	
fortress	1	
fortunate	1	
fortune	1	
fortunes	6	
forty	2	1
forward	7	4
found	26	9
foundation	7	1
foundations	8	1
founded	4	
founders	2	
fountain	7	
four		7
fourscore	1	
fourteen		1
fourteenth		2
fourth		13
fowler	1	
fowls	1	
fragile	1	
fragrant	1	
frail	1	
frame		1
frames	1	
Francis		2
fraud	1	
free	28	7
freed	9	

Key Word	Occurrences Section One	Occurrences Section Two
freedom	21	
freely	2	2
freewill	1	
fremuerunt		*1
frequent		1
frequently		2
fresh	2	
fret	3	
Friday		21
Fridays		9
friend	10	2
friendless	3	
friendly	1	
friends	19	8
fro	3	
frogs	2	
from	704	182
front		1
frost	3	
frosts	1	
fruit	24	1
fruitful	5	2
fruits	11	1
frustrate	2	
frustrates	1	
frustration	1	
fulfill	24	1
fulfilled	3	1
fulfilling	4	
fulfillment	7	
fulfills	1	
full	53	10
fullness	24	
fully	5	1
function		5

Key Word	Occurrences Section One	Occurrences Section Two
functions		2
fundamenta		*1
funeral		3
furnace	1	
furnished	1	
furnishings		7
furore		*2
furrows	3	
further	1	7
furthermore		6
fury	7	
future	6	3
gain	3	
gains	1	
galaxies	2	
Galilee	1	
gall	1	
gallantly	1	
gangs	1	
garden	2	
garment	4	
garments	5	
gasps	1	
gat	1	
gate	8	
gates	14	
gather	13	4
gathered	18	2
gathering	2	3
gathers	2	
gaunt	1	
gave	71	
gaze	3	
gazed	1	1

Key Word	Occurrences Section One	Occurrences Section Two
Gebal	1	
general	1	24
generally		4
generation	47	
generations	20	
generous	3	
generously	2	
Genesis		8
gentes		*2
Gentiles	6	
gentle	2	
get	3	
Ghost	39	19
Ghosts		1
Gideon	1	
gift	31	3
gifts	43	9
Gilead	2	
Gimel		*1
girded	3	
girds	1	
give	415	11
given	104	39
giver	27	1
gives	27	8
givest	3	
giveth	5	1
giving	35	15
glad	52	
gladden	2	
gladly	5	
gladness	22	
glimpses	1	
glistening	2	

Key Word	Occurrences Section One	Occurrences Section Two
gloat	5	
gloom	4	
gloria		18
gloriaris		*1
gloried	1	
glorified	22	
glorify	41	1
glorious	51	1
gloriously	2	
glory	393	8
glow	1	
glowing	1	
gluttony		1
gnash	2	
gnashed	1	
gnats	1	
go	84	8
goals	1	
goats	4	
GOD	9	1
God	1998	143
Godhead		8
godliness	2	4
godly	20	6
godparent		1
godparents		11
gods	27	2
goes	7	5
going	10	1
gold	12	
Golgotha		2
gone	27	1
good	189	28
goodly	3	
goodness	61	1

Key Word	Occurrences Section One	Occurrences Section Two
goods	2	3
goodwill	3	
Gospel	59	80
govern	12	
governance	2	1
governed	9	1
governing		1
government	3	7
governor	5	
governors	1	
gown	1	
grace	205	24
gracefully	1	
graces	1	1
gracious	68	3
graciously	19	
graciousness	1	
graft	2	
grafted	1	1
grain	7	
grandeur	2	
grant	340	1
granted	1	
granting	4	
grants	1	
grapes	1	
grasp	1	
grasped	1	
grass	13	
grateful	3	
gratitude	2	1
grave	29	8
graven	1	
graves	1	
graveside		1

Key Word	Occurrences Section One	Occurrences Section Two
gray	1	
grazed	1	
grazing	1	
great	187	24
greater	4	3
greatest	1	1
greatly	10	1
greatness	15	
greed	1	
greedy	1	
Greek		2
green	13	
greet	3	12
greeting		4
greetings		2
greets		6
grew	1	
grief	11	1
grieve	1	
grieved	3	1
grieving	1	
grievous	1	1
grievously	1	
grip	1	
groan	2	
groaning	4	
gross	2	
ground	20	1
grounded	2	2
group		2
grouped		1
groups		1
grove	1	
grow	17	2
groweth	1	

Key Word	Occurrences Section One	Occurrences Section Two
growing	2	
grown	6	1
grows	2	
growth	2	
grumbled	1	
guarantee	1	
guard	10	
guardian	3	
guidance	4	6
guide	43	
guided	9	
guides	5	
guiding	2	
guile	2	
guilt	7	2
guilty	4	1
gullies	1	
gushed	2	
Habakkuk		2
habitabit		*1
habitat		2
habitation	5	
habitations	2	
habui		*1
had	53	*2
hadst	*1	
haec		*1
Hagarenes	1	
hail	4	
hailstones	3	
hairs	2	
hairy	1	
half	1	
hall		1
hallelujah	24	1

Key Word	Occurrences Section One	Occurrences Section Two
hallowed	28	
halt		1
Ham	4	
Hamath	1	
hammers	1	
hand	164	32
handed	4	1
handful	1	
handiwork	4	
handmaid	2	
handmaiden	2	
hands	90	27
hang	2	
hangings		1
Hannah	1	
happen	5	
happens	1	
happily		1
happiness	1	
happy	33	2
harbor	1	
hard	12	1
harden	2	
hardened	1	
hardness	2	1
hardship	1	
hardships	1	
harm	4	
harmony	5	1
harnessed	1	
harp	13	
harps	1	
hart	1	
harvest	5	4
harvests	3	

Key Word	Occurrences Section One	Occurrences Section Two
has	287	36
hast	*89	
haste	11	
hasten	9	
hastened	1	
hatchets	1	
hate	31	
hated	5	
hateful	3	
hatest	1	
hath	48	20
hatred	11	1
hatreds	1	
haughtily	2	
haughtiness	1	
haughty	4	
haunts	1	
have	1041	80
haven	2	
having	22	7
he	*945	*41
head	27	8
headed	1	
headings		1
headlong	1	
heads	12	
heal	10	1
healed	7	
healer	1	
healing	11	
heals	2	
health	34	4
healthful	1	
heap	4	
hear	161	5

Key Word	Occurrences Section One	Occurrences Section Two
heard	34	5
hearers		1
hearing	1	3
hearken	8	
hears	4	
heart	207	2
hearted	1	
heartfelt	2	
heartily	4	
hearts	146	1
hearty	8	
heat	4	
heathen	9	1
heaven	228	2
heavenly	112	4
heavens	63	
heavily	3	
heaviness	6	
heavy	8	
Hebrew	2	5
Hebrews		10
heed	5	
heeded	1	
heel	1	
heels	2	
height	2	1
heighten	1	
heights	6	
heinous		1
heirs	9	
held	5	3
hell	8	3
helmet	2	
help	160	1
helped	5	

Key Word	Occurrences Section One	Occurrences Section Two
helper	9	
helpers	1	
helpless	4	1
helps	1	
hem	2	
hence	1	
henceforth	3	1
her	*62	*17
heralds	2	
herd	1	
herds	5	
here	*45	*41
hereafter	5	1
hereby		4
Hereford		1
herein		1
heresy	1	
heretofore		1
heritage	8	
Hermon	4	
Herod	2	
heroic		2
hers		*1
Heth		*1
hid	9	
hidden	12	
hide	26	
hides	1	
hiding	1	
Hierome		*1
high	87	1
higher	5	
highest	21	
highly	24	
highway	2	

Key Word	Occurrences Section One	Occurrences Section Two
hilaron		*7
hill	15	
hills	21	
hilltop	1	
hilltops	1	
him	*680	*19
himself	*71	*9
hinder	1	
hindered	2	
hinders		1
his	*1141	*54
historic		2
historical		1
history	4	
hither	1	
hoarfrost	1	
hold	36	19
holdest	1	
holding		1
holds	4	
hole	1	
holies	1	
holiness	40	
holpen	2	
holy	1116	204
homage	1	
home	11	2
homeless	4	
homes	6	
homilies		7
homily		15
homoousios		1
honest	3	
honesty		1
honey	4	

Key Word	Occurrences Section One	Occurrences Section Two
honor	72	1
honorable	1	
honored	4	
honors	2	
honour		1
hoofs	1	
hope	82	1
hoped	1	2
hopes	1	
Horeb	1	
horn	7	
horns	8	
horror	1	
horse	5	
horses	1	
hosanna	17	
hospital		2
host	1	
hosts	27	
hot	7	
hound	1	
hounding	1	
hour	10	
hours	4	
house	66	7
household	12	
houses	1	2
housetops	1	
how	105	2
however		6
howl	1	
human	34	11
humane	1	
humanity	7	

Key Word	Occurrences Section One	Occurrences Section Two
humble	29	2
humbled	14	
humbly	47	
humiliated	1	
humiliation	1	
humilitatem		*1
humility	5	1
hundred		2
hung	3	
hunger	5	
hungry	12	
hunt	1	
hunter	2	
hurl	1	
hurled	6	
hurt	8	
hurteth		1
hurtful	3	
husband	9	11
hushed	1	
hybrid		1
hymn	3	80
hymns		10
hymnus		*1
hypocrisy	2	
I	*1125	*28
ice	2	
identical		1
idiom		2
idleness		1
idol	1	
idolatry		1
idols	9	
if	88	143
ignorance	4	

Key Word	Occurrences Section One	Occurrences Section Two
ignorances	1	
ill	2	
illness	1	2
illuminare		*1
illuminatio		*2
illumination	1	
illumine	4	
illumined	4	
image	25	1
images	1	1
imagination	2	
imaginations	1	
imagine	4	
imitate	2	
immaculate	1	
immaculati		*1
immeasurable	2	
immediately		22
immerses		1
immortal	9	
immortality	4	
impartially	1	
imparts	1	
impatience	1	
impediment	2	
imperishable		1
impiety		1
implore	1	
importance	3	
important		1
imposed		2
impressed	1	
imprisoned	1	
improperly	1	
improve	2	

Key Word	Occurrences Section One	Occurrences Section Two
impurity	1	
imputes	1	
in	*3126	*757
inaccessible	1	
inapplicable		1
inauguration	1	1
incapable		1
incarnate	19	
incarnation	5	24
incense	7	2
incised		1
inclement		1
inclina		*1
incline	23	
inclined	3	1
include	1	7
included	1	12
includes		1
including		8
incomprehensible		4
incomprehensibles		1
inconveniences		1
incorporate	1	
incorporated		1
incorporates		2
incorporating	1	
incorruption		1
increase	29	
increased	3	1
increases	1	
increasing	4	
increasingly		1
indebted		1
indeed	34	

Key Word	Occurrences Section One	Occurrences Section Two
indented		1
independence		6
independent		1
indicate		2
indicated		4
indicates		1
indicating		1
indifference	2	
indifferent		1
indignation	10	
indissoluble		1
individual		1
individually		2
individuals		2
indolent	1	
inducted		3
induction		5
indulgent	1	
industries	2	
industry	1	4
indwelling	4	
ineffable	2	
inestimable	3	
infants	5	3
infect	1	
infection		1
inferior		1
infinite	8	1
infinitely	4	
infirm	2	
infirmities	6	
infirmity	1	
inflamed	2	1
inflict	1	
influence		2

Key Word	Occurrences Section One	Occurrences Section Two
inform		1
inhabitants	2	
inhabited	1	
inhabiteth	1	
inhabits	1	
inherent	1	1
inherit	5	
inheritance	32	
inherited	1	
inheritors	1	
inimicis		*1
iniquities	5	
iniquity	11	
iniquos		*1
initial		1
initiated	1	
initiation		2
injunctions		1
injured	2	
injuries	1	
injury	1	
injustice	3	
injustus		*1
inlaid		1
inmost	1	
innocence	5	
innocent	10	
innocents	2	5
innumerable	4	
inordinate	3	
inquiring	1	1
inquiry		1
insects	1	
insertions		1
inside		2

Key Word	Occurrences Section One	Occurrences Section Two
insight	1	
insignia		3
insipiens		*2
insolence	1	
insolent	1	
insomuch		2
inspiration	9	1
inspire	7	
inspired	6	
installation		1
instance		1
instances		1
instead	3	16
institute	3	
instituted	5	2
institution	2	10
institutions	1	2
instruct	7	1
instructed	3	1
instruction		2
instructive		1
instrument	4	2
instrumental		9
instruments	1	2
integrity	6	
intelligit		*1
intemperate	1	
intend	3	
intended	3	4
intending		2
intends		1
intention	1	4
intentions		1
interceded	1	
intercedes	1	

Key Word	Occurrences Section One	Occurrences Section Two
intercession	3	8
intercessions	4	11
intermingled	1	
interpret	2	
interpretation	1	
interpreting	1	
interrupts		1
interstellar	1	
into	*305	*43
intolerable	1	
intravit		*1
intricate		1
introduce		4
introduced		2
introduction		2
invaluable		1
invent	1	
invented		1
invention		1
invisible	3	1
invisibly		1
invitation	1	7
invitatories		1
invitatory		16
invite	2	
invited		2
invites	1	2
invocarem		*2
invocation		5
invoke	1	
inward	6	
inwardly	5	
iron	5	
is	*1259	*658
Isaac	3	1

Key Word	Occurrences Section One	Occurrences Section Two
Isaiah	1	37
Ishmaelites	1	
island	1	
isles	2	
isolation	1	
Israel	93	6
issue	1	
issued	1	1
it	*483	*235
italics		4
its	*73	*34
itself	*7	*3
ivory	1	
Jabin	1	
jackals	1	
Jacob	38	
jails	1	
James	6	11
January		9
jaws	1	
jealous	1	
jealousy	1	
Jearim	1	
Jehovah		1
Jeremiah		3
Jerusalem	29	3
Jesus	858	21
Job		4
Joel		4
John	9	55
join	8	7
joined	11	4
joining	6	
joins		3

Key Word	Occurrences Section One	Occurrences Section Two
joint	1	1
Jordan	5	
Joseph	7	3
Joshua	1	2
journey	1	
journeys	1	
joy	117	4
joyful	26	
joyfully	6	
joyous	4	
joys	12	
jubilant	1	
jubilate		6
Judaea	1	1
Judah	9	
Judas	2	
Jude	2	2
Judea	1	
judge	46	9
judged	3	
Judges		1
judgement		5
judgements	1	
judica		*3
judicium		*3
judges	3	
judging	2	
judgment	30	
judgments	32	
Judith		1
July		14
June		17
jurisdiction		2
just	35	3
justi		*1

Key Word	Occurrences Section One	Occurrences Section Two
justice	62	8
justification	2	4
justified	3	2
justly	4	
justus		*1
Kadesh	1	
Kalender		1
Kaph		*1
Kedar	1	
keep	141	2
keeper	1	1
keepeth	2	
keeping	7	1
keeps	5	
kept	13	26
keys	1	2
kill	2	
killed	2	
kind	4	2
kindle	7	1
kindled	6	2
kindly	1	
kindness	43	
kindnesses	1	
kindred	1	
kindreds	1	
kinds	2	6
king	84	6
kingdom	138	
kingdoms	5	
kingly	1	
kings	34	3
kingship	2	
Kishon	1	
kissed	1	

Key Word	Occurrences Section One	Occurrences Section Two
knee	3	
kneel	9	16
kneeling	1	16
kneels		4
knees	2	
knit	10	
know	128	3
knowest	5	
knowing	4	
knowledge	45	6
known	75	8
knows	10	2
Kyrie	8	4
Kyries		4
labor	26	5
laborers	1	
laboring	1	
labors	11	
lack	6	
lacking		1
laden	3	
ladies	1	
laetatus		*1
laid	25	4
laity	3	4
lamb	23	2
lambs	1	
Lambeth		2
Lamedh		*1
lament	1	
lamentation	4	
Lamentations		6
lamenting	3	
lamp	6	
lamps		2

Key Word	Occurrences Section One	Occurrences Section Two
land	100	2
lands	16	2
language	2	8
languished	1	
languishes	1	
lantern	3	
large		1
largely		1
larger	2	
lash	1	
last	24	6
lasting		1
late	1	3
lately		2
later		1
Latin		2
latter	1	
laud	3	1
lauda		*1
laudable	2	
laudamus		*3
laudate		*6
laudem		*1
laugh	5	
laughing	2	
laughs	1	
laughter	2	
law	61	8
lawful		4
lawfully	7	4
lawgiver	1	
lawless	1	
laws	11	5
lay	15	67
laying	3	11

Key Word	Occurrences Section One	Occurrences Section Two
lays	3	10
Lazarus	1	
lead	56	9
leader		16
leaders	7	
leadership	4	
leadeth	3	
leading	4	3
leads	9	11
leaf	1	
leaning	1	
leanness	1	
learn	13	
learned	2	
learning	4	
least	1	7
leather	1	
leave	12	1
leaven	6	
leaves	1	2
leaving	1	
Lebanon	5	
lectern	1	5
lectionary		15
led	28	7
left	26	7
legem		*1
legends		1
legislature	1	2
legitimately		1
leisure	2	2
lend		1
lending	2	
length	9	1
lengthen	2	

Key Word	Occurrences Section One	Occurrences Section Two
lengthened		6
lengthening		1
lengthenings		2
lengthens	1	
Lent	2	60
Lenten	1	
less	1	3
Lesson	15	31
Lessons		69
lest	11	
let	558	4
lets	1	
letter		5
letters		3
lettest	2	
levavi		*5
level	3	
Levi	1	
Leviathan	2	
Leviticus		1
liars	1	
libations	1	
liberally		1
liberties	4	
liberty	13	2
lick	1	
licensed		1
lie	22	
lied	1	
lies	10	
life	464	35
lifetime	2	
lift	52	
lifted	17	4
lifting	5	

Key Word	Occurrences Section One	Occurrences Section Two
lifts	7	
light	194	20
lighted		12
lighten	4	
lighter	1	
lighting	3	5
lightly	1	
lightning	3	
lightnings	3	
lights	6	
like	206	13
likeness	9	
likewise	4	7
limbs	1	
limit	2	
limitations		1
limited	1	
limitless	1	
limits	1	
Lincoln		1
line	4	
lines		3
lingered	2	
linked	3	
links	1	
lion	11	
lions	5	
lips	46	4
list		5
listed		9
listen	13	
listens	1	
lit	4	
litany		40
literature		2

Key Word	Occurrences Section One	Occurrences Section Two
little	13	3
liturgical		2
liturgies		1
liturgy	1	50
live	116	3
lived	5	
lively	4	3
lives	242	2
livest	4	
livestock	1	
liveth	165	1
living	66	4
lo	3	
load	1	
loathe	1	
loathing	1	
local		8
locally		2
locust	3	
locusts	1	
locutus		*1
lodge	1	
lodging	2	
lofty	5	
logical		1
loins	2	
loneliness	1	
lonely	5	
long	75	4
longed	1	
longer	11	3
longeth	1	
longing	2	
longs	2	
look	58	2

Key Word	Occurrences Section One	Occurrences Section Two
looked	10	
looking	3	1
looks	5	
loose	1	2
loosed	2	
LORD	786	1
Lord	1645	185
lord	1	
Lords	6	2
lose	4	
losing	1	
loss	5	
lost	11	
Lot	1	
lot	5	
lots	1	
loud	5	3
lovable	1	
love	308	18
loved	57	2
loveliness	1	
lovely	2	
lover	5	
loves	10	
loveth	1	
loving	66	
low	11	
lower	1	
lowliness	4	
lowly	16	
loyal	4	
loyalties	1	
lucerna		*2
Luke	2	28
lurk	1	

Key Word	Occurrences Section One	Occurrences Section Two
lurking	1	
lust	1	2
lusteth		1
lute	2	
lying	10	
lyre	6	
Maccabees		2
made	213	31
Magdelene	3	2
magistrate		4
magistrates	1	1
magna		*1
Magnificat		6
magnificence	1	
magnified	2	
magnify	23	
Magnus		*1
maid	1	
maidens	3	
main		1
maintain	4	2
maintained	1	
maintains	1	
maintenance	2	
majestic		1
majesty	28	4
major		19
make	203	26
Maker	25	1
makes	17	4
makest	2	
maketh	1	
making	8	2
Malachi		3
male	1	1

Key Word	Occurrences Section One	Occurrences Section Two
malice	12	
malicious	1	
maliciously	1	
man	53	43
manage	1	
Manasseh	3	1
Manasses		1
manhood	1	6
manifest	6	
manifestation		1
manifested	8	
manifestly	1	
manifold	7	1
mankind	14	3
manna	1	
manner	6	16
manners	1	2
mansion	2	
mansions		1
mantle	2	
manual		1
manus		*1
manuscripts		2
many	49	13
March		6
marched	2	
margin		1
Mark	2	12
mark	6	1
marked	1	1
marking		1
marks		1
marriage	13	19
marriages		1
married	4	9

Key Word	Occurrences Section One	Occurrences Section Two
marrow	1	
marry		1
Martha	2	
martyr	7	2
martyrdom	4	
martyrs	10	
marvelous	17	
marvelously	1	
marvels	2	
Mary	35	12
mass	1	
Massah	1	
masses		1
master	6	
masters	1	
mastery	1	
material	1	
materials		1
Matins		1
matrimony	7	4
matter	2	5
matters	2	1
Matthew	2	22
Matthias	3	2
mature	1	1
Maundy		4
May		11
may	*911	*672
mayest	*1	
mayors	1	
me	*930	*15
mea		*7
meadows	2	
meal		5
meals		2

Key Word	Occurrences Section One	Occurrences Section Two
mean	22	2
meaning	2	2
means	14	2
meant	2	2
measure	4	
meat	2	
mediation	3	
mediator	7	1
meditate	10	
meditating	1	
meditation	6	2
meek	4	1
meet	12	5
meeting	1	2
meets		1
mei		*4
meis		*2
Melchizedek	1	
melody	3	
melt	3	
melted	1	
melting	1	
melts	4	
Mem		*2
member	4	6
members	21	29
membership	1	
Memento		*1
memor		*1
memorial	9	
memory	5	
men	37	33
mentions		2
meo		*1
meos		*1

Key Word	Occurrences Section One	Occurrences Section Two
mercies	34	
merciful	83	
mercifully	51	
mercy	357	3
mere	3	
Meribah	3	
merit		1
merits	9	
merry	2	
Meshech	1	
message	3	
messengers	3	
Messiah	11	
met	1	
meter		1
method		6
methods		4
metrical		2
meum		*2
meus		*3
Michael		3
mid	2	
Midian	1	
midnight	3	
midst	33	4
might	78	5
mightier	3	
mightily	1	
mighty	63	
mihi		*1
mind	48	4
mindful	11	
minds	16	1
mine	*23	
mingled	1	1

Key Word	Occurrences Section One	Occurrences Section Two
minister	17	44
ministered	2	7
ministering		4
ministers	20	33
ministration	2	8
ministrations	1	1
ministries	8	2
ministry	43	27
mirabilia		*2
miracle	1	
mire	4	
Miriam	1	
mirth	1	
miscarried		1
mischief	1	
misdeeds	1	
misdoings	1	
misereatur		*1
miserere		4
misericordiam		*1
misericordias		*1
misery	12	
misfortune	2	
misfortunes	1	
mislead	1	
mission	12	15
missionary		3
missions		2
mistress	1	
misused	1	
mitre		1
Mizar	1	
Moab	2	
Moabites	1	
mob	1	

Key Word	Occurrences Section One	Occurrences Section Two
mock	2	
mocked	2	
mockers	1	
mockery	1	
model	1	1
models	1	
moderate	1	
modern		1
modernization		1
modernized		1
modes		1
modest	1	1
moisture	1	
molded	2	
molten	1	
monastic		4
Monday		8
money	1	2
monotonous		1
monsters	1	
moon	18	1
moral		1
morally		1
morals		1
more	79	62
moreover		2
morning	3	57
morrow	2	
mortal	15	
mortality	1	
mortals	9	
mortifying		1
Moses	9	4
most	120	21
moth	1	

Key Word	Occurrences Section One	Occurrences Section Two
mother	29	2
mount	9	
mountain	7	
mountains	27	
mounted	4	
mourn	7	4
mourning	1	
mourns	1	
mouth	61	1
mouths	12	
movable		1
move	8	1
moved	12	
movement		1
moves	1	2
moving		1
mown	1	
much	16	5
mud	1	
mule	1	
multiplicati		*1
multiplied	2	
multiplies	1	
multiply	5	
multitude	7	1
multitudes	4	
murder	5	
murmer	1	
muse	1	
music	5	12
musical		2
musicians	1	3
must	*13	13
mute	1	
mutter	1	

Key Word	Occurrences Section One	Occurrences Section Two
mutual	4	
muzzle	1	
my	*1184	*8
myrrh	1	
myself	*12	
mysteries	18	
mystery	24	
mystical	5	
Name	319	14
name	51	19
named	1	2
namely		1
names	5	5
Naphtali	1	
narrative		1
nation	22	8
national		6
nations	106	4
native		1
nativity	2	6
natural	2	7
naturally		1
nature	23	18
natures		4
naught	2	
Nazareth	2	
ne		*2
near	34	4
nearby		1
nearer	1	1
nearly	1	
necessarily		1
necessary	8	27
necessities	7	
necessity	7	6

Key Word	Occurrences Section One	Occurrences Section Two
neck	3	1
necklace	1	
need	21	3
needed	1	2
needlessly		1
needs	16	4
needy	22	
Negev	2	
neglect	1	
neglected	1	3
neglecting		1
negligence	1	
negligences	1	
neighbor	18	
neighboring		2
neighbors	29	1
neither	22	12
nest	1	
nests	2	
net	8	
nethermost	1	
nets	1	
never	56	4
nevertheless	5	1
new	95	68
newly	1	28
newness	9	
news	9	
next	1	
Nicene	3	15
nigh	1	
night	103	
nights	2	
nine		1
ninefold		1

Key Word	Occurrences Section One	Occurrences Section Two
nineteenth		2
ninety		1
ninth		4
nisi		*2
no	169	66
nobis		*1
noble	7	
nobles	2	
nocturn		1
noise	3	
noli		*1
nomen		*1
nomine		*1
non		*4
none	30	6
nonne		*1
noon		1
noonday	4	1
nor	*67	*19
normally		14
north	2	
nos		*1
noses	1	
noster		*3
nostrils	2	
nostrum		*5
not	*584	*146
note	1	2
noted	1	1
nothing	27	3
notice	2	
notified		2
notify		1
notorious	1	
notoriously		1

Key Word	Occurrences Section One	Occurrences Section Two
notus		*1
notwithstanding		3
nouns		1
nourish	6	1
nourished	3	
nourishment	2	
November		14
novit		*1
now	*373	*26
nowhere	1	
numb	1	
number	16	7
numbered	7	8
Numbers		3
numeration		1
Nun		*1
nunc		*8
nuptial		3
nurses	1	1
nursing		1
nurture	4	1
nurtured	1	
O	*1065	*15
oak	1	
oath	7	1
ob		*1
obedience	22	2
obedient	7	
obey	18	1
obeyed	6	
object	1	
objection		3
objects		2
oblation	7	1
oblations	3	2

Key Word	Occurrences Section One	Occurrences Section Two
obligations	2	
oblivion	1	
observance	2	7
observe	5	
observed	1	18
obsolete		2
obtain	21	1
obtained	2	6
obtaining		1
occasion	4	24
occasional		1
occasions	2	59
occupations	4	
occupied	1	
occupy	1	
occur		4
occurred		1
occurence		1
occurs		2
ocean	1	
October		17
oculos		*4
odd		1
odio		*1
oemulari		*1
of	*4768	*2318
off	27	3
offence		1
offences		2
offend	1	1
offended	8	1
offendeth		1
offends	1	
offense	3	
offenses	11	

Key Word	Occurrences Section One	Occurrences Section Two
offer	44	5
offered	22	16
offering	24	3
offerings	12	9
offers	1	
Offertory		42
office	6	53
officers	1	
offices	1	10
officials	1	
officiant		90
officiate		2
officiates		2
officiating		1
offspring	8	1
oft	2	1
often	8	3
Og	2	
oh	*23	
oil	20	11
old	45	37
older		2
oldest		1
olive	2	1
omens	1	
omission		1
omit		1
omits		1
omitted		28
omitting		5
omnes		*3
omnia		*2
on	*338	*287
once	10	11
one	624	226

Key Word	Occurrences Section One	Occurrences Section Two
ones	10	1
only	119	40
open	49	7
opened	16	1
openest	1	
opening		9
openly	2	3
opens	1	
opera		*2
operating		1
operation		2
Ophir	1	
opinion		3
opportunities	1	
opportunity		10
oppress	5	
oppressed	15	2
oppresses	2	
oppression	11	
oppressor	2	
oppressors	3	
optional		4
or	*132	*1121
oratory		2
ordain	8	2
ordained	9	42
ordaining	1	1
order	20	65
ordered	2	9
ordereth	1	
ordering	3	5
orderly		2
orders	2	11
ordinance	1	4

Key Word	Occurrences Section One	Occurrences Section Two
ordinand		24
ordinands		7
ordinarily		4
ordinary		1
ordination	5	14
ordinations		11
ore	1	
Oreb	1	
organ		1
organic		1
organize		1
original		11
originally		1
Orion	2	
ornaments		2
orphan	3	
orphans	5	
other	60	284
others	37	20
otherwise		11
ought	8	14
our	*1874	*76
ours	*3	
ourselves	*58	*5
out	*215	14
outer	1	
outline		4
outside	1	
outward	6	
outwardly	3	
over	117	21
overcame	7	
overcome	8	
overflow	3	
overflowed	1	

Key Word	Occurrences Section One	Occurrences Section Two
overflowing	1	
overrun	1	
overseeing	2	
overtake	3	
overtaken	1	
overthrew	1	
overthrow	1	
overthroweth		1
overthrown	4	
overwhelm	3	
overwhelmed	4	
overwhelms	1	
owl	1	
own	81	21
owned		1
ox	2	
oxen	3	
packs	1	
pagan	1	
page		108
pages		35
paid	1	
pain	23	3
painful		1
painted		1
pains	4	
palace	2	
palaces	1	
pall		2
palm	2	4
palms		3
pant	1	
Pantokrator		1
parable	1	
paradise	9	

Key Word	Occurrences Section One	Occurrences Section Two
paragraph		1
parallelism		2
paratum		*1
parcel	2	
pardon	14	
pardoned	2	
pardoning	2	
pardons	2	1
parent		1
parentheses		5
parents	4	17
parish	3	12
parishes		1
parishioners		1
Parliament		1
parochial		1
part	7	37
partake	2	
partaker	1	
partakers	11	1
partaking		2
parted	4	2
partially		1
participants		1
participate		3
participates		1
participating		1
particular	1	7
particularly	5	3
particulars		1
parties		2
partly		3
partners	1	
parts	5	20
party		3

Key Word	Occurrences Section One	Occurrences Section Two
Paschal	16	17
pass	19	2
passage		10
passages		12
passed	4	1
passeth	3	
passing	3	
passion	24	9
passions		1
Passover	7	5
past	17	1
pastor	12	3
pastoral	2	7
pastors	6	
pasture	10	
pastures	4	
path	14	
paths	11	
pathway	1	
pathways	2	
patience	21	
patient	5	1
patiently	6	
Patri		*3
patriarchs	4	
patron	1	1
patronal		3
pattern	2	1
patterns	1	
Paul	7	6
pause		1
pausing		1
pavilion	2	
pavimento		*1
pay	5	1

Key Word	Occurrences Section One	Occurrences Section Two
payment	1	
pays	1	
Pe		*1
peace	218	46
peaceable	1	1
peaceably	3	
peaceful	3	
peacefully	3	
peak	1	
pedibus		*2
Pelagians		1
pen	1	
penance	1	2
penitence	6	7
penitent	20	21
penitents		1
penitential		16
pens	1	
Pentecost		62
people	320	468
peoples	85	2
Peor	1	
peradventure	1	
perceive	10	
perceives	1	
perfect	45	4
perfected	1	
perfecter	2	1
perfection	6	1
perfectly	11	
perform	9	5
performed	1	2
perhaps	1	
peril	1	1
perilous		1

Key Word	Occurrences Section One	Occurrences Section Two
perils	5	2
period		10
periods		1
perish	22	1
perished	2	
permission		2
permit	1	1
permitted		2
perpetual	11	
perplexity	3	
persecute	7	
persecuted	5	
persecuti		*1
persecutors	4	
perseverance	1	
persevere	10	
persevering	1	
person	6	73
personal		5
persons	29	58
persuaded	3	
pertaining		1
perverse	1	
pestilence	3	
Peter	5	11
petition	4	2
petitions	8	10
Pharaoh	4	
Philadelphia		1
Philip	2	2
Philippians		6
Philistia	3	
Philistines	1	
Phinehas	1	
phos		*7

Key Word	Occurrences Section One	Occurrences Section Two
phrases		1
physical		1
physician	2	
picks		1
Pie		1
piece	1	1
pieces	2	
pierce	1	
pierced	2	
piercing	1	
piety		2
Pilate	14	
pilgrimage	7	
pilgrims	1	
pillar	6	
pillars	1	
pine	1	
pinions	2	
pioneer	1	
pipe	2	
pit	16	
pitied	1	
pits	1	
pity	20	
place	85	96
placed	3	11
places	23	9
placing		4
plague	8	
plain		4
plainest		1
plainly		5
plainness		1
plains	1	
plan	8	1

Key Word	Occurrences Section One	Occurrences Section Two
planets	1	
plans	4	1
plant	3	
planted	8	
planting		1
plants	4	
plaudite		*1
play	3	
played		6
playing	1	
plea	2	
plead	1	
pleaded	1	
pleasant	4	3
please	38	
pleased	9	
pleases	2	
pleasing	6	1
pleasure	10	
pleasures	2	
pledge	12	
pledged	1	
Pleiades	2	
plenteous	3	
plenteousness	1	
plenty	1	
plied	1	
plight	1	
plot	9	
plots	1	
plowed	2	
plowman	1	
plowmen	1	
pluck	3	
plucked	1	

Key Word	Occurrences Section One	Occurrences Section Two
plunder	1	
plundered	2	
plural		2
poetry		2
point	1	2
pointing		1
points		1
poison	1	
polluted	1	
pollution	1	
ponder	5	
pondered	1	
pone		*1
Pontius	14	
pontifical		1
pool	1	
pools	2	
poor	48	5
poorer	4	
popule		*1
portable		1
portals	1	
portent	1	
portents	1	
portio		*1
portion	6	5
portions		6
positions	2	
possess	7	
possesseth		1
possession	6	1
possessions	2	
possible	1	11
postcommunion		18
posterity	1	

Key Word	Occurrences Section One	Occurrences Section Two
postponed		2
posuit		*1
pot	2	
pottery	1	
pounding	2	1
pour	24	1
poured	8	2
pourest	1	
poureth	1	
pouring		1
pours	3	2
poverty	9	
power	208	10
powerful	1	
powers	10	1
practicable		1
practice	1	1
practicing		1
praise	272	9
praised	20	
praises	34	2
praiseworthy	1	
praising	3	
pray	244	5
prayed	6	
prayer	106	240
prayerfully	1	
prayers	53	129
prays	1	4
preach	21	3
preached	2	9
preacher		1
preaches		1
preaching	10	2
precede	2	5

Key Word	Occurrences Section One	Occurrences Section Two
preceded		2
precedence		9
precedes		8
preceding		30
precepts	1	1
precious	18	
preclude		1
predestination		4
prediction	1	
preface		308
prefaces		7
preferences		1
preferred		4
prefix		1
prejudice	6	1
prelude		2
premises		1
preparation	3	1
prepare	20	7
prepared	34	1
prepares	1	1
preparest	1	
preparing		3
prepossessions		1
prerogative		4
presbyter	1	3
presbyterate		1
presbyters	2	10
prescribed		1
presence	92	6
present	39	73
presentation		19
presentations		1
presented	8	27
presenters		8

Key Word	Occurrences Section One	Occurrences Section Two
presenting	3	
presents	2	3
preservation	4	1
preserve	40	
preserved		1
preserver	2	1
preserves	3	
preserveth	1	
preside		8
president	5	2
presides		12
presiding	2	24
press	2	1
pressed	3	
presses	1	
pressure	1	
presume	2	1
presumption	1	
presumptuous	1	
prevail	4	
prevailed	2	
preventing		1
prevention	1	
previously		5
prey	3	
price	2	
priceless	1	1
pride	12	
priest	24	147
priesthood	8	1
priests	17	26
primal	1	
primarily		1
primitive		1
prince	3	

Key Word	Occurrences Section One	Occurrences Section Two
princely	2	
princes	10	4
princess	1	
principal	2	20
principalities		1
principes		*1
principles		3
printed		2
prior		4
prison	4	
prisoners	11	
prisons	1	2
privacy		1
private	2	4
privately		3
privileges	1	1
prized	1	
probably		2
probasti		*2
probe	1	
procedure		1
proceed	4	
proceedeth	1	
proceeding		2
proceeds	6	11
procession	5	17
processional		2
proclaim	51	2
proclaimed	6	
proclaiming	5	
proclaims	6	
proclamation	1	3
procreation	1	
procured	1	
procuring		1

Key Word	Occurrences Section One	Occurrences Section Two
produce	2	
produced		1
profaned	1	
profess	6	
professeth		1
profession		2
professors		1
profit	4	4
profitable	2	2
profundis		2
prohibit		1
prolong	1	
promise	44	3
promised	35	1
promises	17	6
promote	3	1
promoted	1	
promotes	1	
promulgating		1
pronounce	4	5
pronounced	1	3
pronounces		3
pronouncing		1
pronouns		3
proof		1
proper	3	121
properly		5
Propers		7
property	1	2
prophet	3	2
prophets	33	3
propitiation		1
prosper	10	
prosperity	14	1
prospers	1	

Key Word	Occurrences Section One	Occurrences Section Two
prostrate	1	
protect	14	
protected	4	
protection	3	5
protector	2	
protects	1	
Protestant		4
proud	21	
prove	3	
proved	4	3
proverb	1	
Proverbs		1
provide	7	3
provided	2	25
providence	21	
provides	1	3
provision	4	2
provisions	1	1
provocation	1	
provoked	4	
provoking	1	
prowl	2	
prowls	1	
prudent		1
psalm		173
psalmody		6
psalms	4	65
Psalter		15
psaltery	2	
public	7	22
publican		1
publicly		1
publish	2	
published		1
pueri		*1

Key Word	Occurrences Section One	Occurrences Section Two
puff	4	
pull	1	
pulpit	1	4
punish	7	1
punished	6	
punishment	2	
purchase		1
purchased	1	
pure	28	2
purely		1
pureness	3	
Purgatory		2
purge	2	
purged	2	
purified	1	
purify	6	
purpose	12	11
purposed	1	
purposely		1
purposes	8	1
pursue	9	
pursues	1	
pursuit	1	
push	1	
pushed	1	
put	117	5
puts	3	
putting	2	
Q		*124
Qoph		*1
Quadrilateral		2
quaemadmodum		*1
quaerite		*1
qualified		1
quails	1	

Key Word	Occurrences Section One	Occurrences Section Two
quake	2	
quakes	1	
quaking	1	
qualified	3	
quam		*3
quare		*1
quarrel		1
quatrains		2
queen	1	1
quell	1	
quemadmodum		*1
quench	1	1
question		8
questions		3
qui		*6
quia		*1
quick	4	2
quicken	1	1
quickly	5	
quicunque		*1
quid		*4
quiet	4	3
quieted	2	
quieting		1
quietly	1	
quietness	5	
quis		*2
quiver	1	
quo		*1
quomodo		*1
quoniam		*2
quorum		*1
quoties		*1
race	10	2
races	2	2

Key Word	Occurrences Section One	Occurrences Section Two
racked	1	
radiance	6	
radiant	2	
rage	5	
raging	3	
Rahab	1	
railed	1	
rails		1
raiment	2	
rain	12	2
rained	2	
rains	1	
raise	20	
raised	30	3
raising	5	
ram	3	
rams	3	
ran	1	
rank		3
ransom	4	
ramsomed	1	
ramsoms	1	
rapids	1	
rash	2	1
rather	2	13
ratification		1
ravaged	1	
ravening	1	
ravens	1	
razed	1	
razor	1	
re		*1
reach	8	
reached	1	

Key Word	Occurrences Section One	Occurrences Section Two
reaches	5	
reacheth	1	
reaching	2	
read	4	83
reader		55
readers		4
readily	4	
readiness	1	2
reading	25	60
readings		32
reads		22
ready	19	5
reaffirm	5	1
reaffirmation		7
reaffirmed	1	1
realm		6
reap	2	
reaper	1	
reason	8	4
reasonable	6	7
reasons		2
rebel	3	
rebelled	6	
rebelling	1	
rebellion	2	1
rebellious	2	
rebels	1	
reborn	10	
rebuild	3	
rebuilding	1	
rebuilds	1	
rebuke	10	
rebuked	4	1
rebukes	1	
recall	3	

Key Word	Occurrences Section One	Occurrences Section Two
recalled	2	
recalling	4	
recalls		2
recant	1	
receive	93	28
received	18	18
receives	2	1
receiving	3	9
recent		1
reception		9
recitation		6
recite	3	1
recited		5
reciting		1
reckon	1	
reckoned	1	
recognition		1
recognize	9	
recognized		5
recognizing	1	
recommended		4
recompense	1	
reconcile	2	1
reconciled	9	1
reconciler	1	
reconciliation	14	4
reconciling	1	
record	3	
recorded	1	
recount	2	
recounting	1	
recovers		1
recovery	1	3
rector	4	5
rectors		1

Key Word	Occurrences Section One	Occurrences Section Two
recurs		1
red	7	1
redeem	10	
redeemed	29	1
redeemer	16	2
redeeming	10	
redeems	1	
redemption	36	3
redemptive	1	
redressed		1
reeds	1	
reeled	3	
reeling	1	
refer		4
reference		2
references		4
referent		1
referred		3
refers		1
refined	1	
reflect	1	
reform	1	
refrain	1	2
refrained	1	
refrains		2
refresh	2	
refreshed	3	
refreshing	2	
refreshment	4	
refuge	44	
refugees	2	
refugium		4
refuse	1	2
refused	3	
refusing		2

Key Word	Occurrences Section One	Occurrences Section Two
regain		1
regard	8	2
regarded	2	
regards	1	4
regenerate	1	
regenerated		1
regeneration		1
regis		*1
registered		1
regit		*2
regnavit		*3
regular	1	4
regularly		3
reign	19	3
reignest	4	
reigneth	159	
reigning	1	
reigns	193	
rein	1	
reject	1	
rejected	10	
rejection	1	
rejoice	75	1
rejoiced	3	
rejoices	8	
rejoiceth	1	
rejoicing	17	
related	1	2
relating		1
relationship	6	
relatives		1
release	2	
released	1	
relented	1	
relevant		1

Key Word	Occurrences Section One	Occurrences Section Two
relics		1
relied	1	
relief	7	
relieve	7	
relieved	2	
religion	6	5
religious	2	2
religiously		1
rely	4	
remain	7	13
remainder		1
remaining		3
remains	1	8
remedy	1	1
remember	78	
remembered	12	
rememberest	1	
remembering	6	1
remembers	3	
remembrance	42	
remission	13	1
remnant	1	
removal	1	
remove	1	1
removed	2	
rend	3	
render	6	1
rendered		1
rendering	1	2
renders	1	
renew	19	4
renewal	2	13
renewed	17	1
renewing	2	
renews	1	

Key Word	Occurrences Section One	Occurrences Section Two
renounce	7	
renounced	1	
renovated		1
renown	4	
renunciation	3	
repaid	1	
repair	1	
repairing		1
repay	9	
repays	1	
repeat		1
repeated		2
repel	3	
repent	26	1
repentance	21	3
repented	1	
repenteth	1	
repents	1	
repetition		2
repetitions		1
replaced		1
replaces		1
reported		2
repose	2	
represent	4	
representative		3
representatives	4	9
represented	2	1
reproach	12	
repugnant		5
repulisti		*1
request	1	1
requests	1	
require	5	5
required	8	6

Key Word	Occurrences Section One	Occurrences Section Two
requirements	2	
requires		3
requireth		1
requisite		2
rescue	14	
rescued	7	
reserved		8
Resh		*1
residue	1	
resist	5	
resisting	3	
resolution		2
resort	1	1
resound	1	
resounding	1	
resources	3	2
respect	12	1
respectful		1
respective		3
respects		1
respond	1	19
responding	1	
responds	1	4
response	3	14
responses		5
responsibilities	1	4
responsibility	7	2
responsible	1	
responsive	2	1
responsively		3
responsorial		1
rest	66	4
rested	4	
resting	7	1
restitution	2	1

Key Word	Occurrences Section One	Occurrences Section Two
restless	2	
restoration		5
restore	27	
restored	15	2
restores	4	
restoreth	1	
restrain	2	1
restricted		1
resurrection	104	6
retained		1
reticence		1
retreated	1	
retribue		*1
retribuet		*1
return	24	4
returning	2	
returns	1	
reunion		2
reunite	1	
reunited	1	
reveal	6	
revealed	24	3
revealing	3	
reveals	1	
revelation	8	17
revenge	1	
reverence	6	2
reverend		1
reverent		1
reverently	3	2
review		3
reviews		1
revile	4	
reviled	1	
revilings	1	

Key Word	Occurrences Section One	Occurrences Section Two
revised		1
revision		1
revive	6	1
revives	3	
revolt	1	
revolution		1
reward	6	
rewarded	5	
rhyme		1
rich	16	1
richer	4	
riches	15	1
richly	2	
richness	1	
riddle	1	
ride	3	
rider	2	
rides	2	
ridges	1	
right	132	14
righteous	83	4
righteously	1	
righteousness	90	1
rightful	2	
rightly	5	7
rightness	1	
rights	2	
ring	7	6
rings		2
rise	24	2
risen	44	
rises	1	
riseth	1	
rising	14	
rite	4	27

Key Word	Occurrences Section One	Occurrences Section Two
rites	4	14
river	11	
rivers	7	
road	2	
roar	1	
roared	1	
roaring	5	
rob	1	
robbery	1	
robe	1	
robed	1	
rochet		1
rock	28	1
rocked	1	
rocks	1	
rod	6	
Rogation		7
role	1	
roles		2
roll	1	
rolled	1	
Romans		13
Rome		2
Romish		1
roof	4	
room	2	
rooms		1
root	6	
roots	1	
rose	28	1
round	14	
rounds	1	
rouse	1	
roused	1	
rout	1	

Key Word	Occurrences Section One	Occurrences Section Two
routed	1	
royal	4	1
rubbish	1	
rubble	2	
rubrical		1
rubrics		6
rugged	2	
ruin	10	
ruins	4	
rule	21	3
ruled	1	
ruler	10	
rulers	14	2
rules	5	10
rumors	2	
run	13	
rung		1
runneth	1	
running	6	
runs	6	
rural	1	2
Ruth		1
ruthless	1	
Saba	1	
Sabaoth	1	
sabbath	6	
sack	3	
sacrament	26	32
sacramental	2	1
sacraments	43	21
sacred	12	6
sacrifice	54	3
sacrificed	10	
sacrifices	9	1
sad		1

Key Word	Occurrences Section One	Occurrences Section Two
Sadhe		*1
sadness	1	
saepe		*1
safe	15	1
safeguard	1	
safeguarded	1	
safely	3	
safety	16	
sages	1	
said	73	119
saint	3	83
saints	96	40
saith	6	5
sake	92	4
sale	1	
Salem	1	
Salisbury		1
salt	1	
salutare		*1
salutation		11
salvation	104	15
salvum		*2
Samaria	2	
same	89	37
Samekh		*1
Samuel	2	3
sancte		*3
sanctification	2	1
sanctified	9	
Sanctifier	1	
sanctifies	1	
sanctify	16	
sanctifying	1	
sanctuary	10	
Sanctus		3

Key Word	Occurrences Section One	Occurrences Section Two
sand	2	
sandal	2	
sang	1	
sank	1	
sap	1	
Sarah	1	
sat	6	
Satan	6	
satisfaction	1	2
satisfactory		1
satisfied	7	
satisfies	3	
satisfy	9	
satisfying		1
Saturday		17
Saturdays		8
save	67	4
saved	20	5
saves	1	
saving	18	
Savior	148	1
Saviour		3
saw	7	
say	75	54
sayest	1	
saying	25	71
says	9	160
scale	1	
scales	1	
scalp	2	
scandal		1
scatter	3	
scattered	13	
scatterest	1	
scatters	2	

Key Word	Occurrences Section One	Occurrences Section Two
scepter	6	
schemes	6	
schism	1	1
school		2
schools	1	2
scoff	3	
scoffed	1	
scorching	1	
scorn	10	
scorned	1	
scornful	2	
scriptural		1
scripture	6	44
scriptures	22	11
scruple	1	
sculptured	1	
sea	47	1
seal	1	1
sealed	4	1
sealing	2	
search	7	1
searched	3	
searing	1	
seas	11	
season	10	53
seasonable	2	
seasons	2	8
seat	4	
seated	18	6
seating		1
seats	1	
second	5	31
secondly		1
secrecy	1	1
secret	10	1

Key Word	Occurrences Section One	Occurrences Section Two
secretly	5	
secrets	8	
sect		1
section		2
sections		3
secure	3	1
see	91	33
seed	6	
seedtime	1	
seeing	3	
seek	71	2
seekers	1	
seeketh	1	
seeking	8	3
seeks	4	
seem		2
seems		1
seen	21	2
seers	1	
sees	3	1
seest	1	
seize	5	
seized	2	
select		4
selected	3	11
selection		3
selections		8
selective		1
selects		1
self	9	3
selfish	2	
selling	1	
selves	6	
senators	2	
send	38	1

Key Word	Occurrences Section One	Occurrences Section Two
sending	5	
sends	4	
sense	11	2
sensible	1	
sensuality		1
sent	44	2
sentence		7
sentences		15
separate	2	8
separated	1	2
separately		7
separation		1
September		17
Septuagesima		*1
sepulcher	2	
sequence		4
seraphim	2	
serenity	2	
series		1
serious		1
seriously	1	1
seriousness	1	
sermon		25
serpent	4	
servant	135	
servanthood	1	
servants	88	1
serve	97	14
served	11	
serves	1	8
serveth	1	
service	49	179
services		19
serving	5	
servo		*1

Key Word	Occurrences Section One	Occurrences Section Two
session		1
set	99	23
sets	5	7
settest	1	
setting	14	
settled	1	
seven	3	4
seventeenth		2
seventh		8
seventy	1	
several	5	6
severity		1
shade	2	
shadow	22	
shadows	1	
shafts	1	
shake	4	
shaken	10	
shakes	3	
shall	*431	*34
shalt	*20	
shame	36	
shamed	1	
shameful	2	
share	46	4
shared	2	1
sharing	1	
sharp	2	
sharpen	1	
sharpened	3	
sharpness	1	
shatter	1	
shattered	2	
shatters	3	
she	*6	*3

Key Word	Occurrences Section One	Occurrences Section Two
sheaves	3	
Shechem	2	
shed	21	
shedding	1	
sheep	30	
sheepfolds	2	
shelter	5	
shepherd	23	2
shepherded	1	
sherd	1	
shield	22	
shields	1	
Shiloh	1	
Shin		*1
shine	35	1
shined	1	
shines	1	
shining	5	
ships	3	
shook	3	
shoot	4	
shoots	1	
short	4	5
shorten		1
shortened	1	2
shorter		2
shortness	2	1
should	*40	*50
shoulder	1	1
shouldering	2	
shoulders	1	
shout	18	1
shouts	5	
show	79	1
showed	4	

Key Word	Occurrences Section One	Occurrences Section Two
shower	1	
showers	3	
showest	1	
showing	3	
shown	10	2
shows	4	
shrine	1	
shrink	2	
shrubs		1
shun	1	
shut	6	
si		*1
sick	19	19
sickbed	1	
sickness	17	4
side	16	3
sight		6
sigh	1	
sighing	7	
sight	48	
sign	22	10
signature		1
signatures		1
signed		4
significance	1	1
signifies	1	
signify		1
signing		4
signs	11	4
Sihon	2	
silence	16	76
silenced	1	
silent	4	7
silently		1

Key Word	Occurrences Section One	Occurrences Section Two
silver	8	
Simeon		7
similar		22
similarity		1
similarly		1
similis		*1
Simon	4	2
simple	2	2
simultaneously		1
sin	119	34
Sinai	2	
since	17	5
sincere	1	1
sincerity	6	
sinful	4	
sinfulness	1	
sing	94	2
singers	2	2
singing	1	8
single	1	2
singleness	4	
sings	3	11
singular		2
sink	3	
sinking	1	
sinned	21	
sinner	8	
sinners	22	
sinning	2	
sins	188	9
Sirach		1
Sisera	1	
sister	16	
sisters	1	
sit	10	14

Key Word	Occurrences Section One	Occurrences Section Two
sits	7	
sittest	4	
sitteth	4	2
sitting	2	
sixfold		1
sixteenth		3
sixth		11
size		1
skies	5	
skill	5	
skilled	1	
skillful	1	
skillfulness	1	
skin	2	
skip	1	
skipped	2	
sky	5	
slain	3	
slander	3	
slanderer	1	
slanderers	1	
slandering	1	
slanderous		1
slaughter	4	
slave	2	
slavery	1	
slay	3	
sleek	2	
sleep	17	1
sleeping	5	
sleet	1	
slept	1	
slew	3	
slip	2	
slipped	2	

Key Word	Occurrences Section One	Occurrences Section Two
slippery	2	
slips	1	
slow	6	
slumber	4	
small	3	1
smash	1	
smeared	1	
smell	1	
smite	2	
smiters	1	
smitten	1	
smoke	8	
smooth	3	
smoother	1	
snail	1	
snare	10	
snares	6	
snarl	2	
snatch	4	
snow	6	
so	*256	*57
soak	1	
sober	4	
social		12
society	2	
soften	1	
softer	1	
soil	2	
sojourner	2	
sojourners	2	
solace	1	
sold	1	
solemn	8	4
solemnly	6	1
solitary	2	

Key Word	Occurrences Section One	Occurrences Section Two
solitude	1	
solo		*1
Solomon		2
some	14	86
someone	1	
something	1	1
sometimes		3
Son	527	31
song	23	41
songs	9	1
sons	8	3
soon	9	4
sooner	1	
soothe	3	
sorely	4	
sorrow	27	2
sorrowful	4	
sorrowing	1	
sorrows	7	
sorry	11	
sort		2
sorts	1	2
sought	6	
soul	84	4
souls	25	2
sound	20	3
soundness	1	
sounds	2	
source	11	
south	3	
sovereign	2	
sovereignty	1	
sow	1	
sowed	3	
sowing	1	

Key Word	Occurrences Section One	Occurrences Section Two
space	2	
spake	3	
span	2	
spare	10	
sparrow	2	
speak	39	5
speaking	6	1
speaks	7	
spear	1	
spears	1	
special	5	22
specially		1
specific		3
speech	4	1
speed	5	4
speedily	3	1
spell	1	
spelled		1
spend	2	
spent	4	
speravi		*3
spheres		1
spiced	1	
spirit	809	24
spirits	15	
spiritual	19	3
Spiritus		*6
spit	1	
spite	1	
splendid	2	
splendor	17	
split	4	
splits	1	
spoils	2	
spoke	12	1

Key Word	Occurrences Section One	Occurrences Section Two
spoken	12	3
sponsor		1
sponsored		1
sponsors	1	8
sport	1	
spot	1	1
spouse	2	
spread	14	1
spring	3	4
springs	7	
sprung	1	
spurn	1	
spy	4	
squandered	1	
squares	2	
St		*7
staff	4	3
stagger	1	
staggered	1	
stalks	2	
stalls	1	
stand	49	45
standard		2
standeth	2	1
standing	1	58
stands	10	18
star	3	
stare	1	
stars	6	
start	1	
state	5	8
stated		1
statement		4
statements	1	
states	6	9

Key Word	Occurrences Section One	Occurrences Section Two
stature	4	
statute	2	
statutes	28	
stay	4	
steadfast	21	
steadfastly	2	
steadfastness	2	
steady	1	
steal	2	
steel	1	
Stephen	3	3
steps	9	
stetit		*1
steward	1	
stewards	8	1
stewardship		2
sticks	1	
stiffness		1
still	25	6
stillborn	1	
stilled	1	
sting	4	
stink	1	
stir	6	
stirred		1
stirring	2	
stirs	1	
stock	1	
stole	2	5
stone	6	
stones	3	
stony	2	
stood	4	
stooped	1	
stoops	1	

Key Word	Occurrences Section One	Occurrences Section Two
stop	2	
stopped	1	
stops	1	
storehouse	1	
stores	1	
stories		1
stork	1	
storm	5	
stormy	2	
story		2
straight	5	
straightway	1	
strange	3	
stranger	7	1
strangers	6	
strap	1	
stray	4	
strayed	5	
stream	1	
streams	7	
street	1	
streets	2	
strength	116	3
strengthen	37	2
strengthened	17	
strengthening	2	
strengthens	2	
stress	1	
stretch	4	
stretched	10	
stretching	2	
stricken	1	
stride	1	
strife	6	
strike	7	

Key Word	Occurrences Section One	Occurrences Section Two
strikes	1	
string	1	
stringed	1	
strings	3	
strip	1	
strips	1	
strive	5	
strong	29	1
stronger	3	
strongest	1	
stronghold	19	
strongholds	3	
struck	7	
structure		1
struggle	1	
struggles	1	
stubborn	1	2
stubbornness	1	
studied	1	
study	10	2
stumble	5	
stumbled	4	
stumbling	5	
stunned	1	
stupid	2	
subdue	1	
subdues	2	
subject	1	7
subjection	1	
submission	1	
submit	1	1
subsequent		4
subsequently		1
subsistence		1
subsisting		1

Key Word	Occurrences Section One	Occurrences Section Two
substance	7	12
substantial		1
substitute		3
substituted		8
substitutes		11
substituting		2
succeeding		2
succession		2
succeeds	1	
success	2	
successes	1	
succor	3	
Succoth	2	
succulent	1	
such	56	60
sudden	1	
suddenly	9	
suffer	32	4
suffered	27	2
sufferers	1	
suffering	27	1
sufferings	3	
suffice		1
sufficiency		1
sufficient	1	6
sufficiently	1	
suffrages		4
suggest		1
suggested		6
suggestions		1
suit		1
suitability	1	
suitable	5	71
sulphur	1	

Key Word	Occurrences Section One	Occurrences Section Two
sum	2	*1
summary	2	2
summed	1	
summer	6	2
summon	1	
sun	32	
Sunday		209
Sundays		30
sundry	1	
sung		117
sunrise		1
suns	1	
sunset		1
sunt		*1
super		*2
supererogation		2
superstitions		1
superstitious		3
supervising		1
supped	1	
supper	11	11
supplication	12	1
supplications	13	
supplied	1	
supply	2	1
support	9	1
supported	4	
supposed		1
supreme	1	
sure	20	2
surely	24	
surety	1	
surface	1	
surge		*1
surgeons	1	

Key Word	Occurrences Section One	Occurrences Section Two
surging	1	
surpass	1	
surpasses	1	
surpassing	1	
surplice		2
surrender		1
surround	9	
surrounded	5	
surrounding	1	
surrounds	2	
Susanna		1
suspends		1
suspicions	1	
sustain	21	
sustained	4	
sustains	8	
swallow	4	2
swallowed	4	
sware	1	
swarm	1	
swarms	2	
sway	1	
swear	2	1
swearing		1
sweat	1	
sweep	2	
sweet	2	1
sweeter	2	
swell	1	
swept	3	
swerved	1	
swift	3	
swiftly	1	
swooped	1	
sword	20	1

Key Word	Occurrences Section One	Occurrences Section Two
swords	1	
swore	5	
sworn	8	
sycamores	1	
symbol	3	9
symbols		4
symmetry		1
sympathy	1	1
Synodals		1
tabernacle	6	
table	14	29
tables		1
Tabor	1	
take	100	33
taken	20	6
takes	6	7
takest	10	
taking		6
tale	2	
talents	3	
talk		2
talked	1	
talking	2	
tarry	6	
Tarshish	1	
task	1	1
tasks	1	
taste	3	
taught	32	4
taunt	2	
taunted	1	
taunts	4	
Taw		*1
te		*15
teach	38	1

Key Word	Occurrences Section One	Occurrences Section Two
teacher	2	4
teachers	3	
teaches	5	
teacheth	1	
teaching	19	3
teachings	4	
tear	1	1
tears	14	1
teeth	7	1
tell	19	1
telling		1
tells	1	
temperance	1	
tempest	4	
tempestuous	1	
temple	24	
temples	1	
temporal	2	3
temptation	19	
temptations	5	
tempted	7	
ten	9	2
tend	5	1
tender	14	
tendrils	1	
tens	1	
tent	1	
tenth		2
tents	7	
tenure		1
term		3
terms		3
terra		*1
terrible	1	
terrified	2	

Key Word	Occurrences Section One	Occurrences Section Two
terrify	1	
terror	12	
terrors	3	
test	5	
Testament	7	34
Testaments	4	1
tested	5	
testify	1	1
testimonies	4	2
testimony	4	
Teth		*1
Tetragrammaton		1
text		6
texts		4
than	*69	*18
thank	77	2
thankful	11	
thankfully	6	
thankfulness	2	
thanks	200	4
thanksgiving	35	51
thanksgivings	1	26
that	*1384	*259
the	*8609	*5143
thee	*540	*1
their	*639	*88
theirs	*1	
them	*590	*69
themselves	*27	*13
then	*74	*194
thence	2	
theologian		2
Theotokos		1
there	*148	*66
thereafter		8

Key Word	Occurrences Section One	Occurrences Section Two
thereby	2	5
therefore	*72	15
therein	5	4
thereof	1	6
thereto	1	
thereunto		2
thereupon	1	
these	*91	*76
they	*633	*96
thick	2	
thief	2	
thigh	1	
thine	68	
thing	14	13
things	185	37
think	11	1
thinks	1	
third	19	15
thirdly		1
thirst	7	
thirsts	1	
thirsty	5	
thirteenth		2
thirtieth		2
this	*528	*280
thistles	1	
thither	1	
Thomas	2	2
thorns	2	
thoroughly		1
those	*466	*67
thou	*163	*2
though	46	2
thought	22	3
thoughts	22	

Key Word	Occurrences Section One	Occurrences Section Two
thousand	10	2
thousands	6	
threats	1	
three	5	46
threefold		2
threescore	1	
threshold	1	3
throat	5	
throne	26	
thrones	5	
throng	2	
throngs	1	
through	612	43
throughout	23	4
throw	2	
thrown	2	
thrust	2	1
thumb		1
Thursday		7
Thursdays		2
thunder	4	
thunderbolts	3	
thundered	2	
thunders	1	
thus	5	4
thwarts	1	
thy	*788	
tibi		*4
thyself	*5	
tidings	2	
ties	1	
till	5	
timbrel	3	
time	80	55
timely	1	

Key Word	Occurrences Section One	Occurrences Section Two
times	27	28
Timothy		4
tippet		3
tire	1	
title		3
titles		2
to	*3416	*822
Tobias		1
Tobit		1
today	20	
together	79	37
toil	6	
tokens	2	1
told	3	
tomb	5	
tongue	32	6
tongues	11	
too	17	4
took	33	2
tookest	1	
tools		1
top	1	
topple	1	
toppled	1	
toppling	1	
tops	1	
torch	3	
tore	1	
torn	1	
torrent	4	
torrents	1	
toss	3	
tossed	1	
toto		*1
totters	1	

Key Word	Occurrences Section One	Occurrences Section Two
touch	2	
touches	1	1
touching		5
toward	13	1
towards	7	5
tower	4	
towering	1	
towers	2	
town	2	
towns	2	2
trace	1	
trackless	1	
trade	1	
tradition		1
traditional		26
traditionally		2
traditions		3
trains	2	
trample	6	
trampled	1	
trampling	2	
tranquillity	8	
transferred		4
transfiguration		6
transfigured	2	
transformed	1	
transgressions	10	
transgressors	1	
transitory	1	1
translation		1
translations		1
transliterated		1
Transubstantiation		1
trap	4	
trapped	2	

Key Word	Occurrences Section One	Occurrences Section Two
traps	2	
travail	2	
travel	3	
travelers		2
treacherous	2	
treachery	1	
tread	4	
treasure	4	
treated	1	
tree	4	1
trees	10	1
tremble	12	
trembled	2	
trembles	2	
trembling	6	
tresspass	15	
trespasses	15	
trial	11	
trials	1	
tribe	3	
tribes	5	
tribulation	3	
tribulations	1	
tribunal	1	
tribute	4	
tried	4	
trifle	1	
Trinity	14	45
trip	2	
triplets		1
tripped	1	
Trisagion		3
triumph	21	
triumphed	6	
trodden	1	

Key Word	Occurrences Section One	Occurrences Section Two
troop	1	
troth	1	
trouble	47	4
troubled	6	1
troubles	10	
troubling		1
true	88	4
truehearted	1	
truest		1
truly	55	6
trumpet	2	
trumpets	2	
trust	95	2
trusted	12	
trustees		1
trusting	4	
trusts	1	
trustworthy	1	
truth	116	5
truths	2	1
try	2	
tua		*1
tuae		*1
Tuesday		8
tui		*1
tumult	3	
tunc		*1
tuo		*1
turmoil	1	
turn	57	2
turned	26	
turnest	2	
turneth	1	
turns	5	
twelfth		3

Key Word	Occurrences Section One	Occurrences Section Two
twelve	5	3
twentieth		2
twenty	1	19
twice	1	1
twinkling	1	
two	17	51
tyrant	1	
tyrants	2	
Tyre	3	
ultimate		1
ultionum		*1
unable		3
unadvisedly	1	
unawares	1	
unbearable	1	
unborn	5	
unbounded	1	
unceasing	2	
uncertain		2
uncertainties	1	
uncertainty	2	
unchangeable	7	
uncharitable	1	
unchristian		1
unclean		1
uncovered	1	
uncreate		3
uncreated		2
unction	4	1
undefiled		1
undependable	1	
under	68	10
understand	14	5
understanded		2
understandest	1	

Key Word	Occurrences Section One	Occurrences Section Two
understandeth		1
understanding	29	3
understands	1	
understood	6	5
undertake	2	
undertaking		1
undeserved	1	
undivided	2	1
undone	16	
unearned	1	
unemployed	1	2
unending	9	
unfailing	4	2
unfaithful	1	
unfaithfulness	1	
unfamiliar	1	
unfeigned	1	
unfeignedly	3	
unfinished	1	
ungodly	9	2
unhappy	1	
uninfluenced		1
union	12	3
unison		3
unite	4	
united	17	5
unites	1	
uniting	6	1
unity	112	17
universal	5	2
universe	6	
universities	1	
unjust	1	
unjustly	3	
unknown	3	1

Key Word	Occurrences Section One	Occurrences Section Two
unleavened	2	
unless	4	11
unnecessary		1
unpardonable		1
unprepared	1	
unprofitable		1
unread		1
unrestrained		1
unrighteous	1	
unrighteousness	4	
unruly	2	
unsearchable	2	
unseen	6	1
unshaken		1
unspeakable		1
unsteady	1	
untended	1	
until	*28	*18
unto	*126	*12
untrue		1
unveiled	1	
unworthily		1
unworthiness	3	1
unworthy	6	
up	237	10
upheld	1	
uphold	15	
upholds	2	
uplifted	1	
upon	*397	*58
upper	1	
upright	14	
uprightness	3	
uproar	1	
urgent		1

Key Word	Occurrences Section One	Occurrences Section Two
us	*1521	*40
usages		1
use	23	68
used	3	186
useful	1	
usefulness	1	
useless	1	
uses	2	3
using		23
usquequo		*1
usual		14
usually		2
ut		*2
utique		*1
utter	2	
uttered	1	
utterly	8	2
uttermost	6	
utters	1	
vain	14	3
vainglory	2	
vainly		2
valiant	3	
valley	7	1
valleys	3	
vanish	5	
vanished	1	
vanquished	1	
variance	2	
variations		2
varied	1	
variety	1	
various	3	27
varying		2
vast	2	

Key Word	Occurrences Section One	Occurrences Section Two
vault	1	
vaunted	1	
venerate	3	
venerunt		*1
vengeance	4	
veni		6
veniat		*1
Venite		8
venomous	1	
ventured	1	
verba		*1
verbi		*1
verbs		2
vere		*1
verge	1	
verily	1	
verity		1
versa		1
verse		21
verses		12
versicle		9
versicles		3
versification		1
version		9
versions		2
very	27	11
vesper	5	
vespers		1
vessel		10
vessels	3	6
vest		1
vested		6
vestments		2
vesture		4
vicar		1

Key Word	Occurrences Section One	Occurrences Section Two
vicars		2
vice	2	1
victims	3	2
victories	2	
victorious	6	
victory	36	1
vide		*1
view		2
Vigil	2	14
village	1	
villages	1	
vindication	3	
vine	5	
vinegar	1	
vines	2	
vineyard		1
vineyards	1	
violence	11	
violent	4	
vir		*2
virgin	37	5
virtue	7	2
virtues	2	
virtuous	2	
virtute		*1
visible	7	6
visibly		2
vision	4	
visit	12	
visitation	2	3
visited	2	
vitulum		*1
vocal		1

Key Word	Occurrences Section One	Occurrences Section Two
vocalized		1
vocation	7	4
vocations		2
voce		*2
voice	57	5
voices	11	
void		2
voluntary		1
vouchsafe	3	
vow	7	1
vowed	1	
vowel		1
vowels		1
vows	26	18
vult		*1
vulture	1	
wag	1	
waged	1	
waifs	1	
wail	1	
wailing	2	
wait	22	3
waited	2	
waits	5	
wake	5	
waken	2	
waking	3	
walk	47	2
walked	3	
walking	13	
walks	1	
wall	3	
walls	9	
wander	1	

Key Word	Occurrences Section One	Occurrences Section Two
wandered	2	
wandering	1	
wanderings	1	
want	7	
wanting	2	
war	5	1
warden		3
wardens		1
warned	1	
warning	1	
warnings	2	
warped	1	
warrants		1
warranty		1
warrior	7	
warriors	1	
wars	1	1
was	*217	*34
wash	10	
washbasin	1	
washed	5	
washes	1	
washing		1
waste	7	
wasted	3	
wastes	2	
watch	30	
watches	8	
watchful	2	
watching	4	
watchman	1	
watchmen	3	
water	46	23
watercourses	2	
waters	49	6

Key Word	Occurrences Section One	Occurrences Section Two
waves	7	1
Waw		*1
wax	3	
way	108	4
wayfarer	1	
ways	65	3
wayward	1	
we	*1536	*58
weak	9	2
weakness	14	
weaknesses	14	
wealth	8	
weapons	2	1
wear	2	1
wearied	1	
wears	1	
weary	7	
weather	2	1
wedded	1	
wedding	3	3
wedlock	1	
Wednesday		26
Wednesdays		1
weeds	1	
week	6	62
weekday		3
weekdays		23
weekly	2	1
weeks		4
weep	4	
weeping	5	
weigh	1	1
weighing	1	
weighs	3	
weight	2	

Key Word	Occurrences Section One	Occurrences Section Two
weighty		3
welcome	2	
welcomed		1
welfare	4	2
well	38	10
wells	1	
went	19	1
wept	2	1
were	*91	*15
west	3	
whales	2	
what	*188	*11
whatever	7	2
whatsoever	2	2
wheat	2	
when	*196	*169
whence	*1	*1
whenever	*15	*2
where	*92	*15
whereas		*3
whereby	*3	*9
wherefore	*3	*8
wherein	*2	*1
whereof	*3	*7
wherever	*5	
wherewith	*1	*2
whet	1	
whether	4	16
which	*262	*137
while	*42	*14
whipped	1	
whirling	1	
whirlwind	1	
whisper	2	
whispering	1	

Key Word	Occurrences Section One	Occurrences Section Two
white	3	1
whither	3	
Whitsunday		3
who	*1507	*63
whoever	13	
whole	88	11
wholeness	1	
wholesome	3	4
wholly	1	
whom	*142	*4
whoring	1	
whose	*156	*3
whosoever	3	4
why	51	
wicked	104	3
wickedly	1	
wickedness	32	1
wide	7	
widening	1	
widow	3	
widowed	2	
widows	2	
wife	12	12
wild	11	
wilderness	17	
will	890	26
willed		1
willest	2	
willing	6	
willingly	5	2
willingness	1	
wills	10	1
wilt	6	
wily	1	
win	1	

Key Word	Occurrences Section One	Occurrences Section Two
wind	20	
winds	4	
wine	18	36
winged	2	
wings	14	
wink	1	
winter	5	2
wipe	1	2
wiped	2	
wisdom	46	7
wise	12	4
wisely	2	
wiser	2	
wish	4	1
wishes		4
wit		2
with	*1477	*285
withdrawn	1	
wither	4	
withered	4	
withers	1	
withheld	2	
withhold	2	
within	44	11
without	88	20
witness	36	2
witnessed	2	
witnesses	12	5
witnessing	1	
wits	1	
woke	1	
woman	15	11
womb	12	1
women	12	
won	6	

Key Word	Occurrences Section One	Occurrences Section Two
wonder	4	
wonderful	32	
wonderfully	14	
wonders	21	
wondrous	3	
wont	1	
wood	3	
wooden		1
wool	1	
word	163	47
wording		1
words	48	76
work	81	16
worked	2	
worker	2	
workers	5	
working	12	3
works	74	14
world	263	16
worldly	3	1
worlds	7	1
worm	1	
worn	2	2
worse	4	
worship	84	26
worshiped	12	
worshipers	2	
worshipped		2
worshipping		1
worships	2	
worth	4	
worthily	12	2
worthiness	2	
worthless	5	
worthy	35	1

Key Word	Occurrences Section One	Occurrences Section Two
would	*45	*4
wouldest	*3	
wound	48	
wounded	4	
woundeth		1
wounds	4	1
woven	1	
wrap	3	
wrapped	1	
wraps	1	
wrath	20	1
wrathful	4	
wreak	1	
wreath		1
wretched	2	
wretchedness	3	
wretchlessness		1
writ		2
write	2	
writer	1	
writers		1
writhe	1	
writhed	1	
writings		1
written	9	3
wrong	9	2
wrongfully	1	
wrongs	2	
wrought	4	
YAHWEH	2	1
Yahweh	1	1
ye	*81	
yea	7	2
year	2	46
yearly	2	

Key Word	Occurrences Section One	Occurrences Section Two
years	19	7
yesterday	2	
yet	51	21
YHWH		4
yield	3	
yielded		1
Yodh		*1
yoke	3	
yonder	1	
York		1
you	*2494	*35
young	23	9
younger		2
your	*2360	*23
yours	*46	
yourself	*37	*1
yourselves	*6	
youth	9	
Zalmon	1	
Zalmunna	1	
Zayin		*1
zeal	3	
zealous	2	
Zebah	1	
Zebulon	1	
Zechariah		4
Zephaniah		1
Zeeb	1	
Zion	45	
Zoan	2	

Table of Deletions & Retentions

1. Pronouns

All personal, possessive, reflexive, intensive, relative, interrogative, and demonstrative pronouns have been categorically deleted. Indefinite pronouns have been retained.

Personal Pronouns Deleted

he	her	him	I	it	me	she
thee	them	they	thou	us	we	you

Possessive Forms Deleted

her	hers	his	its	mine	my
our	ours	their	theirs	your	yours

Reflexive and Intensive Pronouns Deleted

herself	himself	itself	myself
oneself	ourselves	themselves	thyself
yourself	yourselves		

Relative and Interrogative Pronouns Deleted

that	what	which	who	whom	whose

Demonstrative Pronouns Deleted

that	these	this	those

Commonly Used Indefinite Pronouns Retained

all	another	any	anybody
both	each	either	everybody
few	many	most	neither
nobody	one	other	several
some	someone	such	

2. Commonly Used Prepositions

Prepositions not dealing with action, direction, or time have been cut from the Concordance. Though not included in Section One, the preposition "out" is included in Section Two in the interest of illustrating its archaic usage.

Prepositions Deleted

about	at	but	by	for	in
into	of	on	to	until	unto
upon	with				

Prepositions Retained

above	across	after	against
along	amid	among	around
before	behind	below	beneath
beside	besides	between	beyond
concerning	down	during	except
from	like	off	over
past	since	through	throughout
toward	towards	under	underneath
up	within	without	

3. Conjunctions

All coordinating conjunctions have been deleted. The first half of the construction of correlative conjunctions has been retained, while some subordinating conjunctions have been left for reasons of semantic interest.

Coordinating Conjunctions Deleted

and	but	for	nor	or

Correlative Conjunctions (First Half Retained)

both / and	either / or
neither / nor	whether / or

Commonly Used Subordinating Conjunctions Deleted

after	as	because	before
inasmuch	so	than	that
until	when	whence	whenever
where	whereby	wherefore	wherein
whereof	wherever	wherewith	while

Commonly Used Subordinating Conjunctions Retained

although	how	if	provided
since	though	unless	

4. Articles Deleted

a	an	the

5. Infinitive Deleted

to

6. Auxiliary Verbs Deleted

Most auxiliary verbs have been cut. Other usages of these same words have been retained. Though not included in Section One, the auxiliary verbs "been," "doth," and "must" are included in Section Two in the interest of illustrating their archaic usage.

Usages Deleted

am	are	be	can	cannot	did
didst	do	does	dost	doth	had
hadst	has	hast	hath	have	is
may	mayest	might	shall	shalt	should
was	were	will	would	wouldest	

Other Meanings

Verb Transitive Forms Retained

had	has	hast	hath	have

Noun Forms Retained

might	will

7. Interjections Deleted

O	oh

8. Miscellaneous

The adjective "done," the common adverbs "again," "already," "also," and "therefore," and the auxiliary verbs "been" and "must" appear in Section Two but are not included in Section One. The common adverbs "here," "not," "now," "then," and "there" were deleted from both sections. The gerund forms of the word "doing" were deleted.